Italy

Damien Simonis

Duncan Garwood, Paula Hardy, Alex Leviton,
Josephine Quintero, Miles Roddis, Richard Watkins

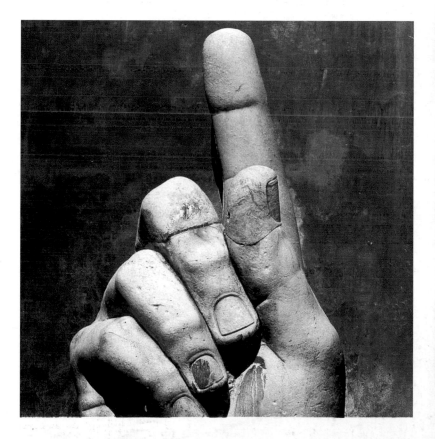

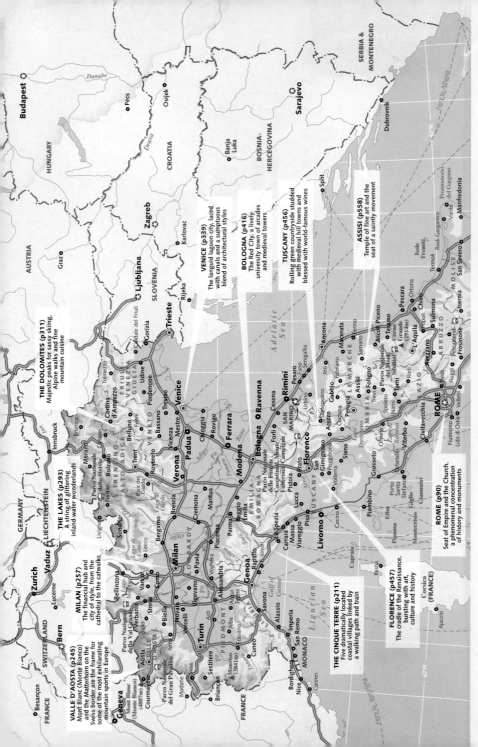

VALLE D'AOSTA (p245)
Mont Blanc (Monte Bianco) and the Matterhorn on the Swiss border are the frame for some of the most exhilarating mountain sports in Europe

MILAN (p257)
The financial hub and city of style, from the cathedral to the catwalks

THE LAKES (p293)
A string of glittering inland water wonderlands

THE DOLOMITES (p311)
Majestic peaks for sassy skiing, Alpine walks and fine mountain cuisine

VENICE (p339)
The languid lagoon city, laced with canals and a sumptuous blend of architectural styles

BOLOGNA (p416)
The Red City, a lively university town of arcades and medieval towers

TUSCANY (p456)
Rolling green countryside studded with medieval hill towns and blessed with world-famous wines

ASSISI (p558)
Temple of fine art and the seat of a saintly movement

THE CINQUE TERRE (p211)
Five dramatically located coastal villages linked by a walking path and train

FLORENCE (p457)
The cradle of the Renaissance, bursting with art, culture and history

ROME (p90)
Seat of Empire and the Church, a phenomenal concentration of history and monuments

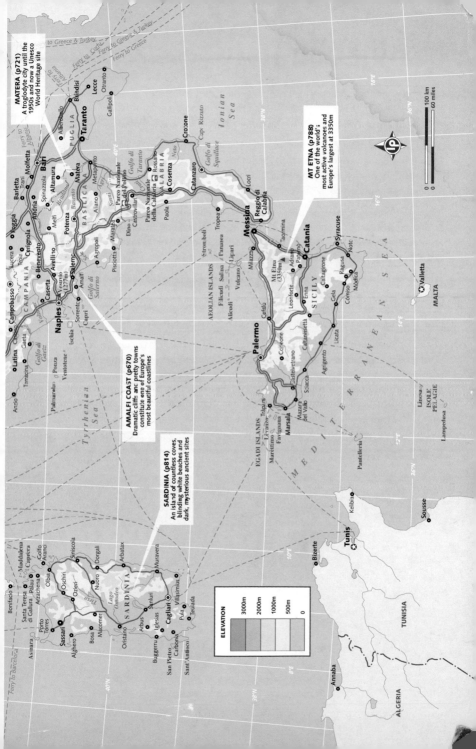

MATERA (p721)
A troglodyte city until the 1950s and now a Unesco World Heritage site

MT ETNA (p788)
One of the world's most active volcanoes and Europe's largest at 3350m

AMALFI COAST (p670)
Dramatic cliffs and pretty towns constitute one of Europe's most beautiful coastlines

SARDINIA (p814)
An island of countless coves, blinding white beaches and dark, mysterious ancient sites

ELEVATION
3000m
2000m
1000m
500m
0

100 km
60 miles

Ferry to Greece & Turkey
Ferry to Greece & Turkey
Ferry to Greece

Lecce
Otranto
Brindisi
Gallipoli

Ionian Sea

Taranto
Bari
Molfetta
Barletta
Trani
Altamura
Andria
Spinazzola
Cerignola
Foggia
Lucera
Troia
PUGLIA
Matera
Metaponto
Golfo di Taranto
Rossano
Crotone
Capo Rizzuto

BASILICATA
Potenza
Melfi
Benevento
Avellino
Campobasso
CAMPANIA
Caserta
Naples
Salerno
Amalfi
Sorrento
Capri
Golfo di Salerno
Vesuvio (1277m)
Ischia
Pisciotta
Agropoli
Maratea
Castrovillari
Sibari
Sinni
Parco Nazionale del Pollino
Parco Nazionale della Calabria
CALABRIA
Cosenza
Catanzaro
Golfo di Squillace
Paola
Locri
Reggio di Calabria
Messina
Tropea
Dino
Alano

Tyrrhenian Sea

Latina
Anzio
Terracina
Gaeta
Golfo di Gaeta
Ponza
Ventotene
Palmarola

AEOLIAN ISLANDS
Stromboli
Salina
Panarea
Filicudi
Alicudi
Lipari
Vulcano

Palermo
Cefalù
Corleone
Castelvetrano
Sciacca
Agrigento
Licata
Gela
Comiso
Modica
Ragusa
Noto
Syracuse
Catania
Paterno
Adrano
Mt Etna (3350m)
Taormina
Milazzo
Leonforte
Enna
Caltagirone
Caltanissetta
SICILY

EGADI ISLANDS
Levanzo
Marettimo
Favignana
Trapani
Marsala
Mazara del Vallo

MEDITERRANEAN SEA

Pantelleria

ISOLE PELAGIE
Linosa
Lampedusa

MALTA
Valletta

Bonifacio
Santa Teresa di Gallura
Palau
La Maddalena
Capraia
Porto Torres
Asinara
Alghero
Sassari
Macomer
Bosa
Ozieri
Olbia
Oschiri
Golfo Aranci
Siniscola
Nuoro
Dorgali
Arbatax
Muravera
SARDINIA
Lago Omodeo
Oristano
Arbus
Buggerru
Carbonia
Iglesias
Sanluri
Villasimius
Cagliari
Pula
Teulada
Sant'Antioco
San Pietro

Ferry to Barcellona

Bizerte
Tunis
TUNISIA
Kelibia
Sousse
Annaba
ALGERIA

Tyrrhenian Sea

Destination Italy

Long before northern Europeans started buying homes in Tuscany they were traversing the Alps to feast on Italy's countless wonders. From Dürer to Dickens, artists, writers, grandees and dandies descended on Italy for the Grand Tour.

United only in 1870, the history of Italy is more a fable book of histories than a single, linear tome. Some seek out the splendour of Imperial Rome and its ancient forbears. These are evident in the city itself, but can also be found in magnificent vestiges such as Verona's Arena, the lava-preserved town of Pompeii and the Greek temples of Paestum and Sicily.

A universe away is the lagoon city of Venice, onetime master of the Med, and the artistic treasures of Medici Florence. The riches extend far beyond the obvious. The roll-call of extraordinary towns great and small is endless: Byzantine Ravenna, medieval Siena, baroque Lecce, the hill towns of Tuscany, Umbria and Le Marche…

Italy is not just an urban adventure. The northern wall of the Alps invites you to indulge in the whole gamut of mountain sports. Ski in Courmayeur or hike in the Dolomites. Sardinia, Sicily, Calabria and southern Puglia boast golden beaches, sparking coves and impossibly clear waters. Island-hop around the Aeolian and Egadi groups off Sicily, or make for distant Lampedusa, closer to Africa than Europe.

Your taste buds will demand attention. The Arabs introduced spaghetti to Sicily but pasta is only the start. In Venice people chomp on *cicheti,* seafood bar snacks, while in Florence they have a penchant for wild boar. Sicily is a font of fish where Arab spice traditions live on. And Tuscan wines are just the tip of the oenological iceberg – pleasures for the palate range from Piedmont's Barolos to Sardinia's Cannonaus.

The Italians are not joking when they call their home *Il Belpaese,* the Beautiful Country. Come see for yourself!

Highlights Italy

Relive past Roman glories at the Colosseum (p110)

JON DAVISON

GLENN BEANLAND

Imagine ancient life at the Roman Forum (p113), once the heart of the Republic

OTHER HIGHLIGHTS

- Race to the Dolomites (p311) for some amazing skiing and walking.
- Jet-set to the cobalt blue waters of the stunning Aeolian Islands (p766).
- Amble along the Cinque Terre (p211), each village clinging defiantly to the steep coastline.

RUSSELL MOUNTFORD

Gaze at Michelangelo's divine Sistine Chapel (p137)

JON DAVISON

Enjoy great views over Sirmione from the tower of the Castello Scaligero (p303)

DENNIS JONES

Dine by the calm waters of Lago di Como (p297)

Peaceful moments about at the ever-popular Lago Maggiore (p293)

MARTIN MOOS

Be dazzled by the elaborate façade of the Basilica di San Marco (p348)

DAMIEN SIMONIS

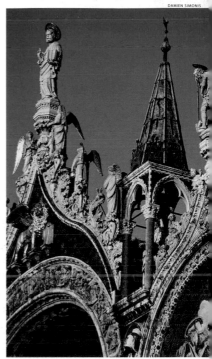

ROBERTO SONCIN GEROMETTA

The ultimate Venetian experience – streaming down the Grand Canal in a gondola (p363)

Paint the town red (and blue and yellow) in the pretty fishing village of Burano (p362)

ROBERTO SONCIN GEROMETTA

David (p473) strikes a pose in the Galleria dell'Accademia

JOHN HAY

BETHUNE CARMICHAEL

Marvel at Italy's greatest concentration of Renaissance art at the Uffizi Gallery (p468)

Enjoy beguiling views from the Ponte Vecchio (p474), as night falls on the River Arno

JOHN ELK III

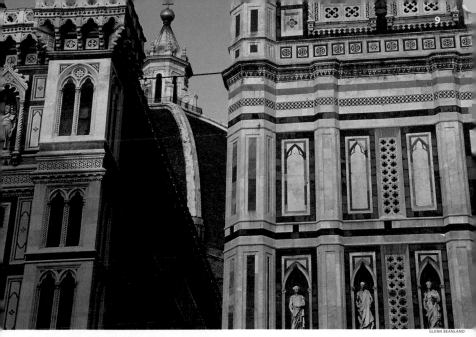

GLENN BEANLAND

Your first glimpse of Florence's Duomo (p460) may well stop you in your tracks

JULIET COOMBE

The Fountain of Neptune (p467) rules Florence's Piazza della Signoria

It's a long way to the top – climbing the Brenta Dolomites (p317)

GARETH MCCORMACK

Step back, look up and take in the visual feast of Orvieto's cathedral (p573)

Welcome to one of the world's most iconic stuff-ups, the Leaning Tower of Pisa (p503)

Explore Matera's *sassi* (p723), made famous in Mel Gibson's film, *The Passion of the Christ*

Stroll along the ancient streets of Pompeii (p654)

PHILIP & KAREN SMITH

STEPHEN SAKS

For whom the bell tolls – the 68m-high bell tower (p712) in Lecce's Piazza del Duomo

Houses hug precipitous cliffs on the Amalfi Coast (p670)

JONATHAN SMITH

12

WAYNE WALTON

Reach up to the heavens, the Tempio di Ercole (p801) at the Valley of the Temples in Agrigento

A Sardinian woman in traditional costume for the Festa del Redentore (p831) in Nuoro

DAMIEN SIMONIS

Relax by the crystal-clear waters of the Golfo di Orosei's Cala Mariolu (p851)

DAMIEN SIMONIS

Contents

Regional Map Contents

The Authors

DAMIEN SIMONIS
Coordinating Author, The Veneto

Damien still remembers listening to crackly shortwave Italian broadcasts years ago on many an Australian midsummer night. It all started in Rome, part of a typical backpacking tour, and carried on as a university obsession. Damien has explored Italy from Bolzano in the north to the island of Lampedusa, way south of Sicily. He has lived in Milan, Florence, Venice and Palermo, and returns frequently for work and (especially) pleasure. Involved with this guide since its 2nd edition, Damien has also written Lonely Planet's *Venice*, *Best of Venice*, *Florence*, *Tuscany* and *Sardinia*.

For this edition of Italy, Damien also updated the Destination, Highlights, Getting Started, Itineraries, Snapshot, History, The Culture, Environment, Directory and Health chapters.

The Coordinating Author's Favourite Trip

For a two-week spring escape, my thoughts turn to the sea and country. A flight to **Genoa** (p193) gets me into position. After a night in the city (and dinner in an old-town trattoria) I make for the **Cinque Terre** (p211), basing myself in **Vernazza** (p213). After three days' unwinding, I move into Tuscany and head for the hills. With spring flowers flourishing, the **Apuane Alps** (p500) are perfect for some hiking. The hard legwork done, it's time for a town-and-country mix, so I move onto **Lucca** (p495) and then venture deeper south to **San Gimignano** (p521) before backing up to **Florence** (p457) and then **Bologna** (p416) for a change of scene and cuisine. I interrupt the return to Genoa along the back roads over the Apennines with a stop in **Parma** (p432).

DUNCAN GARWOOD
Rome & Lazio, Abruzzo & Molise

A writer and aficionado of cheap white wine, Duncan lives in the green hills just south of Rome. His first taste of Italian life came in 1997 when a move to the port of Bari provided a crash-course in the ways of Mediterranean life. Since then Duncan has spent much of his time travelling up and down the peninsula trying to get his head around this most beautiful and complicated of countries. An Italian speaker, he's worked on various Lonely Planet Italy guides, including the *Rome* city guide.

LONELY PLANET AUTHORS

Why is our travel information the best in the world? It's simple: our authors are independent, dedicated travellers. They don't research using just the Internet or phone, and they don't take freebies in exchange for positive coverage. They travel widely, to all the popular spots and off the beaten track. They personally visit thousands of hotels, restaurants, cafés, bars, galleries, palaces, museums and more – and they take pride in getting all the details right, and telling it how it is. For more, see the authors section on www.lonelyplanet.com.

PAULA HARDY
Puglia, Basilicata & Calabria, Sicily

Paula has spent the last five years living in and writing her way around the fringes of the Mediterranean, from a cultural history of Libya to Lonely Planet projects in Italy, Morocco and Spain. This has given her a deep appreciation of the composite oriental and occidental culture that makes southern Italy and Sicily endlessly fascinating, while repeated visits over the years have allowed her to savour the changing colours and contexts of Mediterranean life. When not climbing mountains and volcanoes to work off the worst excesses of Italian restaurants, Paula lives in London and contributes travel articles to the *Telegraph, Independent, Daily Express* and *Wanderlust Travel Magazine*.

ALEX LEVITON
Umbria & Le Marche, Transport

Alex discovered Italy by accident on her way to Africa in 1998. She has since logged seven trips there, six of those with time spent in Umbria. For kicks, she's been known to take seven-hour Italian train journeys to nowhere in particular. After graduating with a master's degree in journalism from UC Berkeley, Alex moved into a tobacco warehouse in Durham, North Carolina, where she is painting her hallway in Venetian plaster and contemplating purchasing Italian-language Scrabble.

JOSEPHINE QUINTERO
Campania, Sardinia

Josephine is a freelance writer specialising in travel and has lived and worked in both California and Kuwait. She has written for food and wine magazines, been a ghostwriter for biographies (and the occasional spy thriller), edited the Kuwait oil magazine *Kuwaiti Digest* and been held hostage in Iraq. Her love for Italy has resulted in regular trips and, to Josephine's delight, her daughter recently moved to northern Italy where a spare room is now kept in perpetual readiness.

MILES RODDIS
Emilia-Romagna & San Marino, Tuscany

This is Miles' third Italian job for Lonely Planet. Having cut his teeth on a swath of Africa from Ghana in the west to Eritrea and Djibouti in the east, he writes these days mostly about Mediterranean lands. Living just across the water in Valencia, Spain, Miles has written or contributed to more than 25 Lonely Planet books including *Europe on a Shoestring* and *Mediterranean Europe*.

RICHARD WATKINS   Liguria, Piedmont & Valle d'Aosta, Lombardy & the Lakes, Trento-Alto Adige, Friuli-Venezia Giulia

Richard's first introduction to Italy came in 1994 when his Ancient History studies at Oxford led him to a brief but captivating stint at the British School in Rome. After leaving university Richard's jobs included teaching English in countries as far afield as Bulgaria and Singapore, compiling rugby results for local newspapers and writing reviews for travel-related websites. Richard's seemingly incurable wanderlust continues, and he has contributed to almost a dozen Lonely Planet titles including *Tuscany & Umbria*, *Rome* and *Europe on a Shoestring*.

Getting Started

You could keep visiting Italy for the rest of your life and still not exhaust all it has to offer. It's a treasure chest of art, a living tableau of human history, a culinary delight and a natural wonder with everything from craggy mountains and glistening glaciers to sparkling seas and golden beaches.

WHEN TO GO

The immediate response is 'any time'! On a more serious note, the best period is April to June. The weather is sunny without being stifling, the countryside bursts with spring flowers, and the flood of summer tourism, largely dictated by school holidays, has yet to crash over the peninsula. Most Italians hit the road in July and August, so those two months – in which prices soar, tempers flare and the country broils – are best avoided.

The vision of Italy as the land of eternal Mediterranean sunshine is a trifle distorted. In the Alps, winters are long and severe. First snowfalls usually occur in November and freak falls in June are not unusual. The ski season is high season in the Alps. Those mountains shield Lombardy from the extremes of the northern European winter, but cloud and rain are common – Milan comes close to being Italy's London.

Florence's position, nestled in a valley surrounded by hills, creates ovenlike conditions in summer. Rome experiences hot summers and mild winters. That tendency continues in the south: in Sicily and Sardinia you can expect very mild winters and long hot summers (a dip in the sea is possible from Easter to October).

Italy's calendar of religious, local and national festivals, along with cultural events, is busy year-round but bulges with possibility from Easter to September; see p862 for more information.

See Climate Charts (p858) for more information.

COSTS & MONEY

Italy isn't cheap, although compared with the UK and northern Europe the situation is not so bad. What you spend on accommodation (your single greatest expense) will depend on various factors, such as location (Turin is pricier than Taranto), season (August is crazy on the coast), the degree of comfort and luck. At the bottom end you will pay €14 to €20 at youth hostels, where meals generally cost €9. The cheapest *pensione* (small hotel) is unlikely to cost less than €25/40 for a basic single/double anywhere from Pisa to Palermo. You can stumble across comfortable rooms with their own bathroom from €50 to €80. Midrange hotels in the more expensive places such as Rome, Florence and Venice can easily cost from €80/120 to €150/200 for singles/doubles.

Eating out is just as variable. In Venice and Milan you tend to pay a lot (and sometimes get little in return), while tourist magnets such as

---

DON'T LEAVE HOME WITHOUT...

- Valid travel insurance (p865).
- Your ID card or passport and visa if required (p871).
- A driving licence and car documents if driving, along with appropriate car insurance (p883).
- A set of smart casual clothes: grimy T-shirts, shorts and dusty sandals don't cut the mustard in bars and restaurants in fashion-conscious Italy.

TOP TENS

Our Favourite Festivals & Events

Italians celebrate in many different ways – from Venice's Carnevale to Siena's equestrian folly, Il Palio, the gamut is enormous. Here is our top 10; for a more comprehensive listing, see p862.

- Carnevale – February; Venice (p364)
- Sa Sartiglia – February; Oristano in Sardinia (p829)
- Corsa dei Ceri (Candles Race) – May; Gubbio in Umbria (p567)
- Processione dei Serpari (Snake-charmers' Procession) – May; Cocullo in Abruzzo (p607)
- Palio delle Quattro Antiche Repubbliche Marinare (Regatta of the Four Ancient Maritime Republics) – May/June; rotates each year between Venice, Pisa, Amalfi and Genoa (p863)
- Umbria Jazz – July; Perugia in Umbria (p548)
- Il Palio (The Banner) – July and August; Siena in Tuscany (p518)
- I Candelieri (The Candlesticks) – August; Sassari in Sardinia (p831)
- Regata Storica (Historic Regatta) – September; Venice (p364)
- Festa di San Gennaro – 16 December, also takes place on the first Sunday in May and 19 September; Naples in Campania (p628)

Must-See Italian Movies

Before you start your real trip, why not embark on a celluloid adventure through Italy with some of the following classics, new and old? See p58 for reviews.

- *Il Postino* (1994) Director: Michael Radford
- *La Dolce Vita* (1960) Director: Federico Fellini
- *Il Gattopardo* (1963) Director: Luchino Visconti
- *Ladri di Biciclette* (1948) Director: Vittorio de Sica
- *La Vita è Bella* (1997) Director: Roberto Benigni
- *Roma Città Aperta* (1945) Director: Roberto Rossellini
- *A Room with a View* (1986) Director: James Ivory
- *Death in Venice* (1971) Director: Luchino Visconti
- *Nuovo Cinema Paradiso* (1988) Director: Giuseppe Tornatore
- *Buongiorno, Notte* (2004) Director: Marco Bellocchio

Top Reads

Before the advent of cinema, writers conveyed the sights, feelings and sensibilities of Italians and their world in print. The following are just the tip of the literary iceberg. See p56 for reviews.

- *Cristo se è Fermato a Eboli* (Christ Stopped at Eboli; 1947) Carlo Levi
- *Il Gattopardo* (The Leopard; 1958) Giuseppe Tomasi di Lampedusa
- *I Promessi Sposi* (The Betrothed; 1827) Alessandro Manzoni
- *Der Tod in Venedig* (Death in Venice; 1930) Thomas Mann
- *Il Nome della Rosa* (The Name of the Rose; 1980) Umberto Eco
- *Il Giorno della Civetta* (The Day of the Owl; 1961) Leonardo Sciascia
- *La Romana* (The Woman of Rome; 1947) Alberto Moravia
- *La Storia* (History; 1974) Elsa Morante
- *Canne al Vento* (Reeds in the Wind; 1913) Grazia Deledda
- *Il Re di Girgenti* (The King of Girgenti; 2001) by Andrea Camilleri

Florence and Rome offer surprisingly affordable options. On average you should reckon on €20 to €40 for a full meal with house wine, although you can still find basic set lunch menus for €10 to €15.

A backpacker sticking religiously to youth hostels, snacking at midday and travelling slowly could scrape by on €40 to €45 per day. Your average midrange daily budget, including a sandwich for lunch and a simple dinner, as well as budgeting for a couple of sights and travel, might come to anything from €100 to €150 a day.

Public transport is reasonably priced, but car hire (p882) is expensive (as is petrol) and is probably best arranged before leaving home. On trains (p884) you can save money by travelling on the slower *regionale* and *diretto* trains.

TRAVEL LITERATURE

HOW MUCH?

Coffee at the bar €0.90-1

Bowl of pasta & pesto €6-10

Gelato €1-2

Local newspaper €0.90

Foreign newspaper €1.50-2.80

City bus/tram ride €1

10-minute taxi ride €8-10

Reams have been written on Italy and it seems like everyone's been at it, from DH Lawrence to Hermann Hesse, from Charles Dickens to Henry James. Much has also been penned in more recent times giving lucid insight into all aspects of the country. A burgeoning genre is the wide-eyed-foreigner-who-went-to-live-in-Tuscany-and-encountered-many-endearing-problems-but-loved-it-all model. And in response is the what-it's-*really*-like-living-in-rural-Italy mode (these books are rarely set in cities). For books on Italian history and society, see p56.

A Season with Verona (Tim Parks) Author of several books on Italy, Parks looks under the country's skin through the prism of Verona's second-rate football team.

A Small Place in Italy (Eric Newby) Long before it became habitual for Anglo-Saxon escapists to settle in Tuscany, one of the grand travel scribblers was there resurrecting a tumbledown farmhouse in the 1960s.

Heel to Toe: Encounter in the South of Italy (Charles Lister) Lister explores the glory and sadness of the south in his trip aboard a clapped-out moped.

Rambling on the Road to Rome (Peter Francis Browne) The author follows, on foot, the road taken a century ago by Hilaire Belloc from Toul in France to Rome and recounted in Belloc's classic *A Path to Rome*.

The Stones of Florence and **Venice Observed** (Mary McCarthy) With deceptive ease and flowing prose, McCarthy opens up all sorts of views on these two *città d'arte* (cities of art).

Too Much Tuscan Sun (Dario Castagno) Had enough of the Tuscany hype? Pick up this Chianti guide's humorous account of trailing around with oddball tourists in Castagno's beloved home turf.

Vanilla Beans & Brodo – Real Life in the Hills of Tuscany (Isabella Dusi) Dusi recounts in great colour life in the Tuscan wine town of Montalcino, her adopted home.

Venice (James Morris) Before he became Jan, Morris wrote this delicious personal ode to the lagoon city, treating with equal dexterity Venice's distant glorious past and troubled present.

INTERNET RESOURCES

Delicious Italy (www.deliciousitaly.com) Here's where to find that cooking course in Venice, learn about *mozzarella di bufala* (buffalo milk cheese) and immerse yourself in Italy's fabulous food and wine.

Ente Nazionale Italiano per il Turismo (www.enit.it) The Italian national tourist body's website has information on everything from local tourist office addresses to gallery and museum details and general introductions to food, art and history.

Italia Mia (www.italiamia.com) The best thing about this site is its mass of links. Click on art and, as well as a list of artists' biographies, you get a host of links to museums, galleries and related items around the country. Elsewhere you can explore everything from Italian cinema to genealogy.

Lonely Planet (www.lonelyplanet.com) Can get you started with summaries on Italy, links to Italy-related sites and travellers trading information on the Thorn Tree.

Trenitalia (www.trenitalia.it) Plan train journeys, check timetables and prices and book tickets on Italy's national railway's website.

Itineraries

CLASSIC ROUTES

CLASSIC CITIES
2 Weeks/Rome to Milan

Two weeks is not a long time to spend in Italy but, with a bit of planning and by seizing the moment, it's possible to undertake a whistle-stop tour of the tried and tested, throwing in a couple of hasty side tours.

Start with three days in the ancient capital of **Rome** (p90), home to the dome of St Peter's, the Sistine Chapel, the Colosseum, Trevi Fountain and more. From Rome push onto **Florence** (p457) for a mind-blowing collection of Italian art in the splendid Uffizi Gallery and elsewhere. Squeeze in a couple of day trips to **Siena** (p513), a labyrinth medieval city, and **Pisa** (p501), with its renowned leaning tower and majestic cathedral. After four days in Tuscany it's time to head north. You might make a one-day stop in **Bologna** (p416), with its graceful monuments, bustling boulevards and great food, before proceeding onto the illustrious jewel of the Adriatic, **Venice** (p339).

Spend three days marvelling at the mosaics of the Basilica di San Marco, exploring the picturesque waterways of the lagoon city and gazing at the grand houses of the Grand Canal. You can then set off west for a one-day stopover to explore the beautiful streets of historic **Verona** (p384), home to the majestic Roman Arena and the fictitious Romeo and Juliet. From there proceed west to the great metropolis of **Milan** (p257), the financial hub of the country blessed with Leonardo da Vinci's *The Last Supper*, and the chic Monte Napoleone area, one of Europe's most exclusive shopping districts.

Rome to Milan, via Florence and Venice, is a breathtaking 935km trip that you can do in a couple of weeks, but which easily merits as much time as you can give it.

FROM TOP TO TAIL: THE GRAND TOUR   1 Month/Milan to Palermo

Thankfully no longer the preserve of aristocratic young men, anyone with time on their hands can make the most of a trip to Italy by starting in the north and working slowly south (or vice versa), taking in all the attractions of a traditional grand tour as you go.

A good starting point is the financial metropolis and shopping capital of Italy, **Milan** (p257), from where you can head north and east to the glittering **Lombard lakes** (p293), then onto elegant **Verona** (p384) and the unique lagoon city of **Venice** (p339).

Take time to sample the architectural and culinary delights of **Bologna** (p416) before progressing to **Florence** (p457) for an art infusion. From there you could loop west to explore the Romanesque jewels of walled-in **Lucca** (p495) and **Pisa** (p501) of Leaning Tower fame. Swing southeast to experience the medieval splendour of **Siena** (p513) before continuing south to the equally enchanting Umbrian hill capital of **Perugia** (p543).

From Perugia let all roads lead you straight to **Rome** (p90) to discover the wonderful ancient city in all its glory before scampering onto **Naples** (p616), the chaotic metropolis of the south and one-time capital of the Kingdom of the Two Sicilies. Don't miss the fascinating ruins of **Pompeii** (p654) and the precipitous cliff-lined **Amalfi Coast** (p670) before setting off east across the bottom of the boot into Puglia to **Lecce** (p710), with its extravagant baroque palaces, and the wild **Penisola Salentina** (p714) coast. Alternatively, opt for the road along the Calabrian coast and the ferry across to the sizzling island of **Sicily** (p745), with its wealth of history, good food, stark landscapes, island hideaways, beautiful beaches and volcanic splendour. Wind up in **Palermo** (p749), the southern island's fascinating capital.

To complete the grand tour you'll need at least a month but you can extend it for as much time as you have available. Traverse a world of different cultures and a treasure chest of art along this 1720km trail from Milan to Palermo.

A CAMPAIGN IN CAMPANIA

1 Week/Naples to Parco Nazionale del Cilento e Vallo di Diano

Exploring the Mezzogiorno makes for an incredible trip, whether you want to live it up in a crazy, chaotic city, ponder the greatness of civilisations long past amid their ancient ruins or explore some of the country's most dazzling coastline.

Sitting in the shadow of Mt Vesuvius, **Naples** (p616) is a thriving metropolis where life is lived at a raucous and anarchic pace. You'll want to devote two days to exploring the city quarters around Spaccanapoli, the grand Museo Archeologico Nazionale and the city's trattorie.

Within striking distance of this fascinating city lie the ruins of two Roman settlements where daily life was frozen in time by a fierce eruption from Vesuvius. **Herculaneum** (p651), once a Roman resort town, is still being excavated and **Pompeii** (p654), Italy's premier tourist attraction offering an enthralling insight into the daily lives of the Romans, needs no introduction. You could devote a day or more to this excursion. Don't even think about leaving the Bay of Naples without making a visit to **Capri** (p642), the island home of spectacular caves, lush vegetation and charming villages. It is a magical place to spend a day or two. The **Amalfi Coast** (p670) is one of Europe's most dramatic coastlines incorporating beautiful towns such as **Positano** (p670), **Amalfi** (p673) and **Ravello** (p676) along its spine-tingling coastal route, while **Paestum** (p680), a shade further south, boasts three Greek temples that are among the best-preserved monuments of Magna Graecia. Nearby, **Agropoli** (p683) makes a handy base for Paestum and the **Parco Nazionale del Cilento e Vallo di Diano** (p682) is good for a nature injection before returning to the chaotic hustle of Naples via a quick stop in **Salerno** (p678).

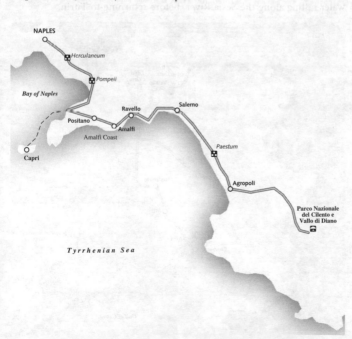

This route is short on kilometres (240km round trip) but high on interest along some of southern Italy's most densely packed coast; one week is barely enough to get to grips with this part of the south.

ROADS LESS TRAVELLED

DISCOVERING PIEDMONT   1 Week/Turin to Monte Rosa

Largely ignored in favour of seemingly more illustrious regions such as
Tuscany and Umbria, Piedmont proffers a surprising palette of options
for all tastes. **Turin** (p224), the regional capital, exudes a certain grandeur
with its proud, elegant centre and charming riverside location. It offers all
the delights of the big city, in marked contrast to the options beyond.

Head southwest for **Saluzzo** (p239), a pretty medieval town at the beginning of one of a number of enticing valleys that lead west into the French
Alps – an option worth taking up if you love nature and have some extra
time. Due east of Saluzzo you enter gastronome territory – the Langhe
hills. The nerve centre of this prestigious wine-making area is **Alba** (p239),
famed for its white truffles. With your own wheels you can explore the
villages that give their names to some fine tipples and tasty meals: **Barolo**
(p242) for noble reds; **Cinzano** (p240) for its tart liquor; or **Cherasco** (p241)
for its gourmet snail dishes. To the north is Alba's medieval arch rival, **Asti**
(p243), another wine centre (this time white). Still more reds are produced
in the verdant **Monferrato** (p243) region to its north.

From here, shoot north along the A26 to **Lago d'Orta** (p296), one of the
prettiest lakes in northern Italy. Think about an overnight stay in the
charming lakeside village of Orta San Giulio. Fans of the Alps could then
head west for **Varallo** (p245) and the Valsesia valley. At the valley's end
you butt up against the walls of the Swiss Alps. You can opt for skiing
or hiking in the shadow of the mighty 4633m-high **Monte Rosa**, or white-
water rafting along the Sesia River, before returning to Turin.

Time your Pied-
mont parade with
seasonal whims:
spring for hiking,
winter for skiing or
September for the
wine, truffle and
food festivals in the
Alba and Asti areas.
This 480km round
trip starting in the
capital, Turin, could
easily be extended
in time and distance
by further explora-
tion of the Alpine
valleys and villages
in the north and
southwest.

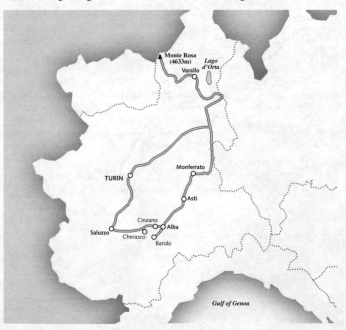

PENETRATING PUGLIA   2 Weeks/Bari to Lecce

For many backpackers, Puglia means little more than a ferry to or out of
Bari or Brindisi on the Italy–Greece route. But the region is rich in sights
and natural beauty, and boasts an addictive cuisine.

Start with the capital, **Bari** (p697), a common arrival point by rail, air
and sea, and head inland for the extraordinary **Castel del Monte** (p697).
From there swivel northeast to the fishing town of **Trani** (p695), which is
dominated by a remarkable Romanesque cathedral.

Further northwest lies the **Promontorio del Gargano** (p689), dotted with
cheerful coastal villages such as **Vieste** (p691), and the inland objective
of pilgrimage for Italians from around the country, **San Giovanni Rotondo**
(p691), home to Padre Pio. You could also consider an excursion to the
Isole Tremiti (p694).

You'll now want to backtrack south for the land of the *trulli* (conical-
roofed stone houses) centred on **Alberobello** (p703). Nearby, **Ostuni** (p706)
and **Martina Franca** (p705) are among Puglia's prettiest towns. Virtually
directly south is the tatty but impressive **Taranto** (p716).

The coast to Taranto's east is sprinkled with some great beaches. Follow them around to **Gallipoli** (p716) and proceed to the east coast of the
Penisola Salentina (p714), a wild, largely untouched area with some long,
quiet beaches, before winding up in **Lecce** (p710), an extravagant baroque
treasure chest.

This route of
680km will take
you the length and
breadth of one of
the south's most
fascinating regions,
a trip that can be
tailored along the
way and takes in
castles, Roman-
esque and baroque
churches, forests,
islands and wild,
empty beaches.

SAMPLING SARDINIA   1 Month/Cagliari to Santa Maria Navarrese

The attractions of Sardinia are no secret to Italians, but the majority of foreign visitors to Italy have yet to include this spectacular island on their itinerary – it is a world apart and the perfect place to combine fascinating historical sites with spectacular scenery and some all-essential beach R&R.

The capital, **Cagliari** (p817), is an attractive city with a hilly medieval town centre and its own lovely beach. Moving up the west coast, you shouldn't miss the **Costa Verde** (p828), a magnificent stretch of coastline that remains unspoilt and offers idyllic spots for swimming and sunbathing. The **Nuraghe Su Nuraxi** (p832) fortress, a vast nuraghic complex dating from 1500 to 400 BC, is just inland. To the northwest, on the **Sinis Peninsula** (p830), you'll encounter the ancient Roman city of **Tharros** (p830), which boasts ruins of significant archaeological interest.

Head north to the charming town of **Bosa** (p833) and its fine beach before continuing on the dramatic coastal road to **Alghero** (p834), a pretty, walled port town and a good base to explore more of the island's superb coast. Swinging east, you can follow the beaches to **Santa Teresa di Gallura** (p841), which is not a bad base for the northeast part of the island, or make for **La Maddalena** (p842), at the heart of a captivating archipelago.

The province of **Nuoro** (p845) has isolated inlets, spectacular gorges, deep caves and wonderful walking trails, and will give you a unique taste of the island's traditional culture. The most spectacular bit of coast, the **Golfo di Orosei** (p845), can either be explored by boat or on foot from **Cala Gonone** (p850) to the north or the more laid-back **Santa Maria Navarrese** (p849), further south. From here, beach-lovers with wheels can complete a slow circuit back to Cagliari along the coast road.

Discover this spectacular island in a leisurely 900km round trip (take as long or as short as you like) starting in the capital, Cagliari.

TAILORED TRIPS

TASTEBUDS ON TOUR

You don't need to go far in Italy to experience *cucina italiana* at its best, but if you're passionate about food and take your wine seriously, a trip to the gastronomic heart of Italy – Emilia-Romagna, Tuscany and Umbria – is a must.

Stock up your cupboards at **Mercato delle Erbe** (p422) in **Bologna** (p416), and complete your store with a bottle of the finest balsamic vinegar from **Modena** (p425). By now you'll be hungry so have your antipasto in one of the most famous of foodie towns, **Parma** (p432), home to Italy's best prosciutto and *parmigiano reggiano* (Parmesan cheese).

For the *primo piatto* (first course) it's off to **Umbria** (p541) for some *umbricelli* pasta served with shaved truffles, or even the elusive *tartufo nero* (black truffle) from around **Norcia** (p572), if you're lucky.

For the *secondo piatto* (second course), sample the famous *bistecca alla fiorentina* (steak) from **Florence** (p457), or *porchetta* (an Umbrian speciality of suckling pig stuffed with its liver, wild fennel and rosemary) in **Perugia** (p543).

Wash it all down with a glass of red wine from the **Chianti** (p511) region or a drop of white from **Orvieto's** (p573) vineyards. Finally, finish off with **Siena's** (p513) *panforte* (a flat, hard cake with candied fruits and nuts), or *cantucci e vin santo* (crisp *biscotti*, or biscuits, dipped in the local sweet wine, *vin santo*), another Tuscan favourite.

WORLD HERITAGE SITES

With its vast historical legacy, it's no surprise that Italy is home to 40 World Heritage sites. They are a grand mix of natural and manmade, but the latter are in the majority. You'll need plenty of time to get around them all (visit http://whc.unesco.org for a comprehensive list), but if you prefer the past in more manageable doses, you could try the following selection of Italy's World Heritage best.

Start at the Roman resort town of **Tivoli** (p180) before pushing onto some of Tuscany's historic towns – take your pick from **Florence** (p457), **Siena** (p513), **San Gimignano** (p521), **Pisa** (p501) and **Pienza** (p529), as all their town centres are designated sites.

From Tuscany it's a short hop to **Modena's** (p425) fine Romanesque cathedral, **Ravenna's** (p444) stunning early Christian and Byzantine mosaics and the splendid Renaissance city of **Ferrara** (p439).

Then turn your attention to **Urbino** (p585), one of Italy's best-preserved and most beautiful hill towns. Finally, finish in **Assisi** (p558), the picturesque home of St Francis, which attracts millions of tourists and pilgrims each year.

SHAKESPEAREAN ITALY

The jury is out on whether Shakespeare actually made it to Italy at all but, with nearly a third of his plays set here, there's no doubt about the importance of the country to the Bard's works.

You don't need to be a literary genius to work out Italy's connection with *The Merchant of Venice*, likewise *The Two Gentlemen of Verona*. But did you know that *The Taming of the Shrew* was set in **Padua** (p375), that *All's Well That Ends Well* has a couple of scenes in **Florence** (p457), and that **Sicily** (p745) features briefly in *The Winter's Tale*?

Rome (p90) has links to a veritable slew of big names: *Antony and Cleopatra, Coriolanus, Cymbeline, Julius Caesar* and *Titus Andronicus,* and let's not forget that *Othello* begins in the grand republic of **Venice** (p339).

But perhaps the most famous are those star-crossed lovers from fair **Verona** (p384), where you can actually visit a house claiming to be Juliet's. It's a shame about one little historical detail: Romeo and Juliet didn't exist!

A VOLCANOLOGIST'S VENTURE

From Naples you can see the brooding **Mt Vesuvius** (p653) in the distance, and this is your first objective – trek to the top and visit the Museo dell'Osservatorio. A little further south you can witness the devastation

caused by the world's best-known volcano disaster in the Roman town of **Pompeii** (p654).

Take a ferry or hydrofoil from Naples direct to **Stromboli** (p774), the dramatic volcano-island in the Aeolian group off northeast Sicily. This is possibly one of the most stunning places in Italy to spend a night or two, especially if the volcano is rumbling!

While in the Aeolian Islands you could pay a visit to the volcanic **Vulcano** (p770), with its crater and mud baths, the pumice mines of the main island, **Lìpari** (p767), and the grottoes of distant **Filicudi** (p775).

From Lìpari board a ferry for Milazzo or Messina, from where you can travel south in the shadow of Italy's most powerful volcanic symbol, **Mt Etna** (p788), to the city of **Catania** (p783), with its unique buildings made of local lava stone. A visit to the brooding Mt Etna itself, perhaps including a guided trip to the nearby **Valle del Bove** (p789) to trail the most recent lava flows, is a must. Ferry connections from Catania facilitate the trip back to Naples.

Snapshot

Spring is a time of reawakening from winter lethargy, and nowhere more so than in mostly sunny Italy. But in 2005 Italians barely had time to think about pulling summer clothes out of storage before the country was rocked by two extraordinary, if perhaps predictable, events.

At around 9.30pm on 2 April, 84-year-old Pope John Paul II died after weeks of illness. The doughty Polish pontiff, immediately dubbed Magnus (The Great) by his cardinals, had reigned over the Catholic Church for 26 years.

Millions flocked to Rome to join endless queues to bid the Pope farewell as he lay in state before his funeral. The simplicity of his coffin was contrasted by the pomp of the occasion, which attracted three US presidents (one current, two former) and a host of leaders from around the planet. Loathed by some for his uncompromising stand on issues such as abortion and contraception, the man also excited fervid support. Crowds gathered for his funeral chanted '*santo subito!*' (sainthood now). By the time he was buried in the crypt of St Peter's, enough miracles had been anecdotally attributed to John Paul II to justify his nomination. If his German friend and successor Pope Benedict XVI (Joseph Ratzinger, elected on 19 April at the age of 78) has anything to do with it, John Paul II will be a saint in record time. On 13 May Benedict announced the opening of the process of beatification. He will find his predecessor a tough act to follow.

He ain't the only one. Italy's attention-seeking right-wing entrepreneur Prime Minister Silvio Berlusconi might as well not have existed in the days following the Pope's death, which occurred on the same weekend as key regional and municipal elections. Thirteen of the country's 20 regions were up for grabs, and Berlusconi's Casa delle Libertà (House of Liberties) alliance was swept aside by the loose centre-left opposition coalition headed by former prime minister and European Commission chief Romano Prodi. Berlusconi's boys hung onto just two strongholds, Lombardy and the Veneto. Berlusconi is determined to stick out his full term and not hold national elections until May 2006.

The openness of divisions among Berlusconi's partners cast a pall over his capacity to govern, something Berlusconi's natural allies outside parliament, the Confindustria employers' body, had already publicly called into question. The match between Berlusconi as Il Cavaliere (The Knight) and Prodi as Il Professore (The Professor), as the local press has long dubbed them, will no doubt be bigger than the Milan football derby.

Berlusconi's time in power has been, erm, colourful. He thinks nothing of disappearing from the public scene for a quick facelift or hair transplant. 'When I look in the mirror, I am happy to see my image reflects how youthful I feel,' he smiles like a Cheshire cat. 'It's also a matter of respect for others,' he concludes in all seriousness.

Swept to power in 2001, Berlusconi has dedicated considerable energy to devising laws apparently aimed at getting him and his cronies off the hook in a series of fraud and corruption trials. However, this didn't stop the judiciary making new fraud charges against him in April 2005.

Berlusconi's decision to contribute troops to the occupation force in Iraq was bitterly contested at home and led to several abductions and killings of Italians. Ever ready with undying declarations of loyalty to his pal in Washington, George W Bush, Berlusconi astonished everyone by announcing that Italy would withdraw from Iraq in September 2005 and

FAST FACTS

Population: 57.3 million

Area: 301,230 sq km

GDP: €1364 billion

GDP per head: €23,500

GDP growth: 0.8%

Inflation: 2.3%

Income from tourism: €150 billion

Unemployment rate: 8.6% (20% in the south)

Average life expectancy: 79

Highest point: Mont Blanc (Monte Bianco) de Courmayeur at 4807m

Annual pasta consumption: 28kg per person (the nearest rival is Switzerland with 10kg per person). Sicilians eat 42kg per person every year!

then denying it. In the end, his wily foreign minister, Gianfranco Fini, announced a partial pullout from February 2006. Fini, head of the once-Fascist Alleanza Nazionale, is seen by many as a future prime minister, although his decision to go against the government and vote for three out of four amendments to a law imposing tight regulations on artificial insemination in June 2005 drew flak from his own party. The referendum on the amendments failed due to insufficient voter turnout.

'The problem isn't the euro, it's Italy'

There is plenty more spectacle where that came from. One response to the problem of clandestine immigration was a deal with Libya in 2004 to set up camps in the desert for the expatriation of illegal immigrants arriving by boat from North Africa. As hundreds disembarked almost daily on the tiny island of Lampedusa in spring 2005, the European Court blocked the expulsions to Libya on human rights grounds.

At home, Berlusconi considers the broad left opposition coalition a vipers' nest of communists and a threat to the nation. The country's judiciary, he thunders, is equally nefarious, riddled with 'politicised' judges (probably communists, too) eager to stop him from doing his good work. In mid-2005 he managed to push through a justice reform bill that, he said, would oblige judges to be less political.

In spite of Berlusconi's credentials as a businessman, and his sparkling optimism, Italy has sunk into a blue funk. The once proud Fiat motor company struggles to avoid implosion and food giant Parmalat has collapsed after €10 billion disappeared down an Enron-style black hole. Spanish and Dutch banks made unprecedented takeover moves on Italian institutions in 2005, a first in the highly protected Italian banking sector. Italian textiles are taking hits from cheap Chinese imports. In May 2005 the country slid into recession. Perma-tanned Berlusconi smiled and blamed the Easter holidays for what he called a technical blip. 'You can't expect productivity to go up when everyone's at the beach,' he quipped. Not so funny were demands from two radical coalition ministers that Italy deal with its problems by pulling out of the euro and returning to the lira. Berlusconi kept mum, the rest of the EU dismissed the remarks as 'absurd' and Prodi commented, 'The problem isn't the euro, it's Italy'.

So much bad news is enough to make you want a cigarette, but not in Italy! In January 2005, the government banned smoking (introducing a series of hefty fines) in all enclosed public areas, from offices, cafés and trains to lifts and halls in private apartment blocks.

One person who probably felt like a cigarette in March 2005 was Riccardo Muti, the mercurial musical director of Milan's La Scala opera house. After 19 years at the opera company's artistic helm, Muti was forced to step down by a revolt among staff.

Bosses of a different kind were also probably reaching for their cigs. Police nabbed Camorra chief Cosimo di Lauro in December 2004. A month later his rival, Raffaelo Amato, was picked up by Spanish cops after he lost €6000 at Barcelona gambling tables. Another Christmas present was the arrest of Calabrian 'ndrangheta boss Antonio Rosmini. These successes don't hide the fact that organised crime remains a huge problem. More than 130 people died in and around Naples in 2004 as rival Camorra gangs tore each other apart.

History

Few countries have been on such a bumpy roller-coaster ride. The Italian peninsula lay at the core of one of the greatest world powers ever known, the Roman Empire; one of the world's great monotheistic religions, Catholicism, has its headquarters in Rome; and it was largely the dynamic city-states of Italy that set the modern era in motion, with their insatiable curiosity for learning and artistic revolution that blossomed with the Renaissance. But Italy has known moments of chaos and suffering, too. The collapse of the Roman Empire brought centuries of disruption. The rise of Europe's nation states from the 16th century left the divided Italian peninsula behind. Italian unity was won in blood, but many Italians have since lived in abject poverty, sparking great waves of internal migration. Only since the economic miracle of the 1960s has Italy truly begun to rise out of the mire. Today it is no superpower but a key, vibrant pillar in the construction of the EU.

A good site for a potted history of Italy from its origins through to the 20th century is www .tricolore.net/history.htm.

PREHISTORIC ITALY

Stone Age nomadic hunter-gatherers were roaming across Italy at least 70,000 years ago and some researchers believe primitive humans may have lived in Sardinia as long as 400,000 years ago.

By around 4000 BC the Neolithic humans entering Italy from the east were bringing with them the art of land cultivation. Agriculture required people to stay in one spot and so fixed settlements emerged. It appears that the Bronze Age reached Italy around 3000 BC.

By 1800 BC Italy had been settled by numerous tribes united by the Indo-European origins of their Italic languages. North of the Apennines the main tribes were the Ligurians (in the northwest), the Raeti (later overrun by the Etruscans) and the Veneti. In Latium (today's Lazio), the dominant tribes were the Latins, who later would come to dominate the entire peninsula. Most of central Italy was inhabited by a group of tribes collectively known as the Umbro-Sabellians; the south was dominated by the Oscans.

THE ETRUSCANS & THE GREEKS

Etruscan culture reached its height from the 7th to the 6th century BC. Etruria was based on city-states mostly concentrated between the Arno and Tiber rivers. Among them were Caere (Cerveteri), Tarquinii (Tarquinia), Veii (Veio), Perusia (Perugia), Volaterrae (Volterra) and Arretium (Arezzo). Most of what we know of the Etruscan people has been deduced from artefacts and paintings unearthed at their burial sights, especially at Tarquinia near Rome.

Another general site on Italian history is www .arcaini.com/ITALY/Italy History/ItalyHistory .html. It covers in potted form everything from prehistory to the postwar period.

While the Etruscans dominated the centre of the peninsula, Greek traders settled in the south in the 8th century BC, setting up a series of independent city-states along the coast and in Sicily that together were known as Magna Graecia. They flourished until the 3rd century BC and the ruins of magnificent Doric temples in Italy's south (at Paestum) and on Sicily (at Agrigento, Selinunte and Segesta) stand as testimony to the splendour of Greek civilisation in Italy.

TIMELINE	c70,000 BC	753 BC
	Palaeolithic hunter-gatherers roam across Italy	According to legend, Romulus founds the city of Rome

SO JUST WHAT DID THE ROMANS DO FOR US?

It is often said that the Romans were not overly original, copying the Greeks in art, literature and science. But they were a canny lot who came up with some practical ideas that can only, however grudgingly, have impressed the folk they went about conquering.

More than anything else, the Romans gave us the loo. Rome's Cloaca Maxima, or Big Sewer, was created in the 8th century BC and is still in use! Romans came up with flushing latrines and regular clean water supply via aqueducts. The Turks can't really claim a patent on Turkish baths, since the idea of steam rooms and hot tubs is Roman. Indeed, the Romans created public and private bath complexes throughout the empire. Fourth century AD Rome had 11 public baths, some 900 private ones and more than 1000 public fountains.

The word 'plumbing' comes from the Latin word for lead, *plumbus*. Even today, old European plumbing uses lead pipes instead of 20th-century replacements such as PVC. Indeed, it took Europeans until well into the modern era to discover the benefits of regular bathing and proper sanitation.

The Romans were great civil engineers and another of their lasting brainwaves was... roads. As the empire grew, so did their ancient system of 'motorways'. Road engineering was an incredible feat of accuracy when you consider that the Romans had no compasses or other modern instruments. With the roads came other bright ideas – postal services and wayside inns. Messages could be shot around the empire in a matter of days or weeks by sending despatch riders. At conveniently spaced locations (not unlike modern truck stops) the riders would exchange their horses for fresh mounts, have a snack and continue on their way. This worked better than many modern postal systems in Europe! The Romans even devised a type of odometer, a cogwheel that engaged with the wheel of a chariot or other vehicle to count every Roman mile travelled.

As the Etruscans spread south of the Tiber a clash was inevitable. The Greeks of Campania overcame them in a sea encounter off Cumae in 535 BC, setting the scene for Etruscan decline. The death knell, however, would come from an unexpected source – the grubby but growing Latin town of Rome.

ROMULUS & A LIKELY STORY

Aeneas, a refugee from Troy whose mother was the goddess Venus, is said to have landed in Italy in 1184 BC and established a kingdom based at Alba Longa. The last of this line produced the twins Romulus and Remus, allegedly sired by Mars himself and suckled by a she-wolf. Romulus then went onto found Rome in 753 BC.

The Oxford History of the Roman World, edited by John Boardman, Jasper Griffin and Oswyn Murray, is a succinct and clearly set out introduction to the history of ancient Rome.

All a shade far-fetched, but somewhere along the line myth gives way to fact. Seven kings are said to have followed Romulus and at least three were historical Etruscan rulers, indicating that Rome was under some degree of Etruscan control. The last of Rome's Etruscan chiefs, Tarquinius, was ejected in 509 BC by disgruntled Latin nobles and the Roman Republic was established.

The republic got off to a rocky start, with infighting in Rome and a struggle to gain ascendancy over neighbouring Latin towns. This accomplished, the Romans decided to deal with the troublesome Etruscans by conquering the town of Veii in 396 BC. In the following century Etruscan cities were either defeated or entered into a peaceful alliance with the increasingly powerful Romans: Etruscan culture and language slowly disappeared.

264–241 BC	218–202 BC
Rome fights the First Punic War against rival Carthage	Hannibal invades Italy and launches the Second Punic War, in which Italy gained territory in Spain

THE REPUBLIC AT WORK

Under the republic, *imperium,* or regal power, was placed into the hands of two consuls who acted as political and military leaders and were elected for nonrenewable one-year terms by an assembly of the people. The Senate, whose members were appointed for life, advised the consuls.

Although from the beginning monuments were emblazoned with the initials SPQR (Senatus Populusque Romanus, or the Senate and People of Rome), the 'people' initially had precious little say in affairs. (The initials are still used and many Romans would argue that little has changed.) Known as plebeian (literally 'the many'), the disenfranchised majority slowly wrested concessions from the patrician class in the more than two centuries that followed the founding of the republic. Some plebs were even appointed as consuls.

Abroad, defeated city-states were not taken over directly; rather they were obliged to become allies. They retained their government and lands but had to provide troops on demand to serve in the Roman army. This increased the republic's military strength, and the protection offered by Roman hegemony induced many cities to become allies voluntarily.

The Romans were a rough-and-ready lot. Rome did not bother to mint coins until 269 BC, even though the neighbouring (and later conquered or allied) Etruscans and Greeks had long had their own currencies. The Etruscans and Greeks also brought writing to the attention of Romans, who found it useful for documents and technical affairs but hardly glowed in the literature department. Eventually the Greek pantheon of gods formed the bedrock of Roman worship.

Roman Sex, by John Clarke, is the result of decades of investigation into Roman eroticism, sexual mores and social attitudes. It is at once a serious anthropological retrospective and an amusing look at a society whose attitudes to sex were very different from our own.

WARS OF EXPANSION

In 264 BC Rome found itself at war with its Mediterranean rival, Carthage (in present-day Tunisia). The bone of contention was Sicily, and when the First Punic War was over in 241 BC, Rome had won control of the island. In the following decades Rome embroiled itself in Greek affairs and marched north to evict the Gauls from the Po valley. By 218 BC all of Italy south of the Alps, except the northwest, was under Roman control.

The Carthaginians came back for more in the Second Punic War (218–202 BC). The young Carthaginian general Hannibal marched across North Africa, Spain and Gaul (modern France) to enter Italy over the Alps. He roamed the peninsula at will and inflicted several defeats on the Romans, but had no access to reinforcements until his brother Hasdrubal arrived in 207 BC.

During the ensuing stalemate, the Romans discovered a military genius of their own to match Hannibal – Publius Cornelius Scipio. Backed by a strong army, the 25-year-old general struck first at Hannibal's power base in Spain and then, in 204 BC, attacked Africa, forcing the Carthaginians to recall Hannibal to defend the capital. In 202 BC Scipio won the decisive Battle of Zama over Hannibal, who committed suicide in exile some 20 years later.

It didn't stop there. By 146 BC all of mainland Greece was under Roman control and an expeditionary force had ended a three-year siege of Carthage and razed the city to the ground. Much of North Africa came under the Roman sphere of influence.

44 BC	31 BC
Conspirators assassinate Julius Caesar after he is proclaimed dictator for life	Octavian defeats Antony and Cleopatra at Actium, Greece

MARK ANTONY'S ILL-FATED EGYPTIAN AFFAIR

After their victory in Greece over Brutus and Cassius, who had assassinated Caesar in 44 BC to revive the Republic, Octavian returned to Rome and Mark Antony departed for the East, where he intended to lead a Roman army against Parthia. Before doing so he summoned the queen of Egypt, Cleopatra VII, for questioning on her alleged aid to Cassius.

Cleopatra turned up to the meeting dressed as Venus, goddess of love, and soon had Antony like a ball of putty in her erotic hand. Rather than set off for military exploits in Parthia, he wandered off to Alexandria for a roll in the hay. Meantime, his wife Fulvia was trying to maintain his influence in Rome, where Octavian's power was growing daily.

Antony finally returned to Italy in 40 BC and agreed with Octavian to divide power. Octavian would rule over Italy and Europe and Antony over Greece and the East. Fulvia had died, so to seal the deal Antony married Octavian's half-sister Octavia.

They moved to Athens and three years later Antony finally departed for Parthia. His campaign was a disaster. Rather than go home to his wife and children in Athens he headed straight for Alexandria, where he proceeded to hand over Roman territory to Cleopatra and declared his son by her the successor to Caesar. All this was too much for Octavian and the Senate, who declared war on Cleopatra and outlawed Antony. Antony led a fleet to Actium, off Greece, in 31 BC, but was soundly defeated – Cleopatra's 60 vessels turned tail almost from the outset. The following year Antony committed suicide. Several weeks later, having failed to seduce Octavian and unwilling to be paraded around the streets of Rome as a defeated enemy, Cleopatra too took her life.

DEMISE OF THE REPUBLIC

As the 2nd century BC drew to a close, Rome slipped into a period of factional strife exacerbated by problems abroad. Germanic tribes moving across northern Europe in search of land challenged Roman authority in client states and attacked Gaul. The result was the rise in political power of the generals and ultimately the proclamation in 82 BC of the dictatorship of Cornelius Sulla. The tendency to appoint dictators and so get around the limits placed on consuls eroded Rome's republican base. In the coming decades power was shared largely under the old pals act, with characters such as Gnaeus Pompeius Magnus (Pompey the Great) dominating the scene. In 59 BC Pompey helped a rising military star, Gaius Julius Caesar, to the consulship, after which he left to conquer Gaul between 58 BC and 51 BC.

Caesar's treatment of the Gauls was mild and the area became his power base. Pompey's jealousy of Caesar's success led to civil war and ultimately to Caesar's proclamation as dictator for life – to all intents and purposes signalling the end of the Republic. He launched a series of reforms, overhauled the Senate and embarked on a building programme (of which the Curia and Basilica Giulia, see p113, remain).

Grown too powerful for even his friends, Caesar was assassinated on the Ides of March (15 March) in 44 BC. One deed in blood seems to beget more and in the years following Caesar's death, his lieutenant, Mark Antony (Marcus Antonius), and his nominated heir, great-nephew Octavian, plunged into civil war against Caesar's assassins. Things calmed down as Octavian took control of the western half of the empire and Antony headed to the east, but when Antony fell head over heels for Cleopatra VII in 31 BC, Octavian finally claimed victory over Antony and Cleopatra.

The colourful life and times of Julius Caesar are examined in greater detail at www.iol.ie/~coolmine/typ/romans/romans6.html.

AD 79	117–38
The massive eruption of Mt Vesuvius all but destroys towns of Pompeii and Herculaneum	The Roman Empire reaches its greatest extent, from Britain to Parthia, under Hadrian

A NEW ORDER

Octavian was left as sole ruler of the Roman world but, remembering Caesar's fate, trod carefully. In 27 BC he surrendered his powers to the Senate, which promptly gave them back. Four years later his position was regularised again, with the Senate voting him the unique title of Augustus (Your Eminence). By 19 BC, with all-important control of the army in his hands, Augustus had cemented his position as virtual emperor of Rome.

The new era of political stability that followed allowed the arts to flourish. Augustus was lucky in having as his contemporaries the poets Virgil, Horace and Ovid, as well as the historian Livy. He encouraged the visual arts, restored existing buildings and constructed many new ones. During his reign the Pantheon was raised and he boasted that he had 'found Rome in brick and left it in marble'.

Augustus reigned for 40 years and things remained stable under his successor Tiberius (AD 14–37). After that, things degenerated quickly. Gaius Caligula (37–45) was plain nutty, Claudius (46–53) unprepossessing but conscientious, and Nero (54–68) hell-bent on upsetting everyone with his obsession with all things Greek. With the provinces in uproar, the Senate impeached Nero, who committed suicide.

Stability was restored with Vespasian (69–79), who made a point of rebuilding the temple on the Capitoline Hill and constructing a huge amphitheatre in Nero's Domus Aurea.

PAX ROMANA

Despite the shenanigans of some wayward emperors, the Empire was never in any serious danger. Indeed, the long period of comparatively enlightened rule that started with Augustus brought about an unprecedented degree of prosperity and security to the Mediterranean. The Empire reached its maximum extent and was, in the main, wisely administered.

By AD 100 the city of Rome is said to have had more than 1.5 million inhabitants and all the trappings of the imperial capital – its wealth and prosperity were obvious in the rich mosaics, marble temples, public baths, theatres, circuses and libraries. An extensive network of aqueducts fed the baths and provided private houses with running water and flushing toilets.

The Empire extended from the Iberian peninsula, Gaul and Britain to a line that basically followed the Rhine and Danube rivers. All of the present-day Balkans and Greece, along with the areas known in those times as Dacia, Moesia and Thrace (considerable territories reaching to the Black Sea), were under Roman control. Most of modern-day Turkey, Syria, Lebanon, Palestine and Israel was occupied by Rome's legions and linked up with Egypt. From there a deep strip of Roman territory stretched along the length of North Africa to the Atlantic coast of what is today northern Morocco. The entire Mediterranean was a Roman lake.

Trajan (98–117) was an experienced general of Spanish birth who conquered the Parthians and devoted considerable energy to the upkeep and building of highways, aqueducts, bridges, canals and ports. He improved the postal system and instituted loans and grants to stimulate agriculture.

For a detailed run-down on Roman emperors from Caesar to Caligula, check out www.roman-emperors.org.

I, Claudius and *Claudius the God*, by Robert Graves, delve into all sorts of aspects of imperial Rome at the time Claudius was in charge.

Gaius Caligula, apart from engaging in incest with his sisters, is also said to have proposed making his horse a consul.

Emperor Constantine I ends persecution of the Christians and grants them freedom to worship

German Odovacar proclaims himself king in Rome, sealing the end of the Roman Empire

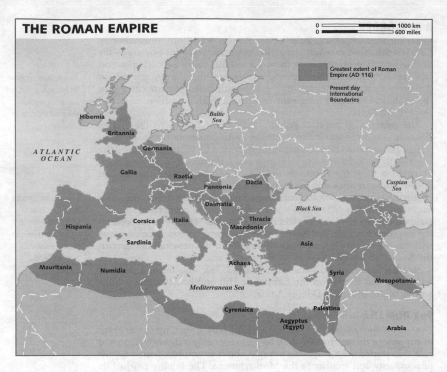

THE ROMAN EMPIRE

0 [===] 1000 km
0 [===] 600 miles

Greatest extent of Roman
Empire (AD 116)

Present day
International
Boundaries

Hadrian (117–38) gave priority to the maintenance of a peaceful and prosperous Empire, well guarded by disciplined garrisons along its long frontiers. In Britain, for instance, he built Hadrian's Wall from the mouth of the River Tyne to the Solway Firth.

The reigns of Antonius Pius (138–61) and the philosopher-emperor Marcus Aurelius (161–80) were stable, but the latter spent 14 years fighting invaders along the Danube and from Parthia, stretching the Empire's resources to the limit. His inept successor, Commodus (180–92), managed to empty the imperial coffers and presided over a series of crises within the Empire as economic stagnation in Italy and Gaul pushed citizens to revolt. When the North African Septimius Severus (193–211) came to power, he was kept busy for four years by civil strife. He subsequently brought a steadying hand to imperial finances and defence.

DECLINE OF THE EMPIRE

By the time Diocletian (284–305) became sole emperor, the world had changed. Autocratic rule was the norm and the military wielded effective power. Attacks on the Empire from without and revolts within had become part and parcel of imperial existence. A disturbing new religious force was also rapidly gaining popularity. Christians had been a harmless minority, but in these trying times it became increasingly easy to target them as a cause

| Lombards invade and occupy northern Italy | Pepin the Short ousts the Lombards and recognises the power of popes over the Papal States |

of the Empire's problems. Although Empirewide persecution occurred rarely, localised campaigns against Christians were not uncommon.

Constantine I (sole emperor 324–337) reversed Diocletian's policy of persecuting Christians, converted to the monotheistic religion and granted Christians full freedom to worship in 313.

Shortly thereafter Constantine founded Constantinople, on the Bosporus in Byzantium, as a new strategic centre, but he still lavished attention on the ageing capital, Rome. His ambitious building programme included churches such as the Basilica di San Lorenzo Fuori-le-Mura (p125), Santa Croce (p127) and Basilica di Costantino (p115) in the Roman Forum and his own triumphal arch, Constantine's Arch.

Constantine's successors were constantly engaged in defensive wars. Valentinian (364–75) and his brother Valens (364–78) split the imperial administration in two, with the elder and more capable Valentian taking the western half. Unity was preserved in name until the death of their successor, Theodosius, in 395. One of his sons, Honorius, ruled the Western Roman Empire, while his other son, Arcadius, ruled the Eastern Roman Empire.

The Roman Marcus Tullio Tiro invented shorthand in 63 BC.

The Western Empire collapsed under the weight of barbarian invasion and ceased to exist in 476 when the German, Odovacar, proclaimed himself king. He was trounced by the Ostrogoth Theodoric in 493, who ruled in Italy until 526.

The Eastern Empire, with its capital in Constantinople, managed to survive. By the time Justinian I (527–65) came to the imperial throne, the Roman Empire (that is, what was left of its eastern half) stretched from parts of present-day Serbia and Montenegro across to Asia Minor, a coastal strip of what is now Syria, Lebanon, Jordan and Israel down to Egypt and a strip of North Africa as far west as modern Libya.

Justinian, however, had a dream. He saw the glory of Rome restored and embarked on a series of wars of reconquest. At the height of his success he had retaken most of Italy and even extended imperial power as far as coastal Spain, but the gains proved short-lived. Within three years of Justinian's death, the Lombard tribes lurking to the north of Italy launched invasions of the peninsula. The Byzantines were left with Ravenna and other pockets along the southeast coast of Italy.

In Rome, the western Church asserted itself as a spiritual and secular force. Pope Gregory I (590–604) set the pattern of Church administration that was to guide Catholic services and rituals throughout history.

LOMBARD ITALY & THE PAPAL STATES

The Lombards were a Swabian people from the lower basin of the Elbe who settled around Milan, Pavia and Brescia and took over the south Italian duchies of Spoleto and Benevento. The Byzantines were left in nominal control over much of the rest.

In an effort to unseat the Lombards, Pope Stephen II invited the Franks to invade Italy, which they duly did in 754 and 756 under the command of their king, Pepin the Short. The popes were, even at this early stage, an incredibly canny lot. The papacy invented the Donation of Constantine, a document in which Constantine I purportedly granted the Church control of the city of Rome and surrounding territories. At this point Rome was theoretically controlled by the Byzantine Duke of Rome. In return for

1130	1240–70
Norman Roger II crowned king of Sicily, creating a united southern Italian kingdom	Italian cities, among them Florence, Genoa, Milan, Pisa and Venice, rise as powerful city-states

the papal blessing and an ill-defined say in Italian affairs, Pepin marched into Italy, defeated the Lombards and at the same time declared the creation of the Papal States (ie territories under the direct political control of the pope), to be made up of hitherto Byzantine-controlled lands.

Pepin's son and successor, Charlemagne, confirmed his father's backing for the Papal States. In return he was crowned emperor by Pope Leo III on Christmas Day 800 and the concept of the Holy Roman Empire came into being. The bond between the papacy and the Byzantine Empire was thus forever broken and political power in what had been the Western Roman Empire shifted north of the Alps, where it would remain for more than 1000 years.

Charlemagne's successors were unable to hold together his vast Carolingian Empire and Italy became a battleground of rival powers and states. The imperial crown was ruthlessly fought over; similarly Rome's aristocratic families engaged in battle for the papacy.

AN OASIS OF CALM

The rise of Islam in Arabia in the 7th century and its spread across North Africa led to a Muslim landing in Sicily, which had been fully occupied only in 902. The Muslims (who were known as Saracens in Italy), a mix of Arabs and Berbers, established a splendid civilisation. The fundamentals of Greek culture were restored and elaborated on by Muslim scholars such as the physician and philosopher Avicenna, the astronomer and geographer Al-Battani and the mathematician Al-Khwarizmi. Cotton, sugar cane, oranges and lemons were introduced in the south, taxes were lower than elsewhere in Italy and the Sicilians lived relatively peacefully under their Arab lords for more than two centuries.

The Arabs introduced spaghetti to Sicily, where 'strings of pasta' were documented by the Arab geographer Al-Idrissi in Palermo in 1150.

The Muslims soon arrived on the mainland, largely as mercenaries in the service of rival southern potentates, mostly Byzantine Greek in orientation if not always politically loyal or tied to Constantinople.

PAPACY VERSUS EMPIRE

Following the demise of the Carolingian Empire in 887, warfare broke out in earnest between north Italian rulers, who were divided in their support of Frankish and Germanic claimants (all of whom were absentee landlords) to the imperial title and throne. Finally, in 962 the Saxon Otto I was crowned Holy Roman Emperor in Rome, the first of a long line of Germanic rulers to hold the post until 1806.

Inevitably, the two protagonists in the creation of this illusory successor to the Roman Empire must end up in conflict. In the course of the 11th century, a heated contest over who had the right to invest bishops in Germany brought the popes and emperors to a stand-off. After Pope Gregory VII excommunicated Emperor Henry IV, the latter literally came to the pope on his knees to beg forgiveness. Gregory thus won enormous political power, since the pope would clearly only nominate bishops friendly to Rome.

In the following two centuries imperial armies, on one pretext or another and frequently with the aim of underlining the Empire's theoretical authority over the cities of northern Italy, would descend on the peninsula with monotonous regularity. This conflict formed the focal point of Italian politics in the late Middle Ages and two camps emerged:

1309	1348
Pope Clement V shifts papacy to Avignon in France, where it remained for almost 70 years	The Black Death (bubonic plague) wreaks havoc across Italy, decimating the population

Guelphs (Guelfi, in support of the pope) and Ghibellines (Ghibellini, in support of the emperor).

NORMAN CONQUEST OF THE SOUTH

As popes and emperors duelled in the north, Christian Norman zealots arrived in southern Italy in the early 11th century. In the following decades they ably exploited local conflicts between Muslim, Byzantine and other independent rulers to gain control. Roger II was crowned king of Sicily in Palermo in 1130, thus creating a unified kingdom of the south.

The Normans assimilated and adapted local culture. The result could be seen in their architecture, in which elements of Romanesque simplicity, Muslim elegance and Byzantine decorative splendour all shone through. King Roger's magnificent Cappella Palatina (in Palermo, p752) and the cathedral at Monreale (just outside Palermo, p761) are excellent examples of the Norman genius for adaptation and fusion.

Norman rule gave way to Germanic as the son of Holy Roman Emperor Frederick I (Barbarossa), Henry, was married to Constance de Hauteville, heir to the Norman throne in Sicily. Barbarossa's grandson, Frederick II, became Holy Roman Emperor in 1220. An enlightened ruler, Frederick, who became known as Stupor Mundi (Wonder of the World), was a warrior and a scholar who also allowed freedom of worship to Muslims and Jews.

Charles of Anjou won the struggle for succession after Frederick II's death, but French dominion brought heavy taxes, particularly on rich landowners who did not accept such measures graciously. Despite his efforts to improve infrastructure, open silver mines and reform administration, the Sicilians loathed him and finally revolted in 1282. The rising came to be known as the Sicilian Vespers. Locals handed the crown to Peter III, the Catalano-Aragonese ruler of the Crown of Aragon (northeast Spain).

For a range of topics on medieval Italy, see www .medioevoitaliano.org. The site contains links to subjects on medieval Italy, mostly in Italian but also in English. You can join special interest forums.

ITALY OF THE COMMUNES

While the south of Italy tended to centralised rule, the north was heading the opposite way. Port cities such as Genoa, Pisa and especially Venice, along with internal centres such as Florence, Milan, Parma, Bologna, Padua, Verona and Modena, became increasingly insolent towards attempts by the Holy Roman Emperors to meddle in their affairs.

The cities' growing prosperity and independence also brought them into conflict with Rome, which found itself increasingly incapable of exercising influence over them. Indeed, at times Rome's control over some of its own Papal States was challenged.

Between the 12th and 14th centuries, these city-states developed new forms of government. Venice adopted an oligarchic, 'parliamentary' system in an attempt at limited democracy. More commonly, the city-state created a *comune* (town council), a form of republican government dominated at first by aristocrats but then increasingly by the wealthy middle classes. The well-heeled families soon turned their attentions from business rivalry to political struggles in which each aimed to gain control of the *signoria* (government).

In some cities, great dynasties, such as the Medici in Florence and the Visconti and Sforza in Milan, came to dominate their respective stages.

1469–92	1506
Florence's Lorenzo de' Medici rules Italy's most flourishing Renaissance city	Work starts on St Peter's Basilica, to a design by Donato Bramante, in Rome

War between the city-states was also a constant, and eventually a few emerged as small regional powers and absorbed their neighbours.

In Florence, prosperity was based on the wool trade, finance and general commerce. Abroad, its coinage, the *firenze* (florin), was king. By dint of war and purchase, Florence acquired control of almost all Tuscany by the 1450s – only Siena and Lucca remained beyond the city's grasp.

In Milan, the noble Visconti family destroyed its rivals and extended Milanese control over Pavia and Cremona, and later Genoa. Giangaleazzo Visconti (1351–1402) turned Milan from a city-state into a strong European power. The policies of the Visconti (up to 1450), followed by those of the Sforza family, allowed Milan to spread its power to the Ticino area of Switzerland and east to the Lago di Garda.

The Milanese sphere of influence butted up against that of Venice. By 1450 the lagoon city had reached the height of its territorial greatness. In addition to its possessions in Greece, Dalmatia and beyond, Venice had expanded inland. The banner of the Lion of St Mark flew across northeast Italy, from Gorizia to Bergamo.

The strength and prosperity of these city-states was always in flux, and at times greater forces wrought havoc on them. Indeed, Europe of the 14th century was a continent ripe for disaster. Population growth, mismanaged agriculture and urban overcrowding lead to famine and paved the way for the horrors of the plague.

In 1348 the first great wave of plague swept across Italy and much of the rest of western Europe, decimating urban centres (Florence is said to have lost three-quarters of its populace) and wreaking havoc in the country as well. The Black Death, as the disease came to be known, remained a constant of life in Europe well into the next century, visiting death and suffering on one region or another with frightening frequency.

History of the Italian People, by Giuliano Procacci, is one of the best general histories of the country in any language. It covers the period from the early Middle Ages until 1948.

HUMANISM

As the 15th century progressed, more universities and private schools were founded to educate a growing army of scholars, diplomats and public servants. A lively intelligentsia emerged, whose protagonists frequently moved from one court to another, enriching their knowledge and scholarly interchange.

As early as the 12th century, Averroës, a Muslim philosopher born in Córdoba (Spain), had resurrected Aristotle's doctrine that immortality was gained through individual efforts towards universal reason. This emphasis on the autonomy of human reason was a revolutionary philosophical position that by the 15th century became known as humanism.

The thirst for classical knowledge was accelerated by the arrival of Greek scholars from Byzantium, fleeing before the Turks (who took Constantinople in 1453). Through them, Western European scholars rediscovered the works of the ancients, especially key figures including Plato and Aristotle. A rigorous scientific approach to learning, frequently flying in the face of Church doctrine, characterised the *studia humanitatis* (study of the humanities).

The Church had grave misgivings about the new learning, which shifted the emphasis away from God to human reason (and hence potentially weakened the Church's authority), but it could do little to stem

1562–63	1571
The Counter-Reformation is launched at the Council of Trent, confirming the split between Catholics and Protestants	Combined European fleet, more than half provided by Venice, defeats Turks in the Battle of Lepanto

A WHOLLY UNHOLY POPE & HIS DANGEROUS CHILDREN

The popes of 15th-century Italy were a different breed. They fought wars to maintain their territories, indulged in political assassination, kept mistresses and had children by them. Most were motivated more by the desire for personal gain or dynastic interest than spiritual concerns.

The Spaniard Rodrigo Borgia, who became Pope Alexander VI in 1492 in probably the most corrupt election in papal history, took the biscuit. He established a notoriously licentious court and throughout his papacy maintained a mistress, Vannozza Catanei, who bore him several infamous offspring – all of whom the pope shamelessly manoeuvred into positions worthy of their descent!

Alexander's son Cesare, who killed his own brother, terrorised Italy in a campaign to consolidate and expand the Papal States. Ruthless, brilliant and an all-round nasty fellow (his victims were often found floating down the Tiber), Cesare's campaign went well until Pope Julius II – a bitter enemy of the Borgia family – came to the throne in 1503. Cesare, stripped of his territories and deported to Spain, died four years later.

His sister, Lucrezia, has gone down in history, perhaps unfairly, as the embodiment of Borgia cruelty, lust and avarice. It is said Pope Alexander was obsessed with his daughter to the point of incest. He ensured that she lived in incredible luxury and considered no man worthy of her. Nevertheless, Lucrezia married several times – one of her husbands was assassinated by Cesare and another was publicly declared impotent by Alexander. She finally ended up with Alfonso d'Este, the duke of Ferrara. In hindsight it appears she was, in the main, an instrument of her father's and brother's machinations rather than a willing participant.

it. The seats of Italian government increasingly sought the prestige of the presence of scholars in their midst. Venice, Florence, Milan and lesser cities frequently thumbed their noses at Rome and sheltered scholars considered heretics by the papacy.

Weakened by the Great Schism of the 14th century, during which the papacy found itself exiled in Avignon from 1309 to 1377 and then with rival popes in Avignon and Rome from 1378 to 1417, the Church was in no position to argue.

THE RENAISSANCE

The Church would indeed embrace aspects of the new learning. Rome had suffered incredible neglect but after the schism the papacy initiated a programme of urban transformation. This coincided with the coming of the Renaissance, the inevitably explosive artistic offshoot of humanism.

The Vatican became one of the greatest Italian patrons of a new wave of artists, sculptors and architects. Donatello, Sandro Botticelli and Fra Angelico all lived and worked in Rome at this time. At the beginning of the 16th century, Pope Julius II asked Bramante to begin work on the second St Peter's Basilica. In 1508 Raphael started painting the rooms in the Vatican now known as Stanze di Raffaello (p136), while between 1508 and 1512 Michelangelo worked on the Sistine Chapel (p137).

Rome, which had a population of 100,000 and was a major centre of political cultural life, was a generous patron, but the impulses for artistic creation and development in Renaissance Italy were multiple. Indeed the real stimulus came from the city-states. Wealth, humanistic thought and artistic revolution went hand in hand.

John Julius Norwich's *A History of Venice* is one of the all-time great works on the lagoon city in English and is highly readable. He has more recently published *Venice: Paradise of Cities*.

In Florence, the Medici family and especially Lorenzo Il Magnifico (the Magnificent), saw diplomatic value and prestige in patronising the fine arts. He enriched the city with the presence, and works, of the greatest artists of the time, particularly Michelangelo. Feudal lords such as Federico da Montefeltro in Urbino and Milan's Francesco Sforza competed with each other for the services of artists, writers, poets and musicians.

The Venice of the Dogi, which had always tended to stand aloof from the rest of Italy, boarded the Renaissance train and a distinctly northern, slightly melancholy, branch of the Renaissance took off.

Not all Italian states experienced the great social blossoming of the Renaissance. In the south, quarrels over power and land between the Visconti family (in league with Alfonso V of Aragon) and the house of Anjou ensured the repression of the liberty and free thinking that had inspired the new sense of creativity and productivity in other parts of the country.

The House of Medici: Its Rise and Fall, by Christopher Hibbert, is a wonderfully told account of Florence's most powerful dynasty, which was born in the splendour of the Renaissance but petered out rather ingloriously.

THE COUNTER-REFORMATION & ITALIAN DECLINE

By the third decade of the 16th century, the broad-minded curiosity of the Renaissance had begun to give way to the intolerance of the Counter-Reformation. Art was one thing, but curious free-thinking quite another. No doubt many in Rome saw humanism as the cause of the Reformation, a term for the movement led by Germany's Martin Luther that aimed to reform the Church (and which led to the rise of Protestantism in its many forms).

The transition was epitomised by the reign of Pope Paul III (1534–49), who – in best Renaissance style – promoted the building of the Palazzo Farnese in Rome (p120) but also, in 1540, sanctioned the establishment of Ignatius Loyola's order of the Jesuits and, in 1542, of the Holy Office. The latter was the final (and ruthless) court of appeal in the trials of suspected heretics and part of the much-feared Inquisition.

Pope Paul III's fanatical opposition to Protestantism and his purging of clerical abuse, as he saw it, resulted in a widespread campaign of torture and fear. In 1559 the Church published the *Index Librorum Prohibitorum* (Index of Prohibited Books) and the persecution of intellectuals and free thinkers intensified.

Two of the great Italian intellectuals to suffer during the Counter-Reformation were Giordano Bruno (1548–1600) and Galileo Galilei (1564–1642). Bruno was a Dominican monk who was forced to flee Italy for Calvinist Geneva, from where he travelled extensively throughout Europe before being arrested by the Inquisition in Venice in 1592. In 1870 the Kingdom of Italy erected a statue of Bruno in Rome's Campo de' Fiori (p120), where he had been burnt at the stake for heresy. Galileo was forced by the Church to renounce his approval of the Copernican astronomical system, which held that the earth moved round the sun rather than the reverse.

The latter years of the 16th century were not all counterproductive. Pope Gregory XIII (1572–85) replaced the Julian calendar with the Gregorian one in 1582, fixing the start of the year on 1 January and adjusting the system of leap years to align the 365-day year with the seasons. In addition, Rome was greatly embellished by the architectural and sculptural achievements of Gian Lorenzo Bernini (1598–1680).

1804	1861
Napoleon creates the Kingdom of Italy, with himself as king of course	House of Savoy's Vittorio Emanuele II proclaimed king of a newly united Italy

By now Italy had ceased to be at the cutting edge of European culture. Italian ports and trade had declined with the discovery of the Americas and the growth of Atlantic trade. Much of Italy was dominated by foreign powers, especially Spain. Madrid's hold was wrenched loose in the wake of the War of the Spanish Succession (1701–14) and Austria moved in to Lombardy and much of the north (except Venice and the Veneto). Tuscany was under the control of the Lorraine dynasty (and closely linked to Austria). The Bourbon dynasty installed in Naples meant the southern kingdom, or what was now known as the Kingdom of the Two Sicilies, had become independent.

THE LONG MARCH TO UNITY

The French Revolution at the end of the 18th century and the rise of Napoleon awakened hopes in Italy of an independent nation. The Napoleonic interlude (he created the Kingdom of Italy in 1804) helped foment the idea that a single Italian state could be created and many Italians hoped this would occur after Napoleon's demise. It was not to be. The reactionary Congress of Vienna restored all the foreign rulers to their places in Italy.

This backward step was bad news, but it did encourage the rapid growth of secret societies comprised, in the main, of disaffected middle-class intellectuals. In the south, the republican Carbonari society pushed hard and often ruthlessly for a valid constitution, leading a revolutionary uprising in Naples in 1820. Several abortive uprisings were put down around the country during the 1830s and 1840s.

In 1848 revolts rocked almost every major city in Europe. In their newspaper, *Il Risorgimento*, nationalist writer Cesare Balbo and Count Camillo Benso di Cavour of Turin pressed for a constitution and published their parliamentary *Statuto* (Statute). Cavour, the prime minister of the Savoy monarchy that ruled Piedmont and Sardinia, became the diplomatic brains behind the Italian unity movement. He conspired with the French and won over British support for the creation of an independent Italy. Meanwhile, revolutionary hero Giuseppe Garibaldi returned from South America. In a daring stroke he and his Red Shirts seized Sicily and Naples from the Bourbons in 1860 and handed them over to the Savoy King Vittorio Emanuele II.

The bloody Franco-Austrian War (which was also known as the war for Italian independence; 1859–61), unleashed in northern Italy, led to the occupation of Lombardy and the retreat of the Austrians to their eastern possessions in the Veneto. With Lombardy and the south in the hands of the Italians, the new Italian kingdom was proclaimed. Tuscany joined in 1861 and Venice was seized in 1866. Rome was wrested from French control only during the Franco-Prussian War in 1870. Italian unity was complete and the parliament moved from its temporary home in Florence to Rome.

The turbulent new state saw violent swings between socialists and the right. Giovanni Giolitti, one of Italy's longest-serving prime ministers (heading five governments between 1892 and 1921) managed to bridge the political extremes and institute male suffrage. Women were denied the right to vote until after WWII.

Alessandro Volta invented the electric battery in 1800 and gave his name to the measurement of electric power.

Swiss Henri Dunant created the Red Cross after witnessing the horrors of the Battle of Solferino during the 1859–61 war.

1915–18	1922
Italy joins Allies against Germany and Austria in WWI, beginning three years' heavy combat	Mussolini and his Fascists march on Rome and take power

WWI

When war broke out in Europe in July 1914, Italy chose to remain neutral despite being a member of the Triple Alliance with Austria and Germany. Italy had territorial claims to make in Trent, the southern Tyrol, Trieste and even in Dalmatia, but the new country's weakness had compelled it to appease its powerful Austrian neighbour.

In April 1915 the government changed its mind and joined the Allies on the understanding that upon the successful conclusion of hostilities Italy would receive the territories it sought. From then until the end of the war, Italy and Austria engaged in a weary war of attrition. When the Austro-Hungarian forces collapsed in November 1918, the Italians marched into Trieste and Trent. But Rome was disappointed by the postwar settlement as not all its claims were met by the Treaty of Versailles.

The young country had been manifestly ill-prepared for this gruesome conflict. Not only did Italy lose 600,000 men, but the war economy had produced a small concentration of powerful industrial barons, while leaving the bulk of the civilian populace in penury. It was an explosive cocktail.

FASCISM & WWII

In 1919 Benito Mussolini, one-time socialist and journalist, founded the Fascist Party, with its hallmarks of the black shirt and Roman salute. These were to become symbols of violent oppression and aggressive nationalism for the next 23 years. After his march on Rome in 1922 and victory in the 1924 elections, Mussolini took full control of the country by 1925.

In 1929 Mussolini and Pope Pius XI signed the Lateran Pact, whereby Catholicism was declared the sole religion of the Italian nation and the Vatican was recognised as an independent state. In return, the papacy finally acknowledged the united Kingdom of Italy.

The great dictator also embarked on an aggressive if inept foreign policy, leading to skirmishes with Greece over the island of Corfu and to military expeditions against nationalist forces in the Italian colony of Libya.

In 1935 Italy sought a new colonial conquest through the invasion of Abyssinia (present-day Ethiopia) from the Italian base in Eritrea, but it took seven months to capture Addis Ababa. The act was condemned by the League of Nations, which imposed limited sanctions on Italy.

Mussolini entered WWII on Germany's side in 1940, a move Hitler must have regretted later. Germany found itself pulling Italy's chestnuts out of the fire in campaigns in the Balkans and North Africa and could not prevent Allied landings in Sicily in 1943. The Italians had had enough of Mussolini and his war and so the king, Vittorio Emanuele III, had the dictator arrested. In September, Italy surrendered and the Germans, who had rescued Mussolini, occupied the northern half of the country and reinstalled the dictator.

The painfully slow Allied campaign up the peninsula and German repression led to the formation of the Resistance. The Nazi response to partisan attacks was savage. In one of the most notorious reprisals, 1830 men, women and children were murdered by the SS at Marzabotto, south of Bologna, in October 1944.

Novelist Rosetta Loy provides a fascinating personal view of life in Rome under the Fascists in *First Words: A Childhood in Fascist Italy*. Loy places special emphasis on the changes wrought by Mussolini's anti-Jewish race laws.

Denis Mack Smith produced one of the most penetrating works on Italy's dictator with his *Mussolini*. Along with Mussolini's career it assesses his impact on the greater evil of the time, Hitler.

For more on the history of Fascist Italy, see www.thecorner.org/hists/total/f-italy.htm. Here you can trace Mussolini's rise to power and the tumultuous years of his rule.

1939	1940
Italy invades and occupies Albania prior to start of WWII	Fascist Italy enters WWII on Nazi Germany's side and invades Greece

Northern Italy was finally liberated in April 1945 and Mussolini was strung up by Resistance fighters in Milan's Piazzale Lotto.

THE REPUBLIC

In the aftermath of war, the left-wing Resistance was disarmed and Italy's political forces scrambled to regroup. The USA, through the economic largesse of the Marshall Plan, wielded considerable political influence and no doubt used this in attempts to keep the left in check.

Immediately after the war three coalition governments succeeded one another. The third, which came to power in December 1945, was dominated by the newly formed right-wing Democrazia Cristiana (DC; Christian Democrats), led by Alcide de Gasperi, who remained prime minister until 1953.

In 1946, following a referendum, the constitutional monarchy was abolished and a republic established. It was not until the elections of April 1948, when the Constituent Assembly had finished its work, that the first government was elected under the new constitution. De Gasperi's DC won a majority and excluded the left from power. Until then, the Partito Comunista Italiano (PCI; Communist Party), led by Palmiro Togliatti, and the Partito Socialista Italiano (PSI; Socialist Party), led by Pietro Nenni, had participated in ruling coalitions.

Until the 1980s the PCI played a crucial role in Italy's social and political development, in spite of being systematically kept out of government. The party, especially under the charismatic leadership of Enrico Berlinguer, steadily increased its share of the poll and always had more card-carrying members than the DC, but the spectre of European communism and the Cold War undermined its chances of participating in government.

Not long after WWII, Norman Lewis penned The Honoured Society, *an intriguing study of Sicily, and in 2000 he returned to the subject, and especially the Mafia, with* In Sicily.

BOOM & THE YEARS OF LEAD

By the early 1950s the country's economy had begun to recover and the Cassa per il Mezzogiorno (State Fund for the South) was formed to inject funds into development projects for the country's poorer regions (including Sicily and Sardinia).

In 1958 Italy became a founding member of the European Economic Community (EEC) and this signalled the beginning of the Economic Miracle, a spurt of growth that saw unemployment drop as industry expanded. A major feature of this period was the development of Italy's automobile industry and, more particularly, of Fiat in Turin, which sparked a massive migration of peasants from the south to the north.

Influenced by similar events in France, in 1967 and 1968 Italian university students rose up in protest. Ostensibly the protests were against poor conditions in the universities, but they were really aimed at authority and the perceived impotence of the left. In 1969 the protests were followed by a series of strikes that continued into 1971.

The 1970s were dominated by the new spectre of terrorism. By 1970, a group of young left-wing militants had formed the Brigate Rosse (Red Brigades). Neo-Fascist terrorists had already struck with a bomb blast in Milan in 1969. The Brigate Rosse was the most prominent terrorist group operating in the country during the Anni di Piombo (Years of Lead) from 1973 to 1980, a period of considerable social unrest and regular protests,

Liposuction was first tried out by Dr Giorgio Fisher, a Roman gynaecologist, in 1974.

1943	1946
Allies land in southern Italy, which later declares armistice and topples Mussolini from power	Italians vote in national referendum to abolish the monarchy and create a republic

especially in the universities. In 1978 the Brigate Rosse claimed their most important victim – former DC prime minister Aldo Moro. His kidnap and murder (the subject of a film, *Buongiorno Notte,* released in 2004) shook the country. They would outdo themselves with the Bologna train station blast in 1980, killing 84 people.

Although much has happened since it was written, Paul Ginsborg's *A History of Contemporary Italy: Society and Politics 1943–1988* remains one of the single-most readable and insightful books on postwar Italy.

Despite the Brigate Rosse, the 1970s was a time of some positive change. In 1970 regional governments with limited powers were formed in 15 of the country's 20 regions (the other five, Sicily, Sardinia, Valle d'Aosta, Trentino-Alto Adige and Friuli-Venezia Giulia already had strong autonomy statutes). In the same year divorce became legal and eight years later abortion was legalised, following antisexist legislation that allowed women to keep their own names after marriage.

THE NERVOUS NINETIES & TANGENTOPOLI

A growth spurt in the 1980s saw Italy become one of the world's leading economies, but by the 1990s a new period of crisis had set in. High unemployment and inflation, combined with a huge national debt and an extremely unstable lira, led the government to introduce draconian measures to cut public spending. A series of left and centre-left governments maintained this tough course in order to join the European monetary union and, in 2001, enter the single currency.

During the 1990s the PCI reached a watershed and split. The old guard now goes by the title Partito Rifondazione Comunista (PRC; Refounded Communist Party), under the leadership of Fausto Bertinotti. The bigger and moderate breakaway wing reformed itself as Democratici di Sinistra (DS; Left Democrats).

While the communists squabbled, the rest of the Italian political scene was rocked by the Tangentopoli ('kickback city') scandal, which broke in Milan in 1992 when a PSI functionary was arrested on bribery charges. A can of worms had been opened and no-one was terribly surprised by what they saw. Led by Milanese magistrate Antonio di Pietro, investigations known as Mani Pulite (Clean Hands) implicated thousands of politicians, public officials and businesspeople. Charges ranged from bribery and receiving kickbacks to blatant theft.

Tangentopoli left two of the traditional parties, the DC and PSI, in tatters and demolished the centre of the Italian political spectrum. At the 1994 national elections, voters expressed their disgust by electing a new right-wing coalition comprised of media magnate Silvio Berlusconi's newly formed Forza Italia (Go Italy) party, the neo-Fascist Alleanza Nazionale (National Alliance) and Umberto Bossi's radical federalist Lega Nord (Northern League). The turbulent Bossi scuppered the alliance, known as the Casa delle Libertà (House of Liberties) nine months later and a series of troubled left and centre-left governments succeeded each other until national elections were called in 2001.

NATO's war with Yugoslavia in 1999 threw Italy into the international spotlight and political squabbling was minimised in the country's attempts to cope with its frontline position. In the end Italy gained brownie points as a competent and faithful ally during the conflict in which it effectively served as a giant aircraft carrier for NATO air raids on Yugoslavia.

1978	1993
Red Brigades kidnap and assassinate the former prime minister Aldo Moro	Lonely Planet publishes the first edition of *Italy*

THE RETURN OF IL CAVALIERE

Shortly after joining the euro in 2001, Rome's centre-left coalition collapsed and Berlusconi (dubbed Il Cavaliere, 'The Knight', in the press) got a second chance. The same coalition as in 1994 swept to power and this time Berlusconi's Forza Italia, which won a remarkable 30% of the vote, did not need to rely on its coalition partners. Anyone on the Left hoping for a repeat of his first short-lived fate at the helm of Italian politics would be sorely disappointed. Heading up a colourful regime, Berlusconi has maintained power in spite of a host of problems, even managing to have all corruption charges levelled against him dropped.

Berlusconi has indeed always maintained that he is a victim of left-wing 'politicised' judges hell bent on breaking this self-made tycoon-cum–prime minister. Caught between a rock and a hard place with corruption charges pending, in 2003 he passed a law giving the prime minister and other top political figures immunity from prosecution in 2003. The law was thrown out by the Constitutional Court in early 2004 and Berlusconi's trial resumed in April that year. Although several of his lieutenants received prison sentences, Berlusconi surprised and frustrated his critics when he was cleared of all charges.

Rome: the Biography of a City, by Christopher Hibbert, is a racy and anecdote-filled account of the long and often secretive past of the Eternal City.

Berlusconi is estimated to control or influence up to 90% of Italy's free TV channels, a situation he promised to rectify when he came to power. The opposite happened. The state-owned TV and radio company, RAI, has come under increasing pressure to toe the government line, leading its president to resign in May 2004, saying that RAI had become a 'mail box' for requests from the government.

Berlusconi promised in 2001 to run Italy like a corporation, chipping away at complex tax and labour laws, a stagnant public service and corruption. His determination to raise the pension age and cut benefits infuriated the left, and continues to do so. The trade unions, having unleashed a general strike over proposed labour law changes in April 2003, took to the streets again in October on the pensions issue. The unions disagree with government (and EU) assertions that the generous pension deal Italians have enjoyed for decades is unsustainable.

The man is nothing if not a character, and he's keen to leave his mark. In 2003 he gave the green light to a controversial project to build mobile dykes to protect Venice from flooding. The project has been mired in crossfire over its viability and environmental impact for decades. Berlusconi also announced a project to build a massive bridge across the Strait of Messina to link the mainland with Sicily. Optimists say it could be opened by 2011. Others say the idea is loopy.

Stuck in an economy that has been performing badly virtually since the late 1990s, Italians reacted with dismay to news of the death in 2002 of Gianni Agnelli, head of the once-mighty but now ailing Fiat car giant. Somehow his passing seemed emblematic of the country's malaise. A little light relief came with the return of the Italian royal family, Vittorio Emanuele & Co. Not with a bang, mind, more with a somewhat tail-between-the-legs whimper. Exiled since the end of WWII, the family was given permission to return by the parliament in 2002.

2001	2005
Silvio Berlusconi's right-wing Casa delle Libertà (Liberties House) coalition wins absolute majority in national polls	Pope John Paul II dies in Rome; Silvio Berlusconi suffers a big defeat in regional elections

The Culture

THE NATIONAL PSYCHE

Voluble, quick-witted, tenacious, stylish, vain, *bons vivants*, sassy, expressive…clichés about the Italian character abound. As with all clichés, there is something to them. Blessed with a land of extraordinary variety, jammed with the testimony of thousands of years of history and some of the world's greatest food and wine, the Italians certainly know how to live.

What constitutes an Italian? From the breezy nonchalance of the self-assured Roman and the laconic Neapolitan to the hard-working Milanese and the German-speaking South Tirolean in the Alto Adige, at times it seems that little really unites these people. They even have a name for their strong regional identity: *campanilismo* (an attachment to the local bell tower). Only when confronted by foreigners does the national pride of the average Italian begin to prevail over strictly local sentiment.

From the fall of the Roman Empire until reunification in 1870, the Italian peninsula was divided into an array of city-states, imperial territories belonging to one foreign nation or another and the Papal States. And so regional loyalties carry the day. The diffidence of northerners to their cousins in the south is eloquent testimony to the sometimes cagey relationship between Italians.

Cagier still is their relationship with the political system. Italians suffer few illusions about a state that seems to offer them little and demand much. Politics, justice and economic interests are all closely woven together, creating a great deal of scepticism in your average Giuseppe or

British journalist Charles Richards takes you through the murky backstage of modern Italian life in *The New Italians*. Packed with surprising revelations, not all of them bad, it's an eye-opener.

OUR THING

For a moment, it might have seemed more like the skyline over wartime Baghdad. One December morning in 2004, squadrons of air force helicopters swarmed over some of Naples' poorest districts as 1000 troops and police swept in to hunt out high-level delinquents in this, one of the heartlands of Italian organised crime. Fifty people were arrested and the operation was declared a grand success. But such is the local power of Italy's Mafia groups that when the police later came to arrest Cosimo di Lauro, one of the heads of the Camorra (the Neapolitan Mafia), the entire neighbourhood held them virtually hostage until reinforcements arrived. In spite of the occasional successes, the fight against organised crime in Italy seems destined to continue indefinitely.

Italy's Mafia comprises five distinct groups: the original Sicilian Mafia, known as Cosa Nostra (Our Thing); the Calabrian 'ndrangheta; the Camorra of Naples; and the two Puglian contributions, the Sacra Corona Unita and La Rosa. Whether operating separately or together, they constitute a formidable economic power. Their combined annual turnover of about €100 billion represents 10% of Italy's GDP, and they are said to control one in five businesses. Even if these figures are inflated, as some observers maintain, they give a pretty good idea of the problem facing the Italian police. All is made worse by the inevitable corruption of politicians, individual judges and cops. Countless costly and seemingly interminable trials of crime figures have ended fruitlessly in the past, lost in the morass of favour-trafficking that blights a significant portion of Italian political life.

These groups are involved in everything from construction and drug-trafficking through to trash. Yes, trash. The Camorra does a nice line in removing industrial waste on the cheap and dumping it on farmland in Campania. Hundreds of square kilometres in Campania have been declared toxic emergency zones as a result. According to the environmental group Legambiente, 'eco-crimes' of this kind represent 10% of organised crime profits in Italy.

Giuseppina on the street. If they can find a way around the frequently silly rules, they will.

LIFESTYLE

In a country where faith in public institutions is tepid at best, the family remains one pillar of society on which Italians continue to depend.

Typically, young Italians will stay at home at least until they have finished their studies or marry. Some remain in the parental home long after they have embarked on careers, only leaving when, married or otherwise, they have a steady job and can afford to buy their own home.

If in Anglo-Saxon countries young and even not-so-young people don't bat an eyelid at sharing apartments with other people, in Italy such arrangements are almost exclusively the domain of students who have moved from another city.

However tightly knit the Italian family may be, it is shrinking. Nearly half of all families have only one child, childless couples are no longer the exception (they made up 19% of households in 2003) and, with an average of 38% of marriages finishing in separation or divorce in 2002, single-parent families continue to grow. A quarter of all households are represented by singles.

The Church is not impressed and the recently deceased Pope John Paul II was never hesitant (Benedict XVI is likely to follow in his footsteps) to remind Italian families of their duty to procreate (sex is not for fun). Politicians agree, although they have an eye more on the future viability of the country's pension system than on morality.

It's not that Italians don't want to have children, or that women choose careers over progeny. Indeed 80% of women over 40 have a child. But they tend to leave it at one. Most families cite financial problems impeding them from having more. It might be that expectations are also higher. Conspicuous consumption of cars, clothes and indispensable accessories such as the latest mobile phones all require fiscal effort. Older folk say people nowadays are too selfish to make the sacrifices involved in having children.

But there is something in the financial argument not to have children. A Eurostat report in 2004 showed that in the years 1996 to 2002, the growth in buying power of Italian blue-collar workers rose just 0% to 7%, while the European average was around 18% (20% to 30% in the UK). Another report in 2004 showed that a typical 35-year-old engineer or production manager might earn as little as €15,000 a year – less than half of that earned by their northern European colleagues. Unfortunately the cost of living in Italy is not half.

The corollary to the low birth rate is the ageing population. Italians (as in the rest of Europe) are living longer and more healthily. As the birth

Midnight in Sicily, by Peter Robb, is a cleverly woven account of Sicily, which aside from its travelogue and culinary sidebars, is above all a revealing look at organised crime on that troubled island.

From his home in Verona, Tim Parks turns his breezy humour to the serious subject of Italian schooling in *Italian Education*.

MUMMY'S BOYS

The rough charm of the unshaven Italian Lothario is an inescapable image. The truth is perhaps a little less alluring.

According to figures published in 2001 and regularly cited in following years, Italian men constitute an *esercito di mammoni* (army of mummy's boys). If you believe the figures, 67.9% of single Italian men remain at home with mum (and dad) up to the age of 34 at least. By contrast, the figure for women is 52%. In the age group 30 to 40, 36.5% of men are still at home with the folks, while just 18% of women are yet to flee the familial nest.

And even after the big move, one in three continue to see *la mamma* every day (usually armed with a big appetite and a dirty washing basket), a habit not always appreciated by spouses!

For a light-hearted look at Italian life and culture, visit www.italiansrus .com. More glitzy and serious, www.italian culture.net has comprehensive information.

rate stays low and the work force begins to shrink, this will mean big problems for the country's generous pension system.

Italy remains a country of conservative mores. While, for example, cohabiting among unmarried couples is becoming more widespread (almost 13% of couples married since 1987 had lived together beforehand) and homosexuality is well tolerated in major cities, the very idea of gay marriages has most politicians choking on their cappuccino.

POPULATION

Italy's population is one of the oldest in the world and if it weren't for immigration it would actually be shrinking. With around 10 million people over 65 (out of a total population of 58 million), Italians are dying more quickly than they're arriving. And, half of those elderly people are living alone.

An average of 2.1 children per woman is needed to keep the population stable, a feat that would require a procreative surge worthy of Casanova. Currently Italian women average 1.3 children a head.

By January 2004 it was estimated some 2.6 million foreigners were living in Italy, but figures are hard to pin down because of the number of illegal residents.

The cities of Rome, Milan and Naples continue to top the population charts, although some figures show a slight drift away from the cities.

SPORT
Football

No other sport in Italy enjoys anything like the saturation media coverage given to *il calcio* (football). Formula One comes the closest but even then only when Ferrari is winning.

Italy produces some of Europe's most exciting football. In the past decade, two of their sides, Turin's Juventus and AC Milan, have dominated the game at home and frequently made it to the finals of Europe-wide competitions. In May 2005 AC Milan snatched defeat from the jaws of victory, losing on penalties to Liverpool (after leading 3–0 at half time) in the Champions League final played in Istanbul.

Check out www.lega-calcio .it, Italy's official football site, for the latest Serie A results. For info in English, try www.channel 4.com/sport/football _italia/magazine.html.

Italy's club teams have traditionally done well in European tournaments – 10 European Cups (eight of them between Milan's AC Milan and Inter teams!) and nine UEFA Cups is the tally so far. The national team, the Azzuri (Blues), are also among the world's best, although a limp showing in the 2002 World Cup didn't impress many. Two years earlier they narrowly lost the final of the European championship to the French who'd also put them out of the 1998 World Cup. Italy has picked up the World Cup three times (1934, 1938 and 1982) and won the European Championship once (1968).

On the home front, the top division, Serie A, is dominated by an elite group of *squadre* (teams) from the north. In the 14 seasons (from 1992 to 2005) Juventus and AC Milan have taken the silverware every season bar two. Indeed, teams from Turin (Juventus and Torino) and Milan (AC Milan and Inter) have utterly dominated the home game, taking 57 championships between them from 1930 to 2005.

Aside from top football, the Italian game also produces plenty of violence. The 2005 Champion's League quarter final between AC Milan and Inter was stopped after Inter fans bombed the field with flares.

The season starts at the end of August and finishes with the Coppa d'Italia (Italy Cup) in June. Below the premier league Serie A come the Serie B, C1 and C2 leagues.

Tickets for games start at about €10 for the lousiest positions and rise to about €70. They are available from official agencies or directly from the stadiums. Check out www.football.it (in Italian). Italy's major stadiums:

San Siro Stadium (Stadio Giuseppe Meazza; ☎ 02 404 24 32; www.sansirotour.com; Via Piccolomini 5, Milan) AC Milan and Inter.

Stadio delle Alpi (☎ 011 739 57 59; Viale Grande Torino, Turin) Juventus and Torino.

Stadio Olimpico (Map p95; ☎ 06 3 68 51; Foro Italico, Viale dei Gladiatori 2, Rome) AS Roma and Lazio.

Stadio San Paolo (☎ 081 239 56 23; Piazzale Vincenzo Tecchio, Naples) Napoli.

Motor Racing

To an Italian there is Formula One and then there is Ferrari – the former furnishes the stage, the latter the spectacle. Led by top driver and seven times champion Michael Schumacher (from Germany), Ferrari is chasing a sixth consecutive title. However, the 2005 season got off to a shaky start, leading many to think that the flaming red cars of Ferrari might have lost their stranglehold over the competition.

Italy hosts two races each year. The Italian Grand Prix is held each September at the Monza race track just north of Milan, while the San Marino Grand Prix (to all intents and purposes, if not technically, an Italian race) is run at the 5km Imola circuit in April or May.

Tickets for the **Autodromo Nazionale Monza** (☎ 039 248 22 12; www.monzanet.it; Parco di Monza, Via Vedano 5) are sold at the track and online. You can also pick them up at the **Automobile Club Italia** (Map p262; ☎ 02 774 51; www.aci.it in Italian; Corso Venezia 43, Milan). Tickets cost from €55 for a spot on the grass to €490 for the best grandstand seat. These one-day tickets are available from July only if spots are vacant. Prior to July, you can purchase three-day tickets instead, which cost €90 and €520, respectively.

Tickets for the San Marino Grand Prix cost from €40 to €450 and are available from the **Consorzio San Marino** (☎ 0549 88 54 31; www.formula1.sm; Contrada Omagnano 20).

For classic-car enthusiasts the **Mille Miglia** (www.millemiglia.it in Italian) takes place in mid-May, with nearly 1000 cars hurtling down from Brescia to Rome and back on a 'Thousand Mile' route.

Skiing

Given Italy's geography it's not surprising that skiing is popular, both as a sport and as an excuse to dress up. For many, to miss *la settimana bianca* (literally 'the white week') in January or February would be as unthinkable as working in August. Most of the chic resorts are in the north and fill up quickly in season. For some of the most popular spots check out Piedmont's Valle di Susa and Valle di Chesone on p236, the Valle d'Aosta on p247, and the Dolomites on p311.

In February 2006 Turin will stage the **Winter Olympics** (www.torino2006.it). Most of the mountain events are scheduled for resorts to the west of the city, while city-centre venues will host the skating and ice hockey.

Cycling

With the suicide in February 2004 of Marco Pantani, winner of the Giro d'Italia and Tour de France in 1998, the world lost one of the great characters of cycling and Italy her leading champion. The Pirate, as he was nicknamed, was disqualified from the 1999 Giro on doping charges, a setback from which he never really recovered.

But other champions are emerging. Names to watch include Damiano Cunego, Gilberto Simoni, Paolo Savoldelli, Danilo di Luca and Paolo

All the latest on fast cars, upcoming races and the all-important points table for the elite of motor racing can be found at www.formula1.com.

Ferrari's Michael Schumacher, the record-breaking seven-times Formula 1 champion, was disqualified from the 1997 championship when he tried to ram Jacque Villeneuve's car off the track in Jerez, Spain.

More than 10 million Italians get around on motorbikes and *motorini* (scooters), but since July 2005 the police have been confiscating them for life from those caught riding without a helmet!

Bettini. Savoldelli pedalled to victory in the 2005 Giro d'Italia, repeating his 2002 exploit.

Rugby Union

If the national football team is considered a dangerous predator, Italy's rugby braves are, by comparison, minnows. And although interest and investment in rugby is growing, Italy has failed to make much of a dent on the world rugby stage. After a creditable second last in the Six Nations Championship in 2004, they picked up the wooden spoon in 2005 (their third in six championships), leaving home supporters more than a little dispirited.

The team play home international games at Rome's **Stadio Flaminio** (☎ 06 368 57 832; Viale Maresciallo Pilsudski). For news and links to other Italian rugby sites, check out the **Associazione Italiana Rugbysti** (www.air.it in Italian). For news in English on Italian rugby, try www.scrum.com.

MULTICULTURALISM

From the 19th century until the 1970s, Italy traditionally had been a country of emigrants. In recent decades the tables have turned and now the migrants are heading for Italy. Long coastlines and uneven policing make it a relatively easy point of entry into Europe. Of the estimated 2.6 million immigrants (about 4.5% of the total population), more than half a million are reckoned to be clandestine. This latter figure changes as many come out of the closet, as it were, and apply to have their situation legalised. By some estimates more than 10% of the Italian population will be made up of immigrants by 2025.

In Italy, as elsewhere in Europe, immigrants will increasingly be needed as the local work force declines because of low birth rates. The question is thus how to promote and organise legitimate immigration flows and put an end to the dangerous free-for-all that now dominates. Presently, people-traffickers launch boats loaded up to the gunnels with illegal immigrants from North Africa (others arrive overland from Eastern Europe) and head to Italy and, the migrants hope, to a better life. Most of the arrivals are men, many fail to find work and remain clandestine, with some turning to crime, helping fuel the slowly rising tide of xenophobia in this otherwise fairly easy-going country.

While there is no doubt that frictions, especially in certain parts of many cities, are real, media hype does not help the issue. Although the flow of illegal immigrants by sea has slowed marginally since 2002, the attention given to it perpetuates the impression of an uncontrolled invasion. Enormous attention was paid, for example, to the decision of a village mayor to enforce a Mussolini-era law banning masks as a way of outlawing the veil on a handful of Muslim residents. Little attention is paid to general reports that most Italians have no problem with Muslim women wearing the veil. With growing fears of international Islamicist terrorism, there is no doubt that Muslims are regarded with growing suspicion.

Tobias Jones' *The Dark Heart of Italy* (2003) is a scathing study of the Berlusconi phenomenon – this fierce critique caused a scandal in Italy. 'What does he know?' critics said. Quite a lot, really.

The new reality on the ground was reflected by moves in 2005 by the Turin city council to give resident foreigners the right to vote in local elections, a move that caused ire in the national government in Rome, which vowed to challenge the moves in court. The council replied that such residents paid local taxes and had the right to have a voice.

Tourists are unlikely to experience racism, although Black tourists have occasionally complained of not always being treated with the courtesy one would expect.

MEDIA

In a country where politics, finance and the law all seem to overlap in a fashion that might leave fans of the Westminster system perplexed, it is hardly surprising that the media is highly politicised.

None of the media are more politicised than the three state TV channels of the RAI. Long divvied up as strongholds of the main political parties, RAI's stations underwent something of an identity crisis with the arrival in power of Silvio Berlusconi, who just happens to be a media mogul in his own right. Berlusconi (the world's 20th-richest human being) and his crew have wielded considerable influence over news content on the RAI channels. At the very least it can be said that in reporting on national politics, the RAI stations have for the most part rolled over.

Curiously, what mild criticism there has been of Berlusconi on TV has come from within his own three Mediaset TV channels! With just one other national channel (apart from options such as MTV and myriad local stations) in competition, Berlusconi has a stranglehold on the country's media machine. For years his promises to distance himself from his own company to avoid a conflict of interest were quietly forgotten. After his nasty regional election shock in April 2005 (see p31), Berlusconi announced a sell off of 17% of Mediaset, with his share dropping to 34%. The most sceptical reaction from critics suggested he was selling because he feared stock would collapse on the market if he lost the next general elections.

Silvio Berlusconi, Italy's prime minister and richest man, is said to be worth a cool €12 billion.

It's not all Berlusconi. The main print media are largely free of his grasp, and range from the right-wing Fiat-owned *La Stampa* to the mildly left Rome-based *La Repubblica*. Fiat also has an interest in the centre-right *Il Corriere della Sera*, based in Milan. Hackles have been raised by talk of relaxing media cross-ownership laws, which could open up the way for Berlusconi (whether prime minister or not) to expand his media power.

RELIGION

Rome is synonymous with Catholicism. The pope lives in the centre of town in his own state called the Vatican. The death of Pope John Paul II and the subsequent election of Benedict XVI in April 2005 propelled this tiny plot of land to the forefront of world consciousness for several weeks – as if it needed more tourist publicity!

The role of religion in modern Italian life appears to be more a matter of form than serious belief. But form counts in Italy and first Communions, church weddings and religious feast days are an integral part of life and are much celebrated occasions. Church attendance stands at about 35% (compared with 70% after WWII), yet around 80% of Italians consider themselves Catholic. As many as 18% declare themselves agnostic or atheist. The biggest problem, as in the rest of the West, is the steady decline in vocations, with ever fewer men signing up for the priesthood.

LOOKING THE PART

In churches you are expected to dress modestly and if the guardians deem your dress indecent you don't get in. Pleading that you've travelled across the world just to see this very church doesn't cut it. This means no shorts (for men or women) or short skirts, and shoulders should be covered. The major tourist attractions, such as St Peter's Basilica (p133) in Rome, Basilica di San Marco (p348) in Venice and Basilica di San Francesco (p558) in Assisi, are particularly strict.

Pilgrimages are big business. Busloads of Italians still crisscross the country to venerate their favourite saint. Particularly popular is Padre Pio (see the boxed text, p691).

Of the non-Catholics in Italy, the Muslims are making the furthest inroads. Boosted by immigration, there are now around 700,000 Muslims in Italy, making Islam Italy's second religion. There is no sign that Italy will follow France's lead in banning the wearing of religious symbols, veils or otherwise, in schools.

At number three are the Jehovah's Witnesses with 400,000 adherents, followed by 360,000 evangelical Protestants at number four.

WOMEN IN ITALY

Italian women continue to make strides in what has long been a male-dominated society. In the majority of married couples aged up to the mid-40s, the woman has a superior qualification to that of her male partner. This is not to say she always has a better job, however: the glass ceiling is still in place, and many women combine work, often part-time, with the raising of a child.

Women may be achieving more in higher education, but the female figure is still openly an object of public sexual exploitation. Long-legged, scantily clad lasses rarely seem to be absent from a host of TV shows. Even serious news magazines, such as *L'Espresso*, frequently find an excuse to have a voluptuous bimbo on the cover.

There is also a considerable difference between the north and the more traditional south, although the gap is closing. Women with children in the north are twice as likely to have a job than their southern counterparts.

ARTS

Here we offer a brief survey of Italy's arts, past and present. See p70 for information on painting and sculpture.

Literature

Italy fairly swarms with writers of all sorts. From the depths of Sicily hails Andrea Camilleri (b 1925), known for his detective thrillers, featuring the maverick detective Montalbano, written in a colourful mix of Italian and Sicilian dialect. Perhaps his most engaging novel is, however, *Il Re di Girgenti* (The King of Girgenti), a fantasy-filled story of the brief reign of peasant king Zosimo over a Sicilian town. One of the great pieces of modern Italian literature is Eugenio Corti's (b 1921) *Il Cavallo Rosso* (The Red Horse), a grand epic set in Italy, Russia and Germany and spanning the years from 1940 to 1974. Up in Tuscany, Antonio Tabucchi (b 1943) has been prolific, but he remains best known for his touching novel *Sostiene Pereira* (According to Pereira), which is set in Lisbon when Portugal lived under a dictatorship. Susanna Tamaro (b 1957) is one of the most successful contemporary Italian women writers. Her latest, *Rispondimi* (Answer Me), is a three-part story that takes a cold look at modern society, with rather ugly scenes of modern selfishness and even cruelty – the reality is stranger than fiction the author claims.

Take a light look at Dante's hell with this on-line personality test. After answering the questions at www.4degreez.com /misc/dante-inferno-test .mv you'll see which circle of hell is appropriate for you. Can't take literature seriously all the time!

Looking back down the centuries, the towering inferno of Italian literature is Dante Alighieri (1265–1321). His *Divina Commedia* (Divine Comedy) was the first major work written in Italian (as opposed to Latin) and tells of the author's journey through hell, purgatory and paradise (on the way taking pot shots at a host of his contemporaries, especially in hell). With a supporting cast of Francesco Petrarca (Petrarch; 1304–74) and Giovanni Boccaccio (1313–75), the 14th century was a boom period.

'Hold on, what about the Romans?' interrupt the Classicists. You can't ignore Cicero (106–43 BC), Virgil (70–19 BC), Ovid (43 BC–AD 17), Horace (65–08 BC) and Livy (61 or 59 BC–AD 17). Of their combined works arguably the most famous is Virgil's *Aeneid*. A rollicking epic, it tells of how Aeneas escapes from Troy only to finish up founding Rome.

Skip forward to the Renaissance and you find that most of the artistic talent was either playing with paint or chipping away at blocks of marble. The 18th and 19th centuries, however, proved more fruitful. A landmark publication in the 1840s was *I Promessi Sposi* (The Betrothed), by Alessandro Manzoni (1785–1873). It's a dense semihistorical novel that uses a love story as cover for political critique.

Meanwhile, south of Manzoni's Milan in Le Marche, Giacomo Leopardi (1798–1837) was morosely penning verse heavy with longing and melancholy. In Florence, Carlo Collodi (1826–90) provided a cheery interlude, creating the world's most famous puppet, *Pinocchio*.

Suffering was a major theme of Primo Levi's work. A Jewish chemist from Turin, his internment in Auschwitz provided the horrific inspiration for his works including *Se Questo é un Uomo* (If This Is a Man), the dignified story of his survival. Born in 1919, Levi committed suicide in 1987.

Fellow Turin writer Cesare Pavese (1908–50) also took his own life, dying the year his greatest novel *La Luna e il Faló* (The Moon and the Bonfire) was published. Carlo Levi (1902–75), the third of this Turin triumvirate, is remembered for his haunting portrayal of southern Italy in *Cristo si é Fermato a Eboli* (Christ Stopped at Eboli), where he was sent into internal exile during the Mussolini years.

A writer of a different ilk, Italo Calvino (1923–85) developed a unique fantastical style. *I Nostri Antenati* (Our Ancestors) is a collection of three ingenious stories, featuring a viscount sliced in half, a baron who lives in the trees and a suit of armour worn by a nonexistent knight.

Modern Rome is represented on the literary map by Alberto Moravia (1907–90), with novels like *La Romana* (The Woman of Rome), and his long-time partner Elsa Morante (1912–85). Her masterpiece is *La Storia* (History), the tough tale of an ill-fated family set against the poverty and desperation of wartime Rome.

Moving offshore, Sardinia and Sicily have thrown up a number of major literary players. Nobel prize–winner Grazia Deledda's (1875–1936) novel *Canne al Vento* (Reeds in the Wind) portrays the difficulties of a Sardinian noblewoman in accepting social changes.

Similarly in *Il Gattopardo* (The Leopard), Giuseppe Tomasi di Lampedusa (1896–1957) describes the decline of Italian unification forces on the feudal order in Sicily. It brilliantly encapsulates the island's wary mentality.

Taking the theme further, Leonardo Sciascia (1921–89) explores the Mafia's hold on Sicily in *Il Giorno della Civetta* (The Day of the Owl), his story of a murder investigation thwarted by the culture of silence.

Murder is also at the heart of the complex bestseller *Il Nome della Rosa* (The Name of the Rose), written by Umberto Eco (b 1932) and made into a film with Sean Connery.

Cinema & TV

Images of Roberto Benigni jumping around like a loon at the 1999 Oscar ceremony, where he won Best Actor for *La Vita è Bella* (Life Is Beautiful), did much for Italy's cinematic profile. However, modern Italian films still lack the verve of former pictures.

The real heyday of Italian film-making was the immediate postwar period when cinematic tradition was shunned in the name of truth. The

Few books have captured the beguiling atmosphere of Venice as well as Salley Vickers' *Miss Garnet's Angel*, the critically acclaimed novel of a retired teacher's discovery of La Serenissima.

Everything you always wanted to know about Italian cinema is at www .cinecitta.it (in Italian).

neorealists – Luchino Visconti (1906–76), Roberto Rossellini (1906–77) and Vittorio de Sica (1901–74) – focused on the everyday struggles of Italy's war-battered citizens, rather than the muscular heroism so beloved of Hollywood.

The slippery art of *arrangiarsi* (getting by) features heavily in Italian films, particularly as a source of humour. The actor Totò (1898–1967) exploited it to great comic effect with his quick Neapolitan wit, while later exponents included three of Italy's most popular actors: Alberto Sordi (1920–2003), Massimo Troisi (1953–94) and Roberto Benigni (b 1952).

Although Italy's acting talent is, and has been, formidable with names like Rudolph Valentino (1895–1926), Marcello Mastroianni (1924–96) and Sophia Loren (b 1934) familiar to most, it's as a producer of films that Italy is better known.

Rome's vast studio complex Cinecittà was founded in 1937 and earned its place in cinematic history when epics such as *Ben Hur* and *Cleopatra* were filmed there. More recently Martin Scorsese used the complex to re-create 19th-century New York for *Gangs of New York*.

The city of Rome itself has provided the background to a number of films. Federico Fellini (1920–94) in particular was inspired by the city. No such urban setting is evident in the spaghetti westerns of Sergio Leone (1929–89); marked by their haunting soundtracks and eerie lack of dialogue these films made the name of both Leone as director and a certain Clint Eastwood.

At the same time, during the 1960s and '70s, Michelangelo Antonioni (b 1912) and Bernardo Bertolucci (b 1940) began to appear on the movie scene and an entire horror-movie industry was born. Output proved to be prolific and full of industrial-strength doses of exploitative sex and violence.

On TV Italy doesn't score so well. Critics point to the quantity of imported quiz shows, the interminable variety shows and daily displays of female flesh as indicators of pretty awful standards. But some fine made-for-TV movies have emerged, too. *La Meglio Gioventù* (The Best of Youth), a six-hour teledrama directed by Marco Tullio Giordana in 2003, won a prize at Cannes for its portrayal of Italy's postwar middle class; it follows the lives of two brothers from the hopeful 1960s to the present. A year earlier, *Perlasca: Un Eroe Italiano* (2002; Alberto Negrin), recounting the story of the Italian version of Oscar Schindler, was a huge hit. Giorgio Perlasca, caught in Fascist Budapest when Italy surrendered in 1943, was a Fascist but not a racist. He embarked on the risky game of pretending to be the Spanish consul, while aiding Jews to escape.

For a sweeping panorama of postwar Italian cinema (and TV) these films cover most angles.

Roma Città Aperta (Rome Open City; 1945; Roberto Rossellini) Set in German-occupied Rome and starring Anna Magnani as a woman who loses her love to Fascism,this film is a gritty testament to courage.

Ladri di Biciclette (Bicycle Thieves; 1948; Vittorio de Sica) A genuinely moving neorealist drama that traces the appalling fortune that follows the central character as he tries to support his family.

I Soliti Ignoti (The Usual Unknowns; 1958; Mario Monicelli) The cast of this classic crime caper runs like a who's who of Italian cinema: Totò, Vittorio Gassman, Marcello Mastroianni and Claudia Cardinale.

La Dolce Vita (1960; Federico Fellini) Who hasn't seen Anita Ekberg cavorting in the Trevi Fountain? She plays Hollywood queen to Mastroianni's journalist in this Roman classic.

Il Gattopardo (The Leopard; 1963; Luchino Visconti) Burt Lancaster stars in this adaptation of Tomasi di Lampedusa's drama of Sicilian nobility. The dance scene is the interminable highlight.

The Good, the Bad and the Ugly (1968; Sergio Leone) Leone's testosterone-laden spaghetti western introduces Clint Eastwood as the nameless gunslinger. It's the best of its type.

La Capa Gira (2000) directed by Alessandro Piva, was a critical and cult success; this film of Bari's sordid underbelly was filmed entirely in dialect. This, along with a thumping soundtrack, makes it a joy to watch *and* listen to.

Sergio Leone's spaghetti westerns were mostly filmed neither in the far West nor in Italy...but in Almería province in southern Spain.

All lingering shots and period costumes, *A Room with a View* (1986; James Ivory) – a romantic tale of love in pre-WW1 Florence – has done more for the city than a thousand tourist brochures.

Death in Venice (1971; Luchino Visconti) Set on the Lido, this is Thomas Mann's melancholy tale of spiritual and physical decay, as well as death of Aschenbach in cholera-ridden Venice.

Nuovo Cinema Paradiso (1988; Giuseppe Tornatore) A small town in Sicily provides the atmospheric backdrop to a young child's relationship with a grizzly projectionist.

Caro Diario (Dear Diary; 1994; Nanni Moretti) This self-indulgent autobiographical piece won Moretti the best director award at Cannes. Writer, actor and director Moretti's spiky personality makes for some entertaining viewing.

Il Postino (The Postman; 1994; Michael Radford) Filmed on the Aeolian Islands and Procida, Massimo Troisi stars in this beautifully shot story of Chilean Pablo Neruda's exile to a southern Italian town.

La Vita è Bella (Life Is Beautiful; 1997; Roberto Benigni) Oscar-winner Benigni took something of a risk with this comedy set in a Nazi concentration camp – it paid off.

Respiro (2003; Emanuele Crialese) A delightful and anything but maudlin story of the less idyllic side of life for a woman on the islet of Lampedusa.

Dopo Mezzanotte (After Midnight; 2003; Davide Ferrario) Set in the cinema museum housed in the extraordinary Mole Antonelliana in Turin, the film is about the lives, hopes and dreams of a group of young misfits, and a musing on cinema.

Buongiorno, Notte (Good Morning, Night; 2004, Marco Bellocchio) An unconventional look at terrorism's futility, recounting the abduction and murder of one-time prime minister Aldo Moro by the Red Brigades, as seen through the eyes of a fictional woman gang member.

Music

Italy and music surely mean one thing – opera. What could be more Italian than Pavarotti singing Verdi?

Cremona-born Claudio Monteverdi (1567–1643) is credited with having created the modern opera form in the early 17th century. And Italy's 18th- and 19th-century opera composers rank with the best. Verdi (1813–1901) might be the most famous but Puccini (1858–1924), Bellini (1801–35), Donizetti (1797–1848) and Rossini (1792–1868) are hardly unknowns.

Great opera requires great opera houses, and Italy doesn't fall short on that score either. La Scala (p273) in Milan, Teatro San Carlo (p635) in Naples, La Fenice (p372) in Venice, Teatro Massimo (p759) in Palermo and Rome's Teatro dell'Opera (p171) all count among the world's premier venues. Verona's Roman Arena (p388) is a splendid setting for summer outdoor performances.

Luciano Pavarotti (b 1935) is the top voice (he has sold more than 100 million discs) but his career is edging to an end: in December 2004 he announced one last long worldwide farewell tour that was set to take him to 40 cities around the planet in the course of 2005 and 2006. Blind tenor Andrea Bocelli (b 1958) also sells well, having carved for himself a niche as a singer of popular classics. Italy boasts two of the world's top conductors in Riccardo Muti (b 1941) and Claudio Abbado (b 1933). The former is probably planning a long holiday after the coup against him in La Scala in 2005 (see p32).

But Italy's musical heritage is not all opera-based. Antonio Vivaldi (1678–1741) created the concerto in its current form, while also composing one of classical music's most popular hits, *Le Quattro Stagioni* (The Four Seasons).

Modern musicians have not met with similar universal success. Part of the reason for this lies in the importance singers attach to lyrics. Singer-songwriters such as Francesco de Gregori, Fabrizio De Andrè, Franco Battiato and Pino Daniele simply don't translate well into English. Seventies idol Lucio Battisti tried to break into the American market but his soft, syrupy material didn't cut it, while rockers Vasco Rossi, Ligabue and Irene Grandi fill home stadiums but offer international audiences nothing new. And who has heard of the…Pooh? It may sound a silly name

Monteverdi wrote what is considered Europe's first great opera, *Orfeo* (Orpheus) in Mantua in 1607. He wound up in Venice, where the world's first public opera houses opened in his lifetime.

Check up on one of the all-time biggest names in opera at www.luciano pavarotti.com.

Antonio Vivaldi, born in Venice, was known as the Red Priest because of his original calling and shock of bright red hair.

for a four-man rock band, but the Pooh are as long-lived as the Stones, belting out albums since 1970 and still touring!

Of the few who have enjoyed success beyond Italy, Zucchero (Adelmo Fornaciari) has had a few hits with his scratchy, bluesy voice. While not such a hit in the Anglo-Saxon market, Eros Ramazzotti and Laura Pausini have regular hits in other Mediterranean countries, especially Spain.

Rappers Jovanotti and Neapolitan group 99 Posse bang out songs with enviable energy and biting social lyrics, Carmen Consoli woos with her silky Sicilian voice and DJs scratch and mix with the best of them. DJ Robert Miles (real name Roberto Concina) may have gone all London-like but his musical schooling was pure Italian. His 2004 album *Mile_Gurtus* was a hit.

Architecture

Italian architecture is more a matter of history than current affairs. True, Renzo Piano (b 1937) is one of the world's top architects (his auditorium in Rome considered an aesthetic and acoustic success), Paolo Portoghesi (b 1931) is highly regarded, and Pier Luigi Nervi (1891–1979) did original things with reinforced concrete, but architecture in Italy isn't what it once was.

Way back in the 8th century BC it was the Greek colonists of Magna Graecia who set the pace, creating an architectural heritage that's still visible in southern Italy. In Sicily, the Valley of the Temples (p801) in Agrigento is a spectacular architectural showcase, while on the mainland Paestum (p680) in Campania and the ruins of Metaponto (p720) in Basilicata are stunning.

Etruscan architecture, mostly aping Greek styles, didn't age so well. The Romans, however, were master builders, taking existing styles and blowing them up to massive proportions. Innovative construction techniques culminated in Rome's Colosseum (p110) and the amphitheatres in Verona (p386) and Capua (p641). The Roman construction legacy stretches across Europe in grand aqueducts (such as Segovia in Spain), walls (Hadrian's in the UK) and temples. Closer to home, you don't need to go past the splendours of the Roman Forum (p113) and the Palatine (p111) in Rome to marvel at the greatness (not to mention solidity) of Roman construction.

It did not end with the fall of Rome. The Byzantine empire in the East – the heir to Rome, with its capital in Constantinople – influenced builders on the Italian peninsula in the early centuries of the Middle Ages. The Byzantine style is most striking in Ravenna and Venice. The Basilica di San Marco (St Mark's Basilica; p348) in the latter is a unique hybrid, mixing elements of Byzantine, Romanesque, Gothic and Renaissance styles.

It was from the Lombard heartland of northern Italy that a strictly Western European style, Romanesque (c 1050–1200), spread across the continent. The style rested on certain simple principles: thick, plain walls, barrel-vaulted roofs and a profusion of semicircles, most notable in doorways, windows and apses. A host of variations on the theme developed, from the sparkling wonders of Tuscan Romanesque, especially in Pisa (p501) and Lucca (p495) to the more sober version found in parts of southern Italy. Trani's cathedral (p695) is a fine example.

The soaring, sky-defying Gothic style that emerged in 12th- and 13th-century France and gradually spread to Italy was another matter altogether. Although the Italian approach to the style was less decoratively lavish (with the exception of Milan's cathedral, p262) than in northern Europe, it nevertheless produced some stunning results. Highlights

Peter Murray's The Architecture of the Italian Renaissance casts a penetrating look into this most brilliant epoch in the country's architectural history, starting from the 13th century.

include the Basilica di San Francesco (p558) in Assisi; Santa Maria Novella (p471) and Santa Croce (p473) in Florence; and the cathedrals of Siena (p516) and Orvieto (p573).

The dome topping the Duomo (p464) in Florence marked the arrival of the early Renaissance. Designed by Filippo Brunelleschi (1377–1446) it was original in concept and construction.

Of the domes that followed few could outdo the design Michelangelo Buonarroti (1475–1564) envisaged for St Peter's Basilica (p133) in Rome. Michelangelo was just one of a number of artists employed by the pope of the day to work on Rome's flagship church; notable names include Raphael (1483–1520), who also lent a hand with a spot of painting in the Vatican, and, a century or so later, Gianlorenzo Bernini (1598–1680), the master of baroque. Bernini, when he wasn't transforming the face of Rome or chipping away at marble, designed the gigantic altar canopy above St Peter's grave.

The Renaissance, too, took many forms, and in the northeast Andrea Palladio adorned Venice and the surrounding territory with churches and mansions of an extraordinary classical harmony. The Chiesa del SS Redentore (p361) and Chiesa di San Giorgio Maggiore (p361) in the lagoon city are two examples.

Baroque also put the Puglian city of Lecce on the architectural map. The most opulent of the city's churches is the Basilica di Santa Croce (p712).

No less elegant, although a little more restrained, were the works produced in the early 18th century. Rome's Spanish Steps (p124), built in 1726, and Trevi Fountain (p123) are two examples offering a foretaste of the neoclassicists. A reaction against the frivolous excesses of baroque, neoclassicism wasn't exactly low-key. The Palazzo Reale di Capodimonte (p626) in Naples, the royal palace designed by Luigi Vanvitelli (1700–73) in Caserta (p640), La Scala (p264) in Milan and Venice's Teatro la Fenice (p351) don't stand out for their sobriety.

This period marks the last great era of Italian architecture. Art Nouveau, known in Italy as *Stile Liberty*, made a brief appearance in the early 20th century before Mussolini charged in with his grandiose vision of manly Fascist architecture – the Roman quarter of EUR (Esposizione Universale di Roma; p130) is a revealing example.

> The Renaissance architectural genius Andrea Palladio's real name was Andrea di Pietro; he started life as a simple stonemason.

Theatre & Dance

The junior members of Italy's arts family, theatre and dance flourish without startling the observer. Depending on your tastes you'll generally find more experimental offerings in Bologna or Milan; Rome tends to the conservative, while Naples enjoys a unique theatrical culture.

Italy's most famous modern playwright is Sicilian Luigi Pirandello (1867–1936). With such classics as *Sei Personaggi in Cerca d'Autore* (Six Characters in Search of an Author), he earned the 1934 Nobel Prize for Literature and influenced a generation of European writers.

Over the water in Naples, Eduardo De Filippo (1900–84) produced a body of often bittersweet work inspired by the everyday struggles of the average Neapolitan; *Sabato, Domenica e Lunedí* (Saturday, Sunday and Monday), a story of family jealousy around the Sunday lunch table, is a good example.

Nobel prize–winner Dario Fo (b 1926) has been writing, directing and performing since the 1950s. His work is laced with political and social critique and has proved popular on London's West End. Hits have included *Morte Accidentale di un Anarchico* (Accidental Death of an Anarchist), *Non si Paga, Non si Paga* (Can't Pay, Won't Pay) and *Mistero Buffo*.

> The Carnevale masks of Venice are inspired by the characters of the *Commedia dell'Arte*, semi-improvised theatre with standard characters that emerged in 14th-century Italy and spread to the rest of Europe.

Dacia Maraini (b 1936) is one of Italy's most important feminist writers. She continues to work as a journalist while her all-women theatre company, Teatro della Maddalena, stages her 30-plus plays. Some of these, including the 1978 *Dialogo di una Prostituta con un suo Cliente* (Dialogue of a Prostitute with Client), have played abroad.

Dance is something that most Italians prefer to do rather than watch. Carla Fracci (b 1936) enjoyed a long, successful dancing career with, among others, the Royal Ballet in England and the American Ballet Theatre, while Alessandra Ferri (b 1963) is today regarded as one of the world's premier ballerinas.

Rudolph Valentino's real name was Rodolfo Pietro Filiberto Guglielmi. He hailed from the small town of Castellaneta in Puglia.

Environment

THE LAND

Italy's distinctive shape makes it one of the most easily recognisable countries in the world. Its long bootlike mainland peninsula protrudes south into the Mediterranean, flanked by two major islands – Sicily (to the south) and Sardinia (to the west) – and a host of smaller ones.

Bound on three sides by four seas (the Adriatic, Ionian, Ligurian and Tyrrhenian), the country has more than 8000km of coastline. Coastal scenery ranges from the low-lying sparkling beaches of Sardinia to the dramatically precipitous cliffs of Amalfi.

More than 75% of Italy is mountainous and two chief ranges dominate the landscape. The Alps stretch 966km from east to west across the northern boundary of the country. The highest mountains are in the western sector with peaks rising above 4500m. The stunning Valle d'Aosta includes Mont Blanc (Monte Bianco; 4807m), Monte Rosa (4633m) and the Matterhorn (Monte Cervino; 4478m), all shared with neighbouring France and Switzerland, and Gran Paradiso (4061m). The eastern sector is lower but no less beautiful. It is here that you'll find the Dolomites, blessed with spectacular scenery. The picture was altered slightly in mid-2004, however, when freak weather caused the collapse of some rocky peaks in the Dolomites. Scientists attributed the erosion to an exceptionally cold winter following the broiling summer of 2003.

The Alpine foothills are bejewelled by a string of grand lakes; the largest include Lago di Garda, Lago di Maggiore and Lago di Como.

More than 1000 glaciers, all in a constant state of retreat, dot the Alpine area. The most well known is the Marmolada glacier on the border of Trentino and Veneto, which is popular with skiers and snowboard enthusiasts.

The second mountain chain, the Apennine (Appennini) range, is often described as the 'backbone' of Italy due to its shape and extent. The range curves roughly south from Genoa to Calabria and runs for 1350km. The highest peak is the Corno Grande (2912m) in the Gran Sasso d'Italia group (Abruzzo).

Only a quarter of Italy's land mass can be described as lowland. One of the largest areas is the Po valley plain. Located at the foot of the Alpine range, the plain is divided by the Po River, which at 628km is the longest river in Italy. The area is heavily populated and industrialised.

Italy has a complex geological history characterised by marked environmental and climatic changes. Around 100 million years ago a huge ocean called the Tethys covered the area now occupied by the peninsula. Gradually the ocean began to recede and various types of materials were deposited, including limestone, dolomite and sandstone, as well as the extensive coral reefs to the northeast from which the Dolomite mountain range was later formed.

The crucial moment in the formation of the Italian peninsula came around 40 million years ago when the African continental plate butted up against the European land mass. The collision forced the edge of the European plate to fold under. Over the centuries the African continent then pushed sheets of the southern European continental plate up to 1000km north over the folds. This process created the Alpine and Apennine chains and explains why some of the higher strata of the Alps are actually older than lower levels.

The biblical story of Noah and the great flood is thought to have originated from geological movements in the Mediterranean more than two million years ago.

EARTHQUAKES & VOLCANOES

A fault line runs through the entire Italian peninsula – from eastern Sicily, following the Apennine range up into the Alps of Friuli-Venezia Giulia in the northeast. It corresponds to the collision point of the European and African continental plates and still subjects a good part of the country to seismic activity. Italy is usually hit by minor quakes several times a year. Central and southern Italy, including Sicily, are occasionally rocked by devastating earthquakes.

The worst quake of the last century was in 1908, when Messina and Reggio di Calabria were destroyed by a seaquake (an earthquake originating under the sea floor) registering 7 on the Richter scale. Almost 86,000 people were killed by the quake and subsequent tidal wave. In November 1980 an earthquake southeast of Naples destroyed several villages and killed 2570 people. An earthquake in the Apennine range in September 1997, which affected Umbria and Le Marche, killed 10 people and caused part of the vaulted ceiling of the Basilica di San Francesco d'Assisi, in Assisi, to collapse, destroying important frescoes. In late 2002 Molise was hit by a quake measuring 5.4 on the Richter scale, which destroyed a primary school in the hill-top town of San Giuliano di Puglia and killed 29 people. A quake of 5.2 on the Richter scale hit the area around Brescia in November 2004 and was felt in Switzerland and Austria.

Italy also has six active volcanoes: Stromboli and Vulcano on the Aeolian Islands; Vesuvius, the Campi Flegrei and the island of Ischia near Naples; and Etna on Sicily. Stromboli and Etna are among the world's most active volcanoes, while Vesuvius has not erupted since 1944. This has become a source of concern for scientists who estimate that it should erupt every 30 years. The longer before the next blast, the more destructive it is likely to be. Some three million people live in the vicinity of the mountain – a disaster waiting to happen.

In 2001 officials were forced to close a tourist area and scientific monitoring station after lava flowed down Etna's southern slopes. Further activity in 2002, including a quake measuring 5.6 on the Richter scale, saw the temporary closure of Sicily's Catania airport. The mountain has been fairly quiet since early 2003. Stromboli was active in the spring of 2003 when an eruption sent around 10 million cu metres of volcanic rock plunging into the sea, setting off an 8m tidal wave that affected areas more than 160km away.

Related volcanic activity produces thermal and mud springs, notably at Viterbo in Lazio and on the Aeolian Islands. The Campi Flegrei, near Naples, is an area of intense volcanic activity, which includes hot springs, gas emissions and steam jets.

Both mountain chains underwent significant erosion, resulting in huge deposits of sand, gravel and clay at their feet and in part preparing the way for the development of lowland areas. By around two million years ago, after the landscape had been shaped and reshaped by the combined forces of continental plate movement and erosion, the Italian peninsula had almost arrived at its present form. The sea level continued to rise and fall with the alternation of ice ages and periods of warm climate, until the end of the last ice age around 10,000 to 12,000 years ago.

Aimed at amateur enthusiasts, Christopher Kilburn and Bill McGuire's *Italian Volcanoes* provides an in-depth account of Italy's key volcanic districts.

WILDLIFE

Italy is not renowned for its wildlife-watching, but you'll be surprised by how many species naturally dwell in the country. If you head for the great outdoors you will have the chance to spot more common mammals such as deer, chamois (mountain goats), ibex, wild boar, wildcats, hedgehogs, hares and rabbits. Touring the many national parks and nature reserves will increase your chances of seeing something a little more unusual.

Animals

There's a bear in there! Along with the 80 Marsican brown bears that roam the Parco Nazionale d'Abruzzo, Lazio e Molise, around 20 brown bears (12 of them born in 2005) are also at large in the Parco Naturale

Adamello-Brenta, partly as a result of their reintroduction from Slovenia. Not everyone is happy. Farmers have seen their hen pens raided and some pasture land is now deemed off limits.

The Parco Nazionale dei Monti Sibillini, straddling Umbria and Le Marche, is home to more than 50 species of mammal, including the wolf, porcupine, wildcat, snow vole and roe deer. As there are more than 150 types of bird inhabiting the park you're sure to see a diversity of colourful plumage and hear a wide range of birdsong. Species include the golden eagle, peregrine falcon and rock partridge. There are also more than 20 types of reptile and invertebrate living in the park, including the Orsini viper and *Chirocephalus marchesoni* (a small, rare crustacean which lives exclusively in the Lago di Pilato).

In the Parco Nazionale delle Dolomiti Bellunesi you should easily spot mouflon sheep and chamois. Rather more elusive are the golden eagle and the rare alpine salamander.

Parco Nazionale Arcipelago Toscano occupies one of the main migratory corridors in the Mediterranean. The islands of Elba, Giglio, Capraia, Gorgona, Pianosa, Giannutri and Montecristo provide endless nesting possibilities for birds. Species include falcons, wall creepers, various types of swallow and the red partridge. Other unusual wildlife includes the tarantula gecko and the endemic viper of Montecristo.

Swordfish, tuna and dolphins are common along the coastline.

The Parco Nazionale del Circeo in Lazio also coincides with the main migratory routes. The park is a good place to spot water birds such as the spoonbill and greater flamingo, as well as rare birds of prey like the peregrine and osprey.

White sharks are known to exist in the Mediterranean (particularly in its southern waters) but attacks are extremely rare.

For a full list of national parks, see p66.

Plants

The long human presence on the Italian peninsula has had a significant impact on the environment, resulting in the widespread destruction of original forests and vegetation and their replacement with crops and orchards. Aesthetically the result is not always displeasing – much of the beauty of Tuscany, for instance, lies in the combination of olive groves, vineyards, fallow fields and stands of cypress and pine.

Italy's plant life is predominantly Mediterranean. Three broad classifications of evergreen tree dominate – ilex (or evergreen oak), cork and pine. The occasional virgin ilex and oak forest still survives in the more inaccessible reaches of Tuscany, Umbria, Calabria, Puglia and Sardinia. These ancient woods are made up of trees that can reach up to 15m high and whose thick canopies block out light to the forest floor, preventing most undergrowth. Most common are ilex stands that have been created, or at least interfered with, by humans. They tend to be sparser than the virgin forest, with smaller trees and abundant undergrowth.

Next to the ilex the most common tree is the cork. Corkwood has been long prized and there is not a cork tree standing today that is part of a virgin forest. Often they are mixed in with ilex and other oaks, although in Sicily and Sardinia it is possible to come across pure cork forests.

There are three types of pine: the Aleppo pine (the hardiest of the three); the domestic pine, especially common in Tuscany and also known as the umbrella pine for the long, flattened appearance of its branches; and the maritime pine, which, in spite of its name, is generally found further inland than the other two!

Try Paul Sterry's *Complete Mediterranean Wildlife* for a general guide to the flora and fauna of the region.

Ancient imports which are an inevitable part of much of the Italian countryside (especially from Tuscany south) are the olive and cypress. The former comes in many shapes and sizes – the most striking of which are the robust trees of Puglia.

Much of the country is covered by *macchia* (maquis), which is a broad term that covers all sorts of vegetation ranging from 2m to as much as 6m in height. Typical *macchia* includes herbs such as lavender, rosemary and thyme, as well as shrubs of the cistus family (gorse, juniper and heather) and, if the soil is at all acidic, broom. Orchids, gladioli and irises flower beneath these shrubs and are colourful in spring.

Where the action of humans and nature has been particularly harsh, or the soil is poor, the *macchia* becomes *gariga,* the very barest of scrub. This is dominated by aromatic herbs such as lavender, rosemary and thyme.

Field Guide to Wildflowers of Southern Europe by Paul Davies and Bob Gibbons is a pocket-sized identification guide covering around 1200 species.

Endangered Species

Changes in the environment, combined with the Italians' passion for *la caccia* (hunting), have led to many native animals and birds becoming extinct, rare or endangered. Hunters constitute a powerful lobby in Italy and continue to win regular referendums on whether hunting should be banned.

In the 20th century 13 species became extinct in Italy, including the alpine lynx. Under laws introduced progressively over the years, many animals and birds are now protected, but the World Wide Fund for Nature (WWF) says 60% of Italy's vertebrates are at risk.

Among those slowly making a comeback after being reintroduced in the wild are the brown bear, which survives only in the Brenta area of Trentino; the Marsican brown bear, which has been reintroduced in Abruzzo; and the lynx, which is extremely rare and found mainly in the area around Tarvisio in Friuli-Venezia Giulia. A handful of them have also been reintroduced in Abruzzo, in the Parco Nazionale d'Abruzzo, Lazio e Molise. Wolves, which are slightly more common, can most easily be seen in the park's enclosure at Civitella Alfedena.

Where to Watch Birds in Italy, published by the Italian League for the Protection of Birds (LIPU), has more than 100 recommendations for species-spotting. Check out their website at www.lipu.it (in Italian). It also has a UK branch at www.lipu-uk.org.

Otters thrive in the Parco Nazionale del Cilento e Vallo di Diano in Campania and the Parco Nazionale della Majella in Abruzzo. Another extremely rare (and possibly extinct) animal is the monk seal; the occasional claimed sighting keeps hopes alive that a few survive in sea caves on the east coast of Sardinia. The magnificent golden eagle was almost wiped out by hunters and now numbers about 300 pairs throughout the country. A colony of griffon vultures survives on the west coast of Sardinia, near Bosa. The bearded vulture, known in Italy as the *gipeto,* has been reintroduced in the Alps.

NATIONAL PARKS

Italy has 21 national parks, with three more on the way, and well over 400 smaller nature reserves, natural parks and wetlands. The national parks cover just over 1.5 million hectares (5% of the country) and Italy's environmentalists are continually campaigning to increase the amount

---

SANCTUARY AT SEA FOR MEDITERRANEAN MAMMALS

An 87,500 sq km area of the Mediterranean between southeast France, northwest Italy and northern Sardinia (encompassing Corsica and the islands around Elba) was set aside in 2002 as a unique protected zone, the Pelagos Sanctuary, for Mediterranean marine mammals. Fin whales and striped dolphins make up 80% of sightings in the area but many other species also cruise through here.

THE RICHEST HERITAGE

Italy has more World Heritage sites than any other country. The 40 sites range from entire old city centres (such as Siena, Naples, Pienza and Florence) through to sites of natural beauty such as the Amalfi Coast, the Cinque Terre and the Aeolian Islands. The latter listing could be threatened if controversial hotel construction plans for the islands of Lipari and Vulcano go ahead. The lists are revised annually in July.

of land that is protected. The parks, reserves and wetlands all play a crucial part in the protection of the country's flora and fauna and there are regular conservation events and open days to promote them. Italy's national parks include:

- Parco Nazionale Arcipelago Toscano (p509) – Tuscany
- Parco Nazionale d'Abruzzo, Lazio e Molise (p607) – Abruzzo
- Parco Nazionale dei Monti Sibillini (p596) – Umbria/Le Marche
- Parco Nazionale del Cilento e Vallo di Diano (p682) – Campania
- Parco Nazionale del Circeo (p189) – Lazio
- Parco Nazionale del Gargano (p690) – Puglia
- Parco Nazionale del Gennargentu e Golfo di Orosei (p848) – Sardinia
- Parco Nazionale del Gran Paradiso (p252) – Piedmont/Valle d'Aosta
- Parco Nazionale del Gran Sasso e Monti della Laga (p604) – Abruzzo
- Parco Nazionale del Pollino (p731) – Basilicata/Calabria
- Parco Nazionale del Vesuvio (p653) – Campania
- Parco Nazionale della Calabria (p734) – Calabria
- Parco Nazionale della Majella (p606) – Abruzzo
- Parco Nazionale della Val Grande Piedmont
- Parco Nazionale dell'Arcipelago di La Maddalena (p842) – Sardinia
- Parco Nazionale dell'Asinara (p840) – Sardinia
- Parco Nazionale dell'Aspromonte (p738) – Calabria
- Parco Nazionale delle Cinque Terre (p212) – Liguria
- Parco Nazionale delle Dolomiti Bellunesi (p391) – The Veneto
- Parco Nazionale delle Foreste Casentinesi, Monte Falterona, Campigna Emilia-Romagna
- Parco Nazionale dello Stelvio (Nationalpark Stilfserjoch; p330) – Trentino-Alto Adige

The official Italian national parks website, www.parks.it, offers comprehensive information on individual parks, useful publications, details of local wildlife, weather forecasts and educational initiatives.

A third of the world's population of Corsican seagulls can be found in the Parco Nazionale Arcipelago Toscano – which explains why it has become the park's mascot.

ENVIRONMENTAL ISSUES

Italy is a dramatically beautiful country, but since Etruscan times humans have left their mark on the environment.

The Italian government's record on ecological and environmental issues has not been good, although in the past few years things have begun to improve. The Ministry for the Environment, created in 1986, is taking an increasingly tougher line on environmental issues, partly in response to EU directives. Italy is committed to many international agreements dealing with issues as wide-ranging as desertification, hazardous wastes, air pollution and marine dumping.

The industrialised north of Italy and most of the country's main cities suffer from high levels of air pollution. Sulphur dioxide levels have been reduced in recent years, primarily by substituting natural gas for coal. But much of the smog and poor air quality can be attributed to the fact that Italy has one of the highest per-capita levels of car ownership in the world. Visible evidence of the damage this causes can be seen on buildings where the stone has become blackened due to consistent exposure to exhaust fumes and emissions.

RESPONSIBLE TRAVEL

Visitors should travel responsibly at all times. Follow these common-sense rules:

- Always dispose of litter thoughtfully.
- Do not discard items that could start a fire (cigarette butts, glass bottles etc) – forest fires are an annual torment.
- Stick to footpaths wherever possible.
- Close gates behind you.
- Do not pick flowers or wilfully damage tree bark or roots – some of the species you see are protected.
- Do not climb on walls or parts of buildings.
- Respect landowners' property and do not trespass into private areas.
- Take care when walking near cliffs – they can be dangerously slippery and quick to crumble.
- Keep noise to a minimum and avoid disturbing wildlife.
- Pay attention to signs and public warnings.

Italian cities (particularly those across the north of the country) frequently undergo smog alerts, when cars are either ordered off the streets or odd/even alternate numberplate days are imposed to halve traffic. With pollution levels dangerously high in some cities in January 2005, Rome and Milan decided to ban cars altogether one Sunday. The sight of central Rome with not one car, but plenty of people on foot, bike and, yes, horseback, had people rubbing their eyes in disbelief.

Rome and Florence are in the vanguard of Italian cities trying to arrest the growing popularity of SUVs (sports utility vehicles). The cost of the annual permit needed to bring a car into central Rome was trebled for SUV owners (to €1000), while in Florence private vehicles (except those of residents) with wheels more than 73cm in diameter are banned from the historic city centre.

For details of Italy's cleanest beaches, see www.blueflag.org.

Other initiatives across the country include car-sharing programmes, voluntary car-free Sundays and the renovation of buildings that have been badly affected by pollution. Many of these measures are taken at a local or regional level.

Away from the city smog, Italy faces plenty of other environmental challenges. Inadequate treatment and disposal of industrial and domestic waste frequently leads to coastal pollution, which means dirty beaches and a murky sea. Areas particularly affected include the Ligurian coast, the northern Adriatic and areas near major cities such as Rome and Naples. However, it is possible to find clean beaches, particularly in southern Puglia, Calabria, Sardinia and Sicily.

The coast suffers in other ways. Since the discovery of beach-side tourism in the 1960s, there has been no shortage of ill-advised building on much of the Italian coast. One area that still boasts some beautiful, as yet unmarred, stretches of coastline is Sardinia, but a rash of development plans have set alarm bells ringing there too.

Following the example of entrepreneur Prime Minister Silvio Berlusconi, who owns a luxury villa on the island, millionaire Renato Soru stood for and won Sardinia's regional governorship in July 2004, partly on a platform of protecting the island's environment. One of his first measures was to freeze all building within 2km of the coast for up to 18 months while a controlled development plan was drawn up. Berlusconi's government in Rome reacted badly, questioning the constitutionality of such a measure (do plans by some of Berlusconi's relatives to build a new resort area south of the Costa Smeralda have anything to do with the central government's indignation?).

Then in early 2005, much to the jubilation of environmentalists, Soru created the Conservatoria delle Coste, a body whose task will be to protect the most beautiful parts of the coast from building speculation. The Italian WWF hailed the initiative as an example for the rest of the country.

The WWF and the national environmental group Legambiente have condemned Berlusconi's plan for the world's longest suspension bridge, to be built between Reggio di Calabria and Messina in Sicily. Environmentalists predict disaster for local sea and bird life, not to mention the danger posed by building such a bridge in a seismic danger area (anyone remember the 1908 quake?). See the boxed text on p742 for more information.

Litter-conscious visitors to Italy will be astounded by the widespread habit of Italians who dump rubbish when and where they like. They might be still more astounded to know that trash is big business for the Mafia. The Naples-based Camorra makes a healthy living from dumping industrial waste in the countryside of Campania, turning large tracts of farmland into toxic traps (see p50).

In addition to the environmental problems caused by humans, the country is affected by many natural hazards, including landslides, mudflows, earthquakes and volcanic eruptions. Environmental groups maintain that some of these natural disasters are exacerbated by human intervention. It seems that the increase in the number of devastating floods in parts of northern Italy and landslides in Campania in recent years are due not only to increased rainfall, but also to deforestation and excessive building near rivers. According to the WWF, a third of Italy's entire coastline is threatened by erosion, largely the result of unfettered construction.

The World Wide Fund for Nature (WWF) has an Italian chapter at www .wwf.it.

Italian Artistic Tradition

Almost all roads in the history of Italian art lead back to Rome – home of both the Caesars and the popes. Over the centuries, art in Italy has invariably been used as a propaganda tool, either in the service of the state or of the church.

Roman art covers a period of well over 1000 years, from Romulus to Constantine, and for most of this time art and politics were intimately connected. Monuments that recognised public service and buildings that met public needs formed the core of early Roman art. Civic leaders of the Roman Republic and, later, of the Roman Empire, were well aware of the potential of art as a means of promoting their own ends.

Constantine's conversion to Christianity, which was adopted as the state religion in AD 313, began the trend of official art being used to glorify the Church rather than the emperor. This trend continued up to and beyond the 15th century and the Renaissance. Glorification of the Church was almost the sole purpose of baroque artists during the Counter-Reformation. The artists of the Renaissance were drawn to the secular art of the early Roman Empire and their adaptation of these classical and Hellenistic forms had more effect on subsequent European art than did early Christian art.

In 20th-century Italy, under Benito Mussolini's dictatorship, art was once again pressed into the service of the state. Mussolini initiated an extensive programme of archaeology in Rome and North Africa, with the express purpose of showing his regime as an extension of imperial Rome. He used ancient Roman symbols for political purposes and had buildings designed in a style of classicism that conveyed imperial grandeur.

Work out your rococo from your Renaissance at www.artcyclopedia.com.

ART & THE INDIVIDUAL

In what art historians call the archaic period, Rome was on the fringe of the Etruscan realm, which had developed its own art forms. However, almost no Roman art has survived from this period. The Roman Republic began with the expulsion of the last Etruscan king in the 6th century BC, but it continued to look over its shoulder for artistic inspiration to the Etruscan heritage or to the Greeks. Roman society was essentially bourgeois and the

---

MUST-SEE WORKS OF ART

It's a hotly debated list but here are our favourites:

- Bernini's *Apollo e Dafne* at the Museo e Galleria Borghese, Rome (p131)
- Byzantine mosaics, Ravenna (p444)
- Frescoes in Basilica di San Francesco, Assisi (p558)
- Giotto's frescoes at Cappella degli Scrovegni, Padua (p375)
- Leonardo da Vinci's *Last Supper*, Milan (p265)
- Michelangelo's *David* at the Galleria dell'Accademia, Florence (p473)
- Michelangelo's *Pietà* in St Peter's Basilica, Rome (p134)
- Michelangelo's Sistine Chapel, Rome (p137)
- Roman mosaics at the Museo Archeologico Nazionale, Naples (p624)
- Veronese's *Convito in Casa di Levi* at the Gallerie dell'Accademia, Venice (p351)

wealthy were supplied with looted originals from the Greek world, which hindered progress in art. But eventually Roman art enlarged upon and almost utterly transformed the Greek tradition.

Unlike Hellenic art, Roman art was essentially secular and inextricably linked with its architectural development. There was much more emphasis on interior space and decoration than on the appearance of the exterior. The challenge was to create and adorn increasingly large and more magnificent interiors to match imperial pride and the growing self-consciousness and importance of the individual.

Apart from their skills in architecture and engineering, the Romans are celebrated for three achievements in art: the development of portraiture, the narrative (most notably seen in historical relief sculpture) and landscape painting.

By the end of the 3rd century BC the Roman portrait was a firmly established tradition. Verism, a type of portraiture often referred to simply as the Republican portrait, is characterised by a stark realism in keeping with the Romans' interest in personality rather than type. It may initially have been inspired by Etruscan examples but is thought to owe much to the custom of storing death masks of family ancestors.

ART IN THE SERVICE OF THE STATE

Art during the Roman Empire was initially dominated by commemorative reliefs of successful generals, and buildings financed by public figures. But soon the Romans found that they needed an art that served the state and not just the individual. Art and architecture were now instruments of propaganda for the state as guided by the imperial family.

Relief sculptures depicting historical events on the walls of public monuments became popular. Particular emperors or members of their families were shown in imposing positions. In contrast to the Greeks, who preferred to tell stories through myth, the Romans liked to depict historical events in a factual and secular way. The prowess of the supreme Roman, the emperor, who represented the grandeur of Rome but was also an individual, was of prime interest. Roman narrative sculpture was thus a particular extension of the trend in Roman portraiture.

Many of the sculptural and architectural works completed in the service of the first emperor, Augustus (63 BC–AD 14), had a propaganda message that was strengthened through associations with classical Greece and the golden age of Athens. Augustus used art to remind the public of his success in fulfilling the visions of Julius Caesar. His style and approach became a model for subsequent emperors because he was able to create a visual means of demonstrating the benefits he had brought to the Roman populace.

His most significant propaganda statement was the Ara Pacis Augustae (Alter of Peace), the altar set up on the Campus Martius in Rome to commemorate the peace that Augustus had finally brought to the Empire. Flanked by tall screens and carved externally with life-sized figures, the altar repeatedly reminds viewers, through myth and allegory as well as representations of contemporary events, of the greatness of the emperor.

Whereas the Ara Pacis depicts space in quite a sophisticated way through details of landscape, the sculptural reliefs on the Basilica Aemilia in the Roman Forum, illustrating the death of Tarpeia, a woman who turned traitor to her own city, are quite flat. These works exemplify two important strains in the art of the period, one idealised and elegant, the other dramatic, intense and direct, and representative of the native Italic, or plebeian, style.

'Augustus used art to remind the public of his success in fulfilling the visions of Julius Caesar'

The Augustan Legacy

The emperors who followed Augustus always had his reputation and plans as a legacy. Each succeeding emperor set a new tone, which gave a special character to the artistic output of his time, although the framework of images and associations that Augustus had set up remained unaltered. The value of continuity for political purposes was put above personal taste.

A century after the reliefs on the Ara Pacis were carved, the whole perspective in portraiture was already undergoing significant and theatrical change. In the Arco di Tito (Arch of Titus, built in AD 81) at the head of the Roman Forum, the emperor is glorified even above Victory, who crowns him, and his chariot is twisted awkwardly to exhibit him in full face.

In the course of its search for new freedoms, Roman historical art seized upon and perfected a convention known as the 'continuous style' – where the same character is repeated from scene to scene in a single undivided composition – a sort of petrified strip cartoon. The convention recurs in Roman reliefs, particularly in mythological stories on sarcophagi of the 2nd and 3rd centuries. The greatest manifestation of this type is the Colonna di Traiano (Trajan's Column), a sculptural document erected in the Roman Forum in AD 113, which records the campaigns and victories of Trajan over the Dacians in a breathtaking continuous spiral, providing a constant reminder of the virtues of the emperor and by extension the success of the state.

A Handbook of Roman Art, by Martin Henig, is a clear, readable introduction to the whole spectrum of Roman art.

The Last Roman Emperor

After 395 the Roman world was divided into an Eastern and a Western Empire. The rule of Constantine marked the end of an era. It was the last fanfare of the pagan empire and the prelude to the Christian state of Byzantium. Constantine turned to works of art, many of them colossal in scope, to proclaim his own importance. But he also initiated the practice of removing sculptures from previous works and erecting them on his own monuments, hoping to acquire some of the honour and appeal of the predecessors whose sculptural panels he reused. The last great monument of Imperial Rome was the Arco di Costantino (Arch of Constantine; p111).

In 330 Constantine made the ancient city of Byzantium his capital and renamed it Constantinople. Though the main imperial centre of gravity now lay in the east, for several centuries the people of Constantinople still thought of themselves as Romans, and the guardians and true practitioners of Roman art. Pagan art traditions continued, though much of the imagery during the 4th century could be seen as imperial rather than pagan.

ART IN THE SERVICE OF THE CHURCH
Byzantine & Early Christian

The city of Constantinople now became the great cultural and artistic centre of Christianity; it was to remain so up to the time of the Renaissance, though its influence on the art of that period was never as fundamental as the art of ancient Rome. Byzantine art grew out of the same background as early Christian art and at times can hardly be separated from it. Christianity de-emphasised the naturalistic aspects of the classical tradition and exalted the spirit over the body. These new expectations joined the requirements of clarity and hierarchy, typical of this period, that were carried over into the art of Byzantium and the early medieval period. But though the Christian emphasis on the immaterial world gave art a new meaning, it did not give it a new style.

The Medieval World

The Italian Middle Ages have often been regarded as simply an age between the Roman Empire and the Renaissance. But such a view makes it very difficult to understand all subsequent Italian history, for Italy as we know it was born in the Middle Ages. The barbarian invasions of the 5th and 6th centuries began a process that turned a unified empire into a land of small independent city-states, the centres of cultural and political life. Italian towns have always managed to incorporate the past into the present with a gradual process of adaptation and transformation. This process can be seen most clearly in the classical buildings adapted to new purposes from the 4th century onwards. Most of this adaptation and reuse of classical buildings, or parts of them, was motivated by convenience – it was easier and cheaper than having to quarry and rebuild. But that wasn't the only motivation. As the emperors had sought to glorify their rule, the bishops of Rome sought to glorify the new Church. However, the conversions played a vital role in preserving many buildings after their original function had disappeared. Ironically, the Renaissance architects were much more destructive, because they were seldom content to adapt ancient buildings to new functions or to reuse marble without having it recarved.

Once more ideas of clarity and simplicity began to outweigh ideals of faithful imitation in art. One of the major influences on art of this time was Pope Gregory the Great (540–604). His declaration that 'painting can do for the illiterate what writing does for those who can read' was aimed at the iconoclasts of Byzantium. But it also had the effect of limiting artists. If the story had to be told as clearly and simply as possible, anything that might divert attention from this main and sacred aim had to be omitted. Thus, at first glance, many pictures of the period look rather stiff and rigid. There is nothing of the mastery of movement and expression that was the pride of Greek art, which had persisted through until Roman times.

> 'Painting can do for the illiterate what writing does for those who can read'

THE ART OF ILLUSION – THE ITALIAN REVOLUTION IN PAINTING

The Byzantine painters in Italy knew how to make use of light and shade and had an understanding of the principles of foreshortening (how to convey an effect of perspective). It only required a genius to break the spell of their conservatism, to venture into a new world and translate the figures of Gothic sculpture into painting. This genius was the Florentine painter Giotto di Bondone (c 1266–1337). Giotto's aims and outlook owed much to the great sculptors of the northern cathedrals, and his methods owed much to the Byzantine masters. But the Italians were convinced that he had initiated an entirely new epoch of art. Giotto's most famous works are frescoes (where paint is applied on a wall while the plaster is still wet). Around 1306 he covered the walls of the Cappella degli Scrovegni (p375) in Padua in northern Italy with stories of the life of the Virgin and Christ. Underneath he painted personifications of virtues and vices such as those sometimes used in northern cathedrals. Giotto's figure of Faith is a painting that gives the illusion of a statue in the round, with its foreshortening of the arm, modelling of face and neck, and deep shadows in the flowing folds of the drapery. Nothing like this had been done for a thousand years. Giotto had rediscovered the art of creating the illusion of depth on a flat surface.

THE WORSHIP OF NATURE

By the 14th century the aims of painting had shifted from telling a sacred story as clearly as possible to representing nature as faithfully as possible. In Italy, particularly in Florence, Giotto's art had changed the whole idea of painting. The old Byzantine manner suddenly seemed stiff and outmoded.

The ideals of the Gothic painters of the north also began to have their effect on the southern masters, particularly in Siena. The greatest Sienese master of Giotto's generation, Duccio (c 1255–1319), successfully breathed new life into the old Byzantine forms instead of discarding them altogether. *The Annunciation* (now in the Uffizi, Florence), painted by Simone Martini and Lippo Memmi in 1333 for an altar in Siena's cathedral, successfully fitted figures into the complicated shape of the panel – an art that was learned from the medieval tradition. But when medieval artists arranged the symbols of the sacred stories to form a satisfying arrangement, they ignored the real shape and proportion of things, forgetting about space altogether. The Sienese artists worked differently, introducing light and shade.

Until this time artists had merely learned the ancient formulas for representing the main figures of the sacred stories and applied this knowledge in new combinations. Now they had to be able to make studies from nature. But soon even the newly acquired mastery of painting such details as flowers or animals did not satisfy them. They wanted to explore the laws of vision and to acquire sufficient knowledge of the human body to build it up in their statues and pictures, as the Greeks and Romans had done. Essentially, medieval art was at an end.

The Conquest of Reality – The Renaissance

In the 14th century the highest praise for an artist was to say his work was as good as that of the ancients. But many believed the northern 'barbarians' had almost destroyed the heritage of art, science and scholarship that had flourished in the classical period. It was time for a rebirth, a *renaissance*, of the glorious past. In Florence, in the first decades of the 15th century, a group of artists and architects deliberately set out to create a new art. Their leader was an architect, Filippo Brunelleschi (1377–1446), whose fame rests partly on an achievement of construction and design. The Florentines wished to have their cathedral crowned by a mighty dome and Brunelleschi devised a method to span the immense space between the pillars. He went on to develop a totally new way of building, using the forms of classical architecture to create harmony and beauty, and his friends extended his interest in classical proportions and values to painting and sculpture.

The Penguin Book of the Renaissance, by JH Plumb, analyses the successes of this astounding movement.

Even the Greeks, who understood foreshortening, and the Hellenistic painters, skilled in creating the illusion of depth, did not know the mathematical laws by which objects appear to diminish as they recede from us. Brunelleschi gave artists the mathematical means of solving this problem, and a whole new perspective.

THE NEW PERSPECTIVE

One of the first paintings made according to these mathematical rules was a wall painting in a Florentine church. *The Holy Trinity, the Virgin, St John & Donors,* in the Basilica di Santa Maria Novella, was painted in around 1428 by Masaccio (1401–28). He not only introduced the technical trick of perspective but used it to frame his figures so that startled viewers felt they were looking through a hole in the wall into a burial chapel with figures that looked like statues. After this the Florentine masters were no longer content to repeat the old formulae handed down by medieval artists. Like the Greeks and Romans they began to study the human body in their studios and workshops by asking models or fellow artists to pose for them.

A website dedicated to the life and works of Michelangelo is at www.michelangelo.com /buonarroti.html.

The greatest sculptor of Brunelleschi's circle was the Florentine master Donatello (c 1386–1466). His marble statue of St George, in the Chiesa di Orsanmichele, in Florence, shows how he wanted to replace the gentle refinement of his predecessors with a vigorous observation of nature. In Siena, Donatello made a bronze relief called *Herod's Feast* (1427) for a font in the Battistero di San Giovanni. To people accustomed to the clear and graceful narrative of Gothic art this must have seemed shocking. Like Masaccio's figures, Donatello's are harsh and angular, their gestures violent.

Thus the Florentine masters had developed a method by which nature could be represented in a picture with almost scientific accuracy. They began with the framework of perspective lines and then they built up the human body through their knowledge of anatomy and the laws of foreshortening. The mastery of science and the knowledge of classical art remained for some time the exclusive possession of the Italian artists of the Renaissance. But the passionate will to create a new art more faithful to nature than anything ever seen before also inspired the artists of the same generation to the north of the country. The Flemish painter Jan van Eyck (c1390–1441) perfected the new technique of oil painting, substituting slow-drying oil for the egg which, until then, had been used to bind coloured pigments. By the first decade of the 16th century, oil paint had become the prime painting medium in Italy.

In Giorgio Vasari's *Lives of the Artists*, the 16th-century painter reflects on the lives of his contemporaries in Florence.

The powers artists had gained now made it impossible to think of art only as a way to convey the meaning of sacred stories; they wanted to use these powers to add to the beauty and grace of life. Fascinated by the idea that art could be used to mirror a fragment of the real world, artists began to experiment and to search for new and startling effects.

NEW PROBLEMS

While artists elsewhere were applying the inventions of the Florentine masters, artists in Florence became aware of the new problems these innovations had created. Though medieval painters were unaware of the rules of draughtsmanship, this enabled them to distribute their figures over the picture in any way they liked in order to create a perfect pattern. Even 14th-century painters such as Simone Martini (c1280–1344) were able to arrange their figures to form a lucid design.

However, as soon as the new concept of making the picture a mirror of reality was adopted, this question of how to arrange the figures was no longer so easy to solve. This was particularly the case with large works such as altar paintings which had to be seen from afar and had to fit into the architectural framework of the whole church. Moreover, they had to present a sacred story to the worshippers in a clear and impressive outline. It was in finding a solution to this problem that Italian art reached its greatest heights a generation later.

HIDDEN AWAY

The full extent of Italy's art heritage is by no means fully documented, and 'new' masterpieces pop up in forgotten, dusty corners with incredible frequency.

Towards the end of 2004 a series of important works was uncovered by researchers. A painting attributed to Raphael was found beneath a later painting, uncovered by restorers working in Gubbio, Umbria, while an unnoticed statue in a church in Puglia was revealed as the work of gifted artist Andrea Mantegna (c 1431–1506). Until then it had been thought that none of Mantegna's sculptures had survived.

Most exciting, however, is the discovery of what may have been the workshop of Leonardo da Vinci, tucked between a military institute and a monastery in Florence. The frescoes bear a strong resemblance to his known work and Vasari's 16th-century work *Lives of the Artists* states that Leonardo used rooms in the building. The jury is still out on the authenticity of the claims.

Perfect Harmony – the High Renaissance

The beginning of the 16th century (the Cinquecento), the time of Leonardo da Vinci (1452–1519) and Michelangelo Buonarotti (1475–1564), of Raphael (1483–1520), Titian (1485–1576) and Correggio (1489–1534), is the most famous period of Italian art. By now cities competed to secure the services of the great artists to beautify their buildings and to create works of lasting fame. The masters vied with each other for the commissions and sought social status to recognise the triumph of their skills.

The spirit of bold enterprise that made Donato Bramante's plan for St Peter's possible is characteristic of the period of the High Renaissance, which produced so many of the world's greatest artists. Nothing seemed impossible to them, and Leonardo da Vinci and Michelangelo Buonarotti set new standards in art of which nobody had ever dreamed.

Among his amazing sketches, Leonardo da Vinci is credited with drawing the world's first parachute, helicopter, aeroplane and car.

The Crisis of Perfection

Around 1520, all lovers of art in the Italian cities seemed to agree that painting had reached the peak of perfection. Michelangelo, Raphael, Titian and da Vinci had actually achieved everything that former generations had tried to do. No problem of draughtsmanship seemed too difficult, no subject matter too complicated. Now artists tried to beat the initiators of perfection at their own game, concentrating on style and tending to neglect meaning; this was derided by later critics as mannerism. But artists such as Il Parmigiano (1504–40) who deliberately sought to create something new and unexpected, even at the expense of the 'natural' beauty established by the great masters, were perhaps the first 'modern' artists.

Leonardo da Vinci: The Flights of the Mind by Charles Nicholl is a gripping biography of the artist.

In the late 16th century two artists of very different natures, who had grown tired of mannerism, took very different approaches to painting in an attempt to break the deadlock caused by the achievements of their predecessors.

Annibale Caracci (1560–1609), from Bologna, had studied the art of Venice and Correggio and was entranced by the work of Raphael. He aimed to recapture something of this art's simplicity and beauty instead of deliberately contradicting it. He created magnificent frescoes of mythological subjects in the Palazzo Farnese (p120). The style followed by Guido Reni and the followers of Caracci, who formulated the programme of idealising nature according to the standards set by classical statues, has often been described as neoclassical. Caracci's *Virgin Mourning Christ* altar painting (now in the Museo Archeologico Nazionale in Naples, p624) is as simple and harmonious as any early Renaissance painting. But the way he used light in a direct appeal to the emotions foreshadowed the new school of art that came to be known as baroque.

Michelangelo Merisi da Caravaggio (1573–1610), the *enfant terrible* of the late-16th-century art world, had no liking for classical models or respect for 'ideal beauty'. Described by the writer Stendhal as a 'great painter…a wicked man' and centuries later by art critic Robert Hughes as 'saturnine, coarse and queer', his paintings were as controversial as his behaviour, and he was condemned by contemporaries for being a 'naturalist'. But his way of handling light and shade to make his scenes glow with an uncompromising honesty has delighted and influenced artists for generations. For more information on Caravaggio, see the boxed text on opposite.

Baroque

The baroque style is perhaps the greatest example of art used to convey concepts – primarily faith in the Church and its doctrines. Designed to combat the rapidly spreading Protestant Reformation and, at the same

ON THE CARAVAGGIO TRAIL

Much of the information that scholars have gathered about Caravaggio's time in Rome has been gleaned from police records. Trouble with the law was a fact of daily life for the artist.

Caravaggio arrived in Rome around 1590 where he gained a reputation for wandering around the streets of the historic centre, from Campo de' Fiori to the Pantheon, brandishing (and sometimes using) a long sword. One of his girlfriends was a prostitute who worked in Piazza Navona and he was arrested on several occasions, once for launching a tray laden with artichokes at a waiter in a restaurant and another time for throwing rocks at the windows of his former landlady's house.

He was, however, fortunate to meet a number of influential churchmen who recognised his artistic genius, provided him with lodgings and introduced him to important dealers and collectors.

The artist fled Rome in 1606 after a ball game in Campo de' Fiori during which he killed his opponent. He spent four years on the run in Naples, Malta and Sicily and died in Porto Ercole in Tuscany at the age of 36.

Caravaggio's paintings were controversial. He used peasants, beggars and prostitutes as his models, giving his Madonnas and saints a realism that was not always well received. On several occasions he had to repaint commissions for churches because the subjects were deemed to be too lifelike: saints would *not* have had such dirty feet.

Several of these rejected works were bought by intuitive private collectors, including Cardinal Scipione Borghese. Borghese is said to have used his influence in the Church (he was a nephew of Pope Paul V) to persuade several religious confraternities, who had commissioned Caravaggio works, to reject the completed paintings for being too 'realistic'. Caravaggio would then be constrained to produce a more acceptable version of the same subject, enabling Borghese to buy the offending work, soon to be considered a masterpiece, at a bargain price.

Caravaggio's work dots Rome. The *Madonna dei Pellegrini* (Madonna of the Pilgrims) in Chiesa di Sant'Agostino (p120) is regarded as one of his most alluring works and features a superbly serene Madonna surrounded by scruffy pilgrims. Two saintly masterpieces in Chiesa di Santa Maria del Popolo (p122) are the *Conversione di San Paolo* (Conversion of St Paul), a daring composition dominated by the rear end of a horse, below which the saint is sprawled, and the *Crocifissione di San Pietro* (Crucifixion of St Peter), which uses dramatic foreshortened figures and depicts the moment when St Peter is tied upside down on the cross.

The Museo e Galleria Borghese (p131) contains six Caravaggios, including the *Ragazzo con Canestro di Frutta* (Boy with a Basket of Fruit), the *Bacchino Malato* (Sick Bacchus) and the famous *Madonna dei Palafrenieri*, commissioned for a chapel in St Peter's but snapped up by Scipione Borghese.

The dramatic *Davide con la Testa di Golia* (David with Goliath's Head) and *San Giovanni Battista*, showing a young St John the Baptist, were apparently given to Borghese by the artist in exchange for clemency from Pope Paul V for the murder he committed in 1606. Another *San Giovanni Battista* is in the Pinacoteca of the Capitoline Museums (p116). The Galleria Nazionale d'Arte Antica (p125) at Palazzo Barberini has a striking *Narcissus* and a gruesome *Giuditta e Oloferne* (Judith and Holofernes). Caravaggio's *Deposizione nel Sepolcro* (Descent from the Cross) is hanging in the Pinacoteca of the Vatican Museums (p135).

time, to emphasise the importance of the Catholic religion, the baroque was blatantly propagandistic; all the visual arts were used to make an appeal to the faithful that was both sensory and emotional.

The essential feature of baroque art was a fundamental ambiguity. Baroque artists proclaimed themselves the heirs of the Renaissance and claimed to accept its norms, but they violated these systematically. Renaissance meant equilibrium, moderation, sobriety, reason, logic – baroque meant movement, desire for novelty, love of the infinite, of contrasts and the bold fusion of all forms of art. It was as dramatic, exuberant and theatrical as the preceding period had been serene and restrained. In fact the term 'baroque' was used by critics of a later period to describe the tendencies of the 17th century that they found to be absurd or grotesque.

The baroque style in Italy is synonymous with Rome and the work of two rivals, Gianlorenzo Bernini (1598–1680) and Francesco Borromini (1599–1667), who helped to make the capital the series of stage sets it appears to be today. Architect Borromini was no longer content with decorating a wall using principles taken from classical architecture. His 'over-the-top' Chiesa di Sant'Agnese in Agone (p119) in Rome's Piazza Navona is a typical baroque church, curved as if it had been modelled in clay, ornate and highly theatrical.

Theatricality is also evident in the work of the great baroque sculptor Bernini, who dared to represent the vision of the Spanish Saint Theresa in a moment of ecstasy, for a side chapel in Santa Maria della Vittoria, Rome. The artist deliberately used this work of religious art to arouse feelings of exultation and mystic transport. In this and many other works he achieved an intensity of facial expression which until then had never been attempted with art. Even his handling of draperies was, at the time, completely new. Instead of letting them fall in dignified folds in the approved classical manner, he made them writhe and whirl to add to the effect of excitement and movement. He was soon imitated all over Europe.

In the decoration of the ceiling of the Jesuit church in Rome, Chiesa del Gesù (p119), Giovanni Battista Gaulli (1639–1709), also known as Baciaccia, a painter of Bernini's following, gives us the illusion that the vault of the church has opened and that we are looking straight into the glories of heaven.

PAST & PRESENT: THE NEW ITALY

Travellers have been visiting Italy for centuries, primarily to admire the glories of her past greatness. Though the Roman past inspired great innovations in Italian art, the modern age could not rival these artistic achievements. By the 18th century, Italy was beginning to rebel against years of foreign rule – first under the French in Napoleon's time and then under the Austrians. But though new ideas of political unity were forming, there was only one innovation in art – the painting and engraving of views, most notably in Venice, to meet the demand of travellers wanting souvenirs. Francesco Guardi's (1712–93) views of the Venetian lagoon show that the spirit of baroque, the taste for movement and bold effects, can express itself even in a simple cityscape.

Despite the slow movement towards Italian unity, at the beginning of the 19th century Italy's cities remained as they had been for centuries – highly individual centres of culture with sharply contrasting ways of life. Music was the supreme art of this period and the age of revolution in politics was an era of chaste refinement in the arts. Not surprisingly, neoclassicism, whose greatest exponent in Italy was the sculptor Antonio Canova (1757–1822), was most at home in the land that had produced classicism itself. Canova renounced movement in favour of stillness, emotion in favour of restraint, illusion in favour of simplicity, and he appealed to connoisseurs throughout Europe, notably Napoleon himself. Canova's most famous work is a daring sculpture of Pauline Bonaparte Borghese as a reclining *Venere Vincitrice* (Conquering Venus), in the Museo e Galleria Borghese (p131) in Rome. But Canova was the last Italian artist to win overwhelming international fame. For some 400 years, Italian architecture, sculpture and painting had played a dominant role in the cultural life of Europe. With the death of Canova in 1822 this supremacy came to an end.

Rudolf Wittkower's *Art & Architecture in Italy 1600–1750* is an excellent reference covering baroque art and architecture.

Modern Movements

The two main developments in Italian art at the outbreak of WWI could not have been more different. Futurism, led by Filippo Tommaso Marinetti (1876–1944) and Umberto Boccioni (1882–1916), sought new ways to express the dynamism of the machine age. Metaphysical Painting, by contrast, looked inwards and produced mysterious images from the subconscious world.

Futurism demanded a new art for a new world and denounced every attachment to the arts of the past. Unlike many other movements, named by antagonistic critics, it chose its own name and was not born out of any dissatisfaction with a particular art form. It started with a general idea that was expressed in words, the first example of the modern artist's manifesto. It was some time before the movement, soon joined by Giacomo Balla (1871–1958) and Gino Severini (1883–1965), found a pictorial vehicle for its ideas. When the first major show of futurist paintings opened in Milan in 1911, it was still the subject matter rather than the style of work that was new. Futurism has thus been described as an art movement that put ideas before style. In this it challenged not only traditional artistic values but also the aesthetic ambitions of most avant-garde art. Some art critics contend that without the Italian futurists, cubism could never have played so big a role in modern art. By showing bright colour joined to cubist broken forms, the Italian futurists encouraged the lesser cubists of Paris to move away from a monochromatic idiom.

Futurism was the last wholly Italian artistic movement. Though it did not last long, it was one of the most radical modern movements, noisily rejecting all traditions and institutions.

Metaphysical Painting also had a short life. Its most famous exponent, Giorgio De Chirico (1888–1978), lost interest in the style after the war, but his work held a powerful attraction for the Surrealist Movement, which developed in France in the 1920s. Stillness and a sense of foreboding are the haunting qualities of De Chirico's *Place d'Italie 1912*, showing disconnected images from the world of dreams in settings that usually embody memories of classical Italian architecture.

Though Giacomo Manzu (1908–91) later revived the Italian religious tradition in sculpture (his best-known work is a bronze door in St Peter's Basilica in Rome), the days when art in Italy was fully employed in the service of the church or the state seem finally to be over and art and the individual has taken on a new meaning in the modern age.

'Futurism has been described as an art movement that puts ideas before style'

Food & Drink

To eat and drink in Italy is to be thrust into the very heart of Italian life. Although this is a country that has exported its food culture around the world, Italian cuisine – *cucina italiana* – as such doesn't exist. Spend any time among the people of, say, Umbria and you'll hear an awful lot about Umbrian cuisine. But Italian cuisine? Well, that's not something they know about. The geography makes for many microclimates and the history for plenty of microcultures. The result is a range of food that is diverse, unexpected and intriguing.

STAPLES & SPECIALITIES

Despite the mind-boggling number of variations that exist, some common staples bind the regions of Italy.

Antonio Carluccio's *Italia* celebrates Italy's regional cuisine and love of good living.

Campania

Naples is home to that most famous of Italian dishes, the pizza, and the general consensus is that smoky, wood-fired Neapolitan pizza is the best in the country. Take note of the basics: *mozzarella di bufala* (buffalo milk mozzarella) and the *conserva di pomodoro* (tomato sauce) are unequalled in flavour and appear in many other dishes besides pizza. A favourite sweet in Naples is *sfogliatella*, layers of flaky pastry with a ricotta filling.

A well-chilled *limoncello* – a sublime lemon liqueur – is the perfect way to end a meal.

Emilia-Romagna

For extensive descriptions of regional specialities and recipes, see www.italianmade.com.

Emilia-Romagna is arguably the gastronomic heart of Italy. Parma is the home of the best prosciutto and also of *parmigiano reggiano* (Parmesan, see the boxed text, p436), while Modena is famed for its balsamic vinegar (see the boxed text, p427). Bologna's offering is *mortadella* sausage.

Also the heartland of fresh pasta, Emilia-Romagna's regional specialities, including *tagliatelle al ragú* (and its prosaic adaptation, the famous spaghetti bolognese), lasagne and tortellini, are among the best-known Italian dishes abroad.

Lazio

The food in this region can sit heavily in the stomach but is no less mouthwatering for it. Traditional pasta dishes include *carbonara* (egg yolk, cheese and pancetta), *alfredo* (butter, cream and Parmesan) and *amatriciana* (tomato and bacon, with a touch of chilli).

Offal is never far from the Roman table, and neither are *carciofi* (artichokes), which are rounder, fleshier and better-tasting than virtually anywhere else in the country. Polish off your meal with a glass of delicate Frascati.

Liguria

The cuisine of this coastal region makes good use of fresh herbs, olive oil and seafood. Culinary specialities include pesto – a delicious sauce of basil, garlic, oil, pine nuts and *pecorino* cheese – which is served with pasta or dolloped into the classic *minestrone alla genovese* (Genoese vegetable soup).

Ligurian olives are small, dark and delicious, without the slightest hint of bitterness.

Lombardy

Lombardy's dishes favour butter over olive oil. Creamy risotto and buttery polenta are staples, and are often eaten instead of pasta. Duck, geese and cured meats also feature strongly.

The classic rice dish is probably *risotto all milanese*, scented with saffron and bone marrow; bone marrow is also the best part of osso buco (braised veal shanks).

Lombardy's cheeses are some of the most interesting in the country, and include gorgonzola, *taleggio* and *grana padano*.

Milan is the home of *panettone*, a yeast-risen sweet bread traditionally eaten at Christmas.

Piedmont

Often delicate and always flavoursome, the cuisine of Piedmont comes alive in autumn with mushrooms and occasional *tartufo bianco* (white truffle) used in a wide variety of dishes.

The Piedmontese also make good use of game birds and animals, including chamois, pheasant, quail and even frogs. Chocolate is another regional speciality, as is coffee: Turin is the home of Lavazza. Nuts are also very good and find their way into *torrone*, a type of nougat, and *amaretti* biscuits.

Piedmont rivals Tuscany for the title of best reds in Italy with big hitters such as Barolo (think chocolate and cherries), Barbaresco and Dolcetto. For whites it offers up crisp Gavi and sparkling Asti.

Puglia

The cuisine of Puglia is simple, often taking a single ingredient, capturing its special qualities and bringing it out to the fore. Vegetable and seafood dishes are the favourites. Try the *orecchiette* (pasta in the shape of 'little ears'), which are traditionally served with *cime di rapa* (turnip tops), or broccoli and anchovies. Another traditional dish is *fave a cicoria*, a puree of dried broad beans served with chicory and drizzled with extra-virgin olive oil.

Puglia's wines are gaining ground; try good-value, classy reds like Salice Salentino and Copertino.

Sardinia

One of the island's best-known dishes is *porcetto* (baby pig roasted on a spit). Try the *carta musica* (a thin, crisp bread eaten warm and sprinkled with salt and oil) and the *bottarga* (dried pressed tuna roe which tops pasta instead of cheese). *Pecorino sardo* is a sharp, aged sheep's-milk cheese of which the Sardi are justifiably proud.

The most money a white truffle ever sold for was UK£28,000 (€39,800) in 2004. For more on the fate of that troubled tuber, see the boxed text on p489.

THE BIGGEST CHEESE BATTLE

Lombardy's *grana padano* and Emilia-Romagna's *parmigiano reggiano* (Parmesan) are squaring up in the battle of the big cheeses. On the face of it these two hard, nutty cheeses may seem pretty similar but, as the marketing board for Parmesan will assure you, they are not!

Parmesan is produced to strict guidelines: the cows only eat local hay and alfalfa, and the cheese is aged for at least 24 months. *Grana padano*, on the other hand, has less time-consuming production techniques and is usually on the shelf after 15 months.

The difference has seen the marketing boards come to blows as *grana padano* tries to shake its 'younger, cheaper Parmesan' image in the tussle to top your tagliatelle. There's only one way to sort it out – buy a bit of both cheeses and make up your own mind.

Sicily

The focus in Sicily is on seafood and fresh seasonal produce. Try the *pesce spada* (swordfish), sliced into thick steaks and grilled, or the Palermo speciality *pasta con le sarde*, with sardines, wild fennel, pine nuts and raisins. Aubergines are popular, as are *capperi* (capers), both of which feature in *caponata*, a vegetable starter. Don't leave the island without trying cassata, a rich sponge cake filled with a cream of ricotta, liqueur and candied fruits.

Sicily is famous for Marsala, a sweet, sherry-like wine that makes an excellent *aperitivo*.

Trentino-Alto Adige

Marcella Hazan's *The Essentials of Classic Italian Cooking* is a must-have on any cook's shelf: the recipes are inspiring.

The cuisine in this region has a considerable Austrian influence, so you will find *canederli* (noodle soup), bread dumplings, goulash and Wiener schnitzel. Local specialities include smoked meats – *speck* (cured, cold-smoked pork belly) is at its best here – and heavy, black-rye bread.

Tuscany

Tuscan specialities are noted for their simplicity and flavour – this is genuine seasonal cuisine. Bread is the essential staple, appearing in bruschetta, used to thicken soups, or appearing in *panzanella* salad, while Tuscan oils are regarded as some of the finest in the world.

In Florence, try *bistecca alla fiorentina*, a huge T-bone steak. Among the other staples of Tuscan cuisine are the popular small white cannellini beans, although all types of beans are widely used. There is also a range of soups, from the simply flavoured *acquacotta* (literally 'cooked water') to rich *minestrone alla fiorentina*, flavoured with pork and chicken giblets. Don't miss *panforte*, Siena's famous Christmas fruitcake.

Tuscan wines are famous the world over, from dark red Chianti and the excellent Brunello di Montalcino to aromatic white Vernaccia di San Gimignano. The dessert wine Vin Santo (literally 'holy wine') is made from semidried grapes.

Umbria

In Umbria, both the *tartufo* and porcini mushrooms are abundant; they turn up in pasta, rice and much more. While many dishes are based upon vegetables, the locals also love their meat. A speciality is *porchetta*, a whole roast piglet stuffed with rosemary.

Chestnuts, lentils and olives are especially good here, as are Umbria's cakes and pastries. Don't miss out on the famous chocolate-coated hazel-nuts called *baci* (kisses).

Orvieto is the best local wine: it's a crisp, medium-bodied white with a tempting summery aroma.

TRAVEL YOUR TASTEBUDS

As well as all the goodies you'll be expecting to find on the menu in Italy, there are a few more unusual items that you may not. In Rome, where the distinct cuisine was founded on the poverty of the general populace, you'll find the fifth quarter – offal – readily available. Order a dish with the word *coratella* in the name and you'll end up with lungs, kidneys and heart. In Florence, *trippa* (tripe) is served up in buns to hungry hordes from mobile vans. Not to be outdone by the French, *carne equine* or *cavallo* (horse) is fairly common, and you'll find *lumache* (snails) in Piedmont.

The Veneto

This region is renowned for its *bollito misto* (boiled meats) and *radicchio* (a bitter red chicory) from Treviso. Don't miss *risotto nero* (risotto coloured and flavoured with black squid ink) or the simpler dish of *risi e bisi* (rice and peas).

Sweet tooths will be relieved to know that the Veneto is also the home of tiramisu (sponge cakes soaked in coffee and Marsala and arranged in layers with mascarpone cheese).

Best known for its white wines, the Veneto's sparkling Prosecco or sprightly Soave will get your evening off to flying start.

As well as being the world's largest producer of wine, Italy is also the largest consumer.

DRINKS

Wine & Spirits

In Italy, *vino* (wine) is an essential accompaniment to any meal and *digestivi* (liqueurs) are a popular way to end one. Italians are very proud of their wines and find it hard to believe that anyone else in the world could produce wines as good as theirs. Many Italians only drink alcohol with meals and the foreign custom of going out for a drink is still considered unusual.

There are four main classifications of wine in Italy:

Denominazione di origine controllata e garantita (DOCG) Classic Italian wines (in theory), subject to strict, traditional production methods and tested for quality.

Denominazione di origine controllata (DOC) Vineyard sites and production methods are still regulated, although the label does not certify quality.

Indicazione geografica tipica (IGT) A term introduced to cover wines from quality regions that are of a style or use grapes that fall outside the DOCG and DOC classifications.

Vino da tavola (table wine) The most basic wines but, as with IGT, this can indicate that the producer is simply operating outside of the DOCG and DOC regulations.

The Slow Food Movement's annually updated *Guide to Italian Wines* is an excellent resource with region-by-region profiles of producers and their wines.

The style of wine varies throughout the country, so make a point of sampling the local produce during your travels. For regional specialities, see p80.

Before dinner Italians might drink a Campari and soda, or a fruit cocktail, usually pre-prepared and often served without alcohol. After dinner, try a shot of grappa (a grape-based liqueur that is either an acquired taste or a relative of paintstripper, depending on your viewpoint), or an *amaro* (a dark liqueur prepared from herbs). If you prefer a sweeter liqueur, try the almond-flavoured *amaretto* or the sweet aniseed *sambuca*. On the Amalfi Coast and the islands of the Gulf of Naples, the fragrant local lemons are used to produce *limoncello*.

Eighty-five percent of Tuscany's wine production is red, while in Umbria the position is reversed; 80% of its wine is white.

Beer

The most common Italian beers are crisp and light Pilsner-style lagers, and younger Italians are happy to guzzle them down with a pizza. The main local labels are Peroni, Dreher and Moretti, all very drinkable and cheaper than the imported varieties. If you want a local beer, ask for a *birra nazionale*, which will be either in a bottle or *alla spina* (on tap).

Coffee

Coffee in Italy isn't like anywhere else in the world: it's better.

An espresso is a small shot of strong black coffee. It is also simply called *un caffè*. You can ask for a *caffè doppio* (a double shot), *caffè lungo* (literally 'long coffee') or *caffè Americano*, although the last two will usually be an espresso with water run through the grinds and they may taste bitter.

A *caffè corretto* is an espresso with a dash of grappa or some other spirit, and a *macchiato* ('stained' coffee) is an espresso with a dash of milk. You can ask for a *macchiato caldo* (with a drop of hot, foamed milk) or *freddo* (with cold milk). On the other hand, *latte macchiato* is warmed milk stained with a drop of coffee. *Caffè freddo* is a long glass of cold, black, sweetened coffee. If you want it without sugar, ask for *caffè freddo amaro*.

Then, of course, there's the cappuccino (*caffè* with frothy milk). If you want it without froth, ask for a *cappuccino senza schiuma*. Italians tend to drink cappuccinos only with breakfast and during the morning, never after meals. You will also find it difficult to convince bartenders to make your cappuccino hot rather than *tiepido* (lukewarm) – overheating the milk destroys its natural sweetness. If you must, ask for your cappuccino *ben caldo* (hot), *molto caldo* (very hot) or *bollente* (boiling) and wait for the same 'tut-tut' response that you'll attract if you order one after dinner.

Variations on the milky coffee menu include a *caffè latte*, a milkier version of the cappuccino with less froth. In summer the *cappuccino freddo*, a bit like an iced coffee, is popular. You will also find *caffè granita*, sweet and strong, which is traditionally served with a dollop of whipped cream.

Tea

Italians don't drink a lot of *tè* (tea) and generally do so only in the late afternoon, when they might take a cup with a few *pasticcini* (small cakes). You can order tea in bars, although it will usually arrive in the form of a cup of warm water with an accompanying tea bag. If this doesn't suit your taste, ask for the water *molto caldo* or *bollente*.

Water

Despite the fact that tap water is reliable throughout most of the country, many Italians prefer to drink bottled *acqua minerale* (mineral water). This is available either *frizzante* (sparkling) or *naturale* (still) and you will be asked in restaurants and bars which type you would prefer. If you just want a glass of tap water, you should ask for *acqua dal rubinetto*, although simply asking for *acqua naturale* will also suffice.

CELEBRATIONS

Italy celebrates an unprecedented number of festivals, many of them coming from each region's pagan past.

People on the peninsula have always celebrated something – whether it be a harvest, a god, a wedding or a birth – and when Christianity arrived the Italians simply put their new god as the figurehead. Most of these festivals were wild affairs: the Saturnalia festival in Roman times was a week of drunken revelry in honour of the god of disorder; it was marked by a pig sacrifice at the start and a human sacrifice at the end. Celebrations these days are more sedate affairs, but they can still be amazing. The biggest times for festivals in Italy these days centre around Natale (Christmas), Pasqua (Easter) and Carnevale (the period leading up to Ash Wednesday, the first day of Lent).

The classic way to celebrate any feast day is to precede it with a day of eating *magro* (lean) because the feast day is usually a day of overindulgence. While just about every festival has some kind of food involved, many of them are only about food. The general rule is that a *sagra* (feasting festival) will offer food, although you'll normally be expected to pay, and at a *festa* (festival or celebration) you may have to bring your own.

WHERE TO EAT & DRINK

A *tavola calda* (literally 'hot table') normally offers cheap, pre-prepared food which showcases local specialities and can include self-service pasta, roast meats, *pizza al taglio* (pizza by the slice) and vegetable dishes.

The delightful *Dear Francesca: An Italian Journey of Recipes Recounted with Love*, by Mary Contini, is a unique book full of recipes and tales of life.

Italy is home to the world's first university of gastronomy. A brainchild of the Slow Food Movement, it aims to preserve gastronomic traditions (see the boxed text, p241).

ITALY'S TOP FIVE

These restaurants are not necessarily the most expensive and they may not carry the most Michelin stars, but these are the places we *really* want to spend our last night in Italy in.

- Cracko-Peck (Milan; p269) – one of Milan's oldest and most revered restaurants.
- Ristorante Duomo (Ragusa; p798) – said to be the best restaurant in Sicily and boy is it good.
- Enoteca Corsi (Rome; p151) – you'd have to look long and hard to beat this bustling, genuine Roman trattoria.
- Osteria Il Ghiottone (Perugia; p550) – unpretentious, simple and delicious.
- Antica Hostaria (Cagliari p822) – one of the strongholds of fine dining in Sardinia.

A trattoria is basically a cheaper version of a *ristorante* (restaurant) with less-aloof service and simpler dishes. A *ristorante* generally has a wider selection of dishes, printed menus, a higher standard of service and higher prices. The problem is that many establishments that are in fact *ristoranti* call themselves trattorie, and vice versa, usually to capture the spirit of the other establishment – sophisticated elegance or rustic charm, respectively. It is best to check the menu, usually posted by the door, for prices. Don't judge the quality of a *ristorante* or trattoria by its appearance. You are likely to eat your most memorable meal at a place with plastic tablecloths in a backstreet, a dingy piazza or on a back road in the country. And don't panic if you find yourself in a trattoria that has no printed menu: they often offer the best and most authentic food.

Al Dente, by William Black, engagingly recounts a gastronomic tour of Italy from its top to its toe.

A pizzeria will, of course, serve pizza but usually also has a trattoria-style menu. An *osteria* is likely to be either a wine bar offering a small selection of dishes with a verbal menu, or a small trattoria.

Bars are popular hang-outs, serving mostly coffee, soft drinks and alcohol. They often sell brioche (breakfast pastry), *cornetti* (croissants), *panini* (bread rolls with simple fillings) and *spuntini* (snacks) to have with your drink. You can round off a meal with a *gelato* (ice cream) from a *gelateria* – a crowd outside is always a good sign.

Most eating establishments have a cover charge (*coperto*; usually from around €1 to €2) and a *servizio* (service charge) of 10% to 15%. Restaurants usually open for lunch from noon to 3pm, but many are not keen to take orders after 2pm. In the evening, opening hours vary from north to south. In the north dinner starts at around 7.30pm, but in Sicily you will be hard-pressed to find a restaurant open before 8.30pm.

Quick Eats

There are numerous outlets where you can buy *pizza al taglio*. You could also try one of the *alimentari* (grocery stores) and ask them to make a *panino* with the filling of your choice.

Fast food is becoming increasingly popular in Italy and you'll find all the usual global chains, but seriously, why bother when Italian fast food – *arancini* (herby, deep-fried rice balls stuffed with meat or cheese) in Sicily, *filetti di baccalà* (dried salted cod) in Rome, and pizza found all over the country – is so good?

VEGETARIANS & VEGANS

While menus around the country have an abundance of vegetable-based dishes, vegetarians need to be aware of misleading names and the fact that many Italians don't think a little bit of prosciutto really counts as meat.

Having said that, most eating establishments do serve a good selection of antipasti (starters) and *contorni* (vegetables prepared in a variety of ways), and the further south you go, the better the vegetable dishes get. Look for the word *magro* (thin or lean) on menus, which usually means that the dish is meatless. Vegans are in for a much tougher time. Cheese is used universally, so you have to say '*senza formaggio*' (without cheese) as a matter of course. Also remember that *pasta fresca* (fresh pasta), which may also turn up in soups, is made with eggs. You'll find vegetarian and vegan restaurants in larger cities, such as Rome and Milan.

EATING WITH KIDS

You'll be hard-pressed to find a children's menu in most Italian restaurants. It's not that kids are not welcome but because, more than anywhere, they are. Local children are treated very much as adults and are taken out to dinner from a very young age. You'll often see families order a *mezzo piatto* (half-plate) off the menu for their smaller members. Virtually all restaurants are perfectly comfortable tailoring a dish to meet your kid's tastes.

High chairs are available in many restaurants, but it would be a lot safer to bring one along if you can. While children are often taken out, and the owner's kids may be seen scrambling about the room, it's expected that kids are well behaved, and disciplined if they are not.

For more information on travelling with your little ones, see p857.

HABITS & CUSTOMS

Italians will rarely eat a sit-down *colazione* (breakfast) – they tend to drink a cappuccino and eat a pastry while standing at a bar.

Pranzo (lunch) is traditionally the main meal of the day and many shops and businesses close for three to four hours every afternoon for the meal and the siesta that is traditionally supposed to follow. A full meal will consist of an antipasto, which can vary from bruschetta to fried vegetables or *prosciutto e melone* (cured ham wrapped around melon). Next comes the *primo piatto* (first course), a pasta or risotto, followed by the *secondo piatto* (second course) of meat or fish. Italians often then eat an *insalata* (salad) or *contorno* (vegetable side dish) and round off the meal with fruit, or occasionally with *dolci* (sweets) and coffee.

Cena, the evening meal, was traditionally a more simple affair, but in recent years habits have been changing because of the inconvenience of travelling home for lunch every day.

In general, Italians are not big snackers, although it is not uncommon for them to have a quick bite – usually a *tramezzino* (sandwich), *merendina* (cake or biscuit) or slice of pizza – halfway through the morning or afternoon.

For an excellent food and travel portal, visit www.deliciousitaly.com; it also lists courses and wine tours.

COOKING COURSES

There are hundreds of cooking and wine-tasting courses in Italy.

Casa Ombuto (www.italiancookerycourse.com) High on the hills of the Casentino valley in Tuscany stands Casa Ombuto. Seven-day courses are run by inspiring tutors in this cave-like *cucina* (kitchen).

International Wine Academy of Roma (Map pp98-9; ☎ 06 699 08 78; www.wineacademy roma.com; Vicolo del Bottino 8) Runs various wine courses. For a half-day introduction to Italy's major wine regions, the variety of grapes grown and tasting techniques expect to pay €150. Three-day courses cost about €550 and include a vineyard visit.

La Cucina del Garga (☎ 055 21 13 96; www.garga.it) Hands-on Tuscan cookery courses, from one to eight days, run by the team from Trattoria Garga (p482) in Florence.

Menfi (www.tastingplaces.com) Published cookery writer Maxine Clark hosts a week-long course in the 18th-century Villa Ravida in Menfi, Sicily. The course is an exploration of the earthy and exotic mix of Sicilian food. Tasting Places also offers courses in Tuscany, Umbria and the Veneto.

Roman Kitchen (Map pp98-9; ☎ 06 679 71 03; www.italiangourmet.com; Via del Plebiscito 112) Cookery writer Diane Seed's courses run four or five times a year from her kitchen in Rome's Palazzo Doria Pamphilj. Week-long courses cost €750, with each lesson running for 3½ hours a day.

EAT YOUR WORDS

Get behind the cuisine scene by getting to know the language. For more on pronunciation guidelines, see p890.

Anna del Conte's *The Gastronomy of Italy* is the definitive tome on Italian food and an essential reference.

Useful Phrases

I'd like to reserve a table.
Vorrei riservare un tavolo.   vo-ray ree-ser-va-re oon ta-vo-lo

I'd like the menu, please.
Vorrei il menù, per favore.   vo-ray eel me-noo per fa-vo-re

Do you have a menu in English?
Avete un menù (scritto) in inglese?   a-ve-te oon me-noo (skree-to) een een-gle-ze

What would you recommend?
Cosa mi consiglia?   ko-za mee kon-see-lya

I'd like a local speciality.
Vorrei una specialità di questa regione. vo-ray oo-na spe-cha-lee-ta dee kwe-sta re-jo-ne

Please bring the bill.
Mi porta il conto, per favore?   mee por-ta eel kon-to per fa-vo-re

Is service included in the bill?
Il servizio è compreso nel conto?   eel ser-vee-tsyo e kom-pre-zo nel kon-to

I'm a vegetarian.
Sono vegetariano/a. (m/f)   so-no ve-je-ta-rya-no/a

I'm a vegan.
Sono vegetaliano/a. (m/f)   so-no ve-je-ta-lya-no/a

Food Glossary

acciughe	a-choo-ge	anchovies
aceto	a-che-to	vinegar
acqua	a-kwa	water
aglio	a-lyo	garlic
agnello	a-nye-lo	lamb
alla griglia	a-la gree-lya	grilled (broiled)
aragosta	a-ra-go-sta	lobster
arancia	a-ran-cha	orange
arrosto/a (m/f)	a-ro-sto/a	roasted
asparagi	as-pa-ra-jee	asparagus
birra	bee-ra	beer
bistecca	bees-te-ka	steak
bollito/a (m/f)	bo-lee-to/a	boiled
burro	boo-ro	butter
caffè	ka-fe	coffee
calamari	ka-la-ma-ree	squid
capretto	ka-pre-to	kid (goat)
carciofi	kar-cho-fee	artichokes
carota	ka-ro-ta	carrot
cavolo	ka-vo-lo	cabbage
ciliegia	chee-lee-e-ja	cherry
coniglio	ko-nee-lyo	rabbit
cotto/a (m/f)	ko-to/a	cooked
cozze	ko-tse	mussels
crudo/a (m/f)	kroo-do/a	raw
fagiolini	fa-jo-lee-nee	green beans

fegato	*fe*-ga-to	liver
finocchio	fee-*no*-kyo	fennel
formaggio	for-*ma*-jo	cheese
fragole	*fra*-go-le	strawberries
fritto/a (m/f)	*free*-to/a	fried
frutti di mare	*froo*-te dee *ma*-re	seafood
funghi	*foon*-ghee	mushrooms
gamberoni	gam-be-*ro*-nee	prawns
granchio	*gran*-kyo	crab
insalata	in-sa-*la*-ta	salad
latte	*la*-te	milk
limone	lee-*mo*-ne	lemon
manzo	*man*-zo	beef
mela	*me*-la	apple
melanzane	me-lan-*dza*-ne	aubergine
melone	me-*lo*-ne	cantaloupe; musk melon; rockmelon
merluzzo	mer-*loo*-tso	cod
miele	*mye*-le	honey
olio	*o*-lyo	oil
oliva	o-*lee*-va	olive
ostriche	*os*-tree-ke	oysters
pane	*pa*-ne	bread
panna	*pa*-na	cream
patate	pa-*ta*-te	potatoes
pepe	*pe*-pe	pepper
peperoncino	pe-pe-ron-*chee*-no	chilli
peperoni	pe-pe-*ro*-nee	capsicum; peppers
pera	*pe*-ra	pear
pesca	*pe*-ska	peach
pesce spada	*pe*-she *spa*-da	swordfish
piselli	pee-*ze*-lee	peas
pollo	*po*-lo	chicken
polpi	*pol*-pee	octopus
pomodori	po-mo-*do*-ree	tomatoes
prosciutto cotto	pro-*shoo*-to *ko*-to	cooked ham
prosciutto crudo	pro-*shoo*-to *kroo*-do	cured ham
riso	*ree*-zo	rice
rucola	*roo*-ko-la	rocket
sale	*sa*-le	salt
salsiccia	sal-*see*-cha	sausage
sarde	*sar*-de	sardines
seppia	*se*-pya	cuttlefish
sgombro	*sgom*-bro	mackerel
spinaci	spee-*na*-chee	spinach
tartufo	tar-*too*-fo	truffle
tè	te	tea
tonno	*to*-no	tuna
trippa	*tree*-pa	tripe
uovo/uova	*wo*-vo/*wo*-va	egg/eggs
uva	*oo*-va	grapes
vino (rosso/bianco)	*vee*-no (*ro*-so/*byan*-ko)	wine (red/white)
vitello	vee-*te*-lo	veal
vongole	*von*-go-le	clams
zucchero	*tsoo*-ke-ro	sugar

Rome & Lazio

If you judged a city by the number of words it has inspired, Rome would surely top the charts. *Caput Mundi* (Capital of the World), the Eternal City, the city to which all roads lead, Rome has been mesmerising visitors for more than 2500 years. An addictive mix of classical culture and baroque beauty, of angry traffic and relentless noise, it's an exhausting place.

Unfortunately, you'll never see it all – there are simply too many churches, monuments, museums and galleries to take in. The trick is not to worry about it. Stroll the streets, have an ice cream, stop for a coffee – do as the Romans do.

Rome is almost as famous for its anarchic traffic as for its instantly recognisable monuments. But to write the city off as chaotic is to overlook its ability to rise up to the big occasion. When Pope John Paul II died in April 2005, the city calmly dealt with millions of mourners who flooded into town, including more than 200 heads of state. It was a bravura performance from a city that has long struggled to balance the demands of a modern working capital with its priceless artistic legacy.

But there's more to Lazio than Rome, even if there's little of Lazio that wasn't once Roman. Since ancient times the rich built villas in the countryside, and towns developed as fiefdoms of noble Roman families. Often ignored by visitors, Lazio is a surprisingly beautiful region, worth at the very least a day trip or two. For a taster, head to Tivoli and the ruins of Hadrian's Villa or to the ancient Roman port at Ostia Antica. Further north and you enter the land of the Etruscans. Not to be missed are the famous tombs of Cerveteri and Tarquinia.

HIGHLIGHTS

- Let Michelangelo's *Pietà* entrance you in **St Peter's Basilica** (p134)
- Get lost in the **Vatican Museums** (p134) en route to the **Sistine Chapel** (p137)
- Dream of ancient glories at the **Roman Forum** (p113), **Palatine** (p111) and **Colosseum** (p110)
- Take a breather in Villa Borghese after visiting the **Museo e Galleria Borghese** (p131)
- Enjoy the paintwork in Tarquinia's **Etruscan tombs** (p182)

★ Tarquinia

★ Rome

- POPULATION: Rome city 2.5 million; Rome province 3.7 million; Lazio 5.1 million
- AREA: Lazio 17,202 sq km

ROME

HISTORY

Rome's origins date to that nether period when myth had not yet become history. The story of the she-wolf suckling Romulus and Remus is a nice legend but few historians accept it as historical fact. What they do acknowledge is that Romulus became the first king of Rome (Roma) on 21 April 753 BC and that the city was an amalgamation of Etruscan, Latin and Sabine settlements on the Palatine (Palatino), Esquiline (Esquilino) and Quirinal (Quirinale) Hills. Archaeological discoveries have confirmed the existence of a settlement on the Palatine in that period.

The Roman Republic was founded in 509 BC and was the major power in the Western world until internal rivalries led to civil war. Julius Caesar went to war with his erstwhile partner Pompey, leaving Mark Antony and Octavian to fight for the top job after Caesar was murdered in 44 BC. Octavian prevailed and, with the blessing of the Senate, became Augustus, the first Roman Emperor.

One of the more stable Roman emperors, he ruled well and the city enjoyed a period of political stability and artistic achievement. Successive rulers such as Tiberius, Caligula and Nero, as well as events such as the Great Fire of AD 64, combined to leave Rome in tatters but the city bounced back. By 100, it had a population of 1.5 million and was the undisputed *Caput Mundi* – the Roman Forum was the centre of municipal life and crowds flocked to the bloodstained Colosseum. But it couldn't last and when, in 330, Constantine moved his power base to Byzantium, Rome's glory days were numbered. In 455 it was routed by the Vandals and in 476 the last emperor of the Western Roman Empire, Romulus Augustulus, was deposed.

By now Rome's Christian roots had taken firm hold. Christianity had been spreading since the 1st century AD thanks to the underground efforts of apostles Peter and Paul and under Constantine it received official recognition. Pope Gregory I (590–604) did much to strengthen the Church's grip over the city and, in 774, its place as centre of the Christian world was cemented when Pope Leo III crowned Charlemagne as Holy Roman Emperor.

The medieval period was marked by continuous fighting by just about anyone capable of raising an army. In the thick of things the Papal States fought their corner as ruthlessly as anyone.

However, in 1309 Pope Clement V decided enough was enough and upped sticks to Avignon, leaving the powerful Colonna and Orsini families to contest control of the city. Once the waters had calmed, Pope Gregory XI returned to Rome in 1377 and, finding the city close to ruins, set up home in the fortified Vatican.

But out of the ruins grew the Rome of the Renaissance. At the behest of the great papal dynasties – the Barberini, Farnese and Pamphilj among others – the leading artists of the 15th and 16th centuries were summoned to work on projects such as the Sistine Chapel and St Peter's Basilica. However, the enemy was never far away, and in 1527 Pope Clement VII took refuge in Castel Sant'Angelo as Charles V's Spanish forces ransacked Rome.

Once again Rome needed rebuilding and it was to the 17th-century baroque masters Bernini and Borromini that the city's patrons turned. With their exuberant churches, fountains and palazzi (mansions), these two bitter rivals changed the face of the city. The building boom following the unification of Italy and the declaration of Rome as its capital also profoundly influenced the look of the city, as did Mussolini and hasty post-WWII expansion.

Rome has always attracted visitors and although mass tourism, in the form of the Grand Tour, only took off in the 18th century, the city has for much of its history attracted vast numbers of pilgrims. Recent years have seen spectacular confirmation of this. Preceded by a vast city clean up, the Jubilee Year in 2000 saw an influx of around 16 million Catholics enter the city, while the death of Pope John Paul II on 2 April 2005 provoked an invasion of more than three million mourners in the space of a week.

ORIENTATION

Rome is a sprawling city but most sights lie within the relatively compact area bounded by the River Tiber to the west and the main

ROME IN...

Two Days

Visit **St Peter's Basilica** (p133), the **Vatican Museums** (p134) and the **Sistine Chapel** (p137). Lunch around **Piazza Navona** (p119), before popping into the **Pantheon** (p117) en route to the **Colosseum** (p110) and the **Roman Forum** (p113). Make a night of it drinking in vibrant **Trastevere** (p168).

After a leisurely breakfast wander over to the **Trevi Fountain** (p123) and **Piazza di Spagna** (p124), where the **Spanish Steps** (p124) provide excellent people-watching. In the nearby **Villa Borghese** (p131), the **Museo e Galleria Borghese** (p131) is a highlight of any visit.

At night, drink in **Campo de' Fiori** (p166) or club it in **Testaccio** (p169).

Four Days

Once you've seen the greatest hits, stroll the streets: check out the designer shops on **Via dei Condotti** (p172), enjoy the quiet of the **Jewish Ghetto** (p120), or marvel at the views from the top of the **Vittoriano** (p117) on Piazza Venezia.

Back on the museum trail, visit the **Capitoline Museums** (p116). After dark, join the student drinkers and fashionable diners in **San Lorenzo** (p167).

One Week

Venture out to **Via Appia Antica** (p128) and the **Catacombs of San Callisto** (p129), or take a day trip: choose between **Ostia Antica** (p178), or the Etruscan treasures of **Cerveteri** (p181) and **Tarquinia** (p181).

train station Stazione Termini to the east, Villa Borghese to the north and the Colosseum to the south. The Vatican City and Trastevere are over the water on the west bank of the Tiber. Distances are not huge and walking is the best way to get around the city.

The city's major transport hub, Stazione Termini (its full name is Stazione Centrale-Roma Termini) is a useful, if unattractive, point of reference. The majority of cheap hotels and *pensioni* (small hotels or guesthouses) are in the area and the main city bus terminus is on Piazza Cinquecento, in front of the station.

From Piazza Cinquecento, Via Cavour leads directly down to the Roman Forum, while from Piazza della Repubblica, a short walk to the west of Stazione Termini, Via Nazionale heads down towards Piazza Venezia. Running north from Piazza Venezia, Via del Corso leads up to Piazza del Popolo and the Villa Borghese. In the area east of Via del Corso you will find the tourist-heavy areas of the Trevi Fountain and Piazza di Spagna; to the west lie the Pantheon and Piazza Navona.

To reach the Vatican from Piazza Venezia head west to Largo di Torre Argentina and continue along Corso Vittorio Emanuele II. Cross the River Tiber, turn left into Via delle Conciliazione and you'll see St Peter's Basilica directly in front of you. The atmospheric quarter of Trastevere is south of the Vatican.

For travelling further afield, national and international trains terminate at Stazione Termini. Intercity buses, however, use Stazione Tiburtina to the east of the city centre. From Termini take Metro Line B in the direction of Rebibbia. Regional buses serving towns in Lazio depart from various points throughout the city, usually corresponding with metro stops.

For further information on getting from Leonardo da Vinci Airport (Fiumicino) to the city centre, see p174.

Maps

The Rome Tourist Board (p94) publishes an excellent pocket-sized city map, *Roma*, which is freely available at the tourist office in Via Parigi. Tourist information kiosks around town also hand out *Charta Roma*, an A3-sized stylised map with the major sights and their opening hours. Otherwise plenty of maps are available at newsstands and bookshops.

ROME & LAZIO

Lonely Planet's *Rome City Map* indicates all principal landmarks, as well as museums, shops and information points, and has a street index.

Editrice Lozzi publishes various city maps: the basic version *Roma* (€3) lists all major streets and bus/tram routes; *Rome Today* (€5.50) comprises a city map, a map of the province of Rome and an enlarged plan of the city centre; and the *Roma Metro-Bus* (€5.50) map details the city's main transport routes.

For maps of ancient Rome try the Lozzi *Archaeo Map* (€4), with a plan of the Roman Forum, Palatine and Colosseum, or *Ancient Rome* (€3.50), published by Electa.

The best road map is the 1:12,500 *Pianta Roma* (€7), published by the Touring Club Italiano.

INFORMATION
Bookshops
Almost Corner Bookshop (Map pp106-7; ☎ 06 583 69 42; Via del Moro 45; ⏲ 10am-1.30pm Mon-Sat, 11am-1.30pm & 3.30-8pm Sun) From the classics to contemporary bestsellers – all in English.

Anglo-American Bookshop (Map pp102-3; ☎ 06 679 52 22; www.aab.it; Via della Vite 102) Literature, travel guides and reference books in English. Also has a kids' section.

Bibli Bookshop (Map pp106-7; ☎ 06 588 40 97; www.bibli.it in Italian; Via dei Fienaroli 28; ⏲ 5.30pm-midnight Mon, 11am-midnight Tue-Sun) Popular with expats for its café, cultural centre and Internet facilities (half/full hour €4/6). Limited selection of books in English.

Feltrinelli International (Map pp102-3; ☎ 06 482 78 78; Via Orlando 84; ⏲ 9am-8pm Mon-Sat, 10am-1.30pm & 4-7.30pm Sun) Slick chain store with tons of fiction, nonfiction, guidebooks and maps in English and other languages.

Libreria del Viaggiatore (Map p104; ☎ 06 688 01 048; Via del Pellegrino 78) Specialising in travel literature, it carries a huge range of maps.

Lion Bookshop (Map pp98-9; ☎ 06 326 54 007; Via dei Greci 33-6) Long-standing English-language bookshop with a little café.

Emergency
Main police station (questura; Map pp102-3; ☎ 06 4 68 61; Via San Vitale 11)

Ufficio Stranieri (Foreigners' Bureau; Map pp102-3; ☎ 06 468 63 216; Via Genova 2; ⏲ 24hr) Thefts can be reported here; also come here for a *permesso di soggiorno* (permit; see p871).

Internet Access
Costs vary but are usually between €3 and €6 an hour, with hefty discounts if you take out a subscription.

Easy Internet Café (Map pp102-3; Piazza Barberini 2; ⏲ 7am-1am) Rates depend on the time of day, but reckon on about €2 for 50 minutes. You can also print digital pictures for €2 per print or download them onto a CD for €5.

Internet Café (Map pp102-3; ☎ 06 445 49 53; Via dei Marrucini 12; per hr €3; ⏲ 9.30am-1am Mon-Fri, 5pm-1am Sat & Sun) Much frequented by students in the San Lorenzo area, east of Termini.

Internet point (Map p104; ☎ 06 683 01 215; Piazza di Firenze 25; per hr €3; ⏲ 8.30am-8.30pm Mon-Fri, 9.30am-5.30pm Sat) Has a photocopy and fax service.

New Internet Point (Map pp106-7; ☎ 06 583 33 316; Piazza Sonnino 27; per hr €4; ⏲ 8am-midnight) Over the road from the tourist Iinformation point in Trastevere.

Sivet Internet Point (Map p104; ☎ 06 688 02 906; Via della Scrofa 73; per hr €3.90; ⏲ 9am-6pm Mon-Fri) Also offers photocopying services and laser printing.

Splashnet (Map pp102-3; ☎ 06 493 82 073; Via Varese 33; per hr €1.50; ⏲ 8.30am-1am summer, 8.30am-11pm winter) Surf while you soak your threads at this laundrette-cum-Internet café near Stazione Termini.

TreviNet (Map pp102-3; ☎ 06 699 22 320; Via in Arcione 103; per hr €3.50; ⏲ 11am-10pm Mon-Sat, 4.30-11pm Sun) Offers student discounts, scanning, free CD-burning, digital and webcam picture downloads, as well as direct connections for laptops.

Internet Resources
ATAC (www.atac.roma.it) Practical information from Rome's public transport company.

Comune di Roma (www.comune.roma.it in Italian) The official website of Rome City Council.

Enjoy Rome (www.enjoyrome.com) Useful advice from an independent tourist agency.

Musei Online (www.museionline.it) Government website with the latest on Italy's museums.

Roma Turismo (www.romaturismo.it) Rome Tourist Board's comprehensive website. Lists all official accommodation options, upcoming events and much more.

Rome Buddy (www.romebuddy.com) An American site that provides down-to-earth advice and dry humour.

Trenitalia (www.trenitalia.com) For train times and online reservations.

Vatican (www.vatican.va) Official site of the Vatican.

Wanted in Rome (www.wantedinrome.com) Classified ads, listings, reviews and ads for upmarket flats.

Laundry
Typically, laundrettes are open from 8am to 10pm daily. A 6kg to 8kg load costs around

€6 to wash and dry. There are several self-service laundrettes in the streets northeast of **Stazione Termini** (Map pp102–3). *Lavasecco* (dry-cleaning) costs range from around €3 for a shirt to €6 for a jacket.

Bolle Blu (Map pp102-3; ☎ 06 447 03 096; Via Milazzo 20b) As well as washing, Bolle Blu provides free Indian tea, Internet access for €2 per hour and left-luggage facilities at €2 for five hours.

Bolle Blu 2 (Map pp102-3; ☎ 06 446 58 04; Via Palestro 59-61) Offers an ironing service and Internet access for €2 per hour. Luggage lockers are available at €3 for 24 hours.

Onda Blu (Map p95; Via Vespasiano 50)

Splashnet (Map pp102-3; ☎ 06 493 80 450; Via Varese 33) Internet access costs €1.50 per hour. Also has luggage storage at €2 per day.

Wash & Dry Lavarapido cnr Via della Pellicla & Vicolo del Piede (Map pp106-7; ☎ 347 096 56 86); Via della Chiesa Nuova 15-16 (Map p104) Student discounts available.

Left Luggage
Near Stazione Termini three laundries provide luggage storage: Bolle Blu, Bolle Blu 2 and Splashnet. See opposite for details.

Fiumicino airport (1st 7hr €2, 7-24hr €3.50; ☺ 7am-11pm) In the international arrivals area on the ground floor.

Stazione Termini (Map pp102-3; 1st 5hr €3.00, 6-12hr per hr €0.60; ☺ 7am-midnight) Lower-ground floor under platform 24.

Libraries
Biblioteca Nazionale Centrale Vittorio Emanuele II (Map pp102-3; ☎ 06 4 98 91; Viale Castro Pretorio 105; ☺ 8.30am-7pm Mon-Fri, 8.30am-1.30pm Sat) Italy's national book repository also has periodicals, newspapers, official acts, drawings, engravings and photographs. Readers need ID to get a day pass.

Media
Il Messaggero (www.ilmessaggero.it in Italian) Pick up Rome's local newspaper which has a weekly listings supplement, *Metro*.

La Repubblica (www.repubblica.it in Italian) Rome-based national newspaper publishes its listings supplement, *Trovaroma*, on Thursdays.

Osservatore Romano (www.vatican.va) Weekly editions of the Vatican's official daily newspaper are published in English.

Roma Cè (www.romace.it in Italian) Rome's best weekly entertainment guide, with a small section in English, comes out on Wednesdays.

Wanted in Rome (www.wantedinrome.it) Expat magazine published on alternate Wednesdays, with classified ads, listings and reviews.

Medical Services
Night pharmacies in the city centre are listed at www.romaturismo.it, in daily newspapers and in pharmacy windows.

Pharmacy Piazza Cinquecento 51 (Map pp102-3; ☎ 06 488 00 19; ☺ 24hr); Stazione Termini (☺ 7.30am-10pm) There is a 24-hour pharmacy on the western flank of Piazza Cinquecento. The Stazione Termini pharmacy is inside the station, on the lower ground floor.

Ospedale Bambino Gesù (Map pp98-9; ☎ 06 6 85 91, first aid for children ☎ 06 685 92 351; Piazza di Sant'Onofrio 4) Rome's paediatric hospital.

Ospedale di Odontoiatria G Eastman (Map p95; ☎ 06 84 48 31; Viale Regina Elena 287b) For emergency dental treatment.

Ospedale San Giacomo (Map pp96-7; ☎ 06 3 62 61; Via A Canova 29) Hospital near Piazza del Popolo.

Ospedale Santo Spirito (Map pp98-9; ☎ 06 6 83 51; Lungotevere in Sassia 1) Hospital near the Vatican; several languages spoken.

Policlinico Umberto I (Map pp102-3; ☎ 06 4 99 71, first aid ☎ 06 499 79 501; Viale del Policlinico 155) Hospital near Stazione Termini.

Money
There's a bank and several currency exchange booths at **Stazione Termini** (Map pp102–3), Leonardo da Vinci Airport and Ciampino Airport. In town, there are numerous exchange booths, including:

American Express (Map pp102-3; ☎ 06 6 76 41; Piazza di Spagna 38; ☺ 8am-7pm Mon-Fri, 8am-1.15pm Sat)

Thomas Cook Travelex (Map pp102-3; ☎ 06 420 20 150; Piazza Barberini 21a; ☺ 9am-7pm Mon-Sat, 9.30am-5pm Sun)

Post
There are post office branches at Piazza dei Capretti 69, Via Terme di Diocleziane 30, Via della Scrofa 61/63 and Via Arenula.

Main post office (Map pp98-9; ☎ 06 679 50 44; Piazza di San Silvestro 20; ☺ 8.30am-6.30pm Mon-Fri, 8.30am-1pm Sat) Collect *poste restante* mail here.

Vatican post office (Map pp98-9; ☎ 06 698 83 406; Piazza San Pietro; ☺ 8.30am-7pm Mon-Fri, 8.30am-6pm Sat) Letters can be posted in blue Vatican post boxes only if they carry Vatican stamps.

Telephone & Fax
There's also hundreds of public payphones dotted about town. Major post offices offer fax services; otherwise, there are numerous private services, usually in *tabacchi* (tobacconist's shops) and stationery stores. You can

make international calls and send emails from the **Centro di Comunicazione** (Map pp102-3; Stazione Termini; 8am-8pm).

Toilets

Your best bet is to nip into a café or bar. However, there are some public toilets at:

Piazza di San Silvestro (Map pp98-9; 10am-7.40pm)
Piazza di Spagna (Map pp98-9; 10am-7.40pm)
Stazione Termini (Map pp102-3; admission €0.70) Lower-ground floor.

Tourist Information

Centro Servizi Pellegrini e Turisti (Map pp98-9; ☎ 06 698 84 466; Piazza San Pietro; 8.30am-7pm Mon-Sat) The Vatican's official tourist office, to the left of the basilica, can provide times of daily Mass but no printed material.
Enjoy Rome (Map pp102-3; ☎ 06 445 18 43; www .enjoyrome.com; Via Marghera 8a; 8.30am-7pm Mon-Fri, 8.30am-2pm Sat) Pick up the useful *When in Rome* city guide from this excellent private tourist office.
Meridiana Information Point (Map pp96-7; ☎ 06 853 04 242; Viale dell'Uccelleria, Villa Borghese; 9am-5pm) For information on Villa Borghese.
Rome Tourist Board (APT; Map pp102-3; ☎ 06 48 89 91; www.romaturismo.it; Via Parigi 5; 9am-7pm Mon-Sat) Has loads of literature on accommodation, itineraries and activities. Also regional maps and guides to Lazio.

The **Comune di Roma** (☎ 06 360 04 399; 9am-7.30pm) runs a multilingual tourist information line and **tourist information points** (9.30am-7.30pm) at **Leonardo da Vinci Airport** (☎ 06 659 54 471; Terminal C, International Arrivals) and at various locations in town:

Castel Sant'Angelo (Map pp98-9; ☎ 06 688 09 707; Piazza Pia)
Piazza Cinquecento (Map pp102-3; ☎ 06 478 25 194) Outside Stazione Termini.
Piazza di San Giovanni in Laterano (Map pp108-9; ☎ 06 772 03 535) Opposite the basilica.
Piazza Navona (Map p104; ☎ 06 688 09 240) Near Piazza delle Cinque Lune.
Piazza Santa Maria Maggiore (Map pp102-3; ☎ 06 474 09 55; Via dell'Olmata)
Piazza Sonnino (Map pp106-7; ☎ 06 583 33 457)
Stazione Termini (Map pp102-3; ☎ 06 489 06 300; 8am-9pm) Opposite platform 4.
Trevi Fountain (Map pp98-9; ☎ 06 678 29 88; Via Marco Minghetti) This tourist point is nearer to Via del Corso than the fountain.
Via dei Fori Imperiali (Map p114; ☎ 06 699 24 307; Piazza del Tempio della Pace)

Via Nazionale (Map pp102-3; ☎ 06 478 24 525) In front of Palazzo delle Esposizioni.

Travel Agencies

CTS (www.cts.it in Italian); Corso Vittorio Emanuele II 297 (Map pp98-9; ☎ 06 687 26 72); Via degli Ausoni 5 (Map pp102-3; ☎ 06 445 01 41) Near La Sapienza university; Via Genova 16 (Map pp102-3; ☎ 06 467 92 71) Italy's official student travel service; offers discounted air, rail and bus tickets to students and travellers under 30. CTS also issues International Student Identity Cards (ISICs). If you're not a student, to get CTS fares you need a CTS card, which costs €28 and is valid for a year.
Enjoy Rome (Map pp102-3; ☎ 06 445 18 43; www .enjoyrome.com; Via Marghera 8a; 8.30am-7pm Mon-Fri, 8.30am-2pm Sat) This tourist office also operates as a travel agency selling discount tickets for air, bus and rail services and dealing with everything from car hire to Vatican tours.
Passaggi (Map pp102-3; Stazione Termini; 7.15am-9pm) Organise all your rail, ferry and car transport here.

DANGERS & ANNOYANCES

Rome is a safe city but, although you're unlikely to be assaulted, petty crime is rife. Pickpockets are active in and around Stazione Termini, at major sights such as the Colosseum and around Piazza di Spagna. Watch out on crowded public transport (bus No 64 from Stazione Termini to St Peter's is notorious). Bag snatchers, particularly on mopeds, are also a nuisance. Always carry bags away from the street side, slung across your body. Similarly, never leave cameras or valuables unguarded, even for a second.

Women travellers may experience unwanted attention, and gropes on crowded buses are not unheard of. It's best to just ignore catcalls, but if you're the victim of wandering hands, make a fuss.

Italians obey road rules with discretion so don't take it for granted that cars and scooters will stop at red lights. The only way to cross the road is to step confidently into the traffic and walk calmly across.

Rome's heavy traffic also means heavy pollution, which can rise to such high levels in summer that elderly people, children and people with respiratory complaints are warned to stay indoors. Check with your hotel for daily information.

For more on dangers and annoyances, see p860.

(Continued on page 110)

GREATER ROME

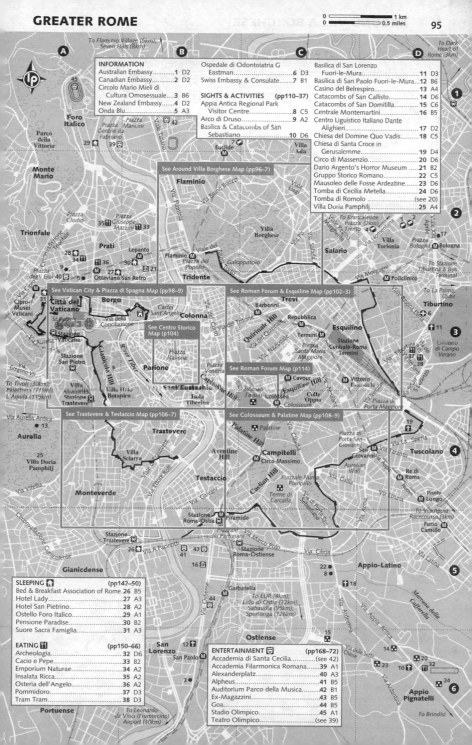

INFORMATION
Australian Embassy...........1 D2
Canadian Embassy...........2 D2
Circolo Mario Mieli di
    Cultura Omosessuale.....3 B6
New Zealand Embassy......4 D2
Onda Blu...........5 A3

Ospedale di Odontoiatria G
    Eastman.................6 D3
Swiss Embassy & Consulate....7 B1

SIGHTS & ACTIVITIES (pp110–37)
Appia Antica Regional Park
    Visitor Centre...........8 C5
Arco di Druso.................9 A2
Basilica & Catacombs of San
    Sebastiano.............10 D6

Basilica di San Lorenzo
    Fuori-le-Mura...........11 D3
Basilica di San Paolo Fuori-le-Mura....12 B6
Casino del Belrespiro.......13 A4
Catacombs of San Callisto....14 D6
Catacombs of San Domitilla....15 C6
Centrale Montemartini......16 B5
Centro Liguistico Italiano Dante
    Alighieri...............17 D2
Chiesa del Domine Quo Vadis....18 C5
Chiesa di Santa Croce in
    Gerusalemme...........19 D4
Circo di Massenzio.........20 D6
Dario Argento's Horror Museum....21 B2
Gruppo Storico Romano....22 C5
Mausoleo delle Fosse Ardeatine....23 D6
Tomba di Cecilia Metella....24 D6
Tomba di Romolo.........(see 20)
Villa Doria Pamphilj........25 A4

SLEEPING (pp142–50)
Bed & Breakfast Association of Rome.26 B5
Hotel Lady...........27 A3
Hotel San Pietrino........28 A2
Ostello Foro Italico.......29 A1
Pensione Paradise.........30 B2
Suore Sacra Famiglia.......31 A3

EATING (pp150–66)
Archeologia...........32 D6
Cacio e Pepe...........33 B2
Emporium Naturae.......34 A2
Insalata Ricca...........35 A2
Osteria dell'Angelo.......36 A2
Pommidoro.............37 D3
Tram Tram.............38 D3

ENTERTAINMENT (pp168–72)
Accademia di Santa Cecilia.......(see 42)
Accademia Filarmonica Romana....39 A1
Alexanderplatz...........40 A3
Alpheus.................41 B5
Auditorium Parco della Musica....42 B1
Ex-Magazzini...........43 B5
Goa...................44 B5
Stadio Olimpico.........45 A1
Teatro Olimpico.........(see 39)

INFORMATION
Austrian Embassy.................................1 F3
Dutch Embassy & Consulate...............2 E2
Meridiana Information Point.................3 F4
Ospedale San Giacomo.........................4 B6
UK Embassy...5 H6

SIGHTS & ACTIVITIES   (pp110–37)
Aerophile Italia...................................6 D5
Bioparco..7 E3
Chiesa di Santa Maria dei Miracoli.......8 B6
Chiesa di Santa Maria del Popolo........9 B5
Chiesa di Santa Maria in Montesanto...10 B6
Explora..11 B4
Galleria Nazionale d'Arte Moderna e
    Contemporanea..............................12 D3
Museo e Galleria Borghese..................13 F4
Museo Nazionale Etrusco
    di Villa Giulia................................14 B3
Villa Borghese....................................15 C4

SLEEPING   (pp142–50)
Hotel de Russie....................................16 B5
Hotel Locarno......................................17 B6
Hotel Tizi..18 H6

EATING   (pp150–66)
Edy...19 C6

DRINKING   (pp166–8)
Caffè delle Arte...............................(see 12)
Canova...20 B5
Rosati...21 B6

ENTERTAINMENT   (pp168–72)
Alien...22 H5
Villa Giulia......................................(see 14)

TRANSPORT   (pp173–7)
I Bike...23 E6
Villa Borghese Car Park.......................24 E6

0 — 200 m
0 — 0.1 miles

E **F** **G** **H**

1

2

3

4

5

6

Parioli

Villa Ada

Villa Grazioli

Piazza Cuba

Piazza Ungheria

Viale dei Parioli

Via A Stoppani

Viale Bruno Buozzi

Via G Antonelli

Via F Siacci

Via Liegi

To Catacombs of Santa Priscilla (750m)

Via G D'Arezzo

Via Cavalieri

Via Aterno

Via M

2

Via U Aldrovandi

Via G Rossini

Piazza G Verdi

Via Nibburo

Viale G Cardosini

Via G Paisiello

3

Viale del Giardino Zoologica

Via S Mercadante Via N Porpora

Via Melburo

Via G Frescobaldi

7

Via Po

Largo N Spinelli

1

Piazza Giardino Zoologico

Via Panorato

Via Basento

Piazzale di Daini

Viale dell'Uccelliera

Viale dei Due Macthronti

Villa Borghese

Villa Torlonia

Largo Aqua Felix

3 ℹ 13
Piazzale del Museo Borghese

4

Piazza di Sienna

Piazza le dei Cavalli Marini

Via di Villa Albani

Via Salaria

Via Pinciana

Via Po

Cavalli Marini

Via G Carsanzio

Isonzo

Via Tevere

Via Salaria

Via Veneto

22

Via Nizza

Via Wolfango Goethe

Piazzale Sienkiewicz

Via Teresa

Via Anieni

5

Via San Paolo del Brasile

Viale del Museo Borghese

Villa Borghese

Via Bergamo

Piazza Fiume

Via Pinciana

Corso d'Italia

Via Campania

Corso d'Italia

Porta Pinciana

Via Pisana

Via Valtellini

Piazzale Brasile

24

Via Calabria

Via Puglie

Via Lucania

Porta Pia

6

23

Largo Federico Fellini

Via Campania

Via Sardegna

Via Romagna

Via Piave

Via Lazio

Via Vittorio Veneto

Via Marche

Via Sicilia

Via Toscana

Via Abruzzi

Via Boncompagni

Via Pietro Canonica

Piazza Sallustio

18

Via Cadorna

5

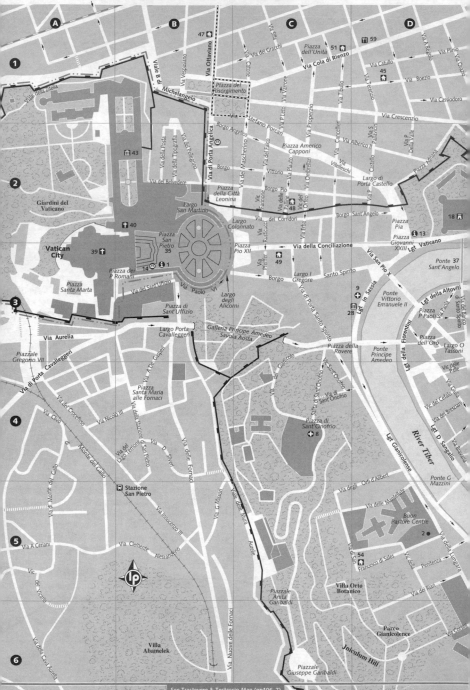

0   200 m
0   0.1 miles

See Around Villa
Borghese Map (pp96–7)

E   F   G   H

Viale Regina Elena

Via Piave

127

Via Goito

122   73
117
100

Via Cernaia

Via Montebello

Via Palestro

Via dei Mille

Via Castro Pretorio

15   1

Piazza
delle Finanze

87   91   Castro
Pretorio

Via Montebello

Via Gaeta

80
10

78

M   Castro
Pretorio

2   2

93

76

Via Volturno

71
116

Piazza dell'
Indipendenza

Via Vittorio Bachelet

Via San Martino della Battaglia

Via Villafranca

96

Città
Universitaria

74

Via Solferino

Via Magenta

Via Vicenza

Via del Mille

67   36

5

Via Marghera

Viale dell'Università

135
138
139

21

47

Via Enrico
de Nicola

Via Marsala

70

4

18

79

Ministero
Difesa
Aeronautica

Viale Castro Pretorio

Via di Castro Pretorio

Via Milazzo

8G

Via Vasse

114
40

Viale P. Gobetti

3   3

Largo di
Villa Peretti   Via L. Einaudi

Piazza
Cinquecento

20

Piazzale
Aldo Moro

46

D'Angiò

136
98
6

M Termini

137

88

Via dei Frentani

Via dei Siculi

11

Via de' Marucci

Stazione
Centrale-Roma
Termini

Via dei Ramni

Piazza
dei Siculi

To CTS (50m)

83
16
110

Via Cavour

14

Via G.
Amendola

125

4   4

Via Tiburtina

Via dei Volsci

62

39

85   G. Giolitti
126

Via Marsala

Via Filippo Turati

Via Cattaneo

Via Rattazzi

Via Giovanni Giolitti

dell'Esquilino

Via Farini

Via degli Equi

103   95
121

65

Piazza
Manfredo
Fanti

Via Principe Amedeo

Via A. Cappellini

Via dei Sabelli

Via dei
Aurum

Via di Porta Labicana

29

Piazza
Santa Maria
Maggiore

72

77

Via Napoleone III

89

Via Mamiani

Largo Sant'
Alfonso

Martino ai Monti   Via di San Vito

Via Carlo Alberto

Via Ricasoli

Via Principe Umberto

Via Giovanni Giolitti

5   5

Largo
Brancaccio   Via dello Statuto

106

Piazza
Vittorio
Emanuele II

Vittorio
Emanuele   M

112

Via Lamarmora

Via dei Pross.

Via Leopardi

111

Parco
di Traiano

Largo
Leopardi

Via Merulana

Via Conte Verde

Via Principe Eugenio

Via di Porta Maggiore

Esquilino

63

Via Buonarroti

Via Machiavelli

Via Foscolo

Piazza
Dante

Via Petrarca

Via Emanuele Filiberto

Via Carlo

Via Nino Bixio

Viale Manzoni

58

Terme di Traiano

Via C. Pascal

Via Ferruccio

Via Giusti

Via C. Botta

Via Giustiniani

Via Alfieri

Via Tasso

Via di Santa Croce in Gerusalemme

La Grance

Piazza
di Porta
Maggiore

6   6

See Colosseum & Palatine Map (pp108–9)

0 _____ 100 m
0 _____ 0.1 miles

A **B** **C** **D**

1

Ponte
Umberto I

Piazza
Cardelli

V dei Prefetti

Piazza di
Firenze

1 @

Via della Scrofa

Via di Monte Brianzo

Via d'Ascanio

Via della Stelletta

Lungotevere Tor di Nona

15
Piazza Ponte
Umberto I

Via dell'Orso

49   27

Via dei Portoghesi

52

Via di Tor di Nona

Via G. Zanardelli

Via dell'Acquasparta

14

Piazza
Lacellotti

Via dei Tre Archi

Via dei Coronari

Piazza
Sant'
Apollinare

8

Piazza
di Sant'
Agostino
Agostino

Via delle Coppelle

Piazza in
Campo Marzio

35

Piazza degli Uffici di Vicario

45

Piazza
delle
Coppelle

44

2

Piazza di
San Salvatore
in Lauro

Piazzella
di San
Simeone

Via della Vetrina

Piazza Tor
Sanguigna

Piazza
delle
Cinque Lune

4

3
@

69

Via San Giovanni d'Arco

Largo
G Toniolo

Piazza
Rondanini

67

Piazza
della
Maddalena

Via delle
Colonnelle

48

L'Arco di Pace

Largo
Febo

Piazza
di Monte-
vecchio

Vic delle Vacche

Vicolo delle Volpe

Via delle Vetrine

Via delle Vacche

64

Piazza
del Fico

54

53

Via di Santa Maria dell'Anima

12

Piazza
Navona
21

Piazza
di San
Luigi
dei Francesi

6

39

Via Giustiniani

Via della Rosetta

Via della Rosetta

60

3

Via Monte
Giordano

59

Via del Corallo

Via de' Banchi Vecchi

Via di Tor Millina

70

10

17

Piazza
Madama

Corso del Rinascimento

31

22

Piazza
della
Rotonda

38

Via della Chiesa Nuova

Via del Teatro Pace

Via del Governo Vecchio

7

Via de Cupis

Piazza
Sant'
Eustachio

20

51

5

Via del Grana

18

11

Via degli Staderari

56

57

Via di Santa Chiara

Via della Palombella

Piazza
della
Minerva

4

Piazza
della
Chiesa
Nuova

Via Sora

Vic Savelli

Piazza
di Pasquino

47

Via del Canestrari

25

Via dei Sediari

66

Via di Teatro Valle

Piazza
Santa
Chiara

28

Corso Vittorio Emanuele II

33

Via del Pellegrino

Via della Cancelleria

Parione

13

Piazza
di San
Pantaleo

68

Piazza
dei Massimi

32

Largo del
Teatro Valle

Sant'Eustachio

Via Arco della
Ciambella

5

Via de' Cappellari

Via di
Montoro

Piazza della Cancelleria

50

40

Via dei Baullari

Vic dei Bovari

46

Largo
dei Chiavari

Piazza
del Paradiso

Corso Vittorio Emanuele II

Piazza
Vidoni

Via del Sudario

65

Largo
di Stimmate

Largo di
Torre Argentina

Corso Vittorio
Emanuele II

6

Via del Monserrato

43

42

Via di Gallo

55

58

9

Campo
de' Fiori

36

63

Via dei Baullari

62

24

23

29

Piazza
del Biscione

Largo
del
Pallaro

Piazza
dei Satiri

26

Via del Monte della Farina

71

Via di Sant'Anna

Largo
Arenula

Via Florida

30

Via San Girolamo
della Carità

16

Piazza Farnese

Via della Corda

Piazza
della
Quercia

61

37

19

Piazza
Capodiferro

Via Giulia

Via dei Farnesi

Via del Mascherone

Via di Polveroni

Via Capo di Ferro

Via dell'Arco del Monte

41

Largo
dei Librari

Piazza del
Monte di
Pietà

34

Via de' Giubbonari

Piazza B.
Cairoli

Via Arenula

Via Paganica

Via del Falegnami

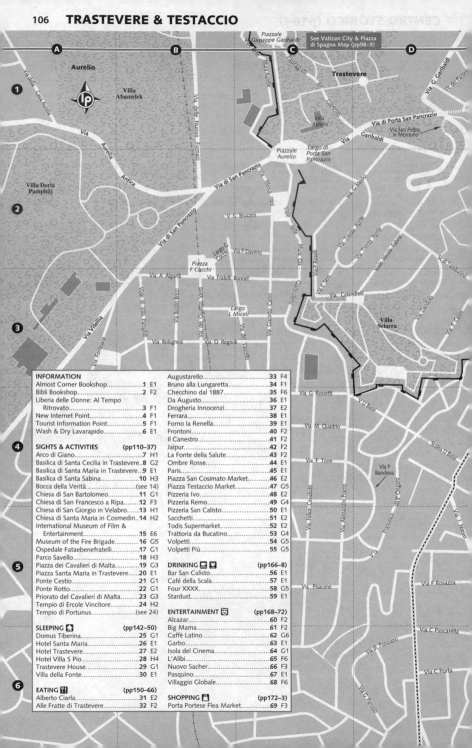

See Vatican City & Piazza di Spagna Map (pp98–9)

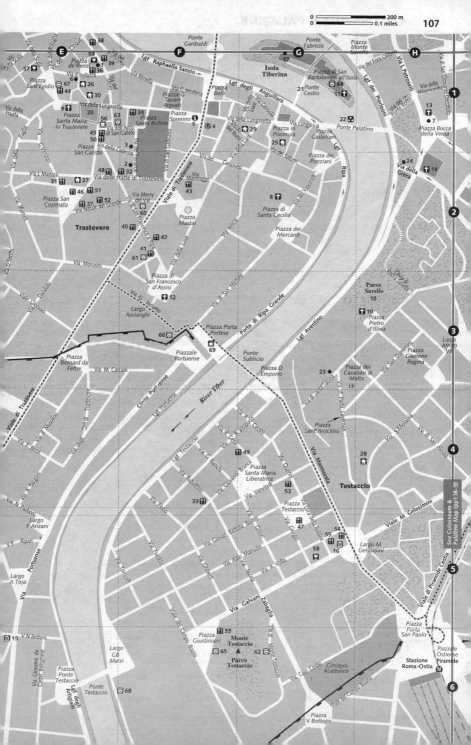

0 — 200 m
0 — 0.1 miles

E **F** **G** **H**

Ponte Garibaldi
Ponte Fabricio
Piazza Monte Savello

Lgt Raphaello Sanzio

Via della Scala
Via della Scala
57
Piazza de' Renzi 59
39
Via Renella
Lgt degli Anguillara
Isola Tiberina
17
Piazza di San Bartolomeo all'Isola
64
Via del Foro Olitorio
Via di San Giovanni Decollato
1

Piazza Sant'Egidio
67 6
44
1
38
Via del Politeama
Via G. Modena
Piazza Belli
21 Ponte Cestio
11
Lgt dei Pierleoni
Lgt de Cenci
Via Portico
13
7
Piazza Bocca della Verità

9
Via della Lungaretta
30
Piazza G Tavani Arguati
Piazza Sonnino
4
Via della Lungaretta
Piazza in Piscinula
25
Ponte Palatino
22
24
Via della Greca
14

Piazza Santa Maria in Trastevere
56
20
34
Piazza Santa Rufina
29
Via della Luce
Piazza Castellani
Lgt
50
45
Via dell'Arco di San Calisto

Piazza San Calisto
3
2
32
Via della Cisterna
Via di San Calisto
Via dei Genovesi
Piazza dei Ponziani
Ripa

48
Via delle fratte di Trastevere
31
27
Via L Manara
43
Via Marmaggi
8
Piazza di Santa Cecilia

Piazza San Cosimato
46
51
37
52
60
Via Natale del Grande
Trastevere
40
Piazza dei Mercanti

Via Merry del Val
Piazza Mastai
42
41
61
Via della Luce
Via Anicia
Via dei Vascelli

Via Morosini
Piazza di San Francesco d'Assisi
12
Via di San Michele
Via di Porta di Ripa Grande

Largo Ascianghi
66
Piazza Porta Portese
69
Parco Savello
18
10
Piazza Pietro d'Illiria
Largo Arrigo VII

Piazza Bernard da Feltre
Via M Cattaneo
Piazzale Portuense
Ponte Sublicio
Piazza D Emporio
23
Piazza dei Cavalieri di Malta
Piazza Giunone Regina

Viale di Trastevere
Clivio Portuense
Lgt Portuense
River Tiber
Lgt Aventino

Via dell'Orti di Trastevere
Via A. Baiamonti
Via N. Palloni
49
Piazza Santa Maria Liberatrice
53
Testaccio
28

Via E. Rezzi
Lgt Testaccio
Via G Bianchi
Via C. Balbo
Via Giovanni Branca
Via Galvani
Via Mastro Giorgio
Via Mamorata

Largo F Anzani
V.P. Ripari
33
Via Rubattino
Piazza Testaccio
47
54
55
16
58
Largo M Gelsomini
Viale M Gelsomini

Largo A Toja
Via Portuense
Via Pacinotti
Via G Battista Bodoni
Via Aldo Manuzio
Via A Volta

Via V N Bettoni
15
Largo GB Marzi
35
Monte Testaccio
65
62
Parco Testaccio
Cimitero Acattolico
Piazza Porta San Paolo
Piazzale Ostiense
Piramide
M

Via Giovanni da Castel Bolognese
Piazza Ponte Testaccio
Ponte Testaccio
Lgt degli Artigiani
68
Piazza Giustiniani
Via Zabaglia
Via Caio Cestio
Viale del Campo Boario
Stazione Roma-Ostia

Piazza V Bottego

See Colosseum & Palatine Map (pp138-9)
Via di Piramide Cestia

1 **2** **3** **4** **5** **6**

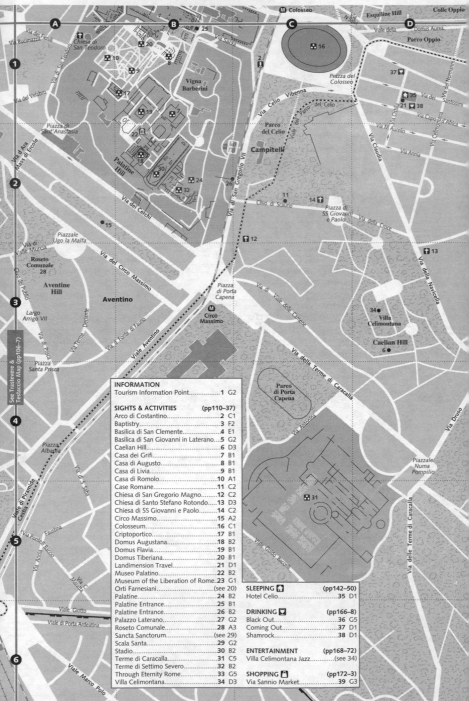

INFORMATION

Tourism Information Point	**1**	G2

SIGHTS & ACTIVITIES (pp110–37)

Arco di Costantino	**2**	C1
Baptistry	**3**	F2
Basilica di San Clemente	**4**	E1
Basilica di San Giovanni in Laterano	**5**	G2
Caelian Hill	**6**	D3
Casa dei Grifi	**7**	B1
Casa di Augusto	**8**	B1
Casa di Livia	**9**	B1
Casa di Romolo	**10**	A1
Case Romane	**11**	C2
Chiesa di San Gregorio Magno	**12**	C2
Chiesa di Santo Stefano Rotondo	**13**	D3
Chiesa di SS Giovanni e Paolo	**14**	C2
Circo Massimo	**15**	A2
Colosseum	**16**	C1
Criptoportico	**17**	B1
Domus Augustana	**18**	B2
Domus Flavia	**19**	B1
Domus Tiberiana	**20**	B1
Landimension Travel	**21**	D1
Museo Palatino	**22**	B2
Museum of the Liberation of Rome	**23**	G1
Orti Farnesiani	(see 20)	
Palatine	**24**	B2
Palatine Entrance	**25**	B1
Palatine Entrance	**26**	B2
Palazzo Laterano	**27**	G2
Roseto Comunale	**28**	A3
Sancta Sanctorum	(see 29)	
Scala Santa	**29**	G2
Stadio	**30**	B2
Terme di Caracalla	**31**	C5
Terme di Settimo Severo	**32**	B2
Through Eternity Rome	**33**	B1
Villa Celimontana	**34**	D3

SLEEPING (pp142–50)

Hotel Celio	**35**	D1

DRINKING (pp166–8)

Black Out	**36**	G5
Coming Out	**37**	D1
Shamrock	**38**	D1

ENTERTAINMENT (pp168–72)

Villa Celimontana Jazz	(see 34)	

SHOPPING (pp172–3)

Via Sannio Market	**39**	G3

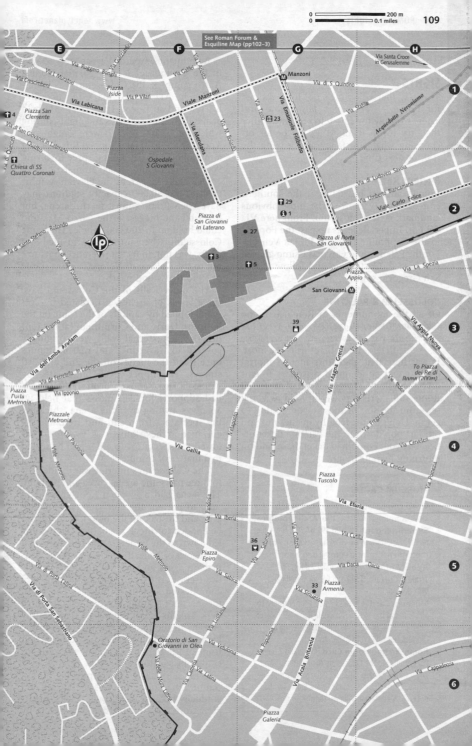

0 ⸻ 200 m
0 ⸻ 0.1 miles

E   F   G   H

See Roman Forum &
Esquiline Map (pp102–3)

Via Santa Croce
in Gerusalemme

Via I. Muratori
Via Ruggero Bonghi
Via Crescimbeni
Via I. Muratori
Piazza
Iside
Via P Villari
Via Labicana
Via Galilei
Viale Manzoni
Manzoni M
Via di S. Quintino
Via Statilia
Acquedotto Neroniano
1

Via Ariosto
Via M. Buiardo
Via Tasso
Via Emanuele Filiberto
23
Via di Ludovico Savoia

Piazza San
Clemente
4
Via di San Giovanni in Laterano
Quattro
Via di Querceti
Ospedale
S Giovanni
Via Merulana

Chiesa di SS
Quattro Coronati

Via Umberto Biancamano
Viale Carlo Felice

29
1
2

Piazza di
San Giovanni
in Laterano
27
Piazza di Porta
San Giovanni
Via La Spezia

Via di Santo Stefano Rotondo
Via di Vila Fonseca

3
5
Piazza
Appio
San Giovanni M

Via di S. Erasmo
Via dell'Amba Aradam
39

Via Appia Nuova
3

Via de Ferretella in Laterano
Via Sannio
Via Amba N
Via Veio
Via Magna Grecia
Via Faleria
Via Fregene
To Piazza
dei Re di
Roma (200m)

Piazza
Porta
Metronia
Via Ipponio
Via Vetulonia
Via Veio
Via Cervelen
4

Piazzale
Metronia
Via Pannonia
Viale Metronio
Via Gallia
Via Licia
Via Pandosia
Via Turi
Via Cilizia
Piazza
Tuscolo
Via Ceneda
Via Pareta
Via Etruria
Via Cutilia

Viale Metronio
Piazza
Epiro
Via Iberia
Via Satrico
Via Saturnia
Via Collazia
36
Via Dacia
Dacia
Via Imea
5

Via di Porta Latina
Via di Porta San Sebastiano
Piazza
Armenia
33
Via Populonia
Via Sinuessa
Via Acaia Britannia

Oratorio di San
Giovanni in Olea
Via Vetulonia
Via Latina
Via Capina
Via delle Mura Latine
Via Cappadocia
6

Piazza
Galeria

(Continued from page 94)

SIGHTS

They say that a lifetime's not long enough for Rome – *Roma, non basta una vita!* There's simply too much to see. And rather than try to do it all, you'd be better off choosing what you fancy and leaving the rest for next time.

Ancient Rome

Rome's ancient heart lies at the southern end of the city centre. The most obvious landmark is the Colosseum. From here Via dei Fori Imperiale leads up past the Forums to the Capitoline Hill and Piazza Venezia. For the Palatine and Circo Massimo go past the Arco di Costantino and follow Via di San Gregorio south.

COLOSSEUM & PALATINE

Of all the monuments in Rome, it is the **Colosseum** (Colosseo; Map pp108-9; ☎ 06 399 67 700; www.pierreci.it; Piazza del Colosseo; admission incl Palatine €8; ⏰ 9am-1hr before sunset) that thrills the most. It was here that gladiators met in mortal combat and condemned prisoners fought off hungry lions. The great symbol of eternal Rome still exerts a powerful hold as you'll see from the size of the crowds waiting to get in. Don't let the lengthy queues put you off: just pop down to the Palatine ticket office, buy your combined ticket there, and on returning march straight in.

MUSEUM CARDS

Three combination tickets are available for sites administered by the **Archaeological Superintendent** (☎ 06 399 67 700; www.pier reci.it). Tickets can be purchased at any of the monuments or museums listed here:

Appia Antica Card (€6, valid 7 days) For the Terme di Caracalla, Tomba di Cecilia Metella and Villa dei Quintili.

Museum Card (€9, valid 7 days) For entrance to all venues of the Museo Nazionale Romano: Palazzo Altemps, Palazzo Massimo alle Terme, Terme di Diocleziano and Crypta Balbi.

Roma Archaeologia Card (€20, valid 7 days) For entrance to the Colosseum, the Palatine, Terme di Caracalla, Palazzo Altemps, Palazzo Massimo alle Terme, Terme di Diocleziano, Crypta Balbi, Tomba di Cecilia Metella and Villa dei Quintili.

Built by the emperor Vespasian (r 69–79) in the grounds of Nero's palatial Domus Aurea complex, the Colosseum was inaugurated in AD 80. To mark the occasion his son and successor Titus (r 79–81) held games that lasted 100 days and nights, during which some 5000 animals were slaughtered. Trajan (r 98–117) later topped this, holding a marathon 117-day killing spree involving 9000 gladiators and 10,000 animals.

Originally known as the Flavian Amphitheatre, the 50,000-capacity stadium may have been Rome's most fearful arena, but it wasn't the biggest – the Circo Massimo could hold up to 200,000 people. The name Colosseum, when introduced in medieval times, was not, in fact, a reference to its size but to the *Colosso di Nerone,* a giant statue of Nero that stood nearby.

The outer walls of the Colosseum have three levels of arches, articulated by columns topped by capitals of the Ionic (at the bottom), Doric and Corinthian (at the top) orders. The external walls were originally covered in travertine, and marble statues once filled the niches on the 2nd and 3rd storeys. The upper level, punctuated by windows and slender Corinthian pilasters, had supports for 240 masts that held up a canvas awning over the arena, shielding the spectators from sun and rain. The 80 entrance arches, known as *vomitoria,* allowed the spectators to enter and be seated in a matter of minutes.

The Colosseum's interior was divided into three parts: the arena, cavea and podium. The **arena** had a wooden floor covered in sand to prevent the combatants from slipping and to soak up the blood. It could also be flooded for mock sea battles. Trap doors led down to the underground chambers and passageways beneath the arena floor. Animals in cages and sets for the various battles were hoisted onto the arena by a very complicated system of pulleys. The **cavea**, for spectator seating, was divided into three tiers: knights sat in the lowest tier, wealthy citizens in the middle and the plebs in the highest tier. The **podium**, a broad terrace in front of the tiers of seats, was reserved for emperors, senators and VIPs.

With the fall of the Empire in the 6th century, the Colosseum was abandoned and gradually became overgrown. Exotic plants grew from seeds inadvertently carried in by

---

GLADIATORS

Gladiatorial fighting originated as an Etruscan funerary rite, as a form of human sacrifice. But by the 1st century BC it had developed into something far more gruesome – big business – and emperors staged increasingly bloodthirsty spectacles; Augustus once showed 5000 pairs of gladiators while Trajan had 9000 perform for him.

The combatants – prisoners of war, slaves or volunteers – were paired off to ensure the greatest spectacle. Thus, one would have a heavy sword and shield and the other, almost naked, would carry a net and trident. Bouts were not necessarily to the death as a defeated gladiator could appeal to the presiding VIP who, if he wanted to curry popular favour, would judge on the basis of the crowd's reaction. Thumbs up meant life, thumbs down death, which the defeated man was expected to face with courage.

Although gambling was technically illegal in Rome, vast sums were wagered on gladiatorial combats. Successful gladiators were popular heroes and lived to enjoy a comfortable retirement, with some running their own training schools.

African and Asian beasts imported for the games. In the Middle Ages, the Colosseum became a fortress, occupied by two of the city's warrior families: the Frangipani and the Annibaldi. Its reputation as the symbol of Rome, the Eternal City, also dates to the Middle Ages, with Bede writing that 'while the Colosseum stands, Rome shall stand, but when the Colosseum falls, Rome shall fall – and when Rome falls, the world will end'.

Damaged several times by earthquakes, it was later used as a source of stone and marble for later generations of builders. Pollution and the vibrations caused by traffic and the metro have also taken their toll.

On the western side of the Colosseum, the **Arco di Costantino** (Map pp108–9) was built to honour Constantine following his victory over rival Maxentius at the battle of the Milvian Bridge (northwest of Villa Borghese) in AD 312.

Just down the road, the **Palatine** (Map pp108-9; ☎ 06 399 67 700; entrances at Piazza di Santa Maria Nova & Via di San Gregorio VII 30; admission incl Colosseum €8; ⊙ 9am-1hr before sunset) is where Romulus killed his brother Remus and founded Rome in 753 BC. Today it's a beautiful area of ruins and great views – ideal for a picnic.

Overlooking the Roman Forum, the Palatine was ancient Rome's poshest neighbourhood; aristocrats sought to build houses here and successive emperors built increasingly opulent palaces. But after Rome's fall, the Palatine fell into disrepair and in the Middle Ages churches and castles were built over the ruins. During the Renaissance, members of wealthy families, most notably Cardinal

Alessandro Farnese, established gardens on the hill.

The largest part of the Palatine, as it appears today, is covered by the ruins of Emperor Domitian's vast complex, which served as the main imperial palace for 300 years. Divided into the Domus Flavia (imperial palace), the Domus Augustana (the emperor's private residence) and a *stadio* (stadium), it was built by the architect Rabirius in the 1st century AD. To do so Rabirius levelled a crest of land and buried many Republican-era houses; some have since been unearthed.

On entering from the Roman Forum follow the path ahead to the ruins of the **Domus Augustana** (Map pp108–9). Originally this residence was built on two levels with rooms leading off a garden courtyard on each floor. You can't get down to the lower level but from above you can see the basin of a fountain and beyond it rooms that were paved with coloured marble. The palace had an elaborate colonnaded façade to the south overlooking the Circo Massimo, from where you get the clearest indication of the grand scale of the complex. Southeast of the Domus Augustana is the **stadio** (Map pp108–9), probably used by emperors for private games and events.

Next to the stadium are the scant remains of baths built by Septimus Severus, the **Terme di Settimio Severo** (Map pp108–9).

The big white building (a former convent) between the Domus Augustana and the Domus Flavia houses the **Museo Palatino** (Map pp108-9; ⊙ 9am-2hr before sunset). Here you'll see artefacts found on the Palatine, some dating to the Palaeolithic and Bronze Ages.

CHEAP THRILLS

With more than 900 churches and some of the world's most famous museums and monuments, you'd expect to spend a fortune sightseeing in Rome. Fortunately, it's possible to enjoy many of the city's sights without spending a penny.

You won't have to fork out anything to visit the Roman Forum, Trevi Fountain, Spanish Steps, Pantheon, Bocca della Verità, or admire the exterior of the Colosseum and Castel Sant'Angelo. All of Rome's churches, many of which contain extraordinary works of art, are also free.

You'll find **Michelangelo** in San Pietro in Vincoli (p122), St Peter's Basilica (p133), Chiesa di Santa Maria Sopra Minerva (p119) and Piazza del Campidoglio (p116); **Bernini** in Chiesa di San Francesco a Ripa (p126), St Peter's Basilica (p133), outside Chiesa di Santa Maria Sopra Minerva (p119), on Ponte Sant'Angelo (p137), at Sant'Andrea al Quirinale (p124) and in the Piazza Navona (p119); and **Caravaggio** in Chiesa di Santa Maria del Popolo (p122), Chiesa di Sant'Agostino (p120) and Chiesa di San Luigi dei Francesi (p120).

North of the Museo Palatino is the **Domus Flavia** (Map pp108–9), once connected to the Domus Augustana. The palace comprised three large halls to the north (the central one of which was the emperor's throne room) and a large *triclinium* (banqueting hall) to the south, which was paved in coloured marble that can still be seen. The Domus Flavia was constructed over earlier edifices. One of these, which can sometimes be visited (ask at the Palatine entrance on Via di San Gregorio VII), is the **Casa dei Grifi** (House of the Griffins; Map pp108–9), so called because of a stucco relief of two griffins in one of the rooms. It is the oldest building on the Palatine and dates from the late 2nd or 1st century BC.

Among the best-preserved buildings on the Palatine is the **Casa di Livia** (Map pp108–9), home of Augustus' wife Livia. Nearby, the **Casa di Augusto** (Map pp108–9) was hubby's pile. Both these houses are being restored and can sometimes be visited, depending on what the archaeologists and restorers are up to.

Next to the Casa di Augusto is the **Casa di Romolo** (House of Romulus; Map pp108–9), where it is thought Romulus and Remus were brought up after their discovery by the shepherd Faustulus. Excavations carried out in the 1940s revealed evidence of supports for wattle and daub huts dating from the 9th century BC.

The **Criptoportico** (Cryptoporticus; Map pp108–9) is south of the Casa di Livia. It's a 128m tunnel built by Nero to connect his Domus Aurea (see left) with the imperial palaces on the Palatine.

The area west of this was once the **Domus Tiberiana** (Tiberius' Palace; Map pp108–9) which Caligula extended further northwards to the Forum; today it is the site of the **Orti Farnesiani** (Map pp108–9), Alessandro Farnese's mid-16th-century gardens. Considered one of Europe's earliest botanical gardens, it's a lovely area of rose gardens and shady pines. Twin pavilions stand at the northern point of the garden, from where the view over the Forum is breathtaking.

Over the road from the Colosseum, the **Domus Aurea** (Golden House; Map pp102-3; ☎ 06 399 67 700; www.pierreci.it; Viale della Domus Aurea; admission €5, plus booking fee €1.50; ☼ 9am-7.45pm Mon, Wed & Sun, booking essential) was Nero's great gift to himself. A monumental exercise in vanity, the vast palace spread over the Palatine, Oppian (Oppio) and Caelian (Celio) Hills. Built after the fire of AD 64 and named after the gold that covered its façade, the Domus Aurea boasted frescoed banqueting halls, nymphaeums, baths and terraces. In the grounds that covered up to a third of the city, wild animals roamed and drank from the artificial lake.

After Nero's death in 68, his successors were quick to remove all trace of his excesses: Vespasian drained the lake and built the Colosseum in its place; Domitian built his palace on the Palatine; and Trajan constructed a bath complex on top of the Oppian Hill (this is this area that has been excavated). Today, it's quite difficult to distinguish between the parts of the original complex and the later baths.

The baths and the underlying ruins were abandoned by the 6th century. During the Renaissance, artists (including Ghirlandaio, Perugino and Raphael) lowered themselves into the ruins in order to study the frescoes and doodle on the walls.

Experts reckon that only about 20% of the palace remains and although excavations are ongoing you can visit some 30-odd underground rooms. The octagonal room at the end of the tour is where Suetonius describes Nero playing the lyre on a revolving stage.

THE FORUMS & AROUND

In ancient Rome, a forum was a shopping mall, civic centre and religious complex all rolled into one. The original Roman Forum got too small around 46 BC and successive emperors built new ones (the Imperial Forums) as demand and vanity required. They were dramatic public spaces, richly decorated and grandly scaled. Today, however, they are ruins, so be prepared to use your imagination or join a guided tour.

As you walk up Via dei Fori Imperiali from the Colosseum you'll see the **Roman Forum** (Foro Romano; Map p114; ☎ 06 3996 77 00; entrances at Largo Romolo e Remo 5-6, Piazza di Santa Maria Nova 53 & Via di Monte Tarpeo; admission free; ☒ 9am-1hr before sunset) on your left. Before going in you might want to fork out €4 for an audioguide or €3.50 for the daily 10.30am tour in English. The tour departs from the Piazza di Santa Maria Nova entrance.

The oldest and most famous of the forums, the Roman Forum grew over the course of 900 years. Originally an Etruscan burial ground, it was first developed in the 7th century BC and expanded to become the gleaming heart of the Roman Republic. Its importance declined after the 4th century until eventually the site was used as pasture land.

In the Middle Ages it was known as the *Campo Vaccino* (literally 'cow field') and extensively plundered for its stone and marble. Note that it was the Romans, not invading barbarians, who dismantled the city in order to build their new palaces, churches and monuments.

During the Renaissance, with the renewed appreciation of all things classical, the Forum provided inspiration for artists and architects. The area was systematically excavated in the 18th and 19th centuries, and the excavations continue.

As you enter the Forum from Via dei Fori Imperiali, to your left is the **Tempio di Antonino e Faustina** (Map p114), erected in AD 141 by the Senate and dedicated to the Empress Faustina and later to the Emperor Antoninus Pius. It was transformed into a church

in the 8th century, so the soaring columns now frame the **Chiesa di San Lorenzo in Miranda** (Map p114). To your right the **Basilica Aemilia** (Map p114), built in 179 BC, was 100m long with a two-storey porticoed façade lined with shops.

At the end of this short path you come to the **Via Sacra**, which traverses the Roman Forum from northwest to southeast. Opposite the basilica stands the **Tempio di Giulio Cesare** (Temple of Julius Caesar; Map p114), erected by Augustus in 29 BC on the site where Caesar's body had been burned 15 years before. Head right up Via Sacra and you reach the **Curia** (Map p114), the building on the right just after the Basilica Aemilia. Once the meeting place of the Roman Senate, it was rebuilt successively by Julius Caesar, Augustus, Domitian and Diocletian, and converted into a Christian church in the Middle Ages. What you see today is a 1937 reconstruction of Diocletian's Curia. The bronze doors are copies – the originals were used by Borromini for the Basilica di San Giovanni in Laterano (see p127).

In front of the Curia is the famous **Lapis Niger** (Map p114), a large piece of black marble that covered a sacred area which legend says was the tomb of Romulus. Down a short flight of stairs (closed to the public) under the Lapis Niger is the oldest-known Latin inscription, dating from the 6th century BC.

At the end of Via Sacra stands the **Arco di Settimio Severo** (Arch of Septimus Severus; Map p114). Erected in AD 203 to celebrate the Roman victory over the Parthians (from modern day Iran), the arch is one of the finest examples of its type in Italy. Nearby, the **Millarium Aureum** (Map p114) marked the very centre of ancient Rome, from which distances to the city were measured.

On your left are the remains of the **Rostrum** (Map p114), an elaborate podium for public speakers. It was here that Shakespeare's Mark Antony made his famous 'Friends, Roman, countrymen…' speech.

The eight granite columns that you see from here are all that remain of the **Tempio di Saturno** (Temple of Saturn; Map p114), one of Rome's most important temples. Inaugurated in 497 BC, it was used as the state treasury and during Caesar's rule contained 13 tonnes of gold, 114 tonnes of silver and 30 million silver coins. Behind the temple and backing onto the Capitoline are (from

ROME & LAZIO

north to south) the ruins of the **Tempio della Concordia** (Temple of Concord; Map p114), the three remaining columns of **Tempio di Vespasiano** (Temple of Vespasian; Map p114) and **Portico degli Dei Consenti** (Map p114).

Marking the centre of Piazza del Foro, the forum's main market and meeting place during the Republican era, is the **Colonna di Foca** (Column of Phocus; Map p114). The last monument erected in the Roman Forum, it was built in AD 608 to honour the Eastern Roman Emperor Phocus, who donated the Pantheon to the Church. To your right are the remains of the **Basilica Giulia** (Map p114), the 1st-century BC headquarters of the Roman civil justice system.

ROMAN FORUM

0 ————————— 200 m
0 ————————— 0.1 miles

INFORMATION		
Tourist Information Point	1	C4

SIGHTS & ACTIVITIES		
Arco di Settimio Severo	2	A4
Arco di Tito	3	C5
Basilica Aemilia	4	B4
Basilica di Costantino	5	C5
Basilica di SS Cosma e Damiano	6	C4
Basilica Giulia	7	A4
Capitoline Museum	(see 25)	
Carcere Mamertino	8	A4
Casa delle Vestali	9	B5
Chiesa di San Lorenzo in Miranda	(see 32)	
Chiesa di Santa Francesca Romana	10	C5
Chiesa di Santa Maria Antiqua	11	B5
Chiesa di Santa Maria in Aracoeli	12	A3
Colonna di Foca	13	A4
Context in Rome	14	D3
Curia	15	B4

Foro di Cesare	16	A3
Imperial Forum (Foro di Augusto)	17	B3
Imperial Forum (Foro di Nerva)	18	B3
Imperial Forums Visitor Centre	19	C4
Lapis Niger	20	B4
Largo Romolo e Remo Entrance	21	B4
Millarium Aureum	22	A4
Museo Centrale del Risorgimento	23	A3
Palazzo Nuovo	24	A3
Palazzo Senatorio	25	A4
Piazza del Campidoglio	26	A4
Piazza di Santa Maria Nova Entrance	27	C5
Portico degli Dei Consenti	28	A4
Rostrum	29	A4
Statue of Marcus Aurelius	30	A4
Statue of Minerva	(see 25)	
Tabularium	(see 25)	
Tempio della Concordia	31	A4
Tempio di Antonino e Faustina	32	A4
Tempio di Castore e Polluce	33	B5

Tempio di Giulio Cesare	34	B4
Tempio di Romolo	35	C4
Tempio di Saturno	36	A4
Tempio di Venere e Roma	37	D5
Tempio di Vespasiano	38	A4
Tempio di Vesta	39	B5
Via di Monte Tarpeo Entrance	40	A4
Vittoriano	41	A3

SLEEPING		
Hotel Forum	42	C3
Hotel Nerva	43	C3

EATING		
Baires	44	C3

DRINKING		
Café dei Musei	45	A4
Cavour 313	46	C3

At the end of the basilica is the **Tempio di Castore e Polluce** (Temple of Castor and Pollux; Map p114), built in 489 BC to mark the defeat of the Etruscan Tarquins and in honour of the Dioscuri (or Heavenly Twins) who miraculously appeared to the Roman troops during an important battle. Look out for the three Corinthian columns. Behind the temple and closed to the public is the **Chiesa di Santa Maria Antiqua** (Map p114), the oldest Christian church in the Forum.

Back towards Via Sacra is the **Casa delle Vestali** (House of the Vestal Virgins; Map p114), home of the virgins who tended the sacred flame in the adjoining **Tempio di Vesta** (Map p114). The six priestesses were selected from patrician families when aged between six and 10. They had to serve in the temple for 30 years and were bound by a vow of chastity during this time. If the flame in the temple went out the priestess responsible would be flogged. If a priestess lost her virginity she was buried alive, since her blood could not be spilled, and the offending man was flogged to death.

Once back on Via Sacra turn left and after the **Tempio di Romolo** (Map p114), you'll see the vast **Basilica di Costantino** (Map p114), also known as the Basilica di Massenzio, on your left. Emperor Maxentius initiated work on the basilica and Constantine finished it in AD 315. A colossal statue of Constantine was unearthed at the site in 1487. Pieces of this statue – a head, hand and foot – are on display in the courtyard of the Palazzo dei Conservatori in the Capitoline Museums (see p116).

Following the path you come to the **Arco di Tito** (Arch of Titus; Map p114), built in AD 81 to celebrate Vespasian and Titus' victories against Jerusalem. In the past, Roman Jews would avoid passing under this arch, the historical symbol of the beginning of the Diaspora.

Connected to the Forum by the Basilica di Costantino is the **Basilica di SS Cosma e Damiano** (Map p114; ☎ 06 699 15 40; entrance at Via dei Fori Imperiale; ⊙ 8am-1pm & 3-7pm), a 6th-century church best known for the vivid mosaics behind the altar. Depicting Jesus flanked by St Peter and St Paul against an electric blue background, they are among the most beautiful in Rome. In a room off the 17th-century cloisters is a vast Neapolitan *presepio* (Nativity scene) dating to the 18th century.

At the eastern end of the Forum, the 9th-century **Chiesa di Santa Francesca Romana** (Map p114; ☎ 06 679 55 28; Piazza di Santa Francesca Romana; ⊙ 9.30am-noon & 3-5pm) incorporates part of the **Tempio di Venere e Roma** (Temple of Venus and Rome; Map p114). Every 9 March Roman taxi drivers park as close as possible to the church to be blessed by Santa Francesca Romana, the patron saint of motorists who lies beneath the altar.

On the other side of Via dei Fori Imperiali, the collection of forums known as the **Imperial Forums** (Fori Imperiali; Map pp102-3; ☎ 06 679 77 86; www.capitolium.org; Via dei Fori Imperiali; tours with guide €7; ⊙ 9am-7pm Apr-Sep, 9am-6pm Oct-Mar) were constructed by Trajan, Augustus, Caesar, Nerva and Vespasian between 42 BC and AD 112.

Unfortunately much of the area was buried in 1933 when Mussolini built Via dei Fori Imperiali between the Colosseum and Piazza Venezia. To visit the forums – except for Foro di Traiano, see below – you'll have to book a guided tour at the **Imperial Forums visitor centre** (Map p114; ☎ 06 679 77 86; Via dei Fori Imperiali; ⊙ 9.30am-6.30pm).

The most extensively excavated of the Imperial Forums is the **Foro di Traiano** (Trajan's Forum; Map pp102-3; ☎ 06 679 00 48; entrance at Colonna di Traiano; admission €3.20; ⊙ 9am-7pm Tue-Sun Apr-Sep, 9am-4.30pm Tue-Sun Oct-Mar). Little remains of the vast 2nd-century precinct except for some pillars that once formed part of the **Basilica Ulpia** (Map pp102-3) and the **Colonna di Traiano** (Trajan's Column; Map pp102-3). The column was erected to mark Trajan's victories over the Dacians (from modern-day Romania) and is decorated with a spiral of reliefs depicting the battles against the Dacian armies. Minutely detailed, the reliefs are regarded as among the finest examples of ancient Roman sculpture. A golden statue of Trajan once topped the column but it was lost during the Middle Ages and replaced with a statue of St Peter.

Mercati di Traiano (Trajan's Markets; Map pp102-3; ☎ 06 679 00 48) comprises the vast semicircular construction that you see from the road. The ancient equivalent of the shopping mall, the markets were spread over three floors of shops and offices. It's temporarily closed to the public. The tall red-brick tower above the market buildings, the **Torre delle Milizie** (Militia Tower; Map pp102-3) was built in the 13th century.

Just to the southeast of Foro di Traiano and markets are the **Foro di Augusto** (Forum of Augustus; Map p114) and the **Foro di Nerva** (Forum of Nerva; Map p114), although very little remains of either complex. The 30m-high wall behind the Foro di Augusto was built to protect it against the fires which frequently swept through the area.

On the other side of Via dei Fori Imperiali, three columns on a raised platform are all that remain of the **Foro di Cesare** (Forum of Caesar; Map p114).

CAPITOLINE HILL

Rising above the Roman Forum, the Capitoline Hill (Campidoglio) has been the seat of Rome's municipal government since ancient times. Topped by **Piazza del Campidoglio** (Map p114), the hill boasts the world's oldest public museums and some great views.

The best way to approach the piazza is via the **Cordonata** (Map pp98–9), Michelangelo's graceful staircase that leads up from Piazza d'Aracoeli. It's guarded at the bottom by two ancient Egyptian granite lions and at the top by statues of Castor and Pollux, salvaged from the nearby Jewish Ghetto in the 16th century.

Designed by Michelangelo in 1538, Piazza del Campidoglio is bordered by three palazzi: Palazzo Nuovo to the left, Palazzo Senatorio straight ahead and Palazzo dei Conservatori on the right. Together, Palazzo Nuovo and Palazzo dei Conservatori house the Capitoline Museums (right), while **Palazzo Senatorio** (admission free; 9am-4pm Sun) houses the city council (bring identification for entry).

In the centre of the square, the bronze equestrian **statue of Marcus Aurelius** (Map p114) is a copy. The original, which dates from the 2nd century AD, has been in Palazzo Nuovo since 1981. The fountain at the base of Palazzo Senatorio's double staircase features a 1st-century statue of **Minerva** in a central niche. On either side of her are statues of two laid-back men representing, on the right, the Tiber and, on the left, the Nile.

To the left of the palazzo is Via di San Pietro in Carcere and, down the stairs, the **Carcere Mamertino** (Mamertine Prison; Map p114; ☎ 06 679 29 02; 9am-12.30pm & 2.30-5.30pm summer, to 2-5pm winter) is where prisoners were put through a hole in the floor to starve to death. St Peter was believed to have been imprisoned here and to have created a miraculous stream of water to baptise his jailers. It's now a church, San Pietro in Carcere.

Marking the highest point of the Capitoline Hill is the 6th-century **Chiesa di Santa Maria in Aracoeli** (Map p114; ☎ 06 679 81 55; Piazza Santa Maria in Aracoeli; 9am-12.30pm & 2.30-5.30pm). The church is accessible from the piazza – go up the steps in the southeastern corner of the square – or more dramatically by way of the 14th-century Aracoeli staircase to the left of the Cordonata. The ruins you see to the left of the staircase are the remains of a Roman apartment block, or **insula** (Map pp98–9), typically used to house the poor.

Built on the site where, according to legend, the Tiburtine Sybil told Augustus of the coming birth of Christ, the church not only offers a quiet haven from the crowds outside but also a fresco by Pinturicchio and, most famously, a statue of the baby Jesus. Unfortunately, the statue you see today is a copy of the original, said to have been carved from wood from the garden of Gethsemane, was stolen in 1994.

The world's oldest national museums, the **Capitoline Museums** (Musei Capitolini; Map pp98-9; ☎ 06 399 67 800; Piazza del Campidoglio; admission without/with exhibition €6.20/€7.80; 9am-8pm Tue-Sun) were founded in 1471 when Pope Sixtus IV donated a few bronze sculptures to the city. Today the collection includes some of ancient Rome's finest treasures, with the emphasis on sculpture.

The main entrance to the museums is in **Palazzo dei Conservatori** (Map pp98–9). Of the sculpture on the 1st floor, the Etruscan *Lupa Capitolina* is the most famous. Standing in the Sala Della Lupe, the 6th-century BC bronze wolf stands over her suckling wards Romulus and Remus. Surprisingly the twins were only added in the 15th century. Another crowd-pleaser is the *Spinario* in Room 3, a delicate 1st-century BC bronze of a boy removing a thorn from his foot.

The inner courtyard contains the mammoth head, hand and foot of the 12m-high statue of Constantine that originally stood in the Basilica di Massenzio in the Roman Forum.

On the 2nd floor the Pinacoteca (Art Gallery) contains paintings by heavyweights such as Titian, Tintoretto, Reni, van Dyck and Rubens. Look out for Caravaggio's sensual *San Giovanni Battista* in the Sala di Santa Petronilla. Painted between 1595 and 1596, it shows

St John the Baptist with his arm looped over a ram's head. This unusual depiction has led some to speculate that the artist's real subject was in fact Isaac and not St John.

A tunnel links Palazzo dei Conservatori to Palazzo Nuovo on the other side of the square via the **Tabularium** (Map p114), ancient Rome's central archive, beneath Palazzo Senatorio.

Palazzo Nuovo (Map p114) is crammed to its elegant rafters with classical sculpture. Highlights include the *Discobolus* in Room 1, a 3rd-century discus thrower to which a pair of legs were added in the 18th century; the Sala dei Filosofi, with its busts of various philosophers, poets and politicians; and the red-marble *Satiro Ridente* (a satyr holding a bunch of grapes), that Nathaniel Hawthorne used for his novel *The Marble Faun*. The star of the show, however, is the *Galata Morente* (Dying Gaul) in Room 8. A Roman copy of a 3rd-century-BC Greek original, it movingly depicts the anguish of a dying Frenchman.

PIAZZA VENEZIA

Bustling Piazza Venezia is dominated by Rome's most visible and hated landmark, the **Vittoriano** (Map p114; ☎ 06 699 17 18; admission free; ⏰ 9.30am-6pm). Romans dismiss it as the 'wedding cake' or 'typewriter' but admit that it's the best address in town: it's the only place from where you can't actually see it. Climb to the top and you'll see what they mean – the views are exceptional.

Built to commemorate Vittorio Emanuele II and unified Italy, it today hosts the tomb of the Unknown Soldier. This means that you can't sit anywhere on the monument, a rule that the hawk-eyed guardians strictly enforce.

In the depths of the building the **Museo Centrale del Risorgimento** (Map p114; ☎ 06 678 06 64; Via din San Pietro in Carcere; admission free; ⏰ 9am-6.30pm Tue-Sun) documents the history of Italian unification. Exhibits include the stretcher on which the wounded Garibaldi was placed at the Battle of Aspromonte.

On the western side of the piazza is the Renaissance **Palazzo Venezia** (Map pp98–9) where Mussolini used to have his official residence. The best way to see the interior is to visit the oft-overlooked **Museo di Palazzo Venezia** (Map pp98-9; ☎ 06 679 88 65; entrance at Via del Plebiscito 118; admission €4; ⏰ 8.30am-7pm Tue-Sat winter) with its superb Byzantine and early Renais-sance paintings and eclectic collection of jewellery, tapestries, ceramics, bronze figurines, arms and armour. Remember to look up occasionally to admire the coffered ceilings.

Actually part of Palazzo Venezia, but facing onto Piazza di San Marco, the **Basilica di San Marco** (Map pp98-9; Piazza di San Marco; ⏰ 7am-1pm & 4-7pm) was founded in the 4th century in honour of St Mark the Evangelist. After undergoing several transformations, the church now has a Renaissance façade, a Romanesque bell tower and a largely baroque interior. The main attraction is the 9th-century mosaic in the apse, which depicts Christ with saints and Pope Gregory IV.

Centro Storico

Bordered by the River Tiber to the west and Via del Corso to the east, the *centro storico* (historic centre) is where you will find some of Rome's great piazzas: Piazza Navona, Campo de' Fiori, Piazza del Popolo, and a whole host of smaller squares. Baroque churches abound and although the Pantheon is a good point of reference it is also a great area to get lost in.

PANTHEON & AROUND

Ancient Rome's best-preserved building, the **Pantheon** (Map p104; ☎ 06 683 00 230; Piazza della Rotonda; admission free; ⏰ 9am-7.30pm Mon-Sat, to 5.30pm Sun) has been standing for some 2000 years. In its current form it dates to around AD 120 when the Emperor Hadrian built the Pantheon over Marcus Agrippa's original temple (27 BC). For centuries, historians read the name Agrippa in the inscription on the pediment and thought that Hadrian's version was, in fact, the 1st-century BC original. When excavations in the 19th century revealed traces of the earlier temple, they realised their mistake.

Although the Pantheon has been a Christian church since 608, Hadrian's temple was dedicated to the classical gods, hence the name Pantheon, a derivation of the Greek words *pan* (all) and *theos* (god). Today you'll find the tombs of kings Vittorio Emanuele II and Umberto I alongside the tomb of the artist Raphael.

From the outside you get no idea of the dimensions of the extraordinary dome that tops the building. Considered the Roman's most important architectural achievement, the dome – the largest masonry vault ever

BUT WAIT, THERE'S MORE

For an alternative tour of Rome's museums you could try the following.

Founded by a French missionary obsessed with life after death, the small **Museum of Souls in Purgatory** (Museo delle Anime del Purgatorio; Map pp98-9; ☎ 06 688 06 517; Chiesa del Sacro Cuore del Gesù, Lungotevere Prati 12; admission free; ☽ 7.30-11am & 4-7pm Mon-Sat) displays pieces of cloth, wooden tables and breviaries allegedly marked with traces of fire from souls languishing in purgatory.

Fans of Italian horror might like **Dario Argento's Horror Museum** (Museo degli Orrori di Dario Argento; Map p95; ☎ 06 321 13 95; Via dei Gracchi 260; admission €3; ☽ 10.30am-1pm & 4-7.30pm Mon-Sat), above a shop dedicated to the Italian director. Here you'll find a small collection of sets and special effects from horror films.

Celluloid history is the theme of the **International Museum of Film & Entertainment** (Museo Internazionale del Cinema e dello Spettacolo; Map pp106-7; ☎ 06 370 02 66; www.mics.pagehere.com in Italian; Via Portuense 101; ☽ guided tours in English by appointment only), which displays souvenirs from Rome's glory days as capital of the cinematic world. It has cameras, projectors, posters for international film productions, as well as an important collection of Italian and European silent films.

There are plenty of famous faces to see at the **Wax Museum** (Museo delle Cere; Map pp102-3; ☎ 06 679 64 82; Piazza dei Santissimi Apostoli 67; admission €6; ☽ 9am-8pm), Rome's equivalent of London's Madame Tussaud's. Ranging from Lenin to Snow White, the 250 figures comprise poets, politicians, murderers and priests.

For those interested in mending books or bodies, there's a **Museum of the Central Institute for Book Pathology** (Museo dell'Istituto Centrale di Patologia del Libro; Map pp102-3; ☎ 06 48 29 11; Via Milano 76; admission free; ☽ 9am-6pm Mon-Fri), which demonstrates book manufacturing and restoration techniques, and a **Museum of the Medical Arts** (Museo Storico dell'Arte Sanitaria; Map pp98-9; ☎ 06 683 52 353; www.doctor33.it/accade/museo in Italian; Lungotevere in Sassia 3; admission €2.60; ☽ 10am-noon Mon, Wed & Fri), with a collection of scary-looking surgical instruments and more than 10,000 books.

There's a **Napoleonic Museum** (Museo Napoleonico; Map p104; ☎ 06 688 06 286; Piazza Ponte Umberto I 1; 9am-7pm Tue-Sun) that traces the rise of the Bonaparte family back to the second Roman Empire. And, to prove that not everyone fiddled while Rome burned, there's a **Museum of the Fire Brigade** (Museo dei Vigili del Fuoco; Map pp106-7; ☎ 06 574 68 08; Via Galvani 2; admission free; ☽ 9.30am-12.30pm & 4.30-7.30pm Tue-Fri, 4.30-7.30pm Sat), which documents the history of Rome's firefighters since the age of Augustus.

The **Museum of the Liberation of Rome** (Museo Storico della Liberazione di Roma; Map pp108-9; ☎ 06 700 38 66; Via Tasso 145; admission free; ☽ 9.30am-12.30pm Sat & Sun, 4-7pm Tue, Thu & Fri) is housed in what was once the headquarters of the notorious SS Kommandatur, where members of the Roman Resistance were interrogated, tortured and imprisoned during WWII. Particularly moving are the messages scrawled on the walls by condemned prisoners.

On a lighter note, the **National Pasta Museum** (Museo Nazionale delle Paste Alimentari; Map pp102-3; ☎ 06 699 11 19; www.pastainmuseum.com; Piazza Scanderberg 117; admission €10; ☽ 9.30am-5.30pm) is the only museum in the world dedicated to more than two millennia of pasta. A highlight is the Neapolitan Room, with its photos of film stars tucking into plates of pasta.

built – is a perfect semisphere (the diameter is equal to the interior height of 43.3m). Light is provided by the oculus – a 9m opening in the dome – and 22 small holes in the marble floor allow any rain that enters to drain away.

Somewhat the worse for wear, the exterior is still imposing, with 16 Corinthian columns (each a single block of stone) supporting a triangular pediment. Rivets and holes in the brickwork indicate where the original marble-veneer panels have been removed.

Over the centuries the temple was consistently plundered and damaged. In the 17th century, for example, Pope Urban VIII had the bronze ceiling of the portico melted down to make the *baldachin* (canopy) over the main altar in St Peter's and 80 cannons for Castel Sant'Angelo. Thankfully, he left the original bronze doors.

Just south of the Pantheon, the Piazza della Minerva is home to Bernini's **Elefantino** (Map pp98–9), a curious and much-loved sculpture of an elephant supporting a 6th-century

BC Egyptian obelisk. On the eastern flank of the square is the 13th-century Dominican **Chiesa di Santa Maria Sopra Minerva** (Map pp98-9; ☎ 06 679 39 26; Piazza della Minerva; ☼ 7am-7pm). Built on the site of an ancient temple to Minerva, this treasure-trove of a church is one of the few examples of Gothic architecture in Rome. Largely restored in the 19th century, it boasts superb frescoes by Filippino Lippi in the Cappella Carafa (c 1489) and, left of the high altar, one of Michelangelo's lesser known sculptures, *Christ Bearing the Cross* (c 1520). The body of Santa Caterina di Siena, minus her head (which is in Siena), lies under the high altar.

Equally, if not more spectacular is the **Chiesa del Gesù** (Map pp98-9; ☎ 06 69 70 01; Piazza del Gesù; ☼ 6am-12.30pm & 4-7.15pm), Rome's first Jesuit church. A magnificent example of Counter-Reformation architecture, it was built between 1551 and 1584 with money donated by Cardinal Alessandro Farnese, who was subsequently said to own the three most beautiful things in Rome: his family palazzo, his daughter and the Church of Gesù.

Although the façade by Giacomo della Porta is impressive, it is the amazing interior that is the real attraction. Designed by Giacomo Barozzi da Vignola, a pupil of Michelangelo, it's an amazing ensemble of gold and marble built to draw worshippers to the Jesuit fold. Works to look out for include the astounding vault fresco by Giovanni Battista Gaulli (who was known as Il Baciccia). His masterful use of perspective is evident as figures appear to tumble from the vault onto the coffered ceiling. Baciccia also painted the cupola frescoes and designed the stucco decoration.

In the Cappella di Sant'Ignazio in the northern transept, St Ignatius Loyola, the founder of the Jesuits, is buried in an opulent marble and bronze tomb with lapis lazuli–encrusted columns. The Spanish saint actually lived in the church from 1544 until his death in 1556. To the east of the church you can visit **Loyola's rooms** (☼ 4-6pm Mon-Sat, 10am-noon Sun) which contain a masterful trompe l'oeil perspective by Andrea del Pozzo.

Nearby, the **Museo Nazionale Romano: Crypta Balbi** (Map pp98-9; ☎ 06 399 67 700; Via delle Botteghe Oscure 31; admission €4; ☼ 9am-7.45pm Tue-Sun) is the latest addition to the Museo Nazionale Romano. Built over the ruins of medieval and Renaissance buildings, which themselves stand over the Theatre of Balbus (13 BC), the museum perfectly illustrates Rome's multilayered history. The artefacts on display include finds from the excavation of the Crypta itself, as well as items taken from the forums, and the Oppian and Caelian Hills.

PIAZZA NAVONA & AROUND
The baroque palazzi, magnificent fountains, street hawkers, buskers and tourists make **Piazza Navona** (Map p104) one of Rome's most captivating public spaces. Laid out on the ruins of an arena built by Domitian in AD 86, it was paved over in the 15th century and for almost 300 years was the city's main market.

Of the piazza's three fountains, it is Bernini's **Fontana dei Quattro Fiumi** (Fountain of the Four Rivers; Map p104), depicting the Nile, Ganges, Danube and Plate, that grabs the most attention. Legend has it that the figure of the Nile is shielding his eyes from the **Chiesa di Sant'Agnese in Agone** (Map p104; ☼ 10am-noon & 4-7pm Tue-Sun), designed by Bernini's bitter rival, Borromini. It's not true, however. Bernini completed his fountain two years before his contemporary started work on the façade and the veiled gesture indicates that the source of the Nile was unknown at the time.

At the northern end of the piazza, the **Fontana del Nettuno** (Map p104) is a 19th-century creation, while the **Fontana del Moro** (Map p104) to the south was originally designed in 1576. The largest building in the square is the 17th-century **Palazzo Pamphilj** (Map p104), built for Pope Innocent X and now home to the Brazilian Embassy.

North of Piazza Navona, the Renaissance and baroque **Museo Nazionale Romano: Palazzo Altemps** (Map p104; ☎ 06 683 35 66; Piazza Sant'Apollinare 46; adult/concession €5/2.50; ☼ 9am-7.30pm Tue-Sun) houses the famous Ludovisi collection.

Cardinal Ludovico Ludovisi, a nephew of Pope Gregory XV, was a ravenous collector of ancient sculpture, which was regularly unearthed in the building boom of Counter-Reformation Rome. He employed leading sculptors – including Bernini and Alessandro Algardi – to repair and 'enhance' the works, replacing missing limbs and sticking new heads on headless torsos.

The museum's prize exhibits (untouched by baroque hands) include the 5th-century BC *Trono Ludovisi*, a carved marble throne that scholars think came from a Greek colony in southern Italy, and the *Galata Suicida*, a dramatic depiction of a Gaul knifing himself to death over a dying woman. The Egyptian collection of the Museo Nazionale Romano is also housed here.

Baroque frescoes provide a decorative backdrop throughout the museum. Landscapes and hunting scenes are seen through trompe l'oeil windows in the Sala delle Prospettive Dipinte (1st floor), and a 15th-century fresco by Melozzo da Forlì in the Sala della Piattaia – once the main reception room of the palazzo – displays a cupboard full of wedding gifts.

A short walk away are two churches that no art-lover should miss. The **Chiesa di Sant'Agostino** (Map p104; ☎ 06 688 01 962; Piazza di Sant'Agostino; ☺ 8am-noon & 4-7.30pm) contains two outstanding works of art: Raphael's fresco of Isaiah and the *Madonna of the Pilgrims* by Caravaggio. Even more dramatic are Caravaggio's three canvases in the **Chiesa di San Luigi dei Francesi** (Map p104; ☎ 06 68 82 71; Piazza di San Luigi dei Francesi; ☺ 8.30am-12.30pm & 3.30-7pm). Collectively known as the St Matthew cycle, they completely upstage the church's opulent baroque interior.

To the south of Piazza Navona, the baroque Palazzo Braschi houses the **Museo di Roma** (Map p104; ☎ 06 671 08 346; www.museodiroma .comune.roma.it; Piazza di San Pantaleo 10; admission €6.20; ☺ 9am-7pm Tue-Sun), devoted to Rome's history from the Middle Ages to the first half of the 20th century. The collection includes photographs, etchings, clothes and furniture, while the extensive collection of paintings includes some interesting depictions of Rome before it was transformed by the building frenzy of the 17th century. There are also enough portraits of popes to satisfy the most conscientious of papal historians.

CAMPO DE' FIORI & AROUND

Noisy and colourful **Campo de' Fiori** (Il Campo; Map p104) has two faces: in the morning it stages Rome's most famous produce market, while at night it fills with trendy diners and young drinkers. Towering over the square is the sinister form of Giordano Bruno, a monk who was burned at the stake for heresy in 1600.

Nearby, in the more tranquil Piazza Farnese, the **Palazzo Farnese** (Map p104) is a magnificent Renaissance building. Started

in 1514 by Antonio da Sangallo, continued by Michelangelo and finished by Giacomo della Porta, it is now the French Embassy. The twin fountains in the square were enormous granite baths taken from the Terme di Caracalla.

South of Campo de' Fiori and Piazza Farnese in the 16th-century **Palazzo Spada** (Map p104; ☎ 06 683 24 09; Piazza Capodiferro €5; ☺ 8.30am-7.30pm Tue-Sun) is Borromini's famous perspective. What appears to be a 25m-long corridor lined with columns leading to a life-size statue is, in fact, only 10m long. The sculpture, which was a later addition, is actually hip-height and the columns diminish in size not because of distance but because they actually get shorter. Upstairs the small art gallery houses the Spada family art collection (acquired by the state in 1926), with works by Andrea del Sarto, Guido Reni, Guercino and Titian.

JEWISH GHETTO & ISOLA TIBERINA

Jews have lived in Rome since the 2nd century BC. In 1555 Pope Paul IV issued a papal bull ordering that they be confined to the Jewish Ghetto, a situation which more or less lasted until the end of the 19th century and was reinstated by the Nazis during WWII. Via del Portico d'Ottavia is the centre of this tightly packed and surprisingly tranquil area.

Housed in Rome's synagogue, the **Museum of Jewish Art** (Map pp98-9; ☎ 06 684 00 661; Lungotevere de' Cenci 15; admission €5.20; ☺ 9am-7.30pm Mon-Thu, 9am-1.30pm Fri & Sun Apr-Sep, 9am-4.30pm Mon-Thu, 9am-1.30pm Fri, 9am-12.30pm Sun Oct-Mar) documents the relations of Rome's Jews with the state of Italy and the Nazis.

To the east of the Ghetto, the **Teatro di Marcello** (Map pp98-9; Via del Teatro di Marcello) was planned by Julius Caesar and built by Augustus in around 13 BC. A 16th-century palazzo was later built onto the original two-storey arcaded theatre.

Follow Via del Teatro di Marcello round as it becomes Via L Petroselli and you eventually come to Piazza Bocca della Verità where you'll find one of Rome's most famous curiosities: the **Bocca della Verità** (Mouth of Truth; Map pp106-7). Legend has it that if you put your right hand in the mouth of this mask-shaped disk while telling a lie the mouth will snap shut and bite your hand off. How such a myth arose over a round piece of marble once used as an ancient manhole cover is anybody's guess.

The mouth lives in the portico of one of Rome's finest medieval churches. The **Chiesa di Santa Maria in Cosmedin** (Map pp106-7; ☎ 06 678 14 19; Piazza Bocca della Verità 18; admission free; ⊗ 9am-1pm & 2.30-6pm) dates to the 8th century, although it was a 12th-century face-lift that gave it its current look. Highlights to look out for include the seven-storey bell tower, the frescoes in the aisles and the beautiful floor heavily decorated with inlaid marble.

Opposite the church are two tiny Roman temples: the round **Tempio di Ercole Vincitore** (Map pp106-7) and the **Tempio di Portunus** (Map pp106-7). Just off the piazza, the **Arco di Giano** (Arch of Janus; Map pp106-7) is a four-sided Roman arch that once covered a crossroads, while the medieval **Chiesa di San Giorgio in Velabro** (Map pp106-7; ☎ 06 692 04 534; Via del Velabro 19; ⊗ 10am-12.30pm & 4-6.30pm) has recently been restored after it was severely damaged by a Mafia bomb attack in 1993.

To reach the **Isola Tiberina** (Map pp106-7), the world's smallest inhabited island, double back up the river to the **Ponte Fabricio** (Map pp98-9), itself a record-breaker: it dates to 62 BC and is Rome's oldest standing bridge. The Isola Tiberina has been associated with healing since the 3rd century BC, when the Romans adopted Aesculapius, the Greek god of healing, as their own and erected a temple to him on the island. Today it's the site of the **Ospedale Fatebenefratelli** (Map pp106-7). The **Chiesa di San Bartolomeo** (Map pp106-7; ⊗ 9am-12.30pm & 3.30-6pm) was built on the island in the 10th century on the ruins

of the Roman temple. It has a Romanesque bell tower and a marble wellhead, believed to have been built over the same spring that provided healing waters for the temple. The **Ponte Cestio** (Map pp106-7), built in 46 BC, connects the island with Trastevere to the south. It was rebuilt in the late 19th century. Also to the south of the island are the remains of the **Ponte Rotto** (Broken Bridge; Map pp106-7), ancient Rome's first stone bridge.

VIA DEL CORSO

Rome's busiest shopping street runs north from Piazza Venezia to Piazza del Popolo.

Just north of Piazza Venezia, **Palazzo Doria Pamphilj** (Map pp98-9; cnr Via del Corso & Via del Plebiscito) is home to the **Galleria Doria Pamphilj** (Map pp98-9; ☎ 06 679 73 23; www.doriapamphilj.it in Italian; entrance at Piazza del Collegio Romano 2; admission €8; ⊗ 10am-5pm Fri-Wed) and one of Rome's finest private art collections, including works by Raphael, Tintoretto, Brueghel and Titian. Elaborate picture galleries – and the stunning private apartments – are crammed from floor to ceiling with paintings, although the most famous of all, Velasquez's portrait of Innocent X, the founder of the collection, dazzles in its own chamber. The excellent audioguide is spoken by a member of the Pamphilj family and is included in the price.

Some way to the north, located behind the Fascist-era Piazza Augusto Imperatore, is the **Ara Pacis Augustae** (Altar of Peace; Map pp98-9; ☎ 06 671 03 887), a monument to the peace that Augustus established both at home and

---

GOVERNMENT RULES

The heart of Italy's government beats in the area around Piazza Colonna. Named after the 30m **Colonna Antonina** (Map pp98-9), erected in AD 180 to commemorate Marcus Aurelius' victories in battle, the square is flanked by the 17th-century **Palazzo Chigi** (Map pp98-9; ☎ 06 677 93 111; www.governo.it in Italian; Palazzo Colonna 370; ⊗ group visits by appointment), the official residence of the Presidente del Consiglio, the Italian prime minister.

In the adjoining piazza the even more impressive **Palazzo Montecitorio** (Map pp98-9; ☎ 06 6 76 01; www.camera.it; Piazza Montecitorio; ⊗ 10am-6pm) is home to the Chamber of Deputies, the lower house of the Italian parliament. Originally designed by Bernini in 1653, it was the seat of the papal courts until 1870 when Rome became capital of Italy and the politicians moved in. The upper house, the Senate, is nearby in **Palazzo Madama** (Map p104; ☎ 06 6 70 61; www.senato.it; Piazza Madama 11; ⊗ 10am-6pm), the 16th-century townhouse of Giovanni de' Medici (who later became Pope Leo X). Guided visits of both palazzi occur on the first Sunday of each month.

The fourth of Italy's great institutional palazzi is the Palazzo del Quirinale (p124), home of the president of the republic.

abroad. One of the most important works in the history of ancient Roman sculpture, the reliefs date to 13 BC. Panels excavated from the 16th century onwards ended up in the Medici collection, the Vatican and the Louvre; in 1937, under Mussolini, the remaining parts were reassembled in the present location. A new, state-of-the-art museum complex designed by Richard Meier is still under construction; inauguration is planned for 21 April 2006.

East of the monument is the rather sorry-looking **Mausoleo di Augusto** (Mausoleum of Augustus; Map pp98-9). This was once one of Rome's greatest monuments, built by Augustus for himself and his family. It was originally faced with marble and was converted into a fortress during the Middle Ages. It served various purposes until Mussolini restored it to its original state in 1936. It's currently closed to the public.

PIAZZA DEL POPOLO

Vast **Piazza del Popolo** (Map pp96–7) was laid out in 1538 at the convergence of the three roads – Via di Ripetta, Via del Corso and Via del Babuino – forming a trident at what was once Rome's northern entrance. Characterised by the two 17th-century baroque churches, **Chiesa di Santa Maria dei Miracoli** (Map pp96–7) and **Chiesa di Santa Maria in Montesanto** (Map pp96–7), it was redesigned in neoclassical style in 1823. In its centre is an obelisk brought by Augustus from Heliopolis, in ancient Greece, and moved here from the Circo Massimo in the mid-16th century. To the east is a ramp leading up to the Pincio Hill, which affords a great view of the city.

The **Chiesa di Santa Maria del Popolo** (Map pp96-7; ☎ 06 361 08 36; Piazza del Popolo; ☼ 7am-noon & 4-7pm Mon-Sat, 8am-1.30pm & 4.30-7.30pm Sun), next to the Porta del Popolo at the northern side of the piazza, is a magnificent repository of art. The first chapel was built here in 1099 to exorcise the ghost of Nero who was buried on this spot and whose ghost was said to haunt the area. Later transformed in the 15th century, it boasts some superb 16th-century vault frescoes by Pinturicchio. In Raphael's Cappella Chigi (completed by Bernini some 100 years later) you'll find a famous mosaic of a kneeling skeleton, while in the Cappella Cerasi, to the left of the altar, hang two Caravaggio canvases: the *Conversion of St Paul* and the *Crucifixion of St Peter*.

East of Via del Corso

Stretching from Stazione Termini and the student area of San Lorenzo in the east to Via del Corso in the west, this busy slice of Rome contains two of its favourite sights: the Spanish Steps and the Trevi Fountain; its most expensive shopping street, Via dei Condotti; and the Italian president's official residence, Palazzo del Quirinale.

ESQUILINE

The largest and highest of Rome's seven hills, the **Esquiline** (Esquilino; Map pp102–3) extends from the Colosseum to Stazione Termini, encompassing Via Cavour (a major traffic artery between Stazione Termini and Via dei Fori Imperiali), the charming residential area of Monti and the Basilica di Santa Maria Maggiore. Much of the hill was covered with vineyards and gardens until the late 19th century, when they were dug up to make way for grandiose apartment blocks.

Pilgrims and art-lovers flock to the **Basilica di San Pietro in Vincoli** (Map pp102-3; ☎ 06 488 28 65; Piazza di San Pietro in Vincoli 4a; ☼ 7am-12.30pm & 3.30-7pm) for two reasons: to see St Peter's chains and to photograph Michelangelo's tomb of Pope Julius II. The church was built in the 5th century specially to house the chains that bound St Peter when he was imprisoned in the Mamertine (see p116). Some time after St Peter's death, the chains were sent to Constantinople for a period before returning to Rome as relics. They arrived in two pieces and legend has it that when they were reunited they miraculously joined together. They are now displayed under the altar.

To the right of the altar is Michelangelo's monumental tomb. At the centre of the work is a well-built Moses (with two small horns sticking out of his head and a magnificent waist-length beard) flanked by statues of Leah and Rachel. Despite its imposing scale it was never actually finished – Michelangelo had originally envisaged 40 statues but got sidetracked with the Sistine Chapel (p137); in the end, Pope Julius II was buried in St Peter's Basilica without the great tomb he had envisioned.

A flight of steps through a low arch leads down from the church to Via Cavour.

Nearby, the **Chiesa di Santa Lucia in Selci** (Map pp102-3; ☎ 06 482 76 23; Via in Selci 82; ☼ 9.30-10.30am Sun) is hidden away in an Augustinian convent. Best known for its 17th-century

Borromini interior, the church dates to some time before the 8th century. It's not open to the public, except for Mass on Sunday morning, but if you ring the bell and ask the resident nuns nicely they'll probably let you in.

One of Rome's four patriarchal basilicas (the others being St Peter's, San Giovanni in Laterano and San Paolo Fuori-le-Mura), the **Basilica di Santa Maria Maggiore** (Map pp102-3; ☎ 06 48 31 95; Piazza Santa Maria Maggiore; ☯ 7am-7pm) was built on the highest point of the Esquiline Hill in the 5th century. Much tampered with over the centuries, its main façade dates to the 18th century, although the mosaics date to the earlier 13th-century façade, the interior is baroque and the bell tower Romanesque. The original form of the vast interior remains intact and the most notable feature is the cycle of 5th-century mosaics in the triumphal arch and nave. If you can see that high, they depict biblical scenes featuring Abraham, Jacob and Isaac to the left, and Moses and Joshua to the right. The sumptuously decorated Cappella Sistina, last on the right, was built in the 16th century and contains the tombs of Popes Sixtus V and Pius V. Opposite is the Cappella Borghese (or Cappella Paolina), also full of elaborate decoration, erected in the 17th century by Pope Paul V. The *Madonna and Child* above the altar is believed to date from the 12th to the 13th century.

At the base of the Esquiline Hill, near the Colosseum, the **Basilica di San Clemente** (Map pp108-9; ☎ 06 704 51 018; Via di San Giovanni in Laterano; church/excavations free/€3; ☯ 9am-12.30pm & 3-6pm Mon-Fri, 10am-12.30pm & 3-6pm Sat & Sun) provides a fascinating glimpse into Rome's multilayered past. Through the courtyard, the 12th-century church at street level was built over a 4th-century church which was, in turn, constructed over a 1st-century Roman house. A pagan 2nd-century temple was later added to the house, which is believed to stand over foundations dating to the Roman Republic.

In the medieval church the 12th-century mosaic in the apse is stunning. It depicts the *Triumph of the Cross*, with 12 doves symbolising the apostles. Figures around the cross include the Madonna and St John, as well as St John the Baptist and other saints.

The church below was mostly destroyed by Norman invaders in 1084 but some faded 11th-century frescoes remain, illustrating the life of San Clemente. Descend further and you'll find yourself walking an ancient lane leading to the Roman house and temple of Mithras.

TREVI FOUNTAIN TO THE QUIRINAL

Immortalised by a frolicking Anita Ekberg in Fellini's film *La Dolce Vita*, the **Trevi Fountain** (Fontana di Trevi; Map pp102-3) is Rome's most famous fountain. The baroque bonanza was designed by Nicola Salvi in 1732 and depicts Neptune's chariot being led by Tritons with sea horses – one wild,

---

A THOUGHT FOR YOUR PENNIES

To toss a coin over your shoulder into the Trevi Fountain is to ensure that one day you'll return. By the same token, a second coin will have you falling in love with an Italian and the third coin will have you marrying him or her. All very romantic, but what happens to the money?

It goes to charity is the official answer. Once a week a team from Rome's electricity company ACEA hoovers up the coins and sends them to Caritas, an Italian charity where volunteers weigh, clean and sort the coins into currencies – coins have been found from up to 58 different countries.

But in 2002 it was revealed that a homeless man known as D'Artagnan had been making up to €1000 a day for 34 years from the Trevi coins. The public was outraged but it wasn't at all clear if he'd broken the law. According to a 1994 high court ruling, taking coins from the fountain was as legal as throwing them in. Magistrates, however, fined D'Artagnan under a 1999 law that banned entering the city's fountains. Unabated he continued until the introduction of the euro put a damper on his scheme – his magnet proved useless on the new coins. The latest legal footnote came in October 2003 when a Roman court ruled that it was no longer a crime to take the coins as they don't belong to anyone.

And in case you're wondering, yes, the coins do add up. On an average day about €1,500 is thrown into the fountain, while in October 2004 visitors chucked away more than €54,000.

one docile – representing the various moods of the sea. The water comes from one of the city's earliest aqueducts and the name 'Trevi' refers to the *tre vie* (three roads) which converge at the fountain.

At the top of the Quirinal (Quirinale) Hill, the **Palazzo del Quirinale** (Map pp102-3; ☎ 06 4 69 91; www.quirinale.it; Piazza del Quirinale; admission €5.20; ☺ 8.30am-12.30pm Sun Sep-Jul, closed holidays) is the official residence of the president of the republic. Built and added to from 1574 to the early 18th century, it was the summer residence of the popes until 1870, when it became the royal palace of the kings of Italy. When the royals were booted out of Italy in 1946 it passed to the president of the new republic.

In the former stables of the palace, the **Scuderie Papali al Quirinale** (Map pp102-3; ☎ 06 69 62 70; www.scuderiequirinale.it; Via XXIV Maggio 16; ☺ exhibitions only) is used for art exhibitions.

The obelisk in the centre of the piazza was moved here from the Mausoleo di Augusto in 1786. It's flanked by the large statues of the Dioscuri, Castor and Pollux, which are Imperial-era copies of 5th-century BC Greek originals.

Along Via del Quirinale are two excellent examples of baroque architecture: the **Chiesa di Sant'Andrea al Quirinale** (Map pp102-3; ☎ 06 489 03 187; Via del Quirinale 29; ☺ 9am-noon & 4-7pm Mon-Fri, 9am-noon Sat), designed by Bernini, and the **Chiesa di San Carlo alle Quattro Fontane** (Map pp102-3; ☎ 06 488 32 61; Via del Quirinale 23; ☺ 10am-1pm & 3-6pm Mon-Fri & Sun, 10am-1pm Sat), by Borromini. Sant'Andrea is considered one of Bernini's masterpieces. He designed it with an elliptical floor plan and with a series of chapels opening onto the central area. Although there is not a whole lot to see at nearby San Carlo, it is important as it was the first church designed by Borromini in Rome. The church stands at the intersection known as Quattro Fontane, named after the late-16th-century fountains at its four corners.

If you've been tramping around the hectic Via Nazionale area, nip into the stripy **San Paolo Entro Le Mure** (Map pp102-3; ☎ 06 420 31 21; cnr Via Nazionale & Via Napoli) for a quiet breather. An American Episcopal church, it's known for its 19th-century mosaics and modern sculpture.

The building you see halfway down Via Nazionale is the 19th-century **Palazzo delle Esposizioni** (Map pp102-3; ☎ 06 474 59 03; www.pala

expo.it), an important cultural centre that's currently closed for restoration.

PIAZZA DI SPAGNA & THE SPANISH STEPS

The favourite flirting ground of Italian teenagers, **Piazza di Spagna** (Map pp98-9) and the famous **Spanish Steps** (Scalinata della Trinità dei Monti; Map pp102-3) have acted as magnets for visitors since the 18th century. The piazza was named after the Spanish Embassy to the Holy See, although the staircase, built with a legacy from the French in 1725, leads to the French church **Trinità dei Monti** (Map pp102-3). At the foot of the steps, the fountain of a sinking boat, the **Barcaccia** (Map pp98-9), is believed to be by Pietro Bernini, father of the famous Gian Lorenzo.

To the right as you face the steps, the **Keats-Shelley House** (Map pp102-3; ☎ 06 678 42 35; www .keats-shelley-house.org; Piazza di Spagna 26; admission €3; ☺ 9am-1pm & 3-6pm Mon-Fri, 11am-2pm & 3-6pm Sat) is the house where Keats died in 1821. Now it's a small museum full of poetic memorabilia.

On the other side of the square, well-heeled shoppers make for the designer stores that line Rome's poshest shopping strip, Via dei Condotti.

VIA VITTORIO VENETO & PIAZZA BARBERINI

Once the haunt of glam film stars and the paparazzi, Via Veneto is no longer the *dolce* centre of Roman *vita*. It's still an impressive tree-lined street but nowadays the overpriced restaurants and cafés are frequented by tourists rather than celebs.

At the bottom of the street near Piazza Barberini is a church with a morbid appeal. There is nothing special about the 17th-century **Chiesa di Santa Maria della Concezione** (Map pp102-3; ☎ 06 487 11 85; Via Vittorio Veneto 27; admission by donation; ☺ 9am-noon & 3-6pm Fri-Wed) but dip into the Capuchin cemetery beneath (access is to the right of the church steps) and you'll be gobsmacked. Everything from the picture frames to the light fittings is made of human bones. Between 1528 and 1870 the Capuchin monks used the bones of 4000 of their departed brothers to create the mesmerising and macabre décor. The message in the last crypt provides food for thought: 'What you are now we used to be; what we are now you will be'.

In the centre of Piazza Barberini is the spectacular **Fontana del Tritone** (Fountain of the Triton; Map pp102–3), created by Bernini in 1643 for Pope Urban VIII, patriarch of the Barberini family. In the northeastern corner, the **Fontana delle Api** (Fountain of the Bees; Map pp102–3) was created by the same artist for the Barberini family, whose crest features three bees.

The grand 17th-century **Palazzo Barberini** (Map pp102-3; Via delle Quattro Fontane) was commissioned by Urban VIII to celebrate the Barberini family's rise to papal power. Many big baroque architects worked on it, including both Bernini and Borromini. Today it houses part of the **Galleria Nazionale d'Arte Antica** (Map pp102-3; ☎ 06 481 45 91; www.galleriaborghese.it; entrance at Via Barberini 18; admission €5; 🕙 9am-7pm Tue-Sun), which includes paintings by Raphael, Caravaggio, Guido Reni, Bernini, Filippo Lippi and Holbein. A highlight is the ceiling of the main salon, entitled the *Triumph of Divine Providence* and painted between 1633 and 1639 by Pietro da Cortona.

PIAZZA DELLA REPUBBLICA & AROUND

The area around **Piazza della Repubblica** (Map pp102–3) is not immediately appealing, but it is here that you will find the bulk of the Museo Nazionale Romano's world-famous archaeological collection.

The complex of baths, libraries, concert halls and gardens that made up the **Terme di Diocleziano** (Diocletian's Baths; Map pp102–3) was the largest of its kind in ancient Rome, covering about 13 hectares, with a capacity to hold 3000 people. Completed in the early 4th century, it fell into disrepair after the aqueduct that fed the baths was destroyed by invaders in about AD 536. Today the ruins constitute part of the **Museo Nazionale Romano: Terme di Diocleziano** (Map pp102-3; ☎ 06 399 67 700; Viale Enrico di Nicola 78; admission €5; 🕙 9am-7.45pm Tue-Sun). Exhibits on the ground and 1st floor include ancient epigraphs, vases, amphorae and household objects in terracotta and bronze. Upstairs you'll find burial objects from Italian protohistory (11th to 6th century BC), while the elegant Renaissance cloister is lined with classical sarcophagi, headless statues, and huge sculptured animal heads from Trajan's Forum.

Michelangelo incorporated the main hall and tepidarium of Diocletian's Baths into the design of the **Basilica di Santa Maria degli Angeli** (Map pp102-3; ☎ 06 488 08 12; Piazza della Repubblica; admission free; 🕙 7am-6.30pm Mon-Sat, 8am-7.30pm Sun), although only the great vaulted ceiling remains from his original plans. The meridian in the transept traces both the polar star and the time of the sun's zenith (visible at noon).

Some of the city's best examples of Roman art are housed in the **Museo Nazionale Romano: Palazzo Massimo alle Terme** (Map pp102-3; ☎ 06 489 03 500; Largo di Villa Peretti 1; admission €6; 🕙 9am-7.45pm Tue-Sun). The ground and 1st floors are given over to sculpture from the 2nd century BC to the 5th century AD. Rejecting realism for glorification, ancient artists presented emperors in various vainglorious poses – check out the depiction of Augustus as Pontifex Maximus in Sala V.

The highlights of the museum, however, are the sensational paintings and mosaics, including frescoes (dating from at least 20–10 BC) from Villa Livia, one of the homes of Augustus' wife. These stunning frescoes, which totally surround you, depict an illusionary garden with all the plants in full bloom.

SAN LORENZO

To the east of Stazione Termini, San Lorenzo is the student heartland of the capital. The one major sight here is the **Basilica di San Lorenzo Fuori-le-Mura** (St Lawrence Outside the Walls; Map p95; ☎ 06 49 15 11; Piazzale del Verano 3; 🕙 3.30-7pm). The only major church to have suffered bomb damage in WWII, it was built by Constantine in the 4th century over the martyred St Lawrence's burial place. Medieval alterations and modern repairs have produced what remains today. Highlights to look out for are the Cosmati floor, the 13th-century frescoed portico, and the catacombs of Santa Ciriaca where St Laurence was buried (ask the sacristan for admission).

Trastevere

One of the most picturesque parts of Rome, Trastevere is over the river from the *centro storico*. Traditionally, it was a poor working-class area but it's increasingly being taken over by wealthy foreigners attracted by the suggestive streets and the abundance of bars, trattorie and cafés.

At the heart of Trastevere is the lovely **Piazza Santa Maria in Trastevere** (Map pp106–7). A prime people-watching spot, it becomes very animated at night when the street sellers are out in force and the crowds of tourists mingle with young locals out for a good time. The fountain in the centre of the square is a 17th-century restoration of the Roman original.

It would be easy to overlook the **Basilica di Santa Maria in Trastevere** (Map pp106-7; ☎ 06 581 48 02; Piazza Santa Maria in Trastevere; ☷ 7.30am-12.30pm & 3.30-7.30pm) nestled in the corner of the piazza. To do so would be a mistake. Said to be the oldest church dedicated to the Virgin Mary in Rome, it boasts some stunning 12th-century mosaics. It was originally built in AD 337 but a major overhaul in 1138 saw the addition of the Romanesque bell tower and frescoed façade.

Inside it's the glittery gold mosaics in the apse that stand out. They depict the Madonna sitting on the right hand of Christ and flanked by various saints. Below this is a series of six 13th-century mosaics by Pietro Cavallini illustrating the life of the Virgin Mary. There are 21 ancient Roman columns, some taken from the Terme di Caracalla, and the wooden ceiling dates to the 17th century.

From Piazza Santa Maria in Trastevere it's a short walk to Piazza Trilussa and the picturesque pedestrian bridge of **Ponte Sisto** (Map pp98-9), which leads back across the Tiber to Via Giulia and Campo de' Fiori.

On the other side of Trastevere, to the east of Viale di Trastevere (the large road on which the No 8 tram drops you off if coming from Largo di Torre Argentina), are two churches worth checking on. The last resting place of Santa Cecilia (the patron saint of music), the **Basilica di Santa Cecilia in Trastevere** (Map pp106-7; ☎ 06 589 92 89; Piazza di Santa Cecilia; church/Cavallini fresco free/€2; ☷ church

9.30am-12.30pm & 4-6.30pm, fresco 10.15am-12.15pm Mon-Fri, 11.15am-12.15pm Sat & Sun) features a stunning 13th-century fresco by Pietro Cavallini. To view the *Last Judgement* go through the convent to the nuns' choir. Beneath the church you can visit the **excavations** (admission €2.50) of Roman houses, one of which might have belonged to Santa Cecilia.

Nearby, towards the end of Via delle Luce, is the **Chiesa di San Francesco a Ripa** (Map pp106-7; Piazza di San Francesco d'Assisi; ☷ 7am-1pm & 4-7.30pm Mon-Fri, 7am-noon & 4-7pm), home to one of Bernini's ecstasy sculptures, *Blessed Ludovica Albertoni*. It's in the fourth chapel on the left.

JANICULUM

Rising up behind Trastevere, the **Janiculum Hill** (Gianicolo; Map pp98-9) is the perfect spot to catch your breath after the crowds below. The views over Rome's rooftops are breathtaking and the kids will be happy playing on the merry-go-round, anchored just off Piazzale Giuseppe Garibaldi. There are also pony rides and a small bar. Puppet shows are often held here on Sundays.

The hill was the scene of one of the fiercest battles in the struggle for Italian unification. In 1849 a makeshift army led by Garibaldi defended Rome against French troops sent to restore papal rule.

On foot it's quite a climb: from Via della Scala in Trastevere turn left up Via Garibaldi and keep on climbing. Otherwise take bus No 870 from Via Paola just off Corso Vittorio Emanuele II near the River Tiber.

The bus will also take you within easy walking distance of the nearby **Villa Doria Pamphilj** (Map p95; Via Aurelia Antica; ☷ sunrise-sunset), Rome's largest park and a lovely spot for a walk and a picnic. The park was laid out in the 17th century for Prince Camillo Pamphilj, cousin of Pope Innocent X. At its centre is the **Casino del Belrespiro** (Map p95), the Prince's summer residence, now used for official government functions.

Southern Rome

The southern quadrant of the city has some of Rome's greatest hits and some lovely lesser-known spots where you really can get off the beaten track. The most obvious landmark here is the Basilica di San Giovanni in Laterano, but you'll also find the extraordinary Terme di Caracalla and, further afield, Via Appia Antica and the catacombs.

THE SAINTLY SEVEN

The number seven is of both geographic and religious relevance in Rome. The city was originally built on seven hills (the Palatine, Capitoline, Aventine, Caelian, Esquiline, Viminal and Quirinal), while the Church recognises seven pilgrim churches. These are the four patriarchal basilicas – St Peter's (p133), San Giovanni in Laterano (opposite), Santa Maria Maggiore (p123) and San Paolo Fuori-le-Mura (p131) – as well as San Lorenzo Fuori-le-Mura (p125), Santa Croce in Gerusalemme (opposite) and San Sebastiano (p129).

SAN GIOVANNI

Founded by Constantine in the 4th century, the **Basilica di San Giovanni in Laterano** (Map pp108-9; ☎ 06 698 86 452; Piazza di San Giovanni in Laterano 4; ⏲ 7am-6.30pm) was the first Christian basilica built in Rome. It is Rome's cathedral and the pope's seat as Bishop of Rome. It has been destroyed by fire twice and rebuilt several times, and the combination of styles adds up to make one hugely impressive church.

The basilica's most eye-catching feature is Alessandro Galilei's huge white façade. A mid-18th-century example of late baroque classicism, it was designed big to convey the infinite authority of the Church. The **bronze doors** were moved here from the Curia in the Roman Forum, while to their right is the Holy Door that is only opened in Jubilee Years. Above the **portico** (porch; built 1736) are 15 colossal statues representing Christ with St John the Baptist, as well as John the Evangelist and the 12 apostles.

The interior has been done up on numerous occasions. In 1425 Martin V had the floor inlaid with stone and mosaic, while in 1646 Borromini turned his baroque talents to the job. His fingerprint is on the pillars in the nave and the sculptural frames around the funerary monuments in the aisles. A Gothic baldachin over the papal altar contains relics that include the heads of Sts Peter and Paul. The apse was rebuilt in the 19th century; its mosaics are copies of the originals.

To the left of the altar, the beautiful **cloister** (admission €2; ⏲ 9am-6pm Apr-Oct, to 5pm Nov-Mar) was built by the Vassalletto family in the 13th century. The columns were once completely covered with inlaid marble mosaics, remains of which can still be seen. On the western side, there's a marble slab supported by four columns that Christians in the Middle Ages thought represented the height of Christ.

There's a second entrance into the basilica on Piazza San Giovanni in Laterano. To the right of the door in Domenico Fontana's 16th-century façade is the **Palazzo Laterano** (Map pp108–9), which was the papal residence until the popes moved to Avignon early in the 14th century. It was largely destroyed by fire in 1308 and most of what remained was demolished in the 16th century. The present building houses offices of the diocese of Rome.

More interesting is the domed **baptistry** (Map pp108-9; admission free; ⏲ 7.30am-12.30pm & 4-7.30pm) to the left of the façade. Like the basilica it was built by Constantine and served as the prototype for later Christian churches and bell towers. Pope Sixtus III gave it its current octagonal shape. A basalt font rests in the centre, beneath a dome decorated with modern copies of frescoes by Andrea Sacchi. The **Cappella di Santa Rufina** is decorated with a faded 5th-century mosaic of vines and foliage, while the vault of **Cappella di San Giovanni Evangelista** has a mosaic of the Lamb of God surrounded by birds and flowers. **Cappella di San Venanzio** and its mosaics were added by Pope John IV in the 7th century.

At the opposite end of Piazza San Giovanni in Laterano is the **Scala Santa** (Holy Staircase; Map pp108-9; admission free; ⏲ 6.15am-noon & 3.30-6.45pm Apr-Sep, 6.15am-noon & 3-6.15pm Oct-Mar) and the **Sancta Sanctorum** (Holy of Holies; Map pp108-9; admission €3; ⏲ 10.30-11.30am & 3.30-4.30pm Apr-Sep, 3-4pm Tue, Thu & Sat Oct-Mar). This is one of the few religious sites in Rome where the attraction is the spiritual atmosphere rather than the amazing art on display. The Scala Santa is said to be the staircase that Jesus walked up in Pontius Pilate's palace in Jerusalem. Consequently you can only climb it on your knees. At the top of the stairs, the Sancta Sanctorum was the popes' private chapel and contains spectacular 13th-century frescoes. The highlight is the *Image of the Most Holy Saviour*, which legend claims was not painted by human hand.

Some way to the east of Piazza di San Giovanni, **Chiesa di Santa Croce in Gerusalemme** (Map p95; ☎ 06 701 47 69; Piazza Santa Croce in Gerusalemme 12; ⏲ 6.30am-12.30pm & 3.30-7.30pm) was founded in AD 320 by St Helena, Constantine's mother. The church takes its name from the Christian relics, including a piece of the cross on which Christ was crucified, which St Helena brought to Rome from Jerusalem. The bell tower was added in 1144, the façade and oval vestibule in 1744.

CAELIAN HILL

The **Caelian Hill** (Map pp108–9) is a peaceful area (always a relative concept in central Rome) rising to the south of the Colosseum. The best picnic spot is the **Villa Celimontana** (Map pp108-9; Via della Navicella; ⏲ sunrise-sunset) park on top of the hill. Nearby there are a number of churches worth popping into.

The circular **Chiesa di Santo Stefano Rotondo** (Map pp108-9; ☎ 06 704 93 717; Via di Santo Stefano

Rotondo 7), built between 468 and 483, is one of Rome's earliest churches. Inside are two rings of antique granite and marble columns. The wall is lined with frescoes depicting the various ways in which saints were martyred. The church is currently closed for restoration.

A short walk to the west and you'll find the **Chiesa di SS Giovanni e Paolo** (Map pp108-9; ☎ 06 700 57 45; Piazza di SS Giovanni e Paolo; ☺ 8.30am-noon & 3.30-6pm Mon-Thu), a 4th-century church dedicated to Sts John and Paul, who were beheaded by Constantine II's anti-Christian successor, Julian, for refusing to serve in his court. Little is left of the original edifice; the façade is 12th century and the over-the-top interior is 18th century.

Beneath the church are excavations of various **Case Romane** (Roman Houses; Map pp108-9; ☎ 06 704 54 544; www.caseromane.it in Italian; admission €6; ☺ 10am-1pm & 3-6pm Thu-Mon). According to tradition the two saints, John and Paul, lived here and evidence has revealed that the houses were used for Christian worship. There are more than 20 rooms, many of them richly decorated. To get to the excavations go past the church and enter the door before the last arch on the right.

Continuing down the hill you'll reach Via di San Gregorio VII. Turn left for the 8th-century **Chiesa di San Gregorio Magno** (Map pp108-9; ☎ 06 700 82 27; Piazza di San Gregorio 1; ☺ 9am-1pm & 2.30-7pm). Built in honour of Pope Gregory the Great on the site where he dispatched St Augustine to convert the British to Christianity, it was remodelled in baroque style in the 18th century. In the Cappella di San Gregorio, at the end of the right aisle, you'll see a stately 1st-century-BC marble throne believed to have been St Gregory's.

One of Rome's most impressive ruins, the **Terme di Caracalla** (Map pp108-9; ☎ 06 575 86 26; Via delle Terme di Caracalla 52; admission €5; ☺ 9am-1hr before sunset Tue-Sat, 9am-1pm Mon) are a striking reminder of the massive scale on which the Roman emperors liked to build. Covering 10 hectares, Caracalla's Baths could hold 1600 people and had shops, gardens, libraries and entertainment. Begun by Antonius Caracalla and inaugurated in AD 217, the baths were used until the 6th century AD. Excavations in the 16th and 17th centuries unearthed important sculptures, which found their way into the Farnese family collection.

From the baths it's just a short walk to the **Circo Massimo** (Map pp108-9). What was

once Rome's largest stadium with room for 200,000 spectators and a 600m track decorated with statues and columns (watch the chariot race in *Ben Hur* for a rough idea) is now a rather sorry stretch of forlorn grass.

AVENTINE HILL

South of the Circo Massimo, the peaceful **Aventine Hill** (Aventino; Map pp108-9) offers stunning views across the river to St Peter's. Via di Valle Murcia and Clivo de Publici are the approaches with the most character. Along the way you'll pass the **Roseto Comunale** (Map pp108-9), a beautiful public rose garden best seen in spring and summer, and, at the top, the pretty, walled **Parco Savello** (Map pp106-7), planted with orange trees.

Next to the park is the beautifully suggestive 5th-century **Basilica di Santa Sabina** (Map pp106-7; ☎ 06 5 79 41; Piazza Pietro d'Illiria 1; ☺ 6.30am-12.45pm & 3.30-7pm). Of particular note is the carved cypress-wood door to the far left as you stand under the 15th-century portico facing the church. Dating from the 5th century, it features panels depicting biblical scenes, including a crucifixion scene that's one of the oldest in existence. Architecture buffs might be interested to know that the 24 Corinthian columns inside the church are Rome's first example of columns that support arches.

Before you head down the hill, pop along to the **Piazza dei Cavalieri di Malta** (Map pp106-7) at the end of Via Santa Sabina. The first building you come to is **Priorato dei Cavalieri di Malta** (Map pp106-7). Look through the keyhole for one of the most unexpected and charming views in Rome: beautifully framed by the lock you'll see St Peter's Basilica.

VIA APPIA ANTICA & THE CATACOMBS

Known to the Romans as the *regina viarum* (queen of roads), **Via Appia Antica** (Appian Way; Map p95) once ran from the Via di Porta San Sebastiano, near the Terme di Caracalla, to Brindisi on the eastern coast of Puglia. It takes its name from the original builder Appius Claudius Caecus who laid the first 90km section of the road in 312 BC. Considered revolutionary because it was almost perfectly straight, it was later extended to reach Brindisi in 190 BC.

An area rich in ancient history – this is where you'll find the catacombs – it's also a great place for a stroll. On Sundays a long section of the road is closed to traffic but be warned that this is when locals and tourists arrive by the coachload.

To get to Via Appia Antica and the catacombs catch one of the following buses: bus No 218 from Piazza San Giovanni in Laterano; bus No 660 from the Colli Albani stop on Metro A; or bus No 118 from the Piramide stop on Metro B. Alternatively, ATAC's daily Archeobus (€8) departs Piazza Venezia every hour (see p141).

If you're planning on really doing the sights think about buying the Appia Antica Card (see the boxed text, p110). Further information on the area is available at the **Appia Antica Regional Park Visitor Centre** (Map p95; ☎ 06 512 63 14; www.parcoappiaantica.org; Via Appia Antica 42; ☻ 9.30am-6pm summer, to 4.30pm winter).

The main attraction along Via Appia Antica are the catacombs – some 300km of tunnels carved out of the soft tufa rock (see the boxed text, below). Corpses were wrapped in simple white sheets and usually placed in rectangular niches carved into the tunnel walls, which were then closed with marble or terracotta slabs.

The largest, most famous and the busiest of the catacombs are the **Catacombs of San Callisto** (Map p95; ☎ 06 513 01 580; Via Appia Antica 110; www.catacombe.roma.it; admission €5; ☻ 8.30am-noon & 2.30-5.30pm Thu-Tue, to 5pm winter, closed Feb). The martyred patron saint of music, Santa Cecilia, was originally buried here although her body was later removed to the Basilica

di Santa Cecilia in Trastevere. Founded at the end of the 2nd century, the catacombs became the official cemetery of the newly established Roman Church. In the 20km of tunnels explored to date, archaeologists have found the sepulchres of some 500,000 people and the tombs of seven popes, who were martyred in the 3rd century.

The **Catacombs of San Sebastiano** (Map p95; ☎ 06 785 03 50; Via Appia Antica 136; admission €5; ☻ 8.30am-noon & 2.30-5.30pm Mon-Sat, to 5pm winter, closed mid-Nov–mid-Dec) were a safe haven for the remains of Sts Peter and Paul during the reign of Vespasian. The first level is now almost completely destroyed but frescoes, stucco work, epigraphs and three perfectly preserved mausoleums can be seen on the 2nd level.

The **basilica** (Map p95; ☎ 06 780 00 47; ☻ 8am-5.30pm Mon-Fri, 8am-7pm Sat, 7am-1pm & 2.30-5.30pm Sun) above them dates from the 4th century and preserves one of the arrows used to kill St Sebastian.

Among Rome's largest and oldest, the **Catacombs of San Domitilla** (Map p95; ☎ 06 511 03 42; www.catacombe.domitilla.it; Via delle Sette Chiese 283; admission €5; ☻ 8.30am-noon & 2.30-5.30pm Wed-Mon summer, to 5pm winter, closed Jan) were established on the private burial ground of Flavia Domitilla, niece of the Emperor Domitian and a member of the wealthy Flavian family. They contain Christian paintings and the underground church of SS Nereus e Achilleus.

ROMAN UNDERWORLD

Rome's extensive network of catacombs were built as communal burial grounds. A Roman law banned burials within the city walls and persecution left the early Christians little choice but to dig.

During periods of persecution, martyrs were often buried in catacombs beside the fathers of the Church and the first popes. However, space was limited and became increasingly sought after. A trade in tomb real estate developed, becoming increasingly cut-throat until Pope Gregory I abolished the sale of graves in 597. However, Christians had already started to abandon the catacombs as early as 313, when Constantine issued the Milan decree of religious tolerance.

Increasingly, Christians opted to bury their dead in catacombs near the churches and basilicas that were being built (often above pagan temples). This became common practice under Theodosius, who made Christianity the state religion in 394.

In about 800, after frequent incursions by invaders, the bodies of the martyrs and first popes were transferred to the basilicas inside the city walls. The catacombs were abandoned and eventually many were forgotten. In the Middle Ages only three catacombs were known. Those of San Sebastiano were the most frequented as a place of pilgrimage, since they had earlier been the burial place of Sts Peter and Paul.

From the mid-19th century onwards, scholars of Christian archaeology began a programme of scientific research and more than 30 catacombs in the Rome area have been uncovered.

Near the city end of Via Appia, the **Chiesa del Domine Quo Vadis** (Map p95; Via Appia Antica; ⏰ 7am-7pm) is built at the point where St Peter, while fleeing Rome, is said to have met a vision of Jesus. Peter asked: 'Domine, quo vadis?' – 'Lord, where are you going?' When Jesus replied he was going to Rome to be crucified again, Peter decided to join him and on his return to the city was immediately arrested and executed. In the centre of the aisle there are two footprints that are supposed to belong to Christ.

Further down the road, **Circo di Massenzio** (Map p95; ☎ 06 780 13 24; Via Appia Antica 153; admission €2.60; ⏰ 9am-5pm Tue-Sun summer, 9am-1pm Tue-Sun winter) is the best preserved of Rome's ancient racetracks. In fact, you can still make out the starting stalls used for chariot races. The 10,000-seat arena was built by Maxentius around AD 309 but was never actually completed and he never got to see a race there. Above the track is the **Tomba di Romolo** (Map p95), a tomb built for Maxentius' son Romulus. The tomb is indefinitely closed for restoration.

A short hop to the south brings you to the famous **Tomba di Cecilia Metella** (Map p95; ☎ 06 780 24 65; Via Appia Antica 161; admission €2; ⏰ 9am-1hr before sunset Tue-Sun). Money talked in the 1st century BC and Cecilia Metella's fabulously wealthy in-laws made sure she was buried in style. The massive cylindrical mausoleum, 11m high and 30m in diameter, encloses a burial chamber that's now roofless. Due to its position, the tomb was converted into a fortress by the Caetani family in the early 14th century.

Not far past it is a section of the original road, excavated in the mid-19th century.

Before leaving the Via Appia area stop off at the **Mausoleo delle Fosse Ardeatine** (Map p95; ☎ 06 513 67 42; Via Ardeatina 174; admission free; ⏰ 8.15am-5pm) for a sobering reminder of the horrors of war. Buried here outside the Ardeatine Caves are 335 Italian prisoners shot by the Nazis in retaliation for a partisan attack. There is also a small **museum** (⏰ 8.15am-4.45pm) dedicated to the Italian resistance to the German occupation.

EUR

Mussolini's Orwellian quarter of giant Fascist buildings (now largely used by government ministries) was designed for an international exhibition in 1942. However, war intervened and the exhibition never took place although it did give its name to the area; EUR stands for Esposizione Universale di Roma.

To get to EUR take Metro B for EUR Palasport. The area merits a visit for its Fascist architecture if nothing else. Check out, for example, the **Palazzo della Civiltà del Lavoro** (Palace of the Workers; Map p130), a square building with arched windows, known as the Square Colosseum.

There are a few museums in the area, of which the **Museo della Civiltà Romana** (Map p130; ☎ 06 592 60 41; Piazza Giovanni Agnelli 10; admission €6.20; ⏰ 9am-6.45pm Tue-Sat, 9am-1pm Sun) is the most impressive. Founded by Mussolini in 1937 to glorify Imperial Rome it boasts a magnificent scale model of the ancient city, its monuments and battles. Kids will love it, which perhaps explains the frequent presence of large groups of Italian school children.

Less captivating is the **Museo Nazionale Preistorico Etnografico Luigi Pigorini** (Map p130; ☎ 06 549 55 21; Piazza Marconi 14; admission €4; ⏰ 9am-8pm), which houses prehistoric artefacts (human bones, mammoth tusks, shells and so on) from around the world.

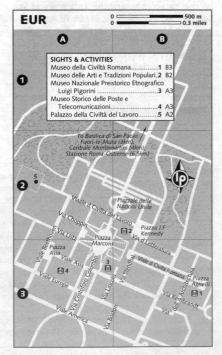

For a surprisingly interesting insight into rural traditions and folk art, head for the **Museo delle Arti e Tradizioni Popolari** (Map p130; ☎ 06 592 61 48; Piazza Marconi 8; admission €4; ☼ 9am-8pm, by appointment only 6-8pm), while the **Museo Storico delle Poste e Telecomunicazioni** (Map p130; ☎ 065 544 20 92; Viale Europa 190; admission free; ☼ 9am-1pm Mon-Fri) uses stamp printing matrixes, telephone and telegraphic equipment to tell the story of Italy's much-maligned postal service.

SAN PAOLO

The **Basilica di San Paolo Fuori-le-Mura** (St Paul's Outside the Walls; Map p95; ☎ 06 541 03 41; Via Ostiense 186; ☼ 7.30am-6.30pm, cloisters closed 1-3pm) is the largest basilica in Rome after St Peter's. Originally built by Constantine on the site where St Paul was buried, it was largely destroyed by fire in 1823.

Among the treasures to survive were the 5th-century mosaics on the triumphal arch, a Romanesque paschal candlestick and the marble tabernacle (c 1285) by Arnolfo di Cambio. Doom-mongers should note the portraits of the popes beneath the nave windows. Legend has it that when there is no space left for the next portrait, the world will fall. There are eight positions left.

The **cloisters** of the adjacent Benedictine abbey also survived the fire. They are masterpieces of Cosmati work, with elaborate mosaic-encrusted columns.

To get to the basilica take the Metro Line B to San Paolo.

Also in the area is the **Centrale Montemartini** (Map p95; ☎ 06 574 80 42; Via Ostiense 106; admission €4.20; ☼ 9.30am-7pm), an outpost of the Capitoline Museums (p116). The former power station houses many pieces that the Capitoline Museums don't have room for. It's particularly striking to see classical sculpture displayed next to industrial remnants, such as diesel engines and giant furnaces.

Northern Rome

The northern part of Rome is less packed with sights than elsewhere but Villa Borghese is a great place to unwind and its gallery is one of the city's must-see sights.

VILLA BORGHESE & AROUND

This beautiful **park** (Map pp96–7), located just northeast of Piazza del Popolo, was once the estate of Cardinal Scipione Borghese. You can enter from Piazzale Flaminio,

from the top of Pincio Hill above the Spanish Steps or from the top of Via Vittorio Veneto. It's a good place to have a picnic or to take children for a run around. You can hire in-line skates (including helmets and kneepads) and bikes.

To overlook the **Museo e Galleria Borghese** (Map pp96–7; ☎ 06 3 28 10; www.ticketeria.it; Piazzale del Museo Borghese; admission €8.50; ☼ 9am-7pm Tue-Sun, prebooking necessary) would be to miss one of the capital's finest art galleries. It's stunning and absolutely worth the hassle of the two-minute phone call you'll need to make to book a ticket. In order to limit numbers, visitors are admitted at two-hourly intervals, so after you've picked up your ticket you'll have to wait for the entry time you were given when you booked.

The collection, including works by Caravaggio, Bernini, Botticelli and Raphael, was formed by Cardinal Scipione Borghese, the most passionate and knowledgeable art connoisseur of his day. Housed in his beautiful 18th-century villa, the collection was bought by the Italian state in 1902. After a 13-year restoration period, it reopened to the public in 1997.

The collection is divided into two parts: the ground-floor museum with its superb sculpture, intricate Roman floor mosaics and stunning frescoes; and the upstairs picture gallery. On the ground floor, in Sala I, you immediately come across Antonio Canova's daring depiction of Napoleon's sister, Paolina Bonaparte Borghese, reclining topless as *Venere Vincitrice* (Victorious Venus). But it's Bernini's spectacular carvings – flamboyant depictions of pagan myths – that really take the breath away. Just look at Pluto's hand pressing into the soft flesh of Persephone's thigh in the *Ratto di Proserpina* (Rape of Persephone; Sala IV) or at Daphne's hands morphing into leaves in the swirling *Apollo e Dafne* (Sala III). A helpless Apollo looks on as Daphne is transformed into a tree.

Six Caravaggio paintings including several early works are in Sala VIII, while upstairs you can gaze on works by Giovanni Bellini, Giorgione, Veronese, Botticelli, Guercino, Domenichino and Rubens, among others. Highlights include Raphael's *Deposizione di Cristo* (Christ Being Taken Down from the Cross; Sala IX) of 1507 and Titian's early masterpiece the *Amor Sacro e Amor Profano* (Sacred and Profane Love; Sala XX).

ROME & LAZIO

For a complete change of period and style, the **Galleria Nazionale d'Arte Moderna e Contemporanea** (Map pp96-7; ☎ 06 323 40 00; www.gnam.arti .beniculturali.it; Viale delle Belle Arti 131, disabled entrance at Via Antonio Gramsci 73; admission €6.50; ☒ 8.30am-7.30pm Tue-Sun) displays works by some of the most important exponents of modern Italian art. Here you'll find canvases by the *macchiaioli* (meaning 'dabbers' and referring to the Italian version of the Impressionists) and the futurists (Boccioni and Balla). A highlight is Rafaello Sernesi's *Roofs in Sunlight*. There's also a well-represented international contingent: Degas, Cezanne, Kandinsky and Henry Moore, among others. The *belle époque* palazzo that houses the museum was built in 1911 for the Rome International Exhibition.

A short walk down Viale delle belle Arti leads to the 16th-century villa of Pope Julius III, home of the **Museo Nazionale Etrusco di Villa Giulia** (Map pp96-7; bookings ☎ 06 82 46 20; www.ticketeria.it; Piazzale di Villa Giulia 9; admission €4; ☒ 8.30am-7.30pm Tue-Sun). If you're at all interested in Etruscan history you'll love it here. There are thousands of exhibits, including those on domestic objects, cooking utensils, terracotta vases and amphorae, and bronze mirrors, and the remains of a horse-drawn chariot. If you're planning on visiting Etruscan sites in Lazio this is the ideal place to bone up on the subject before you go.

Of particular note is the polychrome terracotta statue of *Apollo* found at Veio (currently being restored) and the *Sarcofago degli Sposi* (Sarcophagi of the Betrothed) taken from a tomb at Cerveteri. Both date to the 6th century BC.

If the weight of culture is beginning to tell, or your kids are driving you bonkers, head for the nearby **Bioparco** (Map pp96-7; ☎ 06 360 82 11; www.bioparco.it in Italian; Viale del Giardino Zoologico 1; adult/infant/child €8.50/free/6.50; ☒ 9.30am-6pm 26 Mar–30 Oct, 9.30am-5pm 31 Oct–25 Mar). Rome's zoo has improved a lot in recent years but it's still not exactly inspiring. Quite frankly, there are better ways to spend your money but if you're desperate to see a lion in the centre of Rome there's nowhere else to go.

To the northeast of the park on Via Salaria, the **Catacombs of Santa Priscilla** (☎ 06 862 06 272; www.catacombedipriscilla.com; Via Salaria 430; admission €5; ☒ 8.30am-noon & 2.30-5pm Tue-Sun Feb-Dec) belonged to the Acilii family in the 1st century AD. They were expanded in the 3rd and 4th centuries and became a popular society burial ground with appropriate upmarket decoration, quite a lot of which has survived. The funerary chapel, the Cappella Greca, retains some 3rd-century frescoes of biblical scenes.

Vatican City & Borgo

The world's smallest sovereign state, the **Vatican City** (Città del Vaticano; Map pp98–9) might cover an area of less than 1 sq km but it packs quite a punch. When the pope speaks, his word immediately becomes gospel for the world's one billion Catholics. And what the Vatican City lacks in size it makes up for in wealth – the opulence of St Peter's and the vast collections of the Vatican Museums have to be seen to be believed.

The Vatican regained its independence in 1929 after 68 years as part of the Kingdom of Italy. Under the terms of the Lateran Treaty, signed by Mussolini and Pius XI, the pope was also given sovereignty over the basilicas of San Giovanni in Laterano (as well as the Palazzo Laterano), Santa Maria Maggiore and San Paolo Fuori-le-Mura.

The Vatican has its own postal service, currency, newspaper, radio station and train station (now used only for freight). It also has its own army of Swiss Guards, responsible for the pope's personal security. The corps was established in 1506 by Julius II to defend the Papal States against invading armies. The guards still wear the traditional eye-catching red, yellow and blue uniform and brandish

---

AN AUDIENCE WITH THE POPE

At 11am on Wednesdays, the pope addresses his flock at the Vatican (in July and August he does so in the Castel Gandolfo). For free tickets, go to the **Prefettura della Casa Pontificia** (Map pp98-9; ☎ 06 698 84 631; fax 06 698 85 863; ☒ 9am-1pm), through the bronze doors under the colonnade to the right of St Peter's as you face the basilica. You can apply on the Tuesday before the audience (or, at a push, on the morning of the audience). Alternatively, write to the Prefettura della Casa Pontificia, 00120 Città del Vaticano, or send a fax. Specify the date you'd like to attend and the number of tickets required. If you are staying at a hotel in Rome, the office will forward the tickets there.

ST PETER'S TOMB

Excavations beneath St Peter's, which began in 1940, have uncovered part of the original church and what archaeologists believe is the tomb of St Peter. Today the site of the empty tomb is marked by a shrine and a wall plastered with red.

In 1942 the bones of an elderly, strongly built man were found in a box hidden behind a wall covered by pilgrims' graffiti. After more than 30 years of forensic examination, Pope Paul VI declared the bones to be those of St Peter in 1976. John Paul II had some of the relics transferred to his hospital room when he was recovering from the 1981 assassination attempt. The bones were then returned to the tomb and are kept in hermetically sealed Perspex cases designed by NASA.

The excavations can be visited by appointment only. Apply in person to the **Ufficio Scavi** (Map pp98-9; ☎ 06 698 85 318; scavi@fsp.va; Fabbrica di San Pietro; ☿ 9am-5pm Mon-Fri) or write to the Ufficio Scavi, Fabbrica di San Pietro, 00120 Città del Vaticano, and stipulate the date you'd like to visit. You need to book at least one week ahead; tickets cost €10. Small groups are taken through the excavations most days from 9am to noon and 2pm to 5pm.

unwieldy 15th-century pikes, but forget any idea that they're theatrical props – they are in fact highly trained soldiers.

The first pope to establish a fixed papal residence in the Vatican was Symmachus (498–514), although it wasn't until 1377 that the Vatican palace became the official residence of the pope. Before that pontiffs had lived at the Palazzo Laterano, adjacent to the Basilica di San Giovanni, and, for a short time in the 14th century, in Avignon.

The current look of the Vatican is the culmination of more than a thousand years of chipping and changing. The Leonine walls date to 846 when Leo IV had them put up after a series of Saracen raids, while the Vatican palace, now home to the Vatican Museums, was originally constructed by Eugenius III in the 12th century. Subsequent popes extended it, fortified it and decorated it according to their political and artistic needs.

PIAZZA SAN PIETRO

One of the world's great public spaces, Bernini's massive **Piazza San Pietro** (Map pp98–9) is a breathtaking work of baroque town planning. Laid out in the 17th century as a place for Christians to gather, the piazza was designed to open up before visitors as they escaped the jumble of narrow streets that originally surrounded the area. Mussolini, however, spoiled Bernini's effect when he built the long straight approach road, Via della Conciliazione.

Looked at from above the piazza resembles a giant keyhole: two semicircular colonnades, each of which is made up of four rows

of Doric columns, bound a giant oval that straightens out towards the basilica. On the square there are two points from where you can see all the columns perfectly aligned. Look for the iron paving disks either side of the central obelisk. The ancient Egyptian obelisk was brought to Rome by Caligula from Heliopolis.

ST PETER'S BASILICA

You don't need to be religious to be bowled over by **St Peter's Basilica** (Basilica di San Pietro; Map pp98-9; ☎ 06 698 81 662; www.vatican.va; Piazza San Pietro; basilica admission free, dome with/without lift €7/4; ☿ basilica 7am-7pm Apr-Sep, to 6pm Oct-Mar, dome 8am-5.45pm Apr-Sep, to 4.45pm Oct-Mar). The great basilica is not only huge, but also a monument to artistic genius. On a more prosaic note, remember to dress appropriately if you want to get in – that means no shorts, miniskirts or bare shoulders. Your excuses are unlikely to sway the sartorial guardians stationed on the doors.

The first basilica was built here by Rome's first Christian emperor, Constantine, in the 4th century. Standing on the site of Nero's stadium, the Ager Vaticanus, where St Peter is said to have been martyred and buried between AD 6 and 67, it was consecrated in AD 326.

More than a 1000 years later the basilica had fallen into disrepair. In the mid-15th century Nicholas V took a stab at its reconstruction, but it was not until 1506, when Julius II employed Bramante, that serious work began. Bramante designed a new basilica on a Greek cross plan, with a central dome and four smaller domes. He also oversaw the demolition of much of the old basilica and attracted great criticism for the unnecessary destruction of many of its most precious works of art.

It took more than 150 years to complete the new basilica, now the second biggest in the world (the largest is in Yamoussoukro on the Ivory Coast). Bramante, Raphael, Antonio da Sangallo, Giacomo della Porta and Carlo Maderno all contributed, but it is generally held that St Peter's owes most to Michelangelo, who took over the project in 1547 at the age of 72 and was responsible for the design of the dome.

The façade and portico were designed by Maderno, who took over the project after Michelangelo's death. He was also instructed to lengthen the nave towards the piazza, effectively altering Bramante's original Greek cross plan to a Latin cross.

The cavernous interior (it's 187m long), decorated by Bernini and Giacomo della Porta, can hold up to 60,000 people and contains some spectacular works of art. Chief among them is Michelangelo's superb **Pietà**, at the beginning of the right aisle. Sculpted when he was only 25 years old, this is the only work to carry his signature (on the sash across the Madonna's breast). It is now protected by bulletproof glass after a hammer-wielding vandal attacked it in 1972.

Nearby, the **red porphyry disk** just inside the main door marks the spot where Charlemagne and later Holy Roman Emperors were crowned by the pope.

Dominating the centre of the church is Bernini's 29m-high baroque **baldachin**. Supported by four spiral columns and made with bronze taken from the Pantheon, it stands over the high altar, which itself sits on the site of St Peter's grave. The pope is the only priest permitted to serve at the high altar.

To the right as you face the high altar is a famous bronze **statue of St Peter**, believed to be a 13th-century work by Arnolfo di Cambio. The statue's right foot has been worn down by the kisses and touches of many pilgrims.

Michelangelo's masterpiece **dome** soars 119m above the high altar. Its balconies are decorated with reliefs depicting the *Reliquie Maggiori* (Major Relics): the lance of San Longino, which he used to pierce Christ's side; the cloth of Santa Veronica, which bears a miraculous image of Christ; and a piece of the True Cross, collected by St Helena, the mother of Emperor Constantine.

Entry to the dome is to the far right of the basilica – you'll recognise it by the queues outside. A small lift takes you halfway up but it's still a long climb to the top. Press on though and you'll be rewarded with some stunning views over Rome. It's well worth the effort, but it's also a long and tiring climb and not recommended for those who suffer from claustrophobia or vertigo.

The **Vatican Grottoes** (Sacre Grotte Vaticane; Map pp98-9; ⏰ 7am-6pm Apr-Sep, to 5pm Oct-Mar) below the church contain the tombs of numerous popes, including John Paul II. The entrance is to the right as you approach the papal altar.

VATICAN MUSEUMS

From Piazza San Pietro follow the walls of the Vatican northward to the **Vatican Museums** (Musei Vaticani; Map pp98-9; ☎ 06 698 83 333; www.vatican.va; admission €12, last Sun of month free; ⏰ 8.45am-4.45pm, last admission 3.20pm, Mon-Fri, 8.45am-1.45pm Sat mid-Mar–late Oct & late-Dec–Jan, 8.45am-1.45pm, last admission 12.20pm, Mon-Fri Jan-Mar & Nov–late Dec, 8.45am-1.45pm last Sun of month). The complicated hours change regularly so it's always best to check ahead.

The museums are enormous and you'll never manage to see everything in one go – you'd need several hours just to see the highlights. To make navigation easier there are four colour-coded itineraries which take anything from 45 minutes to five hours. Each itinerary starts at the Quattro Cancelli area, near the entrance, and each one finishes up at the Sistine Chapel, so if you want you can walk straight there. However, bear in mind that you can't backtrack once you are there, so if you want to see, say, the *Stanze di Raffaello* make sure you do so first. Also be prepared to jostle for position in the chapel – it's almost always heaving and there's really not a lot you can do to avoid the crowds.

The *Guide to the Vatican Museums and City,* on sale at the museums, is a worthwhile investment. You can also hire CD audioguides (€5.50).

The Vatican Museums are well equipped for disabled visitors; there are four suggested itineraries, several lifts and specially fitted toilets. Wheelchairs can also be reserved in advance; call ☎ 06 698 83 860. Parents with young children can take strollers into the museums.

The buildings that house the Vatican Museums, known collectively as the Palazzo Apostolico Vaticano, cover an area of 5.5 hectares. Each gallery contains priceless treasures but for a whistle-stop tour get to the Stanze di Raffaello, the Pinacoteca, the Gallerie delle Carte Geografiche (Map Gallery) and, of course, the Sistine Chapel. Unless they're of particular interest you could skim the Museo Gregoriano Profano (Gregorian Museum of Pagan Antiquities), Museo Pio-Cristiano (Pio Christian Museum) and Museo Missionario-Etnologico (Missionary and Ethnological Museum).

What follows is a brief description of some of the museum's major features and highlights.

Among the relatively small number of pictures in the **Pinacoteca** you'll find Raphael's last work, *La Trasfigurazione*, and paintings by Giotto, Bellini, Caravaggio and Leonardo da Vinci, whose *San Gerolamo* was never finished.

Founded by Gregory XVI in 1839, the **Museo Gregoriano Egizio** (Egyptian Museum) contains pieces taken from Egypt in Roman times. The collection is small but there are fascinating exhibits including the *Trono di Rameses II*, part of a statue of the seated king, and sarcophagi dating from around 1000 BC.

The Vatican's enormous collection of ancient sculpture is contained in a series of galleries. The long corridor that forms the **Museo Chiaramonti** contains hundreds of marble busts and statues, while off to the right Pius VII's **Braccio Nuovo** (New Wing) contains some important works. These include a famous statue of Augustus, and a carving depicting the Nile as a reclining god with 16 babies (which are thought to represent the number of cubits the Nile rose when in flood) playing on him.

Housed in the late-15th-century Belvedere Pavilion, **Museo Pio-Clementino** is accessible through the Egyptian Museum or from

MICHELANGELO & THE POPES

Michelangelo Buonarotti came to work in Rome for Pope Julius II, who wanted him to create a grand marble tomb for his own burial. The tomb, which you can see in the **Basilica di San Pietro in Vincoli** (p122), preoccupied Michelangelo for most of his life, but was never completed.

Michelangelo's passion was sculpture and he was reluctant to take on the job for which he is now most famous – the painting of the Sistine Chapel. But when he finally accepted Julius II's commission, he set to work with passionate obsession, dismissing all assistance and working lying down on scaffolding lodged up high under the windows for four years, pushing himself to artistic and physical limits and bickering constantly with the pope who wanted the job finished.

Despite his unhappiness as a Vatican-employed painter, Michelangelo returned to Rome almost 20 years later, at the age of 59, to work on another painting in the Sistine Chapel. This time it was at the request of Pope Clement VI, who wanted the Florentine artist to paint *The Last Judgement* on the altar wall.

When Clement VIII died, his successor, Paul III, was determined to have Michelangelo work exclusively for him. He wanted the Sistine Chapel finished. In 1535 he appointed Michelangelo as chief architect, sculptor and painter to the Vatican.

When *The Last Judgement* was finally completed and unveiled in 1541, it caused quite a scandal. But though Pope Pius IV had Daniele da Volterra, one of Michelangelo's students, add fig leaves and loin cloths to the many nudes, Michelangelo's work was claimed by many to be one of his best, surpassing all the other paintings in the chapel, including his own ceiling frescoes.

The artist spent his last years working – unhappily (he felt that it was a penance from God) – on St Peter's Basilica. He disapproved of the plans that had been drawn up by Antonio da Sangallo the Younger before his death, claiming they deprived the basilica of light, and argued with Sangallo's assistants, who wanted to retain their master's designs. Instead Michelangelo created the magnificent light-filled dome based on Brunelleschi's design for the cathedral in Florence, and a stately façade.

He continued to direct the work until his death on 18 February 1564. The dome and façade of St Peter's were completed to his designs by Vignola, Giacomo della Porta and Carlo Fontana.

the Cortile Ottagono (Octagonal Courtyard), itself part of the museum. To the left as you enter the courtyard is the *Apollo Belvedere*, a 2nd-century Roman copy in marble of a 4th-century BC Greek bronze, considered one of the great masterpieces of classical sculpture. A second unmissable piece is the *Lacoön*, depicting a Trojan priest of Apollo and his two sons in mortal struggle with two sea serpents. This statue was excavated from the Domus Aurea area.

In the **Sala delle Muse** (Room of Muses) is the *Torso Belvedere*, a Greek sculpture from the 1st century BC, which was found in the Campo de' Fiori during the time of Pope Julius II. The sculpture was much admired by Michelangelo and other Renaissance artists. In the **Sala a Croce Greca** (Greek Cross Room) are the porphyry stone sarcophagi of Constantine's daughter, Constantia, and his mother, St Helena.

Up one flight of the Simonetti staircase is the **Museo Gregoriano Etrusco** (Etruscan Museum), containing artefacts from Etruscan tombs in southern Etruria. Of particular interest are those in Room II from the Regolini-Galassi tomb, discovered in 1836, south of

Cerveteri. Those buried in the tomb included a princess, and among the finds on display are gold jewellery and a funeral carriage with a bronze bed and funeral couch.

Magnificent views of Rome can be had from the last room at the end of this wing (through the Sala delle Terracotte). From here you can also get a glimpse down the full drop of Bramante's spiral staircase, which was designed so that horses could be ridden up it.

Through the superb **Galleria delle Carte Geografiche** (Map Gallery) and the **Galleria degli Arazzi** (Tapestry Gallery) are the magnificent **Stanze di Raffaello**, the private apartments of Pope Julius II. Raphael himself painted the Stanza della Segnatura and the Stanza d'Eliodoro, while the Stanza dell'Incendio was painted by his students to his designs and the ceiling was painted by his master, Perugino.

In the Stanza della Segnatura lives one of Raphael's best-known masterpieces, *La Scuola d'Atene* (The School of Athens), featuring philosophers and scholars gathered around Plato and Aristotle. The lone figure in front of the steps is believed to be

---

THE POPE'S DEAD, LONG LIVE THE POPE

Morto un papa se ne fa un altro. The white smoke billowing out of the specially erected chimney could only mean one thing. After one of the shortest conclaves in recent times, the 115 cardinals locked in the Sistine Chapel had elected Pope John Paul II's successor. On 19 April 2005 the 78-year-old Josef Ratzinger became the first German since Vittore II (1055–57), and only the second non-Italian in almost 500 years, to be nominated pope. The first non-Italian, a Pole, had died 17 days before.

News of John Paul II's death was greeted with an outpouring of emotion that Rome has rarely witnessed. More than three million mourners poured into the Vatican to pay their respects to the third-longest serving pope of all time. Pilgrims queued for more than 12 hours to file past Karol Wojtyla's body in St Peter's Basilica, while Church officials hurried to organise the funeral. A masterpiece of diplomatic stage management, the televised funeral was attended by some 205 official delegations and 13 monarchs. The media-savvy John Paul II would surely have approved.

A charismatic and energetic pontiff, John Paul II will best be remembered for his role in the fall of communism. An outspoken supporter of the Polish trade union Solidarnosc, he continued to defend the underdog throughout his papacy. In his latter years he railed against the oppression of developing countries and called on the G8 nations to drop Third World debt. Theologically, however, he was an authoritarian arch-conservative brooking no talk of liberalising the Church's stance on contraception and other social issues.

In this John Paul II was backed to the hilt by Ratzinger, a Bavarian theologian, who since 1981 had been head of the Congregation for the Doctrine of the Faith, the Vatican ministry responsible for, among other things, the Church's line on ethics and morality. Taking the name Benedict XVI, Ratzinger is unlikely to allow a softening of the orthodoxy which he has worked so long to promote.

Michelangelo, who was painting the Sistine Chapel at the time, while the figure of Plato is said to be a portrait of Leonardo da Vinci, with Euclide (lower right) as Bramante. Raphael also included a self-portrait in the lower right corner (he's the second figure from the right). Opposite is *La Disputa del Sacramento* (Disputation on the Sacrament), also by Raphael.

In the Stanza d'Eliodoro is another Raphael masterpiece, *Cacciata d'Eliodoro* (Expulsion of Heliodorus from the Temple), on the main wall (to the right as you enter from the Sala dei Chiaroscuri), which symbolises Julius' military victory over foreign powers. To the left is *Mass of Bolsena,* showing Julius II paying homage to a relic from a 13th-century miracle in the lakeside town of Bolsena (see p187). Next is *Leone X ferma l'invasione di Attila* (Leo X Repulsing Attila), by Raphael and his students. On the fourth wall is *Liberazione di San Pietro* (Liberation of St Peter), which depicts the saint being freed from prison, but is actually an allusion to Pope Leo's imprisonment after the battle of Ravenna (also the real subject of the Attila fresco).

SISTINE CHAPEL

For many the real reason for visiting the museums is to view the remarkable **Sistine Chapel** (Capella Sistina; Map pp98–9). This is the room into which the papal conclave is locked to elect the next pope, although it's better known as home to the most famous works of art in the world: Michelangelo's **frescoes** on the barrel-vaulted ceiling (painted 1508–12), and **The Last Judgement** on the end wall (completed in 1541).

The chapel was originally built in 1484 for Pope Sixtus IV, after whom it is named, but it was actually Julius II who commissioned Michelangelo to decorate it. The great artist was reluctant to take on the job – he considered himself a sculptor not a painter – but started work in 1508. He worked almost entirely alone and fought furiously with his impatient papal boss.

The frescoes down the middle represent nine scenes from the book of Genesis, including the *Division of Day from Night,* the *Creation of Adam,* the *Expulsion of Adam and Eve from the Garden of Eden* and the *Flood.* These main images are framed by the *Ignudi,* athletic male nudes; next to them,

on the lower curved part of the vault, are large figures of Hebrew prophets and pagan sibyls. In the lunettes over the windows are the ancestors of Christ.

The walls of the chapel were also painted by important Renaissance artists, including Botticelli, Domenico Ghirlandaio, Pinturicchio and Luca Signorelli. Anywhere else these frescoes would be the star of the show, but here they're often passed over with little more than a glance. They are, however, magnificent late-15th-century works, depicting events in the lives of Moses and Christ. Botticelli's *Temptation of Christ* and the *Cleansing of the Leper* (the second fresco on the right) is particularly beautiful. The first frescoes in each cycle, the *Finding of Moses* and the *Birth of Christ* by Perugino, were destroyed to make way for *The Last Judgement* – a great controversy at the time.

The Last Judgement, with its dramatic, swirling mass of predominantly naked bodies, depicts the souls of the dead being torn from their graves to face the wrath of God. The subject was chosen by Paul III as a warning to Catholics to toe the line during the Reformation, then sweeping Europe. A work of highly charged emotion, it is said to reflect Michelangelo's tormented faith.

BORGO

The area between the Vatican and the Tiber is known as the Borgo. The major landmark here is **Castel Sant'Angelo** (Map pp98–9; ☎ 06 681 91 11; Lungotevere Castello 50; admission €5; ☻ 9am-8pm Tue-Sun). Originally the mausoleum of Emperor Hadrian, it was converted into a fortress for the popes in the 6th century AD. It was named by Pope Gregory the Great in AD 590, after he saw a vision of an angel above the structure heralding the end of a plague in Rome. The fortress was linked to the Vatican palaces in 1277 by a wall and passageway, often used by popes to escape in times of threat. During the 16th-century sack of Rome by Emperor Charles V, hundreds of people lived in the fortress for months.

Opposite the castle, the **Ponte Sant'Angelo** (Map pp98–9) was built by Hadrian in AD 136 to provide an approach to his mausoleum. It collapsed in 1450 and was subsequently rebuilt, incorporating parts of the ancient bridge. In the 17th century, Bernini and his pupils sculpted the figures of angels which now line this pedestrian-only bridge.

ROME & LAZIO

WALKING TOUR

If you have never been to Rome, or if you have limited time, this tour of selected hits provides an introduction.

Start in Piazza di Trevi, at the iconic **Trevi Fountain** (**1**; p123). City lore has it that during construction a busybody barber criticised the project from the balcony of his shop on the right side of the square. Architect Nicola Salvi got the last laugh though; he blocked the barber's sign and his view with a giant ornament on the balustrade in the shape of a barber's soap pot. Toss a coin over your shoulder into the fountain, then take Via dei Crociferi and Via Sabini down to busy Via del Corso. Cross the road to Piazza Colonna and you enter the political core of the capital. Pass **Palazzo Chigi** (**2**;

> **WALK FACTS**
>
> **Start** Piazza di Trevi
> **Finish** St Peter's Basilica
> **Distance** 3.5km
> **Duration** Three hours

see the boxed text, p121), the official residence of the prime minister, on your right as you make for Piazza Montecitorio and the impressive seat of the Italian Chamber of Deputies, **Palazzo Montecitorio** (**3**; see the boxed text, p121). From the palazzo duck down Via della Guglia and veer right into Via dei Pastini until you emerge in the busy Piazza della Rotonda, where the **Pantheon** (**4**; p117) needs no introduction. Mosey along its eastern flank to Bernini's cute **Elefantino** (**5**; p118), then pop into the 13th-century **Chiesa di Santa Maria Sopra Minerva** (**6**; p119), which might not be one of Rome's most famous churches but can still boast its own Michelangelo sculpture. By now it's coffee time. Take Via della Palombella up to **Piazza Sant'Eustachio** (**7**) and drop into the café of the same name (p167). When suitably refreshed, follow Via degli Straderari to Corso del Rinascimento, drop a quick left followed by a short right and you're into the baroque jamboree that is **Piazza Navona** (**8**; p119). Here you can compare the two giants of Roman baroque: Bernini created the square's most famous fountain, **Fontana**

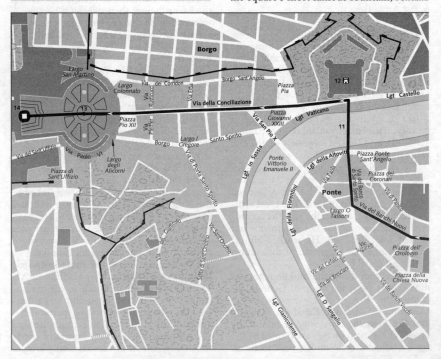

dei Quattro Fiumi (**9**; p119), and his bitter rival Borromini produced the piazza's best-known façade, that of the **Chiesa di Sant'Agnese in Agone** (**10**; p119). Exit the piazza at the southwestern corner and take Via Pasquino through to Via del Governo Vecchio. Keep going straight down this atmospheric street, with its second-hand clothes shops, wine bars and trattorie, until you emerge from its extension Via Banchi Nuovi near the pedestrian-only **Ponte Sant'Angelo** (**11**; p137). Cross the bridge, stopping, or not, to peruse the fake designer gear laid out by the street hawkers, and you'll come face to face with **Castel Sant'Angelo** (**12**; p137). You can't take the secret passageway that connects the castle with the Vatican, but you can follow Via della Conciliazione up to **Piazza San Pietro** (**13**; p133) and the holiest of the holy Catholic churches, **St Peter's Basilica** (**14**; p133).

COURSES
Cooking
Cookery writer Diane Seed runs her **Roman Kitchen** (Map pp98-9; ☎ 06 6/9 71 03; www.italiangourmet.com) either four or five times a year from her kitchen in the Palazzo Doria Pamphilj. Week-long courses cost €750 for 3½ hours of lessons per day, while for a three-day programme expect to pay €450.

Gladiator School
If the idea of dressing up in a short tunic and brandishing a sword turns you on, then the **Gruppo Storico Romano** (Map p95; ☎ 06 516 07 951; www.gsr-roma.com; Via Appia Antica 18) can help. An association of history enthusiasts, it has established Rome's first gladiator school. Courses, open to men and women, last two months and cover both theory and combat. They cost €112 but when you sign on you get a complimentary tunic, pair of sandals, belt, protective glove and wooden sword. Ironically, you'll also need a medical certificate before you're let in the arena – mortal combat is a pastime for the fit and healthy.

Language
There are hundreds of schools offering language courses in Rome. Costs vary from around €340 for a 40-hour, two-week course to about €1400 for a longer six-month course.

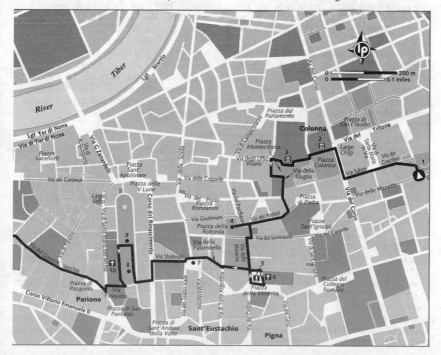

Some schools will also offer accommodation packages. Reputable schools:

Arco di Druso (Map p95; ☎ 06 397 50 984; www
.arcodidruso.com; Via Tunisi 4)

Centro Linguistico Italiano Dante Alighieri (Map
p95; ☎ 06 442 31 400; www.clidante.it; Piazza Bologna 1)

Italiaidea (Map pp102-3; ☎ 06 699 41 314; www
.italiaidea.com; 1st fl, Via dei Due Macelli 47)

**Torre di Babele Centro di Lingua e Cultura
Italiana** (Map pp102-3; ☎ 06 700 84 34; www.torre
dibabele.com; Via Nino Bixio 74)

Wine-Tasting

Refine your palate on one of the courses run by the **International Wine Academy of Roma** (Map pp98-9; ☎ 06 699 08 78; www.wineacademyroma .com; Vicolo del Bottino 8). Learn about Italy's wine regions and tone up your tasting skills on the €150 half-day course. For a more detailed look at the world of wine go for the three-day €550 course which includes a vineyard visit.

ROME FOR CHILDREN

Even with the best will in the world, traipsing around Rome with kids is exhausting. But it need not reach breaking point. You can always arouse your little one's blood lust by taking them to the **Colosseum** (p110) or impressing them with the morbid bone display under the **Chiesa di Santa Maria della Concezione** (p124). There are also the catacombs under **Via Appia Antica** (p128).

There's a museum dedicated to the under 12s. **Explora** (Map pp96-7; ☎ 06 361 37 76; www .mdbr.it; Via Flaminia 82; adult/child €5/7; ⏰ tours depart 9.30am, 11.30am, 3pm & 5pm Tue, Wed, Thu & Fri, 10am, noon, 3pm & 5pm Sat & Sun Oct-Jun, 10am, noon, 3pm & 5pm Tue-Sun Jul & Sep, noon, 3pm & 5pm Tue-Sun Aug) offers kids the chance to turn their hands to a range of activities including weighing fruit on electronic supermarket scales and using TV cameras. It is advisable to book ahead, particularly at weekends; visits last one hour and 45 minutes.

A real kid-pleaser is the **Time Elevator** (Map pp98-9; ☎ 06 977 46 243; www.time-elevator.it; Via dei Santissimi Apostoli 20; adult/child €11/9.20; ⏰ 11am-7.30pm), a 45-minute virtual journey through 3000 years of Roman history; shows occur every 15 minutes. With panoramic screens, flight-simulator technology and a surround-sound system it's a moving experience in the literal sense of the word. It's not recommended for under fives. You'll find this ingenious crowd-pleaser three minutes' walk from Piazza Venezia, just off Via del Corso.

In **Villa Borghese** (p131) there are bikes and inline skates for hire, train rides and Rome's zoo, the **Bioparco** (p132). Kids may enjoy the Sunday puppet shows on Piazzale Giuseppe Garibaldi on the **Janiculum Hill** (p126). **Villa Celimontana** (p127), on the western slopes of the Caelian Hill (the entrance is at Piazza della Navicella), is a lovely public park with a children's playground.

TOURS
Air

Aerophile Italia (Map pp96-7; ☎ 06 321 11 511; www .aerophile.it; Viale del Galoppatoio, Villa Borghese; tickets Mon-Fri €15, Sat & Sun €18; ⏰ 9.30am-sunset) offers balloon ascents over Rome. A tethered hot-air balloon rises to a height of 550m where it floats for 15 minutes before being hauled down again. There are places for up to 30 people on each ascent.

Boat

Battelli di Roma (Map pp98-9; ☎ 06 678 93 61; www .battellidiroma.it; tickets €10; ⏰ tours 10.30am, noon, 3.30pm & 5pm) runs daily boat tours along the Tiber. The 75-minute round trip departs from Ponte Sant'Angelo and covers the stretch down to the Isola Tiberina and then up to Ponte Risorgimento. Tickets are available at Tourist Information Points (see p94). You can also dine on the river: dinner cruises (€43) leave Ponte Sant'Angelo every evening at 8pm and return at about 10.15pm.

Bus

Trambus (Map pp102-3; ☎ 06 469 52 252; www.trambus open.com; Piazza Cinquecento) operates two tour buses: the 110open and the Archeobus. The **110open** (tickets €13; ⏰ tours every 15min 8.40am-8.25pm) is an open-top double-decker bus that departs from the bus terminus outside Termini (platform C), and stops at the Quirinal, Colosseum, Bocca della Verità, Piazza Venezia, Piazza Navona, St Peter's, Piazza Cavour, the Ara Pacis, Trevi Fountain and Via Veneto. Tickets, available on board or from the ticket office on platform D of Piazza Cinquecento, are valid for the day and allow you to pop off and on as you please. There's a multilingual hostess on board, as well as an audioguide in six languages. Journey time is two hours.

The **Archeobus** (tickets €8; ☼ tours hourly 9.45am-4.45pm) is another stop-and-go bus, which takes groups of up to 16 down Via Appia Antica, stopping at points of archaeological interest such as Piazza Venezia, Bocca della Verità, Circo Massimo, Terme di Caracalla, Porta di San Sebastiano, the Catacombs of San Callisto and San Sebastiano and the Tomba di Cecilia Metella. The bus departs from Termini bus terminus and tickets are available as for the 110open service earlier.

Green Line Tours (Map pp102-3; ☎ 06 482 74 80; www.greenlinetours.com; Via Farini 5a) offers up to 19 different tours as far afield as Pompeii and Florence. Buses, all equipped with a multilingual audioguide, depart from Piazza Cinquecento although some tours include hotel pick-ups. The standard 90-minute Shuttle Tour costs €22, while prices for longer half-day tours of Classical, Imperial, Christian and Illuminated Rome start at €31.50. There's also another branch at Piazza Cinquecento.

Stop-n-Go City Tours (Map pp102-3; ☎ 06 478 26 379; www.romecitytours.com; Piazza Cinquecento 44/48; 1-/2-/3-day tickets €12/18/24; ☼ tours hourly 9.30am-5.30pm) offers a range of tours, covering the city centre, Via Appia Antica and the catacombs, Ostia Antica, Tivoli, the Castelli Romani (the hills to the south of Rome) and the Etruscan towns of Cerveteri and Tarquinia. There are nine daily city tours departing from Termini each day. Tickets are available on the bus.

Cycling
Enjoy Rome (Map pp102-3; ☎ 06 445 18 43; www.enjoyrome.com; Via Marghera 8; tours under/over 26 years €20/25) organises afternoon and evening bike tours which are a huge hit, but you have to be between 18 and 35 to participate. The three-hour route includes Villa Borghese, the Bocca della Verità and the Colosseum. Tours are seasonal so check that they're running.

Landimension Travel (Map pp108-9; ☎ 06 700 36 22; www.landimensiontravel.it; Via Ostilia 10; per person in groups of 2/3/4-6 €60/50/40; ☼ tours 9.15am & 3pm) offers tours by electric bicycle. The three-hour tours cover one of four itineraries: Trastevere and environs, Ancient Rome, Appia Antica and Classical Rome. All groups are accompanied by experienced guides and equipment is provided.

Walking
Context in Rome (Map p114; ☎ 06 482 09 11; www.contextrome.com; Via Baccina 40) does archaeological walks in small groups with expert guides, often American students specialising in art history and archaeology. Tours are tailor-made and by prior arrangement only. Itineraries (costs are per group) cover St Peter's (€150, two hours), Ancient Rome (€275, four hours) and Vatican Art (€275, four hours).

Dark Heart of Rome (☎ 338 500 64 24; www.thedarkheartofrome.com; Via Serravalle 27) runs tours of Rome's bloody underbelly. You can visit the site of famous murders, miracles and supernatural mysteries. The 1½-hour night walks depart at 9.20pm from Piazza Vidoni, near Corso Vittorio Emanuele II; tours cost €14.

Enjoy Rome (Map pp102-3; ☎ 06 445 18 43; www.enjoyrome.com; Via Marghera 8) has tours designed for budget travellers. Their three-hour walking tours (under/over 26 years €15/21) cover ancient Rome (by day or night), the Vatican, Trastevere and the Ghetto. Tours to the Catacombs and Appian Way (€30/35) and the Vatican cost extra to cover entrance costs. All guides are native English speakers or hold degrees in archaeology or related areas.

Through Eternity Rome (Map pp108-9; ☎ 06 700 93 36, 0347 336 52 98; www.througheternity.com; Via Sinuessa 8) employs native English speakers to make Rome come alive on their walking tours. Prices are set for the tour rather than per person so to pay less rope in as many friends as you can. Examples of tours include a twilight tour of Renaissance and baroque Rome (€25, 2½ hours), the Vatican Museums and St Peter's (€40, five hours, groups of one to five people) and wine-tasting and dinner in Trastevere (€50, 3½ hours).

FESTIVALS & EVENTS
Rome's calendar bursts with events ranging from colourful traditional celebrations with a religious and/or historical flavour, through to festivals of the performing arts, including opera, music and theatre.

Summer is definitely the best time to visit if you want to catch the best of the festivals. The Estate Romana festival, which runs from June to September, sponsors literally hundreds of events, many of which are staged in spectacular outdoor settings. In autumn, the Romaeuropa festival (dance, theatre and opera) attracts big-name performers.

Easter is also a big time in Rome as Holy Week is celebrated with numerous processions and services. Check with the tourist office for further details.

January
New Year (1 Jan) A candlelit procession in the catacombs.

March/April
Festa di San Giuseppe (Feast of St Joseph; 19 Mar) Celebrated in the Trionfale neighbourhood, between the Vatican and Monte Mario. Little stalls are set up to serve *fritelle* (fried pastries) and there's usually a special market set up near the church of San Giuseppe.

Settimana dei Beni Culturale (Mar/Apr) Public museums and galleries open free of charge during culture week.

Procession of the Cross (Easter) A candlelit procession to the Colosseum on Good Friday evening is led by the pope. At noon on Easter Sunday he gives his traditional blessing from the balcony in St Peter's Square.

Mostra delle Azalee (Exhibition of Azaleas; late Mar/Apr) The Spanish Steps are decorated with masses of pink azaleas.

Rome's Birthday (21 Apr) To celebrate its birthday, the City of Rome provides processions, fireworks and free entry to lots of museums.

May
Primo Maggio (1 May) Rome's May Day rock festival attracts huge crowds and international performers to the traditional venue at the Basilica di San Giovanni in Laterano.

June
Feast of San Pietro e Paolo (Feast of Sts Peter & Paul; 29 Jun) This feast, for the patron saints of the city, includes major celebrations at St Peter's.

Birth of John the Baptist (23-24 Jun) Many celebrate the birth of St John the Baptist, particularly around the Basilica di San Giovanni in Laterano, where special market stalls set up and there's lots of lovely *porchetta* (pork) to eat.

Estate Romana (Jun-Sep)The big event in summer, this is a series of outdoor cultural events and activities for the few people who have remained in the capital.

¡Fiesta! (mid-Jun–Sep) Festival of Latin American food, music and dance on the racecourse on Via Appia.

July
Festa de'Noantri (3rd week in Jul) Based around Trastevere, this traditional working-class festival, originally with food, wine and dancing, is becoming ever-less authentic.

August
Festa della Madonna della Neve (5 Aug) To celebrate the legendary snowfall that fell on 5 August 352, rose petals are showered on celebrants in the Basilica di Santa Maria Maggiore.

September
RomaEuropa (Sep-Nov) Top international artists take to the stage in Rome's autumn festival of theatre, opera and dance.

October
Via dei Coronari Mostra-Mercato (Oct) Antique shops on Via dei Coronari, just off Piazza Navona, open their doors and display their wares.

December
Toy Fair (1st week in Dec) Christmas time in Rome sees a toy fair, with lots of handmade *presepi* (Nativity scenes), bagpipe players, bright lights and fun in Piazza Navona.

Feast of San Silvestro (31 Dec) The pope visits the Chiesa del Gesù and sings the Te Deum, while the mayor presents a chalice to the presiding priest.

Capodanno (31 Dec) Open-air concerts and fireworks mark the New Year. An almost forgotten tradition involves throwing unwanted household appliances off your balcony.

SLEEPING

Following the spruce-up for the year 2000 Jubilee, Rome now has good accommodation options: hotels, *pensioni*, hostels, religious institutions and B&Bs. There are even a few camp sites in the city suburbs. Quality varies but prices are universally high. Reckon on about €20 for a bed in a hostel dorm and anything between €50 and €150 for a double with bathroom in a two-star hotel.

Most of the budget hotels are located in the not-so-beautiful streets around Stazione Termini. Although the area's not as bad as it once was, it's a favourite haunt of pickpockets, and women travelling alone may feel uncomfortable at night. However, accommodation standards are rising and you can find some surprisingly nice places to stay.

For a full immersion in Rome, head for the *centro storico*. Prices are higher, but it's here that you'll really experience the city. Similarly, Trastevere is a picturesque and lively place to stay – just don't expect much peace and quiet. The area around the Vatican is a good compromise if you want somewhere beautiful but less hectic. All these areas are a bus ride or metro journey from Termini.

Although Rome doesn't have a low season as such, the majority of hotels offer discounts in July and August (when many Italians head to the beach) and from November to March (excluding the Christmas and New Year period). Expect to pay top whack in spring and autumn and over the main holiday periods (Christmas, New Year and Easter). You should always book ahead if at all possible. Many hotels will request a faxed confirmation of your reservation together with a credit card number as deposit.

If you don't have a credit card you'll usually be asked to send a money order to cover the first night's stay.

Arrive without a reservation, however, and all's not lost. There's a free **hotel reservation service** (Map pp102-3; ☎ 06 699 10 00; Stazione Termini; ⊙ 7am-10pm) at the main train station (opposite platform 21) and the nearby Enjoy Rome (p94) tourist office can also book a room for you. Whatever you do, though, don't follow the people hanging around at the train station who claim to be tourism officials and offer to find you a room. Chances are they'll lead you to some dump for which you'll end up paying way over the official rates.

For official rates, check the list on www .romaturismo.it. Unless otherwise indicated, prices quoted in the hotel reviews are maximum prices for a room with a bathroom.

Accommodation Options

BED & BREAKFAST

A recent trend, B&B is becoming increasingly popular in Rome and there are now more than 850 officially listed operators. Many of the newer places are effectively *pensioni*, meaning that you get your own keys and can come and go as you like. The Rome Tourist Board (p94) publishes a full list.

The following are agencies specialising in B&B accommodation.

Bed & Breakfast Italia (Map pp98-9; ☎ 06 688 01 513; www.bbitalia.it; Corso Vittorio Emanuele II 282) Rome's longest-established B&B network has accommodation in three categories: 2 Crowns is €37.70/30.50 single/double per person with shared bathroom; 3 Crowns €50.60/43.40 single/double with bathroom; 4 Crowns €66.60/57.80 luxurious single/double with bathroom. You can view and book all apartments online.

Bed & Breakfast Association of Rome (Map p95; ☎ 06 553 02 248; www.b-b.rm.it; Via A Pacinotti 73) Has more than 100 properties on its books. Other than rooms in B&Bs, they also organise short-term rentals of fully furnished flats, usually for a minimum of three nights. Single rooms start at €54, doubles €76. Online viewing and booking is available.

Cross Pollinate (www.cross-pollinate.com) An online agency. Rooms are categorised by type (single, double etc), with a picture for each one and a location map available. To reserve a room, type in your credit card details and you'll have confirmation in 24 hours. Per person prices start at €50 for a single room and €30 for a double.

HOSTELS

Associazione Italiana Alberghi per la Gioventù (AIG; Map pp102-3; ☎ 06 487 11 52; www.ostellionline.org; Via Cavour 44; ⊙ 8am-5pm Mon-Fri), the Italian youth hostel association, has information about all the youth hostels in Italy and will assist with bookings to stay at universities during summer. You can also join Hostelling International (HI) here.

RELIGIOUS INSTITUTIONS

Not surprisingly Rome is well furnished with religious institutions, many of which offer cheap(ish) rooms for the night. Bear in mind, though, that all religious institutions have strict curfews and the accommodation, while clean, is of the basic, no-frills variety. It's always wise to book well in advance. For a list of institutions, check out www.santasu sanna.org/comingToRome/convents.html.

RENTAL ACCOMMODATION

Apartments near the centre of Rome are not cheap (bank on around €900 per month for a studio apartment or a small one-bedroom place, with bills on top of that). However, for a longer stay they can often work out cheaper than an extended hotel sojourn. For a mini-apartment in a hotel block, go online at www.romaturismo.it and check out the section marked residences.

Several of the English-language bookshops in Rome have noticeboards where people looking for accommodation or offering a room on a short- or long-term basis place their messages. Try the Almost Corner Bookshop (p92) in Trastevere, or Feltrinelli International (p92), near Piazza della Repubblica. Another option is to check the classified ads in *Wanted in Rome* (published fortnightly on Wednesday) or *Porta Portese* (published twice weekly on Tuesday and Friday).

There are many estate agencies specialising in short-term rentals in Rome, which charge a fee for their services. You will also be asked for a deposit of up to one month's rent. Agencies are listed in the telephone directory under *agenzie immobiliari*.

CAMPING

All of Rome's camp sites, including the two listed here, are someway out of the centre.

Flaminio Village (☎ 06 333 26 04; www.villaginflaminio.it; Via Flaminia Nuova 821; person/tent/car €10.30/6.60/4.90, bungalows from €54; P ⊠) In the Parco Regionale di Veio to the north of the city, this site has just about everything you might need, including its own bar and restaurant. Take Metro A (direction Battistini) to Flaminio, change to the Roma-Nord train line and get off at Due Ponti station, about 150m from the camp site. After midnight night bus No 24 stops just outside the entrance.

Seven Hills (☎ 06 303 10 826; www.sevenhills.it; Via Cassia 1216; per person/tent/car €9.50/6/4.50; P ⊠) Kids will love the minizoo (with peacocks, rabbits and deer) at this 5-hectare camp site in Rome's northern suburbs. Older campers might prefer the disco/pub. Catch Metro A to Valle Aurelia, then take FM3 for La Giustiniana. From there it's about a 1km walk.

Ancient Rome
MIDRANGE
Hotel Celio (Map pp108-9; ☎ 06 704 95 333; www.hotelcelio.com; Via dei Santissimi Quattro 35c; s €120-250, d €170-310, ste €290-600; ⊠) A charming hotel located near the Colosseum, the Hotel Celio manages to get away with a décor that combines frescoes, mosaic floors and trompe l'oeil. The midsized rooms, complete with mod cons and flat-screen TVs, are themed on the Renaissance artists after whom they're named. On the roof garden, the minigym is the perfect place to sweat over photos of Sophia Loren.

Hotel Nerva (Map p114; ☎ 06 678 18 35; www.hotelnerva.com; Via Tor de'Conti; s €80-160, d €100-220; ⊠) You can sleep undisturbed here even as the crowds flock to the Imperial Forums not two yards away. The rooms are all soundproofed and even if they're not the biggest in Rome, they're discreetly decorated and comfortable. The management are also very friendly and go out of their way to help. Two rooms have facilities for disabled travellers.

TOP END
Hotel Forum (Map p114; ☎ 06 679 24 46; www.hotelforum.com; Via Tor de'Conti 25; s €145-220, d €220-330; P ⊠) The reception of this businesslike hotel resembles a Victorian gentleman's club: heavy wood panelling, antiques and a formal staff kitted out in tails and ties. Rooms are predictably well furnished but the hotel's best asset is its delightful roof-garden restaurant with views over the nearby forums.

Centro Storico
BUDGET
Pensione Panda (Map pp98-9; ☎ 06 678 01 79; www.hotelpanda.it; Via della Croce 35; s/d €48/68, with bathroom €65/98) There are many hotels in the centre of Rome. Not many, however, are so cheap and so central. Some 50m from the Spanish steps, the Panda is one of the capital's best budget *pensioni*; it has pretty rooms with arched ceilings and hospitable English-speaking staff.

MIDRANGE
Hotel Teatro di Pompeo (Map p104; ☎ 06 687 28 12; www.hotelteatrodipompeo.it; Largo del Pallaro 8; d €190; ⊠) Built on top of a theatre that Pompey constructed in 55 BC (now the breakfast room), this smart family-run hotel is in the suggestive area near Campo de' Fiori. Particularly atmospheric are the rooms on the 3rd floor, with their sloping wood-beamed ceilings and tasteful décor. Last-minute special deals are available.

Hotel Portoghesi (Map p104; ☎ 06 686 42 31; www.hotelportoghesiroma.com; Via dei Portoghesi 1; s €120-145, d €150-185; ⊠) Beautifully positioned in a picturesque street of craft shops and jewellers, the Portoghesi extends a warm welcome. Not only are the staff friendly and helpful but the rooms are comfortable and the roof terrace is a great place to escape the bustle of the *centro storico* below. The hotel operates a no-smoking policy throughout.

Albergo Abruzzi (Map p104; ☎ 06 679 20 21; www.hotelabruzzi.it; Piazza della Rotonda 69; s €130-155, d €175-195) Directly opposite the Pantheon, nowhere in Rome can boast a more impressive (or noisier!) location. Recently renovated, the highly popular Abruzzo is smarter than it once was and rooms now have parquet floors and satellite TV. The management, however, hasn't changed and is as friendly as ever.

Hotel Navona (Map p104; ☎ 06 686 42 03; www.hotelnavona.com; Via dei Sediari 8; s €90-110, d €125-140) Officially, this is a one-star hotel but don't be fooled – it's a cut above your average *pensione*. Rooms vary in quality; some are big and bright, others are very small, and the décor is largely ad hoc, with an antique desk here and a plastic lamp there. But what you're really paying for here is the location, a skip and a jump from Piazza Navona.

Albergo del Sole (Map p104; ☎ 06 687 94 46; www.solealbiscione.it; Via del Biscione 76; s/d €65/95, with bathroom €85/120; P) The oldest hotel in Rome, this place dates to 1462. It's been done up since then, although the complex warren of corridors and low wood-beamed ceilings give credence to its Medieval architecture. There's nothing special about the basic rooms although the 2nd-floor roof terrace is a definite plus. Parking is €18 to €21; credit cards are not accepted.

Hotel Campo de' Fiori (Map p104; ☎ 06 688 06 865; www.hotelcampodefiori.com; Via del Biscione 6; s/d €100/140, 2-/4-person apt €150/230) Currently undergoing a thorough makeover, Hotel Campo de' Fiori should be sparkling new when you arrive. Rooms occupy a six-storey palazzo, to which a lift is being added, while apartments are dotted around the area just off Campo de' Fiori.

Hotel Forte (Map pp98-9; ☎ 06 320 76 25; www .hotelforte.com; Via Margutta 61; s €113-160, d €140-230; ☒) A stone's throw from Piazza di Spagna, the popular Hotel Forte is a bright place decorated in faux-classic style. The public spaces are choc-a-bloc with fake antiques – Via Margutta is famous for its many antique shops – and the corridors are lined with columns. The rooms don't escape the classical theme either.

Hotel Pomezia (Map p104; ☒ /fax 06 686 13 71; hotelpomezia@libero.it; Via dei Chiavari 13; s €105-55, d €125-75; ☒) They're a friendly bunch here, and although there's nothing special about the accommodation it's a nice place to stay. Rooms are simple, if a little anonymous, with inoffensive yellow walls and light-wood bedside tables. One room is equipped for disabled travellers. Breakfast is included.

Hotel Ponte Sisto (Map pp98-9; ☎ 06 686 31 368; www.hotelpontesisto.it; Via dei Pettinari 64; s €95-180, d €150-310; ℗ ☒ ▢) Housed in an 18th-century palazzo, this city-centre delight offers stylish rooms and suggestive views. Pick of the panoramas is the view from the only room on the 6th floor; look through the oval window to the Janiculum Hill and St Peter's.

Suore di Santa Brigida (Map p104; ☎ 06 688 92 596; brigida@mclink.it; entrance at Via Monserrato 54; s/d €100/180) The sisters of Santa Brigida offer simple, no-frills rooms in the house where the Swedish St Brigid died in 1373. This place is beautifully located in Piazza Farnese.

TOP END

Hotel Santa Chiara (Map p104; ☎ 06 687 29 79; www .albergosantachiara.com; Via di Santa Chiara 21; s/d €143/215) For a three-star hotel, the Santa Chiara

makes quite a first impression: dramatic Venetian chandeliers, marble columns and classical statues. The rooms, however, are decorated with more modest modern trappings. Some have small balconies overlooking the narrow side streets, although those around the internal courtyard are quieter.

Grand Hotel de la Minerve (Map pp98-9; ☎ 06 69 52 01; www.grandhotelminerve.it; Piazza della Minerva 69; s/d €400/455; ☒) Bernini's *Elefantino* trumpets the presence of the grand old Minerve, one of Rome's top hotels. A stately old pile, it will appeal to those with traditional tastes in luxury. Rooms are all individually decorated; some have original 17th-century wood-beamed ceilings, others have vaulted ceilings and four-poster beds.

East of Via del Corso

BUDGET

Welrome Hotel (Map pp102-3; ☎ 06 478 24 343; www .welrome.it; Via Calatafimi 15-19; s €40-100, d €50-110) The maternal owner of the Welrome has a personal mission to look after her guests: not only does she take huge pride in her small, spotless hotel but she enthusiastically points out the cheapest places to eat, tells you where not to waste your time and what's good to do. Families should go for the huge room named after Piazza di Spagna.

Beehive (Map pp102-3; ☎ 06 447 04 553; www.the -beehive.com; Via Marghera 8; dm €20, d with shared bathroom €70) A far cry from your usual hostel, this place is bright, airy and decorated with considerable flair. The corridors are lined with pop art and original paintings (left by artist guests), while the blue and orange plastic furniture is funky and fun. Rooms, needless to say, are spotless and the kitchen pristine. You must book ahead as walk-ins are not accepted and party animals positively discouraged. Check-in is after 3pm.

Alessandro Downtown Hostel (Map pp102-3; ☎ 06 443 40 147; www.hostelalessandro.com; Via Carlo Cattaneo 23; dm €17) Travellers speak well of this slick hostel near Stazione Termini. With a 24-hour reception, laundry facilities and large bar area, it's a professional operation staffed by helpful English speakers. Beds are in eight- to 12-people dormitories.

Fawlty Towers (Map pp102-3; ☎ 06 445 03 74; www .fawltytowers.org; Via Magenta 39; dm €22, s/d €39/55, with bathroom €66/82) On the 5th floor – cross your fingers that the lift is working – this popular hostel-cum-*pensione* offers dorms and basic but clean rooms. A particularly attractive feature is the sunny rooftop terrace. To bag a dorm bed in summer you have to call (either in person or by phone) at 9pm the night before.

Hotel Castelfidardo (Map pp102-3; ☎ 06 446 46 38; www.hotelcastelfidardo.com; Via Castelfidardo 31; s/d €50/70, with bathroom €60/80) One of Rome's most elegant one-star hotels, Castelfidardo is just off Piazza dell'Indipendenza. Gleaming halls lead to good-sized spacious rooms furnished with simple taste and the English-speaking staff go out of their way to help.

Hotel Lazzari (Map pp102-3; www.hotellazzari.com) In the same building and under the same management as Hotel Castelfidardo, Hotel Lazzari offers more of the same.

Hotel Des Artistes (Map pp102-3; ☎ 06 445 43 65; www.hoteldesartistes.com; Via Villafranca 20; dm €15-24, d €59-186) Run by an enthusiastic young couple, Des Artistes is a place for all budgets with everything from dormitory beds to a suite with a small living room. Rooms are decked out in wood and gold with faux-antique furniture and three-star trappings such as TV and computer connections. A rooftop terrace is open until 1am.

Hotel Tizi (Map pp96-7; ☎ 06 482 01 28; fax 06 474 32 66; Via Collina 48; s/d with shared bathroom €45/60, d with bathroom €70) Staying at this humble *pensione* is more like sleeping in a large family home than in a hotel. There's nothing remotely flash about the rooms although they are light, spacious and scrupulously clean. Check for discounts in low season and for stays of more than five days. This hotel only accepts cash.

Hotel Sweet Home (Map pp102-3; ☎ 06 488 09 54; www.hotelsweethome.it in Italian; Via Principe Amedeo 47; s €41-51, with bathroom €50-93, d €61-72, with bathroom €82-103) The old pictures, dark corridors and air of fading gentility give Hotel Sweet Home a charm that many of the slicker big hotels lack. Rooms vary in size and comfort although those facing away from the street are larger and quieter.

Hotel Katty (Map pp102-3; ☎ /fax 06 444 12 16; Via Palestro 35; s/d €47/62, with bathroom €69/83) Some of the rooms at this brisk, efficient *pensione* are big, others are small, some have bathrooms, some don't. But all are clean, unfussy and full of character. The owner insists that you'll rarely pay the maximum prices quoted here.

Papa Germano (Map pp102-3; ☎ 06 48 69 19; www .hotelpapagermano.it; Via Calatafimi 14a; dm €20-26, s/d with shared bathroom €45/75, d €68-100; ⚇) A decent budget option, Papa Germano enjoys a bubbly atmosphere thanks to its English- and French-speaking staff. The dorm décor leaves a bit to be desired, unless you like green and pink-rose wallpaper, but the beds are comfortable enough and the bathrooms clean.

YWCA (Map pp102-3; ☎ 06 488 04 60; foyer.roma@ ywca-ucdg.it; Via Cesare Balbo 4; s/d €37/62, with bathroom €47/74, tr & q per person €26) Hidden behind the morning market stalls, the YWCA is open to men, women and couples and offers some of the cheapest rooms in the centre, including two singles equipped for disabled travellers. It's popular so book well ahead although night owls should note that there's a midnight curfew. No credit cards.

Albergo Giusti (Map pp102-3; ☎ 06 704 53 462; s.annagiusti@tiscali.it; Via Giusti 5; s/d €45/78) Run by the sisters of Sant'Anna, this B&B option is in a convent in the side streets near the Basilica di Santa Maria Maggiore. The hospitable but rather stern nuns welcome families, groups and lone travellers. Curfew is 10.30pm.

Hotel Cervia (Map pp102-3; ☎ 06 49 10 57; www .hotelcerviaroma.com; Via Palestro 55; dm €20, s/d €35/60, with bathroom €59/80) Managed by two chatty ladies, the Cervia has basic furnished rooms with high-vaulted ceilings, and four- and five-bed dorms on the 3rd floor. Free cots are provided for kids under two; breakfast is €3.

Hotel Restivo (Map pp102-3; ☎ 06 446 21 70; info@ hotelrestivo.com) Run by the same people as the Hotel Cervia, Hotel Restivo is on the 2nd floor of the same building.

Freedom Traveller Hostel (Map pp102-3; ☎ 06 478 23 862; www.freedom-traveller.it; Via Gaeta 25; dm €17-22, d €50-60; ⚇) As much a meeting point for travellers as a traditional hostel, this busy place is laid-back, lively and brash. It serves English breakfasts, and organises movie nights, pizza parties, pub crawls and city tours. There's a terrace as well as free Internet in the reception area.

Hostel Beautiful (Map pp102-3; ☎ 06 446 58 90; www.hostelbeautiful.com; Via Napoleone III 35; dm €20; ⚇) One of a plethora of hostels in the Termini area, the Beautiful is not exactly that but it's clean, friendly and popular. There's a maximum of five beds per dormitory, a small kitchen and common room (which has Internet), no lock-out and no curfew.

Pop Inn Hostel (Map pp102-3; ☎ 06 495 98 87; www .popinnhostel.com; Via Marsala 80; dm €16-25, s/d from €46/52, s with shared bathroom €41-90, d with shared bathroom €42-92) A perennial favourite with backpackers, the Pop Inn is laid-back, lively and a little tatty round the edges. Rock music fills the common rooms and the multilingual staff are friendly.

MIDRANGE

Hotel Venezia (Map pp102-3; ☎ 06 445 71 01; www .hotelvenezia.com; Via Varese 18; s/d €118/160) The smartest hotel in the scruffy Termini area, the Venezia oozes style. But despite its classy demeanour – picture antique furniture and attractive fabrics – it's a wonderfully unstuffy place and the multilingual staff are charming and efficient. Rooms are tastefully decorated and those on the top floor each have their own balcony. Prices drop by about 10% in the low season.

Residenza Cellini (Map pp102-3; ☎ 06 478 25 204; www.residenzacellini.it; Via Modena 5; d €145-240, ste €165-260) With only six vast rooms, the Cellini is ideal for honeymooners or those after a quiet getaway. Situated in a nondescript building near Piazza della Repubblica, the six beautifully appointed rooms each have parquet floors, antique furniture and fine fabrics. Fresh flowers adorn the bright hall.

58 Le Real B&B (Map pp102-3; ☎ 06 482 35 66; www.58viacavour.it; Via Cavour 58; r €70-110, ste €100-120; 🖾) The owners of this small B&B have gone to great lengths to mix modern convenience with refined décor. No two rooms are the same: eg room 22 has a small kitchen, while room 21 boasts gold walls, a walnut bedstead and an elaborate chandelier. The apartment is covered with original works of art and the panoramic views from the sun terrace are quite something.

Hotel Locarno (Map pp96-7; ☎ 06 361 08 41; www .hotellocarno.com; Via della Penna 22; s/d €120/190) This lovely old Art Deco palace, near Piazza del Popolo, is a friendly, and cheaper, alternative to some of the more impersonal topend hotels. A throwback to more elegant times, rooms are furnished with parquet, heavy curtains and the odd gilt-framed mirror. It's consistently popular with tourists and business travellers.

Hotel Oceania (Map pp102-3; ☎ 06 482 46 96; www.hoteloceania.it; Via Firenze 38; s €80-120, d €100-155) You'll need to book early to bag a room at this superfriendly small hotel. The red carpet is always out in the Oceania's two top-floor apartments and the rooms are all large and

inviting. The thoughtful extras, like English newspapers and modem plugs for those with laptop computers, earn extra points.

Hotel Modigliani (Map pp102-3; ☎ 06 428 15 226; www.hotelmodigliani.com; Via della Purificazione 42; s €147-185, d €158-198) A quick glance in the guest book at the Modigliani reveals recurring phrases such as 'loved this place' and 'charming staff'. Run by an artist and his musician partner, it is indeed a friendly and helpful hotel. The rooms are pleasant (one has a view of St Peter's) and there's a quiet internal courtyard ideal for evening drinks.

Hotel Columbia (Map pp102-3; ☎ 06 488 35 09; www .hotelcolumbia.com; Via del Viminale 15; s/d €118/160; 🖾) The sister hotel of the Hotel Venezia (left) makes a good impression with its brick-floored reception and pleasantly decorated rooms even if, beneath the smart veneer, there are signs of wear and tear. The roof terrace is a favourite place for evening drinks.

Hotel Mozart (Map pp98-9; ☎ 06 360 01 915; www .hotelmozart.com; Via dei Greci 23/B; s €119-170, d €165-235) Despite its modest entrance the Hotel Mozart is surprisingly big. Large and classically attired public spaces lead through to light and spacious rooms. Topping everything is a beautiful roof.

Hotel Gabriella (Map pp102-3; ☎ 06 445 01 20; www .gabriellahotel.com; 1st fl, Via Palestro 88; s €80-120, d €150; 🖾) A very welcoming family-run place, this two-star hotel offers considerable comfort. The plush blue fabrics and mosaic bathroom tiling create a stylish ambience for which you could easily pay more.

Hotel d'Este (Map pp102-3; ☎ 06 446 56 07; www .hotel-deste.com; Via Carlo Alberto 4b; s €50-120, d €60-140;

ROME & LAZIO

P) Very close to the Piazza Santa Maria Maggiore, Hotel d'Este combines comfort with character. However, it's about to be renovated so whether the chandeliers, wood panelling and brass bedsteads survive remains to be seen. The 1st-floor roof garden will surely remain.

Hotel Dolomiti (Map pp102-3; ☎ 06 49 10 58; www .hotel-dolomiti.it; Via San Martino della Battaglia 11; s €65-90, d €85-135;) One of two hotels in the same building run by the same friendly family, Hotel Dolomiti has airy rooms decorated with simple efficiency. There's a small bar and English, French and Spanish are spoken.

TOP END

Aleph (Map pp102-3; ☎ 06 42 29 01; www.boscolohotels .com; Via di San Basilio 15; r €310-561, ste €750) To step into the red light of this über-chic hotel is to enter a vision of hell. Inspired by Dante's *Divine Comedy*, the sexy décor features acres of black marble, two life-size models of Samurai warriors and lots of red leather. Rooms provide the heaven part of the Dante-esque theme with modern furniture set against large black-and-white photos of Rome.

Radisson SAS (Map pp102-3; ☎ 06 44 48 41; www .radissonsas.com; Via Fillipo Turati 171; r €200-285;) Formerly the Hotel Es, the first of Rome's new wave of designer hotels has changed hands but kept its look. That means from the outside it has all the allure of a multi-storey car park, on the inside there are swathes of bright space and a spectacular polychromatic inner atrium.

Hotel de Russie (Map pp96-7; ☎ 06 32 88 81; www .roccofortehotels.com; Via del Babuino 9; s from €410, d from €600; P) This is where the Hollywood A-list bunk up when in town: Cruise, Spielberg, de Caprio and Diaz have all stayed here. It's famous for its minimalist opulence and spectacular terraced gardens.

Hotel Scalinata di Spagna (Map pp102-3; ☎ 06 679 30 06; www.hotelscalinata.com; Piazza della Trinità dei Monti 17; s €150-300, d €160-320;) Enjoying one of Rome's premier locations – at the top of the Spanish Steps – and with prices to match, Scalinata di Spagna is a surprisingly informal place. It's something of a warren with low corridors leading off to smallish old-fashioned rooms, some of which offer views over Rome's rooftops. Room No 18 has a private terrace and connects with an adjoining room to make a family suite.

Trastevere

La Foresteria Orsa Maggiore (Map pp98-9; ☎ 06 684 01 724; www.casainternazionaledelledonne.org in Italian; Via San Francesco di Sales 1a; per person €26-62) This is a women-only guesthouse in a beautifully restored 16th-century convent. It is run by the *Casa Internazionale delle Donne* (International Women's House). Most of the 11 functional rooms on the 2nd floor face an internal garden and there's a communal room with TV, newspapers and a library.

Villa della Fonte (Map pp106-7; ☎ 06 580 37 97; www .villafonte.com; Via della Fonte d'Olio 8; s/d €110/160;) In a quiet little corner of Trastevere, Villa della Fonte is a delightful B&B-style pad. It has five stylish but small rooms decorated with a monastic simplicity that perfectly suits the 17th-century building. The tight corridors are lined with black-and-white photos of cheeky street urchins while outside the sunny garden terrace is the perfect place for forty winks.

Hotel Santa Maria (Map pp106-7; ☎ 06 589 46 26; www.hotelsantamaria.info; Vicolo del Piede 2; s €135-165, d €155-210; P) Go through the green gate and you enter a tranquil haven. Housed in a spacious 17th-century cloister, the Santa Maria has 19 hacienda-style rooms around a delightful courtyard garden. Cool and classy, the rooms are simple and attractive, combining wrought-iron bedsteads, earth-coloured floor tiling and cream walls. The attentive management is young, polite and English speaking.

Trastevere House (Map pp106-7; ☎ /fax 06 588 37 74; www.trasteverehouse.it; Vicolo del Buco 7; s €65-95, d €95-140) Tucked away in a lovely little piazza, this quaint little hotel is housed in a historic palazzo. Although the wood beams and heavy wooden shutters are not original they are in theme and add a touch of character to the small rooms.

Domus Tiberina (Map pp106-7; ☎ /fax 06 580 30 33; www.domustiberina.com; Via in Piscinula 37; s €65-95, d €95-140) In the quiet end of Trastevere (always a relative concept here), this snug little hotel has rooms decorated with majolica tiles, floral designs and wooden furniture. It won't be to everyone's taste but the place has character and the staff are cordial.

Hotel Trastevere (Map pp106-7; ☎ 06 581 47 13; info@hotel trastevere.com; Via L Manara 24a-25; s/d €80/103) Overlooking the market square of Piazza San Cosimato, this place offers good value for money. Rooms are modern and comfy and even if they lack character, they are at least a bargain.

Southern Rome

Hotel Villa S Pio (Map pp106-7; ☎ 06 574 52 31; www.aventinohotels.com; Via S Melania 19; s/d €130/220; P ⊠) One of five turn-of-the-century villas that make up the Aventino group of hotels, the Villa S Pio is a bright and spacious hotel in a quiet residential area. Rooms are huge with parquet and classical décor, there's black marble in the bathrooms and the leafy garden contains at least one statue of the Madonna. There are also facilities for disabled people.

Northern Rome

Ostello Foro Italico (Map p95; ☎ 06 323 62 67; www.ostellionline.org; Viale delle Olimpiadi 61; dm €17) Near the Stadio Olimpico in the north of the city, Rome's one official youth hostel is well equipped if nothing flash: there's a bar, self-service restaurant and a garden, but no kitchen. Bookings must be made one month in advance, otherwise you have to turn up at 10am. However, you can't enter the dorm until 2pm and there's a midnight curfew. Take Metro A to Ottaviano and then bus No 32 to the Foro Italico.

Vatican City & Borgo
BUDGET
Hotel San Pietrino (Map p95; ☎ 06 370 01 32; www.sanpietrino.it; Via Giovanni Bettolo 43; s €38-48, d €68-98; ⊠ 🖳) When this hotel establishes itself on the scene its prices will shoot up. As it stands it's exceptional value for money. The 12 rooms are beautifully decorated with cream walls and terracotta floors, the dark-wood furniture fits in well, and the extras – TV and DVD player, ADSL Internet connection – are unusual for a place in this category. Highly recommended.

Colors Hotel (Map pp98-9; ☎ 06 687 40 30; www.colorshotel.com; Via Boezio 31; dm/s €23/60, d €80-100; 🖳) An excellent hostel-cum-*pensione*, Colors is run by the hospitable folk at Enjoy Rome (p94). It's a relaxed place with bright sunny rooms and a fully equipped kitchen. There's no curfew and no lock-out period. At the time of writing, seven new rooms were being constructed on the 3rd floor. They will be slightly more expensive, in the €90 to €100 bracket, but will all have private bathrooms and TVs.

Hotel Lady (Map p95; ☎ 06 324 21 12; fax 06 324 34 46; 4th fl, Via Germanico 198; s/d with shared bathroom €60/85, d €130-180) A homely old-school *pensione*, the Hotel Lady is a warm and inviting place. All the rooms are slightly different and even if they're on the small side they're comfortable and spotlessly clean. Ask for room No 4 or 6, both of which still have their original beamed ceilings. The eccentric owner and his wife don't speak English, but will merrily chat to you in Italian.

Hotel Joli (Map pp98-9; ☎ 06 324 18 54; www.hoteljoliroma.com; 6th fl, Via Cola di Rienzo 243; s €45-72, d €70-108) Families with children will feel at home at this laid-back place where the owners' kids cheerfully run around. Situated on the 6th floor, rooms come with ceiling fans and some boast views of St Peter's dome. Those on the inside are, however, quieter. Bathrooms are small and the lack of a shower curtain can lead to flooding. Book well in advance.

Pensione Paradise (Map p95; ☎ 06 360 04 331; www.pensioneparadise.com; Viale Giulio Cesare 47; s/d €55/90) The owner extends a warm welcome to all his guests at this simple, no-frills *pensione*. Near the Lepanto metro stop, it has bright rooms with terracotta-tiled floors and basic furniture. For the price it's a good bet.

Suore Sacra Famiglia (Map p95; ☎ 06 397 23 844; fax 06 397 23 792; Viale Vaticano 92; s/d €30/52) Within a stone's throw of the entrance to the Vatican Museums, this convent is among the cheapest places to stay in this elegant neck of Rome. The sisters are welcoming and you're free to come and go as you please as long as you're back by midnight.

MIDRANGE
Hotel Bramante (Map pp98-9; ☎ 06 688 06 426; www.hotelbramante.com; Via delle Palline 24; s €100-160, d €150-220; ⊠) Tucked away in a sidestreet behind St Peter's, this is a charming place to stay. The original 16th-century building was designed by the Swiss architect Domenico Fontana, who lived in it until he was expelled from Rome by Pope Sixtus V. The low wood-beamed ceilings top rooms decorated with antique furniture and discreet modern trappings.

Hotel Amalia (Map pp98-9; ☎ 06 397 23 356; www.hotelamalia.com; Via Germanico 66; s €59-130, d €89-210; ⊠) Spread over five floors, the Amalia offers bright and spacious rooms with all the mod cons, including air-con and bathrooms bedecked in fake marble. It's a particularly good bet in low season when prices drop considerably.

Hotel Florida (Map pp98-9; ☎ 06 324 18 72; www .hotelfloridaroma.it; 2nd fl, Via Cola di Rienzo 243; s/d with shared bathroom €30/55, s €50-80, d €60-120; ❄) In this small, quiet lodging on the 2nd floor the red carpet leads to decent-sized rooms which come with air-con included in the price (except for those rooms which share a bathroom).

TOP END

Hotel Columbus (Map pp98-9; ☎ 06 686 54 35; www .hotelcolumbus.net; Via della Conciliazione 33; s €100-200, d €160-320; P ❄) Any closer to St Peter's and you'd be bunking down with the pope. This 15th-century Renaissance palazzo is quiet and surprisingly homely given its history and proportions. Public rooms have frescoes by Pinturicchio and guestrooms are comfortable, if unoriginal in look.

EATING

Rome has a wide selection of trattorie, restaurants and pizzerias. Generally, the places around Stazione Termini are to be avoided if you want to pay reasonable prices for good-quality Italian food, although there are exceptions and it is the best area for ethnic food. Rome is not big on international cuisine but you can find restaurants, albeit very few, specialising in Indian, Chinese, African, Japanese and Mexican cooking.

For an altogether more rewarding experience head either to the centre or the university enclave of San Lorenzo. An up-and-coming area to the east of Termini, it boasts a number of highly regarded restaurants and an inviting vivacious buzz.

The *centro storico* is teeming with places to satisfy all tastes and most pockets. It's difficult to find genuine bargain prices around Piazza Navona or Campo de' Fiori but you may decide that the stunning backdrop is worth a few extra euros. Trastevere is always a favourite area, both with locals and visitors, although it's becoming increasingly difficult to find genuine old-school trattorie as the lure of tourist lucre leads to an emphasis on numbers served rather than quality.

The neighbourhoods around Monti provide local and ethnic eats, while for hardcore Roman cuisine the two best areas are the Ghetto, where Roman Jewish cuisine

abounds, and Testaccio, the spiritual home of offal and the more grisly side of *cucina romana* (Roman cooking).

Many restaurants close down for several weeks during the traditional summer holiday month of August, although council laws state that they must consult with local colleagues to ensure that a similar business is open no more than 300m away.

Ancient Rome

Da Ricci (Map pp102-3; ☎ 06 488 11 07; Via Genova 32; pizzas €8; ☺ 9pm-midnight Tue-Sun) Also known as Est! Est!! Est!!!, this place started up as a wine shop in 1905 and 100 years later is the capital's oldest pizzeria. The pizzas are Neapolitan style and some claim the slightly thicker crusts make them the best in town. It's a boisterous place full of cheerful students and large groups of noisy diners.

La Cicala e La Formica (Map pp102-3; ☎ 06 481 74 90; Via Leonina 17; 1st/2nd courses €8/10 ☺ Mon-Sat) A laid-back little restaurant with outdoor seating in the summer and a warm barrel-vaulted interior, this is a lovely place to eat. There are no great innovations on the menu, rather a homely pride in simple food that's well prepared. Come at lunch and the €10 set menu is a bargain. Expect classics such as bruschetta, pasta and aubergines and *frittata* (an omelette cooked with various fillings).

Il Posto Accanto (Map pp102-3; ☎ 06 474 30 02; Via del Boschetto 36a; 1st/2nd courses €9/16; ☺ closed lunch Sat & Sun) One of a number of restaurants along pretty Via del Boschetto, this is a fine place to dine. It's small – there're only 25 places – and instantly memorable: turquoise walls adorned with copious quantities of fruit and veg are not easy to forget. The food is excellent and house specialities include artichokes, homemade ravioli and fish. It's not entirely necessary to book but it's probably a good idea.

Mexico al 104 (Map pp102-3; ☎ 06 474 27 72; Via Urbana 104; set menus €16 & €19.50) Hidden in heavy ivy foliage is the entrance to this small Mexican restaurant. To aficionados of the cuisine it offers little new, but in the centre of Rome it's something of a novelty. The set menus offer a combination of tacos, burritos, tamales and enchiladas and the small setting is suggestive – not perhaps of Acapulco, but suggestive nonetheless.

Il Guru (Map pp102-3; ☎ 06 489 04 656; Via Cimarra 4-6; set menus €15, €18 & €19) If you're dying for an Indian this is as good a place as any. The décor is the usual mix of elephants and embroidered drapes and the menu offers tandooris (cooked in a proper tandoori oven), curries and vegetable mixes. It's a friendly place and the prices are reasonable.

For a slab of meat as big as Sicily, the brash Argentine chain restaurant **Baires** (Map p114; ☎ 06 692 02 164; Via Cavour 315; salads €8, steaks €12) is the right place. Specialising in meat any which way – steaks, sausages, spare ribs – it also has a range of soups and salads. It's often full of rowdy groups so romantic diners should try elsewhere. There's another **branch** (Map p104; ☎ 06 686 12 93; Corso del Rinascimento 1) near the Pantheon.

Centro Storico
BUDGET
Da Tonino al Governo Vecchio (Map p104; ☎ 06 687 70 02; Via del Governo Vecchio 18; 1st/2nd courses €5/7) You'll find no cheaper place for a sit-down meal in the centre of Rome. Despite a recent makeover Tonino's is still wonderfully modest with fading pictures hanging on white walls. There is a menu but more likely the waiter will simply ask what you want. You can't really go wrong – everything's pretty good – but if you want a recommendation, go for the *pasta alla gricia* (pasta with bacon and cheese).

Pizzeria da Baffetto (Map p104; ☎ 06 686 16 17; Via del Governo Vecchio 114; pizzas about €8; ☒ 6.30pm-midnight) For a pizza experience *alla romana* (Roman style), join the queue outside this famous pizzeria and wait to be squeezed into whatever table space is next available. The pizzas themselves are of the thin-crust Roman variety (as opposed to the deeper pan Neapolitan version) and are served bubbling hot from the wood-fired oven. Expect to be hurried on your way once you've finished.

Filetti di Baccalà (Map p104; ☎ 06 686 40 18; Largo dei Librari 88; meals about €15; ☒ 6.30-10.30pm Mon-Sat) For a slab of fried *baccalà* (salted cod), head to Rome's best-loved fish and chipper. Try the fish sticks accompanied by deep-fried veggies or the antipasti and salads. Everything's cheap and tasty.

Insalata Ricca (salads/pastas €6/6.50); Largo dei Chiavari 85 (Map p104; ☎ 06 688 03 656); Piazza Pasquino 72 (Map p104; ☎ 06 683 07 81); Via FP Calboli 50-52 (Map p95; ☎ 06 375 13 941) There's nothing particularly Roman about this fast-food joint, which

specialises in salad and pasta, but it's central, cheap and popular with locals. King-size salads range from a simple basil, tomato and mozzarella *caprese* to a lobster, prawn and scampi *pescatore*.

MIDRANGE
Da Sergio alla Grotta (Map p104; ☎ 06 686 42 93; Via delle Grotte 27; 1st/2nd courses from €6/9; ☒ Mon-Sat) Near the Campo de' Fiori, this atmospheric trattoria attracts office workers, labourers, screaming kids and tourists in equal measure. The menu is classic Roman – think *cacio e pepe* (pecorino cheese and ground black pepper), *carbonara*, *amatriciana* (with pancetta, tomato and chilli) – and the portions are huge. The meat dishes are also excellent with large steaks grilled over hot coals. In the summer there are a few tables outside.

Alfredo e Ada (Map pp98-9; ☎ 06 687 88 42; Via dei Banchi Nuovo 14; full meals €20; ☒ Mon-Fri) Once you've found a seat at this tiny, unmarked trattoria, all you need do is wait. You don't need to bother with a menu as you get what Ada puts in front of you. This will probably be something simple like pasta with tomato sauce followed by sausage and lentils or beef and red bean stew. Ask for a pudding and out comes Ada's legendary biscuit tin with whatever she's got inside. There's no coffee and no credit cards.

Ditirambo (Map p104; ☎ 06 687 16 26; Piazza della Cancelleria 74; 1st/2nd courses €8/15; ☒ Tue-Sun & dinner

Mon) Just off Campo de' Fiori, Ditirambo enjoys a deserved reputation for tasty, innovative cooking. Here you can warm yourself with a lentil, porcini mushroom and chestnut soup or experiment with veal served with powdered coffee. Like all serious places it changes its menu to accommodate the freshest of ingredients and makes all its own bread and pasta. It is unpretentious and very popular, so make sure you book a table.

Albistrò (Map pp98-9; ☎ 06 686 52 74; Via dei Banchi Vecchi 140a; 1st/2nd courses €9/12; ☾ dinner Thu-Tue) A charming little bistro, Albistrò continues to win plaudits for its unique brand of international cuisine. This ranges from regional Italian to oriental with fish curries sharing menu space with quiches and steaks. Each dish is original, and beautifully presented, and you can ask about its origins and seek advice on the wines in Italian, French or English. Albistrò is excellent value for money. It's essential to book on weekends.

Armando Al Pantheon (Map p104; ☎ 06 688 03 034; Salita dei Crescenzi 31; 1st/2nd courses €8/11; ☾ lunch & dinner Mon-Fri, lunch Sat) A warm, family-run trattoria within a stone's throw of the Pantheon, Armando's is a traditional place that serves excellent Roman cuisine. As an alternative to pasta, the *zuppa di orzo con funghi porcini e tartufo* (barley soup with mushrooms and truffle) is a minor meal in itself while for hardcore meat eaters the *trippa alla romana* (Roman tripe) is a classic.

Sora Margherita (Map pp98-9; ☎ 06 687 42 16; Piazza delle Cinque Scole 30; 1st/2nd courses €7/8; ☾ lunch Tue-Sun) This hole-in-the-wall eatery is not what it started out as – a cheap kitchen for hungry locals – as the word's been out for some time. But if you want hearty pasta and delicious Jewish fare at excellent prices, get down to Sora's in the Ghetto. The service is pure Roman – brusque but not quite unfriendly – and the décor nonexistent (formica tables and wobbly chairs), but still you'll need to queue to get in.

L'Orso 80 (Map p104; ☎ 06 686 49 04; Via dell'Orso 33; 1st/2nd courses €9/15; ☾ Tue-Sat) If you could find them, Tom Cruise, Nicole Kidman and Brad Pitt would all attest to L'Orso's legendary antipasto spread. You can pick'n'mix from mozzarella, risotto balls, prosciutto, roasted vegetables, meatballs, beans, salads and marinated mushrooms. If that doesn't fill you up, the chargrilled meat and pizzas are excellent.

Da Giggetto (Map pp98-9; ☎ 06 686 11 05; Via del Portico d'Ottavia 21-2; 1st/2nd courses €8/12; ☾ Tue-Sun) Right next to the Portico d'Ottavia, Da Giggetto is famous for its Roman-Jewish cooking. Particularly good are the fried starters such as *carciofi alla giudia* (lightly fried artichokes) and *fiore di zucca* (courgette flowers fried and flavoured with anchovies). One of the best-known restaurants in the Ghetto, it's not a snooty place although service can be gruff.

Le Pain Quotidien (Map pp98-9; ☎ 06 688 07 727; Via Tomacelli 18; tartines €8, brunch €18.50; ☾ 9am-midnight Tue-Sun) Specialising in French baguettes, quiches and salads, this faux-rustic place might be as French as the Colosseum but it's still a fun spot to eat. You can either grab a sandwich at the bar or break the freshly baked bread with everyone else at the long wooden tables. It's a trendy spot so expect queues.

TOP END

La Rosetta (Map p104; ☎ 06 686 10 02; Via della Rosetta 8-9; 1st/2nd courses €18/20; ☾ Mon-Fri, dinner Sat) Some say this is the best fish restaurant in town, others that it's one of the best. Whatever the verdict, you'll eat memorably, and expensively, here. Considered one of the top chefs in Italy, Massimo Riccioli serves up classics such as *linguine ai frutti di mare* (flat spaghetti with seafood), as well as personal innovations like *moscardini* (baby octopus) with mint. Booking is essential.

Osteria dell'Ingegno (Map pp98-9; ☎ 06 678 06 62; Piazza della Pietra 45; 1st/2nd courses €10/13; ☾ Mon-Sat) A smart, modern-looking restaurant with wicker chairs and a bright interior, this is a favourite of Italian politicians. The emphasis is on vegetarian food but turkey, tuna and steak feature among the seconds. Menus change seasonally but signature dishes include a delicious salad of fresh buffalo mozzarella, baby chicory and anchovies, and *farfalle* (butterfly-shaped pasta) with leeks and saffron.

Boccondivino (Map p104; ☎ 06 683 08 626; Piazza in Campo Marzio 6; 1st/2nd courses €13/20; ☾ Mon-Sat) The Roman columns that flank the entrance to this swank modern restaurant are original. Inside, it's a different story with faux marble, metal chairs with fake zebra skin and snazzy lighting. The contemporary cuisine features new takes on Italian classics and although the menu often changes you can expect innovative versions of *carpaccio* (raw beef), risotto and steak.

Piperno (Map pp98-9; ☎ 06 688 06 629; Via Monte de' Cenci 9; 1st/2nd courses €10/18; ☼ Tue-Sat & lunch Sun) It's a novel experience to ask a waiter in a white jacket and bow tie to bring you his *palle del Nonno* (Grandpa's balls). But the ricotta and chocolate puffs are one of the signature dishes of this historic restaurant. Specialising in Roman-Jewish cuisine, it's turned deep-frying into an art form. For proof try the mixed platter of deep-fried fillets of *baccalà*, stuffed courgette flowers, vegetables and mozzarella cheese.

East of Via del Corso
BUDGET
Indian Fast Food (Map pp102-3; Via Mamiani 11; ☎ 06 446 07 92; curries €6.50; ☼ 11am-4pm & 5-10.30pm) A genuine Indian takeaway just off Piazza Vittorio Emanuele, this place might not look much but it has great curries and spicy samosas. The fare is displayed for easy picking – just point to what you want – and you can either take it away with you or sit at one of the white plastic-topped tables under the neon lighting.

Ristofer (Map pp102-3; Via Marsala 13; meals €7) You can sit down here and eat a plate of pasta and a main course and still have change from €10. Technically it's the railworkers' canteen but it's open to the public; just go through the massive wooden doors, grab a tray and take your pick. It's not gourmet food but it's cheap and filling.

Moka (Map pp102-3; ☎ 06 474 22 11; Via Giovanni Giolitti 34; pastas from €5; ☼ 24hr) To the right of platform 24 as you look out towards the trains of Termini, Moka is a snack bar that serves food at all hours. Plonk yourself on a metal chair and tuck into a plate of *antipasto di mare* (a seafood starter) or plunge into a plate of spaghetti with tomato sauce. There's also a selection of salads and *panini* (filled bread rolls).

MIDRANGE
Difronte a (Map pp98-9; ☎ 06 678 03 55; Via della Croce 38; 1st/2nd courses €7/9; ☼ noon-midnight Tue-Sun) A newcomer to Rome's fashionable shopping district, Difronte a is colourful, funky and fun. A styled jumble of bare brick, yellow and red walls, wrought iron and protruding lights on wires, it offers huge portions of Italian food at very reasonable prices. There's a good

selection of bruschetta and pasta, including a lip-smacking *orecchiette* (ear-shaped pasta) with prawns, pesto and cream.

Colline Emiliane (Map pp102-3; ☎ 06 481 75 38; Via degli Avignonesi 22; 1st/2nd courses €9/15; ☼ Sat-Thu) This welcoming trattoria just off Piazza Barberini flies the flag for Emilia-Romagna, the Italian province that has gifted the world with Parmesan cheese, balsamic vinegar, bolognese sauce and Parma ham. The food here bears no resemblance to the healthy offerings of the Mediterranean diet. Instead it's all about cream, veal, homemade pasta and scrummy pasta fillings such as mashed pumpkin.

Il Chianti (Map pp102-3; ☎ 06 678 75 50; Via del Lavatore 81-82; 1st/2nd courses €9/15; ☼ Mon-Sat) As a general rule the restaurants around the Trevi Fountain dish up overpriced tourist fare. This pretty ivy-clad wine bar is an exception. Serving a selection of imaginative salads (eg pine nuts, cinnamon, pear and blue cheese), pastas and meat dishes, it's a great place to eat as you watch the world go by. At least it is in summer when tables spill out onto the piazza outside.

Africa (Map pp102-3; ☎ 06 494 10 77; Via Gaeta 26-28; mains €10; ☼ Tue-Sun) In the multicultural area around Stazione Termini, Africa is an Ethiopian and Eritrean restaurant favoured by expats and curious Romans. Use your fingers to dig into falafel and *sambusa* (a cross between a spring roll and a samosa) and scoop up meat and vegetables with soft, spongy *injera* bread.

Tram Tram (Map p95; ☎ 06 447 02 585; Via dei Reti 44; 1st/2nd courses €8/12) Taking its name from the trams that rattle past outside, Tram Tram is popular with a young trendy set, and is recommended by just about everyone. A warm and friendly trattoria, it specialises in seafood and vegetables from southern Italy so expect dishes like *orecchiette con vongole e broccoli* (pasta with clams and broccoli) and swordfish served in various guises. There are also mains without fish for vegetarians.

Il Dito e la Luna (Map pp102-3; ☎ 06 494 07 26; Via dei Sabelli 49-51; 1st/2nd courses €8/10; ☼ dinner Mon-Sat) This bistro-style restaurant serves up an excellent Sicilian-inspired menu. Signature dishes include anchovies marinated in orange juice, a savoury tart made with onions and melted Parmesan and *caponata* (a sort of Sicilian ratatouille). It also has a decent wine list.

Arancia Blu (Map pp102-3; ☎ 06 445 41 05; Via dei Latini 55-65; 1st/2nd courses €8/10; ☺ dinner) In San Lorenzo, Arancia Blu has been flying the flag for high-quality vegetarian food for some years. Taking a nouvelle approach, it offers dishes like *spaghetti alla chitarra con tartufo nero e pecorino* (thick spaghetti with black truffle and spicy cheese) and a range of interesting salads and soups. Service can be snooty although the soft lighting and wood ceilings are attractive.

Shaki (Map pp98-9; ☎ 06 679 16 94; Via Mario de Fiori 29a; salads €9.50) Shaki is something of a hybrid: an oriental minimalist wine bar that serves Mediterranean snacks. Right in the heart of the posh shopping district, it's a hip place for a glass or two of wine and a tasty salad. Ingredients are fresh and the best of the salads are the simplest, think mozzarella, Parma ham and cherry tomatoes.

Gioia Mia (Map pp102-3; ☎ 06 488 27 84; Via degli Avignonesi 34; 1st/2nd courses €6.50/7, pizzas €7; ☺ Mon-Sat) Also known as Pisciapiano – actually a Tuscan wine and not a reference to the neon cherub pissing into a wine glass above the bar – this is a no-frills, old-school pizzeria-cum-trattoria. Tablecloths are red and white and the antipasti dishes are laid out to tempt you. It's best known, however, for its pizzas – which aren't bad, they're not great either – and lively atmosphere.

Pommidoro (Map p95; ☎ 06 445 26 92; Piazza dei Sanniti 44; 1st/2nd courses €8/9; ☺ Mon-Sat) A favourite of Italian film director Pierpaolo Pasolini, this San Lorenzo institution continues to attract celebs – check out the signed photos of Nicole Kidman and Roman pin-up Sabrina Ferilli. What they come for is the informal atmosphere and affordable local cuisine.

Mario (Map pp98-9; ☎ 06 678 38 18; Via della Vite 55; 1st/2nd courses €8/13; ☺ Mon-Sat Sep-Jul) Tuscan cooking relies on earthy ingredients: beans, game and huge slabs of meat. This is what you get at Mario's, a long-standing trattoria that serves a constant stream of locals and tourists. Try the *ribollita* (bread soup) or, if you and your partner can stomach it, a massive steak *fiorentina*. It's a snip at €40 for two.

Edy (Map pp96-7; ☎ 06 360 01 738; Vicolo del Babuino 4; 1st/2nd courses €9/14; ☺ Mon-Sat) Although Edy's is no longer the neighbourhood trattoria that it once was, it still cooks a pretty mean plate of pasta. The house speciality is *spaghetti al cartoccio*, a silver-foil parcel of pasta and

seafood, although you might be tempted by the *ravioli al tartufo* (ravioli with truffle) or, on a cold day, the sausages and lentils.

Naturist Club – L'Isola (Map pp98-9; ☎ 06 679 25 09; 4th fl, Via delle Vite 14; set menus €14; ☺ Mon-Fri) A veggie haven leading a double life: at lunch it's a semi–self service vegetarian eatery serving pies and wholegrain risottos; by night it's a restaurant with fish as the speciality. The food is good and the décor cheerful with red chairs set to candle-lit tables. Diners are asked to book for the evening.

TOP END

'Gusto (Map pp98-9; ☎ 06 322 62 73; Piazza Augusto Imperatore 9; lunch buffet €10, 1st/2nd courses €10/18) A huge warehouse-style eatery with its own foodie shop, 'Gusto was one of the first designer restaurants to appear in Rome. On the ground floor waiters buzz around topping up the salad bar and flinging out Neapolitan-style pizzas, while upstairs the pace is slower and the cooking more refined. Mixing Italian staples with oriental touches, dishes include lamb with coconut milk, and shellfish salad with exotic fruit.

Bistrò (Map pp102-3; ☎ 06 447 02 868; Via Palestro 40; 1st/2nd courses €12/18; ☺ dinner Mon-Sat) An elegant barrel-vaulted restaurant, Bistrò is one of the few upmarket eateries in the scruffy Termini area. Despite its studied bistro-look – check the lovely zinc-topped bar – the menu is very Italian with Roman classics such as *carbonara* appearing alongside *gnocchetti vongole e tartufo* (little gnocchi with clams and truffles).

Trastevere
BUDGET

Dar Poeta (Map pp98-9; ☎ 06 588 05 16; Vicolo del Bologna 46; pizzas €7; ☺ dinner) Tucked away in an atmospheric side street, Dar Poeta is famous for its thick pizzas, great bruschette and salads. But its *pièce de résistance* is without doubt the calzone stuffed with ricotta and Nutella. It's a rumbustuous place so expect to queue, using elbows if and when necessary.

Pizzeria Ivo (Map pp106-7; ☎ 06 581 70 82; Via di San Francesco a Ripa 158; pizzas from €5; ☺ Wed-Mon) One of Trastevere's, if not Rome's, most famous pizzerias, Ivo has been serving Roman pizzas, meaning a thin and crunchy base, for some 40 years. As you'd expect it's a popular place so get there early for a table or jostle for position outside.

Pizzeria San Calisto (Map pp106-7; ☎ 06 581 82 56; Piazza San Calisto 9a; pizzas from €5.20; ☉ Tue-Sun) Another well-known pizzeria, this is an excellent spot to people-watch while you wait. There's a lengthy list of bruschette and *crostini* and more than 30 toppings for pizzas so big they hang off the edge of your plate.

MIDRANGE
Alle Fratte di Trastevere (Map pp106-7; ☎ 06 583 57 75; Via delle Fratte di Trastevere 50; 1st/2nd courses €7/9; ☉ Thu-Tue) A warm welcome, delicious food and a pleasant setting are the three fundamentals of your successful trattoria. Alle Fratte scores top marks in each. English-speaking staff dish out generous portions of classics like *orecchiette a cacio e pepe* (pasta with pecorino cheese and pepper – OK, the real Roman recipe uses spaghetti) and main courses of roasted fish and escalopes. Linger as long as you like over coffee and liqueurs.

Bruno alla Lungaretta (Map pp106-7; ☎ 06 580 98 62; Via della Lungaretta 68-70; 1st/2nd courses €9/12; ☉ Mon-Sat) Terracotta floor tiles and original wood beams provide a lovely setting for the tasty Roman cooking served here. Reliable favourites to consider include homemade gnocchi with a wild boar sauce, steak with balsamic vinegar and, to finish, rich chocolate mousse. To drink you can choose from some 100 labels on the wine list.

Da Augusto (Map pp106-7; ☎ 06 580 37 98; Piazza de'Renzi 15; 1st/2nd courses €6/8; ☉ lunch & dinner Mon-Fri & lunch Sat Sep-Jul) For an old-fashioned Trastevere meal, plonk yourself at one of Augusto's tables and order from the menu of Roman classics. The waiters will bark at you – bark back – and dish out plates of fettuccine, *rigatoni all'amatriciana* and *stracciatella* (clear broth with egg and Parmesan).

Jaipur (Map pp106-7; ☎ 06 580 39 92; Via di San Francesco a Ripa 56; curries €8; ☉ Tue-Sun & dinner Mon) Despite looking like every other Indian restaurant in Rome, Jaipur is actually a cut above the average. There's nothing special about the choice of tandoori dishes, tikka masalas and rogan joshs, they simply taste better than most. Vegetarians can opt for a special *degustazione* menu for two (€38).

Ombre Rosse (Map pp106-7; ☎ 06 588 41 55; Piazza Sant'Egidio 12; pastas & salads €8; ☉ 7am-2.30am Mon-Sat, 5pm-2.30am Sun) Next to the Pasquino cinema, this bar-cum-pub serves crunchy salads and filling *panini*, and a hefty selection of liqueurs. The young, attractive staff work hard

to supply the sunglass-toting Romans and weary tourists who make up the clientele.

TOP END
Alberto Ciarla (Map pp106-7; ☎ 06 581 86 68; Piazza San Cosimato 40; taster menus €50, €74 & €84; ☉ dinner Mon-Sat) A contender for the title of top fish restaurant in Rome, Ciarla's is a mix of stunning seafood and oddly garish interior design. Still, the food should do the talking and by any standards it screams. Recipes tend to be simple – eg fried molluscs and prawns or marinated salmon – but the results are mouth watering.

Ferrara (Map pp106-7; ☎ 06 583 33 920; Via del Moro 1a; 1st/2nd courses €9/18; ☉ Mon-Sat) This *enoteca* (wine bar) is spread over three elegant, whitewashed levels. Predictably, wine takes centre stage and the list is encyclopaedic, satisfying everybody from serious connoisseurs to enthusiastic amateurs. Foodies won't be disappointed though, the food is high quality and imaginative. Booking is recommended.

Paris (Map pp106-7; ☎ 06 581 53 78; Piazza San Calisto 7a; 1st/2nd courses €10/18; ☉ Tue-Sat & lunch Sun) A Roman restaurant of the old school, Paris is still the best place outside the Ghetto to sample true Roman Jewish cuisine. The delicate *fritto misto con baccalà* (deep-fried vegetables with salt cod) is memorable and on Tuesdays and Fridays the *minestra di arzilla ai broccoli* (skate soup with broccoli) is unique.

Southern Rome
Volpetti Più (Map pp106-7; ☎ 06 574 43 06; Via A Volta 8) One of the few places in town where you can sit down and eat well for under €10, Volpetti Più is a sumptuous *tavola calda* (literally 'hot table'). Here you'll find pizza, pasta, soup, meat, vegetables and fried nibbles. The quality is as impressive as the quantity and the booming cooks who dish out the food are always willing to explain what everything is (albeit in Italian).

Pizzeria Remo (Map pp106-7; ☎ 06 574 62 70; Piazza Santa Maria Liberatrice 44; pizzas €6; ☉ dinner Mon-Sat) The most famous pizzeria in Testaccio, Remo is said by many to serve the best Roman pizza in town. An institution in this neck of the woods, it's utterly without frills (you make your order by ticking your choices on a sheet of paper), incredibly noisy and fun if you're up for it.

Trattoria da Bucatino (Map pp106-7; ☎ 06 574 68 86; Via Luca della Robbia 84; 1st/2nd courses €7/9; ☉ Tue-Sun)

A popular Testaccio eating place, da Bucatino is decorated with a mix of photos, paintings, empty Chianti bottles and a stuffed boar's head. Fortunately, the food is more conventional. The antipasto buffet is excellent and there's a good selection of pasta dishes, which are served in huge portions. Main courses are chalked up daily depending on what the chef has got to hand.

Augustarello (Map pp106-7; ☎ 06 574 65 85; Via Giovanni Branca 98; 1st/2nd courses €6/8; ☼ Mon-Sat) No place for a vegetarian, this is an offal place. In fact, it's menu is largely, although not exclusively, made up of the *quinto quarto* (the fifth quarter, or insides of a cow). There are those who delight in *pajata* (veal calf intestines) and *coda alla vaccinara* (oxtail) and those who don't, and if you don't you're probably better off eating elsewhere. If it's your thing, however, you'll love it here.

Checchino dal 1887 (Map pp106-7; ☎ 06 574 38 16; Via di Monte Testaccio 30; full meals about €55; ☼ Tue-Sat) Situated within a cow's tail of Rome's former abattoir, it's no surprise to discover that offal – from calves' heads to pigs' trotters and sweetbreads – dominates the menu. If you can't stomach this Roman soul food there are a number of less demanding alternatives. Wash it all down with a wine from the well-stocked cellar.

Archeologia (Map p95; ☎ 06 788 04 94; Via Appia Antica 139; 1st/2nd courses €12/17; ☼ Wed-Mon) Way out in Via Appia Antica, this is by far the best restaurant in this touristy area. An elegant eatery housed in an ancient country house, it offers such mouthfuls as *fettucine al fileto di cernia con finocchio selvatico* (fettucine pasta with grouper and wild fennel), which, fortunately, is easier to eat than say.

Vatican City & Borgo

Cacio e Pepe (Map p95; ☎ 06 321 72 68; Via Avezzana 11; 1st/2nd courses €6/7; ☼ Mon-Fri & lunch Sat) To call this hole-in-the-wall old-school eatery a trattoria would be to give it airs beyond its size and humble demeanour. But don't be fooled, the home cooking is exceptional. In fact, Romans will put up with freezing winter temperatures to sit outside and dig into staples such as *spaghetti alla carbonara* and meatballs, rather than wait to eat inside.

Osteria dell'Angelo (Map p95; ☎ 06 372 94 70; Via G Bettolo 24; 1st/2nd courses €8/10, set menus €25; ☼ lunch Tue-Fri & dinner Mon-Sat) Just a few minutes' walk from the Vatican, this is a hugely popular

neighbourhood trattoria with solid wooden furniture, photos of Angelo's rugby-playing heroes, a sociable atmosphere and robust versions of Roman favourites like *tonnarelli cacio e pepe* (pasta with spicy cheese and pepper), tripe and braised oxtail. You'll need to book in advance.

Quick Eats

Rome has no shortage of *alimentari* (delicatessens) where you can normally get a *panino* (about €3) made up for you. Alternatively, there are hundreds of *pizza a taglio* outlets for a takeaway slice of pizza (about €3 depending on the size). Bars often serve *tramezzini* (premade refrigerated sandwiches, about €4), which will cost more if you sit down. There are also any number of bakeries that are good for a cheap snack.

Antico Forno (Map pp102-3; ☎ 06 679 28 66; Via delle Muratte 8; ☼ 7am-9pm) A minisupermarket near the Trevi Fountain, this place has a well-stocked deli counter where you can choose a filling for your freshly baked *panini*. There's also a good selection of focaccia and pizza.

Forno di Campo de' Fiori (Map p104; ☎ 06 688 06 662; Campo de' Fiori 22; ☼ 7am-1.30pm & 5.30-8.30pm Mon-Wed, Fri & Sat) One of the capital's most famous and sweet-smelling bakeries, the Forno di Campo de' Fiori now operates two outlets. In one you'll find cakes, tarts and sweet nibbles; in the other, right opposite, stock up on bread of all shapes and sizes and pizza sold by the metre. Aficionados swear by the *pizza bianca* (with olive oil and salt) although the *pizza rossa* (with tomato) is just as good.

Forno la Renella (Map pp106-7; ☎ 06 581 72 65; Via del Moro 15-16; ☼ 9am-9pm) The wood-fired ovens at this historic Trastevere bakery have been firing for decades, producing a delicious daily batch of pizza, bread and biscuits. To help you choose there's a list of seasonal ingredients on a board outside.

Frontoni (Map pp106-7; ☎ 06 581 24 36; Viale di Trastevere; ☼ 10am-1am Mon-Sat, 5am-midnight Sun) Frontoni offers a huge range of sandwich fillings that you can have with a simple *panino* or in *pizza bianca*. It also has good *pizza a taglio* with novel toppings such as ham and fig. For a choice of hot pastas, vegetable side dishes and salads (about €4), head upstairs to the restaurant.

(Continued on page 165)

ROME METRO AND CITY RAILWAYS MAP

CHRISTOPHER GROENHOUT

Statue at Piazza Navona (p119), Rome

Trevi Fountain (p123), Rome

MARTIN MOOS

St Peter's Basilica (p133), Vatican City

ALLAN MONTAIN

MARTIN MOOS

Ceiling of Villa d'Este (p180), Tivoli

JEFFREY BECOM

Medusa door knocker,
Viterbo (p183)

Villa Adriana (p180), Tivoli

WITOLD SKRYPCZAK

Riomaggiore (p213), the Cinque Terre

Wine-growing regions, Asti (p243)

Mont Blanc (p247), Valle d'Aosta

Cathedral (p262), Piazza del Duomo, Milan

MARTIN MOOS

Lago di Como (p297), Lombardy

DENNIS JONES

Shop window of Tiffany & Co (p275),
Golden Quad, Milan

MARTIN MOOS

Roman Area (p386), Verona

JULIET COOMBE

Ponte di Rialto (p347), Venice

ROBERTO SONCIN GEROMETTA

Regata Storica (Historic Regatta; p364), Grand Canal, Venice

ROBERTO SONCIN GEROMET

Cathedral (p426), Modena

Cycling past Piazza Maggiore (p418), Bologna

MARTIN HUGHES

Byzantine mosaics, Basilica di San Vitale (p444), Ravenna

HANNAH LEVY

JON DAVISON

Isola d'Elba (p509), Tuscany

Wine barrels, near Montalcino
(p528)

ALAN BENSON

NICK TAPP

Apuane Alps (p500), Tuscany

Fonte Gaia (p515), Piazza del Campo, Siena

JOHN

(Continued from page 156)

Zi' Fenizia (Map pp98-9; ☎ 06 689 69 76; Via di Santa Maria del Pianto 64; ⊙ Fri-Wed, closed Fri & Sat afternoons & Jewish holidays) A kosher place in the Ghetto, Aunty Fenizia is known for her delicious *pizza a taglio*. There's no cheese on the pizzas but with some 40 toppings on offer you hardly miss it.

Fantasia del Pane (Map pp102-3; ☎ 06 495 83 37; Via Goito 9; ⊙ 7am-2.30pm & 4.30-7.30pm, closed Sat afternoon) In the Termini area, this swish bakery rustles up a mean slice of pizza, as well as some mighty fine bread.

Other *pizza a taglio* outlets to try:

Pizza a Taglio (Map p104; Via Baullari 140) Between Campo de' Fiori and Corso Vittorio Emanuele II.

Pizza a Taglio (Map pp102-3; Via delle Muratte 14) Near the Trevi Fountain.

Pizza Farcita (Map pp98-9; Corso Vittorio Emanuele II 273)

Self-Catering

For deli supplies and wine, shop at *alimentari*, which are generally open 7am to 1.30pm and 5pm to 8pm every day except Thursday afternoon and Sunday (during the summer months they will often close on Saturday afternoon instead of Thursday).

For fresh fruit and vegetables, there are hundreds of outdoor markets, notably:

Campo de' Fiori (Map p104)

Piazza San Cosimato Market (Map pp106-7) In Trastevere.

Piazza Testaccio (Map pp106-7)

Piazza Vittorio Emanuele (Map pp102-3)

Via del Lavatore (Map pp98-9) Near the Trevi Fountain.

Supermarkets are few and far between but you can stock up at:

Conad (Map pp102-3; Stazione Termini)

DeSpar (Map p104; Via Giustiniani 18b-21) Near the Pantheon.

Sir (Map pp102-3; Piazza dell'Indipendenza 28)

Todis (Map pp106-7; Via Natale del Grande 24) In Trastevere.

The following are some of Rome's finer food shops.

Volpetti (Map pp106-7; ☎ 06 574 23 52; www.volpetti.com; Via Marmorata 47) A deli with a website means serious attention is paid to the food

---

CAKES, PASTRIES & ICE CREAM

Rome and ice cream go together like a house on fire. To taste for yourself try the following places.

San Crispino (Map pp98-9; ☎ 06 679 39 24; Via della Panetteria 42; ⊙ noon-12.30pm Mon, Wed, Thu & Sun, noon-1.30am Fri & Sat) Critics claim San Crispino serves the best ice cream in town. The cream-based flavours – ginger, whisky, pistachio – are particularly good, along with the fruit sorbets.

Gelateria Giolitti (Map p104; ☎ 06 699 12 43; Via degli Uffici del Vicario 40; ⊙ 7am-midnight) Said to have been Pope John Paul II's favourite, the *marrons glacè* (glacé chestnuts) is one of Giolitti's 70 flavours. There's also a great selection of cakes and pastries.

Gelateria della Palma (Map p104; ☎ 06 688 06 752; Via della Maddalena 20; ⊙ 8am-1am) A warning to parents: don't take kids in here unless you want to spend a lot. There are lollipops, sweets and chocolates and that's before you get to the ice cream. The house speciality is the *meringata* (ice cream with pieces of meringue).

La Fonte della Salute (Map pp106-7; ☎ 06 589 74 71; Via Marmaggi 2-6; ⊙ 10am-1.30am, to 2am Fri & Sat) Generous scoops, superb fruit flavours and soy- and yoghurt-based *gelati* are the trademarks of this Trastevere *gelateria*.

For cakes and pastries.

Bernasconi (Map p104; ☎ 06 688 06 264; Piazza B Cairoli 16) A small and uninspiring bar that serves excellent *cornetti* (croissants usually filled with jam, Nutella or custard).

Bella Napoli (Map p104; ☎ 06 687 70 48; Corso Vittorio Emanuele II 246a) Try the *sfogliatelle* (ricotta-filled sweet pastry), a Neapolitan speciality that's good any time of the day.

La Dolceroma (Map pp98-9; ☎ 06 689 21 96; Via del Portico d'Ottavia 20d) A tiny shop selling sticky Austrian strudels, cakes and pastries, muffins and chocolate fudge cake.

Il Forno del Ghetto (Map pp98-9; ☎ 06 68 76 37; Via del Portico d'Ottavia 1b) The all-female team in this tiny kosher bakery produce a legendary ricotta-and-damson tart.

Panella l'Arte del Pane (Map pp102-3; ☎ 06 487 24 35; Largo Leopardi 2-10) Near the Basilica di Santa Maria Maggiore, this place tempts with a devilish display of cakes, tarts, pastries, bread and pizza.

Sacchetti (Map pp106-7; Piazza San Cosimato 61) Gems include a chestnut-and-cream confection called *monte bianco* and *granita di caffè*, a slushy coffee-flavoured ice drink topped with cream.

here. You'll find everything from smelly ageing cheese to fresh homemade pasta, salami, and veggie pies. If you want to have a ham sent home, get online if you can't make it to Testaccio.

Volpetti alla Scrofa (Map p104; ☎ 06 688 06 335; Via della Scrofa 31-32) An Aladdin's den of delicacies including Belgian beer, French champagne, Italian truffles, sausage and cheese. It's also a *tavola calda* so you can eat here (a set menu of pasta, veg and fruit is €8.50).

Castroni (Map pp98-9; ☎ 06 687 43 83; Via Cola di Rienzo 196) Near the Vatican, Castroni is a favourite with expats for its international food (for Brits baked beans and salad cream, for Aussies Vegemite). It also has a good selection of gourmet food, both packaged and fresh.

Drogheria Innocenzi (Map pp106-7; ☎ 06 581 27 25; Piazza San Cosimato 66; ☾ 6.30am-1.30pm & 4.30-8pm Mon-Wed, Fri & Sat) An old-fashioned food store with sacks of rice, cornflakes, honey, *limoncello* (lemon liqueur) and gourmet chocolates. And quite a lot besides.

Billo Bottarga (Map pp98-9; ☎ 06 581 27 25; Via Sant'Ambrogio 20) In the Ghetto, this store specialises in kosher food and is famous for its *bottarga* (roe of tuna or mullet).

Trimani (Map pp102-3; ☎ 06 446 96 61; Via Goito 20) Among the 4000 labels sold at Rome's biggest *enoteca* are wines from all over the world.

Trimani winebar (Map pp102-3; ☎ 06 446 96 30; Via Cernaia 37b) Round the corner from Trimani.

La Bottega del Cioccolato (Map pp102-3; ☎ 06 482 14 73; Via Leonina 82) A small and devilishly tempting chocolate shop, this is not the place to go if you're hungry. The homemade chocs are beautifully displayed in old-fashioned glass cabinets.

For organic food and herbal products head for:

Emporium Naturae (Map p95; ☎ 06 375 11 415; Viale delle Milizie 7a) Near the Vatican.

Il Canestro (Map pp106-7; ☎ 06 574 62 87; Via San Francesco a Ripa 105) In Trastevere.

L'Albero del Pane (Map pp98-9; ☎ 06 686 50 16; Via di Santa Maria del Pianto 19) In the Jewish quarter.

DRINKING

Rome has a well-developed bar and café culture and a growing but still fairly small pub scene. For coffee connoisseurs there are any number of cafés, ranging from neon-lit hole-in-the-walls to painfully chic glamour hang-outs.

Much of the action is in the *centro storico*. Campo de' Fiori is especially popular with young revellers and it's here that you'll find the major drinking going on. The alleyways around Piazza Navona also have some trendy late-night hang-outs, ranging from elegant wine bars to English-style pubs. Trastevere is another pub-heavy area where locals and tourists mingle merrily. To get away from the tourist scene, head for San Lorenzo, east of Stazione Termini, where students crowd into the various pubs.

Ancient Rome

Café dei Musei (Map p114; ☎ 06 326 51 236; Capitoline Museums, Piazza del Campidoglio 19) A lovely spot to take a break from the wonders of the Capitoline Museums and relax with a drink. From the terrace the views of ancient Rome are stunning.

Shamrock (Map pp108-9; ☎ 06 679 17 29; Via Capo d'Africa 26d) This place is popular with an international crowd, this Irish pub serves Guinness on tap and has darts and pay TV for those unmissable games of footy.

Centro Storico

Bar della Pace (Map p104; ☎ 06 686 12 16; Via della Pace 5) Publishers looking for images of *la dolce vita* would be hard pushed to find a better picture than the Bar della Pace. In the foreground, sharply dressed beauties sip on their drinks, while behind them ivy cascades down the façade of the Art Nouveau café.

Bar del Fico (Map p104; ☎ 06 687 55 68; Piazza del Fico 24) If the beautiful people go to the Bar della Pace round the corner, the capital's well-heeled bohemians come here. It's a laid-back place where you can while away the hours reading the newspaper, playing chess or even having the odd drink or two. The pace heats up as the sun goes down.

Jonathan's Angels (Map p104; ☎ 06 689 34 26; Via della Fossa 18) No shrinking violet, Jonathan, ex-circus acrobat, rules the roost in this, his unique creation. A temple to everything that glitters and glows, it's lit by fairy lights and boasts the most amazing loo in Rome. A drink here is one you won't forget in a hurry.

Trinity College (Map pp98-9; ☎ 06 678 64 72; Via del Collegio Romano 6) A big booming pub just off busy Via del Corso, Trinity College has a good selection of imported beers and excellent bar food. It gets packed to overflowing at weekends so groups of single men might have trouble getting past the bouncers.

L'Angolo Divino (Map p104; ☎ 06 686 44 13; Via dei Balestrari) This charming wine bar, with wooden beams and terracotta floors, has been run by the same family for three generations. It's a lovely place for a quiet glass of excellent wine, a nibble of cheese or a light meal. Between 10.30am and 8pm there's 5% off wine sold by the glass.

Caffè Sant'Eustachio (Map p104; ☎ 06 686 13 09; Piazza Sant'Eustachio 82) Famed throughout Rome for its coffee, this place does a great *gran caffè*, a creamy coffee made by beating the first drops of espresso and several teaspoons of sugar into a frothy paste, then adding the rest of the coffee on top.

Camilloni a Sant'Eustachio (Map p104; ☎ 06 686 49 95; Piazza Sant'Eustachio 54-5) Just over the square from its namesake, this place also serves a serious espresso. It's also well known for its pastries, so if you're in the neighbourhood have breakfast here.

Il Goccetto (Map pp98-9; ☎ 06 686 42 68; Via dei Banchi Vecchi 14) An old-fashioned *enoteca* with a dark interior and bottles lining the wooden walls, Il Goccetto is an atmospheric spot for a drop. Join the regulars at the bar and choose from the 20 or so wines served by the glass or go the whole hog and order a bottle from the selection of international and Italian vintages.

Vineria (Map p104; ☎ 06 688 03 268; Campo de' Fiori) On Campo de' Fiori, Vineria is also known as Da Giorgio. Once the gathering place of the Roman literati, today it's an unpretentious place to savour wine or guzzle beer. Like all the bars on the Campo, it gets very full and unless you get in early it'll be find standing room only.

Il Nolano (Map p104; ☎ 06 687 93 44; Campo de' Fiori 11) Taking its name from Giordano Bruno da Nola, the hooded monk in the square, Il Nolano is an arty wine bar that's often used for art exhibitions and book presentations. Note the tables made from second-hand materials and the old wooden cinema seats.

Sloppy Sam's (Map p104; ☎ 06 688 02 637; Campo de' Fiori 9-10) Noisy, brash and usually full of drinking students, Sloppy Sam's is a recognised stop on most city pub crawls. If you want to get hammered in like-minded company, then this is the place for you.

La Tazza d'Oro (Map p104; ☎ 06 679 27 68; Via degli Orfani 84-6; ☼ Mon-Sat) Regulars at this temple

to coffee are among the choosiest in the capital. They know what a good coffee should taste like and they won't take nothing less. A speciality is the *granita di caffè*, a coffee-flavoured slush puppy.

Rosati (Map pp96-7; ☎ 06 322 58 59; Piazza del Popolo 5) According to Roman lore the Rosati is the hang-out of the left-wing chattering classes, while their right-wing counterparts head to the **Canova** (Map pp96-7; ☎ 06 361 22 31; Piazza del Popolo 16) over the square. Whatever, the Rosati is an elegant, if expensive, place for an early evening drink or ice cream.

Caffè Farnese (Map p104; ☎ 06 688 02 125; Via dei Baullari 106) According to Goethe, Piazza Farnese is one of the world's most beautiful squares. Judge for yourself from the vantage of a streetside table at this unassuming café, a great spot for people-watching.

Bartaruga (Map pp98-9; ☎ 06 689 22 99; Piazza Mattei 9) A celebrity hang-out, Bartaruga is decked out in a baroque ensemble of oriental furniture and velvet fabrics. VIPs come here for the cocktails and sounds, which range from soul to techno.

East of Via del Corso

Rive Gauche 2 (Map pp102-3; ☎ 06 445 67 22; Via dei Sabelli 43) One of the most popular pubs in San Lorenzo, Rive Gauche is nearly always full of students, foreigners and assorted friends. A vibrant and animated spot, it offers little in the way of entertainment other than drink but creates a buzz that's genuinely infectious. Be warned, however, it's a big place, gets very full, and has only one tiny loo.

Cavour 313 (Map p114; ☎ 06 678 54 96; Via Cavour 313; snacks €10; ☼ 10am-2.30pm & 7.30pm-12.30am) One of the oldest wine bars in Rome, Cavour 313 has an extensive wine list of about 1200 labels, including Californian and Australian wines. To nibble with your wine the cheese board is superb, and soups are served both hot and cold.

Newscafé (Map pp102-3; ☎ 06 699 23 473; Via della Stamperia 72) Decked out in sleek steel and wood with black-and-white photos on the walls and glossy mags strewn carefully on the tables, this is the place to grab a paper and look cool reading it. Sip at the bar inside or casually adjourn to a table outside.

Fiddler's Elbow (Map pp102-3; ☎ 06 487 21 10; Via dell'Olmata 43) Near the Basilica di Santa Maria Maggiore, this was one of the first wave of Irish pubs to open in Rome some 20 years ago. It attracts a mixture of international residents and Romans, many of whom want to try out their English on native speakers.

Caffè Greco (Map pp98-9; ☎ 06 679 17 00; Via dei Condotti 86) Keats and Casanova were among the early regulars at this historic café. It opened in 1760 and although it's still going strong it's of more interest for its history than anything it serves. The coffee's OK, the food expensive and the service coldly professional.

Babington's English Tea Rooms (Map pp98-9; ☎ 06 678 60 27; Piazza di Spagna 23) For a bastion of England that's more Jane Austen than Tony Blair, Babington's has been serving Earl Grey by the fireside since the 19th century. But while time has stood still the prices haven't: for a full high tea of sandwiches, crumpets and cakes expect to fork out €24.

Trastevere

Café della Scala (Map pp106-7; ☎ 06 580 37 63; Via della Scala 4) This small, laid-back café is the sort of place you come for a quiet drink only to end up some hours later trying to remember how to walk. The cocktails are ferocious. With measures poured by eye, waiters usually err on the side of generosity to produce industrial-strength drinks that pack one hell of a punch.

Stardust (Map pp106-7; ☎ 06 583 20 875; Vicolo dei Renzi 4) A well-known Trastevere watering hole, Stardust is loved for its smoky jazz atmosphere – there's often live music – although the bar staff are as happy playing Rossini as Louis Armstrong. It's open in the afternoon for tea and serves snacks in the early evening but the real buzz kicks in after 10pm. At weekends there's brunch with bagels and American coffee.

Bar San Calisto (Map pp106-7; ☎ 06 583 58 69; Piazza San Calisto) To look at, this down-at-heel bar is nothing special. In fact, it's far from inviting as crowds of punks, travellers, red-eyed dealers and alcoholics swill about outside. But it's famous for its chocolate: drunk hot with cream in winter, eaten as ice cream in summer. You can always pick up a cheap bottle here and plonk yourself in the nearby Piazza Santa Maria in Trastevere.

Friends Art Café (Map pp98-9; ☎ 06 581 61 11; Piazza Trilussa 34) It's all high-tech stainless steel and attitude at this swish spot. Full of young Romans dressed to the nines, it's not the place to bumble into in your shorts

looking for pints of bitter; cocktails and brightly coloured aperitifs are much more the thing.

Southern Rome

Four XXXX (Map pp106-7; ☎ 06 575 72 96; Via Galvani 29) Despite its name, Four XXXX is more Latin than Oz. True, there is still Castlemaine XXXX beer on tap and steak on the menu but the atmosphere is more tequila and fajitas. The sounds range from samba to soul.

Northern Rome

Caffè delle Arte (Map pp96-7; ☎ 06 326 51 236; Via Gramsci 72/75) Part of the Galleria Nazionale d'Arte Moderna e Contemporanea in the middle of Villa Borghese, this café is a favourite for family outings. There are tables outside on a lovely terrace and it's a great place for Sunday brunch.

ENTERTAINMENT

To entertain yourself in Rome it's often enough to park yourself at a streetside table and watch the world go by. But that's not to say that there's nothing going on. The city's cultural calendar is well established and proposes a host of alternatives, particularly in the summer when the Estate Romana (see p141) festival sponsors hundreds of theatre, cinema, opera and music events. Many performances take place in parks, gardens and church courtyards, with classical ruins and Renaissance villas providing atmospheric backdrops. Autumn is also full of cultural activity with specialised festivals dedicated to dance, drama and jazz.

The clubbing scene is less cutting edge than in London, say, or Berlin, but head down to Testaccio late on a Saturday night and you'll find a buzzing, excitable vibe.

Roma C'è (€1) is Rome's most comprehensive listings guide, and comes complete with a small English-language section; it's published every Wednesday. Two other useful guides are: *Metro*, a Thursday supplement to *Il Messaggero*; and *Trovaroma*, also out on Thursdays, which comes with *La Repubblica*. Both papers also carry daily cinema, theatre and concert listings. The English-language magazine *Wanted in Rome* also contains listings of festivals, exhibitions, dance shows, classical-music events, operas and cinema releases. It's published every other Wednesday. Useful websites include www.romace.it

(in Italian), www.romaturismo.it and www .comune.roma.it.

Tickets for big events are available from: **Hello** (Map pp102-3; ☎ 800 90 70 80, 06 808 83 52; www.amitonline.it in Italian; Stazione Termini; ☼ 10am-6.40pm Mon-Fri, 10am-3pm Sat) On the Via Giovanni Giolitti side of Stazione Termini. Accepts cash payments only. **Orbis** (Map pp102-3; ☎ 06 474 47 76; Piazza dell'Esquilino 37; ☼ 9.30am-1pm & 4-7.30pm Mon-Fri, 9.30am-1pm Sat) Near Basilica di Santa Maria Maggiore.

Nightclubs & Live Music

Clubs cover most tastes ranging from dressy glam hang-outs to converted warehouses with big-name DJs. Most places open around 10.30pm or 11pm and continue through to the early hours. Admission charges clearly vary, but expect to pay anything from €5 to €25, which may or may not include a drink. The best clubbing is in Testaccio.

Goa (Map p95; ☎ 06 574 82 77; Via Libetta 13; ☼ Oct-May) Trend-setting industrial décor, plasma screens and heavy-duty bouncers keep Goa at the forefront of Italian clubbing. National and international DJs queue up to spin house, electronic and experimental sounds. One Sunday a month Goa goes gay with 'Gorgeous Goa' and one Friday it's lesbian night with 'Venus Rising'.

Ex-Magazzini (Map p95; ☎ 06 575 80 40; Via Magazzini Generali 8) A huge and very trendy disco bar in a converted warehouse full of beautiful Romans dancing to trance, pop and breakbeat downstairs. Upstairs, the exhausted darlings chill out on plush sofas. Expect to queue and occasional live performance.

Alien (Map pp96-7; ☎ 06 841 22 12; Via Velletri 13) Pure disco, Alien constantly changes its look to keep up with the newest fads. In its latest apparition the look is lounge minimalism and the music is house. Theme nights range from fetish to revival and on Saturday Alien goes gay.

Qube (☎ 06 438 54 450; Via di Portonaccio 212) Spread over three floors, Qube is Rome's largest disco. Attracting an up-for-it crowd, it hosts live performances, cabaret nights and, at least once a week (usually Friday), gay nights. The sounds are largely mainstream commercial.

Alpheus (Map p95; ☎ 06 574 78 26; Via del Commercio 36) Alpheus defies most labels. Its three halls host everything from Argentine tango on Sundays to house, hip-hop, rock and soul. Gay nights are regular and well supported.

Il Locale (Map p104; ☎ 06 687 90 75; Vicolo del Fico 3) Much frequented by city celebs, Il Locale is one of the best venues for live music in the centre. Just off fashionable Via del Governo Vecchio (near Piazza Navona), it's a small, informal place, so expect to queue on Friday and Saturday nights. Once in, make sure to sample one of their colourful cocktails.

Caffè Latino (Map pp106-7; ☎ 06 572 88 556; Via di Monte Testaccio 96) Latin American music is huge in Rome and this Testaccio club is the place to hear it. There's live music most nights before DJs take over, spinning acid jazz, funk and yes, you guessed it, South American music.

Black Out (Map pp108-9; ☎ 06 704 96 791; Via Saturnia 18) One of Rome's historic, and most popular, rock clubs, Black Out regularly hosts national and international bands. The music ranges from heavy metal to ska with occasional bursts of punk, indie and goth.

Villaggio Globale (Map pp106-7; ☎ 06 575 72 33; Lungotevere Testaccio 2) Rome's former slaughterhouse now houses a multipurpose entertainment village. Run by the Villaggio Globale *centro sociale* (social centre; originally a squat but now a slick business operation), it stages concerts and theatrical performances, as well as offering a whole host of courses. Many big names like to perform here to return to their counterculture roots.

Brancaleone (☎ 06 820 00 959; Via Levanna 11) One of the top venues on the Rome music scene, this *centro sociale* serves up an eclectic range of music. There are regular drum-and-bass and house sets, Thursday is reggae night and Saturdays tend to be electronic. It's hip, hard and cutting edge.

Gay & Lesbian Venues

Details of Rome's gay and lesbian bars and clubs are provided in gay publications and through local gay organisations (see p170 for more details).

Coming Out (Map pp108-9; ☎ 06 700 98 71; Via San Giovanni in Laterano 8) With a name like this, Coming Out couldn't be anything but a gay and lesbian bar. A relaxed, mainly young place, it hosts occasional gigs, and for amateur crooners karaoke from Wednesday to Sunday.

Hangar (Map pp102-3; ☎ 06 488 13 97; Via in Selci 69) A historic landmark on Rome's gay map, Hangar has been attracting punters of all ages for over 20 years. The varied clientele (both Italian and foreign) includes a significant number of gym bunnies. The American owner, John Moss, has recently added a dark room.

L'Alibi (Map pp106-7; ☎ 06 574 34 48; Via di Monte Testaccio 44) For years regarded as Rome's premier gay spot, L'Alibi now attracts a mixed crowd. Spread over two floors it offers conventional house and disco music and a great roof terrace.

Edoardo II (Map pp98-9; ☎ 06 699 42 419; Vicolo Margana 14) Named after Christopher Marlowe's 16th-century tragedy, this place is done up like a medieval torture chamber. There's no dancing, or torturing, it's just a bar – but if you're on the pull, it's a top spot.

Garbo (Map pp106-7; ☎ 06 583 20 782; Vicolo di Santa Margherita 1a) Tucked away in a quiet corner of Trastevere, Garbo is a candlelit cocktail bar catering to couples rather than cruisers. The atmosphere is relaxed and welcoming.

Classical Music

The city's abundance of atmospheric settings makes Rome a great place to catch a classical concert. The Auditorium Parco della Musica is a startlingly modern complex that combines architectural innovation with perfect acoustics. Free concerts are often held in many of Rome's churches, especially at Easter and around Christmas and New Year. Seats are available on a first-come, first-served basis and the programmes are generally excellent. Check newspapers and listings for programmes.

Rome's two major classical music organisations are the **Accademia di Santa Cecilia** (Map p95; ☎ 06 808 20 58; www.santacecilia.it; Viale Pietro de Coubertin 34) and the **Accademia Filarmonica Romana** (Map p95; ☎ 06 320 17 52; www.filarmonica romana.org; Piazza Gentile da Fabriano 17). The former organises a year-round programme, characterised by short festivals dedicated to a single composer. The Santa Cecilia orchestra is often joined by world-class international performers for concerts at the Auditorium Parco della Musica or, in summer, at Villa Giulia (Map pp96–7).

Auditorium Parco della Musica (Map p95; ☎ 06 8 02 42, box office ☎ 06 808 20 58; www.musicaperroma .it; Viale Pietro de Coubertin) Designed by Italy's top architect Renzo Piano, the auditorium comprises three concert halls and a 3000-capacity open-air arena. Of the three halls, the largest, the 2,800-seat Sala Santa Cecilia, is home to the Santa Cecilia orchestra. To

---

GAY & LESBIAN ROME

Rome is essentially a conservative city and although homosexuality is well tolerated, the gay scene is not a patch on that of many other international capitals. The year 2000 was, however, a watershed as the city hosted World Pride, a week-long festival of parties and events, in the middle of the Roman Catholic Jubilee Year.

Rome's main cultural and political gay organisation is the **Circolo Mario Mieli di Cultura Omosessuale** (Map p95; ☎ 06 541 39 85; www.mariomieli.it in Italian; Via Efeso 2a), off Via Ostiense near the Basilica di San Paolo Fuori-le-Mura, which organises debates, cultural events and social functions. It also runs free AIDS/HIV testing and a care centre. Its website has information and listings of forthcoming events, both social and political, including Rome Pride, which takes place every year in June. Mario Mieli also publishes a free monthly magazine AUT, available from gay bookshops and organisations.

The national organisation for lesbians is **Coordinamento Lesbiche Italiano** (Map pp98-9; ☎ 06 686 42 01; cli_network@iol.it; cnr Via San Francesco di Sales & Via della Lungara, Trastevere), also known as the Buon Pastore Centre. The centre has a women-only hostel, La Foresteria Orsa Maggiore (p148).

Rome has several gay bars and discos and there is even a gay beach near Ostia. The lesbian scene is less active, although there are various associations that organise events.

Two good sources of information are the **Libreria Babele** (Map pp98-9; ☎ 06 687 66 28; Via dei Banchi Vecchi 116), an exclusively gay and lesbian bookshop, and the lesbian **Libreria delle Donne: Al Tempo Ritrovato** (Map pp106-7; ☎ 06 581 77 24; Via dei Fienaroli 31d), in Trastevere. Both carry details of forthcoming events.

Other useful listings guides are Pride (€3.10), a national monthly magazine, AUT (free) – both available at gay and lesbian organisations and in bookshops – and the international gay guide, Spartacus. You can also go online at www.gay.it/guida/Lazio/Roma (in Italian).

get to the auditorium take Tram 2 from Piazzale Flaminio or, from Stazione Termini, bus M, which departs every 15 minutes between 5pm and the end of the last performance.

Teatro Olimpico (Map p95; ☎ 06 320 17 52; www .teatroolimpico.it in Italian; Piazza Gentile da Fabriano 17) The Accademia Filarmonica Romana holds its season here. The programme features mainly chamber music, with some contemporary concerts and multimedia events.

Opera

Rome's opera season starts in December and continues until June. Tickets are expensive: the cheapest upper-balcony seats start at around €22 and prices go up to €120. First-night performances cost more.

In the summer, opera is performed outdoors, often at the Terme di Caracalla (Map pp108–9).

Teatro dell'Opera (Map pp102-3; ☎ 06 481 602 87 06; www.opera.roma.it in Italian; Piazza Beniamino Gigli; ☺ box office inquiries 9am-2pm Mon-Fri) Often considered a poor cousin of La Scala in Milan or San Carlo in Naples, Rome's opera house may not blow you away with its acoustics but it certainly makes an impression. The Fascist-era façade hides a 19th-century fres coed interior with acres of stucco, red velvet and gilt. The theatre also hosts a number of ballet performances.

Jazz & Blues

Romans, like all Italians, adore jazz, and there are a host of excellent venues around the city.

Alexanderplatz (Map p95; ☎ 06 397 42 171; Via Ostia 9) A dark, smoky kinda place as befits its billing as Rome's top jazz joint, Alexanderplatz has live music most nights often featuring big name performers, both Italian and foreign. In July and August the club moves to the grounds of Villa Celimontana for the Villa Celimontana Jazz (Map pp108–9), one of Rome's popular summer festivals.

Big Mama (Map pp106-7; ☎ 06 581 24 51; Via San Francesco a Ripa 18) Aficionados of the blues will enjoy Big Mama. Since 1984 this Trastevere institution has been playing host to the world's top bluesmen, although it also serves rock, jazz and funk.

La Palma (☎ 06 435 99 029; Via Giuseppe Mirri 35) Insiders rate this place on a par with Alex-

anderplatz as a jazz venue. It's a bit of a hike from the centre but it's worth it for the top-quality Monday and Friday jazz nights.

New Orleans Café (Map pp102-3; ☎ 06 420 14 785; Via XX Settembre 52) Surrounded by government ministries and banks, this city-centre bar is a good bet for live jazz. The regular concerts are well advertised and popular. If there's no concert on, however, the atmosphere can be stilted.

Theatre

There are over 80 theatres in the city, many of them worth visiting as much for the architecture and decoration as for the production itself. In summer the **Miracle Players** (☎ 06 446 98 67; www.miracleplayers.org) perform classic English dramas such as *Everyman* and *Julius Caesar,* usually in abridged form, near the Roman Forum and other open-air locations. Performances are usually free.

Teatro Valle (Map p104; ☎ 06 688 03 794; Via del Teatro Valle 23a) A perfectly proportioned theatre proposing a variable programme that occasionally includes contemporary works with English-language subtitles or translated into Italian.

Arte del Teatro Studio (Map pp102-3; ☎ 06 444 13 75; Via Urbana 107) The English Theatre of Rome puts on a mix of contemporary one-act plays and full-length dramas in English every Friday.

Teatro Argentina (Map p104; ☎ 06 688 04 601; www.teatrodiroma.net in Italian; Largo di Torre Argentina 52) The official home of the Teatro di Roma, the Teatro Argentina stages major theatre and dance productions.

Cinemas

Of Rome's 80-odd cinemas only a handful show films in the original language (marked VO or *versione originale* in listings). Expect to pay around €8, with some discounts on Wednesdays.

Pasquino (Map pp106-7; ☎ 06 580 36 22; Piazza Sant'Egidio) In the heart of Trastevere, the three-screen Pasquino shows daily films in English. They range from blockbusters to art-house flicks.

Alcazar (Map pp106-7; ☎ 06 588 00 99; Via Merry del Val 14) On Monday you can see films in English or with English subtitles.

Nuovo Sacher (Map pp106-7; ☎ 06 581 81 16; Largo Ascianghi 1) Owned by Italian film director Nanni Moretti, it shows films in their original language (not necessarily English) on Monday and Tuesday.

Warner Village Moderno (Map pp102-3; ☎ 06 477 79 202; Piazza della Repubblica 45) Film premieres are often held at this multiplex, which screens Hollywood blockbusters (both in English and Italian) and major release Italian films.

A popular form of entertainment in the hot Roman summer is outdoor cinema.

Isola del Cinema (Map pp106-7; ☎ 06 583 33 113; www.isoladelcinema.com) Independent arty films are shown on the Isola Tiberina in July and August.

Massenzio (☎ 06 428 14 962; www.massenzio.it in Italian) Old classics and current releases are shown on a huge outdoor screen. The location changes every year but a favourite spot is opposite the Colosseum.

Sport

A trip to Rome's impressive football stadium, the **Stadio Olimpico** (Map p95; ☎ 06 3 68 51; Foro Italico, Viale dei Gladiatori 2), provides a memorable experience. Throughout the season (September to May) there's a game on most Sundays involving one of the city's two teams, AS Roma (the *giallorossi*, yellow and reds) or Lazio (the *biancazzuri*, white and blues). Tickets cost from €15 to €65 and can be bought at the Lottomatica (lottery centres), the stadium, ticket agencies or at one of the many Roma or Lazio stores around the city: try **AS Roma Store** (Map pp98-9; ☎ 06 692 00 642; Piazza Colonna 360) or **Lazio Point** (Map p114; ☎ 06 648 26 688; Via Farini 34).

To get to the stadium take Metro Line A to Ottaviano and then bus No 32.

SHOPPING

There's really no better way of mingling with the locals than (window) shopping on a Saturday afternoon. For top-of-the-range designer clobber, head for the area around Piazza di Spagna (Map pp98–9) and in particular Via dei Condotti, Via Frattina, Via delle Vite and Via Borgognona.

Moving down a euro or two, Via Nazionale (Map p114), Via del Corso (Map pp98–9) and, near the Vatican, Via Cola di Rienzo (Map pp98–9) are good for midrange clothing, while second-hand threads can be found along Via del Governo Vecchio (Map p104), just off Piazza Navona.

If you're looking for antiques or an unusual gifts, try Via dei Coronari (Map p104)

or Via Margutta (Map pp96–7), where the shops often resemble art galleries and the prices exhibit no mercy.

If you can time your visit to coincide with the *saldi* (sales), you'll pick up some great bargains, although you'll need to be up for some bare-knuckle shopping. Winter sales run from early January to mid-February and the summer sales from July to early September.

For information on food and wine shops, see p165.

Antique Photos & Prints

Alinari (Map pp98-9; ☎ 06 679 29 23; Via Alibert 16a) Photographic prints of Rome reproduced from 19th-century glass-plate negatives by the Alinari brothers.

Nardecchia (Map p104; ☎ 06 686 93 18; Piazza Navona 25) Check out Nardecchia for antique prints, including 18th-century etchings of Rome by Giovanni Battista Piranesi.

Clothing, Shoes & Leather Goods

The big designer names need no introduction; all are located around Via dei Condotti and the Spanish Steps.

Armani (Map pp98-9; ☎ 06 699 14 60; Via dei Condotti 77)

Artigianato del Cuoio (Map pp98-9; ☎ 06 678 44 35; 2nd fl, Via Belsiana 90) An unmarked leather workshop that'll do bags, belts and luggage to your own design in 24 hours.

Bruno Magli (Map pp98-9; ☎ 06 692 02 264; Via dei Condotti 6) Shoes and leather accessories.

Dolce & Gabbana (Map pp98-9; 06 679 22 94; Piazza di Spagna 94-95)

Fendi (Map pp98-9; ☎ 06 69 96 61; Via Borgognona 36-40)

Furla (Map pp98-9; ☎ 06 692 00 363; Piazza di Spagna 22) For bags in colourful leather.

Gucci (Map pp98-9; ☎ 06 679 04 05; Via dei Condotti 8)

Just Cavalli (Map pp98-9; ☎ 06 679 22 94; Piazza di Spagna 82-83) Threads by one of Italy's most contemporary designers.

La Perla (Map pp98-9; ☎ 06 699 41 934; Via dei Condotti 79) Luscious silk lingerie.

Louis Big Shoes (Map pp102-3; ☎ 06 679 16 77; Via Cavour 309) Shoes for the larger foot.

Mandarina Duck (Map pp102-3; ☎ 06 678 64 14; Via Due Macelli 59) Trendsetting bags in high-tech fabrics.

Max Mara Via dei Condotti 17 (Map pp98-9); Via Frattina 28 (Map pp98-9; ☎ 06 679 36 38)

Moschino (Map pp98-9; ☎ 06 678 11 44; Via Borgognona 32a) Provocative clothes from iconoclastic Italian designer.

Prada (Map pp98-9; ☎ 06 679 08 97; Via dei Condotti 92-95)

Valentino (Map pp98-9; ☎ 06 678 36 56; Via dei Condotti 13)

Versace (Map pp98-9; ☎ 06 678 05 21; Via del Bocca di Leone 26/27)

Designer Goods & Homewares

Art'è (Map p104; ☎ 06 683 39 07; Piazza Rondanini 32) Colourful plastic lamps, clocks and Alessi kitchenware share elegant shelf space.

C.U.C.I.N.A. (Map pp98-9; ☎ 06 679 12 75; Via Mario de' Fiori 65) For state-of-the-art stainless-steel kitchenware.

Leone Limentani (Map pp98-9; ☎ 06 683 07 000; Via Portico d'Ottavia 47) An Aladdin's cave of kitchen and tableware, expensive porcelain and bargain-basement knick-knacks.

Spazio Sette (Map p104; ☎ 06 686 97 08; Via dei Barbieri 7) Funky modern furniture displayed over three floors in a former 17th-century cardinal's palace.

'Gusto (Map pp98-9; ☎ 06 323 63 63; Piazza Augusto Imperatore 7) Part of the food hall of the same name (see p154), this cool culinary store sells a wide selection of cookbooks and some painfully hip kitchen utensils.

Markets

Porta Portese flea market (Map pp106-7; Piazza Porta Portese) Sunday morning in Rome means this flea market. With thousands of stalls selling everything from rare books to spare bike parts, it gets extremely busy so beware of pickpockets.

Via Sannio market (Map pp108-9; Via Sannio; ☒ to 1pm Mon-Sat) For second-hand clothes and cheap shoes, head to the weekday market, near San Giovanni Metro station (Line A).

Shopping for Children

Bertè (Map p104; ☎ 06 687 50 11; Piazza Navona) A giant Pinocchio guards the door to this expensive toy shop. It's famous for its wooden dolls and puppets.

Città del Sole (Map p104; ☎ 06 687 54 04; Via della Scrofa 65) A parent's dream: imaginative and well-made toys with hardly an electronic gadget in sight.

La Cicogna (Map pp98-9; ☎ 06 678 69 77; Via Frattina 138) Designer togs for kids.

Stationery, Arts & Crafts

Ditta G Pozzi Via del Gesù 74-5 (Map pp98-9; ☎ 06 678 44 77); Via Pie di Marmo 38/41 (Map pp98-9; ☎ 06 679 36 74) Artists have been getting their oil paints, brushes, pens and pencils from Ditta G Pozzi since 1825.

Vertecchi (Map pp98-9; ☎ 06 679 01 55; Via della Croce 72) For upmarket pens and paper, and fine art materials.

GETTING THERE & AWAY
Air

Rome's main airport is **Leonardo da Vinci** (FCO; Map p179; ☎ 06 659 55 571; www.adr.it), commonly known as Fiumicino. The second smaller airport, **Ciampino** (CIA; Map p179; ☎ 06 794 94 225; wwwadr.it), is used by many low-cost airlines and charter flights. For details on getting to and from the airports, see p174.

Bus

Long-distance national and international buses use the bus terminus on Piazzale Tiburtina, in front of Stazione Tiburtina. Take Metro Line B from Stazione Termini to Tiburtina.

Cotral buses (☎ 800 15 00 08; www.cotralspa.it in Italian) serve the Lazio region and depart from numerous points throughout the city, depending on their destination. The company is linked with Rome's public transport system, which means that you can buy one *biglietto integrato regionale giornaliero* (BIRG) ticket that covers city buses, trams, metro and train lines, and regional buses and trains (see the boxed text, p178).

Car & Motorcycle

Driving to the centre of Rome is not the easiest thing in the world to do. There are traffic restrictions, one-way systems, an almost total lack of street parking and a huge number of manic drivers. Still, if you're up for it, it's quite a rush.

Rome is circled by the Grande Raccordo Anulare (GRA) to which all major autostrade (motorways) and *strade statali* (SS, major state roads) connect. Approaching Rome from the north on the A1 autostrada get off at the Roma Nord exit; from the south use Roma Sud. After a few kilometres, you'll find yourself nearing the GRA. From the GRA the most important roads are:

Via Cassia (SS2) From Ponte Milvio this runs northwest to Viterbo, Siena and Florence.

Via Flaminia (SS3) Parallels Via Cassia before forking off northeast to Terni, Foligno and over the Apennines into Le Marche, ending on the Adriatic coast at Fano.

ROME & LAZIO

Via Salaria (SS4) Heads north from near Porta Pia in central Rome to Rieti and into Le Marche, ending at Porto d'Ascoli on the Adriatic coast.

Via Tiburtina (SS5) Links Rome with Tivoli and Pescara, on the coast of Abruzzo.

Via Casilina (SS6) Heads southeast to Anagni and into Campania, terminating at Capua near Naples.

Via Appia Nuova (SS7) Heads south, via Ciampino airport and the Castelli Romani, into Campania, then crosses the Apennines into Basilicata, through Potenza and Matera to Taranto in Puglia and finally on to Brindisi.

Via Cristoforo Colombo From near Porta San Sebastiano (the start of Via Appia Antica) south to EUR and then Ostia.

Via del Mare/Via Ostiense (SS8) Via del Mare heads southwest to Ostia; it becomes Via Ostiense on the city side of the GRA.

Via Aurelia (SS1) Heads northeast from the Vatican, following the Tyrrhenian coast to Pisa, Genoa and France.

From the GRA, take the autostrada Roma-Fiumicino for Leonardo da Vinci (Fiumicino) airport and the A24 autostrada for the Parco Nazionale d'Abruzzo, Lazio & Molise and Pescara.

Train

Almost all trains arrive at and depart from Stazione Termini (Map pp102–3). There are regular connections to other European countries, all the major cities in Italy and many smaller towns.

The **train information office** (Map pp102-3; ☾ 7am-9.45pm) at Stazione Termini is very helpful, though it's often crowded and you have to take a ticket and wait your turn (English is spoken). They cannot, however, make reservations. These must be made at the main ticket and reservation windows in the front hall. Alternatively go online at www.trenitalia.com or find one of the many travel agencies that has an FS or *biglietti treni* (train tickets) sign in the window. Another way to reserve or buy tickets is to use the automatic ticket machines, where you can pay with cash, credit or ATM card.

If you're doing a lot of rail travel you can buy an official Trenitalia *orario* (timetable, €4) at most newsstands in and around the station.

Remember to validate your train ticket in the yellow machines on the station platforms before you get on your train. If you don't you may be fined, and it's worth noting that claiming ignorance rarely works anymore.

Rome's other principal train stations are Stazione Tiburtina, Stazione Roma-Ostiense (Map p95) and Stazione Trastevere (Map p95).

GETTING AROUND
To/From the Airport

Fiumicino is about 30km southwest of the city centre and is well connected to it. Getting to and from Ciampino is more time consuming by public transport even if it's only 15km southeast of the centre. However, several low-cost airlines, namely Ryanair and easyJet now offer a shuttle service to/from Ciampino airport. Operated by **Terravision** (☎ 06 794 94 572; www.terravision.it), buses depart from Via Marsala outside of Stazione Termini two hours before each scheduled flight, and from Ciampino soon after the arrival of each flight. Buy your tickets (€8 single, €13.50 return) from the **Hotel Royal Santina** (Map pp102-3; Via Marsala 22), opposite the bus stop, or at Ciampino airport. For details on public transport links, see below.

BUS

From 11.30pm to 6am, Cotral run an hourly bus from Stazione Tiburtina (accessible by bus No 42N from the main bus station on Piazza Cinquecento, in front of Termini) to Fiumicino airport (€5) via Termini. Buy your ticket on the bus.

If you arrive at Ciampino, Cotral buses (5.45am to 10.30pm, €1) will take you to the Anagnina Metro station, from where you can get to Stazione Termini. Buy your bus ticket from the *tabacchi* inside the airport. Alternatively get a Cotral bus (€1) to Ciampino train station from where regular trains connect with Stazione Termini (€1.70).

Alternatively catch a **Schiaffini bus** (www.schiaffini.com) to Ciampino train station from where regular trains connect with Stazione Termini (€1.70). Departures are approximately every forty minutes between 6am (7.20am on Sunday) and 11.35pm; tickets, available on the bus, cost €1.

If you miss the bus and it's after 11pm, you'll have to fork out for a taxi, which will cost about €39 plus surcharges for luggage.

CAR

If you've decided to hire a car (p176) follow the signs for Rome out of the Leonardo da Vinci airport and onto the autostrada. Exit the autostrada at EUR, then follow the *centro* signs (they look like a bull's eye) to reach Via Cristoforo Colombo, which will take you directly into the centre of Rome.

From Ciampino, it is easier: exit the airport, turn right onto Via Appia Nuova and follow it to the centre.

TAXI

Official taxis leave from outside the arrivals hall at Fiumicino. They are white or yellow and have the letters SPQR on their door. As a rule insist on the metered fare rather than an agreed price as it leaves less room for misunderstanding. A taxi to the centre of Rome from Fiumicino costs from €40 to €60 (including surcharges for the airport, your luggage and depending on the time of day or night). If anyone approaches you in the terminal offering a taxi, say no – they're breaking the law.

Several private companies run shuttle services which work out about the same price as a taxi but are usually a lot more comfortable. **Airport Connection Services** (☎ 06 338 32 21; www.airportconnection.it) has two prices: €20 for one person and €30 for two people. A six-person minivan costs €55. Shuttles run between 7am and 7pm with hotel pick-up included in the price. You'll need to book at least a day in advance.

Airport Shuttle (☎ 06 420 14 507; www.airport shuttle.it) offers transfers to/from Fiumicino in a minivan for €26 for one person, then €6 for each additional passenger up to a maximum of eight. From Fiumicino into Rome there's also an €11 surcharge. To/from Ciampino costs €42 for one to two people, with €6 for each additional person. A 30% surcharge is added between 10pm and 7am.

TRAIN

Fiumicino airport is easy to get to by train. The *Leonardo Express,* the direct Fiumicino–Termini train costs €9.50 (€11 on board) and takes about 30 minutes. It departs and arrives from platform 27 at Termini (a 400m walk from the main concourse). The first departure is at 5.52am, then trains run half-hourly until the last one at 10.52pm.

From Fiumicino, trains start at 6.37am and run half-hourly until 11.37pm. If you want to get to Termini don't take the train for Orte or Fara Sabina. These slower trains stop at Trastevere, Ostiense and Tiburtina stations

but not Termini. They cost €5 and run every 15 minutes (hourly on Sundays and public holidays) from 5.57am to 11.27pm, and from Tiburtina from 5.06am until 10.36pm.

Tickets for the *Leonardo Express* are available at Termini from *tabacchi* and newsstands in the station, at vending machines or at the **Alitalia desk** (near platform 22; ☯ 9am-7.30pm). At Fiumicino, get tickets from the vending machines or the ticket desks at the rail terminus.

Car & Motorcycle

Roman traffic is notorious and driving or riding here requires skills that aren't often taught in driving lessons. A cool head, nerves of steel and a primordial sense of survival also help. As a general rule, worry about what's in front of you, leaving those behind you to think about your rear!

Most of the *centro storico* of Rome is closed to normal traffic. You're not allowed to drive in the centre from 6.30am to 6pm Monday to Friday and 2pm to 6pm Saturday unless you're a resident or have special permission. You'll also need to watch out for the increasing number of no-traffic Sundays and days when circulation is limited to vehicles with odd/even number plates.

All 22 streets accessing the 'Limited Traffic Zone' (ZTL) have been equipped with electronic-access detection devices. If you're staying in this zone, contact your hotel, which will fax the authorities with your number plate, thus saving you a €68.25 fine. For further information, check www.sta.roma.it (in Italian) or call ☎ 06 571 18 333 from 8am to 6pm Monday to Friday and 2pm to 6pm Saturday.

Parking in the city is no fun. Blue lines denote pay-and-display spaces with tickets available from meters (coins only) and *tabacchi*. Costs vary but in the centre expect to pay €1 per hour between 8am and 8pm (11pm in some parts). Traffic wardens are vigilant and fines of up to €68.25 are common. If you're really unlucky you could find your car's been clamped or towed away. If so, call the **traffic police** (☎ 06 6 76 91) who can tell you where to go to collect it. You'll have to pay about €100 to get it back, plus a hefty fine.

The city's most convenient car park is at Villa Borghese (Map pp96–7); entry is from Piazzale Brasile at the top of Via Vittorio Veneto. There's also supervised car parks at

Stazione Termini (Map pp102–3); at Piazzale dei Partigiani, just outside Stazione Ostiense (Map p95); and at Stazione Tiburtina. Costs vary from €1.15 to €2.50 per hour.

CAR HIRE

The major car-rental companies all have representatives in Rome.

Avis (24hr bookings ☎ 800 86 30 63; www.avisauto noleggio.it in Italian); Ciampino airport (☎ 06 793 40 195); Fiumicino airport (☎ 06 650 11 531); Stazione Termini (Map pp102-3; ☎ 06 481 43 73)

Europcar (central bookings ☎ 800 01 44 10; www.europ car.com); Ciampino airport (☎ 06 793 40 387); Fiumicino airport (☎ 06 650 10 287); Stazione Termini (Map pp102-3; ☎ 06 488 28 54)

Hertz (www.hertz.com); Ciampino airport (☎ 06 650 10 256); Fiumicino airport (☎ 06 592 27 42); Stazione Termini (Map pp102-3; ☎ 06 474 03 89)

Maggiore National (central bookings ☎ 848 86 70 67; www.maggiore.it); Ciampino airport (☎ 06 793 40 368); Fiumicino airport (☎ 06 650 10 678); Stazione Termini (Map pp102-3; ☎ 06 488 00 49)

MOTORCYCLE & BICYCLE HIRE

Flying round Rome on a scooter is a memorable, if hairy, experience. If you'd prefer to cycle, be careful, Romans are not used to seeing bicycles on the roads. As a beginner you may be wise to venture forth on a Sunday, when much of central Rome is closed to traffic. A useful map is *Roma in Bici*, which details bike paths and itineraries and is available from the Rome Tourist Board (p94).

To hire a scooter you'll need a credit card and photo ID; for a bike, ID is usually sufficient. You may also have to leave a cash deposit. Reliable operators include:

Appia Antica Regional Park Visitor Centre (Map p95; ☎ 06 512 63 14; Via Appia Antica 42; bikes per hr/day €3/10)

Bici e Baci (Map pp102-3; ☎ 06 482 84 43; www .bicibaci.com; Via del Viminale 5; per day bikes €11, scooters from €19, 500cc motorbikes €95)

Cyclò (Map pp102-3; ☎ 06 481 56 69; www.scooterhire .it; Via Cavour 80; per day bikes €12, scooters from €32)

I Bike (Map pp96-7; ☎ 06 322 52 40; Villa Borghese underground car park, 3rd sector, Via Vittorio Veneto 156; scooters per day €60)

Treno e Scooter Rent (Map pp102-3; ☎ 06 489 05 823; Stazione Termini; per day bikes €9.50, scooters from €31)

Public Transport

Rome's public transport system includes buses, trams, a metro and a suburban train

network. Tickets are valid for all forms of transport and come in various forms. The simplest is the *biglietto integrato a tempo* (BIT), which costs €1 and is valid for 75 minutes. In that time you can use as many buses or trams as you like but the metro only once. Daily tickets cost €4 (ask for a *biglietto giornaliero*), a three-day ticket €11 and weekly tickets €16; children up to 1m tall, or under four, travel free. Note that tickets do not include routes to Fiumicino airport.

You can buy tickets at *tabacchi*, newsstands and from vending machines at main bus stops. They must be purchased before you get on the bus or train and then validated in the yellow machine once on the bus or tram, or at the entrance gates for the metro. You risk a €52 fine if you're caught without a validated ticket.

BUS & TRAM

Rome's buses and trams are run by **ATAC** (☎ 800 43 17 84; www.atac.roma.it). The **main bus station** (Map pp102-3; Piazza Cinquecento) is in front of Stazione Termini, where there's an information booth (on the stand in the centre of the piazza). Largo di Torre Argentina, Piazza Venezia and Piazza San Silvestro are other important hubs. Buses generally run from about 5.30am until midnight, with limited services throughout the night on some routes. Pick up a free transport map from the ATAC information booth at the main bus station. Useful routes:

H Stazione Termini, Via Nazionale, Piazza Venezia, Largo di Torre Argentina, Ponte Garibaldi, Viale Trastevere and into the western suburbs.

No 170 Stazione Termini, Via Nazionale, Piazza Venezia, Via del Teatro Marcello and Bocca della Verità (then south to Testaccio and EUR).

No 175 Stazione Termini, Piazza Barberini, Via del Corso, Teatro di Marcello, Aventine Hill and Stazione Ostiense.

No 23 Piazzale Clodio, Piazza Risorgimento, Ponte Vittorio Emanuele II, Lungotevere, Ponte Garibaldi, Via Marmorata (Testaccio), Piazzale Ostiense and Basilica di San Paolo.

No 40 Express Stazione Termini, Via Nazionale, Piazza Venezia, Largo di Torre Argentina, Chiesa Nuova, Piazza Pia (for Castel Sant'Angelo) and St Peter's.

No 492 Stazione Tiburtina, San Lorenzo, Stazione Termini, Piazza Barberini, Piazza Venezia, Corso Rinascimento, Piazza Cavour, Piazza Risorgimento and Cipro-Vatican Museums (Metro Line A).

No 590 Follows the route of Metro Line A and has special facilities for disabled passengers.

No 64 Stazione Termini to St Peter's. It takes the same route as the No 40 Express but is more crowded and has more stops.
No 660 Largo Colli Albani, Via Appia Nuova and Via Appia Antica (near Tomba di Cecilia Metella).
No 714 Stazione Termini, Piazza Santa Maria Maggiore, Piazza San Giovanni in Laterano and Viale delle Terme di Caracalla (then south to EUR).
No 8 Tram Largo di Torre Argentina, Trastevere, Stazione Trastevere and Monteverde Nuovo.
No 910 Stazione Termini, Piazza della Repubblica, Via Piemonte, Via Pincians (Villa Borghese), Piazza Euclide, Palazzetto dello Sport and Piazza Mancini.

ELECTRIC BUS
In an effort to minimise pollution, the city has established several electric bus lines.
116 Via Vittorio Veneto, Piazza Barberini, Piazza di Spagna, Corso Rinascimento, Campo de' Fiori, Piazza Farnese, Via Monserrato, Via Giulia, Terminal Gianicolo, Campo de' Fiori, Corso Rinascimento, Piazza della Rotonda, Piazza Colonna, Piazza Barberini and Via Vittorio Veneto.
117 Piazza San Giovanni in Laterano, Piazza del Colosseo, Via dei Serpenti, Largo Tritonem, Piazza di Spagna, Piazza del Popolo, Via del Corso, Piazza Venezia, Piazza del Colosseo, Via Labicana and Piazza San Giovanni in Laterano. Weekdays only.
119 Piazza del Popolo, Via del Corso, Largo Goldoni, Piazza Venezia, Via del Tritone, Piazza Barberini, Via Veneto, Piazza Barberini, Piazza di Spagna, Via del Babuino and Piazza del Popolo (on Saturday and Sunday it ends at Via Vittorio Veneto).

METRO & TRAIN
Rome's two metro lines, Line A and Line B, cross at Termini, the only point at which you can change from one line to the other. Trains run approximately every five to 10 minutes between 5.30am and 11.30pm (one hour later on Saturday). However, as of January 2005 and for three years, Line A is closing for engineering works at 9pm every night. To replace it there are two temporary bus lines: MA1 from Battistini to Arco di Travertino and MA2 from Viale G Washington (off Piazzale Flaminio) to Anagnina.

All the metro stations on Line B have wheelchair access, except for Circo Massimo, Colosseo and Cavour (direction Laurentina). On Line A Cipro-Musei Vaticani Station is one of the few stations equipped with such facilities.

In addition to the metro, Rome has an overground rail network. It is useful only if you are heading out of town to the Castelli Romani (p188), the beaches at Lido di Ostia or the ruins at Ostia Antica (p178).

NIGHT BUS
Rome's night bus service is pretty comprehensive: there are more than 20 lines, most of which pass Termini and/or Piazza Venezia. Usually departures occur every 30 minutes, with buses marked with an N after the number. Night bus stops have a blue owl symbol.

The most useful routes:
29N Piramide (Piazzale Ostiense), Ponte Vittorio Emanuele II, Piazza Risorgimento, Viale Belle Arti, Piazza Ungheria, Viale Regina Margherita, Piazza Porta Maggiore, Piazza Porta San Giovanni, Piazza del Colosseo and Piramide.
40N Same route as Metro Line B.
55N Same route as Metro Line A.
78N Piazzale Clodio, Piazzale Flaminio, Piazza Cavour, Corso Rinascimento, Via delle Botteghe Oscure (Largo di Torre Argentina), Piazza Venezia, Via Nazionale and Stazione Termini.

Taxi
Rome's taxi drivers are no better or worse than in any other city. Some will try to fleece you, others won't. To minimise the risk make sure your taxi is licensed and metered, and always go with the metered fare, never an arranged price. Daytime trips within the centre of Rome can cost anywhere from €5 to €20. Any more and you're probably being taken for a ride.

If you have a problem, get the driver's name and licence number from the plaque on the inside of the rear door and call his/her taxi company, the number of which will be on the outside of the driver's door.

Hailing a cab doesn't work in Rome. You must either wait at a taxi rank or telephone for one. In the *centro storico* you can find these at: Largo di Torre Argentina, the Pantheon, Corso del Rinascimento and Piazza Navona, Piazza di Spagna, Largo Goldoni, Piazza del Popolo, Piazza Venezia, the Colosseum, at Piazza GG Belli in Trastevere and near the Vatican at Piazza del Pio XII and Piazza Risorgimento. Remember, though, that when you call for a cab, the meter is switched on straight away and you pay for the cost of the journey from wherever the driver receives the call. To phone, try:
☎ 06 35 70
☎ 06 66 45
☎ 06 88 22
☎ 06 41 57
☎ 06 49 94
☎ 06 55 51

LAZIO

With a capital like Rome it's not surprising that the rest of Lazio is somewhat overshadowed. But get out of the capital and you'll discover a region that's not only beautiful – hilly in the north, parched and rugged in the south – but also rich in history and culture.

The most obvious place to start is Ostia Antica, imperial Rome's ruined port town. Similarly impressive are the ruins of Emperor Hadrian's palatial complex (Villa Adriana) near Tivoli. Both are an easy day trip from Rome.

To see something *really* old, however, head north to Etruria, the ancient land of the Etruscans. Cerveteri and Tarquinia were important centres and it's here that you'll find some strange and beautiful Etruscan tombs. Nearby, Viterbo retains enough of its medieval core to show what it must have been like in its 13th-century golden age.

In summer overheated Romans cool down at the volcanic lakes of Bolsena and Bracciano, both a better option than the polluted and overcrowded beaches to the west of Rome. Still, if it's the sea you want, head south to the long sandy beaches of Sabaudia and Sperlonga.

Wine buffs will enjoy Frascati, the smartest of the towns in the Castelli Romani Hills, just south of Rome. Further afield the dramatic monasteries at Subiaco and Monte Cassino are architecturally audacious as well as historically important.

Almost everywhere in Lazio is accessible by public transport, usually by bus in the hilly interior, but you will need plenty of patience to travel this way. Your own wheels will certainly make things easier. However, be warned that Romans are great day trippers and in the warmer months Sunday traffic can be appalling as thousands choreograph their return to Rome to coincide with everyone else's.

OSTIA ANTICA

Founded by the Romans in the 4th century BC at the mouth of the River Tiber, Ostia became a great port and later a strategic centre for defence and trade. Decline arrived in the 5th century AD when barbarian invasions and the outbreak of malaria led to the abandonment of the city, and its slow

---

CHEAP BUS & TRAIN TICKETS

The best way to travel by public transport in Lazio is to arm yourself with a daily *biglietto integrato regionale giornaliero* (BIRG) ticket. These tickets allow unlimited travel on all city and regional transport, including buses, trains (but not including Fiumicino airport services), trams and, in Rome, the metro. They're priced according to zones: the most expensive, zone 7, costs €10.50; the cheapest, zone 1, €2.50. Tickets are available from *tabacchi*.

---

burial – up to 2nd-floor level – in river silt, thanks to which it's survived so well. Pope Gregory IV re-established the town in the 9th century AD.

Information about the town and ruins is available from the Rome Tourist Board office in Rome (see p94), or online at www.ostiaantica.net.

There is a good café and bookshop within the ruins complex, which makes an atmospheric spot for a picnic, even if technically you're not allowed to bring food into the site.

Sights

The beautifully preserved **ruins** (☎ 06 563 58 099; www.itnw.roma.it/ostia/scavi in Italian; Viale dei Romagnoli 717; admission €4.20; ☺ 8.30am-6pm Tue-Sun Apr-Oct, to 5pm Tue-Sun Mar, to 4pm Tue-Sun Jan, Feb, Nov & Dec) are spread out and you'll need a few hours to do them justice.

In contrast to Pompeii, which was a wealthy resort town, Ostia was a busy working port and the clearly discernible ruins of restaurants, laundries, shops, houses and public meeting places give a good impression of what life must have been like. The main thoroughfare, the **Decumanus Maximus**, runs over 1km from the city's entrance (the Porta Romana) to the Porta Marina, which originally led to the sea. Behind the restored **theatre**, built by Agrippa and later enlarged to hold 3000 people, is the **Piazzale delle Corporazioni**, the offices of Ostia's merchant guilds, which display well-preserved mosaics depicting the different interests of each business.

The 2nd-century **Casa di Diana** is a pristine example of ancient Rome's high-density housing, built when space was at a premium.

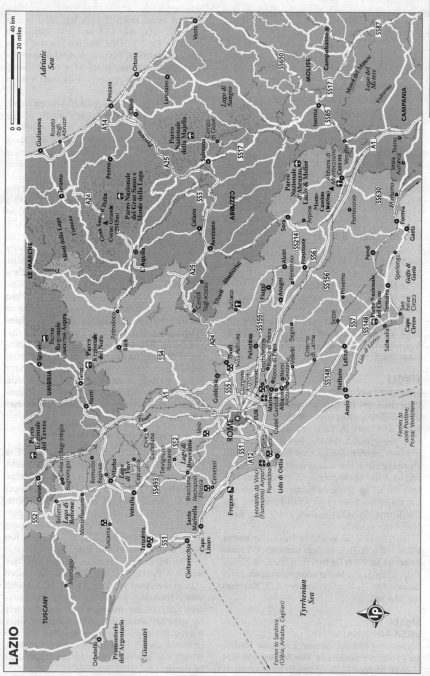

LAZIO

Nearby, the **Thermopolium** bears a striking resemblance to a modern bar.

Ostia once had several baths complexes, including the **Terme di Foro**, which were also equipped with a roomful of stone toilets (the *forica*) which still remain pretty much intact.

Continue along Via dei Dipinti to reach the **museum** (⌚ 9am-1.30pm & 2.15-6.30pm Tue-Sun Apr-Oct, 9am-5.30pm Tue-Sun Mar, 9am-4.30pm Tue-Sun Jan, Feb, Nov & Dec), which houses statues and sarcophagi excavated on site.

Near the entrance to the excavations is the **Castello di Giulio II** (☎ 06 563 58 024; Piazza della Rocca; guided tours free; ⌚ 9am-12.45pm Tue-Sun, 2.30-4.15pm Tue & Thu), an impressive example of 15th-century military architecture.

Getting There & Away

From Rome, take Metro Line B to Piramide, then the Ostia Lido train from Stazione Porta San Paolo (next to the metro station). Trains leave about every half-hour and the trip takes approximately 30 minutes. It is covered by the standard BIT tickets (see p176).

The ruins are also easy to reach by car. Take Via del Mare, which runs parallel to Via Ostiense, and follow the signs for the *scavi* (ruins).

TIVOLI

pop 49,254 / elev 225m

Pass through Rome's scruffy eastern suburbs and you soon come to the busy hilltop town of Tivoli. A Roman resort and summer playground for the Renaissance rich, it's best known for its two Unesco World Heritage sites: the monumental Villa Adriana and the 16th-century Villa d'Este. The latter with its terraced gardens and ornate fountains is easier to get to and prettier, but the former is what makes a day trip here really worthwhile.

Information is available from the **tourist office** (☎ 0774 31 12 49; Largo Garibaldi; ⌚ 8.30am-2.30pm Tue-Sat, 3-6pm Tue-Thu), near the Cotral bus stop, or from the **tourist information point** (Piazza Nazione Unite; ⌚ 10am-3pm Mon-Wed & Fri, 10am-5pm Thu, Sat & Sun).

Sights

VILLA ADRIANA

Something of a misnomer, Emperor Hadrian's summer residence **Villa Adriana** (☎ 0774 53 02 03; admission €6.50; ⌚ 9am-1hr before sunset) is more a small town than a big villa. It was built between AD 118 and 134 and, even given the excess of the Roman Empire, it set new standards of luxury. A model near the entrance gives you some idea of the scale of the original complex, which you'll need several hours to explore.

A great traveller and enthusiastic architect, Hadrian personally designed much of the complex, taking inspiration from buildings he'd seen around the world. The **Pecile**, a large porticoed pool area where you now enter and where the emperor used to stroll after lunch, was a reproduction of a building in Athens. Similarly, the **Canopo** is a copy of the sanctuary of Serapis near Alexandria, with a long canal of water, originally surrounded by Egyptian statues, representing the Nile.

To the east of the pecile is one of the highlights of the complex, Hadrian's private retreat, the **Teatro Marittimo**. Built on an island in an artificial pool, it was originally a minivilla accessible only by swing bridges, which the emperor would have raised when he felt like a dip. Nearby, the fish pond is encircled by an underground gallery where Hadrian liked to wander. There's also nymphaeums, temples and barracks, and a museum displaying the latest discoveries from ongoing excavations. Archaeologists have found features such as a heated bench with steam pipes under the sand and a network of subterranean service passages for horses and carts.

VILLA D'ESTE

More impressive outside than in, **Villa d'Este** (☎ 0774 31 20 70; Piazza Trento; admission €6.50; ⌚ 8.30am-6.30pm Tue-Sun Apr-Sep, 8.30am-4.30pm Tue-Sun Oct-Mar) is a former Benedictine convent that Lucrezia Borgia's son, Ippolito d'Este, transformed into a sumptuous pleasure palace in 1550. From 1865 to 1886 it was home to Franz Liszt and inspired his composition *Fountains of the Villa d'Este*.

The Mannerist frescoes in the villa are worth a fleeting glance but it's the elaborate garden that you come for: terraces with water-spouting gargoyles, shady pathways and spectacular fountains powered solely by gravitational force. One fountain once played the organ, another imitated the call of birds. Don't miss the Rometta fountain, which has reproductions of the landmarks of Rome.

Getting There & Away

Tivoli is 30km east of Rome and is accessible by Cotral bus from outside the Ponte Mammolo station on Metro Line B. Buses depart at least every 20 minutes and the one-hour journey costs €1.60.

To get to Villa Adriana take the CAT shuttle bus No 4X from Largo Garibaldi in Tivoli town centre to the entrance of the villa.

By car you can either take Via Tiburtina or, to save yourself some time, the Rome–L'Aquila autostrada (A24).

ETRUSCAN SITES

The north of Lazio was an important Etruscan stronghold. Dating to around 800 BC, the Etruscans developed a highly cultured society using sophisticated architectural and artistic techniques which the Romans later adapted and claimed as their own. They were a major thorn in Roman flanks until the 3rd and 4th century BC when successive waves of legionnaires swept aside the last Etruscan defences.

For the best Etruscan treasures, head to Tarquinia and Cerveteri, two of the major city-states in the Etruscan League. Ideally do this while reading DH Lawrence's *Etruscan Places* in *DH Lawrence and Italy* (published by Penguin).

Cerveteri

pop 29,373 / elev 81m

Although it's pretty enough, the real reason to come to Cerveteri is to visit its Unesco-listed Etruscan tombs.

Ceveteri, or Kysry to the Etruscans and Caere to Latin-speakers, was one of the most important commercial centres in the Mediterranean from the 7th to the 5th century BC. However, as Roman power grew so Cerveteri's fortunes faded, and in 358 BC the city was annexed by Rome.

The first half of the 19th century saw the first tentative archaeological explorations in the area and in 1911 systematic excavations began in earnest.

For information about the site, pay a visit to the **tourist information point** (☎ 06 995 52 637; Piazza Aldo Moro; ✆ 10am-12.30pm & 4.30-6.30pm) at the top of the hill, near the *centro storico*. From here you can get an hourly shuttle bus (€0.80 one way) to the **Necropoli di Banditaccia** (Banditaccia Necropolis; ☎ 06 994 00 01; Via del Necropoli; admission €4; ✆ 9am-7pm Tue-Sun summer, 9am-4pm

Tue-Sun winter), the tomb complex 2km out of town. The tombs are built into *tumoli* (mounds of earth with carved stone bases), laid out in the form of a town, with streets, squares and terraces of 'houses'. The result is a strange and haunting landscape. Signs indicate the path to follow and some of the major tombs, including the 4th-century-BC **Tomba dei Rilievi**, are decorated with painted reliefs of cooking implements and other household items.

Treasures taken from the tombs can be seen in the Vatican Museums (p134) and Museo Nazionale Etrusco di Villa Giulia (p132) in Rome, and in Cerveteri's medieval town centre at the **Museo Nazionale di Cerveteri** (☎ 06 994 13 54; Piazza Santa Maria; admission €4; ✆ 9am-7pm Tue-Sun). On the same square is the **Antica Locanda Le Ginestre** (☎ 06 994 06 72; Piazza Santa Maria 5; 1st/2nd courses €10/18; ✆ Tue-Sun), a family-run restaurant whose food induces diners to travel from Rome. Pasta and desserts are all homemade and the imaginative dishes are prepared with organically grown local produce.

Cerveteri is easily accessible from Rome by Cotral bus (75 minutes, half-hourly) from outside the Lepanto stop on Metro Line A. Buy the regional 24-hour ticket (BIRG) for €6. By car take either Via Aurelia (SS1) or the Civitavecchia autostrada (A12) and exit at Cerceteri-Ladispoli. The journey should take approximately 40 minutes.

Tarquinia

pop 15,472 / elev 169m

Further up the coast, Tarquinia is the most famous of Lazio's Etruscan centres. It is best known for its beautiful painted tombs, it also has the best Etruscan museum outside of Rome and a suggestive medieval quarter. Legend suggests that the town was founded towards the end of the Bronze Age in the 12th century BC. Later home to the Tarquin kings of Rome before the creation of the Roman Republic, it reached its prime in the 4th century BC, before a century of struggle ended with surrender to Rome in 204 BC.

ORIENTATION & INFORMATION

Whether travelling by car or bus, you arrive at the medieval gate, the Barriera San Giusto, just outside the main entrance to the town. The **tourist information office** (☎ 0766 85

63 84; info@tarquinia@apt.it; Piazza Cavour 1; ⏰ 8am-2pm Mon-Sat) is on your left as you walk through the medieval ramparts.

SIGHTS

Within a stone's throw of the Barriera San Giusto, the 15th-century Palazzo Vitelleschi houses the impressive **Museo Nazionale Tarquiniese** (☎ 0766 85 60 36; Piazza Cavour; admission €4, incl necropolis €6.50; ⏰ 8.30am-7.30pm Tue-Sun). Located within the museum you will find frescoes removed from nearby excavations, including a beautiful terracotta frieze of winged horses (the Cavalli Alati, which are currently being restored), sarcophagi, jewellery and some plates whose saucy illustrations would surely have put the Etruscans off their peas (they're in Sala 6 on the ground floor). Also on the ground floor, in Sala 9, the *sarcofogo con cerbiatto* is a model of 4th-century BC workmanship, showing a half-naked reclining woman holding a plate from which a long-necked dog (the *cerbiatto*) is drinking.

To see the famous painted tombs *in situ*, however, head for the **necropolis** (☎ 0766 85 63 08; admission €4, incl Museo Nazionale Tarquiniese €6.50; ⏰ 8.30am-7.30pm summer, 8.30am-2pm winter), just a 2km hike out of town (from Piazza Cavour take Via Umberto I, pass through the Porta Romana and follow Via IV Novembre until you see the tombs on your left). Almost 6000 tombs have been excavated since the first digs in 1489, of which 60 are painted. Now protected by Unesco, the tombs have suffered centuries of exposure and are now maintained at constant temperatures. They are visible only through glass partitions. On any given day only a selection are open for viewing by the public. There are some beautiful hunting scenes in the Tomba della Caccia e della Pesca, while the Tomba dei Tori, one of the oldest tombs, has scenes of Achilles in action, as well as a smattering of smut.

Back in town, the medieval centre is a pleasant place for a stroll and offers some sweeping views of the rolling countryside from the top of Alberata Dante Alighieri above Piazza Matteoti.

If you have a car, you can get to the scarce remains of the Etruscan acropolis of **Tarxuna**, on the crest of Civita Hill nearby, where a large temple, the **Ara della Regina**, has been excavated.

SLEEPING & EATING

It's a long day trip from Rome to Tarquinia; if you prefer to stay overnight it's advisable to book ahead.

Hotel San Marco (☎ 0766 84 22 34; www.san-marco.com; Piazza Cavour 18; s/d €50/65) Opposite the Museo Nazionale Tarquiniese, this friendly little hotel has bright, unfussy rooms on top of a gaudy American-style bar. It's not the most peaceful spot in town.

Hotel all'Olivo (☎ 0766 85 73 18; info@hotel-allolivo.it; Via Togliatti 13/15; s/d with breakfast €50/80, pizzas from €6, 1st/2nd courses from €7/8) In the newer part of town downhill from the historic centre, the Hotel all'Olivo is a bland modern structure with bland modern rooms. On the plus side, rooms are comfortable and the hotel restaurant serves huge helpings of delicious food.

Tuscia Tirrenica (☎ 0766 86 42 94; www.campingtuscia.it; Viale delle Nereidi; person/tent/car €10/9/5; ⏰ May-Sep; 🐾) On the coast 5km from the medieval town, this is a big, well-equipped camp site. Among the facilities there's a swimming pool, supermarket and tennis court.

Trattoria Arcadia (☎ 0766 85 55 01; Via Mazzini 6; 1st/2nd courses from €5/6) Tucked away in a dark side street, this simple trattoria is one of many in the *centro storico* that serves platefuls of tasty pasta and the usual array of meat dishes.

GETTING THERE & AWAY

From Rome, Cotral buses leave approximately every hour from the Saxa Rubra station on the Ferrovia Roma-Nord train line arriving at the Barriera San Giusto. The 1½-hour journey costs €3.80.

By car, take the autostrada for Civitavecchia and then the Via Aurelia (SS1). Tarquinia is about 90km northwest of Rome.

CIVITAVECCHIA

pop 50,068

There's no compelling reason to come to Civitavecchia other than to take a ferry to Sardinia. It's not an unpleasant place, there's simply not much to do. Established by Emperor Trajan in AD 106, it was later conquered by the Saracens, but regained importance as a papal stronghold in the 16th century. The medieval town was almost completely destroyed by bombing during WWII.

In 1995 Civitavecchia hit Italian headlines when a statue of the Madonna started crying tears of blood. Tests revealed that the tears were in fact human blood and although the Vatican has yet to rule on the authenticity of the miracle, the statue still attracts crowds of pilgrims. To join them take a Line A bus from the city centre to Pantano, 5km away, and ask for the Chiesa di Sant'Agostino.

Orientation & Information

The port is about a 400m walk from the train station. As you leave the station, turn right into Viale Garibaldi and follow the road along the seafront. Near the Michelangelo fortress at the western end of the seafront there's a **tourist information point** (☎ 0766 2 53 48; Viale Garibaldi; ☺ 8.30am-1pm Mon-Sat, 3-6pm Tue, Wed & Fri).

Getting There & Away

TO/FROM ROME

Cotral buses from Rome to Civitavecchia leave from outside the Lepanto station on Metro Line A about every 40 minutes. Journey time is nearly two hours and tickets cost €3.50. Alternatively, trains run regularly between Civitavecchia and Stazione Termini in Rome (€4.10, 1¼ hours, every 30 minutes).

By car, take the A12 autostrada from Rome.

FERRIES TO/FROM SARDINIA

From Civitavecchia, ferries sail for Olbia (eight hours), Arbatax (10 hours) and Cagliari (14 to 17 hours) in Sardinia. Departure times and prices change every year so you should always check ahead. All fares quoted are for a 2nd-class deck ticket.

Tirrenia (☎ 199 12 31 99; www.tirrenia.it) sails to Olbia (low/high season €15.80/17.90), Arbatax (low/high season €20.70/25.75) and Cagliari (low/high season €24.40/30.55). Add €2.55 tax to these prices when departing from Civitavecchia.

For Olbia, **Moby** (☎ 199 30 30 40; www.moby.it) also has ferries (from €17 to €40) and fast ferries (€25 to €54).

Tickets can be purchased at travel agencies and at the Stazione Marittima in Civitavecchia. If travelling in high season be sure to book well in advance.

Trenitalia also runs two daily ferries to Olbia; the fare is about €15 but you cannot book in advance and availability cannot be guaranteed.

VITERBO

pop 59,354 / elev 327m

Despite sustaining heavy bomb damage in WWII, Viterbo is Lazio's best-preserved medieval town and makes a good base for exploring the region's hilly north. For travellers with less time, it's an easy and rewarding day trip from Rome.

Founded by the Etruscans and eventually taken over by Rome, Viterbo developed into an important medieval centre, and in the 13th century became the residence of the popes. Papal elections were held in the Gothic Palazzo dei Papi where, in 1271, the entire college of cardinals was briefly imprisoned. The story goes that after three years of deliberation the cardinals still hadn't elected a new pope. Mad with frustration, the Viterbesi locked the dithering priests in a turreted hall and starved them into electing Pope Gregory X.

Apart from its historical appeal, Viterbo is famous for its therapeutic hot springs. The best known is the sulphurous Bulicame pool, mentioned by Dante in the *Divine Comedy*.

Orientation

Viterbo's walled *centro storico* is small and best covered on foot. From Stazione Porta Roma it's a short walk along Viale Armando Diaz to Porta Romana, one of the city's medieval gates. Go through it and follow Via Giuseppe Garibaldi down to Piazza Fontana Grande. Keep going along Via Cavour and you arrive at Piazza del Plebiscito, the core of the historic centre. Here you have three choices: turn right into Via Roma and its extension Corso Italia, an elegant shopping street; take Via San Lorenzo for the Cathedral and Palazzo dei Papi; or continue down Via F Ascenzi to Piazza Martiri d'Ungheria – most of the hotels are in the area northeast of this huge and unlovely square.

The intercity bus station is somewhat inconveniently located at Riello, which is a few kilometres out of town.

Information

Internet Italia (☎ 0761 30 93 73; Via Cavour 73; per hr €2.40; ☺ 10am-9pm Mon-Fri, 10am-8pm Sat)
Post office (☎ 0761 30 48 06; Via F Ascenzi) Opposite the tourist office.
Tourist information office Stazione Porta Romana (☎ 0761 30 47 95; www.provincia.vt.it in Italian; Via

ROME & LAZIO

VITERBO

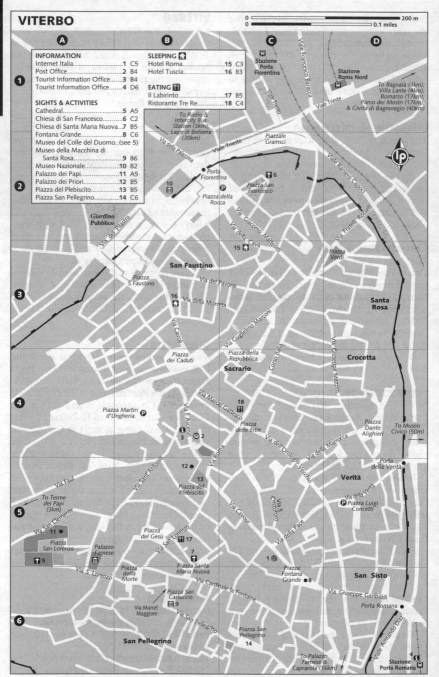

INFORMATION	
Internet Italia	1 C5
Post Office	2 B4
Tourist Information Office	3 B4
Tourist Information Office	4 D6

SIGHTS & ACTIVITIES	
Cathedral	5 A5
Chiesa di San Francesco	6 C2
Chiesa di Santa Maria Nuova	7 B5
Fontana Grande	8 C6
Museo del Colle del Duomo	(see 5)
Museo della Macchina di Santa Rosa	9 B6
Museo Nazionale	10 B2
Palazzo dei Papi	11 A5
Palazzo dei Priori	12 B5
Piazza del Plebiscito	13 B5
Piazza San Pellegrino	14 C6

SLEEPING	
Hotel Roma	15 C3
Hotel Tuscia	16 B3

EATING	
Il Labirinto	17 B5
Ristorante Tre Re	18 C4

Romiti; 9.30am-1pm & 3-6pm); Via F Ascenzi (☎ 0761 32 59 92; 10am-1pm & 4-6pm Mon-Sat) Ask for the useful booklet *Ospitalità Tuscia*.

Sights

PIAZZA DEL PLEBISCITO

Flanked by elegant palazzi, this Renaissance piazza is dominated by the imposing **Palazzo dei Priori** (Piazza del Plebiscito; admission free; 9am-1pm & 3-6pm). Now home to the town council, it's worth a quick look for the 16th-century frescoes which colourfully depict Viterbo's ancient origins. You'll find the best in the Sala Regia on the 1st floor. Outside, the elegant courtyard and fountain were added two centuries after the palazzo was built in 1460.

CATHEDRAL & PALAZZO DEI PAPI

For an idea of how rich Viterbo once was, head to Piazza San Lorenzo, the religious heart of the medieval city. It was here that the cardinals came to vote for their popes and pray in the 12th-century **cathedral** (Cattedrale di San Lorenzo; ☎ 0761 32 54 62; Piazza San Lorenzo), currently closed for restoration. Built originally to a simple Romanesque design, it owes its current Gothic look to a 14th-century makeover. Next door, the **Museo del Colle del Duomo** (admission incl Sala del Conclave in Palazzo Papale €3; 9.30am-12.30pm & 3.30-5.30pm) displays a small collection of religious artefacts.

On the northern side of the square, the 13th-century **Palazzo dei Papi** (☎ 0761 34 17 16) was built to entice the papacy away from Rome. Head up the stairs to the graceful Gothic *loggia* (colonnade) to peer into the **Sala del Conclave**, the hall where five popes were elected. To get inside you'll need to phone to arrange a time.

CHIESA DI SANTA MARIA NUOVA

The oldest church in Viterbo, the Romanesque **Chiesa di Santa Maria Nuova** (Piazza Santa Maria Nuova; 10am-1pm & 3-5pm) was restored to its original form after bomb damage in WWII. Of particular note are the cloisters, which are believed to date from an earlier period.

MEDIEVAL QUARTER

The remarkably well-preserved medieval quarter lies to the south of Via Cardinale la Fontaine. Wander down Via San Pellegrino with its low-slung arches and claustrophobic grey houses to the pint-sized but perfectly formed **Piazza San Pellegrino**.

While in the area, pop into the **Museo della Macchina di Santa Rosa** (☎ 0761 34 51 57; Via San Pellegrino 60; admission €1; 10am-1pm & 4-7pm Wed-Sun) to learn how the Viterbesi let their hair down. The museum documents the history of the Machine of St Rose, the 30m-high construction that is carted around town at the annual festival on 3 September.

OTHER SIGHTS

For a shot of Etruscan culture, head to the **Museo Nazionale** (☎ 0761 32 59 29; Piazza della Rocca; admission €2; 8.30am-7.30pm Tue-Sun) by the northern entrance to the town. Not a big place, it has an interesting collection of Etruscan artefacts taken from local digs and, on the 1st floor, an impressive series of statues dedicated to the Muses.

A short walk away from the museum is the **Chiesa di San Francesco** (☎ 0761 34 16 96; Piazza San Francesco; 8am-noon & 3.30-7pm), a Gothic church containing the tombs of two popes: Clement IV (died 1268) and Adrian V (died 1276); both are lavishly decorated, notably that of Adrian, which features Cosmati work.

On the other side of town, the **Museo Civico** (☎ 0761 34 82 75; Piazza Crispi; admission €3; 9am-7pm Tue-Sun) features yet more Etruscan goodies and a small art gallery, the highlight of which is Sebastiano del Piombo's *Pietà*.

In the piazza of the same name, the unimaginatively titled **Fontana Grande** (Big Fountain) is the oldest and largest of Viterbo's Gothic fountains.

Sleeping & Eating

Hotel Roma (☎ 0761 22 72 74; fax 0761 30 55 07; Via della Cava 26; s/d €42/60; P) A friendly family-run hotel, this modest place near Piazza della Rocca has slightly fading brown rooms that lack style but do the job. If you're coming by car it's worth paying the €5 for parking.

Hotel Tuscia (☎ 0761 34 44 00; www.tusciahotel .com; Via Cairoli 41; s/d €52/80; P) A step up in price and comfort, the rooms at the three-star Tuscia are large and light, if uninspired. Some have balconies overlooking the unexceptional Via Cairoli. Parking is available on request and costs an extra €7.

Ristorante Tre Re (☎ 0761 30 46 19; Via Macel Gattesco 3; 1st/2nd courses €6/7) A historic Viterbo trattoria, the Tre Re dishes up steaming plates of local specialities. None is more typical than the *acquapazza Viterbese*, a scalding soup of chicory, potatoes and tomatoes with a poached egg swimming on top. Portions are huge and the prices very reasonable.

Il Labirinto (☎ 0761 30 70 26; Via San Lorenzo 46; pizzas €5.50, 1st/2nd courses €6/7) Despite the brick arches and wood-beamed ceiling this place is strangely characterless. Having said that, it serves decent enough food. Pizzas are massive, antipasti tasty and the pasta typically Roman – so expect dishes such as *carbonara* and *all'amatriciana*.

Getting There & Away

From Rome, Cotral buses (€3.30, 1½ hours, every 30 minutes) depart from the Saxa Rubra station on the Ferrovia Roma-Nord train line. Catch the train to Saxa Rubra from Piazzale Flaminio (just north of Piazza del Popolo). In Viterbo, make sure to get off at Porta Romana otherwise you'll find yourself at the intercity bus station at Riello, a few kilometres northwest of the town. If this happens, catch city bus No 11 into town.

By car, Viterbo is a straight drive up Via Cassia (SS2: about 1½ hours). Enter the old town through the Porta Romana onto Via Giuseppe Garibaldi, which becomes Via Cavour. The best bet for parking is either Piazza Martiri d'Ungheria or Piazza della Rocca.

Direct, if slow, Trenitalia trains depart hourly from Rome's Ostiense, Trastevere and San Pietro stations for Stazione Porta Romana. The journey takes at least 1½ hours and costs €4.10.

AROUND VITERBO

Viterbo's thermal springs are about 3km west of town. The easiest to get to are the **Terme dei Papi** (☎ 0761 35 01; www.termedeipapi .it in Italian; Strada Bagni 12; pool Mon-Sat €12, Sun €15; ⏱ year-round), where you can take a dip in the sulphurous pool, have an invigorating massage (from €22) or treat yourself to a gloopy mud bath (about €60). Take city bus No 2 from Piazza Martiri d'Ungheria.

You won't find much mud in the magnificent gardens at **Villa Lante**, 4km northeast of Viterbo at Bagnaia. Considered among the finest Renaissance gardens in Italy they form part of the large public **park** (☎ 0761 28 80 08; admission €2; ⏱ 8.30am-1hr before sunset Tue-Sun) that surrounds the 16th-century villa. To get to Bagnaia take city bus No 6 from Piazza dei Caduti in Viterbo.

Similarly Renaissance in look and style is the grandiose **Palazzo Farnese** (☎ 0761 64 60 52; admission €2; ⏱ 8.30am-6.45pm Tue-Sun) at Caprarola, southeast of Viterbo. Designed by Vignal and decorated by some of the finest Mannerist artists of the day, it makes quite an impression. Not to miss are the frescoes by Taddeo and Federico Zuccari in the Sala del Concilio di Trento. Seven buses daily leave from the Riello bus station just outside Viterbo for Caprarola; the last bus returns at 6.35pm from Caprarola. Tickets cost €1.60.

At Bomarzo, 17km northeast of Viterbo, the **Parco dei Mostri** (☎ 0761 92 40 29; admission €8; ⏱ 8am-sunset) will entertain children and adults alike. The park of the 16th-century Palazzo Orsini is peopled by gigantic and grotesque sculptures, including an ogre, giant and even a dragon. Also of interest here are the octagonal *tempietto* (little temple) and the crooked house, built without using right angles. From Viterbo, catch the Cotral bus from near Viale Trento to Bomarzo (€1.60, five daily), then follow the signs to Palazzo Orsini.

Images of **Civita di Bagnoregio** feature in hundreds of publicity posters for the province of Viterbo. An abandoned village stuck on top of a huge rock in the middle of a barren ravine, it certainly makes a great picture. However, it's not quite as abandoned as it seems. Its original inhabitants might have deserted *en masse* after erosion led many buildings to collapse, but it has since been restored and is becoming an increasingly popular tourist attraction.

There's not much to do other than enjoy the views and breathe the surreal air, but if you want to stay the night book one of the three rooms at the **Civita B&B** (☎ 0761 76 00 16; Via della Fraticella 4; d €68), a warm little place above the Trattoria Antico Forno. Run by the same people, the trattoria serves a decent, if unexciting, tourist menu (€15).

The only way to reach the village is by a footbridge from Bagnoregio (north of Viterbo). There's a car park at the base of the walkway (€1 per hour) or you can catch one of the shuttle buses from Piazza Battaglini in Bagnoregio to the bridge. There are seven daily Cotral buses going between Viterbo and Bagnoregio (€1.60).

THE LAKES

Sunk into the volcanic landscape north of Rome are several lakes, all of which are attractive summer destinations. Less crowded than Lazio's beaches, they still get very busy, particularly on hot weekends.

Lago di Bracciano

Taking its name from the pretty cobbled town of Bracciano, Lago di Bracciano has for centuries provided Rome with drinking water. For information on the lake and its environs, ask at the **tourist information kiosk** (☎ 06 998 40 062; Piazza IV Novembre; ⊗ 9am-1pm Tue-Sun & 3-6pm Tue & Thu) in Bracciano's town centre.

Most people come to mess around in the water but if you need a castle to visit, head for the **Castello Orsini-Odelscalchi** (☎ 06 998 04 348; Piazza Castello; admission €6; ⊗ 10am-noon & 3-5pm Tue-Sun), built by the Orsini family in the late 15th century.

On the northern edge of the lake is the picturesque town of Trevignano Romano, with its fetching waterfront and modest beach.

There's no shortage of trattorie here. **Trattoria del Castello** (☎ 06 998 04 339; Piazza Mazzini 1; 1st/2nd courses €6/7), opposite the entrance to the castle in Bracciano, plays Blondie and Blink 182 on the stereo and serves imaginative dishes prepared with fresh ingredients. Particularly yummy is the *tonnarelli cacio, pepe e cozze* (pasta with cheese, pepper and mussels).

Vino e Camino (☎ 06 998 03 433; Piazza Mazzini 11; 1st/2nd courses from €9/9; ⊗ Tue-Sun) is a little more upmarket. This *enoteca* offers a carefully selected wine list to accompany the lovingly prepared regional classics that constitute much of the menu. Typical dishes include *pasta con la zucca* (pasta with pumpkin), *porchetta* (roast suckling pig) and *millefoglie al caffè* (a cake of thin sheets of puff pastry divided by layers of coffee cream).

A simple day trip from Rome, Bracciano is easy to get to by bus. Hourly Cotral coaches depart from outside the Lepanto Metro station in Rome arriving in Piazza Pasqualetti, east of the town centre. The 45-minute trip costs €2.

By car, take Via Braccianense (SS493) for Bracciano, or take Via Cassia (SS2) and then follow the signs to Trevignano Romano.

Lago di Bolsena

A short 30km hop from Viterbo, the Lago di Bolsena is the largest of Lazio's lakes. The main town is Bolsena itself, a charming place which, despite a heavy hotel presence, retains its medieval character.

Like many Italian towns, Bolsena has a miracle story. In 1263 a priest saying Mass got the surprise of his life when blood began to drip from the bread he was blessing. Science was unable to disprove the miracle and Pope Urban IV promptly founded the festival of **Corpus Domini** to celebrate: each June the townspeople hold a 3km procession and decorate the town with flowers.

For details of the festival and other information, go to the **tourist office** (☎ 0761 79 99 23; Piazza Matteoti; ⊗ 9.30am-12.30pm & 3.30-6.30pm daily May-Sep, 9.30am-12.30pm Mon-Sat Oct-Apr) at the bottom of the medieval quarter.

You can see four stones stained with the miraculous blood in the 11th-century **Chiesa di Santa Cristina** (☎ 0761 79 90 67; Piazza Santa Cristina; ⊗ 7.15am-12.45pm & 3.30-7.45pm Easter-Sep, 7.15am-12.30pm & 3-5.45pm Oct-Easter) in the medieval quarter. Beneath the church, the **catacombs** (admission €4; ⊗ 9.30am-noon & 3.30-6.30pm Easter-Sep, 9.30-11.30am & 3-5pm Oct-Easter) are noteworthy for a number of tombs that are still sealed.

To enjoy some spectacular views over the lake, climb up to the **Castello Monaldeschi** (☎ 0761 79 86 30; admission €3.50, panoramic walkway €2; ⊗ 10am-1pm & 4-8pm Tue-Sun summer, 10am-1pm & 3-6pm Tue-Sat winter) at the top of the hill. Originally built between the 13th and 16th centuries, the castle was pulled down by the locals in 1815 to prevent it from being taken by an invading Luciano Bonaparte. It now houses the **Museo Territoriale del Lago di Bolsena**, which is dedicated to the area's volcanic geology.

There are many hotels and camp sites by the lake.

Villaggio Camping Lido (☎ 0761 79 92 58; person/tent/car €6.10/11.50/2.60; ▣), on the lakeside, is a large camp site 1.5km from Bolsena. A self-sufficient place, it has shops, a restaurant and pizzeria and a host of sports facilities, such as tennis courts and a swimming pool.

An easy walk from the medieval quarter, the **Hotel Columbus** (☎ 0761 79 90 09; www.atihotels.it in Italian; Viale Colesanti 27; s €47-69, d €56-87) is a smart three-star pile by the lake. Rooms are modern, carpeted and for the area pretty good value for money.

If you're touring the area by car and you don't mind a drop of plonk, it's worth stopping off at **Montefiascone**, home of Est, Est, Est white wine. Local history has it, or at least the wine labels claim, that on his travels a monk wrote 'est' (it is) to indicate the places where the wine was good. On arriving at Montefiascone he was so overcome by the quality of the wine that he exclaimed 'Est! Est! Est!'. Stock up at the **Cantina di Montefiascone** (☎ 0761 25 11 30; Via Grilli 2; ⏱ 8am-1pm & 3-7pm), just off the main SS2 road into town.

From Viterbo, there are Cotral buses to Bolsena (€2, 50 minutes, hourly) leaving from the bus station at Riello. On Sunday there is only one bus that leaves around 9am (returning at around 6pm). By car, take the Via Cassia (SS2) and follow the signs.

CASTELLI ROMANI

About 20km south of Rome, the Colli Albani (Alban Hills) and their 13 towns are collectively known as the Castelli Romani. Since early Roman days they've provided a green refuge from the city and today Romans still flock to the area on hot summer weekends. The most famous towns are Castel Gandolfo, where the pope has his summer residence, and Frascati, famous for its crisp white wine.

Frascati is an easy train ride from Rome and makes a rewarding day trip. A good point of reference is the busy Piazzale Marconi, where you'll find the **tourist office** (☎ 06 942 03 31; Piazzale Marconi 1; ⏱ 8am-1pm Mon-Sat, 4-7pm Wed & Fri summer, 3-6pm Wed & Fri winter).

The large villa you see rising above the square is the 16th-century **Villa Aldobrandini**, designed by Giacomo della Porta and built by Carlo Maderno. Although the villa is not open to the public you can still have a wander in the **gardens** (⏱ 9am-1pm & 3-5pm Mon-Fri) once you have picked up a permit from the tourist office.

For a place to stay in Frascati, the **Hotel Panorama** (☎ 06 942 18 00; hotelpanoramafrasc@tisca li.it; Piazza Carlo Casini 3; s/d €50/65) lives up to its name with five white rooms offering views over Rome and beyond.

If you've got a car head up to the ruins of ancient **Tusculum**. Not a whole lot remains of this once imposing town except for a small amphitheatre, a crumbling villa and a small stretch of road leading up to the city. However, the grassy hilltop is a popular spot to do some walking and it commands some fine views.

A short drive away at **Grottaferrata** there's a 15th-century **abbey** (abbazia; ☎ 06 945 93 09; Viale San Nilo; admission free; ⏱ 8.30am-12.30pm & 4-6.30pm Tue-Sat, 8.30-10am & 4-6.30pm Sun), founded in the

11th century and now home to a congregation of Greek monks and a small museum.

Continuing southwest brings you to **Castel Gandolfo**, a smart hilltop *borgo* overlooking Lago di Albano. Dominating the town is the pope's summer residence which although closed to the public still attracts coachloads of tourists. The small *centro storico* is a lovely place for an evening stroll, and for those that are romantically inclined the **Antico Ristorante Pagnanelli** (☎ 06 936 00 04; Via A Gramsci 4; 1st/2nd courses €10/16; ⏱ Wed-Mon) is ideal. With fantastic views over the lake, high-class cuisine and a 3000-label wine list, it's a memorable place to dine. To save a return journey to Rome, pop next door for a room at **Pagnanelli Lucia** (☎ 06 936 14 22; Via A Gramsci 2; d €90).

The smaller of the two volcanic lakes in the Castelli, **Lago di Nemi** has spawned numerous legends. In ancient times it was the centre of a cult to the goddess Diana while today rumours circulate of black magic rites. Tourist officials, however, prefer to direct you to the **Museo delle Navi Romani** (☎ 06 939 80 40; Via Diana; admission €2; ⏱ 9am-6pm), built by Mussolini to house two Roman boats found in the lake. You can grab a bite to eat at the clifftop **Trattoria la Sirena del Lago** (☎ 06 936 80 20; Via del Plebiscito 26; 1st/2nd courses €7/8), where the pasta is tasty and the local wine refreshing.

Most of the towns of the Castelli Romani are accessible from Rome by Cotral bus from the Anagnina station on Metro Line A. Access between them, though, is wellnigh impossible. Trains also leave from Stazione Termini for Frascati (€1.70, 30 minutes, hourly), Castel Gandolfo (€1.70, 40 minutes, hourly) and Albano Laziale (€1.70, 50 minutes, hourly), from where you can catch a bus to Lago di Nemi.

PALESTRINA

Once an important Roman town, Palestrina stands on the slopes of Monte Ginestro, one of the foothills of the Apennines. For much of its Roman existence it was dominated by the **Santuario della Fortuna Primigenia**, a massive sanctuary dating back to the 2nd century BC. Originally built on six terraced levels and topped by a circular temple with a statue of the goddess Palestrina, it would have covered much of what is now the town's *centro storico*. However, the sanctuary has largely been built over and in the 17th century the **Palazzo Colonna Barberini** was built on its highest point. The palazzo today houses the **Museo Nazionale Archeologico Prenestino** (☎ 06 953 81 00; Piazza della Cortina; admission €3; ☽ 9am-8pm) and its important collection of Roman artefacts. Of particular interest is the spectacular Nile mosaic, a masterpiece of Hellenistic art, which came from the most sacred part of the temple (where the cathedral with its Romanesque belfry now stands). It depicts the Nile in flood from Ethiopia to Alexandria.

The **tourist office** (☎ 06 957 31 76; Piazza Santa Maria degli Angeli 2; ☽ 9am-1pm & 3-7pm) is located close to the Museo Nazionale Archeologico Prenestino in the town centre.

Palestrina is also renowned as the birthplace of the 16th-century choral composer Giovanni Pierluigi da Palestrina. His former home, the **Casa di Palestrina** (☎ 06 953 80 83; www.fondpalestrina.org; admission €2.50; ☽ 9.30am-12.30pm Tue-Sun), is now a museum as well as an important music library.

Palestrina is accessible from Rome by Cotral bus (€2, 55 minutes, half-hourly) from the Anagnina stop on Metro Line A. By car it's a straightforward 39km along Via Prenestina (SS155).

ANAGNI & ALATRI

These two hilltop towns are in the rugged, hilly area known as the Ciociara, 40 minutes' drive southeast of Rome. Both are worth a stop if you're passing through, but if you've time or energy for only one, go to **Anagni**. The birthplace of several medieval popes, its major drawcard is the 11th-century Lombard-Romanesque **cathedral** (☎ 0775 72 83 74; Via Leone XII; ☽ 9am-1pm & 4-7pm Apr-Sep, 9am-1pm & 3-6pm Oct-Mar) and more specifically the beautifully frescoed **crypt** (admission €3; ☽ entry every 15min) underneath. The vibrantly colourful frescoes were painted by Benedictine monks in the 13th century and are considered fine examples of their genre. The crypt's pavement, along with the cathedral's above, was laid by Cosmati.

Alatri was an important place during the 6th and 4th centuries BC. Its ancient 25-hectare acropolis is ringed by huge walls from the 6th-century BC, built by the town's original inhabitants, the Ernici. The atmospheric streets around the central Piazza Santa Maria Maggiore are ideal for an evening stroll.

From Rome, you'll have to change at Colleferro to get to Anagni by bus. Cotral buses for Colleferro (€2.80, 1¼ hours, eight

daily) leave from the Anagnina stop on the Metro Line A. From Colleferro, buses depart hourly for Anagni (€1, 45 minutes).

To get to Alatri, take a train to Anagni-Fiuggi (€3.30, one hour, hourly) and then the Cotral bus to Alatri (€1, hourly).

By car, both towns are signposted from the A1 Rome–Naples autostrada.

ALONG THE COAST

Unless you're after bumper-to-bumper traffic jams, polluted water and crowds of poscurs on the pull you'll be disappointed with the beaches nearest Rome: Fregene and the Lido di Ostia. The coast further south, however, is a much nicer prospect. Sabaudia and Sperlonga both boast long sandy beaches and cleaner water.

Sabaudia

Not a particularly attractive place in itself, Sabaudia is the centre of the **Parco Nazionale del Circeo** (www.parcocirceo.it in Italian; Via Carlo Alberto 107; ☽ 9.30am-1pm & 5-7pm), an 800-hectare area of sand dunes, rocky coastline, forest and wetlands. The **visitor centre** (☎ 0773 51 13 85) can provide details on activities available in the area including fishing, bird-watching, walking and cycling.

Cotral buses for Sabaudia leave from outside the Laurentina station on Metro Line B. Tickets cost €3.80.

Sperlonga

The small coastal town of Sperlonga is almost entirely given over to tourism. But that shouldn't necessarily put you off as the whitewashed *centro storico* is a trendy spot to hang out in (in summer, at least) and there are two inviting sandy beaches either side of a rocky promontory. There's a small **tourist office** (☎ 0771 55 70 00; Corso San Leone 22; ☽ 8am-2pm Mon-Fri, 2.30-5.30pm Tue & Thu) at the top of the hill.

Other than the beach, the main attraction is the **Grotta di Tiberio** (admission €2; ☽ 8.30am-7.30pm), a cave with a circular pool used by the emperor Tiberius. The remains of his villa are in front of the cave. Statues found in the cave are housed in the nearby museum.

For a place to stay and somewhere to eat, try one of the places listed below.

Albergo Major (☎ 0771 54 92 44; Via Romita I 4; s €60-90, d €80-120), just off the main seafront road into town, has decent-enough rooms and excellent facilities for beach bunnies: tone up on your tan in the solarium before heading to the hotel's private beach area.

To treat yourself to seafood so fresh it virtually wriggles off the plate, head to **Agli Archi** (☎ 0771 5 43 00; Via Ottaviano 17; 1st & 2nd courses €10), up in the medieval quarter. Signature dishes include a tantalising *linguine agli scampi* (long pasta with scampi) and *zuppa di cozze* (mussel soup).

To get to Sperlonga from Rome, take a regional train (not the intercity) from Stazione Termini to Fondi (€5.60, 1¼ hours, about 20 daily). From here, get the connecting **Piazzoli** (☎ 0771 51 90 67) bus to Sperlonga (€1, 10 minutes, eight daily).

Sperlonga is 120km from Rome by car. Take the Via Pontina (SS148) and follow signs to Terracina and then Sperlonga.

ISOLE PONTINE

Although not exactly a secret, this group of small islands between Rome and Naples is largely overlooked by international tourists. Things are changing, however, and increasing numbers of foreigners are joining the hordes of Italian visitors who holiday on Ponza and Ventotene – the only two inhabited islands. Prices are not cheap though, and budget travellers would do well to avoid the peak summer months of July and August. Note that many places shut down in winter.

The history of the islands goes back a long way. Homer refers to Ponza in the *Odyssey*, while in Roman times they were a favourite retreat for emperors and courtiers. But as the Roman Empire declined, the islands were left vulnerable to violent attacks by the Saracens and by groups from mainland Italy and the nearby Aeolian Islands. Unfaithful wives, promiscuous daughters and persecuted Christians counted among the large number of people exiled to the islands at this time.

A later golden age came in the 18th century. However, commerce flourished at the expense of the natural habitat, which was largely destroyed in the locals' rush to build and to cultivate. Today Ponza is ecologically still in pretty poor shape: there's a lot of erosion caused by terraced farming and birdhunting is virtually an obsession; migrating

---

BLAZE THE BENEDICTINE TRAIL

It's a strange but appropriate fact that St Benedict is the patron saint of engineers and speleologists. Appropriate because the father of Western monasticism actually spent three years holed up in a cave in Subiaco, a small town 63km east of Rome. Fleeing the vice that had so disgusted him as a student in Rome, he sought the gloom of the grotto to meditate and pray. During this time he attracted a large local following which eventually provoked the ire of his fellow friars and forced him onto the road.

There are today two monasteries that make the hike to Subiaco worthwhile. The first and most important is the spectacular **Monastery of St Benedict** (☎ 0774 8 50 39; ◷ 9am-12.30pm & 3-6.30pm), carved into the rock over the famous cave. Apart from its stunning setting, described by Petrarch as 'the edge of Paradise', the monastery boasts some amazingly colourful 13th- to 15th-century frescoes. Halfway down the hill from the monastery is the **Monastery of St Scholastica** (☎ 0774 8 55 25; ◷ 9am-12.30pm & 3.30-7pm), where Italy's first book was printed in 1465.

From Subiaco, St Benedict headed south until, it's said, three ravens led him to the top of Monte Cassino. Here, in 529 AD, he founded the Abbey that was to be his home until he died in 547 AD. One of the medieval world's most important Christian centres, the monumental **Abbey** (☎ 0776 31 15 29; ◷ 8.30am-12.30pm & 3.30-5pm summer, Sun winter) has been destroyed and rebuilt several times throughout its history, most recently in 1953. During WWII the Abbey was central to German efforts to stop the Allied push north. After almost six months of bitter fighting the Allies finally bombed the Abbey in May 1944 in a desperate attempt to break through. The graves of more than 1000 Polish soldiers are laid out in the Polish War Cemetery opposite the Abbey.

It's difficult to get to the monasteries in Subiaco by public transport: take a Cotral bus to Subiaco (€3.10, 1¼ hours, 29 daily) from Ponte Mammolo on Metro Line B in Rome; then it's a demanding but scenic 5km walk east of town.

For Cassino take a train from Stazione Termini (€6.70, two hours, 29 daily) and then one of the infrequent shuttle buses from Piazza San Benedetto up to the Abbey.

birds pass over on their journey between Europe and Africa. However, the islands are now under national park protection.

There is a **tourist information office** (☎ 0771 8 00 31; Via Molo Musco; ⏲ 9am-1pm & 3.30-7.30pm Apr-Sep, 9.30am-1pm Sat & Sun Oct-Mar) near the ferry embarkation point on Ponza. Exit the ferry and follow the waterfront to your left until you've virtually come full circle. On Ventotene, go to the private travel agency **Bemtilem** (☎ 0771 8 53 65; Piazza Castello 16) for information.

Sleeping & Eating

Many of the locals rent out individual rooms to tourists for much less than hotels and you'll find them touting at the port; otherwise go to the tourist information office for an authorised list. All the following places are on Ponza.

Hotel Mari (☎ 0771 80 1 01; www.hotelmari.com; Corso Pisacane 19; s/d/apt €78/148/228; ⏲ Mar-Oct) You can lie on your bed and watch the ferries pull into port at this friendly seafront hotel. Rooms are simple with few outstanding features; for the sea views you'll pay an extra €30.

Gennarino a Mare (☎ 0771 8 00 71; Via Dante 64; r €130-245, 1st/2nd courses €15/20) When Hollywood film stars drop by they don't slum it with the rest of us, they get their launches to drop them off at the terrace of this famous sea-

food restaurant. Upstairs there are 12 small but stylish rooms overhanging the sea.

Tutti Noi (☎ 0771 82 00 44; Via Dante; 1st/2nd courses €8/8.50) One of a number of trattorie on the seafront, this modest eatery serves superb seafood. To whet your appetite go for the *antipasti di mare*, a huge plate of crab, octopus and marinated salmon. To follow, the *linguine allo scoglio*, thin spaghetti with a fishy tomato sauce, is just as good.

Getting There & Around

Ponza and Ventotene are accessible by car ferry or hydrofoil from Anzio, Terracina or Formia. Timetable information is available from most travel agents and, in summer, from the Rome section of *Il Messaggero* and *Il Tempo* newspapers. Prices vary according to the point of departure, but from Terracina the three-hour daily crossing costs €25 (return).

There's a hydrofoil that runs between Ponza and Ventotene. In both cases get information from the port or the Pro Loco office.

Cars and large motorbikes are forbidden on Ponza in summer, but there's a good local bus service (tickets €1). Otherwise, you can rent a scooter at the port for about €30 per day.

Liguria, Piedmont & Valle d'Aosta

This northwestern corner of the country is a microcosm of Italy's best. This extraordinary area of Italy has traditionally been the country's political, economic and intellectual powerhouse. Liguria, Piedmont and Valle d'Aosta each have their own distinct identity, culture and history, and all reward deeper exploration. The slim coastal crescent of Liguria offers inviting Riviera resorts, picture-postcard seaside villages and some of the country's finest white wines, while its museum-studded capital, Genoa, has undergone something of a renaissance since taking on the mantle of European City of Culture for the year of 2004.

Piedmont is the traditional home of Risorgimento (the 19th-century movement to unify Italy's disparate states) and Italy's industrial achievements. In fact, Piedmont has had such success in industry that it is now second only to Lombardy in industrial production, making it one of Italy's wealthiest regions. This is reflected in the area's food and wine. Piedmont is home to the Slow Food Movement, beautiful risottos, white truffles and many more delights. There are also vineyards producing prestige reds such as Barolo and Barbaresco. The region's capital, Turin, is best known for its baroque architecture, cars and its delectable chocolate. The city will be thrust into the international spotlight in 2006 when it hosts the Winter Olympics.

At the feet of Mont Blanc and the Matterhorn, is the Valle d'Aosta, a quiet valley of hilltop castles and quaint mountain villages where a version of French (and German in parts) is spoken alongside Italian. There are plenty of on- and off-piste adventures to be had in the ski resorts both here and in northern Piedmont, while mountain bikers and walkers seeking one more trail better than the last won't be disappointed.

HIGHLIGHTS

- Raise a glass of prestigious **Barolo** (p242) or celebrate with a bubbly **Asti** (p243)
- Take a leisurely tour of the Cinque Terre villages near **La Spezia** (p211)
- Visit the **Musei di Strada Nuova** (p197) in Genoa or Turin's **Museo Nazionale del Cinema** (p230)
- Explore Genoa's eccentric **Museo delle Culture del Mondo** (p200)
- Go **whale-watching** (p202) in the Ligurian Sea
- Ski the **Milky Way** (p238) or legendary off-piste **Valle d'Aosta** (p247)
- Master orange-dodging at Ivrea's **Carnival** (p244)

- POPULATION: Liguria 1.5 million; Piedmont 4.2 million; Valle d'Aosta 120,909
- AREA: Liguria 5413 sq km; Piedmont 25,399 sq km; Valle d'Aosta 3262 sq km

LIGURIA

Stretching from Tuscany to the French border, alluring Liguria has been attracting sun-, sand- and sea-lovers ever since the days of the ancient Romans. The poets Byron and Shelley frolicked in the waves here back in the early 1800s, and were soon followed by armies of foreign holiday-makers who flocked to upmarket Anglo-inspired resorts such as San Remo and Bordighera. A later generation of moneyed jet-setters found glitzy Portofino more to their liking.

However, there is more to Liguria than just beaches. The regional capital, Genoa, is awash with excellent museums and art galleries as well as some outstanding restaurants, while the mountainous hinterland hides hilltop villages and holds plenty of scope for walkers. The Unesco-listed Cinque Terre villages, west of La Spezia, are a pure delight.

GENOA

pop 604,730

Visitors' first impressions of Genoa (Genova) are often unfavourable, whether they bus from the airport into town through the ugly industrial sprawl, or arrive at the frenetic, scruffy train stations. Genoa doesn't display its charms so easily, but given the chance to wander, explore and discover this historic, cosmopolitan and fascinating port town, you may find yourself staying much longer than you ever expected.

In the wider world, Genoa is perhaps best known as the birthplace of Christopher Columbus (1451–1506). The 500th anniversary of his discovery of America was marked with an Expo in 1992, an event which transformed the ancient Genoese harbour from a decaying backwater into a glitzy showpiece for the city. Genoa-born architect Renzo Piano was the man behind the brilliant face-lift that left Genoa with a clutch of lasting portside attractions. Genoa was named European City of Culture in 2004, an accolade that spurred on yet more renovations and additions to the cityscape, including several new museums and a metro system. Genoa celebrates another of its favourite sons, the legendary violinist Paganini, with annual music festivals.

At the heart of its old town, Genoa's infamous labyrinth of *caruggi* (dark narrow alleys), punctuated with medieval churches and Renaissance palaces, bears witness to the back-stabbing dramas and intrigues of Genoa's golden age and the bickering dynasties that made the city the spellbinding place it is today.

History

Genoa, founded in the 4th century BC, possibly derives its name from the Latin *ianua* (door). An important Roman port, it was later occupied by Franks, Saracens and the Milanese. A famous victory over Venice in 1298 led to a period of rapid growth, but quarrels between the Grimaldis, Dorias, Spinolas and other noble families of the city caused much internal disruption.

Genoa's glory days came in the 16th century, when it was known as *La Superba* (literally 'the proud' or 'haughty'). Under the rule of Imperial Admiral Andrea Doria, it benefited from Spain's American fortunes by financing Spanish exploration. This golden age lasted into the 17th century and produced many magnificent palaces filled with great works of art – the glint of gold attracted masters such as Rubens, Caravaggio and Van Dyck, whose works still adorn the city's galleries. Galeazzo Alessi (1512–72), who designed many of the city's splendid buildings, is regarded as one of the greatest architects of 16th-century northern Italy. The Age of Exploration came as a terrible blow and as the Mediterranean's mercantile importance declined so did Genoa's.

Genoa was a leading participant in the Risorgimento, and during WWII it was the first northern city to rise against Nazi occupation and the Italian Fascists towards the close of the war, liberating itself before the arrival of Allied troops.

After the war the city expanded rapidly along the coast, although, by the 1970s, decline had set in as big industries folded and port activity decreased. However, since the 1992 Expo, things have improved, with vast amounts being spent on returning the historic port area to its former glory and further city-wide renovations.

Orientation

Genoa stretches along the coast for 30km and is served by 15 train stations. The centre is tucked between the two main stations, Stazione Principe and Stazione Brignole. The main shopping strip, Via XX Settembre,

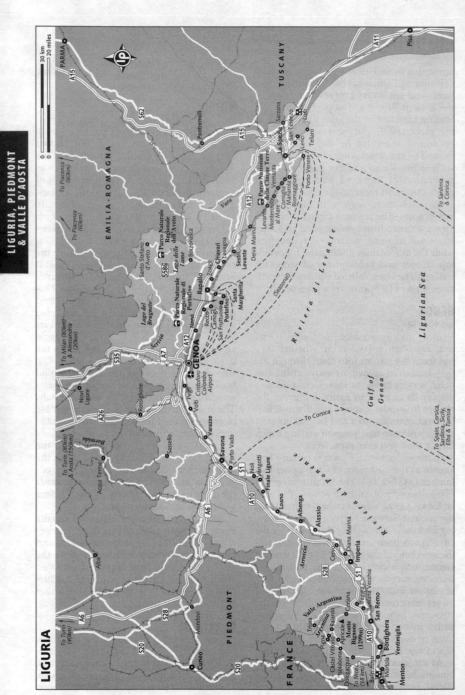

starts a short walk southwest of Stazione Brignole and spills into the city's focal point, Piazza de Ferrari. West towards the port and stretching around the waterfront towards Stazione Principe you will find the oldest Genoese quarters.

Information

BOOKSHOPS

La Feltrinelli (Map pp198-9; ☎ 010 54 08 30; Via XX Settembre 231-233r) English-language novels on the 1st floor.
Libreria Porto Antico (Map pp198-9; ☎ 010 251 8422; Palazzina Milo, Porto Antico) Good selection of English-language novels, tourist books on Genoa, maps and Lonely Planet titles.
Touring Club Italiano Genoa (TCI; Map pp198-9; ☎ 010 56 21 35; info@in-centro.it; Via XX Settembre 19r) More maps and guides.

EMERGENCY

Police station (Map pp198-9; ☎ 010 5 36 61; Via Armando Diaz 2)

INTERNET ACCESS

First-time users need a passport to register at these places; online access costs around €3 to €4 an hour.
Libreria Mondadori (Map pp198-9, Via XX Settembre 16a; per hr €3) On 1st floor of Coin department store.
Nonedove Internet Point (Map pp198-9; ☎ 010 570 48 78; cnr Corso Buenos Aires & Piazza Borgo Pila; ☼ 9.30am-8.30pm)
Touring Club Italiano Genoa (TCI; Map pp198-9; ☎ 010 56 21 35; Via XX Settembre 19r; ☼ 10am-7.30pm Mon-Fri, 10am-1.30pm & 3-7.30pm Sat)

LAUNDRY

La Maddalena (Map pp198-9; Via della Maddalena 2; ☼ 8am-8pm)
Le Bolle di Sapone (Map pp198-9; Molo Ponte Morosini 26; ☼ 6am-11pm)

LEFT LUGGAGE

Expect to pay around €3 for 24 hours.
Stazione Brignole (Map pp198-9; Piazza Giuseppe Verdi; ☼ 7am-9pm)
Stazione Principe (Map pp198-9; Piazza Acquaverde; ☼ 6am-midnight)

MEDICAL SERVICES

Ghersi (Map pp198-9; ☎ 010 54 16 61; Corso Buenos Aires 18) Night pharmacy.
Guardia Medica (☎ 010 35 40 22) Emergency doctor.
Ospedale San Martino (Map p196; ☎ 010 55 51; Largo Rosanna Benci 10) Hospital.

MONEY

Banks riddle Via Fieschi, which is off Via XX Settembre. Likewise, there are ATMs throughout the city.

POST

Post office Main post office (Map pp198-9; Piazza Piccapietra 67-9; ☼ 8am-6.30pm Mon-Sat); Stazione Principe (Map pp198-9; ☼ 8am-6.30pm Mon-Fri, 8am-12.30pm Sat)

TOURIST INFORMATION

There are the following tourist information booths.
Airport (☎ 010 601 52 47; iat.aeroporto@apt.genova.it; ☼ 9.30am-1.30pm & 2.30-5.30pm Mon-Sat, 10am-1.30pm & 2.30-5pm Sun)
City centre (Map p196; ☎ 010 24 87 11; www.apt.genova.it; Piazza Giacomo Matteotti; ☼ 9am-1pm & 3-6pm)
Ferry terminal (Map pp198-9; ☎ 010 246 36 86; ☼ 9.30am-12.30pm & 1.30-5.30pm)
Porto Antico In front of Magazzini del Cotone (Map pp198-9; ☼ 9am-8pm); Piazza delle Feste (Map pp198-9; ☼ 9am-8pm) Run by the port authorities.
Stazione Principe (Map pp198-9; ☎ 010 246 26 33; ☼ 9.30am-1pm & 2.30-6pm Mon-Sat)

TRAVEL AGENCIES

Geotravels (Map pp198-9; ☎ 010 59 28 37; geotravels@statcasale.com; Piazza della Vittoria 30r)
Pesci Viaggi e Turismo (Map pp198-9; ☎ 010 56 49 36; pesciros@tin.it; Piazza della Vittoria 94r)
Touring Club Italiano (TCI; Map pp198-9; ☎ 010 595 52 91; negozio.genova@touringclub.it; Palazzo Ducale, Piazza Giacomo Matteotti 62r)

Sights

PIAZZA DE FERRARI

With its Art Nouveau **Palazzo della Borsa** (closed to the public) – the former stock exchange – Palazzo Ducale, the neoclassical Teatro Carlo Felice and **Museo dell'Accademia Ligustica di Belle Arti** (Map pp198-9; ☎ 010 58 19 57; Largo Pertini 4; adult/child €3/2; ☼ 3-7pm Tue-Sun), exhibiting 14th to 20th-century artworks, this square is the place to start.

The main entrance to the **Palazzo Ducale** (Map pp198-9; ☎ 010 557 40 00; www.palazzoducale.genova.it in Italian; Piazza Giacomo Matteotti 9; admission varies; ☼ exhibitions 9am-9pm Tue-Sun) is on adjoining Piazza Giacomo Matteotti. Once the seat of the city's rulers, today it hosts a few small, specialist museums and archives, including the **Museo del Jazz** (Map pp198-9; ☎ 010 58 52 41; www.italianjazzinstitute.com in Italian; admission by reservation only; ☼ 4-7pm Mon-Sat) with its collection

GENOA

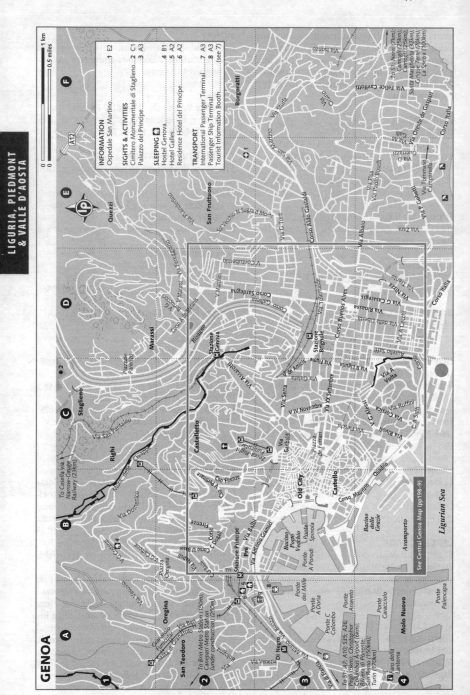

INFORMATION	
Ospedale San Martino	1 E2
SIGHTS & ACTIVITIES	
Cimitero Monumentale di Staglieno	2 C1
Palazzo del Principe	3 A3
SLEEPING 🛏	
Hostel Genova	4 B1
Hotel Galles	5 A2
Residence Hotel del Principe	6 A2
TRANSPORT	
International Passenger Terminal	7 A3
Passenger Ship Terminal	8 A3
Tourist Information Booth	(see 7)

LIGURIA, PIEDMONT & VALLE D'AOSTA

of original recordings. Also here are temporary art exhibitions, a bookshop, café and a few restaurants (see p204). You can wander around the building's neoclassical atrium, flanked by two porticoed courtyards. Its medieval **Torre Grimaldina** was a prison for upper-class troublemakers under the Republic.

CATTEDRALE DI SAN LORENZO

Genoa's **cathedral** (Map pp198-9; Piazza San Lorenzo; �---8am-7pm), with its black-and-white striped Gothic marble façade, fronted by twisting columns and crouching lions, is breathtaking. It was consecrated in 1118, but its two bell towers and cupola weren't built until the 16th century.

Inside, the **Cappella del San Giovanni Battista** (built from 1450–65) once housed relics of St John the Baptist. Above the central doorway there's a great lunette with a painting of the Last Judgement, the work of an anonymous Byzantine painter of the early 14th century. Look out for the unexploded British bomb, which luckily failed to detonate when it hit the cathedral in 1941. In the sacristy, the **Museo del Tesoro** (Map pp198-9; ☎ 010 247 18 31; adult/child €5.50/4.50; �---tours 9am-noon & 3-6pm Mon-Sat) preserves various dubious holy relics, including the medieval Sacro Catino, a glass vessel once thought to be the Holy Grail. Other artefacts include the polished quartz platter upon which Salome is said to have received John the Baptist's head, and a fragment of the True Cross.

CHIESA DEL GESÙ

Heading southeast from the cathedral you'll come across the baroque **Chiesa del Gesù** (Map pp198-9; Piazza Giacomo Matteotti). Built in 1597 on the foundations of a medieval church, it became the seat of the Jesuit order in Genoa, and is decked out with the usual gilded plasterwork and rich marble. More interestingly though, it is the proud possessor of two works by Rubens, the *Circoncisione,* which hangs over the main altar, and the *Miracoli di San Ignazio,* displayed in a side chapel. Also worth noting is the *Assunta* by Guido Reni, on the opposite side of the church.

PORTA SOPRANA & CASA DELLA FAMIGLIA COLOMBO

A short stroll southeast from the Chiesa del Gesù brings you to the only remaining section of the city's 12th-century defensive walls. **Porta Soprana** was built in 1155, but what you see today is a restored version – as is **Casa della Famiglia Colombo** (Map pp198-9; ☎ 010 246 53 46; Piazza Dante; admission free; �---9am-noon & 2-6pm Sat & Sun), the alleged birthplace of Christopher Columbus.

VIA GARIBALDI

Skirting the northern edge of what was once the city limits, the pedestrianised Via Garibaldi (formerly called the Strada Nuova; www.stradanuova.it) was planned by Galeazzo Alessi in the 16th century. It quickly became the city's most elite and fashionable quarter, lined with the magnificent palaces of Genoa's wealthiest citizens. Today, three of these palaces, collectively known as the **Musei di Strada Nuova**, hold the city's finest collection of Old Masters. Combined tickets for the Palazzo Rosso and Palazzo Bianco (adult/child €7/5) must be purchased at the **bookshop** (☎ 010 246 77 86; �---9am-7pm Tue-Sun) inside Palazzo Doria-Tursi.

Palazzo Rosso (Map pp198-9; ☎ 010 247 63 51; www.museopalazzorosso.it; Via Garibaldi 18; �---9am-7pm Tue-Fri, 10am-7pm Sat & Sun) displays an extensive assemblage of paintings, including several portraits by Van Dyck of the local Brignole-Sale family, while other standouts include Guido Reni's *San Sebastiano* and Guercino's *La Morte di Cleopatra.* Veronese, Dürer and Bernardo Strozzi are also represented, while the sumptuous, frescoed rooms are also worth pausing over.

Opposite, **Palazzo Bianco** (Map pp198-9; ☎ 010 247 63 51; www.museopalazzobianco.it; Via Garibaldi 11; �---9am-7pm Tue-Fri, 10am-7pm Sat & Sun) features works by Flemish, Dutch, Spanish and Italian artists. Rubens' *Venere e Marte* and Van Dyck's *Vertumna e Pomona* are among the highlights, which also include works by Hans Memling, Filippino Lippi and Murillo, as well as 15th-century religious icons.

One exit from the Palazzo Bianco leads across the roof terrace into neighbouring **Palazzo Doria-Tursi** (Map pp198-9; ☎ 010 247 63 51; Via Garibaldi 9; admission free; �---9am-7pm Tue-Fri, 10am-7pm Sat & Sun), where you will find the Sala Paganiniana, a one-room museum displaying personal effects of the legendary violinist Niccolò Paganini. Pride of place goes to his famous instrument, the 'Canone', made in Cremona in 1743. One lucky musician gets to play the maestro's violin during October's Paganiniana festival. Other artefacts on

LIGURIA, PIEDMONT & VALLE D'AOSTA

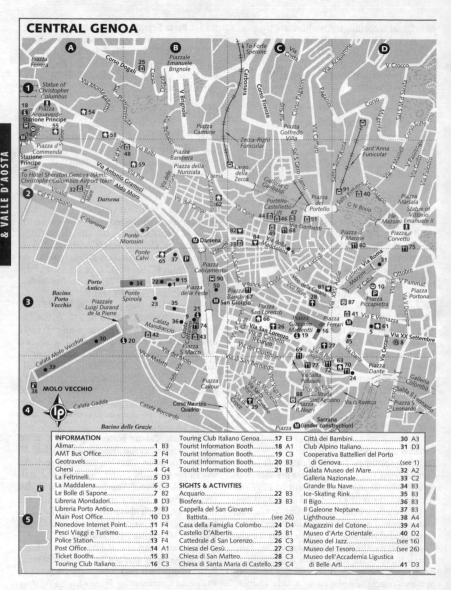

CENTRAL GENOA

INFORMATION		Touring Club Italiano Genoa........17 E3		Città dei Bambini........................30 A3
Alimar.................................1 B3		Tourist Information Booth........18 A1		Club Alpino Italiano..................31 D3
AMT Bus Office....................2 F4		Tourist Information Booth........19 C3		Cooperativa Battellieri del Porto
Geotravels...........................3 F4		Tourist Information Booth........20 B3		di Genova.............................(see 1)
Ghersi.................................4 G4		Tourist Information Booth........21 B3		Galata Museo del Mare............32 A2
La Feltrinelli.......................5 D3				Galleria Nazionale...................33 C2
La Maddalena.....................6 C3		**SIGHTS & ACTIVITIES**		Grande Blu Nave.....................34 B3
Le Bolle di Sapone................7 B2		Acquario...............................22 B3		Ice-Skating Rink......................35 B3
Libreria Mondadori..............8 D3		Biosfera................................23 B3		Il Bigo....................................36 B3
Libreria Porto Antico............9 B3		Cappella del San Giovanni		Il Galeone Neptune.................37 B3
Main Post Office.................10 D3		Battista................................(see 26)		Lighthouse.............................38 A4
Nonedove Internet Point.....11 F4		Casa della Famiglia Colombo....24 D4		Magazzini del Cotone.............39 A4
Pesci Viaggi e Turismo.........12 F4		Castello D'Albertis..................25 B1		Museo d'Arte Orientale............40 D2
Police Station......................13 F4		Cattedrale di San Lorenzo........26 C3		Museo del Jazz.......................(see 16)
Post Office..........................14 A1		Chiesa del Gesù.....................27 C3		Museo del Tesoro....................(see 26)
Ticket Booths......................15 B3		Chiesa di San Matteo..............28 C3		Museo dell'Accademia Ligustica
Touring Club Italiano...........16 C3		Chiesa di Santa Maria di Castello..29 C4		di Belle Arti............................41 D3

show include letters, musical scores and his travelling chess set. The palace has housed Genoa's town hall since 1848.

The most elaborate façade on the street belongs to the recently renovated **Palazzo Lomellino** (Map pp198-9; ☎ 010 595 70 60; www.palazzolomellino.org; Via Garibaldi 7; admission free; ⏱ 10am-7pm Tue-Sun), dating from 1563. The grey-blue

exterior is festooned with stucco adornments, while the internal courtyard is dominated by an elaborate 18th-century nymphaeum, or fountain. Upstairs, the remarkably preserved 17th-century frescoes by Bernardo Strozzi were only uncovered in 2002, after languishing for almost 300 years behind a false ceiling. They depict allegories of the

LIGURIA, PIEDMONT & VALLE D'AOSTA

0 _____ 200 m
0 _____ 0.2 miles

SLEEPING
Albergo Carola	52	E2
Albergo Fiume	53	F3
Hotel Acquaverde	54	A1
Hotel Aquila & Reale	55	A1
Hotel Assarotti	56	E2
Hotel Astoria	57	E2
Hotel Balbi	58	A1
Hotel Bologna	59	B2
Hotel Brignole	60	F3
Hotel Bristol Palace	61	D3
Hotel Cairoli	62	B2
Hotel Cristoforo Colombo	63	D4
Hotel Moderno Verdi	64	B2
Jolly Hotel Marina	65	B3
Locanda di Palazzo Cicala	66	C3

EATING
A Ved Romanengo	67	C3
Antica Cantina I Tre Merli	68	C2
Café degli Specchi	69	C3
Café di Barbarossa	70	D4
Cantine Squarciafico	(see 66)	
Cuxinn-E	71	E3
Da Yang	72	C4
Enoteca Sola	73	F5
I Tre Merli	74	B3
Mangini	75	D2
Mentelocale	(see 10)	
Mentelocale Café	(see 16)	
Mercato Orientale	76	E3
Pizzeria di Vico dei Biscotti	77	C4
Ristorante Pizzeria Number 1	(see 64)	
Standa	78	E4
Taverna Da Michele	79	G4
Trattoria da Maria	80	D2

DRINKING
Britannia Pub	81	C3
La Madeleine Café Teatro	82	C2
Maddox Rock Café	83	F4
Quattro Canti	84	C2

ENTERTAINMENT
FNAC	85	E3
Multi-Sala Ariston	(see 30)	
Ricordi Mediastore	86	E3
Teatro Carlo Felice	87	D3
Teatro della Tosse	88	C4

TRANSPORT
AMT Bus Stop	89	F3
AMT Information Office	(see 92)	
Bus Terminal	90	B3
Funicolare St Anna	91	D2
Main AMT Bus Terminal	92	F4

Museo delle Culture del Mondo	(see 25)	
Museo Luzzati	42	B3
Museo Nazionale dell'Antartide	43	B3
Palazzo Bianco	44	C2
Palazzo della Borsa	45	D3
Palazzo Doria-Tursi	46	C2
Palazzo Ducale	(see 16)	
Palazzo Lomellino	47	C2
Palazzo Reale	48	B2
Palazzo Rosso	49	C2
Palazzo San Giorgio	50	B3
Palazzo Spinola	51	C2
Porta Soprana	(see 24)	
Torre Grimaldina	(see 16)	

'New World', in homage to the palace's one-time owners, the Centurione family, who had financed Columbus's voyages to the Americas. Guided tours take place on Sunday afternoons; phone for reservations and prices.

Palazzo Spinola (Map pp198-9; Via Garibaldi 5) was built between 1558 and 1576 for Angelo Spinola, Emperor Charles V's banker. Appropriately, today it is home to Deutsche Bank. The palace has magnificent frescoes in its courtyard.

A short walk east of Via Garibaldi, a path from Piazza Corvetto twists through terraced gardens to the **Museo d'Arte Orientale** (Map pp198-9; ☎ 010 54 22 85; Piazzale Mazzini 1; adult/

MUSEUM CARD

Serial museum-goers should pick up the Card Musei (Museum Card), which comes in 24-hour (€9), 24-hour plus city bus ticket (€10), three-day (€15) and, for the really committed, annual (€30) versions. The card gives free admission to around 20 of Genoa's museums and discounted access to several more. You can buy it at various locations, including the Palazzo Doria-Tursi bookshop (p197), Palazzo Ducale (p195) and the Acquario (right). For more details, see www.museigenova.it.

child €4/2.80; 9am-1pm Tue-Fri, 10am-7pm Sat & Sun). With some 20,000 items, including porcelain, bronzes, costumes and musical instruments, it's one of Europe's largest collections of Japanese art. Heading southwest, elegant **Via Roma**, with its Art Nouveau boutiques, and adjacent glass-covered **Galleria Mazzini**, is Genoa's finest shopping street. It links Piazza Corvetto with Piazza de Ferrari.

OLD CITY

Medieval Genoa is famous for its historic maze of *caruggi* – twisting lanes and dank, odoriferous blind alleys spill in a bewildering spaghetti formation across the oldest part of Genoa. Its core is bounded by Porta dei Vacca, the waterfront streets Via Cairoli, Via Garibaldi and Via XXV Aprile, and the Porta Soprana around the inland periphery. Most of the old city's lowlife (prostitution, drugs and so on) is concentrated in the zone west of **Via San Luca**, with Piazza Banchi at its southern end. East of the piazza is **Via Orefici**, where you'll find market stalls.

The **Palazzo Reale** (Map pp198-9; 010 271 01; www.palazzorealegenova.it in Italian; Via Balbi 10; adult/child €4/free; 9am-7pm Thu-Sun, 9am-1.30pm Tue & Wed) features Renaissance works and terraced gardens. A combined ticket costs €6.50 and also covers admission to the **Galleria Nazionale** (Map pp198-9; 010 270 53 00; www.palazzospinola.it; Piazza Superiore di Pellicceria 1; adult/child €4/free; 9am-8pm Tue-Sat, 2-8pm Sun). The latter, a 16th-century mansion, was owned by the Spinolas, one of the Republic's most formidable dynasties. Their ancestral home displays Italian and Flemish Renaissance art.

Towering over the western end of town, **Castello D'Albertis** houses the unique **Museo delle Culture del Mondo** (Museum of World Cultures; Map pp198-9; 010 272 38 20; www.castellodalbertis genova.it; Corso Dogali 18; adult/child €6/5; 10am-5pm Oct-Mar, 10am-6pm Apr-Sep). The commanding neo-Gothic pile was built in 1892 on the ruins of a much older castle for the globe-trotting Capitano Enrico D'Albertis, who hauled back all manner of random 'curiosities' from his extensive sea voyages. These now form a kind of old-fashioned Victorian museum of a museum; where else could you find a stuffed platypus, a fragment of the Great Wall of China and a handful of sand from San Salvador (Columbus' first discovery in the New World) in the same cabinet? A modern extension displays pre-Columbian ceramics and textiles from the Americas, and traditional musical instruments. If you don't fancy the climb up to Corso Dogali, there's a lift from Via Balbi (€0.50) that deposits you right across from the castle gates.

Further west, on the waterfront, is the **Palazzo del Principe** (Map p196; 010 25 55 09; www.palazzodelprincipe.it; Via Adua 6; adult/child €6.20/4.65; 10am-5pm Tue-Sun), once home of the famed 16th-century admiral, Andrea Doria. The sumptuous Renaissance interiors, with their frescoes, tapestries, furniture and paintings, have been thoughtfully restored, and the formal gardens provide a calm respite from the city bustle.

Doria himself lies entombed in his family church, **Chiesa di San Matteo** (Map pp198-9; Piazza San Matteo), which was founded in 1125.

Also worth a visit is the Romanesque **Chiesa di Santa Maria di Castello** (Map pp198-9; Via Santa Maria di Castello) with its wonderful fresco of the *Annunciation* by Giusto di Ravensburg.

PORTO ANTICO

Genoa's ancient **port** (www.portoantico.it) was given a thorough overhaul in 2004 and is now one of the city's main attractions, for both tourists and promenading locals. Unfortunately, nothing can detract from the Sopraelevata, the flyover that slashes straight through the old port area. Just back from the waterfront, frescoed **Palazzo San Giorgio** (Map pp198-9; Piazza Caricamento) was built in 1260 and became a prison in 1298; inmate Marco Polo worked on *Il Milione* within its walls. Today, it hosts occasional exhibitions.

Genoa's **Acquario** (Aquarium; Map pp198-9; 010 234 56 78; www.acquariodigenova.it; Ponte Spinola; adult/

child €13/8; ⊗ 9.30am-7.30pm Mon-Wed & Fri, 9.30am-10pm Thu, 9.30am-8.30pm Sat & Sun Sep-Jun, 9.30am-11pm Jul & Aug) is one of the city's main attractions. Sharks are among the 5000 animals swimming in six million litres of water, in tanks that are protected by 25cm-thick glass. Grande Nave Blu, the adjoining floating barge, takes visitors on a voyage through the Age of Discovery and into a Madagascan rainforest.

Right beside the aquarium, the **Biosfera** (Map pp198-9; ☎ 335 599 0187; Ponte Spinola; adult/child €4/3; ⊗ 9.30am-sunset Tue-Sun) is a humid mini-ecosystem with tropical plants, butterflies and birds living in a big glass ball designed by Renzo Piano.

Further along is another Piano-designed feature **Il Bigo** (Map pp198-9; Calata Cattaneo; adult/child €3/1.50; ⊗ 10am-5pm Tue-Sun Jan-Feb & Oct, 10am-6pm Tue-Sun Mar-May & Sep, 2-8pm Mon, 10am-11pm Tue-Sun Jul-Aug, 10am-5pm Sat & Sun Nov-Dec), which hoists a cylindrical cabin 200m into the air, giving its occupants a bird's-eye view of the Porto Antico. Behind it is an **ice-skating rink** (Map pp198-9; ☎ 347 486 0524; Piazza delle Feste; adult/child €7/6; ⊗ 8am-midnight Mon-Fri, 10am-2am Sat, 10am-midnight Sun).

An unexpected waterfront attraction is the **Museo Nazionale dell'Antartide** (Map pp198-9; ☎ 010 254 36 90; www.mna.it; Palazzino Millo, Calata Cattaneo; adult/child €5.30/4.30; ⊗ 9.45am-5.30pm Tue-Sun Jun-Sep, 9.45am-5.30pm Tue-Fri, 10am-6pm Sat & Sun Oct-May). The only museum in Europe entirely dedicated to the great white continent provides a wealth of information on its unique geology and biology.

Walking west along Calata Mandraccio you pass **Porta Siberia** (built in 1550), a city gate named after *cibaria*, a derivation of the Italian word for food (alluding to the port's grain warehouses). Inside, exhibitions of the works of Genoese artist and scenographer Emanuele Luzzati fill the **Museo Luzzati** (Map pp198-9; ☎ 010 253 03 28; www.museoluzzati.it in Italian; Calata Mandraccio; adult/child €5/4; ⊗ 9.30am-5.30pm Tue-Fri, 10.30am-6.30pm Sat & Sun, 9.30am-10.30pm 1st Fri of month).

Further west are the **Magazzini del Cotone**, one-time cotton warehouses that have since been converted into an entertainment area with a multiplex cinema, games arcade and shops. On the 1st floor, the **Città dei Bambini** (Map pp198-9; ☎ 010 247 57 02; www.cittadeibambini.net in Italian; Magazzini del Cotone; adult/child €5/6; ⊗ 10am-6pm Tue-Sun Oct-Jun, 11.30am-7.30pm Jul-Sep) is an interactive area aimed at showing kids aged three to 14 the wonders of play, science and technology. A sweeping view of Porto Antico and its **lighthouse** (built in 1543) can be enjoyed from Molo Vecchio, the western-

---

THE GENIUS OF GENOA

Niccolò Paganini (1782–1840) was the greatest violinist of his age. Extracting chords, arpeggios and rhythms hitherto undreamed of, the Genoese musician revolutionised violin technique with his use of harmonics and left-handed pizzicato. He was also a virtuoso on the guitar and a prolific composer, writing six concertos, 24 quartets for violin, viola, guitar and other strings, 12 sonatas for violin and guitar, and a long list of further sonatas in a career that took him to every corner of Italy and all of Europe's great stages.

In 1798 Paganini ran away from his tyrannical father, ending up in Lucca where he scraped together a living giving concerts. Loose women and gambling became part of the 16-year-old's life for a short while, leading on more than one occasion to him pawning his violin to pay off a debt.

Between 1805 and 1813 Paganini worked for the princess of Lucca as the court violinist and in 1828 he performed for the first time in Vienna – a coup that coincided with a public defence of himself in the *Revue Musicale*, intended to squash rumours claiming that the maestro was, in fact, demonically inspired.

Diabolical rumours did not diminish Paganini's popularity, although the adjectives 'capricious', 'greedy', 'mean' and 'egotistical' were regularly associated with his name. At the height of his fame in the late 1820s, everything from hats and shawls to foodstuffs were named after him. Hundreds of adoring fans mobbed him when he left concert halls, while Chopin and Liszt applied much of what they learned from Paganini's genius to the piano.

Paganini spent his last days in Nice, now in France, where he died penniless in 1840, four years after blowing his entire fortune on a failed casino venture in Paris.

most tip of the peninsula, behind Magazzini del Cotone.

Just to the west of the Porto Antico stands the gigantic glass box that is the **Galata Museo del Mare** (Map pp198-9; ☎ 010 234 56 55; www.galata museodelmare.it in Italian; Calata di Mari 1; adult/child €12/5; ⏲ 10am-7.30pm Mar-Jul & Sep-Oct, 10am-7.30pm Sat-Thu, 10am-10pm Fri Aug, 10am-6pm Tue-Sun Nov-Feb). Genoa's newest museum traces the history of seafaring from earliest times through the ages of sail and steam to the present day, with reconstructions and multimedia resources.

After that, kids might enjoy a little snoop around **Il Galeone Neptune** (Map pp198-9; Molo Ponte Calvi; adult/child €5/3; ⏲ 10am-6pm), a cartoonish mock-up of a 17th-century galleon, used in the 1986 Roman Polanski film *Pirates*. It's moored alongside the Jolly Hotel Marina (see p204).

OTHER SIGHTS

The high country, leaning protectively over the city, bears a 13km-long scar of city walls,

built between 1626 and 1632 to shield the port's landward side. These Mura Nuove (New Walls) covered a much larger area than their 12th-century predecessors, which stretched west to the lighthouse, east to Piazza della Vittoria and north to the 490m-high **Forte Sperone**, the largest of the remaining defensive forts. The fortress hosts plays and concerts in summer.

The easiest way to reach the walls is by cable car from Largo della Zecca to Righi, which is at 300m. From Largo Giorgio Caproni (the square in front of Righi cable-car station), trails lead to Forte Sperone. Contact **Club Alpino Italiano** (CAI; Map pp198-9; ☎ 010 59 21 22; www.cailigure.it in Italian; Galleria Mazzini 7/3, Via Roma) for more information.

A narrow-gauge railway snakes from the **Stazione Genova** (Map pp198-9; ☎ 010 83 73 21; www .ferroviagenovacasella.it in Italian; Via alla Stazione per Casella 15) 25km north to **Casella** (one way/return €2/3, one hour, 405m, eight to 12 daily), a village in the Scrivia Valley. The railway has been in operation since 1929 and offers passengers great views of Genoa's forts and the **Cimitero Monumentale di Staglieno** (Map p196; ☎ 010 87 01 84; Piazzale Resasco; ⏲ 7.30am-5pm), a monumental cemetery dating from 1851. Revolutionary Giuseppe Mazzini (1805–72) and Constance Lloyd (1858–98), who was Oscar Wilde's wife, are buried here. However, the main draw for visitors is its wealth of exquisite, sentimental or just overblown funerary sculptures. For details, pick up the free *Art Itineraries in Staglieno* brochure from tourist offices. To visit the cemetery take bus No 34 from Stazione Principe.

Tours

Information and tickets for boat trips are available from the **ticket booths** (Map pp198-9; ☎ 010 25 67 75; Ponte Spinola; ⏲ 9.30am-6.30pm Sep-Jun, 9am-8pm Jul & Aug) beside the aquarium at Porto Antico.

Port tours (45 minutes) run by **Cooperativa Battellieri del Porto di Genova** (Map pp198-9; ☎ 010 26 57 12; www.battellierigenova.it in Italian; Calata degli Zingari; adult/child €6/4) depart at 10am from Ponte Spinola. From July to September it also runs excursions to Portofino (adult/child €15/10), Vernazza in the Cinque Terre (adult/child €23/15) and Porto Venere (adult/child €25/18). **Alimar** (Map pp198-9; ☎ 010 25 67 75; www.ali mar.ge.it in Italian; Calata degli Zingari) runs 45-minute harbour tours year-round (adult/child €6/

WHALE-WATCH LIGURIA

There's no guarantee that you'll see one. In fact, those aboard whale-spotting excursions organised by the Cooperativa Battellieri del Porto di Genova (see right) are advised to bring binoculars.

Trips, run in consultation with the World Wide Fund for Nature (WWF) who plant a biologist on board, sail from Genoa into a 96,000-sq-km protected zone wedged between the Côte d'Azur (France) and Tunisia. Some eight cetacean species are known to exist here, the long-finned pilot whale, sperm whale and Risso's dolphin among them. Its striped dolphin population peaks at 25,000 in summer. Its whale population is estimated at 2000.

Whale-spotting **expeditions** (☎ 010 26 57 12; www.whalewatchliguria.it; Calata degli Zingari; adult/child from Genoa €33/18, from Savona €30/15, from Alassio €28/15) that run between May and September depart at 9am from Genoa's Porto Antico and at 10.30am from Savona's Pontile Marinetta several times a month, most frequently in July and August. Check the website for exact days and details for Alassio. Advance reservations by telephone are obligatory.

free), and boat trips to Monterosso in the Cinque Terre (€23), Portofino/San Fruttuoso (€15) and Portovenevre (€25) between April and September.

Festivals & Events

The **Premio Paganini** is an international violin competition held in September, and more musical events take place during October's **Paganiniana** festival. Exact dates and venues change each year.

Genoa is one of four historical maritime cities that race each other in the **Pallo delle Quattro Antiche Repubbliche Marinare** (Regatta of the Four Ancient Maritime Republics) in June. The city will host its next race in 2008.

Sleeping

BUDGET

Budget hotels are spread around town, with perhaps the greatest concentration found along Via Balbi and the surrounding area.

Hostel Genova (Map p196; ☎ 010 242 24 57; hostel ge@iol.it; Via G Costanzi 120; dm/s/d from €15/22/40; ☻ reception 9am-3.30pm & midnight-7am Feb–mid-Dec; ℗) Dorms have eight beds and some quadruple rooms have disabled facilities at Genoa's only hostel, 2km north of the old centre in Righi. Rates include breakfast and sheets. Catch bus No 40 from Stazione Brignole to the end of the line or No 35 from Stazione Principe to Stazione Brignole, and then connect with No 40.

Albergo Carola (Map pp198-9; ☎ 010 839 13 40; Via Groppallo 4; s/d from €21/33, with bathroom from €35/41) Albergo Carola's clean, well-kept rooms can be found on the 3rd floor of a lovely old building near Stazione Brignole.

Hotel Cairoli (Map pp198-9; ☎ 010 246 14 54; www .hotelcairoligenova.com; Via Cairoli 14/4; s/d from €52/73; ℗ ✂) The dozen rooms in this 3rd-floor hotel are clean and simple, and worth more than the two stars bestowed on them. There's a rooftop terrace where guests can lounge in the evenings. Breakfast is €8 extra.

Also worth considering:

Albergo Fiume (Map pp198-9; ☎ 010 59 16 91; Via Fiume 9r; s/d €45/60)

Hotel Balbi (Map pp198-9; ☎ 010 247 21 12; hotel balbi@inwind.it; Via Balbi 21; s/d from €20/40, with bathroom from €30/50)

Hotel Bologna (Map pp198-9; ☎ 010 246 57 72; Piazza Superiore del Roso 3; s/d from €21/35, d with bathroom from €35; ℗)

MIDRANGE

Hotel Acquaverde (Map pp198-9; ☎ 010 26 54 27; www.hotelacquaverde.it; Via Balbi 29; s/d/tr Nov-Mar €35/75/95, Apr-Oct €50/100/130; ℗ ✂) This simple place on the top three floors of a restored 17th-century townhouse has plain, serviceable rooms and is reasonably priced.

Hotel Assarotti (Map pp198-9; ☎ 010 88 58 22; www.hotelassarotti.it; Via Assarotti 40c; s/d/tr from €45/70/85; ℗ ✂ 🖥) This family-run two-star hotel offers a bit of a getaway from the hubbub of central Genoa. Bus No 36 links the hotel with Piazza de Ferrari and Via XX Settembre.

Hotel Cristoforo Colombo (Map pp198-9; ☎ 010 251 36 43; www.hotelcolombo.it; Via di Porta Soprana 27; s/d/tr from €50/80/110) Christopher Columbus is a charming choice in a good central location in the old city. Advance reservations are essential.

Hotel Brignole (Map pp198-9; ☎ 010 56 16 51; www.hotelbrignole.com; Via del Corallo 13r; s/d/tr €68/85/95; ℗ ✂ 🖥) Near Stazione Brignole, this is a decent midrange choice with the usual comforts and amenities, though it's functional rather than fancy.

Hotel Galles (Map p196; ☎ 010 24 62 820; www .hotelgallesgenova.com; Via Bersaglieri d'Italia 13; s/d/tr €65/85/105; ℗ ✂) Hotel Galles is a friendly three-star hotel offering newly renovated rooms with wooden floors, comfy beds and large gleaming bathrooms. Thankfully, the double-glazed windows cuts out most of the noise from the nearby flyover.

Residence Hotel del Principe (Map p196; ☎ 010 26 16 98; residencedelprincipe@virgilio.it; Via Andrea Doria 10; s/d €70/90; ℗ ✂) Smart modern rooms in neutral tones are offered by this grand-looking place just down the road from Stazione Principe. The handy location means it books up quickly.

Hotel Aquila & Reale (Map pp198-9; ☎ 010 25 61 32; fax 010 26 55 11; Piazza Aquaverde 1; s/d €70/100; ℗ ✂) Opposite Stazione Principe, the Aquila has a certain faded *fin de siècle* ambience, with its scattering of antique furnishings, potted ferns and uniformed staff. Rooms are cosy, if perhaps a little old-fashioned for some.

Hotel Astoria (Map pp198-9; ☎ 010 87 33 16; www .hotelastoria-ge.com; Piazza Brignole 4; s/d from €70/90; ℗ ✂) Dating from 1860, the Astoria is a quiet hotel with a warm ochre façade. Rooms, which lead onto frescoed public lounges, have been recently renovated and come with huge gleaming bathrooms.

AUTHOR'S CHOICE

Locanda di Palazzo Cicala (Map pp198-9; ☎ 010 251 88 24; http://palazzocicala.it; Piazza San Lorenzo 16; s/d/tr/ste from €125/170/210/240; P ⊠ ⬚) With just six rooms on the 1st floor of a 16th-century palace right opposite the Duomo, the Locanda di Palazzo Cicala is one of Genoa's best-located hotels. The palazzo has recently been completely restored, and while the grand 18th-century stucco façade has been retained, the interior has been given a thoroughly contemporary, minimalist make-over.

The spacious, high-ceilinged rooms are kitted out with stylish designer furnishings, including lamps by Jasper Morrison, chairs by Ron Arad and ultramodern toilets by Philippe Stark, as well as fax machines, PCs and modems. Pushchairs, cots, toys and other parental paraphernalia are available for those with kids in tow and there's a very good restaurant on the ground floor (see right).

TOP END

Hotel Moderno Verdi (Map pp198-9; ☎ 010 55 32 104; www.modernoverdi.it; Piazza Giuseppe Verdi 5; s/d/tr from €135/190/220; P ⊠) Handy for Brignole Stazione, the Moderno Verdi is an upmarket choice built in the Liberty style. Rooms are tastefully furnished and have modern amenities including modem points, while most singles come with queen-sized beds.

Hotel Sheraton Genova (Map pp198-9; ☎ 010 6 54 91; www.sheratongenova.com; Via Pionieri e Aviatori d'Italia 44; s/d €130/160; P ⊠ ⬚) Beside the airport, 6km west of the centre, the Sheraton is handy for those early departures or late arrivals. It's a giant glassy structure with all the mod cons, including a gym and shuttle bus to whisk you into the city.

Jolly Hotel Marina (Map pp198-9; ☎ 010 25 11 320; www.jollyhotels.com; Molo Ponte Calvi; s/d €180/220; P ⊠) The pastel pink Jolly Hotel juts out merrily into the harbour on its own pontoon, and provides all amenities associated with this upmarket nationwide chain. All rooms have balconies, where you can sit and watch the yachts in the bay or the traffic speeding along the adjacent flyover.

Hotel Bristol Palace (Map pp198-9; ☎ 010 59 25 41; www.hotelbristolpalace.com; Via XX Settembre 35; s/d/ste low season €130/150/450, high season €269/370/600; P ⊠ ⬚) Housed in a late-19th-century mansion on Genoa's main shopping street, the Bristol Palace oozes *belle époque* style and elegance, with large, airy rooms and original antique furnishings. Prices vary dramatically during the year.

Eating

Don't leave town without sampling pasta doused in *pesto Genovese* (a sauce of basil, garlic, Parmesan and pine nuts), *torta pasqualina* (a spinach, ricotta cheese and egg tart), *pansotti* (spinach-filled ravioli with a thick, creamy hazelnut sauce) and, of course, focaccia and *farinata* (flat bread).

RESTAURANTS

Ristorante Pizzeria Number 1 (Map pp198-9; ☎ 010 54 18 85; Piazza Giuseppe Verdi 21r; pizzas €5-8; ☙ lunch & dinner Mon-Sat) This busy, unpretentious place opposite Stazione Brignole serves up a big menu of pizzas and pasta dishes, and is also an amenable spot for a beer or two.

Taverna Da Michele (Map pp198-9; ☎ 010 59 36 71; Via della Libertà 41r; pizzas €5-8, mains €10-12; ☙ lunch & dinner Mon-Fri, dinner Sat & Sun) Enjoy a pizza beneath creeping vines at this little-known spot with a peaceful green terrace – a rarity in this traffic-crazy city.

Enoteca Sola (Map pp198-9; ☎ 010 59 45 13; Via Carlo Barabino 120r; mains €9-15; ☙ Mon-Sat Sep-Jul) Dine in style at this fabulous wine shop. The wine list is extensive, the staff knowledgeable and typical Genoese dishes, including the house speciality *stoccafisso alla Genovese* (stockfish), star on the handwritten menu.

Cuxinn-E (Map pp198-9; ☎ 010 595 98 39; Via Galata 35r; 1st courses €5.50-8, 2nd courses €6.50-11; ☙ Mon-Sat) Traditional Genoese fodder might well be cooked up at Cuxinn-E, but its minimalist modern décor – all aglow in warm amber and ochre – makes a refreshing change from the rustic, bottle-lined norm.

Cantine Squarciafico (Map pp198-9; ☎ 010 247 08 23; Piazza Invrea 3r; mains €10-12; ☙ lunch & dinner Sep-Jul) In the same historic building as the Locanda di Palazzo Cicala (see left), this inviting restaurant offers a changing daily menu of traditional Ligurian cuisine, including lots of pasta (with *pesto Genovese*, of course), fish and beef dishes. Plus there's an extensive wine selection.

Mentelocale (Map pp198-9; ☎ 010 595 96 48; www.mentelocale.it in Italian; Palazzo Ducale, Piazza de Ferrari; mains €10-15; ☙ lunch & dinner) A modern fusion restaurant inside the Palazzo Ducale serving up a varied and interesting menu, with an emphasis on fresh fish and vegetables. Tuna with sesame and lime, tempura prawns and chicken curry are just some of the tasty items presented for your delectation.

I Tre Merli (Map pp198-9; ☎ 010 246 44 16; www .itremerli.it; Palazzina Millo, Porto Antico; mains €12-20; ☺ lunch & dinner) This pleasant portside eatery serves up some excellent Ligurian cuisine, including vegetable pies, pasta and fish, as well as a good choice of local wines. The *pansotti di magro in salsa di noci* (herb ravioli with walnut sauce) is particularly good.

Antica Cantina I Tre Merli (Map pp198-9; ☎ 010 247 40 95; Vico dietro il Coro della Maddalena 26r; mains €15-20; ☺ lunch & dinner Mon-Fri & dinner Sat) Under the same management as I Tre Merli, this is an altogether more intimate little place, tucked down an alley off Via Garibaldi. Meaty Ligurian fare is on the menu, along with some fine local *vino*.

Pizzeria di Vico dei Biscotti (Map pp198-9; ☎ 010 251 89 90; Vico dei Biscotti 4; pizzas €6-8; ☺ lunch & dinner) This big pizza place is a reliable spot to fill up on a *quattro stagione* (four seasons) and a beer or two, and is particularly busy in the evenings.

Da Yang (Map pp198-9; ☎ 010 247 53 49; Via di Porta Soprana 25r; mains €5-8; ☺ noon-3pm & 7pm-midnight) This little Chinese restaurant offers a good-value fixed lunch menu (€6.50), and while not exactly a gourmet treat, it's tasty and the place is open when many other restaurants are closed.

Trattoria da Maria (Map pp198-9; ☎ 010 58 10 80; Vico Testa d'Oro 14; lunch menus €9) Off Via XXV Aprile, Trattoria da Maria exudes a simple charm with its checked tablecloths (often hanging outside to dry), handwritten menu and especially the hearty dishes served by granny in a pinny.

CAFÉS

Café degli Specchi (Map pp198-9; ☎ 010 246 81 93; Via Salita Pollaiuoli 43r; mains about €7-10; ☺ Mon-Sat) Genoa's Café of Mirrors is an Art Deco joint where the literati hung out in the 1920s. Its original vaulted interior was used as a backdrop for some scenes in Dino Risi's film *Scent of a Woman* (1974). Drop by in the early evening and enjoy a free buffet with your apéritif.

Café di Barbarossa (Map pp198-9; ☎ 010 246 50 97; Piano di Sant'Andrea 21-3r; mains €10) This simple but stylish café-cum-bar basks in the shade of towering 12th-century Porta Soprana. It is tucked in the basement of a palace dating back to 1250 and has a red-brick cellar.

Mentelocale Café (Map pp198-9; ☎ 010 595 96 48; Palazzo Ducale, Piazza Giacomo Matteotti 9; lunch menus about €12) Newspapers to read, designer chairs to pose in and computer terminals feature in this ultramodern café.

Most cake shops sell *kranz* (honey-glazed raisin bread baked in a twist and topped with sugar crystals) and *pandolce Genovese* (traditional Genoese fruit bread). Genoa's finest are **Mangini** (Map pp198-9; ☎ 010 56 40 13; Piazza Corvetto 3r), dating to 1876, and **A Ved Romanengo** (Map pp198-9; ☎ 010 247 29 15; Via Orefici 31-33), open since 1805. Both have small sit-down areas.

SELF-CATERING

One of the larger and more central supermarkets is **Standa** (Map pp198-9; Via XX Settembre 46-54r; ☺ 8am-8pm Mon-Sat, 3.30-7.30pm Sun), on the corner of Via Cesarea. It also has a takeaway bakery.

Drinking

Britannia Pub (Map pp198-9; ☎ 010 247 45 32; Vico della Casana 76r; ☺ noon-late Mon-Sat) This British style, old-world pub with its green wooden façade offers a variety of imported beers, as well as a light lunch menu, including pasta, salads and hamburgers.

MARKET DAY

The most evocative and economical place to shop for everything from fresh fruit and vegetables to cheeses, meat and a plentiful assortment of fish, is Genoa's venerable **Mercato Orientale** (Map pp198-9; entrances at Via XX Settembre 75r & Via Galata). Flower stalls are grouped in front of the covered market on Via XX Settembre. In the old town, fruit and veg stalls are set up on Piazza Banchi and Via degli Orefici, immediately east.

Works by local artists and second-hand books can be picked up from the open air stalls beneath the arcades on Piazza Colombo, a pretty square at the southern foot of Via Galata. On the first Saturday and Sunday of the month from October to July, an antique market fills the interior courtyards of Palazzo Ducale.

Quattro Canti (Map pp198-9; ☎ 010 25 29 97; Via Ai Quattro Canti di San Francesco 28) This old-city bar dishes up *panini,* bruschetta and good music to a mellow crowd.

Maddox Rock Café (Map pp198-9; ☎ 010 56 58 96; Via Malta 15) American-style Maddox shakes a mean apéritif, matched by an endless supply of complimentary pizza slices, tortilla chips and olives. Sport is shown on a big screen.

La Madeleine Café Teatro (Map pp198-9; ☎ 010 246 53 12; Via della Maddalena 103) A red-brick interior greets drinkers at this fabulous café theatre-cum-music bar where live bands blast their stuff from 10pm most nights.

Entertainment

Tickets for cultural and sporting events are sold at box offices inside **Ricordi Mediastore** (Map pp198-9; ☎ 010 54 33 31; Via alla Porta degli Archi 88-94) and **FNAC** (Map pp198-9; ☎ 010 29 01 11; Via XX Settembre 58). English-language films are shown at **Multi-Sala Ariston** (Map pp198-9; ☎ 010 247 35 49; Vico San Matteo 14-16).

Take in a play or opera at **Teatro Carlo Felice** (Map pp198-9; ☎ 010 538 12 24/7; www.carlofelice.it in Italian; Passo Eugenio Montale 4), Genoa's four-stage opera house. Casanova walked the boards at **Teatro della Tosse** (Map pp198-9; ☎ 010 247 07 93; www.teatrodellatosse.it in Italian; Piazza Renato Negri 4), the city's oldest theatre, dating back to 1702.

Getting There & Away

AIR

Regular domestic and international flights use **Christopher Columbus airport** (Aeroporto Internazionale di Cristoforo Colombo; GOA; Map p196; ☎ 010 601 54 10; www.airport.genova.it), 6km west of the city in Sestri Ponente.

BOAT

Ferries sail to/from Spain, Sicily, Sardinia, Corsica and Tunisia from the **international passenger terminal** (terminal traghetti; Map p196; 24hr information ☎ 166 152 39 393; www.porto.genova.it; Via Milano 51). Only cruise ships use the 1930s passenger ship terminal on Ponte dei Mille.

Fares listed below are for one-way, low/high season deck-class tickets. Ferry operators based at the international passenger terminal include:

EneRnaR (☎ 899 20 00 01) Ferries to/from Sardinia (Palau €35/60) April to September.

Grandi Navi Veloci (☎ 800 46 65 10, 010 254 65; www.gnv.it) Ferries to/from Sardinia (Porto Torres

year-round €34/75, Olbia June to September €38/77) and year-round to/from Sicily (Palermo €70/110).

Moby Lines (☎ 010 254 15 13; www.mobylines.it) Ferries year-round to/from Corsica (Bastia €17/32) and Sardinia (Olbia €35/65).

Tirrenia (☎ 800 82 40 79; www.tirrenia.it) Ferries and high-speed boats year-round to/from Sardinia (Porto Torres €25/50, Olbia €28/38, Cagliari July to September €45), with connections to Sicily.

From June to September, **Cooperativa Battellieri del Golfo Paradiso** (☎ 018 577 20 91; www.golfoparadiso.it in Italian; Via Scalo 3) operates boats from the Porto Antico to Camogli (one way/return €9/11), Portofino (€9/11), the Cinque Terre (€15.50/23.50) and Porto Venere (€19/25) on the Riviera di Levante.

BUS

Buses to international cities use the main AMT bus terminal on Piazza della Vittoria, as do buses to/from Milan's Malpensa airport (€16, two hours, twice daily) and other inter-regional services. Tickets are sold at both Geotravels and Pesci Viaggi e Turismo (see p195).

TRAIN

Genoa is linked by train (intercity fares are quoted) to Turin (€16, 1¾ hours, seven to 10 daily), Milan (€13, 1½ hours, up to eight daily), Pisa (€16, two hours, up to eight daily) and Rome (€36, 5¼ hours, six daily). It makes little difference which of the two train stations (Principe or Brignole) you choose, except for trips along the two Rivieras. However, going west to San Remo (€7.70, 2¼ to three hours, five daily) and Ventimiglia (€8.80, 2½ hours, six daily) there are more departures from Stazione Principe.

Getting Around

TO/FROM THE AIRPORT

AMT's line No 100 departs from the **AMT bus stop** (☎ 010 558 24 14) on Piazza Giuseppe Verdi, outside Stazione Brignole (€3, 30 minutes, every 20 minutes 5.30am to 11pm). It stops at Stazione Principe en route to the airport. Tickets can be bought from the driver or from a machine at the bus stop outside the airport.

PUBLIC TRANSPORT

AMT (☎ 800 085 352, 010 599 74 14; www.amt.genova.it in Italian) operates buses throughout the city and there is an **AMT information office** (Map pp198-9; Piazza della Vittoria; 🕑 7.15am-6pm Mon-Fri, 7am-7pm Sat & Sun) at the bus terminal. Bus line No 383 links Stazione Brignole with Piazza de Ferrari and Stazione Principe. A ticket valid for 90 minutes costs €1 (10-ticket carnet €9.50) and an all-day ticket costs €3. Tickets can be used on main-line trains within the city limits (as far as Nervi and Voltri), as well as on the brand-new **metro** (www.genovametro.com), still partly under construction at the time of research. Six of the planned 10 stations were up and running in 2005: Brin, Stazione Principe, San Giorgio, Di Negro, Piazza de Ferrari and Darsena.

AROUND GENOA
Nervi
Around 7km east of the centre of Genoa, Nervi is a former fishing village which has now been subsumed into the city's urban sprawl. Despite its suburban status, Nervi has maintained much of the peaceful seaside resort atmosphere that made it so popular with 19th-century holiday-makers. In the bad old days of scurvy, Nervi supplied most of the lemons used by the British navy.

SIGHTS
A combined ticket (€7) gives access to all three museums in Nervi.

The **Galleria d'Arte Moderna** (☎ 010 372 60 25; Via Capolungo 3; adult/child €6/5; 🕑 10am-7pm Tue-Sun) displays an important collection of 19th- and 20th-century paintings, with a concentration on Italian artists such as Filippo De Pisis, Arturo Martini and Rubaldo Merello.

Raccolte Frugone (☎ 010 32 23 96; Via Capolungo 9; adult/child €4/2.80; 🕑 9am-7pm Tue-Fri, 10am-7pm Sat & Sun), housed in the Villa Grimaldi Fassio, overlooks the leafy, squirrel-filled Parchi di Nervi. The Frugone collection consists of more 19th- and early 20th-century Italian art, including Eduardo Rubino's sensual marble nude, *Il Risveglio*, and paintings by Alessandro Milesi, Pietro Fragiacomo and American artist Richard E Miller.

The **Museo Giannettino Luxoro** (☎ 010 32 26 73; Via Mafalda di Savoia 3; adult/child €4/2.80; 🕑 9am-1pm Tue-Fri, 10am-1pm Sat) has a rich collection of 18th-century clocks, silverware, ceramics and furniture displayed in a splendidly restored villa, alongside paintings from the period.

SLEEPING & EATING
Nervi is an easy day trip from the city centre, but there are several hotels if you wish to escape the urban hubbub.

Hotel Bel Sito (☎ 010 372 80 60; heler77@hotmail.com; Via Capolungo 12; s/d €45/70; 🕑 Dec Oct; **P**) The two-star Bel Sito is an attractive, homely choice in a peaceful spot located opposite the Raccolte Frugone museum.

Hotel Astor (☎ 010 372 84 86; www.astorhotel.it; Viale delle Palme 16; s/d from €130/160; **P**) Nestled quietly on a lovely avenue lined with orange trees, palms and 19th-century villas, the bland modern box of the Astor looks a little out of place, but nevertheless, it offers a good standard of service and accommodation.

Chandra Bar (☎ 010 860 36 40; Passeggiata Garibaldi 26r; mains €7-12; 🕑 3pm-2am Tue-Sat, 11.30am-2am Sun) This busy seafront place serves up a varied menu of curries, pasta and fresh fish, plus Thai and Brazilian cuisine on different days. It also provides live music.

Pegli
Like Nervi, Pegli is a former seafront village that now lies within the city boundaries of Genoa, roughly 9km west of the centre. It's well worth a quick trip out to Pegli for its two museums and the lovely parks.

The **Museo di Archeologia Ligure** (☎ 010 698 10 48; www.museoarcheologicogenova.it; Via Pallavicini 11; adult/child €4/free; 🕑 9am-7pm Tue-Fri, 10am-7pm Sat & Sun), in the striking Villa Pallavicini, holds displays of locally excavated artefacts from the prehistoric through to the Roman period, as well as a collection of Egyptian antiquities.

Maritime matters are covered in the **Museo Navale** (☎ 010 696 98 85; www.museonavale.it; Villa Doria, Piazza Bonavino 7; adult/child €4/free; 🕑 9am-1pm Tue-Fri, 10am-7pm Sat & Sun), with an exhibition of models, photographs and other reminders of the days of sail.

Also worth a wander are the **Parco Villa Pallavicini** (☎ 010 66 68 64; Via Pallavicini; admission €3.50; 🕑 9am-7pm Apr-Sep, 9am-5pm Oct-Mar), with its formal lawns, lakes and glasshouse, and the neighbouring **Giardino Botanico** (☎ 010 66 68 64; admission €3.50; 🕑 9am-12.30pm Tue-Sun), home to a small collection of exotic plants.

A combined ticket for both museums and both gardens costs €8.

Getting There & Away
Both Nervi and Pegli are best reached by frequent trains from Genoa's Stazione Brignole

(both €1, 20 to 25 minutes). Buses, using the same ticket, can take twice as long.

RIVIERA DI LEVANTE

Once you get beyond Genoa's portside sprawl, the coastline east of the city rapidly opens up to present some of the loveliest seaside towns and villages in Italy, from jet-set Portofino and classy Santa Margherita to the delightful Cinque Terre, pretty almost to the point of tweeness. Hugely popular with both Italian and foreign tourists, this area offers dramatic scenery and exhilarating walking opportunities. At the far end of this stretch of coastline, Porto Venere and Lerici, with their poetic associations, are also rewarding destinations.

Camogli
pop 5737

Wandering Camogli's alleys and cobbled streets, 25km east of Genoa, it is hard not to be taken aback by the painstaking trompe l'oeil decoration. The main esplanade, Via Garibaldi, is a colourful place, especially on the second Sunday in May when fishermen celebrate the **Sagra del Pesce** (Fish Festival) with a big fry-up – hundreds of fish are cooked in 3m-wide pans along the busy waterfront. Camogli, meaning 'house of wives', takes its name from the days when the women ran the town while their husbands were at sea.

From here, boats nip across to the **Punta Chiappi**, a rocky outcrop on the Portofino promontory where you can swim and sunbathe. The **tourist office** (☎ 0185 77 10 66; iat .camogli@apt.genova.it; Via XX Settembre 33; ☧ 9am-12.30pm & 3.30-6pm Mon-Sat, 9am-1pm Sun) has a list of diving schools and boat-rental places.

SLEEPING & EATING
If you'd like to stay, the best place in town is **Hotel Cenobio dei Dogi** (☎ 0185 72 41; www.cenobio .com; Via Cuneo 34; s/d low season from €108/150, high season from €151/203; ⓟ ⓧ ⓡ), set in a 16th-century villa. Pricey restaurants and cafés line the waterfront and Piazza Colombo; delve down the lanes away from the water to escape the lunchtime crowd and get a better deal.

GETTING THERE & AWAY
Tigullio (☎ 0185 23 11 08) runs buses to/from Rapallo and Santa Margherita (both €1, every 20 minutes) from the bus stop just past the tourist office on Via XX Settembre.

Camogli (€2, 30 minutes from Stazione Principe, hourly) is on the Genoa–La Spezia train line.

Year-round, the Cooperativa Battellieri del Golfo Paradiso (p206) runs boats to and from Punta Chiappi (one way/return €4/6), San Fruttuoso (€5.50/8), Portofino (€8/12, June to September), Porto Venere (€13/20, June to September) and the Cinque Terre (€12/19, June to September).

San Fruttuoso

Fascinating San Fruttuoso, 5km southeast of Camogli, is dominated by the **Abbazia di San Fruttuoso di Capodimonte** (☎ 0185 77 27 03; adult/ child €4/2.50; ☧ 10am-6pm Jun-Sep, 10am-4pm Tue-Sun Mar-May & Oct, 10am-4pm Sat & Sun Dec-Feb). The Benedictine abbey was built as a final resting place for Bishop St Fructuosus of Tarragona (who was martyred in Spain in 259), and rebuilt in the mid-13th century with the assistance of the Doria family, who used it as a family crypt. It fell into decay with the decline of the religious community, and in the 19th century was divided into small living quarters by local fishermen.

In 1954 a bronze statue of Christ was lowered 15m to the sea bed by locals as a tribute to divers lost at sea and to bless the waters. Dive to see it or view it from a boat if the waters are calm (the Cooperativa Battellieri del Golfo Paradiso, p206, can provide details). A religious ceremony is held over the statue each August.

San Fruttuoso is only accessible on foot from Camogli or Portofino – a stiff but exhilarating 5km-long cliffside walk that takes up to 2½ hours one way from either town – or by boat year-round from Camogli; it's only accessible from Portofino, Rapallo and Santa Margherita in summer.

Portofino
pop 550

Glamorous Portofino, 38km east of Genoa, is Liguria's most exclusive seaside resort and has long been popular with artists, writers and the international jet set. The poet Petrarch and writers Guy de Maupassant and Truman Capote found inspiration here, and in its 1950s and '60s heydays, a myriad of Hollywood luminaries dropped by for the odd photo opportunity. The huddle of pink and yellow houses around the tiny harbour is the picture-postcard Riviera at its best, although these days the place is almost wholly given over to top-end tourism. There are a rash of designer boutiques, should you find yourself running low on Gucci or Cartier, and expensive cafés where fur-coated ladies in shades sip apéritifs and gaze out to sea.

The **tourist office** (☎ /fax 0185 29 291; Via Roma 35; 10am-1pm & 1.30-4.30pm Tue-Sun) has plenty of information on Portofino and its protected green surrounds.

SIGHTS & ACTIVITIES

At the port a flight of stairs signposted 'Salita San Giorgio' leads past the **Chiesa di San Giorgio** to **Castello Brown** (☎ 0185 26 71 01; www.portofinoevents.com; Via alla Penisola 13a; adult/child €3.50/free; 10am-7pm Apr-Sep, 10am-5pm Oct-Mar). The Genoese-built castle saw action against the Venetians, Savoyards, Sardinians and Austrians and later fell to Napoleon. In 1867 it was bought by the British diplomat Montague Yeats Brown, who transformed it into a grand family home. The visit takes in several rooms housing some of Brown's furniture, and temporary exhibitions. The fabulous tiled staircase is one of the showpieces of the neogothic interior, while there are great views from the garden. For a better outlook continue for another 300m or so along the same track to the **lighthouse**.

Sailing boats and motorboats can be hired from **Giorgio Mussini & Co** (☎ 0185 26 93 27; Calata Marconi 38) in summer. **Garage Portofino Motonoleggio** (☎ 0185 26 90 39; Piazza della Libertà 27) rents mountain bikes (around €15 per day) and the tourist office distributes free maps of **walking** and **biking** trails around the Monte di Portofino (610m) in the Parco Naturale Regionale di Portofino.

Heading north along the coastal road is the **Abbazia della Cervara** (Abbazia di San Girolamo; ☎ 800 65 21 10; www.cervara.it; Lungomare Rossetti, Via Cervara 10; guided tours 10am, 11am & noon 1st & 3rd Sun of month Mar-Oct), built in 1361 and surrounded by formal gardens. Benedictine monks lived here from the 14th to the 18th century, during which time they played host to three popes and a saint (Catherine of Siena), while the French king, François I, spent a less convivial time here as a prisoner after the 1525 Battle of Pavia. French Trappist monks arrived in the 19th century, but the abbey has been a private residence since 1937. Guided tours (by reservation only)

take in the gardens, 15th-century chapterhouse, 16th-century cloister and the Saracen Tower built to safeguard the abbey against Saracen attacks in the 1500s.

SLEEPING & EATING

Don't expect to find any bargains in pricey Portofino.

Eden (☎ 0185 26 90 91; www.hoteledenportofino.com; Vico Dritto 18; s/d low season €130/180, high season €200/250; P) This pleasant, family-run hotel, with just 12 immaculate rooms, is on a quiet side street not far from the harbour front, and has a small palm-filled garden.

Piccolo Hotel (☎ 0185 26 90 15; www.dominapiccolo.it; Via Duca degli Abuzzi 31; d low/high season €140/235; P) The Little Hotel comes in the guise of a three-storey villa with signature palm trees and a tiny beach. It's a short walk from the port.

Hotel Splendido (☎ 0185 26 78 01; www.splendido.orient-express.com; Salita Baratta 16; s/d/ste low season from €501/856/1364, high season from €584/982/1572; P) The splendid Hotel Splendido is a former monastery set in the hills above the port, and has been Portofino's plushest hotel since the 1950s; the Duke and Duchess of Windsor, Burton and Taylor, and Bogart and Bacall are just some of the celebrity couples who've laid their heads here over the years. The sunny, spacious rooms have all been individually designed, and some come with balconies. Prices quoted are for half board.

The Hotel Splendido also runs the portside **Splendido Mare** (☎ 0185 26 78 06; Via Roma 2; s/d/ste low season from €410/473/893, high season from €512/591/1061; P).

Ö Magazin (☎ 0185 26 91 78; Calata Marconi 34; mains €15-20) Decked out like the cabin of a boat, this waterfront eatery is a tad more authentic than the rest. Look for the handful of tables romantically perched away from it all at the far end of the port.

Bar Mariuccia (☎ 0185 26 90 80; Piazza Martiri Olivetta 27) is a good place for a cappuccino, right on the square. As usual, you'll pay more if you sit outside.

GETTING THERE & AROUND

Portofino is an easy bus ride from Santa Margherita (see p210 for details).

From April to October, Servizio Marittimo del Tigullio (p211) runs daily ferries from Portofino to San Fruttuoso (one way/return €5.50/8) and Santa Margherita (€3.50/6).

Motorists must park at the village entrance and pay €4.50/12 every one/three hours (cash only) for the privilege.

Santa Margherita

pop 10,600

Once the home to a coral-fishing fleet that roamed as far afield as Africa, Santa Margherita, 32km southeast of Genoa, is known for its orange blossoms and lace. In a sheltered bay on the eastern side of the Portofino promontory on the Golfo di Tigullio, its waterfront is a jumble of one-time fishing cottages, elegant hotels with Liberty façades and moored million-dollar yachts.

ORIENTATION

From the **train station** (Via Roma), head downhill to the palm tree–clad port, then along Corso Doria to Piazza Vittorio Veneto, from where most buses depart. Boat trips depart from the jetty off the adjoining square, Piazza Martiri della Libertà.

INFORMATION

Internet point (☎ 0185 29 30 92; liguriacom@tigullio.it; Via Giunchetto 39; per hr €4)

Post office (Via Giunchetto 45; ✆ 8am-6pm Mon-Fri, 8am-1.15pm Sat)

Tourist office (☎ 0185 28 74 85; www.apttigullio .liguria.it; Via XXV Aprile 2b; ✆ 9.30am-12.30pm & 2.30-5.30pm Mon-Sat).

SIGHTS

Lemon trees, palms and other flora typical of Santa Margherita's hot climate grow in the parklands surrounding the 17th-century **Villa Durazzo** (☎ 0185 29 31 35; entrances at Piazzale San Giacomo 3, Via San Francesco d'Assisi 3 & Via Principe Centurione; admission free; ✆ 9.30am-6.30pm Mar-Oct, 9.40am-4.30pm Nov-Feb). The villa itself is closed to visitors.

In the centre of town, the baroque **Basilica Della Rosa** (Piazza Caprea), built in 1658, boasts the usual gaudy interior.

Sailing, water-skiing, scuba diving and walking opportunities abound, especially in the **Parco Naturale Regionale di Portofino**, which has its **headquarters** (☎ 0185 28 94 79; it.parcodiportofino@libero.it; Viale Rainusso 1) in Santa Margherita.

SLEEPING

Fasce (☎ 0185 28 64 35; www.hotelfasce.it; Via Luigi Bozzo 3; s/d/tr €88/98/125; P ✖) Tucked off a Corso Matteotti sidestreet, this two-star Anglo/Italian-run hotel has 16 clean and cosy modern rooms, a roof terrace for sunbathing and free bicycles to borrow.

Hotel Laurin (☎ 0185 28 99 71; www.laurinhotel.it; Lungomare Marconi 3; s €88-125, d €129-178; P ✖ ⛱) This Best Western quayside hotel provides the usual four-star comforts, including a 3rd-floor swimming pool and a gym. It also has its own private patch of sand.

Imperial Palace Hotel (☎ 0185 28 89 91; www .hotelimperial.com; Via Pagana 19; s/d low season from €157/267, high season from €187/314; P ✖ ⛱) The five-star Imperial is an historic 19th-century Liberty villa in the heart of town, and was the venue for the signing of the 1922 Treaty of Rapallo between Germany and Russia. It's set in a large seafront park and has a gym and heated seawater pool. Sea-view rooms are dearer.

EATING & DRINKING

Trattoria dei Pescatori (☎ 0185 28 67 47; Via Bottaro 43-44; mains €20-25; ✆ Wed-Mon) This simple but soulful seafood restaurant dates back to 1911 and serves pricey rustic dishes with a fishy flavour. *Moscardini affogati* (stewed baby octopus) is a speciality.

Ristorante Palma (☎ 0185 28 74 36; Piazza della Libertà 9; mains €7-10; ✆ lunch & dinner) Pizzas loom large on the menu at this central restaurant, though there are plenty of fish and meat dishes if you've had enough of them.

Bar Colombo (☎ 0185 28 70 58; Via Pescino 13; ✆ Tue-Sun) Do what Burton, Taylor and other Hollywood greats did and pass a few hours at this historic Art Nouveau place on the waterfront.

Zinco of London (☎ 0185 28 04 31; Via Pescino 6; pizzas €9, mains about €15; ✆ Thu-Tue) This 'American bar' and art café with large windows overlooking the central square is a cool spot for a cocktail.

GETTING THERE & AROUND

Tigullio Trasporti (☎ 800 01 48 08; www.tigullio trasporti.it in Italian) runs buses to/from Porto fino (€1, every 20 minutes) and Camogli (€1.10, every 30 minutes). Buy tickets at its **information kiosk** (☎ 0185 28 88 34; Piazza Vittorio Veneto) at the bus terminal. Tickets bought from the driver will cost slightly more.

By train, there are hourly services to/from Genoa (€2.10, 35 minutes) and La Spezia (€3.80, 1½ hours).

Servizio Marittimo del Tigullio (☎ 0185 28 46 70; www.traghettiportofino.it; Via Palestro 8/1b) runs seasonal ferries to/from Portofino Venere (one way/return €18/28.50), San Fruttuoso (€8/12.50), Portofino (€4.50/7) and Rapallo (€15/22).

Get around by **taxi** (☎ 0185 28 79 98), bicycle or moped – hire the latter two from **Noleggio Cicli e Motocicli** (☎ 330 87 86 12; Via XXV Aprile 11; per 4hr/day €7/10; ☺ Mon-Sat).

Rapallo
pop 29,360

Rapallo, overlooking the Gulf of Tigullio, gets particularly busy on Thursday when market stalls fill central Piazza Cile. Bright blue changing cabins line the town's sandy beach and lend the palm tree–studded waterfront an old-fashioned air. The little castle by the sea, built in 1550, hosts art exhibitions.

With its Roman origins Rapallo boasts a bridge supposedly used by Hannibal during the Carthaginian invasion of Italy in 218 BC. In the 19th century the town became known for its lace and was a popular destination for wintering tourists from Britain.

Since 1934 a **cable car** (☎ 0185 27 34 44; funivia .rapallo@libero.it; Piazzale Solari 2; one way/return €5.20/ 7.75; ☺ 9am-12.30pm Mon-Fri, 8.30am-12.30pm Sat & Sun Mar-Oct) has trundled up to **Santuario Basilica di Montallegro** (612m), a sanctuary built on the spot where, on 2 July 1557, the Virgin Mary was reportedly sighted. Walkers and mountain bikers can follow an old mule track (5km, 1½ hours) to the hill-top site. The **tourist office** (☎ 0185 23 03 46; Lungo Vittorio Veneto 7; ☺ 9.30am-12.30pm & 2.30-5.30pm Mon-Sat) has details of other walks in the area and stocks walking maps.

SLEEPING & EATING
Hotel L'Approdo (☎ 0185 23 45 45; www.approdohotel .it; Via San Michele di Pagana 160; s/d low season €49/98, high season €72/144; P ⛱) With its commanding hillside position, this is a smart, modern place with great sea views and sunny rooms, some fitted for disabled access.

Hotel Miro (☎ 0185 23 41 00; www.hotelmiro.net; Lungomare Vittorio Veneto 32; s/d low season €67/77, high season €110/130; P ⛱) On the seafront, the 10-room Hotel Miro occupies a 19th-century townhouse, and has retained much of its historical character. Half and full board are available.

The waterfront is lined with places to eat, drink and snack. Try **Parla Come Mangi**

(☎ 0185 23 49 93; Corso Italia 60), a fabulous wine, cheese and sausage shop.

GETTING THERE & AWAY
Tigullio Trasporti (☎ 800 01 48 08, 0185 23 11 08; www .tigulliotrasporti.it in Italian; Piazza delle Nazioni) runs regular buses to/from Santa Margherita (€1, every 20 minutes) and Camogli.

Servizio Marittimo del Tigullio runs year-round boats to/from Santa Margherita (one way/return €2/3), Portofino (€5/8) and San Fruttuoso (€7.50/12.50), and seasonal boats to Genoa (€11/15.50), the Cinque Terre (€17/26) and Porto Venere (€17/26).

Chiavari to Levanto

The stretch of coast between the Portofino promontory and the Cinque Terre can be a letdown, wedged as it is between two such beautiful spots. It does have some of the Riviera di Levante's best beaches, although the rash of resorts – **Chiavari**, **Lavagna**, **Sestri Levante**, **Deiva Marina** and **Levanto** – get packed out in summer.

Inland you can breathe fresh mountain air in the **Parco Naturale Regionale dell'Aveto**, a nature reserve at the northern end of the **Val d'Aveto**. The tranquil valley starts 12km north of the coast in **Borzonasca**. Heading north, **Santo Stefano d'Aveto** (population 1281) is a small cross-country skiing centre and the main village in the valley. Between the two is **Lago delle Lame**, a glacial lake whose shallow waters have preserved fir-tree stumps from 2500 years ago. Information on walks in the area is covered by the **park office** (☎ 0185 34 03 11; Via Marre 75a) in Borzonasca and Santo Stefano d'Aveto's **tourist office** (☎ 0185 880 46; Piazza del Popolo 1).

Chiavari (population 27,536), with an arcaded old town, 12km east of Santa Margherita, is the main access point inland; by car, follow the signs in town for Carasco. The Chiavari **tourist office** (☎ 0185 532 51 98; Corso Assarotti 1) is opposite the train station.

Cinque Terre

Clinging defiantly to the steep coastline west of La Spezia, the five villages that make up the Cinque Terre – Monterosso, Vernazza, Corniglia, Manarola and Riomaggiore – are among the most charming in Italy. This Unesco World Heritage site encompasses a national park and protected marine area, and offers several walking paths allowing you to explore the stunning scenery at your own leisure. Each village is linked by train.

The mountains, covered by terraced vineyards and 7000km of dry-stone walls, drop precipitously into the Mediterranean. Wine growers use monorail mechanisms to ferry themselves up and the grapes down, while olive groves festoon the lower slopes. Tourism long ago overtook fishing and viniculture as the mainstay industry (100 hectares are farmed today, compared to 1400 in its heyday), prompting fears for these unique lands; if the terraced hillsides are not worked, they will quite literally slide into the sea.

Although the **Parco Nazionale delle Cinque Terre** was created in 1999, it was not until 2002 that any real protective measures were taken. Information centres have now been set up and walkers pay to use trails that the park authorities close when numbers get too great.

Hotels are scarce but numerous villagers have rooms to rent: look for signs reading *camere* (rooms) or *affittacamere* (rooms for rent).

INFORMATION

National park offices sell the Cinque Terre Card (€3), valid for 24 hours and allowing unlimited use of walking paths. Cards covering rail travel also cover trails; a one-/three-/seven-day pass costs €5.40/13/20.60 (child €2.70/6.50/10.30). For online information, check out www.cinqueterre.it and www.cinqueterre.com. The park offices sell maps and have information on walking and cycling in the area.

Parco Nazionale office Cinque Terre (☎ 0187 92 06 33; www.parconazionale5terre.it in Italian; Piazza Rio Finale 26; ❧ 6.30am-8pm Oct-Apr, 6.30am-10pm Jun-Sep) Has Internet access per 10 minutes €0.80; Corniglia (☎ 0187 81 25 23; ❧ 7am-8pm); La Spezia (☎ 0187 74 35 00; ❧ 7am-8pm) Internet access per 10 minutes €0.80; Manarola (☎ 0187 76 05 11; ❧ 7am-8pm); Monterosso (☎ 0187 81 70 59; ❧ 7am-8pm); Vernazza (☎ 0187 81 25 33; ❧ 7am-8pm) The Cinque Terre office is the main one and is outside Riomaggiore train station.

MONTEROSSO
pop 1566

Monterosso is the most developed of the Cinque Terre villages, offering a good choice of hotels and restaurants. Huge statues are

---

LOVERS' LANE

The **Via dell'Amore** (Lovers' Lane; ☎ 0187 92 10 26; viadellamore@libero.it; ❧ 9am-9pm) is a well-paved coastal path linking Manarola with Riomaggiore (1km), lined with picnic areas and stone benches. At either end steps lead up from the train station to the path – checkpoints along the way ensure no-one sneaks by without a €3 trail pass.

The Via dell'Amore is part of the 12km-long *sentiero azzurro* (blue trail; trail No 2) that runs the length of the coast between Monterosso and Riomaggiore. Unlike Lovers' Lane (which is flat, well-paved and suited to walkers of all abilities, including children and wheelchairs and prams), the rest of the footpath is only for the sure footed and well equipped. The first stretch between Monterosso and Vernazza (4km) is particularly difficult – lots of ups and downs – and is the least scenic. Further east, dramatic coastal views and pretty little coves with crystal-clear water delight on the Corniglia to Manarola route (3km).

---

embedded into the rocks overlook one of the region's few beaches, a long, narrow stretch of coarse sand and pebbles.

Monterosso has several hotels to choose from, including the pleasant beachfront **Hotel La Spiaggia** (☎ 0187 81 75 67; www.laspiaggiahotel.com; Via Lungomare 98; s/d €100/130; P ⊠), a renovated 19th-century building with its own stretch of beach.

Alternatively, try the four-star **Hotel Palme** (☎ 0187 82 90 13; www.hotelpalme.it; Via 4 Novembre 18; d/tr from €155/202; P ⊠), a bright modern place with a lovely palm-filled garden.

On the seafront, **Enoteca 5 Terre** (☎ 0187 81 80 63; Lungomare Fegina 92-94) is an amenable spot to sip a glass or two of the local wine (around €2), and there is a well-stocked shop attached. In the historic centre **Enoteca Internazionale** (☎ 0187 81 72 87; Via Roma 62) and **Cantina du Sciacchetrà** (☎ 0187 81 78 28; Via Roma 7) are two of several wine bars where the Cinque Terre's renowned white wines can be tasted and bought.

Also worth trying are the local anchovies. Enjoy the tasty little fishes fresh from the sea, fried, raw with lemon juice, pickled in brine or in a *tian* (oven-baked with potatoes and tomatoes).

VERNAZZA
pop 1065

Vernazza's tiny harbour is a delight, so perfectly quaint you'll think you've wandered onto a film set. The small waterfront piazza seems to be the village focus, watched over by the rather gloomy harbour-side **Chiesa di Santa Margherita**, which has stood since 1318. The ruins of an 11th-century castle overlook the water on the other side of the port. Heading inland, the road is choked with vineyards and lemon groves.

Vernazza's main cobbled street, Via Roma, links seaside Piazza Marconi with the train station. **L'Eremo sul Mare** (☎ 339 268 5617; Via Gerai; d €90; 🔀) is a charming cliffside villa with just three rooms and a lovely sun terrace.

On the main street, there are several little cafés, while one of the best places to try traditional Cinque Terre seafood is **Trattoria Gianni Franzi** (☎ 0187 82 10 03; Piazza Matteotti 5; mains €10-12; 🕐 lunch & dinner). Fish dishes are also served at **Trattoria da Sandro** (☎ 0187 81 22 23; Via Roma 69; mains €10).

CORNIGLIA

Balanced precariously along a ridge high above the sea, Corniglia offers a picturesque scene of four-storey houses, narrow lanes and stairways woven into a hill by **La Torre**, a medieval lookout. From the central square, Via Fieschi cuts through the village heart to **Belvedere Santa Maria**, another lookout with a coastal panorama. In summer, minibuses shuttle tourists between the station and village – otherwise, it is a strenuous 363-step zig-zag uphill.

Dai Fera' (☎ 0187 81 23 23; Via alla Marina 39; d from €60) offers clean and simple rooms close to the seafront.

MANAROLA

More grapes are grown around Manarola than any other Cinque Terre village. At the northern end of steep Via Discovolo, you'll come upon **Piazzale Papa Innocenzo IV**, dominated by a bell tower and used as a defensive lookout in the Middle Ages. Opposite, the **Chiesa di San Lorenzo** dates from 1338 and houses a 15th-century polyptych. Fit visitors can follow a path off nearby Via Rollandi that leads through vineyards to the top of the mountain.

Hotel Ca' d'Andrean (☎ 0187 92 00 40; www.cadandrean.it; Via Discovolo 101; s/d €70/88) is a friendly,

family-run hotel that occupies an old olive mill with a relaxing garden planted with lemon trees. There's a bar, and breakfast is included. Small reductions are sometimes offered outside the summer season.

The Cinque Terre's only hostel, **Ostello 5 Terre** (☎ 0187 92 02 15; www.cinqueterre.net/ostello; Via Riccobaldi 21; dm low/high season €17/22, q low/high season €68/88; 🕐 reception low season 7am-1pm & 4pm-midnight, high season 7am-1pm & 5pm-1am; 💻), rents out mountain bikes, kayaks and snorkelling gear. Each single-sex, six-bed dorm has its own bathroom. Lockout times are 10am to 4pm or 5pm.

Marina Piccola (☎ 0187 92 01 03; www.hotelmarinapiccola.com; Via Lo Scalo 16; s/d from €83/105, mains about €12), the Little Marina, overlooks Manarola's little marina no less. *Zuppa di datteri* (date soup) and a shoal of fish dishes are the house specialities. Some of the rooms have sea views.

RIOMAGGIORE
pop 1789

A mess of houses slithering down a ravine to form the main street, Riomaggiore is the main village in the Cinque Terre. Tiny fishing boats bob by the shore or sit stacked on the small waterside square when seas are rough. Outside the train station – a short walk through a tunnel or ride in a lift from town – murals depict the hard work of Cinque Terre farmers who, over the centuries, built the Cinque Terre with their bare hands.

Marine life can be viewed through a mask with the **Cooperative Sub 5 Terre** (☎ 0187 92 05 96; Via San Giacomo), a diving centre that rents out snorkels and canoes/kayaks. Walkers with a keen eye for nature should make a beeline for the **Torre Guardiola** (☎ 0187 76 00 52; 🕐 9am-1pm Aug, 9am-1pm & 4-7pm Feb-Jul, Sep & Oct), a nature observation and bird-watching centre located on **Fossola Beach**, immediately southeast of Riomaggiore marina. From the centre a botanical walking trail leads along the coast.

A clutch of B&Bs, and room and apartment rental agencies litter Via Colombo, including:

Edi (☎ 0187 92 03 25; Via Colombo 111)
La Dolce Vita (☎ 0187 76 00 44; Via Colombo 120)
La Locanda Ca' dei Duxi (☎ 0187 92 00 36; www.duxi.it; Via Colombo 36; d low/high season from €60/90; P 🔀)

Locanda dalla Compagnia (☎ 0187 76 00 59; Via del Santuario 32; d €80; P 🔀) At the top of the road, it's an unmissable bright yellow house with green shutters, right beside the 16th-century Oratoria di Santa Maria Assunta.

There are a number of basic places to eat along the main street, including **Pizzeria Veciu Muin** (☎ 0187 92 04 87; Via Colombo 83; pizzas €7-8; 🕑 lunch & dinner Tue-Sun).

GETTING THERE & AROUND

The Cinque Terre's saving grace is its lack of motorised traffic. Cars are not allowed beyond village entrances, meaning a hefty hourly parking fee (about €1) and a strenuous hike of 1km or more. In some villages, park authorities run minibus shuttles (one way/return €1.50/2.50) between the car park and village entrance.

The easiest way to get to the Cinque Terre is by the Genoa–La Spezia train service, which trundles along the coast every 15 to 30 minutes between 6.30am and 10pm. Unlimited 2nd-class rail travel between Levanto and La Spezia is covered by the Cinque Terre Card (see p212).

In summer Cooperativa Battellieri del Golfo Paradiso (p206) runs boats to the Cinque Terre from Genoa.

Seasonal boat services to/from Santa Margherita (one way/return €14/21) are handled by Servizio Marittimo del Tigullio (p211).

From late March to October, La Spezia–based Navigazione Golfo dei Poeti (p216) runs daily shuttle boats between all of the Cinque Terre villages (except Corniglia).

La Spezia
pop 91,279

La Spezia, 100km southeast of Genoa, sits at the head of the gulf of the same name – also known as the Gulf of Poets in deference to Byron, Dante, DH Lawrence, Shelley, George Sand and many others drawn here by its beauty.

The construction from 1860 to 1865 of Italy's largest naval base propelled La Spezia from minor port to provincial capital, its street grid and venerable public buildings largely a product of that time. Today it's a busy working town, dominated by the still-significant naval presence, though its clutch of museums make it worth a stopover. It's also a useful base for excursions to the Cinque Terre, Porto Venere and beyond.

INFORMATION
Caffetteria Italia (Via Prione 315; per hr €2) Internet access.
Police station (☎ 0187 56 71; Viale Italia 497)
Post office (☎ 0187 79 61; Piazza di Giuseppe Verdi; 🕑 8am-6.30pm Mon-Sat)
Tourist office (☎ 0187 25 43 11; www.aptcinqueterre .sp.it; Viale G Mazzini 47; 🕑 9am-1pm & 2.30-5.30pm Mon-Sat, 9am-1pm Sun)

SIGHTS

La Spezia's star attraction is the **Museo Amedeo Lia** (☎ 0187 73 11 00; www.castagna.it/mal; Via Prione 234; adult/child €6/3; 🕑 10am-6pm Tue-Sun), a fine-art museum in a restored 17th-century friary. The collection covers the 13th to 18th centuries and includes paintings by masters such as Tintoretto, Montagna, Titian and Pietro Lorenzetti. Also on show are Roman bronzes and ecclesiastical treasures such as Limoges crucifixes and illuminated musical manuscripts.

Next door to the museum, the Palazzina delle Arti dates back to the 19th century. Inside, the **Museo del Sigilio** (☎ 0187 77 85 44; Via Prione 236; adult/child €3/2; 🕑 4-7pm Tue, 10am-noon & 4-7pm Wed-Sun) displays more than 1500 seals dating from the 4th millennium BC to the present day.

The **Castello di San Giorgio** (☎ 0187 75 11 42; www.castagna.it/sangiorgio; Via XXVII Marzo; adult/child €5/3; 🕑 9.30am-12.30pm & 3-6pm Wed-Mon Oct-Mar, 9.30am-12.30pm & 5-8pm Wed-Mon Apr-Sep) presents an assortment of local archaeological artefacts from the prehistoric through to the medieval period, including architectural fragments from Roman Luni (see p217) and ancient Ligurian statue-stelae.

A collection of mostly Italian abstract art can be viewed at the **Centro Arte Moderna e Contemporanea** (☎ 0187 73 45 93; Piazza Cesare Battisti 1; adult/child €6/4; 🕑 10am-1pm & 3-7pm Tue-Sat, 11am-7pm Sun), which also stages temporary exhibitions.

A ticket covering admission to all these museums costs €12 and is valid for 72 hours. You can purchase a ticket from any of the participating museums.

Next to La Spezia's naval base is the **Museo Tecnico Navale** (Naval Museum; ☎ 0187 78 30 16, Viale Amendola 1; admission €1.55; 🕑 8.30am-6pm Mon-Sat, 10.15am-3.45pm Sun), founded in 1870. It hosts a phalanx of *polene* (colourful busts or statuettes that graced the prows of vessels) and lots of model ships. The naval base

LA SPEZIA

0   400 m
0   0.2 miles

To Police Station
(1km); A15; Lerici
(10km); Tellaro (13km);
Parma (120km)

To Genoa
(100km)

To Cinque
Terre (20km);
Porto Venere
(23km)

Naval Base

Naval
Port

To Corsica;
Sardinia

To Coastal
Towns

To Genoa

To
Coastal
Towns

SLEEPING
Albergo Teatro..............................**8** B3
Hotel Firenze e Continentale.....**9** A1
Hotel Genova................................**10** B2
Hotel Venezia...............................**11** A1

EATING
Nettare e Ambrosia......................**12** B3
Trattoria Da Vito...........................**13** A2
Vicolo Intherno.............................**14** B3

DRINKING
Le Rune..**15** B3

SIGHTS & ACTIVITIES
Castello di San Giorgio.................**4** B2
Centro Arte Moderna e
Contemporanea..........................**5** B3
Museo del Sigilio.........................**6** B2
Museo Tecnico Navale..................**7** B4

INFORMATION
Caffetteria Italia.............................**1** A2
Post Office.....................................**2** C2
Tourist Office.................................**3** C3

TRANSPORT
ATC Bus for Porto Venere.........**16** B3
ATC Buses for Sarzana & Lerici..**17** A1
Ferry Terminal..............................**18** D3
Happy Lines.................................**19** D3
Navigazione Golfo dei Poeti......**20** C3

---

itself only opens to the public for one day of the year – 19 March, the festival of the town's patron saint, Joseph.

SLEEPING

Albergo Teatro (☎ 0187 73 13 74; www.albergoteatro .it; Via Carpenino 31; s/d with shared bathroom low season €20/35, high season €28/46, d with bathroom low/high season €45/61) Cheap and down-to-earth sums up La Spezia's Theatre Hotel where spartan rooms ensure a sound sleep nonetheless. It's predictably popular, so book ahead.

Hotel Venezia (☎ 0187 73 34 65; Via Paleocapa 10; s/d/tr low season €42/62/78, high season €51/87/103) Orange trees front this modern three-star hotel where a mustard-coloured façade shields a hotchpotch of furnishings inside.

Hotel Genova (☎ 0187 73 29 72; www.hotelgenova .it; Via F Rosselli 84; s/d €70/105; ✕) A charming exterior dresses a modern interior at this pleasant if unremarkable three-star pad, on a quiet pedestrian street off the main drag.

Hotel Firenze e Continentale (☎ 0187 71 32 00; www.hotelfirenzecontinentale.it; Via Paleocapa 7; s/d from €70/100; ✕) The three-star Florence is a smart but slightly stuffy place that has retained some of its early 1900s style. It is close to the train station.

EATING & DRINKING

Trattoria Da Vito (☎ 0187 77 07 65; Via Prione 287; pizzas €5-8; ✕ lunch & dinner) This tiny family-run place on the main street is a dependable place for fresh pizzas.

Vicolo Intherno (☎ 0187 239 98; Via della Canonica 22; mains €8-10; ☽ Tue-Sat) Sit around solid wooden tables beneath a hefty beamed ceiling and wash down the *torte di verdure* (Ligurian vegetable pie) or stockfish with a choice of local vintages.

Nettare e Ambrosia (☎ 0187 73 72 52; Via Fazio 85 & 86; mains €10-15; ☽ Mon-Sat) It might appear a tad shabby and simple from the outside, but Nectar & Ambrosia is *the* place to sample great wines in an authentic La Spezian atmosphere. Its largely fish-based cuisine is equally inspiring.

Le Rune (☎ 0187 75 18 87; Via Sapri 69; ☽ 7am-3am) This busy 'Celtic' pub also doubles as a tea room and café, and offers live music and tarot card readings in the evenings.

GETTING THERE & AWAY

Towns close to La Spezia can only be reached by buses run by **Azienda Trasporti Consortile** (ATC; ☎ 800 32 23 22; www.atclaspezia.it in Italian); these include Porto Venere (€1.35, up to five daily from Via Domenico Chiodo), Lerici (€1.35, two or three daily from the train station) and Sarzana (€1.50, two or three daily from the train station).

La Spezia is on the Genoa–Rome railway line and is also connected to Milan (€22, three hours, four daily), Turin (€20, three hours, several daily) and Pisa (€6.85, 50 minutes, almost hourly). The Cinque Terre and other coastal towns are easily accessible by train – tickets cost about €1.10 each stop.

Navigazione Golfo dei Poeti (☎ 0187 96 76 76; www.navigazionegolfodeipoeti.it; Passeggiata C Morin) runs boat services to Genoa, as well as other coastal towns.

From April through to October, **Happy Lines** (☎ 0187 56 44 28; Via Maralunga 45), with a ticket booth at the **ferry terminal**, runs daily ferries to Bastia in Corsica.

Porto Venere
pop 4120

Historic Porto Venere, with its riddle of narrow lanes, pretty harbour front and Byronic associations, is a pleasing spot to relax and enjoy some of the fine local seafood. The Romans built Portus Veneris as a base en route from Gaul to Spain, and in later years, Byzantines, Lombards, the Genovese and Napoleon all recognised its importance.

The **tourist office** (☎ 0187 79 06 91; www.porto venere.it; Piazza Bastreri 7; ☽ 10am-noon & 3-6pm Thu-Tue Apr-Sep) sells a couple of useful maps and walking guides in English. Outside the hectic summer season, Porto Venere is something of a ghost town.

From the waterfront, narrow steps and cobbled paths lead uphill to the **Chiesa di San Lorenzo** (built in 1130). In the church's shadow lies **Castello Doria** (adult/child €2.60/1.50; ☽ 10.30am-1.30pm & 2.30-5.30pm Fri-Sun), built in the 16th century as part of the Genoese Republic's defence system and offering magnificent views from its terraced gardens.

At the end of the quay a Cinque Terre panorama unfolds from the rocky terraces of **Grotta Arpaia**, a former haunt of Byron, who once swam across the gulf from Porto Venere to Lerici. George Sand also stayed here. Traces of a pagan temple have been uncovered on the quay, inside **Chiesa di San Pietro**, which was built in 1277 in the typical Genoese Gothic fashion with black-and-white bands of marble. Just off the promontory lie the tiny islands of **Palmaria**, **Tino** and **Tinetto**.

SLEEPING & EATING

Albergo Genio (☎/fax 0187 79 06 11; Piazza Bastreri 8; s/d low season €65/83, high season €76/88; ☽ mid-Feb-mid-Jan) This small, seven-room hotel is simple but atmospheric. From Piazza Bastreri, scale the spiral stairs in the round tower to get here. Breakfast (alfresco beneath the vines in summer) costs an extra €6.

Grand Hotel Portovenere (☎ 0187 79 26 10; ghp@rphotels.com; Via Garibaldi 5; d low/high season from €85/125; P X 🖵) This fabulous four-star oasis of charm and luxury, inside what was once a 12th-century monastery, is Porto Venere's grand choice.

A half-dozen or so restaurants line Calata Doria, by the sea. A block inland Porto Venere's main old-town street, Via Cappellini, proffers several tasty choices.

Antica Osteria del Caruggio (☎ 0187 79 06 17; Via Cappellini 94; mains about €10; ☽ lunch & dinner Fri-Wed) Sample razor-clam soup and other traditional dishes at this old-world place crammed with antique knick-knacks.

Fish is the main feature of the menu at **Ristorante del Pescatore** (☎ 0187 79 80 15; Via Olivo 33; mains €10-12; ☽ lunch & dinner), while lighter meals, including perch ravioli, can be had at tiny **Bar La Piazzetta** (Via Capellini 56; mains €6-8; ☽ lunch & dinner). It's also a nice spot for a quiet drink and a browse through the papers left out for customers.

GETTING THERE & AWAY

Porto Venere is served by daily buses from La Spezia.

From late March to October, La Spezia-based Navigazione Golfo dei Poeti (opposite) sails from Porto Venere to/from Lerici (return €8, six daily), La Spezia (return €6), the Cinque Terre (return €14 to €20) and Portofino (return €24, mid-June to mid-September). It also runs boat excursions to Palmaria, Tino and Tinetto (€8).

Lerici & Around
pop 10,847

At the southeastern end of the Riviera di Levante, 10km from La Spezia, Lerici is an exclusive summer refuge for wealthy Italians. Magnolia, yew and cedar trees grow in its 1930s public gardens, and pool-clad villas cling to the cliffs along the beach. For outstanding views make your way on foot or by public lift to the 12th-century Castello di Lerici, home to the ferociously fascinating **Museo Geopaleontologico** (☎ 0187 96 90 42; Piazza San Giorgio 1; adult/child €4.60/3.10; ◷ 10.30am-12.30pm Tue-Fri mid-Oct–mid-Mar, 10.30am-12.30pm Tue-Fri, 2.30-5.30pm Sat & Sun mid-Mar–Jun, 10.30am-12.30pm & 6.30pm–midnight Tue-Sun Jul-Aug, 10.30am 1pm & 2.30 6pm Tue-Sun Sep–mid-Oct). Earthquakes, robots and dinosaurs all feature in the museum's futuristic exhibits.

Lerici's **tourist office** (☎ 0187 96 73 46; Info@ aptcinqueterre.sp.it; Via Biaggini 6; ◷ 9am-1pm & 2.30-5.30pm Mon-Sat, 9am-1pm Sun) can advise on walking and cycling in the area. There are a number of hotels to choose from, including the attractive seafront **Hotel Shelley** (☎ 0187 96 82 04; www.hotelshelley.it; Lungomare Biaggini 5; s/d from €100/130; Ⓟ 🌠), with sunny rooms and a private stretch of sand. Half- and full-board deals are available.

From Lerici a scenic 3km coastal stroll leads north to **San Terenzo**, a seaside village with a sandy beach and Genoese castle. The Shelleys stayed at the waterfront Villa Magni (closed to visitors) in the early 1820s and Percy drowned here when his boat sank off the coast in 1822 on a return trip from Livorno.

Another coastal stroll, 4km south, takes you past magnificent little bays to **Tellaro**, a fishing hamlet with pink-and-orange houses cluttered about narrow lanes and tiny squares. Weave your way to the **Chiesa San Giorgio**, sit on the rocks and imagine an octopus ringing the church bells – which, according to legend, it did to warn the villagers of a Saracen attack.

Val di Magra

Southeast of La Spezia the Magra Valley forms the easternmost tongue of Ligurian territory. **Sarzana** (population 20,120), a short bus or train ride from La Spezia, was an important outpost of the Genoese republic. In its cathedral you can see the world's oldest crucifix painted on wood.

Enthusiasts of archaeology should head to **Luni** (☎ 0187 668 11; adult/child €2/free; ◷ 9am-7pm Tue-Sun), 6km southeast of Sarzana. Established as a Roman colony in 177 BC, it thrived as a wealthy trading centre until the Middle Ages, when the port began to silt up, encouraging the spread of malaria. The town was finally abandoned in 1204. Excavations have revealed an amphitheatre, forum, temples and houses, along with some remarkable mosaic floors and frescoes.

Nature walks abound in this pretty region, much of which is protected by the **Parco di Montemarcello-Magra**, which has an **information centre** (☎ 0187 69 10 71; www.parcomagra.it in Italian; Via Paci 2) in Sarzana.

RIVIERA DI PONENTE

Stretching southwest from Genoa to France, this part of the Ligurian coast is more built-up than the eastern side, although upmarket old-style resorts such as Imperia and Bordighera still charm the visitors here. San Remo, famous for its flowers and music festival, is the main coastal hotspot, while the mountains, hiding a warren of hill-top villages, promise cool air and pretty walking and driving circuits.

Savona
pop 61,910

When you approach Savona from either the southwest or northeast, it is the sprawl of the port's facilities that strikes you first – a sprawl that scarcely matches the chaos of its long-time rival, Genoa. The two cities were steady opponents from the time of the Punic Wars and the Genoese destroyed the town in 1528, proving their dominance.

The **tourist office** (☎ 019 840 23 21; iatsavona@ infocomm.it; Via Guidobono 23; ◷ 9am-12.30pm & 3-6pm Mon-Sat, 9am-12.30pm Sun) is near Savona's sandy beach.

Savona's medieval centre, dominated by the baroque **Cattedrale di Nostra Signora Assunta**, still survives, as does Savona's lumbering **Fortezza del Priamàr** (Piazza Priamàr), built in 1528 to protect the town. Within the fortress's impressive walls are an art gallery displaying 16th- to 20th-century works, a couple of sculpture museums and the **Civico Museo Storico Archeologico** (☎ 019 82 27 08; Piazza Priamàr; adult/child €2/1; ☼ 10am-noon & 4-6pm Tue-Sat, 4-6pm Sun), displaying archaeological treasures.

Restaurants, trattorie and cafés line Via Paleocapa.

SAR (☎ 0182 215 44) and **ACTS** (☎ 019 220 11) buses, departing from Piazza del Popolo and the train station, are the best options for reaching points inland. Bus No 2 links the train station and the fortress. On foot, Via Collodi and Via Don Minzoni lead from the station across the River Letimbro towards Piazza del Popolo, from where Via Paleocapa runs to the marina.

Trains run along the coast to Genoa (€2.95, 45 minutes, almost hourly) and San Remo (€5.35, 1¾ hours, eight daily).

Corsica Ferries (☎ 019 21 55 11) runs up to three boats daily between Savona's Porto Vado and Corsica.

Finale Ligure
pop 12,300

With a good beach and affordable accommodation, Finale Ligure is a handy base for exploring the Riviera di Ponente. Its historic centre, known as Finalborgo – a clutter of twisting alleys behind medieval walls – is set back from the coast on the River Pora. Finale Marina, on the waterfront, is where most hotels and restaurants languish, while Finale Pia – towards Genoa – runs along the River Sciusa and is more suburban.

From the train station at Piazza Vittorio Veneto, at Finale Marina's western end, walk down Via Saccone to the sea and the **tourist office** (☎ 019 68 10 19; iatfinale@italianriviera.com; Via San Pietro 14; ☼ 9am-12.30pm & 3-6.30pm Mon-Sat, 9am-noon Sun). The promenade along Via San Pietro and Via Concezione, plus the pedestrian Via Roma, are crammed with places to eat.

SAR (☎ 0182 215 44) buses yo-yo every 30 minutes along the coast to/from Savona (€2, 50 minutes), stopping en route in Finalborgo (€1, five minutes) and Noli (€1.25, 20 minutes). Buses use the stop in front of the train station.

Albenga
pop 22,760

Albenga's medieval centre sets it apart from the resorts further west.

Settled as far back as the 5th century BC, Albenga grew from its Roman roots to become an independent maritime republic during the Middle Ages. In the 13th century it threw in its lot and formed an alliance with Genoa.

The **tourist office** (☎ 0182 55 84 44; iatalbenga@italianriviera.com; Viale Martiri della Libertà 1; ☼ 9am-12.30pm & 3-6.30pm Tue-Sat) has plenty of useful information on the town.

Albenga's **Museo Diocesano di Arte Sacra** (Via Episcopio 5; adult/child €3/1; ☼ 10am-noon & 3-6pm Tue-Sun), featuring a painting by Caravaggio, is near a 5th-century **baptistry** and Romanesque **cathedral**.

A collection of 1st-century amphorae, recovered in 1950 from the wreck of a Roman cargo vessel found 4km offshore, is displayed in the **Museo Navale Romano** (Roman Naval Museum; ☎ 0182 512 15; Piazza San Michele 12; adult/child €3/1; ☼ 10am-12.30pm & 2.30-6pm Tue-Sun).

From the train station at Piazza Matteotti, turn left and then left again beneath the railway bridge, then bear east along tree-lined Viale Italia to get to the sea. To get to the historic centre from Piazza Matteotti, walk straight ahead (west) along Viale Martiri della Libertà.

Albenga is served by trains and SAR buses (the main stop is on Piazza del Popolo) along the coast.

Alassio
pop 11,365

In addition to 3km of white beaches, pretty Alassio boasts its own variety of *baci* (literally 'kisses'), sugary concoctions comprising two biscuit whirls sandwiched together with chocolate cream.

The **tourist office** (☎ 0182 64 70 27; iatalassio@italianriviera.com; Via Mazzini 68) can assist you with hotel reservations. The **regional tourist office** (☎ 0182 64 711; www.italianriviera.com; Viale Gibb 26) is another useful source of information on Alassio and its surrounds.

Narrow alleys cut from Via XX Settembre to the beach. A couple of streets inland, between the sea and the Art Nouveau train station, is the **Muretto di Alassio**, a wall of fame engraved with visiting luminaries' autographs. Hemingway's is on the façade of the building opposite at Corso Dante 312 (a legendary café in the 1930s).

Alassio was once a popular destination for wealthy sun-seeking Britons in the 19th century, and should you decide to stay, the **Villa della Pergola** (☎ 0182 64 04 14; www.villadel lapergola.it; Via Privata Montagù 9/1; s/d/ste €150/180/200; P) recaptures some of the style and luxury enjoyed by the upper-class Victorians. Built in the 1880s by Sir Daniel Hanbury, this peaceful mansion has just six rooms with classic English furnishings, and is set in a huge park planted with eucalyptus, pine and olive trees. The minimum stay is two nights. Cheaper sleep is available at the three-star **Hotel dei Fiori** (☎ 0182 64 05 19; www.hoteldeifiori-alas sio.it; Viale Marconi 78; d low/high season €48/85; ✷).

Imperia
pop 39,518

Dominated by lines of hothouses on the surrounding hillside, Imperia is the main city of Liguria's westernmost province, commonly known as the Riviera dei Fiori because of the area's flower-growing industry, which is among Italy's most extensive. Imperia was founded in 1923 by Mussolini when he bridged the River Impero and unified the towns of Porto Maurizio (west) and Oneglia (east) – they still retain the air of separate towns. The resort's outlying apartment blocks are hardly appealing, but Porto Maurizio – the older of the two – dominated by a large neoclassical cathedral, merits an afternoon stroll.

From Porto Maurizio train station, go uphill to Viale Matteotti or through an underpass to the waterfront, which eventually leads to Corso Garibaldi. The **tourist office** (☎ 0183 66 01 40; Viale G Matteotti 37) can advise on accommodation, including the resort's numerous camping grounds.

San Remo
pop 50,834

San Remo came to the forefront in the 19th century as a resort for Europe's leisured high society, with a particularly high contingent coming from Britain and Russia; Tsarina Maria Alexandrovna (mother of the last tsar, Nicholas II) once held court here. Today, the self-styled 'City of Flowers' may not be quite so grand or exclusive, but it is a busy and likeable town, and makes a good base for exploring the Riviera.

The ancient heart of San Remo, La Pigna (literally 'Pine Cone'), is a muddled maze of streets just north of Corso Matteotti, San Remo's main strip. Corso Matteotti runs westwards and at Piazzale Battisti it meets Corso Imperatrice, while eastwards it turns into Corso Giuseppe Garibaldi, which itself then transforms into Corso Felice Cavallotti, where you'll find the train station.

INFORMATION

Get your hands on *Rivieri dei Fiori News*, a free monthly newspaper available at the tourist office. For more information about the area, check out www.sanremoguide.com, www.sanremonet.com and www.sanremo manifestazioni.it (in Italian).

Hospital (☎ 0184 53 61; Via Giovanni Borea 56)
Police station (☎ 0184 5 90 81; Via del Castillo 5)
Post office (Via Roma 156; ✷ 8am-6pm Mon-Sat)
Tourist office (☎ 0184 59 059; www.rivieradeifiori.org; Largo Nuvoloni 1; ✷ 8am-7pm Mon-Sat, 9am-1pm Sun)

SIGHTS & ACTIVITIES

The **Chiesa Russa Ortodossia** (☎ 0184 53 18 07; Via Nuvoloni 2; admission €1; ✷ 9.30am-noon & 3-6pm) was built for the Russian community that followed Tsarina Maria to San Remo. The Russian Orthodox church – with its onion shaped domes and pale blue interior – was designed in 1906 by Alexei Shchusev who, 20 years later, planned Lenin's mausoleum in Moscow. These days it's used as an exhibition space for Russian icons. Nearby, high above Corso Matteotti, is the famous **casino** (Corso degli Inglesi), built in 1905 for the expat big-spenders and still going strong.

A stroll along shop-lined Corso Matteotti brings you to the sumptuous **Palazzo Borea d'Olmo** (☎ 0184 53 19 42; Corso Matteotti 143; admission free; ✷ 9am-noon & 3-6pm Tue-Sat), built during the 15th century, which today houses the **Museo Civico**. Several rooms, some with fine frescoed ceilings, hold small displays of local prehistoric and Roman archaeological finds, paintings and temporary exhibitions. Highlights include Maurizio Carrega's *Gloria di San Napoleone*, painted in 1808 as a sycophantic homage to the Corsican despot of the same name, and bronze statues by Franco Bargiggia. From here you can cut west through the narrow streets to get to **La Pigna**.

Go northeast along Corso Matteotti to reach Italy's principal **flower market** (Via Frantoi

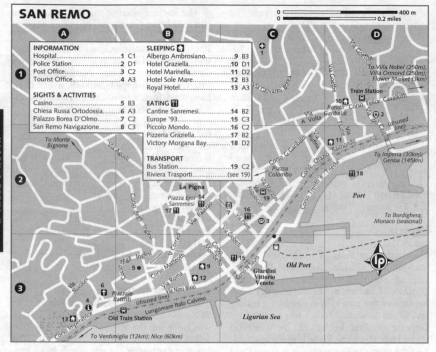

SAN REMO

0 ————————— 400 m
0 ————————— 0.2 miles

INFORMATION
Hospital.............................1 C1
Police Station....................2 D1
Post Office........................3 C2
Tourist Office....................4 A3

SIGHTS & ACTIVITIES
Casino...............................5 B3
Chiesa Russa Ortodossia...6 A3
Palazzo Borea D'Olmo.......7 C2
San Remo Navigazione......8 C3

SLEEPING
Albergo Ambrosiano............9 B3
Hotel Graziella.................10 D1
Hotel Marinella................11 D2
Hotel Sole Mare...............12 B3
Royal Hotel.....................13 A3

EATING
Cantine Sanremesi.............14 B2
Europe '93......................15 C3
Piccolo Mondo.................16 C2
Pizzeria Graziella.............17 B2
Victory Morgana Bay..........18 D2

TRANSPORT
Bus Station......................19 C2
Riviera Trasporti............(see 19)

To Villa Nobel (250m);
Villa Ormond (250m);
Flower Market (3km)

Train Station

To Monte Bignone

To Imperia (30km);
Genoa (145km)

La Pigna

Piazza Eroi Sanremesi

Piazza Colombo

Port

To Bordighera;
Monaco (seasonal)

Old Port

Giardini Vittorio Veneto

Piazzale Battisti   (disused line)

Old Train Station

Lungomare Italo Calvino

Ligurian Sea

To Ventimiglia (12km); Nice (60km)

Canaii; ☼ 6-8am Jun-Oct), 3km east of town – go to watch the frenetic bidding. Further east still, Corso Felice Cavallotti leads to a clutch of elegant villas. The Moorish **Villa Nobel** (Corso Felice Cavallotti 112), to the east of the city centre, is the former home of Alfred Nobel, the Swedish inventor of dynamite who bestowed his name on the Nobel Prize. Occasional art exhibitions are held in **Villa Ormond** (☎ 0184 50 57 62; Corso Felice Cavallotti 51; admission free; ☼ gardens 8am-7pm), better known for its Japanese gardens.

San Remo Navigazione (☎ 0184 50 50 55; Corso Nazario Sauro), at the old port, runs twice-daily 1½-hour boat trips to Bordighera (adult/child €12/6 March–September).

FESTIVALS & EVENTS
San Remo hosts a number of major events, starting off with the colourful **Corso Fiorito** (Flower Parade), held over two days in January. The **Festival di San Remo** (www.festivaldisanremo.com in Italian), a festival of Italian music, has been going since 1951, and attracts top talent from both Italy and overseas each March.

San Remo is also famous for its rallies (www.sanremorally.it), kicking off with the **Rally Storico** in April, a race for cars made between 1931 and 1981. The **Rally Classic** takes place in May, while the big **Rally e San Remo**, first held in 1926, is run in October every three years; the next is due in 2006.

SLEEPING
San Remo has no shortage of hotels, although summer and festival times can be awkward and many places shut in September.

Albergo Ambrosiano (☎ 0184 57 71 89; www.hotel ambrosiano.it; Via Roma 36; d low/high season from €40/80) This friendly 4th-floor hotel is one of the best deals in town. Its eight rooms are clean and spacious, although those with lots of luggage may find the miniature lift something of a challenge.

Hotel Graziella (☎ 0184 57 10 31; fax 0184 57 00 43; Rondò Garibaldi 2; s/d/tr €50/60/70) Handy for the train station, Graziella is an attractive villa set back from the road in a pretty garden.

Hotel Sole Mare (☎ 0184 57 71 05; fax 0184 53 27 78; Via Carli 23; s/d/tr/q low season €57/77/100/120, high season €54/89/122/145; P ❄) Sole Mare is a bright and airy option on the 4th floor of a blue-painted building.

Hotel Marinella (☎ 0184 50 59 00; www.hotel marinella.it in Italian; Via Rufina 21; s/d from €50/80; 🖳) Just across the road from the seafront, the Marinella is a good midrange choice with its own restaurant. Rooms are light and modern, and have their own balconies.

Royal Hotel (☎ 0184 53 91; www.royalhotelsanremo .com; Corso Imperatrice 80; s/d low season from €125/185, high season from €214/314; P 🖳 🖳 🖳) The elegant five-star Royal opened its doors in 1872 and remains San Remo's finest hotel. With its large gardens, pools, tennis court, minigolf and children's playrooms, it's like a resort in itself, and rooms are tastefully traditional.

EATING
Cheap trattorie fill the old-town alleys around Piazza Eroi Sanremesi and open-air snack bars stud the length of Corso Nazario Sauro, the promenade overlooking the old port.

Europe '93 (☎ 0184 50 14 10; Via Nino Bixio 47; pizzas €6-8; 🕑 lunch & dinner) Fresh, good-quality oven-baked pizzas are the stock in trade of this smart little place near the seafront.

Victory Morgana Bay (☎ 0184 59 16 20; Corso Trento e Trieste 16; mains €8-12; 🕑 11am-3pm Tue, 11am-2am Wed-Mon) This upmarket 'yachting café' boasts an enviable seafront location and serves up a varied menu of salads, *panini*, fish and grills, with occasional live music in the evenings.

Cantine Sanremesi (☎ 0184 57 20 63; Via Palazzo 7; 1st/2nd courses from €5/7; 🕑 Tue-Sun) Try the local cuisine at this old tavern, about the only place in San Remo with a time-worn character. The *stoccafisso alla sanremasa* (stockfish with tomato and potatoes) is delicious.

Piccolo Mondo (☎ 0184 50 90 12; Via Piave 7; mains from €10; 🕑 Mon, Tue, Thu & Fri) Feast on *trippe alla ligure* (Ligurian tripe), *polpo con patate* (octopus with potatoes) or osso buco (veal shanks) at San Remo's most traditional dining spot. What's cooking depends on what's at the market.

Pizzeria Graziella (☎ 0184 50 20 88; Piazza Eroi Sanremesi 49; mains €7-8; 🕑 lunch & dinner) This simple place serves up a big menu of pizzas and pasta dishes and offers a reasonable three-course 'tourist menu' (€12).

GETTING THERE & AROUND
Riviera Trasporti (☎ 0184 59 27 06; Piazza Colombo 42) buses leave from the bus station for the French border, Imperia (€1.80, 45 minutes, at least hourly) and inland destinations such as Taggia (25 minutes, at least hourly).

From San Remo's labyrinthine underground train station on Corso Felice Cavallotti there are trains to/from Genoa (€7.70, three hours, hourly), Ventimiglia (€1.60, 15 minutes, hourly) and stations in between.

Valle Argentina
The Silver Valley stretches from **Taggia** (population 13,622), a charming place a few kilometres inland from the San Remo–Imperia road, into thickly wooded mountains that seem light years from the coastal resorts. Quaint villages abound in this neck of the woods, each seeming even more impossibly perched on a hill crest than the one before.

Buses from San Remo head as far as **Triora** (population 425; elevation 776m), which is 33km north of San Remo. This haunting medieval village, the scene of celebrated witch trials and executions in the 16th century, dominates the surrounding valleys and the trip is worth the effort. Gruesome tales of witches being burned alive are portrayed in its **Museo Etnografico e della Stregoneria** (Museum of Ethnography & Witchcraft; Corso Italia 1; adult/child €2/1; 🕑 2.30-6pm Mon-Fri, 10.30am-noon & 2.30-6pm Sat & Sun Oct-Apr, 3-7pm Mon-Fri, 10.30am-noon & 3-7pm Sat & Sun Jun, Jul & Sep, 10.30am-noon & 3-7pm Aug).

Triora's **tourist office** (☎ 0184 9 44 77; Corso Italia 7) has information on the valley.

Valle Nervia
From Triora, a stunning 25km-long series of hairpin bends brings you to **Pigna** (population 989; elevation 280m) in the upper Valle Nervia. Riddled with alleys and narrow streets crisscrossing in all directions, the medieval village is a delight to get lost in. Its fortified neighbour and traditional rival, **Castel Vittorio** (population 395; elevation 420m), 5km to the southeast, is equally medieval.

Isolabona (population 690; elevation 106m), a former stronghold of the Doria family 10km south of Castel Vittorio, is dominated by a half-ruined 15th-century castle where concerts are held in summer. From here you can pick up the scenic drive from Ventimiglia to San Remo on the coast.

A frequent visitor to the **Dolceacqua** (population 1943; elevation 51m) Monet painted the medieval village's plentiful palazzi several times. The Doria's family castle tops off the old upper part of the village on the left bank of the River Nervia. Theatre performances are held here in July and August. Cross the late-medieval, single-span bridge, 33m wide, to get to Il Borgo, Dolceacqua's newer quarters. The **tourist office** (☎ 0184 20 66 66; www.dolceacqua.it; Via Barberis Colombo 2) has a list of places where you can taste and buy the village's well-known Rossese, ruby-red wine. Black olives are grown in abundance here.

Buses (four to six daily) link Ventimiglia with Pigna, Castel Vittorio, Apricale, Isolabona and Dolceacqua; Ventimiglia's tourist office has updated schedules (see below).

Bordighera
pop 10,487
A few kilometres west of San Remo is the built-up town, Bordighera. Apart from being a one-time favourite haunt of rich British seaside-lovers – the collection of charming hotels and a British cemetery attest to this – Bordighera's fame rests on a centuries-old monopoly of the Holy Week palm business. The Vatican selects its branches exclusively from the palms along the promenade Lungomare Argentina. The **tourist office** (☎ 0184 26 23 22; Via Vittorio Emanuele 172) can give you details on accommodation.

Ventimiglia
pop 26,725
Those arriving from the snazzier side of the French Riviera will probably find Ventimiglia a bit of a letdown. The town is fairly bland and the beach grey and pebbly. However, it's a useful base for jaunts into the hinterland. Typically in this frontier area, French seems to have almost equal status with Italian.

Corso Genova is the main eastern exit from the city, while its continuation to the west, Via Cavour, runs past the **tourist office** (☎ /fax 0184 35 11 83; Via Cavour 61; ⏰ 9am-12.30pm & 3-7pm Mon-Sat) and into France.

Ventimiglia's **Area Archeologica** (Roman ruins; admission free; ⏰ 3-5.30pm Sat & Sun), on the eastern edge of town, includes an amphitheatre and baths dating from the 2nd and 3rd centuries when the town was known as Albintimulium. Its medieval town, riddled with steep and twisting alleyways and crowned with a

12th-century **cathedral** (Via del Capo), looms on a hill on the western bank of the River Roia.

The sea-facing **Hotel Seagull** (☎ 0184 35 17 26; www.seagullhotel.it; Passeggiata Marconi 24; s/d from €60/75; 🅿) is in a quiet, scenic spot on the opposite (west) side of the River Roia from the town centre. Both half- and full-board options are offered.

Gran Caffè Cavour (Via Cavour 43b; fixed price menus €8.90; ⏰ lunch & dinner) is a cheap and cheerful eatery that offers fixed two-course meals with wine. It is regularly packed out.

Those with their own transport should consider picking up a copy of the free booklet *Le Vie dei Sapori e dei Colori* (Routes of Flavours and Colours) from the tourist office. It details, in English, French, German and Italian, three scenic routes accessible from Ventimiglia.

The blue route (18km) follows the Val Roia north to the village of Olivetta San Michele on the French border; the red route (24km) runs along the Val Nervia, through Dolceacqua and Pigna towards Castel Vittorio; and the green route (33km) twists northeast through olive groves and vineyards to the village of Bajardo (elevation 910m). A fourth track, the yellow route (16km), links Bordighera with the little hillside village of Seborga (elevation 517m).

From the **train station** (Via della Stazione), Corso della Repubblica leads to the beach. Trains connect Ventimiglia with Genoa (€8.80, two to 3½ hours, hourly), Nice (50 minutes, hourly) and into France.

Villa Hanbury
Overlooking the coast just by the small village of **Mortola** are the **Giardini Botanici Hanbury** (☎ 0184 22 95 07; adult/child €7.50/4; ⏰ 9.30am-6pm mid-Jun–mid-Sep, 9.30am-5pm mid-Sep–mid-Oct & Mar–mid-Jun, 9.30am-4pm mid-Oct–Feb). Established in 1867 by the wealthy English businessman Sir Thomas Hanbury, this unique 18-hectare estate hosts a varied array of native and exotic flora, including a palm grove, Australian forest and citrus orchard, along with a section of Roman road. Today it's under the care of the University of Genoa, and is recognised as an internationally important botanical collection. Take bus No 1a from Via Cavour in Ventimiglia; the bus goes on to the Ponte San Lodovico frontier post, from where you can walk down to the Balzi Rossi on the French border.

PIEDMONT

The historical home of Italian unity and Italian industry, Piedmont (Piemonte) stretches along the French and Swiss borders, drawing influences from both countries. The regional capital, Turin, with its grand squares, elegant arcades and cultured café society, is a fascinating city brimming with some of the country's very best museums and galleries. Much of Italy's industrial boom last century had its roots in and around Turin where Fabbrica Italiana di Automobili Torino (Fiat) started making cars. Today, Piedmont is second only to Lombardy in industrial production and

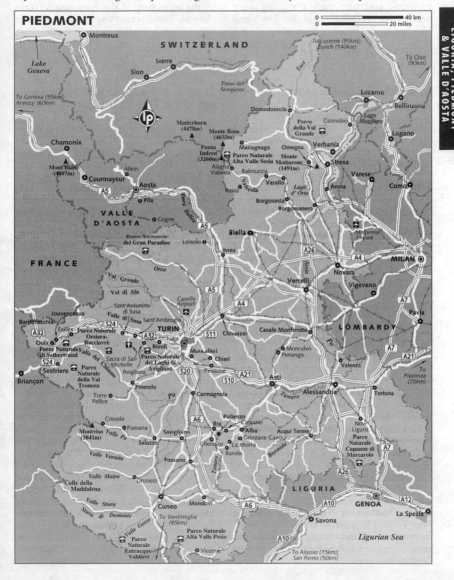

PIEDMONT

is one of the country's wealthiest areas. International attention will be focused on the region in 2006 when the XX Winter Olympic Games get underway.

Piedmont is famous for its food and wine, including pricey but excellent Barolo and sparkling Asti. White truffles, hazelnuts and chocolate are other highly regarded local products, and with such a rich culinary heritage it's no wonder that the Slow Food Movement, dedicated to promoting the art of real cooking and fresh, traditional ingredients, has its international headquarters here. The region accounts for two-thirds of Italy's rice production, and risotto is a favourite local dish. You need never have a bad meal in Piedmont!

The area's other main attraction is the Grande Traversata delle Alpi, a walk of more than 200km through the Alps from the Ligurian border to Lago Maggiore in the northeast of the region.

Activities

For walkers the big hike is the two-week Grande Traversata delle Alpi (GTA), starting near Viozene in southern Piedmont and following a network of Alpine *rifugi* (mountain huts) north through the province of Cuneo, the Valle di Susa and the Parco Nazionale del Gran Paradiso. It continues across the north of the region before ending on the banks of Lago Maggiore at Cannobio. Tourist offices and regional branches of Club Alpino Italiano have maps, itineraries, and lists of *rifugi* (which are generally open from July to September).

Horse riding is a popular summertime activity here. Many places organise treks and less-demanding rides through some of the region's valleys and national parks. A popular approach is to book a place in an *agriturismo* (farm-stay accommodation) where horse riding is an option. Contact **Agriturismo Piemonte** (☎ 011 53 49 18; www.agriturismopiemonte.it in Italian; Via Lagrange 2) in Turin for a list of 100-plus farms that offer a range of activities, accommodation and dining opportunities.

Some of Europe's most fashionable Alpine **skiing** pistes and greatest peaks – Mont Blanc and the Matterhorn – are spitting distance from Turin. The generous sprinkling of Piedmontese resorts and villages in between the great mountains will host the 2006 Winter Olympics.

TURIN

pop 900,985 / elev 240m

At the confluence of the rivers Po and Dura, Turin (Torino) is a regal baroque city of wide boulevards, covered arcades, grand public buildings and palatial coffee houses, all indicative of its important past and wealthy and cultured present. Famous worldwide as the repository of the eponymous Turin Shroud, Turin is also known for producing cars, chocolate, coffee and vermouth – Fiat, Ferrero Rocher, Lavazza, Cinzano and Martini are local institutions, while Turin is also the home town of Nutella and Tic-Tacs.

In addition, Turin has an enviable roll call of top-class museums, such as the Museo Egizio and Museo Nazionale del Cinema, that can justly lay claim to being among the very best of their kind anywhere. Meanwhile, its galleries hold some of Italy's most important art collections. Although much of the industrial and suburban sprawl west and south of the centre is predictably awful, there's an enormous green belt in the hills east of the Po River, proffering splendid views to the snow-covered Alps to the west and north. The city is also rapidly shedding its old industrial image. Preparations for the 2006 Winter Olympics have engendered a real civic pride and set a building boom in motion, with a new metro system currently under construction.

History

It is unclear whether the ancient city of Taurisia began as a Celtic or Ligurian settlement. It was destroyed by Hannibal in 218 BC, and the Roman colony of Augusta Taurinorum was established here almost two centuries later. In succeeding years, Goths, Lombards and Franks tramped through the city. In 1563 the Savoys abandoned their old capital of Chambéry (now in France) to set up court in Turin, which pretty much shared the dynasty's fortunes thereafter. The Savoys annexed Sardinia in 1720, but Napoleon virtually put an end to their power and occupied Turin in 1798. Turin suffered Austrian and Russian occupation before Vittorio Emanuele I restored the House of Savoy and re-entered Turin in 1814. Nevertheless, Austria remained the true power throughout northern Italy until unification, when Turin became the capital (1861–64), an honour it then passed onto Florence.

Turin adapted quickly to its loss of political significance, becoming first a centre for industrial production during the early 20th century and later a hive of trade-union activity. Giants such as Fiat lured hundreds of thousands of impoverished southern Italians to Turin and housed them in vast company-built and -owned suburbs such as Mirafiori to the south. Fiat's owners, the Agnelli family (who also happen to own the champion Juventus football club, Turin's local newspaper and a large chunk of the national daily *Corriere della Sera*), is one of Italy's most powerful establishment forces. These days, Turin is Italy's second-largest industrial city after Milan.

Orientation

Stazione Porta Nuova is currently the main point of arrival, although most trains will be using the revamped Stazione Porta Susa, once its construction is complete in 2007. Busy Corso Vittorio Emanuele II is the main tram and bus route, running southeast to northwest, while Via Roma links the station (southwest) with Piazza Castello (northeast). Piazza Carlo Felice, the square in front of the station, and Via Nizza, which continues southwest past the station, are the main axes of Turin's seedier side.

The Mole Antonelliana dominates the horizon to the east, while vast Piazza Vittorio Veneto leads up to the mighty River Po. The city's nightlife is centred round the riverside Murazzi del Po and the Quadrilatero Romano, the old-town patch of Turin west of Piazza Castello.

Information

BOOKSHOPS

Libreria Druetto (☎ 561 91 66; drulib@tin.it; Via Roma 227) Art, architecture and design books.
Libreria Luxemburg (☎ 011 561 38 96; Via Battisti 7) Anglo-American bookshop.
Touring Club Italiano (☎ 011 562 72 07; Via San Francesco d'Assisi 3) Excellent range of maps and guides.

EMERGENCY

Police station (☎ 011 5 58 81; Corso Vinzaglio 10)

INTERNET ACCESS

1PC4YOU (☎ 011 83 59 08; Via Giuseppe Verdi 20g; per hr €6; ☯ 9am-10pm Mon-Sat, noon-10pm Sun)
FNAC (☎ 011 511 67 11; Via Roma 56; per 30/60min €2/3; ☯ 9.30am-8pm Mon-Sat, 10am-8pm Sun)

Internet Train (☎ 011 54 30 00; Via Carlo Alberto 18; per 30min €3; ☯ 9.30am-10pm Mon-Fri, 9.30am-8pm Sat) Free surfing 1pm to 1.30pm and 7pm to 7.30pm.

INTERNET RESOURCES

Extra Torino (www.extratorino.it) Comprehensive, up-to-date listings guide in English.
Visit Turin 2006 (www.visitturin2006.com) Ideas on what to see and do in the city.

LAUNDRY

Lav@sciuga (www.lavasciuga.torino.it; ☯ 8am-10pm) There are several branches around town, at Piazza della Repubblica 5, Via Sant'Anselmo 9 and Via Vanchiglia 10, which also provide free Internet access for customers.

LEFT LUGGAGE

Stazione Porta Nuova (opposite platform No 16; 1st 12/next 12hr €3/2; ☯ 6am-midnight)

MEDICAL SERVICES

Farmacia Boniscontro (☎ 011 53 82 71; Corso Vittorio Emanuele II 66; ☯ 3pm-12.30am) Night pharmacy.
Ospedale Mauriziano Umberto I (☎ 011 5 08 01; Largo Turati 62) Hospital.
Pharmacy (☎ 011 518 64 67; Stazione Porta Nuova; ☯ 7am-7.30pm)

MONEY

A bank, ATM and exchange booth can all be found within Stazione Porta Nuova. Other banks dot Via Roma and Piazza San Carlo. A 24-hour automatic banknote change machine can be found outside **Banca CRT** (Piazza CLN) and another in front of **Banca San Paolo** (Via Santa Teresa 1g).

POST

Post office (Via Alfieri 10; ☯ 8.30am-7pm Mon-Fri, 8.30am-1pm Sat)

TOURIST INFORMATION

There is only one central phone number for tourist offices.
Airport tourist office (☎ 011 53 51 81; ☯ 8.30am-10.30pm)
Atrium Città (☎ 011 53 51 81; www.atriumtorino.it; Piazza Solferino; ☯ 9.30am-7pm) Multimedia resources on Turin, event/concert reservations, plus café.
Atrium Torino 2006 (☎ 011 53 51 81; www.turismo torino.org; Piazza Solferino; ☯ 9.30am-7pm) Main tourist office, Olympic information and museum.
Circolo Culturale Maurice (☎ 011 521 11 16; www .mauriceglbt.org in Italian; Via della Basilica 3-5) Gay and lesbian information and happenings.

LIGURIA, PIEDMONT & VALLE D'AOSTA

TURIN

Corso Francia

To Docks Home, Castello di Rivoli (12km); Valle di Susa (52km)

Piazza Statuto

Via San Domenico

Via Giuseppe Garibaldi

Via Pessalacqua

Stazione Porta Susa

Piazza XVII Dicembre

Corso Inghilterra

Giardino Cittadella

Via San Valfrè

Via de Sonnaz

To Bus Station (700m); Hospital (6km)

Corso Vittorio Emanuele II

Via Magenta

Via Montevecchio

Corso Re Umberto

Corso Stati Uniti

To Ospedale Mauriziano Umberto I (1km); Palazzina di Caccia di Stupinigi (10km); Museo di Arte e Ammobiliamento Storia (10km); Asti (60km); Alba (65km); Genoa (170km)

Corso Turati

TORINO CARD

Serious sightseers can invest €15/17 in a Torino Card, valid for 48/72 hours and covering admission to most monuments and museums in town, a ride up the Mole Antonelliana panoramic lift, a return trip on the Sassi-Superga cable car, and all public transport costs including ATM boats on the River Po and the Turismo Bus Torino (see p232). It also offers discounts for some guided tours and theatres. You can buy the card at tourist offices.

Informacittà (☎ 011 442 28 88; Via Palazzo di Città 9a; ☺ 8.30am-6pm Mon-Fri, 9am-1pm Sat) City information service.

Stazione Porta Nuova office (☎ 011 53 51 81; ☺ 9.30am-7pm)

TRAVEL AGENCIES
CTS Viaggi (☎ 011 812 45 34; Via Montebello 2h) Student and youth travel.

Sights
PIAZZA CASTELLO
At the heart of the city, Turin's grandest square shelters a wealth of museums, theatres and cafés in its porticoed promenades. Essentially baroque, the piazza was laid out from the 14th century to serve as the seat of dynastic power for the House of Savoy. The piazza is dominated by Palazzo Madama, a part-medieval, part-baroque castle built in the 13th century on the site of the old Roman gate. It was named after Madama Reale Maria Cristina, the widow of Vittorio Amedeo I, who lived here in the 17th century. Today, part of the palace houses the **Museo Civico d'Arte Antica** (☎ 011 442 99 12; Piazza Castello), currently closed for restoration but it may possibly reopen in 2006.

In the northwestern corner of the square is the baroque **Chiesa di San Lorenzo** (Piazza Castello), designed by Guarino Guarini. The richly complex interior compensates for the spare façade.

Statues of the mythical twins Castor and Pollux guard the entrance to the **Palazzo Reale** (☎ 011 436 14 55; Piazza Castello; adult/child €6.50/free; ☺ 8.30am-7pm Tue-Sun), and according to local legend, also watch over the border between the sacred and diabolical halves of the city (see the boxed text, opposite). Quite an

austere building erected for Carlo Emanuele II around 1646, its lavishly decorated rooms house an assortment of furnishings, porcelain and other knick-knacks. The surrounding **Giardino Reale** (Royal Garden; admission free; ☺ 9am-1hr before sunset), east of the palace, was designed in 1697 by André le Nôtre, who also created the gardens at Versailles.

The entrance to the Savoy **Armeria Reale** (Royal Armoury; ☎ 011 54 38 89; Piazza Castello) is under the porticoes just right of the palace gates. It contains what some claim to be Europe's best collection of arms. It's closed for renovation and should reopen sometime in 2006.

Under the porticoes in Piazza Castello's northeastern corner, you will find the **state archives** (1730–34), **prefecture** (1733–57), and the **Teatro Regio Torino** and **Teatro Piccolo Regio**.

DUOMO DI SAN GIOVANNI
Turin's **cathedral** (Piazza San Giovanni), built between 1491 and 1498 on the site of three 14th-century basilicas, houses the famous Shroud of Turin (see the boxed text, p231). The **Cappella della Santa Sindone** (built 1668–94), the rightful home since 1694 of the cloth in which Christ's body was supposedly wrapped after his crucifixion, has been closed for restoration since 1997 when it was severely damaged by fire. A copy of the cloth is on permanent display in front of the cathedral altar.

The Romanesque **bell tower**, that stands alone to the left of the cathedral, was designed by Juvarra and built in 1723. Just to the north lie the remains of a 1st-century **Roman amphitheatre**, while a little further to the northwest lie **Porta Palatina**, the red-brick remains of a Roman-era gate. Just across the road is the **Museo d'Antichità** (Museum of Antiquity; ☎ 011 521 22 51; Via XX Settembre 88c; adult/child €4/free; ☺ 9am-7pm Tue-Sun), displaying antiquities amassed by the Savoy dynasty, including Etruscan urns, Roman bronzes and Greek vases, alongside assorted locally excavated archaeological finds.

MUSEUMS
Baroque Palazzo Carignano was the birthplace of Carlo Alberto and Vittorio Emanuele II, and the seat of united Italy's first parliament from 1861 to 1864. You can see the parliament as part of the **Museo Nazionale del Risorgimento Italiano** (☎ 011 562 11 47; Via Accademia delle Scienze 5; adult/child €5/3.50; ☺ 9am-7pm

Tue-Sun), which has an extensive display of arms, paintings and documents tracing the turbulent century from the revolts of 1848 to WWII.

One of the major players of the Risorgimento, Camillo Benso di Cavour, was born and died at **Palazzo Cavour** (☎ 011 53 06 90; Via Camillo Cavour 8; adult/child €6.50/free; 10am-7.30pm Tue-Sun). The baroque palace dates to 1729 and can be visited only during temporary exhibitions.

On the same street as Palazzo Carignano is **Palazzo dell'Accademia delle Scienze** (Via Accademia delle Scienze 6), home to the **Museo Egizio** (☎ 011 561 77 76; www.museoegizio.org in Italian; adult/child €6.50/free; 8.30am-7.30pm Tue-Sun). Established in the late 18th century, it's considered to have one of the best collections of ancient Egyptian treasures outside Cairo and London. In the same building is **Galleria Sabauda** (☎ 011 561 83 91; adult/child €4/free; 8.30am-7.30pm Tue-Sat mid-Sep–May, 8.30am-7.30pm Tue-Fri, 8.30am-11pm Sat Jun–mid-Sep), housing the Savoy family's incredible collection of art, which includes works by Van Dyck, Rembrandt, Poussin, Tintoretto and Jan Brueghel. A combination ticket that covers admission to both museums costs €8 for adults (children are free).

Those who can't get enough of the Holy Shroud should drop by **Museo della Sindone** (☎ 011 436 58 32; www.sindone.it in Italian; Via San Domenico 28; adult/child €5.50/2.50; 9am-noon & 3-7pm). Despite its informative displays and assortment of associated artefacts, such as the first camera used to photograph the cloth (in 1898), the museum does little to unravel the mystery of the Holy Shroud. Guided tours are in Italian only; ask for a free English-language audioguide.

A menagerie of stuffed animals is on show at the **Museo Regionale di Scienze Naturale** (Natural Science Museum; ☎ 011 432 30 80; Via Giovanni Giolitti 36; adult/child €5/2.50; 10am-7pm Wed-Mon), inside a monumental 17th-century hospital with four inner courtyards and a chapel.

Further afield, the **Galleria Civica d'Arte Moderna e Contemporanea** (GAM; ☎ 011 562 99 11; www.gamtorino.it; Via Magenta 31; adult/child €7.50/4; 9am-7pm Tue-Sun) is dedicated to 19th- and 20th-century artists, including De Chirico, Otto Dix and Klee. More modern-art exhibitions are held in **Palazzo Bricherasio** (☎ 011 517 18 11; www.palazzobricherasio.it in Italian; Via Lagrange 20; adult/child €6.50/free, audioguide 1/2 people €3.50/5; 2-8pm Mon, 9am-8pm Tue & Wed, 9am-11pm Thu-Sun). The art gallery, in a 17th-century palace, has hosted surrealist Dalí and been 'wrapped' by Christo and Jeanne-Claude in its time.

If gleaming autos get your pulse racing, head for the **Museo dell'Automobile** (☎ 011 67 76 66; www.museoauto.it in Italian; Corso Unità d'Italia 40; adult/child €5.50/4; 10am-6.30pm Tue, Wed, Fri & Sat, 10am-10pm Thu, 10am-8.30pm Sun). Among

---

TURIN IN BLACK & WHITE

As many Turinese will proudly tell you, Turin is a truly magical city. Some maintain that it is in fact *two* magical cities, White Turin and Black Turin, governed by the forces of good and evil respectively. Occult lore claims that the city stands at a particularly powerful intersection of mystic energies, forming one of the corners of a white magic triangle along with Lyon and Prague, as well as one of the points on a black magic triangle, completed by London and San Francisco. Added to this, Turin is also at the confluence of two mighty rivers: the Po, which has been identified with the male power of the Sun; and the Dora, linked with the female power of the Moon.

The 'black heart' of Turin is, allegedly, Piazza Statuto, near Stazione Porta Susa. Used by the Romans as a necropolis, and the site of the medieval city's gallows, it's perhaps no wonder that this spot should have negative connotations – it's even said that the Gates of Hell themselves lie beneath this outwardly unremarkable square...

Following this magical city map, the boundary between the black and white cities runs unseen between the statues of the Dioscuri (Castor and Pollux), which guard the entrance to the Palazzo Reale, while the 'white heart' of Turin is in the vicinity of Piazza Castello, towards the Giardino Reale. This, of course, is the historic centre of the old city, and what better representation of positive energy could there be than the Holy Shroud, kept in the nearby Duomo?

If you want to learn more about this fascinating aspect of Turin, tag along on the Magic Turin tour, run by Somewhere (p232).

its 400 engineering marvels are one of the first Fiats, and the Isotta Franchini driven by Gloria Swanson in the film *Sunset Boulevard*. Take bus No 34 from beside Stazione Porta Nuova.

PIAZZAS

It is the great squares and elegant boulevards that lend Turin its air of reserved majesty. Via Roma, Turin's main shopping thoroughfare since 1615, stretches south from Piazza Castello to Stazione Porta Nuova and was built by Mazzucchetti in 1865.

Walking south from Piazza Castello, you emerge on Piazza San Carlo. Known as Turin's drawing room, and home to several renowned cafés, the square is surrounded by characteristic porticoes (central Turin has some 18km of them) and is capped at its southern end by two baroque churches, **Chiesa di San Carlo** and **Chiesa di Santa Cristina**. At the time of research, the square itself was just one great hole in the ground, as work on a subterranean car park was underway. Further down Via Roma you reach Piazza Carlo Felice, with a pleasant little garden at its centre that has recently had a bit of a make-over.

Now the main axis of Turin's seedier side of life, Via Nizza and the surrounding area is worth exploring but is dodgy territory at night. If you do happen to be wandering around here, head east a few blocks to admire the Oriental strangeness of the 19th-century **synagogue** (Via San Pio V).

VIA PO & AROUND

Trendy cafés are strung out along and around Via Po, which connects Piazza Castello with the river by way of Piazza Vittorio Veneto.

Turin's single most remarkable sight is the **Mole Antonelliana** (Via Montebello 20). Intended as a synagogue when it was started in 1862, this extraordinary structure – 167m tall – is the symbol of Turin, and appears on the Italian two-cent coin. Capped by an aluminium spire it is engineering as art form. Inside you'll find the absorbing **Museo Nazionale del Cinema** (☎ 011 812 56 58; www.museonazionaledelcinema.org; adult/child €5.20/free; ☼ 9am-8pm Tue-Fri & Sun, 9am-11pm Sat), which takes visitors on an interactive tour through cinematic history, from the earliest magic lanterns, stereoscopes and other optical toys to the present day. Movie

memorabilia, including Marilyn Monroe's black lace bustier, Peter O'Toole's robe from *Lawrence of Arabia* and the coffin used by Bela Lugosi's *Dracula* is on display. At the heart of the museum is the vast Temple Hall, surrounded by 10 'chapels' devoted to various film genres. There are, of course, plenty of films to watch, from vintage peepshows such as *Seminary Girls* (1897) to contemporary avant-garde animation, as well as endless buttons to push. The glass **Panoramic Lift** (adult/child €4/3, lift & museum tickets €6.80/2.60) silently whisks visitors 85m up to the Mole's stunning roof terrace in 59 seconds.

Walking southwest along the River Po, you come to **Castello del Valentino** (closed to the public), a mock French-style chateau built in the 17th century. The carefully designed French-style **Parco Valentino** surrounding the chateau opened in 1856 and is one of the most celebrated parks in Italy. A little further southwest is the *faux*-medieval **Rocca** (Castle; Viale Virgilio 107; adult/child €3/2; ☼ 9am-7pm Oct-Mar, 9am-8pm Apr-Sep) and **village** (admission free), collectively known as **Borgo Medievale**. They were built for the Italian General Exhibition in 1884.

Southeast of the Piazza Vittorio Veneto, across the Po, is the **Chiesa di Gran Madre di Dio** (closed to the public), built from 1818 to 1831 to commemorate the return of Vittorio Emanuele I from exile. Some claim it's yet another secret repository for the Holy Grail.

LINGOTTO

Around 3km south of the city centre is the **Lingotto Fiere** (☎ 011 664 41 11; www.lingottofiere.it; Via Nizza 294), Turin's shiny congress and exhibition centre. Fiat cars were produced here until 1982, after which the factory was transformed by top architect Renzo Piano into the cutting-edge complex seen today. Two of the city's finest hotels, Le Meridien Lingotto and Le Meridien Art + Tech, are housed here, as well as the **Pinacoteca Giovanni e Marella Agnelli** (☎ 011 006 27 13; Via Nizza 230; adult/child €4/2.50; ☼ 9am-7pm Tue-Sun), with paintings by, among others, Canaletto, Renoir, Manet, Matisse and Picasso. To get here, take bus No 34 or 35 from Stazione Porto Nuova.

BASILICA DI SUPERGA

In 1706 Vittorio Amedeo II promised to build a basilica to honour the Virgin Mary if Turin was saved from besieging French

THE HOLY SHROUD

The *Sindone* (Holy Shroud) is Catholicism's greatest icon of faith, luring millions of pilgrims to Turin when it is publicly displayed every few years. Only the pope and the bishop of Turin can decide when the sacred cloth will next be hauled out – its last public appearance was in 2000.

For centuries experts and fanatics have argued over the authenticity of the Shroud of Turin, said to be the burial cloth in which Jesus' body was wrapped. Tests in 1981 uncovered traces of human blood (type AB) and pollen from plants known to exist around Jerusalem. Cynics claim the shroud is a medieval fake; carbon dating carried out in 1988 seemed to confirm this, tying it to the 13th century. However, most agree that the white cloth – 4.37m long and 1.10m wide – was woven in the Middle East.

How the image of a human body – with fractured nose, bruised right cheek, lance wound in the chest, scourge marks on the back, thorn wounds on the forehead and nail wounds on both wrists and feet – was formed on the cloth remains the biggest mystery. Some have suggested that the Shroud was in fact the first ever attempt at photography (using a camera obscura) by Leonardo da Vinci.

The first mention of a Holy Shroud comes from AD 944, when such an object was kept in Constantinople. This, apparently, was looted during the sack of that city by Crusaders in 1204, and by 1453 it was in the hands of Duke Louis of Savoy. He stowed it away in a silver casket in Chambéry, now in France. The tie dye–style brown patterns visible on it today were caused by a fire in 1532 that saw a drop of hot silver fall into the casket and through the folded layers. Safe-guarded in Turin since 1578, the shroud is now laid out flat in a vacuum-sealed box, which in turn is stored in a controlled atmosphere. Since the death of former King Umberto II in 1983, the shroud has officially been the property of the Vatican.

and Spanish armies. The city was indeed saved, and architect Filippo Juvarra built the church on a hill across the River Po. It became the final resting place of the Savoys, whose lavish tombs make for interesting viewing. In 1949 a plane carrying the entire Turin football team crashed into the basilica in thick fog. At the rear of the church, you'll find their tomb lies.

To get there take tram No 15 from Piazza Vittorio Veneto to the Sassi-Superga stop on Corso Casale, then walk 20m to **Stazione Sassi** (☎ 800 01 91 52; Strada Communale di Superga 4; ☽ 9am-noon & 2-8pm Mon & Wed-Fri, 7am-midnight Tue, 9am-8pm Sat), the cable-car station from where an original tram dating back to 1934 rattles the 3.1km up the hillside (18 minutes, hourly).

LA PALAZZINA DI CACCIA DI STUPINIGI

This little palace set in formal gardens beyond Mirafiori was once the Savoys' hunting lodge. The Juvarra creation, a rococo delight, was designed for Vittorio Amedeo II in 1729. Many parts of the building are in original condition and the rest is slowly being restored. Artworks and furniture from Savoy palaces are displayed in the **Museo di Arte e Ammobiliamento Storia** (☎ 011 358 12 20;

adult/child €6.20/5.20; ☽ 10am-6pm Tue-Sun Apr-Oct, 9am-5pm Tue-Sun Nov-Mar).

Take bus No 4 from along Via San Secondo (near Stazione Porta Nuova) or along its southbound route from Piazza della Repubblica to Piazza Calo Marlo, then bus No 41 to the palace.

CASTELLO DI RIVOLI

The preferred residence of the Savoy family from the 14th century onwards lies outside central Turin in Rivoli. The 17th-century **castle** (☎ 011 956 52 22; www.castellodirivoli.org; Piazza Mafalda di Savoia; adult/child €6.50/free; ☽ 10am-5pm Tue-Thu, 10am-9pm Fri-Sun, free guided tours 3.30pm & 6pm Sat, 11am, 3pm & 6pm Sun) now contains the **Museo d'Arte Contemporanea**, which displays works by Italian and foreign artists, including Franz Ackermann, Gilbert and George and Frank Gehry.

Take GTT bus No 36 from Piazza Statuto to Rivoli bus station, then bus No 36n or any No 36 marked 'Castello' up the hill. Journey time is about one hour (€1.25).

Tours

The tourist office runs guided city tours following changing themes, such as Literary Turin (€6, 1½ hours), departing on Saturday at 6pm from the Atrium office. General city tours (€6) leave at 10am on Saturdays, but are conducted only in Italian.

Contemporary art lovers should pick up the free *L'Arte Contemporanea* brochure from tourist offices, which maps out a self-guided walking tour taking in Turin's most striking public art installations.

Turismo Bus Torino (1-day tickets adult/child €5/3; 10am-6pm) is a hop-on, hop-off bus service, run by public transport company GTT, that has an on-board hostess and serves 14 different points around central Turin. Buy tickets on board or at tourist offices.

GTT also operates **Navigazione sul Po** (adult return €3.10) boat trips on the River Po. Boats to the Borgo Medievale in Parco Valentino and on to Moncalieri depart from **Imbarco Murazzi** (Murazzi del Po 65) four times a day Tuesday to Saturday and seven times a day on Sundays from May to September, with fewer departures at other times of the year.

Somewhere (011 668 05 80; www.somewhere.it) is a private operator that runs some intriguing themed tours, including Magic Turin (€20, Thursday and Saturday at 9pm) and Underground Turin (€25, Wednesday and Friday at 8.30pm), exploring lesser-known aspects of the city. There are various pick-up points – see the website for details.

Festivals & Events

The star turn of Turin's festival scene is **Cioccolatò** (www.cioccola-to.com in Italian), a two-week celebration of all things cocoa-related held each March, with tastings, sculpture competitions and numerous stalls selling sweet confectionary around the city centre.

The biennial **Salone Internazionale del Gusto** is an international five-day festival of food and wine, organised by Slow Food (see p241), with traditional producers from around the world showcasing and selling their wares in a huge street market. The next event is in October 2006.

Festival Internazionale di Film con Tematiche Omosessuali (www.turinglfilmfestival.com), held in April, is a five-day international gay and lesbian film festival.

Sleeping

BUDGET

Ostello Torino (011 660 29 39; hostelto@tin.it; Via Alby 1; dm B&B €14, f per person €13-17; mid-Jan–mid-Dec) Turin's 76-bed hostel, 1.8km from the train station, can be reached by bus No 52 (No 64 on Sunday) from Stazione Porta Nuova. Family rooms have their own bathroom and the dormitories sleep three to eight. A nightly heating charge of €1 is charged between October and April. Non-HI cardholders can buy a one-night stamp or annual card on arrival.

Hotel Versilia (/fax 011 65 76 78; Via Sant'Anselmo 4; d with shared/private bathroom €45/55) This simple but comfortable place stands opposite the synagogue near Stazione Porta Nuova and represents reasonable value.

Hotel Bologna (011 562 02 90; www.hotelbologna srl.it in Italian; Corso Vittorio Emanuele II 60; s/d €60/85) Just across from Stazione Porta Nuova, this busy two-star hotel, run by a couple of friendly old ladies, is a good bet. Rooms are neat and modern and come with extra-big showers. Rooms overlooking the neighbouring restaurant can be noisy, however.

Albergo Sila (011 54 40 86; Piazza Carlo Felice 80; s/d with shower €43/55, s/d with shower & toilet €55/68) Decent, clean rooms are found on the 3rd floor of this porticoed building, handy to Stazione Porta Nuova.

Villa Rey (/fax 011 819 01 17; Strada Val San Martino Superiore 27; person/tent/car €5/4/1.10; Mar-Oct) Take bus No 61 from Piazza Stazione Porta Nuova to the end of the line, then bus No 54 from the corner of Corso Casale and Corso Gabetti to get to this camping ground in the hills east of the River Po.

MIDRANGE

Hotel Montevecchio (011 562 00 23; montevecchio@ email.it; Via Montevecchio 13; s/d low season €58/75, high season €68/88;) Hovering between budget and midrange, this family-run place in a quiet residential area is hard to beat for a sound night's sleep.

Hotel Roma e Rocca Cavour (011 561 27 72; www.romarocca.it; Piazza Carlo Felice 60; s €49-86, d €68-105, tr €71-117;) Run by the same family since it was established in 1854, this is one of Turin's most historic hotels, handily located opposite the Porta Nuova train station. 'Economy' rooms share bathrooms and are smaller and more basic than the modern 'comfort' rooms, which have tasteful antique furnishings. Breakfast costs €7.50.

Hotel Piemontese (011 669 81 01; www.hotel piemontese.it; Via Berthollet 21; s/d from €69/89;) This Best Western outlet is a charming Liberty hotel which stands proudly on a quiet street a brief stroll away from Stazione Porta Nuova. Pricier rooms with Jacuzzi and hydromassage are available.

Hotel Dogana Vecchia (☎ 011 436 67 52; fax 011 436 71 94; Via Corte d'Appello 4; s/d from €88/105; P) Mozart and Verdi were among the more distinguished guests to stay at this elegant, three-star pad, an inn dating from the 17th century.

Hotel Solferino & Artuá (☎ 011 517 53 01; www .hotelartua.it; Via Brofferio 1 & 3; s/d from €100/125; P 💻) In a grand old townhouse, Artuá is one of two hotels run by the same team, just off the grand and leafy Corso Re Umberto I. Ride the fantastic old wooden lift with glass doors to the 4th floor. A laptop is available at reception for guests to use in their room.

Hotel Boston (☎ 011 50 03 59; www.hotelbos tontorino.it; Via Massena 70; s/d/ste from €92/116/140; P 😧 💻) The austere classical façade of the Boston gives no inkling of what's going on inside. The public areas are filled with modern art, including original works by Warhol, Lichtenstein, Aldo Mondino and others, along with goldfish bowls in the shape of giant wine glasses and various other installations. Rooms are individually designed, and come with their own original artworks and big round bathtubs, while service is impeccable.

Victoria Hotel (☎ 011 561 19 09; www.hotelvic toria-torino.com; Via Nino Costa 4; s/d from €107/154; 😧) Marble-clad walls, chintzy sofas and lots of wood panelling add to the charm of this English country–style hotel, beautifully placed on a pedestrian lane around the corner from the congress centre.

Hotel des Artistes (☎ 011 812 44 16; www.des artisteshotel.it; Via Principe Amedeo 21; s/d €130/180; P 😧) Bright, spacious rooms decorated in contemporary style are on offer at the Hotel des Artistes. Rates fluctuate (watch for 'special offers' on its website) and can drop by 20% on non-holiday weekends.

Hotel Genio (☎ 011 650 57 71; www.hotelgenio.it; Corso Vittorio Emanuele II 47; s/d Mon-Thu €103/140, Fri-Sun €67/90; P 😧) This Best Western hotel is tucked beneath the arcades, not far from Stazione Porta Nuova. It has a slight air of faded grandeur, and weekend prices are reasonable for what's on offer.

TOP END
Grand Hotel Sitea (☎ 011 517 01 71; sitea@thi.it; Via Carlo Alberto 35; s/d low season €115/155, high season

€190/255; P 😧) This top-notch oasis of calm and sophistication is apparently where the champion Juventus football team is put up when in town.

Turin Palace Hotel (☎ 011 562 55 11; www.thi .it; Via Sacchi 8; s/d €225/277; P 😧 💻 ✕) Established in 1872, this is Turin's last word in late-19th-century luxury, with its spacious and tastefully decorated rooms.

The four-star **Le Meridien Lingotto** (☎ 011 664 20 00; www.lemeridienlingotto.it; Via Nizza 262; d €125-270, ste €285-450; P 😧) occupies part of the historic Fiat car factory, which was built in the 1920s and renovated by architect Renzo Piano in the late 1980s. The factory's original full-length windows have been retained, allowing light to flood the large, stylish rooms. There's also a snazzy restaurant overlooking a tropical garden. The five-star annex, **Le Meridien Art + Tech** (d €150-390, ste €1000-3000; P 😧), takes the luxury level up another notch, with furniture by Gio Ponti and Philippe Stark for the style-conscious guest. The former car-testing circuit on the roof, which featured in the classic 1969 film *The Italian Job*, has been converted into a jogging track for guests.

Eating

Turin's cuisine is heavily influenced by the French, and the massive migration of southern Italians to the city brought traditions of cooking unmatched anywhere else in the north. Try *risotto alla Piemontese* (with butter and cheese) or *zuppa canavesana* (turnip soup), and finish with a Savoy favourite, *panna cotta* (kind of like an Italian crème caramel).

RESTAURANTS
Pepino (☎ 011 54 20 09; Piazza Carignano 8; buffet lunch €14.50; 🕐 lunch) Arrive early if you want to bag a table at this little restaurant, which offers a very popular fixed-price lunchtime buffet. Choose from a changing selection of cold meats, salads, pasta and vegetables, and finish off with some delectable desserts (you can try up to three different types). Sunday is especially busy. The ice-cream lolly was invented at Pepino's in 1937, and they're still regarded as the best in town.

Brek (☎ 011 53 45 56; Piazza Carlo Felice 22; 1st/2nd courses about €3/7; 🕐 11.30am-3pm & 6.30-10.30pm) This ever-busy branch of the national buffet chain offers one of the best deals in town.

SWEET TORINO

Peyrano (☎ 011 53 87 65; www.peyrano.com; Corso Vittorio Emanuele II 76), creator of Dolci Momenti a Torino (Sweet Moments in Turin) and *grappini* (chocolates filled with grappa), is Turin's most famous chocolate house. Others include **Gerla** (Corso Vittorio Emanuele II 88) and **Giordano** (Piazza Carlo Felice 69).

Turin's best-known confectioner, **Leone** (www.pastiglieleone.it), has made sweets since 1857, and is renowned for its little boxes of *pastiglie* (lozenges) in a variety of flavours including orange blossom, green tea and absinthe, as well as less esoteric herbal concoctions. Most cafés have a selection on their counters.

If ice cream's your thing, then try **Caffè Miretti** (☎ 011 53 36 87; Corso Giacomo Matteotti 5), where flavours include orange cream, chestnut and amaretto.

Choose from a selection of salads, pasta, grilled meats and desserts and fill your own glass with either wine or beer on tap. It's excellent value and consequently packs out around lunchtime.

Pizzeria Stars & Roses (☎ 011 516 20 52; Piazza Paleocapa 2; pizzas €7-9) The list of pizzas on offer at this stylish place is lengthy and adventurous, with toppings including salmon and whisky or caviar and vodka.

Fratelli La Cozza (☎ 011 85 00 99; Corso Regio Parco 39; pizzas from €5) This legendary pizzeria is famous as much for its owner – Turinese comic TV presenter Piero Chiamretti – as its delicious Napoli-inspired pizzas.

Kettepare (☎ 011 88 35 15; Via San Massimo 4; 1st/2nd courses about €5/6; ☽ lunch & dinner) This cosy little restaurant and bar is a big hit with lunching locals, who pop in for the well-priced pasta and grills.

Kirkuk Kafè (☎ 011 53 06 57; Via Carlo Alberto 16bis; mains €5-7; ☽ 6.30pm-midnight Mon & Tue, noon-3pm & 6.30pm-midnight Wed-Sat) Sit on silk cushions or on regular chairs, and treat your taste buds to some Kurdish, Turkish, Iraqi and Iranian cuisine. Call to book as it's very popular and very small.

I Tre Galli (☎ 011 521 60 27; Via Sant' Agostino 25; meals about €15) This place is spacious, rustic and full of light. Most people come for the wine and its fantastic array of apéritif snacks served on a buzzing pavement terrace.

Montagne Viva (☎ 011 521 78 82; Piazza Emanuele Filiberto 3a; meals about €15; ☽ Mon-Sat) Piedmontese fare (honey, meats, wine) can be sampled in a variety of dishes cooked with strictly local farm produce at this innovative *agriturismo* restaurant, run by the regional consortium for typical agricultural products.

Mare Nostrum (☎ 011 839 45 43; Via Matteo Pescatore 16; mains €18-20; ☽ dinner) If it's seafood you're searching for, then come to Mare Nostrum, Turin's most respected fish restaurant. Only the best and freshest ingredients make up the pricey but exceptional menu.

Restaurant del Cambio (☎ 011 54 66 90; Piazza Carignano 2; mains about €20; ☽ lunch & dinner Mon-Sat) Crimson velvet, glittering chandeliers, baroque mirrors and an air of timeless elegance greet you at this grand dame of the Turin dining scene, once patronised by Count Cavour and other leading lights. It first opened its doors in 1757, and classic Piedmont cuisine still dominates the menu. Bookings and smart dress are advised.

CAFÉS

Partly due to Turin's legacy of French and Austrian involvement, the city has a flourishing café life. In the early evening all these places lay out a succulent banquet of snacks to accompany aperitifs.

Caffè San Carlo (☎ 011 53 25 86; Piazza San Carlo 156; 1st/2nd courses from €5.50/7; ☽ noon-3pm & 7-11pm) Host to a gaggle of Risorgimento nationalists and intellectuals in the 1840s, this sumptuous café, dating back to 1822, is where suited folk network today. It offers cocktails, toasted snacks and 28 types of coffee.

Caffè Mulassano (☎ 011 54 79 90; Piazza Castello 15; mains about €10; ☽ lunch & dinner) Mulassano (built 1907–09) is an Art Nouveau gem, with a marble floor, mirrored walls, a coffered ceiling – and just four tables. As in days gone by, the theatre mob from nearby Teatro Regio adore this relic.

Baratti & Milano (☎ 011 561 30 60; Piazza Castello 27; mains about €10-15; ☽ lunch & dinner) Elegant Baratti & Milano, with a stunning interior dating back to 1858, serves coffee, cakes and light lunches, and is particularly famous for its delicious chocolate – both the drinking and bar form. Crowds flock here on Sunday to buy cakes, sweets and biscuits from its old-fashioned shop counter.

Platti (☎ 011 506 90 56; Corso Vittorio Emanuele II 72; lunch menus €15.50) The original Art Nouveau interior (1870) remains firmly intact at this sweet-laden coffee, cake and liquor shop. Skip the noisy terrace and have lunch inside beneath the gold leaf.

Caffè Torino (☎ 011 54 51 18; Piazza San Carlo 204; mains from €12.50; ☘ lunch & dinner) Torino has served coffee beneath its chandelier-lit frescoed ceiling since 1903. Stand with the gaggle of Turinese at the bar or pay a fortune for silver service – a glass of wine costs €6.80. When leaving, rub your shoe across the brass bull embedded in the pavement for good luck.

Al Bicerin (☎ 011 436 93 25; Piazza della Consolata 5; ☘ lunch & dinner) Cavour, Dumas et al came here to drink *bicerin* (€4), a hot mix of coffee, chocolate, milk and cream. Other chocolate treats cooked up at this café, which dates back to 1763, include chocolate on toast, and hot chocolate with ice cream. Its terrace at the foot of a 14th-century church bell tower is one of Turin's most peaceful.

Caffè Elena (☎ 011 812 33 41; Piazza Vittorio Veneto 5; ☘ Thu-Tue) Easily the trendiest of Turin's historic bunch, Elena lures the beautiful people with its wood-panelled interior and Starck-designed chairs on a terrace overlooking one of the city's busiest squares. The wine list runs to some 700 or so names.

Pastis (☎ 011 521 10 85; Piazza Emanuele Filiberto 9; ☘ 9am-3.30pm & 6pm-2am) Food design is what this boldly painted café-cum-bar prides itself on. It's a pleasant spot for a cocktail beneath the trees outside.

Mood (☎ 011 566 08 09; Via Battisti 3e; ☘ 8am-9pm Mon-Sat) Flick through design and art books while sipping a cappuccino at this modern library-café.

Drinking

The main drinking spots are the riverside area around Piazza Vittoria Veneto and the so-called Quadrilatero Romano district east of Piazza Savoia.

Lobelix (☎ 011 436 72 06; Via Corte d'Appello 15f; ☘ Mon-Sat) This leafy terrace sits beneath trees on Piazza Savoia and is a favourite place for apéritifs – its banquet of snacks from 6pm is one of Turin's most extravagant.

Frog (☎ 011 440 77 36; Via Mercanti 19; ☘ Tue-Sun) The Frog is a large music bar and restaurant with a typical pub-style interior – dark wooden panelling, table lamps, curtains etc.

Taberna Libraria (☎ 011 83 65 05; Via Bogino 5; ☘ 10am-9pm) The mainstay of this new-style

enolibreria (wine bookshop) is its excellent array of wines available to taste and buy. A definite highlight for oenophiles.

Vinicola Al Sorij (☎ 011 83 56 67; Via Matteo Pescatore 10c; ☘ 6pm-2am Mon-Sat) Another wine bar hot on the trail of Turin's more moneyed crowd, this tiny spot just behind Piazza Vittorio Veneto has a cellar of more than 500 different wines.

San Tommaso 10 (☎ 011 53 42 01; Via San Tommaso 10; ☘ 8am-7pm Mon-Sat) Coffee aficionados should make a beeline for this little place, the original Lavazza coffee house. It offers a staggering assortment of inventive flavoured and spiced coffees, plus the regular stuff. If in doubt over what to choose, try the house speciality, the espresso, a curiously thick drink that you eat yoghurt-like with a spoon.

Entertainment

Entertainment listings are included in *Torino Sette*, the Friday insert of the newspaper **La Stampa** (www.lastampa.it in Italian). Cinema, theatre and exhibition listings are also included in its daily *Spettacoli Cronaca* section. Also worth picking up at the tourist office and in many bars around town is the free 80-page **News Spettacolo** (www.newspettacolo.com in Italian), a weekly booklet listing several hundred entertainment venues.

Tickets for rock concerts are sold at the **Ricordi Media Store** (☎ 011 562 11 56; Piazza CLN 251). For other events, go to the tourist office on Piazza Solferino (see p225).

NIGHTCLUBS & LIVE MUSIC

Turin's clubbing district centres on Murazzi del Po (also called Lungo Po Murazzi), the arcaded riverside area stretching between Pontes Vittorio Emanuele I and Umberto I. Names to look for:

Alcatraz (☎ 011 83 69 00; Murazzi del Po 37)
Jammin' (☎ 011 88 28 69; Murazzi del Po 17-19; ☘ from midnight)
Pier 7-9-11 (☎ 011 83 53 56; Murazzi del Po 7-11)

Most are open from 9pm to late and cover charges vary depending on the night. Away from the city centre there is a twinset of thumping venues.

Docks Home (☎ 011 28 02 51; Via Valprato 68) is the real star of Turin's music scene; it's set in a converted 1912 warehouse complex to the west of the city. House music dominates and exhibitions are sometimes held here.

The other big name in the dance and music circuit, **Hiroshima Mon Amour** (HMA; ☎ 011 317 66 36; Via Bossoli 83; admission free–€15), plays everything from folk and punk to tango and techno.

CINEMAS

Near the Mole Antonelliana, **Cinema Massimo** (☎ 011 812 56 58; Via Giuseppe Verdi 18; admission €7) offers an eclectic mix of films, mainly in English or with subtitles. One of its three screens only shows classic films.

THEATRE

Teatro Regio Torino (☎ 011 881 52 41; www.teatro regio.torino.it in Italian; Piazza Castello 215; ☯ ticket office 10.30am-6pm Tue-Fri, 10.30am-4pm Sat, 1hr before performances) Sold-out performances can sometimes be watched for free on live TV in the adjoining **Teatro Piccolo Regio** (☎ 011 881 52 41) where Puccini premiered *La Bohème* in 1896.

Getting There & Away
AIR

Turin airport (TRN; ☎ 011 567 63 61; www.turin-air port.com), 16km northwest of the city centre in Caselle, is served by connections to European and national destinations. Several budget no-frills airlines fly here.

BUS

Most international, national and regional buses terminate at the **bus station** (☎ 011 433 25 25; Corso Castelfidardo). You can also get to Milan's Malpensa airport from here.

TRAIN

The main train station is **Stazione Porta Nuova** (Piazza Carlo Felice), until 2007. Regular daily trains connect Turin with Milan (€16, 1¾ hours), Aosta (€7, two hours), Venice (€26, five hours), Genoa (€16.85, 1¾ hours) and Rome (€45, seven hours). Most also stop at **Stazione Porta Susa** (Corso Inghilterra).

Getting Around
TO/FROM THE AIRPORT

Sadem (☎ 011 300 01 66; www.sadem.it in Italian) runs buses to the airport from Piazza Carlo Felice (€5, 40 minutes), also stopping at Stazione Porta Susa (30 minutes). Buses depart every 30 minutes between 5.15am and 10.30pm (6.30am and 11.30pm from the airport). Single tickets cost €5 and are

sold at **Confetteria Avvignano** (Piazza Carlo Felice 50) right behind the bus stop.

CAR & MOTORCYCLE

Motoring information, road maps and guides are provided by the **Automobile Club Torino** (ACT; ☎ 011 5 77 91; Via San Francesco da Paola 20a). Major car-rental agencies have offices at Stazione Porta Nuova and the airport.

PUBLIC TRANSPORT

The city boasts a dense network of buses, trams and a cable car run by **Gruppo Torinese Trasporti** (GTT; ☎ 800 01 91 52; www.gtt.to.it in Italian), which also has an **information office** (☯ 7am-9pm) at Stazione Porta Nuova. Buses and trams run from 6am to midnight and tickets cost €0.90 (€12.50 for a 15-ticket carnet, €3 for a one-day pass). Parts of Turin's new metro system should be up and running by 2006, and it is hoped that it will be completed by 2007. See www.metrotorino.it for progress reports.

TAXI

Centrale Radio (☎ 011 57 37)
Radio Taxi (☎ 011 57 30)

VALLE DI SUSA & VALLE DI CHISONE

Alpine scenery and snow-laden slopes draw a steady stream of skiers to the legendary Via Lattea (Milky Way), two parallel valleys immediately west of Turin. The more northern of the two, Valle di Susa, meanders past a magnificent abbey, the old Celtic town of Susa and a clutch of pretty mountain villages. Its southern counterpart, the Valle di Chisone, is pure ski resort–territory where slick Sestriere reigns.

During the ski season and in summer, Turinese flock here in droves for the fresh mountain air. The main Italy–France highway (S24) and railway line roar furiously along the Valle di Susa, making this traffic-busy valley easily accessible by both public transport and car.

Many of the events in the 2006 Winter Olympics will be held in resorts along these valleys.

Sacra di San Michele

Perched on a hill above the road from Turin is the **Sacra di San Michele** (☎ 011 93 91 30; adult/child €2.50/1.50; ☯ 9.30am-12.30pm & 3-5pm Tue-Fri 9.30am-noon & 2.40-5pm Sat & Sun mid-Oct–mid-Mar,

9.30am-12.30pm & 3-6pm Tue-Fri, 9.30am-noon & 2.30-6pm Sat & Sun mid-Mar–mid-Oct), a mean and moody Gothic-Romanesque abbey which has kept sentry atop Monte Pirchiriano (962m) since the 10th century. Inside, don't miss the so-called 'Zodiac Door', a 12th-century door-way sculpted with cheeky *putti* (winsome cherubs) pulling each other's hair. Sunday mass is celebrated at noon and 6pm, and concerts are held on Saturday evenings in summer; ask at the Avigliana tourist office for details.

The only way to get to the abbey from **Avigliana** (population 10,500), the abbey's closest town 12km west (and a 26km train ride from Turin, €1.50, 20 minutes), is by car or, for fit and experienced walkers, on foot.

Avigliana's **tourist office** (☎ 011 932 86 50; avigliana@montagnedoc.it; Piazza del Popolo 2; ☑ 9am-noon & 3-6pm Mon-Fri, 9am-noon Sat) has route maps and information on walking and mountain biking in the area, including around the two lakes and marshlands in the **Parco Naturale dei Laghi di Avigliana**. This protected area is on the town's western fringe. The best place to eat in Avigliana is **Trattoria Croce Bianca** (☎ 011 932 81 91, Via XX Settembre 56; mains €12-14; ☑ lunch & dinner Tue-Sun), which serves up a variety of local meaty dishes.

A 30km-long circular bike trail loops from Avigliana to the abbey and back. By foot the shortest walk is actually from Sant'Ambrogio, a village further west, where an old mule track leads from the foot of the hill to the abbey – a strenuous 90-minute climb. Another route passes by **Il Sentiero dei Franchi** (☎ 011 96 31 747; ilsentierodeifranchi@tiscali.it; Borgata Cresto 16; mains €6-7; ☑ 9am-3pm & 7pm-midnight Wed-Mon), a hiker-friendly bar and restaurant in Borgata Cresto (a 2km climb above Sant'Antonino di Susa) where you can grab a plate of home-dried salami or tasty spinach gnocchi. Advance reservations are essential.

Susa & Oulx
On the busiest route between Turin and France, **Susa** (population 6579; elevation 205m) started life as a Celtic town (a Druid well remains as testimony) before falling under the Roman Empire's sway. The important Roman ruins make it a pleasant stop on the way to the western ski resorts. In addition to the remains of a Roman **aqueduct**, a still-used **amphitheatre** and the triumphal

Arco d'Augusto, dating from 9 BC, the town's early 11th-century **cathedral** is among Piedmont's rare medieval survivors.

Worth a brief pit stop is the forbidding **Forte di Exilles** (☎ 0122 5 82 70; adult/child €5/1.50; ☑ 10am-7pm Tue-Sun Apr-Sep, 10am-2pm Oct-Mar), overlooking the quiet village of Exilles 15km west of Susa. Its military role only ended in 1943. Opening days vary so check with the **tourist office** (☎ /fax 0122 62 24 70; Corso Inghilterra 39; ☑ 9am-noon & 3-6pm) in Susa.

Nothing much in itself, **Oulx** (population 2638; elevation 1070m), 21km west of Susa, is the main stepping stone to the ski resorts of the Milky Way. Its **tourist office** (☎ 0122 83 15 96; oulx@montagnedoc.it; Piazza Garambois 2; ☑ 9am-noon & 3-6pm) is one of the valley's largest and can help with accommodation, walking and cycling itineraries.

Around 5km east of Oulx, **Jouvenceaux** is a quiet hamlet with the tiny but striking **Chiesa di San Antonio**; its outside is unusually covered with restored 15th-century frescoes, including St Christopher and a scene of the Last Judgement. If you want to stay, try cosy **Chalet Chez Nous** (☎ 0122 85 97 82; www.chaletchez nous.it; Frazione Jouvenceaux 41; s/d €70/100; P).

Sapav buses (☎ 800 80 19 01, 0122 62 20 15; www.sapav.com in Italian) connect Susa with Oulx (20 minutes), Avigliana (35 minutes), Turin (1¼ hours) and the Milky Way resorts.

Bardonecchia
pop 3084 / elev 1312m
At the head of the Susa valley and right on the French border, Bardonecchia is the last stop in Italy before the Fréjus Tunnel, and a centre for cross-country skiing. It's very popular with weekending Turinese skiers, as evidenced by the ample supply of ugly holiday apartment blocks, but it does have a pleasant old town that makes a good base for exploring this corner of the country.

The **tourist office** (☎ 0122 990 32; www.monta gnedoc.it; Viale della Vittoria 4; ☑ 9am-12.30pm & 2.30-7pm Mon-Sat) has loads of local information.

There are lots of hotels. The most central option is **Hotel Tabor** (☎ 0122 99 98 57; www.hotel-tabor.it; Via Stazione 6; s/d half board from €60/90; P), while **La Nigritella** (☎ 0122 98 04 77; www.lanigritella.it; Via Melezet 96; s/d half board from €42/84; P) is a more traditional alpine-style chalet just outside town.

There are several trains a day to Turin (€5, one hour) and stations in between.

Sestriere & the Milky Way

pop 885 / elev 2035m

Conceived by Mussolini and built by the Agnelli clan of Fiat fame in the 1930s, Sestriere ranks among Europe's most glamorous ski resorts – no less due to its enviable location in the eastern realms of the vast Via Lattea ski domain. The area embraces 400km of pistes and five interlinked ski resorts: Sestriere, Sauze d'Oulx (1509m), Sansicario (1700m), Cesano Torinese (1350m) and Claviere (1760m) in Italy; and Montgenèvre (1850m) in neighbouring France. This prestigious area entices both skiers and boarders of all abilities with its enormous range of slopes and exceptionally reliable snow conditions. In February 2006 it will stage several of the big events in the Winter Olympics, including alpine skiing, freestyle skiing and bobsleigh.

Sestriere's **tourist office** (☎ 0122 75 54 44; www.sestriere.it; Via Louset; ⏰ 9am-12.30pm & 2.30-7pm) has mountains of information on every conceivable summer and winter sport, including **heli-skiing**, **bobsledding** and **mushing**, **golfing** on Europe's highest golf course, **walking**, **free-climbing** and **mountain biking**. It also makes hotel reservations, although only a couple of three-star hotels open out of season. There are small tourist offices in **Sauze d'Oulx** (☎ 0122 85 80 09; Piazza Assietta 18; ⏰ 9am-12.30pm & 3-6.30pm) and **Claviere** (☎ 0122 87 88 56; claviera@montagnedoc.it; Via Nazionale 30).

A six-day ski pass covering the entire Milky Way domain costs €138/155 in low/high season and skiing lessons start at €32 per hour for private tuition. More information is available online at www.vialattea.it.

Sestriere's central square, Piazza Fraiteve, is loaded with sports shops and places to eat and drink, including the popular pizzeria the **Pinky** (☎ 0122 76 441; Piazza Fraiteve 5n; pizzas €4-6) and the trendier **Sestriere Café** (☎ 0122 77 106; Piazza Agnelli 1; mains €7-8).

Sapav buses (☎ 800 80 19 01, 0122 75 54 44; www.sapav.com in Italian) connect Sestriere with Cesana (€2.10, 25 minutes), Oulx (€3, 45 minutes) and Turin (€5.10, two to three hours) up to five times daily.

SOUTHERN PIEDMONT

Prepare for gastronomic overload; southern Piedmont seems almost custom-made for gourmets. Here you'll find the international headquarters of the Slow Food Movement and the University of Gastronomic Sciences, while quality red wines such as Barolo and Barbaresco, sparkling white wines, hazelnuts, precious white truffles and mushrooms are among the gustatory pleasures this region dishes up.

Better still, it remains relatively unexplored. Numerous valleys slice paths westwards to France and the mountains provide excellent walking, cycling and skiing.

Cuneo & Around

pop 54,642 / elev 543m

Cuneo is a mildly interesting provincial capital with a small but pleasant old town in the northern wedge of the city. Its **tourist office** (☎ 0171 69 32 58; www.cuneotourism.com; Via Roma 28; ⏰ 9.30am-12.30pm & 3-6.30pm Mon-Sat) has plenty of information and can help with suggestion for accommodation.

From here a clutch of valleys radiate west towards the southern French Alps. The longest, the **Valle Stura**, leads 70km to the Colle della Maddalena (1996m), a mountain pass linking Italy with France. When snowfalls are good, skiing is possible, both here and on the bare-rock mountain slopes characteristic of the more southern **Valle Gesso**. Northwest of Cuneo, the dead-end **Valle Maira** climbs past the pretty medieval

---

MARTINI & ROSSI

The first homemade vermouth was sold in Turin by Cinzano back in 1757, while in 1786 one Antonio Carpano concocted a wine-based apéritif flavoured with alpine herbs, which came to be known as Punt e Mes. However, it was the Turinese duo, Martini (an alcohol salesman) and Rossi (a distillery supplier), who really put the beverage on the map. They teamed up in the 1850s and created a wine and liqueur distillery of their own in 1879. What happened after that can be discovered at the **Museo Martini di Storia dell'Enologia** (☎ 011 941 92 17; Piazzale Luigi Rossi 1; admission free; ⏰ 2-5pm Tue-Fri, 9am-noon & 2-5pm Sat & Sun Sep-Jul), about 20km southeast of Turin in Pessione. The museum is housed in the cellars of an 18th-century villa. One of Martini's largest production plants is also here but guided tours and tasting sessions have to be arranged in advance.

village of **Dronero** (population 7035; elevation 622m).

Cuneo's big plus is transport, with regular trains from its central train station, at Piazzale Libertà, to Saluzzo (€2.45, 35 minutes, up to six daily), Turin (€5, 1¼ hours, up to eight daily), San Remo (€5.90, 2¼ hours, three daily), Ventimiglia (€4.85, two hours, around four daily) and Nice (2¾ hours, at least six daily) in France. There is a second train station for the Cuneo–Gesso line, serving small towns in that valley to the southwest.

Saluzzo
pop 15,740 / elev 395m

Once a feisty medieval stronghold, Saluzzo, 32km north of Cuneo and 60km south of Turin, maintained its independence until the Savoys won it in a 1601 treaty with France. One of its better-known sons was General Carlo dalla Chiesa, whose implacable pursuit of the Mafia led to his assassination in the early 1980s.

The **tourist office** (☎ 0175 467 10; iat@comune .saluzzo.it; Piazza dei Mondagli 5; 9am-12.30pm & 3-6.30pm Mon-Sat, 9am-noon & 3-7pm Sun Apr-Sep, 9am-12.30pm & 2-5.30pm Mon-Sat, 9am-noon & 2-6pm Sun Oct Mar) can help with accommodation.

The burnt-red tiled rooftops of Saluzzo's charming old town make a pretty picture from the top of the **Torre Civica** (☎ 0175 414 55; Via San Giovanni; admission €2.50, incl Museo Civico di Casa Cavassa €5; 9.30am-12.30pm & 2.30-6.30pm Thu-Sun Mar-Sep, same hr Sat & Sun Oct-Feb), a 15th-century tower where the town administration once sat. The Marchesi, Saluzzo's medieval rulers, meted out justice from **La Castiglia** (Piazza Castello), the sombre castle nearby; while the **Museo Civico di Casa Cavassa** (☎ 0175 414 55; Via San Giovanni 5; adult/child €4/2, incl Torre Civica €5; 10am-1pm & 2-6pm Thu-Sun Apr-Sep, 10am-1pm & 2-5pm Tue & Wed Oct-Mar) is a fine example of a 16th-century noble's residence.

SLEEPING & EATING
Hotel Astor (☎ 0175 455 06; fax 0175 474 50; Piazza Garibaldi 39; s/d €65/93;) Ring the bell to enter this three-star hotel, overlooking one of the main squares in the new part of town but just a few minutes' walk from Saluzzo's medieval heart.

Trattoria Përpôin (☎ 0175 423 83; Via Spielberg 19-27; s/d from €45/70, menus €12-25;) Enjoy the hearty home cooking at shared tables in this

cheerful hotel-cum-restaurant. There is no hotel reception; call ahead if you intend on arriving outside restaurant opening hours.

GETTING THERE & AWAY
There are **buses** (☎ 0175 437 44) from Saluzzo to/from Turin (€3.50, 1½ hours, hourly). Otherwise, take a train to Cuneo (€2.45, 30 minutes, up to six daily), from where there are connections for Turin.

Alba
pop 29,834 / elev 172m

Solid red-brick towers rise above the heart of Alba, a medieval wine town famed for its gastronomy, particularly its in-demand white truffles.

Alba's prosperous heydays were in the 15th and 16th centuries, and the town fell under Savoy control in 1628. During WWII, citizens proclaimed it an independent republic, which lasted 23 days, after it was liberated from the Nazis by partisans.

Alba's **tourist office** (☎ 0173 3 58 33; www.lang heroero.it; Piazza Medford 3; 9am-12.30pm & 2.30-6.30pm Mon-Fri, 9am-12.30pm Sat) sells walking maps and runs a B&B booking service.

With so many picturesque vineyards to check out and wine cellars to visit, **cycling** and **walking** in the surrounding Langhe hills is a true pleasure.

Alba's truffles are celebrated each October/November with a **truffle fair**, while its other claim to fame is its **donkey race** (Palio degli Asini) also held in October. The race was inaugurated in 1932 to mock nearby Asti, Alba's rival in all things, including wine production. Hazelnuts harvested here end up in Gianduiotti chocolates and in the nutty chocolate spread Nutella, produced in Alba by Ferrero.

SLEEPING & EATING
Albergo Leon d'Oro (☎ /fax 0173 44 19 01; Piazza Marconi 2; s/d €28/45, with bathroom €45/60) Overlooking the fresh food market, the Golden Lion's white wooden shutters hide a flower-filled interior terrace and spotlessly clean, if old-fashioned, rooms.

Ai Portici (☎ 0173 348 58; www.aiporticialba.it in Italian; Via Roma 6; s/d €40/55) This charming little hotel near the train station has just four cosy rooms with antique furnishings.

Vincafé (☎ 0173 36 46 03; Via Vittorio Emanuele II 12; cheese & meat platters €8-16) This contemporary wine bar cooks up a splendid feast of mixed cheese and meat platters in a vaulted stone cellar, and the wine list stretches beyond the 350 mark.

Via Vittorio Emanuele II, Alba's main street and pedestrian zone, is lined with cafés and delicatessens selling fresh truffles – black and white – in season. Out of season, opt for a wedge of *crutina al tartufo* (a hard cheese with specks of black truffle).

GETTING THERE & AROUND

From the **bus station** (☎ 800 99 00 97; Corso Matteotti 10) there are frequent buses to/from Turin (€3.70, 2¼ hours, up to 10 daily) and sporadic buses to/from Barolo (€1.80, 25 minutes, two daily) and other surrounding villages.

From Alba's **train station** (Piazza Trento e Trieste) there are hourly trains to/from Turin (€4/5.30 via Bra/Asti, 50 minutes, hourly). From the station walk left along Corso Bandiera and its continuation, Corso Matteotti, to reach the tourist office.

Around Alba

Some of Italy's best reds come from the gently rolling Langhe hills around Alba. Barbaresco, Barolo and La Morra – named after the surrounding tiny villages that produce them – are big names to look for. Some of the most sought-after wines are stashed away in the prestigious Cavour Regional Piedmontese wine cellar in **Castello Grinzane Cavour** (☎ 0173 26 21 59; Piazza Castello 5; admission €3.50; ⌚ tours 10am-5.30pm Wed-Mon), one of many hill-top castles in this area, 5km south of Alba. The Italian statesman Camillo Cavour lived here in the 1850s.

CINZANO

The famous alcoholic beverage, Cinzano, is concocted and bottled 10km west of Alba in Cinzano, below the hill-top Santa Vittoria d'Alba area on the busy S231. The monstrous distilling plant of United Distillers & Vintners (UDV) cannot be visited individually but you can try to hook up with a group and organise a pre-arranged tour of the **Villa Cinzano** (☎ 0172 47 71 11) and its vast cellars. Artefacts chronicling the history of the company that started as a small distilling operation in Turin's hills in 1757 are displayed in the villa, a former hunting lodge of King Carlo Alberto.

TIME FOR TRUFFLES

When autumn comes to Piedmont, it's time to *andare a funghi* (mushroom-pick). Mushrooms, especially the popular *porcini* (boletus) and the harder to find *tartufo* (truffle), also known as *Tuber magnatum*, are considered something of a delicacy. Black truffles are precious, but it is the white truffle of Alba *(Tuber magnatum pico)* – which can range from white with pink veins to brownish-grey in colour – that is the most prized of all.

The white truffle is celebrated in the town of Alba each year with the **Fiera del Tartufo Bianco d'Alba** (Alba White Truffle Fair), held every Saturday and Sunday for four weeks from early October to early November. The open-air truffle feast – open to everyone – fills Piazza Medford, while truffle and mushroom traders haggle over whopping 2kg slabs of *porcini* and fist-sized truffles at the market in Coro della Maddalena (Maddalena Courtyard). The fair ends with a worldwide white truffle auction at Castello Grinzane Cavour.

BRA

pop 28,300

The provincial market town of Bra, around 15km west of Alba, is best known as the headquarters of the Slow Food Movement, the international organisation that promotes the joy of real, properly prepared food, and supports small producers around the world.

Bra's **tourist office** (☎ 0172 43 01 84; www.comune .bra.cn.it in Italian; Via Moffa di Lisio 14; ⌚ 9am-1pm & 3-6pm Mon-Fri, 9am-noon Sat & Sun Mar-Nov) has heaps of information on the town and the region.

The biennial **Cheese festival**, held over three days in September (the next one is in 2007), takes over the town and attracts huge numbers of visitors – more than 150,000 at the last count. Around 4km southeast of Bra is the village of Pollenzo, once an important Roman settlement and today home to the Università di Scienze Gastronomiche (see the boxed text, opposite). The most obvious reminder of Roman Pollentia is the circle of 18th-century houses that perfectly follows the ground-plan of the amphitheatre.

Besides its foodie associations, Bra is also famous for its rich architecture. During the

17th and 18th centuries, the town underwent something of a baroque building boom, the best example of which is the **Chiesa di San Andrea** (Piazza Caduti), designed by Bernini. At the northern edge of town, the **Santuario della Madonna dei Fiori** (Viale Madonna dei Fiori) is an impressive baroque/neoclassical chapel complex devoted to the Madonna, who supposedly appeared here in 1336.

The **Museo Civico Artistico-Storico** (☎ 0172 42 38 80; Palazzo Traversa, Via Parpera 4; admission free; ☻ 3-6pm Tue-Thu, 10am-noon & 3-6pm Sat & Sun 2nd week of month) has eclectic displays including Roman artefacts, 18th-century paintings and medieval weaponry, while the **Museo Civico di Storia Naturale** (☎ 0172 41 20 10; Via Craveri 15; admission free; ☻ 3-6pm Tue-Sun) is the place to go for fossils, minerals and stuffed birds.

Sleeping & Eating

Albergo Dell'Agenzia (☎ 0172 45 86 00; www.albergo agenzia.it; Via Fossano 21, Pollenzo-Bra; s/d/ste from €155/195/290; ℗ ⓡ) The charming and unique Albergo Dell'Agenzia is part of the same complex that houses the Università di Scienze Gastronomiche in the quiet village of Pollenzo. The rooms are spacious and elegantly furnished with huge beds, walk-in wardrobes and sparkling clean bathrooms. Prince Charles, among others, has stayed here and with a restaurant run by people who really know their business, a well-stocked wine cellar and a park, what more could you ask for?

Hotel Cavalieri (☎ 0172 42 15 16; www.hotelcava lieri.net; Piazza Arpino 37; s/d low season €85/95, high season €105/115; ℗ ⓧ) The four-star Cavalieri is a big modern place with neat, bright rooms and large bathrooms. It also has a good restaurant, and guests can use the sports complex next door, which has tennis courts, swimming pools, football pitches and more.

Osteria del Boccondivino (☎ 0172 42 56 74; www .boccondivinoslow.it in Italian; Via Mendicità Istruita 14; mains €10-15; ☻ lunch & dinner Tue-Sat) Attached to the Slow Food headquarters, this homely little restaurant lined with wine bottles was the first eatery opened by the nascent movement, back in 1984. The food is predictably fresh and excellent, and the menu, featuring local Langhe cuisine, changes daily.

Getting There & Away

From the train station on Via Vittorio Veneto several trains link Bra with Turin daily (€3.50, one hour), via Carmagnola. Buses also run from here to Pollenzo (€0.80, 15 minutes, Monday to Saturday morning).

CHERASCO

pop 7140 / elev 288m

Lumache (snails) are an integral part of Langhe cuisine, and nowhere more so than in Cherasco, Italy's self-proclaimed snail capital located 23km west of Alba. The molluscs are not actually farmed here (it's too cold) but simply marketed and sold.

SLOW DOWN...& STUDY

Don't mention burgers and fries around this part of the world – they take food seriously here. In 1986 the **Slow Food Movement** (www.slowfood.com) was founded in Bra, in response to what was seen as an increasingly globalised, frenetic lifestyle and unhealthy eating habits. Now spread worldwide, the nonprofit organisation has 82,000 members in 107 countries, where it supports agricultural biodiversity, regional gastronomic traditions and small-scale local farmers and producers, as well as food festivals such as the Cheese festival in Bra and Salone del Gusto in Turin. The Slow Food **international headquarters** (☎ 0172 41 96 11; www.slowfood.it; Via della Mendicità Istruita 14) is in Bra and has free brochures and books for sale for those keen to learn more.

In addition, Slow Food has founded the **Università di Scienze Gastronomiche** (University of Gastronomic Sciences; www.unisg.it) which has campuses in Pollenzo, near Bra, and Colorno, in the province of Parma. In Pollenzo, the **main site** (☎ 0172 45 84 19; Piazza Vittorio Emanuele 9) occupies a former royal palace, and accepted its first 70 students in October 2004 for three-year courses in gastronomy and food management. The complex has an excellent **restaurant** (☎ 0172 45 84 22; www.guidoristorante.it; ☻ Tue-Sat) serving the very best regional cuisine, a hotel (Albergo Dell'Agenzia) and the **Banca del Vino** (☎ 0172 45 84 18; www.bancadelvino.it in Italian), a vast wine cellar opened in 2005 and intended as a major 'library' of Piedmontese and Italian wines. Free guided tastings are offered; phone ahead for reservations.

Snails in this neck of the woods are never served as a starter or curled up in their shells. Rather, they are dished up *nudo* (shell-less). They can be pan-fried, roasted, dressed in an artichoke sauce or minced inside ravioli. Dishes typical to Piedmont include *lumache al barbera* (snails simmered in Barbera red wine and ground nuts) and *lumache alla Piemontese* (snails stewed with onions, nuts, anchovies and parsley in a tomato sauce).

Two tasty trattorie to try these dishes at are **La Lumaca** (☎ 0172 48 94 21; cnr Via San Pietro & Via Cavour; mains €8-10; ☧ noon or 12.30-2pm & 8-9.30pm Wed-Sun) and **Osteria della Rosa Rossa** (☎ 0172 48 81 33; Via San Pietro 31; mains €8; ☧ 12.30-2pm & 8-9pm Fri-Tue). Advance reservations are essential at both.

The **Istituto Internazionale di Elicicoltura** (☎ 0172 48 92 18; www.lumache-elici.com; Via Vittorio Emanuele 55) has more heliciculture (snail-farming) facts.

Cherasco is also known for its Sunday antique markets, held three times a year, plus several other specialised markets devoted to furniture, ceramics, motorcars and local produce. The **tourist office** (☎ 0172 48 85 52; Palazzo Comunale; www.cherasco2000.com in Italian) has details.

BAROLO
pop 680

'Robust', 'velvety', 'truffle-scented with orange reflections' and the 'wine of kings and king of wine' are among the compliments piled onto the extraordinary red wine produced around Barolo, 20km southwest of Alba. The village celebrates wine fairs in mid-September and October, and you can taste and buy wine in the **Enoteca Regionale del Barolo** (☎ 0173 5 62 77; www.baroloworld.it; ☧ 10am-12.30pm & 3-6.30pm Fri-Wed) inside Castello di Barolo.

No, you aren't drunk. **Capella Sol LeWitt-David Tremlett** (☎ 0173 28 25 82), a chapel on top of a vine-covered hill between Barolo and **La Morra**, really is painted all the colours of the rainbow. Built by a farmer in 1914, the ruined church (never consecrated) was restored and painted with symmetrical patterns in red, blue, green, yellow and orange by British and American artists in 1999. The chapel is 1.6km southeast of La Morra along a dirt track, signposted off Via Roma at the southern end of the village. It can be

---

L'INSIEME

If you want to visit some of the Barolo vineyards and try some of their excellent produce, contact **L'Insieme** (☎ 0173 50 92 12; www.linsieme.org; Cascina Nuova 51, La Morra), an association of nine small independent winemakers who have banded together to share their knowledge and create some premium wines, while ploughing back some of the profits into international charities. Members such as **Mauro Veglio** (☎ 3336 72 49 68; www.mauroveglio.com; Frazione Annunziata, Cascina Nuova 50, La Morra) will be happy to give you a tour and free tasting. Though not cheap (reckon on €30 or more for a bottle), wine sold at the cellar door will cost you a lot less than in a wine shop back in the city. More economical bottles of Nebbiolo and Barbera d'Alba are also for sale. Phone ahead for reservations and directions; you'll need your own transport, and roads and villages are poorly signposted.

---

accessed from Barolo too. You need your own wheels to get there.

EASTERN & NORTHERN PIEDMONT

East of Turin sits Asti, a name most people link with the sparkling white wine. From here wide plains fan out north to Ivrea and northeast towards Milan. Apart from the gentle green hills and vineyards of Monferrato, this is a largely barren landscape typical of eastern and northern Piedmont. In fact, approaching Vercelli (with a population 480,015), a large town on the west bank of the River Sesia, the land becomes so flat (and soggy) that rice – no fewer than 100 different varieties – is grown. Following the river north past Varallo to Monte Rosa and the Swiss frontier, flat plains begin to fizzle out and Alpine slopes kick in. Skiing, walking, biking and white-water rafting are among the many ways to explore this mountainous terrain.

The last main stop in northern Piedmont before Switzerland is **Domodossola** (population 18,650; elevation 277m), a once attractive pre-Alpine town swallowed up by suburban sprawl. From here you can jump aboard a charming train to the Swiss town of Locarno.

Asti

pop 71,536 / elev 123m

Long synonymous with sparkling wine, Asti is the capital of the Italian bubbly industry, and although perhaps not a visually exciting town, its medieval core is worth a quick lookover. Asti became a Roman colony in 89 BC, and after existing as an independent city-state in the 13th and 14th centuries, it was passed around between Spain, Austria, France and finally the Savoys, prior to unification. During the late 13th century the region became one of Italy's wealthiest, with 150-odd towers springing up in Asti alone to show off different families' wealth. Only 12 remain today; one of them, 38m-tall **Torre Troyana o Dell'Orologio** (☎ 0141 39 94 60; Piazza Medici; ☼ 10am-1pm & 4-7pm Apr-Sep, 10am-1pm & 3-6pm Sat & Sun Oct), can be scaled.

Since the 1850s the grapes grown on the largely flat plains around Asti have produced Italy's top sparkling wine – Asti (better known, incorrectly since 1993, as Asti Spumante). The sweet white wine is best drunk young and at a chilled 6°C to 8°C, like its less-fizzy cousin Moscato d'Asti. There are numerous places to sample it, either in town or out of town in Asti's 9120 hectares of vineyards tended by 6800 wine growers. The **tourist office** (☎ 0141 53 03 57; www.terredasti .it; Piazza Alfieri 29; ☼ 9am-1pm & 2.30-6.30pm Mon-Sat, 9am-1pm Sun) has a complete list.

September's flurry of wine festivals offers ample tasting opportunities; the 10-day **Douja d'Or** (a *douja* being a terracotta wine jug unique to Asti) is followed by the one-day **Delle Sagre** food festival on the 2nd Sunday of the month, which attracts staggering numbers of visitors. The **Palio**, held on the third weekend in September, sees 21 jockeys race their horses around Piazza Alfieri.

At Asti's chaotic Wednesday and Saturday morning markets on Piazza Alfieri and Piazza Campo del Palio, everything from clothes and fresh food to lawnmowers and tractors is sold.

SLEEPING & EATING

Hotel Reale (☎ 0141 53 02 40; www.hotel-reale.com; Piazza Alfieri 6; s/d from €75/110; ☒) This grand old hotel occupies a majestic 18th-century mansion right in the heart of town, and provides all the mod cons you'd expect.

Hotel Cavour (☎ 0141 53 02 22; Piazza Marconi; s/d from €39/58) Asti's budget option is a small family-run place opposite the train station. The rooms are simple but clean and the welcome is friendly.

Tacaband (☎ 0141 53 09 99; Via al Teatro Alfieri 5; mains €10; ☼ noon-2pm & 8-9.30pm Thu-Tue) Pick and choose from 500 different wines at this select wine bar, next to the theatre off pedestrian Corso Alfieri. To aid the tasting process it offers a good-value range of fixed lunchtime menus during the week (€12 to €18).

3 Bicchieri (☎ 0141 32 41 37; Piazza Statuto 37; salads €3.80-5.20, mixed platters €6; ☼ 7.30am-late Tue-Sun) Although housed inside a 16th-century tower, the interior of this place is strictly contemporary. Platters of *bresaola* (dried seasoned meat), mixed salami and cheese are proffered and, naturally, there's a good choice of wine.

GETTING THERE & AWAY

Asti is on the Turin–Alessandria–Genoa railway line and is served by regular trains (hourly) in both directions. Journey time is 30 to 55 minutes to/from Turin (€3.50) and 1¾ hours to/from Genoa (€5.75).

Monferrato

'Bright', 'young' and 'intensely red' is how critics sum up the Barbera del Monferrato wines produced in Monferrato, a cluster of wine-producing villages spread between Asti and **Casale Monferrato** (population 38,500; elevation 116m), 20km to the northeast. Little visited and beautiful, this green pocket is ideal wine-tasting territory.

At the **Cooperativa Sette Colli** (☎ 0141 91 72 06; www.vinisettecollimoncalvo.it in Italian; ☼ 9am-noon & 3-6pm Mon-Sat, 9am-noon Sun) in Moncalvo, 15km north of Asti along the S457, you can also do free wine-tasting or buy. Otherwise many of the dozens of *agriturismi* in this rural region run informal cellar tours; the **Consorzio Operatori Turistici Asti e Monferrato** (☎ 0141 53 03 57; www.terredasti.it in Italian; Piazza Alfieri 29) in Asti has a list.

Very much a family affair, the **Tenuta del Barone** (☎ 0141 91 01 61; Via Barone 18, Penango; www.tenutadelbarone.com; s/d B&B low season €44/62, high season €55/77.50, dinner with wine €25; ℗) is a rambling farm dating from 1550 that has been converted into a cheery B&B. Sleep in the old stables and feast on huge amounts of homemade food cooked up by Mamma. Penango, 2km from Moncalvo, is signposted from Moncalvo's southern end.

Locanda del Sant'Uffizio (☎ 0141 91 62 92; santuffizio@thi.it; Strada Sant'Uffizio 1, Cioccaro di Penango; s/d €158/215; P ⌧ 🖳 🕭) is a haven of peace in the form of a restored 17th-century convent with 4 hectares of working vineyards. Stylish rooms – some with original frescoes – reflect the colour of the flowers after which they are named.

Ivrea

pop 25,100

The pleasant but outwardly unexciting town of Ivrea, 55km northeast of Turin, is famous for typewriters and oranges, and explodes in early February as it celebrates the chaotic festival, Battaglia delle Arance (see the boxed text, below).

Ivrea's **tourist office** (☎ 0125 61 81 31; www.can avese-vallilanzo.it in Italian; Corso Vercelli 1; ☯ 9.30am-12.30pm & 2.30-6pm Mon-Fri, 10am-noon & 3-6pm Sat) has more information.

The River Dora Baltea runs through the centre of town, neatly dividing the historic old town (north bank) from the new town (south bank). The old town holds the most

interest for visitors with its arcaded squares and medieval red-brick **castle** (☎ 0125 444 15; Piazza Castello; admission €2; ☯ 10am-noon & 3-6pm Sun May-Oct), which functioned as a prison between 1750 and 1970. The nearby **Duomo** (Piazza Duomo) dates from the 11th century.

Olivetti – founded by local entrepreneur Camillo Olivetti (1868–1943) in Ivrea in 1896 – manufactured typewriters in the new town in the 1950s and 1960s. Today its Bauhaus-inspired factory and offices with their giant glass façades form part of **MAAM** (Museo a Cielo Aperto dell'Architettura Moderna; ☎ 0125 64 18 15; Via Jervis 26; admission free; ☯ museum 24hr, info centre 9am-1pm Tue-Sat), an open-air museum of modern architecture. Seven numbered information panels in English lead visitors on a tour of the Olivetti building façades (all still in use).

SLEEPING & EATING

Trattoria Residence Monferrato (☎ 0125 64 10 12; monferrato@iol.it; Via Gariglietti 1; s/d €45/55, mains €7; ☯ Mon-Sat, lunch Sun) Typical Piedmontese cuisine characterises this excellent-value

---

THE BATTLE OF ORANGES

The story goes that, back in the 12th century, a miller chose Violetta, another miller's pretty young daughter, for his wife. But Ranieri, the wicked Count of Biandrate, reserved for himself the right to the first round with any local woman who was about to be married. The miller's daughter was so upset by this that she sparked a revolt against the tyrant by the impoverished townspeople. On foot and armed only with stones, they launched themselves against the count's troops, pelting them as they rode around the town in horse-drawn carts. This desperate uprising went down in the town's folk history and centuries later provided an excuse for rival gangs from different parts of town to stage an annual riot around the town's carnival.

When Napoleon occupied this part of Italy in the early 1800s, his administrators ordered everyone to wear red revolutionary bonnets. They also put a stop to the fatal brawling, ordering that from then on the re-enactment of the famous uprising was to be carried out with oranges.

And so today, for three consecutive days, nine teams of 'revolutionaries' (3500 people in all) pound each other with 400,000kg of oranges imported from Sicily for the occasion. *Anyone* slipping on the slimy carpet of squashed orange without some kind of red headgear is considered fair game for a massive orange assault by the 'rebel' squads.

The Battle of Oranges is part of the **Ivrea Carnival**, which traditionally starts on the Thursday before Lent with a masked ball on Piazza Ottinetti. On Saturday evening the *mugnaia* (miller's daughter) is presented to the town, along with the other costumed medieval characters, and Napoleonic troops parade through town amid fireworks and torchlight. The next morning the so-called 'distribution of beans' on Piazza Maretta is followed by the solemn 'Preda in Dora' ceremony, where the town leader throws a stone into the Dora River to symbolise the town's uprising against tyrannical feudal rule. Sunday afternoon sees the main costumed procession with drums, flag bearers and a band – and the start of the orange battles! The final battle on Shrove Tuesday is followed on Ash Wednesday by a great open-air feast of polenta and salted cod in the Borghetto quarter of town. This marks the start of Lent.

trattoria with a handful of kitchenette-equipped rooms above. Its eight-dish anti-pasti (nine if you opt for snails too), costing €15.50, is a meal in itself and ensures you'll never forget the place.

Albergo Nord (☎ 0125 401 35; Corso Nigra 53; s/d from €35/46) Basic but clean rooms are offered by this modest family-run establishment near the train station.

Enoteca Vino e Dintori (☎ 0125 64 12 23; Via Arduino 126; ☿ Tue-Sat) This traditional wine bar hosts thematic tasting evenings on Fridays and Saturdays, focusing on regional specialities (risotto evenings are quite frequent) as well as wine.

GETTING THERE & AWAY

From Ivrea's train station on the corner of Corso Jervis and Corso Nigra in the new town, there are direct trains to/from Aosta (€3.50, one hour, hourly), Chivasso (€2.45, 30 minutes, at least hourly) and Turin (€3.90, one hour, up to eight daily). Both the historic centre and MAAM are an easy walk from here.

Varallo

pop 7795 / elev 451m

Varallo marks the start of the Valsesia, one of the less-crowded Piedmontese valleys that, together with the Valle d'Aosta's Val d'Ayas and Val di Gressoney, forms part of the Monte Rosa ski area. White-water rafters, canoeists and kayakers take to the Sesia's wild rapids from May to September.

The **tourist office** (☎ 0163 56 44 04; www.turismo valsesiavercelli.it in Italian; Corso Roma 38; ☿ 9am-1pm & 2.30-6.30pm Mon-Fri, 9.30am-1pm & 2.30-7pm Sat) has lots of information on Varallo and its surrounds and has details on white-water sport associations along the valley, including Varallo's **Accadueo Scuola di Sport Fluviali** (☎ 347 58 36 888; www.accadueo-sesia.it in Italian; Crevola Varallo).

The Passion of Christ dramatically unfolds at Varallo's **Sacro Monte di Varallo** (☎ 0163 539 38; riservasacromonte@laproxima.it; admission free), a series of 45 chapels dating back to the 16th century. Inside each numbered chapel, life-size statues capture a biblical episode, often in bloody detail, be it the original sin, Herod's massacre of Bethlehem's innocents or Christ's crucifixion. Work started on the first chapel in 1491 and the entire project took 250 years to complete. The wooded complex, above the town, is protected by the

Riserva Naturale Speciale del Sacro Monte di Varallo. In summer a **cable car** (one way €2) links the Sacro Monte with Piazza G Ferrari in town.

Autoservizi Novarese (☎ 011 90 31 003) operates buses from Varallo to Turin (€6.25, 2¼ hours, two daily). For information on buses to/from Alagna Sesia (one hour, up to five daily) contact **ATAP** (☎ 015 84 88 411).

VALLE D'AOSTA

Covering just 3262 sq km and with a population of only 120,589, the Valle d'Aosta is the smallest – and wealthiest – region in Italy. It enjoys self-governing status, meaning that 90% of local taxes are spent within the province. Its inhabitants, known as Valdostans, speak a Franco-Provençal patois, with French sharing equal rights with Italian. To the east, the Walser villagers cling to their German dialect, Tich.

Neolithic and early Bronze Age remains have been discovered in the Valle d'Aosta and early Roman sites dot the valley. For a century the Valle d'Aosta was part of the French kingdom of Bourgogne, and later fell under the sway of Napoleon. The region was incorporated into the new Kingdom of Italy in 1861. Under Mussolini's regime massive immigration from other parts of Italy was encouraged in an attempt to bury the region's separate identity, but after WWII many Valdostans considered ceding from Italy altogether to rejoin France. This was a move that came to nothing in the end because the high degree of autonomy the Valdostans wished to retain for their province was unacceptable to the centralised French government. The fact that the Valle D'Aosta was then a rather poor rural area didn't help either.

Always an important passageway through the Alps, the valley is lined with castles. The opening of the Mont Blanc Tunnel in 1965 connected Courmayeur at the western end of the valley with the French resort of Chamonix – and transformed a quiet valley into a major road-freight thoroughfare and premier skiing area.

Valle d'Aosta cuisine makes liberal use of the local cheese *fontina* (see p250) and polenta. Traditional dishes include *seupa valpellinentze* (thick soup of cabbage, bread,

VALLE D'AOSTA

LIGURIA, PIEDMONT & VALLE D'AOSTA

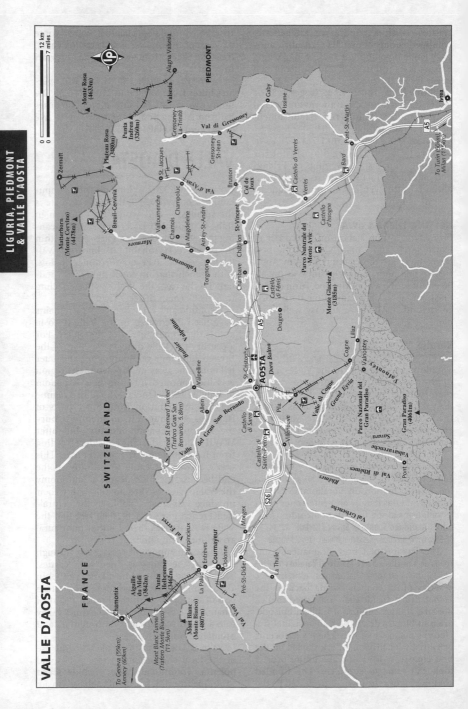

12 km
7 miles

PIEDMONT

To Turin (30km);
Milan (175km)

A5

Ivrea

Monte Rosa
(4633m)

Valsesia

Alagna Valsesia

Gaby

Issime

Pont-St-Martin

Val di Gressoney

Gressoney-
La-Trinité

Bard

Zermatt

Plateau Rosa
(3480m)

Punta
Indren
(3260m)

Gressoney-
St-Jean

Castello di Verrès

Verrès

St-Jacques

Val d'Ayas

Matterhorn
(Monte Cervino)
(4478m)

Breuil-Cervinia

Brusson

Col de
Joux

Castello
d'Issogne

Parco Naturale del
Monte Avic

Marmore

Valtournenche

Champoluc

Chamois

La Magdeleine

Antey-St-André

Châtillon

St-Vincent

Valtournenche

Torgnon

Chambave

Castello
di Fénis

Drugea

Monte Glacier
(3185m)

Cogne

Lillaz

SWITZERLAND

Valpelline

Bionaz

Great St Bernard Tunnel
(Traforo Gran San
Bernardo, 5.8km)

Valpelline

Allein

Valle del Gran San Bernardo

St-Cristophe

Dora Baltea

AOSTA

A5

Pila

Castello
di Sarre

Castello
di Sainte-Pierre

Villeneuve

Valle di Cogne

Grand Eyvia

Vainontey

Valnontey

Parco Nazionale del
Gran Paradiso

Gran Paradiso
(4061m)

Savara

Valsavarenche

Rhêmes

Val di Rhêmes

Pont

FRANCE

Chamonix

Aiguille
du Midi
(3842m)

Punta
Helbronner
(3462m)

Mont Blanc Tunnel
(Traforo Monte Bianco)
(11.5km)

Mont Blanc
(Monte Bianco)
(4807m)

To Geneva (55km);
Annecy (60km)

Planpincieux

Entrèves

La Palud

Val Ferret

Courmayeur
Dolonne

Pré-St-Didier

Morgex

Val Veny

La Thuile

S26

Val Grisenche

Val Grisenche

beef broth and *fontina*), and *carbonada con polenta* (another soup traditionally made with the meat of the chamois although beef is now generally used). The valley is also home to small, government-subsidised co-operative vineyards, producing some excellent and much sought-after wines, though these are rarely available outside the region.

Valle d'Aosta shares Europe's highest mountain, Mont Blanc (Monte Bianco, 4807m), with France and the Matterhorn (Monte Cervino, 4478m) with Switzerland. It also takes in the Gran Paradiso (4061m), which it shares with Piedmont.

Activities

The mountains in Valle d'Aosta ensure formidable **downhill skiing**, with thundering off-piste opportunities for experienced skiers. Courmayeur (where cable cars glide to the French resort of Chamonix) and Breuil-Cervinia (from where you can ski to Zermatt, Switzerland) are by far the best-known resorts, but smaller spots such as Pila (immediately south of Aosta) and the Valtournenche and Val di Gressoney resorts all offer scenic off the beaten track skiing for intermediates and beginners. The Valle di Cogne, in Parco Nazionale del Gran Paradiso, and the Val di Gressoney, at the southern foot of Monte Rosa, are leading **cross-country skiing** centres.

Information on ski schools, mountain guides and ski-lift passes for individual resorts are detailed under Activities in the respective resort sections. A three-/six-day lift pass covering the entire Valle d'Aosta, Alagna Valsesia (Piedmont) and Zermatt (Switzerland) costs €97/182. An Around Mont Blanc pass is valid in the Four Valleys skiing area (Switzerland), Chamonix (France) and Valle d'Aosta and covers six days of skiing (€220). Various other passes, including full-season passes, are available. For more information, see www.skivallee.it.

While expert mountaineers set off across the ice to tackle Mont Blanc from Courmayeur, walkers should settle for one of the dozens of half- and full-day **walks** and rambles at lower altitudes offered by the region. Many trails in the valley are suitable for **mountain biking** and there are some particularly interesting nature trails in the Parco Nazionale del Gran Paradiso (p253). Details on walks, huts and mountain guides are listed under Activities in the respective resort sections.

AOSTA

pop 34,193 / elev 565m

Aosta, the so-called 'Rome of the Alps', is the Valle d'Aosta's capital and only major city. As usual in these northern border regions, there's a markedly 'un-Italian' feel to the place, which has more of a Swiss aura of orderliness and reserve. Aosta boasts some important Roman remains, but otherwise attractions are thin on the ground. However, good transport links make it a natural jumping-off point to the region's 11 valleys and their green wonders.

Information

Banks abound on and around the Piazza Chanoux.

Aosta tourist office (☎ 0165 23 66 27; www.regione.vda.it/turismo; Piazza Chanoux 2; ☼ 9am-1pm & 3-8pm Jun-Sep, 9am-1pm & 3-8pm Mon-Sat, 9am-1pm Sun Oct-May) Provides information on the entire region, including comprehensive accommodation lists.

Change Exact (Via E Aubert 77; ☼ 10am-1pm & 2.30-6.30pm Mon-Sat) Currency exchange and Western Union money transfer.

Farmacia Centrale (☎ 0165 26 22 05; Piazza Chanoux 35) Pharmacy.

Hospital (☎ 0165 3041; Viale Ginevra 3)

Police station (☎ 0165 26 21 69; Corso Battaglione Aosta 169) West of the town centre.

Post office (Piazza Narbonne; ☼ 8.15am-6pm Mon-Fri, 8.15am-1pm Sat)

A BOVINE BEAUTY QUEST

Every October thousands of Valdostans gather in Aosta to watch the cow fights. Known traditionally as the Bataille de Reines (Battle of the Queens), the event is organised along the lines of a beauty contest. Knockouts start around the valley in March, when locals from across the region prime their best bovines for battle, and end with the Aosta-based finals on the third Sunday in October, when the queen of the cows is crowned. This might seem a bit strange, but it is a tradition from the days when cows returning from mountain fields would tussle with each other. The losing cow is not injured and the match ends when one pulls away.

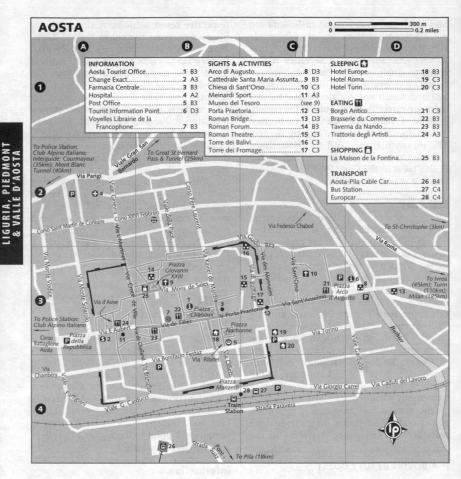

AOSTA

0 ──────────────── 300 m
0 ──────────────── 0.2 miles

INFORMATION	
Aosta Tourist Office..................1	B3
Change Exact..........................2	A3
Farmacia Centrale.....................3	B3
Hospital................................4	A2
Post Office............................5	B3
Tourist Information Point.............6	D3
Voyelles Librairie de la Francophone.............7	B3

SIGHTS & ACTIVITIES	
Arco di Augusto......................8	D3
Cattedrale Santa Maria Assunta...9	B3
Chiesa di Sant'Orso.................10	C3
Meinardi Sport........................11	A3
Museo del Tesoro.............(see 9)	
Porta Praetoria......................12	C3
Roman Bridge........................13	D3
Roman Forum.........................14	B3
Roman Theatre.......................15	C3
Torre dei Balivi......................16	C3
Torre dei Fromage..................17	C3

SLEEPING 🛏	
Hotel Europe........................18	B3
Hotel Roma.........................19	C3
Hotel Turin.........................20	C3

EATING 🍴	
Borgo Antico........................21	C3
Brasserie du Commerce.............22	B3
Taverna da Nando...................23	C3
Trattoria degli Artisti..............24	A3

SHOPPING 🛍	
La Maison de la Fontina............25	B3

TRANSPORT	
Aosta-Pila Cable Car................26	B4
Bus Station..........................27	C4
Europcar.............................28	C4

Tourist information point (☎ 0165 25 53 43; Piazza Arco di Augusto; ☻ 10am-2pm & 3-7pm Mar-Jan) Books hotels in Aosta and around. Touch-screen monitors outside provide local hotel details if it's closed.

Voyelles Librairie de la Francophone (☎ 0165 4 36 49; info@librairiedelafrancophone.it; Via de Tillier 28; per hr €1.50) French bookshop with Internet access.

Sights
ROMAN RUINS

Deemed the city's symbol, the **Arco di Augusto** (Piazza Arco di Augusto) has been strung with a crucifix in its centre since medieval times. From Piazza Arco di Augusto, nip east across the River Buthier bridge to view the cobbled **Roman bridge** – still in use since the 1st century. Then backtrack west 300m along Via

Sant'Anselmo to **Porta Praetoria**, the main gate to the Roman city.

Heading north along Via di Bailliage takes you to Aosta's **Roman theatre** (Via Porta Praetoria; admission free; ☻ 9am-6.30pm Oct-Feb, 9am-8pm Mar-Sep); it's located down a dust track. Part of its 22m-high façade is still intact. In summer, performances are held in the better-preserved lower section. All that remains of the **Roman forum**, another couple of blocks west, beneath Piazza Giovanni XXIII, is a colonnaded walkway known as **Criptoportico**. The foreboding **Torre dei Balivi**, a former prison, marks one corner of the Roman wall and peers down on the smaller **Torre dei Fromage** (☎ 0165 44 23 38; admission free; ☻ 9.30am-noon & 2.30-6.30pm Tue-Sun) – named after a family rather than a cheese – which today hosts temporary art exhibitions.

CATTEDRALE SANTA MARIA ASSUNTA
Aosta's **cathedral** (Piazza Giovanni XXIII; ☺ 6.30am-noon & 3-7pm) has a neoclassical façade that belies the impressive Gothic interior. Inside, the carved 15th-century walnut-wood choir stalls are particularly beautiful. Two mosaics on the floor, dating from the 12th to the 14th centuries, are also worth studying, as are the religious art treasures displayed in the **Museo del Tesoro** (☎ 0165 40 413; adult/child €2.10/0.75; ☺ 9-11.30am & 3-5.30pm Mon-Sat, 8.30-10am & 10.45-11.30am Sun Apr-Sep, 8.30-10am, 10.45-11.30am & 3-5.30pm Sun Oct-Feb), located in the cathedral's deambulatory.

CHIESA DI SANT'ORSO
This **church** (Via Sant'Orso; ☺ 10am-12.30pm & 1.30-5pm Mon-Fri, 10am-12.30pm & 1.30-6pm Sun Oct-Feb, 9am-7pm Mar-Jun & Sep, 9am-8pm Jul & Aug) dates back to the 10th century but was altered on several occasions, notably in the 15th century when Giorgio di Challant of the ruling family ordered the original frescoes covered and a new roof installed. Remnants of these frescoes can be viewed by clambering up into the cavity between the original and 15th-century ceilings. The interior and the magnificently carved choir stalls are Gothic, but excavations have unearthed the remains of an earlier church, possibly dating from the 8th century. The Romanesque cloister, with its ornately carved capitals representing biblical scenes, is to the right of the church.

Activities
SKIING
The small resort of Pila (1800m), accessible by **Aosta–Pila cable car** (☎ 0165 36 36 15; www.pila.it; half-/full-day pass €20/28; ☺ mid-Dec–mid-Apr) from Aosta or an 18km drive south, is quick and easy to reach from the town. Its 70km of runs, served by 13 lifts, form one of the valley's largest ski areas. Its highest slope, in the shadow of Gran Paradiso, reaches 2700m and sports a snow park with a half pipe, jump and slide for boarders. The ski station is a village of sorts, but services such as the tourist office, police and medical services are handled from Aosta. For details on ski passes covering here and other resorts in the Valle d'Aosta, see p247.

WALKING & MOUNTAIN BIKING
The lower slopes leading down from Pila into the Dora Baltea valley provide easy picturesque walks and rides. Mountain bikes can be transported for free on the **Aosta–Pila cable car** (adult one way/return €2.60/4.20; ☺ 8am-12.15pm & 2-5pm or 6pm Jun-Aug) and mountain bikers can buy a one-day pass (transport only, €13), allowing unlimited use of the cable car and chairlifts. The tourist office gives advice on mountain biking itineraries and walking trails and has lists of Alpine guides and mountain accommodation.

Recommended walking clubs that, among other things, organise treks and provide mountain guides include:

Club Alpino Italiano (CAI; ☎ 0165 4 01 94; www.caivda.it in Italian; Corso Battaglione Aosta 81; ☺ 6.30-8pm Tue, 8-10pm Fri) West of the city centre.

Interguide (☎ 0165 4 09 39; www.interguide.it in Italian; Via Monte Emilius 13; ☺ 6.30-8pm Tue, 8pm-10pm Fri) West of the city centre.

Meinardi Sport (☎ 0165 4 06 78; Via E Aubert; ☺ 3-7.30pm Mon, 9am-12.30pm & 3-7.30pm Tue-Sat) A well-stocked sports shop with walking supplies and maps.

Festivals & Events
The **Fiera di Sant'Orso**, the annual wood fair held around Porta Praetoria on 30 and 31 January, honours the town's patron saint. Craftspeople from all over the valley gather to display their carvings and present an item to the saint at the Chiesa di Sant'Orso.

Sleeping
Aosta isn't exactly over-supplied with hotel accommodation, and what there is tends to be pretty nondescript. Cheaper (and often more charming) lodgings lie in the hinterland. Aosta can easily be visited from Cogne, 24km south of Aosta on the northern fringe of the Parco Nazionale del Gran Paradiso; see p253 for accommodation details.

Hotel Roma (☎ 0165 408 21; hroma@libero.it; Via Torino 7; s/d from €38/65; P) There's something slightly 1970s about the Roma, but it is a friendly, reasonably priced option just outside the old Roman walls. Breakfast is €6.

Hotel Turin (☎ 0165 445 93; www.hotelturin.it; Via Torino 14; s/d low season from €44/57, high season from €60/92; P) The Turin is a modern boxy affair east of the old walls, and provides regulation three-star comforts.

Hotel Europe (☎ 0165 23 63 63; www.ethotels.com; Piazza Narbonne 8; s/d from €60/84; P) The central,

VALDOSTAN CHEESE

A curious cross between Gouda and Brie best sums up *fontina*, Valdostans' favourite cheese honoured with its own DOP (designation of protected origin) since 1996. It must be made from the full-cream unpasteurised milk of Valdostan cows that have grazed on pastures up to 2700m above sea level. One hundred litres of milk makes 10kg of cheese. During a period of three months it matures in underground rock tunnels, it is turned daily and brushed and salted on alternate days. This and other age-old traditions can be discovered first-hand at the **Valpelline Visitors' Centre** (☎ 0165 7 33 09; Frissonière; admission free; 🕙 8.30am-12.30pm & 2.30-6.30pm Mon-Fri, 9am-noon & 3-6pm Sat & Sun mid-Jun–mid-Sep, 9am-noon & 2.30-5.30pm Mon-Fri mid-Sep–mid-Jun). To get to the centre from Aosta, follow the SR28 for 7km north to Valpelline, turn east towards Ollomont and after 1.5km turn west along a mountain road to Frissonière.

In Aosta, **La Maison de la Fontina** (☎ 0165 23 56 51; Via Mons de Sales 14; 🕙 Mon-Sat), a cheese shop established in 1937, stocks an outstanding selection of regional cheese, including Stravecchio di Montagna, an extremely strong, salty and potent hard cheese – eat it *before* asking how it is made.

four-star Europe is a perfectly comfortable if rather anonymous place, with the usual business hotel features.

Eating

Plenty of open-air café terraces spring up on sunbaked Piazza Chanoux in summer.

Taverna da Nando (☎ 0165 444 55; Via de Tillier 41; pizzas €4-7, set menus €12-28; 🕙 Tue-Sun) Nando's seems to have an obsession with polenta and veal, which dominate the menu. Pizzas are good value and the 'tourist menus' aren't bad either.

Brasserie du Commerce (☎ 0165 3 56 13; Via de Tillier 10; mains €8-12, set menus about €25; 🕙 lunch & dinner) One of Aosta's best eating spots, the Brasserie serves up excellent local cuisine, with a good range of antipasti and lots of cheesy and polenta-filled dishes. The three-course set menus will satisfy the biggest of appetites, and service is cheery.

Borgo Antico (☎ 0165 422 55; Via Sant'Anselmo 143; mains €10-20, menus from €22.50; 🕙 lunch & dinner Tue-Sun) Lots of pasta and grills adorn the menu at the Borgo, which also offers rather pricey set three-course 'tourist menus' – fish, meat and vegetarian options are available.

Trattoria degli Artisti (☎ 0165 4 09 60; Via Maillet 5-7; mains €7.50-12; 🕙 Tue-Sat) It's polenta time again at this cosy little trattoria, tucked down an alleyway off Via E Aubert. It serves plenty of traditional regional cuisine, much of which seems to involve cheese.

Getting There & Away

Buses to Milan (€13, 1½ to 3½ hours, two daily), Turin (€8, two hours, up to 10 daily)

and Courmayeur (€3, one hour, up to eight daily) leave from Aosta's **bus station** (☎ 0165 26 20 27; Via Giorgio Carrel), virtually opposite the train station. To get to Breuil-Cervinia, take a Turin-bound bus to Châtillon (30 minutes, eight daily), then a connecting bus (one hour, seven daily) to the resort.

Aosta's train station, on Piazza Manzetti, is served by trains from most parts of Italy via Turin (€7, two to 2½ hours, more than 10 daily).

Aosta is on the A5, which connects Turin with the Mont Blanc Tunnel and France. Another exit road north of the city leads to the Great St Bernard Tunnel and onto Switzerland.

Getting Around

Aosta's walled centre is closed to private cars. Shuttle buses run through town from the train station. Book a **taxi** (☎ 0165 3 18 31) or hire your own wheels from **Europcar** (☎ 0165 4 14 32) at the train station.

AOSTA VALLEY CASTLES

If you need a break from the slopes, the Aosta valley is peppered with Gothic castles just waiting to be explored. Each castle is within view of the next, and messages used to be transferred along the valley by flag signals. From Aosta follow the scenic S26 that runs parallel to the busy A5.

East from Aosta is the magnificently restored **Castello di Fénis** (☎ 0165 76 42 63; adult/child €5/free; 🕙 9am-6.30pm Mar-Jun & Sep, 9am-7.30pm Jul & Aug, 10-11.30am & 2-4.30pm Wed-Sat & Mon, 10-11.30am & 2-5.30pm Sun Oct-Feb). Formerly owned by the

Challant family, it features rich frescoes. It was never really used as a defensive post but served as a plush residence.

Past St-Vincent is the sober **Castello di Verrès** (☎ 0125 92 90 67). More like the real thing, this castle does sentinel duty high on its rocky perch. It's closed until September 2006.

Around 1km southwest of the River Dora Baltea, below the town of Verrès, is the 15th-century **Castello d'Issogne** (☎ 0125 92 93 73; adult/child €5/free; ☟ 9am-6.30pm daily Mar-Jun & Sep, 9am-7.30pm daily Jul & Aug, 10am-noon & 1.30-4.30pm Thu-Sat & Mon & Tue, 10am-noon & 1.30-5.30pm Sun Oct-Feb). This building was a castle, although you would hardly know it – it looks more like a stately home.

Further down the valley still, towards Pont-St-Martin, the fortress of **Bard** (closed) was a no-nonsense military outpost given short shrift by Napoleon on his first campaign into Italy. Once you are at Pont-St-Martin, you could strike north to **Castel Savoia** in Gressoney-St-Jean; see p255.

Heading west from Aosta towards Mont Blanc, you quickly hit **Castello di Sarre** (☎ 0165 25 75 39; adult/child €5/free; ☟ 9am-6.30pm Mar-Jun & Sep, 9am-7.30pm Jul & Aug, 10am-noon & 1.30-4.30pm Tue-Sat, 10am-noon & 1.30-5.30pm Sun Oct-Feb). Built in 1710 on the remains of a 13th-century fort, King Vittorio Emanuele II bought it in 1869 to use as a hunting residence. The Savoys sold the castle in 1972 and it now serves as a museum of the royal presence in the region.

Castello di Saint-Pierre (☎ 0165 90 34 85; adult/child €3/1.50; ☟ 9am-7pm Apr-Sep), home to a natural history museum, is the last main sight of interest on Aosta's castle route.

COURMAYEUR

pop 2976 / elev 1224m

Set against the backdrop of Mont Blanc and with much of the original village intact, Courmayeur is one of the Valle d'Aosta's more picturesque, and more expensive, skiing resorts. It's a good base for walking or biking excursions in summer, but there are few sights as such.

The resort has more than 140km of downhill and cross-country ski runs and a feast of summer activities, including skiing, horse riding, hang-gliding, canoeing and 280km of footpaths in the mountains. Year-round a cable car links La Palud, near Courmayeur, with Punta Helbronner (3462m) on

Mont Blanc – an extraordinary 20-minute ride. From here another cable car (April to September only) takes you on a breathtaking 5km transglacial ride across the Italian border to the Aiguille du Midi (3842m) in France (from where the world's highest cable car transports you into the French ski resort of Chamonix).

Information

Ambulance (☎ 0165 84 46 84)
Ospedale Regionale d'Aosta (hospital; ☎ 0165 30 42 56)
Tourist office (☎ 0165 84 20 60; www.courmayeur.net in Italian; Piazzale Monte Bianco 13; ☟ 9am-12.30pm & 3-6.30pm)

Activities

The **Società delle Guide Alpine di Courmayeur** (☎ 0165 84 20 64; www.guidecourmayeur.com; Piazzale Monte Bianco 14), founded in 1859, is Italy's oldest guiding association. In winter its guides lead adventure seekers off-piste, up frozen waterfalls and on heli-skiing expeditions. In summer, rock climbing, canyoning, canoeing, kayaking and hiking are among its many activities. The association's dramatic history is unravelled in the **Museo Alpino Duca degli Abruzzi** (☎ 0165 84 20 64; Piazza Henry 2; admission free).

SKIING

Courmayeur is served by four cable cars, two gondolas and numerous drag lifts, all run by **Funivie Courmayeur Mont Blanc** (☎ 0165 84 66 58; www.courmayeur-montblanc.com; Strada Regionale 47). Skiing lessons with the **Scuola di Sci Monte Bianco** (☎ 0165 84 24 77; www.scuolascimontebianco.com in Italian; Strada Regionale 51), founded in 1922, start at €30 for a one- to three-hour private or group lesson. For advanced skiers the legendary Vallée Blanche off-piste descent from Punta Helbronner into Chamonix (France) is a must. Ability aside, an experienced guide is essential for the challenging 24km-long run.

SWIMMING

For an exhilarating summertime experience take a heady dive into Courmayeur's open-air alpine **swimming pool** (☎ 0165 84 66 58; adult/child under 5 €10/free, pool & return cable-car admission €16/free; ☟ 9.30am-5.30pm mid-Jun–early Sep), tucked in the heart of the mountains at the top of the Courmayeur cable car on Plan Checrouit (1709m). Admission to the pool includes use of the sauna.

WALKING & MOUNTAIN BIKING

In July and August the Courmayeur and Val Veny **cable cars** (☎ 0165 84 66 58; one way/return €6/10) and the Maison Vieille **chairlift** (☎ 0165 84 66 58; one way/return €4/5) whisk walkers and mountain bikers up into the mountains; transporting a bike is free. All three run from around 9.15am to 1pm and 2.15pm to 5.15pm from June to August.

The **La Palud–Punta Helbronner cable car** (☎ 0165 8 99 25; www.montebianco.com in Italian; return €31; ⏰ 8.30am-12.40pm & 2-4.30pm) departs every 20 minutes in each direction. From mid-station 2173m-high **Pavillon du Mt Fréty** (return €12), nature-lovers can take a flowery stroll around the **Giardino Alpino Saussurea** (☎ 0165 8 99 25; adult/child €2/1.50; ⏰ 9.30am-6pm Jul-Sep). From this Alpine garden – Europe's highest at 2175m – the stunning views of the Mont Blanc range alone make a visit worthwhile. Walking trails around here are numerous and many fall within the **Pavillon du Mt Fréty Nature Oasis**, a protected zone of 1200 hectares tucked between glaciers and populated by ibexes (wild goats), marmots and deer.

Even if it's sweltering in the valley be prepared for temperatures as low as −10°C at **Punta Helbronner** (3462m). Take heavy winter clothes and sunglasses and head up early in the morning to avoid the heavy weather that often descends onto the summit area in the early afternoon. Bring your passport (and check if you need a visa) if you intend to make the glacial crossing (return to Aiguille du Midi/Chamonix €17.50/39) into France.

Mountain bikes can be hired at **Noleggio Ulisse** (☎ 0165 84 22 55), in front of the Courmayeur chairlift, or **Lo Caraco** (☎ 0165 84 41 52; Via Roma 150) in town. Hire costs around €10 a day.

Those seeking a guide should contact the Società delle Guide Alpine di Courmayeur (see p251) or the **Associazione Accompagnatori della Natura Courmayeur-Mt Blanc** (☎ 0165 86 21 40; Strada La Palud 1).

Sleeping & Eating

Peak-season accommodation in Courmayeur can cost up to 50% more than in low season, but hotel rates in towns along the valleys – La Palud, Dolonne, Entrèves, La Saxe, Plan Ponquet, Pré-St-Didier, Val Ferret, and Morgex – soar less dramatically. For mountain-hut accommodation ask the tourist office for a list of *rifugi*. In the old part of Courmayeur quality food shops and restaurants line Via Roma.

Rifugio Pavillon (☎ 0165 84 40 90; Pavillon du Mt Fréty; ⏰ 10am-5pm Dec-Oct) At a heady height of 2173m and promising a dramatic mountain panorama from any deck chair you flop on, this mountain bar-café-restaurant makes an exhilarating lunch stop for those travelling up to Punta Helbronner or walking around Mt Fréty. It has 24 dorm beds should your legs refuse to shift another inch.

Hotel Crampon (☎ 0165 83 23 85; www.crampon .it; Via Villette 8; s/d/tr low season €45/70/90, high season €90/130/160; ⏰ Dec-Mar & Jul-Sep; P ▣) Located on a quiet side street in the centre of town, the family-run Crampon offers cosy rooms and a relaxing garden. In winter, a free shuttle bus whisks you to the cable-car station.

Camping Monte Bianco La Sorgente (☎ 0165 86 90 89 summer, 0165 84 82 09 winter; www.camping lasorgente.net; Peuterey-Val Veny; person/tent/car from €4.50/3.50/4.50, bungalow 2/4 people €35/65; P ▣) This well-equipped camping ground, in the middle of a forest 5km from Courmayeur, has a great range of budget accommodation and runs a host of activities for campers. Some bungalows have their own kitchen.

Getting There & Away

Three trains daily from Aosta terminate at Pré-St-Didier, with bus connections (20 to 30 minutes, eight to 10 daily) to **Courmayeur bus station** (☎ 0166 84 13 97; Piazzale Monte Bianco) outside the tourist office. There are up to eight direct Aosta–Courmayeur buses daily (€3, one hour) and long-haul buses serve Milan (€18, 4½ hours, three to five daily) and Turin (€9, 3½ to 4½ hours, two to four daily).

Immediately north of Courmayeur, the 11.5km-long Mont Blanc Tunnel leads to Chamonix (France).

PARCO NAZIONALE DEL GRAN PARADISO

Gran Paradiso was Italy's first national park, established in 1922 after Vittorio Emanuele II gave his hunting reserve to the state. By 1945 the ibex had been almost hunted to extinction and there were only 419 left in the park. Today, as the result of a conservation policy, almost 4000 live here.

The national park incorporates the valleys around the Gran Paradiso (4061m), three of which are in the Valle d'Aosta: the Valsavarenche, Val di Rhêmes and the beautiful Valle di Cogne. On the Piedmont side of the mountain, the park includes the valleys of Soana and Orco.

The main stepping stone into the park is the lovely village-resort of **Cogne** (population 1474; elevation 1534m), a former iron-ore mining village on the park's northern fringe which, since the late 1970s, has devoted itself to greener activities. It is also known for its lace-making.

Information

The **tourist office** (☎ 0165 7 40 40; www.cogne.org in Italian; Piazza Chanoux 36; ☺ 9am-12.30pm & 2.30-5.30pm Mon-Sat) has stacks of information on the park and a list of emergency contact numbers.

The **Consorzio Gran Paradiso Natura** (☎ 0165 92 06 09; www.granparadisonatura.it; Loc Trépont 91, Villeneuve) has tourist information. The park's Turin-based **headquarters** (☎ 011 86 06 211; Via Della Rocca 47; ☺ 9am-noon & 1-5pm Mon-Sat) can also help.

Activities

Excellent cross-country skiing trails line the Valle di Cogne, one of the Valle d'Aosta's most picturesque, unspoiled valleys. There are 80km of well-marked cross-country trails in Cogne, also the starting point for 9km of downhill slopes. A one-/two-day ski pass covering the use of Cogne's single cable car, chairlift and drag lift costs €18/30. Skiing lessons are offered by the **Scuola Italian Sci Gran Paradiso ski** (☎ 0165 / 43 00; Piazza Chanoux 38).

Come summer, more than 1000 species of Alpine flora and butterflies typical to these mountains can be discovered at the fascinating **Giardino Alpino Paradisia** (☎ 0165 7 41 47; adult/child €2.50/1.50; ☺ 9.30am-12.30pm & 2.30-6.30pm Jun–mid-Sep), an Alpine botanical garden in Valnontey (1700m). Otherwise, consider hooking up with a naturalist through the **Associazione Guide della Nature** (☎ 0165 7 42 82; Piazza Chanoux 36, Cogne; ☺ 9am-noon Mon, Wed & Sat). Between July and September it runs a rash of half- and full-day guided walks.

From Cogne an easy walking trail (3km) leads southeast through forest to Lillaz and its waterfall. Another path (2.8km) meanders through grassland south to Valnontey. From the top of the **Cogne–Montzeuc cable car** (☎ 0165 7 40 08; one way/return €4/6; ☺ 9am-noon & 2-5.30pm Jul–mid-Sep) there's a nature trail (4km) with information panels and 15 observation posts. The main point of departure for the Gran Paradiso peak is Pont in the Valsavarenche.

For guides, contact the **Società Guide Alpine di Cogne** (☎ 0165 7 42 82; geoabel@libero.it; Piazza Chanoux 40, Cogne).

Sleeping

Wilderness camping is forbidden in the park, but there are 11 alpine *rifugi*; the tourist office has a list. Hotels are plentiful in Cogne, but those seeking true peace and tranquillity should plump for Valnontey, 3km south.

La Barme (☎ 0165 74 91 77; www.hotellabarme.com; Valnontey; d half board low/mid/high season €90/98/120; **P**) What was a traditional stone-and-wood dairy in the 1830s has been transformed into a delightful 15-room hotel with wooden furnishings and a roaring winter fire. The hotel rents cross-country skis in winter and mountain bikes in summer. The minimum stay is three nights.

Hotel Bellevue (☎ 0165 7 48 25; www.hotelbelle vue.it; Via Grand Paradis 22, Cogne; d low/mid/high season €140/170/230, 2-person chalet €220/270/320; ☺ mid-Dec–mid-Oct; **P** **⊠**) Cogne's top four-star choice is a fabulous, green-shuttered mountain hideaway from the 1920s. Its old-world charm, complete with weighty cow bells strung from hefty old beams, bathtubs with legs, cheese cellars and complimentary afternoon tea, is sure to delight. The price includes admittance to the health spa, and mountain bikes and snow shoes are available. You'll pay 10% more for stays of less than three nights.

Camping Lo Stambecco (☎ 0165 7 41 52; www .campinglostambecco.com; Valnontey; person/tent/car €5/4/3; ☺ May-Sep; **P**) Bang in the heart of the park, this well-run and friendly site should keep most campers smiling. Rent wheels or blades from its sister hotel, La Barme.

Getting There & Around

There are up to seven buses daily to/from Cogne and Aosta (50 minutes), from where many more services can be picked up. Cogne can also be reached by cable car from Pila.

Valley buses (up to 10 daily) link Cogne with Valnontey (€0.80, five minutes) and Lillaz (€0.80, five minutes).

VALTOURNENCHE

Stretching from the Valle d'Aosta to the Matterhorn (4478m), the 25km-long Valtournenche is synonymous with **Breuil-Cervinia** (2050m), a ski resort that – despite its modern façade – offers some of Europe's finest skiing. Skiing into Zermatt (Switzerland) or simply viewing what English poet Byron described as 'Europe's noble rock' is unforgettable. Smaller skiing areas include **Antey-St-André** (1080m), **La Magdeleine** (1644m) and **Valtournenche** (1524m), 9km south of Breuil-Cervinia. Nature-lovers seeking a flashback in time should make a beeline for **Chamois** (1800m), a mountain hamlet accessible only by cable car or on foot.

Information

There are tourist offices here:
Antey-St-André (☎ 0166 54 82 66; antey@monte cervino.it; Piazza A Rolando 1; ☾ 9am-noon & 3-6.30pm)
Breuil-Cervinia (☎ 0166 94 91 36; www.cervinia.it; Via Carrel 29; ☾ 9am-noon & 3-6.30pm)
Valtournenche (☎ 0166 9 20 29; valtournenche@mont ecervino.it; Via Roma 45; ☾ 9am-noon & 3-6.30pm)

Activities

Plateau Rosa (3480m) and the Little Matterhorn (3883m) in the Breuil-Cervinia ski area offer some of Europe's highest skiing, while the Campetto area has introduced the Valle d'Aosta to night skiing. A couple of dozen cable cars, four of which originate in Breuil-Cervinia, serve the 200km of downhill pistes that can be skied here. A one-/seven-day ski pass covering Breuil-Cervinia and Valtournenche costs €32/188. There are numerous rates and add-ons that are listed at www.cervinia.it.

Contact Breul-Cervinia's **Scuola di Sci del Breuil Cervinia** (☎ 0166 94 09 60; www.scuolascibreuil .com) or **Scuola Sci del Cervino** (☎ 0166 94 87 44; www.scuolacervino.com) for skiing and snowboarding lessons, and its mountain guide association **Società Guide del Cervino** (☎ 0166 94 81 69; www.guidedelcervino.com; Via J Antoine Carrel 20) to make the most of the Matterhorn's wild off-piste opportunities.

Between July and September several cableways and lifts to Plateau Rosa continue to operate, allowing the truly dedicated to ski all year round. In October cableways only run on the weekend.

Basic walking maps are available at the information offices, but if you want to tackle the Matterhorn you need to be properly dressed and equipped. Get a 1:25,000 walking map, such as the Instituto Geographico Central (IGC) map No 108 (available from bookshops in Aosta, see p248), and consider a guide – contact the Società Guide del Cervino in Breuil-Cervinia.

Sleeping & Eating

Rifugio Guide del Cervino (☎ 0166 9 21 01; giorgio .carrel@galactica.it) Breathtakingly nestled at the height of 3480m on Plateau Rosa, this mountain hut gets crammed with skiers in winter and walkers in summer. Ride the Plateau Rosa cable car to get here. At full moon it throws dinners, followed by a torch-lit ski descent down into Breuil-Cervinia.

Hotel Pub Grivola (☎ 0166 94 82 87; Breuil-Cervinia; s/d from €55/70, mains €12-15) Well-placed at the top of Breuil-Cervinia's main pedestrian street, this three-star hotel-restaurant-bar caters to all tastes.

Hotel Punta Maquignaz (☎ 0166 94 91 45; www .puntamaquignaz.com; Breuil-Cervinia; half board per person low/mid/high season €70/95/105) Half board is a must at this handsome four-star hulk of a hotel, complete with stacked logs in the hallway alongside cow bells and bear skins.

Getting There & Away

Savda (☎ 0165 36 12 44) operates buses from Breuil-Cervinia to Châtillon (one hour, seven daily), from where there are connecting buses to/from Aosta and trains to other destinations in Italy. Longer-haul seasonal bus services from Breuil-Cervinia include to/from Turin, Milan and Genoa.

VALLE D'AYAS, VAL DI GRESSONEY & VALSESIA

East of Valtournenche, the Val di Gressoney, Val d'Ayas and Valsesia (in Piedmont) snake splendidly north to the feet of majestic Monte Rosa. It was to these southern Monte Rosa valleys that the Walsers – an ethnic group of German descent – migrated from Switzerland's Valais region in the 13th century.

Today, the Val di Gressoney and Valsesia remain Walser strongholds; German is the mother tongue of many in these rural climes where village names are written trilingually and quaint Walser *Stadel* (wood-slatted houses built from larch on short stilts) dot the hillsides. Walsers don traditional dress each year on Midsummer's Day (24 June) to celebrate mass. Other Walser traditions can be discovered in the small **Museo Walser** (☎ 0163 92 29 88; admission free; ☾ 2-6pm Sat & Sun Sep-Jun, 2-6pm Mon Jul, 10am-noon & 2-6pm Aug), in Piedmont, on Alagna Valsesia's northern edge.

In the Valle d'Ayas, **Champoluc**, at the head of the valley, is the main resort, although **Brusson** also makes a handy base for those seeking easy half-day ambles. Pretty lakeside **Gressoney-St-Jean** (population 816; elevation 1385m) and **Gressoney-La-Trinité** (population 306; elevation 1637m), a few kilometres north, are the main villages in the Val di Gressoney. The more sprawling Valsesia helter-skelters big-dipper style all the way from the relatively low-lying ski resort of **Alagna Valsesia** (1191m) in the north to urban Vercelli, 50km west of Milan.

For more information, see www.monterosa-ski.com.

Information

There are several tourist offices.
Alagna Valsesia (☎ 0163 92 29 88; www.alagna.it; Piazza Grober 1) The main information source for mountain activities in the Valsesia.
Brusson (☎ 0125 30 02 40; infobrusson@aiatmonterosa .com; Piazza Municipio 2; ☽ 9am-noon & 3-6pm Mon-Sat, 9am-12.30pm & 2-5pm Sun)
Champoluc (☎ 0125 30 71 13; www.aiatmonterosa .com; Via Varasc 16; ☽ 9am-12.30pm & 4-7pm Jan-Apr, 9am-12.30pm & 3-6pm May-Dec)
Gressoney-La-Trinité (☎ 0125 36 61 43; infogresso neylatrinite@libero.it; Piazza Tache; ☽ 9am-12.30pm & 4-7pm Jan-Apr, 9am-12.30pm & 3-6pm May-Dec)
Gressoney-St-Jean (☎ 0125 35 51 85; www.aiatmonte rosawalser.it; Villa Deslex; ☽ 9am-12.30pm & 2.30-6.30pm Mon-Sat, 9am-12.30pm & 2.30-6pm Sun)

Sights

Before heading to the hills, brush up on your Alpine fauna at Gressoney-St-Jean's **Museo Regionale della Fauna Alpina** (☎ 0125 35 54 06; adult/child €3/free; ☽ 9am-12.30pm & 3-6pm Thu-Tue), at the southern end of the village.

Queen Margherita picked Gressoney-St-Jean as the location for **Castel Savoia** (☎ 0125 35 53 96) in 1894, a fairytale mansion enjoyed by the Italian royals well into the 1900s; it's currently closed for renovation.

Activities

The Ayas, Gressoney and Sesia valleys form **Monterosa Ski**, a ski area sporting 180km of downhill runs (best suited to intermediate skiers) and 38 ski lifts. From Alagna Valsesia a cable car climbs to Punta Indren (3260m).

Of the three valleys the Val di Gressoney is the place to cross-country ski; the 25km-long Gressoney-St-Jean piste takes skiers past Castel Savoia and dozens of traditional Walser houses. Lower down the valley the 15km-long trail linking the villages of Gaby

and Issime is an easy one to do, and picturesque at that.

Walks abound in this neck of the woods. In summer you can ride a cable car from Gressoney-La-Trinité to Lago Gabiet, an Alpine lake (elevation 2357m) from where numerous trails can be picked up. The tourist offices have more details as well as lists of local mountain guides.

Sleeping & Eating

Rifugio Gabiet (☎ 0125 36 62 58; fax 0125 80 61 52; Lago Gabiet; d half board low/high season €72/80; ☽ mid-Dec–mid-Apr & mid-Jun–mid-Sep) This attractive mountain hotel, named after the family who opened it several decades ago, stands tall and alone at 2880m. It peers down on Lago Gabiet and can be reached by cable car from Gressoney-La-Trinité. Its 25 cosy double rooms are generally filled by walkers, heli-skiers and other mountain enthusiasts. You can dine here too.

Hotel Petit Prince (☎ 0125 30 66 62; www.hotel petitprince.com; Route Tchavagnod 1, Antagnod; d low/high season per person from €49/65; P 🖥) This charming Alpine chalet-style hotel is set on a quiet mountainside location above Champoluc. The smart modern rooms all have balconies, and the homely lounge is the perfect place to relax over a drink or two in the evenings. The attached restaurant, *L'Etoile*, serves top local cuisine with some innovative extras: try the blue-cheese ice cream.

Hotel Genzianella (☎ 0125 30 71 56; www.hotel genzianella.it; Place de la Grotte 5, St Jacques; s/d low season from €40/62, high season from €75/130; P 🖥) Get away from it all in the tiny hamlet of St Jacques, just outside Champoluc. The Genzianella is a peaceful place with cosy rooms and its own well-regarded restaurant.

Hotel Castor (☎ 0125 30 71 17; www.hotelcastor.it; Via Ramey 2, Champoluc; s half board €55-93 d half board €100-170; P) In the heart of town, the Castor is a big chalet style affair popular with British tour groups. It has a large bar and neat grounds. Prices vary throughout the year.

Getting There & Away

Trains running through Aosta stop in St-Vincent and Verrès, from where you can catch a bus to the Ayas or Gressoney valleys. **Valdostana Impresa Trasporti Automobilistici** (☎ 0125 96 65 46) operates buses from Verrès train station to Champoluc (€2.10, one hour, up to nine daily).

LIGURIA, PIEDMONT & VALLE D'AOSTA

Lombardy & the Lakes

Stretching from the Alps to the lush plains of the River Po, Lombardy (Lombardia) is a geographically diverse and wealthy region, which has long been popular with northern European visitors for its blue lakes and beautiful scenery. Chic Milan is the regional capital, Italy's financial centre, a shopper's paradise and the main gateway to Lombardy, renowned worldwide for its fashion shows. Beyond the metropolis, the region is peppered with attractive towns, each with a distinct character inherited from the times of the independent city-states: Mantua, with its Renaissance architecture; Cremona, forever linked to the age-old craft of violin-making; and Bergamo, Brescia and Pavia with their air of affluent civility are all worthy destinations. North of Milan, Como, on the southern edge of Lago di Como, is one of northern Italy's jewels – its urbane and cosmopolitan atmosphere and slight whiff of lingering *belle époque* charm draws a steady stream of international tourists. Equally enchanting lakes, such as Lago d'Orta and Lago di Garda, are also firmly on the tourist trail.

Lombardy formed part of the Roman province of Gallia Cisalpina (Cisalpine Gaul) before it fell to the Lombards. Interference by the Franks under Emperor Barbarossa in the 12th century ended when the cities united under the Lega Lombarda (Lombard League). After the League collapsed, Lombardy was divided between the Visconti, Sforza, Gonzaga and Scaliger dynasties and was later invaded by the Venetians, Habsburgs and Napoleon.

Lombard cuisine relies heavily on rice and polenta and features butter, cream and cheese from its Alpine pastures and Lombardy's sparkling wines are among Italy's best; the Franciacorta red is mellow, while the white is fruity and dry.

HIGHLIGHTS

- Take in a performance at Milan's **La Scala** (p264)
- Traverse the blue waters of **Lago Maggiore** (p293)
- Eat out at Milan's **Craco-Peck** (p269), Bergamo's **Ristorante Da Vittorio** (p282) & Mantua's **Ristorante Masseria** (p292)
- Stroll along **Lago di Como** (p2970) with a *gelato* (ice cream)
- Discover Mantua's fabulous **Palazzo Ducale** (p289)
- Visit Lago di Garda's Disney-style **amusement parks** (p304)
- Admire Leonardo's **The Last Supper** (p265)
- Explore the peaceful Roman ruins at **Sirmione** (p303)

★ Lago Maggiore
★ Lago di Como
★ Bergamo
★ Lago di Garda
★ Milan
★ Sirmione
★ Mantua

■ POPULATION: 9.1 million	■ AREA: 23,835 sq km

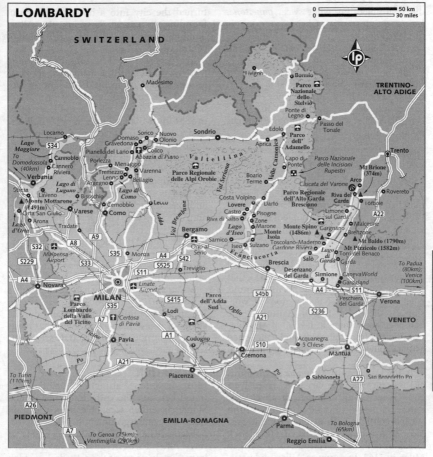

LOMBARDY

LOMBARDY & THE LAKES

MILAN

pop 1.3 million / elev 122m

Milan (Milano) is synonymous with style. This frenetic metropolis is Italy's economic engine room, the powerhouse of world design and Paris' arch rival on the catwalk. Milan is home to the country's stock market and most of Italy's major corporations. The nation's largest concentration of industry is also here. This excess of wealth and status, coupled with the natural showiness of the Milanese has hardly endeared these city slickers to other Italians, especially those from Turin, Rome or further south, who often regard them as insufferably smug.

Milan is strictly for city-lovers. It's a huge, sprawling place, noisy, traffic-ridden, harried and stressful. For its size, it doesn't have too many big sights, although Da Vinci's *The Last Supper* is one of the world's great art icons and the Castello Sforzesco is certainly one of the drawcards of this part of Italy. However, shopping is *the* thing to do here, and pretentious posers aplenty throng the streets of the Golden Quad, where the world's top fashion designers hawk their high-end wares. The city is also top of most international music tour programmes, its clubbing scene is hot and hip, and theatre and cinema flourish in this oasis of sophistication.

Food is another Milan joy. Historical cafés where Verdi and other eminent composers dined are plentiful, while sweet *panettone*, Italy's quintessential Christmas cake, is modelled after the lofty domes of a Lombard cathedral. Milan's over-decorated cathedral, incidentally, is the world's fourth largest.

The slick efficiency and dynamism of Milan is impossible to deny, and while it may be an expensive place to stay, no visit to northern Italy should bypass it. Just don't come in August when the stifling heat forces many wilting locals to flee.

HISTORY

Milan is said to have been founded by Celtic tribes who settled along the River Po in the 7th century BC. In 222 BC Roman legions marched into the territory, defeated the Gallic Insubres tribe and occupied the town, which they called Mediolanum (literally 'middle of the plain'). Mediolanum's key position on the trade routes between Rome and northwestern Europe ensured its continued prosperity and it was here in AD 313 that Emperor Constantine made his momentous edict granting Christians freedom of worship. By the end of the 4th century, Rome had been abandoned in favour of Mediolanum by the Imperial court, and functioned as the capital city of the collapsing Western empire.

In the 11th century a *comune* (town council) was formed. The city-state, ruled by a council including members of all classes, entered a period of rapid growth but soon started conflicts with neighbouring towns. Holy Roman emperor, Barbarossa (Frederick I), exploited these local disputes and besieged Milan in 1162. In response, Milan and its allies formed the Lega Lombarda and exacted revenge in 1176.

From the mid-13th century the city was governed by a succession of dynasties – the Torrianis, the Viscontis and finally the Sforzas. It fell under Spanish rule in 1535 and passed to Austria in 1713.

Napoleon made Milan the capital of his Cisalpine Republic in 1797 and, five years later, of his Italian Republic, crowning himself king of Italy in 1805. Austria returned in 1814 but troops under Vittorio Emanuele II and Napoleon III quickly crushed the Austrian forces in 1859 and Milan became part of the nascent Kingdom of Italy.

After WWI Mussolini, then in Milan as editor of the socialist newspaper *Avanti!*, turned the city into a hotbed of fascism, founding the Fascist Party in 1919. Allied bombings during WWII destroyed much of central Milan.

The post-war period saw quick economic recovery in Milan, but neofascist terrorist groups sprang up in the 1960s, and in December 1969 a bomb exploded in a Milan bank, killing 16 people. In the late 1980s, protest by Milan's business and political leaders against inefficient and corrupt government in Rome and subsidies directed to the south spawned the separatist party, the Lega Nord (Northern League). In 1992 the Tangentopoli scandal broke, implicating thousands of Milanese politicians, officials and businesspeople, fashion designers Gianni Versace and Giorgio Armani among them. A year later a Sicilian Mafia terrorist bomb exploded outside Milan's contemporary art museum and in 1995 fashion tycoon Maurizio Gucci was shot dead outside his office on the same street.

Milan's self-made-big shot (and Italy's richest man) Silvio Berlusconi was elected Italian prime minister in 2001, and despite all his legal and financial wrangles, has managed to survive, becoming Italy's longest-serving post-war premier.

ORIENTATION

Most of Milan's attractions are concentrated between the cathedral and Castello Sforzesco, either accessible from the train stations by underground railway, the Metropolitana Milanese (MM). Other parts of town likely to be frequented are Brera – immediately north of the cathedral – which encompasses many galleries and fashionable shopping streets; Navigli to the south; and the Porta Garibaldi area north of town where the city's fashionable Corso Como bars and clubs lie.

INFORMATION
Bookshops

American Bookstore (Map p262; ☎ 02 87 89 20; Via M Camperio 16; ⏰ 1-7pm Mon, 10am-7pm Tue-Sat) English-language novels and nonfiction, including lots of art books and Lonely Planet guides.

English Bookshop (Map pp260-1; ☎ 02 469 44 68; www.englishbookshop.it; Via Mascheroni 12) English titles.

La Scala Bookstore (Map p262; ☎ 02 869 22 60; www.lascalabookstore.com; Piazza della Scala) Opera books, CDs and DVDs.

Rizzoli (Map p262; ☎ 02 864 61 071; Galleria Vittorio Emanuele II) Unbeatable range of translated works by Italian writers and Italy-inspired travel literature in its basement, along with English- and French-language novels.

Touring Club Italiano (Map p262; ☎ 02 535 99 71; Corso Italia 10) Guidebooks and walking maps.

Emergency

Foreigners' police office (Map p262; ☎ 02 6 22 65 58; Via Montebello 26)

Police station (Map p262; ☎ 02 6 22 61; Via Fatebenefratelli 11)

Internet Access

Extremelot (Map pp260-1; ☎ 02 454 91 469; Ripa di Porta Ticinese 9, per hr €5) Seemingly never full and definitely the most comfortable.

Internet Enjoy (Map pp260-1; ☎ 02 835 72 25; Alzaia Naviglio Pavese 2; per hr €3.10; ☯ 9am-1am Mon-Sat, 8pm-1am Sun) Sit in a blue booth and surf.

Le Point Contact (Map pp260-1; ☎ 02 671 01 061; Via Pergolesi 21; per hr €4; ☯ 9am-10pm) Cheap telephone-calling centre with Internet access.

Virgin Megastore (Map p262; ☎ 02 880 01 200; Duomo Centre, Piazza del Duomo 8; ☯ 10am-midnight) Buy a one-/two-hour coded slip of paper for €2/4 from the sales desk and wait until a computer frees up; type in the code (valid one month) to access the Net.

Laundry

Washing costs around €3.50/6 per 7/16kg.

Onda Blu (Map pp260-1; Via Savona 1; ☯ 9am-10pm)

Lavanderia self service (Map pp260-1; Via Tadino 4; ☯ 8am-9pm)

Left Luggage

Stazione Centrale (Map pp260-1; ☯ 6am-1.30am; 1st 12hr €3)

Stazione Nord (Map pp260-1; ☎ 800 55 77 30; ☯ 5.15am-11.30pm; 24hr €4) Safety-deposit lockers next to the Malpensa Express ticket office.

Stazione Porta Garibaldi (Map pp260-1; 24hr €4; ☯ 7am-8.30pm)

Media

The comprehensive listings guide, *Milano è Milano*, sold at the tourist office for €3, is worth buying. The online edition of **Hello Milano** (www.hellomilano.it) is meatier than its monthly print edition (free). **Easy Milano** (www.easymilano.it) is another dual print/electronic publication for Anglophones. The free Italian newspapers distributed on the underground are handy for what's-on listings.

Medical Services

24-hour pharmacy (Map pp260-1; ☎ 02 669 09 35; Stazione Centrale)

Farmacia Carlo Erba (Map p262; ☎ 02 87 86 68; Piazza del Duomo 21; ☯ 9pm-8.30am) All-night pharmacy.

Milan Clinic (Map p262; ☎ 02 760 16 047; www.milanclinic.com; Via Cerva 25) One of several private clinics with English-speaking doctors.

Ospedale Maggiore Policlinico (Map p262; ☎ 02 5 50 31, foreigners ☎ 02 550 33 171; Via Francesco Sforza 35) Hospital.

Money

There are currency-exchange offices at both airports and a couple on the western side of Piazza del Duomo.

American Express (Map p262; ☎ 02 721 04 010; Via Larga 4; ☯ 9am-5.30pm Mon-Fri)

Banca Cesare Ponte (Map p262; Piazza del Duomo 19) There's a 24-hour automatic banknote-exchange machine here and at Stazione Centrale.

Banca Commerciale Italiana (Map p262; Piazza della Scala) A 24-hour booth with currency-exchange machine and ATMs.

Post

Central post office (Map p262; Piazza Cordusio; ☯ 8am-7pm Mon-Fri, 8.30am-noon Sat)

Stazione Centrale (Map pp260-1; Piazza Duca d'Aosta; ☯ 8am-7pm Mon-Fri, 8.30am-12.30pm Sat)

Tourist Information

Tourist office Via Marconi 1 (Map p262; ☎ 02 725 24 301; www.milanoinfotourist.com; ☯ 8.45am-1pm & 2-6pm Mon-Sat, 9am-1pm & 2-5pm Sun) The central office; Linate airport (Map p257; ☎ 02 702 00 443; ☯ 9am-5pm Mon-Fri); Malpensa airport (Map p257; ☎ 02 748 67 213; ☯ 9am-5pm Mon-Fri); Stazione Centrale (Map pp260-1; ☎ 02 725 24 360; ☯ 8am-7pm Mon-Sat, 9am-noon & 1.30-6pm Sun)

Travel Agencies

CIT (Map p262; ☎ 02 863 70 227; milano.gve@cititalia.net; Galleria Vittorio Emanuele II; ☯ 9am-7pm Mon-Fri, 9am-1pm & 2-6pm Sat) Plane, train and boat reservations –

INFORMATION DIAL-UP

Call these local information numbers (Italian only) for location, opening times and anything else you want know about:

Cinemas & Museums (☎ 1101)
Hotels & ATMs (☎ 1102)
Pharmacies (☎ 1100)

MILAN

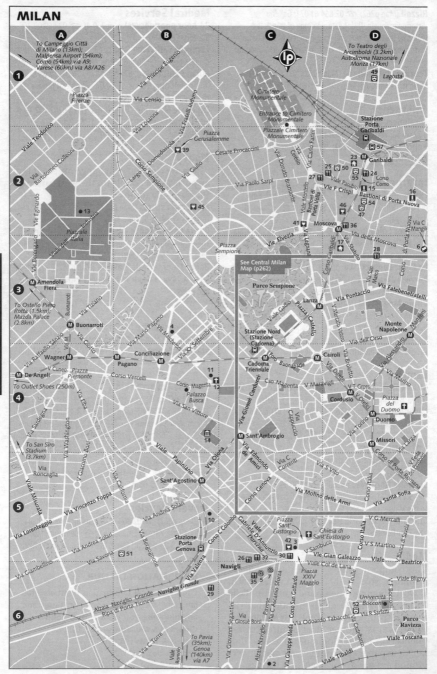

0   500 m
0   0.3 miles

INFORMATION
24-Hour Pharmacy.................1 E1
Centro d'Iniziativa Gay-Arci
    Gay Milano........................2 C6
CTS.......................................3 C5
English Bookshop...................4 B3
Extremelot.............................5 C6
French Consulate....................6 D3
Internet Enjoy........................7 C6
Lavanderia Self Service...........8 E3
Le Point Contact....................9 F2
Onda Blu.............................10 B5
Voyage Wasteels...............(see 1)

SIGHTS & ACTIVITIES
Cenacolo Vinciano................11 B4
Chiesa di Santa Maria delle
    Grazie..............................12 B4
Fiera di Milano.....................13 A2
Museo Nazionale della
    Scienza e della Tecnica.....14 B4
Porta Garibaldi.....................15 D2
Porta Nuova.........................16 D2

SLEEPING
Carlyle Brera........................17 D3
Hotel Del Sole......................18 F2
Hotel Poerio.........................19 F3
Hotel St George....................20 E2
Hotel San Tomaso................21 F3
Roy's Bed & Breakfast...........22 F1
Una Hotel Tocq....................23 D2

EATING
1U Corso Como Café.............24 D2
Antica Trattoria della Pesa.....25 D2
Brellin.................................26 C5
Fabbrica...............................27 C2
La Latteria...........................28 D3
Le Vigne.............................29 B6
Mercato Comunale................30 C5
New Gandhi.........................31 F2
Officina 12...........................32 C5
Pattini & Marinoni................33 F2
Pizzeria Spontini..................34 F2
Ponte Rosso........................35 C6
Princi: Il Bread & Breakfast....36 D2
Rossi...................................37 G3
Viel.....................................38 F2

DRINKING
Absolut Ice Bar....................39 B2
Artdeco Café.......................40 F3
ATM....................................41 C2
Café Viarenna......................42 C5
Kooka Bar............................43 F5
Lelephante...........................44 F3
Loco Bar.........................(see 42)
Makia..................................45 B2
Radetzky.............................46 D2

ENTERTAINMENT
Anteo Cinema.......................47 D2
Arcobaleno Film Centre.........48 E3
Blue Note............................49 D1
Gasoline..............................50 D2
Mexico................................51 B5
Propaganda.........................52 D6
Rolling Stone.......................53 F4
Shocking.........................(see 54)
Teatro Smeraldo...................54 D2
Tocqueville 13......................55 D2

SHOPPING
Corso Como 10.................(see 24)

TRANSPORT
AWS Bici Motor....................56 F1
Bus Station..........................57 D2
Malpensa Shuttle..................58 F1

To Alcatraz (600m);
Bergamo (60km);
Brescia (106km) via A4

Via Schiaparelli

Sondrio

Stazione Centrale

Viale Brianza

V. Giovanni, V. Pergolesi

Via Andrea Doria

Caiazzo

Gioia

Piazza Duca d'Aosta

Centrale FS

Via Napo Torriani

Via Vitruvio

Via Benedetto Marcello

Via Dom. Scarlatti

Via Settembrini

Via Lazzaro Palazzi

Via Privata Pergolesi

Viale Gran Sasso

Piazza Aspromonte

Via Cesare Correnti

Via N. Piccini

Viale Lombardia

Piola

To Autodromo Nazionale Monza (19km)

Lima

Corso Buenos Aires

Via C.B. Morgagni

Via Abruzzi

Via Cappuccio

Via San Gregorio

Viale Tunisia

Repubblica

Bastioni di Porta Venezia

Turati

Via D. Majno

Porta Venezia

Via Lambro

Via Melzo

Via Filippo Juvara

Via Spallanzani

Via Castelmorrone

Viale Romagna

Via Lombardia

Venezia

Viale Piave

Palestro

Via delle Spiga

Dataland

Corso Venezia

Via Senato

Viale Luigi Majno

Via Lecco

Via Poerio

San Babila

V. Borgogna

Via Pietro Mascagni

Corso Indipendenza

Corso Plebisciti

Piazzale Susa

Via Cappuccini

V. Battisti

Via Francesco Sforza

Corso di Porta Vittoria

Via Filippo Corridoni

Porta Vittoria

Via della Commenda

Via Archimede

Via Macedonio Melloni

Via Fiori

Via Pinamonte da Vimercate

Viale Bianca Maria

Viale Premuda

Via Marcona

Piazza Emilia

Piazza Giuseppe Grandi

Viale Campania

Via Tito Livio

Crocetta

Via A. Lamarmora

Corso XXII Marzo

Istituto Europeo di Design

Largo Marinai d'Italia

Stazione Porta Vittoria

To Linate Airport (3.7km); Brescia (113km) via S11

Corso di Porta Romana

Corso di Porta Vigentina

d'Este

Via A. Filippetti

Viale Sabotino

Viale Isonzo

Via Fogazzaro

Via Bergamo

Via Lazio

Via Comelico

Viale Umbria

Via Sottocorno

Via Augusto Anfossi

Viale Regina Margherita

Via Monte Nero

Piazzale F Martini

Piazzale Libia

Via Pier Lombardo

Via S.Luttuada

Via Rosolino Pilo

Via P.L. da Palestrina

Via Sigieri

Via Cirene

Piazza Insubria

Via Lodovico il Moro

Corso Lodi

Via Muratori

Via Crema

Via G Bellezza Via G Romano

Via Palladio

Via Brembo

Lodi TIBB

Porta Romana

Via Leo Longanesi

To I Magazzini Generali (800m)

Via Tito Livio

Viale Molise

Viale Puglia

E   F   G   H

1   2   3   4   5   6

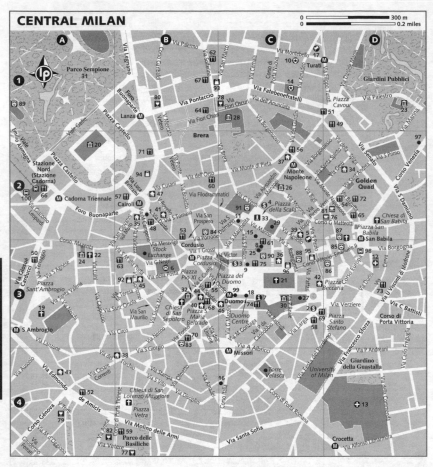

CENTRAL MILAN

LOMBARDY & THE LAKES

but none by email or telephone! You'll need to visit the office in person. Also has a currency-exchange service.
CTS (Map pp260-1; ☎ 02 837 26 74; Corso di Porta Ticinese 100) Student and budget travel.
Voyages Wasteels (Map pp260-1; ☎ 02 669 00 20; Galleria di Testa, Stazione Centrale)

DANGERS & ANNOYANCES
Pickpockets and thieves haunt Milan's main shopping areas, train stations and busiest public-transport routes. Pay particular attention on metro Line 3 between the Stazione Centrale and Duomo stops.

Beware the bird-seed sellers on Piazza del Duomo who flog seeds to unsuspecting tourists by sneakily popping seed in their pockets, prompting pigeons to dive-bomb

the victim, who is then encouraged to buy seed to escape further bombardment.

SIGHTS
Cathedral
Milan's impressive navel, **Piazza del Duomo** (Map p262), home to Milan's most visible monument, the cathedral, has been Milan's social, geographical and pigeon centre since medieval times.

Commissioned in 1386 by Gian Galeazzo Visconti, the **cathedral** holds a congregation of up to 40,000. The first glimpse of this late-Gothic wonder is memorable, with its marble façade (under renovation) shaped into pinnacles, statues and pillars, the whole held together by a web of flying buttresses.

Some 135 spires and 3200 statues – built between 1397 and 1812 – are crammed onto the roof and into the façade. The central spire, 108m tall, is capped by a gilded copper statue of the **Madonnina** (literally 'our little Madonna'), the city's traditional protector. The surrounding forest of spires, statuary and pinnacles distracts from an interesting omission – the cathedral has no bell tower.

The brass doors at the front bear the marks of bombs that fell near the cathedral during WWII. High above the altar is a nail, said to have come from Christ's cross, which is displayed once a year in September. Originally lowered using a device made by Leonardo da Vinci called the *nigola*, the nail is now retrieved by more modern means. The *nigola* is stored near the roof on the right-hand side as you enter the cathedral by the main entrance off Piazza del Duomo. Next to the main entrance a stairwell leads to an early Christian **Battistero di San Giovanni** (admission €1.50; ⏰ 9.30am-5.15pm Tue-Sun), the baptistry that predates the Gothic church.

The **crypt** (admission free) displays the remains of San Carlo Borromeo, who died in 1584, in a glass casket, while off to the side, the **treasury** (admission €1; ⏰ 9.30am-1.30pm & 2-6pm Mon-Sat, 1.30 3.30pm Sun) has a small and quite missable collection of liturgical vessels.

The 165-step climb to the **cathedral roof** (admission €4; ⏰ 9am-5.20pm) is worth the effort for the pigeon-eye view of the city centre. The **lift** (admission €6; ⏰ 9am-5.20pm) is kinder on the thigh muscles. Entrances to both are outside the cathedral on the northern flank.

Shorts and uncovered shoulders are not allowed inside the cathedral.

Around the Cathedral

The southern side of Piazza del Duomo is dominated by the **Palazzo Arcivescovile** and **Palazzo Reale**, the traditional seats of Milan's ecclesiastical and civil rulers from the 11th and 12th centuries. At the **Museo del Duomo** (Map p262; ☎ 02 86 03 58; Piazza del Duomo 14; adult/child €6/3; ⏰ 10am-1.15pm & 3-6pm), in the palace's left wing, you can study the six centuries of cathedral history in a lot more detail.

Virtually destroyed in bombing raids during WWII, the cruciform **Galleria Vittorio Emanuele II** – known as *il salotto di Milano* (Milan's drawing room) thanks to its elegant cafés (see the boxed text, p270) – leads north off Piazza del Duomo. The covered arcade, designed by Giuseppe Mengoni, was one of the first buildings in Europe to employ mainly iron and glass as structural elements. The four mosaics around the central octagon represent Europe, Africa, Asia and North America. Rub the sole of your shoe across the bull's worn-away testicles for good luck.

Southwest of the Piazza del Duomo, the **Pinacoteca Ambrosiana** (Map p262; ☎ 02 80 69 21; www.ambrosiana.it; Piazza Pio XI 2; adult/child €7.50/4.50; 10am-5.30pm Tue-Sun) is one of the city's finest galleries. It contains Italy's first real still life, Caravaggio's *Canestro di Frutta* (Fruit Basket), as well as works by Tiepolo, Titian and Raphael. Da Vinci's *Musico* (Musician) is also on show.

La Scala & Around

Walk north through the Galleria Vittorio Emanuele II from Piazza del Duomo to Piazza della Scala, dominated by a **monument** dedicated to Leonardo da Vinci, and Milan's legendary opera house, **La Scala** (Teatro alla Scala). The fabulous playhouse opened on 3 August 1778, was practically destroyed during WWII but reopened in 1946 under the baton of Arturo Toscanini, who returned to Milan from New York after a 15-year absence. Learn more at the **Museo Teatrale alla Scala** (right) and see p273 for ticket details.

Palazzo Marino, between Piazza della Scala and Piazza San Fedele, was begun in 1558 by Galeazzo Alessi and is a masterpiece of 16th-century residential architecture. Milan's municipal council has sat here since 1859. There are more than 60 other grand palaces scattered about the city centre – a far cry from the several hundred that stood at the end of the 19th century.

Northeast, **Museo Poldi-Pezzoli** (Map p262; ☎ 02 79 48 89; www.museopoldipezzoli.it; Via Alessandro Manzoni 12; adult/child €6/4; 10am-6pm Tue-Sun) hosts an eclectic assemblage of porcelain, jewellery, tapestries, antique furniture and paintings, including Botticelli's *Madonna and Child* among others.

Museo Teatrale alla Scala

This enchanting **museum** (Map p262; ☎ 02 43 35 35 21; www.teatroallascala.org; Piazza Scala; adult/child €5/4; 9am-12.30pm & 1.30-5pm), inside the opera house, takes theatre-lovers on a whirlwind tour of La Scala's fabulous past. Precious collections of antique musical instruments, curtain designs and theatrical costumes worn by Maria Callas and other greats are among the memorabilia to be seen, and the visit also takes in a peek at the theatre itself, if there are no rehearsals or performances on.

Castello Sforzesco

At the northern end of Via Dante stands the imposing **Castello Sforzesco** (Map p262; ☎ 02 884 63 700; www.milanocastello.it; Piazza Castello; adult/child €3/1.50, after 2pm Fri free; castle grounds 7am-6pm or 7pm, museums 9am-5.30pm Tue-Sun). Originally a Visconti fortress, it was later home to the mighty Sforza dynasty that ruled Renaissance Milan. Leonardo da Vinci helped design the defences. Today, it shelters several excellent museums.

A vast collection of Lombard sculptures is displayed in the **Museo d'Arte Antica**, where you will also find the private ducal chambers and Michelangelo's last, unfinished work, entitled *Pietà Rondanini*. In the **Pinacoteca e Raccolte d'Arte** is an applied arts display and a picture gallery, featuring works by Bellini, Tiepolo, Mantegna, Correggio, Titian and van Dyck. Another museum is devoted to ancient Egyptian treasures, while the **Museo della Preistoria** displays a collection of local archaeological finds from the Palaeolithic era to the Iron Age. The **Museo degli Strumenti Musicali** enchants visitors with its vintage musical instruments.

Behind the red-brick castle **Parco Sempione** is a 47-hectare park featuring a neoclassical arch, a neglected arena inaugurated by Napoleon in 1806 and the Torre Branca (1933), a 103m-tall steel tower near the rather ugly Palazzo dell'Arte.

Palazzo di Brera

Just east of Castello Sforzesco, the sprawling 17th-century Palazzo di Brera houses the **Pinacoteca di Brera** (Map p262; ☎ 02 894 21 146; Via Brera 28; adult/child €5/2.50; 8.30am-7.15pm). Its extensive treasury of paintings has grown since the gallery was inaugurated at the start of the 19th century, with Andrea Mantegna's masterpiece *The Dead Christ* being one of the better-known works on display. Raphael, Bellini, Rembrandt, Goya, Caravaggio and van Dyck are others represented.

The Last Supper

One of the most famous art images in the world, Leonardo da Vinci's wonderful mural depicting the Last Supper decorates one wall of the **Cenacolo Vinciano** (Map pp260–1), the refectory adjoining **Chiesa di Santa Maria delle Grazie** (Map pp260-1; Corso Magenta; ☼ 8.15am-7pm Tue-Sun). Painted between 1495 and 1498, Leonardo's work captures the moment when Jesus uttered the words 'One of you will betray me'. The word *cenacolo* means refectory, the place where Christ and the 12 Apostles celebrated the Last Supper, and is also used to refer to any mural depicting this scene.

Restoration of *The Last Supper* began in 1977 and was completed in 1999. Centuries of damage from floods, bombing and decay had left the mural in a lamentable state. The method employed by restorers in the 19th century caused the most damage – their alcohol and cotton-wool technique removed a layer from the painting. Even so,

Leonardo must take some of the blame, as his experimental mix of oil and tempera was not durable. The Dominicans did not help matters in 1652 by raising the refectory floor, callously chopping off a lower section of da Vinci's scene – including Jesus' feet.

To see **The Last Supper** (☎ 02 894 21 146; www.cena colovinciano.org; adult/child €6.50/free, plus booking fee €1.50) you have to book ahead by phone; call at least three or four days in advance if you want to guarantee a ticket. Once through to an operator, you'll be allotted a visiting time and a reservation number which you present 30 minutes before your visit at the refectory ticket desk. Turn up late and your ticket will be resold.

The ticket desk at the refectory rents out audioguides (one/two people €2.50/4.50) in English. English-language guided tours (€3.25) take place at 9.30am and 3.30pm Tuesday to Sunday. Again, reservations are necessary.

South of Castello Sforzesco

Housed in the Monastero Maggiore, a 9th-century Benedictine convent rebuilt in the

LOMBARDY & THE LAKES

AMBROSE & AUGUSTINE

When the future St Ambrose (Sant'Ambrogio) was appointed bishop of Milan in 374 his credentials were hardly in order – he hadn't even been baptised. Yet this former governor of Liguria had impressed everyone with his skills in umpiring between the Catholics and the Christian Arians that denied Christ's oneness with God (so slick was he with his words that he was dubbed 'the honey-tongued doctor'), so he received all the sacraments and the mitre in an unusually accelerated procedure.

At that time Milan was the effective capital of the western half of the crumbling Roman Empire and Ambrose became a leading figure in imperial politics. He and the emperor of the Western Roman Empire, Gratian, embarked on a crusade to eradicate paganism and the Arian heresy.

His influence grew to such an extent that he was later able to challenge the authority of Theodosius – the eastern emperor and guarantor of the Western Empire after Gratian's assassination – with impunity. In one incident the emperor ordered Christians to rebuild a synagogue they'd burned. Ambrose demanded the order be revoked and, threatening to stir-up popular feeling, convinced the emperor to see things his way.

Into this heady atmosphere stepped another future saint, Augustine of Hippo, born at Thagaste, North Africa, in 354. Augustine, who had dallied with the Manichee heresy and Neo-Platonism, was drawn to Milan to meet the widely respected and renowned orator Ambrose and hear him preach, and it was in a Milan garden in 386 that he resolved to abandon his secular career and his marriage, and convert to Catholicism. He was baptised by Ambrose the following year and returned to North Africa in 388, where he wrote two of the greatest works of Christian literature, the *Confessions* and the *City of God*.

Ambrose presaged the Church's future political role in European affairs and inspired the composition of the *Te Deum*. He died in 397. Augustine, who was made Bishop of Hippo in 396, died during the Vandal siege of that city in 430, but his influence on the Christian Church continued for centuries, and his writings are still considered masterpieces of prose.

1500s, the **Civico Museo Archeologico** (Map p262; ☎ 02 864 50 011; Corso Magenta 15; adult/child €2/1, after 2pm Fri free; ⏲ 9am-5.30pm Tue-Sat, 9am-5pm Sun) has substantial Roman, Greek, Etruscan and medieval sections. Adjoining it is **Chiesa di San Maurizio** (Map p262) with 16th-century frescoes by Bernardino Luini.

A short stroll south is the Romanesque **Basilica di Sant'Ambrogio** (Map p262; Piazza Sant'Ambrogio 15), dedicated to Milan's patron saint, St Ambrose (see the boxed text, p265). Founded in the 4th century by Ambrose, Bishop of Milan, the church on Piazza Sant'Ambrogio has been repaired, rebuilt and restored several times since and is a hotchpotch of styles. The shorter of the two bell towers dates to the 9th century, as does the remarkable ciborium (freestanding canopy over the altar) under the dome inside. The saint himself is buried in the crypt.

To discover Leonardo da Vinci's seemingly endless skills and interests, check the fascinating displays at the **Museo Nazionale della Scienza e della Tecnica** (Map pp260-1; ☎ 02 48 55 51; www.museoscienza.org; Via San Vittore 21; adult/child €7/5; ⏲ 9.30am-5pm Tue-Fri, 9.30am-6.30pm Sat & Sun), which has exhibitions on everything from clock- and guitar-making to electricity and astronomy.

Around Piazza Cavour
The **Civica Galleria d'Arte Moderna** (GAM; Map p262; ☎ 02 760 02 819; Via Palestro 16; ⏲ 9am-5.30pm Tue-Sun), in the 18th-century Villa Reale which Napoleon temporarily called home, has a wide collection of 19th-century works, including many from the Milan's neoclassical period. More recent works can be enjoyed in the neighbouring **Padiglione d'Arte Contemporanea** (PAC; Map p262; ☎ 02 760 09 085; www.comune.milano.it/pac; Via Palestro 14; adult/child €5.20/2.60; ⏲ 9.30am-5.30pm Tue-Wed & Fri & Sat, 9.30am-9pm Thu, 9.30am-7.30pm Sun).

TOURS
The tourist office sells tickets for three-hour city bus tours (€47, including admission to *The Last Supper*). Bus tours depart at 3pm from Piazza Duomo. They also sell tickets for the tourist trams (€20), which depart three times daily from Piazza Castello for a spin around the main sights.

Zani Viaggi (☎ 02 86 71 31; www.zaniviaggi.it) runs a variety of coach tours in and around the city, including day trips to Lake Garda (€45),

Verona (€45) and Venice (€68), as well as trips to Gardaland amusement park (p304) for €33, including admission. Trips depart from Piazza Castello and Stazione Centrale.

FESTIVALS & EVENTS
The **Festa di Sant'Ambrogio** on 7 December is Milan's biggest feast day. Celebrations take place at the **Fiera di Milano** (Map pp260-1; ☎ 800 82 00 29, 02 480 08 061; www.fieramilano.com; Largo Domodossola 1), the trade, conference and exhibition centre northwest of the city. La Scala marks the solemn occasion by opening its opera season on this day.

The first 10 days of June are devoted to the **Festa del Naviglio**, a smorgasbord of parades, music and other performances. The **Milan Jazz Festival** rocks through the city in November. Make the tourist office your first port of call for finding out more about these and other festivals and events. See the boxed text on p275 for information on the international fashion and furniture shows.

Centro d'Iniziativa Gay – ArciGay Milano (Map p262; ☎ 02 541 22 225; www.arcigaymilano.org in Italian; Via Bezzeca 3), the main point of contact for gays and lesbians, organises Milan's annual Gay Pride march.

SLEEPING
Milan's hotels are among the most overpriced in Italy and finding any room (let alone a cheap one) can be a real challenge. Unless you book months in advance, you have virtually no chance of finding a bed during the fashion weeks and other fairs and exhibitions, when hotels happily inflate their already high prices to often ridiculous levels. The tourist office distributes *Milano Hotels*, an annual listings guide (free) to Milan's 350-odd hotels, and can put you in touch with accommodation agencies that make hotel reservations. However, unless you absolutely have to stay in town, or money is no object, there are far more attractive and affordable places to rest up within easy commuting distance of Milan: Como (p299), Cremona (p288) and Bergamo (p282) are all worth trying.

Around Stazione Centrale
Although handily placed, some budget hotels in the Stazione Centrale area double quietly (or perhaps not so quietly) as brothels. Places not appearing to sport a dual trade are listed here.

Roy's Bed & Breakfast (Map pp260-1; ☎ 0347 76 63 9 85; Via Ponte Seveso; d/tr €55/70, d with bathroom €70) On the western flank of Stazione Centrale, Roy's offers just three light, modern and breezily decorated rooms on the 1st floor of an old townhouse. The room's are clean, friendly and good value, and advance bookings are recommended.

Hotel San Tomaso (Map pp260-1; ☎ 02 295 14 747; hotelsantomaso@tin.it; Viale Tunisia 6; s/d from €40/65, d with bathroom €75) Hotel San Tomaso has pretty basic but acceptable rooms, and friendly English-speaking staff. Should it be full, there's another similar hotel in the same building.

Hotel Poerio (Map pp260-1; ☎ 02 295 22 872; Via Poerio 32; s/d from €50/75) Tucked down a quiet residential street, Hotel Poerio is the city's most peaceful budget option.

Hotel Del Sole (Map pp260-1; ☎ 02 295 12 971; www.delsolehotel.com; Via Gaspare Spontini 6; s/d €50/85) Wend your way up the spiral mirrored staircase to the 1st-floor reception where a smile greets travellers. Rooms are spartan, but OK for an overnight stay. Prices quoted here are maximum rates – they do vary, depending on how full or empty the hotel is.

Hotel St George (Map pp260-1; ☎ 02 29 51 03 75, www.hotelstgeorge.it; Viale Tunisia 9; s/d from €95/110; P 🅿) The four-star St George is a fairly characterless modern hotel on a busy road, although it's rooms are comfortable enough. However, prices more than double during fair periods, or any other time designated as 'high season'.

Around the Cathedral
BUDGET
Hotel Nuovo (Map p262; ☎ 02 86 46 44 44; fax 02 86 46 05 42; Piazza Beccaria 6; s/d €30/50, d/tr with bathroom €100/135) The only real budget option in this area, Hotel Nuovo is a rare find indeed. Just off Piazza del Duomo, it offers simple but clean rooms in a very central spot, and, consequently, books up quickly.

MIDRANGE
Hotel Gritti (Map p262; ☎ 02 80 10 56; www.hotel gritti.com; Piazza Santa Maria Beltrade 4; s/d/tr €99/142/197; P 🅿) Half-way down Via Torino from the cathedral, this reasonable three-star place overlooks a fairly quiet square and often has rooms available when others don't.

Hotel Vecchia Milano (Map p262; ☎ 02 87 50 42; hotelvecchimilano@tiscalinet.it; Via Borromei 4; s/d

€110/160) Old-world charm exudes from 'Old Milan', appropriately placed in an atmospheric cobbled street off Via Torino.

Hotel Ariston (Map p262; ☎ 02 720 00 556; ariston@brerahotels.com; Largo Carrobbio 2; s/d/tr €155/ 220/235; P 🅿 🅿 🅿) Ariston is Milan's first ecological hotel – purified air in hotel rooms, purified water in the herbal teas at breakfast, natural fibres in the mattresses, recyclable paper and biodegradable cleaning products throughout, and a free bicycle at the door for guests to breathe in all those Milanese traffic fumes.

Hotel Spadari (Map p262; ☎ 02 720 02 371; www.spadarihotel.com; Via Spadari 11; s/d/ste €168/218/ 368; P 🅿 🅿 🅿) Perfectly located just a short stroll from the cathedral, Spadari has 38 rooms all kitted out with designer furniture and original paintings by contemporary artists. Very cool, very chic.

Hotel London (Map p262; ☎ 02 720 20 166; hotel .london@traveleurope.it; Via Rovello 3; s/d €90/130, with bathroom €100/150; 🅿) Off Via Dante, two-star Hotel London looks swanky but charges reasonable rates for central Milan. At these prices, you may as well pay the little extra to have your own bathroom.

Hotel Pierre Milano (Map p262; ☎ 02 72 00 05 81; www.hotelpierremilano.it; Via Edmondo De Amicis 32; s/d from €160/220; P 🅿 🅿) On a quiet street on the edge of the city centre, Pierre Milano offers intimate luxury, with artfully designed interiors and large, restful rooms.

Una Hotel Cusani (Map p262; ☎ 800 60 61 62, 02 85 601; www.unahotels.it; Via Cusani 13; s/d Mon-Fri from €198/234, d Sat & Sun from €178; 🅿 P) Halfway between the Duomo and Castello Sforzesco, the Cusani is a huge modern chain hotel offering all the expected four-star comforts. Parking costs a not inconsiderable €26 per night.

Genius Downtown (Map p262; ☎ 02 720 94 644; hotelgenius@tiscali.it; Via Porlezza 4; s/d/tr from €99/155/ 180; 🅿 🅿) In a quiet alley off Via Camperio, Milan's Genius hotel is a stone's throw from Castello Sforzesco. The newspaper delivered to your room each morning is a nice touch (take your pick when you check-in).

TOP END
Hotel de la Ville (Map p262; ☎ 02 879 13 11; Via Hoepli 6; www.delavillemilano.com; s/d/ste €282/328/485; P 🅿 🅿) Unattractive from the outside but stunning inside, Hotel de la Ville has long seduced show-business types and fashion

celebrities. The décor is that of 'high-class English dwellings' (to quote its own brochure) and rooms are spacious and elegant.

Grand Hotel et de Milan (Map p262; ☎ 02 72 31 41; www.grandhoteletdemilan.it, Via Alessandro Manzoni 29; s/d/ste from €275/330/690; P ✕ ▣) Milan's most prestigious hotel – an eclectic mix of Art Nouveau and Art Deco dating from 1863 – was home to Giuseppe Verdi for the last few years of his life. The name-dropping doesn't stop there, however; Ernest Hemmingway, Maria Callas and Caruso are also proudly listed as past guests in the hotel's publicity bumf. Much of the original furniture remains in suites No 105 and No 106 where Verdi lived.

Grand Hotel Duomo (Map p262; ☎ 02 88 33; www .grandhotelduomo.com; Via San Raffaele 1; s/d Mon-Thu from €235/320, Fri-Sun from €190/280; P ✕ ▣) Sipping tea amid orange trees on the roof terrace or admiring paintings by Brunelleschi are but some of the pleasures awaiting guests inside this beautiful marbled palace built in 1860. Breakfast is another €15.

Four Seasons Hotel (Map p262; ☎ 02 770 88; www .fourseasons.com/milan; Via Gesù 6/8; d/ste from €500/740; ✕ ✕ ▣) With a location right in the heart of the fashion district, the Four Seasons is undoubtedly one of Milan's most luxurious accommodation options. Occupying a renovated 15th-century convent, it retains some of the historical ambience, including medieval architectural elements and frescoes, while most of the predictably elegant rooms look over the cloistered courtyard, and come with lavish marble bathrooms. Little extras include a limousine service and personal valets.

Around Porta Garibaldi

Una Hotel Tocq (Map pp260-1; ☎ 02 620 71; una.tocq@ unahotels.it; Via A De Tocqueville 7d; d from €163; P ✕ ▣ ☀) It might be part of a luxurious four-star Italian hotel chain but Una Hotel Tocq is Milan's temple to contemporary design. Its hip location between the city's most happening bars and clubs lures famous faces. Week-day high-season prices jump around €100.

Carlyle Brera (Map pp260-1; ☎ 02 29 00 38 88; car lyle@brerahotels.it; Corso Garibaldi 84; s/d €255/290; P ✕ ▣) Brera's four-star hotel has all the mod cons, including high-speed Internet, free bike rental and an à la carte pillow menu. Choose from eight different shapes

and stuffings upon arrival including the 'sleep in a meadow' pillow filled with aromatic herbs, moulded foam and traditional goose down.

Out of Town

There are a couple of good budget options towards the outer edge of town.

Ostello Piero Rotta (☎ 02 392 67 095; ostellomi lano@aiglombardia.it; Via Martino Bassi 2; B&B €18.50; ☽ reception 7-9am & 3.30pm-1am) The city's only HI hostel is a two-minute walk south along Viale Angelo Salmoiraghi from the QT8 underground stop. HI cards are compulsory.

Campeggio Città di Milano (☎ 02 482 00 999; www.parcoaquatica.com in Italian; Via G Airaghi 61; person/tent/car €8/6/6, 2-/3-/4-person bungalow from €40/50/62; ☽ Feb-Nov) This camping ground, a good few kilometres west of the centre, keeps campers happy with its wide range of facilities and a water amusement park. Take the underground to the De Angeli station, then bus No 72 from Piazza de Angeli to the Di Vittorio stop, from where it is a 400m walk to the camping ground. By car, leave the Tangenziale Ovest at San Siro-Via Novara.

EATING

Milan has some of Italy's finest, and most expensive restaurants, but with a city this size there's a huge, cosmopolitan choice of eateries. At the bottom end of the scale, sandwich bars and fast-food joints litter the streets around the cathedral and Stazione Centrale, while fashion houses have begun opening up exclusive cafés and restaurants attached to their stores around the Golden Quad.

The city has a strong provincial cuisine. Polenta is served with almost everything and *risotto alla milanese* (with saffron and bone marrow) dominates the first course of many restaurant menus. Meaty dishes include *fritto misto alla milanese* (fried slices of bone marrow, liver and lung), *busecca* (sliced tripe boiled with beans) and *cotoletta alla milanese* (breaded veal). Milan is also the home of *panettone* (fruity Christmas cake) and *colomba*, a dry, dove-shaped cake first baked in the 6th century and traditionally eaten with a sweet dessert wine.

Bar snacks are a Milanese institution, with most bars laying out their fare from around 6pm daily.

Restaurants

AROUND THE CATHEDRAL

Trattoria da Pino (Map p262; ☎ 02 760 00 532; Via Cerva 14; mains €6, lunch €13; ☷ 8am-8pm Mon-Fri, 8am-4pm Sat) Nowhere can you beat the cost to quality ratio dished up at this authentic trattoria where strangers dine at shared tables. Its three-course lunch menu is built solely from hearty homemade cooking and includes wine or water.

Farinella (Map p262; ☎ 02 89 09 50 84; Foro Buonaparte 71; pizzas €7-9, mains about €10; ☷ lunch & dinner) Bamboo, designer light-shades and black-and-white photographs adorn this swish modern place serving pizzas, pasta, salads and more. Settle down with a cocktail in the adjoining bar before dining, or, if you are here during 'happy hour' (6pm to 8pm), the generous free buffet should satisfy most appetites.

Paper Moon (Map p262; ☎ 02 796 083, 02 760 22 297; Via Bagutta 1; mains €15; ☷ Mon-Sat) Minimalist Paper Moon lures a well-dressed crowd. Its fresh asparagus (in season) topped with two fried eggs is appealing, as is its grilled cheese served piping hot and gooey on a bed of rocket.

Boccondivino (Map p262; ☎ 02 86 60 40; Via Giosuè Carducci 17; mains €15-18; ☷ 8pm-midnight Mon-Sat) Dine here for a gastronomic voyage through Italy – pick from 40 different cheeses, dozens of smoked and dried meats and over 900 wines. Sign up for a wine-tasting course if the whole experience leaves you feeling somewhat inadequate.

Antica Osteria Milanese (Map p262; ☎ 02 86 13 67; Via M Camperio 12; mains €11-13; ☷ lunch & dinner) Some places don't change as this traditional, frill-free trattoria, popular with lunching businessmen, testifies. The *meneghina alla griglia al Grand Marnier* (Milanese sponge cake soaked in liqueur and then baked) is a sweet speciality.

BRERA

Hip Via Fiori Chiari is well known for its summer pavement terraces.

La Rosa Nera (Map p262; ☎ 02 659 89 72; Via Solferino 12; mains €12-15; ☷ lunch & dinner Thu-Tue) With its plush red-velvet benches, nude portraits and vague Art Nouveau style, 'The Black Rose' is an atmospheric restaurant choice. Risotto, pasta, fish and pizzas fill the varied menu, and the wine is good, if a little expensive at around more than €20 a bottle.

La Latteria (Map pp260-1; ☎ 026597653; Via San Marco 24; mains €10-13; ☷ 12.15-2.30pm & 7.30-9.30pm Mon-Fri) This pocket-sized trattoria might have been around for what seems like centuries but nothing has changed – thankfully. Original white-and-blue bar tiles, flowery wallpaper and about a dozen tables add up to one very charming, very tasty lunch spot.

Il Coriandolo (Map p262; ☎ 02 869 32 73; Via dell'Orso 1; mains €12-16; ☷ lunch & dinner) Dine on delicious *risotto alla vecchia maniera milanese* (literally 'old Milanese risotto') as you sit beneath an ornate moulded ceiling at this upmarket restaurant, on the edge of Brera.

Tintero (Map p262; ☎ 02 86 14 18; Via Q Sella; mains about €15; ☷ lunch & dinner) A bold interior paying homage to contemporary design contrasts starkly with the traditional exterior of this popular restaurant, near the Castello Sforzesco. In the summer, sit on the flowery pavement terrace and watch cars whiz by.

AROUND STAZIONE CENTRALE

New Gandhi (Map pp260-1; ☎ 02 29 41 40 08; www.newgandhi.it; Via Benedetto Marcello 93; mains €9-12; ☷ lunch & dinner Tue-Sun & dinner Mon) Escape pasta and pizza at this authentic Indian restaurant that dishes up the usual range of curried meat and veg. The fixed lunch menus (vegetarian/

AUTHOR'S CHOICE

Craco-Peck (Map p262; ☎ 02 87 67 74; craco-peck@peck.it; Via Victor Hugo 4; mains €30; ☷ lunch & dinner Mon-Sat) One of Milan's oldest and most revered restaurants, Craco-Peck, under the same management as the nearby Peck gourmet food store (p271), has gained an enviable international reputation for the quality of its cuisine, and boasts two Michelin stars. Carlo Cracco is one of Italy's leading young chefs, and he has put together an exceptional menu of traditional Milanese cooking with some innovative twists. Breaded veal, pork, saffron risotto, ham and truffles feature, along with unusual dishes such as pig snout with prawns and green tomatoes, and there are some 1800 different wines (from around €20) to choose from. There are just two small dining rooms, and reservations are essential. Those with deeper pockets still might try the *degustazione* (taster) menu (€165).

LOMBARDY & THE LAKES

HISTORICAL CAFÉS

These institutions are classic places for breakfast, lunch or an apéritif in the company of a lavish array of never-ending hors d'oeuvres.

Cova (Map p262; ☎ 02 760 05 578; Via Monte Napoleone 8) Founded in 1817 by a soldier in Napoleon's army, this elegant tearoom has stood in Monte Napoleone since 1950 (the original was destroyed during WWII).

Marchesi (Map p262; ☎ 02 87 67 30; Via S M alla Porta 11a) The legendary marchioness has been in the cake-and-coffee business since 1824. Her heavily wood-panelled interior shelters luscious displays of chess and draughtboards made from chocolate.

Il Salotto (Map p262; Galleria Vittorio Emanuele II; pizzas €10, mains €15) Milan's 'drawing room' is a bit of a tourist trap, with a five-language menu, harassed waiters and outrageous prices for the privilege of sitting in this historical location.

Zucca in Galleria (Map p262; ☎ 02 864 64 435; Galleria Vittorio Emanuele II 21; mains €15-20) Milan's most historic café overlooks Piazza del Duomo and displays a glittering mosaic interior dating from 1867.

---

meat €7.50/8.50) come with coffee and wine, and are excellent value. Six-course dinner menus start at €15.

NAVIGLI & PORTA TICINESE

Eating options abound in this area, renowned for its late opening hours and innovative cuisine cooked up by a mixed bag of chefs. Canalside Ripa di Porta Ticinese makes for a particularly tasty evening stroll.

Le Vigne (Map pp260-1; ☎ 02 837 56 17; Ripa di Porta Ticinese 61; mains about €6) Those seeking nothing more than a feast of local cheese and wine are heartily welcomed at Le Vigne.

Brellin (Map pp260-1; ☎ 02 581 01 351; Alzaia Naviglio Grande 14; mains €14; ✆ 12.30-2.30pm & 7pm-2am Mon-Sat, noon-3pm Sun) The main draw of Brellin is its canalside flower-filled garden – unique among Milanese restaurants. Dark wooden panels furnish the less-appealing interior.

Officina 12 (Map pp260-1; ☎ 02 894 22 261; www.officina12.it in Italian; Alzaia Naviglio Grande 12; mains €12; ✆ 7pm-2am Tue-Sat, 12.30-3pm & 7pm-midnight Sun) The new kid on this attractive waterfront block is a modern affair with a red interior. Its cobbled patio overlooking the canal is

veryy appealing and it has a snazzy 'American bar' (happy hour is 7pm to 9.30pm).

Ponte Rosso (Map pp260-1; ☎ 02 837 31 32; Ripa di Porta Ticinese 23; mains €15; ✆ Thu-Sat & Mon-Wed) The Red Bridge is run by a wine and balsamic vinegar connoisseur who also collects corkscrews and cocktail shakers. Attempt to order anything less than the four-course dining experience and you'll be frowned upon.

CORSO COMO

Antica Trattoria della Pesa (Map pp260-1; ☎ 02 655 57 41; Viale Pasubio 10; mains €15-20; ✆ Mon-Sat) A traditional trattoria with the signature, bottle-filled windows, lures a chic crowd thanks to its location a step away from the Corso Como nightlife scene. The place has been feeding hungry Milanese since 1880.

Cafés

Milan's café scene is a mix of old (see the boxed text, left) and new.

Emporio Armani Caffè (Map p262; ☎ 02 72 31 86 80; Via Croce Rossa 2; mains around €10, Sun brunch €22; ✆ noon-4.30pm) Attached to Armani's flagship store, this chic spot is where jewellery-jingling ladies and Japanese tourists are served salads and pasta dishes by impeccably groomed waiters.

10 Corso Como Café (Map pp260-1; ☎ 02 29 01 35 81; Corso Como 10; salads €18-20; ✆ 11am-9pm) This terribly stylish café lures models as well as other beautiful people with its snacks and exclusive atmosphere. It's a little mannered and pretentious, but still unique, if you don't mind parting with €5 for a cup of herbal tea.

Caffè della Pusteria (Map p262; ☎ 02 894 02 146; Via Edmondo de Amicis 22; salads €4-7; ✆ lunch) With an old-fashioned, jazz-inspired interior and a terrace beneath vines this place manages to lure a young and trendy crowd to this busy lunchtime café.

Other central venues to slam espresso shots or linger over an apéritif and bar snacks:

Bar Centro (Map p262; ☎ 02 760 01 415; Corso G Matteotti 3) Eclectic décor and cocktail-quaffing crowd.

Sunflower Bar (Map p262; ☎ 02 760 22 754; Via Pietro Verri 8) Terrace bar beneath arches.

Quick Eats

Brek (Map p262; ☎ 02 65 36 19; Piazza Cavour; mains €6-8; ✆ lunch & dinner) This nationwide canteen-style restaurant never disappoints. Well-priced salads, pasta, grills and soups are on offer, as well as cheap wine and beer on tap.

NICE ICES

Feeling hot and bothered? Cool down with a *gelato* (ice cream).

Gelateria le Colonne (Map p262; ☎ 02 837 22 92; Corso di Porta Ticinese 75; ice creams €2; ♥ Thu-Tue) Expect to queue at this tiny 'artisan' ice-cream bar, with flavours including rice, amaretto and orange blossom. The genepi sorbet (an Alpine herb) is a standout.

Rossi (Map pp260-1; ☎ 02 73 04 92; Viale Romagna 23; ♥ Wed-Mon) Rossi is reckoned to be Milan's ice-cream queen – if the crowds are anything to go by, it could be true.

Viel (♥ 8am-2am Wed-Mon) Duomo (Map p262; Via Manzoni 3e); Stazione Centrale (Map pp260-1; ☎ 02 295 16 123; Corso Buenos Aires 15; ice creams €2) Ice creams and *frullati di frutta* (fruit shakes) are packed with fruit, as the lush fruity displays waiting to be mushed up testify.

Poker (Map p262; ☎ 02 58 307 530; Piazza Santo Stefano 5; mains €3-4; ♥ 7am-5pm Mon-Sat) Rub elbows with a Milanese workforce at this cheap and cheerful self-service restaurant, a stone's throw from the cathedral.

Armandola (Map p262; ☎ 02 760 21 657; Via della Spiga 50; pastas €5-6; ♥ lunch & dinner) Shoppers can indulge in a bowl of pasta standing up at this delicatessen shop. Pick the right day and white Alba truffles might just end up on your plate (at a price).

Coco's (Map p262; ☎ 02 454 83 253; Via San Prospero 4; mains €4-6; ♥ lunch & dinner) Italy's first vegetarian chain fries up veggie burgers and other yummy soul food in a soulful wooden interior.

Pizzeria Spontini (Map pp260-1; ☎ 02 204 74 44; Via Gaspare Spontini; pizza slices €4, pastas €4) This busy little pizza joint has cooked up the best pizza in the Stazione Centrale area – and much of Milan – since 1953. Munch standing up or on the move.

Flash (Map pp260-1; ☎ 02 583 04 489; Via Bergamini 1; pizzas €10; ♥ 24hr) This pizzeria on the corner of Via Larga draws a young crowd. Unusually for a place that never closes, its pizzas are worth the trip any time of day or night.

Fabbrica (Map pp260-1; ☎ 02 655 27 71; Via Pasubio 2; pizzas €10; ✕) With its low-hanging steel table lamps and brown-paper table mats, trendy Factory exudes a definite industrial feel. The pizzeria is nicely located near the Corso Como bars and clubs.

Self-Catering

Via Speronari, just off Piazza del Duomo, is the best street around the cathedral for bread, cakes, salami, cheese, fruit and wine.

Peck (Map p262; ☎ 02 802 31 61; www.peck.it in Italian; Via Spadari 7-9; ♥ 3-7.30pm Mon, 8.45am-7.30pm Tue-Sat) Established in 1883, Peck is one of Europe's most prestigious gourmet-food outlets, famous for its homemade ravioli, 3200 variations of *parmigiano reggiano* (Parmesan) and wine cellar. Everything edible is available on the ground floor, while upstairs there's a wine bar and tea room. They also run the upmarket Craco-Peck restaurant across the road (see p269).

Centro Botanico (Map pp260-1; ☎ 02 2901 3254; www.centrobotanico.it in Italian; Piazza San Marco 1; ♥ 10am-2.30pm & 3.30-8pm Mon-Fri, 10am-8pm Sat, 1-7.30pm Sun) Organic produce of all kinds can be yours at this green haven.

Princi: Il Bread & Breakfast (Map p262; ☎ 02 659 90 13; Via Moscova 52; ♥ 7am-9pm Mon-Sat, 8am-10pm Sun) This busy bakery and coffee bar sells slices of pizza and focaccia (priced by weight) to eat in or on the move. There's also a superb choice of cakes, bread and fresh pasta. There are several other branches around town.

Pattini & Marinoni (♥ 7am-8pm Mon-Sat); Stazione Central (Map pp260-1; Corso Buenos Aires 53); Stazione Nord (Map p262; Piazza Cadorna 10); Brera (Map p262; Via Solferino 5) This bread shop sells great breads, cakes and pizza slices. The Brera branch gets especially busy.

Stock up on supermarket produce at the **Superfresco Standa** (Map p262; Via della Palla 2a) and fresh fruit, veggies and fish at the covered market, **Mercato Comunale** (Piazza XXIV Maggio; ♥ 8.30am-1pm Mon-Thu, 4-7.30pm Fri, 8.30am-1pm & 3.30-7.30pm Sat).

DRINKING

There is a trio of spots in particular to search for a drink, music and a madding Milanese crowd in a chic and trendy setting. Most bars open until 2am or 3am and a beer can cost anything from €5 to €10. Many places serve food, too.

Heading towards the Stazione Centrale, **Lelephante** (Map pp260-1; ☎ 02 295 18 768; Via Melzo 22; ♥ Tue-Sun) and **Artdeco Café** (Map pp260-1; ☎ 02 295 24 720; Via Lambro 7) are a twin set of hip bars.

Brera

Le Trottoir (Map p262; ☎ 02 80 10 02; Corso Garibaldi 1; mains about €4-5; ♥ lunch & dinner) Aspiring artists hang wild art on the walls of this wacky bar. Its small stage hosts alternative bands (often jazz) and simple food of the pasta and salad kind is dished up upstairs.

Jamaica (Map p262; ☎ 02 87 67 23; Via Brera 32) Lap up Brera street life on the pavement terrace of this ageing bar where artists and intellectuals have lamented the world's woes since 1921.

Navigli & Porta Ticinese

Several bars in this canalside area float alongside Via Ascanio Sforza, but there's plenty of others to choose from.

Coquetel (Map p262; ☎ 02 836 06 88; Via Vetere 14; ✆ 8am-2am) Closed but a few hours a day, this relaxed and laid-back bar lies on the southern fringe of Milan's central ring. Its pavement terrace, at the end of a dead-end street on the grassy edge of Parco delle Basiliche, makes it an ideal summertime spot.

Tabloid (Map p262; ☎ 02 894 00 709; Corso di Porta Ticinese 60; ✆ 6pm-4am) A panther and leopard guard the entrance to this cocksure disco bar where misted windows hide what happens inside. One thing is sure – dress up or look good to get in here. Don your dancing shoes, Friday to Sunday.

Le Biciclette (Map p262; ☎ 02 581 04 325; Via Torti 1; ✆ 6pm-2am Mon-Sat, 12.30-4.30pm & 6pm-2am Sun) In a converted bicycle workshop with a well-worn mosaic floor, Le Biciclette is an ode to two wheels. 'Cuisine, art & design' is the house motto, brunch is served on Sunday and art exhibitions change monthly.

Kooka Bar (Map pp260-1; ☎ 02 54 12 25 07; www .kookabar.net in Italian; Piazzale Libia 3; ✆ 6pm-2am Tue-Sat, 3pm-2am Sun) East of the Navigli district is Kooka Bar, which, as the name might suggest, has a complement of Australian staff and a good stock of Australian wines behind the bar. Pool tables and live televised sports add to the matey expat atmosphere.

Corso Como

This fashionable patch is conveniently close to Stazione Porta Garibaldi and is laden with many of Milan's best nightclubs (opposite).

Radetzky (Map pp260-1; ☎ 02 657 26 45; Corso Garibaldi 105; ✆ 7pm-2am) This long-favoured haunt is a must for one drink, purely to absorb its marbled and minimal Art Deco interior.

Makia (Map pp260-1; ☎ 02 336 04 012; Corso Sempione 28) Furnishings at this drinks and food bar reflect the latest in contemporary design, and it is popular with media types.

ATM (Map pp260-1; ☎ 02 655 23 65; Bastioni di Porta Volta 15) The ungainly bunker sandwiched between speeding cars on a traffic island was an ATM terminal until Milanese glamour queens transformed it into the chic place it is today.

Absolut Ice Bar (Map pp260-1; ☎ 02 89 07 85 31; www .townhouse.it/icebar; Piazza Gerusalemme 12; ✆ 6pm-midnight Mon-Fri) Ice from Sweden's Torne River has been shipped to Milan to create this crystal cavern inside the Townhouse 12 Hotel. Everything, including the sofas, light fittings and glasses, are carved out of 400 tonnes of pure, translucent ice. Kept at a constant -5ºC, this cool bar serves up only vodka and fruit juice, which, at €17 a shot, will certainly take your breath away. Cloaks, boots and gloves must be donned upon entry, and visits are timed to a maximum of 30 minutes per person. Reservations are essential, but credit cards are not accepted.

ENTERTAINMENT

Milan has some of Italy's top clubs, several cinemas screening English-language films and a fabulous year-round cultural calendar, topped off by La Scala's opera season. The main theatre and concert season opens in October.

Other than those mentioned in this guide, there are at least another 50 active theatres in Milan; check the newspapers and ask at the tourist office. The latter also stocks *Milano Mese*, the free monthly entertainment guide (in English) – an essential reference for culture buffs.

For club listings, **Corriere della Sera** (www.cor riere.it in Italian) runs a reasonable supplement, **ViviMilano** (www.corriere.it/vivimilano in Italian), on Wednesday. **La Repubblica** (www.repubblica.it in Italian) counters on Thursday with *Tutto Milano*. Both papers run cinema listings.

Cinemas

English-language films are shown at the following cinemas. Tickets at all three cost €7/4 for evening/afternoon screenings.

Anteo (Map pp260-1; ☎ 02 659 77 32; www.anteo spaziocinema.com in Italian; Via Milazzo 9)

Arcobaleno Film Centre (Map pp260-1; ☎ 02 294 06 054; Viale Tunisia 11)

Mexico (Map pp260-1; ☎ 02 489 51 802; www.cinema mexico.it in Italian; Via Savona 57).

Live Music

Blue Note (Map pp260-1; ☎ 0269016888; www.bluenote
milano.com in Italian; Via Pietro Borsieni 37; tickets €23-30;
☼ 10am-1pm & 2-7pm Mon, 10am-1pm & 2pm-midnight
Tue-Fri, 2pm-midnight Sat, 7-11pm Sun) hosts top-
class jazz acts from around the world.

Propaganda (Map pp260-1; ☎ 02 583 10 682; Via
Castelbarco 11; ☼ Thu-Mon) and **Rolling Stone** (Map
pp260-1; ☎ 02 73 31 72; www.rollingstone.it in Italian;
Corso XXII Marzo 32; ☼ Thu-Sun) are live rock-band
venues to watch out for.

All the biggest names play at **Alcatraz**
(see below), **Mazda Palace** (☎ 02 334 00 551; Viale
Sant'Elia 33), near the San Siro stadium, and
Filaforum (☎ 02 48 85 71; www.filaforum.it in Italian),
further out of town. To get to the latter,
take the MM2 line to Romolo and pick up a
special shuttle bus laid on for concerts.

Box Tickets (see the boxed text, right) sells
tickets for concerts at all these venues.

Nightclubs

Milan boasts dozens of places to dance, although the scene for Milanese social butterflies revolves around 10 or so clubs, generally
open until 3am or 4am Tuesday to Sunday.
The Corso Como area is particularly well
endowed with fashionable venues. Cover
charges vary from €10 to €20.

La Banque (Map p262; ☎ 02 869 96 565; www
.labanque.it in Italian; Via Porrone 6; ☼ Tue-Sun) Among
the most central of clubs, this was a bank before the clerks moved out and the clubbers
moved in.

Old Fashion Café (Map p262; ☎ 02 805 62 31;
www.oldfashion.it in Italian; Viale Emillio Alemagna 6;
☼ 9pm-4am Tue-Sat) Look for the discreet red
canopy at the rear of the Palazzo dell'Arte
to uncover this club where the fashion-
conscious mingle. DJs mix most nights.

Alcatraz (☎ 02 690 16 352; Via Valtellina 21) An excellent live-concert venue north of the centre
near the Cimitero Monumentale, Alcatraz is
transformed into one of the city's biggest
clubs on Friday and Saturday nights.

I Magazzini Generali (☎ 02 552 11 313; Via Pietra-
santa 14; ☼ 10/11pm-4am Wed-Sun) This thumping
space, happily housed in a 1930s converted
warehouse, is a fair hike south of the city
centre. House and hip hop dominate.

Other fashionable clubs on Corso Como
where face control counts:
Gasoline (Map pp260-1; ☎ 02 290 13 245; Via Bonnet
11a; admission €16; ☼ Thu-Sun) Gay-friendly hangout
popular with the fashion-scene set.

Shocking (Map pp260-1; ☎ 01 265 51 240; www.shock
ing club.net in Italian; Bastioni di Porta Nuova 12) Tucked
beside Teatro Smeraldo, this place draws a student crowd.
Tocqueville 13 (Map pp260-1; ☎ 02 290 02 973; Via
A de Tocqueville 13; ☼ Tue-Sun) On the ground floor of
an unattractive high-rise, this place also has a restaurant,
open from 9pm.

Opera & Theatre

The legendary **La Scala** opera house is synonymous with Milan itself. The opera
season runs from November through to
July but – with the exception of August –
you can see theatre, ballet and concerts
here year-round. The theatre has recently
undergone a thorough renovation, and
reopened in December 2004. Opera also
plays at the **Teatro degli Arcimboldi** (☎ 02 72
00 37 44; Viale dell'Innovazione) in Milan's Bicocca
district. To get here, take a train from either Stazione Centrale or Stazione Porta
Garibaldi to Stazione di Greco Pirelli (five
to six minutes) or hop aboard a shuttle
bus, departing every five minutes between
6.45pm and 7pm from Piazza del Duomo.
A regular ATM underground ticket covers
either journey.

WHERE TO SCORE TICKETS

Tickets for concerts, sporting events and
the theatre can be booked through **Ticket
One** (☎ 02 39 22 61, 840 05 27 20; www.ticket
one.it) or **Ticket Web** (☎ 02 760 09 131; www
.ticketweb.it). **Milano Concerti** (☎ 02 487 02
726) only handles ticketing for international
rock concerts. **Box Tickets** (☎ 02 847 09
750; www.boxtickets.it in Italian) sells tickets
for musicals at Teatro Smeraldo, sporting
events at the San Siro stadium and pop
concerts at Milan's live music venues (for
more details, see left).

In Milan itself, try the following ticket
offices inside:
FNAC (Map p262; ☎ 02 72 08 21; fnac@
ticketweb.it; Via della Palla 2)On Via Torino.
Messaggerie Musicali (Map p262;
☎ 02 79 55 02; Galleria del Corso 20) With an
entrance on Corso Vittorio Emanuele II.
Ricordi Mediastore (Map p262; ☎ 02 864 60
272; www.ricordimediastores.it in Italian; Galleria
Vittorio Emanuele II)
Virgin Megastore (Map p262; ☎ 02 880 01
200; Duomo Centre, Piazza del Duomo 8)

Getting hold of opera tickets (€10 to €215) requires luck and perseverance. About two months before the first performance, tickets can be bought by telephone on ☎ 02 86 07 75 (24 hours) and online at www.teatro allascala.org; these tickets carry a 20% surcharge. One month before the first performance, any remaining tickets are sold (for a 10% surcharge) at the main **La Scala box office** (Map p262; ☎ 02 72 00 37 44; www .teatroallascala.org; Galleria Vittorio Emanuele; ☼ noon-6pm). On the actual day of the performance, tickets for any unsold seats – a very rare occurrence – are sold (at half-price). There is also a self-ticketing machine in the La Scala Bookstore (p258). To find out what tickets are available when, consult the computer terminal in the La Scala box office or look online.

Musicals are staged at **Teatro Smeraldo** (Map pp260-1; ☎ 02 290 06 767; www.smeraldo.it in Italian; Piazza XX Aprile 10).

Sport
The Italian Grand Prix tears around the **Autodromo Nazionale Monza** (☎ 039 248 22 12; www.monzanet.it; Parco di Monza, Via Vedano 5) in September. The track, 20km north of central Milan, can be reached along Viale Monza from Piazzale Loreto.

Milan's two football clubs, AC Milan and FC Internazionale Milano (known simply as Inter) play on alternate Sundays in season at the **San Siro stadium** (Stadio Giuseppe Meazza; ☎ 02 404 24 32; www.sansirotour.com; Via Piccolomini 5; museum €7, museum & guided tour adult/child €12.50/10; ☼ nonmatch days 10am-5pm), built in 1926. To get here, take tram No 24, bus No 95, 49 or 72, or the underground to the Lotto station (MM1), from where a free shuttle bus can run you to the stadium. Tickets are available at the stadium or, for AC Milan matches, from **Milan Point** (Map p262; ☎ 02 894 22 711; Corso San Gottardo 2) and branches of the Cariplo bank. For Inter matches, try Banca Popolare di Milano branches or Ticket One (see the boxed text, p273).

SHOPPING
High-priced high fashion can be consumed in Milan's Golden Quad (see the boxed text, opposite). Streets for fashion that's more

GOLDEN QUAD

0   200 m
0 ──────────────── 0.1 miles

SHOPPING 🛍️
Armani (Casualwear)..................1 B3	Damiani........................9 A2
Armani (Kids' & Formal Wear).....2 B3	Diffusione Tessile................10 B3
Armani Accessories....................3 B1	Dolce & Gabbana.............11 B1
Armani........................(see 23)	Dolce & Gabbana.............12 B2
Bally..........................4 B2	Emporio Armani...............13 A1
Barbara Bui....................5 A1	Factory Store Valextra........14 B3
Calvin Klein................(see 28)	Fausto Santini................15 B2
Cartier........................6 A2	Fratelli Rossetti...............16 B2
Chanel........................7 B2	Gio Moretti....................17 B2
D-Magazine....................8 A1	Gio Moretti (Babywear)......18 B2
	Gucci.........................19 A2
	Gucci.........................20 A2
	Hermès.......................21 B1
	I Pinco Pallino...............22 B1
	Kenzo........................23 B2
	Luis Vuitton..................24 B2
	Mariella Burani..............25 B2
	Moschino.....................26 B1
	Moschino.....................27 B2
	Moschino.....................28 B3
	Nilufar.......................29 B1
	Paul Smith....................30 A1
	Prada.........................31 B2
	Prada (Lingerie)..............32 B2
	Prada (Shoes).................33 B2
	Prada (Women's Collection)...34 B1
	Ralph Lauren..................35 B2
	Roberto Cavalli...............36 B1
	Salvatore Ferragamo.....(see 25)
	Semoneta......................37 B1
	Sergio Rossi & Camper....(see 4)
	Tiffany & Co..................38 B1
	Trussardi......................39 B2
	Valentino......................40 A1
	Versace........................41 A2
	Yves St Laurent................42 A2

FASHION & DESIGN

Milan's meteoric rise to European fashion and design capital rode on a wave of creative activity that the city witnessed from the 1960s. With the departure of many haute-couture fashion houses from Florence in the mid-1950s, coupled with the emergence of a new mass market in high fashion, Italy's largest fashion show – a twice-yearly Florentine event since 1951 – made a leap to the industrial north.

The first international fashion show waltzed down Milan's catwalk in 1971. In 1982 Milan-born designer Giorgio Armani revolutionised the industry with his more wearable and affordable *prêt à porter* ('ready to wear') collection. The Giorgio Armani empire set another precedent in 2000 with the opening of its flagship store, Milan's **Emporio Armani** (Map p274; ☎ 02 723 18 630; Via Alessandro Manzoni 31) – 6000 sq metres of space pioneering designer shopping for fashion, flowers and wine 'under one roof'. Former Italian *Vogue* contributor Carla Sozzani had already experimented with the idea in 1991 with the launch of the seriously trendy **10 Corso Como** (see p270), a cutting-edge art gallery, fashion shop and restaurant rolled into one.

Gucci (Map p274; ☎ 02 77 12 71; Via Monte Napoleone 5 & 27), the industry's other big name, moved to Milan in 1951, launching the birth of Milan's legendary **Golden Quad** (Quadrilatero d'Oro; Map p274) – a quadrangle of pedestrian streets, sketched out by Via della Spiga, Via Sant'Andrea, Via Monte Napoleone and Via Alessandro Manzoni, and crammed with boutiques of some of the world's best-known and popular designers: Prada, Versace, Dolce & Gabbana, Gianfranco Ferrè, Chanel, Moschino, Hermès, Kenzo, Trussadi and Paul Smith are all here, to give you but a small taste. For glittering gold and diamonds you can't go past a visit to **Tiffany & Co** (Map p274; Via della Spiga 19a), **Cartier** (Map p274; cnr Via Montenapoleone & Via Gesù) or **Damiani** (Map p274; Via Montenapoleone 10), Italy's leading diamond house. **Semoneta** (Map p274; Via della Spiga) is the place to go for the snazziest ladies' gloves.

There are numerous discount-fashion outlets around the city, and beyond, for the more thrifty fashionista, including **D-Magazine** (Map p274; ☎ 02 76 00 60 27; Via Montenapoleone 26) and **Emporio Isola** (Map p262; ☎ 02 805 46 66) for men's and women's clothes, **Barbara Bui** (Map p274; ☎ 02 29 06 02 16; Via Alessandro Manzoni 45) for women's fashions, **Diffusione Tessile** (Map p274; ☎ 02 76 00 08 29; Galleria San Carlo 6) for Max Mara clothing, **Outlet Shoes** (☎ 02 40 69 03; Via Martinetti 6) for, naturally, shoes and **Factory Store Valextra** (Map p274; ☎ 02 76 00 34 59; Via Cerva 11) for leather goods. Bigger outlets, including those for designers Armani, Dolce & Gabbana, Trussadi and others, are located outside the city. The tourist office has a free map and further details about these stores.

The Milan fashion shows are seasonal. The world's top designers unveil their ready-to-wear women's collections in February/March and September/October, while the men's fashion show takes place in January and June/July. Shows last 10 to 12 days and are held at the Fiera di Milano.

Milan is also the world's design capital but you wouldn't know it unless you search it out. Showrooms and galleries are spread throughout the city and most products are made for export. The latest designs are unveiled each year at the five-day Salone Internazionale del Mobile (Furniture Fair), hosted by Milan at the Fiera dei Milano since 1961. Magazines with listings to look out for at newspaper stands include *Domus* and *La Casa Bella,* both founded by Gio Ponti (1891–1979) – considered the architect of Italian design – in 1928; and *Interni,* a monthly design magazine published since 1954.

The original beanbag created by Milan's Zanotta in 1968, Panton chairs, the Milan-designed Carlton stack of shelves (1972) produced by the Milanese furniture house Memphis, and the lush-lipped Bocca sofa form part of the awe-inspiring collection at **Galleria Mode** (Map p262; Via San Paolo 1). **Nilufar** (Map p274; Via della Spiga 32) is another place dealing exclusively in rare and original furniture designed between 1950 and 2000. **Area Design** (☎ 02 869 84 584; Via Borromei 11) deals in designer furniture made between the 1960s and 1980s. Notable designs to come out of the world's design capital in the 1990s included Ron Arad's Bookworm book shelf, produced in 1994 by Milanese pioneer of plastic **Kartell** (☎ 02 659 79 16; Via Carlo Porta 1) and one of the many pieces sold in its large white flagship store.

LOMBARDY & THE LAKES

affordable lie behind the cathedral around Corso Vittorio Emanuele II, and between Piazza della Scala and Piazza San Babila.

In the 1960s Giorgio Armani dressed the windows of Milan's main department store **La Rinascente** (Map p262; Piazza del Duomo; 9am-10pm Tue-Sat, 10am-8pm Sun) before setting up his own fashion empire.

An array of designer consumables is sold at **Corso Como 10** (Map pp260-1; 02 29 00 26 74; Corso Como 10) including clothes, perfume, crockery and lamps. Upstairs there's a book and music store.

Markets fill the canal-side Viale Papiniano in the southwest of the city on Tuesday and Saturday mornings. There is a flea market in Viale Gabriele d'Annunzio on Saturday and an antique market in Brera on Via Fiori Chiari that is held every third Saturday of the month.

A huge market where you can buy absolutely anything is held on the last Sunday of each month on the Alzaia Naviglio Grande and Ripa di Porta Ticinese.

GETTING THERE & AWAY
Air
Most European and other international flights use **Malpensa airport** (www.malpensa.com), 50km northwest of the city. Most (but not all) domestic and a handful of European flights use **Linate airport** (www.sea-aeroportimilano.it), 7km east of the city centre. An increasing number of budget airlines also use **Orio al Serio airport**, near Bergamo.

For all flight information, call 02 748 52 200 (both Malpensa and Linate airports).

Bus
Bus stations are scattered throughout the city so unless you know exactly where you are going, you're much better off travelling by train.

Buses (which are operated by numerous different companies) to many national as well as international destinations leave from the **bus station** (Map pp260-1; 02 63 79 01; Piazza Sigmund Freud) opposite the main entrance to the Stazione Porta Garibaldi. **Eurolines** (02 637 90 299; Piazza Sigmund Freud) has a ticketing desk here.

Train
You can catch a train from **Stazione Centrale** (Map pp260-1; Piazza Duca d'Aosta) to all major cities

in Italy. Check schedules at its **information office** (147 88 80 88; 7am-9pm). Daily trains (intercity train fares are quoted here) run to and from Venice (€22, 3½ hours), Florence (€23, 3½ hours), Genoa (€14.50, 1½ hours), Turin (€18, 1½ hours), Rome (€44, 5¾ hours) and Naples (€53, eight hours). This is also a good point to pick up international connections to/from Switzerland (with the Cisalpino train) and France (with the TGV).

Ferrovie Nord Milano (FNM) trains from **Stazione Nord** (Map p262; Stazione Cadorna, Piazza Luigi Cadorna) connect Milan with Como (€3.40, one hour, hourly) and Desanzano (€6.30, 1¼ hours, hourly). Regional services to many towns northwest of Milan are more frequent from **Stazione Porta Garibaldi** (Map pp260-1; Piazza Sigmund Freud).

GETTING AROUND
To/From the Airport
LINATE AIRPORT
From Milan's Piazza Luigi di Savoia, in front of the Stazione Centrale, **Autostradale** (02 33 91 07 94; www.autostradale.com in Italian) also runs buses to Linate airport (adult/child one way €2.50/1.40, 25 minutes, every 1½ hours between 5.40am and 9.35pm). Tickets are sold on board by the driver. You can also get local ATM bus No 73 (€1 one way, 20 minutes, about every 15 minutes between 5.30am and 8pm) from Piazza San Babila (on the corner of Corso Europa). In addition, Autostradale operates a regular service between Linate and Malpensa airports (adult/child €9/4.50, one hour 10 minutes).

MALPENSA AIRPORT
The **Malpensa Express** (02 20 222; www.malpensaexpress.it; ticket office 7am-8pm) train links Stazione Nord with Malpensa airport (adult/child one way €9/4.50, if purchased on train €11.50/7.50, adult/child day return €12/6, 40 minutes, every 30 minutes).

The airport is also served by **Malpensa Shuttle** (Map pp260-1; 02 585 83 185; www.malpensa-shuttle.com; ticket office 7am-9pm) coaches, departing from Piazza Luigi di Savoia, outside Stazione Centrale (every 20 minutes 5am to 10.30pm). A one-way ticket per adult/child costs €5/2.50 for the one-hour journey. A taxi from Malpensa into Milan will cost at least €65.

ORIO AL SERIO AIRPORT

Autostradale (☎ 02 33 91 07 94; www.autostradale.com in Italian) runs buses roughly every 90-minutes between 4.15am and 10pm from Piazza Luigi di Savoia to Orio al Serio airport (adult/child €6.70/3.35, one hour), near Bergamo.

Bicycle

Hire a bicycle for around €5 a day from **AWS Bici Motor** (Map pp260-1; ☎ 02 670 72 145; Via Ponte Seveso 33), on the corner of Via Schiaparelli.

Car & Motorcycle

Entering central Milan by car is a major headache and public transport is a far preferable option. Street parking costs €1.50 per hour in the city centre (€2 per five hours after 8pm). To pay, buy a SostaMilano card from a tobacconist, scratch off the date and hour, and display it on your dashboard. Underground car parks charge €5 for the first two hours and between €1.50 to €2 per hour after that.

Motoring information is provided by the **Automobile Club Italia** (ACI; Map p262; ☎ 02 774 51; Corso Venezia 43). Hertz, Avis, Maggiore and Europcar have offices at Stazione Centrale and both airports. You can also purchase tickets for the Italian Grand Prix here – for details, see p53.

Public Transport

Milan's public transport system, run by **ATM** (☎ 800 80 81 81; www.atm-mi.it) is efficient. The underground consists of four underground lines (red MM1, green MM2, yellow MM3 and blue Passante Ferroviario) which run 6am to midnight.

A ticket costs €1 and is valid for one underground ride or up to 75 minutes travel on ATM buses and trams. You can buy a book of 10 tickets (five double-journey tickets) for €9.20 or unlimited one-/two-day tickets for bus, tram and MM costing €3/5.50. The tickets are sold at underground stations, tobacconists and newspaper stands around town.

Free public-transport maps are available from ATM's **Info Point** (☺ 7.45am-8.15pm Mon-Sat) in the Duomo underground station.

Taxi

Don't bother trying to hail taxis – they don't stop. Head for a taxi rank or call ☎ 02 40 40, ☎ 02 69 69 or ☎ 02 85 85.

SOUTH OF MILAN

PAVIA

pop 73,893 / elev 77m

Pavia is an industrial and agricultural centre on the banks of the River Ticino, known for its university. Originally the Roman Ticinum, Pavia rivalled Milan as the capital of the Lombard kings until the 11th century. Like many northern cities, Pavia became a pawn of power politics as the Renaissance dawned. Spain occupied it in the early 16th century, followed immediately by the Austrians from the early 18th century. Interrupted by a few years of Napoleonic French control from 1796, Austrian rule lasted until 1859.

The province produces about one-third of Italy's rice, making Pavia a good place to try out some risotto dishes.

Information

Banca Nazionale del Lavoro (Via Mentana)

CTS (☎ 0382 3 51 95; Via Bossolaro 27) Student and youth travel.

Farmacia Fapa (Corso Strada Nuova 100) Historic pharmacy (1828) with night service.

Ospedale San Matteo (☎ 0382 50 11; Piazza Golgi 2) Hospital.

Police station (☎ 0382 51 21; Viale Rismondo 68)

Post office (Piazza della Posta 2; ☺ 8.30am-7pm Mon-Sat)

Tourist office (☎ 0382 2 21 56; www.apt.pavia.it in Italian; Via Fabio Filzi 22; ☺ 8.30am-12.30pm & 2-6pm Mon-Sat)

Sights

OLD TOWN

Pavia once boasted around 100 medieval **watchtowers**; the trio on Piazza di Leonardo da Vinci is all that remains today. The forbidding **Castello Visconteo** looms over the northern end of medieval Pavia. Only ever used as a palatial residence, rather than a defensive fortress, the castle was built in 1360 for Galeazzo II Visconti and now houses the **Museo Civico** (☎ 0382 30 48 16; museocivici@comune .pv.it; Viale XI Febbraio; adult/EU-citizen child €6/free; ☺ 10am-6pm Tue-Sun).

The museum is divided into several sections, with archaeological, ethnographic and art collections, and displays on medieval Pavia and the Risorgimento (the Italian reunification period).

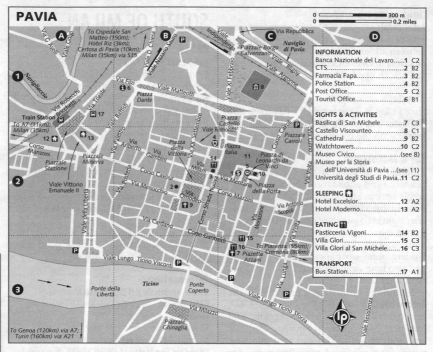

PAVIA

INFORMATION	
Banca Nazionale del Lavaro......1	C2
CTS...........................2	B2
Farmacia Fapa..................3	B2
Police Station..................4	B2
Post Office.....................5	C2
Tourist Office..................6	B1

SIGHTS & ACTIVITIES	
Basilica di San Michele..........7	C3
Castello Viscounteo.............8	C1
Cathedral.....................9	B2
Watchtowers..................10	C2
Museo Civico..............(see 8)	
Museo per la Storia	
dell'Università di Pavia ...(see 11)	
Università degli Studi di Pavia..11	C2

SLEEPING	
Hotel Excelsior................12	A2
Hotel Moderno.................13	A2

EATING	
Pasticceria Vigoni..............14	B2
Villa Glori....................15	C3
Villa Glori al San Michele.......16	C3

TRANSPORT	
Bus Station....................17	A1

The medieval centre is dominated by the **Università degli Studi di Pavia** (University of Pavia; ☎ 0382 50 41; www.unipv.it in Italian; Corso Strada Nuova 65), founded as a school in the 9th century. It became a university in 1361, and counts Christopher Columbus among its notable graduates. The self-taught physicist Alessandro Volta, inventor of the electric battery, lectured here. Discover other facts in the **Museo per la Storia dell'Università di Pavia** (☎ 0382 2 97 24; Corso Strada Nuova 65; ☼ 3.30-5pm Mon, 9.30am-noon Fri), the small museum in the academic complex.

The old town's other landmark is the **cathedral**, a short walk south of the university along pedestrian Corso Strada Nuovo. Work started on the hulk of a church – topped by Italy's third-largest dome – in 1488 but it wasn't completed until the 19th century. Both da Vinci and Bramante contributed to the church's design. In 1989 its bell tower collapsed, killing four people.

Continuing south along Corso Strada Nuova, and then east along Corso Garibaldi brings you to the **Basilica di San Michele** (Piazzetta Azzani 1), built in the Romanesque style in 1090.

Emperor Frederick Barbarossa was crowned Holy Roman Emperor here in 1155.

CERTOSA DI PAVIA

One of the most notable buildings produced during the Italian Renaissance was Pavia's splendid **certosa** (charterhouse; ☎ 0382 92 56 13; Viale Monumento; admission by donation; ☼ 9-11.30am & 2.30-4.30pm Tue-Sun Oct-Mar, 9-11.30am & 2.30-5.30pm Tue-Sun Apr, 9-11.30am & 2.30-6pm Tue-Sun May-Sep), a Carthusian monastery about 10km north of Pavia. Founded by Gian Galeazzo Visconti of Milan in 1396 as a private chapel for the Visconti family and a home for 12 monks, the Certosa soon became one of northern Italy's most lavish buildings.

The interior is Gothic, although some Renaissance decoration is evident. In the former sacristy is a giant sculpture, dating from 1409 and made from hippopotamus teeth, including 66 small bas-reliefs and 94 statuettes. Behind the 122 arches of the larger cloisters are 24 cells, each a self-contained living area for one monk. Several are open to the public.

SGEA buses to Milan stop at the Certosa. See opposite for details.

LOMBARDY & THE LAKES

Sleeping

Hotel Excelsior (☎ 0382 2 85 96; www.excelsiorpa
via.com; Piazzale Stazione 25; s/d €54/78; P ⊠ ☐)
Standard three-star comforts make the Excelsior, across from the train station, a reasonable choice, and some rooms are fitted
for disabled access. Breakfast is €6 extra.

Hotel Riz (☎ 0382 58 02 80; www.hotelrizpavia.com;
Via dei Longobardi 3, San Genesio; s/d €68/91; P ⊠)
The Riz, located around 3km north of the
centre in San Genesio, is a stylish modern
place with big rooms. It's a popular choice
with international business travellers.

Hotel Moderno (☎ 0382 30 34 01; www.hotel
moderno.it; Viale Vittorio Emanuele 41; s/d/tr/ste €105/140/
154/225; P ⊠) The four-star Hotel Moderno
is Pavia's upmarket choice, nestled in an old
family palazzo from the 19th century. Its 53
rooms are all smartly furnished in contemporary style and there's a fitness centre and
free bike rental for guests.

Eating

Cafés abound beneath the arches on Piazza
della Vittoria.

Pasticceria Vigoni (☎ 0382 2 21 03; Corso Strada
Nuova 110) Sample a slice of *torta paradiso* (literally 'paradise cake') at Pasticceria Vignoni,
a cake shop and tearoom dating to 1878 in
front of the university.

Villa Glori (☎ 0382 2 07 16; Via Villa Glori 10; mains
€10-12; ⏲ Wed-Mon) Feast on Pavian culinary
pleasures on a cobbled terrace.

Villa Glori al San Michele (Piazzetta Azzani) Taste
local vintages at this place, a wine bar run
by the same team as Villa Glori.

Getting There & Around

SGEA buses (☎ 0382 42 20 45; www.sgea.it in Italian) linking **Pavia bus station** (Via Trieste) and
Viale Bligny in Milan (€2.75, 35 minutes,
seven daily) stop en route at the Certosa di
Pavia (€1.20, 10 minutes, seven daily). To
reach the charterhouse (about a 10-minute
walk) from the bus stop, turn right at the
traffic lights and continue straight ahead.
Pavia–Milan buses continue onto Malpensa
airport (€10, 1½ hours). Updated schedules
are on the SGEA website.

Direct trains depart from the Pavia train
station to Milan (€2.70, 30 minutes, up to
eight daily), Genoa and beyond.

Pavia is small and easy enough to get
around. Bicycles are popular and most summers the city council plants several bicycle

stands – including at Hotel Moderno and
the university – around town, from where
cyclists can borrow free bikes.

EAST OF MILAN

BERGAMO

pop 117,415 / elev 249m

Virtually two cities, Bergamo's walled hilltop
città alta (upper town) is surrounded by the
città bassa (lower town), a sprawling modern
addition to this magnificent former outpost
of the Venetian empire. Although Milan's
skyscrapers to the southwest are visible on
a clear day, historically Bergamo was more
closely associated with Venice, which was in
control of the city for 350 years until Napoleon arrived. Although long dominated
by outsiders, Bergamo has retained a strong
sense of local identity, perhaps demonstrated
most colourfully by the local dialect, which is
almost incomprehensible to visitors.

Bergamo, with its wealth of medieval,
Renaissance and baroque architecture, is one
of Italy's lesser-known highlights, although
more and more tourists are now 'discovering' this lovely spot thanks to the increase in
budget airline traffic into Orio al Serio airport, just 4km southeast of the city. Several
small ski resorts speckle the Bergamo Alps
around the town.

Information

You'll find several banks in the lower town
and on Via Colleoni, near the upper town
tourist office.

CTS (☎ 035 24 41 67; bergamo@cts.it; Via Pignolo
16a; ⏲ 9.30am-12.30pm & 3-7pm Mon-Fri, 9.30am-
12.30pm Sat)

Galleria Internazionale del Libro (☎ 035 23 01 30;
Via XX Settembre 83) Travel guides and English-language
novels.

Lavanderia self service (Via Angelo Maj 39b;
⏲ 7.30am-8pm)

Libreria di Dimetra (☎ 035 21 00 86; Viale Papa
Giovanni XXIII 28) Walking and cycling guidebooks (in
Italian) and city maps.

Ospedale Riuniti (☎ 035 26 91 11; Largo Barozzi 1)

Police station (☎ 035 27 61 11; Via Alessandro Noli)

Post office lower town (Via Masone 2a; ⏲ 8.30am-7pm
Mon-Sat); upper town (Via S Lorenzo; ⏲ 8.30am-2pm
Mon-Fri, 8.30am-12.30pm Sat)

Tourist office lower town (☎ 035 21 02 04; www.apt
.bergamo.it; Viale Vittorio Emanuele II 20; ⏲ 9am-

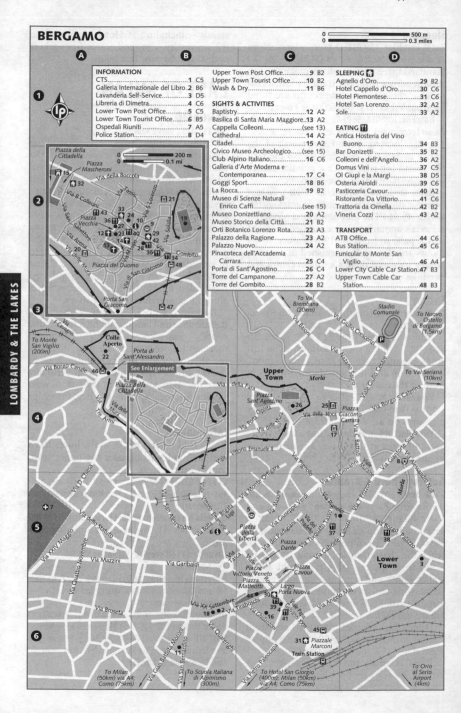

BERGAMO

INFORMATION
CTS..1 C5
Galleria Internazionale del Libro.2 B6
Lavanderia Self-Service............3 D5
Libreria di Dimetra.....................4 C6
Lower Town Post Office..............5 C5
Lower Town Tourist Office...........6 B5
Ospedali Riuniti..........................7 A5
Police Station.............................8 D4

Upper Town Post Office.............9 B2
Upper Town Tourist Office........10 B2
Wash & Dry..............................11 B6

SIGHTS & ACTIVITIES
Baptistry..................................12 A2
Basilica di Santa Maria Maggiore.13 A2
Cappella Colleoni....................(see 13)
Cathedral.................................14 A2
Citadel.....................................15 A2
Civico Museo Archeologico......(see 15)
Club Alpino Italiano..................16 C6
Galleria d'Arte Moderna e
   Contemporanea....................17 C4
Goggi Sport..............................18 B6
La Rocca..................................19 B2
Museo di Scienze Naturali
   Enrico Caffi...........................(see 15)
Museo Donizettiano.................20 A2
Museo Storico della Città.........21 B2
Orti Botanico Lorenzo Rota......22 A3
Palazzo della Ragione..............23 A2
Palazzo Nuovo.........................24 A2
Pinacoteca dell'Accademia
   Carrara................................25 C4
Porta di Sant'Agostino.............26 C4
Torre del Campanone...............27 A2
Torre del Gombito....................28 B2

SLEEPING 🛏
Agnello d'Oro..........................29 B2
Hotel Cappello d'Oro...............30 C6
Hotel Piemontese.....................31 C6
Hotel San Lorenzo....................32 A2
Sole...33 A2

EATING 🍽
Antica Hosteria del Vino
   Buono.................................34 B3
Bar Donizetti 35 B2
Colleoni e dell'Angelo.............36 A2
Domus Vini...............................37 C5
Ol Giupi e la Margi..................38 D5
Osteria Airoldi.........................39 C6
Pasticceria Cavour...................40 A2
Ristorante Da Vittorio..............41 C6
Trattoria da Ornella.................42 B2
Vineria Cozzi...........................43 A2

TRANSPORT
ATB Office................................44 C6
Bus Station...............................45 C6
Funicular to Monte San
   Vigilio..................................46 A4
Lower City Cable Car Station.47 B3
Upper Town Cable Car
   Station.................................48 B3

LOMBARDY & THE LAKES

12.30pm Mon & Fri, 9am-12.30pm & 2.30-4pm Tue-Thu);
upper town (☎ 035 24 22 26; iat.bergamo@apt.bergamo
.it; Vicolo Aquila Nera 2; ☯ 9am-12.30pm Mon & Fri,
9am-12.30pm & 2.30-4pm Tue-Thu)
Wash & Dry (Via San Bernardino 11d; ☯ 7.30am-8pm)

Sights
PIAZZA VECCHIA
Medieval Bergamo's heart is based around
a lovely piazza adorned with some splendid
architecture. The white porticoed building
on Via B Colleoni, which forms the northern side of the piazza, is the 17th century
Palazzo Nuovo, now a library. Turn south and
you face the imposing arches and columns
of the **Palazzo della Ragione**, built in the 12th
century. The lion of St Mark is a reminder
of Venice's long reign. Note the sun clock
in the pavement beneath the arches. Next
to the palace, the **Torre del Campanone** (Piazza
Vecchia; adult/child €1/0.50; ☯ 10.30am-4pm Sat & Sun Nov-
Feb, 10am-12.30pm & 2-6pm Tue-Fri, 10am-6pm Sat & Sun
Mar, Apr & Oct, 10am-8pm Sat & Sun May-Sep) tolls the
old 10pm curfew. Scale the tower for some
wonderful views.

Tucked in behind these secular buildings
is the core of Bergamo's spiritual life, the
Piazza del Duomo. Of more interest than
the modest baroque **cathedral** (☎ 035 21 02 23;
Piazza del Duomo; ☯ 7.30-11.45am & 3-6.30pm) is the
neighbouring **Basilica di Santa Maria Maggiore**
(☎ 035 22 33 27; Piazza del Duomo; ☯ 9am-12.30pm
& 2.30-5pm Mon-Fri, 9-11am & 2.30-5pm Sat, 9-11am &
2.30-6pm Sun), a Romanesque church begun
in 1137. Gaetano Donizetti, a 19th-century
composer and son of Bergamo, is buried
here. The gaudy Renaissance **Cappella Colleoni**
(☎ 035 21 00 61; Piazza del Duomo; ☯ 9am-12.30pm
& 2-4.30pm Tue-Sun Nov-Mar, 9am-12.30pm & 2-6.30pm
Tue-Sun Apr-Oct) is an extravagant addition to
the church.

The octagonal **baptistry** was built inside the
Basilica di Santa Maria Maggiore in 1340 but
moved outside in the late 19th century.

CITADEL
The upper city's western tip is filled by the
defensive hulk of Bergamo's **citadel**, occupied today by two small museums, the **Museo
di Scienze Naturali Enrico Caffi** (☎ 035 39 94 42;
msnbg@tiscalinet.it; Piazza Citadella 10; admission free;
☯ 9am-noon & 2-6pm Tue-Fri, 9am-7.30pm Sat & Sun Apr-
Sep, 9am-12.30pm & 2.30-5.30pm Tue-Sun Oct-Mar), with
its collection of stuffed animals and fossils,
and the **Civico Museo Archeologico** (☎ 035 24 28

39; Piazza Citadella 12; admission free; ☯ 9am-12.30pm
& 2.30-6pm Tue-Sun), chronicling local history
from the prehistoric through to the Lombard period, with some interesting Roman
frescoes and mosaics on show.

MUSEO STORICO DELLA CITTÀ
In the former Convento di San Francesco
(founded in the 13th century), this **museum**
(☎ 035 24 71 16; www.museostoricobg.org; Piazza Mercato del Fieno 6a; admission free; ☯ 9am-1pm & 2-5.30pm
Tue-Sun) recounts the city's past, with emphasis on the period 1797 to Italian unification
in the 1860s.

MUSEO DONIZETTIANO
A collection of furnishings and belongings
of Bergamo's favourite musical son, Gaetano
Donizetti (1797–1848), including his piano
and manuscripts, can be seen at the **Museo
Donizettiano** (☎ 035 39 92 69; Via Arena 9; admission free;
☯ 10am-1pm Mon-Fri, 10am-1pm & 2.30-5pm Sat & Sun).

LOOKOUTS
A stroll downhill along Via Colleoni and Via
Gombito takes you past **Torre del Gombito**, a
12th-century tower. Carry on along medieval
Bergamo's main street towards the cable-car
station and then turn left to **La Rocca** (adult/child
€1/0.50; ☯ 10.30am-4pm Sat & Sun Nov-Feb, 10am-6pm
Sat & Sun Mar, Apr & Oct, 10am-8pm Sat & Sun May-Sep),
a fortress set in a park. The views from the
park (☯ 9am-8pm Apr-Sep, 10am-6pm Oct & Mar, 10am-
4pm Nov-Feb) are worth the effort, as is a stroll
around the fortress.

For more spectacular views, trudge uphill
along Colle Aperto and bear left (following
the yellow signs) up a steep flight of stone
steps to Bergamo's **Orti Botanico Lorenzo Rota**
(☎ 035 39 94 66; Scaletta di Colle Aperto; ☯ 9am-noon &
2-5pm Mar & Oct, 9am-noon & 2-6pm Tue-Fri, 9am-7pm Sat
& Sun Apr-Sep). More than 900 species grow in
the hillside botanical garden.

PINACOTECA DELL'ACCADEMIA CARRARA
If you have the time, make sure you visit
the art gallery of **Accademia Carrara** (☎ 035 39
96 43; www.accademiacarrara.bergamo.it in Italian; Piazza Giacomo Carrara 82a; adult/child Mon-Sat €2.58/free;
☯ 9.30am-1pm & 3-6.45pm Tue-Sun Apr-Sep, 9.30am-1pm
& 2.30-5.45pm Tue-Sun Oct-Mar), reached on foot
from the upper town through **Porta di Sant'
Agostino** and down Via della Noca. Founded
in 1780, it contains an impressive range of
Italian masters. Raphael's *San Sebastiano* is

definitely one of the highlights, but other artists represented include Botticelli, Canaletto, Mantegna and Titian.

On the opposite side of the square is the **Galleria d'Arte Moderna e Contemporanea** (GAMeC; ☎ 035 39 95 28; www.gamec.it; Piazza Giacomo Carrara; admission free; ✆ 10am-1pm & 3-7pm Tue-Sat, 10am-7pm Sun), which displays the academy's small permanent collection of modern works by Italian artists such as de Chirico, de Pisis and Gentilini. Admission prices and opening hours vary for temporary exhibitions.

Activities

Club Alpino Italiano (CAI; ☎ 035 24 42 73; www.cai bergamo.it in Italian; Via Ghislanzoni 15) has information about winter sports, walking and gentle strolls in the nearby Bergamo Alps. It also runs a small library specialising in walking and outdoor activity plus other mountain-related titles. Buy anything you forgot to pack at **Goggi Sport** (Via XX Settembre 73-77).

Guided climbing expeditions up frozen waterfalls, sheer rock faces or mere mountains are run by the **Scuola Italiana di Alpinismo** (☎ 035 32 30 511; www.guidealpinebergamo.it in Italian; Via San Bernardino 145).

Sleeping

Bergamo has a reasonable stock of hotels, but they do tend to fill up quickly and advance bookings are recommended.

LOWER TOWN

Nuovo Ostello di Bergamo (☎ 035 36 17 24; www .ostellodibergamo.it; Via Galileo Ferraris 1; dm/s/d with breakfast €15/20/46; ✆ reception 7am-midnight; P 🖥) Bergamo's neat, 54-bed hostel is about 4km north of the train station. Take bus No 14 from Largo Porta Nuova or follow Viale Giulio Cesare north past the stadium and take the fourth turn on the right after crossing the large Circonvallazione Fabriciano intersection.

Hotel San Giorgio (☎ 035 21 20 43; www.san giorgioalbergo.it; Via San Giorgio 10; s/d €30/50, s/d/tr/q with bathroom €50/65/80/100) This basic two-star place, around 400m southwest of the train station, is one of the cheaper options in town and offers clean, simple rooms.

Hotel Piemontese (☎ 035 24 26 29; www.hotel piemontese.com; Piazzale G Marconi 11; s/d Mon-Thu €80/115, s/d Fri-Sun €75/100; P 🞨 🖥) Facing the train station, Hotel Piemontese is a handily located hotel with the regulation three-star

comforts and facilities. Cheaper rates are offered in January, February and August.

Hotel Cappello d'Oro (☎ 035 23 25 03; www.bw hotelcappellodoro-bg.it; Viale Papa Giovanni XXIII 12; s/d from €155/185; P 🞨 🞨) This four-star Best Western outpost is one of Bergamo's more upscale choices, with comfort and service levels that are hard to beat.

UPPER TOWN

Bergamo's most charming options – each with a superb restaurant – are on the hill.

Hotel San Lorenzo (☎ 035 23 73 83; www.hotel sanlorenzobg.it; Piazza Mascheroni 9a; s/d from €75/95; P 🞨) San Lorenzo offers quiet and comfortable rooms in a thoughtfully renovated old building overlooking Piazza Mascheroni.

Sole (☎ 035 21 82 38; fax 035 24 00 11; Via B Colleoni 1; d €75) Soulful Sole is just off Piazza Vecchia. Simple lino floors, coupled with big windows and brightly coloured bedspreads, lend rooms a country feel. There's also a garden restaurant.

Agnello d'Oro (☎ 035 24 98 83; Via Gombito 22; s/d €52/92; 🞨) With the incredible clutter of objects adorning every wall, this 17th-century spot could easily pass for an eccentric antique shop. Rooms are attractive and you can dine al fresco in summer.

Eating

The Bergamaschi are passionate about polenta and eat it as a side dish or dessert – *polenta e osei* are little cakes filled with jam and topped with yellow icing and chocolate birds. Bergamo contributed *casonsèi*, a ravioli stuffed with meat, to the Italian table and the area is noted for its fine red wines, including Valcalepio.

LOWER TOWN

Ristorante Da Vittorio (☎ 035 21 80 60; Viale Papa Giovanni XXIII 21; meals €45-95; ✆ lunch & dinner, closed Wed Sep-Dec) With its two Michelin stars, Vittorio is officially the best restaurant in town, and regarded as one of the best in Italy. The air of epicurean elegance is enhanced with a uniformed doorman, and fish, mushroom and truffle dishes feature among the house specialities.

Osteria Airoldi (☎ 035 24 44 23; Viale Papa Giovanni XXIII 18) This bright, breezy and spacious wine bar/coffeehouse is a modern break from the traditional norm. Perch on a bar stool or splay out on a low bench.

Ol Giupì e la Margì (☎ 035 24 23 66; Via Borgo Palazzo 22; mains €10-12; ☺ lunch Sun, lunch & dinner Tue-Sat Sep-Jul) Taste some true Bergamo delicacies in this authentic brick-vaulted restaurant, where waiters in traditional garb serve up dishes such as fried sausages, risotto and roast rabbit with grappa and polenta.

Domus Vini (☎ 035 21 08 67; Passagio Canonici Lateranensi, Via Torquato Tasso 70; ☺ 10am-2.30pm & 5.30pm-midnight Tue-Sat, 9.30am-2.30pm Sun) This stylish wine bar, tucked beneath arches of the cloistered Chiostro di Santo Spirito, prides itself on its foie gras, fresh meats, rare cheeses and chocolates.

UPPER TOWN

Dining is tasty but not cheap in medieval Bergamo.

Pasticceria Cavour (☎ 035 24 34 18; Via Gombito 7a; mains from €10; ☺ Thu-Tue) Plump little cherubs frescoed on the walls add to the charm of this late 19th-century tearoom where the sweet-toothed have splurged since 1850. Come Sunday, plump for brunch (€16) or a choice of fish and meat dishes from its all-day buffet.

Bar Donizetti (☎ 035 24 26 61; Via Gombito 17a; ☺ Wed-Mon) Wine, cheese and cold cuts are the prime temptations of this shop-cum-bar and lunchtime spot where you can dine al fresco in a stunning loggia overlooking the upper town's main street.

Trattoria da Ornella (☎ 035 23 27 36; Via Gombito 15; mains from €10; ☺ lunch & dinner Fri-Wed) *Polenta taragna* (polenta cooked with butter, cheese and a choice of rabbit, chicken or veal) is the house speciality at this traditional no-frills eating house.

Antica Hosteria del Vino Buono (☎ 035 24 79 93; Piazza Mercato delle Scarpe; mains €8-9; ☺ Tue-Sun) Feast on cheese-sprinkled *casoncelli* (homemade pasta cushions filled with a spicy sausage meat and laced with a buttery sage sauce) followed by a plate of *polenta del Bergami* (polenta and mushrooms) – two dishes typical to Bergamo – at this authentic inn.

Colleoni e dell'Angelo (☎ 035 23 25 96; www .colleonidellangelo.com in Italian; Piazza Vecchia 7; mains from €15; ☺ Tue-Sun) This upmarket place offers inventive local cuisine prepared by highly regarded chef Pierangelo Cornaro, including vinegar-scented pigeon breast with apple salad, veal in black truffle sauce, and lobster. The pricey six-course *Menu Gourmand* (€58) may be a bit rich for some

people, but there are more manageable pasta dishes, too.

Getting There & Away
AIR
The local airport, **Orio al Serio** (☎ 035 32 63 23; www.orioaeroporto.it), is 4km southeast of the train station. There are daily flights to/from London Luton and Stansted, Glasgow, Liverpool, Paris Beauvais and Amsterdam, among others, as well as less frequent services to Dublin, Berlin, Tallinn and other European cities with budget airlines. Flights also link up with Rome, Naples, Cagliari and Palermo.

BUS
From Bergamo's bus station on Piazzale G Marconi, **SAB** (☎ 035 24 02 40; www.sab-autoservizi .it in Italian) operates services to the lakes and mountains as well as to/from Milan's Piazza Castello (€5, every half-hour).

TRAIN
From the Piazzale Marconi train station, there are almost hourly trains to/from Milan's Stazione Centrale (€4.50, 45 minutes) and less-frequent trains to Brescia (€4, 50 minutes, four daily) and Cremona (€6, two hours, two daily).

Getting Around
TO/FROM THE AIRPORT
ATB buses (☎ 035 23 60 26) operates buses to/from Orio al Serio airport, departing every 20 minutes from Bergamo bus station. A one-way ticket costs €1.50 and journey time is 10 minutes. The airport is also served by direct buses from Milan and Brescia – see p277 for details.

PUBLIC TRANSPORT
ATB buses also serve the city. Bus No 1 connects the train station with the cable car to the upper city and Colle Aperto. From the latter, either bus No 21 or a second cable car continues uphill to San Vigilio. Bus No 3 runs from Porta di Sant'Alessandro in the upper city to Via Pietro Paleocapa in the lower city. Buy tickets, valid for 75 minutes' travel on buses and cable cars for €1 from machines at the train and cable-car stations; a 10-ticket carnet costs €7.50 and an all-day ticket allowing unlimited travel is available for €2.50. A three-day ticket costs €5.

All the major car-rental agencies can be found at Orio al Serio airport.

Avis (☎ 035 31 01 92)
Europcar (☎ 035 31 86 22)
Hertz (☎ 035 31 12 58)
Sixt (☎ 035 31 88 62)

VALTELLINA

Covering the band of Alps across Lombardy's north, the Valtellina is one of Italy's less attractive Alpine regions, although it does have some acceptable skiing and is well set up for walking.

The **Valtellina tourist board** (www.valtellinaonline.com) has tourist information points in the following towns:

Aprica (☎ 0342 74 61 13; infoaprica@provinica.so.it; Corso Roma 150)
Livigno (☎ 0342 05 22 00; www.livignoweb.com; Via de la Gesù 65)
Madesimo (☎ 0343 5 30 15; infomadesimo@provinicia .so.it; Via alle Scuole)
Sondrio (☎ 0342 51 25 00; infovaltellina@provincia .so.it; Via Trieste 12)

See Lonely Planet's *Walking in Italy* for more guidance. For information on the Alpine ski resort of Bormio, in Valtellina's far eastern realms, see the Parco Nazionale dello Stelvio on p330.

Trains leave Milan for Sondrio (€7.75, two hours, hourly), a regional transport hub from where buses connect with the resorts and towns.

BRESCIA

pop 194,700 / elev 149m

First impressions of Brescia, especially for those arriving at the scruffy train and bus stations at the seedy, rough-edged southern end of town, are not likely to be favourable. However, Brescia is the provincial capital and a major transport hub, and its student life gives the place a bit of buzz. The historic centre is more attractive, and there are also a few museums and Roman remains well worth seeing.

When the Romans took control of the Gallic town in 225 BC, Brescia already had centuries of now obscure history behind it. The Carolingians took over in the 9th century, and were followed by a millennium's worth of outside rulers. As revolutionary fervour swept Europe in 1848–49, Brescia was dubbed 'The Lioness' for its 10-day

uprising against Austria – an unsuccessful prelude to its participation in the movement towards Italian unification a decade later.

Risotto, beef dishes and *lumache alla bresciana* (snails cooked up with Parmesan cheese and fresh spinach) are common in Brescia and the region offers many good wines, including those from Botticino, Lugana and Riviera del Garda. A free booklet, *Strada dei Vini Bresciani del Garda* (in Italian) available from the tourist office, gives details on the local wine route for drivers.

Information

Brixia Web (☎ 030 375 93 31; www.brixiaweb.it in Italian; Via Antiche Mura 6a; per hr €4; 11am-8pm Mon-Fri, 11am-7.30pm Sat, 2-7pm Sun) Users need a passport to gain access.
Ospedale Civile (☎ 030 3 99 51; Piazzale Ospedale) Hospital.
Police station (☎ 030 3 74 41; Via Botticelli)
Post office (Piazza della Vittoria; 8.30am-7pm Mon-Sat)
Tourist office Corso Zanardelli 34 (☎ 030 4 34 18; www .bresciaholiday.com; 9am-12.30pm & 3-6pm Mon-Fri, 9am-12.30pm Sat) Main tourist office; Piazza della Loggia 6 (☎ 030 240 03 57; 9.30am-6.30pm Mon-Sat)

Sights

CASTLE

Brescia's historic centre is dominated by a hill, **Colle Cidneo**, crowned with a rambling **castle** which has been the core of the city defences for centuries. **Torre Mirabella**, the main round tower, was built by the Viscontis in the 13th century. The castle hosts two mildly diverting museums, the **Museo delle Armi Antiche** (☎ 030 29 32 92; adult/child €3/1; 9.30am-1pm & 2.30-5pm Tue-Sun Oct-May, 10am-5pm Tue-Sun Jun-Sep), with its extensive collection of vintage weaponry, and the **Civico Museo del Risorgimento** (☎ 030 441 76; adult/child €3/1; 9.30am-1pm & 2.30-5pm Tue-Sun Oct-May, 10am-5pm Tue-Sun Jun-Sep), dedicated to the history of Italian unification.

CATHEDRALS & PIAZZAS

The most compelling of all Brescia's religious monuments is the 11th-century **Duomo Vecchio** (Old Cathedral; Piazza Paolo VI; 10am-noon & 3-7pm Tue-Sun), a rare example of a circular-plan Romanesque basilica, built over a 6th-century church. Interesting features include fragmentary floor mosaics and the elaborate sarcophagus of Bishop Berado Maggi

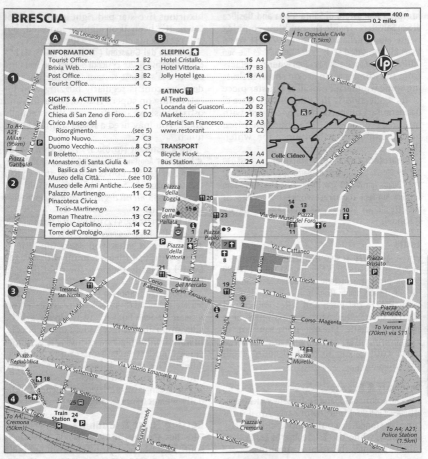

(1308). Next door, the **Duomo Nuovo** (New Cathedral; Piazza Paolo VI; ☼ 7.30am-noon & 4-7pm) dating from 1604, dwarfs its ancient neighbour but is of less interest. Also on the square is **Il Broletto**, the medieval town hall with an 11th-century tower.

Northwest of Piazza Paolo VI is the **Piazza della Loggia**, dominated by the squat 16th-century loggia in which Palladio had a hand. The **Torre dell'Orologio**, with its exquisite astrological timepiece, is modelled on the one in Venice's Piazza San Marco.

Finally, the Fascist-era **Piazza della Vittoria** is worth a look. Laid out in 1932 by Piacentini, the square and its buildings (like the post office) are a perfect example of the period's rather severe monumentalism.

ROMAN RUINS & MUSEUMS

Significant evidence of the Roman presence in Brescia remains. Along Via dei Musei are the now partly restored and impressive remains of the **Tempio Capitolino** (admission free, ☼ 10am-4pm), a Roman temple built by the Emperor Vespasian in AD 73. The **Palazzo Martinengo** (☎ 030 280 79 34; Via dei Musei 28; ☼ 9.30am-7.30pm Tue-Sun), opposite the small 18th-century **Chiesa di San Zeno di Foro** (Piazza del Foro), is the majestic host to temporary art exhibitions. Admission fees vary.

About 50m east of the Tempio Capitolino along Via dei Musei, cobbled Vicolo del Fontanon leads to the well-preserved ruins of a **Roman theatre**. Continuing east you'll reach Brescia's most intriguing sight – the jumbled **Monastero di Santa Giulia and Basilica di San Salvatore**. Inside the rambling complex is the **Museo della Città** (☎ 030 297 78 34; Via dei Musei 81b; adult/child €8/4; ⏰ 9.30am-5.30pm Tue-Sun Oct-May, 10am-6pm Tue-Sun Jun-Sep) where artefacts from the Roman town are on show, including some wonderful mosaics. The star piece of the collection is the 8th-century **Croce di Desiderio**, a Lombard cross encrusted with hundreds of jewels. The museum often hosts temporary exhibitions, for which there is a separate charge.

Pinacoteca Civica Tosio-Martinengo (☎ 030 377 49 99; Via Martinengo da Barco 1; adult/child €3/1; ⏰ 9.30am-1pm & 2.30-5pm Tue-Sun Oct-May, 10am-5pm Tue-Sun Jun-Sep) features works by artists of the Brescian school, as well as works by Raphael.

Tours

For a quick spin around Brescia's historic heart, jump aboard the **tourist tram** (☎ 030 377 52 07; www.centoterre.it in Italian; adult/student €6/5; ⏰ departs hourly 10am-4pm), which departs from Piazza del Foro and takes you round all the main sites, with a possibility of a stop at the castle. The one-hour tour comes with commentary (in Italian), and the tram ticket entitles you to a €2 discount at all city museums.

Festivals & Events

The **International Piano Festival** (www.festivalmic helangeli.it in Italian) held from early April until June, is staged in conjunction with nearby Bergamo, while the **Estate Aperta** festival of music occupies the summer months.

Sleeping & Eating

Hotel Cristallo (☎ 030 377 24 68; info@hotelcristallobr escia.com; Viale della Stazione 12a; s/d €55/80) Convenient for the bus and train stations, Cristallo is a slightly dowdy but reasonable three-star choice with friendly staff. Reception is on the 1st floor.

Jolly Hotel Igea (☎ 030 442 21; www.jollyhotels .it; Viale della Stazione 15; s/d Mon-Fri €116/152, Sat & Sun €80/115; 🖳 🅿) Just a stone's throw from the train station, this modern branch of the nationwide chain offers spotless, tastefully furnished rooms with all the mod cons you would wish for.

Hotel Vittoria (☎ 030 28 00 61; www.hotelvitt oria.com; Via X Giornate 20; s/d/ste €166/217/274; 🖳) Brescia's top place to lay your head is this luxurious five-star pad right in the heart of town. It's been thoroughly renovated, but still retains much of its 1930s elegance.

Locanda dei Guasconi (☎ 030 377 16 05; Via Beccaria 11; mains €10-20; ⏰ lunch & dinner Tue-Sun) One of Brescia's finest restaurants, the Locanda dei Guasconi is regularly buzzing with locals dining on superb risotto, pasta, fish and ostrich dishes, and the wine list is equally good. You may need a reservation, even for lunch.

www.restorant (☎ 030 375 22 54; www.restorant .it; Vicolo Sant' Agostino 3b; mains €10-13; ⏰ noon-1.30pm & 8pm-2am Mon-Sat) Looks count at this stylish fish restaurant. Seafood-lovers should not miss the €33 *menù degustazione di pesce* (fish taster menu).

Al Teatro (☎ 030 44 251; Via Mazzini 36; pizzas €5-8; ⏰ lunch Tue, lunch & dinner Wed-Sat) If a big pizza and a beer is what you seek, this bright, unpretentious little restaurant with a vague Laurel & Hardy theme is the right place to head for.

Osteria San Francesco (☎ 030 29 04 75; Tresanda San Nicola 13; mains €8-10, set dinner menu €20; ⏰ lunch & dinner Tue-Sun) Tucked away down a little alley opposite the tiny Chiesa di San Nicola, this authentic place serves hearty regional cuisine and attracts a discerning local clientele. The meaty three-course set meals, with wine, are good value.

For fresh fruit and veggies head for the daily **market** (Piazza del Mercato).

Getting There & Around

The **bus station** (☎ 030 44 915; Via Solferino) is southwest of the city centre. From here **SAIA Trasporti** (☎ 030 230 88 11; www.saiatrasporti.it in Italian) buses serve Verona (€7, two hours, 10 to 14 daily) via Desenzano del Garda (€3, 50 minutes) and Sirmione (€3.60, one hour), and Cremona (€4, 1¼ hours, hourly).

The train station is around a 10-minute walk from the city centre along Corso dei Martiri della Libertà and Viale della Stazione. There are regular trains to and from Milan (€7.40, 50 minutes), Cremona (€3.95, one hour), Bergamo (€3.75, 30 minutes) and Venice (€10, 2¼ hours).

From June to September, you can pick up a free bicycle from the **bicycle kiosk** (⏰ 7.30am-8.30pm) in front of the train station on Piazzale Stazione. The tourist office has a list of other pick-up and drop-off points around town.

CREMONA

pop 71,420 / elev 45m

Home of the Stradivari violin, Cremona jealously maintains its centuries-old status as premier exponent of the delicate art of making the perfect stringed instrument. All of the great violin-making dynasties started here – Amati, Guarneri and Stradivari – and there are plenty of opportunities to get acquainted with the art of violin making. A wealthy, independent city-state for centuries, Cremona also boasts some fine architecture, including a magnificent cathedral. Antique stalls line Piazza della Pace and the courtyard of the Palazzo Comunale on Sundays.

Information

Banca Popolare di Cremona (Piazza del Comune) 24-hour banknote-exchange machine and ATM.
Hospital (☎ 0372 40 51 11; Largo Priori)
Police station (☎ 0372 40 74 27; Via Tribunali 6)
Post office (Via Verdi 1; ⏰ 8.30am-5.30pm Mon-Fri, 8.30am-noon Sat)
Tourist office (☎ 0372 232 33; Piazza del Comune 5; ⏰ 9am-12.30pm & 3-6pm Mon-Sat, 9am-12.30pm Sun Jul & Aug)

Sights

PIAZZA DEL COMUNE

Medieval Cremona, like most Lombard towns, was an independent *comune* until the 14th century, when the Viscontis of Milan added it to their growing collection. To maintain the difference between the secular and spiritual, buildings connected with the Church were erected on the eastern side of the square, and those concerned with secular affairs were constructed across the way.

The **cathedral** started out as a Romanesque basilica but, by the time it was finished in 1190, it was heavily overtaken by Gothic modishness (best demonstrated by its Latin cross-shaped ground plan). The cathedral's façade is largely faithful to the original concept. Inside there are paintings by Renaissance masters Boccaccio Boccaccino, Giulio Campi and Gian Francesco Bembo, although perhaps most interesting are the partial frescoes uncovered in the early 1990s, including a vast scene of the Crucifixion above the central doorway.

The cathedral's most prized possession is the 'Holy Thorn' relic, allegedly from the

LOMBARDY & THE LAKES

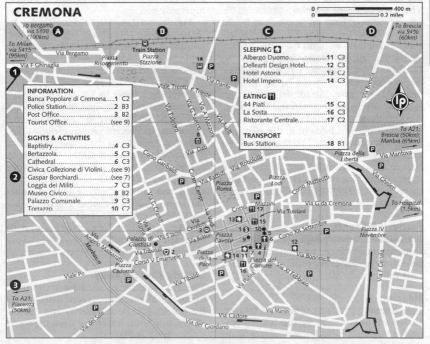

INFORMATION
Banca Popolare di Cremona.....1 C2
Police Station........................2 B3
Post Office...........................3 B2
Tourist Office....................(see 9)

SIGHTS & ACTIVITIES
Baptistry.............................4 C3
Bertazzola...........................5 C3
Cathedral.............................6 C3
Civica Collezione di Violini.....(see 9)
Gaspar Borchiardi................(see 7)
Loggia dei Militi...................7 C3
Museo Civico.......................8 B2
Palazzo Comunale..................9 C3
Torrazzo............................10 C2

SLEEPING
Albergo Duomo......................11 C3
Dellearti Design Hotel...........12 C3
Hotel Astoria......................13 C2
Hotel Impero.......................14 C3

EATING
44 Piati............................15 C2
La Sosta...........................16 C3
Ristorante Centrale...............17 C2

TRANSPORT
Bus Station........................18 B1

Crown of Thorns worn by Jesus Christ, and donated to the church by local boy Pope Gregory XIV in 1591. It's kept behind bars in the Capella delle Reliquie. In the crypt, meanwhile, the robed and masked body of Cremona's 12th-century patron saint, San Omobono Tucenghi, is on show in a glass casket.

The adjoining 111m-tall **torrazzo** (bell tower; adult/child €4/3, incl baptistry €5/4; ☺ 10am-1pm Tue-Fri, 10am-1pm & 2.30-6pm Sat & Sun), with its great zodiacal clock, is connected to the cathedral by a Renaissance loggia, the **Bertazzola**. On the other side of the cathedral is the 12th-century **baptistry** (adult/child €2/1, incl Torrazzo €5/4; ☺ 10am-1pm & 2.30-6pm Tue-Sun), which houses some architectural fragments including a 12th-century figure of the Archangel Gabriel that once perched on the roof of the baptistry.

Across the square is **Palazzo Comunale** and, to its south, the smaller porticoed **Loggia dei Militi**; both date to the 13th century. The former was, and remains, the town hall; the latter housed the town's militia.

MUSEUMS & VIOLINS
The **Civica Collezione di Violini** (☎ 0372 205 02; Palazzo Communale, Piazza del Comune 5; adult/child €6/3.50, incl Museo Civico €10/5; ☺ 9am-6pm Tue-Sat, 10am-6pm Sun) features items from the Stradivari workshop. The **Museo Civico** (☎ 0372 312 22; Via Ugolani Dati 4; adult/child €7/4, incl Civica Collezione di Violini €10/5; ☺ 9am-6pm Tue-Sat, 10am-6pm Sun) holds yet more Stradivari violins, as well as instruments by Amati and Guarneri. Also on show is a varied collection of art, and archaeological finds from the vicinity.

Gaspar Borchiardi (☎ 0372 3 19 69; Loggia dei Militi, Piazza San Antonio) is one of several violin- and bow-making workshops sprinkled in the streets around the Piazza del Comune. Cremona has some 90-odd in all; the tourist office has a list.

Festivals & Events
Triennale Internazionale degli Strumenti ad Arco (International Stringed Instrument Expo) is held in Cremona every third October; the next will be in 2006.

Sleeping
Albergo Duomo (☎ 0372 352 42; fax 0372 45 83 92; Via Gonfalonieri 13; s/d €45/65; ✗ Ⓟ) Just a few steps from Cremona's cathedral and ablaze with

wrought-iron flower boxes in spring, Albergo Duomo is a pleasant place, with cosy modern rooms. It also runs its own pizzeria.

Hotel Astoria (☎ 0372 46 16 16; fax 0372 46 18 10; Via Bordigallo 19; s/d €45/70; ✗ Ⓟ) Down a small lane near Piazza Cavour, rooms brandish three-star mod cons.

Hotel Impero (☎ 0372 41 30 13; www.hotelimpero .cr.it; Piazza della Pace 21; s/d from €61/110; ✗ ▢ Ⓟ) The four-star Impero, located on a pretty piazza in the centre of town, comes with large rooms and the standard corporate comforts.

Dellearti Design Hotel (☎ 0372 231 31; www .dellearti.com; Via Bonomelli 8; s/d/ste from €95/135/155; ✗ Ⓟ) The achingly arty Dellearti is Cremona's trendiest hotel, with rotating displays of contemporary paintings and photographs scattered around. There's a Turkish bath and a gym, and of course, the rooms are suitably chic and restful.

Eating
Cremona's gifts to Italian cuisine include *bollito* (boiled meats) and *cotechino* (boiled pork sausage) both with polenta. *Mostarda*, often served with *bollito*, is fruit in a sweet mustardy goo.

44 Piati (☎ 0372 46 18 67; Via Torriani 11; mains €4-5; ☺ lunch & dinner) This cheery self-service restaurant in the heart of town offers excellent value, with a changing menu of cafeteria standards and cheap drinks and desserts.

La Sosta (☎ 0372 45 66 56; Via Sicardo 9; mains €10; ☺ lunch & dinner Tue-Sat, lunch Sun Sep-Jun) Surrounded by violin-makers' workshops, this is a beautiful place to feast on regional delicacies. Its *gnocchi vecchia cremona* (old Cremona gnocchi) is the house speciality.

Ristorante Centrale (☎ 0372 2 87 01; Vicolo Pertusio 4; mains €8-10; ☺ lunch & dinner Fri-Wed) Centrale is a popular spot, oozing history and charm, where you can try a variety of local dishes and some fresh local cheese. The restaurant does not accept credit cards.

Open-air market stalls on the Piazza della Pace sell fresh fruit and vegetables every morning.

Getting There & Away
The city can be reached by train from Milan (€5.25, one hour, several daily), Mantua (€4.40, one hour, hourly) and Brescia (€3.95, one hour, hourly) or from the south by changing at Piacenza.

MANTUA

pop 47,970

On the shores of Lago Superiore, Lago di Mezzo and Lago Inferiore (a glorified widening of the River Mincio) is Mantua (Mantova), a serene and beautiful city. Part of its waters are protected by the Parco del Mincio but industrial sprawl from a booming petrochemical industry has scarred the surrounding countryside.

Mantua was settled by the Etruscans in the 10th century BC and prospered under Roman rule. The most famous of the Latin poets, Virgil, was born just outside the modern town in 70 BC. The city fell into the hands of the Gonzaga dynasty in 1328, under whose rule it flourished, attracting the likes of Andrea Mantegna, Petrarch, Antonio Pisanello and Rubens. The Scottish scholar, swordsman and playboy James Crichton – better known as the 'Admirable Crichton' – was drawn to the opulent Gonzaga court, only to be killed in a duel at the age of just 22 in 1582, while Shakespeare's Romeo found his fateful poison in a Mantuan apothecary. The golden days of 'La Gloriosa' came to an abrupt end when Austria took control in 1708. Habsburg troops were in control (aside from the Napoleonic interlude at the end of the 18th century) until 1866, when Mantua finally rejoined Italy.

Over a million pigs a year are reared in the province of Mantua. Try *salumi* (salt pork), pancetta (salt-cured bacon), *prosciutto crudo* (salt-cured ham) and risotto with the locally grown *vialone nano* rice. Pasta-wise, *tortelli di zucca* (pumpkin-stuffed cushions of square pasta) is *the* dish, while *risotto alla pilota* (risotto with minced pork) and *luccio* (pike) are also very popular. The sweet-toothed will enjoy *torta sbrisolona* (a hard, biscuit-like cake with almonds). Wines such as red Rubino dei Morenici Mantovani from the hills around Lago di Garda are highly palatable.

Information

Banks, with ATMs, are scattered throughout the city centre.

Bit & Phone (☎ 0376 22 05 94; Via S Bettinelli 21; per hr €4; ☻ 10am-10pm Thu-Tue) Internet access.

Hospital (☎ 0376 20 14 34; Via Albertoni)

Police station (☎ 0376 20 51; Piazza Sordello 46)

Post office (Piazza Martiri di Belfiore; ☻ 8.30am-7pm Mon-Sat) Also has currency exchange and an ATM inside.

Tourist office (☎ 0376 32 82 53; www.aptmantova.it in Italian; Piazza Mantegna 6; ☻ 8.30am-12.30pm & 3-6pm Mon-Sat, 9.30am-12.30pm Sun)

Sights

PALAZZO DUCALE

Also known as the Reggia dei Gonzaga after the long-time rulers of Mantua, the **Palazzo Ducale** (☎ 0376 35 21 00; www.mantovaducale.it; Piazza Sordello 40; adult/EU-citizen child €6.50/free; ☻ 8.45am-7.15pm Tue-Sun) occupies a great chunk of the city's northeastern corner. Its walls hide three squares, fifteen courtyards, a park and 500-odd rooms. The centrepiece is **Castello di San Giorgio**, overflowing with artworks collected by the Gonzaga family. The highpoint is Andrea Mantegna's **Camera degli Sposi**, a wonderful series of frescoes executed by the master between 1465 and 1474 in one of the castle's towers. The trompe l'oeil oculus adds a playful touch to the more formal family scenes. Among the many other rooms worth pausing over are the **Sala del Pisanello**, decorated with unfinished 15th-century frescoes of Arthurian legends by the eponymous Pisanello, the heavily frescoed **Sala di Troia** and the **Camera dello Zodiaco**, with its magnificent deep-blue ceiling festooned with figures from the Zodiac. Equally bizarre is the 18th-century **Sala del Fiumi**, a Habsburg-era folly with artificial grottoes covered in shells and mosaic.

CHURCHES

The baroque cupola of **Basilica di Sant' Andrea** looms above the city. Designed by Leon Battista Alberti in 1472, Mantua's principal house of worship safeguards a much-disputed relic; golden vessels said to hold earth soaked by the blood of Christ. Longinus, the Roman soldier who speared Christ on the cross is said to have scooped up the earth and buried it in Mantua after leaving Palestine. Today, these containers rest beneath a marble octagon in front of the altar, and are paraded around the town in a grand procession on Good Friday. There is no dispute, though, about the tomb of the painter Andrea Mantegna, also to be found inside the basilica.

South of the basilica, across 15th-century colonnaded Piazza delle Erbe, is the 11th-century Romanesque **Rotonda di San Lorenzo** (Piazza delle Erbe; admission free; ☻ 10am-1pm & 3-6pm Mon-Fri, 10am-6pm Sat & Sun), sunk below the level

MANTUA

INFORMATION

Bit & Phone............................	**1** B3
Police Station........................	**2** E3
Post Office............................	**3** D4
Tourist Office........................	**4** D3

SIGHTS & ACTIVITIES

Basilica di Sant'Andrea............	**5** D3
Casa di Rigoletto...................	**6** E2
Castello di San Giorgio............	**7** F2
Cathedral.............................	**8** E2
Imbarco Motonavi Andes............	**9** F2
Motonavi Andes......................	**10** E2
Museo Archeologico.................	**11** E2
Museo Tazio Nuvolari e	
Learco Guerra......................	**12** E3
Palazzo Broletto....................	**13** D3
Palazzo della Ragione..............	**14** D3
Palazzo Ducale......................	**15** E2
Rotonda di San Lorenzo............	**16** D3
Torre della Gabbia.................	**17** E3

SLEEPING

Albergo Bianchi Stazione..........	**18** B3
Hotel ABC Superior.................	**19** B3
Hotel Due Guerrieri................	**20** E2
Rechigi Hotel.......................	**21** D4

EATING

Caffè Borsa..........................	**22** C4
Caravatti............................	**23** E3
Clos Wine Bar.......................	**24** D3
Freddi Agnoli.......................	**25** C4
La Ducale...........................	**26** D3
Locanda dell'Orologio..............	**27** D3
Ristorante Masseria................	**28** D3
Vecchia Milano.....................	**29** E2

TRANSPORT

Bus Station..........................	**30** A4

Lago di Mezzo

Lago Superiore

Lago Inferiore

To Verona (40km);
Brescia (65km)

To San Benedetto Po &
(21km);to-Parma (60km)

To San Benedetto Po
(60km)

Boats to San
Benedetto Po &
Venice

To Palazzo
Te (300m)

To S Bonfanti (200m)

To Hospital
(200m)

To Santuario di
Santa Maria delle
Grazie (8km);
Sabbioneta
(35km);
Cremona (65km)

of the square and believed to stand on the site of a Roman temple dedicated to Venus. In the **Palazzo della Ragione**, which runs the length of the square from the Rotonda and was once the seat of secular power in the city, you can see exhibitions of varying interest (usually free).

The **cathedral** (Piazza Sordello 16) pales before the magnificence of the basilica. The façade was erected in the mid-18th century, while the decoration inside was completed by Giulio Romano after a fire in 1545.

On Lago Superiore, 8km from Mantua in Grazie di Curtatone, is the Lombard Gothic–style **Santuario di Santa Maria delle Grazie** (☎ 037 63 10 02; Grazie di Curtatone), built in 1406 in thanks for the end of the Black Death. Inside are 53 life-size papier-mâché statues.

PIAZZE

Past the 13th-century Palazzo della Ragione is **Palazzo Broletto**, which dominates neighbouring Piazza Broletto. In a niche on the façade is a seated figure wearing a doctor's cap, which is said to represent Virgil. Carved in the 13th century, it became known as **Vecia Mantua**, the city's symbol.

Speed fans might enjoy the **Museo Tazio Nuvolari e Learco Guerra** (☎ 0376 32 79 29; Piazza Broletto 9; adult/child €3/2; ☯ 10am-1pm & 3.30-6.30pm Fri-Wed Apr-Oct, 10am-1pm & 3.30-6.30pm Sat & Sun Nov, Dec & Mar), dedicated to local cycling and motor-racing stars of the early 20th century.

Enter Piazza Sordello from the south and on your left you have the grand house of the Gonzagas' predecessors, the Bonacolsi clan. Hapless prisoners used to be dangled in a cage from the tower, aptly called the **Torre della Gabbia** (Cage Tower). Behind the cathedral lies **Casa di Rigoletto** (☎ 0376 44 94 62; Piazza Sordello; admission free; ☯ 10am-12.30pm & 3-6pm), which Verdi used as a model set for most of his operas.

Opposite, inside what was once a market, is the one-roomed **Museo Archeologico** (☎ 0376 32 92 23; Piazza Castello 5; admission free; ☯ 8.30am-6.30pm Tue-Sat, 8.30am-1.30pm Sun). Prehistoric and Roman artefacts from the region are on display, though there's little information in anything but Italian.

PALAZZO TE

Mantua's other Gonzaga palace, **Palazzo Te** (☎ 0376 32 32 66; Viale Te; adult/child €10/7; ☯ 1-6.30pm Mon, 9am-6.30pm Tue-Fri, 9am-8pm Sat & Sun),

at the southern edge of the centre, is a grand 16th-century villa built by Giulio Romano. It has many splendid rooms, including the **Camera dei Giganti**, one of the most fantastic and frightening creations of the Renaissance, adorned with dramatic frescoes depicting Jupiter's destruction of the Titans. It also houses a modern art collection and an Egyptian museum.

Activities

Motonavi Andes (☎ 0376 32 28 75; www.motonaviandes .it in Italian; Via San Giorgio 2) organises 1¼-hour boat tours of the lakes (adult/child €10/8), five-hour excursions to San Benedetto Po (adult/child €18/15) and day trips to Venice (adult/child €68/57). Boats arrive/depart from the **Imbarco Motonavi Andes**, behind Castello di San Giorgio on Lago di Mezzo's shore.

The tourist office stocks an excellent booklet in English detailing cycling itineraries along the Po River, in the **Parco del Mincio** (☎ 0376 36 26 57; Via Marangoni 36) and around the lakes. One route takes cyclists around Lago Superiore to the Santuario di Santa Maria delle Grazie (left). In town, **S Bonfanti** (☎ 0376 22 09 09; Viale Piave 22b; ☯ 8.30am-12.30pm & 2.30-7.30pm Mon-Sat) rents bicycles.

For an informative stroll visit the **Parco dell Scienza** (☎ 0376 33 83 37; Viale Mincio), a riverside promenade stretching along the shore of Lago di Mezzo, from Porta San Giorgio to Porta Molina. Information panels and various gadgets along the way illustrate various physical and scientific phenomena in a kid-friendly fashion.

THE CHASTE & ROYAL POET

Dryden called Virgil 'the chastest and royalest of poets'. Born 70 years before Christ on his parents' farm just outside Mantua, Virgil, the city's favourite son, was one of ancient Rome's greatest poets. Of the three works he left behind, *The Aeneid* is the most exalted. An epic in the great tradition of the ancient Sumerian myth *Gilgamesh*, and Homer's *Iliad* and *Odyssey*, the tale is a fantastic account of the foundation of Rome, loaded with symbolism and told with unsurpassed virtuosity. The inspiration of countless poets since, Virgil comes to life as Dante's 'sweet master' in the *Divine Comedy*, 14 centuries after Virgil's death.

Festivals & Events

For five days each September, central Mantua is taken over by the **Festivaletteratura** (Literature Festival), with readings, author discussions and open-air bookstalls.

Sleeping

Hotel ABC Superior (☎ 0376 32 33 47; Piazza Don Leoni 25; s/d from €45/65; ✗ P) Right opposite the train station, this hotel is a reasonable, and very convenient option. The grubby stairways are a bit off-putting but rooms are perfectly clean and comfortable.

Albergo Bianchi Stazione (☎ 0376 32 64 65; www.albergobianchi.com; Piazza Don Leoni 24; s/d from €60/80; ✗ P) Next door to the ABC, the Bianchi is another three-star place which offers a similar, if perhaps slightly smarter, setup. Some rooms look out onto a private garden at the back.

Hotel Due Guerrieri (☎ 0376 32 15 33; Piazza Sordello 52; d €110; P ✗) The gleam might well have rubbed off this ageing hotel's three stars a while back but its impressive location at the feet of Torre del Gabbia makes it a worthy midrange option.

Rechigi Hotel (☎ 0376 32 07 81; www.rechigi.com; Via Pier Fortunato Calvi 30; s/d €114/202; P ✗ 🖳) A stark marble interior provides the stunning backdrop for the Le Corbusier designer chairs and contemporary art displayed at this fabulous four-star, art hotel.

Eating

Open-air cafés abound on Piazze Sordello, Broletto and Erbe.

Ristorante Masseria (☎ 0376 36 53 03; Piazza Broletto 7; mains €8-12; ✗ lunch & dinner Sat-Tue & Thu, dinner Fri) With its great central location, friendly service and excellent local cuisine, Masseria is one of Mantua's best restaurants. The pumpkin ravioli is particularly good, as is the wine. The building dates from the 13th century, and an added bonus for diners is the early 15th-century fresco of medieval Mantua, the oldest depiction of the city in existence. It was only rediscovered during renovations in 1981.

Locanda dell'Orologio (☎ 0376 36 97 57; Piazza delle Erbe 15; mains from €12; ✗ lunch & dinner) One of a group of places to eat al fresco on this square, Locanda is known for its designer décor and refreshing use of vegetables.

Vecchia Milano (☎ 0376 32 97 20; Piazza Sordello 26; mains €9-10; ✗ Thu-Tue) Dine on Mantua's

favourites at this old-world *osteria* (simple trattoria-style restaurant), including the famous *tortelli di zucca* (pumpkin-filled pasta cushions).

Clos Wine Bar (☎ 0376 36 99 72; www.closwinebar.it; Corte del Sogliari 3; mains €9; ✗ 10am-10pm Tue-Sun) This innovative wine bar-cum-eating space is Mantua's most contemporary choice. Heave open the giant glass door to discover a minimalist interior with a high ceiling.

Caffè Borsa (☎ 0376 32 60 16; Corsa della Libertà 6; ✗ 7am-midnight Mon-Thu, 7-2am Fri-Sun) For a contemporary choice away from the tourist zone, try Borsa, with its contrasting Kartell- and Liberty-style chairs and resident DJ who spins discs at the weekend.

Buy a *torta sbrisolona* and other sweet Mantuan specialities from **Caravatti** (Piazza delle Erbe 18) or **La Ducale** (Via Pier Fortunato Calvi 25), both dating from 1865.

Shopping

Markets stalls selling everything from fruit, flowers, pots, pans and clothes to useless clutter fill Piazze Sordello, Broletto and Erbe and their surrounding streets on Thursday morning.

Getting There & Around

From the **bus station** (Piazzale A Mondadori), **APAM** (☎ 0376 32 72 37) operates buses to/from Sabbioneta (see opposite) and San Benedetto Po (see opposite). Azienda Provinciale Trasporti Verona (ARV) buses head to Peschiera del Garda on Lago di Garda (see p303).

From the **train station** (Piazza Don Leoni), there are direct trains to/from Cremona, Milan and Verona.

AROUND MANTUA
Sabbioneta

Some 30km southwest of Mantua, the surreal town of Sabbioneta was created in the 16th century by Vespasiano Gonzaga Colonna in a failed attempt to build Utopia. The idea was to create a city that was *misura d'uomo* or 'made to man's measure'.

Within the heavily restored star-shaped walls are four 16th-century monuments to visit. Sabbioneta's **ticket office** (☎ 0375 22 10 44; www.comune.sabbioneta.mn.it in Italian; Piazza d'Armi 1; ✗ 10am-1pm & 2-5.30pm), inside Palazzo Giardino, sells tickets covering admission to all four monuments (adult/child €8/3.50) and doles out maps and general information on the town. Tickets for individual sites all cost €3.

Of these, the **Teatro all'Antica** (Antique Theatre; ☽ 10am-1pm & 2.30-6pm Tue-Fri, 10am-1pm & 2-7pm Sat Apr-Sep; 10am-1pm & 2.30-5.30pm Tue-Fri, 10am-1pm & 2.30-6pm Sat & Sun Oct-Mar), constructed in the years 1588 to 1590, with statues of Olympic gods topping a loggia held up by Corinthian pillars, and the 90m-long **Galleria degli Antichi** (Gallery of the Ancients), constructed in the years 1583 to 1584, with its frescoed walls and painted wood ceiling, are the most interesting. The duke of Sabbioneta resided in **Palazzo Giardino** (Garden Palace), built from 1578 to 1588 and ruled the dukedom from the 1554 **Palazzo Ducale** (Ducal Palace). The *galleria* and the palazzi all have the same opening hours as the Teatro all'Antica.

The **tourist office** (☎ 0375 5 20 39; www.sabbioneta.org in Italian; Via Vespasiano Gonzaga 27; ☽ 10am-12.30pm & 2.30-5.30pm) has information on other Sabbioneta sights, including a 19th-century **synagogue** (Via Bernardino Campi 1; adult/child €2.30/1; ☽ 10am-12.30pm & 2.30-5.30pm Sat & Sun) and the **Museo A Passo d'Uomo** (☎ 0375 22 02 99; adult/child €3/1; ☽ 3.30-6.30pm Wed & Thu, 9.30am-12.30pm Fri, 10.30am-12.30pm & 2.30-7.30pm Sat & Sun), which includes a treasury, with a Golden Fleece medallion found in the tomb of Vespasiano Gonzaga.

APAM (☎ 0376 23 03 46) buses link Sabbioneta with Mantua (€5.50, 50 minutes, up to five daily).

San Benedetto Po

This Benedictine **abbey** (☎ 0376 62 00 25; Piazza Matteotti; ☽ church 7.30am-12.30pm & 3-7pm, cloisters 8am-7pm) in this small Po valley town, 21km southeast of Mantua, was founded in 1007. Little remains of the original buildings, although the Chiesa di Santa Maria still sports a 12th-century mosaic. The star attraction is the Correggio fresco, which was discovered in the refectory in 1984.

There are buses to the town from Mantua (€2.50, 35 minutes, around 10 daily).

THE LAKES

Where the Lombard plains rise into the Alps, northern Italy is strung with a necklace of blue lakes, which have been a longtime playground for the Milanese rich and tourists from all over northern Europe.

LAGO MAGGIORE

A captivating lake, Maggiore (also known as Lago Verbano) is stunning in parts, although its shores are flatter and less spectacular than its pre-Alpine counterparts. Fed principally by the Rivers Ticino and Tresa, this lovely lake is about 65km long and lures crowds in July and August. Stresa is the main lakeside town.

Getting There & Around

Buses leave from the waterfront at Stresa for destinations around the lake and elsewhere, including Milan, Novara and Lago d'Orta. The daily Verbania Intra-Milan bus service operated by **SAF** (☎ 0323 40 15 26; www.safduemila.com in Italian) links Stresa with Arona (€1.75, 20 minutes), Verbania Pallanza (€1.75, 20 minutes), Verbania Intra (€1.75, 25 minutes) and Milan (€5.60, 1½ hours).

Stresa – the main town on the lake – sits on the Domodossola–Milan train line and is well served by hourly trains from both Milan (€6.95, one hour) and Domodossola (€2.65, 30 minutes).

Ferries and hydrofoils around the lake are operated by **Navigazione Lago Maggiore** (☎ 0323 303 93, 800 55 18 01; www.navigazionelaghi.it in Italian), which has its main ticket office and landing stage next to the Stresa **tourist office** (Piazza Marconi 14-16). Boats connect Stresa with Arona (adult/child return €8/4, 40 minutes), Angera (€8/4, 35 minutes), Baveno (€5/2.60, 20 minutes) and Pallanza (€7/3.60, 35 minutes). Various one-day passes are also available – a ticket covering Isola dei Pescatori, Isola Bella and Isola Madre costs €9/5 per adult/child, and a ticket covering Isola dei Pescatori plus the Villa Taranto is €10/5 per adult/child. More expensive one-day passes include admission to the various villas, too. Services are reduced in autumn and winter.

The only car ferry connecting the western and eastern shores for motorists sails between Verbania Intra (the Swiss end of Verbania) and Laveno. Ferries run every 20 minutes; and one-way transport costs €4 for a small car and driver or €2.90 for a bicycle and cyclist.

A good trip is the circular excursion from Stresa to Domodossola by train, from where you get a charming little train to Locarno (in Switzerland – remember to take your passports) and a ferry back from Locarno to Stresa. The 'Lago Maggiore Express' package deal costs €27/13.50 per adult/child; get your tickets from Navigazione Lago Maggiore.

Stresa
pop 4885 / elev 205m

On the lake's western shore, and officially in the province of Piedmont, Stresa has long been popular with a moneyed British and German crowd, and has been likened to an English tearoom – pretty, prim and proper but also a little staid. Out of season it's dead, and hotels tend to shut up over winter. It's commonly marketed as a base for visiting the Borromean Islands (see right), although they can easily be reached from other resorts around the lake too.

Hemingway was one of many writers to seek inspiration on Maggiore's shores. He first set foot in Stresa in 1918 to convalesce from a war wound, and part of one of his novels, *A Farewell to Arms*, is set here.

INFORMATION
Banks and ATMs abound on Corso Italia, the road running along Stresa's waterfront.

Post office (Via Anna Bolongaro 44; 8.30am-7pm Mon-Fri, 8.30am-1pm Sat)

Tourist office (0323 313 08; proloco.stresa@libero.it; Piazza Marconi 16; 10am-12.30pm & 3-6.30pm Mar-Oct, 10am-12.30pm & 3-6.30pm Mon-Fri, 10am-12.30pm Sat Nov-Feb)

SIGHTS & ACTIVITIES
Apart from visiting the Borromean Islands (right), activities include riding the **Funivia Stresa-Mottarone** (0323 302 95; Piazzale della Funivia; adult return Alpino/Mottarone €6.50/11.50; departs every 40min 9.20am-5pm) to the top of 1491m-high Monte Mottarone. The cable car takes 40 minutes to reach the top. At the Alpino mid-station (803m), 700 Alpine species flourish in the **Giardino Botanico Alpinia** (0323 302 95; adult/child €1.50/1.20; 9.30am-6pm Tue-Sun Apr–mid-Oct), a botanical garden dating from 1934.

The mountain itself offers good **biking** trails as well as **walking** opportunities. **Mountain bikes** (0323 303 99; www.bicico.it) can be rented from the lower Stresa cable-car station. Rates include a helmet and road book detailing a 25km panoramic descent (two to three hours) from the top of Mottarone back to Stresa. A one-way trip with a bike on the cable car to Alpino/Mottarone costs €5.50/9.

Walkers should ask at the cable-car station for a copy of *Trekking on the Slopes of*

Mont Mottarone, a free brochure compiled by the Club Alpino Italiano (CAI), which outlines a two-hour walk from Stresa to the Giardino Botanico Alpinia and a four-hour walk to the top of Mottarone. Walks further afield are mapped out in the free multilingual *Nature Hikes* brochure, available at tourist offices.

Most winters, skiers and snowboarders can cruise down the gentle slopes of Mottarone from late December to early March. **Skiing** is limited to five green and two blue slopes. Gear can be hired from the station at the top of Mottarone. A one-day ski pass costs €16.

Parco Zoologico di Villa Pallavicino (0323 324 07; adult/child €6.70/4.70; 9am-6pm Mar-Nov), at the southern end of Stresa, is a kid-friendly park where the exotic birds and animals can roam relatively freely.

SLEEPING & EATING
There are 40 camping grounds up and down the lake's western shore; the tourist office has a list.

Hotel Luina (0323 302 85; luinastresa@yahoo.it; Via Garibaldi 21; s/d from €31/49) In the heart of Stresa's cobbled streets, Luina is a simple but friendly place with quiet rooms and a restaurant. Some have a lake view.

Hotel Elena (0323 310 43; www.hotelelena.com; Piazza Cadorna; s/d from €57/68) Adjoining a café, old-fashioned Hotel Elena is slap-bang on Stresa's pedestrian central square. Rooms are small but well kept and each has a balcony overlooking the square.

Grand Hotel des Iles Borromees (0323 93 89 38; www.borromees.it; Corso Umberto I; s/d from €277/374; P X) Rockefeller, Bernard Shaw, Hemingway, Clark Gable and Mussolini are among the illustrious guests to have stayed at Stresa's most fabulous hotel, built in 1861 and furnished precisely as it would have been in the *belle époque*.

Osteria degli Amici (0323 304 53; Via Anna Maria Bolongaro 33; pizzas €4-8, mains from €10) Dine under vines on one of Stresa's most delightful terraces. Expect to queue as it's always packed.

Borromean Islands
The Borromean Islands (Isole Borromee) can be reached from various points around the lake but Stresa and Baveno are the best departure points. The four islands – Bella,

Madre, Pescatori (or Superiore) and San Giovanni – form the lake's most beautiful corner. San Giovanni is off-limits to tourists.

Bella was named after Carlo III's wife, the *bella* (beautiful) Isabella, in the 17th century and has courted a number of famous holiday-makers – Wagner, Stendhal, Byron and Goethe among them. **Palazzo Borromeo** (☎ 0323 305 56; www.borromeoturismo.it in Italian; adult/child €9/4; ⏰ 9am-5.30pm mid–Mar-Sep, 9am-5pm Oct) is its main drawcard. Built in the 17th century for the Borromeo family, the sumptuous palace contains works by Tiepolo and Van Dyck, as well as Flemish tapestries and sculptures by Canova. Mussolini tried to stave off WWII here at the Conference of Stresa in April 1935. The fossilised boat displayed behind glass in one of the palace grottoes is 3000 years old. The actual grottoes – studded with pebbles from the lake bed – took 25 years to complete. What's left of the island swarms with stalls selling ice cream, pizzas and tacky souvenirs.

Madre provides fertile ground for Italy's tallest palm trees. The entire island is taken up by the fabulous, 16th- to 18th-century **Palazzo Madre** (☎ 0323 312 61; adult/child €8.50/4; ⏰ 9am-5.30pm Apr-Sep, 9am-5pm Oct) and its sumptuous peacock-filled gardens which are even more lavish than those of Palazzo Borromeo. Highlights of the interior include Countess Borromeo's doll collection, a neoclassical puppet theatre designed by a scenographer from Milan's La Scala and smaller theatre with a cast of devilish marionettes. A combined ticket covering admission to the Borromeo and Madre palaces costs €12/7 per adult/child.

Apart from an 11th-century apse and a 16th-century fresco hanging in the **Chiesa di San Vittore**, there are no real sights to see on **Pescatori**, making it most visitors' port of call for lunch. Despite the many places to eat, there are no snack stalls and the tiny island retains some of its original fishing-village atmosphere. Count on eating and paying, much the same in whichever waterfront restaurant you plump for – grilled fish 'fresh from the lake' for around €14. If you want to stay on the island, the romantic **Albergo Verbano** (☎ 0323 304 08; www.hotelverbano.it; s/d/tr €100/148/170; ⏰ Mar-Dec) is a pleasant spot. Rooms, with wrought-iron bedsteads, are all named after flowers.

Western Shore
SIGHTS
It was the once-fortified Rocca di Arona in **Arona** (population 15,900), 20km south of Stresa that French novelist Stendhal vividly depicted in prose after witnessing its demolition in 1800. Ruins of the 9th-century fortress and an early Romanesque chapel are all that remain in the vast parkland today (off-limits to visitors). Below the castle, an attractive waterfront unfolds with an appealing line-up of smart cafés where you can enjoy a view of the magnificent Rocca di Angera across the water.

The **tourist office** (☎ 0322 24 36 01; Piazzale Duca d'Aosta; ⏰ 9am-12.30pm & 3-6pm Mon-Fri, 9am-12.30pm Sat) is opposite the train and bus stations. Rocca di Angera is a medieval castle whose magnificent walls today shelter the 12-room **Museo della Bambola** (Dolls Museum; ☎ 0331 93 13 00; adult/child €6.50/4; ⏰ 9.30am-12.30pm & 2-6pm Apr-Sep, 9.30am-12.30pm & 2-5pm Oct).

Heading towards Switzerland, **Verbania** (population 30,300), the biggest town on the lake and actually in Piedmont, offers plenty of accommodation in most classes. Split into three districts, it is Verbania Intra – the Swiss end with an attractive old town and car ferry terminal and on the waterfront in Verbania Pallanza – the middle chunk – that are of the most interest. In Pallanza the green fingered can stroll the grounds of the late-19th-century **Villa Taranto** (☎ 0323 40 45 55; www.villa taranto.it; adult/child €8/5.50; ⏰ 8.30am-7.30pm mid–Mar-Oct). In 1931 royal archer and Scottish captain Neil McEacharn bought the villa from the Savoy family and planted some 20,000 species over 30 years, creating what are today considered among Europe's finest botanical gardens.

Boats stop at Pallanza and at the landing stage in front of the villa. There's a **tourist office** (⏰ 9am-12.30pm & 2-5.30pm Fri-Sun) at the car ferry terminal and on the waterfront in **Verbania Pallanza** (☎ 0323 50 32 49; Corso Zanitello 6-8; ⏰ 9am-12.30pm & 3-6pm Mon-Sat, 9am-12.30pm Sun).

Cannero Riviera (population 1200) is a tranquil lakeside village. Just off the coast lie some tiny islets that, before being taken over by the Borromeo family in the 15th century, served as a den for thieves who operated in the area during the 12th century.

More interesting is **Cannobio** (population 5100), 5km short of the Swiss border. The tiny toy town's spotless cobblestone streets retain something of a village flavour. It has an active sailing and surfing school, **Tomaso Surf & Sail** (☎ 0323 7 22 14; www.tomaso.com) next to a patch of gritty beach at the village's northern end, and mountain bikes can be hired per hour/day for €3/11 from **Cicli Prezan** (Viale Vittorio Veneto 9), opposite the **tourist office** (☎ / fax 0323 7 12 12; Viale Vittorio Veneto 4; ☼ 9am-noon & 4.30-7pm Mon-Fri, 9am-noon Sat & Sun).

SLEEPING

Ostello Verbania (☎ 0323 50 16 48; Via alle Rose 7, Verbania; dm with breakfast €18.50; ☼ reception 7am-11am & 3.30-11.30pm Mar-Oct & Christmas) Backpackers should make a beeline for Verbania's only hostel. Rates include sheet hire.

Hotel Pironi (☎ 0323 7 21 84; hotel.pironi@cannobio .net; Via Marconi 35, Cannobio; s/d from €80/130) Languishing in a 15th-century palazzo amid Cannobio's cobbled maze, this is one of several charming hotels in Cannobio.

EATING

Ostello del Castello (☎ 0323 51 65 79; Piazza Castello 9, Verbania Intra; mains €12-18; ☼ Mon-Sat) With its flower-topped pergola terrace overlooking a quaint old-town square, Ostello del Castello's location – 20m from the ferry port – is hard to beat. Wine is plentiful and dishes are rustic and regional.

Arona has a trio of trendy waterfront places:

Café de la Sera (☎ 0322 24 15 67; Lungo Lago Marconi 85; mains €7-8; ☼ lunch & dinner) Mellow café offering a simple choice of four dishes for each course.

Gym Café (☎ 0322 24 36 84; Lungo Lago Marconi 47; mains €7-10) For those who prefer a 1950s US-diner feel.

Ul Boc (☎ 0322 446 58; Lungo Lago Marconi 71; mains €10 ☼ 8am-3am Thu-Tue) With a dazzling Art Deco–inspired décor.

LAGO D'ORTA

Only 15km long and about 2.5km wide, Lago d'Orta is entirely within the Piedmont region and is separated from its more celebrated eastern neighbour, Lago Maggiore, by Monte Mottarone. Orta is surrounded by lush woodlands and, unlike the larger lakes, the area does not swarm with visitors year-round.

The main town on the lake is **Orta San Giulio** (population 1133; elevation 293m), an idyllic spot with no real sights but lots of cobbled lanes to stroll and medieval squares to sip coffee on. From the main waterfront square,

regular launches make the short trip to the **Isola San Giulio**, named after a Greek evangelist who apparently rid the island of an assortment of snakes and monsters late in the 4th century. The island, dubbed the 'island of silence', is dominated by the 12th-century **Basilica di San Giulio**, from where a single footpath – La Via del Silenzio (The Way of Silence) – encircles the island. There is one museum, the **Museo del Regio Esercito Italiano** (☎ 0322 90 52 24; adult/child €5/2.60; ☼ 9.30am-6pm), dedicated to military history from 1861 to 1945, and a small pebble beach.

Sacro Monte, behind Orta San Giulio, is dotted with some 20 small chapels dedicated to St Francis of Assisi. It makes for a pleasant stroll above the town. Another lakeside spot, accessible by boat from Orta San Giulio, is **Omegna**, popular for its Thursday market. The small village of **Armeno**, at the foot of Monte Mottarone, is worth visiting, not least for its umbrella museum. From here, the narrow road that perilously wiggles to the mountain peak (and down to Stresa on Lago Maggiore) makes for a splendid drive.

Sleeping & Eating

Piccolo Hotel Olina (☎ 0322 90 56 56; Via Olina 40; s/d €50/70) One of Orta's cheaper options, rooms here are cosy but charming. There are self-catering apartments to rent too, plus a tasty restaurant.

Hotel San Rocco (☎ 0322 91 19 77; www.hotelsan rocco.it; Via Gippini 11; s/d from €153/221; P ✄ ▯ ▤) Giuseppine nuns lived a life of seclusion at this 17th-century convent until 1960, when it was transformed into a luxurious hotel. Moor your motorboat outside and cruise into this pool-filled oasis of luxury.

Villa Crespi (☎ 0322 91 19 02; www.slh.com/crespi; s/d from €140/200; P ✄ ▯ ▤) Secular decadence was lived out to the full by the 19th-century industrialist Benigno Crespi who made a fortune trading cotton – and had this Oriental extravaganza built in 1879. Its lavish gardens and opulent Moorish interior are breathtaking.

Getting There & Away

Orta Miasino train station, a short walk from the centre of Orta San Giulio, is just off the Novara–Domodossola train line.

Navigazione Lago d'Orta (☎ 0322 84 48 62) runs boats to numerous other lakeside spots from its landing stage on Piazza Motta to Isola

San Giulio (single/return €1.50/3), Omegna (€3.50/5) and Pella (€2/3.50). Island boats simply leave when there are sufficient passengers to warrant the five-minute crossing.

LAGO DI COMO

Marie Henri Beyle first set foot on the shores of Lake Como (also known as Lago Lario) as a 17-year-old conscript under Napoleon. Years later, as Stendhal, he wrote in *La Chartreuse de Parme* that the blue-green waters of the lake and grandeur of the Alps made it the most beautiful place in the world. The hordes of Italian and foreign tourists who have flocked here ever since suggest he was onto something. Local luminaries include the Roman writers Pliny the Elder and Pliny the Younger, and Alessandro Volta, who invented the modern battery.

This immense body of water, which sprawls in an upside down 'Y' shape at the foot of the Rhaetian Alps, is enchantingly beautiful. **Isola Comacina**, the lake's sole island, is where Lombard kings took refuge from invaders. Although it might look desperately inviting, Lago di Como's waters are murky and swimming is not advised.

Getting There & Around

The Como-based **Società Pubblica Trasporti** (SPT; ☎ 031 24 72 47; www.sptcomo.it in Italian) operates regular buses around the lake departing from the bus station. Key routes include Como–Colico (1½ hours, three to five daily), via all the villages on the western shore mentioned in this section (some with a change of bus in Menaggio); Menaggio–Lugano (one hour, hourly), via Lago di Piano; Como–Bellagio (one hour, hourly); and Como–Erba–Lecco (one hour, almost hourly). Further afield there are buses to and from Como and Bergamo (€6, 2¼ hours, around six daily); Como and Malpensa airport (€13, one hour, three daily); and Menaggio and Malpensa airport (€13, two hours, one or two daily). Updated schedules are online.

Como's main train station (usually listed as Como San Giovanni on train timetables) is the lake's main point of arrival and departure. Trains from Milan's Stazione Centrale (€3.40, one hour, at least hourly) stop here and continue on into Germany. Trains from Milan's Stazione Nord (€3.40, one hour, hourly) use Como's lakeside Stazione FNM (listed on timetables as Como Nord Lago).

From Lecco, local trains run the length of the less-popular eastern shore.

Ferries operated by Como-based company **Navigazione Lago di Como** (☎ 031 57 92 11, ☎ 800 55 18 01; www.navigazionelaghi.it in Italian; Piazza Cavour) criss-cross the lake year-round departing from the jetty at the northern end of Piazza Cavour. Hydrofoils only sail April to September. Single ferry fares range from €1.40 (Como–Cernobbio) to €7.80 (Como–Lecco). A whole host of other tickets are available, including those for day cruises with lunch and those which include admission to various lakeside villas.

Motorists can cross the lake with a car ferry on the western shore at Cadenabbia and on the eastern shore at Varenna. There are also limited car ferries from Bellagio to Cadenabbia, Menaggio and Varenna.

Como

pop 82,890 / elev 202m

Elegant Como, 50km north of Milan, is the main access town to the lake and sits at the base of the 146 sq km body of water. It has relatively few attractions in its own right, although the lakeside location is stunning, its narrow pedestrian lanes are a pleasure to explore, and there are numerous bars and cafés where you can relax with a cold drink on a balmy day. However, come summertime, the town is packed out with British and German tourists. Como makes a good base for exploring the fairytale lakeside villages, and is a much more attractive and affordable, place to stay than Milan.

INFORMATION

Banca d'Italia (Via Boldoni 15) Currency exchange and ATM.

Bar Black Panther (031 24 30 06; Via Garibaldi 59; ☺ 7am-midnight Tue-Sun) Has free Internet access for customers.

Ospedale Sant'Anna (☎ 031 58 51 11; Via Napoleona 60) Hospital.

Police station (☎ 031 31 71; Viale Roosevelt 7)

Post office Via T Gallio 6 (☺ 8.30am-7pm Mon-Sat) Main post office; also has currency exchange; Via Vittorio Emanuele II 99 (☺ 8.30am-12.30pm Mon-Sat)

Tourist office (☎ 031 330 01 11; www.lakecomo.org; Piazza Cavour 17; ☺ 9am-1pm & 2.30-6pm Mon-Sat)

SIGHTS & ACTIVITIES

From Piazza Cavour, the main square overlooking the water, walk south along arcaded

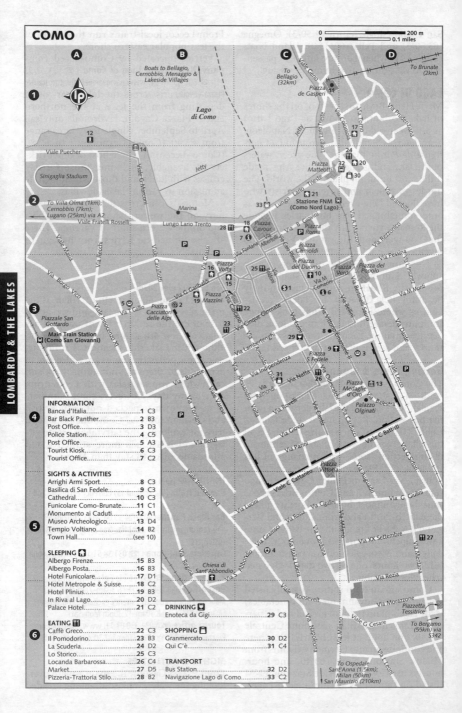

COMO

0 _____ 200 m
0 _____ 0.1 miles

LOMBARDY & THE LAKES

INFORMATION
Banca d'Italia....................................**1** C3
Bar Black Panther.............................**2** B3
Post Office...**3** D3
Police Station....................................**4** C5
Post Office...**5** A3
Tourist Kiosk.....................................**6** C3
Tourist Office....................................**7** C2

SIGHTS & ACTIVITIES
Arrighi Armi Sport............................**8** C3
Basilica di San Fedele.......................**9** C3
Cathedral...**10** C3
Funicolare Como-Brunate................**11** C1
Monumento ai Caduti......................**12** A1
Museo Archeologico........................**13** D4
Tempio Voltiano...............................**14** B2
Town Hall....................................(see 10)

SLEEPING 🏠
Albergo Firenze................................**15** B3
Albergo Posta...................................**16** B3
Hotel Funicolare..............................**17** D1
Hotel Metropole & Suisse................**18** C2
Hotel Plinius.....................................**19** B3
In Riva al Lago.................................**20** D2
Palace Hotel.....................................**21** C2

EATING 🍴
Caffè Greco......................................**22** C3
Il Pomodorino..................................**23** B3
La Scuderia......................................**24** D2
Lo Storico...**25** C3
Locanda Barbarossa.........................**26** C4
Market...**27** D5
Pizzeria-Trattoria Stilo....................**28** B2

DRINKING 🍷
Enoteca da Gigi...............................**29** C3

SHOPPING 🛍
Granmercato.....................................**30** D2
Qui C'è...**31** C4

TRANSPORT
Bus Station.......................................**32** D2
Navigazione Lago di Como..............**33** C2

Via Caio Plinio to Como's marble-faced **cathedral** (Piazza del Duomo), built between the 14th and 18th centuries. Elements of baroque, Gothic, Romanesque and Renaissance styles are crowned with a high octagonal dome. Next to it the polychromatic **town hall** was altered in 1435 to make way for its sacred neighbour. Continue south to get to the 6th-century **Basilica di San Fedele** (Via Vittoria Emanuele II), named after the saint who brought Christianity to the Como region. The basilica's unusual layout is noteworthy – a circular building with three naves and three apses, which has been likened to a clover-leaf. Its 16th-century rose window and medieval frescoes add to its charm. The façade dates from 1914.

Heading south along the same street is the **Museo Archeologico** (☎ 031 27 13 43; Piazza Medaglie d'Oro; adult/child €3/free; 🕑 9.30am-12.30pm & 2-5pm Tue Sat, 10am-1pm Sun), containing significant remains from prehistoric and Roman times. Garibaldi stayed in the palace opposite for a while. Continuing a block south, you come up against Como's **city walls**, rebuilt in 1162 following their demolition by the Milanese in 1127 who forced Como to surrender, destroy all its buildings (save its churches) and walls, and become dependent on Milan until Barbarossa came along in 1152.

An alternative walk from Piazza Cavour is westward along the shore to the **Templo Voltiano** (☎ 031 57 47 05; Viale Marconi; adult/child €3/free; 🕑 10am-noon & 3-6pm Tue-Sun Apr-Oct, 10am-noon & 2-4pm Nov-Mar), a lakeside neoclassical temple built in 1927. Inside is an exhibition on the life of Como-born electric-battery inventor Alessandro Volta (1745–1827), after whom the electric unit is named. The **Monumento ai Caduti** (War Memorial; Viale Puecher 9), nearby, is a classic example of Fascist architecture and dates to 1931.

Northeast along the waterfront, past Piazza Matteotti and the train station, is the **Funicolare Como-Brunate** (☎ 031 30 36 08; Piazza de Gasperi 4; adult/child one way €2.35/1.55, return €4.05/2.60; 🕑 6am-midnight summer, 6am-10.30pm winter), a cable car built in 1894. It takes seven minutes to reach hilltop **Brunate** (720m), a quiet village offering splendid views, but watch out for the cars on those winding narrow roads. Brunate's baroque **Chiesa di San Andrea** (Piazza della Chiesa), with its pink exterior and giant bell peeking out of the bell tower, is hard to miss. In **San Maurizio**, a short walk away, scale

143 steps to the top of the lighthouse, built in 1927 to mark the centenary of Alessandro Volta's death. A shuttle bus (€1) links the two hamlets. Back down the hill, the tourist office has ample walking and cycling information. Pick up any gear you forgot to pack from **Arrighi Armi Sport** (☎ 031 26 22 95; Via Indipendenza 20).

SLEEPING

Villa Olmo (☎ 031 57 38 00; Via Bellinzona 6; dm with breakfast €13.50; 🕑 Mar-Nov) Como's hostel fronts the lake, 1km from the main train station and 20m from the closest bus stop. Take bus No 1, 6, 11 or 14. HI cards are obligatory.

In Riva al Lago (☎ 031 30 23 33; www.InrIva.Info; Piazza Matteotti 4; s/d from €28/39, with bathroom from €40/52; **P**) Don't be deceived by this hotel's unassuming exterior, right behind the bus station. The hotel's recent refurbishment has transformed it into an attractive budget option, and the rooms are tastefully furnished, some with original wood beams.

Albergo Posta (☎ 031 26 60 12; www.hotelposta.net; Via G Garibaldi 2; s/d from €42/52; **P**) In the heart of Como, the simple but comfortable Posta offers good value. Some rooms have balconies overlooking the street, and there's a popular restaurant on the ground floor. Breakfast is €7.50 extra.

Hotel Plinius (☎ 031 27 30 67; www.hotelplinius .com; Via G Garibaldi 33; s/d/tr from €47/67/90; **P** 🕸) Under the same management as Albergo Posta, Plinius is an outwardly ugly modern place with decent rooms and the usual three-star amenities.

Hotel Funicolare (☎ 031 30 16 06; Via Coloniola 8; s/d €47/74) Funicolare is a basic two-star hidden away on a quiet lane not far from the cablecar station. It's a little old-fashioned, but rooms are perfectly clean and acceptable.

Locanda Milano (☎ 031 336 50 69; www.locanda milano.it in Italian; Via Alessandro Volta 62, Brunate; s/d May-Mar from €62/77.50, Apr €77/93; **P**) If you find Como too touristy, get away from it all in the hilltop village of Brunate, where Locanda Milano offers cosy, restful rooms above its well-regarded restaurant (meals around €18 to €20).

Palace Hotel (☎ 031 30 33 03; www.palacehotel.it; Lungo Lario Trieste 16; s/d/ste from €105/155/215; **P** 🕸) Como's grandest hotel choice, the Palace is an imposing neoclassical villa set in its own leafy grounds overlooking the lake. It's recently undergone a thorough refit, and both rooms and public areas reflect that *belle époque* elegance.

Hotel Metropole & Suisse (☎ 031 26 94 44; www .hotelmetropolesuisse.com; Piazza Cavour 9; s/d/ste €141/ 170/214; ☒ ℗) Dating from 1892, the stylish Metropole & Suisse exudes old-world charm, and occupies a prime lakeside location. Rooms are neat and spacious, some with lake views.

Albergo Firenze (☎ 031 30 03 33; www.albergo firenze.it; Piazza Volta 16; s/d €78/125; ☒ ℗) This attractive hotel offers 44 bright and spotless rooms (including four with disabled access) above a women's clothes shop on Piazza Volta. Reception is on the 1st floor.

EATING & DRINKING

Locanda Barbarossa (☎ 031 275 34 21; Via Odelschalchi 10; pizzas €6-9; ⏲ lunch & dinner Tue-Sun) This smart little brick-vault restaurant and bar is the perfect choice for cheap and filling pizzas and pasta dishes.

La Scuderia (☎ 031 30 43 22; Piazza Matteotti 4; mains €10; ⏲ lunch & dinner) Tucked behind the bus station, this popular trattoria cooks up a tasty local cuisine and has lots of grilled fish on its menu.

Pizzeria-Trattoria Stilo (☎ 031 26 12 38; Lungo Lario Trento 11; pizzas about €5-7; ⏲ lunch & dinner) Another cheap and cheerful place with a huge list of traditional and more adventurous pizzas, Stilo occupies the 1st floor of a lakefront building, offering some fine views.

Il Pomodorino (☎ 031 24 03 84; Via 5 Giornate 62b; mains €7-12; ⏲ lunch & dinner) Hidden away on a quiet pedestrian lane, Il Pomodorino's orange walls and bizarre art installations and décor are a surprise. But it's hugely popular and you may have to wait to be seated in the evenings. There's an extensive menu of pizzas, as well as fish and meat dishes, and an internal courtyard for sunnier days.

Ristorante Bellavista (☎ 031 22 10 31; Piazza Bonacossa 2, Brunate; mains €11-13; ⏲ lunch & dinner Wed-Mon) Ride the cable car up to Brunate to dine in this peaceful historic villa with great views over the lake. Fresh fish, pasta, steaks and turkey are on the varied menu, and service is quick and friendly.

Lo Storico (☎ 031 26 01 93; Via Juvara 14; mains €18-30; ⏲ dinner Mon-Sat) A plush, historic restaurant serving up top-notch fish dishes, with swordfish, lobster, octopus, sea urchins and other denizens of the deep listed on its pricey marine menu.

Enoteca da Gigi (☎ 031 26 31 06; www.enoteca gigi.com in Italian; Via Luini 48; ⏲ 9am-1pm & 2.30-8pm Mon-Fri, 9am-9pm Sat, 11am-9pm Sun) An impressive array of wines, vintage whiskies and grappas line the walls of this sociable wine shop and bar, along with olive oils and balsamic vinegars. Drop by in the evening for a glass of Prosecco or a sauvignon blanc (from €2) and enjoy the free, freshly prepared bruschetta.

Self-caterers can stock up on supplies at: **Granmercato** (Piazza Matteotti 3; ⏲ 8.30am-1pm Mon, 8.30am-1.30pm & 3.30-7.30pm Tue-Fri, 8am-7.30pm Sat) **Market** (Via Mentana 15) **Qui C'è** (Via Natta 43; ⏲ 8am-1.30pm & 2.30-8pm Mon-Sat, 9.30am-1pm Sun)

Western Shore

Lago di Como's western shore stretches a handsome 80km from Como (south) to Sorico (north), from where you can continue north into Switzerland or head east into Trentino-Alto Adige (see p309). The wiggly S340 snakes along Como's shore for most of the way, making driving or cycling along this route an invigorating experience.

In **Cernobbio**, art exhibitions can be viewed in the 19th-century **Villa Erba** (☎ 031 34 91; www .villaerba.it in Italian; Largo Luchino Visconti).

From Cernobbio a lower lakeside road (Via Regina Vecchia) skirts the lakeshore, past a fabulous row of 19th-century villas around **Moltrasio** and a couple of charming lunchtime spots on Laglio's north fringe. A few kilometres further north in **Argegno**, venture into the mountains with the **Funivia Argegno-Pigra** (one way/return €2/3; ⏲ 8am-noon & 2-6pm Apr, Jun & Sep, 8am-noon & 2-7pm Jul & Aug, 8am-noon & 2-5pm Oct-Mar). The cable car makes the five-minute climb to the 860m-high village of Pigra every 30 minutes.

Scenes from *Stars Wars Episode II* were filmed at **Villa del Balbianello** (☎ 0344 5 61 10; adult/child €5/2.50; ⏲ gardens 10am-12.30pm & 3.30-6.30pm Tue, Thu & Fri, 10am-6pm Sat & Sun Apr-Oct), a villa built by Cardinal Angelo Durini in Lenno in 1787. Visitors are only allowed to walk the 1km from the Lenno landing stage to the estate on Tuesday and at weekends; other days, you have to take a **taxi boat** (☎ 333 410 38 54) from Lenno.

In **Tremezzo** (population 1300), pergolas knitted around orange trees and some of Europe's finest rhododendrons, azaleas and camellias (April to May) bloom in the botanical gardens of 17th-century **Villa Carlotta** (☎ 0344

4 04 05; Riva Garibaldi; adult/child €6.50/free; 🕙 9am-6pm Apr-Sep, 9-11.30am & 2-4.30pm Mar & Nov). The villa, strung with paintings and tapestries, takes its name from the Prussian princess who was given the place as a wedding present by her mother in 1847. The Tremezzo **tourist office** (☎ 0344 4 04 93; infotremezzo@tiscalinet.it; Via Statale Regina; 🕙 9am-noon & 3.30-6.30pm Wed-Mon Apr-Oct) adjoins the boat jetty.

Motorists can cross the lake by car ferry in Cadenabbia, 3km south of **Menaggio** (population 3200). A popular centre for walking, the **tourist office** (☎ 0344 3 29 24; www.menaggio.com; Piazza Garibaldi; 🕙 9am-noon & 3-6pm Mon-Sat) sells several excellent brochures on walking and biking. The hostel (see right) rents bikes and arranges treks around Lago di Piano in the Val Menaggio, a remote valley connecting Lago di Como with Lake Lugano in Switzerland. The small lake is protected by the **Riserva Naturale Lago di Piano**. Three marked nature trails, 4km to 5.3km long, encircle the lake and the **visitors centre** (☎ 0344 7 49 61; riservalagopiano@yacc.it; Via Statale 117, Piano di Porlezza; 🕙 9am-noon Mon, Tue & Sat, 2-4pm Wed May-Oct), on the lake's northern shore, rents mountain bikes (€5 per hour) and arranges guided visits on foot (€2.50) and on horseback (€30).

SLEEPING

The lake offers literally hundreds of accommodation possibilities. The stand outs (from south to north) are listed.

Albergo Centrale (☎ 031 51 14 11; www.albergo-centrale.com; Via Regina 39, Cernobbio; s/d low season €50/85, high season €75/120; P 🅿️) A typical wood-shuttered place, this pretty little choice away from the water on Cernobbio's main street has a flowery terrace, a red-brick cellar, a tavern serving pizzas baked in a wood-fired oven and 19 cosy rooms. High-season prices jump around €30.

Villa d'Este (☎ 031 34 81; www.villadeste.it; Via Regina 40, Cernobbio; d from €630; P 🅿️ 🖥️ 🛥️) This splendid 120-year-old villa, Lago di Como's most famous hotel, is the last word in lakeside luxury. Rooms are dressed in Como silk and its outdoor pool floats on the lake.

Hotel Villa Marie (☎ 0344 4 04 27; www.hotelvillamarie.com; Via Regina 30, Tremezzo; s/d from €75/90; P 🅿️ ✖️ 🛥️) A short stroll south from Tremezzo's boat jetty, this stunning three-star, 19th-century villa hotel has a charming lakeside terrace and light, spacious rooms. The lake-view doubles cost €110.

Grand Hotel Tremezzo (☎ 0344 4 24 91; www.grandhoteltremezzo.com; Via Regina 8, Tremezzo; d/ste low season from €220/330, high season from €300/446; P 🅿️ 🖥️ 🛥️) A glass lift whisks guests from the lake shore up to one of Lago di Como's most romantic hotels. The lovely Liberty-style hotel opened its doors in 1910 and today remains family run. Its vast gardens are magnificent.

Ostello La Primula (☎ 0344 3 23 56; www.menaggiohostel.com; Via IV Novembre 106, Menaggio; dm with breakfast €13.50, f 4-6 beds €14; 🕙 reception 8-10am & 4-10pm mid-Mar–early Nov; P 🅿️) La Primula is a top-notch hostel, with great facilities, though dorms themselves are rather plain. You can rent a bicycle or kayak (€11 per day) and there's a pleasant garden.

Camping OK La Rivetta (☎ 0344 7 07 15; www.campingoklarivetta.com; Via Calbiga 30, Porlezza; person/site low season €4.50/9, high season €5.50/11, 2-/4-person bungalow low season from €40/55, high season from €45/62; 🕙 Apr-Oct; P 🛥️) This clean, green and peaceful camping ground, 2km east of Porlezza in the Riserva Naturale Lago di Piano, offers good facilities. Some bungalows are equipped for disabled guests, and there's a playground and video arcade for the kids.

EATING

Many eateries are dotted around the lake; a few interesting choices are listed.

Tom & Jerry (☎ 031 34 23 17; Via Regina 33b, Cernobbio; mains €10-12; 🕙 10am-3pm & 5.30pm-midnight Thu-Tue) This wine bar and restaurant, decked out 1950s style, is an atmospheric spot to try some fantastic wines. There's also a lovely garden overlooking a quiet park.

Red & White (☎ 0344 4 00 95; Via Portici Sampietro 18, Tremezzo) Red & White is an authentic wine bar where you can sample local wines over lunch. Its hot chocolate is thick enough to eat with a spoon. Omelettes and pastas are on the brief menu.

Alberghetto e La Cucina della Marianna (☎ 0344 4 30 95; www.la-marianna.com; Via Regina 57, Cadenabbia di Griante; s/d from €55/74, meals €20; 🕙 Wed-Mon) Freshly baked bread and a lakeside terrace are highlights of this tempting trattoria where Paola cooks up traditional lake cuisine.

Eastern Shore

Como's eastern shore is the least scenic – the lakeside S36 is an old military road and a motorway blasts its way along the entire 40km length from just north of Colico (north) to

Lecco (south), en route to the Lombardian capital. The **Abbazia di Piona** (9am-noon & 2.15-4.45pm), a Cistercian abbey, is a pocket of peace about 10km south of Colico. From the lakeside S36, follow the mountain road for 2.5km; the last stretch is cobbled.

Pretty **Varenna** (population 850), 13km south, is crowned by a castle and studded with extravagant villas. The gardens of **Villa Monastero** (0341 83 12 81; Piazza Venin 1; adult/child €2/1.50; 9am-6pm Mar-Oct), a former monastery, and **Villa Cipressi** (0341 83 01 13; Via IV Novembre 18; adult/child €2/1.50; 9am-7pm Mar-Oct) can both be visited. Magnolias, camellias and yucca trees are among their floral wonders. To get to both villas from Piazzale Martiri Libertà, the square next to the boat jetty, follow the **lakeside promenade** around the shore then bear left (inland) up the steps to Piazza San Giorgio, the village square. Both villas are signposted from here.

The **tourist office** (0341 83 03 67; www.varennaitaly.com; Piazza Venini 1; 10am-noon & 3-5pm Tue-Sat, 10am-noon Sun) offers information on the plentiful sleeping and eating options on the lake's eastern shore. Try **Villa Cipressi** (0341 83 01 13; Via IV Novembre 18; www.hotelvillacipressi.it; s/d from €80/120;), with its light, spacious rooms in a delightful setting. At the lakeside **Vecchia Varenna** (0341 83 07 93; www.vecchiavarenna.it; Contrada Scoscesa 10, Varenna; mains €15-16; Tue-Sun Feb-Dec) you can dine on fresh perch, pike and trout, as well as rabbit, duck, and, less appealing, braised donkey.

Southern Shore

The so-called 'southern shore' (the V stretch of Lago di Como's Y) embraces the pearl of the lake, **Bellagio** (population 3000) – a pretty little town sitting square on the point where the lake's western and eastern arms split and head south. The 32km drive to Como (west) is itself rewarding; the 22km trip down the eastern side towards Lecco is less so.

The lavish gardens of **Villa Serbelloni** (031 95 15 55; Via Garibaldi 8; adult/child €6.50/3; tours 11am & 4pm Tue-Sun Apr-Oct) cover much of the promontory on which Bellagio sits. Visits are by guided tour only and tours are limited to 16 people; tickets are sold 10 minutes in advance from the small **tourist office** (Piazza Chiesa 14) near the church. Garden-lovers can also stroll the grounds of neoclassical **Villa Melzi D'Eril** (339 644 68 30; Via Melzi D'Eril; adult/child €5/3; 9am-6pm Mar-Oct), built in 1808 for one of

Napoleon's associates and known in horticultural circles for its springtime azaleas and rhododendrons.

Bellagio **tourist office** (031 95 02 04; Piazza Mazzini; www.bellagiolakecomo.com; 9am-noon & 3-6pm Apr-Oct, Mon & Wed-Sat Nov-Mar), next to the boat landing stage, has loads of information on water sports, mountain biking and other lake activities.

Bellagio boasts a couple of outstanding spots to sleep.

Residence La Limonera (031 95 21 24; www.residencelalimonera.com; Via Bellosio 2; 2-/3-/4-person apt Nov-Mar €60/78/85, Apr-Oct €100/130/135;) This elegant villa in an old lemon grove has been divided into 11 spacious and thoughtfully furnished self-catering apartments. It's a peaceful place in the centre of town.

La Pergola (031 95 02 63; www.lapergolabellagio.it; Piazza del Porto 4; s/d/tr from €70/120/135, mains €10; restaurant Wed-Mon;) Scenically set in the fishing hamlet of Pescallo, on the eastern shore of the Bellagio promontory, La Pergola peers towards Lecco from its 16th-century waterfront perch. Its terrace restaurant adds to its natural old-world charm.

Grand Hotel Villa Serbelloni (031 95 02 16; www.villaserbelloni.com; Via Roma 1; s/d from €165/250;) This lovely villa was built in 1852 and has been a grand hotel since 1872. A private landing stage, beach, tennis courts, fitness centre, sauna, poolside restaurant and beauty farm are but some of the luxurious facilities available.

LAGO DI GARDA

Lago di Garda is the largest, most overdeveloped, least scenic – and ironically most popular – of the Italian lakes. Lying between the Alps and the Po valley, the 370-sq-km pool of murky water enjoys a temperate climate and is revered by windsurfers across Europe for its extraordinary Ora (southerly) and Peler (northerly) winds. At its northern reaches the lake is hemmed in by craggy mountains and resembles a fjord. As the lake broadens towards the south, it takes on the appearance of an inland sea.

Villages liberally stud the shoreline. The lake's trio of towns – the picturesque but tourist-filled **Sirmione** on the particularly crowded southern shore, **Gardone Riviera** on its western edge and **Riva del Garda**, a popular base for walking in the nearby Alps at the lake's quieter northern end – form a neat triangle around the lake. Windsurfers hang out around Torbole and Malcesine, two windy windsurfing spots south of Riva del Garda on the eastern shore. From the latter, walkers and mountain bikers can ride a state-of-the-art glass bubble of a cable car up to **Monte Baldo** (2200m), from where trails abound. In winter you can ski on its slopes.

Getting There & Around

From Desenzano del Garda train station, **ARV** (☎ 045 805 79 11) runs buses to Riva del Garda (€5.40, two hours, up to six daily) via Salò (30 minutes), Gardone Riviera (35 minutes) and Limone sul Garda (1½ hours). Peschiera del Garda train station is on the Riva del Garda–Malcesine–Garda–Verona ARV bus route, with hourly buses to both Riva (€4.90, 1½ hours) and Verona (€3, 20 minutes). Buses also run to/from Mantua (1¼ hours, up to eight daily) from Peschiera del Garda train station. The Riva del Garda–Milan (€11, 3¾ hours, three daily) bus route operated by **Società Italiana Autoservizi** (SIA; ☎ 02 864 62 350; www.sia-autoservizi.it in Italian) also serves Limone, Gardone Riviera, Salò and Brescia; find bus schedules and fares online. **Atesina** (☎ 046455 23 85; www.atesina.it in Italian) runs hourly buses from Riva del Garda to/from Arco (€1, 20 minutes), Rovereto (€2.80, 45 minutes) and Trent (€3.90, 1¾ hours).

The lake is served by train stations in Desenzano del Garda and Peschiera del Garda, both on the Milan–Venice train line with almost hourly trains in each direction. **Navigazione sul Lago di Garda** (☎ 030 914 95 11, 800 55 18 01; www.navigazionelaghi.it in Italian; Piazza Matteotti 2, Desenzano del Garda) operates passenger ferries year-round between all towns mentioned in this section and others. Motorists can cross the lake using the car ferry that yo-yos between Toscolano-Maderno (9km north of Salò on the western shore) and Torri del Benaco (8km north of Garda on the eastern shore), or seasonally between Limone (11km south of Riva del Garda on the western shore) and Malcesine (15km south of Riva on the eastern side). Lakeside ticketing booths and tourist offices have timetables. Transporting a small car/bicycle on either ferry route costs €5.60/4.10 one way. Passenger one-way fares on a ferry/hydrofoil range from €1.40/2.70 (Riva–Torbole) to €9.30/12.60 (Riva–Peschiera). A one-day ticket allowing unlimited travel

costs €22.40/11.20 per adult/child and a day ticket covering the lower/upper half of the lake only is €14.60/12.60 (child €7.30/6.30).

Sirmione
pop 6500 / elev 68m

The Roman poet Catullus celebrated Sirmione, a narrow peninsula jutting out from the southern shore of the lake, as the 'jewel of all islands', and his name is still invoked in connection with the place. It is a popular bathing spot and jammed tight with tourists but does retain a comparatively relaxed atmosphere. The area of interest, guarded by a castle, is an islet attached by a bridge to the rest of the peninsula.

The **tourist office** (☎ 030 91 61 14; Viale Marconi 8; ☾ 9am-9pm Apr-Oct) adjoins a bank and the bus station. Motorised vehicles are banned from the historic centre.

SIGHTS & ACTIVITIES

The colossal Roman villa-complex known as the **Grotte di Catullo** (☎ 030 91 61 57; adult/child €4/free; ☾ 8.30am-7pm Tue-Sun Mar-Oct, 8.30am-5pm Tue-Sun Oct-Feb) has no direct link with the Roman poet, dating from around two centuries after his death, although Catullus and his family did have a villa hereabouts. The extensive ruins ramble over the northern tip of the peninsula, and the opulent lifestyles of the villa's wealthy inhabitants can be glimpsed in the onsite museum, filled with the highest-quality frescoes, marbles and household artefacts.

Castello Scaligero (☎ 030 91 64 68; adult/child €4/2; ☾ 9am-12.30pm & 3-6pm Mon-Fri, 9am-12.30pm Sat) was built by Verona's ruling family, the Scaligeri, as a stronghold on the lake in 1250. There's not a lot inside but there are great views from the tower.

From the jetty near the castle, all sorts of vessels will make any manner of trip around the lake – at a price – and an array of water activities can be arranged. Massages, saunas and other sensuous delights can be enjoyed at the **Terme di Sirmione** (☎ 030 9 99 04 23, 800 80 21 25; www.termedisirmione.com; Piazza Virgilio 1).

You can rent mountain bikes/50cc scooters for around €10/35 per day from **Adventure Sprint** (☎ 030 91 90 00; Via Brescia 15; ☾ 9am-6.30pm).

SLEEPING

There's over 90 hotels crammed into Sirmione, many of which close from the end of

October to March. Four camping grounds lie near the town and the tourist office can advise on others around the lake.

Camping Sirmione (☎ 030 91 90 45; www.camping -sirmione.com; Via Sirmioncino 9, Colombane; person/tent/ tent & car low season €6/6/9, high season €9/8/14, 2/4-bed chalets low season €45/65, high season €70/100; P ⓑ) This attractive, well-kept site at the base of the peninsula has smart, modern chalets and good facilities including a restaurant, shop and waterskiing school.

Hotel Catullo (☎ 030 990 58 11; www.hotelcatullo. it; Piazza Flaminia 7; r from €55; ⓧ) One of Sirmione's oldest hotels, dating back to 1888, the pink-hued Catullo occupies a prime lakeside location, with a lovely garden and smart, contemporary rooms. Half and full board are available (from €65/75), while lake-view rooms cost €5 extra.

Hotel du Lac (☎ 030 91 60 26; www.hoteldulac sirmione.com; Via XXV Aprile 60; s/d from €62/83; ⓧ ⓑ) With glorious views over Lake Garda, Hotel du Lac is a good midrange choice with a waterfront garden. Rooms are plain but comfortable, and all have balconies.

Baia Blu Hotel Sirmione (☎ 030 919 61 84; www .baiabluhotel.com; Viale Marconi 31; d low/high season €90/150; P ⓧ ⓑ) Four-star comforts are on hand at the Baia Blu, with its spacious, very blue rooms, which all come with lake views. It also has a well-equipped 'wellness centre'.

Palace Hotel Villa Cortine (☎ 030 990 58 90; www.hotelvillacortine.com; Via Grotte 6; s/d from €300/420; P ⓧ ⓛ ⓑ) This five-star neoclassical villa, built in the 1880s, rests in a lovely park. Half board and a minimum stay of three nights is compulsory in high season.

EATING
There are loads of takeaway food outlets to be found, especially around Piazza Carducci, where the bulk of cafés, ice-cream parlours and restaurants are located.

Bar Fantastico (Via Santa Maria Maggiore 2) This traditional little bar, seemingly free of tourists, is a fine place to try a glass of local wine on tap.

Wara Warda (☎ 030 91 62 87; Piazza Carducci 9/10; pizzas €8) Sit in relative tranquillity and watch the mayhem of Sirmione's main square and boat dock. The pizzas are particularly tasty, authentic and laden with cheese.

Antica Trattoria La Speranzana (Via Dante 16; 1st/ 2nd courses €8/15) This lovely little trattoria near the church is tucked well away from the

waterfront circus – eat in peace on a quiet terrace, between olive trees by the lake.

Around Sirmione
Sirmione is 5km east of **Desenzano del Garda** (population 24,385), a useful transport hub, but of little interest in itself. Further north from Desenzano is **Salò** (population 9980) which gave its name to Mussolini's puppet republic in 1943, after the dictator was rescued from the south by the Nazis.

Larger-than-life dinosaurs, pirate ships, roller coasters, a puppet theatre and a dolphinarium are part of the excitement at the kid-orientated **Gardaland** (☎ 045 644 97 77; www.garda landit; day tickets adult/child €24/20; ⓨ 10am-6pm Apr–mid-Jun & last 2 weeks of Sep, 9am-midnight mid-Jun–mid-Sep, 9am-6pm Sat & Sun Oct). It's just outside Desenzano and is the largest amusement park in Italy. Multiday tickets are also available.

Next door, **CanevaWorld** (☎ 045 696 99 00; www .canevaworld.it; Via Fossalta 1) features an **aqua park** (adult/child €18/15; ⓨ 10am-7pm mid-May–mid-Sep), **medieval shows** (adult/child €22/14; ⓨ 1-2 daily Apr-Sep) as well as a **Rock Star Café** (ⓨ 6pm-2am), jammed packed with rock and roll memorabilia. CanevaWorld's **Movie Studios** (adult/ child €18/15; ⓨ 10am-7pm mid-Mar–Sep) can also be found next door. Stunt-packed Rambo- and Zorro-action shows that thrill audiences are part of the attractions here. Exact opening times vary slightly throughout the year, so check the website for details.

In Disney fashion, both parks have onsite hotels; contact them directly for customised packages.

Free buses shuttle visitors the 2km to both parks to/from Peschiera del Garda train station.

Gardone Riviera
pop 2520 / elev 85m
On the western edge of the lake at the head of a small inlet is Gardone Riviera, once one of the lake's most elegant holiday spots. No longer quite so fashionable, it lures the crowds today with **Il Vittoriale** (☎ 0365 29 65 11; www.vittoriale.it; Piazza Vittoriale; adult/child Il Vittoriale €7/4, Il Vittoriale & grounds or Museo della Guerra €11/8, Il Vittoriale, grounds & Museo della Guerra €16/11; ⓨ grounds 8.30am-8pm Tue-Sun Apr-Sep, 9am-5pm Tue-Sun Oct-Mar, Il Vittoriale & Museo della Guerra 9.30am-7pm Tue-Sun Apr-Sep, 9am-1pm & 2-5pm Tue-Sun Oct-Mar). This fabulous estate belonged to Italy's controversial poet and ultranationalist, Gabriele

d'Annunzio (1863–1938), who moved here in 1922 because, he claimed, he wanted to escape the world which made him ill.

Visits to d'Annunzio's house are by guided tour only (in Italian, 25 minutes, departures every 10 minutes). **Museo della Guerra** (War Museum) records d'Annunzio's WWI antics – one of his most triumphant and more bizarre feats was to capture a battleship from the fledgling Yugoslavia shortly after WWI when Italy's territorial claims had been partly frustrated in postwar peace talk. In July and August, classical concerts, ballets, plays and operas are staged in the **open-air theatre** (☎ 0365 29 65 19) in the villa grounds.

Gardone's **Giardino Botanico Fondazione André Heller** (☎ 336 41 08 77; Via Roma; adult/child €6/3; 9am-6pm Mar–mid-Oct) were laid out in 1900 and redesigned in the late 1990s by multimedia artist André Heller. They include sculptures by Keith Haring, Roy Lichtenstein and others, and some 8000 plant species grow here.

The **tourist office** (☎ 0365 2 03 47; www.brescia holiday.com; Corso Repubblica 8; 9am-12.30pm & 3.30-6.30pm Jul-Sep, 9am-12.30pm & 3.30-6.30pm Fri & Sat & Mon-Wed, 9am-12.30pm Thu Oct-Jun) stocks a wealth of information on lake accommodation and activities.

At the 1903 waterside palace, the **Villa Fiordaliso** (☎ 0365 2 01 58; www.villafiordaliso.it; Via Zanardelli 150, d from €250, P ⬛ ⬛ ⬛) has historically furnished rooms are named after various flowers. D'Annunzio lived here from 1921 to 1923, as did Mussolini's mistress, Clara Petacci, in 1943. The villa also has an acclaimed restaurant.

The waterfront is lined with plenty more places to eat, drink and be merry.

Trattoria Agli Angeli (☎ 0365 2 08 32; Piazza Garibaldi 2; s/d from €45/80; meals €20), en route to Il Vittoriale, is a pretty little trattoria overlooking a quintessentially Italian piazza. It has a handful of simple rooms above.

Around Gardone Riviera

About 12km north of Gardone, just past the car ferry port at Toscolano-Maderno, is **Gargnano** (population 3004) where Mussolini was based during the short life of his Repubblica Sociale Italiana (or Repubblica di Salò). He was guarded by German SS units and the republic was, in fact, fictitious, as northern Italy was occupied territory after Italy signed an armistice with the Allies in September

1943. The republic lasted until 25 April 1945 when the last German troops were finally cleared from Italy. Mussolini was killed three days later near Lago di Como.

Without a doubt the finest place to stay on the entire lake is the **Grand Hotel a Villa Feltrinelli** (☎ 0365 79 80 00; www.villafeltrinelli.com; Via Rimembranza 38; d from €735; P ⬛ ⬛ ⬛), a fairytale villa built as a lakeside residence for the Feltrinelli family in 1892 and host to Mussolini before his fall from glory. Guests are waited on hand and foot by their own personal butler.

Riva del Garda
pop 14,725 / elev 70m

Riva del Garda, on the lake's northern edge, officially in the neighbouring province of Trentino, has a pleasant old centre of cobbled lanes and squares. Links with the Germanic world are evident, not just in the sheer number of German and Austrian tourists, but also in the town's history. Riva was part of Habsburg Austria until it was incorporated into Italy after WWI and was annexed briefly by Nazi Germany in the closing years of WWII. Central European figures such as Nietzsche, Kafka and Thomas Mann rested at Riva.

Riva, along with Torbole (see p306), is a popular windsurfing spot and has several schools that run courses, hire out equipment and so on. The main **tourist office** (☎ 0464 55 44 44; Giardini di Porta Orientale 8; 9am-noon & 3-6.15pm Mon-Sat Apr–mid-Jun, 9am-noon & 3-6.15pm Mon-Sat, 10am-noon & 3-6.30pm Sun mid-Jun–Sep, 9am-noon & 2.30-5.15pm Mon-Fri Oct-Mar) and its **kiosk** (☎ 0464 55 07 76; Lungolago d'Annunzio 4c; 9am-noon & 3-6.15pm Apr-Oct), overlooking Piazza Catena where the boats dock, both have a list. They can also advise you on everything from climbing and paragliding to wine-tasting and touring flea markets.

Riva is a popular starting point for walks around **Monte Rocchetta** (972m), which dominates the northern end of Lago di Garda. Immediately south of the village, the shore is laced by a long shingle beach, overlooked by a wide green park.

SIGHTS

Guarding the waterfront is the **Museo Civico** (☎ 0464 57 38 69; Piazza Cesare Battisti 3; adult/child €3/1.50; 9.30am-12.30pm & 2.30-6.30pm Tue-Sun), a typical city museum inside the Rocca di

Riva built in 1124. The castle presents photographic exhibitions, an art gallery and also various archaeological finds from Arco.

The 34m-tall **Torre Apponale** is Riva's other century post. Scale its steep 165 steps for a stunning panorama. The sturdy 13th-century square tower is topped by an angel-shaped weather vane and is named after *ponale* – the southwest direction of the port that it faces. Tickets for the Museo Civico also cover admission to the tower.

About 3km north of town and a pleasant 45-minute stroll is **Cascata del Varone** (☎ 0464 52 14 21; adult/child €4/free; ☼ 10am-12.30pm & 2-5pm Mar, Oct & school holidays Nov-Feb, 9am-6pm Apr & Sep, 9am-7pm May-Aug). The impressive 100m waterfall is fed by the Lago di Tenno, a tiny lake northwest of Lago di Garda.

SLEEPING & EATING

Riva's hotel reservation centre **Consorzio Garda Trentino Hotel** (☎ 0464 55 36 67; www.gardatrentino hotels.com; Via Bastoni 7) makes free reservations for hotels with three or more stars.

Campeggio Bavaria (☎ 0464 55 25 24; camping bavaria@yahoo.it; Viale Rovereto 100; person/tent/car from €9/6/5; **P**) One of four camping grounds dotting Riva's lakeside, this one is part of the Marco Segnana Surf Center (see right) and is generally packed out with surfers and mountain bikers.

Albergo Ancora (☎ 0464 52 21 31; hotelancora@ riavdelgarde.com; Via Montanara 2; s/d from €55/88) This is a satisfying two-star option, tucked well away from the boat-clambering crowds. Unlike most other lake hotels, it sports no half-board deals but does give guests 15% discount in its tasty restaurant.

Hotel Sole (☎ 0464 55 26 86; www.hotelsole.net; Piazza 3 Novembre 35; s/d low season from €74/96, high season from €106/190) This smart four-star establishment, once patronised by Nietzsche, is a reasonable option, but it has clearly seen better days. Rooms with a lake view cost more.

Riva has dozens of takeaway places and delicatessens for picnic supplies, as well as a mind-boggling choice of lakeside cafés, pastry shops and *gelaterie* (ice-cream shops). For exceptional pizzas, head straight to **Bella Napoli** (☎ 0464 55 21 39; Via Armandi Diaz 29; pizzas €5-10), away from the water.

Around Riva del Garda

There is plenty to see and do around Riva del Garda. Northbound, the 20-minute stroll through olive groves from the medieval village of **Arco** (population 14,438) to **Castello di Arco** (☎ 0464 51 01 56; adult/child €3/1.50; ☼ 10am-7pm Apr-Sep, 10am-4pm Oct-Mar) limbers up the muscles for the more strenuous terrain awaiting walkers a few kilometres north.

Anyone looking for some outdoorsy exertion should contact **Friends of Arco** (☎ 3331 661 401; www.friendsofarco.it; Via Fabbri 18, Arco), a mountain-guide service offering a huge range of courses and excursions, from gentle day trips taking in the local botany to multiday adventure courses, including canyoning, trekking climbing and ski mountaineering. Three-day base or advanced rock-climbing courses cost €150, three-day gentle ski-mountaineering in the Dolomites costs €126, while three days of river trekking will cost you €214. Food and accommodation is not included.

TORBOLE
pop 5000 / elev 67m

Host to the **World Windsurf Championships** in June or July, and a huge **Surf Festival** at the end of May, this is *the* place to ride the wind. Garda-fan Goethe described Torbole as 'a wonder of nature, an enchanting sight', and indeed the village still retains much of its original fishing-village charm. Picturesque strolls aside, most people come here to surf.

The **Marco Segnana Surf Center** (☎ 0464 50 59 63; www.surfsegnana.it; Foci del Sarca), with bases at lakeside Lido di Torbole in Torbole and on Porfina beach in Riva del Garda, is a large surfing centre (board rental per hour/day from €16/40, three-hour beginner/advanced lessons €55/68) which rents catamarans (per hour/half day €35/85) and mountain bikes (per hour/day €5/15), too. Sports gear can be picked up at **Flipper** (☎ 0464 50 50 72; Via Matteotti 57b), a well-equipped sports shop.

The **tourist office** (☎ 0464 50 51 77; Via Lungolago Verona 19; ☼ 9am-noon & 3-6.30pm Jun-Sep, 9am-noon & 3-6.30pm Mon-Sat Oct-May) has a complete list of surfing schools, distributes free mountain-bike and walking maps and has information on accommodation.

MALCESINE

Garda's other surfing centre, 15km south, is a village of cobbled streets crowned by the **Castello e Museo Scaligero** (☎ 045 740 08 37; Via Castello; adult/child €4/1; ☼ 9.30am-7pm Apr-Nov, 9am-6pm Sat & Sun Dec-Mar), immortalised by Goethe. Inside the castle walls there are stunning lake views and a couple of natural-history museums to be seen, as well as a collection of Goethe's books. Olives harvested around here are turned into extra-virgin olive oil by the **Consorzio Olivicoltori di Malcesine** (☎ 045 740 12 86; Via Navene).

Malcesine's other must-do is the **Funivia Malcesine-Monte Baldo** (☎ 045 740 02 06; adult/child under 1.4m return €15/12; ☽ 8am-7pm), a cable car that offers an eagle-eye mountain view from its rotating glass cabins during its panoramic 10-minute journey up to 1790m. Pick up trail information and maps from Malcesine **tourist office** (☎ 045 740 00 44; wwww.malcesinepiu .it; Via Capitanato; ☽ 9am-noon & 3-6pm Mon-Sat) and rent a mountain bike from **Furioli Bike** (☎ 045 740 00 89; Piazza Matteotti). In winter you can ski on Monte Baldo.

The shuttered **Albergo Aurora** (☎ 045 740 01 14; www.aurora-malcesine.com; Piazza Matteotti 10; d low/high season €35/41; **P**) is an exceptionally good-value, one-star choice in the cobbled village heart of the town. Nearby is **Osteria Santo Cielo** (Piazza Quirico Turazza; ☽ 8am-2am), an atmospheric wine bar with no more than half-a-dozen tables inside and a few more outside on the tiny cobbled square.

LAGO D'ISEO

Lago d'Iseo is the least known and least at-tractive of the lakes. Shut in by mountains, it is scarred by industry and a string of tun-nels at its northeastern end around **Castro** and **Lovere**, although driving through the blasted rock face at the water's edge can be enjoyable. Heading south, the **Franciacorta** – a patch of rolling countryside that produces good wine – spills around the lake shore, while the mountainous hinterland offers interesting walking possibilities.

Riva di Solto (population 825) and **Sarnico** (population 5875), with its lovely Liberty villas towards the southern end of the lake, are a couple of fairly unspoilt villages on the western shore with a sprinkling of hotels and restaurants.

The River Oglio winds up to the lake through the **Valle Camonica** between two na-tional parks. Walking is the main attraction both here and around **Marone** on the eastern shore, from where a road winds into the mountains to **Zone**. Small and quiet **Sulzano** (population 1475), 12km south of Marone, is linked by ferry to the lake island of Monte Isola.

Getting There & Around

SAB (☎ 035 28 90 00; www.sab-autoservizi.it in Italian) buses trundle between Sarnico and Bergamo (50 minutes, up to six daily), and trains link Iseo train station with Brescia (€2.70, 30 minutes, hourly).

Navigazione sul Lago d'Iseo (☎ 035 97 14 83; www .navigazionelagoiseo.it) operates up to eight ferries daily between (south to north) Sarnico, Iseo, Monte Isola, Lovere and Pisogne. Single fares range from €1.75 (Sulzano–Peschiera Maraglioli on Monte Isola) to €5.50 (Iseo–Lovere). In winter there are substantially fewer sailings.

Iseo

pop 8383 / elev 198m

A pleasant, if rather quiet, spot fronting the southern end of the lake, Iseo boasts the first monument erected to Garibaldi. South of the small town lies a 2-sq-km protected wetland, formed from 18th-century peat beds. In late spring the pools are smothered in water lilies.

From Iseo you can catch a boat to **Monte Isola** (www.monteisola.com), Europe's largest lake island at 5 sq km. Few vehicles are allowed on the streets – cycling is the preferred means of getting around, making the fishing village a peaceful place to stay. Ask at Iseo **tourist office** (☎ 030 98 02 09; Lungolago Marconi 2) for de-tails of the 15km-long trail – suitable for both cyclists and walkers – that encircles the island.

Motorists have to dump their cars on the other side of the water before heading to the island's camping ground **Campeggio Monte Isola** (☎ 030 982 52 21; Via Croce 144; person/tent from €4.20/7.80; ☽ year-round).

Iseolago Hotel (☎ 030 98 89 91; www.iseolagohotel .it; Via Colombera 2; s/d low season €89/131, high season €108/166; **P** ☒ ☒) is beautifully situated in landscaped grounds that lead down to the lake, while the spacious, parquet-floored rooms, two restaurants and two pools live up to four-star standards.

Ostello del Porto (☎ 035 983 52 90; Via Paglia 70, Lovere; dm/d €16.50/39; **P** ☐), on the northern shore of the lake in Lovere, is a new hostel, in a renovated steel factory, offering clean, en-suite rooms, all with lake views.

Valle Camonica

The Valle Camonica weaves its way from the north of Lago d'Iseo to the vast **Parco** dell'Adamello and, further north, to the **Parco Nazionale dello Stelvio**. The area borders on Trentino-Alto Adige and takes in the better parts of the Lombard Alps. The two national parks offer many walks and are dotted with Alpine huts to rest up.

About halfway between Darfo and Edolo, lovers of rock art will have a field day. The **Parco Nazionale delle Incisioni Rupestri** (☎ 0364 4 21 40; adult/child €5/2.50; ☺ 9am-6.30pm Tue-Sun summer, 8.30am-4.30pm Mon-Fri & 9am-4.30pm Sat & Sun winter), at Capo di Ponte, is a 30-hectare open-air museum containing a representative array

of rock engravings going as far back as the Bronze Age. The valley is littered with such carvings.

The area north of Edolo offers some reasonable winter **skiing**, particularly near Ponte di Legno, at the northern end of the valley, and the nearby Passo del Tonale. Brescia's tourist office (see p284) stocks plenty of walking, camping and mountain-hut information. In the valley there are tourist offices at **Darfo Boario Terme** (☎ 0364 53 16 09; Piazza Einaudi 2) and **Ponte di Legno** (☎ 0364 9 11 22; Corso Milano 41).

Trentino-Alto Adige

Italy's northernmost region, the autonomous twin province of Trentino-Alto Adige stretches from the shores of Lake Garda in the south to the Austrian border in the north, incorporating much of the Dolomite range.

The marriage of Trentino and Alto Adige has at times created friction, with some extreme elements in Alto Adige calling for secession from Italy. It's also something of a schizophrenic region, incorporating two vastly different provinces. Trentino is historically and culturally Italian, despite an uneasy century under Habsburg rule, while Alto Adige, also known as South Tyrol (Südtirol), was an integral part of Austria until it was ceded, along with Trentino, to Italy at the end of WWI. German language and culture dominate the province to this day. Less than a third of the population favour Italian as their first language, while Ladin, an ancient Latin-based language, is spoken by a tiny minority, whose strongholds include the Val Badia and Val Gardena.

Trent, Trentino's capital, is an attractive, easy-going city with a long history, and is the most convenient base for exploring the region. Riva del Garda to the south is a relaxing lakeside resort, while the more active can take advantage of some of the best ski slopes in the Alps in the west of the province.

Enter Bolzano, the capital of Alto Adige, and you might think you've crossed the border into Austria, with German street signs, Tirolean architecture and locals chatting away in German over frothy beer and sausages, giving the place a distinctly un-Italian atmosphere. Dubbed 'Italy's Christmas Capital' for its festive yuletide market and snowy winter beauty, it's a great place from which to launch forays into Alto Adige's lovely hidden valleys.

HIGHLIGHTS

- Bear-watch in Spormaggiore at the **Parco Naturale Adamello-Brenta** (p320)
- Discover the elusive **Ladins** (p332)
- Meet Bolzano's ice man, **Ötzi** (p327)
- Smell the grass with a **hay bath** (p331)
- Walk and ski in the **Dolomites** (p311)
- Take time out for the museums and galleries of **Trent** (p314) and **Rovereto** (p317)
- Indulge in solid, beery Germanic fare at restaurants such as **Bolzano's Hopfen & Co** (p327) and Merano's **Forsterbräu** (p329)

- POPULATION: 943,000
- AREA: 13,613 sq km

TRENTINO-ALTO ADIGE

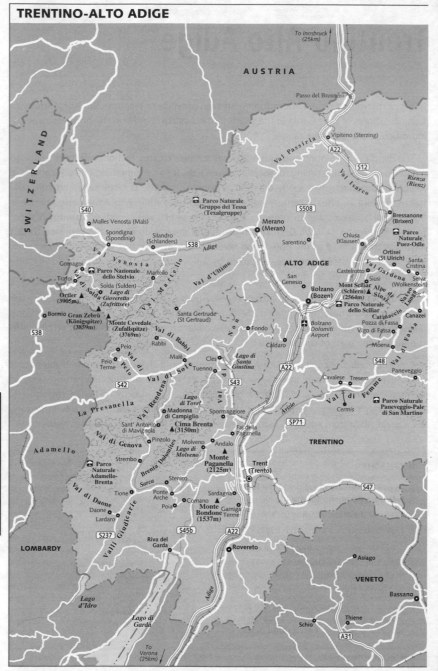

AUSTRIA

To Innsbruck
(25km)

Passo del Brennero

Vipiteno (Sterzing)

SWITZERLAND

Val Passiria

A22

S12

Rienza
(Rienz)

Parco Naturale
Gruppo del Tessa
(Texalgruppe)

S40

Malles Venosta (Mals)

S508

Bressanone
(Brixen)

Spondigna
(Spondinig)

Silandro
(Schlanders)

Merano
(Meran)

Chiusa
(Klausen)

Parco
Naturale
Puez-Odle

S38

Adige

Sarentino

Ortisei
(St Ulrich)

Santa
Cristina

Val Venosta

Val d'Ultimo

ALTO ADIGE

Val Gardena

Selva
(Wolkenstein)

Gomagoi

Martello

San
Genesio

Castelrotto

Siusi

Sasso
Lungo

Trafoi

Parco Nazionale
dello Stelvio

Bolzano
(Bozen)

Mont Sciliar
(Schlern) ▲
(2564m)

Alpe di
Siusi

Solda (Sulden)

Val Martello

Lago di
Gioveretto
(Zufrittsee)

Val d'Isarco

Ortler
(3905m)

Catinaccio

Parco Naturale
dello Sciliar

Santa Gertrude
(St Gertraud)

Bormio Gran Zebrù
(Königspitze)
(3859m)

Monte Cevedale
(Zufallspitze)
(3769m)

Bolzano
Dolomiti
Airport

Pozza di Fassa

Canazei

Vigo di Fassa

S38

Val di Rabbi

Fondo

Moena

Peio

Non

Val di Fassa

Rabbi

Caldaro

Peio
Terme

Malè

Cles

Lago di
Santa
Giustina

S48

Paneveggio

Val di Sole

Tuenno

A22

Cavalese

Tresero

Peio

S42

S43

SP71

Val di Femme

Parco Naturale
Paneveggio-Pale
di San Martino

La Presanella

Lago
di Tovel

Spormaggiore

Avisio

Cermis

Madonna
di Campiglio

Val Rendena

Sant' Antonio
di Mavignola

Cima Brenta
(3150m)

Far della
Paganella

TRENTINO

Pinzolo

Molveno

Andalo

Val di Genova

Lago di
Molveno

Adamello

Strembo

Brenta Dolomites

Monte
Paganella
(2125m)

Trent
(Trento)

Parco
Naturale
Adamello-
Brenta

Sarca

Stenico

Sardagna

S47

Tione

Val di Daone

Ponte
Arche

Comano

Monte
Bondone
(1537m)

Garniga
Terme

Poia

Daone

Valli Giudicarie

A22

Lardaro

S237

S45b

Riva del
Garda

Rovereto

Asiago

LOMBARDY

VENETO

Bassano

Lago
d'Idro

Schio

Thiene

Lago di
Garda

Adige

To
Verona
(25km)

A31

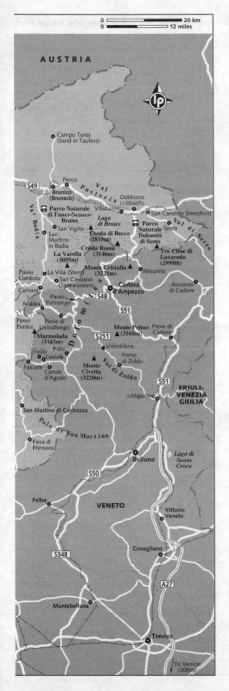

Information

The provincial tourist offices in Trent (p314) and Bolzano (p325) stock loads of practical information, including updated lists of *rifugi* (mountain huts) and B&B farmhouses. The regional Trentino Tourist Board (p314) in Trent also has an office in **Milan** (☎ 02 864 61 251; apt.milano@trentino.to; Piazza Diaz 5).

Activities

SKIING IN THE DOLOMITES

The Dolomites boast innumerable excellent ski resorts, including fashionable (and pricey) Cortina d'Ampezzo, Madonna di Campiglio, San Martino di Castrozza and Canazei, as well as the extremely popular resorts of the Val Gardena.

Both accommodation and ski facilities are abundant in the area and you have plenty of scope to choose between downhill and cross-country skiing, as well as *sci alpinismo*, which combines skiing and mountaineering skills on longer excursions. Snowboarding and most other winter sports are also equally well catered for.

High season runs from mid-December to early January and then February to mid-March.

Ski passes range from those covering the use of lifts in one resort and its immediate neighbours (ideal if you've only one or two days or don't intend venturing far) to the **Dolomiti Superski** (www.dolomitisuperski.com) pass, which allows access to 464 lifts and some 1220km of ski runs across 12 regions. It costs around €95/167 for a three-/six-day pass (in high season €108/190). Prices for passes

MOUNTAIN EMERGENCIES

Many towns and resorts have local telephone numbers (listed in Information sections in this guide) to call for mountain rescue. However, wherever you are, calling ☎ 118 will get you out of trouble. Before setting out always check out the weather forecast, snow conditions and **avalanche warnings** (☎ 0461 23 89 39; www.meteotrent ino.it); snow reports are updated at 1pm daily. The **14th Delegation-SAT Alpine Rescue team** (☎ 0461 23 31 66; Via Manci 57), the largest of 35 Alpine rescue stations staffed by 350 volunteers in the region, is based in Trent.

TRENTINO-ALTO ADIGE

covering individual resorts and areas are listed throughout this chapter.

Several ski schools operate at every resort; they all offer boarding lessons, as well as classic downhill skiing. A six-day course (three hours of group tuition per day) costs about €130, and private lessons average €30 to €40 per hour. In more expensive resorts, such as Cortina, prices can jump much higher.

Tourist offices abound across the region, but the best for getting general information, including more on ski-pass prices and accommodation packages, are those in Trent (p314) and Bolzano (p325).

WALKING IN THE DOLOMITES

The Dolomites, stretching across Trentino-Alto Adige into the Veneto, provide the most spectacular and varied opportunities for walkers in the Italian Alps – from half-day rambles to more demanding routes that require mountaineering skills.

Trails are generally well marked with numbers on red-and-white painted bands (on trees and rocks along the trails) or inside different coloured triangles for the Alte Vie (High Routes). Numerous *rifugi* offer overnight lodging and meals. Tourist offices usually have maps with roughly marked trails, but walkers planning anything more than the most basic itinerary should buy detailed walking maps from bookshops (listed under Information in the relevant town sections).

Those wanting to undertake guided walks or tackle more difficult trails that combine mountaineering skills with walking (with or without a guide) can seek information at Guide Alpine (mountain guide) offices in the region (also listed under the relevant town sections).

For more on walking in the Dolomites, see Lonely Planet's *Walking in Italy* guide.

Preparations

The walking season runs from the end of June to the end of September (sometimes into October, depending on the weather). Note that most mountain huts close from mid-September.

Among the many maps available are the *carte topografiche per escursionisti* maps published by Tabacco at a scale of 1:25,000. These topographic maps provide extensive details of trails, altitudes and gradients, as well as marking all mountain huts, and are widely available in bookshops throughout the region. Maps in the equally reputable Kompass series are also widely available.

Always check the weather predictions before setting out (see the boxed text, p311), ensure you're prepared, have the correct gear and the correct equipment for high-altitude conditions and set out early. The weather can change suddenly in the Alps, even in hot August when it can dramatically turn cold and wet, especially in the afternoon.

Walking Areas

The best areas for walking in the Dolomites:
Alpe di Siusi, Sciliar and Catinaccio group All accessible from Siusi and Castelrotto.
Brenta group (Brenta Dolomites) Accessible from Molveno or Madonna di Campiglio.
Cortina The area around here straddles Alto Adige and the Veneto and features the magnificent Parco Naturale di Fanes-Sennes-Braies and, to the south, Monte Pelmo, Monte Civetta and the Val di Zoldo area.
Pale di San Martino Accessible from San Martino di Castrozza and Fiera di Primiero.
Sella group Accessible from the Val Gardena, Val Badia, Pieve di Livinallongo and the Val di Fassa.
Sesto group (Sesto Dolomites) North of Cortina towards Austria, accessible from San Candido or Sesto in Val Pusteria.

AN ALPINE CORAL REEF

The Dolomites are, in fact, ancient coral reefs reconstituted as Alpine peaks. Accounting for a vast portion of the eastern Alps, the spiky peaks take their name from French geologist De Dolomieu, the first to identify their composition of sedimentary limestone formed from calcium carbonate and magnesium. Around 100 million years ago, the entire area was covered with tropical forest and a shallow, warm sea. After millions of years, the sea receded at the same time as the Alps were being formed, raising what had once been the seabed to heights of between 2000m and 3000m. During the Ice Age, the coral reefs and rocks were eroded by glaciers that, together with normal atmospheric erosion, shaped the fantastic and spectacular formations seen in the Dolomites today. It is not unusual to find marine fossils among the pinnacles, towers and dramatic sheer drops of these mountains.

Val di Genova and the Adamello group Both accessible from Madonna di Campiglio (the Brenta and Adamello groups form the Parco Naturale Adamello-Brenta).

There are four Alte Vie in the Dolomites, each taking up to two weeks. Routes link existing trails and incorporate new trails which make difficult sections easier to traverse.

Each route links a chain of *rifugi*, and you can opt to only walk certain sections.
Alta Via No 1 Crosses the Dolomites from north to south, from Lago di Braies to Belluno.
Alta Via No 2 Extends from Bressanone to Feltre and is known as the 'High Route of Legends' because it passes through Odle, the mythical kingdom of ancient Ladin fairytales.
Alta Via No 3 Links Villabassa and Longarone.
Alta Via No 4 Goes from San Candido to Pieve di Cadore.

The Alte Vie are marked by numbers inside triangles – blue for No 1, red for No 2 and orange/brown for No 3; No 4 is marked by numbers on red-and-white bands. Booklets with the routes in detail are available at most tourist offices in the region.

OTHER ACTIVITIES
Summer pastimes include mountain biking, hang-gliding and rock climbing. Tourist offices can help find trails, bike-rental outlets and hang-gliding schools and pass on information. Mountain guide associations (see Information in the relevant town sections) organise guided excursions, ranging from family rambles to challenging walks taking several days at high altitudes.

Getting There & Around
Bolzano airport (p327) in the region is only served by a couple of European flights. Otherwise the nearest airports are Verona, Bergamo and Innsbruck (Austria) from where trains run south to Bolzano.

Public transport is managed by two main companies: **Trentino Trasporti** (☎ 0461 82 10 00; www.ttspa.it in Italian) in Trentino and **Servizi Autobus Dolomiti** (SAD; ☎ 800 846 047; www.sii.bz.it) in Alto Adige. The main towns and many ski resorts can be reached directly from major Italian cities including Rome, Florence, Bologna, Milan and Genoa. Information about these services is available from tourist offices and bus stations throughout Trentino-Alto Adige, or from bus stations in the respective cities.

TAKING MUSIC TO NEW HEIGHTS

Every summer Trentino's regional tourist board organises free high-altitude concerts, embracing everything from classical and blues to jazz, ethnic and funk sounds.

Most performances start at 2pm, allowing audiences ample time to ramble uphill to the venue, which is always a *rifugio* or mountain pass. Some venues are better reached with the aid of the local Alpine guide – most run free guided treks to the concert.

The culturally inclined who prefer a tad more wrist action can limber up with a spot of wine-tasting in a traditional Trentino wine cellar, followed by an evening concert. Local wine can likewise be sampled during the musical events held in a *malghe* – an Alpine hut on a hill where butter and cheese are traditionally made.

For more information, call ☎ 0461 83 90 00, look online at www.trentino.to, or contact the tourist office in Trent (p314).

TRENTINO

TRENT
pop 108,577 / elev 194m
The fresh and laid-back capital of Trentino, Trent (Trento to the locals) is a perfect starting point for forays into the province and the neighbouring Parco Naturale Adamello-Brenta. Its tourist offices have extensive information on the town and Trentino, and its public-transport network is efficient and extensive. Trent is an attractive city, with its long, rich history at the meeting point between Italian and Germanic cultures has left it with a wealth of fine architecture, as well as several museums well worth pausing over. At the heart of town, Piazza del Duomo, with its playful Renaissance fountain and looming cathedral, is a gem. Heading south, vineyards are strung the length of the pretty road linking Trent with Rovereto (see p317).

Known by the ancient Romans as Tridentum, Trent later passed from the Goths to the Lombards and was eventually annexed by the Holy Roman Empire when it became known as Trento or Trient. From 1027 until 1803 it was an Episcopal principality during

TRENTO CARD

To get the most out of your visit to Trent, consider buying the Trento Card, available in 24-/48-hour versions (€9/14). Freebies offered by the card include access to city museums, city tours, unlimited public transport, a ride on the Funivia Trento-Sardagna, guided tours and tastings at wine cellars in the region, and various other discounts. Cardholders can also take advantage of the special deals offered by some local hotels. Cards are sold at the tourist office and some participating museums.

a period marked by political and territorial conflict with the rulers of Tirolo. The Council of Trent (1545–63) considered restructuring the Catholic Church in the wake of Protestantism and formed the basis of the Counter-Reformation here.

Information

BOOKSHOPS

Ancora Libreria (Via Santa Croce 35) Has Kompass walking maps.
Libreria Viaggeria (☎ 0461 23 33 37; Via S Vifilio 20) Excellent travel bookshop.
Rizzoli (Corso III Novembre) English-language novels in its basement.
Touring Club Italiano (☎ 0461 22 11 61; Via Garibaldi 27) Maps and guides galore.

EMERGENCY

Police station (☎ 0461 89 95 11; Piazza della Mostra)

INTERNET ACCESS

Wireless Internet Café Olimpia (☎ 0461 98 24 45; Via Belenzani 33; per hr €5; 7am-9pm Mon & Tue, 7am-midnight Wed-Sat)

LEFT LUGGAGE

Main train station (per hr €1; 8.30am-12.15pm & 1.30-5.30pm)

MEDICAL SERVICES

Guardia Medica (☎ 0461 91 58 09) Emergency doctor.
Hospital (☎ 0461 90 31 11; Largo Medaglie d'Oro 9) Hospital southeast of the centre.

MONEY

You'll find plenty of banks with ATMs in the centre of town.

POST

Post office (Via Calepina; 8.30am-6.30pm Mon-Fri, 8am-12.30pm Sat)

TOURIST INFORMATION

Tourist office (☎ 0461 98 38 80; www.apt.trento.it; Via Manci 2; 9am-7pm Mon-Sat)
Trentino Agritur (☎ 0461 23 53 23; Via Aconcio 13; 9am-5pm Mon-Fri) Info point for *agriturismo* (farm-stay accommodation), places to eat and activities in the Trentino countryside.
Trentino Tourist Board (☎ 800 010 545, 0461 49 73 53; www.trentino.to; Via Romagnosi 11)

Sights

Flanked by a Romanesque **cathedral** (6.40am-12.15pm & 2.30-8pm) and the 13th-century **Palazzo Pretorio** and its tower, Piazza del Duomo is the natural place to start a tour of Trent. Host to the Council of Trent, the dimly lit cathedral displays fragments of medieval frescoes inside its transepts. Two colonnaded staircases flank its nave, and the foundations of an early Christian church form part of an archaeological area.

Illuminated manuscripts, paintings depicting the Council of Trent, liturgical vestments and other 15th- to 19th-century treasures all form part of the awe-inspiring collection in the **Museo Diocesano** (☎ 0461 23 44 19; Piazza del Duomo 18; adult/child €3.50/0.50, archaeological zone €1/free, 1st Sun of month free; 9.30am-12.30pm & 2.30-6pm Wed-Mon), inside the former bishop's residence of Palazzo Pretorio. Admission to the museum also includes entry to the cathedral's archaeological zone and treasury.

On the other side of the piazza are two Renaissance houses, with fresco-decorated façades, called the **Casa Cazuffi-Rella**. The 18th-century, cherub-swathed **Fontana di Nettuno** gushes in the piazza's centre. Southeast of here is the **Museo Tridentino di Scienze Naturali** (Natural Science Museum; ☎ 0461 27 03 11; www.mtsn.tn.it in Italian; Via Calepina 14; adult/child €2.50/1.50; 9am-12.30pm & 2.30-6pm Tue-Sun), with exhibits on the local flora, fauna and fossil records.

A short walk north of the Piazza del Duomo, subterranean Trent can be explored at the fascinating **Tridentum La Città Sotterranea** (☎ 0461 23 01 71; Piazza Battisti; adult/child €2/1; 9am-noon & 2.30-6pm Tue-Sun Sep-May, 10am-noon & 2.30-7pm Jun-Aug), where archaeological remains of the Roman city can be viewed close up.

A stroll northeast through pedestrian streets takes you to **Castello del Buonconsiglio**

TRENT

| 0 | 200 m |
| 0 | 0.1 miles |

INFORMATION

Ancora Libreria	**1** D4
Libreria Viaggeria	**2** D3
Police Station	**3** D2
Post Office	**4** D3
Rizzoli	**5** D4
Touring Club Italiano	**6** D3
Tourist Office	**7** C3
Trentino Agritur	**8** D1
Trentino Tourist Board	**9** D3
Wireless Internet Café Olimpia	**10** D3

SIGHTS & ACTIVITIES

Badia di San Lorenzo	**11** C2
Casa Cazuffi-Rella	**12** C3
Castello del Buonconsiglio	**13** D2
Cathedral	**14** C3
Fontana di Nettuno	**15** C3
Magno Palazzo	(see 13)
Museo di Arte Moderna e Contemporanea	**16** B4
Museo Diocesano	**17** D3
Museo Tridentino di Scienze Naturali	**18** D3
Palazzo Pretorio	(see 17)
Società degli Alpinisti Tridentini	**19** D2
Sportler	**20** D3
Tridentum La Città Sotterranea	**21** D3

SLEEPING

Albergo Aquila d'Oro	**22** C3
Grand Hotel	**23** D2
Hotel America	**24** D3
Hotel Venezia	(see 22)
Ostello Giovane Europa	**25** C2

EATING

Al Volt	**26** D4
Due Giganti	**27** D3
Pedavena	**28** D4
Pizzeria 77	**29** C3
Pizzeria Primavera	**30** D2
Supermercato Trentino	**31** D4

TRANSPORT

| Funivia Trento-Sardagna | **32** B3 |
| Intercity Bus Station | **33** C2 |

(☎ 0461 23 37 70; www.buonconsiglio.it; Via Bernardo Clesio 5; adult/child €5/2.50; ☷ 9am-noon & 2-5pm Tue-Sun Oct-Mar, 9am-noon & 2-5.30pm Tue-Sun Apr-Sep), home of the bishop-princes who ruled Trent until 1803. The fortified complex incorporates the **Castelvecchio**, the original 13th-century castle, the Renaissance bishops' residence **Magno Palazzo**, and a varied collection of art and antiques. It also hosts temporary exhibitions.

Near the train station, the 12th-century **Badia di San Lorenzo** (Via Pozzo 2; ☷ 6.30am-noon & 3-7pm), once attached to a long-gone monastery, is worth a look for its cross vault festooned with red stars and its bronze statue of Padre Pio. The abbey was badly damaged by WWII bombing and again during the 1966 floods, but has now been faithfully restored.

Housed in the regal Palazzo delle Albere is Trent's small **Museo di Arte Moderna e Contemporanea** (MART; ☎ 0461 23 48 60; Via Roberto da Sanseverino 45; adult/child €5/3, incl MART in Rovereto €10; ☷ 10am-6pm Tue-Sun), part of MART in Rovereto (see p317). Works displayed inside include 19th- and early 20th-century impressionist and symbolist paintings by Trentino artists, the most impressive being Luigi Bonazza's huge triptych, *La Leggenda di Orfeo* (1905). Look out for the colourful fragmentary frescoes on the walls, too.

Around 8km south of town, near the tiny Mattarello airport, is **Museo dell' Aeronautica Gianni Caproni** (☎ 0461 94 48 88; www.museocaproni .it in Italian; Via Lidorno 3; adult/child €2.50/1.50; ☷ 9am-1pm & 2-5pm Tue-Fri, 10am-1pm & 2-6pm Sat & Sun), a branch of the Natural Science Museum with a collection of vintage airplanes, including early biplanes. To get here, you'll need your own transport.

Activities

From Trent you can ride the **Funivia Trento-Sardagna** (☎ 0461 23 21 54; Via Montegrappa 1; one way €0.90) cable car to Sardagna, a pleasant year-round strolling territory. From here 15km of winding road by car (there's no public transport available) brings you to the small ski station of **Vaneze di Monte** (1350m), connected by cable car to its higher counterpart **Vasòn** – where most ski schools and ski-hire shops are – and the gentle slopes of 1537m-high **Monte Bondone** (www.montebon done.it). The latter is criss-crossed by 37km of cross-country ski trails and nine downhill runs. Its slopes are more famed in the region, however, for their extraordinary grass (see the boxed text, p331). One-/two-day ski passes start from around €20/36. On weekends between December and March, Skibus Monte Bondone, run by Trentino Trasporti, wends its way from Trent to Vaneze (€0.90 one way). For walking information, including itineraries and *rifugi* in Trentino, contact the local **Società degli Alpinisti Tridentini** (SAT; ☎ 0461 98 18 71; Via Manci 57; ☒ 8am-noon & 3-7pm Mon-Fri).

Sportler (☎ 0461 98 12 90; Via Mantova 12) is a sports shop with a vast array of goods, including mountain bikes, for sale.

Tours

The tourist office runs guided tours of the city centre (adult/child €3/free), departing from in front of the tourist office at 3pm on Saturday. Tours of the Castello del Buonconsiglio (adult/child €3/free) depart from the tourist office on Saturday at 10am. For self-guided walking or cycling tours in the city and the wider province, pick up one of the excellent free brochures, *Trento Itineraries*, at the tourist office, following themes such as nature, history and 'vineyards and castles'.

Festivals & Events

Costumed parades, craft and produce fairs, raft races, historical re-enactments, music and fireworks are among the merry-makings during the **Feste Vigiliane**, a week-long festival celebrating the feast of St Vigil (Trent's patron saint) in mid-June. Much tastier still

is the annual **Polenta Festival**, which is held on the last weekend of September to celebrate Trent's most traditional culinary dish. Trent's **Christmas Market**, which takes over Piazza di Fiera from the end of November till Christmas Eve, is the best in the region.

Sleeping

Drop into Trentino Agritur's office (p314) for information on B&Bs on farms and other idyllic rural settings outside of town.

Ostello Giovane Europa (☎ 0461 26 34 84; info@ gayaproject.org; Via Torre Vanga 9; dm €15-18, s/d €25/40; ☒ reception 7.30am-11am & 3-11pm) Travellers of any age can stay at this clean, modern and pleasingly central hostel. Mountain views, cheap canteen food and excellent bathrooms facilities are other assets. HI cards are obligatory.

Hotel Venezia (☎ /fax 0461 23 41 14; Piazza del Duomo 45; s/d from €45/55) This 1950s-style hotel is split across two buildings; rival Albergo Aquila d'Oro forms the filling in the sandwich. It is a simple, central hotel with basic rooms that are comfortable enough for a short stay, and the location is convenient.

Albergo Aquila d'Oro (☎ 0461 98 62 82; www.aquila doro.it in Italian; Via Belenzani 76; s/d from €60/70; ☒) This quiet, family-run hotel with 20 rooms is spitting distance from the hubbub of the central square.

Hotel America (☎ 0461 98 30 10; www.hotelamerica .it; Via Torre Verde 50; s/d/tr €65/98/114; P ☒) This pastel pad is situated at the end of a busy road not far from the train station. Rooms are large and comfortable and the buffet breakfast is excellent. The hotel also offers

---

AUTHOR'S CHOICE

Hotel Villa Madruzzo (☎ 0461 98 62 20; www.villamadruzzo.it; Via Ponte Alto 26, Cognola; s/d from €62/102; P) If identikit glass-and-concrete city-centre boxes are getting you down, this palatial place 3km northeast of Trent in the hillside village of Cognola might just be the place to relax and recharge. Far grander than its three stars would suggest, historic Villa Madruzzo was once home to Cardinal Madruzzo, and is set in vast flower-filled gardens. The 50 rooms are all individually decorated with antique furnishings, and the very highly regarded restaurants dishes up local specialities.

neat, self-contained apartments for longer stays (minimum one week, €350 per week).

Grand Hotel (☎ 0461 27 10 01; www.boscolohotels .com; Via Alfieri 1; d from €100; 🅿 🖳 ⊠ 🅿) Convenient for the train station, the Grand is a huge modern chain hotel, which looks pretty bland on the outside, but once inside, the comfort and facilities are probably the best in town.

Eating

Due Giganti (☎ 0461 23 75 15; Via Simonino 14; mains about €4, dinner buffet €6.80; 🕑 noon-2.30pm & 6.30-10pm) Locals flock to this cheap 'all you can eat' self-service restaurant, where you can pile your plate with pizza, salads and chips. It's remarkably good value and the €13.80 Sunday lunch buffet is especially popular. Children under 1m tall eat free.

Al Volt (☎ 0461 98 37 76; Via Santa Croce 16; mains about €8-10; 🕑 Fri-Wed & dinner Thu) A simple yet soulful place, Al Volt has specialised in *piatti tipici trentini* (literally 'typical Trent plates') since 1894. Pick from a couple of first courses and five or six seconds. Finish off your meal with *strudel della nonna* (grandma's strudel).

Pedavena (☎ 0461 98 62 55; www.birreriapedav ena.com in Italian; Piazza di Fiera 13; mains about €7-8; 🕑 Wed-Mon) You can't beat this 1920's brewery for that German beer-hall feeling, complete with stags' heads mounted on the wall and cheap, hearty food. Sausages, tripe and pasta fill the menu, and you can round it off with a glass of Lag's Bier.

Pizzeria Primavera (☎ 0461 23 98 40; Via Suffragio 92; pizzas €6-8; 🕑 lunch & dinner) This cosy pizzeria is a bit of a tight squeeze, but if you're in search of simple, filling fare, it's a good bet.

Pizzeria 77 (☎ 0461 23 72 09; Via Verdi 77; mains about €7-8; 🕑 lunch & dinner) This popular local hangout with long shared tables is a cheap and cheerful place for good-value pizzas, pasta and risotto dishes.

Supermercato Trentino (Corso III Novembre 4-6) Pick up picnic supplies here.

Getting There & Away

Regular trains connect Trent's **train station** (Piazza Dante) with Verona (one hour, hourly), Venice (2½ hours, up to six daily), Bologna (3¼ hours, four daily) and Bolzano (€2.20, 30 minutes, at least hourly). The Trent–Malè train line (the station is next to the main station) connects the city with Cles in the Val di Non.

From the **bus station** (Via Andrea Pozzo), local bus company **Trentino Trasporti** (☎ 0461 82 10 00; www.ttspa.it in Italian) runs buses to and from various destinations, including Madonna di Campiglio (€4), San Martino di Castrozza (€5.60), Molveno (€3.20), Canazei (€5.30) and Rovereto (€2.60).

ROVERETO
pop 34,200
For contemporary art-lovers, the 15km trip south from Trent to Rovereto is a must. Its **Museo d'Arte Modern e Contemporanea** (MART; ☎ 0464 43 88 87; www.mart.trento.it in Italian; Corso Bertini 43; adult/child €8/5, incl MART in Trent €10; 🕑 10am-6pm Tue-Thu, Sat & Sun, 10am-9pm Fri) displays dozens of priceless pieces from the early 20th century to the present day, including Andy Warhol's *Four Marilyns* (1962), Tom Wesselman's *Seascape* (1966), several Picassos and various wrapped creations by Christo. Temporary exhibitions fill the 2nd floor of the building – a work of art in itself with its monumental glass dome designed by Swiss-born architect Mario Botta.

The **Museo Storico Italiano Della Guerra** (Italian War Historical Museum; ☎ 0464 43 81 00; Via Castelbarco 7; adult/child €5.50/2; 🕑 8.30am-12.30pm & 2-6pm Tue-Sun) is worth a peek, as is the **Campana della Pace** (Bell of Peace; adult/child €1/0.50; 🕑 9am-noon & 2-6pm Nov-Feb, 9am-noon & 2-7pm Mon-Fri, 9am-7pm Sat & Sun Apr-Jul & Sep, 9am-7pm Aug), a bell of peace cast in 1924 from bronze canons from the 19 countries that fought in WWI. The 3.36m-tall bell – the world's largest ringing bell – tolls every evening around 9pm from its perch atop Miravelle Hill on Rovereto's eastern fringe. To get here, follow the signs in town from Via Santa Maria.

The **tourist office** (☎ 0464 43 03 63; www.apt .rovereto.tn.it; Corso Rosmini 6a; 🕑 8.30am-12.15pm & 2.30-6pm Mon-Fri) has lots of information on the town.

In the medieval heart of old Rovereto, **Scala della Torre** (☎ 0464 43 71 00; Via Scala della Torre 7; mains about €10) is a cosy decades-old trattoria and *birraria* (pub), and is the place to feast on typical mountain fare.

Buses run regularly to Trent (€2.60, 30 minutes).

BRENTA DOLOMITES
Northwest of Trent and part of the Parco Naturale Adamello-Brenta, this majestic group of peaks is isolated from the main body of

the Dolomites and provides dramatic walking opportunities, best suited to those keen to test their mountaineering skills. Harnesses and ropes are essential for most of the high-altitude trails, including one of the group's most famous trails, Via Bocchetta di Tuckett; opened up by 19th-century climber Francis Fox Tuckett from Molveno to Cima Brenta, and including gruelling sections of *vie ferrate* (trails with permanent steel cords).

Lakeside Molveno and Madonna di Campiglio make suitable bases from which to delve into the Brenta Dolomites (Dolomiti di Brenta). The wiggly S421, S237 and S239 linking Molveno to Madonna make for a scenic, if perilous, drive.

Molveno

pop 1080 / elev 864m

This pretty village, just 38km northwest of Trent by road, sits in a picturesque position by Lago di Molveno, overshadowed by the towering Brenta Dolomites. It became famous in the 19th century as a base for British and German mountaineers who came to open up trails into the group. In winter, skiers and snowboarders skim down the slopes of **Monte Paganella** (2125m), linked by cable car to **Andalo** (population 1026), 4km northeast of Molveno, and **Fai della Paganella** (population 900), 10km north.

INFORMATION

Andalo tourist office (☎ 0461 58 58 36; www.apt andalo.com; Piazza Dolomiti 1; ⏱ 9am-12.30pm & 3.30-7pm Mon-Sat, 9.30am-12.30pm Sun)

Fai della Paganella tourist office (☎ 0461 58 31 30; info@aptfaidellapaganella.com; Via Villa; ⏱ 9am-12.30pm & 3.30-7pm Mon-Sat, 9.30am-12.30pm Sun)

Guardia Medica (☎ 0461 58 56 37; ⏱ 8pm-8am) Night-time medical aid.

Molveno Iniziative Turistiche (☎ 0461 58 60 86; Piazza Marconi 1; ⏱ 9am-12.30pm & 3-6.30pm Mon-Fri) Hotel reservations, information on the Molveno Card and mountain-bike itineraries.

Molveno tourist office (☎ 0461 58 69 24; www.apt molveno.com; Piazza Marconi 5; ⏱ 9am-12.30pm & 3-6.30pm Mon, Wed, Fri & Sat, 9am-12.30pm Tue & Thu, 9.30am-12.30pm Sun)

Tourist medical service (☎ 0461 58 60 45) Daytime medical aid.

ACTIVITIES

Cyclists, mountain bikers and walkers needing a guiding hand should contact Molveno's

Guide Alpine Brenta Est (☎ 0461 58 69 24, 329 582 41 46; guidealpine@aptdolomitipagnella.com; Piazza Marconi 1; ⏱ 8.30-10pm Jul & Aug). It can organise rock climbing and guided walks in summer and ski-mountaineering, frozen waterfall climbing and snow-shoeing excursions in the Parco Naturale Adamello-Brenta in winter.

The Paganella ski area is accessible from Andalo (by cable car) and Fai della Paganella (by chair lift). It has two cross-country skiing trails and 50km of downhill ski slopes, ranging from beginner-friendly greens to heart-thumping blacks. Plenty of sports shops in Andalo and Fai della Paganella rent gear. A Skipass Paganella allowing unlimited use of the resort's one cable car, chairs and drag lifts costs €15.50/18.50/21 for two/three/four hours (high season €17.50/21/23) or €24/46/63 for one/two/three days (high season €30/53.50/78). The Skirama and Super-skirama Adamello-Brenta passes (opposite) are both valid here, as is the Dolomiti Super-ski pass (p311).

From the top of Molveno village, a two-seater **cable car** (☎ 0461 58 69 81; one way/return €5/5.50) transports you in two stages up to Pradel (1400m), from where trail No 340, which is a pleasant and easy one-hour walk, leads to the **Rifugio Croz dell'Altissimo** (☎ 0368 98 92 42; ⏱ Jun-Sep) at 1430m. Several other trails, of varying difficulty, start off from here. Tourist offices have complete lists of mountain huts.

SLEEPING & EATING

There are numerous farmhouses to sleep in and eat at around Molveno, best suited for self-transporting travellers looking for a bit of peace and quiet – to find them, ask at the tourist office (left).

Almost a dozen hotels in Molveno subscribe to the Molveno Card scheme – guests staying at these hotels are entitled to free mountain-bike hire, among other things. Most hotels only open between Christmas and New Year, for Mardi Gras in February and from Easter to mid-October. Full board is generally obligatory in December, July and August. Prices can vary throughout the year, with the highest rates in August. The following places to stay are all part of this scheme.

Camping Spiaggia (☎ 0461 58 69 78; camping@ molveno.it; Via Lungolago 25; per person €5-9, tent & car €8-14.50; ⏱ year-round, reception 9am-noon & 2-7pm)

Rates at Molveno's lakeside camp site, include free admission to the neighbouring outdoor swimming pool, tennis court and table-tennis tables, as well as to the numerous forms of on-site entertainment. Prices are at their highest in July and August.

Hotel Belvedere (☎ 0461 58 69 33; www.belvedere online.com; Via Nazionale 9; d half board per person from €51; year-round; P ⊠ ⊠) The Belvedere offers the best value and some of the best facilities and is also one of a handful of hotels to keep its doors open all year. Mountain-bike rental is free to guests and a bus shuttles skiing guests from the hotel to Andalo in season. There's also a 'wellness centre' offering massages, manicures and the like, and a gym. Full board is an extra €12 per person.

Hotel Alexander Cima Tosa (☎ 0461 58 69 28; www .alexandermolveno.com; Piazza Scuole 7; s/d half board from €54/90; P ⊠) In the centre of town, Alexander is a big modern place with spacious rooms, most with balconies, and an attractive sun terrace.

Hotel Nevada (☎ 0461 58 69 70; www.hotelnevada .it; Via Paganella 23; s/d half board from €44/80; P ⊠) The Nevada is another good central choice with lake views. Rooms, with stripped wood flooring, have balconies and there's a big garden and a gym.

Fai della Paganella also has several decent places to rest up, including the modern **Hotel Montana** (☎ 0461 58 31 82; www.hotelmontana .net; Via Battisti 8b; s/d from €40/60; P ⊠), which has mountain bikes and ski equipment for hire and runs a shuttle bus to the slopes.

GETTING THERE & AWAY
From Molveno, **Trentino Trasporti** (☎ 0461 82 10 00) runs buses to Trent (€3.20, 3½ hours, up to nine daily) and services to Madonna di Campiglio (€8.50) and Riva del Garda (€5.50) on Lago di Garda.

Madonna di Campiglio & Pinzolo
elev 1522m
One of the top ski resorts in the Alps, Madonna di Campiglio (known locally simply as Madonna) sprawls along the Val Rendena on the northwestern side of the Brenta Dolomites. Less expensive, family-orientated Pinzolo is 16km south of the resort. Austrian emperor Franz Joseph and his wife were frequent visitors to Madonna at the end of the 19th century – an era relived in late February when fireworks blaze and costumed

pageants waltz through town during the annual Habsburg Carnival.

As with most resorts in the region, Madonna and Pinzolo are ghost towns out of season.

INFORMATION
Guardia Medica (☎ 0465 44 08 81, 0465 80 16 00) Emergency doctor.
Madonna tourist office (☎ 0465 44 75 01; www .campiglio.to; Via Pradalago 4; 9am-12.30pm & 3-7pm Mon-Sat, 10am-1pm Sun)
Pinzolo tourist office (☎ 0465 50 10 07; www.pinzolo .to; Piazzale Ciciamimo; 9am-noon & 3-6.30pm Mon-Sat, 9am-noon Sun)
Tourist medical service (☎ 0465 44 30 73) Only functions in season.

SIGHTS & ACTIVITIES
A network of chair lifts and several **cable cars** (☎ 0465 44 77 44) take skiers and boarders from Madonna to its numerous ski runs and a snowboarding park (with half pipe, slide park and boarder cross) in winter, and to walking and mountain-biking trails in summer. In Pinzolo there is just one **cable car** (☎ 0465 50 12 56; www.funiviepinzolo.it in Italian; Via M Bolognini 84; 8.30am-12.30pm & 2-6pm mid-Dec–Apr & Jun–mid-Sep), which climbs the mountain to 2100m-high Doss del Sabion (one way/return €5/8, 20 minutes), stopping at midstation Pra Rodoni (1530m; €5/6, 10 minutes) en route. Mountain bikes can be hired at this cable-car station in summer.

In winter, a one-/three-/six-day ski pass for Madonna di Campiglio costs €31/85/145 (high season €34/90/156). Five-day Skirama Adamello-Brenta passes covering either resort, plus one day in the other, are also available (low/high season €126.50/152). The less restrictive Superskirama Adamelo-Brenta pass, available from one to 14 days, covers both resorts, as well as others in the valley; as an example, for three/seven days it costs €95/178 (high season €105/202).

There are plenty of walking opportunities in the area, too. Particularly enchanting are the guided walks (€10) to a traditional Alpine pasture hut in the national park, run once on Wednesday mid-July to September, by the tourist office and Parco Naturello Adamello-Brenta. Reserve a place at Madonna tourist office.

In Campo Carlo Magno, 2km north of Madonna, the **Cabinovia Grostè** (one way/return €9/14;

☺ 8.30am-12.30pm & 2-5pm mid-Dec–Apr & Jun–mid-Sep) cable car takes walkers up, in two stages, to the Passo Grostè (2440m), from where you can set off into the Brenta Dolomites. The Via delle Bocchette (trail No 305) – the *via ferrato* for which the Brenta group is famous – also leaves from the cable-car station. Only experienced mountaineers with the correct equipment should attempt it. Otherwise, take trail No 316 to **Rifugio del Tuckett** (☎ 0464 44 12 26; ☺ mid-Jun–mid-Sep) and Q Sella (2271m). From there take trail No 328 and then No 318 to the **Rifugio Brentei** (☎ 0465 44 12 44) at 2182m. All trails heading higher into the group from this point cross glaciers and need special equipment.

Pinzolo's 16th-century **Chiesa di San Vigilio** merits a visit for its external painting entitled *La Danza Macabra* (The Dance of Death). North of Pinzolo is the entrance to the **Val di Genova**, often described as one of the Alps' most beautiful valleys. A series of spectacular waterfalls along the way enhances its reputation as great walking country. Four mountain huts strung out along the valley floor make overnight stays an option – Pinzolo tourist office has details.

Descending into the **Val Rendena**, a few kilometres southwest of Madonna, brings you to the **Valli Giudicarie** area near Lardaro. The area is not served by public transport and you need your own car to explore the spectacular side valleys here. The 25km-long **Val di Daone** road, just southwest of Lardaro, brings you to a reservoir, from where a two-hour stroll along the reservoir edge ends at the peaceful 1918m-high **Rifugio Val di Fumo** (☎ 0465 67 45 25; ☺ mid-Jun–mid-Sep), at the foot of the imposing Carè Alto in the Adamello group. This old-style 1960s mountain hut recalls the mountain-lovers' paradise before tourists discovered the Dolomites. This, and most other huts in the region, are managed by the Trent-based Società degli Alpinisti Tridentini (p316).

SLEEPING & EATING

There are few budget options in Madonna and most insist on full or half board, while some may be reluctant to accept bookings for less than seven days at busy times of year.

Most hotels are open mid-December to Easter, and mid-June to mid-September.

PARCO NATURALE ADAMELLO-BRENTA

The Italian Alps' last remaining brown bears mingle with ibex, red deer, marmots and chamois in Trentino's largest protected area, the 620-sq-km Parco Naturale Adamello-Brenta, dotted with more than 80 lakes and the Admello glacier, one of the largest in Europe. Brown bears can be viewed at close quarters at the **Centro Visitatori Spormaggiore** (☎ 0461 65 36 22; Via Alt Spaur 6; admission free; ☺ 9.30am-12.30pm & 3-6.30pm Mon-Fri, 10am-noon & 2-6pm Sat & Sun) in **Spormaggiore** (population 1176), 15km northeast of Molveno. Some of the park's dozen or so brown bears live in a large enclosure at the bear-watching visitors centre – park authorities closely monitor the others with the aid of radio collars.

Some 82 bird species nest in the Parco Naturale Adamello-Brenta. Spot some around the banks of Lago di Tovel, set deep in a forest some 30km north of Spormaggiore in the park's heart. An easy walking trail encircles the lake (one hour). The lakeside **visitors centre** (☎ 0463 45 10 33; ☺ 9am-1pm & 2-6pm Jul & Aug, 9am-1pm & 2-6pm Sat & Sun Sep) has extensive information on other walks in the park. Those keen to learn more about local animal life should make time to visit the **Centro Visitatori Fauna** (☎ 0465 62 20 75; adult/child €2.50/1.50; ☺ 10am-noon & 2-6pm Mon-Sat, 9am-noon & 2-7pm Sun Jul-Sep), in the park's southern realms in **Daone** (population 591), 45km south of Madonna di Campiglio and 50km west of Riva del Garda in Lombardy. The fauna centre organises numerous nature walks and activities in summer. At other times, only groups of fifteen or more are admitted, by reservation.

More information on the park, including lists of mountain huts, Alpine guides, and walking and mountain-biking maps and itineraries can be obtained from the helpful **visitors centre** (☺ 9am-noon & 4-8pm Apr-Sep) in **Sant'Antonio di Mavignola**, 15km south of Madonna di Campiglio, or from the **park headquarters** (☎ 0465 80 46 37; www.parcoadamellobrenta.tn.it in Italian; Via Nazionale 12; ☺ 8.30am-noon & 2-7pm Jul & Aug, 8.30am-noon & 4-6pm Mon-Fri Sep-Jun), a few kilometres south in **Strembo** (population 442).

Camping Parco Adamello (☎ 0465 50 17 93; info@ campingparcoadamello.it; Carisolo; person/tent & car low season €7/8, high season €9/12; ☺ year-round; **P**) This camp site, 1km north of Pinzolo, sits amid mountains in the national park, making it a natural starting point for walking and cycling forays into nature.

Hotel Bellavista (☎ 0465 50 11 64; www.bellavista net.com in Italian; Pinzola; s/d from €47/80, half board per person per week low/high season from €273/399; ☺ year-round; **P**) Pinzolo's 57-room 'Beautiful View' hotel – one of the few hotels to open all year – is a modern place with plain but comfortable rooms done out with a lot of brown wood.

Hotel Crozzon (☎ 0465 44 22 22; www.hotelcrozzon .com; Viale Dolomiti di Brenta 96, Madonna; s/d half board per person from €65/100; **P**) This friendly, modern hotel in Madonna offers bright, clean rooms and it has its own restaurant. Full board is another €10 per person; prices in winter can double.

Hotel Alpina (☎ 0465 44 10 75; www.alpina.it; Via Sfulmini 5, Madonna; s/d full board from €80/120; **P**) Another Alpine-style hideaway, Alpina is a reasonable three-star option. The minimum stay is three nights, and there are special deals on offer for stays of one week or more.

GETTING THERE & AWAY
Madonna di Campiglio and Pinzolo are accessible by bus from Trent and Milan (3¾ hours, one daily in each direction from mid-December to March). From mid-December to mid-April **shuttle buses** (☎ 0465 50 10 07) run from Milan's Malpensa and Linate airports and Verona's Villafranca airport to and from Madonna and Pinzolo. All bus trips cost around the €1 to €2 mark.

VAL DI NON, VAL DI SOLE & VALLE DI PEIO

The **Val di Non** is a picturesque valley of apple orchards and castles accessible from Trent via the Trent–Male train or bus. The main town is **Cles**, dominated by Castel Cles. The **tourist office** (☎ 0463 42 13 76; Corso Dante 30; ☺ 9am-noon Mon, 9am-noon & 3-6pm Tue-Sat) is just off the main road through town, and there is another in the nearby village of **Fondo** (☎ 0463 83 01 33). You may want to stay here on your way north, although accommodation choices are limited.

West from Cles, the scenic S42 thrusts motorists into the **Val di Sole**, a pretty valley

which traces the course of the River Noce. The tourist office in **Malè** (☎ 0463 90 12 80; www.valdisole.net; Piazza Regina Elena 19; ☺ 9am-noon & 3.30-6.30pm Mon-Sat, 10am-noon Sun) has extensive information for the entire valley, and can advise you on walking trails and ski facilities in the area. The three-star **Liberty Hotel Malè** (☎ 0463 90 11 05; www.libertyhotelmale .it; Piazza Garibaldi 33; s/d full board from €56/88; **P**) is one of a handful of good-quality hotels in the village. Half board is just €4 less per person.

From **Peio Terme** (Pejo Terme; 1393m) in the **Valle di Peio**, chair lifts operate to the Rifugio Doss dei Cembri (2400m), from where expert mountaineers scale great heights to reach Monte Vioz (3645m) and the edge of the Forni glacier. If that sounds like too much exertion, you can relax at the **Terme di Pejo** (☎ 0463 75 32 26; www.termepejo.it; Via delle Acque Acidule 3, Peio), a three-star hotel and spa complex which offers a variety of spa treatments and 'wellness packages', including weight-loss and anti-stress programmes lasting from one week. Contact them for details and prices.

Ferrovia Trent–Malè buses (☎ 0463 90 11 50) connect Peio Terme with Madonna di Campiglio and Malè. Malè is on the Trent–Malè train line (1½ hours, eight daily).

PALE DI SAN MARTINO
elev 1467m

Hopping east across the Brenner motorway (A22), which brutally slices through the region, one comes up against the imposing range, Pale di San Martino – mountains so stark and grey-white they virtually glow in the dark. Noted for its Alpine vegetation and wildlife, including roe deer, chamois, marmots, wildfowl and birds of prey such as the golden eagle, this impressive mountain range is embraced by the Parco Naturale Paneveggio Pale di San Martino. At its feet huddles **San Martino di Castrozza**, a small but popular Trentino skiing resort and walking spot.

Equally popular, and offering more facilities, is **Cavalese** (population 3600; elevation 1000m), a small town wedged in the floor of the **Val di Fiemme** from where skiers take a cable car up to the Cermis ski area (2229m) and beyond. To take a break from the snow, you can visit the **Centro Arte Contemporanea Cavalese** (☎ 0462 23 54 16; www.artecavalese.it; Palazzo

Firmian, Piazzetta Rizzoli 1; admission free; ⏱ 3.30-7.30pm Fri-Sun), with its well-presented collection of modern art.

There are plenty of places to stay in Cavalese, one of the best being the four-star **Hotel Grünwald** (☎ 0462 34 03 69; www.hotelgrunwald.it; Via Bresadola 3; d from €140; P ⏷). Otherwise, the tourist office can help.

Information

Cavalese tourist office (☎ 0462 24 11 11; www.apt fiemme.tn.it; Via Bronzetti 60; ⏱ 9am-noon & 3.30-7pm Mon-Sat)
Parco Naturale Paneveggio-Pale di San Martino's visitors centre (☎ 0439 76 88 59; parcopan.org; Via Laghetto, San Martino)
San Martino tourist office (☎ 0439 76 88 67; www .sanmartino.com; Via Passo Rolle 165; ⏱ 9am-noon & 3-7pm Mon-Sat, 9.30am-12.30pm Sun)
Tourist medical service San Martino (☎ 0439 76 87 39); Fiera di Primiero (☎ 0439 76 20 60)

Activities

San Martino is surrounded by excellent ski runs which, together with those in the Val di Fiemme, form part of the extensive Superski Dolomiti region. In winter, ski buses connect the valley with the various runs. In summer, a chair lift and cable car from San Martino whisks walkers to the Rifugio Rosetta (2600m), from where several trails (some easy, some requiring mountaineering skills) can be picked up.

Maps of the Pale di San Martino's well-marked walking trails are available at the tourist offices (above). Alternatively, try the Parco Naturale Paneveggio-Pale di San Martino's visitors centre, or head 16km north to **Paneveggio** where the park also runs a visitors centre. A 1.2km trail leads from the visitors centre to the **Area Faunistica del Cervofauna**, a nature area where you can watch deer. At the park's impressive headquarters in the **Villa Welsperg** (⏱ 9.30am-12.30pm & 2-5pm) in Val Canali, suspended aquariums illustrate the park's water life and there are exhibitions dedicated to the flora and fauna. The villa itself was built in 1853 and is surrounded by stunning gardens. To get to the villa, follow the southbound S50 from San Martino di Castrozza for 14km and in the village of Fiera di Primiero bear east along a narrow road for a couple of kilometres. After the hamlet of Tonadico, bear left (north) to the villa.

The tourist offices act as contact points for local Alpine guide groups which organise, among other things, mountaineering ascents on Pala di San Martino, Cima della Madonna and Sass Maor, a 120km-long, high-altitude skiing excursion.

Sleeping & Eating

Local food is served at various *malghe* around San Martino, since transformed into highly atmospheric little restaurants.

Malga Venegiota (☎ 0462 57 60 44; Via Rioni 1, Tonadico; ⏱ Tue-Sun Jun-Sep) Typical dishes guaranteed to excite (see the boxed text, p328) are dished up at this authentic mountain inn at 1824m in Tonadico. The restaurant is accessible in summertime by road or on foot from Passo Rolle via a three-hour return trail from Malga Juribello, or by a shorter trail incorporating the Baita Segantini chair lift.

Agritur Darial (☎ 0462 81 47 05; www.agritur darial.it; Via Cavada 61; s/d B&B from €34/56, half board from €37/62; P) High on a hill (1100m) with a herd of goats, 4km east of Cavalese in Tesero, this working farm offers stunning views of the Val di Fiemme and excellent local cuisine, including, naturally, lots of fresh goats cheese. Evocative extras include a Finnish sauna, roaring fire and maybe even some yodelling.

Hotel Madonna (☎ 0439 6 81 37, 800 200 822; www.hotelmadonna.it; Via Passo Rolle 72; s/d full board low season from €44/80, high season from €52/94) Spend a night at San Martino's former post house dating to 1906. Run by the Poggi family from Bologna since the 1950s, the Madonna has 25 comfortable rooms overlooking the main street.

Grand Hotel des Alpes (☎ 0439 76 90 69; www .hoteldesalpes.it; Via Passo Rolle 18; s/d B&B from €60/88, full board from €76/120; P ⏹ ⏸ ⏷) San Martino's four-star option is a classy place to stay. Breakfast in the chandelier-lit Salle degli Archi (Archer's Room), dine at Il Cervo (The Deer) or enjoy a less formal, heartier meal at La Canisela (The Path). Prices vary throughout the year, and between June and September there is a one-week minimum stay.

Getting There & Away

Trentino Trasporti buses run to San Martino from Trent (€5.60) and Canazei (via Predazzo).

CANAZEI & AROUND

This popular ski resort in the **Val di Fassa** is surrounded by the striking peaks of the Gruppo di Sella to the north, the Catinaccio (Rosengarten; 2981m) to the west and the Marmolada (3342m) to the southeast. **Canazei** (population 1809; elevation 1465m) and the villages along the valley to **Moena** (population 2662; elevation 1114m), 15km south, are geared towards summer and winter tourism, although some locals still make a traditional living from dairy farming. Pozza di Fassa and neighbouring Vigo di Fass remain strongholds of Ladin culture (see the boxed text, p332).

Those who'd rather flee the tourist flock can always head east from Moena, across the Passo San Pellegrino (1918m) into the **Valle del Biois**, where more rural pastures hold a couple of delicious places to sleep and eat. An eastbound journey from Canazei takes you across the breathtaking **Passo Pordoi** – complete with 27 hairpin bends – and into the Val Badia.

Information

Information on the **Valle del Biois** (www.trevalli .com) is doled out by the tiny tourist offices in Caviola and Falcade.

Canazei tourist office (☎ 0462 60 11 13; www.fassa .com; Piazza Marconi 5; ⏱ 8.30am-12.15pm & 3-6pm Mon-Sat, 10am-12.30pm Sun).

Caviola tourist office (☎ 0437 59 01 16; fax 0437 59 01 16; Via Lungo Tegosa 8; ⏱ 10.30am-12.30pm & 4-5pm Mon-Fri)

Falcade tourist office (☎ 0437 59 92 41; falcade@ infodolomiti.ti; Corso Roma 1; ⏱ 9am-12.30pm & 3.30-6.30pm)

Val di Fassa tourist office (☎ 0462 60 23 66; Strèda de Dolèda 10, Canazei; ⏱ 8.30am-12.15pm & 3-6pm Mon-Sat, 10am-12.30pm Sun) Information on the whole valley.

Sights & Activities

Possibilities for skiing include 120km of downhill and cross-country runs, as well as challenging Alpine tours and the Sella Ronda ski circuit (p324). Dolomiti Superski passes are valid, alongside cheaper passes specific to the Val di Fassa which cost €70/121 for three/ six days. The Tre Valli ski pass (from €80/145 for a three-/six-day pass) covers the Fassa, Biois and San Pellegrino valleys. In summer, you can ski down the Marmolada glacier.

Walkers can approach the Catinaccio group from Vigo di Fassa, 11km southwest

of Canazei. The best approach to the Gruppo di Sella (p324) is from Passo Pordoi, where a cable car goes to almost 3000m. Any gear you forgot to pack can be picked up in Canazei at the **Tecnica** (Via Roma 24) sport shop.

Canazei's green surrounds offer ample rambles for less-experienced walkers. Ask at the tourist office for a copy of the English-language brochure, *Low-level Walks in the Fassa Valley*, which outlines 29 walks in the Val di Fassa (1.5km to 8km long). Of particular interest are those incorporating visits to old Ladin landmarks such as the **Botega da Pinter** (☎ 0462 57 35 74; Via Dolomiti 4; ⏱ 10am-noon & 4-7pm Mon-Sat mid-Jun–mid-Sep), an authentic reconstruction of a cooper's workshop 17km south of Canazei in Moena, and 16th-century **La Sia** (☎ 0462 60 23 23; Via Pian Trevisan; ⏱ 9am-noon & 3-6pm Mon-Fri mid-Mar–mid-Dec), a sawmill in Penia, 3km east of Canazei along the narrow S641.

Staff at the tourist office can also advise on mountain-bike trails. In Canazei, **Detomas Fiorenzo** (☎ 0462 60 24 47; Via Pareda 31) is one of several sports shops renting bicycles, as well as skis and snowboards. The tourist office has several brochures detailing bike-riding itineraries.

Sleeping & Eating

CANAZEI

Hotels and restaurants are generally open from mid-December to Easter and again for the short summer season from June to mid-September.

Camping Catinaccio Rosengarten (☎ 0462 76 33 05; www.catinacciorosengarten.com; Via Avisio 15, Pozza di Fassi; person/tent/car low season €6.70/3/3, high season €8.50/3.50/3, 2-/4-bed bungalows from €36.50/85; **P**) This huge site in Pozza di Fassi has a selection of wood and brick bungalows if canvas isn't your thing, and lots of facilities and activities on hand, including archery, football, gymnastics classes and a baby club. They also offer guided mountain excursions.

Hotel Engel (☎ 0462 60 24 95; Strèda del Ciuch 10; d per person from €40; **P**) This big Alpine chalet-style affair offers good three-star comforts, and all rooms have balconies. In winter, the minimum stay is one week.

Garni Stella Alpina (☎ 0462 60 11 27; www.stella -alpina.net; Via Antermont 4; B&B per person from €34-52; **P** **✗**) This charming Alpine hotel with just seven rooms has a traditional Ladin atmosphere with mod cons including a sauna and Jacuzzi. There's also a vaulted cellar for tasting wine.

Osteria La Montanara (☎ 0462 60 13 52; Via Dolomiti 147-151; mains about €10) As well as full-blown meals, this cosy inn cooks up a tasty range of well-topped bruschette (when in season) until 1am.

VALLE DEL BIOIS

There is a trio of three-star hotels on Via Pineta (the S346) just west of Caviola in Falcade.

Pensione Rondinella (☎ 0437 59 01 22; fax 0437 59 01 22; Via Lungo Tegosa, Fedèr; s/d from €20/35; ☾ Jul-Apr) What you see is what you get at this simple, down-to-earth B&B with 11 rooms in the tiny hamlet of Fedèr, 2km from Caviola, signposted west of Canale d'Agordo off the S346. Rooms with balconies afford stunning views.

Tabià (☎ 0437 59 04 34; Fedèr; mains from €7; ☾ Wed-Mon) Authentic, homemade cuisine is cooked up at this fabulous, family-run *tabià* (hay barn) which serves wholesome food, such as ravioli stuffed with pear and gorgonzola, and mushroom-laced *pansotti* (triangle-shaped ravioli) with fried cheese.

Getting There & Away

Canazei can be reached by bus from Trent (€5.30) and by SAD bus from Bolzano and the Val Gardena. Buses do not cross the high mountain passes (such as Passo di Sella) in winter.

GRUPPO DI SELLA

The Sella group, in the western Dolomites, straddles the border between Trentino and Alto Adige, close to Cortina d'Ampezzo in the Veneto and the spectacular Parco Naturale di Fanes-Sennes-Braies. To the west is the spiky Sasso Lungo (Langkofel; 3181m), which extends to the Alpe di Siusi in Alto Adige. To the east is the Val Badia and its main town, Corvara, while to the south lies the Val di Fassa.

Skiers can complete the tour of the Sella in a single day on the famous network of runs known as the **Sella Ronda**. The long and challenging route (23.1km covered by runs and 13.5km by ski lifts) is only suitable for speedier skiers with some experience, a good level of fitness and lots of luck with the weather. Tourist offices can give you a leaflet that describes the clockwise and anticlockwise

routes, kicking off from Selva (1565m; see p331) no later than 10am. Portavescovo, at 2495m, is the highest point. You'll need a Dolomiti Superski pass (p311).

For serious walkers there is a summer version of the same leaflet detailing the circular route that takes roughly eight hours to complete. Both the Sella and Sasso Lungo walking trails can be reached from Canazei or the Val Gardena resorts by bus to Passo di Sella or Passo di Pordoi. Passo di Sella (2244m) is a mountain pass laced with hairpin bends. From the equally hair-raising Passo di Pordoi (2239m) a cable car takes you to Sasso Pordoi (2950m). Digest the breathtaking views from the café terrace of the **Rifugio Maria** (☎ 0462 60 11 78), then pick up the Alta Via No 2 trail which crosses the group, heads down to the Passo Gardena and continues into the Parco Naturale Puez-Odle.

For more information on the Sella, see Val Gardena on p331 and Val Badia on p334.

ALTO ADIGE

You could be forgiven for thinking you were no longer in Italy upon entering Alto Adige (Südtirol), and in fact this orderly Alpine fairyland owes much more to its largely Austrian heritage than it does to its recent Italian history. German has equal status with Italian, and you will see, and hear, both languages wherever you go in this region. Streets all have Italian and German names – sometimes they're very different, which can get confusing – and hotels and restaurants occasionally go by two names. The Italian versions have been used here. There's even a small political party intent on reunification with Alto Adige's neighbour to the north.

The capital, Bolzano, is a pretty and likeable town, with a distinct Austrian atmosphere, while Alto Adige is a year-round attraction for skiers, climbers and walkers, or those just looking to appreciate its natural splendour, relax in a hay bath or one of the region's more conventional spas.

For local news, views and events, pick up a copy of the local Italian daily, **Alto Adige** (www.altoadige.it in Italian); *Dolomiten,* which is published daily in German; or for culturally inquisitive souls, *La Usc di Ladins* (see the boxed text, p332).

BOLZANO

pop 97,300 / elev 265m

Provincial capital Bolzano (Bozen) is unmistakably Austrian. German competes with Italian on street signs, restaurant fronts and in conversations you'll hear in town. Both languages are compulsory subjects in school but otherwise there are precious few reminders of Italian rule here. The town's small historic centre, with its lovely Tirolean architecture and arcaded streets, harbours numerous outdoor cafés, restaurants and pubs, as well as some fine museums, one of which is now home to the famous Ötzi the Iceman (see the boxed text, p327).

Settled in the Middle Ages, Bolzano was an important market town that became a pawn in the power battles between the bishops of Trent and the counts of Tirolo. During the first decades of the 19th century it passed, with the rest of the Tirolo, from Bavaria to Austria to Napoleon's Kingdom of Italy and, finally, again to Austria. Along with the rest of the Südtirol, Bolzano was ceded to Italy after WWI and was declared the capital of the province in 1927.

Bolzano is linked by a cable car to **San Genesio** (1087m), 10km northwest by a wiggly road; **Renon**, several kilometres east; and **Colle di Villa** (1181m), 4km south. The Colle di Villa cableway is the world's oldest – you can view the original gondola at the upper terminal.

Information

Banks riddle the centre and a currency-exchange booth is at the train station.

Green & Clean (Via Garibaldi 24; ☼ 6am-midnight) Self-service laundrette.

Hospital (☎ 0471 90 81 11; Via Lorenz Böhler) Out of the centre towards Merano.

Left luggage (train station, Piazza Stazione; 1st 12hr €2, then per 2-5hr €1; ☼ 8am-6.30pm)

Police station (☎ 0471 97 60 00, ☎ 0471 94 76 80; Via Marconi 33)

Post office (Via della Posta; ☼ 8am-6.30pm Mon-Fri, 8am-1pm Sat)

Tourist office (☎ 0471 30 70 00; www.bolzano-bozen.it; Piazza Walther 8; ☼ 9am-6.30pm Mon-Fri, 9am-12.30pm Sat)

Sights & Activities

Start a sightseeing tour of the town with the Gothic **cathedral** (Piazza Parrocchia; ☼ 9.45am-noon

BOLZANO

0   200 m
0   0.1 miles

INFORMATION
Green & Clean.................................1 C3
Police Station..................................2 A3
Post Office......................................3 B2
Tourist Office..................................4 B2

SIGHTS & ACTIVITIES
Castel Mareccio...............................5 A1
Cathedral..6 B2
Chiesa di Domenicani........................7 A2
Chiesa di Francescani........................8 B1
Club Alpino Italiano..........................9 B2
Giacomelli Sports............................10 A2
Museo Archeologico dell'Alto
Adige..11 A2
Museo di Scienze Naturali Alto
Adige..12 C1
Sportler Velo..................................13 C2

SLEEPING 🛏
Hotel Figl.....................................14 B2
Hotel Greif....................................15 B2
Parkhotel Laurin.............................16 C2
Stadt Hotel Città.............................17 B2

EATING 🍴
Cavallino Bianco/Weiss Rössl.....18 B1
Hopfen & Co..................................19 B2
Lounge Exil Cafe.............................20 B2
Market..21 B2
Nadamas.......................................22 B2

TRANSPORT
Bike Rental Stall.............................23 B3
Intercity Bus Station.......................24 B3

TRENTINO-ALTO ADIGE

MUSEUM CARD

Serious sightseers would do well to pick up the Museum Card (€2.50), valid for an entire year. It gives discounted access to Castel Roncolo and five museums in Bolzano, plus a discount on city tours. The Museum Card is available at the tourist office and from participating museums.

& 2-5pm Mon-Fri, 9.45am-noon Sat) and the nearby **Chiesa dei Domenicani** (Piazza Domenicani; ☼ 9.30am-6pm Mon-Sat), with its cloisters and chapel featuring 14th-century frescoes of the Giotto school. Take a walk along arcaded **Via Portici**, through the charming Piazza delle Erbe, the daily fresh-produce market, to reach the 14th-century **Chiesa di Francescani** (Via dei Francescani). It features beautiful cloisters and a magnificent Gothic altarpiece, carved in 1500 by Hans Klocker, in the Cappella della Beata Vergine (Chapel of the Blessed Virgin).

Bolzano's top attraction is the **Museo Archeologico dell'Alto Adige** (☎ 0471 32 01 00; www.iceman.it; Via Museo 43; adult/child under 6 yrs €8/free; ☼ 10am-5pm Tue, Wed & Fri-Sun, 10am-7pm Thu) displaying an important collection of regional treasures, including prehistoric and Roman remnants from the area. However, the real star of the show is Ötzi, the Iceman (see the boxed text, opposite). The amazingly intact mummified body, decorated with mysterious tattoos, was discovered in the Similaun glacier in September 1991 and dates back over 5000 years. The so-called iceman's clothing and equipment is on display, while his body is kept in a separate, temperature-controlled room with a tiny window to peer through. Frustratingly, information is only in German and Italian.

Alto Adige's wondrous flora, fauna and geology can be discovered at the **Museo di Scienze Naturali Alto Adige** (☎ 0471 41 29 64; www.museonatura.it; Via dei Bottai 1; adult/child €5/3.50; ☼ 10am-6pm Tue-Sun). The centrepiece is its gigantic saltwater aquarium.

Bolzano's surrounds have several castles worth the trek, including the 12th-century **Castel Mareccio** (Schloss Maretsch; ☎ 0471 97 66 15; mareccio@comune.bolzano.it; Via Claudia dè Medici 12; guided tours €4; ☼ tours 11.30am & 4.30pm Tue), north along Via della Roggia from Piazza delle Erbe. The **Castel Roncolo** (☎ 0471 32 98 08; roncolo@comune.bolzano.it; Via Castel Ried; adult/child €8/5.50; ☼ 10am-6pm

Tue-Sun), also known as Schloss Runkelstein, is out of town on the road to Sarentino (Sarnthein). Built in 1237, it is renowned for its rare 14th-century frescoes depicting scenes from secular literature of the day like the tale of Tristan and Isolde. **Shuttle buses** (☎ 0471 32 98 08) link Piazza Walther with Castel Roncolo between 10am and 6pm at weekends. **Castel Firmiano** (☎ 0471 63 31 45) was built on a military site dating back to AD 945; it's currently closed for restoration. A bike is an invigorating means of getting around to all three castles.

Bolzano's three cable cars whisk skiers and walkers into the mountains. **Funivia del Colle** (☎ 0471 97 85 45; Piazza Campiglio; one way/return €2.10/2.60) **Funivia del Renon** (☎ 0471 97 84 79; Via Renon; one way/return €2.50/3.50) 500m east of the train station. **Funivia San Genesio** (☎ 0471 97 84 36; Via Sarentino; one way/return €2/3.20)

Walkers and cyclists can buy gear at **Sportler Velo** (☎ 0471 97 77 19; Via Grappoli 56), or **Giacomelli Sports** (Via Museo 20a).

Tours

The tourist office organises two-hour guided walking tours of the old historic centre (€4, three times weekly, in Italian and German only).

The tourist office also organises guided expeditions of a gentle nature around Bolzano at weekends and during holidays from April to early November. A half-/full-day walk costs €10/14 and places must be reserved in advance. For more serious hikes in Alto Adige, contact local walking club **Club Alpino Italiano** (☎ 0471 97 81 72; Piazza delle Erbe 46; ☼ 11am-1pm & 5-7pm Tue-Fri).

Sleeping

Hotel Figl (☎ 0471 97 84 12; www.figl.net; Piazza del Grano 9; s/d from €75/98; P) Peering out across a pretty piazza, Figl is a fine midrange option with bright, modern rooms. Breakfast is €5.

Hotel Greif (☎ 0471 31 80 00; www.greif.it; Piazza Walther; s/d from €132/165; P) Hotel Greif's 33 light and spacious rooms have each been decorated by a different contemporary artist, and come with a laptop and free Internet access. Tasteful furnishings and marble bathrooms add to the glamour.

Stadt Hotel Città (☎ 0471 97 52 21; www.hotel citta.info; Piazza Walther 21; s/d/tr from €87/118/145;

ÖTZI THE ICEMAN'S LAST MEAL

In 1991 tourists in the mountains near the Italo-Austrian border stumbled across the body of a prehistoric hunter, remarkably well preserved in ice, together with weapons, leather clothing and a basket. The hunter subsequently became known as Ötzi, the Iceman. DNA testing on Ötzi shows that, before he was killed by a rival's arrow (found lodged in his left shoulder) he had last dined on a healthy serving of venison, probably ibex or red deer.

The body, the oldest frozen mummy yet found, was taken to Innsbruck, in Austria, where scientists dated it to around 3000 BC. This forced re-evaluation of when the Bronze Age arrived in Italy, which until this discovery had been put at around 1800 BC.

The Austrians were intent on keeping the body until surveyors confirmed that the site of its discovery is 11m inside the Italian border. In 1998 after a six-year custody battle, the Iceman was transported to Bolzano, where museum curators have created a refrigerated showcase to keep him in the same frozen state that preserved his body for 5000 years.

🔀 ❌ Ⓟ) Right in the heart of town, overlooking the main square, the Stadt Hotel dates from 1914 but has been thoroughly modernised, with neat, spacious rooms.

Parkhotel Laurin (☎ 0471 31 30 00; www.laurin.it; Via Laurin 4; s/d/ste from €115/165/280; Ⓟ 🔀 🖳 🐾) The Laurin has been Bolzano's choicest hotel since 1910, and enjoys an enviable setting in its own lush gardens in the centre of town. Rooms are spacious and individually styled, with large marble bathrooms and original artworks. The piano bar hosts jazz concerts on Friday evenings, while the restaurant is also one of Bolzano's best.

Eating & Drinking

The best restaurants in Bolzano specialise in Tirolean-style Austrian dishes such as *speckknödelsuppe* (bacon-dumpling soup), complemented with a red St Magdalener or Lagrein wine.

Hopfen & Co (☎ 0471 30 07 88; Piazza delle Erbe 17; mains about €5-8; 🕙 9.30am-1am Mon-Sat) Step back into Habsburg Austria at this venerable, 800-year-old inn which serves up hearty portions

of traditional dishes including sauerkraut and sausages cooked in beer. The bar is a pokey, smoky, dark wood-panelled affair, fine for sampling the cloudy, unfiltered beer which is brewed on the premises in a couple of gleaming copper vats, but the restaurant is in a separate smoke-free room.

Lounge Exil Cafe (☎ 0471 97 18 14; Piazza del Grano 2a) A young, fun place to hang out, this industrial café is the place to sip cocktails, drink tea or munch on a salad.

Nadamas (☎ 0471 98 06 84; Piazza delle Erbe; mains €9-12; 🕙 lunch & dinner Mon-Sat) Thai, Moroccan and various combinations of cuisines are on offer at Nadamas. Curries, couscous and salads are the order of the day.

Cavallino Bianco/Weiss Rössl (☎ 0471 97 32 67; Via dei Bottai 6; mains €10; 🕙 8am-1am Mon-Sat) Extremely popular and reasonably priced, the 'White Horse' serves up a wide choice of traditionally meaty treats, plus there's some decent vegetarian options.

Pick up fruit, vegetables, bread, cheese and meats from the morning **market** (Piazza delle Erbe; 🕙 Mon-Sat).

Getting There & Around

Bolzano airport (Aeroporto di Bolzano; ☎ 0471 25 52 55; info@abd-airport.it) is served by a couple of daily flights to Rome, Munich, Olbia and Cagliari.

Buses run by **SAD** (www.sad.it) leave from the **bus station** (☎ 800 846 047; Via Perathoner) for destinations throughout the province, including Val Gardena (up to 12 daily), Brunico (up to 10 daily), Val Pusteria (four or five daily) and Merano (55 minutes, hourly between 6.10am and 11.25pm). SAD buses also head for resorts outside the province, including Cortina d'Ampezzo. Updated timetables are on the SAD website.

Bolzano **train station** (Piazza Stazione) is connected by hourly trains with Merano (40 minutes), Trent (€2.20, 30 minutes) and Verona (2½ hours), from where trains to dozens of other cities can be picked up.

You can also catch a train from Bolzano to Brunico (€6.80, 1½ hours, six daily) in the Val Pusteria.

Bicycles can be picked up for free at the **open-air stall** (☎ 0471 99 75 78; Via della Stazione 2; 🕙 7.30am-8pm Easter-Oct) near the train station; you may need to leave a deposit. The tourist office also rents bikes for €5 per day (plus €10 deposit).

FANTASTIC FOOD

Try out some of the following for an authentic taste of Trentino-Alto Adige, and wash it all down with a chilled mug of Forst, the local beer brewed in Merano.

Canederli Germanic Alto Adige's answer to pasta: large bread dumplings, known in German as *knödel*.

Cotto e cren Cooked ham with horseradish; *salsa al cren* is a sausage variation, and both are antipasti.

Formaggio grigio A most interesting cheese from the Val Pusteria, concocted from unpasteurised milk and guaranteed to thrill. The Gasthof-Albergo Oberraut near Brunico is one of the few farms where one can still sample it; season with apple vinegar, olive oil and salt.

Gulasch A thinner version of spicy Hungarian goulash, either served as a soup or with *canederli* as a steamy main course.

Polenta e coniglio Game dishes are popular in Trentino-Alto Adige; this one includes rabbit, cooked up with polenta.

Polenta e crauti Cornflour meal and sauerkraut, two staple ingredients in the kitchens of Trentino-Alto Adige.

Risotto ai funghi Risotto laced with *brisa* mushrooms, locally picked and known for their extraordinarily strong and distinctive flavour.

Spàtzle Little flour and egg dumplings, topped with melted gorgonzola make a tasty antipasto or are dished up alongside meat as a main course.

Strangolapreti Spinach-flavoured gnocchi.

Strudel A tasty desert of sliced and cooked apples rolled in a thick pastry.

Trippa alla parmigiana Tripe with Parmesan cheese.

MERANO

pop 34,235 / elev 323m

Merano (Meran) is a picturesque little town, with a typically Tirolean centre – clean, sedate and well tended – that throngs with tourists in season. The town has long been known for its spa treatments, and the state-of-the-art Terme di Merano, a thermal-bath complex offering a wide range of therapeutic and beauty programmes, is a big draw year-round. The town neighbours the Parco Naturale Gruppo del Tessa, the Parco Nazionale dello Stelvio and the spectacular Ortles mountain range, making Merano a handy stopover on the way to higher altitudes.

Orientation & Information

The train and bus stations are a 10-minute stroll from the centre. Exit the train station, turn right into Via Europa and at Piazza Mazzini take Corso Libertà – past the tourist office and several banks with ATMs – to reach the historic centre. Pedestrianised Via dei Portici is the main shopping street.

Emergency mountain rescue (☎ 0473 22 23 33, 118)

Ospedale Civile Tappeiner (☎ 0473 26 33 33; Via Rossini 5) For medical emergencies.

Post office (Via Roma 2) On the other side of the River Passirio from the old town.

Tourist office (☎ 0473 23 52 23; www.meraninfo.it; Corso Libertà 35; ☺ 9am-12.30pm & 2-6pm Mon-Fri, 9.30am-12.30pm Sat)

Sights

The historic centre of town surrounds arcaded Via dei Portici and Piazza del Duomo – take any of the streets off Corso Libertà near the tourist office (leading away from the river).

Exhibits chronicle 200 years of female fashions at the **Museo della Donna** (☎ 0473 23 12 16; Via dei Portici 68; adult/child €3.60/2.60; ☺ 10am-noon & 2-5pm Mon-Fri, 10am-12.30pm Sat Jan-Oct, 10am-6pm Sat-Mon Nov & Dec), with plenty of period costumes and accessories. The **Museo Civico** (☎ 0473 23 60 15; Via delle Corse 42; adult/child €2/1.50; ☺ 10am-5pm Tue-Sat, 10am-1pm Sun Sep-Jun, 4-7pm Sun Jul & Aug), meanwhile, focuses on local archaeology, history and art, and counts a rare death mask of Napoleon among its collection. The third in the museum trio, the **Museo Ebraico** (☎ 0473 23 61 27; Via Schiller 14; admission free; ☺ 3-6pm Tue & Wed, 9am-noon Thu, 3-5pm Fri) is housed in Merano's synagogue, built in 1901. The museum recounts the history of the town's Jewish population from the early 19th century through to WWII.

Of Alto Adige's many castles, **Castello Principesco** (☎ 0473 23 01 02; Via Galilei; adult/child €2/1.50; ☺ 10am-5pm Tue-Sat, 10am-1pm Sun) – home to the Tirol princes from 1470 – is one of the better maintained. Vast landscaped gardens with numerous exotic plants, an aviary and some 100,000 tulips (when in season) surround **Castel Trauttmansdorff** (www.trauttmansdorff

.it; Via San Valentino 51a), a mid-19th-century castle where Empress Sissi stayed while taking the waters at Merano. Inside, the **Touriseum** (Tourism Museum; ☎ 0473 27 01 72; www.touriseum.it; garden & museum adult/6-17 yrs/under 6 yrs €9.50/7/free; ☺ 9am-6pm mid-Mar–mid-Nov, 9am-9pm May-Sep) tells the historical tale of Alpine tourism.

Beer-lovers will enjoy a tour of the **Forst Brewery** (☎ 0473 26 01 11; Forst), just outside Merano. The tourist office has details; tours are by advance reservations only.

Activities

The recently renovated **Terme Merano** (Therme Meran; ☎ 0473 25 20 00; www.kurbadmeran.it; Piazza Terme 1; swimming pools 2hr adult/child €8.50/4.50, all day €11.50/7.50; ☺ 9am-10pm) is an ultramodern spa and 'wellness' centre, boasting a staggering 25 indoor and outdoor pools. Treatments on offer include herbal baths, massages, facials and reflexology. Prices start at €99 for the 'Grape Power' treatment including a grape-seed bath, grape-oil massage and thermal bath, rising to €365 for a three-day detox programme. The spa complex is also home to a restaurant and a four-star hotel (which wasn't open at the time of research, but may be by now).

Some 6km east of town, the **Funivia Val di Nova** (adult half-/full-day ski pass €16/22; ☺ 9am-noon & 1.15-5pm) cable car, operated by **Funivie Monte Ivigna** (☎ 0473 23 48 21; www.meran2000.com in Italian; Via Val di Nova 37), carries winter-sports enthusiasts up to Piffling in **Merano 2000**, a small ski station at 2000m, with 40km of slopes served by five chair lifts, a gondola and a couple of drag lifts. Skiing on the mountain is limited and is best suited to beginners. Bus No 1A links Merano train station with the Val di Nova cable car.

The tourist office runs guided walks between July and September, and distributes a free map, marked up with various parks and walks, including the popular Passeggiata Tappeiner which kicks off on Via Laurin and meanders for 4km around Monte Benedetto (514m) before dropping down to the banks of the River Passirio. The **chair lift** (☎ 0473 92 31 05; Via Laurin; ☺ 9am-6pm Sep-Jun, 9am-7pm Jul & Aug), next to the start of the footpath, links Merano with the village of **Tirolo**, from where a **cable car** (☎ 0473 92 34 80) carries on up the mountain to **Muta**. Another itinerary, the Passeggiata Gilf, makes for a pleasant riverside stroll – a different

---

MERAN CARD

If you're going to be in town a while, you might find the **Meran Card** (www.meran card.com) useful. Valid for three (adult/child €25/12.50) or seven days (€46/23), it gives free access to museums, buses and lifts. It's available from the tourist office.

---

poem is carved on each of the 24 wooden benches lining the footpath.

Walking, cycling and other sports gear can be picked up at sports shop, **Sportler** (☎ 0473 21 13 40; Via dei Portici 272).

Sleeping

Pension Ausserweindlhof (☎ /fax 0473 23 42 03; www.rolbox.it/ausserweindlhof; Via Cava 2; s/d from €26.40/53; P ☒) Nestled among vineyards and orchards in quiet countryside around 3km east of town, this friendly little *pensione* has clean, plain rooms, and the pool and sauna are unexpected bonuses. There is a 10% discount for stays of three nights or more.

Hotel Westend (☎ 0473 44 76 54; www.westend .it; Via Speckbacher 9; s/d B&B low season from €49/80, half board from €61/104, s/d B&B high season from €73/128; P ☒) At the western end of the riverside promenade, the regal façade of Hotel Westend shines in all its mustard-and-gold loveliness, framed by a flowery garden. Rooms are large and modern, and there are free bikes if you fancy a ride round town.

Hotel Conte di Merano (☎ 0473 23 21 81; www .contedimerano.it; Via delle Corse 78; s/d B&B low season from €54/88, high season from €64/108; P) This grandiose place is near Via dei Portici and has lovely rooms. Half board costs €10 extra per person, while in low season a minimum stay of three nights is required.

Grand Hotel Palace (☎ 0473 27 10 00; www.pal ace.it; Via Cavour 2; s/d from €170/224; P ☒ ☒) The five-star Palace is Merano's finest hotel, set in beautifully kept grounds. As you would expect, rooms are grand, spacious and tastefully furnished, and for those quiet, contemplative moments, there's a reading room and even a chapel. Spa facilities are also offered – see the website for a price list.

Eating

Forsterbräu (☎ 0473 23 65 35; Corso della Libertà 90; mains about €10; ☺ Wed-Mon) Set around an atmospheric courtyard, this typically Tirolean restaurant cooks up a lovely *gulaschsuppe* (goulash soup) and a choice of fresh trout dishes. The place is actually part of the Forst brewery, making a pint of Forst beer and a plate of *speck* (smoked pork) an attractive proposition.

Bistro 7 (☎ 0473 21 06 36; Via dei Portici 232; mains about €10-20; ☺ 8.15am-1am) One of Merano's coolest hangouts is Bistro 7, a café/restaurant/cocktail bar. The restaurant serves up a high standard of pasta, fish and meat dishes, while the café can be a splendid spot for a leisurely breakfast.

Vinoteca Pizzeria Relax (☎ 0473 23 67 35; Via Cavour 31; pizzas about €6-8; ☺ noon-2.30pm & 6pm-12.30am) This bottle-lined bar and restaurant is a great place to try a glass or two of Alto Adige's fine wines, and the pizzas aren't bad either.

La Veneta (☎ 0473 22 02 57; Via Monastero 2; mains €7-10; ☺ lunch & dinner) Reacquaint yourself with good Italian cuisine at this traditional trattoria, serving pasta and risotto dishes in a big garden. Tripe and veal are perhaps less appealing house specialities. Upstairs, there are 10 rooms if you want to stay (B&B €28 per person).

Alto Adige's famed *speck* as well as other meats and sausages are sold at **Gögele** (Via dei Portici 77-83).

Getting There & Around

SAD buses connect Merano **bus station** (Piazza Stazione) with Monte San Caterina and other villages that give access to the Tessa group, as well as to Silandro and the valleys leading into the Parco Nazionale dello Stelvio and the Ortles range.

Bolzano (€2.20, almost hourly) is an easy 40-minute journey from Merano **train station** (Piazza Stazione).

Pick up a free pair of wheels (you'll require a small deposit) from the open-air stand marked **Noleggio Biciclette-Fahrradverleih** (☺ 9am-7pm Mon-Sat Mar-Sep), located next to the bus station.

PARCO NAZIONALE DELLO STELVIO

If you can tear yourself away from the Dolomites this national park offers even more fantastic walking possibilities: at low altitudes in the pretty valleys of Val d'Ultimo, Val Martello and Val di Solda and at high altitudes on spectacular peaks such as the Gran Zebrù (3859m), Cevedale (3769m) and the breathtaking Ortler (3905m), all part of the Ortles range. There is a network of well-marked trails, including routes over some of the range's glaciers. The park incorporates one of Europe's largest glaciers, the Ghiacciaio dei Forni.

The glaciers permit year-round skiing and there are well-serviced runs at Solda and the Passo della Stelvio (2757m); the latter is the second-highest pass in the Alps and is approached from the north from the hamlet of **Trafoi** (1543m) on one of Europe's most spectacular roads, a series of tight switchbacks covering 15km, with some very steep gradients. The road is famous among cyclists, who flock to the park every summer to tackle the ascent.

With the highest slopes at 3012m, good snow is assured season-long. The **Bormio tourist office** (☎ 0342 90 33 00; www.bormioonline .com; Via Roma 131b, Bormio) is an unbeatable source of information on the entire park; its website is exhaustive.

The Parco Nazionale dello Stelvio straddles both Alto Adige and Trentino and can be approached from Merano (from where you have easy access to the Val d'Ultimo, Val Martello, Val di Solda and the Passo Stelvio), or from the Val di Sole in Trentino, which gives easy access to the Valle di Peio and the Val di Rabbi.

Bormio

elev 1125m

Immediately south of the Passo della Stelvio is this pretty little ski resort, with its well-preserved historical centre, speckled with medieval churches. The town, which hosted the 2005 Alpine World Skiing Championships, has been famous for its curative springs since Roman times, and Charlemagne, Leonardo da Vinci and Garibaldi are just a few of the luminaries among the hordes of visitors drawn here by the waters over the centuries.

Today, the **Bormio Terme** (☎ 0342 90 13 25; www .bormioterme.it; Via Stelvio 10; adult/child 1hr €12/7, 5hr €28/19; ☺ 9am-10pm Mon, Wed & Fri, 9am-8pm Thu, Sat & Sun) offers various spa treatments. The prices given include access to the pools, mud pool, sauna, Turkish bath and solarium.

If you're after a bit of rest and relaxation, try the four-star **Hotel Bagni Vecchi** (☎ 0342 91 01 31; www.bagnidibormio.it; Via Statale Stelvio; s/d half board from €139/170; P ☁ ✕), a luxurious 12-room spa complex on the site of an old

TRENTINO-ALTO ADIGE

HAY BATHS

A *bagno di fieno* (hay bath) is just what it says it is – a good long soak in the hay. South Tiroleans have been doing it for centuries.

The grass that grows on the lower slopes of the Siusi Alps (1800m to 2200m) is reputed to make the best bath. In summer, the mountain meadows' heady cocktail of grasses, aromatic plants and medicinal herbs, such as lavender and thyme, are cut when damp and left to ferment for several days. Then it's bath time.

Swaddled in a sheet, bathers immerse themselves in a 'trough' of hay, freshly watered and warmed, for between 15 minutes to an hour. As the bath heats up, bathers sweat. Obesity, back-ache, gout, rheumatism and lumbago are among the ills a hay bath is said to soothe.

Hay baths are said to originate from the very simple concept of farmers taking a quick and refreshing snooze on their freshly cut hay. Founded in 1903 great-grandfather Kompatscher of today's **Hotel Heubad** (Hotel Hay Bath; ☎ 0471 72 50 20; www.hotelheubad.com; Via Sciliar 12, Fiè di Sopra; d half board per person low/high season from €59/70, s supplement per day €6; ☯ Apr-Oct; Ⓟ 🗙 🛋), 12km northeast of Bolzano in the mountain hamlet of **Fiè allo Sciliar** (800m), opened South Tirol's first hay-bathing station. Guests today can opt for one of several packages (a four-/seven-/10-day stay with half board and three/six/eight hay baths and massages costs from €380/690/960) but anyone can drop by for a one hour hay bath (€30), as well as various massages, manicures, pedicures and so on. Advance reservations ensure a successful soak.

Roman bathing site, with no less than 30 hot springs, and a host of spa treatments available to guests. The minimum stay is two nights, and prices include unlimited spa access.

Val di Solda

The village of **Solda** (1906m), at the head of the Val di Solda, is a small ski resort and a base for walkers and climbers in summer. Challenging trails lead you to high altitudes, including trail No 28, which crosses the Madriccio pass (3123m) into the Val Martello. Solda **tourist office** (☎ 0473 61 30 15) has information on accommodation and activities. Between October and Christmas the village all but shuts down.

SAD buses connect Solda with Merano Monday to Friday during the summer only; you need to change at Spondigna.

Val Martello

This picturesque valley is a good choice for relatively low-altitude walks, with spectacular views of some of the park's high peaks.

The real beauty of the valley is that it is unspoiled by ski lifts and downhill ski runs. In the winter there is excellent cross-country skiing, and climbers can attempt the valley's frozen waterfalls from January to March.

People with children might like to take trail No 20 up into the Val di Peder. It is an easy walk with some lovely picnic spots along the way and the chance to see animals, including chamois and deer.

The road into the valley is open year-round, and SAD bus 107 runs to **Martello** village from Silandro.

VAL GARDENA

An enchanting Alpine valley, Val Gardena is hemmed in by the towering peaks of the Parco Naturale Puez-Odle, the imposing Gruppo di Sella and Sasso Lungo, and the gentle slopes of the Alpe di Siusi, the largest high plain in the Alps. It is one of the most popular skiing areas in the Alps because of the relatively reasonable prices and excellent facilities offered by the valley's main towns – **Ortisei** (population 5500; elevation 1236m), **Santa Cristina** (population 1760; elevation 1428m) and **Selva** (population 2500; elevation 1563m). Its ski runs throng with snow fiends in winter, while warmer months see walkers flock to trails at both high and low altitudes.

Along with Val Badia, the Val Gardena has managed to preserve the ancient Ladin language and culture, and a rich tradition of colourful legends (for more details see the boxed text, p332). The ancient tradition of woodcarving is nurtured here and the valley's artisans are famed for their statues, figurines, altars and toys. Beware of mass-produced imitations.

TRENTINO-ALTO ADIGE

THE LADIN TRADITION

Ladin language and culture can be traced back to around 15 BC, when the people of the Central Alps were forcibly united into the Roman province of Rhaetia. The Romans, of course, introduced Latin to the province, but the original inhabitants of the area modified the language to such an extent that by the 5th century it had evolved into an independent Romance language, known as Rhaeto-Romanic. At one point the entire Tirol was Ladin but today the language and culture are confined to the Val Gardena and the Val Badia where, in the 1981 census, about 90% of locals declared that they belonged to the Ladin language group. Along with German and Italian, Ladin is taught in schools, and the survival of the Ladin cultural and linguistic identity is protected by law. **La Usc di Ladins** (www.lauscdiladins.com in Ladin & Italian) is the local Ladin-language newspaper.

Ladin culture is rich in vibrant poetry and legends, and peopled by fairies, elves, giants and heroes. Passed on by word of mouth for centuries, and often heavily influenced by Germanic myths, many of these legends were once in danger of being lost. In the early 1900s journalist Carlo Felice Wolff, who had lived most of his life in Bolzano, spent 10 years gathering and researching the local legends, listening to the old folk, farmers and shepherds recount the legends and fairytales. The legends he eventually published were reconstructed from the many different versions he gathered.

The magic of these myths is rekindled in Ortisei's **Museo Ladin** (☎ 0471 79 75 54; Piazza San Antonio; admission free; ☉ 10am-noon & 3-7pm Tue-Sun Jul & Aug, 3-6.30pm Tue-Fri Jun, Sep & Oct, 3-6.30pm Tue & Fri Nov-Apr) – not to be confused with the other Museo Ladin in the Tor Castle. The museum has particularly good sections on flora and fauna specific to the Ladin lands, and local woodcarving. Ask here or at the tourist office for information on woodcarving courses run in the town in July and August. Of a similar ilk is the **Museo Ladin di Fascia** (☎ 0462 76 01 82; museo@istladin.net; Via Milano 5; admission free; ☉ 10am-noon & 3-7pm Jul & Aug, 3-7pm Tue-Sat Sep-Jun), in Pozza di Fassa in the Val di Fassa. The **Institut Cultural Ladin** (☎ 0462 76 42 67; www.istladin .net; Via della Chiesa 6), in neighbouring Vigo di Fassa, was set up in 1975 to safeguard the Ladin language and culture and holds an extensive library and film archive. It also runs Ladin language courses, mainly aimed at locals.

The state-of-the-art **Museo Ladin** (☎ 0474 52 40 20; www.museumladin.it; Via Tor 72; adult/child €5.50/ 2.75; ☉ 10am-6pm Tue-Sat, 2-6pm Sun mid-Mar–Oct, 2-6pm Wed-Fri end-Dec–mid-Mar) inside 12th-century Tor Castle, some 15km south of Brunico in San Martino in Badia (S244) is the largest of the three museums, packed with informative multimedia displays.

Information

Ortisei tourist office (☎ 0471 79 63 28; info@val-gar dena.net; Via Rezia 1; ☉ 8.30am-12.30pm & 2.30-6.30pm Mon-Sat, 8.30am or 10am-noon & 5-6.30pm Sun)
Santa Cristina tourist office (☎ 0471 79 30 46; fax 0471 79 31 98; Via Chemun 9; ☉ 8am-noon & 2.30-6.30pm Mon-Sat, 8.30am or 9.30am-noon Sun)
Selva tourist office (☎ 0471 79 51 22; fax 0471 79 42 45; Via Mëisules 213; ☉ 8am-noon & 3-6.30pm Mon-Sat, 8.30am or 9am-noon & 4.30pm or 5-6.30pm Sun)
Tourism Val Gardena (www.gardena.org)
Tourist medical service Ortisei (☎ 0471 79 77 85); Selva (☎ 0471 79 42 66)

Activities

In addition to its own fine downhill ski runs, the valley forms part of the Sella Ronda, a network of ski runs connecting the Val Gardena, Val Badia, Livinallongo and Val di Fassa (for which you will need a Dolomiti Superski pass). Ski passes covering the use of 81 lifts in the Val Gardena are marginally cheaper – €28/82/144 for one/three/six days (high season €31/90/158).

Areas such as the Vallunga, near Selva, offer cross-country skiing. There are stunning trails around Forcella Pordoi and Val Lasties in the Gruppo di Sella, and on the Sasso Lungo.

This is also a walkers' paradise with endless possibilities, from the challenging Alte Vie of the Gruppo di Sella and the magnificent Parco Naturale Puez-Odle, to picturesque strolls for walkers of all abilities in spots such as the Vallunga. Those seeking guidance can contact the nearest office of the **Scuola di Alpinismo Catores** (www.catores .com; ☉ summer only) in **Ortisei** (☎ 0471 79 82 23;

TRENTINO-ALTO ADIGE

Piazza della Chiesa; ☑ 5.30-7pm) or **Santa Cristina** (☎ 0471 79 30 99; Piazza Dosses; ☑ 5.30-7pm). Both Alpine guide schools can organise botanical walks, as well as climbing courses, glacier excursions and treks.

In summer cable cars carry walkers into the mountains from all three towns in the valley. From Ortisei you can ride a cable car to Seceda which, at 2456m, offers a memorable view – one of the most spectacular in the Alps – of the Gruppo di Odle, a series of spiky pinnacles. From Seceda trail No 2a passes through a typical Alpine environment; lush, green sloping pastures dotted with wooden *malghe*, used by herders as summer shelters.

Sleeping & Eating

Tourist offices have full lists of eating and sleeping options in the valley.

Hotel Posta Al Cervo (☎ 0471 79 51 74; www .hotelpostaalcervo.com; Via Meisules 116, Selva; d B&B per person low/high season from €31/37, half board from €38/55; P ☒) Right in the centre of town, the Posta al Cervo is a friendly and reasonably priced little place with cosy, woody rooms and a fine restaurant serving Ladin and Italian cuisine.

Hotel Alpenheim (☎ 04/1 /9 65 15; www.alpen heim.it; Via Grohmann 54, Ortisei; s/d half board from €65/114; P ☒ ☒) The Alpenheim is a smart four-star establishment luxuriating in large, well-manicured grounds. Room décor is a trifle bland, but all come with balconies, and there's a full programme of inhouse spa treatments on offer. Various package deals are available.

Hotel Maria (☎ 0471 79 70 47; www.hotelmaria .cc; Via Rezia 49, Ortisei; s/d from €61/112; P) In Ortisei's pedestrian heart, Maria is a spotless modern option in a renovated townhouse. Guests are offered free use of nearby swimming pools and tennis courts.

Hotel Adler (☎ 0471 77 50 00; www.hotel-adler.com; Via Rezia 7, Ortisei; s/d from €109/196; P ☒ ☐ ☒) Offering a 'water world' with various pools, oriental and Turkish baths, and an original Ladin farmstead where you can relax in a hay bath, a 'fitness world' with a gym and steam baths, and a programme of Ayurvedic treatments, the four-star Adler is a haven for the sore and the tired, or for those who just want to relax in style. There's also a lounge, library and a kids' club with playrooms and guided activities. For much of

the year, full-board seven-day packages are obligatory.

Ristorante Concordia (☎ 0471 79 62 76; Via Roma 41, Ortisei; mains about €10-12; ☑ lunch & dinner) Considered to be one of Ortisei's best restaurants, Concordia serves fresh homemade pasta and other Italian standards in a wood-panelled dining room.

Getting There & Around

The Val Gardena is accessible from Bolzano by SAD bus, as well as from Canazei (summer only). Regular buses connect the towns along the valley and you can reach the Alpe di Siusi by either bus or cable car. Full timetables are available at the tourist offices.

In winter the Val Gardena Ski Express is a shuttle bus service linking the various villages and lifts in the valley; a €2 ticket covers a week's unlimited travel.

ALPE DI SIUSI & PARCO NATURALE DELLO SCILIAR

There's something magical about the view across the Alpe di Siusi to the Sciliar, as the green undulating pastures end dramatically at the foot of these towering peaks. It is a particularly spectacular scene in an area that certainly doesn't lack views. The Alpe di Siusi (1700m to 2200m), the largest plateau in Europe, forms part of what is known as the Altipiano dello Sciliar, which also incorporates the villages of **Castelrotto** and **Siusi**, lower down at about 1000m.

There is something for walkers of all ages and expertise in this area. The gentle slopes of the Alpe di Siusi are perfect for families with kids, and you won't need much more than average stamina to make it to the **Rifugio Bolzano** (☎ 0471 61 20 24) at 2457m, just under Monte Pez (2564m), the Sciliar's summit. If you're after more challenging walks, the jagged peaks of the Catinaccio group and the Sasso Lungo are nearby. These mountains are famous among climbers worldwide. There are also several *vie ferrate* and plenty of good trails for mountain bikers. The Catinaccio group can also be approached from the Val di Fassa.

Alpe di Siusi tourist offices in **Castelrotto** (☎ 0471 70 63 33; www.castelrotto.org; Piazza Kraus 1), **Siusi** (☎ 0471 70 70 24; Via Sciliar 8) and **Compaccio** (☎ 0471 72 79 04) have heaps of information on winter activities such as downhill skiing, ski-mountaineering, cross-country skiing and walking trails (with snow shoes) in the area – part of the Superski Dolomiti network.

The Altipiano dello Sciliar is accessible by SAD bus from Bolzano, the Val Gardena and Bressanone. By car, exit the Brenner motorway (A22) at Bolzano Nord or Chiusa. From May to October the roads of the Alpe di Siusi are closed to normal traffic. Tourists with a hotel booking in the zone can obtain a permit from the Compaccio tourist office, allowing them to drive between 4pm and 10am. Organise your pass before arriving in the area; ask your hotel for assistance. A regular bus service operates from Castelrotto and Siusi to Compaccio, and from there onto the Alpe di Siusi.

VAL BADIA

Along with the Val Gardena, Val Badia is one of the last strongholds of the ancient Ladin culture and language. Many Ladin legends are set on the nearby Fanes high plain, which forms part of the magnificent Parco Naturale di Fanes-Sennes-Braies. This is one of the most evocative places in the Dolomites and can be reached easily from the Val Badia, either on foot or by cable car from Passo Falzarego.

Towns in the valley – Colfosco (1645m), La Villa (1433m), San Cassiano (1537m) and Corvara (1568m) – together form the Alta Badia ski area.

CORVARA

pop 1268 / elev 1568m

The central town of the Ladin tribes, Corvara is an amenable place with plenty of accommodation. Primarily a ski resort, it is also an excellent base for walkers wanting to tackle the peaks enclosing the Alta Badia. Of the Alta Badia's 130km of slopes, it is the Gran Rosa ski slope, 4.5km north of Corvara in La Villa, that is undoubtedly the most legendary.

Information

Associazione Guide Alpine Val Badia (☎ 0471 83 68 98; guide.valbadia@rolmail.net; Via Burje) For advice on skiing, heli-skiing, ice climbing and advanced walking trails. Phone lines are only manned between 6pm and 7pm.

Corvara tourist office (☎ 0471 83 61 76; www.alta badia.org; Via Col Alt 36; ☼ 8am-noon & 3-6pm Mon-Fri, 9am-noon & 3-6pm Sat, 10.30am-12.30pm Sun) A good source of information.

Helicopter mountain rescue (☎ 0471 79 71 71,118)
Hospital (☎ 0474 58 11 11) The closest public hospital is in Brunico.

Activities

Corvara is located on the much-vaunted Sella Ronda – a four-valley downhill ski circuit which, tackled from either direction, takes in 90 minutes of lifts and 120 minutes of skiing – and is part of the Dolomiti Superski network (see p311). A cheaper Alta Badia ski pass, restricted to Alta Badia's 130km of slopes, costs €30/87/153 for one/three/six days (high season €34/99/173); passes are sold at the **ski pass office** (☎ 0471 83 63 66; Via Col Alt 88c). Ski schools are listed online at www .altabadiaski.com.

From the Passo Falzarego mountain pass (2105m), 20km east of Corvara, a cable car ascends into the Parco Naturale di Fanes-Sennes-Braies. Alternatively, pick up trail No 12 from near La Villa or trail No 11, which joins Alta Via No 1 at the Capanna Alpina, a few kilometres off the main road between Passo Valparola and San Cassiano. Either trail takes you up to the Alpe di Fanes and the two *rifugi*, Lavarella and Fanes.

A combination of cable car and chair lift will take you from Corvara up the Gruppo di Sella at Vallon (2550m), where you'll get a spectacular view across to the Marmolada glacier. From Vallon you can traverse the Sella or follow the trail that winds around the valley at the top of the chair lift.

Horse riding, mountain biking and hanggliding are other popular valley activities. A tandem flight with paragliding school **Centro Volo Libero Alta Badia** (☎ 0471 84 75 92; www.cvl-alta badia.com in Italian & German; Via Bosc da Plan 46) in La Villa costs €65. Corvara tourist office has a list of places where you can hire mountain bikes.

Sleeping & Eating

Most hotels open early December to early April and mid-June to early October. All the places listed double as reasonable eating options.

Posta Zirm Hotel (☎ 0471 83 61 75; www.postazirm .com; Via Col Alt 95; s/d half board low season from €90/160, s/d high season from €115/210; P R) Corvara's largest and most prominent hotel – at the top of the street next to the Sport Kostner shopping complex – dates from 1808 and has a popular restaurant and tavern.

Hotel Marmolada (☎ 0471 83 61 39; www.hotel -marmolada.com; Via Col Alt 80; s/d half board from €58/100; **P**) This large wooden structure, opposite the main ski-pass office, is a charming place to stay in summer or winter. Its restaurant dishes up solid regional fare.

La Perla (☎ 0471 83 10 00; www.romantikperla.it; Via Col Alt 105; d half board per person from €182; **P**) Corvara's 'romantik hotel' is a four-star oasis of luxury. Excellent food and wine dished up in traditional, 18th-century Ladin-style restaurant are among its many sensory delights.

Getting There & Away

From the bus stop in front of the Posta Zirm Hotel on Via Col Alt, **SAD buses** (☎ 800 84 60 47; www.sii.bz.it) link Corvara with Bolzano (€6.80, 2½ hours, up to five daily in season) and Brunico (€4.90, 1¼ hours, eight daily). Less-frequent services link Corvara with the Val Gardena, Passo Sella and Passo Pordoi, Canazei and the Passo Falzarego. Buses reroute in winter to avoid crossing high mountain passes.

CORTINA D'AMPEZZO

pop 6570 / elev 1224m

Across the Fanes-Conturines range from the Val Badia is the queen of the Dolomites, Cortina d'Ampezzo. Italy's most famous, fashionable and expensive ski resort, Cortina is situated in the Veneto, but has been included here because of its central location. Despite the high-flyer status, there is reasonably priced accommodation to be found if you know where to look and book well in advance.

Situated in the Ampezzo bowl, Cortina is surrounded by some of the most stunning mountains in the Dolomites, including (in a clockwise direction) Cristallo, the Gruppo di Sorapiss-Marmarole, Antelao, Becco di Mezzodi-Croda da Lago, Nuvolau-Averau-Cinque Torri and Tofane. To the south are the Pelmo and the Civetta. Facilities for both downhill and cross-country skiing are first class, and the small town's population swells dramatically during the ski season; great walking and climbing possibilities crowd out the town in summer, too.

Information

Croce Bianca (☎ 0436 27 71) Emergency medical aid.
Post office (Largo Poste 20; ⏱ 8.30am-6.30pm Mon-Fri, 8.30am-1pm Sat)

Tourist office (☎ 0436 32 31; www.infodolomiti.it; Piazzetta San Francesco 8; ⏱ 9am-12.30pm & 3.30-6.30pm)

Activities

Cortina offers some first-rate skiing, especially for advanced skiers whose hearts could well skip a beat when they stand at the top of the legendary Staunies black mogul run at 3000m. Of the resort's nine cable cars, two cars whisk walkers and skiers straight into the mountains from downtown Cortina: the two-stage **Funivia Cortina-Faloria** (☎ 0436 25 17; Via G Marconi; one way/return €10/14) links the town with the Faloria ski area at 2123m, and the three-stage **Funivia Cortina-Tofana di Mezzo** (☎ 0436 50 52; Via dello Stadio; one way/return €22/34) climbs to 3130m. Lifts generally run 9am to 5pm daily mid-December to early April, and from June to September or early October. Ski passes are sold at the **ski pass office** (☎ 0436 86 21 71; Via G Marconi 15), while the Dolomiti Superski ski pass also covers the resort.

Dog sledding, scaling frozen waterfalls, and ice skating inside Cortina's **Olympic Ice Stadium** (☎ 0436 43 80; Via dello Stadio; ⏱ 10.30am-12.30pm & 3.30-5.30pm mid-Dec–Mar) are some of the other winter sports to try out. The **Gruppo Guide Alpine Cortina** (☎ 0436 86 85 05; www.guide cortina.com; Corso Italia 69a) organises the usual rock-climbing courses and guided walks for adults, plus history and nature excursions and courses for kids.

Not far from Cortina, and accessible by Dolomiti Bus in summer, are the Tre Cime di Lavaredo, one of the world's most famous climbing locations and a panoramic place to walk. The fact that you can arrive by bus literally at the foot of the Tre Cime means the area is very busy in the high season.

Sleeping & Eating

International Camping Olympia (☎ 0436 50 57; www .campingolympiacortina.it; person/tent & car from €4.50/7; **P**) Pitch your tent at 1283m at this friendly site, 4km north of Cortina in Fiames. There's space for 300 tents, or book well ahead of time and snag one of 25 beds in a bungalow. Local bus services connect the town with International Camping Olympia at Fiames and Pocol.

Pensione Fiames (☎ 0436 23 66; fax 0436 57 33; Via Fiames 13; s/d from €30/40) This *pensione*, 4km north of Cortina in Fiames, has garden and breakfast terrace. It's cheap and basic but cosy enough.

Hotel Montana (☎ 0436 86 04 98; www.cortina
-hotel.com; Corso Italia 94; s/d from €48/72) Right beside the church, the central Montana is an
unbeatable two-star deal.

Baita Fraina (☎ 0436 36 34; www.baitafraina.it; Via
Fraina 1; d B&B per person low/high season from €39/65;
☽ Tue-Sun Jul-Sep & Dec–mid-Apr) This family-run
B&B, 3km from the centre, is as popular for
its kitchen as for its seven homelike rooms
with mountain views. Feast on delights such
as beetroot-stuffed ravioli, spinach gnocchi,
venison and duck.

Getting There & Away
From Cortina **bus station** (Via G Marconi), SAD
buses run to Dobbiaco (45 minutes, twice
daily), where you can change for Brunico
and Bolzano. **Dolomiti Bus** (www.dolomitibus.it in
Italian) serves Pocol (€1.40, 15 minutes, nine
daily), Passo Falzarego (€1.40, 20 minutes,
nine daily) and Belluno (€4.90).

VALZOLDANA
Valzoldana lies just 20km south of Cortina. It's also south of the imposing Civetta
(3220m) and Pelmo (3168m) groups, yet it
has none of the tourist trappings displayed by
its more illustrious neighbour. The Zoldani
once made their living by exploiting the
local resources – metal deposits and water –
to make nails for the Venetian Republic;
until 1890, that is, when a flood destroyed
their makeshift smithies. Many people left
the region and emigrated to Munich and
Vienna, setting up as travelling ice-cream
and sorbet salesmen; today many of their
descendants run famous ice-cream parlours
the world over. Since the 1970s the profits
from these commercial activities have fostered the growth of the tourism industry.

Modern **ski runs** hug the Civetta group at
Zoldo Alto. About 80km of runs link the
valley to the Dolomiti Superski network,
allowing skiers to reach the Sella and Marmolada groups. In the lower valley around
Forno di Zoldo, the landscape is unchanged,
the prices and crowds have been kept under
control and the food is authentic and excellent. On foot, take advantage of an extensive
network of **walking paths**. Six days takes the
more experienced on a round trip through
unspoiled woodland beneath the peaks of
less famous mountains like Sfornioi, Bosconero and Pramper. For more information
on summer and winter activities and places

to stay, contact the Valzoldana tourist office
in **Forno di Zoldo** (☎ 0437 78 73 49; fornodizoldo@
infodolomiti.it; Via Roma 1) or in **Zoldo Alto** (☎ 0437
78 91 45; zoldoalto@infodolomiti.it; Mareson).

Sleeping & Eating
There are numerous hotels and camp sites
in the valley, where you can eat too.

Rifugio Casera di Bosconero (☎ 0437 78 73 49;
☽ Jun-Sep) Walkers can ask at the tourist office about this mountain hut, only accessible
by foot. At 1457m, in the conifer forest at the
foot of the mountain of the same name, it is
accessible from Forno on the path marked
490A or from Lago di Pontesi on paths 490
or 485 – both are good half-day walks.

Casa Rosada (☎ 0437 79 42 26; casarosada@dolomiti
.it; Pralongo, Forno di Zoldo; 1-/2-/3-person apt per week
from €170/210/260) This beautiful flower-be-
decked mountain chalet provides a real
getaway for those happy to cook for themselves. Weekly forays in the forest are organised and a free shuttle bus runs guests
year-round to and from the lifts.

Getting There & Away
The valley is served by the S251 that descends
from the Forcella Staulanza pass (1789m) in
the north to Longarone in the southeast.
Coming from the south, leave the S51 at
Longarone, following signs to Cortina, and
then turn left onto the S251.

VAL PUSTERIA & THE SESTO DOLOMITES
On the Dolomites' northern edge, the Val
Pusteria is bordered by the magnificent
Parco Naturale di Fanes-Sennes-Braies and,
further north, by the Parco Naturale delle
Dolomiti di Sesto, which includes some of
the area's most famous peaks – among them
the Tre Cime di Lavaredo. The valley is easily reached from the Val Badia and Cortina
d'Ampezzo along the spectacular Valle di
Landro. Its main centre, **Brunico** (population 13,700; elevation 835m), is a pleasant
market town, which neighbours the tiny ski
resort of **Plan de Corones** (2275m) and has excellent transport connections for excursions
into Parco Naturale di Fanes-Sennes-Braies.
More picturesque options are the quaint **San
Candido** (population 3112; elevation 1175m),
just 9km from Austria, or **Sesto** (population
1938; elevation 1311m), at the base of the
Sesto Dolomites.

Information

Brunico tourist office (☎ 0474 55 57 22; www
.bruneck.com; Piazza Municipio 7; ⊙ 9am-12.30pm &
3-6pm Mon-Fri, 9am-noon Sat)
Plan de Corones tourist office (☎ 0474 55 54 47;
www.kronplatz.com; Via Michael Pacher 11a; ⊙ 8am-
noon & 2-6pm Mon-Sat, 10am-noon Sun)
San Candido tourist office (☎ 0474 91 31 49; Piazza
del Magistrato; ⊙ 8am-noon & 3.30-6.30pm Mon-Fri,
8am-noon Sat)
Sesto tourist office (☎ 0474 71 03 10; Via Dolomiti;
⊙ 8am-noon & 2-6pm Mon-Sat, 10am-noon Sun)

Activities

Easy to get to from the Val Pusteria is beautiful Lago di Braies, a perfect spot for a leisurely
lakeside stroll. More serious walkers might
like to tackle part of the Alta Via No 1, which
starts here. Parco Naturale di Fanes-Sennes-
Braies is more easily approached from the
Val Badia or from Passo Falzarego.

At the other end of the valley, towards
Austria, are the Sesto Dolomites, where there
are some spectacular trails. The Valle Campo
di Dentro, near San Candido, and the Val
Fiscalina, near Sesto, are criss-crossed with
trails – both walking and cross-country skiing. From the Val Fiscalina it's a long but easy
walk along trail No 102 to Rifugio Locatelli
(2405m), from where you will be able to get
a great view of the Tre Cime di Lavaredo.
Most trails around the Tre Cime are easy
enough for inexperienced walkers and families, although they get very crowded in July
and August with walkers on the tourist trail.

From May to October, adventure seekers
can take a spin on a raft with **Rafting Club
Activ** (☎ 0474 67 84 22; Via Valle Aurina 22), 12km
north of Brunico in Campo Tures. River
kayaking, canyoning and waterfall climbing
are among the wet activities run by the club.
Count on paying about €50 per person for a
half day of white-water rafting.

Plan de Corones, 4km south of Brunico, offers ample green and blue runs, making it
ideal for beginners. The station is linked by
cable car to Brunico. The Dolomiti Superski
pass can be used here, and gear can be hired
in Brunico and Plan de Corones.

Mountain bikes can be hired at **Trojer
Biciclette** (☎ 0474 91 32 16; Via Herzog Tassilo 2a) or
Papin Sport (☎ 0474 91 34 50; Via Freising 9) in San
Candido for around €15 a day. **Kronplatz Bike**
(☎ 0474 55 21 86, 348 735 03 68; www.kronplatzbike.it;
Via Ahmtaler 19) in Brunico is a fully fledged

mountain-biking club, and should be the
main contact for bikers seeking a mountain
guide or organised expedition. In Brunico,
sports shop **Sportler** (☎ 0474 55 60 23; Via Centrale)
sells cycling gear, as well as walking equipment, maps and guides.

Sleeping & Eating

The best places to rest up and feast are
around Brunico and San Candido.

Hotel Blitzburg (☎ 0474 55 57 23; www.blitzburg
.it; Via Europa 10; s/d half board from €55/100; P) In
the centre of Brunico, this atmospheric old
place offers big, bright rooms at a reasonable rate and has a sauna for guest use.

Rubner Hotel Rudolf (☎ 0474 57 05 70; www
.hotel-rudolf.com; Riscone; d/ste half board per person from
€69/78; P ⚐) This lovely Alpine idyll at the
foot of Mount Kronspatz has light, restful
rooms, a fully equipped spa with pools,
steam baths and more, and an excellent
restaurant cooking up traditional Tirolean
cuisine. The minimum stay here is three
nights.

Cavallino Bianco/Weisses Roessl (☎ 0474 91 31 35;
www.weissesroessl.com; Via Duca Tassilo 1, San Candido; d half
board per person from €75; ⊙ Wed-Mon; P ⚐ 🖥 ⚐)
This charming option, in a 17th-century
house next to the village church, is a perfect
place to eat then sleep. A spa, fitness centre,
pool and cinema for kids are perks. Again,
there's a three-night minimum stay.

Hotel Grauerbär (☎ 0474 91 31 15; www.hotel
grauerbaer.com; Via Rainer 2, San Candido; s/d half board
from €70/108; P ⚐ ⚐) Four stars and a history dating back to 1462 add up to one very
lovely place to stay. The hotel is on a quiet
pedestrian street in San Candido and guests
have free use of the village swimming pool.

Getting There & Away

SAD buses travel to Brunico (€4.90, 45 minutes, hourly) and Cortina (one hour, four
daily) from San Candido. From Bolzano,
there are buses to and from Merano, Val
Badia, San Vigilio di Marebbe and Val Gardena (on the Innsbruck bus). From either
town sporadic buses and trains go to Dobbiaco, from where buses run to Lago di
Braies.

The Val Pusteria is reached by train from
Bolzano via Fortezza (where a change is
then necessary). Brunico and San Candido
are 40 minutes and 1¼ hours from Fortezza,
respectively.

The Veneto

Most travellers to the Veneto are so dazzled by Venice they neglect the rest. But it's well worth setting aside a few days to behold Giotto's extraordinary frescoes in Padua and perhaps to take in an opera at Verona's Roman Arena. Even without the opera, how can you pass up on the romantic city of *Romeo and Juliet*?

Vicenza, Palladio's home town and repository of some of his architecture, is well worth a stopover, perhaps on your way to the northern reaches of the Veneto and the chic ski slopes of Cortina d'Ampezzo. Strike out from the big centres and you discover the pleasant city of Treviso, home of Benetton and a charming riverside medieval core, and Belluno, a great base for walks in the staggering eastern Dolomites.

The region's cuisine is founded on rice and corn-based polenta. Risotto is cooked with almost everything the countryside and lagoon have to offer – from baby peas to baby crabs. One of the Veneto's best-known contributions to the Italian table is tiramisu, a dessert of mascarpone cheese, coffee, Marsala, sponge and chocolate. The single most popular tipple is Prosecco, a generic bubbly that flows freely in bars across the region. The Bellini, a cocktail of Prosecco and peach nectar, has come a long way since Giuseppe Cipriani first mixed one at Harry's Bar in Venice in the 1950s, but most locals prefer a biting afternoon *spritz* – the classic early evening apéritif in the Veneto, made of one part Prosecco, one part soda and one part bitters (such as Campari or the slightly sweeter Aperol).

HIGHLIGHTS

- Check out the modern art of the **Peggy Guggenheim Collection** (p354) and **Ca' Pesaro** (p356)
- Discover glass and old lace at **Murano** (p361) and **Burano** (p362)
- Sample fabulous seafood with a meal in one of Venice's **osterie** (p368)
- Tour Palladio's villas, from the **Brenta Riviera** (p375) to **Vicenza** (p380)
- Judge Giotto's frescoes at Padua's **Cappella degli Scrovegni** (p375)
- Enjoy a summertime open-air opera at Verona's magnificent **Roman Arena** (p386)
- Ride in a **gondola** (p363) or just wander alongside them
- Witness the marvellous mosaics in Venice's **Basilica di San Marco** (p348) and Torcello's **Santa Maria Assunta** (p362)
- Walk in the Alpine pastures of the **Dolomites** (p391)

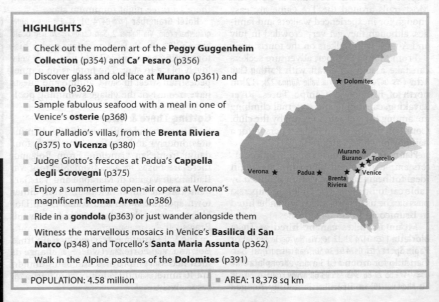

- POPULATION: 4.58 million
- AREA: 18,378 sq km

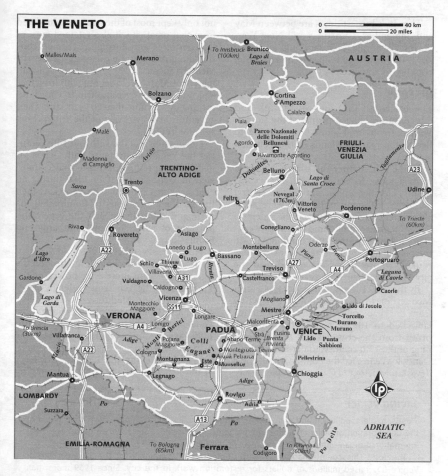

VENICE

pop 64,000 (city), 270,000 (mainland)

Perhaps no other city in the world has inspired the superlatives heaped upon Venice (Venezia to the natives) by travellers and writers throughout the centuries.

Forget that Venice is no longer a great maritime republic but rather a city besieged by rising tides and decay.

Today, Byron would probably be reluctant to take a dip in the murky Grand Canal (Canal Grande) after a late-night tryst but the thoughts of Henry James are as true as they were a century ago: 'Dear old Venice has lost her complexion, her figure, her reputation, her self-respect; and yet, with it all, has so puzzlingly not lost a shred of her distinction.' La Serenissima Repubblica (Most Serene Republic) remains a singular phenomenon.

The secret to discovering the romance and beauty of Venice is to *walk*. Parts of the Cannaregio, Dorsoduro and Castello *sestieri* (districts) are empty of tourists, even in the high season. You can become lost for hours in the narrow, winding streets between the Ponte dell'Accademia and Stazione di Santa Lucia (train station), where the signs that point towards San Marco and the Ponte di Rialto rarely seem to make sense (although, in their own way they do) – but what a way to pass the time!

The city's busiest times are between May and September, Christmas and New Year, during Carnevale (February) and at Easter, but it is always a good idea to make a hotel booking in advance.

HISTORY

The barbarian invasions of the 5th and 6th centuries obliged people of the Roman Veneto towns and along the Adriatic to flee to the marshy islands of the Venetian lagoon.

In the 6th century the islands began to form a loose federation, with each community electing representatives to a central authority, although its leaders were actually under the sway of Byzantine rulers in Ravenna. Byzantium's hold over Italy weakened in the early 8th century and in AD 726 the people of Venice elected their first doge (duke), whose successors would lead the city for more than 1000 years.

By the late 11th century, Venice was a great Mediterranean merchant power, prospering from the chaos caused by the First Crusade launched in 1095. The city continued to profit from the crusades and at the beginning of the 13th century, under Doge Enrico Dandolo, Venice led the Fourth Crusade on a devastating detour to Constantinople. Venice not only kept most of the treasures plundered from that great city, it also retained most of the territories won during the crusade, consolidating its maritime might in the Eastern Mediterranean. In 1271 the young Venetian merchant Marco Polo set out with his father and uncle on an overland trip to China, returning by sea more than 20 years later. Their adventure was symbolic of the enterprising spirit of Venice.

During much of the 13th and 14th centuries the Venetians struggled with Genoa for maritime supremacy, a tussle that culminated in Genoa's defeat in 1380 during an epic siege at Chioggia. The Venetians then turned their attentions to dominating the mainland, capturing most of the Veneto and portions of what are now Lombardy and Emilia-Romagna.

However, several events beyond Venetian control began to have a telling effect on the lagoon city. The increasing power of the Turks forced the Venetians to deploy forces to protect their Mediterranean interests. The fall of Constantinople in 1453 and the Venetian territory of Morea (in Greece) in 1499 gave the Turks control of access to the Adriatic Sea.

Worse still in the long term, the discovery of the Americas in 1492 and the rounding

---

SAVING VENICE

Floods, neglect, pollution and many other factors (including pigeon poop) have contributed to the degeneration of many of Venice's monuments and artworks. Since 1969 a group of private international organisations, under the aegis of Unesco, has worked to repair the damage.

The Joint Unesco–International Private Committees Programme for the Safeguarding of Venice has raised millions of dollars for restoration work in the city. Since 1969 more than 100 monuments and 1000 works of art have been restored. Major projects have included the Chiesa di Madonna dell'Orto, the façade of the Chiesa di San Zulian, Chiesa di San Francesco della Vigna, Chiesa di Santa Maria Formosa, Chiesa di San Chiesa di San Nicolò dei Mendicoli, Basilica di Santa Maria Assunta on Torcello, the Loggetta of the Campanile in Piazza San Marco, the Palazzo Ducale's Porta della Carta, the Old Jewish Cemetery on the Lido and the bronze equestrian statue of Bartolomeo Colleoni in Castello.

Funding comes from 29 private and charitable organisations from Italy and a dozen other countries. Apart from restoration work, the programme finances specialist courses for trainee restorers in Venice. Among the higher-profile groups is the UK's Venice in Peril Fund, whose honorary chairman is Viscount Norwich, one of the best-known historians of Venice in English. For UK£50 a year you can join **Venice in Peril** (☎ 020-7736 6891; www.veniceinperil.org; Unit 4 Hurlingham Studios, Ranelagh Gardens, London SW6 3PA). The fund is presently helping to restore the Emiliana chapel on San Michele (expected to cost UK£250,000).

Important though the work of these organisations is in keeping Venice's difficulties in the public eye, more than 90% of the finance for restoration and related projects in Venice since 1966 has come from the Italian government.

of Africa's Cape of Good Hope in 1498 by Portuguese explorer Vasco da Gama opened up new trade routes that would eventually supplant the Mediterranean and allow European importers to avoid Venetian taxes and duties.

Even so, Venice long remained a formidable power. The *dogi*, the Signoria (a council of 10 high ministers that effectively constituted the executive arm of government) and, later, the much-feared judicial Consiglio dei Dieci (Council of Ten) ruled with an iron fist. They headed a complex system of councils and government committees, of which the Maggior Consiglio (Great Council) was the equivalent of parliament. The doge, an elected leader, was the head of state and generally the most powerful individual in government, but a complex set of checks and balances limited his power and ensured that Venice was ruled by a tight-knit oligarchy. A decree of 1297 virtually closed off membership of the Maggior Consiglio to all but the most established patriarchal families.

For security reasons, Venetians were encouraged to spy on each other wherever the Venetian Republic had an interest. Acts considered detrimental to the interests of the state were punished swiftly and brutally. Trials were rarely public but executions commonly so – the classic location was between the columns bearing the statues of the Lion of St Mark and St Theodore on Piazzetta San Marco. On occasion, though, a body would just turn up on the street as a potent example to other potentially wayward citizens.

Venice was remarkably cosmopolitan, its commerce attracting people of all nationalities, from Parisians to Persians. And although Venice limited the commercial and social activities of its Jewish community, which it concentrated in what was one of Europe's earliest ghettos, it did nothing to stifle Judaism. Similarly, the Armenians were permitted religious freedom for centuries and were given protection during the infamous Inquisition.

The city's wealth was made all the more conspicuous by the luxury goods traded and produced there. Venice had a European monopoly on the making of what is now known as Murano glass, its merchants had reintroduced the art of making mosaics,

and Venetian artisans made fine silks and delicate lace.

But even as her people wallowed in their well being, Venice was on the wane. Turkey and the Papal States made gains at the Republic's expense during the 16th and 17th centuries, and in 1669 Venice lost Crete (its last Mediterranean stronghold) to the Turks after a 25-year battle.

Finally, in 1797 the Maggior Consiglio abolished the constitution and opened the city's gates to Napoleon, who in turn handed Venice over to the Austrians. Napoleon returned in 1805, incorporating the city into his Kingdom of Italy, but it reverted to Austria after his fall. The movement for Italian unification spread quickly through the Veneto and, after several rebellions, Venice was united with the Kingdom of Italy in 1866. The city was bombed during WWI but suffered only minor damage during WWII, when most attacks were aimed at the neighbouring industrial zones of Mestre and Porto Marghera.

The city's prestige as a tourist destination grew during the 19th century as it was surpassed as a trade port by Trieste. Today, Venice's modest permanent population (less than half that of the 1950s) is swollen by up to 20 million visitors each year, the majority of them day-trippers.

ORIENTATION

Venice is built on 117 small islands and has some 150 canals and 409 bridges. Only three bridges cross the Grand Canal: the Ponte di Rialto, the Ponte dell'Accademia and the Ponte dei Scalzi. A fourth bridge should already be in place but the Ponte di Calatrava, between Piazzale Roma and Fondamenta di Santa Lucia (for the train station), has been beset by problems and seems to be a long way off opening.

Stretching away to the north and south are the shallow waters of the Laguna Veneta, dotted by what seems a crumbling mosaic of islands, islets and rocks. Among them, Murano, Burano and Torcello are all of interest and lie to the north. Acting as a breakwater to the east, the long and slender Lido di Venezia stretches 10km south, followed by another similarly narrow island, Pellestrina, which reaches down to the sleepy town of Chioggia. The latter marks where the mainland closes off the lagoon to the south.

THE VENETO

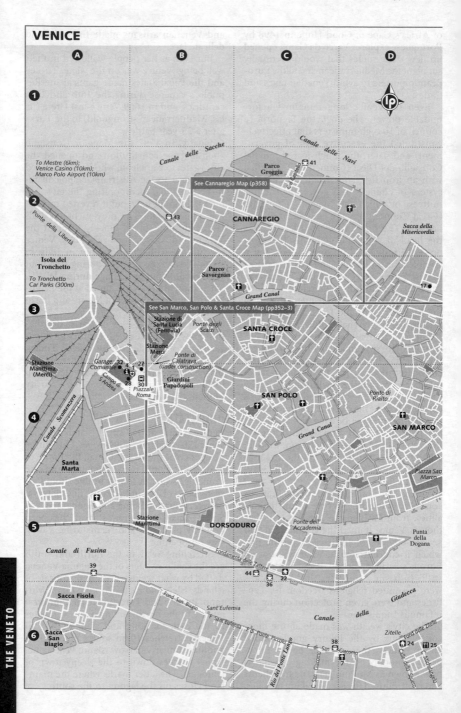

VENICE

To Mestre (6km);
Venice Casino (10km);
Marco Polo Airport (10km)

Ponte della Libertà

Isola del
Tronchetto

To Tronchetto
Car Parks (300m)

Stazione
Marittima
(Merci)

Canale Scomenzera

Santa
Marta

Canale delle Sacche

Canale delle Navi

Parco
Groggia

See Cannaregio Map (p358)

CANNAREGIO

Sacca della
Misericordia

Parco
Savorgnan

Grand Canal

See San Marco, San Polo & Santa Croce Map (pp352–3)

Stazione di
Santa Lucia
(Ferrovia)

Ponte degli
Scalzi

SANTA CROCE

Stazione
Merci

Ponte di
Calatrava
(under construction)

Garage
Comunale

Campo di
S'Andrea

Piazzale
Roma

Giardini
Papadopoli

SAN POLO

Ponte di
Rialto

SAN MARCO

Grand Canal

DORSODURO

Ponte dell'
Accademia

Piazza San
Marco

Punta
della
Dogana

Stazione
Marittima

Fondamenta delle Zattere

Canale di Fusina

Sacca Fisola

Fond San Biagio

Sant'Eufemia

F Sant'Eufemia

F di Ponte Piccolo

Giudecca

Canale della

Zitelle

Fond delle Zitelle

Sacca
San
Biagio

Rio del Ponte Lungo

F di San Giacomo

C San Giacomo

Giacomo

F di San

THE VENETO

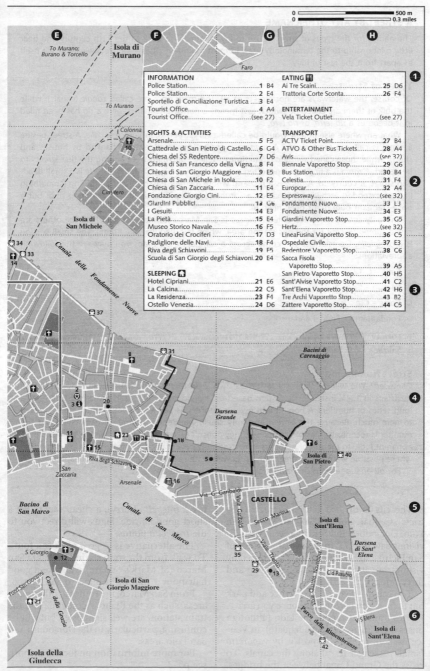

INFORMATION
Police Station	**1**	B4
Police Station	**2**	E4
Sportello di Conciliazione Turistica	**3**	E4
Tourist Office	**4**	A4
Tourist Office	(see	27)

SIGHTS & ACTIVITIES
Arsenale	**5**	F5
Cattedrale di San Pietro di Castello	**6**	G4
Chiesa del SS Redentore	**7**	D6
Chiesa di San Francesco della Vigna	**8**	F4
Chiesa di San Giorgio Maggiore	**9**	E5
Chiesa di San Michele in Isola	**10**	F2
Chiesa di San Zaccaria	**11**	E4
Fondazione Giorgio Cini	**12**	E5
Giardini Pubblici	**13**	G6
I Gesuiti	**14**	E3
La Pietà	**15**	E4
Museo Storico Navale	**16**	F5
Oratorio dei Crociferi	**17**	D3
Padiglione delle Navi	**18**	F4
Riva degli Schiavoni	**19**	F5
Scuola di San Giorgio degli Schiavoni	**20**	E4

SLEEPING
Hotel Cipriani	**21**	E6
La Calcina	**22**	C5
La Residenza	**23**	F4
Ostello Venezia	**24**	D6

EATING
Ai Tre Scaini	**25**	D6
Trattoria Corte Sconta	**26**	F4

ENTERTAINMENT
Vela Ticket Outlet	(see	27)

TRANSPORT
ACTV Ticket Point	**27**	B4
ATVO & Other Bus Tickets	**28**	A4
Avis	(see	32)
Biennale Vaporetto Stop	**29**	G6
Bus Station	**30**	B4
Celestia	**31**	F4
Europcar	(see	32)
Expressway	(see	32)
Fondamento Nuovo	**33**	L3
Fondamente Nuove	**34**	E3
Giardini Vaporetto Stop	**35**	G5
Hertz	(see	32)
LineaFusina Vaporetto Stop	**36**	C5
Ospedale Civile	**37**	E3
Redentore Vaporetto Stop	**38**	C6
Sacca Fisola Vaporetto Stop	**39**	A5
San Pietro Vaporetto Stop	**40**	H5
Sant'Alvise Vaporetto Stop	**41**	C2
Sant'Elena Vaporetto Stop	**42**	H6
Tre Archi Vaporetto Stop	**43**	B2
Zattere Vaporetto Stop	**44**	C5

THE VENETO

A STREET BY ANY OTHER NAME

The names for the types of street in use today in Venice go back to the 11th century and bear little relationship to the terminology used in most mainland cities – Venice always did see itself as apart from the rest of Italy.

Types of Streets

Of course, the waterways are not streets at all. The main ones are called *canale* (canals), while the bulk of them are called *rio* (which just means a narrower canal). Where a *rio* has been filled in it becomes a *rio terrà*, or *rio terà*.

What anywhere else in Italy would be called a *via* (street) is, in Venice, a *calle*. A street beside a canal is called a *fondamenta*. A *ruga* or *rughetta* is a smaller street flanked by houses and shops, while those called *salizada* (sometimes spelled *salizzada*) were among the first streets to be paved. A *ramo* is a tiny side lane, often connecting two bigger streets. A *corte* is a small dead-end street or courtyard. A quay is a *riva* and where a street passes under a building (something like an extended archway) it is called a *sotoportego*. A *piscina* is not a swimming pool but a once-stagnant pool that's been filled in.

The only square in Venice called a *piazza* is San Marco (St Mark's Square); all the others are called *campo* (except for the bus station area, which is called Piazzale Roma). The small version is a *campiello*. Occasionally you come across a *campazzo*. On maps you may see the following abbreviations:

- Calle – C, Cl
- Campo – Cpo
- Corte – Cte
- Fondamenta – Fond, Fondam, F
- Palazzo – Pal
- Salizada – Sal, Saliz

Street Numbering

Confused? You will be. Venice also has its own style of street numbering, introduced by the Austrians in 1841. Instead of a system based on individual streets, each *sestiere* (district) has a long series of numbers. A hotel might give its address as San Marco 4687, which doesn't seem to help much. Because the *sestieri* are fairly small, wandering around and searching out the number is technically feasible and sometimes doesn't take that long. But there is precious little apparent logic to the run of numbers – frustration is never far away. Most streets are named, so where possible we provide street names as well as the *sestiere* number in this chapter.

For other suggestions on navigational aids, see opposite.

The city is divided into six *sestieri* (districts): Cannaregio, Castello, San Marco, San Polo, Dorsoduro and Santa Croce. These divisions date to 1171. In the east, the islands of San Pietro and Sant'Elena, largely ignored by visitors, are attached to Castello by two and three bridges respectively.

You can drive your car to Venice and park but there is nowhere to drive once you arrive. Ferries transport cars to the Lido (although buses there are more than adequate). In Venice itself all public transport is by *vaporetto* (small passenger ferry) along the canals. To cross the Grand Canal between the bridges, use a *traghetto* (ferry), a cheap way to get a short gondola ride. Signs will direct you to the *traghetto* points.

The alternative is to go *a piedi* (on foot). To walk from the train station to Piazza San Marco (St Mark's Square) will take a good half-hour – follow the signs to San Marco.

From San Marco, the routes to other main areas, such as the Rialto, Accademia and the train station, are well signposted but can be confusing, particularly in the Dorsoduro and San Polo areas.

For more information on local transport, see p373.

Maps

Aside from Lonely Planet's *Venice* map, one of the best maps is *Venezia*, produced by the Touring Club Italiano (scale 1:5000). If you plan to stay for the long haul, *Calli, Campielli e Canali* (Edizioni Helvetica) is for you. This book is the definitive street guide and will allow you to locate to within 100m any Venetian-style address you need.

INFORMATION
Bookshops

Giunti al Punto (Map p358; ☎ 041 275 01 52; Campo San Geremia, Cannaregio 282; ☻ 9am-8pm Mon & Tue, 9am-9pm Wed & Thu, 9am-10pm Fri & Sun, 9am-midnight Sat) Late-night readers in need of a paperback (several languages are catered for) can head here any day of the week.
Studium (Map pp352-3; ☎ 041 522 23 82; Calle de la Canonica 337a) A good selection of English-language guides and books on Venice.

Emergency

Police station (Map pp342-3; ☎ 041 271 57 72; Fondamenta di San Lorenzo, Castello 5053) Head here if you have been robbed.

Internet Access

Internet point (Map pp352-3; ☎ 041 71 46 66; Calle dei Preti, Dorsoduro 3812a; per hr €9; ☻ 9.15am-8pm Mon-Sat)
Planet Internet (Map p358; ☎ 041 524 41 88; Rio Terà San Leonardo, Cannaregio 1519; per hr €8; ☻ 9am-midnight)
World House (Map pp352-3; ☎ 041 528 48 71; www.world-house.org; Calle della Chiesa, Castello 4502; per hr €8; ☻ 10am-11pm)

Laundry

Orange Laundry (Map pp352-3; www.laundry.it; Calle Chioverette, Santa Croce 665b; 8kg wash €3, 12kg dry €2; ☻ 7.30am-10.30pm)
Speedy Wash (Map p358; Rio Terà San Leonardo, Cannaregio 1520; 8kg wash €4.50, 15kg dry €3; ☻ 8am-11pm)

Lost Property

If you lose stuff in Venice it may well be gone forever, but you could try the checking out the local **police station** (Map pp342-3; ☎ 041 522 45 76; Vigili Urbani) on Piazzale Roma. Otherwise the following numbers might be useful:
ACTV (☎ 041 272 21 79) Public transport.
Marco Polo airport (☎ 041 260 92 22)
Municipio (☎ 041 274 81 11) Town hall.
Train station (☎ 041 78 55 31)

Medical Services

Current information on late-night pharmacies is listed in *Un Ospite di Venezia* (A Guest in Venice; available from tourist offices and some hotels) and daily newspapers such as *Il Gazzettino* or *La Nuova Venezia*.
Ospedale Civile (Map pp352-3; ☎ 041 529 41 11; Campo SS Giovanni e Paolo 6777) This is the main hospital. For emergency treatment, go straight to the *pronto soccorso* (casualty) section, where you can also get emergency dental treatment.
Ospedale Umberto I (☎ 800 501 060; Via Circonvallazione 50) A modern mainland hospital in Mestre.

Money

You will find several bank branches, most with ATMs, in the area around Ponte di Rialto and San Marco. Numerous bureaux de change are scattered across the city and at the train station.
American Express (Map pp352-3; ☎ 041 520 08 44; Salizada San Moisè, San Marco 1471; ☻ 9am-5.30pm Mon-Fri, 9am-12.30pm Sat) It has an ATM for American Express cards.
Travelex Piazza San Marco (Map pp352-3; ☎ 041 528 73 58; Piazza San Marco 142; ☻ 9am-6pm Mon-Sat, 9.30am-5pm Sun); Rialto (Map pp352-3; Riva del Ferro 5126)

Post

Main post office (Map pp352-3; Salizada del Fondaco dei Tedeschi; ☻ 8.30am-6.30pm Mon-Sat) Near the Ponte di Rialto. Stamps are available at windows in the central courtyard. There is something quite special about doing your postal business in this former trading house. Stand by the well in the middle and try to imagine the bustle as German traders and brokers shuffled their goods around on the ground floor or struck deals in their quarters on the upper levels back in the republic's trading heyday.

Telephone

There is a bank of **telephones** (Map pp352-3; Calle Galeazza) near the post office. You will also find phones at the train station. Unstaffed phone offices can be found at:
Cannaregio (Map pp352-3; Strada Nova)
San Marco (Map pp352-3; Calle San Luca 4585)

Tourist Information

Azienda di Promozione Turistica (APT; central information line ☎ 041 529 87 11; www.turismovenezia.it) has several branches around Venice that can provide information on the town and the province:
Chioggia (☎ 041 40 10 68; www.chioggiatourism.it; Lungomare Adriatico 101, Sottomarina; ☻ 8.30am-6.30pm) Reduced hours in winter.

Lido (Gran Viale Santa Maria Elisabetta 6a; ◯ 9am-12.30pm & 3.30-6pm Jun-Sep)

Marco Polo airport (arrivals hall; ◯ 9.30am-7.30pm)

Piazzale Roma (Map pp342-3; ◯ 9.30am-6.30pm) Next to Garage Comunale. Operates shorter hours from November to March.

Piazza San Marco (Map pp352-3; Piazza San Marco 71f; ◯ 9am-3.30pm Mon-Sat) The main tourist office. Staff will assist with information on hotels, transport and things to see and do in the city.

Stazione di Santa Lucia (Map pp352-3; ◯ 8am-6.30pm) Open as late as 8pm in summer.

Venice Pavilion Infopoint (Map pp352-3; Venice Pavilion; ◯ 10am-6pm) Also an APT branch; next to Giardini ex Reali, a quick walk from Piazza San Marco.

The useful monthly booklet *Un Ospite di Venezia*, published by a group of Venetian hoteliers, is sometimes available from tourist offices (and some hotels). Ask also for *Leo*, a free monthly magazine with articles in Italian and English and a handy listings insert, *Bussola*.

You can contact the tourist offices of the **Sportello di Conciliazione Turistica** (Map pp342-3; ☎ 041 529 87 10; complaint.apt@turismovenezia.it; Fondamenta di San Lorenzo, Castello 5050; ◯ 8.30am-1.30pm Mon-Fri) with complaints, although it doesn't promise much more than to listen.

Travel Agencies

CTS (Map pp352-3; ☎ 041 520 56 60; www.cts.it in Italian; Calle Foscari, Dorsoduro 3252) The main Italian student and youth travel organisation.

Gran Canal Viaggi (Map pp352-3; ☎ 041 271 21 11; Calle del Lovo, San Marco 4759/4760)

SIGHTS

After wafting down the Grand Canal, you will want to organise yourself to see some of the cream of Venice's countless extraordinary sights. The following section is roughly divided into the city's *sestieri*, and together forms a circuit through the city, starting and ending in Piazza San Marco.

Grand Canal

Described by the French writer Philippe de Commines in the 15th century as 'the finest street in the world, with the finest houses', the Grand Canal is a little dilapidated these days but still rivals the world's great boulevards. It weaves for 3.5km through the city like a huge, back-to-front 'S', with a depth

of about 6m and a width ranging from 40m to 100m. Taking a *vaporetto* is the only way to see the incredible parade of buildings, including more than 100 palazzi, which date from the 12th to the 18th centuries. Board *vaporetto* No 1 at Piazzale Roma and try to grab a seat on the deck at the back.

Perhaps by the time you have this book in your hands you should pass first under the new **Ponte di Calatrava** (Map pp352-3), a daring bridge designed by the Spanish architect Santiago Calatrava. More likely all you will see are the protruding bits on either end of the canal waiting patiently for the middle section to be fitted.

Not far past the train station are the **Ponte dei Scalzi** (Map pp352-3) and the Canale di Cannaregio (the city's second-largest canal) and just after the Riva di Biasio stop (to the right) is one of the most celebrated Veneto-Byzantine buildings, the **Fondaco dei Turchi** (Map pp352-3). Once a Turkish warehouse and now housing the Museo Civico di Storia Naturale (Natural History Museum), the building is recognisable by the three-storey towers on either side of its colonnade.

The canal continues past the Rio di San Marcuola to **Palazzo Vendramin-Calergi** (Map p358) on the left. Richard Wagner died here in 1883 and it is now a fine Renaissance home for the casino (p371).

Further on and to the right, just after the San Stae stop, is **Ca' Pesaro** (Map pp352-3), Baldassare Longhena's baroque masterpiece (built between 1679 and 1710). Longhena died worrying about the cost of the building and it was only completed after his death. It now houses the Galleria d'Arte Moderna and Museo d'Arte Orientale.

Shortly after, to the left, is the **Ca' d'Oro** (Golden House; Map pp352-3), acclaimed as the most beautiful Gothic building in Venice. To the right, as the boat turns for the Ponte di Rialto, is the **pescaria** (fish market; Map pp352-3) on Campo della Pescaria, built in 1907 (though there has been a fish market on the site for centuries).

On the right, just after the *pescaria*, are the **Fabbriche Nuove** (Map pp352-3), built in 1555 by Jacopo Sansovino as a courthouse. Next door is the city's produce market and then the **Fabbriche Vecchie** (Map pp352-3), built in 1522 to house markets and offices. Just before the Ponte di Rialto, on the left bank, the **Fondaco dei Tedeschi** (Map pp352-3) was

THE VENETO

once the most important trading house on the canal and now serves as the main post office. It was rebuilt after a fire in 1505 and frescoes by Titian and Giorgione (remnants of which are on view in the Ca' d'Oro) once adorned its façade.

The stone **Ponte di Rialto** (Map pp352–3) was built in the late 16th century by Antonio da Ponte, who had won the commission over architects including Palladio. The Renaissance **Palazzo Grimani** (Map pp352–3), on the left after the bridge and just before the Rio di San Luca, was designed by Sanmicheli. Further along the same bank, the **Palazzo Corner-Spinelli** (Map pp352–3) was designed in the same period by Mauro Cordussi. On the right, as the canal swings sharply to the left, is the late-Gothic **Ca' Foscari** (Map pp352–3), commissioned by Doge Francesco Foscari. One of the finest mansions in the city and the seat of the university, it is followed on the left by the 18th-century **Palazzo Grassi** (Map pp352–3). Owned by Fiat until early 2005, it was renowned as a cultural and exhibition centre; it is hoped that this will continue. Opposite, the massive **Ca' Rezzonico** (Map pp352–3), designed by Baldassare Longhena, houses a fine collection of 18th-century art.

You're now approaching the last of the canal's bridges, the wooden **Ponte dell'Accademia** (Map pp352–3), built in 1930 to replace a metal 19th-century structure. Past it and on the right is the unfinished **Palazzo Venier dei Leoni** (Map pp352–3), where American heiress Peggy Guggenheim lived until her death in 1979. It is home to her collection of modern art. Two buildings along is **Palazzo Dario** (Map pp352–3) built in 1487 and recognisable by the multicoloured marble façade and its many chimneys. It is said to be cursed.

On the left bank, at the Santa Maria del Giglio stop, is **Palazzo Corner** (Map pp352–3), an imposing, ivy-covered residence also known as the Ca' Granda and designed in the mid-16th century by Jacopo Sansovino. On the right, before the canal broadens into the expanse facing San Marco, is Baldassare Longhena's **Chiesa di Santa Maria della Salute** (Map pp352–3), which takes central place in many a postcard of the city.

San Marco

Napoleon thought **Piazza San Marco** (Map pp352–3) to be the 'finest drawing room in Europe'. Enclosed by the basilica and the arcaded Procuratie Vecchie and Nuove, the square plays host to competing flocks of pigeons and tourists. Stand and wait for the bronze *Mori* (Moors) to strike the bell of the 15th-century **Torre dell'Orologio** (Map

---

MAKING HIS MARK

The story goes that an angel appeared to the Evangelist Mark when his boat put in at Rialto while on his way from Aquileia to Rome. The winged fellow informed the future saint that his body would rest in Venice (which didn't exist at this point!). When Mark died some years later, it was in Alexandria in Egypt. In 828 two Venetian merchants persuaded the guardians of his Alexandrian tomb to let them have the corpse, which they then smuggled onto their ship.

You've got to ask yourself why the merchants bothered with such a strange cargo. Well, in those days, any city worthy of the name had a patron saint of stature. Venice had St Theodore (San Teodoro), but the poor old fellow didn't really cut the mustard in the Christian hierarchy. An Evangelist, though, would be something quite different. Did Doge Giustinian Partecipazio order this body-snatching mission? Whatever the truth of this tale, it seems that *someone's* putrid corpse was transported to Venice and that everyone rather liked to think St Mark was now in their midst. St Theodore was unceremoniously demoted and the doge ordered the construction of a chapel to house the newcomer. That church would later become the Basilica di San Marco. St Mark was symbolised in the Book of Revelation (the Apocalypse) as a winged lion and this image came to be synonymous with La Serenissima Repubblica (Most Serene Republic).

Legend also has it that, during the rebuilding of the basilica in 1063, the body of St Mark was hidden and then 'lost' when its hiding place was forgotten. In 1094 when the church was consecrated, the corpse (which must have been a picture of frailty by this time) broke through the column in which it had been enclosed. 'It's a miracle!' the Venetians cried. Or just dodgy plasterwork? St Mark had been lost and now was found. A grateful populace buried the remains beneath the basilica's high altar, where they now lie.

DISCOUNTS ON ADMISSION

Rolling Venice Concession Pass

If you are aged between 14 and 29, pick up the Rolling Venice card (€3), which offers significant discounts on food, accommodation, entertainment, public transport, museums and galleries. You can get the card at tourist offices, ACTV public transport ticket points and Vela information and ticket stands. Two of the latter are located in front of the train station (Map pp352–3) and the Venice Pavilion Infopoint (Map pp352–3). The Rolling Venice map lists all the hotels, restaurants, shops, museums, cinemas and theatres where the card entitles you to reductions.

Other Discounts

Admission to state museums is free for EU citizens under 18 or over 65. In Venice this means just a handful of locations: the Gallerie dell'Accademia, the Ca' d'Oro and the Museo d'Arte Orientale. Admission to these is also free for non-EU citizens 12 years old and under.

A handful of museums and galleries offer discounts for students and seniors regardless of where they are from. It never hurts to ask.

Special Tickets

A Museum Pass covers admission to the Palazzo Ducale, Museo Correr, Museo Archeologico, Libreria Nazionale Marciana, Torre dell'Orologio, Ca' Rezzonico, Museo Vetrario on Murano, Museo del Merletto on Burano, Palazzo Mocenigo (Map pp352–3), the Casa di Goldoni and Ca' Pesaro. The ticket costs €15.50 (students aged 15 to 29 pay €10) and can be purchased from any of these museums. It is valid for three months.

You can also buy a Museum Card for €11 (student/child €5.50/3) that covers the Palazzo Ducale, Museo Correr, Museo Archeologico and Libreria Nazionale Marciana only.

Further options include an €8 (student €4.50) ticket for Ca' Rezzonico, Palazzo Mocenigo and the Casa di Goldoni, and a €6 (student €4) ticket for the Murano and Burano museums. When Palazzo Fortuny finally fully opens it will be grouped with Ca' Pesaro at €6 (student €4). Another cumulative ticket groups the Gallerie dell'Accademia, the Ca' d'Oro and the Museo d'Arte Orientale (adult/child €11/5.50).

An organisation called **Chorus** (☎ 041 275 04 62; www.chorusvenezia.org), involved in the upkeep of Venice's most artistically significant churches, offers visitors a special ticket (adult/senior & student up to 29 years €9/6) providing admission to 15 outstanding churches. The ticket is valid for a year. Otherwise, admission to the individual churches concerned is €2.50. The churches are Santa Maria Gloriosa dei Frari, Santa Maria del Giglio, Santo Stefano, Santa Maria Formosa, Santa Maria dei Miracoli, San Polo, San Giacomo dell'Orio, San Stae (Map pp352–3), Sant'Alvise (Map p358), La Madonna dell'Orto, San Giovanni Elemosinario, I Gesuiti, San Pietro di Castello (Map pp342–3), Il Redentore and San Sebastian. The ticket is available from any of the churches. Among the most worthwhile to visit are Santa Maria Gloriosa dei Frari, San Giacomo dell'Orio, Santo Stefano, San Polo and Santa Maria dei Miracoli.

pp352–3), which rises above the entrance to the Marzarie (Mercerie in Italian), the main thoroughfare from San Marco to the Rialto. Or sit and savour an expensive coffee at Florian or Quadri (p370), 18th-century cafés across from each other on the piazza.

The **Basilica di San Marco** (St Mark's Basilica; Map pp352–3; ☎ 041 522 52 05; www.basilicasanmarco.it; Piazza San Marco; admission free; ☻ 9.45am-5.30pm Mon-Sat, 2-4.30pm Sun & holidays) embodies a magnificent blend of architectural and decorative styles, dominated by the Byzantine style and ranging through Romanesque to Renaissance.

Note that modest dress is essential for visiting the basilica. This means covering your arms and wearing skirts or pants at least down to the knees. The 'underdressed' will be turned away, no matter how long they have queued. You will not be allowed in with any kind of bags or backpacks either. The side entrance of the Ateneo San Basso, on Calle San Basso, just off Piazzetta San dei Leoni, has free **baggage storage** (Map pp352–3; ☻ 9.30am-5.30pm) where you can leave your bags before you join the queue for the basilica (there's a one-hour limit). In the

Ateneo San Basso you can also see a video on the basilica.

You can try booking an entry time to the basilica at least two days in advance on the Web at www.alata.it (if it's working!) to avoid queuing.

The original church, a chapel built to house the purported remains of the evangelist St Mark (see the boxed text, p347), was destroyed by fire in 932 and rebuilt, but in 1063 Doge Domenico Contarini decided it was poor in comparison to the splendid Romanesque churches being raised in mainland cities and had it demolished.

The new basilica, built on the plan of a Greek cross, with five bulbous domes, was modelled on Constantinople's (later destroyed) Church of the Twelve Apostles and consecrated in 1094. It was actually built as the doges' private chapel and remained so until it became Venice's cathedral in 1807.

For more than 500 years, the doges enlarged and embellished the church, adorning it with an incredible array of treasures plundered from the East, in particular from Constantinople, during the crusades.

The arches above the doorways in the **façade** boast fine mosaics. The one on the left, depicting the arrival of St Mark's body in Venice, was completed in 1270. The three arches of the main doorway are decorated with Romanesque carvings, dating from around 1240.

On the loggia (balcony) above the main door are copies of four gilded bronze horses; the originals, on display inside, were stolen and brought to Venice when Constantinople was sacked in 1204, during the Fourth Crusade. Napoleon moved them to Paris in 1797 but they were returned following the collapse of the French Empire.

Through the doors is the **narthex**, or vestibule, its domes and arches decorated with mosaics, mainly dating from the 13th century. The oldest mosaics in the basilica, dating from around 1063, are in the niches of the bay in front of the main door from the narthex into the church proper. They feature the Madonna with the Apostles.

The **interior** of the basilica is simply dazzling; if you can take your eyes off the glitter of the mosaics, take time to admire the 12th-century marble pavement, a geometrical whimsy which has subsided in places, making the floor uneven.

The lower level of the walls is lined with precious Eastern marbles and above this decoration the extraordinary feast of gilded **mosaics** begins. Work started on the mosaics in the 11th century and continued until well into the 13th century. More were added in the 14th and 15th centuries in the baptistry and side chapels and, as late as the 18th century, still more mosaics were being added or restored.

To the right of the high altar is the entrance to the sanctuary. St Mark's body is contained in a sarcophagus beneath the altar. Behind the altar is the exquisite **Pala d'Oro** (admission €1.50; ☉ 9.45am-5pm Mon-Sat, 2-5pm Sun & holidays Apr-Sep, 9.45am-4.45pm Mon-Sat, 1-4.45pm Sun & holidays Oct-Mar), a gold, enamel and jewel-encrusted altarpiece made in Constantinople for Doge Pietro Orseolo I in 976. It was enriched and reworked in Constantinople in 1105, enlarged by Venetian goldsmiths in 1209 and reset again in the 14th century. Among the almost 2000 precious stones that adorn it are emeralds, amethysts, sapphires, rubies and pearls.

The **Tesoro** (Treasury; admission €2; ☉ 9.45am-5pm Mon-Sat, 2-5pm Sun & holidays Apr-Sep, 9.45am-4.45pm Mon-Sat, 1-4.45pm Sun & holidays Oct-Mar), accessible from the right transept, contains most of the booty from the 1204 raid on Constantinople, including a thorn said to be from the crown worn by Christ.

Through a door at the far right end of the narthex is a stairway which leads up to the **Galleria** (Museo di San Marco; Map pp352-3; admission €3; ☉ 9.45am-5pm Apr-Sep, 9.45am-4.45pm Oct-Mar), which contains the original gilded bronze horses and the **Loggia dei Cavalli**. The *galleria* affords a wonderful view of the church's interior, while the loggia has equally splendid vistas of the square.

The basilica's mosaics are best seen when illuminated: on weekdays from 11.30am to 12.30pm and during some of the weekend Masses.

The basilica's 99m-tall **Campanile** (Bell Tower; Map pp352-3; adult/child €6/3; ☉ 9.45am-8pm Jul-Sep, 9.30am-5pm Apr-Jun, 9.45am-4pm Oct-Mar), built in the 10th century, collapsed on 14 July 1902 and was rebuilt brick by brick. The views from the top are spectacular.

The former residence and offices of the Procurators of St Mark (responsible for the upkeep of the basilica), the **Procuratie Vecchie** (Map pp352-3), were designed by Mauro

Codussi and occupy the entire northern side of Piazza San Marco.

On the south side of the piazza are the **Procuratie Nuove** (Map pp352–3), planned by Jacopo Sansovino and completed by Vincenzo Scamozzi and Baldassare Longhena. Napoleon converted this building into his royal palace and demolished the church of San Geminiano at the western end of the piazza to build the wing commonly known as the Ala Napoleonica, which housed his ballroom.

The Ala Napoleonica is now home to the **Museo Correr** (☎ 041 240 52 11; www.musei civicivenezianі.it; Piazza San Marco 52; ⏱ 9am-7pm Apr-Oct, 9am-5pm Nov-Mar), dedicated to the art and history of Venice. Through this museum you also access first the **Museo Archeologico**, which houses an impressive, if somewhat repetitive, selection of ancient sculptures, and then the **Libreria Nazionale Marciana**. Described by Palladio as the most sumptuous palace ever built, the Libreria was designed by Jacopo Sansovino. It takes up the entire western side of the Piazzetta di San Marco. Inside, the main reading hall is a sumptuous 16th-century creation, its ceiling decorated by a battalion of artists, including Veronese. For admission prices for these museums, see boxed text, p348.

Stretching from Piazza San Marco to the waterfront, the **Piazzetta di San Marco** (Map pp352–3) features two columns bearing statues of the Lion of St Mark and St Theodore (San Teodoro), the city's two patron saints. Originally a marketplace, the area was also a preferred location for public executions and political meetings.

The **Palazzo Ducale** (Doges' Palace; Map pp352-3; ☎ 041 271 59 11; www.museicivicveneziani.it; Piazzetta di San Marco; ⏱ 9am-7pm Apr-Oct, 9am-5pm Nov-Mar) was, as the name suggests, the doges' official residence, but also the seat of the Republic's government, bureaucracy and main prisons. Established in the 9th century, the palace began to assume its present form 500 years later with the decision to build the massive Sala del Maggior Consiglio for the council members, who ranged in number from 1200 to 1700. It was inaugurated in 1419. For admission prices, see the boxed text, p348. An optional audioguide is available for €5.50.

The palace's two magnificent Gothic façades in white Istrian stone and pink Veronese marble face the water and Piazzetta di San Marco. Much of the building was damaged by fire in 1577 but it was restored by Antonio da Ponte (who designed the Ponte di Rialto).

The former main entrance (and now exit), the 15th-century **Porta della Carta** (Paper Door), to which government decrees were fixed, was carved by Giovanni and Bartolomeo Bon. Leading from the courtyard, the **Scala dei Giganti** (Giants' Staircase) by Antonio Rizzo takes its name from the huge statues of Mars and Neptune, by Jacopo Sansovino, which flank the landing.

Past Sansovino's **Scala d'Oro** (Golden Staircase) is a labyrinth of rooms, including the **Sala delle Quattro Porte** (Hall of the Four Doors) on the 3rd floor, where ambassadors would be requested to await their ducal audience. The room's ceiling was designed by Palladio and the frescoes are by Tintoretto. Off this room is the **Anticollegio** (College Antechamber), featuring four Tintorettos and the *Ratto d'Europa* (Rape of Europa) by Veronese. Through here, the ceiling of the splendid **Sala del Collegio** (College Hall) features a series of works by Veronese. Next is the **Sala del Senato** (Senate Hall), graced by yet more Tintorettos.

The route takes you to the immense **Sala del Maggior Consiglio** (Grand Council Hall) on the 2nd floor. It is dominated at one end by Tintoretto's *Paradiso* (Paradise), one of the world's largest oil paintings, measuring 22m by 7m. Among the many other paintings in the hall is a masterpiece, the *Apoteosi di Venezia* (Apotheosis of Venice) by Veronese, in one of the central ceiling panels. Note the black space in the frieze on the wall depicting the first 76 doges of Venice. Doge Marin Falier would have appeared there had he not lost his head for treason in 1355.

Next, you will find yourself crossing the small, enclosed **Ponte dei Sospiri** (Bridge of Sighs; Map pp352–3) to reach the 'new prisons' (built when those in the Palazzo Ducale proved insufficient). The bridge is named because of the sighs prisoners tended to make on their way into the dungeons. The poor unfortunate souls to make this dismal crossing must have been well behaved indeed not to give more vigorous vent to their displeasure.

The **Itinerari Segreti** (Secret Itineraries; ☎ 041 520 90 70; adult/student/child €12.50/7/4; ⏱ tours in English

9.55am, 10.45am & 11.35am, Italian 9.30am & 11.10am, in French 10.20am, noon & 12.25pm) is a 1½-hour guided tour that takes an intriguing look at lesser-known nooks of the palace. You pass from civil servants' offices to a torture chamber, the Inquisitor's office and upstairs to the **Piombi** (Leads; prison cells beneath the roof of the building). Here prisoners froze in winter and sweltered in summer. Giacomo Casanova got five years but managed to escape. You also get an explanation of the engineering behind the ceiling of the immense Sala del Maggior Consiglio below.

Around San Marco

The **Marzarie** (Mercerie; Map pp352–3), a series of streets lined with shops, connects Piazza San Marco and the Rialto in a tortuous manner. The **Chiesa di San Salvador** (Map pp352–3; 9am-noon & 4-6pm Mon-Sat, 4-6pm Sun Jun-Aug, 9am-noon & 3-6pm Mon-Sat, 3-6pm Sun Sep-May), built on a plan of three Greek crosses laid end to end, features Titian's *Annunciazione* (Annunciation), at the third altar on the right as you approach the main altar. Behind the main altar itself is another of his contributions, the *Trasfigurazione* (Transfiguration).

The area immediately west of Piazza San Marco is a rabbit warren of streets and alleys lined with exclusive shops, where you might pick up some interesting gifts and souvenirs, such as watercolours of the city, marbled paper and carnival masks.

First raised in 1792, the **Teatro La Fenice** (☎ 041 78 66 11; www.teatrolafenice.it; Campo San Fantin 1965; adult/student & senior guided tours €7/5) is one of the world's finest opera houses. Well, it might be. It was reopened in late 2003, carefully restored and equipped with the latest technology after fire gutted it in 1996. For the guided tour you must book ahead by phone or in person and you should reckon on a couple of days' waiting time. Tour times are volatile – you will be told when trying to book what times on what days tours are available.

Duck up north to admire and climb the graceful 15th-century external spiral staircase at the **Palazzo Contarini del Bovolo** (Map pp352–3; ☎ 041 271 90 12; Corte del Bovolo 4299; adult/child €3/2.50; 10am-6pm Apr-Oct, 10am-4pm Sat & Sun Nov-Mar, 10am-4pm daily Christmas & Carnevale).

A few blocks south is Calle Larga XXII Marzo, from where you can turn right for the **Chiesa di Santa Maria del Giglio** (Map pp352-

3; admission €2.50; 10am-5pm Mon-Sat, 1-5pm Sun), also known as Santa Maria Zobenigo. Its baroque façade features maps of European cities as they were in 1678. Go onto Campo Santo Stefano (aka Campo Francesco Morosini) and the Gothic **Chiesa di Santo Stefano** (Map pp352-3; 10am-5pm Mon-Sat, 1-5pm Sun) is on your right (the entry is on the western side). Of note are three paintings by Tintoretto in the little **museum** (admission €2.50): *Ultima Cena* (Last Supper), *Lavanda dei Piedi* (Washing of the Feet) and *Orazione nell'Orto* (Agony in the Garden). Outside, the church's bell tower leans disconcertingly.

At the bottom end of the square, poke your nose into **Palazzo Franchetti** (Map pp352-3; ☎ 041 240 77 11; Campo Santo Stefano 2842; adult/student €7/5; 2-7pm Mon-Sat, 11am-7pm Sun & holidays), a fine and eclectically decorated 16th-century Venetian mansion that frequently hosts exhibitions.

Dorsoduro

The **Gallerie dell'Accademia** (Map pp352-3; ☎ 041 522 22 47, bookings ☎ 041 520 03 45; www.gallerieaccademia.org in Italian; Campo della Carità 1050; adult/EU citizen 18-25/child under 12 & EU citizen under 18 or over 65 €6.50/3.25/free, video/audioguides €4/6; 8.15am 2pm Mon, 8.15am 7.15pm Tue-Sun) is a must for anyone with even a passing interest in art. The former church and convent of Santa Maria della Carità, with additions by Palladio, hosts a collection that follows the progression of Venetian art from the 14th to the 18th centuries.

Room 1 contains works by the early 14th-century painter Paolo Veneziano, including the *Incoronazione di Maria* (Coronation of Mary). The main feature of Room 2, which covers the late 15th and early 16th centuries, is Carpaccio's altarpiece *Crocifissione e Apoteosi dei 10,000 Martiri del Monte Ararat* (Crucifixion and Apotheosis of the 10,000 Martyrs of Mt Ararat). It also contains works by Giovanni Bellini. Rooms 4 and 5 feature Andrea Mantegna's *San Giorgio* (St George), several paintings of the Madonna and Child by Giovanni Bellini and Giorgione's fabulous *La Tempesta* (The Storm). Rooms 6 to 10 contain works of the High Renaissance, including Tintoretto and Titian, but one of the highlights is Paolo Veronese's *Convito in Casa di Levi* (Feast in the House of Levi) in Room 10. Originally called *Ultima Cena* (Last Supper), the painting's name was changed because the Inquisition objected to

THE VENETO

SAN MARCO, SAN POLO & SANTA CROCE

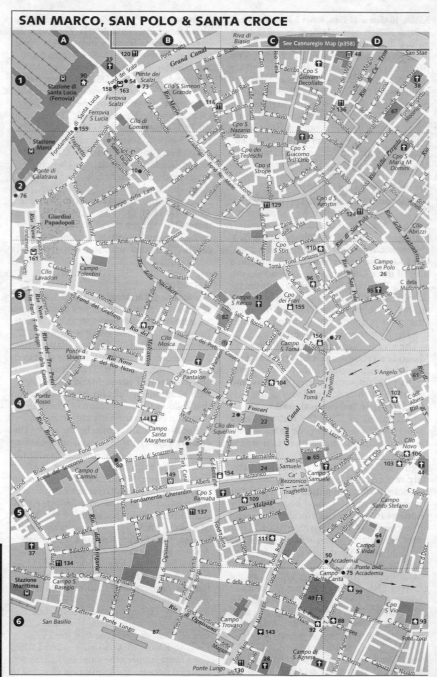

See Cannaregio Map (p358)

THE VENETO

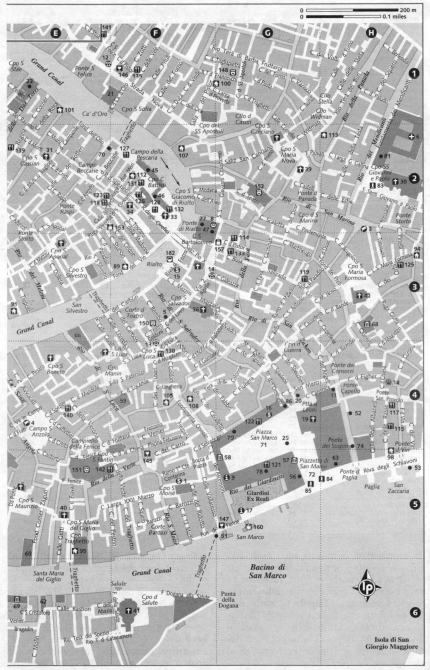

its depiction of characters such as drunkards and dwarfs. The room also contains one of Titian's last works, a *Pietà*. In Room 13 are a number of works by the 18th-century painter Giambattista Tiepolo. Giovanni Bellini and Carpaccio appear yet again in subsequent rooms and the collection ends in Room 24 with Tiepolo's beautiful *Presentazione di Maria al Tempio* (Presentation of Mary at the Temple).

Peggy Guggenheim called the unfinished Palazzo Venier dei Leoni, a short stroll east of the Gallerie dell'Accademia, home for 30 years until her death in 1979. She left behind the **Peggy Guggenheim Collection** (Map pp352-3; ☎ 041 240 54 11; www.guggenheim-venice.it; Palazzo Venier dai Leoni 701; adult/senior/student €10/8/5; ☼ 10am-6pm Wed-Mon) of works by her favourite modern artists, representing most of the major artistic movements of the 20th century.

THE VENETO

Picasso, Mondrian, Kandinsky, Ernst, Chagall, Klee, Miró, Pollock, Brancusi, Dalí, Magritte and Bacon are all represented. Take a wander around the sculpture garden (which includes works by Moore, Giacometti and Ernst), where Miss Guggenheim and many of her pet dogs are buried.

Dominating the entrance to the Grand Canal, the beautiful **Chiesa di Santa Maria della Salute** (Map pp352-3; ☎ 041 522 55 58; www.marcianum.it/salute in Italian; Campo della Salute 1/b; sacristy admission €1.50; ☼ 9am-noon & 3.30-6pm) was built in the 17th century in honour of the Virgin Mary, who was believed to have delivered the city from an outbreak of plague that had killed more than a third of the population. From inside Baldassare Longhena's octagonal main church you access the Great Sacristy, where Titian and Tintoretto left their mark. Every year, on 21 November, a procession takes place from Piazza San Marco to the church to give thanks for the city's good health.

The Fondamenta delle Zattere, more simply known as the **Zattere** (Map pp352–3), runs along the Canale della Giudecca from Punta della Salute to the old Stazione Marittima (ferry terminal). It is a popular spot for the traditional evening *passeggiata* (stroll). The main sight is the 18th-century Santa Maria del Rosario, or **Chiesa dei Gesuati** (Map pp352-3; Fondamenta delle Zattere 909; admission €2.50; ☼ 10am-5pm Mon-Sat, 1-5pm Sun), designed by Giorgio Massari. Tiepolo's ceiling frescoes tell the story of San Domenico (St Dominic). At the end of the Zattere, over Rio di San Basegio, the **Chiesa di San Sebastian** (Map pp352-3; Campo San Sebastian 1687; admission €2.50; ☼ 10am-5pm Mon-Sat, 1-5pm Sun) was the local church of Paolo Veronese, who provided most of the paintings and lies buried in the church.

The 17th- and 18th-century **Ca' Rezzonico** (Map pp352–3), which faces the Grand Canal, houses the **Museo del Settecento Veneziano** (Museum of the 18th Century; ☎ 041 241 01 00; www.museiciviciveneziani.it; Fondamenta Rezzonico 3136; adult/student/child €6.50/4.50/2.50; ☼ 10am-6pm Wed-Mon Apr-Oct, 10am-5pm Wed-Mon Nov-Mar). Designed by Baldassare Longhena and completed by Massari, it was home to several notables over the years, including the poet Robert Browning. A broad staircase by Massari ascends from the ground floor to the main floor and onto the ballroom, a splendid hall dripping with frescoes and richly furnished

with 18th-century couches, tables and ebony statues. Particularly noteworthy is Tiepolo's ceiling fresco in the Sala del Trono (Throne Room), the *Allegoria del Merito tra Nobiltà e Virtù* (Allegory of Merit Between Nobility and Virtue).

Tiepolo also had a hand in the 16th-century **Scuola Grande dei Carmini** (Map pp352-3; ☎ 041 528 94 20; Campo Santa Margherita 2617; adult/student €5/4; ☼ 9am-6pm Mon-Sat, 9am-4pm Sun Apr-Oct, 9am-4pm daily Nov-Mar), near the church of the same name, just west of Campo Santa Margherita. Of its numerous works of art, the nine ceiling paintings by Tiepolo in the Salone Superiore (upstairs) depict the virtues surrounding the Virgin in Glory.

San Polo & Santa Croce

The massive **Chiesa di Santa Maria Gloriosa dei Frari** (Map pp352-3; Campo dei Frari, San Polo 3004; admission €2.50; ☼ 9am-6pm Mon-Sat, 1-6pm Sun), rich in art, is one of the highlights of a visit to Venice. It was built for the Franciscans in the 14th and 15th centuries and decorated by an illustrious array of artists in the Gothic style. Titian, who is buried in the church, is the main attraction. His dramatic *Assunta* (Assumption; 1518) over the high altar represents a key moment in his rise as one of the city's greatest artists. It was praised unreservedly by all and sundry as a work of inspired genius. Another of Titian's masterpieces, the *Madonna di Ca' Pesaro*, hangs above the Pesaro altar (in the left-hand aisle, near the choir stalls).

Just behind the bulk of the Frari is another Venetian treasure chest. Built for the Confraternity of St Roch in the 16th century and decorated with more than 50 paintings by Tintoretto, the **Scuola Grande di San Rocco** (Map pp352-3; ☎ 041 523 48 64; Campo San Rocco, San Polo 3052; adult/18-26/under 18 €5.50/4/free; ☼ 9am-5.30pm Easter-Oct, 10am-4pm Nov-Easter) is Venice's artistic equivalent of a 2kg box of Ferrero Rocher chocolates.

After winning a competition (also in the field was Paolo Veronese) Tintoretto devoted 23 years of his life to decorating the building. The overwhelming concentration of his paintings is too much for the average human to digest. Chronologically speaking, you should start upstairs (Scarpagnino designed the staircase) in the Sala Grande Superiore. Here you can pick up mirrors to carry around to avoid getting a sore neck while inspecting the ceiling paintings (which

THE VENETO

depict Old Testament episodes). Around the walls are scenes from the New Testament. A handful of works by other artists (such as Titian, Giorgione and Tiepolo) can also be seen. Downstairs, the walls of the confraternity's assembly hall feature a series on the life of the Virgin Mary, starting on the left wall with the *Annunciazione* (Annunciation) and ending with the *Assunzione* (Assumption) opposite.

A short walk east and across the Rio di San Tomà is the 15th-century **Casa di Goldoni** (Map pp352–3; ☎ 041 275 93 25; www.museicivicivenezianii .it; Calle Nomboli, San Polo 2794; adult/senior, student & child €2.50/1.50; ⚐ 10am-5pm Mon-Sat Apr-Oct, 10am-4pm Mon-Sat Nov-Mar), where Venice's greatest playwright, Carlo Goldoni, was born in 1707. The house is worth a visit and Goldoni fans will find a host of material on the playwright's life and works.

Heading towards the Ponte di Rialto from the Chiesa di Santa Maria Gloriosa dei Frari, you soon arrive in the vast **Campo San Polo** (Map pp352–3), the city's largest square after San Marco. Locals bring their children here to play so if you are travelling with small kids they might appreciate some social contact while you take a cappuccino break. The square is rounded off in its southwest corner by the **Chiesa di San Polo** (Map pp352–3; Campo San Polo 2115; admission €2.50; ⚐ 10am-5pm Mon-Sat, 1-5pm Sun), of note mostly for Tiepolo's *Via Crucis* cycle in the sacristy.

The area around the **Ponte di Rialto** (Map pp352–3), bursting with life as the scene of the daily produce market, was one of the earliest settled locations in Venice. Rialto, or *rivo alto*, means high bank, and the spot was considered one of the safest in the lagoon. There has been a market here for almost 1000 years – the **Fabbriche Vecchie** (Map pp352–3) along the Ruga degli Orefici and the **Fabbriche Nuove** (Map pp352–3), running along the Grand Canal, were built by Scarpagnino after a fire destroyed the old markets in 1514.

Although there has been a bridge at the Rialto since the foundation of the city, the present stone construction by Antonio da Ponte was completed in 1592.

Virtually in the middle of the market, off the Ruga degli Orefici, is the **Chiesa di San Giacomo di Rialto** (Map pp352–3). According to local legend it was founded on 25 March 421, the same day as the city. Nearby is the recently restored **Chiesa di San Giovanni Elemosinario**

(Map pp352–3; Ruga Vecchia San Giovanni, San Polo 477; admission €2.50; ⚐ 10am-5pm Mon-Sat, 1-5pm Sun), a beautiful Renaissance church built on the site of an earlier one by Antonio Abbondi after a disastrous fire in 1514 destroyed much of the Rialto area. You would hardly know that the church was here, crammed as it is into the surrounding housing. The frescoes inside the dome are by Pordenone.

From Campo San Polo you could – instead of making for the Rialto – head north and then west in the general direction of Stazione di Santa Lucia. Several sights make this a worthwhile option, and you can always double-back towards the Rialto afterwards.

Tintoretto fans will want to visit the **Chiesa di San Cassian** (Map pp352–3; Campo San Cassian; ⚐ 9am-noon Tue-Sun), northwest of the Rialto. The sanctuary is decorated with three of his paintings, *Crocifissione* (Crucifixion), *Risurrezione* (Resurrection) and *Discesa nel Limbo* (Descent into Limbo).

The beautifully restored Renaissance **Ca' Pesaro** (Map pp352–3; ☎ 041 524 06 95; www.museicivici veneziani.it; Fondamenta de Ca' Pesaro, Santa Croce 2076; adult/senior, student & child €5.50/3; ⚐ 10am-6pm Tue-Sun Apr-Oct, 10am-5pm Tue-Sun Nov-Mar), further north and facing the Grand Canal, has housed the **Galleria d'Arte Moderna** since 1902. The collection lays a heavy emphasis on Italian and particularly Venetian art from the late 19th and first half of the 20th centuries. But these works are interspersed with some engaging international collections covering a broad range. Many of the works were purchased from the Venezia Biennale art festival over the years and artists include De Chirico, Miró, Chagall, Kandinsky, Klee, Klimt and Moore. The **Museo d'Arte Orientale**, in the same building on the top floor, is a fascinating old-time collection of Edo-period art and objects from Japan, including a notable set of warriors' armour. Also on show are Chinese porcelain and Indonesian shadow puppets.

Continuing northwest past the Chiesa di San Stae, you'll find the **Fondaco dei Turchi** (Map pp352–3), a 12th-century building used as a warehouse by Turkish merchants and now housing the **Museo Civico di Storia Naturale** (Natural History Museum; ☎ 041 275 02 06; www.museicivi civeneziani.it; Salizada del Fontego dei Turchi 1730; admission free; ⚐ 10am-6pm Sat & Sun). Partially opened, the main display contains finds from desert archaeological expeditions in North Africa, notably an Ouransaurus skeleton and remains of a 12m-long prehistoric crocodile.

South from the Fondaco dei Turchi in a broad leafy *campo* stands the 13th-century **Chiesa di San Giacomo dell'Orio** (Map pp352-3; Campo San Giacomo dell'Orio, Santa Croce 1457; admission €2.50; ⏰ 10am-5pm Mon-Sat, 1-5pm Sun). It is one of the few good examples of Romanesque architecture (albeit somewhat disguised by later Gothic additions) in Venice. In front of the main altar is a wooden crucifix by Veronese and on the wall at the rear of the central apse, a rare work by Lorenzo Lotto, *Madonna col Bambino e Santi* (Madonna with Child and Saints).

Cannaregio

The long pedestrian thoroughfare connecting the train station and Piazza San Marco crawls with tourists – few venture off it into the peaceful back lanes. By the time you read this, the **Ponte di Calatrava** (Map pp352-3), Venice's flash fourth bridge across the Grand Canal linking Fondamenta di Santa Lucia (and hence the train station) with Piazzale Roma, might be up and useable. Don't hold your breath though, as engineering errors have set the project back incalculably.

The Carmelite **Chiesa dei Scalzi** (Map pp352-3; Fondamenta dei Scalzi 55; ⏰ 7-11.45am & 4-6.45pm Mon-Sat, 7.45am-12.30pm & 4-7pm Sun & holidays) is next to the train station. There are some damaged frescoes by Tiepolo in the vaults of two of the side chapels.

Along the Rio Terà Lista di Spagna, the otherwise uninspiring 18th-century **Chiesa di San Geremia** (Map p358; Campo San Geremia 274; ⏰ 8.30am-noon & 4-6.30pm Mon-Sat, 9.30am-12.15pm & 5.30-6.30pm Sun & holidays) holds the body of Santa Lucia, who was martyred in Syracuse in AD 304. Her body was stolen by Venetian merchants from Constantinople in 1204 and moved to San Geremia after the Palladian church of Santa Lucia was demolished to make way for the train station.

Venice has the dubious honour of having furnished the world with a new and sinister word after the area called the Ghetto. Most easily accessible from the Fondamenta di Cannaregio, through the **Sotoportego del Ghetto** (Map p358), this is often touted as the world's first ghetto, which is not wholly true. While the name was new, the concept of keeping Jews herded into one quarter of town was not (as Spanish Jews well knew). This

area in Venice was once a *getto* (foundry), a word whose pronunciation later changed and took on a whole new meaning.

The city's Jewish population was ordered to move to the small island, the *Getto Novo* (Ghetto Nuovo, or New Foundry), in 1516. They were locked in at night by Christian soldiers and forced to follow a set of rules limiting their social and economic activities. They did retain full freedom of religious expression. Extreme overcrowding combined with building height restrictions means that some apartment blocks have as many as seven storeys but with low ceilings. In 1797 after the fall of the Venetian Republic, Jews were allowed to leave the Ghetto Nuovo to live wherever they chose.

The **Museo Ebraico** (Map p358; ☎ 041 71 53 59; www.ghetto.it; Campo del Ghetto Nuovo, Cannaregio 2902b; adult/student €3/2; ⏰ 10am-7pm Sun-Fri Jun-Sep, 10am-4.30pm Sun-Fri Oct-May, except Jewish holidays) contains a modest collection of Jewish religious silverware. The guided **tours** (adult/student incl Museo Ebraico €8.50/7; ⏰ half-hourly or hourly from 10.30am Sun-Fri, except Jewish holidays) of the Ghetto and three of its *scholas* (synagogues) that leave from the museum are highly recommended. The three synagogues visited on the tours are the **Schola Canton** (Map p358), **Schola Italiana** (Map p358) and either the **Schola Levantina** (Map p358) during the summer or the **Schola Spagnola** (Map p358) in winter. Also inquire at the museum about guided tours to the old Jewish cemetery on the Lido.

Cross the iron bridge from the Campo di Ghetto Nuovo to reach the Fondamenta degli Ormesini and turn right. This is a truly peaceful part of Venice, almost empty of tourists. There are some interesting bars and a couple of good restaurants along the *fondamenta*. Not far away from here, the 14th-century **Chiesa della Madonna dell'Orto** (Map p358; Campo della Madonna dell'Orto 3520; admission €2.50; ⏰ 10am-5pm Mon-Sat, 1-5pm Sun) was Tintoretto's parish church and contains many of his artworks. Among them are the *Giudizio Finale* (Last Judgement), *Adorazione del Vitello d'Oro* (Adoration of the Golden Calf) and the *Apparizione della Croce a San Pietro* (Vision of the Cross to St Peter). On the wall at the end of the right aisle is the *Presentazione di Maria al Tempio* (Presentation of the Virgin Mary in the Temple). Tintoretto is buried with other family members in the church.

CANNAREGIO

INFORMATION	Schola Levantina..............11 B3	**DRINKING**
Giunti al Punto...............1 A4	Schola Spagnola..............12 B3	Osteria agli Ormesini...........19 C3
Planet Internet...............2 B4	Schola Tedesca...............(see 7)	Paradiso Perduto..............20 D3
Speedy Wash.................3 B4	Sotoportego del Ghetto........13 B3	
		ENTERTAINMENT
SIGHTS & ACTIVITIES	**SLEEPING**	Casanova....................21 A4
Chiesa della Madonna dell'Orto.....4 D2	Alloggi Gerotto Calderan.......14 A4	Casinò di Venezia.............22 C4
Chiesa di San Geremia........5 B4	Ca' Pozzo...................15 B3	
Chiesa di Sant'Alvise.........6 C2		
Museo Ebraico...............7 B3	**EATING**	
Palazzo Vendramin-Calergi.....(see 22)	Billa Supermarket.............16 D4	
Parco Savorgnan.............8 A4	Gam Gam...................17 B3	
Schola Canton...............9 B3	Sahara....................18 D3	
Schola Italiana..............10 B3		

Further east the Jesuit church, known popularly as **I Gesuiti** (Map pp342-3; ☎ 041 528 65 79; Salizada dei Specchieri 4880; ☑ 10am-noon & 4-6pm), and more properly as Santa Maria Assunta, dates from the early 18th century. Its baroque interior features walls with inlaid marble in imitation of curtains. Titian's *Martirio di San Lorenzo* (Martyrdom of St Lawrence) is first on the left as you enter the church, balanced by Tintoretto's *Assunzione della Vergine* (Assumption of the Virgin) in the northern transept. Across the street is the tiny 12th-century **Oratorio dei Crociferi** (Map pp342-3; ☎ 041 271 90 12; Campo dei Gesuiti 4095; admission €2; ☑ 3.30-6.30pm Fri & Sat Apr-Oct), brimming with frescoes and paintings by Palma il Giovane.

From here you could head south towards the Grand Canal for the 15th-century **Ca' d'Oro** (Golden House; Map pp352-3; ☎ 041 520 03 45; www.cadoro.org in Italian; Calle di Ca' d'Oro 3932; adult/student/child under 12 & EU citizen under 18 or over 65 €5/2.50/free; ☑ 8.15am-2pm Mon, 8.15am-7.15pm Tue-Sun), so named for the gilding that originally decorated the sculptural details of the façade. Visible from the Grand Canal, the façade stands out from the remainder of the edifice, which is rather drab by comparison. Ca d'Oro houses the **Galleria Franchetti**, an impressive collection of bronzes, tapestries and paintings. On the 2nd floor you can see a series of fragments of frescoes saved from the outside of the Fondaco dei Tedeschi (p346). All but one are by Titian. The other, a nude work by Giorgione, is the most striking.

As you move east, stop by the utterly charming **Chiesa di Santa Maria dei Miracoli** (Map pp352-3; Campo dei Miracoli 6074; admission €2.50; ☼ 10am-5pm Mon-Sat, 1-5pm Sun), a Renaissance chocolate box designed by Pietro Lombardo and seemingly lathered in magnificent sculptures. Pietro and his son Tullio Lombardo executed the carvings on the choir.

From here it is a quick hop eastwards over a couple of bridges into the neighbouring *sestiere* of Castello.

Castello

In Campo SS Giovanni e Paolo you are confronted by the proud equestrian bronze statue of Bartolomeo Colleoni, one of Venice's more loyal mercenary mainland commanders. It is as though he stands guard in front of the huge Gothic **Chiesa dei SS Giovanni e Paolo** (Map pp352-3; ☎ 041 523 59 13; Campo SS Giovanni e Paolo; admission €2.50; ☼ 9.30am-7pm Mon-Sat, 1-7pm Sun), founded by the Dominicans and built to rival the Franciscans' Chiesa di Santa Maria Gloriosa dei Frari (p355) in size and grandeur. Work started on the church, also known by its Venetian name of San Zanipolo, in 1333, but it was not consecrated until 1430. Its vast interior is divided simply into a nave and two aisles, separated by graceful, soaring arches. The beautiful stained-glass window (the largest in Venice) in the southern transept was made in the 15th century in Murano to designs by various artists, including Bartolomeo Vivarini and Girolamo Mocetto.

Around the walls, many of the tombs of 25 doges were sculpted by prominent Gothic and Renaissance artists. Look out for Giovanni Bellini's polyptych of *San Vincenzo Ferreri* (St Vincent Ferrer) over the second altar of the right aisle. In the Cappella del Rosario, off the northern arm of the transept, is a series of paintings by Paolo Veronese, including ceiling panels and an *Adorazione dei Pastori* (Adoration of the Shepherds) on the western wall.

At right angles to the main façade of the church is the rather more eye-catching marble frontage of the former **Scuola Grande di San Marco** (Map pp352-3). Pietro Lombardo and his sons worked on what was once one of the most important of Venice's religious confraternities (which now constitutes the entrance to the city's main hospital). Codussi put the finishing touches on this Renaissance gem.

Almost directly south is another enchanting square, full of life and chatter and presided over by the church that gives it its name, the **Chiesa di Santa Maria Formosa** (Map pp352-3; Campo Santa Maria Formosa 5267; admission €2.50; ☼ 10am-5pm Mon-Sat, 1-5pm Sun). Rebuilt in 1492 by Mauro Cordussi on the former site of a 7th-century church, it contains an altarpiece by Palma Giovane depicting Santa Barbara. Just across a walkway off the southern end of the *campo* is the 16th-century **Palazzo Querini-Stampalia** (Map pp352-3). The mansion was donated to the city in 1868 by the Count Gerolamo Querini. On the 2nd floor, the **Museo della Fondazione Querini-Stampalia** (☎ 041 271 14 11; www.querinistampalia.it in Italian; Campiello Querini Stampaglia 5252; adult/student & senior €6/4; ☼ 10am-6pm Tue-Thu & Sun, 10am-10pm Fri & Sat) has a collection of paintings and Venetian furniture.

East of Campo SS Giovanni e Paolo stands what to all intents and purposes seems the twin tower of the Campanile in Piazza San Marco. It is in fact the bell tower of the **Chiesa di San Francesco della Vigna** (Map pp342-3; ☎ 041 520 61 02; Campo San Francesco della Vigna 2786; ☼ 8am-12.30pm & 3-7pm). Designed and built by Jacopo Sansovino, this Franciscan church is named for the vineyard that once thrived on the site. Its façade was designed by Palladio and inside, just to the left of the main door, is a triptych of saints by Antonio Vivarini.

Not at all otherworldly is the site of the **Arsenale** (Map pp342-3), the greatest medieval shipyards in all Europe and source of wonder to all who visited. The dockyards were founded in 1104 and at their peak were home to 300 shipping companies and employed up to 16,000 people, capable of turning out a new galley a day. Covering 32 hectares and enclosed by fortifications, the Arsenale was a symbol of Venice's maritime supremacy. Napoleon wrecked it in 1797 but it was later rebuilt and remained in use until WWI as a shipyard for the Italian navy. The Renaissance gateway surmounted by the Lion of St Mark commemorates the Christian victory over the Turkish fleet in the Battle of Lepanto in 1571. You can enter the vestibule and peer through to the interior of the Arsenale. It can be open as early as 7am and is generally shut by 5pm. You get the chance to see more of the Arsenale when temporary exhibitions are held.

A SINKING CITY

Venice can be flooded by high tides during winter. Known as *acque alte,* these mainly occur between November and April (especially in November and December), flooding low-lying areas such as Piazza San Marco. The serious floods are announced several hours before they reach their high point by 16 sirens throughout the city and islands. The wailing of the sirens is becoming an increasingly common part of the Venetian winter.

In some areas you can see the water rising up over the canal border, although most of the water actually bubbles up through drains. Buy a pair of *stivali di gomma* (Wellington boots, or gumboots) and continue sightseeing. *Passarelle* (raised walkways) are set up in Piazza San Marco and other major tourist areas (you can pick up a brochure with a map of the *passarelle* at the tourist office) and the floods usually last only a few hours. If the flood level exceeds 1.2m you can be in trouble, as even the walkways are no use.

Since 1900 Venice has sunk by more than 23cm, partly due to rising sea levels and partly due to subsidence. Climate change could cause a general global rise in sea levels of 40cm to 60cm by 2100, which would make the city uninhabitable if no preventative measures are taken.

And the canals are incredibly polluted. Until the years after WWII, the Adriatic Sea's natural tidal currents flushed the lagoon and kept the canals relatively clean. But the dredging of a 14m-deep canal in the 1960s, to allow tankers access to the giant refinery at Porto Marghera, changed the currents. Fears of an oil spill in the lagoon populate the nightmares of many a Venetian ecologist.

As though all this were not enough, the salt water has also been corroding the foundations of the city's buildings (not the pylons upon which most of the city rests). Alarm bells have been ringing and eminent persons have warned that if efforts are not made to counteract the effects of corrosion, canal-side buildings could start to collapse.

The good news, perhaps, is that in 2002 Rome finally gave the go-ahead for a controversial project to install 79 mobile barriers at the lagoon entrance. They will be activated when floods of 1.1m above mean sea level (which occur on average about five times a year) threaten the lagoon. Work will not be completed before 2011. The Mose project, as it is known, is the centrepiece of a wide series of measures aimed to protect the city. Breakwaters out to sea and a project to raise the waterfront edge of Piazza San Marco are other elements of the plan. If none of this works, the city could be doomed.

Museo Storico Navale (Map pp342–3; ☎ 041 520 02 76; Riva San Biagio 2148; admission €1.55; ⏰ 8.45am-1.30pm Mon-Fri, 8.45am-1pm Sat), located towards the Canale di San Marco on the far side of the Rio dell'Arsenale, covers the Republic's maritime history with a huge exhibition of paraphernalia, model boats, costumes and weapons. Among the exhibits is a gondola which once belonged to Peggy Guggenheim. The ticket for the museum also gets you into the **Padiglione delle Navi** (Ships Pavilion; Map pp342–3), on Fondamenta della Madonna near the entrance to the Arsenale. Of the various boats on display, the most outstanding is the *Scalé Reale,* an early 19th-century ceremonial vessel last used in 1959 to bring the body of the Venetian Pope Pius X to rest at the Basilica di San Marco.

At the eastern edge of Venice, the residential back lanes of Castello are worth wandering to see how the locals live. Beyond, the **Giardini Pubblici** (Map pp342–3), heart of the city's Biennale art festival, and the islands of **San Pietro** and **Sant'Elena** are pools of peace far removed from the busy heart of Venice.

From the Museo Storico Navale you can meander west towards San Marco along the waterside **Riva degli Schiavoni** (Map pp342–3), long the main landing stage of La Serenissima and still abuzz today. About halfway along is the Chiesa di Santa Maria della Pietà, known simply as **La Pietà** (Map pp342–3), where Vivaldi was concert master in the early 18th century. If you find it open, look for the ceiling fresco by Tiepolo.

An unusual façade makes the 15th-century **Chiesa di San Zaccaria** (Map pp342–3; ☎ 041 522 12 57; Campo San Zaccaria 4693; ⏰ 10am-noon & 4-6pm Mon-Sat, 4-6pm Sun) unique. Most of the Gothic façade is by Antonio Gambello, while the upper part, in Renaissance style, is by Codussi. On the second altar of the northern aisle is Giovanni

THE VENETO

Bellini's *La Vergine in Trono col Bambino, un Angelo Suonatore e Santi* (The Virgin Enthroned with Jesus, an Angel Musician and Saints). Admission to the Cappella di Sant'Anastasia is €1.

Venice was known for its religious tolerance. Among those to find refuge here were Slavs, mostly from across the Adriatic. They established the **Scuola di San Giorgio degli Schiavoni** (Map pp342-3; ☎ 041 522 88 28; Calle dei Furlani 3259a; admission €3; ☺ 9.30am-12.30pm & 3.30-6.30pm Tue-Sat, 9.30am-12.30pm Sun Apr-Oct, 10am-12.30pm & 3-6pm Tue-Sat, 10am-12.30pm Sun Nov-Mar) in the 15th century. The walls of the ground-floor hall are decorated with superb paintings by Vittore Carpaccio, depicting events in the lives of the three patron saints of Dalmatia: George, Tryphone and Jerome. The image of St George dispatching the dragon to the next life is particularly graphic.

Giudecca
Originally known as the *spina longa* (long fishbone) because of its shape, Giudecca's present name probably derives from the word Zudega (from *giudicato*, or the judged), which was applied to families of rebellious nobles at one time banished from Venice and later allowed to return. Some suggest the name refers to the Jews who lived here prior to the creation of the Ghetto. Rich Venetians later came of their own accord to build villas on the island. Its main attraction is the **Chiesa del SS Redentore** (Map pp342-3; Campo del SS Redentore 194; admission €2.50; ☺ 10am-5pm Mon-Sat, 1-5pm Sun), built by Palladio in 1577 after the city was saved from a savage outbreak of plague. On the third Saturday in July the doge would pay a visit to the church, crossing the canal from the Zattere on a pontoon bridge. The Festa del Redentore (Feast of the Redeemer; p364) remains one of the most important on Venice's calendar of events. Nos 41, 42, 82 and N (night) *vaporetti* call at several stops along Giudecca and run in both directions (ie towards San Marco and Piazzale Roma).

San Giorgio Maggiore
On the island of the same name, Palladio's **Chiesa di San Giorgio Maggiore** (Map pp342-3; ☎ 041 522 78 27; ☺ 9.30am-12.30pm & 2.30-6.30pm May-Sep, 9.30am-12.30pm & 2.30-4.30pm Oct-Apr) enjoys one of the most prominent positions in Venice and, although the church inspired mixed

reactions among the architect's contemporaries, it had a significant influence on architecture at the time. Built between 1565 and 1580, the church has an austere interior, which is an interesting contrast to its bold façade. Its art treasures include works by Tintoretto: an *Ultima Cena* (Last Supper) and the *Raccolta della Manna* (Shower of Manna) on the walls of the high altar, and a *Deposizione* (Deposition) in the Cappella dei Morti (Chapel of the Dead). Take the lift (€3) to the top of the 60m-high bell tower for an extraordinary view. It is also possible, on weekends, to join the one-hour guided tour of the adjacent **Fondazione Giorgio Cini** (Map pp342-3; ☎ 041 524 01 19; www.cini.it; adult/senior & child 7-12/child under 7 €12/10/free; ☺ 10am-4.30pm Sat & Sun), housed in a former monastery built around the church.

Nos 82 and N (night) *vaporetti* call at San Giorgio Maggiore and run in both directions (ie towards San Marco and Piazzale Roma).

San Michele
The city's cemetery was established on **Isola di San Michele** under Napoleon. Until then, Venetians had been buried in parish plots across town, not a very salubrious solution, as Napoleon's public administrators realised. The **Chiesa di San Michele in Isola** (Map pp342-3), begun by Codussi in 1469, was among the city's first Renaissance buildings.

Nos 41 and 42 *vaporetti* between Fondamente Nuove and Murano call in at San Michele.

Murano
The people of Venice have been making crystal and glass (the difference between the two lies in the amount of lead employed) since as early as the 10th century. The art had come from the Middle East to Italy in Roman times, but Venice's artisans learned much from their contemporaries in the East, whose secrets were brought back by merchants. The industry was moved to the island of Murano in the 13th century because of the fire hazard to the city.

Venice developed a European monopoly on the production of what is now known as Murano glass and the methods of the craft were such a well-guarded secret that it was considered treason for a glass-worker to leave the city. The incredibly elaborate pieces produced by artisans today can range from the beautiful to the grotesque – but, as the Italians would say, '*i gusti son gusti*' (there's no accounting for taste)! Watching the glass-workers in action is certainly captivating. You can see them in several outlets along Fondamenta dei Vetrai and a couple on Calle Bressaggio. Look for the *Fornace* (Furnace) sign.

The **Museo Vetrario** (☎ 041 73 95 86; www.musei civiciveneziani.it; Fondamenta Giustinian 8; adult/senior, student & child €4/2.50; ☺ 10am-5pm Thu-Tue Apr-Oct, 10am-4pm Thu-Tue Nov-Mar) traces the story of Venetian glass-making from its earliest days and contains some exquisite pieces from down the centuries.

The nearby **Chiesa dei SS Maria e Donato** (☎ 041 73 90 56; Campo San Donato; ☺ 9am-noon & 3.30-7pm Mon-Sat, 3.30-7pm Sun) is a fascinating example of Veneto-Byzantine architecture. Founded in the 7th century and rebuilt 500 years later, the church was first dedicated to the Virgin Mary. It was rededicated to San Donato after his bones were brought here from Cephalonia, along with those of a dragon he had supposedly killed (four of the 'dragon' bones hang behind the altar). The church's mosaic pavement and the impressive mosaic of the Virgin Mary in the apse date from the 12th century.

The island is most easily reached by the regular *vaporetto* No 42 (No 41 the other way) from Fondamente Nuove, Ferrovia and other stops. Or take the No 5 from San Zaccaria or the DM from Tronchetto.

Burano

Famous for its lace industry, Burano is a pretty fishing village, its streets and canals lined with bright, pastel-coloured houses. The **Museo del Merletto** (☎ 041 73 00 34; www.mu seiciviciveneziani.it; Piazza Galuppi 187; adult/senior, student & child €4/2.50; ☺ 10am-5pm Wed-Mon Apr-Oct, 10am-4pm Wed-Mon Nov-Mar), the island's lace-making museum, is housed in the former lace-making school (which shut in 1970). If you plan to buy lace on the island, choose with care as these days not all of it is locally made.

Take the LN ferry from the Fondamente Nuove to Burano.

Torcello

The delightful island of Torcello, with its overgrown main square and sparse, scruffy-looking buildings and monuments, was at its peak from the mid-7th to the 13th centuries,

when it was the seat of the Bishop of Altinum and home to some 20,000 people. Rivalry with Venice and a succession of malaria epidemics systematically reduced the island's splendour and its population. Today, fewer than 80 people call the island home.

The island's Veneto-Byzantine cathedral, **Santa Maria Assunta** (☎ 041 270 24 64; Piazza Torcello; cathedral €3, bell tower €2, incl both & Museo di Torcello €6; ☺ 10.30am-6pm Mar-Oct, 10am-5pm Nov-Feb), should not be missed. Founded in the 7th century and rebuilt in the 11th century, it was Venice's first cathedral. On the cathedral's western wall is a vast mosaic depicting the Last Judgement, but its great treasure is the mosaic of the Madonna in the semidome of the apse. Starkly set on a pure gold background, the figure is one of the most stunning works of Byzantine art you will see in Italy. Climb the bell tower for lovely views across the island and beyond.

The adjacent, tiny **Chiesa di Santa Fosca** (☺ 10am-4.30pm) was founded in the 11th century to house the body of Santa Fosca. Across the square, in the Palazzo del Consiglio, is the **Museo di Torcello** (☎ 041 270 24 64; Piazza Torcello; admission €2, incl cathedral & bell tower €6; ☺ 10.30am-5.30pm Tue-Sun Mar-Oct, 10am-5pm Tue-Sun Nov-Feb), telling the history of the island. Part of the collection is in the adjacent **Palazzo dell'Archivio**. Both buildings date from the 13th century and together they formed the nerve centre of temporal power in Torcello.

To reach the island take an LN ferry from Fondamente Nuove to Burano and change to the T ferry.

The Lido

The main draw here is the beach, but the water can be polluted and the public areas are often unkempt. Some of the beaches at the southern end of the island, such as those at Alberoni, are an exception. If you want to stay closer to the northern end of the island (and the *vaporetto* stops), you will pay a small fortune (up to €10 for a sun-lounger and €60 for a change room per day) to hire a chair and umbrella in the more easily accessible and cleaner areas of the beach.

The Lido forms a land barrier between the lagoon and the Adriatic Sea. For centuries the doges trekked out here to perform Venice's Marriage to the Sea ceremony by dropping a ring into the shallows, celebrating Venice's close relationship with the sea.

THE VENETO

The Lido became a fashionable seaside resort around the late 19th century and its more glorious days are depicted (in admittedly melancholy fashion) in Thomas Mann's novel *Death in Venice*. The rows of modern holiday apartments and hotels that fill in summer ensure the beaches are crowded, but the Lido is not quite the fashionable draw it once was.

The snappy **Palazzo del Cinema** hosts the Venice International Film Festival each September (see p364). You might trundle through on your way south to Chioggia via Pellestrina. From central Venice, the Lido can be reached by various *vaporetti*, including the Nos 1, 51, 52, 61, 62, 82, N, and the vehicle ferry from Tronchetto.

Chioggia

Chioggia lies at the southern end of the lagoon and is the second-most important city in it after Venice. Invaded and destroyed by the Venetian Republic's maritime rival, Genoa, in the late 14th century, the medieval core of modern Chioggia is a crumbly but not uninteresting counterpoint to its more illustrious patron to the north. In no way cute like Murano or Burano, Chioggia is a firmly practical town, its big fishing fleet everywhere in evidence. If your time is limited in Venice, you can live without Chioggia – the trip can take up to two hours. City bus Nos 1, 2, 6 and 7 connect Chioggia with the Sottomarina, saving you the 15-minute walk.

From the Lido, bus No 11 leaves from Gran Viale Santa Maria Elisabetta, outside the tourist office; it boards the car ferry at Alberoni and then connects with a boat at Pellestrina for Chioggia (the whole trip costs €5 one way). Or you can take the more prosaic overland bus from Piazzale Roma (€4, one hour). The **tourist office** (☎ 041 40 10 68; www.chioggiatourism.it; Lungomare Adriatico 101; ☼ 8.30am-6.30pm, shorter hrs winter) is on the waterfront at the Sottomarina.

ACTIVITIES

A gondola ride is the quintessence of romantic Venice, although at €73 for 50 minutes (€91 from 8pm to 8am) the official price is a rather hefty return from the clouds to reality. The rates are for a maximum of six people – less romantic but more affordable. After the first 50 minutes you pay in 25-minute increments (€37, or €47 after 8pm). Several

travellers have reported successfully negotiating below the official rates (definitely possible if business is slow), so get your haggling skills in order!

Gondolas are available near main canals all over the city, and can be booked by phoning ☎ 041 528 50 75 or calling in at various gondola *stazi* (stops) such as those in **Rialto** (☎ 041 522 49 04) and at the **train station** (☎ 041 71 85 43).

COURSES

Ca' Macana (Map pp352-3; ☎ 041 522 97 49; www.camacana.com; Calle delle Botteghe, Dorsoduro 3172) is a workshop that runs a pair of short courses (2½ hours each) in mask-making and decorating for groups of between 10 to 55. The courses cost between €23 and €56.50 (plus VAT) per person, depending on numbers.

Fondazione Giorgio Cini (Map pp342-3; ☎ 041 524 01 19; www.cini.it; Isola di San Giorgio Maggiore) organises seminars and specialist courses on subjects relating to the city and its culture, such as music, art and restoration.

Istituto Venezia (Map pp352-3; ☎ 041 522 43 31; www.istitutovenezia.com; Campo Santa Margherita, Dorsoduro 3116a) offers language and one- and two-week courses on subjects as diverse as cooking, wine and Burano lace. Four weeks (80 hours) of intensive language classes cost €600.

VENICE FOR CHILDREN

Venice isn't for art-lovers and hopeless romantics alone. The city is varied enough to keep even the most recalcitrant juniors interested at least some of the time. Some of the stuff grown-ups like, such as gondola and *vaporetto* rides, taking time out on a beach or a good *gelato*, will also appeal to kids.

Understandably most of the museums and galleries will leave the little 'uns cold, but some of them may work. Boys should get a kick out of the boats and model ships at the Museo Storico Navale (p360). The sculpture garden at the Peggy Guggenheim Collection (p354) may prove an educational distraction while you indulge your modern art needs.

Climbing towers is usually a winner. Try the Campanile in Piazza San Marco (p349) or the bell tower at San Giorgio Maggiore (p361).

Parco Savorgnan (part of Palazzo Savorgnan; Map p358) and the Giardini Pubblici (p360) have swings and the like.

THE VENETO

Discounts are available for children (usually aged under 12) on public transport and for admission to some museums, galleries and other sights.

TOURS

You can join free tours for a biblical explanation of the mosaics in the Basilica di San Marco. They are arranged by the Patriarcato (the church body in Venice) and take place in Italian at 11am Monday to Saturday. Tours in English are at 11am on Monday, Thursday and Friday, and in French at the same time on Thursday. This timetable is subject to change. For more information, call ☎ 041 270 24 21 from 10am to noon, Monday to Friday. Consult *Un Ospite di Venezia* for details of other visits to churches and sights in the city.

Travel agencies and hotel receptions can put you onto groups that run walking tours in Venice, among them **Venice Events** (☎ 041 523 99 79; www.veniceevents.com; Frezzaria, San Marco 1827) and **Venice Walks & Tours** (☎ 041 520 86 16; www.tours-italy.com). They both offer several two-hour walking tours at €20 a person and boat tours along the Grand Canal (€40 per person).

FESTIVALS & EVENTS

The major event of the year is **Carnevale**, when Venetians don spectacular masks and costumes for a 10-day street party in the run-up to Ash Wednesday. The starting dates for Carnevale in the next few years are 21 February 2006, 13 February 2007 and 29 January 2008.

The city next hosts the **Palio delle Quattro Repubbliche Marinare** (Regatta of the Four Ancient Maritime Republics) in June 2007. The former maritime republics of Genoa, Pisa, Venice and Amalfi take turns to host this colourful event.

Much more than Carnevale, which is to a great extent the preserve of tourists, the Venetians celebrate the **Festa del Redentore** on the third weekend of July. Gondola regattas and other activities serve as the build-up to a spectacular midnight fireworks display. A pontoon bridge is slung between Fondamenta delle Zattere and Giudecca to allow pilgrims to walk across to the Chiesa del SS Redentore. The feast day was inaugurated in 1577 to give thanks for deliverance from a bout of the plague.

The **Regata Storica** (Historic Regatta) is a series of gondola and other traditional boat races along the Grand Canal preceded by a spectacular parade of boats decorated in 15th-century style. It is held on the first Sunday in September.

The **Venice Biennale**, a major exhibition of international visual arts, started in 1895 and was held every even-numbered year from the early 20th century onwards. However, the 1992 festival was postponed until 1993 so there would be a festival on the Biennale's 100th anniversary in 1995. It is held from June to October/November in permanent pavilions in the Giardini Pubblici (Map pp342–3), as well as in other locations (in particular the Arsenale) throughout the city. The next one is in 2007. Major art exhibitions are held at locations throughout the city. Every other year the city hosts a less well known but equally prestigious architecture Biennale.

The **Venice International Film Festival** (Mostra del Cinema di Venezia), Italy's version of Cannes, is organised by the Biennale and is held annually in late August/early September at the Palazzo del Cinema on the Lido.

In November, in a procession over a pontoon bridge to the Chiesa di Santa Maria della Salute, the **Festa della Madonna della Salute** gives thanks for the city's deliverance from plague in 1630.

SLEEPING

Venice is one of the most expensive cities in Italy to stay overnight, although a fever of hotel openings has taken the heat out of price inflation since 2002. Even in the depths of the low season you won't find more than about half-a-dozen places offering singles/doubles with shared bathroom for less than €45/70. A decent budget double with private bathroom can easily cost from €100 up in high season. Most places include breakfast (often quite unsatisfactory) whether you like it or not.

Some hotels have the same prices year-round while others drop them when things are slow. Low season for the average Venetian hotelier means November, early December, January and the period between Carnevale and Easter. For some there is a dip in July and August as well. Some of the more expensive hotels operate further price differentials: weekend rates can be higher than during the week. Rooms with views (especially of the Grand Canal) are generally more expensive than those without.

Most of the top hotels are around San Marco and along the Grand Canal but it is possible to find bargains tucked away in tiny streets and on side canals in the heart of the city. A huddle of cheapies lies in wait near the train station. A growing selection of better-located budget and midrange options are spread across the city.

It's advisable to book well in advance year-round in Venice but particularly in May, September, during Carnevale and other holidays (such as Easter, Christmas and New Year) and at weekends.

The **Associazione Veneziana Albergatori** (Venice Hoteliers Association; Map pp352-3; in Italy ☎ 800 843 006, from abroad ☎ 39 041 522 22 64; www.veneziasi .it; ✆ 8am-10pm Easter-Oct, 8am-9pm Nov-Easter) has offices at the train station, in Piazzale Roma and at the Tronchetto car park. The staff will book you a room but you must leave a small deposit as well as pay a minimal booking fee.

Budget travellers have the option of the youth hostel on Giudecca and a handful of other dormitory-style arrangements, some of them religious institutions. They mostly open in summer only.

San Marco
BUDGET
Locanda Casa Petrarca (Map pp352-3; ☎ /fax 041 520 04 30; Calle delle Schiavine, San Marco 4386; s/d to €65/110) A family-run place high up in an ancient apartment building and one of the nicer budget places in the San Marco area. To get here, find Campo San Luca, follow Calle dei Fuseri, take the second left and then turn right into Calle Schiavone.

MIDRANGE
Locanda Orseolo (Map pp352-3; ☎ 0415204877; www.loc andaorseolo.com; Corte Zorzi 1083; s/d €170/240; ✖ ▢) With 15 splendidly renovated rooms in a key location close to the Bacino Orseolo, a kind of gondola terminal behind the Piazza San Marco, this is a beautiful gem run by attentive young staff.

Locanda Fiorita (Map pp352-3; ☎ 0415234754; www .locandafiorita.com; Campiello Novo 3457a; s/d €80/130; ✖) Set on a quiet square just back from the broad Campo Santo Stefano, this higgledy piggledy-looking house contains a handful of simple rooms, some of which look

onto the square. Nice touches include the Venetian-style furnishings, reproduction artwork and tapestries. It has more rooms in a nearby annexe, Ca' Morosini.

Locanda Antico Fiore (Map pp352-3; ☎ 041 522 79 41; www.anticofiore.com; Corte Lucatello 3486; s/d to €125/145; ✖ ▢) This charming, completely restored hotel is located in an 18th-century palazzo. The front door is on a narrow *rio* just in from the Grand Canal, so you could arrive in style by water taxi at this modestly priced place. Inside you will find cosy lodgings over a couple of floors. All rooms are tastefully decorated (with tapestries and timber furniture) and each has a different colour scheme.

Locanda Art Deco (Map pp352-3; ☎ 041 277 05 58; www.locandaartdeco.com; Calle delle Botteghe 2966; d €160; ✖ ▢) Art Deco has bright, white-washed rooms with exposed timber-beam ceilings. Iron bedsteads are attached to particularly comfy beds with orthopaedic mattresses – no chance of backache in Venice if you stay in this enticing little hideaway.

TOP END
Gritti Palace (Map pp352-3; ☎ 041 79 46 11; www .starwood.com/grittipalace; Campo Traghetto 2467; d €500-2500; ✖) One of the grand old dames of Venetian living. This luxury property, the façade of which fronts the Grand Canal, is one of the most famous hotels in Venice. You'll be mixing with royalty and celebs in a wide variety of rooms crammed with antique furniture.

Dorsoduro
BUDGET
Hotel Galleria (Map pp352-3; ☎ 041 523 24 89; www .hotelgalleria.it; Campo della Carità 878a; s/d €75/105, d with bathroom to €150) The only one-star hotel right on the Grand Canal near the Ponte dell'Accademia. Space is a tad tight, but the décor is welcoming in this 17th-century mansion. If you can get one of the rooms on the canal side, how can you possibly complain?

Locanda Ca' Foscari (Map pp352-3; ☎ 041 710 401; www.locandacafoscari.com; Calle Marcona 3887b; s/d €62/93; ✆ mid-Jan–Nov) For a simple, family-run lodging house close to the Frari and Campo Santa Margherita, this is not a bad choice. A little aged, it nonetheless offers reasonably sized rooms (except the single), some with their own bathroom.

MIDRANGE

Pensione Accademia Villa Maravege (Map pp352-3; ☎ 041 521 01 88; www.pensioneaccademia.it; Fondamenta Bollani 1058; s €125, d €183-275; ✖) Set in lovely gardens right on the Grand Canal and just a few steps away from the Gallerie dell'Accademia, this fine 17th-century villa has grand sitting and dining rooms, capped by splendid timber ceilings. Rooms are simple but elegant, some with four-poster beds and timber floors.

Albergo agli Alboretti (Map pp352-3; ☎ 041 523 00 58; www.aglialboretti.com; Rio Terà Antonio Foscarini 884; s/d €105/180; ✖ 🖳) This place almost feels like an inviting mountain chalet when you step inside. The management is friendly and the rooms are tastefully arranged and mostly of a good size. The restaurant comes highly recommended.

La Calcina (Map pp342-3; ☎ 041 520 64 66; www.lacalcina.com; Fondamenta Zattere ai Gesuati 780; s/d €106/186; ✖) John Ruskin stopped in here while he wrote *The Stones of Venice* in 1876. This charming hotel has a smidgen of garden attached and looks across to Giudecca. The immaculate rooms with parquet floors and timber furnishings are sober but charming. Some have small terraces attached and others have views over the Canale della Giudecca.

Locanda San Barnaba (Map pp352-3; ☎ 041 241 12 33; www.locanda-sanbarnaba.com; Calle del Traghetto 2785-6; s/d €110/170; ✖) This 13-room hotel has been elegantly carved out of a fine mansion. Rooms are well equipped and some face directly onto the canal. A small terrace graces the top of the building, and there's a small canal-side garden for breakfast or evening drinks.

TOP END

Ca' Pisani Hotel (Map pp352-3; ☎ 041 240 14 11; www.capisanihotel.it; Rio Terà Antonio Foscarini 979a; d €260-354; ✖) Named after the hero of the siege of Chioggia in 1380, the staid façade of this centuries-old building belies the self-conscious design interior, filled with 1930s and 1940s furnishings as well as items especially made for the hotel. The rooms, some with exposed-beam ceilings, are elegant, well equipped and full of pleasing decorative touches.

DD.724 (Map pp352-3; ☎ 041 277 02 62; www.dd724.it; Ramo de Mula 724; d €240-300, ste €340; ✖ 🖳) Another slick designer digs. The seven rooms and suites are individually tailored, with features such as LCD TV and home cinema. The hotel looks onto the gardens of the Peggy Guggenheim Collection and a narrow *rio*.

San Polo & Santa Croce

BUDGET

Hotel dalla Mora (Map pp352-3; ☎ 041 71 07 03; www.hoteldallamora.it; Salizada San Pantalon, Santa Croce 42a; s/d €60/90; ✖) Dalla Mora sits on a small canal just off Salizada San Pantalon. The hotel has clean, airy rooms, some with lovely canal views, and there is a terrace.

Hotel Alex (Map pp352-3; ☎ 041 523 13 41; www.hotelalexinvenice.com; Rio Terà, San Polo 2606; s/d €46/72, d with bathroom €99) Over three floors, this quiet hotel midway between the Frari and Campo San Polo offers an affordable place to lay your head. Rooms are mostly well lit and of a good size.

MIDRANGE

Ca' Angeli (Map pp352-3; ☎ 041 523 24 80; www.caangeli.it; Calle del Traghetto de la Madonneta, San Polo 1434; s/d €180/290; ✖) Hidden down a narrow *calle* and facing the Grand Canal is this superb Escher-like house, with a variety of rooms filled with antique furniture. Among the best are one with canal views and another with roof terrace. The sunny, canal-side reading room is delicious. Cash only.

Pensione Guerrato (Map pp352-3; ☎ 041 528 59 27; http://web.tiscali.it/pensioneguerrato; Ruga due Mori, San Polo 240a; d €95, with bathroom €125) It is worth seeking out this place, hidden away amid

---

AUTHOR'S CHOICE

Oltre il Giardino (Map pp352-3; ☎ 041 275 00 15; www.oltreilgiardino-venezia.com; Fondamenta Contarini, San Polo 2542; d €220-380; ✖ 🖳) Back in 1922, Alma Mahler (the composer Gustav's wife), who was then living with writer Franz Werfel, bought this magical house and garden for 100,000 lire. Today's owners have turned it into a beautifully relaxed home away from home, with timber floors, exquisitely chosen furniture and just six rooms, all of them different. One on the ground floor has a private corner of the garden. Sun streams into those on the top floor. The garden creates a sense of having a private piece of heaven. Prices vary according to the room.

THE VENETO

the Rialto markets. It's housed in a former convent, which had also served as a hostel for knights heading off on the Third Crusade. From some of the spacious, light rooms you can at least catch glimpses of the Grand Canal. Some frescoes have been uncovered and the attic rooms are delightful.

Hotel San Cassiano (Map pp352-3; ☎ 041 524 17 68; www.sancassiano.it; Calle della Rosa, Santa Croce 2232; s/d €200/360; ✸ 🖥) The 14th-century Ca' Favretto houses a mixed selection of rooms (and an incredibly mixed range of prices). The better ones are high-ceilinged doubles overlooking the Grand Canal. The building is a wonderful old pile with stone doorways along the staircases. Grab a balcony table over the canal for breakfast.

Antica Locanda Sturion (Map pp352-3; ☎ 041 523 62 43; www.locandasturion.com; Calle Sturion, San Polo 679; s €170, d €240-300; ✸) Two minutes from the Ponte di Rialto, this place has been a hotel on and off since the 13th century (when it was the Hospitium Sturionis). The best of its 11 rooms are the two generous suites overlooking the canal.

Cannaregio
BUDGET
Residenza Ca' Riccio (Map pp352-3; ☎ 041 528 23 34; www.cariccio.com; Rio Terà dei Birri 5394a; s/d €83/99; ✸ 🖥) This 14th-century residence has been lovingly restored, with exposed brick and stonework, timber ceiling beams and polished burnt red floor tiles. Most rooms look out onto a garden or courtyard.

Alloggi Gerotto Calderan (Map p358; ☎ 041 71 53 61; Campo San Geremia 283; s/d/tr/q €42/88/108/125) For a simple, budget deal this place has several advantages. It offers a large range of rooms with a commensurately bewildering battery of prices depending on size, views and whether there is a private bathroom. Most rooms have pleasing views over the square.

MIDRANGE
Locanda Leon Bianco (Map pp352-3; ☎ 041 523 35 72; www.leonbianco.it; Corte Leon Bianco 5629; d with Grand Canal view €200) Three wonderful rooms (out of eight) look right onto the Grand Canal. The undulating *terrazzo alla Veneziana* (Venetian-style floor using a marble chip and plaster mix) and heavy timber doors with their original locks lend the rooms real charm. There are no singles but the price drops in small rooms without canal views.

Ca' Pozzo (Map p358; ☎ 041 524 05 04; www.capozzo venice.com; Sotoportego Ca' Pozzo 1279; s/d €160/210; ✸ 🖥) A small-scale haunt of designer touches, this guesthouse is buried deep down a blind alley. Tastefully designed rooms each have modern artworks. In some you will find exposed ceiling beams, in others tiled floors.

Hotel Giorgione (Map pp352-3; ☎ 041 522 58 10; www.alberghi-venezia.hotelgiorgione.com; Calle Larga dei Proverbi 4587; s/d €173/265, ste €400; ✸) A welcoming hotel with comfortable, if in some cases rather small, rooms mostly in a 15th-century mansion. At the centre of the hotel is a peaceful courtyard. You can take breakfast outside and sip drinks on the 1st-floor terrace.

Castello
BUDGET
Foresteria Valdese (Map pp352-3; ☎ 041 528 67 97; www.diaconiavaldese.org/venezia; Palazzo Cavagnis, Castello 5170; dm €22, d €58-75) A rambling old mansion near Campo Santa Maria Formosa. Double rates depend on the room and whether or not it has a bathroom. Breakfast is included. Book well ahead.

MIDRANGE
La Residenza (Map pp342-3; ☎ 041 528 53 15; www.venicelaresidenza.com; Campo Bandiera e Moro 3608; s/d €100/160; ✸) This grand 15th-century mansion presides over a square in the Castello area. The main hall upstairs makes quite an impression with its candelabras, elaborate decoration and distinguished furniture. The rooms are rather more restrained but they're good value.

TOP END
Hotel Danieli (Map pp352-3; ☎ 041 522 64 80; www.starwood.com/luxury; Riva degli Schiavoni 4196; s/d from €434/690, ste €825-2648; ✸ 🖥) Hotel Danieli opened in 1822 in the 14th-century Palazzo Dandolo (it was then known as the Royale). Just wandering into the grand foyer – all arches, sweeping staircases and balconies, is a trip down through centuries of splendour. Dining in the Terrazza Danieli rooftop restaurant is a feast for the eyes and palate and heartily recommended.

Giudecca & the Islands
BUDGET
Ostello Venezia (Map pp342-3; ☎ 041 523 82 11; fax 041 523 56 89; Fondamenta della Croce 86, Giudecca; dm with breakfast €18.50; ⏰ check-in 1.30-11.30pm) The

one HI hostel in Venice is located in a peaceful spot on Giudecca. Evening meals are available for €9. Catch *vaporetto* Nos 41, 42 or 82 from the train station or Piazzale Roma to Zitelle.

TOP END

Hotel Cipriani (Map pp342-3; ☎ 041 520 77 44; www.hotel cipriani.it; Giudecca 10; s €335-825, d €625-815, ste €1090-4750; ⚹ 🖳 🏊) Set in the one-time villa of the Mocenigo family, surrounded by lavish grounds and pools, with unbeatable views across the lagoon. It occupies virtually the whole eastern chunk of Giudecca.

San Clemente Palace (☎ 041 244 50 01; www .sanclemente.thi.it in Italian; Isola San Clemente; s/d €370/410, ste €600-1900 ⚹ 🖳 🏊) This former island monastery and madhouse south of Giudecca is now a luxury hotel with 205 rooms, two swimming pools, tennis courts, a golf course, conference space and wonderful gardens. A private shuttle boat runs to the hotel from the Alilaguna airport boat stop at San Zaccaria.

Excelsior (☎ 041 526 02 01; www.starwood.com/west in; Lungomare Guglielmo Marconi 41, Lido; s/d €340/445; ☺ May-Oct; 🅿 ⚹ 🖳 🏊) A fanciful Moorish-style property that's long been the top address on the Lido. The Oriental theme continues in its luxurious rooms, many of which look out to sea or across the lagoon to Venice.

Camping

Camping grounds on the mainland south of Mestre and along the Litorale del Cavallino coast at the north end of the lagoon are another option. The tourist office has a full list of grounds in addition to those listed here.

Marina di Venezia (☎ 041 530 25 11; www.marina divenezia.it; Via Montello 6, Punta Sabbioni; person/tent €7.80/22.80; ☺ late Apr–Sep; 🅿) On the Litorale de Cavallino, this place has just about everything, from a private beach to a shop, cinema and playground. It also has bungalows. One of the ground's bars and a *gelateria* are wi-fi areas. You can get the *vaporetto* from Punta Sabbioni to Fondamente Nuove (Cannaregio), on the north shore of Venice, via Burano and Murano.

Campeggio Fusina (☎ 041 547 00 55; www.camping -fusina.com; Via Moranzani 79, Località Fusina; person/tent & car €7/14; 🅿) This camping ground is reasonably well equipped. You can eat at the restaurant and the bar hums on summer nights.

The most direct link with Venice is on the LineaFusina *vaporetto* straight into Venice (Zattere stop), which costs €5/9 one way/ return. A local bus (No 11) runs between the camping ground and the train station in Mestre. Some travellers have reported being disturbed at night by summertime discos in the area.

EATING

Venice is about the most expensive city in Italy for eating out, so you may find yourself resorting to *panini* or *tramezzini* (sandwich triangles) that cost from around €1.50 for lunchtime snacks.

Search out the little trattorie and *osterie* (simple restaurant, often with a bar) tucked away along side lanes and canals or dotted about squares away from the main tourist centres. Many bars serve filling snacks with lunchtime and predinner drinks. A Venetian *osteria* is a cross between a bar and a *trattoria*, where you can sample *cicheti* (bar snacks), generally washed down with an *ombra* (small glass of wine). Some *osterie* also serve full meals.

Better areas to look for places to eat include the backstreets of Cannaregio and San Polo, as well as around Campo Santa Margherita in Dorsoduro. A few good spots lurk about in Castello and San Marco.

Restaurants & Osterie
SAN MARCO

Ai Rusteghi (Map pp352-3; ☎ 041 523 22 05; Campiello del Tentor 5513; mini panini €1.20; ☺ 8am-9.30pm Mon-Sat) In a quiet back square away from the hubbub, this is the perfect stop for a great range of little filled panini and wine.

Osteria alla Botte (Map pp352-3; ☎ 041 520 97 75; Calle Bissa 5482; meals €25-30; ☺ Mon-Wed, Fri & Sat & lunch Sun) This spirited backstreet *bacaro* (bar/ eatery) near the Ponte di Rialto is ideal for munching *cicheti* over a glass of Prosecco. You can also take a seat for a robust meal.

Vino Vino (Map pp352-3; ☎ 041 241 76 88; Ponte delle Veste 2007a; meals €25; ☺ Wed-Mon) A popular bar/*osteria* near Teatro La Fenice. The menu changes daily and the preprepared food is reasonable. The *sarde in saor* (fried, marinated pilchards) are good and the wine list is endless.

Vini da Arturo (Map pp352-3; ☎ 041 528 69 74; Calle dei Assassini 3656; meals €80; ☺ Mon-Sat) Welcome to one of this fishy city's few meat emporiums.

No prawns here, just tender slabs of land-going animals' flesh, healthy vegetable sides and sloshings of fine wine in an ageless half-hidden restaurant.

DORSODURO

Ristorante la Bitta (Map pp352-3; ☎ 041 523 05 31; Calle Lunga San Barnaba 2753a; meals €35-40; ☺ dinner Mon-Sat) The short and regularly changing menu is dominated by a few first courses (try the *gnocchi con zucche ricotta affumicata*, or gnocchi with pumpkin and smoked ricotta) and tempting meat dishes, all presented in a romantic setting.

Osteria da Toni (Map pp352-3; ☎ 041 523 82 72; Fondamenta San Basegio 1642; meals €20-30; ☺ Tue-Sun) This is an excellent spot for a canal-side workaday lunch. Or head inside and grab a spot where you can sit amid all the bustle and crowded tables. The daily menu is limited to a few pasta options followed by a handful of fish and meat mains.

SAN POLO & SANTA CROCE

All'Arco (Map pp352-3; ☎ 041 520 56 66; Calle dell'Arco, San Polo 436; cicheti €1.50-3; ☺ Mon-Sat) Just the place if you are looking for a locals' spot for downing a few *cicheti* and a glass or two of wine.

Cantina do Mori (Map pp352-3; ☎ 041 522 54 01; Soto portego dei do Mori, San Polo 429; snacks €3-4; ☺ 8am-8.30pm Mon-Sat) Hidden away near the Ponte di Rialto is this traditional institution, which has been serving up snacks and wine since the 15th century. It is known for such items as its *francobolli* (literally 'stamps'), tiny stuffed bread snacks.

Vecio Fritolin (Map pp352-3; ☎ 041 522 28 81; Calle della Regina, Santa Croce 2262; meals €45-50; ☺ Tue-Sun) There's a touch of class to dining here. Unfailingly fresh ingredients are used to create a combination of classic and inventive local and more broadly Italian cuisine. Both the desserts and bread are homemade and renowned around town.

Osteria La Zucca (Map pp352-3; ☎ 041 524 15 70; Calle del Tentor, Santa Croce 1762; meals €30-35; ☺ Mon-Sat) La Zucca is an excellent option for frustrated vegetarians. The menu is a Med mix and even the vegetable side orders are inspired.

Muro Vino e Cucina (Map pp352-3; ☎ 041 523 47 40; Campo Cesare Battisti, San Polo 222; meals €45-50; ☺ 4pm-1am Mon-Sat) Upstairs from the designer bar scene take a seat in a gleaming industrial-style setting. The Bavarian cook prepares everything from traditional Venetian dishes

to Bavarian snags. The chef likes to play a little with the food, which has a refreshing modern touch.

Naranzaria (Map pp352-3; ☎ 041 724 10 35; Campo San Giacometto di Rialto, San Polo 130; meals €30-40; ☺ Tue-Sun) A hip hangout for sushi, light dishes and a wine or two. Nibble and jabber downstairs, take an upstairs table with a Grand Canal view or, in summer, sit out on the terrace overlooking the canal.

Ganesh Ji (Map pp352-3; ☎ 041 71 90 84; Fondamenta Rio Marin, San Polo 2426; meals €20-25, set menus €23; ☺ Fri-Tue & dinner Thu) A rare, exotic flavour in Venice. Fancy a quick curry? Forget it. But a good slow one can be had on the pleasant canal terrace. Ganesh Ji serves up authentic dishes at reasonable prices.

Da Fiore (Map pp352-3; ☎ 041 72 13 08; Calle del Scaleter, San Polo 2202; meals €130-150; ☺ Tue-Sat) This recipient of a Michelin star lurks behind an unprepossessing shop front that belies the Art Deco interior. Traditional dishes, such as *risotto ai scampi* (lobster risotto) and *bigoli in salsa* (thick spaghetti with sauce), are prepared with optimum care. Reservations are necessary.

CANNAREGIO

Osteria dalla Vedova (Map pp352-3; ☎ 041 528 53 24; Calle del Pistor 3912; meals €30-35; ☺ Mon-Wed, Fri, Sat & dinner Sun) One of the oldest *osterie* in Venice. The 'Widow's Hostelry' (also known as Trattoria Ca d'Or) offers excellent, modestly priced food, mostly from the sea. Wander in for the *cicheti*, a cornucopia of snacks from battered artichokes to *folpeti* (teensy deep-fried octopi).

Sahara (Map p358; ☎ 041 72 10 77; Fondamenta della Misericordia 2520; meals €20-25; ☺ 7pm-2am Mon-Fri, 11am-3pm & 7pm-2am Sat & Sun) Good Middle Eastern food is served here and you can even clap along to a display of belly dancing on Saturday night.

Gam Gam (Map p358; ☎ 041 71 52 84; Calle del Ghetto Vecchio 1123; meals €30; ☺ noon-10pm Sun-Thu & lunch Fri) Good if you like Israeli-style falafels and other Middle Eastern delicacies, with the occasional variation on Italian food.

Vini da Gigio (Map pp352-3; ☎ 041 528 51 40; Fondamenta della Chiesa 3628a; meals €50-60; ☺ Wed-Sun) Come to try some of Vini da Gigio's stock of fine wines and good cooking. The *gnocchetti con scampi e pesto* (little dumplings with prawns and pesto) might be followed by grilled fish.

THE VENETO

CASTELLO

Al Vecio Penasa (Map pp352-3; ☎ 041 523 72 02; Calle delle Rasse 4587; panini & snacks €3-5; ☑ 6.30am-11.30pm) There's an excellent selection of sandwiches and snacks at quite reasonable prices in this rapid-movement bar and eatery.

Alla Rivetta (Map pp352-3; ☎ 041 528 73 02; Ponte San Provolo 4625; meals €20-25; ☑ Tue-Sun) One of the few restaurants near Piazza San Marco that can be recommended. It has long been on the tourist list of 'must' places to eat but you can still get edible seafood for not unreasonable prices. Even a few of the local gondoliers eat here.

Enoteca Mascareta (Map pp352-3; ☎ 041 523 07 44; Calle Lunga Santa Maria Formosa 5138; meals incl wine €35; ☑ 7pm-2am Fri-Tue) Now in the hands of local character Mauro Lorenzon, the 'Little Mask' is a relaxed spot for anything from a mixed platter of cheese and cold meats to a limited range of hot meals, all washed down with a fine selection of wines.

Trattoria Corte Sconta (Map pp342-3; ☎ 041 522 70 24; Calle del Pestrin 3886; meals €50; ☑ Tue-Sat) The chefs prepare almost exclusively seafood, fresh from the market and served up in a charming garden (or indoors). The secret is well out now, so book ahead and expect an upward creep in prices.

GIUDECCA

Ai Tre Scaini (Map pp342-3; ☎ 041 522 47 90; Calle Michelangelo 53c, Giudecca; meals €25; ☑ Fri-Sun, Tue, Wed & lunch Mon) *The* popular local eatery. It's a no-nonsense place for seafood and other goodies. You can dine in the garden out back.

TORCELLO

Locanda Cipriani (☎ 041 73 01 50; Piazza Santa Fosca 29, Torcello; meals €50-80; ☑ lunch Wed-Mon & dinner Sat Feb-Dec) An exclusive, leafy culinary hideaway dating to 1946. Ernest Hemingway ate (and drank) here.

CHIOGGIA

Osteria Penzo (☎ 041 40 09 92; Calle Larga Bersaglio 526, Chioggia; meals €35-40; ☑ Wed-Sun & lunch Mon) One of several good-value restaurants specialising mostly in seafood in Chioggia, serving up piping-hot local dishes based entirely on the fleet's catch.

Cafés

If you can cope with the idea of paying from €5 for a coffee plus an extra €5 surcharge for the cheesy orchestra, spend an hour or more sitting at an outdoor table at the centuries-old Florian or Quadri and enjoy the atmosphere of Piazza San Marco. Or drop the music altogether and soak up the atmosphere inside.

Caffè Florian (Map pp352-3; ☎ 041 520 56 41; Piazza San Marco 56/59; ☑ 10am-midnight Thu-Tue Apr-Oct, 10am-11pm Thu-Tue Nov-Mar) The more famous of the two. Lord Byron and Henry James used to take breakfast here (separately).

Caffè Quadri (Map pp352-3; ☎ 041 522 21 05; Piazza San Marco 120; ☑ 9am-midnight Tue-Sun) In much the same league as Florian, and equally steeped in history. Upstairs is one of the city's luxury restaurants.

Gelaterie

Ice-cream prices range from about €1 for a small cup to €3 for a big cone. Prices don't vary much but the generosity of serves can. The following are among some of the best *gelaterie* in Venice.

Alaska (Map pp352-3; ☎ 041 71 52 11; Calle Larga dei Bari, Santa Croce 1159; ☑ 8am-1pm & 3-8pm)

Boutique del Gelato (Map pp352-3; ☎ 041 522 32 83; Salizada San Lio, Castello 5727; ☑ 10am-8.30pm Sun-Fri, 10am-9.30pm Sat)

Gelateria Nico (Map pp352-3; ☎ 041 522 52 93; Fondamenta Zattere, Dorsoduro 922; ☑ 6.45am-10pm Fri-Wed)

Quick Eats

Brek (Map pp352-3; ☎ 041 244 01 58; Rio Terà Lista di Spagna, Cannaregio 124; meals €10-15; ☑ 7.30am-10.30pm) A much better place to do cheap fast-ish food than the average burger joint. You can get decent full meals at lunch and dinner and snacks throughout the day.

Spizzico (Map pp352-3; Campo San Luca, San Marco 4475/4476; pizza slices €3.50; ☑ 9am-11pm Mon-Sat) Not a bad chain if you're after a quick slice of pizza.

Self-Catering

The best fresh produce **markets** (Map pp352–3) take place on the San Polo side of the Ponte di Rialto. Grocery shops, where you can buy salami, cheese and bread, are concentrated around Campo Beccarie, which happens to lie next to the **pescaria** (Map pp352–3), the city's main fish market.

Billa Supermarket (Map p358; Strada Nova, Cannaregio 3660; ☑ 8.30am-8pm Mon-Sat, 9am-8pm Sun) is a well-stocked and handy supermarket option for self-caterers.

DRINKING

Al Bottegon (Map pp352-3; ☎ 041 523 00 34; Fondamenta Maravegie 992; ⊗ 8.30am-8.30pm Mon-Sat) This is a classic, oldtime Venetian wine bar that hasn't changed in decades. It also happens to serve up some great *panini* to munch on with your Prosecco.

Caffè (Map pp352-3; ☎ 041 528 79 98; Campo Santa Margherita 2693; ⊗ 7am-1am Mon-Sat) A lively, hip student bar with snacks. It is known to locals as the *caffè rosso* because of the red sign. This square is one of the most happening in town with several good bars to choose from.

Centrale (Map pp352-3; ☎ 041 296 06 64; Piscina Frezzaria 1659b; cocktails €9-12; ⊗ 6.30pm-2am Mon-Sat) Exposed brick walls, emerald green lighting, deep lounges and chilled music make this the closest thing to Manhattan in San Marco.

Fiddler's Elbow (Map pp352-3; ☎ 041 523 99 30; Corte dei Pali 3847; ⊗ 5pm-1am Thu-Tue) This representative of the Irish bar genre in Venice sets up a few tables outside on the square. Several other Irish pubs are dotted about town.

Osteria agli Ormesini (Map p358; ☎ 041 71 58 34; Fondamenta degli Ormesini 2710; ⊗ 7.30pm-2am Mon-Sat) Oodles of wine and 120 types of bottled beer are on offer in one knockabout little place. It's something of a student haunt and tipplers spill out onto the *fondamenta* to enjoy their ambers.

Paradiso Perduto (Map p358; ☎ 041 72 05 81; Fondamenta della Misericordia 2539; meals €25; ⊗ Thu-Mon) The place has lost a little of its oomph since it changed hands, but Lost Paradise can still be a rollicking spot for a few drinks at its long benches, and live music at the weekends is usually assured. You can eat here, too.

Harry's Bar (Map pp352-3; ☎ 041 528 57 77; Calle Vallaresso 1323; cocktails €10-12; ⊗ noon-11pm) As well as being one of the city's most notable restaurants, Harry's is first and foremost a bar. Everyone who is anyone and passing through Venice usually ends up here sooner or later. Have a Bellini in the place of its invention!

ENTERTAINMENT

The Venice Carnevale (p364) is one of Italy's best-known festivals, but exhibitions, theatre and musical events continue throughout the year in Venice. Check the monthly listings magazine *VeNews*. At the tourist office ask for the free *Un Ospite di Venezia* and *Leo* magazines.

Casinos

Casinò di Venezia (Map p358; ☎ 041 529 71 11; www .casinovenezia.it; Palazzo Vendramin-Calergi, Cannaregio 2040; admission €5; ⊗ 3.30pm-2.30am) The elegant gambler's preferred haunt in the heart of Venice.

Venice Casino (☎ 041 529 71 11; www.casinovene zia.it; Ca' Noghera, Via Triestina 222, Tessera; admission €5; ⊗ 11am-4.30am Sun-Fri, 11am-6am Sat) Italy's premier mainland gambling house, out near the airport. A free shuttle bus to the casino operates from Piazzale Roma.

Cinemas

Summer Arena (Campo San Polo) A cinema-under-the-stars during held July and August. It often features British and American films but they are generally dubbed. About the only chance to catch cinema in the original language is during the September film festival (see p364).

Cinema Giorgione Movie d'Essai (Map pp352-3; ☎ 041 522 62 98; Rio Terà di Franceschi, Cannaregio 4612; adult/student €7/4.50) This modern cinema frequently presents quality movies, not just Hollywood schlock.

Nightclubs

Casanova (Map p358; ☎ 041 524 06 64; Rio Terà Lista di Spagna 158/a; ⊗ 10pm-4am Tue & Thu-Sat) A quick stumble from the train station, this is about the only place in Venice that can vaguely call itself a club, complete with mirror balls. The music is mainstream and on occasion it can hop.

Round Midnight (Map pp352-3; ☎ 041 523 20 56; Fondamenta dello Squero, Dorsoduro 3102; ⊗ 10.30pm-4am Mon-Sat Sep-May) The dancing cove to head for after you've finished hanging about on Campo Santa Margherita. You can sip all sorts of cocktails and even get a snack. The music tends to be acid jazz and Latin.

Many young locals go to one of a handful of clubs on the mainland in and around Mestre. In summer, Jesolo and its beach (to the north of the lagoon) is where most of the action takes place.

Theatre, Opera & Classical Music

Tickets are available directly from the theatre concerned, usually one hour before the show. To book in advance you can call or go online as indicated under individual entries.

You can purchase tickets for the majority of events in Venice at **Vela** (☎ 041 24 24; www

.hellovenezia.it, www.velaspa.com) outlets, which are part of the ACTV. Vela has kiosks in front of the train station, at Piazzale Roma and the Venice Pavilion Infopoint.

Teatro La Fenice (Map pp352-3; ☎ 041 786 5 75; www.teatrolafenice.it; Campo San Fantin, San Marco 1977; tickets €20-1000) The grand opera theatre of Venice is back in action. Destroyed by fire in 1996, it was reopened at the end of 2003, reproducing its old look but with the latest in theatre technology (and safety equipment).

Teatro Malibran (Map pp352-3; ☎ 041 786 5 11; www.teatrolafenice.it; Calle del Teatro, San Marco 5870; tickets €10-95) The bijou, restored 17th-century Teatro Malibran shares the opera and classical concert load with the Fenice.

Teatro Goldoni (Map pp352-3; ☎ 041 240 20 11; www.teatrostabileveneto.it; Calle Teatro Goldoni, San Marco 4650b; tickets €6-42) Named after the city's greatest playwright, this is the main drama theatre in Venice. It's not unusual for Goldoni's plays to be performed here – what more appropriate location?

SHOPPING
You can expect most shops hoping to sell to tourists to open all weekend during the high season (Easter to September).

The main shopping area for clothing, shoes, accessories and jewellery is in the narrow streets between San Marco and the Rialto, particularly the Marzarie and around Campo San Luca. The more upmarket shopping area is west of Piazza San Marco.

Classic gift options include Murano glass and Burano lace, Carnevale masks and lovely *carta marmorizzata* (marbled paper).

Marco Polo (☎ 041 73 99 04; www.marcopologlass.it; Fondamenta Manin 1, Murano) One of the handful of larger, reliable glass merchants in Murano, Marco Polo offers you the opportunity of seeing the masters at work, a large display of traditional glassware, as well as a quasi-museum of contemporary art in glass by international creators.

Ca' Macana (Map pp352-3; ☎ 041 520 32 29; Calle delle Botteghe, Dorsoduro 5176) One of the best stores and workshops in Venice producing Carnevale masks.

Aliani (Map pp352-3; ☎ 041 522 49 13; Ruga Vecchia di San Giovanni, San Polo 654) An outstanding collection of cheeses and other delicatessen products have long made Aliani a favoured gastronomic stop in the Rialto area. You will also find a range of wines.

Legatoria Polliero (Map pp352-3; ☎ 041 528 51 30; Campo dei Frari, San Polo 2995) A traditional exponent of the art of Venetian bookbinding with (and without) marbled paper.

Mazzon Le Borse (Map pp352-3; ☎ 041 520 34 21; Campiello San Tomà, San Polo 2807) An unassuming store and workshop, Mazzon le Borse is a great place to shop for handmade leather bags and accessories.

Vivaldi Store (Map pp352-3; ☎ 041 522 13 43; Salizada del Fontego dei Tedeschi 5537; ⏱ 9.30am-7.30pm Mon-Sat, 11am-7pm Sun) Can't get the sounds of Vivaldi out of your mind? If you need a CD of music related to Venice, pop by here. Cristiano Nalesso specialises in all things Venetian.

GETTING THERE & AWAY
Air
Venice's modern **Marco Polo airport** (VCE; ☎ 041 260 92 60; www.veniceairport.it) is 12km outside Venice and just east of Mestre (it also sometimes goes by the name of the nearby settlement of Tessera). Some flights, notably Ryanair's budget services, use the minuscule **San Giuseppe airport** (TSF; ☎ 0422 31 53 31), about 5km southwest of Treviso and 30km (about an hour's drive through traffic) from Venice. Airport bus services link both airports with Venice and Mestre, and the Alilaguna fast ferry runs from Marco Polo airport. For more details, see opposite.

Boat
Apart from Mediterranean cruise ships that call in, a couple of companies run regular ferries to Venice from Greece and Croatia. Contact **Minoan Lines** (www.minoan.gr) or **Venezia Lines** (www.venezialines.com).

Bus
ACTV (☎ 041 24 24; www.actv.it) local buses leave from the **bus station** (Map pp342–3) on Piazzale Roma for surrounding areas, including Mestre and Chioggia. There are ticket offices on Piazzale Roma and in front of the **train station** (Map pp342–3).

ATVO (Azienda Trasporti Veneto Orientale; ☎ 041 520 55 30) operates buses to destinations all over the eastern part of the Veneto. A handful of other companies have the occasional service to more distant locations but to get to most places in Italy the train is an easier option. Tickets and information are available at the ticket office on Piazzale Roma.

THE VENETO

Car & Motorcycle

The A4 connects Trieste with Turin, passing through Mestre (and hence Venice). Take the Venice exit and follow the signs for the city. From the south, take the A13 from Bologna, which connects with the A4 at Padua.

Once you cross the bridge from Mestre, the Ponte della Libertà, cars must be left at one of the huge car parks on Piazzale Roma or on the island of Tronchetto. Parking is not cheap and you will pay €18 or more for every 24 hours. Parking stations in Mestre are cheaper.

The following all have offices on Piazzale Roma, as well as at Marco Polo airport.

Avis (Map pp342–3; ☎ 041 523 73 77, in Italy ☎ 199 10 01 33)

Europcar (Map pp342–3; ☎ 041 523 86 16)

Expressway (Map pp342–3; ☎ 041 522 30 00)

Hertz (Map pp342–3; ☎ 041 528 40 91)

Train

The train station, **Stazione di Santa Lucia** (Map pp352–3), is directly linked by train to Padua (€2.50 to €8.95, 30 to 40 minutes, three or four hourly), Verona (€6.10 to €12.65, 1¼ to 2¼ hours, two hourly), Milan, Trieste and Bologna, and is easily accessible from the cities of Florence and Rome. You can also reach Venice by rail from major points in France, Germany, Austria, Switzerland, Slovenia and Croatia.

GETTING AROUND
To/From the Airports

The **Alilaguna** (www.alilaguna.com) airport fast ferry costs €10 to/from Venice or the Lido and €5 to/from Murano. You can pick it up at the Zattere or near Piazza San Marco, in front of the **Giardini Ex Reali** (Map pp352–3).

The standard water taxi rate for the ride between Piazzetta di San Marco and Marco Polo airport is €45. To/from the Lido costs €55. Keep an eye out for night and baggage surcharges.

ATVO (☎ 041 520 55 30) buses run to the airport from Piazzale Roma (€3, 20 minutes, 27 to 30 daily).

Eurobus (☎ 041 541 51 80) buses connect with flights at Treviso's San Giuseppe airport. The trip to/from Piazzale Roma takes 65 minutes and costs €4.50 (€8 return, but the ticket is valid for one week only).

Traghetto

The poor man's gondola, *traghetti* are used by locals to cross the Grand Canal where there is no nearby bridge. There is no limit (except common sense) on the number of passengers who can stand. The *traghetto* ride costs €0.50.

Traghetti are supposed to operate from about 9am to 6pm between Campo Traghetto (near Santa Maria del Giglio) and Calle de Lanza; Calle Mocenigo Casa Vecchia, further north, and Calle Traghetto; and Campo Santa Sofia and Campo della Pescaria, near the produce market.

Several other *traghetto* routes operate from 9am to noon only. They include Stazione di Santa Lucia to Fondamenta San Simeon Piccolo; Campo San Marcuola to Salizada del Fondaco dei Turchi; Fondamenta del Vin to Riva del Carbon, near the Ponte di Rialto; Campo San Samuele, north of the Ponte dell'Accademia, and Calle del Traghetto; and Calle Vallaresso to Punta della Dogana. Some of these may on occasion not operate at all (as was the case with the latter two in 2005).

VENICE CARD

A much-touted all-inclusive transport and sights card, **Venice Card** (☎ 041 24 24; www.venicecard .it) can save a little hassle but represents no financial saving over alternatives (indeed it can work out to be more costly).

There are two types of Venice Card. The blue card gives you unlimited use of ferries and buses throughout the Venice municipality for one, three or seven days. It also gives you free access to the public toilets (which otherwise cost €0.50) scattered around town.

The orange version throws in the Musei Civici (City Museums) for free (for more information, see the boxed text, p348).

The junior (those aged under 30) blue card costs €9/22/49 for one/three/seven days, while the senior version costs €14/29/51. The junior orange card costs €18/35/61 and the senior version €28/47/68. The three- and seven-day passes are cheaper if purchased online.

Vaporetto

The city's main mode of public transport are *vaporetti*. A car ferry (No 17) transports vehicles from Tronchetto, near Piazzale Roma, to the Lido. From Piazzale Roma, *vaporetto* No 1 zigzags down the Grand Canal to San Marco and then the Lido. It is a great introduction to Venice to travel this way but there are faster lines if you are in a hurry.

Tickets can be purchased from the ticket booths at most landing stations and at Vela outlets. Generally tickets are validated when they are sold to you, which means they are for immediate use. If they are not validated, or if you request them not to be (so that you can use them later on), you are supposed to validate them in the machines at each landing station before you get on the boat. If not, you could be fined. You can also buy tickets when boarding (at a slightly higher price). You will be charged double if you have lots of luggage.

Catching these things can be confusing. Sometimes boats going both ways call at the same stop; occasionally boats have limited stops (for instance ferries heading down the Grand Canal from Piazzale Roma and Ferrovia sometimes only go as far as the Rialto). At the bigger stops (like Ferrovia) different landings are set aside for the different routes *and* directions.

Single *vaporetto* tickets cost €3.50 (plus €3.50 for luggage!), even if you only ride to the next station. A 24-hour ticket is better value at €10.50 for unlimited travel. Better still are the three-day (€22) tickets. Rolling Venice pass holders (see p348) can get the three-day ticket for €15. For information on the Venice Card, see p373. Routes and route numbers can change, so the following list is a guide only.

DM (Diretto Murano) Piazzale Roma–Ferrovia–Murano and back.

LN (Laguna Nord) San Zaccaria (Pietà)–Lido–Litorale del Cavallino (Punta Sabbioni)–Treporti–Burano–Mazzorbo–Murano (Faro)–Fondamente Nuove and back.

T Torcello–Burano (half-hourly service) and back from 7am to 8.30pm.

No 1 Piazzale Roma–Ferrovia–Grand Canal (all stops)–Lido and back.

No 3 Fast circular line: Tronchetto–Ferrovia–San Samuele–Accademia–San Marco–Tronchetto (summer only).

No 4 Fast circular line in reverse direction to No 3 (summer only).

No 5 San Zaccaria–Murano and back.

No 11 Lido–Pellestrina and back.

No 13 Fondamente Nuove–Murano–Vignole–Sant'Erasmo–Treporti and back.

No 17 Car ferry: Tronchetto–Lido and back (extends to Punta Sabbioni in summer).

No 18 Murano–Vignole–Sant'Erasmo–Lido and back (summer only).

No 20 San Zaccaria–San Servolo–San Lazzaro and back.

No 24 Mestre (Darsena Via Torino)–Rialto and back. A limited commuter service that runs not more than four times a day and not necessarily year-round.

No 31 Pellestrina–Chioggia and back (part of the No 11 bus line from Lido).

No 41 Circular line: Piazzale Roma–Sacca Fisola– Giudecca–San Zaccaria–San Pietro–Fondamente Nuove–Murano–Ferrovia.

No 42 Circular line in reverse direction to No 41.

No 51 Circular line: Piazzale Roma–Santa Marta–Zattere–San Zaccaria–Lido–San Pietro–Fondamente Nuove–Ferrovia.

No 52 Circular line in reverse direction to No 51.

No 61 Limited-stops weekdays only circular line: Piazzale Roma–Santa Marta–San Basilio–Zattere–Giardini–Sant'Elena–Lido.

No 62 Limited-stops weekdays only circular line, reverse direction to No 61.

No 82 San Zaccaria–San Marco–Grand Canal (all stops)–Ferrovia–Piazzale Roma–Tronchetto–Zattere– Giudecca–San Giorgio. A Limitato San Marco or Limitato Piazzale Roma sign means it will not go beyond those stops. Sometimes it goes only as far as Rialto. In summer the line extends from San Zaccaria to the Lido.

N All-stops night circuit: Lido–Giardini–San Zaccaria–Grand Canal (all stops)–Ferrovia–Piazzale Roma–Tronchetto–Giudecca–San Giorgio–San Zaccaria (starts around 11.30pm; last service around 5am).

N A second night service (aka NMU) from Fondamente Nuove to Murano – this has three or four runs from midnight.

N A third night run, this time a nocturnal version of the Laguna Nord service (aka NLN) – a handful of services between Fondamente Nuove and Burano, Mazzorbo, Torcello, Sant'Erasmo and Treporti.

Water Taxis

Venetian water taxis ain't cheap, with an €8.70 flagfall, an extra €6 if you order one by telephone, €1.30 per minute thereafter and various other surcharges that can make a gondola ride look cheap. Up to 15 people can ride in a taxi, but that can be rather uncomfortable.

There are jetties outside the train station and on **Rio Novo** (Map pp352–3).

AROUND THE VENETO

THE BRENTA RIVIERA

Dotted along the River Brenta, which passes through Padua and spills into the Venetian lagoon, are more than 100 villas built over the centuries by wealthy Venetian families as summer homes; most are closed to the public. The most outstanding are **Villa Foscari** (1571), built by Palladio at Malcontenta, and **Villa Pisani**, also known as the Villa Nazionale, at Strà, which was built for Doge Alvise Pisani. It was used by Napoleon and was the site of the first meeting between Hitler and Mussolini. ACTV buses running between Padua and Venice stop at or near the villas. Those that open generally do so with widely varying timetables from May to the end of September. Ask at the tourist offices in Venice for the latest details. See p384 for information on other Venetian villas.

You can take full-day tours along the River Brenta. The luxurious **Burchiello** (☎ 049 820 69 10; www.ilburchiello.it; one way adult/child 12-18/child 6-12/child under 6 €62/44/31/free; ⏰ Mar-Oct) barge plied the River Brenta from Venice to Padua in the 17th and 18th centuries. Today's rather more modern version cruises up and down the river between Venice and Strà (the price includes tours of Villa Foscari and Villa Barchessa Valmarana). Departures from Venice (Riva degli Schiavoni) are on Tuesday, Thursday and Saturday; those from Strà are on Wednesday, Friday and Sunday. Shuttle buses connect Strà and Padua's main bus station. Other companies also operate tours along the Brenta, including **I Batelli del Brenta** (☎ 049 876 02 33; www.battellidelbrenta.it; half- & full-day tours €33-53), offering similar tours at similar prices. Ask at the Venice or Padua tourist offices for more details.

PADUA

pop 206,000

The city of St Anthony and home to Italy's second-oldest university, Padua (Padova to the locals) is also the site of one of the most remarkable works of late Gothic art (prefiguring the Renaissance) in Northern Italy. Just 37km west of Venice, this dynamic student town, with its arcaded streets and fetching medieval centre, deserves at least a day trip from the lagoon city.

The Veneti tribes of the northeast established a town here even before the Romans arrived, but Patavium was then all but wiped off the map by Lombard invaders in AD 602. The city grew again as a powerful and wealthy city-state in the 13th and 14th centuries under the Carrara clan, who set up the *studium* (university) but who were also involved in incessant skirmishes with neighbours. Venice brought an end to this when it occupied Padua and its territories in 1405.

Information

Complesso Clinico Ospedaliero (☎ 049 821 11 11; Via Giustiniani 1) Hospital.

Feltrinelli International (Via San Francesco 14) For books in various languages.

Internet Point In Collegio (☎ 049 65 84 84; Via Petrarca 9; membership fee €2, 1st hr €6, then per hr €3; ⏰ 10am-2am Mon-Fri, 4-8pm Sat, 2-8pm Sun)

Police station (☎ 049 83 31 11; Riviera Ruzante 11)

Post office (Corso Garibaldi 33; ⏰ 8.30am-6.30pm Mon-Sat)

Tourist information booth (☎ 049 875 30 87; Piazza del Santo; ⏰ Mar-Oct)

Tourist office (www.turismopadova.it); train station (☎ 049 875 20 77; ⏰ 9am-7pm Mon-Sat, 9am-noon Sun); Vicolo Pedrocchi (☎ 049 876 79 27; ⏰ 9am-1.30pm & 3-7pm Mon-Sat)

Sights

The **Padova Card** (€14) is a pass that's valid for 48 hours and allows you to visit the Cappella degli Scrovegni (plus €1 booking fee), Musei Civici agli Eremitani, Palazzo della Ragione, Museo del Risorgimento e dell'Età Contemporanea (which includes the Caffè Pedrocchi), the baptistry in the cathedral, the Orto Botanico, a couple of minor chapels and Petrarch's House in Arquà Petrarca. It's available from tourist offices and the monuments concerned. A family museum card valid for 15 days for two adults and two children for all the above except the Orto Botanico costs €25.

CAPPELLA DEGLI SCROVEGNI

Art-lovers visit Padua just to see the lively Giotto frescoes in this **chapel** (☎ 049 201 00 20; www.cappelladegliscrovegni.it; Giardini dell'Arena; adult/child €12/8, Mon €8/5, plus booking fee €1; ⏰ 9am-7pm) in the Giardini dell'Arena, just a five-minute walk from the train station. Enrico Scrovegni commissioned its construction in 1303 as a

PADUA

0   400 m
0   0.2 miles

To A4 (5km)

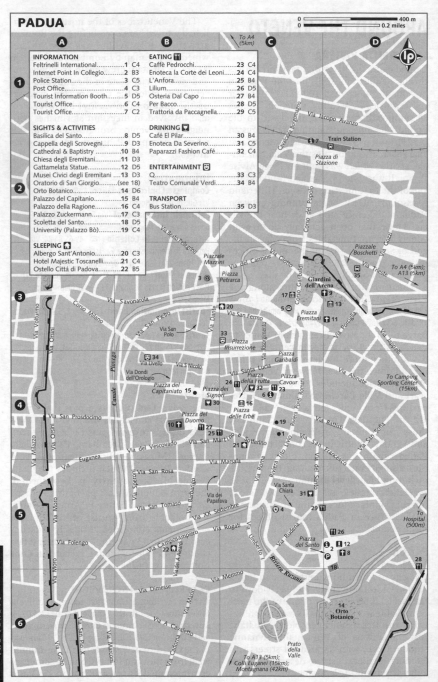

INFORMATION
Feltrinelli International...............1 C4
Internet Point In Collegio.........2 B3
Police Station...........................3 C5
Post Office...............................4 C3
Tourist Information Booth.......5 D5
Tourist Office............................6 C4
Tourist Office............................7 C2

SIGHTS & ACTIVITIES
Basilica del Santo.....................8 D5
Cappella degli Scrovegni...........9 D3
Cathedral & Baptistry 10 B4
Chiesa degli Eremitani............11 D3
Gattamelata Statue.................12 D5
Musei Civici degli Eremitani ...13 D3
Oratorio di San Giorgio.......(see 18)
Orto Botanico..........................14 D6
Palazzo del Capitanio..............15 B4
Palazzo della Ragione.............16 C4
Palazzo Zuckermann...............17 C3
Scoletta del Santo...................18 D5
University (Palazzo Bò)............19 C4

SLEEPING
Albergo Sant'Antonio.............20 C3
Hotel Majestic Toscanelli........21 C4
Ostello Città di Padova...........22 B5

EATING
Caffè Pedrocchi......................23 C4
Enoteca la Corte dei Leoni......24 C4
L'Anfora..................................25 B4
Lilium.....................................26 D5
Osteria Dal Capo.....................27 B4
Per Bacco...............................28 D5
Trattoria da Paccagnella.........29 C5

DRINKING
Café El Pilar............................30 B4
Enoteca Da Severino...............31 C5
Paparazzi Fashion Café...........32 C4

ENTERTAINMENT
Q..33 C3
Teatro Comunale Verdi...........34 B4

TRANSPORT
Bus Station..............................35 D3

Via Jacopo Avanzo

Train Station
Piazza di Stazione

Via Gozzi

Piazzale Boschetti
Via Trieste
To A4 (5km);
A13 (5km)

Corso del Popolo

Canale del Piovego

Via Beato Pellegrino

Piazzale Mazzini

Via del Carmine

Via Giotto

Giardini dell'Arena

Piazza Petrarca

Corso Garibaldi

Piazza Eremitani

Via Porciglia

Via Jappelli

Corso Milano

Via Savonarola

Via Dante

Via San Pietro

Via San Polo

Via San Fermo

Piazza Insurrezione

Via Livello

Via S Nicolò

Via Dondi dell'Orologio

Piazza del Capitaniato

Piazza dei Signori

Piazza della Frutta

Piazza Cavour

Piazza Garibaldi

Via Santa Lucia

Via Altinate

To Camping Sporting Center (15km)

Via Roma

Riviera Tito Livio

Riviera Ponte Romani

Via San Francesco

Via San Sofia

Piazza del Duomo

Piazza delle Erbe

Via San Martino e Solferino

Via del Santo

Via Battisti

Via del Vescovado

Via Marsala

Via Euganea

Via San Prosdocimo

Via Orsini

Via Miazzo

Via Volturno

Via San Rosa

Via Speroni

Via Barbarigo

Via dei Papafava

Via San Tomaso

Via XX Settembre

Via Santa Chiara

To Hospital (500m)

Via Rogati

Via Umberto I

Via Camposampiero

Via de M Aleardi

Piazza del Santo

Via Rudena

Riviera Ruzante

Via Folengo

Via Moro

Via San Pio X

Via Marconi

Via Cadorra

Via Dimesse

Via Maini

Via A Cavaletto

Via Memmo

Orto Botanico

Prato della Valle

To A13 (5km);
Colli Euganei (15km);
Montagnana (42km)

resting place for his father, who was denied a Christian burial because of his money-lending practices. Giotto's remarkable fresco cycle, probably completed between 1304 and 1306, illustrates the lives of Mary and Christ and is arranged in three bands. Among the most famous scenes in the cycle is the *Bacio di Giuda* (Kiss of Judas). The series ends with the *Ultima Cena* (Last Supper) on the entrance wall and the Vices and Virtues are depicted around the lower parts of the walls. Keep in mind the era when the frescoes were painted – Giotto was moving well away from the two-dimensional figures of his medieval contemporaries. Effectively he was on the cusp between Gothic art and the remarkable creative explosion that was still decades away – the Renaissance. Booking 24 hours in advance by phone or online is obligatory and visitors can spend a maximum 15 minutes inside the chapel. It's sometimes open until 10pm.

At the adjacent **Musei Civici agli Eremitani** (☎ 049 820 45 50; Piazza Eremitani 8; adult/child €10/5, incl Cappella degli Scrovegni €12/5; ☼ 9am-7pm Tue-Sun) the collection of 14th- to 18th-century Veneto art and largely forgettable archaeological artefacts includes a crucifix by Giotto.

On the same ticket as the above museum you can visit the nearby early 20th-century **Palazzo Zuckermann**, which is home to an extensive applied and decorative arts museum and a private collection on the 2nd floor dominated by a treasure chest of ancient coins.

CHIESA DEGLI EREMITANI

Completed in the early 14th century, this Augustinian **church** (☎ 049 875 64 10; Giardini dell'Arena; ☼ 8.15am-6.45pm Mon-Sat, 10am-noon & 4-7pm Sun & holidays Mar-Oct, 8.15am-6.15pm Mon-Sat, 10am-1pm & 4.15-7pm Sun & holidays Nov-Feb) was painstakingly rebuilt after it was bombed in WWII. The remains of frescoes created by Andrea Mantegna during his twenties are displayed in a chapel to the left of the apse. Most were wiped out in the bombing, the greatest single loss to Italian art during the war. The *Martirio di San Jacopo* (Martyrdom of St James), on the left, was pieced together from fragments found in the rubble of the church while the *Martirio di San Cristoforo* (Martyrdom of St Christopher), opposite, was saved because it had been removed before the war.

HISTORIC CENTRE

Via VIII Febbraio leads you to the **university** (☎ 049 827 30 47; Via VIII Febbraio; adult/student & child €3/1.50; ☼ 9.15am-12.15pm Tue, Thu & Sat, 3.15-6.15pm Mon, Wed & Fri), the main part of which is housed in the Palazzo Bò ('ox' in Veneto dialect – it's named after an inn that previously occupied the site). Established in 1222, the university is Italy's oldest after the one in Bologna. Europe's first anatomy theatre was opened here in 1594 and Galileo Galilei taught here from 1592 to 1610. The main courtyard and its halls are plastered with the coats of arms of the great and learned from across Europe. There are three guided tours a day, which are included in the admission price.

Continue along to Piazza delle Erbe and Piazza della Frutta, which are separated by the grand Gothic **Palazzo della Ragione** (☎ 049 820 50 06; Piazza delle Erbe; adult/child €8/4; ☼ 9am-7pm Tue-Sun), also known as the Salone for the grand hall on its upper floor.

West from here is Piazza dei Signori, dominated by the 14th-century **Palazzo del Capitanio**, the former residence of the city's Venetian ruler. South of the palazzo is the city's **cathedral** (☎ 049 66 28 14; Piazza del Duomo; ☼ 7.30am-noon & 3.30-7.30pm Mon-Sat, 7.45am-1pm & 3.45-8.30pm Sun & holidays), built from a much altered design of Michelangelo's. The 13th-century Romanesque **baptistry** (☎ 049 65 69 14; Piazza del Duomo; adult/child €2.50/1; ☼ 10am-6pm) features a series of frescoes of Old and New Testament scenes by Giusto de' Menabuoi, influenced by Giotto.

PIAZZA DEL SANTO

At the south end of the old centre stands the majestic Basilica di Sant'Antonio, or simply the **Basilica del Santo** (☼ 6.30am-7pm Nov-Feb, 6.30am-7.45pm Mar-Oct), which houses the corpse of the town's patron saint, St Anthony of Padua (1193–1232), and is an important place of pilgrimage. Construction of what is known to townspeople as Il Santo began in 1232. The saint's tomb, bedecked by requests for his intercession to cure illness and thanks for having done so, is in the Cappella del Santo, in the left transept. Look out for the saint's relics in the apse. The sculptures and reliefs of the high altar are by Donatello, master sculptor of the Florentine Renaissance. He remained in town long enough to carry out the Gattamelata equestrian statue that still dominates Piazza del Santo in 1453. This magnificent representation of the 15th-century Venetian mercenary leader Erasmos da Narni (whose nickname, Gattamelata, translates as 'Honeyed Cat') is considered the first great bronze of the Italian Renaissance.

On the south side of the piazza lies the **Oratorio di San Giorgio** (☎ 049 875 52 35; admission incl Scoletta del Santo €2; ⏱ 9am-12.30pm & 2.30-7pm Apr-Sep, 9am-12.30pm & 2.30-5pm Oct-Mar), the burial chapel of the Lupi di Soranga family of Parma, with 14th-century frescoes. Next door is the **Scoletta del Santo**, containing works believed to be by Titian.

Just south of Piazza del Santo, the **Orto Botanico** (☎ 049 827 21 19; adult/child €4/3; ⏱ 9am-1pm & 3-6pm Apr-Oct, 9am-1pm Mon-Sat Nov-Mar), laid out in 1545, is purportedly the oldest botanical garden in Europe.

Sleeping

Koko Nor Association (☎ 049 864 33 94; www.bb kokonor.it; Via Selva 5) This association can help you to find B&B-style accommodation in family homes as well as furnished apartments (they have 15 places on the books in Padua and four in the surrounding area) for around €60 to €70 for two people. The tourist office can provide a list of about 30 B&Bs.

Hotel Majestic Toscanelli (☎ 049 66 32 44; www2 .goldgate.it/hoteltoscanelli; Via dell'Arco 2; s/d to €115/172; ✖ P) Hidden away in a leafy corner of one of the lanes that twist away from Piazza delle Erbe, the hotel boasts classy rooms in various styles (ranging from Imperial to what the owners call '19th-century English') and complete with all the usual mod cons. The Toscanelli opened in 1946 in what was once Padua's Jewish quarter.

Albergo Sant'Antonio (☎ 049 875 13 93; www.hotel sanantonio.it; Via San Fermo 118; s/d €62/82; ✖) The comfortable, airy rooms here are a good deal. It has some cheaper ones with shared bathrooms.

Ostello Città di Padova (☎ 049 875 22 19; Via dei A Aleardi 30; dm with breakfast €15) Not bad as far as hostels go. To get there take bus Nos 3, 8 or 12 from the train station to Prato della Valle and ask for directions. Dorms have 16 bunk beds and the hostel also has some family rooms (€16.50) with four bunk beds and bathroom.

Camping Sporting Center (☎ 049 79 34 00; www .sportingcenter.it; Via Roma 123, Montegrotto Terme; per person/tent €7.50/10.70; ⏱ Mar–mid-Nov; 🏊) The only camping ground in the province of Padua, this place is about 15km away from the city centre. It's big and boasts a swimming pool, access to spa facilities, shops and just about anything else your heart might desire. The ground can be reached by city bus M from the train station.

Eating

Osteria Dal Capo (☎ 049 66 31 05; Via degli Obizzi 2; meals €30; ⏱ Tue-Sat & dinner Mon) This carefully maintained *osteria* is known throughout town as the perfect spot for quality traditional Veneto cooking. Try the *bavette ai frutti di mare* (a seafood pasta dish), or classics ranging from *zuppa di pesce* (fish soup) to *spezzatino di puledro* (chunky horse stew).

Per Bacco (☎ 049 875 46 64; Piazzale Pontecorvo 10; meals €30-35; ⏱ Tue-Sun) It's away from the centre but a visit repays the effort needed to get here. The warm timber and yellow décor creates a romantic mood. The menu changes regularly and tends to combine the traditional with a little inventive spark. You might try the duck carpaccio or dove done in liquorice.

Enoteca la Corte dei Leoni (☎ 049 875 00 83; Via Pietro d'Abano 1; meals €45; ⏱ Tue-Sat, dinner Mon & lunch Sun) A modern temple of wine, also offering a fine-dining experience. In summer, book a table in the courtyard (where jazz concerts are also occasionally staged). The food is excellent if a little nouvelle in terms of portions.

Trattoria da Paccagnella (☎ 049 875 05 49; Via del Santo 113; meals €30; ⏱ Mon-Sat) A comfortably elegant setting for fine Veneto cuisine, especially duck and game meats. How about *fagottini al radicchio di Treviso e pancetta croccante* (pasta bundles with red Treviso lettuce and crispy bacon) followed by *petto d'anatra al melograno* (duck breast with pomegranate)?

Caffè Pedrocchi (☎ 049 878 12 31; www.caffeped rocchi.it; Via VIII Febbraio 15; ⏱ 9am-10pm Sun-Wed, 9am-1am Thu-Sat) Fronted by a spruced-up neoclassical façade, this café has been in business since the 19th century. It was one of Stendhal's favourite haunts and remains a classy Padua coffee stop.

Lilium (☎ 049 875 11 07; Via del Santo 181; ⏱ 7.30am-8pm winter, 7.30am-10pm Tue-Sun summer) A fine pastry shop that offers wonderful gelato and delicious sweet things.

L'Anfora (☎ 049 65 66 29; Via dei Sconcin 13; meals €25-30; ♥ Mon-Sat) A good-natured place where locals crowd the bar for a wine or two and perhaps a few snacks. Or you can sit down for a hearty meal. Fancy some tripe?

Drinking
There are several traditional spots around Piazza delle Erbe for taking the evening *spritz*. In summer especially, hundreds of people clutching their favourite tipples spread out across the square in the early evening. Much the same thing happens on a reduced scale on Piazza dei Signori.

Café El Pilar (☎ 049 65 75 65; Piazza dei Signori 8; ♥ 8.30am-1am Mon-Sat) Beautiful people and others converge here and around nearby Piazza del Duomo for the evening *spritz*.

Enoteca Da Severino (☎ 049 65 06 97; Via del Santo 44; ♥ 10am-1.30pm & 5-9pm Mon-Sat) Wine-lovers are beckoned to taste tipples from around the region and beyond. The walls of this tiny wine bar are lined with bottles and appreciative drinkers spill out into the street in the warmer months.

Paparazzi Fashion Café (☎ 049 875 93 06; Via Marsilio da Padova 17; ♥ 8.30am-2am Mon-Sat) A young cool crowd gathers here, all sunglasses at night and designer stubble, low red lights, black and white décor and dark drinking corners.

Entertainment
Teatro Comunale Verdi (☎ 049 877 70 11; www .teatrostabileveneto.it; Via Livello 32) Works of classic Italian and occasionally foreign theatre are staged here, ranging from local Veneto hero Goldoni to Goethe or more modern playwrights such as Brecht. It's a grand old theatre in the round but pretty much everything is performed in Italian.

Q (☎ 049 875 16 80; www.q-bar.it; Via Dotto 3; ♥ 7pm-4am Tue-Sun) Q could be the place for you if you want a less staid evening. This is about the most central club in Padova (several others are scattered about in the suburbs and countryside).

Getting There & Away
BUS
Regular **SITA buses** (☎ 049 820 68 44) from Venice (€2.90, 45 to 60 minutes) arrive at Piazzale Boschetti, 200m south of the train station.

From Padua you can get buses to Montegrotto Terme, the Colli Euganei and as far afield as Genoa. Often you are better off with the train.

CAR & MOTORCYCLE
The A4 (Turin–Milan–Venice–Trieste) passes to the north, while the A13, which connects the city with Bologna, starts at the southern edge of town. The two motorways are connected by a ring road.

TRAIN
The easiest way to Padua from Venice is by train (€2.50 to €8.95, 30 to 40 minutes). Regular trains proceed from Padua to Bologna, Vicenza, Verona, Milan and beyond. The station is about 500m north of Cappella degli Scrovegni, from where it's a further 1km to the city centre. Local buses run into the centre from in front of the train station.

AROUND PADUA
Colli Euganei
Southwest of Padua, along the A13 or the SS16, the Colli Euganei (Euganean Hills) are dotted with vineyards and good walking trails: ask at the Padua tourist office for information about trails and accommodation. As you move around, you will encounter numerous villages, along with the occasional castle and abbey scattered about the countryside.

If you are driving (which you pretty much have to as public transport is abysmal in the area), follow the signposted *Strada dei Vini dei Colli Euganei* (Euganean Hills Wine Rd), which will take you on a tour of many vineyards. Pick up a map and itinerary from the tourist office in Padua.

HOT SPRINGS
The area is also famous for its hot springs or *terme*. The water passes underground from the low mountains of the Prealps north of Padua, where it is heated to more than 85ºC and collects mineral salts. This water then bubbles up in the Colli Euganei area. The two main spa centres are Abano Terme and Montegrotto Terme.

For information, approach the tourist offices in **Abano Terme** (☎ 049 866 90 55; Via Pietro d'Abano 18) and **Montegrotto Terme** (☎ 049 79 33 84; Viale Stazione 60). Between the two towns, there are more than 100 hotels with hot springs facilities.

THE VENETO

ARQUÀ PETRARCA

This quiet, hilly medieval village in the southern Colli Euganei was where Italy's great poet Petrarch (Petrarca) chose to spend the last five years of his life. You can visit his **house** (☎ 0429 71 82 94, Via Valleselle 4, Arquà Petrarca; adult €3; ☒ 9am-noon & 3-6.30pm Tue-Sun Mar-Oct, 9am-noon & 2.30-5pm Tue-Sun Nov-Feb), which is set in cheerful gardens and contains various bits and bobs that purportedly had something to do with the scribe. Buses run here from Este and Monselice, both a short distance to the south. Up to three daily buses from Padua (€2.65, 55 minutes) run a route to Este that takes them through here.

Monselice

pop 17,470

An easy train trip south from Padua, Monselice was once wrapped in no fewer than five protective layers of fortifications. The main point of interest here is the restored **castle** (☎ 049 7 29 31; adult/child €5.50/3; ☒ 1hr guided tours 9am-noon & 3-6pm Tue-Sun Apr-Nov). The complex contains buildings raised between the 11th and 15th centuries. To get here, take the Padua–Montagnana train (20 minutes).

Este

pop 16,700

Heading west from Monselice along the road to Mantua (Mantova), this town is yet another in the chain of fortified strongholds in the area. Padua's Carrara clan were assiduous fortress builders – it seems they had a good number of enemies to keep at bay. Although the walls of their castle are in reasonable shape, the inside is pretty much a ruin. On the bumpy lane that climbs northwards behind the castle is the **Villa Kunkler**, where Byron settled for a year or so in 1817. Shelley also stayed here.

You'll find a couple of hotels here and the town is on the train line linking Montagnana (10 minutes), Monselice (10 minutes) and Padua (30 minutes).

Montagnana

pop 9330

About 12km west of Este rise the magnificent defensive perimeter walls, dating to the 13th and 14th centuries, of this fortified plains town. Of all the Veneto's walled towns, this is the most impressive – there are almost 2km of walls studded with 24 towers and four gates. Once inside, however, there's not an awful lot to see.

Ostello Rocca degli Alberi (☎ 0429 8 10 76; Castello degli Alberi, Montagnana; dm €11.50; ☒ Apr–mid-Oct) is a unique HI youth hostel housed in a former watchtower of the town's extraordinary walls, and close to the town's train station.

The train from Padua (€3, 50 minutes) runs via Monselice and Este.

VICENZA

pop 110,000

Vicenza is a centre of Italian textile manufacturing and a leader in the development and production of computer components, making it one of the country's wealthiest cities. Most tourists come to Vicenza to see the work of Palladio, who was particularly busy here.

Vicenza flourished as the Roman Vicentia. In 1404 it became part of the Venetian Republic. Testimony to the close ties between the lagoon city and Vicenza are the many Venetian Gothic mansions here.

Orientation

From the train station, in the gardens of Campo Marzo, Via Roma heads into Piazzale de Gasperi. From here, the main street, Corso Andrea Palladio, leads right through to the heart of town.

Information

Main post office (Contrà Garibaldi 1; ☒ 8.30am-6.30pm Mon-Sat)

Ospedale Civile (☎ 0444 99 31 11; Viale Ferdinando Rodolfi 37) Hospital.

Police station (☎ 0444 54 33 33; Viale Giuseppe Mazzini 213)

Tourist office (www.vicenzae.org); Piazza dei Signori (☎ 0444 54 41 22; Piazza dei Signori 8; ☒ 10am-2pm & 2.30-6.30pm); Piazza Matteotti (☎ 0444 32 08 54; Piazza Matteotti 12; ☒ 9am-1pm & 2-6pm)

Sights

Piazza Castello contains several grand edifices, including the oddly truncated **Palazzo Porto-Breganze** on the south side, designed by Palladio and built by Scamozzi (one of the city's leading 16th-century architects). Its couple of outsized columns look strange now but had the building been completed it would have been one of the city's most imposing. Corso Andrea Palladio runs northeast from the square and is lined with fine buildings.

VICENZA

0   400 m
0   0.2 miles

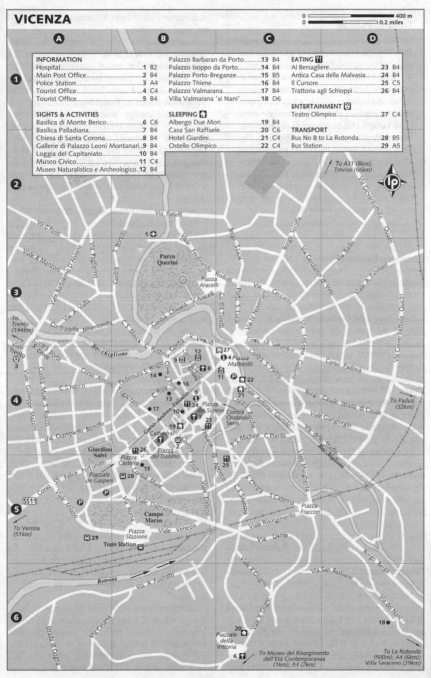

INFORMATION
Hospital...1 B2
Main Post Office................................2 B4
Police Station......................................3 A4
Tourist Office.......................................4 C4
Tourist Office.......................................5 B4

SIGHTS & ACTIVITIES
Basilica di Monte Berico....................6 C6
Basilica Palladiana.............................7 B4
Chiesa di Santa Corona....................8 B4
Gallerie di Palazzo Leoni Montanari..9 B4
Loggia del Capitaniato....................10 B4
Museo Civico......................................11 C4
Museo Naturalistico e Archeologico..12 B4

Palazzo Barbaran da Porto.........13 B4
Palazzo Isoppo da Porto............14 B4
Palazzo Porto-Breganze...............15 B5
Palazzo Thiene..............................16 B4
Palazzo Valmarana.......................17 B4
Villa Valmarana 'ai Nani'............18 D6

SLEEPING
Albergo Due Mori.........................19 B4
Casa San Raffaele.........................20 C6
Hotel Giardini...............................21 C4
Ostello Olimpico...........................22 C4

EATING
Al Bersagliere...............................23 B4
Antica Casa della Malvasia.........24 B4
Il Cursore......................................25 C5
Trattoria agli Schioppi.................26 B4

ENTERTAINMENT
Teatro Olimpico............................27 C4

TRANSPORT
Bus No 8 to La Rotonda..............28 B5
Bus Station...................................29 A5

TICKETS PLEASE

Several combined ticket options are available. The Card Musei costs €7 and gives you entry to the Teatro Olimpico, Museo Civico (Palazzo Chiericati) and the Museo Naturalistico e Archeologico (admission is with combined ticket only). For €8 you can also visit the obscure **Museo del Risorgimento** (Viale X Giugno 115), southeast of the train station, dedicated to Italian reunification. The Card Musei e Palazzi (€11) gets you entry to all these, the Gallerie di Palazzo Leoni Montanari and Palazzo Barbaran da Porto. There is a family card for the museums and Teatro Olimpico (€3) for three family members and up. All are valid for three days.

Piazza dei Signori is dominated by the immense **Basilica Palladiana** (☎ 0444 32 36 81; ✆ 9am-5pm Tue-Sun), on which Palladio started work in 1549 over an earlier Gothic building (the slender 12th-century bell tower is all that remains of the original structure). Palladio's **Loggia del Capitaniato**, at the northwest side of the piazza on the corner of Via del Monte, was left unfinished at his death.

Contrà Porti, which runs northwards from Corso Andrea Palladio, is one of the most majestic streets in Vicenza. A No 12, **Palazzo Thiene** (☎ 0444 54 21 31; admission free; ✆ 9am-noon & 3-6pm Wed & Fri, 9am-noon Sat May-Sep, 9am-noon & 3-6pm Tue & Wed Oct-Apr) by Lorenzo da Bologna, was originally intended to occupy the entire block. You must book ahead to visit and the entrance to the palazzo is on Contrà San Gaetano Thiene. Palladio's **Palazzo Barbaran da Porto** (☎ 0444 32 30 14; adult/student €5.50/3.50; ✆ 10am-6pm Tue-Sun) at No 11 features a double row of columns. A World Heritage–listed building, it is richly decorated and home to a museum and study centre devoted to Palladio. It frequently hosts architecture exhibitions. Palladio also built the **Palazzo Isoppo da Porto** at No 21, which is unfinished. His **Palazzo Valmarana** (Corso Antonio Fogazzaro 18) is considered one of his more eccentric creations.

North along Corso Andrea Palladio and left into Contrà di Santa Corona is the **Chiesa di Santa Corona** (✆ 8.30am-noon & 3-6pm Tue-Sun, 4-6pm Mon), established in 1261 by the Dominicans to house a relic from Christ's crown of thorns. Inside are the *Battesimo di Gesù* (Baptism of Christ) by Giovanni Bellini and

Adorazione dei Magi (Adoration of the Magi) by Paolo Veronese.

Corso Andrea Palladio ends at the **Teatro Olimpico** (☎ 0444 22 28 00; ✆ 9am-7pm Tue-Sun Jul & Aug, 9am-5pm Tue-Sun Sep-Jun), started by Palladio in 1580 and completed by Scamozzi after the former's death. Considered to be one of the purest creations of Renaissance architecture, the theatre design was based on Palladio's studies of Roman structures. Scamozzi's remarkable street scene, stretching back from the main façade of the stage, is modelled on the ancient Greek city of Thebes. Since its restoration in 1934, the theatre has become a prized performance space for opera and drama.

The nearby **Museo Civico** (☎ 0444 32 13 48; Palazzo Chiericati, Piazza Matteotti 37/39; ✆ 9am-7pm Tue-Sun Jul & Aug, 9am-5pm Tue-Sun Sep-Jun), housed in yet another Palladian edifice, contains works by local artists as well as by the Tiepolos and Veronese. The **Museo Naturalistico e Archeologico** (☎ 0444 32 04 40; Contrà di Santa Corona 4; ✆ 9am-7pm Tue-Sun Jul & Aug, 9am-5pm Tue-Sun Sep-Jun) has a modest collection of local ancient artefacts.

The sober baroque façade of the **Gallerie di Palazzo Leoni Montanari** (☎ 800 57 88 75; www .palazzomontanari.com; Contrà di Santa Corona 25; adult/ student €3.50/2.50; ✆ 10am-6pm Fri-Sun) hides an extravagant interior. For a long time a private mansion and bank, it now contains a collection of more than 400 Russian icons (top floor) and mostly 18th-century Venetian paintings (1st floor), including some by Canaletto and Pietro Longhi. There are frequent temporary exhibitions, too.

The **Basilica di Monte Berico** (☎ 0444 32 09 98; Piazzale della Vittoria; ✆ 6.15am-12.30pm & 2.30-7.30pm Mon-Sat, 6.15am-8pm Sun & holidays), set on top of a hill south of the city centre, presents magnificent views. It was built in the 18th century to replace a 15th-century Gothic structure, itself raised on the supposed site of two appearances by the Virgin Mary in 1426. An impressive 18th-century colonnade runs uphill to the church, roughly parallel to Viale X Giugno. Bus 18 (€1) runs here from Via Roma.

A 20-minute walk part of the way back down Viale X Giugno and then east along Via San Bastiano will take you to the **Villa Valmarana 'ai Nani'** (☎ 0444 54 39 76; Via dei Nani 2/8; admission €6; ✆ 10am-noon & 3-6pm Wed, Thu, Sat & Sun, 3-6pm Tue & Fri mid-Mar–early Nov), which

THE VENETO

features brilliant frescoes by Giambattista and Giandomenico Tiepolo. The 'ai Nani' (dwarfs) part of the name refers to the statues perched on top of the gates surrounding the property.

A path leads on to Palladio's Villa Capra, better known as **La Rotonda** (☎ 0444 32 17 93; Via Rotonda 29; admission La Rotonda €6, gardens €3; ♥ villa 10am-noon & 3-6pm Wed Mar-Nov, gardens 10am-noon & 3-6pm Tue-Sun Mar-Nov). It is one of the architect's most admired (and copied) creations, having served as a model for buildings across Europe and the USA. The name comes from the low dome that caps this square-based structure, each side fronted by the columns of a classical façade. Bus No 8 heading for Debba or Lumignano (€1.50) from Via Roma stops nearby.

Sleeping

Villa Saraceno (☎ 0444 89 13 71; Landmark Trust In UK ☎ 01628-825925; www.landmarktrust.org.uk; Via Finale 8, Finale di Agugliaro; villa UK£295-795; ⊠) This restored 16th-century Palladian country villa is a noble choice of lodgings, with room for up to 16 people (rates are to rent the entire building). Aside from the magnificent setting, it has a pool. Parts of the building can be visited by the public (2pm to 4pm Wednesday April to October). Buses run to Finale di Agugliaro from Vicenza.

Casa San Raffaele (☎ 0444 54 57 67; albergosan raffaele@tin.it; Viale X Giugno 10; d with breakfast €65; ☒ P) Located in a former convent behind the colonnade leading to Monte Bèrico, this is a charming spot to spend the night and the best choice in the lower budget range.

Hotel Giardini (☎ 0444 32 64 58; www.hotelgiard ini.com; Viale Antonio Giuriolo 10; s/d with breakfast €103/129; ☒ P) A rather modern hotel (with decidedly little in the way of gardens), this is nevertheless a perfectly comfortable and handy choice for the heart of the town.

Albergo Due Mori (☎ 0444 32 18 86; www.hotel duemori.com; Contrà do Rode 26; s/d to €45/77) Near Piazza dei Signori, this is a central cheapie with basic but attractive, and in most cases, fairly spacious rooms (it even has a suite). Some cheaper doubles (€52) have use of a common bathroom and the hotels offers disabled access.

Ostello Olimpico (☎ 0444 54 02 22; ostello.vicenza@ tin.it; Viale Antonio Giuriolo 7/9; dm/s €15.50/19; ♥ 7.30-9.30am & 3.30-11.30pm) An HI youth hostel in a fine building right by the Teatro Olimpico.

Eating

Al Bersagliere (☎ 0444 32 35 07; Contrà Pescheria 11; meals €35; ♥ Mon-Sat) A traditional *osteria* where you can eat *cicheti* at the bar or proceed to the cosy little tables for seasonal cooking (watch for the mushrooms in autumn). The *bigoli al ragù d'anatra* (thick spaghetti in duck sauce) is scrummy.

Antica Casa della Malvasia (☎ 0444 54 37 04; Contrà delle Morette 5; meals €25; ♥ Tue-Sun) This establishment has been around since 1200. In those days it was the local sales point for Malvasia wine imported from Greece by Venetian merchants, who usually gathered here in the evenings to sample the goods. Drinking is still a primary occupation in a locale that has changed little over the centuries – on offer is an array of 80 types of wine (especially Malvasia varieties) and around 100 types of grappa (the grape-based white liqueur now produced all over Italy but which has its medieval origins in the Veneto, especially in and around the town of Bassano del Grappa).

Il Cursore (☎ 0444 32 35 04; Stradella Pozzetto 10; meals €25-30; ♥ Wed-Mon & dinner Sun) Food has been served up here since the 19th century and it remains a great spot for local dishes such as *spaghetti col baccalà mantecato* (spaghetti with salted cod, garlic and parsley).

Trattoria agli Schioppi (☎ 0444 54 37 01; Contrà Castello 26; meals €30; ♥ Mon-Fri & lunch Sat) Hearty meat dishes are served up here, including *fegato alla veneziano* (calf's liver with onions) and *baccalà alla vicentina* (a local cod favourite).

Drinking

On summer afternoons and evenings the central squares fill with people who gather for the *aperitivo*, that lingering evening tipple, and to chat. The tourist office has a list of bars and clubs, mostly out of the centre.

Entertainment

Teatro Olimpico (☎ 800 323 285, 0444 22 28 01; www .olimpico.vicenza.it; Corso Andrea Palladio) is the stage for theatre, classical music concerts and other performances.

Concerts are held in summer at the Villa Valmarana 'ai Nani' – check at the tourist office for details, for this and other concerts in the summer Concerti in Villa Estate programme.

Vicenza Jazz is an annual jazz festival held in May.

THE VENETO

Getting There & Away

BUS

FTV (☎ 0444 22 31 15) buses leave from the bus station, just near the train station, for Thiene, Asiago (in the hilly north of the province), Bassano and towns throughout the nearby Monti Berici (Berici Hills).

CAR & MOTORCYCLE

The city is on the A4 connecting Milan with Venice. The SS11 connects Vicenza with Verona and Padua, and this is the best route if you want to hitchhike. There is a large car park near Piazza Castello and the train station.

TRAIN

Regular trains arrive from Venice (€3.85 to €8.95, 45 minutes to 1½ hours) and Padua (€2.50 to €8.30, 15 to 25 minutes).

AROUND VICENZA

As Venice's maritime power waned in the 16th century, the city's wealthy inhabitants turned their attention inland, acquiring land to build sumptuous **villas**. Forbidden from building castles by the Venetian senate, which feared a landscape dotted with well-defended forts, Vicenza's patricians joined the villa construction spree. Many of the thousands that were built remain, albeit frequently run down and closed to the public.

The tourist office in Vicenza can provide reams of information about the villas, including an illustrated map, *Ville dal 1400 al 1800*.

Drivers should have little trouble planning an itinerary. One possibility is to take the SS11 south of Vicenza to Montecchio Maggiore and then onto Lonigo and Pojana Maggiore. From there head north for Longare and back to Vicenza. A return trip of 100km, the route takes in about a dozen villas.

If you are without a car, take the FTV bus north from Vicenza to Thiene, passing through Caldogno and Villaverla, and then continue onto Lugo. Villa Godi-Valmarana, now known as the **Malinverni**, at Lonedo di Lugo, was Palladio's first villa.

VERONA

pop 256,000

Wander the streets of Verona on a winter's night and you might believe the tragic love story of Romeo and Juliet to be true. Beyond the Shakespearean hyperbole, however, you'll find plenty to keep you occupied in one of Italy's most beautiful cities. Known as *piccola Roma* (little Rome) for its importance in imperial days, its truly golden era came during the 13th and 14th centuries under the Della Scala family (also known as the Scaligeri). The period was noted for the savage family feuding of which Shakespeare wrote in his play.

Orientation

Old Verona is small and it's easy to find your way around. Buses leave for the centre from outside the train station, south of town; otherwise, walk north, past the bus station, and along Corso Porta Nuova to Piazza Brà, 1.5km away. From the piazza, walk along Via G Mazzini and turn left at Via Cappello to reach Piazza delle Erbe.

Information

Banca Popolare di Bergamo (Piazza Brà) One of several banks with a currency-exchange machine.

Guardia Medica (☎ 045 807 56 27; ☽ 8pm-8am) Medical services; the staff usually come to you.

Internet Etc (☎ 045 800 02 22; Via Quattro Spade 3b; per hr €5.50; ☽ 2.30-8pm Mon, 10.30am-8pm Tue-Sat)

Main post office (Piazza Viviani 7; ☽ 8.30am-6.30pm Mon-Sat)

Onda Blu (Via XX Settembre 62a; wash €3.50, dry €3.50; ☽ 8am-10pm) Laundry.

Ospedale Civile Maggiore (☎ 045 807 11 11; Piazza A Stefani) Hospital northwest of Ponte Vittoria.

Police station (☎ 045 809 04 11; Lungadige Galtarossa 11) Near Ponte Navi.

Tourist office (www.tourism.verona.it); train station (☎ 045 800 08 61; ☽ 9am-6pm Mon-Sat, 9am-3pm Sun); Verona-Villafranca airport (☎ 045 861 91 63; ☽ 9am-6pm Mon-Sat May-Aug, 11am-5pm Mon-Sat Sep-Apr); Via degli Alpini (☎ 045 806 86 80; Via degli Alpini 9; ☽ 9am-7pm Mon-Sat, 9am-3pm Sun)

Sights

Remember that a lot of sights are closed, or open in the afternoon only, on Monday. If you are only planning to spend a day here, make it any other day of the week. There is a joint ticket, the Verona Card (one/three days is €8/12) for getting into all the main sights (available at sights and tobacconists). With it you can use town buses and enter all the main monuments and churches, and get reduced admission on a few places of lesser importance.

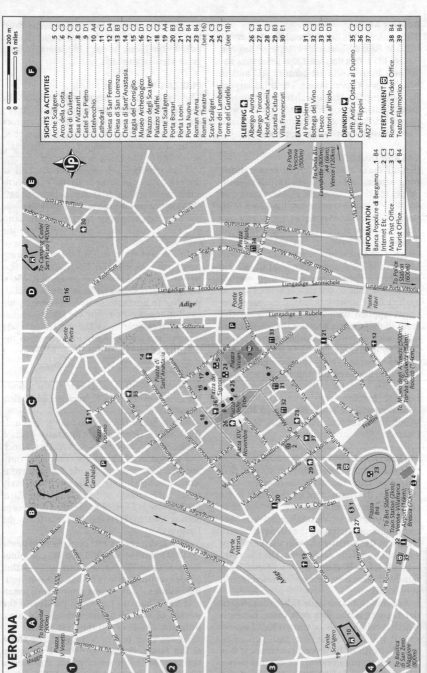

VERONA

SIGHTS & ACTIVITIES	
Arche Scaligere	5 C2
Arco della Costa	6 C3
Casa di Giulietta	7 C3
Casa Mazzanti	8 C3
Castel San Pietro	9 D1
Castelvecchio	10 A4
Cathedral	11 C1
Chiesa di San Fermo	12 D4
Chiesa di San Lorenzo	13 B3
Chiesa di Sant'Anastasia	14 C2
Loggia del Consiglio	15 C2
Museo Archeologico	16 D1
Palazzo degli Scaligeri	17 C2
Palazzo Maffei	18 C2
Ponte Scaligero	19 A4
Porta Borsari	20 B3
Porta Leoni	21 D4
Porta Nuova	22 B4
Roman Arena	23 B4
Roman Theatre	(see 16)
Scavi Scaligeri	24 C3
Torre dei Lamberti	25 C3
Torre del Gardello	(see 18)
SLEEPING	
Albergo Aurora	26 C3
Albergo Torcolo	27 B4
Hotel Accademia	28 B3
Locanda Catullo	29 B3
Villa Francescati	30 E1
EATING	
Al Pompiere	31 C3
Bottega del Vino	32 C3
Il Desco	33 D3
Trattoria all'Isolo	34 D3
DRINKING	
Caffè Antica Osteria al Duomo	35 C2
Caffè Filippini	36 C3
M27	37 C3
ENTERTAINMENT	
Roman Arena Ticket Office	38 B4
Teatro Filarmonico	39 B4
INFORMATION	
Banca Popolare di Bergamo	1 B4
Internet Etc	2 C3
Main Post Office	3 B3
Tourist Office	4 B4

ROMAN ARENA

This pink marble Roman **amphitheatre** (☎ 045 800 32 04; Piazza Brà; adult/child €3.10/2.10; ⏰ 9am-7pm Tue-Sun, 1.45-7.30pm Mon, 8am-3.30pm during opera season) was built in the 1st century AD and is now Verona's opera house. The third-largest Roman amphitheatre in existence, it can seat around 20,000 people. It is remarkably well preserved, despite a 12th-century earthquake that destroyed most of its outer wall.

CASA DI GIULIETTA

Just off Via G Mazzini, Verona's main shopping street, is **Casa di Giulietta** (Juliet's House; ☎ 045 803 43 03; Via Cappello 23; adult/student/child €4/3/1; ⏰ 8.30am-7.30pm Tue-Sun, 1.45-7.30pm Mon). Romeo and Juliet may have been utterly fictional but here you can swoon beneath what popular myth says was her balcony (or, if in need of a new lover, approach a bronze statue of Juliet and rub her right breast for good luck). Others have made their eternal mark by adding to the slew of scribbled love graffiti (and more disgusting messages on paper applied with chewing gum) on the walls of the house, a practice the town council vowed to halt (seemingly with limited success) in 2004.

If the theme excites you, you could also seek out the **Tomba di Giulietta** (Juliet's Tomb; ☎ 045 800 03 61; Via del Pontiere 35; adult/student €2.60/1.50; ⏰ 8.30am-7.30pm Tue-Sun, 1.45-7.30pm Mon). Also housed here is the **Museo degli Affreschi**, which has a collection of frescoes of minor interest.

PIAZZA DELLE ERBE

Originally the site of a Roman forum, this piazza remains the lively heart of the city. Although the permanent market stalls in its centre detract from its beauty, the square is lined with some of Verona's most sumptuous buildings, including the baroque **Palazzo Maffei**, at the north end, with the adjoining 14th-century **Torre del Gardello**. On the eastern side is **Casa Mazzanti**, a former Della Scala family residence. Its fresco-decorated façade stands out.

Separating Piazza delle Erbe from Piazza dei Signori is the **Arco della Costa**, beneath which a whale's rib is suspended. Legend says it will fall on the first 'just' person to walk beneath it. In several centuries, it has never fallen, not even on the various popes who have paraded beneath it. Ascend the

nearby 12th-century **Torre dei Lamberti** (☎ 045 803 27 26; admission by lift/on foot €3/2, incl Arche Scaligere €4/3; ⏰ 9am-7.30pm Tue-Sun, 1.30-7.30pm Mon) for a great view of the city.

PIAZZA DEI SIGNORI

The 15th-century **Loggia del Consiglio**, the former city council building at the northern end of this square, is regarded as Verona's finest Renaissance structure. It is attached to the **Palazzo degli Scaligeri**, once the main residence of the Della Scala family.

Through the archway at the far end of the piazza are the **Arche Scaligere** (Via Arche Scaligere; admission incl Torre dei Lamberti by lift/on foot €4/3; ⏰ 9.30am-7.30pm Tue-Sun, 1.45pm-7.30pm Mon Jun-Sep), the elaborate tombs of the Della Scala family. You can see them quite well from the outside.

In the courtyard behind the Arche, *scavi* (excavation work) has been done on this part of medieval Verona. You enter the **Scavi Scaligeri** (⏰ 10am-7pm Tue-Sun) through a building used to host important photographic exhibitions. You pay for the latter (admission charges vary), as the excavations are not in themselves overly interesting to the uninitiated.

CHURCHES

A combined entrance ticket to all the following churches costs €5. Otherwise, admission to each costs €2.

North from the Arche Scaligere stands the Gothic **Chiesa di Sant'Anastasia** (Piazza di Sant'Anastasia; ⏰ 9am-6pm Mon-Sat, 1-6pm Sun), which was started in 1290 but not completed until the late 15th century. Inside are numerous works of art including, in the sacristy, a lovely fresco by Pisanello of *San Giorgio che Parte per Liberare la Donzella dal Drago* (St George Setting Out to Free the Princess from the Dragon).

The 12th-century **cathedral** (Piazza del Duomo; ⏰ 10am-5.30pm Mon-Sat, 1.30-5.30pm Sun) combines Romanesque (lower section) and Gothic (upper section) styles and has some intriguing features. Look for the sculpture of Jonah and the Whale on the south porch and the statues of two of Charlemagne's paladins, Roland and Oliver, on the west porch.

At the river end of Via Leoni, the **Chiesa di San Fermo** (Stradone San Fermo; ⏰ 10am-6pm Mon-Sat, 1-6pm Sun) is actually two churches: a Gothic church was built in the 13th century over the original 11th-century Romanesque structure. The **Chiesa di San Lorenzo** (Corso Cavour; ☺ 10am-6pm Mon-Sat, 1-6pm Sun) is near the Castelvecchio and the Basilica di San Zeno Maggiore (below) is further to the west.

CASTELVECCHIO

Southwest from the Piazza delle Erbe is the 14th-century fortress of Cangrande II (of the Della Scala family), on the banks of the River Adige. The fortress was severely damaged by bombing during WWII and restored in the 1960s. Today it houses a **museum** (☎ 045 806 26 11; Corso Castelvecchio 2; adult/student/child €4/3/1; ☺ 8.30am-7.30pm Tue-Sun) and it showcases a diverse collection of paintings, jewellery, frescoes and medieval artefacts. Among the paintings are works by Pisanello, Giovanni Bellini, Tiepolo, Carpaccio and Veronese. Also of note is a 14th-century equestrian statue of Cangrande I. The **Ponte Scaligero**, spanning the River Adige, was rebuilt after being destroyed by WWII bombing.

BASILICA DI SAN ZENO MAGGIORE

A masterpiece of Romanesque architecture, this **church** (Piazza San Zeno; ☺ 8.30am-6pm Mon-Sat, 9am-12.30am & 1.30-6pm Sun Mar-Oct, 8.30am-1pm & 1.30-5pm Tue-Sat, 9am-12.30pm & 1.40-5pm Sun, 8.30am-noon & 3-5pm Mon Nov-Feb), in honour of the city's patron saint, was built mainly in the 12th century, although its apse was rebuilt in the 14th century and its bell tower, a relic of an earlier structure on the site, was started in 1045. The basilica's magnificent rose window depicts the Wheel of Fortune. Before going inside, take a look at the sculptures on either side of the main doors. The highlight inside is Mantegna's *Maestà della Vergine* (The Majesty of the Virgin Mary), above the high altar. But the interior of this mighty church is festooned with remarkable frescoes, dating from the 12th to the 15th centuries. St Zeno's eerily lit and robed corpse can be seen at the back of the crypt.

ACROSS THE RIVER

Across Ponte Pietra is a **Roman theatre**, built in the 1st century AD and still used today for concerts and plays. Take the lift at the back of the theatre to the convent above, which has an interesting collection of Greek and Roman pieces in the **Museo Archeologico** (☎ 045 800 03 60; Regaste Redentore 2; adult/child €2.60/1.50; ☺ 8.30am-7.30pm Tue-Sun, 1.45-7.30pm Mon).

On a hill behind the theatre and museum is the **Castel San Pietro**, built by the Austrians on the site of an earlier castle.

Sleeping

If you are having problems finding a hotel room, you could try calling the **Cooperativa Albergatori Veronesi** (☎ 045 800 98 44; www.cav.vr.it). It offers rooms starting with two-star hotels and the service is free. If you want to try a local homestay, check **Verona Bed and Breakfast** (www.veronabedandbreakfast.it). Be aware that it has nothing on offer in the old centre. You can pick up the list at tourist offices.

Villa Francescati (☎ 045 59 03 60; fax 045 800 91 27; Salita Fontana del Ferro 15; dm with breakfast €15; ☺ 7am-11.30pm) A beautiful HI youth hostel housed in a 16th-century villa not far from the camping ground. The gardens are gorgeous and it has family rooms too. Meals cost €9 but there are no cooking facilities. Catch bus No 73 (weekdays) or No 90 (Sundays and holidays) from the train station.

Locanda Catullo (☎ 045 800 27 86; locandacatullo@tiscali.it; Via Valerio Catullo 1; s/d with shared bathroom €40/55, d with bathroom €65) A good cheapie with friendly management and clean, straightforward rooms. At these rates it's about the best value in town.

Albergo Torcolo (☎ 045 800 38 71; www.hoteltorcolo.it; Vicolo Listone 3; s/d €75/108; ☒ ℗) A quiet little building barely 50m off Piazza Brà, this spot has a variety of rooms. Some of the most attractive feature wrought-iron bed heads and timber ceiling beams.

Albergo Aurora (☎ 045 59 47 17; www.hotelaurora.biz; Piazza XIV Novembre 2; s/d to €116/158) The better rooms in this sprawling, central hotel are spacious and comfortable and many have been given a bit of sprucing up. The terrace is a pleasant spot for a drink and a little sun.

Hotel Accademia (☎ 045 59 62 22; Via Scala 12; s/d €162/250; ☒ 🖳 ℗) For a touch of class in the heart of the chic shopping end of the old town, this is a classic choice. Through a grand neoclassical entrance you sashay on up to your rooms, with plush easy chairs and crisp, bright décor. The hotel has its own restaurant and conference area.

Camping Castel San Pietro (☎ 045 59 20 37; www.campingcastelsanpietro.com; Via Castel San Pietro 2; person/tent €5.50/10.50; ☺ mid-May–mid-Oct) Not a bad camping ground, away from the bustle of the town below. Sites are leafy and you can relax on the two grand terraces. There's a minimarket, washing machines and other comforts. Catch bus No 41 or 95 from the train station.

Eating

Bottega del Vino (☎ 045 800 45 35; Vicolo Scudo di Francia 3a; meals €50; ⏲ Wed-Mon) A must visit if wine is your thing, the staff at this age-old wine cellar serve up some fine food, too. The wine list is endless and your choice will be served with all the ceremony you might expect at an upmarket wine-tasting. The cost of your meal can vary wildly depending on your choice of tipple. If nothing else, wander in to this perennially busy dining hall – the frescoes alone, complemented by shelf loads of ancient bottles, are worth the effort.

Il Desco (☎ 045 801 00 15; Via Dietro San Sebastiano 7; meals €120-150; ⏲ Tue-Sat & lunch Sun) Rated one of the best restaurants in all of Italy and a Michelin-star winner, this is a refined dining option for meticulously prepared local cuisine.

Al Pompiere (☎ 045 803 05 37; Vicolo Regina d'Ungheria 5; meals €35; ⏲ Tue-Sat & dinner Mon) The fireman's (pompiere) hat is still on the wall, along with a host of black-and-white photos from down the years. On display is a rich assortment of cheeses that you can try before tucking into, say, a plate of bigoli con le sarde (chunky spaghetti with sardines) followed by some hearty pastissada de caval, a horse-meat dish typical of Verona.

Trattoria all'Isolo (☎ 045 59 42 91; Piazza dell'Isolo 5a; meals €25-30; ⏲ Thu-Tue) Across the river in what feels like a more genuine, less touristy Verona, all'Isolo offers good local cooking. In this tiny eatery just about anything the staff make with bigoli is bound to please. They also do various things with horse and even donkey meat.

Drinking

Caffè Antica Osteria al Duomo (☎ 045 800 45 05; Via Duomo 7; ⏲ noon-2pm & 7-10pm Mon-Wed, Fri & Sat) A cosy centuries-old tavern with mandolins, balalaikas and other stringed instruments hanging on the wall. Pop in for a drop of fragolino (the local sweet strawberry wine). They also serve light meals.

Caffè Filippini (☎ 045 800 45 49; Piazza delle Erbe 26; ⏲ 8am-2am Thu-Tue) Where else do you want to be on a sunny afternoon than sitting at

an outdoor table at this classic Verona bar sipping the house speciality, a Filippini (a mix of vermouth, gin, lemon and ice)?

M27 (☎ 045 803 42 42; Via G Mazzini 27a; ⏲ 9am-2am Tue-Sun) A young, hip Veronese crowd is attracted to this angular bar. Whether for morning coffee or evening cocktails they perch on designer stools in a squeaky-clean, polished ambience. Or they head upstairs, where, among other things, they find a smokers' section, now of prime importance to puffers in suddenly smoke-free Italy.

You can get a list of clubs from the tourist offices but all but two are in the countryside around Verona and the two in town are a reasonable trek from the centre. A classic is **Rococó** (☎ 347 239 12 03; Via Basso Acquar 61; ⏲ 10pm-4am Thu-Sun). The club has a touch of decorative Oriental luxury and the music ranges from hip-hop and R&B nights to world music and soul. All washed down with colourful cocktails.

Entertainment

Roman Arena (☎ 045 800 51 51; www.arena.it; ticket office Ente Lirico Arena di Verona, Via Dietro Anfiteatro 6b; tickets €15-150; ⏲ opera season Jul-Sep) Tickets are available online and at travel agents around the country.

Teatro Filarmonico (☎ 045 800 51 51; www.arena .it; Via dei Mutilati 4) This 18th-century theatre, just south of Piazza Brà, is also run by the Ente Lirico Arena di Verona. A winter programme of ballet and opera dominates the proceedings, but you might just as easily come across a jazz night.

Getting There & Away

AIR

Verona-Villafranca airport (VRN; ☎ 045 809 56 66) is 12km outside town and accessible by bus to/from the train station (€4.50, 15 minutes, every 20 minutes from 6am to 11pm). Flights arrive here from all over Italy and some European cities, including Amsterdam, Barcelona, Berlin, Brussels, London and Paris. Ryanair flies in from several cities to **Brescia** (☎ 030 965 65 99; www.aeroportidelgarda .it) to the west. Airport buses connect the train station with Brescia airport (€11/16 one way/return, one hour).

BUS

The main intercity bus station is in front of the train station, in an area known as

Porta Nuova. Although buses serve many big cities, they are generally only a useful option for those needing to reach provincial localities not served by train.

CAR & MOTORCYCLE
Verona is at the intersection of the Serenissima A4 (Turin–Trieste) and Brennero A22 motorways.

TRAIN
Verona has rail links with Milan, Mantua, Modena, Florence and Rome. There are also regular trains serving destinations in Austria, Switzerland and Germany (10 daily to/from Munich). The trip to/from Venice is easiest by train (€6.10 to €12.65, 1¼ to 2¼ hours).

Getting Around
AMT (city transport) bus Nos 11, 12, 13 and 14 (bus Nos 91 or 92 on Sunday and holidays) connect the train station with Piazza Brà (tickets cost €1 and are valid for an hour). Otherwise, it's a 20-minute walk along Corso Porta Nuova. Buy tickets from newsagents and tobacconists before you board the bus.

TREVISO
pop 80,700
Touted by the locals as little Venice, Treviso is the home of the Benetton fashion dynasty (along with *radicchio*, a tart red lettuce) and is blessed with a pretty historic centre. This much-overlooked town dates to Roman times and was long the most faithful of Venice's subject cities.

Treviso is an easy day trip from Venice or a fine stop on the way north to Belluno and the Dolomites. If you're coming to Venice with Ryanair, it's worth considering stopping overnight here on your way in or out.

Orientation
From the train station head north along Via Roma (over the canal), past the bus station and across the bridge (the nicely placed McDonald's on the river is an unmistakable landmark) and keep walking straight ahead along Corso del Popolo. At Piazza della Borsa veer left down Via XX Settembre and you arrive in the heart of the city, Piazza dei Signori.

Information
Tourist office (☎ 0422 54 76 32; http://turismo.provin cia.treviso.it; Piazzetta Monte di Pietà 8; ⏱ 9am-12.30pm & 2-6pm Tue-Fri, 9.30am-12.30pm & 3-6pm Sat & Sun, 9am-12.30pm Mon) Adjacent to Piazza dei Signori.

Sights & Activities
The tourist office promotes Treviso as the *città d'acqua* (city of water) and compares it to Venice. While the River Sile, which weaves through the centre, and the handful of canals are quite beautiful in parts, the comparisons are more touching than realistic.

That said, it is delightful to wander around the city. Piazza dei Signori is dominated by the fine brick **Palazzo dei Trecento**, the one-time seat of city government beneath whose (unfortunately glassed-in) vaults you can stop for coffee and a bite. The medieval main street is the porticoed Via Calmaggiore, leading to the **cathedral** (Piazza del Duomo; ⏱ 7.30am-noon & 3.30-7pm Mon-Fri, 7.30am-1pm & 3.30-8pm Sat & Sun), a massive structure whose main source of interest lies in the frescoes inside by Il Pordenone (1484–1539).

Backtrack to Piazza dei Signori and head east (around and behind the Palazzo dei Trecento) and you will soon find yourself in a warren of lanes that leads to five delightful bridges across the Canal Cagnan. This runs roughly north–south (you'll run into the colourful fish market along the way)

BUSTING WITH WINE

Sheltered beneath glass under the grand portico in front of the Palazzo dei Trecento is a weather-worn bust of a woman cupping voluminous breasts in her hands. This Fontana delle Tette (Tit Fountain) was erected in central Treviso by the town's governor (or *podestà*) in 1559. From the fountain's nipples sprang forth abundant water from the nearby Canal Cagnan but each year, when a new *podestà* took office, the water was replaced by wine, red from one breast and white from the other, for three festive days. This practice continued until the humourless Napoleon arrived and put an end to Venetian rule in 1797. A modern replica has been set up in a small courtyard just off Calle del Podestà, but alas the heady wine days are gone for good.

and spills into the River Sile at a pleasant corner where part of the city walls remain intact. Treviso is a comparatively leafy town and this is particularly the case at some points along the canal. You can also see the occasional mill wheel (the one by Vicolo Molinetto still turns).

While on the east side of the canal make a beeline for the **Museo Civico di Santa Caterina** (☎ 0422 54 48 64; Via di Santa Caterina; admission €3; ◷ 9am-12.30pm & 2.30-6pm Tue-Sun). The church and its attached convent now house many of the city's treasures. The highlight is the church itself, which boasts remarkable frescoes attributed to Gentile da Fabriano (an artist who worked in the early 15th century), along with other artists. The beautiful 15th-century **Cappella degli Innocenti** (Chapel of the Innocents), added by the endowment of a wealthy patron, contains frescoes carried out by two unknown masters and of such a freshness that it seems they were completed yesterday. To these have been added the extraordinary fresco cycle by Tomaso da Modena (1326–79) on the life and martyrdom of St Ursula (Santa Orsola or Orseola), recovered late in the 19th century from an already partly demolished church.

Over two floors of the former convent is part of the eclectic collection of Luigi Bailo, a 19th-century friar who made it his life work to collect ancient artefacts and artworks to preserve the memory of Treviso's past. At the time most townsfolk thought him an eccentric. Today they owe him a debt of thanks. The collection starts with an archaeological section, proceeds with Romanesque statuary (including a rather striking terracotta funereal monument to some town toff, featuring the said toff in repose), and continues with a series of single paintings by Lotto, Titian, Tintoretto, Guardi and others (including among them three portraits by Rosalba Carrera).

Tomaso also left frescoes in the imposing **Chiesa di San Nicolò** (Via San Nicolò; ◷ 7am-noon & 3.30-6pm), on the other side of town. The star attraction here is the **Sala del Capitolo dei Domenicani** (☎ 0422 32 47; Piazzetta Benedetto XI 2; admission by donation; ◷ 8am-6pm) in the seminary alongside the church. Enter and follow the directions across a cloister to the room, adorned with the portraits of 40 Dominican friars by Tomaso da Modena, all intent on copying illuminated manuscripts. One of

them, on the right as you enter, has a magnifying glass in his hand. This 14th-century depiction of a reading glass is thought to be the first ever.

In summer, you can take a day-long **boat cruise** (☎ 0422 78 86 63; per person €22) on the *Silis* or *Altino* down the Sile to the Venetian lagoon and back. The tours are by reservation only; call or ask at the tourist office. Boats do not leave from Treviso, but from several other villages along the river just southeast of Treviso.

Sleeping & Eating

Albergo Campeol (☎ 0422 5 66 01; www.albergo campeol.it in Italian; Piazza Ancilotto 4; s/d €52/85) A nicely maintained place in a restored building that spreads around a quiet little pedestrian square just off Piazza dei Signori. It's about the only decent central choice and three of the doubles have canal views.

Ristorante al Dante (☎ 0422 59 18 97; Piazza Garibaldi 6; meals €20-25; ◷ Mon-Sat) An excellent budget eating option where you can sidle up to the bar for a host of *cicheti* or dine at one of the teeny tables. In summer you can sit outside and gaze across to the river. Typically people pop in for bar snacks and Prosecco, or perhaps a crisp Friuli white.

All'Antico Pallone (☎ 0422 54 08 57; Vicolo Rialto 5; meals €20-25; ◷ Mon-Sat) Just left off Via XX Settembre on your way to Piazza dei Signori lurks this traditional wine and *cicheti* den. Other snacks include a good range of sandwiches and a limited array of dishes. Take up a spot at one of the timber tables and select your wine, with choices concentrating on the Veneto region but including labels from all over Italy.

Muscoli's (☎ 0422 58 33 90; Via Pescheria 23; dishes €6-8; ◷ Mon-Sat) This old-style no-nonsense *osteria* with timber beams and knockabout tables out the back gets a mixed crowd of locals in for a glass or three of wine, a few snacks and the occasional dish in the dining area out the back, which looks over the Canal Cagnan. There is no menu – the barman will just rattle off whatever is on offer for the day. Or you could pick up a quick serve of *fritto misto in scartosso* (Venetian fish and chips, without the chips) to take away.

Piola (☎ 0422 54 02 87; www.piola.it; Via Carlo Alberto 11; pizzas €5-7; ◷ noon-2.30pm & 7pm-1am Mon-Fri, 7pm-2am Sat, 6.30pm-1am Sun) A hip little bar-cum-pizzeria, where you can sit outside on a little terrace or bury yourself in the dimly lit innards of the bar with Treviso's night crowd. The pizzas are good and you have a wide choice of toppings. This place has done well, opening branches as far away as Brazil – another local business success story!

Shopping

Treviso claims Luciano Benetton, the clothing manufacturer, as its favourite son. You will find a huge **Benetton** (☎ 0422 55 99 11; Piazza dell'Indipendenza 5; 9.15am-12.30pm & 3.30-7.30pm Tue-Sat, 3.30-7.30pm Sun-Mon) shop in the centre of town; factory outlets around the outskirts of town are the strict preserve of Benetton employees.

Getting There & Away

Ryanair uses Treviso's tiny **San Giuseppe airport** (TSF; ☎ 0422 31 53 31), about 5km southwest of Treviso. Local bus No 6 runs past the airport into the centre of town.

The bus station is on Lungosile Mattei, near the train station in Piazzale Duca d'Aosta. ACTV buses connect Treviso with Venice and La Marca buses link it to other towns in the province such as Conegliano (€2.00, 45 minutes) and Vittorio Veneto (€3.40, one hour five minutes).

It often makes better sense to get the train. The journey from Venice (€2.05) takes 25 to 30 minutes. Other trains connect the town with Belluno (via Conegliano and Vittorio Veneto), Padua and major cities to the south and west.

By car, take the SS53 for Venice and Padua.

BELLUNO

pop 35,000

Belluno is a beautiful town at the foot of the Dolomites. If you start early enough, you could just about combine it with Treviso in a day trip from Venice, either by train or bus. Better still, hang around for a few days and use it as a base to explore the mountains. For further information walking in the Dolomites, see p312.

Orientation

Buses arrive at Piazzale della Stazione, in front of the train station. From here take Via Dante (which becomes Via Loreto) and then turn left at the T-junction down Via Matteotti into the central Piazza dei Martiri.

Information

Tourist office (☎ 0437 94 00 83; Piazza del Duomo 2; 9am-12.30pm & 3.30-6.30pm) Produces a feast of information on walking, trekking, skiing and other sporting activities.

Sights & Activities

Although no notable monuments await inspection, a wander around the old town is pleasant. The main square (really a broad pedestrian avenue), **Piazza dei Martiri** (Martyrs' Square), takes its name from four partisans hanged here in the dying stages of WWII.

The heart of the old town is formed by **Piazza del Duomo**, dominated on one side by the early 16th-century Renaissance **Cattedrale di San Martino**, the **Palazzo Rosso**, from about the same period, and the **Palazzo dei Vescovi**. The latter's tower is one of three that belonged to the original, but long gone, 12th-century structure.

For most, the reason for reaching Belluno is as a starting point for activities in the mountains, from **walking** in summer to **skiing** in winter. Stretching away to the northwest of Belluno is the **Parco Nazionale delle Dolomiti Bellunesi**, a beautiful national park laden with opportunities for those who want some fresh mountain air.

Six **Alte Vie delle Dolomiti** (high-altitude walking trails in the Dolomites) pass through the territory surrounding Belluno and along them you will find *rifugi* (mountain huts). Route No 1 in particular has *rifugi* where you can stay at the end of a day's walking. Route No 1 stretches between Belluno and Lago di Braies.

Sleeping & Eating

Ostello Imperina (☎ 0437 6 24 51; ostelloimperina@inwind.it; Località Le Miniere; dm with breakfast €15.50; 7-10am & 3.30-11.30pm Apr-Sep) The nearest youth hostel, 35km northwest of Belluno at Rivamonte Agordino, within the Parco Nazionale delle Dolomiti Bellunesi. In this cabin there are some family rooms, too. You must call ahead in April and May. You can get there on the Agordo bus (50 minutes) from Belluno.

A handful of hotels dot the town, as well as some B&Bs and *affittacamere* (like a B&B but without breakfast). Plenty more lodging options are scattered about the surrounding towns and villages.

Hotel Al Ponte della Vittoria (☎ 0437 92 52 70; www.alpontedellavittoria.com; Via Monte Grappa 1;

s/d €45/70; (P)) Located just across the bridge
from the centre of town, this hotel is a
reasonable deal with good-sized but plain
rooms. The half board, at €47/80 for a single/
double, is pretty good value. The restaurant
serves up hearty fare.

Albergo Cappello e Cadore (☎ 0437 94 02 46;
www.albergocappello.com; Via Ricci 8; s/d €70/100; 🍴
(P)) In a restored mid-19th-century establishment just off Piazza dei Martiri in the
centre of town, this is a somewhat more
comfortable option, although the dominant
rose coloured décor of the public spaces is
a little off-putting. Rooms sparkle without
having any of the charm you might expect
from a building this age.

La Taverna (☎ 0437 2 51 92; Via Cipro 7; meals €25-30;
🕙 Mon-Sat) Here you have the option of snack-
ing at the bar or proceeding through to the
restaurant area, where you will be treated to
hearty cooking. Around Christmas it serves
a local speciality – a snail and eel combo that
won't be to everyone's taste!

Getting There & Away

Dolomiti Bus (☎ 0437 94 12 37) buses depart
from in front of the train station, on the
western edge of town, for Agordo, Cortina
d'Ampezzo, Feltre and smaller towns in the
mountains and south of town.

Trains from Venice (€6.10, one hour 55
minutes) run here via Treviso. They are
none to regular and you will have to change
once along the way. Some run from Mestre instead and go via Padova (where you
change – it takes an eternity).

By car you can take the A27 motorway
from Venice (Mestre) or follow the state
roads via Treviso. The latter can be time-
consuming because of heavy traffic.

Friuli-Venezia Giulia

Germanic, Slavic and Italian influences converge in this easternmost corner of northern Italy and, though it's one of the country's smaller regions, Friuli-Venezia Giulia's distinct character and varied and engaging landscapes make it a fascinating place to explore. The region also produces some of Italy's best white wines, especially along the Slovenian border area known as the Colli Orientali.

The intriguing borderland city of Trieste is still on the fringes of most tourist trails, but thanks to its international airport and easy access to Slovenia and Croatia, numbers of visitors are growing. With its wealth of Austro-Hungarian architecture and Viennese coffee-house culture, Trieste is unlike any other Italian city (and a worthy destination in its own right), while Aquileia, with its spectacular Roman mosaics, is a must for anyone interested in the ancient world. The region's second-largest city, Udine, is best known for its Palladian architecture, and has some rewarding museums. The Adriatic coast consists largely of lagoons and flat wetlands, much favoured by birdlife, as well as the hugely popular seaside resorts of Grado and Lignano. North, towards the Austrian border, the stunning area of Il Carnia attracts skiers in winter and walkers in summer.

Historically, Friuli-Venezia Giulia has been invaded, occupied and generally trampled upon by several warlike nations, all of whom left their indelible marks on the landscape. Roman rule gave way to the Visigoths, Attila's Huns, the Lombards and Charlemagne's Franks, and by 1797 the region was under Habsburg control. Most of Friuli joined Italy in 1866, but it was not until after WWI, when many of Italy's 700,000 dead fell in Friuli-Venezia Giulia, that Gorizia, Trieste, Istria and Dalmatia were included. Italy retained Trieste after WWII, but was obliged to cede Dalmatia and the Istrian Peninsula to Tito's Yugoslavia.

HIGHLIGHTS

- Check out fabulous Roman mosaic floors in **Aquileia** (p406)
- Discover Archduke Maximilian's seaside castle at **Miramare** (p402)
- Sample the beery Germanic buffets and Viennese-style cafés of **Trieste** (p399)
- Enjoy sun, sand and sea at **Grado** (p407) and **Lignano** (p408)
- Bird-spot around the **Grado lagoons** (p407) and the **Laguna di Marano** (p408)
- Ski, hike and bike ride in the northern **Il Carnia region** (p412)

★ Il Carnia

Aquileia ★
Lignano ★ Laguna ★ Grado ★ Miramare ★
di Marano Trieste ★

| ■ POPULATION: 1.1 million | ■ AREA: 7845 sq km |

TRIESTE

pop 209,557

Sitting at the end of the extreme eastern spit of Italy between the Adriatic Sea and Slovenia, Trieste has an atmosphere and character all of its own. The faded grandeur of its imposing and largely homogenous neoclassical architecture is a sharp reminder of its days as the great southern port of the Austro-Hungarian Empire during the 18th and 19th centuries, and the Habsburg spirit still lingers amid Trieste's elegant squares, palaces and Viennese-style coffee houses.

Unfairly bypassed by many tourists, Trieste is a vibrant city with a lively cultural scene and some fine museums, churches and Roman remains worth pausing over. It also offers a good base for exploring this stretch of coastline, which hosts treasures such as Castello Miramare (p402). Meanwhile, its international airport makes it a convenient gateway for forays into the neighbouring countries of Slovenia or Croatia.

History

According to one misty legend, Trieste was founded by Japhet, son of the biblical Noah, while another legend grants founding-father status to Tergeste, a companion of Jason (of Argonaut fame). More prosaically, however, the Roman colony of Tergeste (possibly simply meaning 'market town') was established in 178 BC and it rapidly became a wealthy trading port. The Goths, Byzantines and the

Lombards followed in succeeding centuries, and in 1202 the city fell to the Venetians. Trieste battled for, and won, its independence, but in 1382 voluntarily accepted the overlordship of Austria, as defence against bellicose Venice. The city remained under Austrian rule until 1918.

The 18th and 19th centuries were a prosperous era for the cultured, cosmopolitan Habsburg port. Sigmund Freud, James Joyce and Italo Svevo came here to think and write, while two of Verdi's operas (*Il Corsaro* and *Stifelio*) were premiered here. In 1945 the Allies occupied Trieste pending the settlement of Italy's border disputes with Belgrade, remaining until 1954.

Orientation

Trieste's main bus and train stations are at the northern edge of town. To the west lies the port and the Adriatic Sea, while to the south, Borgo Terasiano centres on the photogenic Canal Grande. The vast Piazza dell'Unità d'Italia forms the heart of the city, watched over by the Colle di San Giusto to the east, topped with its 15th-century castle.

Information

There are currency-exchange booths at the train and bus stations and ferry terminal, and banks abound on Corso Italia.

Hospital (☎ 040 399 11 11; Piazza dell'Ospedale)
Left luggage (per hr €1); bus station (Piazza della Libertà; ☺ 6.15am-8.30pm Mon-Fri, 6.30am-1pm Sat & Sun); train station (Piazza della Libertà; ☺ 7am-8pm)
Police station (☎ 040 379 01 11; Via Tor Bandena 6)
Post office (Piazza Vittorio Veneto 1; ☺ 8am-7pm Mon-Sat)
Regional tourist office (☎ 040 36 52 48; www.regione.fvg.it in Italian; Via Rossini 6; ☺ 9am-1pm Mon-Fri)
SmileNet (☎ 040 322 02 04; Piazza dello Squero Vecchio 1c; per 15min €2; ☺ 10am-1pm & 3-9pm Mon-Fri)
Trieste tourist office (☎ 040 347 83 12; www.trieste tourism.it; Piazza dell'Unità d'Italia 4b; ☺ 9.30am-7pm)

Sights

COLLE DI SAN GIUSTO

With commanding views across the city and the sea, this hill is topped by a sturdy 15th-century **castello** (currently closed for renovation), largely built over earlier fortifications by the city's medieval Venetian rulers. Apart from wandering around the walls, you can visit the **Lapidario Tergestino** (☎ 040

T FOR YOU

Busy sightseers might want to take advantage of the **T For You** card, available in 24- and 48-hour versions (€8/10), which gives free admission to all civic museums, free bus travel and a free seat on the Trieste by Bus tour (see p398). It also offers discounts at city hotels, restaurants and theatres, plus various other benefits, all listed in the complimentary *Trieste Ti Aspetta* booklet. The cards can be bought at the tourist office, museums and at Castello Miramare.

---

30 93 62; Piazza della Cattedrale 3; admission free; ☺ 9am-1pm Mon-Sat). It houses a small collection of statuary and architectural fragments.

Just below the castle, stands a WWI **war memorial**, sculpted in 1935 in the severe Fascist style, stands as the focal point of a small park.

The **Basilica di San Giusto**, completed in 1400, is the synthesis of two earlier Christian basilicas, and is a blend of the Ravenna and Byzantine styles. The interior contains 13th-century frescoes and a mosaic from the same period depicting St Justus, the town's patron saint. The Virgin and Child and the Apostles appear on another wonderfully preserved mosaic, dating from the 12th century.

One intriguing feature of the basilica is the chapel, known as the Escorial Carlista, containing the tombs of nine members of the Spanish royal family; after a factional dynastic struggle in Spain in the 1830s, Carlos V fled and set up the 'Carlist' court in Trieste, which survived until 1874. The last Spanish royal interred here, though, was Francisco José de Habsburg, as recently as 1975.

Down the road, the **Civico Museo di Storia ed Arte ed Orto Lapidario** (History & Art Museum & Stone Garden; ☎ 040 31 05 00; Piazza delle Cattedrale 1; adult/child €2/1; ☺ 9am-1pm Tue & Thu-Sun, 9am-7pm Wed) displays locally retrieved artefacts from the Roman and medieval periods.

To get here, take bus No 24 from the train station. Otherwise, walk up from the waterfront area, following Via F Venezian, Via San Michele and Via San Giusto.

CENTRAL TRIESTE

The area of straight boulevards to the north of Corso Italia, known as Borgo Teresiano, were designed by Austrian urban planners

TRIESTE

TRANSPORT

Agemar	52 D2
Bus Station	53 D1
Samer & Co Shipping	54 C3
Samer & Co Shipping	55 D3
Tram to Villa Opicina & Camping Pian del Grisa	56 E2

INFORMATION

Hospital	1 F3
Police Station	2 D3
Post Office	3 D2
Regional Tourist Office	4 D2
SmileNet	5 C3
Trieste Tourist Office	6 C3

SIGHTS & ACTIVITIES

Acquario Marino	7 B4
Arco del Riccardo	8 D4
Basilica di San Giusto	9 D4
Basilica di San Silvestro	10 D4
Castello di San Giusto	11 D4
Chiesa di Santa Maria Maggiore	12 D4
Chiesa di Sant'Antonio Taumaturgo	13 E2
Chiesa di Santo Spiridione	14 D2
Civico Museo di Storia ed Arte & Orto Lapidario	15 D4
Lapidario Tergestino	16 D4
Museo Civico di Storia Naturale	17 C4
Museo d'Arte Orientale	18 C3
Museo della Communità Ebraica Carlo e Vera Wagner	19 E3
Museo Joyce	(see 7)
Museo Postale e Telegrafico della Mitteleuropa	20 C4
Museo Revoltella	21 D3
Museo Svevo	(see 17)
Roman Theatre	22 D4
War Memorial	23 D4

SLEEPING

Albergo Alla Posta	23 E2
Grand Hotel Duchi d'Aosta	24 C3
Hotel Alabarda	25 D2
Hotel Colombia	26 E1
Hotel Italia	27 D1
Hotel James Joyce	28 C3
Hotel Milano	29 E1
Novo Hotel Impero	30 D2
Nuovo Albergo Centro	31 D2

EATING

Al Barattolo	32 E2
Alimentazione BM	33 D3
Buffet Da Mario	34 E2
Buffet Da Pepi	35 D3
Buffet da Siora Rosa	36 C4
Buffet Rudy	37 E2
Caffè degli Specchi	38 C3
Caffè San Marco	39 F2
Caffè Stella Polare	40 D3
Caffè Tommaseo	41 D3
Circus	42 E3
Enoteca Bischoff	43 D3
Euro Spesa	(see 25)
Pasticceria Pirona	44 E4
Trattoria al Nuovo Antico Pavone	45 B4
Trattoria Da Giovanni	46 E2

DRINKING

Duke	47 F4
TNT Pub	48 E3

ENTERTAINMENT

Casa della Musica	49 C4
Teatro Miela	50 D2
Teatro Verdi	51 C3

in the 18th century for Empress Maria Theresa. The pretty **Canal Grande**, running through this area, marks the northern end of the harbour. The striking Serbian Orthodox **Chiesa di Santo Spiridione**, on the street of the same name, was completed in 1868 and sports some glittering mosaics. The eastern end of Piazza San Antonio Nuovo is dominated by the enormous neoclassical Catholic **Chiesa di Sant'Antonio Taumaturgo** (1842).

At its western end, Corso Italia runs into the vast **Piazza dell'Unità d'Italia**, an elegant triumph of Austro-Hungarian town planning. A stroll south brings you to the waterfront **Acquario Marino** (☎ 040 30 62 01; Riva Nazario Sauro 1; adult/child €3/2; 🕑 9am-7pm Tue-Sun Apr-Sep, 9am-1pm Tue-Sun Nov-Mar) where you can view some of the denizens of the Adriatic deep, as well as more tropical fish. The former **fish market** (1913), which fills the southern half of the building, is slowly being developed as a future exhibition space. The waterfront ends at the **Lanterna**, now a disused 19th-century lighthouse.

Behind Piazza dell'Unità d'Italia are the well-preserved remains of the **Roman theatre** (Via del Teatro Romano), built between the 1st and 2nd centuries AD. Concerts are occasionally held here during summer. The **Arco di Riccardo** (Via del Trionfo) is an earlier Roman remnant, one of the old town gateways dating from 33 BC. Nearby, the baroque **Chiesa di Santa Maria Maggiore**, next door to the minute Romanesque **Basilica di San Silvestro**, is a cavernous but unremarkable church, where the main point of interest is the tiny painting by Sassoferrato of the *Madonna della Salute*.

MUSEUMS

Trieste's premier museum, **Museo Revoltella** (☎ 040 675 43 50; www.museorevoltella.it; Via Diaz 27; adult/child €5/3; 🕑 9am-1.30pm & 4-7pm Wed-Mon), was founded in 1872, in the city-centre palace that was once home to the extremely wealthy Baron Pasquale Revoltella. The original furnishings have been retained and restored, and the baron's flamboyant tastes hang heavily in the gaudy rooms, with their chandeliers, gilded plaster, silk wallpaper and gold curtains. His personal collection of 19th-century Italian paintings and marble sculptures of nudes is on show here. The modern section of the museum holds a more extensive assemblage of late 19th- and 20th-century works by Triestine, Italian and international

RISIERA DI SAN SABBA

The Risiera di San Sabba was once a rice-husking plant at the southern end of Trieste. In 1944 the Germans, with local Fascist help, built a crematorium here and turned it into Italy's only extermination camp. It is believed 20,000 people perished here, including 5000 of Trieste's 6000 Jews. Yugoslav partisans closed it when they liberated the city in 1945, and 20 years later it became a national monument and **museum** (☎ 040 82 62 02; Via Valmaura, Ratto della Pileria; admission free; 🕑 9am-7pm). You can get there by catching bus No 10.

artists. Highlights include Urbano Nono's arresting statue group, *Belisario*, and the huge canvas *Beethoven* by Balestrieri Lionello. There are also minor works by De Chirico and Morandi.

The **Museo d'Arte Orientale** (☎ 040 322 07 36; Via San Sebastiano 1; adult/child €3/2; 🕑 9am-1pm Tue & Thu-Sun, 9am-7pm Wed) exhibits an important collection of Chinese porcelain and Japanese prints, drawings, musical instruments and weaponry, spread out over four floors.

Philatelists might like to have a quick peek at the unusual **Museo Postale e Telegrafico della Mitteleuropa** (☎ 040 676 42 54; Piazza Vittorio Veneto 1; adult/child €1.55/1; 🕑 9am-1pm) in the post-office building, with exhibitions on the history of the postal system in Habsburg times.

Three small museums call the **Biblioteca Civica** (Public Library; Piazza Hortis 4) home. The **Museo Civico di Storia Naturale** (☎ 040 30 18 21; 3rd fl; adult/child €3/2; 🕑 8.30am-1.30pm Tue-Sun) displays a musty array of stuffed animals and bones, while the **Museo Joyce** (☎ 040 675 81 83; 2nd fl; admission free; 🕑 10am-noon Mon-Fri) and the adjacent **Museo Svevo** (☎ 040 675 81 82; 2nd fl; admission free; 🕑 10am-1pm Mon-Sat, 10am-noon Sun) hold equally dry exhibitions of documents relating to the writers James Joyce and Italo Svevo, who both lived and worked in the city.

Memories of Trieste's Jewish heritage have been preserved at the **Museo della Comunità Ebraica Carlo e Vera Wagner** (☎ 040 63 38 19; Via del Monte 5; adult/child €5.21/3.10; 🕑 4-7pm Tue, 10am-1pm Fri, 5-8pm Sun), which has a small exhibition of liturgical items and photographs.

Animal life typical to the unusual karstic terrain of Trieste can be observed at the **Speleovivarium** (☎ 040 30 67 70; Via Guido Reni 2c;

admission free; 🕙 10am-noon Sun mid-Oct–mid-Jun), a didactic science museum housed in an old air-raid shelter.

Nearby on the waterfront, located in a restored 19th-century wharf building, is Trieste's **Museo del Mare** (Sea Museum; ☎ 040 30 49 87; Via Campo Marzio 5; adult/child €3/2; 🕙 8.30am-1.30pm Tue-Sun), tracing the history of navigation and commercial fishing in the region.

Activities

If you fancy a quick dip, the state-of-the-art **Aquamarina** (☎ 040 30 11 00; www.2001team.com in Italian; Molo Fratelli Bandiera 1; adult/child pool admission €5.90/4.60; 🕙 7.40am-10.20pm Mon, Wed & Fri, 10.20am-1pm & 3.40-6.20pm Tue & Thu, 7.40am-7.20pm Sat, 7.40am-1pm Sun), near the Lanterna, is the place to go. It has a range of activities and treatments on offer, including aquarobics classes, a gym, saunas and Turkish baths.

Tours

Trieste by Bus (☎ 040 4 41 44; adult/child under 10 yrs €5.20/free; 🕙 2pm Sat) city tours depart from in front of the train station and take 2½ hours, including a 30-minute stop at the Colle di San Giusto. Buy tickets at the Club Eurostar office in the train station.

The tourist office also runs thematic **walking tours** (in Italian and German only). Advance bookings are essential; phone for details of prices and routes.

Literary travellers can follow in the footsteps of James Joyce (1882–1941) with the free English-language *Joyce: Triestine Itineraries* brochure, available at the tourist office. The Dublin-born writer lived in Trieste from 1904 to 1915, completing *A Portrait of the Artist as a Young Man* and *Dubliners* and beginning *Ulysses* here. Fans of Trieste's rather lugubrious literary hero, Italo Svevo (1861–1928), can pick up the *Svevo: Triestine Itineraries* brochure (in English) here as well.

Festivals & Events

The annual, week-long **Trieste Film Festival** (www.alpeadriacinema.it) attracts an international crowd every January, with screenings in a number of locations.

The first Sunday of May sees the **Maratona d'Europa** (www.bavisela.it), one of Italy's big running events, while the **Barcolana** (www.barcolana .it) is a major sailing competition that takes place on the second Sunday in October; free

concerts, live music and other assorted festivities take over the city for the three days leading up to the event.

Sleeping
BUDGET

Budget accommodation isn't Trieste's strong point, and you will have to head out of town if you're looking for a dorm bed.

Nuovo Albergo Centro (☎ 040 347 87 90; www .hotelcentrotrieste.it; Via Roma 13; s/d from €32/45, with bathroom from €48/68; 🖳 P) Right in the heart of Trieste, this small family-run hotel is great value for money, and offers fresh, newly renovated rooms.

Hotel Alabarda (☎ 040 63 02 69; www.hotelala barda.it; Via Valdirivo 22; s/d from €35/50, with bathroom from €52/70; P) This acceptable two-star hotel has a variety of bright, clean rooms on the 3rd floor of an old townhouse.

Ostello Tergeste (☎ 040 22 41 02; www.ostelloter geste.it; Viale Miramare 331; dm with breakfast €13; 🕙 reception 7am-11.30pm) This HI hostel by the sea, 7km northwest of town, is a stone's throw from Castello Miramare (see p402). Separate male and female dorms house between four and 20 beds. Guests must evacuate between 10am and 1pm, and curfew is at 11.30pm.

Ostello Scout (☎ 040 22 55 62; info@ostelloscout.it; Via di Prosecco 381, Prosecco; dm €10; P) This basic place is in Prosecco, located 7km north of Trieste. The accommodation is simple and functional, and, as the name suggests, aimed at scout and school groups, but reasonable half-board (€23.50) and full-board (€33.50) options are available for those staying at least three days. Breakfast is €3.50.

Agriturismo Horse Farm (☎ 040 22 69 01; www .horsefarm.it; Basovizza 338; s/d/tr from €42/68/88; P) Get away from it all at this charming farmstead outside the tiny village of Basovizza, which is very close to the Slovenian border and around 8km east of Trieste. It's a working farm, producing salami and pancetta, among other things, and they also organise horse-riding and mountain-biking excursions in the surrounding countryside.

Camping Imperial Carso (☎ 040 20 04 59; www .campingimperialcarso.it; Aurisina Cave 551; person/tent/car from €3.70/4/4.50; P 🐾) This well-equipped site is pleasantly located amid woodland just outside the village of Aurisina, about 12km north of Trieste. It has a playground and grocery store and offers a variety of sports activities, as well as a free shuttle bus to the seaside, 4km away. Prices rise by about a third in July and August.

Camping Pian del Grisa (☎ 040 21 31 42; www .piandelgrisa.it; Via Contovello 226, Opicina; person/tent/car from €4.80/2.50/2.80; [P] [🅂]) This large three-star site, 5km north of Trieste, has excellent facilities, including tennis and basketball courts. Also on offer are guided mountain-biking expeditions and scuba-diving trips, and plenty of advice and information on other sporty activities in the area. Take tram No 2 or bus No 4 from Piazza Oberdan.

MIDRANGE

Novo Hotel Impero (☎ 040 36 42 42; www.hotelimp erotrieste.it; Via S Anastasio 1; s/d/tr from €70/95/125; [🅇] [P]) The imperious Novo Hotel Impero is a grand neoclassical edifice facing the train station. It's a comfortable and conven-ient three-star choice, with a touch of faded Austro-Hungarian elegance lingering amid the stucco and chandeliers.

Hotel Italia (☎ 040 36 99 00; www.hotel-italia.it; Via della Geppa 15; s/d €80/95; [🅇] [P]) This is one of those indistinguishable but pleasant three-star options, conveniently close to the train station. Rooms are quiet and comfortable, which is all you really need.

Albergo Alla Posta (☎ 040 36 52 08; www.albergo postatrieste.it; Piazza Oberdan 1; s/d/tr from €98/130/155; [🅇]) This stylish place combines a pleasant old-world feel with state-of-the-art amen-ities. The rooms are restfully decorated in neutral tones, while pets are welcome for an extra €15 per night.

Hotel Milano (☎ 040 36 96 80; www.hotel-milano .com; Via Ghega 17; s/d/tr from €75/100/125; [🅇] [P] [🖳]) The Milano is a spotlessly modern and stand-ardised kind of place, but comfort and ser-vice can't be faulted. Prices vary throughout the year; expect to pay about 25% more in summer. Discounts are sometimes available for stays of three nights or more.

Hotel Colombia (☎ 040 36 91 91; www.hotelcolom bia.it; Via Geppa 18; s/d Mon-Thu from €110/140, Fri-Sun from €90/115; [🅇] [🅇] [🖳]) The Colombia is a smart four-star hotel with plush, comfortable rooms, including some with disabled access, and a vaguely arty theme going on. For the week-end rate, a minimum stay of two nights is required.

Hotel James Joyce (☎ 040 31 10 23; www.hotel jamesjoyce.com; Via dei Cavazzeni 7; s/d from €55/80) Tucked away down a side street in the cen-tre of town, this small hotel occupies a newly

renovated 18th-century building. The stark white rooms with tiled floors are a touch spartan, but it's bright and clean and in a good location.

TOP END

Grand Hotel Duchi d'Aosta (☎ 040 760 00 11; www .grandhotelduchidaosta.com; Piazza dell'Unità d'Italia 2; s/d/ste Mon-Thu from €214/285/340, s/d Fri-Sun from €114/165; [🅇] [P] [✕]) If you're looking for style and tradition, look no further than the four-star Duchi d'Aosta, Trieste's grandest hotel. The commanding location on the city's main square is unbeatable, and the rooms, some fitted for disabled access, have all the modern facilities you could desire. The hotel restaur-ant, Harry's Grill, offers fine local cuisine, and guests have free access to the private beach of the Hotel Riviera & Maximilian's (see above) at Miramare, which is under the same management.

Hotel Greif Maria Theresia (☎ 040 41 01 15; www.greifgroup.net; Viale Miramare 109; s/d/ste Mon-Thu €230/275/350, s/d Fri-Sun €140/190; [🅇] [P] [🅂] [🖳]) Polished wood floors, elegant period furnish-ings and an air of calm efficiency greet you at this pleasingly relaxed seaside hotel, a few kilometres north of the city hustle and bustle. There's a gym and sauna, as well as a 4th-floor restaurant with panoramic sea views.

Hotel Riviera & Maximilian's (☎ 040 22 45 51; www.hotelrivieraemaximilian.com; Strada Costiera 22; s/d/ ste from €68/99/125; [🅇] [P] [🅂]) Another smart sea-side retreat around 9km north of town, this attractive hotel with just 20 rooms, includ-ing some with disabled access, is a popular place with its own private beach. Prices do vary throughout the year, however. Pets are welcome.

Residence Maximilian's (☎ 040 22 45 51; www .residencetrieste.com; Strada Costiera 33; ste per week/ month from €630/1950; [🅇] [P]) Under the same management as the Hotel Riviera, this place offers fully equipped and serviced suites with small kitchens for longer stays (minimum one week).

Eating
RESTAURANTS

Al Barattolo (☎ 040 63 14 80; Piazza San Antonio Nuovo 2; pizzas from €6; [☽] lunch & dinner) Facing Piazza San Antonio Nuovo, this ever-busy pizzeria is a good place to know about, especially on Sunday or mid-afternoon when most other places are closed.

Trattoria al Nuovo Antico Pavone (☎ 040 30 38 99; Riva Grumala 2; mains about €8-12; ☺ lunch & dinner Mon-Sat) Fresh fish in many forms, along with regulation pasta, adorns the menu at this cosy harbour-front trattoria.

Trattoria Da Giovanni (☎ 040 63 93 96; Via San Lazzaro 14; mains from €7; ☺ Mon-Sat Sep-Jul) This trattoria mixes old with new – legs of ham dangling from the stark white ceiling add a dramatic touch. Dishes are traditional and generally pretty pig-centric.

Circus (☎ 040 63 34 99; Via San Lazzaro 9b; dishes €4.50; ☺ 8am-9pm Mon-Sat) The slogan of this fun-oriented café/restaurant is 'Drinkjokecommunitypeoplefoodmusicjoyfriendlysnack'. It is dressed up like a circus big top and flaunts a jazzy kind of feeling, serving the usual pub grub and salads.

CAFÉS

Trieste's coffee culture has a long pedigree.

Caffè San Marco (☎ 040 36 35 38; Via Cesare Battisti 18; mains about €10) This café, rebuilt after WWI, is by far the most atmospheric – a favourite with students, chess players and newspaper rustlers.

Caffè Tommaseo (☎ 040 36 26 66; www.caffetom maseo.com; Riva III Novembre; 1st/2nd courses from €5.50/ 11.50; ☺ 8am-12.30am) One of Trieste's most historic cafés, dating from 1830, Tommaseo is a smart place for lunch, with a menu dominated by beef and fish dishes. The *belle époque* interior has been carefully renovated, while sculpted cherubs in the moulded ceiling and lots of mirrors add a Viennese feel.

Pasticceria Pirona (☎ 040 63 60 46; Largo della Barriera Vecchia 12) James Joyce sought inspiration at this cake shop and café that's guaranteed to please the sweetest tooth.

Caffè Stella Polare (☎ 040 63 27 42; Via Dante 14) This old-world place on the corner of Piazza San Antonio is an appealing pit-stop for pre-prandial cocktails or just a quick espresso.

Caffè degli Specchi (☎ 040 36 57 77; Piazza dell' Unità d'Italia 7) Caffè degli Specchi first opened its doors back in 1839, and has been a fashionable spot for coffee-sipping Triestines ever since. It's an attractive place to relax with a glass of wine or two and the outdoor seats on the square are quickly snapped up by locals.

BUFFETS

Buffets are a Triestine institution, serving up cheap and authentic local food. Expect lots of boiled bacon, sausages and beer.

Buffet Rudy (☎ 040 63 94 28; Via Valdirivo 32; mains €7-10; ☺ lunch & dinner Mon-Sat) Bratwurst and beer are the order of the day at Buffet Rudy, where you can tuck into a plate of German sausages and sauerkraut and wash it down with one of the powerful Bavarian brews on tap. Boiled bacon and venison with polenta also feature on the heavily meaty menu.

Buffet Da Pepi (☎ 040 36 68 58; Via Cassa di Risparmio 3; mains about €7-10; ☺ Mon-Sat) Come to Da Pepi for a traditional meal of boiled meat and beer – not recommended for vegetarians. All kinds of porky joints and offal have been cooked up here since 1897.

Buffet Da Mario (☎ 040 63 93 24; Via Torrebianca 41; mains from €4; ☺ Mon-Sat) Fried squid, sardines, and a host of the usual meaty snacks can be yours at this typical cheap buffet.

WHERE TO FEAST ON FRIULIAN FODDER

Friulian cuisine has been influenced by many cultures but poverty has contributed the most. One typical dish, *brovada*, sees you eating turnips fermented with the dregs of pressed grapes, while *brodetto* is a simple fish soup. Otherwise, gnocchi (potato, pumpkin or bread dumplings) are popular, as are *cialzons* (a ravioli-gnocchi hybrid stuffed with everything from cheese to chocolate) or sausages and *bolliti* (boiled meats) dished up with polenta and *cren*, a rather strong horseradish. *Jota* is a thick soup of beans and sauerkraut.

Buffets (the local interpretation of a basic Italian *osteria* or wine bar with food) are the places to munch on all these dishes, and Trieste is particularly well endowed with them. Wines from the eastern hills of Friuli, stretching from near the city on the Slovene border up into the Alps, are considered the region's tastiest and are best sampled in a *frasca* or *locanda* (rustic, family-run wine bar).

Coffee, the coda to any Friulian feast, can be drunk *à la resentin* (coffee in a cup rinsed with grappa). A *gocciato* or *goccia* is a Triestine espresso or *americano* with a dash of foamed milk floating dead-centre on top. Stirring in sugar without disturbing the milk is an acquired art.

SELF-CATERING

Shop for basics at **Euro Spesa** (Via Valdirivo 13 & 22); fruit and veg at the daily **market** (Piazza del Ponterosso); pasta, pesto, honey and grappa at **Alimentazione BM** (Via San Nicolò 17); and wine at **Enoteca Bischoff** (☎ 040 63 14 22; Via Mazzini 21), a wine cellar dating from 1796.

Drinking

TNT Pub (☎ 040 66 11 16; Via Ginnastica 46; ☯ 11am-2.30pm & 6pm-1am) This vaguely British-style pub out near the hospital has a range of beers on tap and also serves up reasonable food.

Duke (☎ 040 63 93 80; Via Vidali 2b) In the same area as TNT, the Duke is another very popular nightspot for locals in search of beery entertainment.

Entertainment

Trieste's leading theatre and opera house is the **Teatro Verdi** (☎ 040 672 21 11; www.teatroverdi-trieste.com; Piazza Verdi 1), which was designed by Matteo Pertsch, the architect of Milan's La Scala. The main concert and opera season runs from October to May, while the International Festival of Light Opera takes place here in July and August. The Slovene side of Trieste life finds expression at the **Teatro Sloveno** (☎ 040 63 26 64; Via Petronio 4) just southeast of the centre, while the **Teatro Miela** (☎ 040 36 51 19; www.miela.it in Italian; Piazza Duca degli Abruzzi 3) stages an eclectic mix of events including plays, concerts, cabaret and film screenings.

Getting There & Away

AIR

Friuli-Venezia Giulia airport (TRS; ☎ 0481 77 32 24; www.aeroporto.fvg.it; Via Aquileia 46), also known as Ronchi dei Legionari or Trieste Airport, is 33km northwest of Trieste near Monfalcone. Direct daily flights to/from Munich and London Stansted and less frequent services to Belgrade arrive and depart from here, as do domestic flights to/from Rome and Milan.

BOAT

Ferries use the **Stazione Marittima** (ferry terminal; Molo dei Bersaglieri 3) in town. **Agemar** (☎ 040 36 37 37; Piazza Duca degli Abruzzi 1a) sells tickets for the car ferry that sails twice weekly to/from Durres in Albania (deck seat one way low/high season €60/80, small car low/high season €95/120). Ferries to Greece now all leave from Venice (see p372).

From mid-June to late September, **Samer & Co Shipping** (☎ 040 670 27 11; www.samer.com; Piazza dell'Unità d'Italia 7) sells tickets for motorboats along the coast to/from Grado (one way/return €6.45/12.90, 55 minutes, one daily), Lignano (€7.25/14.45, 1¼ hours, one daily) and various points along the Istrian coast in Slovenia and Croatia. It also has a **ticketing desk** (☎ 040 30 35 40; stazione.marittima@samer.com; Molo dei Bersaglieri 3) at the ferry terminal itself. Tickets are sold at the terminal 45 minutes before departure.

BUS

National and international buses operate from the **bus station** (☎ 040 42 50 20; Via Fabio Severo 24). Services include Udine (€4.50, 1¼ hours, at least hourly) and destinations in Slovenia and Croatia such as Ljubljana (€11, 2¾ hours, once daily Monday to Saturday), Zagreb (€12, five hours, once daily Monday to Saturday) and Dubrovnik (€55, 15 hours, once daily). Bus ervices to Belgrade (€50, 10 hours, once daily) and Sofia, in Bulgaria (€59, 15 hours, twice daily), are operated by **Florentia Bus** (☎ 040 42 50 20; www.florentiabus.it); tickets can be bought at Coop Rossana, Via Flavia Gioia 2, near the bus station.

TRAIN

The **train station** (☎ 147 8 80 88; Piazza della Libertà 8) serves trains going to Gorizia (€3, 50 minutes, hourly), Udine (€5.95, 1½ hours, hourly), Venice (€12, two hours, at least hourly) and Rome (€50.39, 7½ hours, twice daily).

Getting Around

Bus No 30 connects the train station with Via Roma and the waterfront, bus No 24 goes to/from Castello di San Giusto, bus No 36 links Trieste bus station with Miramare, and Villa Opicina is served by tram No 2 or bus No 4. A single/double journey ticket costs €0.90/1 and a one-day ticket is available for €3.

Bus No 51 runs to the airport approximately every 30 minutes between 4.30am and 10.35pm from Trieste bus station (€2.75, one hour). Buses are operated by the Gorizia-based **APT** (Azienda Provinciale Trasporti Gorizia; ☎ 800 955 957; www.aptgorizia.it in Italian).

Shuttle boats link the Stazione Marittima with Muggia year-round (one way/return €2.80/5, 30 minutes, six to 10 boats sail daily), and Barcola (€1.75, 20 minutes, five or six daily) and Grignano (€2.80, 55 minutes, five or six daily) from mid-April to mid-October. For more information, contact the public-transport company **Trieste Trasporti** (☎ 800 016 675; www.triestetrasporti.it in Italian).

AROUND TRIESTE

A short coastal trip northwest takes you to the **Riviera di Barcola**, a busy stretch of coast guarded by the 70m-high **Faro della Vittoria** (☎ 040 41 04 61), a lighthouse built in 1927 as a memorial to local sailors who perished in WWI. You can normally climb the monument for panoramic views of the bay, but it's closed for renovation.

Miramare

At the riviera's northern end, 7km northwest of Trieste, **Castello Miramare** (☎ 040 22 41 43; www.castello-miramare.it; adult/EU citizens 18-25/child €4/2/free, audioguide €3.50; ☼ 9am-7pm Mon-Sat, 8.30am-7pm Sun Apr-Sep, 9am-6pm Mar & Oct, 9am-5pm Nov-Feb) rises romantically over the waves. The ostentatious neogothic castle was the brainchild of Archduke Maximilian of Austria, and construction began in 1855. Sadly, Maximilian didn't live to see his project completed. He accepted an offer to become Emperor of Mexico in 1864, only to be deposed in 1866 and executed by firing squad. His widow, Carlotta, went mad and moved to Belgium, where she died in 1927.

Downstairs, several rooms have been preserved much as they were during Maximilian's day, including his cabin-like ground-floor bedroom and peaceful library with its full complement of tomes, marble busts and magnificent sea views. The blue-silk wall coverings display the archducal emblems – anchors, crowns and pineapples – while elsewhere, rich red wallpaper and drapes carry the poignant symbol of the Imperial Mexican eagle.

Upstairs, the magnificent Throne Room (which was never used as such) is plastered with portraits of Habsburg royalty. Also on this floor is a suite of rooms once used by Duke Amadeo of Aosta and his family in the 1930s, and furnished in a very different Art Deco style. Unfortunately, like the castle's first occupant, grandiose high office and an untimely death overseas came to Amadeo. He was appointed Viceroy of Ethiopia by Mussolini in 1937, and five years later died of malaria in a British POW camp in Kenya. After WWII, Castello Miramare was used as the headquarters of the US military administration, which stayed until 1954.

The castle is set in 22 hectares of lush **gardens** (admission free; ☼ 9am-7pm Mar-Oct, 9am-5pm Nov-Feb), which contain a variety of rare and exotic trees, as well as formal lawns and ponds. Maximilian was particularly interested in matters botanical and had heated greenhouses built in the grounds. Today, they are home to the **Parco Tropicale** (☎ 040 22 44 06; www.parcotropicale.it in Italian; adult/child €6.50/3.50; ☼ 10am-6pm Mar-Oct, 10am-4pm Nov-Feb) where tropical butterflies, hummingbirds, parrots and other brightly hued birds can be viewed close up.

The waters here are protected by the Riserva Naturale Marina di Miramare and swimming is forbidden. The reserve's **visitors centre** (☎ 040 22 41 47; www.riservamarinamiramare.it in Italian; ☼ 9am-12.30pm & 2.30-6.30pm Apr-Sep, 9am-12.30pm & 2-5pm Tue-Wed & Fri-Sun Oct-Mar), in the Castelletto, opposite the Parco Tropicale, has tanks containing live fish, sponges and other local marine residents on show, and organises snorkelling and diving expeditions.

Aspiring scientists (young and old) might enjoy a trip around the fascinating multimedia exhibitions at the **Science Centre Immaginario Scientifico** (☎ 040 22 44 24; www.immaginarioscientifico .it in Italian; Riva Massimiliano e Carlotta 15; adult/child €5/3.50; ☼ 10am-8pm Sun Sep-Jun, 7-11pm Fri, 10am-9pm Sat & Sun Jul & Aug), an interactive science museum in Grignano Mare, next to Miramare. Bus No 36 links Trieste train station with Miramare and Grignano Mare (the last stop).

Muggia
pop 13.340

South along the coast, a 5km trip past Trieste's industrial outskirts (including the Illy coffee-roasting plant) and around the Baia di Muggia brings you to this fortified fishing village with a 14th-century castle. Boats sail between Muggia and Trieste (see opposite) and Slovenia is just 4km south from here.

Muggia has plenty of hotels should you wish to stay, including the smart **Hotel San Rocco** (☎ 040 33 01 00; www.hotelsanrocco.com; Strada per Lazzaretto 2; s/d from €75/115; **P**). The tourist office in Trieste has a full list.

Il Carso

Inland, the leggy strip of land between the coast and the Slovenian border is known as **Il Carso** (Carso Heights), a name pertaining to the geological make-up of this white calcareous tableland, potholed with caves and riddled with doline (sinkholes created when caves collapse).

Flora and fauna can be observed at close quarters at the **Carsiana Giardino Botanico** (☎ 040 22 95 73; adult/child €3/2; ☼ 10am-noon Tue-Fri Nov-Mar, 10am-noon Tue-Fri, 10am-1pm & 3-7pm Sat & Sun Apr-Oct) in Sgonico.

Near Villa Opicina, 5km northeast of Trieste, is the **Grotta Gigante** (☎ 040 32 73 12; www .grottagigante.it in Italian; adult/child €7/5; ☼ guided tours half-hourly 10am-6pm Apr-Sep, hourly 10am-4pm Mar & Oct, hourly 10am-noon & 2-4pm Nov-Feb). At 107m high, 280m long and 65m wide, this is the world's largest accessible cave – the dome of St Peter's Cathedral could easily fit inside. Coloured globes light up the interior with its awe-inspiring stalagmites, one a towering 12m tall. Take bus No 42 from Trieste's Piazza Oberdan, or tram No 2 – the scenic choice that has covered the 5.2km journey since 1902 – from the same square to Villa Opicina, then bus No 42 to the cave.

Local ethnographic tradition comes to life at the **Casa Carsico** (☎ 040 32 71 24; Rupingrande 31; admission free; ☼ 11am-12.30pm & 3.30-6pm Sun & holidays Apr-Nov) in Rupingrande, north of Villa Opicina. The plateau's most important folk festival, **Nozze Carsiche** (Karstic Wedding), is held every two years for four days at the end of August, 2km southeast of Rupingrande in a 16th-century fortress in **Monrupino**.

With the exception of Villa Opicina, you will need your own transport to explore Il Carso.

GORIZIA
pop 35,570 / elev 86m

Slap bang on the frontier between the Latin and Slavic worlds, Gorizia, like much of Friuli-Venezia Giulia, doesn't feel particularly Italian, and in fact only joined the Italian state after WWI, when it was ceded by Austria. Most locals speak Italian and Slovenian, and road signs are in both languages. Its handful of so-so attractions wouldn't normally invite a detour, but its unique borderline location makes it worth a quick visit, if only for the opportunity to pop over to Slovenia for an hour or two. The twin town of Gorizia-Nova Gorica is still split by a manned border, but community relations between the two sides are good and buses regularly ferry locals and curious tourists back and forth. It's an easy day trip from Udine, but don't decide to come on a Monday – almost everything is closed, including shops.

The city hosts a **jazz festival** each year in March.

History

Settled before the arrival of the Romans, the hilltop castle and surrounding town were always on the periphery of someone else's empire – Roman, Holy Roman and, from the early 16th century, that of the Austrian Habsburgs. Apart from a brief spell under Venice, Gorizia first came under Italian control after WWI. In the wake of WWII, Italy and Yugoslavia drew a line (in the form of a fence) through the city in 1947, leaving most of the old city in Italian hands, and spurring Tito's followers to erect the soulless Nova Gorica on the other side. In 1991 Gorizia became next-door neighbour to an independent Slovenia.

When Slovenia joined the EU in 2004, the forbidding fence between the two nations was torn down, but perfunctory border checkpoints and controls will continue to operate for as long as Slovenia is not party to the Schengen Convention.

Information

Cartlibreria Antonini (Via Mazzini 1316) Bookshop with maps and guides.
Post office (cnr Corso Verdi & Via Oberdan)
Tourist office (☎ 0481 53 57 64; www.gorizia-turismo .it; Corso Italia 9; ☼ 9.30am-1pm & 3-6pm Mon-Fri, 10am-1pm & 3-6pm Sat)

Sights

BORGO CASTELLO

Gorizia's main sight is its **castle** (☎ 0481 53 51 46; Borgo Castello 36; adult/child €3/free, exhibitions €4-9/free; ⏲ 9.30am-1pm & 3-7.30pm Tue-Sun Apr-Oct, 9.30am-6pm Tue-Sun Nov-Mar), the original nucleus of the town. It has undergone several transformations and was restored in the 1920s after suffering serious damage in WWI.

Beneath the main fortress, within the castle walls, is the **Museo della Grande Guerra** (☎ 0481 53 39 26; Borgo Castello 15; adult/child €3.50/free; ⏲ 9am-7pm Tue-Sun Apr–mid-Sep, 10am-1pm & 2-7pm Tue-Sun mid-Sep–Mar), where the gory and tragic tale of WWI trench warfare on the Italian/Austrian front is told.

Next door, the **Museo della Moda e delle Arti Applicate** (Museum of Fashion & Applied Arts; ☎ 0481 53 39 26; Borgo Castello 15; ⏲ 9am-7pm Tue-Sun Apr–mid-Sep, 10am-1pm & 2-7pm Tue-Sun mid-Sep–Mar) presents a far prettier picture, with a collection of the finery of the well-to-do of the 19th and early 20th centuries. Admission to the war museum covers the fashion museum too.

PIAZZA TRANSALPINA

The wire fence between Italy and the former Yugoslavia (now Slovenia) once ran through the middle of this piazza, but in 2004 the dispiriting Cold War relic was finally pulled down, amid much ceremony and celebration, to create a new, communal square. At its heart is a vast mosaic circle, with the international border line running through it, so you're now free to stand with a foot in each country, with Nova Gorica train station in front of you. However, there is no official border crossing here, so do not even try to walk beyond the confines of the piazza; Slovenian police still keep a lookout for straying tourists.

CHURCHES

The most outstanding of Gorizia's churches is the **Chiesa di Sant'Ignazio** (Piazza della Vittoria), which was built from 1654–1724, topped by onion-shaped domes. The 14th-century **Chiesa di Santo Spirito**, by the castle, is worth a peek, as is Gorizia's 18th-century **synagogue** (☎ 0481 53 21 15; Via Ascoli 19; admission free; ⏲ 6-8pm Tue & Thu summer, 5-7pm Tue & Thu winter, 10am-1pm 2nd Sun of month). Inside is a small exhibition dedicated to Jews in Gorizia and the Gorizian philosopher Carlo Michelstaedter (1887–1910), a writer who committed suicide aged

23 after finishing his best-known work, *La persuasione e la rettorica* (Persuasion and Rhetoric).

Sleeping & Eating

Albergo Alla Transalpina (☎ 0481 53 02 91; www .hotel-transalpina.com; Via Caprin 30; s/d from €45/70; **P**) This three-star hotel stands in a unique position, overlooking the Italian/Slovenian border on the open Piazza Transalpina. Rooms are light and airy and there's a good restaurant attached. Breakfast is €5 extra.

Euro Diplomat Hotel (☎ 0481 8 21 66; www.euro diplomathotel.it; Corso Italia 63; s/d €65/100; **P**) In the centre of town, this is one of those big boxy affairs that could be anywhere, but it's a smart, modern place offering soft beds and all expected facilities.

Cafés are plentiful on Corso Italia, the main street in the new part of town, while the old-town streets below the castle and around the covered **food market** (Via Verdi 30) are the best places to find trattorie.

Pizzeria Al Lampione (☎ 0481 3 27 80; Via Pellico 7; pizzas €5-8; ⏲ lunch & dinner) One of the few places open on a Monday, the Lampione is a friendly trattoria set back from the road. A huge range of pizzas is on offer, as are pasta, meat and fish dishes.

Alla Luna (☎ 0481 53 03 74; Via Oberdan 13; mains about €10-12; ⏲ lunch & dinner Tue-Sun) Original ceramic tiles on the walls, a beamed ceiling and knick-knacks galore add a rustic touch to this historic family-run trattoria, dating from 1876. The cushioned window seats are particularly cosy, and the cold meat and cheese platters are delicious.

Getting There & Away

From the **bus station** (Via IX Agosto), off Corso Italia, buses operated by the **APT** (☎ 800 955 957; www.aptgorizia.it in Italian) run to Nova Gorica bus station (Avtobusna Postaja Nova Gorica; €1, 25 minutes), from where you can get buses to destinations across Slovenia. Other bus services go to and from Aquileia (€3.25, two hours, six daily), Friuli-Venezia Giulia airport (€2.30, 35 minutes, 10 daily) and Palmanova (€2.75, 2½ hours, up to eight daily).

The **train station** (Piazzale Martiri Libertà d'Italia), about 1km southwest of the centre at the end of Corso Italia, has regular connections to/from Udine (€2.75, 30 minutes, at least hourly) and Trieste (€3.25, 50 minutes, hourly).

AROUND GORIZIA

The **Collio hills** around Gorizia produce some of Italy's finest white wines – among the first in Italy to be awarded a *denominazione di origine controllata* (DOC; controlled origin denomination) in 1968 (see p83). The tourist office in Gorizia has a list of cellars where you can taste, buy and drink the local vintage. Otherwise, contact the **Movimento Turismo del Vino Friuli-Venezi Giulia** (☎ 0432 28 95 40; www.mtvfriulivg.it), which has comprehensive information on all of the region's wincrics.

More sobering are the monuments to WWI soldiers, built here during the 1930s. The remains of 57,200 soldiers who died during WWI rest inside the **Sacrario di Oslavia** (☼ 8am-noon & 2-4.45pm Oct-Mar, 9am-12.30pm & 2.30-4.45pm Apr-Sep), 5km north of Gorizia.

The **Redipuglia Memorial**, beside the S305 near Redipuglia and 15km south of Gorizia, shelters the remains of over 100,000 soldiers from the Italian Third Army. An on-site **museum** (☎ 0481 48 90 24; admission free; ☼ 8am-noon & 2-4.45pm Tue-Sat Oct-Mar, 8.30am-noon & 1.30-5pm Tue-Sun Apr-Sep) relates the history of the Great War, and there are fortified trenches and other warfare remnants to be seen at the foot of the monstrous 22-tier hillside memorial. Originally built on a much smaller scale next to the museum, the memorial was not deemed pompous enough by Mussolini, who had the entire thing rebuilt (and 100,000 soldiers' remains shifted across the street) in 1937.

The area is sprinkled with other monuments, including one atop **Monte di San Michele**, 10km south of Gorizia near San Martino del Carso, the scene of particularly bloody encounters (you can still wander through the battlefield today).

APT buses link Gorizia and Oslavia, and Redipuglia can be reached by train from Gorizia (€1.80, 15 minutes, at least hourly).

PALMANOVA
pop 5380 / elev 26m

If you flew over it, you'd see what makes this town so special. Built 10km north of Aquileia in 1593 by the Venetians, Palmanova is a fortress in the form of a nine-pointed star – a fact that is hard to see once you're inside the town. Napoleon and the Austrians made later use of it, and to this day the Italian army maintains a garrison here.

From hexagonal Piazza Grande, sitting at the centre of the star, six roads radiate out through the old town to the defensive walls, the city's real attraction. Head along one of the spokes, Borgo Udine, to uncover local history in the **Civico Museo Storico** (☎ 0432 92 91 06; propalma@libero.it; Borgo Udine 4; adult/child €1/0.50; ☼ 9.30am-12.30pm Thu-Tue), inside the Palazzo Trevisan. The museum also acts as a tourist office and has information on secret-tunnel tours that wind beneath the city walls.

The **Museo Storico Militare** (☎ 0432 92 35 35; Borgo Cividale Dongione di Porta Cividale; admission free; ☼ 9am-noon & 2-4pm Tue-Sat, 9am-noon Sun winter, 9am-noon & 4-6pm Tue-Sat, 9am-noon Sun summer) is inside the Porta Cividale, one of three monumental entrances to the fortified town. The military museum traces the history of troops stationed in Palmanova from 1593 to WWII.

The family-owned **Albergo Ristorante Roma** (☎ 0432 92 84 72; www.hotelromapalmanova.it; Via Borgo Cividale 27; s/d/tr from €36/52/66; P) is a simple but perfectly comfortable place, and the only hotel fortunate enough to sit within the city walls.

Cafés stud central Piazza Grande; they include **Caffè Torinese** (Piazza Grande 9; ☼ 7am-2am Thu-Tue), which cooks up some succulent salads and *panini* (bread rolls with filling), as well as cheese and ham platters, to be enjoyed with some local wine.

Palmanova is a bus ride from Gorizia, Udine and Aquileia.

AQUILEIA
pop 3433

Founded in 181 BC, Aquileia was one of the largest and richest cities of the Roman Empire, with a population as high as 100,000 at its peak, and was a major trading link between Rome and the East. Aquileia was also an important centre for early Christianity in Europe, and a patriarchate was founded here in the 4th century. Destroyed by Attila's Huns in AD 452, the town never regained its former status, although the construction of the basilica in the 11th century ensured its religious importance for centuries. Aquileia was under Austrian rule from 1509 until 1918, and was listed as a Unesco World Heritage site in 1998.

A relatively tiny town – with the largest Palaeo-Christian mosaic floor in Europe – Aquileia lies at the eastern end of the Venetian plains. Guided tours of its extraordinary

Roman sights are organised by the **tourist office** (☎ 0431 9 10 87; www.aquileiaturismo.info in Italian; Piazza Capitolo 4; ☼ 9am-5pm) and more information can be found at www.aquileia.it.

Sights

Aquileia's star attraction is without doubt the Latin cross–shaped **basilica** (Piazza Capitolo; admission free; ☼ 9am-1pm & 2-5pm Mon-Fri, 9am-5pm Sat & Sun), rebuilt after an earthquake in 1348. The entire floor of the church is covered with one of the largest and most spectacular Roman-era mosaics in the world. The 760-sq-m floor of the basilica's 4th-century predecessor is protected with transparent glass walkways, allowing visitors to wander above the long-hidden images, which include episodes from the story of Jonah and the whale, the Good Shepherd, various sea creatures and birds and portraits of, presumably, the wealthy Roman patrons of this early Christian church. Equally remarkable treasures fill the basilica's two crypts. The 9th-century **Cripta degli Affreschi** (Crypt of Frescoes; adult/child incl Cripta degli Scavi €2.60/free) is adorned with faded 12th-century frescoes depicting the trials and tribulations of saints, while the **Cripta degli Scavi** (Excavations Crypt; adult/child incl Cripta degli Affreschi €2.60/free) reveals more mosaic floors in varying states of preservation. Images include birds, goats and foliage, as well as more peculiar subjects such as a lobster in a tree and a fight between a tortoise and a chicken. Images here were destroyed or badly damaged by the erection of the basilica's 73m-high **bell tower**, built in 1030 with stones from the Roman amphitheatre.

Scattered remnants of the Roman town include extensive ruins of the **Porto Fluviale** (River Port; Via Sacra; admission free; ☼ 8.30am-1hr before sunset), the old port, which once linked the settlement to the sea. Also free to visit are the partially restored remains of houses, markets, sections of road and the **Forum** on Via Giulia Augusta.

Locally excavated statues, pottery, glassware and jewellery are displayed in the **Museo Archeologico Nazionale** (☎ 0431 9 10 16; Via Roma 1; adult/EU citizens 18-25/child €4/2/free; ☼ 8.30am-2pm Mon, 8.30am-7.30pm Tue-Sun), one of northern Italy's most important collections. One intriguing artefact is the gilded bronze head of an emperor dating from the 3rd century AD, which at some point was violently hacked off its owner's body and discarded.

It has been suggested that this is a representation of Emperor Maximinus, who was killed during a siege in Aquileia in AD 238. Tombstones and mosaics are on show in the gardens, where a separate building houses the hull of a Roman ship.

Aquileia's **Museo Paleocristiano** (☎ 0431 9 11 31; Piazza Pirano; admission free; ☼ 8.30am-1.45pm) exhibits more early Christian mosaic floors and tombstones from the surrounds.

Festivals & Events

Local chefs cook up Roman-inspired dishes during Aquileia's annual Roman-food festival, known as **A Tavola con gli Antichi Romani** (At Table with the Ancient Romans) held in July or August; ask at the tourist office for what's cooking where.

Sleeping & Eating

Ostello Domus Augusta (☎ 0431 9 10 24; www.ostello aquileia.it; Via Roma 25; dm/s/d with breakfast €16.50/23/36; ☼ reception 7.30am-12.30pm & 2-11.30pm; ▢ P) This gleaming new hostel has some 92 beds, shared out between dorms that sleep up to six people, and regular singles and doubles. There's a small garden to relax in and bikes for rent. The hostel is closed from 10am to 2pm.

Camping Aquileia (☎ 0431 9 10 42; www.camping aquileia.it; Via Gemina 10; person/site low season €4.40/7.30, high season €6.50/9.50; ☼ mid-May–mid-Sep; P ▨) Camping Aquileia is a big family-friendly place north of the centre, opposite the Porto Fluviale. It also rents three- and four-bed bungalows with a kitchenette (from €38), which get booked up quickly.

Albergo Aquila Nera (☎ 0431 9 10 45; Piazza Garibaldi 5; s/d €30/60, d with bathroom €70; P) This clean and simple little place, with its whitewashed façade and shutters, is centrally located and offers good-value half- and full-board deals.

Hotel Restaurant Patriarchi (☎ 0431 91 95 95; www.hotelpatriarchi.it; Via Giulia Augusta 12; s/d from €44/74; P) This three-star choice is a stone's throw from the basilica and is the best place in town. Its wine cellar is well stocked and the chef is a dab hand at fish dishes. Half- and full-board options are available.

Getting There & Away

SAF buses link Aquileia with Grado (€1.50, 15 minutes, at least hourly), Palmanova (€1.85, 30 minutes, up to eight daily) and Udine

(€2.75, 1¼ hours, up to eight daily). Daily buses to/from Gorizia (€3.25, two hours, six daily) are handled by the Gorizia-based **APT** (☎ 800 955 957; www.aptgorizia.it in Italian).

GRADO
pop 8872

The popular beach resort of Grado, 14km south of Aquileia, is spread out along a narrow island backed by lagoons. The small medieval centre, crisscrossed by narrow *calli* (lanes), is dominated by the Romanesque **Basilica di Sant'Eufemia** (Campo dei Parriarchi) and the nearby remains of a 4th- to 5th-century church **mosaic** (Piazza Biagio Marin). The beachfront is lined with *belle époque* mansions, beach huts and thermal baths. From October to April, though, the place is dead.

Small *casoni* (reed huts), built for fishermen during winter, dot the tiny islands surrounding Grado. In summer some can be visited by boat (2½ hours, adult/child €15/8); the **tourist office** (☎ 0431 87 71 11; www .gradoturismo.info in Italian; Viale Dante Alighieri 72; ☷ 8am-1pm & 2-5pm Sat-Thu, 8am-1pm Fri Apr-Oct, closed Sat & Sun Nov-Mar) has details. Many of the islands are protected nature reserves and off-limits to tourists.

Each year on the first Sunday in July, a votive procession, with a statue of the Virgin Mary on board, sails from Grado to the **Santuario di Barbana** (☎ 0431 8 04 53), an 8th-century church on an island 5km east. Grado fishermen have done this since 1237 when the Madonna of Barbana saved their town from the plague. Boats link the sanctuary with Grado (adult/child return €4/2.50, three to eight times daily from April to October, and twice daily on Sunday from November to March).

Sleeping & Eating

Grado has an abundant supply of hotels, although there are no real budget options and many close down outside the summer season. Prices are at their highest during August. **Grado Promhotels** (☎ 0431 8 29 29; Riva Zaccaria Gregori 9; ☷ 9am-12.30pm & 3-6.30pm) is a local agency that can book you into hotels and apartments if you have any problems.

Albergo Alla Spiaggia (☎ 0431 8 48 41; www.albergo allaspiaggia.it; Via Mazzini 2; s/d from €54/108, half/full board per person from €63/68; ☷ Apr-Oct; P ☷) This late-1920s Art Deco hotel sports a quintessential seaside façade, with a sparkling white

bar and blue tables and chairs adorning each balcony. It sits bang on the seafront and has a lovely garden.

Hotel Metropole (☎ 0431 87 62 07; www.gradohotel .com; Piazza San Marco 15; s/d/tr/ste from €64/94/129/136; ☷ P) The historic Metropole, with its commanding harbourside location, dates back to 1900 and is still one of Grado's finest hotels. Prices vary throughout the year.

Hotel Helvetia (☎ 0431 87 39 30; www.hotelhel vetiagrado.it; Viale Kennedy 15; s/d from €45/74, half/full board per person from €45/52; ☷ P) The three-star Helvetia is one of the cheaper choices in town. It's set back a little from the sea, but it's a neat, modern place and all rooms have balconies.

Hotel Ville Bianchi (☎ 0431 8 01 69; www.ville bianchi.it in Italian; Viale Dante Alighieri 50; d full board per person €110; ☷ Apr-Oct; ☷ P) This imposing *fin de siècle* hotel occupies an enviable position right on the beachfront. The grand yellow-and-white villa has been thoroughly restored and offers spacious, modern rooms.

Al Canevon (☎ 0431 8 16 62; Calle Corbatto 11; mains €11-13; ☷ lunch & dinner Thu-Tue) In the heart of the old town, this busy, slightly touristy place serves a menu dominated by fish, with a few meat dishes thrown in.

Agli Artisti (☎ 0431 8 30 81; Campiello Porta Grande 2; 1st courses €6.20, 2nd courses €5-11; ☷ Wed-Sun) On the old-town fringe, this pretty little spot cooks up good-quality regional cuisine.

Getting There & Away

Grado is served by regular buses to and from Aquileia (€1.50, 15 minutes, at least hourly) and Udine (€3.25, 1¼ hours, 12 daily).

AROUND GRADO

Riserva Naturale Regionale della Valle Cavanata protects a 1920s fish-farming area and extraordinary birdlife in the eastern part of the lagoon; more than 230 bird species have been observed visiting the reserve, including the greylag goose and many wading birds.

Further east, the final 15km stretch of the River Isonzo's journey into the Adriatic flows through the **Riserva Naturale Regionale Foce dell'Isonzo**, a 2350-hectare nature reserve where visitors can bird-watch or horse ride, cycle and walk around salt marshes and mud flats. Reserve passes are sold at the **visitors centre** (☎ 0432 99 81 33; www.foceisonzo.it; adult/child €2/1; ☷ 9am-5pm Fri-Wed) in Isola della Cona in the reserve.

LAGUNA DI MARANO

The Marano Lagoon sprawls, in all its natural grandeur, immediately west of the Laguna di Grado. Frequented more by birdlife than human life, this wet spot is accessible by just a couple of gravel roads.

Pretty little **Marano Lagunare** (population 2100), a Roman fishing port that was later fortified, is the only settlement on the lagoon shore and a perfect hideaway. Peace and quiet is ensured by two nature reserves – the 1377-hectare **Riserva Naturale della Foci dello Stella**, protecting the marshy mouth of the River Stella, and the **Riserva Naturale della Valle Canal Nuovo**, a 121-hectare reserve in a former fishing valley.

Bird-watching is the main activity at the **visitors centre** (☎ 0431 6 75 51; Via delle Valli 2), shared by the two reserves in a traditional fisherman's reed hut.

LIGNANO

The Lignano area is a busy and traditional seaside resort. Occupying the tip of a peninsula facing Laguna di Marano to the north and the open Adriatic Sea to the south, **Lignano Sabbiadoro** (population 6543) sits at the northern head of three adjoining resorts. **Lignano Pineta**, 1km south, went up in the 1950s, while **Lignano Riviera**, the newest of the three at the mouth of the River Tagliamento, is marketed as the most nature-friendly.

Huge numbers of Italian and foreign tourists descend on the sandy beaches of the peninsula each summer, and there are plenty of family-friendly attractions and activities to keep them amused at every turn. Every imaginable water sport is on hand, and there are a couple of funfairs, a zoo and amusement parks. The biggest and most popular of these is **Gulliverlandia** (☎ 0431 42 31 33; www .gulliverlandia.it; Via San Giuliano 13, Lignano Sabbiadoro; adult/child €15/12; ☻ 10am-6pm May-Sep) which has an aquarium, circus, seal shows and various funfair rides to keep kids happy. Nearby is **Aquasplash** (☎ 0431 42 88 26; www.aquasplash.it in Italian; Viale Europa; adult/child €17/13; ☻ 10am-6.30pm May-Sep), a huge water park featuring rides, slides and pools.

Each of the three resorts has a good variety of accommodation on offer. In Sabbiardo, **Pension Orchidea** (☎ 0431 7 15 58; Via Latisana 122; s/d from €27/54; ☒ Ⓟ) offers simple, clean and homy accommodation at a good price, while portside **Hotel La Goletta** (☎ 04317

12 74; www.hotelgoletta.it; Viale Italia 44; s/d from €38/64) is another reasonable choice.

A more modern alternative in Pineta is the **Hotel San Francisco** (☎ 0431 42 22 34; www.hotel sanfrancisco.it; Viale delle Palme 40; s/d from €39.50/68; ☒ Ⓟ), where bright, peaceful rooms all come with balconies. Guests have use of a private beach, and bikes are available for rent. The minimum stay is three nights.

In Riviera, try four-star **Hotel Meriadanus** (☎ 0431 42 85 61; www.hotelmeriadanus.it; Viale della Musica 1; s/d from €57/90; ☒ Ⓟ ☒), a quiet place with an attractive garden.

All of these hotels offer half- and fullboard options. Prices vary throughout the year; expect to pay about a third more in July and August.

The tourist offices in **Sabbiadoro** (☎ 0431 7 18 21; www.aptlignano.it; Via Latisana 42) and **Pineta** (☎ 0431 42 21 69; Via dei Pini 53; ☻ Jun-Sep) can help with reservations, while the website www .lignano.it is a good source of information.

Lignano Sabbiadoro is linked by bus to Udine (€4.50, 1½ hours, several daily).

UDINE

pop 95,936 / elev 114m

The region's second-largest city, Udine is no tourist hotspot, but it's a busy, cultured place with some decent museums and galleries and photogenic Renaissance architecture, warranting a day or two of anyone's time. The city's convoluted history has left it heir to an odd mix of Italian, Slavic and Germanic influences, and some inhabitants still speak the local dialect, as dual street names (in dialect and Italian) testify.

The Romans founded Udine as a waystation. By the early 15th century, when it first came under Venetian control, Udine had grown into a city to rival nearby Cividale del Friuli and Aquileia. Napoleon's lieutenants briefly took control in the early 1800s, followed by the Austrians, who held the city until 1866, when it joined Italy. Udine survived WWII intact, but an earthquake in 1976 caused heavy damage and cost hundreds of lives – see the boxed text, p413. The great Renaissance painter Giambattista Tiepolo lived here for many years, leaving a number of works behind.

Information

There is a bank and ATM opposite the train station at the southern foot of Via Roma, and plenty more on and around Piazza del Duomo.

Hospital (☎ 0432 55 21; Piazza Santa Maria della Misericordia 15) About 2km north of the centre.

Libreria Carducci (☎ 0432 50 27 86; Piazza XX Settembre 16; ☺ Mon-Sat) Travel guides and maps aplenty.

Police station (☎ 0432 59 41 11; Via della Prefettura 16)

Post office Via Vittorio Veneto 42 (☺ 8.30am-7pm Mon-Sat) The main post office; Via Roma 25 (☺ 8.30am-2pm Mon-Fri, 8.30am-1pm Sat) Branch post office.

Tourist office (☎ 0432 29 59 72; www.udine-turismo .it; Piazza I Maggio 7; ☺ 9am-1pm & 2-5pm Mon-Thu, 9am-1pm & 2.30-5.30pm Fri & Sat, 10am-1pm Sun)

Sights

PIAZZA DELLA LIBERTÀ & AROUND

A gem of the Renaissance, Piazza della Libertà lies at Udine's old-town heart. The 15th-century **Palazzo del Comune** (Town Hall), also known as the Loggia del Lionello after its architect, is a clear reminder of Venetian influence, as is the **Loggia di San Giovanni** opposite, which features a clock with Moorish figures that strike the hours.

The **Arco Bollani** (Bollani Arch), next to the Loggia di San Giovanni, was designed by Andrea Palladio in 1556 and leads up to the castle used by the Venetian governors. The **castle** (built in the mid-16th century after an earthquake in 1511 destroyed the previous castle) now houses the **Galleria d'Arte Antica** (☎ 0432 27 15 91; adult/child €2.65/1.80, Sun mornings free; ☺ 9.30am-12.30pm & 3-6pm Tue-Sun), with works by Caravaggio, Carpaccio and Tiepolo. Admission includes a visit to the **Museo Archeologico** (Archaeological Museum), also in the castle. There's little information in anything but Italian. The 12th-century **Chiesa di Santa Maria del Castello** on the hill used to stand within the medieval castle walls.

CATHEDRAL & AROUND

Heading south from Piazza della Libertà down Via Vittorio Veneto, you reach Piazza del Duomo and Udine's 13th-century Romanesque-Gothic **cathedral**, with several frescoes by Tiepolo displayed in the **Museo del Duomo** (☎ 0432 50 68 30; admission free; ☺ 9am-noon & 4-6pm Tue-Sat, 4-6pm Sun). Across the street is the **Oratorio della Purità**, with a beautiful ceiling painting of the Assumption by Tiepolo. Ask in the cathedral for a guided tour (free) of the oratory.

South of Piazza del Duomo sits the 13th-century **Chiesa di San Francesco** (Largo Ospedale

Vecchio; adult/child €5/3.50; ☺ exhibitions 9am-noon & 3.30-7pm Tue-Sun). Although once one of Udine's most striking churches, it is now used as a gallery and is open only during exhibitions.

GALLERIA D'ARTE MODERNA

The **Modern Art Gallery** (☎ 0432 29 58 91; Piazzale Paolo Diacono 22; adult/child Mon-Sat €2.60/1.80, admission free Sun; ☺ 9.30am-12.30pm & 3-6pm Tue-Sat, 9.30am-12.30pm Sun), north of the centre, was established in 1885 after a rich Udinese merchant died and left his estate to the city. It features works by well-known 20th-century Italian artists, such as De Chirico, Severini and Morandi.

Sleeping

Those seeking farmhouse accommodation around Udine should contact **Agriturismo del Friuli Venezia-Giulia** (☎ 0432 20 26 46; www .agriturismofvg.com; Via Gorghi 27).

Hotel Principe (☎ 0432 50 60 00; www.principe-hotel .it; Viale Europa Unita 51; s/d/tr Mon-Fri from €69/99/119, Sat & Sun from €59/79/99; ✖ P) Set back from the busy road in a thankfully quiet courtyard, Principe is a smart and friendly option that's handy for the train station.

Hotel Europa (☎ 0432 29 44 46; fax 0432 51 26 54; Viale Europa Unita 47; s/d from €47//75; ✖ P ☐) On the main road, next door to the Principe, the Europa is a slightly older place, now looking a little worn. However, it's acceptable for a short stay.

Ambassador Palace Hotel (☎ 0432 50 37 77; www .ambassadorpalacehotel.it; Via Carducci 46; s/d/ste €110/ 140/190; ✖ P) This smart four-star choice provides a touch of understated elegance in a good central location, and rooms are spacious and restful.

Astoria Hotel Italia (☎ 0432 50 90 70; www.hotel astoria.udine.it; Piazza XX Settembre 24; s/d/ste from €74/ 111/156; ✖ P) This hotel is a solid midrange choice with all the usual comforts of those could-be-anywhere-in-the-world places favoured by business travellers.

Hotel Friuli (☎ 0432 23 43 51; friuli@hotelfriuli .udine.it; Viale Ledra 24; s/d from €52/88; ✖ P) Under the same management as the Astoria, the Friuli is a big modern three-star place on the outskirts of the city centre. The rooms are plain but comfortable and it has a well-regarded restaurant.

Eating

Several open-air cafés and restaurants are dotted around Piazza Matteotti and the

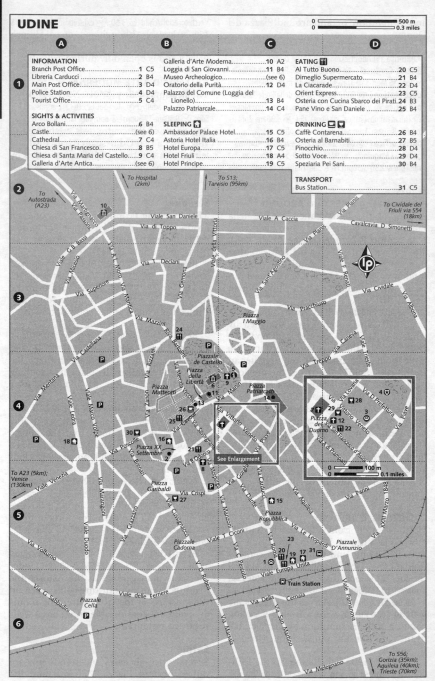

UDINE

0 ————— 500 m
0 ————— 0.3 miles

INFORMATION
Branch Post Office.............................1 C5
Libreria Carducci...............................2 B4
Main Post Office................................3 D4
Police Station....................................4 D4
Tourist Office.....................................5 C4

SIGHTS & ACTIVITIES
Arco Bollani......................................6 B4
Castle...(see 6)
Cathedral..7 C4
Chiesa di San Francesco.....................8 B5
Chiesa di Santa Maria del Castello.....9 C4
Galleria d'Arte Antica....................(see 6)

Galleria d'Arte Moderna..................10 A2
Loggia di San Giovanni...................11 B4
Museo Archeologico.....................(see 6)
Oratorio della Purità.......................12 D4
Palazzo del Comune (Loggia del
    Lionello).....................................13 B4
Palazzo Patriarcale..........................14 C4

SLEEPING
Ambassador Palace Hotel................15 C5
Astoria Hotel Italia 16 B4
Hotel Europa...................................17 C5
Hotel Friuli......................................18 A4
Hotel Principe..................................19 C5

EATING
Al Tutto Buono...............................20 C5
Dimeglio Supermercato...................21 B4
La Ciacarade...................................22 D4
Orient Express.................................23 C5
Osteria con Cucina Sbarco dei Pirati..24 B3
Pane Vino e San Daniele 25 B4

DRINKING
Caffè Contarena..............................26 B4
Osteria al Barnabiti.........................27 B5
Pinocchio.......................................28 D4
Sotto Voce.....................................29 D4
Speziaria Pei Sani...........................30 B4

TRANSPORT
Bus Station......................................31 C5

surrounding pedestrian streets. Don't wait too late to eat out, as the city starts closing down for the night around 10pm.

Orient Express (☎ 0432 51 08 84; Viale Europa Unita 61; pizzas €5-9; ☽ lunch & dinner) Done out with lots of wood panelling and antique-style light fittings to imitate the train buffet cars of old, this is a good spot for well-priced pizzas and a good variety of meat and fish dishes. A children's menu is also offered.

Osteria con Cucina Sbarco dei Pirati (☎ 0432 2 13 30; Riva Bartolini 12; mains about €8; ☽ lunch & dinner) Quite what pirates are doing in this part of the world isn't too clear, but the theme is abandoned indoors, where pots, pans, saws, clogs, saddles and other assorted junk hang from the walls and ceiling. Typical meaty Friulian fare fills the brief menu.

La Ciacarade (☎ 0432 51 02 50; Via San Francesco d'Assisi 6; mains about €10; ☽ Mon-Fri) Ham hunks hung above the bar and giant bowls of fresh strawberries, cherries and other seasonal fruits entice diners to eat at this authentic trattoria.

Pane Vino e San Daniele (☎ 0432 29 99 34; Piazzetta Lionello 12; 1st/2nd courses from €6.50/11; ☽ lunch & dinner) Bread, wine and prosciutto from San Daniele (see p412) make this an authentic lunch spot. Bands set the joint jiving on Friday and Saturday evenings.

Self-caterers can buy all the run-of-the-mill foodstuffs at **Dimeglio Supermercato** (Via Bonaldo Stringher), and regional cheese, meat and ready-made dishes from the delicatessen **Al Tutto Buono** (☎ 0432 50 42 70; Via Roma 56).

Drinking

Sotto Voce (☎ 0432 2 18 10; Via Vittorio Veneto 23) Calling itself an 'American fashion bar', this small drinking spot is popular with youngish locals chatting over apéritifs before dinner.

Caffè Contarena (☎ 0432 51 27 41; Via Cavour 11; ☽ Mon-Sat) An Art Deco interior offset by a wooden ceiling and weathered leather chairs lures a mixed crowd to this stunning café beneath the porticoes of Palazzo d'Aronco on Piazza della Libertà. An enoteca (wine bar) adjoins the café.

Pinocchio (☎ 0432 50 63 94; Via Lovaria 3a; ☽ 8am-3pm & 6pm-2am Tue-Sat) Hip Pinocchio is a blues café and music bar with a sprawling bar, low lights and thumping music.

Speziaria Pei Sani (☎ 0432 50 50 51; Via Poscolle 13; ☽ 10am-9pm Mon-Sat) Walls are bottle-lined with wine after wine and grappa after grappa

at this superb wine bar. Sit on the pavement terrace outside and taste the best of Friuli.

Osteria al Barnabiti (☎ 338 393 62 14; Piazza Garibaldi; ☽ Mon-Sat) Rough around the edges it might be, but this typical osteria offers wine drinkers the quintessential drinking experience, day or night.

Getting There & Away

From the **bus station** (☎ 0432 50 69 41; Viale Europa Unita 31) services operated by SAF (☎ 800 91 53 03, 0432 60 81 11; www.saf.ud.it) go to/from Trieste (€4.80, 1¼ hours, hourly), Aquileia (€2.75, 1¼ hours, up to eight daily), Lignano Sabbiadoro (€4.50, 1½ hours, nine to 11 daily) and Grado (€3.25, 1¼ hours, 12 daily). Buses also link Udine and Friuli-Venezia Giulia airport (€3.25, one hour, hourly).

From Udine's **train station** (☎ 0432 89 20 21; Viale Europa Unita) services run to Trieste (€5.95, 1½ hours, hourly), Venice (€6.85, 2½ hours, several daily) and Gorizia (€2.75, 30 minutes, hourly).

VILLA MANIN

True contemporary art lovers will adore the exhibitions at **Villa Manin** (☎ 0432 90 66 57; www .villamanin.it; Piazza Manin 10; adult/child €8/5; ☽ museum 9am-12.30pm & 3-6pm Tue-Sun, park 9am-5pm Tue-Fri, 9am-6pm Sat & Sun Easter-Oct), a villa in **Passariano**, 30km southwest of Udine. Home to the wealthy Manin family from the 1600s until as late as the 1990s (when the last count died heirless), the vast mansion is surrounded by 19 hectares of manicured gardens. A victorious Napoleon Bonaparte turned it into his headquarters in 1797 and it was here that the Treaty of Campoformido (1797), which saw the Venetian empire swallowed up by the Habsburgs, was signed. Exhibition opening hours and admission fees vary, so call in advance.

CIVIDALE DEL FRIULI

pop 11,375 / elev 138m

Lucky Cividale del Friuli, with its small medieval centre, has survived several devastating earthquakes since being founded by Julius Caesar in 50 BC.

Lying 15km northeast of Udine, Cividale is most picturesque where the 15th-century **Ponte del Diavolo** (Devil's Bridge) crosses the emerald-green River Natisone. Blown up by retreating Italian troops in 1917, the bridge was rebuilt after the war. Legend says that the devil himself threw the 22m-high stone bridge into the river at an earlier point in its history.

Walk through the cobbled lanes to the **Tempietto Longobardo** (Longobardo Temple; ☎ 0432 70 08 67; Borgo Brossano; adult/child €2/1; ⏰ 9.30am-12.30pm & 3-6.30pm Mon-Sat, 9.30am-1pm & 3-7.30pm Sun). Also known as the Oratorio di Santa Maria in Valle, this church is an exquisite example of Lombard artwork. To the west, the 16th-century **cathedral** (Piazza del Duomo) houses the **Museo Cristiano** (Christian Museum; ☎ 0432 70 12 11; admission free; ⏰ 9.30am-noon & 3-7pm Mon-Sat, 3-7pm Sun), where the star attraction is the 8th-century Altar of Ratchis, with its fascinating naive carvings.

Also worth a look-over is the nearby **Museo Archeologico** (☎ 0432 70 07 00; Piazza del Duomo 13; admission €4; ⏰ 9am-2pm Mon, 8.30am-7pm Tue-Sun) housing a collection of Roman and medieval sculptures and tombstones.

The **tourist office** (☎ 0432 73 14 61; arpt_cividale@regione.fvg.it; Corso Paolino d'Aquileia 10; ⏰ 9am-1pm & 3-5pm Mon-Fri), near the Devil's Bridge, has plenty of information on walks around Cividale.

Discover Friuli (☎ 339 724 5055; www.discoverfriuli.com; Via Manzoni 28) is a private company offering a wide range of cultural and gastronomic tours of the region, from half- and full-day sightseeing excursions to multiday themed tours. The four-day wine tour of the Colli Orientali and Aquileia areas (May and October) costs €525 per person, including accommodation, while four-day cookery trips cost around €655. All tours will pick up/drop off in Udine.

One of the more enticing places to stay is the peaceful **Locanda Al Castello** (☎ 0432 73 32 42; www.alcastello.net; Via del Castello 12; s/d €75/110; Ⓟ), housed in a former Jesuit monastery around 1km from the historic centre. It has its own restaurant (closed Wednesday).

Trains connect Cividale with Udine (€1.70, 15 minutes, at least hourly) and Trieste (€3.85, 1½ hours, up to eight daily).

SAN DANIELE DEL FRIULI
pop 7750

So exquisitely sweet it practically melts in your mouth, prosciutto San Daniele is raw ham taken from the hind leg of a black pig and salted and cured from 12 to 18 months. Locals from San Daniele, the village from which it originates, located 20km northwest

of Udine, parade down the streets disguised as hams in August during the **Aria di Festa**, a four-day festival held to celebrate their world-famous ham. Almost 15% of all prosciutto consumed in Italy is from San Daniele.

There are no less than 27 *prosciuttifici* in the village, although the most you'll get to see of these large industrial ham-curing plants is a 30-minute tour of the curing room where the hams are hung to air. The **tourist office** (☎ 0432 94 07 65; www.infosandaniele.com; Via Roma 3; ⏰ 9.30am-12.30pm Wed-Sat) has a list of *prosciuttifici* that accept visits; advance reservations are essential.

There are, of course, many establishments from which to buy the prized local products; try **Prosciutti Coradazzi** (☎ 0432 95 75 82; www.coradazzi.com; Via Kennedy 128; ⏰ closed morning Mon, afternoon Sat & Sun) or **Bottega del Prosciutto** (☎ 0432 95 70 43; Via Umberto I 2). For a light lunch of prosciutto San Daniele wrapped around *grissini* (bread sticks), or just a platter of the wafer-thin sliced ham, look no further than the simple **Bar Municipio** (☎ 0432 95 50 12; Via Garibaldi 21; ⏰ Sun-Fri). **Ristorante Al Boschetto** (☎ 0432 95 44 85; Via Frittalon 12; mains about €20; ⏰ lunch & dinner Fri-Tue, lunch Wed) is an upmarket choice, also known for its *risotto di miele* (honey risotto).

You will need your own transport to get to San Daniele. Three cycling itineraries (each 22km) lead cyclists through the hills around the village; ask at the tourist office for itinerary details.

IL CARNIA

North of Udine's earthquake zone, the lowlands give way to Alpine country on the way to Austria. The region is known generically as Il Carnia, after the people who settled here around the 4th century BC, and its attractions are walking, cycling and skiing.

The eastern half is characterised by forbidding and rocky bluffs along the valley to **Tarvisio** (population 5240; elevation 754m), an alpine walking and skiing resort 7km short of the Austrian border and 11km from Slovenia, also known for its Saturday market. There are several places to stay in and around the town. Try the Alpine-style **Hotel Edelhof** (☎ 0428 64 40 25; Via Diaz 11; s/d from €45/90; Ⓟ), which also offers half- and full-board deals.

You can **ski** around Tarvisio but most of the Friuli-Venezia Giulia resorts lie in

THE EPICENTRE OF AN EARTHQUAKE

On 6 May 1976 an earthquake measuring 6.5 on the Richter scale ripped through the medieval village of **Venzone** (population 2306), one of a cluster of villages in Il Gemonese, a little-known pocket of land 30km north of Udine in the Tagliamento Valley. The strongest seismic shockwave lasted more than 90 seconds, killing 989 people and injuring another 3000 across an area of 5000 sq km in northern Friuli. For Venzone, at the centre of the quake, the final blow came on 15 September 1976 when a second earthquake struck. The blast, 6.1 on the Richter scale, demolished what little remained of the shell-shocked village. That same year the village of rubble was redeclared an historic national monument.

With the exception of a ruined church on Via Alberton del Colle, which stands as a memorial to the 42 Venzone villagers who died, medieval Venzone has since been rebuilt stone by stone. Two churches, the city walls, gates and dozens of quaint town houses – such as the one housing the **tourist office** (☎ 0432 98 50 34; Via Glizoio di Mels 5/4; ♥ Apr-Sep) – have all been raised from the rubble.

The surrounding villages of **Trasaghis** (population 2550) and **Gemona del Friuli** (population 11,137) were also destroyed by the 1976 earthquakes. In Gemona, stubs of the outer walls and the steps leading up to the altar are all that remain of the once-stunning 15th-century **Chiesa di Santa Maria** (Via Cavour). Gemona makes a handy base for exploring the region, and has a **tourist office** (☎ 0432 98 14 41; Piazza del Municipio 5; ♥ Apr-Sep). Should you wish to stay, **Hotel Willy** (☎ 0432 98 17 33; Via Bariglaria 164; s/d/tr/q €50/75/90/106; 💻 P) is a well-priced place with a gym, sauna and restaurant.

Neighbouring **Bordano** (population 811), another victim, has since reinvented itself as one of Europe's largest butterfly centres. Some 1500 butterfly species (500 of which are nocturnal) flutter around **Monte San Simeone** (1505m), while in town, more than 400 species of tropical butterflies are bred at the **Casa delle Farfalle** (☎ 0432 98 81 35; www.casaperlefarfalle.it; Via Canada 1; adult/child €6.50/4.50; ♥ 9.30am-12.30pm & 2-4pm Mar & Oct, 9.30am-noon & 2-5.30pm Apr-Sep).

Il Carnia's more attractive, verdant western half. In a rough curve from west to east, names to watch out for include Piancavallo, Forni di Sopra, Ravascletto-Zoncolan and Sella Nevea. Downhill pistes best suited to beginners and intermediates start at 1700m.

Most towns in the region will have a couple of hotels; Udine's tourist office (p408) has a list. Those intent on **walking**, **cycling** or **biking** in the region should also pick up itinerary information there. Alternatively, contact the tourist offices in **Barcis** (☎ 0427 76 30 00; Piazza V Emanuele II 5), **Forni di Sopra** (☎ 0433 88 67 67; Via Cadore 1), **Piancavallo** (☎ 0434 65 51 91; Piazzale della Puppa) or **Tarvisio** (☎ 0428 21 35; www .tarvisiano.org; Via Roma 10).

Tarvisio is connected by train to Udine (€6.20, 1¾ hours, up to 10 daily).

Emilia-Romagna & San Marino

The geography's simple: Emilia to the west, Romagna to the east and Bologna, the region's biggest city, bang in the middle.

Emilia-Romagna's architectural riches are mostly from the Renaissance. Its past is a family history: the Farnese in Parma and Piacenza, the Este in Ferrara and Modena, the Bentivoglio in Bologna; each leaving its legacy in stone and brick and patronising the finest artists of the day. In much earlier times, Ravenna, its breathtaking mosaics rivalled only by those of Istanbul, was capital of the Byzantine Empire's western regions.

Bologna, the regional capital, was one of Europe's most important medieval cities; its university is the continent's oldest and has turned out the likes of Erasmus, Copernicus and Dante. It is also Italy's food capital, drawing on fresh produce from the fertile Po valley and adding tortellini and lasagne to the Italian table and international cooking vocabulary.

From Bologna, you can make day trips to Ferrara, Modena and Parma, all once important Renaissance towns. Rimini, with its beaches and summer nightlife, is one of Italy's premier sun spots, while the tiny republic of San Marino, invaded daily by armies of tourists, offers fine hilltop views.

Travel between Emilia-Romagna's main towns is easy; an efficient train line runs east–west, paralleled for much of its length by autostrada.

HIGHLIGHTS

- See red in **Bologna** (p416), with its magnificent red-brick monuments and more than 40km of elegant arcades
- Discover **Ravenna's** (p444) shimmering early Christian mosaics
- Dream on with a visit to **Galleria Ferrari's** (p429) grand prix–winning racing cars in Maranello
- Check out the Romanesque splendour of the stone carvings of Modena's **cathedral** (p426)
- Visit a **Parmesan cheese factory** (p436) in Parma
- Join in the wacky fun of Ferrara's annual **Buskers' Festival** (p441)

■ POPULATION: Emilia-Romagna 4 million; San Marino 27,800	■ AREA: Emilia-Romagna 22,121 sq km; San Marino 61 sq km

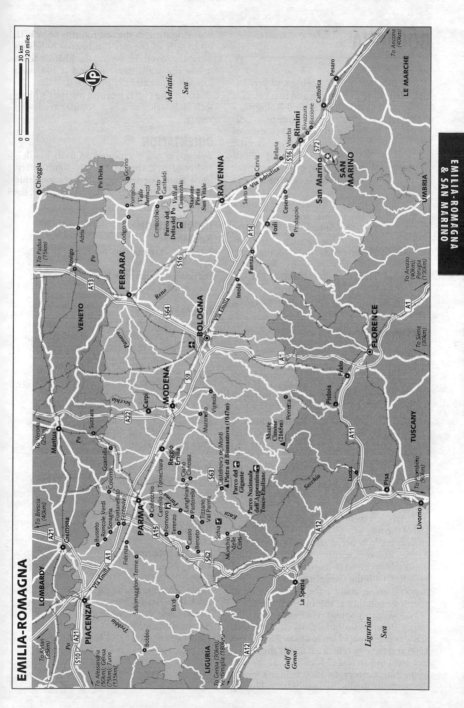

EMILIA-ROMAGNA & SAN MARINO

BOLOGNA

pop 373,000

If you think red brick's boring and provincial, then come to Bologna and marvel. Not for nothing is it known as Red Bologna, a sobriquet that reflects both the hue of its politics (until fairly recently it was a bastion of the Democratici di Sinistra, the democratic party of the left) and the dominant colour of its elegant monuments, plus more than 40km – yes, that's 40km – of arcades and porticos.

The university is still something of a source of student agitation, albeit scarcely a squeak compared to the protest heyday of the 1970s. Together with one of the country's better organised gay communities, the students add a dynamism that's missing in smaller Emilian towns. The city administrators chip in with an unstinting and imaginative arts programme to keep even the most demanding culture-buff well occupied.

HISTORY

Bologna started life in the 6th century BC as Felsina. For two centuries it was the capital of the Etruscan Po valley territories until tribes from Gaul took over, renaming it Bononia. They lasted another couple of hundred years before surrendering to the Romans' northward march. As the Western Empire crumbled, Bologna was successively sacked and occupied by Visigoths, Huns, Goths and Lombards.

The city reached its pinnacle as an independent commune and leading European university around the 12th century. Wealth brought a building boom and every well-to-do family left its mark by erecting a tower – 180 of them in all, of which 15 still stand. The endless tussle between the papacy and Holy Roman Empire for control of northern Italy inevitably involved Bologna. The city started by siding with the Guelphs (who backed the papacy), going against the Ghibellines, but adopted neutrality in the 14th century.

Following a popular rebellion against the ruling Bentivoglio family, when their palace was razed, papal troops took Bologna in 1506 and the city remained under their control until the arrival of Napoleon at the end of the 18th century. In 1860 Bologna joined the newly formed Kingdom of Italy. During heavy fighting in the last months of WWII, up to 40% of the city's industrial buildings were destroyed. However, the historic town inside the walls survived and it has been lovingly and carefully preserved.

Today the city is a centre for Italy's high-tech industries and is a popular trade-fair venue.

ORIENTATION

Bologna is easily explored on foot. Via dell' Indipendenza, the main north–south artery, leads from the train and bus stations into Piazza del Nettuno and Piazza Maggiore, the heart of the city.

INFORMATION

Bookshops

Feltrinelli – International bookshop (☎ 051 26 80 70; Via Zamboni 7b)

Feltrinelli – Italian bookshop (☎ 051 26 68 91; Piazza di Porta Ravegnana 1)

Internet Access

Caffè 14 Luglio (☎ 051 27 02 83; Piazza Calderini 6; per hr €6; ⊙ 9am-9pm Mon-Sat) Two stations available.

Ethnoland (☎ 051 420 47 00; Via Amendola 15c; per hr €3; ⊙ 8am-8.30pm) Three stations available.

Net Arena (Via de' Giudei 3d; per hr €3.50; ⊙ 10am-midnight Mon-Fri, 10am-8pm Sat, 4-9pm Sun) The largest of the three.

Laundry

iWash (Via G Petroni 38; ⊙ 9am-9pm)

Onda Blu (Via Saragozza 34a/b; ⊙ 6am-11pm)

Medical Services

Ospedale Maggiore (☎ 051 647 81 11; Via Emilia Ponente) West of the city centre.

Post

Main post office (Piazza Minghetti)

Tourist Information

ArciGay il Cassero (☎ 051 6 49 44 16; www.cassero.it in Italian; Via Don Minzoni 18)

Centro Servizi per i Turisti (☎ 800 85 60 65; ⊙ 10am-2pm & 3-7pm Mon-Sat, 10am-2pm Sun) Co-located with the main tourist office. Makes hotel bookings free of charge in associated hotels.

Tourist office (☎ 051 24 65 41; www.bolognaturismo .info); airport (⊙ 8am-8pm Mon-Sat, 9am-3pm Sun); bus station (9am-1pm & 3-7pm Mon-Sat); Piazza Maggiore 1 (⊙ 9am-8pm) Main office; train station (⊙ 8.30am-7.30pm Mon-Sat)

BOLOGNA

0 ____ 400 m
0 ____ 0.2 miles

INFORMATION

Caffè 14 Luglio.	1 C4
Centro Servizi per I Turisti.	(see 11)
CTS.	2 B1
Ethnoland.	3 B1
Feltrinelli-International	
Bookshop.	4 B1
Feltrinelli-Italian Bookshop.	5 B1
IWash Laundrette.	6 D3
Main Post Office.	7 B2
Main Tourist Office.	8 B1
Net Arena.	9 B1
Onda Blu.	10 B4
Tourist Office.	11 A1

SIGHTS & ACTIVITIES

Basilica di San Domenico.	12 C4
Basilica di San Petronio.	13 A2
Basilica di Santo Stefano.	14 C3
Cattedrale di San Pietro.	15 A1
Chiesa di San Francesco.	16 B3
Chiesa di San Giacomo	
Maggiore.	17 D3
Collezioni Comunali d'Arte.	(see 23)
Le Due Torri.	18 B1
Museo Civico Archeologico.	19 B2
Museo Civico Medioevale e del	
Rinascimento.	20 A1
Museo Morandi.	(see 23)
Neptune's Fountain.	21 A1
Oratorio di Santa Cecilia.	22 D3
Palazzo Comunale.	23 A1
Palazzo del Podestà.	(see 11)
Palazzo del Re Enzo.	24 A1
Palazzo dell'Archiginnasio.	25 A2
Palazzo Poggi.	(see 27)
Pinacoteca Nazionale.	26 D2
Santi Vitale e Agricola.	(see 14)
Torre degli Asinelli.	(see 18)
University.	27 D2

SLEEPING 🛏

Albergo delle D'apperie.	28 B1
Albergo Garisenda.	29 B1
Albergo 'panorama'.	30 B3
Hotel Commercianti.	31 A2

Hotel Corona d'Oro 1890.	32 B1
Hotel Novecento.	33 A2
Hotel Orologio.	34 A2
Hotel Roma.	35 A2
Hotel Ross ni.	36 D3

EATING 🍴

Bass' Otto.	37 B3
Diana.	38 C2
Drogheria della Rosa.	39 D4
Gelateria delle Moline.	40 C2
La Brace.	41 D3
La Sorbetteria Castiglione.	42 B3
Mercato delle Erbe.	43 B3
Pizzeria Altero.	44 B1
Produce Market.	45 B1
Tamburini.	46 B1
Trattoria da Danio.	47 A3
Trattoria da Gianni.	48 B1

DRINKING 🍷

Bravo Caffe.	49 D2
Café de Paris.	50 B2
Café le Palais.	51 B2
Cantina Bentivoglio.	52 C2
Le Stanze.	53 C2
Marsalino.	54 C2
Osteria de Sole.	55 A1
Osteria L'Infedele.	56 D3
Rosa Rose.	(see 48)

ENTERTAINMENT 🎭

Arena del Sole.	57 C2
Chet Baker Jazz Club.	58 B2
Cinema Capital.	59 C1
Cinema Odeon.	60 D2
Corto Maltese.	61 C2
Kinki.	62 B1
Teatro Comunale.	63 D2
Teatro Duse.	64 D4

TRANSPORT

Europcar.	65 B1
Hertz.	66 B1
Main Bus Station.	67 B1
Senzauto.	68 C1

Travel Agencies

CTS (☎ 051 23 75 01; Largo Respighi 2) Student travel organisation.

SIGHTS

The *Bologna dei Musei* card (one/three days €12/16), on sale at the main tourist office and participating museums, allows admission to seven of the city's major attractions, including Collezioni Comunali d'Arte, Museo Civico Medioevale e del Rinascimento and Museo Civico Archeologico, among others. Children up to 14 years old go free.

Piazze Maggiore & del Nettuno

Some of Bologna's most graceful medieval and Renaissance monuments fringe Piazza Maggiore and the adjoining Piazza del Nettuno. At the centre of Bologna's old city, this pair of bustling pedestrianised squares are a focal point of city life, with Bolognesi flocking to the cafés and gathering around the mime artists and buskers who perform on the uneven stone pavement.

NEPTUNE'S FOUNTAIN

Between the two piazze stands a mighty bronze fountain of **Neptune**, sculpted in 1566 by a Frenchman known to posterity as Giambologna. The four cherubs represent the winds and the four sirens, water spouting from every nipple, symbolise the four known continents of the pre-Oceania world.

PALAZZO COMUNALE

The Palazzo Comunale (aka the Palazzo D'Accursio) lines the western flank of the two piazze. Its immense central staircase, attributed to the Renaissance architect Donato Bramante, was built wide enough for horse-drawn carriages to chauffeur their occupants up to the 1st floor. The left side of the building was the residence of the Accursio family and, from the 16th to 19th centuries, home to the Papal Legate. Above the main entrance is a bronze statue of Pope Gregory XIII, a native of Bologna responsible for the Gregorian calendar. Within the building are two art collections.

The **Collezioni Comunali d'Arte** (☎ 051 20 36 29; admission €4; ☽ 9am-6.30pm Tue-Sat, 10am-6.30pm Sun) includes paintings, sculpture and furniture originally in private collections. From here, you get a magnificent view over Piazza Maggiore.

The splendid **Museo Morandi** (☎ 051 20 36 29; admission €4; ☽ 10am-6pm Tue-Sun) contains more than 200 paintings, watercolours, drawings and prints spanning the career of the 20th-century Bolognese artist Giorgio Morandi.

Outside the palazzo are three large panels bearing photos of hundreds of local partisans killed in the resistance to German occupation, many executed at this very spot. Such displays are relatively common in the towns of Emilia-Romagna, which was a centre of fierce partisan activity.

PALAZZO DEL RE ENZO

Across from Palazzo Comunale, this **palace**, open only during exhibitions, is named after King Enzo of Sicily, who was confined here for 20 long years in the 13th century.

PALAZZO DEL PODESTÀ

Beneath this fine example of Renaissance architecture and behind the cafés facing Piazza Maggiore, there's a whispering **gallery** where two perpendicular passages intersect. Stand diagonally opposite someone and whisper: the acoustics are amazing. Notice how this medieval tower, a considerable feat of engineering, doesn't rest on the ground but on the pillars of the vault. It too is open only during exhibitions.

BASILICA DI SAN PETRONIO

Named after the city's patron saint, San Petronio, the **basilica** (☽ 7.30am-1pm & 2.30-6pm) was started in 1392 but, for political reasons, was never finished.

Originally intended to be larger than the first St Peter's in Rome (the structure was destroyed to make way for Rome's present basilica), San Petronio was effectively truncated by the papacy, which decreed it could not be larger than St Peter's and that much of the land should be used for a university. The façade is incomplete and if you walk along Via dell'Archiginnasio, on the eastern side of the basilica, you can see semiconstructed apses poking out oddly. Yet despite the papal interdiction, the basilica is still the fifth-largest in the world and an example of Gothic-style architecture at its best.

The central doorway, carved in 1425 by Jacopo della Quercia, features a beautiful Madonna and Child and scenes from the Old and New Testaments. The chapels inside contain frescoes by Giovanni da Modena and Jacopo di Paolo. A giant brass sundial, designed by Cassini in 1656, stretches along the floor of the eastern aisle.

Marginalised and just up the street, Bologna's cathedral, **Cattedrale di San Pietro** (Via dell'Independenza 9-13; ☼ 7.30am-noon & 4-6.15pm Mon-Sat, 8am-12.30pm & 3.30-6.15pm Sun), is very much the poor relation having been ravaged and redeveloped many times over the centuries.

Museo Civico Archeologico

Just east of the basilica, the **archaeological museum** (☎ 051 2 75 72 11; Via dell' Archiginnasio 2; admission €4; ☼ 9am-6.30pm Tue-Sat, 10am-6.30pm Sun) has well-displayed and well-documented Egyptian and Roman artefacts and one of Italy's best Etruscan collections, which is less well presented. Highlights of the latter are two burial chambers unearthed near the city.

Palazzo del Archiginnasio

The site of the city's university from 1563 to 1805 (notice the professors' coats of arms adorning the walls, surrounded by the appropriately more modest plaques of appreciative students), this **palace** (☎ 051 27 68 11; Piazza Galvani 1; admission free; ☼ 9am-1pm Mon-Sat) has a 17th-century anatomy theatre, crafted entirely from wood. The canopy above the lecturer's chair is supported by skinless figures. The theatre, together with many of the building's frescoes, was destroyed during WWII and completely rebuilt.

Museo Civico Medioevale e del Rinascimento

Within the Palazzo Ghilisardi-Fava, which has some fine frescoes by Jacopo della Quercia, this **museum** (☎ 051 20 39 30; Via Manzoni 4; admission €4; ☼ 9am-6.30pm Tue-Sat, 10am-6.30pm Sun) houses a collection of battle armour, bronze statues and medieval coffin slabs.

Le Due Torri

The two slender and seemingly precarious leaning towers that rise above Piazza di Porta Ravegnana are unmistakable landmarks. The taller one, all 97.6m of it, is the **Torre degli Asinelli** (admission €3; ☼ 9am-6pm, to 5pm winter). Built by the family of the same name in 1109, it has 498 steps that you can climb (despite the 1.3m lean) for a marvellous view over the city. The Garisenda family was even less cautious with foundations when erecting its own tower, originally designed to compete with its neighbour and later sized down to 48m because of its 3.2m lean. Wisely, given such a tilt, it's closed to the public.

University Quarter

Northeast of the towers, along Via Zamboni, is the **Chiesa di San Giacomo Maggiore** (Piazza Rossini; ☼ 6.45am-noon & 4-6pm). Built in the 13th century and remodelled in 1722, it's notable for the Bentivoglio chapel, with frescoes by Lorenzo Costa and an altarpiece by Francesco Raibolini (known as Il Francia).

The same pair were mainly responsible for the striking late-15th-century cycle of 10 frescoes describing the life of St Cecilia in the adjacent **Oratorio di Santa Cecilia** (☼ 10am-1pm & 3-7pm, to 6pm winter).

The **university** has a whole range of museums (Ships and Old Maps, Military Architecture, Obstetrics, Anatomy of Domestic Animals, Astronomy and much more) open to the public and mostly within the **Palazzo Poggi** (☎ 051 2 09 99 88; www.unibo.it/musei-universitari in Italian; Via Zamboni 33). Visit its website or call by the palazzo for a catalogue. The main tourist office also carries a list.

Pinacoteca Nazionale

North of the university, this **art gallery** (☎ 051 4 21 19 84; Via delle Belle Arti 56; admission €4; ☼ 9am-7pm Tue-Sun) concentrates on works by Bolognese artists from the 14th century onwards. The extensive exhibits include several works by Giotto, as well as Raphael's *Ecstasy of St Cecilia*. El Greco and Titian are also represented, but by comparatively little-known works.

Basilica di Santo Stefano

From the two towers, head southeast along Via Santo Stefano, a residential area for Bologna's wealthy and lined with the elegant façades of their palazzi.

The **basilica** (Via Santo Stefano 24; ☼ 9am-12.15 & 3.30-6.30pm) is in fact a group of four churches remaining from an original seven. On the right stand the 11th-century Romanesque **Chiesa del Crocefisso** (Crucifix) and the octagonal **Chiesa del Santo Sepolcro** (Holy Sepulchre), whose shape suggests it started life as a baptistry. The Chiesa del Crocefisso houses the bones of San Petronio. Legend has it that the basin in the small courtyard is the one in which Pontius Pilate washed his hands after he condemned Christ to death. In actual fact it's an 8th-century Lombard artefact.

Santi Vitale e Agricola (8am-noon & 3.30-7.30pm Mon-Sat, 9am-12.30pm & 4.30-8pm Sun) is the city's oldest church. Incorporating recycled Roman masonry and carvings, the bulk of the building dates from the 11th century. The considerably older tombs of two saints in the side aisles once served as altars. From the **Capilla della Santa Trinità** you can pass to the modest medieval colonnaded cloister, off which lies a small **museum** with a limited collection of paintings and frescoes.

Basilica di San Domenico

The **basilica** (Piazza San Domenico 13; 7am-1pm & 3.30-7.30pm) was erected in the early 16th century to house the remains of San Domenico, founder of the Dominican order, who died in 1221 soon after opening a convent on this very site.

The **Cappella di San Domenico** in the south aisle contains the saint's elaborate sarcophagus, incised with vigorous reliefs illustrating scenes from his life. Designed by Nicola Pisano in the late 13th century, the chapel was worked on by a host of artists over the following couple of centuries. Michelangelo carved the angel on the right of the altar when he was only 19. San Domenico's skull is in a reliquary behind the sarcophagus. There's a small **museum** behind the main altar. Notice, too, the intricately executed wooden tableaux of the choir stalls.

When Mozart spent a month at the city's music academy, he occasionally played the church's organ.

Chiesa di San Francesco

Outside the east end of this **church** (Piazza San Francesco; 7am-noon & 3-7pm) is a trio of elaborate tombs of the *glossatori* (university law professors). The church was one of the first in Italy to be built in the French Gothic style. Inside is the tomb of Pope Alexander V and a remarkable 14th-century marble altarpiece, reworked in the 19th century, depicting sundry saints, their higher ranks seemingly impaled upon slender stalagmites, and scenes from the life of St Francis.

Basilica Santuario della Madonna di San Luca

You can see this hilltop **basilica** (46 Via di San Luca; 7am-12.30pm & 2.30-7pm, to 5pm in winter) from most parts of the city. Built in the mid-18th century, it houses a representation of the Virgin Mary, supposedly painted by Saint Luke (hence the place's name) and transported from the Middle East to Bologna in the 12th century.

The sanctuary lies about 4km southwest of the city centre and is connected to the city walls by the world's longest portico, held aloft by 666 arches, beginning at Piazza di Porta Saragozza, itself southwest of the centre. Take bus No 20 from the city centre to Villa Spada, from where you can continue by minibus (buy the €2.60 return ticket on board) to the sanctuary.

To stretch the legs, continue one more stop on bus No 20 to the Meloncello arch and walk the remaining 2km under the arches.

TOURS

Three outfits offer guided walking tours of the city in English.

GAIA (051 2 96 00 05; www.guidebologna.com) Meets 10.30am Wednesday, Saturday and Sunday outside the main tourist office.

Le Guide d'Arte (051 2 75 02 54) Meets 3pm Saturday and Sunday outside the main tourist office.

Prima Classe (347 894 40 94) Meets 11am Monday and Friday, and 4pm Tuesday and Thursday beside Neptune's fountain.

You do not need to book and all charge €13 per person.

Prima Classe also has two-hour **cycle tours** (tours incl bike rental €18) of Bologna's cultural high spots. Call to reserve your spot; there's a minimum of three participants for tours to begin.

An increasing number of hotels, including several of those we recommend, participate in the tourist office's Room with a View scheme, offering free two-hour guided walking tours on Sunday mornings. Reserve through your hotel.

FESTIVALS & EVENTS

Each summer the city sponsors a three-month festival of open-air events involving museums and galleries, the university, and local and national performers. Bologna's tourist offices carry programme details.

SLEEPING

Bologna's busy trade-fair calendar means that hotels are often heavily booked, especially during spring and autumn. The city's top-end hotels cater primarily to business folk; when there are no fairs on, some offer discounts of up to 50% and attractive weekend rates.

Budget

Ostello Due Torri-San Sisto (☎ 051 50 18 10; hostel bologna@hotmail.com; Via Viadagola 5 & 14; dm/d with breakfast €15/34; 💻) A pair of HI-affiliated hostels, barely 100m apart, out in the country 6km north of the heart of town. Take bus Nos 93 (Monday to Saturday, daytime), 301 (Sunday) or 21B (daily, after 8.30pm) from Via Irnerio or Via Marconi.

Centro Turistico Città di Bologna (☎ 051 32 50 16; www.hotelcamping.com; Via Romita 12/4a; person/site €7/12; 🏊) This very swish camping ground with all the creature comforts is on the north side of town, 6km from the main station. Take bus No 68 from the bus station.

Midrange

Albergo delle Drapperie (☎ 051 22 39 55; albergo drapperie@libero.it; Via delle Drapperie 5; s €60-100, d €75-135; 🏊) Barely 100m from Piazza Maggiore, this place has been freshly and comprehensively renovated. The rooms are attractively furnished and contemporary ceiling trescoes are a creative variant on a traditional feature. You can rent a bike (don't attempt to force your car down narrow, bustling Via delle Drapperie) for €5 per day.

Albergo Garisenda (☎ 051 22 43 69; garisenda@ garisenda.fastwebnet.it; 3rd fl Galleria del Leone 1, Via Rizzoli 9; s/d/tr from €50/70/100, d/tr with bathroom €95/120) The Garisenda has just seven rooms, some looking out over the leaning towers. Breakfast, included in the price, may be modest but the coffee is real and freshly expressed from the burbling machine – something too often absent from much grander establishments. The entrance is within a covered shopping gallery off Via Rizzoli.

Albergo Panorama (☎ 051 22 18 02; www.hotelpan oramabologna.it; 4th fl, Via Livraghi 1; s/d/tr/p €55/70/85/95; 🏊) This is a family-owned hotel where three generations play their part in the running. The rooms are large, airy and spotless and some have great views if you crane your neck ever so slightly.

Hotel Rossini (☎ 051 23 77 16; www.albergorossini .com; Via dei Bibiena 11; s/d €42/70, with bathroom €70/100; 🕐 closed mid-Jul–mid-Aug; 🏊) Located down a quiet street in the heart of the university area its 21 rooms, some with air-con, are maintained to high standards and the welcome is friendly.

Hotel Roma (☎ 051 22 63 22; www.hotelroma.biz; Via Massimo d'Azeglio 9; s/d with breakfast €120/150; Ⓟ 🏊) Upmarket and over a century in business, Hotel Roma offers superior comfort right in the heart of town, although the bedrooms' floral wallpaper and fabrics are a just mite overpowering. Parking is €16.

Top End

The company **Bologna Art Hotels** (☎ 051 7 45 73 35; www.bolognarthotels.it) operates four delightfully renovated top-end options in central Bologna (listed below) with the same central reservations number. The prices listed for each hotel include breakfast; parking is €28.

Hotel Commercianti (☎ 051 7 45 75 11; Via de' Pignattari 11; s €135-300, d €155-320; Ⓟ 🏊 💻) Tucked away down an inconspicuous back alley, where the bas-relief figures on the walls of the Basilica di San Petronio gawp into the 1st-floor windows, lies this hotel. It occupies the restored 12th-century building that was Bologna's first town hall.

Hotel Corona d'Oro 1890 (☎ 051 7 45 76 11; Via Oberdan 12; s €135-300, d €155-320; Ⓟ 🏊) With its gloriously luminous central atrium, marble bathrooms and Art Nouveau décor this hotel speaks of a different, more recent heritage. Push the boat out that little bit more and request deluxe room 214, whose balcony overlooks the interior patio.

Hotel Orologio (☎ 051 7 45 74 11; Via IV Novembre 10; s €135-300, d €155-320; Ⓟ 🏊 💻) Exquisitely furnished – not the least of its charms are the wrought-iron beds – the Orologio occupies a lovely old palazzo. Its eponymous clock, up in the tower, considerably doesn't strike during the night. Readers report a particularly satisfying breakfast.

Hotel Novecento (☎ 0517 45 73 11; Piazza Galileo 4/3; s €135-300, d €155-320; 🏊) Just as stylish and comfortable as the above options, this hotel replicates the best of 1930s design.

EATING

Red Bologna is also called La Grassa (The Fat), a term referring to the richness of the cuisine rather than the girth of its inhabitants, though the Bolognesi are indeed deadly serious about their food. Just look at the way all things edible, especially pasta, bread and cheeses, are displayed with such style in the shop windows.

EMILIA-ROMAGNA & SAN MARINO

The best pasta is *tirata a mano*, hand-stretched and rolled with a wooden pin, not a machine, and a good many Bolognesi restaurants still roll their own. It is cooked in many ways and eaten with a multitude of sauces. Spaghetti bolognese, that favourite student culinary standby, originated here – though the Bolognesi call the meat sauce *ragù* and prefer to mix it with tagliatelle. *Mortadella*, known sometimes as Bologna sausage or baloney, also hails from the area. The hills nearby produce the light, fizzy Lambrusco red and a full, dry Sauvignon.

If you're after economical eating, the university district northeast of Via Rizzoli is well endowed with reasonable restaurants and trattorie.

Restaurants

Bass' Otto (☎ 051 23 25 11; Via Ugo Bassi 8; meals about €15; ☒ Sun-Fri) Bass Eight styles itself as 'Ristorante Free Flow', an apt description of this busy self-service joint, particularly popular with lunch-time crowds.

Pizzeria Altero (☎ 051 22 66 12; Via Ugo Bassi 10; pizza slices €0.60-1.20; ☒ 8.30am-10pm Mon-Sat, noon-11pm Sun) This place is one of Bologna's best bets for tasty *pizza al taglio* (by the slice). Elbow your way through the throng that regularly crams into this tiny pizzeria for a stand-up snack or order takeaway at the fast-service window.

La Brace (☎ 051 23 56 56; Via San Vitale 15; pizzas €4-7.50, mains €7-18) Broken into intimate dining areas by wooden partitions this restaurant has youthful portraits of James Dean, Marlon Brando, Brigitte Bardot and Mick Jagger gazing down on you as though the years have never passed. The restaurant's strength, from antipasti through to mains, is emphatically fish with a particularly impressive range of starters; to sample a variety

---

AUTHOR'S CHOICE

Trattoria da Gianni (☎ 051 22 94 34; Via Clavature 18; mains €9-13.50; ☒ Tue-Sat & lunch Sun) Down a side alley, its walls bedecked with testimonials and press cuttings and its tables adorned with fresh flowers, da Gianni is well worth seeking out, especially for its homemade pasta. Twirl their *tagliatelle al ragù* around your fork or sip the *tortellini in brodo* (tortellini in broth).

---

go for their *antipasto di mare*, a selection from the sea.

Drogheria della Rosa (☎ 051 22 25 29; Via Cartoleria 10; meals about €35; ☒ Mon-Sat) Occupying a former pharmacy, Drogheria della Rosa's shelves are still stacked with apothecaries jars and bottles. It's an agreeably informal place (witness the case upon case of wine lining the stairs that descend to the subterranean toilets). There's no printed menu but the staff will happily run through the day's choices in English.

Tamburini (☎ 051 23 47 26; Via Caprarie 1; meals about €20; ☒ lunch Mon-Sat) Mainly a **delicatessen** (☒ 8.30am-7pm Mon-Sat), Tamburini has been in business for more than 70 years and sells some of Bologna's finest food products. The bistrot also offers a *very* classy version of the self-service genre, where dishes vary daily.

Trattoria da Danio (☎ 051 55 52 02; Via San Felice 50a; mains €4.50-11.50; ☒ daily) Almost 70 years in business, da Danio is full of locals who return time and again for delicious mains and pasta, including tortellini stuffed with pumpkin. The set menu at €11.50 is exceptional value.

Diana (☎ 051 23 13 02; Via dell'Indipendenza 24; mains €12-18; ☒ Tue-Sun) This is a stylish long hall of a place, with white-jacketed waiters and crystal chandeliers, offering fine cuisine. To take the pain out of ordering, go for their trolley of roast meats, freshly sliced at your table, then select from the tempting dessert trolley as it's wheeled by.

Gelaterie

La Sorbetteria Castiglione (Via Castiglione 44; ☒ Tue-Sun) This place makes truly world-beating ice cream (see the proudly displayed certificate for the Premio Speciale, the special award they received at the Concorso Internationale Gelatissimo 2003). You can see the ice cream being churned at the rear of the shop.

Gelateria delle Moline (Via delle Moline 13b; ☒ Wed-Mon) Primarily a student hangout, here you can have your ice cream slapped between focaccia or biscuits. Or just take it neat – and it doesn't come much neater…

Self-Catering

For the freshest fruit and vegetables in town, drop into the **Mercato delle Erbe** (Via Ugo Bassi 27; ☒ Mon-Sat), Bologna's main covered market.

The tight maze of streets, east of Piazza Maggiore, is rich in speciality food shops, including Tamburini (opposite), and has a daily **produce market** (Via Clavature 12).

DRINKING

Via del Pratello, just off Via Ugo Bassi, is a student haunt – understandably since it abounds in cheap bars, *birrerie* (pubs), *osterie* (traditionally, wine bars serving some food) and trattorie. If funds are running low, you can always join the swig-from-the-bottle student groups who throng Piazza Verdi on warm evenings.

Osteria del Sole (Vicolo Ranocchi 1d; ☺ 8am-2pm & 7.30-9pm Mon-Sat) First open for business in the 15th century this is the last place left in Bologna that maintains the centuries-old tradition of the *osteria* strictly as a watering hole. Hours, in principle as above, are erratic.

Osteria L'Infedele (☎ 0335 669 23 61; Via Gerusalemme 5a; snacks €5.15-6.50, glass of wine from €2.50; ☺ Tue-Sun) L'Infedele is a cosy place to hang out with a glass of wine or for a light meal; the friendly staff and excellent background jazz are bonuses.

Rosa Rose (☎ 051 22 50 71; Via Clavature 18) This place, near Trattoria da Gianni, quite simply buzzes. It's pleasant for a cocktail or coffee, *panino* (bread rolls with simple fillings) or pasta – if you can fight your way to a table amid the throngs of regulars.

Café le Palais (☎ 051 6 48 69 63; Via de' Musei 40e) Just off Piazza Maggiore, here you can join Bologna's beautiful people for a glass of wine (from €3.50) in the plush, mirrored interior or on the terrace beneath the broad colonnade.

Cantina Bentivoglio (☎ 051 26 54 16; www.cantina bentivoglio.it; Via Mascarella 4b; ☺ 8pm-2am) Call it a wine bar (this bottle-lined cellar has more than 500 labels to choose from), restaurant (a good meal will set you back about €25, not including wine) or jazz club (there's live music nightly), snug Cantina Bentivoglio makes for a great night out.

Bravo Caffè (☎ 051 26 61 12; Via Mascarella 1; mains €9-11; ☺ from 7pm Mon-Sat) Bravo Caffè, with warm red lighting, good wine and cool background music, is another smart place for a drink or snack. It too features regular live jazz from Monday to Thursday.

Marsalino (☎ 051 23 86 75; Via Marsala 13d) Tiny, arty and chameleonlike Marsalino is a tearoom from 4pm, metamorphoses into a cocktail/wine bar from 6pm, then, at 8pm, becomes a modest restaurant.

Le Stanze (☎ 051 22 87 67; Via Borgo San Pietro 1) This place pulls in a cool, trendy, young clientele. The frescoed walls and ceiling of this former chapel of a patrician's palazzo, friendly staff and good music, sometimes live, give Le Stanze an agreeable ambience – although the drinks and surroundings are more appealing than the food.

Café de Paris (☎ 051 23 49 80; Piazza Minghetti; ☺ 8am-3am Mon-Sat, 10am-3am Sun) One of the 'in'-est of Bologna's many 'in' places. It has a small terrace, shielded from the street, a reasonable selection of draught beers and mixes some mean cocktails.

ENTERTAINMENT

A Guest of Bologna, available from tourist offices and some hotels, is a useful bimonthly guide to what's on, as is the monthly information sheet in Italian *Invito in Provincia*, especially for the cultural scene. Both are free. The monthly **2night Magazine** (www.2night .it in Italian) has more information about clubbing and live music. *Bonews* (€2.50), available from newsstands, is the most comprehensive guide.

Cinemas

Cinema Lumière (☎ 051 2 19 53 11; www.cinetecadi bologna.it; Via Azzo Gardino 65; admission €6) Just to the northwest of the city centre Cinema Lumière is an excellent two-screen public-sector cinema, run by the municipality, that shows arthouse films in their original version.

Cinema Odeon (☎ 051 22 79 16; Via Mascarella 3; admission €5) and **Cinema Capital** (☎ 051 24 10 02; Via Milazzo 1; admission €5) screen films in English on Thursday and Tuesday, respectively. The day may vary, so do phone ahead to check. Both normally close in summer, when filmgoers flock to the city's outdoor cinemas.

Nightclubs

Bologna has one of Italy's liveliest night scenes, bolstered by its active student population. Cantina Bentivoglio (left) is one of the best jazz venues in town. The other, **Chet Baker Jazz Club** (☎ 051 22 37 95; www.chetbaker .it in Italian; Via Polese 7a; ☺ Mon-Sat), has live music Tuesday to Saturday from 10pm.

Corto Maltese (☎ 051 22 97 46; Via Borgo San Pietro 9/2a; ☺ 9pm-3am) A stylish, popular disco/bar with nightly DJs who mix funk, rhythm and blues. Monday is Erasmus night – a weekly night which several bars offer to draw in

EMILIA-ROMAGNA & SAN MARINO

Erasmus students, usually with cut-price drinks and other student-friendly activities.

Kinki (☎ 051 5 87 51 78; Via Zamboni 1a; admission about €15; ☷ Thu-Sat) A longtime favourite disco, welcoming to lesbians and gays, where house music prevails.

Villa Serena (☎ 051 6 15 67 89; Via della Barca 1; admission free; ☷ 9pm-3am Thu-Sat) West of the city centre, offering three floors of film screenings and music, live and canned. A comfortable garden provides relaxed outdoor chilling areas.

Theatre & Opera
Bologna has an active cultural scene year-round. **Teatro Comunale** (☎ 051 52 99 99; Piazza Verdi), where Wagner's works were heard for the first time in Italy, is Bologna's main venue for opera and concerts. **Arena del Sole** (☎ 051 27 07 90; Via dell'Indipendenza 44) puts on mainly modern classics while **Teatro Duse** (☎ 051 23 18 36; Via Cartoleria 42) has a varied programme of classical and contemporary theatre.

SHOPPING
Bologna's main shopping streets are Via Ugo Bassi, Via Rizzoli, Via Marconi, Via dell'Indipendenza, Via Massimo d'Azeglio, Via Farini and Via San Felice. You can safely leave your wallet behind on Thursday afternoons, when all shops are shut.

On Friday and Saturday there's a flea and antique market at the Parco della Montagnola that seeps into Piazza del Otto Agosto.

GETTING THERE & AWAY
Air
International destinations from Bologna's **Guglielmo Marconi airport** (BLQ; ☎ 051 647 96 15; www.bologna-airport.it), about 6km northwest of the city at Borgo Panigale, include London Gatwick (British Airways, three daily); London Stansted (EasyJet, one daily); Paris (Alitalia and Air France, five daily); Frankfurt (Lufthansa and British Midland, four daily); and Amsterdam (KLM, three daily).

Ryanair flies twice daily between London Stansted and **Forlì** (☎ 0543 47 49 21; www.forli-airport.it), 70km southeast of Bologna. **Buses** (www.e-bus.it; tickets €10) run to/from Bologna's bus station to coincide with flights.

Bus
Buses for Ferrara (€3.30, one hour, hourly) leave from the **bus station** (☎ 051 29 02 90) off

Piazza XX Settembre, just east of the train station. For most other regional destinations, the train's a better option.

Car & Motorcycle
The city is linked to Milan, Florence and Rome by the A1 Autostrada del Sole. The A13 heads directly to Ferrara, Padua and Venice, and the A14 to Rimini and Ravenna. Bologna is also on the Via Emilia (S9), which connects Milan to the Adriatic coast. The S64 goes to Ferrara.

Most major car-hire companies are represented both at the airport and in town. City offices include **Europcar** (☎ 051 24 71 01; Via G Amendola 12f) and **Hertz** (☎ 051 25 48 30; Via G Amendola 16a).

Train
The train station is at the northern end of the city. A journey anywhere within 100km of Bologna costs a maximum of €3.60. There are regular trains to Ravenna (€4.70) and Ferrara (€2.90).

Bologna is a major transport junction for northern Italy and has several daily services to Florence (€7.75), Rome (€28.45) and Milan (€22.75).

GETTING AROUND
Aerobus (€4.50) connects the city with the airport. It leaves from the main train station every 15 minutes from 5.30am to 11.10pm.

Bologna has a commendably efficient bus system, run by **ATC** (☎ 051 29 02 90; www.atc.bo.it). It has information booths at the main train station and on Via Marconi. Buses No 30 and 21 are among several that connect the main train station with the city centre.

Much of the city centre is off-limits to traffic – and is all the more visitor-friendly for it. If you're staying in the heart of town, your hotel can provide a permit (per day €7) which entitles you to 24 hours' parking within the *cordon sanitaire* (official no-car boundary).

Should you be footsore, the best way to get around the centre is by bike. You can hire one at the train station from **Senzauto** (☎ 051 25 14 01; 12/24hr €6/9; ☷ 7-11am & noon-8pm Mon-Fri), down the ramp at the far end of the vast cycle park just east of the station.

To book a taxi, phone ☎ 051 37 27 27 or ☎ 051 53 41 41.

WEST OF BOLOGNA

MODENA
pop 177,000

Modena – whose Piazza Grande, cathedral and tower are all classified as Unesco World Heritage sites – is the birthplace of Luciano Pavarotti, Italy's favourite tenor. Nearby are car manufacturers Ferrari, Maserati and De Tomaso, who all do their bit to make this town one of the most affluent cities in the country.

Some 40km northwest of Bologna, Modena was one of a series of Roman garrison towns established along the Via Emilia in the 2nd century BC.

It was an obscure little place until it became a free city in the 12th century and then passed to the Este family late in the following century. Prosperity came when it was chosen to be the capital of a much-reduced Este duchy in 1598, after the family lost Ferrara to the Papal States. Apart from a brief Napoleonic interlude, the Este family ran the town until Italian unification in the 19th century.

Orientation

Via Emilia is Modena's main drag. The street slices through the centre of town from west to east. Flanking it to the south and north are Piazza Grande and Piazza Mazzini, the town's principal squares.

EMILIA-ROMAGNA & SAN MARINO

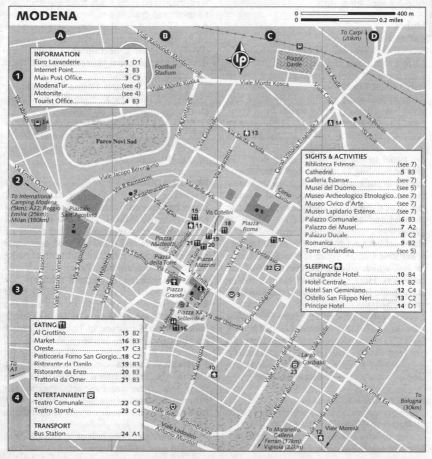

MODENA

INFORMATION
Euro Lavanderie..................1 D1
Internet Point......................2 B3
Main Post Office.................3 C3
ModenaTur.......................(see 4)
Motorsite........................(see 4)
Tourist Office.....................4 B3

SIGHTS & ACTIVITIES
Biblioteca Estense...............(see 7)
Cathedral...........................5 B3
Galleria Estense.................(see 7)
Musei del Duomo..............(see 7)
Museo Archeologico Etnologico...(see 7)
Museo Civico d'Arte..........(see 7)
Museo Lapidario Estense......(see 7)
Palazzo Comunale..............6 B3
Palazzo dei Musei..............7 A2
Palazzo Ducale...................8 C2
Romanica............................9 B2
Torre Ghirlandina..............(see 5)

SLEEPING
Canalgrande Hotel.............10 B4
Hotel Centrale....................11 B2
Hotel San Geminiano.........12 C4
Ostello San Filippo Neri.....13 C2
Principe Hotel.....................14 D1

EATING
Al Grottino.........................15 B2
Market................................16 B3
Oreste................................17 C3
Pasticceria Forno San Giorgio...18 C2
Ristorante da Danilo...........19 B3
Ristorante da Enzo.............20 B3
Trattoria da Omer...............21 B3

ENTERTAINMENT
Teatro Comunale...............22 C3
Teatro Storchi....................23 C4

TRANSPORT
Bus Station........................24 A1

Information
Euro Lavanderie (31 Via Piave; ☒ 8am-10pm)
Internet point (☎ 059 21 20 96; Piazza Grande 34;
per hr €4; ☒ 10am-8pm)
Main post office (Via Emilia 86)
ModenaTur (☎ 059 22 00 22; www.modenatur.net; Via
Scudari 8-10; ☒ 9am-1pm & 3-6.30pm) Beside the tourist
office, ModenaTur can turn its hand to most things –
booking accommodation without a fee, buying opera
tickets, or arranging a visit to a balsamic vinegar producer,
private collection of vintage racing cars or a *parmigiano
reggiano* dairy.
Tourist office (☎ 059 20 66 60; www.comune.modena
.it – click on *turista*; Via Scudari 12; ☒ 3-6pm Mon,
9.30am-12.30pm & 3-6pm Tue-Sat, 9.30am-12.30pm Sun)
Carries a guide for disabled visitors, *Muoversi nella Città di
Modena* – it's in Italian but with clear symbols indicating
wheelchair access to main sights.

Sights
CATHEDRAL
Started in 1099 and dedicated to Modena's
patron saint, San Geminiano, this **cathedral**
(Piazza Grande; ☒ 7am-12.30pm & 3.30-7pm) is one of
Italy's finest Romanesque places of worship.
Around the façade are engagingly naive and
vivid bas-reliefs depicting scenes from Genesis. They're the work of the 12th-century
sculptor Wiligelmo who – a rare practice
in those times – autographed his work (see
the panel to the left of the main door), as
did the building's architect, Lanfranco (signing off in the main apse). Among the many
vigorous carvings, both sacred and secular,
are typical medieval themes depicting the
months and agricultural scenes. Much of
Wiligelmo's work has been removed to the
Musei del Duomo (☎ 059 4 39 69 69; Via Lanfranco
6; adult/child €3/2; ☒ 9.30am-12.30pm & 3.30-6.30pm
Tue-Sun), which adjoins the north side of the
cathedral. Here, you can hire an excellent
audioguide (€1) covering both the museum
and cathedral.

The early 13th-century **Torre Ghirlandina**
(admission €1; ☒ 9.30am-12.30pm & 3-7pm Sun Apr-Jul &
Sep-Oct) – another degree or two and it would
out lean Pisa's – rises to 87m, culminating
in a slender Gothic spire. Facing it is the
elegant façade of the **Palazzo Comunale**.

PALAZZO DEI MUSEI
There are several galleries within the **Palazzo
dei Musei** (☎ 059 20 01 25; Piazzale Sant'Agostino).

The **Galleria Estense** (admission €4; ☒ 8.30am-
7.30pm Tue-Sun) features most of the Este family

collection: a rich, well-displayed diachronic
collection of the main schools of northern
Italy from late medieval times to the 18th
century. There are also some fine Flemish
works and a canvas or two by Velázquez,
Correggio and El Greco for good measure.

The **Biblioteca Estense** (admission €2.60; ☒ 9am-
1pm Mon-Sat), essentially a research library, has
one of Italy's most valuable collections of
books, letters and manuscripts including the
Bible of Borso d'Este, its 1200 pages vividly
illustrated by Ferrarese artists.

A combined ticket (€4) gives you entry to
the **Museo Archeologico Etnologico** (☒ 9am-noon
Tue-Sat, 3-6pm Tue & Sat, 10am-1pm & 3-6pm Sun) and
the **Museo Civico d'Arte** (☒ 9am-noon Tue-Sat, 3-6pm
Tue & Sat, 10am-1pm & 3-6pm Sun). In addition to
well-displayed local finds from Palaeolithic
to medieval eras, the museum has exhibits
from Africa, Asia, Peru and New Guinea.
Most interesting among the Museo Civico
d'Arte's eclectic collection are the sections
devoted to traditional paper making, textiles
and musical instruments.

The **Museo Lapidario Estense** (admission free;
☒ 8am-7pm) displays Roman and medieval
stonework, including sarcophagi.

A *biglietto cumulativo* (combined ticket,
€6) gives entry to most galleries and museums within the Palazzo dei Musei and also
to the Musei del Duomo.

PALAZZO DUCALE
Started in 1634 for the Este family, this
heavy baroque edifice is now Modena's military academy, located on Piazza Roma. Its
scrubbed, fresh-faced, heel-clicking cadets in
their trim hats and multicoloured uniforms
look as if they've marched right off a Quality Street chocolate box. Fancy dress apart,
they're considered Italy's crack soldiers.

Courses
Romanica (☎ 059 24 56 51; www.romanica.it; Via Castel-
maraldo 45) runs courses in Italian language
and culture for non-native speakers.

Festivals & Events
During the **Serate Estensi** in late June and
early July, there are banquets, jousts and
other early Renaissance fun as the good folk
of Modena don period costume and let their
hair down.

Modena celebrates balsamic vinegar, the
nectar it gave to the world, with **Balsamico È**, a

series of exhibitions, events and tastings from mid-May to early June.

Sleeping

Ostello San Filippo Neri (☎ 059 23 45 98; hostelmod ena@hotmail.com; Via Santa Orsola 48-52; dm/d €14.50/32; 🖳) Modena's hostel is conveniently central and HI-affiliated.

International Camping Modena (☎ 059 33 22 52; www.internationalcamping.org; Via Cave di Ramo 111, Bruciata; person/site €6/11; ⊗ year-round) A well-endowed camping ground, 5km west of the city in Bruciata. Take bus No 19.

Hotel San Geminiano (☎ 059 21 03 03; previ dan@tiscali.net; Viale Moreali 41; d €58, s/d with bathroom €47/78; P 🖳) Southeast of the city centre and recently renovated, this hotel is an easy 15-minute stroll from Piazza Grande. Run by a young couple, it's child-friendly and offers free parking. Readers recommend the separately run restaurant below. All prices include breakfast.

Principe Hotel (☎ 059 21 86 70; www.hotelprincipe .mo.it in Italian; Corso Vittorio Emanuele II 94; s/d/tr with breakfast €70/102/125; 🔀 🖳) This makes an excellent midrange choice. Rooms are large and comfortable though you may prefer to stuff the bouquet of plastic flowers under the bed. Weekend rates are a particular snip.

Hotel Centrale (☎ 059 21 88 08; www.hotelcentrale .com; Via Rismondo 55; s/d €40/80, s/d/tr with bathroom €80/130/175; P 🔀) In the very heart of town,

Centrale is a welcoming hotel that offers comfortable if somewhat pricey rooms (parking is an extra €10). The bedroom wallpaper is a little gloomy and the prints of Dionysian romps may not be to everyone's taste…

Canalgrande Hotel (☎ 059 21 71 60; www.canal grandehotel.it; Corso Canalgrande 6; s/d/tr with breakfast €120/172/205; P 🔀 🖳) This remains a venerable Modenese institution despite its rather dowdy exterior. It's a cosy place to stay with antique furniture, frescoes overhead, stucco in plenty and a leafy, tranquil terrace leading into a garden at the rear. Parking is €10.50 and there's wi-fi.

Eating & Drinking

Like Bologna and Parma, Modena produces an excellent *prosciutto crudo* (cured ham). The city's gastronomic speciality is *zampone* (stuffed pig's trotter), something of an acquired taste that's well worth the effort. Modena also brews the bulk of Italy's prized balsamic vinegar, a rich aromatic condiment. Tortellini is another speciality, as is Lambrusco, a lively, sparkling, too often underestimated red, to be drunk chilled and with everything.

You'll find a selection of the city's better bars on and around Via Emilia, near the cathedral.

Oreste (☎ 059 24 33 24; Piazza Roma 31; mains €10-15; ⊗ closed Sun dinner & Wed) This place has

---

A TASTE WORTH WAITING FOR

Real *aceto balsamico* from Modena is a rare and beautiful thing. Commercial balsamic vinegar, as sold around the world, bears little relation to its upmarket cousin. Balsamic vinegar is made by boiling up vats of must (unfermented grape juice) from Trebbiano (white) and Lambrusco (red) vines grown in a closely defined area around Modena. The must is filtered, placed in a large oak barrel, then over many years decanted and transferred into smaller barrels made of different woods that are stored in farmhouse lofts. The summer temperature in these lofts can reach 50°C, so much of the must evaporates (after 25 years, 100kg of must will have rendered down to 1kg) and the remainder becomes ever darker and stickier.

Aceto balsamico tradizionale di Modena is aged for at least 12 years, and *aceto balsamico tradizionale di Modena extravecchio* for at least 25. Compared with other vinegars, it's sweet and dense, complex and lingering. The older the vinegar, the thicker and more intensely flavoured it becomes.

Balsamic vinegar remains very much a cottage industry, monitored tightly by a consortium that maintains quality, does all the bottling and controls the quantity that is produced.

Don't waste it in a salad. Drip a couple of drops onto a sliver of Parmesan cheese or a fresh strawberry. The extra flavour the merest dribble imparts to vanilla ice cream is enough to make you squirm.

ModenaTur (see opposite) can arrange a free visit to a local producer – English-speaking if you're lucky.

tradition, charm and superb cuisine. The current owner's father, knocking 90 years old, still potters around while his son gives a detailed and impassioned breakdown of the dishes of the day. Light floods in through the large windows though the décor rather reflects the era when dad was in his prime.

Al Grottino (☎ 059 22 39 85; Via Taglio 26; pizzas €5.50-8, mains €6.50-18; ☻ Thu-Tue) This is a popular pizza joint and restaurant where you can eat cheap or go for something more subtle. The tables are cleared, reset and reoccupied in the wink of an eye under the benign, watchful gaze of the paunchy owner. It also does takeaways.

Trattoria da Omer (☎ 059 21 80 50; Via Torre 33; pastas & mains €7.50; ☻ Mon-Sat) A friendly family trattoria serving wonderful Modenese and Ferrarese traditional pasta and mains. Just try the *tortellini fiocchi di neve* (snowflakes), which really do melt in the mouth.

Ristorante da Enzo (☎ 059 22 51 77; Via Coltellini 17; meals €20-30; ☻ Mon-Sat) You're greeted with skeins of delicious fresh, homemade pasta as you enter this restaurant. Long-established and highly regarded, its other speciality is dishes featuring balsamic vinegar such as

the *scaloppina all'aceto balsamico* (€8.25). The more adventurous might like to gnaw on another local and house speciality, *zampone di Modena con fagiolini* (pigs' trotters with beans).

Ristorante da Danilo (☎ 059 22 54 98; Via Coltellini 31; pastas €6.50, mains €13-15; ☻ Mon-Sat) Just up the street from da Enzo, this place is equally impressive. Try the *pappardelle con lepre* (wide ribbon pasta with hare) – and, no, 'Waiter, there's a hare in my pasta' jokes don't go down well. What does slip down quite delightfully is the house carafe red, the local Sangiovese. Fragrant and the colour of garnets, it enhances anything meaty. Save a cranny for the delicious homemade desserts.

Pasticceria Forno San Giorgio (☎ 059 22 35 14; Via Taglio 6; ☻ Tue-Sun) This place has been satisfying the sweet tooths of Modena with its cakes and pastries for well over a century. It's a great spot for coffee and cake or a snack.

Modena has a good fresh-produce **market** (☻ Mon-Sat), which has its main entrance on Via Albinelli.

Entertainment

During July and August, the Piazza Grande makes a great venue for outdoor concerts and ballet.

Teatro Comunale (☎ 059 20 69 93; Corso Canalgrande 85) is where most opera performances take place and **Teatro Storchi** (☎ 059 20 69 93; Largo Garibaldi 15) offers mainly drama.

Shopping

On the fourth Saturday and Sunday of every month, except for July and December, a giant antiques fair is held in Parco Novi Sad.

Getting There & Around

The **bus station** (☎ 059 22 22 20) is on Via Fabriani. **ATCM** (☎ 059 41 67 11; www.atcm.mo.it in Italian) and other companies connect Modena with most towns in the region.

The train station is at the north end of the action area, fronting Piazza Dante. Train destinations include Bologna (€2.50, 30 minutes), Parma (€3.25, 30 minutes) and Milan (€14.80, two hours).

The city is at the junction of the A1 Autostrada del Sole, connecting Rome with Milan, and the A22, which heads north to Mantua, Verona and the Brenner pass.

VRRM, VRRM

Sleek, purring, sexy and infinitely stylish, so many of the racers and luxury sports cars that turn heads around the world – Lamborghini, Maserati, De Tomaso, and Ferrari with its prancing black horse logo – are assembled around Ferrara and Modena.

On Sundays during April and May, a selection of the very latest models give a sassy feel to the sober confines of Modena's Piazza Grande. More venerable models get an extended outing during May's **Mille Miglia** (www.millemiglia.it), a vintage car race that roars through the streets of Ferrara and Modena, then onto the chequered flag in Brescia. May also sees the Modena Cento Ore (100 Hours) Classic, a four-day event for historic cars that starts and finishes in Modena.

Galleria Ferrari (opposite) is open daily. You can also visit the Ferrari factory, those of other legendary names and vintage car museums by appointment. Call **Motorsite** (☎ 059 21 82 64; www.motorsite.it; Via Scudari 10) in Modena for more information.

ATCM's bus No 7 links the train station with the bus station and city centre.

At the train station and other venues, you can hire a bike (6.30am to 8pm Monday to Friday) for a very reasonable €0.60 per hour (and an even more reasonable €0.30 for the third hour and beyond) or, if you don't fancy a little pedal-pushing, an electric bicycle at €1.30 per hour.

For a taxi, call ☎ 059 37 42 42.

AROUND MODENA
Galleria Ferrari

The legendary Enzo Ferrari died in 1988 but his factory in **Maranello**, 17km south of Modena, continues to turn out world-beating racing and sports cars that we mere-mortal motorists can only dream of. **Galleria Ferrari** (☎ 0536 94 32 04; Via Dino Ferrari 43; adult/child €12/9; ☼ 9am-7pm May-Sep, 9am-6pm Oct-Apr) is essentially the company's museum and historical archive. It has the largest collection of Ferraris on show in the world, has a couple of simulators and sells a host of memorabilia to satisfy the most avid Ferrari fan.

Carpi
pop 62,600

Once the centre of the Pio family territories, old Carpi is agreeably constructed in the characteristic local red brick. A mere 20km north of Modena, it's easily reached by train.

Its sights come on a gargantuan scale. The massive **Palazzo Pio**, externally elegant yet run down within, stretches the eastern length of one of Italy's biggest squares, Piazza dei Martiri. To its south is a little jewel of a 19th-century theatre but you'll be lucky to find it open. A rank of porticos runs along the piazza's western flank, while the salmon pink and gleaming white façade of the 16th-century **cathedral** sits benignly over its northern end. Just behind and east of Palazzo Pio, a huge brick tower overwhelms the remaining elements of the tiny **Chiesa di Santa Maria del Castello** (Piazzale Re Astolfo). Pop in to enjoy its carved marble pulpit and 15th-century frescoes – again, if you find the church open.

REGGIO EMILIA
pop 144,300

Also known as Reggio nell'Emilia, the town started life in the 2nd century BC as a Roman colony along the Via Emilia, which

still slices through it. Much of Reggio was built by the Este family during the 400 years it controlled the town, beginning in 1406.

The cheese we know in English as Parmesan ('of Parma'), is called more accurately in Italian *parmigiano reggiano*, reflecting the fact that production straddles both provinces.

Reggio's churches and museums are really only for ardent ecclesiastical and archaeological buffs. All the same, it has a pleasant-enough centre and the town is a practical base for exploring the Apennines to the south.

Information
Post office (Via Sessi 3)

Qui Qua (☎ 0522 40 61 72; Piazza Fontanesi 4a/b; per hr €6; ☼ 9am-7.30pm Mon- Sat)

Telecom office (Galleria San Rocco 8f) On the south side of Piazza della Vittoria.

Tourist office (☎ 0522 45 11 52; www.municipio.re.it /turismo; Piazza Camillo Prampolini 5c; ☼ 8.30am-1pm & 2.30-6pm Mon-Sat, 9am-noon Sun Sep-Jul, 8.30am-1.30pm Mon-Sat Aug) On the main square.

Sights
The city's few sights are concentrated around Piazza del Monte (formerly Piazza Cesare Battisti), Piazza Camillo Prampolini and also Piazza San Prospero.

CHURCHES
Reggio's **cathedral** (Piazza Camillo Prampolini; ☼ 8am-12.30pm & 4-7.30pm) is wedged between the latter two piazze. Built in the 13th century in the Romanesque style, it was almost completely remodelled 300 years later.

The clean-lined façade of the 15th-century **Chiesa di San Prospero** (☼ 8am-12.30pm & 4-7.30pm), on the piazza of the same name, is guarded by a royal pair of red marble lions and their four cubs. Its striking octagonal bell tower was built in 1537.

The baroque **Basilica della Ghiara** (Corso Garibaldi 44; ☼ 10am-noon & 4-5.30pm Mon-Sat, 3.30-5.30pm Sun) has frescoes by 17th-century Emilian artists that merit more than a glance.

PALAZZO DEL MUNICIPIO
Within the 14th-century **town hall**, on the south side of Piazza Camillo Prampolini, is the **Sala del Tricolore**, the room where the Italian flag was devised during a conference which established Napoleon's short-lived Cispadane Republic in 1797.

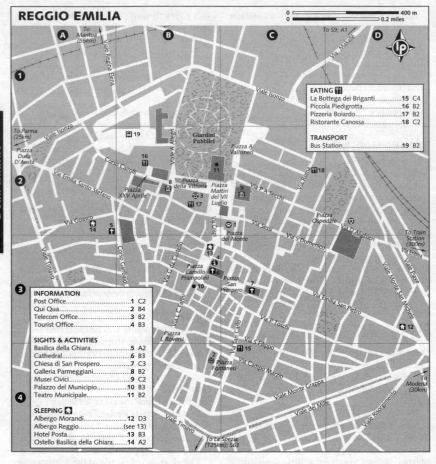

REGGIO EMILIA

EATING
La Bottega dei Briganti..............15 C4
Piccola Piedigrotta....................16 B2
Pizzeria Boiardo.........................17 B2
Ristorante Canossa....................18 C2

TRANSPORT
Bus Station................................19 B2

INFORMATION
Post Office...................................1 C2
Qui Qua.......................................2 B4
Telecom Office.............................3 B2
Tourist Office...............................4 B3

SIGHTS & ACTIVITIES
Basilica della Ghiara......................5 A2
Cathedral.....................................6 B3
Chiesa di San Prospero..................7 C3
Galleria Parmeggiani.....................8 B2
Musei Civici..................................9 C2
Palazzo del Municipio..................10 B3
Teatro Municipale.......................11 B2

SLEEPING
Albergo Morandi........................12 D3
Albergo Reggio......................(see 13)
Hotel Posta................................13 B3
Ostello Basilica della Ghiara.......14 A2

TEATRO MUNICIPALE
On the north side of Piazza Martiri del VII
Luglio, this imposing building with a bevy of
muses and goddesses teetering on the edge of
its roof could almost be a royal palace. Built
in 1857 as an opera house, it is now used for
dance, opera and theatre performances.

MUSEUMS
The **Musei Civici** (☎ 0522 45 64 77; Via PA Secchi 2;
admission free; ☺ 9am-noon Mon-Fri, 9am-noon & 3-7pm
Sat, 10am-1pm & 3-7pm Sun) houses a collection of
mainly 18th-century artworks and archaeological discoveries. **Galleria Parmeggiani** (☎ 0522
45 10 54; Corso Cairoli 2; admission free; ☺ 9am-noon Tue-Fri,
9am-noon & 3-7pm Sat & Sun) has some worthwhile
Italian, Flemish and Spanish pieces, which
includes an El Greco, plus a heterogeneous
collection of costumes and armoury.

Sleeping
Hotel Posta (☎ 0522 43 29 44; www.hotelposta.re.it; Piazza del Monte 2; s/d with breakfast €135/180; P ✕ ▯)
This place makes a superb top-end choice.
Once the residence of the Este family, and
later the Palazzo del Capitano del Populo
(governor's residence), this venerable inn
has been accommodating travellers for almost five centuries. Each of the 39 rooms
is individually decorated; ask for one overlooking Piazza Camillo Prampolini. Parking
is €12. Rooms at **Albergo Reggio** (www.albergoreg
gio.it; s/d €75/95) the Posta's attractive 16-room
annexe 50m away, have cooking facilities.

EMILIA-ROMAGNA
& SAN MARINO

Albergo Morandi (☎ 0522 45 43 97; www.albergo morandi.com in Italian; Via Emilia San Pietro 64; s/d/tr with breakfast €67/100/126; P ✿) A friendly, family-run three-star hotel, handy for the train station. You'll need to make a reservation except in July and August, when everyone's at the coast.

Ostello Basilica della Ghiara (☎ 0522 45 23 23; fax 0522 45 47 95; Via Guasco 6; dm/d with breakfast €14/32) Reggio's conveniently central, HI-affiliated and fairly disorganised hostel occupies an ex-monastery.

Eating

There's a market, including fruit and veg, each Tuesday and Friday on Reggio's central squares. Typical local snacks include *erbazzone* (herb pie with cheese or bacon) and *gnocco fritto* (fried salted dough), the best is as light as air.

Ristorante Canossa (☎ 0522 45 41 96; Via Roma 37; meals €30-35; ☺ Thu-Tue Aug-Jun) Ristorante Canossa, where the pasta is homemade, is one of few places in town serving excellent Reggiano cuisine. Dither between the *tortelli di zucca* (pumpkin tortelli) or *tortelli d'erba alla reggiana* (tortelli with local herbs).

La Bottega dei Briganti (☎ 0522 43 66 43; Via San Carlo 14b; pastas €6.70, mains €9.50-13.25; ☺ Mon-Sat) This *birreria/osteria* has a wonderful conspiratorial atmosphere and a small leafy courtyard. It serves up excellent pasta and risotto dishes.

Pizzeria Boiardo (☎ 0522 45 42 35; Galleria Cavour 3f; pizzas €4.30-7.75; ☺ Thu-Tue) In a covered gallery just south of Piazza della Vittoria, Boiardo offers both pizza and straightforward meals. The wood-fired oven also burns at lunch time.

Piccola Piedigrotta (☎ 0522 43 49 22; Piazza XXV Aprile 1b; pizzas €3.60-5.50, pastas from €5.50; ☺ Tue-Sun) A small pizzeria/trattoria that makes tasty pizzas and simple pasta dishes in an informal setting. It also does takeaways.

Getting There & Around

Bus operator **ACT** (☎ 0522 43 16 67; www.actre.it in Italian) serves the city and region from the bus station in Viale A Allegri. Destinations include Carpi (€3.30, one hour, 10 daily) and Castelnovo ne' Monti (€4, 1¼ hours, at least 12 daily).

The train station is east of the town centre. Frequent trains serve all stops on the Milan–Bologna line including Milan (€13.10, 1½

hours), Parma (€1.95, 15 minutes), Modena (€1.95, 15 minutes) and Bologna (€5.80, 45 minutes).

Reggio Emilia is on the Via Emilia (S9) and A1 autostrade. The S63 is a tortuous but scenic route that takes you southwest across the Parma Apennines to La Spezia on the Ligurian coast.

For a taxi, call ☎ 0522 45 25 45.

AROUND REGGIO EMILIA

Southwest of the city along the scenic S63 are the Apennines and the Parco del Gigante, part of the **Parco Nazionale dell'Appennino Tosco-Emiliano** (www.appenninoreggiano.it). Among several signed walking trails, well served by *rifugi* (mountain huts), the most extensive is the Matilda Way, a four- to seven-day trek from Ciano, in the Enza valley near Canossa, to San Pellegrino in Alpe, just over the border in Tuscany.

The tourist office at **Castelnovo ne' Monti** (☎ 0522 81 04 30; www.reappennino.it; Via Roma 33c; ☺ 9am-1pm Mon-Sat year-round, 3-6pm Mon, Wed, Fri Mar-Oct) has bags of information about open-air activities and sells *Parco del Gigante*, a handy map of the area at 1:25,000 with trails indicated, and *Ciclopista Ippovia del Gigante*, a good guide for cyclists. For a more gentle outing, ascend or walk around the **Pietra di Bismantova** (1047m), a huge limestone outcrop 2.5km from town and a popular venue for climbers.

A pair of medieval castles once owned by Matilda, countess of Canossa, merit a detour, as much for their views as for their architectural interest. The castle of **Canossa** (☎ 0522 87 71 04; Via del Castello; admission free; ☺ 9am-12.30pm & 3-7pm Tue-Sun Apr-Oct, 9am-4.30pm Tue-Sun Nov-Mar) built in 940 and then rebuilt in the 13th century, is where Matilda famously reconciled the excommunicated Holy Roman Emperor Henry IV with Pope Gregory VII in 1077. May your visit be more pleasant than that of poor Henry who, as legend has it, stood outside, barefoot in the snow, for three days as penance for having insulted His Holiness. Largely ruined, the castle has a small museum.

From Canossa you can see across to the castle of **Rossena** (☎ 0522 51 15 76; admission by guided tour €4.50; ☺ 3-7pm Sat, 11am-7pm Sun Mar-Oct, 2.30-5.30pm Sun Nov-Feb), better preserved but less accessible. By road 4.5km away, it's much nearer as the crow flies.

For a good base to explore the Po valley area north of Reggio Emilia, settle on **Guastalla**, where there's a 25-bed HI-affiliated youth hostel, **Ostello Quadrio Michelotti** (☎ 0522 83 92 28; lunetia@tin.it; Via Lido Po 11/13; B&B €12.50; ☺ Apr–mid-Oct). Both trains and buses run here from Reggio Emilia.

PORRETTA

The tiny thermal-spring town of Porretta Terme, known simply as Porretta, lies about 50km southwest of Bologna in the Apennines. Traditionally a sleepy resort for people wanting to take advantage of the therapeutic mineral waters, the town has in recent years become a draw for soul-music lovers from across Europe. Each year over three nights in July, the town hosts the **Porretta Soul Festival** (www.porrettasoul.it), a tribute to Otis Redding and a celebration of the popular Memphis sound.

Porretta's **tourist office** (☎ 0534 2 20 21; ☺ 8.30am-2.30pm Mon-Sat) is on Piazza Libertà.

Hotel Santoli (☎ 053 42 32 06; www.hotelsantoli .com; Via Roma 3; s/d €77/120) is a comfortable four-star, family-run hotel that's particularly green, with both a roof garden and a secluded garden at ground level. Il Bassotto, the hotel restaurant, serves up a variety of imaginative dishes.

Trattoria Toscana (☎ 053 42 22 08; Piazza della Libertà 7; s/d with bathroom €30/43, meals from €15; ☺ Tue-Sun) is another good place to sample Emilian cuisine, and Tuscan, too. It also rents rooms.

Trains run to Porretta from Bologna and Florence.

PARMA

pop 165,000

Of the Emilian cities west of Bologna, Parma is the pick of the crop. Straddling the banks of Torrente Parma, a tributary of the Po, it's a well-off, orderly city. Bicycles rule in the squares and cobbled lanes of the old town centre and the surrounding countryside is home not only to *parmigiano reggiano* and Parma ham (Italy's best prosciutto), but also to the massive Barilla pasta factory, a scattering of castles and a few threading walking tracks. No doubt inspired by such plenty, Verdi composed many of his greatest works here and Stendhal immortalised the city in his classic French novel, *La Chartreuse de Parme.*

History

Originally Etruscan, Parma achieved importance as a Roman colony astride what would become the Via Emilia. As Roman authority dwindled, the town passed onto the Goths, then the Lombards and then the Franks.

In the 11th century Parma threw in its lot with the Holy Roman Empire against the papacy and even furnished two antipopes. In the following centuries internal squabbling largely determined the city's turbulent fate, as it fell successively to the Visconti family, the Sforzas, the French and finally – sweet revenge – the papacy.

The Farnese family ruled Parma in the pope's name from 1545 to 1731, when the Bourbons took control, making Parma one of the pawns in Europe's power games. Don Philip of Bourbon, son of Spain's Philip V, and his wife, Louise Elisabeth, daughter of France's Louis XV, ushered in a period of peace and frenetic cultural activity. Following Napoleon's incursions into northern Italy at the beginning of the 19th century, Parma entered a period of instability that ended only with Italian unification. Some 60 years later, the barricades went up as Parma became the only Emilian city to oppose the infamous 1922 march on Rome by Mussolini's blackshirts.

Orientation

From the train station, Via Verdi leads south to the green turf of Piazza della Pace. Continue south along Via Garibaldi for Piazza Garibaldi, Parma's main square.

Information

Euro Lavanderia (Via Massimo d'Azeglio 108; ☺ 7.30am-10.30pm)

InformaGiovani (☎ 0521 21 87 49; ☺ 9am-1pm & 3-7pm Mon, Tue & Thu-Sat, 9am 1pm Wed) Beside the tourist office, has information for young people and disabled travellers.

Main post office (Via Melloni) Off Via Garibaldi.

Police station (☎ 0521 21 94; Borgo della Posta 14)

Polidoro Web (per hr €5); Galleria Polidoro 6b (☎ 0521 20 64 78; off Via Mazzini; ☺ 10am-8pm Mon-Sat); Via Maestri 4b (☎ 0521 39 14 83; ☺ 10am-10pm Mon-Fri, 10am-7.30pm Sat)

Tourist office (☎ 0521 21 88 89; http://turismo.comune .parma.it/turismo; Via Melloni 1a; ☺ 9am-7pm Mon-Sat, 9am-1pm Sun) Just off Piazza della Pace. Will store your bags during working hours.

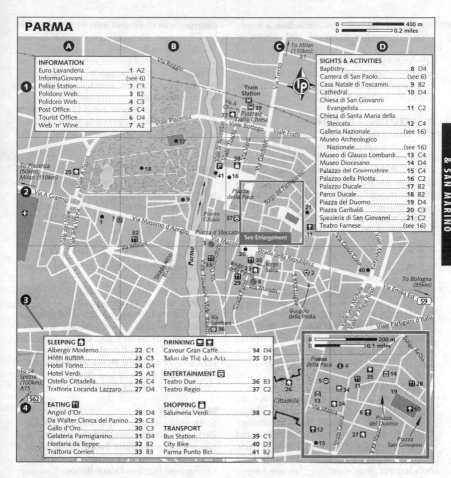

PARMA

EMILIA-ROMAGNA & SAN MARINO

Web 'n' Wine (Via Massimo d'Azeglio 72d; per hr €5; 10am-8pm Mon-Sat) Check your email with a glass of fine wine at your elbow.

Sights
PIAZZA DEL DUOMO

Externally, Parma's **cathedral** (Piazza del Duomo; 9am-12.30pm & 3-7pm), consecrated in 1106, is classic Lombard-Romanesque. Internally, by contrast, the gross gilded pulpit and ornate lampholders clamped onto delicate pillars all shout high baroque bombast. You need to look up high for baroque at its best – in the dome, Correggio's *Assumption of the Virgin* amid a swirl of cherubims' limbs and, above the central nave, the Mannerist frescoes attributed to Lattanzio Gambara. Take time

to look at the restored wood inlay in the sacristy and, in the southern transept, Benedetto Antelami's highly stylised yet intensely moving sculpture, *Descent from the Cross*, completed in 1178.

Antelami was also responsible for the striking pink-marble **baptistry** (admission €4; 9am-12.30pm & 3-6.30pm) on the south side of the piazza. Typically octagonal on the outside, it's divided into 16 segments within. Started in 1196, it wasn't completed until 1307 after several interruptions (most notably when the supply of pink Verona marble ran out).

The **Museo Diocesano** (☎ 0521 20 86 99; Vicolo del Vescovado 3a; admission €3; 9am-12.30pm & 3-6.30pm), in the cellars of the former bishop's palace, displays statuary from the cathedral and exterior of the baptistry, including a finely sculpted, pensive Solomon with Sheba at his side. There's also a large, well-preserved 5th-century early Christian mosaic, which was discovered under Piazza del Duomo.

A combined ticket (€5) allows entry into the baptistry and Museo Diocesano.

PALAZZO DELLA PILOTTA

The hulk of this immense palazzo, shattered by WWII air raids, looms over Piazza della Pace. Built for the Farnese family between 1583 and 1622, and supposedly named after the Spanish ball game of pelota that was played within its walls, it now houses a trio of cultural sites.

Galleria Nazionale (☎ 0521 23 33 09; admission incl Teatro Farnese €6; ☉ 8.30am-1.45pm Tue-Sun) includes works by local artists Antonio Correggio and Francesco Parmigianino, plus Fra Angelico, Canaletto and El Greco. The **Teatro Farnese**, a copy of Andrea Palladio's Teatro Olimpico in Vicenza, is constructed entirely out of wood and was almost completely rebuilt after WWII bombing.

The **Museo Archeologico Nazionale** (☎ 0521 23 37 18; admission €2; ☉ 8.30am-1.30pm Tue-Sun) displays Roman artefacts discovered around Parma and Etruscan finds from the Po valley.

PIAZZA GARIBALDI

On the site of the ancient Roman forum, Piazza Garibaldi is at Parma's heart. On its north side, the façade of the 17th-century **Palazzo del Governatore**, nowadays municipal offices, sports a giant sundial, added in 1829. Behind the palace in the **Chiesa di Santa Maria della Steccata** (Piazza Steccata 9; ☉ 9am-noon & 3-6pm) is some of Parmigianino's most extraordinary work, especially the stunning frescoes on the arches, high above the altar. Many members of the ruling Farnese and Bourbon families lie buried in this church, which is known to locals simply as La Steccata.

CHIESA DI SAN GIOVANNI EVANGELISTA

Just east of the cathedral, this **church** (Piazzale San Giovanni; ☉ 8am-noon & 3-7.45pm) and the adjoining **monastery** (☉ 8.30am-noon & 3-6pm) rose in the early 16th century on the site of a 10th-century original. The monastery sells all sorts of oils and unguents distilled by the monks. The church's ornate baroque façade was grafted on a century later and the magnificent decoration of the cupola –

disgracefully ill-lit and unapproachable – is by Correggio. Parmigianino's contribution includes the adornment of the chapels.

Just around the corner, the **Spezieria di San Giovanni** (Borgo Pipa 1; adult/child €2/1; ☉ 8.30am-1.45pm Tue-Sun), the monastery's ancient pharmacy, is all dark woodwork, bottles and jars.

For more Correggio, head for the **Camera di San Paolo** (☎ 0521 23 33 09; Via Melloni; adult/child €2/free; ☉ 8.30am-1.45pm Tue-Sun), near the tourist office, in the convent of the same name.

MUSEO DI GLAUCO LOMBARDI

Waterloo meant different things to different people. While Napoleon headed into miserable exile, his second wife, Marie-Louise of Austria, fared better. After her heady few years as Empress of all France, she was left with the dukedom of Parma, Piacenza and Guastalla. She ruled until 1847, with a level of moderation and good sense uncommon for the time.

Several of her belongings, including a portrait of her great husband, ended up in the hands of town notable and collector Glauco Lombardi. An eclectic assortment of Lombardi's treasures and other objects illustrative of life in Parma over the past few centuries now fill the **Museo di Glauco Lombardi** (☎ 0521 23 37 27; Via Garibaldi 15; adult/child €4/free; ☉ 9.30am-3.30pm Tue-Sat, 9am-6.30pm Sun).

WEST BANK

Stretching along the west bank of the River Parma (l'Oltretorrente) are the pleasant set-piece gardens of **Parco Ducale** (☉ 6am-midnight Apr-Sep, 7am-8pm Oct-Mar), laid out in 1560 around the Farnese family's **Palazzo Ducale**; these days it's the local police station.

At the southeastern corner of the park is the **Casa Natale di Toscanini** (☎ 0521 28 54 99; Via R Tanzi 13; admission €2; ☉ 9am-1pm & 2-6pm Tue-Sun), birthplace of Italy's greatest modern conductor, Arturo Toscanini (1867–1957). It has a small museum dedicated to the maestro's life and music. If in a musical frame of mind, you could also visit the tomb of Niccolò Paganini, 2km further south in the Cimitero della Villetta.

POST OFFICE

Even if you don't need a stamp, poke your nose into Parma's Art Deco main **post office** (Via Melloni), as ornate as the best of Italian railway stations and almost as big.

IS THERE A CONDUCTOR IN THE HOUSE?

Toscanini trained primarily as a cellist at Parma's Conservatory, graduating at 18 with maximum honours in both composition and the cello. His first overseas gig was in Brazil as a humble member of the orchestra accompanying a visiting Italian opera troupe. Relations became strained between the singers and the Brazilian conductor until one night in Rio de Janeiro when, as the audience began to hiss and boo, the conductor stormed off stage and into the night. Toscanini, still only 19, took up the baton and conducted that night's performance of Verdi's *Aida* entirely from memory. Thus began, almost by accident, the career of one of music's most illustrious orchestral directors.

Sleeping

Trattoria Locanda Lazzaro (☎ 0521 20 89 44; Via XX Marzo 14; s €35, s/d with bathroom from €42/60) This place has seven small, pleasant rooms and a new owner who's gradually making each room even more agreeable. You might not find anyone around outside of restaurant hours (see right).

Hotel Torino (☎ 0521 28 10 46; www.hotel-torino .it; Via Mazza 7; s/d with breakfast €82/125; P ⊠ ⌨) Just off Piazza della Pace, Torino is a good midrange choice, popular with performers from the nearby Teatro Regio. Room 404, which can accommodate up to four, has a huge double-sided balcony. Parking is €12.

Albergo Moderno (☎ 0521 77 26 47; info@century hotel.it; Via A Cecchi 4; s/d €32/60, with bathroom €55/70) This place couldn't be handier for the train station and is a reasonable choice in a town that's short on economical accommodation. However, each bedroom's reproduction paintings in heavy gilt frames may oppress a little until you douse the light.

Hotel Button (☎ 0521 20 80 39; hotelbutton@tin .it; Borgo Salina 7; s/d/tr with breakfast €78/110/138; P ⊠) Right in the heart of town, just off Piazza Garibaldi, Hotel Button is a sedate and tranquil place. It has a 24-hour bar and room service, should you fancy a little late-night roistering. Parking is €13.

Hotel Verdi (☎ 0521 29 35 39; www.hotelverdi.it; Viale A Pasini 18; s/d €162/214; P ⊠ ⌨) Verdi has 20 tastefully furnished bedrooms, each with a safe and a marble bathroom. Over the road is leafy Parco Ducale and there's an excellent separately managed restaurant, Santa Croce, next door.

Ostello Cittadella (☎ 0521 96 14 34; ostellocittadel la@libero.it; Parco Cittadella 5; dm €10.50, person/site €7/11; ☻ Apr-Oct) The city's small HI-affiliated youth hostel lies within the walls of a giant former fortress and accommodates 25 people in four-bed dorms. Take bus No 9 or 12 from the train station or city centre. There's also an equally tiny camping ground.

Eating

Angiol d'Or (☎ 0521 28 26 32; Vicolo Scutellari 1; mains around €15, degustation menu €40; ☻ closed Sun dinner & Tue) In the shadow of the cathedral, this is a smart candlelit place with crisp cream tablecloths and an impressive wine cellar. Savour the *stracetti di manzo saltati nel Lambrusco* (thin strips of beef sautéed in wine).

Gallo d'Oro (☎ 0521 20 88 46; Borgo Salina 3; mains €7.50-8.50; ☻ Mon-Sat) Gallo d'Oro has an agreeably retro décor with arty photos of long-faded movie stars and 1950s covers from *La Gazzetta del Sporto* and *Marie-France*. One of Parma's best informal trattorie, where booking is essential, it serves up consistently good Emilian cuisine, including delicious cold meats (just watch the accountant–cum–meat slicer lovingly carve the slices of meat and set them out).

Trattoria Corrieri (☎ 0521 23 44 26; Via Conservatorio 1-3; mains €7-8; ☻ closed dinner Sun) Under the same ownership as the Gallo d'Oro and just as rich in character, you'll eat equally well here.

Trattoria Locanda Lazzaro (☎ 0521 20 89 44; Via XX Marzo 14; meals €22-28; ☻ daily Easter-Nov, closed Thu & dinner Sun Nov-Easter) Located in the hotel of the same name (see left) this restaurant does an original *risotto de pere e gorgonzola* (risotto with pear and gorgonzola cheese) and meaty mains from all the major quadrupeds, including horse. The dining room could do with a coat of paint yet is freshened up with real plants. Doodle on your place mat and – who knows? – your creation may make it up on the walls, together with the idle sketches of so many previous diners.

Da Walter Clinica del Panino (☎ 0521 20 63 09; Borgo Palmia 2; ☻ Mon-Sat) This place has small, basic tables and the neon lights glare – yet

---

THE BIG CHEESE

Imitated but never matched, *parmigiano reggiano* (Parmesan) is the king of Italy's cheeses. It has been made in the area around Parma for more than 700 years and is so valuable that wheels of the cheese were once accepted as currency.

The cheese is made with skimmed evening milk and full cream morning milk, which is poured into copper vats, cultured, heated and then stirred with a giant paddle. The cheesemakers delve into the vats – hairy arms and all – to check the consistency of the curd, then heave it out into cheesecloth. Each lump of curd is cut in two, shaped into a wheel form (which also imparts the distinctive *parmigiano* 'branding' on the rind) and left in brine for more than a month before being aged for at least one and often two or more years. The regulating consortium checks every single cheese for quality before it is sold.

For a free two-hour **visit** (8.30-10.30am Mon-Fri) to a Parmesan cheese factory, call the **Consorzio del Parmigiano Reggiano** (☎ 0521 29 27 00; www.parmigiano-reggiano.it) to book.

---

it's just what a fast-food joint should be. The staff is cheerful, there are more than 100 varieties of snacks and sandwiches on offer (just tick/check the menu they pass to you) and prices are very reasonable.

Gelateria Parmigianino (☎ 0521 23 84 22; Via Cavour 39b) One of several tempting *gelaterie* in the centre.

Hostaria da Beppe (☎ 0521 20 65 08; Via Imbriani 51b; set menu €21, mains €9.50-14.50; Tue-Sat) This is the place for a classy meal tucked away from the main streets. The pasta's homemade and the house speciality is risotto with osso buco.

Drinking

Salon de Thé des Arts (☎ 0521 20 60 06; Borgo del Parmigianino 5b; Tue-Sun) A stylish little place that has a huge selection of teas to revive and refresh the weariest of travellers, accompanied by sweet or savoury crepes (€7), or a handful of the scrummy homemade chocolates.

Cavour Gran Caffè (☎ 0521 20 62 23; Via Cavour 30b; Mon-Sat) This café makes a pleasant drinks

stop, whether on the terrace or inside beneath the colourful frescoes and glinting chandelier.

Entertainment

Parma's opera, concert and theatre season runs from about October to April.

Teatro Regio (☎ 0521 03 93 93; Via Garibaldi 16a) offers a particularly rich programme of music and opera, even by exacting Italian standards, while the **Teatro Due** (☎ 0521 23 02 42; Via Salnitrara 10) presents the city's top drama.

In summer, the city sponsors several outdoor music programmes.

Shopping

It would be a shame to leave Parma without a few local delicacies tucked away in your bag. **Salumeria Verdi** (Via Verdi 6c; Mon-Sat) is one of several great one-stop delicatessens with dangling sausages, shelves of Lambrusco wines, slabs of Parma ham and wheel upon wheel of *parmigiano reggiano*.

Getting There & Away

TEP (☎ 800 97 79 66; www.tep.pr.it in Italian) operates buses throughout the region, including into the Apennines. There are up to six buses daily to/from Busseto (€3.15, 1¼ hours), via Soragna (€2.65, one hour), leaving from Piazzale dalla Chiesa in front of the train station.

Frequent trains connect Parma with Milan (€11.50, 1¼ hours), Bologna (€4.70, one hour), Brescia (€5.75, two hours), Modena (€3.25, 30 minutes) and Piacenza (€3.25, 30 minutes).

Parma is on the A1 connecting Bologna and Milan and just east of the A15, which runs to La Spezia. The Via Emilia (S9) passes right through town.

Getting Around

Leave your car at the underground car park on Viale Toschi or park it beside one of the many meters near the station and along the main roads around the historic centre, from which motor traffic is banned.

Parma Punto Bici (☎ 0521 28 19 79; www.parma -puntobici.it; Viale Toschi; 9.30am-1pm & 3-6.30pm), an admirable initiative of the municipality, rents out bicycles (per hour €0.70) and electric bikes (per hour €0.90). Or hire a bike from **City Bike** (☎ 0521 23 56 39; Viale Mentana 8a; per half/full day €5/8).

For a taxi, call ☎ 0521 25 25 62.

AROUND PARMA
Verdi Country

A pleasant day tour northwest of Parma takes in a couple of the province's more than 20 castles, plus four buildings closely associated with Verdi, Parma's most famous son.

Sitting in a murky moat, 19km northwest of Parma, the **Rocca Sanvitale di Fontanellato** (☎ 0521 82 90 55; Fontanellato; adult/child €7/2.50; ⏰ 9.30-11.30am & 3-6pm Apr-Oct, 9.30-11.30am & 3-5pm Tue-Sun Nov-Mar) was constructed in the 16th century by the family of the same name. Conceived more as a pleasure dome than a military bastion, it has some vivid frescoes by Parmigianino. Admission is by guided tour only (in Italian).

Nine kilometres further northwest is Soragna, site of the **Rocca Meli Lupi** (☎ 0524 59 79 64; adult/child €7/3.50; ⏰ 9-11am & 3-6pm Tue-Sun Mar-Oct, 9-11am & 2.30-5.30pm Tue-Sun Nov-Feb). Constructed in 1385 and resembling more a stately home than a fortress, it's a fine example of early baroque and has retained its original period furniture. There are hourly guided tours in Italian.

The **Casa Natale di Giuseppe Verdi** (☎ 0524 9 74 50; adult/child €4/3; ⏰ 9.30-noon & 3-6.30pm Tue-Sun Mar-Oct, 9.30am-12.30pm & 2.30-5.30pm Tue-Sun Nov-Feb), site of the humble home where Giuseppe Verdi came into the world in 1813, is 5km further on in the hamlet of Roncole Verdi.

Next stop is **Busseto**, with its splendidly ornate **Teatro Verdi** (☎ 052 49 24 87; adult/child €4/3; ⏰ 9.30am-noon & 3-6.30pm Tue-Sun Mar-Oct, 9.30am-12.30pm & 2.30-4.30pm Tue-Sun Nov-Feb) on Piazza Verdi. Admission is by guided tour only.

Also facing Piazza Verdi is **Casa Barezzi** (☎ 0524 93 11 17; Via Roma 119; admission €3; ⏰ 10am-12.30pm & 3-6.30pm Tue-Sun Mar-Oct, 10am-12.30pm & 2.30-5.30pm Tue-Sun Nov-Feb), home of the composer's patron and father-in-law. It is the site of Verdi's first concert and is packed with Verdi memorabilia.

Verdi's villa, **Sant'Agata** (☎ 0523 83 00 00; Via Verdi 22; adult/child €6/free; ⏰ 9am-noon & 2.30-6.30pm mid-Feb–mid-Oct, 9.30-11.30am & 2.30-4.30pm mid-Oct–mid-Feb), where he composed many of his major works, sits in the countryside 5km northwest of Busseto.

A combined ticket for the first three Verdi venues costs €8/6.50 per adult/child. An alternative at €13/11 allows entry to all four. For more information on the Verdi sights, contact Busseto's **tourist office** (☎ 0524 924 87; www.bussetolive.com in Italian; Piazza Verdi 10; ⏰ 9.30am-1pm & 3-6.30pm Apr-Sep, 9.30am-1pm & 2.30-5.30pm Tue-Sun Oct-Mar).

TEP buses from Parma run along this route up to six times a day from Monday to Saturday.

South into the Apennines

A pair of tempting routes lead south of Parma to cross the Apennines into northwest Tuscany. Alternatively, you could explore either as a half-day outing from Parma.

The first roughly follows the River Parma towards **Langhirano**, famed for its high-quality hams. About 5km short of the town and 18km from Parma rises the majestic **Castello di Torrechiara** (☎ 0521 35 52 55; adult/child €3/free; ⏰ 8.30am-6.45pm Tue-Sun Apr-Sep, 8am-3.15pm Tue-Fri, 9am-4.15pm Sat & Sun Oct-Mar), which offers staggering views towards the Apennines. It's one of many castles built or rebuilt by Pier Maria Rossi in the 15th century. Here, he romped with his lover Bianca Pellegrini in the exquisitely frescoed Camera d'Oro (Golden Room), where he (or more frequently she?) could look at a map of all his castles on the ceiling.

From Langhirano, follow the road down the west bank of the Parma, crossing the river at Pastorello and continuing to **Tizzano Val Parma**, a charming Apennine village that offers pleasant walking in summer and reasonable winter skiing at **Schia**, which is 10km further on.

Further south still, the heights around **Monchio delle Corti** offer views as far as La Spezia on a good day. It's a possible base for exploring some of the 20 glacial lakes that dot the southern corner of the province at the border with Tuscany.

The mountains here are crisscrossed with **walking** and **cycling** tracks and dotted with *rifugi*. An interesting trekking challenge is to follow a section of the signed **Romea**, or **Via Francigena**, an ancient pilgrim route heading south to Rome via the villages of Collecchio, Fornovo, Bardone, Terenzo, Cassio and Berceto, each with its small Romanesque church. The tourist office in Parma (p432) can advise on maps and accommodation.

Castello Bardi (⏰ 10am-7pm Jul-Aug, 2-7pm Mon-Sat & 10am-7pm Sun Jun & Sep, 2-6pm Sat & 10am-6pm Sun Mar-May & Oct, 2-5pm Sat & 10am-5pm Sun Nov), about 65km southwest of Parma (not on the above route), also merits a mention. Soaring above the surrounding town, it dates from

898, although most of the present structure was built in the 15th century.

PIACENZA
pop 97,300

In the northwestern corner of Emilia, just short of the Lombardy frontier, Piacenza, a prosperous town, is pleasant enough for a brief stop if you're prepared to persevere through its dreary industrial outer suburbs.

The train station is on the eastern edge of the old town, an easy 20-minute walk from the central square, Piazza dei Cavalli.

Information

Internet Train (☎ 0523 31 27 72; Via Cittadella 36; per hr €4.30; ☷ 10am-10pm Mon-Sat)

Tourist office (☎ 0523 32 93 24; iat@comune.piacenza .it; Piazza dei Cavalli 7; ☷ 9am-1pm & 5-8pm Tue-Sun Apr-Sep, 9am-1pm & 5-8pm Tue-Sat Oct-Mar) In the southeastern corner of the main square.

Sights

Piazza dei Cavalli (Square of the Horses) is dominated by the impressive brick and marble 13th-century town hall, also known as Il Gotico, the subtle brickwork of its upper storeys is as delicate as embroidery.

The riders astride the pair of magnificent bronze horses that seem to stand guard over the square are the Farnese dukes Alessandro and his son Ranuccio. Cast by Francesco Mochi, these equestrian statues date from 1625.

The 12th-century Lombard-Romanesque **cathedral** (Via XX Settembre; ☷ 7am-noon & 4-7pm) harmoniously blends white and pink marble, mellow sandstone and red brick. Some of the dome frescoes are by Guercino. The nearby **Basilica di Sant'Antonino** (Piazza Sant'Antonino; ☷ 8am-noon & 4-6.30pm Mon-Sat, 8am-12.30pm & 8-9.30pm Sun) was built in the 11th century on the site of an earlier church. Its peculiar octagonal tower is claimed to be the oldest of its type in Italy.

The **Palazzo Farnese** (☎ 0523 32 82 70; Piazza Citadella; admission €5.60; ☷ 8.45am-1pm Tue-Sat, 3-6pm Fri, Sat, 9.30am-1pm & 3-6pm Sun), a mammoth structure, was started in 1558 but never fully completed. It houses the Pinacoteca, an art gallery, and four little museums, of archaeology, carriages, Italian unification and the main one, the **Museo Civico** with its bizarre Etruscan Fegato di Piacenza, a sheep's liver in bronze that was used for divining the future. Admission to the palazzo includes entry to all the museums.

A few blocks south of Piazza dei Cavalli, the **Galleria Ricci Oddi** (☎ 0523 32 07 42; Via San Siro 13; admission €4; ☷ 10am-noon & 3-6pm Tue-Sun) contains a respectable collection of Italian art and sculpture from the 18th century onwards.

Sleeping & Eating

Hotel Nazionale (☎ 0523 71 20 00; www.hotelna zionale.it; Via Genova 35; s/d with breakfast from €68/85; P ☒ ☐) This hotel is about 1km southwest of Piazza dei Cavalli (follow Corso Vittorio Emanuele II, which becomes Via Genova). With more than 70 years in business, it has 78 well furnished if rather small rooms. You may want to invest an extra €15 for a superior grade double, a larger room with a small lounge. Parking is €13.

Grande Albergo Roma (☎ 0523 32 32 01; www .grandealbergoroma.it; Via Cittadella 14; s/d with breakfast €130/175; P ☒ ☐) Stylishly furnished, conveniently central and soundproofed, with a superb 7th-floor breakfast terrace. There's also a free gym and sauna (€8) for fitness freaks, and wi-fi. Parking is €16. It runs a highly regarded restaurant, **Piccolo Roma** (mains €15-22; ☷ closed Sat & dinner Sun).

Santa Teresa (☎ 0523 32 57 86; Corso Vittorio Emanuele II 169b/c; mains €6-9) A popular bar though nothing fancy, Santa Teresa has a small restaurant at the rear serving good, modestly priced local cuisine including *pisarei e fasô* (€5.50), a satisfying fusion of red beans and the local pasta.

Antica Osteria del Teatro (☎ 0523 32 37 77; Via Verdi 16; mains €26-30; ☷ Tue-Sat) In an altogether different price bracket, this place is one of Emilia's finest restaurants, set in a restored 15th-century palace. To avoid the agony of making difficult decisions from the enticing menu, you might want to go for the traditional menu (€57) or *menù degustazione* (€70). Or plump for the *treccia di branzino* (steamed, garnished sea bass, €26).

Getting There & Around

The bus station is on Piazza Citadella. However, the train is a more convenient way to travel for most destinations. There are direct train services to/from Milan (€6.55, 45 minutes), Turin (€9, two hours), Cremona (€2.50, 30 minutes), Parma (€3.25, 30 minutes) and Bologna (€11.40, 1½ hours).

Piacenza is just off the A1 linking Milan and Bologna and the A21 joining Brescia and Turin. The Via Emilia (S9) also runs past Piacenza on its way to Rimini and the Adriatic Sea.

Bus Nos 2, 4 and 6 run between the train station and Piazza dei Cavalli.

EAST OF BOLOGNA

FERRARA

pop 130,200

For Lucrezia Borgia (see the boxed text, p43), marriage into the Este family brought several disadvantages, not least among them the move to this Po valley city, just south of the modern border with Veneto. Close to the river and wetlands, in winter Ferrara can be cold, grey and shrouded in banks of fog. But winter doesn't last and Ferrara retains much of the austere splendour of its Renaissance heyday, back when it was strong enough to keep both Rome and Venice at arm's length.

History

The Este dynasty ruled Ferrara from 1260 to 1598, its political and military prowess matched by intense cultural activity. Petrarch, Titian, Antonio Pisanello and poets Torquato Tasso and Ludovico Ariosto are just some of the luminaries who spent time here under the patronage of the Este dukes.

When the House of Este fell in 1598, Pope Clement VIII claimed the city, only to preside over its decline. Ferrara recovered importance during and after the Napoleonic period, when it was made chief city of the lower River Po. Today's local government has carefully restored much of the centre, which was battered during WWII.

Ferrara was the birthplace of Girolamo Savonarola (see the boxed text, p468), the fanatical Dominican monk whose statue with its manic eyes and posturing arms presides over the square that bears his name.

Orientation

Viale Cavour slices northwest–southeast from Porta Po near the train station to Piazza Medaglie d'Oro. It passes Ferrara's splendid castle, at whose feet spread old Ferrara's three principal piazze – Savanorola, del Castello and della Repubblica.

Information

Ferrara Internet Point (Via Adelardi 17; per hr €4; 11am-11pm Mon-Fri, 11am-7pm Sat)

Guardia Medica (☎ 0532 20 31 31) Emergency doctor.

Main post office (Viale Cavour 27)

Police station (☎ 0532 29 43 11; Corso Frcole I d'Este 26)

Speedy Web (☎ 0532 24 80 92; Corso Porta Po 37; per hr €4; 9am-2pm & 4-7pm Mon-Sat)

Tourist office Viale Cavour (☎ 0532 20 93 70; www .ferrarainfo.com; 9am-1pm & 2-6pm Mon-Sat, 9.30am-1pm & 2-5pm Sun) In the main courtyard of Castello Estense; Piazza Municipale (☎ 0532 41 94 74)

Sights

CASTELLO ESTENSE

This imposing **castle** (☎ 0532 29 92 33; Viale Cavour; adult/child €6/free; 9.30am-5.30pm Tue-Sun) was started in 1385 for Nicolò II d'Este, primarily to defend the family from its riotous subjects who at one point rebelled over tax increases. Later it became the dynasty's permanent residence.

Although sections are now used as government offices, many of the rooms, including the royal suites, are open for viewing. Highlights are the Sala dei Giganti (Giants' Room) and Salone dei Giochi (Games Salon) – with frescoes by Camillo and Sebastiano Filippi – the Cappella di Renée de France and the claustrophobic dungeon. Here, in 1425, Duke Nicolò III d'Este had his young second wife, Parisina Malatesta, and his son, Ugo, beheaded after discovering they were lovers, providing the inspiration for Robert Browning's *My Last Duchess*.

For an additional €1 you can go up the tower.

PALAZZO MUNICIPALE

Linked to the castle, the 13th-century crenellated **town hall** also once contained Este family apartments. Nowadays, it's largely occupied by administrative offices but you can wander around its twin courtyards. The entrance is watched over by copper statues of Nicolò III and his less wayward son, Borso – they're 20th-century copies but none-the-less imposing.

CATHEDRAL

Take your time gazing at the superb three-tiered marble façade of the **cathedral** (Piazza Cattedrale; 7.30am-noon & 3-6.30pm Mon-Sat, 7.30am-12.30pm & 3.30-7.30pm Sun). Its upper part is a

EMILIA-ROMAGNA & SAN MARINO

FERRARA

graphic representation of the final judgement and heaven and hell (notice the four
figures clambering out of their coffins, just
below). Astride a pair of handsome lions at
the base squat an oddly secular duo, mouths
agape at the effort of holding it all up.

Along the south side is an attractive colonnaded medieval merchants' gallery.

Highlights of the **Museo della Cattedrale**
(☎ 0532 24 49 49; Via San Romano; adult/child €5/free;
🕑 9am-1pm & 3-6pm Tue-Sun), just opposite, include a serene Madonna statue by Jacopo
della Quercia, a couple of vigorous Cosimo
Tura canvases of St George and the dragon
and the Annunciation, and some witty bas-
reliefs illustrating the months of the year.

MUSEUMS & GALLERIES

You can buy a combined ticket for €8, giving you entry to the following museums: Museo della Cattedrale, Palazzina di Marfisa d'Este, Palazzo Schifanoia and Museo Lapidario.

The **Palazzo dei Diamanti** (Palace of the Diamonds), named after the diamond-shaped stones decorating its façade, was built for Sigismondo d'Este late in the 15th century. Regarded as the family's grandest palazzo, it is now home to the **Pinacoteca Nazionale** (☎ 0532 20 58 44; Corso Ercole I d'Este 21; adult/child €4/free; ☽ 9am-2pm Tue-Wed, Fri & Sat, 9am-7pm Thu, 9am-1pm Sun), which houses works by artists of the Ferrarese and Bolognese schools. Regrettably for a national museum, labelling of the exhibits is exclusively in Italian.

If you read Italian, drop into the **Museo del Risorgimento e della Resistenza** (☎ 0532 24 49 49; Corso Ercole I d'Este 19; admission €3; ☽ 9am-8pm Tue-Sun) next door to the Palazzo dei Diamanti. The museum showcases a fascinating collection of documents, proclamations and posters from WWII.

Lucrezia Borgia spent many of her days in Ferrara at what is now the **Casa Romei** (☎ 0532 24 03 41; Via Savonarola 30; adult/child €2/free; ☽ 8.30am-7.30pm Tue-Sun), a typical Renaissance house with a peaceful inner patio.

The **Palazzina di Marfisa d'Este** (☎ 0532 24 49 49; Corso Giovecca 170; adult/child €3/free; ☽ 9am-1pm & 3-6pm Tue-Sun), a patrician palace built in 1559, has ornate decorations and furnishings and a shady garden.

The 14th-century **Palazzo Schifanoia** (☎ 0532 24 49 49; Via Scandiana 23; adult/child €5/free; ☽ 9am-6pm Tue-Sun) is a sumptuous Este residence on Via Scandiana. The Salone dei Mesi (Room of the Months) is clad with vigorous, animated frescoes of the months and seasons by Francesco del Cossa. Sadly, all but one wall, illustrating September to December, are very deteriorated. A ticket also gives entry to the nearby **Museo Lapidario** (Via Camposabbionario 23; ☽ 9am-6pm Tue-Sun), a small, undocumented collection of Roman and Etruscan stele, tombs and inscriptions.

Within the **Palazzo di Ludovico il Moro** is the **Museo Archeologico Nazionale** (☎ 0532 6 62 99; Via XX Settembre 124; adult/child €4/free; ☽ 9am-2pm Tue-Sun). The palazzo was built by Biagio Rossetti for the duke of Milan and the collection of Etruscan artefacts and Attic vases is well worth a look.

CITY WALLS & VAULTS

Although not terribly impressive, most of the 9km of ancient city walls are more or less intact and some parts are walkable. Alternatively, hire a bike and cycle the perimeter (ask at the tourist office for its free booklet the *Seven Bicycle Routes in the Province of Ferrara;* Itinerary 1 describes the circuit).

Within the city walls, take a short diversion southwards from Piazza Trento Trieste along the attractively colonnaded Via San Romano and stroll beneath the arches that span Via Volte. This lane once ran parallel with the riverbank until the Po changed its course and merchants slung covered bridges over the river to connect the family home and warehouse.

Festivals & Events

On the last Sunday of May each year, the eight *contrade* (districts) of Ferrara compete in **Il Palio**, a horse race that momentarily turns Piazza Ariostea into medieval bedlam. Claimed to be the oldest race of its kind in Italy, the first official competition was held in 1279. For more background, check www .paliodiferrara.it.

The annual week-long **Ferrara Buskers' Festival** (☎ 0532 24 93 37; www.ferrarabuskers.com), held in late August, attracts buskers from around the globe, with the city paying travel and accommodation expenses for 20 lucky invited performers.

Sleeping

Accommodation is usually easy to find, although many hotels close during August.

Hotel de Prati (☎ 0532 24 19 05; www.hoteldeprati .com; Via Padiglioni 5; s/d with breakfast €75/110; ☒) In a quiet lane within a stone's throw of the castle, de Prati is a splendid, tasteful, family place. Rooms have wrought-iron bedsteads, antique furniture and selected prints of works by Ferrara Renaissance painters. The corridors, by contrast, are enlivened by changing exhibitions of contemporary art.

Albergo Annunziata (☎ 0532 20 11 11; www.an nunziata.it; Piazza della Repubblica 5; s/d with breakfast €120/190; P ☒ ☐) It's attested that no less a lover than Casanova slept here – 'spent the night' might be more accurate. Then, this luxury hotel, bright with flowers and rich in all creature comforts (including free bicycle use and wi-fi), was but a simple locanda. Bang opposite the castle, its

EMILIA-ROMAGNA
& SAN MARINO

AUTHOR'S CHOICE

Locanda Borgonuovo (☎ 0532 21 11 00; www.borgonuovo.com; Via Cairoli 29; s/d with breakfast €55/95; P ⊠ 🖳) Locanda Borgonuovo is a four-room gem of a B&B. And what a B it is! Ample, varied and rich in local produce including homemade cakes and jams, it will see you through way beyond lunch time. The welcome is ultrafriendly and informed, bicycles are free for guests and there's a delightfully frondy, shaded patio, where tortoises Tara and Ferrari maintain a stately pace. There's also a pair of apartments (€85 to €95) next door, which can accommodate from two to five guests. Reservations are imperative. Parking is €5.

rooms have magnificent views, whichever way they face. It also has six exquisitely restored apartments (per day with breakfast €180 to €220). Parking here costs €7 and there's wi-fi.

Hotel Europa (☎ 0532 20 54 56; www.hoteleuropa ferrara.com; Corso Giovecca 49; s/d/tr with breakfast €74/115/140; P ⊠ 🖳) Hotel Europa, despite successive renovations, retains its period charm. Constructed in the 19th century, it has some rooms with disabled facilities and others that still have their original ceiling frescoes. It also has a couple of apartments (€115) with cooking facilities. Ask for a peep at the guestbook, it is signed by luminaries such as Benito Mussolini, the Khedive of Egypt, Emile Zola and Alexandre Dumas. To inspire sweet singing in the shower, reserve room No 4, where Verdi once slept. The hotel provides bicycles for free; parking costs €8.

Pensione Artisti (☎ 0532 76 10 38; Via Vittoria 66; s/d €21/38, d with bathroom €55) Cheery, family-run and just a few minutes' walk south of the cathedral. There's a small cooking area for guest use on two of its three floors. If you want an en suite (only three of the 20 bedrooms have them), be sure to book.

Estense (☎ 0532 75 23 96; campeggio.estense@libero .it; Via Gramicia 76; person/site €5/6.50; year-round) Ferrara's only camping ground is just outside the city walls. Take bus No 1 or 5 from the train station to Piazzale San Giovanni and follow the signs.

Estense (☎ 0532 20 42 27; hostelferrara@hotmail .com; Corso Rossetti 24; dm/d with breakfast €17/36)

Ferrara's HI-affiliated youth hostel, confusingly also called Estense, is within easy walking distance from the centre and has cheap public parking just behind.

Eating

Ferrara's cuisine is typical of the Emilia-Romagna region, incorporating meats and cheeses. One local speciality is *cappellacci di zucca*, a pasta pouch filled with pumpkin that looks like a small, floppy hat. Another is *pampota*, a kind of gingerbread cake, stuffed with nuts and coated in dark chocolate.

Quel Fantastico Giovedì (☎ 0532 76 05 70; Via Castelnuovo 9; mains about €13; Thu-Tue) This place is well off the beaten tourist track and worth every step of the way. It's one of those restaurants where you won't find a normal, round plate. Portions are on the small side but exquisite, and the ample wine list is a leather-bound tome. The beamed rooms are sponged in orange and cool jazz warbles in the background.

Antica Trattoria Volano (☎ 0532 76 14 21; Via le Volano 20; mains €8-12; Sat-Thu) Just beyond the city walls, this trattoria is a favourite with discerning Ferrarese who come to savour its freshly rolled house pasta and to relax in its attractive rear garden.

Il Ciclone (☎ 0532 21 02 62; 1st fl, Via Vignatagliata 11; pizzas €3.50-8, mains about €13; Tue-Sun) Il Ciclone is a friendly pizzeria and restaurant that specialises in fish dishes. You can go simple and select from around 50 varieties of pizza or try à la carte. Dip your fork into the delightful *risotto alla pescatore* (fish risotto).

Al Brindisi (☎ 0532 20 91 42; Via Adelardi 11; pastas from €6.50, mains about €10, glass of wine from €2.50; Tue-Sun) This splendid *osteria*-cum-*enoteca* (wine bar) is just the place for a glass of Romagna's finest wine and a hearty snack or even a full meal. Dating from 1435, its walls are lined with dusty vintage wine bottles and it claims among its past guests both Titian and Benvenuto Cellini.

Trattoria il Mandolino (☎ 0532 76 00 80; Via Carlo Mayr 83; mains about €8; lunch Mon & Wed-Sun) The place for Ferrarese home cooking where the genial hostess will talk you through her delights of the day in English. Lasagne so light that it melts in your mouth and *cappellacci di zucca* are two of the treats in store.

Ristorante Max (☎ 0532 20 93 09; Piazza della Repubblica 16; meals €40-50; closed Mon & lunch Sun)

Max, also warmly recommended and staffed by a young, friendly team, has a menu that's short, creative and almost exclusively fishy. The wine list is equally carefully selected. Leave a cranny for a platter of its own rich dark chocolates.

Self caterers can stock up at the **covered market** (Via Vegri; ☉ 7am-1.30pm Mon-Sat).

Drinking

Pasticceria Leon d'Oro (☎ 0532 20 93 18; Piazza Cattedrale 2-10; ☉ Thu-Tue) One of a trio of excellent *pasticcerie* facing the cathedral, Leon d'Oro offers the best views from its terrace, which makes an ideal drink or snack stop.

Café Teatro (☎ 0532 20 59 15; Corso Giovecca 1; ☉ Tue-Sun) Smart early evening drinkers spill onto the street from tiny Café Teatro, which overlooks the castle.

Il Messisbugo (☎ 0532 76 40 60; Via Carlo Mayr 79; ☉ 7pm-2am Tue-Sun) Il Messisbugo also regularly overflows, and is livelier than Teatro and a popular student haunt.

Getting There & Around

The bus station is on Via Rampari San Paolo. **ACFT** (☎ 0532 59 94 11; www.acft.it in Italian) buses operate services within the city (single ride €0.83, four-ride carnet €2.70) and to surrounding towns such as Comacchio (€3.80, 1¼ hours, eight daily), as well as to the Adriatic beaches (some of these leave from the train station).

The train is the better option for Bologna (€2.90, 15 to 30 minutes) and Ravenna (€4.20, 1¼ hours).

Most traffic is banned from the city centre. ACFT buses No 1, 2 and 9 run from the train station to the city centre.

For a taxi, call ☎ 0532 900 900.

Even better, get in the saddle and join the hundreds of other wheelers in what is, if you discount the jarring effect of the cobbles on tender loins, Italy's most cycle-friendly city. Among places where you can rent bikes (per hour/three hours/day around €2/6/10) are:

Itinerando (Piazzale Kennedy 6-8)
Pirani e Bagni (Piazza Stazione)
Roberto Ceragioli (Piazza Travaglio 4)
Romanelli (Via Luna 10)

PO DELTA

The Po Delta (Foci del Po) is where the Po River spills into the Adriatic Sea. Straddling Emilia-Romagna and the Veneto, it makes a pleasant day trip from either Ferrara or Ravenna. A battery of *lidi* (small beach resorts), backed by pine woods, offer coastal fun. The **Parco del Delta del Po** (www.parcodeltapo.it) is one of Europe's largest wetlands. It embraces a pair of alluring lagoons: the Valli di Comacchio and Valle Bertuzzi. With more than 300 species nesting or passing through, it's a small paradise for ornithologists. Comacchio's annual **Bird-watching Fair** (☎ 0533 68 11 80; www .podeltabirdfair.it) in late April is, understandably, the largest event of its kind in Europe.

In summertime, the mosquitoes are maneaters; slap on the insect repellent and consider mosquito nets if you're camping.

Sights

ABBAZIA DI POMPOSA

This **abbey** (☎ 0533 71 91 10; Codigoro; admission Mon-Sat €4, Sun free; ☉ 8.30am-7pm), 50km east of Ferrara, is one of Italy's oldest Benedictine endowments. The monk Guido d'Arezzo reputedly invented the musical scale here, and in its time the abbey was one of Italy's foremost cultural centres. Its decline began in the 14th century, and in 1652, vespers were sung for the last time. The nave of its church has elaborate mosaic paving and is adorned with frescoes from the 14th-century Bologna school and artworks by Vitale di Bologna. There's also a small museum.

The abbey stages a classical music festival **Rassegna di Musica Clasica** each July.

COMACCHIO

Thin canals thread their way through this delightful little fishing village. The Trepponti (Triple Bridge), constructed in 1635, arches its back over a trio of them. The **tourist office** (☎ 0533 31 01 61; Piazza Folegatti 28; ☉ 9.30am-12.30pm & 4-6.30pm Tue-Sun Mar-Oct, 10am-12.30pm & 3.30-5.30pm Fri-Sun Nov-Feb) is in Piazza Folegatti.

Enjoy fish or eels – a speciality of the lagoons – at one of the many tempting restaurants overlooking the canals. Or install yourself on the terrace of **La Barcaccia** (☎ 0533 31 10 81; Piazza XX Settembre 41; mains €12-18.50; ☉ Tue-Sun), right beside the cathedral. It too specialises in grilled eel and does fine seafood and fish platters.

Activities

The Comacchio tourist office and other seasonal equivalents carry a wealth of information about **cycling** itineraries, **walking**, horse riding and boat excursions – the savvy way to explore the delta.

The 132km Destra Po cycle route follows the banks of the river from west of Ferrara to the sea. Pick up the free *Destra Po* leaflet from any tourist office. Also pack away *Seven Bicycle Routes in the Province of Ferrara*, which has a detailed description of two-day runs within the park, and *Bicideltapo*, which has even more suggestions.

Those into bird-watching should arm themselves with the pamphlet *Birdwatching in the Po Delta Park: Map & Itineraries* and also the eminently practical and detailed *Where to Go Birdwatching in the Po Delta* by Bob Scott, published locally.

RAVENNA

pop 136,600

Celebrated for the early Christian and Byzantine mosaics that adorn its churches and monuments (eight of which are Unesco World Heritage sites), Ravenna was the capital of the Byzantine Empire's western regions during the reign of Emperor Justinian and Empress Theodora.

The city had been the capital of the Western Roman Empire ever since 402, when the ineffectual Emperor Honorius moved his court from Rome because Ravenna's surrounding malarial swamps made it easier to defend from northern invaders. However, the barbarians simply walked around him and marched into Rome in 410. Honorius was unable or unwilling to react, preferring to vegetate in Ravenna until his death in 423, and the city finally followed 50 years later.

The Byzantines arrived in 540 and ruled until the Lombards conquered the city in 752. Venetians controlled Ravenna from 1441 to 1509, when it was incorporated into the Papal States.

Under the Romans, Goths and Byzantines, Ravenna gradually rose to become one of the most splendid Mediterranean cities. Its mosaics, described by Dante in his *Divine Comedy* as a symphony of colour, are matched only by those of Istanbul. The city is close to Adriatic beaches, but they aren't the coast's most attractive.

Orientation

From the train station, on the eastern edge of town in Piazzale Farini, it's a short walk along Viale Farini and its continuation, Via Diaz, into central Piazza del Popolo. From here, nearly everything of interest is within easy walking distance.

Information

Foto Expert (Via Massimo d'Azeglio 3/d; per hr €2; 9am-1pm & 3.30-7.30pm Mon-Fri, 9am-1pm Sat) Surely Italy's cheapest Internet access.

Post office (Piazza Garibaldi)

Police station (☎ 0544 29 91 11; Via Berlinguer 10-20)

Splash (Via Candiano 16; 7am-10pm) A laundry over the tracks, just south of the train station.

Telecom office (Via G Rasponi 22)

Tourist office Via Salara 8/12 (☎ 0544 3 54 04; www .turismo.ravenna.it in Italian; 8.30am-7pm Mon-Sat Apr-Sep, to 6pm Oct-Mar, 10am-4pm Sun year-round) The main tourist office; Via delle Industrie 14 (☎ 0544 45 15 39; 9.30am-12.30pm & 3-6pm Apr-Sep, 9.30am-12.30pm & 2.30-5.30pm Oct-Mar) At the Mausoleo di Teodorico.

Sights

The website www.ravennamosaici.it gives information, both historical and practical, about Ravenna's main sights.

BASILICA DI SAN VITALE

The **basilica** (Via San Vitale; 9am-7pm) was consecrated in 547 by Archbishop Maximian. Its sombre exterior hides a dazzling internal feast of colour. The mosaics on the side and end walls represent scenes from the Old Testament. To the left, Abraham prepares to sacrifice Isaac in the presence of three angels. The one on the right portrays the death of Abel and the offering of Melchizedek. Inside the chancel, two magnificent mosaics depict the Byzantine Emperor Justinian with San Massimiano (left) and a particularly solemn and expressive Empress Theodora, who was his consort (right).

MAUSOLEO DI GALLA PLACIDIA

The **mausoleum** (Via San Vitale; 9am-7pm) was constructed for Galla Placidia, the half-sister of Emperor Honorius, who initiated construction of many of Ravenna's grandest buildings, although it's unlikely that she ever lay here. The light inside, filtered through alabaster windows, is dim yet, supplemented by a single central lamp, is sufficient enough to illuminate the city's oldest mosaics.

MUSEO NAZIONALE

Ravenna's main **museum** (☎ 0544 3 44 24; Via San Vitale; admission €4; 8.30am-7.30pm Tue-Sun) has

RAVENNA

INFORMATION
Foto Expert	1 B2
Post Office	2 B2
Splash	3 D3
Telecom Office	4 B3
Tourist Office	5 D1
Tourist Office	6 B2

SIGHTS & ACTIVITIES
Basilica dello Spirito Santo	(see 9)
Basilica di San Vitale	7 B2
Basilica di Sant'Apollinare Nuovo	8 C3
Battistero degli Ariani	9 C2
Battistero Neoniano	10 B3
Cathedral	11 B3
Chiesa di San Francesco	12 C3
Cooperativa Mosaicisti	13 B1
Giardino Rasponi	14 B3
Mausoleo di Galla Placidia	15 B2
Mausoleo di Teodorico	16 D1
Mosaic Art School	17 C3
Museo Arcivescovile	18 B3
Museo Nazionale	19 B2
Teatro Alighieri	20 C2
Tomba di Dante	21 C3

SLEEPING
Albergo Cappello	22 B2
Albergo Ristorante al Giaciglio	23 C2
Hotel Centrale Byron	24 B2
Hotel Ravenna	25 D2

EATING
Bizantino	26 B2
Ca' de Vèn	27 B3
Covered Market	(see 26)
Gelateria Cavour	28 B2
La Gardela	29 B2
L'Oste Bacco	30 B2

DRINKING
Cabiria	31 B2
Fellini Scalino Cinque	32 B2
Locanda del Melarancio	33 B3

TRANSPORT
Bus Station	34 D2
Cooperativa Sociale la Formica	35 D2
Punto Bus	36 D2

a wealth of accumulated pottery, bronzes, icons and vestments plus a greater concentration of portraits of the Madonna and Child, of very variable quality, than you're ever likely to see elsewhere. Monks began this collection of prehistoric, Roman, Christian and Byzantine artefacts in the 18th century and various items from later periods have been added.

CATHEDRAL, MUSEO ARCIVESCOVILE & BATTISTERO NEONIANO

The town's **cathedral** (Via G Rasponi) was built in 1733 after its 5th-century predecessor was destroyed by an earthquake. It is fairly unremarkable but the small adjoining **Museo Arcivescovile** (Episcopal Museum; Piazza Arcivescovado;

9am-7pm) contains an exquisite 6th-century ivory throne of Middle Eastern origin and some beautiful mosaics.

Even more impressive, and still *in situ,* are the mosaics of the baptism of Christ and the apostles on the domed roof of neighbouring **Battistero Neoniano** (Via Battistero; 9am-7pm). Thought to have started life as a Roman bathhouse (and there's a certain watery logic here since baptism at the time was by total immersion) it was converted into a baptistry in the 5th century.

Giardino Rasponi (admission free; 9am-12.45pm & 3.30-7.45pm), just beside Piazza Kennedy, is a small, scented herb garden where you can rest your feet awhile in the shadow of the cathedral.

TICKETS & TIMES

There are three combined tickets on offer in Ravenna. The first (€7.50), valid for seven days, gives entry to the five main monuments – Basilica di San Vitale, Mausoleo di Galla Placidia, Basilica di Sant'Apollinare Nuovo, Museo Arcivescovile and Battistero Neoniano. There's no individual admission price for these monuments.

Another ticket (€5) lets you into Mausoleo di Teodorico and the Museo Nazionale. Pay an extra €1.50 and this final ticket also includes the Basilica di Sant'Apollinare in Classe, about 5km southeast of town. Each of these sites has its own admission price.

The opening times we list are good for April to September and tend to be longer than those for the rest of the year.

The Basilica di San Vitale, Mausoleo di Galla Placidia and Museo Nazionale are all in the same complex, which has its main entrance on Via San Vitale.

To see the mosaics in a different light, do the rounds at night. They're open and illuminated 9pm to 11.30pm every evening during July and August.

TOMBA DI DANTE

Much of Dante's *Divine Comedy* was written right here in Ravenna. Following his exile from Florence in 1302, Dante came to live in Ravenna, where he stayed until his death in 1321. To this day Florence still supplies the oil for the lamp that burns continually in his tomb, as a perpetual act of penance for having exiled him. The 18th-century **tomb** (Via Dante Alighieri 9; admission free; ☽ 8.30am-6pm), beside **Chiesa di San Francesco** (☽ 7am-noon & 2.45-7pm), merits a detour to see the mosaic floor, shimmering beneath its flooded crypt. A mound placed over Dante's sarcophagus during WWII to protect it from air raids is proudly marked, and the area around the tomb has been declared a – albeit much abused – *zona di silenzio* (area of silence).

Another literary great, Lord Byron, briefly lived in a house on nearby Piazza di San Francesco.

Near the tomb, stop and pause to admire the clean, neoclassical façade of the **Teatro Alighieri**, Ravenna's main theatre, just beside Piazza Garibaldi.

MAUSOLEO DI TEODORICO

This two-storey **mausoleum** (Via delle Industrie 14; admission €2; ☽ 8.30am-7pm), built in 520, is a considerable feat of construction with its huge blocks of stone, uncemented by any mortar, and broad dome, 11m in diameter. At the heart of the mausoleum is a Roman basin of porphyry, for all the world appearing like a giant bath, that was recycled as a sarcophagus.

OTHER CHURCHES

The **Basilica di Sant'Apollinare Nuovo** (Via di Roma; ☽ 9am-7pm), originally built by the Goths in the 6th century, is a must see. The exquisite mosaic on the right (south) wall of the nave depicts a procession of 26 martyrs heading towards Christ in Majesty with his apostles. On the left wall is a complementary and equally expressive procession of virgins, bearing offerings to the Madonna.

Behind the **Basilica dello Spirito Santo**, just off Via Diaz, is the **Battistero degli Ariani** (Via degli Ariani; admission free; ☽ 8.30am-7.30pm). Like the Battistero Neoniano, its dome has a breathtaking mosaic depicting the baptism of Christ.

Five kilometres southeast of the city centre is the **Basilica di Sant'Apollinare in Classe** (☎ 0544 47 35 69; Via Romea Sud, Classe; admission €2; ☽ 8.30am-7.30pm Mon-Sat, 1-7.30pm Sun). The basilica was built in the 6th century on the burial site of Ravenna's patron saint, who converted the city to Christianity in the 2nd century. The highlight of this harmonious construction is a brilliant, star-spangled mosaic in the apse. To get there take bus No 4 or the train to Classe.

Courses

The **Mosaic Art School** (☎ 335 561 84 85; www.mosaic-tiles.com; Via F Negri 14) offers intensive five-day courses across all levels in the art of mosaics.

Fifty years in the business, the **Centro Internazionale di Studi per l'Insegnamento del Mosaico** (Cisim; ☎ 0544 45 03 44; www.mosaico.ravenna.it; Via M Monti 32, Bassente) runs an intensive one-week mosaic course from late June to early September.

The **Cooperativa Mosaicisti** (☎ 0544 3 47 99; www.coopmosaico.it; Via Fiandrini 1), in the grounds of the Museo Nazionale and less immediately welcoming than the others, also runs mosaic courses.

Festivals & Events

Riccardo Muti, director of Milan's La Scala, has close ties with Ravenna and is intimately involved each year with the **Ravenna Festival** (☎ 0544 24 92 44; www.ravennafestival.org), one of Italy's top music events, with recitals from mid-June to late July.

Stars of the jazz scene come to Ravenna in the second half of July for **Ravenna Jazz** (☎ 0544 40 56 66). Check out **Crossroads** (www .crossroads-it.com in Italian), a trimonthly magazine, for information about who's currently performing on Ravenna's active jazz scene.

Sleeping

Albergo Ristorante al Giac-ciglio (☎ 0544 3 94 03; www.albergoalgiaciglio.com in Italian; Via Rocca Brancaleone 42; s/d/tr €38/43/53, with bathroom €43/65/75) A welcoming, economical, family-run 16-room hotel. It's a great budget option and also has a good **restaurant** (pastas from €5.50, mains about €10, tourist menu €15; ☼ dinner) that makes its own pasta and specialises in Romagnan food, with fresh fish and seafood on Friday. There's also a vegetarian menu (€15).

Albergo Cappello (☎ 0544 21 98 13; www.albergo cappello.it; Via IV Novembre 41; s/d with breakfast from €93/110; P ☼ ☐) In a 15th-century townhouse, Cappello has seven lovely, ample rooms with intricately painted wooden ceilings and traces of *fresco*. Enterprisingly renovated, what's new – such as the innovative lighting from vast moons overhead and standard lamps sprouting bulbs in all directions – blends harmoniously with the antique. It runs a superb **restaurant** (mains €17-18, degustation menu €30; ☼ closed Sun dinner & Mon), too. Parking is €14.

Hotel Centrale Byron (☎ 0544 3 34 79; www.hotel byron.com; Via IV Novembre 14; s/d from with breakfast €65/108; ☼ ☐) This place offers all the comforts you'd expect from a three-star hotel from its polished brass door onwards. A mere 20 paces from Piazza del Popolo, it couldn't be more central.

Hotel Ravenna (☎ 0544 21 22 04; hotelravenna@ ravennablu.it; Viale Maroncelli 12; s/d €40/55, s/d/tr with bathroom €48/73/98; P) Hotel Ravenna is another family-run hotel. Convenient for the station, it's clean, pleasant and welcoming. Rooms are large and there's free parking for guests.

Ostello Dante (☎ 0544 42 11 64; Via Nicolodi 12; dm/d with breakfast €13.50/30) HI-affiliated, Ostello Dante is in a modern building 1km east from the train station. In an excellent initiative that

ought to be copied by every hotel in the land, it has small box safes (€0.20) near reception where you can stash your valuables. Take bus No 1 from town or the train station.

The closest camping sites are on the coast at Marina di Ravenna (take ATM bus No 70 or follow the S67 from the town centre).

Camping Piomboni (☎ 0544 53 02 30; www.camp ingpiomboni.it; Viale della Pace 421; person/site €7/10.90; ☼ Easter–mid-Sep) Eight kilometres from Ravenna, this camping ground is convenient for the beach and set in shady pinewood. Take bus No 70 from Ravenna.

Eating

For a couple of highly recommended hotel-restaurant options, see left.

Ca' de Vèn (☎ 0544 3 01 63; Via Corrado Ricci 24; mains €9-13.50; ☼ Tue-Sun) As much an *enoteca* as a restaurant, it has a short but splendid menu that changes weekly. The vast, high-roofed eating area has been in turn a lodging house, spice shop and wine cellar (just *look* at all those bottles of rare Emiliagna wines on the shelves; you're unlikely to be able to afford to buy any but current best vintages are available at around €2.50 a glass).

L'Oste Bacco (☎ 0544 3 53 63; Via Salara 20; mains €7-13; ☼ Wed-Mon) A truly inventive little place, normally packed to the gunnels with discerning locals. It's well worth the effort of deciphering the handwritten list of daily specials. As a starter, plump for the *frittata ai porri dolci* (omelette with leeks).

La Gardela (☎ 0544 21 71 47; Via Ponte Marino 3; meals €18-25; ☼ Fri-Wed) An elegant yet informal eatery whose specialities include *cappalletti romagnoli al ragù* (hat-shaped pasta with meat sauce, €5.20).

Gelateria Cavour (☎ 0544 3 60 08; Via Cavour 42; ice creams €1.50-2.75) For a sweet finale, head for Gelateria Cavour.

Bizantino (Piazza Andrea Costa; mains €4.10-5, menus €6.20 & €7.50; ☼ lunch Mon-Fri) A popular self-service restaurant inside the main entrance of the covered market, this is the place for a quick, economical lunch-time bite.

Self-caterers and sandwich-fillers should stock up at the city's **covered market** (Piazza Andrea Costa).

Drinking

Cabiria (Via Mordani 8; ☼ 6pm-2am Mon-Sat) A wine bar with a terrace on a quiet, cobbled street that attracts drinkers of all ages.

Fellini Scalino Cinque (Piazza Kennedy 15) This brings life to the dourly functional Casa del Mutilato di Guerra that broods over the piazza. It's a chameleon of a place: a lunch-time restaurant, then a place for afternoon tea, it puts on its party gear around 6pm and rocks till way past midnight. There's a DJ on Tuesday and on weekends.

Locanda del Melarancio (☎ 0544 21 52 58; Via Mentana 33) Change out of your ripped jeans and flip flops to enjoy Locanda del Mela-rancio, a very smooth place for an apéritif or more. It's at the junction of Gardini, Gui-doni and Gordoni streets (try explaining that at speed to a taxi driver after a couple of cocktails).

Getting There & Around

Ryanair flies twice daily between London (Stansted) and Forlì, 35km southwest of Ravenna.

ATM buses depart from Piazzale Farini for towns along the coast. **Punto Bus** (☎ 0544 68 99 00), on the piazza, is ATM's information and ticketing office. An in-town journey costs €0.75 and a *biglietto turistico* (tourist ticket), valid for three days, is €3.

Frequent trains connect the city with Bologna (€4.70), Ferrara (€4.20; change here for Venice, €8.95), Faenza (€2.50), Rimini (€2.90) and the south coast.

Ravenna is on a branch of the A14 Bologna to Rimini autostrada. The S16 (Via Adriatica) heads south to Rimini and on down the coast. The main car parks are east of the train station and north of the Basilica di San Vitale.

To its immense credit, Ravenna runs a free bicycle-hire service for visitors. Simply pick up a key from the main tourist office, borrow a bike from one of the several cycle parking stalls around town and return it to the same rack. Red bikes are for residents, yellow for visitors.

Cooperativa Sociale la Formica (☎ 0544 3 70 31; 7am-8pm Mon-Sat), which operates from a shed just south of the station, acts as a left-luggage office and rents out bikes (per hour/day €1/7.75).

FAENZA

This Romagnola town has been producing high-grade ceramics for hundreds of years and gave us the word faïence (tin-glazed earthenware). A 30-minute train ride from Ravenna, its vast **Museo Internazionale delle Ceramiche** (☎ 0546 69 73 11; Viale Baccarini 19; adult/child €6/3; 9am-7pm Tue-Sat, 9.30am-1pm & 3-7pm Sun Apr-Oct, 9am-1.30pm Tue-Fri, 9.30am-5.30pm Sat & Sun Nov-Mar) displays a treasure-trove of pots, plates and finest tableware from around the world and across the centuries.

Faenza's **tourist office** (☎ 0546 2 52 31) is at Piazza del Popolo 1.

RIMINI
pop 129,700

The extensive beach and Rimini's frenetic nightlife pull in holiday-makers by the tens of thousands to this Adriatic fun spot; young folk flock here every weekend from as far away as Rome. In summer, the town, with more than 100 discos and clubs to choose from, bursts with Italian and, in-creasingly, foreign holiday-makers in search of a free scrap of beach and nocturnal fun and games. Even so, and in spite of all the frenzy, Rimini remains a family-holiday destination for many Italians.

Its old city centre was hugely battered by 400 allied bombing raids in WWII but enough remains to warrant a snoop around.

Federico Fellini, Italy's exuberant film di-rector and winner of more than 10 Oscars, hails from Rimini. He and his wife and fre-quent star, the haunting Giulietta Masina, lie side by side in the town cemetery.

History

Originally Umbrian, then Etruscan, and then the important Roman colony of Arimi-num, Rimini sits at the centre of the Riviera del Sole. The city continued to change hands throughout the Middle Ages, knowing Byz-antine, Lombard and papal rule before end-ing up in the hands of the Malatesta family in the 13th century. At the beginning of the 16th century, Cesare Borgia added the city to his list of short-lived conquests but Rimini soon succumbed to Venice, then the Papal States. Rimini, finally its own master, joined the Kingdom of Italy in 1860.

Orientation

The train station is at the northern edge of the small historic quarter, which is bounded by Corso Giovanni XXIII to the west and Corso d'Augusto, itself punctuated by old Rimini's two main squares, Piazza Tre Mar-tiri and Piazza Cavour. Wherever you are,

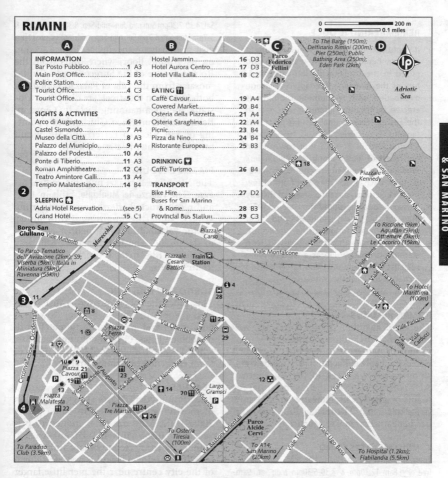

RIMINI

INFORMATION		SLEEPING
Bar Posto Pubblico	1 A3	Adria Hotel Reservation (see 5)
Main Post Office	2 B3	Grand Hotel 15 C1
Police Station	3 A3	
Tourist Office	4 C3	Hostel Jammin 16 D3
Tourist Office	5 C1	Hotel Aurora Centro 17 D3
		Hotel Villa Lalla 18 C2
SIGHTS & ACTIVITIES		
Arco di Augusto	6 B4	EATING
Castel Sismondo	7 A4	Caffè Cavour 19 A4
Museo della Città	8 A3	Covered Market 20 B4
Palazzo del Municipio	9 A3	Osteria della Piazzetta 21 A4
Palazzo del Podestà	10 A4	Osteria Saraghina 22 A4
Ponte di Tiberio	11 A3	Picnic 23 B4
Roman Amphitheatre	12 C4	Pizza da Nino 24 B4
Teatro Amintore Galli	13 A4	Ristorante Europea 25 B3
Tempio Malatestiano	14 B4	
		DRINKING
		Caffè Turismo 26 B4
		TRANSPORT
		Bike Hire 27 D2
		Buses for San Marino & Rome 28 B3
		Provincial Bus Station 29 C3

walk in an easterly direction and you can't fail to hit a beach.

Information

Bar Posto Pubblico (☎ 0541 2 98 28; Corso Giovanni XXIII 20a; per hr €3; ☻ 7.30am-midnight Mon-Sat Jun Sep, 2-10pm Sun Oct-May) Internet facilities.

Guardia Medica (☎ 0541 70 57 57) Emergency doctor.

Hospital (☎ 0541 70 51 11; Viale Luigi Settembrini 2) Southeast of the centre.

Main post office (Corso d'Augusto)

Police station (☎ 0541 35 31 11; Corso d'Augusto 192)

Tourist office Parco Federico Fellini 3 (☎ 0541 5 69 02; www.riminiturismo.it; ☻ 8.30am-7pm Easter–mid-Sep, 8.30am-7pm Mon-Sat mid-Sep–Easter) The main office; train station (☎ 0541 5 13 31; Parco Federico Fellini; ☻ 8.30am-7pm Easter-Oct, 10am-4pm Mon-Sat

Nov-Easter) There are also three beachfront kiosks, open in summer only.

Sights & Activities

CASTEL SISMONDO

At the southwestern corner of the old town, the **castle** (Piazza Malatesta; ☻ exhibitions only), also known as the Rocca Malatestiana, takes its name from Sigismondo, one of the Malatesta family who ruled for a couple of centuries until Cesare Borgia took over in 1500. Sigismondo wasn't your ideal ruler: Pope Pius II – himself no angel – burned his effigy in Rome and condemned him to hell for an impressive litany of sins that included rape, murder, incest, adultery and severe oppression of the people.

REMEMBERING IL DUCE

It might seem a little odd that Italy's great dictator, Benito Mussolini, was born and raised in the traditionally left-wing territory of the Romagna. Predappio, a village overloaded with monumental buildings erected by its most infamous son, is also the Fascist leader's final resting place; his remains were buried here in 1957. About 15km south of Forlì (a dull town 45km northwest of Rimini along the Via Emilia), Predappio is the scene of pro-Fascist celebrations each year, when the faithful few mark 31 October, the anniversary of the day Mussolini became prime minister in 1922. Many of the young skinheads and older die-hards, before donning the black shirt, probably forget that their beloved icon started his political life as a card-carrying socialist and journalist who rarely missed a chance to wave the red flag.

ROMAN REMAINS

The **Arco di Augusto** (Arch of Augustus) was erected in 27 BC at the southeastern end of Corso d'Augusto. At the Corso's western end is the **Ponte di Tiberio** (Tiberius' Bridge), slung across the creek in the 1st century AD. You can also visit the insubstantial remains of a **Roman amphitheatre** (cnr Viale Roma & Via Bastioni Orientali). The former Roman forum lies beneath Piazza Tre Martiri.

TEMPIO MALATESTIANO

Tempio Malatestiano (Via IV Novembre 35; admission free; ☒ 8am-12.30pm & 3.30-6.30pm Mon-Sat, 9am-1pm & 3.30-7.30pm Sun) of the Malatesta clan is Rimini's grandest monument. Dedicated to St Francis, the church was transformed in the 15th century to house the tomb of Sigismondo Malatesta's beloved mistress, Isotta degli Atti. Most of the unfinished façade is by the Florentine Leon Battista Alberti, one of the period's great architects. The side chapels are separated from the single wide nave by marble balustrades topped by tubby cherubs. The chapel nearest the altar on the south side has a fine fresco by Piero della Francesca.

MUSEO DELLA CITTÀ

Rimini's town **museum** (☎ 0541 2 14 82; Via Tonini 1; adult/child €4/2.50; ☒ 10am-12.30pm & 4.30-7.30pm Mon-Sat, 4.30-7.30pm Sun mid-Jun–mid-Sep, 8.30am-12.30pm & 5-7pm Mon-Sat, 4-7pm Sun mid-Sep–mid-Jun) is worth a visit primarily for the archaeological section on its ground floor, where finds from the Roman House of the Surgeon and splendid mosaics from the villa of Palazzo Diotallevi, both just down the street, are displayed. Upstairs, there's a haunting Pietà by Giovanni Bellini and Domenico Ghirlandaio's painting of San Vicenzo Ferreri and supplicant members of the Malatesta family.

PIAZZA CAVOUR

The city's finest palazzi hug this central piazza. The **Palazzo del Municipio**, built in 1562 and reconstructed after being razed during WWII, abuts the imposing 14th-century Gothic **Palazzo del Podestà**; neither are open to the public. The **Teatro Amintore Galli** only went up in 1857 in the feverish years leading to unification.

BORGO SAN GIULIANO

This old fisherfolk's quarter is just north of the Ponte di Tiberio bridge. Nowadays gussied up and arty, it's a little patchwork of cobbled lanes, up-and-coming trattorias, wine bars and trim terraced houses, many of them enlivened by painted murals.

BEACHES

The Rimini riviera boasts a staggering 40km of mostly sandy beaches, in some places 200m wide. Most are either rented to private companies, which in turn rent space to bathers, or connected to hotels. Indeed, the only free sand you'll find is a stretch north of the city centre near the pier little larger than a couple of beach towels.

The typical daily charge for an umbrella and a pair of loungers is around €15, including access to changing rooms and showers. Though the price may sting, these private areas are well worth it if you have children. All have bars and small playgrounds and most organise special activities. Several offer windsurfing courses and board hire.

All of Rimini's beaches bear the coveted EU blue flag as an indication of their cleanliness, and pollution levels are monitored daily.

THEME PARKS

Rimini isn't just for sun-lovers and socialites; the coast abounds in theme parks at various points on the naffness scale for kids and their suffering parents. **Italia in Miniatura** (☎ 0541 73 20 04; www.italiainminiatura.com; Via Popilia 239, Viserba SS16 km 197; adult/child €14/10; ☿ 9am-midnight Jul & Aug, 9am-7.30pm Apr-Jun & Sep, 9am-sunset Sat & Sun Oct-Mar), west of the city in Viserba, is a collection of reproductions of the best bits of Italy, such as scale models of some 120 buildings facing Venice's Grand Canal and Piazza San Marco. Take bus No 8 from the Rimini train station or Viserba.

Fiabilandia (☎ 0541 37 20 64; Via Cardano 15, Rivazzurra di Rimini; adult/child €15/10; ☿ 10am-midnight Jul & Aug, 10am-7pm Apr-Jun & Sep), southeast of the city centre is a fantasy park full of weird and wonderful settings such as Fu-Ming's Oriental Labyrinth and the Valley of the Gnomes. Take bus No 9 from Rimini's train station.

Among several dolphinariums in the area is **Delfinario Rimini** (☎ 0541 5 02 98; Lungomare Tintori 2; adult/child €9/6; ☿ Easter-Sep), beside Rimini's public beach.

Those of an aeronautical bent will be flying high at the **Parco Tematico dell'Aviazione** (☎ 0541 75 66 96; Via S Aquilina 58; adult/child €8/6.50; ☿ 9am-7pm), beside the road leading to San Marino. With more than 40 planes including MiGs, a DC3 once owned by Clark Gable and a Gloucester Javelin, plus a variety of weapons used to shoot them down, it's a great place for all those who've never quite grown up. Take bus No 7.

For more harmless flying things, pay a visit to **Eden Park** (☎ 0541 72 06 38; Via Popilia 345-47; adult/child €4/3; ☿ 9am-sunset), a sanctuary for exotic birds and animals at Torre Pedrera in the northern beach area.

Waterparks in and around Rimini include **Aquafàn** (☎ 0541 60 30 50; Via Pistoia, Riccione; adult/child €19/12; ☿ 10am-6.30pm mid-Jun–mid-Sep) at Riccione, about 15km south of town. Take bus No 42, 45 or 51 from Riccione station.

The biggest, newest and most imaginative of the parks, **Oltremare** (☎ 0541 42 71; Via Ascoli Piceno 6, Riccione; adult/child €21/16; ☿ 10am-midnight Jul & Aug, 10am-6pm Apr, 10am-6.30pm May-Jun & Sep), also in Riccione, has a wealth of displays about the earth, oceans and all sorts of disparate themes. To get here, take bus No 42, 45 or 51 from Riccione train station.

Tours

In summer, there are free multilingual guided walking **tours** (☎ 0541 5 54 14; ☿ Tue mid-Jun–mid-Sep) of the old quarter. Just turn up at the

Museo della Città's **public relations office** (Corso d'Augusto 158) at 9am.

Festivals & Events

Paganello, held over a long weekend in March, is an international Frisbee moot.

On 21 June, the longest day of the year, Rimini stays up late to celebrate **Gradisca** with dancing, fireworks and eating; it's estimated that revellers consume some two tonnes of grilled sardines and 12,000L of local Sangiovese wine in that one night.

In summer, the **Rimini Jazz Festival** (☎ 0541 5 10 11; riminidixieland@libero.it) is held outdoors beside the main Marina Centro beach area every year, while September's more sedate **Sagra Malatestiana Music Festival** brings in top classical conductors and performers.

Sleeping

In July and August accommodation can be difficult to find and very expensive since proprietors often make full board compulsory. In winter many of Rimini's 1500 hotels close and the city is dead. In summer touts, sanctioned by the tourist office, frequent intersections on the outskirts of the city and offer rooms at so-called bargain rates. It is much better and more reliable to book through **Adria Hotel Reservation** (☎ 0541 5 33 99; Piazzale Federico Fellini 3), a neighbour of the main tourist office.

Most hotels are boarded up outside the main season. Those we recommend here are open year-round. During August, prices increase absurdly so we've generally indicated both high- and low-season extremes.

Hostel Jammin (☎ 0541 39 08 00; www.hosteljammin.com; Viale Derna 22; dm €16-18, d/tr with bathroom €38/57; ☐) HI-affiliated and freshly opened this place is more hotel than hostel, its rooms accommodating from two to four. Run by a hyper-friendly young team, it's down a quiet street yet within easy strolling distance of the beach. Bikes are free for guests and there's a great roof terrace from which you can just glimpse the sea. The tariff includes breakfast, and there's wi-fi.

Hotel Villa Lalla (☎ 0541 5 51 55; www.villalalla.com; Viale Veneto 22; s €34-73, d €52-130; P ☒ ☐) Villa Lalla looks from the exterior like the post-WWII private villa it once was. Now a tautly managed hotel, its rates outside high season are very reasonable and include breakfast. It's well worth paying a little extra for the better rooms, which are indeed markedly superior. And, from mid-May to mid-September when the restaurant's open, it is a good idea to invest in half board or full board (a mere €4 and €8, respectively). Bikes are free for guests; parking is €4.

Hotel Marittima (☎ 0541 39 25 25; www.hotelmarittima.it; Viale Parisano 24; s/d with breakfast €48.50/81; P ⊠ 🖵) Quiet yet only a couple of blocks from the beach, Marittima is an excellent midrange choice. Rooms are trim and the breakfast room and bar are light, bright and airy. Parking is €5.

Hotel Aurora Centro (☎ 0541 39 10 02; fax 0541 39 16 82; Via Tobruk 6; s/d €35/60; P) Run by a welcoming, exuberant elderly couple, this is an excellent economical choice, handy for the beach and with a well-stocked downstairs bar.

Camping Italia Rimini (☎ 0541 73 28 82; www.campingitaliarimini.it; Via Toscanelli 112, Viserba; person/site €8.50/14; ☼ mid-May–Sep) One of a wide choice of camping grounds, this area is wooded, shady and about 1km northwest of the city centre. Take bus No 4.

Grand Hotel (☎ 0541 5 60 60; www.grandhotelrimini.com; Parco Federico Fellini; s/d with breakfast from €180/240; P ⊠ 🖵) The Grand Hotel exudes old-world charm. 'A fable of riches, luxury and oriental splendour' – that's how Fellini regarded the Grand Hotel when he was a boy. Adolescent overstatement it might have been but the five-star Grand remains truly that with its lovely terrace, pool, vast shady garden and attentive service.

Eating

For fast food, nothing beats a *piadina*, a toasted half-moon of unleavened bread with a savoury filling – Romagna's retort to the wrap.

Ristorante Europa (☎ 0541 2 87 61; Viale Roma 51; mains €16-20.50; ☼ Mon-Sat) With silver candlesticks on the tables, cascading bouquets of dried flowers and leaves, a couple of pouting goldfish and nightlights flickering around the perimeter, Ristorante Europa verges on the decadent. And the acclaimed cuisine is just as wicked...

Picnic (☎ 0541 2 19 16; Via Tempio Malatestiano 3; pizzas €4-7, mains €8-13; ☼ Tue-Sun) Like so many Rimini restaurants, Picnic is particularly strong on fish and seafood. Try the *spaghetti allo scoglio* (with seafood), perhaps followed by the *grigliata mista* (a platter of fish) grilled to perfection. Good food – and

it's really very good – comes slowly here (inexcusably slowly, the last time we ate there) so dine with a good friend or an equally palatable book.

Osteria Saraghina (☎ 0541 78 37 94; Via Poletti 32; seafood pastas €7-13, mains €12-15; ☼ Tue-Sun) Here you will find fish and seafood throughout the menu. The quality is excellent, the venue agreeable and the staff friendly – plus the view of Castel Sismondo is a bonus.

Osteria della Piazzetta (☎ 0541 78 39 86; Vicolo Pescheria 5; meals €25-35; ☼ Mon-Sat) This place offers typical Romagna cuisine, served up in hearty portions. Be sure to sample the *strozzapreti misto funghi e salsiccia* (short-strand pasta with mushrooms and finely chopped sausage).

Pizza da Nino (Via IV Novembre 9) As simple as they come, Pizza da Nino bakes tasty, instant, takeaway pizza by the slice and *piadine* from €1.20.

Osteria Tiresia (☎ 0541 78 18 96; Via XX Settembre 41; ☼ dinner Tue-Sun) For that very special occasion. You'll leave at least €100 lighter but with a wonderful feeling in your tum after one of the finest meals you're ever likely to taste, consumed in agreeably – and paradoxically – peasant-rustic surroundings.

Caffè Cavour (☎ 0541 78 51 23; Piazza Cavour 13) Attractive and angled between the main square and Rimini's former marketplace, this makes a good pit stop for cappuccino or *panini* throughout the day.

For self-catering or picnic provender, load up at Rimini's **covered market** (Via Castelfidardo).

Drinking

Barge (☎ 0541 2 26 85; Lungomare Tintori 13) Barge, along the beachfront, is a Romagnola version of the Irish pub. Good music (DJ or live), drinks and food are a magnet for all the fashionable 20-somethings. Draft Guinness at a bargain €3 a pint is far from the least of its charms.

Caffè Turismo (☎ 0541 2 27 15; Piazza Tre Martiri 3) Caffè Turismo isn't the tourist trap its name might imply. Designer cool, all glass and mellow olive-green, its *the* place for watching the beautiful people of Rimini strut their stuff. The single giant footsteps toilet is a nod towards an earlier tradition...

Entertainment

Discotecas and clubs come and go (in winter very few are open at all). Ask at the tourist office for your type of club and also about the special summer-service buses that go to the clubs. In summer, the coast north and south of Rimini positively throbs and pounds, all along its length.

Le Cocoricò (☎ 0541 60 51 83; Via Chieti 44, Riccione; admission €26) Rimini coast's most famous club, Le Cocoricò, is 15km south in Riccione. Underground, techno and house music rule. Go there with 2000 of your closest friends – you'll all fit.

Paradiso Club (☎ 0541 75 11 32; www.paradiso club.it in Italian; Via Covignano 260; admission €19) An equally vast club in Rimini with two dance floors, seven bars and there's a restaurant too. The music's eclectic and anything goes.

Getting There & Away

Ryanair flies twice daily between London (Stansted) and Forlì airport, 50km northwest of Rimini. Buses run to the airport from Rimini's train station to coincide with flights.

There are regular buses to towns all along the coast, including Riccione (No 11) and Cattolica (Nos 11 and 125). Buses run from Rimini's train station to San Marino (return €6.20, 45 minutes, six to eight daily) and there's also a daily direct bus to/from Rome (€24.60, 5¼ hours).

Trains run frequently down the coast to Ancona (€7.65), Bari (€33.85), Lecce (€47.80) and Taranto (€47.90). Up the line, they service Ravenna (€2.90), Bologna (€6.45) and then onto Milan (€26.90).

You have a choice of the A14 (south into Le Marche or northwest towards Bologna and Milan) or the toll-free but quite often clogged S16 autostrada.

Getting Around

TRAM (www.tram.rimini.it in Italian) buses operate throughout the city. In August, the Blue Line are special late-night buses with onboard music connecting the out-of-town clubs with the city centre, train station and camping grounds. They run all through the night until 6am and for €3 you can hop on and off at will. If you're a seriously dedicated clubber, pick up a seven-night pass for €2.

For a taxi, ring ☎ 0541 5 00 20.

An open-air stall on Piazzale Kennedy, one of several cycling options, rents out city bikes (per hour €3) and mountain bikes (per hour €4).

SAN MARINO

pop 27,730
What did King Arthur say of Camelot in Monty Python's *The Holy Grail*? 'It is a silly place.' Lying 657m above sea level and only 10km from the Adriatic Sea as the crow flies, the 61-sq-km Repubblica di San Marino, Europe's third-smallest state after the Vatican and Monaco, seems a little on the silly side, too. One can only speculate what Mexico's consul does here – or, indeed, his homologue, the San Marino Honorary Consul in Honolulu – and you're unlikely to ever see a greater density of kitsch souvenir stands. This said, the old town is pleasant enough if you catch it at a quiet time and the views all around are simply spectacular.

If you're in Rimini, think of it as just another of the beach resort's theme parks. You can take pictures of the republic's soldiers, buy local coinage and send mail with San Marino stamps. Avoid weekends, especially in summer, when the town is clogged with visitors.

History

Several legends describe the founding of this hilly city-state, including one about a stonecutter who was given the land on top of Monte Titano by a rich Roman woman whose son he had cured. What's attested is that the inhabitants of the mountain republic are the inheritors of 1700 years of revolution-free liberty; 'Welcome to the Country of Freedom', the signs proclaim. Everybody has left San Marino well alone. Well almost. Cesare Borgia took possession early in the 16th century, but his rule was short-lived as he died soon after. In 1739 one Cardinal Giulio Alberoni took over the republic but the pope backed San Marino's independence and the cardinal was sent packing.

During WWII the republic of San Marino remained neutral and played host to 100,000 refugees until 1944, when the Allies marched into the town. San Marino joined the European Council in 1988 and the UN in 1992.

This tiny republic has some bizarre regulations (see the boxed text, p454) and citizenship is passed on only through the male line. A 1999 referendum to change this law was not passed.

Orientation

Perched on a clifftop, the old part of San Marino, the only element of any interest, is essentially one main street. Enter via the Porta San Francesco, ascend Via Basilicius to Piazza Titano, keep climbing another 50m to Piazza Garibaldi, turn left up Contrada del Collegio, go to the end of Contrada del Omagnano or parallel Contrado del Pianello – then stop short or you'll fall over the cliff. That's it. You've done the capital of this nation state.

Information

Post office (Viale Antonio Onofri 87; ⏰ 8.15am-4.30pm Mon-Fri)

Tourist office (☎ 0549 88 29 14; www.visitsanmarino .com; Contrada del Collegio; ⏰ 8.30am-6.30pm)

Sights & Activities

You might want to spend some time in San Marino's small **state museum** (☎ 0549 88 38 35; Piazza Titano 1; adult/child €3/free; ⏰ 8am-8pm Apr–mid-Sep,

> ### GOLD-DIGGERS KEEP OUT
>
> The Republic of San Marino has laws to stop foreign gold-diggers snatching its supply of rich, elderly men. After several incidences of young foreigners marrying elderly San Marino residents for their money, regulations were introduced banning female domestic staff aged under 50. In the words of a spokesperson for the San Marino congress: 'It's a question of sovereignty and of the measures that a small state takes to protect itself.'

9am-5pm mid-Sep–Mar) even if most of the more interesting exhibits, which are impressively displayed, come from outside the republic. Or take a squint at the **Palazzo Pubblico** (admission €3). Or just wander along the well-kept city walls and perhaps poke around the two fortresses, **Rocca Guaita** and **Rocca Cesta** (admission to each €3; ⏰ 8am-8pm Apr–mid-Sep, 9am-5pm mid-Sep–Mar), which has a small museum of old weapons. Otherwise, there are several other private minimuseums after your money – museums of modern weapons, instruments of torture, wax dummies and a reptilarium/aquarium.

Combine your pleasures and you can buy a ticket for the state museum and Palazzo Pubblico for €4.50. For the same price, you can also get one giving admission to the two forts.

Stamp collectors can pick up current issues at the post office and browse or buy back issues of stamps from **Ufficio Filatelico-Numismatico** (Piazza Garibaldi 5).

To stretch the legs and enjoy superb views through the trees before mixing it with the throng, leave your vehicle in car park No 3, beside the radio and TV station on the south side of town, and walk the narrow footpath along the crest.

Sleeping & Eating

There are several camping grounds signposted off the main road (S72) running through the republic from Rimini.

Albergo Diamond (☎ /fax 0549 99 10 03; Contrada del Collegio 50; d €55) has six spacious rooms above a large, busy restaurant...should you miss the last bus out.

Food is not one of San Marino's strong points and the best thing about some of the

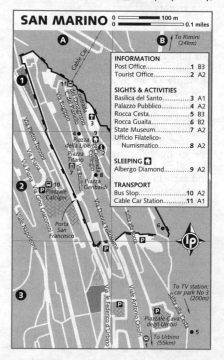

SAN MARINO

0 _____ 100 m
0 _____ 0.1 miles

INFORMATION	
Post Office.....................1	B3
Tourist Office.................2	A2

SIGHTS & ACTIVITIES	
Basilica del Santo..............3	A1
Palazzo Pubblico...............4	A2
Rocca Cesta....................5	B3
Rocca Guaita...................6	B2
State Museum..................7	A2
Ufficio Filatelico-	
Numismatico.................8	A2

SLEEPING 🏠	
Albergo Diamond...............9	A2

TRANSPORT	
Bus Stop.......................10	A2
Cable Car Station............11	A1

cafés is the views. The centre is well endowed with places offering set meals starting at around €15.

Shopping

Buy nothing is probably the best advice. 'Welcome to Fred's Spirits: cheap booze and free drinks' proclaims one come-on. Fred and his fellow traders claim to sell cut-price alcohol but you'd want to be sure what your poison is worth in Italy before buying here in the belief that you're getting duty-free bargains.

Getting There & Away

Buses run to/from Rimini (return €6.20, 45 minutes, six to eight daily), arriving at the parking station in Piazzale Calcigni, better known as Piazzale delle Autocorriere. The S72 leads up from Rimini.

If you arrive by car, leave it at one of the numerous car parks (Nos 6 and 7 are the highest) and walk or take the series of stairs and elevators to the town. If all the town car parks are full, you'll have to park near the *funivia* (cable car, return €3.10) and take it to the centre.

EMILIA-ROMAGNA
& SAN MARINO

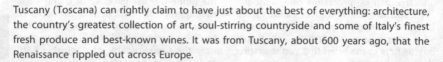

Tuscany

Tuscany (Toscana) can rightly claim to have just about the best of everything: architecture, the country's greatest collection of art, soul-stirring countryside and some of Italy's finest fresh produce and best-known wines. It was from Tuscany, about 600 years ago, that the Renaissance rippled out across Europe.

The works of Michelangelo, Leonardo da Vinci and so many other 14th- to 16th-century Tuscan masters remain models for artists to this day. Tuscan architects such as Brunelleschi and Leon Battista Alberti have had an enduring influence on the course of architecture. Dante, Petrarch and Boccaccio planted the seeds for a unified Italian language with their vigorous literature. Most people are drawn to Tuscany by the artistic splendours of Florence and Siena or to view the Leaning Tower of Pisa. But Tuscany also harbours some of Italy's most impressive hill towns and there's great scope for walking, notably among the gentle green hills and valleys of Il Chianti or, for more vigorous striding, the Apuane Alps.

In the south, Etruscan sites around Saturnia and Sovana take you away from the mainstream tourist itinerary. And the southern coast boasts some pleasant beaches, especially on the Monte Argentario peninsula and Elba island. Travelling in Tuscany is easy. The A1 and main train line ensure good north–south connections, and major areas are easily accessible by public transport. However, a car does give you much greater flexibility.

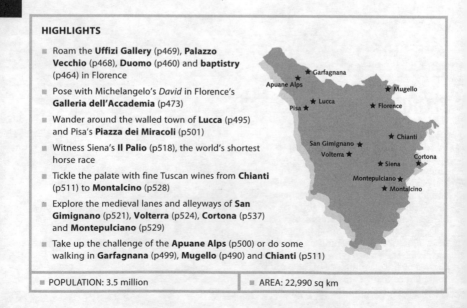

HIGHLIGHTS

- Roam the **Uffizi Gallery** (p469), **Palazzo Vecchio** (p468), **Duomo** (p460) and **baptistry** (p464) in Florence
- Pose with Michelangelo's *David* in Florence's **Galleria dell'Accademia** (p473)
- Wander around the walled town of **Lucca** (p495) and Pisa's **Piazza dei Miracoli** (p501)
- Witness Siena's **Il Palio** (p518), the world's shortest horse race
- Tickle the palate with fine Tuscan wines from **Chianti** (p511) to **Montalcino** (p528)
- Explore the medieval lanes and alleyways of **San Gimignano** (p521), **Volterra** (p524), **Cortona** (p537) and **Montepulciano** (p529)
- Take up the challenge of the **Apuane Alps** (p500) or do some walking in **Garfagnana** (p499), **Mugello** (p490) and **Chianti** (p511)

- POPULATION: 3.5 million
- AREA: 22,990 sq km

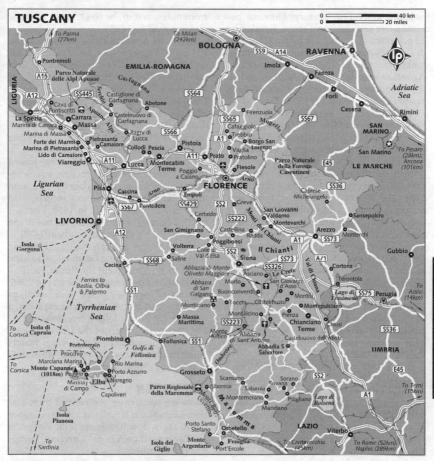

FLORENCE

pop 353,000

Beside the banks of the River Arno and set among low hills clad in olive groves and vineyards, Florence (Firenze) is immediately captivating. Cradle of the Renaissance and home of Machiavelli, Michelangelo and the Medici, the city seems unfairly over-blessed with art, culture and history.

Despite the traffic and stifling summer heat, Florence attracts millions of tourists each year. The French writer Stendhal was so dazzled by the magnificence of the Basilica di Santa Croce that he was barely able to walk for faintness. He's not the only one to have

felt overwhelmed by the beauty of the city – Florentine doctors reputedly treat a good dozen cases of 'Stendhalismo' each year.

You need at least four or five days to do Florence any justice at all.

HISTORY

Controversy still reigns over who founded Florence. The most commonly accepted story holds that Julius Caesar founded Florentia around 59 BC, making it a strategic garrison on the narrowest crossing of the Arno and thus controlling the Via Flaminia, which linked Rome to northern Italy and Gaul. But archaeological evidence suggests an earlier village, founded perhaps by the Etruscans of Fiesole as early as 200 BC.

In the early 12th century, Florence became a free *comune* (town council), ruled by 12 *priori* (consuls) assisted by the Consiglio di Cento (Council of One Hundred), drawn mainly from the prosperous merchant class. Agitation among differing factions led to the appointment of a foreign head of state, known as the *podestà*, in 1207.

The first conflicts between two of the factions, the pro-papal Guelphs (Guelfi) and the pro-imperial Ghibellines (Ghibellini), started in the mid-13th century, with power passing from one to the other for almost a century.

In the 1290s the Guelphs split into two factions: the Neri (Blacks) and Bianchi (Whites). When the Bianchi were defeated, Dante was among those driven into exile in 1302. As the nobility lost ground the Guelph merchant class took control, but trouble was never far away. The great plague of 1348 halved the city's population and the government was rocked by growing agitation from the lower classes.

In the late 14th century Florence was ruled by a caucus of Guelphs under the leadership of the Albizi family. Among the families opposing them were the Medici, who substantially increased their clout when they became the papal bankers.

In the 15th century, Cosimo de' Medici emerged as the head of the opposition to the Albizi and eventually became Florence's ruler. His eye for talent saw a whole constellation of artists such as Alberti, Brunelleschi, Lorenzo Ghiberti, Donatello, Fra Angelico and Fra Filippo Lippi flourish under his patronage. Many of the city's finest buildings are testimony to his taste.

The rule of Lorenzo il Magnifico (1469–92), Cosimo's grandson, ushered in the most glorious period of Florentine civilisation and of the Italian Renaissance. His court fostered a great flowering of art, music and poetry, turning Florence into the cultural capital of Italy.

Lorenzo kept up the family tradition by sponsoring artists such as Botticelli and Domenico Ghirlandaio and encouraging Leonardo da Vinci and a young Michelangelo.

Not long before Lorenzo's death in 1492, the Medici bank failed and the family was driven out of Florence. The city fell under the control of Girolamo Savonarola (see the boxed text, p468), a Dominican monk who led a puritanical republic until, after falling from public favour, he was tried as a heretic and executed in 1498.

After the Spanish defeated Florence in 1512, the Emperor Charles V married his daughter to Lorenzo's great-grandson Alessandro de' Medici, whom he made duke of Florence in 1530. Seven years later Cosimo I de' Medici, one of the last truly capable Medici rulers, took charge, becoming grand duke of Tuscany after Siena fell to Florence in 1569 and ushering in more than 150 years of Medici domination of Tuscany.

In 1737 the grand duchy of Tuscany passed to the French House of Lorraine, which retained control, apart from a brief interruption under Napoleon, until it was incorporated into the Kingdom of Italy in 1860. Florence briefly became the national capital but Rome assumed the mantle permanently in 1870.

Florence was severely damaged during WWII by the retreating Germans, who blew up all its bridges except the Ponte Vecchio. Devastating floods ravaged the city in 1966, causing inestimable damage to its buildings and artworks. In 1993 the Mafia exploded a massive car bomb, killing five, injuring 37 and destroying a part of the Uffizi Gallery. Just over a decade later, the gallery is undergoing its biggest-ever expansion, which will double its exhibiting area.

ORIENTATION

However you arrive, the central train station, Santa Maria Novella, is a good reference point. From it, a 10-minute walk along Via de' Panzani, then Via de' Cerretani brings you to the cathedral.

From Piazza di San Giovanni, next to the cathedral, Via Roma leads to Piazza della

---

THE RED & THE BLACK

Florence has two parallel street-numbering systems: red or brown numbers (which have 'r' for *rosso*, red, after the number) indicate commercial premises; black or blue ones are for private residences.

To compound the confusion, black or blue numbers may denote whole buildings while each red/brown one refers to one commercial entity – and a building may have several. It can turn you purple if you're in a hurry hunting for a specific address.

Repubblica and continues as Via Calimala and then Via Por Santa Maria to the Ponte Vecchio.

From the cathedral take Via de' Calzaiuoli to get to Piazza della Signoria, the historic seat of government, and the Uffizi Gallery on its south side, overlooking the River Arno.

INFORMATION
Bookshops
Feltrinelli International (Map p466; ☎ 055 21 95 24; Via Cavour 12-20r) Good selection in English and major European languages.

Paperback Exchange (Map pp462-3; ☎ 055 247 81 54; www.papex.it; Via Fiesolana 31r) Great range of new and secondhand books in English.

Emergency
Police station (Map pp460-1; ☎ 055 4 97 71; Via Zara 2) Has a foreigners' office.

Tourist police (Polizia Assistenza Turistica; Map pp462-3; ☎ 055 20 39 11; Piazza dei Ciompi, Via Pietrapiana 50r)

Internet Access
Internet point (Map p466; ☎ 055 24 07 80; Borgo degli Albizi 66r; per hr €3)

Internet Train (per hr about €4); beneath Stazione di Santa Maria Novella (Map pp462-3; ☎ 055 239 97 20); Borgo San Jacopo 30r (Map p466; ☎ 055 265 79 35); Via dei Benci 36r (Map pp462-3; ☎ 055 263 85 55); Via dell'Oriuolo 40r (Map p466; ☎ 055 263 89 68); Via Guelfa 24a (Map p466; ☎ 055 21 47 94) Over 10 branches.

Internet Resources
City of Florence (www.comune.firenze.it) Useful portal for information on the city.

Florence for Fun (www.florenceforfun.org) Fun, good for accommodation and museum bookings, well tuned in to Florence's nightlife.

Studentsville (www.studentsville.it) City life from a student perspective.

Laundry
Wash & Dry (☎ 800 23 11 72; ⏰ 8am-10pm); Via de' Serragli 87r (Map pp462-3); Via dei Servi 105r (Map pp462-3); Via del Sole 29r (Map p466); Via della Scala 52-54r (Map pp462-3); Via Nazionale 129r (Map pp462-3)

Medical Services
All'Insegna del Moro (Map p466; ☎ 055 21 13 43; Piazza di San Giovanni 28; ⏰ 24hr) Pharmacy.

Dr Stephen Kerr (Map p466; ☎ 055 28 80 55; www .dr-kerr.com; Via Porta Rossa 1; ⏰ clinic 3-5pm Mon-Fri) Resident British doctor.

Tourist medical service (Map pp460-1; ☎ 055 47 54 11; Via Lorenzo il Magnifico 59; ⏰ 24hr) Has doctors who speak English, French and German.

Money
American Express (Map p466; ☎ 055 5 09 81; Via Dante Alighieri 22r)

Travelex (Map p466; ☎ 055 28 97 81; Lungarno degli Acciaiuoli 6r)

Post
Main post office (Map p466; Via Pellicceria)

Telephone
Most public telephones accept both coins and phonecards (from €5, available from tobacconists and newsstands). Private call centres are much cheaper.

Tourist Information
Amerigo Vespucci airport (Map pp460-1; ☎ 055 31 58 74; ⏰ 7.30am-11.30pm) Two kilometres northwest of the city.

Azione Gay e Lesbica (Map pp462-3; ☎ 055 22 02 50; www.azionegayelesbica.it in Italian; Via Pisana 32r)

Consorzio ITA (Informazione Turistiche Alberghiere; Map pp462-3; ☎ 055 28 28 93; fax 055 247 82 32; Stazione di Santa Maria Novella; ⏰ 8.45am-9pm) Offers basic tourist information and books accommodation.

Libreria delle Donne (Map pp462-3; ☎ 055 24 03 84; Via Fiesolana 2b) For information to tune you into Florence's lesbian scene.

Tourist office Borgo Santa Croce 29r (Map p466; ☎ 055 234 04 44; ⏰ 8.30am-7pm Mon-Sat Apr-Sep, to 5pm Oct-Mar, 8.30am-2pm Sun year-round); Piazza della Stazione 4 (Map pp462-3; ☎ 055 21 22 45; ⏰ 8.30am-7pm Mon-Sat, 8.30am-2pm Sun); Via Cavour 1r (Map pp462-3; ☎ 055 29 08 32; www.firenzeturismo.it; ⏰ 8.30am-6.30pm Mon-Sat, 8.30am-1.30pm Sun) Main tourist office.

Travel Agencies
CTS (Map pp462-3; ☎ 055 28 95 70; www.cts.it in Italian; Via de' Ginori 25r) The Florence branch of this national youth-travel organisation.

SIGHTS
Florence can seriously overwhelm. We won't even *try* to compete with the battalions of literati and other nobs who've spilled rivers of ink reaching for an original superlative.

The city just swarms with sights, mostly within walking distance of each other. All we can do here is point and steer you through the most unmissable of the shouldn't-be-misseds. For sexier detail, pick up Lonely

TUSCANY

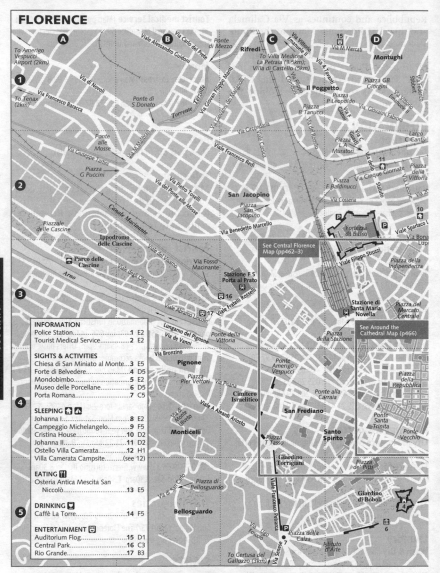

FLORENCE

Planet's *Tuscany & Umbria.* To delve even deeper, pack its *Florence.*

As with everywhere in Italy, museums and monuments tend to close on Monday, though since Florence is a year-round, week-through tourist destination, major monuments open daily. The tourist office has a comprehensive list of opening hours.

Piazza del Duomo & Around

You'll probably already have glimpsed the sloping, brown-tiled dome to Florence's **Duomo** (Map p466; ☎ 055 230 28 85; ☟ 10am-5pm Mon-Wed & Fri, 10am-3.30pm Thu, 10am-4.45pm Sat, 1.30-4.45pm Sun) as it peeks through the crowded streets around the square. All the same, your first glimpse of the cathedral's tiered

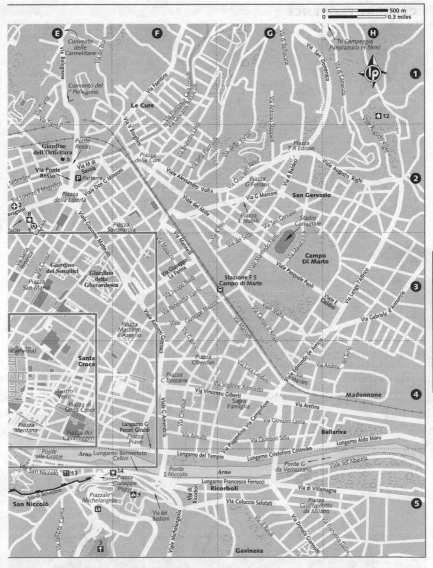

pink, white and green marble façade will stop you in your tracks.

The cathedral was begun in 1296 by the Sienese architect Arnolfo di Cambio and it took almost 150 years to complete. The façade is neo-Gothic, built in the 19th century to replace Arnolfo di Cambio's uncompleted original, which was pulled down

in the 16th century. Inside, the cathedral is decorated with beautiful frescoes by Vasari and Federico Zuccari, and the stained-glass windows by Donatello, Andrea del Castagno, Paolo Uccello and Lorenzo Ghiberti positively glow.

The cathedral's vast interior (it is 155m long and 90m wide) and its sparse decoration

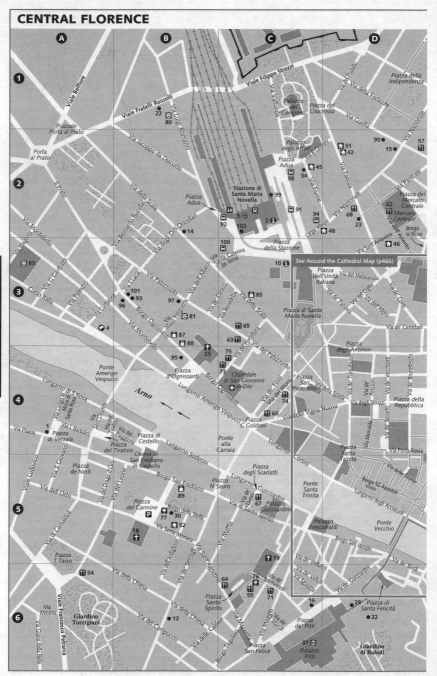

CENTRAL FLORENCE

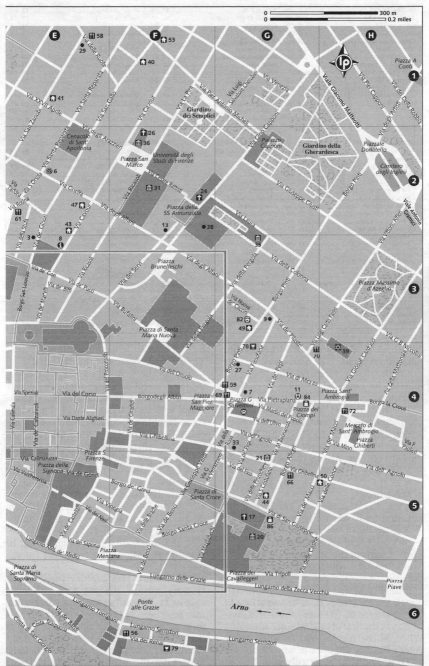

TUSCANY

TUSCANY

can come as a surprise after the visually tumultuous façade. The sacristies on either side of the altar feature enamelled terracotta lunettes by Luca della Robbia over their doorways.

The two frescoes in the northern aisle commemorate the *condottieri* (mercenary leaders) Sir John Hawkwood and Niccolò da Tolentino, who fought for Florence in the 14th century. Also in the northern aisle is a painting of Dante, including a depiction of the *Divine Comedy*, by Domenico di Michelino.

A stairway near the main entrance of the cathedral leads you to the **crypt** (admission €3; 10am-5pm Mon-Fri, 10am-4.45pm Sat), with Brunelleschi's tomb and excavations that have unearthed parts of the 5th-century Basilica di Santa Reparata, which originally stood on the site.

Brunelleschi won a public competition to design the enormous **dome** (entrance at Porta dei Canonici; admission €6; 8.30am-7pm Mon-Fri, 8.30am-5.40pm Sat), the first of its kind since antiquity. When Michelangelo went to work on St Peter's Basilica (Basilica di San Pietro, see p133) in Rome, he reportedly said: 'I go to

build a greater dome, but not a fairer one'. The entrance is outside the cathedral.

In 1334 Giotto designed and began building the graceful 82m-high **campanile** (bell tower; Map p466; Piazza del Duomo; admission €6; 8.30am-7.30pm) with its 414 steps, but died before he could complete it. Andrea Pisano and Francesco Talenti continued the work. The first tier of bas-reliefs around the base, carved by Pisano but possibly designed by Giotto, depicts the 'Creation of Man and the Arts and Industries'. The bas-reliefs on the second tier illustrate the planets, cardinal virtues, the arts and the seven sacraments. The sculptures of the prophets and sibyls in the niches of the upper storeys are copies of works by Donatello and other artists; the originals can be found in the Museo dell'Opera del Duomo (see p465).

The mainly 11th-century Romanesque **baptistry** (battistero; Map p466; Piazza San Giovanni; admission €3; noon-7pm Mon-Sat, 8.30am-2pm Sun) may have been built as early as the 5th century on the site of a Roman temple. One of the oldest buildings in Florence, it's dedicated, like many such constructions in Italy, to St John the Baptist and counts Dante

QUEUE JUMPING

You can skip (or at least shorten) some of the museum queues in Florence by booking ahead. In summer especially, long queues can mean a sticky wait of up to four hours!

For €3 extra per museum you can book a ticket in advance to any of the *musei statali* (state museums), which include the Uffizi Gallery, Palazzo Pitti, Museo del Bargello, Galleria dell'Accademia, Museo Archeologico and Cappelle Medicee. Simply (though not necessarily swiftly: you may find yourself in a long phone queue) phone **Firenze Musei** (☎ 055 29 48 83; www.firenzemusei.it; 8.30am-6.30pm Mon-Fri, 8.30am-12.30pm Sat). When you arrive at the site at the allotted time, quote your booking number, pay and smile smugly at the perspiring hordes.

For the Uffizi you can also buy tickets in advance at the gallery itself (also €3 for each ticket supplement).

Weekend a Firenze (www.weekendafirenze.com) is an online service for booking museums, galleries, shows and tours. You pay €4.80 on top of the normal ticket price; reserve at least three days in advance. Print out the email confirmation they send and present it on the day of your visit. Many major hotels will also book entry tickets for you.

---

among the famous who have been dunked and baptised in its font.

The octagonal structure is chiefly famous for its gilded bronze doors, particularly the celebrated 15th-century eastern portals facing the cathedral, the *Gate of Paradise* (Porta del Paradiso) by Lorenzo Ghiberti. The bas-reliefs on its 10 panels depict scenes from the Old Testament.

The southern door, executed by Pisano and completed in 1330, is the oldest. The bas-reliefs on its 28 compartments deal predominantly with the life of St John the Baptist. The northern door is by Ghiberti, who won a public competition in 1401 for its design, and its main theme is also St John the Baptist.

Some of the doors are copies; the original panels are gradually being restored and will be displayed in the Museo dell'Opera del Duomo.

Within the baptistry, the 13th-century vibrant mosaics of the dome, created by artists from Venice, depict, among other themes, *Christ in Majesty* and the *Last Judgement*.

The **Museo dell'Opera del Duomo** (Map p466; Piazza del Duomo 9; admission €6; 9am-7.30pm Mon-Sat, 9am-1.40pm Sun) mainly features sculptural treasures from the cathedral. Displays include the equipment used by Brunelleschi to build the dome, as well as his death mask. On the mezzanine floor is Michelangelo's *Pietà*, which he intended for his own tomb. Vasari recorded in his *Lives of the Artists* that, dissatisfied with both the quality of the marble and of his own work, Michelangelo broke up the unfinished sculpture, destroying the arm and left leg of the figure of Christ. A student

of Michelangelo's later restored the arm and completed the figure of Mary Magdalene.

Eight of the original 10 panels from the baptistry's *Gates of Paradise* can also be found on display.

The most striking of Donatello's several carvings are the haunted gaze of his *Prophet Habakkuk,* originally in the bell tower, and his wooden carving of a gaunt, desolate *Mary Magdalene.* Also on the 1st floor, a pair of exquisitely carved *cantorie* (singing galleries) by Donatello and Luca della Robbia face each other, musicians and children at play adding a refreshingly frivolous touch amid so much sombre piety.

From the Cathedral to Piazza della Signoria

From Piazza del Duomo take Via de' Calzaiuoli to reach the **Chiesa di Orsanmichele** (Map p466; Via Arte della Lana). Originally a grain market, the church was formed in the 14th century when the arcades of the market building were walled in. Statues of the city guilds' patron saints adorn the exterior. Commissioned over a period of two centuries, they represent the work of many Renaissance artists. Some statues are now in the Museo

EUROPEANS DO IT CHEAPER

If you carry an EU passport (and you'll need to have it with you) and are under 18 or over 65, admission to Florence's state museums is free. EU citizens aged between 18 and 25 pay half price.

TUSCANY

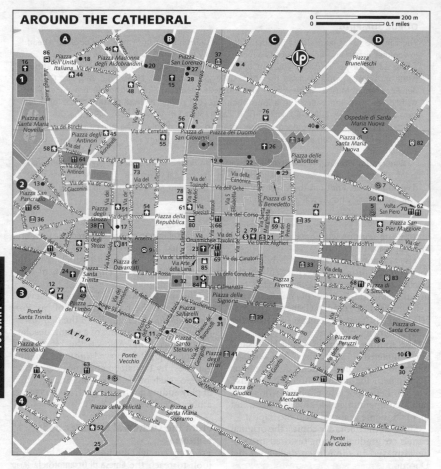

AROUND THE CATHEDRAL

del Bargello but many splendid pieces remain, including Lorenzo Ghiberti's bronze *Saint Matthew* and a copy of Donatello's *St George*. It was closed for renovations the last time we visited.

Northwest is the **Piazza della Repubblica**, originally the site of a Roman forum and heart of the medieval city. Today's buildings, for the most part constructed in the late 19th century, are home to Florence's most fashionable and expensive cafés.

If you head east from the piazza and turn right into Via Santa Margherita, you'll find the **Casa di Dante** with a small **museum** (Map p466) tracing Dante's life; it's currently closed for renovation. Continuing east on Via del Corso will bring you to the **Palazzo dei Pazzi**,

which is attributed to Guiliano da Maiano. These days it's used as offices but you're free to peek into the courtyard.

The 1254 **Palazzo del Bargello** (Map p466), also known as the Palazzo del Podestà, was originally the residence of the chief magistrate. It then became a police station, during which time many unfortunates were tortured near the well in the centre of the medieval courtyard, the site of the city's gallows. This gaunt building now enjoys a happier destiny as home to the excellent **Museo del Bargello** (Map p466; ☎ 055 238 86 06; Via del Proconsolo 4; admission €4; ☑ 8.15am-1.50pm Tue-Sat &, 2nd & 4th Sun of month), which houses Italy's most comprehensive collection of Tuscan Renaissance sculpture.

Several works by Michelangelo grace the ground floor, notably his drunken *Bacchus* (executed when the artist aged 22), a marble bust of *Brutus* and the *Tondo Pitti,* a large roundel of the Madonna and Child with the infant St John. Other works of particular interest are Benvenuto Cellini's rather camp marble *Ganimede* (Ganymede) and his *Narciso* (Narcissus), along with Giambologna's *Mercurio Volante* (Winged Mercury).

Don't miss Donatello's stunning bronze *David* on the 1st floor, the first freestanding sculpture since the time of antiquity to depict a fully nude man. Among many other works by Donatello are *San Giorgio* (St George), originally on the façade of the Chiesa di Orsanmichele, and the *Marzocco,* Florence's heraldic lion that once stood proud in the Piazza della Signoria.

The **Mercato Nuovo** (Map p466; Via Porta Rossa), a loggia (open gallery) built in the mid-16th century to house the city's gold and silver, has fallen on hard times and today is home to tacky souvenir and leather stalls. At its southern end is the Fontana del Porcellino (Piglet Fountain). Rub the porker's snout, throw a modest coin into the fountain and – so goes the legend – you're bound to return to Florence.

Head towards Via de' Tornabuoni and go north for the **Palazzo Strozzi** (Map p466; Piazza degli Strozzi), which is one of Florence's most impressive Renaissance palazzi. Although the palace was never completed, the three finished façades in heavy rusticated *pietra forte* (literally 'strong stone', a local sandstone), designed by Benedetto da Maiano, speak naked power. Inside is a grand but somewhat gloomy courtyard. Today the palazzo is used for art exhibitions.

Just along the road is the altogether more delicate **Palazzo dei Rucellai** (Map p466; Via della Vigna Nuova), designed by Alberti, with its frieze and incised irregular blocks.

Piazza della Signoria

The hub of the city's political life through the centuries and surrounded by some of its most celebrated buildings, this Piazza della Signoria resembles an outdoor sculpture gallery. Ammannati's huge **Fountain of Neptune** spurts beside the Palazzo Vecchio, at the entrance of which stand copies of Michelangelo's *David* (the original is in the Galleria dell'Accademia) and Donatello's *Marzocco,* the heraldic Florentine lion (the original is in the Museo del Bargello). An equestrian statue of Cosimo I de' Medici by Giambologna prances in the centre of the piazza. Look on the ground for the bronze plaque marking the spot where Savonarola was hanged and burnt at the stake in 1498.

TUSCANY

TUSCANY

SAVONAROLA

The Renaissance was a time of extraordinary contrasts. Artists, writers and philosophers of great talent flourished against a backdrop of violence, war, plague and extreme poverty.

In Florence the court of Lorenzo il Magnifico was among the most splendid and enlightened in Europe. Yet in the streets, and increasingly in Lorenzo's court itself, people had begun to listen intently to the fanatical preachings of a Dominican monk called Girolamo Savonarola.

Born in Ferrara, Savonarola moved to Florence, where he preached against luxury, greed, corruption of the clergy and the Renaissance itself. To him the Church and the world were corrupt and its rulers oppressors.

In 1494, when the Medici were expelled from Florence and a republic proclaimed, Savonarola was appointed its legislator. Under his severe, moralistic lead the city underwent a kind of religious reform.

But his enemies were many and powerful. The corrupt Borgia Pope Alexander VI excommunicated Savonarola for preaching against him. Then, as the Florentine public turned cold on the evangelistic preacher, he came under attack from the Franciscan monks and began to lose the support of his dwindling political allies.

After refusing to undergo ordeal by fire, Savonarola was arrested. On 22 May 1498 in Piazza della Signoria (today a plaque marks the spot) he was hung and burnt at the stake for heresy and his ashes were thrown into the Arno.

Loggia della Signoria (Map p466), built in the late 14th century as a platform for public ceremonies, eventually became a showcase for sculptures. To the left of the steps is Benvenuto Cellini's magnificent bronze statue of *Perseo* (Perseus) brandishing the head of Medusa. To the right is Giambologna's Mannerist *Rape of the Sabine Women*, his final work.

Palazzo Vecchio (Map p466; ☎ 055 276 82 24; Piazza della Signoria; admission €6; ☺ 9am-7pm Fri-Wed, 9am-2pm Thu), built by Arnolfo di Cambio between 1298 and 1314, is the traditional seat of Florentine government. Its **Torre d'Arnolfo**, 94m high and crowned with striking crenellations, is as much a symbol of the city as the cathedral.

Created for the Signoria, which was the highest level of Florentine republican government, the Palazzo Vecchio became Cosimo I de' Medici's palace in the mid-16th century, before he moved to the Palazzo Pitti. The Medici commissioned Vasari to reorganise the interior and create a series of sumptuous rooms. Upstairs from Michelozzo's beautiful courtyard, just inside the entrance, the lavishly decorated apartments begin. The **Salone dei Cinquecento** was the meeting room of the 'parliament' during Savonarola's time. It was later used for banquets and festivities and features frescoes by Vasari and his apprentices, glorifying Florentine victories over arch rivals Pisa and Siena. The monumental

statuary includes a graphic series on the *Labours of Hercules* by Vincenzo de' Rossi and Michelangelo's *Genio della Vittoria* (Genius of Victory) statue, originally destined for Rome and Pope Julius II's tomb.

Vasari designed the intimate yet equally sumptuous little **studiolo** (Francesco I's study), decorated by a team of top Florentine Mannerist artists, that leads off the vast hall.

There follows a series of rooms, each one dedicated to a senior member of the Medicis, the décor of which blares their glory in a heavy-handed manner until you reach, on the 2nd floor, the **Sala dei Gigli** (Room of the Lilies), named after its frieze of fleur-de-lys, the symbol of the French monarchy. Look up at its remarkable coffered ceiling and enjoy Donatello's powerful carving of *Guiditta e Oloferne* (Judith and Holofernes). Just off this hall are the chancery, where Machiavelli plotted for a while, and the map room, intriguing for both cartophiles and the simply curious, its panels painted with maps, often very rudimentary, of the known world of the time.

From the Palazzo Vecchio you can climb up to the battlements for fine views over the city.

Uffizi Gallery

The **Palazzo degli Uffizi**, designed and built by Vasari in the second half of the 16th century at the request of Cosimo I de' Medici, originally housed the city's administrators, judiciary and guilds. It was, in effect, a government office building (*uffizi* meaning offices).

Vasari also designed the Corridoio Vasariano, a long private corridor that links the Palazzo Vecchio and the Palazzo Pitti (p474) through the Uffizi Gallery and across Ponte Vecchio. Cosimo's successor, Francesco I, commissioned the architect Buontalenti to modify the upper floor of the palazzo to house the Medici's growing art collection. Thus, indirectly, the first steps were taken to turn it into an art gallery.

THE GALLERY

The **Uffizi Gallery** (Map p466; ☎ 055 238 86 51; Piazza degli Uffizi 6; admission €6.50; ☉ 8.15am-6.50pm Tue-Sun) houses the Medici family's private collection, bequeathed to Florence in 1743 by the last of the family, Anna Maria Ludovica, on condition that it never leave the city. The Uffizi, although by no means the biggest art gallery around, houses the world's single greatest collection of Italian and Florentine art.

Sadly, several of its artworks were destroyed and others badly damaged when a car bomb planted by the Mafia exploded outside the gallery's west wing in May 1993. Documents cataloguing the collection were also destroyed.

Partly in response to the bombing, but even more to the gallery's immense popularity (more than 1.5 million visitors march through every year, compared to a mere trickle of 100,000 annually in the 1950s!), restoration and reorganisation will lead to what promoters refer to as the 'Nuovi Uffizi'.

The gallery as it stands now is arranged to illustrate the evolving story of Italian and, in particular, Florentine art.

Given the crowds (you can easily find yourself queuing for up to four hours to get to the ticket window), consider booking ahead (see the boxed text, p465). Alternatively, turn up an hour before opening time and queue to guarantee yourself entry or plan to visit later in the day, when lines and waiting times tend to be shorter.

Since there's such a wealth of treasures competing for your attention, investing in an audioguide (one/two persons €4.65/6.20) makes sound sense, especially if it is your first visit.

On the ground floor of the gallery are the restored remains of the 11th-century **Chiesa di San Piero Scheraggio**, closed to the public at the time of writing.

Upstairs in the gallery proper, the first accessible rooms feature works by Tuscan masters of the 13th and early 14th centuries. The stars of Room 2 are three paintings of the *Madonna in Maestà* by Duccio di Buoninsegna, Cimabue and Giotto. All three were formerly altarpieces in Florentine churches. Looking at them in this order, you can sense the transition from Gothic to the precursor of the Renaissance.

Room 3 traces the Sienese school of the 14th century. Of particular note is Simone Martini's shimmering *Annunciazione* (Annunciation), considered a masterpiece of the school.

Room 7 features artworks by painters of the early-15th-century Florentine school, which pioneered the Renaissance. There is one panel (the other two are in Paris' Louvre and London's National Gallery) from Paolo Uccello's striking *La Battaglia di San Romano* (Battle of San Romano). In his efforts to create perspective he directs the lances, horses and soldiers to a central disappearing point. Other works include Piero della Francesca's portraits of *Battista Sforza* and *Federico da Montefeltro*.

Room 9 is devoted largely to Antonio de Pollaiuolo. His series of six virtues is followed by an addition by Botticelli (*Fortezza* or Strength). Here the clarity of line and light, and the humanity in the face, set it apart from Pollaiuolo's work, making the canvas a taster for the Botticelli Rooms, Nos 10 to 14, considered to be the gallery's most

---

NUOVI UFFIZI

With an investment of €60 million and a planned, perhaps optimistic, completion date in late 2007, the Uffizi is set to double in size over the next few years. So the disposition of paintings and rooms that we describe here may change radically during the life span of this book.

While work is in progress, you're likely to find several galleries closed and others newly opened. Check the illuminated signboard by the main entrance for the order of the day.

spectacular. Highlights include the ethereal *La Nascita di Venere* (The Birth of Venus) and *Allegoria della Primavera* (Allegory of Spring). Contrast these with his *Calunnia* (Calumny): for some a disturbing reflection of Botticelli's loss of faith in human potential as he aged, for others a deliberate reining in of his free spirit in order not to invite the attentions of the puritanical Savonarola.

Room 15 features Da Vinci's *Annunciazione*, painted when he was a student of Verrocchio. Quite different but equally arresting in its swirling composition is his unfinished *Adorazione dei Magi*.

Room 18, the Tribuna, houses the celebrated *Medici Venus*, a 1st-century-BC copy of a 4th-century-BC sculpture by the Greek sculptor Praxiteles. The room also contains portraits of various members of the Medici family.

The great Umbrian painter Perugino, who studied under Piero della Francesca and later became Raphael's master, is represented in Room 19, as is Luca Signorelli. Piero di Cosimo's *Perseo Libera Andromeda* is full of fantastical whimsy with beasts and flying heroes. Room 20 features works from the German Renaissance, including Dürer's *Adorazione dei Magi*. Room 21, with a heavily Venetian leaning, has works by Giovanni Bellini and his pupil Giorgione, along with a few by Vittorio Carpaccio.

The star of Room 25 is Michelangelo's dazzling *Tondo Doni*, which depicts the Holy Family. The composition is highly unusual, with Joseph holding Jesus on Mary's shoulder as she twists around to watch him. The colours are so vibrant and the lines so clear, it seems almost photographic. This masterpiece of the High Renaissance leaps out at you as you enter, demanding attention.

In Room 26 are works by Raphael, including his *Leo X*, remarkable for the richness of colour (especially the reds) and detail. Also on display are works by Andrea del Sarto. Room 27 is dominated by the sometimes disquieting works of Florence's two main Mannerist masters, Pontormo and Rosso Fiorentino.

Room 28 boasts eight Titians, including *Venere d'Urbino* (Venus of Urbino). His presence signals a shift in the weighting to representatives of the Venetian school. Rooms 29 and 30 contain works by comparatively minor painters from the north of Italy but

Room 31 has some powerful paintings by Venice's Paolo Veronese, especially his *Sacra Famiglia e Santa Barbara* (Holy Family and St Barbara). In Room 32 it's Tintoretto's turn to star.

Room 35 comes as a bit of a shock as you are confronted with the enormous and sumptuous canvases of Federico Barocci (1535–1612) from Urbino. Rooms 36 and 37 are part of the exit while the adjoining Room 38 houses the extraordinary restored *Annunciazione* by Siena's Simone Martini and Lippo Memmi.

Room 41 represents mostly non-Italian masters including Rubens, Van Dyck and Spain's Diego Velázquez. Pause before the two enormous tableaux by Rubens, seeping with violence and power, representing the French King Henri IV at the Battle of Ivry and his triumphal march into Paris. The beautifully designed Room 42 (long closed but you can peek in), with its exquisite coffered ceiling and splendid dome, is filled with Roman statues.

Room 43 has a pair of contrasting canvases by Caravaggio, with his bold play of light and shade, notably his *Il Sacrificio d'Isacco*. Rembrandt and other Dutch masters feature in Room 44 while Room 45 takes us back to Venice, with 18th-century works by Canaletto, Guardi, Tiepolo, Crespi and the two Longhi, along with a couple of stray pieces by the Spaniard Goya.

CORRIDOIO VASARIANO

When Cosimo I de' Medici's wife bought the Palazzo Pitti and the family moved into their new digs, they wanted to maintain their link – literally – with what from now on would be known as the Palazzo Vecchio. So Cosimo commissioned Vasari to build the **Corridoio Vasariano** (Map p466), an enclosed walkway traversing the distance between the two palaces that would allow the Medicis to wander between each in privacy. At the time of writing, the passageway wasn't open to the public. For an update, contact Firenze Musei (see the boxed text, p465).

Santa Maria Novella & Around

West of the Uffizi is the **Ponte Santa Trinita**, rebuilt after being destroyed during WWII. Michelangelo is believed to have drawn the original plan of the bridge, which was executed by Ammannati. To its north is **Via**

de' Tornabuoni, one of the city's most fashionable streets, lined with Renaissance mansions and classy shops including Ferragamo, Gucci and Armani.

The 14th-century **Chiesa di Santa Trinita** (Map p466; Piazza Santa Trinita; 🕑 8am-noon Mon-Sat, 4-6pm daily) has eye-catching frescoes depicting the life of St Francis by Domenico Ghirlandaio in Cappella Sassetti (in the south transept). Lorenzo Monaco, who was Fra Angelico's master, painted the altarpiece of the *Annunciation* in the fourth chapel of the south aisle and also the frescoes on the chapel walls.

Northwest from Ponte alla Carraia is the 13th-century **Chiesa di Ognissanti** (Map pp462-3; Borgo Ognissanti; 🕑 7am-12.30pm & 4-8pm Mon-Sat, 4-8pm Sun). The church, with its typically baroque façade, was much altered in the 17th century. Inside are older treasures: a pair of frescoes by Domenico Ghirlandaio and Botticelli's *San Augustin*. Seek out Ghirlandaio's fresco, above the second altar on the right, of the Madonna della Misericordia, protector of the Vespucci family. Amerigo Vespucci, the Florentine navigator who gave his name to the American continent, is supposed to be the young boy whose head peeks between the Madonna and the old man. Ghirlandaio's masterpiece the *Last Supper* covers most of a wall in the former monastery's refectory, reached via the cloister.

The **Basilica di Santa Maria Novella** (Map p466; ☎ 055 21 59 18; Piazza di Santa Maria Novella; admission €2.50; 🕑 9am-5pm Mon-Thu & Sat, 1-5pm Fri & Sun) was begun in the late 13th century as the Dominican order's Florentine base. It was largely completed by around 1360 but work on its façade and interior continued well into the 15th century. The lower section of the green and white marble façade is transitional from Romanesque to Gothic, while the upper section and the main doorway were designed by Alberti and completed around 1470. The highlight of the Gothic interior, halfway along the north aisle, is Masaccio's superb fresco of the Trinity (1428), one of the first artworks to use the then newly discovered techniques of perspective and proportion.

The first chapel to the right of the altar, the **Cappella di Filippo Strozzi**, features lively frescoes by Filippino Lippi depicting the lives of St John the Evangelist and St Philip. Another important work is Ghirlandaio's series of frescoes behind the main altar,

painted with the help of artists who may have included the young Michelangelo. Relating the lives of the Virgin Mary, St John the Baptist and others, the frescoes are notable for their depiction of Florentine life during the Renaissance. Brunelleschi's crucifix hangs above the altar in the **Cappella Gondi**, the first chapel left of the choir.

The cloisters (the entrance is on the left of the façade) feature some of the city's best frescoes. The **Chiostro Verde** (Green Cloister) is so named because green is the predominant colour of the fresco cycle by Paolo Uccello. The impressive **Cappellone degli Spagnuoli** (Spanish Chapel) contains some frescoes by Andrea di Bonaiuto.

San Lorenzo Area

The Medici commissioned Brunelleschi to rebuild the **Basilica di San Lorenzo** (Map p466; Piazza San Lorenzo; admission €2.50; 🕑 10am-5pm Mon-Sat) in 1425, on the site of a 4th-century basilica. Considered one of the most harmonious examples of Renaissance architecture, it was the Medici family church and many family members are buried here. The two bronze pulpits were started by Donatello, who died before they were completed. He is buried in the chapel featuring Fra Filippo Lippi's *Annunciation*. Brunelleschi also designed the adjoining **Sagrestia Vecchia** (Old Sacristy), the interior of which was decorated in the main by Donatello.

From another entrance off Piazza San Lorenzo, you can enter the church's peaceful cloisters. A staircase leads from the main entrance up to the **Biblioteca Laurenziana Medicea**, nowadays restricted to researchers burrowing through its 10,000 volumes. Commissioned by Cosimo de' Medici to house the Medici library, its real attraction is Michelangelo's magnificent vestibule and staircase, which are accessible to all.

Enter the **Cappelle Medicee** (Medicean Chapels; Map p466; ☎ 055 238 86 02; admission €6; 🕑 8.15am-4.50pm Tue-Sat & alternate Sun) through Piazza Madonna degli Aldobrandini. **Cappella dei Principi** (Princes' Chapel) is sumptuously decorated with marble and semiprecious stones. It was the principal burial place of the Medici rulers. The graceful and simple **Sagrestia Nuova** (New Sacristy) was Michelangelo's first architectural work. His exquisite sculptures *Night and Day, Dawn and Dusk* and *Madonna with Child* adorn the Medici tombs.

Just off Piazza San Lorenzo is the extraordinary **Palazzo Medici-Riccardi** (Map p466; ☎ 055 276 03 40; Via Cavour 3; admission €4; ☉ 9am-7pm Thu-Tue). Since only seven visitors are allowed in at a time and for a maximum of seven minutes – you have to admire the symmetry – it is essential to reserve your slot in advance.

Typical of the Florentine Renaissance style, the palace was designed by Michelozzo for Cosimo de' Medici in 1444. The principal Medici residence until 1540, the palace was the prototype for other buildings in the city, such as the Palazzo Pitti and Palazzo Strozzi, before being remodelled by its new owners, the Riccardi family, in the 17th century. The chapel upstairs has a series of wonderfully detailed, serene frescoes by Benozzo Gozzoli, whose ostensible theme of the *Journey of the Magi* is but a slender pretext for portraying members of the Medici clan in their best light. A couple of hundred years later, the Riccardis built the sumptuously decorated Sala di Luca Giordano, commissioning the eponymous artist to adorn the ceiling with his complex *Allegory of Divine Wisdom* (1685).

San Marco Area

Piazza San Marco is at the heart of the university area. Flanking it are a now deconsecrated Dominican **convent** and **Chiesa di San Marco** (Map pp462–3), where you'll find the **Museo di San Marco** (Map pp462-3; ☎ 055 238 86 08; Piazza San Marco 1; admission €4; ☉ 8.15am-1.50pm Tue-Fri, 8.15am-6.50pm Sat, 2nd & 4th Sun & 3rd & 5th Mon of month). Dip into the church, founded in 1299, rebuilt by Michelozzo in 1437 and again remodelled by Giambologna some years later, but you're really here for the splendours of the adjoining convent.

Famous Florentines who called the convent home include the painters Fra Angelico and Fra Bartolommeo, as well as Sant' Antoninus and Girolamo Savonarola (see the boxed text, p468). Fra Angelico, who painted the radiant frescoes on the convent walls, and Savonarola were of the same religious order, the latter arriving in Florence almost 30 years after the painter's death in 1455. The convent is a museum of Fra Angelico's works, many moved here in the 19th century. Among the better-known works are his *Deposizione di Cristo* and *Pala di San Marco*, an altarpiece for the church, paid for by the Medici family. The walls of the upstairs cells,

painted *in situ* (if you're using a museum guide, look carefully for the faded numbers on each door), carry several masterpieces, including the magnificent *Madonna delle Ombre* (Virgin of the Shadows), on the external wall between cells No 25 and 26.

From Piazza San Marco, a right turn into Via Cesare Battisti brings you to the **Chiesa della SS Annunziata** (Map pp462-3; Piazza della SS Annunziata; ☉ 7.30am-12.30pm & 4-6.30pm), which was established in 1250 by the founders of the Servite order and rebuilt by Michelozzo and others in the mid-15th century. The church is dedicated to the Virgin Mary and in the ornate tabernacle, to your left as you enter the church from the atrium, is a so-called miraculous painting of the Virgin. No longer on public view, the canvas is attributed to a 14th-century friar and legend says it was completed by an angel. Also of note are frescoes by Andrea del Castagno in the first two chapels on the left of the church, a fresco by Perugino in the fifth chapel, and the frescoes in Michelozzo's atrium, particularly the *Birth of the Virgin* by Andrea del Sarto and the *Visitation* by Jacopo Pontormo. Within the church's official opening hours, you'll need to time it just right in order to squeeze yourself in between each morning's seven masses.

Also in the university district, the beautiful **Piazza della SS Annunziata**, where Giambologna's equestrian statue of Grand Duke Ferdinando I de' Medici commands the scene, usually teems with students rather than tourists. On the piazza's southeastern side, **Spedale degli Innocenti** (Map pp462-3; ☎ 055 249 17 08; Piazza della SS Annunziata 12; admission €2.60; ☉ 8.30am-2pm Thu-Tue) was founded in 1421 as Europe's first orphanage (hence the 'innocents' in its name). Brunelleschi designed the portico, which Andrea della Robbia decorated with terracotta medallions of babies in swaddling clothes. At the north end of the portico, the false door surrounded by railings was once a revolving door where unwanted children were left. A good number of people in Florence with surnames such as degli Innocenti, Innocenti and Nocentini can trace their family tree only as far back as the orphanage. A small gallery inside features works by Florentine artists, including Luca della Robbia and Domenico Ghirlandaio, whose striking *Adorazione dei Magi* is at the right end of the hall.

About 200m southeast of the piazza is the **Museo Archeologico** (Map pp462-3; ☎ 055 23 57 50; Via della Colonna 38; admission €4; ☺ 2-7pm Mon, 8.30am-7pm Tue & Thu, 8.30am-2pm Wed & Fri-Sun). Its rich collection of finds, including most of the Medici hoard of antiquities, plunges you deep into the past and offers an alternative to all that Renaissance splendour. On the 1st floor you can either head left into the ancient Egyptian collection or right for the smaller section on Etruscan and Greco-Roman art.

The former is an impressive collection of sculpture, various coffins, tablets inscribed with hieroglyphics and a remarkable array of everyday objects. The first two rooms of the Etruscan section hold various funeral urns. Particularly noteworthy is the marble *Sarcofago delle Amazzoni* (Sarcophagus of the Amazons) from Tarquinia.

Moving on you'll enter a gallery lined with cabinets positively that's stuffed with bronze statuettes and miniatures, dwarfed by the outstanding, growling *Chimera*, lion-like with a supplementary goat and snake head. Less allegorical, more literal, and yet almost as compelling, is the life-size statue, *Arringatore* (Orator).

The 2nd floor is rich in Greek sculpture and ceramics, and Greek and Roman bronzes. Pause awhile to outstare the magnificent snorting *Medicci Riccardi* stallion's head in Room 1.

The excellent **Galleria dell'Accademia** (Map pp462-3; ☎ 055 238 86 09; Via Ricasoli 60; admission Sep-Nov €6.50, Dec-Aug €8; ☺ 8.15am-6.50pm Tue-Sun) displays paintings by Florentine artists spanning the 13th to 16th centuries. Its main draw is Michelangelo's **David**, perhaps the world's most famous statue, which was carved from a single block of marble when the artist was only 29. Originally in the Piazza della Signoria, the colossal statue now stands in an alcove at the end of the main hall on the ground floor.

Santa Croce Area

Piazza di Santa Croce, today lined with souvenir shops, was used for the execution of heretics in Savonarola's day. Attributed to Arnolfo di Cambio, the Franciscan **Basilica di Santa Croce** (Map pp462-3; Piazza di Santa Croce; admission incl Museo dell'Opera €4; ☺ 9.30am-5.30pm Mon-Sat, 1-5.30pm Sun) was started in 1294 on the site of a Franciscan chapel; the façade and bell tower were added in the 19th century. The

three-nave interior of the basilica is grand, if austere. The floor is paved with the tombstones of famous Florentines of the past 500 years, while monuments to the particularly notable were added along the walls from the mid-16th century.

Along the southern wall is Michelangelo's tomb, designed by Vasari, and a cenotaph dedicated to Dante, whose remains, in fact, are in Ravenna (see p446). Further along is a monument to the 18th-century dramatist and poet Vittorio Alfieri by Antonio Canova, a monument to Machiavelli and a gilded bas-relief *Annunciation* by Donatello.

The Cappella Castellani, a chapel to the right of the south transept, is painted from top to toe with frescoes by Agnolo Gaddi. In the Cappella Baroncelli, at the end of the south transept, frescoes by his father, Taddeo Gaddi, depict the life of the Virgin. Agnolo Gaddi also painted the frescoes above and behind the altar.

West of the sacristy, the Capella dei Medici has a fine two-tone altarpiece in glazed terracotta by Andrea della Robbia. Between the two is the Scuola del Cuoio (leatherwork school; see p486).

The Bardi and Peruzzi chapels, to the right of the chancel, are clad in rich frescoes by Giotto. In the central chapel of the northern transept (also a Bardi chapel) hangs a wooden crucifix by Donatello.

Brunelleschi designed the serene cloisters just before his death in 1446. His **Cappella dei Pazzi** (Map pp462–3), at the end of the first cloister, with its harmonious lines and restrained terracotta decoration, is a masterpiece of Renaissance architecture.

The **Museo dell'Opera di Santa Croce** (Map pp462-3; ☺ 9am-7.30pm Mon-Sat, 9am-1.40pm Sun), in the southwest corner of the first cloister, features a crucifix by Cimabue, restored after it was severely damaged during the disastrous 1966 flood, when more than 4m of water inundated the Santa Croce area.

Michelangelo owned the **Casa Buonarroti** (Map pp462-3; ☎ 055 24 17 52; Via Ghibellina 70; admission €6.50; ☺ 9.30am-2pm Wed-Mon) but never lived in it. The Michelangelo memorabilia housed here mostly consists of copies of his works and portraits of the master.

To the right of the ticket window is an archaeological display of items collected by the Buonarroti family, including some interesting Etruscan pieces. Beyond this room

TUSCANY

are some paintings done in imitation of Michelangelo's style, plus some glazed terracotta pieces by the della Robbia family.

Upstairs, you can admire a detailed model of Michelangelo's design for the façade of the Basilica di San Lorenzo – as close as the church ever came to getting one. Michelangelo also completed a couple of marble bas-reliefs and a crucifix. Of the reliefs, *Madonna della Scala* (Madonna of the Steps) is thought to be his earliest work.

The Oltrarno

Literally 'Beyond the Arno', the Oltrarno takes in all of Florence south of the river.

PONTE VECCHIO

This 14th-century bridge has twinkled with the glittering wares of jewellery merchants since the time Ferdinando I de' Medici ordered them here to replace the often malodorous presence of the town butchers who used to toss unwanted leftovers into the river. It was the only bridge not to be blown up by the Nazis in 1944; some say on Hitler's express orders, others that the German commander disobeyed those very orders (yet still wreaked havoc by razing the medieval quarters at either end). Views of and from the bridge are every bit as beguiling as you might expect.

PALAZZO PITTI

Begun in 1458 for the Pitti family, rivals of the Medici, the original nucleus of the **palace** (Map pp462-3; ☎ 055 238 86 14; Piazza de' Pitti) took up the space encompassing the seven sets of windows on the 2nd and 3rd storeys. Ironically, Cosimo I de' Medici and Eleonora de Toledo acquired the palace in 1549. It remained the official residence of Florence's rulers until 1919, when the Savoy royal family handed it over to the state. Combined entry to the palace and all galleries and museums costs €10.50 (after 4pm €7.75) or you can pick and choose; quoted here are individual prices for each of the palace's five museums, of which the Galleria Palantina is by far the most significant.

The **Galleria Palatina** (Palatine Gallery; admission incl Royal Apartments €6.50; ⊗ 8.15am-6.50pm Tue-Sun) houses paintings from the 16th to 18th centuries, hung in lavishly decorated rooms, mostly collected by the Medici and their grand ducal successors.

Beyond the resplendent **Sala Bianca** (White Room), with its ornate 18th-century stucco ceiling and crystal chandeliers, are the **Royal Apartments**, a series of sickeningly furnished and decorated rooms, where the Medici and their successors lived, slept and received their guests. The style and division of tasks assigned to each room is reminiscent of Spanish royal palaces, all heavily bedecked with drapes, silk and chandeliers. Each room has a colour theme, ranging from aqua green to deep wine red to dusty mellow yellow.

The paintings hanging in the gallery itself don't follow any particular chronological or thematic sequence and canvases tend to hop about, so simply stop and marvel where the fancy takes you.

Tuscan masters include Fra Filippo Lippi, Sandro Botticelli, Giorgio Vasari and Andrea del Sarto (well represented with a canvas in just about every room). There are more than 10 works by Raphael and a similar profusion by Titian (especially in the **Sala Venere**; Venus Room). Caravaggio features with his striking *Amore Dormiente* (Love Sleeping) in the **Sala dell'Educazione di Giove** (Education of Jupiter Room).

Tintoretto, Paolo Veronese, Jose Ribera, Bravo Murillo, Rubens, Velazquez and Van Dyck are other significant Italian and foreign painters represented here.

The palace's other galleries and museums are worth a look if you have plenty of time. The **Galleria d'Arte Moderna** and **Galleria del Costume** (admission €5; ⊗ 8.15am-1.50pm Tue-Sat & alternating Sun & Mon) have common opening hours and tariffs. The Modern Art Gallery covers mostly Tuscan works from the 18th to the mid-20th century while the Costume Museum has high-fashion apparel from the 18th and 19th centuries.

A *biglietto cumulativo* (combined ticket; €4) gives entry to the palace's superb Renaissance **Giardino di Boboli** (Boboli Gardens; Map pp462-3; ⊗ 8.15am-7.30pm Jun-Aug, to 6.30pm Mar-May & Sep-Oct, to 4.30pm Nov-Feb), laid out in the mid-16th century and, observing the same hours, the **Museo delle Porcellane** (Map pp460–1). At the southern limit of the gardens and offering great views over the palace complex and Florentine countryside, it has a rich collection of Sevres, Vincennes, Viennese and Meissen china and porcelain, gathered over the centuries by the illustrious tenants of Palazzo Pitti.

Entered from the garden courtyard, the **Museo degli Argenti** (Silver Museum; ☺ 8.15am-7.30pm Jun-Aug, to 6.30pm Mar-May & Sep-Oct, to 4.30pm Nov-Feb) displays glassware, silver and semiprecious stones from the Medici collections.

Also within the gardens, which are occasionally a venue for classical-music concerts in the summer, is the **Grotta del Buontalenti** (Map pp462–3), a fanciful artificial grotto designed by the eponymous artist. Within its recesses a fleshy Venus by Giambologna rises from the waves.

At the top of the hill, the rambling fortifications of the **Forte di Belvedere** (Map pp460–1), built by the Grand Duke Ferdinando I towards the end of the 16th century to protect the Palazzo Pitti, were closed for renovations when we last visited.

PIAZZALE MICHELANGELO
The breathtaking panorama from this vast esplanade is marred only by the cheap souvenir stalls at your back. It's best approached by a steep 10-minute walk up the wiggly road, paths and steps that climb from the riverside and Piazza Giuseppe Poggi.

An easier but less rewarding alternative is to hop aboard bus No 13, which sets out from Stazione di Santa Maria Novella and crosses Ponte alle Grazie.

CHURCHES
The Oltrarno has three churches that are well worth seeking out.

The magnificent Romanesque **Chiesa di San Miniato al Monte** (Map pp460-1; off Viale Galileo Galilei; ☺ 8am-7.30pm May-Oct, 8am-noon & 3-6pm Nov-Apr), where building started in the 11th century, is a steep 10-minute climb up from Piazzale Michelangelo. The church's multicoloured marble façade, depicting Christ between the Virgin and San Miniato (a local Christian martyr), was tacked onto the building a few of centuries later.

Inside are 13th- to 15th-century frescoes on the south wall and intricate inlaid marble designs all down the length of the nave, leading to a fine Romanesque crypt. The raised choir and presbytery have an intricate marble pulpit and screen, rich in intricate geometrical designs. The **sacristy**, in the southeast corner, features marvellously bright frescoes depicting the life of St Benedict. The four figures in its cross vault represent the Evangelists.

Slap-bang in the middle of the nave is the bijou **Capella del Crocefisso**, to which Michelozzo, Agnolo Gaddi and Luca della Robbia all contributed.

The **Cappella del Cardinale del Portogallo**, beside the north aisle, features a tomb by Antonio Rossellino and a gorgeous terracotta ceiling by Luca della Robbia.

Come around 4.30pm (winter) or 5.30pm (summer) and you can hear the monks' Gregorian chant wafting up from the crypt. Bus No 13 stops nearby.

The 13th-century **Basilica di Santa Maria del Carmine** (Map pp462-3; Piazza del Carmine) was all but destroyed by fire in the late 18th century. Fortunately the fire managed to spare the magnificent frescoes by Masaccio in the **Cappella Brancacci** (☎ 055 276 82 24; admission €4; ☺ reservation only 10am-5pm Wed-Sat & Mon, 1-5pm Sun), entered via the cloister to the right of the church. A maximum of 30 visitors are allowed into the chapel at a time and, such is the chapel's popularity, you have to reserve in advance. Considered the painter's finest work, the frescoes with their vibrant colours had an enormous influence on 15th-century Florentine art. Masaccio painted them in his early 20s but interrupted the task to go to Rome, where he died aged only 28. Filippino Lippi completed the cycle some 60 years later. Masaccio's contribution includes the *Expulsion of Adam and Eve from Paradise* and *The Tribute Money* on the cappella's upper left wall.

Basilica di Santo Spirito (Map pp462-3; Piazza Santo Spirito; ☺ 10am-noon & 4-5.30pm Mon-Sat, 11.30-noon Sun, closed Wed afternoon), one of Brunelleschi's last commissions, is beautifully planned, with a colonnade of 35 columns and a series of semicircular chapels. The chapels' works of art include a *Madonna and Saints* by Filippino Lippi in the right transept. In the equally harmonious sacristy is a poignantly tender wooden crucifix (it's not often you see Christ with a penis) attributed to Michelangelo.

Certosa del Galluzzo
From Porta Romana at the southern tip of the Oltrarno area, follow Via Senese south about 3km to the village of Galluzzo and the **Certosa del Galluzzo** (Map pp460-1; ☎ 055 204 92 26; ☺ 9am-noon & 3-6pm Tue-Sun Apr-Sep, to 5pm Oct-Mar), its remarkable 14th-century monastery. The Carthusian order of monks once had

50 monasteries around Italy but these days inhabit only two. The Certosa del Galluzzo passed into Cistercian hands in 1955.

The certosa can be visited only in a guided group (only in Italian). The Gothic hall of the **Palazzo degli Studi** has a small collection of art, including five somewhat weathered frescoes by Pontormo. The **Basilica di San Lorenzo**, with 14th-century origins, has a Renaissance exterior. To one side of it is the **Colloquio**, a narrow hall with benches. Here the Carthusian monks were permitted to break their vow of silence once a week, though they got a second chance on Mondays when allowed to leave the monastery grounds for a gentle stroll.

You end up in the **Chiostro Grande**, biggest of the complex's three cloisters and flanked by 18 monks' cells decorated with busts from the della Robbia workshop.

Bus No 37 from Stazione di Santa Maria Novella passes nearby.

COURSES

Florence has more than 30 schools offering courses in Italian language and culture. Others put on courses in art, including painting, drawing, sculpture and art history, and several offer cooking classes.

Language

The main tourist office in Via Cavour (see p459) has a list of schools running language courses. Below is a list of well-established institutions.

British Institute of Florence (Map p466; ☎ 055 267 78 200; www.britishinstitute.it; Piazza Strozzi 2) This much-respected institution has been operating since 1917.

Centro Lingua Italiana Calvino (CLIC; Map pp462-3; ☎ 055 28 80 81; www.clicschool.it; Viale Fratelli Rosselli 74)

Centro Lorenzo de' Medici (Map pp462-3; ☎ 055 28 73 60; www.lorenzodemedici.it; Via Faenza 43)

Istituto di Lingua e Cultura Italiana Michelangelo (Map pp462-3; ☎ 055 24 09 75; www.michelangelo -edu.it; Via Ghibellina 88)

Istituto Europeo (Map p466; ☎ 055 238 10 71; www .istitutoeuropeo.it; Piazzale delle Pallottole 1)

Linguaviva (Map pp462-3; ☎ 055 29 43 59; www .linguaviva.it; Via Fiume 17)

Scuola Leonardo da Vinci (Map p466; ☎ 055 26 11 81; www.scuolaleonardo.com; Via Bufalini 3)

Other

Many of the above language schools also offer supplementary courses in art history, cooking, fashion and music. The schools below specialise in such activities.

Accademia Italiana (Map pp462-3; ☎ 055 28 46 16; www.accademiaitaliana.com; Piazza de' Pitti 15) Language, culture and a wide range of design programmes in Italian including graphics, textile, fashion etc.

Cordon Bleu (Map pp462-3; ☎ 055 234 54 68; www .cordonbleu-it.com; Via di Mezzo 55r) Good choice for gourmet cookery.

Florence Dance Center (Map pp462-3; ☎ 055 28 92 76; www.florencedance.org in Italian; Borgo della Stella 23r) Courses in classical, jazz and modern dance.

Istituto per l'Arte e il Restauro Palazzo Spinelli (Map p466; ☎ 055 24 60 01; www.spinelli.it; Borgo Santa Croce 10) Restoration (anything from paintings to ceramics), interior and graphic design, gilding and marquetry.

La Cucina del Garga (☎ 055 21 13 96; www.garga.it) Hands-on Tuscan cookery courses, from one to eight days, run by the team from Trattoria Garga (p482).

FLORENCE FOR CHILDREN

Buy each of the younger kids a copy of *Fun in Florence* by Nancy Shroyer Howard. With do-and-find sections for major sites such as the cathedral and Uffizi courtyard, they can be happily employed while the grown-ups go round gawping at the boring bits.

Older children can get to grips with the city in a stimulating way by delving into *Florence, Just Add Water*, and *Florence: Playing with Art* by Maria Salvia Baldini.

Other books to keep them occupied include *Florence for Kids* from Edizioni Lapis, plus, for older kids, *Florence for Teens* and *Florence: A Young Traveller's Guide*.

There's a small **playground** (Map pp462–3) in Piazza Massimo d'Azeglio, about 650m east of the cathedral. Beside the River Arno, about 1.2km west of Stazione di Santa Maria Novella, is the **Parco delle Cascine** (Map pp460–1), a massive public park. And right in the heart of Piazza dell Repubblica is a constantly turning merry-go-round (carousel).

Mondobimbo (Map pp460-1; ☎ 055 553 29 46; Via Ponte Rosso; admission €5; ✆ 10am-midnight May-Sep, 10am-7pm Oct-Apr) is a well-stocked playground with everything from bouncy castles to a minirailway, aimed at kids aged two to 10.

TOURS
Bus

CAF Tours (Map p466; ☎ 055 21 06 12; www.caftours .com; Via Sant'Antonino 6r) do coach tours of the city (€39 to €82) and nearby towns such as Lucca and Pisa.

Cycling

Florence by Bike (Map pp462-3; ☎ 055 48 89 92; www
.florencebybike.it; Via San Zanobi 120-122r) does a day
tour (32km) of the Chianti area (including
bike, equipment and lunch €73.50).

Bicycle Tuscany (☎ 055 22 25 80; www.bicycletuscany
.com) does regular tours (21km) in the Tuscan
country (with transport, bike and equipment,
including lunch and a winery visit €60).

I Bike Italy (☎ 055 234 23 71; www.ibikeitaly.com)
offers a 25km tour around Fiesole or a 50km
circuit around Il Chianti (each €70). Both are
as much gastronomic as sporty and include
shuttle bus, lunch, and bike and gear hire.

Accidental Tourist (☎ 055 69 93 76; www.accidental
tourist.com) offers fairly gentle half-day walking
(€70) and cycling (€75) tours, plus cookery
classes (€80).

Walking

Walking Tours of Florence (Map p466; ☎ 055 264 50
33; www.artviva.com; Piazza Santo Stefano 2) organises
several excellent three-hour walks of the
city (€20 to €39) led by specialists. They can
also plot specific walks to suit your personal
needs and tastes – at a price – and offer
half-day guided cycle tours (€40, 14km).

Mercurio Tours (☎ 055 21 33 55; www.mercurio-italy
.org) offers a range of visits within and beyond
the city. Reserve by phone, or in person at
Amici del Turismo (Via Cavour 36r).

Florence Walks & Tours (☎ 800 50 11 72; www.tours
-italy.com) does a three-hour walk (€20, Monday
to Saturday). Just turn up at 9.50am outside
the Louis Vuitton shop in Piazza Strozzi.

FESTIVALS & EVENTS

Florence is rich in festivals. One that always
goes off with a bang is the **Scoppio del Carro**
(Explosion of the Cart), in which a cart full of
fireworks is exploded in front of the cathedral
on Easter Saturday.

On 24 June, the **Festa di San Giovanni** (Festival of St John) is celebrated with almost-
anything-goes Calcio Storico medieval football matches which are played on Piazza di
Santa Croce. It ends with a fireworks display
over Piazzale Michelangelo.

The **Festa delle Rificolone** (Festival of the
Paper Lanterns), during which a procession
of drummers, *sbandieratori* (flag-throwers),
musicians and others in medieval dress winds
its way from Piazza di Santa Croce to Piazza
della SS Annunziata, celebrating the eve of
Our Lady's birthday on 7 September.

The **Internazionale Antiquariato**, a major antiques fair attracting exhibitors from across
Europe, is held every two years at the Palazzo
Strozzi. The **Maggio Musicale Fiorentino** in Florence is a major music festival (see p485).

SLEEPING

There are more than 200 one- and two-star
hotels alone in Florence. All the same, it's
prudent to book ahead between mid-April
and October.

The Consorzio ITA (see p459) office at
Stazione di Santa Maria Novella can make
reservations for a small fee.

The prices we quote are for the high season
(roughly Easter to mid-October). Outside
these months, many midrange and top-end
hotels offer some very juicy bargains. Lots of
hotels also dip their prices in the hot months
of July and August.

Hotels and *pensioni* are concentrated in
three main areas: near Stazione di Santa
Maria Novella, near Piazza di Santa Maria
Novella and in the old city between the
Arno and the cathedral.

Accommodation Options

Such organisations can book you into their
member hotels but rarely drop below two
stars and some take their cut from both the
client and hotel.

Florence Promhotels (☎ 055 55 39 41, 800 86 60 22;
www.promhotels.it; Viale Volta 72)

Top Quark (☎ 055 33 40 41, 800 60 88 22; www.family
hotels.com; Viale Fratelli Rossi 39r)

RENTAL ACCOMMODATION

These three bodies specialise in B&Bs, *affittacamere* (rooms for rent) and short-stay
apartments.

Florence & Abroad (Map pp462-3; ☎ 055 48 70 04;
www.florenceandabroad.com; Via San Zanobi 58) Specialises in short- and medium-term rental accommodation in
Florence and the Fiesole area for those with a fairly liberal
budget.

Associazione Bed & Breakfast Affittacamere (AB&BA;
☎ 055 654 08 60; www.abbafirenze.it; Via P Mastri 26)

Gente di Toscana (☎ 0575 52 92 75; www.gentedi
toscana.it; Via S Michele, Scandicci)

CAMPING

There are three camping options in and
around Florence.

Campeggio Michelangelo (Map pp460-1; ☎ 055
681 19 77; www.ecvacanze.it; Viale Michelangelo 80;

person/car/tent/€9.50/6/4.50; ☻ year-round) The closest camp site to the city centre, just off Piazzale Michelangelo, south of the River Arno. Big and comparatively leafy, it's handy for the historic quarter though the steep walk back may have you panting. Take bus No 13 from Stazione di Santa Maria Novella.

Villa Camerata (Map pp460-1; ☎ 055 60 14 51; fax 055 61 03 00; Viale Augusto Righi 2-4; person/tent €6/5) Beside the HI-affiliated hostel of the same name (p481) and in a green setting. Space for tents is decidedly limited but is more generous for campervans.

See p489 for details of the third camp site, Campeggio Panoramico in the hills near Fiesole.

East of Stazione di Santa Maria Novella
BUDGET
Ostello Archi Rossi (Map pp462-3; ☎ 055 29 08 04; www.hostelarchirossi.com; Via Faenza 94r; dm from €18.50, s €28.50; 🖵) This is a well-run private hostel conveniently close to Stazione di Santa Maria Novella. Decorated with frescoes by local art students and guests' graffiti, it's well equipped, with washing machines and microwaves. You can make reservations via the website. Includes breakfast.

MIDRANGE
Residenze Johlea I & II (Map pp462-3; ☎ 055 463 32 92; www.johlea.it; Via San Gallo 76 & 80; s €70, d €95-105; ✄) Near neighbours, each of these two places offers tasteful, impeccable, individually decorated rooms with dinky minifridges. For extra space, ask for the suite in No 76 (€115); breakfast is included with all rooms. No 80, which acts as reception for both, has a gorgeous little roof terrace, that's accessible to all guests. Reservations are essential between March and November.

Antica Dimora (Map pp462-3; ☎ 055 462 72 96; www.anticadimorafirenze.it; 2nd fl, Via San Gallo 72; s €90-110, d €130-145; ✄) Dimora is the Johleas' recently opened sister B&B, just down the road. Four of its six rooms have sybaritic four-poster beds and all are large and adorned with reproductions of old black-and-white prints. It has wi-fi and breakfast is included.

Johanna I (Map pp460-1; ☎ 055 48 18 96; Via Bonifacio Lupi 14; s/d €60/95); **Johanna II** (Map pp460-1; ☎ 055 47 33 77; Via Cinque Giornate 12; d €80-95) The same consortium as the Antica Dimora (above) also runs an equally attractive pair of nearby,

more modest B&Bs. For more information, consult www.johanna.it.

Hotel Azzi (Map pp462-3; ☎ 055 21 38 06; www .hotelazzi.it; Via Faenza 56; s/d €60/90, with bathroom €70/110) Hotel Azzi, with its attractive terrace, is popular among artists, visiting musicians and actors. You may be lucky enough to coincide with one of the hotel's gastronomic and musical soirées. Rooms are comfortable with freshly upgraded bathrooms; ask for one away from noisy Via Faenza. All come with breakfast.

Cristina House (Map pp460-1; ☎ 055 48 31 45; www.cristinahouse.it; 2nd fl, Via Leone X 2; d with shower/ bathroom & breakfast €100/120; ✄) A wonderfully cosy five-room place down a quiet street, just north of busy Viale Spartaco Lavagnini. You can be one of the family as the ever-helpful Cristina's children play beneath a display of postcards sent by satisfied guests from around the globe. Or you can retire to the seclusion of your large, trim room.

Hotel Le Cascine (Map pp462-3; ☎ 055 21 10 66; fax 055 21 07 69; www.hotellecascine.it; 1st fl, Largo Alinari 15; s €50-120, d €90-170; Ⓟ ✄ 🖵) Le Cascine is a three-star place with young, friendly staff. It is one of the better choices in an area overburdened with hotels. The rooms are attractively furnished and some have balconies. All rooms include breakfast.

Hotel Désirée (Map pp462-3; ☎ 055 238 23 82; www .desireehotel.com; Via Fiume 20; s/d €70/120; Ⓟ ✄) This is a very personable hotel. The 18 spick-and-span, high-ceilinged rooms, many overlooking a tranquil, leafy rear courtyard, have mosaic floors and are tastefully furnished. Parking is €20.

Hotel Accademia (Map p466; ☎ 055 29 34 51; www .accademiahotel.net; Via Faenza 7; s/d/tr with breakfast €85/150/190; Ⓟ ✄ 🖵) In an 18th-century mansion, the Accademia has impressive stained-glass doors, carved wooden ceilings and a marble staircase that tempts you to do your best Ginger Rogers or Fred Astaire impersonation. Bedrooms are pleasant with parquet floors. Parking is €25.

Hotel Bellettini (Map p466; ☎ 055 21 35 61; www .hotelbellettini.com; 2nd fl, Via de' Conti 7; s/d/tr €100/ 140/180; Ⓟ ✄ 🖵) A delightful, welcoming hotel with around 30 bright, well-furnished rooms; try for one with a view of the Basilica di San Lorenzo. The Bellettini has an equally attractive, slightly more expensive annexe nearby. Valet parking will set you back €23 to €27.

Hotel Casci (Map pp462-3; ☎ 055 21 16 86; www
.hotelcasci.com; 2nd fl, Via Cavour 13; s/d with breakfast
€110/150; P ⌘ 🖳) Casci is a friendly family
hotel within a 15th-century mansion where
the décor is attractively olive green. For a
relaxing soak, choose a room with one of the
recently installed shell-shaped baths. Look
up at the fresco as you take breakfast, which
includes fresh espresso coffee. Parking is €23
to €27.

Hotel Globus (Map pp462-3; ☎ 055 21 10 62; www
.hotelglobus.com; Via Sant'Antonino 24; s/d/tr €70/100/150;
P ⌘ 🖳) A cosy, stylish hotel that once belonged to the composer Rossini, it comes recommended by several readers. All 23 rooms
have free Internet access via the TV, some
have good views over the city and the showers have hydromassage. Parking is €21.

TOP END

Hotel Monna Lisa (Map pp462-3; ☎ 055 247 97 51;
www.monnalisa.it; Borgo Pinti 27; s/d/tr with breakfast
€180/290/415; P ⌘) Hotel Monna Lisa is in a
fine Renaissance palazzo. Most of the furnishings and paintings are of the period, many
of them family heirlooms. Nonchalantly on
display are works by Giovanni Dupré, the
19th-century sculptor, whose relatives still
own the hotel. Some rooms overlook the
bijou private garden, bedecked with flowers,
where you can enjoy a buffet breakfast in
summer. Parking is €15.

Hotel Il Guelfo Bianco (Map pp462-3; ☎ 055 28
83 30; www.ilguelfobianco.it; Via Cavour 29; s €135, d from
€180; P ⌘ 🖳) This hotel has 40 attractive,
comfortable rooms, all including breakfast.
Room No 124 is a charming double with its
own private terrace. There are some fine antiques and – an original touch for Florence –
quality contemporary art adorns the public
areas and bedrooms. Valet parking is €24.

Around Piazza di Santa Maria Novella

Hotel Scoti (Map p466; ☎ 055 29 21 28; www.hotelscoti
.com; 2nd fl, Via de' Tornabuoni 7; s/d €65/85) Within a
16th-century palazzo on Florence's smart-
est shopping strip, Hotel Scoti remains one
of Florence's most attractive, well-priced
choices. With welcoming Italian-Australian
owners, its rooms, furnished with antique
pieces, are full of character and the common sitting room with its floor-to-ceiling
frescoes and chandelier is a little gem.

Grand Hotel Baglioni (Map p466; ☎ 055 2 35 80;
www.hotelbaglioni.it; Piazza dell'Unità Italiana 6; s €188-

270, d €261-375; P ⌘ 🖳) Grand Hotel Baglioni has a mellow tone, with wooden beams
and staircase and public areas made of
pietra serena, the soft grey stone typical of
many Florentine monuments. The rooftop
terrace restaurant and garden have stirring
views over the city. Parking is €35 to €40.

Hotel Abaco (Map p466; ☎ 055 238 19 19; www
.abaco-hotel.it; 2nd fl, Via dei Banchi 1; d €65, with shower
€75, with bathroom €90; P ⌘ 🖳) A simple, well-
maintained establishment with just seven
rooms, three with a bathroom, all named
after a Renaissance artist and furnished in
high baroque style. In low season they'll
rent a double for one person (€50 to €65).
There's a €5 supplement for air-con; valet
parking is €24.

Pensione Ferretti (Map p466; ☎ 055 238 13 28;
www.pensioneferretti.it; Via delle Belle Donne 17; s/d/tr
€52/82/110, with bathroom €65/102/130; P 🖳) Hidden away on a tiny, quiet intersection, Ferretti is a modest hotel with a friendly, family
feel to it. Rooms have ceiling fans and the
off-peak rates are substantially lower than
high season's. Parking is €21; breakfast is
included.

Between the Cathedral & the Arno

BUDGET

Hotel Orchidea (Map p466; ☎ 055 248 03 46; www
.hotelorchideaflorence.it; 1st fl, Borgo degli Albizi 11; s/d
with shared bathroom €55/75) A fine, homely, old-
fashioned *pensione* in a grand mansion. Its
seven rooms are simple, well maintained
and rich in character.

Hotel San Giovanni (Map p466; ☎ 055 28 83 85;
www.hotelsangiovanni.com; Via de' Cerretani 2; s/d/tr
€55/75/97, d/tr with bathroom €95/120; P) Once
part of the bishop's private residence (see
the traces of fresco in several rooms), Hotel
San Giovanni has charming, often spacious
rooms with parquet flooring. Six of the nine
rooms have views of the cathedral; all include breakfast. This place has the same
Italian-Australian owners as Hotel Perseo
(see p480), where you can take breakfast
and also check in if no-one answers here.
Valet parking is €24.

Hotel Dalí (Map p466; ☎ 055 234 07 06; www
.hoteldali.com; 2nd fl, Via dell'Oriuolo 17; s/d €40/60, d
with bathroom €75, extra bed €20; P) A spruce,
simple, warmly recommended hotel, run
by a friendly, helpful young couple. Some
rooms overlook the serene inner courtyard.
One bedroom can squeeze in up to six, so

bring the gang. There's free parking, rare as icebergs in Florence.

Hotel Cestelli (Map p466; ☎ 055 21 42 13; www .hotelcestelli.com; Borgo SS Apostoli 25; s/d €40/65, d with bathroom €80; P) This hotel has new owners who have whirled through, repainting and refurbishing. Room No 4 (€100 plus €20 per person) is vast (stick your head out the window and you get a view of the Arno) and can accommodate up to four. The only things smoking in this friendly place are the joss sticks, beloved of Alessio, the dynamic proprietor. Valet parking is €20.

MIDRANGE

Hotel Perseo (Map p466; ☎ 055 21 25 04; www.hotel perseo.it; 3rd fl, Via de'Cerretani 1; d/tr/q with breakfast €95/120/140; P 🗶 🖵) This place was radically renovated in 2005 and offers greater comfort than its sister, Hotel San Giovanni (p479), a well-lobbed stone's throw away. The décor is befittingly arty with original canvases by the owner and one or two by long-forgotten, impecunious students who, in the harsh days after WWII, would leave a painting in lieu of rent. Parking is €24.

Pensione Maria Luisa de' Medici (Map p466; ☎ 055 28 00 48; 2nd fl, Via del Corso 1; d/tr €68/110, with bathroom €95/125) This *pensione*, in a 17th-century mansion, is tastefully furnished and rich in antiques. You can dip into the doctor-owner's equally impressive collection of coffee-table art volumes. You'll sleep soundly, protected by his superb collection of winged angels and cherubims that keep watch over the corridors. The rooms are enormous: most can easily accommodate four, some even five people; breakfast is included.

Hotel Bavaria (Map p466; ☎ 055 234 03 13; www .hotelbavariafirenze.it; Borgo degli Albizi 26; s/d €50/70, d/tr with bathroom €98/113) Bavaria is within the 16th-century Palazzo di Ramirez di Montalvo. The rooms (including breakfast) are furnished with fine antique pieces. With its warm ochre colours, low wooden ceilings and flexible pricing, it makes an excellent choice. Reservations are imperative, especially between April and July.

Hotel Pendini (Map p466; ☎ 055 21 11 70; www .hotelpendini.net; 4th fl, Via degli Strozzi 2; s €80-110, d €110-150; P 🗶 🖵) A homely 42-room family-owned place where rooms are furnished with antiques and reproductions. Some of the rooms look out over Piazza della Repubblica. Parking is €24.

TOP END

Relais Uffizi (Map p466; ☎ 055 267 62 39; www.relais uffizi.it; 2nd fl, Chiasso del Buco 16; s/d/tr from €120/180/220; P 🗶) A stylish small hotel, hidden away down an alley (Chiasso de' Baroncelli), in a 16th-century building, a mere pigeon hop from Piazza della Signoria (parking is €30). From its breakfast room there are unparalleled views of the seething square. The large, tastefully furnished bedrooms have four-poster beds.

Hotel Helvetia & Bristol (Map p466; ☎ 055 2 66 51; www.royaldemeure.com; Via dei Pescioni 2; s/d from €275/440; P 🗶 🖵) Deservedly five-star, this hotel is distinguished by the elegance of its *belle époque* setting and the discreet yet warm charm of its staff. Each of its 67 rooms is swathed in rich fabrics, fine antiques abound and bathrooms are of Carrara marble. Guests who've savoured its charm include Bertrand Russell, Pirandello and Stravinsky. Parking costs €30 to €35.

Savoy (Map p466; ☎ 055 2 73 51; www.hotelsavoy.it; Piazza della Repubblica 7; s/d from €300/460; P 🗶 🖵) The Savoy is a beguiling mix; the 107 spacious bedrooms in this most classic of buildings have a fresh, contemporary feel. If you aren't on your knees after a day of sightseeing, its fitness centre offers exercise – with heart-stopping views from its windows.

Santa Croce & East of the Centre

Hotel Wanda (Map pp462-3; ☎ 055 234 44 84; www .hotelwanda.it; Via Ghibellina 51; s/d/tr €70/88/119, d/tr with bathroom €119/140; 🗶) Hotel Wanda is a welcoming, tranquil, somewhat higgledy-piggledy place. Its large rooms, many with ceiling frescoes, are much airier and lighter than the dowdy façade would suggest. For a fun night, request Room 13: it is lined with old mirrors. Breakfast is included.

Hotel Dante (Map pp462-3; ☎ 055 24 17 72; www .hotel-dante.it; Via S Cristofano 2; s/d €88/120; ℗ ▢ 😊) Down a quiet street right by the Basilica di Santa Croce, Hotel Dante is popular with visiting actors, as the photogallery of smiling faces beside reception attests. Fully 50% of its rooms have a kitchen – ideal for families, dining in or eschewing the pricey breakfast (€12). Parking costs €10 to €15 and there's wi-fi.

The Oltrarno

Ostello Santa Monaca (Map pp462-3; ☎ 055 26 83 38; www.ostello.it; Via Santa Monaca 6; dm €17; ▢) Once a convent, Santa Monaca is warmly recommended. At this friendly hostel, run by a cooperative, guests get a special deal at a nearby restaurant. There's a laundrette, guests' kitchen (you'll need your own equipment) and free safe deposit at reception. Reservations by email or letter.

Hotel la Scaletta (Map p466; ☎ 055 28 30 28; www .hotellascaletta.it; top fl, Via de' Guicciardini 13; s/d with breakfast €90/140; 😊 ▢) La Scaletta has new owners, who have improved upon what was already a delightful place, full of rambling corridors over three levels, within a 15th-century palazzo. It's worth the room rate simply for the great 360-degree view from the roof terrace and you're scarcely 100m from both the Ponte Vecchio and Palazzo Pitti.

Around Florence

Ostello Villa Camerata (Map pp460-1; ☎ 055 60 14 51; florenceaighostel@virgilio.it; Viale Augusto Righi 2-4; dm €18, d/tr/q with bathroom €44/54/66; ℗ ▢) An HI-affiliated hostel that occupies a converted 17th century villa. Surrounded by extensive grounds, it must rank as one of Italy's most beautiful. Breakfast included. To get here, get on bus No 17, 17B or 17C (30 minutes, every half-hour) from the southwest side of Stazione di Santa Maria Novella.

EATING

Simplicity and quality sum up Tuscany's cuisine and Florence offers the widest choice. Here, rich green Tuscan olive oil, fresh fruit and vegetables, tender meat and, of course,

the classic wine Chianti are so often the basics of a good meal.

Meat-eaters might want to take on the challenge of the local carnivore's classic, *bistecca alla fiorentina*, a huge slab of prime Florentine steak. It usually costs around €40 per kilo, which is quite adequate for two.

East of Stazione di Santa Maria Novella
BUDGET

Nerbone (Map pp462-3; ☎ 055 21 99 49; Mercato Centrale San Lorenzo; mains €5; ☷ 7am-2pm Mon-Sat) As simple as they come and just inside the central market's western entrance, Nerbone has been serving steaming lunchtime platters since 1872. The handwritten menu changes daily. Start with the particularly substantial *ribollita* (a rich, chewy vegetable soup) and round off a hearty lunch with *biscotti di Prato* (crunchy almond biscuit/cookie) served with a shot of Vin Santo (sweet dessert wine). Friday is fish day.

Mario (Map pp462-3; ☎ 055 21 85 50; Via Rosina 2; mains about €6, pastas €3.50-4.50; ☷ lunch Mon-Sat) In business for more than 50 years, Mario is a bustling bar and trattoria that attracts a mix of market workers and others in search of a guaranteed cheap, filling lunch. It's well worth the wait you'll probably have before lunching elbow-to-elbow with the person next to you.

Il Vegetariano (Map pp462-3; ☎ 055 47 50 30; Via delle Ruote 30r; meals about €15; ☷ lunch & dinner Tue-Fri, dinner Sat & Sun) One of the few veggie options in town, this place has a great selection of fresh food, salads and mains. There's always a vegan option and the chalked-up menu changes regularly, reflecting what's freshest at the market.

MIDRANGE

Ristorante Lobs (Map pp462-3; ☎ 055 21 24 78; Via Faenza 75-77r; mains about €25) A superb fish restaurant that offers always fresh, exclusively Mediterranean fish and seafood. The setting has maritime frescoes and, appropriately, salmon-pink walls. At lunchtime they do a selection of pasta specials for just €7. Sluice it all down with the Soave wine from Italy's northeast.

I Tozzo di Pane (Map pp462-3; ☎ 055 47 57 53; Via Guelfa 94r; mains €8-15; ☷ Tue-Sat & dinner Mon) A simple neighbourhood place, run by a young, friendly team where cool jazz warbles in the background. For starters, go for

TUSCANY

the *zuppa toscana*, a thick gruel of vegetables and barley. Although not to all tastes, the *trippa alla Fiorentina* (tripe) follows on a treat. The small rear garden is a pleasant retreat from the street in summer.

Around Piazza di Santa Maria Novella

Ostaria dei Centopoveri (Map pp462-3; ☎ 055 21 88 46; Via del Palazzuolo 31r; meals €35-40; ✆ Wed-Sun & dinner Tue) The 'hostel of the hundred poor people' is a quality dining option and a congenial spot in a not-so-congenial part of town. On offer are creative variations on traditional Tuscan food in a down-to-earth setting.

Between the Cathedral & the Arno

Trattoria Coco Lezzone (Map p466; ☎ 055 28 71 78; Via Parioncino 26r; mains €9.50-15.50; ✆ Mon-Sat) This trattoria is another cheerful, homely spot. No credit cards, no coffee, just very good food; this tiny place knows its clients believe it's good and doesn't make unnecessary concessions. *Ribollita* is the house speciality and Friday is fresh-fish day.

Cantinetta Antinori (Map p466; ☎ 055 29 22 34; Piazza degli Antinori 3; snacks €9-12, mains about €20; ✆ Mon-Fri) On the ground floor of 15th-century Palazzo Antinori, Cantinetta Antinori is a suave place where the waiters communicate in tactful sotto voce. Sit at the attractive polished wooden bar or look down upon your fellow quaffers from the upstairs balcony.

Trattoria Garga (Map pp462-3; ☎ 055 239 88 98; Via del Moro 48r; mains €21-25; ✆ dinner Tue-Sun) Trattoria Garga, with more than 25 successful years in business, offers imaginative, creative fare. It also does cookery courses, where you can learn to make a dish you might have just eaten, as well as gastronomic tours of Tuscany (see p476).

L'Osteria di Giovanni (Map pp462-3; ☎ 055 28 48 97; Via del Moro 22; mains €8.50-15.50; ✆ closed lunch Tue) This is a very recent addition to Florence's gourmet options, run with flair by a father and son team, fresh from years of culinary triumph in Siena. Get along there quickly before the word spreads…

Da il Latini (Map p466; ☎ 055 21 09 16; Via dei Palchetti 6r; mains €10-20; ✆ Tue-Sat) This is a popular Florentine favourite – so much so that you may find yourself waiting in line since they don't take reservations. It's well worth hanging around; the wine list is impressive and the food largely Tuscan but the dining

area speaks of Spain with all those legs of ham dangling from the ceiling.

Trattoria dei 13 Gobbi (Map p462-3; ☎ 055 21 32 04; Via del Porcellana 9r; mains €10-12.50; ✆ Tue-Sun) This trattoria is low-ceilinged and snug, its bucolic setting matched by the plant-filled rear courtyard. Beef and pork dishes figure prominently so be prepared to ease out your belt a notch.

Trattoria Sostanza (Map pp462-3; ☎ 055 21 26 91; Via del Porcellana 25r; mains €8.50-12.50; ✆ Mon-Fri) Trattoria Sostanza, with its simple décor and tiled walls, is another authentic Tuscan eatery that simmers up a mean minestrone. Another favourite of the house is the *petti di pollo al burro* (chicken breasts in butter).

Ristorante Self-Service Leonardo (Map p466; ☎ 055 28 44 46; Via de' Pecori 35r; mains €4-5; ✆ Sun-Fri) A refectory-style option, this is hard to beat if you're wanting to eat a full meal while pinching the pennies.

Santa Croce & East of the Centre
BUDGET

Koo-cli-Koo (Map pp462-3; ☎ 055 234 22 01; Borgo Pinti 2r, cnr Via dell'Oriuolo; sandwiches €1.50-3, dishes €5; ✆ noon-10pm Mon-Fri & lunch Sat) One of Italy's rare hole-in-the-wall vegetarian takeaways. Run by a cheerful family, its food, which is laid all out before you so you can pick and choose, is both wholesome and tasty.

Antico Noè (Map p466; ☎ 055 234 08 38; Volta di San Piero 6r; panini €3.80-4.50, mains €8-13; ✆ noon-midnight Mon-Sat) A legendary place, just off Piazza San Pier Maggiore, with two sections: a takeaway sandwich bar with juicy cold cuts and, just next door, a cosy little restaurant where you can enjoy fine cooking and mellow wine to slow jazz and blues tunes.

Ruth's (Map pp462-3; ☎ 055 248 08 88; Via Luigi Carto Farini 2a; meals about €12; ✆ Sun-Thu, lunch Fri & dinner Sat) Located beside Florence's synagogue, Ruth's serves up tasty dishes, at once kosher and vegetarian. For a variety of savours, try the *gran piatto di Ruth per due* (the translation, 'big Ruth's dish for two', does the svelte owner a disservice). This filling mixed platter (€18 for two) includes couscous, felafel, filo-pastry pie and potato salad.

Ramraj (Map pp462-3; ☎ 055 24 09 99; Via Ghibellina 61r; set menus €8; ✆ Tue-Sun) Ramraj offers takeaway or eat-in Indian specialities. The set menu comes in vegetarian and carnivore variants or you can select from the ample range on display.

MIDRANGE

Trattoria Cibrèo (Map pp462-3; ☎ 055 234 11 00; Via de' Macci 122r; starters €5, mains €13; ☒ Tue-Sat Sep-Jul) An excellent-value trattoria where dried red peppers dangle like coral necklaces from the ceiling. It uses the same kitchens as its namesake, the expensive restaurant next door, and offers the same, although much more restricted, menu. Bring cash and come early: they take neither reservations nor credit cards.

Ristorante Natalino (Map pp462-3; ☎ 055 28 94 04; Borgo degli Albizi 17r; mains €11-16; ☒ Mon-Sat) Ristorante Natalino, in a long-deconsecrated church, has been around for well over a century. It's a friendly, informal place where you'll eat well, whether in the small dining area beside the bar or the attractive vaulted interior. If it features (the menu changes regularly), savour the fried calves' liver with sage – and leave a corner for the tempting homemade desserts.

Osteria de' Benci (Map p466; ☎ 055 234 49 23; Via de' Benci 13r; mains €10-15; ☒ Mon-Sat) Dining is a pleasure beneath this restaurant's vaulted ceiling. The young team changes the menu monthly and serves up well-prepared fare, including good honest slabs of *carbonata di chianina*, which is even more tender and succulent than the ubiquitous *bistecca alla fiorentina*.

TOP END

Ristorante Cibrèo (Map pp462-3; ☎ 055 234 11 00; Via de' Macci 118; starters €18, mains €34; ☒ Tue-Sat Sep-Jul) Next door to the fine trattoria of the same name, Cibrèo is justifiably famous in Florence and way beyond. Warm timber dominates the décor and the table settings are an indicator of the class that this place exudes. Reservations are essential.

The Oltrarno

BUDGET

Trattoria Casalinga (Map pp462-3; ☎ 055 21 86 24; Via de' Michelozzi 9r; mains about €5; ☒ Mon-Sat) This trattoria is a cheerful, family-run place where you can get a filling meal with wine at bargain-basement prices. Don't expect to linger as there's usually a queue of expectant diners eager to take over your table.

I Tarocchi (Map pp462-3; ☎ 055 234 39 12; Via dei Renai 12-16r; pizzas, 1st & 2nd courses €6-8; ☒ Tue-Fri & dinner Sat & Sun) I Tarocchi serves excellent pizzas and its first courses alone are enough to

satisfy most people's hunger. Plant yourself on the pavement terrace or snuggle up on one of the inside benches.

MIDRANGE

Trattoria Cammillo (Map p466; ☎ 055 21 24 27; Borgo San Jacopo 57r; mains €13-17; ☒ Thu-Mon) Trattoria Cammillo is a traditional type of place, its walls crowded with canvases, and the ample menu changes every day. It remains a very Florentine haunt whose staff, bow-tied and aproned, offer discreet service with a smile. If it's on, go for the juicy roast pork: the crackling is as stiff as the waiters' starched shirts.

Borgo Antico (Map pp462-3; ☎ 055 21 04 37; Piazza Santo Spirito 6r; salads & pizzas €7, mains about €15) Borgo Antico enjoys a great summer location beside a bustling piazza. Try one of the big, leafy salads (one of several vegetarian options), tuck into a pizza or choose from the menu, which changes daily.

Al Tranvai (Map pp462-3; ☎ 055 22 51 97; Piazza Tasso 14r; mains €8-12; ☒ Mon-Fri) This place is a wonderful, rustic Tuscan eatery where you can eat nudged up with the locals at the interior tables or out on the terrace. Since it's so deservedly popular, you'd be wise to reserve your small space.

Osteria Antica Mescita San Niccolò (Map pp460-1; ☎ 055 234 28 36; Via San Niccolò 60r; meals about €25; ☒ Mon-Sat) This is a fine little eating hideaway where the food is tasty, authentic and home-style. Throw in a good bottle from the huge range of Tuscan tipples and you'll have a great meal. The lunch buffet (€10) is especially good value.

Osteria Santo Spirito (Map pp462-3; ☎ 055 238 23 83; Piazza Santo Spirito 16r; meals about €30) This *osteria* (simple trattoria-style restaurant) offers a slightly higher-quality meal than most of the bustling haunts across the square. Built on two floors, it spills onto the piazza in summer. Try the gnocchi with soft cheese *gratiné* and truffle oil (€9).

Ristorante Beccofino (Map pp462-3; ☎ 055 29 00 76; Piazza degli Scarlatti 1r; 1st/2nd courses to €10/20; ☒ Tue-Sun) Beccofino is both innovative restaurant and stylish *enoteca* (wine bar) with more than 50 wines on offer by the glass. It's decidedly *nouvelle* chic; the giant terracotta fish skeleton splayed over one wall may induce a shudder and the stainless-steel, floor-lit toilets are far from the least of its charms.

TUSCANY

TOP END

Borgo San Jacopo (Map p466; ☎ 055 28 16 61; Borgo San Jacopo 62r; mains €18-25; ☒ dinner Wed-Mon) The Borgo San Jacopo is another very stylish recent arrival, all gleaming glass and stainless steel. It's just as innovative as you'd expect from an offshoot of the equally hip Gallery Hotel Art (see the boxed text, p480).

Gelaterie

Gelateria Vivoli (Map p466; ☎ 055 29 23 34; Via dell' Isola delle Stinche 7) Choose from a broad range of creamy *gelati*.

Festival del Gelato (Map p466; ☎ 055 29 43 86; Via del Corso 75r) Just off Piazza della Repubblica, with more than 70 flavours on offer, it should satisfy even the most demanding child.

Perchè No? (Map p466; ☎ 055 239 89 69; Via dei Tavolini 19r; ☒ Wed-Sun) This *gelateria*, in business for around 70 years, does excellent ices.

Quick Eats

Fiaschetteria Vecchio Casentino (Map p466; ☎ 055 21 74 11; Via dei Neri 17r; ☒ Tue-Sun) Casentino does a magnificent array of snacks and more than 30 different kinds of *panini*, all under €6.50. It also carries a good selection of wines by the glass.

Il Nilo (Map p466; ☎ 055 24 16 99; Volta di San Piero 9r; ☒ noon-10pm) Zaki from Cairo, the man with the widest grin in town, does tasty *shawarma* and felafel sandwiches (€2.50 or €3.50) to takeaway or munch on the spot.

Self-Catering

Mercato Centrale San Lorenzo (Map pp462-3; Piazza del Mercato Centrale; ☒ 7am-2pm Mon-Sat) This

---

AUTHOR'S CHOICE

I Fratellini (Map p466; ☎ 055 239 60 96; Via dei Cimatori 38r; panini €2.10) It may be little more than a hole in the wall and you have to eat in the street but the best quick snack place in all of Europe is I Fratellini. You'll never see *panini*, fresh filled as you order, whipped up so quickly as at this wonderful, seething place, established in 1875. Just watch the deft backhand pass from maker to wine pourer. There's no seating and etiquette requires that you leave your empty glass on one of the two wooden shelves on the wall outside.

---

central market is a cornucopia of delights for self-caterers and sandwich fillers.

Pasta Fresca Morioni (Map pp462-3; ☎ 055 239 61 73; Via Palazzuolo 56r) A tiny *pasticceria* where you can see the team inside turning out the freshest of pasta in many different guises.

DRINKING
Cafés

Gilli (Map p466; ☎ 055 21 38 96; Piazza della Repubblica 39r; ☒ Wed-Sun) One of several historic cafés around the square, Gilli has been serving up good coffee since 1733. It's very reasonably priced if you stand at the bar.

Rinascente (Map p466; Via Speziali 13-23r) Enjoy a coffee (€3 to €5) at the rooftop café of this department store, just off Piazza della Repubblica, while savouring stunning views of the square and cathedral way below.

Bars

Astor Caffè (Map p466; Piazza del Duomo 5r) You could take breakfast here then return some 12 hours later to mix with the nocturnal crowd who gather around for loud music and cocktails, opposite the solemn walls of the cathedral. Keep an eye on the giant red clock so closing time doesn't sneak up on you...

Capocaccia (Map p466; Lungarno Corsini 12-14r; ☒ noon-1am) This is where Florence's beautiful people gather, especially on balmy spring and summer evenings, for a riverside nibble and a cocktail or two. Tuesday is sushi night and the DJ takes over at 11pm each evening.

Mayday (Map p466; ☎ 055 238 12 90; Via Dante Alighieri 16r; ☒ 8pm-2am Mon-Sat) Mayday is strong on theme nights and often runs an art exhibition. The two *ragazzi* who run the place have an amazing collection of CDs, sometimes supplemented with live music.

Rex Caffè (Map pp462-3; ☎ 055 248 03 31; Via Fiesolana 25r) Another top stop on the cocktail circuit, this is a hip place to sip your favourite mixed concoction against a background of an illuminated world map.

Cabiria (Map pp462-3; ☎ 055 21 57 32; Piazza Santo Spirito 4r; ☒ 11am-2am Wed-Mon) A popular café by day, Cabiria converts into a busy music bar at night. In summer, the buzz extends onto Piazza Santo Spirito, which becomes a stage for an outdoor bar and regular free concerts.

La Dolce Vita (Map pp462-3; ☎ 055 28 45 95; Piazza del Carmine 6r; ☒ 5pm-2am Tue-Sun) Just a piazza away from Santo Spirito, this place attracts a very stylish crowd, especially on weekends. At other times, it is usually a quiet spot to enjoy a cocktail.

Zoe (Map pp462-3; ☎ 055 24 31 11; Via dei Renai 13r; ⏰ 8.30pm-1am Mon-Sat, 6.30pm-1am Sun) With its innards glowing red and bedecked with art exhibitions which change monthly, this bar heaves as its squadrons of punters, mostly young locals, spill out onto the street.

Caffè La Torre (Map pp460-1; ☎ 055 68 06 43; Lungarno Benvenuto Cellini 65r) This place has reasonably priced drinks. You can hang out into the wee hours, listening to music ranging from jazz to Latin rhythms.

ENTERTAINMENT

Several publications list the city's major festivals, as well as theatrical and musical events.

Turismonotizie is a bimonthly published by the tourist office; nominally it's €0.50 but it's often available free. *Informacittà* is a monthly freebie. Check the website, www.informacittafirenze.it (in Italian), for the latest updates. *Eventi* is a free monthly flyer listing major events that's compiled by the tourist office, who also produce the annual brochure *Avventimenti*, which covers major events in and around the city.

Florence Concierge Information is a more compendious privately published free bimonthly that runs a good what's-on website, www.florence-concierge.it, with plenty of links.

Firenze Spettacolo, the city's definitive entertainment publication, is available monthly for €1.75 at bookstalls.

Box Office (Map pp462-3; ☎ 055 21 08 04; www.boxol.it; Via Luigi Alamanni 39; ⏰ 10am-7.30pm Tue-Sat, 3.30-7.30pm Mon) is a handy centralised ticket outlet. You can reserve in person, by phone or online.

You can book tickets for the theatre, football matches and other events online through **Ticket One** (www.ticketone.it).

Live Music & Nightclubs

Some of the bigger venues are well outside the town centre. Depending on who's playing, admission costs from nothing to more than €10 – the drinks will cost you on top of that (at least €5 for a beer).

Jazz Club (Map pp462-3; ☎ 055 247 97 00; Via Nuova de'Caccini 3; drinks about €7; ⏰ 9.30pm-1am Sun-Thu, 9.30pm-2am Fri & Sat Oct-May) Florence's tiptop

strictly jazz venue stages some quality acts, both local and from wider afield, in an atmospheric vaulted basement. A 12-month compulsory membership is €5.

Tenax (Map pp460-1; ☎ 055 30 81 60; www.tenax.org; Via Pratese 46; admission to €25; ⏰ Tue-Sun) One of the city's more popular nightclubs, Tenax is well out to the northwest of town. It is also Florence's major venue for Italian and international acts. Catch bus No 29 or 30 from Stazione di Santa Maria Novella to get there. You'll need a taxi or a lift to get home.

Auditorium Flog (Map pp460-1; ☎ 055 49 04 37; Via M Mercati 24b; admission free-€12) Another major venue for bands, this is in the Rifredi area, quite a way north of the city centre. It's not as big as Tenax (in any sense) but there's a reasonable stage and dance area. Catch bus No 8 or 14 from Stazione di Santa Maria Novella.

Central Park (Map pp460-1; ☎ 055 35 35 05; Via Fosso Macinante 2-6; drinks about €8; ⏰ Tue-Sun) This is one of the city's most popular clubs. As you wander from one of the five dance areas to another, you can expect a general range of music from Latin and pop through to house. In the summertime, dance inside or under the stars.

Rio Grande (Map pp460-1; ☎ 055 33 13 71; Viale degli Olmi; admission before/after 1am €16/20; ⏰ Tue-Sat) Rio Grande has three dance spaces offering house, funk and mainstream commercial music and puts on regular theme nights; Thursday is usually salsa and Caribbean.

Cinemas

Surprisingly for such a cosmopolitan city, very few cinemas in Florence show subtitled films *(versione originale)*.

Odeon Cinehall (Map p466; ☎ 055 21 40 68; Piazza Strozzi) The city's main cinema usually screens subtitled films on Monday, Tuesday and Thursday.

Cinema Fulgor (Map pp462-3; ☎ 055 238 18 81; Via Maso Finiguerra 22r) Screens English-language films on Thursday evenings.

Theatre & Classical Music

Teatro Comunale (Map pp462-3; ☎ 800 11 22 11; Corso Italia 16) The venue for concerts, opera and dance, organised by the **Maggio Musicale Fiorentino** (www.maggiofiorentino.com), which also runs an international concert festival at the theatre in May and June.

TUSCANY

Teatro Verdi (Map p466; ☎ 055 21 23 20; www
.teatroverdifirenze.it; Via Ghibellina 99) Hosts drama,
opera, concerts and dance.

Teatro della Pergola (Map p466; ☎ 055 2 26 41;
Via della Pergola 18) The **Amici della Musica** (☎ 055
60 74 40; www.amicimusica.fi.it) organises concerts
here from October to April.

In summer especially, concerts of chamber music are held in churches across the city. The prestigious Orchestra da Camera Fiorentina (Florentine Chamber Orchestra) performance season runs from March to October.

SHOPPING

Milan, say serious shoppers, has the best clothes and Rome has the best shoes. But Florence, all concur, has the greatest variety of goods. It's where some of the greats of fashion such as Gucci and Ferragamo first entered the rag trade.

Designer Goods

The main shopping area is between the cathedral and the Arno, with boutiques concentrated along Via Roma, Via de' Calzaiuoli and Via Por Santa Maria, leading to the goldsmiths that line Ponte Vecchio. Window-shop along Via della Vigna Nuova and Via de' Tornabuoni, where top designers, such as Yves Saint-Laurent, Ferragamo, Versace, Gucci, and Valentino, sell their wares.

At **Stockhouse Il Giglio** (Map pp462-3; ☎ 055 21
75 96; Borgo Ognissanti 86r) and **Stockhouse One Price**
(Map pp462-3; ☎ 055 28 46 74; Borgo Ognissanti 74r),
just along the road, designer labels are sold at tempting discount rates.

Factory Outlets

The tourist office has a list of designer outlet stores, offering discounts of up to 50%, around Florence. Some are single-brand, but most bunch up several designers.

The Mall (Via Europa 8, Leccio Reggello; ☯ 10am-7pm
Mon-Sat, 3-7pm Sun) The biggest outlet by far. To get there, a bus (€2.60, 9am and 12.30pm Monday to Friday and 9am on Saturday) runs from the SITA bus station (opposite), returning at noon and 5pm. For truly dedicated bargain sniffers, CAF Tours (p476) runs a bus (€19) on Tuesday, Wednesday and Saturday that allows a couple of hours at both the Prada outlet and the Mall. If you are driving take the A1 towards Rome, then the Incisa exit and follow signs for Leccio.

Markets

Coming down to earth, in terms of both price and quality, the **open-air market** (9am-
7.30pm Tue-Sun) that sprawls around the Piazza San Lorenzo and up towards the Mercato Centrale offers leather goods, clothing and jewellery at low prices, as well as foodstuffs. Quality varies hugely. You can say the same and more for the goods being hawked at the similarly cheap and cheerful Mercato Nuovo (p467). It's open 9am to 7.30pm Tuesday to Sunday).

Mercato dei Pulci (flea market; Map p462-3; Piazza
dei Ciompi) This market, off Borgo Allegri, is an amazing clutter of junk and bric-a-brac with the odd worthwhile antique waiting to be discovered. There's an especially big one that brings in vendors from all around on the last Sunday of the month.

Specialist Shops

High fashion apart, Florence also has some very swanky specialist shops.

For gold and jewellery, browse the shops on either side of the Ponte Vecchio. Name locations include **Gherardi** (No 8r) and **Vettori**
(No 37r).

Scuola del Cuoio (Map pp462-3; ☎ 055 24 45 33; Via
di San Giuseppe 5r) Lovers of leather will enjoy this training school (you can also enter from the Basilica di Santa Croce), where you can watch leatherworkers fashioning goods and buy their wares. Elsewhere, Via de' Gondi and Borgo de' Greci (both Map p466) are lined with leather shops.

**Oficina Profumo-Farmaceutica di Santa Maria
Novella** (Map pp462-3; ☎ 055 21 62 76; Via della Scala
16) Follow your nose at the risk of suffering olfactory orgasm. This pharmacy, originally established by the Dominicans, has been producing all manner of unguents, balms, soaps and scents ever since 1612. You may sniff at the prices when you see them…

Pineider (Map p466; ☎ 055 28 46 55; Piazza della Signo-
ria) Florence is also famous for its beautifully patterned paper, which is stocked in many stationery and speciality shops throughout the city and at the markets. Pineider is a particularly classy purveyor of paper and has been in business since 1774.

Pusateri (Map p466; ☎ 055 21 41 92; Via de' Calzaiuoli
25r) A wonderful specialist shop that sells stylish gloves.

Twisted (Map pp462-3; ☎ 055 28 20 11; Borgo San
Frediano 21r) Jazz fiends should make a pilgrim-

age to Twisted, which has an outstanding collection of jazz recordings and posters.

GETTING THERE & AWAY
Air
Amerigo Vespucci (Map pp460-1; ☎ 055 37 34 98), 5km northwest of the city centre, caters for domestic and a handful of European flights. See p459 for details on the airport's tourist information office.

Aeroport Galileo Galilei (p506) is much larger and one of the north's main international and domestic airports. Nearer to Pisa, it's an hour away by car or regular train service.

Bus
The **SITA bus station** (Map pp462-3; ☎ 800 37 37 60; www.sita-on-line.it in Italian; Via Santa Caterina da Siena 15) is just to the west of Piazza della Stazione. SITA and Tra-in share a direct, rapid service to/from Siena (€6.50, 1¼ hours, at least hourly), or you can change in Poggibonsi (€4.30, 50 minutes, every 30 minutes) where there are also connecting buses for San Gimignano (€5.90, 1¼ hours, 12 daily). Buses for Siena also run via Poggibonsi and Colle di Val d'Elsa (1¼ hours, hourly), where you can change for Volterra (€6.95, 1½ hours, four daily).

Direct buses serve Arezzo, Castellina in Chianti, Faenza in Emilia-Romagna, Grosseto, Greve, Radda and other smaller cities throughout Tuscany.

Several bus companies, including **CAP** (Map pp462-3; ☎ 055 21 46 37) and **COPIT** (Map pp462-3; ☎ 800 57 05 30) operate from Largo Alinari, at the station end of Via Nazionale. Services to nearby towns include Prato (€2.40, 45 minutes, every 15 minutes) and Pistoia (€3, 50 minutes, hourly).

Lazzi (Map pp462-3; ☎ 055 35 10 61; www.lazzi .it in Italian; Piazza Adua 1), next to the Stazione di Santa Maria Novella, runs buses to/from Prato (€2.40, 45 minutes, hourly), Pistoia (€3, 50 minutes, 10 daily), Lucca (€4.70, 1½ hours, frequent) and Pisa (€6.20, two hours, hourly).

Lazzi forms part of the Eurolines network of international bus services. You can, for instance, catch a bus to Barcelona, Paris, Prague or London.

Car & Motorcycle
Florence is connected by the A1 northwards to Bologna and Milan and southwards to Rome and Naples. The Autostrada del Mare (A11) links the city with Prato, Lucca, Pisa and the coast, and a *superstrada* (no tolls) joins the city with Siena.

The much more picturesque SS67 connects the city with Pisa to the west and Forlì and Ravenna to the east.

Train
The **train information office** (Map pp462-3; ☒ 7am-9pm) is in the southwest corner of the main foyer at Stazione di Santa Maria Novella. There's a left luggage office on platform 16.

Florence is on the Rome–Milan line. There are regular trains to/from Rome (€29.50, 1½ to two hours), Bologna (€13.20, one hour), Milan (€28.90, 2¾ to 3¼ hours) and Venice (€26.60, three hours). To get to Genoa (€16.60) change in Pisa (€5, 1¼ hours, 40 daily) and in Milan for Turin (€34.65).

Frequent regional trains run to Prato (€1.60), Pistoia (€2.60) and Lucca (€4.60).

GETTING AROUND
To/From the Airports
Vola in Bus (€4, 20 minutes, every 30 minutes from 6am to 11pm) is a shuttle bus service between the SITA bus station and Amerigo Vespucci airport. A taxi costs around €20.

Trains (€5.40, 1½ hours) leave Stazione di Santa Maria Novella for Galileo Galilei airport near Pisa about every hour until 5pm. If there's nothing direct, take a train to Pisa, from where there are more frequent connections.

Bicycle
Cycling around Florence is one way to beat the traffic – though the cobbles may rattle your bones.

Florence by Bike (p477) rents out bikes from €7.50/13/32 per five hours/day/three days and scooters from €23/31/81. If you're in Florence for some months, consider investing in a new bike with their sell and repurchase plan.

Alinari (Map pp462-3; ☎ 055 28 05 00; www.alinari rental.com; Via Guelfa 85r; ☒ daily Mar-Oct, Mon-Sat Nov-Feb) rents bikes from €7/12/45 per five hours/day/week. They also hire out scooters (€22/28/140) and motorbikes (per hour/day from €10/55).

The Via dei Benci branch of Internet Train (p459) rents town bikes (per half-/full day €6/12).

Car & Motorcycle

Casual traffic is banned from the heart of town. Cyclopean cameras snap your numberplate as you enter and fines for transgressors are savage. Parking anywhere can induce apoplexy; the only practical advice is to dump your vehicle as soon as you can. A few hotels have their own facilities while many, including quite modest establishments, have a special arrangement with a nearby private garage. It's expensive: a typical fee for 24 hours varies from €15 to more than €50. Valet parking, increasingly on offer, normally costs no extra.

There are car parks around the city centre fringe. The cheapest options for a longer stay are the ones in Parterre and Piazza della Calza, over the river in Oltrarno. Both cost €1.50 per hour or €15 for a 24-hour period.

If you're unlucky enough to have your car towed away, phone ☎ 055 78 38 82.

A bunch of car-rental agencies cluster together in the Borgo Ognissanti area. Among the biggies:

Avis (Map pp462-3; ☎ 199 10 01 33; Borgo Ognissanti 128r)

Europcar (Map pp462-3; ☎ 800 82 80 50; Borgo Ognissanti 53-57r)

Hertz (Map pp462-3; ☎ 199 11 22 11; Via Maso Finiguerra 33r)

A couple of local competitors are **Happy Rent** (Map pp462-3; ☎ 055 239 96 96; Borgo Ognissanti 153r), who also rent out motorbikes and scooters, and **Thrifty Rental** (Map pp462-3; ☎ 055 28 71 61; Borgo Ognissanti 134r).

Public Transport

Buses of **ATAF** (Azienda Trasporti Area Fiorentina; ☎ 800 42 45 00; www.ataf.net) service the city centre, Fiesole and other areas on the city's periphery.

You'll find bus stops for several main routes around the Stazione di Santa Maria Novella. Some of the most useful lines operate from one just outside its southeastern exit. These include:

No 7 For Fiesole.

No 13 For Piazzale Michelangelo.

No 70 For the cathedral and the Uffizi (night bus).

A network of dinky little electric *bussini* (minibuses) operates around the centre of town from Monday to Saturday. You can get a map of all bus routes, published by ATAF, from tourist offices.

Tickets for buses and *bussini* cost €1 and a handy *biglietto multiplo* (four-journey ticket) is €3.90; a day pass is €4.50. If you are hanging around Florence longer, you might want to invest in a weekly ticket (€16) or *mensile* (monthly) at €31.

Taxi

For a taxi, call ☎ 055 42 42 or ☎ 055 43 90.

AROUND FLORENCE
Fiesole

Perched in the hills about 8km northeast of Florence, between the valleys of the Rivers Arno and Mugnone, Fiesole and its scattered villas have attracted the likes of Boccaccio, Marcel Proust, Gertrude Stein and Frank Lloyd Wright, all drawn by the lush olive groves and valleys – not to mention the spectacular view of Florence spread out below.

Fiesole, for long the most important city in northern Etruria, was founded in the 7th century BC by the Etruscans. An easy half-day outing from Florence, it's a fabulous spot for a picnic and short walk. Avoid Sunday when half of Florence invades.

The **tourist office** (☎ 055 59 87 20; Via Portigiani 3; ⏰ 9am-6pm Mon-Sat, 10am-1pm & 2-6pm Sun Apr-Oct, 9am-5pm Mon-Sat, 10am-4pm Sun Nov-Mar) is just off Piazza Mino da Fiesole, the heart of the village.

SIGHTS & ACTIVITIES

A combined ticket (€6.70) gives you entry to Fiesole's main sights: Museo Bandini and Zona Archeologica.

Museo Bandini (☎ 055 5 94 77; Via Dupré; ⏰ 10am-7pm daily Apr-Sep, 10am-5pm Wed-Mon Oct-Mar) has an impressive collection of early Tuscan Renaissance works, including Taddeo Gaddi's *Annunciation*.

Opposite the museum, **Zona Archeologica** (⏰ 9.30am-7pm Apr-Sep, 9.30am-5pm Wed-Mon Oct-Mar) features a 1st-century-BC Roman theatre, which is the venue for the Estate Fiesolana, a series of concerts and performances held between June and August. Also in the complex are a small Etruscan temple and Roman baths. Its little archaeological museum, with exhibits from the Bronze Age to the Roman period, is worth a look.

Far in time and style from the Renaissance splendours of the valley below, the **Museo Primo Conti** (☎ 055 59 70 95; Via Dupré 18; admission €3; ⏰ 9am-2pm), about 300m north of the piazza, was the home of the eponymous avant-garde 20th-century artist and houses more than 60 of his paintings.

For a five-star panorama, head 200m up steep Via S Francesco to a small viewpoint. If you're planning a picnic or just want a refreshing walk, pick up the tourist office brochure *Parco di Montefeceri*, which describes four easy walks from 1.5km to 3.5km.

SLEEPING & EATING

Campeggio Panoramico (☎ 055 59 90 69; www.florencecamping.com; Via Peramonda 1; person/site €10.50/15.75; ⊠) Larger and cooler than the camp sites in Florence and, with panoramic views of the city, makes a seductive alternative. It has a bar, restaurant and pool.

Hotel Villa Aurora restaurant (☎ 055 5 93 63; Piazza Mino da Fiesole 39; meals about €45) On the main square, you'll eat very well here, whether in the lavish indoor dining room or on one of the open-air terraces with the superb sweeping panorama of the plain below.

Trattoria Le Cave di Maiano (☎ 055 5 91 33; Via Cave di Maiano 16; meals about €30; ⊠ closed lunch Mon) Alternatively, drop down to this trattoria in Maiano. This favourite with Florentines is a fine spot for traditional meat dishes. There are several intimate, interconnecting dining rooms and, for optimum views of the surrounds, external terraces.

GETTING THERE & AWAY

Take ATAF bus No 7 from Stazione di Santa Maria Novella in Florence. If you're driving,

Fiesole's signed from Florence's Piazza della Libertà.

Medici Villas

The Medicis built several opulent villas in the countryside around Florence as their wealth and prosperity grew during the 15th and 16th centuries. Nowadays, enclosed by the city's suburbs and industrial sprawl, most are easily reached by ATAF bus from Stazione di Santa Maria Novella. A combined ticket (€2) allows you to see two of the finest, Villa Medicea La Petraia and di Castello.

Villa Medicea La Petraia (☎ 055 45 26 91; Via della Petraia 40; ⊠ 8.15am-sunset, closed 2nd & 3rd Mon of month) is about 3.5km north of the city. Commissioned by Cardinal Ferdinando de' Medici in 1576, this former castle was converted by Buontalenti and features a magnificent garden. Take bus No 28.

Villa Medicea di Castello (☎ 055 45 47 91; Via di Castello 47; ⊠ 8.15am-sunset, closed 2nd & 3rd Mon of month), further north, is Lorenzo il Magnifico's summer home. You can only visit the park. Again, take bus No 28.

Access to the **Villa Medicea di Careggi** (☎ 055 427 95 01; Viale Pieraccini 17; admission free; ⊠ 9am-6pm Mon-Fri, 9am-noon Sat), where Lorenzo il Magnifico breathed his last in 1492, is limited as the building is used as administrative offices for the local hospital. ATAF bus No 14C from Stazione di Santa Maria Novella runs past the villa.

Another Medici getaway was the **Villa di Poggio a Caiano** (☎ 055 87 70 12; Piazza Medici; villa/

NO TRUFFLING MATTER

In late 2004, a consortium headed by Zafferano, a Michelin-star Italian restaurant in London, shelled out UK£28,000 (€39,800) at a charity auction for a prized 850g Tuscan white truffle, a mud-clogged, knobbly lump of fungus about the size of a child's brain. 'Earthy, sexy and an aphrodisiac' is how Enzo Cassini, the restaurant manager, described his prize. Earthy, undoubtedly, and perhaps an aphrodisiac to some; it's rich in a chemical that's almost identical to a sex hormone secreted by a male pig.

The head chef, one Andy Needham, reverentially placed this ball of pungent scent, in form not unlike a dinosaur turd, within the restaurant fridge, locked it, pocketed the keys and flew off for four days of holiday. His return left a bitter taste as he discovered within the fridge one sad, seeping and decidedly 'off' truffle. Making the best of a bad bungle, he interred it in his back garden.

But the truffle was still not at peace. This king of its kind merited a more regal burial so it was flown back to its native Tuscany. There, attended by guards in medieval costume and to the throb of a drum, it was solemnly buried in the grounds of the Castello di Cafaggiolo, 25km north of Florence and its final resting place – unless, that is, some feisty sow should come snuffling by...

TUSCANY

grounds €2/free; ⊙ tours hourly 8.30am-6.30pm Jun-Aug, 8.30am-sunset Sep-May, closed 2nd & 3rd Mon of month). About 15km from Florence on the road to Pistoia, this mansion is set in magnificent sprawling gardens. Its interior is sumptuously decorated with frescoes and furnished much as it was when it functioned as a royal residence of the Savoys. Take the COPIT bus (return €4, 30 minutes) which runs between Florence and Pistoia; it stops right outside.

Il Mugello

The area northeast of Florence leading up to the border with Emilia-Romagna is known as the Mugello. In it are some of Tuscany's most traditional villages, interspersed with elegant second homes for fortunate Florentines. The valley through which the River Sieve winds is one of Tuscany's premier wine areas.

In Borgo San Lorenzo, **Comunità Montana del Mugello** (☎ 055 849 53 46; Via Togliatti 45), **Associazione Turismo Ambiente** (☎ 055 845 87 93; Piazza Dante 29) and **Borga Informa** (☎ 055 845 62 30; infoborgo@tin.it; Villa Pedori Giraldi) are all useful sources of information about the area. The last two can arrange accommodation and excursions in the area.

The Medici originated from the Mugello and held extensive property in the area. Several Medici family castles, villas and palaces dot the area but most are closed to the public. Take the SS65 northwards from Florence to get here.

Near Vaglia, about 5km north of Pratolino, the **Parco della Villa Medici-Demidoff** (☎ 055 40 91 55; admission €2.60; ⊙ 10am-8pm Thu-Sun Apr-Sep, 10am-6pm Sun Mar & Oct) is a lovely romantic garden, built around a long-demolished Medici villa. After about 12km turn right for glimpses of **Trebbio**, then **Cafaggiolo**, further along the same road. Originally a fortress, Cafaggiolo was converted into a villa by Michelozzo in 1451. Neither places are open to the public.

The Mugello area makes for some pleasant walking. *Sorgenti Firenze Trekking* (SOFT; Florence Springs Trekking) is a network of signed day or half-day trails crisscrossing the area. *Mugello, Alto Mugello, Val di Sieve*, produced by SELCA, is a decent map for hikers at 1:70,000 (its trail No 8 is an easy 3½-hour round-trip walk, starting from the villa at Cafaggiolo and passing by Trebbio).

NORTHERN & WESTERN TUSCANY

PRATO

pop 174,600

Virtually enclosed within Florence's urban and industrial sprawl and a mere 17km to its northwest, Prato is one of Italy's main textile centres. Tuscany's second-largest town after Florence, it has the country's biggest concentration of Chinese immigrants, many now second- or even third-generation Pratese. Founded by the Ligurians, the city fell to the Etruscans, then the Romans.

As early as the 11th century it was an important centre for wool production. Continuing the tradition, textiles, together with leather working, are to this day Prato's main industries. It's worth dropping in on your way to the more picturesque cities of Pistoia, Lucca and Pisa or as a half-day trip from Florence.

Orientation

Prato's compact historical heart is girdled by near-intact city walls. Its nucleus is Piazza S Maria delle Carceri. The main train station (Prato Stazione Centrale) lies east of the city centre.

Information

Tourist office (☎ 0574 2 41 12; www.prato.turismo .toscana.it; Piazza S Maria delle Carceri 15; ⊙ daily Apr-Sep, 9am-1.30pm & 2.30-6.30pm Mon-Sat Oct-Mar)

Sights

A combined ticket (€5), bought at any of the three sites, gives entry to the Museo di Pittura Murale, Museo dell'Opera del Duomo and Castello dell'Imperatore.

CATHEDRAL

The 12th-century **Cattedrale Santo Stefano** (Piazza del Duomo; ⊙ 7.30am-noon & 3.30-7pm) has a typically Pisan-Romanesque façade. Unadorned but for a terracotta lunette by Andrea della Robbia, it's banded in white-and-green Tuscan marble, a pattern you'll also come across in Siena, Pistoia and Lucca.

What's unique about this cathedral is its protruding exterior, **Pulpito della Sacra Cintola**, which juts out over the piazza to the right of the main, western entrance. The original

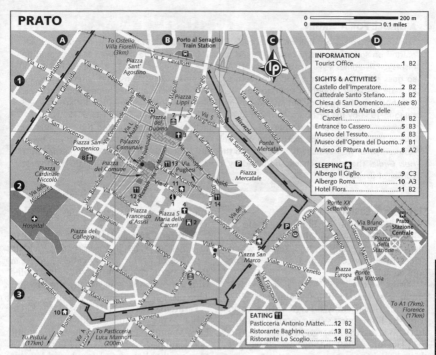

eroded panels of the pulpit, designed by Donatello and Michelozzo in the 1430s, are in the **Museo dell'Opera del Duomo** (☎ 0574 2 93 39; Piazza del Duomo 49; admission €3; ☑ 9.30am-12.30pm & 3-6.30pm Mon & Wed-Sat, 9.30am-12.30pm Sun).

MUSEO DEL TESSUTO

Prato's **textile museum** (☎ 0574 61 15 03; Via Santa Chiara 24; adult/child €4/2; ☑ 10am-6pm Mon & Wed-Fri, 10am-2pm Sat, 4-7pm Sun) devotes itself to textiles throughout the ages. It highlights the achievements of the local cloth industry but you will also find examples of textiles (some from as early as the 3rd century) from around Italy and Europe, and as far afield as India, China and the Americas.

MUSEO DI PITTURA MURALE

This small but impressive **museum** (☎ 0574 44 05 01; Piazza San Domenico; admission €5; ☑ 9am-1pm Mon & Wed-Sat, 3-6pm Fri & Sat), within the Chiesa di San Domenico, houses a collection of largely Tuscan paintings. Among the artists are Filippo Lippi, Paolo Uccello and Bernardo Daddi, with his touchingly naive polyptych of the miracle of the Virgin's girdle (see the

boxed text, p492). Enjoy, too, the 14th- to 17th-century frescoes and graffiti.

CHIESA DI SANTA MARIA DELLE CARCERI & AROUND

Built by Giuliano da Sangallo towards the end of the 15th century, the high, graceful interior of this **church** (Piazza Santa Maria delle Carceri; ☑ 7am-noon & 4-7pm) was a prototype for many a Renaissance church in Tuscany. The glazed terracotta frieze and, above it, medallions of the Evangelists are by Andrea della Robbia and his team.

On the same piazza, **Castello dell'Imperatore** (☎ 0574 3 82 07; Piazza Santa Maria delle Carceri; admission €2; ☑ 9am-1pm Apr-Sep), Prato's castle, was built in the 13th century by the Holy Roman Emperor Frederick II. It's an interesting enough example of military architecture but, with its bare interior, only really worth dropping into if you're carrying a combined ticket.

Just down the road is the **Cassero** (Viale Piave; admission free; ☑ 10am-1pm & 4-7pm Wed-Mon), a long, much-restored medieval covered passageway that originally allowed access from the castle to the city walls.

A GIRDLE FOR A VIRGIN

You don't often see a pulpit on the *outside* of a cathedral. But Prato's is rather special. It was grafted on so that the *sacra cintola* (sacred girdle), believed to be the Virgin Mary's, could be displayed five times a year (Easter, 1 May, 15 August, 8 September and 25 December). The Virgin, so goes the story, gave the girdle (or belt) to St Thomas. Generations later, after the Second Crusade, a soldier brought it to Prato from Jerusalem. In medieval times huge importance was attached to such holy relics. But just how many girdles did Mary have? Another, declared the real thing in 1953 by the Orthodox Patriarch of Antioch, is stored in the Syrian city of Homs.

Among the magnificent frescoes inside the church, look for those behind the high altar by Filippo Lippi, depicting the martyrdom of St John the Baptist and St Stephen (which was being restored when we last visited). Seek out too those by Agnolo Gaddi depicting the *Legend of the Holy Girdle*. They're in a chapel, bordered by intricate wrought-iron screens, at the northwest corner of the nave.

Sleeping & Eating

Within easy reach of Florence, Prato is worth considering as an alternative base to the big city, especially in high season when prices in Florence rise and places can be booked solid.

Albergo Il Giglio (☎ 0574 3 70 49; albergoilgiglio@ tin.it; Piazza San Marco 14; s/d €41/60, with bathroom €58/72; 🛇) This is a friendly *albergo* with a cosy, could-be-home guest sitting room. The family (who also own Albergo Roma) have run the place since 1969 so they have clearly got the mix right.

Albergo Roma (☎ 0574 3 17 77; albergoilgiglio@tin .it; Via G Carradori 1; s/d €55/60; 🛇) A one-star joint, Albergo Roma has 12 modest rooms but they are spruce, clean and excellent value for your euro. Ask for one at the back as the hotel overlooks a busy road.

Hotel Flora (☎ 0574 3 35 21; www.hotelflora.info; Via B Cairoli 31; s/d with breakfast €95/150; 🅿 🛇 🖵) An attractive three-star midrange option in the heart of town. All 31 bedrooms have been recently renovated and the small, enclosed roof terrace offers good views over town. Parking is €10.

Ostello Villa Fiorelli (☎ 0574 69 76 11; cspsrl@ interfree.it; Parco di Galceti, Via di Galceti 64; dm/d €14.50/35) Prato's HI-affiliated youth hostel, served by bus No 13, is some 3km north of Piazza del Duomo.

Ristorante Lo Scoglio (☎ 0574 2 27 60; Via Verdi 42; pizzas from €6, meals about €20; 🕑 Tue-Sun) Ristorante Lo Scoglio has a wide-ranging menu that offers everything from pizza to fresh fish.

Ristorante Baghino (☎ 0574 2 79 20; Via dell'Accademia 9; meals €18-23; 🕑 Mon-Sat) This restaurant is in much the same vein as Lo Scoglio but offers more stylish surroundings and carries a decent wine list.

Pasticceria Antonio Mattei (☎ 0574 2 57 56; Via Ricasoli 20; 🕑 Tue-Sat & mornings Sun) Pick up a packet of *cantucci*, also called *biscotti di Prato*, a crunchy, rusk-like biscuit studded with almonds that you usually dip in wine. This place makes them on the spot.

Pasticceria Luca Mannori (☎ 0574 2 16 28; Via Lazzarini 2; 🕑 Wed-Mon) Just outside the city walls, Luca Mannori serves altogether more subtle cakes and pastries. On two occasions, Signor Mannori has been proclaimed world champion in international confectionery competitions – his *torta sette veli* (tart of the seven veils) is a true *pièce de résistance*.

Getting There & Around

CAP and Lazzi buses operate regular services to/from Florence (€2.40, 45 minutes, every 15 minutes) departing from Prato Stazione Centrale train station.

By car, take the A1 Calenzano exit or the A11 Prato turn-off.

Prato is on the Florence–Bologna and Florence–Lucca train lines. Sample fares and destinations include to Florence (€1.50, 25 minutes, every 10 minutes), Bologna (€7.45, one hour, 20 daily), Lucca (€4.10, one hour, 20 daily) and Pistoia (€1.50, 20 minutes, every 30 minutes).

PISTOIA

pop 84,200

Pistoia is a pleasant city that sits snugly at the foot of the Apennines. Only 45 minutes northwest of Florence by train, it deserves more attention than it normally gets. Although Pistoia has grown well beyond its

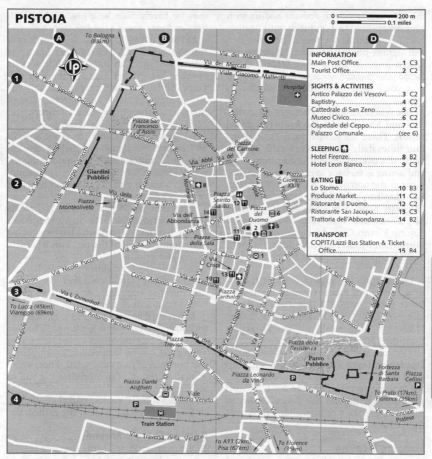

PISTOIA

0   200 m
0   0.1 miles

INFORMATION
Main Post Office.....................1 C3
Tourist Office...........................2 C2

SIGHTS & ACTIVITIES
Antico Palazzo dei Vescovi.....3 C2
Baptistry................................4 C2
Cattedrale di San Zeno...........5 C2
Museo Civico..........................6 C2
Ospedale del Ceppo................7 C2
Palazzo Comunale................(see 6)

SLEEPING
Hotel Firenze..........................8 B2
Hotel Leon Bianco..................9 C3

EATING
Lo Storno..............................10 B3
Produce Market.....................11 C2
Ristorante Il Duomo...............12 C2
Ristorante San Jacopo............13 C3
Trattoria dell'Abbondanza......14 B2

TRANSPORT
COPIT/Lazzi Bus Station & Ticket
   Office.................................15 B4

---

medieval ramparts – and is now a world centre for the manufacture of trains – its historic centre is well preserved. Here, in the 16th century, the city's metalworkers created the pistol, which was named after the city.

On Wednesday and Saturday mornings, Piazza del Duomo and the streets surrounding it become a veritable sea of blue awnings and jostling shoppers as Pistoia hosts a lively market.

Orientation

From the train station, head north along Via XX Settembre, eventually turning right into Via Cavour. Via Roma, branching off the northern side of Via Cavour, takes you to the main square, Piazza del Duomo.

Information

Main post office (Via Roma 5)
Tourist office (☎ 0573 2 16 22; www.pistoia.turismo .toscana.it in Italian; Piazza del Duomo 4; ⏲ 9am-1pm & 3-6pm Mon-Sat) Occupies part of the Antico Palazzo dei Vescovi.

Sights

Most of Pistoia's visual wealth is concentrated in Piazza del Duomo. The Pisan-Romanesque façade of the **Cattedrale di San Zeno** (Piazza del Duomo; ⏲ 8.30am-12.30pm & 3.30-7pm) boasts a lunette of the Madonna and Child by Andrea della Robbia, who also made the glazed tiles that line the barrel vault of the main porch. Inside is the remarkable silver **altarpiece of San Giacomo**. It was begun in the 13th century, with artisans adding to it over the ensuing two centuries until Brunelleschi contributed the final touch, the two half-figures on the left side. However, it's locked away in the gloomy **Cappella di San Jacopo** (adult/child €2/0.50) off the north aisle. To visit, you'll need to track down some church official.

The venerable building between the cathedral and Via Roma is the **Antico Palazzo dei Vescovi**. There are guided tours (in Italian) four times daily through the wealth of artefacts, discovered during restoration work and dating as far back as Etruscan times. Reserve at the tourist office. Across Via Roma is the **baptistry** (admission free; 🕙 8am-6pm Tue-Sun). Elegantly banded in white-and-green marble, it was started in 1337 to a design by Andrea Pisano. Closed for extensive renovations when we last passed through, it should again be open to the public by the time you read this.

Dominating the eastern flank of the piazza, the Gothic **Palazzo Comunale** houses the **Museo Civico** (☎ 0573 37 12 96; Piazza del Duomo; adult/child €3.10/1.55; 🕙 10am-7pm Tue-Sat, 9.30am-12.30pm Sun), with works by Tuscan artists from the 13th to 20th centuries.

The splendidly rich portico of the nearby **Ospedale del Ceppo** (Piazza Giovanni XXIII) will stop even the monument-weary in their tracks; the unique terracotta frieze by Giovanni della Robbia depicts the *Seven Works of Mercy*, while the five medallions represent the *Virtues*.

Sleeping & Eating

If you're driving, the hotels we recommend can provide a pass entitling you to free street parking, from 9pm to 9am, or you can arrange private garage parking (around €5).

Hotel Leon Bianco (☎ 0573 2 66 75; www.hotelleonbianco.it; Via Panciatichi 2; s/d €60/100; P ✗ ▯) A friendly, family-owned hotel, by far the most venerable in town, which has operated as an inn since the 15th century. Rooms are spacious and comfortable.

Hotel Firenze (☎ 0573 2 31 41; www.hotel-firenze.it; Via Curtatone e Montanara 42; s/d with breakfast €60/80; P ✗ ▯) The Hotel Firenze has large, simple rooms with fridges. Although a little colourless and glum, the facilities are just fine.

If you're looking for a place to eat or to rest your feet over a drink, Via del Lestrone

may be barely 50m long but, packed with bars and eateries, it's the one to prowl.

Lo Storno (☎ 0573 2 61 93; Via del Lastrone 8; meals from €20; 🕙 Wed-Sat & lunch Tue) This place has a long pedigree: an *osteria* of one sort or another has existed here for the past 600 years. Today, the chef prepares a continually changing array of dishes in full view of the guests, the atmosphere is cheery and bustling and portions are large.

Trattoria dell'Abbondanza (☎ 0573 36 80 37; Via dell'Abbondanza; mains from €7-9; 🕙 Fri-Tue & dinner Thu) This little trattoria, down a quiet passageway off Piazza Spirito Santo, has a frequently changing menu and offers a good selection of soups and pasta.

Ristorante San Jacopo (☎ 0573 2 77 86; Via Crispi 15; meals about €20; 🕙 Tue-Sat & lunch Sun) San Jacopo has new owners, who have respected and retained most of the previous à la carte menu and continue to serve great Tuscan dishes. House specialities include *baccalà alla Livornese* (salted cod) and *maccheroni alla Pistoiese* (macaroni as you have never tasted it, in a duck sauce).

Ristorante Il Duomo (☎ 0573 3 19 48; Via Bracciolini 5; mains about €5; 🕙 noon-3pm Mon-Sat) This is a cheap, self-service, buffet-style place where your plate can be heaped high with generous portions of pasta and salad. There's also a small selection of main dishes – if you've still a spare cranny.

There's a small **produce market** (🕙 Mon-Sat) in Piazza della Sala, west of the cathedral.

Getting There & Around

Buses connect Pistoia with Florence (€3, 50 minutes, hourly) and local towns in Tuscany. The main ticket office and departure point for COPIT and Lazzi buses is opposite the train station.

The city is on the A11 and the SS64/SS66, which head northeast for Bologna and northwest for Parma, respectively. Bus Nos 10 and 12 both connect the train station with the cathedral.

Trains link Pistoia with Florence (€2.80, 45 minutes, every 30 minutes), Prato (€1.50, 20 minutes, every 30 minutes), Lucca (€3.20, 45 minutes, more than 20 per day), Pisa (€4.10, 1¼ hours, five direct daily) and Viareggio (€4.10, one hour, hourly).

If you leave your vehicle in the car park by Piazza Cellini, there's a shuttle bus (return €1) into the centre of town.

LUCCA

pop 81,900

Hidden behind imposing Renaissance walls, Lucca, an essential stopover on any Tuscan tour, also makes a charming base for exploring the Apuane Alps and the Garfagnana.

Founded by the Etruscans, Lucca became a Roman colony in 180 BC and a free *comune* (self-governing city) during the 12th century, when it enjoyed a period of prosperity based on the silk trade. In 1314 it briefly fell under the control of Pisa but under the leadership of local adventurer Castruccio Castracani degli Antelminelli, the city regained its freedom and remained an independent republic for almost 500 years.

Napoleon ended all this in 1805, when he created the principality of Lucca and placed one of the seemingly countless members of his family in need of an Italian fiefdom (this time his sister Elisa) in control. Twelve years later the city became a Bourbon duchy, before being incorporated into the Kingdom of Italy.

Lucca remains a strong agricultural centre. The long periods of peace it has enjoyed explain the almost perfect preservation of the city walls, which were rarely put to the test.

Orientation

From the train station on Piazza Ricasoli, just outside the city walls, walk west to Piazza Risorgimento then through Porta San Pietro. Head north along Via Vittorio Veneto, over immense Piazza Napoleone and on to Piazza San Michele, the centre of town.

Information

Two useful portals are www.luccatourist.it and www.in-lucca.it.

Armonie Lucchesi (Via del Gocifisso 4; per 15min incl drink €3; 🕑 9.30am-1pm & 3.30-8pm) Internet access.

Copisteria Paolini (Via Catalani 28; per hr €4.80; 🕑 8am-9pm Mon-Fri, 8am-noon Sat) Internet access.

Main post office (Via Vallisneri 2)

Niagara (Via Michele Rosi 26; 🕑 8am-10pm) Laundry services.

Tourist office Piazza Napoleone (☎ 0583 91 99 41; 🕑 10am-7pm Apr-Oct, 10am-1pm Nov-Mar); Piazza Santa Maria 35 (☎ 0583 91 99 31; 🕑 9am-8pm Apr-Oct, 9am-1pm & 3-6pm Nov-Mar); Piazzale Verdi (☎ 0583 58 31 50; 🕑 9am-7pm Easter-Oct, 9am-5.30pm Nov-Easter) The main tourist office rents bicycles and stocks an excellent city audioguide in English (one/two persons €9/14).

Sights

BIRD'S-EYE LUCCA

Huff and puff your way up the 207 steps of the **Torre delle Ore** (Via Fillungo; admission €3.50; 🕑 9am-7pm Mar-Sep, to 5pm Oct-Feb), which is a 13th century clock tower whose possession was hotly contested by rival families in medieval days. Or else attack the 230 equally steep stairs of the tower of the **Palazzo Guinigi** (Via Sant'Andrea; adult/child €3.50/2.50; 🕑 9am-midnight May-Sep, to 7.30pm Mar-Apr, to 5pm Oct-Feb), where a tiny coppice of self-seeded Holm oak trees offers welcome shade.

Whichever one you choose, the sweeping overview of the city, once you make the top, is stunning.

CATHEDRAL

Lucca's mainly Romanesque **cathedral** (Piazza San Martino; admission free; 🕑 9.30am-6.45pm Apr-Sep, 9.30am-4.45pm Oct-Mar), dedicated to San Martino, dates from the 11th century. The exquisite façade was constructed in the prevailing Lucchese-Pisan style. Each of the multitude of columns in its upper section is different. The reliefs over the left doorway of the portico are believed to be by Nicola Pisano.

The interior was rebuilt in the 14th and 15th centuries with a Gothic flourish. Matteo Civitali designed the pulpit and, in the northern aisle, the 15th-century *tempietto* (small temple) contains the **Volto Santo**. Legend has it that this simply fashioned image

---

SO WHO'S THE LADY IN THE TOMB?

Ilaria del Carretto, the young second wife of the 15th-century lord of Lucca, Paolo Guinigi, died during childbirth when only 24. Distraught, her husband commissioned Jacopo della Quercia, perhaps the most accomplished sculptor of his day, to carve her tomb.

So, for centuries, has gone the story…

But recent research has thrown a dark shadow over this image of the grieving, loving husband. It's been suggested that the reclining marble form in fact represents Caterina Antelminelli, one of four local maidens engaged to Paolo – all of whom died before their wedding day.

Now *there's* a story that could have given the tabloids of the day a feeding frenzy.

TUSCANY

LUCCA

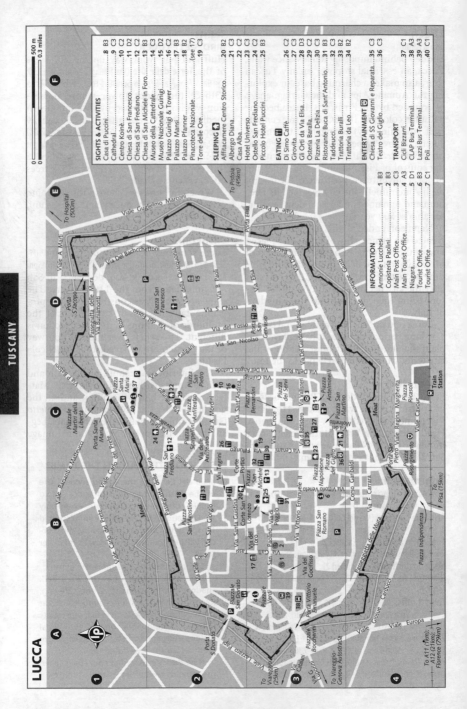

SIGHTS & ACTIVITIES
Casa di Puccini	8	B3
Cathedral	9	C3
Centro Koine	10	C2
Chiesa di San Francesco	11	D2
Chiesa di San Frediano	12	C2
Chiesa di San Michele in Foro	13	B3
Museo della Cattedrale	14	C3
Museo Nazionale Guinigi	15	D2
Palazzo Guinigi & Tower	16	D2
Palazzo Mansi	17	B3
Palazzo Pfanner	18	B2
Pinacoteca Nazionale	(see 17)	
Torre delle Ore	19	C3

SLEEPING
Affittacamere Centro Storico	20	B2
Albergo Diana	21	C3
Casa Alba	22	C3
Hotel Universo	23	C3
Ostello San Frediano	24	C2
Piccolo Hotel Puccini	25	B3

EATING
Di Simo Caffè	26	C2
Girovita	27	C3
Gli Orti da Via Elisa	28	D3
Osteria Baralla	29	C3
Pizzeria La Delizia	30	B3
Ristorante Buca di Sant'Antonio	31	B3
Taddeucci	32	C3
Trattoria Buralli	33	B2
Trattoria da Leo	34	B2

ENTERTAINMENT
Chiesa di SS Giovanni e Reparata	35	C3
Teatro del Giglio	36	C3

TRANSPORT
Cicli Bizzarri	37	C1
CLAP Bus Terminal	38	A3
Lazzi Bus Terminal	39	B3
Poli	40	C1

INFORMATION
Armonie Lucchesi	1	B3
Copisteria Paolini	2	B3
Main Post Office	3	C2
Main Tourist Office	4	A3
Niagara	5	D1
Tourist Office	6	B3
Tourist Office	7	C1

TUSCANY

of Christ on a wooden crucifix, dated to the 11th century, was carved by Nicodemus, who witnessed the crucifixion. A major object of pilgrimage, every 13 September the crucifix is carried in procession through the streets. In the **sacristy** (admission €2, incl Museo della Cattedrale €6), the cool marble tomb of Ilaria del Carretto is a masterpiece of funerary sculpture.

The cathedral's many artworks include a magnificent *Last Supper* by Tintoretto, over the third altar of the south aisle.

The adjacent **Museo della Cattedrale** (☎ 0583 49 05 30; Via Arcivescovato; adult/child €4/2.50; ☷ 10am-6pm Easter-Oct, to 2pm Mon-Fri, to 5pm Sat & Sun Nov-Easter) has a well-displayed collection of religious art.

CHIESA DI SAN MICHELE IN FORO

Equally dazzling is this Romanesque **church** (Piazza San Michele; ☷ 9am-noon & 3-6pm, to 5pm Oct-Mar), built on the site of its 8th-century precursor over a period of nearly 300 years, beginning in the 11th century. The exquisite wedding-cake façade is topped by a figure of the Archangel Michael slaying a dragon. Look for Andrea della Robbia's *Madonna and Child* in the first chapel of the south aisle.

Languidly lording it over Piazza Cittadella, Puccini the maestro still sits, cast in bronze, with a cigarette dangling from his slender fingers, oblivious and in defiance of recent legislation. Just to the north of this square is the **Casa di Puccini** (☎ 0583 58 40 28; Corte San Lorenzo 9), the composer's modest house, preserved in much the same way as he left it, his glasses and pen poised on the desk beside the piano where he wrote *Madame Butterfly* and much of his later work. It was closed for renovations when we last tried to pay our respects.

VIA FILLUNGO

Lucca's busiest street, Via Fillungo, threads its way through the medieval heart of the old city. It's a fascinating mix of smart boutiques, restaurants and buildings of great charm and antiquity – often occupying the same space; just look up, above the street level bustle.

The **Piazza Anfiteatro** is a huge oval just east of Via Fillungo. The houses, raised upon the foundations of the one-time Roman amphitheatre, retain the shape of this distant original. Nowadays, pavement cafés and restaurants jostle to accommodate one another around the edges of the square – or, rather, ellipse.

A short walk further east is **Piazza San Francesco** and the attractive 13th-century **church** of the same name. Along Via della Quarquonia is the Villa Guinigi, home to the **Museo Nazionale Guinigi** (☎ 0583 49 60 33; adult/child €4/free; ☷ 8.30am-7.30pm Tue-Sat, to 1.30pm Sun) and the city's art museum, where there is a collection of paintings, sculptures and archaeological finds.

West of Via Fillungo, the façade of the **Chiesa di San Frediano** (Piazza San Frediano; ☷ 9am-noon & 3-6pm, to 5pm Oct-Mar) has a unique (and much-restored) 13th-century mosaic in a markedly Byzantine style. That's not the only anomalous feature – pause to check your bearings. Unlike just about every other church this side of Jerusalem, the apse faces *west*, away from the Holy City.

The main feature of the beautiful basilica's interior is **Fontana Lustrale**, a 12th-century baptismal font decorated with sculpted reliefs, just to the right as you enter. Behind it is an *Annunciation* by Andrea della Robbia. Note, too, the fine capitals, many of which were recycled from the Roman amphitheatre nearby.

To retreat temporarily from an excess of churches and Renaissance splendour, dip into the nearby 17th-century **Palazzo Pfanner** (☎ 340 923 30 85; Via degli Asili 33; adult/child €2.50/1.50, incl garden €4/3; ☷ 10am-6pm Mar–mid-Nov). A staircase leads to the sumptuously furnished living area. In the ornate 18th-century garden, the only one of substance within the city walls, you pass between a guard of honour of statues representing Greek and Roman deities. Incidentally, the eponymous Felix Pfanner, may God rest his soul, was an Austrian émigré who first brought beer to Italy – and brewed it in the palazzo's cellars.

The 17th century **Palazzo Mansi** (Via Galli Tassi 43), a wonderful piece of rococo excess (that elaborate, gilded bridal suite must have inspired *such* high jinks in its time), houses the smallish **Pinacoteca Nazionale** (☎ 0583 5 55 70; admission €4; ☷ 8.30am-7.30pm Tue-Sat, 8.30am-1.30pm Sun) with paintings of the same period and some lively frescoes.

CITY WALLS

Take time out from monument bashing to walk, jog or cycle all 3km of the rim of the city's walls, raised in the 16th and 17th centuries. You won't be alone and you'll get some great Peeping Tom glimpses into the lives of those below.

Courses

The **Centro Koinè** (☎ 0583 49 30 40; www.koinecenter .com; Via A Mordini 60) offers Italian language and cultural courses.

Festivals & Events

The city that gave birth to both Puccini and Boccherini has admirably catholic musical tastes. For more than 50 years the nearby village of Torre del Lago has been holding its annual **Puccini Festival**, spanning July and August. While Lucca's annual **Summer Festival**, held in July, pulls in top performers such as Oasis, David Bowie, Jamiroquai, Rod Stewart and Elton John.

Sleeping

Ostello San Frediano (☎ 0583 46 99 57; info@ostel lolucca.it; Via della Cavallerizza 12; dm/d €16.50/43; 🖳) This excellent HI-affiliated hostel with its 148 beds in voluminous rooms occupies a vast former schoolhouse. It has a bar, albeit intermittently staffed, and a reasonable restaurant.

Affittacamere Centro Storico (☎ 0583 49 07 48; www.affittacamerecentrostorico.com; Corte Portici 16; d without/with bathroom €80/120) This is a B&B with aspirations. Friendliness itself, it's a great option smack in the heart of town. There's no curfew (you get your own front-door key) and all rooms are equipped with a small fridge and safe. Low season rates are significantly cheaper.

Albergo Diana (☎ 0583 49 22 02; www.albergodiana .com; Via del Molinetto 11; d with/without bathroom €67/47; 🅿 🖳) Albergo Diana is a family-run, two-star hotel with nine slightly chintzy but satisfying rooms (parking is an extra €4). For more comfort, consider the nearby annexe (s/d including air-con €75/95), previously the family home. The two ground-floor rooms are equipped for handicapped guests.

Casa Alba (☎ 0583 49 53 61; www.casa-alba.com; 2nd fl, Via Fillungo 142; s/d €45/55, with bathroom €70/80; 😵) Casa Alba is where Antipodean travellers will feel at home; the delightful owner has spent many years in Australia. Her five rooms are small but sunny, washed in pastel colours with arty prints and fridges. Reservations are essential from Easter to October,

and winter prices are substantially lower. Breakfast is included.

Piccolo Hotel Puccini (☎ 0583 5 54 21; www.hotel puccini.com; Via di Poggio 9; s/d €60/85; 🅿) This hotel is a stylish, friendly three-star with a glossy marble lobby. Its 14 modern rooms have all the trimmings and the location, within spitting distance of Piazza San Michele, is unbeatable. Parking costs €18.

Hotel Universo (☎ 0583 49 36 78; www.universo lucca.com; Piazza del Giglio 1; s/d with breakfast €100/140) Hotel Universo. built in 1857, sits on an attractive tree-lined square and offers old-fashioned charm with modern service. The rooms offer views of either the equally venerable Teatro del Giglio or the cathedral.

Eating

Gli Orti da Via Elisa (☎ 0583 49 12 41; Via Elisa 17; mains €7-9; 🕑 dinner Thu-Tue) This is a crowded, popular trattoria and pizzeria where you'll find locals and transient visitors tucking into pizzas and generous mains, or working their way through the regularly changing set menu (€24).

Ristorante Buca di Sant'Antonio (☎ 0583 5 58 81; Via della Cervia 3; mains about €15; 🕑 Tue-Sat & lunch Sun) Founded in 1782, this restaurant is all white-washed rooms, old beams, tiled floors and copper pots. The dishes seem deliciously innovative but are touted as traditional Luccan cuisine. Savour, for example, the ricotta and leek pie with chickpea sauce.

Trattoria Buralli (☎ 0583 95 06 11; Piazza Sant' Agostino 9; 🕑 Thu-Tue) This trattoria is an intimate local favourite that makes few concessions to outsiders. You can play it easy and go for the à la carte menu with English translation. It's better, however, to throw a wild card and pluck one of the five different menus (around €16). Friday night is veggie night, when they offer a four-course meat-free menu for €18.50.

Trattoria da Leo (☎ 0583 49 22 36; Via Tegrimi 1; mains €8-10; 🕑 Mon-Sat) A wonderful, bustling, noisy trattoria, Da Leo attracts a mixed clientele of students, workers and ladies taking a break from shopping. Save a small corner for the *torta di fichi e noci* (fig and walnut tart). In summer the shaded outside seating comes into its own.

Di Simo Caffè (☎ 0583 49 62 34; Via Fillungo 58) With its grand bar and *gelateria*, Di Simo Caffè was once patronised by Puccini and his coterie (the maestro would tickle the ivories of the piano at the entrance to the dining area). In season, it spoons out some mean ice creams. Year-round, go for the leafy salads and mains (€8), cakes and world-beating coffees. And hey, you'll never come across a more subtly camouflaged toilet door, indistinguishable from the wooden panelling that surrounds it. Take your leave early…

Osteria Baralla (☎ 0583 44 02 40; Via dell Anfiteatro 5-9; mains €9.50-13; ❥ Mon-Sat) This *osteria* has pleasing pink-brick vaulting and sotto voce piped jazz. Rich in Tuscan specialities, it carries a good range of wines by the glass. Go meat, go red in tooth and claw; the roast lamb, for example, is cooked to perfection with all its juices intact. Service is swift and needs to be; the place is a firm Lucchese favourite.

Girovita (☎ 0583 46 94 12; Piazza Antelminelli 2; salads & pastas €6.50; ❥ Tue-Sun) Girovita is a pleasant, predominantly veggie place from whose piazza seating you get a picture-postcard view of the cathedral's façade.

Pizzeria La Delizia (☎ 0583 44 05 22; Via Fillungo 5) For pizza by the slice, join lots of others for a quick fill-up at La Delizia.

Taddeucci (Piazza San Michele 34; ❥ Fri-Wed) You shouldn't leave town without sampling a slice of *buccellato*, a cross between a biscuit and a bun, typical of Lucca. You won't find it fresher than at Taddeucci, a fine *pasticceria* where it's made on the premises.

Entertainment

The local English-language monthly *Grapevine* (€2), carried by tourist offices, has a useful what's on section.

Teatro del Giglio (Piazza del Giglio) Lucca's prime venue for opera and theatre.

Chiesa di SS Giovanni e Reparata (Piazza San Martino) Musical recitals also take place here. Pick up *Lucca Musica*, a free monthly, from the tourist office for details of what's in store.

Getting There & Away

CLAP buses (☎ 0583 58 78 97) serve the region, including destinations in the Garfagnana such as Castelnuovo (€3.30, 1½ hours, eight daily).

Lazzi (☎ 0583 58 48 76) runs hourly buses to Florence (€4.70, 1½ hours) and Pisa (€2.20, 45 minutes). It has four daily services to La Spezia (€5.20, three hours) and six services to Marina di Carrara (€3.50, two hours) via

Marina di Massa. Both companies operate from Piazzale Verdi.

The A11 runs westwards to Pisa and Viareggio and eastwards to Florence. The SS12, then the SS445 from Forno, links the city with the Garfagnana.

Lucca is on the Florence–Pisa–Viareggio train line and there are also services into the Garfagnana. There are frequent trains to/from Pisa (€2.10, 25 minutes) and Florence (€4.60, 1½ hours) via Pistoia (€3.20, 45 minutes) and Prato (€4.10, one hour).

Getting Around

Most cars are banned within the city walls and you can expect a few hard stares if you attempt to drive in. This said, most hotels will give you a permit entitling you to park in spaces for residents (indicated by yellow lines).

CLAP electric buses connect the station, Corso Garibaldi and Piazzale Verdi but it's just as easy and more pleasurable to walk.

Lucca is a very bike-friendly town. You can hire cycles from **Poli** (☎ 0583 49 37 87; Piazza Santa Maria 42), nearby **Cicli Bizzarri** (☎ 0583 49 60 31; Piazza Santa Maria 32) and the tourist office in Piazzale Verdi. Rates are about €2.25 per hour, €11 per day.

For a taxi, call ☎ 0583 95 52 00.

AROUND LUCCA

The **Parco de Pinocchio** (☎ 0572 42 93 42; adult/child €9/7; ❥ 8.30am-sunset), a tribute to Italy's naughtiest and best-selling fictional character, is in a pine forest just outside the village of **Collodi**, 15km east of Lucca. With a series of mosaics recounting the main episodes in the puppet's life, as well as statues and tableaux, it's as much a treat for grown-ups as it is for kids.

LA GARFAGNANA

The heart of the Garfagnana is the valley formed by the River Serchio and its tributaries. It's an excellent area for walking, horse riding and a host of other outdoor pursuits. Historically a region of net migration as villagers left to lead less harsh lives on the plains, it's now revitalised thanks to tourism and to the paper mills that whir outside most valley towns.

The main bases for outdoor activities are the charming little spa town of **Bagni di Lucca** – where the **Circolo dei Forestieri** (☎ 0583

8 60 38; Piazza Jean Varraud 10; tourist menus €10, mains €6; ✷ closed lunch Mon & Tue Easter-Oct) makes a splendid, excellent-value lunch stop – and **Castelnuovo di Garfagnana**.

In Castelnuovo, the **Centro Visite Parco Alpi Apuane** (☎ 0583 64 42 42; www.parks.it/parco.alpi.apu ane; Piazza delle Erbe 1; ✷ 9am-1pm & 3-7pm Jun-Sep, to 5.30pm Oct-May) is well documented with maps and brochures. Its pamphlet *Apuan Alps: A World to Get to Know* gives details of *rifugi* (mountain huts) and walks.

Also in Castelnuovo, **Consorzio Garfagnana Turistica** (☎ 0583 64 44 73; www.garfagnanaturistica .info; Via della Centrale 2; ✷ 9am-1pm & 2.30-7pm Mon-Sat) can reserve accommodation (opening hours sometimes vary). Its free booklet *Garfagnana Trekking* describes a 10-day route while *Garfagnana a Cavallo* details guided horse treks. *Garfagnana by Bicycle* (€16.50) comes in a handy wallet form and describes more than 25 cycle trips for all levels of fitness.

Cartadel Turismo Rurale della Garfagnana e Valle del Serchio, a free map available from the tourist office, has detailed multilingual suggestions for hikes and driving routes in the region. For general reading, *Valley Garfagnana & the Serchio Valley*, produced by the Lucca tourism authority, is a much more substantial volume. For a general overview, pick up their free booklet *Garfagnana & the Serchio Valley*.

APUANE ALPS

This mountain range rears up between the coastal Versilia Riviera and, inland, the vast valley of the Garfagnana. Altitudes are relatively low compared to the real Alps further north, but the Apuane Alps offer great walking possibilities, often with spectacular views of the coastline and Ligurian Sea. Lonely Planet's *Walking in Italy* describes a couple of enjoyable multiday routes. Francesco Greco's *The Alps of Tuscany* describes in detail many more.

You will find a good network of marked walking trails and *rifugi*. To guide your steps, pick up *Alpi Apuane Settentrionali*, published by the Massa and Carrara tourist offices with trails and *rifugi* marked up, or *Alpi Apuane*, produced by Edizione Multigraphic of Florence. Both are at 1:25,000.

MASSA & CARRARA

The province of Massa and Carrara stretches towards Tuscany's northwestern limit. Inland, Massa, its administrative centre, has

---

CARRARA'S MARBLE

For centuries, marble (derived from the Greek *marmaros*, meaning shining stone) has been hewn and shaped as a luxury material for sculpture and prestige construction. And Carrara has long been the world's largest extractor.

It's amazing that there's any mountain left. The Romans first hacked into the hillside (look for the initials of the early quarrymen, chiselled into the rock to indicate stakes and claims). Their tools and extraction techniques remained largely unchanged until the 19th century, when gunpowder was introduced.

Wasteful and destructive, gunpowder was eventually replaced by the helicoidal thread, a thick hawser that ground its way through the rock like a cheese cutter paring off Parmesan. Nowadays, towering cranes operate diamond-cutting chains that slice off huge cubes that litter the mountain like some giant kid's building blocks.

The workshops of Carrara still turn out their share of *putti* (winsome cherubs), Madonnas and the like, but most marble these days is shipped abroad in huge blocks, to be worked elsewhere. Then again, several international sculptors we won't name have had a chip knocked off the old block and a corner or two rounded in order to fashion their next oeuvre into rough shape.

The **Museo del Marmo** (☎ 0585 84 57 46; Viale XX Settembre; adult/child €4.50/2.50; ✷ 10am-6pm Mon-Sat May-Jun & Sep, 10am-8pm Mon-Sat Jul-Aug, 9am-5pm Oct-Apr) is opposite the stadium, halfway between Carrara and Marina di Carrara. With descriptive panels in English, it has more marble in more varieties than you will have ever seen before and describes extraction from chisel-and-hammer days to the 21st century's high-powered industrial quarrying.

Head 5km north of town to visit the **Cava di Fontiscritti**, a working quarry, where the guy who runs the souvenir shop has a small private **marble museum** (☎ 0585 7 09 81; admission free; ✷ 9am-7pm).

little to entice you. The towns' beachfront extensions, Marina di Massa and Marina di Carrara, are both popular with holidaying Italians.

Just look at the snowcapped mountains dominating Carrara, at the foothills of the Apuane Alps, even in high summer – but it's all an illusion and really marble, field upon field of it, in vast quarries that eat into the hills. The texture and purity of Carrara's white marble is unrivalled. Michelangelo selected blocks from here for many of his masterpieces. More recently, Henry Moore would pick his way through the jumble of rocks and cutoffs in search of the perfect piece.

There's a **tourist office** (☎ 0585 63 25 19; Via Garibaldi 41d; ☻ 9am-1pm Tue-Sat, 3-6pm Tue & Thu) in Marina di Carrara.

Ostello Apuano (☎ 0585 78 00 34; ostelloapuano@ hotmail.com; Viale delle Pinete 237, Marina di Massa; dm €10; ☻ mid-Mar–Sep) is an attractive HI-affiliated youth hostel right on the seafront at Partaccia, just north of Marina di Massa. From Carrara train station catch bus No 53, marked Via Avenza Mare.

Both Massa and Carrara are accessible from the A12 and the SS1 Via Aurelia; signs direct you to the quarries and attractions.

PISA
pop 89,000

Once, it briefly, a maritime power to rival Genoa and Venice, Pisa now draws its fame from an architectural project gone terribly wrong: its Leaning Tower (Torre Pendente). But the world famous tower is only one of a trio of Romanesque splendours on the green carpet of the Piazza dei Miracoli – a serious rival to Venice's Piazza San Marco for the title of Italy's most memorable square.

Pisa has a centuries-old tradition as a university town and still swarms with students.

History

Possibly of Greek origin, Pisa became an important naval base under Rome and remained a significant port for many centuries. The city's so called golden days began late in the 9th century when it became an independent maritime republic and a rival of Genoa and Venice. The good times rolled on into the 12th and 13th centuries, by which time Pisa controlled Corsica, Sardinia and most of the mainland coast as far south as Civitavecchia. Most of the city's finest

buildings date from this period, when the distinctive Pisan-Romanesque architectural style flourished.

Pisa's support for the Ghibellines during the tussles between the Holy Roman Emperor and the pope brought the city into conflict with its mostly Guelph Tuscan neighbours, including Siena, Lucca and Florence. The real blow came when Genoa's fleet defeated Pisa in devastating fashion at the Battle of Meloria in 1284. After the city fell to Florence in 1406, the Medici encouraged great artistic, literary and scientific endeavours and re-established Pisa's university. Galileo Galilei, the city's most famous son, later taught at the university.

Orientation

Stazione Pisa Centrale, the main train station, is at the southern edge of town. The main intercity bus station is on nearby Piazza Sant'Antonio. The medieval centre is about 800m north, across the River Arno. Piazza dei Miracoli (also known as Piazza del Duomo) is about another 650m north.

Information

Internet Planet (☎ 050 83 07 02; Piazza Cavallotti 3-4; per hr €3.10; ☻ 10am midnight Mon Fri, 10am 8pm Sat, 3-8pm Sun)

Koinè Internet Point (☎ 050 83 07 01; Via dei Mille 3-5; per hr €3; ☻ 10am-midnight Mon-Fri, 1pm-midnight Sat & Sun)

Main post office (Piazza Vittorio Emanuele II)

Onda Blu (☎ 800 86 13 46; Via San Francesco 8a; ☻ 8am 10pm) Laundry facilities.

Tourist office airport (☎ 050 50 37 00); Piazza dei Miracoli 1 (☎ 050 56 04 64; ☻ 9am-6pm Mar-Sep, 9.30am-5pm Oct-Feb); Piazza Vittorio Emanuele II 16 (☎ 050 4 22 91; ☻ 9am-7pm Mon-Fri, to 1.30pm Sat) The main tourist office is the Piazza dei Miracoli branch, just north of the Leaning Tower, beside the ticket office.

Sights
PIAZZA DEI MIRACOLI

The Piazza dei Miracoli ranks as one of the world's loveliest squares. Set among its sprawling lawns is one of Europe's most extraordinary concentrations of Romanesque splendour: the cathedral, the baptistry and the Leaning Tower, all financed with the loot and booty brought back to the city after Pisa beat the Arabs in Sicily. The piazza teems with people: students studying or at play, local workers eating lunch and tourists, many

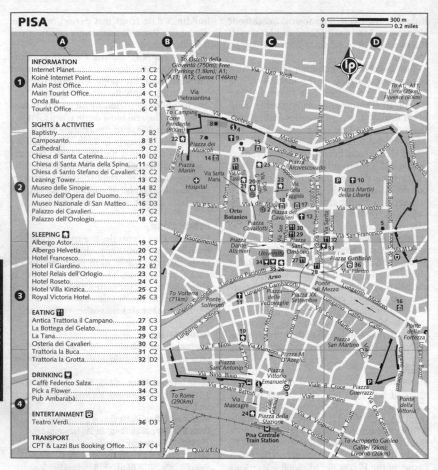

PISA

0   300 m
0   0.2 miles

To Ostello della
Gioventù (750m); Free
Parking (1.8km); A1;
A11; A12; Genoa (146km)

Via Ugo Rindi

To A1; A11;
Lucca (25km);
Florence (80km)

Via
Pietrasantina

To Camping
Torre
Pendente
(800m)

Via Contessca

Matilde

Strada (S12) Statale

Piazza dei
Miracoli

Via Cardinale P. Maffi

Piazza
Arcivescovado

Via San Zeno

Via Vittorio Veneto

Via Galli
Tassi

Via Santa
Maria

Piazza
Manin

Via Roma

Via Capponi

Piazza
della
Faggiola

Piazza Martiri
della Libertà

Via Filippo Buonarotti

Via Santa
Hospital

Via P Salvi

Via dei Mille

Orto
Botanico

Piazza dei
Cavalieri

Via San Lorenzo

Via Santa
Cecilia

Piazza
Cavallotti

Via San Francesco

Via
Risorgimento

Piazza
Dante
Alighieri

University

Piazza
Sant'
Antonio

Piazza Garibaldi

Via M Lalli

Via Palestro

To Volterra
(71km)

Lungarno Simonelli

Ponte
Solferino

Lungarno Pacinotti

Arno

Lungarno Gambacorti

Piazza
delle
Vettovaglie

Piazza XX
Settembre

Ponte
di Mezzo

Lungarno Mediceo

Via San Martino

Ponte
della
Fortezza

Lungarno Fibonacci

Lungarno Buozzi

Via C Mazzini

Corso Italia

Via San Martino

Piazza
San Martino

Via F. Niosi

Via Manzoni

Piazza M
D'Azeglio

Via Nino Bixio

Piazza
Sant'Antonio

Piazza
Vittorio
Emanuele II

Viale B Croce

Piazza
Guerrazzi

Ponte
della
Vittoria

To Rome
(290km)

Via Cesare Battisti

Via
Mascagni

Viale
Gramsci

Viale
Bonaini

Via A Vespucci

Via Carlo Cattaneo

Piazza della
Stazione

Via F. Corridoni

Pisa Centrale
Train Station

To Aeroporto Galileo
Galilei (2km);
Livorno (20km)

Quarantola

(a fun one, this) getting snapped as they extend their arms ta'i chi–like so the shot suggests they're pushing the tower over.

You may also care to indulge in one of the wonderfully kitsch tower souvenirs, ranging from the inevitable cigarette lighters to the infinitely more exciting glowing, flashing lamps.

There's a staggered pricing system for admission to the main sights. A single monument or museum costs €5 while €6 admits you to two. Another option (€8.50) – which we recommend as it can eliminate a lot of queuing – gives entry to four (the two museums, baptistry and Campo Santo cemetery). A huffing, puffing trip up the Leaning Tower is a hefty €15. Bring the kids while they're

small; under 10s go free everywhere except the tower, from which those under eight are excluded for safety reasons.

Opening times for these sights are of Machiavellian complexity. In the following section we quote the summer and winter 'extremes'. For the times of the day, call ☎ 050 56 05 47, a number covering all monuments and museums.

CATHEDRAL

The majesty of Pisa's **cathedral** (Piazza dei Miracoli; admission Mar-Oct €2, Nov-Feb free; ☉ 10am-5.30pm Mon-Sat, 1-5.45pm Sun Mar-Oct, to 7.45pm Apr-Sep; 10am-12.30pm & 3-4.45pm Mon-Sat, 3-4.30pm Sun Nov-Feb) made it a model for Romanesque churches throughout Tuscany and even Sardinia.

Begun in 1064, it's clad inside and out with alternating bands of dark green and cream marble that were to become characteristic of the Pisan-Romanesque style.

The main façade has four exquisite tiers of columns diminishing skywards. The vast interior has 68 columns in classical style. The bronze doors of the transept, facing the Leaning Tower, are by Bonanno Pisano. The 16th-century bronze doors of the main entrance were designed by the school of Giambologna to replace the wooden originals, destroyed in a fire in 1596, after which the interior was also mostly redecorated. Enjoy the depth of detail that Giovanni Pisano imparted to the vibrant early 14th-century marble pulpit in the north aisle, which he spent 10 years of his life working on. Above the altar, a striking mosaic of *Christ in Majesty,* completed by Cimabue in 1302, stares down upon visitors.

LEANING TOWER

Only a limited number of visitors are allowed to go up the **Leaning Tower** (Torre Pendent; www.opapisa.it/boxoffice; Piazza dei Miracoli; admission €15; 8am-8pm Apr-Sep, 9am-5pm or 6pm Mar-Oct) each day. To be sure you're one of them reserve well in advance, either via the website or in person. See the boxed text (below) for more information.

WHY THE LEANING TOWER LEANS

Welcome to one of the world's greatest cockups. The cathedral's *campanile* (bell tower) first started to lean when its architect, Bonanno Pisano, had completed only three tiers. Shifting soil is the most favoured explanation and the 'leaning tower' continued to incline by an average of 1mm every year. Over the years several solutions to stop the lean were tried without success. Then in 1998, cables were wrapped around the 3rd storey and attached to A-frames. This held the tower in place while workers removed small portions of soil on the northern side to create a counter-subsidence. It did the trick and the famous lean lost 40cm. The lean is now 4.1m off the perpendicular (once it was 5m) but, more importantly, the slippage that first caused the tower to lean has finally been arrested.

BAPTISTRY

The unusual round **battistero** (Piazza dei Miracoli; 8am-7.30pm Apr-Sep, 9am-5.30pm Mar & Oct, 9am-4.30pm Nov-Feb) was started in 1153 by Diotisalvi, remodelled and continued by Nicola and Giovanni Pisano more than a century later and finally completed in the 14th century – hence the hybrid architectural styles. The lower level of arcades is in Pisan-Romanesque style and the pinnacled upper section and dome are Gothic. Inside, Nicola Pisano carved the beautiful pulpit (compare it with the one that his son, Giovanni, made for the cathedral), while in 1246 Guido da Como chiselled the octagonal white marble font, as big as a moderate swimming pool and used in its time for baptism by total immersion. The acoustics beneath the dome are remarkable; risk a low whisper and hear it resound. Climb the stairs to the gallery for a great overview.

CEMETERY

They say that behind the white wall of this exquisite **Camposanto** (Piazza dei Miracoli; 8am-7.30pm Apr-Sep, 9am-5.30pm Mar & Oct, 9am-4.30pm Nov-Feb) is soil shipped from Calvary during the crusades, which is reputed to reduce cadavers to skeletons within days. During WWII Allied artillery badly damaged or destroyed many of the cloisters' precious frescoes. Among those saved and displayed in the Fresco Room are the *Triumph of Death* and *Last Judgement,* attributed to an anonymous 14th-century painter known as 'The Master of the Triumph of Death'. Many of the more interesting sarcophagi are of Greco-Roman origin, recycled as the last resting place of prominent Pisans in the Middle Ages.

MUSEO DELLE SINOPIE

This **museum** (Piazza dei Miracoli; 8am-7.30pm Apr-Sep, 9am-5.30pm Mar & Oct, 9am-4.30pm Nov-Feb) houses vast reddish brown sketches drawn onto walls as outlines for frescoes – and revealed in the cemetery after the WWII artillery raids. Now restored to the best degree possible, these *sinopie* give a fascinating insight into the process of creating a fresco.

MUSEO DELL'OPERA DEL DUOMO

This **museum** (Piazza dei Miracoli; 8am-7.30pm Apr-Sep, 9am-5.30pm Mar & Oct, 9am-4.30pm Nov-Feb) has a profusion of artworks from the cathedral, tower and baptistry, including a magnificent ivory carving of the *Madonna and Child* by Giovanni Pisano (Room 11).

THE CITY

From Piazza dei Miracoli, head south along Via Santa Maria and turn left at Piazza Cavallotti for the splendid **Piazza dei Cavalieri**, remodelled by Vasari in the 16th century. **Palazzo dell'Orologio**, located on the northern side of the piazza, occupies the site of a tower where, in 1288, Count Ugolino della Gherardesca, along with his sons and grandsons, were starved to death on suspicion of having helped the Genovese enemy at the Battle of Meloria, an incident recorded in Dante's *Inferno*. **Palazzo dei Cavalieri**, on the northeastern side of the piazza, was redesigned by Vasari and features remarkable graffiti decoration.

The piazza and palazzo are both named for the Knights of Santo Stefano, a religious and military order founded by Cosimo de' Medici. Their church, **Chiesa di Santo Stefano dei Cavalieri** (Piazza dei Cavalieri; admission €1.30; 10am-7pm Mar-Oct, 11am-4.30pm Mon-Sat, 11.30am-5.30pm Sun Nov-Feb), was also designed by Vasari. **Chiesa di Santa Caterina** (Piazza Martiri della Libertà; 10.30am-6.30pm Mon-Sat, 1-6.30pm Sun), north of Via San Lorenzo, is a fine example of Pisan-Gothic architecture and contains works by Nino Pisano.

Wander south to the area around Borgo Stretto, the city's medieval heart. East along the waterfront boulevard, Lungarno Mediceo, is the **Museo Nazionale di San Matteo** (050 54 18 65; Lungarno Mediceo; admission €4; 8.30am-7pm Tue-Sat, 8.30am-1pm Sun), a fine gallery featuring, in particular, works by Giovanni and Nicola Pisano, Masaccio and Donatello.

Cross the Ponte di Mezzo and head west to reach the **Chiesa di Santa Maria della Spina** (Lungarno Gambacorti; admission €1.50; 10am-1.30pm & 2.30-6pm Tue-Fri, 10am-7pm Sat & Sun Mar-Oct, 10am-2pm Tue-Sun Nov-Feb). Built in the early 14th century to house a thorn from Christ's crown, this tiny church beside the Arno is refreshingly intimate after the megaweights of the Piazza dei Miracoli.

Tours

Il Navicello (050 50 31 08; www.ilnavicello.it in Italian) does boat trips (adult/child €4/5) that cruise the River Arno and other excursions, including fishing trips.

Festivals & Events

On 17 June, the Arno comes to life with the **Regata Storica di San Ranieri**, a rowing competition commemorating the city's patron saint. The night before on 16 june, Pisa celebrates the **Luminaria**, when some 50,000 candles and blazing torches glow, making the night-time city bright with light.

For the **Gioco del Ponte** (Game of the Bridge), on the last Sunday in June, two groups in medieval costume battle it out over the Ponte di Mezzo.

The **Palio delle Quattro Antiche Repubbliche Marinare** (Regatta of the Four Ancient Maritime Republics) sees a procession of boats and a dramatic race between the four historical maritime rivals: Pisa, Venice, Amalfi and Genoa. The event rotates between the four towns: it's Pisa's turn in 2006, then Venice (2007), Genoa (2008) and Amalfi (2009). Although usually held in June, it has on occasion been delayed as late as September.

Sleeping

Hotel Francesco (050 55 41 09; www.hotelfrancesco .com; Via Santa Maria 129; s/d €95/115;) With an ideal location (parking apart!) on the main bar/restaurant drag, Francesco is a small and welcoming 13-room hotel that's recently had a total revamp, imparting a slick modern look. There are views over the nearby botanical gardens.

Albergo Helvetia (050 55 30 84; Via Don Gaetano Boschi 31; s/d €35/45, d with bathroom €62) On a quiet street, Helvetia is a particularly welcoming, family place run by an engaging young couple. Some rooms overlook the appealingly quirky, tousled courtyard and garden where cacti abound.

Hotel Roseto (050 4 25 96; www.hotelroseto.it; Via Mascagni 24; s/d/tr €57/72/90;) This hotel is the handiest of all for the train station and a late-night arrival. With cosy if unspectacular rooms and a small garden, it continues to be great value for your euro.

Hotel il Giardino (050 56 21 01; www.pisaonline .it/giardino; Piazza Manin 1; s/d with breakfast €70/110;) The Giardino has sparkling, well-maintained rooms with lots of shiny light-coloured wood and a classy, cool colour scheme. Enjoy breakfast on the tranquil upstairs terrace with the city walls and dome of the Baptistry in full view.

Hotel Villa Kinzica (050 56 04 19; www.hotel villakinzica.it; Piazza Arcivescovado 2; s/d/tr with breakfast

€78/108/124; (P) (X)) Once a private villa, Hotel Villa Kinzica has been tastefully revamped into a gracious hotel. Its 34 attractive rooms have bags of character – and some rooms even boast views of the Leaning Tower as a bonus.

Albergo Astor (☎ 050 4 45 51; www.hotel-astor .com; Via Manzoni 22; d with/without bathroom €75/60) An easy walk from the train station, Astor is a good-value, two-star family hotel that has recently been comprehensively redecorated, inside and out.

Royal Victoria Hotel (☎ 050 94 01 11; www.royal victoria.it; Lungarno Pacinotti 12; s/d €67/77, s/d/tr with bath-room €108/128/138; (P) (X) (□)) The Royal Victoria Hotel offers old-world luxury accompanied by warm, attentive service (and there's the modern touch of wi-fi). The doyen of Pisan hotels, run by the Piegaja family for five generations, represents excellent value for money (breakfast is included in the price). Ecologically friendly, it rents out bicycles to guests for €5 per day and whizzy little Smart cars for a mere €15 per day, plus mileage. Parking is €18.

Hotel Relais dell'Orologio (☎ 050 83 03 61; www .hotelrelaisorologio.com; Via della Faggiola 12-14; s/d with breakfast from €200/300, (P) (X)) Pisa's newest and only five-star hotel occupies a tastefully restored 14th-century noble tower house. Its 21 rooms, some with original frescoes, each have their individual décor and are elegantly furnished with lashings of white linen and antique mirrors. The large, tranquil rear patio is an extra bonus. Parking costs €20.

Ostello della Gioventù (☎ /fax 050 89 06 22; Via Pietrasantina 15; dm/d €15/42) This is a rambling non-HI hostel, just north of the city centre, beside a murky stream where mosquitoes breed in summer. Take bus No 3 from the train station or town centre.

Camping Torre Pendente (☎ 050 56 17 04; www .campingtoscana.it/torrependente; Via delle Cascine 86; per-son/tent/car €8/6.50/4.50; (Y) Apr–mid-Oct; (🚲)) About 1km northwest of Piazza dei Miracoli, this camp ground isn't Tuscany's most attractive but it does boast a supermarket, restaurant and small pool.

Eating

Being a university town, Pisa has a good range of eating places, especially around Borgo Stretto, Piazza Dante Alighieri and the university, and, increasingly, the popular

student area on and around Via San Martino, south of the Arno.

La Tana (☎ 050 58 05 40; Via San Frediano 6; meals €10-14; (Y) Mon-Sat) With friendly service and affordable prices, La Tana is a popular venue for students and staff from the nearby university. Its fare is served up on rustic wooden tables and you can snuggle down in the booths. If you are in a rush to get back to some serious monument bashing, go for the *pasta veloce* (speedy meal, €7), which comes all on one plate.

Osteria dei Cavalieri (☎ 050 58 08 58; Via San Frediano 16; (Y) Mon-Fri & dinner Sat) Like La Tana this *osteria* also offers a high-speed, one-dish lunchtime special (€11) – and what a dish. Prized by locals in the know, the *osteria* also has a shortish but enticing and original choice of dishes, including *carpac-cio di polpi* (octopus carpaccio). Although the size of portions may require a siesta afterwards, the set meals (€25 to €30) are worth the blowout and the wine list is just as impressive.

Trattoria La Buca (☎ 050 56 06 60; Via Galli Tassi 6; mains €6.50-11, pizzas €7) Another favourite with both Pisans and visitors alike. Convenient for the Piazza dei Miracoli, its rear garden lets you switch off from a temporary excess of the Romanesque.

Antica Trattoria il Campano (☎ 050 58 05 85; Via Cavalca 19; mains €10-14; (Y) Thu-Tue) This is a styl-ish trattoria beside Pisa's earthy fruit and veg market, with an adventurous Tuscan menu. For starters go for the vast *tagliere del Re* (minimum two people €12): 'It's a surprise,' says the menu but we'll let you into the secret – you get a wonderfully rich platter of 12 kinds of Tuscan antipasti. Dine downstairs beneath vaulted arches or up-stairs under the bare rafters.

Trattoria La Grotta (☎ 050 57 81 05; Via San Francesco 103; mains €13-15; (Y) Mon-Sat) La Grotta is, as the name suggests, indeed a cavelike place that serves up good portions of Tus-can fare. The creative menu changes at least monthly, reflecting what's in season.

La Bottega del Gelato (Piazza Garibaldi) This *gelateria* dollops out seriously creamy ice cream. Head for this place, located near the river, and join the constant queue, in winter and summer alike.

There's an animated open-air morning **food market** (Piazza delle Vettovaglie), off Borgo Stretto.

Drinking

There are several stylish bars hugging Via Oberdan and Borgo Stretto. Otherwise, head south of the river, where casual student hangouts abound.

Caffè Federico Salza (Borgo Stretto 46; daily Apr-Oct, Tue-Sun Nov-Mar) A long-established café popular with Pisa's shirt-and-tie sophisticates, who prop up the amply stocked bar. It also tempts with a tantalising selection of cakes, *gelati* and chocolates.

Pick a Flower (Via Serafini Angolo) Has a great moody atmosphere with candlelight, good wines by the glass and tapas. The outside terrace attracts a lively chic crowd.

Pub Ambarabà (Vicolo della Croce Rossa 5; Wed-Mon) A popular bar that specialises in sassy cocktails and international beer. There are also light veggie snacks and Internet access on offer.

Entertainment

The **Teatro Verdi** (☎ 050 94 11 11; Via Palestro 40) regularly offers opera, dance and theatre.

Getting There & Away

AIR

The city's **Aeroporto Galileo Galilei** (☎ 050 50 07 07; www.pisa-airport.com), about 2km south of the city centre, is Tuscany's main international airport and handles flights to most major European cities.

Daily destinations include to London Gatwick (British Airways), London Stansted (Ryanair), Liverpool (Ryanair), Coventry, Doncaster/Sheffield and Bournemouth (Thomsonfly).

BUS

Lazzi and CPT share a common booking office on Piazza Sant'Antonio.

Lazzi (☎ 050 46 2 88) operates hourly services to Lucca (€2.20, 45 minutes, 30 daily) and Florence (€6.20, two hours, hourly). Change at Lucca for services to Prato, Pistoia, Massa and Carrara.

CPT (☎ 050 50 55 11) runs to Volterra (€4.50, two hours, 10 daily) and Livorno (€2.30, 45 minutes, every 30 minutes).

CAR & MOTORCYCLE

Pisa is close to both the A11 and A12. The SS67 is a toll-free alternative for Florence, while the north–south SS1, the Via Aurelia, connects the city with La Spezia and Rome.

TRAIN

Pisa is connected to Florence and is also on the Rome–La Spezia train line. Destinations include Florence (€5, 1¼ hours, 40 daily), Rome (€21.30, three to four hours, 20 daily), Livorno (€1.70, 15 minutes, hourly), Pistoia (€4.10, 1¼ hours, five daily) and Lucca (€2.10, 25 minutes, around 20 daily).

Getting Around

For the airport, take a train from Stazione Pisa Centrale (€1, five minutes, 15 per day), or CPT bus No 3, which passes through the city centre and past the train station on its way to the airport.

CPT bus Nos 3 and 4 run between the train station and cathedral.

There's a huge free car park about 2km north of Piazza dei Miracoli with frequent shuttle buses to the centre (return €1.60). When we last passed through, a cavernous subterranean car park was being gouged out beneath Piazza Vittorio Emanuele II and may now be ready to swallow your vehicle.

For a taxi, call ☎ 050 54 16 00.

LIVORNO

pop 156,200

Livorno, still occasionally called by its bizarre anglicised name, Leghorn, was hammered hard in WWII. Its postwar building programme may be charitably described as unimaginative. Frankly, it's a bit of a dump, a place to pass through if you're catching a boat for Sardinia or Corsica.

Orientation

From the main train station on Piazza Dante, 1km east of the city, walk westwards along Viale Carducci, Via de Larderel, then Via Grande into central Piazza Grande, Livorno's main square.

Information

Caffè Grande (Via Grande 59; per hr €5; 7am-11pm Jun-Sep, Wed-Mon Oct-May) Internet place with four computers upstairs.

Main post office (Via Cairoli 46)

Niagara (Borgo dei Cappuccini 13) Laundry.

PC Planet (☎ 0586 82 95 16; Via Giuseppe Garibaldi 110; per hr €4.15; 9.30am-1pm & 3.30-8pm Mon-Sat) Internet access.

Tourist kiosk (☎ 0586 20 46 11; www.costadeglietruschi.it; Piazza del Municipio; 10am-1pm & 3-6pm Mon-Sat Apr-Oct, 9am-5pm Mon-Sat Nov-Mar)

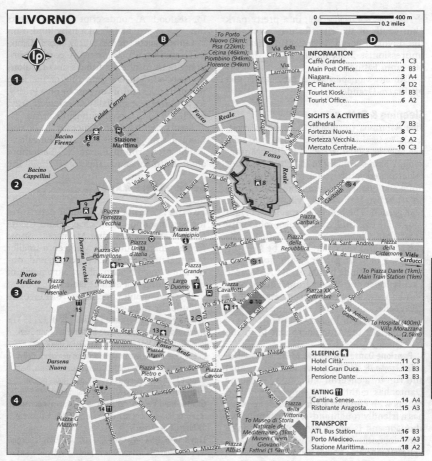

LIVORNO

INFORMATION	
Caffè Grande	1 C3
Main Post Office	2 B3
Niagara	3 A4
PC Planet	4 D2
Tourist Kiosk	5 B3
Tourist Office	6 A2

SIGHTS & ACTIVITIES	
Cathedral	7 B3
Fortezza Nuova	8 C2
Fortezza Vecchia	9 A2
Mercato Centrale	10 C3

SLEEPING	
Hotel Città'	11 C3
Hotel Gran Duca	12 B3
Pensione Dante	13 B3

EATING	
Cantina Senese	14 A4
Ristorante Aragosta	15 A3

TRANSPORT	
ATL Bus Station	16 B3
Porto Mediceo	17 A3
Stazione Marittima	18 A2

Tourist office (☎ 0586 89 53 20; ⏲ Jun-Sep) Near the main ferry terminal, Stazione Marittima.

Sights

The 95m-long **Mercato Centrale** (Via Buontalenti), Livorno's magnificent late-19th-century neo-classical food market, miraculously survived Allied WWII bombing intact. For us, it's the finest site in town, both architecturally and gastronomically.

The **Fortezza Nuova** (admission free), in the area known because of its small canals as Piccola Venezia (Little Venice – oh please!), was built for the Medici family in the late 16th century. The interior is now a park and little remains of the fort except for the sturdy outer walls.

Close to the waterfront is the city's other fort, the **Fortezza Vecchia** (Old Fort), constructed 60 years earlier on the site of an 11th-century building. With huge vertical cracks and bits crumbling away, it looks as though it might give up and slide into the sea at any moment.

Museo di Storia Naturale del Mediterraneo (☎ 0586 26 67 11; Via Roma 234; adult/child €10/5; ⏲ 9am-1pm Tue-Sat & 3-7.30pm Tue, Thu & Sun), 1km south of the city, has recently undergone a huge face-lift and is now much more friendly and hands-on. The star of the show remains a 20m-long skeleton of 'Annie', a common whale.

The **Museo Civico Giovanni Fattori** (☎ 0586 80 80 01; Via San Jacopo in Acquaviva 65; admission €4;

(⊙ 10am-1pm & 4-7pm Tue-Sun), in a pretty park 1km south of the city, features works by the Livorno-based 19th-century Italian-impressionist Macchiaioli school, led by Giovanni Fattori.

The city's unspectacular **cathedral** is just off Piazza Grande.

Sleeping & Eating

Villa Morazzana (☎ 0586 50 00 76; www.villamoraz zana.it; Via Curiel 110; hostel dm/d €18/44, hotel s/d/tr with bathroom €50/75/100; [P] [◻]) Villa Morazzana, 2.5km southeast of the city, is at once HI-affiliated youth hostel, friendly informal hotel and quality restaurant, all packed into an attractive 18th-century villa with a huge rear garden. The hotel's 11 spacious, bright rooms are each individually decorated with great flair. Choose room 201 with its sylvan scene and you could almost be sleeping al fresco in your garden. Both hostel and hotel rates include breakfast. Its Ristorante Lavilla (open for dinner from Thursday to Sunday) offers gourmet cuisine and keeps a great cellar of wines and whiskies. Bus No 3 runs hourly from Piazza Grande. If you're driving, take the Montanero exit from the A12.

Pensione Dante (☎ 0586 89 34 61; 1st fl, Via degli Scali d'Azeglio 28; s/d €35/40) Overlooking a canal and run by a cheerful old couple, Pensione Dante has eight large, simply furnished rooms with corridor bathrooms. The place has a friendly rough-and-tumble family feel about it and is not a bad option if you're euro-economising.

Hotel Gran Duca (☎ 0586 89 10 24; www.granduca.it in Italian; Piazza Micheli 16; s/d with breakfast €86/124, mains about €12-14; [P] [⊠]) This hotel is built into the old protective walls of the port. Rooms are fully equipped and, for fitness freaks, there's the added bonus of a Jacuzzi, Turkish bath and fitness centre. It's right opposite the port and has a decent restaurant.

Hotel Città (☎ 0586 88 34 95; www.hotelcitta.it; Via di Franco 32; s/d €83/108; [P] [⊠] [◻]) Hotel Città, family owned and friendly, is a tempting three-star option in the heart of town. It looks unprepossessing from the outside but rooms, although smallish, are just fine and come equipped with a fridge and a safe. Parking is €13.

Ristorante Aragosta (☎ 0586 89 53 95; Piazza dell'Arsenale 6; mains €8-12.30; ⊙ Mon-Sat) Right on the waterfront, Aragosta is the place to head

for seafood. A nondescript exterior masks inner pleasures, mainly of a fishy kind.

Cantina Senese (☎ 0586 89 02 39; Borgo dei Cappucini 95; meals from €25; ⊙ Mon-Sat) A popular, unpretentious local eatery that's also fabulous for seafood. Squeeze onto one of the long wooden tables and, if you pass by on a Friday, try the Livornese speciality *cacciucco di pesce*, a rich fish soup served with garlic bread.

Load up with fresh produce for the boat at Livorno's magnificent Mercato Centrale.

The area around Piazza XX Settembre abounds in bars and cafés.

Getting There & Away

BOAT

Livorno is a major port. Regular departures for Sardinia and Corsica leave from Calata Carrara, beside Stazione Marittima. Some ferries depart from Porto Mediceo, a smaller terminal near Piazza dell'Arsenale, and others from Porto Nuovo, about 3km north of the city along Via Sant'Orlando.

Ferry companies operating from Livorno include the following:

Corsica Ferries & Sardinia Ferries (☎ 019 21 55 11; www.corsicaferries.com, www.sardiniaferries.com; Stazione Marittima) Heads to Bastia in Corsica (deck class €25 to €32, four hours, two or three services per week, daily in summer) and Sardinia (deck class to Golfo Aranci, near Olbia, €25 to €37, six hours express, nine hours regular ferry, four services per week, daily in summer).

Grandi Navi Veloci (☎ 0586 40 98 04; www.grimaldi .it; Porto Nuovo) Goes to Palermo in Sicily (deck class €80; 17 hours, three weekly).

Lloyd Sardegna (☎ 0565 22 23 00; www.lloydsardegna .it; Porto Nuovo) Goes to Olbia in Sardinia (€26, 11 hours, daily).

Moby (☎ 199 30 30 40; www.moby.it; Stazione Marittima) Ferries depart for Bastia in Corsica (€15 to €29, three to four hours) and Olbia in Sardinia (€20 to €49, eight to 12 hours).

Toremar (☎ 199 12 31 99; www.toremar.it in Italian; Porto Mideceo) Heads to Isola di Capraia (€10.50, 2½ hours, daily).

BUS

ATL buses (☎ 0586 88 42 62) depart from Largo Duomo for Cecina (€2.90, one hour, every 30 minutes), Piombino (€6.20, 2¼ hours, six daily) and Pisa (€2.30, 45 minutes, every 30 minutes).

CAR & MOTORCYCLE

The A12 runs past the city, while the SS1 connects Livorno with Rome.

TRAIN

Livorno is on the Rome–La Spezia line and is also connected to Florence and Pisa. Sample destinations and fares include Rome (€14.30 to €24.70, three to four hours, 12 daily), Florence (€5.90, 1½ hours, 16 daily) and Pisa (€1.70, 15 minutes, hourly).

Trains are a lot less frequent to Stazione Marittima, the station for the ports, but buses to and from the main train station run quite regularly.

Getting Around

ATL bus No 1 runs from the main train station to Porto Mediceo. To reach Stazione Marittima, take bus No 7 or electric bus No PB1, PB2 or PB3. All pass through Piazza Grande.

ELBA

pop 30,100

Napoleon should have considered himself lucky to be exiled to such a pretty spot as the Isola d'Elba. Arriving in May 1814, he escaped within the year and went onto meet his Waterloo.

Nowadays tourism has firmly supplanted iron-ore mining, for centuries Elba's main earner. More than a million visitors a year willingly allow themselves to be marooned here. They come to swim in its glorious blue waters, lie on the beaches and eat fine food. Others are drawn by Elba's mountainous terrain, which offers challenging treks and staggering views. Just 28km long and 19km across at its widest point, Elba is well equipped for visitors, with plenty of hotels and camp sites. Together with Tuscany's other offshore islands, it's included within the **Parco Nazionale Arcipelago Toscano** (www.islepark.it), Europe's largest marine protected area. Elba's main towns are Portoferraio on the island's northern side and Marina di Campo in the south.

If you can, avoid August when the island gets unpleasantly crowded and reservations are essential.

Information

Associazione Albergatori Isola d'Elba (☎ 0565 91 55 55; www.albergatorielbani.it; Calata Italia 20, Portoferraio) The island's professional hotel association, it can reserve accommodation.

Elba Link (www.elbalink.it) Carries lots of useful information about the island.

Info Park Are@ (☎ 0565 91 94 94; Viale Elba, Portoferraio; ⏰ 8am-8pm daily Jun-Sep, Mon-Sat Oct-May) Information office of the Parco Nazionale Arcipelago Toscano.

Tourist office Marina di Campo (☎ 0565 97 79 69; Piazza dei Granatieri; ⏰ Jun-Sep); Portoferraio (☎ 0565 91 46 71; www.aptelba.it; Calata Italia 43; ⏰ 8am-8pm Mon-Sat, 8am-2pm Sun Easter-Oct, 8am-6pm Mon-Sat Oct-Easter) Called the Agenzia per il Turismo dell'Archipelago Toscano; the Portoferraio branch is near the ferry port. The one at Marina di Campo is a small seasonal office.

Activities

If you're here for an active time, pick up the multilingual tourist office leaflet *Lo Sport Emerge del Mare*. It has a useful map and lists walking and cycling trails plus where to sign on for scuba diving, windsurfing and other watery activities.

Isola d'Elba, at 1:25,000 and published by Edizioni Multigraphic, and *Isola d'Elba*, at 1:35,000 from Vivaldi Editori, both have recommended routes for walkers and cyclists overprinted. *Isola d'Elba: Itinerari tra Storia e Natura* at 1:25,000 has a multilingual key and the most stimulating range of walks superimposed. The Vivaldi Editori edition also has descriptions in English of 10 walks and six mountain-bike routes around the island. **Il Libraio** (☎ 0565 91 71 35; Calata Mazzini 10), on the waterfront beside the old town, stocks them.

Portoferraio

SIGHTS

From the ferry terminal, the old town, enclosed by a medieval wall and protected by a pair of brooding fortresses, is a bit less than a kilometre along the foreshore. Here you'll encounter the **Villa dei Mulini** (☎ 0565 91 58 46; Piazzale Napoleone; adult/child €3/free; ⏰ 9am-7pm Mon & Wed-Sat, 9am-1pm Sun), Napoleon's home while he was emperor of this small isle, with its splendid terraced garden and library. During his brief Elban exile, he certainly didn't want for creature comforts – contrast his Elba lifestyle with the simplicity of his camp bed and travelling trunk when he was on the campaign trail.

The **Villa Napoleonica di San Martino** (☎ 0565 91 46 88; adult/child €3/free; ⏰ 9am-7pm Wed-Sat, 9am-1pm Sun), where Napoleon occasionally dropped in, is set in hills about 5km southwest of town. Modest by Napoleonic standards, it is dominated by the overbearing mid-19th-century gallery at its base, built to house his memorabilia.

A combined ticket for both villas is €5.

SLEEPING & EATING

In the height of summer many hotels operate a compulsory half-board policy.

Albergo Ape Elbana (☎ 0565 91 42 45; apelbana@ elba2000.it; Salita de' Medici 2; s €40-60, d €55-95; **P** ☒) This is in the old town, open all year and overlooking Piazza della Repubblica (where hotel guests can park for free). This buttercoloured building is the island's oldest hotel, where guests of Napoleon are reputed to have stayed. The position is its best point as rooms, while large, are a little soulless.

Villa Ombrosa (☎ 0565 91 43 63; www.villaombrosa .it; Via De Gasperi 3; s/d with breakfast €91/182; **P**) Another of the very few hotels on the island that is open year-round. With a great location overlooking the sea and Spiaggia delle Ghiaie, it also has its own small private beach. Half board, considerably more creative than many hotels' bland buffet fare, is obligatory in summer.

Acquaviva (☎ 0565 91 91 03; www.campingacquaviva .it; person/tent/car €12/13/3; ☽ mid-Mar–mid-Oct) About 4km west of town is Portoferraio's nearest camp site. A great choice for sunsets over the sea, it's about as close as you can get to the beach without getting your feet wet.

Stella Marina (☎ 0565 91 59 83; Banchina Alto Fondale; meals €23-35) Stella Marina is a justifiably popular fish and seafood restaurant. Stuck in a car park beside the Toremar ferry jetty and looking unpromising from the exterior, its cuisine is fine and imaginative though drinks are overpriced.

Emanuel (☎ 0565 93 90 03; Enfola; menus €18-27, mains €14-17; ☽ Easter-Nov) At road's end on Capo Enfola, Emanuel offers splendid views over the water. Enjoy a lingering dinner on its beachfront terrace, shaded by a magnificent fig tree. The cuisine is consistently good. Fish and seafood dominate but there are always a couple of inventive meat dishes and a vegetarian option.

Marciana Marina

Almost 20km west of Portoferraio, Marciana Marina, unlike so many brash, modern marinas, is a place with roots and character. Fronted by some pleasant pebble beaches, it makes a fine base for attacking the island's best walking trails.

Casa Lupi (☎ /fax 0565 9 91 43; Località Ontanelli 35; s/d €30/70; ☽ closed Jan-early Mar) is about half a kilometre inland on the road to Marciana. Beside a vineyard, with a garden of peach trees and rose bushes, it's a small hotel in peaceful surroundings. Rooms are no-frills but comfortable and clean.

Ristorante Loris (☎ 0565 9 94 96; Via XX Settembre 29; pizzas €5-8, mains €9-15; ☽ Tue-Sun) is a promising seafood venue where all the pastas and desserts are homemade. Try, for something special, the *ravioli all'astice* (lobster ravioli in a pepper and Parmesan sauce).

Osteria del Piano (☎ 0565 90 72 92; Via Provinciale 24; meals about €25) is about halfway between Portoferraio and Marciana Marina, on the road just outside Procchio. They too make all their own pasta and serve up some astonishing concoctions, such as black-and-white spaghetti in a lobster sauce.

Around Marciana Marina

A twisting 4km ascent brings you to the attractive inland village of Poggio, with its steep, cobbled alleys and stunning views of Marciana Marina and the coast.

Albergo Monte Capanne (☎ /fax 0565 9 90 83; Via dei Pini 13; s/d €26/46, d with bathroom €52; ☽ Apr-Oct) is a great little mountain retreat where you're assured of a robust, cheery welcome. If it gets too warm for you on the coast, chill out here in the hinterland. The terrace is large and ivy-clad and rooms, with swoony views of the coast way below, are cosy.

Some 750m south of the nearby village of Marciana, a **cable lift** (☎ 0565 90 10 20; one way/return €9/13), with open-barred cabins that look like parrot cages, operates in summer and whisks you almost to the summit of Monte Capanne with views, on a clear day, as far as Corsica.

Marina di Campo

Marina di Campo, on the south side of island, is Elba's second-largest town. Curling around a picturesque bay, its small fishing harbour adds character to what is otherwise very much a holiday town. Its beach of bright, white sand pulls in holidaymakers by the thousands; coves further west, although less spectacular, are more tranquil.

Albergo Thomas (☎ 0565 97 77 32; www.elba thomashotel.com; Viale degli Etruschi 32; per person with breakfast €32-59; ☽ mid-Mar–Oct; **P**), a three-star hotel attractively set among pine trees and a short walk from the beach, is one of the more affordable options in the town itself.

Porto Azzurro & Capoliveri

Dominated by its fort, which was built in 1603 by Philip III of Spain and is now a prison, Porto Azzurro is a pleasant resort town close to some excellent beaches.

Albergo Villa Italia (☎ 0565 9 51 19; villaitalia@info elba.it; Viale Italia 41; d/tr/q with breakfast €80/90/105; ☺ mid-Mar–Oct; P) is a clean and friendly, family-run place. The 12 bedrooms are small but spruce and about the cheapest in town. It's on a fairly noisy road yet scarcely 200m from the beach.

Ristorante Cutty Sark (☎ 0565 95 78 21; Piazza del Mercato 25; meals €25-35; ☺ Wed-Mon) has a mainly seafood menu with a couple of concessions to carnivores. Savour the *ravioloni all'Ammiraglia*, large ravioli filled with courgettes (zucchini) and shrimp meat, and bathed in a shrimp and tomato sauce.

From Porto Azzurro, take a short trip south to Capoliveri, one of the island's little hill-top surprise packets. Wander its narrow streets and enjoy the giddy views before trying out one of the nearby beaches such as Barabarca, accessible only by a steep track that winds down the cliff, and Zuccale, more easily reached and perfect for a family outing.

Getting There & Away

Elba is an agreeable one-hour ferry journey from Piombino. If you arrive in Piombino by train, take a connecting train on to the port. Boats to Portoferraio are the most frequent, while some call in at Rio Marina, Marina di Campo and Porto Azzurro.

Boats are run by **Moby** (☎ 199 30 30 40; www .moby.it) and **Toremar** (☎ 199 12 31 99; www.toremar .it in Italian). Unless it is a summer weekend or the middle of August, when queues can form, simply buy a ticket at the port. Fares (€6 to €9.50 per person, €20.70 to €49 per small car) vary according to the season.

Toremar also operates a passenger-only hydrofoil service (€10, 40 minutes) all year-round, and, between June and August, a fast vehicle and passenger service (two people/car from €69.20 return) to Portoferraio.

Getting Around

You can scream around Elba by mountain bike or scooter. Typical high season daily rates are city bikes €15, mountain bikes €24, mopeds €30 and scooters (100 to 125cc) €40. Don't bother with a vehicle: the roads are already overclogged with cars in summer.

Two Wheels Network (TWN; ☎ 0565 91 46 66; www .twn-rent.it; Viale Elba 32, Portoferraio), one of several car-rental outlets, rents bikes, scooters and even kayaks.

Elba's bus company, **ATL** (☎ 0565 91 43 92), runs an efficient trans-island service. Pick up a timetable from the main **bus station** (Viale Elba, Portoferraio). From Portoferraio (the bus terminal is almost opposite the Toremar jetty), there are at least seven runs daily (all €2) to/from Marciana Marina, Marina di Campo, Capoliveri and Porto Azzurro. A day pass costs €7 and a six-day run-around is €19.

In Portoferraio, call ☎ 0565 91 51 12 for a cab.

CENTRAL TUSCANY

IL CHIANTI

Il Chianti, as the gentle hills and valleys between Florence and Siena are called, produces some of the country's best-marketed wines – it's not called Chiantishire for nothing. The most well known is Chianti Classico, a blend of white and red grapes, which is sold under the Gallo Nero (Black Cockerel/Rooster) symbol.

The area is split between the provinces of Florence (Chianti Fiorentino) and Siena (Chianti Sienese). The lovely Monti del Chianti rising into the Apennines mark the area's eastern boundary.

It's a land of rolling hills, olive groves and vineyards. Among them stand Romanesque churches, known as *pievi*, and the many castles of Florentine and Sienese warlords. But perhaps the hype has been just a trifle overdone. There's plenty of more spectacular country to be seen in other areas of Tuscany (around Pitigliano or up in the Apuane Alps, for example). Let's not put you off, but the Tuscan countryside by no means begins and ends in Il Chianti.

Many explore Il Chianti by bicycle and it's also gentle walking country. Pack a copy of *Chianti Classico: Val di Pesa-Val d'Elsa*, a map at 1:25,000 with walking trails superimposed. Lonely Planet's *Walking in Italy* describes a three-day classic of its own that passes through Greve and Radda.

Budget accommodation is limited. Wherever you stay, you'll need to book well ahead since this is a popular area for tourists year-round.

For some useful links, check out www .chiantionline.com.

Greve

Around 20km south of Florence on the SS222, Greve is the first good base for exploring the area. Its unusual triangular Piazza Matteotti, surrounded by porticoes, is an interesting provincial version of a Florentine piazza. At its heart stands a statue of Giovanni da Verrazzano, a local boy made good and discoverer of New York harbour. He's commemorated there by the Verrazzano Narrows bridge (the good captain lost a 'z' from his name somewhere in the mid-Atlantic), linking Staten Island to Brooklyn and indelibly printed in the soul and on the soles of every runner who's done the New York marathon.

If good wines tickle your palate, hit town for Greve's annual wine fair, held during the first or second week of September.

The **tourist office** (☎ 055 854 62 87; Viale Verrazzano 59; ☼ 9.30am-1pm & 2.30-7pm) is on the main street. **Chianti Slow Travel** (☎ 055 854 62 99; www .chiantiechianti.it in Italian; Piazza Ferrante Mori 1) can book accommodation and arrange visits to local wineries.

Greve has a couple of good hotels, both with quality restaurants.

Albergo Giovanni da Verrazzano (☎ 055 85 31 89; www.verrazzano.it, Piazza Matteotti 28; s/d €68/90, with bathroom €86/105; ☼ closed 1st 3 weeks Feb; ▯) is a pleasant three-star family hotel, run by the same family for three generations. Some of its 10 rooms overlook the main square.

Albergo Del Chianti (☎ 055 85 37 63; www.albergo delchianti.it; Piazza Matteotti 86; d with breakfast €75; ☼ mid-Mar–mid-Nov; ☒ ▨) is another three-star hotel, also on Greve's central piazza. It has a pool, garden and attractive breakfast bar.

Macelleria Falorni (☎ 055 85 30 29; Piazza Matteotti 69-71) is a butcher, renowned throughout Tuscany for its prime quality meat, including the traditional *cinta senese* pork. The two huge chopping tables outside its door give a clue to what is happening inside…

The place to enjoy similar quality, carefully selected meats (see the gleaming scales and slicer on the counter as you enter) is **Mangiando Mangiando** (☎ 055 854 63 72; Piazza Matteotti 80; mains €9.50-14), an intimate little restaurant with heavy wooden tables and chairs and friendly service. Since capacity is quite limited, do reserve.

Le Cantine di Greve in Chianti (☎ 055 854 64 04; Piazza delle Cantine; ☼ 10am-7pm) is a vast *enoteca* with more than 1200 varieties of Chianti and other wines on sale. It blends tradition and 21st-century technology; buy yourself a prepaid wine card (from €10), stick it into one of the taps that dispense around 150 different wines and your tipple trickles out. To get there follow the signs from Piazza Matteotti.

Castellina

The huge cylindrical silos at the entry to Castellina may make you think you've hit the industrial zone by mistake. In fact, they're brimming with Chianti Classico, the wine that, together with tourism, brings wealth to this small community, long ago a frontier town between warring Siena and Florence. From the southern car park, take Via Ferruccio, then turn almost immediately right to walk into town beneath the tunnel-like **Via del Volte**. This medieval street, originally open to the elements, then encroached upon by shops and houses, is now a long, vaulted, shady tunnel, particularly welcome in the summertime.

Castellina's **tourist office** (☎ 0577 74 13 92; www.essenceoftuscany.it; Via Ferruccio 26; ☼ 10am-1pm & 2-6pm daily Mar-Nov, 10am-1pm & 2-4pm Mon-Sat Dec & Feb), towards the northern end, is an enterprising place that rents bikes, books accommodation and arranges visits to wineries. They'll even lay on a cookery class for a small group.

Albergo Squarcialupi (☎ 0577 74 11 86; www.pal azzosquarcialupi.com; Via Ferruccio 22; d with breakfast from €110; ☼ mid-Mar–Oct; ▣ ☒ ▯ ▨) has large, airy rooms in a much adapted 15th-century palazzo that's full of character. It has a small bar and *enoteca* and outside there's a lovely terrace and garden with a pool.

La Capannuccia (☎ 0577 74 11 83; d with breakfast €90-120; ▨), at the end of a 1.5km dirt road with no other building in sight, is the ultimate Tuscan getaway. Its five rooms are attractively furnished with antiques, there's a cosy lounge and the hosts couldn't be more welcoming. Reserve in the morning for one of the gourmet dinners (about €25). To get there, follow signs from Bar Pietra

Fitta (near to km39 on the SS222, north of Castellina).

At **Antica Trattoria La Torre** (☎ 0577 74 02 36; Piazza del Comune 15; mains from €6; ☒ Sat-Thu, closed 2nd half Feb) the Stiaccini family, now in its fourth generation, continues to rustle up traditional Chianti fare, using prime ingredients. Dine in the large, beamed interior or on the ample terrace in the shadow of the fortress.

Pick up a bottle or two of the classic nectar at **Antica Fattoria la Castellina** (☎ 0577 74 04 54; Via Ferruccio 26) or simply browse the dusty collection of vintage wines. It runs a two-hour seminar, including tasting, on the secrets of Chianti Classico.

Radda

Radda, 11km east of Castellina, makes a good base for a couple of days' walking. The **tourist office** (☎ 0577 73 84 94; Piazza Castello 6; ☒ 10am-1pm & 3-7pm Mon-Sat, 10.30am-12.30pm Sun Mar-Oct, 10.30am-12.30pm & 3.30-6.30pm Mon-Sat Nov-Feb) occupies an ex-convent. It has a couple of route descriptions (in English) of half-day walks and can advise on winery visits.

The nucleus of the village is the Piazza Ferrucci, where the 16th-century **Palazzo del Podestà**, its façade emblazoned with shields and escutcheons, faces the village church, whose *Christ in Majesty* over the main portal is now sadly all but effaced by the elements.

Da Giovannino (☎ 0577 73 80 56; Via Roma 6-8; s/d €50/60) is a charming family-run hotel in the centre of town, complete with wood-beamed ceilings and views of the countryside. The cosy bar below does tasty snacks and pasta dishes. They also have a couple of apartments (d €75).

Palazzo Leopoldo (☎ 0577 73 56 05; www.palazzo leopoldo.it; Via Roma 33; d with breakfast from €180; ☒ Feb-Dec; P ☒ ☐ ☒), where Leopold, Archduke of Tuscany, stayed briefly in 1837 (hence the name), is nowadays a charming hotel with 17 individually furnished and decorated rooms. Buffet breakfast is served in the original setting of the palazzo's 18th-century kitchen. Its restaurant, La Perla del Palazzo, has a lovely terrace and garden with staggeringly beautiful views.

Getting Around

The picturesque SS222, known as the Strada Chiantigiana, runs between Florence and Siena. You can bus hop but having your own wheels makes exploration much easier.

SITA buses connect Florence and Greve (one hour, every 30 minutes), with one daily bus continuing to Radda (1½ hours) and one heading to Castellina (1½ hours).

SIENA

pop 52,800

Siena is one of Italy's most enchanting cities. While Florence, its historical rival, saw its greatest flourishing during the Renaissance, Siena's artistic glories are earlier and Gothic.

The medieval centre bristles with majestic buildings, such as the Palazzo Comunale on Il Campo, the main square, while its profusion of churches and small museums harbour a wealth of artwork. Budget in a couple of days to really savour the city and its rich treasures. Or make it more than two; Siena also makes a great base for exploring central Tuscany, especially the five-star medieval towns of San Gimignano and Volterra. One problem: accommodation of any kind is difficult to find in summer, unless you book ahead, and well-nigh impossible during Il Palio, the city's famous twice-yearly festival.

History

According to legend, Siena was founded by the son of Remus, and the symbol of the wolf feeding the twins Romulus and Remus is as ubiquitous in Siena as in Rome. In reality the city was probably of Etruscan origin, although it wasn't until the 1st century BC, when the Romans established a military colony there called Sena Julia, that it began to grow into a proper town.

In the 12th century, Siena's wealth, size and power grew along with its involvement in commerce and trade. Its rivalry with neighbouring Florence also grew proportionately, leading to numerous wars during the first half of the 13th century between Guelph Florence and Ghibelline Siena. In 1230 Florence besieged Siena and catapulted dung and donkeys over its walls. Siena's revenge came at the Battle of Montaperti in 1260 but victory was short-lived. Only 10 years later the Tuscan Ghibellines were defeated by Charles of Anjou and for almost a century Siena was allied to Florence, the chief town of the Tuscan Guelph League (supporters of the pope).

This was when Siena, ruled by the Council of Nine (a bourgeois group constantly

SIENA

0 |————————| 200 m
0 |————————| 0.1 miles

A

INFORMATION
Internet Train.................................1 B6
Internet Train.................................2 C5
Libreria Senese...............................3 B5
Main Post Office............................4 B4
Meg@web.......................................5 D6
Onda Blu...6 B5
Tourist Office..................................7 B5
Wash & Dry....................................8 C5

SIGHTS & ACTIVITIES
Baptistry...9 B5
Basilica di Santa Maria dei Servi.......10 D6
Casa di Santa Caterina..................11 A4
Cathedral......................................12 B5
Chiesa di San Domenico...............13 A5
Chiesa di San Francesco................14 C4
Fonte Gaia....................................15 B5
Loggia dei Mercanti......................16 B5
Museo Civico........................(see 19)
Museo dell'Opera Metropolitana...17 B5
Oratorio di San Bernardino...........18 C4
Palazzo Comunale........................19 B5
Palazzo Piccolomini......................20 C5
Palazzo Salimbeni.........................21 B4

B

Palazzo Spannocchi.......................22 B4
Palazzo Tantucci............................23 B4
Palazzo Tolomei............................24 B5
Pinacoteca Nazionale....................25 B6
Santa Maria della Scala.................26 A6
Scuola Leonardo da Vinci.............27 A4
Torre del Mangia.....................(see 19)
Università per Stranieri..................28 C5

SLEEPING
Albergo Bernini.............................29 A4
Albergo Cannon d'Oro..................30 B4
Chiusarelli......................................31 A4
Hotel Antica Torre.........................32 D6
Hotel Duomo................................33 A6
Hotel Le Tre Donzelle....................34 B5
Locanda Garibaldi.........................35 B5
Pensione Palazzo Ravizza..............36 A6
Piccolo Hotel Etruria......................37 B5
Siena Hotels Promotion.................38 A4

EATING
Al Marsili......................................39 B6
Antica Osteria da Divo..................40 A5
Cane e Gatto................................41 D6

C

Consorzio Agrario Siena................42 B4
Il Carroccio...................................43 B5
La Chiacchera...............................44 A4
Nannini...45 B5
Osteria Castelvecchio....................46 B6
Osteria da Cice.............................47 B6
Osteria Le Logge...........................48 C5
Pizzicheria de Miccoli....................49 B6
Ristorante il Capriccio..............(see 36)
Trattoria La Torre..........................50 C5
Trattoria Tullio ai Tre Cristi...........51 C4

ENTERTAINMENT
Cinema Moderno..........................52 B4

SHOPPING
La Cantina in Piazza......................53 B5
Siena Ricama.................................54 B5

TRANSPORT
Local Bus Station..........................55 A3
Perozzi Noleggi.............................56 A3
Perozzi Noleggi.............................57 A3
Sena...58 A3
Tra-in....................................(see 58)

TUSCANY

bickering with the aristocracy), enjoyed its greatest prosperity. It was the Council that directed the construction of so many of the fine buildings in the Sienese-Gothic style that give the city its striking appearance, including lasting monuments such as the cathedral, the Palazzo Comunale and Il Campo itself.

The Sienese school of painting had its origins at this time with Guido da Siena and reached its peak in the early 14th century, when artists such as Duccio di Buoninsegna and Ambrogio Lorenzetti were at work.

A plague outbreak in 1348 killed two-thirds of the city's 100,000 inhabitants and led to a period of decline.

At the end of the 14th century, Siena came under the control of Milan's Visconti family, followed in the next century by the autocratic patrician Pandolfo Petrucci. Under Petrucci the city's fortunes improved somewhat until the Holy Roman Emperor Charles V conquered it in 1555 after a two-year siege that left thousands of people dead. He handed the city over to Cosimo I de' Medici, who barred the inhabitants from operating banks and thus severely curtailed Siena's power.

Siena was home to Santa Caterina, one of Italy's most famous saints. But saints don't make money. Today Siena relies on tourism for its prosperity and the success of its Monte dei Paschi di Siena bank, founded in 1472 and now one of the city's largest employers.

In 1966 Siena was the first European city to banish motor traffic from its heart. To stroll its arteries, unclogged by carbon monoxide and unthreatened by speeding vehicles, is not the least of the town's pleasures.

Orientation

Historic Siena, still largely surrounded by its medieval walls punctuated by the eight original city gates, is small and easily tackled on foot, although the way streets swirl in semicircles around Il Campo may confuse you. At the city's heart is this gently sloping square, around which curve its main streets: the Banchi di Sopra, Via di Città and Banchi di Sotto.

If the rather cramped tourist office map is not adequate for you, invest in a copy of the *Siena* (Litografia Artistica Cartografia; €5.50) map at 1:7000 and with a street index.

Information

Internet Train Via di Città 121 (per hr €6); Via di Pantaneto 57 (per hr €6; ☺ 8am-8pm Sun-Fri) Also a popular café with wi-fi.

Libreria Senese (☎ 0577 28 08 45; Via di Città 62-66) Has a good stock of English, Dutch and German books. Also sells international newspapers.

Main post office (Piazza Matteotti 1)

Meg@web (☎ 0577 4 49 46; Via di Pantaneto 132; per hr €6; ☺ 10am-11pm Mon-Sat, 3-9pm Sun) Internet access.

Onda Blu (Via del Casato di Sotto 17; ☺ 8am-10pm) Laundry.

Tourist office (☎ 0577 28 05 51; www.terresiena.it; Piazza del Campo 56; ☺ 9am-7pm) Can help to reserve accommodation.

Wash & Dry (Via di Pantaneto 38; ☺ 8am-10pm)

Sights
IL CAMPO

The magnificent, scallop-shaped, slanting Piazza del Campo has been the town's civic centre ever since the Council of Nine staked it out in the mid-14th century. The square's paving is divided into nine sectors, representing the members of the Council of Nine. In the upper part of the square is the 15th-century **Fonte Gaia** (Happy Fountain). The original panels by Jacopo della Quercia are severely weathered and those that clad the fountain are reproductions.

At the lowest point of the piazza, the spare, elegant **Palazzo Comunale** is also known as the Palazzo Pubblico, or town hall. Entry to the ground-floor central courtyard is free. From the palazzo soars its graceful bell tower,

---

SAFE COMBINATIONS

Siena has a bewildering permutation of combined tickets. The distribution, when we last visited, was as follows:

- Museo Civico & Torre del Mangia (€10).

- Museo Civico, Santa Maria della Scala, Palazzo Papesse (€10, valid for two days).

- Museo dell'Opera Metropolitana, Oratorio di San Bernardino, Battistero di San Giovanni (€10, valid for three days).

- Museo Civico, Santa Maria della Scala, Palazzo Papesse, Museo dell'Opera Metropolitana, Battistero di San Giovanni and Oratorio di San Bernardino – the bumper bundle (€16, valid for seven days), though it does not include Torre del Mangia.

the **Torre del Mangia** (admission €6; ⏰ 10am-7pm mid-Mar–Oct, 10am-4pm Nov–mid-Mar), 102m high, completed in 1297.

The lower level of the palazzo's façade features a characteristic Sienese-Gothic arcade. Inside is the **Museo Civico** (☎ 0577 29 22 63; adult/student €7/4.50; ⏰ 10am-7pm mid-Mar–Oct, 10am-5.30pm Nov–mid-Mar), occupying rooms richly decorated by artists of the Sienese school.

Of particular note is Simone Martini's famous *Maestà* (Virgin Mary in Majesty), on display in the Sala del Mappamondo. Completed in 1315, it features the Madonna beneath a canopy surrounded by saints and angels and is his first known canvas. In the Sala dei Nove are Ambrogio Lorenzetti's didactic frescoes depicting *Allegories of Good and Bad Government*, contrasting the harmony of good government with the alas, much deteriorated – maybe there's a message there – privations and trials of those subject to bad rule. The chapel has delightful frescoes by Taddeo di Bartolo depicting the life of the Virgin.

CATHEDRAL

The **cathedral** (☎ 0577 4 73 21; Piazza del Duomo; admission €3; ⏰ 10.30am-7.30pm Mon-Sat, 1.30-6.30pm Sun Mar-Oct, 10.30am-6.30pm Mon-Sat, 1.30-5.30pm Sun Nov-Feb) is one of Italy's greatest Gothic churches. Begun in 1196, it was completed by 1215, although work continued on features such as the apse and dome well into the 13th century. The magnificent façade of white, green and red polychrome marble was begun by Giovanni Pisano – who completed only the lower section before his death – and finished towards the end of the 14th century. The mosaics in the gables are 19th-century additions. The statues of philosophers and prophets by Pisano above the lower section are copies; the originals are in the adjacent Museo dell'Opera Metropolitana.

In 1339 the city's leaders planned to enlarge the cathedral and create one of Italy's biggest churches. Known as the Nuovo Duomo (New Cathedral), the remains of this project are on Piazza Jacopo della Quercia, on the eastern side of the cathedral. The daring plan, to build an immense new nave with the present church becoming the transept, was scotched by the plague of 1348.

The most precious feature of the cathedral's interior is the inlaid marble floor, decorated with 56 panels depicting historical and biblical subjects. The earliest ones are graffiti designs in simple black-and-white marble, dating from the mid-14th century. The latest, panels in coloured marble, were created in the 16th century. The most valuable are kept covered and are revealed only from 7 to 22 August each year.

Other draw cards include the exquisitely crafted marble and porphyry pulpit by Nicola Pisano, aided by his equally talented son, Giovanni. Also seek out the bronze statue of St John the Baptist by Donatello, in a chapel off the north transept.

Through a door from the north aisle is another of the cathedral's jewels, the **Libreria Piccolomini**, built to house the books of Enea Silvio Piccolomini, better known as Pius II. The walls of the small hall have vividly coloured narrative frescoes by Bernardino Pinturicchio, depicting events in the life of Piccolomini.

MUSEO DELL'OPERA METROPOLITANA

This **museum** (☎ 0577 28 30 48; Piazza del Duomo 8; admission €6; ⏰ 9am-7.30pm mid-Mar–Sep, 9am-6pm Oct, 9am-1.30pm Nov–mid-Mar), also known as Museo dell'Opera del Duomo, is in what would have been the southern aisle of the nave of the Nuovo Duomo.

Among its great artworks, which formerly adorned the cathedral, are the 12 statues of prophets and philosophers by Giovanni Pisano that decorated the façade. The museum's main draw is Duccio di Buoninsegna's striking early 14th-century *Maestà*, which is painted on both sides as a screen for the cathedral's high altar. The front and back have now been separated and the panels depicting the story of the Passion hang opposite the *Maestà*. Other artists represented are Ambrogio Lorenzetti, Simone Martini and Taddeo di Bartolo, and there's also a rich collection of tapestries and manuscripts.

For a great panoramic view – and a touch of physical exertion to counterbalance so much aesthetic exercise – haul yourself up the 131 steps that lead, via a very narrow corkscrew stairway, to the top of the façade of the putative Nuovo Duomo.

BAPTISTRY

Just north of the cathedral and down a flight of stairs is the **battistero** (Piazza San Giovanni; admission €3; ⏰ 9am-7.30pm mid-Mar–Sep, 9am-6pm Oct, 10.30am-1pm & 2-5pm Nov–mid-Mar).

While the baptistry's Gothic façade has remained unfinished, the interior is richly decorated with frescoes. The centrepiece, both literally and figuratively, is a marble font by Jacopo della Quercia, decorated with bronze panels in relief and depicting the life of St John the Baptist. Artists include Lorenzo Ghiberti (*Baptism of Christ* and *St John in Prison*) and Donatello (*Herod's Feast*).

SANTA MARIA DELLA SCALA
In the basement of this former **pilgrims' hospital** (☎ 0577 22 48 11; Piazza del Duomo 2; admission €6; ☑ 10.30am-6.30pm Apr-Oct, 10.30am-4.30pm Nov-Mar) are copies and touched-up reproductions of Jacopo della Quercia's magnificent frescoes for Il Campo's Fonte Gaia. The Sala dei Pellegrinaio is clad in vivid secular frescoes (quite a relief after so much spirituality all around town) by Domenico di Bartolo, lauding the good works of the hospital and its patrons. There's also a collection of Roman and Etruscan remains.

PINACOTECA NAZIONALE
Within the 15th-century Palazzo Buonsignori, this **art gallery** (☎ 0577 28 11 61; Via San Pietro 29; adult/child €4/free; ☑ 8.15am-7.50pm Tue-Sat, 8.15am-1.15pm Sun, 8.30am-1.30pm Mon) is a showcase for the greatest of Sienese artists. Look for the *Madonna col Bambino* (Madonna with Child) by Simone Martini, and a series of Madonnas by Ambrogio Lorenzetti.

CHIESA DI SAN DOMENICO
Within this imposing **church** (Piazza San Domenico; ☑ 7.30am-1pm & 3-6.30pm), Santa Caterina di Siena took her vows. In the **Cappella di Santa Caterina**, off the south aisle, are frescoes by Sodoma depicting events in her life – and her head, in a 15th-century tabernacle above the altar. She died in Rome, where most of her body is preserved, but, in line with the bizarre practice of collecting relics of dead saints, her head was returned to Siena. In a small window box to the right of the chapel are her desiccated thumb and the nasty-looking whip that she flogged herself with for the wellbeing of the souls of the faithful.

For more of Santa Caterina – figuratively speaking – visit **Casa di Santa Caterina** (☎ 0577 28 08 01; Costa di Sant'Antonio 6; admission free; ☑ 9am-12.30pm & 3-6pm), where the saint was born and lived with her parents plus, says the legend, 24 siblings. The rooms, converted into small

chapels in the 15th century, are decorated with frescoes and paintings by many Sienese artists, including Sodoma.

OTHER CHURCHES & PALAZZI
Loggia dei Mercanti, the 15th-century triple-arched balcony where merchants used to plot deals, is just northwest of Il Campo. From here, strike east along Banchi di Sotto until you pass **Palazzo Piccolomini**, a Renaissance palazzo housing the city's archives. Further east are the 13th-century **Basilica di Santa Maria dei Servi** (Via die Servi), with frescoes by Pietro Lorenzetti in a chapel off the north transept, and 14th-century **Porta Romana**.

On the south side and worth a detour is **Chiesa di Sant'Agostino** (Prato di Sant'Agostino; admission €2; ☑ 10.30am-1.30pm & 3-5.30pm mid-Mar-Oct). The second altar on the south aisle has a superb *Adoration of the Crucifix* by Perugino while the Piccolomini chapel's jewel is Sodoma's *Adoration of the Magi*.

Return to Il Campo and head north on Banchi di Sopra, past Piazza Tolomei, which is dominated by the 13th-century **Palazzo Tolomei**. Further along, Piazza Salimbeni is bound to the north by **Palazzo Tantucci**, Gothic **Palazzo Salimbeni** (the prestige head office of Monte dei Paschi di Siena bank) to the east and, on the third flank, Renaissance **Palazzo Spannocchi**, from where 29 finely carved busts stare down at you from beneath the eaves.

Northeast of here, along Via dei Rossi, is **Chiesa di San Francesco**, with its vast single nave. It has suffered over the years from a devastating 17th-century fire and use as army barracks. It was being further disturbed by massive works in the square that spreads before it when we last passed by. Beside the church is the **Oratorio di San Bernardino** (☎ 0577 28 30 48; Piazza San Francesco 9; admission €3; ☑ 10.30am-1.30pm & 3-5.30pm mid-Mar-Oct) with its small museum of religious artworks.

Courses
LANGUAGE & CULTURE
Università per Stranieri (University for Foreigners; ☎ 0577 24 01 15; www.unistrasi.it; off Via di Pantaneto 45) offers various courses in Italian language and culture.

Two other reputable Italian language schools also offer supplementary cultural – and even culinary – options: **Scuola Leonardo da Vinci** (☎ 0577 24 90 97; www .scuolaleonardo.com; Via del Paradiso 16)

Società Dante Alighieri (☎ 0577 4 95 33; www.dante alighieri.com; Via Tommaso Pendola 37) Southwest of the city centre.

MUSIC

Accademia Musicale Chigiana (☎ 0577 2 20 91; www .chigiana.it; Via di Città 89) offers classical music courses every summer, as well as seminars and concerts performed by visiting musicians, teachers and students as part of the Settimana Musicale Senese.

Within the Fortezza Medicea, **Associazione Siena Jazz** (☎ 0577 27 14 01; www.sienajazz.it; Piazza Libertà), one of Europe's foremost institutions of its type, offers courses in jazz.

Tours

Treno Natura (☎ 0577 20 74 13; www.ferrovieturistiche .it; ⊙ May, early Jun, Sep & Oct) is a great way to see the stunning scenery of the Crete Senese, south of Siena. The line dates back to the 19th century but trains are now run exclusively for tourists and staffed by volunteers. The route loops from Siena through Asciano, across to the Val d'Orcia and Stazione di Monte Antico and then back to Siena. Trains stop at Asciano and Monte Antico and connect with the service from Florence. They run for only about 20 days each year so do check the website or ask in advance at the tourist office. Round-trip

tickets cost €15 if you're hauled by a diesel, €25 if it's a steam train.

Festivals & Events

The Accademia Musicale Chigiana (left) mounts the **Settimana Musicale Senese** in July and the **Estate Musicale Chigiana** in July, August and September. Concerts in these series are frequently held in the magnificent settings of the Abbazia di San Galgano (p527), about 20km southwest of the city, and Abbazia di Sant'Antimo (p529), near Montalcino. For information, call ☎ 0577 2 20 91.

In July and August, the city hosts **Siena Jazz**, an international festival promoted by the Associazione Siena Jazz (left), with concerts at the Fortezza Medicea and various sites throughout the city.

In November, the **Festa di Santa Cecilia**, a series of concerts and exhibitions, takes place to honour Cecilia, patron saint of musicians.

Sleeping

The tourist office makes reservations free of charge for *affitacamere* (rooms for rent) and hotels of three stars and above. You can also book in person (administration charge €2) or online through **Siena Hotels Promotion** (☎ 0577 28 80 84; www.hotelsiena.com; Piazza Madre di Calcutta 5; ⊙ 9am-8pm Mon-Sat Mar-Oct, 9am-7pm Nov-Feb), located near Chiesa di San Domenico.

IL PALIO

This spectacular event is held twice-yearly on 2 July and 16 August. Dating from the Middle Ages, it features a series of colourful pageants, and a wild horse race around Il Campo.

Ten of Siena's 17 *contrade* (town districts) compete for the coveted *palio* (silk banner). Each *contrada* has its own traditions, symbol and colours plus its own church and *palio* museum – rivalry is razor keen.

Il Campo becomes a racetrack, with a ring of packed dirt around its perimeter serving as the course. From about 5pm representatives from each *contrada* parade in historical costume, all bearing their individual banners. For scarcely one exhilarating minute, the 10 horses and their bareback riders tear three times around Il Campo with a speed and violence that make your hair stand on end.

Even if a horse loses its rider, it's still eligible to win. There is only one rule: riders mustn't tug at the reins of other horses.

Join the crowds in the centre of Il Campo at least four hours before the start (7.45pm in July, 7pm in August) if you want a place on the rails. If you can't find a good vantage point, don't despair; the race is televised live (the Sienese exact a huge fee from the national TV network, RAI, for screening rights), then played back repeatedly throughout the evening.

A day or two earlier, you might see jockeys and horses trying out in Il Campo – almost as good as the real thing. Between May and October, **Cinema Moderno** (☎ 0577 28 92 01; Piazza Tolomei; admission €5.25; ⊙ 9.30am-5pm) runs a mini-epic 20-minute film of Siena and Il Palio that will take your breath away.

Hotel Antica Torre (☎ 0577 22 22 55; anticatorre@ email.it; Via Fieravecchia 7; d €113; ✗) This has only eight rooms (so do book weeks in advance) and its bathrooms are scarcely large enough to swing a flannel. But this snug place – all exposed beams and brickwork, tucked into a 16th-century tower and hidden down a side street – is a jewel. Haul yourself to the top floor for the best views.

Locanda Garibaldi (☎ 0577 28 42 04; Via Giovanni Duprè 18; d €75, set menu €20, mains €7-9) With seven big, bright rooms, furnished with flair, the whole place has an individual, funky feel. The twinkly eyed jovial host and his wife also run the well-patronised ground-floor restaurant (open Sunday to Friday).

Albergo Bernini (☎ 0577 28 90 47; www.albergo bernini.com; Via della Sapienza 15; d €62, s/d with bathroom €78/82) A welcoming, family-run hotel (owner Mauro is a professional accordion player who often squeezes out a few tunes for guests). Its tiny terrace has views across to the cathedral and the Chiesa di San Domenico. For space and views, choose room No 11. Reservations are essential from April to October.

Albergo Cannon d'Oro (☎ 0577 4 43 21; www .cannondoro.com; Via dei Montanini 28; s/d €75/95; P ✗) A trim, attractive and excellent-value hotel. Don't be deterred by the golden cannon (the very one that gave the place its name) trained upon you as you debouch from a narrow alley to face the otherwise amicable reception desk. A few of the rooms have air-con; parking is €15.

Both of the following fine hotels observe a 12.30am curfew. However, many other hotels don't, so the street outside can be noisy in summer.

Hotel Le Tre Donzelle (☎ /fax 0577 22 39 33, Via delle Donzelle 5; s/d €33/46, d with bathroom €60) Central, friendly and popular, this was originally constructed as a tavern in the 13th century. Rooms are clean and simple and the shared bathrooms are spotless.

Piccolo Hotel Etruria (☎ 0577 28 80 88; www.hotel etruria.com; Via delle Donzelle 3; s/d/tr €50/80/105; ✗) Another equally welcoming family hotel, just off Il Campo. The air-con whooshing into its large, pleasant rooms is a plus in summer and there's a central light, airy sitting area.

Chiusarelli (☎ 0577 28 05 62; www.chiusarelli.com; Viale Curtatone 15; s/d with breakfast €80/120; P ✗ 🖳) Chiusarelli has been functioning continuously since 1870. It has a pleasant, spacious breakfast room and the rooms are attractive.

The rear ones are for lovers of quiet and, on alternate Sundays in season, lucky football fans: they overlook the stadium where Siena, regularly propping up Serie A, play home matches.

Pensione Palazzo Ravizza (☎ 0577 28 04 62; www .palazzoravizza.it; Pian dei Mantellini 34; s/d/tr with breakfast from €130/160/220; P ✗ 🖳) Occupies a delightful Renaissance palazzo with frescoed ceilings and carefully selected antique furniture. Service is courteous and efficient, there's a small, leafy garden and their Ristorante il Capriccio is worth crossing town for.

Hotel Duomo (☎ 0577 28 90 88; www.hotelduomo .it; Via di Stalloreggi 38; s/d/tr with breakfast €104/130/171; P ✗ 🖳) An attractive 18th-century palazzo with a small 1st-floor terrace and tastefully decorated rooms, several offering views of the cathedral.

Hotel Santa Caterina (☎ 0577 22 11 05; www .hscsiena.it; Via Piccolomini 7; s/d with breakfast to €105/155; P ✗) An elegantly renovated 18th-century villa just outside the city walls, a stone's throw beyond the Porta Romana. It's a tranquil haven; rooms are tastefully furnished, the breakfast room is light and airy and there's a lovely shaded garden with open views to the surrounding hills. Parking is €12.

Siena Colleverde (☎ 0577 28 00 44; Via Scacciapen-sieri 47; person/site €7.75/7.75; ☽ mid-Apr–mid-Oct; 🚊) A good camp site 2km north of the historical centre. Take bus No 3 or No 8 from Piazza Gramsci or Viale Tozzi.

Ostello Guidoriccio (☎ 0577 5 22 12; Via Fiorentina 89, Località Stellino; per person €13.50) All rooms are doubles at Siena's HI-affiliated youth hostel, about 2km northwest of the city centre. Take bus No 10, 15 or 35 from Piazza Gramsci, or No 4 or 77 from the train station.

Eating

According to the Sienese, most Tuscan cuisine has its origins here. Among many traditional dishes are *ribollita*, *panzanella* (summer salad of soaked bread, basil, onion and tomatoes), *pappardelle con la lepre* (ribbon pasta with hare) and the juicy charcoal-grilled beef steaks of the Chianina. *Panforte* (a rich cake of almonds, honey and candied fruit) was originally created as tucker for crusaders to the Holy Land.

RESTAURANTS

Osteria Le Logge (☎ 0577 4 80 13; Via del Porrione 33; mains €15-18; ☽ Mon-Sat) Le Logge changes its

TUSCANY

menu of creative Tuscan cuisine almost daily. In the downstairs dining room, once a pharmacy, bottles of wine are arrayed in cases, floor to ceiling, like books in a library (there are more than 18,000 more in the cellars so you won't go thirsty) and there's also a large streetside terrace.

Trattoria La Torre (☎ 0577 28 75 48; Via di Salicotto 7-9; mains €6.50-10, tourist menus €20; ☽ Fri-Wed) This trattoria has only 10 tables. It's an intimate family-run place, in a vaulted cellar just off Il Campo, where the food is rustled up in full view of diners. There's fresh homemade pasta and portions are generally formidable; do keep space for one of the delightful homemade desserts.

Cane e Gatto (☎ 0577 28 75 45; Via Pagliaresi 6; meals about €65; ☽ dinner Fri-Wed) The name Dog & Cat might suggest that you're in for a pub lunch. Far from it. It's one of Siena's finest restaurants, with prices that reflect its quality. Avoid making a decision by rolling with the regularly changing seven-course *menù degustazione* (taster menu) or just pick a selection from it.

Ristorante il Capriccio (☎ 0577 28 17 57; Pian dei Mantellini 32; mains €9-16; ☽ Thu-Tue) The restaurant in Pensione Palazzo Ravizza offers fine cuisine and the chance to eat either in its wood-panelled dining room or outside in the wonderful garden.

Antica Osteria da Divo (☎ 0577 28 43 81; Via Franciosa 29; mains €16-19; ☽ Sun-Fri) This place plays background jazz that is as smooth as the walls are rough-hewn. At the lower, cellar level you're dining amid Etruscan tombs. The inventive menu includes dishes like tarragon-scented lamb followed by girth-widening goodies such as a pistachio and vanilla pie with raspberry sauce.

La Chiacchera (☎ 0577 28 06 31; Costa di Sant'Antonio 4; pastas €4-4.50, mains €5-6; ☽ daily Easter-Oct, Wed-Mon Nov-Easter) La Chiacchera is a tiny, informal restaurant run by a young staff. It offers a great menu of local specialities and the wooden tables on a quiet pedestrian street make it a good lunch venue.

Osteria da Cice (☎ 0577 28 80 26; Via San Pietro 32; mains €7-11.50, tourist menus €12; ☽ Tue-Sun) This place is also in the hands of a friendly team, which reflects its mainly youthful clientele. Come to Osteria da Cice for an informal, relaxed meal. The menu has plenty of vegetarian options among its *primi piatti* (first courses).

Il Carroccio (☎ 0577 4 11 65; Via Casato di Sotto 32; pastas €6.50-7, mains €12-15; ☽ Thu-Mon & lunch Tue) This restaurant does exceptional pasta. Try the *pici*, a kind of thick spaghetti typical of Siena, followed by the *tegamate di maiale* (pork with fennel seeds). The Carroccio is a member of the Slow Food Movement (see the boxed text, p241) – always a good sign.

Trattoria Tullio ai Tre Cristi (☎ 0577 28 06 08; Vicolo di Provenzano 1; mains €13-17; ☽ Thu-Tue) This has been a place for hungry Sienese for nigh on 170 years – so the service is, perhaps understandably, sometimes on the slow side. This apart, it's a delightful place: wood panelled, brick-vaulted and tucked away down a clearly signed side alley.

Osteria Castelvecchio (☎ 0577 4 95 86; Via di Castelvecchio 65; mains €9.50; ☽ Mon-Sat) Highly regarded by locals, Castelvecchio has a couple of attractive bare-brick rooms. Those with rumbling tummies should opt for the constantly changing *menù degustazione* (€25). It's also a good spot for veggies, with at least four meatless dishes normally on offer.

Al Marsili (☎ 0577 4 71 54; Via del Castoro 3; mains €11-17; ☽ Tue-Sun) Al Marsili is one of the city's classiest restaurants, where white-smocked waiters dish up traditional Sienese cuisine like *pici alla casareccia* (*pici* with a meat and mushroom sauce). The restaurant also offers more innovative dishes such as gnocchi in a duck sauce.

CAFÉS

Nannini (Banchi di Sopra 22) Always crowded, Nannini is something of a Sienese institution, baking its finest cakes and serving up good coffee with speed and panache.

SELF-CATERING

Pizzicheria de Miccoli (☎ 0577 28 91 84; Via di Città 93-95) Richly scented, de Miccoli has windows festooned with sausages, piled-up cheeses and porcini mushrooms by the sackful.

Consorzio Agrario Siena (Via Pianagini 13) For its part, this is a rich emporium of local food and wines.

Drinking

Enoteca Italiana (Fortezza Medicea; ☽ noon-1am Tue-Sat, to 8pm Sun) Northwest of the city centre within the fortress walls; the former munition cellars have been artfully transformed into a classy *enoteca* that carries more than 1500 labels.

Shopping

See opposite for details about two specialist food shops.

La Cantina in Piazza (Via del Casato di Sotto 24; ⊗ closed Wed afternoon) A very well-endowed wine shop, ideal for a picnic special or a case to lug home or have freighted.

Siena Ricama (☎ 0577 28 83 38; Via di Città 61) Promotes the crafts of Siena, in particular embroidery.

Wednesday market (⊗ 7.30am-1pm) Spreads all around Fortezza Medicea and seeps towards the Stadio Comunale. One of Tuscany's largest, it's great for foodstuffs, cheap clothing or just aimless browsing.

Getting There & Away

BUS

The local bus station is in Piazza Gramsci. **Tra-in** (☎ 0577 20 42 46) or SITA express buses race up to Florence (€6.50, 1¼ hours, up to 30 daily). Other regional Tra-in destinations include San Gimignano (€5.20, 1¼ hours, 10 daily, direct or change in Poggibonsi), Montalcino (€3.25, 1½ hours, six daily) and Montepulciano (€4.45, 1¾ hours).

Sena (☎ 0577 28 32 03; www.sena.it) buses run to/from Rome (€17.50, three hours, eight daily) and Milan (€25, 4¼ hours, three daily) and there are seven buses daily to Arezzo (€5, 1½ hours).

Both Tra-in and Sena have ticket offices underneath the piazza, where there's also a left-luggage office.

CAR & MOTORCYCLE

For Florence take the SS2, the *superstrada,* or the more attractive SS222, also known as the Strada Chiantigiana, which meanders its way through the hills of Chianti.

TRAIN

Siena isn't on a major train line so buses are generally a better alternative. By train, change at Chiusi for Rome and at Empoli for Florence.

Getting Around

Tra-in operates city bus services (€0.90). Bus Nos 8, 9 and 10 run between the train station and Piazza Gramsci. Cars are banned from the town centre, though visitors can drop off their luggage at the hotel, then get out. **Perozzi Noleggi** (☎ 0577 28 83 87; Via dei Gazzani 16-18) rents mountain bikes (per day/week

€10/50) and 50cc scooters (€26/150). If there's no-one in the showroom, pop round the corner to Via del Romitorio 5.

There are large car parks at the Stadio Comunale and around the Fortezza Medicea, both just north of Piazza San Domenico. There's also another big one at Il Campo, south of the centre.

For a taxi, call ☎ 0577 4 92 22.

SAN GIMIGNANO

pop 7150

As you crest the hill coming from the east, the 14 towers of this walled town look like a medieval Manhattan. And when you arrive you might well feel that half of Manhattan has moved in. Within easy reach of both Siena and Florence, San Gimignano is a tourist magnet. Come in winter or early spring to indulge your imagination a little; in summer you'll spend your time dodging fellow visitors. Even then though, you'll discover a different, almost peaceful San Gimignano once the last bus has pulled out.

There's good reason for such popularity. The towers, which once numbered 72, were symbols of the power and wealth of the city's medieval families. San Gimignano delle Belle Torri (meaning 'of the Fine Towers' - though they're actually almost devoid of design and rather dull unless sheer height impresses you) is surrounded by lush, productive land and the setting is altogether enchanting.

Originally an Etruscan village, the town was named after the bishop of Modena, San Gimignano, who is said to have saved the city from Attila the Hun. It became a *comune* in 1199, but continually fought with Volterra. Internal battles between the Ardinghelli (Guelph) and Salvucci (Ghibelline) families over the next two centuries caused divisions. Most of the towers were built during this period; in the 13th century, one *podestà* (town chief) forbade the building of towers higher than his own 51m pile. In 1348 plague wiped out much of the population and weakened the nobles' power, leading to the town's submission to Florence in 1353. Today, not even the plague would deter the summer swarms.

Orientation

From the main gate, Porta San Giovanni, at the southern end of the town, Via San Giovanni heads northwards to central Piazza

TUSCANY

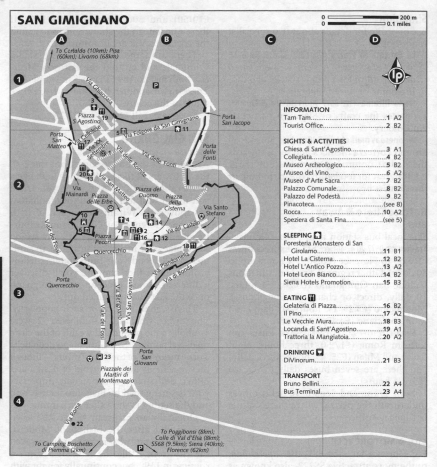

SAN GIMIGNANO

INFORMATION
Tam Tam..1 A2
Tourist Office..2 B2

SIGHTS & ACTIVITIES
Chiesa di Sant'Agostino....................3 A1
Collegiata..4 B2
Museo Archeologico.........................5 B2
Museo del Vino...................................6 A2
Museo d'Arte Sacra...........................7 B2
Palazzo Comunale.............................8 B2
Palazzo del Podestà..........................9 B2
Pinacoteca.......................................(see 8)
Rocca...10 A2
Speziera di Santa Fina...................(see 5)

SLEEPING
Foresteria Monastero di San
   Girolamo...11 B1
Hotel La Cisterna.............................12 B2
Hotel L'Antico Pozzo.......................13 A2
Hotel Leon Bianco...........................14 B2
Siena Hotels Promotion..................15 B3

EATING
Gelateria di Piazza...........................16 B2
Il Pino..17 A2
Le Vecchie Mura...............................18 B3
Locanda di Sant'Agostino.............19 A1
Trattoria la Mangiatoia..................20 A2

DRINKING
DiVinorum..21 B3

TRANSPORT
Bruno Bellini......................................22 A4
Bus Terminal......................................23 A4

della Cisterna and the connecting Piazza del Duomo. From here the other major thoroughfare, Via San Matteo, extends to the principal northern gate, Porta San Matteo.

Information

Tam Tam (☎ 0577 90 71 00; Via XX Settembre 4b; per hr €6; ⏰ 10am-7pm Apr-Oct, 2-7pm Nov-Feb) For Internet.

Tourist office (☎ 0577 94 00 08; www.sangimignano .com in Italian; Piazza del Duomo 1; ⏰ 9am-1pm & 3-7pm Mar-Oct, 9am-1pm & 2-6pm Nov-Feb)

Sights

COLLEGIATA

The 13th century **Palazzo del Podestà** and its tower, the **Torre della Rognosa**, look across to the town's Romanesque **cathedral** (adult/child

€3.50/1.50; ⏰ 9.30am-7.30pm Mon-Fri, 9.30am-5pm Sat, 12.30-5pm Sun Apr-Oct, 9.30am-5pm Mon-Sat, 12.30-5pm Sun Nov–mid-Jan & Mar). Access is up a flight of steps. Its bare façade belies the remarkable 14th-century frescoes that stripe the interior walls like some vast medieval comic strip.

Along the northern aisle are key moments from the Old Testament by Bartolo di Fredi. Opposite, covering the walls of the south aisle, Barna da Siena illustrates New Testament scenes. On the inside wall of the façade, extending onto adjoining walls, Taddeo di Bartolo probably scared the daylights out of pious locals with his gruesome depiction of the Last Judgement. The **Cappella di Santa Fina** is adorned with

MONEYSAVERS

If you're an assiduous sightseer, two combined tickets may be worth your while. One (adult/child €7.50/5.50) gives admission to the Palazzo Comunale and its Museo Civico, the archaeological museum and some secondary sights. The other (adult/child €5.50/2.50) gets you into the Cathedral and nearby Museo d'Arte Sacra.

naive and touching frescoes by Domenico Ghirlandaio depicting events in the life of the saint, and a quite superb alabaster and marble altar picked out in gold.

Across the square, the **Museo d'Arte Sacra** (☎ 0577 94 03 16; Piazza Pecori 1; adult/child €3/1.50; ☽ 9.30am-7.30pm Mon-Fri, 9.30am-5pm Sat, 12.30-5pm Sun Apr-Oct, 9.30am-5pm Mon-Sat, 12.30-5pm Sun Nov-mid-Jan & Mar) has some fine works of religious art, collected, in the main, from the town's churches.

PALAZZO COMUNALE

From the internal courtyard, climb the stairs to the **Pinacoteca** (☎ 0577 99 03 12; Piazza del Duomo; adult/child museum & tower €5/4; ☽ 9.30am-7pm Mar-Oct, 10am-5pm Nov-Feb), which features paintings from the Sienese and Florentine schools of the 12th to 15th centuries. In the main room, the great poet **Sala di Dante** addressed the town's council, urging it to support the Guelphs' cause. The room contains an early 14th-century fresco of the *Maestà* by Lippo Memmi. Climb up the palazzo's **Torre Grossa** for a spectacular view of the town and surrounding countryside.

MUSEUMS

At San Gimignano's recently opened **Museo del Vino** (Wine Museum; ☎ 0577 94 12 67; Rocca di Montestaffoli; admission free; ☽ 11am-7pm Thu-Mon, 3-7pm Wed Mar-Oct), inside the town's fortress, a sommelier is on hand to lead an informed – and paid – tasting of some of the choice local white wines.

The recently opened **Museo Archeologico** (☎ 0577 94 03 48; Via Folgore da San Gimignano 11; adult/child €3.50/2.50; ☽ 11am-5.30pm mid-Mar–mid-Dec) complex is home to the town's small archaeological museum, **Speziera di Santa Fina**, a reconstructed 16th-century pharmacy and herb garden and a **modern art gallery** that in itself merits a visit.

OTHER SIGHTS

From the **Rocca**, what remains of the town's fortress, there are great views over the surrounding countryside.

At the northern end of the town is the **Chiesa di Sant'Agostino** (Piazza Sant'Agostino; ☽ 7am-noon & 3-7pm Apr-Oct, to 6pm Nov-Mar). Its main attraction is the fresco cycle in the apse by Benozzo Gozzoli, depicting the saint's life.

Sleeping

In high summer San Gimignano can be as unpromising for accommodation as that Christmas Eve in Bethlehem. This said, **Siena Hotels Promotion** (☎ 0577 94 08 09; www.hotelsiena .com; Via San Giovanni 125; ☽ Mon-Sat) will book hotels and some *affittacamere* for callers-in (for a €2 fee) or online via their website. The tourist office, for its part, will reserve a wider range of *affittacamere* and also *agriturismi* (farm-stay accommodation) if you call by in person.

Two highly recommended hotels flank Piazza della Cisterna, the main square. In both, you pay a little more for superb views.

Hotel La Cisterna (☎ 0577 94 03 28; www.hotel cisterna.it; Piazza della Cisterna 24; s/d/tr with breakfast €75/95/125, ☒ ☐) This hotel is in a splendid 14th-century building with vaulted ceilings and chandeliers. Nearly 100 years in business, it offers truly 21st-century comfort in quiet, spacious, comfortable rooms. Like a view of the square? Or how about vistas across the valley? You can take your pick.

Hotel Leon Bianco (☎ 0577 94 12 94; www.leon bianco.com; Piazza della Cisterna 13; s/d/tr with breakfast from €75/105/145; ☒ ☐) Leon Bianco faces La Cisterna across the square and also occupies a 14th-century mansion. This smoothly run hotel is equally welcoming and friendly with a pretty inner courtyard and breakfast patio.

Foresteria Monasterio di San Girolamo (☎ 0577 94 05 73; Via Folgore da San Gimignano 26-32; per person €25; ☒) This is an excellent budget choice. Run by friendly nuns, it has basic but spacious, comfortable rooms, all with bathrooms and sleeping two to five people. Check-in/out is 9.30am to 12.15pm and 3.30pm to 5.30pm.

Hotel L'Antico Pozzo (☎ 0577 94 20 14; www .anticopozzo.com; Via San Matteo 87; s/d/tr with breakfast from €100/135/165; ☽ closed 1st 2 weeks Nov; ☒ ☐) L'Antico Pozzo is named after the old softly illuminated *pozzo* (well), just off the lobby. Each room has its own personality, with thick stone walls, high ceilings, wrought-iron

TUSCANY

beds, frescoes, antique prints and peach-coloured walls. Room 20 has a magnificent domed ceiling.

Camping Boschetto di Piemma (☎ 0577 94 03 52; www.boschettodipiemma.it; person/tent/car €6.40/6/2.80; ☺ year-round) Two kilometres south of town at Santa Lucia, this is the nearest camp site. Buses stop right outside.

Eating

Trattoria la Mangiatoia (☎ 0577 94 15 28; Via Mainardi 5; mains around €15; ☺ Wed-Mon Feb-Oct) This is a highly regarded trattoria, serving tempting, mainly regional fare. With candles flickering and classical music in the background, share it with that special someone. You can hold hands after dark on the delightful summer patio.

Le Vecchie Mura (☎ 0577 94 02 70; Via Piandornella 15; meals €25-30; ☺ dinner Wed-Mon) Le Vecchie Mura is a wonderful spot, especially if you snap up a terrace table on a warm summer's night. The food competes with the phenomenal view of rolling green hills and Le Vecchie Mura carries more than 12 varieties of San Gimignano wine. Choose from a delicious selection of *primi piatti* such as *gnocchi con tartufo e formaggio* (gnocchi with truffles and cheese) – book ahead to guarantee that panorama.

Il Pino (☎ 0577 94 04 15; Via Cellolese 8-10; mains €14-16; ☺ Fri-Wed) Il Pino is spruce, vaulted and airy with fresh flowers on each table. Service is friendly and attentive and the menu, including several truffle-based specialities, can rival any in town. The desserts, all made on the premises, are dinner's final temptation.

Gelateria di Piazza (☎ 0577 94 22 44; Piazza della Cisterna 4; ☺ Mar–mid-Nov) This gelateria looks modest but, as the pictures around the wall attest, many celebrities have closed their lips around one of its rich ice creams ('All the family thought the ice cream was delicious,' attested one Tony Blair). There's a variant based on Vernaccia, the local wine, and if you want to be more adventurous, saffron cream.

Locanda di Sant'Agostino (☎ 0577 94 31 41; Piazza Sant'Agostino 15; bruschette from €4; ☺ daily Mar-Nov, Tue-Sun Dec-Feb) This is a pleasant spot for a relatively quiet drink, crispy salad and a sample from the repertoire of 49 *bruschette*.

Each Thursday morning there's a **produce market** (Piazza della Cisterna & Piazza del Duomo).

Drinking

DiVinorum (Piazza della Cisterna 30; ☺ 11am-midnight daily Mar-Oct, Fri-Sun Nov-Feb) Housed in cavernous former stables, this is a cool wine bar run by local lads. In summer, sip your drink on the tiny outdoor terrace with stunning valley views.

Getting There & Around

The **bus terminal** (Piazzale dei Martiri di Montemaggio) is beside Porta San Giovanni. They run to/from Florence (€5.90, 1¼ hours, 12 daily) and Siena (€5.20, one to 1½ hours, 10 daily). A few buses are direct but most require a change at Poggibonsi. The tourist office has timetables.

For Volterra (€4.30, 1½ hours, four daily Monday to Saturday) you need to change in Colle di Val d'Elsa, and maybe also in Poggibonsi, which has the closest train station.

From Florence or Siena, take the SS2 to Poggibonsi, then the SS68 via Colle di Val d'Elsa.

There's a shuttle service for hotel guests from the car parks (per hour €2) outside the city walls, beside and below Porta San Giovanni. You'll find free parking in the new parts of town, just northwest of the old centre.

Bruno Bellini (☎ 0577 94 02 01; Via Roma 41) rents mountain bikes (€15 per day) and scooters (from €31 per day).

VOLTERRA

pop 11,400

Perched high on a rocky plateau, 29km southwest of San Gimignano, Volterra's well-preserved medieval ramparts give the town a forbidding air, while the gentle Tuscan countryside rolling out for miles around provides the perfect contrast. The city has long had a strong alabaster industry, a legacy from the Etruscans.

The Etruscan settlement of Velathri was an important trading centre and remained so under the Romans, who renamed it Volaterrae. A long period of conflict with Florence started in the 12th century and ended only when the Medici took possession of the city in the 15th century.

Orientation & Information

Whichever one of the four main gates you enter, the road will lead you to central Piazza dei Priori.

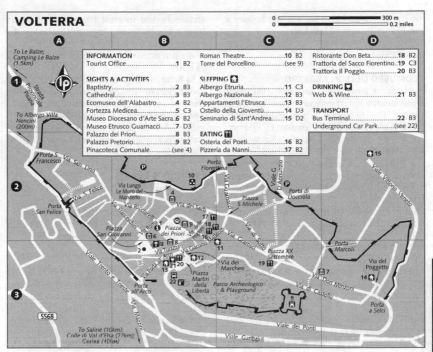

VOLTERRA

Tourist office (☎ 0588 8 72 57; www.volterratur.it; Piazza dei Priori 19-20; ☀ 9am-1pm & 2-7pm Apr-Oct, 10am-1pm & 2-6pm Nov-Mar) Offers a free hotel-booking service and rents out a good town audioguide (€5).

Sights

PIAZZA DEI PRIORI & AROUND

Piazza dei Priori is ringed by austere medieval mansions. The 13th-century **Palazzo dei Priori** (admission €1; ☀ 10.30am-5.30pm daily mid-Mar–Oct, 10am-5pm Sat & Sun Nov–mid-Mar), the oldest seat of local government in Tuscany, is believed to have been a model for Florence's Palazzo Vecchio (p468). Highlights are a fresco of the Crucifixion by Piero

Francesco Fiorentino on the staircase, the magnificent cross-vaulted council hall and a small antechamber on the 1st floor giving a bird's-eye view of the piazza below.

Palazzo Pretorio dates back to the same era. From it thrusts the **Torre del Porcellino** (Piglet's Tower), so-named because of the wild boar protruding from its upper section.

The **cathedral** (Piazza San Giovanni; ☀ 8am-12.30pm & 3-6pm) was built in the 12th and 13th centuries. Highlights include a small fresco, the *Procession of the Magi* by Benozzo Gozzoli, behind a terracotta Nativity group tucked away in the oratory at the beginning of the north aisle. There is also an exquisite 15th-century tabernacle by Mino da Fiesole that rises above the high altar. Just west of the cathedral, the 13th-century **baptistry** features a small marble font by Andrea Sansovino.

Nearby, the **Museo Diocesano d'Arte Sacra** (☎ 0588 8 62 90; Via Roma 1; ☀ 9am-1pm & 3-6pm mid-Mar–Oct, 9am-1pm Nov–mid-Mar) merits a peek for its collection of ecclesiastical vestments, gold reliquaries and works by Andrea della Robbia and Rosso Fiorentino. The **Pinacoteca Comunale** (☎ 0588 8 75 80; Via dei Sarti 1; ☀ 9am-7pm mid-Mar–Oct, 8.30am-1.45pm Nov–mid-Mar) houses a modest collection of local art.

For admission prices, see the boxed text on p525.

ECOMUSEO DELL'ALABASTRO

As befits a town that has hewn the rock from nearby quarries ever since Etruscan times, Volterra has its own **alabaster museum** (☎ 075 98 73 06; Via dei Sarti 1; admission €3; ☽ 11am-5pm daily mid-Mar–Oct, 9am-1.30pm Sat & Sun Nov–mid-Mar), which shares the same building as the Pinacoteca Comunale. On the ground floor are contemporary creations, including a finely chiselled mandolin and a bizarre fried egg, while on the two upper floors are choice examples from Etruscan times onwards and a re-created artisan's workshop.

MUSEO ETRUSCO GUARNACCI

In terms of content, this is one of Italy's finest **Etruscan museums** (☎ 0588 8 63 47; Via Don Minzoni 15; ☽ 9am-7pm mid-Mar–Oct, 8.30am-1.45pm Nov–mid-Mar). Sadly, it's still very much old-style didactic in tone, badly labelled and stuffy. You really need to invest an extra €3 in their multilingual audioguide.

All exhibits were unearthed locally. They include a vast collection of some 600 funerary urns carved mainly from alabaster and tufa and are displayed according to subject and period. Be selective, they all start to look the same after a while. The best examples (those dating from later periods) are on the 2nd and 3rd floors.

Original touches are the Ombra della Sera bronze *ex voto*, a strange, elongated nude figure that would fit harmoniously in any museum of modern art, and the urn of the Sposi, a terracotta rendering of an elderly couple, their faces depicted in portrait fashion rather than the usual stylised manner.

See the boxed text, p525, for admission information.

OTHER SIGHTS

On the city's northern edge lies the **Roman theatre** (☽ 10.30am-5.30pm daily mid-Mar–Oct, 10am-4pm Sat & Sun Nov–mid-Mar), a well-preserved complex complete with a Roman bathhouse.

The **Fortezza Medicea**, built in the 14th century and altered by Lorenzo il Magnifico, is nowadays a prison (you can't enter unless you plan to stay for a while). To its west is the pleasant **Parco Archeologico**. Little of

archaeological interest has survived, apart from a few battered Etruscan tombs but it's a good place for a picnic.

A combined ticket (€2) gives you entry to both.

Le Balze, a deep eroded limestone ravine about 2km northwest of the city centre, has claimed several churches since the Middle Ages as the buildings tumbled into its deep gullies. A 14th-century monastery, perched on the precipice, seems perilously close to continuing the tradition.

Festivals & Events

On the third and fourth Sundays of August, the citizens of Volterra roll back the calendar some 600 years, take to the streets in period costume and celebrate **Volterra AD 1398** with gusto and all the fun of a medieval fair.

Sleeping

Seminario di Sant'Andrea (☎ 0588 8 60 28; fax 0588 9 07 91; Viale Vittorio Veneto 2; d with/without bathroom €36/28; P) Still an active church retreat, this place is peaceful, if a mite dilapidated, with vaulted ceilings and 60 large, clean rooms. Open to all comers, it's a mere 600m or so from Piazza dei Priori, has free parking and makes an excellent budget choice.

Albergo Etruria (☎ 0588 8 73 77; Via Giacomo Matteotti 32; www.albergoetruria.it; s/d €60/80; ☽ Feb-Dec) Etruria is a pleasant, cosy hotel, recently taken over by two ladies with grand plans. The bathrooms have been freshly tiled and refurbished. Look for the remains of an Etruscan wall upstairs and savour the fine views from the roof garden – a genuine garden with lawns and bushes.

Albergo Nazionale (☎ 0588 8 62 84; www.albergonazionalevolterra.it; Via dei Marchesi 11; s/d/tr €50/69/80) Nazionale is a late-19th-century hotel where DH Lawrence once stayed. Rooms vary in size and style and some have balconies; room 403, with a pair of them, is your best option. Meals in its summertime restaurant are simple, solid and uncomplicated; the reception desk betrays the same qualities.

Albergo Villa Nencini (☎ 0588 8 63 86; www.villa nencini.it; Borgo S. Stefano 55; s/d with breakfast €60/83; P ☐ ☑) A tranquil family hotel, Villa Nencini is a mere 200m beyond Porta S Francesco yet a world away from the town's summer bustle. Choose the original 17th-century mansion or the recently constructed wing. Grounds are shady, views across the valley magnificent and, with access to its restaurant and impressive collection of wines, you're fully self-sufficient.

Appartamenti l'Etrusca (☎ 0588 8 40 73; letrusca@ libero.it; Via Porta all'Arco 37-41; 1-/2-/3-person apt €40/70/80) Unlike most such rental companies, this place is happy to take you in for even a single night. The exterior of this late-Renaissance building gives no hint of all the mod cons within.

Camping le Balze (☎ 0588 8 78 80; Via di Mandringa 15; person/tent/car €6/4/2; ☼ Easter-Oct; ☒) The closest camp site to town has a swimming pool and sits right on Le Balze.

Eating

Ristorante Don Beta (☎ 0588 8 67 30; Via Giacomo Matteotti 39; menus €13-18, mains €10-12; ☼ Tue-Sun) With four truffle-based *primi piatti* and five *secondi* (second courses) enhanced by their fragrance, this restaurant is the place to sample the prized fungus, which abounds – in so far as it abounds anywhere in the woods around Volterra. Do check on the price first. Or else, choose the local *ciandoli alle noci,* little spring-shaped whorls of pasta in a walnut sauce. The only downside is the flickering, if sotto voce, TV in the corner.

Trattoria del Sacco Fiorentino (☎ 0588 8 85 37; Piazza XX Settembre 18; mains €8-14; ☼ Thu-Tue) This is a great little vaulted trattoria that serves up imaginative dishes with a happy selection of local wines. Try the *coniglio in salsa di aglio e vin santo* (rabbit cooked in a garlic and dessert-wine sauce) or the mouthwatering gnocchi with baby veg.

Trattoria il Poggio (☎ 0588 8 52 57; Via Porta all'Arco 7; meals about €20; ☼ Wed-Mon) Il Poggio is a popular restaurant where the cheery wait-staff bustle around and find time to chat with the regulars while the electric dumb-waiter merely raises your food from the sub-terranean kitchen. There's a good set menu, an outdoor terrace and rich dishes such as risotto with clams, scampi and rocket.

Osteria dei Poeti (☎ 0588 8 60 29; Via Giacomo Matteotti 55; mains €8-16, tourist menus €12; ☼ Fri-Wed) Also extremely popular with locals, Osteria dei Poeti is another typical Tuscan rustic restaurant, all pleasing mellow brickwork and golden arches. The cuisine, however, is delightfully out of the ordinary. For starters, opt for the *antipasto del poeta,* a rich assortment of canapés, cheeses and cold cuts.

Pizzeria da Nanni (☎ 0588 8 40 47; Via delle Pregioni 40; pizzas €6-7; ☼ Mon-Sat) A hole-in-the-wall-plus – the plus being the excellent pizzas that Nanni spatulas from his oven, while sustaining a vivid line of backchat, notably with his long suffering wife.

Drinking

Web & Wine (Via Porta all'Arco 11-13; ☼ 7am-1am daily Mar-Oct, Wed-Mon Nov-Feb) At once an Internet point (Web access is €4 per hour), a stylish *enoteca* (with a good selection of tipples), a snack stop and hip designer café with underlit Etruscan remains. Surf your way through a foamy cappuccino while checking your inbox.

Getting There & Around

Driving and parking inside the walled town are more or less prohibited. Park in one of the designated areas around the circumference, most of which are free. There's a paying four-level underground car park beneath Piazza Martiri della Libertà, which is also the bus terminal.

The tourist office carries bus and train timetables. **CPT buses** (☎ 0588 8 61 86) connect the town with Saline (€1.55, 20 minutes, frequent) and its train station. From Saline, 9km to the southwest, there are bus connections for Pisa (€5.05, two hours) and Cecina (€3.20), to which there's also a train link.

For San Gimignano (€4.30, 1½ hours), Siena (€4.45, 1½ hours) and Florence (€6.95, two hours), change at Colle di Val d'Elsa (€2.25, 50 minutes), to where there are four runs daily except Sunday.

By car, take the SS68, which runs between Cecina and Colle di Val d'Elsa.

ABBAZIA DI SAN GALGANO

About 20km southwest of Siena on the SS73 is the 13th-century **San Galgano abbey** (☎ 0577 75 67 00; admission free; ☼ 8am-7.30pm), a fine Gothic ruin that still speaks strongly of its illustrious past. The monks of this former Cistercian abbey were among Tuscany's most powerful, forming the judiciary and acting as accountants for the *comune* of Volterra and Siena. They presided over disputes between the cities, played a significant role in the construction of the cathedral in Siena and built themselves an opulent church.

Nowadays, the walls still stand but the roof collapsed a long time ago. The Accademia

Musicale Chigiana in Siena sponsors concerts at the abbey during the summertime (see p518).

On a hillock overlooking the abbey is the tiny, round Romanesque **Cappella di Monte Siepi**, built for the local soldier and saint San Galgano, who lived his last years here as a hermit. A real-life 'sword in the stone' is under glass in the floor of the chapel, plunged there, legend has it, by San Galgano to indicate his renunciation of worldly life.

LE CRETE

Southeast of Siena, this area of rolling clay hills is a feast of classic Tuscan images: bare ridges topped by solitary cypress trees, hills silhouetted one against another as they fade into the misty distance, their gently undulating flanks scored here and there by steep ravines, as scarred and eroded as any cowboy's badlands. Its most harmonious valley, the Val d'Orcia, is the latest Italian area to be declared a Unesco World Heritage site. Hire a car or bike in Florence or Siena and spend a few days pottering around Le Crete, a Tuscan dialect word meaning clay. In summer, you could book your passage on the Treno Natura (p518).

Abbazia di Monte Oliveto Maggiore (☎ 0577 70 76 11; admission free; ✆ 9.15am–noon & 3.15-6pm Apr-Oct, to 5pm Nov-Mar), a 14th-century monastery, is still a retreat for around 40 monks. Frescoes by Signorelli and Sodoma decorate the Great Cloister, illustrating events in the life of the ascetic St Benedict.

MONTALCINO

pop 5100

A pretty town, perched high above the Orcia valley, Montalcino is best known for its wine, the Brunello, a rich red that has gained considerable international fame. There are plenty of wine cellars around town where you can taste and buy Brunello (a bottle costs a minimum of €20 – we did say it was special!) as well as other local wines such as Rosso di Montalcino.

If you're a jazz-loving oenophile, you'll savour the town's annual **Jazz & Wine festival**, held in the second and third weeks of July.

The **tourist office** (☎ 0577 84 93 31; www.prolocomontalcino.it in Italian; Costa Municipio 1; ✆ 10am-1pm & 2-5.40pm Apr-Oct, closed Mon Nov-Mar) is just off Piazza del Popolo, the main square. It can tell you which vineyards are open for tastings.

Sights

Museo Civico e Diocesano d'Arte Sacra (☎ 0577 84 60 14; Via Ricasoli 31; adult/child €4.50/3; ✆ 10am-1pm & 2-5.50pm Tue-Sun), just off Piazza Sant'Agostino, occupies a former monastery. In addition to canvases by Andrea di Bartolo, Sano di Pietro and others, it has a fine collection of painted wooden sculptures by the Sienese school.

Within the 14th-century **fortress** (☎ 0577 84 92 11; admission free; ✆ 9am-8pm Apr-Oct, to 6pm Nov-Mar) is an *enoteca* where you can sample and buy local wines. To walk the ramparts (though the view is almost as magnificent from the courtyard) buy a ticket (adult/child €3/1.50) at the bar.

A combined ticket giving full access to the museum and fortress costs €6.

There's a vigorous **Friday market** on and around Via della Libertà.

Sleeping & Eating

Il Giardino (☎ /fax 0577 84 82 57; Piazza Cavour 4; s/d €45/53) An excellent-value, friendly, family-run, two-star hotel. Occupying a venerable building overlooking Piazza Cavour, its décor has a distinct 1970s feel.

Hotel Il Giglio (☎ 0577 84 81 67; www.gigliohotel.com; Via S Saloni 5; s/d/tr €60/90/105; **P**) Montalcino's oldest hotel, recently substantially renovated, is another family concern. Rooms have comfortable wrought-iron beds – each gilded with a painted *giglio* (lily) – and all doubles have wonderful panoramic views. Il Giglio also has a small annexe (s/d €48/65), just up the street and a couple of apartments (two to four people €70 to €90). Room 1 has an enormous terrace that comes at no extra cost.

Both hotels have restaurants that are well worth a visit.

Hotel Vecchia Oliviera (☎ 0577 84 60 28; www.vecchiaoliviera.com; Angolo Via Landi 1; d with breakfast from €150; **P** **⊠** **⚛**) Just beside the Porta Cerbaia, this is a former olive mill, tastefully restored with earthy colours and terracotta tiles. Tranquil (it's at the very limit of the town), each of its rooms is individually decorated. The back patio has stunning views.

Taverna Il Grappolo Blu (☎ 0577 84 71 50; Scale di Via Moglio 1; meals €17-25) The chef here does ingenious things with local ingredients; try the juicy *coniglio al brunello* (rabbit cooked in Brunello wine).

Getting There & Away

Regular Tra-in buses (€3, 1½ hours, six daily) run to/from Siena.

ABBAZIA DI SANT'ANTIMO

This beautiful isolated Romanesque **church** (☎ 0577 83 56 59; Castelnuovo dell'Abate; ☺ 10.30am-12.30pm & 3-6.30pm Mon-Sat, 9-10.30am & 3-6pm Sun) lies in a broad valley just below the village of Castelnuovo dell'Abate. It's best visited in the morning, when the sun streams through the east windows.

The exterior, built in pale travertine stone, is simple but for the stone carvings set in the bell tower and apsidal chapels. Inside, take time to study the capitals of the columns lining the nave, especially the one representing Daniel in the lion's den (second on the right as you enter).

Three daily buses (€1, 15 minutes) connect Montalcino with the village of Castelnuovo dell'Abate. From here, it is an easy walk to the church.

PIENZA

pop 2250

Pienza, too often dismissed as Montepulciano's little sister, is well worth visiting for its own sake.

Information

Tourist office (☎ 0578 74 90 71; ☺ 9.30am-1pm & 3-6.30pm) On Piazza Pio II, the heart of this tiny village, within the Palazzo Comunale. It rents a 50-minute audioguide (one/two persons €5/8).

Sights

Spin 360 degrees and you've taken in Pienza's major monuments. Gems of the Renaissance and all constructed in a mere three years between 1459 and 1462, they're grouped around Piazza Pio II. The square is named after the pope who, in one of the earliest examples of town planning, commissioned the architect Bernardo Rossellino to rebuild the little town of his birth.

Highlights of the **cathedral** (☺ 8.30am-1pm & 2.15-7pm), with its Renaissance façade, are a superb marble tabernacle by Rossellino and five altarpieces, all by Sienese artists.

Palazzo Piccolomini, Padre Pio II's country residence, is considered to be Rossellino's masterpiece. From its loggia, there's spectacular panoramic views over the Val d'Orcia below.

Palazzo Borgia, also called the Palazzo Vescovile, houses Pienza's small **Museo Diocesano** (☎ 0578 74 99 05; adult/child €4.50/2.50; ☺ 10am-1pm & 3-6pm Wed-Mon mid-Mar–Oct, Sat & Sun Nov–mid-Mar) with paintings of the Sienese school and some striking 16th-century Flemish tapestries.

Almost a monument in its own right, the pungent **Bottega del Naturalista** (Corso Rossellino 16) has a truly mouthwatering choice of cheeses, in particular the renowned ewe's milk *pecorino di pienza*.

MONTEPULCIANO

pop 13,900

Set atop a narrow ridge of volcanic rock, Montepulciano looks down upon the superb countryside of the Valdichiana. A producer of some of the region's finest wines, including the highly reputed *vino nobile*, it's the perfect place to spend a quiet day or two.

Orientation

The town sheers off to the left and right from the main street, which rises steeply southwards from Porta al Prato to the Piazza Grande and fortress beyond. The 750m walk may leave you breathless but, bordered by the town's finest buildings, it is well worth the exercise.

Information

Strada del Vino Nobile di Montepulciano Information Office (☎ 0578 71 74 84; www.stradavinonobile.it; Piazza Grande 7; ☺ 10am-1pm & 3-7pm Mon-Sat Mar-Oct, to 6.30pm Nov-Feb) Among other activities, it arranges wine tours and tastings and leads an unstrenuous country walk, culminating in lunch. Can also book accommodation.

Tourist office (☎ 0578 75 73 41; www.prolocomontepulciano.it; Piazza Don Minzoni; ☺ 9.30am-12.30pm & 3-8pm Easter-Jul & Sep-Oct, 9.30am-8pm Aug, 9.30am-12.30pm Mon-Sat & 3-6pm Sun Nov-Easter) Can also reserve accommodation, has a couple of Internet points (per hr €4) and sells local bus tickets, plus train tickets for destinations throughout Italy.

Sights

Most of the main sights are clustered around Piazza Grande, although the town's streets harbour a wealth of palazzi, fine buildings and churches.

From the **Porta al Prato**, walk south along Via di Gracciano nel Corso. At the upper end of Piazza Savonarola is the **Colonna del**

Marzocca, erected in 1511 to confirm Montepulciano's allegiance to Florence. It's topped by a splendid stone lion, which is as squat as a pussycat.

Among several noble residences lining the main street is the **Palazzo Bucelli** at No 73, whose lower façades are recycled Etruscan and Latin inscriptions and reliefs. The **Palazzo Cocconi**, nearly opposite at No 70, was also designed by Sangallo.

Continuing up Via di Gracciano nel Corso, you will find Michelozzo's **Chiesa di Sant'Agostino** (Piazza Michelozzo; ⌚ 9am-noon & 3-6pm). Opposite, a medieval **tower house** is topped by the town clock, which strikes the hours, and the bizarre figure of Pulcinella (Punch of Punch and Judy fame).

Continue up the hill and turn right at the Loggia di Mercato, first left into Via del Poggiolo, then left again into Via Ricci. In the Gothic Palazzo Neri-Orselli is the **Museo Civico** (☎ 0578 71 73 00; Via Ricci 10; adult/child €4.15/2.60; ⌚ 10am-7pm Tue-Sun Aug, 10am-1pm & 3-6pm Tue-Sun Sep-Jul). The small collection features terracotta reliefs by the della Robbia family and Gothic and Renaissance paintings.

Overlooking Piazza Grande, which is the town's highest point, is the **Palazzo Comunale** (admission free; ⌚ 9am-1.30pm Mon-Sat). Built in the 13th-century Gothic style and remodelled in the 15th century by Michelozzo, it still functions as the town hall. From the top of its **tower** (admission €1.55; ⌚ Apr-Oct) on a clear day, you can see as far as the Monti Sibillini to the east and the Gran Sasso to the southeast (entry is on the 2nd floor).

Opposite is the **Palazzo Contucci** and its extensive wine cellar, **Cantine Contucci** (☎ 0578 75 70 06; ⌚ 8am-12.30pm & 2.30-6.30pm), which is open for visiting and sampling.

The 16th-century **cathedral** (Piazza Grande; ⌚ 9am-noon & 4-6pm) has an unfinished façade. Above the high altar is a lovely triptych by Taddeo da Bartolo of the Assumption.

Prominently positioned in the valley below is the domed **Chiesa di San Biagio** (Via di San Biagio; ⌚ 9am-12.30pm & 3-7pm summer, to 6pm winter), a fine Renaissance church built by Antonio da Sangallo the Elder; its highlight is a stunning marble altarpiece.

Sleeping & Eating

Meublé Il Riccio (☎ 0578 75 77 13; www.ilriccio.net; Via Talosa 21; s/d €75/85; P ✶ ▯) This is a gorgeous yet tiny hotel, with only six bedrooms, that occupies a Renaissance palazzo just off Piazza Grande. Rooms are cosy and the communal areas and porticoed courtyard are a delight in themselves.

Albergo Il Marzocco (☎ 0578 75 72 62; www.albergoilmarzocco.it; Piazza Savonarola 18; s/d with breakfast €60/95) The same family has run this hotel for more than a century. Rooms in this 16th-century building are large, comfortable and well furnished. Those with a balcony and views come at no extra cost.

Bellavista (☎ 0578 75 73 48, ☎ 0347 823 23 14; bellavista@bccmp.com; Via Ricci 25; d €50-65) If you are on a budget, Bellavista is an excellent choice. Nearly all of its 10 double rooms have fantastic views. No-one else lives here so phone ahead in order to be met and given a key. If you've omitted this stage, there's a phone in the entrance lobby from where you can call.

Trattoria Diva e Maceo (☎ 0578 71 69 51; Via di Gracciano nel Corso 90; meals €20-28; ⌚ Wed-Mon) This is a simple, uncomplicated trattoria, popular with locals, that carries a good selection of wines from the region.

Borgo Buio (☎ 0578 71 74 97; Via Borgo Buio 10; meals €30-40; ⌚ Sat-Thu) Borgo Buio has a menu that could scarcely be shorter. But then the quality of the cuisine could hardly be higher at this rustic, low-lit restaurant that also functions as an *enoteca*.

La Grotta (☎ 0578 75 74 79; Via San Biagio 2; meals €45-55; ⌚ Thu-Tue) Opposite the church of San Bagio, La Grotta is Montepulciano's finest restaurant. Inside this 15th-century building the dining is appropriately elegant while the tables in the garden are tempting for a summer lunch.

Caffè Poliziano (☎ 0578 75 86 15; Via di Voltaia nel Corso 27) Established as a café in 1868, Poliziano has had a chequered past: at times café-cabaret, minicinema, grocery and, once again since 1990, an elegant café, it has been lovingly restored to its original form by the current owners.

Getting There & Around

Tra-in runs five buses daily between Montepulciano and Siena (€4.45, 1¾ hours) via Pienza. Regular LFE buses connect with Chiusi (€2, 50 minutes, every 30 minutes) and continue to Chiusi-Chianciano Terme train station.

Chiusi-Chianciano Terme, 18km southeast and on the main Rome–Florence line, is the most convenient train station (rather than Stazione di Montepulciano, which has very infrequent services).

By car, take the Chianciano Terme exit from the A1 and follow the SS146. Cars are banned from the centre. There's car parks near the Porta al Prato, from where mini-buses weave their way to Piazza Grande.

SOUTHERN TUSCANY

MAREMMA

The Maremma extends along Tuscany's coast from just north of Grosseto to its southern border with Lazio, embracing the Parco Regionale della Maremma and Monte Argentario. Fronting the coast, it's an area of long sandy beaches and reclaimed marshland, crisscrossed by dikes and drainage ditches. Inland are the extraordinary hill towns of Sovana, Sorano and Pitigliano, each rich in Etruscan remains.

PARCO REGIONALE DELLA MAREMMA

This spectacular **nature park** (admission €6-8) includes the Monti dell'Uccellina, which drops to a magnificent stretch of unspoiled coastline. The main **visitors centre** (☎ 0564 40 70 98; www.parcomaremma.it; ✆ 7.30am-6.30pm Jul-Sep, 8.30am-1.30pm Oct–mid-Mar, 8.30am-4pm mid-Mar–Jun) is in Alberese, on the park's northern edge. Park access is limited to 11 signed walking trails, varying from 2.5km to 12km. Entry (by ticket bought at the visitors centre) varies according to whether a minibus transports you to your chosen route. Depending upon your trail, you stand a chance of spotting deer, wild boar, foxes and hawks.

The **Centro Turismo Equestre Il Rialto** (☎ 0564 40 71 02), 600m north of the visitors centre, offers guided canoe outings (adult/child €16/8, three hours) and horse-riding trips (€33) and also rents mountain bikes (€3/8 per hour/day).

To restore your energy after a walk, **Il Mangiapane** (☎ 0564 40 72 63; mains €7-9), beside the Centro Turismo Equestre Il Rialto, has a shaded wooden terrace where you can munch on a snack or something more substantial, including homemade pasta.

MONTE ARGENTARIO

Once an island but long ago linked to the mainland by a couple of extensive sand bars, the rugged Monte Argentario is popular with holidaying Romans and almost neglected by the rest of the world.

Orbetello

Sitting in the middle of three isthmuses, Orbetello speaks of Mediterranean lands further west. The main attraction is its **cathedral** (Piazza della Repubblica; ✆ 9am-noon & 3-6pm), which has retained its 14th-century Gothic façade despite being remodelled in the Spanish style in the 16th century. Other reminders of the Spanish garrison that was stationed in the city for nigh on 150 years include the Viceroy's residence on Piazza Eroe dei Due Mondi, the fort and the city walls, parts of which are the original Etruscan fortification.

Porto Santo Stefano

This one-time fishing port, like its neighbour Port'Ercole, now devotes itself in the main to tourism, much of it upmarket.

INFORMATION

Il Galeone (Lungomare dei Navigatori 40; per hr €5; ✆ 8am-midnight) A bar with a couple of Internet points.
Tourist office (☎ 0564 81 42 08; www.lamaremma.info; Piazzale Sant'Andrea; ✆ 9am-1pm & 3 5pm Mon-Sat) At the eastern end of the port.

ACTIVITIES

If you have wheels, follow signs for the Via Panoramica, a circular route offering great coastal views across to the hazy whaleback of the **Isola del Giglio**, Tuscany's second-largest island after Elba, across the water. For another spectacular drive, take a right turn 6km east of Porto Santo Stefano, up the signed road leading to **Convento dei Frati Passionisti**, a convent with sensational views across to the mainland.

There are plenty of reasonable pebbly beaches, one of the most popular is the long strip of **Feniglia**, northeast of Port'Ercole.

Toremar and Maregiglio sail regularly (adult/child return €10.60/5.40) to the Isola del Giglio, which makes a pleasant day trip.

SLEEPING

Pensione Weekend (☎/fax 0564 81 25 80; Via Martiri d'Ungheria 3; d from €55) This is a true gem. It was undergoing extensive renovation when we last visited so prices may have risen. The friendly, polyglot owner can give you a voucher entitling you to a 20% reduction at Lo Sfizio (p532).

TUSCANY

Albergo Belvedere (☎ /fax 0564 81 26 34; Via del Fortino 51; s/d with breakfast €60/100; ☯ May-Oct) This hotel is a luxury complex, 1km east of the harbour. Overlooking the water, it has its own private beach.

Hotel Torre di Cala Piccola (☎ 0564 82 51 11; www .torredicalapiccola.com; Cala Piccola; s/d/tr with breakfast €270/356/420; ☯ Apr-Oct; P ✕ 🖵) A self-contained complex built around an old Spanish watchtower, this hotel is 8km southwest of Porto Santo Stefano. Here, you can leave the crowds in your wake and enjoy spectacular seascapes in one of their luxury bungalows. A minibus transports you down the hillside to the hotel's private beach.

Camping Feniglia (☎ 0564 83 10 90; camping.feni glia@virgilio.it; person/site €9/12; ☯ year-round) In Feniglia, about 1.5km north of Port'Ercole, this camping ground is just 50m from the sea. The trouble is, most of the ground is occupied by permanently planted caravans and family tents.

EATING

Lo Sfizio (☎ 0564 81 25 92; Lungomare dei Navigatori 26; pizzas from €5.50, meals €22-30; ☯ daily Apr-Oct, Tue-Sun Nov-Mar) With its corny fish-theme décor and bar of blinking lights, this looks unpromising. But what draws in diners are the very reasonably priced fish and seafood dishes and the friendly informality of its staff.

Il Veliero (☎ 0564 81 22 26; Via Panoramica 149-151; meals €30-35; ☯ Tue-Sun Feb-Dec) This is an excellent restaurant, high above the port, that serves the freshest of fare from the sea – the owner's father runs a fish shop in town. It's a steep climb (head up the steps, guarded by a terracotta lion, just above Pensione Weekend) but well worth the exertion, especially if you've reserved a table at the small terrace with its plunging view.

Il Moletto (☎ 0564 81 36 36; Via del Molo 52; ☯ Thu-Tue) Among several enticing quayside seafood restaurants, Il Moletto wins for its location. At this wooden cabin, set apart from the rest at the end of a mole, you can dine beside a picture window or on the jetty as the evening breeze cools your pasta.

Trattoria Da Siro (☎ 0564 81 25 38; Corso Umberto 100; meals €30-35; ☯ Tue-Sun) Overlooking the waterfront, Da Siro also manages that same mix of well-prepared fish and seafood, spiced with an impressive seascape.

Pizzeria da Gigetto (☎ 0564 81 44 95; Via del Molo 9) For a great view without paying panoramic prices, grab a pizza from this pizzeria and munch it on the waterfront terrace, then finish off with an ice cream from Bar Gelateria Chioda, right next door.

GETTING THERE & AWAY

Frequent **Rama buses** (☎ 0564 85 00 00) connect most towns on Monte Argentario with downtown Orbetello (€1.50, 20 minutes) and continue to the train station. They also run to Grosseto (€3.40, one hour, up to four daily).

By car follow signs for Monte Argentario from the SS1.

ETRUSCAN SITES
Terme di Saturnia

This **thermal spa** (☎ 0564 60 01 11; www.termedi saturnia.it; day admission €16, 3pm-closing €12, parking €3; ☯ 9.30am-7.30pm Apr-Sep, 9.30am-5.30pm Oct-Mar) is about 2.5km south of the village of Saturnia. You can happily spend a whole day dunking yourself in the hot pools and signing on for some of the ancillary activities such as the alluring 'four-hand massage shower' or, for that light-as-air feeling, the 'infiltration of gaseous oxygen to reduce excess fat'.

On the other hand, if you just fancy a quick dip, head left down a dirt lane 700m south of the Terme turn-off and frolic for free in the warm waters that cascade down a gentle waterfall.

Pitigliano

Pitigliano seems to grow organically from the high rocky outcrop that towers over the surrounding countryside. The main monuments are within a stone's throw of Piazza Garibaldi, where you'll find the **tourist office** (☎ 0564 67 11; ☯ 10.20am-1pm & 3-7pm Tue-Sun Apr-Oct, 10.20am-1pm & 2-6pm Tue-Sun Nov-Mar).

SIGHTS

Off the square are an imposing 16th-century **viaduct** and the 13th-century **Palazzo Orsini** (☎ 0564 61 44 19; adult/child €2.50/1.50; ☯ 10am-1pm & 3-7pm Tue-Sun, to 5pm Oct-Mar). The latter's small museum houses a cluttered collection of ecclesiastical objects, assembled, you get the feeling, as much to fill the vast empty space as for any aesthetic merit.

Opposite is the altogether more organised **Museo Archeologico** (☎ 0564 61 40 67; Piazza della Fortezza; adult/child €2.60/1.55; ☯ 10am-1pm & 4-7pm Tue-Sun Apr-Sep, 10am-1pm & 3-6pm Tue-Sun Oct-Mar), with a rich display of finds from local Etruscan sites. They're well displayed but the descriptive panels are only in Italian.

Only the tall bell tower remains as a reminder of the Romanesque original of Pitigliano's **cathedral**, with its baroque façade and unexceptional interior.

The town's medieval lanes and steep alleys are a delight to wander, particularly around the small **Ghetto** quarter. Take Via Zuccarelli and turn left for **La Piccola Gerusalemme** (☎ 0564 61 60 06; Vicolo Manin 30; adult/child €2.50/1.50; 🕙 10am-12.30pm & 4-7pm Sun-Fri May-Oct, 10am-12.30pm & 3-5.30pm Sun-Fri Nov-Apr). The area fell into disrepair with the demise of Pitigliano's Jewish community at the end of WWII and was practically rebuilt from scratch in 1995. A visit includes the tiny, richly adorned synagogue and a small museum of Jewish culture, including the old bakery, kosher butchers and dyeing shops.

There are some spectacular walks around Pitigliano. The base of the rocky outcrop is stippled with Etruscan tomb caves carved into the soft tufa, many of them recycled as storage cellars. From there, you can follow a signed trail (about 6km) to Sovana.

SLEEPING & EATING

Albergo Guastini (☎ 0564 61 60 65; www.albergoguastini.it; Piazza Petruccioli 16; s/d/tr €36/62/80, meals about €25; 🕙 closed mid-Jan–mid-Feb) Pitigliano's only hotel is particularly friendly and welcoming. Perched on the edge of the cliff face, many of its rooms have marvellous views. Its highly regarded restaurant also merits a visit.

Osteria Il Tufo Allegro (☎ 0564 61 61 92; Vico della Costituzione 2; mains €13-17.50; 🕙 Thu-Mon, dinner Tue & Wed) Just off Via Zuccarelli. The aromas emanating from its kitchen should be enough to draw you into the cavernous chamber, carved out of the tufa rock foundations.

Il Forno (Via Roma 16) Pick up a stick or two of *sfratto*, a gorgeously sticky local confection made of honey and walnuts, from this place. Counterbalance the sweetness with a glass or two of the town's excellent dryish Bianco di Pitigliano wine.

GETTING THERE & AWAY

Rama buses (☎ 0564 61 60 40) go between Pitigliano and Grosseto's train station (€5.50, two hours, four daily). They connect Pitigliano with Sorano (€2.45, 15 minutes, seven daily) and Sovana (€2.45, 20 minutes, one daily).

Sovana

Sovana is really little more than a one-street village of butterscotch-coloured sandstone – but, gosh, it's pretty. The **tourist office** (☎ 0564 61 40 74; 🕙 10am-1pm & 3-7pm daily Mar-Nov, Fri-Sun Dec-Feb) is in the Palazzo Pretorio.

Opposite, the **Chiesa di Santa Maria** is a simple square-shaped Romanesque church with some rich Renaissance frescoes and, over the altar, a magnificent 9th-century ciborium, or canopy, in white marble.

Walk west along Via del Duomo to reach the imposing Gothic-Romanesque **cathedral**. Although largely rebuilt in the 12th and 13th centuries, the original construction dates back to the 9th century. The striking portal on the north wall is pieced together from fragments of this earlier building – or, as some would maintain, from a pagan temple.

Sovana was the birthplace of Pope Gregory VII; at the eastern end of the village are a cluster of medieval mansions and the remains of a fortress that belonged to his family.

Within the **Necropoli di Sovana** (admission €5.50; 🕙 9am-7pm daily mid-Mar–Oct, 9am-5pm Fri-Sun Nov–mid-Mar), 1.5km south of the village, are Tuscany's most significant Etruscan tombs, the grandest of which is the **Tomba Ildebranda**, the only surviving temple-style tomb.

The area is famous for its *vie cave*, deep, narrow sunken walkways carved into the rock by the Etruscans. Drovers' roads? Ceremonial passages? Trenches for safe movement in time of attack? To this day no-one knows their purpose. The most spectacular can be as much as 20m deep and run for up to 1km. You'll pass a typical one 500m west of Pitigliano on the road to Sovana.

Taverna Etrusca (☎ 0564 61 61 83; www.sovanahotel.it; Piazza Pretorio 16; s/d €60/80; 🕙 Feb-Dec) is a three-star hotel whose simple but attractive rooms have stripped wooden floors. Its **restaurant** (mains €10-12; 🕙 Thu-Tue), in the hands of a new and vastly experienced cook, serves mainly Tuscan specialities and always has at least one vegetarian option.

Albergo Scilla (☎ 0564 61 65 31; www.scilla-sovana.it; Via R Siviero 1-3; d with breakfast €92; 🅿 🔀) has eight terracotta-and-white rooms with marshmallow-soft pillows and attractive wrought-iron beds, mosaic bathrooms and a quiet garden. Across the road you can enjoy fine fare at its attractively glassed-in restaurant, **Ristorante**

dei Merli (meals about €35; ☼ Tue-Sun), which also has vegetarian options.

Sorano

Sorano is something of the poor relation of the three hill towns. High on a rocky spur, its houses, many of which are nowadays unoccupied, seem to huddle together in an effort not to shove one another off their precarious perch. The town's main attraction is the partly renovated **Fortezza Orsini** (Piazza Cairoli; admission €2; ☼ 10am-1pm & 3-7pm Apr-Sep, 10am-1pm & 2.30-5pm Fri-Sun Oct-Mar).

A few kilometres out of Sorano on the road to Sovana is the **Necropoli di San Rocco**, another Etruscan burial area.

EASTERN TUSCANY

AREZZO

pop 92,450

Heavily bombed during WWII, Arezzo is not exactly one of Tuscany's prettiest cities. That said, the small medieval centre packs some inspiring highlights: the sloping Piazza Grande, the Pieve di Santa Maria and, of course, the five-star frescoes by Piero della Francesca in the Chiesa di San Francesco. The setting for much of Roberto Benigni's Oscar-winning film *Life Is Beautiful*, it's well worth a visit, easily accomplished as a day trip from Florence.

Arezzo, in its time an important Etruscan town, was later absorbed into the Roman Empire. A free republic as early as the 10th century, it supported the Ghibelline cause in the violent battles between pope and emperor and was eventually subjugated by Florence in 1384.

It's also the birthplace of the Renaissance poet Petrarch, who popularised the sonnet format, penning his verses in both Latin and Italian, and Giorgio Vasari, the prolific painter and architect who contributed so much to Renaissance Florence.

Arezzo stages a huge and highly reputed antiques fair, pulling in more than 500 exhibitors and spreading over the Piazza Grande and surrounding streets, on the first weekend of every month.

North of town is the Parco Nazionale delle Foreste Casentinesi, a wooded national park that takes in some of the Apennines' most spectacular scenery.

Orientation

From the train station on the southern edge of the walled city, pedestrianised Corso Italia leads to the Piazza Grande, Arezzo's nucleus.

Information

Centro di Accoglienza Turistico (☎ 0575 40 35 74; Via Ricasoli; ☼ 9.30am-5.30pm Apr-Sep, to 7pm Jul-Aug, 10am-5pm Oct-Mar)

Eutelia (Via Guido Monaco 61; per hr €1.50; ☼ 9am-9pm) Internet access and cheap international phone calls.

Post office (Via Guido Monaco 34)

Tourist office (☎ 0575 2 08 39; www.apt.arezzo.it; Piazza della Repubblica 28; ☼ 9am-1pm & 3-7pm Mon-Sat, 9am-1pm Sun Apr-Sep, 9am-1pm & 3-6.30pm Mon-Sat Oct-Mar) Can reserve accommodation for personal callers (fee €3).

Sights & Activities

CHIESA DI SAN FRANCESCO

Gracing the apse of this 14th-century **church** (Piazza San Francesco; ☼ 8.30am-noon & 2-6.30pm) is one of the greatest works of Italian art, Piero della Francesca's fresco cycle of the *Legend of the True Cross*. This masterpiece relates in 10 episodes a highly coloured subsequent history of the cross on which Christ was crucified.

You can get some sense of the frescoes from beyond the cordon in front of the altar, but to really appreciate them up close you need to plan ahead for a **visit with audioguide** (reservations ☎ 0575 35 27 27; www.pierodellafrancesca .it; admission €6; ☼ every 30min 9am-6.30pm Mon-Sat, 1-5pm Sun Apr-Oct, 9am-5.30pm Mon-Sat, 1-5pm Sun Nov-Mar). Since only 25 people are allowed in every half-hour, it's essential to prebook by phone or at any of the sites that participate in the combined ticket scheme. The ticket office is at Piazza San Francesco 4.

PIEVE DI SANTA MARIA

This 12th-century **church** (Corso Italia 7; ☼ 8am-1pm & 3-7pm May-Sep, 8am-noon & 3-6pm Oct-Apr) has a magnificent Romanesque arcaded façade, in form reminiscent of the cathedral at

---

COMBINED TICKETS

You can buy a combined ticket (€14) giving entry to the Piero della Francesca frescoes in the Chiesa di San Francesco, plus Museo Archeologico, Museo Statale d'Arte Medievale e Moderna and Casa di Vasari at any of the four venues.

AREZZO

INFORMATION
Centro di Accoglienza Turistico.....**1** B2
Eutelia...**2** A4
Post Office...**3** B3
Tourist Office....................................**4** A4

SIGHTS & ACTIVITIES
Casa di Petrarca...............................**5** C3
Casa di Vasari...................................**6** B2
Cathedral...**7** C2
Chiesa di San Domenico.................**8** B2
Chiesa di San Francesco.................**9** B3
Museo Archeologico.....................**10** B4

Museo Statale d'Arte
   Medievale e Moderna.......**11** B2
Palazzo della Fraternità dei
   Laici.......................................**12** C3
Palazzo delle Logge Vasariane..**13** C3
Pieve di Santa Maria...............**14** C3
Roman Amphitheatre...............**15** B4

SLEEPING 🛏
Cavaliere Palace.......................**16** B3
Hotel Continentale..................**17** A3
Hotel Patio...............................**18** B3
La Terrazza...............................**19** B3

EATING 🍴
Antica Trattoria da Guido......**20** B3
La Buca di San Francesco......**21** B3
La Lancia d'Oro.......................**22** C3
La Torre di Gnicche.................**23** C3
La Tua Piadina.........................**24** B3
Ristorante Logge Vasari.........**25** C3
Trattoria il Saraceno...............**26** B3

TRANSPORT
Bus Station...............................**27** A3

TUSCANY

Pisa, yet without the glorious marble facing. Over the central doorway are lively carved reliefs representing the months of the year. The 14th-century bell tower with its 40 apertures is something of an emblem for the city. The monochrome of the interior's warm, grey stone is relieved by Pietro Lorenzetti's fine polyptych, *Madonna and Saints,* beneath the semidome of the apse.

PIAZZA GRANDE & AROUND
The porticoes of **Palazzo delle Logge Vasariane**, completed in 1573, overlook this cobbled piazza. In the northwest corner, **Palazzo della Fraternità dei Laici**, with its churchlike façade, was started in 1375 in the Gothic style and finished after the onset of the Renaissance.

Via dei Pileati leads to **Casa di Petrarca**, the poet's former home.

CATHEDRAL
Arezzo's **cathedral** (Piazza del Duomo; 🕑 6.30am-12.30pm & 3-6.30pm) was started in the 13th century yet was not completed until well into the 15th century. In the northeast corner, left of the main altar, an exquisite fresco of *Mary Magdalene* by Piero della Francesca is dwarfed in size, but not beauty, by the rich marble reliefs of the tomb of Bishop Guido Tarlati.

CHIESA DI SAN DOMENICO & AROUND
The short detour to the **Chiesa di San Domenico** (Piazza San Domenico 7; 🕑 8.30am-7pm) is a must in

order to see its haunting *Crucifixion* – one of Cimabue's earliest works, painted around 1265 – which rears above the main altar. To the west, the **Casa di Vasari** (☎ 0575 40 90 40; Via XX Settembre 55; adult/child €2/1; ☼ 8am-7.30pm Mon & Wed-Sat, 8.30am-1pm Sun) was built and sumptuously decorated (overwhelmingly so in the case of the Sala del Camino, the Fireplace Room) by the architect himself; ring the bell if the door's closed.

Down the hill, the **Museo Statale d'Arte Medievale e Moderna** (☎ 0575 40 90 50; Via San Lorentino 8; admission €4; ☼ 8.30am-7.30pm Tue-Sun) houses works by local artists, including Luca Signorelli and Vasari, spanning from the 13th to 18th centuries.

MUSEO ARCHEOLOGICO & ROMAN AMPHITHEATRE

East of the train station, the **archaeological museum** (☎ 0575 2 08 82; Via Margaritone 10; admission €4; ☼ 8.30am-7.30pm) is in a convent overlooking the remains of a **Roman amphitheatre** (admission free; ☼ 7.30am-8pm, to 6pm Nov-Mar). Among the highlights of the museum, which has a sizable collection of Etruscan and Roman artefacts, is an exquisite tiny portrait of a bearded man executed on glass in the 3rd century AD.

CENTRO DI ACCOGLIENZA TURISTICO

The centre, which also serves as a tourist office (see p534), hires out audioguides on Arezzo (adult/child per day €5/3) together with an accompanying map. It also projects *Arezzo da Vedere*, a 15-minute audiovisual show (adult/child €2/1.50) that gives a vivid overview of the city.

Sleeping

Villa Severi (☎ 0575 29 90 47; www.peterpan.it; Via F Redi 13; dm/d €15/35; ☼ year-round) A non-HI youth hostel, Villa Severi is northeast of town in a wonderfully restored and spacious villa overlooking the countryside. Take bus No 4 from Piazza Guido Monaco.

La Terrazza (☎ 0575 2 83 87; laterrazza@lycos.it; 5th fl, Via Guido Monaco 25; s/d with breakfast €35/50) With shared bathrooms, La Terrazza is welcoming and excellent value. Essentially a couple of stylish apartments on two floors, its five rooms are large and light, there's a kitchen for guest use and the landlady bakes the tastiest of cakes. Go down the passage beside Blockbuster.

Cavaliere Palace (☎ 0575 2 68 36; www.cavaliere hotels.com; Via Madonna del Prato 83; s/d with breakfast €93/135; **P** ☒) This place is a reliable four-star choice, barely 100m from the station, that offers a friendly welcome. Rooms, while unexciting, are snug, well soundproofed and more than adequate. Parking is €13.

Hotel Patio (☎ 0575 40 19 62; www.hotelpatio.it; Via Cavour 23; s/d/ste from €130/176/224; **P** ☒) This is Arezzo's most characterful hotel, with seven themed rooms, each dedicated to one of Bruce Chatwin's travel books. Each has original furnishings from the various countries represented, including Australia, China and Morocco. Valet parking is €18.

Hotel Continentale (☎ 0575 2 02 51; www.hotel continentale.com; Piazza Guido Monaco 7; s/d €67/98; **P** ☒ ☐) A modern, central three-star option, with comfy, spotless rooms. There's individual Internet access in every room, a bar that tempts you to linger and a roof terrace with fine views. Valet parking costs €15.

Camping Le Ginestre (☎ 0575 36 35 66; Via Ruscello 100; person/site €8/13; ☼ year-round) This is the nearest camp site. Take LFI bus No S2, in the direction of Viciomaggio.

Eating

Antica Trattoria da Guido (☎ 0575 2 37 60; Via Madonna del Prato 85; meals from €18; ☼ Mon-Sat) Wood-panelled and with ochre walls, this is an economical family-run trattoria that serves up excellent home-style food. Its short handwritten menu changes regularly, according to what's best in the market.

Trattoria Il Saraceno (☎ 0575 2 76 44; Via G Mazzini 3a; mains €6.50-10.50; ☼ Thu-Tue) Sixty years in business, this trattoria serves quality, varied Tuscan fare at very reasonable prices. The impressive wine collection, to suit all palates and pockets, is arrayed around every wall and they also do pizzas (from €5).

La Buca di San Francesco (☎ 0575 2 32 71; Via San Francesco 1; mains €8-9.50; ☼ Wed-Sun & lunch Mon) La Buca, arched and vaulted, is all soft angles and shapes, its walls decorated with alluring frescoes. Mains are good value and it does three fixed menus (€13, €16 and €19), styled *frate*, *abate* and *priore* (friar, abbot and prior), as befits a restaurant that nudges against the church of San Francesco.

La Torre di Gnicche (☎ 0575 35 20 35; Piaggia San Martino 8; mains about €9; ☼ Thu-Tue) Just off Piazza Grande, this is a fine traditional restaurant offering a rich variety of antipasti. Choose from the ample range of local *pecorino* cheeses, accompanied by a choice red from its extensive wine list.

These next two restaurants, each with a terrace under the loggia that looks down over Piazza Grande, are run by two brothers.

La Lancia d'Oro (☎ 0575 2 10 33; Piazza Grande 18-19; mains €11-13; ☷ Tue-Sat & lunch Sun) This is a sophisticated place with fresh flowers on the tables and where your order is supplemented by excellent snacks and titbits that arrive unannounced. There's a jolly, waggish waiter, while the interior, painted with swags and green-and-white stripes, makes you feel like you're dining in a marquee.

Ristorante Logge Vasari (☎ 0575 30 03 33; Via Vasari 19; mains €12-14; ☷ Wed-Mon) This restaurant has two pleasant interior rooms and serves equally delectable cuisine. You'll leave satisfied and satiated if you treat yourself to the innovative *menu degustazione* (€36).

La Tua Piadina (☎ 0575 2 32 40; Via de' Cenci 18) A justifiably popular takeaway place hidden away down a side street, where you can get a range of hot and tasty *piadine*, the Emilia version of the wrap, from around €3.

Piazza Sant'Agostino comes alive each Tuesday, Thursday and Saturday with the city's produce market.

Getting There & Away

Bus services from Piazza della Repubblica include to Cortona (€2.60, one hour, over 10 daily), Sansepolcro (€3, one hour, seven daily) and Siena (€5, 1½ hours, seven daily). For Florence, you're better off hopping on the train.

Arezzo is on the Florence–Rome train line with frequent services to Rome (€20.70, two hours) and Florence (€10.10, 1½ hours). Trains also call by Cortona (€2.10, 20 minutes, hourly). Arezzo is just a few kilometres east of the A1 and the SS73 heads east to Sansepolcro.

SANSEPOLCRO
pop 15,750

Sansepolcro is an important stop on an itinerary of Piero della Francesca's work. Between the two, make a brief stop in Monterchi to see the artist's famous fresco **Madonna del Parto** (Pregnant Madonna; ☎ 0575 7 07 13; Via della Reglia 1; adult/child €3.10/free; ☷ 9am-1pm & 2-7pm Tue-Sun Apr-Sep, to 6pm Oct-Mar). A sensitive touch: pregnant women also get free admission.

Sansepolcro is the birthplace of Piero della Francesca. The artist left town when quite young and returned in his seventies to work on his treatises, including his seminal *On Perspective in Painting*.

There's a small **tourist office** (☎ 0575 74 05 36; infosansepolcro@apt.arezzo.it; Via Matteoti 8; ☷ 9am-1pm & 3.30-6.30pm Apr-Sep, 9.30am-12.30pm & 3.30-5.30pm Mon-Sat, 9.30am-12.30pm Sun Oct-Mar) in town.

Within the **Museo Civico** (☎ 0575 73 22 18; Via Aggiunti 65; adult/child €6.20/3; ☷ 9am-1.30pm & 2.30-7.30pm Jun-Sep, 9.30am-1pm & 2.30-6pm Oct-May), just round the corner from the tourist office, are a couple of Piero della Francesca masterpieces: his *Resurrection*, and the *Madonna della Misericordia* polyptych, where the Virgin spreads her protective cloak over the painting's benefactors.

The **Locanda Giglio & Ristorante Fiorentino** (☎ 0575 74 20 33; Via I Pacioli 60; s/d/tr with breakfast €45/70/95, meals €20-25; P ✄) is an exceptionally friendly hotel and restaurant that's been in the same family for four generations. The four hotel rooms with their oak floors, underfloor lighting and period furniture recovered from the family loft have been imaginatively renovated by Alessia, an architect and youngest of the family (ask for La Torre with a lovely low bed and the best of the views), while Dad, Alessio, still runs the restaurant with panache. The pasta's homemade and the imaginative menu changes with the seasons (Alessio tells you with pride that there'll never be a freezer in *his* kitchen).

SITA buses link Sansepolcro with Arezzo (€3, one hour, seven daily) and there are several trains daily to Perugia (€4.40, 1¾ hours).

CORTONA
pop 22,300

Set high on a hillside cloaked in olive groves, Cortona offers stunning views across the Tuscan countryside. In the late 14th century Fra Angelico lived and worked here, and fellow artists Luca Signorelli (1450–1523) and Pietro da Cortona (1596–1669) were both born within the walls.

Large chunks of *Under the Tuscan Sun*, the soap-in-the-sun film of the book by Frances Mayes, were shot in Cortona. (You'll look in vain, though, for the fountain in which the eccentric Englishwoman cavorts; it was built specially for the occasion.)

A full week of merriment in May or June (the date varies to coincide with Ascension day) culminates in the Giostra dell'Archidado, a crossbow competition first held in the Middle Ages. Among other festivities, contestants from the city's traditional neighbourhoods dress up in medieval garb to compete for the *verretta d'oro* (golden arrow).

Orientation

Piazzale Garibaldi, on the southern edge of the walled city, is where buses arrive. From it, there are sensational views across the plain to Lago di Trasimeno. From the piazzale, walk straight up Via Nazionale – about the only flat street in the whole town – to Piazza della Repubblica, the main square.

Information

Pensieri Grandi e Piccoli (Via Guelfa 36; per hr €5; 🕑 10am-1pm & 2-6pm Mon-Sat) An eccentric souvenir shop with two Internet terminals.

Tourist office (☎ 0575 63 03 52; Via Nazionale 42; 🕑 9am-1pm & 3-7pm Mon-Sat, 9am-1pm Sun May-Sep, 9am-1pm & 3-6pm Mon-Fri, 9am-1pm Sat Oct-Apr)

Sights

Brooding over lopsided Piazza della Repubblica is the **Palazzo Comunale**, built in the 13th century, renovated in the 16th and once again in the 19th. To the north is attractive **Piazza Signorelli** and, on its north side, 13th-century **Palazzo Casali**, whose rather plain façade was added in the 17th century. Inside is the **Museo dell'Accademia Etrusca** (☎ 0575 63 04 15; Piazza Signorelli 9; adult/child €4.20/1.50; 🕑 10am-7pm Apr-Oct, 10am-5pm Tue-Sun Nov-Mar), which displays substantial local Etruscan finds, including an elaborate 2nd-century BC oil lamp.

Little is left of the original Romanesque character of the **cathedral**, northwest of Piazza Signorelli. It was completely rebuilt late in the Renaissance and again, indifferently, in the 18th century. Its true wealth lies in the **Museo Diocesano** (☎ 0575 6 28 30; Piazza del Duomo 1; adult/child €5/1; 🕑 10am-7pm Apr-Oct, 10am-5pm Tue-Sun Nov-Mar) in the former church of Gesù. Its fine collection includes works by Luca Signorelli and a beautiful *Annunciation* and *Madonna* by Fra Angelico.

Wriggle up through a sleepy warren of steep cobbled lanes in the eastern part of town to the largely 19th-century **Chiesa di Santa Margherita** (Piazza Santa Margherita; 🕑 7.30am-noon & 3-7pm Apr-Oct, 8.30am-noon & 3-6pm Oct-Apr).

Within is the ornate 14th-century tomb of Cortona's patron saint, Margherita – whose remains, in fact, are in the coffin above the main altar. It's a stiff climb, but worth it – and it is worth pushing even further uphill to the forbidding **Fortezza Medicea** (☎ 0575 60 37 93; adult/child €3/1.50; 🕑 10am-6pm May-Sep), Cortona's highest point, with stupendous views over the surrounding countryside.

Courses

Polymnia (☎ 0575 61 25 82; www.polymnia.net; Vicolo Boni 18) offers Italian language courses and related cultural and social activities for non-native speakers.

Tours

Cortona Wellness (☎ 0575 60 31 36; www.cortonawellness.it in Italian) organises guided four- to five-hour hikes (around €15 per person) in the spectacular countryside around the town.

Sleeping

Hotel San Michele (☎ 0575 60 43 48; www.hotelsanmichele.net; Via Guelfa 15; s/d with breakfast from €83/134; 🕑 mid-Mar–Dec; Ⓟ 🐾) Just off Piazza della Repubblica, San Michele is Cortona's finest hotel. Primarily Renaissance but with elements dating from the 12th century and modifications over subsequent centuries, it's like a little history of Cortona in stone. Rooms are airy, spacious and exquisitely furnished. Parking is €11.

Hotel Italia (☎ 0575 63 02 54; www.planhotel.com /hitalia; Via Ghibellina 5/7; s/d/tr with breakfast €75/100/125; 🐾) Italia, recently taken over and extensively renovated by the new owners, is in a 17th-century palazzo just off Piazza della Repubblica. Rooms have traditional cross-beamed ceilings and are decorated in warm orange and ochre colours. Views are breathtaking from the roof-level breakfast room.

Ostello San Marco (☎ 0575 60 13 92; ostellocortona@libero.it; Via Maffei 57; dm/d with breakfast €12/32; 🕑 year-round) Cortona's HI-affiliated hostel is in a former monastery, a short, steep walk east of Piazzale Garibaldi. It's a fairly run-down and ill-cared for place, despite the impressive premises.

Eating

Osteria del Teatro (☎ 0575 63 05 56; Via Maffei 2; mains €8.50-15; 🕑 Thu-Tue) This *osteria*, in a grand converted palazzo, has friendly service and fresh flowers on every table. Featuring in just about every Italian gastronomic guide, its walls are clad with photos of actors who have played and dined in town. In summer, try the *ravioli ai fiori di zucca* (pumpkin-flower ravioli). Downsides are the over-obtrusive music and that staple of 'Italian' restaurants outside Italy – a giant phallus of a pepperpot that the waitress handles with difficulty.

Ristorante Tonino (☎ 0575 63 05 00; Piazza Garibaldi 1; meals about €30-35; ☯ Wed-Sun & lunch Mon) This place has magnificent views as far as Lago di Trasimeno from its summer terrace and specialises in antipasti. Try the *ravioli al tartufo e pecorino* (ravioli with truffles and *pecorino* cheese).

Pane e Vino (☎ 0575 63 10 10; Piazza Signorelli 27; ☯ Tue-Sun) Pane e Vino is a huge and hugely popular dining hall, right in the heart of town. For a quick snack of regional specialities, go for the *piatto del cacciatore* (the hunter's platter of wild boar, deer, goose and turkey). There are more than 500 wines to choose from and most of the pasta (€5.20 to €6) is homemade.

Trattoria Dardano (☎ 0575 60 19 44; Via Dardano 24; meals €15-20; ☯ Thu-Tue) This is just one of half a dozen reliable, no-nonsense trattorie that line Via Dardano.

Bottega della Pasta Fresca (Via Dardano 29) Self-caterers should stock up at this glorious little hole-in-the-wall shop that makes its own pasta.

There's a Saturday **market** (Piazza Signorelli), which sells farmers' products.

Getting There & Around

From Piazzale Garibaldi, LFI buses connect the town with Arezzo (€2.60, one hour, over 10 daily), via Castiglion Fiorentino.

The nearest train station on the main Rome–Florence line is about 6km away at Camucia–Cortona, to which shuttle buses (€1, 15 minutes) run at least hourly. Destinations include Arezzo (€2.10, 20 minutes, hourly), Florence (€6.50, 1½ hours, hourly), Rome (€8.90, 2¼ hours, every two hours) and Perugia (€2.70, 40 minutes, over 12 daily).

The tourist office has timetables and sells both bus and train tickets.

By car the city is on the north–south SS71 that runs to Arezzo. It's also close to the SS75 that connects Perugia to the A1.

TUSCANY

Umbria & Le Marche

A magical landscape of mountains, dotted with olive trees, draped by grape vines, its summits studded with hill towns, both Umbria and Le Marche offer superb art and architectural treasures that reflect thousands of years of history and culture. The Etruscans and Romans left their mark as did the popes, who conquered the independent city *comuni* (town councils) that grew out of the Middle Ages and ruled a network of Papal States across central Italy.

Despite the network of roads, the area has not yet bowed to the tyranny of tourism and an astonishing amount of the landscape appears to have remained unchanged for centuries.

In Umbria, which gave birth to more than its fair share of saints and painters, the beautifully preserved medieval towns of Perugia, Gubbio and Todi, St Francis' home town of Assisi and the extraordinary cathedral in Orvieto seem to hover under the same hazy light that inspired the medieval masters. To the east, Le Marche hugs the Adriatic coast with its international port city of Ancona and beach resorts, but its charm mostly lies in the hills with exquisite, undiscovered treasures such as Urbino, a preserved Renaissance city deemed a World Heritage site; Macerata and its spectacular Arena Sferisterico; and Ascoli Piceno, which rivals any Italian town with its sheer abundance of history.

After having enough of art and history, head to the mountains – the Monti Sibillini – to walk or wander, to glide or ski, ride bikes or horses along deserted tracks, climb rocks or spy rare species of birds and flowers in the superbly maintained national parks.

HIGHLIGHTS

- Swing to cool **Umbria Jazz** (p548) in the heat and heart of cultured Perugia
- Stay at a serene luxury ecohostel in the middle of the activity-happy **Lago di Trasimeno** (p556)
- Explore the life of St Francis and his spiritual and artistic influence in the magnificent **Basilica di San Francesco** (p558) in Assisi
- Hike, bike, ski or camp the forested peaks of the mystical **Monti Sibillini** (p596)
- Marvel at the Duke of Montefeltro's Ideal City – **Urbino** (p585) – the Renaissance in microcosm
- Fifty years of tradition has perfected Umbria's best *gelato* at the unassuming **Bar Pianegiani** (p557) in unhurried Todi

★ Urbino

★ Perugia

Lago di ★ ★ Assisi
Trasimeno

Monti
Sibillini
★

★ Todi

- POPULATION: Umbria 840,482; Le Marche 1.4 million
- AREA: Umbria 8,456 sq km; Le Marche 9,691 sq km

UMBRIA

Every inch of Umbria is ancient. The landscape of rolling hills and meandering country roads has been perfected over three millennia. The only province in Italy that borders neither the sea nor another country, Umbria has retained many traditions. You'll see grandmothers in aprons making pasta by hand and front doors that haven't been locked in a century. In spring the countryside is splashed with red, pink, yellow, purple and blue wild flowers. In summer it explodes with the vibrant yellow of the sunflowers harvested to make cooking oil. The rolling mountains of the Apennines in the north and east descend into hills, many capped by medieval towns, and eventually flatten out into lush valleys along the River Tiber.

Perugia, a short distance west and the region's capital, is a stunning city of great cultural traditions that enjoys a lively nightlife fired by the city's two universities, including a Università per Stranieri (University for Foreigners). Spoleto offers an international arts festival, Gubbio practically begs for hours and hours of aimless wandering, Assisi is perhaps tied to its famous son more than any other place on Earth.

This is a land of tastes and flavours. Nature is fundamental to the Umbrian. Umbria even has a special department – l'Assessorato alle Politiche Agricole e Forestali della Regione dell'Umbria – to protect and promote products typical of the area. Umbrian cuisine is simple but delicious and based on locally grown ingredients, perfected over the centuries. *Tartufo* (truffle) is used in sauces, pasta and rice dishes. Umbria's *porcini* (a type of mushroom) can be added to pasta or rice, but are best eaten as 'steaks'. Orvieto's golden wines and the Sagrantino of Montefalco are respected throughout Europe.

History

Prehistoric remains, conserved largely in the Archaeological Museum in Perugia, reveal a human presence here as far back as the Palaeolithic and Neolithic periods. Around 1000 BC the Oscan-Umbrians swept into the region. Later, the Etruscans settled the western bank of the Tiber, founding the towns of Perugia and Orvieto, and eventually creating 12 powerful city-states. But the Umbrian civilisation really began to decline when it came into contact with Rome. By the end of the 2nd century BC Rome had all the towns of Umbria under its control and had initiated great public works such as the Via Flaminia, which joined Rome with the upper Adriatic. Remains of the Roman period can still be seen in Perugia, Assisi, Foligno, Gubbio, Todi, Spoleto, Narni and Terni.

The Saracen invasions of the 5th and 6th centuries ended Roman rule and caused the Umbrians to retreat to fortified medieval hill towns such as Gubbio and Todi.

With the barbarian hordes constantly at the gates, Christianity found fertile terrain and began to flourish. One of the first religious buildings in Umbria, the church of Sant'Angelo, was built in Perugia between the 5th and 6th century.

St Benedict was born in Norcia in 480 and, a few centuries later, the Benedictine monastic order was founded at San Pietro in Perugia. From the first centuries of the late medieval period and throughout the 13th and 14th centuries, monasticism spread throughout Umbria.

By the 11th century the main cities in the region had become independent city-republics, united in a strong spiritual current generated by the religious movements. But domination by the Goths, the Lombards and various ruling families, as well as centuries of Guelph–Ghibelline rivalry, led to a long decline that left Umbria ripe for papal rule from the early 16th century.

In the 14th century, *signorie,* or dominions ruled by powerful noble families, flourished.

TOP FIVE OTHERWORLDLY EXPERIENCES

- Get in touch with the spirit of St Francis in his **crypt** (p560) at sunrise.
- Commune with fairies and talking wolves at **Monti Sibillini** (p597).
- Teeter precariously up Mt Ingino in a **birdcage funicular** (p565) in Gubbio.
- Spend a day in the biblical **Medieval Gardens** (p547) in Perugia – be sure to bring an apple.
- Descend into the Ancona abyss at the **Grotte di Frasassi** (p589).

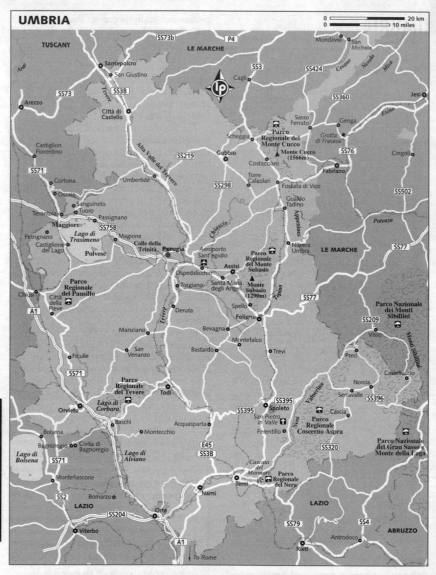

UMBRIA

But eventually all of Umbria came to be controlled as part of the Papal States, and remained so until the 19th century.

National Parks & Reserves

Umbria shares the beautiful Parco Nazionale dei Monti Sibillini with Le Marche (see p596). Filled with waterfalls, walking trails, camp sites and the odd wolf, this is a world away from the vineyards and medieval art that make up the rest of central Italy. Check the official website at www.sibillini.net for more on activities and accommodation.

East of Gubbio, the Parco Regionale del Monte Cucco is dotted with caves, many of which can be explored, and is well set up for

---

USEFUL WEBSITES ON UMBRIA

These websites will help you navigate your way through Umbria.

Bella Umbria (www.bellaumbria.net) This is the most comprehensive website on Umbria; the Events and Traditions page allows you to search for festivals by either town or date.

TourinUmbria (www.tourinumbria.org) A complete listing of accommodation, restaurants and itineraries accessible to travellers with physical disabilities.

Umbria2000 (www.umbria2000.it) The official Umbrian tourist website.

Umbria Trasporti (www.umbriatrasporti.it) Useful for train and bus information; you can also dial ☎ 800 512 141 while in Italy to get instant information.

---

walkers, rock climbers and horse riders. For more information on the park, visit www .parks.it/parco.monte.cucco.

Getting Around

Getting around Umbria on public transport requires some forethought. Conversely, having a car is a hindrance in several congested hill towns. The best way to see Umbria is to take the train or bus to Assisi, Spoleto, Perugia, Orvieto or Gubbio and rent a car for a week and wander through the countryside.

Extensive bus routes, state train services and the private **Ferrovia Centrale Umbra** (Umbrian Central Railway; FCU; ☎ 075 57 54 01; www.fcu.it in Italian) make most areas of the region easily accessible. For general Umbria transport information, call ☎ 800 512 141 (you will rarely be connected to someone who speaks English, but if you're well practised in Italian numbers, and can tell them the city, they'll usually patiently tell you the prices and times of day that trains leave) or check out the website at www.umbriatrasporti.it (the 'English version' button is practically hidden just under the main heading). For information and ticket sales for local and out-of-town services, call ☎ 800 892 021, or the FCU.

PERUGIA
pop 153,857

One of Italy's best-preserved medieval hill towns, Perugia is also a hip student town with a never-ending stream of cultural events, restaurants to try and concerts to attend.

Perugia has a lively and bloody past. The Umbrii tribe inhabited the surrounding area and controlled land stretching from present-day Tuscany into Le Marche, but it was the Etruscans who founded the city, which reached its zenith in the 6th century BC. It fell to the Romans in 310 BC and was given the name Perusia. During the Middle Ages the city was racked by the internal feuding of the Baglioni and Oddi families and violent wars against its neighbours. In the mid-13th century Perugia was home to the Flagellants, a curious sect whose members whipped themselves as a religious penance. In 1538 the city was incorporated into the Papal States under Pope Paul III, remaining under papal control for almost three centuries. It was during this time as a Guelph city that Perugia warred against many of its neighbouring towns.

Perugia has a strong artistic and cultural tradition. In the 15th century it was home to fresco painters Bernardino Pinturicchio and his master Pietro Vannucci, who was to teach Raphael. This city also attracted the great Tuscan masters Fra Angelico and Piero della Francesca. Today, the Università per Stranieri, established in 1925, offers courses in Italian and attracts thousands of students from all over the world.

Orientation

Old Perugia's main strip, Corso Vannucci (named after the artist Pietro Vannucci, known as Perugino), runs south to north from Piazza Italia (where buses and taxis congregate) through Piazza della Repubblica and finally ends in the heart of the old city at Piazza IV Novembre, bound by the cathedral and the Palazzo dei Priori. Most places listed in this chapter are just a short walk from this gathering point. Intercity buses will drop you off at Piazza dei Partigiani, from where you can take the *scala mobili* (escalator) up to Piazza Italia. From the train station (officially called Perugia Fontivegge but the sign simply reads 'Perugia') take bus No 7, 11 or 15 to Piazza Italia. Perugia's local transport service is run by Azienda Perugina della Mobilità (APM).

Information
BOOKSHOPS

La Libreria (☎ 075 573 50 57; Via Oberdan 52; ☻ 9am-8pm Mon-Sat, 9am-1pm & 4.30-8pm Sun) Stocks

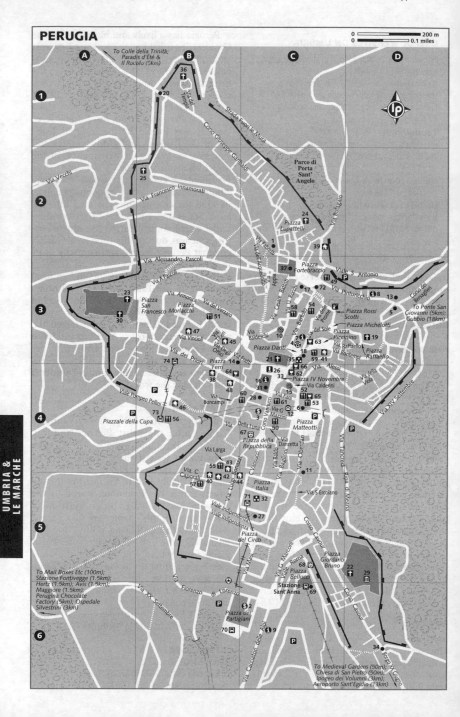

PERUGIA

0 — 200 m
0 — 0.1 miles

UMBRIA &
LE MARCHE

INFORMATION

67 Laundry	1	C2
ATM	2	C6
Banca del Umbria	3	C4
Centro Omnitel	4	C3
CTS	5	D3
Farmacia San Martino	6	C4
Il Periscopio	7	C3
InformaGiovani	8	D3
InfoUmbria	9	C6
Internet Point	10	C3
La Libreria	11	C4
Main Post Office	12	C4
Onda Blu	13	D3
Police Station	(see 16)	
Solidarietà Totale	14	B3
Tempo Reale	15	C4
Tourist Office	16	C4

SIGHTS & ACTIVITIES

Arco Etrusco	17	C3
Associazione Umbria Jazz	18	C3
Cappella di San Severo	19	D3
Cassero di Porta Sant'Angelo	20	B1
Cathedral	21	C3
Chiesa di San Domenico	22	D5
Chiesa di San Francesco al Prato	23	A3
Chiesa di Sant'Agostino	24	C2
Chiesa San Francesco delle Donne	25	B2
Collegio del Cambio	(see 31)	
Collegio della Mercanzia	(see 31)	
Fontana Maggiore	26	C4
Galleria Nazionale dell'Umbria	(see 31)	
Giardini Carducci	27	C5
Istituto Europeo di Arti Operative	28	C4
Museo Archeologico Nazionale dell'Umbria	29	D5
Oratorio di San Bernardino	30	A3
Palazzo dei Priori	31	C4
Palazzo della Provincia	32	C5
Piazza IV Novembre	33	C4
Porta San Pietro	34	D6
Pozzo Etrusco	35	C3
Rocca Paolina	(see 32)	
Sala dei Notari	(see 31)	
Tempio di Sant'Angelo	36	B1
Università per Stranieri	37	C3

SLEEPING

Anna	38	B4
Atena Service	39	C2
Casa Spagnoli	40	B5
Centro Internazionale per la Gioventù	41	C3
Eden	42	B5
Fortuna	43	B4
La Rosetta	44	B5
Morlacchi	45	B3
Paola	46	B4
Primavera Mini Hotel	47	B3
Priori	48	B4

EATING

Augusta Perusia Cioccolato	49	C3
Caffè di Perugia	50	C4
Caffè Morlacchi	51	B3
Coop	52	C4
Covered Market	53	C4
Il Falchetto	54	C3
Il Segreto di Pulcinella	55	B4
La Cambusa	56	B4
Osteria Il Ghiottone	57	B5
Pizzeria Etrusca	58	C3
Pizzeria Mediterranea	59	C3
Ristorante Il Bacio	60	C4
Sandri	61	C4

DRINKING

Bar Centrale	62	C4
Bottega di Vino	63	C3
Cinastik	64	B4
La Terrazza	65	C4
Shamrock Pub	66	C4

ENTERTAINMENT

Cinema Teatro del Pavone	67	C4
Velvet	68	C5

TRANSPORT

Ferrovia Centrale Umbra	69	C6
Intercity Bus Station	70	B6
Rocca Paolina Scale Mobile	71	C5
Scooty Rent	72	C3
Via dei Priori Scale Mobile	73	B4
Via dei Priori Scale Mobile	74	B3

a selection of English-language books, as well as maps and Lonely Planet guidebooks.

EMERGENCY

Police station (☎ 075 572 32 32; Palazzo di Priori)

INTERNET ACCESS

Over a dozen Internet cafés have popped up, most charging around €1.50 per hour. If you'll be spending some time in Perugia, buy an *abbonamento* discount card from the café you frequent the most. They usually cost €12 for 10 hours.

Tempo Reale (☎ 075 573 55 33; Via del Forno 17; 8am-10pm) Central, friendly, with high-speed connection and ample opening hours.

INTERNET RESOURCES

Perugia Online (www.perugiaonline.com) Information on accommodation, food, history, activities and sights.

Umbria Online (www.umbriaonline.com) Has a link to every town in Umbria, with some great info on Perugia.

LAUNDRY

Consider staying at Casa Spagnoli Bed & Breakfast (p549), where they'll do your laundry free of charge if you stay over two nights. Both the following options cost an incredibly pricey €3 each to wash and dry.

67 Laundry (Via Pinturicchio; 8am-10pm) Sells single serves of detergent.

Onda Blu (Corso dei Bersaglieri 4; 9am-10pm)

LEFT LUGGAGE

Train station (per bag 1st 12hr €3, next 12hr €2; 6.30am-7.30pm)

MEDIA

A must-have for students or anyone staying in Perugia for longer than a few hours is the English-language *The Little Blue Book*, available free at many locations, including Teatro del Pavone and newsstands around town. Find restaurant and housing suggestions, side trips and a description of the local characters.

The Comune di Perugia's monthly publication *Viva Perugia – What, Where, When* (€0.80 from newsstands) lists events, transport schedules and useful information.

MEDICAL SERVICES

Emergency doctor (☎ 075 3 40 24) Weekends and nights.

Farmacia San Martino (Piazza Matteotti 26; 24hr) Pharmacy.

Ospedale Silvestrini (☎ 075 75 81; S Andrea della Frate) Hospital with emergency services.

MONEY

Many banks line Corso Vannucci. All have ATM machines. Cashing travellers cheques inside usually garners a 2% to 5% service charge. There is also an ATM at Stazione Fontivegge.

POST

Mail Boxes Etc Via D'Andreotto 71 (☎ 075 50 17 98); Via della Pallotta 2b/5 (☎ 075 3 60 80) Both are between the train station and town. Instead of lugging a heavy suitcase, send your packages home FedEx, Airborne Express or DHL.

Main post office (Piazza Matteotti; ☼ 8am-6.30pm Mon-Sat)

TELEPHONE

Centro Omnitel (☎ 075 572 37 78; Piazza Danti 17) Buy your indispensable Italian *telefonino* here, or, if you have a GSM compatible phone, purchase an Italian SIM card to pop in your own phone. You can then purchase *ricarica* (recharge) cards in denominations of €10, €15, €20 or €50 for more talk time.

Tempo Reale (☎ 075 573 55 33; Via del Forno 17; ☼ 8am-10pm) Phone calls cost €0.11 a minute to the US, Canada, UK, Australia and most places in Europe. South Africa is €0.16. Internet here costs €1.20 an hour.

TOURIST INFORMATION

Il Periscopio (☎ 075 573 08 08; Via del Sole 6) This privately run tourist-information service also books cooking, Italian-language, painting and ceramics courses.

InformaGiovani (☎ 075 572 06 46; www.comune .perugia.it/informagiovani in Italian; Via Idalia 1; ☼ 10am-1.30pm Mon-Fri, 3.30-5pm Mon-Wed) Assists young travellers and students living in Perugia with information on Italian culture, work opportunities, education and travelling abroad. Young people should come here just to gaze at the flyers offering apartments for rent, band gigs etc. Free Internet use for clients. The office is off Via Pinturicchio.

InfoUmbria (☎ 075 57 57; www.infoumbria.com in Italian; Largo Cacciatori delle Alpi 3; ☼ 9am-1.30pm & 2.30-6.30pm Mon-Fri, 9am-1pm Sat) Private Info-Umbria, also known as Infotourist, offers information on all of Umbria, and is a fantastic resource for *agriturismi* (farm-stay or country-inn accommodation), festivals, sights, hotels and general information. Internet costs €1 for 30 minutes. It's near the Piazza dei Partigiani intercity bus station.

Solidarietà Totale (☎ 075 572 31 75; Via A Fratti 18) Information on gay and lesbian events.

Tourist office (☎ 075 573 64 58; info@iat.perugia.it; Palazzo dei Priori, Piazza IV Novembre 3; ☼ 8.30am-1.30pm & 3.30-6.30pm Mon-Sat & 9am-1pm Sun) Opposite the cathedral. Most of the staff at Umbrian tourist offices do not speak English.

TRAVEL AGENCIES

CTS (☎ 075 572 70 50; Via del Roscetto 21) Specialises in budget and student travel and sells International Student Identity Cards (ISIC) to students studying at the university.

Sights

HISTORIC CENTRE

The centre of Perugia – and therefore the centre of Umbria – is **Piazza IV Novembre**. For thousands of years, it was the meeting point for the ancient Etruscan and Roman civilisations. In the medieval period, it was the political centre of Perugia. Now students and tourists come here to eat *gelato*.

At the northern end of the piazza is the **cathedral** (☎ 075 572 38 32; Piazza IV Novembre). Although a church has been on this land since the 900s, the version you see was begun in 1345 from designs created by Fra Bevignate in 1300. Building of the cathedral continued until 1587, and the doorway was built in the late 1700s; however, the main façade was never completed. Inside you'll find dramatic Gothic architecture, an altarpiece by Signorelli and sculptures by Duccio. The **steps** in front of the cathedral's pink façade is where all of Perugia seemingly congregates.

In the middle of the Piazza IV Novembre stands the **Fontana Maggiore** (Great Fountain). It was designed by Fra Bevignate, but it was left to father-son team Nicola and Giovanni Pisano to build the fountain between 1275 and 1278. Along the edge are bas-relief statues representing scenes from the Old Testament (including Eve seducing Adam), the founding of Rome, the 'liberal arts', and a griffin and a lion. Look for the griffin all over Perugia – it's the city's symbol.

At the southern end of the piazza starts the block-long **Palazzo dei Priori** (Corso Vannucci 1), a virtual cornucopia of the best museums Umbria has to offer. Start in the stunning **Galleria Nazionale dell'Umbria** (National Gallery of Umbria; ☎ /fax 075 574 14 00; adult/concession/EU citizen under 18 & over 65 €6.50/3.50/free; ☼ 8.30am-7.30pm, closed 1st Mon of month), entered on Corso Vannucci, an art historian's dream come true, with 30 rooms of art dating as far back as the 13th century, as well as rooms dedicated to works from home-town heroes Perugino and Pinturicchio.

The three other **museums** (☼ 9am-12.30pm & 3-7pm Mon-Sat summer, often closed winter afternoons) in the palazzo include the gilded **Collegio del Cambio** (Exchange Guild; ☎ 075 572 85 99), which consists of three rooms: the Sala dei Legisti (Legislative Chamber), with wooden stalls carved by Zuccari in the 17th century; the Sala dell'Udienza (Audience Chamber), with frescoes by Perugino; and the Chapel of San

Giovanni Battista, painted by Giannicola di Paolo, a student of Perugino's. The **Collegio della Mercanzia** (Merchant's Guild; ☎ 075 573 03 66) highlights an older audience chamber, from the 13th century, covered in wood panelling by northern craftsmen. A combined ticket for both *collegi* is €4/3 adult/concession. The **Sala dei Notari** (Notaries' Hall; ☎ 075 574 12 74; admission free) was built between 1293 and 1297 and is where the nobility met. The arches supporting the vaults are Romanesque, covered with frescoes depicting biblical scenes and Aesop's fables. To reach the hall, walk up the steps from the Piazza IV Novembre.

At the southern end of Corso Vannucci is the tiny **Giardini Carducci**, with lovely views of the countryside. The gardens stand atop a once-massive 16th-century fortress, now known as the **Rocca Paolina**, built by Pope Paul III in the 1540s and standing over a medieval quarter formerly inhabited by some of the city's most powerful families. Destroyed by the citizens of Perugia after Italian unification, the ruins remain a symbol of defiance against oppression. A series of *scale mobili* run through the Rocca and you can wander around inside the ruins, which are often used for art exhibitions.

You'll think you have left the city altogether at the **Medieval Gardens** (guided tour information ☎ 075 585 64 32; Borgo XX Giugno 74; admission free; ☼ 8am-6.30pm), behind the Chiesa di San Pietro, 300m southeast of the city. These gardens date back to the medieval period at a time when monasteries were creating gardens full of biblical symbolism. Bring a picnic, pick up a brochure (in English) from the university to tour through each numbered stop, and make a day of it. Guided tours are free, but there's no guarantee you'll get someone who speaks English, as tours are usually given by graduate students from the university (and they occur extremely sporadically).

In front of the medieval gardens is the 10th-century **Chiesa di San Pietro** (☎ 075 3 47 70; Borgo XX Giugno; ☼ 8am-noon & 4pm-sunset), entered through a frescoed doorway in the first courtyard. The interior is an incredible mix of gilt and marble and contains a *Pietà* by Perugino. Many of the paintings in this church depict biblical women.

You can buy a combined ticket called the **Perugia City Museum Circuit** (adult/senior/child €2.50/2/1), which is valid for one week, at any of the three following sights. First, you can venture down into the 3rd-century-BC **Pozzo Etrusco** (Etruscan Well; ☎ 075 573 36 69; Piazza Danti 18; ☼ 10.30am-1.30pm & 2.30-6.30pm Apr-Oct, 10.30am-1.30pm & 2.30-4.30pm Nov-Mar). The 36m-deep well was the main water reservoir of the Etruscan town. The second stop is the **Cappella di San Severo** (☎ 075 573 38 64; Piazza Raffaello; ☼ 10.30am-1.30pm & 2.30-6.30pm Apr-Oct, 10.30am-1.30pm & 2.30-4.30pm Nov-Mar), decorated with Raphael's *Trinity with Saints* (thought by many to be his first fresco) and frescoes by Perugino. The third museum included is the **Cassero di Porta Sant'Angelo** (panoramic tower; ☎ 075 573 36 69; Porta Sant'Angelo; ☼ 11am-1.30pm & 3-6.30pm Apr-Oct, 11am-1.30pm & 3-5pm Nov-Mar). The panoramic view facing back on to Perugia is the main reason to come out here, plus it offers a historical briefing of the three city walls.

Walking down towards the Università per Stranieri takes you to an **Arco Etrusco** (Etruscan Arch), one of two ancient city gates. The official name is the Arco d'Augusto, named after the Roman emperor Octavian. Its lower section is Etruscan, dating from the 3rd century BC; the upper part is Roman and bears the inscription 'Augusta Perusia'. The loggia on top dates from the Renaissance.

North along Corso Giuseppe Garibaldi is the **Chiesa di Sant'Agostino** (Piazza Lupattelli; ☼ 8am-noon & 4pm-sunset), with a beautiful 16th-century choir by sculptor and architect Baccio d'Agnolo. Small signs forlornly mark the places where artworks once hung before they were carried off to France by Napoleon and his men. Further north along the same thoroughfare, Via del Tempio branches off to the Romanesque **Tempio di Sant'Angelo** (☎ 075 57 22 64; Via Sant'Angelo; ☼ 10am-noon & 4-6pm), said to stand on the site of an ancient temple. The columns inside the round church were taken from earlier buildings. Be sure to look for hidden symbolism carved into the walls.

Along Corso Cavour, the **Chiesa di San Domenico** (☎ 075 573 15 68; Piazza Giordano Bruno; ☼ 8am-noon & 4pm-sunset), built in the early 14th-century, is the city's largest church. Its Romanesque interior, lightened by the immense stained-glass windows, was replaced by austere Gothic fittings in the 16th century. Pope Benedict XI, who died after eating poisoned figs in 1325, lies buried here. The adjoining convent is the home of the **Museo Archeologico Nazionale dell'Umbria** (☎ 075

572 71 41; Piazza Giordano Bruno 10; adult/concession/EU citizen under 18/over 65 €2/1/free; ❤ 8.30am-7.30pm Tue-Sun, 2.30-7.30pm Mon), which has an excellent collection of Etruscan pieces and a section on prehistory. The most important item in the collection is the *Cippo Perugino*, the Perugian Memorial Stone, a travertine stone with one of the longest Etruscan language engravings.

OUT OF TOWN

Around 5km southeast of the city, at Ponte San Giovanni, is the **Ipogeo dei Volumni** (☎ 075 39 33 29; Via Assisana; adult/concession/child & EU citizen under 18 €3/1.50/free; ❤ 9am-1pm & 3.30-6.30pm Sep-Jun, 9am-12.30pm & 4.30-7pm Jul-Aug), a 2nd-century-BC Etruscan burial site. An underground chamber contains a series of recesses holding the funerary urns of the Volumnio family. The grounds are a massive expanse of partially unearthed burial chambers with several buildings housing the artefacts that weren't stolen. Take a train or APM bus No 3 from Piazza Italia to Ponte San Giovanni and walk west from there. By car, take the Bonanzano exit heading south on the E45.

Get in touch with your inner Willy Wonka at the **Perugina chocolate factory** (☎ 075 527 67 96; Van San Sisto; admission free; ❤ 8.30am-1pm & 2-5pm Mon-Fri). Granted, you'll learn more than you'd ever want to know about the business practices of a chocolate company, but you get as many free samples as you could ever possibly ingest at once, and there's a shop filled with all sorts of chocolate goodies. Take bus No 7 almost to the end of the line and ask the bus driver to let you off at 'La Perugina'.

Courses

The list of courses available to locals and foreigners in and around Perugia could constitute a book in itself. You can learn Italian, take up ceramics, study music or spend a month cooking. The tourist office has details of all available courses.

The **Università per Stranieri** (University for Foreigners; ☎ 075 5 74 61; www.unistrapg.it; Palazzo Gallenga, Piazza Fortebraccio 4) was set up in 1932 by Benito Mussolini to improve the image of Italy abroad. It worked pretty well. This incredibly popular university offers courses in language, literature, history, art, music and architecture, to name a few. A series of degree courses are available, as well as one-, two- and three-month intensive language courses and advanced and refresher courses

for teachers of Italian abroad. The most basic language course costs €233 per month.

Istituto Europea di Arti Operative (☎ 075 573 50 22; www.ieao.it in Italian; Via dei Priori 14; ❤ 10am-12.30pm) runs courses in fashion, industrial and interior design, graphic design, architecture, restoration, drawing and painting. All classes are taught in Italian.

Tours

From April until September, **Guide in Umbria** (☎ 075 573 29 33; www.guideinumbria.com in Italian; Info-Umbria office, Largo Cacciatori delle Alpi 3) offers small eight-person coach tours to surrounding towns in Umbria. If you don't want to rent a car or your schedule doesn't fit in with the train or bus times, this is a perfect solution. Prices are reasonable, from €20 to €39 for a full-day trip. The tours visit Assisi, Orvieto and Gubbio, but they're especially beneficial for places such as the Valnerina or the areas around Lago di Trasimeno because you'll be able to see things that wouldn't be accessible without a vehicle.

Contact Il Periscopio (p546) for day-long cooking or art courses.

Festivals & Events

Perugia – and Umbria in general – has no less than 80 gazillion events, festivals, concerts, summer outdoor movies and *sagre* (traditional festivals). Not surprisingly, most festivals are between May and October, but tourist offices will have a list of all the festivals throughout the year.

Chill out to the world-famous **Umbria Jazz** (☎ 075 573 24 32; www.umbriajazz.com), attracting performers like BB King, Patti LaBelle, Buena Vista Social Club and Chick Corea. Tickets cost from €5 to €50, but you needn't spend a dime to tune in; jam sessions spill out onto the streets and in cafés throughout the day and into the wee hours, including a late night New Orleans Brass Band finale. InfoUmbria (p546) can help you to book accommodation and tickets.

Sagra Musicale Umbra (Holy Music Festival; ☎ 075 572 13 74; www.sagramusicaleumbra.com in Italian) is one of the oldest music festivals in Europe. Begun in 1937, the festival is held in Perugia in mid-May and features world-renowned conductors and musicians.

In January and June, the **Amici della Musica** (☎ 075 572 52 64; www.amicimusicapg.it) organise a series of classical music concerts in some of

UMBRIA &
LE MARCHE

Perugia's most atmospheric venues. Students with ID can get tickets for under €10.

For ballet–lovers, there are performances in Perugia and around from January to April, organised by the **Fondazione Umbria Spettacolo** (☎ 075 572 67 64; www.balletumbria.com in Italian).

For tickets for performances by the Amici della Musica and Fondazione Umbria Spettacolo, buy online, over the phone, or inquire at the tourist office.

Serious chocoholics might be willing to put up with the overwhelming crowd scene at **Eurochocolate**, which occurs from mid- to late October each year. Hundreds of booths associated with chocolate set up for the week, plying their wares to the addicted.

Sleeping

Perugia has a fine array of hotels and *pensioni* (small hotels or guesthouses), and is a good place to stay if you're using public transport for the entire time or just part of your trip. You can get a 10-pass bus ticket (€7.20) to travel to the train station and take one- or two-day trips to virtually anywhere in Umbria, and many places in Tuscany. There's no reason to stay outside the historic centre; it's noisier, less charming and not much cheaper.

High-season rates are listed here, but almost every hotel offers a discount during the low season, which varies from place to place, but is usually January to March, November to early December and possibly August.

RENTAL ACCOMMODATION

Be warned that apartment services in Perugia have a reputation for ripping people off. One such scam is to find all sorts of fake problems requiring the hefty security deposit they've already retained, leaving the traveller, who has to catch a train in an hour, no choice but to count it up as experience.

Atena Service (☎ 075 573 29 92; www.atenaservice .com; Via del Bulagaio 38) can arrange accommodation from €200 per month for a shared room in an apartment, and from €550 per month for a one-bedroom apartment to yourself.

Il Periscopio (p546) can also arrange rental accommodation.

There are several ways to go about it yourself. Ask at the tourist office, which can help with pricier weekly accommodation. On Wednesday and Saturday, check *Cerco e Trovo* for apartment listings. Be sure to

call before noon, as rooms go quick. Once in town, you can check posted flyers at the Università per Stranieri (opposite) or at Informa-Giovani (p546) for rental accommodation.

BUDGET
Hotels & B&Bs

Casa Spagnoli Bed & Breakfast (☎ 075 573 51 27, 340 350 38 93; www.perugiaonline.com/bbspagnoli; Via Caporali 17; s/d/tr with shared bathroom & breakfast €37/56/68) Feel like you're staying with your long-lost Italian third cousins at this comfortable and spacious private home. Join in on the Wednesday night yoga class or talk politics with the international Spagnolis, who speak fluent Italian, Spanish, French and English. It offers a small weekly discount and it's perfectly located near Piazza Italia, so it makes an ideal base for exploring Umbria by public transport from Perugia. If you stay two days or more, they'll even do your laundry for free!

Morlacchi (☎ 075 572 03 19; morlacchi@tiscalinet.it; Via Tiberi 2; s €40, s/d €54/65) This friendly, family-run two-star hotel is a popular choice, so phone ahead for reservations. Offers good discounts in the off season.

Paola (☎ 075 572 38 16; Via della Canapina 5; s/d €33/52) It's a great bet if you want use of your own kitchen without the lockout of the hostel. Eight simply furnished rooms. Take bus No 6 or 7 heading towards Piazza Italia and get off at the Pellini car park. Signs will point you up the steps to the right. From the city centre, walk down Via dei Priori.

Also available:

Anna (☎ /fax 075 573 63 04; annahotel@hotmail.com; Via dei Priori 48; s/d €30/48, with bathroom from €40/62; **P**) An eclectic 4th-floor walk up.

Eden (☎ 075 572 81 02; fax 075 572 03 42; Via C Caporali 9; s/d/tr €40/60/77, breakfast €5) There isn't much else in this hotel's favour other than it being cheap and central.

Camping & Hostels

The city has two camp sites, both in Colle della Trinità, 5km northwest of the city and reached by taking bus No 9 from Piazza Italia (ask the driver to drop you off at the Superal supermarket, from where it's a 300m walk to the camp sites).

Paradis d'Été (☎ 075 517 31 21; www.emmeti.it /Welcome/Umbria/Perugia/Alberghi/Paradis/; Via del Mercato 29a, Str Fontana, Colle della Trinità; person/tent/car €6.20/4.65/2.85; ☼ year-round; ☒) This camp site has 50 well-shaded sites in a park-like setting with good facilities and a swimming pool. If you're tentless, you can rent a bungalow for up to six people (€41 to €96 depending on the season and how many people).

Il Rocolo (☎ /fax 075 517 85 50; ilrocolo@ilrocolo.it; Str Fontana 1n, Loc Colle della Trinità; person/tent/car €6/5/2.50; ☺ mid-Apr–Sep) Il Rocolo has over 100 sites with a bit of shade and all the standard facilities, including an on-site restaurant, minimarket, *bocce* (bowls) and playground. It's 6km from the city centre, near highway E-45. A minibus makes the journey back and forth several times a day.

Centro Internazionale per la Gioventù (☎ /fax 075 572 28 80; www.ostello.perugia.it; Via Bontempi 13; dm €12, sheets €1.50; 🖳) If the 9.30am to 4pm lockout and the midnight curfew (*no* exceptions) don't scare you off, then you'll appreciate the sweeping countryside view and wafting sounds of church bells from the hostel's terrace, where guests often gather after making dinner in the well-stocked kitchen. Enjoy the 16th-century frescoed ceilings.

MIDRANGE

Primavera Mini Hotel (☎ 075 572 16 57; www.prima veraminihotel.com; Via Vincioli 8; s/d/tr €48/70/90) This central and quiet hotel run by a dedicated English- and French-speaking mother and daughter team is a fabulous find, quietly tucked in a corner. The surrounding magnificent views complement the bright and airy rooms and common areas. All rooms come with private bath, telephone and TV. Hopefully, they won't find out how much more they should be charging.

Fortuna (☎ 075 572 28 45; www.umbriahotels.com; Via Luigi Bonazzi 9; s/d/tr with breakfast €86/124/167; 🐾 🖳) In a location both quiet and central, this spotlessly clean hotel is partially housed in a building dating back to the 1300s. Ancient stone, frescoes and Venetian plaster walls gracefully accompany comfortable new furnishings, parquet floors and thankfully modern bathrooms.

Priori (☎ 075 572 91 55; www.hotelpriori.it; Via dei Priori; s/d with breakfast €66/95; P) Have breakfast on the stunning rooftop terrace. Parking is €15/25 for a small/large car.

TOP END

La Rosetta (☎ /fax 075 572 08 41; www.perugiaonline .com/larosetta; Piazza Italia 19; s/d/tr €79/120/160; P 🐾) You'll be so close to the centre of Perugia you can practically crawl to most sights. Although the building is hundreds of years

old, the décor includes pieces from both the 18th century and the 1920s. Updated with computer outlets, Sky TV and modern showers, and offering conference space and meeting rooms, La Rosetta is a business hotel where travellers are just as comfortable. La Rosetta has got a few parking spots that are free to its guests, but once these are taken, you'll have to park in a parking garage which costs €20.

Eating

Because of the great number of students and tourists, the amount of places to eat in Perugia is staggering. A pizzeria is around every corner, and there are dozens of restaurants. There's not a lot of choice, though: most serve an extremely similar array of Umbrian pasta, such as *strangozzi* (a square-shaped spaghetti-like pasta) and meat dishes such as *cinghiale* (wild boar), but a few excellent restaurants stand out for their food, value, location, or all three.

RESTAURANTS

Il Falchetto (☎ 075 573 17 75; Via Bartolo 20; mains €7-13; ☺ Tue-Sun) In a great location just behind the cathedral, this restaurant (named 'the eagle') offers some of Perugia's better dishes. Try the house speciality, *falchetto verde*, a spinach and gnocchi dish served as a bubbling hot casserole (€8.50).

Il Segreto di Pulcinella (☎ 075 573 62 84; Via Larga 8; ☺ Tue-Sun) The only 'real' Neapolitan pizza in Perugia, it has a dazzling array of pies from the simplest *margherita* to those piled with olives, artichokes or meat. It also features Perugia's best array of salads (€2.70 to €6.20), with ingredients like mascarpone and pears, and loads of pasta dishes including

---

AUTHOR'S CHOICE

Osteria Il Ghiottone (☎ 075 572 77 88; Via Caporali 12; mains €8; ☺ Thu-Tue) With age comes taste at this quiet place. Aldo has run his restaurant for almost two decades, and his family has been creating their own olive oil for almost 200 years. The restaurant is unpretentious, simple and serves delicious food. Be sure to try any of the fresh pasta Aldo makes by hand, such as *umbricelli alle ghiottone* (€8.35). For €12 take home a litre of the family olive oil.

the rich *caramelle al zafferano* (noodles in a creamy sweet saffron sauce; €8.50).

La Cambusa (☎ 075 572 13 83; Via dei Priori 82; mains €8; ☺ Wed-Mon) This inexpensive and reliable restaurant is mostly populated by the locals. It specialises in seafood dishes, including a swordfish *carpaccio* (thinly sliced meat, dressed and eaten raw) and the best *calamari fritti* (fried calamari) in town.

Ristorante Il Bacio (☎ 075 572 09 09; Via Boncampi 6; mains €11; ☺ Thu-Tue) A cavernous pizzeria and restaurant that serves decent pizza at decent prices, but its selling point is that it's one of the only late-night restaurants in the historic centre, open until 12.30am.

CAFÉS

Many of the restaurants that line Corso Vannucci open up street cafés in the warmer months. You're paying for atmosphere so don't worry if the food isn't the best you've ever had.

Sandri (☎ 075 572 41 12; Corso Vannucci 32; ☺ 10am-8pm) Just try to walk by this café, a Perugian staple, without having your mouth water at the sight of chocolate cakes and candied fruit.

Caffè Morlacchi (☎ 075 572 17 60; Piazza Morlacchi 8; ☺ 8am-1am Mon-Sat) Bring your bongo drum and leftist rhetoric to this most hip of establishments. Serves international light fare and drinks to students, professors and foreigners.

Caffè di Perugia (☎ 075 573 18 63; Via Mazzini 10; ☺ noon-3pm & 7pm-midnight Wed-Mon) This is the fanciest café in town and makes delectable desserts, all on display. It also serves a fine array of basic pasta and meat dishes.

QUICK EATS

Pizzeria Mediterranea (☎ 075 572 13 22; Piazza Piccinino 11/12; pizzas from €4.50; ☺ Wed-Thu) Very trendy and in a good location, Mediterranea can get fairly busy at times so be prepared to queue.

Pizzeria Etrusca (☎ 075 572 07 62; Via Ulisse Rocchi 31; pizzas from €4) Etrusca is a popular student haunt.

For another great pizza option, check out Il Segreto di Pulcinella (opposite).

Augusta Perusia Cioccolato (☎ 075 573 45 77; Via Pinturicchio 2; ☺ 10.30am-8pm Mon-Sat) Handmade chocolate bars come in boxes with old paintings of Perugia. If they make it that long, you can bring them home as welcome gifts.

It serves wonderful homemade *gelato*, including flavours such as mascarpone, baci, pinoli, cinnamon and, of course, chocolate.

SELF-CATERING

Coop (Piazza Matteotti; ☺ 9am-8pm) The largest grocery store in the historic centre. You can buy all sorts of pasta, vegetables and staples here, as well as prepared food from the deli.

Covered market (☺ 7am-1.30pm Mon-Sat) Below Coop is this market, slightly hidden down a staircase from Piazza Matteotti, where you can buy fresh produce, bread, cheese and meat.

Drinking

Bottega di Vino (☎ /fax 075 571 61 81; Via del Sole 1; ☺ wine bar 6pm-1am Mon-Sat, wine shop 9am-1pm & 4-8pm Mon-Sat) Flaming torches light the way and a fire burns on the terrace. Inside, live jazz and hundreds of bottles of wine lining the walls add to the romance of the setting. You can taste dozens of Umbrian wines, and can then purchase them from the wine bar with the help of sommelier-like experts.

Cinastik (☎ 075 572 09 99; Via dei Priori 36; ☺ 6.30pm-2.30am Mon-Sat) Feel very much like you're on the continent in this swanky hot spot. Downstairs pumps with sultry music and the mixed drinks flow. Upstairs is a little quieter (make sure you check out the coolest bathrooms in Perugia).

Shamrock Pub (☎ 075 573 66 25; Piazza Danti 18; ☺ 6pm-2am) For late-night drinks, sample a Guinness at the Shamrock, down an appropriately dank but atmospheric alley off Piazza Danti.

Bar Centrale (Piazza IV Novembre 35; ☺ 7am-11pm) A popular meeting place for students, with outdoor tables under umbrellas where you can sit with a *panini* and watch the students on the cathedral steps.

La Terrazza (Via Matteotti 18a; ☺ summer only) Sit in the park and continue to enjoy the view of the sun setting over the Umbrian hillside, or head into a darkened pub for a drink? Here you can have both. On the back terrace of the building that houses the Coop and covered markets is this open-air bar, perfect for an evening *aperitivo*.

Entertainment

Much of Perugia's nightlife parades outside the cathedral and around Fontana Maggiore. Practically every night, hundreds of local and foreign students congregate here, playing guitars and drums and chatting with friends. Tourists mix in easily, slurping *gelati* and enjoying this version of outdoor theatre. When the student population grows, the Università per Stranieri offers a bus that leaves from Palazzo Gallenga for some of the clubs on the outskirts of town that are difficult to get to on foot (especially since the *scale mobili* stop running just after midnight). Check with the university for details.

Cinema Teatro del Pavone (☎ 075 572 49 11; Corso Vannucci 67) On Monday nights, this cinema runs films in their original language for €4 (students €3.50).

Velvet (☎ 075 572 13 21; www.velvetfashioncafé.com; Viale Roma 20) Come to where the beautiful people play and party. It doesn't open until after midnight, but you can party here until the wee hours.

Shopping

Antiques market (Piazza Italia & Giardini Carducci) If you're lucky enough to be in Perugia on the last weekend of the month, spend a few hours in the antiques market around the Piazza Italia and in the Giardini Carducci. It's a great place to pick up old prints, frames, furniture, jewellery, postcards, stamps etc. The second week of January sees steep discounts, as prices can be reduced by as much as 75%.

Umbria Terra Viva (Piazza Piccinino) On the first Sunday of each month in Piazza Piccinino (heading towards Via Bontempi from the cathedral) is this market, where you can buy naturally and organically grown traditional Umbrian products at less-than-gourmet prices.

Getting There & Away

AIR

About 13km east of Perugia, **Aeroporto Sant' Egidio** (☎ 075 59 21 41; www.airport.umbria.it) offers flights to Milan all year-round, plus seasonal summer flights to Denmark, Sardinia and Mallorca.

A taxi one way or round trip to Sant'Egidio costs €25 (yes, both trips cost the same price regardless). Sulga buses (tickets €2.60) coincide with the three daily Alitalia flights to Milan. They leave Piazza Italia at 5.20am, 10.20am and 4.10pm (stopping at the train station five minutes later, and the airport 25 minutes after that). Coming back, flights leave the airport at 11.34am, 4.55pm and

10.40pm. It's a tight connection but Alitalia expects several customers to be on the bus with you.

BUS

To most towns, it doesn't pay to the take long-distance buses (*interurbano* as opposed to local or *urbano* buses) in terms of time or price, but several towns are easier reached by bus than train. Buses rarely run on Sundays.

Intercity buses leave from Piazza dei Partigiani (take the *scale mobili* from Piazza Italia). **Sulga** (☎ 800 099 661; www.sulga.it in Italian) heads from Partigiani to Rome (€14.50, three hours, five daily) continuing onto Fiumicino airport (€19.20, 3¾ hours, leaving Partigiani at 6.33am, 7.30am, 8.30am or 9am, 2.30pm and 5.30pm). Heading to Perugia from Fiumicino, simply cross the street from the international terminal. Buses leave from the airport at 12.30pm, 2.30pm, 4.30pm and 5pm. Sulga also operates the Perugia to Florence service (€9.80, 2½ hours), which runs once daily (except Sunday) in each direction, leaving Perugia at 7.30am and Florence at 6pm (from Piazza Adua at Santa Maria Novella).

APM (☎ 800 512 141, 075 57 31 707; www.apmper ugia.it in Italian) and **SSIT** (☎ 0742 67 07 46; www .spoletina.com) buses leave from Piazza dei Partigiani for Deruta (€2.40, 25 minutes, nine daily), Torgiano (€1.60, 25 minutes, six daily), Assisi (€2.80, 55 minutes, 10 daily), Todi (€4.40, one hour 20 minutes, four daily), Gubbio (€4, one hour 10 minutes, about eight daily), Gualdo Tadino (€4.80, one hour 25 minutes, six daily), the Lake Trasimeno towns (€2.40 to €4.40, 30 minutes to one hour 10 minutes, six to eight daily) and Norcia (€6.80, 2½ hours, one at 2pm). Check the TV monitors above the terminals. It's best to take the train to Spello, Foligno, Spoleto, Orvieto or Assisi.

Current train and bus routes, company details and timetables are listed in the monthly booklet *Viva Perugia* (€0.80), available at *tabacchi* (tobacconists) and tourist offices.

CAR & MOTORCYCLE

From Rome, leave the A1 at the Orte exit and follow the signs for Terni. Once at Terni, take the S3B-E45 for Perugia. From the north, exit the A1 at Valdichiana and take dual carriageway S75B for Perugia. The S75 to the east connects the city with Assisi.

You'll find three car-rental companies at the main train station:

Avis (☎ /fax 075 500 03 95; alvalrent@hotmail.com; ⏰ 8.30am-1pm & 3.30-7pm Mon-Fri, 8.30am-1pm Sat) Run by an English-speaking family in their third generation as Avis employees. Rates cost about €233 for a manual transmission (about €400 per week for an automatic). Smart cars are available for about €40 a day.

Hertz (☎ 075 500 24 39; hertzperugia@tiscali.it; ⏰ 8.30am-1pm & 3.30-7pm Mon-Fri, 8.30am-1pm Sat)

Maggiore (☎ 075 500 74 99; www.maggiore.it in Italian; ⏰ 8.30am-1pm & 3.30-7pm Mon-Fri, 8.30am-1pm Sat)

Give **Scootyrent** (☎ 075 572 07 10, 333 102 65 05; www.scootyrent.com; Via Pinturicchio 76) a call for scooter hire. For about €20 a day, you can feel like a real Italian, transporting yourself and taking your life in your hands, all at the same time.

TRAIN

The main train station, **Stazione Fontivegge** (☎ 848 88 88 08), is on Piazza Vittorio Veneto, 1.5km west of the city centre and easily accessible by frequent buses from Piazza Italia. The ticket office is open from 6.30am to 8.10pm, but you can buy tickets at the automated machines any time of day with a credit card or cash. There are services to Rome (€10.15 to €18.45, 2¼ to three hours, seven daily), Florence (€7.90 to €12.50, two hours, every other hour or so), Assisi (€1.65, 20 minutes, hourly), Gubbio (€4.80, 1½ hours, seven daily), Spello (€1.95, 30 minutes, hourly) and Arezzo (€4.50, one hour 10 minutes, every two hours).

FCU (☎ 075 57 54 01; www.fcu.it in Italian; Stazione Sant'Anna, Piazzale Bellucci) are adorably graffittied 'Thomas the Tank Engine' trains which stop at many tourist destinations. Take the train to Terni to switch to Rome. Unlike every other Italian train, validate your ticket on board.

Take the FCU to Deruta (€1.25, 20 minutes, 14 daily), Fratta Todina/Monte Castello di Vibio (€2.05, 40 minutes, 18 daily), Todi (€2.55, 50 minutes, 18 daily) or Terni (€4.40, 1½ hours, 17 daily). The Sansepolcro line heads to Umbertide (€2.05, 45 minutes, 19 daily) and Città di Castello (€3.05, one hour 10 minutes, 16 daily).

Getting Around
BUS

It's a steep climb uphill from the train station, so a bus ride is highly recommended, especially for those with luggage. The city bus costs €0.80 (€0.65 for seniors) and takes you as far as Piazza Italia in the historic centre. Be sure to validate your ticket upon boarding or you will be fined on the spot if. If you haven't bought a ticket, you can buy one on the bus for €1.50. Bus Nos 6 and 7 are the most immediate, but bus Nos 11, 13 and 15d will also get you to Piazza Italia. Buy your bus ticket from the small green bus kiosk in front of the train station, in Piazza Italia, or at one of the many *tabacchi* throughout the city. If you're going to stick around for a while, buy a 10-ticket pass for €7.20.

An airbus connects Piazza Italia with the Aeroporto Sant'Egidio (see opposite).

CAR & MOTORCYCLE

If you arrive in Perugia by car, following the Centro signs along the winding roads up the hill will bring you to Piazza Italia. Driving and parking in Perugia is expensive. Most of the city centre is largely closed to normal, nonresidential traffic, although tourists may drive to their hotels to drop off luggage. Rumour has it that parking police are more lenient on tourist cars, but if you park illegally for too long you run the risk of getting towed. Perugia has six paid car parks: Piazza Partigiani (the most central and convenient), Viale Pellini, Mercato Coperto, Briglie di Braccio, Viale Sant'Antonio and Piazzale Europa. The free car park is located at Piazza Cupa. *Scale mobili* or *ascensori* (lifts) lead from each car park towards the city centre, but take note: they don't operate 24 hours, and usually stop between about midnight or 1am and 6am or 7am.

Parking fees cost €0.80 to €1.05 per hour (24 hours a day). If you intend to use the car park a lot, buy a tourist *abbonamento* (unlimited parking-ticket pass) from the ticket office at the car park for about €7.75 for the first day and €5.20 for each successive day. For general parking information, contact **SIPA** (☎ 075 572 19 38).

Call the **Deposito Veicoli Rimossi** (☎ 075 577 53 75) if your car has been towed; be prepared to pay around €105 to retrieve it.

The best bet is simply to rent a car on your way out of Perugia.

TAXI

For a taxi, dial ☎ 075 500 48 88 between 6am and 2am (24 hours, July to August). A ride from the city centre to the main train station will cost about €10.

TORGIANO

Fans of wine and olive oil will appreciate this town, a monument to these two most important Umbrian, and indeed Italian, products. Torgiano is famous throughout the world for its fine wines, and the Lungarotti family, the closest thing Umbria has to a ruling noble family these days, owns many of the local vineyards, the excellent wine museum and the second of Umbria's two five-star hotels.

Sights & Activities

Established by the Lungarotti Foundation, the **Museo del Vino** (☎ 075 988 02 00; Corso Vittorio Emanuele 31; admission €4, incl Museo dell'Olivo e dell'Olio €7; ◷ 9am-1pm & 3-7pm summer, to 6pm winter) traces the history of the production of wine in the region back to Etruscan times. Displays of utensils, graphic art, wine containers and production techniques fill 20 rooms in the 16th-century palazzo. Guided tours in English, Spanish, French, German or Japanese can be arranged for groups but must be booked ahead.

With support from research institutes in Italy and abroad, the Lungarotti family helped organise the **Museo dell'Olivo e dell'Olio** (☎ 075 988 03 00; Via Garibaldi 10; admission €4; ◷ 9am-1pm & 3-7pm summer, to 6pm winter), which opened in 2000. Contained in a series of medieval houses, the museum traces the production cycle of the olive, outlines its biology, and documents the culture and use of olives and how they relate to the economy, the landscape, religion, medicine, diet, sport, crafts and traditions.

Festivals & Events

In the second half of November, the **Banco d'Assaggio dei Vini** – a dedicated wine-tasting demonstration – is an important event on the international calendar.

Sleeping & Eating

Le Tre Vaselle (☎ 075 988 04 47; www.3vaselle.it; Via Garibaldi 48; r €160-260; Ⓟ Ⓧ Ⓧ Ⓡ) Known throughout the country for its refinement, this Lungarotti-run hotel and restaurant is one of Torgiano's main draws. The hotel has disappointed some who didn't think the service matched the prices, but the amenities

are many: Jacuzzi tubs or exercise bikes in several rooms, inviting common areas with fireplaces, games tables and plush couches for reading and relaxing. The restaurant has hardly met a diner it didn't impress. The meals are as artfully presented as they are delicious. It will cost dearly, around €70 per person, but this is the top-rated restaurant in all of Umbria.

DERUTA

pop 7400

About 15km south of Perugia on the SS3bis-E45 to Terni, Deruta is famed for its richly coloured and intensely patterned pottery. The Etruscans and Romans worked the clay around Deruta but it was not until the bright blue and yellow metallic-oxide majolica glazing technique was imported from Majorca in the 15th century that the ceramics industry took off. Thus, ceramics in the area came to be known as Majolica.

Prices in Deruta can be lower or higher than towns like Gubbio or Assisi, but know what you're getting (ie either quality handmade items at boutique outlets or massproduced factory knockoffs). Many of the larger operations are mass-produced in a factory. The prices will be lower, but so will the quality. For the best quality, head to a smaller shop that follows the centuries-old Deruta traditions. Try **Maioliche Nulli** (☎ /fax 075 97 23 84; Via Tiberina 142), where Rolando Nulli creates each item by hand, while his brother Goffredo finishes them with intricate paintings, specialising in classic medieval designs. If they're not busy and you ask nicely in Italian, they might even bring you downstairs and teach you to throw a bowl on the wheel.

You can get a taste for the genuine article at the **Museo Regionale della Ceramica** (☎ /fax 075 971 10 00; Largo San Francesco; adult/concession/child under 6 €3/2/free; ◷ 10am-1pm & 3-6pm or 7pm, closed Tue winter), in the former Franciscan convent. The history of the production of pottery in Deruta from the 14th century until the beginning of the 20th century is presented here, along with an explanation of the development of the special glaze, including some splendid examples.

Contact the **tourist office** (☎ 075 971 0043; Piazza dei Consoli) for accommodation. APM buses connect the town with Perugia (€1.95, 30 minutes, six daily).

LAGO DI TRASIMENO

Lake Trasimeno is extremely popular for two groups of travellers: weekly villa or *agriturismo* denizens who flit about the surrounding Umbrian and Tuscan sunflower-covered hillsides sampling wines and olive oils, and Dutch families on camp-site holidays at the lakeside beaches.

So far, the villa-goers and the Dutch seem to get along fairly well, and most everyone calmly enjoys the water sports, local cuisine, never-ending walking trails and Umbria's best hostel, located on its own practically private island.

Orientation

Bypass Passignano, the area's main tourist hot spot for holidaying Italians, if you want any relaxation, and head to Castiglione del Lago or one of the area's smaller towns or islands. A car is helpful, but you can get there and around using public transport and bicycles (many camp sites and hotels offer rentals).

Information

Tourist office (☎ 075 965 24 84; www.castiglionedellago .it; Piazza Mazzini 10, Castiglione del Lago; ☼ 8.30am-1pm & 3.30-7pm Mon-Sat & 9am-1pm Sun) Advises on *agriturismi*, as well as walking and biking trails and water sports.

Sights & Activities

Many people visit this lake district to indulge in water sports, walking and horse riding. But many also go for the culinary delights. The locals are very proud of their excellent produce, most notably their high-quality DOC wines (see p83) and DOP (Denominazione d'Origine Protetta, or Protected Denomination of Origin) olive oils. If you are interested in following the Strade del Vino (Wine Route) of the Colli del Trasimeno (Trasimeno Hill district), the **Associazione Strada del Vino Colli del Trasimeno** (☎ 075 58 29 41; www.montitrasimeno.umbria .it in Italian; Comunità Montana, Via S Bonaventura 10, Perugia) produces a brochure with suggested itineraries. You can also pick up this brochure at the tourist office in Castiglione del Lago. Look out, too, for *Trasimeno a Tavola*, the guide to local restaurants, which includes sample menus and price guides; it's also available from the tourist office.

On Wednesday morning, enjoy a pleasant wander through the **market** in Castiglione del Lago.

Castiglione del Lago's attractions include the **Palazzo della Corgna** (☎ 075 965 82 10; Piazza Gramsci; admission incl Rocca del Leone adult/concession €3/2; ☼ 10am-1pm & 4-7.30pm summer, 9.30am-4.30pm Sat & Sun winter), an ancient ducal palace. A covered passageway connects the palace with the 13th-century **Rocca del Leone**, an excellent example of medieval military architecture.

The lake's main inhabited island – **Isola Maggiore**, near Passignano – was reputedly a favourite with St Francis. The hill-top **Chiesa di San Michele Arcangelo** contains a Crucifixion painted by Bartolomeo Caporali dating from around 1460. You can also visit the mostly uninhabited island and environmental lab at Isola Polvese (see p556) for a day trip.

Ask at one of the tourist offices for a booklet of walking and horse-riding tracks. Horse-riding centres include the **Poggio del Belveduto** (☎ 075 82 90 76; www.poggiodelbelveduto .it; Via San Donato 65, Loc Campori di Sopra in Passignano), which also offers archery courses.

Sleeping

For a full list of places to stay in this area, pick up a brochure from the local tourist office, check out www.umbria2000.it, or consult the *Umbria Infotourist Map* available from the InfoUmbria office (see p546),

---

HANNIBAL VS THE ROMANS

During the second Punic War between Rome and Carthage, Lake Trasimeno was the site of one of the deadliest battles in all of Roman history. Roman troops led by Consul Calus Flaminius were set up in what is now the town of Tuoro. Quite the wartime strategist, Carthaginian general Hannibal made it look as if he was nonchalantly passing by (with 50,000 troops, 9000 horses and 37 elephants) in the direction of Rome. Hannibal's men even lit a series of torches far from the lake, leading Flaminius' men to believe the Carthaginians were too far away to be a threat. Under the cover of the lake's typical misty morning, Hannibal ambushed so expediently that the Romans hardly had time to suit up, killing over three-fifths of Flaminius' 25,000-strong army. A local stream ran with the blood of Flaminius and his soldiers for three straight days, earning it the name *Sanguinetto* (the Bloody).

where they will also help you to make hotel reservations.

Fattoria Il Poggio (☎ 075 965 95 50; www.fattoria isolapolvese.com; Isola Polvese; dm/f with breakfast €15/17, full meals €10; ☽ 1 Mar–30 Oct, reception closed 3-7pm; ☒ ▣) Besides being impeccably run, you would hardly ever know you're staying in an HI youth hostel. Dorm, doubles and family rooms all with views of the surrounding lake. It takes some preplanning, but those who don't mind catching a ferry back by 7pm will be rewarded handsomely with a family-style meal in an environmentally equipped former barn on their own private island. After dinner, enjoy a drink with new international friends over the sunset or a game of table tennis. Kayaks, private beaches, games, TV with DVDs, laundry room, 14th-century ruins and a nearby environmental lab are just a part of the offerings. Groups can book in the off season by appointment only.

Il Torrione (☎ 075 95 32 36; www.trasinet.com/iltor rione; Via delle Mura 4/8, Castiglione del Lago; r €55-65) These artistically minded hosts have found the best location in town for their tranquil oasis. Each room is decorated with artwork painted by the owner. A private garden overlooks the lake, complete with chaise lounges from which to watch the sunset.

Camping Badiaccia (☎ 075 965 90 97; www.badiac cia.com; Via Trasimeno I 91, Bivia Borghetto; person/tent/car/dog €6.50/6/2/2, 3-/6-person bungalows €35-93; ▣ ▣ ☒) Practise your Dutch while playing tennis, table tennis or *bocce*, eating at the surprisingly good *ristorante*/pizzeria, or swimming in one of three pools (one hydro-massage and just for adults). The camp site is paradise for families, but the childless will equally enjoy renting a kayak, bicycle or paddleboat, working out at the fitness room, using the laundry facilities and the beachfront location. For a small fee, they'll pick you up at the Terontola train station; the camp site is located just south of the SS75 on the SS71.

La Torre (☎ 075 95 16 66; www.trasinet.com/latorre; Via Emanuele 50, Castiglione del Lago; s/d €50/75, breakfast €5; ▣ ☒) The price is right at this central three-star hotel, a renovated palace. The rooms are a tad sterile but fully outfitted with TV, minibar and telephone,

Eating

The main specialities of the Trasimeno area are *fagiolina* (little white beans), olive oil and wine. In addition, you'll find many fish dishes such as *carp in porchetta* (cooked in a wood oven with garlic, fennel and herbs) and *tegamaccio*, a kind of soupy stew of the best varieties of local fish, cooked in olive oil, white wine and herbs.

La Cantina (☎ 075 965 24 32; Via Emanuele 93, Castiglione del Lago; mains €6.60-13.20; ☽ Tue-Sun) Not only is the well-priced restaurant fabulous – a stately interior with a lovely outdoor terrace for summer dining – but there's also an adjacent *magazzino* (shop) where you can sample and buy the area's best wine, olive oil and treats. Try the delicious trout with local *fagiolina* (€8.20).

L'Acquario (☎ 075 965 24 32; Via Vittoria Emanuele 69, Castiglione del Lago; set menu €25; ☽ Thu-Tue) This rather refined restaurant is a great place to try out the local *carp in porchetta* fresh from the lake or have an appetizer of eel in *tegamaccio*.

Da Settimio (☎ 075 847 60 00; Via Lungolago Alicata, San Feliciano; mains €6-21.50; ☽ Fri-Wed Jan-Oct; ▣ ☒) If you stay on Isola Polvese, you'll most likely pass by this restaurant near the ferry terminal in San Feliciano. It doesn't look like much, but locals know it as the best fish restaurant in the area, handed down from father to son for four generations. Try the *risotto alla pescatora* (fisherman's risotto) or the appetiser of 'fried little fishies'.

Getting There & Around

APM buses connect Perugia with Passignano (€2.80, one hour, five daily) and Castiglione del Lago (€4.40, one hour 20 minutes, eight daily). Passignano is also served by regular trains from Perugia (€2.05, 25 minutes, hourly) via Terontola, making it the most accessible part of the lake.

APM (☎ 075 82 71 57) also operates ferry services. The company has offices on the waterfront at each town, where you can pick up a timetable. In the high season, hourly ferries head from Passignano to Castiglione del Lago (€4, 40 minutes), San Feliciano to Isola Polvese (€2.80, 10 minutes) and Castiglione del Lago to Isola Maggiore (€3.50, 30 minutes). Ferries stop running at 7pm.

You can hire bicycles at most camp sites, Fattoria Il Poggio (left) or at these outlets:
Cicli Valentini (☎ /fax 075 95 16 63; Via Firenze 68b, Castiglione del Lago)
Marinelli Ferrettini Fabio (☎ /fax 075 95 31 26; Via B Buozzi 26, Castiglione del Lago)

TODI

pop 17,000

Originally an Etruscan frontier settlement, Todi ended up as a prosperous commune in the early Middle Ages – a prosperity reflected in the grandness of its central Piazza del Popolo. Set atop a craggy hill, it seems to have ignored the 21st century.

Information

Paolo M Fedrighini Centro Grafica Digitale (☎ 075 894 22 27; Piazza Umberto 1/17; per 15min €1.55) Internet access.

Post office (☎ 075 894 24 26; ⏲ 8am-6.30pm Mon-Fri, 8am-12.30pm Sat)

Tourist office (☎ 075 894 33 95; www.todi.umbria 2000.it; ⏲ 9.30am-1pm & 3-6pm Mon-Sat, 10am-1pm Sun & holidays)

Sights

Just try to walk through the **Piazza del Popolo** (Piazza of the People) without feeling compelled to sit on medieval building steps and write a postcard home. The lugubrious 13th-century **Palazzo del Capitano del Popolo** (☎ 075 895 62 16; Piazza del Popolo; admission €3.10; ⏲ 10.30am-1pm & 2-6pm Apr-Aug, 10.30am-1pm & 2-5pm Tue-Sun Mar & Sep, 10.30am-1pm, 2-4.30pm Tue-Sun Oct-Feb) features an elegant triple window and houses the city's recently restored *pinacoteca* (picture gallery) and archaeological museum.

The **cathedral** (☎ 075 894 30 41; Piazza del Popolo; ⏲ 8.30am-12.30pm & 2.30-6.30pm), at the northwestern end of the square, has a magnificent rose window and intricately decorated doorway. The crypt dating back to the 8th century is worth visiting for the inlaid wooden stalls in the chancel.

Wander through Todi's medieval labyrinth and pop into some of the other churches, including the lofty **Tempio di San Fortunato** (Piazza Umberto 1; admission free; ⏲ 9.30am-12.30pm & 3-6pm), with frescoes by Masolino da Panicale and the tomb of San Jacopone, Todi's beloved patron saint.

Just outside the city walls is the late Renaissance **Chiesa di Santa Maria della Consolazione**, designed by Donato Bramante in 1508 but not completed until 99 years later.

Festivals & Events

The **Todi Festival**, held for 10 days each July/August, is a mixture of classical and jazz concerts, theatre, ballet and cinema. Ask at the tourist office for details.

Sleeping

There are only five hotels – all three or four stars – in Todi. The budget-conscious may want to consider staying at a religious house or contacting the tourist office for B&Bs.

Pensionato SS Annunziata (☎ 075 894 22 68; www .monasterosmr.com; Via San Biagio 2; s/d/tr with breakfast €35/70/105) Get away to this tranquil retreat within the city walls. Set around a lovely garden, all rooms come with private bath and bed linens, and some with furnishings from the 1400s. Try to catch a meal with your hosts, nuns from the Mary's Servant of Repair order.

Villa Luisa (☎ 075 894 85 71; www.villaluisa.it; Via A Cortesi 147; s/d with breakfast €80/120; Ⓟ Ⓧ Ⓔ) This place is outside the city walls on the bus line coming in from the train station, but it's set in its own park-like grounds with a pool, lift and restaurant.

Casa per Ferie Luigi Crispolti (☎ 075 894 53 37; www.crispoltiferie.it in Italian; Via Cesia 96; s/d with breakfast €33/52) You'll feel a bit like Little Orphan Annie in this former religious house turned orphanage, but it's clean, directly in town and cheap.

Eating

Ristorante Umbria (☎ 075 894 27 37; Via Santa Bonaventura 13; mains €9-23; ⏲ Thu-Tue) This restaurant, as its name suggests, serves local dishes. It's reasonably expensive but worth it for the view from the terrace.

Antica Hosteria de la Valle (☎ 075 894 48 48; Via Ciuffelli 17/19/21; mains €11; ⏲ Tue-Sun) Most of the time you'll be dining here with the locals. Pasta is homemade and delicious, but the traditional *farro* (an ancient grain) soup (€7) should not be missed.

Getting There & Away

APM (☎ 075 50 67 81) bus line E12 leaves from Perugia's Piazza Partigiani (€4.80, one hour) every hour or so, but only four reach Piazza Jacopone in the city centre. The rest stop at

---

AUTHOR'S CHOICE

Bar Pianegiani (☎ 075 894 23 76; Corso Cavour 40; ⏲ 6am-midnight) Just like Clark Kent, this nondescript neighbourhood bar puts on an innocent front to conceal the magic that lies beneath. The best *gelato* in Umbria, nay, perhaps on Earth, calls Pianegiani's home.

Piazza Consolazione, where it's possible to take city bus A or B or walk uphill 2km. Heading back to Perugia from Piazza Jacapone are five buses a day at 6.35am, 12.42pm, 1.30pm, 3.38pm and 4.58pm (Monday to Saturday). There is one daily service to Orvieto (€4.40, 1½ hours) at 5.50am, which returns at 2.05pm.

Todi is on the **FCU** (☎ 075 57 54 01; www.fcu.it in Italian) train line, which runs through Deruta to Perugia (€2.55, 50 min, 18 daily). Although the train station is 3km away, city bus C runs there (€0.80, 20 minutes) once an hour, every other hour on Sundays. By road, Todi is easily reached on the SS3B-E45, which runs between Perugia and Terni, or take the Orvieto turnoff from A1 (the Milan–Rome–Naples route).

ASSISI

pop 25,000

St Francis was born here in 1182 and spent most of his adult life preaching around this area of Umbria (see the boxed text, p560).

Assisi is the quintessentially quaint and tranquil Italian hill town. In fact, it is so quaint and tranquil that millions upon millions of tourists and religious pilgrims come to Assisi every year, collectively appreciating its quaintness and tranquillity.

However, the town somehow manages to retain its calming, almost spiritual lustre. Wander off the main streets and Assisi can feel surprisingly personal, even in the busy summer months.

Orientation

Piazza del Comune is the centre of Assisi. At the northwestern edge of this square, Via San Paolo and Via Portica both eventually lead to the Basilica di San Francesco. Via Portica also leads to the Porta San Pietro and the Piazzale dell'Unità d'Italia, where most intercity buses stop, although APM buses from smaller towns in the area terminate at Piazza Matteotti. Train riders arrive at Piazza Matteotti by shuttle bus (€0.80) from Santa Maria degli Angeli.

Information

Banks are a dime a dozen in Assisi. Many congregate around the Piazza del Comune and all offer ATMs.

Acquazzura (☎ 075 804 09 27; Via San Bernadino Siena 6, Santa Maria degli Angeli) A self-service laundromat

between the train station and basilica in Santa Maria degli Angeli.

Branch tourist office (☎ 075 81 67 66; ☾ Easter-Nov) Just outside Porta Nuova.

Ospedale di Assisi (☎ 075 813 92 27) Hospital about 1km southeast of Porta Nuova in Fuori Porta.

Police station (☎ 075 81 28 20; Piazza del Comune)

Post office Porta Nuova (☾ 8.10am-6.25pm Mon-Fri, 8.10am-1pm Sat & Sun); Porta San Pietro (☾ 8.10am-6.25pm Mon-Fri, 8.10am-1pm Sat & Sun)

Sabatini Sandro (Via Portica 29b; per 30min €3; ☾ 8am-8pm) Internet facilities.

Tourist office (☎ 075 81 25 34; info@iat.assisi.pg.it; Piazza del Comune 22; ☾ 8am-6.30pm Mon-Sat, 10am-1pm & 2-5pm Sun summer, 8am-2pm & 3-6pm Mon-Sat, 9am-1pm Sun winter)

Sights

BASILICA DI SAN FRANCESCO

The **Basilica di San Francesco** (☎ 075 81 90 01; Piazza di San Francesco) has a separate **information office** (☎ 075 819 00 84; www.sanfrancescoassisi.org; ☾ 9am-noon & 2-5pm Mon-Sat) opposite the entrance to the lower church.

The basilica saw heavy damage and four deaths during a series of earthquakes on 26 September 1997. Years of painstaking restoration – including piecing together frescoes from crumbled bits, some not much larger than a grain of sand – will probably go on until at least 2010.

The basilica was built on a hill known as Colle d'Inferno (Hell Hill). People were executed at the gallows here until the 13th century. St Francis asked his followers to bury him here in keeping with Jesus, who had died on the cross among criminals and outcasts. The area is now known as Paradise Hill.

The **upper church** (☾ 8.30am-6.50pm Easter-Nov, to 6pm Nov-Easter, to 7.15pm holidays) was built just after the lower church, between 1230 and 1253, and the change in style and grandiosity is readily apparent. One of the most famous pieces of art in the world is the 28-part fresco circling the walls. The fresco has been attributed to Giotto and his pupils for hundreds of years, but the question of who produced it is now under debate within the art-historian community. The fresco starts just to the right of the altar and continues clockwise around the church. Above each image is a corresponding biblical fresco with 28 corresponding images from the Old and New Testament (possibly painted

ASSISI

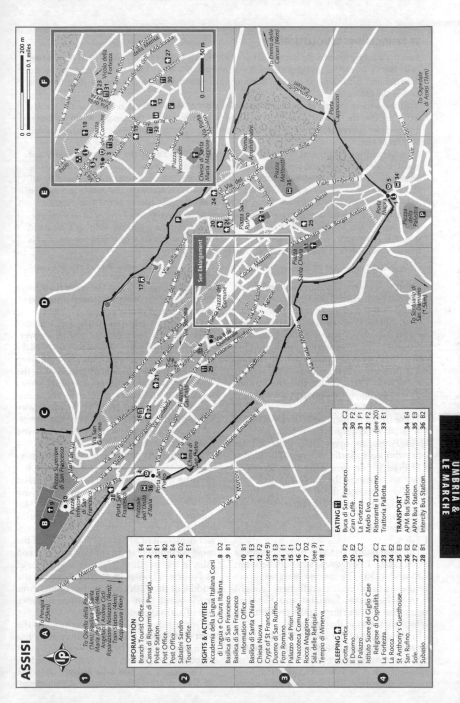

ST FRANCIS THE REVOLUTIONARY

Born the wealthy son of a cloth merchant in 1182, Francis (Francesco in Italian) filled his younger years with wild parties and daydreams about becoming a great knight. In his mid-20s he did head off into battle against Perugia, but a gradual religious awakening was to steer him to a different noble calling.

At the ancient church of San Damiano, he heard the voice of Jesus on the crucifix: Francis, repair my church. He took cloth from his father's shop to sell for the repairs. When his father dragged him in front of the bishop for punishment, Francis stripped off his clothes and renounced his former life.

He walked the countryside, wearing simple robes and preaching the virtues of poverty and equal respect for popes and lepers alike. He had a special affinity with animals and it's said he once preached to a flock of birds who stayed completely still until he said they could fly off. Many people were attracted to Francis' lifestyle and within a few years, he developed the first order of Frati Minori (Friars Minor) that, after his death, became known as the Franciscans.

Francis spent his remaining years living out what would become the Franciscan vows of poverty, chastity and obedience. In 1224, at age 43, he received the stigmata, realizing a dream to truly feel Jesus' suffering. Three years later, he died lying on the floor of a mud hut among his brothers and sisters of the order and his beloved Lady Poverty.

by Giotto, or Pietro Cavallini, who might or might not have painted the fresco cycle). The frescoes in the basilica literally revolutionised art in the Western world. All the gold leaf and flat iconic images of the Byzantine and Romanesque periods were eschewed for natural backgrounds, people of all classes, and a human, suffering Jesus. This was in keeping with Francis' idea that the human body was 'brother' and the earth around him mother and sister.

These fresco painters were the storytellers of their day, turning biblical passages into *Bibliae Pauperum*: open public Bibles for the poor, who were mostly illiterate. The scenes in St Francis' life were tied to the scenes as a way to translate the Bible through images. For instance, the fifth fresco shows St Francis renouncing his father, while the corresponding biblical fresco shows the disobedient Adam and Eve in the Garden of Eden.

The **lower church** (☾ 6.30am-6.50pm Easter-Nov, to 6pm Nov-Easter, to 7.15pm holidays) was built between 1228 and 1230. The stained-glass windows are the work of master craftsmen brought in from Germany, England and Flanders during the 13th century, and were quite an architectural feat at that time.

In the centre of the lower church, above the main altar, are four frescoes attributed to Maestro delle Vele, a pupil of Giotto, that represent what St Francis called 'the four greatest allegories'. The first was the victory of Francis over evil, and the other three were the precepts his order was based on: poverty, obedience and chastity.

Lorenzetti's triptych in the left transept ends with his most famous and controversial, *Madonna Who Celebrates Francis*. Mary is seen holding the baby Jesus and indicating with her thumb towards St Francis. On the other side of Mary is the apostle John, whom we're assuming is being unfavourably compared with Francis. In 1234 Pope Gregory IX decided that the image was not heretical because John had written the gospel, but Francis had lived it.

Cimabue was the most historically important painter who worked in this church because he was the only artist to get a first-hand account from St Francis' two nephews, who had personally known the saint. In the *Madonna in Majesty*, in the right transept, much has been tampered with, but Cimabue's intact depiction of St Francis is considered the most accurate. Francis appears peaceful and calm in this painting. The first biographer of St Francis, Thomas of Celano, wrote in the middle of the 13th century that Francis was an eloquent man, of cheerful countenance and of a kindly aspect.

Downstairs from the lower church is the **crypt of St Francis**, where the saint's body has been laid to rest. There are seats for quiet reflection, but it can get pretty crowded.

The basilica's **Sala delle Reliquie** (Relics Hall; ☎ 075 81 90 01; ☾ 9am-6pm daily, 1-4.30pm holidays) contains items from St Francis' life, including his simple tunic and sandals and fragments of his celebrated *Canticle of the Creatures*. The most important relic here is the Franciscan Rule parchment, the *Book of Life* composed by Francis.

CHURCHES

Basilica di Santa Chiara (☎ 075 81 22 82; Piazza Santa Chiara; ☼ 6am-noon & 2-7pm summer, to 6pm winter) is 13th-century Romanesque, with steep ramparts and a striking façade. The white and pink stone that makes up the exterior here (the same stone that makes many buildings in Assisi look like they glow in the sunlight) came from nearby Subasio. The daughter of an Assisian nobleman, St Clare was a spiritual contemporary of St Francis and founded the Sorelle Povere di Santa Chiara (Order of the Poor Ladies), now known as the Poor Clares. She is buried in the church's crypt. The Byzantine cross that is said to have spoken to St Francis is also housed here.

From the basilica, take Via San Francesco back to Piazza del Comune, once the site of a partially excavated **Foro Romano** (Roman Forum; ☎ 075 81 30 53; Via Portica; adult/child incl Pinacoteca €3/2; ☼ 10.30am-1.30pm & 2-6pm summer, to 5pm winter). Some of the shops on the piazza open their basements to reveal Roman ruins. The **Chiesa Nuova** (☎ 075 81 23 39; Piazza Chiesa Nuova; ☼ 6.30am-noon & 2.30-6pm summer, 6.30am-noon & 2-6pm winter) was built by King Philip III of Spain in the 1600s on the spot reputed to be the house of St Francis' family. Mass is said daily at 7am, with an extra service on holidays at 10am.

The **Tempio di Minerva**, facing Piazza del Comune and Palazzo dei Priori, is now a church but retains its impressive pillared façade. Wander into some of the shops on the piazza, which open their basements to reveal Roman ruins. The city's **Pinacoteca Comunale** (☎ 075 81 20 33; Palazzo Vallemani, Via San Francesco 10; adult/child incl Foro Romano €3/2; ☼ 10am-1pm & 3-6pm 16 Mar–15 Oct, 10am-1pm & 3-5pm 16 Oct–15 Mar) displays Umbrian Renaissance art and frescoes from Giotto's school.

Dominating the city is the massive 14th-century **Rocca Maggiore** (☎ 075 81 52 92; Via della Rocca; admission €2; ☼ 10am-sunset), a hill fortress offering fabulous views over the valley and across to Perugia.

The 13th-century Romanesque **Duomo di San Rufino** (☎ 075 81 60 16; Piazza San Rufino; ☼ 7am-noon & 2-7pm), remodelled by Galeazzo Alessi

in the 16th century, contains the fountain where St Francis and St Clare were baptized. The façade is festooned with grotesque figures and fantastic animals.

FRANCISCAN SITES

Around 1.5km south of the Porta Nuova, the **Santuario di San Damiano** (☎ 075 81 22 73; admission free; ☼ 10am-noon & 2-6pm summer, 10am-noon & 2-4.30pm winter, vespers 7pm summer & 5pm winter) was built on the spot where St Francis first heard the voice of Jesus and where he wrote his *Canticle of the Creatures*. You can visit the original convent founded by St Clare in 1212 here, as well as its cloisters and refectory.

About 4km east of the city is **Eremo delle Carceri** (☎ 075 81 23 01; admission free; ☼ 6.30am-7.15pm Easter-Nov, to sunset Nov-Easter), the hermitage that St Francis retreated to after hearing the word of God. The *carceri* (prisons) are the caves that functioned as hermits' retreats for St Francis and his followers. Apart from a few fences and tourist paths, everything remains as it was in St Francis' time, and a few Franciscans live here in a monastery built in the 15th century. Eremo delle Carceri is a great jumping-off point for walks through Monte Subasio.

A quick walk from the train station is the imposing **Basilica di Santa Maria degli Angeli** (☎ 075 8 05 11; Santa Maria degli Angeli; ☼ 6.30am-8pm), built between 1565 and 1685 around the first Franciscan monastery and tiny Porziuncola Chapel. Perugino fans will appreciate his intact Crucifixion, painted on the rear wall. St Francis died at the site of the **Cappella del Transito** on 3 October 1226.

Activities

St Francis buffs and nature buffs will appreciate the plethora of strolls, day hikes and overnight pilgrimage walks leading into and out of Assisi. The tourist office has several maps for those on such a peregrination, including a route that follows in St Francis' footsteps to Gubbio (18km).

A popular spot for hikers is nearby **Monte Subasio**. Local bookstores sell all sorts of walking and mountain-biking guides and maps for the area and the tourist office can help with brochures and maps as well.

Bicycle rentals are available at **Angelucci Andrea Cicli Riparazione Noleggio** (☎ 075 804 25 50; VG Becchetti 31) in Santa Maria degli Angeli and at Ostello della Pace (p562).

UMBRIA & LE MARCHE

Courses

Accademia della Lingua Italiana Corsi di Lingua e Cultura Italiana (☎ /fax 075 81 52 81; www.aliassisi.it; Via San Paolo 36) runs a variety of courses, including Italian language, culture, singing, painting and cooking. It also offers free preparation for the CILS (Italian teacher abroad) course. There's a maximum of 12 students per class and costs start at about €280 for two weeks of instruction.

Festivals & Events

The **Festa di San Francesco** falls on 3 and 4 October and is the main religious event in the city. **Settimana Santa** (Easter Week) is celebrated with processions and performances. The colourful **Festa di Calendimaggio** celebrates spring in medieval fashion and starts the first Thursday after 1 May.

Sleeping

Assisi has a phenomenal amount of rooms for rent but in peak periods, such as Easter, August and September, and during the Festa di San Francesco, you will need to book accommodation well in advance.

The tourist office has a complete list of private rooms, religious institutions (of which there are 17), flats and *agriturismi* options in and around Assisi and can assist with bookings in a pinch. Otherwise, keep an eye out for *camere* (rooms for rent) signs as you wander the streets.

BUDGET

Ostello della Pace (☎ 075 81 67 67; www.assisihostel .com; Via Valecchie 177; dm with breakfast €15, half/full board €24.50/33.50; ♥ closed 10 Jan–1 Mar; ℗ ▯) Assisi's HI youth hostel is lovingly family-

---

AUTHOR'S CHOICE

St Anthony's Guesthouse (☎ 075 81 25 42; atoneassisi@tiscalinet.it; Via Galeazzo Alessi 10; s/d/ tr with breakfast 35/55/75; ℗) Look for the iron statue of St Francis feeding the birds and you've found your Assisian oasis. Rooms are austere but welcoming and several have balconies with take-your-breath-away views. Gardens, ample parking, an 800-year-old breakfast salon and an ancient Door of Death make this a heavenly choice. Like most religious accommodation, it has a two-night minimum and 11pm curfew.

---

run, in a beautiful and quiet location and has great pillows. It's on the shuttle-bus route between Santa Maria degli Angeli and Assisi. There's a laundry room for guests. Full and half board available.

Grotta Antica (☎ 075 81 34 67; www.bellaumbria .net/hotel-grottaantica; Via Macelli Vecchi 1; s/d €30/40) The price is not a mistake. Perfectly located on a tiny side street less than 30m from the Palazzo del Comune, it's a wonder these rooms are also clean and hospitable. Abele speaks fluent English and Spanish and takes care of the seven simple rooms and the restaurant of the same name (see opposite).

La Rocca (☎ 075 81 22 84; www.hotelarocca.it; Via Porta Perlici 27; s/d/tr/q €39/46/65/73; ▧) At some point in our lives we all might ask ourselves: 'What do I value more in life – a hairdryer and the possibility of a good view or a guaranteed quiet night's sleep?' If the former, ask for '*una camera con una panorama*' and wear earplugs if the downstairs restaurant and bar looks hopping.

Sole (☎ 075 81 23 73, ☎ 075 81 29 22; www.assisi hotelsole.com; Corso Mazzini 35; s/d €24/42, s/d/tr with bathroom €42/62/83) This comfortable little hotel has 35 rooms, in renovated 15th-century buildings, now on both sides of the street. There are direct-dial phones in every room, a TV room and lounge, restaurant, lift and bar.

Il Duomo (☎ 075 81 27 42; www.hotelsanrufino.it; Vicolo San Lorenzo; s/d €42/52) Owned by the same folks who run the two-star San Rufino, this is a lovely one-star choice on a quiet alleyway just a stone's throw from the Piazza del Comune. For this price there aren't too many extras, but the nine rooms are understandably popular, so book ahead.

Istituto Suore del Giglio Case Religiose di Ospitalità (☎ /fax 075 81 22 67; Via San Francesco 13; s/d €27/42) There's well over a dozen religious institutions that offer rooms, but this one is centrally located, has an incredibly friendly staff (including several English-speaking Zambian nuns) and a terrace with a lovely view calming enough to inspire a religious experience. Two rooms even have their own balconies and there are several family rooms with up to five beds. Look for the sign that reads: Casa di Ospitalità 'Maria Immacolata'. Curfew is 10.30pm.

MIDRANGE

Il Palazzo (☎ 075 81 68 41; www.hotelilpalazzo.it; Via San Francesco 8; s/d €90/135) The rooms in this lovely

15th-century palazzo, half of which is occupied by the owners (descendants of the original occupants), have been restored in the simple elegance that Italians are famous for: white walls, terracotta floors, a few pieces of fine old furniture in splendidly carved wood, and beautiful carpets. Despite its central position the hotel is also very quiet and filled with light. The only disadvantage is that there are a lot of stairs to negotiate.

La Fortezza (☎ 075 81 24 18; www.lafortezzahotel .com; Vicolo della Fortezza 2b; r with/without breakfast €65/52) A comfortable, charming and intimate hotel run by the Chiocchetti family behind their restaurant, just off Piazza del Comune.

San Rufino (☎ 075 81 28 03; www.hotelsanrufino .it; Via Porta Perlici 7; s/d/tr €42/52/66, breakfast €5) A small hotel owned by the same family as Il Duomo, this is around the corner and just as quiet. Sweetly decorated rooms all come with direct-dial phones and TVs. It also offers cradles for babies.

TOP END

Subasio (☎ 075 81 22 06; www.umbria.org/hotel/suba sio; Via Frate Elia 2; s/d/ste with breakfast €114/181/233; P 🞱) Feel like a star at this most gracious of Assisian hotels. The rooms are furnished in Florentine Renaissance style, and distinguished former guests include Greta Garbo and Charlie Chaplin.

Eating

RESTAURANTS

In a twist, most of Assisi's better restaurants (even the more inexpensive ones) are part of hotels.

Trattoria Pallotta (☎ 075 81 26 49; Vicolo della Volta Pinta; mains €6.80-15; 🞱 Wed-Mon) Head through the Volta Pinta (Painted Vault) off Piazza del Comune, careful not to bump into someone as you gaze at the 16th-century frescoes above you, into this gorgeous setting of vaulted brick walls and wood-beamed ceilings. They cook all the Umbrian classics here: rabbit, homemade *strangozzi*, even pigeon. The two-star hotel is a good bet.

Grotta Antica (☎ 075 81 34 67; Vicolo Buscatti 6; mains €5-8.50) Abele – hotel proprietor, lawyer and chef – is from Liguria, so you can rest assured that although there are only a handful of menu items, you needn't look past the pesto dishes for a cheap and filling main course. His prices on wine can't be beat anywhere in Assisi.

Buca di San Francesco (☎ 075 81 22 04; Via Brizi 1; mains €14; 🞱 Tue-Sun) Sample traditional Umbrian dishes and specialities of the house in a medieval setting. Choose from bruschette, local sausage, *spaghetti alla buca*, gnocchi and homemade desserts.

Medio Evo (☎ 075 81 30 68; Via Arco dei Priori 4; mains about €12; 🞱 Thu-Tue) Traditional Umbrian dishes are served in fabulous vaulted 13th-century surroundings. The early 6.45pm opening time is geared for, and highly appreciated by, non-Italian tourists.

Ristorante il Duomo (☎ 075 81 27 42; Vicolo San Lorenzo; pizzas €3-7.50, mains €4.50-9) Pizza is the stronghold of this restaurant. Several pages on the menu are dedicated to all toppings and varieties.

La Fortezza (☎ 075 81 24 18; Via della Fortezza 2b; mains €9; 🞱 Fri-Wed) This family-run restaurant off Piazza del Comune serves traditional Umbrian dishes, as well as those from Trentino, and a good selection of local wines. Credit cards are accepted.

CAFÉS

Gran Caffè (☎ 075 815 51 44; Corso Mazzini 16; 🞱 8am-midnight) This elegant place has the most fabulous *gelati*, mouth watering pastries and cakes, and a great selection of drinks. Try the *tè freddo alla pesca* (iced tea with peach) on a hot day, or choose from a selection of delicious hot chocolates and coffee when the weather is cool. Remember it costs much more to sit.

Shopping

Assisi is a good town for shopping as many shops stay open during siesta. The closer you get to the Basilica, the tackier the souvenirs – Franciscan friar shot glasses and nuns playing poker – but meander off the beaten path for leather, ceramics and clothing. Open-air markets take place in Piazza Matteotti on Saturday and Santa Maria degli Angeli on Monday.

Getting There & Away

Although Assisi's train station is 4km west in Santa Maria degli Angeli, it is the better option as it is cheaper and more frequent than the bus. A constant shuttle bus (€0.80) runs between the train station and the APM bus station on Piazza Matteotti (tickets are available in the *tabacchi* at the station and in town). It is on the Foligno–Terontola line

UMBRIA & LE MARCHE

with regular services to Perugia (€1.65, 30 minutes, hourly). You can change at Terontola for Florence (€9, 1¾ to 2¾ hours, 10 daily) and at Foligno for Rome (€9 to €14.30, two to 2½ hours, hourly).

Buses run to Perugia (€2.80, 50 minutes, eight daily) and Gubbio (€4.80, one hour 10 minutes, 11 daily) from the intercity bus station on Piazza dell'Unità d'Italia. Take Sulga to Florence (€11, 2½ hours, one daily at 7am) and Rome's Stazione Tiburtina (€14.50, 3¼ hours, three daily).

To reach Assisi from Perugia by road, take the SS75, exit at Ospedalicchio and follow the signs.

Getting Around

A shuttle bus (€0.80) operates every half-hour between Piazza Matteotti and the train station. Normal traffic is subject to restrictions in the city centre and daytime parking is all but banned. Six car parks dot the city walls (they are connected to the centre by orange shuttle buses), or head for Via della Rocca where, for the price of a short but fairly steep walk, you should be able to find free parking.

For a taxi, dial ☎ 075 81 31 00.

SPELLO

pop 7600

Sometimes it seems like it's just not possible for the next Umbrian town to be any prettier than the last. And then you visit Spello. It's often passed by as tourists head to nearby Assisi or Perugia, but the proliferation of arched stone walkways and hanging flower-pots make it well worth a visit, especially in spring when the whole bloomin' town smells of flowers.

Orientation & Information

The train station is about 500m from the Piazza Kennedy entrance, scattered with remnants of the town's former Roman glory days as Hyspellum. Just past the Chiesa di Sant' Andrea on the far side of Piazza Matteotti is the local **tourist information office** (Pro Loco; ☎ /fax 0742 30 10 09; prospello@libero.it, Piazza Matteotti 3; ☾ 9.30am-12.30pm & 3.30-5.30pm) It can provide you with a list of accommodation and has maps of walks in the surrounding area, including an 8km walk across the hills to Assisi. Purchase a city map here for €0.50.

Sights

The town revolves around the Piazza Matteotti, where you'll find the gloomy **Chiesa di Sant'Andrea** (Piazza Matteotti; ☾ 8am-7pm) where you can admire Pinturicchio's *Madonna with Child and Saints*. A few doors down is the 12th-century **Chiesa di Santa Maria Maggiore** (Piazza Matteotti; ☾ 8.30am-12.30pm & 3-7pm summer, 8.30am-12.30pm & 3-6pm winter) and the town's real treat, Pinturicchio's beautiful frescoes in the **Cappella Baglioni** (inside the church). Also of note is the chapel's exquisite floor (dating from 1566). Head up to the Porta dell'Arco for the sweeping Umbrian view you've been waiting for.

Festivals & Events

The people of Spello celebrate the feast of **Corpus Domini** in June (the date changes each year) by skilfully decorating stretches of the main street with fresh flowers in colourful designs. Come on the Saturday evening before the Sunday procession to see the floral fantasies being laid out (from about 8.30pm) and participate in the festive atmosphere. The Corpus procession begins at 11am Sunday.

Sleeping

Residence San Jacopo (☎ 0742 30 12 60; www.residencesanjacopo.it in Italian; Via Borgo di Via Giulia 1; apt from €93) Seven hundred years of history exude from these seven mini-apartments. With invitingly rustic furniture, kitchenettes and a town centre location, visitors will feel like residents after just a day or two. Great weekly rates.

Del Prato Paolucci (☎ 0742 30 10 18; Via Brodolini 4; s/d €45/70; P) Don't expect anything special, but these are the least expensive rooms in town. You will, however, have a perfectly acceptable bathroom, TV and phone, and a few rooms have views. Call ahead and the gregarious owners will pick you up at the train station.

Il Cacciatore (☎ 0742 65 11 41; fax 0742 30 16 03; Via Giulia 42; s/d/tr 55/85/100) This place has a great restaurant (closed Monday) with a large terrace, perfect for a summer lunch, and rooms furnished in business casual.

Getting There & Away

Spello is directly on the train line between Perugia and Foligno, so trains run at least hourly to Perugia (€2.05, 30 minutes), Assisi (€1.15, 10 minutes) and Foligno (€0.80,

15 minutes). Spello is on the SS75 between Perugia and Foligno. The station is often unstaffed, so buy your tickets at either the self-service ticket machine or Bar dell' Angelo around the corner on Viale Gugliemi Marconi.

AROUND SPELLO

Wine drinkers will want to spend at least a day in and around this region. The medieval hamlet of **Bevagna** comes to life in the last week of June for the Mercato delle Gaite, where old-world taverns open up and many medieval-era handicrafts are brought back to life. The town was recently voted the most beautiful village in Italy by census takers, who also appreciated the village's safe atmosphere where children play in the streets and everyone can walk to work. For visitors, Romanesque churches, wine bars and a dearth of tourists add to the charm. For one-stop shopping, check in with the amiable Assù at **Enoteca Piazza Onofri** (☎ 0742 36 19 20; www .enotecaonofri.it; ☺ Thu-Tue); she runs a restaurant and good-value hotel in addition to her wine shop.

Around 7km to the southeast, **Montefalco** is also known as the Ringhiera dell'Umbria (Balcony of Umbria) for its expansive views, but it is the wonderful Sagrantino red wine that brings people in by the wine-tasting carload. The medieval town has no less than four *enoteche* (wine bars) in the Piazza del Comune alone.

GUBBIO

pop 32,000

Seated on the steep slopes of Monte Ingino overlooking a picturesque valley, the many centuries-old palazzi of Gubbio exude a warm ochre glow. For travellers who want to get not too far off the beaten path, Gubbio is one part romance, two parts history, a taste of art, a dash of gastronomy and a pinch of adventure. On 15 May the entire town erupts in a splendiferous Renaissance competition, the Corsa dei Ceri.

Gubbio is famous for its Eugubian Tablets, which date from 300 to 100 BC and constitute the best existing example of ancient Umbrian script. An important ally of the Roman Empire and a key stop on the Via Flaminia, the town declined during the Saracen invasions. In the 14th century it fell into the hands of the Montefeltro family of Urbino (p585) and was later incorporated into the Papal States.

Orientation

The city is small and easy to explore. The immense traffic circle known as the Piazza Quaranta Martiri, at the base of the hill, is where buses to the city terminate, and it also has a large car park. The square was named in honour of 40 local people who were killed by the Nazis in 1944 in reprisal for partisan activities. From here it is a short, if somewhat steep, walk up Via della Repubblica to the main square, Piazza Grande, also known as the Piazza della Signoria. Or, you can take the lift from the Piazza del Podestà to the Palazzo Ducale and the cathedral. Corso Garibaldi and Piazza Oderisi are to your right as you head up the hill.

Information

Easy Gubbio (☎ 075 922 00 66; Via della Repubblica 13) Travel assistance.
Hospital (☎ 0 75 923 91; Piazza Quaranta Martiri)
Police station (☎ 075 927 37 70; Via XX Settembre 97)
Post office (☎ 075 927 37 73; Via Cairoli 11; ☺ 8.10am-5pm Mon-Sat)
Tourist office (☎ 075 922 06 93; info@iat.gubbio.pg.it; www.gubbio-altochiascio.umbria2000.it; Piazza Oderisi; ☺ 8.30am-1pm & 3-6pm Mon-Sat, 9.30am-12.30pm Sun)

Sights

FUNIVIA COLLE ELETTO

Although the **Basilica di Sant'Ubaldo** – where you'll find the body of St Ubaldo, the 12th-century bishop of Gubbio – is a perfectly lovely church, the adventure is in the getting there. Take the **Funivia Colle Eletto** (☎ 075 922 11 99; adult/child return €5/4; ☺ 9am-7.30pm Jul-Aug, 9.30am-1.15pm & 2.30-5.30 or 7pm Mar-Jun, Sep & Oct, 10am-1.15pm & 2.30-5pm Nov-Feb, closed Wed winter), where your first rule is to believe the sweaty man when he tells you to stand on the dot. He will then throw you into a moving metal contraption that looks frighteningly like an open-topped human birdcage. You're whisked instantly away on a cable car that looks more like a precarious ski lift, dangling dozens of metres above a rocky hill (bring a camera, but hold tight). The ride up is as frightening as it is utterly beautiful. There's a restaurant on top of the hill and the aforementioned church, but the nicest way to spend the day is to bring a picnic and have a wander.

GUBBIO

CATHEDRAL & PALAZZO DUCALE

Via Ducale leads up to the 13th-century pink **cathedral** (Via Federico da Montefeltro; donations welcome; 9am-5pm Mon-Sat, 9am-1pm Sun), with a fine 12th-century stained-glass window and a fresco attributed to Bernardino Pinturicchio. Opposite, the 15th-century **Palazzo Ducale** (075 927 58 72; Via Federico da Montefeltro; adult/concession €2/1; 8.30am-7pm Mon & Wed-Fri, 9am-10.30pm Sat & Sun) was built by the Duke of Montefeltro family as a scaled-down version of their grand palazzo in Urbino; its walls hide an impressive Renaissance courtyard.

MUSEUMS, CHURCHES & PALAZZI

Just below the Funivia Colle Eletto is the **Museo della Ceramica a Lustro e Torre Medioevale di Porta Romana** (075 922 11 99; Via Dante 24; admission €2.50; 9am-1pm & 3.30-7pm). The *a lustro* ceramic style has its origins in 11th-century Muslim Spain. On the 2nd floor, ceramics from prehistoric times share space with medieval and Renaissance pieces. There's also a collection of crossbows from the 18th century, some that have a target range as far as 50m. Check out the really un-fun-looking

chastity belt on the 4th floor and appreciate the fact that you are alive today instead of 300 years ago.

Gubbio's most impressive buildings look out over **Piazza Grande**, where the heart of the Corsa dei Ceri event takes place. The piazza is dominated above all by the 14th-century **Palazzo dei Consoli**, attributed to Gattapone. The crenellated façade and tower can be seen from all over the town. The building houses the **Museo Civico** (075 927 42 98; Piazza Grande; adult/concession incl gallery €4/2.50; 10am-1pm & 3-6pm Apr-Oct, 10am-1pm & 2-5pm Nov-Mar), which displays the Eugubian Tablets, discovered in 1444. The seven bronze tablets are the main source for research into the ancient Umbrian language. Upstairs is a picture gallery featuring works from the Gubbian school. Across the square is the **Palazzo del Podestà**, also known as the Palazzo Pretorio, built along similar lines to its grander counterpart. Now the city's active town hall, the impressive vaulted ceilings might be peeked at if you ask nicely.

Perugia's Fra Bevignate is said to have designed the **Chiesa di San Francesco** (Piazza Quaranta

Martiri; 7.15am-noon & 3.30-7.30pm). It features impressive frescoes by a local artist, Ottaviano Nelli. Built in a simple Gothic style in the 13th century, it has an impressive rose window. Wander into the **Chiostro della Pace** (Cloister of Peace) in the adjoining convent to view some ancient mosaics and meander around the peaceful garden.

In the western end of the medieval section is the 13th-century **Palazzo del Bargello**, the city's medieval police station and prison. In front of it is the **Fontana dei Pazzi** (Fountain of Lunatics), so-named because of a belief that if you walk around it three times, you will go mad. On summer weekends the number of tourists actually carrying out this bizarre ritual is indeed cause for concern about their collective sanity.

ROMAN GUBBIO

Southwest of Piazza Quaranta Martiri, off Viale del Teatro Romano, are the overgrown remains of a 1st-century-AD **Teatro Romano** (075 922 09 22; admission free; 8.30am-7.30pm Apr-Sep, 8am 1.30pm Oct-Mar). In the summer, check with the tourist office about outdoor concerts held here.

Festivals & Events

The **Corsa dei Ceri** (Candles Race) is a centuries-old event held each year on 15 May to commemorate the city's patron saint, Sant'Ubaldo. It starts at 5.30am and involves three teams, each carrying a *cero* (these 'candles' are massive wooden pillars weighing about 400kg, each bearing a statue of a 'rival' saint) and racing through the city's streets. This is one of Italy's liveliest festivals and warrants inclusion in your itinerary.

On the last Sunday in May, there's the annual **Palio della Balestra**, an archery competition involving medieval crossbows, in which Gubbio competes with its neighbour San Sepolcro. The festival carries over all year in tourist shops alive with crossbow paraphernalia.

Sleeping

Many locals rent rooms to tourists, so ask at the tourist office about *affittacamere* (rooms for rent). You can also get a brochure there which lists hotels, camp sites and restaurants in the area with current prices.

Città di Gubbio & Villa Ortoguidone (075 927 20 37; fax 075 92 76 20; Loc Ortoguidone; person/tent €8.50/9, 2-person apt €40-83, 4-person apt €80-166; Easter-Sep;) For camping, try this site in Ortoguidone, a southern suburb of Gubbio, less than 3km south of Piazza Quaranta Martiri along the SS298 (Via Perugina). There are also stunning apartments in an old stone manor house with TVs, beautiful wooden furnishings and private bathrooms. July and August visits require a one-week stay.

Residenza Le Logge (075 927 75 74; www.pagine gialle.it/residenzalelogge in Italian; Via Piccardi 7-9; s/d/tr with breakfast €47/70/80) This is one of those rare little perfect locations, where you'll either appreciate the great value or feel luxurious on a tight budget. Decorated throughout with homy antiques and comfortable beds, it's quiet, tranquil and central. Three rooms feature great garden views, but the view of Gubbio is also beautiful. During summer, you can take your breakfast in the garden. Ask for the room with the gracious blue-and-white porcelain-and-ceramic bathtub big enough to park a Fiat in.

Locanda del Duca (/fax 075 927 77 53; www.um briatravel.com/delduca/locandadelducaeng.htm; Via Piccardi 1; s/d/tr/q €42/57/67/77) One of the cheapest hotels in town, Locanda del Duca has just seven rooms, all with pleasant polished wood interiors and grand wooden doors. Some rooms have views of the Palazzo dei Consoli or the river.

Bosone Palace (075 922 06 88; www.mencarelli group.com; Via XX Settembre 22; s/d with breakfast €77/110, ste with breakfast €165-195;) Fancy a fresco with your breakfast? How about staying in a room once frequented by Dante Alighieri? The patrician Bosone family enjoyed Dante as a guest several times. The place went through a complete renovation in 2005 to move from three-star to four-star category, deservedly so. All rooms have minibars, satellite TV and phones in the bathroom, and many have gorgeous views of the surrounding valley. For the experience of a lifetime, upgrade to a Renaissance Suite.

Grotta dell'Angelo (075 927 17 47; grottadell angelo@jumpy.it; Via Gioia 47; s/d/tr €52/75/90; closed part of Jan) While it is mostly a popular restaurant with all sorts of truffle dishes and a beautiful garden, the Grotta dell'Angelo also serves up a few basic rooms for rent.

Eating

Taverna del Lupo (075 927 43 68; Via Ansidei 21; mains €16; Tue-Sun) Il Lupo was the wolf that

St Francis domesticated, who supposedly came back to this restaurant to dine. The wolf made an excellent choice. The atmosphere is sophisticated if a bit stiff. Most ingredients are local, fresh and meals deserve at least two hours to properly savour.

Ristorante Il Campanone (☎ 075 927 60 11; Via Piccardi 21; mains €7-14.50; ✆ Thu-Tue) In a cavernous vaulted restaurant just a few blocks from Piazza Grande. Meals are as rich as they are delicious; decidedly popular is the veal with pear and truffle appetizer (€9) and for a main course, puff pastry with beef, local cheese and tomatoes, and basil (€13).

Ristorante Fabiani (☎ 075 927 46 39; Piazza Quaranta Martiri 26; mains €6.80-16.50; ✆ Wed-Mon) A fabulous spot to sit in the back patio and enjoy the garden for a few hours. The selection here is vast, and they offer a rotating €15 tourist menu or a €20 *menù gastronomico* of whatever is in season. Stop in on Thursday or Friday for their fish specials.

Shopping

Leo Grilli Arte (☎ 075 922 22 72; Via dei Consoli 78; ✆ 9.30am-1pm & 3-7pm Tue-Sun) In the Middle Ages, ceramics were one of Gubbio's main sources of income and there are some fabulous contemporary samples on sale in this crumbly 15th-century mansion.

Getting There & Around

APM buses run to Perugia (€4, one hour 10 minutes, eight daily), Gualdo Tadino (€2.40, 50 minutes, 10 daily) and Umbertide (€2.80, 50 minutes, three daily). Buses depart from Piazza Quaranta Martiri.

The closest train station is at Fossato di Vico, about 18km southeast of the city. Hourly APM buses connect the station with Gubbio (€2.20, 30 minutes), although there are delays of up to an hour between train and bus connections. From Fossato di Vico, hourly trains take about 30 minutes to Foligno (€2.55), where you can switch for other cities.

By car or motorcycle, take the SS298 from Perugia or the SS76 from Ancona, and follow the signs. Parking in the large car park in Piazza Quaranta Martiri costs €0.50 per hour.

Walking is the best way to get around, but APM buses connect Piazza Quaranta Martiri with the funicular station and most main sights.

PARCO REGIONALE DEL MONTE CUCCO

East of Gubbio, Parco Regionale del Monte Cucco is a haven for outdoor activities and is also dotted with caves, many of which can be explored. It is well set up for walkers, rock climbers and horse riders, and has many hotels and *rifugi* (mountain huts). **Costacciaro**, accessible by bus from Gubbio (€2.20, 30 minutes) via Scheggia or Fossato di Vico, is a good base for exploring the area and is the starting point for a walk to the summit of Monte Cucco (1566m).

Monte Cucco is a fantastic place to go caving. The Monte Cucco karst system is the largest in Italy and the fifth deepest in the world (922m). Sinkholes, wells and dolines create unique geological formations and lush habitats for various species of birds and plants.

The Club Alpino Italiano (C I) produces a walking map, *Carta dei Sentieri Massiccio del Monte Cucco* (€12), for sale in local bookshops and at newsagents. The free booklet *Monte Cucco Park: Country Walks through History* is available in English at *rifugi* and tourist offices throughout Umbria. Use this as a guide to the best of Umbria's nature and history. The booklet describes in detail 11 walks in the area, taking you through some of Umbria's most picturesque terrain, which is more alpinelike than the typical rolling hillside. The guide also details the estimated time needed while walking at a good pace (most take at least four hours and are far from civilization, so take lots of water and emergency supplies just in case), the presence of water sources on the trail and a thorough map of each route. If you don't have your walking gear, Tour #6 is a 62km driving route through ancient abbeys and monasteries in the region.

Centro Escursionistico Naturalistico Speleologico (☎ 075 917 04 00; www.cens.it in Italian; Via Galeazzi 5, Costacciaro) can help you with information about exploring local caves, walking and mountain-bike routes, and set you up with rafting and cross-country skiing expeditions. You can get information at the **park office** (☎ 075 917 73 26; parco.montecucco@libero.it; Villa Anita, Via Matteotti 52, Sigillo) about the area, as well as hang-gliding and walking trips. Online, look for information at www.parks.it/parco .monte.cucco.

The **Campeggio Rio Verde** (☎ 075 917 01 38; www .campingrioverde.it in Italian; adult/child/tent/car €5/3/

4.50/2.50) camp site offers horse riding (€13 per hour, during summer), rock climbing and speleology (cave exploration). It's 3km west of Costacciaro. Many *agriturismo* establishments in the area can also arrange horse riding. Don't even consider coming here on a weekend in August – the rates more than quintuple. A good mountain inn is the **Rifugio Escursionistico Dal Lepre** (☎ /fax 075 917 77 33; Pian del Monte, Sigillo, Montecucco; r with breakfast €15), also featuring a decent restaurant.

It is possible to hire mountain bikes at the **Coop Arte e Natura** (☎ 075 917 07 40; Via Stazione 2) in the village of Fossato di Vico, about 8km southeast of Costacciaro.

SPOLETO

pop 37,360

Each June and July, this otherwise quiet town takes centre stage for an international parade of drama, music, opera and dance (see p571). If you plan to visit Spoleto during the festival, book accommodation and tickets months in advance. When the festival ends, Spoleto goes back to sleep, but it's nonetheless an enchanting town to spend a day or two exploring.

Orientation

The old part of the city is about 1km south of the main train station; take the orange shuttle bus (€0.80) marked A, B or C for Piazza della Libertà in the centre, where you'll find the tourist office and the Roman-era theatre. Piazza del Mercato, a short walk northeast of Piazza della Libertà, marks the engaging heart of old Spoleto. Between here and Piazza del Duomo you'll find the bulk of the city's monuments and some fine shops.

Information

A Tutta Birra (☎ 348 241 18 40; Via di Fontesecca 7; ☼ noon-11pm Wed-Mon) Internet facilities; you can also get a connection at Pizzeria Zeppelin (p572).

Ospedale di Madonna di Loretta (☎ 0743 21 01; Via Madonna di Loreto) Hospital.

Police (113 Viale Trento e Trieste)

Post office (☎ 0743 20 15 20; entrance off Viale Giacomo Matteotti; ☼ 8am-6.30pm Mon-Fri, 8am-12.30pm Sat)

Tourist office (☎ 0743 23 89 20/1; info@iat.spoleto .pg.it; Piazza della Libertà 7; ☼ 9am-1pm & 4-7pm Mon-Sat, 10am-1pm Sun summer, 9am-1pm & 3.30-6.30pm Mon-Sat winter)

Sights

ROMAN SPOLETO

Make your first stop the **Museo Archeologico** (☎ 0743 22 32 77; Via S Agata; adult/concession/child €4/2/ free; ☼ 8.30am-7.30pm), located on the western edge of Piazza della Libertà. It holds a well-displayed collection of Roman and Etruscan bits and bobs from the area. Then step outside to view the mostly intact 1st-century **Teatro Romano** (Roman Theatre), which often hosts live performances during the summer. Check with the museum or the tourist office.

East of Piazza della Libertà, around the Piazza Fontana, are more Roman remains, including the **Arco di Druso e Germanico** (Arch of Drusus and Germanicus; sons of the Emperor Tiberius), which marks the entrance to the old forum. The excavated **Casa Romana** (Roman House; ☎ /fax 0743 4 64 34; Via di Visiale; adult/ child €2/1; ☼ 10am-8pm daily 16 Mar–15 Oct, 10am-1pm & 3-6pm Wed-Mon 16 Oct–15 Mar) dates from the 1st century.

CHURCHES

A short walk north through Piazza del Municipio takes you to the 12th-century **Chiesa di Sant'Eufemia** (☎ 0743 23 10 22; Via A Saffi; adult/child €3.10/1.55; ☼ 10am-12.30pm & 3.30-7pm summer, 10am-12.30pm & 3.30-6pm winter). Set within the grounds of the archbishop's palazzo, it is notable for its *matronei*, galleries set high above the main body of the church to segregate the female congregation.

From here, it is a quick stroll northeast to the **cathedral** (☎ 0743 4 43 07; Piazza del Duomo; ☼ 7.30am-12.30pm & 3-6pm summer, 7.30am-12.30pm & 3-5pm winter), consecrated in 1198 and remodelled in the 17th century. Inside, the first chapel to the right of the nave was decorated by Bernardino Pinturicchio, and Annibale Carracci completed an impressive fresco in the right transept. The frescoes in the domed apse were executed by Filippo Lippi and his assistants. Lippi died before completing the work and Lorenzo de Medici travelled to Spoleto from Florence and ordered Lippi's son, Filippino, to build a mausoleum for the artist. This now stands in the right transept of the cathedral.

The spectacular closing concert of the Spoleto Festival is held on the piazza.

OTHER SIGHTS

Inside the town hall on Piazza del Municipio is the **Pinacoteca Comunale** (☎ 0743 21 81; Piazza

SPOLETO

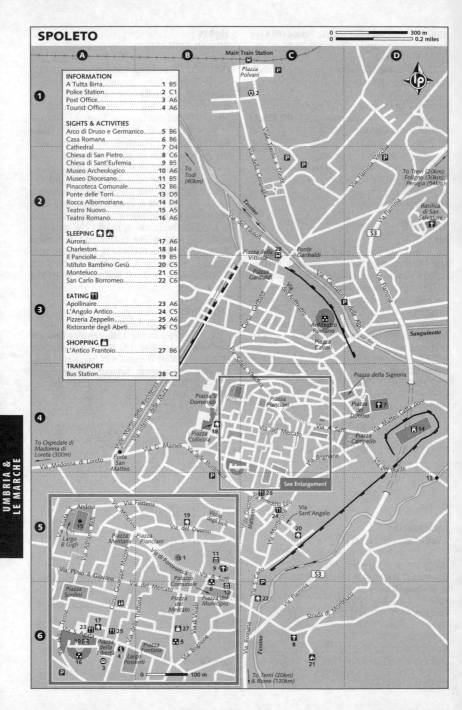

0   300 m
0   0.2 miles

INFORMATION	
A Tutta Birra............................1	B5
Police Station.........................2	C1
Post Office.............................3	A6
Tourist Office.........................4	A6

SIGHTS & ACTIVITIES	
Arco di Druso e Germanico.........5	B6
Casa Romana...........................6	B6
Cathedral...............................7	D4
Chiesa di San Pietro..................8	C6
Chiesa di Sant'Eufemia...............9	B5
Museo Archeologico.................10	A6
Museo Diocesano....................11	B5
Pinacoteca Comunale...............12	B6
Ponte delle Torri.....................13	D5
Rocca Albornoziana................14	D4
Teatro Nuovo.........................15	A5
Teatro Romano.......................16	A6

SLEEPING	
Aurora...................................17	A6
Charleston.............................18	B4
Il Panciolle............................19	B5
Istituto Bambino Gesù..............20	C5
Monteluco.............................21	C6
San Carlo Borromeo................22	C6

EATING	
Apollinaire............................23	A6
L'Angolo Antico......................24	C5
Pizzeria Zeppelin....................25	A6
Ristorante degli Abeti..............26	C5

SHOPPING	
L'Antico Frantoio....................27	B6

TRANSPORT	
Bus Station............................28	C2

0   100 m

del Municipio; adult/child incl tour €2/1; 10am-1pm & 3-6pm Tue-Sun). It is a sumptuous building, with some impressive works by Umbrian artists.

The **Rocca Albornoziana** (/fax 0743 22 30 55; Piazza Campello; adult/child incl tour €4/3; 10am-8pm summer & weekends, 10am-1pm & 3-6pm late Mar-Jun, Sep & Oct, closed Nov–early Mar) dominates the city. It's a former papal fortress that until 1982 was a high-security prison housing such notables as Pope John Paul II's attempted assassin, Ali Agca. Reservations for tours are essential as entry is only by guided tour.

An hour-long stroll or an all-day hike can be made along the Via del Ponte to the **Ponte delle Torri**, erected in the 14th century on the foundations of a Roman aqueduct. Cross the bridge and follow the lower path, Strada di Monteluco, to reach the **Chiesa di San Pietro** (0743 4 48 82; Loc San Pietro; admission free; 9.30am-11am & 3.30-6.30pm). The 13th-century façade, the main attraction of the church, is liberally bedecked with sculpted animals.

Festivals & Events

The Italian-American composer Gian Carlo Menotti conceived the **Festival dei Due Mondi** (Festival of Two Worlds) in 1958. Now simply known as the Spoleto Festival, it has given the town a worldwide reputation.

Events at the festival, held over three weeks from late June to mid-July, range from opera and theatre performances to ballet and art exhibitions, in the Rocca Albornoziana and **Teatro Nuovo** (Largo B Gigli) and the cathedral, among other places. Tickets cost €5 to €200, but most are in the €20 to €30 range. The most famous performances sell out as early as March or April, but you can still buy tickets that week for many shows. There are usually several free concerts in various churches.

For details, phone 800 565 600 or look for further details and book tickets online at www.spoletofestival.it.

Sleeping

The city is well served by cheap hotels, *affittacamere*, hostels and camp sites, although if you're coming for the festival you will need to book a room months in advance.

BUDGET

Monteluco (/fax 0743 22 03 58; Loc San Pietro; www.geocities.com/monteluco2002; person/tent €5/6; Apr-Sep) This leafy, quiet camp site is just behind the Chiesa di San Pietro. It's an easy 15- to 20-minute walk from the town centre and less than a kilometre from the aqueduct and several good walking trails. The restaurant at the camp site is good enough to bring locals out.

Istituto Bambino Gesù (0743 4 02 32; Via Sant' Angelo 4; s/d with breakfast €28/50) The combined age of these enterprising nun/B&B proprietors might be older than the 16th-century convent itself. Get in touch with your monastic side in these bare-bones cells, containing no more than a bed, a dresser and a postage stamp–sized bathroom. But the price is right, the views are simply amazing and the dead-silent, pitch-black nights will guarantee a good night's sleep.

Il Panciolle (/fax 0743 4 56 77; Via del Duomo 3; s/d with bathroom from €45/60;) Comfortable enough for those used to nicer hotels and a splurge for hostellers, this Spoleto mainstay is in a good position between the cathedral and the Piazza del Mercato. The rooms facing the street can be a tad loud. Hairdryers, TVs and comfortable bedding in all rooms. Ask for a parking pass.

San Carlo Borromeo (0743 22 53 20; www.geocities.com/sancarloborromeo; Via San Carlo; s/d/tr with breakfast 35/52/72;) The least atmospheric of the hotels listed, the convenience, price and free car park make it a safe bet. The back rooms are quieter and have a view of Monteluco, but all are clean, functional and spacious. Disability access. Small pets welcome.

MIDRANGE

Charleston (0743 22 00 52; www.hotelcharleston.it; Piazza Collicola 10; s/d/tr/ste with breakfast €59/79/110/149;) With a sauna and a fireplace, as well as an outdoor terrace, the Charleston is an enticing location in both winter and summer. Named after Charleston, South Carolina (home of a sister Spoleto Festival), the hotel is covered in distinguished modern art and provides wine-tastings or *aperitivos* every evening. The 17th-century building has been thoroughly renovated with double-paned windows and some rooms come with VCRs or bathtubs. The wood-beamed attic suite is worth the splurge.

Aurora (0743 22 03 15; www.hotelauroraspoleto.it; Via Apollinaire 3; s/d €50/80;) Just off Piazza della Libertà, the Aurora is very central and fabulous value. The staff is friendly and will help you plan your Spoleto itinerary. Some rooms have pleasant balconies and breakfast is excellent.

Eating

Apollinaire (☎ 0743 22 32 56; Via S Agata 14; tasting/veggie menu €30/35; ☼ Wed-Sun) California cuisine meets Umbrian tradition. Somehow this restaurant manages to figure out that squid-ink pasta does go with pesto and crayfish, and rabbit feels quite at home in a black olive sauce. No matter what, save room for dessert. The menu changes seasonally but you are constantly enveloped in low wood-beamed ceilings and candlelight flickering against brick.

L'Angolo Antico (☎ 0743 4 90 66; Via Monterone 109; mains €8-14; ☼ Tue-Sun) Dine with a full set of armour under a vaulted beam ceiling in this family-run *ristorante* and pizzeria. Nothing fancy on the menu, just good filling *strangozzi alla spoletina* (local pasta in fresh tomato sauce) and *scallopine al limone* (pork in a lemon sauce).

Ristorante degli Abeti (☎ 0743 22 00 25; Via Benedetto Egio 3/5; mains €6.50-17; ☼ Wed-Mon) Get your red meat and cream fix here. Not the place for dieters or vegetarians, the menu offers sinfully rich piles of artery-thickeners, such as *pappardelle con cinghiale e tartufo* (pasta with wild boar and truffles) and *prosciutto di cinghiale* (ham with wild boar).

Pizzeria Zeppelin (☎ 0743 4 77 67; Corso Giuseppe Mazzini 81; pizzas & snacks €0.80-3; ☼ 10.30am-9.30pm) A meeting point in town, here you can get a filling slice of pizza for less than €1, plus check your email (one hour costs €3)

Shopping

L'Antico Frantoio (☎ 0743 4 98 93; Via Arco di Druso 8) Sandra has been cooking up her own sauces for several decades now. She sells them at this gourmet store, along with cheeses, salami, pasta, *lenticchie* (lentils) and all sorts of Umbrian goodies. A conveniently placed grocer is just next door, selling fresh olive bread and drinks with which to plan your Spoleto picnic.

Getting There & Around

From the train station, take city buses A–E for €0.80 (make sure the bus reads 'Centro'). The local **Società Spoletina di Imprese Trasporti** (SSIT; ☎ 0743 21 22 08/9; www.spoletina.com) buses depart from the near the train station. Long-distance buses are rare as the train is so

convenient, but you'll need a bus to get to Norcia and the Valnerina (€4.40, one hour, six daily) or Cascia (€4.40, one hour 10 minutes, six daily). Buses to Monteluco run in summer only (€0.80, 15 minutes, hourly).

Trains from the main **station** (☎ 0743 4 85 16; Piazza Polvani) connect with Rome (€6.85 to €11.60, one to 2½ hours, hourly), Ancona (€7.90 to €13.15, two hours, 10 daily), Perugia (€3.50, one hour, seven daily) and Assisi (€2.55, 40 minutes, hourly – take care not to land on one of the €9.10 Eurostars).

NORCIA & THE VALNERINA

The Valnerina is a valley, and the fortified medieval village of Norcia is the valley's main town and a transport hub of sorts.

Like the rest of the Valnerina, Norcia has suffered from many earthquakes over the centuries; several buildings were damaged in 1997. For tourist information, visit the **Casa del Parco** (☎ 0743 81 70 90; Via Solferino 22; ☼ 9.30am-12.30pm & 3-6pm Mon-Fri, 9.30am-12.30pm & 3.30-6.30pm Sat & Sun).

Festivals & Events

The last weekend in February plus the first weekend are March is dedicated to the **Mostra Mercato del Tartufo Nero** (black truffle market) and to the display of black truffles, with lots of music and folkloric festivities.

Activities

The Casa del Parco has information on walking and other activities in the surrounding area. To hang-glide or paraglide, head for Castelluccio.

The area forms part of the **Parco Nazionale dei Monti Sibillini**. Buy Kompass map No 666 (scale 1:50,000) of walking trails, available from the Casa del Parco.

To learn hang-gliding, contact **Pro Delta** (☎ 0743 82 11 56; www.prodelta.it/eng/main.htm; Via delle Fate 3) in Castelluccio; it opens in summer only. No credit cards are accepted, but readers have enthused about the courses. Another school is **Fly Castelluccio** (☎ 0736 25 56 30; Via Iannella 32, Ascoli Piceno, Le Marche). A beginners course of five days will cost about €400 at both organisations.

To hire bikes, try **Associazione Pian Grande** (☎ 0743 81 72 79, 0743 81 70 22; Pian Grande di Castelluccio di Norcia), which is open mostly in the afternoons from Easter to October. They can also arrange horse riding.

PIAN GRANDE

Mountainous perfection lies in the fields just east of Norcia. A steep 26km drive will bring you to the mystical Monti Sibillini (p596), awash with flowers during the spring and snow during the winter.

Perched above the Pian Grande is the tiny hill-top village of **Castelluccio**, where you can still see goats wandering through the ancient cobblestone streets. The town is famous for its *lenticchie* (lentils), and *pecorino* and ricotta cheeses. The sole hotel is **Albergo Sibilla** (☎ /fax 0743 82 11 13; Via Pian Grande 2; s/d €29/45), with 11 rooms, some with a view to die for, and a good restaurant downstairs.

Sleeping & Eating

Norcia produces the country's best salami – in fact the word 'Norcineria' is synonymous with 'butcher' throughout all of Italy. This is also a stronghold of the elusive black truffle.

Hotel Grotta Azzura (☎ 0743 81 65 13; www.bianconi.com; Via Alfieri 12; s €37-88, d €44-125, mains €7-19) An 18th-century palazzo with suits of armour in the reception, this hotel can be a fabulous deal during the week and off season, but don't even think of coming here on a Saturday in August. The restaurant, Ristorante Granaro del Monte, is well known throughout the region. It is a tad touristy, but the food is still excellent and comes in great piles of truffles, *porcini* and sausages. In the winter, sit inside next to the grand fireplace.

Da Benito (☎ 0743 81 66 70; guelsnc@virgilio.it; Via Marconi 5; s €27-40, d €30-75) This is a friendly one-star hotel within the city walls. There are eight modest rooms above a family-run restaurant.

ORVIETO

pop 21,600
The entire town is placed precariously on a cliff made of the area's tufaceous stone, a craggy porous limestone that seems imminently ready to crumble under the weight of Orvieto's magnificent Gothic cathedral (or, at least under all the tourists who are now drawn to see it). Just off a main autostrada, Orvieto can get a bit crowded with summer bus tours, but they're all here for good reason.

Orientation

Trains pull in at Orvieto Scalo and from here you can catch bus No 1 up to the old town or board the funicular to take you up the steep hill to Piazza Cahen.

Those with cars should head to a free lot behind the train station (at the roundabout in front of the station head in the direction of 'Arezzo' and turn left into the large parking lot). There's plenty of parking space in Piazza Cahen and in several designated areas outside the old city walls. The Orvieto Unica Card (below) will buy you five hours of free parking at the former Campo della Fiera and take you on an *ascensore* (lift) into the city centre.

Information

ATC (☺ 8am-1.15pm & 4-6pm Mon-Fri) Tourist office, beside the train station. Also sells the Orvieto Unica Card.
Caffè Montanucci (0763 34 12 61; Corso Cavour 21; per 30min €3.10; ☺ Thu-Tue) Pick up a supply of chocolate or a *panini* at this café (see p577), while you surf the Internet.
Doctor (☎ 0763 30 18 84)
Hospital (☎ 0763 30 71) In the Ciconia area, east of the train station.
Libreria dei Sette (☎ 0763 34 44 36; Corso Cavour 85; ☺ 9am-1pm & 4-8pm) Stock up on a collection of maps, English-language books or Lonely Planets (in Italian).
Police station (☎ 0763 39 21 11; Piazza Cahen)
Post office (☎ 0763 34 09 14; Via Largo M Ravelli; ☺ 8.10am-4.45pm Mon-Sat)
Tourist office (☎ 0763 34 17 72; info@iat.orvieto.tr.it; Piazza del Duomo 24; ☺ 8.15am-1.50pm & 4-7pm Mon-Fri, 10am-1pm & 3-6pm Sat, Sun & holidays)

Sights

If you plan to spend more than a day in Orvieto consider buying the **Orvieto Unico Card** (adult/concession valid 1 yr €12.50/10.50). It entitles its owner to entrance to the four biggest attractions (the Cappella di San Brizio, Museo Claudio Faina e Civico, Orvieto Underground and Torre del Moro), five hours' free car parking at the train station or a return trip on the cable car and city buses, and offers discounts at many shops and restaurants in town. It can be purchased at the parking lot Campo della Fiera, the attractions listed earlier, the tourist office or the funicular parking lot.

CATHEDRAL

Little can prepare you for the visual feast that is the **cathedral** (☎ 0763 34 11 67; Piazza del

ORVIETO

INFORMATION
ATC.....................................1 F1
Libreria dei Sette.................2 C2
Police Station.......................3 E1
Post Office...........................4 C2
Tourist Office.......................5 C3

SIGHTS & ACTIVITIES
Cathedral.............................6 C3
Chiesa di San Giovenale.....7 A2

Chiesa di Sant'Andrea.............8 B2
La Rocca.................................9 E1
Museo Archeologico Nazionale..10 D3
Museo Claudio Faina e Civico...11 C3
Museo d'Arte Moderna Emilio
    Greco............................(see 14)
Museo dell'Opera del Duomo..(see 14)
Orvieto Underground............12 C3
Palazzo del Popolo.................13 C2
Palazzo Papale.......................(see 10)

Palazzo Soliano....................14 C3
Parco delle Grotte...............(see 12)
Pozzo di San Patrizio............15 E1
Torre del Moro....................16 C2

Duomo; ☾ 7.30am-12.45pm year-round, 2.30-7.15pm Apr-Sep, 2.30-6.15pm Mar & Oct & 2.30-5.15pm Nov-Feb). Started in 1290, this remarkable edifice was originally planned in the Romanesque style but, as work proceeded and architects changed, Gothic features were incorporated into the structure. The black-and-white marble banding of the main body of the church is overshadowed by the rich rainbow colours of the façade. A harmonious blend of mosaic and sculpture, plain stone and dazzling colour, it has been likened to a giant outdoor altar screen.

Pope Urban IV ordered that the cathedral be built following the Miracle of Bolsena in 1263, when a priest who was passing through the town of Bolsena (near Orvieto) had his doubts about transubstantiation dispelled when blood began to drip from the Host onto the altar linen while he celebrated mass. The linen was presented to Pope Urban IV in Orvieto. He also declared the new feast day of Corpus Domini.

The building took 30 years to plan and three centuries to complete. It was probably started by Fra Bevignate and later additions

were made by Lorenzo Maitani (responsible for Florence's cathedral), Andrea Pisano and his son Nino Pisano, Andrea Orcagna and Michele Sanicheli. The great bronze doors, the work of Emilio Greco, were added in the 1960s.

Inside, Luca Signorelli's fresco cycle *The Last Judgement* shimmers with life. Look for it to the right of the altar in the **Cappella di San Brizio** (admission €3; ☾ closed during Mass). Signorelli began work on the series in 1499, and Michelangelo is said to have taken inspiration from it. Indeed, to some, Michelangelo's masterpiece runs a close second to Signorelli's work. The **Cappella del Corporale** (admission free; ☾ 7.30am-12.45pm & 2.30-7.15pm summer, varies winter, closed during Mass) houses the blood-stained altar linen of the miracle, preserved in a silver reliquary decorated by artists of the Sienese school. The walls feature frescoes depicting the miracle, painted by Ugolino di Prete Ilario.

AROUND THE CATHEDRAL
Next to the cathedral is the **Museo dell'Opera del Duomo** (☎ 0763 34 24 77; Palazzo Soliano, Piazza del

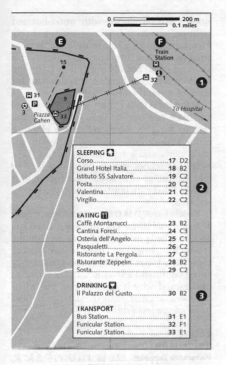

0   200 m
0   0.1 miles

Train Station

To Hospital

Piazza Cahen

SLEEPING 🏠

Corso	17	D2
Grand Hotel Italia	18	B2
Istituto SS Salvatore	19	C2
Posta	20	C2
Valentina	21	C2
Virgilio	22	C2

EATING 🍴

Caffè Montanucci	23	B2
Cantina Foresi	24	C3
Osteria dell'Angelo	25	C1
Pasqualetti	26	C2
Ristorante La Pergola	27	C3
Ristorante Zeppelin	28	B2
Sosta	29	C2

DRINKING 🍷

Il Palazzo del Gusto	30	B2

TRANSPORT

Bus Station	31	E1
Funicular Station	32	F1
Funicular Station	33	E1

Duomo; admission €5; 🕙 10am-noon Tue & Thu, 11am-1pm & 3-6pm Sat & Sun), which houses a clutter of religious relics from the cathedral, as well as Etruscan antiquities and works by artists such as Simone Martini and the three Pisanos: Andrea, Nino and Giovanni.

Museo d'Arte Moderna Emilio Greco (☎ 0763 34 46 05; Palazzo Soliano, Piazza del Duomo; adult/child €2.50/1.50; 🕙 10.30am-1pm & 2-6.30pm Tue-Sun Apr-Sep, 10.30am-1pm & 2-5.30pm Tue-Sun Oct-Mar) displays a collection of modern pieces by Emilio Greco, the creator of the cathedral's bronze doors. A full-fare €5.50 (concession €4) combined ticket also includes admission to the Pozzo di San Patrizio.

Around the corner in the **Palazzo Papale** you can view Etruscan antiquities in the **Museo Archeologico Nazionale** (☎ /fax 0763 34 10 39; Palazzo Papale, Piazza del Duomo; adult/concession €3/1.50; 🕙 8.30am-7.30pm). The much more interesting **Museo Claudio Faina e Civico** (☎ 0763 34 15 11; www.museofaina.it; Piazza del Duomo 29; adult/concession €4.50/3; 🕙 9.30am-6pm Apr-Sep, 10am-5pm Tue-Sun Oct-Mar), opposite the cathedral, houses one of Italy's most important collection of Etruscan archaeological artefacts, as well as some

significant Greek ceramic works, mostly found near Piazza Cahen in tombs dating back to the 6th century BC. There are guided tours at 11am and 4pm (3pm October to March) and an interactive trip for kids.

OTHER SIGHTS & ACTIVITIES

Head northwest along Via del Duomo to Corso Cavour and the **Torre del Moro** (Moor's Tower; ☎ 0763 34 45 67; Corso Cavour 87; adult/concession €2.80/2; 🕙 10am-8pm May-Aug, 10am-7pm Mar, Apr, Sep & Oct, 10.30am-1pm & 2.30-7pm Nov-Feb). Climb all 250 steps for sweeping views of the city. Back on ground level, continue west to Piazza della Repubblica, and to the 12th-century **Chiesa di Sant'Andrea** (Piazza della Repubblica; 🕙 8.30am-12.30pm & 3.30-7.30pm) and its curious decagonal bell tower. The piazza, once Orvieto's Roman forum, is at the heart of what remains of the medieval city.

North of Corso Cavour, the 12th-century Romanesque-Gothic **Palazzo del Popolo** presides over the piazza of the same name. At the northwestern end of town is the **Chiesa di San Giovenale** (Piazza Giovenale; 🕙 8am-12.30pm & 3.30-6pm), a church constructed in the year 1000. Its Romanesque-Gothic art and later frescoes from the medieval Orvieto school are an astounding contrast.

Standing watch at the town's easternmost tip is the 14th-century fortress known as **La Rocca**, part of which is now a public garden. To the north of the fortress, the **Pozzo di San Patrizio** (St Patrick's Well; ☎ 0763 34 37 68; Viale Sangallo; adult/concession €4.50/3.50; 🕙 10am-6.45pm Apr-Sep, to 5.45pm Sep-Apr) is a well that stands as a testament to the hardy disposition of the townsfolk. More than 60m deep, it is lined by two spiral staircases (for water-bearing mules) and a Latin inscription that reads: 'What nature denied for defence, in this case water, was added by the work of man'.

The coolest place in Orvieto – literally – is the **Orvieto Underground** (☎ 0763 34 06 88, ☎ 339 733 27 64; Parco delle Grotte; adult/concession €5.50/3.30; 🕙 tours 11am, 12.15pm, 4pm & 5.15pm daily Mar-Jan, Sat & Sun Feb), a series of 440 caves used for millennia by locals for various purposes. The tours (with English- or German-speaking guides) take you through several that were used back through the centuries as WWII bomb shelters, refrigerators, wells and, during many a pesky Roman or Barbarian siege, as dovecotes to trap their usual one-course dinner: pigeon (still seen on local restaurant menus as *palombo*). Tours leave from in front of the tourist office. Hint: during the summer, take the 12.15pm tour. You'll enjoy the year-round temperature of 12°C to 15°C, while most museums and shops are closed.

Festivals & Events

Umbria Jazz Winter takes place from the end of December to early January, with a great feast and party on New Year's Eve. Ask at the tourist office for a programme of events. See p548 for details of the summer jazz festival.

Sleeping

Orvieto does not lack for hotels, and visitors will benefit from the highly competitive pricing. It's always a good idea to book ahead in summer or at the weekend or if you're planning to come over New Year when the Umbria Jazz Winter festival is in full swing.

BUDGET

Porziuncola (☎ 0763 34 13 87; Loc Cappuccini 8; dm €10-12; P) With only eight beds in two separate single-sex rooms, you'd do best to call ahead. Take bus No 5 from Piazza Cahen to the Cappuccini neighbourhood, just a few kilometres away.

Istituto SS Salvatore (☎ /fax 0763 34 29 10; www .argoweb.it/istituto_sansalvatore; Via del Popolo 1; s/d €35/55) Practise your Italian with these jovial nuns. There is a 10.30pm curfew, but the place is comfortable and clean and there's a lovely garden. Singles don't have bathrooms.

Posta (☎ 0763 34 19 09; www.orvietohotels.it; Via L Signorelli 18; s/d €31/43, with bathroom €37/56) Rooms in this stolid, rather ramshackle but impressive 16th-century building are endearing, as if your quirky great aunt with the big hoop earrings had decorated them. Great fluffy blankets.

Valentina (☎ /fax 0763 34 16 07; valentina.z@tiscali net.it; Via Vivaria 7; s/d/tr with breakfast €50/65/85, apt €130) As if being set back on a quiet street wasn't enough, the rooms are also soundproof, casually elegant and spacious. Valentina lives downstairs with two friendly dogs. All rooms have private bathrooms, TVs and hairdryers, and laundry service is available.

MIDRANGE

Corso (☎ /fax 0763 34 20 20; www.hotelcorso.net; Corso Cavour 343; s/d €60/82; ❷ 💻) Set a bit further away from the cathedral than most other hotels, this is nevertheless an excellent choice.

Rooms are enveloped with wood-beamed ceilings, terracotta bricks or antique cherry furniture, allowing one to describe them as snug rather than tiny. The breakfast buffet is an extra €6.50 but it's worth it to sit on the outdoor terrace. There's a 10% discount for stays of more than two nights.

Grand Hotel Italia (☎ 076 334 32 75; www.grand hotelitalia.it; Via di Piazza del Popolo 13; s/d with breakfast €80/130; P) The rooms reflect the elegance of the 19th-century building, many with superb views and a few with balconies. Take note that school groups often stay here to take advantage of its conference rooms, so it can get filled with boisterous teenagers every so often.

Virgilio (☎ 0763 34 18 82; www.hotelvirgilio.it; Piazza del Duomo 5; s/d €62/85) This three-star hotel has an unrivalled position on Piazza del Duomo. It has clean, bright and basic rooms; most of these have views that are so spectacular they could command admission. It's not hard to understand why it's so popular, but when the rooms are that small, the staff could stand to be a little less gruff.

Eating
RESTAURANTS

Ristorante Zeppelin (☎ 0763 34 14 47; Via Garibaldi 28; mains €24; ☯ closed dinner Sun) This natty place has a cool 1920s atmosphere, jazz on the stereo and a long wooden bar where Ingrid Bergman would have felt right at home. It serves creative Umbrian food, including well-priced tasting menus for vegetarians (€25), children (€20), truffle-lovers (€40) and traditionalists (€25). Ask about their day-long cooking courses.

Sosta (☎ 0763 34 30 25; Corso Cavour 100a; mains €5) This extremely simple self-service restaurant actually serves up some very good pizza and pasta. It's cafeteria style so you order as much or as little as you like, including meat and vegetable dishes. Students get a discount.

Osteria dell'Angelo (☎ 0763 34 18 05; Piazza XXIX Marzo 8a; mains €22; ☯ Tue-Sun) Judged by local food writers to be one of the best restaurants in Umbria, this is certainly an elegant place. Your meal is being cooked by the winner of the 2000 'Chef to Watch' competition. The banana soufflé with a rum-and-cream sauce is recommended and the wine list is extensive.

Ristorante La Pergola (☎ 0763 34 30 65; Via dei Magoni 9b; mains €9; ☯ Thu-Tue) The food at this restaurant is typically Umbrian – good and filling – but the real draw here is dining in the flower-filled garden in the back. If you can, try the *cinghiale*.

CAFÉS
Caffè Montanucci (☎ 0763 34 12 61; Corso Cavour 21; dishes from €3.60; ☒ Thu-Tue) An affable one-stop shop for espresso, *gelato*, *panini*, Internet access and the best part: the wall o' chocolate. There are hundreds of chocolate bars from all over the world piled up on a few of the tables, causing the mouths of many passers-by to water.

Cantina Foresi (☎ /fax 0763 34 16 11; Piazza del Duomo 2) A family-run café serving up *panini* and sausages, washed down with wines from the ancient cellar.

GELATERIE
Pasqualetti (☎ 0763 34 10 34; Piazza del Duomo 14) This *gelateria* serves mouth-watering *gelato*, plus there are plenty of tables on the piazza for you to gaze at the magnificence of the cathedral while you gobble.

Drinking
Il Palazzo del Gusto (☎ 0763 39 35 29; www.orvieto congusto.it; Via Ripa Serancia I 16; wine tastings €5-11; ☒ 11am-1pm & 3-5pm winter, 11am-1pm & 5-7pm summer) This Etruscan subterranean wine cellar is as infused with atmosphere as it is with yeast. Several tunnels have been redecorated for wine tastings and parties. Peek behind the glass doors for a look at ancient Etruscan tunnels. Check with the tourist office as to when they're open for tastings.

Shopping
Despite being a tourist town, the quality of the local products is still high. Look out for shops selling ceramics, lace and delicious sample packs of local wines, sausages, olive oil, cheeses and mushroom products. Explore and enjoy.

Getting There & Away
Buses depart from the station on Piazza Cahen and make a stop at the train station as well. Cotral buses connect the city with Viterbo in Lazio (€2.80, 1½ hours, seven daily) and Bagnoregio (€1.65, one hour, seven daily), where you can take a bus into Civita di Bagnoregio (p186). **ATC buses** (☎ 0763 34 22 65) run to Todi (€4.40, one hour, at 2.05pm

returning at 5.50am), while **SIRA** (☎ 0763 417 30 053) runs a daily bus service to Rome at 8.10am Monday to Saturday, and at 7.10am on Sunday (€5.15, 1½ hours).

Trains travel to Rome (€6.85, 1¼ hours, hourly) and Florence (€10.10 to €17.15, 1½ to 2½ hours, hourly), Perugia (€6.10, 1¼ hours, at least every other hour). The city is on the A1, and the SS71 heads north to Lago di Trasimeno.

Getting Around
A century-old funicular connects Piazza Cahen with the train station, with carriages leaving every 10 to 15 minutes from 7.15am to 8.30pm daily (€0.80 or €0.90 including the bus from Piazza Cahen to Piazza del Duomo). Bus No 1 also runs up to the old town from the train station (€0.80). Once in Orvieto, the easiest way to see the city is on foot, although ATC bus A connects Piazza Cahen with Piazza del Duomo and bus B runs to Piazza della Repubblica.

For a taxi, dial ☎ 0763 30 19 03 or swing by Piazza Matteotti.

LE MARCHE

Those in the Italian know have been tossing around the idea of Le Marche as the next Tuscany. It's got it all: a dramatic coastline quickly rising to sloping hillsides and finishing off with jagged mountain peaks. The hundreds of enchanting towns that cling to the hill tops are teeming with an astonishing heritage of ancient churches, splendid monuments and priceless art treasures that have been largely ignored by travellers. The capital, Ancona, has been a maritime port since the Greeks discovered it centuries ago and it still ferries thousands of goods and people back and forth to far-off destinations: Albania, Turkey, Greece, Croatia. But it's further inland where you can visit some of Italy's most splendid ancient cities: Urbino, the Renaissance in microcosm; the stunningly beautiful but undiscovered Ascoli Piceno; and lovely little Macerata. In Pesaro you'll find the sea, ancient archaeology and throngs of pale sun-seekers in Speedos. Magical Monti Sibillini stands out from the central Apennines, often swathed in mystical fog and dusted with snow, even in the summer months.

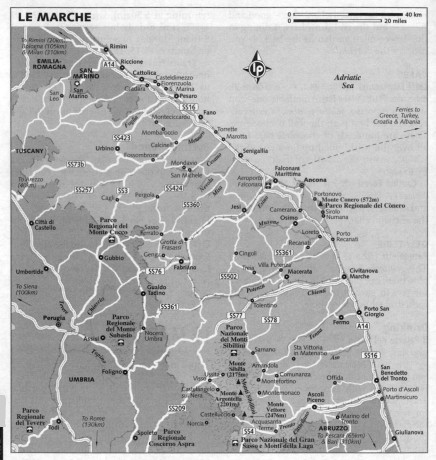

LE MARCHE

Adriatic Sea

History

Not much is known about the first inhabitants of Le Marche, who lived along the coast as far back as 23,000 years ago. The first archaeological evidence is from the Piceni tribe (whose 3000-year-old artefacts can be seen in the Museo Archeologico in Ascoli Piceno). The Romans invaded the region early in the 3rd century BC, and dominated the area for almost 700 years. At the fall of the Roman Empire, Le Marche was sacked by the Goths, Vandals, Ostrogoths and, finally, the Lombards.

In the middle of the 8th century AD, Pope Stephen II decided to call upon foreigners to oust the ungodly Lombards. The first to lead the charge of the Frankish army was

Pepin the Short, but it was his rather tall son Charlemagne who finally took back control from the Lombards for good. On Christmas Day 800 AD, Pope Leo III crowned him emperor of the Holy Roman Empire. However, he was never recognized as such by the Eastern Byzantine church, which had control of much of Le Marche's Adriatic coast at the time.

After Charlemagne's death, Le Marche entered into centuries of war, anarchy and general Dark Ages mayhem. In central Italy, two factions developed, that of the Guelphs – who backed papal rule – and the Ghibellines – who backed rule by the emperor. The Guelph faction eventually won out and Le Marche became part of the Papal States, held under close watch by a succession of popes, while much of Europe was busy enjoying the Renaissance. It stayed there until Italian unification in 1861.

National Parks & Reserves

In the 1980s and '90s mass tourism, almost all concentrated on the coast, threatened to encroach on several natural areas. In response, Le Marche developed no less than 10 national and regional parks or protected areas, including the stunning Monti Sibillini in the far west Apennines and the coastal beauty of the Parco Regionale di Monte Conero near Ancona.

The Le Marche Regional Office of Tourism publishes some excellent free brochures and booklets on camping, *agriturismo* and other accommodation options, as well as details on the various parks themselves. You can pick up this information (although most of it is in Italian) at the main tourist office in Ancona or check out www.turismo.marche.it.

Getting There & Around

Drivers have two options on the coastline: the A14 autostrada (main highway) or the SS16 *strada statale* (state highway). Inland roads are either secondary or tertiary and much slower. Regular trains ply the coast on the Bologna–Lecce line and spurs head to Macerata and Ascoli Piceno, but it requires some forethought and help from the tourist board to travel between inland towns.

ANCONA

pop 100,000

Most people only spend enough time in Ancona to catch a ferry elsewhere. And they're not making a bad choice. However, Ancona is developing its tourist infrastructure and although fairly grimy and tattered, the town does have more than enough sights for you to warrant an extra day or two here.

A major point of trade with the east since the Middle Ages, Ancona remains the mid-Adriatic's largest port, doing a healthy business in tourism as well as road freight. The old centre of Ancona was heavily bombed in WWII but today the provincial capital, which supports a major university, is a fascinating mixture of ancient and modern and is also a very congenial base for exploring the national park and nearby towns.

Orientation

There are two distinct parts to Ancona: the modern sprawl around the train station, and the old centre further up the hill. All trains arrive at the main station on Piazza Nello e Carlo Rosselli, though a few continue 1.5km north to the ferry terminal. There are several hotels near Piazza Roma and a cluster around the main train station. What remains of the old town stretches in an arc around the waterfront.

If you arrive by ferry, walk from Largo Dogana, near the ferry terminal, uphill southeast to the central Piazza Roma and east to the city's grand Piazza Cavour to hit the centre of town.

When you exit the station, bus Nos 1 and 4 will take you to the port and the centre of town. Cross past the first bus lane to the covered bus stop with a sign that reads Porto/Centro. Tickets are available at all *tabacchi* for €0.90.

MAPS

You will find plenty of maps of Ancona and the surrounding area at the excellent newsstand at the main train station or at bookshops, hotels and newsstands around town.

Information

BOOKSHOPS

Gulliver Librerie (☎ 071 207 39 43; Corso Giuseppe Garibaldi 35; ☼ 10am-2pm & 4-8pm Mon-Fri, 10am-1pm & 5-8pm Sat & Sun) Carries maps and books in English, French and Spanish.

EMERGENCY

Police station (☎ 071 2 28 81; Via Giovanni Gervasoni 19) South of the city centre.

INTERNET ACCESS

Internet centre (☎ 071 280 08 56; Corso Carlo Alberto 82; ☼ 9.30am-12.30pm & 4pm-late Tue-Sat)
World Wide Media Centre (Piazza Roselli 5a; per hr €3) Across from the train station.

INTERNET RESOURCES

Regione Le Marche (www.le-marche.com) The official tourist-office website; also has useful information on Ancona, including accommodation and sights.

LAUNDRY

Laundrette (Corso Carlo Alberto 76; wash €3, dry €3; ☼ 8am-10pm Mon-Sat)

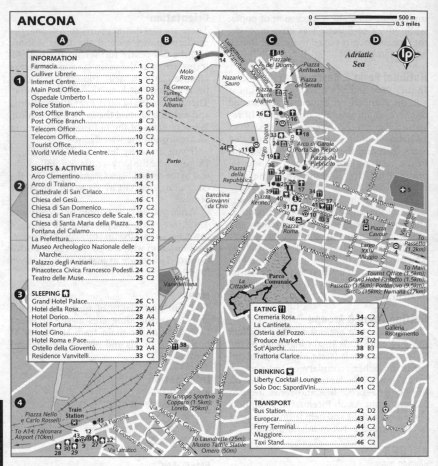

ANCONA

INFORMATION
Farmacia	1	C2
Gulliver Librerie	2	C2
Internet Centre	3	C2
Main Post Office	4	D3
Ospedale Umberto I	5	D2
Police Station	6	D4
Post Office Branch	7	C1
Post Office Branch	8	C2
Telecom Office	9	A4
Telecom Office	10	A4
Tourist Office	11	C2
World Wide Media Centre	12	A4

SIGHTS & ACTIVITIES
Arco Clementino	13	B1
Arco di Traiano	14	C1
Cattedrale di San Ciriaco	15	C1
Chiesa del Gesù	16	C1
Chiesa di San Domenico	17	C1
Chiesa di San Francesco delle Scale	18	C2
Chiesa di Santa Maria della Piazza	19	C2
Fontana del Calamo	20	C2
La Prefettura	21	C2
Museo Archeologico Nazionale delle Marche	22	C1
Palazzo degli Anziani	23	C1
Pinacoteca Civica Francesco Podesti	24	C2
Teatro delle Muse	25	C2

SLEEPING
Grand Hotel Palace	26	C1
Hotel della Rosa	27	A4
Hotel Dorico	28	A4
Hotel Fortuna	29	A4
Hotel Gino	30	A4
Hotel Roma e Pace	31	C2
Ostello della Gioventù	32	A4
Residence Vanvitelli	33	C2

EATING
Cremeria Rosa	34	C2
La Cantineta	35	C2
Osteria del Pozzo	36	C2
Produce Market	37	D2
Sot'Ajarchi	38	B3
Trattoria Clarice	39	C2

DRINKING
Liberty Cocktail Lounge	40	C2
Solo Doc: SapordiVini	41	C2

TRANSPORT
Bus Station	42	D2
Europcar	43	A4
Ferry Terminal	44	C2
Maggiore	45	A4
Taxi Stand	46	C2

LEFT LUGGAGE

Ferry terminal (1st 2 days free) For ferry passengers.
Train station (per bag 1st 12hr €3, next 12hr €2; 24hr) Self-service lockers.

MEDICAL SERVICES

Farmacia Centrale (Corso Mazzini 1)
Ospedale Umberto I (☎ 071 596 30 16; Piazza Capelli 1) Hospital.

POST

Post office cnr Via Ciriaco Pizzecolli & Via della Catena (8.10am-5.30pm Mon-Fri, 9am-12.30pm Sat); ferry terminal (8.10am-5.30pm Mon-Fri, 9am-12.30pm Sat); Largo XXIV Maggio (8.15am-7pm Mon-Sat) The main post office is at Largo XXIV Maggio; the other two locations are post office branches.

TELEPHONE

Telecom office (Piazza Roma 26; ☎ 7am-10pm) The Internet is also available.

TOILETS

Ferry terminal (admission free)
Train station (admission €0.52, shower incl towel & soap €5.16; 24hr)

TOURIST INFORMATION

Tourist office (www.turismo.marche.it); ferry terminal (☎ 071 20 11 83; 8am-8pm Tue-Sat, 2-8pm Sun & Mon 1 Jun–15 Sep); Via Thaon de Revel 4 (☎ 071 35 89 91; 9am-2pm & 3-6pm Mon-Fri, 9am-1pm & 3-6pm Sat, 9am-1pm Sun summer) The main tourist office (on Via Thaon de Revel) is inconveniently placed at the eastern end of town. Take bus 1/4 to Piazze IV Novembre. You'll need to buy a ticket (€0.90, valid one hour) from a *tabacchi*. The tourist office is just past the Grand Hotel Passetto. By bus from Piazza Cavour it's about five minutes, otherwise it's a pleasant 30-minute walk. It has shorter operating hours in winter.

Sights

The elegant Piazza del Plebiscito has been Ancona's meeting spot since medieval times. The piazza is flanked by the baroque **Chiesa di San Domenico** (Piazza del Plebiscito; ☺ 7.15am-12.30pm & 4-7pm), containing the superb *Crucifixion* by Titian and *Annunciation* by Guercino. That gigantic statue in front is Pope Clement XII, who was honoured by the town for giving it free port status. The fountain in front is from the 19th century, but head instead along Corso Mazzini, where you will see the 16th-century **Fontana del Calamo**, 13 masked spouts supposedly representing effigies of those who had been beheaded.

The ornate **Teatro delle Muse** (☎ 071 5 25 25; www.teatrodellemuse.org; Via della Loggia), built in 1826, has a neoclassical façade of six Ionic columns which meld with Greek friezes portraying Apollo and the Muses.

The **Pinacoteca Civica Francesco Podesti** (☎ 071 222 50 41; Via Ciriaco Pizzecolli 17; adult/concession €4/3; ☺ 9am-7pm Tue-Fri, 9am-1pm Mon, 8.30am-6.30pm Sat, 3-7pm Sun) displays artworks spanning six centuries, from artists including Guercino, Carlo Crivelli, Lorenzo Lotto and Titian, plus many modern pieces.

A bit further north along Via Ciriaco Pizzecolli and off to the right is **Chiesa di San Francesco delle Scale**, noteworthy for its 15th-century Venetian-Gothic doorway by Orsini. Check out the ancient waterway below or ascend the many steps to the bell tower. Beyond the church is Vanvitelli's **Chiesa del Gesù** (Church of Jesus), which is nearly always closed. Nearby, in the **Palazzo degli Anziani**, is the economics faculty of the city's 13th-century university.

The **Museo Archeologico Nazionale delle Marche** (☎ 071 20 26 02; Via Ferretti 6; adult/concession/child €4/2/free; ☺ 8.30am-7.30pm Tue-Sun, closed Mon except holidays) is in the 16th-century Palazzo Ferretti, where the ceilings are covered with original frescoes and bas-reliefs. Although not the most thoughtfully laid-out display, artefacts range from Greek and Etruscan back to the Bronze and Neolithic Ages. You'll have the open Roman ruins across the way to yourself most days.

Museo Tattile Statile Omero (☎ 071 281 19 35; www.museoomero.it; Via Tiziano 50; admission free; 9am-1pm & 3-7pm Tue-Sat) is the only museum of its kind in all of Europe, this is one museum where you're supposed to touch the art. All of its sculptures have been created for the blind in order to feel the representations of Roman statues, the Parthenon and St Peter's, as well as Michelangelo's David. Children will also enjoy the interactive quality. What's more, their website has been translated into Esperanto.

CATTEDRALE DI SAN CIRIACO

Via Giovanni XXIII leads up Monte Guasco to Piazzale del Duomo, where there are sweeping views of the city and the port. Here, the **Cattedrale di San Ciriaco** (☎ 071 20 03 91; Piazzale del Duomo; admission free; ☺ 9am-noon & 3-7pm summer, to 6pm winter) sits grandly atop the site of an ancient Pagan temple, jimmied together with Byzantine, Romanesque and Gothic features. The small **museum** (☎ 071 5 26 88; Piazzale del Duomo 9; admission by donation; ☺ 4-6pm summer, book in winter) by the cathedral holds the 4th-century sarcophagus of Flavius Gorgonius, a masterpiece of early Christian art. You can take bus No 11, which runs from Piazza Roma to Piazza Repubblica, or get your exercise walking up the rather steep hill.

WATERFRONT

North of Piazza Dante Alighieri, at the far end of the port, is the **Arco di Traiano** (Trajan's Arch), erected in 115 BC by Apollodorus of Damascus in honour of the Roman Emperor Trajan. Luigi Vanvitelli's **Arco Clementino** (Clementine's Arch), inspired by the former and dedicated to Pope Clement XII, is further on, near Molo Rizzo. You'll find the small Piazza Santa Maria and the disused, tumbledown **Chiesa di Santa Maria della Piazza**, which retains scraps of 5th- and 6th-century pavement mosaics. The large building is the **Mole Vanvitelliana**, designed by Luigi Vanvitelli in 1732 for Pope Clementine. It is now the magnificent venue for some major exhibitions. Call ☎ 071 222 50 31 for details.

Festivals & Events

Ancona Jazz takes place in October. The **Premio Marche** is an international exhibition of contemporary art held in November and December. The festival of the city's patron saint, San Ciriaco, takes place in May. Check with the tourist office for details.

Sleeping

BUDGET

Ostello della Gioventù (☎/fax 071 4 22 57; Via Lamaticci 7; dm €15; ☒ closed midnight-6.30am & 11am-4.30pm) Ancona's HI-youth hostel is divided into a male and female floor with spotless four- to six-person bedrooms and separate bathrooms.

Hotel Gino (☎/fax 071 4 21 79; hotel.gino@tiscalinet.it; Via Flaminia 4; s/d with breakfast €30/45; ℙ ☒ ☒) Fairly comfortable, conveniently located and there's a telephone and TV in each room. Plus, there's that low-priced hotel rarity: a hairdryer. Ask for a parking permit if you have a car.

Hotel Dorico (☎ 071 4 30 09; www.paginegialle.it/htl dorico; Via Flaminia 8; s/d/tr with breakfast €35/45/55) Despite its position on the busy road, this hotel is reasonably quiet, clean and comfortable. Slightly worn, but there are showers, a telephone and a TV in every room.

MIDRANGE

Residence Vanvitelli (☎ 071 207 65 76, 338 27 92 87; www.residencevanvitelli.it; Piazza Saffi; studio/1-/2-room apt per night €60/75/90, per week €350/450/550; ℙ ▯) Tucked away in a tiny piazza no more than a 10-minute walk from most of Ancona's sights is this comfortable, quiet and modern rental. All flats include kitchenettes, fax and TV, and the bed linens are changed every other day.

Hotel Fortuna (☎ 0714 26 63; www.hotelfortuna.it; Piazza Rosselli 15; s/d/tr with breakfast €52/83/98; ℙ ☒ ▯) The nicest of the train station area hotels, this hotel is outfitted with simple furnishings in sparkling clean surroundings and deliciously plush towels. The breakfast buffet is enormous for Italian standards, complete with fruit, eggs and homemade torte (and can be served in your room for a €3 charge).

Hotel della Rosa (☎ 071 4 13 88, 071 4 26 51; www.hoteldellarosa.it in Italian; Piazza Roselli 3; s/d/tr with breakfast €63/88/93; ☒ ▯) This comfortable hotel has been recently refurbished in 'business bland' with direct-dial phones and satellite TV (with CNN). Wheelchair access is available, but most rooms have the oddest placed toilets, so tall people are cautioned.

Hotel Roma e Pace (☎ 071 20 20 07; www.hotelroma epace.it; Via Giacomo Leopardi 1; s/d/tr €50/85/110; ℙ ☒ ▯) It's as central as it gets and has frescoes

by Cherubini gracing the ceiling, but street noise, the rude service and often smoky rooms make the location almost not worth it. Ask to see a room before plunking down your money, as quality varies dramatically. Internet costs €1.50 per 15 minutes.

TOP END

Grand Hotel Passetto (☎ 071 3 13 07; www.hotel passetto.it; Via Thaon de Revel 1; s/d/f/ste with breakfast €115/175/190/215; ℙ ☒ ☒) Modern in an elegant rather than a harsh way, this three-storey hotel has 55 rooms, most with either sea view, terrace, Jacuzzi, four-poster iron bed or some combination of the four. Rooms are decorated in sleek white with non-hotel-like art on the walls. Stroll five seconds to the *ascensore* to get to the beach or cross the street to their restaurant, reputedly the best in town (see opposite). Substantial discounts can be had on weekends and around holidays.

Grand Hotel Palace (☎ 071 20 18 13; www.hotel ancona.it; Lungomare Luigi Vanvitelli 24; s/d with breakfast from €110/150; ☒ closed Christmas; ℙ ☒) Many of the rooms have a beautiful sea view, but the breakfast salon is the prime port-watching area (if you can tear your eyes away from the table full of sweet and savoury delectables). All of the luxurious and light-filled rooms have their own bath, telephone and satellite TV. Snacks and drinks are available in the antique lounge each afternoon.

Eating

RESTAURANTS

La Cantineta (☎ 071 20 11 07; Via Gramsci 1/C; mains €5.20-13) Off Piazza del Plebiscito, the upstairs restaurant offers checked tablecloths, a constantly going TV and cheap and filling meals. It specialises in seafood, including local salted fish, which is best sampled over pasta as *tagliatelle allo stoccafisso* (€6.50).

Trattoria Clarice (☎ 071 20 29 26; Via Traffico 6; mains €5.20-11; ☒ Tue-Sun) Ancona is not noted for its food and this restaurant serves up just the basics. However, it manages to be locals' favourite restaurant in the city centre. It's off Piazza Kennedy.

Osteria del Pozzo (☎ 071 207 39 96; Via Bonda 2; mains €7) This small place is just off Piazza del Plebiscito and serves good, reasonably priced food in a convivial atmosphere.

Sot'Ajarchi (☎ 071 20 24 41; Via Guglielmo Marconi 93; mains €25-50; ☒ Mon-Sat) This small restaurant under the *portici* (arcade) in front of the port specialises, not surprisingly, in fish. For your *primo piatto* (first course) try the *pasta alla marinara* or the *minestra di seppie* (cuttlefish soup), follow it up with a main course such as the recommended *guazzetto*, and finish off with a simple homemade dessert like *zuppa inglese* (liquor-soaked sponge) and some *biscottini* dipped into *vin santo* (little biscuits in wine).

Passetto (☎ 071 3 32 14; Piazza 1V Novembre 1; mains €16; ❧ Tue-Sun, dinner only Sun & Aug) Run by the same owners as the Grand Hotel Passetto, this is well-known as Ancona's best restaurant. It's quite apt that it specialises in seafood, as it is well placed overlooking the sea.

Cremeria Rosa (☎ 071 20 34 08; Corso Mazzini 61) A cafeteria, bar and *gelateria* all in one, it's also on the main drag, perfect for people-watching while eating a sundae as big as your whole head.

SELF-CATERING

Produce market (Corso Giuseppe Mazzini 130; ❧ 5am-8pm Mon-Sat) This is a picnickers' Mecca. Dozens of booths line this green metal-and-glass-enclosed bazaar. Freshly baked pastries and bread, locally produced cheese and meat, and everything else you would need for a picnic (including plastic cups) are sold here.

Drinking

Liberty Cocktail Lounge (☎ 071 20 34 84; Via Traffico 7-10; ❧ 11am-2am Thu-Tue) The hot spot in town, this Art Deco–inspired café would have made Picasso feel right at home. Asia-influenced artwork, Tiffany glass lamps and a classy Bohemian crowd will make you want to paint the scene and sell it as a framed poster. It's off Piazza Kennedy.

Solo Doc: SapordiVini (☎ 339 241 34 16; Corso Giuseppe Mazzini 106; ❧ 7am-10pm Mon-Fri, 8am-1pm & 4pm-2am Sat) While away hours on a warm day outside at this café and bar under the Italian version of a tented harem. Bar tables and plush low couches seat the young hip crowd as well as visitors. Or just stroll by and enjoy the piped-in jazz, dance or world music.

Getting There & Away

AIR

Falconara airport (AOI; www.ancona-airport.it in Italian; ☎ 071 2 82 71) has been recently expanded, and this easily accessible airport now takes flights from Munich, Paris, London, Barcelona, Milan, Rome, Florence and Timisoara.

See p874 for more information on low-cost carriers such as E Vola Via or Ryanair.

BUS

Most provincial and regional buses depart from Piazza Cavour but many originate first at the train station, including buses to Falconara. See the table below for destinations.

Destination	Cost (€)	Duration	Frequency
Falconara airport	1	40min	every 45min
Loreto	1.85	40min	hourly
Macerata	2.75	1½hr	6 daily
Numana	1.45	40min	hourly
Portonovo	0.90	30min	6 daily Jun-Aug
Recanati	2.25	1hr	hourly
Senigallia	1.50	1hr	hourly
Urbino	5.60	2½hr	2pm Mon-Sat

CAR & MOTORCYCLE

Ancona is on the A14, which links Bologna with Bari. The SS16 coastal road runs parallel to the autostrada and is a more pleasant toll-free alternative if you're not looking to get anywhere fast. The SS76 connects Ancona with Perugia and Rome.

FERRY

Ferry operators have booths at the ferry terminal or check with an agency in town. Ferries operate to Greece, Croatia, Albania and Turkey.

TRAIN

Ancona is on the Bologna–Lecce line, so take note of whether you're taking a Eurostar or not, as there can be a substantial supplement. For more information, call ☎ 848 88 80 88 (not available from mobile phones) between 7am and 9pm. See the table below for train destinations.

Destination	Cost (€)	Duration	Frequency
Bari	32-35	4hr	twice daily (3.50am & 10.51am)
Bologna	11-22	1¾-3hr	hourly
Florence	21-30	3-4hr	hourly (excl 11.40am-1.15pm)
Milan	20-34	3hr	hourly (excl 8.40-10.40am)
Pesaro	4-9	30-50min	hourly
Rome	14-22	2¾hr	7 daily

Getting Around

Conero Bus service J runs roughly every hour from the train station to the airport, from 6.05am to 8.30pm Monday to Saturday and seven times a day on Sunday (€1.10, 25 to 45 minutes). The bus labelled 'Ancona–Aeroporto' does the trip during August and on Sunday and public holidays.

There are about six Conero Bus services, including No 1/4 which connects the main train station with the ferry terminal and Piazza Cavour (€0.80); look for the bus stop with the big signpost displaying Centro and Porto.

For a taxi, telephone ☎ 071 4 33 21.

You'll find **Europcar** (☎ 071 20 31 00) across from the train station and **Maggiore** (☎ 071 4 26 24) 40m to the left as you walk out.

AROUND ANCONA
Parco Naturale del Monte Cònero

This park extends 5800 hectares around Monte Cònero in the province of Ancona and takes in the beautiful coastal towns of Portonovo (9.5km south of Ancona), Sirolo (22km from Ancona) and Numana (a further 2km southeast) as well as Camerano, further inland. With its mountains and rolling hills, many species of birds and well-maintained walking tracks, it offers wonderful opportunities for all sorts of seaside and rural activities (as well as some great places for eating and drinking).

INFORMATION

Campeggio Club Adriatico (☎ /fax 071 13 43 71; Viale della Vittoria 37, Ancona) For more information on suggested itineraries within the park and areas especially equipped for camping or caravanning.

Consorzio del Parco del Conero (☎ 0719 33 11 61; www.parks.it/parco.conero; Via Vivaldi 1/3, Sirolo) For information on the park itself or to arrange guided tours.

Visitors centre (☎ /fax 071 933 18 79; Via Peschiera 30a, Sirolo) Offers the same services as the *consorzio*.

EATING

There are a few rather good restaurants in Parco Naturale del Monte Cònero.

Portonovo

Laghetto (☎ 071 801 11 83; Via Portonovo; mains €30-35; ☽ closed Mon winter & Jan-Mar) Situated in a wooden chalet a few steps away from the sea, Laghetto provides great meals and great service.

Susci Bar al Clandestino (☎ 071 80 14 22; Via Portonovo, Loc Poggio; ☽ mid-May–mid-Sep) Susci Bar Al Clandestino serves food that is highly recommended by Italy's food critics. There's no formality here and after a swim in the beautiful Baia di Portonove, you can drop in for a taste of its Mediterranean sushi or some tapas.

Giacchetti (☎ 071 80 13 84; Via Portonove 171; mains €40; ☽ closed Mon winter & Nov-Mar) Has been serving great seafood dishes for years.

Hotel Fortino Napoleonico (☎ 071 80 14 54; Via Poggio 1; mains €50; ☽ Tue-Sun Feb-Dec) An upmarket place where you can dine elegantly on dishes comprising good fresh seafood.

Sirolo

Rocco (☎ /fax 071 933 05 58; Via Torrione 1; mains €45-55; ☽ Wed-Mon, closed mid-Oct–Easter) A lovely place run by passionate young cooks who base their excellent dishes on local fresh fish.

Hostaria Il Grottino (☎ 071 933 12 18; Via dell' Ospedale 9; ☽ Fri-Mon & Wed, closed Nov & 15-30 Jan) Comfortable and popular – you'd be wise to book.

Numana

Saraghino (☎ /fax 071 739 15 96; Via Litoranea 209, Loc Martelli; mains €45; ☽ Tue-Sun Mar-Jan) Gaze out to sea with a glass of excellent wine and one of the superb and creative dishes – artichokes with gorgonzola, *tagliatelle con scampetti* (pasta with lobster), *vongole e pomodoro fresco* (clams with fresh tomato) – prepared by one of Italy's celebrated up-and-coming young chefs, Roberto Fiorini.

Costarella (☎ 071 736 02 97; Via IV Novembre 35; mains €55; ☽ Wed-Mon Easter-Nov) You'll find this delightful little place at the top of a steep flight of steps in the middle of the town. The dishes are based on local produce, fish of course, and seasonable vegetables. The antipasti are definitely worth sampling.

Loreto

Thousands of Catholic pilgrims travel here every year because of the belief that angels transferred the house of the Virgin Mary from Palestine to this spot towards the end of the 13th century. The basilica that was built over the site was begun in 1468, on Gothic lines, and later expanded and added to by some Renaissance luminaries, including Bramante, to become today's **Santuario della Santa Casa** (☎ 071 97 01 04, 071 97 68 37; Piazza della Madonna; ☽ 6.15am-12.30pm & 2.30-8pm).

For a meal, try **Andreina** (☎ 071 97 01 24; Via Buffolareccia 14; mains €30; ☾ Wed-Mon Aug-Jun). This rustic little restaurant has a certain elegance to it. Meat dishes and local wines are the speciality, although other dishes such as the omelettes with black truffles are definitely worth trying, too.

Loreto lies about 28km south of Ancona and can be reached easily by bus. Loreto train station (on the Bologna–Lecce line) is a few kilometres away, but shuttle buses connect it with the town centre.

URBINO
pop 6000

Urbino is the jewel of Le Marche and one of the best-preserved and most beautiful hill towns in Italy. It enjoyed a period of great splendour under the Montefeltro family from the 12th century onwards, and reached its zenith under Duca Federico da Montefeltro. The Duke gathered together all the great artists, architects and scholars of his day to create a sort of Renaissance think tank. The town's splendour was made official by Unesco, who deemed the entire city centre a World Heritage site.

By the mid-16th century, central Italy was ruled by the pope; only the duchy of Urbino remained autonomous. The city and its territories were now reigned over by the Della Rovere family, since the Montefeltro family had been left without heirs. The Della Rovere family was, however, linked to the papacy. Two of its members were elected popes (Sisto IV and Giulio II), and Francesco Maria I Della Rovere became commander of the pontifical army.

The town can be a pain to reach by public transport, but should not be missed. The area to the north, particularly the winding road to San Marino and on into Emilia-Romagna, is a treat and there are plenty of hotels in the small towns along the way.

Orientation

Buses arrive at Borgo Mercatale, at the western edge of the city. To get to the city centre, head up Via Mazzini or take the €0.25 *ascensore* to Teatro Sanzio. The entire city is walled, so drivers are advised to drop their cars at one of several car parks (all marked on the map). Take care to not park at Piazzale Roma on Saturday, as there is a market on Sunday and your car *will* be towed.

MAPS

You can buy the useful *Urbino Mini-guide con pianta* (in English) for €2 from the Piazza Mercatale information point, or from various newspaper and magazine shops in the old town. The main tourist map, *Urbino: Pianta della Città*, is more than sufficient for most travellers.

Information

Banca Nazionale di Lavoro (Via Vittorio Veneto 53) ATM and exchange facilities.
Netgate (☎ 0722 24 62; Via G Mazzini 17; ☾ 10am-11pm Mon-Fri, noon-11pm Sat, noon-10pm Sun; per 30min/1hr €2.50/4) Internet facilities.
Ospedale Civile (☎ 0722 30 11; Via Bonconte da Montefeltro) Hospital located about 1.5km north of the city centre.
Pharmacy (Piazza della Repubblica 9)
Police station (☎ 0722 3 51 81; Piazza Mercatale)
Post office (☎ 0722 37 79 17; Via Bramante 18; ☾ 8.30am-6.30pm Mon-Sat)
Tourist information point (☾ 6.30am-8.30pm) Find it at the entrance to the lift that takes you from the main car park and bus station in Piazza Mercatale to the old town uphill.
Tourist office (☎ 0722 26 13; fax 0722 24 41; Via Puccinotti 3; ☾ 9am-1pm Mon-Sat, 9am-1pm & 3-6pm Sun & holidays from May-Sep) Visitors have 10 minutes of free Internet.

Sights
PALAZZO DUCALE

The grand residence of Urbino's ruling dynasty was completed in 1482 and is one of Italy's most complete early Renaissance palazzi. **Palazzo Ducale** (☎ 0722 32 26 25; Piazza Duca Federico; adult/concession €4/2; ☾ 8.30am-7.15pm Tue-Sun, 8.30am-2pm Mon) houses the **Galleria Nazionale delle Marche**, **Museo Archeologico**, **Museo della Ceramica** and **Sotterranei**.

From Corso Garibaldi you get the best view of the complex with its unusual Facciata dei Torricini, a three-storey loggia in the form of a triumphal arch, that's flanked by circular towers.

A monumental staircase, one of Italy's first, leads to the *piano nobile* (literally 'noble floor') and the Ducal Apartments. The best-preserved room is Duca Federico's Studiolo. The most famous of the paintings on display is Piero della Francesca's masterpiece, *The Flagellation*. Another highlight is the remarkable portrait of Federico and his son Guidobaldo, which is attributed to Spanish

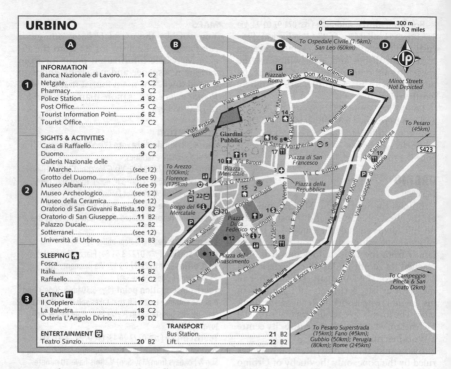

artist Pedro Berruguete. The collection also includes a large number of drawings done by Federico Barocci.

CHURCHES

Rebuilt in the early 19th century in neoclassical style, the interior of Urbino's **Duomo** (Piazza Duca Federico; ☉ 7.30am-1pm & 2-7pm) commands much greater interest than its austere façade. Particularly memorable is Federico Barocci's *Last Supper*. The basilica's **Museo Albani** (☎ 0722 28 50; admission incl the Grotto del Duomo €3; ☉ 9am-1pm & 2-7pm) contains further paintings, including Andrea da Bologna's *Madonna del Latte* (Madonna Breastfeeding). Be sure to check out the subterranean **Grotto del Duomo** while you're there.

The 14th-century **Oratorio di San Giovanni Battista** (☎ 0347 671 11 81; Via Barocci; admission €2; ☉ 10am-12.30pm & 3-5.30pm Mon-Sat, 10am-12.30pm Sun) features brightly coloured frescoes by Lorenzo and Giacomo Salimbeni. A few steps away, the **Oratorio di San Giuseppe** (☎ 0347 671 11 81; Via Barocci; admission €2; ☉ 10am-12.30pm & 3-5.30pm Mon-Sat, 10am-12.30pm Sun) boasts a stucco *Nativity* by Federico Brandani.

CASA DI RAFFAELLO

North of the Piazza della Repubblica you'll find the 15th-century **Casa di Raffaello** (☎ 0722 32 01 05; Via Raffaello 57; adult/student €3/1; ☉ 9am-1pm & 3-7pm Mon-Sat, 10am-1pm Sun), the house where Raphael spent his first 16 years.

On the 1st floor is possibly one of Raphael's first frescoes, a Madonna with child.

Courses

Università di Urbino (☎ 800 462 446; www.uniurb .it; Via Saffi 2) offers an intensive one-month course in language and culture for foreign students during August for €460. The school can also arrange accommodation in apartments, *agriturismi* or private homes starting at €170.

Festivals & Events

In May Urbino decks itself out in flowers for the **Urbino Città Fiorita** festival. The **Urbino Jazz Festival** takes place in June, while in July the **International Festival of Ancient Music** occurs. The **Festa dell' Duca** takes place on the second Sunday in August, when the town's streets become the setting for a costume procession and the re-enactment of a tournament on horseback. Europe's only kite-flying competition is held here on the first Sunday in September. Check with the tourist office for up-to-date details.

Sleeping

The tourist office can provide a full list of private rooms and other accommodation options.

Locanda della Valle Nuova (☎ /fax 0722 33 03 03; www.vallenuova.it; La Cappella 14, Sagrata di Fermignano; per person with breakfast €48; 🕑 mid-Jun–mid-Nov; P 🖳 🕿) Ecology and comfort co-exist in perfect balance at this six-room working *agriturismo*. Also an organic restaurant, Locanda della Valle Nuova grows an incredible array of fruit, vegetables, grains and wine grapes plus raises naturally fed cattle and hens. Enjoy a horse ride or a home-grown truffle. It is about 20 minutes from Urbino, but the English-speaking owners will assist you with transport and visiting the local towns. There's a minimum three-night stay; no credit cards.

Fosca (☎ 0722 2 54 21; fax 0722 26 00; Via Raffaello 67; s/d €21/35) On the 4th floor of an ancient building is this simple *pensione*. Six rooms share two bathrooms of dubious cleanliness (try to grab the one en suite) but each has a sink. Rooms are drab but at this price, you'll forgive them for not buying better towels.

Campeggio Pineta (☎ 0722 47 10; fax 0722 47 34; Via San Donato, Loc Cesana; person/tent €5.50/12; 🕑 Easter-Sep) Only 2km from the city centre, this camp site is located amid a luscious surrounding of trees.

Italia (☎ 0722 27 01; www.albergo-italia-urbino.it; Corso Garibaldi 32; s with breakfast €45-65, d with breakfast €65-115, extra bed €25; 🕿) Set behind the Palazzo Ducale, the Italia could not be better positioned. All the mod cons are available, but the tile floors and white walls might make it too modern for some.

Raffaello (☎ 0722 47 84; www.albergoraffaello.com; Via Santa Margherita 38/40; s/d with breakfast €70/115; 🕿) The imposing marbled entrance of this former seminary makes way for plain but comfortable rooms outfitted with TVs, minibars and radios. Some rooms have fantastic views of the palace, so try to snag one with a balcony. The proprietors will transport guests to and from any of the car parks or bus stations in town.

Also recommended:

San Domenico (☎ 0722 26 26; www.viphotels.it; Piazza Rinascimento 3; s/d 103/165; P 🕿 🖳)

Eating

Don't miss the *strozzapreti*, available in most restaurants. These worm-like shreds of pasta were designed to choke priests, but they're delicious.

Osteria L'Angolo Divino (☎ 0722 32 75 59; Via Sant'Andrea 14; mains €9.50-18.50; 🕑 Thu-Mon Nov-Sep) This subterranean *enoteca* just oozes atmosphere. Arched brick alcoves overflow with wine bottles, available for tastings. Even teetotallers will enjoy this place, as the menu boasts simple but perfectly flavoured pasta specialities, including the much better tasting than it sounds *pasta nel sacco* (pasta in a sack), which is fresh pasta coated with eggs and breadcrumbs.

La Balestra (☎ 0722 29 42; Via Valerio 16; pizzas €2.50-7, mains €7-14; 🕑 dinner-midnight) This spot is popular with Urbino's literati and university students as it's as cosy as it is cheap. Try their speciality, *pappardelle del duca* (thick ribbon pasta) or the famous *strozzapreti*.

Il Coppiere (☎ 0722 32 23 26; Via Santa Margherita 1; mains €8-14) A great place to try simple local fare such as black truffle ravioli (€8) or grilled lamb (€8).

Entertainment

The arts come alive in Urbino during the summer season.

The grand old 19th-century **Teatro Sanzio** (☎ 0722 22 81; Corso Garibaldi) hosts plays and concerts, particularly from July to September. Pick up a brochure at the main tourist office.

Getting There & Around

The Pesaro-based company **Soget** (☎ /fax 0721 54 96 20) runs up to 15 services daily between Urbino and Pesaro (€2.05 at bars in Piazza Matteotti, €3.05 on board, 55 minutes). **Bucci** (☎ 0721 3 24 01) runs two buses per day to Rome (€17.85, five hours) at 6am and 3pm.

Take the bus to Pesaro to pick up trains (see p589).

An autostrada and the S423 connect Urbino with Pesaro, while the S73B connects the town with the SS3 heading for Rome. Most motor vehicles are banned from the walled city. **Taxis** (☎ 0722 25 50) and shuttle buses operate from Piazza della Repubblica and Piazza Mercatale. There are car parks outside the city gates. Note that there is no parking on Piazzale Roma on Saturday morning as it's market day.

PESARO

pop 90,000

Pesaro is in an incredible location set up against the beach with undulating hills offering expanses for outdoor activities spreading out on either side. Too bad thousands of Speedo-clad northern Europeans come here for five months out of the year to lie like sardines along a beautiful strip of beach backed by an equally ugly strip of high-rise concrete hotels. However, Pesaro has a beautiful medieval centre with fabulous shopping. It was also the birthplace of the composer Rossini, who loved his hometown so much he willed his possessions to it when he died.

Orientation

The train station is in the far western edge of downtown, about 2km from the beach. From the train station, walk along Viale del Risorgimento, through the Piazza Lazzarini, where the name switches to Via Branca, Via Rossini and finally Viale della Repubblica, which ends at the waterfront and the tourist office in Piazza della Libertà.

Information

Guardia Medica Turistica (☎ 0721 2 13 44; Viale Trento 300) Medical services.

Left luggage (per bag 1st 12hr €3, next 12hr €2) At the train station.

Pesaro Urbino Tourism (www.turismo.pesarourbino .it) Has excellent information in English, with maps, hotels and sights.

Police station (☎ 0721 42 551; Via Giordano Bruno 5)

Post office (☎ 0721 3 31 58; Piazza del Popolo; ☒ 8.15am-7.40pm Mon-Sat)

Tourist information (☎ 800 563 800) This number provides information, sometimes in English.

Tourist office (☎ 0721 6 93 41; www.comune.pesaro .ps.it in Italian; Piazzale della Libertà 11; ☒ 9am-1pm & 3.30-6.30pm Mon-Sat, 9am-1pm Sun summer, 9am-1pm Mon, Wed, Fri & Sat, 3-6pm Tue & Thu winter) Pick up its free Handy Guide, in English.

Sights & Activities

The 15th-century **Palazzo Ducale**, dominating Piazza del Popolo, housed the ruling Della Rovere family. Today it houses bureaucracy and is closed to the public. The splendid windows that grace its façade are by Domenico Rosselli.

Check out the town's combined **Musei Civici**, **Museo delle Ceramiche** and **Pinacoteca** (☎ 0721 38 75 41; Piazza Toschi Mosca 29; adult/under 25 €7/4; ☒ 9.30am-12.30pm Tue-Sun year-round, 4-7pm Thu & Sun Sep-Jun, 5-8pm Wed & Fri-Sun, 5-11pm Tue & Thu Jul & Aug). Pesaro's ceramic tradition dates back to the 1300s and the museum boasts an impressive display from the last 700 years. The Pinacoteca houses Giovanni Bellini's magnificent altarpiece depicting the coronation of the Virgin.

In 1792 the composer Rossini was born in a typical Pesaro house that is now known as the **Casa Rossini** (☎ 0721 38 73 57; Via Rossini 34; adult/under 25 €4/3; ☒ 9.30am-12.30pm Tue-Sun & 4-7pm Thu-Sun). Follow the history of Rossini and opera through the early 19th century via a series of prints, personal effects and portraits.

The **Chiesa di Sant'Agostino** (Corso XI Settembre; admission free; ☒ 8am-7pm) features some intricate 15th-century inlaid-wood choir stalls. The modest **Museo Oliveriano** (☎ 0721 3 33 44; Via Mazza 97; admission free; ☒ 4-7pm Mon-Sat Jul & Aug, 9.30am-12.30pm Mon-Sat Sep-Jun on request) contains archaeological finds from a nearby Iron Age necropolis, including coins, medals and a child's tomb.

Festivals & Events

Pesaro hosts the **International Festival of New Cinema** in June. In honour of its most famous son, the town also hosts the **Rossini Opera Festival** (☎ 0721 380 02 94; www.rossinioperafestival.it; Via Rossini 24; ☒ box office 10am-1pm & 3-5pm Mon-Fri) around town each summer.

Sleeping

The majority of hotels close down from October until around Easter. Most places are square concrete blocks from the 1960s, uninspired but close to or on the beach. The best time to go is September or May, when you have the weather but not the hordes of sun-seeking tourists. For a room, contact the **Associazione Pesarese di Albergatori** (☎ 0721 6 79 59; www.apahotel.it; Viale Marconi 57) or try the tourist office.

Marinella (☎ 0721 5 57 95; www.campingmarinella .it; SS Adriatica km 244, Loc Fossosejore; per person €7.80, bungalows d/tr/q €60/70/103; ☒ Easter-Sep) Drift off to the sound of waves breaking on the beach in your seaside tent. A casual restaurant is on site, as well as a market, beach volleyball, washing machines, showers and lots of child-friendly activities.

Ostello Sejore (☎ 0721 39 09 30; www.ostellosejore .it; Strada Panoramica Ardizio 232; dm/d €14/32; � reception 9am-noon & 6-8pm; P) Perched on a hill overlooking the beach, this hostel's balcony garners a lovely view. Dorm rooms are clean and doubles have en suite. They rent bicycles for €5 a day or €20 for the week. It's a fairly stringently run but private operation.

Leonardo Da Vinci (☎ 0721 3 37 33; www.leonardo davincihotelpesaro.it; Viale Trieste 54; per person €32.50-62.50; �YMay-Sep; P ⊠ ⊠) One of the best locations of the mass seaside tourism hotels. You get a choice between lying out at the pool or walking 15 steps further to snooze under one of many umbrellas along the beach. Every room has a small balcony; most have sea views. They offer half or full board so you'll always get at least breakfast and the lunchtime buffet.

Athena (☎ 0721 3 01 14; fax 0721 3 38 78; Viale Pola 18; s/d from €35/50; �Yyear-round) It's walking distance from the beach and the medieval town, and the price is about as low as it gets in Pesaro. Make sure to ask to see a room, as some have bathrooms that double as showers.

Eating

Felici e Contenti (☎ 0721 3 20 60; Via Cattaneo 37; mains €7.50-17; �Yclosed Sat morning & Mon) When a restaurant names itself 'Happily Ever After', you can bet you'll retire for the evening both happy and content. Their speciality is fish, but pasta also makes a memorable entrance on the menu. The atmosphere is more sophisticatedly urban than many other Pesaro restaurants and it's located on a quiet side street in the medieval centre.

Polo (☎ 0721 37 59 02; Viale Trieste 231; mains €8-16.50; �YTue-Sun) Polo's a fairly hip and popular establishment which serves a good mix of Italian and international food (and an extraordinary variety of grappa).

C'Era Una Volta (☎ 0721 3 09 11; Via Cattaneo 26; pizzas from €3.50; �YTue-Sun) The raucous atmosphere is almost as fun as the pizzas, topped with peas, artichokes, *speck*, pancetta, or even *patate fritti* (chips). No glass of wine is more than €2.80 and an enormous array of pasta dishes can be had for under €7.50.

There are food shops and a produce market on Via Branca, behind the post office.

Entertainment

Teatro Rossini (☎ 0721 3 31 84; Piazza Lazzarini) hosts a series of symphony concerts throughout the year. For information, contact the **Ente Concerti** (☎ 0721 3 24 82; enteconcerti@libero.it; Via Branca 93).

Getting There & Around

The main bus station is on Piazza Matteotti. **AMI** (☎ 0721 28 91 45, 0721 37 48 62) buses connect Pesaro with Cattolica (€1.10, 45 minutes, hourly), Fossosejore (€0.60, 15 minutes, half-hourly) and most small towns in the region. **Bucci** (☎ 0721 3 24 01) operates a service to Ancona (€2.95, one hour 20 minutes, four daily) and to Rome at 6am daily (€19.35, four hours 40 minutes). Buses make the return journey from Rome at 4pm. **Soget** (☎ 0721 37 13 18) runs up to 10 buses daily to Urbino (€1.90, 55 minutes).

Pesaro is on the Bologna–Lecce train line and you can reach Rome (€15.45 to €23.90, four hours, nine daily) by changing trains at Falconara Marittima, just before Ancona. There are hourly services to Ancona (€3.10, 40 minutes), Rimini (€3.80, 30 minutes) and Bologna (€7.50, two hours). Catch the Ancona-bound train for Fano (€1.80, 10 minutes) and Senigallia (€2.30, 25 minutes). By car, Pesaro is on the A14 and the SS16.

AMI buses connect the train station with Piazza Matteotti, including bus Nos 1, 3, 4, 5, CD and CS. For a taxi in the centre, telephone ☎ 0721 3 14 30; at the train station, call ☎ 0721 3 11 11.

GROTTE DI FRASASSI

In September 1971 a team of climbers stumbled across an aperture in the hill country around Genga, about 50km southwest of Ancona, which turned out to be the biggest known cave in Europe, containing a spectacle of stalactites and stalagmites, some of them 1.4 million years old.

The **grotte** (☎ 0732 9 00 80; www.frasassi.com; adult/concession/child under 6 & disabled persons €12/11/ free; � 8.30am-6.30pm Aug, 9.30am-6pm Mar-Jul & Sep-Oct, hours vary Nov, Dec & Feb, closed most of Jan) now has a 1.5km-long trail laid through five chambers where professional guides take you through a 70-minute tour. **Ancona Abyss**, the first chamber, is almost 200m high, 180m wide and 120m long. The ticket area and car park are just outside San Vittore Terme, and the entrance to the caves is

600m further west. Call ahead, as there is an insanely complex schedule.

For €26 to €36 you can have a more challenging experience that lasts for three hours and involves passing across 30m chasms and crawling on your hands and knees along narrow passages and tunnels. Book in advance. To stay overnight, there are a couple of hotels in San Vittore Terme and Genga.

To reach the caves from Ancona, take the SS76 off the A14 or catch the train for Genga (€2.95, 45 minutes, four daily), about 2km from the caves' ticket area; a shuttle bus runs from the train station in summer.

MACERATA

pop 42,800

Macerata has been growing as a bustling hill town for 3000 years, when the Picena tribe first settled the region in the 10th century BC. It's easy to stroll through, has many good sights and offers a fabulous selection of accommodation (including a tidy-as-a-pin youth hostel).

Orientation

Piazza della Libertà is the focal point of the medieval city, contained within the 14th-century walls above the sprawl of the more modern development. Intercity buses arrive at the huge Giardini Diaz below. An underground pass leads to a lift that takes you to the bottom of Via XX Settembre in the old town. Follow this road through Piazza Oberdan and along Via Gramsci to reach Piazza della Libertà and the tourist office. If you arrive by train, bus No 6 links the train station, which is south of the city centre, to Piazza della Libertà. Other buses climb up Viale Leopardi.

There is parking virtually right around the city walls and you may even find a space on one of the main squares inside the old city.

Information

Info Point Macerata (☎ 0733 23 43 33; Piazza Mazzini 12a) Information on visiting Sferistico and brochures on the area. Opens sporadically.

Internet centre (☎ 0733 26 44 04; Piazza Mazzini 52; per hr €2.50)

Marche Voyager (www.le-marche.com/Marche) Tourist website from the Le Marche Region Tourism Department.

Ospedale Civile (☎ 0733 25 72 13; Via S Lucia) Hospital.

Police station (☎ 0733 2 54 11; Piazza della Libertà 15)

Portal of the Province of Macerata (www.provincia .mc.it/tourism_eng.asp) Government tourist website for the province.

Post office (Piazza Oberdan 1-3; ☺ 8.15am-7.30pm Mon-Sat)

Telecom office (☎ 0733 26 01 32; Galleria del Commercio 24; ☺ 9am-1pm & 4-7pm)

Tourist office (☎ 0733 23 48 07; iat.macerata@regione .marche.it; Piazza della Libertà 9; ☺ 10am-1pm & 3-6pm Mon-Fri, 10am-1pm Sat & Sun)

Sights & Activities

The city centre starts at the **Loggia dei Mercanti**, next to the tourist office in the Piazza della Libertà. Built in the 16th century, the open-air building housed travelling merchants selling their wares to the area's villagers. Across the square is the **Teatro Lauro Rossi**, (☎ 0733 25 63 06; fax 0733 23 52 72; Piazza della Libertà 21; admission from €19; ☺ tours 9am-1pm & 5-8pm Mon-Fri), an elegant theatre built in 1774 for the musical enjoyment of the nobility which now allows well-dressed riffraff to attend.

In Piazza Vittorio Veneto, at the end of the main boulevard Corso della Repubblica, you will find a museum triumvirate in the Palazzo Ricci: the **Museo Civico**, the **Museo delle Carrozze** and the **Pinacoteca** (☎ 0733 25 63 61; Piazza Vittorio Veneto 2; admission free; ☺ 9am-1pm & 4-7.30pm Tue-Sat, 9am-1pm Sun). The latter has a good collection of early Renaissance works, including a 15th-century Madonna by Carlo Crivelli. The Museo delle Carrozze (carriage museum) houses an extensive collection of 18th- to 20th-century coaches. The Museo Civico contains Roman and Piceni archaeological remains. As if this wasn't enough, there's also the Municipal Library, which boasts 300,000 texts, many ancient maps and medieval manuscripts.

The 16th-century **Palazzo Ricci** (☎ 0733 26 14 84; Via D Ricci 1; admission free; ☺ 4-6pm Tue & Thu, 10am-noon Sat) houses a collection of 20th-century Italian masters such as Giorgio De Chirico, Giacomo Balla, Gino Severini, Fortunato Depero and Renato Guttoso. In July and August it is the venue for a national exhibition of 20th-century Italian art.

During the summer (or even off season, just for a visit) be sure to check out the **Arena Sferisterio** (☎ 0733 23 07 35; www.sferisterio.it; Piazza Mazzini 10; admission €2, shows €15-100; ☺ 9.30am-1pm & 4-8pm summer, 10.30am-1pm & 5-8pm Mon-Sat winter), which resembles an ancient Roman arena

MACERATA

INFORMATION		Museo delle Carrozze......................(see 9)	**EATING** 🍴
Info Point Macerata...........................**1** D3		Palazzo del Comune.......................**10** C2	Da Secondo.......................................**17** C2
Internet Centre..................................**2** C3		Palazzo Ricci....................................**11** B3	Da Silvano...**18** C3
Police Station.....................................**3** C2		Pinacoteca....................................(see 9)	Istanbul Kebab..................................**19** D3
Post Office..**4** B3		Teatro Lauri Rossi............................**12** C3	Osteria dei Fiori...............................**20** C3
Telecom Office...................................**5** C2			
Tourist Office.....................................**6** C2		**SLEEPING** 🛏	**TRANSPORT**
		Arcadia...**13** D3	APM Buses..**21** D2
SIGHTS & ACTIVITIES		Arena..**14** D3	Bus Station.......................................**22** A2
Arena Sferisterio...............................**7** D3		Lauri...**15** B2	Lift..**23** A3
Loggia dei Mercanti..........................**8** C2		Ostello Asilo Ricci...........................**16** D3	
Museo Civico......................................**9** B3			

but was built between 1819 and 1829. Between 15 July and 15 August every year it is a venue for the Stagione Lirica, one of Italy's most prestigious musical events, which attracts big operatic names. Tickets run from €15 to €100. Inquire at the tourist office for programme details.

On the outskirts of town are many archaeological remains from **Helvia Recina**, a Roman town 5km north of Macerata, which was destroyed by the Goths.

Festivals & Events

During the week leading up to the first Sunday in August, in nearby Treia, you can witness the annual **Disfida del Bracciale**, a festival that revives the tradition and folklore surrounding the 19th-century game. *Bracciale* involves players hitting leather balls with spiked wooden hand guards that look like a cross between a torture device and a pine cone.

Sleeping

Le Case (☎ 0733 23 18 97; www.ristorantelecase.it; Locanda Mozzavinici 16; d/ste with breakfast €125/200; P 🛏 🔊)

In a restored monastery a few kilometres from the centre, this is a marvellous place to eat fantastic food and drink great wine without breaking the bank. You can then sleep it off in gilded 'country house' rooms in the middle of the verdant Le Marche countryside. It also offers what Italians have unfortunately decided to name a 'Beauty Farm', which is a collection of a pool, hot tub, sauna and treatment rooms for massages and the like. To forget that you've been carrying a 10kg bag for two weeks, ask for a shiatsu or Ayurvedic massage with Sergio.

Ostello Asilo Ricci (☎ /fax 0733 23 25 15; ostello asiloricci@cssg.it; Via dell'Asilo 36; s/d/tr/q with breakfast €22.50/40/54.50/58; 🔊) Housed in a restored school a stone's throw from the town centre, this quiet hostel has spacious rooms painted in a vibrant orange Venetian plaster and is so tidy that the sheets are even ironed. To bathe, you simply use showerheads next to private toilets.

Arena (☎ 0733 23 09 31; www.itwg.com/macerata; Vicolo Sferisterio 16; s/d €45/75; P) One of the best breakfasts of any two-star hotel around. The designer was hopefully fired after picking out the wallpaper and fabric, but other than that, the rooms are comfortable. There's a hairdryer *and* a towel warmer, and they have several rooms for people with disabilities.

Lauri (☎ /fax 0733 23 23 76; www.gestionihotels.it; Via T Lauri 6; s/d/tr/q with breakfast 45/70/90/110; 🔀) Arched hallways lead to 30 plain but amply outfitted rooms, complete with *frigobar* (the adorable Italian word for a minibar), towel warmer, cable TV, scrolled iron beds and not horribly awful showers. Singles are nice value.

Arcadia (☎ 0733 23 59 61; www.gestionihotels.it; Via Matteo Ricci 134; s/d/tr €60/90/110; P 🔀) This pleasant little hotel in a quiet street not far from the cathedral gives three-star comfort at very reasonable prices. There's room for just six cars in their garage so book ahead.

Eating

Da Secondo (☎ 0733 26 09 12; Via Pescheria Vecchia 26/28; mains €7.80-18; 😊 Tue-Sun) *The* place in Macerata to try the local cuisine. Follow the town's history through photos covering the walls as well as in the regional ingredients: *pecorino* (sheep's-milk cheese), *tartufo* (truffles) and osso buco with *porcini* mushrooms. In summer, dine on the romantic outdoor terrace.

Osteria dei Fiori (☎ 0733 26 01 42; Via Lauro Rossi 61; mains €6-13; 😊 Mon-Sat, closed mid-Aug–mid-Sep) Recommended by several readers. Favourites include polenta, risotto, lamb chops drenched in aromatic herbs and the lentil soup with *crostini* (croutons).

Istanbul Kebab (☎ 0733 23 81 60; Viale Trieste 6; mains €3-5; 😊 8am-2am, to midnight Sun) A tiny takeaway (only five seats) serving practically 24 hours a day, it's a tasty and inexpensive break from pasta, just in case one so desires.

Da Silvano (☎ 0733 26 02 161; Piaggia delle Torre 15; fixed-priced menu €30; 😊 Tue-Sun) A popular restaurant on a steep set of stairs, Da Silvano serves traditional Marchigiani dishes in a comfortable atmosphere.

Getting There & Around

Macerata is off the main railway line, which ensures its tranquillity but requires at least one change, either in Civitanova Le Marche for most easterly routes (including Ancona and some trains from Rome) or the more time-consuming Fabriano to the west (including Umbria, Tuscany and most trains from Rome). The **train station** (☎ 0733 24 03 54) is located at Piazza XXV Aprile 8/10. Good

connections include Ancona (€4, 1 hour 20 minutes, hourly), Rome (€13.25, four to 5½ hours, seven daily) and Ascoli Piceno (€4, one to 2½ hours, 11 daily); change trains in San Benedetto del Tronto or Porto d'Ascoli and Civitanova Marche.

Buses can be a better option to Perugia (€12, 2½ hours, 8.30am daily) and onto Florence (€19, 4½ hours), also heading to Rome (€18.50, 4¼ hours, three daily) and Ancona (€3.20, 1½ hours, 10 daily). Ask at the tourist office for timetables, which are also available at the bus terminal in **Giardini Diaz** (☎ 0733 23 09 06).

The local orange **APM** (☎ 0733 2 93 51) bus Nos 6A, 6B, 7, 8 or 11 will take you into town from the train station. They start at either Rampa Zara or Piazza della Libertà.

You'll find **taxis** (☎ 0733 23 35 70) for hire at Piazza della Libertà, at the **train station** (☎ 0733 24 03 53), as well as at **Giardini Diaz** (☎ 0733 23 13 39).

The SS77 connects the city with the A14 to the east and roads for Rome in the west.

ASCOLI PICENO
pop 55,000

Dominated by nearby mountains leading into the Apennines, Ascoli Piceno's art, history and traditions rival many of the better-known towns in Italy. Its old centre is quite extensive. Largely constructed in local travertine stone and laid out according to the traditional Roman model, it reached its zenith during the Renaissance, but has many interesting reminders of its medieval and more ancient past.

Ascoli Piceno was probably settled by the Piceni tribe in the 6th century BC. The salt trade eventually brought the city into contact with the Romans, to whom it finally fell in 268 BC. By the 6th century AD, the Goths and then the Lombards were in control. The city flourished in the Middle Ages, despite being ransacked by the troops of Holy Roman Emperor Frederick II after a long siege in 1242.

Orientation

The old town and its modern extension are separated by the Castellano River. The train station is in the new town, east of the river. From the station, turn right into Viale Indipendenza and head west across Ponte Maggiore, along Corso Vittorio Emanuele and

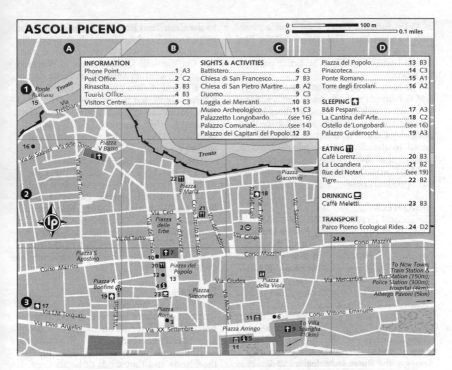

ASCOLI PICENO

INFORMATION		SIGHTS & ACTIVITIES		Piazza del Popolo.............13 B3
Phone Point.....................1 A3		Battistero.........................6 C3		Pinacoteca........................14 C3
Post Office......................2 C2		Chiesa di San Francesco......7 B3		Ponte Romano..................15 A1
Rinascita.........................3 B3		Chiesa di San Pietro Martire...8 A2		Torre degli Ercolani............16 A2
Tourist Office..................4 B3		Duomo............................9 C3		
Visitors Centre................5 C3		Loggia dei Mercanti..........10 B3		SLEEPING
		Museo Archeologico.........11 C3		B&B Pespani....................17 A3
		Palazzetto Longobardo.....(see 16)		La Cantina dell'Arte...........18 C2
		Palazzo Comunale............(see 14)		Ostello de'Longobardi......(see 16)
		Palazzo dei Capitani del Popolo.12 B3		Palazzo Guiderocchi...........19 A3
				EATING
				Café Lorenz......................20 B3
				La Locandiera...................21 B2
				Ruc dei Notari.................(see 19)
				Tigre...............................22 B2
				DRINKING
				Caffè Meletti.....................23 B3
				TRANSPORT
				Parco Piceno Ecological Rides...24 D2

past the cathedral. Head for Piazza Giudea, then Piazza Viola, which takes you to Piazza Fausto Simonetti just behind Piazza del Popolo, the heart of the medieval city. The walk takes around 15 minutes.

MAPS

The Provincia di Ascoli Piceno, in conjunction with the Istituto Geografico D'Agostini, publishes a useful road map for the province, with information in English. Parco Piceno publishes a free map (available at the tourist office) of the historical centre of Ascoli, with an index of monuments and streets. You can also pick up a copy of the *Pianta della Città* (Map of the City), published by the *comune*, at the main tourist office. The map indicates places of interest, parking areas and hotels within the city.

Information

City of Ascoli Pisceno (www.comune.ascoli-piceno.it) A consortium interested in promoting the area. Has information on events and festivals.

Hospital (☎ 0736 35 81; Monticello) Located 4km east of town.

Phone point (☎ 0736 25 23 70; Piazza Bonfine 6; per hr €2; ☻ 9am-12.45pm & 3-9pm) Has Internet and does phonecalls to the UK, US and Australia for €0.15 per minute.

Police station (☎ 0736 35 51 11; Viale della Repubblica 8)

Post office (☎ 0736 24 22 85; Via Crispi; ☻ 8am-6.30pm Mon-Fri, 8am-2.30pm Sat)

Rinascita (☎ 0736 25 96 53; www.rinascita.it in Italian; Piazza Roma 7) This lovely bookshop has it all: English language books, a whole Lonely Planet section (in Italian), lots of maps and a lovely café to while away an afternoon.

Tourist office (☎ 0736 25 30 45; iat.ascolipiceno@regione.marche.it; Piazza del Popolo; ☻ 9am-12.30pm & 3-6.30pm Mon-Fri, 9am-1pm Sat & Sun) The main council-run office.

Visitors centre (☎ 0736 29 82 04; Piazza Arringo 7; ☻ 9.30am-12.30pm & 3.30-6.30pm) Focuses on the *pinacoteca* (art gallery) but is also available for all other tourist needs.

Sights

PIAZZA DEL POPOLO

The heart of medieval Ascoli and the town's forum in Roman times, Piazza del Popolo is dominated on the western side by the 13th-century **Palazzo dei Capitani del Popolo**. The seat of Ascoli's rulers, it was burned to the ground

UMBRIA & LE MARCHE

in 1535 during a bitter local feud and rebuilt 10 years later. The statue of Pope Paul III above the main entrance was erected in recognition of his efforts to bring peace to the town.

The beautiful **Chiesa di San Francesco** (☎ 0736 25 94 46; Piazza del Popolo; ⊙ 7am-12.30pm & 3.30-8pm) was started back in 1262 and features a 15th-century wooden crucifix and 16th-century works by Cola dell'Amatrice. Virtually annexed to the church is **Loggia dei Mercanti**, built in the 16th century by the powerful guild of wool merchants, who displayed their products here.

PINACOTECA
The second-largest art gallery in Le Marche is inside the 17th-century **Palazzo Comunale** on Piazza Arringo, southeast of Piazza del Popolo. The **Pinacoteca** (☎ 0736 29 82 13, 0736 29 82 04; Piazza Arringo; adult/concession/child €5/3/2; ⊙ 8.30am-12.30pm & 2.30-7pm summer) boasts 400 works, including paintings by van Dyck, Titian, Carlo Crivelli and even an etching by Rembrandt. The gallery was founded in 1861 with works taken from churches and religious orders that were suppressed in the wake of Italian unification. Across Piazza Arringo, the **Museo Archeologico** (☎ 0736 25 35 62; Piazza Arringo; adult/under 18 €2/free; ⊙ 8.30am-7.30pm Tue-Sun) has a collection of implements used by the ancient Piceni tribe.

DUOMO
On the eastern flank of Piazza Arringo, Ascoli's **Duomo** (☎ 0736 25 97 74; Piazza Arringo; ⊙ 7am-12.30pm & 4-8pm) was built in the 15th century over a medieval building and dedicated to St Emidio, patron saint of the city. In the **Cappella del Sacramento** is what is considered by critics to be Carlo Crivelli's best work, the *Polittico*, a polyptych executed in 1473. The **crypt of Sant Emidio** has a set of mosaics any ceramicist will appreciate, but be sure to look through the locked gates at the ancient tunnels.

The **battistero** (baptistry) – next to the cathedral and something of a traffic barrier today – has remained unchanged since it was constructed in the 11th century.

VECCHIO QUARTIERE
The town's Vecchio Quartiere (Old Quarter) stretches from Corso Mazzini (the main thoroughfare of the Roman-era settlement) to the Castellano River. Its main street is the picturesque Via delle Torri, which eventually becomes Via Solestà; it's a perfect spot to wander. On Via delle Donne (Street of Women) is the 14th-century **Chiesa di San Pietro Martire** (☎ 0736 25 52 14; Piazza V Basso; ⊙ 7.30am-12.30pm & 3.30-7pm), dedicated to the saint who founded the Dominican community at Ascoli. The chunky Gothic structure houses the Reliquario della Santa Spina, containing what is said to be a thorn from Christ's crown.

The 40m-high **Torre degli Ercolani** located on Via dei Soderini, west of the Chiesa di San Pietro Martire, is the tallest of the town's medieval towers. **Palazzetto Longobardo**, a 12th-century Lombard-Romanesque defensive position and now the Ostello dei Longobardi, a youth hostel (see below for details), abuts the tower. Just to the north is the well-preserved **Ponte Romano**, a single-arched Roman bridge.

Festivals
With all the medieval festivals in Italy, when one of them receives an accolade for best historical reenactment, there's probably a pretty good reason. Ascoli's **Quintana**, held the first Sunday in August, brings out thousands and thousands of locals dressed in the typical costume of the 12th and 13th centuries: knights in suits of armour, ladies in velvet and lace. Processions and flag-waving contests take place throughout July and August, but the big draw is the Quintana day's joust, when the town's six *sestiers* (or quarters) face each other in a joust.

Sleeping
For a town with not many hotels, Ascoli has a good range of accommodation. Tourist offices have lists of other accommodation options, including rooms and apartments, *agriturismi* and B&B options in outlying districts.

Ostello dei Longobardi (☎ 0736 26 18 62; fax 0736 25 91 91; Via dei Soderini 26; dm €14) You'll feel right at home gnawing on a turkey drumstick or participating in leech-sponsored bloodletting inside what's left of the 11th- and 12th-century stone palace-turned-youth hostel. Remember that comfort and warmth were invented after the Middle Ages, so don't expect much from the plumbing and ask for an extra blanket in the winter. Two single-sex rooms sleep just eight each.

B&B Pespani (☎ 320 80 82 705; incontridiolan
za@libero.it; Via LM Torquato 6; s/d with breakfast €25/40)
Staying here is like staying with long-lost
family who will most likely become newly
found friends. He teaches theatre and mime,
she teaches yoga and dance, and they both
speak good English. Their two sons have
decorated the house with artwork on every
available service. The bathroom facilities will
be shared, but so will many cross-cultural
discussions.

La Cantina dell'Arte (☎ 0736 25 57 44; fax 0736
25 51 91; Rua della Lupa 8; s/d/tr/q €30/40/50/60) Thirteen simple rooms all come with private
bath and the quad even has a tiny balcony.
Even though it's tucked onto a side street,
bring earplugs, as soundproofing techniques
haven't improved much since the building's
inception in 1748.

Palazzo Guiderocchi (☎ 0736 24 40 11; www.palazzo
guiderocchi.com; Via Cesare Battisti 3; r with breakfast
€159-190, ste with breakfast €219-250; P ✗) Not
many places offer the history, atmosphere
and comfort of this 12th-century palace.
Fully restored, it maintains the romance of
six-metre vaulted ceilings on the 1st floor,
low wood-beamed ceilings on the 2nd, and
frescoes and several original doors throughout. Graceful period furnishings fit alongside thankfully modern bathrooms and
palatial but cosy beds. Best of all, the price
can drop by over half in the off season, on a
Sunday or when rooms are empty.

Eating

Plan your heart attack around Ascoli's favourite gastronomic son: *olive all'ascolana*
(olives stuffed with veal and then deep-
fried). Almost every restaurant in Ascoli, as
well as the surrounding area, serves them.
And after you've had your meal try their
mistra, an after-dinner drink made with
aniseed, liquorice and distilled secrets.

Café Lorenz (☎ 0736 25 99 59; Piazza del Popolo 5;
snacks & gelati €2-6, drinks & wine €2-5; ✿ 10am-2pm)
Head upstairs for a convivial drink or a light
dinner. But the main reason to come here
again and again: Lorenz sells takeaway *olive
all'ascolana* for €3.

La Locandiera (☎ 0736 26 25 09; Via Goldoni 2; mains
€5.50-14; ✿ Tue-Sun) This friendly trattoria,
with vaulted brick ceilings, is popular with
locals and great value for money. Sample the
antipasti: the dishes just keep coming, and
are always linked to seasonal produce.

Rua dei Notari (☎ 0736 26 36 30; Via Cesare Battisti 3;
mains €10-15) Perfect for a special meal, this elegant restaurant possesses old-world charm
in an elegant modern setting. Dishes present
as artfully as the modern paintings covering
the walls. There are meat and pasta dishes
as well as starters, including fried goodies
ascolana and *pecorino* with local honey (€8).
A fabulous deal is the *prix fixe* (fixed-price
menu).

Tigre (☎ 0763 34 10 00; Viale Indipendenza; ✿ 8.45am-
12.45pm & 4-8pm, closed Sun & mornings Mon) The most
central of Ascoli's supermarkets, this location
has a deli and a good wine selection.

Drinking

Caffè Meletti (☎ 0736 25 96 26; Piazza delle Popolo;
✿ 8am-7pm) From the shade of the ancient
portico you can sip a coffee or the famous
anisette as you gaze onto the perfect Italian piazza. Or sit inside to enjoy the statu-
esque carved wood stairway and bar. It was
once a popular spot for the likes of Ernest
Hemingway and Jean Paul Sartre. The café,
founded in 1907, fell into disrepair but has
since been completely restored to its former
glory.

Getting There & Away

Buses leave from Piazzale della Stazione, in
front of the train station in the new part
of town, east of the Castellano river. **Start**
(☎ 0736 34 22 43) runs buses to Rome (€10.85,
three hours, four daily). In Rome, Start
buses leave from Viale Castro Pretorio 84,
near Stazione Termini. **Mazzuca** (☎ 0736 40 22
67) serves Montemonaco (€2.60, 1½ hours,
three daily), Amandola (€2.20, one hour 10
minutes, three daily) and other towns near
the Monti Sibillini range. At 6.30am daily,
Amadio (☎ 0736 34 23 40) runs a service to Florence (€23.10, 6¼ hours) via Perugia (€15.50,
4¼ hours) and Siena (€20.85, 5½ hours).

A spur train line connects Ascoli Piceno
with Porto d'Ascoli (€1.90, 35 minutes) every
hour and San Benedetto del Tronto (€2.40,
40 minutes), both of which are on the Bologna to Lecce line. From San Benedetto there
are half-hourly trains to Ancona (€4.30, one
hour 10 minutes). Ask at the train station
for a free timetable brochure (*orario*) for Le
Marche trains.

From the A14 motorway, exit at San
Benedetto del Tronto and follow the *superstrada* (expressway) for Ascoli Piceno. From

Rome, take the Antique Salaria or A2 motorway L'Aquila-Teramo. Follow the state road Piceno–Aprutina for Ascoli Piceno.

Getting Around

Most of the tranquil historic centre of Ascoli Piceno is closed to motor traffic. Locals walk or cycle and visitors can have free use of a bicycle for the duration of their stay if they present ID to **Parco Piceno Ecological Rides** (☎ 0736 26 32 61; Corso Mazzini 224).

MONTI SIBILLINI

Covering both the western reaches of Le Marche and up and over the Apennine border with Umbria is the mystical Monti Sibillini. The **Parco Nazionale dei Monti Sibillini** contains over 10 peaks that rise to a height of above 2000m and there are countless wildflowers, ancient towns, wild wolves and soaring peregrine falcons veiled in the valleys below. For tourist purposes, the region is divided into four slopes for all tastes: flowering, magic, sacred, historical. Take your pick and explore.

The area is a paradise for anyone interested in outdoor activities. Walking trails crisscross the area. Mountain hostels known as *rifugi* welcome hikers every few kilometres or so with a restaurant and a warm bed (maps are available at any local tourist office).

On both the Le Marche and Umbria sides you'll find hang-gliding and horseback riding. During the winter, several towns offer Central Italy's best skiing: Sarnano, Bolognola, Ussita, Acquacanina and Castelsantangelo sul Nera. For the most adventurous among us, there is a nine-day mountain trek covering the length of the entire range.

Amandola is one of the prettiest villages in Le Marche. Although there is no cheap accommodation, there are quite a few options in surrounding localities. Just south is Montefortino, a good base for accessing Montemonaco, at the base of Monte Sibilla, a place for serious walkers (but not public transport users). One of the better known hikes is the Gola dell'Infernaccio (Gorge of Hell), which is a relatively simple but spectacular walk.

To reach the range, take the SS4 from Ascoli Piceno and follow the signs. Buses connect the area with Ascoli Piceno and various cities throughout Le Marche.

Information

Sarnano tourist office (☎ 0733 65 71 44; iat.sarnano@regione.marche.it; Largo Ricciardi 1; ☽ 8.30am-1pm Mon-Fri) in Sarnano has walking and climbing information and details of accommodation in the park.

There are 15 'Casa del Parco' visitors information centres, several of which are open daily, including **Amàndola** (☎ /fax 0736 84 85 98; Via Indipendenza 73). Each tourist office carries a plethora of books, maps, brochures and guides to satisfy every cultural or natural interest, from monastery to mountain-biking trails.

Check out www.sibillini.net, the area's official website, which is mostly translated into English and has loads of information on camping and hotels, hikes, outdoor activities and services.

Activities

Il Maneggio Le Querce (☎ /fax 0733 65 82 11; C da Bisio, Sarnano), found in the province of Macerata, can arrange horse riding and courses in equitation.

Sleeping & Eating

Rifugio Casali (☎ 0737 9 95 90; Ussita; dm with breakfast €35; P) One of a dozen *rifugi* in the Monti Sibillini national park, this one has three dorm-style bedrooms, each with a bathroom and hot shower. The *rifugi* is open July and August, and around the Christmas and New Year period; the rest of the year it is open by appointment.

Casa Rosi (☎ 0763 85 00 23; www.casarosi.it; Via Montazzolini 8, Montefortino; d per person €30) Enjoy the warm hospitality offered by the English owners (who will even make you a full English breakfast). Three cosy rooms are furnished in pine, making for the full mountain-cabin feel.

Sibilla (☎ 0736 85 61 44; Via Roma 52, Montemonaco; s/d with breakfast €27/47; ☽ year-round; P) This friendly, family-run place has 10 rooms, all with private bathrooms.

Castel di Luco Hotel & Restaurant (☎ 0736 80 23 19; www.casteldiluco.com; Castel di Luco, Acquasante Terme; r €159, mains €31; P) Between the park and Ascoli is the village of Acquasante Terme and the gloriously antediluvian Castel di Luco Hotel & Restaurant, the sort of place you'd want to spend a honeymoon, or a lifetime. Most of the structure is exactly as it was in AD 1052, the first record of its existence.

MAGIC MOUNTAINS

Sibylline: the very word has become synonymous with occult and mysterious things, and for centuries the rugged, wild world of the Monti Sibillini has stirred the imagination of writers. In the Middle Ages, this mountain range of 20 summits was know as a realm of demons, necromancers and fairies. The name derives from the famous legend of Sibyl, thought to be able to foresee the future and reputed to live in a cave below Mt Sibylla, one of the three highest peaks of the range.

Whether or not you believe these ancient stories, you can't help but be entranced by the magic of these mountains that straddle Umbria and Le Marche. As you climb, the vegetation changes, from oaks, European hops and flowering ashes, to beechwoods higher up. Higher still you find rough grazing land and rare, precious species of flowers like Apennine edelweiss. In the summer, the northernmost part of the park is filled with blooming orchids, liliaceae, narcissuses and alpine aster. The creatures that live in the mountains are just as wild. There are wolves, wild cats, roe deer and porcupines, while golden eagles, goshawks, sparrowhawks and peregrine falcons soar overhead.

The 70,000 hectares set aside in 1993 as a national park also contain other evocative reminders of an ancient world. There are abbeys and medieval towns nestling at the bottom of the mountains, and churches with late-Gothic frescoes, castles and lookout towers erected by valley dwellers to defend themselves against Saracen raids. In the valley of the Fiastroe River is the Grotta dei Fratti (The Friars' Cave), an impressive ravine hollowed out by water which served as a refuge in the 11th century for the Clareno monks. Norcia – the birthplace of St Benedict, the patron saint of Europe – is the starting point for many excursions including to the Abbey of Sant Eutizio, in the *comune* of Preci, founded at the end of the 5th century and famous for the skills the monks developed In healing the sick with medicinal herbs from the Sibillini Mountains.

Three suites open up to exposed-brick walls, wood-beamed ceilings and wrought-iron furnishings. The vaulted fresco restaurant (closed Sunday evening and Monday) is worth a visit just to walk down its staircase, carved out of the fortress' ancient rock.

Montespino (☎ /fax 0736 85 92 38; Montefortino Cerratana; person/tent €4.15/6.20, 2-/4-/6-bed bungalow €26/39/47; ☽ Jun-Sep, weekends only mid-Sep–Dec; **P** ☒) With a view of Monte Conero and surrounded by a forest full of trees, this camp site seems like it's in the middle of nowhere but it's just a few kilometres off the SS78 between Macerata and Ascoli Piceno. Full service with a restaurant, bar, market, *bocce* court, swimming pool and children's games.

Quattro Stagioni (☎ 0733 65 11 47; www.camping4 stagioni.it; Loc Forseneta, Sarnano; 2 people & caravan/tent €23, extra person €5, child €3, 4-person bungalows €60; **P** ☒) Fabulously located just outside of Sarnano, this family-friendly camp site has two separate pools for adults and children, table tennis, a discotheque and courts for just about everything: *bocce*, tennis and soccer. They're open all year and have a restaurant, market and pizzeria. During high season they offer instruction in swimming,

horse riding and even aerobics classes. Bungalows come with kitchenettes and have full bathroom.

SENIGALLIA
pop 30,000
Senigallia's aptly named **Spiaggia di Velluto** (Velvet Beach) is reputedly one of the best *lidi* (bathing beaches) on the Adriatic coast.

The **tourist office** (☎ 071 792 27 25; iat.senigallia@ regione.marche.it; Piazzale Morandi 2; ☽ 9am-1pm & 3.30-6.30pm Mon-Sat, mornings Sun in summer) is located between Velvet Beach and the train station.

Apart from sun, sea and sand, the main draw is the **Rocca Roveresca** (☎ 071 6 32 58; Piazza del Duca; admission €2.05; ☽ 8.30am-7.30pm Tue-Sun), whose four stout, crenellated towers make it hard to miss. Its plush Renaissance interior makes a visit well worthwhile.

Sleeping & Eating
If you're having trouble finding a room, try the **Associazione Alberghi e Turismo** (☎ 071 6 53 43; Viale IV Novembre 2).

Albergo Eleonora (☎ 071 792 73 73; fax 071 65 94 82; Lungomare G Marconi 2; s/d from €20.65/41.30; ☎ year-round) This fairly anonymous red high rise is on the waterfront, close to the train station. It's friendly and has a handy bar and restaurant downstairs. There's compulsory full board in August at €46.50 per person.

Liana (☎ 071 6 52 06; fax 071 792 17 50; Lungomare Leonardo da Vinci 54; person/tent from €4.65/13.45) This camp site, just north of Spiaggia di Velluto, has slightly better facilities.

Spiaggia di Velluto (☎ /fax 071 6 48 73; Lungomare Leonardo da Vinci; person/tent from €4.40/13.45) This camp site is about 3km south of Senigallia, right on the beach.

Getting There & Away

All buses stop at the main train station, which is in the town centre on Via Rafaele Sanzio. Bucci buses operate along the SS16 coastal road to Ancona (€1.50, 35 minutes, 25 daily), Fano (€1.50, 30 minutes, five daily) and Pesaro (€1.70, 50 minutes, four daily). Plenty of trains also service the same stretch.

Abruzzo & Molise

Abruzzo and neighbouring Molise offer some of Italy's least-explored countryside. And it's this wild landscape of stark Apennine peaks and dark valleys, of ancient forests and brooding castles that's the real reason to visit. In few other places in Italy can you find such solitude.

But that's not to say that tourism has bypassed the area. It hasn't. The Parco Nazionale d'Abruzzo, Lazio & Molise attracts some two million visitors annually, while further east the heavily developed Adriatic resorts swell with sunseekers every August. Inland, however, the pace is slower and the infrastructure less obtrusive.

Abruzzo and Molise boast three national parks encompassing some 3350 sq km of the Apennines. Here a small number of wolves and bears roam free, and although you're unlikely to meet one, it adds an edge to know that you might. A vast outdoor playground, the parks provide great hiking with trails ranging from gentle strolls along lush valley floors to hardcore mountain routes. In winter, the slopes snow over and skiers take to the pistes.

With a history of poverty and neglect, neither region is as culturally rich as its more illustrious neighbours, but there are gems to be found. The Romanesque Basilica di Santa Maria di Collemaggio in L'Aquila and the Byzantine frescoes of the Abbazia di San Vincenzo Volturno, northwest of Isernia, are both striking examples of artistic expression.

The two regions (known collectively as the Abruzzi until they were divided in 1963) are among Italy's most earthquake prone. In 2002 a quake killed 29 people in the small hilltop town of San Giuliano di Puglia, while one of the area's worst disasters struck in 1915, when a massive jolt left 30,000 people dead.

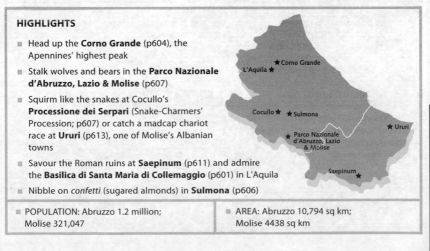

HIGHLIGHTS

- Head up the **Corno Grande** (p604), the Apennines' highest peak
- Stalk wolves and bears in the **Parco Nazionale d'Abruzzo, Lazio & Molise** (p607)
- Squirm like the snakes at Cocullo's **Processione dei Serpari** (Snake-Charmers' Procession; p607) or catch a madcap chariot race at **Ururi** (p613), one of Molise's Albanian towns
- Savour the Roman ruins at **Saepinum** (p611) and admire the **Basilica di Santa Maria di Collemaggio** (p601) in L'Aquila
- Nibble on *confetti* (sugared almonds) in **Sulmona** (p606)

★ Corno Grande
L'Aquila ★
Cocullo ★ ★ Sulmona
★ Ururi
Parco Nazionale d'Abruzzo, Lazio & Molise
Saepinum ★

- POPULATION: Abruzzo 1.2 million; Molise 321,047
- AREA: Abruzzo 10,794 sq km; Molise 4438 sq km

ABRUZZO & MOLISE

ABRUZZO

More spectacular than its southern neighbour Molise, Abruzzo is home to two of the Apennine's highest mountains. Towering above the regional capital, L'Aquila, the Corno Grande (2914m) is the highest point of the Gran Sasso d'Italia, a massif of sawtooth summits and 1000m-high precipices; to the southeast the Monte Amaro (2795m) dominates the ominous Majella range.

Although best known for its dramatic mountains, Abruzzo's landscape is surprisingly diverse: there are ancient forests in the Parco Nazionale d'Abruzzo, Lazio & Molise, a vast plain to the east of Avezzano and a sandy coastline with excellent swimming in summer.

Many towns retain a medieval look. Chief among them, L'Aquila and Sulmona are well worth visiting, while the numerous hilltop castles and isolated, sometimes abandoned, *borghi* (villages) can exude a sinister charm – they're the perfect setting for a Gothic horror story.

In fact, ancient Abruzzo was famed for its witches, wizards and snake-charmers – members of a tribe known as the Marsi, who lived around modern-day Avezzano. Even today, snakes feature in a bizarre annual festival (see p607) in the mountain village of Cocullo, near Sulmona.

L'AQUILA
pop 69,160 / elev 720m

A city of grey stone and biting winters, L'Aquila is hard to warm to. Icy winds whistle in from the Gran Sasso d'Italia and the dour architecture adds little cheer. However, don't be discouraged – it is worth exploring and as the evening sun casts an opaque rose light over the surrounding mountains you'll probably find your spirits rising.

Legend has it that the city was founded by the Swabian King Frederick II and built by his son Conrad IV in 1254. The original citizens of L'Aquila (meaning 'the eagle' – a reference to the eagle in the Swabian coat of arms) were drawn from 99 villages, and each village was required to build its own piazza, church and fountain. Earthquakes have des-

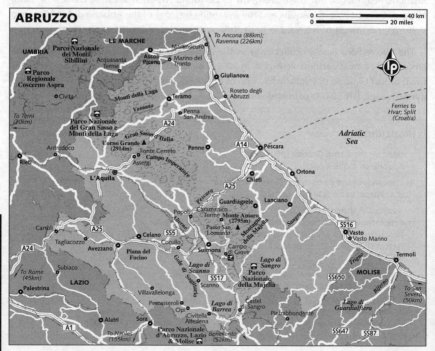

troyed most of the original churches and piazze but a fountain, Fontana delle 99 Cannelle, survives along with the town-hall bell, which chimes 99 times every evening.

L'Aquila's people have a rebellious spirit, but have frequently backed the wrong horse. In 1423 the city endured a 13-month siege by the Aragonese for supporting the Anjou in the fight for the Kingdom of Naples. L'Aquila rose against Spanish rule twice in the 16th and 17th centuries and both times the city was crushed. The 1703 earthquake all but finished off L'Aquila. Revolt finally proved fruitful when, in 1860, the city was made regional capital for its efforts towards national unity.

Orientation

Your best point of reference is Piazza del Duomo in the *centro storico* (historic centre). All the city sights are within easy walking distance and the piazza is directly linked to the bus terminal by a 500m escalator-cum-walkway. From the piazza, the centre's main street, Corso Vittorio Emanuele runs north, while to the south its continuation, Corso Federico II, leads down to the Villa Comunale park.

L'Aquila's train station is west and downhill of the city centre. Bus Nos 5 and 8 will take you into town. Get off at Via XX Settembre, from where it's a short walk up Corso Federico II to Piazza del Duomo.

Information

Banca SanPaolo (☎ 0862 66 81; Corso Vittorio Emanuele 61) One of several banks along Corso Vittorio Emanuele with an ATM.
Duomo.net (☎ 0862 2 18 93; Via Cimino 19; per hr €3; ☺ 9am-midnight Mon-Sat, 4pm-midnight Sun) For Internet access and international phone calls.
Hospital (☎ 0862 36 81; Località Coppito)
L'Aquila City (www.laquila.com in Italian) Uninspiring but comprehensive site with lots of useful information.
Pharmacy (Farmacia; ☎ 0862 2 61 91; Corso Vittorio Emanuele 15; ☺ 9am-1pm & 4-7.30pm Mon-Fri)
Police station (☎ 0862 43 01; Via Strinella 2)
Post office (☎ 0862 63 73 10; Piazza del Duomo 39; ☺ 8am-6.30pm Mon-Sat)
Tourist office Piazza Santa Maria Paganica 5 (☎ 0862 41 08 08; ☺ 8am-1pm & 3-6pm Mon-Fri, 8am-1pm Sat Oct-May, 8am-1pm Sun Jun-Sep) Main tourist office; Via XX Settembre 8 (☎ 0862 2 23 06; ☺ 9am-1pm & 3-6pm Mon-Fri, 9am-1pm Sat Oct-May, 9am-1pm & 4-7pm Mon-Sat, 9am-1pm Sun Jun-Sep)

Sights

FORTE SPAGNOLO

L'Aquila's 16th-century castle stands at the northeastern corner of the *centro storico*. Known locally as the **Forte Spagnolo** (Spanish Fort), it was built after an unsuccessful rebellion against the city's Spanish rulers in 1528. The austere geometry, steep blanched battlements and now-empty moat were designed by the Valencian architect Pirro Luis Scrivà and commissioned by Don Pedro de Toledo, the hated Spanish viceroy of Naples and de facto ruler of L'Aquila.

Offering wonderful views over the Gran Sasso d'Italia, the castle today houses the **Museo Nazionale d'Abruzzo** (☎ 0862 63 31; Castello Cinquecentesco; admission €4; ☺ 9am-8pm Tue-Sun), L'Aquila's premier museum. Here you will find a collection of local religious art and the skeleton of a million-year-old mammoth, unearthed near the city in 1954.

CHURCHES

A beautiful landmark, the **Basilica di Santa Maria di Collemaggio** (☎ 0862 2 63 92; Viale di Collemaggio; ☺ 8.30am-1pm & 3-8pm Mon-Fri, 8.30am-8pm Sat & Sun), is one of Abruzzo's most famous churches. Its square pink-and-white quilt-pattern façade beautifully combines Romanesque and Gothic architecture – note the rose windows and imposing central portal. In contrast, the gloomy interior is cold and stark.

Consecrated in 1288, the basilica became an important religious centre in 1294 when the church's founder, Pietro del Morrone, was crowned pope here. An unworldly ex-hermit, Pope Celestine V was ill-equipped for the papacy and lasted only a few months. Forced to abdicate by conniving cardinals, he was imprisoned by his successor, Pope Boniface VIII, and died in 1296. As founder of the Celestine order, he was canonised seven years later and his tomb lies inside the basilica.

To the north, the **Basilica di San Bernardino** (☎ 0862 2 22 55; Piazza San Bernardino; ☺ 7am-noon & 4-6pm Mon-Sat, 4-6.30pm Sun) is a lavish affair. Dating from the 15th century, it has undergone various face-lifts over the centuries, the most important of which followed the 1703 earthquake. The three-tiered Renaissance façade of classical columns and elegant arches is matched in opulence by the rich baroque interior. Of note are the detailed

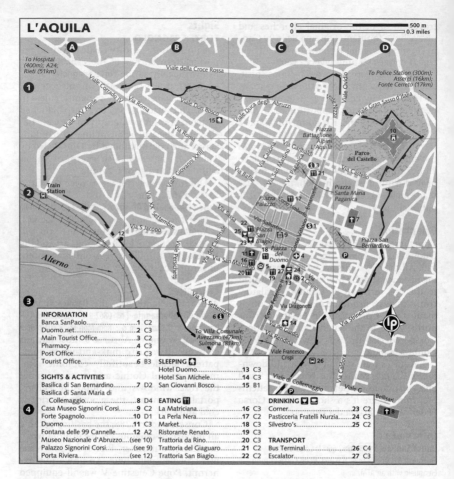

reliefs on San Bernadino's mausoleum, the work of local artist Silvestro dell'Aquila. San Bernadino, originally from Siena, died in L'Aquila in 1444.

Forming one side of Piazza del Duomo, L'Aquila's **Duomo** (Piazza del Duomo; ☒ 8.30am-noon & 4.30-7pm) is one of the city's many earth-quake victims. Rebuilt many times since the 13th-century, today it boasts little more than an unexceptional neoclassical façade.

CASA MUSEO SIGNORINI CORSI
The beautifully preserved **Palazzo Signorini Corsi** houses the Corsi family's considerable collection of religious art and period furniture. To see how the city's aristocracy once lived, head for this small **museum** (☎ 0862 41 09

00; Via Patini 42; adult/child €3.10/2.10; ☒ 4-7pm Tue-Fri, 10am-1pm & 4-7pm Sat & Sun) in the city centre.

FONTANA DELLE 99 CANNELLE
A monument to L'Aquila's magic number 99, this is the city's most emblematic sight. The **Fountain of the 99 Spouts** is, however, a misnomer – there are, in fact, only 93 spewing gargoyles. Surrounded by a wall of pink-and-white stone, the 13th-century fountain is one of the few supplies of freshwater that has proved reliable in the city's seismic past. The source of the water remains a mystery but on more than one occasion it's proved a lifesaver to the people of L'Aquila. The fountain lies to the west of the centre, near the **Porta Riviera**, one of the city's four medieval gates.

LA PERDONANZA

Thanks to the forgiving nature of L'Aquila's favourite pope, you can now wipe your spiritual slate clean every year at La Perdonanza (the Pardon).

L'Aquila's festival *par excellence* goes back to 1294 and the day when Pietro del Morrone was crowned Pope Celestine V in the Basilica di Santa Maria di Collemaggio. In an act of unprecedented largesse, Celestine, a former hermit, granted plenary indulgence to everyone present who had confessed and taken Communion.

Since then, every 28 August, the pardon has been repeated. In a solemn ceremony, the mayor of L'Aquila reads Celestine's original decree, and a cardinal nominated by the Vatican orders the Porta Santa (Holy Door) to be opened. For the next 24 hours the faithful stream through in their thousands, confident that all who cross the threshold will be absolved of their sins.

The grand door-opening ceremony is preceded by a 1000-strong costumed procession (from Piazza Palazzo to the Basilica di Santa Maria di Collemaggio) and a week of highly charged celebrations.

Sleeping

Accommodation in L'Aquila is thin on the ground, so it's always best to book ahead.

San Giovanni Bosco (☎ 0862 6 39 31; Viale Don Bosco 6; s/d with bathroom €25/45) A short walk out from the centre, this religious institution offers the cheapest beds in town. Rooms are basic and clean but not for night owls, as there's an 11pm curfew.

Hotel Duomo (☎ 0862 41 08 93; www.hotel-duomo it; Via Dragonetti 6; s/d with bathroom €60/78; ℗) A charming and discreet little hotel just off Piazza del Duomo, the Duomo is as welcoming as it is comfortable. The burnt-sienna floor tiles and dark-wood furniture give the rooms a central Italian feel, while the mod cons provide the comfort. Car parking costs €5 in the hotel's nearby car park or €3 for a street permit.

Hotel San Michele (☎ 0862 42 02 60; www.stmich elehotel.it; Via dei Giardini 6; s/d with bathroom & breakfast €65/90; ℗) Noise from the nearby Villa Comunale park is unlikely to keep you awake at night, as all the rooms at this modern hotel have been soundproofed. Furnished with parquet floors and unexciting décor, they leave little lasting impression. Parking is an extra €8.

Eating

There are any number of restaurants and trattorie in the city centre. Most stick to traditional specialities, which include *maccheroni alla chitarra* (thick, homemade macaroni) and *agnello* (lamb). Fruit and veg are sold at the weekday **market** (Piazza del Duomo).

La Perla Nera (☎ 0862 41 34 79; Piazza Palazzo 5; pizza slices €2.50) A great place to join the locals for a quick lunchtime snack. There's a good range of pizzas, calzone and fried croquettes.

La Matriciana (☎ 0862 2 60 65; Via Arcivescovado 5/a; 1st/2nd courses from €6/6.50; ⏰ Mon-Sat) La Matriciana is a typical low-key trattoria. The décor is instantly forgettable and the menu made up of traditional pastas and meat-based dishes. However, the food is good, the prices are reasonable and the lone waiter works hard to feed his hungry diners. According to Italian custom, fish is served on Fridays: try the pasta with scampi (the real crustacean, not the bread-crumbed version) and the *baccalà* (cod).

Trattoria da Rino (☎ 0862 2 52 80; Via San Marciano 2; 1st/2nd courses from €5/6; ⏰ Tue-Sun) A family affair, Da Rino is a relaxed place to eat. There are no surprises to be had here, just hearty portions of warming Abruzzo classics. Expect *spaghetti alla chitarra al ragù* (homemade spaghetti with a meat sauce) and lamb served in various guises. The house red is cheap and although not great it's perfectly drinkable.

Trattoria del Giaguaro (☎ 0862 2 40 01; Piazza Santa Maria Paganica 4; 1st/2nd courses €6/8; ⏰ lunch Mon & Wed-Sun) A favourite of lunching locals, this well-established trattoria fills quickly around 1.30pm, so get in good and early. Tried and tested staples include *zuppa di legumi* (a thick pulse soup) and osso buco (veal shank).

Other eating options include **Trattoria San Biagio** (☎ 0862 2 21 39; Piazza San Biagio 4; 1st/2nd courses about €6/8; ⏰ Mon-Sat) and **Ristorante Renato** (☎ 0862 2 55 96; Via dell'Indipendenza 9; 1st/2nd courses from €6/7; ⏰ Mon-Sat), both of which serve good regional cuisine.

Drinking

Pasticceria Fratelli Nurzia (☎ 0862 2 10 02; Piazza del Duomo 74) One of the city's historic *pasticcerie*, this café-cum-cake shop serves goodies concocted in the Nurzia family business since 1835. The house speciality is the *caffè Nurzia*, a coffee to which cream and chocolate are liberally added.

Corner (Via Cavour 2; ⏰ 7pm-2am) For an early evening apéritif the Corner is a friendly pub-cum-bar that's popular with the fashionable 30-something set.

Silvestro's (☎ 347 616 50 23; Via Sassa 24; ⏰ 7pm-2am Tue-Sun) Not far away from the Corner, bar staff pull the pints at this large wood-panelled Irish pub.

Entertainment

An annual season of weekly concerts is held between October and May by, among others, the **Società Aquilana dei Concerti** (☎ 0862 41 41 61). If you're in town during summer, ask about the special open-air concert, ballet and drama performances, staged at various locations including the Basilica di San Bernadino, the Basilica di Santa Maria di Collemaggio and the courtyard of the Forte Spagnolo.

Getting There & Away

Perhaps the best way to get to L'Aquila is by bus – the connections are both efficient and comprehensive.

ARPA (☎ 0862 41 28 08, in Rome ☎ 06 442 33 928; www.arpaonline.it in Italian) runs buses to Rome's Stazione Tiburtina (€8.90, 1¾ hours, 19 daily), Sulmona (€4.50, 1½ hours, 10 daily) and Pescara (€7.30, 2½ hours, 10 daily). All buses leave from the main **bus terminal** (Viale di Collemaggio).

By train, the town is accessible from Rome (€10.20, four hours, 10 daily), via Sulmona or Terni, and from Pescara (€6.10, 2½ hours, eight daily), via Sulmona.

PARCO NAZIONALE DEL GRAN SASSO E MONTI DELLA LAGA

You don't have to go far from L'Aquila before you're into the spectacular mountain scenery of the Parco Nazionale del Gran Sasso e Monti della Laga. One of Italy's biggest parks, it extends for 1500 sq km, spilling over into Lazio and Le Marche. The park's predominant feature is its jagged rocky landscape through which Europe's southernmost glacier, the Calderone, cuts its slow course.

The **park office** (☎ 0862 605 22 48; www.gransasso lagapark.it in Italian; Via del Convento 1; ⏰ 10.30am-1pm & 4-6pm Mon-Fri) is in Assergi, some 10km northeast of L'Aquila. It carries information and a park map in English. For walking, pick up the IGN map *Parco Nazionale del Gran Sasso* at 1:25,000 at the park office in Assergi.

There is a **funivia** (cable car; ☎ 347 271 85 79; weekdays/weekends €10/13; ⏰ 8.45am-4.15pm Mon-Fri, 8.30am-4.15pm Sat & Sun) leaving Fonte Cerreto every 30 minutes for **Campo Imperatore** (2117m), a desolate highland plain where Mussolini was briefly imprisoned in 1943. Here you can trek in summer and ski in winter (a daily ski pass costs €16 Monday to Friday and €22 on Saturday and Sunday).

One of the most popular trekking routes is the surprisingly straightforward climb to the top of **Corno Grande**. Rated moderate to demanding, the 9km *via normale* (normal route) starts in the main parking area at Campo Imperatore and heads to the summit at 2914m. The trail should be relatively free of snow from early June to late September/early October. For more details, see Lonely Planet's *Walking in Italy*.

The park has a network of *rifugi* (mountain huts) for walkers. Hotel accommodation is limited and expensive, but there is a camp site and a hostel.

Camping Funivia del Gran Sasso (☎ 0862 60 61 63; Fonte Cerreto; person/tent/car €6.20/4.70/1; ⏰ mid-May–mid-Sep) is a handy base for walking, and is also the nearest camp site to L'Aquila. Alternatively, jump on the cable car and ride up to the **Ostello Campo Imperatore** (☎ 0862 40 00 11; Campo Imperatore; per person €15; ⏰ year-round), a hostel offering bunk beds in rooms of two or four.

To get to the park by public transport take bus No 76 (€0.80, 20 minutes, hourly) from L'Aquila to Piazza Santa Maria Paganica, and then a Linea M bus to Assergi and Fonte Cerreto (€0.80, 20 minutes, 13 daily).

SULMONA

pop 25,276 / elev 400m

An atmospheric medieval town, Sulmona is prosperous and charming. Hemmed in by mountains, its dramatic surroundings loom darkly over the suggestive *centro storico*. Easily covered in a day, it makes a good base for exploring southern Abruzzo.

Despite its medieval appearance, Sulmona's origins predate the Romans. Though no-one is absolutely sure, the consensus is that it was founded by Solimo, a companion of Aeneas. The poet Ovid was born here in 43 BC, and later in the Middle Ages Sulmona became an important commercial centre.

The source of much of Sulmona's wealth is the *confetti* industry – the production of sugar almonds which are presented to guests at Italian weddings.

Orientation

The walled *centro storico* is easy to navigate. Most sights are on or near the main street, Corso Ovidio, which runs from the Villa Comunale, a small park beside Piazzale Tresca, to the impressive Piazza Garibaldi. It's a five-minute stroll and is closed to traffic outside business hours. About halfway down the *corso* (main street) is Piazza XX Settembre.

The train station is about 2km northwest of the historic centre; the half-hourly bus A runs between the two.

Information

3D Sistemi (☎ 0864 21 20 47; Piazza Plebiscito 2; per 15min €1.50; ☾ 9am-1pm & 4 7.30pm Mon Wed, Fri & Sat) For Internet access.

Council tourist office (☎ 0864 21 02 16; www.comune .sulmona.aq.it in Italian; Palazzo dell'Annunziata, Corso Ovidio; ☾ 9am-1.30pm & 4-8pm)

Tourist office (☎ 0864 5 32 76; Corso Ovidio 208; ☾ 9am-1pm Mon- Fri & alternate Sat, 3-6pm Mon, Wed & Fri Apr-Sep, 9am-1pm & 4-7pm Mon-Sat, 9am-1pm Sun May-Aug)

Sights

The most impressive of the palazzi that line the Corso Ovidio is the 16th-century **Palazzo dell'Annunziata** (Corso Ovidio), which is a harmonious blend of Gothic and Renaissance architecture. Over the years it has been a hospital, pharmacy, magistrate's court and school; nowadays it houses the small **Museo Civico** (☎ 0864 21 02 16; Corso Ovidio; admission €1; ☾ by appointment). Here you will find artefacts ranging from Roman mosaics to Renaissance sculpture, coins and prints. Adjoining the palazzo is a baroque church of the same name, originally dating from 1320 but rebuilt after the 1703 earthquake.

Nearby, the **Piazza XX Settembre**, with its statue of Ovid (see the boxed text, below), is a popular meeting point.

Continuing along Corso Ovidio you come to **Piazza Garibaldi**. Pass under the arches of the 13th-century **aqueduct** and go down the steps to Sulmona's grandest square. The piazza is the scene of a colourful market every Wednesday and Saturday morning and its most famous feature is the austere Renaissance **Fontana del Vecchio** (Fountain of the Old One). Some say that the bearded face from which the water spews is that of Solimo, the founder of Sulmona. Elsewhere on the piazza, the 14th-century **Chiesa di San Filippo Neri** (Piazza Garibaldi; ☾ 10am-1pm & 4-7pm) boasts an impressive Gothic façade, while nearby, on the adjacent Piazza del Carmine, the Romanesque portal is all that remains of the **Chiesa di San Francesco della Scarpa**, destroyed in the 1703 earthquake.

OVID

Ovid was never meant to be a poet. Born into a wealthy Sulmona family in 43 BC, the young Publius Ovidius Naso was shipped off to Rome to study rhetoric and carve out for himself a comfortable career in politics. But once in the capital he fell in with the literary set and began to write poetry. Ovid's early erotic verse, such as *Amores* and *Ars Amatoria* (the Art of Love), gained him quick popularity in Roman high society.

Considered his masterpiece, *Metamorphoses* is a kind of extended cover version of a whole gamut of Greek myths, culminating in descriptions of Caesar's transformation into a star and the apotheosis of Augustus, who was ruler at the time. This last piece of sycophancy did not stop the emperor from banishing him to the Black Sea in AD 8. The reason why remains a mystery, although Ovid himself alludes to a *carmen et error* (a poem and his behaviour). He died in Tomi, in modern-day Romania, 10 years later.

Ovid's work was much studied by medieval scholars and gave rise to many myths. He was said to have turned men into birds and women into trees, and to have transformed himself into a black dog or werewolf to talk to demons. Equally outlandish was the legend that he could read with his feet.

In Sulmona, sweet-making becomes art at the **Fabbrica Confetti Pelino**, the most famous of the sugared-almond manufacturers. Housed in the egg-blue factory is the **Museo dell'Arte Confettiera** (☎ 0864 21 00 47; Via Stazione Introdacqua 55; admission free; ☺ 9.30am-12.30pm & 3.30-6.30pm Mon-Sat), about a 1km signposted walk from the Porta Napoli, at the southern end of Corso Ovidio.

Sleeping & Eating

Hotel Italia (☎ 0864 5 23 08; Piazza Salvatore Tommasi 3; s/d €25/43, with bathroom €33/54) Some hotels just never change and Hotel Italia is one such place. As you enter the elegant old palazzo the tone is set by the life-sized model of a medieval lady. The interior of marble columns and dark corridors is wonderfully ramshackle, and the rooms themselves are decent enough, if a little rough around the edges.

Albergo Ristorante Stella (☎ 0864 5 26 53; www .hasr.it in Italian; Via Panfilo Mazara 18; s/d with bathroom & breakfast €40/70) When we last visited this was a simple *pensione* full of character. It's since been done up and although it's gained in comfort – rooms have parquet floors, TVs and phones – it's lost some of its old-fashioned charm. Rates, however, are reasonable, it's very central and the owners are welcoming.

Ristorante Italia (☎ 0864 3 30 70; Piazza XX Settembre 23; 1st/2nd courses about €6/7; ☺ Tue-Sun) Absolutely without any pretensions, the relaxed Ristorante Italia serves up large portions of good workaday food. Particularly fine is the grilled meat washed down with a glass or three of red wine. The service is friendly as the maternal patrons insist that their diners eat well.

Napul'è (☎ 0864 3 31 20; Vico delle Colle 5; pizzas from €5; ☺ Tue-Sun) With the TV on in the corner and the *pizzaiolo* (pizza-maker) popping out to chat with his mates, this simple pizzeria is not the place for a romantic tête-à-tête. But if you're after a tasty pizza and a refreshing beer, it'll do just fine.

Drinking

Gran Caffè (☎ 0864 3 30 12; Piazza XX Settembre 12-14) As you sip your cappuccino at this fashionable café, ponder Ovid's words written over the bar: '*et Venus in vinis ignis in igne fuit*'. Roughly translated this reads: 'Wine turns the heart to love and sparks it into fire'.

Shopping

Corso Ovidio is lined with any number of *confetti* shops. As good as any is **Confetteria Maria Di Vito** (☎ 0864 559 08; Corso Ovidio 187) where you'll find a wide selection of *confetti* and *torrone*, a chewy nougat confection.

Getting There & Away

ARPA (☎ 0864 21 04 69; www.arpaonline.it in Italian) buses leave from a confusing array of points, including Villa Comunale, the train station, and beneath the Ponte Capograssi. To find out which stop you need, ask the **tobacconist** (Piazza XX Settembre 18), which is the official ticket sales point.

ARPA buses link Sulmona to L'Aquila (€4.50 one way, one hour, nine daily), Pescara (€5.10 one way, one hour, seven daily), Scanno (€4.40 one way, one hour, nine daily) and other nearby towns. **Satam** (☎ 0871 34 49 69) runs services to Naples (€14, 2½ hours, four daily).

Sulmona is just off the A25 Rome to Pescara autostrada if you are travelling by car. Or, from L'Aquila, follow the SS17 south.

Trains link the town with L'Aquila (€3.60, one hour, 10 daily), Pescara (€3.60, 1¼ hours, 19 daily), Rome (€9, 2½ hours, seven daily) and Naples (€12.40, 4½ hours, three daily).

From the train station take bus A for the centre.

PARCO NAZIONALE DELLA MAJELLA

Easily accessible from Sulmona, the 750-sq-km Parco Nazionale della Majella encompasses more than 60 mountains. Of these, 30 exceed 2000m and Monte Amaro (2795m) is the second highest in the Apennines. Pliny the Elder described the Majella as the 'Father of all Mountains', but for some reason it's now known as the 'Mother of all Mountains'. Among the bleak summits live some 30 wolves, 20 bears and 50 chamois.

For further information, contact the **park headquarters** (☎ 0871 80 00 23; www.parks.it/parco .nazionale.majella; Via Occidentale 6; ☺ 9.30am-1pm & 5-8pm) in Guardiagrele. By public transport the best way to get to Guardiagrele is via Pescara, from where ARPA buses depart four times daily. The 80-minute journey costs €3.30.

COCULLO

A largely unexceptional village, Cocullo stages one of Italy's weirdest festivals. On the first Thursday in May villagers celebrate the feast of San Domenico by adorning a statue of the saint with jewels, banknotes and live snakes. The statue is carried through the village by fearless bearers, who are also bedecked with writhing reptiles. The festival, said to have pagan origins, is known as the **Processione dei Serpari** (Snake-Charmers' Procession). The procession begins at noon and continues throughout the afternoon.

Cocullo has no accommodation, but is accessible by ARPA bus from Sulmona (€1.50, 20 minutes, four daily). You can also reach Cocullo by train from Celano (€2, 35 minutes, five daily). Ask at either of the tourist offices in Sulmona for details (p605), as the usually scant services are increased for the festival.

SCANNO

pop 2093 / elev 1050m

Scanno is the perfect picture of a hilltop village – a remote medieval *borgo* set amid stunning scenery. It's also a very popular tourist destination and the increasing number of hotels and holidaymakers is an irrefutable fact. In fact, much of the reward in visiting Scanno is getting there. The exhilarating drive up from Sulmona takes you through the Gole di Sagittaro (Sagittarius Gorges) and past the tranquil Lago di Scanno.

Long a centre of wool production and for centuries an exclusive supplier to the Franciscan order, Scanno was 'discovered' after WWII by photographers who, fascinated by the use of traditional costume, heralded the village as an example of traditionalism in a modern world. Even today it's still possible to see a handful of elderly women in costume.

Information

Tourist office (☎ 0864 7 43 17; Piazza Santa Maria della Valle 12; ☺ 9am-1pm & 4-7pm Mon-Sat, 9am-1pm Sun mid-May–Sep, 9am-1pm & 3-6pm Mon-Sat Oct–mid-May) On the edge of the medieval town centre.

Sleeping & Eating

There are plenty of hotels, most of which insist on at least half board in August and July. Many close in winter.

Pensione Nilde (☎ 0864 7 43 59; Viale del Lago 101; s €16-31, d €40-56; ☺ year-round) The cheapest *pensione* in town, the Nilde sits on the side of the road rising up to the village. It has modest rooms, some of which face across to the medieval centre.

Pensione Grotta dei Colombi (☎ 0864 7 43 93; Viale dei Caduti 64; s/d €35/50, half/full board per person high season €50/55) For a room with a view head to this friendly place on the edge of the *centro storico*. Rooms are decorated with rustic simplicity and the spacious public spaces are bright and welcoming.

Ristorante Gli Archetti (☎ 0864 7 46 45; Via Silla 8; taster menus €35; ☺ Wed-Mon) The menu at this elegantly rustic and much-vaunted restaurant changes according to the season, but classic dishes include a mousse of seasonal vegetables and steak cooked in Montepulciano red wine. For pud, the little tarts with ricotta, nuts and saffron are very tempting.

Trattoria Lo Sgabello (☎ 0864 74 74 76; Via dei Pescatori 45; 1st/2nd courses €7/9) If you haven't seen any costume-clad locals in the village, check out the photos that line the walls at this bright trattoria. Down the stairs from the *centro storico,* it specialises in regional cooking so expect plenty of lamb, *maccheroni alla chitarra* and bucketloads of red wine.

Getting There & Away

ARPA (☎ 0864 21 05 32) buses connect Scanno with Sulmona (€4.40, one hour, nine daily).

Autolinee Schiappa (☎ 0864 7 43 62) buses depart from Stazione Tiburtina in Rome for Scanno (€13.40, 2½ hours) at noon, 3pm, 5.45pm and 9.15pm.

PARCO NAZIONALE D'ABRUZZO, LAZIO & MOLISE

The oldest and most popular of Abruzzo's regional parks, the Parco Nazionale d'Abruzzo, Lazio & Molise is one of the few places in Italy where it's possible to see bears in the wild. Since it was established in 1923, the park has been at the forefront of Italy's conservation movement and, along with the neighbouring Parco Nazionale della Majella, is the last refuge of the Marsican brown bear and Apennine wolf. At the last count there were around 80 bears, 40 wolves, 600 indigenous Abruzzo chamois and 10 lynx living wild.

The largely mountainous 1100-sq-km park is circled by an external protected area of 1500 sq km.

Orientation & Information

A convenient base is the touristy town of Pescasseroli or, if you prefer somewhere more low-key, nearby Civitella Alfedena.

ABRUZZO & MOLISE

In Pescasseroli (elevation 1167m) the **park information office** (☎ 0863 911 32 42; Vico Consultore 1; 🕑 10am-2pm & 3-5.30pm Tue-Sun) has loads of useful information, including a *Carta Turistica* (€6) with walking routes and *rifugi* highlighted on the map. There's also a **tourist office** (☎ 0863 91 04 61; Via Piave 2; 🕑 9am-1pm & 3-6pm Mon-Sat, 9am-1pm Sun) and a **Centro di Visita** (☎ 0863 91 07 15; Viale Colli d'Oro; admission €6; 🕑 10am-2pm & 3-5.30pm Tue-Sun), with a small museum and zoo.

Less hectic than Pescasseroli, Civitella Alfedena (elevation 1121m) lies on the park's eastern edge above Lago di Barrea. Here you will find a combined park information and visitor centre, the **Centro Lupo** (Wolf Centre; ☎ 0864 89 01 41; museum €3; 🕑 9.40am-1pm & 3-7pm Tue-Sun). At the small museum here there's an open-air corral where a few wolves prowl in semicaptivity.

Activities

This is trekking territory, with well-marked trails ranging from easy family jaunts to serious hikes. Information is readily available from the park information offices, which also organise guided tours. Alternatively, go online at www.parcoabruzzo.it (in Italian), where you'll find suggested itineraries for walkers and cyclists of all levels.

Sleeping & Eating

Albergo Prato Rosso (☎ 0863 91 05 42; Via della Chiesa 14, Pescasseroli; d/tr with bathroom €50/55) A tiny homy affair, this is a far cry from the large three-star hotels that constitute much of Pescasseroli. Right in the heart of town, it has small comfortable rooms complete with creature comforts and paper-thin walls – so hope for quiet neighbours!

Campeggio dell'Orso (☎ 339 334 90 17; person/tent €3.10/4.15; 🕑 year-round) In a wood by a river, this camp site couldn't really get much closer to nature. About 1km south of Pescasseroli, it has all the basic facilities.

Albergo La Torre (☎ 0864 89 01 21; www.albergola torre.com; Via Castello 3, Civitella Alfedena; s €25-36, d €39-52, full meals about €20) Tucked away in the picturesque centre of Civitella Alfedena, this walkers' favourite is exactly what you need after a day's hiking in the mountains. It's warm, friendly and the food is hot and hearty.

Campeggio Wolf (☎ 0864 89 03 60; Via Nazionale, Civitella Alfedena; person/tent/car €6.50/7/4; 🕑 Apr-Oct) A large but relatively subdued camp site, Campeggio Wolf is conveniently situated in the heart of Civitella. It has games for the kids and a restaurant for parents.

Pizzeria San Francisco (☎ 0863 91 06 50; Via Isonzo 1, Pescasseroli; pizzas about €6) If you're in Pescasseroli during the snowy winter this is one of the few places open. It's a large informal place where locals nip in for a takeaway, and large bubbling pizzas are prepared in the wood-burning oven.

Getting There & Away

Pescasseroli, Civitella Alfedena and other villages in the park are linked by five daily **ARPA** (☎ 0864 21 04 96) buses to Avezzano (€3.90, 1½ hours), from where you can change for L'Aquila; and to Castel di Sangro (€3.30, 1¼ hours) for connections to Sulmona. Between mid-June and mid-September, three daily ARPA buses run between Stazione Tiburtina in Rome and Pescasseroli. Tickets cost €11.

PESCARA

pop 121,728

Abruzzo's largest city, Pescara is a heavily developed seaside resort and commercial centre. It's not an unpleasant place but unless you're coming for the beaches there's not a whole lot to do. However, it is the region's main transport hub so you might find yourself passing through.

Pescara's one cultural drawcard is the annual **jazz festival** (☎ 085 692 00 57; tickets from €10), held in the second half of July at the Teatro D'Annunzio. It attracts some big-name international performers and enthusiastic audiences.

Orientation & Information

From the train and intercity bus stations on Piazzale della Repubblica, the beach is just a short walk down Corso Umberto I.

The **tourist office** (☎ 800 50 25 20; Corso Vittorio Emanuele II 301; 🕑 9am-1pm Mon-Fri) is just off Piazzale della Repubblica. Look for the large Abruzzo Promozione Turismo logo.

Sights

If you've got a little time on your hands, the **Museo delle Genti d'Abruzzo** (☎ 085 451 00 26; Via delle Caserme 22; adult/child €5/2; 🕑 9am-1pm Mon-Sat, 3.30-6pm Tue & Thu, 4-7pm Sun Sep-Jun, 9am-1pm Mon-Fri & 9.30pm-12.30am Tue-Sun Jul-Aug) tells the story of local peasant culture.

Near the seafront, the **Museo d'Arte Moderna Vittoria Colonna** (☎ 085 428 37 59; Piazza Primo Maggiore; admission free; ☷ 9am-1pm & 3.30-8.30pm Mon-Sat, 9am-1pm & 4-8pm Sun) is more like a community centre than a modern art gallery. Look out for the Picasso and Miró among the small collection.

Sleeping & Eating

Albergo Planet (☎ 085 421 16 57; Via Piave 142; s/d €25/40, with bathroom €30/50) Don't expect a red-carpet welcome at this no-frills one-star hotel. The rooms are fine – the punk pink wallpaper could be classified as a definite feature – and the location near the train station is convenient.

Hotel Alba (☎ 085 38 91 45; www.hotelalba.pescara .it; Via Michelangelo Forti 14; s/d with bathroom & breakfast €60/90; ☷ P) Smarter on the outside than in, Hotel Alba offers functional rooms and fading décor. The mod cons, including satellite TV, all work and some bathrooms have the added interest of a mirrored ceiling. Parking costs an extra €8.

Pinguino (☎ 085 6 28 69; Corso Manthonè 36; pizzas from €4, 1st/2nd courses from €5/7) Across the river, on one of Pescara's trendiest streets, Pinguino functions as both a restaurant and a pizzeria. The speciality of the house is the unusual pizzas with toppings such as lemon and yoghurt.

Cantina di Jozz (☎ 0854 51 88 00; Via delle Caserme 61; meals about €25; ☷ Tue-Sat & lunch Sun) Foodies highly rate this place which serves traditional Abruzzese food in a convivial atmosphere. Meals are served according to the changing daily menu, with the chef serving tableside from large steaming pots on a trolley. It's a good idea to book.

AUTHOR'S CHOICE

La Vongola (☎ 085 37 42 36; Lungomare G Matteotti 54; 1st/2nd courses from €8/12) One of several restaurants on the seafront, La Vongola specialises in fish, and even if you're on a budget it's worth a splurge. The *risotto pescatore*, cooked with fresh clams, scampi and a naughty touch of chilli, is a lovely warm-up for the *fritto misto*, a selection of assorted fish lightly fried in crisp batter. The house white is really very drinkable, but if you want help choosing a bottle the tireless staff will happily advise you.

Getting There & Away

AIR
Pescara airport (PSR; ☎ 085 432 42 00; www.abruzzo -airport.it) is 3km out of town and easily reached by bus No 38 (€0.90, 20 minutes, every 15 minutes) from Corso Vittorio Emanuele II in front of the train station. **Ryanair** (www.ryan air.com) operates a daily flight to/from London Stansted.

BOAT
A jetfoil runs daily to Croatia's island of Hvar and onto Split (called Spalato in Italian; one way €64 to €84, 4¾ hours) between mid-June and late September. For information, contact **Agenzia Sanmar** (☎ 0854 51 08 73; www.sanmar.it; Lungomare Giovanni XXIII Papa 1) at the port.

BUS
ARPA (www.arpaonline.it in Italian) buses leave from Piazzale della Repubblica for L'Aquila (€7.30, two hours, 10 daily), Sulmona (€5.10, 1¼ hours, four daily) and many other destinations in Abruzzo. Buses also run to Naples (€19, 4½ hours, four daily) and Stazione Tiburtina (€15, 2¾ hours, four daily) in Rome. Timetables are posted at the **ARPA ticket office** (☎ 085 421 50 99) on the piazza.

CAR & MOTORCYCLE
Heading along the coast, you can choose between the A14 or the SS16; the latter hugs the coast more closely. Both the A25 and SS5 lead towards Rome, L'Aquila and Sulmona.

TRAIN
Pescara is on the main train line along the Adriatic coast. There are direct trains to:

Destination	Cost (€)	Duration (hrs)	Frequency
Ancona	11.05	1¾	26 daily
Bari	20.50	3	19 daily
Bologna	23.65	3½	16 daily
L'Aquila (via Sulmona)	6.10	2½	10 daily
Rome	11.30	3½	6 daily
Sulmona	3.60	1¼	frequent

AROUND PESCARA
Hidden away in **Chieti**, a windy hilltop town 18km south of Pescara, lies the region's most important museum. Housed in a 19th-century villa in the Villa Comunale park the

Museo Archeologico Nazionale (☎ 0871 33 16 68; adult/child €4/2; ☯ 9am-8pm Tue-Sun) displays a fantastic collection of local finds. The ground floor is dominated by stupendous Roman sculpture and a collection of 15,000 coins dating from the 4th century BC to the 19th century. Upstairs the so-called *Warrior of Capestrano*, a 6th-century funerary statue, steals the show.

Nearby and much better signposted is the **Complesso Archeologico la Civitella** (☎ 0871 63137; adult/child €4/2; ☯ 9am-8pm Tue-Sun) a modern archaeological museum built round a Roman amphitheatre. Exhibits include weapons and pottery dating back to the Iron Age.

Regular buses (€0.90, 40 minutes, every 20 minutes) link Chieti with Piazzale della Repubblica in Pescara.

VASTO

pop 34,000 / elev 144m

On Abruzzo's southern coast, Vasto is a historic hilltop town with a well-preserved medieval quarter and superb sea views. Five kilometres downhill is the modern resort of **Vasto Marina**, a strip of hotels and restaurants fronting a long sandy beach. Very busy in summer, the Vasto Marina virtually closes down between October and March.

Much of Vasto's *centro storico* dates from the 15th century, a golden period in which the city was known as 'the Athens of the Abruzzi'.

Orientation & Information

The *centro storico* lies to the east of Corso Garibaldi, Vasto's main street. An imposing landmark is the boarded-up Castello Caldoresco, the 15th-century castle on Piazza G Rossetti.

The **tourist office** (☎ 0873 36 73 12; Piazza del Popolo 18; ☯ 9am-1pm & 3-6pm Mon-Fri) is a short walk east of the central Piazza G Rossetti.

Sights

From Piazza G Rossetti, Corso de Parma leads down to Piazza del Popolo and two of the town's main sights. The 13th-century **Cattedrale di San Giuseppe** (☎ 0873 36 71 93; Via Buonconsiglio 12; ☯ 8.30am-noon & 4.30-7pm) is a lovely low-key example of Romanesque architecture, while the nearby **Palazzo d'Avalos** is pure Renaissance. Today the palazzo houses the **Museo Civico** (☎ 0873 36 77 73; Piazza del Popolo) and the town's eclectic collection of ancient bronzes, glasswork and paintings by local artists; the museum is currently closed for restoration.

Sleeping & Eating

The tourist office can provide accommodation lists for Vasto and Vasto Marina.

Hotel San Marco (☎ 0873 6 05 37; fax 0873 699 52; Via Madonna dell'Asilo 4; s/d with bathroom €35/60; ☯ year-round) Up in Vasto proper, this friendly two-star hotel is just off Corso Garibaldi. The rooms are currently rather old-fashioned, with dated décor and tired wallpaper, but they are about to be revamped so you may well find them sparkling and new.

Hostaria del Pavone (☎ 0873 6 02 27; Via Barbarotta; 1st/2nd courses from €8/12; ☯ Wed-Mon) Tucked away in the *centro storico* this highly regarded restaurant is a bit more than your average *osteria* (a simple trattoria-style restaurant). Specialising in seafood – although the grilled meat is also pretty good – the menu varies according to the catch of the day. Signature dishes include stuffed calamari, *orecchiette* (ear-shaped pasta) with clams and asparagus, and *brodetto alla vastese,* the local fish soup.

Getting There & Away

By car Vasto is on the A14 autostrada and the SS16, both of which run up the Adriatic coast.

The train station (Vasto–San Salvo) is about 2km south of Vasto Marina. Regular trains run to Pescara (€5.55, one hour, 10 daily) and Termoli (€4, 1¼ hours, 12 daily). From the station take bus No 1 or 4 (€0.75, 15 minutes, half-hourly) for Vasto Marina and town centre.

MOLISE

One of Italy's forgotten areas, Molise invariably suffers comparison with the more spectacular Abruzzo. Over much of the bleak countryside lies a palpable air of abandon and the towns are largely unexciting. However, with a car, or industrial doses of patience, you can enjoy this most unglamorous and ancient of regions.

Life in Molise goes back to prehistoric times. Excavations in Isernia have unearthed the oldest human settlement in Europe – a 700,000-year-old village, which makes the

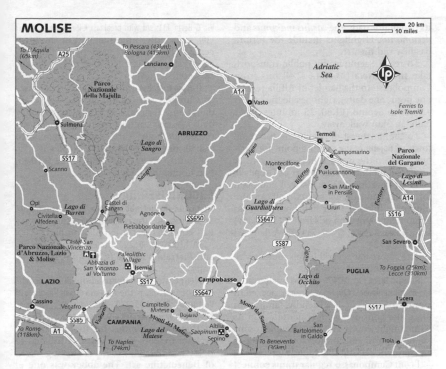

Samnite village at Pietrabbondante and the Roman ruins at Saepinum seem positively modern. The Abbazia di San Vincenzo al Volturno is famous for its Byzantine frescoes, while the Monti del Matese provide good skiing, hiking and cycling. On the coast the small beach resort of Termoli is a jumping-off point for the Isole Tremiti (see p694).

CAMPOBASSO

pop 50,991 / elev 701m

There's very little reason to come to Campobasso, unless you're passing through en route to Saepinum. Molise's regional capital and a transport hub, it's an uninspiring modern city best known for its *carabinieri* (military police) training school.

There's a hard-to-find **tourist office** (☎ 0874 41 56 62; Piazza della Vittoria 14; ⏰ 8am-2pm Mon-Sat) west of Piazza Vittorio Emanuele II. To reach it from the train station, turn left into Via Cavour, right into Corso Bucci and left again into Corso Vittorio Emanuele and it's over the road from the Max Mara shop.

In the *centro storico*, the churches of **San Bartolomeo** (Salita San Bartolomeo) and **San Giorgio**

(☎ 0874 31 14 24; Viale della Rimembranza; ⏰ by appointment) are fine examples of Romanesque architecture. The **castle**, now a military weather station, is striking from a distance but less impressive close up. More worthwhile is the small **Museo Samnitico** (Samnite Museum; ☎ 0874 41 22 65; Via Chiarizia 12; admission free; ⏰ 9am 1pm & 3-7pm Tue-Sun), with artefacts from local sites.

Trasporti Molise (☎ 0874 49 30 80) has buses to Rome (€11.90, three hours, seven daily). Otherwise there are trains to Isernia (€2.80, one hour, 16 daily), Termoli (€4.05, 1¾ hours, eight daily) and Naples (€9, three hours, four daily).

AROUND CAMPOBASSO

Overlooked by the **Monti del Matese** (Matese Mountains), the ruins of the Roman town of **Saepinum** (admission free) are among the best preserved and least visited in Italy. Although a tough destination to get to if you're without wheels, it is well worth the effort. An unimportant provincial town, Saepinum survived into the 9th century before being sacked by Arab invaders. The walled town retains three of its four original gates and its two main roads, the *cardus maximus* and *decamanus*. Highlights include the forum, basilica and theatre.

To reach Saepinum by public transport, take the **Larivera** (☎ 0874 6 47 44) bus from Campobasso to the hamlet of Altilia (€1.20, one hour, one daily), right beside the site, or a train to Sepino (€1.60, 25 minutes, three daily), a 3km walk away.

To the northeast of Saepinum, the small town of **Bojano** is the starting point for various walks in the wooded hills, while further up in the mountains the resort of **Campitello Matese** (elevation 1430m) is well equipped for winter and summer sports. You can hire mountain bikes (€3 per half-hour) and ski equipment (boots and skis from €13 per day) from **Galeassi Sport** (☎ 0874 78 41 80). A daily ski pass costs €24.

The resort has several hotels, but they're not for the budget conscious.

Rifugio Jezza (☎ 0874 78 41 88; full board per person €30-65, full meals about €20; ☯ year-round), decked in simple rustic décor, is a friendly, family-run place and considerably less spartan than its name might imply. The plain double rooms are both warm and comfortable, and there's a restaurant serving filling local fare.

From Campobasso regular trains connect with Bojano (€1.60, 30 minutes, 10 daily), while **Autolinee Micone** (☎ 0874 78 01 20) runs a daily bus up to Campitello Matese (one hour).

ISERNIA

pop 21,263 / elev 423m

Hit repeatedly by earthquakes over the years, Isernia is a dreary workaday place with one claim to fame – in 1979 road workers unearthed what turned out to be Europe's oldest human settlement. Work on the 700,000-year-old site is ongoing and, although the excavations are closed to the public, you can visit by calling the **site office** (☎ 0865 41 35 26).

If you don't make it to the site itself, the small **Museo Santa Maria delle Monache** (☎ 0865 41 51 79; Corso Marcelli 48; admission €2; ☯ 8am-7.30pm) is the next best thing. Exhibits include piles of elephant and rhino bones, fossils and stone tools.

The **tourist office** (☎ 0865 39 92; 6th fl, Palazzo della Regione, Via Farinacci 9; ☯ 8am-2pm Mon-Sat) has information on the town and province.

If you have to stay the night, head for the **Hotel Sayonara** (☎ 0865 5 09 92; www.sayonara.is.it;

Via G Berta 131; s/d with breakfast €45/70, lunch/dinner €10), a friendly three-star pad in the town centre. The rooms are modern and the adjacent restaurant is fine for an unspectacular two-course meal.

Trasporti Molise (☎ 0874 49 30 80) runs buses to Campobasso (€2.85, 50 minutes, eight daily) and Termoli (€6.35, 1¾ hours, three daily). Trains connect Isernia with Sulmona (€6.90, 2¼ hours, three daily), Campobasso (€2.80, one hour, 16 daily), Naples (€5.75, 1¾ hours, seven daily) and Rome (€10.15, two hours, five daily).

AROUND ISERNIA

Just outside **Pietrabbondante**, 26km northeast of Isernia, are the remains of a 2nd-century BC Samnite theatre-temple complex.

SATI (☎ 0874 60 52 20) buses connect Isernia and Pietrabbondante (€2, 35 minutes, nine daily).

Near **Castel San Vincenzo**, about 30km northwest of Isernia, is the **Abbazia di San Vincenzo al Volturno** (☎ 0865 95 52 46; admission free; ☯ 9am-noon & 3-5pm daily summer, Sat & Sun only winter), a Benedictine abbey famous for the magnificent cycle of frescoes in the crypt. Attributed to Epifanio (824–842) they are striking works of Benedictine art. The abbey was one of the foremost monastic and cultural centres in 9th-century Europe before it fell prey to earthquakes and Arab raiders. Rebuilt numerous, times it's now home to a community of American nuns.

Larivera (☎ 0874 6 47 44) buses run between Isernia and Castel San Vincenzo (€1.50, 1½ hours, four daily), a 1km walk from the abbey.

TERMOLI

pop 30,669

Molise's top seaside resort, Termoli boasts a long sandy beach, a twee town centre and year-round ferries to the Isole Tremiti. The town's most famous landmark, Frederick II's 13th-century Swabian **castle** (closed to the public) guards entry to the tiny *borgo*, a tangle of narrow streets, medieval houses and souvenir shops. From the castle follow the road up and you come to Piazza Duomo and the 12th-century **cathedral** (☎ 0875 70 80 25; Piazza Duomo; ☯ on request), a fine example of Puglian-Romanesque architecture.

The **tourist office** (☎ 0875 70 39 13; Piazza Bega 42; ☯ 8am-noon Mon-Sat, 3-6.30pm Mon & Wed & 4.50-

TERMOLI TIME

Sitting at 42° longitude and 15° latitude, as confirmed by the calculations of Francesco Porro on 1 April 1898, Termoli is where Italian and Central European Time is set. The actual line of measurement, the 15th meridian, passes through a crumbling tower known as the Mulino a Vento (Windmill), which today forms the centrepiece of a hideous block of flats on the Rio Vivo.

The idea of international time zones was formally accepted in Washington, DC, in 1884 – prior to that each country operated on its own time – and adopted a year later. Taking the Greenwich meridian as the central axis, zones were established at intervals of 15°.

The Italian government accepted this system on 1 November 1893 and Termoli found itself the timekeeper for the entire peninsula and beyond.

6.30pm Tue, Thu & Fri) is tucked away in a car park behind a small shopping gallery, 100m east of the train station.

Sleeping & Eating

Accommodation for the budget conscious can be tight and in winter much of Termoli simply shuts down.

Pensione Osteria San Giorgio (☎ 0875 70 43 84; Corso Fratelli Brigida 20-22; s/d with bathroom €42/62; ☯ year-round) One of the cheapest places in town, this modest *pensione* has simple, uncluttered rooms and serves up decent food in the *osteria*. It's on a lively street near the castle so it may get a bit noisy in high summer. There are discounts of up to €10 in the low season.

Hotel Meridiano (☎ 0875 70 59 46; www.hotel meridiano.com; Lungomare Cristoforo Colombo 524; s/d with bathroom €82/62; ☯ year-round; P) This large concrete pile overlooking the sea road is nicer inside than out. Many of the large bright rooms overlook the sea and the service is efficient and friendly.

Cala Saracena (☎ 0875 5 21 93; SS Europa 2, 174; 2 people with tent & car €26; ☯ Jun–mid-Sep) A beachfront camp site just out of town, the Saracena is one of various camp sites along the SS16 Adriatica–Pescara road (also known as Europa 2). To get here take a local bus from the train station.

La Nuova Mangiatoia (☎ 0875 71 41 04; Via Frentana 3; 1st/2nd courses from €6/7) Although you can also eat meat in the atmospheric brick-vaulted dining room, the seafood here is particularly good. The cold seafood antipasto bursts with flavour and the grilled fish has a pleasant wood-smoke aftertaste. The only gripe: bigger portions please.

Getting There & Away
BOAT

Termoli is the only port with daily year-round ferries to the Isole Tremiti (p694). The service is operated by **Adriatica Navigazione** (☎ 0875 70 53 43) and leaves Termoli at 9am every day except Tuesday and Saturday, when it sails at 8am; it heads back at 4.20pm. Between June and August, **Navigazione Libera del Golfo** (☎ 0875 70 48 95; www.navlib.it) and **Navigargano** (☎ 0875 70 59 90) also operate services. Buy your ticket from each company's kiosk at the ferry terminal. The return fare is €25.60.

BUS

Termoli's intercity bus station is beside Via Martiri della Resistenza. **SATI buses** (☎ 0874 6 50 50) link Termoli with Campobasso (€3, 1¼ hours, hourly) and Pescara (€3, 1¼ hours, three daily). **Trasporti Molise** (☎ 0875 70 39 37) serves Isernia (€6.35, 1¾ hours, three daily), while **Cerella** (☎ 0873 39 11 68) runs buses to Rome (€12.90, three hours, one daily) and Naples (€10.50, three hours, two daily).

CAR & MOTORCYCLE

Termoli is on the A14 and SS16, which follow the coast north to Pescara and south to Bari. The SS87 links Termoli with Campobasso.

TRAIN

Trains serve Bologna (€35, 5¼ hours, 10 daily), Lecce (€32, five hours, eight daily) and stations along the Adriatic coast.

ALBANIAN TOWNS

Several villages to the south of Termoli form an Albanian enclave which dates back to the 15th century. These include **Campomarino**, **Portocannone**, **San Martino in Pensilis** and **Ururi**. Although the inhabitants shrugged off their Orthodox religion in the 18th century, they still use a version of Albanian that's incomprehensible to outsiders. However, it's for their *carressi* (chariot races) that the villages are best known. Each year Ururi (3 May),

ABRUZZO & MOLISE

Portocannone (the Monday after Whit Sunday) and San Martino in Pensilis (30 April) all stage a no-holds-barred **chariot race**. The chariots (more like carts) are pulled by bulls and hurtle round a traditional course urged on by villagers on horseback.

In the case of Ururi, three teams take to the 4km course to compete for the honour of carrying the relics of the Santa Croce (Holy Cross) through the village. The night

before the race all the cart drivers, bulls and the horse riders are blessed by the local priest.

SATI buses connect Termoli with Porto cannone (€1, 20 minutes, 14 daily), San Martino in Pensilis (€1, 25 minutes, 10 daily) and Ururi (€1, 35 minutes, four daily).

To get to Campomarino from Termoli take one of the frequent Larivera buses (€1, 20 minutes, 32 daily).

Campania

Campania can't be summed up in a glib phrase or two. This region has the lot it seems: fabulous coastal scenery, forgotten mountains, ancient sites and glossy resorts. And that's not even counting Naples, with its edgy in-your-face vitality that stays with you long after the photos have been developed. Nearby there is still more drama: about 700,000 people live in the shadow of Mt Vesuvius, the heady backdrop to the Bay of Naples, with Pompeii and Herculaneum the ancient victims.

Further down the coast, the Greek temples of Paestum are among the best preserved in the world, while, to the west of Naples, Lago d'Averno (Lake Avernus), in the Campi Flegrei, was believed to be the entrance to the ancient underworld. Legend abounds in Campania. Homer, Ulysses, Virgil and other characters of classical mythology have all left their mark. Stories tell how sirens lured sailors to their deaths off Sorrento, and of islands inhabited by mermaids. Travel down the bewitching Amalfi Coast or out to the magical islands that vividly reflect the extremities of this region. Just a 45-minute ferry ride from Naples, tiny Procida is tranquil and relatively unknown, while nearby Capri has a moneyed gloss and is home to Italy's most luxurious hotels, restaurants and shops.

Back on the mainland, coastal mountains plunge into the sea in a stunning vertical landscape of precipitous crags, forests and resort towns. On the downside, in summer hordes pile in, blocking roads and pushing prices sky-high. Still, console yourself with a *limoncello* (lemon liqueur), and head back to Naples for a pizza. They're the best in the world.

HIGHLIGHTS

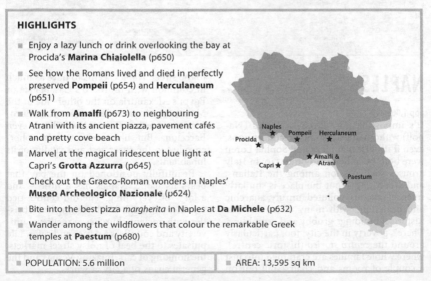

- Enjoy a lazy lunch or drink overlooking the bay at Procida's **Marina Chiaiolella** (p650)
- See how the Romans lived and died in perfectly preserved **Pompeii** (p654) and **Herculaneum** (p651)
- Walk from **Amalfi** (p673) to neighbouring Atrani with its ancient piazza, pavement cafés and pretty cove beach
- Marvel at the magical iridescent blue light at Capri's **Grotta Azzurra** (p645)
- Check out the Graeco-Roman wonders in Naples' **Museo Archeologico Nazionale** (p624)
- Bite into the best pizza *margherita* in Naples at **Da Michele** (p632)
- Wander among the wildflowers that colour the remarkable Greek temples at **Paestum** (p680)

■ POPULATION: 5.6 million	■ AREA: 13,595 sq km

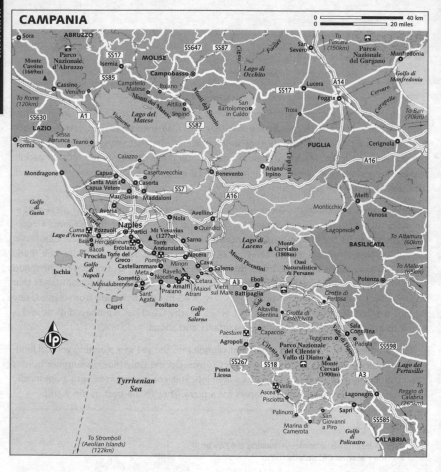

NAPLES

pop 1,008,419

It's impossible to approach Naples (Napoli) without at least some preconceptions, even if it's just that pizza and Sophia Loren were both born here. No other city in Italy arouses such passion among the Italians, and everything about the place is similarly intense: raucous, polluted, unruly, anarchic and deafening, with many of its majestic historical buildings grubby and crumbling. There's poverty in the city, too, particularly around the *centro storico* (historic centre), where whole families are crammed into just a couple of rooms and chairs spill out on to the street. Naples seems to have as much in common with Morocco's Casablanca or Egypt's Alexandria on the other side of the Mediterranean as it does with fellow European ports such as Genoa, Marseilles or even Barcelona. But, like these cities, its coherence lies in the sheer zest and vitality of its inhabitants.

Beautifully positioned on the bay that bears its name, Naples has a little – and a lot – of everything. The old centre, tied together with high-level washing lines, bristles with ancient churches, a medieval university and countless eateries and cafés. Life pulsates to the beat of noisy street markets, the honking of cars, buzzing Vespas and the general chaos of a city at work.

But while this is all relatively harmless, there is a nasty side. The Neapolitan Mafia, the Camorra, thrives, specialising in bank hold-ups and controlling the local fruit and vegetable markets, prostitution and the massive *toto nero* (illegal football pools). More worrying still, in 2004 over 100 people were killed by the Camorra, the highest level of violence recorded since the 1980s.

This, despite the successful facelift the city has received over the past decade under former left-wing mayor Antonio Bassolino and his successor, Rosa Iervolino. Improvements to the infrastructure include an ambitious €3.8 billion metro extension, due for completion in 2011, and the pedestrianisation of Via Chiaia. There are similar plans to ban traffic from areas in the historic centre, which should be welcomed by everyone – except the taxi drivers, that is.

HISTORY

Soon after founding Cumae (Cuma) in 1000 BC, colonists from Rhodes established a settlement on the western side of Mt Vesuvius. Centuries later, Phoenician traders from present-day Lebanon and Greeks were attracted by the coast's splendour and so expanded the settlement, christening it Neapolis (New City). It thrived as a centre of Greek culture and later, under Roman rule, became something of a VIP resort, a favourite of emperors Pompey, Caesar and Tiberius.

After successive waves of invasion by the wild Goths and a couple of spells associated with Byzantium, Naples remained an independent dukedom for about 400 years until captured by the Normans in AD 1139. They, in turn, were replaced by the German Hohenstaufens, whose Swabian dynasty lasted until 1266 and gave the city many new institutions, including its university. After the defeat and death of Manfred, king of Sicily, at the battle of Benevento in 1266, Charles I of Anjou took control of the Kingdom of Sicily and turned Naples into its de facto capital. Following a period of disorder, the Angevins were succeeded in 1442 by the Spanish house of Aragón, under whom the city came to prosper. Alfonso I of Aragón, in particular, introduced new laws and promoted the arts and sciences.

In 1503 Naples and the Kingdom of Sicily were absorbed by Spain, which sent viceroys to to rule as virtual dictators. Despite their heavy-handed rule, Naples flourished artistically and acquired much of its splendour during this period. Indeed it continued to bloom when the Spanish Bourbons re-established Naples as the capital of the Kingdom of the Two Sicilies in 1734 (which encompassed part of the Italian peninsula and Sicily from the mid-15th to mid-19th centuries). Aside from a Napoleonic interlude under Joachim Murat (1806–15), the Bourbons remained until unseated by Garibaldi and the Kingdom of Italy in 1860, when Naples was a serious but unsuccessful contender for capital of the new nation.

The city was heavily damaged during more than 100 bombing raids in WWII and the effects can still be seen on many monuments around the city. The Allies subsequently presided over a fairly disastrous period of transition from war to peace; many observers have since attributed the initial boom in the city's organised crime, at least in part, to members of the occupying forces. A severe earthquake in 1980 and the dormant Vesuvius looming to the east remind Neapolitans of their city's vulnerability and have undoubtedly contributed to their endemic fatalism and hedonistic lifestyle.

ORIENTATION

Naples stretches along the waterfront and is divided into *quartieri* (districts). Stazione Centrale (the main train station) and the bus station are off Piazza Garibaldi, east of Spaccanapoli, the ancient heart of Naples. Piazza Garibaldi and its side streets form an enormous, unwelcoming transport terminus and street market. Not surprisingly, this area is also the city's red-light district and is distinctly seedy, with many cheap hotels doubling as brothels.

A wide shopping street, Corso Umberto I, skirts the southern edge of Spaccanapoli, aligned southwest from Piazza Garibaldi to Piazza Bovio. From here Via A Depretis runs to the huge Piazza Municipio, dominated by the Castel Nuovo. From the waterfront behind the castle, ferries sail to the bay islands, Palermo and other long-distance destinations.

The Palazzo Reale (the former royal palace), next to the castle, stands over Piazza Trento e Trieste. Naples' main street, Via Toledo, leads north from the square, briefly becomes Via Roma, passes alongside Piazza

CAMPANIA

NAPLES

INFORMATION
CTS...1 F3
Every Tour...............................2 E4
Feltrinelli................................3 E4
Feltrinelli................................4 D5
Internet Point..........................5 E4
Internetbar...............................6 E3
Main Tourist Office..................7 D5
My Beautiful Laundrette...........8 E3
Navig@ndo...............................9 E3
Ospedale Loreto-Mare............10 H3
Pharmacy................................11 H2
Police Station.........................12 E4
Post Office..............................13 E4
Tourist Information Office.........14 A5
Tourist Information Office.........15 E3
Tourist Information Office.........16 H2
Tourist Information Office.........17 E4

SIGHTS & ACTIVITIES
Acquario.................................18 C5
Basilica del Carmine Maggiore..19 G3
Basilica di San Giorgio Maggiore..20 F3
Basilica di Santa Chiara.........(see 15)
Biblioteca Nazionale..............(see 49)
Cappella di San Severo............21 F3
Castel dell'Ovo.......................22 E6
Castel Nuovo..........................23 E4
Castel Sant'Elmo....................24 D4
Cathedral................................25 F2
Certosa di San Martino............26 D4
Chiesa del Gesù Nuovo............27 E3
Chiesa di San Domenico Maggiore..28 F3
Chiesa di San Francesco di Paola..29 E5
Chiesa di San Paolo Maggiore...30 F2

Chiesa di Sant'Angelo a Nilo......31 F3
Chiesa di Sant'Anna dei Lombardi...32 E3
Chiesa di SS Filippo e Giacomo...33 F3
Chiesa e Pinacoteca dei Girolamini..34 F2
Chiesa e Scavi di San Lorenzo
   Maggiore..............................35 F2
Fontana dell'Immacolatella.......36 E6
Fontana di Nettuno..................37 E4
Museo Archeologico Nazionale...38 E2
Museo Civico Gaetano Filangieri..39 F3
Museo Civico...........................(see 23)
Museo del Palazzo Reale.........(see 49)
Museo del Tesoro di San Gennaro...40 F2
Museo di Mineralogia, Zoologia e
   Antropologia.........................41 F3
Museo Nazionale della Ceramica
   Duca di Martina.....................42 C4
Museo Nazionale di San Martino...(see 26)
Museo Pignatelli......................43 C5
Napoli Sotterranea..................44 F2
Ospedale delle Bambole...........45 F3
Palazzo Cuomo........................(see 39)
Palazzo di Carafa di Maddaloni...46 F3
Palazzo Filomarino..................47 F3
Palazzo Marigliano..................48 F3
Palazzo Reale..........................49 E5
Port'Alba................................50 E3
University of Naples.................51 E3

SLEEPING
6 Small Rooms........................52 E3
Albergo Duomo.......................53 F3
B&B Cappella Vecchia.............54 D5
B&B Morelli.............................55 D5
B&B Santa Lucia.....................56 E5

Belle Arti Resort......................57 E2
Chiaja Hotel de Charme............58 D5
Costantinopoli 104...................59 E3
Donnalbina 7...........................60 F3
Grand Hotel Oriente................61 E4
Grand Hotel Parker's...............62 C5
Grand Hotel Santa Lucia.........63 E6
Hotel Bellini............................64 F2
Hotel Belvedere......................65 D3
Hotel Caravaggio....................66 F2
Hotel Casanova.......................67 G2
Hotel Il Convento....................68 E4
Hotel Ideal..............................69 H2
Hotel Luna Rossa....................70 G2
Hotel Miramare.......................71 E5
Hotel Nuovo Rebecchino.........72 G2
Hotel Pignatelli.......................73 F3
Hotel Pinto-Storey..................74 C5
Hotel Plaza.............................75 G2
Hotel Rex...............................76 E6
Hotel San Francisco al Monte...77 D4
Hotel Toledo...........................78 E4
Hotel Zara..............................79 G2
Napolit'amo............................80 E4
Palazzo Turchini......................81 E4
Pensione Margherita...............82 C4
Pensione Ruggiero..................(see 74)
Portalba 33..............................83 E3
Sansevero D'Angri...................84 E3

To Catacombe Di San Gennaro (500m); Palazzo Reale Di Capodimonte (900m); Parco di Capodimonte (900m)

Orto Botanico

To Piazza Carlo III (200m); A1; A3; Capodichino Airport (4km); Caserta (25km)

To Pompeii (25km)

To Aeolian Islands (207km); Milazzo (270km); Palermo (309km); Cagliari (426km); Tunisia (715km);

To Procida (19km); Sorrento (20km); Forio (25km); Capri (27km); Ischia (33km)

0   600 m
0   0.4 miles

DRINKING 🍷 🍸

Dai Lazzarella	105	E3
Caffè dell'Epoca	106	E3
Caffè Gambrinus	107	E5
Intra Moenia	(see 94)	

ENTERTAINMENT 🎭

Box Office	(see 115)	
Cinema Amedeo	108	C5
Club Live Music	109	A6
Kinky Bar	110	E3
New Age Disco	111	F2
Otto Jazz Club	112	D4
Teatro San Carlo	113	E5
Velvet Zone	114	E3

SHOPPING 🛍

Galleria Umberto 1	115	E4
Limoné	(see 44)	

EATING 🍴

Amor e Fantasia	85	E5
Bersagliera	86	E6
Caprese	87	B4
Castello	88	C5
Da Michele	89	G3
Di Bruno	90	C5
D.M. L.U.I.S.E.	91	E4
Donna Teresa	92	C3
Dora	93	C5
Il Caffè Arabo	94	E3
Kukai	95	E5
La Cantina della Sapienza	96	E2
La Cantinella	97	E5
La Locanda del Grifo	98	F2
La Sfogliatella	99	H2
Lombardi a Santa Chiara	100	E3
Pizzeria Sorbillo	101	F3
Ristorante Bellini	102	E3
Trattoria da Carmine	103	F2
Trianon	104	G3

TRANSPORT 🚌

Alibus For Airport	116	F4
ANM Bus Information Office	117	G2
ANM Information Kiosk	118	G2
Avis Car Rental	119	H2
Bar Clizia	120	H3
Funicolare di Chiaia	121	C4
Funicolare di Mergellina	122	A6
Funicolare di Montesanto	123	D3
Funicolare Station	124	C3
Funicolare Station	125	C4
Funicolare Station	126	C4
Funicolare Centrale	127	E4
Hertz Car Rental	128	H3
Intercity & ANM Bus Station	129	G2
Molo Beverello	130	F5
SITA Bus Stop	131	H3
SITA Bus Stop	132	G4
SNAV & Alilauro Hydrofoil Terminal	133	B6
Tourcar	134	E4

Dante, on the western boundary of Spaccanapoli, then undergoes three more name changes before reaching the Parco di Capodimonte, north of the centre.

The extensions of two of Naples' more original streets, Via San Biagio dei Librai (which becomes Via Benedetto Croce at its western end) and Via dei Tribunali, both eventually meet Via Roma. Much of Naples' street life, artisans and a host of good, cheap restaurants can be found in this area. Via San Biagio dei Librai is part of an almost straight run from near Stazione Centrale through Spaccanapoli to the foot of the hilltop Vomero district.

To the south and west of the city extend broad boulevards and majestic squares leading to the districts of Santa Lucia and Mergellina. Above it all sits Naples' upper–middle class in the relative calm of Vomero, a natural balcony with grand views across the city and the bay to Vesuvius.

INFORMATION
Bookshops
Feltrinelli Piazza dei Martiri (☎ 081 240 54 11); Via San Tommaso d'Aquino 15 (☎ 081 552 14 36) For a selection of books in English, including Lonely Planet titles; a second smaller branch is just off Via Toledo.

Emergency
To report a stolen car, call ☎ 081 794 14 35.
Police station (☎ 081 794 11 11; Via Medina 75) There is an office for foreigners here.

Internet Access
Internet Point (☎ 081 497 60 90; Vico Tre Re a Toledo 59a; per 30min €1; ❤ 9am-9pm Mon-Sat) Also an agent for Western Union.
Internetbar (☎ 081 29 52 37; Piazza Bellini 74; per hr €3; ❤ 9am-2am Mon-Sat, 8pm-2am Sun) A real bar where you can sup a cocktail while cruising the Net.
Navig@ndo (☎ 081 193 600 30; Via Santa Anna di Lombardi 28; per hr €2; ❤ 9.30am-9.30pm)

Internet Resources
Around Naples (www.napoli.com) General Naples site.
I Naples (www.inaples.it) The official tourist-board site.
Neapolitan Way (www.napolinapoli.com) Useful general Naples site.

Laundry
My Beautiful Laundrette (☎ 081 542 21 62; Via Montesanto 2; per 6kg €7; ❤ 9am-8.30pm Mon-Sat) There's also an Internet point (per hr €3).

Medical Services
Ambulance (☎ 081 752 06 96, 112)
Guardia Medica (❤ 24hr) Phone numbers for doctors are in the listings guide Qui Napoli.
Ospedale Loreto-Mare (☎ 081 254 27 01; Via Amerigo Vespucci) Hospital.

Money
Every Tour (☎ 081 551 85 64; Piazza Municipio 5-6) Represents American Express, changes money and is an agent for Western Union.

Post
Post office (☎ 081 551 14 56; Piazza Matteotti; ❤ 8.15am-7pm Mon-Sat)

Tourist Information
Tourist information office Piazza dei Martiri 58 (☎ 081 40 53 11; ❤ 8.30am-2.30pm Mon-Fri) Main tourist office; Mergellina train station (☎ 081 761 21 02; ❤ 9am-7.30pm Mon-Sat, 9am-1.30pm Sun); Piazza del Gesù Nuovo (☎ 081 552 33 28; ❤ 9am-8pm Mon-Sat, 9am-3pm Sun); Stazione Centrale (☎ 081 20 66 66; ❤ 9am-7.30pm Mon-Sat, 9am-1.30pm Sun); Via San Carlo 7 (☎ 081 40 23 94; ❤ 9am-8pm Mon-Sat, 9am-3pm Sun) More useful than the main tourist office, these branches stock the essential bilingual brochure Qui Napoli plus a city map and guides to major monuments.

Travel Agencies
CTS (☎ 081 552 79 60; Via Mezzocannone 25) An efficient student travel centre.

DANGERS & ANNOYANCES
Naples has a certain reputation and, even though you're unlikely to encounter Mafia shoot-outs, petty crime can be a problem. Be especially vigilant for moped bandits and pickpockets on crowded transport. Also, if you are shopping at the markets around Piazza Garibaldi, be wary of the digital camera scam reported by several readers. In short, you are shown a superb camera with all the fancy gizmos but, hand your money over, and what you will end up with is an empty box. You should also watch out for groups of dishevelled-looking women and children asking for money.

Car and motorcycle theft is rife, so think twice before bringing a vehicle into town and never leave anything in the car, particularly at night.

Travellers should be careful about walking alone in the streets late at night, particularly near Stazione Centrale and Piazza Dante.

Never venture into the dark sidestreets at night unless you are in a group. The area west of Via Toledo and as far north as Piazza Carità, though safe enough during daylight hours, can also be threatening after dark.

SIGHTS

To make the most of your time and money in Naples (and indeed the entire Campania region), the **Campania artecard** (☎ 800 600 601; www.campaniartecard.it) is an excellent investment. A cumulative ticket that covers museum admission and transport, it comes in various forms. In Naples itself, a three-day ticket (€13) gives free admission to two participating sites, a 50% discount on others and free transport in Naples, including the Alibus trip from the airport to the city centre, and the Campi Flegrei. Other options range from €25 to €28 and cover sites as far afield as Pompeii and Paestum. Cards can be bought at train stations, newsagents, participating museums, via the Internet or through the call centre.

Spaccanapoli

CATHEDRAL

Built on the site of earlier churches, which were themselves preceded by a temple to the god Neptune, this grand **cathedral** (☎ 081 44 90 97; Via Duomo; ☿ 8am-12.30pm & 4.30-7pm Mon-Fri, 8am-12.30pm & 4.30-7.30pm Sat, 8am-1.30pm & 5-7.30pm Sun) was begun by Charles I of Anjou in 1272. Largely destroyed in 1456 by an earthquake, it's undergone numerous alterations. More recently, fascinating ancient remains, including an ancient gymnasium, have been uncovered during the construction of the Duomo metro stop. Within the cathedral, above the wide central nave, is an ornately decorated coffered ceiling.

Central to Naples' religious (some would say superstitious) life is the 17th-century baroque **Cappella di San Gennaro** (Chapel of St Gennaro). Within the chapel are the skull and a couple of phials of the congealed blood taken from San Gennaro, the city's patron saint. He was martyred at Pozzuoli, west of Naples, in AD 305 and tradition holds that his blood liquefied in these phials when his body was transferred back to Naples. For information of the mysterious San Gennaro festival, see p628.

The next chapel eastwards contains an urn with the saint's bones, cupboards full of femurs, tibias and fibulas and a stash of other grisly relics. Below the high altar is the **Cappella Carafa**, also known as the Crypt of San Gennaro, a Renaissance chapel.

Halfway down the north aisle and beyond the 17th-century **Basilica di Santa Restituta** is the fascinating **archaeological zone** (admission €3; ☿ 9am-noon & 4.30-7pm Mon-Sat, 9am-noon Sun). The tunnels beneath lead you deep into the remains of the site's original Greek and Roman buildings. Here, too, is the **baptistry**, the oldest in Western Europe, with its remarkably fresh 4th-century mosaics.

Inaugurated in early 2004, the **Museo del Tesoro di San Gennaro** (☎ 081 29 49 80; Via Duomo 149; admission incl multilingual audioguide €5.50; ☿ 9am-6.30pm Tue-Sat, 9.30am-7pm Sun) contains an impressive collection of intricate works of silver, together with jewellery, busts, statues and paintings donated to Naples' patron saint over the centuries by the city's wealthier citizens.

AROUND THE CATHEDRAL

Opposite the cathedral is the entrance to the **Chiesa e Pinacoteca dei Girolamini** (☎ 081 44 91 39; ☿ 9.30am-12.30pm & 2-5.30pm Mon-Sat, 9.30am-12.30pm Sun), a rich baroque church with two façades, currently closed for restoration. A small gallery in the adjoining convent is open, however, and features paintings from the 16th to 18th centuries.

Duck around the corner into Via dei Tribunali and to the left in Piazza San Gaetano you will come across the **Chiesa e Scavi di San Lorenzo Maggiore** (☎ 081 211 08 60; Piazza San Gaetano; admission €4; ☿ 9.30am-5.30pm Mon-Sat, 9.30am-1.30pm Sun). The interior of the church, begun in the 13th century, is French Gothic. Catherine of Austria, who died in 1323, is buried here in an impressive mosaic-covered tomb. You can pass through to the cloisters of the neighbouring convent, where the poet Petrarch stayed in 1345. Beneath the complex are the *scavi* (excavations) of the original Graeco-Roman city, with a remarkably well-preserved main street lined with shops, including a butcher, a bakery and an ancient tax office; heartily recommended.

Across Via dei Tribunali is the **Chiesa di San Paolo Maggiore** (Piazza San Gaetano 76; ☿ 9am-1pm). It was built in the late 16th century on the site of a Roman temple and the opulent interior houses the Sanctuary of San Gaetano. For details of Napoli Sotterranea (Underground Naples), see p628.

While you are in the area check out the **Basilica di San Giorgio Maggiore** (Via Duomo 237; 8am-noon & 5-7pm Mon-Sat, 8am-1pm Sun). It's situated where Via San Biagio dei Librai meets Via Duomo and is worth a quick look for its classical and relatively austere – at least by Neapolitan standards – interior.

Across the road and down on the corner of Via Lucrezia Di Alagno is the 15th-century **Palazzo Cuomo**, built by Tuscan artists. The building was moved several metres in 1881 when the street was widened. It now contains the **Museo Civico Gaetano Filangieri** (☎ 081 20 31 75; Via Duomo), currently closed for restoration.

VIA SAN BIAGIO DEI LIBRAI

Don't miss the **Ospedale delle Bambole** (Dolls' Hospital; Via San Biagio dei Librai 81). Even if you don't happen to have a doll that needs urgent medical attention, it has a quirky charm. There are many intriguing artisan shops on this street and its continuation, Via Benedetto Croce, as well as the parallel Via dei Tribunali to the north and the labyrinth of side alleys. You will come across not only goldsmiths and other jewellers, but also the makers of the famously elaborate Neapolitan *presepi* (Nativity scenes).

At No 39, two blocks west of the Dolls' Hospital, is the **Palazzo Marigliano**. Behind the grubby façade is a magnificent Renaissance entrance hall. Carrying on westwards you pass **Palazzo di Carafa di Maddaloni** and **Chiesa di SS Filippo e Giacomo** with their contrasting baroque and classical styles.

AROUND PIAZZA SAN DOMENICO MAGGIORE

Chiesa di Sant'Angelo a Nilo (☎ 081 420 12 22; entrance at Vico Donnaromita 15; 10am-noon & 2-4pm Mon-Fri) sits beside Via San Biagio dei Librai, its façade benignly presided over by a quartet of tubby gilt cherubs. Built in 1385 and remodelled in the 18th century, it contains the monumental Renaissance tomb of Cardinal Brancaccio, to which Donatello contributed.

Where Via San Biagio dei Librai becomes Via Benedetto Croce, in the piazza bearing its name, stands the Gothic **Chiesa di San Domenico Maggiore** (Piazza San Domenico Maggiore 8a; 8am-noon & 5-7pm), which was completed in 1324 by the Dominican order and much favoured by the Aragonese nobility. The interior of the church, a cross between baroque and 19th-century neo-Gothic, features some fine examples of Renaissance sculpture. In the sacristy are 45 coffins of the princes of Aragón and other nobles.

The deceptive simplicity of the exterior of **Cappella di San Severo** (Via de Sanctis 19; admission €5; 10am-5.40pm Mon-Sat, 10am-1.10pm Sun), on a narrow lane east of the church, is a dazzling contrast to the treasure chest of allegorical sculpture inside. For instance, Giuseppe Sanmartino's *Cristo Velato* (Veiled Christ), still confounds experts who cannot agree on how he created the apparently translucent veil. Also intriguing is Corradini's *Pudicizia* (Modesty), which is more erotic than modest. The chapel contains the tomb of the princes of Sangro di San Severo.

AROUND PIAZZA DEL GESÙ NUOVO

From Piazza San Domenico Maggiore, Via Benedetto Croce continues west, following the course of the old Roman main street. Croce, Italy's foremost philosopher and historian in the first half of the 20th century, lived and died in **Palazzo Filomarino**, a grand Renaissance building on the right at No 12 just before you reach Via S Sebastiano.

Across Via S Sebastiano is **Basilica di Santa Chiara** (☎ 081 552 62 09; Via Santa Chiara 49; 9.30am-1pm & 4.30-5.30pm Mon-Fri, 9.30am-1pm Sat & Sun), one of Naples' principal medieval monuments, and its adjacent convent. Built by the Angevins in the 14th century it suffered from subsequent earthquakes and baroque alterations. Since WWII, when incendiary bombs burned the church and destroyed many of its works of art, it has been returned more or less to its original Gothic appearance. Within the **nuns' cloisters** (admission €4; 9.30am-1pm & 2.30-5.30pm Mon-Sat, 9.30am-1pm Sun), behind the church, is a long parapet entirely covered in decorative ceramic tiles, depicting landscapes and scenes from the nuns' lives.

A few steps west, Piazza del Gesù Nuovo opens before you with its ornate freestanding *guglia* (obelisk). The 16th-century **Chiesa del Gesù Nuovo** (☎ 081 551 86 13; Piazza del Gesù Nuovo; 6.45am-1pm & 4-7.30pm), on the northern side of the piazza, is one of the city's greatest examples of Renaissance architecture. The interior was redecorated in Neapolitan baroque style after a fire in 1639.

The 15th-century **Chiesa di Sant'Anna dei Lombardi** (☎ 081 551 33 33; Piazza Monteoliveto; 8.30am-12.30pm Tue-Sat), southwest of Piazza del Gesù Nuovo, features fine Renaissance

VORACIOUS COLLECTING, FARNESE STYLE

It was Cardinal Alessandro Farnese who founded the Farnese collection. On becoming Pope Paul III in 1534, he began by gathering art treasures for the Vatican, then turned his attention to embellishing the family seat, Palazzo Farnese, in Rome. Through papal influence, the Farnese family monopolised excavations around the city. In 1540 the *Toro Farnese* (Farnese Bull) was discovered near the Terme di Caracalla (p128) and installed in the gardens of Palazzo Farnese. It remained there until 1787, when it was moved to Naples' Museo Archeologico Nazionale, now the home of other famous Farnese treasures such as *Venere Callipigia* and *Ercole a riposo*.

This particular pope's vow of celibacy didn't prevent him from fathering four children. One of the most interesting paintings at the Palazzo Reale di Capodimonte is an unfinished portrait by Titian of Paul III with his two grandsons – Ottavio, who became the Duke of Parma and Piacenza, and Gran Cardinale Alessandro, who later became a serious collector in his own right. Alessandro continued the collection, commissioning works from Michelangelo, El Greco and other contemporary painters of renown.

The collection was transferred to Capodimonte from the Farnese family's power base in Parma and Piacenza in 1759. Many paintings were sold off in the 19th century, when the entire remaining collection was transferred to what is now the Museo Archeologico Nazionale. The paintings were returned to Capodimonte in 1957.

sculpture, including a superb terracotta *Pietà* (1492) by Guido Mazzoni.

AROUND PIAZZA DEL CARMINE

On the waterfront in Piazza del Carmine, the **Basilica del Carmine Maggiore** was the scene of the 1647 Neapolitan Revolution led by Masaniello. Each year on 16 July a fireworks display celebrates the festival of the Madonna by simulating the burning of the bell tower.

South of Spaccanapoli

CASTEL NUOVO

When Charles I of Anjou took over Naples and the Swabians' Sicilian kingdom, he found himself to be in control not only of his new southern Italian acquisitions, but also of possessions in Tuscany, northern Italy and Provence (France). It made sense to base the new dynasty in Naples, rather than Palermo in Sicily, and Charles launched an ambitious construction programme to expand the port and city walls. His plans included converting a Franciscan convent into the castle that still stands in Piazza Municipio. Also called the Maschio Angioino, the **Castel Nuovo** (New Castle) has crenellated round towers that make it one of the most striking buildings in Naples.

The castle was erected in three years from 1279 but what you see today is the result of renovations by the Aragonese two centuries later, as well as a meticulous restoration effort prior to WWII. The heavy grey stone that dominates the castle was imported from Mallorca in Spain. The two-storey Renaissance triumphal arch at the entrance, the Torre della Guardia, commemorates the triumphal entry of Alfonso I of Aragón into Naples in 1443.

Spread across several halls on three floors is the **Museo Civico** (☎ 081 795 58 77; admission €5; ☻ 9am-7pm Mon-Sat, 9am-2pm Sun). The 14th- and 15th-century frescoes and sculptures on the ground floor are of the most interest. The other two floors display paintings, either by Neapolitan artists or with Naples or Campania as subjects, covering the 17th to the early 20th centuries.

Nearby on Via Medina is the **Fontana di Nettuno**, by Bernini, dating from 1601. Originally situated on Piazza Bovio, it has been moved to allow construction of the metro to continue on its former site.

PIAZZA TRENTO E TRIESTE

One of Naples' more elegant squares, Piazza Trento e Trieste, is fronted on the northeastern side by Italy's largest opera house, the sumptuous **Teatro San Carlo** (☎ 081 797 21 11; Via San Carlo 98; guided tours €5; ☻ 9am-6pm), famed for its perfect acoustics. Locals will proudly boast that it was built in 1737, predating its northern rival, Milan's La Scala, by 41 years. Inaugurated on 4 December 1737 by King Charles VII, it was severely damaged by a fire in 1816 and rebuilt by Antonio Niccolini, the same architect who a few years before had

CAMPANIA

added the façade. From the outside there are no clues as to the opulence of the six-level red and gold interior. Twenty-minute tours depart from the San Carlo shop every 20 minutes and are conducted in various languages, including English.

Across Via San Carlo is one of the four entrances to the palatial glass atrium of the **Galleria Umberto I** shopping centre opened in 1900. A twin to the Galleria Vittorio Emanuele II in Milan (see p264), it's worth a look for its impressive marble floor and structural engineering but it probably won't detain you for long. A favoured haunt of street vendors and housing a few anonymous shops and cafés, it retains little of the refined air that it breathed in the early 20th century.

PALAZZO REALE

Facing the grand Piazza del Plebiscito, this magnificent **palace** (☎ 081 794 40 21; entrance at Piazza Trento e Trieste; admission €4; ✆ 9am-8pm Thu-Tue) was built around 1600. It was completely renovated in 1841 and suffered extensive damage during WWII. The statues of the eight most important kings of Naples were inserted into façade niches in 1888.

From the courtyard a huge double staircase leads to the royal apartments. These apartments house the **Museo del Palazzo Reale**, a rich collection of furnishings, porcelain, tapestries, statues and paintings.

The palace is also home to the **Biblioteca Nazionale** (National Library; ☎ 081 40 12 73; admission free; ✆ 9am-7.30pm Mon-Fri, 9am-1.30pm Sat), which includes the vast Farnese collection brought to Naples by Charles of Bourbon, with at least 2000 papyri discovered at Herculaneum and fragments of a 5th-century Coptic Bible. Visitors should bring ID for a security check by staff.

CHIESA DI SAN FRANCESCO DI PAOLA

At the western end of Piazza del Plebiscito, this dominating church was begun by Ferdinand I in 1817 to celebrate the restoration of his kingdom after the Napoleonic interlude. Flanked by semicircular colonnades, the church is based on the Pantheon and is a popular wedding spot.

Toledo & Quartieri Spagnoli

MUSEO ARCHEOLOGICO NAZIONALE

The magnificent **archaeological museum** (☎ 081 44 01 66; Piazza Museo Nazionale; admission €6.50; ✆ 9am-7.30pm Wed-Mon) displays treasures forming one of the most comprehensive collections of Graeco-Roman artefacts in the world. Originally a cavalry barracks and later the seat of the city's university, the museum was established by Charles of Bourbon (also known as Charles III of Bourbon) in the late 18th century. It houses the rich collection of antiquities Charles inherited from his mother, Elizabeth Farnese, as well as the treasures that had been discovered at the sites of Pompeii and Herculaneum. The museum also contains the Borgia collection of Etruscan and Egyptian relics.

To avoid getting lost in its rambling galleries (numbered in Roman numerals) invest €7.50 in the bilingual *Guida di Orientamento* or, to concentrate on the highlights, €4 for an audioguide in English.

Many items of classical sculpture from the Farnese collection, including the famous *Toro Farnese* (Farnese Bull), are displayed on the ground floor. Sculpted in the early 3rd century AD, the *Toro Farnese*, probably a Roman copy of a Greek original, is an enormous group of figures depicting the death of Dirce, Queen of Thebes, who was tied to a bull and torn apart over rocks in Greek mythology. Carved from a single block of marble, it was later restored by Michelangelo.

On the mezzanine floor are mosaics, mostly from Pompeii, including the *Battle of Alexander*, the best-known depiction of the great Macedonian emperor. It once paved the floor in the Casa del Fauno at Pompeii and is now just one of a series of remarkably detailed and lifelike pieces.

The 1st floor of the museum is largely devoted to a treasure-trove of discoveries from Pompeii, Herculaneum, Stabiae and Cumae (Cuma). The items range from huge murals and frescoes to a pair of gladiator helmets, household items, ceramics and glassware – even egg cups. Galleries 86 and 87 house an extraordinary collection of vases from mixed origins, many carefully reassembled from fragments. In the basement is a small Egyptian collection. Note that at the time of writing renovations were being carried out on the museum. These are anticipated to continue until early 2007 and means that certain galleries may be temporarily closed with no prior notice.

The **Gabinetto Segreto** (Secret Room) reopened to the public in 2000 after decades of being accessible only to the seriously scientific. The ancient smut on display includes an intriguing statue of Pan up to no good with a nanny goat and nine paintings depicting erotic positions, which served as a menu for brothel clients.

Santa Lucia

The so-called **Castel dell'Ovo** (Castle of the Egg; ☎ 081 764 05 90; Borgo Marinaro; admission free; ✹ 9am-6pm Mon-Fri, 9am-1pm Sat & Sun) is on the small rocky Borgo Marinaro, off Santa Lucia. Built in the 12th century by the Normans on the site of a Roman villa, the castle became a key fortress in the defence of Campania. According to myth, the castle owes its name to Virgil. The Roman poet was said to have buried an egg on the site where the castle now stands, ominously warning that when the egg breaks the castle will fall.

The **Fontana dell'Immacolatella**, at the end of Via Partenope, dates from the 17th century and features statues by Bernini and Naccherini.

Lungomare Caracciolo

West of Santa Lucia, Via Partenope spills into Piazza della Vittoria, marking the beginning of the Riviera di Chiaia. This boulevard runs beside the **Villa Comunale**, a large park marked on its seaward side by Via Francesco Caracciolo, which is closed to traffic on Sunday mornings and taken over by strollers, skaters, scooters and joggers.

Within the park is the **acquario** (aquarium; ☎ 081 583 32 63; Villa Comunale; adult/child €1.50/1; ✹ 9am-6pm summer, 9am-5pm Mon-Sat, 9am-2pm Sun winter). Founded in the late 19th century by German naturalist Anton Dohrn, this is Europe's oldest aquarium. Its 30 tanks contain some 200 species of sea life, taken exclusively from the Bay of Naples.

Close by is the **Museo Pignatelli** (☎ 081 761 23 56; Riviera di Chiaia 200; admission €2.10; ✹ 9am-2pm Tue-Sun), an old patrician residence that once belonged to the Rothschild family. It contains mostly 19th-century furnishings, china and other moderately interesting knick-knacks. A pavilion set in the villa's handsome gardens houses a coach museum.

Vomero

The Vomero (*vom*-e-ro) hill, visible from all over the city, is a serene and well-to-do residential quarter that rises above all the chaos below. Dominated by the foreboding Castel Sant'Elmo and the stunning Certosa di San Martino, it's an area of spectacular views and tree-lined streets, new shops and smart restaurants. Three cable-car railways connect Vomero and the city (p637).

CASTEL SANT'ELMO

Commanding spectacular views across the city and bay, this star-shaped **castle** (☎ 081 578 40 30; Largo San Martino; admission €1; ✹ 8.30am-7.30pm Tue-Sun) was built into the tufa rock of the hill by the Spanish in 1538. Impressive though it is, the austere castle has seen little real military action. The biggest blow it received came in 1587 when a bolt of lightning hit the castle's stock of gunpowder, killing some 150 people. It has, however, seen plenty of prisoners: a longtime jail, its dungeons were used as a military prison until the 1970s. The admission times and price can vary when the castle is being used for exhibitions.

CERTOSA DI SAN MARTINO

Barely 100m from the castle lies this Carthusian monastery, established in the 14th century and rebuilt in the 17th century in Neapolitan baroque style. It houses the excellent **Museo Nazionale di San Martino** (☎ 081 578 17 69; Via Tito Angelini; admission €6; ✹ 8.30am-7.30pm Tue-Sun), which features a section on naval history, an area dedicated to the history of the Kingdom of Naples and an extensive art collection. Of particular interest is the Sezione Presepiale, several rooms devoted to a collection of Neapolitan *presepi* carved in the 18th and 19th centuries. These range from the minuscule – a Nativity scene in an ornately decorated eggshell – to the massive. The most famous piece, the Cucinello *presepe*, covers one wall of what used to be the monastery's kitchen. Angels fly down to a landscape of rock houses and shepherds, all crafted out of wood, cork and terracotta. Don't miss the monastery's church and the rooms that flank it which contain a feast of frescoes and paintings by some of Naples' most important 17th-century artists. The Grand Cloister is also a beautiful space of manicured gardens, marble statues and white porticoes. There is a magnificent view from here and from Largo San Martino, the square outside the monastery's main entrance.

CAMPANIA

VILLA FLORIDIANA

In a city decidedly short of green space, this public **park** (admission free; 🕑 9am-1hr before sunset Tue-Sun) is a tonic, spreading down the slopes from Via D Cimarosa in Vomero to Mergellina. The stately home at its lower, southern end was built in 1817 by Ferdinand I for his wife, the Duchess of Floridia. Today it contains the **Museo Nazionale della Ceramica Duca di Martina** (☎ 081 578 84 18; admission €2.50; 🕑 8.30am-2pm Tue-Fri, 9am-2pm Sat & Sun), which has an extensive collection of European, Chinese and Japanese china, ivory, enamels and Italian majolica.

Capodimonte

PALAZZO REALE DI CAPODIMONTE

Work on a new palace for Charles of Bourbon started in 1738 and took almost a century to complete. On the northern edge of the city, the distinctive pinky orange and grey palace is set in the extensive **Parco di Capodimonte** (admission free; 🕑 8am-1hr before sunset), which once formed an aristocratic hunting ground. Extensively restored, the palace now houses the **Museo e Gallerie di Capodimonte** (☎ 081 749 91 11; Parco di Capodimonte; adult/child €7.50/6.50; 🕑 8.30am-7.30pm Tue-Sun), which displays the important Farnese collection (see the boxed text, p623). The paintings hang in the royal galleries on the 1st floor and are divided into periods and schools. The extensive collection boasts works by, among many others, Bellini, Botticelli, Caravaggio, Correggio, Masaccio and Titian. One of its most famous paintings is Masaccio's *Crocifissione* (Crucifixion). Other highlights are Bellini's *Trasfigurazione* (Transfiguration), and nine canvases by Titian.

In the recently opened **Galleria della Cose Rare** (Gallery of Rare Objects) you can imagine how the dinner table of Cardinal Alessandro Farnese might have looked. His blue majolica table service has his coat of arms embossed in gold on every piece, while the elaborate centrepiece depicting Diana the huntress can be used as a goblet by taking off the stag's detachable head.

Also on the palazzo's 1st floor are the **royal apartments**, with an extensive collection of armour, ivories, bronzes, porcelain and majolica, tapestries, as well as many other works of art. Room 51, the *Salottino di Porcellana,* is a sheer study of tasteless extravagance, boasting more than 3000 pieces of porcelain.

The *salottino* was originally created between 1757 and 1759 for the Palazzo Reale in Portici but was transferred to Capodimonte in 1867.

The 2nd-floor galleries display work by Neapolitan artists from the 13th to the 19th centuries, plus some spectacular Belgian tapestries depicting episodes from the Battle of Pavia.

The museum is spread over three floors and 160 rooms and to see the whole place in one day is simply impossible. You'd need at least two days to start getting to grips with the place. For most people though, a full morning is sufficient for a shortened 'best of' tour.

CATACOMBE DI SAN GENNARO

Dating from the 2nd century, the **catacombs** (☎ 081 741 10 71; Via di Capodimonte 16; admission €5; 🕑 1hr guided tours 9am, 10am, 11am & noon) house a mix of tombs, corridors and broad vestibules held up by columns and arches, and are decorated with early Christian frescoes and mosaics. This was an important pilgrimage site in the 5th century, when San Gennaro's body was brought here.

WALKING TOUR

You'll never walk all of Naples in a day but the itinerary we describe here will give you a brief overview of the fascinating *centro storico.*

Beginning from Piazza Garibaldi, head a short way down Corso Umberto I before veering right into Via Egiziaca a Forcella. After crossing Via P Colletta, follow the street as it veers leftwards and merges into Via Vicaria Vecchia. Where it meets the busy cross street, Via Duomo, stands the **Basilica di San Giorgio Maggiore** (**1**; p622) on your left and, two blocks northwest up Via Duomo, stands the **cathedral** (**2**; p621), with the **Museo del Tesoro di San Gennaro** (**3**; p621) next door. Opposite the cathedral is the entrance to the **Chiesa e Pinacoteca dei Girolamini** (**4**; p621).

Walk back southeast to where you emerged onto Via Duomo. Turn right off Via Duomo into Via San Biagio dei Librai, one of the liveliest roads in Spaccanapoli and one of the original Roman streets. On your way, you'll pass the **Ospedale delle Bambole** (**5**; p622), or Dolls' Hospital; the **Chiesa di SS Filippo e Giacomo** (**6**; p622); and the **Chiesa di Sant'Angelo a Nilo** (**7**; p622).

The rear of the imposing **Chiesa di San Domenico Maggiore** (8; p622) abuts onto the café-fringed, pedestrianised piazza of the same name. At the heart of the square is a *guglia*, a kind of ground-level, richly carved baroque steeple or obelisk, topped by a statue of the good saint himself. The colourfully tiled **Cappella di San Severo** (9; p622) is just off this square in a lane east of the church; the graffiti is a real shame. This chapel is home to the stunning *Cristo Velato* (Veiled Christ), as beautiful a sculpture as any in Naples.

Walk back to Via Benedetto Croce and continue westwards, past **Palazzo Filomarino** (10; p622), then the **Basilica di Santa Chiara** (11; p622) as far as Piazza del Gesù Nuovo and **Chiesa del Gesù Nuovo** (12; p622). Backtrack from the square to the first intersection and turn left along Via S Sebastiano. At the next intersection on your left, a short street leads down to **Port'Alba (13)**, a city gate built in 1625, then to Piazza Dante. Back on route and ahead of you is Piazza Bellini and, further ahead, Piazza Luigi Miraglia, from which Via dei Tribunali leads east. You're now walking along the *decamanus*, or main street, of the original Greek, and later

Roman, town. Two-thirds of the way along Via dei Tribunali stood the Greek agora, or central market and meeting place, in what is now **Piazza San Gaetano (14)**.

A great place to rest your weary feet is back in one of Piazza Bellini's several cafés. While you're at it you could inspect the remains of the ancient Greek city walls under the square. From the square, an easy walk north along Via Santa Maria di Costantinopoli brings you to the unmissable **Museo Archeologico Nazionale (15**; p624).

NAPLES FOR CHILDREN

Apart from the castles and catacombs, the aquarium, the never-dull street life – and the ice cream – there are a number of attractions that might appeal to children.

Within the University of Naples is the museum complex, the **Musei di Mineralogia, Zoologia e Antropologia** (☎ 081 253 51 62; Via Mezzocannone 8; admission to each museum €0.70; ☼ 9am-1.30pm & 3-5pm Mon, 9am-1.30pm Tue-Sun Sep-Jul). The Museo di Mineralogia features minerals, meteorites and quartz crystals collected from the Vesuvius region. The Museo di Zoologia is the most child-friendly of the three, while the Museo di Antropologia, across the courtyard, is also worth peeking into for its prehistoric relics.

Città della Scienza (Science City; ☎ 081 372 37 28; www.cittadellascienza.it; Via Coroglio 104; adult/child €7/6; ☼ 9am-5pm Tue-Sat, 10am-7pm Sun) takes its visitors on an interactive exploration of the world around us. Features examine natural

WALK FACTS

Start Piazza Garibaldi
Finish Museo Archeologico Nazionale
Distance 4 km
Duration About four hours

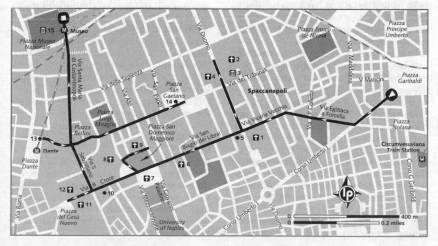

phenomena, the science behind modern communication and, in the planetarium (€2), the night sky. To get here take the metro to the Cavalleggeri d'Aosta stop then walk for around 1.5km (follow the signs) or take bus No C10.

Edenlandia (☎ 081 239 40 90; www.edenlandia.it in Italian; Viale Kennedy 76; adult/child under 1.1m €4/ free, day pass incl all attractions €8.50; ☼ 5pm-midnight Mon-Fri, 10.30am-midnight Sat & Sun Jun-Sep), Naples' historic amusement park, has more than 200 attractions. Take the westbound Ferrovia Cumana from Stazione Cumana and get off at the Edenlandia station.

Situated on the westernmost tip of Posillipo, **Parco Virgiliano** (Viale Virgilio; ☼ 8am-1hr before sunset) offers some of the best views in the whole city and you can also spy Capri, Procida and Ischia and, of course, Mount Vesuvius on a clear day. There are swings and slides for the kids and some well-tended paths for family strolls, plus an ice-cream stand or two.

TOURS

Tourcar (☎ 081 552 04 29; Piazza Matteotti) is just one of several companies that organise excursions to the Bay of Naples islands, the Amalfi Coast and Pompeii, Herculaneum and Vesuvius. A tour to Pompeii costs €43, Capri is €78 and a Naples city tour costs €30.

For something headily different, dip underground at **Napoli Sotterranea** (Underground Naples; ☎ 081 29 69 44; www.napolisotterranea.org; Piazza San Gaetano 68, entrance beside church; guided tours €9.30; ☼ 1½hr tours at noon, 2pm & 4pm Mon-Wed, Fri, 9pm Thu, 6pm Sat & Sun), for a guided tour that takes you 40m below the city to explore the network of passages and caves. These were originally hewn by the Greeks to extract the soft tufa stone used in construction, then extended by the Romans as water conduits. Clogged up with illegally dumped refuse over the centuries, they were used as air-raid shelters in WWII. Part of the tour takes place by candlelight via extremely narrow passages – not suitable for expanded girths! The second part of the tour is up at street level with a visit to the remains of a nearby Roman theatre which, until a few years ago, was hidden below a motorbike workshop.

Citysightseeing Napoli (adult/child €18/9) is a hop-on-hop-off open-top bus with three different city tours and pick-up points at main sights throughout the city.

FESTIVALS & EVENTS

Naples' main festivals honour San Gennaro. On the first Sunday in May, 19 September and 16 December each year, thousands gather to pray in the cathedral for the **Festa di San Gennaro**, to witness the saint's blood, held in two phials, liquefy: a miracle believed to save the city from potential disasters. The saint is said to have saved the city from calamity on numerous occasions – although the miracle spectacularly failed to occur in 1941 when Vesuvius erupted.

Other festivals include the **Madonna del Carmine**, held on 16 July in Piazza del Carmine, which culminates in a fireworks display, and the **Madonna di Piedigrotta** (5 to 12 September). At Christmas, thousands of elaborate *presepi* are erected around the city.

Neapolis Rock Festival, held at the height of summer, attracts top international acts. It's held west of town, down by the beach at Arenile di Bagnoli.

SLEEPING

The choice of accommodation is vast and varied, including gorgeous *palazzi*, exec-style hotels and small family-run B&Bs.

Budget hotels are particularly prevalent in and around seedy Piazza Garibaldi and the Mercato quarter. Rest assured, the hotels listed here are safe and reliable and, unlike several in this district, do not have rooms rented by the hour.

To really absorb the heart and soul of Naples, head for the *centro storico*, where there's plenty of atmospheric yet comfortable places to stay and you'll have many of the city's sights within easy walking distance.

For more upmarket, sophisticated surroundings, Santa Lucia and Chiaia are suitably elegant, while, for a more detached view of the city, take a cable car up to tranquil Vomero with its spectacular views.

The closest camp sites are in Pozzuoli to the west and Pompeii to the east.

Mercato
BUDGET

Hotel Zara (☎ 081 28 71 25; www.hotelzara.it; 2nd fl, Via Firenze 81; s/d €45/65; ☒ ☐) Recently revamped, the rooms here have a crisp new look with shiny natural wood and off-white furnishings. There is a handy book exchange and bright sitting room where breakfast is served for an extra €4.

Hotel Luna Rossa (☎ 081 554 87 52; www.hotel lunarossa.it; Via G Pica 20-22; s/d €60/90) A good example of how you can euro-economise by staying in this part of town. This slick quality hotel is run by the daughter of a Neapolitan musician and each room is named after a local song, with the lyrics framed so you can practise warbling in the shower. Decorated in various hues of pink, the rooms are ultra-comfortable.

Hotel Casanova (☎ 081 26 82 87; www.hotelcasanova.com; Corso G Garibaldi 333; s/d €18/39, with bathroom €26/51.50) The world-weary owner of this hotel doesn't quite live up to the name: his son runs Hotel Zara with a lot more zip. But the rooms are large and neat and the flowery roof terrace is an added plus.

MIDRANGE

Hotel Nuovo Rebecchino (☎ 081 26 80 26; www .nuovorebecchino.it; Corso G Garibaldi 356; s/d €105/160; P ⊠ 🖳) Oozing with Neapolitan charm, manager Rosario can help with tours and city advice. Recently revamped rooms are solid Regency style and hung with 19th-century prints. There is free Internet access and a sunny breakfast room where you can opt for the full bacon and eggs deal, upon request.

Hotel Ideal (☎ 081 26 92 37; www.albergoideal.it; Piazza Garibaldi 99; s/d €65/100; P ⊠) A short stagger from the train station, this hotel is handy if you've just arrived and are weighed down – or just plain weary. The Ideal's large rooms are washed in warm salmon tones with grand brass beds.

Hotel Plaza (☎ 081 563 61 68; www.hotelplazanapoli .it; Piazza Principe Umberto, 23; s/d €87/110; P ⊠ 🖳) This slick modern hotel in a gracious 19th-century building has rooms with double-glazing, balconies and Internet access. The bathrooms are a dazzle of Med-blue mosaic tiles and there is the choice of a cooked or continental breakfast.

Centro Storico
BUDGET

6 Small Rooms (☎ 081 790 13 78; www.at6smallrooms .com; Via Diodata Lioy 18; dm/d €18/55) It's a slog to the top floor but, once there, you'll probably stay a while. Run by an Australian-Italian couple, this place has a hip communal feel with a large chill-out living room and kitchen. There are colourful murals throughout.

Hotel Bellini (☎ 081 45 69 96; fax 081 29 22 56; Via San Paolo 44; s/d €51/77) Just off one of the liveliest

stretches of Via dei Tribunali, Bellini is full of Neapolitan charm. In other words, not everything works, the furnishings are old-fashioned and you can string your washing up outside the window. The manager Alessandro speaks excellent English.

Albergo Duomo (☎ 081 26 59 88; www.hotelduomo napoli.it; Via Duomo 228; s/d €40/65) As the name suggests, this place is situated in the shadow of the cathedral. Despite the disarmingly shabby entrance, the pale pink rooms are large and airy, if a little anonymous. Book ahead as rooms get snapped up quickly.

Donnalbina 7 (☎ 081 195 678 17; www.donnalbina7 .it; Via Donnalbina 7; s/d €65/90; ⊠) If Ikea opened a B&B it would probably look something like this. Brand new and fairly priced, this hotel's rooms are slick, modern and minimalist, with spot lighting and lashings of white offset by pale grey tiles and burgundy walls. Breakfast is served in your room, fresh from the *pasticceria* (cake shop) across the road.

MIDRANGE

Hotel Pignatelli (☎ 081 658 49 50; www.hotelpignatelli napoli.com in Italian; Via San Giovanni Maggiore Pignatelli 16; s/d €50/90) It is not often you can gaze up at 15th-century beamed ceilings with frescoes at this price. Other indulgences include gracious brass beds, two-person sized showers and tasteful butter-coloured walls twinned with terracotta tiles.

Sansevero D'Angri (☎ 081 790 10 00; www.sansevero doria.it in Italian; Piazza VII Settembre 28; d/ste €110/150; ⊠ 🖳) Staying at D'Angri is like sleeping in a genuine palace – not surprising given that Vanvitelli, the original architect, also designed the royal palace at Caserta. The public rooms with original frescoes are particularly sumptuous. Check out the turquoise-and-gold boudoir and the frescoed hall of mirrors where occasional concerts are held. The bedrooms are of a good size but, in comparison, they're fairly plain.

Belle Arti Resort (☎ 081 557 10 62; www.belle artiresort.com; Via Santa Maria di Costantinopoli 27; s/d €80/100; ⊠ 🖳) This exquisite B&B boutique hotel opened in November 2004 in a baronial 17th-century palazzo. The quasi-Sistine ceiling frescoes are just lovely, especially the water nymphs in Room 112. The antique wardrobes are happily combined with more modern touches, including large marbled bathrooms, free ADSL Internet use and minibars.

CAMPANIA

Portalba 33 (☎ 081 549 32 51; www.portalba33.it; Via Port'Alba 33; s/d €120/150; ☒) Truly original, this five-room B&B is contemporary yet elegant, extravagant yet tasteful. There are fake-fur bedspreads, an antique rocking horse, in-room bathtubs, strange shag-style seats in primary colours and a personal gym. It is hard to describe (can you tell?) – check the website for pics.

Costantinopoli 104 (☎ 081 557 10 35; www.costan tinopoli104.it; Via Santa Maria di Costantinopoli 104; s/d €145/170; ☒ ☒) A real oasis of calm in the centre of town, this 19th-century villa has had a shiny chic update. The rooms are large and minimalist with just enough soft furnishings for comfort. A massive Art Deco stained-glass window looks onto a swimming pool surrounded by mature palms and greenery.

TOP END

Hotel Caravaggio (☎ 081 211 00 66; www.caravag giohotel.it; Piazza Riario Sforza 157; s/d €130/200; ℗ ☒ ☒) Right in the pulsating heart of the old city, within confessional distance of the cathedral, this former 17th-century palace artfully combines the old with the new. Rooms are painted bright primary colours and feature high ceilings, original stone arches and honey-coloured terracotta tiles.

Grand Hotel Oriente (☎ 081 551 21 33; www.ori ente.it; Via A Diaz 44; s/d €155/220; ℗ ☒ ☒) Despite the charmless modern exterior, this hotel's facilities and comfort are up there with the best of them. Rooms sport a green-and-blue theme; the beds are king size, there's ADSL access and wonderful views from the upper floors.

Toledo & Vomero

BUDGET

Pensione Margherita (☎ 081 556 70 44; Via D Cimarosa 29; s/d €35/62) Expect a homy welcome and no-frills, but adequate, accommodation at this place just a short cable-car jaunt up from the centre. The views are far from humdrum – over Capri and Sorrento.

MIDRANGE

Napolit'amo (☎ 081 552 36 26; www.napolitamo.it; Via Toledo 148; s/d €72/95; ℗ ☒) A palatial hideaway right on this throbbing shopping street, this family-run former 16th-century palace retains much of the atmosphere of its former glory days. Welcome nods to the present,

however, include parking, double-glazing and free Internet access for guests.

Hotel Toledo (☎ 081 40 68 71; www.hoteltoledo .com; Via Montecalvario 15; s/d €85/140; ℗ ☒ ☒) A tastefully renovated smart city hotel with dark-wood furnishings coupled with a warm earthy colour scheme. Mod cons include satellite TV, free Internet use and minibars. Lemon and palm trees adorn the roof terrace, which overlooks the lively Quartieri Spagnoli.

Hotel Il Convento (☎ 081 40 39 77; www.hotelil convento.com; Via Speranzella 137a; s/d €145/175; ☒) Named after the neighbourhood convent, this well-restored 16th-century building combines cream colours and dark wood with occasional original brickwork – pity about the plastic flowers. Cough up €210 to bag the room with the private roof terrace.

Hotel Belvedere (☎ 081 578 81 69; Via Tito Angelini 51-59; s/d €100/120; ☒) Location, location, location – this hotel is high above the city and the views over the rooftops to Vesuvius are breathtaking. There's a pretty garden with lemon trees but the rooms are fairly drab by comparison. Readers have told us that the staff can be less than friendly.

TOP END

Grand Hotel Parker's (☎ 081 761 24 74; www.grand hotelparkers.com; Corso Vittorio Emanuele I 34; s/d €225/260; ℗ ☒ ☒) Named after the British marine biologist George Parker Bidder, who owned the hotel up until 1908, Parker's is a stately pile. It is luxuriously decorated with antiques, chandeliers and gilt-framed oil paintings, and the piano bar and roof terrace afford

---

AUTHOR'S CHOICE

Palazzo Turchini (☎ 081 551 06 06; www .palazzoturchini.it; Via Medina 21-22; s/d €130/150; ☒ ☒) Wake up to the sound of bubbling water from the adjacent grand fountain on Via Medina. This gorgeous 17th-century palazzo has been given a deft upbeat look with soothing pastel tones, parquet floors, Internet access in the rooms and hydro-massage bathtubs. The flower-flanked roof terrace is the morning spot for cappuccino and *sfogliatelle* (pastry with ricotta filling). An adjacent restaurant is planned, along with some classy suites which will have hydromassage baths.

swoonsome views of Chiaia and the Bay of Naples.

Hotel San Francisco al Monte (☎ 081 251 24 61; Corso Vittorio Emanuele I 328; s/d €240/270; **P** 🞨 🖳 🎇) The monks' cells at this 16th-century monastery have been converted into splendid rooms, all with views over the bay. The ancient cloisters contain an open-air bar, and the barrel-vaulted corridors are cool and atmospheric. A rambling garden and swimming pool on the 7th floor complete the look.

Chiaia & Santa Lucia
BUDGET

B&B Santa Lucia (☎ 081 245 74 83; www.borgosanta lucia.net; Via Santa Lucia 90; s €70/d €80-90) A 50m Frisbee throw from the seafront, this sparkling new B&B could do with a bit of colour to offset the clinical white and light-wood colour scheme, but the good-sized rooms are comfortable and have fridges. You'll pay €10 more for an ocean view, which is quite costly just for the colour blue.

Pensione Ruggiero (☎ 081 66 35 36; Via Martucci 72; s/d €70/90) This grand old building is very central for the Via dei Mille shops. The rooms are unpretentious and bright; go for a view of the bustling piazza if you can.

MIDRANGE

B&B Morelli (☎ 081 245 22 91; www.bbmorelli49.it; Via Domenico Morelli 49; s/d €65/95) A fun place to stay, especially for fans of cinema memorabilia and pop culture. There are posters throughout, advertising Fellini classics and Almodovar films and sharing wall space with contemporary divas like Madonna. Add to this the dazzle of classical Florentine floor tiles and colourful knick-knacks and you have a real one-off at the right price.

B&B Cappella Vecchia (☎ 081 240 51 17; www.cap pellavecchia11.it; Vico SM a Cappella Vecchia 11; s/d €65/110; 🞨 🖳) Chic and modern, this B&B's rooms are colourful and upbeat, with tasteful artwork on the walls and a large communal sitting room with books, Internet access and plenty of slouching space. Bike hire and tours can be arranged.

Chiaja Hotel De Charme (☎ 081 41 55 55; www .hotelchiaia.it; Via Chiaia 216; s/d €95/140; 🞨 🖳) This classy boutique hotel is run by the grandson of the former marquis owner. Next door used to be a brothel and the six rooms are now a separate fun wing with an appropriate floral and flirty look. Overall, however, the décor

is refined elegance, and you can languish in a private Jacuzzi for a few euros more.

Hotel Rex (☎ 081 764 93 89; www.hotel-rex.it; Via Palepoli 12; s/d €105/125; 🞨 🖳) There's a pleasing old-fashioned air about this hotel near the seafront. The rooms are large with heavy, dark furniture, chandeliers and balconies. There is no dining room, meaning that breakfast has to be served in your room, which is a shame.

Hotel Pinto-Storey (☎ 081 68 12 60; www.pinto storey.it; 4th & 5th fl, Via Martucci 72; s/d €85/125; 🞨) A laid-back hotel lies behind the charming Art Deco entrance. Tastefully restored, the rooms are spacious and welcoming while the location is perfect for a little retail therapy at the nearby Via dei Mille shops.

TOP END

Hotel Miramare (☎ 081 764 75 89; www.hotelmira mare.com; Via N Sauro 24; s/d €199/249; 🞨 🖳) Built in the classic Liberty style in 1914, this grand hotel has a gracious old-fashioned feel on the ground floor with its overstuffed sofas, marble statues, plush rugs and piano. The recently refurbished rooms are stylish and colourful, while the roof garden is a delight of flowers, hammocks and sea views.

Grand Hotel Santa Lucia (☎ 081 764 06 66; www .santalucia.it; Via Partenope 46; s/d €240/300; 🞨 🖳 🎇) In a prime situation across from the Borgo Marinaro, this elegant hotel dates back to 1906. Grand tapestries, oil paintings and the Regency-style carpeted rooms exhibit impeccable taste; the roof-garden swimming pool has superb sea views.

EATING

A bad eating experience in Naples is rare. The lust for life here shows in the superb food, with many restaurants several generations old. The Neapolitans don't believe in drizzle and fusion; the best cuisine is deliciously simple and traditional, and based on fresh seasonal ingredients. The pizza was created here and nowhere on earth will you eat it better (see the boxed text, p633). Topped with mozzarella cheese and fresh tomato sauce, it's standard fare. *Misto di frittura* – courgette (zucchini) flowers, deep-fried potato and aubergine (eggplant) – tempts from tiny stalls in tiny streets, as does mozzarella *in carozza* (deep-fried in bread).

Seafood, in particular clams and mussels, is a Neapolitan speciality. The cakes are simply unbeatable and even the coffee tastes better in Naples.

Aside from the ubiquitous pizzerie, you will see trattoria or *osteria* signs. These are inexpensive, family-owned restaurants, often with a chalked-up menu outside the door. Don't be put off by simple décor. Neapolitans have their priorities right and believe in spending more money on their ingredients and cooking than on decorating the dining room.

Mercato

Da Michele (☎ 081 553 92 04; Via Cesare Sersale 1; pizzas €5-7) This is probably the most famous pizzeria in Naples but you would never know it (until you taste the pizza), as the interior is dingy and old-fashioned. Founded in 1870, Da Michele only makes two types of pizzas: *margherita* (tomatoes, basil and mozzarella) or *marinara* (tomatoes, garlic and oregano) – and they've had a long time to get it right. You can't make a booking; just turn up, take a ticket and wait your turn.

Trianon (☎ 081 553 94 26; Via P Colletta 42-6; pizzas from €5) Simply decorated with black-and-white photos of old Naples and an institution in Neapolitan circles – film director Vittorio de Sica and comic actor Totò were regulars – this historic pizzeria does its city proud. On the dough since 1923, it is still tossing pizzas with the best of them. Expect queues (the word is out).

Centro Storico

Pizzeria Sorbillo (☎ 081 44 66 43; Via dei Tribunali 32; pizzas from €5) Another popular pizza parlour that vies for the city's No 1 spot. There are now three generations of the Sorbillo family, all in the pizza business in Italy or the

US. More has been invested in the *pizzaioli* (pizza-makers) than interior finery. Inside it's basic and rustic, with a corner TV permanently switched to the football channel. There's a massive choice ranging from a margherita to the regal seafood special.

Il Caffè Arabo (☎ 081 442 06 07; Piazza Bellini; snacks from €3) This place shares the same atmosphere as the trendier surrounding bars and cafés, but a glass of wine is half the price and the Middle Eastern nibbles are good value, too. The menu includes falafel, hummus, *fuul* (a bean-based dip), kebabs and a brave attempt at curry (more like a vegetable stew). Service can be slow, so bring a book.

Trattoria da Carmine (☎ 081 29 43 83; Via dei Tribunali 330; meals from €11) All the right ingredients are here: homely atmosphere, nononsense food and attentive old-fashioned service. The menu is limited – often a good sign – and includes a hearty and delicious *penne alla sorrentina* (penne, mozzarella and tomatoes). The walls are papered with black-and-white photos of Naples and its characters (there are plenty).

Ristorante Bellini (☎ 081 45 97 74; Via Santa Maria di Costantinopoli 79-80; 330; full meals from €20) Pasta portions are served on a grand scale and the fish is as fresh as the morning catch. Try the vermicelli with clams and mussels (€9). Bellini's waiters are from the elderly cummerbund school of service, which contributes to the value-for-money vibe.

Lombardi a Santa Chiara (☎ 081 552 07 80; Via Benedetto Croce 59; meals about €25; ☯ Tue-Sun) A classy restaurant, Lombardi's faded grandeur provides a cosy setting for classic pizzas and Neapolitan dishes. Vegetarians also have plenty of choice, especially in the antipasti, where courgettes, artichokes and fresh buffalo mozzarella are artfully combined.

La Cantina della Sapienza (☎ 081 45 90 78; Via della Sapienza 40; meals from €14) For those preferring pared-down simplicity to culinary acrobatics, dishes here change according to what's on sale in the market. With its strung-up washing outside, this place has a real neighbourhood feel. Enjoy such Neapolitan staples as the classic *pizza bianca* topped with nothing more than a drizzle of extra virgin olive oil and crunchy sea salt.

La Locanda del Grifo (☎ 081 442 08 15; Via F del Guidice 14; meals about €22) Sit on the elegant outdoor terrace under an enormous cream-coloured awning. Start with a plate of mozzarella and

---

THE PERFECT PIZZA

Naples and Rome vie for pizza supremacy, yet their two products could scarcely be more different. Pizza in Naples has a soft doughy base, while your true Roman pizza usually has a very thin crust.

Neapolitans regard their version as the authentic one – after all, they will argue, their forefathers invented pizza in the 18th century. Pizzerie in Naples serving the 'real thing' have a sign on the door: *la vera pizza napoletana* (the real Neapolitan pizza). It's not just for show – to merit the seal of approval a pizza-maker has to conform to strict requirements. For a *margherita*, named after Queen Margherita (1851–1926), wife of King Umberto of Savoy), the cheese must be mozzarella (preferably made from buffalo milk), the olive oil extra virgin and the salt from the sea. Rolling pins are banned (the dough must be tossed by hand) and the pizza has to be cooked in a wood-fired oven at a temperature of between 215°C and 250°C.

Do your own research. For just about the best pizza in Naples, head for Da Michele (opposite) near Stazione Centrale. In Rome, try Pizzeria Remo (p155) in Testaccio. *Buon appetito!*

---

prosciutto and end up with the perfectly moist *torta caprese* made with chocolate and hazelnuts. Afterwards, waddle around the corner to one of the classy cafés on Piazza Bellini for a *limoncello* nightcap.

Toledo & Vomero

D.M. L.U.I.S.E. (☎ 081 41 53 67; Via Toledo 266-288; meals about €10) The palm-fringed terrace here at the more elegant end of Toledo is a prime people-watching spot. A good spot for fussy families, this place has a lavish buffet of delectable-looking fare, including spinach pie, fried pizza, risotto, lasagne and more salad choices than you can shake a carrot stick at.

Caprese (☎ 081 55 87 58; Via Luca Giordano 25; meals from €10) This place has a real Caribbean feel, with outside terraces surrounded by colourful flowerbeds, rubber plants and palm trees, plus a bubbling fountain or two. The young team at the helm equals a lively joshing vibe. The *ravioli caprese* (spinach-filled ravioli with a tomato sauce) comes highly recommended.

Donna Teresa (☎ 081 556 70 70; Via Michele Kerbaker 58; meals from €14) This swing-a-cat-size dining room has just eight tables. Family run, Donna Teresa has a limited menu that changes daily. There are usually a couple of nonpasta dishes such as chicken with tomato sauce or meatballs. It's hugely popular; you'll be lucky to get a table at lunchtime (and you can't book).

Chiaia & Santa Lucia

Kukai (☎ 081 41 19 05; Via Carlo De Cesare 55-56; sushi from €4; ✆ Tue-Sun) A real one-off in these parts.

The owner is well-travelled and authenticity is his thing. Even the most savvy sushi fan will not be able to fault the presentation and taste of such Japanese staples as California rolls, sushi mix, sashimi and temaki. The dining room has an appropriate light-wood Zen feel.

Castello (☎ 081 40 04 86; Via Santa Teresa a Chiaia 38; meals from €18; ✆ Mon-Sat Sep-Jul) Despite the grand name, you don't have to spend big to eat here; the dishes are delicious, original and well priced. Pasta choices include *pappardelle* (wide ribbon pasta) with courgette flowers and mussels. It's hard to fault this place, right down to the friendly owners and red-check tablecloths, not to mention the homemade desserts.

Di Bruno (☎ 081 251 24 11; Riviera di Chiaia 213-214; meals from €25; ✆ Tue-Sun) Papa used to run two famous restaurants, but has now scaled down to one with the next generation helping out. The linguine are made daily and feature in the *pasta alla Bruno* signature dish, doused with a rich sauce of mushrooms, ham, courgettes and cream. The candlelit dining room is perfect for locked-eyes-over-a-cocktail time.

Dora (☎ 081 68 05 19; Via Ferdinando Palasciano 30; meals from €40) At the top of yet another skinny washing-hung street, Dora's exterior looks remarkably mundane. In fact, this is one of Naples' most famous seafood restaurants and is always chock-full. Surrounded by breezy blue-and-white tiles and old nautical memorabilia, tuck into dishes like *frittura di pesce* (fried fish) and exceptional fresh prawns.

Bersagliera (☎ 081 764 60 16; Borgo Marinaro 10-11; meals about €40; ✆ Wed-Sun & dinner Tue) Dating

CAMPANIA

from 1923, the palatial dining room with its magnificent carved ceiling has a photo gallery of star diners including Ingrid Bergman and Sophia Loren. Whet your palate on the clam and mussel soup, followed by *taglierini* (fine ribbon pasta) with baby octopus, black olives and tomatoes, or risotto with gorgonzola. There are dreamy views of the bay from the elegant terrace.

La Cantinella (☎ 081 764 86 84; Via Cuma 42; meals about €45) Arguably Naples' most famous restaurant, La Cantinella, with linen-dressed tables and professional service, is famed for its creative approach to classic recipes. Choose from a stomach- (and wallet-) grumbling menu that includes wonderful dishes such as *tagliata di manzon* (entrecôte and rocket in a spicy aromatic sauce). The lengthy and interesting wine list yields some excellent quaffs.

Amor e Fantasia (☎ 081 764 70 40; Via Raffaele Morghen 12; meals about €20; ☽ Wed-Mon) On a lively pedestrian street close to the sea, this restaurant may sound like an S&M club, but the only fantasy you can expect here is its signature dish, *scaloppina fantasy*, a kind of glorified English fry-up with sausage and smoked cheese (instead of chips) which is belly-filling and good. The outside seating has a summer Mediterranean feel with its red geraniums and palms.

DRINKING
Intra Moenia (☎ 081 29 07 20; Piazza Bellini 70) Arty, literary, left-leaning with a mixed gay and hetero clientele, Intra Moenia is a great place to pass an hour or two pondering one of Naples' more beautiful piazze. It also has a small bookshop and Internet access.

Caffè dell'Epoca (☎ 081 29 17 22; Via Santa Maria di Costantinopoli 81-82; ☽ Mon-Sat) Across the road from Piazza Bellini, next to a newspaper kiosk, this stylish café has been serving its wonderful coffee since 1886.

Caffè Gambrinus (☎ 081 41 41 33; Via Chiaia 12) Naples' oldest and most stylish café (with, perhaps, the oldest and grumpiest waiters), Caffè Gambrinus remains the haunt of artists, intellectuals and musicians. The classic Liberty interior also has a counter selling delicious cakes and pastries.

Bar Lazzarella (☎ 081 551 00 05; Calata Trinità Maggiore 7-8) A popular watering hole just off Piazza del Gesù Nuovo, this is an ideal spot to watch the night-time crowds drift by.

ENTERTAINMENT
To check out the club and music scene, pick up the monthly *Qui Napoli* at the tourist offices or a local newspaper. You can buy tickets for most sporting and cultural events at **Box Office** (☎ 081 551 91 88; Galleria Umberto I 15-16). Ask here or at the tourist office about what's happening during your stay.

Each May the city authorities organise *Maggio dei Monumenti*, a month of concerts and cultural activities in various museums and monuments around town; most of these are free. From May until September there are also open-air concerts in various locations. The tourist offices have details.

Nightclubs & Live Music
Young, hip Neapolitans tend to loaf around the city's many piazze, particularly Piazza del Gesù Nuovo and Piazza San Domenico Maggiore, before moving onto the clubs. Most of the bars spill out onto the pavement, especially these days given Italy's strict no-smoking policy.

Kinky Bar (☎ 081 552 15 71; Via Cisterna dell'Olio 21) Not what you might expect, this reggae bar attracts a lively, mainly student crowd. In summer the Kinky crew organises beachside parties and reggae concerts.

Velvet Zone (☎ 347 810 73 28; Via Cisterna dell'Olio 11; admission & 1st drink about €10; ☽ 11pm-6am) Different night, different sound; you'll hear an eclectic mix of hip-hop, rock, techno, pop and more here.

New Age Disco (☎ 081 29 58 08; Via Atri 36; admission €8; ☽ 10pm-2am Tue-Sun) Something of a gay favourite, this place bangs out everything from '80s revival music to industrial and techno.

Club Live Music (Salita della Grotta 10) In an evocative setting burrowed into the hillside in Mergellina, this club generally lives up to its name. It heats up early for Naples with a queue forming by 9.30pm.

Otto Jazz Club (☎ 081 552 43 73; Piazzetta Cariati 23) West of Piazza Trento e Trieste, this is a long-established place that mostly features Neapolitan jazz.

Palapartenope (☎ 081 570 68 06; Via Barbagallo 115) Given its size, Naples has a feeble choice of live-music venues; most of the bigger acts play at the big, if bland, Palapartenope, which seats over 8000.

Arenile di Bagnoli (☎ 081 230 30 50; Via Nuova Bagnoli 10; admission €10; ☽ 10pm-5am May-Sep) This huge complex has several bars and cabanas where you can dance. It's also the venue for the annual Neapolis Rock Festival.

Cinemas
Cinema Amedeo (☎ 081 68 02 66; Via Martucci 69; admission €6.70) shows original-language films on Thursday nights.

Theatre
There are year-round concerts and performances of opera and ballet at **Teatro San Carlo** (☎ 081 797 21 11; Via San Carlo 98; tickets from €20). Unfortunately for visitors, most tickets are sold on a seasonal, subscription basis with relatively few left over for individual purchase. See p623 for more information about this famous opera house.

Sport
It's now a long time since Napoli (the local football team), led by the genius of Maradona, won the national championship, and the team had to fight hard in the 2003–04 season, only to be relegated to Serie C1 due to bankruptcy. They have since been bailed out by Italian film producer, Aurelio De Laurentis, and a promotion back to Serie B seems likely by the 2006 season. Home matches are played at the **Stadio San Paolo** (ticket information ☎ 081 239 56 23; Piazzale Vincenzo Tecchio) in the western suburb of Mostra d'Oltremare, usually on Sunday. If the opposition's any good tickets are very hard to come by. To get there take the metro to Campi Flegrei.

SHOPPING
Neapolitans like to shop almost as much as they like to eat. And, in this city they can happily combine both; the open-air markets are some of the best in Italy, as are the numerous delicatessens and *pasticcerie*. Would-be *limoncello* fans can have a free taste at **Limonè** (☎ 081 29 94 29; Piazza San Gaetano 72), where it's made on the premises using traditional methods.

Naples is world-renowned for its gold and Christmas items such as *presepi* and *pastori* (shepherds). The Nativity scenes can take on huge proportions, becoming fantastic models of the whole of Bethlehem. Most artisans are in Spaccanapoli, in particular along Via San Gregorio Armeno. The tiny objects and figurines range from the sublime to the supremely kitsch. You can buy an exquisite hand-carved Virgin Mary, a tiny roast pig, a baby Jesus with a flashing halo or go all-out with a 25-piece biblical scene complete with running water!

The city's more exclusive shops are in Santa Lucia, behind Piazza del Plebiscito, along Via Chiaia to Piazza dei Martiri and down towards the waterfront.

If you want to avoid much of the chaos and energy on the streets (not easy in Naples), don't hit the main shopping strips on a Saturday morning. And for the best bargains and one-of-a-kind deals, stick to the smaller shops rather than department stores.

TOP FIVE SHOPPING STRIPS

- **Via Toledo** – head for the grander southern pedestrianised end of the avenue with its swanky Galleria Umberto I, classy shops, and dressed-to-be-seen strollers.
- **Via dei Tribunali** – just a few hundred metres long but the stretch between Via San Paolo and Via Atri with its colourful neighbourhood shops has real earthy appeal. These include the butcher, baker, fishmonger, deli, newsagent, plus a couple of churches, much-loved restaurants, fruit and veg stalls, baby-wear shop and, to round it all off, a funeral parlour.
- **Via Chiaia** – another love-to-shop strip with cute boutiques, high-fashion shops, fancy jewellers, homewares stores and upper-crust delis.
- **Via San Gregorio Armeno** – a concentrated double line of workshops and stores selling Naples' traditional Nativity figurines located off Via dei Tribunali at Piazza San Gaetano. Watch the number of zeros on the price tag; they can be surprisingly pricey for something so itsy.
- **Via Calabritto** – all the big names in the designer world cosy up together in this Beverly Hills–style pedestrian street, including Armani, Louis Vuitton, Gucci, Spatarelli, Tod's, Cartier, Cesare Paciotti and Valentino. Window shopping just doesn't get any better than this. To get here, head for Piazza dei Martiri (bus C25) and turn left by Piazza Calabritto.

CAMPANIA

GETTING THERE & AWAY

Air

Capodichino airport (NAP; ☎ 081 789 62 59; www
.gesac.it), about 8km northeast of the city centre, is southern Italy's main airport, linking
Naples with most Italian and several major
European cities.

Airlines represented:

Air Berlin (☎ 0180 573 78 00; www.airberlin.de) Has
weekly flights from Naples to Hanover in August and
September.

Air France (☎ 848 88 44 66; www.airfrance.it in Italian)
Daily to Paris.

Alitalia (☎ 081 709 33 33, international flights ☎ 848
86 56 42) Internal flights and international connections via
Rome and Milan.

British Airways (☎ 848 81 22 66; www.ba.com) Daily
to London Gatwick.

British Midland (☎ 0870 607 05 55; www.flybmi.com)
Regular flights from Edinburgh, Glasgow, Heathrow &
Manchester.

Easyjet (☎ 0871 750 01 00; www.easyjet.com) Daily to
London Stansted, Basel (Switzerland), Berlin and Paris.

Boat

Ferries and hydrofoils leave for Capri, Sorrento, Ischia, Procida and Forio from Molo
Beverello (the jetty) in front of the Castel
Nuovo. Note that ferry and hydrofoil services are affected by sea conditions, which
frequently lead to last-minute cancellations.

Longer-distance ferries for destinations
like Palermo, Cagliari, Milazzo, the Aeolian
Islands and Tunisia leave from the Stazione
Marittima, next to Molo Beverello.

Alilauro and SNAV also operate hydrofoils to the islands of Ischia, Procida and
Capri from Mergellina.

Qui Napoli lists current timetables for
Bay of Naples services.

Tickets for shorter journeys can be bought
at the ticket booths on Molo Beverello and
at Mergellina. For longer journeys try the offices of the ferry companies or travel agents.

A list of the routes serviced follows. The
fares, unless otherwise stated, are for a high-
season, deck-class single. The reduction for
a return journey isn't significant.

Alilauro (☎ 081 761 10 04; www.alilauro.it in Italian)
Operates hydrofoils to Ischia (€12) and Forio (€13).

Caremar (☎ 081 551 38 82; www.caremar.it in Italian)
Serves Capri (ferry/hydrofoil €5.60/10.50), Ischia
(€5.60/10.50) and Procida (€4.50/7.60).

Linee Lauro (☎ 081 552 28 38; www.lineelauro.it in
Italian) Linked with Alilauro, it has ferries to Ischia (€8)

and a year-round service at least weekly to Tunis in Tunisia
(deck class €82 to €125, *poltrona* or airline-style seat €88
to €128, bed in shared cabin €100 to €134). It also has
direct runs to/from Sardinia and Corsica in summer. Fares
for the latter two destinations are deck class €36 to €75,
bed in shared cabin €50 to €90.

Metro del Mare (☎ 199 44 66 44; www.metrodelmare
.com) This relatively new service operates ferries along
the coast to Sorrento (€4), Amalfi (€9), Positano (€8) and
Capri (€8).

Navigazione Libera del Golfo (NLG; ☎ 199 44 66 44;
www.navlib.it in Italian) Runs hydrofoils to/from Capri (€12)
year-round and ferries to/from Amalfi (€9, summer only).

Siremar (☎ 081 580 03 40; www.siremar.it in Italian) Part
of the Tirrenia group, Siremar operates boats to the Aeolian
Islands and Milazzo (€43.88). The service is up to six times a
week in summer, dropping by a third in the low season.

SNAV (☎ 081 428 51 11; www.snav.it) Runs hydrofoils
to Capri (€12), Procida (€8.80) and Ischia (€12). In summer
there are daily services to the Aeolian Islands. SNAV also
operates Sicilia Jet (€31 to €68.50), which foams down the
coast to Palermo daily from mid-April to September.

Tirrenia (☎ 199 12 31 99; www.tirrenia.it) Has a weekly
boat to/from Cagliari (deck class €26 to €32, cabin with
shower €56 to €76). The service increases to twice weekly
in summer.

Bus

Most buses for Italian and some European
cities leave from Piazza Garibaldi in front of
Stazione Centrale. Check destinations carefully or ask at the information kiosk in the
centre of the piazza because there are no
signs.

Maco (☎ 080 310 51 85) has buses to Bari (€20,
three hours). **Miccolis** (☎ 099 735 37 54) runs to
Taranto (€14.25, four hours), Lecce (€24,
5½ hours) and Brindisi (€21.50, five hours),
while **CLP** (☎ 081 531 17 07) serves Foggia (€9.50,
two hours), Perugia (€28, 1¾ hours) and also
Assisi (€30, 4¾ hours).

You can buy tickets and catch **SITA** (☎ 081
552 21 76; www.sita-on-line.it in Italian) buses either
from the port, Varco Immacolatella, or from
Via G Ferraris, near Stazione Centrale; you
can also buy tickets at **Bar Clizia** (Corso Arnaldo
Lucci 173).

Within Campania, SITA runs buses to
Pompeii (€2.20, 40 minutes) and several
other towns on the Amalfi Coast, including
Amalfi (€9, 2¼ hours), Positano (€8, two
hours) and Salerno (by motorway).

Casting wider, SITA also links Naples
with Bari (€20, three hours) and operates a
service to Germany, including to Dortmund

(€110) via Munich and Stuttgart (both €88), Frankfurt (€97) and Düsseldorf (€110.50).

Car & Motorcycle

Naples is on the major north–south Autostrada del Sole, numbered A1 (north to Rome and Milan) and A3 (south to Salerno and Reggio di Calabria). The A30 skirts Naples to the northeast, while the A16 heads northeast to Bari.

When approaching the city, the motorways meet the Tangenziale di Napoli, a major ring road around the city. The ring road hugs the city's northern fringe, meeting the A1 for Rome and the A2 to Capodichino airport in the east and continuing towards Campi Flegrei and Pozzuoli and the west.

Train

Naples is the rail hub for southern Italy. For information, call ☎ 89 20 21. The city is served by *regionale*, *diretto*, Intercity and super-fast Eurostar trains. They arrive and depart from **Stazione Centrale** (☎ 081 554 31 88) or Metropolitana Stazione Garibaldi (on the lower level). There are up to 30 trains daily to/from Rome.

The **Circumvesuviana**(☎ 081 772 24 44, Corso G Garibaldi), about 400m southwest of Stazione Centrale (take the underpass from Stazione Centrale), operates trains to Sorrento via Ercolano, Pompeii as well as other towns along the coast. There are about 40 trains daily running between 5am and 10.30pm (reduced services on Sunday). A ticket to Pompeii costs €2.30, to Sorrento it's €3.20, while to Herculaneum it costs €1.70.

GETTING AROUND
To/From the Airport

For the airport there are two possibilities: **ANM** (☎ 800 63 95 25) bus No 3S (€1, 30 minutes, every 15 minutes) from Piazza Garibaldi, or the **Alibus** airport bus (€3, 20 minutes, at least hourly) from Piazza Municipio; tickets can be bought on the bus.

A taxi to the centre (Piazza Garibaldi or thereabouts) will set you back about €16.

Bus & Tram

Most city ANM buses operating in the central area depart from and terminate in Piazza Garibaldi. To locate your stop you'll probably need to ask at the information kiosk in the centre of the square.

There are four frequent routes (R1, R2, R3 and R4) that connect to other (less frequent) buses running out of the centre. Some useful services:

R1 From Piazza Medaglie d'Oro to Piazza Carità, Piazza Dante and Piazza Bovio.
R2 From Stazione Centrale, along Corso Umberto I, to Piazza Bovio, Piazza Municipio and Piazza Trento e Trieste.
R3 From Mergellina along the Riviera di Chiaia to Piazza Municipio, Piazza Bovio, Piazza Dante and Piazza Carità.
R4 From San Giovanni to Piazza Vittoria via Piazza del Municipio and Via Nuova Marina.
No 3S From Piazza Municipio along Corso Umberto I to Piazza Garibaldi and on to the airport.
No 24 From the Parco Castello and Piazza Trento e Trieste along Via Toledo, Via Roma to Capodimonte.
No 137R From Piazza Dante north to Capodimonte, further north and then back to Piazza Dante.
No 201 From Stazione Centrale to the Museo Archeologico Nazionale and on to Piazza Municipio and Via San Carlo.
No 404 destra A night bus operates from midnight to 5am (hourly departures) from Stazione Centrale through the city centre to the Riviera di Chiaia and on to Pozzuoli, returning to Stazione Centrale.
Tram No 1 Operates from east of Stazione Centrale, through Piazza Garibaldi, the city centre and along the waterfront to Piazza della Vittoria.
Tram No 29 Travels from Piazza Garibaldi to the city centre along Corso G Garibaldi.

Up-to-date timetables can be found in the *Qui Napoli* free guide available from the tourist office.

Cable-Car Railway

Three of Naples' four cable-car railways connect downtown with Vomero:
Funicolare Centrale Ascends from Via Toledo to Piazza Fuga.
Funicolare di Chiaia Travels from Via del Parco Margherita to Via D Cimarosa.
Funicolare di Montesanto Climbs from Piazza Montesanto to Via Raffaele Morghen.

The fourth, Funicolare di Mergellina, connects the waterfront at Via Mergellina with Via Manzoni. Giranapoli tickets are valid for one trip only on the cable-car railways.

Car & Motorcycle

The constant honk of impatient motorists, the blue lights of ambulances and police cars flashing past, the car behind a constant 10cm from your rear end, one-way streets and traffic lights that nobody ever observes –

forget driving in Naples unless you have a death wish. Park your car at one of the car parks, most of which are staffed, and walk around the city centre. The two main car parks are well signposted and located at Stazione Centrale (Piazza Garibaldi) and at the main port, Stazione Marittima.

In addition to the anarchic driving, car theft is a major problem in Naples.

Both **Avis** (☎ 081 761 13 65; Corso Arnaldo Lucci 203) and **Hertz** (☎ 081 20 62 28; Via G Ricciardi 5) have offices at the airport and near Stazione Centrale. Or try the national company **Maggiore** (☎ 081 552 19 00), which has branches within both the station and the airport.

It's impossible to hire a moped in Naples because of the high incidence of theft.

Metro

Naples' **metro** (www.metro.na.it in Italian) is being extended and by 2006 should cover Corso Umberto I and Piazza Municipio, with a line to the airport due for completion in 2007. By 2011, 10 different metro lines should be operating throughout the city, including a line that will link the centre with Capodimonte. Currently there are just two lines.

Linea 1 Runs north from Piazza Dante, stopping at Museo (for Piazza Cavour and line two), Salvator Rosa, Cilea, Piazza Vanvitelli, Piazza Medaglie d'Oro and seven stops beyond.

Linea 2 Runs from Gianturco, just east of Stazione Centrale, with stops at Piazza Garibaldi (for Stazione Centrale), Piazza Cavour, Montesanto, Piazza Amedeo, Mergellina, Piazza Leopardi, Campi Flegrei, Cavaleggeri d'Aosta, Bagnoli and Pozzuoli.

To reach Cuma (€1.70) take Linea 2 to Montesanto and change to the Circumflegrea line. Cuma is the second-last stop on this line. There are frequent daily services.

Public Transport

Naples has a single-ticket system that covers all public transport. Tickets must be validated before travel via a stamping machine that will print the date and time. There are two types of ticket: UnicoNapoli (Naples only) and UnicoCampania, which covers the surrounding areas. The UnicoNapoli single trip costs €1 and is valid for one hour, a day ticket costs €3 and a weekend ticket €9. UnicoCampania tickets work on a zone system, varying between €1 and €5.90 depending on distance. You can buy tickets at stations, ANM booths and tobacconists.

Taxi

Official taxis are white, metered and bear the Naples symbol, the Pulcinella (with his distinctive white cone-shaped hat and long hooked nose), on their front doors. There are taxi stands at most of the city's main piazze or you can call one of the five taxi cooperatives such as **Napoli** (☎ 081 556 44 44) or **Consortaxi** (☎ 081 552 52 52). There's a baffling range of supplements: €2.10 flag fee, €1.60 extra on Sundays and holidays, €2.10 more between 10pm and 7am, €0.50 for every piece of luggage in the boot (trunk) and €1.60 for transporting a small animal (so leave your gerbil at home). Because of traffic delays, even a short trip may end up costing more than you anticipated. Always ensure the meter is on.

AROUND NAPLES

CAMPI FLEGREI

The area west of Naples is called the Campi Flegrei (Phlegraean – or 'Fiery' – Fields), a classical term for the volcanic activity that has made it one of the globe's most geologically unstable areas. It was partly through the Campi Flegrei, which include the long-settled towns of Pozzuoli, Baia and Cuma, that Greek civilisation arrived in Italy. The poet Homer believed the area to be the entrance to Hades, fiery Hell, and Virgil wrote of it in the *Aeneid*. St Paul also briefly put in here and found time to give a sermon. Now part of suburban Naples, it retains several reminders of the ancient Greeks and Romans. Easily accessible by public transport or car, it makes a worthwhile day visit.

Pozzuoli

The first town that emerges beyond Naples' dreary suburbs is Pozzuoli, which is not much of an improvement. However, there are some impressive Roman ruins here and the town has a suitably illustrious history. Established by the Greeks in 530 BC and later renamed Puteoli (Little Wells) by the Romans, Pozzuoli was once one of the Mediterranean's most important ports.

The **tourist office** (☎ 081 526 66 39; Piazza Matteotti 1a; 9am-3.30pm) is beside the Porta Napoli gate, a five-minute walk downhill from the metro station. Ask for the information-heavy brochure, *Welcome to Campi Flegrei*.

It's also worth investing €4 in a cumulative ticket that covers the Tempio di Serapide, the Solfatara crater and the archaeological sites of Baia and Cuma.

Just east of the port, you can gaze down upon the **Tempio di Serapide** (Temple of Serapis), so-named because a statue of the Egyptian god Serapis was found among its ruins. In fact it was the town market with, archaeologists reckon, skilfully designed toilets at either side of the eastern apse. It has been badly damaged over the centuries by seismic activity, which raises and lowers the ground level over long periods. As a result, the church of **Santa Maria delle Grazie**, some 400m away, is sinking at a rate of around 2cm a year.

Head northeast along Via Rosini to the ruins of the **Anfiteatro Flavio** (☎ 081 526 60 07; Via Terracciano 75; admission €4; 9am-1hr before sunset Wed-Mon), dating from the 1st century BC and reasonably well preserved. This is the third-largest amphitheatre in Italy, with seating for over 20,000 spectators, and it could be flooded, like many amphitheatres, for mock naval battles. In AD 305 seven Christian martyrs were thrown to the wild beasts here. Depressingly they survived only to be beheaded later.

Continue northeast up Via Rosini, which becomes Via Solfatara and leads to the desolate **Solfatara crater** (☎ 081 526 23 41; www.solfatara.it; Via Solfatara 161; admission €5; 8.30am-7pm) after about 2km. To get here you can catch any city bus heading uphill. Known to the Romans as the Forum Vulcani (home of the god of fire), you could almost fry an egg on the steaming grey-yellow ground here. Eerie silent jets or fumaroles are emitted leaving the air pungent with sulphurous fumes. Some of the fumaroles have been covered artificially with brick, creating a clammy, sauna-like environment; others are just left open. Famed as a health resort from classical times up until the 20th century, Pozzuoli has several camp sites which are the nearest ones to Naples (the alternatives are in Pompeii, east of the city). They're much of a muchness and full to the gills in summer. One that stands out from the usual tented villages is **Camping Vulcano Solfatara** (☎ 081 526 74 13; www.solfatara.it; Via Solfatara 161; person/tent/car €9/5.40/6.50; Apr-Oct;), shrouded in greenery and with excellent facilities. It is 750m from the Pozzuoli metro station.

Baia & Cuma

About 7km west of Pozzuoli is **Baia**, once a fashionable Roman bathing resort known for its debauchery. Its extensive remains are now submerged some 100m from the shore. At weekends between April and September you can view them from a glass-bottomed boat run by the **Associazione Aliseo** (☎ 081 526 57 80; admission €7.75). All year-round, however, you can view the elaborate Nymphaeum, complete with statues, jewels, coins and decorative pillars dredged up and reassembled in the small **Museo Archeologico dei Campi Flegrei** (☎ 081 523 37 97; Via Castello; admission €4; 9am-5pm Tue-Sat, 9am-7pm Sun). The vast castle that houses the museum was constructed in the late 15th century by the house of Aragón as a defence against possible French invasion. The castle served as a military orphanage during most of the 20th century. Entry is valid for two days and also includes admission to the ruins at Baia, Pozzuoli and Cuma.

Cuma (known to the ancient Greeks as Cumae), some 10km northwest of Pozzuoli, was the earliest Greek colony on the Italian mainland. Make sure to visit the **Antro della Sibilla Cumana** (Cave of the Cumaean Sybil) within the **Acropoli di Cuma** (☎ 081 854 30 60; Via Montecuma; admission €4; 9am-2hr before sunset), an awesome 130m-deep cave.

Inland and 5km from Pozzuoli is the **Lago d'Averno** (Lake Avernus), one of three crater lakes and the mythical entrance to the underworld where Aeneas descended to meet his father. These days one of its more earthly appeals is as a great spot for a picnic.

Portici

Southeast of Naples in the unlovely suburb of Portici is the **Museo Nazionale Ferroviario Pietrarsa** (☎ 081 567 21 77; www.microsys.it/pietrarsa; Via Pietrarsa; admission free; 9am-2pm), Europe's largest railway museum. Covering 36,000 sq metres, exhibits tell the fascinating story of the construction of Italy's railway network. To get here take the Trenitalia train from Stazione Centrale to Pietrarsa-San Giorgio a Cremano.

Getting There & Away
BOAT

There are frequent car and passenger ferries from Pozzuoli to the islands of Ischia and Procida, run by a variety of companies.

Typical prices are €2.60 to Procida and €5.60 to Ischia – more if you take the hydrofoil option.

BUS
Archeobus (☎ 800 00 16 16) departs hourly from 9am to 7pm from the Tempio di Serapide in Pozzuoli for Baia, Bacoli and Cuma.

CAR & MOTORCYCLE
Take the Tangenziale ring road and swing off at the Pozzuoli exit. Less swift but more scenic is taking Via Francesco Caracciolo along the Naples waterfront to Posillipo, then onto Pozzuoli.

TRAIN
Ferrovia Cumana serves Pozzuoli, Baia and Cuma, while the metro runs as far as Pozzuoli, from where you can take Bus 12 for Cuma.

CASERTA
pop 74,850

Dominating this otherwise nondescript town, 22km north of Naples, is the gigantic Palazzo Reale – a good enough reason to stop here.

Founded in the 8th century by the Lombards on the site of a Roman emplacement atop Monte Tifata, Caserta expanded onto the plains below from the 12th century onwards. The construction of the Bourbons' grand palace assured the town an importance it would otherwise never have known.

Star Wars fans will naturally know that George Lucas used the palace for the interior shots of Queen Amidala's royal residence in both *Star Wars Episode 1: The Phantom Menace* and *Star Wars Episode 2: Attack of the Clones.*

Caserta's **tourist office** (☎ 0823 32 11 37; Palazzo Reale; ☒ 8.30am-3.40pm Mon-Sat) is near the entrance to the palace gardens.

Sights
The **Palazzo Reale** (Royal Palace; ☎ 0823 44 74 47; admission €6; ☒ 8.30am-7pm Tue-Sun), more commonly known as the Reggia di Caserta, is one of Italy's most visited historical sites. It's invaded by tourists in the holidays and by school groups during term time – expect crowds.

Work started on the palace in 1752 after Charles of Bourbon, ruler of Naples, decided he wanted a palace just as big and fancy as Versailles. Neapolitan Luigi Vanvitelli was commissioned for the daunting job and built a palace not just equal to Versailles, but even bigger!

The building, with a façade that stretches 250m and contains 1200 rooms, 1790 windows and 34 staircases, is homage to a vanity of massive proportions. You enter by Vanvitelli's immense staircase and follow a route through the royal apartments, elaborately decorated with tapestries, furniture and crystal. Beyond the library is a room containing a vast collection of *presepi*, composed of hundreds of hand-carved Nativity pieces.

To clear the head afterwards, a walk in the elegant landscaped **grounds** (☒ 8.30am-2hr before sunset Tue-Sun) has a curative effect. They stretch out for some 3km to a waterfall and fountain of Diana and, most famously, to the **Giardino Inglese** (English Garden; tours every hr Tue-Sun) with its intricate pathways, exotic plants, pools and cascades – all very much in fashion at the time. The weary can cover the same ground in a pony and trap (from €5) or for €2 you can bring a bike into the park. A picnic is another good idea. Last entry is one hour before closing.

Your ticket gives entry to the royal apartments, grounds, Giardino Inglese and a **museum** (☒ 8.30am-12.30pm Tue-Sun) of local archaeological finds. Within the palace there's also the **Mostra Terrea Motus** (admission free with Palazzo Reale ticket; ☒ 9am-6pm Tue-Sun), illustrating the 1980 earthquake that devastated the region. At the end of all this you can restore your energy in the palace's cafeteria and restaurant.

There's a good guidebook, the *Royal Palace of Caserta and the Old Town* (from €1 to €5, depending on your bargaining prowess), which the persistent vendors will thrust upon you.

Getting There & Away
CPTC buses connect Caserta with Naples' Piazza Garibaldi (€2.80) about every 30 minutes between 8am and 8pm. Some Benevento services also stop in Caserta. The town is on the main train line between Rome (€10.50) and Naples (€3.10). Both bus and train stations are near the Palazzo Reale entrance, which is signposted from each. If you're driving, follow the signs for 'Reggia'.

AROUND CASERTA

In the surrounding urban spread there are a few historic gems.

In San Leucio, around 2km northwest of Caserta, the Complesso Monumentale Belvedere houses the **Museo di Archaeologia Industriale** (☎ 0823 30 18 17; guided tours €4; ❨ 5 tours per day Mon-Sat). Dating from the late 18th century, this industrial complex was a pet project of King Ferdinand to house the poor and employ them in a silk factory. To get here take bus No 107 from the Caserta train station.

About 10km to the northeast of Caserta (take CPTC bus No 10) lies semi-deserted **Casertavecchia**, the original medieval hill-top town, with its ruined 9th-century castle and magnificent domed 12th-century **cathedral** (❨ 9am-1pm & 3.30-6pm).

The modern city of ancient Capua, **Santa Maria Capua Vetere**, about 12km west of Caserta, was populated by the Etruscans, the Samnites and later the Romans. The ruins include an **amphitheatre** (☎ 0823 79 88 64; admission €4; ❨ 9am-5.30pm Tue-Sun) from the 1st century AD. The largest amphitheatre in Italy after the Colosseum in Rome, it is famous as the starting point for the gladiators' revolt led by Spartacus in 71 BC. There are also the remains of the **Arco d'Adriano** (Hadrian's Arch), under which passed the Via Appia, and a **Mithraic temple** used for initiations into the mysterious Mithraism cult.

Most of the artefacts from the area are now housed in the **Museo Provinciale Campano** (☎ 0823 96 14 02; www.museocampano.it; Via Roma 68; admission €4.30; ❨ 9am-1.30pm Mon Sat, 9am-1 Sun), which is located in the modern town of Capua. Regular CPTC buses run from the Caserta train station to Santa Maria Capua Vetere (€1, 30 minutes).

BENEVENTO

pop 63,232

Surrounded by the green hills of the Apennines, Benevento is a provincial capital about 60km northeast of Naples. After a period as a Lombard duchy, when it controlled much of southern Italy, the town was transferred to the control of the papacy in the 11th century and remained mostly under papal rule until 1860.

The **tourist office** (☎ 0824 31 99 38; Piazza Roma 11; ❨ 8.30am-1.45pm & 2.45-6pm) is well stocked and central.

Sights

The town was heavily bombed in WWII and the Romanesque **cathedral** with its elaborate façade had to be largely rebuilt. Southwest of the cathedral is a restored Roman theatre dating from Hadrian's time. The **Arco di Traiano** (Trajan's Arch), built in AD 114, commemorates the opening of the Via Traiano, while the **obelisk** (Piazza Matteotti) marks the Napoleonic invasion of Italy.

The **Chiesa di Santa Sofia**, near the piazza, adjoins what was once a Benedictine abbey. Founded in AD 762, its main entrance dates from the 12th century. The abbey contains the **Museo Sannio** (☎ 0824 2 18 18; Piazza Santa Sofia; admission €3; ❨ 9am-1pm Tue-Sun), which houses remnants of a temple dedicated to the Egyptian goddess Isis, dating from AD 88, along with some impressive archaeological finds.

Sleeping & Eating

Hotel President (☎ 0824 31 67 16; www.hotelpresident benevento.it; Via GB Perasso 1; s/d €85/120) The most convenient hotel for the museum and town centre, the President's rooms have stripy fabrics, white walls and lots of shiny dark wood. While not desperately characterful, it's comfortable enough. There are conference facilities for briefcase hods.

Teatro Gastronomico (☎ 0824 546 05; Via Traiano 65; meals about €25; ❨ Tue-Sun) Next to the triumphal arch, this place lives up to its name with a flamboyant interior decorated like a stage set. Live it up with delicious gnocchi and saucy pasta dishes.

Getting There & Away

FBN buses (☎ 0824 2 49 61) and **Ferrovia Benevento trains** (☎ 0824 32 07 11) both operate direct services between Benevento and Naples. The train station is a good half-hour slog from the town centre and sights. Buses also link Benevento with Rome and Campobasso. Benevento is on the SS7 (Via Appia) and close to the A16.

AVELLINO & AROUND

About 50km east of Naples is the town of Avellino. The **tourist office** (☎ 0825 7 47 32; www .eptavellino.it in Italian; Piazza Libertà 50) is helpful, although a day in town is plenty.

The mountainous area southwest of Avellino, particularly around the towns of Quindici and Sarno, was the scene of horrific mud slides in 1998, where over 130 people

CAMPANIA

died. The immediate cause was excessive rainfall but irresponsible deforestation of the area and unauthorised building on the surrounding hills also contributed much to the disaster.

The area's main attraction is the vertiginous summit of the **Monte Vergine** and the **sanctuary** devoted to the Virgin Mary, north of the city. A young pilgrim, Guglielmo di Vercelli, erected a church here in the 12th century and so began a tradition of pilgrimage that continues to the present day. His remains were finally laid to rest in the crypt of the modern basilica in 1807.

From the summit (1493m) you can spy Naples on a clear day, and the twisting drive up from Avellino is thrilling – or terrifying – depending on your state of mind. In winter there's limited skiing at Lago di Laceno, about 30km southeast of Avellino.

Avellino has buses to Naples every 20 minutes. In summer buses go from Avellino to Monte Vergine and the sanctuary.

BAY OF NAPLES

CAPRI

pop 7270

Capri is a legendary idyll and it's possibly the most mispronounced place in Italy. Unlike the car, the stress is on the first syllable (*ca*-pri), not the second.

A day-tripper's paradise, Capri is heavily geared to tourism, with up to 5000 visitors a day stepping off the boats in midsummer. It's also a confirmed spot on the Mediterranean celebrity circuit, which means wallet-slimming prices all round. Take the time to explore beyond the effortlessly cool cafés and designer boutiques, however, and Capri retains the Med-island charm of grandiose villas, peeling stucco, overgrown vegetable plots and banks upon banks of brilliantly coloured bougainvillea.

History

Already inhabited in the Palaeolithic period, Capri was subsequently occupied by the Greeks. The Romans, for their part, had taste; Emperor Augustus made the island his private playground and Tiberius retired there in AD 27. Augustus is believed to have founded the world's first palaeontological museum, in the Villa Augustus, to house

fossils and Stone Age artefacts unearthed by his workers.

Tiberius, a victim of historian Tacitus' pen, has gone down in history as something of a fiend on the island and until modern times his name has been equated with evil by the islanders.

Throughout history the people of Capri and Anacapri have been at loggerheads and are always ready to trot out their respective patron saints to ward off the *malocchio* (evil eye) of their rivals.

Orientation

About 5km from the mainland at its nearest point, Capri is a mere 6km long and 2.7km wide. As you approach, there's a great camera shot of Capri town with the dramatic slopes of Monte Solaro (589m) to the west.

All hydrofoils and ferries arrive at the Marina Grande, a commercialised transport hub. Buses chug between the port and the towns of Capri and Anacapri, and a cable car links the marina with Capri town (see p648 for more details on getting around). Otherwise, follow Via Marina Grande for a twisting 2.25km calf-wrenching climb. Turn left (east) at the junction with Via Roma for the centre of Capri town or right (west) for Via Provinciale di Anacapri, eventually becoming Via G Orlandi as it reaches the town of Anacapri.

Information

EMERGENCY

Police station (Map p644; ☎ 081 837 72 45; Via Roma 70, Capri)

INTERNET ACCESS

Capri Internet Point (Map p643; ☎ 081 837 32 83; Via De Tommaso 1, Anacapri; per hr €4) Also sells international newspapers.

INTERNET RESOURCES

Anacapri Life (www.anacapri-life.com) Offers a fairly good overview of shops, hotels and sights with links to useful sites for events, transport etc.

Capri.net (www.capri.net) A comprehensive guide to accommodation on Capri.

Capri Tourism (www.capritourism.com) The official tourist board website, with lots of useful stuff like restaurants, special events and transport.

MEDICAL SERVICES

Hospital (☎ 081 838 11 11; Marina Piccola 2)

CAPRI

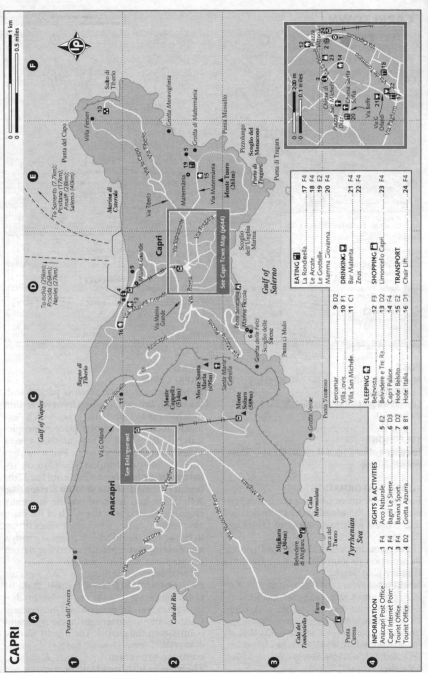

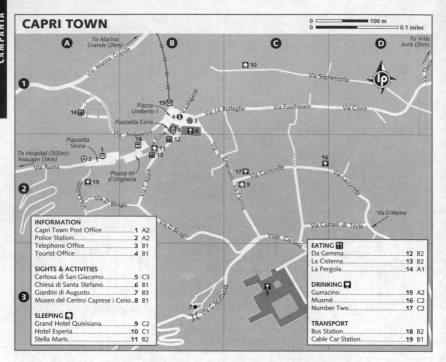

CAPRI TOWN

INFORMATION	
Capri Town Post Office	1 A2
Police Station	2 A2
Telephone Office	3 B1
Tourist Office	4 B1
SIGHTS & ACTIVITIES	
Certosa di San Giacomo	5 C3
Chiesa di Santa Stefano	6 B1
Giardini di Augusto	7 B3
Museo del Centro Caprese i Cerio	8 B1
SLEEPING	
Grand Hotel Quisisiana	9 C2
Hotel Esperia	10 C1
Stella Maris	11 B2

EATING	
Da Gemma	12 B2
La Cisterna	13 B2
La Pergola	14 A1
DRINKING	
Gurracino	15 A2
Musmé	16 C2
Number Two	17 C2
TRANSPORT	
Bus Station	18 B2
Cable Car Station	19 B1

POST

Anacapri post office (Map p643; ☎ 081 837 10 15; Via
De Tommaso 8)
Capri town post office (Map p644; ☎ 081 978 52 11;
Via Roma 50)

TELEPHONE

Telephone office (Map p644; ☎ 081 837 54 47; Piazza
Umberto 1, Capri)

TOURIST INFORMATION

Each tourist office can provide a free stylised map of the island and a more detailed
one (€0.80) with town plans of Capri and
Anacapri.

For accommodation listings and general
information pick up a copy of *Capri È* and
Guida Agli Alberghi.
Tourist office Marina Grande (Map p643; ☎ 081 837
06 34; ♥ 8.30am-8.30pm Jun-Sep, 9am-1pm & 3.30-
6.45pm Mon-Sat Oct-May); Capri town (Map p644; ☎ 081
837 06 86; Piazza Umberto I; ♥ 8.30am-8.30pm
Jun-Sep, 9am-1pm & 3.30-6.45pm Mon-Sat Oct-May);
Anacapri (Map p643; ☎ 081 837 15 24; Via G Orlandi 59;
♥ 8.30am-8.30pm Jun-Sep, 9am-3pm Mon-Sat Oct-Dec
& Mar-May)

Sights
CAPRI TOWN

In high season, Capri town is packed with
the stylish and rich, ranging from wafer-thin
trendy teens to Gucci-clad grans with a Pek-
ingese accessory. The best place to people-
watch is from one of the cafés on Piazza
Umberto I (also known as the Piazzetta), but
stick to one drink unless you plan on re-
mortgaging your house. Check out the 17th-
century domed **Chiesa di Santo Stefano** (Map
p644; ♥ 8am-8pm) here, where the languidly
reclining patricians to the south of the main
altar seem to mirror some of the roués sitting
in the square. Beside it is a reliquary with a
saintly bone that reputedly saved Capri from
the plague in the 19th century.

Head down Via D Birago or Via V Emanu-
ele to **Certosa di San Giacomo** (Map p644; ☎ 081 837
62 18; Viale Certosa; admission free; ♥ 9am-2pm Tue-
Sat, 9am-1pm Sun), an impressive 14th-century
Carthusian monastery with cloisters and
paintings in the chapel. The nearby **Giardini
di Augusto** (Gardens of Augustus; Map p644; ♥ sunrise-
sunset) were founded by Caesar Augustus.
The view is just breathtaking, looking out

to sea over the **Isole Faraglioni** (Map p643), limestone pinnacles which are home to a rare blue lizard. The **Museo del Centro Caprese i Cerio** (Map p644; ☎ 081 837 66 81; Piazzetta Cerio 5; admission €2.60; ☼ 10am-1pm Tue, Wed, Fri & Sat, 3-7pm Thu) has a library with some English books and journals about the island, as well as a fossil collection.

VILLA JOVIS & AROUND

A stiff hour's walk east of the town centre along Via Tiberio leads to the one-time residence of Emperor Tiberius, **Villa Jovis** (Jupiter's Villa; Map p643; ☎ 081 837 06 34; Via Tiberio; admission €2; ☼ 9am-1hr before sunset), also known as the Palazzo di Tiberio. The largest and also best-preserved of the island's Roman villas, it was a vast pleasure complex in its heyday and included imperial quarters, entertainment areas, grand halls, gardens and woodland.

The stairway behind the villa leads to the **Salto di Tiberio** (Tiberius' Leap; Map p643); Tiberius' simple solution for getting rid of his exes (girls and boys, the younger the better) was to throw them off the cliffs at the end of the garden.

A pleasant walk down Via Matermania leads to the **Arco Naturale** (Map p643), a rock arch formed by the pounding sea. Doubling back to the first crossroads, you can turn left down a series of steps and follow the path south, then west, back into town, enjoying heady views of Punta di Tragara and Isole Faraglioni.

ANACAPRI & AROUND

Many visitors are lured to **Villa San Michele** (Map p643; ☎ 081 837 14 01; Viale Axel Munthe; admission €5; ☼ 9am-6pm May-Sep, 10.30am-3.30pm Nov-Feb, 9.30am-4.30pm Mar, 9.30am-5pm Apr & Oct) by the words of its most famous inhabitant, Swedish doctor Axel Munthe. The eclectic house he built on the ruined site of a Roman villa remains immortalised in his book the *Story of San Michele*. Just north of Piazza Vittoria, the villa houses Roman sculptures from the period of Tiberius' rule (AD 14–37). The pathway behind offers superb views over Capri. The (often closed) stairway of 800 steps leading from the town was the only link between Anacapri and the rest of the island until the construction of the mountain road in the 1950s, which helps explain somewhat the historic rift between the two towns.

From Piazza Vittoria, take the **chair lift** (Map p643; lift €6; ☼ 9.30am-sunset Mar-Oct, 10.30am-3pm Nov-Feb) to the top of **Monte Solaro** (Map p643), with its stunning views. From Anacapri a bus runs regularly to **Faro**, which is less crowded and boasts one of Italy's tallest lighthouses.

GROTTA AZZURRA

Capri's craggy coast is studded with more than a dozen sea caves, none as stunning, or as famous, as the **Grotta Azzurra** (Blue Grotto; Map p643; admission €4; ☼ 9am-1hr before sunset). Two Germans, writer Augustus Kopisch and painter Ernst Fries, are credited with discovering the grotto in 1826. Further research, however, revealed Emperor Tiberius had built a quay here around AD 30, complete with a *nymphaeum* (shrine to the water nymph) – an interesting décor idea for your bathroom, but sadly no longer visible here.

Far from being an overblown tourist attraction, the grotto's mysterious iridescent blue light is pure magic. Apparently it is caused by the refraction of sunlight off the sides of the 1.3m-high entrance, coupled with the reflection off the white sandy bottom.

Boats leave to visit the cave from the Marina Grande (€16.30), including the rowing boat in (€4.30) and admission fee (€4); allow a good hour. The singing 'captains' are included in the price, so there's no need to tip. The grotto is closed if the sea is too choppy, so before embarking check that it is open with the nearby Marina Grande tourist office (see opposite).

Activities

Capri is water-sports heaven. For scuba diving, contact **Sercomar** (Map p643; ☎ 081 837 87 81; www.caprisub.com; Via Colombo 64, Marina Grande). **Bagni Le Sirene** (Map p643; ☎ 081 837 69 70; Marina Piccola) hires out canoes and motorised dinghies and can take you water-skiing. For catamarans and sailboards, contact **Banana Sport** (Map p643; ☎ 081 837 51 88; Via Marina Grande 12). Expect to pay around €200 for a motorised dinghy for the day and €110 for a three-dive package.

The main places to swim are **Bagno di Tiberio**, a small inlet west of Marina Grande, where the emperor himself dipped, and a rocky area at Marina Piccola. There are also plenty of hiking opportunities. Contact the tourist offices (opposite) for details of routes, which are mostly classed as moderate to easy.

Festivals & Events

The island's main secular festival, the **Gruppo Folkloristico Caprese** takes place from 1 to 6 January, with local folk groups performing in Piazza Diaz, Anacapri and in Piazza Umberto I.

Sleeping

Hotel space is at a premium in summer and many places close in winter. There are few really cheap rooms at any time of the year; however, if you are able to cough up a few extra euros, there are some magnificent options in the middle to upper-price range, including a couple of Italy's most luxurious hotels.

Camping is forbidden and offenders are often prosecuted. You might want to inquire at the tourist offices about renting a room in a private home.

MARINA GRANDE

Hotel Italia (Map p643; ☎ 081 837 06 02; fax 081 837 03 78; Via Marina Grande 204; s/d €90/100; ☺ Apr-Nov) A homely hotel with grandma around and a hallway of family knick-knacks. Rooms have high ceilings, antiques and a welcoming spare-room feel. There are pretty shady gardens and the use of the pool across the street.

Belvedere e Tre Re (Map p643; ☎ 081 837 03 45; www.belvedere-tre-re.com; Via Marina Grande 238; s/d €100-130; ☺ Apr-Nov; ☒ P) Five minutes' walk uphill from the port, this hotel could do with an update (tossing out the plastic flowers would be a start). On the plus side, the rooms are generous with beach views and there's a sun-bronzing terrace on the roof.

CAPRI

Hotel Belsito (Map p643; ☎ 081 837 87 50; www.hotel belsito.com; Via Matermania 9-11; s/d €80/180; ☒) The colour of aged wine, this low-rise hotel is a real star. There are dreamy views of the Marina Piccola from the light, airy rooms, plus a shady terrace restaurant. Located between the Piazzetta and the Arco Naturale, it's a delightful stroll to both.

Hotel Esperia (Map p644; ☎ 081 837 02 62; fax 081 837 09 33; Via Sopramonte 41; s/d with breakfast €140/170; ☒) The peeling façade, grand columns and giant urns lend an air of faded elegance to this 19th-century villa. Rooms are large and may be a bit floral for some. There are good-sized terraces with sea views, plus a restaurant.

Grand Hotel Quisisiana (Map p644; ☎ 081 837 07 88; www.quisi.com; Via Camerelle 2; s/d with breakfast from €280/330; ☒ ☐ ☒) At Capri's most prestigious address, a short strut from the Piazzetta, you can up the overnight cost to €800 for a palatial duplex. The Quisisiana compound includes pools, subtropical gardens, restaurants and bars. There's a fitness centre and spa in case you get bored with playing idle rich.

Stella Maris (Map p644; ☎ 081 837 04 52; fax 081 837 86 62; Via Roma 27; s/d €60/95) This dowdy small hotel gets away with its pricing due to its central position, just off the classy Piazzetta. The rooms are small and basic. The owner's son speaks English and can be a bit more welcoming than weary old dad.

ANACAPRI

Capri Palace (Map p643; ☎ 081 978 01 11; Via Capodimonte 2b, Anacapri; s/d with breakfast from €230/290; ☒ P ☒) Overlooking the Bay of Naples, this recently renovated luxury hotel is a real special-occasion place. The interior is classic Mediterranean and some rooms have their own terraced garden and private pool. The constant piped classical music could irritate those seeking peace and quiet.

Bellavista (Map p643; ☎ 081 837 14 63; www.bella vistacapri.com; Via Orlandi 10; s/d €90/164; ☺ Apr-Oct; ☒ ☒) A grand dame among hotels here, Bellavista is over 100 years old. The rooms are large and have love 'em or hate 'em '60s-style tile floors with enormous leaf or flower patterns. There are tennis courts and a large formal restaurant with wonderful views.

Eating

Unlike most popular resorts, it's hard to find a bad restaurant here but then, this *is* Italy, and Capri has long catered to the more discerning tourist. The island's culinary gift to the world is *insalata caprese*, a salad of fresh tomato, basil and mozzarella bathed in olive oil.

Many restaurants, like the hotels, close in the winter.

CAPRI

La Pergola (Map p644; ☎ 081 837 74 12; Via Traversa Lo Palazzo 2; meals about €22; ☺ Thu-Tue Nov-Sep) The owner Giancarlo is also the chef – always a good sign. The food is excellent and innovative with dishes like green ravioli in a lemon-cream sauce (€7); the lemons are grown right here. There's a vine-shaded terrace with town and sea views. It's hard to find: persevere and follow the signs.

La Cisterna (Map p644; ☎ 081 837 56 20; Via M Serafina 5; pizzas from €5, meals about €22; ☉ Mar-Jan) The kitsch artwork on the walls somehow adds to the unpretentiousness of this trattoria, which has been family-run for some 18 generations. Solid traditional dishes such as pasta with beans and veal cutlet braised in lemon feature. Rumbling tummies won't go hungry: the portions are huge.

Le Grottelle (Map p643; ☎ 081 837 57 19; Via Arco Naturale 13; full meals about €25; ☉ Apr-Oct) For a touch of grotto dining, Le Grottelle is the place. Tucked inside a couple of small caves 200m before the Arco Naturale (p645), this place is high on atmosphere and has uncomplicated, tasty dishes including grilled fish, chicken and rabbit.

Da Gemma (Map p644; ☎ 081 837 04 61; Via M Serafina 6; meals about €30; ☉ Tue-Sun Mar-Dec) There's a couple of oddities on the menu (such as marmalade omelette) at this famous Capri restaurant that's papered with photographs of diner celebrities such as John Lennon and Graham Greene. One of Capri's originals, it opened 55 years ago and is now run by Gemma's granddaughter. There's an intimate trattoria feel with hanging plants and appealing clutter about the place.

ANACAPRI

La Rondinella (Map p643; ☎ 081 837 12 23; Via G Orlandi 295; full meals about €18) Apparently Graham Greene was a fan of La Rondinella, which has been family run for 50 years. A 10-minute walk from the centre, this place has a relaxed rural feel. There's a tempting antipasti buffet and the salads are generous and good. Chef Michele's *linguine alla ciammura* is a delicious original with a creamy white sauce of anchovies, garlic and parsley.

Le Arcate (Map p643; ☎ 081 837 33 25; Via de Tommaso 24i; meals about €20; ☉ year-round) Le Arcate has a large covered terrace with hanging baskets, sunny yellow tablecloths and terracotta tiles. The discerning reception folk at Capri Palace eat here. Pizzas and pasta dishes are the speciality, the latter including a tasty *tagliatelle* with shrimp and lemon sauce. It's open all year for the locals – another good sign.

Mamma Giovanna (Map p643; ☎ 081 837 20 57; Via Boffe 3-5; meals about €25) With a lovely position on the picturesque Piazza A Diaz, this family-run restaurant dishes up homemade pasta dishes like *pennette* with fresh tomatoes and grilled aubergines, and a lavishly portioned seafood spaghetti.

Drinking
CAPRI

The scene in Capri tends to be expensive and can be surprisingly tacky. Your best bet is to revamp your hip weekend wardrobe (old jeans and a T-shirt simply won't do) and hang out in the central piazze. Alternatively, you can take refuge in one of the numerous watering holes. **Guarracino** (Map p644; ☎ 081 837 05 14; Via Castello 7; ☉ 8pm-4am) is a pleasant spot for a drink.

Shake a leg at the clubs **Musmé** (Map p644; ☎ 081 837 60 11; Via Camerelle 61b) or **Number Two** (Map p644; ☎ 081 837 70 78; Via Camerelle 1), a short stroll down the street and a favourite for cosmetically startled celebs.

ANACAPRI

Sit around in one of the cafés on Piazza A Diaz or shoot pool at **Bar Materita** (Map p643; Via G Orlandi 140). For classier nightlife, glad-rag it down to **Zeus** (Map p643; ☎ 081 837 11 69; Via G Orlandi 103; ☉ 10-5am), which has cabaret and dance music and might just get your blood rushing. Typical cover charges hover around €20 (they accept credit cards).

Shopping

Ceramic tiles and anything lemony are the big sellers. Shops abound, but always make sure to check the quality.

On the lemon front, the island is famous throughout the world for its lemon-scented perfume and *limoncello*.

Limoncello Capri (Map p643; Via Capodimonte 27) This place produces some 70,000 bottles of the lemony tipple annually. It also claims to be the birthplace of *limoncello*. Apparently, the grandmother of current owner Vivica made the tot as an after-dinner treat for the guests in her hotel, some 100 years ago.

The perfumeries are everywhere or, if your ship has come in, you might like to pick up a little number from one of the designer shops on Via Camerelle in Capri town.

Getting There & Away

See Naples (p636) and Sorrento (p669) for details of year-round ferries and hydrofoils to the island. In summertime there's also a

CAMPANIA

hydrofoil service to/from Salerno (€14.50), Positano (€14) and Amalfi (€14.50).

Getting Around

There is no car hire on the island and, between March and October, you can only bring a vehicle here if it's either registered outside Italy or hired at an international airport. It's not advisable, as driving conditions are pretty fraught.

Instead, hop on a **SIPPIC bus** (☎ 081 837 04 20; ticket €1.30, day pass €6.70) which runs from Marina Grande (departing from just west of the pier) to Capri, Anacapri, the Grotta Azzurra and Faro. Buses run between Capri and Anacapri until past midnight. A cable car links Marina Grande with Capri. It is swifter than the bus and also costs €1.30.

From Marina Grande, a taxi ride costs around €15 to Capri and €20 to Anacapri; from Capri to Anacapri costs about €10. Call ☎ 081 837 05 43 in Capri and ☎ 081 837 11 75 in Anacapri. The tourist offices have details of scooter hire.

ISCHIA

pop 18,020

The volcanic outcrop of Ischia is the largest island in the bay. It's an odd combination of bland thermal-spa hotels, filled with elderly Germans, and spectacular scenery with forests, vineyards and picturesque small towns.

Ischia only attracts a fraction of the ice cream–eating, cappuccino-swilling day trippers that head daily for Capri from Naples in summer. Perhaps someone should tell them that the beaches are a lot better here.

History

Ischia was one of the first Greek colonies in the 8th century. The Greeks called the island Pithekoussai after the *pithos* (pottery clay) found there. In 1301 there was a vast eruption of the now-extinct Monte Arso volcano, forcing the inhabitants to flee to the mainland, where many remained permanently.

The Spanish took Ischia, along with Naples, in 1495 and controlled the island until the 18th century when France was in brief occupation, followed by the British. There were fierce battles, including the bombardment of the Castello Aragonese, the scars still evident today. Like so many of these islands during the 19th century, Ischia was a political prison.

Orientation

Ferries dock at Ischia Porto, the main tourist centre. It's about a 2km walk from the pier to Ischia Ponte, which has the atmosphere of an upmarket Naples neighbourhood, its narrow streets lined with all manner of shops, restaurants and cafés.

Information

Bay Watch (☎ 081 333 10 96; Via Iasolino 37) Not a lifeguard operation with Pamela Anderson lookalikes, but it can assist with accommodation and tours.
Ischia Online (www.ischiaonline.it) Excellent Internet resource.
Tourist office (☎ 081 507 42 31; Via Iasolino, Banchina Porto Salvo; ⏰ 9am-2pm & 3-8pm Mon-Sat)

Sights & Activities

In Ischia Ponte the **Castello Aragonese** (☎ 081 99 28 34; admission €8; ⏰ 9.30am-7pm) is a spectacularly situated Aragonese castle complex, comprising a 14th-century cathedral, several smaller churches and a weapons museum.

Whether you have a green thumb (or not), **La Mortella** (☎ 081 98 62 20; Via F Calese 35, Forio; admission €8; ⏰ 9am-7pm Tue, Thu, Sat & Sun Apr-Nov) cannot fail to inspire. Designed by Russell Page, the garden at La Mortella echoes the Moorish gardens of Granada's Alhambra in Spain, with more than 1000 rare and exotic plants from all over the world. The gardens were established by Sir William Walton, the late British composer, and his wife, who made La Mortella their home in 1949. You can drink Fortnum & Mason's tea in the café and classical concerts are held in the gardens every summer.

A fairly strenuous uphill walk from the village of Fontana brings you to the top of **Monte Epomeo** (788m), the island's highest point, with superb views of the Bay of Naples.

Among the island's better beaches is **Lido dei Maronti**, just south of Barano. For exploring the watery depths, contact **Captain Cook** (☎ 335 636 26 30) or **Ischia Diving Center** (☎ 081 98 50 08; Ischia Porto) in Ischia's port, or **Roja Diving Center** (☎ 338 762 01 45) in Sant'Angelo; all have equipment for hire and run courses. A single dive will cost from €30.

Leap on the saddle at **Club Sportivo Ippico** (☎ 081 90 85 18; Via Mario d'Ambra, Forio). Guided treks vary in cost depending on the number of riders, but start from around €24 for two hours.

Sleeping

Most hotels close in winter, and prices normally drop considerably in those that stay open. In addition to the hotels listed below, there are the spa hotels, most of which only take half- or full-board bookings. The tourist office can supply you with a list.

Hotel Conchiglia (☎ 081 99 92 70; Via Chiaia delle Rose; s/d €40/80) An excellent price for this Sant'Angelo location. The rooms are old-fashioned with loads of character – just like owner Gennaro, who met his American wife when she arrived here after a Lonely Planet recommendation. There are balconies, fans, interesting paintings and a good restaurant.

Il Gabbiano (☎ /fax 081 90 94 22; SS Forio-Panza 162, Forio; B&B per person €16; ☷ Apr-Oct) Monastically basic, this hostel is still one of the best around. Near the beach, it has bedrooms sleeping two, four or six, all with balconies and great sea views.

Hotel Semiramis (☎ 081 90 75 11; www.hotelsem iramisischia.com; Spiaggia di Citara, Forio; d with breakfast €100; ☷ Apr-Oct; ☒ ☒) This newish hotel has a tropical-style pool surrounded by palms. Rooms here are large and beautifully tiled in the traditional yellow-and-turquoise pattern. Run by friendly Giovanni and his German wife, the hotel's garden is glorious, with fig trees, vineyards and distant sea views.

Hotel Casa Celestino (☎ 081 99 92 13; www.casa celestino.it; Via Chiaia delle Rose; Sant'Angelo; s/d €90/160, ☷ Jan-Oct; ☒) On the pedestrian walkway down to the headland, this hotel complements the setting perfectly with lashings of brilliant blue paint. The rooms are sparely furnished and enlarged by the spacious balconies with sun-loungers.

Hotel La Sirenella (☎ 081 99 47 43; www.lasirenella .net; Corso Angelo Rizzoli 41, Lacco Ameno; s/d with breakfast €62-124; ☷ Apr-Oct; ☒) This family-owned hotel has recently been done up with classy good taste. You can practically roll out of bed onto the beach here and most rooms have big balconies with sea-and-sand views. Bright primary colour décor gives the place a sunny Med feel.

Mezzatorre Resort & Spa (☎ 081 98 61 11; www .mezzatorre.it; Via Mezzatorre 23, Forio; d from €290; ☒ ☒ ☒) Surrounded by a 2.8-hectare park, this resort oozes luxury. It has all the modern-day facilities, like spa and tennis courts, in a tranquil country-castle setting. The rooms are decorated in earthy colours; some have private garden and Jacuzzi. Check out the

infinity swimming pool above the beach for the ultimate film-star setting.

Camping Internazionale (☎ 081 99 14 49; fax 081 99 14 72; Via Foschini; person/tent/car €9/10/8; ☷ Apr-Sep) Close to Ischia Porto, this is the best choice of the three camp sites on the island. The sites are shady with mature trees.

Eating

La Baia el Clipper (☎ 081 333 42 09; Via Porto 116, Ischia Porto; meals about €40) A young lovers' setting located in the port, La Baia is now run by the second generation and today's catch is proudly displayed at the entrance. Indulge in your dress-code daydreams – it's that kind of place.

Lo Scoglio (☎ 081 99 95 29; Via Cava Ruffano 58, Sant'Angelo; meals about €28) Dramatically jutting out over the sea beside a pretty beach cove, this is a great place for sunsets and seafood. Mussel soup, butterfly noodles with salmon, and grilled bass, are examples of the fishy fare on the menu. Sunday lunchtime is a popular weekly event.

Umberto a Mare (☎ 081 99 71 71; Via Soccorso 1, Forio; mains from €15; ☷ Mar-Dec) In the shadow of the Spanish mission–style Soccorso church, this place has the choice of a café-bar or a more formal restaurant where the menu changes according to the season. A set four-course menu costs €59 or go à la carte with rich mamma-like pasta dishes such as penne with lobster and asparagus.

Getting There & Away

See p636 for details of hydrofoils and ferries. You can catch ferries direct to Capri (€12) and Procida (€3) from Ischia, as well as to Naples (€8) and destinations on the Amalfi Coast.

Getting Around

The main bus station is in Ischia Porto. There are two principal lines: the CS (Circo Sinistra; Left Circle) and CD (Circo Destra; Right Circle), which circle the island in opposite directions, passing through each town and leaving every 30 minutes. Buses pass near all hotels and camp sites. A single ticket, valid for 90 minutes, costs €1.20, while a ticket valid from 6am to 6pm is €4. Taxis and micro-taxis (scooter-engined three-wheelers) are also available.

If you want to hire a car or scooter for the day, there are plenty of rental firms. In

CAMPANIA

addition to hiring out cars (from €32 per day) and mopeds (€25 to €35), **Fratelli del Franco** (☎ 081 99 13 34; Via A De Luca 133) also has mountain bikes (around €10 per day). You can't take a rented vehicle off the island.

PROCIDA
pop 10,770

The confetti pinks, whites and yellows of Procida's tiny cubic houses cluttered along the waterfront are an evocative first introduction to the island. Exploring further does little to detract from that first image.

Procida is the smallest of the main islands in the Bay of Naples and, even in the height of summer, doesn't attract the numbers of tourists welcomed by its more famous neighbours. Nightlife hasn't caught on here yet, either. Procida is an island for those seeking to escape the crowds while still providing a perfect toe-in-the-Med experience.

Orientation & Information

The Marina Grande is the hop-off point for ferries and hydrofoils and forms most of the tourist showcase. Procida's **tourist office** (☎ 081 810 19 68; Via Roma; ⏰ 9.30am-1pm & 3.30-7pm Mon-Sat May-Sep, 9.30am-1pm Mon-Sat Oct-Apr) is next to the Caremar ticket office. However, infinitely more useful is the **Graziella Travel Agency** (☎ 081 896 91 91; Via Roma 117), nearby, which can help with accommodation and boat trips and has a much better free map. A useful website that includes accommodation and ferry timetables is www.procida.net.

Sights & Activities

The best way to explore the island is on foot – it's only about 4 sq km – or by bike. However, the island's narrow roads can be clogged with cars – one of its few drawbacks. Don't miss the unspoilt fishing port of **Marina Corricella**, a 10-minute walk from Marina Grande or the swankier **Marina Chiaiolella** with its harbour of yachts, rather than fishing boats.

The 16th-century **Palazzo Reale d'Avalos**, recently used as a prison, dominates the island but is now all but abandoned. More interesting is the **Abbazia San Michele Arcangelo** (☎ 081 896 76 12; Via Terra Murata 89; admission €2; ⏰ 9.45am-12.45pm year-round & 3-5.30pm May-Oct), about a 1km uphill walk from the Marina Grande. Within the complex are a church, a small museum with some arresting paintings, and a honeycomb of catacombs.

The **Procida Diving Centre** (☎ 081 896 83 85; www.vacanzeaprocida.it/framediving01-uk.htm; Via Cristoforo Colombo 6) runs diving courses and hires out equipment. Budget €32 for a single dive and €60 for a full day. You can charter a yacht from **Bluebone** (☎ 081 896 95 94; www.isoladiprocida.it/bluebone; Via Roma 117) for around €550 per person, per week.

Festivals & Events

On Good Friday there's a colourful **procession of the Misteri**. A wooden statue of Christ and the *Madonna Addolorata*, along with lifesized tableaux of plaster and papier mâché illustrating events leading to Christ's crucifixion, are carted across the island. Men dress in blue tunics with white hoods, while many of the young girls dress as the Madonna.

Sleeping

Hotel Casa Gentile (☎ 081 896 75 75; Via Marina Coricella 88; d €95, meals about €25; ⏰ Apr-Sep) It's hard to miss this shocking-pink cubic hotel in desperate need of sun-bleaching. The rooms have cool tiles and green modular-style furniture with fans and TVs. There's a large communal terrace overlooking the picturesque harbour, boat service to the nearby beach and a decent seafood restaurant.

Hotel Celeste (☎ 081 896 74 88; www.hotelceleste.it; Via Rivoli 6, Marina di Chiaiolella; d €72; ⏰ Apr-Sep; 🅿) Overlooking sweet orange groves, this German-run hotel is open-plan and eco-friendly, and features the first solar panels on the island. Rooms are bright and functional, and there's a home-style garden, a solarium and terraces.

Hotel Crescenzo (☎ 081 896 72 55; www.hotelcrescenzo.it; Via Marina di Chiaiolella 33; s/d €70/95, meals about €30; 🅿) There are just 10 rooms here; choose between a view of the bay or a balcony. The blue-and-white décor is suitably nautical and the restaurant out front is popular with a boisterous local crowd.

Camp sites are dotted around the island: the tourist office has a list.

Eating

Graziella (☎ 081 896 74 79; Via Marina Corricella 14; mains about €6; ⏰ Apr-Oct) Graziella offers a memorable dining experience with its bay view, piles of fishing nets, sleek cats and a backdrop of marshmallow-coloured houses. The menu here includes a spicy *penne alla siciliana* (pasta with a spicy tomato and chilli sauce) and grilled chicken with a sweet-chilli sauce.

Osteria del Gallo (☎ 081 810 19 19; Via Roma s/n, Marina Grande; meals about €20) Enjoy no-nonsense *antipasti di mare* (seafood antipasti; €9) and fish dishes. Owner Matteo has the ruddy reassuring look of a well-seasoned fisherman and will give you a good welcome.

Il Galeone (☎ 081 896 96 22; Via Marina Chiaiolella; meals about €25) This large wood-decked restaurant, a seagull swoop from the harbour, has a large, if predictable, menu of fresh off-the-boat *frutti di mare* (seafood). Try the *pesce all'acqua pazza* (fresh fish cooked with tomatoes, garlic and parsley).

Getting There & Around

Procida is linked by boat and hydrofoil to Ischia (€3, 45 minutes), Pozzuoli and Naples (see p636 for more details). There is a limited bus service (€0.80), with four lines radiating from Marina Grande. Bus No L1 connects the port and Marina Chiaiolella. The small open micro-taxis can be hired for two to three hours for about €35, depending on your bargaining ability. Contact the

Graziella Travel Agency (☎ 081 896 91 91; Via Roma 117) for details on bicycle hire.

SOUTH OF NAPLES

HERCULANEUM & ERCOLANO

Ercolano is a dismal Neapolitan suburb 12km southeast of Naples which, ironically, is home to one of Italy's most magnificent excavations – Herculaneum. This former Roman fishing and port town had a population of about 4000 and its position and charm made it a popular resort for wealthy Romans and Campanians. Sadly, developers have ensured that modern Ercolano is swiftly bypassed by blinkered tourists heading straight for the archaeological site.

History

The fate of Herculaneum paralleled that of nearby Pompeii. Destroyed by an earthquake in AD 63, the city was completely submerged in the AD 79 eruption of Mt Vesuvius. The difference was that Herculaneum was buried by a river of volcanic mud, not the *lapilli*

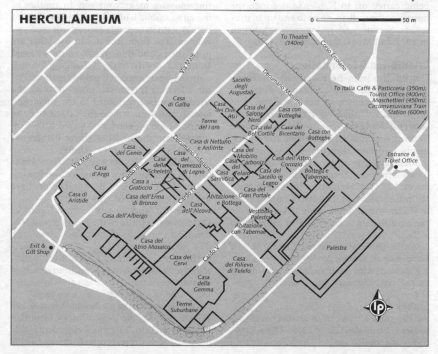

CAMPANIA

CONSTIPATED PIGEONS ONLY PLEASE...

According to local experts, pigeons represent a serious threat to the conservation of the ancient Roman ruins in Herculaneum. Apparently the acidity of their droppings seriously damages the structures and ancient decorated surfaces. They are also constantly pecking at the wooden beams and the carbonised wooden fixtures. The solution may lie in fellow feathered friends: Harris hawks are to be employed to persuade the pigeons to seek an alternative home. Training is a delicate task, however, as the hawks must be sufficiently well fed so as not to attempt to eat the pigeons, but not so overfed that they do not chase them away.

(burning fragments of pumice stone) and ash that rained on Pompeii and helped preserve it. The town was rediscovered in 1709 and amateur excavations were carried out intermittently until 1874, with many finds being carted off to Naples to decorate the houses of the well-to-do or to end up in museums. Serious archaeological work began in 1927 and excavation continues today.

Orientation & Information

Get off the train here dutifully clutching your cut-price double-whammy Pompeii-Herculaneum entrance ticket and you're in for a shock. Unlike Pompeii, there are no souvenir stands or cold-water kiosks here to greet you, just urban squalor and a curious lack of signs directing you to the site.

Resist the urge to turn around and climb back on the train. Instead, head for the main street, Via IV Novembre, which leads from the train station, at the town's eastern edge, to Piazza Scavi and the main ticket office for the excavations – an easy, if dreary, 600m walk.

At the **tourist office** (☎ /fax 081 788 12 43; Via IV Novembre 82; ☺ 9am-2pm Mon-Sat) you can pick up a brochure with an inadequate map of the ruined city, and very little else.

Sights

At the **ruins** (☎ 081 739 09 63; admission €10, incl Pompeii & 3 minor sites €18; ☺ 8.30am-7.30pm Apr-Oct, 8.30am-5pm Nov-Mar) be prepared for some of the houses to be closed, although an attendant may be around to open them; don't feel obliged to tip.

Follow the path running above and around the site, then descend through a short tunnel to emerge beside the **Terme Suburbane** (Suburban Baths), among the best-preserved Roman baths anywhere in Europe, with deep pools, stucco friezes and bas-reliefs looking down upon marble seats and floors.

The site is divided into 11 *insulae* (islands) carved up in a classic Roman grid pattern. The two main streets, Decumano Massimo and Decumano Inferiore, are both crossed by Cardo III, IV and V.

The **Casa d'Argo** (Argus House) is a well-preserved example of a Roman noble family's house, complete with porticoed garden and *triclinium* (dining area).

The most extraordinary mosaic to have survived intact is in the *nyphaeum* (fountain and bath) of the **Casa di Nettuno e Anfitrite** (House of Neptune & Amphitrite; Cardo IV). The warm colours in which the two deities are depicted hint at how lavish the interior of other well-to-do households must have been. For more fine mosaics make your way to another of the city's public baths, **Terme del Foro** (Forum Baths), with its separate sections for men and women. The floor mosaics in the latter are in pristine condition. While women passed from the *apodyterium* (changing rooms; note the finely executed naked figure of Triton adorning the mosaic floor) through the *tepidarium* (warm room) to the *caldarium* (steam bath), men had the added bracing option of the *frigidarium* – a cold bath. You can still see the benches where bathers sat and the wall shelves for clothing.

Casa del Atrio Mosaico (House of the Mosaic Atrium; Cardo IV), an impressive mansion, also has extensive floor mosaics – time and nature have left the floor buckled and uneven.

Behind it, and accessible from Cardo V, **Casa dei Cervi** (House of the Deer) is probably the most imposing of the nobles' dwellings. The two-storey villa, built around a courtyard, contains murals and still-life paintings. In the courtyard is a diminutive pair of marble deer assailed by dogs and an engaging statue of a drunken Hercules peeing.

Casa del Gran Portale (cnr Decumano Inferiore & Cardo V) is named after the elegant brick Corinthian columns that flank its main entrance. Inside are some well-preserved wall paintings.

Sacello degli Augustali, in its time a school, retains a pair of lively and well-preserved murals.

Off the main street is **Casa del Bicentenario** (Bicentenary House; Decumano Massimo), so-named because it was excavated 200 years after digging at Herculaneum first began. A crucifix found in an upstairs room is evidence that there might have been Christians in the town before AD 79.

Northwest of the ruins are the remains of a **theatre** (Corso Ercolano), dating to the Augustan period.

Sleeping & Eating

You'll do better staying in Naples or Sorrento and making the easy rail journey to Herculaneum than staying in Ercolano.

Italia Caffè & Pasticceria (☎ 081 732 14 99; Corso Italia 17) is a humble café with far from humble cakes; pick up a bag-full for your train journey.

Getting There & Away

By far the easiest way to get from central Naples or Sorrento to Ercolano (and also to Pompeii, which many visitors cover in the same day) is by the Circumvesuviana train (see p637). The fare from Naples costs €1.70. By car take the A3 from Naples, exit at Ercolano Portico and follow the signs to car parks near the site's entrance.

MT VESUVIUS

This legendary volcano dominates the landscape, looming ominously over Naples and its environs. Although not as active as Mt Etna in Sicily, **Mt Vesuvius** (Vesuvio; 1281m) is anything but extinct and scientists consider more eruptions a sure thing. After the last blow in 1944 its plume of smoke, long a reminder of the peril, disappeared. This may have eased the minds of some, but for those living in the shadow of Vesuvius; the question is not if, but when (see the boxed text, right).

Vesuvius' name is aptly derived from the Greek *besubios* or *besbios*, meaning 'fire'. The volcano erupted with such ferocity on 24 August AD 79 that it all but destroyed the towns of Pompeii and Herculaneum and pushed the coastline out several kilometres. Subsequent years have witnessed regular displays of the mountain's wrath, the more destructive being those of 1631,

1794 (when the town of Torre del Greco was destroyed), 1906 and, most recently, 1944. Vesuvius is now a national park and a Unesco Biosphere Reserve.

Trasporti Vesuviani (☎ 081 559 31 73) buses run from Ercolano train station to Vesuvius car park (€3.10 return, buy your ticket on the bus). There's then a 1.5km walk (allow 30 to 45 minutes) to the **summit area** (admission €6) and crater rim. Buses depart from Ercolano train station at 9.30am, 10.30am, 11.50am, 12.50pm and 1.50pm. They return to the station at 11.35am, 1pm, 1.55pm, 3pm and 4.10pm. All services leave Pompeii 30 minutes earlier. Be warned that when weather conditions are bad they shut the summit path and suspend bus departures. By car, exit the A3 at Ercolano Portico and follow the signs for Parco Nazionale de Vesuvio. A licensed taxi from Ercolano costs about €31 for four people.

Watch out for a couple of scams. Readers have reported independent bus owners in Ercolano lying about public transport times and charging ludicrous sums to get you up and down. And the little old couple who thrust walking sticks at visitors to help them on the push to the summit aren't doing it for charity, as they will make very clear when you descend.

Pack a sweater as it can be chilly up top, even in summer. Sunglasses are useful against

---

WE'LL PAY YOU TO MOVE

Italian officials are trying to persuade locals to move away from the slopes of Vesuvius by offering them cash payments of €30,000. About 700,000 people live in the shadow of the volcano – a 7km red zone that would be at immediate risk if the volcano erupted. The last eruption was nearly 60 years ago and scientists say that although Vesuvius is sleeping like a baby at the moment, they should be ready for danger. The first payout took place in July 2004 and, to date, 3276 applications have been received. Many locals are still refusing to budge, however, as the money offered would only cover about a quarter of the cost of a new two-bedroom flat. To give the project further publicity, the scheme was featured in three episodes of Italy's popular police drama *La Squadra* in September 2004.

CAMPANIA

ASHES, FIRE & BRIMSTONE

One of the most vivid accounts of the eruption of Vesuvius is by Pliny the Younger, writing to the historian Tacitus. In it, Pliny describes how his uncle, Pliny the Elder, renowned as an early naturalist, met his death:

'He embraced his terrified friend, cheered and encouraged him and, thinking he could calm the latter's fears by showing his own composure, gave orders that he was to be carried to the bathroom. After his bath he lay down and dined; he was quite cheerful, or at any rate pretended he was, which was no less courageous.

Meanwhile on Mt Vesuvius broad sheets of fire and leaping flames blazed at several points, their bright glare emphasised by the darkness of the night. My uncle tried to allay the fears of his companions by repeatedly declaring that these were nothing but bonfires left by the peasants in their terror, or else empty houses on fire in the districts they had abandoned. Then he went to rest and certainly slept, for as he was a stout man his breathing was rather loud and heavy and could be heard by people coming and going outside his door. By this time the courtyard leading to his room was full of ashes mixed with pumice stones so that its level had risen; if he had stayed in the room any longer he would never have got out. He was wakened and came out to join Pomponianus and the rest of the household who had sat up all night. They debated whether to stay indoors or take their chance in the open, for the buildings were now shaking with violent shocks and seemed to be swaying to and fro as if torn from their foundations. Outside on the other hand, there was the danger of falling pumice stones, even though these were light and porous; however, after comparing the risks they chose the latter. As a protection against falling objects they put pillows on their heads tied down with cloths.

Elsewhere there was daylight by this time but they were still in darkness, blacker and denser than any ordinary night, which they relieved by lighting torches and various kinds of lamp. My uncle decided to go down to the shore and investigate on the spot the possibility of escape by sea but he found the waves still wild and dangerous. They spread a sheet on the ground for him to lie down and he repeatedly asked for cold water to drink. Then the flames and smell of sulphur, giving warning of the approaching fire, drove his companions to flight and roused him to stand up. He stood leaning on two slaves and then suddenly collapsed, I imagine because the dense fumes choked his breathing by blocking his windpipe, which was constitutionally weak and narrow and often inflamed. When daylight returned on the 26 – two days after he had last been seen – his body was found intact, uninjured and still fully clothed as though he were in sleep rather than in death.'

Pliny the Younger

the swirling ash and trainers or walking shoes are more practical than sandals or flip-flops (thongs).

On the winding route up to the crest, visit the **Museo dell'Osservatorio Vesuviano** (Museum of the Vesuvian Observatory; ☎ 081 6 10 84 83; www .ov.ingv.it in Italian; admission free; ☯ 10am-2pm Sat & Sun), which tells the history of 2000 years of Vesuvius-watching.

POMPEII
pop 25,900
The victim of the world's most famous volcano disaster, Pompeii is the most important archaeological site in Europe. About 2.3 million people pile in every year, making the

magnificent ruins seem as crowded as the ancient streets must once have been. Ever since Pliny the Younger described the eruption of Vesuvius in AD 79, (see the boxed text, above) the city has been the stuff of books – scholarly and frivolous – and a perfect subject for the big screen. It offers the richest insight into the daily life of the Romans and parts are extraordinarily familiar – like the 89 food takeaways. Allow at least three hours to cover the site.

Less than a kilometre down the road from the ruins, the pleasant modern town of Pompeii boasts a second big crowd-puller: the Santuario della Madonna del Rosario (Sanctuary of Our Lady of the Rosary), a famous place of miracles that attracts pilgrims from all over Italy.

History

The eruption of Vesuvius wasn't the first disaster to strike the Roman port of Pompeii. In AD 63 it was devastated by an earthquake. Following a rapid rebuild, it was just beginning to recover when lightning struck again. On 24 August AD 79 Vesuvius blew its top bigtime, burying the city under a layer of *lapilli* and killing some 2000 of the city's 20,000 inhabitants.

This, some might suggest, was a tragically appropriate destiny for a town that had been founded on prehistoric lava from the very same Vesuvius. The origins of Pompeii are uncertain, but it seems most likely that it was founded in the 7th century BC by the Campanian Oscans. Throughout the next seven centuries the city fell to the ancient Greeks and the Samnites before becoming a Roman colony in 80 BC.

After its catastrophic demise some 160 years later, the city gradually receded from the public eye until 1594, when the architect Domenico Fontana stumbled across the ruins while digging a canal. However, short of recording the find, he took no further action.

Exploration proper finally began in 1748 under the king of Naples, Charles of Bourbon, and continued systematically into the 19th century. Giuseppe Fiorelli, who worked for the Italian government from 1858, is credited with most of the major discoveries.

Most of the ancient city has now been unearthed but work continues and new finds are still being made, such as the series of erotic frescoes unveiled in 2000.

Today, many of the more spectacular mosaics and murals sit in the Museo Archeologico Nazionale in Naples (p624) and other museums around the world. This is an unfortunate by-product of overtourism and underfunding, which have been eroding the original 66-hectare site.

Orientation

The Circumvesuviana drops you at Pompeii Scavi–Villa dei Misteri station, beside the main Porta Marina entrance. By car, signs – and energetic touts – direct you from the A3 to the *scavi* and car parks. There are several camping sites, hotels and restaurants in the vicinity, although the choice is better in the adjacent modern town of Pompeii.

Information

First-aid post (Via T Ravallese)
Pompeii Online (www.pompeii.it in Italian)
Police booth (Piazza Esedra)
Post office (Piazza Esedra)
Tourist office Porta Marina (☎ 081 850 72 55; Piazza Porta Marina Inferiore 12; ☽ 8am-3.30pm Mon-Sat); Pompeii town (☎ 081 850 72 55; Via Sacra 1; ☽ 8am-3.30pm Mon-Sat Oct-Mar, 8am-7pm Mon-Sat Apr-Sep)

Sights
THE RUINS

Porta Marina is nowadays the principal entrance to the **ruins** (☎ 081 857 53 47; www.pompeii sites.org; admission €10, incl Herculaneum & 3 minor sites €18; ☽ 8.30am-7.30pm Apr-Oct, 8.30am-5pm daily Nov-Mar). Audioguides (€6.50) are available but a good guidebook is still a useful tool since it's easy to miss some of the more important sites. Last entry to the ruins is 6pm from April to October; 3.30pm November to March.

The original town was encircled by a wall punctuated by towers and eight gates. Entering by the southwest sea gate, **Porta Marina**, which was considerably closer to the water before the eruption, you pass the **Tempio di Venere** (Temple of Venus) on the right. Originally one of town's most lavish temples, its position made it the target of repeated pillaging, leaving it in the abandoned state you see today.

Further along Via Marina, on the left, you pass the striking **Tempio di Apollo** (Temple of Apollo), the oldest of Pompeii's religious buildings, to enter the **foro** (forum), the centre of the city's life. South of this, opposite Tempio di Apollo, is the **basilica**, the city's law courts and exchange. Dating back to the 2nd century BC, it was one of Pompeii's greatest buildings. Among the fenced-off ruins to the left as you enter are some delightfully gruesome body casts.

The forum, which incidentally was closed to cart traffic, is surrounded by the **Tempio di Giove** (Temple of Jupiter), one of whose two flanking triumphal arches remains; the **market**, where you can see the remains of a series of shops; and the **Edificio di Eumachia**, featuring an imposing marble doorway.

Continue down Via Marina which, after the Edificio, becomes Via dell'Abbondanza, until you reach Via dei Teatri on your right.

CAMPANIA

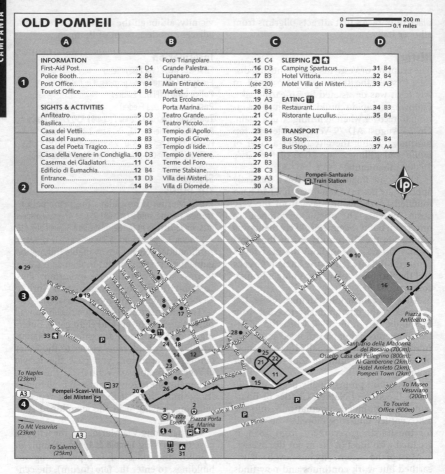

OLD POMPEII

0 _____ 200 m
0 _____ 0.1 miles

INFORMATION
First-Aid Post..........................1 D4
Police Booth...........................2 B4
Post Office.............................3 B4
Tourist Office.........................4 B4

SIGHTS & ACTIVITIES
Anfiteatro..............................5 D3
Basilica.................................6 B4
Casa dei Vettii........................7 B3
Casa del Fauno.......................8 B3
Casa del Poeta Tragico.............9 B3
Casa della Venere in Conchiglia..10 D3
Caserma dei Gladiatori............11 C4
Edificio di Eumachia................12 B4
Entrance...............................13 D3
Foro.....................................14 B4

Foro Triangolare.....................15 C4
Grande Palestra......................16 D3
Lupanaro..............................17 B3
Main Entrance.....................(see 20)
Market..................................18 B3
Porta Ercolano.......................19 A3
Porta Marina.........................20 B4
Teatro Grande........................21 C4
Teatro Piccolo........................22 C4
Tempio di Apollo.....................23 B4
Tempio di Giove......................24 B3
Tempio di Iside.......................25 C4
Tempio di Venere....................26 B4
Terme del Foro.......................27 B3
Terme Stabiane......................28 C3
Villa dei Misteri......................29 A3
Villa di Diomede.....................30 A3

SLEEPING
Camping Spartacus.................31 B4
Hotel Vittoria.........................32 B4
Motel Villa dei Misteri..............33 A3

EATING
Restaurant............................34 B3
Ristorante Lucullus..................35 B4

TRANSPORT
Bus Stop...............................36 B4
Bus Stop...............................37 A4

This leads to the **Foro Triangolare** and the city's theatre district. To your left is the entrance to the **Teatro Grande**, originally built in the 2nd century BC and which was capable of seating up to 5000 spectators. Adjoining it is the more recent **Teatro Piccolo**, also known as the Odeion. The **Caserma dei Gladiatori** (Gladiators' Barracks), behind the theatres, is surrounded by a portico of around 70 columns.

From the pre-Roman **Tempio di Iside** (Temple of Isis), rebuilt after the AD 63 earthquake and dedicated to the Egyptian goddess, turn left back to Via dell'Abbondanza, which intersects with Via Stabiana. **Terme Stabiane** is a 2nd-century BC bath complex complete with *frigidarium, apodyterium, tepidarium* and *caldarium*. In some you can still see the

original tiling and murals. Several body casts are located here.

Towards the northeastern end of Via dell' Abbondanza, **Casa della Venere in Conchiglia** (House of the Venus Marina) has recovered well from the WWII bomb that damaged it in 1943. Its highlight is the striking fresco of the goddess lounging in an unusually large conch shell.

Hidden away in the green northeastern corner of the city lies the grassy **anfiteatro**, the oldest-known Roman amphitheatre. Built in 70 BC, it was at one time capable of holding up to 20,000 bloodthirsty spectators. The nearby **Grande Palestra** is an athletics field with an impressive portico and, at its centre, the remains of a swimming pool.

It was here that the young men of the emperor's youth associations worked out.

Return along Via dell'Abbondanza and then turn right into Via Stabiana (which becomes Via del Vesuvio) to see some of Pompeii's grandest houses. Turn left into Via della Fortuna to meet, on your right, **Casa del Fauno** (House of the Faun), which featured a magnificent mosaic, that can now be seen at the Museo Archeologico Nazionale (p624) in Naples.

A couple of blocks further along Via della Fortuna is the **Casa del Poeta Tragico** (House of the Tragic Poet), with some decent mosaics still *in situ*. Nearby, the **Casa dei Vettii** (Vicolo di Mercurio) sports some well-preserved paintings and statues. Across the road from Casa del Fauno, along Vicolo Storto, is the **Lupanaro**, Pompeii's top brothel with murals indicating the services on offer. And what better place for the young rakes to wash away their sins than the **Terme del Foro** (Forum Baths), a short walk away on Via Terme.

From the Terme del Foro you can continue to the end of Via Terme and turn right into Via Consolare, which takes you out of the town through Porta Ercolano at Pompeii's northwestern edge. Once past the gate you pass **Villa di Diomede**; turn right and you will come to **Villa dei Misteri**, one of the most complete structures left standing in Pompeii. The *Dionysiac Frieze*, the most important fresco still on site, spans the walls of the large dining room. One of the largest paintings to remain from the ancient world, the fresco depicts the initiation of a bride-to-be into the cult of Dionysus, the Greek god of wine.

The **Museo Vesuviano** (☎ 081 850 72 55; Via Bartolomeo 12; admission free; ☼ 8am-2pm Mon-Sat), located southeast of the excavations, contains an interesting array of artefacts.

SANTUARIO DELLA MADONNA DEL ROSARIO

Dominating modern Pompeii's centre, the **Sanctuary of Our Lady of the Rosary** (Piazza Bartolo Longo; ☼ 6.30am-2pm & 3-6.30pm) was consecrated in 1891, some 15 years after the miracle that guaranteed its fame. In 1876 a young girl was cured of epilepsy after praying in front of the painting *Virgin of the Rosary with Child*, above the main altar. News spread rapidly and to this day the painting is the subject of popular devotion.

The sanctuary is flanked by a freestanding 80m-high **campanile** (bell tower; ☎ 081 850 70 00; ☼ 9am-1pm & 3-5pm).

Tours

The tourist offices warn against the dozens of unauthorised guides who swoop on tourists, charging exorbitant prices for brief and generally inaccurate tours. Authorised guides wear identification tags and belong to one of four cooperatives:

Cast (☎ 081 856 42 21)
Casting (☎ 081 850 07 49)
Gata (☎ 081 861 56 61)
Promo Touring (☎ 081 850 88 55)

The official price for a two-hour tour, regardless of whether you're alone, in a couple or in a group of up to 25, is €94.

Sleeping

Pompeii is best visited on a day trip from Naples, Sorrento or Salerno, as once the excavations close there's little to do and the area around the site becomes decidedly seedy.

Ostello Casa del Pellegrino (☎ /fax 081 850 86 44; Via Duca d'Aosta 4; dm with breakfast €15) A stone's throw from the Santuario in a low-rise ex-convent just off Pompeii town's main square, this HI youth hostel has good, if basic facilities in dormitories, or rooms for five or six people.

Motel Villa dei Misteri (☎ 081 861 35 93; www .villadeimisteri.it; Via Villa dei Misteri 11; d €75; ☒ ☒) There's two types of room here: the motel-style rooms around the pool (good if you have kids who swim) and those in the main building. There's a mildly scuffed air about the whole place, but the price is excellent given the location, the air-con and, above all (in summer), the pool.

Hotel Vittoria (☎ 081 536 90 16; www.pompeihotel vittoria.com; Piazza Porta Marina Inferiore 2; s/d with breakfast €50/90; ☒) Hotel Vittoria sits 200m from the Porta Marina entrance to the ruins. Recently refurbished, it successfully combines the *fin de siècle* grandeur of the public areas with up-to-date comforts, like showers and baths, and the toe-curling cosy feel of plush carpeting throughout.

Hotel Amleto (☎ 081 836 10 04; www.hotelamleto .it; Via B Longo 10; d with breakfast €130; ☒) Elegant-themed rooms in the new town with antiques, chandeliers and magnificent trompe l'oeil.

Camping Spartacus (☎ 081 862 40 78; www.camping spartacus.it; Via Plinio 117; person/tent/car €6/3/2, bungalows from €60; 🖳) The first camp site to open here 25 years ago, Spartacus is greener than some, with huge eucalyptus and pine trees. About 200m from the excavations entrance, the cabins are neat and comfortable. There's Internet, a supermarket, bar and pizzeria on site.

Eating
There's a **restaurant** (Via di Mercurio; pastas from €6) within the ruins with a reasonable daily buffet. Otherwise, there are plenty of places outside the gates and in modern Pompeii.

Al Gamberone (☎ 081 850 68 14; Via Piave 36; mains from €8; ☯ Wed-Mon) Near Pompeii's main church in an elegant part of town, this restaurant has plenty of pasta choice, plus good seafood dishes including brandy-doused prawns. Sit under lemon and orange trees in summer.

Ristorante Lucullus (☎ 081 861 30 55; Via Plinio 129; mains from €7; ☯ Wed-Mon) Set back from the street down along an oleander-fringed drive, Ristorante Lucullus has shady palms, Roman statues and several friendly cats. Specials here include *fettucine alla boscaiola* (flat pasta with a sauce of tomatoes, mushrooms and peas) and a vast choice of mix-and-match *contorni* (vegetables).

Getting There & Away
BUS
SITA (081 552 21 76) operates regular bus services between Naples and Pompeii (€2.30, 40 minutes), while **CSTP** (☎ 089 48 70 01) runs buses from Salerno. **Marozzi** (☎ 089 87 10 09) offers services between Rome and Pompeii. The drop-off/pick-up point in Pompeii is just outside the main entrance to the ruins. **Trasporti Vesuviani** (081 559 25 82) runs regular services to Vesuvius from Piazza Esedra.

CAR & MOTORCYCLE
Take the A3 from Naples, a trip of about 23km, or you could spend hours weaving through narrow streets and traffic snarls. Use the Pompeii exit and follow the signs to Pompeii Scavi. Car parks are clearly marked and vigorously touted.

TRAIN
From Naples, take the Circumvesuviana train (€2.30) for Sorrento and get off at Pompeii Scavi–Villa dei Misteri station.

SORRENTO
pop 17,429
An unashamed resort, Sorrento remains a lively yet genteel town. Even the souvenirs are a cut above the normal overpriced tat, with plenty of stuck-in-a-time-warp shops selling ceramics, lacework and inlaid-wood items. The main drawback is the lack of a proper beach; the town straddles the cliffs with superb wraparound views to Naples and Mt Vesuvius. According to Greek legend, the Sirens, mythical provocateurs of pure voice and dodgy intent, lurked in these parts. Sailors of antiquity were powerless to resist the beautiful song of these charming maidens-cum-monsters who would lure them and their ships to their doom. Homer's Ulysses escaped their lure by having his oarsmen plug their ears with wax and by strapping himself to his ship's mast as he sailed past.

Less dangerous now, Sorrento is packed to the gills in high summer, predominantly with British and German holiday-makers. If you do tire of the crowds, Marina Piccola is a maritime Waterloo Station, with ferries and hydrofoils regularly whizzing off to Positano (p670), Amalfi (p673), Capri (p642), Ischia (p648) and Naples (p616).

Orientation
Piazza Tasso, bisected by Sorrento's main street, Corso Italia, is the social epicentre, and is built over a ravine. It's about a 300m walk northwest of the train station, along Corso Italia. If you arrive at Marina Piccola, walk south along Via Marina Piccola then climb the heart-thumping 200 steps or so to reach the piazza. Corso Italia becomes the SS145 en route east to Naples and, heading west, changes its name to Via Capo.

Information
Acampora Travel (☎ 081 878 48 00; Piazza Angelina Lauro 12) Represents American Express.
Deutsche Bank (Piazza Angelina Lauro 22-29) The bank has an ATM.
Hospital (☎ 081 533 11 11; Corso Italia 1)
Police station (☎ 081 807 44 33; Corso Italia 236)
Post office (☎ 081 878 14 95; Corso Italia 210; ☯ 8am-6.30pm Mon-Fri, 8am-12.30pm Sat)
Sorrento Info (☎ 081 807 40 00; Via Tasso 19; per 30min €3; ☯ 10am-1.30pm & 4-8pm Mon-Sat Nov-Apr, 10am-1.30pm & 5-10.30pm Mon-Sat May-Oct) Internet access.
Sorrento Tourism (www.sorrentotourism.it) Good information on the town.

SORRENTO

INFORMATION		
Acampora Travel	1	C3
Deutsche Bank	2	C3
Hospital	3	A4
Police Station	4	D3
Post Office	5	D3
Sorrento Info	6	B4
Telephone Office	7	C3
Tourist Office	8	B3

SIGHTS & ACTIVITIES		
Cathedral	9	B4
Chiesa di San Francesco	10	B3
Daytours	11	C4
Museo Bottega	12	B4
Museo Correale	13	D3
Palazzo Correale	(see 13)	

Sic Sic	14	C3
Villa Comunale	15	B3

SLEEPING		
Grand Hotel Excelsior Vittoria	16	C3
Hotel Capri	17	D3
Hotel Loreley et Londres	18	D3
Hotel Michelangelo	19	D3
Pensione Linda	20	D4

EATING		
Circolo dei Forestieri	(see 8)	
Monde Bio	21	D3
O'Parrucchiano	22	B4
Ristorante il Buco	23	C3
Ristorante Sant'Antonino	24	B4
Zi 'ntonio	25	C3

DRINKING		
Bollicine	26	B4
Café Latino	27	B4
Fauno Bar	28	C4

ENTERTAINMENT		
Teatro Tasso	29	B3

SHOPPING		
Gargiulo & Jannuzzi	30	C4

TRANSPORT		
Bus Station	31	C4
Ferry & Hydrofoil Terminal	32	B3
Sorrento Rentacar	33	C3

Telephone office (☎ 081 807 33 17; Piazza Tasso 37)
Tourist office (☎ 081 807 40 33; Via Luigi De Maio 35;
⊙ 8.45am-6.15pm Mon-Sat) In the Circolo dei Forestieri
(Foreigners' Club), it provides the excellent information
magazine *Surrentum*.

Sights & Activities

The gleaming white façade of the **cathedral**
(Corso Italia; ⊙ 7.30am-noon & 4.30-8.30pm) gives no
hint of the exuberance housed within the interior. A striking Crucifixion sits above the
main altar and the triple-tiered bell tower
rests on an archway with three magnificent
classical columns.

Within the 18th-century **Palazzo Correale**,
with its gracious murals, is the **Museo Correale**
(☎ 081 878 18 46; Via Correale; admission €6; ⊙ 9am-
2pm Wed-Mon), containing a small collection
of 17th- and 18th-century Neapolitan art
and an assortment of Greek and Roman artefacts. The gardens have great bay views
and steps tripping down to the shore. More
art plus stunning 19th century marquetry
furniture can be enjoyed at the newer **Museo
Bottega** (☎ 081 878 12 03; Via San Nicola 28; admission
€8; ⊙ 10am-1pm, 3pm-6.30pm Mon-Sat) with its suitably gorgeous 18th-century palatial setting
featuring frescoed vaults and hand-painted
wallpaper.

Views from the **Villa Comunale** park are
breathtaking, and equally impressive from
the gardens of the beautiful, if modest, cloister of the **Chiesa di San Francesco** (⊙ 8am-1pm &
2-8pm) by the park entrance.

Stroll along Corso Italia, which is closed to traffic in the centre between 10am and 1pm and 7pm to 7am, and through the narrow streets of the old town.

If you're after a beach, head for **Marina Grande** (a 700m walk west from Piazza Tasso), which has small strips of sand. The jetties nearby sport ubiquitous umbrellas and deck chairs that cost up to €15 per day; toddler-friendly it is not. **Bagni Regina Giovanna**, a 2km walk west along Via Capo (or take the bus for Massalubrense), is more picturesque, set among the ruined Roman villa Pollio Felix. To the east is a small beach at Marinella.

Tours

Sic Sic (☎ 081 807 22 83; Marina Piccola; ☖ May-Oct) hires out a variety of boats (starting at around €20 an hour) and organises boat cruises.

Daytours (☎ 081 878 19 84; Corso Italia) offers tours to the Amalfi Coast and Bay of Naples, including Positano (€28), Pompeii (€36) and Capri (€52).

Festivals & Events

The **Sorrento Film Festival**, regarded to be the most important in the country for Italian-produced cinema, is held annually around November.

The city's patron saint, Sant'Antonio, is remembered on 5 February each year with processions and huge markets. The saint is credited with having saved Sorrento during WWII when Salerno and Naples were heavily bombed.

Sleeping

Most accommodation is in the town centre or clustered along Via Capo, the coastal road west of the centre. Be sure to book your bed early for the summer season.

Hotel Michelangelo (☎ 081 878 12 51; www.michel angelohotel.it; Corso Italia 275; d with breakfast €192; ☒ ☒) A shiny modern hotel with marble and terracotta floors, decent art and elegant spacious rooms. The whole place has a warm Mediterranean feel and is well placed for shopping and the beach.

Hotel Capri (☎ 081 878 12 51; www.albergocapri.it; Corso Italia 212; s/d €90/140; ☖ Mar-Oct; ☒) Just across from the Hotel Michelangelo, the Capri is elegantly decorated with antique lemon-and-blue tiles and a profusion of plants and flowers. The hotel is better placed for shopping than for sand in between the toes.

Hotel Loreley et Londres (☎ 081 807 31 87; fax 081 532 90 01; Via Califano 12; d €98; ☖ Mar-Nov) A grand old building looking directly onto Mt Vesuvius, this hotel occupies one of the best sites in town. The interior is faded and floral, with a slight institutional feel. There is a vast terrace bar/restaurant overlooking the sea: perfect for sipping a cocktail at sunset.

Hotel Désiré (☎ /fax 081 878 15 63; Via Capo 31b; s/d with breakfast €60/90; ☖ Mar-Dec) Overlooking the sea, this relaxed hotel has tastefully decorated sunny rooms, a TV lounge, panoramic roof terrace and its very own lift down to the rocky beach. The rates are competitive for all these comforts, and the hotel is well sited for both shops and the sea.

Pensione Linda (☎ /fax 081 878 29 16; Via degli Aranci 125; s/d €50/75) Its suburban setting may be mildly off-putting but it's only a short stroll into town. The rooms are clean and reasonably sized, and some also have balconies. The modern bathrooms have excellent water pressure, a definite plus in these parts.

Grand Hotel Excelsior Vittoria (☎ 081 807 10 44; www.exvitt.it; Piazza Tasso 34; s/d from €235/270) The grand dame of Sorrento, this gracious old hotel sits aloof in its extensive, carefully tended gardens, once the site of a villa belonging to the Emperor Augustus. There are mosaic floors, marble staircases, podgy nymphs and busts of ancient Romans on the terrace. It offers the luxury of a bygone age at 21st-century prices.

Eating

Mondo Bio (☎ 081 807 56 94; Via degli Aranci 146; snacks from €3; ☖ 10am-3pm Mon-Sat) There's just a few tables at this organic-vegetarian shop and restaurant. On offer are tofu burgers, seitan steaks plus lots of healthy alternatives to pizza and pasta, especially for nondairy folk.

Ristorante Il Buco (☎ 081 878 23 54; Rampa Marina Piccola 5; meals about €40) Though Il Buco is a former wine cellar used by monks, there is nothing monastic about the cuisine, which is extravagant and innovative, with dishes like ravioli in a fish, pumpkin and pepper sauce. Outside, the stone archway is one of the city's four main gates that led into ancient Sorrento.

(Continued on page 669)

Piazza del Duomo, Orvieto (p573)

Palazzo Ducale (p585), Urbino

The Apennines and Montefortino (p596), Le Marche

Western ridge of the Corno Grande (p604), Abruzzo

Aqueduct and Piazza Garibaldi (p605), Sulmona

Parco Nazionale d'Abruzzo, Lazio & Molise (p607), Abruzzo

MARTIN MOOS

View of Mt Vesuvius (p653) across Naples

JEAN-BERNARD CARILLET

Chiesa del Gesù Nuovo (p622),
Naples

Neapolitan pizza (p633), Naples

JEAN-BERNARD CARILLET

Procida (p650), Bay of Naples

BILL WASSMAN

ROBERTO SONCIN GEROMETTA

Sant'Andrea Cathedral (p674), Amalfi

Tempio di Nettuno (p681), Paestum

ROBERTO SONCIN GEROMET

Trulli (p702), Puglia

OLIVER STREWE

BETHUNE CARMICHAEL

Bronze doors of the Cathedral
(p695), Trani

Calabrian coastline (p729)

BECCA POSTERINO

DALLAS STRIBLEY

Volcanic mud pools (p770), Vulcano

Mosaics, Cattedrale di Monreale (p761), Monreale

BETHUNE CARMICHAEL

Mt Etna (p788), Sicily

CHRISTOPHER WC

L'ARTE RINNOVA I POPOLI E NE RIVELA LA VITA
VANO DELLE SCENE IL DILETTO OVE NON MIRI A PREPARAR L'AVVENIRE

WAYNE WALTON

Teatro Massimo (p754), Palermo

ALAN BENSON

Fishing boats, Syracuse (p790)

Chiesa di San Giorgio (p797), Mòdica

WAYNE WALTON

Life-savers, Poetto beach (p821), Cagliari

Cattedrale di Santa Maria (p834), Alghero

Grotto near Cala Luna (p851), Golfo di Orosei

Porto Cervo (p843), Costa Smeralda

(Continued from page 660)

O'Parrucchiano (☎ 081 878 13 21; Corso Italia 67; meals about €20; ☺ Thu-Tue) The narrow entrance to this place does little to prepare you for the massive greenhouse setting within. Dating back to 1868 and still in the same family, this place claims to have invented cannelloni, so go for this dish (rather than the 'fried peasant and pork sausages' which is also on the menu!). This is traditional grub in general and well priced, considering the seriously heady setting.

Ristorante Sant'Antonino (☎ 081 877 12 00; Via Santa Maria delle Grazie 6; pizzas from €4.60, meals about €20) The owner, Luigi, is married to an English woman, which helps to explain the diverse menu (and the choice of frozen or fresh chips). There are 12 salads, risotti, savoury crepes, pizza and pasta dishes, plus three reasonably priced set menus. It's in a lovely country-cute setting, with tables surrounded by greenery and lemon trees.

Zi 'ntonio (☎ 081 878 16 23; Via Luigi De Maio 11; meals about €20) A traditional Italian atmosphere prevails in this low-light restaurant with its tiled pictures and dizzy ceiling studded with ceramic plates. The menu includes a heap of rice dishes, including risotto with lobster or with wild mushrooms. There is a daily buffet with a 20-plus choice of tasty-looking dishes.

Circolo dei Forestieri (Foreigners' Club; ☎ 081 877 32 63; Via Luigi de Maio 35; meals about €20) A home-away-from-home for nostalgic Brits, Circolo dei Forestieri enjoys one of Sorrento's most spectacular views. The food is only so-so but good for those who are suffering from potato withdrawal (have them fried or baked). Alternatively, just sip a drink and ogle the view along with the lobster-pink tourists on their holidays.

Drinking

As well as the inevitable Irish-theme pubs, Sorrento has some appealing Med-style bars and, particularly in the main piazze, some classic meet-and-greet cafés.

Bollicine (☎ 081 878 46 16; Via dell'Accademia 9) You can sample Campanian and other wines by the glass at this snug wine-buffs' bar. Nibble on the local specialities, cheeses or cold meats.

Café Latino (☎ 081 878 37 18; Via Pietà 12; ☺ 10am-2am Apr-Sep) Come here to sip a Mary Pickford (rum, pineapple, grenadine and maraschino) and enjoy a cosy little chat with your mate. It's in a lovely garden setting under orange and lemon trees.

Fauno Bar (☎ 081 878 11 35; Piazza Tasso; ☺ Dec-Oct) More a classic café than a bar, Fauno has a vast outside terrace well served by black-bibbed waiters. It's a bit pricey (cocktails cost €8) but always packed out with locals, so there's lots to look at.

Entertainment

Outdoor concerts are held during the summer months in the cloisters of the Chiesa di San Francesco.

Teatro Tasso (☎ 081 807 55 25; Piazza San Antonio; ☺ 9.30pm Mon-Sat Mar-Oct) If you're thrilled by The Sound of Music, you might enjoy Sorrento Musical (€21). It's a potpourri of Neapolitan songs, including a sing-along with 'O Sole Mio' and 'Torna a Sorrento', plus many other less-overworked Neapolitan numbers.

Shopping

Shoppers will enjoy browsing the squeeze-by pedestrian alleys north of Corso Italia and west of Piazza Tasso which are lined with all kinds of shops, including the classic **Gargiulo & Jannuzzi** (☎ 081 878 10 41; Viale Enrico Caruso 1) dating from 1863. Elderly shop assistants will guide you through the three-floor haven where locally made crafts are beautifully displayed, and include embroidered lace, pottery and marquetry items. Shipping can be arranged.

Getting There & Away

SITA buses serve the Amalfi Coast and Sant'Agata, leaving from outside the Circumvesuviana train station. Buy tickets at the station bar or from shops bearing the blue SITA sign. At least 12 buses a day run between Sorrento and Amalfi (€2.40), looping around Positano (€1.30); more than 10 buses a day also run to Ravello (€1).

Circumvesuviana trains run every half-hour between Sorrento and Naples (€3.20), via Pompeii and Ercolano (€1.80 to each).

Linee Marittime Partenopee (☎ 081 807 18 12) runs up to 10 hydrofoils daily to and from Capri (€19 return, 20 minutes) and at least six to and from Naples (€15 return, 35 minutes), while **Caremar** (☎ 081 807 30 77) has three fast-ferry sailings daily to and from Capri (€11.40 return, 25 minutes). All depart from

CAMPANIA

the port at Marina Piccola, where you can also buy your tickets.

Getting Around

Bus Line C runs from Piazza Tasso to the port at Marina Piccola. Tickets cost €1 for 90 minutes are available from tobacconists, newsagents and bars.

Sorrento Rentacar (☎ 081 878 13 86; Corso Italia 210a) is one of several rental companies hiring out scooters (€38) and cars (from €60 per day).

For a taxi, call ☎ 081 878 22 04.

AMALFI COAST

One of the most breathtaking coastlines in Europe, the Amalfi Coast (Costiera Amalfitana) stretches 50km east from Sorrento to Salerno. A narrow asphalt ribbon, itself a feat of road building as spectacular as the views, winds along cliffs that drop down to crystal-clear blue waters and passes through the beautiful towns of Positano and Amalfi. Peering down from its lofty lookout is the stunning hillside village of Ravello. In summer the coast is jam-packed with wealthy tourists, prices are inflated and finding a room is next to impossible; you are much better off coming during the spring and autumn. The Amalfi Coast all but shuts down during winter; unless otherwise noted the restaurants and hotels listed here are open year-round.

When planning your itinerary, you may find www.amalfiscoast.com a useful Web source.

Activities

In the hills, dozens of small paths and stairways connect the coastal towns with mountainside villages. Useful information can be found in Lonely Planet's *Walking in Italy*, which has a chapter featuring the best walks around the Amalfi Coast and Sorrento peninsula; *Landscapes of Sorrento and the Amalfi Coast*, by Julian Tippett, with clear descriptions of over 60 mainly short walks in the area; and *Strade e Sentieri* (€6.50; in Italian only), a worthwhile general guide. The most reliable map to walk by is the Club Alpino Italiano's *Monti Lattari, Penisola Sorrentina, Costiera Amalfitana: Carta dei Sentieri* (€7.75) at a scale of 1:30,000.

Getting There & Away

BOAT

Linee Marittime Partenopee (☎ 081 807 18 12) operates year-round ferries and hydrofoils between Sorrento and Naples. Other companies, such as **Metró Del Mar** (☎ 19 944 66 44; www.metrodelmare.com) operate only in summer, with hydrofoils between Naples and Sorrento (€4), Amalfi (€9) and Positano (€8).

BUS

SITA (☎ 081 552 21 76) operates a service along the SS163 between Sorrento and Salerno with buses leaving about every hour. Buses also connect Rome and the Amalfi Coast, terminating in Salerno.

CAR & MOTORCYCLE

The coastal road is magnificent – as a passenger. To drive it can be something of a white-knuckle ride, as bus drivers nonchalantly edge their way round hairpin bends, jauntily tooting at every turn.

From Naples take the A3, then, just after Pompeii, branch off for Castellammare and follow the signs for Sorrento. At Meta you can continue to Sorrento or, if your destination's further east, bypass the town by taking a short cut over the hills, thus saving yourself a good 30 minutes. To join the coastal road from Salerno, follow the signs for Vietri Sul Mare or Amalfi.

TRAIN

From Naples you can either take the Circumvesuviana to Sorrento or a Trenitalia train to Salerno, then continue along the Amalfi Coast, either eastwards or westwards, by SITA bus.

POSITANO

Positano is, arguably, the most picturesque and photographed of the coastal towns. However, it's not for those with dodgy pins as, where most towns have streets, Positano has steps. Lots of them. The town is steeply stacked with expensive boutiques and houses whose pastel colours – peach, pink, terracotta and white – lend it a faintly theatrical feel. Look close, however, and Positano is reassuringly real with crumbling stucco, streaked paintwork and even, on occasion, the faint whiff of drains.

There certainly is something special about the place and this is reflected, predictably, in

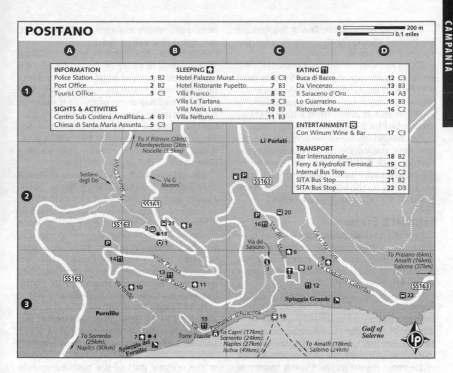

POSITANO

0   200 m
0   0.1 miles

INFORMATION		
Police Station	1	B2
Post Office	2	B2
Tourist Office	3	C3

SIGHTS & ACTIVITIES		
Centro Sub Costiera Amalfitana	4	B3
Chiesa di Santa Maria Assunta	5	C3

SLEEPING		
Hotel Palazzo Murat	6	C3
Hotel Ristorante Pupetto	7	B3
Villa Franco	8	B2
Villa La Tartana	9	C3
Villa Maria Luisa	10	B3
Villa Nettuno	11	B3

EATING		
Buca di Bacco	12	C3
Da Vincenzo	13	B3
Il Saraceno d'Oro	14	A3
Lo Guarracino	15	B3
Ristorante Max	16	C2

ENTERTAINMENT		
Con Winum Wine & Bar	17	C3

TRANSPORT		
Bar Internazionale	18	B2
Ferry & Hydrofoil Terminal	19	C3
Internal Bus Stop	20	C2
SITA Bus Stop	21	B2
SITA Bus Stop	22	D3

the prices, which tend to be a lot higher than elsewhere on the coast.

Orientation

Positano is split in two by a cliff bearing the Torre Trasita (tower). West of this is the smaller, less-crowded Spiaggia del Fornillo beach area and the less-expensive side of town; east is Spiaggia Grande, backing up to the town centre.

Navigating is easy, if steep. Via G Marconi, part of the SS163 Amalfitana, forms a huge hairpin around and above the town, which cascades down to the sea. From it, one-way Viale Pasitea makes a second, lower loop, ribboning off Via G Marconi from the west towards the town centre then climbing back up as Via Cristoforo Colombo to rejoin Via G Marconi and the SS163.

Information

Con Winum Wine & Bar (☎ 089 81 14 61; Via Rampa Teglia 12; per 30min €2; ☒ 8am-3am Apr-Oct) For Internet access at a central location; it's also a wine bar (see p673)
Police station (☎ 089 87 50 11; cnr Via G Marconi & Viale Pasitea)

Post office (cnr Via G Marconi & Viale Pasitea)
Tourist office (☎ 089 87 50 67; Via del Saracino 4; ☒ 8am-2pm & 3.30-8pm Mon-Sat year-round, 3.30-8pm Jul & Aug) At the foot of the Chiesa di Santa Maria Assunta steps.

Sights & Activities

Positano's most famous, and pretty much only, official tourist sight is the **Chiesa di Santa Maria Assunta** (Piazza Flavio Gioia; ☒ 8am-midday & 3.30-7pm), its ceramic dome gleaming under the sun. Inside, regular classical lines are broken by pillars topped with gilded Ionic capitals, while winged cherubs peek from the top of every arch. Above the main altar is a 13th-century Byzantine Black Madonna and Child.

With the church done, it's time to head for the nearby beach. Hiring a chair and umbrella on the fenced-off areas of the **beaches** costs around €15 per day, but the crowded public areas are free. **Boating** isn't cheap either. On Spiaggia Grande expect to pay from €12 an hour for a rowing boat or €22 for a small motorboat (cheaper rates are offered for half- or full-day rental).

For **diving** enthusiasts, **Centro Sub Costiera Amalfitana** (☎ 089 81 21 48) operates from the Spiaggia del Fornillo.

If you're a keen walker and reasonably fit, set aside a day for the classic **Sentiero degli Dei** (Path of the Gods; five to 5½ hours). It follows the steep, well-defined paths linking Positano and Praiano, from where you can catch a bus back along the coastal road.

For staggering views with much less effort, stroll the Via Positanesi d'America, the cliffside path that links the two beaches. At the end of a long walk reward yourself with a cold drink on the beachfront terrace of the Hotel Ristorante Pupetto (see below).

Festivals & Events

Lovers of classical music may want to time their visit to coincide with the **Summer Music**, an annual international chamber-music festival held in Positano at the end of August or in early September.

Sleeping

Positano has plenty of hotels, particularly in the pricier categories. Cheaper accommodation is more limited and usually booked well in advance for summer. Ask at the tourist office about rooms or apartments in private houses.

Villa Maria Luisa (☎ 089 87 50 23; www.pensione marialuisa.com; Via Fornillo 42; s/d €40/65; Mar-Nov) A lovely little hotel, the Maria Luisa has quirky old-fashioned rooms. It's well worth paying the €5 extra for a private terrace as there are magnificent views of the bay. The Falstaffian owner, Carlo, speaks several languages and is very friendly – so are the three cats.

Villa Nettuno (☎ 089 87 54 01; www.villanettuno positano.it; Viale Pasitea 208; s/d €70-80) It is worth tackling the last few steps to find this charming hotel hidden among the foliage. Go for one of the rooms in the 300-year-old part of the building with the frescoed wardrobes and private communal terrace. The hotel's other rooms are still good value and have more modern bathrooms, but the cheapish furniture is a letdown and the new tiling is seriously naff.

Hotel Ristorante Pupetto (☎ 089 87 50 87; fax 089 81 15 17; pupetto@starnet.it; Via Fornillo 37; s/d €90/150; Apr-Dec) This place is right beside Spiaggia del Fornillo, and you can just about tumble onto the beach from all its rooms (which have lovely sea views). You can also eat at the

restaurant, which has a mainly fishy menu, plus good (enough) pizzas.

Villa Franca (☎ 089 87 56 55; www.villafrancahotel .it; Viale Pasitea 318; d €190; Apr-Nov;) An immaculate boutique hotel with a sparkling blue-and-white Mediterranean feel. The rooftop pool has some of the best views in town. The rooms are small but chic, with tiled frescoes, balconies and more good views. There's a small downstairs bar, plus a gym, if you need any more exercise than walking down and up the steps to the beach.

Villa La Tartana (☎ 089 81 21 93; www.villalatartana .it; Via Vicolo Vito Savino 6-8; d €150; Apr-Sep;) A former apartment block on a tiny sidestreet, La Tartana's main disadvantage is the lack of lift (elevator) although, at these prices, you'll probably get your cases lugged up for you. Go for a room on the 3rd floor with huge verandas overlooking the beach. There are bright floral-designed tiles, pretty floral bed heads and bathrooms decorated in earthy tones with a shower and full-size bathtub.

Hotel Palazzo Murat (☎ 089 87 51 77; www.pal azzomurat.it; Via Dei Mulini 23; s/d with breakfast from €205/290;) This 18th-century palace has a palatial arched entrance lined with palms and giant urns. There are just five rooms in the original part of the building and 26 in the newer bit. The décor in both is exquisite, with antiques, original oil paintings and plenty of glossy marble. The gardens are pretty as a picture, with bottlebrush, banana trees, Japanese maple and pine trees.

Eating

Most restaurants are overpriced and many close over the winter, making a brief reappearance for Christmas and New Year.

Il Saraceno d'Oro (☎ 089 81 20 50; Viale Pasitea 254; pizzas about €6, meals €24; Mar-Oct) This highly popular eatery scores well on all counts – food, service, price and décor; the complimentary end-of-meal glass of *limoncello* is a nice touch. The pizzas are excellent, the profiteroles sublime – try them in chocolate sauce or lemon cream.

Da Vincenzo (☎ 089 87 51 28; Viale Pasitea 172-178; meals about €24 Mar-Oct) Family-run since 1959, this restaurant's ebullient father-son duo wait tables with gusto, while wife Marcela does her bit in the kitchen. House specials include *panzarotti* (small fried pastry squares with mozzarella and ham) and *peperoni ripieni* (red peppers stuffed with olives and cheese).

Il Ritrovo (☎ 089 87 54 53; Via Montepertuso 77, Montepertuso; meals about €22; ☼ Thu-Tue) High up in the hills and with lofty sea views, this trattoria is decorated throughout with bunches of tomatoes and, not surprisingly, they show up frequently on the menu as well. Owner Salvatore was a construction worker until his love of food led to this culinary success story around nine years ago.

Buca Di Bacco (☎ 089 811 461 Viale Del Brigantino 35-37; snacks/mains from €3/6) The most popular snack bar and restaurant in town, Buca Di Bacco covers most taste buds and budgets. You can pick up an inexpensive well-stuffed *panino* (bread roll) or sweet pastry here, or enjoy pricier sit-down service at La Pergola restaurant, with a menu including risotto, seafood and good-sized salads.

Ristorante Max (☎ 089 87 50 56; Via dei Mulini 22; meals about €38; ☼ Mar-Nov) Smock-and-beret types will love the setting here: the dining room is within an art gallery, with paintings ranging from renaissance style to modern impressionist. There are set menus and specials of the day such as ravioli with clams and asparagus, and courgette flowers stuffed with ricotta and salmon.

Lo Guarracino (☎ 089 87 57 94; Via Positanesi d'America; meals about €30; ☼ Mar-Nov) On the cliff-side path connecting Positano's two beaches, Lo Guarracino dishes up simply tasty dishes.

Entertainment

Con Winum Wine & Bar (☎ 089 81 14 61; Via Rampa Teglia 12; ☼ 8am-3pm, Apr-Oct) This snazzy wine bar, art gallery and Internet café in one has live jazz on Friday and Saturday in summer. This place attracts boatloads of snappily dressed Italians; the wine list is a serious one with Mondavi Rothschild – a snip at €550 a bottle.

Getting There & Around

SITA buses to Amalfi and Sorrento leave from the top of Via Colombo and the top of Viale Pasitea, outside the Bar Internazionale from where you purchase the tickets.

Positano is a snakes-and-ladders town. If your knees can handle it, there are dozens of narrow alleys and stairways that make walking relatively easy and joyously traffic-free. Otherwise a small orange bus follows the lower ring road every half-hour, passing along Viale Pasitea, Via Cristoforo Colombo and Via G Marconi. Stops are clearly

marked and you buy your ticket (€0.80) on board. It passes by both SITA bus stops.

Depending on the time of year, between one and five hydrofoils or ferries operate daily between Positano and resorts on the Amalfi Coast and the Bay of Naples, including Naples (€8), Salerno (€11), Amalfi (€5), Procida (€10) and Sorrento (€5).

AROUND POSITANO
Nocelle
elev 450m

This tiny, still relatively isolated village lies east of Positano. It's accessible by road or, more interestingly, by a short walking track from the end of Positano's Via Mons S Clinque. Before heading back have lunch at **Trattoria Santa Croce** (☎ 089 81 12 60; meals about €20) and enjoy the panoramic views from its terrace. In summer the place is open for both lunch and dinner; at other times of the year it's best to phone and check in advance. Buses link Nocelle and Positano, running roughly every half-hour in summer.

Praiano

The coastal town of Praiano is less scenic than Amalfi but has more accommodation options and a lovely beach.

Along the coastal road east of Praiano, **Hotel Pensione Continental** (☎ 089 87 40 84; www.continental.praiano.it; Via Roma 21; s/d €65/90) is backed by a pretty garden with winding steps that lead to the beach. The rooms are sparkling blue and white and set among groves of lemon, olive and palm trees. Apartments are also available and the complex includes a smart restaurant with decent pasta dishes. There's a handy SITA bus stop right outside.

AMALFI
pop 5528

It is astonishing to think that pretty little Amalfi was once a maritime superpower with a population of more than 70,000. The latter is particularly hard to get one's head around – Amalfi is in a tight little cove and clearly too small for that many people. The explanation is chilling. Most of the old city, and its populace, simply slid into the sea during a 1343 earthquake.

Today, although the resident population numbers a modest 5500 or so, the numbers swell significantly once again during summer, when camera-slung tourists pour in

CAMPANIA

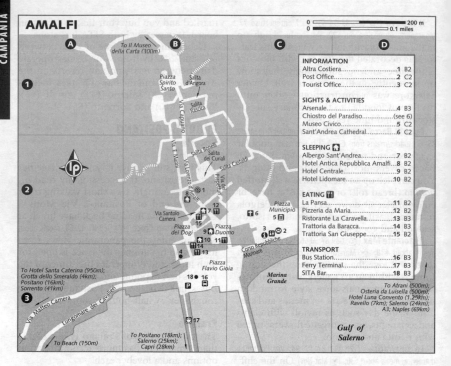

INFORMATION	
Altra Costiera..............................1 B2	
Post Office..................................2 C2	
Tourist Office..............................3 C2	

SIGHTS & ACTIVITIES	
Arsenale.....................................4 B3	
Chiostro del Paradiso..............(see 6)	
Museo Civico..............................5 C2	
Sant'Andrea Cathedral..............6 C2	

SLEEPING	
Albergo Sant'Andrea...................7 B2	
Hotel Antica Repubblica Amalfi...8 B2	
Hotel Centrale............................9 B2	
Hotel Lidomare.........................10 B2	

EATING	
La Pansa...................................11 B2	
Pizzeria da Maria......................12 B2	
Ristorante La Caravella.............13 B3	
Trattoria da Baracca..................14 B3	
Trattoria San Giuseppe.............15 B2	

TRANSPORT	
Bus Station...............................16 B3	
Ferry Terminal..........................17 B3	
SITA Bar...................................18 B3	

by the coach-load. Take an easy stroll eastwards to neighbouring Atrani via a picturesque tangle of backstreets and steps. You are greeted by a pared-down Amalfi with whitewashed alleys, arches and a humble, yet handsome, piazza. You will leave hundreds of tourists behind as well.

Orientation

Most of Amalfi's hotels and restaurants are located around Piazza Duomo or along Via Lorenzo d'Amalfi and its continuation, Via Capuano, which snakes northwards from the cathedral.

Information

Altra Costiera (☎ 089 873 60 82; www.altra.costiera .com; Via Lorenzo d'Amalfi 34; per hr €3) Provides Internet access, accommodation referral and arranges walking and other tours.

Post office (Corso Repubbliche Marinare) Next door to the tourist office.

Tourist office (☎ 089 87 11 07; Corso Repubbliche Marinare 19; ⏰ 8.30am-1.30pm & 3-5.15pm Mon-Fri, 8.30am-12.30pm Sat) Has little useful information but some pretty brochures.

Sights & Activities

The **Sant'Andrea Cathedral** (☎ 089 87 10 59; Piazza del Duomo; ⏰ 9am-7pm Apr-Jun, 9am-9pm Jul-Sep, 9.30am-5.15pm Oct & Mar, 10am-1pm & 2.30-4.30pm Nov-Feb) makes an imposing sight at the top of its sweeping flight of stairs. The cathedral dates in part from the early 10th century, and its distinctive humbug-striped façade has been rebuilt twice, most recently at the end of the 19th century. Although the building is a hybrid, the Arabic-Norman style of Sicily predominates, particularly in the two-tone masonry and bell tower. The interior is mainly baroque and the altar features some fine statues together with mosaics from the 12th and 13th centuries.

The adjoining 13th-century **Chiostro del Paradiso** (admission €2.50; ⏰ 9am-7pm Apr-Jun, 9am-9pm Jul-Sep, 9.30am-5.15pm Oct & Mar, 10am-1pm & 2.30-4.30pm Nov-Feb) was built in Arabic style to house the tombs of prominent citizens.

The small, one-room **Museo Civico** (☎ 089 87 10 66; Piazza Municipio; admission free; ⏰ 8.30am-1pm Mon-Fri), behind Corso Republicche Marinare is in the town-hall building, contains the Tavole Amalfitane (an ancient manuscript

---

THE PAPER'S ARRIVED

Italian society has always been bureaucratic, and it was the demand for endless quantities of legal documents that first brought paper to Amalfi. In the 12th century, Amalfi traders were active in the Arab world, where a new-fangled invention, paper, was already proving more practical than heavy parchment. The merchants learned paper-making techniques and brought these back to Amalfi, where the ready supply of water from the surrounding mountains provided a crucial ingredient.

The basic process for making paper was simple. In the first stage, rags of linen, cotton and hemp were beaten by heavy wooden mallets, powered by a hydraulic wheel, to form a pulp. This pulp was then diluted with water and spread thinly over wire frames. The water was drained off and the resulting sheet placed on a bed of woollen felt. An operator would then build up a 'lasagne' of felt and pulp sheets before placing the whole lot under a press. The squashed paper sheets were placed directly on top of each other to create a 'post', which was left to dry before treatment with animal gelatine and smoothing by hand.

Refinements in the process arrived with more sophisticated machinery, but the fundamental process remained unchanged for centuries, keeping Amalfi well supplied with paper, much to the joy of the region's army of bureaucrats, lawyers and notaries.

---

draft of Amalfi's maritime code) and other historical documents. Ask at the window halfway up the entry stairs for a guide sheet in English. The former republic's restored **Arsenale** (Via Matteo Camera; admission free; 9am-8pm Easter-Sep) is the only ship-building depot of its kind in Italy.

Up in Valle dei Mulini, an easy walk from town, is **Il Museo della Carta** (Paper Museum; 0328 318 86 26; Via delle Cartiere; admission €3.10; 10am-6pm), set up in a paper mill dating from the 13th century (see the boxed text, above).

The ceramics shops which you will see mostly clustered about Piazza Duomo reflect Amalfi's traditional promotion of this craft.

In Conca dei Marini, about 4km along the coast towards Positano, is the **Grotta dello Smeraldo** (admission €5; 9am-7pm Mar-Oct, 9am-4pm Nov-Feb), a grotto so named for the emerald colour of its sandy floor. SITA buses pass by but it's more fun to take one of the boats that run frequently from Amalfi in season (€5 return; allow 1½ hours). At the grotto, as at the Marina Grande area and Spiaggia Santa Croce, you can hire boats for around €24.

The paths and stairways that thread the hills behind Amalfi and up to Ravello make for grand walking.

Festivals & Events
On 24 December and 6 January, skin-divers make a traditional pilgrimage to the ceramic crib in the Grotta dello Smeraldo.

The **Palio delle Quattro Repubbliche Marche**, which rotates between the cities of Amalfi,

Venice, Pisa and Genoa, is held on the first Sunday in June. Amalfi's turn comes round again in 2009.

Sleeping
Albergo Sant'Andrea (089 87 11 45; Via Santolo Camera; s/d €45/75;) Situated about as close to the cathedral as possible without attending confession, Sant'Andrea's rooms are fairly underwhelming but the price is right for this bang-in-the-centre location. The on-site restaurant is handy for sudden hunger pangs.

Hotel Lidomare (089 87 13 32; www.lidomare.it; Largo Duchi Piccolomini 9; s/d with breakfast €50/110;) It's like stepping into an ancestral home at this lovely family-run hotel. The spacious rooms have a real air of gentility, with their appealingly haphazard décor, old-fashioned tiles and fine old antiques. Some rooms have Jacuzzi bathrooms and sea views.

Hotel Antica Repubblica Amalfi (089 87 363 10; www.starnet.it/anticarepubblica; Vico Dei Pastai 2; s/d with breakfast €90/135;) Another hotel that has recently invested in an interior makeover. Warm terracotta tiles are tastefully twinned with traditional Amalfi squares of blue, yellow and apple green, and all rooms have a deft strip of stencilling. Breakfast is served on the panoramic rooftop terrace.

Hotel Centrale (089 87 26 08; www.hotelcen traleamalfi.it; Largo Piccolomini 1; s/d €120/135;) There are striking views of the cathedral from this exquisite boutique hotel which has recently benefited from a total spruce-up. The bright green-and-blue tilework gives the place a

CAMPANIA

vibrant fresh look, while the balconies allow you to discreetly people-watch couples out for a romantic piazza stroll, bless 'em.

Hotel Luna Convento (☎ 089 87 10 02; www.luna hotel.it; Via Pantaleone Comite 33; s/d €190/210; 🌐 🔲) This former convent was founded by St Francis in 1222 and has been a hotel for some 170 years. Rooms in the original building are in the former monks' cells, but there's nothing pokey about the bright tiles and white decoration with balconies and seamless sea views. The newer wing is equally beguiling, with religious frescoes over the bed (to stop any misbehaving). There are two restaurants and a sea-level swimming pool.

Hotel Santa Caterina (☎ 089 87 10 12; www.hotel santacaterina.it; Strada Amalfitana 9; d from €350; 🌐 🔲) Lounge by the saltwater pool, work out in the gym or simply enjoy one of the loveliest gardens in southern Italy at one of its top hotels. Located just outside the town, Hotel Santa Caterina sits on a clifftop commanding fabulous sea views from all the rooms. There is even a Romeo and Juliet suite for honeymooners. There's a private beach, pool and fitness centre.

Eating

Trattoria San Giuseppe (☎ 089 87 26 40; Salita Ruggiero II 4; pizzas from €5, meals about €25; 🕑 Fri-Wed) Earthy and inexpensive, this restaurant is hidden away under an arch in Amalfi's labyrinthine alleyways. There can be a whiffy smell from the antique drains, but the dining room within is cooled by a couple of lazy fans. Some say the pizza here is the best in town. There's a no-fuss pasta choice as well.

Ristorante La Caravella (☎ 089 87 10 29; Via Matteo Camera 12; meals about €45; 🕑 Wed-Mon Jan–mid-Nov) At this Michelin-star restaurant, traditional Amalfi recipes are given a nouvelle zap. The creamy interior attracts a discreet, classy crowd for such lush tuck as black ravioli with cuttlefish and scampi. Poor famished souls can go for the €65 six-course set menu. There's a head-spinning 15,000-bottle wine cellar here, too.

La Pansa (☎ 089 87 10 65; Piazza Duomo 40; 🕑 Wed-Mon) This elegant café on the main piazza has been in the Pansa family for five generations. Choose from a selection of died-and-gone-to-heaven cakes and pastries.

Pizzeria da Maria (☎ 089 87 18 80; Via Lorenzo d'Amalfi 16; pizzas €6, meals about €25) Da Maria attracts a dedicated crowd ranging from off-

the-yacht Neapolitans to local taxi drivers. Head chef Enzo is suitably flamboyant and will explain the dishes to you in rapid Italian. Not the place for a quiet meal, there's a permanent pianist as well. The food is good and traditional, and the portions are huge.

Trattoria da Baracca (☎ 089 87 12 85; Piazza dei Dogi; meals about €20, tourist menus €15.50; 🕑 Thu-Tue) The genial waiters at this seafood restaurant seem to genuinely enjoy their job, rather than merely angling for a tip. There are stripy blue awnings, fishing-boat murals and a fish soup that's reckoned to be very good indeed.

Osteria da Luisella (☎ 089 87 10 87; Piazza Umberto, Atrani; meals about €20; 🕑 10am-3am Thu-Tue) The charismatic owner Franco has recently opened this wine bar–restaurant and Internet café in this prime piazza setting. The menu is traditional and changes according to the season but usually includes big pasta dishes such as *caporalessa*, a delicious baked concoction with aubergines, tomatoes and cheese. There is a lengthy wine list as well.

Getting There & Away

SITA buses run from Piazza Flavio Gioia to Sorrento (€2.40, more than 12 daily) via Positano (€1.30); Salerno (€1.80, at least hourly); and Naples (€3.10, eight daily). You can buy tickets and check current schedules at **SITA Bar** (Piazza Flavio Gioia).

Between Easter and mid-September there are daily ferry sailings to Salerno (€4), Naples (€9), Positano (€5) and the islands of Capri (€11 return) and Ischia (€16.50 return).

RAVELLO

pop 2524 / elev 350m

Ravello is a small stylish place that is largely pedestrianised and thickly coated with tourists in summer. Over the years the town has attracted such elite celebs as DH Lawrence, Gore Vidal, EM Forster and Greta Garbo (who apparently eloped here). Ravello sits like a natural balcony overhanging Amalfi and the nearby towns of Minori and Maiori, and is a delightful place for a wander with its spectacular views. The 7km drive from Amalfi up to the Valle del Dragone passes through the soaring mountains and deep ravines that characterise the area.

Ravello's **tourist office** (☎ 089 85 70 96; www .ravellotime.it; Piazza Duomo 10; 🕑 9am-8pm Mon-Sat Jun-Sep, 9am-6pm Oct-May) has a colour pamphlet, *Ravello, The City of Music*, packed full with information, as well as suggested walking itineraries around the town.

Sights & Activities

The town's 11th-century **cathedral** (Piazza Duomo; 8.30am-1pm & 3-8pm) features an impressive marble pulpit with six lions crouched at its base. The **museum** (admission €2) is located in the crypt and contains religious artefacts.

Overlooking the piazza is **Villa Rufolo**, the past residence of German composer Richard Wagner, who wrote the third act of *Parsifal* here. The villa was built in the 13th century for the wealthy Rufolos and was home to several popes, as well as Charles I of Anjou. The villa's 19th-century **gardens** (089 851 76 57; admission €5; 9am-6pm) make an inspirational setting for the town's annual programme of classical music (below).

East of Piazza Duomo is the 20th-century **Villa Cimbrone** (admission €5; 9am-6pm), set in magnificent gardens. Worth the admission price for the lovely views alone, Villa Cimbrone's highlight is the cliff-hanging **Terrazzo dell'Infinito**, lined with classical busts.

You can also visit the town's vineyards: the small **Casa Vinicola Caruso** (Via della Marra), **Vini Episcopio** (Hotel Palumbo, Via Toro) and **Vini Sammarco** (Via Nazionale). If you prefer a touch of the hard stuff, visit **Giardini di Ravello** beside Vini Sammarco, or **Profumi di Ravello** (Via Trinità), where the famous *limoncello* is produced. Whatever tickles your palate, don't forget that it is a hairy, hairpin ride back to the coast.

Festivals & Events

Ravello's programme of classical music begins in March and continues until late October. It reaches its crescendo in the **Festival Musicale di Ravello** (www.ravellofestival.com) held in the second half of July, when international orchestras and special guests play a repertoire that always features Wagner. Tickets start at €20 and can go as high as €130 for some performances. For information and reservations, contact the **Ravello Concert Society** (089 85 81 81; www.ravelloarts.org). The concerts are held in the gardens of the Villa Rufolo (above).

Ravello's patron saint, San Pantaleon, is recalled with fun and fireworks in late July.

Sleeping

Book well ahead for summer – especially if you're planning a visit during the Festival Musicale in July.

Hotel Toro (/fax 089 85 72 11; www.hoteltoro .it; Via Wagner 3; s/d with breakfast €74/105; Easter-Nov;) Just off central Piazza Duomo, the Hotel Toro is a tasteful place to stay although the clang of the cathedral bells may disturb your beauty sleep. The rooms have soothing terracotta or light marble tiles and cream furnishings, while the grassy, walled garden is a delightful place for a sundowner treat.

Palazzo Sasso (089 81 81 81; www.palazzosasso .com; Via San Giovanni del Toro 28; d from €260; Mar-Oct;) This stunning pale pink 12th-century palace became a hotel in 1880, providing refuge for Wagner and, later, Ingrid Bergman. Creatively refurbished with brushes of colour from the Moorish palette and coupled with tasteful antiques, it's a stunner. There are 44 rooms and suites, most with Jacuzzis and dreamy views.

Graal (089 85 72 22; www.hotelgraal.it; Via della Repubblica 8; s/d €59/98;) Although the public areas could do with updating, the rooms are tastefully decorated with plenty of sun-and-sea colours reflecting the balcony views. There are good-sized bathrooms and the downstairs restaurant has a good reputation in town.

Eating

Cumpà Cosimo (089 85 71 56; Via Roma 44-6; meals about €30) This is a family affair: meat comes fresh from hubby's butcher shop, vegetables and fruit are home-grown, and even the house wine is home-brew. Mama Netta is smiley and welcoming, and will happily explain the menu in her best English. Dishes include rabbit with tomatoes, penne with hot peppers and tomatoes, and a delicious grilled crayfish.

Ristorante Palazzo della Marra (089 85 83 02; Via della Marra 7; meals €35-40; Wed-Mon Apr-Sep) Splash out and you may possibly enjoy the best meal of your trip here. The food is a snip above the competition, both in quality and price, and you can't really fault the 12th-century building for style. Dishes include smoked duck with fennel cream, beef fillet in thyme and, to round it off, tiramisu with cream of pistachio.

Take Away Pizza (089 85 76 05; 41 Viale Parco della Rimembranza) If you're pushed for time or simply want to chew on a pizza, drop in to Take Away Pizza where there are 36 pizza choices to select from.

Getting There & Away

SITA operates about 15 buses daily between Ravello and Amalfi (€1, 25 minutes). By car, turn left (north) about 2km east of Amalfi. Vehicles, thankfully, are not permitted in Ravello's town centre but there is plenty of space in the supervised car parks on the perimeter.

FROM AMALFI TO SALERNO

The 20km drive to Salerno, though marginally less exciting than the 16km stretch westwards to Positano, is exhilarating and dotted with a series of little towns, each worth a brief look around and each a potential base.

Atrani, just round a headland, is a pretty extension of Amalfi with a little beach. Further on are the towns of **Minori** and **Maiori**. Although lacking much of the charm of their better-known partners up the road, both have plenty of hotels and Maiori has a decent-sized beach. Perhaps most attractive is the fishing village of **Cetara**.

Shortly before you reach Salerno, you pass through **Vietri sul Mare**, set on a rise with commanding views over its larger neighbour and a good place to buy local ceramics. The town has plenty of workshops and showrooms and there are some good buys if you shop around.

SALERNO

pop 141,724

Salerno may seem like a bland big city after all those oh-so-pretty Amalfi towns but the place has a charming, if gritty, individuality, with a tumbledown medieval quarter and pleasant seafront promenade. One of southern Italy's many victims of earth tremors and landslides, it was also left in tatters by the heavy fighting that followed the 1943 landings of the American 5th Army, just to the south of the city. It is also an important transport junction and makes an excellent base for exploring the Amalfi Coast (p670) to the west, and Paestum (p680) and the Costiera Cilentana (p682) to the southeast.

Originally an Etruscan and later a Roman colony, Salerno flourished with the arrival of the Normans in the 11th century. Robert Guiscard made it the capital of his dukedom in 1076 and, under his patronage, the Scuola Medica Salernitana was renowned as one of medieval Europe's greatest medical institutes.

Orientation

Salerno's train station is on Piazza Vittorio Veneto, at the eastern end of town. Most intercity buses stop here and there are a number of hotels nearby. Salerno's main shopping strip, the car-free Corso Vittorio Emanuele, leads off northwest to the medieval part of town. Running parallel is Corso Garibaldi, which becomes Via Roma as it heads out of the city for the Amalfi Coast. Tree-lined Lungomare Trieste, on the waterfront, changes its name to Lungomare Marconi at the massive Piazza della Concordia on its way out of town, southeast towards Paestum.

Information

There's a Banca Nazionale del Lavoro ATM at the train station. You'll find several banks with ATMs on Corso Vittorio Emanuele.

Interlanguage Point (☎ 089 75 35 81; 1st fl, Corso Vittorio Emanuele 14; per 25min €1.50, 30min €2; 🕑 9am-1pm & 3.30-9pm Mon-Sat) Internet access.

Mail Box (Via Diaz 19; per 25min €1.50; 🕑 9am-1.30pm & 5.30-8pm Mon-Sat) Internet access.

Ospedale Ruggi d'Aragona (☎ 089 67 11 11; Via San Leonardo) Hospital.

Police station (☎ 089 61 31 11; Piazza Amendola)

Post office (Corso Garibaldi 203)

Salernocity (www.salernocity.com in Italian)

Salerno Memo (www.salernomemo.com in Italian)

Tourist office (☎ 089 23 14 32; Piazza Vittorio Veneto; 🕑 9am-2pm & 3-8pm Mon-Sat)

Sights

CATHEDRAL

The city's **cathedral** (☎ 089 23 13 87; Piazza Alfano; 🕑 10am-6pm), built by the Normans under Robert Guiscard in the 11th century and remodelled in the 18th century, sustained severe damage in the 1980 earthquake. It's dedicated to San Matteo (St Matthew), whose remains were reputedly brought to the city in 954 and buried in the crypt. With its 28 Greek columns, most of them plundered from Paestum, it has a decidedly classical air.

The **Cappella delle Crociate** (Chapel of the Crusades) was so-named because crusaders' weapons were blessed here. It has the 11th-century pope Gregory VII interred under the altar.

Next door on the northern side of the cathedral is the **Museo Diocesano** (☎ 089 23 91 26; Largo del Plebiscito 12; admission free; 🕑 9am-6pm), which has a modest collection of artworks,

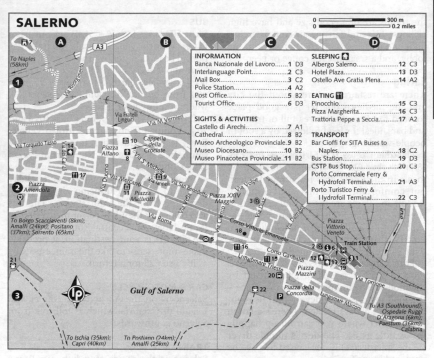

SALERNO

0 ─────── 300 m
0 ─────── 0.2 miles

INFORMATION	
Banca Nazionale del Lavoro......1	D3
Interlanguage Point................2	C3
Mail Box............................3	C2
Police Station.......................4	A2
Post Office..........................5	B2
Tourist Office.......................6	D3

SIGHTS & ACTIVITIES	
Castello di Arechi.................7	A1
Cathedral..........................8	B2
Museo Archeologico Provinciale.9	B2
Museo Diocesano................10	B2
Museo Pinacoteca Provinciale..11	B2

SLEEPING	
Albergo Salerno...................12	C3
Hotel Plaza........................13	D3
Ostello Ave Gratia Plena.......14	A2

EATING	
Pinocchio..........................15	C3
Pizza Margherita..................16	C3
Trattoria Peppe a Seccia.......17	A2

TRANSPORT	
Bar Cioffi for SITA Buses to	
Naples...........................18	C2
Bus Station........................19	D3
CSTP Bus Stop....................20	C3
Porto Commerciale Ferry &	
Hydrofoil Terminal.............21	A3
Porto Turistico Ferry &	
Hydrofoil Terminal.............22	C3

Gulf of Salerno

To Naples (58km)

To Borgo Scacciaventi (8km); Amalfi (24km); Positano (37km); Sorrento (65km)

To Ischia (35km); Capri (40km)

To Postiano (74km); Amalfi (25km)

Piazza Amendola

Piazza Alfano

Piazza Mercanti

Piazza Malteotti

Piazza XXIV Maggio

Corso Vittorio Emanuele

Corso Garibaldi

Lungomare Trieste

Piazza Mazzini

Piazza della Concordia

Piazza Vittorio Veneto

Train Station

Via Torrione

Lungomare Marconi

To A3 (Southbound); Ospedale Ruggi D'Aragona (6km); Paestum (36km); Calabria

---

including items from the Norman period
and a few fragments of Lombard sculpture.

CASTELLO DI ARECHI

A steep walk to the **Castello di Arechi** (☎ 089 22
72 37; Via Benedetto Croce; admission free; ☻ 7am-noon &
4-7.30pm) along Via Risorgimento is rewarded
with good views, if you can ignore the industrial sprawl beneath you. Arechi II, a
Lombard duke of Benevento, built the castle
over a Byzantine fort. Last renovated by the
Spanish in the 16th century, its slow decline
has been arrested by modern restoration.

MUSEUMS

The **Museo Archeologico Provinciale** (☎ 089 23 11 35;
Via San Benedetto 28; admission free; ☻ 9am-8pm Mon-Sat)
contains archaeological finds from around
the region, including some particularly fine
classical pieces.

Deep in the heart of the medieval quarter,
the small **Museo Pinacoteca Provinciale** (☎ 089
258 30 73; Via Mercanti 63; admission free; ☻ 8am-2pm
& 3-8pm Tue-Sat, 9am-1pm Sun, 1-8pm Mon) houses an
interesting collection dating from the Renaissance right up to the first half of the 19th

century. There are some fine canvases by
local boy Andrea Sabatini da Salerno and
an assortment of works by foreign artists
living in the area.

Sleeping

Ostello Ave Gratia Plena (☎ 089 79 02 51; fax 089 40 57
92; Via dei Canali; dm with breakfast €16, d B&B per person
€17) This highly recommended HI hostel is
light, airy and pristine. It's in a former 16th-
century convent, and you can look directly
down into the adjacent church through windows where the nuns used to follow Mass,
thus avoiding eye contact with men.

Hotel Plaza (☎ /fax 089 22 44 77; www.plazasalerno
.it; Piazza Vittorio Veneto 42; s/d €63/95) This hotel has
gone through three generations and, finally,
the drab brown-and-cream colour scheme
is getting a re vamp. A slight exaggeration
perhaps: the bathrooms have sparkling turquoise and white tiles but the brand-new
carpets are still the colour of mud! The location is good, though, and there's a lift.

Albergo Salerno (☎ 089 22 42 11; www.albergo
salerno.com; 5th fl, Via G Vicinanza 42; s/d €55/60; ☒) This
place looks discouraging from the outside but

the rooms are of a good size and have high ceilings, TVs and fans or air-con. There's a light and cheery sitting area, adjacent to the lobby, and a small bar for coffee or beer.

Eating

There are restaurants throughout the city and the medieval quarter is a good place to head for. It's a lively area full of trattorie and bars, ideal for food followed by a spot of people-watching.

Pinocchio (☎ 089 22 99 64; Lungomare Trieste 56-582; meals about €20; ☻ Sat-Thu) Frequented by locals in the know, this restaurant is clean but comfortably informal and cluttered. Rodolf and Paula are the second generation running the place. There are no specials as such, but the *scaloppine ai funghi limone o vino* (veal and mushrooms with a lemon or wine sauce) is especially good.

Pizza Margherita (☎ 089 22 88 80; Corso Garibaldi 201; pizzas & mains from €5) Don't be put off by the modern streamlined look to this place – the food inspires utter devotion in its regulars and it's always packed. There's a lavish lunch buffet where you can fill up happily for as little as €4. The devil's tumble dryer (ie the microwave) is never used here, so be prepared to wait.

Trattoria Peppe a Seccia (☎ 089 22 05 18; Via Antica Corte 5; meals about €15) There's a great southern Italian atmosphere here with the tables sprawled out into this tiny medieval piazza, surrounded by equally ancient houses hung with multicoloured washing. The choices are pizza, pasta and gnocchi and, because this place attracts mainly locals, you can bet on the standard being high.

Drinking

There are numerous bars and pubs along Via Roma and dotted throughout the medieval quarter. Join the locals in their daily *passeggiata* (evening stroll) and see where they stop off for a drink; it's probably the best recommendation you could have.

Getting There & Away
BOAT

Ferries run from Salerno's Porto Turistico to Positano and Amalfi from April to October, while departures for Capri and Ischia leave from the Porto Commerciale. Hydrofoils to these destinations also run in summer. Contact the tourist office for current schedules.

BUS

Most **SITA buses** (☎ 089 40 51 45) set out from Piazza Vittorio Veneto, beside the train station. Those that follow the Amalfi Coast leave about every hour. The exception is the Naples service, which departs every 25 minutes from outside **Bar Cioffi** (Corso Garibaldi 134), where you buy your ticket.

CSTP (☎ 089 48 70 01) operates bus Nos 4 and 50 to Pompeii from Piazza Vittorio Veneto. For Paestum and other towns along the southern coast take bus No 34 from Piazza della Concordia.

Buonotourist runs an express weekday service to Rome's Fiumicino airport (€25), departing from the train station. The bus also passes by the EUR-Fermi metro stop in Rome. However, if central Rome (rather than the airport) is your destination, it probably makes more sense to take the train, especially as it's also €25 for a return.

CAR & MOTORCYCLE

Salerno is on the A3 between Naples and Reggio di Calabria, which is toll free from Salerno southwards.

TRAIN

Salerno is the major stop between Rome (€20), Naples (€2.90) and Reggio di Calabria (€28.60), and is served by all types of trains. It also has good train links with inland towns and the Adriatic coast. The tourist office (p678) can provide the necessary timetable.

Getting Around

Walking is the most sensible option if you're staying in the heart of Salerno. Bus No 41 runs from the train station to the cathedral.

PAESTUM

One of the enduring images of southern Italy is that of three Greek temples standing in fields of wild red poppies. The trio are among the best-preserved monuments of Magna Graecia, as the Greeks called their colonies in southern Italy and Sicily. The small town of Paestum nearby is close to some of Italy's better beaches and just south of where US forces landed in 1943.

Paestum, or Poseidonia as the city was originally called (in honour of Poseidon, the Greek god of the sea), was founded in the 6th century BC by Greek settlers and fell under Roman control in 273 BC, becoming an important trading port. The town was hit by the successive blows of the retreat of the Roman Empire, periodic outbreaks of malaria and savage raids by the Saracens, and was gradually and understandably abandoned. Its temples were rediscovered in the late 18th century by road builders – who proceeded to plough their way right through the ruins. However, the road did little to alter the state of the surrounding area, which remained full of malarial swamps, teeming with snakes and scorpions, until well into the 20th century.

Such days are long past and Paestum is these days a Unesco World Heritage site that is easily covered on foot. The **tourist office** (☎ 0828 81 10 16; www.paestumtourism.it in Italian; Via Magnia Grecia 887; ☽ 9am-5pm May-Jul, 9am-8pm Aug, 9am-4pm Mon-Sat, 9am-1pm Sun Sep-Apr) has a lot of useful information.

The most economical way to enjoy Paestum is to buy a combined entrance ticket (€6.50), which covers both temples and the museum.

Sights
THE RUINS
At the **ruins** (admission €4; ☽ 9am-1hr before sunset), the first temple you meet on entering the site from the northern end, near the tourist office, is the 6th-century-BC **Tempio di Cerere** (Temple of Ceres). The smallest of the three temples, it served for a time as a Christian church.

As you head south you can pick out the basic outline of the large rectangular **forum**, the heart of the ancient city. Among the partially standing buildings are a vast domestic housing area, an Italic temple, the Greek theatre, Bouleuterion (where the Roman senate used to meet) and, further south, the amphitheatre – through which that infamous road was ploughed.

The **Tempio di Nettuno** (Temple of Neptune), dating from about 450 BC, is the largest and best preserved of the three temples; only parts of its inside walls and roof are missing. Almost next door, the so-called **basilica** (in fact, a temple to the goddess Hera) is Paestum's oldest-surviving monument. Dating from the middle of the 6th century BC and with nine columns across and 18 along the sides, it's indeed a majestic building. Just to its east you can, with a touch of imagination, make out remains of the temple's sacrificial altar.

In its time the city was ringed by an impressive 4.7km of walls, subsequently built and rebuilt by both Lucanians and Romans. The most intact section is south of the ruins themselves.

Tickets to the ruins are sold at the main entry point or, in winter, from the museum. Here you can also hire an audioguide (€4).

MUSEO DI PAESTUM
This well-appointed **museum** (☎ 0828 81 10 23; admission €4; ☽ 9am-7pm, closed 1st & 3rd Mon of month), just east of the site, houses a collection of much-weathered *metopes* (bas-relief friezes), including 33 of the original 36 from the Tempio di Argive Hera, about 9km north of Paestum, of which virtually nothing else remains.

Sleeping & Eating
Accommodation tends to be pricey and in summer is absolutely heaving. Think about Salerno or Agropoli as alternatives.

Hotel Villa Rita (☎ /fax 0828 81 10 81; www.hotel villarita.it; Zona Archeologica 5; s/d €60/75; ☽ Mar-Oct; ☒ ℗) Set back from the main road in 2 acres of grounds, this place is a tranquil haven (aside from the birdsong) in the midst of the summer-holiday chaos. Rooms are rustic and there is a good restaurant. The hotel is also conveniently close to the ruins.

Camping Villaggio dei Pini (☎ 0828 81 10 30; Via Torre; www.campingvillaggiodeipini.com; 2 people & tent €20.50, 2-person bungalows per week from €300) This place can tick all the right boxes for family camping, with a volleyball/football pitch, private beach, playground, pizzeria, snack bar and live entertainment. Prices vary according to the season. Bungalows are also available for a minimum of one week.

As with accommodation, restaurants tend to inflate their prices during the summer months. There are a few cafés and snack bars and a couple of restaurants along Via Magnia Grecia, which slices between the temples and the museum.

Ristorante Nettuno (☎ 0828 81 10 28; Via Principe di Piemonte; meals about €20) For something more special, try Ristorante Nettuno, just outside the southern walls. Guarding the southeastern entry to the ruins, visitor-friendly Nettuno offers elegant dining at reasonable prices. The mozzarella here is particularly good and you know it's fresh as the sweet smell of buffalo wafts in from the farm just down the road.

Getting There & Away

CSTP (☎ 800 01 66 59) and **SCAT** (☎ 0974 83 84 15) buses run hourly from Salerno's Piazza della Concordia to Paestum and on to Agropoli.

If you're driving you could take the A3 from Salerno and exit for the SS18 at Battipaglia. Better, however, and altogether more pleasant is the Litoranea, the minor road that hugs the coast. From the A3 take the earlier exit for Pontecagnano and follow the signs for Agropoli and Paestum, which is 36km from Salerno.

Paestum is on the train line from Naples and Salerno to Reggio di Calabria. Most trains stop at Stazione di Capaccio, closer to the new town (about 6km from the site) and less frequently at Stazione di Paestum, less than 1km from the temples. Trains are less frequent than CSTP buses. Ask at the tourist office for current timetables.

PARCO NAZIONALE DEL CILENTO E VALLO DI DIANO

The wild and empty highlands of the Parco Nazionale del Cilento e Vallo di Diano are the perfect antidote to the holiday mayhem along the coast. Occupying the area southeast of Salerno up to the regional borders with Basilicata and Calabria, it is a little-explored area that boasts barren beauty and a number of worthwhile sights. The only problem is transport: without your own you will need plenty of time. For information, ask at the tourist office in Paestum (p681).

The WWF has a wildlife sanctuary, **Oasi Naturalistica di Persano** (☎ 0828 97 46 84; ☺ Sep-Apr), about 20km northeast of Paestum on the River Sele. It's mainly wetlands and is home to a wide variety of birds, both resident and seasonal. Signs direct you there from the SS18.

There's also two cave systems well worth exploring. The **Grotte di Pertosa** (☎ 0975 39 70 37; www.grottedipertosa.it in Italian; short/long tours €5/8; ☺ 9am-7pm Apr-Oct, 9am-4pm Nov-Mar), 40km northeast of Paestum, were discovered in the late 19th century. The tour takes you through 1700m of caves bristling with stalagmites and stalactites. A SITA bus leaves at about 9am from Salerno's Piazza Vittorio Veneto; an-

other will take you back in the afternoon. By car take the A3 southbound from Salerno. The caves are 9km from the Petina exit.

Nearer to Paestum, the **Grotte di Castelcivita** (☎ 0828 97 55 24; www.grottedicastelcivita.it; tours €8; ☺ departs 10am, 11am, noon, 1.30 & hourly to 6.30pm mid-Mar-Oct, 10am, 11.30am, 1.30pm, 3pm & 4.30pm Oct-mid-Mar) are where Spartacus is said to have taken refuge following his slave rebellion in 71 BC. There is a **De Rosa bus** (☎ 0828 94 10 65) that departs from Capaccio Scalo at 9.30am and returns at 4.30pm. By car from Paestum it's about 20km; take the SS18 towards Salerno and follow the signs.

In the opposite direction, down the A3 towards Calabria, just beneath the village of Padula, is the **Certosa di San Lorenzo** (☎ 0975 77 85 49; admission €4; ☺ 9am-7.30pm) which merits a detour. Also known as the Certosa di Padula, this vast monastery has had a turbulent history. Begun in the 14th century and modified over the centuries, it was abandoned in the 19th century, then suffered further degradation as a children's holiday home and later a concentration camp. Many of the monks who lived here were from wealthy aristocratic families and no expense was spared in its construction – as the restored elaborate chapels, huge central courtyard and wood-panelled library reveal.

Mafia junkies might find the **Museo Joe Petrosino** (☎ 0975 773 95; www.joepetrosino.org in Italian; Via Giuseppe Petrosino; admission €2; ☺ 10am-1pm & 3-6pm mid-Mar-Sep) particularly interesting. Up in Padula, the unexceptional village house where this early fighter against the US Mafia was born contains a small museum recording 'la vita e morte di un detective' (the life and death of a detective). Petrosino was gunned down in 1909 by the leader of the local clan as he returned to his native country. Lamanna buses run from Salerno to Padula and (less frequently) to Teggiano.

COSTIERA CILENTANA

Southeast of the Gulf of Salerno, the coastal plains begin to give way to wilder, jagged cliffs and unspoilt scenery, a taste of what lies further on in the stark hills and mountains of Basilicata and the more heavily wooded peaks of Calabria. This southernmost tract of the Campania littoral doesn't really lend itself to summer seaside frolics, although snorkellers will appreciate some of the rocky points. Despite an irregular splattering of camp sites and holiday accommodation, the beaches are not as popular as those further northwest or those southeast in Basilicata and Calabria. CSTP buses leave Salerno for Sapri, on the regional boundary between Campania and Basilicata. Trains heading south from Salerno also stop at most towns on the Costiera Cilentana (Cilento Coast). By car take the SS18, which connects Agropoli with Velia via the inland route, or the SS267, which hugs the coast.

AGROPOLI

Popular with holidaying Italians in summer, this otherwise tranquil coastal town has a charmingly shabby medieval core. Perched on a high promontory overlooking the sea, the town is topped by a crumbling old castle, like a cherry on a cake. A rewarding stop, it makes an excellent base for Paestum and the beaches to the northwest.

There is a **tourist office** (☎ 0329 622 77 54; Corso Garibaldi 38; ⏰ 10.30am-1pm & 3.30-7.30pm Mon-Sat) on the main shopping street.

There are plenty of accommodation options in town – the tourist office can provide you with a list and tell you which months they are open.

Ostello La Lanterna (☎ /fax 0974 83 83 64; lanterna@cilento.it; Via Lanterna 8; dm with breakfast €11; ⏰ mid-Mar–Oct) At Agropoli's northern extremity, this friendly HI hostel is just a two-minute walk from the beach and is homely and relaxed. There are also beds available in family rooms (€11.50) and an evening meal for €7.50.

Hotel Carola (☎ 0974 82 64 22; www.hotelcarola.it; Via Pisacane 1; s/d €62/80; 🖥 🅿) This 19th-century grand hotel has a few rooms with original tiles and an old-fashioned feel – far nicer than the modern equivalent. A shuttle runs to the local beach and the restaurant is highly rated.

Pizzeria U'Sghiz (☎ 0974 82 45 82; Piazza Umberto I; pizzas from €2.50) Purists will blanch, but the pizzas here are made with wholemeal flour – an original touch that works. Served ready-cut, the pizzas come with the topping specified and nothing else, so if you want tomato or mozzarella you'll have to ask for them.

Camping Torino (☎ /fax 0828 81 18 51; Via Litoranea Linora; 2-person sites high season €32; ⏰ Mar-Sep) About

6km north of Agropoli along the Litoranea road, this camp site beside the beach has all the facilities and is a short drive from Paestum.

VELIA

The Greek settlement of Elea, now Velia, was founded in the mid-6th century BC and later became a popular spot for wealthy Romans. The **ruins** (☎ 0974 97 23 96; admission €2; ⏰ 9am-6pm Mon-Sat) here are considerably smaller than those at Paestum and in a far worse state. They are worth a visit only if you have the time.

Albergo Elea (☎ /fax 0974 97 15 77; Via Elea 69; s/d €36/72, half board per person €35), in nearby Ascea, is a pleasant, simply furnished hotel, conveniently near the water. Prices can drop considerably outside of summer.

The train station for Ascea is at Marina di Ascea. To get to the ruins from there, wait for a local bus to Castellamare di Velia.

SOUTH TO SAPRI

From Ascea to Sapri, a dowdy seaside town a few kilometres short of Basilicata, the road climbs, dips and curves its way through country that, while not Italy's prettiest, is rarely dull and at times is spectacular. The beaches along this part of the coast are good and the water usually crystal clear.

Pisciotta, 12km southeast of Ascea, is an attractive medieval village that clings to the mountainside.

Agriturismo San Carlo (☎ /fax 0974 97 61 77; Via Noce 8; s/d with breakfast €35/70) is a real jewel of a place. The charming whitewashed building houses gorgeous rooms with original beams, wooden shutters and elegant brass beds. A working farm, you can savour the olive oil produced here from the local Pisciotta olive trees.

Another 25km or so further on, southeast of the resort town of **Palinuro** (in and around which are camp sites and several hotels), are some striking white-sand **beaches**. A little further still, where the road turns steeply inland to pass through San Giovanni a Piro, is **Marina di Camerota**, which has a small medieval centre. From there it's another 25km to Sapri. If you get this far you should really make the effort to continue the short distance into Basilicata.

Puglia, Basilicata & Calabria

Italy's deep south is well off the beaten track and is frequently dismissed by refined and affluent northerners as the land of *terroni* (peasants). Yet the south is terribly ancient and even more secretive. Its history can be traced back some 8000 years; writer Carlo Levi, exiled here, sensed its dark and enduring paganism, calling it 'that other world...which no-one may enter without a magic key'.

If Puglia is a land without shadows, a luminous landscape of plateaus and plains set against a sun-spotted sea, then Calabria and Basilicata are defined by their crush of mountains and the deep shadows of their canyons and gorges. Magical it may be, but there is plenty to regret – the stark suburban sprawl of Brindisi and Reggio, and the industrial development around Potenza and Taranto, are eyesores on a grand scale.

Above all, southern Italy has not – yet – been overexposed. Its widely distributed sights and attractions force one to travel outside the comfort zone, engaging with the landscape and people on a level impossible in more sophisticated urban centres. Venture into these parts and you'll be rewarded with an unforgettable experience that will challenge your comfortable preconceptions of just what modern Italy is all about.

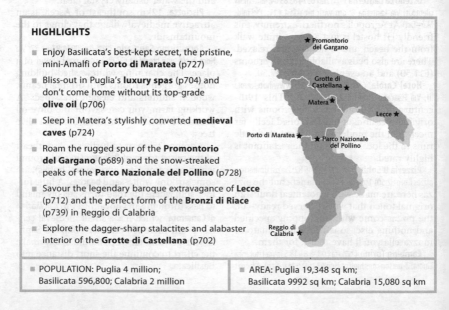

HIGHLIGHTS

- Enjoy Basilicata's best-kept secret, the pristine, mini-Amalfi of **Porto di Maratea** (p727)

- Bliss-out in Puglia's **luxury spas** (p704) and don't come home without its top-grade **olive oil** (p706)

- Sleep in Matera's stylishly converted **medieval caves** (p724)

- Roam the rugged spur of the **Promontorio del Gargano** (p689) and the snow-streaked peaks of the **Parco Nazionale del Pollino** (p728)

- Savour the legendary baroque extravagance of **Lecce** (p712) and the perfect form of the **Bronzi di Riace** (p739) in Reggio di Calabria

- Explore the dagger-sharp stalactites and alabaster interior of the **Grotte di Castellana** (p702)

★ Promontorio del Gargano

★ Grotte di Castellana

★ Matera

★ Lecce

★ Porto di Maratea ★ Parco Nazionale del Pollino

★ Reggio di Calabria

- POPULATION: Puglia 4 million; Basilicata 596,800; Calabria 2 million

- AREA: Puglia 19,348 sq km; Basilicata 9992 sq km; Calabria 15,080 sq km

PUGLIA, BASILICATA & CALABRIA

PUGLIA

Puglia, the 'heel' of Italy's boot, sits between two seas, the Adriatic to the east and Ionian to the south. This strategic position, combined with more than 800km of difficult-to-defend coastline, has shaped the region's history. In the Middle Ages Puglia's ports celebrated returning crusaders and subsequently reaped the whirlwind of vengeful Saracen armies. Today the coastline continues to influence Puglia's politics as scores of illegal immigrants land at Bari and Brindisi.

The wind-eroded cliffs of Puglia constitute some of the country's most lovely coastline, from the dramatic Promontorio del Gargano (Gargano Promontory) to the hidden beaches of the Penisola Salentina (Salentine Peninsula). Geologically speaking the region has more in common with Croatia than with the rest of Italy; its glittering limestone precipices and emerald-green waters are utterly unforgettable.

To get the best out of Puglia, and indeed the whole of the south, your own transport is an advantage and, at times, essential.

History

Many say the only true civilisation of the south was that of the Greeks, who founded a string of settlements along the Ionian coast in the 8th century BC. Their major city was Taras (Taranto), which was settled by Spartan exiles who dominated the region until they were defeated by the Romans in 272 BC. Less than 100 years later, in 190 BC, the Romans completed Via Appia, the road which ran from Rome to the port of Brindisi.

Since then 'brute races' have flung themselves at the province one after the other. The Normans left their fine Romanesque churches, the Swabians their fortifications and castles, and the Spanish their bold baroque buildings epitomised in golden Lecce. No-one, however, is able to place the origins of the strange 16th-century, conical roofed stone houses, the *trulli*, which are unique to Puglia.

Following Mussolini's seizure of power in 1922 in the aftermath of WWI, the south became the frontline in Mussolini's 'Battle for Wheat', an initiative that was aimed at making Italy self-sufficient when it came to food. Even today the south (and especially Puglia) is covered in wheat fields, olive groves and fruit arbours, providing a huge amount of the raw produce found on the Italian table. It's hardly surprising then that popular celebrity chef Antonio Carluccio is Puglia born and bred.

PUGLIA, BASILICATA & CALABRIA

A TASTE OF PUGLIA

Puglia is a food- and wine-lover's paradise – no matter how hard you try, it's difficult to eat badly here. Many of the basic elements in the Italian kitchen originate from Puglia – a huge proportion of Italy's fish is caught off the Puglian coast, 80% of Europe's pasta is produced here and up to 80% of Italy's olive oil originates in Puglia and Calabria.

Tomatoes, broccoli, chicory, fennel, figs, melons, cherries and grapes are just some of the choice fruits and vegetables you'll find. Almonds, grown near Ruvo di Puglia, are used in many traditional cakes and pastries.

Like their Greek forbears, the folk of Puglia eat a lot of *agnello* (lamb) and *capretto* (kid). The meat is usually roasted or grilled with aromatic herbs, or served in tomato-based sauces.

Fish and seafood are abundant. Raw fish (such as anchovies or baby squid) marinated in olive oil and lemon juice is not uncommon. *Cozze* (mussels) are prepared in a variety of ways. One recipe from the Bari area, *tiella alla barese*, has mussels baked with rice and potatoes.

Bread and pasta are both fundamental to the Puglian diet, with per-capita consumption at least double that of the USA. You'll find *orecchiette* (small ear-shaped pasta, sometimes called *strascinati*) in most places, often served with vegetable toppings. Other common Puglian pasta shapes are *cavatelli* and *capunti*.

Many quality wines are produced on the Penisola Salentina (the Salice Salentino is one of the best of the region's reds), in the *trulli* area around Locorotondo, and in the plains around Foggia and Lucera. Some of Italy's best rosé wines hail from Puglia and perfectly complement the local cuisine.

PUGLIA, BASILICATA & CALABRIA

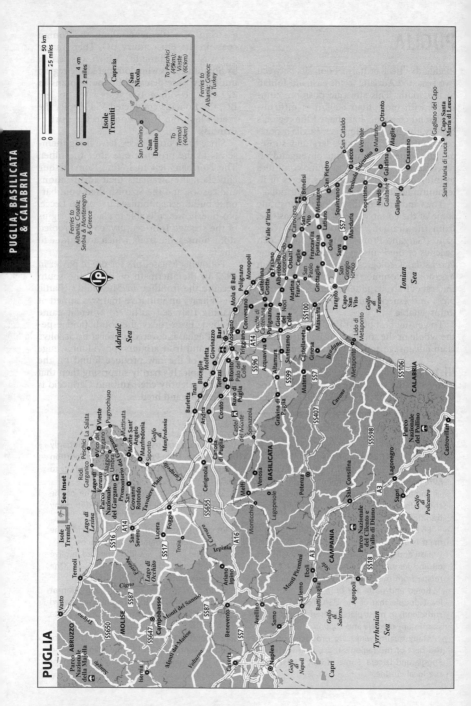

FOGGIA

pop 155,000

If you enter Puglia from the north you descend from the lush pastures of Molise to the sun-baked flatness of the Tavoliere plain, a huge, golden wheat-producing expanse. At its centre is the ugly provincial capital of Foggia, its name derived from its famous *fovea* (grain stores). It was one of the favourite towns of Frederick II (1194–1250), and his heart was kept here in a casket until the massive earthquake of 1731 destroyed the town and everything in it. Later, Foggia became a strategic airbase in WWII, suffering extensive bomb damage that is largely responsible for the shabby construction that defines the modern town.

There is little to detain the visitor here other than connections with San Giovanni Rotondo and the Promontorio del Gargano. The nearby towns of Troia and Lucera are also worth a visit.

Orientation

Train and bus stations face Piazza Vittorio Veneto, on the north rim of the town. Viale XXIV Maggio leads south into Piazza Cavour. On or around the Viale are several hotels, restaurants and shops, as well as the post and telephone offices. From Piazza Cavour, Via Lanza leads to Corso Vittorio Emanuele II and what remains of the old quarter.

Information

Police station (☎ 0881 66 81 11; Via Gramsci Antonio 1)
Post office (Viale XXIV Maggio)
Tourist office (☎ 0881 72 36 50; 1st fl, Via Senatore Emilio Perrone 17; ✆ 8am-1.30pm Mon-Fri) From Piazza Cavour, head south along Corso P Giannone. Take the third left turning into Via Cirillo and go straight on until Piazzale Puglia – Via Perrone is on the right.

Sights

The **cathedral** (☎ 0881 77 34 82; off Corso Vittorio Emanuele II; ✆ 7am-12.30pm & 5-8pm) is Foggia's only noteworthy sight. Built in the 12th century, the lower section remains true to the original Romanesque style. The top half, exuberantly baroque, was grafted on after the earthquake in 1731. Most of the cathedral's treasures were lost in the quake but you can see a Byzantine icon preserved in a chapel inside the church. Legend has it that in the 11th century, shepherds discovered the icon lying in a pond over which burned three flames. These flames are now the symbol of the city.

The **Museo Civico** (☎ 0881 72 62 45; Piazza Nigri; admission free; ✆ 8am-1pm Sun-Fri & 3.30-7pm Tue & Thu) houses archaeological finds and folk crafts from the province.

Sleeping

Hotel Cicolella (☎ 0881 56 61 11; www.hotelcicolella.isnet.it; Viale XXIV Maggio 60; s/d €152/200; ✖) This rust red–coloured Foggia landmark, founded more than 100 years ago, is a delightful blend of old-world charm spiced with contemporary efficiency. The rooms come with all the requisite mod cons and the restaurant serves excellent local cuisine.

Hotel Europa (☎ 0881 72 10 57; www.hoteleuropafoggia.com; Via Monfalcone 52; s/d €93/135; ✖ ✖) About 50m from the train station, this place has very comfortable rooms even if the common areas are rather dated. For a few euros more you can enjoy the suites, which are larger and decked out in some style.

Albergo Venezia (☎ 0881 77 09 03; fax 77 09 04; Via Piave 40; s/d €50/65) Rooms at this conveniently central hotel have all the charm of a doctor's waiting room. However, they're functional and reasonable value for money.

Eating

Because it is not a tourist town, Foggia has a number of excellent and reasonably priced restaurants. There are several trattorie in the sidestreets west of Viale XXIV Maggio.

Ristorante L'Angolo Preferito (☎ 0881 70 85 90; Via Trieste 21; meals €20) The menu, which changes every day and is announced by the waiter, makes heavy use of local produce – good news, as Foggia is in the middle of farm country. The dishes are simple, well cooked and tasty.

Ristorante Margutta (☎ 0881 70 80 60; Via Piave 33; meals €25) This friendly family restaurant near Albergo Venezia is very popular and often full. It specialises in fish dishes and offers a small but select menu.

Also well recommended is the romantic **La Locanda di Malì** (☎ 0881 72 39 37; Via Arpi 86; meals €20-25; ✆ Wed-Sun Sep-Jul).

Getting There & Around

BUS

Buses depart from Piazzale Vittorio Veneto, from in front of the train station, for towns throughout the province of Foggia.

PUGLIA, BASILICATA & CALABRIA

DETOUR: TROIA

Go out of your way to visit Troia (20km south of Foggia), set on a gentle hill surrounded by a crinoline of emerald-green fields. It has a magnificent **cathedral** (Piazza Episcopio), one of the oldest in Puglia (begun in 1093), which gracefully combines Arab-inspired Byzantine artistry with the blind arcades and lozenge motifs of Pisan Romanesque. The 13th-century rose window is one of the finest in Italy, created in Frederick II's time and influenced by the highly developed sense of geometry in Islamic art. The simplicity of the blind arcading around the base is in marked contrast to sculpted gargoyles above and the finely wrought 12th-century bronze doors with their dragon handles.

Inside the church is tall and elegant. It's divided into three narrow aisles lined by columned arches topped with sculpted capitals. The sculpture on the pulpit is also superb and it is worth seeking out the rich treasury.

For somewhere to stay try the no-frills **Albergo Alba d'Oro** (☎ 0881 97 04 25; Viale Kennedy 28; s/d €30/46; 🞉). It's about 10 minutes' walk to the centre. Ring the bell to gain entry.

Regular Ferrovie del Gargano buses link Troia and Foggia (€1.50, 50 minutes).

SITA (☎ 0881 77 31 17; www.sita-on-line.it in Italian) runs buses to Vieste (€4.90, 2¾ hours, five daily) via Manfredonia (€1.80, 50 minutes), Monte Sant'Angelo (€3.60, 1½ hours, five daily), San Giovanni Rotondo (€2.60, one hour, half-hourly), Lucera (€1.30, 30 minutes, five daily) and Campobasso in Molise (€5.70, 1½ hours, two daily).

Ferrovie del Gargano (☎ 0881 72 51 88; www.ferro viedelgargano.com in Italian) has frequent services to Manfredonia (€1.80, 45 minutes) and Troia (€1.50, 50 minutes).

Tickets for both companies are available from the tobacconist at the train station or from the bar opposite, under the Cinema Ariston sign.

CLP (in Naples ☎ 081 531 17 06) runs direct buses connecting Foggia with Naples (€9, two hours, six daily) – they're a faster option than the train. Buy your ticket on board.

CAR & MOTORCYCLE
Take the SS16 south for Bari or north for the Adriatic coast, Termoli and Pescara. The Bologna–Bari A14 also passes Foggia. For Naples, take the SS655, which links with the east–west A16.

TRAIN
There are frequent Eurostar train services from Foggia to Bari (1st/2nd class €18/14, 1¼ hours) and onto Brindisi (€30/23, 2½ hours) and Lecce (€32/24, 2¾ hours). Northwards, up to 10 trains daily head for Ancona (€37/27, 3½ hours) and Bologna (€53.50/40, five hours), with fewer services going to Milan (€68/50.50, seven hours, six daily).

LUCERA
pop 35,100 / elev 219m
Lucera has a curious history. Founded by the Romans in the 4th century BC, the settlement had pretty much run out of steam by the 13th century and was practically abandoned. Then, following his excommunication by his bitter rival Pope Gregory IX, Frederick II decided to bolster his support base in Puglia by importing some 20,000 Sicilian Arabs into town, simultaneously diminishing the headache Arab bandits were causing him in Sicily.

It was an extraordinary move by the Christian monarch, even more so because Frederick allowed the new Muslim inhabitants of Lucera the freedom to build mosques and practice their religion freely a mere 290km from the Holy See at Rome. Frederick was mightily pleased with himself and spent considerable time in Lucera (as well as at his castles at Andria, Trani and Foggia), handpicking his famous Saracen bodyguard from its inhabitants.

History, however, was not so kind; when the town was taken by the rabidly Christian Angevins in 1269, every Muslim who failed to convert was slaughtered.

Sights
Lucera's historical significance is obvious when you set eyes on the enormous **castle** (admission free; 🕙 8am-2.30pm & 4-8pm Tue-Sun), one of the finest that Frederick built in Puglia. It stands 14km northwest of Lucera on a rocky hillock surrounded by a perfect pentagonal wall which is guarded by 24 towers.

The banqueting table from the castle has found its way into the **cathedral** (☺ 8am-noon & 4-7pm), where it now does duty as an altar. The cathedral was originally Lucera's Great Mosque but Charles II of Anjou remodelled it in 1300 into Puglia's only Gothic cathedral. The Gothic **Chiesa di San Francesco** (☺ 8am-noon & 4-7pm) was erected at the same time and incorporates numerous recycled materials from Lucera's poorly maintained 1st-century-BC **Roman amphitheatre** (admission free; ☺ 8am-2.30pm & 4-8pm Tue-Sun). You will find the amphitheatre on the eastern outskirts of town.

Sleeping

Hotel La Balconata 2 (☎ 0881 52 09 98; www.labalconata.it; Via Ferrovia 15; s/d €40/65; ✷ P) Lucera's only hotel is just outside the old city gate. It is a friendly place and offers rooms decorated with an eye for style. The views over the seemingly endless plains of the Tavoliere are impressive.

The hotel also owns and acts as reception for the more economical **Albergo Al Passetto** (Piazza del Popolo; s/d €30/50), on the inside of the city gate.

Getting There & Away

Lucera is easily accessible from Foggia by SITA buses (€1.30, 30 minutes, five daily), which terminate in Piazza del Popolo, or by Ferrovia del Gargano buses, which cover the same route.

MANFREDONIA

pop 57,500

Founded by the Swabian king Manfred (1231–66), Frederick II's illegitimate son, this rapidly developing industrial town has little to attract tourists other than a majestic castle and transport connections to the Promontorio del Gargano.

Intercity buses and trains both terminate in central Piazza Marconi. From there, semi-pedestrianised Corso Manfredi leads to Piazza del Popolo after 300m and to the **tourist office** (☎ 0884 58 19 98; Piazza del Popolo 11; ☺ 8.30am-1.30pm Mon-Fri).

Sights

Guarding the far end of the *corso* (main street) is the town's **castle** (☎ 0884 58 78 38; Corso Manfredi; admission €2.50; ☺ 8.30am-7.30pm daily, closed 1st & last Mon of month). The building was started

by Manfred and completed by Charles of Anjou. The **Museo Archeologico Nazionale del Gargano**, within the castle, displays local finds of Daunian provenance, in particular a series of carved grave slabs.

About 2km south of town is **Siponto**, an important port from Roman to medieval times, when it was abandoned in favour of Manfredonia because of earthquakes and malaria. Apart from the beaches, the only thing of interest is the distinctly Byzantine-looking 11th-century Romanesque **Chiesa di Santa Maria di Siponto**.

Sleeping & Eating

Hotel Sipontum (☎ /fax 0884 54 29 16; Viale di Vittorio 229; s/d €26/41) This hotel won't win any marks for glamour, but the rooms are clean. To get here take bus No 2 from the centre and it's virtually the last building on the left before you leave town.

Ristorante Coppolarossa (☎ 0884 58 25 22; Via dei Celestini 13; meals €26-31) This jovial family-run restaurant comes highly recommended. Specialising in seafood, it grills, fries and boils with panache, producing dishes of high quality. As a starter the seafood buffet (€7) is difficult to top.

Il Baraccio (☎ 0884 558941; Corso Roma 38; meals €30; ☺ noon-3.30pm Fri-Wed) Despite its modern décor, Il Baraccio is a traditional trattoria serving up local specialities such as octopus salad. It has a good reputation that it lives up to.

Getting There & Away

Regular trains and both **SITA** (☎ 0881 77 31 17) and **Ferrovie del Gargano** (☎ 0881 72 51 88) buses connect Manfredonia with Foggia (€1.80, 50 minutes), while SITA has buses daily to and from Vieste (€2.85, 1¾ hours, seven daily). There are also frequent buses daily to and from Monte Sant'Angelo (€0.80, 30 minutes). Get tickets and timetable information from Bar Impero on Piazza Marconi, where all services leave from.

PROMONTORIO DEL GARGANO

The Promontorio del Gargano (Gargano Promontory) is one of the most beautiful areas in southern Italy. Characterised by white limestone cliffs, calcareous grottoes, a crystal-clear green sea and ancient forests, the 'spur' of the Italian boot has more in common with Dalmatia than with the rest of Italy. It is also a place of creeping urbanisation which was thankfully halted in 1991 by the creation of the **Parco Nazionale del Gargano**. Aside from its magnificent display of flora and the primeval forests of Quarto, Spigno and Umbra, the park takes in the no-holds-barred miracle town of San Giovanni Rotonda (see the boxed text, opposite) and the historic pilgrimage destination of Monte Sant'Angelo. The peninsula's seaside towns of Vieste and Peschici are popular summer destinations.

The main park office, **Ente Parco Nazionale del Gargano** (☎ 0884 56 89 01; www.parcogargano.it in Italian; Via Abate 121; ⏱ 9.30am-12.30pm & 3-6pm Tue & Thu), can be found in Monte Sant'Angelo. Here they can organise guided walks and tours in the forest and throughout the peninsula.

Foresta Umbra

Although the Parco Nazionale del Gargano takes in most of the peninsula, only a small portion of this, the Foresta Umbra (Forest of Shadows), is truly wild. The forest is the last remnant of Puglia's ancient forests, and shades the peaks of the promontory's mountainous interior with a blanket of Aleppo pines, oak and beech. Walkers and mountain bikers will find plenty of well-marked trails within the forest's 15,000 hectares and there are several picnic areas.

At the Villaggio Umbra, in the heart of the forest, the Corpo Forestale dello Stato runs a visitors centre housing a small **museum and nature centre** (☎ 0884 56 09 44; admission €1; ⏱ 9am-5pm Jun-Sep).

Specialist tour operators within the Promontorio del Gargano zone also organise excursions. Based in Foggia, **Blue Animation Team** (☎ 0881 70 86 66; Vico Cervo 3) leads five-hour night-time walks (€20) and four-hour mountain-bike rides (€18). Prices include minibus transfer, equipment hire and picnic. From Vieste, **Agenzia Sol** (☎ 0884 70 15 58; www.solvieste.it; Via Trepiccioni 5) leads trekking and biking excursions.

La Chiusa delle More (☎ 330 54 37 66; www.lachiusadellemore.it; Vallo dello Schiaffo; B&B/full board per person €80/100; ⏱ May-Aug; Ⓟ Ⓧ Ⓡ) lets you get away from the cramped coast and escape to an attractive stone-built *agriturismo* (farm-stay accommodation) where you can dine on home-grown produce and enjoy the panoramic views from your poolside lounger. In July and August weekly stays are obligatory.

Monte Sant'Angelo
pop 13,800 / elev 796m

You know as soon as you arrive in Monte Sant'Angelo that it's important. You know because the hustlers move in, pushing everything from car-parking space to kitsch religious souvenirs. But these rogues have been operating for centuries, for as long as pilgrims have been coming to this isolated mountain town overlooking the south coast of the Gargano. The object of devotion is the Santuario di San Michele. Here, in AD 490, St Michael the Archangel is said to have appeared in a grotto before the Bishop of Siponto. He left behind his scarlet cloak and instructions not to consecrate the site, as he had already done so himself. Thus began one of the most important pilgrimage sites in Europe.

During the Middle Ages, the sanctuary marked the end of the pilgrims' Route of the Angel, which began in Normandy and passed through Rome. In AD 999 the Holy Roman Emperor Otto III made a pilgrimage to the sanctuary to pray that prophecies about the end of the world in the year 1000 would not be fulfilled. The sanctuary's fame grew after the widely predicted apocalypse proved to be a damp squib.

SIGHTS

As you descend the steps to the **Santuario di San Michele** (admission free; ⏱ 7.30am-7.30pm daily Jul-Sep, 7.30am-12.30pm & 2.30-7pm Apr, Jun & Oct, to 5pm Nov-Mar) note the graffiti, some of it the work of 17th-century pilgrims. St Michael is said to have left a footprint in stone inside the grotto, so it became customary for pilgrims to carve outlines of their feet and hands and leave accompanying messages.

Finely etched Byzantine bronze and silver doors, cast in Constantinople in 1076, open into the grotto itself. Inside, a 16th-century statue of the archangel covers the site of his footprint.

Once outside, head down the short flight of steps opposite the sanctuary to the **Tomba di Rotari** (admission €0.60), which is, in fact, not a tomb but a 12th-century baptistry with a deep basin sunk into the floor for total immersion. You enter the baptistry through the façade of the **Chiesa di San Pietro**, with its intricate rose window; it's all that remains of the church, destroyed by a 19th-century earthquake. The Romanesque portal of the

PUGLIA, BASILICATA & CALABRIA

THE WORLD'S MOST MARKETED MONK

On 16 June 2002 the most recognisable monk in Italy took his place in the pantheon of saints. Before an estimated 300,000 devotees, Padre Pio (1887–1968) became the 457th saint to be canonised by Pope John Paul II.

To permit this, the Church had, of course, to have a proven miracle; reputation doesn't cut it with the Vatican. Step forward a seven-year-old boy who in February 2000 had defied medical opinion and made a miraculous recovery from meningitis. Apparently the good father had appeared to the comatose boy, telling him he'd be cured. No sooner said than done. Pio's long reputation as a miracle-worker was thus rubber-stamped.

Padre Pio spent most of his life in **San Giovanni Rotondo** where he arrived in 1916 as an ailing Capuchin priest in need of a cooler climate. San Giovanni Rotondo was then a tiny, isolated medieval village in the heart of the Gargano, but as Pio's fame grew so the village underwent something of a miraculous transformation, expanding well beyond its original limits. These days, about eight million pilgrims a year pile into town.

The tomb of Padre Pio lies in the modern **sanctuary** (admission free; ☉ 5.30am-8pm), within which is his **cell** (☉ 7.30am-noon & 3.30-6.30pm). The sanctuary is at the heart of a vast complex that also includes the Home for the Relief of Suffering, one of Italy's premier hospitals (established by Pio), and a new church, still under construction, which will seat over 7000 faithful.

SITA buses run daily to and from Monte Sant'Angelo and serve both Manfredonia and Foggia.

---

adjacent 11th-century **Chiesa di Santa Maria Maggiore** has some fine bas-reliefs. Within are some well-preserved medieval frescoes.

The serpentine alleys and jumbled houses of this town are perfect for a little aimless ambling. Commanding the highest point is a Norman **castle** (admission €1.80; ☉ 8am-7pm Jul-Aug, 9am-1pm & 2.30-6pm Sep-Jun) with Swabian and Aragonese additions. Take time, too, to head for the **belvedere**, a specially situated building that gives visitors sweeping views of the coast.

SLEEPING & EATING

Surprisingly, in a place that teems with visitors, the accommodation here is limited.

In a complex 1km downhill from the historic centre are two hotels offering similar facilities at identical prices.

Hotel Sant'Angelo (☎ 0884 56 55 36; www.hotelsantangelo.com; Via Pulsano; s/d €52/73; P ⓡ) The recent addition to the duo, this hotel has a wonderful panoramic balcony where its restaurant meals are served.

Rotary Hotel (☎ 0884 56 21 46; Via Pulsano; s/d €52/73; P ⓡ) The rooms are standard but the views over the rock-strewn landscape are anything but.

La Jalantuúmene (☎ 0884 56 54 84; Piazza de Galganis 5; menus €25; ☉ Wed-Mon) This restaurant is justifiably recommended by everyone who visits it. It serves excellent fare, accompanied by a long, select wine list, in picturesque

surroundings. In summer, tables spill into the petite piazza.

Don't leave town without tasting the local sweets, *ostie ripiene* (or 'stuffed hosts') – two wafers, like the hosts used at Mass, with a filling of caramelised almonds.

GETTING THERE & AWAY

Monte Sant'Angelo can be accessed by **SITA** (☎ 0881 77 31 17) bus from Foggia (€3.60, 1½ hours, five daily), Manfredonia (€0.80, 20 minutes, 15 daily) and Vieste (€3.90, two hours, five daily). Buy your tickets from Bar Esperia next to the sanctuary.

Vieste
pop 13,500

Vieste is the capital of the Gargano. It has one of the most spectacular beaches on the promontory, a wide yellow-sand strip backed by sheer white cliffs and overshadowed by the towering Scoglio di Pizzomunno, an enormous monolith of rock. Unsurprisingly it is the Gargano's most popular seaside resort, and is a bright little place in summer. In winter, it more or less closes down.

The most attractive place to stay is the historic centre, although resort-style hotels stretch north and south of the town. The better beaches are to the south, between Vieste and Pugnochiuso, and to the north towards Peschici, particularly in the area known as La Salata.

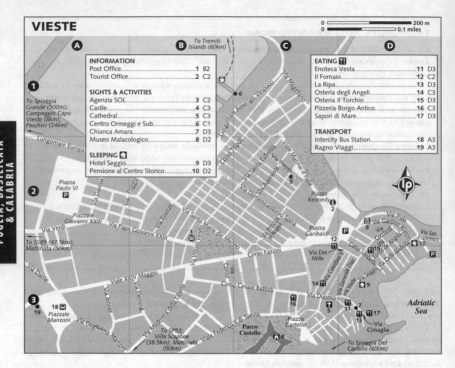

VIESTE

INFORMATION
Post Office..................................1 B2
Tourist Office..............................2 C2

SIGHTS & ACTIVITIES
Agenzia SOL...............................3 C2
Castle...4 C3
Cathedral....................................5 C3
Centro Ormeggi e Sub................6 C1
Chianca Amara............................7 D3
Museo Malacologico...................8 D2

SLEEPING
Hotel Seggio...............................9 D3
Pensione al Centro Storico........10 D2

EATING
Enoteca Vesta............................11 D3
Il Fornaio....................................12 C2
La Ripa......................................13 D3
Osteria degli Angeli...................14 C3
Osteria Il Torchio.......................15 C3
Pizzeria Borgo Antico................16 D3
Sapori di Mare..........................17 D3

TRANSPORT
Intercity Bus Station..................18 A3
Ragno Viaggi..............................19 A3

ORIENTATION

From Piazzale Manzoni, where intercity buses terminate, a 10-minute walk east along Via XXIV Maggio, which becomes Corso Fazzini, brings you to the old town and the attractive promenade of the Marina Piccola.

INFORMATION

Post office (Piazza Vittorio Veneto) Has several public telephones.

Tourist office (☎ 0884 70 88 06; Piazza Kennedy; ☷ 8am-1.30pm Mon-Fri & 4-7pm Tue-Thu Oct-Apr, 8am-1.30pm & 3-9pm Mon-Sat May-Sep) The pink tourist office is at the southern end of the Marina.

SIGHTS & ACTIVITIES

Vieste is primarily a beach resort and has only a few sights of interest located in the winding medieval streets of the historic centre.

Head up to the **Chianca Amara** (Bitter Stone; Via Cimaglia), on which thousands of citizens were beheaded when the Turks sacked Vieste in the 16th century. Nearby, at the town's highest point, is a **castle** built by Frederick II. It's now occupied by the military and closed to

the public, though the tourist office can organise guided tours. The **cathedral** is Puglian-Romanesque but it underwent alterations in the 18th century. You can browse around the **Museo Malacologico** (Mollusc Museum; ☎ 0884 70 55 12; Via Pola 8; admission free; ☷ 9.30am-noon & 5pm-midnight), which contains a huge collection of seashells from all over the world.

At the port, **Centro Ormeggi e Sub** (☎ 0884 70 79 83; ☷ May-Sep) offers diving courses in English and rents out sailing boats and motorboats. From May to September you can also hop on one of the fast boats and day trip it to the Isole Tremiti (p694).

The best beaches, such as Cala San Felice and Cala Sanguinaria, can be found south of Vieste. However, if you don't have your own transport, Spiaggia del Castello is easily accessible, only 1km south of town.

To get off the beach for a day or two, take one of the tours offered by **Agenzia SOL** (☎ 0884 70 15 58; www.solvieste.it; Via Trepiccioni 5). They arrange a whole host of walking and cycling opportunities in the Foresta Umbra. They also hire out mountain bikes (per day/week from €10/50) and cars (per day from €46).

SLEEPING

Most of Vieste's many hotels and *pensioni* are scattered along the beachfront roads north and south of town. Camp sites (as many as 80) abound, particularly along Lungomare E Mattei to the south.

Villa Scapone (☎ 0884 55 92 84; www.villascapone .it; Litoranea Mattinata-Vieste 11.5km; s/d €91/140; Apr-Oct; P 🐾 🅿) An attractive villa fantastically sited on the cliffs between Mattinata and Vieste. The hotel terraces and sundecks tumble seawards and all 24 rooms have stunning sea views. The sliver of beach and sea can be reached through the rocks and is totally secluded.

Hotel Seggio (☎ 0884 70 81 23; www.emmeti.it/ Hseggio; Via Veste 7; s/d €95/140; Apr-Oct; P 🐾 🅿) A lemon-yellow palazzo in the historic centre of Vieste. It has a seafront location and its pretty pool and sunbathing terrace are right at the sea's edge. The rooms are small but it is family run and has a warm Italian feel to it. Parking costs €5 per day.

Pensione al Centro Storico (☎ 0884 70 70 30; www.viesteonline.it/cstorico; Via Mafrolla 32; s/d €40/65; Easter-Oct) Old-fashioned hospitality is offered at this historic *pensione* (small hotel). In a former convent in the old quarter, it has large, high-ceilinged rooms and some very busy tilework. The terrace, where breakfast is served, offers magnificent views over the port.

Campeggio Capo Vieste (☎ 0884 70 63 26; www .capovieste.it; Litoranea Vieste-Peschici Km 8; person/tent/car €10/13.50/4.50; Apr-Oct) This camp site is at La Salata, between Vieste and Peschici, and accessible by Ferrovie del Gargano bus. There are tons of activities, including tennis, a sailing school and kite- and wind-surfing.

EATING

Sapori di Mare (☎ 0884 70 79 79; Via Judeca 30; meals €22; Jun-Sep) At the end of Via Cimaglia in the old town, this is a panoramic spot for a fish dinner or just a cool drink while savouring the glorious view of sea and coastline.

Osteria Il Torchio (☎ 0884 70 71 58; Via Arcaroli 8; meals €20; Mar-Oct) Take up a pew at the long benches in this *osteria* (simple trattoria-style restaurant) and tuck into some surprisingly fine food – simple ingredients with great flavour. Try the *capelli di prete*, fresh ravioli stuffed with cheese and delicately flavoured with sage. This place fills up with a young crowd after 10pm.

Enoteca Vesta (☎ 0884 70 64 11; Via Duomo 14; meals €25) If your wine is as important as your food this is the place for you. This restaurant, housed in a cave, maintains a magnificent selection of Puglian wines which can be savoured in the cool vaulted interior.

Osteria degli Angeli (☎ 0884 70 11 12; Via Celestino V 50; meals €20; late-May–Sep) Near the cathedral, this is a friendly restaurant offering fine cooking. A house speciality worth trying is *troccoli dell'angeli* (pasta with prawns).

La Ripa (☎ 0884 70 80 48; Via Cimaglia 16; meals from €25; Mar-Oct) A kitsch little grotto resembling a minimuseum, the Ripa is an atmospheric place to kick back your heels to the mellow sounds of Eartha Kitt. Seafood is the house speciality, although the cooking is fairly average.

For a pizza or snack, head to the **Pizzeria Borgo Antico** (☎ 0884 70 24 82; Corso Cesare Battisti 11; pizza & beer €11), or **Il Fornaio** (Via Fazzini 1), near the entrance to the old town.

GETTING THERE & AROUND

Vieste's port is just north of the old town, about a five-minute walk from the tourist office. In summer several companies, including **Adriatica** (☎ 199 12 31 99; www.adriatica.it), run boats to the Isole Tremiti. Tickets can be bought at the portside. Boats run during Easter week and there is at least one boat daily from June to September (€27 return, 1½ hours).

Many companies also offer tours of the caves that pock the Gargano coast. A typical three-hour tour costs around €10.

Buses operated by **SITA** (☎ 0881 77 31 17) run between Vieste and Foggia (€4.75, 2¾ hours, five daily) via Manfredonia, while **Ferrovie del Gargano** (☎ 0881 72 51 88) buses connect the town with Peschici (€1.50, 30 minutes, 10 daily) and other towns on the promontory. Buses terminate at Piazzale Manzoni and timetables are posted outside **Ragno Viaggi** (☎ 0884 70 15 28) on the square. Services connecting coastal towns are frequent in summer and almost nonexistent at other times of the year.

Agenzia SOL (see opposite) also sells bus and boat tickets.

Peschici
pop 4300

On a rocky outcrop, Peschici is an attractive whitewashed town that cascades down the hillside to a choppy, green sea. It is also a fast-developing resort, but remains relatively unspoilt and has a cheerful, family-friendly atmosphere. The wide sandy beaches fill up in summer, so book well in advance. Peschici is also one of the embarkation points for the Isole Tremiti.

ORIENTATION & INFORMATION

The medieval and more interesting part of town clings to the clifftop at the point of the bay, while the newer parts extend inland and around the bay. In winter, buses terminate beside Chiesa di San Antonio. For the rest of the year, the terminal is beside the sports ground, uphill from the town's main street, Corso Garibaldi. Turn right into the *corso* and walk straight ahead to reach the old town.

There is a small **tourist office** (☎ 0884 96 27 97; Corso Garibaldi 57; ☉ 10.30am-12.30pm & 5.30-7.30pm Mon-Fri, 10.30am-12.30pm Sat) with useful accommodation information.

SLEEPING & EATING

Peschici has several hotels and *pensioni* but many insist upon a minimum of half board. Numerous camp sites dot the coast east and west of Peschici.

Locanda al Castello (☎ 0884 96 40 38; Piazza Castello 29; s/d €50/80, half/full board per person €55/70; P ⊠) Arriving at this cheerful place is kind of like entering a family home. The welcome is genuine and the atmosphere unstuffy. Situated right by the cliffs, it is definitely the pick of the old quarter. It also runs a decent restaurant (meals €18) and a neighbouring pizzeria (evenings only).

Hotel Timiana (☎ /fax 0884 96 43 21; Viale Libeta 73; full board per person €45-78; ☉ mid-Apr–mid-Sep; P ⊠ ⊠) Set in its own pine-rich grounds 800m from the sea, Timiana has cool white rooms ideal for an afternoon siesta. It offers a free shuttle bus to the beach and serves delicious local dishes in its restaurant.

Baia San Nicola (☎ /fax 0884 96 42 31; www.baia sannicola.it; person/tent/car €9/8.50/4.50; ☉ mid-May–mid-Oct) The best camp site, 2km out of town on the road towards Vieste.

Ristorante La Taverna (☎ 0884 96 41 97; Traversa di Via Castello 6; meals from €20) If you're tall you'll need to mind your head as you stoop into this cosy, character-filled place just off Via Castello, in the heart of the old town. The old boys who cook here like to see that their customers eat well.

GETTING THERE & AWAY

Ferrovie del Gargano serves Peschici. It runs buses to and from Vieste (€1.50, 30 minutes, seven daily) and has daily services to and from San Severo (€4.60, two hours, five daily), with connections to and from Foggia via Rodi Garganico. From April to September (daily from June), boats leave Peschici's port for the Isole Tremiti. For boat tickets and information, go to:

Agrifoglio Tour (☎ 0884 96 27 21; Piazza Sant'Antonio 3)
CTM Compagnia de Navigazione (☎ 0884 96 42 34; Corso Umberto I)

ISOLE TREMITI

pop 400

Tell an Italian you are going to the Isole Tremiti (Tremiti Islands) and chances are they will look at you enviously and start wistfully enthusing about the islands' beauty. It's no exaggeration either, as the three islands that make up this small archipelago, 36km north of the Promontorio del Gargano, are stunning.

The beauty, however, is hard to appreciate in July and August when some 100,000 holidaymakers pile onto the islands. Out of season the islands are magical, though most tourist facilities close down as the few permanent residents resume their quiet and isolated lives.

Easily defensible, **San Nicola** was always the administrative and residential centre of the islands, while the lusher **San Domino** was used to grow crops. Nowadays, most of the islands' accommodation and other facilities are on San Domino. The third island, **Capraia**, is totally uninhabited.

Your boat will arrive at either San Domino or San Nicola. Don't panic if you've been dropped off on the wrong island; small boats regularly make the brief crossing (€1.50, one way).

Sights & Activities

In 1010 Benedictine monks founded the **Abbazia e Chiesa di Santa Maria** (Abbey and Church of St Maria) on San Nicola, and for the next 700 years the islands were ruled by a series of wealthy abbots who accumulated great treasures in the monastery complex. Although the church retains a weather-worn Renaissance portal and a fine 11th-century floor mosaic, its other treasures have been variously stolen or destroyed throughout its troubled history. The one exception is a painted wooden Byzantine crucifix brought to the island in AD 747 and a black Madonna, which was probably transported here from Constantinople in the Middle Ages.

For those more interested in the striking beauty of the islands, San Domino should be their island of choice. It is greener than San Nicola and wilder due to the fact that it was uninhabited for most of its history, leaving its marvellous coastline in almost pristine condition. It has the islands' only sandy beach, **Cala delle Arene**, and there are several small coves where you can swim in the amazingly clear waters. The other great activity is taking a boat trip (€10 from the port) around the island to explore the grottoes, the largest of which, **Grotta del Bue Marino**, is 46m long. A tour around all three islands costs €16. To hire a motorised rubber dinghy, call ☎ 347 938 70 51 and expect to pay about €70 a day.

If you're feeling energetic, a walking track around the island starts at the far end of San Domino village, beyond Pensione Nassa. Alternatively, you could hire a bicycle from Jimmy Bike at Piazzetta San Domino.

The third of the Isole Tremiti, Capraia, is completely uninhabited. Birdlife is plentiful and the flocks of seagulls make an impressive spectacle. There is no organised transport to the island as there's nothing to do once you get there, but if your curiosity gets the better of you, negotiate a trip with a local fisherman.

Sleeping & Eating

In summer you'll need to reserve well in advance. Out of season, phone to check that your chosen hotel is open. In the high season most hotels insist on full board – not a bad idea, since eating options are limited.

Al Faro (☎ 0882 46 34 24; annalisalisci@tin.it; Via della Cantina Sperimentale, San Domino; half board per person €58-73) To get to this colourful place follow the only road up from the port and go straight for about 1km. Half board is obligatory but you'll realise it's a good deal when you sample the excellent local cooking, which continues many of the monastery's culinary traditions.

Hotel Gabbiano (☎ 0882 46 34 10; www.hotel-gabb iano.com; Piazza Belvedere, San Domino; half/full board per person €70/90) Situated on the tiny piazza in San Domino, this hotel offers decent rooms

with the usual three-star trappings and a terrace restaurant overlooking San Nicola.

To stock up on picnic fodder, **La Bottega dei Sapori** minimarket, opposite Al Faro, makes hearty *panini* (bread rolls with filling).

Getting There & Away

Boats for the Isole Tremiti depart from several points on the Italian mainland; see p693, opposite and p613 for more information.

TRANI

pop 53,350

Trani is known as the 'Pearl of Puglia' and its magnificent portside cathedral is one of the region's most photogenic churches and a seriously good reason for visiting this charming town. During the Middle Ages the town rivalled Bari in importance, and became a major embarkation point for merchants going to and from the Near East. Its business interests grew so large that the noble burghers of the town devised the very first maritime code, the Ordinamenta Maris (1063), to help regulate their business interests.

Some 40km northwest along the coast from Bari, it makes an ideal base for exploring this part of Puglia – Barletta, Molfetta and Castel del Monte are all within easy reach.

Orientation & Information

The **train station** (Piazza XX Settembre) is also the point of departure for most provincial buses. From it, Via Cavour leads through tree-lined Piazza della Repubblica, the main square, to Piazza Plebiscito and the public gardens. Turn left for the small picturesque harbour and the cathedral.

The helpful **tourist office** (☎ 0883 58 88 30; 1st fl, Palazzo Palmieri, Piazza Trieste; ☼ 8.30am-1.30pm Mon-Fri, 3-6pm Tue & Thu) is about 200m south of the cathedral.

Sights

Started in 1097 on the site of a Byzantine church, the **cathedral** (☎ 0883 58 24 70; Piazza del Duomo; ☼ 8am-noon & 5-8pm daily Jun-Sep, 8.15am-12.15pm & 3.15-6.30pm Mon-Sat, 9am-12.45pm & 4-7pm Sun Oct-May), dedicated to St Nicholas the Pilgrim, was not completed until the 13th century. It is gorgeously sited on the edge of the harbour, the elegant profile of its *campanile* accentuated by the blue background. The original bronze doors (now on display inside the church) were cast by Barisano da Trani, an accomplished 12th-century artisan who also cast the doors of the cathedral at Ravello as well as the side doors of the cathedral at Monreale.

The grand interior of the cathedral is stunningly simple in Norman style. Near the main altar, take a look at the remains of a 12th-century floor mosaic, similar in style to the one at Otranto. Below the church is the crypt, a forest of ancient columns, where the bones of St Nicholas are kept beneath the altar.

The crypt opens onto the Byzantine Chiesa di Santa Maria della Scala, which itself sits on the Ipogèo San Leucio, a chamber believed to date from the 6th century.

Two hundred metres north of the cathedral is Trani's other major landmark, the vast 13th-century **castle** (☎ 0883 50 66 03; Piazza Manfredi 16; admission €2; ۞ 8.30am-7.30pm) built by Frederick II. There is little of interest within the castle due to the fact that it was used as a prison until recently.

Sleeping

Hotel Regia (☎/fax 0883 58 44 44; Piazza del Duomo 2; s/d €130/150; ۞) This hotel is magnificently located just across the road from the cathedral in the 18th-century Palazzo Filisio. The rooms are understated and stylish, with high ceilings, parquet flooring and perfectly suited elegant furniture. What's more, there's a good restaurant (meals €27).

Albergo Lucy (☎ 0883 48 10 22; www.albergolucy .com; Piazza Plebiscito 11; s/d €36/50) This charming hotel in a restored 17th-century palazzo offers huge rooms full of character. The vaulted ceilings are high, letting in plenty of light, and the décor is unobtrusive. It's ideally located close to the port.

Eating

Torrente Antico (☎ 0883 48 79 11; Via Fusco 3; meals €35; ۞ lunch Tue-Sun) In Trani it is tempting to hover only around the port, but this restaurant is a good reason to plunge into the backstreets. The cooking is pure Puglia, making good use of high-quality produce, and the wine list is excellent.

La Darsena (☎ 0883 48 73 33; Via Statuti Marittimi 98; meals €25; ۞ Tue-Sun) This stylish restaurant is lined with pictures of Puglia in its former days. It occupies part of the Palazzo Palumbo-Quercia. No prizes for guessing that the seafood is particularly good.

Pizza l'Ancora (☎ 0347 803 46 18; Via Banchina al Porto 10; pizzas €5, meals €15-18; ۞ Thu-Tue) The food at this easygoing seaside venue is plentiful and tasty. Given the location, much of the menu is given over to fish, and the seafood salad as an antipasto makes a great meal opener.

Also recommended is the popular trattoria **Ristorante La Nicchia** (☎ 0883 48 20 20; Via S Gervasio 69; meals €18; ۞ Fri-Wed).

Getting There & Away

Buses operated by **STP** (☎ 0883 49 18 00) connect Trani with points along the coast and inland, including Barletta (€1, 20 minutes, hourly) and Andria (€1, 20 minutes, eight daily). Services depart from in front of **Bar Desirée** (☎ 0883 49 10 30; Piazza XX Settembre), where timetables and tickets are available.

In July and August, a bus departs from Trani at 8.30am and connects with the 9am service from Andria to Castel del Monte. The first return run to Andria leaves the castle at 3pm.

The SS16 runs through Trani, linking it to Bari and Foggia, or you can hook up with the A14 Bologna–Bari autostrada.

Trani is on the main train line between Bari (€2.58, 45 minutes, hourly) and Foggia (€4.60, one hour, hourly) and is easily reached from towns along the coast.

AROUND TRANI
Barletta

Barletta's crusading history is a lot more exotic than the modern-day town. Crusaders embarked for the Holy Land from Barletta's down-at-heel port, while King Richard the Lionheart had a hand in the building of Barletta's cathedral, which was the principal seat of the Archbishop of Nazareth for some 600 years (1291–1891).

Barletta's main curiosity, however, is the huge 4th-century bronze Colossus that now stands in the town centre.

ORIENTATION & INFORMATION

From the train station, go down Via Giannone and through the municipal gardens. Turn right along Corso Garibaldi to reach Barletta's centre. From the bus station on Via Manfredi, walk to Piazza Plebiscito and turn right to meet Corso Vittorio Emanuele.

There is a **tourist office** (☎ 0883 33 13 31; Corso Garibaldi 208; ۞ 8.30am-2pm & 5-7pm Tue & Thu) in the town centre.

SIGHTS

Right in the centre on Corso Vittorio Emanuele stands the 5m-high Roman **Colossus**. It is the largest-surviving Roman bronze in the world and is thought to depict the emperor Marcian, whose Triumphal Column still stands in Istanbul where the statue was cast.

The Colossus was actually stolen by the Venetians in 1203 after the sack of Constantinople, but the ship carrying it foundered off the coast of Barletta and the statue washed ashore. For years it lay untouched – Barletta's inhabitants were too superstitious to go near it – but it was finally brought to the city centre where its missing hands and legs were restored. Green with verdigris, it stands stolidly before the 12th-century **Basilica del Santo Sepolcro** (not usually open to the public).

From here Corso Garibaldi leads down to the 12th-century **cathedral** (Corso Garibaldi; ☒ during Mass), which is among the region's better-preserved examples of Puglian-Romanesque style.

As with every town in Puglia, Barletta has a fortified **castle** (☎ 0883 57 83 20; Piazza Corvi; admission €4; ☒ 9am-1pm & 3-7pm Tue-Sun). It is one of Italy's largest, and Frederick II launched the Third Crusade from its council chamber. It now houses a display of Sicilian puppets and the castle's art collection, which includes over 90 works by Barletta's famous son, Giuseppe De Nittis.

FESTIVALS & EVENTS

Disfida di Barletta (Challenge of Barletta) is one of Italy's best-known medieval pageants. Held on the last Sunday in July, it re-enacts a duel between 13 Italian and 13 French knights on 13 February 1503. The home side won and the chivalrous French decamped.

GETTING THERE & AWAY

From the bus station located on Via Manfredi, **Ferrovie del Gargano** (☎ 0881 72 51 88) buses link Barletta with Foggia (€4.20, two hours, frequent); there are regular **STP** (☎ 0883 49 18 00) buses to Trani (€1, 20 minutes), Molfetta (€2.80, 50 minutes) and Bari (€3.35, one hour).

Barletta is on both the Bari–Foggia Trenitalia coastal train line and the Bari–Nord train line. It's easily accessible from Trani and other points along the coast, as well as inland towns.

Castel del Monte

Castel del Monte (☎ 0883 56 99 97; adult/child €3/free; ☒ 9am-6pm) is one of southern Italy's most prominent and talked-about landmarks. Rising from a hilltop, it's visible for miles around and is now a Unesco World Heritage site.

Nobody really knows why Frederick II built it or why he adopted such a peculiar octagonal design. As far as anyone knows, nobody has ever lived there and there is no town or strategic crossroads nearby. It was obviously not built to defend anything, as it has no moat or drawbridge, no arrow slits or trapdoors for boiling oil. It's full of annoying brain-teasers.

Some theories claim that according to the geometric symbolic beliefs of the mid-13th century, the octagon represented the union of the circle and square, of God-perfection (the infinite) and man-perfection (the finite). The castle was therefore nothing less than a celebration of the relationship between man and God. Others claim it was just a simple hunting lodge.

Whichever way you choose to look at it, the castle is unique. It is perfectly octagonal with eight octagonal towers. Completely restored, its interconnecting rooms have decorative marble columns and fireplaces, and the doorways and windows are framed in corallite stone, which once covered the entire lower floor.

The car park (€2.60) is over 1km from the castle entrance. A free shuttle bus runs between the two.

Without a car, travelling to the Castel del Monte is a real pain. The least difficult way is by bus from Andria. From July to mid-September buses depart from Piazza Municipio in Andria at 8.30am, 1.45pm and 4.30pm. The first return is at 3pm. Andria is within easy reach of Trani by bus, or of Bari via the Bari–Nord train.

The Andria–Spinazzola bus (several per day) also passes close to the castle – ask the driver to let you off. For more information, see opposite.

BARI

pop 315,000

Bari is an exasperating city, choked with traffic, full of noise and fury and reassuringly commercial. It is Puglia's capital and one of the most prosperous cities of the south, and you certainly get a sense that the

PUGLIA, BASILICATA & CALABRIA

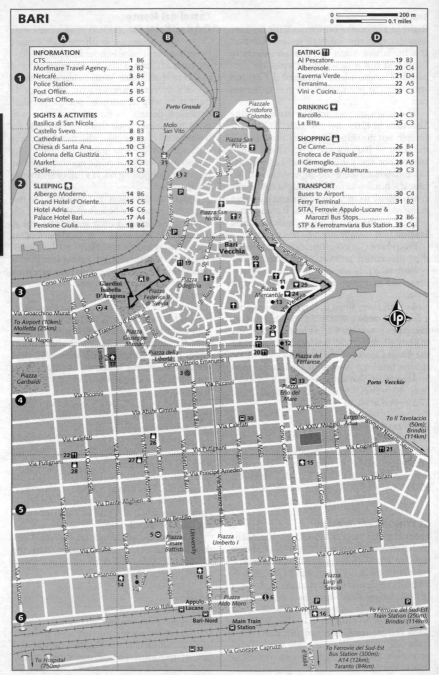

BARI

0 ——————— 200 m
0 ——————— 0.1 miles

INFORMATION
CTS	1	B6
Morfimare Travel Agency	2	B2
Netcafé	3	B4
Police Station	4	A3
Post Office	5	B5
Tourist Office	6	C6

SIGHTS & ACTIVITIES
Basilica di San Nicola	7	C2
Castello Svevo	8	B3
Cathedral	9	B3
Chiesa di Santa Ana	10	C3
Colonna della Giustizia	11	C3
Market	12	C3
Sedile	13	C3

SLEEPING
Albergo Moderno	14	B6
Grand Hotel d'Oriente	15	C5
Hotel Adria	16	C6
Palace Hotel Bari	17	A4
Pensione Giulia	18	B6

EATING
Al Pescatore	19	B3
Alberosole	20	C4
Taverna Verde	21	D4
Terranima	22	A5
Vini e Cucina	23	C3

DRINKING
Barcollo	24	C3
La Bitta	25	C3

SHOPPING
De Carne	26	B4
Enoteca de Pasquale	27	B5
Il Germoglio	28	A5
Il Panettiere di Altamura	29	C3

TRANSPORT
Buses to Airport	30	C4
Ferry Terminal	31	B2
SITA, Ferrovie Appulo-Lucane & Marozzi Bus Stops	32	B6
STP & Ferrotramviaria Bus Station	33	C4

Baresi are singularly focused in the pursuit of prosperity – just check out the designer shops along Via Abate Gimma.

All this, together with its huge university population, makes Bari completely untouristy – a double-edged sword of sorts. On the one hand you will eat and shop well alongside a demanding local clientele, but you will be driven nearly insane by the hysterical rush hour, which seems to last all day, and you won't find any interesting hotels. Still, in recent years, the authorities have been making a considerable effort to rejuvenate the buzzing warren of Bari Vecchia (historic old town) and this is certainly where you should head if you are spending a few days in the city.

Orientation

Orient yourself from Piazza Aldo Moro in front of the main train station in the newer, 19th-century section of the city. From the square, it's about 1km northwards to Bari Vecchia, the old town where all the major monuments are located.

The newer part of Bari is on a grid plan. Any of the streets heading north from Piazza Aldo Moro will take you to Corso Vittorio Emanuele II, separating old and new cities, and onto the ferry terminal. Wide and imposing Corso Cavour is a popular shopping strip.

Information

There are plenty of banks, including one with an ATM at the station. There's a currency exchange booth at the ferry terminal, but you may well find that exchange rates are better in town.

CTS (☎ 080 521 32 44; Via Fornari 7) Good for student travel and discount flights.
Guardia Medica (☎ 080 543 70 04) A 24-hour emergency line for a call-out doctor.
Hospital (☎ 080 547 31 11; Piazza Giulio Cesare)
Morfimare Travel Agency (☎ 080 578 98 11; Corso Antonio de Tullio 36-40) Represents American Express.
Netcafé (☎ 080 524 17 56; Via Andrea da Bari 11; per hr €4; 🕑 9am-10pm Mon-Fri, 9am-1.30pm Sat) Internet.
Police station (☎ 080 529 11 11; Via Gioacchino Murat 4)
Post office (Piazza Cesare Battisti; 🕑 8am-6.30pm Mon-Fri, 8am-12.30pm Sat)
Puglia Turismo (www.pugliaturismo.com)
Tourist office (☎ 080 524 23 61; aptbari@pugliaturismo.com; 1st fl, Piazza Aldo Moro 33a; 🕑 8am-2pm Mon-Fri plus 3-6pm Tue & Thu)

Dangers & Annoyances

Petty crime is a problem in Bari, so take all the usual commonsense precautions. Don't leave anything in your car, don't display money or valuables and watch out for bag-snatchers on mopeds. Be careful in the dark internal streets of Bari Vecchia at night, although there is now a high police presence patrolling the area at the weekend.

Sights

BARI VECCHIA

Covering the narrow peninsula adjacent to the port, Bari Vecchia is an atmospheric labyrinth of tight, uneven alleyways. Squeezed into this small area are 40 churches and more than 120 shrines – if you can find them, for Bari Vecchia's town plan is famous throughout Italy for its mazelike effect.

You could start your exploration of Bari Vecchia with the chaotic **market** alongside the Piazza del Ferrarese. Stumble out of that and walk north to Piazza Mercantile, fronted by the **Sedile**, the medieval headquarters of Bari's Council of Nobles. In the square's northeast corner is the **Colonna della Giustizia** (Column of Justice), to which, says tradition, debtors were tied.

Northwest past the small **Chiesa di Santa Ana** is the **Basilica di San Nicola** (☎ 080 573 71 11; Piazza San Nicola), which was one of the first Norman churches in the south. It is the finest example of Puglian-Romanesque style and was built specifically to house the relics of St Nicholas (better known as Father Christmas), which were stolen from Turkey in 1087 by Baresi fishermen. His remains, embalmed in manna liquid, are said to have miraculous powers and so the basilica remains an important place of pilgrimage.

From here a brief walk south via Strada D Carmine – both street and monument signing are all but nonexistent – brings you to the 12th-century **cathedral** (Piazza Odegitria). Built over the original Byzantine church, the cathedral retains its basilica plan and Eastern-style cupola. The severely plain walls are punctuated with deep arcades and the eastern window is ornamented with plant and animal motifs.

CASTELLO SVEVO

Just beyond the perimeter of Bari Vecchia broods the **Castello Svevo** (Swabian Castle; ☎ 080 528 61 11; Piazza Isabella d'Aragona; admission €2;

(🕙 8.30am-7.30pm Tue-Sun). Originally, a Norman structure was built over the ruins of a Roman fort. Frederick II then incorporated parts of the Norman castle into his own design, including two towers that still stand. The bastions, with corner towers overhanging the moat, were added in the 16th century during Spanish rule. Inside you'll find the **Gipsoteca**, a collection of plaster copies of Romanesque monumental decoration. Most of the castle is closed to the public.

Festivals & Events

Festa di San Nicola (Festival of St Nicholas) is Bari's biggest annual shindig, celebrating the arrival of St Nicholas' relics in Bari. It's held on the closest weekend to 2 and 3 May. On Saturday evening a procession leaves the castle for the Basilica di San Nicola, where the delivery of St Nicholas' bones to the Dominican friars is re-enacted. The next day a fleet of boats carries the statue of St Nicholas along the coast and the evening ends with a massive fireworks competition.

Sleeping

Bari is a big commercial town and its many overpriced hotels cater to a largely business clientele.

Palace Hotel Bari (☎ 080 521 65 51; www.palace hotelbari.it; Via Lombardi 13; s/d €175/235; 🅿 ⊠ 🖳) Despite its sinfully ugly concrete exterior, the Palace Hotel is an oasis of hushed luxury in a chaotic city. However, you will pay a premium price for the plush comfort of its quiet rooms. Its rooftop restaurant, the Murat (meals €30), is one of the best in the city and enjoys fantastic views over the old town.

Grand Hotel d'Oriente (☎ 080 524 40 11; Corso Cavour 32; s/d €110/260; 🅿 ⊠) Originally this grand old hotel catered to wealthy merchants from the Balkans and Far East, hence the name. An imposing building on busy Corso Cavour, it combines modern efficiency with the elegance of the Titanic era.

Hotel Adria (☎ 080 524 66 99; www.adriahotelbari .com; Via Zuppetta 10; s/d €80/120; 🅿 🖳 ⊠) Recently renovated, the Adria offers comfortable bright, modern rooms away from the noisy traffic in the centre. It is quite awkward to get to by car but there is parking opposite the hotel and it is very convenient for the train station.

Albergo Moderno (☎ 080 521 33 13; Via Crisanzio 60; s/d €60/85; 🅿 ⊠) Rooms here are trim and clean, if a touch sterile. They come with a small kitchenette and stove. Breakfast is an extra €6.

Also recommended near the train station is the family-run **Pensione Giulia** (☎ 080 521 66 30; Via Crisanzio 12; s/d €42/55, with bathroom €52/65).

Eating

Alberosole (☎ 080 523 54 46; Corso Vittorio Emanuele 13; meals €30; 🕙 Tue-Sun Sep-Jul) This first-rate restaurant is on the main street dividing the old and new town. The atmosphere is intimate and the service is exceptionally good, as is the imaginative Puglian cuisine. Reservations are recommended.

Terranima (☎ 080 521 97 25; Via Putignani 213; meals €25-30; 🕙 lunch Mon-Sun Sep-Jul) Peep through the lace curtains into the cool, dark interior of this rustic trattoria. Its short and select menu attracts a sleek business crowd and the period furnishings create an intimate atmosphere.

Taverna Verde (☎ 080 554 08 70; Largo Adua 19; meals from €18; 🕙 Mon-Sat) This low-ceilinged and stylish place is very popular. The food, as you'd expect, is good, if not exceptional. Try Puglia's most famous dish – fava bean puree with chicory.

Al Pescatore (☎ 080 523 70 39; Piazza Federico di Svevia 6-8; meals €25) You can't leave Bari without trying the fish. The boats go out in the morning and by lunchtime the best of the catch is on your plate at Al Pescatore. In particular, the grilled squid is memorable.

Il Tavolaccio (☎ 080 558 86 36; Via Petroni 53; meals €15-20; 🕙 Wed-Mon) The waiter will propose a little antipasto to start you off. Say yes and you'll still be eating half an hour later. Portions are huge at this modest trattoria and if you make it to the pasta dishes, the seafood options are good. Excellent value for money.

Vini e Cucina (☎ 338 212 03 91; Strada Vallisa 23; meals €10) Grab a seat at this cult eatery in Bari Vecchia and mix with fishermen and students alike. The food is basic and filling and served by the one indefatigable waiter. You'll remember your meal here!

If you're self-catering or stocking up for a ferry journey, pass by the **market** (Piazza del Ferrarese).

Drinking

Of an evening Piazza Mercantile in Bari Vecchia is the centre of the pub scene. Every night Bari's young and beautiful congregate in the square; some drinking at the various pubs, others just hanging out. Your best bet is to grab a beer wherever and join them.

Barcollo (☎ 080 521 38 89; Piazza Mercantile 69/70; cocktails €5.50) For a taste of things to come in Bari Vecchia, duck into the über-chic Barcollo where you lounge on blood-red banquettes, supping a cocktail and nibbling exquisitely presented hors d'oeuvres.

La Bitta (Via Re Manfredi) For something more down to earth try La Bitta, a pub popular with the English in town.

Shopping

Bari is a great place to stock up on Puglian specialities before you head home.

De Carne (Via Calefati 128) For some fine regional produce head for the venerable delicatessen De Carne, which has a huge range to choose from, as well as some tasty take-out dishes.

Il Germoglio (Via Puntignani 204) Organic jams and cheeses.

Enoteca de Pasquale (Via Marchese di Montrone 87) Stock up on Puglian wines.

Il Panettiere di Altamura (Via Argiro 12) For Altamura's famous bread and *biscotti* (biscuits).

Getting There & Away

AIR

In April 2005 Bari opened its new **airport** (BRI; ☎ 080 583 52 00; www.seap-puglia.it) for the estimated 3½ million passengers who will be coming through here in the next 15 years.

Given the improved infrastructure an increasing number of national and budget airlines now fly into Bari, including Alitalia, British Airways, Hapag-Lloyd Express, Lufthansa and Ryanair. **Alitalia** (☎ 848 86 56 41; www.alitalia.com), **AirOne** (☎ 848 84 88 80; www.flyairone.it) and **Alpi Eagles** (☎ 899 89 98 44; www.alpieagles.com) run a range of domestic services to and from Bologna, Catania (Sicily), Florence, Milan, Palermo, Rome and Venice. **Ada Air** (www.adaair.com) flies daily to Tirrana in Albania.

BOAT

Ferries run from Bari to Greece, Albania, Serbia and Montenegro. All boat companies have offices at the ferry terminal, accessible from the main train station by bus No 20. Fares to Greece are generally more expensive than those available from Brindisi. Once you

FERRY CROSSINGS FROM BARI

Destination	Cost (€) seat/cabin/car	Duration (hr)
Bar, Montenegro	55/68/78	9
Cephalonia, Greece	69/187/80	19
Corfu, Greece	81/130/80	11
Durrës, Albania	70/90/100	8
Igoumenitsa, Greece	81/130/80	10-12
Patras, Greece	81/130/80	15½

have bought your ticket and paid the embarkation tax (per person or car to Greece, Serbia and Montenegro €8, per person or car to Albania €2.85), you'll get a boarding card, which must be stamped by the police at the ferry terminal. Tariffs can be as much as one third cheaper outside the peak period of mid-July to late August. Bicycles normally travel free.

The main companies and the routes they served at the time of writing are as follows:
Adriatica (☎ 199 12 31 99; www.adriatica.it) To and from Durrës (Durazzo) in Albania. Daily departure at 11pm year-round.

Montenegro Lines (☎ 080 578 98 27; www.morfimare.it) Reservations via Morfimare Travel Agency (see p699); heads to Bar in Montenegro. Six ferries per week (Sunday to Friday). Daily departure at 10pm.

Superfast (☎ 080 528 28 28; www.superfast.com) To Igoumenitsa and Patras (Patrassa) in Greece. Daily departure at 8pm year-round. Superfast is the only company that accepts Eurail, Eurodomino and Inter-Rail passes (you have to pay only port taxes and a high-season supplement, if applicable).

Ventouris Ferries (☎ 080 521 76 09; www.ventouris.gr) To Igoumenitsa, Patras, Corfu and Cephalonia. Regular ferries. Also daily ferries to and from Durrës (Albania).

BUS

Intercity buses leave from several locations around town.

From Via Giuseppe Capruzzi, on the south side of the main train station, **SITA** (☎ 080 579 01 11; www.sita-on-line.it in Italian) covers local destinations. This is also the departure point for **Ferrovie Appulo-Lucane** (☎ 080 572 52 28) serving Matera (although the train is infinitely more practical), plus **Marozzi** (☎ 080 505 82 80; www.marozzivt.it in Italian) buses for Rome (€30, eight hours, day departures only – the overnight bus departs from Piazza Aldo Moro) and other long-distance destinations.

Piazza Eroi del Mare is the terminal for **STP** (☎ 080 555 93 05) buses serving Andria (€3.35, one hour, seven daily), Barletta (€3.35, one hour, frequent) and Trani (€2.85, 45 minutes, frequent). **Ferrotramviaria** (☎ 080 523 22 02) buses also leave from here for Andria and Ruvo di Puglia.

Buses operated by **Ferrovie del Sud-Est** (FSE; ☎ 080 542 65 52; www.fseonline.it in Italian) leave from Largo Ciaia, south of Piazza Aldo Moro, for Brindisi (€6.20, 2½ hours, four daily) and Taranto (€4.60, 1½ hours, six daily). They also run frequently to Alberobello (€3.10, 1½ hours), Grotte di Castellana (€2.10, one hour), Martina Franca (€3.60, 1½ hours) and Ostuni (€4.10, two hours).

CAR & MOTORCYCLE

Bari is on the A14 autostrada, which heads northwest to Foggia, south to Taranto and connects with the A16 to Naples at Canosa di Puglia. Exit at Bari–Nord to reach the centre of town.

TRAIN

A whole network of train lines connects Bari with the wider world.

From the main **train station** (☎ 080 89 20 21) Eurostar trains go to Milan (€37.70, 8½ hours) and Rome (€36, five hours). There are frequent services to cities across Puglia, including Foggia (€6.80, 1½ hours), Brindisi (€6.50, 1¼ hours), Lecce (€7.50, 2¼ hours) and Taranto (€6.50, 1¼ hours).

Of the private train services, the **Ferrovia Bari-Nord** (☎ 080 578 95 11) connects the city with the airport (€0.80, at least 20 daily), continuing to Bitonto, Andria and Barletta.

The **Ferrovie Appulo-Lucane** (☎ 080 572 52 28) line links Bari with Altamura (€2.60, one hour, hourly), Matera (€3.60, one hour 20 minutes, 10 daily) and Potenza (€7.80, 3½ hours, four daily).

FSE trains (☎ 080 546 24 45; www.fseonline.it in Italian) head for Alberobello (€3.10, 1½ hours, hourly), Martina Franca (€4, two hours, hourly) and Taranto (€6.20, 2½ hours, six daily), leaving from the station in Via Oberdan – cross under the train tracks south of Piazza Luigi di Savoia and head east along Via Giuseppe Capruzzi for about 500m.

Getting Around

To get to the airport take the Alitalia bus (€4.15), which leaves from the main train station

80 minutes before most flight departures. On its way, it calls by the airline's office at Via Calefati 37.

Central Bari is quite compact – a 15-minute walk will take you from Piazza Aldo Moro to the old town. For the ferry terminal take bus No 20 from Piazza Aldo Moro. A single journey costs €0.80 and a day pass is €1.80.

Street parking is hell. There's a large free parking area just south of the main port entrance, otherwise there is a large multistorey car park between the main and Ferrovie del Sud-Est train stations and one on Via Zuppetta opposite Hotel Adria. They charge €11 per day.

TRULLI COUNTRY

Southwest of Bari the Valle d'Itria embraces the towns of Alberobello, Locorotondo, Cisternino, Martina Franca and Ostuni. It is a place of rolling green hills, criss-crossed by low-slung dry-stone walls, where vineyards and country lanes preserve a wonderfully rustic character. Small farms, clusters of *trulli* and large *masseria* (fortified estates) dot the landscape, providing some of Puglia's finest accommodation. Its main draw is the *trulli* – curious, circular, whitewashed houses with distinctive grey-slate conical roofs. They can be found all over the Valle d'Itria from Conversano to Ostuni, but they mass together in Alberobello. **Long Travel** (www.long-travel.co.uk) specialises in renting out converted *trulli* holiday homes.

Grotte di Castellana

Definitely worth the hassle of getting to, these spectacular limestone **caves** (☎ 800 21 39 76, 080 499 82 11; www.grottedicastellana.it; Piazzale Anelli; ◷ 8.30am-7pm Apr-Oct, 9.30am-12.30pm Nov-Mar), 40km southeast of Bari, are Italy's longest natural subterranean network. The interlinked galleries, first discovered in 1938 by Franco Anelli, contain incredible stalactite and stalagmite formations – look out for the jellyfish, the bacon and the stocking. The highlight is the Grotta Bianca (White Grotto), a cavern of eerie white alabaster hung with stiletto-thin stalactites.

There are two tours in English: a 1km, 50-minute tour that does not include the Grotta Bianca (every hour on the half hour, €8); and the full 3km, two-hour tour that does (every hour on the hour, €13). The temperatures inside the cave averages 15°C so take a light jacket. Visit, too, the **Museo Speleologico Franco Anelli** (admission free; 9am-noon & 3-6pm) or book a visit to the **osservatorio astronomico** (☎ 080 499 82 11; admission €2), which offers wonderful views of the surrounding countryside. Both are near the caves.

The grotto can be reached by rail from Bari on the FSE Bari–Taranto train line. Get off at Castellana Grotte (€2.60, one hour, hourly). From the station there are local buses to the caves, 2km away.

Alberobello
pop 10,900

Named after the primitive oak forest *Arboris Belli* that once covered this entire area, Alberobello has become a victim of its own *trulli* fame. It encompasses the extraordinary Zona dei Trulli, a dense mass of 1500 of these beehive-shaped houses and is now classified a Unesco World Heritage site. In summer (May to October) the town is saturated as coachloads of tourists pile into *trulli* homes, drink in *trulli* bars and shop in *trulli* shops.

Out of season one can enjoy the rather elegant town in general peace and quiet, and savour something of the real rural roots of the *trulli*.

ORIENTATION
Alberobello is divided into the old and new town. The new town is perched on a hilltop, while the Zona dei Trulli lies on the opposite (south) slope. It consists of two adjacent neighbourhoods, the Rione Monti and the Rione Aia Piccola.

If you park in Lago Martellotta, follow the steps up to the Piazza del Popolo where the Belvedere Trulli offers an excellent view over the whole higgledy-piggledy picture.

INFORMATION
Internet point (☎ 080 432 29 42; Corso Trieste 30; per 15min €1.50)

Tourist information office (Monte Nero 1; 10am-1pm & 4-6pm, to 8pm summer) Local office in the Zona dei Trulli.

Tourist office (☎ 080 432 51 71; Piazza del Popolo; 9.30am-12.30pm Mon-Fri) In the Casa d'Amore, just off the main square.

SIGHTS
There are not many sights as such in town, it is more a case of walking around while admiring the eccentricity of it all. Within the quarter of **Rione Monti** over 1000 *trulli* cascade down the hillside. To its east, on the other side of Via Indipendenza, is **Rione Aia Piccola**. It's much less commercialised, with a respectable 400 *trulli*, many of which are still used as family dwellings.

None of the *trullo* date back beyond the 14th century and their origin is unknown. They are made from limestone blocks collected in the nearby fields and are constructed without a single trowelful of mortar. This, it is said, was a tax-dodging device. In the past when the tax collector passed, the *trulli* inhabitants simply dismantled their houses, leaving them free from any house duties. Once the collector was safely distant, up the houses would go again. The best way to experience the *trulli* is to stay in one (see below).

In the modern part of town, the 16th-century **Trullo Sovrano** (☎ 080 432 60 30; Piazza Sacramento; admission €1.30; 10am-7pm Apr-Oct, shorter hrs Sun winter) has been converted into a museum illustrating the history of the *trulli*.

SLEEPING & EATING
Alberobello is an excellent base for touring the surrounding countryside and it is a unique experience to stay in your very own *trullo*.

Trullidea (☎ 080 432 38 60; www.trullidea.it; Via Monte Nero 15; 2/4 people with breakfast per week low season €425/634, high season €566/825) A series of 25 *trulli* homes renovated to a high standard in Alberobello's Trulli Zone. They are available on a self-catering, B&B, half- or full board basis and you can also get involved in lots of other activities such as the grape harvest and cookery lessons.

Hotel Lanzillotta (☎ 080 432 15 11; www.minotel.com; Piazza Ferdinando IV 31; s/d €45/60; P) This recently restructured hotel just off Piazza del Popolo is a good non-*trulli* choice. A friendly welcome awaits and the rooms, eight of which have bathtubs, are decent. It also serves a mean three-course dinner of local specialities for about €13.

Camping dei Trulli (☎ 080 432 36 99; www.campingdeitrulli.com; Via Castellana Grotte, 1.5km; person/tent/car €6/5/2.50, bungalows per person €28; P) This well-equipped camp site is just 1.5km out of town on Via Castellana Grotte. It has a restaurant, market, two swimming pools, tennis courts and bicycle hire.

La Cantina (☎ 080 432 34 73; Via Lippolis 9; meals €20; ☺ Wed-Mon Jul-Sep) In a town full of tourist traps this is a refreshingly good local restaurant serving extremely fresh food. It may not look like much from the exterior but it has a lovely interior where you can watch the chef at work in the open kitchen. The seasonal vegetables are a real highlight.

Also recommended is **Il Poeta Contadino** (☎ 080 432 19 17; Via Independenza; meals €35; ☺ Tue-Sun Oct-Jun, daily Jul & Sep) found in the centre of Alberobello.

GETTING THERE & AWAY

Alberobello is easily accessible from Bari (€3.10, 1½ hours, hourly) on the FSE Bari–Taranto train line. From the station, walk straight ahead along Via Mazzini, which becomes Via Garibaldi, to reach Piazza del Popolo.

Locorotondo

pop 14,100

Right in the heart of Puglia's wine country, Locorotondo is yet another *trulli* centre, although it is not half as commercialised as Alberobello. It takes its name from the circular plan of the town, a gleaming white constellation on the Murge plateau. Meander through its warren of streets, paved with smooth ivory-coloured stones, and chance upon its sun-baked centrepiece, the church of **Santa Maria della Graecia**. Otherwise find a bench in the **Villa Comunale**, a communal garden from where you can enjoy panoramic views of the surrounding valley.

You simply can't come to Locorotondo without sampling the local Spumante. You can do this at the local winery, **Cantina del Locorotondo** (☎ 080 431 16 44; www.locorotondodoc .com; Via Madonna della Catena 99). Ask for Oronzo Mastro for English-speaking tours.

Il Palmento (☎ /fax 080 438 34 04; www.ilpalmento .com; Contrada Cupa 161; ste low/high season €230/290; P ♨) is a top-notch, self-contained hamlet of 12 *trulli* suites that looks like a pixie village. It is set in luxuriant gardens with two pools, a play area and tennis courts. Each *trullo* has its own kitchen although the barrel-vaulted restaurant serves good local cuisine. It is 5km south of Locorotondo.

If you're lucky you'll come across the charming trattoria **U'Curdunn** (☎ 080 431 70 70; Via Dura 19; meals €20; ☺ Tue-Sun) in the historic centre. Its interior is cool and dark after the bright white alleyways and the food uses all organic produce. Good service and a buzzing atmosphere.

Locorotondo is easily accessible from Bari (€3.60, one hour 40 minutes, hourly) on the FSE Bari–Taranto train line.

Cisternino

pop 12,050

The further south you travel in Puglia the stronger the Greek influence becomes obvious on its whitewashed towns. A case in point is the terraced jumble of Cisternino in its landscape of olive trees. It has a pretty communal garden with scenic vistas next to which is its 13th-century **Chiesa Matrice** and **Torre Civica**. If you take Via Basilioni next to

---

SOUTHERN SYBARITES

Now that budget airlines are flying into Bari, you can take advantage of a quick spa break in Puglia. Many of these spas are in Puglia's impressive *masseria* (fortified farmhouses) and clustered conveniently between Fasano and Ostuni (about 45 minutes' drive from Bari).

Top of the list is Ostuni's **La Sommità Relais Culti** (☎ 0831 30 59 25; www.lasommita.it; Via Scipione Petrarolo 7; s/d €180/330; P ♨ ♨), from Milanese lifestyle-brand Culti. Its stunning modern style perfectly complements the purity of form of its ancient barrel vaults.

The more bohemian **Masseria Torre Coccaro** (☎ 080 482 93 10; www.masseriatorrecoccaro.com; Contrada Coccaro 8, Savelletri di Fasano; s/d €249/349; P ♨ ♨) has a subterranean Aveda spa carved out of caves once used for livestock, while the rooms are in converted hay lofts.

For those who like their spas on a grand scale with a grand price tag look no further than the **Masseria San Domenico** (☎ 080 482 77 69; www.masseriasandomenico; Strada Litoranea 379, Savelletri di Fasano; s/d €265/400; P ♨ ♨). The imposing 15th-century building used to be the headquarters of the Knights of Malta and it is surrounded by a sea of manicured olive groves. The thalassotherapy spa uses San Domenico's own range of olive-oil products in many of its treatments.

the tower you can amble along an elegant route right to the central piazza, Vittorio Emanuele.

Cisternino has a grand tradition of *fornello pronto* (ready-to-go roast or grilled meat) and in numerous butcher's shops and trattorie you can select a cut of meat which is promptly roasted or grilled on the spot. Try it at **Trattoria La Botte** (☎ 080 444 78 50; Via Santa Lucia 47; meals €20).

Cisternino is accessible, via Martina Franca, from Bari (€4.60, two hours, three daily) on the FSE Bari–Taranto train line.

Martina Franca
pop 48,800
Martina Franca has one of the finest old quarters in Puglia, a genteel collection of meandering lanes graced with fine baroque buildings. It was founded in the 10th century by refugees fleeing the Arab invasion of Taranto, although it only really started to flourish in the 14th century when Philip of Anjou granted it tax exemptions (*franchigie*, hence the name Franca). It became so wealthy that it acquired a castle and defensive walls complete with 24 solid bastions. The modern-day town is as comfortable and content as its historic counterpart and is a prosperous wine-producing centre.

ORIENTATION & INFORMATION
The FSE train station is downhill from the historic centre. Go right along Viale della Stazione, continuing along Via Alessandro Fighera to Corso Italia; continue to the left along Corso Italia to Piazza XX Settembre.

The **tourist office** (☎ 080 480 57 02; Piazza Roma 37; ⏰ 9am-1pm & 5.30-7.30pm Mon-Fri, 9am-12.30pm Sat) occupies a couple of rooms within the enormous Palazzo Ducale.

SIGHTS
Passing under the baroque **Arco di Sant'Antonio** at the western end of pedestrianised Piazza XX Settembre, you emerge into Piazza Roma, flanked by the 17th-century **Palazzo Ducale**, a vast edifice now used as municipal offices.

From the piazza, follow the fine Corso Vittorio Emanuele, lined with baroque townhouses, to reach Piazza Plebiscito. This is the heart of the historic centre and it is dominated by the exuberant baroque façade of the 18th-century **Basilica di San Martino** (Piazza Plebiscito), its centrepiece the good St Martin

himself, swinging a sword and sharing his cloak with a beggar.

FESTIVALS & EVENTS
Festival della Valle d'Itria (Valley d'Itria Festival) is an annual feast for music-lovers as the town hosts international performances of opera, classical and jazz. For information, phone the **Centro Artistico Musicale Paolo Grassi** (☎ 080 480 51 00) in the Palazzo Ducale. It's held late July to early August.

SLEEPING
Park Hotel San Michele (☎ 080 480 70 53; www .parkhotelsm.it; Viale Carella 9; s/d €72/112; ✖ P ☐) Set in a leafy garden, this is Martina's top hotel. The rooms are light and the décor is minimalist. Given the slick service and comfort, the prices are reasonable. The hotel is linked to the Agriturismo Centrone Piccolo, where you can have lunch or take a couple of cookery lessons.

I Paesi della Luce (☎ 080 430 15 88; www.ipaesidella luce.it; Via Vittorio Emanuele 14; 2-/4-person apt per day €55/65-80, per week €360-400/430-520) A tempting selection of apartments for rent in the old town. The flats are charmingly decorated with flagstones floors, solid wooden furniture and antique beds with extravagant wrought-iron frames. The buildings are historical treasures, with barrel vaulting and cool white interiors.

EATING
Il Ritrovo degli Amici (☎ 080 483 92 49; Corso Messapia 8; meals €25; ⏰ lunch Tue-Sun Mar-Jan) An excellent restaurant with a convivial atmosphere well oiled by the region's fine Spumante wines. The specialities here are its salamis and the sausages.

Ciacco (☎ 080 480 04 72; Via C Ugolino; meals about €20; ⏰ lunch Tue-Sun) Dive into Martina's historic centre to find Ciacco, a traditional restaurant with white-clad tables and a cosy fireplace, serving up Puglian cuisine in a modern key. It's located opposite the communal gardens.

Villaggio In (☎ 080 480 50 21; Via Arco Grassi 8; meals €20) This is a decidedly classy joint where you can dine downstairs then clamber up to the rooftop piano bar, which often has live music at weekends.

GETTING THERE & AROUND
To get to Martina Franca, take the **FSE** (☎ 080 480 80 20) train from Bari (€4, two hours,

hourly) or Taranto (€2.10, 40 minutes, 10 daily). FSE buses also connect Martina Franca with Alberobello (€1.10, 30 minutes, five Monday to Saturday) and Lecce (€5.70, two hours, seven daily).

Bus Nos III and IV connect the FSE train station, down on the plain, with Piazza XX Settembre.

Ostuni

pop 32,800

The white beacon of Ostuni, draped across its three hills, marks the end of the Trulli region and the beginning of the hot, dry Penisola Salentina. Ostuni is encircled with ramparts and its warren of tightly packed streets twist around a dramatic 15th-century **cathedral**. In the last few years Ostuni has become rather chic and now has some excellent restaurants and stylish bars.

ORIENTATION & INFORMATION

From Piazza della Libertà, where the new town meets the old, take Via Cattedrale to the cathedral. From the piazza in front of the cathedral, turn right for a view across the olive groves to the Adriatic Sea – or turn left to get agreeably lost in Ostuni's whitewashed lanes.

AUTHOR'S CHOICE

Il Frantoio (☎ 0832 33 02 76; www.trecolline .it; SS16, km 874; s/d €103/206; **P**) An utterly charming whitewashed farmhouse still very much in operation producing high-quality organic olive oil. As the owners still live and work in the farmhouse the atmosphere is real country house. Even if you aren't staying, book yourself in for one of the marathon nine-course Sunday lunches (€49 including copious amounts of wine), or a balmy, candlelit dinner in the courtyard. The food is unbelievable, and as each course arrives so does a basket of ingredients to explain the delicacies before you. Check out the family album on the website and you'll get some idea of what a warm and welcoming place it is.

You will need a car to reach this *masseria* as it lies 5km outside Ostuni along the SS16 in the direction of Fasano. You will see the sign on your left-hand side when you reach the km 874 sign.

Ostuni's **tourist office** (☎ 0831 30 12 68; Corso Mazzini 8; ☻ 8.30am-1.30pm & 5.30-8.30pm Mon-Fri, 8.30am-1.30pm & 6.30-8.30pm Sat, shorter hrs winter) is just off Piazza della Libertà.

SIGHTS & ACTIVITIES

The **Museo di Civiltà Preclassiche della Murgia** (☎ 0831 33 63 83; Via Cattedrale 15; admission €1.50; ☻ 8.30am-1pm Tue-Sat, 3.30-7pm Tue-Thu, 3.30-7pm Sun Apr-Oct, Tue & Thu Nov-Mar) is housed in the Convento delle Monacelle. Many of the finds come from the Palaeolithic burial ground, which is now the **Parco Archeologico e Naturale di Arignano**, and can be visited by appointment (ask at the museum). Onsite you can see the 25,000-year-old star of the show, Delia. She was pregnant at the time of her death and her well-preserved skeleton was found in a local cave.

Ostuni is absolutely surrounded by olive groves so this is the place to pick some of the region's DOC 'Collina di Brindisi' direct from producers such as **Oleificio Cooperativa Coltivatori** (☎ 0831 30 16 98; Corso Mazzini). A 750ml bottle costs €5.

FESTIVALS & EVENTS

Ostuni's annual feast day, **La Calvalcata**, is held on 26 August and is a lavish event featuring large processions of horsemen dressed in red-and-white uniforms.

SLEEPING & EATING

Albergo Tre Torri (☎ 0831 33 11 14; Corso Vittorio Emanuele II 298; s/d €36/48, with bathroom €41/54) A 10-minute walk from Ostuni's busy old town is this cheerful, homely little hotel. The owners offer a warm welcome and the rooms are unobtrusively decorated. You can also enjoy the panoramic views of the town.

Osteria Piazzetta Cattedrale (☎ 0831 33 50 26; Via Arcidiacono Trinchera 7; meals €25) Tucked under an arch opposite Ostuni's cathedral is this tiny little hostelry serving up some magical food. The antipasti is simply exquisite and includes a melt-in-your-mouth courgette soufflé and the divine burrata cheese (apparently a favourite of the Shah of Iran). The service is attentive and the atmosphere deeply contented. It is tiny so be sure to make a reservation.

Osteria del Tempo Perso (☎ 0831 30 33 20; Gaetano Tanzarella Vitale 47; meals from €28) A rustic restaurant in a former bakery, this place serves great Puglian food, the speciality being the roasted meats. Face the cathedral's south wall, turn right through an archway into Largo Giuseppe Spennati and follow signs to the restaurant.

GETTING THERE & AROUND
STP buses run between Ostuni and Brindisi (€2.30, 50 minutes, six daily) about every two hours, arriving in Piazza Italia in the newer part of Brindisi. They also connect the town with Martina Franca (€3.60, 45 minutes, five daily). Trains run frequently to and from Brindisi (€2.60, 25 minutes) and Bari (€4.10, one hour 10 minutes). A local bus covers the 2.5km between the station and town, running every half-hour.

You can rent a bicycle from **Alba Travel Agency** (☎ 339 866 43 66; Largo Bianchieri 2; per day/week €13/35).

BRINDISI
pop 88,500
Brindisi is southern Italy's busiest merchant and passenger port. It was the end of the ancient Roman road, Via Appia, down whose weary length trudged legionnaires and pilgrims, crusaders and traders all heading to Greece and the Near East. These days very little has changed except now Brindisi's pilgrims are sun-seekers rather than soul-seekers, and they are still on their way to Greece.

Horror stories about thieves and touts ready to relieve you of your luggage and money and whip you off to dodgy hotels haven't helped Brindisi. But in reality it really isn't that bad; there is simply very little to do other than wait for your ferry – it's more boring than dangerous. But the crush of the quayside retains an enervating energy and, if you care to linger, the small historic centre is a good place to while away some time.

Orientation
The new port is east of town, across the Seno di Levante at Costa Morena, in a bleak industrial wilderness.

The old port is located about 1km from the train station along Corso Umberto I, which leads into Corso Garibaldi. There are numerous takeaway food outlets and places to eat along the route, as well as a bewildering array of ferry companies and travel agencies.

Information
Corso Umberto I and Corso Garibaldi bristle with currency-exchange offices and banks.
Ferries (www.ferries.gr) Details of ferry fares and timetables to Greek destinations.
Hospital (☎ 0831 53 71 11; SS7 for Mesagne) Southwest of the centre.
Internet point (Corso Garibaldi 97; per hr €2; ☒ 9am-1pm & 3-9pm) New centre with fast computers. Very convenient.
Photocenter (Corso Umberto I 114; per hr €4; ☒ 9am-1pm daily, 4.30-8.30pm Tue-Fri & Sun) Has Internet.
Police station (☎ 0831 54 31 11; Via Perrino 1)
Post office (☎ 0831 47 11 11; Piazza Vittoria; ☒ 8am-6.30pm Mon-Fri, 8am-12.30pm Sat)
Tourist office (☎ 0831 52 30 72; Viale Regina Margherita 44; ☒ 8.30am-2pm & 3.30-7pm Mon-Fri, 8.30am-1pm Sat)

Dangers & Annoyances
Since the breakup of Yugoslavia and the advent of war in Iraq, Italy's Adriatic ports have borne the brunt of illegal immigration. This has resulted in some disturbing reports of racial harassment by the authorities at key entry points like Brindisi. While this is not the norm it is something to be aware of while travelling this route.

In summer, theft can be a problem with so many inviting backpacks and bags lying around. Nothing of the remotest interest to a thief should be left unattended. Women are advised to be careful alone at night.

With regards to ticket scams, the safest strategy is to deal directly with a reputable ferry company. Readers also report that some less scrupulous travel agents will assure you that your Eurail or Inter-Rail pass is invalid or that the quota is full in order to sell you a full-price ticket. Check with the ferry company.

Sights
For the Romans, as for travellers today, Brindisi was the end of the line or, more specifically, of Via Appia, which stretched cross-country from Rome. For centuries, two great **columns** marked the end of the imperial highway. One was presented to the town of Lecce back in 1666 as thanks to Sant'Oronzo for having relieved Brindisi of the plague. The other is *in situ* and has finally shed its scaffolding after years of restoration. What has been revealed is a rather delicate, gleaming white column at the top of a sweeping set of sun-whitened stairs. Legend has it that the

BRINDISI

0 ——————— 200 m
0 ——————— 0.1 miles

INFORMATION
Internet Point.................................1 D2
Photocenter....................................2 B4
Post Office.......................................3 C3
Tourist Office..................................4 C2

SIGHTS & ACTIVITIES
Cathedral...5 C2
Monument to Italian Sailors.........6 D1
Museo Archeológico.....................7 C2
Palazzo Balsamo............................8 C2
Porta dei Cavalieri Templari.........9 C2
Roman Column..............................10 C2
Tempio di San Giovanni al Sepolcro..11 C2

SLEEPING
Grande Albergo Internazionale........12 C2
Hotel Altair....................................13 D3
Hotel Majestic...............................14 B4
Hotel Orientale.............................15 C3
Hotel Regina.................................16 B4

EATING
Il Giardino......................................17 C2
Market...18 C3
Supermarket..................................19 D2
Trattoria Pantagruele....................20 C2

TRANSPORT
Appia Travel...................................21 D2
Blue Star Ferries............................22 D3
Boats to Monument of Italian Sailors..23 C1
Buses for Costa Morena.................24 D2
FSE & STP Bus Stops.....................25 B4
Hellenic Mediterranean Lines........26 C3
Italian Ferries.................................27 D3
Marmara Lines...............................28 C3
Old Ferry Terminal........................29 D2
Skenderbeg Lines..........................30 D3

Seno di
Ponente

Castello
Svevo

Viale dei Mille

To Chiesa di Santa
Maria del Casale (4km)

To Hospital
(2km)

Piazza
Francesco
Crispi

Train
Station

Piazza
Cairoli

Largo
Palumbo

To Superstrada (1.7km);
Airport (7km);
Lecce (38km);
Taranto (70km);
Bari (100km)

To Fragline
(150m); Costa
Morena (7km)

To Police
Station (200m)

Piazza
del
Duomo

Porto
Interno

Piazza
Vittorio
Emanuele

Piazza
Vittoria

Piazza
del
Popolo

Seno di
Levante

Roman poet Virgil died in a house near here after returning from a voyage to Greece.

In the small historic quarter, the modest **cathedral** (Piazza del Duomo) was originally built in the 11th century but substantially remodelled about 700 years later. You can get a flavour of what it might have looked liked from the nearby **Porta dei Cavalieri Templari**, a fanciful portico with pointy arches which is all that remains of the Knights Templar's main church. Their other church, the **Tempio di San Giovanni al Sepolcro** (Via San Giovanni) is a square brown bulk of Norman stone conforming to the circular plan much loved by the Templars.

Abutting the north side of the cathedral is the small **Museo Archeológico** (☎ 0831 22 14 01;

Piazza del Duomo 8; admission free; ☼ 9am-1pm Tue-Sun, 3.30-6.30pm Tue, Thu & Sat) containing Brindisi's Punta del Serrone bronzes – a find of nearly 3000 bronze sculptures and fragments in Hellenistic Greek style. Across the tranquil square is the **Palazzo Balsamo**, which has a fine loggia.

Brindisi's main sight is the **Chiesa di Santa Maria del Casale**, 4km north of the centre towards the airport. Built by Prince Philip of Taranto around 1300, the church is a melange of Puglian Romanesque, Gothic and Byzantine styles, but the frescoes inside definitely take their cue from the rich Byzantine tradition. The immense *Last Judgement* on the entrance wall is the work of Rinaldo di Taranto, and is full of blood and thunder. Ring the bell at the gate to gain entry. To get there, follow Via Provinciale San Vito around the Seno di Ponente bay. Alternatively, take the airport bus.

A pleasant diversion is to take one of the regular boats (€1.20 return) on Viale Regina Margherita across the harbour to the **Monument to Italian Sailors**. It was erected by Mussolini in 1933 and from its terrace you can enjoy a wonderful view of Brindisi's waterfront.

Sleeping

Grande Albergo Internazionale (☎ 0831 52 34 73; www.albergointernazionale.it; Viale Regina Margherita 23; s/d €145/190; **P** 🕮) Brindisi's top hotel, this early 19th-century palace was built for English merchants on their way to and from Bombay and the Raj. It has great views over the harbour, and it is very convenient for the ferry.

Hotel Orientale (☎ 0831 56 84 51; Corso Garibaldi 49; s/d €90/120; 🕮 **P**) Brindisi's best modern hotel is right in the centre of the *corso*. The décor is unimaginative but the rooms are functionally comfortable and the reception is very efficient.

Hotel Regina (☎ 0831 56 20 01; www.hotelregina web.com; Via Cavour 5; s/d €70/90; 🕮 **P**) Ignore the tired façade and crass 1980s black-and-chrome décor in the reception and you'll find the Regina a comfortable place to pass the night. It also has a useful private garage.

Hotel Altair (☎ 0831 56 22 89; Via Giudea 4; s/d €20/37, d with bathroom €50) Hidden away in a side-street off Corso Garibaldi, this modest hotel has old-style high-ceilinged rooms. It's ideal for early morning departures as the port bus stop is less than five minutes' walk away. Breakfast is an additional €2.50.

Hotel Majestic (☎ 0831 59 79 41; www.ht-majestic.it; Corso Umberto I 151; s/d €88/125; 🕮 **P**) This hotel is convenient for the train station. It's a good deal at weekends, when rates fall by 20%.

Eating

Trattoria Pantagruele (☎ 0831 56 06 05; Via Salita di Ripalta 1; meals €15-20; 🕒 lunch Mon-Sat) Named after the satirical character from Rabelais, this rather highbrow little trattoria is highly regarded and very popular. It is very handy for the port and serves up excellent fish and grilled meats, as well as yummy homemade desserts. In the summer, tables fill the little piazza outside.

Il Giardino (☎ 0831 22 40 26; Via Tarantini 14-18; meals €25; 🕒 lunch Tue-Sun) For a touch more sophistication head to Il Giardino (previously La Lanterna). Established over 40 years ago in a restored 15th-century palazzo, it has a delightful garden and boasts an impressive list of local wines.

For supplies for the boat trip, stock up at the colourful fresh-food **market** (Piazza Mercato; 🕒 mornings Mon-Sat), just behind the post office, or at the **supermarket** (Corso Garibaldi 106).

Getting There & Away

AIR

From **Papola Casale** (BDS; www.seap-puglia.it), Brindisi's small airport, there are internal flights to and from Rome, Naples, Milan, Bologna and Pisa. The airport is served mainly by Alitalia and AirOne, although there are now direct flights from London Stansted with Ryanair.

Major and local car-rental firms are represented at the airport and there are regular buses to Lecce (€2, 45 minutes, six daily).

BOAT

Ferries, all of which take vehicles, leave Brindisi for Greek destinations including Corfu, Igoumenitsa, Patras and the Ionian Islands. From Patras there is a bus to Athens. Boats also service Albania (daily) and Turkey (seasonal).

Most ferry companies operate only in summer. All have offices at Costa Morena (the new port), and the major ones also have offices in town. There's a €8 port tax for each person and car. Check-in at least two hours before departure or you risk losing your reservation (a strong possibility in the high season).

Blue Star Ferries (☎ 0831 56 22 00; www.bluestarferries .com; Corso Garibaldi 65) To and from Igoumenitsa, mostly via Corfu. Sailing is possible year-round (Wednesday to Monday).

Fragline (☎ 0831 54 85 40; www.fragline.gr; Via Spalato 31) To Corfu and Igoumenitsa. Ferries run April to September.

Hellenic Mediterranean Lines (☎ 0831 52 85 31; www.hml.gr; Corso Garibaldi 8) To Corfu, Igoumenitsa and Patras (April to October) and the Ionian Islands (July and August). The largest and most reliable of the lines, Hellenic Mediterranean accepts Eurail and Inter-Rail passes (€15 supplement is payable in July and August). If you intend to use your pass, it is best to reserve in advance in high season.

Italian Ferries (☎ 0831 59 08 40; www.italianferries.it; Corso Garibaldi 96-98) To and from Corfu and Paxos. Italian

FERRY CROSSINGS FROM BRINDISI

Destination	Cost (€) seat/cabin/car	Duration (hr)
Cesme, Turkey	80/110/145	7
Corfu	58/90/55	12
Igoumenitsa, Greece	60/90/63	9-12
Patras, Greece	73/94/70	15-20
Vlore, Albania	60/70/60	8½

Ferries accepts Eurail and Inter-Rail passes for tickets bought at the town centre office, entitling you to reduced rates. For Eurail passholders there is a €20 surcharge in July and August.
Marmara Lines (☎ 0831 56 86 33; www.marmaralines .com; Corso Garibaldi 19) Twice-weekly ferry to Cesme (Turkey). Departs Saturday and Wednesday at 11pm.
Skenderbeg Lines (☎ 0831 52 54 48; www.skenderbeg lines.com; Corso Garibaldi 88) Ferries to and from Vlore (Valona; in Albania), Monday to Saturday.

BUS
Buses operated by **STP** (☎ 0831 54 92 45) connect Brindisi with Ostuni (€2.30, 50 minutes, six daily) and Lecce (€2, 45 minutes, two daily), as well as towns throughout the Penisola Salentina. Most leave from Via Bastioni Carlo V, in front of the train station. **FSE** (☎ 099 477 46 27) buses serving local towns also leave from here.

Marozzi runs to Rome's Stazione Tiburtina (€32.55, nine hours, four daily) and Pisa and Florence (€52, 14 hours, one daily), leaving from Viale Arno. **Appia Travel** (☎ 0831 52 16 84; Viale Regina Margherita 8-9) sells tickets.

CAR & MOTORCYCLE
For the new ferry terminal, follow signs for Costa Morena from the autostrada. Allow plenty of time to board your ferry.

TRAIN
Brindisi is on the main Trenitalia train line. It has regular local services to Bari (€6.20, Eurostar – one hour, *regionale* – one hour 40 minutes), Lecce (€8.50 Eurostar, 40 minutes) and Taranto (€3.65, one hour 10 minutes). Other destinations include Milan (€63.50, 9½ hours) and Rome (€38, six hours).

Getting Around
A free minibus operated by Portabagagli connects the train station and old ferry terminal with Costa Morena. It departs two

hours before boat departures. You'll need a valid ferry ticket.

To reach the airport take the free shuttle bus from the old ferry terminal.

LECCE
pop 105,000

As you stare open-mouthed at the madcap baroque architecture in the city centre, it's almost difficult not to laugh. So joyously extravagant is the stonework that it's either grotesquely ugly or splendidly beautiful; 18th-century traveller Thomas Ashe thought it was 'the most beautiful city in Italy', but the Marchese Grimaldi said the façade of Santa Croce made him think a lunatic was having a nightmare. The local stone actually encourages extravagance; it starts off particularly malleable yet soon after being quarried it hardens, making it the perfect building and sculpting material.

A centre of learning, Lecce, sometimes referred to as the 'Florence of the south', is a university town with deep roots, style, grace – and plenty of student cafés and bars. Convenient for both the Adriatic and Ionian Seas, it makes a great base for exploring the Penisola Salentina.

Orientation
The train station is about 1km southwest of Lecce's historic centre. The town centre's twin main squares are Piazza Sant'Oronzo and Piazza del Duomo, linked by pedestrian Corso Vittorio Emanuele. From the station, walk straight ahead along Viale Oronzo Quarta, which becomes Via B Cairoli, then bear left into Viale Paladini.

Information
You'll find several banks on and around Piazza Sant'Oronzo.
Ambulance (☎ 0832 22 86 30)
Clioinformazione (Via Fazzi 11; per hr €4; ☽ 9am-1pm & 4-8pm Mon-Fri, 9am-1pm Sat) Internet place central and popular with students.
CTS (☎ 0832 30 18 62; Via G Palmieri 89) Travel agency for youth bargain fares.
Hospital (☎ 0832 66 11 11; Via San Cesario) About 2km south of the centre on the road to Gallipoli.
Libreria Mondadori (Piazza Sant'Oronzo 45/46; ☽ 10am-1pm & 4.30-9pm Mon-Fri, 10am-1pm & 5-10.30pm Sat & Sun) Well-stocked bookshop with plenty of maps and guides to the city, plus some lovely illustrated books.

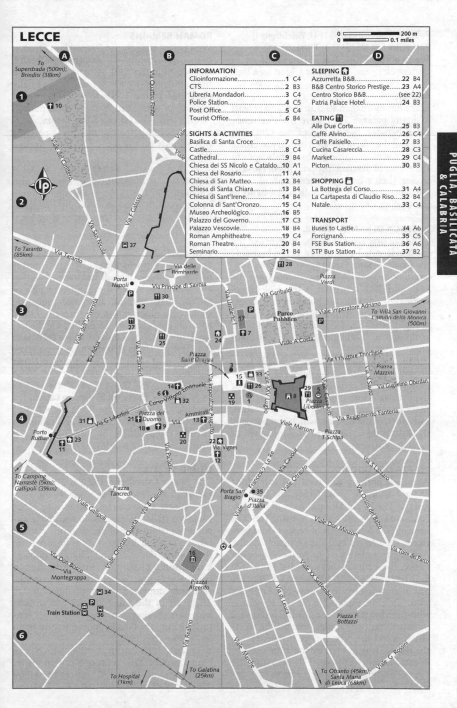

LECCE

INFORMATION		
Clioinformazione	1	C4
CTS	2	B3
Libreria Mondadori	3	C4
Police Station	4	C5
Post Office	5	C4
Tourist Office	6	B4

SIGHTS & ACTIVITIES		
Basilica di Santa Croce	7	C3
Castle	8	C4
Cathedral	9	B4
Chiesa dei SS Nicolò e Cataldo	10	A1
Chiesa del Rosario	11	A4
Chiesa di San Matteo	12	B4
Chiesa di Santa Chiara	13	B4
Chiesa di Sant'Irene	14	B4
Colonna di Sant'Oronzo	15	C4
Museo Archeológico	16	B5
Palazzo del Governo	17	C3
Palazzo Vescovile	18	B4
Roman Amphitheatre	19	C4
Roman Theatre	20	B4
Seminario	21	B4

SLEEPING		
Azzurretta B&B	22	B4
B&B Centro Storico Prestige	23	A4
Centro Storico B&B	(see 22)	
Patria Palace Hotel	24	B3

EATING		
Alle Due Corte	25	B3
Caffè Alvino	26	C4
Caffè Paisiello	27	B3
Cucina Casareccia	28	C3
Market	29	C4
Picton	30	B3

SHOPPING		
La Bottega del Corso	31	A4
La Cartapesta di Claudio Riso	32	B4
Natale	33	C4

TRANSPORT		
Buses to Castle	34	A6
Forcignanò	35	C5
FSE Bus Station	36	A6
STP Bus Station	37	B2

PUGLIA, BASILICATA & CALABRIA

Police station (☎ 0832 69 11 11; Viale Otranto 1)
Post office (☎ 0832 24 35 36; Piazza Libertini)
Tourist office (☎ 0832 24 80 92; Corso Vittorio
Emanuele 24; ☿ 9am-1pm Mon-Sat & 3-5pm Tue & Thu)

Sights

Lecce has more than 40 churches and at least
as many palazzi. They were built or renovated between the middle of the 17th century and the end of the 18th century to create
one of the most unified urban landscapes in
Italy. Two of the main proponents of *barocco
leccese* (Lecce baroque) were Antonio and
Giuseppe Zimbalo, who both had a hand in
the Basilica di Santa Croce.

BASILICA DI SANTA CROCE

Little can prepare you for the opulence of the
most celebrated example of Lecce baroque,
the **Basilica di Santa Croce** (☎ 0832 24 19 57; Via Umberto I; ☿ 8am-1pm & 4-7.30pm). Throughout the
16th and 17th centuries, a team of artists
worked to decorate the building and its extraordinarily ornate façade. It is best viewed
at night, when the swirls and shadows of its
sculpture are highlighted to extraordinary
effect.

The interior is more conventionally Renaissance and definitely deserves a quick
look if you can recover from the impact of
the exterior. Giuseppe Zimbalo also left his
mark in the former Convento dei Celestini,
just north of the basilica, which is nowadays
the **Palazzo del Governo**, the headquarters of
local government.

PIAZZA DEL DUOMO

Although nothing can rival the splendour
of the Basilica di Santa Croce, the baroque
feast of Piazza del Duomo feels like a self-
contained city within a city. During times of
invasion the inhabitants of Lecce would bar-
ricade themselves into the compact square.
Although modest by comparison to Santa
Croce, the 12th-century **cathedral** (☎ 0832 30
85 57; Piazza del Duomo; ☿ 6.30am-noon & 5-7.30pm) is
one of the finest works of Giuseppe Zimbalo,
who was also responsible for the towering,
68m-high **bell tower**. The cathedral is unusual
in that it has two façades, one on the western end and the other, more ornate, facing
the piazza. It is framed by the 15th-century
Palazzo Vescovile (Episcopal Palace) and the
18th-century **Seminario** (☿ exhibitions only), designed by Giuseppe Cino.

ROMAN REMAINS

Well below the level of Piazza Sant'Oronzo
is the 2nd-century-AD **Roman amphitheatre**,
discovered in the 1901 by workmen digging
the foundations for a new bank. It was finally
excavated in the 1930s to reveal a perfect
horseshoe with seating for 15,000 people.
Nearby, rises the **Colonna di Sant'Oronzo**, a statue of Lecce's patron saint who is perched
precariously on the second pillar of Appian
Way.

Within the small **Roman theatre** (☎ 0832 24
61 09; Via Ammirati; admission €2.60; ☿ 10am-1pm), also
uncovered in the 1930s, is an equally small
museum, with some wonderfully preserved
frescoes and mosaics, transferred from local
sites.

CHURCHES

On Corso Vittorio Emanuele, the interior
of 17th-century **Chiesa di Sant'Irene** (☿ 8-11am
& 4-6pm Mon-Sat) boasts a magnificent pair of
mirror-image baroque altarpieces, squaring
up to each other across the transept. Other
baroque churches of interest include the last
work of Giuseppe Zimbalo, **Chiesa del Rosario**
(Via G Libertini); **Chiesa di Santa Chiara** (Piazza Vittorio
Emanuele), with every niche a swirl of twist-
ing columns and ornate statuary; and, 200m
to its south, the **Chiesa di San Matteo** (Via dei
Perroni 29). The **Chiesa dei SS Nicolò e Cataldo** (Via
San Nicola), along from the Porta Napoli, was
built by the Normans in 1180 and rebuilt in
1716 by the prolific Cino, who retained the
Romanesque rose window and portal.

OTHER SIGHTS

The **Museo Archeològico** (☎ 0832 24 70 25; Viale
Gallipoli; admission free; ☿ 9am-1.30pm Mon-Fri, 3-6pm
Tue-Thu) sets a wonderful example to other
southern Italian museums. In the lovely air-
conditioned interior of the museum you can
browse through 10,000 years of history from
Palaeolithic and Neolithic bits and bobs to
a handsome display of Greek and Roman
coins, jewels, pots, weaponry and ornaments,
all neatly displayed in chronological order.
The stars of the show are the Messapians,
who were making jaunty jugs and bowls centuries before the Greeks arrived to give them
any pottery lessons.

Lecce's 16th-century **castle**, which was
built around a 12th-century Norman tower,
is not open to the public unless there is a
temporary exhibition.

Tours

Medius Terrae (☎ 0832 36 46 13, 320 049 90 52; www
.medius-terrae.com) is a small cultural association
run by Davide Torsello and Melinda Pap-
pova, who have crafted a series of tours that
put you in touch with local craftsmen, artisans, cheese-makers, musicians and shepherds. They also run a language course in
connection with Italianoit Language School
in Bologna – see the website for details.

Weekly courses including accommodation, transfers, food and workshops work
out at €900.

Sleeping

Lecce has a budding B&B scene, which offers
the best-value accommodation in town.

Patria Palace Hotel (☎ 0832 24 51 11; www.patria
palacelecce.com; Piazzetta Riccardi; s/d €175/190; ✂ 💻)
Right in the middle of barmy baroque territory, this top-end option has all the requisite
comforts. Each of the rooms is decorated
differently and the shady roof terrace boasts
views over the Basilica di Santa Croce.

B&B Centro Storico Prestige (☎ 0832 30 88 81;
www.bbprestige-lecce.it; Via Santa Maria del Paradiso 4; s/d/
ste €40/70/80; [P] 💻) Run by the irrepressible
Renata, the Prestige is a home away from
home. Rooms are light and airy and beautifully finished, Renata is great company and
there is a pretty communal terrace with views
over San Giovanni Battista.

Centro Storico B&B (☎ 0832 24 28 28; www.bedand
breakfast.lecce.it; Via Vignes 2b; s/d €35/57; [P] ✂)
Mind your head as you stoop to enter this
16th-century palazzo. Rooms in this charming hideaway are more comfortable than the
price would suggest and all have a private
balcony. There's also a nifty terrace for sunbathing. The same family own the **Azzurretta
B&B** (☎ 0832 24 22 11; www.bblecce.it; Via Vignes 2; s/d
€35/57; [P] ✂), on the same floor in the same
building.

Camping Namasté (☎ 0832 32 96 47; www.camping
-lecce.it; Via Novoli; person/tent/car €5/8/8) Just over
4km out of town is the 35,000-sq-m camp
site Camping Namasté. It forms part of an
organic farm and runs yoga classes on site.
To get to Namasté take bus No 26 from the
train station.

Eating

RESTAURANTS

Cucina Casareccia (☎ 0832 24 51 78; Viale Colonnello
Archimede Costadura 19; meals €20; ✆ lunch Tue-Sun)

Reserve a table at this unique restaurant, actually the downstairs rooms of a house, and
put yourself in the capable hands of Carmela
Perrone. She'll whisk you through a dazzling
array of Salentine dishes from the true *cucina
povera* (literally 'cooking of the poor').

Picton (☎ 0832 33 23 83; Via Idomeneo 14; meals €35;
✆ Tue-Sun) This restaurant is housed in an old
palazzo with a cool barrel-vaulted interior
and a refreshing internal garden. The cuisine combines Salentine favourites such as
fish, mushrooms and herbs in exciting new
recipes, some more successful than others.

Alle due Corti (☎ 0832 24 22 23; www.alleduecorti
.com; Corte dei Giugni 1; meals €15-20) For a taste of
the sunny Salentina, this laid-back restaurant
stands out. The menu is classical Puglian
with plenty of fresh fruit, vegetables and
homemade pasta. Don't worry if you don't
understand the menu (written in dialect) as
the waiter explains everything.

Villa Giovanni Camillo della Monica (☎ 0832 45
84 32; Via SS Giacomo e Filippo 40; meals €20; ✆ Wed-
Mon Feb-Dec) Set in the courtyard of a renovated palazzo, this restaurant is charmingly
elegant. The beautifully presented food –
sea bream wrapped in aubergine, steak with
asparagus – matches the surroundings.

Pick up your own ingredients at Lecce's
fresh-produce **market** (Piazza Libertini; ✆ mornings
Mon-Sat).

CAFÉS

Like all university towns, Lecce has a vibrant
café culture.

Caffè Alvino (☎ 0832 24 74 36; Piazza Sant'Oronzo 30)
Enjoy your cappuccino and watch the world
pass by in the beautiful piazza. The café also
serves a decent *rustica*, a confection of puff
pastry, mozzarella cheese and tomato.

Caffè Paisiello (☎ 0832 30 14 04; Via G Palmieri 72)
Sample the pastries or ice cream here as you
sip your chosen drink.

Shopping

Lecce's streets are lined with pretty boutiques, well-stocked bookshops and inviting
delicatessens.

La Cartapesta (☎ 0832 24 34 10; Via Vittorio Emanuele
27) Lecce is famous for its papier-mâché – in
fact the tradition was invented here. You can
buy yourself some of the handcrafted figurines (including a commemorative model of
Pope John Paul II) in this, Claudio Riso's
workshop.

Natale (☎ 0832 25 60 60; Via Trinchese 7) A fabulous confectioner where the windows gleam with jewel-like treats, candied fruits, liqueurs, truffles, pannacotta and dark chocolate cakes that pool like oil slicks on golden plates.

La Bottega del Corso (☎ 0832 24 98 66; Via Libertini 52) A well-stocked deli full of typical produce and freshly baked breads.

Getting There & Away

STP (☎ 0832 35 91 42) runs buses connecting Lecce with towns throughout the Penisola Salentina, including Santa Maria di Leuca and Galatina, departing from Via Adua (although it is much more convenient to travel by train).

FSE (☎ 0832 34 76 34) runs buses to towns including Gallipoli (€2.10, one hour, four daily), Otranto (€2.10, one hour, two daily), Taranto (€4.60, two hours, frequent) and Brindisi (€2, 45 minutes, two daily), leaving from Via Torre del Parco.

Brindisi is 30 minutes away from Lecce by motorway and the SS7 leads to Taranto.

There are frequent trains heading to Bari (1st/2nd class €16/12, 2¼ hours) via Brindisi (€10.50/8, 40 minutes), and daily services to and from Rome (€60.50/43, seven hours, six daily) and Bologna (€71/53, 8½ hours, nine daily). For Naples (€48, six hours), change in Caserta.

FSE trains also depart from the main station for Otranto and Martina Franca.

Getting Around

The historic centre of Lecce is best seen on foot. However, if you are staying a couple of days you may want to hire a bike from **Forcignanò** (☎ 0832 30 60 62; Piazza d'Italia 2/3) at Porta San Biagio. The bikes cost €1.50/10 per hour/day.

Among others, bus Nos 1, 2 and 4 run from the train station to Viale Marconi.

PENISOLA SALENTINA

After Sicily and Sardinia, the Penisola Salentina (Salentine Peninsula) is considered by some to be the third island of Italy. It is hot, dry, cut off and remote, retaining a real flavour of its Greek past. Here the lush greenery of the Valle d'Itria gives way to ochre-coloured fields hazy with wildflowers and immense olive groves. The sun-baked towns are shuttered and hushed although they come alive in the summer months.

Galatina
pop 27,900

Nowhere is the Salentine's Greek past so evident as in the town of Galatina, 18km south of Lecce, where Greek was still spoken up until the early 20th century. It is almost the only place where the ritual of *tarantulism* (a frenzied dance meant to rid the body of tarantula-bite poison) is still practised. The tarantella folk dance evolved from it, and each year on the feast day of St Peter and St Paul (29 June), the ritual is performed at the (now deconsecrated) church dedicated to the saints.

The town's real drawcards are the frescoes of the **Basilica di Santa Caterina d'Alessandria** (☺ 7am-noon & 4.30-8pm summer, 7am-noon & 3.30-6pm winter). It was built by the Franciscans, whose patroness was the French Marie d'Enghien de Brienne. Married to Raimondello Orsini del Balzo, the Salentine's wealthiest noble, she had plenty of cash to splash out on its interior decoration. It is not clear who the artists Marie employed really were; they could have been itinerant painters down from Le Marche and Emilia, or southerners who had been sent north to absorb the latest Renaissance innovations. Whoever they were, they left behind a unique legacy of frescoes depicting stories from the Old and New Testament that cover nearly the entire interior of the basilica. Bring a torch.

If you want to stop overnight try the romantic **Hotel Palazzo Baldi** (☎ 0836 56 83 45; www .hotelpalazzobaldi.com in Italian; Via Corte Baldi 2; s/d €125/200). There are three specially priced rooms at €80/100 per single/double.

FSE runs regular trains between Galatina and Lecce (€1.30, 30 minutes, hourly).

OTRANTO
pop 5350

The ancient nucleus of Otranto, a tightly packed centre of car-free lanes, still shines on its hill. Otranto was Italy's main port to the Orient for a thousand years and as a result has suffered a brutal history. There are fanciful tales that King Minos was here and St Peter is supposed to have celebrated the first Western Mass at the top of the hill.

One thing we can be certain of is the Sack of Otranto in 1480, when 18,000 Turks besieged the town and killed 800 faithful Christians who refused to convert.

Today the blood and gore are a thing of the past and the only fright you'll get is the number of people on Otranto's scenic beaches during the summer months.

The **tourist office** (☎ 0836 80 14 36; Piazza Castello; ⏲ 9am-1pm & 3-8pm Mon-Fri Jun-Sep, 9am-1pm Mon-Fri Oct-May) faces the castle.

Sights

Otranto's premier attraction is the audacious mosaic in the Romanesque **cathedral** (⏲ 8am-noon & 3-7pm Apr-Sep, 8am-noon & 3-5pm Oct-Mar). First built by the Normans in the 11th century and subsequently subjected to a facelift or two, the magnificent cathedral is a forest of slender pillars and carved capitals. Underfoot is a vast 12th-century floor mosaic occupying the whole of the nave. It is a technicolour vision of heaven and hell, a bizarre syncretism of the classics, religion and plain superstition. It was executed by a young monk called Pantaleone, who thought nothing of aligning Adam and Eve with Diana the huntress and Hercules, King Arthur and Alexander the Great, along with a whole menagerie of monkeys, snakes and sea monsters.

It is amazing that it has survived at all, as the Turks stabled their horses here when they beheaded the martyrs of Otranto on a stone now preserved in the altar of the side chapel to the right of the main altar. If you're ghoulish you can inspect their skulls in the glass cases that line the walls.

Just opposite the cathedral is the small **diocesan museum** (admission €1; ⏲ 10am-noon & 4-8pm Apr-Sep, 10am-noon & 3-6pm Oct-Mar) where you can see segments of a 4th-century Roman mosaic, which was recently discovered under the cathedral floor.

Within the tiny **Chiesa di San Pietro** (⏲ 10am-12.30pm & 3-6pm Apr-Sep, 10am-noon & 3-6pm Oct-Mar) are more vivid Byzantine frescoes. It is signposted off the *corso*.

The Aragonese **castle** (Piazza Castello; admission free except during exhibitions; ⏲ 9am-1pm Mon-Fri), at the eastern edge of town beside the port, is typical of the squat, thick-walled forts you'll find in coastal towns throughout Puglia.

Sleeping

Masseria Montelauro (☎ 0836 80 62 03; www.masseria montelauro.it; Strada Otranto-Uggiano; s/d €145/220; ⓟ ⊠ ▣ ▨) Who said all the best hotels were in the Valle d'Itria? The truth is there are some real gems around Otranto, such as the Masseria Montelauro. The 27 rooms are a romantic fantasy, the pool a clear blue square in the inner courtyard and you will often find guests in Zen-like stances practising t'ai chi on the lawns.

Hotel Albania (☎ /fax 0836 80 11 83; www.hotel albania.com; Via S Francesco di Paola 10; s/d €70/120; ⓟ ⊠) A big, white modern hotel opposite the Otranto channel. There are great views from the rooms, which are all cool and modern – perfect for Otranto's blazing summer.

Hotel Meublé (☎ /fax 0836 80 19 52; Porto Craulo 13; d €65-85) Situated within five minutes' walk of the beach, this modest place is ideally suited for a summer stay. Its patio makes for a lovely spot to sample their pizza, prepared in a wood oven.

Eating

Da Sergio (☎ 0836 80 14 08; Corso Garibaldi 9; meals €15-20; ⏲ Thu-Tue Mar-Dec) Try the excellent fish in Otranto's best fish restaurant, where jolly yellow tables abut the *corso*. The clientele is generally local and unfortunately foreign travellers don't get such good service.

Vecchio Otranto (☎ 0836 80 15 75; Corso Garibaldi 98; meals €30; ⏲ Thu-Tue Mar-Dec) Dive into the cool cavern like interior of Vecchio Otranto where you can sample a whole host of fishy delicacies including a delicious salted seafood risotto.

Getting There & Away

Otranto can be reached from Lecce by FSE train (€2.50, one hour), or by bus (€3.10, 50 minutes).

Marozzi (☎ 0836 80 15 78) buses run daily to and from Lecce (€2.10, one hour, three daily). They depart from the port.

For travel information and reservations, head to **Ellade Viaggi** (☎ 0836 80 15 78; www.ellade viaggi.it in Italian; Via Guglielmotto d'Otr 33) at the port.

AROUND OTRANTO

The road south from Otranto takes you along a wild coastline. The land here is rocky, and when the wind is up you can see why it is largely treeless. Many of the towns here started life as Greek settlements, although there are few monuments to be seen. When you reach the resort town of **Santa Maria di Leuca**, you've hit the bottom of the heel of Italy and the dividing line between the Adriatic and Ionian Seas. The Ionian side of the Penisola Salentina in particular is spattered with reasonable beaches. There are few cheap hotels in the area but camp sites abound along the coast.

GALLIPOLI
pop 20,300
Jutting into the Ionian Sea 39km southwest of Lecce, Gallipoli is actually an island connected to the mainland and modern city by a bridge. An important fishing centre, it has a history of strong-willed independence, being the last Salentine settlement to succumb to the Normans in the 11th century.

Information
The **tourist office** (☎ 0833 26 25 29; Piazza Imbriani 9; ☺ 9am-noon & 5-9pm Jul-Aug, 9am-1pm Mon-Fri & 4-6pm Tue & Thu Sep-Jun) is just over the bridge.

Sights
The entrance to the medieval island-town is guarded by an Angevin **castle**. Just opposite, below the ramp leading to the island, is a **fish market** that makes up for its small size with great variety and gusto.

Right in the heart of the old town is the 17th-century baroque **cathedral** (☎ 0833 26 19 87; Via Antonietta de Pace; ☺ during Mass), adorned with paintings by local artists. A little further west is the small **Museo Civico** (☎ 0833 26 42 24; Via Antonietta de Pace 51; admission free; ☺ 9am-12.30pm Tue-Sun).

Back over the bridge and just in the modern part of town is the **Fontana Antica**. Reconstructed in the 16th century from a Greek original, this fountain's much-weathered sculptured figures tell a steamy tale of incest and bestiality.

Sleeping & Eating
Palazzo del Corso (☎ 0833 26 40 40; www.hotelpalaz zodelcorso.it; Corso Roma 145; s/d €180/205; ❄ ▯) A gem of hotel on the *corso* before you enter the old town. Its rooms are a decorative treat, but the real attraction is the roof garden which overlooks the tiny marina, where you lounge on your sunbed before having a dip in the hydromassage tub!

Hotel Al Pescatore (☎/fax 0833 26 36 56; Riviera Colombo 39; s/d €60/90 ❄) In the old town, Al Pescatore has 16 spacious rooms set around an atrium full of vegetation. Half board is compulsory during August (€80 per person).

Some rooms even have views of the port and there's also a fiendishly popular restaurant (meals €20 to €25).

Il Bastione (☎ 0833 26 38 36; Riviera N Sauro 28; meals €25-30) Located on the old sea wall overlooking the beach, this restaurant is a good place for fish, which you can enjoy on the panoramic roof terrace.

Getting There & Away
FSE buses and trains link Gallipoli to Lecce (€2.10, one hour, four daily).

TARANTO
pop 200,400
Break through the industrial horror show with which Taranto presents its visitors and you will find a vivacious historic centre. Founded in the 7th century BC by exiles from Sparta, the city was christened Taras and grew to become one of the wealthiest and most important colonies of Magna Graecia, with a peak population of 300,000. The fun finished, however, in the 3rd century BC when the Romans marched in, changed its name to Tarentum and set off a two-millennia decline in fortunes.

Taranto, along with La Spezia, is Italy's major naval base, and the presence of young sailors is emblematic of a city that has always looked to the sea. In fact, one of the city's more esoteric claims to fame is that it is alleged to be the point where the first cat landed on European shores.

Orientation
Taranto neatly splits into three. The old town is on a tiny island, lodged between the port and train station to the northwest and the new city to the southeast. Italy's largest steel plant occupies almost the entire western half of the city. The more expensive hotels, tourist office and banks are in the grid-patterned new city.

Information
Chiocciolin@it (☎ 099 453 80 51; Corso Umberto I 85; per hr €5; ☺ 9am-1pm & 4.30-9pm Tue-Sat, 4.30-9pm Mon) Internet access.
Hospital (☎ 099 453 24 07; Via Bruno)
Police station (☎ 099 454 51 11; Via Anfiteatro 8)
Post office (☎ 099 470 75 91; Lungomare Vittorio Emanuele III)
Tourist office (☎ 099 453 23 97; Corso Umberto I 113; ☺ 9am-1pm & 5-7pm Mon-Fri, 9am-noon Sat)

TARANTO

INFORMATION		
Chiocciolin@.it	1	C3
Hospital	2	D4
Police Station	3	C3
Post Office	4	C4
Tourist Office	5	C3

SIGHTS & ACTIVITIES		
Castello Aragonese	6	B3
Cathedral	7	A2
Fish Markets	8	A2
Museo Nazionale	9	C3
Palazzo del Governo	10	C3
Palazzo Pantaleo	11	A2
Temple of Poseidon	12	B3
Valigia Travel	13	D3

SLEEPING		
Europa Residence Hotel	14	B3
Hotel Akropolis	15	A2
Hotel Pisani	16	C3

EATING		
Caffè Italiano	17	C3
Market	18	B3
Ponte Vecchio	19	A1
Ristorante al Gambero	20	A1
Ristorante Marc'Aurelio	21	C3
Trattoria al Gatto Rosso	22	C3

TRANSPORT		
Autolinee Miccolis Ticket Office	23	C3
Buses to Lecce	24	D3
Marino Autolinee Ticket Office	(see 23)	
Marozzi Ticket Office	(see 23)	

PUGLIA, BASILICATA & CALABRIA

Dangers & Annoyances

Ironically in a town that welcomed Europe's first cat, stray dogs can be a nuisance. This is particularly true around the old town, which itself can be quite sinister after dark.

Sights

CITTÀ VECCHIA

Just like Naples and Palermo, Taranto has an old town that retains a gritty atmosphere of deep decay and, at the same time, an irrepressible energy and ballsiness that precludes pity. It may be temporarily down at the heel but it certainly isn't down and out, as the city is now investing considerable funds into rehabilitating its old palaces and monuments.

Taranto has a curious city plan where the old town is perched on a small island dividing the Mar Piccolo (Small Sea; an enclosed lagoon) and the Mar Grande (Big Sea). It's a peculiar geography that means that everywhere you go you are surrounded by blue sea and blue sky. Guarding the swing bridge that joins the old and new town, the 15th-century **Castello Aragonese** (☎ 099 775 34 38; ☺ by appointment 9am noon), at the island's southern extreme, is an impressive structure, its sturdy bulwark jutting out to sea with the waves lashing its base. It's occupied by the Italian navy and can only be visited by appointment. Opposite you will see the remaining columns of what was once Taranto's Temple of Poseidon. Legend has it that his son,

Taras, founded the city when he rode into its harbour on the back of a dolphin.

Buried in the old town is the 11th-century **cathedral** (Via del Duomo), one of Puglia's oldest Romanesque buildings and an extravagant treat. Its baroque Cappella di San Cataldo (to whom the cathedral is dedicated) is an absolute riot of frescoes and polychrome marble inlay.

Taranto's real essence lies in its fabulous **fish markets** on Via Cariati, where all the rich variety of Taranto's morning catch is on noisy display.

NEW TOWN

Taranto's new town is a very pleasant surprise. It has a truly urbane atmosphere, with its sleek shopping streets shooting off the impressive palm-planted Piazza Garibaldi which is dominated by the gigantic rust-red 1920s **Palazzo del Governo**.

Unfortunately good things can not be said for the interminable ongoing renovation work of the **Museo Nazionale** (☎ 099 453 21 12; Corso Umberto I 41). It is a real shame, as this archaeological museum is one of the most important in Italy and houses, among other ancient artefacts, an impressive collection of antique gold jewellery. You can get some idea of its scandalously hidden treasures by visiting the temporary display in **Palazzo Pantaleo** (☎ 099 471 84 92; Corso Vittorio Emanuele II; admission €2; ☒ 8.15am-7.15pm) located in the old town.

Tours

Valigia Travel (☎ 099 459 43 74; www.valigiatravel.it; Corso Umberto I 139a) is a travel agency offering some great day trips in Taranto, such as the two-hour gander around Taranto by boat (€7 per person), or the guided archaeological tour in the old town (€20 per person). The agency also does a host of tours in the surrounding province.

Festivals & Events

Le Feste di Pasqua (Holy Week) is a time of high emotion. On Holy Thursday thousands of people gather to witness the Procession of the *Addolorata* (Sorrowful) and on Good Friday they watch the Procession of the Mysteries – when sinister-looking bearers clad in Ku Klux Klan–like robes carry statues representing the Passion of Christ around town.

Sleeping

In the past, Taranto's better hotels were confined to the eastern edge of the city, but now there are couple of very stylish new offerings in, or close to, the atmospheric old town.

Hotel Akropolis (☎ 099 470 41 10; www.hotel akropolis.it; Vico I Seminario 3; s/d €100/160; ☒ ☐) Finally there's a converted palazzo in the heart of the old town. The Akropolis has got it all right, from the tremendous view from its terrace over the terracotta rooftops of the old town to the original tiled floors of its 13 individually decorated bedrooms.

Europa Residence Hotel (☎ 099 452 59 94; www .hoteleuropaonline.it; Via Roma 2; s/d €77/130; ☒) If you don't want to be in the old town, this is the next best thing after the Akropolis. The Europa is located right on the sea edge overlooking the traffic going to and fro beneath the swing bridge. Inside the hotel is modern and comfortable and most of the rooms have uninterrupted sea views.

Hotel Pisani (☎ 099 453 40 87; fax 099 470 75 93; Via Cavour 43; s/d €25/46) The best budget option is Hotel Pisani in the new town, although the rooms can be a bit gloomy.

Eating

Come to Taranto to eat, if for nothing else. It has been famous for its seafood since antiquity, the speciality being its shellfish and gorgeously fleshy oysters.

Ponte Vecchio (☎ 099 470 63 74; Via Fontana 61; meals €20-25; ☒ Wed-Mon) This is a very smart little restaurant with a terrace overlooking the marina. It's not far away from the fish market, so you know that what you're eating is as fresh as the morning's catch.

Ristorante al Gambero (☎ 099 471 11 90; Piazzale Democrate; meals €25; ☒ Tue-Sun) There are some who say Al Gambero, the grand old master of Tarantino dining, isn't what it once was. No matter, it's still pretty good and so near to the sea you can almost point to the fish you want.

Trattoria al Gatto Rosso (☎ 099 452 98 75; Via Cavour 2; meals €15; ☒ Tue-Sun) A relaxed and unpretentious trattoria which has a real touch of class – heavy tablecloths, deep wine glasses and the like. It is located in the new town and is very popular with discerning businessmen so it can get very busy.

Ristorante Marc'Aurelio (☎ 099 452 78 93; Via Cavour 17; meals €15-18) Popular with the locals, this excellent restaurant serves fantastic and abundant antipasto. You can follow this with a pizza prepared in the wood-fired oven or with one of the tempting pasta dishes.

Caffè Italiano (☎ 099 452 17 81; Via D'Aquino 86a; salads €4, meals €10) For something completely different and for a taste of modern Taranto head to this über-stylish café on Via d'Aquino. It has an excellent deli counter serving all manner of salads, omelettes, calzone and sandwiches. It's also a great coffee and juice bar.

There's a fresh-produce **market** (Piazza Castello; ☒ mornings Mon-Sat) just west of the Ponte Girevole.

Getting There & Around

Buses heading north and west depart from Porto Mercantile; those going south and east leave from Via Magnaghi in the new city.

FSE (☎ 099 477 46 27) buses connect Taranto with Bari (€4.60, two hours, eight Monday to Saturday, one Sunday), leaving from the Porto Mercantile, as well as smaller towns in the area. Infrequent **SITA** (☎ 099 829 50 86) buses leave from Porto Mercantile for Matera and Metaponto. **STP** (☎ 0832 39 30 11) and FSE buses connect Taranto with Lecce (€2.60, two hours, five Monday to Saturday).

Marozzi (☎ 099 459 40 89) has express services to and from Rome's Stazione Tiburtina (€36.60, six hours, four daily), leaving from Porto Mercantile. **Marino Autolinee** (☎ 080 311 23 35) does a run through the night to Milan (€46, 11 hours, one daily). **Autolinee Miccolis** (☎ 099 735 37 54) runs daily to and from Naples (€13.45, four hours, three daily) via Potenza (€7.25, two hours). The ticket office for all three companies can be found at Corso Umberto I 67.

It is far preferable, and only around €10 dearer, to travel by train on all of these long-distance routes. Both **Trenitalia** (☎ 89 20 21) and **FSE** (☎ 099 471 59 01) trains connect Taranto with Brindisi (€3.65, 1¼ hours, frequent) and Bari (€6.20, 1¼ hours, frequent), as well as Naples (€20.40, 4½ hours, four daily) and Rome (1st/2nd class Eurostar €53/36, six hours, five daily).

AMAT (☎ 099 4 52 67 32) bus Nos 1/2, 3 and 8 run between the train station and the new city.

For a taxi, call ☎ 099 7 30 47 34. There is metered parking in Piazza Garibaldi (€0.80 per hour).

BASILICATA

Basilicata is Italy's last true wilderness, a chaotic landscape of tremendous mountain ranges, dark forested valleys and villages so melded to the rockface that sometimes you don't know they are there at all. However, Basilicata has suffered unfairly, if unintentionally, at writer Carlo Levi's hand. The title of his superb book, *Christ Stopped at Eboli*, which documented the harsh life of Basilicata's poverty-stricken peasants, suggested that Basilicata was a land beyond the hand of God, a wild and unloved place controlled by outlaw bandits and enthralled by pagan magic. As the rest of Italy modernised, Basilicata languished, the most underdeveloped region in Italy – Levi's depiction of the realities and the subsequent stereotypes that arose have proved hard to shake despite the discovery of Western Europe's largest oil field 30km south of Potenza in 1996, which should have changed the stereotype of Basilicata as a poor wild region beyond commercial development.

However, Basilicata's remote atmosphere and tremendous landscape is finally beginning to attract the attention of travellers. Mel Gibson's controversial film, *The Passion of Christ*, brought the extraordinary *sassi* caves of Matera to the world's attention, while Maratea is fast making a name for itself as one of Italy's most chic seaside resorts. Likewise, the purple-hued mountains of the interior are impossibly grand, a wonderful destination for naturalists; particularly grand are the soaring peaks of the Lucanian Apennines and the Monte Pollino National Park.

History

Basilicata spans Italy's 'instep' with brief strips of coastline touching the Tyrrhenian and Ionian Seas. It was known to the Greeks and Romans as Lucania (a name still heard today) after the Lucani tribe who lived here as far back as the 5th century BC. The Greeks also prospered here, settling along the coastline at Metapontum and Erakleia, but things started to go wrong under the Romans, when the region fell foul of Hannibal, the ferocious Carthaginian general.

In the 10th century the region was renamed by the Byzantine Emperor, Basilikòs

(976–1025), who overthrew the Saracens in Sicily and the south and reintroduced Christianity. This pattern of war and overthrow continued throughout the Middle Ages right up until the 19th century as the Normans, Hohenstaufens, Angevins and the Bourbons constantly tussled over its strategic location. As talk of the Italian unification began to gain ground in the 19th century, Bourbon-sponsored loyalists took to Basilicata's mountains to oppose political change. Ultimately they became the much-feared bandits of local lore who make constant and scary appearances in writings from the late 19th and early 20th centuries by Norman Douglas, Craufurd Ramage and George Gissing – Basilicata's earliest tourists.

IONIAN COAST

Unlike the tremendous Tyrrhenian coast, the Ionian coast is a listless affair of flat, unaggressive seashore and large tourist resorts. However, the Greek ruins at Metaponto and Policoro give a picture of the enormous influence of Magna Graecia in southern Italy. It is particularly worth making the effort to see the two on-site museums, which are stuffed full of well-organised exhibits.

Metaponto

Metaponto's Greek ruins might not be as picturesque as those of Paestum in neighbouring Campania, but they are impressive in that this is the only site where archaeologists have managed to map the entire urban plan. Settled by Greeks in the 8th and 7th centuries BC, Metapontum was probably an outpost of Sibari (see p735) and acted as a buffer between them and aggressive Taranto. Its most famous resident was Pythagoras, who founded a school here after being banished from Crotone (in what is now Calabria) towards the end of the 6th century BC.

From the train station, go straight ahead for 500m to a roundabout. About 1.5km to your right (east) is the **Parco Archeològico** (admission free) and to your left, is the **Museo Archeológico Nazionale** (☎ 0835 74 53 27; Via Aristea 21; admission €2.50; ☺ 9am-7pm). In the park you can see what remains of a **Greek theatre** and the Doric **Tempio di Apollo Licio**, but the real draw is the museum, which houses artefacts from Metapontum and other sites.

After Pythagoras died, his house and school were incorporated into the Temple of Hera. The remains of the temple – 15 columns and sections of pavement – are known as the **Tavole Palatine** (Palatine Tables), since knights, or paladins, are said to have gathered there before heading to the Crusades. It's a little way north, just off the highway – to find it follow the sliproad for Taranto onto the SS106.

Modern Metaponto's only real attraction is a sandy beach, **Lido di Metaponto**, which is completely swamped in summer. It's about 3km east of the train station.

Accommodation in Metaponto is not that great. There are lots of bog-standard seaside hotels but prices are high and in summer everything is booked up, while in winter everything closes. A better alternative is the huge, 7-hectare **Camping Magna Grecia** (☎ 0835 74 18 55; Via Liolo; person/tent/car high season €6.75/7.25/2.60; ☒), 800m from the sea.

SITA (☎ 0835 38 50 07) buses run to Metaponto from Matera (€2.70, one hour, up to five daily) and from Taranto's Porto Mercantile. The town is on the Taranto to Reggio di Calabria line, and trains connect with Potenza, Salerno and occasionally Naples. The station is 3km west of the Lido di Metaponto. If you don't want to walk, wait for one of the regular SITA buses to pass by on the way to the beach.

Policoro
pop 15,250

If you get as far as Metaponto, consider continuing about 21km southwest along the coast to Policoro, originally the Greek settlement of Erakleia. The ruins are no more impressive than those of Metaponto but it's worth visiting for the wonderful **Museo della Siritide** (☎ 0835 97 21 54; Via Colombo 8; admission €2.50; ☒ 9am-8pm Wed-Mon, 2-8pm Tue). It has a fabulous display of artefacts excavated in the area, where you can work your way from 7000 BC through the jewellery, ornament and dress of the Lucanians to the mirrors and vases of the Greeks and then to the spears and javelins of the Romans who put paid to them all. There are also two complete tombs with skeletons surrounded by the objects and jewellery with which they were buried.

SITA buses run down the coast from Metaponto to Policoro but are frequent only in summer.

MATERA
pop 58,250 / elev 405m

Matera is absolutely unique. In no other city do you come face to face with such powerful images of Italy's lost peasant culture. Its famous *sassi* – stone houses carved out of and into the twin ravines that slice through town – tell of a poverty now difficult to imagine in a developed European country, a clichéd image of rudimentary human civilisation that made it Mel Gibson's location of choice for the film, *The Passion of the Christ*.

Disguised in the deep ravine on whose edge the new town is set, Matera's dramatic appearance is hidden until you round the corner of Via d'Addozio. In the early evening this all-encompassing view of the Sasso Barisano is magical, a jumble of glowing tufa-stone houses hugging the limestone hill which they cover entirely; from its pinnacle rises the elegant campanile of the cathedral. It is a view that fills you with anticipation.

History

Matera's cave dwellings are the most extensive and complete troglodyte complex in the Mediterranean, and one of the oldest inhabited human settlements in the world. Until the 20th century the *sassi* were pretty successful dwellings. What started out as simple grottoes were extended and enlarged to become homes. An ingenious system of canals regulated the flow of water and sewage, and small hanging gardens lent a splash of colour. They were so prosperous, in fact, that Matera became the capital of Basilicata in 1663, a position it held until 1806 when the accolade moved further north to Potenza. In the decades that followed an unsustainable increase in population led to the habitation of unsuitable grottoes – originally intended as animal stalls – which lacked both light and running water.

By the 1950s more than half of Matera's population lived in the *sassi*, a typical cave sheltering an average of six children despite an infant mortality rate of 50%. Carlo Levi's impassioned writings about the town told of how the wretched inhabitants would beg

PUGLIA, BASILICATA & CALABRIA

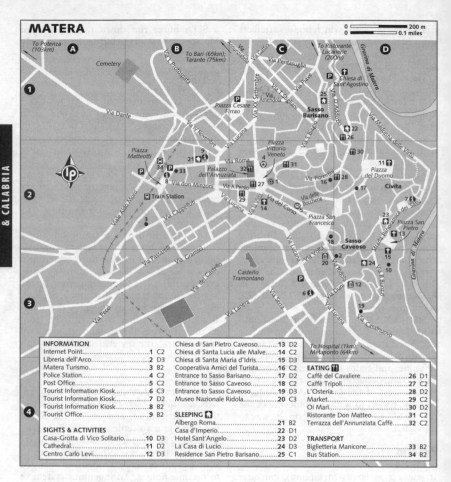

MATERA

INFORMATION	
Internet Point.....................................1	C2
Libreria dell'Arco............................2	D3
Matera Turismo................................3	B2
Police Station..................................4	C2
Post Office.......................................5	C2
Tourist Information Kiosk...............6	C3
Tourist Information Kiosk...............7	B2
Tourist Information Kiosk...............8	B2
Tourist Office...................................9	B2
SIGHTS & ACTIVITIES	
Casa-Grotta di Vico Solitario.........10	D3
Cathedral...11	D2
Centro Carlo Levi............................12	D3

Chiesa di San Pietro Caveoso.........13	D2
Chiesa di Santa Lucia alle Malve....14	C2
Chiesa di Santa Maria d'Idris.........15	D3
Cooperativa Amici del Turista........16	C2
Entrance to Sasso Barisano............17	D2
Entrance to Sasso Caveoso.............18	C2
Entrance to Sasso Caveoso.............19	D3
Museo Nazionale Ridola..................20	C3
SLEEPING	
Albergo Roma..................................21	B2
Casa d'Imperio.................................22	D1
Hotel Sant'Angelo...........................23	D2
La Casa di Lucio...............................24	D3
Residence San Pietro Barisano........25	C1

To Hospital (1km); Metaponto (64km)	
EATING	
Caffè del Cavaliere...........................26	D1
Caffè Tripoli.....................................27	C2
L'Osteria..28	D2
Market...29	D2
Oi Marì...30	D2
Ristorante Don Matteo....................31	B2
Terrazza dell'Annunziata Caffè.......32	C2
TRANSPORT	
Biglietteria Manicone......................33	B2
Bus Station......................................34	B2

passers-by not for money but for quinine to stave off the deadly malaria. Such publicity finally galvanised the authorities into action and in the late 1950s, about 15,000 inhabitants of the *sassi* were forcibly relocated to new government housing schemes.

In 1993 Matera's *sassi* were declared a Unesco World Heritage site. Ironically, the town's history of outrageous misery has now made it Basilicata's leading tourist attraction and the *sassi* are now undergoing systematic and stylish renovation.

Orientation

A short walk down Via Roma from the train and bus stations off Piazza Matteotti brings you to the Piazza Vittorio Veneto, the pedestrianised heart of town. The two *sassi* ravines open up to its east and southeast.

MAPS

It is easy enough to find your own way around the *sassi*. Arm yourself with the map *Matera: Percorsi Turistici* (€1.30), which describes in English four well-signposted itineraries. It is available from **Libreria dell'Arco** (Via Ridola 37).

Information

Basilicata Turistica (www.aptbasilicata.it)
Guardia Medica (☎ 0835 24 35 38) A 24-hour call-out doctor.
Hospital (☎ 0835 24 32 12; Via Montesaglioso) 1km southeast of the centre.

Internet point (☎ 0835 34 61 12; Piazza Vittorio Veneto 49; per hr €4; 🕒 8am-1pm & 5-8.30pm Tue-Sat)
Matera Turismo (Ferula Viaggi; ☎ 0835 33 65 72; www.materaturismo.it; Via Cappelluti 34) A tourist co-operative dedicated to promoting Basilicata. It operates as a travel agency and also runs good cultural, walking, wine-tasting and gastronomic tours.
Police station (☎ 0835 33 46 27; Piazza Vittorio Veneto)
Post office (☎ 0835 33 05 74; Via del Corso 1; 🕒 8am-6.30pm Mon-Fri, 8am-12.30pm Sat)
Sassiweb (www.sassiweb.it) Extensive website with everything you need to know about Matera: hotels, tours, history and lots of fascinating images.
Tourist information kiosk (☎ 0835 24 12 60; kiosks at Via Madonna delle Virtù, Piazza Matteotti & Via Lucana 🕒 9.30am-12.30pm & 4-7pm summer) Run by the Comune di Matera.
Tourist office (☎ 0835 33 19 83; www.materaturismo .it; Via De Viti De Marco 9; 🕒 9am-1pm Mon-Sat & 4-6.30pm Mon & Thu)

Sights & Activities
THE SASSI
From the shaded belvedere of Piazza Vittorio Veneto you will have a bird's-eye view of the deep limestone ravine lined with caves, some dating as far back as the 8th century BC. The two *sassi* districts are the northwest-facing **Sasso Barisano** and the more impoverished, northeast-facing **Sasso Caveoso**. They are extraordinary; riddled with serpentine alleyways and staircases, dotted with over 150 *chiese rupestri* (cave churches) side by side with some 3000 habitable caves where façades are often adorned with baroque and classical motifs.

Although you can easily navigate the *sassi* on your own, engaging a qualified guide does have its benefits. A guide can take you straight to the most interesting sites and offer a great deal of background. They also hold the keys to many of the more interesting cave churches. For some reliable guided itineraries, see (p724).

Of the two *sassi* areas, Caveoso is the more picturesque, including the highlights of **Chiesa di San Pietro Caveoso** (Piazza San Pietro, Sasso Caveoso) and the richly frescoed rock churches of **Santa Maria d'Idris** and **Santa Lucia alle Malve**. A couple of *sassi* have been refurbished as they were when the last inhabitants occupied them. The more interesting of the two is the **Casa-Grotta di Vico Solitario** (off Via B Buozzi; admission €1.50), which has an engaging multilingual audio explanation describing the living conditions of a typical cave house, which included a room for manure and a section for a pig and a donkey!

The *sassi* are accessible from several points around the centre of Matera. There is an entrance just off Piazza Vittorio Veneto. Alternatively, take Via delle Beccherie to Piazza del Duomo and follow the tourist itinerary signs to enter either Barisano or Caveoso. Sasso Caveoso is also accessible from Via Ridola by the stairs next to Albergo Italia.

For a great photograph of the *sassi* head out of town on the Taranto–Laterza road and follow signs for the *chiese rupestri*. This road takes you up on the Murgia plateau to the location of the crucifixion in *The Passion of the Christ,* from where you have fantastic views of the plunging ravine and Matera.

TOWN CENTRE
Piazza Vittorio Veneto is the centre of town and the great *passeggiata* (a stroll, usually in the evenings) meeting point. It is surrounded by elegant churches and richly adorned palazzi, all of which have their backs to the *sassi*, an attempt by the bourgeois to block out the shameful poverty that they once represented. Further excavations here have yielded more ruins of Byzantine Matera, including a rock church, a castle, a large cistern and numerous houses. You can gaze down to the site from the piazza.

The relatively sedate exterior of the 13th-century Puglian-Romanesque **cathedral** (Piazza del Duomo) ill-prepares you for the neobaroque excess within: ornate carved capitals, sumptuously decorated chapels and tons of gilding everywhere; it's currently closed for restoration. Matera's patron saint, the *Madonna della Bruna,* is hidden within the older church, **Santa Maria di Costantinopoli**, which can be accessed from the cathedral if it's open. Her saint's day on 2 July is the region's most important festival (see p724).

The **Museo Nazionale Ridola** (☎ 0835 31 00 58; Via Ridola 24; admission €2.50; 🕒 9am-8pm Tue-Sun & 2-8pm Mon) occupies the 17th-century convent of Santa Chiara and has a collection of primarily prehistoric and classical artefacts. A little south, on Piazzetta Pascoli, is the **Centro Carlo Levi** (☎ 0835 31 42 35; Palazzo Lanfranchi; admission €2; 🕒 9am-1pm & 3.30-7pm Tue-Sun). It houses paintings by Levi, including the enormous mural, *Lucania '61,* which depicts peasant life in Matera in biblical technicolour.

Tours

There are plenty of official guides to the *sassi* – the tourist office has details – otherwise you can get in touch with guides through www.sassiweb.it. Alternatively, contact the **Cooperativa Amici del Turista** (☎ 0835 33 03 01; www.materaturistica.it; Via Fiorentini 28-30) or Matera Turismo (see p723). Matera Turismo can also arrange some very good treks on the Murgia plateau and down the ravine.

A very reliable English-speaking guide is **Amy Weideman** (☎ 339 282 36 18). A half-day tour for two people costs €35.

Festivals & Events

In the **Sagra della Madonna della Bruna** (2 July) a colourful procession transports the Madonna from the cathedral on an ornately decorated papier-mâché float. When the procession is finished (and once the statue has been removed), it is time for the *assalto al carro*, when the crowd descends on the cart and tears it to pieces in order to take away the precious relics.

Sleeping

Since the publicity circus surrounding *The Passion of the Christ* left town, Matera has been overhauling its rickety tourist infrastructure and now boasts a plethora of unique – and very stylish – accommodation in the *sassi* districts.

La Casa di Lucio (☎ 0835 31 27 98; www.lacasadilucio.it; Via San Pietro Caveoso 66; s/d/tr/q/ste €90/120/140/160/250; 🞩) A residence rather than a hotel, La Casa di Lucio has seven bohemian

---

AUTHOR'S CHOICE

Hotel Sant'Angelo (☎ 0835 31 40 10; www.hotelsantangelosassi.it; Piazza San Pietro Caveoso; s/d €90/120; 🞩) Where else can you bed down in a Unesco World Heritage site, especially one as stylish as the Hotel Sant' Angelo, which has taken nearly 14 years to renovate? The other very special feature of this hotel is its unbeatable position overlooking the wild ravine with the pretty Chiesa di San Pietro Caveoso and the Idris rock in the foreground. The rooms (you are free to select the one you like) are spacious and elegantly furnished with antiques and heavy white linens, and the atmosphere is deeply tranquil and relaxing.

---

apartments decorated with an eclectic mix of modern furnishings, bold paint finishes and unexpected prints. Highlights include the gorgeous restaurant, the view of the Idris rock and Murgia plateau from the communal terrace and the cute majolica tiled bar.

Residence San Pietro Barisano (☎ /fax 0835 34 61 91; www.residencesanpietrobarisano.it; Rione San Biagio 52/56; s/d €80/150; 🞩) Just how cool can a cave be? Your very own apartment is styled with modern furniture, sleek wood, ergonomic chairs and very goodlooking stainless-steel kitchens. Here the walls retain that grotto-like feel with all their lumps and bumps although the bathrooms are thankfully very modern.

Casa d'Imperio (☎ 0835 33 05 03; www.casadimperio.it; Via d'Addozio 39; s/d €60/80; 🞩) A very quirky B&B converted by a Roman artist, and boy does it show in the décor – expect lots of oriental rugs, original paintings and *objets d'art* dotted around the place.

If you don't want to stay in the *sassi* the best hotel is the neat **Albergo Roma** (☎ /fax 0835 33 39 12; Via Roma 62; s/d €28/40), which is also convenient for the train station.

Eating

Ristorante Don Matteo (☎ 0835 34 41 45; Via San Biagio 12; meals €30-35) A very small, very discreet restaurant presided over by the charming Don Matteo himself. The service is absolutely impeccable and the poetic menu is full of delicious surprises, including mama's own *melanzane* (aubergine) recipe and some fine roast-meat dishes.

Ristorante Lucanerie (☎ 0835 33 21 33; Via San Stefano 61; meals €25; 🕓 lunch Tue-Sun) Lucanerie is out of the *sassi* and tucked in a backstreet, and you can be sure of getting great food at reasonable prices in this popular restaurant. It specialises in regional cooking, making use of local produce. Reservations are recommended, particularly over the weekend.

L'Osteria (☎ 0835 33 33 95; Via Fiorentini 58; meals €15-18) Down in the Sasso Barisano, this is the perfect spot for intimate dining as there are only six tables. The cuisine is of the homemade, hearty school and the service is friendly. A typical dish is the *capunti e fagioli*, white beans and pasta simmered in a pork stock.

Terrazza dell'Annunziata Caffè (☎ 0835 33 65 25; Piazza Vittorio Veneto; sandwiches/salads €4/5) An amazingly quiet place right on the main piazza.

This café is actually the roof terrace of the old convent Palazzo dell'Annuziata (now converted into a cinema and public library). Take the lift on the main piazza and enjoy panoramic views over Matera.

Oi Marí (☎ 0835 34 61 21; Via Fiorentini 66; pizzas/pastas from €3.50/6.50) Just down the road from L'Osteria, this place sells itself as a stylish Neapolitan pizzeria – and with some justification as the setting is original, the pizzas well prepared and the prices reasonable.

For a light snack, ice creams, coffee or a liqueur (strictly Amaro Lucano, of course) try **Caffè del Cavaliere** (off Via Fiorentini, Sasso Barisano) or **Caffè Tripoli** (Piazza Vittorio Veneto 17).

There's a daily fresh-produce **market** (Via A Persio) just south of Piazza Vittorio Veneto.

Getting There & Away
BUS
The bus station is just north of Piazza Matteotti, near the train station. **SITA** (☎ 0835 33 28 62) runs buses connecting Matera with Taranto (€4.40, 1½ hours, six daily) and Metaponto (€2.70, one hour, up to five daily), as well as many small towns in the province. **Grassani** (☎ 0835 72 14 43) has buses to Potenza (€5.35, two Monday to Saturday).

Marozzi (in Rome ☎ 06 225 21 47; www.marozzivt.it) runs three buses every day from Rome to Matera. A joint SITA and Marozzi service leaves at 10.35pm daily for the northern cities of Siena, Florence and Pisa, via Potenza. Advance booking is essential.

Buy your ticket for all services except Grassani (pay on the bus) at the **Biglietteria Manicone** (☎ 0835 33 28 62; Piazza Matteotti 3-4).

CAR & MOTORCYCLE
Matera's narrow alleys and steep contours are no place for a vehicle. It's better to leave your car north of the *sassi* area and continue on foot. Central Piazza Vittorio Veneto is pedestrianised.

There are three major guarded car parks around town on Via Lucana, Piazza Matteoti and Piazza Cesare Firrao. Parking here costs €5 per day.

TRAIN
Ferrovie Appulo-Lucane (FAL; ☎ 0835 33 28 61) runs regular trains (€3.65, 1½ hours, at least 12 daily) and buses (€3.70, four to six daily) to and from Bari. For Potenza, take a FAL bus to Ferrandina and connect with a Trenitalia

train, or head to Altamura to link up with FAL's Bari–Potenza run.

POTENZA
pop 68,800 / elev 819m
The best way to see Potenza is quickly and by night. That way you will avoid the sight of some of the most brutal housing blocks you're ever likely to see. Badly damaged in repeated earthquakes (the last one was in 1980), Potenza has lost most of its medieval buildings. In addition, Basilicata's regional capital is the highest in the land, making it cloyingly hot in summer and bitterly cold in winter. However, the town is a convenient transport hub.

The centre of town straggles east to west across a high ridge. To the south lie the main Trenitalia and Ferrovie Appulo-Lucane train stations, connected to the centre by bus Nos 1 or 10.

The **tourist office** (☎ 0971 27 44 80; www.aptbasilicata.it; Piazza XVIII Agosto; ✆ 8am-2pm Mon-Fri & 4-7pm Tue & Thu) is central.

Sights
Potenza's sights, such as they are, are in the old centre of town, which is at the very top of the hill; to get there, take the elevators from Piazza Vittorio Emanuele II. The ecclesiastical highlight is the **cathedral**, originally erected in the 12th century but rebuilt in the 18th. The elegant Via Pretoria, flanked by a boutique or two, makes a pleasant traffic-free stroll, especially during the convivial *passeggiata*. North of the town centre is the **Museo Archeológico Provinciale** (☎ 0971 44 48 33; Via Ciccotti; admission free; ✆ 9am-1pm Tue-Sun & 4-7pm Tue-Thu), which houses a collection of artefacts discovered in the region.

Sleeping & Eating
Grande Albergo Potenza (☎ 0971 41 02 20; albergo@libero.it; Corso XVIII Agosto 46; s/d €73/100; ✖ ⬜) If you have to overnight in Potenza, this is the place to console yourself. A quality hotel with all the creature comforts, it adds a much-needed touch of style to the town and has impressive views of the valley.

Antica Osteria Marconi (☎ 0971 5 69 00; Viale Marconi 233; meals €20; ✆ lunch Tue-Sun) A fantastic restaurant – one of the best in Basilicata, serving a range of traditional soups such as *minestra di fave e cicoria* (broad bean and chicory soup), as well as homemade pasta.

The ambience is suitably cosy in winter and there is an eat-out summer terrace.

Getting There & Away

BUS

Various companies operate from different locations in town; the tourist office has a comprehensive list of destinations and services.

Grassani (☎ 0835 72 14 43) has buses to Matera (€5.35, one hour, two daily). **SITA** (☎ 0971 50 68 11) has daily services to Melfi, Venosa and Maratea. Buses leave from Via Appia 185 and also stop near the Scalo Inferiore Trenitalia train station.

Liscio (☎ 0971 5 46 73) serves destinations including Rome (€17, 4½ hours, one daily) and Naples (€7.50, two hours, three daily), via Salerno (€5.40, 1½ hours).

CAR & MOTORCYCLE

Potenza is connected to Salerno in the west by the A3. Metaponto lies southeast along the SS407, the Basentana. For Matera, take the SS407 and then turn north onto the SS7 at Ferrandina.

TRAIN

To pick up a train on the main Trenitalia line from Taranto to Naples, go to **Potenza Inferiore** (☎ 0971 20 21). There are regular services to and from Taranto (€10.90, two hours), Salerno (€5.75, 1¾ hours) and Foggia (€10.90, two hours). To get to Matera (€3.35, one hour, frequent), change to an **FAL** (☎ 0971 41 15 61) bus at Ferrandina on the Metaponto line. For Bari (€12.35, three hours, three daily), use the **Ferrovie Appulo-Lucane** (☎ 0971 41 15 61) at Potenza Superiore station.

MELFI

pop 16,400

Melfi has an impressive history, even if the modern town is unprepossessing. It was a favourite residence of Frederick II, who loved to hunt the nearby wooded slopes of Monte Vulture, shacking up in his huge Melfi castle or further south at the stark, barrack-like structure of **Castello di Lagopesole** (donations welcome; ☾ 9.30am-1pm & 4-7pm Mar-Sep, 3-5pm Oct-Feb). Before Frederick, Melfi's castle was already famous. The Norman knight, Robert Guiscard, was crowned Duke of Apulia and Calabria here, and Pope Urban II declared the First Crusade within its walls in 1089. Nowadays, the castle is home to the **Museo**

Nazionale del Melfese (☎ 0972 23 87 26; admission €2.50; ☾ 9am-8pm Tue-Sun, 2-8pm Mon), which has an excellent collection of artefacts found in the area, some dating from the 8th century BC. Seek out the impressive 2nd-century AD Roman sarcophagus, housed in a small room within the southeast tower. Melfi's **cathedral**, which has been repeatedly shaken by earthquakes, has a fine gilded wooden ceiling and maintains its 12th-century bell tower.

Melfi is 53km north of Potenza and it can be reached from there by a daily bus and train.

VENOSA

pop 12,200

The pick of the area's towns, Venosa, about 25km east of Melfi, used to be a thriving Roman colony and was the birthplace of the poet Horace. Tourist information is available at **Minutiello Viaggi** (☎ 0972 3 25 69; Largo Baliaggio 5).

The town's main square, Piazza Umberto I, is dominated by a 15th-century Aragonese castle which contains a small **archaeological museum** (☎ 0972 3 60 95; Piazza Umberto I; admission €2.50; ☾ 9am-8pm Wed-Mon, 3-8pm Tue). The collection is centred around the finds from the nearby excavations of Roman Venusia, which chart the history and culture of the city. The museum also treasures human bone fragments dating as far back as 300,000 years ago. Although not much to look at, these are the oldest examples of human life found in Europe.

To wander around the **Roman settlement** (admission free; ☾ 9am-1hr before sunset Wed-Mon) head for the northeastern end of town. Next to the ruins is the intriguing **Abbazia della Santissima Trinità** (☎ 0972 3 42 11), the largest monastic complex in Basilicata. It was erected above the Roman temple in around 1046 by the Benedictines and predates the Norman invasions. Within the complex are the abbey palazzo and a pair of churches, one never completed. The earlier church is thought to contain the tomb of the mighty the Robert Guiscard (d 1085) and his much-feared brothers William Bras-de-Fer, Drogo and Humphrey.

Hotel Orazio (☎ /fax 0972 3 11 35; Vittorio Emanuele 142; s/d €36/50) is a 17th-century palace complete with antique majolica tiles and marble floors. The high-ceilinged, graciously decorated rooms are overseen by a pair of grandmotherly ladies who do all they can to make your stay comfortable. The terrace has beautiful views of the valley.

Venosa can be reached by a daily bus from Potenza.

APPENNINO LUCANO

The Appenino Lucano (Lucanian Apennines) rear up sharply just south of Potenza. They cut Basilicata in half, protecting the lush Tyrrhenian Coast and leaving the Ionian shores of Basilicata and Calabria gasping in the semi-arid heat. Careening along its hair-raising roads through the broken spine of mountains can be nerve-wracking and arduous, but if you're looking for drama a drive through these soaring peaks can be the highlight of any trip.

Writer and political activist Carlo Levi was exiled by the Fascist regime to this isolated region in 1935. He lived and is buried in the tiny hilltop town of **Aliano**, where little has changed over the last 75 years. The aching hardship of peasant life which Levi wrote about so graphically is still clear to see in this utterly rural environment. A collection of Levi memorabilia is on display at **Museo Carlo Levi** (☎ 0835 56 80 30); phone to gain entry.

More spectacular than Aliano are the two mountaintop villages of **Castelmezzano** (elevation 985m) and **Pietrapertosa** (elevation 1088m). They are the highest villages in Basilicata and look like something out of a fairytale, wreathed as they often are in cloud tendrils. In Castelmezzano the houses huddle along an impossibly narrow ledge which falls away in vertigo-inducing gorges to the Caperrino River. If it's at all possible, Pietrapertosa is even more dramatic than Castelmezzano. The Saracen fortress at its pinnacle is so difficult to spot because it is actually carved out of the mountain.

You can spend an eerie night in Pietrapertosa in the simple *pensione* **Albergo Il Frantoio** (☎ 0971 98 31 90; albfrontoio@tiscalinet.it; Via M Torraca 15/17; s/d €24/35, d full board €46). Don't miss the totally authentic Lucano restaurant **Al Becco della Civetta** (☎ 0971 98 62 49; Vicolo I Maglietta 7; meals €15; ☽ Wed-Mon) in Castelmezzano.

Aliano is accessible by SITA bus from Matera, with a change in Pisticci Scalo. You will need your own car to visit the villages of Castelmezzano and Pietrapertosa.

TYRRHENIAN COAST

Basilicata's sliver of the Tyrrhenian coast is short (about 20km) but sweet. Squeezed between Calabria and Campania's Cilento peninsula, it shares the same beguiling characteristics, hidden coves and grey sandy beaches backed by majestic coastal cliffs. The SS18 threads a spectacular route along the mountains to the coast's star attraction, the charming seaside town of Maratea.

Maratea
pop 5300

Situated high on a hilltop overlooking the sparkling Gulf of Policastro, Maratea is Italy's well-kept secret. Sophisticated Italians escape here to enjoy the charming town, its elegant hotels and relatively quiet sandy beaches. For once responsible town planning has checked the worst excesses of coastal development, leaving this tiny little enclave as one of the most beautiful spots on the Tyrrhenian coast.

SIGHTS & ACTIVITIES

Maratea is actually a jumbled collection of different communities, each with their own character. Right at the heart of these hamlets is the exquisitely pretty **Porto di Maratea**, clustered like a mini-Amalfi around its tiny harbour. Sleek yachts and bright-blue fishing boats bob in the water overlooked by a muddle of colourful houses framed by rich green cypress forests. Further along the coast is the sophisticated **Marina di Maratea**, which reflects the local policy of 'nonaggressive tourism' with its strictly controlled, low-level development. Uphill the remnants **Maratea Superiore** are all that remains of the original 8th-century BC Greek colony; and then there is the pretty 13th-century medieval *borgo* (small town) of **Maratea Inferiore**. The whole medley of bar-studded piazzas, wriggling alleys and interlocking houses is overlooked by a 70ft-high, gleaming white statue of Christ the Redeemer.

The deep green hillsides that encircle this tumbling conurbation offer excellent walking trails and there are a number of easy day trips to the surrounding hamlets of the **Acquafredda di Maratea** and **Fiumicello**, with a wide sandy beach. You will find the **tourist office** (☎ 0973 87 69 08; Piazza Gesù 40; ☽ 8am-2pm & 4-6pm Mon-Fri, 9am-1pm & 5-8pm Sun Jul-Aug, shorter hrs Sep-Jun) in Fiumicello.

PUGLIA, BASILICATA & CALABRIA

Centro Sub Maratea (☎ 0973 87 00 13; Via Santa Caterina 28, Maratea) offers diving courses for all levels, while **Maratea Mare Service** (☎ 0973 87 69 76; Porto di Maratea) rents boats; ask for Franco.

In July Maratea hosts a summer music festival and you can catch many of the events at Fiumicello.

A worthwhile day trip from Maratea if you have your own car is to pretty **Rivello** (479m). Perched on a high hill overlooking the Noce River, it has an interesting Byzantine history evident in the tiny tiled cupolas and frescoes of its gorgeous churches.

SLEEPING

Maratea is one of the most stylish resorts in the south, with accommodation to match. In 2003 the resort was awarded a Blue Flag classification for the cleanliness of its water and beaches.

Hotel Villa Cheta Elite (☎ 0973 87 81 34; Via Timpone 46; s/d half board €90/180, with sea view €103/206; ⊙ 23 Apr–Nov; P ✗) This is a charming Art Nouveau villa in the hamlet of Acquafredda. The broad terrace commands spectacular views of the Gulf of Policastro and as one-time home to the aristocratic Morsicano family, the rooms retain their faded antique charm.

Locanda delle Donne Monache (☎ 0973 87 74 87; www.mondomaratea.it; Via Mazzei 4; s/d €195/270; ⊙ May-Oct; P ✗ ⊠) Overlooking the medieval *borgo*, this converted convent is a beautiful place to stay, a hotchpotch of vaulted corridors, terraces and gardens. All the rooms are elegantly decorated in pastel shades and many have quaint wrought-iron balconies overlooking the town.

Hotel Villa delle Meraviglie (☎ /fax 0973 87 78 16; www.costadimaratea.com/villadellemeraviglie/; Contrada Ogliastro; s/d €90/150; ⊙ Mar-Oct; P ✗ ⊠) A pretty, modern villa set in a pine-shaded garden overlooking the sea. The 16 double rooms keep it nice and intimate and the facilities are excellent for this price.

Hotel Martino (☎ 0973 87 91 26; www.hotelmartino .net; Via Citrosello 16; half board per person low/high season €52/95; P ✗ ⊠) A recommended hotel, and one of the few to remain open out of season.

EATING

Taverna Rovita (☎ 0973 87 65 88; Via Rovita 13; meals €30; ⊙ Wed-Mon mid-Mar–Dec) Right in the historic centre, this tavern is just off the main

piazza. Rovita specialises in hearty local fare putting the rich ricotta, aubergines and meat of the surrounding woodlands to good use. It also has an excellent seafood menu.

Za Mariuccia (☎ 0973 87 61 63; Via Grotte 2; meals €25; ⊙ Fri-Wed Feb-Dec) A stylish seafood eatery in Maratea Porto with tables overlooking the sea. Fresh, fresh fish served up in every imaginable way, in risottos, pastas, *crudo* (raw) and simply filleted and fried. Truly excellent service makes it a meal to remember.

La Bussola (☎ 0973 87 68 63; Via Santavenere 43; pizzas €10; ⊙ Tue-Sun) A welcoming pizzeria in Fiumicello. The *pizzaiolo* (pizza cook) knows his trade and prepares pizzas that are cooked just long enough to acquire that wonderful smoked flavour.

GETTING THERE & AWAY

SITA (☎ 0971 50 68 11) buses link Maratea to Potenza. They also run up the coast to Sapri in Campania and south to Praia a Mare in Calabria. Local buses (€0.80) connect the coastal towns and Maratea train station with the old centre of Maratea, running frequently in summer. Intercity and regional trains on the Rome–Reggio di Calabria line stop at Maratea train station, below the town.

PARCO NAZIONALE DEL POLLINO

The **Pollino National Park** (www.parcopollino.it in Italian) is Italy's largest national park and the richest repository of flora and fauna in southern Italy. It covers 196,000 hectares, divided equally between Basilicata and Calabria, and has long acted like a rocky curtain, cutting Calabria off from the rest of Italy.

The two main areas of interest in the park are the Pollino Massif (2267m), in the park's centre, and the Monti di Orsomarso (1987m), in the southwest (in Calabria). These sheer mountains, often snowbound, are blanketed by forests of oak, alder, maple, beech, pine and fir trees which filter the harsh southern sun and protect the delicately budding peonies and orchids which form a spectacular mantle of colour after the snow melts. The park is most famous, however, for its ancient *pino loricato* pine trees, which are only found here and in the Balkans. The oldest specimens reach 40m in height and their scaly, grey trunks look like arboreal sculptures against the huge bald rocks.

Walkers in the park can enjoy varied landscapes from deep river canyons to alpine meadows, and the park still protects a rare stock of roe deer, wild cats, wolves, birds of prey and the endangered otter, *Lutra lutra*.

The SS653 cuts across the park and is the best route to take if you want to explore unique Albanian villages such as **San Paolo Albanese** and **San Costantino**. These isolated and unspoilt communities fiercely maintain their mountain culture and the villages are a great place to purchase rare handicrafts still produced by local artisans – wooden crafts in **Terranova di Pollino**, alabaster in **Latronico** and wrought iron in **Sant'Arcangelo**.

Orientation & Information

The main centre of the park is **Rotonda** (elevation 626m), which is accessible from the A3 and SS19. Here you will find the official park office, **Ente Parco Nazionale del Pollino** (☎ 0973 66 93 11; Via delle Frecce Tricolori 6; ⊗ 9.30am-1pm & 4-5.30pm Mon-Fri). For an English-speaking guide, contact Giuseppe Cosenza at Asklepios (see below).

The Carta Excursionistica del Pollino Lucano (scale 1:50000), produced by the Basilicata tourist board, is a useful driving map. It is quite elusive but you should be able to find a copy at the tourist offices in Rotonda, Matera or Maratea. Another very interesting large-scale map is the Parco Nazionale del Pollino map which you can get hold of at the park office in Rotonda and in Matera from Matera Turismo. It shows all the main routes through the park and includes some useful information on the park, its flora and fauna and the park communities. Both maps are free.

Sleeping & Eating

The park website lists all accommodation and refuges available in the park.

Picchio Nero (☎ 0973 9 31 70; www.picchionero.com; Via Mulino 1; s/d €50/60; ℗) The chalet-style Picchio Nero in Terranova di Pollino is the most popular hotel for hikers in the park. It is family run and very cosy and friendly, and can help arrange any number of excursions in the park.

Asklepios (☎ 347 263 14 62; www.asklepios.it; Contrada Barone 9; s/d €20/40; ℗) Despite its rather dour exterior, the Asklepios, in Rotonda, is the place to stay for walkers as it is run by Giuseppe Cosenza, one of the only English-speaking guides in the Pollino. There are only three rooms so advance booking is essential.

Two of the most highly regarded restaurants in the Pollino are the **Luna Rossa** (☎ 0973 9 32 54; Via Marconi 18; meals €15; ⊗ Thu-Tue) in Terranova di Pollino and **Da Pepe** (☎ 0973 66 12 51; Corso Garibaldi 13; meals €20; ⊗ Tue-Sun) in Rotonda. Both serve an impressive menu of local specialities heavy on gamey meats and fresh vegetables.

Getting There & Away

It is virtually impossible to navigate the park without your own vehicle. Bus services are severely limited and almost nonexistent outside high summer.

CALABRIA

A tough ancient land, Calabria shows visitors two very different sides. There is the obvious and appalling eyesore of the urban landscape, all uncontrolled building and unfinished breeze blocks, yet there is also the striking rustic beauty of Calabria's hinterland. Within its parameters Calabria boasts three national parks: the Pollino in the north, the Sila in the centre and the wild Aspromonte in the south. Its beaches are among Italy's best and its ancient hilltop towns appear to grow out of the mountains themselves.

Calabria has suffered from the unhealthy miscegenation between European and government subsidies (aimed to develop the south) and dark Mafia opportunism. The number of half-finished buildings is all too evident, even if not all of them are uninhabited. In fact, the half-finished exteriors often mask well-furnished flats where families live happily, untroubled by invasive house taxes.

Somehow its failure to win the charm offensive has preserved the regional integrity of Calabria's people, their communities, their food and crafts. In returning the visitor to Italy's decidedly unromantic rural roots Calabria provides a healthy reality check on the Italian myth – as Norman Douglas said in *Old Calabria* (published 1915), 'Most of us come to Italy too undiscerning, too reverent…too stuffed with Renaissance ideals and Classical lore'. Calabria will certainly cure you of that.

History

Calabria's history dates back to Palaeolithic times, although it was the Greeks from Sicily

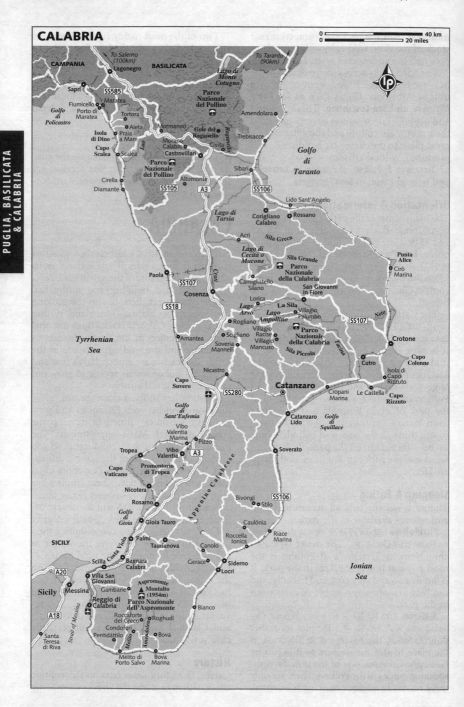

CALABRIA

0 ─────── 40 km
0 ─────── 20 miles

CAMPANIA

To Salerno (100km)
Lagonegro

BASILICATA

To Taranto (90km)

Lago di Monte Cotugno

Sapri

SS585

Maratea

Fiumicello
Porto di Maratea

Golfo di Policastro

Tortora

Parco Nazionale del Pollino

Amendolara

Aieta
Praia a Mare

Mormanno

Gole del Raganello

Isola di Dino

Capo Scalea

Scalea

Morano Calabro

Castrovillari

Civita

Trebisacce

Golfo di Taranto

Parco Nazionale del Pollino

Cirella

Altomonte

SS105

A3

Sibari

SS106

Diamante

Lido Sant'Angelo

Lago di Tarsia

Corigliano Calabro

Rossano

Acri

Sila Greca

Punta Alice

Lago di Cecita o Mucone

Sila Grande

Cirò Marina

Parco Nazionale della Calabria

Paola

SS107

Camigliatello Silano

San Giovanni in Fiore

Cosenza

Lorica

SS18

Lago Arvo

La Sila

Villagio Palumbo

SS107

Neto

Lago Ampollino

Rogliano

Villagio Racise

Parco Nazionale della Calabria

Crotone

Tyrrhenian Sea

Amantea

Scigliano

Soveria Mannelli

Villagio Mancuso

Sila Piccola

Tacina

Cutro

Capo Colonne

Nicastro

Isola di Capo Rizzuto

Capo Suvero

SS280

Catanzaro

Cropani Marina

Le Castella

Capo Rizzuto

Golfo di Sant'Eufemia

Catanzaro Lido

Golfo di Squillace

Vibo Valentia Marina

Pizzo

Tropea

Vibo Valentia

A3

Soverato

Capo Vaticano

Promontorio di Tropea

Nicotera

Bivongi

SS106

Rosarno

Stilo

Golfo di Gioia

Caulónia

Gioia Tauro

Roccella Ionica

Palmi

Canolo

Riace Marina

SICILY

Tauriánova

Scilla

Costa Viola

Gerace

Siderno

Ionian Sea

Bagnara Calabra

Locri

A20

Villa San Giovanni

Aspromonte
Montalto (1954m)

Messina

Gambarie

Sicily

Reggio di Calabria

Parco Nazionale dell'Aspromonte

Bianco

A18

Roccaforte del Greco

Roghudi

Santa Teresa di Riva

Condofuri
Pentidáttilo

Bova

Mélito di Porto Salvo

Bova Marina

Strait of Messina

Amendolea

Melito

who first settled, founding a colony at what is now Reggio di Calabria. Remnants of this colonisation, which spread along the Ionian coast and featured Sibari and Crotone as the star settlements, are still visible today. The fun didn't last though and in 202 BC the cities of Magna Graecia all came under Roman control. Stripping the countryside of its handsome forests, the Romans did irreparable geological damage. Without the protection of the trees navigable rivers became fearsome *fiumare* (torrents) dwindling to wide, dry, drought-stricken riverbeds in high summer.

Later the malarial swamplands along the coast and Saracen raids forced the population inland, creating Calabria's dramatic hilltop villages and towns. These impregnable communities weathered successive invasions by the Normans, Swabians, Aragonese and Bourbons, and remained largely untouched and undeveloped.

Although the brief Napoleonic incursion at the end of the 18th century and the arrival of Garibaldi and Italian unification inspired hope for change, Calabria remained a virtually feudal region.

One of the byproducts of this history was the growth of banditry and later pervasive organised crime. Calabria's Mafia, known as the 'ndrangheta, incites fear in much of the region's population, although tourists are rarely the target of its aggression. For many, the only answer has been to get out and, for at least a century, Calabria has seen its young people migrate to the north or abroad in search of work.

Getting There & Around

Lamezia Terme airport (Sant'Eufemia Lamezia; SUF; ☎ 0968 41 41 11), 63km south of Cosenza and 36km west of Catanzaro, serves Calabria as a whole. At the junction of the A3 and SS280 motorways, it links the region with major Italian cities and is also a destination for charters from northern Europe.

You can get pretty much anywhere by public transport but it is not always fast or easy.

PARCO NAZIONALE DEL POLLINO

You enter Calabria through this enormous national park, which straddles the border with Basilicata. On Calabria's side of the park is the awesome peak of Monti di Orsomarso

and the spectacular canyon of the Gole del Raganello near **Civita**, one of a number of genuine market towns in and around the park. Civita, like many of the villages in the Pollino, has a fascinating history of Albanian immigration and its tiny **Museo Etnico Arbëreshe** (☎ 0981 7 31 50; Piazza Municipio; ⏰ 5-7pm Jun-Sep) is stuffed with interesting photos and artisanal work. Other towns worth visiting are **Castrovillari** and **Morano Calabro**. Naturalists should also check out the wildlife museum **Centro Il Nibbio** (☎ 0981 3 07 45; Vico Il Annunziata 11; adult/concession €3/2; ⏰ 9.30am-1pm & 4-8.30pm) in Morano, where the whole ecosystem of the Pollino is carefully explained.

If you have the nerve, one of the most beautiful experiences in the Calabrian Pollino is to go white-water rafting down the spectacular Lao River. You can arrange rafting, as well as canoeing, canyoning, trekking and mountain biking at **Centro Lao Action Raft** (☎ 0985 2 14 76; www.laoraft.it; Via Lauro 10/12) and **Aventure Lao** (☎ 0985 2 08 93; www.raftinglao.com; Corso Mediterraneo 337) in Scalea which is on the Tyrrhenian coast.

Located in Castrovillari, **Locanda di Alia** (☎ 0981 4 63 70; www.alia.it; Via Jetticelle 55; s/d €70/90; 🅿 🍴 🛜) offers bungalow-style accommodation. It is famous for its **restaurant** (meals €30-40; ⏰ Mon-Sat), one of the best in Calabria, where you can sample traditional recipes full of Calabrian peppers, pork, figs, anise and honey.

Agriturismo Colloreto (☎ 347 323 69 14; fax 0981 3 12 55; www.colloreto.it; Fratelli Coscia; s/d €45/65) is a pretty and unpretentious *agriturismo* near Morano Calabro. Its setting is gorgeous, the rooms are comfortable and stylish and there are a host of activities from riding and walking to fishing and rafting.

Public transport in this part of the park is virtually nonexistent. A car is a really a must for getting around.

COSENZA

pop 72,300 / elev 238m

Cosenza's medieval core is Calabria's best-preserved historic centre, the one piece of history that has managed to escape the constant earthquakes that have levelled almost everything else in the region. It is very picturesque once you find your way into it, through the hideous urbane sprawl that fans out in all directions. It rises above the confluence of the Crati and Busento rivers, its

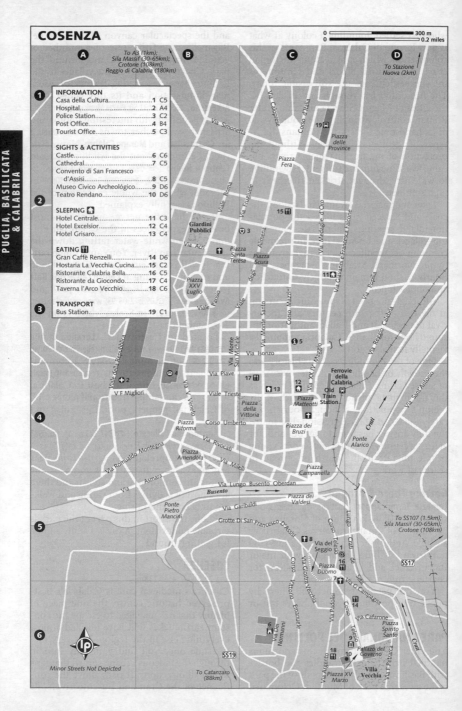

COSENZA

PUGLIA, BASILICATA & CALABRIA

INFORMATION
Casa della Cultura............................1 C5
Hospital..2 A4
Police Station..................................3 C2
Post Office.......................................4 B4
Tourist Office...................................5 C3

SIGHTS & ACTIVITIES
Castle...6 C6
Cathedral...7 C5
Convento di San Francesco
 d'Assisi..8 C5
Museo Civico Archeológico............9 D6
Teatro Rendano.............................10 D6

SLEEPING
Hotel Centrale...............................11 C3
Hotel Excelsior..............................12 C4
Hotel Grisaro.................................13 C4

EATING
Gran Caffè Renzelli.......................14 D6
Hostaria La Vecchia Cucina..........15 C2
Ristorante Calabria Bella...............16 C5
Ristorante da Giocondo................17 C4
Taverna l'Arco Vecchio.................18 C6

TRANSPORT
Bus Station....................................19 C1

narrow alleyways, some no more than steep stairways, snaking round once-elegant mansions right up to the hilltop castle.

In the past Cosenza was a sophisticated and lively city and these days its university draws students from throughout the province and its theatre hosts an excellent opera season. Cosenza is also the gateway to the rolling mountains of La Sila and is major transport hub.

Orientation

The main drag, Corso Mazzini, runs south from Piazza Fera (near the bus station) and intersects Viale Trieste before meeting Piazza dei Bruzi. What little there is of accommodation, food, banks and tourist assistance is all within about a 10-minute walking radius of this intersection. Head further south and cross the Busento River to reach the medieval part of town.

Information

Casa della Cultura (☎ 0984 79 02 71; Corso Telesio Bernardino 98; per 1hr free; ☿ 8am-8pm Mon-Sat) Internet access.

Hospital (☎ 0984 68 11; Via F Migliori)

Police station (☎ 0984 89 11 11; Via Frugiuele 10)

Post office (☎ 0984 2 24 03; Vla V Veneto)

Tourist office (☎ 0984 2 74 85; www.aptcosenza.it; 1st fl, Corso Mazzini 92; ☿ 8am-1.30pm Mon-Fri & 2-5pm Mon-Wed) The website is more helpful than the office.

Sights

Cosenza's handful of sights are all located in the old town, which you enter by crossing the River Crati over the Ponte M Martire. Head up elegant Corso Telesio to the 12th-century **cathedral** (Piazza del Duomo; ☿ during Mass), rebuilt in a restrained baroque style in the 18th century. Inside it is fairly unexceptional except for a copy of an exquisite 13th-century Byzantine Madonna in a chapel off the north aisle.

From the cathedral, you can take the steps up Via del Seggio through a little medieval quarter before turning right to reach the 13th-century **Convento di San Francesco d'Assisi**. Otherwise head on up the *corso* to Piazza XV Marzo, an appealing square fronted by the Palazzo del Governo and the handsome neoclassical **Teatro Rendano**.

Tucked into the piazza's northwest corner is the Accademia Cosentina and, within it, the city's one-room **Museo Civico Archeológico**

(☎ 0984 81 33 24; admission free; ☿ 9am-1pm Mon-Fri). South of the piazza stretches the shady **Villa Vecchia**, a huge, welcome oasis of green.

From here the long and winding Corso Vittorio Emanuele heads up to the **castle** (Piazza Frederico II; admission free; ☿ 8am-8pm) built by the Normans and left in disarray by several earthquakes. Little of interest remains but the view helps makes the steep ascent worthwhile.

Sleeping

Accommodation is a problem in Cosenza, as the city isn't geared for tourism. The few hotels are expensive and far away from the historic centre.

Hotel Centrale (☎ 0984 7 57 50; fax 0984 7 36 84; Viale Mancini; s/d €78/115; ℗ ✖ 🖳) Aimed at the business market, rooms are bland and well equipped. What is not bland is the eyecatching Dalì-inspired sofa, the orange centrepiece of a striking reception.

Hotel Excelsior (☎ /fax 0984 7 43 83; Piazza Matteotti 14; s/d €40/60; ℗) The reception of this once-grand station hotel retains the dimensions of its more illustrious past. The rooms are large, practical and, above all, good value for your euro. The private garage costs €5 per 24 hours.

Hotel Grisaro (☎ 0984 2 79 52; fax 0984 2 78 38; Viale Trieste 38; s/d €36/52) Another reliable city-centre option is Grisaro; the main entrance is on Via Monte Santo.

Eating

Hostaria La Vecchia Cucina (☎ 0984 2 94 39; Via Miceli 21; meals €25) Given that Cosenza is not on the sea, it's pretty amazing what the cooks here manage to do with fish. The *spaghetti alle vongole* (spaghetti with clams) is given a unique twist. Try it!

Ristorante Calabria Bella (☎ 0984 79 35 31; Piazza del Duomo; meals €20) Also in the old town, Calabria Bella offers excellent food in an intimate atmosphere. Much patronised by discerning locals, it specialises in Calabrian cuisine.

Ristorante da Giocondo (☎ 0984 2 98 10; Via Piave 53; meals from €15; ☿ Mon-Sat) For a no-frills plate of pasta this small family restaurant is a good bet. Prices are reasonable and the location is very handy for the hotels around the old station.

Taverna l'Arco Vecchio (☎ 0984 7 25 64; Piazza Archi di Ciaccio 21; meals €25; ☿ Mon-Sat) The sister restaurant of La Vecchia Cucina, this family concern is tucked away deep in the old town. It has attractive, low-ceilinged rooms and serves tasty local dishes.

Gran Caffè Renzelli (☎ 0984 2 68 14; Corso Telesio 46) This venerable café, which bakes its own gooey cakes and desserts, has been run by the same family for five generations. Sink your teeth into the *torroncino torrefacto,* a confection of sugar, spices and hazelnuts, or *varchiglia alla monocale* (chocolate and almond cake).

Getting There & Away

The main bus station is northeast of Piazza Fera. Services leave for Catanzaro (€4.15, 1½ hours, eight daily), Paola (€2.60, 40 minutes, 10 daily) and towns throughout La Sila area. **Autolinee Preite** (☎ 0984 41 30 01) has half-a-dozen buses heading daily along the north Tyrrhenian coast, and **Autolinee Romano** (☎ 09 62 21 7 09) serves Crotone, as well as larger cities like Rome and Milan.

Cosenza is located off the A3 autostrada. The SS107 connects the city with Crotone and the Ionian coast, across La Sila.

The main Trenitalia train station, **Stazione Nuova** (☎ 0984 2 70 59), is about 2km northeast of the city centre. Trains go to Reggio di Calabria (€11.60, two hours 40 minutes, 15 daily), Naples (€20.50, 3½ hours, 13 daily) and Rome (€33, 5½ hours, 12 daily), as well as most destinations around the Calabrian coast.

The **Ferrovie della Calabria** (www.ferroviedella calabria.it) line, which has its terminal beside the old train station, serves La Sila and other small towns around Cosenza. This is a very scenic train route.

Getting Around

Amaco (☎ 0984 30 80 11) bus Nos 15, 16 and 28 link the centre and Stazione Nuova, the main train station.

For a taxi, call ☎ 0984 2 88 77.

LA SILA

La Sila is very un-Mediterranean-like; in fact it is more like England on an unusually sunny day, with lots of green rolling hills, dappled forests and large blue lakes with cavorting day-trippers enjoying themselves. The Sila is actually divided into three areas: the Sila Grande, Sila Greca (to the north) and the Sila Piccola (near Catanzaro), in total covering an area of 32,125 acres. Its highest peaks, covered with tall Corsican pines, reach 2000m, high enough for thick snow in winter. This makes it a popular skiing destination and in summer the climate is coolly alpine with carpets of wildflowers in spring and mushroom-hunting in autumn. At is very peak is the Bosco di Gallopani (Forest of Gallopani), which is now within the protection of the **Parco Nazionale della Calabria**.

Between November and February (the ski season) and July and August you will need to make reservations in advance. Sadly, there are few *rifugi* (mountain huts) and camping in the national parks is forbidden.

Good-quality information in English is a scarce commodity in these parts. As good a starting point as any is the **Calabrian National Park office** (☎ 0984 57 97 57) in Camigliatello Silano while, for what they're worth, there are **tourist offices** (in Camigliatello Silano ☎ 0984 57 80 91; in Lorica ☎ 0984 99 70 69). A useful Web resource is www.portalesila.it.

There are numerous souvenir stalls and bars throughout the park sell simple maps detailing walking itineraries.

Sila Towns

The main towns of the Sila are Camigliatello Silano and San Giovanni in Fiore. Ordinary enough in summer, **Camigliatello Silano** looks quite cute under snow. It is a popular local skiing resort but doesn't host any international competitions. A few lifts operate on Monte Curcio, about 3km to the south. Other lifts can be found near **Lorica**, on pretty Lago Arvo.

The main town of the Sila, however, is **San Giovanni in Fiori**. Its name, which means Saint John in the Flowers, gives some indication of how pretty it must once have been, an alpine Shangri-la away from the heat-haze of the coast. These days, however, San Giovanni is a terrible mess, one of the worst examples of Calabria's uncontrolled building. However, it retains its reputation as a quality craft centre famous for its Armenian-style carpets and tapestry.

About 10km south of San Giovanni in Fiore, **Villagio Palumbo** (☎ 0962 49 30 17) is a resort on Lago Ampollino. There are two similar ventures further south on the road to Catanzaro: **Villaggio Racise** and **Villaggio Mancuso**. All hotels within the resort offer weekend package deals including food and accommodation and are set up for outdoor activities such as cross-country skiing and horse riding.

The Sila's largest lake is Lago di Cecita o Mucone near Camigliatello.

Sleeping

The best places to stay in the Sila are around its pretty lakes. Otherwise Camigliatello is the base of choice in winter.

Park Hotel 108 (☎ 0521 64 81 08; www.charmerelax .it/cosenza-hotel.html; Via Nazionale 86, Lorica; s/d €72/120) One of the most attractive hotels in the Sila, the modern Park Hotel is set on the banks of Lake Avro surrounded by dark-green pines. The rooms are very spacious and decorated with a touch more class than the average Sila pad, but it is the views that are really special.

Hotel Aquila & Edelweiss (☎ 0984 57 80 44; fax 0984 57 87 53; Viale Stazione 11; s/d full board per person €98/82) This three-star hotel is in Camigliatello. Inside it is wood panelled, cosy and welcoming despite its rather stark façade.

For camping try **Villaggio Turistico Lago Arvo** (☎ /fax 0984 53 70 60; Passo della Cornacchia; site per person €4) and **Camping Lorica** (☎ 0984 53 70 18; site per person €5), beside the lake in Lorica.

SOMETHING SPECIAL

B&B Calabria (☎ 349 878 18 94; www.bedand breakfastcalabria.it; s/d €25/40) Break through the invisible curtain of Calabrese reserve by staying in this unique B&B. It is well off the beaten track in the hamlet of Scigliano, which looks out over endless forested vistas. Owner Raphael is an architect trying to inject some vision into the Calabrese construction scene, while his wife Esther runs the modest B&B with grace and efficiency. What's more their enthusiasm for Calabria is infectious – they will give you tips on good shops, great eating places, pack you picnics, lend you their mountain bikes and regale you will some hilarious stories of life in a real Italian village. No wonder this place receives such good word of mouth. To reach it take the Altilia-Grimaldi exit off the A3 and follow the signs to Scigliano (10km). Otherwise take the Ferrovie della Calabria from Cosenza (€2.70, one hour, five daily).

Shopping

The forests of La Sila yield a wondrous variety of wild mushrooms, both edible and poisonous. Sniff around the **Antica Salumeria Campanaro** (Piazza Misasi 5) in Camigliatello Silano; it is a temple to all things fungoid, an emporium of rich odours, fine meats, cheeses, pickles and wines, rivalled in richness, if not in size, by its neighbour, La Casa del Fungho.

Getting There & Away

Camigliatello Silano and San Giovanni in Fiore are both accessible by Ferrovie della Calabria buses (about 10 daily) along the SS107, which links Cosenza and Crotone, or by the twice-daily train running between Cosenza and San Giovanni in Fiore.

IONIAN COAST

With its flat coastline and wide sandy beaches, the Ionian coast has borne the brunt of some very ugly development. With few exceptions the coast is one long, uninterrupted string of resorts, all extremely busy in the summer months. Outside the summer months (June to September) these places shut down and a desolate air hangs over them.

Sibari

About 4km south of the modern town of Sibari is what's left of what was once the seat of the ancient Sybarites, those luxury-loving Greeks renowned for their wealth and excessive love of pampering. You can visit the **remains** (admission free; ☺ 9am–1hr before sunset) – 90% of them beneath reclaimed farmland and bisected by the highway. It was destroyed by a jealous Crotone in the 6th century BC, and excavations since the 1960s have brought only a glimmer of its glory to light. The small **Museo Archeológico della Sibaritide** (admission €2; ☺ 9am-7.30pm, closed 1st & 3rd Mon of month) is 7km from the site (signposted off the autostrada) and can't compare with the riches at Metaponto and Policoro further north.

The coastline from Sibari to Crotone is the region's least developed, partly because the beaches are not terribly good.

Rossano

Rossano, 24km northwest of Sibari, is really two towns – Lido Sant'Angelo, a standard beach resort and coastal extension of the town of Rossano Scalo, and the more interesting original hill town, 6km inland.

The transformation over such a short climb is remarkable. The snaking road takes you through green countryside and seemingly back in time to the atmospheric old town, once an important Italian link in the Byzantine Empire's chain.

Various reminders of Rossano's ties to the ancient city of Constantinople remain. In the central aisle of the **cathedral** is a 9th-century Byzantine fresco of the Madonna and Child, nowadays encased within an ornate polychrome baroque structure. For more proof, visit the **Museo Diocesano** (☎ 0983 52 52 63; admission €3.10; ☼ 9.30am-12.30pm & 4-7pm Tue-Sun), next door, which houses a precious 6th-century codex containing the gospels of St Matthew and St Mark in Greek. If it's closed, ask at Cooperativa Neilos, opposite the cathedral beside the phone kiosk.

Rossano is on the Taranto to Reggio di Calabria train line. From town, the SS177 is a pretty (but long) drive across La Sila to Cosenza.

Crotone
pop 60,000

Calabria's major industrial centre and the region's only Ionian port, Crotone is an ancient city. About 10km north of Isola di Capo Rizzuto, it was founded by the Greeks in 710 BC and reached its zenith in the following century, when it was a major power famed for the beauty of its women and the metaphysics of Pythagoras. There remains precious little to see today.

There is a **tourist office** (☎ 0962 2 31 85; Via Torino 148; ☼ 8.30am-1pm Mon-Sat, 3-7pm Mon & Wed) in the city centre.

The **Museo Archeológico Statale** (☎ 0962 90 56 25; Via Risorgimento 120; admission €2; ☼ 9am-7.30pm, closed 1st & 3rd Mon of month) is one of Calabria's better museums. Nearby is a restored 16th-century **castle** (☎ 0962 92 15 35; Via Risorgimento; admission €2; ☼ 9am-1pm & 3-7pm Tue-Sat, 9am-12.45pm Sun). Typical of the cylindrically towered fortresses erected by the Aragonese in southern Italy, it nowadays houses a small **museum**.

With no evident signposts, **Hotel Capitol** (☎ 0962 2 55 20; Piazza Umberto I; s/d €62/73; P ✸) can be difficult to find, hidden as it is behind a crumbling façade. But the hotel has plenty of character. The reception area is

gigantic and the rooms have high ceilings and simple décor.

A good local restaurant, famed for its Calabrian sweets, is **Casa di Rosa** (☎ 0962 2 19 46; Via Cristoforo Colombo 17; meals €20; ☼ Mon-Sat Feb-Nov).

Le Castella

Le Castella is at the south of one of the few protected areas along this coast, rich in Greek history as well as nature. The shoreline is a protected marine reserve.

The impressive 16th-century Aragonese **castle** was built on the site of an ancient Greek fort (Il Phrourion) and is linked to the mainland by a short causeway. Constructed in the 3rd century BC, it was designed to protect Crotone in the wars against Pyrrhus. At the time of writing the castle was closed to visitors. For further information check out www.riservamarinacaporizzuto.it.

The **Albergo L'Aragonese** (☎ 0962 79 50 13; Via Discesa Marina; half/full board per person €47/58) overlooks the castle. It has a popular restaurant where a full meal costs about €20.

Da Annibale (☎ 0962 79 50 04; Via Duomo 35; meals €25-30) is one of the best fish restaurants along this coast. The catch of the day is always the best bet.

The area offers some of the best camping along the Ionian coast. There are around 15 camp sites near Isola di Capo Rizzuto to the north. A good choice is **La Fattoria** (☎ 0962 79 11 65; fax 0962 95 78 95; Via del Faro; person/tent €8/8; ☼ Jun-Sep), about 1.5km from the sea.

North of Isola di Capo Rizzuto is the **Capo Colonne**, marking the site of the Greek fortress complex of Hera Lacinia. Only a solitary column belonging to a Doric temple remains to testify to the spot's former splendour.

Gerace

A stunning example of a medieval hill town, Gerace is worth a detour for the views alone – on the one side the Ionian Sea, on the other the dark, silent mountains of the interior. About 10km inland from Locri on the SS111, it is becoming something of a routine stop on the tourist circuit. It boasts Calabria's largest Romanesque **cathedral**, high up in the town. First laid out in 1045, later alterations have robbed it of none of its majesty.

For a taste of traditional Calabrian cooking, **Ristorante a Squella** (☎ 0964 35 60 86; Viale della Resistenza 8; meals €15) is the place. Modest and welcoming, it makes for a great lunch-time stop – afterwards you can wander down the road admiring the views.

Further inland is **Canolo**, a small hamlet seemingly untouched by the 20th century. Buses connect Gerace with Locri and also Canolo with Sidernia.

CATANZARO
pop 95,000 / elev 320m

The best view of Catanzaro is of it fading into the distance as you leave town. A grim mountaintop city 12km inland from the Ionian coast, it replaced Reggio di Calabria as the regional capital in the early 1970s. Scarcely anything remains of its Byzantine origins or medieval architecture, thanks to the usual combination of earthquakes and WWII bombs. Other than transport con-nections, there's precious little to draw you here.

Orientation

The train station for the Ferrovie della Cala-bria (FC) is just north of the city centre. Walk southwards along Via Indipendenza

for Piazza Matteotti, the main square, from where Corso Mazzini takes you further south. The main Trenitalia train station is about 2km south and downhill from the centre – you can take a local bus or the cable car from Piazza Roma.

Information

CTS (☎ 0961 72 45 30; Via Indipendenza 26) Travel agency for budget journeys.
Hospital (☎ 0961 88 31 11; Viale Pio X) North of town.
Police station (☎ 0961 88 91 11; Piazza Cavour)
Post office (Piazza Prefettura; ⏱ 8.10am-6pm Mon-Sat)
Tourist office (☎ 0961 74 17 64; 2nd fl, Galleria Mancuso, Via Spasari 3; ⏱ 8.30am-1pm Mon-Fri, 3-5pm Mon & Wed)

Sights
CITY CENTRE

There really isn't a lot to see. The **cathedral** was almost completely rebuilt after the last war and is quite ordinary. Nearby, the **Chiesa di San Domenico del Rosario** contains several attractive Renaissance paintings by com-parative unknowns but is rarely open. More impressive, at least externally, is the baroque

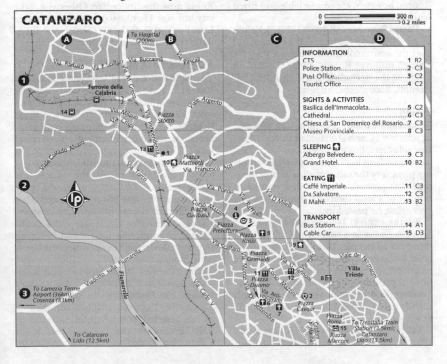

CATANZARO

INFORMATION
CTS..1 B2
Police Station..........................2 C3
Post Office...............................3 C2
Tourist Office...........................4 C2

SIGHTS & ACTIVITIES
Basilica dell'Immacolata............5 C2
Cathedral.................................6 C3
Chiesa di San Domenico del Rosario...7 C3
Museo Provinciale....................8 C3

SLEEPING
Albergo Belvedere.....................9 C3
Grand Hotel............................10 B2

EATING
Caffé Imperiale........................11 C3
Da Salvatore...........................12 C3
Il Mahé...................................13 B2

TRANSPORT
Bus Station.............................14 A1
Cable Car...............................15 D3

Basilica dell'Immacolata with its marble-clad columns.

The city's **Museo Provinciale** (☎ 0961 72 00 19; Villa Margherita; admission free; ☯ 10am-1.30pm & 3.30-5.30pm Tue-Fri, 10am-1.30pm Sat, 9am-12.30pm Sun) has finally re-opened after years of restoration. Situated just inside the Villa Trieste, a green oasis worth a stroll in its own right, it houses a large collection of Greek and Roman coins, some local archaeological finds and various modern works by Calabrian artists.

CATANZARO LIDO

To soak up the sun head for Catanzaro Lido (previously known as Catanzaro Marina), 13.5km away down on the coast. One of the Ionian coast's major resorts, it's heavily developed but less tacky than many others and the beaches stretching off in both directions are among the best on this coast.

Sleeping

Grand Hotel (☎ 0961 70 12 56; fax 0961 74 16 21; Piazza Matteotti; s/d €75/105; ☐ ☒) If it's all about location, this characterless hotel standing in the middle of a road junction wins zero points. Rooms, however, are comfortable and fitted with all the mod cons.

Albergo Belvedere (☎ /fax 0961 72 05 91; Via Italia 33; s/d €24/40, with bathroom €33/54) Looking out over the surrounding hills, this is a friendly enough stopover. Rooms are functional and clean, as the pervading smell of industrial-strength floor cleaner suggests.

Eating

Da Salvatore (☎ 0961 72 43 18; Via Salita del Rosario 28; pizzas from €3, meals €11) Hidden down a narrow sidestreet, this unpretentious restaurant serves excellent local dishes as well as tempting pizza. Try the *salsiccia alla Palanca* (sausage with greens), a unique dish named in honour of a local football hero who ate this every time he passed by.

Il Mahé (☎ 0961 74 60 34; Via Indipendenza 55; meals €18; ☯ Mon-Sat & dinner Sun) Il Mahé is all things to all people. Downstairs, there is a good *rosticceria* (where you can get all sorts of grilled and roast meats). Upstairs functions as pizzeria and restaurant. Also on the 1st floor (in the evenings only) is a bar with nightly entertainment, including live music at weekends.

Caffè Imperiale (☎ 0961 74 32 31; Corso Mazzini 159) A *belle époque* café on Catanzaro's main

thoroughfare, this place is a favoured spot for a weekend ice cream. The coffee and cakes aren't bad either.

Getting There & Away

Buses run by **Ferrovie della Calabria** (☎ 0961 89 61 11; www.ferroviedellacalabria.it) terminate beside the Ferrovie della Calabria train station. They serve Catanzaro Lido, other cities on the Ionian coast, La Sila and towns throughout the province – notably Cosenza (€4.15, 1½ hours, eight daily) and Vibo Valentia (€3.15, two hours, four daily).

Ferrovie della Calabria runs trains between the city and Catanzaro Lido, where you can pick up a Trenitalia train for Reggio di Calabria or head northeast along the Ionian coast.

From the Catanzaro city Trenitalia station, trains connect with Lamezia Terme, Reggio di Calabria and Cosenza, as well as Naples, Rome, Milan and Turin.

Getting Around

Catanzaro's cable car (tickets €0.80) rises from the Trenitalia train station to Piazza Roma near the city centre. Otherwise, take city bus Nos 11, 12, 40 or 41. The Circolare Lido bus connects the city centre, the Trenitalia train station and Catanzaro Lido.

ASPROMONTE MASSIF

The **Parco Nazionale dell'Aspromonte** (www.aspromonte.it), notorious as a hiding place used by Calabrian kidnappers, rises sharply inland from Reggio di Calabria. Its highest peak, **Montalto** (1955m), is dominated by a huge bronze statue of Christ and offers sweeping views across to Sicily.

Subject to frequent mudslides and carved up by torrential rivers, the mountains themselves are bald, stark and arid, possessing an awesome beauty that captivated artist Edward Lear in the late 19th century. These underwater rivers keep the peaks covered in coniferous forests and in spring a burst of flowers soften the otherwise harsh landscape.

The extremes of the weather and landscape have resulted in some extraordinary villages, like **Pentidàttilo** and **Roghudi**, which cling limpet-like to the rockface and are now all but deserted. It is beautiful, unexplored walking country and the park has some trails colour-coded for ease of navigation.

For more information, contact the **tourist office** (☎ 0965 74 32 95; Piazza Carmelo Mangeruca) in **Gambarie**, the main town of the park. Another excellent source of information is the co-operative **Naturaliter** (www.naturaliterweb.it), based in **Condofuri**. It can help arrange excellent walking and donkey treks and can place you in B&Bs throughout the region.

Otherwise make sure you stay at **Azienda Agrituristica Il Bergamotto** (☎ 0965 72 72 13, 347 601 23 38; Condofuri Marina; s/d €45/55) where Ugo Sergi can also arrange excursions. The rooms are simple and the food delicious.

To reach Gambarie, take ATAM city bus No 127 or No 128 from Reggio di Calabria (€1.90, 1½ hours, three daily). Most of the roads inland from Reggio eventually hit the main SS183 road that runs north to the town.

REGGIO DI CALABRIA
pop 180,400

There are two reasons to follow the long, long road that leads to Reggio, the last stop on the mainland. The first is to get a boat to Sicily, the second to see the world-famous Greek statues, the Bronzi di Riace. Neither of these activities will take you far from the waterfront, which is good news because it's the only part of town worth seeing.

In fact, Reggio's seafront pedestrian promenade is a lovely place to wander, as the orange lights of Sicily sparkle so close, coyly tempting you to visit. Unfortunately, any romance in the air is lost the moment you turn away from the sea to behold Reggio's monstrous urban sprawl.

Rocked repeatedly by earthquakes – the most recent devastation was in 1908 – this once-proud ancient Greek city has plenty of other woes, including organised crime. You may notice an unusually large police presence, especially around the law courts in Piazza Castello.

Orientation

Stazione Centrale, the main train station, is at the southern edge of town on Piazza Garibaldi, where most buses also terminate. Walk north along Corso Giuseppe Garibaldi, the city's main street, for the tourist office, shopping and other services. The *corso* has long been a kind of de facto pedestrian zone in the evening, as streams of locals parade in the ritual *passeggiata*.

Nowadays, however, it faces strong competition from the promenade running parallel to it along the shoreline, Corso Vittorio Emanuele III.

Information

Hospital (☎ 0965 39 71 11; Via Melacrino)
Police station (☎ 0965 41 11 11; Corso Giuseppe Garibaldi 442)
Post office (☎ 0965 31 51 11; Via Miraglia 14)
Tourist office (☽ 8am-1.30pm Mon-Fri & 3-5pm Mon & Wed); Via Roma 3 (☎ 0965 2 11 71) The main tourist office; airport (☎ 0965 64 32 91); Corso Giuseppe Garibaldi 329 (☎ 0965 89 20 12); Stazione Centrale (☎ 0965 2 71 20)

Sights

Reggio was virtually rebuilt after the 1908 earthquake that devastated southern Calabria, leaving few historic buildings or significant sights. The one major exception is Reggio's **Museo Nazionale** (☎ 0965 81 22 55; Piazza de Nava; admission €4; ☽ 9am-8pm, closed 1st & 3rd Mon of month), with its wealth of finds from Magna Graecia. Its greatest glory and one of the world's finest examples of ancient Greek sculpture are the **Bronzi di Riace**, two bronze statues discovered near Riace in 1972. After three painstaking years of restoration in Rome and Florence they were returned to Reggio where they now have their own earthquake-proof room in the basement of the museum. Here they stand on a central dais, posed for physical effect, inscrutable, determined and fierce. Larger than life, they depict the Greek obsession with the body beautiful, their perfect form more godlike than human. No-one knows who they are meant to be – whether man or god – and even their provenance is a mystery although they date from around 450 BC.

Aside from the bronzes, the top floor of the museum exhibits canvases, primarily by southern Italian artists, in one of the Mezzogiorno's best collections. It's well worth investing in an audioguide (€3.60, available in English).

The town's gleaming white **cathedral** (Piazza del Duomo), just off Corso Garibaldi, was rebuilt in Romanesque style from the rubble of the 1908 earthquake. Just to its northeast, on Piazza Castello, are a pair of stolid towers, virtually all that remains of a 15th-century Aragonese **castle**.

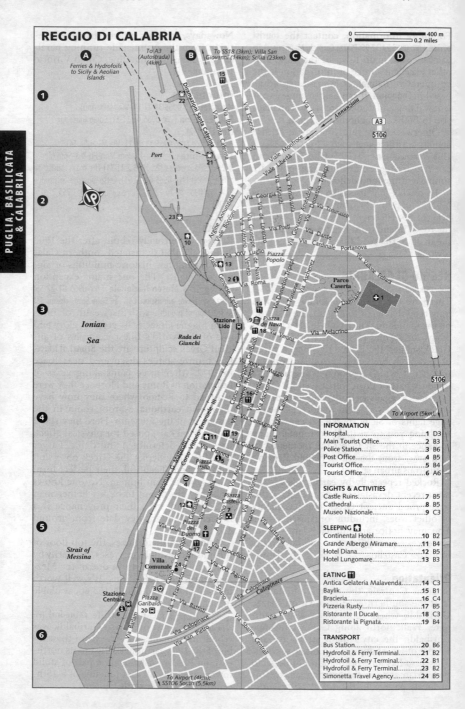

REGGIO DI CALABRIA

PUGLIA, BASILICATA & CALABRIA

To A3 (Autostrada) (4km)

Ferries & Hydrofoils to Sicily & Aeolian Islands

To SS18 (3km); Villa San Giovanni (14km); Scilla (23km)

Port

Ionian Sea

Rada dei Giunchi

Strait of Messina

Stazione Lido

Stazione Centrale

Piazza Popolo

Piazza de Nava

Piazza Italia

Piazza Castello

Piazza del Duomo

Piazza Garibaldi

Villa Comunale

Parco Caserta

To Airport (5km)

To Airport (4km); SS106 South (5.5km)

INFORMATION

Hospital	1 D3
Main Tourist Office	2 B3
Police Station	3 B6
Post Office	4 B5
Tourist Office	5 B4
Tourist Office	6 A6

SIGHTS & ACTIVITIES

Castle Ruins	7 B5
Cathedral	8 B5
Museo Nazionale	9 C3

SLEEPING

Continental Hotel	10 B2
Grande Albergo Miramare	11 B4
Hotel Diana	12 B5
Hotel Lungomare	13 B3

EATING

Antica Gelateria Malavenda	14 C3
Baylik	15 B1
Braceria	16 C4
Pizzeria Rusty	17 B5
Ristorante Il Ducale	18 C3
Ristorante la Pignata	19 B4

TRANSPORT

Bus Station	20 B6
Hydrofoil & Ferry Terminal	21 B2
Hydrofoil & Ferry Terminal	22 B1
Hydrofoil & Ferry Terminal	23 B2
Simonetta Travel Agency	24 B5

Sleeping

Finding a room should be easy, even in summer, since most visitors to Reggio pass straight through on their way to Sicily.

Grande Albergo Miramare (☎ 0965 81 24 44; www .montesanohotels.it; Via Fata Morgana 1; s/d €115/150; P 🔀) Built in 1929 the Miramare is the only *belle époque* hotel in town, and is Reggio's most character-filled accommodation choice. Recently taken over by Montesano hotels, it is currently being totally refurbished and is due for completion in 2006.

Hotel Lungomare (☎ 0965 2 04 86; Via Zerbi 13; www.hotellungomare.rc.it; s/d €78/102; P 🔀) The neat, freshly painted exterior of this period hotel is a welcome sight amid the carnage of Reggio's new buildings. It reflects the efficient and courteous service you will receive inside and the comfortable, modern rooms. Good value for Reggio.

Hotel Diana (☎ 0965 89 15 22; fax 0965 2 40 61; Via Vitrioli 12; s/d/tr €27.50/55/74) It's difficult to miss this interesting city-centre hotel – look out for the three neon signs. If you're lucky (or not) the owner will bash out a melody on the spectacularly out-of-tune piano on the vast downstairs patio.

Continental Hotel (☎ 0965 2 49 90; www.hotelcon tinentalrc.it; s/d €70/80; P 🔀) Barely 50m from the terminal and most convenient for the ferry.

Eating

RESTAURANTS

Baylik (☎ 0965 4 86 24; Vico Leone 3; meals €25-30; 🕑 Fri-Wed) The best fish we sampled while in Calabria makes this awkwardly located restaurant worth the effort. The calamari is so fresh your knife glides through it like butter and there is a dazzling array of other fish dishes. There is no menu as such but the staff are very friendly and can help by recommending things.

Ristorante Il Ducale (☎ 0965 89 15 20; Corso Vittorio Emanuele III 13; meals €30-40) Go up the regal red carpet and treat yourself to dinner with a view. Overlooking the seafront, this is the place to push the boat out and enjoy some stylish Calabrian cooking.

Bracieria (☎ 0965 2 93 61; Via Demetrio Tripepi 81-83; meals €18) This place is trying to be a little too rustic for it to be the genuine article but the food is the real thing. Specialising in grilled meat and fish, it also serves an amazingly good *sapori della Calabria* antipasto comprising brilliant ricotta and chilli-hot bruschetta.

Ristorante la Pignata (☎ 0965 2 78 41; Via Demetrio Tripepi 122; meals €25) Homemade pasta dishes are the house specialities here. Try the *strozzapreti al ragù di carne selvaggina* (pasta in game sauce). It's really very good.

QUICK EATS

For a quick bite, there are plenty of places to buy a snack along Corso Giuseppe Garibaldi. The following are recommended.

Pizzeria Rusty (Via Crocefisso) Next to the cathedral, this pizzeria serves pizza by the slice from €1.10 and tempting fried nibbles.

Antica Gelateria Malavenda (☎ 0965 89 14 49; cnr Via Romeo & Via Giovanni Amendola) For the town's richest ice cream, you can't surpass this long-established Reggio favourite.

Getting There & Away

AIR

Reggio's **airport** (Aeroporto Civile Minniti; REG; ☎ 0965 64 05 17) is at Ravagnese, about 5km to the south. Alitalia and/or Air One fly to and from Rome, Milan and Bergamo, and the occasional charter flight drops by. In town, Alitalia is represented by **Simonetta travel agency** (☎ 0965 33 14 44; Corso Giuseppe Garibaldi 521).

BOAT

Boats for Messina in Sicily leave from the port (just north of Stazione Lido). In high season there are up to 20 hydrofoils per day (€2.90/4.50 one way/return). In low season, there may be as few as two sailings. Some boats continue to the Aeolian Islands.

Services are run by a variety of companies including **Navigazione Generale Italiana** (NGI; ☎ 335 842 77 84), **Meridiano** (☎ 0965 81 04 14) and **Trenitalia** (☎ 0965 89 20 21), with NGI running up to 12 car ferries daily on this route. Prices for cars are €8 one way (passengers don't pay extra), and for foot passengers €1.50.

Ferries for cars and foot passengers cross to Messina around the clock from Villa San Giovanni, 20 minutes further north along the rail line. Both **Caronte** (☎ 0965 79 31 31) and **Tourist Shipping** (☎ 0965 75 14 13) run regular ferries throughout the year. To transport a medium-sized car costs €18/30.50 one way/return, valid for 60 days (passengers don't pay extra); the price for motorcycles is €5 each way. The crossing takes 25 minutes and departs every 20 minutes.

BUS

Most buses terminate at Piazza Garibaldi, in front of the Stazione Centrale. Several different companies operate to towns in Calabria and further beyond. **ATAM** (☎ 0965 62 01 29, 800 43 33 10) serves the Aspromonte Massif, with regular bus No 127 to Gambarie (€2.50, 1½ hours, three daily). **Salzone** (☎ 0965 75 15 86) has bus services to Scilla (€1.24, 45 minutes, six daily). **Lirosi** (☎ 0966 5 75 52) has daily departures to Rome (€35, eight hours, three daily) and Catanzaro (€6, 2½ hours, three daily).

CAR & MOTORCYCLE

The A3 ends at Reggio di Calabria. If you are continuing further south, the SS106 hugs the coast round the 'toe', then heads north along the Ionian Sea.

TRAIN

Trains stop at **Stazione Centrale** (☎ 89 20 21) and less frequently at Stazione Lido, near the museum. Reggio is the terminus for daily trains to and from Milan (€76.50 Eurostar, 12½ hours, nine daily), Rome (€47 Eurostar, 6½ hours, eight daily) and Naples (€32, 5¼ hours, two daily). There are also services for Turin, Florence and Venice but for a wider choice change at Paola (at least 15 daily). Regional services run daily to Catanzaro and Sapri and, less frequently, to Cosenza and Bari.

Getting Around

Orange local buses run by **ATAM** (☎ 0965 62 01 29, 800 43 33 10) cover most of the city. For the port, take bus Nos 13 or 125 from Piazza Garibaldi outside Stazione Centrale. The Porto–Aeroporto bus (No 125) runs from the port via Piazza Garibaldi to the airport and vice versa (€0.80 for up to 90 minutes of travel). Buy your ticket at ATAM offices, tobacconists or newsstands.

TYRRHENIAN COAST

The region's western seashore is a mixture of the good, the bad and the ugly. The Autostrada del Sole (A3) is one of Italy's great coastal drives. It twists and turns through an impossibly dramatic landscape, with mountains to left and right, and huge swathes of dark-green forest and flashes of cerulean-blue sea. But the Italian penchant for cheap summer resorts has taken its toll here, too, and certain stretches are despoiled with badly built hotels and awful stacks of flats.

Out of season, most hotels, camp sites and tourist villages close. In summer many of the hotels are full, although you should have an easier time with the camp sites.

Most coastal towns are on the main train line between Reggio and Naples, and the SS18 road hugs the coast for much of the way. The A3 from Reggio di Calabria to Salerno runs further inland.

TO BRIDGE OR NOT TO BRIDGE

While wooing the nation on his way to victory in the 2001 general elections, Silvio Berlusconi made many promises. One of the more modest promise was to sweep aside thousands of years of geography and bridge the 3km strait that divides Sicily from the Italian mainland.

To do this planners have come up with a €6 billion project to build the world's longest suspension bridge between Reggio di Calabria and Messina. With a total length of 3.7km it will require two 382m towers to support the record-breaking 3300m span. Currently, the Akashi Kaikyo bridge in Japan holds the title with a span of 1991m.

Construction is set to start in spring 2007 with completion due around 2012. That's assuming all concerned agree on the money: 60% will hopefully come from the private sector, the rest from the EU/Italian government.

It's a plan, it seems, that doesn't convince everyone. Environmentalists, in particular, are outraged. The Strait of Messina, they say, supports a finely balanced marine ecosystem that will be completely destroyed; migratory birds will have to find another flight path; and where on earth will workers dump the estimated eight million tons of soil they'll dig up?

Add to this the fact that the area is seriously earthquake prone, and you begin to see why previous governments have quietly let the idea drift away.

The Mafia, of course, will have nothing to do with the partitioning of some of the biggest construction contracts ever awarded in Italy...

Scilla

Scilla comes as a breath of fresh air after the urban mayhem of Reggio and Villa San Giovanni. A picturesque and lively summer town, it marks the beginning (or end if you're travelling southwards) of a striking stretch of coastline. The highlands of the Aspromonte extend to the coast and the views from the cliffs across to Sicily fuel the imagination.

Scilla's highpoint is a rock at the northern end of town that was said to be the lair of Scylla, the mythical six-headed sea monster who drowned sailors as they tried to navigate the Strait of Messina. Swimming off the town's beach is today somewhat safer, as is life for the fisherfolk who operate out of the small port.

Albergo le Sirene (☎ 0965 75 40 19; Via Nazionale 55; s/d €28/48) is a friendly and homely *pensione* that offers plain rooms. In recompense some of them are illuminated by great views over the water to Sicily. There is also a large terrace, which boasts the same views and is ideal for observing the evening *passeggiata* along the promenade.

Promontorio di Tropea

The Promontorio di Tropea, 50km north of Scilla, stretches from Nicotera in the south to Pizzo at the northern end. It is fondly called the Violet Coast after its rose-tinted sunsets. It boasts some of Italy's best sandy beaches and crystal-clear seas and is the regular summer destination for thousands of Italian holidaymakers. This does little to dim the captivating beauty of **Tropea**, the most famous town on this promontory, its old town perched operatically on a rock above an emerald-green sea. The **tourist office** (☎ 0963 6 14 75; Piazza Ercole; ⏰ 9am-1pm & 4-8pm) is in the centre of the old town. Most of the 10 or so hotels close for winter.

Dozens of tourist villages and hotels, most of which are open from May to October, cater to the bulk of visiting tourists.

Hotel Residence Costa Azzurra (☎ 0963 66 31 09; www.hotelcostazzurra.com; full board per person low/high season €48/85; 🐾) is a small, stylish family-run hotel offering beach access and the full gamut of facilities including a children's play area, two pools, tennis and windsurfing. Rooms are scattered throughout the lush gardens.

Hotel Villaggio Stromboli (☎ 0963 66 90 93; www .hotelstromboli.it; full board per person low/high season

€48/85; P ⛱ 🏊) is situated on a beautiful bay 4km northeast of Capo Vaticano. It's a goodlooking holiday village looks towards the island of Stromboli (complete with volcano). It also has villas from €38 to €95 in high season.

A short walk from the city centre leads you to the buzzing pizzeria-cum-trattoria **Ristorante Pizzeria Don Rocco** (☎ 0963 60 70 67; Largo Duomo; meals €15). Frequented by the locals and visitors alike, the atmosphere is convivial and the food is excellent. In particular, Don Rocco do exciting things with tomato and octopus.

Also recommended is the fish restaurant **Osteria del Pescatore** (☎ 0963 60 30 18; Via del Monte 7; meals €25; ⏰ 7.30pm-late Thu-Tue), where the small menu is given over to fried and grilled fish.

Vibo Valentia

pop 33,800

About 8km south of Pizzo, up high and slightly inland, is the long-established town of Vibo Valentia, good for a brief roam and a useful transport hub. The **tourist office** (☎ 0963 4 20 08; Via Forgiari; ⏰ 7.30am-1.30pm Mon-Fri, 2.30-5pm Mon & Wed) is just off Corso Vittorio Emanuele (behind the Galleria Vecchia). Above the town is its **castle**, built by the Normans and later reinforced by both Frederick II and the Angevins. From it, there's a sweeping panorama of coast, inland hills and, on a clear day, the volcanic island of Stromboli. It houses an excellent small **museum** (☎ 0963 4 33 50; admission €2; ⏰ 9am-7pm), which has a wealth of well-displayed artefacts from Hipponion, the original Greek settlement, and Roman Valentia, which superseded it.

A coastal railway runs around the promontory from Rosarno and Nicotera to Vibo Valentia Marina and Pizzo. **SAV** (☎ 0963 611 29) buses also connect most resorts with Tropea and Pizzo.

Pizzo

pop 8700

Pizzo is famous for two things: Italy's best *tartufo*, a type of chocolate ice-cream ball, and the bizarre **Chiesa di Piedigrotta**, an underground cave full of carved stone statues. It was carved into the tufa rock by Neapolitan shipwreck survivors in the 17th century. The church was later added, as was the statue of Fidel Castro! Nowadays it's slowly crumbling which gives it an even more spooky feeling. You will find it immediately north of town.

In town, the 16th-century **Chiesa Matrice di San Giorgio** (Via Marconi) houses the tomb of Joachim Murat, king of Naples (r 1808–15), killed when he was defeated by the Austrians and the Bourbons were restored to the Neapolitan throne. Although he was the architect of various enlightened reforms, the locals showed no great concern when Murat was imprisoned and executed here. To witness a re-enactment of Murat's trial and death, head to the 15th-century **Castello Murat** (☎ 0963 53 25 23; admission €1; ☼ 9am-1pm & 3-10pm Jun-Sep), located just south of Piazza della Repubblica.

Wander through Piazza della Repubblica, at the heart of the picturesque old centre of Pizzo, before settling in at of one of the square's many gelateria terraces for a cold drink or ice-cream fix.

Paola
pop 17,100

The 80km of coast from Pizzo northwards to Paola is mostly overdeveloped and ugly. Paola is the main train hub for Cosenza, about 25km inland, and is a large, comparatively nondescript place.

Watched over by a crumbling castle, the town's main attraction is the **Santuario di San Francesco di Paola** (☎ 0982 58 25 18; admission free; ☼ 6am-1pm & 2-6pm). The saint lived and died in Paola in the 15th century, and the sanctuary that he and his followers carved out of the bare rock has for centuries been the object of pilgrimage. More interesting, however, is the pleasant cloister of the monastery (still in use today), planted with roses and surrounded by naive wall paintings depicting the saint's truly incredible miracles. The original church contains an ornate reliquary of the saint. Also within the complex is a modern basilica, built to mark the second millennium.

There are several hotels near the station but it might be preferable to stay in towns further north along the coast.

Praia a Mare

Diamante and Cirella mark the southern end of a largely uninterrupted stretch of wide, grey pebbly beach that continues north for about 30km to Praia a Mare, just short of Basilicata. Backed by rows of camp sites and growing development projects, the coast lacks much of the scenic splendour to the north in Basilicata or indeed south towards Reggio di Calabria.

A couple of kilometres short of the border with Basilicata, Praia a Mare is a modern resort town. There is a **tourist office** (☎ 0985 7 25 85; Via Amerigo Vespucci 6; ☼ 8am-1pm Mon-Sat) with information on the **Isola di Dino**, just off the coast and famed for its sea caves. To visit the caves expect to pay around €5 for a guided tour from the old boys who operate off the beach. Alternatively, ask at the tourist office.

La Mantinera (☎ 0985 77 90 23; www.lamantinera .it; full board per person low/high season €39/92; ☼ mid-Apr–Sep; P ✄ ✄) is 300m from the beach. It's a huge tourist village at the southern end of town that runs a slick operation and is full of life during the summer months. It offers a range of accommodation, including bungalows (low/high season €280/800 per week) and camping (two people, tent and car low/high season €14/38).

Autolinee Preite (☎ 0984 41 30 01) operates five or six buses daily in each direction between Cosenza and Praia a Mare. **SITA** (☎ 0971 50 68 11) goes north to Maratea and Potenza. Regular trains also pass for Paola and Reggio di Calabria.

Aieta & Tortora

The hill villages of **Aieta** and **Tortora**, about 12km and 6km inland, respectively, from Praia, belong to another world. About three daily **Rocco** (☎ 0985 76 53 12) buses serve both villages. The towns are precariously perched upon ridges that must have been hard-going before asphalt days. Aieta is higher than Tortora and the journey constitutes much of the reward for going there. When you arrive, walk up to the 16th-century **Palazzo Spinello** at the end of the road and take a look into the ravine behind it – it's a great view.

Sicily

In Sicily it seems like the sun shines brighter, the shadows are darker, and life is simultaneously full of intense physical pleasures and bitter-sweet disappointments. As Luigi Barzini so aptly noted, Sicily distils the very best and worst of all things Italian, like the rich sediment that you find in the bottom of a glass of fine wine. Overloaded with art treasures, undersupplied with infrastructure and half-crippled by corruption, Sicily possesses some confusing social topography. Visitors to the island will find themselves struggling to reconcile architectural beauty with modern squalor, artistic excellence with moral ambivalence, the rational with the purely sensual. If you can't accept contradictions, you won't understand Sicily.

After some 25 centuries of foreign domination, Sicilians are heir to an impressive cultural legacy, from the refined architecture of Magna Graecia to the startling artistic fusion of Arab craftsmanship and Norman austerity. Complexity of culture is only matched by stunning natural beauty and diversity of landscape; rolling hills and valleys, brooding Etna, kilometres of aquamarine coastline and a necklace of encircling islands. Barely a third the size of Ireland, Sicily manages to retain the illusion of being a small continent in a large sea.

These days a new generation of Sicilians are waking up to the potential of their extraordinary island and are loathe to remain trapped in the past. New ventures are seeing aristocratic entrepreneurs prising open the doors of some of Europe's finest palazzi and villas while sensitive *agriturismi* are shedding light on some of Sicily's hidden rural treasures and national parks. From volcano-trekking to island hedonism, mountain hideaways to some heavyweight urban culture, Sicily is a fascinating and infinitely varied destination.

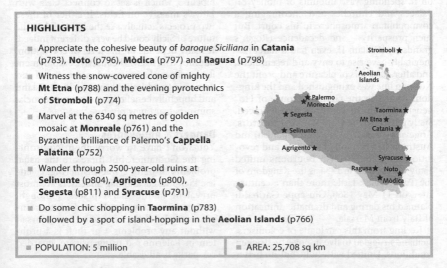

HIGHLIGHTS

- Appreciate the cohesive beauty of *baroque Siciliana* in **Catania** (p783), **Noto** (p796), **Mòdica** (p797) and **Ragusa** (p798)

- Witness the snow-covered cone of mighty **Mt Etna** (p788) and the evening pyrotechnics of **Stromboli** (p774)

- Marvel at the 6340 sq metres of golden mosaic at **Monreale** (p761) and the Byzantine brilliance of Palermo's **Cappella Palatina** (p752)

- Wander through 2500-year-old ruins at **Selinunte** (p804), **Agrigento** (p800), **Segesta** (p811) and **Syracuse** (p791)

- Do some chic shopping in **Taormina** (p783) followed by a spot of island-hopping in the **Aeolian Islands** (p766)

Stromboli ★
Aeolian Islands
★ Palermo
Monreale
★ Segesta   Taormina ★
Mt Etna ★
★ Selinunte   Catania ★
Agrigento ★
Syracuse ★
Ragusa ★ Noto ★
Mòdica ★

■ POPULATION: 5 million	■ AREA: 25,708 sq km

SICILY

History

All Mediterranean nations have contributed to Sicily's history, but ultimately the island's two deep-rooted cultural reference points are Magna Graecia (south and east Sicily) and Moorish north Africa (north and west). This fundamental divide originates from the island's first inhabitants – the Sicani who came from north Africa and settled in northern Sicily, the Siculi from Latium (Italy) who settled the east, and the Elymni from Greece in the south. The subsequent colonisation of the island by Carthaginians from north Africa and Greeks (in the 8th and 6th centuries BC respectively) only compounded this cultural divide through decades of war, during which powerful opposing cities – such as Palermo and Tràpani in the northwest and Catania, Syracuse and Agrigento in the southeast – struggled to dominate the island.

Although inevitably part of the Roman Empire, it was not until the Arab invasions of AD 831 that Sicily truly came into its own. Trade, farming and mining were all fostered under Arab influence and Sicily soon became an enviable prize for European opportunists. Capturing Messina in 1061, Robert Guiscard and his brother Roger I of Hauteville were such men. Carving up the island between them, they began what was soon to become Sicily's most magnificent era.

Impressed by the cultured Arab lifestyle, Roger shamelessly borrowed and improved on it, spending vast amounts of money on palaces and churches and encouraging a cosmopolitan atmosphere in his court. But such prosperity – and decadence (Roger's grandson, William II, even had a harem) – inevitably gave rise to envy and resentment, and after 400 years of pleasure and profit the Norman line was extinguished and the kingdom passed to the German House of Hohenstaufen. In the centuries that followed, Sicily passed to the Holy Roman Emperors, Angevins (French), Aragonese (Spanish) and Austrians in a turmoil of rebellion and revolution until the Spanish Bourbons united Sicily with Naples in 1734 as the Kingdom of the Two Sicilies. Little more than a century later, on 11 May 1860, Giuseppe Garibaldi planned his daring and dramatic unification of Italy from Marsala.

Reeling from this catalogue of colonisers, Sicilians struggled to live in poverty-stricken conditions. Unified with Italy, but no better off, nearly one million men and women emigrated to the USA between 1871 and 1914, before the outbreak of WWI. Ironically, the Allies (seeking Mafia help in America for the reinvasion of Italy) helped in establishing the Mafia's post-war stranglehold on Sicily that was to plague the country right up until the 1990s. In the absence of suitable administrators they invited Don Calógero Vizzini to do the job – under Mussolini the same man had been locked up as one of the most undesirable *mafiosi*. When Sicily became a semi-autonomous region (1948) with its own parliament and legislative powers, Mafia control extended right to the heart of politics with subversive support of the Christian Democrat Party, and the country plunged into a 50-year silent civil war from which it only started to emerge after the anti-Mafia maxi-trials of the 1990s.

Although no-one would be so foolish as to suggest that the power of the Mafia is a thing of the past, Sicilians themselves are less enthralled by the organisation. The thuggery and violence of the 1980s has also considerably diminished. At street level this has resulted in some positive improvements to Sicily's infrastructure and services in the form of small private enterprise. What's more, two major projects look set to have a huge impact on the island; the long proposed bridge over the Messina straits (see the boxed text, p742) and a 520km-long gas pipeline, which is set to connect Gela with Libya's massive oil fields. If either of these two projects actually see the light of day, the future of Sicily could be very different indeed. It really depends on the level of corruption, but the positives will be massive employment for local people, increased international and domestic (read Italian) interest in the island and hopefully beneficial economic and social spin-offs from new revenue.

Dangers & Annoyances

You won't have to worry about confronting the Godfather, but there are the usual problems of petty crime in the bigger cities. Pickpockets and bag-snatchers are most prevalent in the marketplaces, although, having said that, you only need a little common sense and street savvy to enjoy yourself without any problems. Car theft is a problem in Palermo, so using private, guarded car parks is advisable.

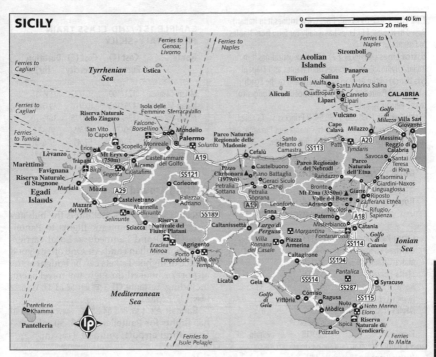

Getting There & Away

AIR

The island is not served by intercontinental flights and only a limited number of airlines fly direct to Sicily – most require a transfer in Rome or Milan. **Alitalia** (www.alitalia.com) is the main carrier, but a range of other airlines also offer competitive rates. These include Air Berlin, Air Malta, British Airways, British Midland, Evolavia, Hapag-Lloyd Express, JMC, Lufthansa and Ryanair. Most charter flights only operate during high season (generally May to October). See p759 and p787 for further details.

BOAT

Regular car and passenger ferries cross the strait between Villa San Giovanni (Calabria) and Messina. Hydrofoils run by the railways and Ustica Lines connects Messina directly with Reggio di Calabria. See Messina (p778) and Reggio di Calabria (p741) for further information.

Sicily is also accessible by ferry from Naples Genoa, Livorno and Cagliari, as well as from Malta and Tunisia. Prices are at their most expensive between June and September. Tickets can be booked through each company or at travel agencies. In summer you will need to book several weeks in advance. Offices and telephone numbers for the ferry companies are listed in the Getting There & Away sections of the relevant cities.

Grandi Navi Veloci (www.gnv.it); Genoa (☎ 010 58 93 31); Palermo (☎ 091 58 74 04); Livorno (☎ 058 640 98 94) Luxury ferries servicing Palermo from Livorno and Genoa.

Grimaldi Ferries (☎ 081 49 64 44; www.grimaldi-ferries .com) A new service connecting Palermo with Tunis. The call centre is in Naples.

Siremar (☎ 091 749 31 11, general information ☎ 199 123 199; www.siremar.it in Italian) Local operator with services from Palermo to Ùstica, Milazzo to the Aeolian Islands, Tràpani to the Egadi Islands and Pantelleria, and Porto Empèdocle (Agrigento) to the Pelagic Islands.

Tirrenia (☎ 199 12 31 99; www.tirrenia.it) The main company servicing the Mediterranean. It runs Palermo–Cagliari, Palermo–Naples, Tràpani–Cagliari and Tràpani–Tunisia services.

Trenitalia (☎ 090 66 16 74; www.trenitalia.it) Runs boats from Villa San Giovanni and Reggio di Calabria to Messina.

TTT Lines (☎ 095 746 21 87; www.tttlines.it in Italian) Based in Naples, TTT Lines has a daily car ferry from Naples to Catania.

Ustica Lines (☎ 0923 2 22 00; www.usticalines.it in Italian) Hydrofoil-only services from Naples and Tràpani (via Ùstica) to the Aeolian Islands, Tràpani to the Egadi Islands and Pantelleria, and Porto Empèdocle (Agrigento) to the Pelagic Islands.

Virtu Ferries (☎ 356 31 88 54; 8 Princess St, Ta'Xbiex, Malta) Runs ferries from Malta to Catania and Pozzallo, just south of Syracuse, between March and October.

SAMPLE 1ST-/2ND-CLASS TRAIN FARES ITALY-SICILY

Route	Cost (€) Eurostar	Cost (€) Intercity	Duration (hr)
Milan-Catania	121/100	102/72	15½-18
Milan-Messina	125/100	100/70	12½-13
Milan-Palermo	126/105	111/78	16½-20
Rome-Catania	80/70	63/45	9½-11
Rome-Messina	70/60	57/41	7½-9
Rome-Palermo	85/74	74/53	10-12

MAINLAND ITALY-SICILY FERRY CROSSINGS

Route	Cost (€) adult seat/car	Duration (hr)
Genoa-Palermo	79/133	20
Livorno-Palermo	64/94	17
Malta-Catania	83/130	3
Malta-Pozzallo	55/92	1½
Naples-Palermo	40/85	11
Naples-Catania	28/76	7½
Naples-Tràpani	83 (hydrofoil only)	6½
Reggio di Calabria-Messina	2.80/18	25min
Tunisia-Tràpani	52/85	11

BUS
Major companies that run long-haul services from Rome or Naples to Sicily include **Interbus** (Segesta; ☎ 091 616 90 39; www.interbus.it) and **SAIS Autolinee** (☎ 091 616 60 28; www.saisautolinee.it). All these services enter Sicily through Messina and continue on to either Catania or Palermo.

It is essential to make an advance reservation on these buses, especially in the high season. Contact details and costs are listed throughout this chapter.

TRAIN
Direct trains run from Milan, Florence, Rome, Naples and Reggio di Calabria to Messina and on to Palermo, Catania and other provincial capitals – the trains are transported from the mainland by ferry from Villa San Giovanni. Although it's more expensive, it is preferable to travel this route on Eurostar (ES) trains, rather than Intercity (IC), as they tend to keep better time and the quality of the service is significantly higher.

Getting Around

AIR
Palermo's Falcone-Borsellino is the hub airport for regular domestic flights to Pantelleria (PNL) and Lampedusa. Local carriers Alitalia, Meridiana and Air One offer a good choice of flights. Tickets can be bought at the airport or booked through any travel agent, including **Sestante CIT** (☎ 091 58 63 33; Via della Libertà 12, Palermo).

Gandalf Air (☎ 848 84 88 80; www.gandalfair.it) has flights for Pantelleria (€30, 50 minutes) from Birgi airport, south of Tràpani.

BUS
Bus services within Sicily are provided by a variety of companies. Buses are usually faster if your destination is not on the main (read 'coastal') train line, although trains tend to be cheaper on the major routes. In small towns and villages tickets are often sold in bars or on the bus.

CAR & MOTORCYCLE
There is no substitute for the freedom your own vehicle can give you, especially when getting to places not well served by public transport. The roads are generally good and autostrade (motorways) connect most major cities. There is a cheap – and worthwhile – toll to use the A18 along the Ionian coast (see the boxed text, p778, for costs).

TRAIN
The coastal train service is very efficient, and the run between Palermo and Agrigento is generally OK. However, train services to towns in the interior can be infrequent and slow, and it is best to do some research before deciding between the train and the bus. The service from Noto to Ragusa, for

instance, can be very picturesque but also very slow.

Trenitalia (www.trenitalia.com) is the partially privatised train system. Intercity (IC) trains are the fastest and most expensive, while the *regionale* is the slowest. All tickets must be validated before you board your train.

PALERMO

pop 680,000
Palermo is a city of compelling contradictions, difficult to define yet impossible to ignore. It is a typical city of the Mediterranean south; outwardly faded, shabby, noisy and dusty, while inwardly seething and sexy. At one time an Arab emirate and seat of a Norman kingdom, it became Europe's grandest city in the 12th century, but in recent years its fame, or should we say notoriety, has originated more from headline-grabbing assassinations, criminal and civic corruption and depressing decrepitude.

But behind the decay, Palermo is a beautiful city with a reserve of cultural, architectural and historical wealth to rival any of Europe's great capitals. The city's role as a crossroads between the east and west has resulted in an intoxicating cultural cross-fertilisation that finds its best expression in the city's architectural mix, a unique fusion of Byzantine, Arab, Norman, Renaissance and baroque. Palermitans themselves have inherited the intriguing looks and social rituals of their cosmopolitan past.

Like their city, Palermitans can be demanding. But you will also find them to be warm, friendly and enthusiastic consumers of life's pleasures, both simple and sophisticated. To get to know them demands a certain level of attention and engagement, but like getting to know the city itself, the resulting rewards are worth the effort.

ORIENTATION

Palermo is a large but manageable city. Via Maqueda is the central street, extending from the train station in the south through Via Ruggero Settimo to the grand Piazza Castelnuovo in the north. Here it turns into Viale della Libertà, a wide leafy boulevard lined with late-19th-century apartment blocks, which marks the beginnings of the modern half of the city.

Via Maqueda is bisected by Corso Vittorio Emanuele, running east to west from the port of La Cala to the Cathedral and Palazzo dei Normanni. The intersection, known as the Quattro Canti (Four Corners), divides the historic centre into four traditional quarters that contain the majority of Palermo's sights. Parallel to Via Maqueda runs Via Roma, the second main street of the old town and a cheap and popular high street. A one-way system rotates traffic north up Via Roma from the train station and south down Via Maqueda.

INFORMATION
Bookshops
Several newsstands around Piazza Verdi sell foreign newspapers.

Feltrinelli (☎ 091 58 77 85; Via Maqueda 395) Palermo's best bookshop with a good foreign-language section as well as city maps, guides to the city and full-colour coffee-table books.

Emergency
Ambulance (☎ 091 30 66 41)
Main police station (theft & lost documents ☎ 091 21 01 11, foreigners office ☎ 091 651 43 30; Piazza della Vittoria) Where you should report thefts and other petty crimes.

Internet Access
Should you need it there is also Internet access at the ferry terminal and airport.

Aboriginal Café (☎ 091 662 2229; www.aboriginalcafe .com; per hr €5; Via Spinuzza 51; 🕙 11am-1pm & 2pm-3am Tue-Sat) An Australian-style bar that doubles as an Internet café. Conveniently located but doesn't have that many terminals.
Internet point (Corso Vittorio Emanuele; per hr €2; 🕙 9am-10pm) Very convenient and reasonably priced. The 10 fast computers get very busy in the late afternoon to early evening.

Left Luggage
Train station (per bag 1st 5hr €3.80, then per hr €0.20; 🕙 7am-11pm)

Medical Services
Farmacia da Naro (☎ 091 58 58 69; Via Roma 207; 🕙 24hr)
Ospedale Civico (☎ 091 666 11 11; Via Carmelo Lazzaro) The main hospital. Offers first aid as well.

Money
There are plenty of ATMs scattered throughout the city. There are exchange offices open

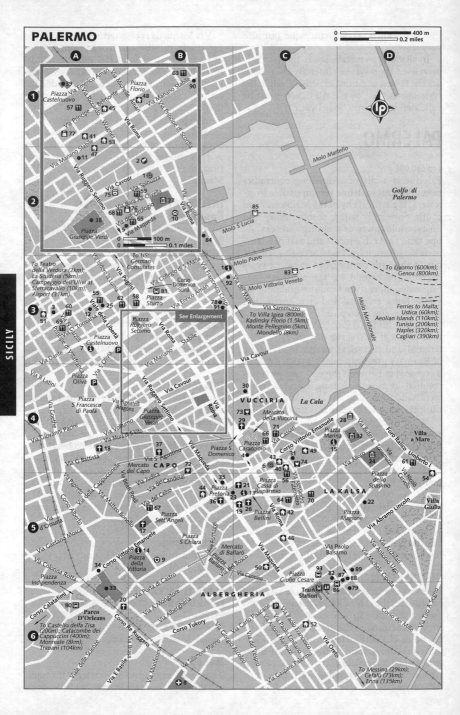

PALERMO

SICILY

outside normal banking hours at the airport (8am to 7pm Monday to Saturday) and train station (8am to 8pm).

Post

Post office (Palazzo delle Poste; Via Roma 322; ⏰ 8.30am-6.30pm Mon-Fri, 8.30am-12.30pm Sat) This monolithic post office is one of the few Fascist buildings in Palermo. Smaller branch offices can be found at the train station and on Piazza Verdi.

Telephone

Telephone booths are dotted throughout the city, particularly at the train station and ferry terminal and around the main piazzas.

Tourist Information

Tourist information booth (⏰ 9am-2pm & 3-8pm Mon-Thu, 8.30am-8.30pm Fri & Sat, 9am-1pm & 3-7pm Sun) These can be found on Molo Piave, Via Cavour, Piazza Bellini, Piazza Marina and Piazza della Vittoria.

Tourist office (www.palermotourism.com in Italian); airport (☎ 091 59 16 98; ⏰ 8am-noon); Piazza Castelnuovo 35 (☎ 091 605 81 11; ⏰ 8.30am-2pm & 2.30-6pm Mon-Fri); train station (☎ 091 616 59 14; ⏰ 8.30am-2pm & 2.30-6pm Mon-Fri, 8.30am-2pm Sat) The office at Piazza Castelnuovo is the main tourist office. It has plenty of brochures on Palermo and the island, the most useful being the bi-monthly Agenda. Helpfulness of staff varies greatly.

Travel Agencies

The following agencies can book train, ferry and air tickets.

CTS (☎ 091 611 07 13; www.cts.it in Italian; Via Nicolò Garzilli 28g) A branch of the national youth travel agency. Also offers tours of the city and island.

Record Viaggi (☎ 091 611 09 10; Via Marino Stabile 168)

Sestante CIT (☎ 091 58 63 33; Via della Libertà 12)

SIGHTS

Around the Quattro Canti

The busy intersection of Corso Vittorio Emanuele and Via Maqueda marks the **Quattro Canti** (Four Corners), the centre of the oldest part of town, neatly bisecting the historic nucleus into four manageable sectors.

Nearby **Piazza Pretoria** is the civic heart of Palermo where a crowd of imposing churches and buildings (most of which were under scaffolding at the time of writing) surround the ornate **Fontana Pretoria**. This huge fountain fills the piazza with its tiered basins, crammed with sculptures, rippling out in concentric circles. The city bought the fountain in 1573 in a bid to outshine the newly crafted Fontana di Orione installed in Messina. It was proudly positioned in front of the Palazzo Pretoria (Municipal Hall), though the flagrant nudity of the leering nymphs proved too much for Sicilian churchgoers attending the grandly formal **San Giuseppe dei Teatini**, and they prudishly dubbed it the Fountain of Shame.

Closing off the eastern side of the square is the **Chiesa di Santa Caterina** (Discesa dei Giudici), Palermo's finest church with a typically Sicilian story. It's held in trust by seven aged Dominican nuns who keep the door firmly bolted; it's opened once a year on St Catherine's Day (25 November) when the public gets the briefest glimpse of its fabulous trompe l'oeil frescoes, stucco statuary and amethyst and lapis altars.

More famous than Santa Caterina and easily accessible is the popular **La Martorana** (Chiesa di Santa Maria dell'Ammiraglio; Piazza Bellini 3; ☉ 8am-1pm & 3.30-5.30pm Mon-Sat, 8.30am-1pm Sun) just around the corner. Originally planned as a mosque, this 12th-century structure was the brainchild of King Roger's Syrian Emir, George of Antioch. In 1433 the church was given over to a pesky set of Benedictine nuns, founded by Eloisa Martorana (hence its nickname), who set about tearing down the Norman apse, reworking the exterior and adding their own frescoed chapel at the expense of the wonderful gold mosaic work. Fortunately, two of the original mosaics to survive are the portraits of George of Antioch and the one of Roger II receiving his crown from Christ (the only portrait of him to survive in Sicily).

Where La Martorana preserves its interior, the small pink-domed **Chiesa di San Cataldo** (Piazza Bellini 3; admission €1; ☉ 9.30am-12.30pm Mon-Sat) is almost bare inside. Its main interest, however, lies in the Arab-Norman style of its exterior – the bijoux domes, solid square shape, the blind arcading and delicate tracery.

Albergheria

West along Corso Vittorio Emanuele, past the waving palms in Piazza delle Vittoria, rises the fortress palace of **Palazzo dei Normanni** (Palazzo Reale; ☎ 091 705 70 03; Piazza Indipendenza 1; adult/concession incl the Cappella Palatina €5/2.50; ☉ 8.30am-noon & 2-5pm Mon-Sat, 8.30am-noon Sun), once the centre of a magnificent medieval court and now the seat of the Sicilian parliament.

Downstairs, just off the three-tiered loggia is Palermo's premier tourist attraction, the **Cappella Palatina** (Palatine Chapel; ☎ 091 705 47 49; ☉ 8.30am-11.45am & 3-5pm Mon-Sat, 8.30am-1.30pm Sun), designed by Roger II in 1130. With every inch of its interior inlaid with precious marbles and exquisite mosaics (coloured glass onto which gold leaf has been applied) the chapel has a jewel-like quality. The mosaics, the bulk of which recount the tales of the Old Testament, are incredibly sophisticated, capturing expression, detail and movement with extraordinary grace and accuracy. Other scenes recall Palermo's pivotal role in the Crusades, an ironic reference given the fact that the chapel was decorated by Muslim artists. The wooden *muqarnas* ceiling – unique in a Christian church – is a masterpiece of honeycomb carving.

This is one of the busiest tourist sites in Palermo so be prepared to queue as custodians limit the number of visitors entering the chapel at any one time. It can be a frustrating process but don't let yourself be put off Palermo's finest sight.

South of the palazzo, you can find a tranquil refuge from the crowds in the peaceful Norman cloisters of the **Chiesa di San Giovanni degli Eremiti** (Via dei Benedettini; ☉ 9am-7pm Mon-Sat, 9am-1pm Sun & holidays).

Behind the splendours of the Palazzo dei Normanni lies the run-down district of Albergheria, a poor and ramshackle quarter once inhabited by the Norman court officials and now home to a growing number of illegal immigrants who are revitalising its alleyways. It is also the location of Palermo's busiest street market, the **Mercato di Ballarò** (Piazza Ballarò), which throbs with activity well into the early evening. It is a fascinating place full of wildly different people; groups of Tunisian men sit around drinking coffee or beer, cook shops and soup kitchens serve up the cheapest possible meals and even some of the traditional stalls now cater for burgeoning new markets for exotic produce like yams and pawpaws.

Il Capo

On 5 May 1072 the Norman 'wolf' Robert Guiscard seized Palermo, thus beginning the city's most prosperous era. Ambitious builders, the Normans gave birth to the extraordinary Arab-Norman style unique to Sicily. Chief among these is the **Cathedral** (☎ 091 33 43 76; www.cattedrale.palermo.it; Corso Vittorio Emanuele; ☉ 9.30am-5.30pm), an extraordinary feast of geometric patterns, ziggurat crenellations, majolica cupolas and blind arches. It's set back from the street, and the foreground

SICILIAN STREET FOOD

Boy, do these people know how to eat. They're at it all the time, when they're shopping, on the way to work, on the way home from work, when they're discussing business, or at any other time of the day. What they're enjoying is the *buffitieri* – little hot snacks prepared at stalls and meant to be eaten on the spot, just like they were in the market places of Sicily's Greek cities. You should give it a go.

Kick off the morning with a *pane e pannelle*, Palermo's famous chickpea fritters. Or you might want to go for the potato croquettes, the *sfincione* (a spongy, oily pizza topped with onions and caciocavallo cheese) or even *scaccie* (discs of bread dough spread with a filling and rolled up into a pancake). In summer, people have a freshly baked brioche filled with a type of ice cream flavoured with fruits, coffee or nougat.

From 4pm onwards you can pick up some barbecued offal like *stigghiola* (goat intestines filled with onions, cheese and parsley) or the Palermo favourite, *frittole* (a soup made from meat, marrow and fat). While in Catania you can buy all manner of *impanata* (bread-dough snacks) stuffed with meat, vegetables or cheese alongside the unique *arancino* (a deep-fried rice ball stuffed with meat, tomato and vegetables).

Another notorious street snack is *pani cu'la mensa* (a bread roll stuffed with sautéed beef spleen). You'll be asked if you want it *schietta o maritata* ('single or married'). If you choose *schietta* the roll will only have ricotta in it before being dipped into boiling lard. It is only the 'married' roll that has the meat in it!

planted with palms; the Oriental impact is enough to skew one's compass to thinking it's somewhere in the East. The interior, although impressive in scale, is a marble shell, a sadly unexotic resting place for the royal Norman tombs. The **crypt and treasury** (adult/concession €2/1.50; ☺ 9am-5.30pm Mon-Sat) contain various jewels belonging to Queen Costanza of Aragon, a bejewelled Norman crown and, most bizarrely, a tooth extracted from Santa Rosalia, the patron saint of Palermo.

Bordering Albergheria, the Capo is another web of interconnected streets and blind alleys. It too has its own street market, **Mercato del Capo**, running the length of Via Sant'Agostino. Like Ballarò it is a seething mass of colourful activity during the day. You can also pop your head into the madly marbled **Chiesa della Concezione** (Via Porta Carini; ☺ 9am-noon & 4-6pm Mon-Sat) along the way.

The centrepiece of the quarter is the imposing monastery of **Sant'Agostino** (☺ 7am-noon & 4-6pm Mon-Sat, 7am-noon Sun). Redecorated by the rich Scláfani family, the interior sports putti statues by Giacomo Serpotta, while the older cloister is decorated in a similar style to that of Monreale (p761).

La Vucciria

Plunge into the streets heading towards the old harbour of La Cala and you'll find architectural gems of a completely different nature to those in Il Capo. The **Oratorio del Rosario di Santa Zita** (Via Squarcialupo; admission free; ☺ 9am-1pm Mon-Sat), the **Oratorio del Rosario di San Domenico** (Via dei Bambinai 2; admission free) and the **Oratorio di San Lorenzo** (Via dell'Immacolatella; admission free; ☺ 9am-noon Mon-Fri) were used by nobles as social clubs and are an incredibly showy display of 17th-century status and wealth. Covered in a preposterous riot of stuccowork by Giacomo Serpotta, they represent the excessive love of ornamentation favoured by Palermitan nobles. The Oratorio del Rosario di San Domenico is temporarily closed.

In stark contrast the shabby streets of Vucciria mark the medieval chasm between rich and poor that existed in Sicily right up until the 1950s. Amid the alleys is Palermo's most notorious street market, **Mercato della Vucciria** (Piazza Caracciolo), although these days the Vucciria is slowly dying, abandoned by downtown shoppers in favour of the Ballarò and Capo markets. A couple of vendors still cling onto what was once a heaving den of crime and activity – a scene of bounty immortalised by the artist Renato Guttuso (1912–87) in his most famous painting *La Vucciria* (1974).

Walking north and crossing Via Roma will bring you to the **Museo Archeologico Regionale** (☎ 091 611 68 05; Via Bara all'Olivella 24; adult/concession €4.50/2; ☺ 8.30am-6.45pm Tue-Sat, 9am-1.30pm Sun & Mon). Housed in a Renaissance monastery,

SICILY

the galleries of this museum surround a lovely inner courtyard and display some of Sicily's most valuable Greek and Roman artefacts. The most important rooms are ranged around the courtyard and display numerous treasures from Selinunte, most notably a series of metopes (decorative friezes) depicting favourite classical scenes full of humour and energy. In one, Hercules fights a wilting Amazon while Actaeon is devoured by his hounds. In another, Perseus gleefully beheads the Gorgon, and the Cercopes twins, hung upside-down, laugh at the sunburnt bum of Hercules. The museum also has good wheelchair access.

La Kalsa

Due to its proximity to the port, La Kalsa was subjected to carpet-bombing during WWII, leaving it derelict and run down. Mother Teresa considered it no better than the Third World and established a mission here. Thankfully, this galvanised the authorities into action and the quarter is now undergoing extensive restoration.

The arterial Via Alloro hides the wonderful **Galleria Regionale Siciliana** (Palazzo Abatellis; ☎ 091 623 00 11; Via Alloro 4; adult/concession €4.50/2; ☯ 9am-1pm & 2.30-7pm Tue-Fri, 9am-1pm Sat-Mon). Full of treasures and paintings from the Middle Ages to the 18th century, it gives a great insight into Sicilian painting – something sadly lacking in more recent years – and numbers among its treasures the famously terrifying *Trionfo della Morta* (Triumph of Death), a 15th-century fresco by an unknown artist, and the exquisite white marble bust of *Eleonora d'Aragona* by Francesco Laurana. The gallery also holds a range of temporary exhibitions.

Just behind the gallery is the **Complessa di Santa Maria dello Spasimo** (☎ 091 616 14 86; Via Spasimo; admission free; ☯ 9am-midnight), originally a church and convent and the only example of Northern Gothic in Sicily. Its elegant polygonal apse and tall slender nave have stood for centuries without a roof. Nowadays it's used as an exhibition space and a concert venue. It's sensational to visit at night.

Striking out from Palazzo Abatellis in the opposite direction up Via IV Aprile will bring you to the gentrified **Piazza Marina** with its small but perfect **Giardino Garibaldi**. The largest palazzo on the square is the imposing 14th-century **Palazzo Chiaramonte Steri**

(☎ 091 33 41 39; Piazza Marina; ☯ exhibitions only). In the 17th century it was the headquarters of the Inquisition and miserable heretics were burnt to death in the quiet garden outside.

Just around the corner from Piazza Marina you will find the **Museo Internazionale delle Marionette** (☎ 091 32 80 60; www.museomario nettepalermo.it in Italian; Via Butera 1; adult/concession €3/1.50; ☯ 9am-1pm & 4-7pm Mon-Fri, 9am-1pm Sat), set up by the Association for the Conservation of Popular Traditions. The museum houses over 3000 puppets, marionettes, glove puppets and shadow figures collected from Palermo, Catania and Naples, as well as many from places such as China, India, southern Asia, Turkey and Africa. A show is staged every Friday at 5.30pm; the museum has a detailed programme.

The 19th-Century City

North of Piazza Giuseppe Verdi, Palermo takes on a more cosmopolitan look. Here there are some glorious examples from the last golden age of Sicilian architecture when neoclassical and Art Nouveau styles were all the rage.

One of the most important buildings of the period was **Teatro Massimo** (☎ 091 605 35 55; www.teatromassimo.it; Piazza Giuseppe Verdi; guided tours adult/concession €3/2; ☯ 10am-3.30pm Tue-Sun), commissioned to celebrate the unification of Italy. The project took some 22 years to complete (1875–97) and was undertaken by Giovanni Battista Basile and subsequently his son, Ernesto. Nowadays the theatre is an iconic Palermo landmark and its volatile history speaks eloquently about the conflicting powers that struggle for supremacy in Palermitan society – civic pride and cultural creativity pitted against the stultifying effects of Pirandellian bureaucracy and Mafia control, which is said to have been responsible for the extraordinary 24 years it took to restore. Appropriately, the closing scene of *The Godfather: Part III*, with its visually stunning juxtaposition of high culture and low crime, drama and death, was filmed here.

Teatro Politeama-Garibaldi (bookings ☎ 091 605 33 15; Piazza Ruggero Settimo; ☯ performances only Nov-May) is Palermo's second theatre. Designed by architect Giuseppe Damiani Almeyda between 1867 and 1874, it has the same imposing circular layout as the Teatro Massimo and features a striking façade that looks like a triumphal arch topped by a huge bronze chariot.

Beyond Piazza Ruggero Settimo the broad boulevard of Viale della Libertà is lined with late-19th-century mansion blocks. Head up here for a sybaritic experience at Palermo's **Hammam** (☎ 091 32 07 83; www.hammam.pa.it in Italian; Via Torrearsa 17d; admission €30; ☼ 10am-10pm, men only Tue, Thu & Sat, women only Mon, Wed & Fri), a luxurious marble-lined Moorish bathhouse where you can indulge in a vigorous scrubdown, a mean sauna and many different types of massages and therapies. There is a one-off charge (€7) for slippers and a hand glove.

The Suburbs

A short bus or car journey west from Piazza Castelnuovo leads to **Castello della Zisa** (☎ 091 652 02 69; Piazza Guglielmo il Buono; adult/concession €2.50/1; ☼ 9am-7pm Mon-Fri, 9am-1pm Sat & Sun). With stalactite vaults, latticework windows and even a wind chamber to protect the Emir from the hot African sirocco, the villa deserves its name, which comes from the Arabic *al aziz*, meaning 'magnificent'. Today it houses a museum of Arab crafts. Take bus No 124 from Piazza Ruggero Settimo.

The morbid **Catacombe dei Cappuccini** (☎ 091 21 21 17; Via Cappuccini 1; admission €1.50; ☼ 9am-noon & 3-5.30pm), located south of the *castello*, is where the mummified bodies and skeletons of some 8000 Palermitans, who died between the 17th and 19th centuries, are on show! Earthly power, sex, religion and professional status are still rigidly distinguished; men and women occupy separate corridors and within the women's area there is a first-class section for virgins. The sight is nothing short of bizarre, with corridors of skeletal Palermitans still dressed in their best, if faded, velvets and silks.

FESTIVALS & EVENTS

Palermo's biggest annual festival, **U Fistinu**, celebrates the patron saint of the city, Santa Rosalia. The saint's relics are paraded through the city amid four days of partying during 10 to 15 July.

In February, Sicily's oldest **Carnevale** is held in the suburb of Termini Imerese. Decorated floats and enormous papier-mâché figures parade the streets.

At Easter, **Settimana Santa** (Holy Week) is the year's major religious festival and is celebrated virtually all over the island. In Palermo there are Greek Orthodox celebrations at La Martorana (p752).

Palermo di Scena is a series of music, cinema, theatre and ballet programmes held throughout the summer.

During the **Festa di Morgana** (www.museomario nettepalermo.it in Italian) puppeteers from all over the world gather at Museo Internazionale delle Marionette. Dates vary each year so check out the website.

SLEEPING

Compared with the rest of Italy, Sicilian accommodation is reasonably priced, but prices do vary according to season and demand. For this reason it is always better (especially in the budget category) to call and book in advance. Most budget options can be found on Via Roma towards the train station. All the midrange and top-end hotels are located north of the Quattro Canti. Between June and October you will need to book in advance.

Parking usually costs an extra €10 to €15 per day.

Budget

Albergo Ariston (☎ 091 33 24 34; www.aristonpalermo .it; Via Marino Stabile 139; s/d €40/58; ✺) This place continues to offer excellent value for money in a prime location at the top end of town. Don't be put off by the run-down appearance of the building and the lift – inside, this little *pensione* is spick-and-span and the service (Italian-speaking only) is friendly and polite.

Ambasciatori Hotel (☎ 091 610 66 881; www.ven ere.it/palermo/ambasciatori; Via Roma 111; s/d €75/98; P ✺) Despite its location on the busy Via Roma, this hotel gets the thumbs up from most travellers. Located on the 5th floor of an old palazzo, the rooms are surprisingly quiet and comfortable. Best of all, breakfast (which admittedly is a bit spartan) is served on a rooftop terrace with views over Palermo's rooftops. The hotel's only drawback is the inconvenient parking.

Artepalermo (☎ 091 32 57 80, 338 131 17 09; www .marjoleinwortmann.com; Vicolo Madonna del Cassaro 7; s/d €30/45) A fantastic deal right in the historic centre. Marjolein is a delightful and cultured hostess who speaks a staggering seven languages. The two comfortable rooms, both with balcony, are cool and airy; you can also make yourself at home in the kitchen and sunbathe on the roof terrace (complete with shower). A friendly and informal place, but beware of the hike up to the 5th floor.

Hotel Orientale (☎ 091 616 57 27; prenotazioni@ albergoorientale.191.it; Via Maqueda 26; s/d €40/50, with bathroom €50/70; **P**) The dramatic, arcaded courtyard of this decaying Palermo building is a great start to this hotel. Renovated in 2003, the Orientale now offers reasonable-value rooms furnished with wrought-iron beds and modern en suite shower rooms. Check out the lovely frescoed ceiling of the library.

Campeggio dell'Ulivi (☎ 091 53 30 21; Via Pegaso, Sferracavallo; per person €7; ☾ year-round) In the suburb of Sferracavallo, this is the best camp site near Palermo. Take bus No 615 from Piazza Vittorio Veneto at the top of Via delle Libertà, which drops you outside the camp site. Price includes shower and electricity.

Midrange

Ai Cartari (☎ 091 611 63 72; www.aicartari.com; Via Alessandro Paternostro 62; s/d €55/110; **P** ⊠ 🖳) Live like a Palermitan in one of these two nicely decorated suites (each of which sleeps up to five people). Your front door opens on to the cute Piazza San Francesco d'Assisi, and Palermo's most famous *focacceria*, Antica Focacceria di San Francesco, is just on your doorstep.

Hotel Tonic (☎ 091 605 53 38; www.hoteltonic.com; Via Marino Stabile 126; s/d €80/100; ⊠) Towards the top of town, very close to Piazza Giuseppe Verdi, this small townhouse hotel deserves its good reputation. All staff speak English and the hotel is comfortably furnished and well run. The room prices remain the same year-round.

Hotel del Centro (☎ 091 617 03 76; www.hoteldel centro.it; Via Roma 72; s €52-75, d €72-95; **P** ⊠ 🖳) A big, busy hotel on Via Roma. It is tastefully decorated throughout, the management is efficient and it's conveniently close to the station. It's been known not to accept credit cards so check beforehand.

Hotel Elite (☎ 091 32 93 18; www.hotelelite.info; Via Mariano Stabile 136; s/d €70/90; **P** ⊠ 🖳) Beyond its chichi décor and questionable latter-day frescoes, Hotel Elite is good value for money and offers a range of services, including laundry and Internet. It is located with a bunch of other hotels in what looks like an office block. Follow the signs.

Hotel Letizia (☎ 091 58 91 10; www.hotelletizia .com; Via dei Bottai 30; s/d/tr €85/134/155; ⊠ 🖳) Near the port of La Cala, this charming hotel is situated just off Piazza Marina. Each of the 13 bedrooms is individually decorated with baroque-style furnishings and the wooden floors and low ceilings give it a cosy feel.

Jolly Hotel (☎ 091 616 50 90; www.jollyhotels.it; Foro Italico Umberto I; s/d €143/177; **P** ⊠ 🐾) The Jolly is a rather bland chain hotel but it has a seafront location and good facilities, not least of which is one of the only pools in Palermo (open from 15 May to 30 September). The only drawback – it is a bit of a hike from the historic centre, although they do loan out bikes.

Hotel Joli (☎ 091 611 17 65; www.hoteljoli.com; Via Michele Amari 11; s/d €78/108; ⊠) Another reliable three-star hotel, although it lacks soul and some of the huge rooms are cavernous rather than luxurious. Some do have nice balconies over Piazza Florio.

Hotel Sausele (☎ 091 616 13 08; www.hotelsausele .it; Via Vincenzo Errante 12; s/d €56/92; **P** ⊠) Despite the chaotic décor in the foyer, the Sausele is a pretty professional small hotel. It is in an excellent location for those who want to use public transport to get around Sicily. The rooms are spartan but clean.

Top End

Villa Igiea (☎ 091 54 76 54; www.cormorano.net/sgas /villaigiea; Salita Belmonte 43; s/d/ste €177/277/498; **P** ⊠ 🐾) This magnificent five-star hotel, 3km north of the city centre, is Palermo's luxury hotel *par excellence*. A sumptuous Art Nouveau–style villa, it is situated in its own terraced gardens, complete with a private beach. Prices drop by 50% in low season.

Hotel Principe di Villafranca (☎ 091 611 85 23; www.principedivillafranca.it; Via G Turrisi Colonna 4; s/d/ste €130/185/268; **P** ⊠ 🖳) This hotel is situated just off Via della Libertà in one of the most exclusive areas of Palermo. It's furnished throughout with Sicilian antiques and expensive linens and has a first-rate restaurant, cosy library and cutting-edge gym.

Centrale Palace Hotel (☎ 091 33 66 66; www.cent ralepalacehotel.it; Corso Vittorio Emanuele 327; s/d €162/182; **P** ⊠) This 18th-century palazzo is one of Palermo's most elegant hotels with a superb location in the heart of the historic centre. The hotel offers a high level of service and the rooms are stylish, though the beds could be wider and more comfortable.

Grand Hotel e des Palmes (☎ 091 602 81 11; www
.amthotels.com; Via Roma 398; s/d €130/190; ☐ ☒)
Opened in 1874, the Grand Hotel is one of
Palermo's most historic hotels. Like a royal
court it has been the scene of intrigue, li-
aisons, and double-dealings throughout Palermo's history, although it was abandoned
by the elite in the 1970s in favour of Villa
Igiea. The grand salons still impress with
their chandeliers and gigantic mirrors while
the rooms are sumptuously decked out.

EATING

One of Sicily's best-kept secrets is its ancient cuisine, a mixture of spicy and sweet
flavours. Palermo's most famous dish is the
tasty *pasta con le sarde*, with sardines, fennel,
peppers, capers and pine nuts. Cakes and
pastries are works of art – try the *cannoli*,
tubes of pastry filled with cream, ricotta or
chocolate – and like the Spaniards, Sicilians
have a penchant for marzipan. Sicilians are
late eaters and restaurants rarely start to fill
up until 9.30pm.

Restaurants
BUDGET

Antica Focacceria di San Francesco (☎ 091 32 02 64,
Via A Paternostro 58; meals €10-15; ☺ Tue-Sun) A Palermitan institution, this atmospheric place is
one of the city's oldest eating houses (opened
1834). It hosted the first Sicilian parliament
and was a favourite haunt of notorious Mafia
boss 'Lucky' Luciano. It serves an age-old
Palermitan snack – a *panino* (filled roll) with
milza (veal innards) and ricotta cheese.

Trattoria Basile (Focacceria del Massimo; ☎ 091
33 56 28; Via Bara all'Olivella 76; meals €5-10; ☺ noon-
3.30pm Mon-Sat) This place just off Piazza Verdi
is a popular, unpretentious trattoria. Slices
of pizza, sandwiches and daily pasta dishes
provide simple but filling fare. Try to avoid
the really busy period between 1pm and 2pm
when every workman in town is trying to
get his plate of pasta.

Zia Pina (Via Cassaro 69; meals €5; ☺ noon-3.30pm
Mon-Sat) A raffish little place in deepest Vucciria. Walk through the kitchen past the piles
of fresh produce to take a pew at a ubiquitous plastic table. Then take the plunge with
your rusty Italian to order up a wonderfully
fresh feast.

Pizzeria Italia (☎ 091 58 98 85; Via dell'Orologio 54;
pizzas €6-8; ☺ 7-11pm Mon-Sat) Palermo's oldest
pizzeria still does a roaring trade in thin-

crust pizzas dripping with steaming cheeses
and the freshest cherry tomatoes.

El-Maghreb (Via Bara all'Olivella 75; shawarma €3; ☺ 7-
11pm Tue-Sun) A Tunisian kebab house serving
shawarma (pita breads filled with lamb and
salad) and *tagen* (a meat or vegetable stew).
Situated just on the corner of Piazza Olivella,
playing loud Arabic music, this is one of the
more lively spots in Palermo.

MIDRANGE

L'Acanto (☎ 091 32 04 44; Via Torrearsa 10; meals €25-
30) New-town elegance together with in-
ventive cooking makes L'Acanto one of the
most fashionable restaurants around town
with the young professional crowd. In summer tables are set out back on the patio and
fill up around 10pm.

Kursaal Kalhesa (☎ 091 616 22 82; www.kursaal
kalhesa.it; 21 Foro Umberto I; lunch/dinner €15/25; ☺ Tue-
Sat, lunch Sun & dinner Mon) Recline on silk cushions
sipping a cocktail beneath the soaring vaulted
ceilings before tucking into some of Palermo's best cuisine on the outdoor restaurant
terrace. There is also a good programme of
jazz and live music, usually on Wednesday or
Thursday at 10pm.

Trattoria Biondo (☎ 091 57 36 62, Via Carducci 15,
meals €25; ☺ Thu-Tue) Be prepared to brave the
stares as you ring the bell to gain entry to this
trattoria. You are on native turf here and the
atmosphere, well-oiled with a fine wine list,
is darkly intimate. It is a great place to sample Palermitan classics such as *pesce spada*
(swordfish) or *pasta con le sarde*.

Shakespeare (☎ 091 749 52 05; Salita Artale 5; meals
€25; ☺ Thu-Tue) Polished wooden floors and
white moulded-plastic chairs are a surprising modern twist in this tiny restaurant behind the Cathedral. The second surprise is
the sumptuous cooking – sea bass in rich
tomato sauce, prawns in filo pastry or fillet
steak with asparagus – that ushers from the
kitchen.

Capricci di Sicilia (☎ 091 32 77 77; Via Instituto Pignatelli 6; meals €20-25; ☺ Tue-Sun) Tucked behind
the colonnade on the left of Piazza Sturco,
this intimate little restaurant takes great
pride in the typical Sicilian dishes it serves
up. Pastas are flavoured with sardines, broccoli and sea urchins, and there is a good
selection of antipasti and Sicilian wine.

Moon Indian Restaurant (☎ 091 338 524 79
01; Via Mariano Stabile 35; meals €15-20; ☺ Mon-Sat)
For all those travellers who have eaten one

too many pizzas or bowls of pasta, Moon Restaurant is a fantastic Indian alternative. The English-speaking proprietors are undertaking a brave venture in the unadventurous Sicilian restaurant scene but they are charming and their sweet little restaurant deserves to succeed.

Trattoria Stella (☎ 091 616 11 36; Via Alloro 104; meals €24; ❨ Tue-Sun, closed 2 weeks Aug) Situated in the courtyard of the old Hotel Patria, hung with fragrant jasmine, the Stella is a popular local restaurant. In summer the tables fill the old courtyard and the food is hearty Sicilian fare.

TOP END

Osteria dei Vespri (☎ 091 617 16 31, Piazza Croce dei Vespri 6; meals €40; ❨ Mon-Sat) A quality tavern serving delectable dishes to rival those of any top European restaurant. In summer sit out under the shadow of the venerable palazzo where Visconti filmed parts of *Il Gattopardo*.

Sant'Andrea (☎ 091 33 49 99; Piazza Sant'Andrea 4; meals €30-35; ❨ Wed-Mon winter, Mon-Sat summer) Tucked in its little piazzetta (where you can sit in summer), the Sant'Andrea remains a romantic hideaway. It has now also earned itself a Michelin star for its delicious food, the ingredients of which come straight from the Vucciria market. It has a unique atmosphere and was the haunt of writer Peter Robb while he researched *Midnight in Sicily*.

La Scuderia (☎ 091 52 03 23; Viale del Fante 9; meals €35-40; ❨ Mon-Sat, closed 2 weeks Aug) The imaginative cuisine in this highly regarded restaurant is complemented by its pretty flower-filled terrace. Despite being 5km outside of Palermo at the foot of Monte Pellegrino, tables here are sought after and reservations are recommended.

Il Firriato (☎ 091 53 02 82; Via G Turrisi Colonna 4; meals €30; ❨ Mon-Sat) Although Il Firriato is the restaurant for Hotel Principe di Villafranca (p756) it is also open to the public and can be accessed from the street. Its limited menu is a sign of the care they take over each dish – the roast lamb is particularly delicious and the desserts are to die for.

Cafés

There are innumerable cafés with outdoor tables where you can linger over breakfast or lunch; the following are just a handful of the better ones.

Antico Caffè Spinnato (☎ 091 58 32 31; Via Principe di Belmonte 107-15) A sophisticated tea salon serving every imaginable Sicilian drink, ice cream and cake. It is the haunt of every professional in town and the homemade hamburgers are too good for words.

Il Baretto (☎ 091 32 96 40; Via XX Settembre 43; salad & sandwiches €4-8; ❨ Mon-Sat) Rich young Palermitans dressed head to toe in designer labels, ladies with serious hairdos and eccentric old men with panamas and shades all congregate here for their light lunch.

Andrea di Martino (☎ 091 58 59 90; Via Mazzini 54; burgers €6-8) A very busy, large café just off Viale della Libertà serving cocktails and fast food. In the evenings its outdoor tables are swamped.

DRINKING

Sicilian nightlife is somewhat sedate and introverted, centred more on restaurants and private parties. Most good bars and dance venues are in the newer part of Palermo although Piazza Olivella and Piazza Magione are both popular places to hang out. In summer, everyone decamps to Mondello Lido by the sea. On week nights almost nothing moves in Palermo.

Kandinsky-Florio (☎ 091 637 56 11; Discesa Tonnara; ❨ 8pm-late) For that special evening out head to this former *tonnara* (tuna processing plant) which is situated on a small harbour at Arenella. This pizzeria/restaurant is a great place to while away the hot summer nights dancing and drinking on its beautiful terrace. However, it is a bit of a hike from the centre of town.

Mi Manda Picone (☎ 091 616 06 60; Via A Paternostro 59; meals €20-25; ❨ 8pm-1am) In a fabulous 13th-century building and with summertime seating in the beautiful Piazza San Francesco, this excellent wine bar serves hearty platters of cheese and *charcuterie*.

I Candelai (☎ 091 32 71 51; Via dei Candelai 65; ❨ Thu-Sat) This converted furniture warehouse features live music, impromptu theatre, art exhibitions and a booming sound system which pumps out mainstream rock. The audience is largely over-sexed, over-styled teenagers and 20-somethings.

I Grilli Giù (☎ 091 58 47 47; Piazza Cavalieri di Malta 11) A gay-friendly cocktail bar (and restaurant) northeast of the Vucciria market where you can sip a cocktail and listen to the latest DJ sounds.

IL TEATRO DEI PUPI

Since the 18th century, puppet shows have entertained workers and children with their chivalric tales of intrigue and derring-do. The tales centred around the legends of Charlemagne's heroic knights, Orlando and Rinaldo, while the extended cast included the fair Angelica, the treacherous Gano di Maqonza and forbidding Saracen warriors. Effectively the soap operas of their day, puppet theatres expounded the deepest sentiments of life – unrequited love, treachery, thirst for justice and the anger and frustration of the oppressed. A puppet could speak volumes where a person could not.

Carved from beech, olive or lemon wood, the puppets stand some 1.5m high although their height and construction depend on their provenance. In Palermo, puppets have wire joints, enabling them to swing swords and behead dragons more effectively. Good puppeteers are judged on the dramatic effect they can create – lots of stamping feet and a gripping running commentary – and on their speed and skill in directing the battle scenes.

ENTERTAINMENT

The daily paper *Il Giornale di Sicilia* has a listing of what's on. The tourist information booths also have programs and listings.

Lo SpasImo (☎ 091 616 14 86; Via Spasimo) This cultural centre in the bombed-out remains of a church (see p754) hosts art exhibitions and live concerts.

Teatro Massimo (☎ 091 605 31 11; Piazza Verdi 9) Ernesto Basile's Art Nouveau masterpiece stages opera, ballet and music concerts. Its programme runs from October to May.

Teatro Politeama Garibaldi (☎ 091 605 32 49; Piazza Ruggero Settimo) The main venue for music and ballet. The season runs from November to May.

Teatro della Verdura (☎ 091 688 41 37; Viale del Fante) A summer-only programme of ballet and music in the lovely gardens of the Villa Castelnuovo.

Cuticchio Mimmo (☎ 091 32 34 00; www.figlidar tecuticchio.com; Via Bara all'Olivella 52; adult/child €5.15/ 2.60; ⏰ 6.30pm Sat & Sun Sep-Jul) A good break for young kids, and the elaborate old puppets will endear themselves to adults, too (see the boxed text, above). In the same street you can visit the **workshop** (Via Bara all'Olivella 48–50) where they're made.

You can also catch performances at the Museo Internazionale delle Marionette (see p754).

SHOPPING

Via Bara all'Olivella is good for arts and crafts. Here you will find the puppet workshop of the Cuticchio family, **Il Laboratorio Teatrale** (Via Bara all'Olivella 48-50).

Palermo is most famous for its elaborate marzipan sweets, the best of which are produced by **Antico Caffè Spinnato** (☎ 091 58 32 31; Via Principe di Belmonte 107-115); for more details, see opposite. To stock up on Sicilian wines check out the huge selection at **Mi Manda Picone** (opposite) or more centrally at **Mangia** (☎ 091 58 76 51; Via Principe di Belmonte 116).

GETTING THERE & AWAY
Air

Falcone-Borsellino airport (PMO; ☎ 091 702 01 11) is at Punta Raisi, around 31km west of Palermo. For 24-hour information on domestic flights, telephone **Alitalia** (airport ☎ 091 601 92 50, office ☎ 091 601 93 33; www.alitalia.com; Viale della Libertà 39). For international flights, call the main airport number.

At any time of year, it's possible to find charter flights between Palermo and major European cities. From the UK **British Midland** (www.flybmi.com) operates flights out of Heathrow and **Ryanair** (www.ryanair.com) flies from Stansted. Germany's **Hapag-Lloyd Express** (www .hlx.com) has flights from German cities into Palermo and the new budget airline carrier, **Evolavia** (www.evolavia.com), does twice-weekly flights from Paris Charles de Gaulle.

It is also the hub airport for regular domestic flights to the islands of Pantelleria and Lampedusa. Local carriers **Alitalia** (www .alitalia.com), **Meridiana** (☎ 199 11 13 33; www.meridi ana.it) and **Air One** (☎ 199 20 70 80; www.flyairone.it) offer a good choice of flights at competitive prices (a one-way fare is usually between €25 and €30).

Boat

The Stazione Marittima (ferry terminal) is located off Via Francesco Crispi. Ferries depart regularly from Molo Vittorio Veneto for Cagliari (Sardinia), Genoa, Livorno and Naples. Buy tickets from any travel agency in town.

Grandi Navi Veloci (☎ 091 58 79 39; www.gnv.it in Italian; Calata Marina d'Italia) Ferries from Palermo to Genoa (€83, 20 hours, one daily) and Livorno (€68, 17 hours, three weekly).

Grimaldi Ferries (in Naples ☎ 081 49 64 44; www .grimaldi-ferries.com; Calata Marina d'Italia) Ferries from Palermo to Tunis (€79, 14 hours, one weekly).

Siremar (☎ 199 12 31 99; www.siremar.it in Italian; Via Francesco Crispi 118) Ferries (€11, 2½ hours, one daily) and summer-only hydrofoils (€16, 1¼ hours, two daily) from Palermo to Ùstica and the Aeolian Islands (Palermo–Lìpari, €32, four hours).

Tirrenia (☎ 199 12 31 99, 091 602 11 11; www.tirrenia .it in Italian; Calata Marinai d'Italia; ☒ 8.30am-12.30pm & 3.30pm-8.45pm Mon-Fri, 3.30pm-8.45pm Sat, 5pm-8.45pm Sun) Services from Palermo to Cagliari on Sardinia (€39, 13 hours, one weekly) and an overnight ferry to Naples (€41, nine hours, one daily). The office is located at the port to the right of the main entrance.

Ustica Lines (☎ 0923 87 38 13; www.usticalines.it in Italian) Summer-only hydrofoil service to the Aeolian Islands (Palermo–Lìpari, €31, four hours, one daily).

Bus

The main intercity bus station is around Via Paolo Balsamo, east of the train station. Sicily's buses are privatised and different routes are serviced by different companies all with their own ticket offices.

Numerous companies besides the ones listed here service points throughout Sicily and most have offices in the Via Paolo Balsamo area. Their addresses and telephone numbers, as well as destinations, are listed all in the *Agenda Turismo*, available from the tourist office.

Azienda Siciliana Trasporti (AST; ☎ 091 680 00 32; www.aziendasicilianatrasporti.it; Via Rosario Gregorio 46) Services to Catania and the southeast including buses to Ragusa (€13.40, four hours, four daily Monday to Saturday, two on Sunday).

Cuffaro (☎ 091 616 15 10; www.cuffaro.it; Via Paolo Balsamo 13) Has daily buses to Agrigento (€7.20, 2½ hours, seven daily Monday to Saturday).

SAIS (☎ 091 617 11 41; Via Paolo Balsamo 20) Runs services to Cefalù (€4.20, one hour, two daily), Catania (€12.50, 2½ hours, 17 daily Monday to Saturday), Enna (€8.70, 1¾ hours, six daily) and Messina (€13.30, 3¼ hours, hourly).

Segesta (☎ 091 616 90 39; www.segesta.it; Via Paolo Balsamo 26) Runs very frequent services to Tràpani (€7.80, two hours, eight daily).

Car & Motorcycle

Palermo is accessible on the A20-E90 toll road from Messina (only partially completed) and from Catania (A19-E932) via Enna (this route is quicker). Tràpani and Marsala are also easily accessible from Palermo by motorway (A29), while Agrigento and Palermo are both linked by the SS121, a good state road through the interior of the island.

Car hire is not cheap in Sicily and it pays to book your rental online before you leave home. In Sicily a week's car hire will cost anything from €300 to €500 so shop around. Often the larger companies offer good deals. All the hire companies are represented at the airport and listed in the tourist information booklet *Agenda Turismo*. **Avis** (at airport ☎ 091 59 16 84, at Via Francesco Crispi 115 ☎ 091 58 69 40; www.avis.com) has a branch in town as does the local firm **Sicily by Car** (☎ 091 58 10 45; www .sbc.it; Via Marino Stabile 6a), which also rents out scooters (€25 per day).

Train

Regular trains leave for Messina (via Milazzo; €10.55 to €14.65, 3½ hours, every 30 minutes), Catania (€11.25 to €14.10, 3½ hours, two daily or change at Messina), Syracuse (€16.90 to €19.91, change at Messina or Catania, six to 10 hours, five daily) and Agrigento (€6.70, 2½ hours, 11 daily), as well as nearby towns such as Cefalù (€3.85, 50 minutes, five daily). There are also intercity trains to Reggio di Calabria, Naples and to Rome. Train timetable information is available in English at the station. In summer the **ticket office** (☎ 091 603 30 88; ☒ 7am-8.45pm) gets very busy, so allow enough time before you depart for purchasing tickets.

GETTING AROUND
To/From the Airport

A half-hourly bus service run by **Prestia e Comandè** (☎ 091 58 04 57) transfers passengers from the airport to the centre of town, dropping people off outside the Politeama Garibaldi theatre and the train station. Tickets for the 45-minute journey cost €5 and are available on the bus. Return journeys to the airport run with similar frequency and pick up at the same points. This is by far the best way to travel to or from the airport.

An hourly train service, the Trinacria Express, also runs from the airport to the central station (€4.50, every 45 minutes). There are plenty of taxis outside the airport and the fare for the same trip is about €50.

Bus

Palermo's orange **city buses** (AMAT; ☎ 091 35 01 11; www.amat.pa.it) are frequent but often overcrowded and slow due to the traffic. Ask at the tourist booths around town for a leaflet detailing the different lines; most stop at the train station. Tickets must be purchased before you get on the bus and are available from tobacconists or the booths at the terminal. They cost €1 and are valid for up to two hours.

There are two small buses – Linea Gialla and Linea Rossa – that operate in the narrow streets of the *centro storico* and can be useful if you are moving between tourist sights and your feet need a rest.

For buses to Monreale (No 389) head to the bus stop at Piazza Indipendenza.

Car & Motorcycle

If you have dealt with Rome or Naples in your own vehicle, Palermo will present no difficulties. Theft of, and from, vehicles is a problem, however, and you are advised to use one of the attended car parks around town if your hotel hasn't got parking space. You will be looking at around €10 to €16 per day.

AROUND PALERMO

Palermo is as exhausting as it is energising, and visitors will welcome a break from the raucous city. Three excellent excursions nearby are the beaches of Mondello, the island of Ùstica and the medieval brilliance of the mosaics at Monreale.

MONDELLO

Set in the lee of Monte Pellegrino is the beach resort of Mondello, full to bursting point with Palermitan teenagers, gaudy beach toys and pushchairs. It's great fun after the intensity of the city. Originally a muddy, malaria-ridden port, Mondello only really became fashionable in the 19th century, when people came to the seaside in their carriages, thus warranting the huge Art Nouveau pier which dominates the seafront and where most of the beaches are private (two sun-loungers and an umbrella is €9). However, there is

a wide swathe of public beach with all the prerequisite pedaloes (standard ones are €9, with slide €12 per hour) and jet skis (€55 per 20 minutes) for hire.

Given its easygoing seaside feel, Mondello is an excellent alternative base for families. The **Addaura Hotel** (☎ 091 684 22 22; www.addaura.it; 4452 Lungomare Cristoforo Colombo; s/d €80/120; P ☒ ☒) and the **Splendid Hotel La Torre** (☎ 091 45 02 22; www.latorre.com; 11 Piano Gallo; s/d €95/124, d with sea view €155; P ☒ ☒) are two good options, both with access to the beach. Or check out **Il Banano** (☎ 091 45 40 11; www.ilbanano.com; Via Stesicoro 3; s/d €37/74; P).

There are numerous seafood restaurants and snack stalls along the avenue, but Mondello's most famous restaurant is the classy **Charleston** (☎ 091 45 01 71; Viale Regina Elena; meals €35-40; ☽ Thu-Tue), located in an Art Nouveau palace with a wide terrace jutting out over the sea. Eating here is a real event so put on your best outfit and make a reservation.

To get to Mondello take bus No 806 from Piazza Sturzo in Palermo.

MONREALE

Inspired by a vision of the Virgin and driven by earthly ambition, William II set about building the **Cattedrale di Monreale** (☎ 091 640 44 13; Piazza del Duomo; ☽ cathedral 8am-6pm, treasury 9.30am-noon & 3.30-5.30pm), located 8km southwest of Palermo. Living in the shadow of his grandfather, Roger II, who was responsible for the cathedral in Cefalù and the Cappella Palatina in Palermo, and vying with his rival Walter of the Mill (the Palermitan archbishop), William was determined to build a cathedral greater than anything that had gone before. The result was the magnificent Monreale, considered the finest example of Norman architecture in Sicily, incorporating Norman, Arab, Byzantine and classical elements.

The interior, completed in 1184, ranks as one of the most impressive creations of the Italian Middle Ages. A catalogue of shimmering mosaics depict a poor man's Bible of Old Testament stories from the Creation of Man to the Assumption, a total of 42 different episodes. What strikes one is the wonderful naivety of the style, a complete contrast to the sophisticated realism of the Cappella Palatina. Here the child-sized scenes depict classic storybook images; Noah's huge ark perches atop the waves, while Christ heals a

SICILY

leper afflicted with wildly exaggerated sores and blotches.

Outside the cathedral is the entrance to the **cloister** (admission €4.50; ☺ 9am-7pm Mon-Sat, 9am-1.30pm Sun), a tranquil courtyard with an overwhelming Oriental flavour. Around the perimeter elegant Romanesque arches are supported by an exquisite array of slender columns alternately decorated with mosaic. Each capital is different and taken together they represent a unique sculptural record of medieval Sicily. The capital of the 19th column on the west aisle depicts William II offering the cathedral to the Madonna.

To reach Monreale (€1, 35 minutes, half-hourly) take bus No 389 from Piazza Indipendenza in Palermo. A word of warning: this bus, which is nearly always crowded, is notorious for pickpockets.

ÙSTICA

Another easy overnight trip from Palermo is to the tiny volcanic island of Ùstica, which became Italy's first marine reserve in 1986. This island (8.7 sq km) is actually the tip of a submerged volcano, and as a result the surrounding waters are a feast of fish and coral, ideal for snorkelling, diving and underwater photography. In July the island hosts the **International Festival of Underwater Activities** which draws divers from around the world. However, the best months to visit are June and September when the wild coastline and dazzling grottoes can be appreciated without the crowds.

The most rewarding dive sites are the **Secca Colombara** to the north of the island and the **Scoglio del Medico** to the west. Note that Zone A of the marine reserve is a protected area. Fishing, diving and even swimming are all forbidden in this area without permission from the Marine Reserve Visitors Centre, which can organise diving excursions into the zone. For landlubbers the rugged coastline can be enjoyed from a series of coastal paths, the most scenic passing through pine woods up to the summit of **Guardia di Mezzo** (248m) before descending to the best part of the coast at **Spalmatore** where you can swim in natural rock pools.

The **Marine Reserve Visitors Centre** (Centro Accoglienza; ☎ 091 844 94 56; Piazza Umberto 1; ☺ 8am-1pm & 4-6pm Mon-Fri, 8am-2pm Sat & Sun Oct-May, 8am-9pm Jun-Sep) is the centre of the village and can advise on room rentals, activities, boat trips and dive centres (most of which are open from April to October).

Sleeping & Eating

There are a total of eight hotels, plus several *affittacamere* (rooms for rent) on Ùstica.

Grotta Azzurra (☎ 091 844 90 48; www.framonho tels.com; Contrada San Ferlicchio; d/ste €126/226; ✖ ☒) Dominating the clifftop above the Grotta Azzurra, all rooms have a romantic terrace overlooking the sea. The rocky beach of the hotel is equipped with a swimming pool and a hydromassage.

Hotel Clelia (☎ 091 844 90 39; www.hotelclelia.it; Via della Vittoria 5; s/d €83/145) A neat little three-star hotel in a central location. Welcoming management and a good restaurant.

Mamma Lia (☎ 091 844 94 07; Via San Giacomo 1; meals €20-25; ☺ Apr-Sep) This is the best of the town centre's numerous eating options; it is very popular so bookings are essential.

Getting There & Around

Siremar (☎ 091 874 93 111; Piazza Capitano Longo 9) operates a year-round car ferry (€11, 2½ hours, one daily) from Palermo. From June to September additional hydrofoils are run (€16, 1¼ minutes, two daily). The office is in the centre of Ùstica.

From June to the end of September you can also pick up the Tràpani–Favignana–Ùstica–Naples hydrofoil, run by **Ùstica Lines** (www.usticalines.it) three days a week. The journey from Naples to Ùstica takes four hours and costs €66 one way.

Orange minibuses make a round trip of the island; they leave from the town hall (€1, half-hourly). Alternatively you could hire a moped at the **Hotel Ariston** (☎ 091 844 90 42; Via della Vittoria) from around €25 per day.

TYRRHENIAN COAST

The stretch of coast between Palermo and Milazzo is an almost uninterrupted line of tourist resorts. Between June and September the well-worn roads carry a steady stream of holidaymakers to and from the coastline's manifold attractions. The best of these include the two massive natural parks of the Madonie and Nébrodi mountains, the sweeping beaches around Capo d'Orlando and Capo Tindari, and Cefalù, a resort town second only to Taormina.

SICILY

PARCO NATURALE REGIONALE DELLE MADONIE

This 40,000-hectare park between Palermo and Cefalù incorporates the Madonie mountain range and some of the highest mountains in Sicily after Mt Etna. The highest peak in the range is Pizzo Carbonara (1979m), and the wild, wooded slopes are home to wolves, wildcats and eagles. Forests cover vast areas of the mountains and include the near-extinct Ancient Nébrodi fir trees that have survived since the last Ice Age. In summer, *agriturismi* (farm stays) arc a good way of exploring the area and its cuisine, which is significantly different from that of the coast. Specialities include roasted lamb and goat, cheeses, grilled mushrooms and aromatic pasta with *sugo* (sauce).

The park is actually an inhabited area, rather than simply a nature reserve – so you can combine walking with visits to some of the more interesting towns like **Castelbuono**, capital of the Madonie and a centre of fine restaurants and excellent pastry shops such as **Fiasconaro** (www.fiasconaro.com; Piazza Margherita 10), where you can buy regional specialities such as manna cake and Turk's head. Other towns worth a visit are **Petralia Sòprana** and **Petralia Sottana**. And in winter, **Piano Battaglia** is the only place in Sicily, other than Etna, where you can ski.

Information

The body responsible for the park is **Ente Parco delle Madonie** (☎ 0921 68 40 11; www.parco dellemadonie.it; Corso Paolo Agliata 16), which has its headquarters in Petralia Sottana and a branch office in Cefalù. It has information about transport and accommodation in the park and also stocks the 1:50,000 *Madonie/ Carta dei Sentieri e del Paesaggio* map, which highlights the park's walking trails.

Sleeping

There are several *rifugi* (mountain huts) in the park and some good *agriturismo* possibilities. Due to the nature of the area most hotels have their own restaurants and many only offer half-board accommodation.

Relais Santa Anastasia (☎ 0921 67 22 33; www .santa-anastasia-relais.it; Contrada Santa Anastasia, Castelbuono; d/ste €200/350; P ≋) A simply gorgeous 12th-century abbey set in a working estate, with beautiful rooms, exquisite attention to detail, fabulous food and wine from the

vineyards. It is 9km from Castelbuono in the direction of Cefalù.

Donalegge al Castellazzo (☎ 0921 56 22 89; www .donalegge.com; 9km along SS120 Polizzi Generosa; B&B/half board per person €60/85; P ✖ ▯ ≋) An unusual farm stay boasting sleek modern furnishings inside an ancient stone farmhouse. Guided walks, horse-riding, mushroom-hunting, olive-picking and cheese-making are just some of the activities you can get stuck into.

Luigi Orestano (☎ /fax 0921 66 21 59; www.rifugio orestano.com/orestano; Località Piano Zucchi; B&B/full board per person €28/45) A large refuge halfway between Piano Battaglia and Cefalù. It is run by the Mogavero family, whose guides can help you with trails and itineraries.

Eating

Nangalarruni (☎ 0921 67 14 28; 5 Via Alberghi delle Con-fraternite, Castelbuono; meals €30; ☽ Thu-Tue) The gastronomic equivalent of the Relais Santa Anastasia, famous throughout Sicily for its mushrooms, pistachio cream, roast meats (including wild boar) and vegetable dishes.

Tenuta Gangivecchio (restaurant ☎ 0921 64 48 04, hotel ☎ 0921 68 91 19; Contrada Gangi Vecchia; half board per person €56.80; ☽ Sep-Jun; P) Another *agriturismo* run by the Tornabene family, which has published a number of highly regarded cookery books. You will find it just outside the town of Gangi.

Trattoria-Pizzeria 'da Salvatore' (☎ 0921 68 01 69; Piazza San Michele 3, Petralia Sòprana; pastas & pizzas €6-8; ☽ Wed-Mon) A tiny trattoria with a wood-burning pizza oven and bags of semola flour propped up around the place. There is no menu at lunchtime, but the generous antipasto of grilled vegetables, pungent cheeses and olives is delicious. Pizzas are an evening-only affair.

Getting There & Away

Getting around the Madonie by bus is a time-consuming business. **SAIS** (☎ 091 616 60 28) runs services from Palermo to Cefalù and most of the mountain towns, including Castelbuono, Geraci Siculi, Gangi, Isnello and Gibilmanna. The most frequent services run to the larger town of Castelbuono (€1.80, 45 minutes, seven daily Monday to Saturday) and the popular Gibilmanna (€1.20, 20 minutes, three daily Monday to Saturday).

If you are planning on travelling in the Madonie it is worth considering car hire for a couple of days from Cefalù or Palermo.

SICILY

CEFALÙ

pop 26,000

This quaint little fishing village sitting in the shadow of La Rocca (Rock) has long been the north coast's favourite holiday spot. Its popularity is reflected in the number of tour buses that hit town daily during summer and fill the streets long into the night. However, despite the crowds, the winding medieval streets, stunning setting, sandy beaches, good nightlife and great shopping continue to lure a steady stream of beautiful people.

From the train station, turn right into Via Moro to reach Via Matteotti and the old town. If you are heading for the beach, turn left and walk along Via Gramsci, which in turn becomes Via V Martoglio.

Information

There are plenty of ATMs in town along Corso Ruggero. It's not a good idea to exchange money at any of the *cambi* (exchange) booths around town as they generally charge higher commissions than banks. You can also change money at the post office, where rates are pretty good.

You can find public telephones dotted throughout town and along the *lungomare* (seafront road).

Ambulance (☎ 0921 42 45 44)

Bacco on Line (☎ 0921 42 17 53; www.baccoonline.it; Corso Ruggero 38; per 30min €2.50) Only one computer. Also a very nice deli and wine shop.

Banca S Angelo (Via Roma; ⏱ 8.30am-1.30pm & 2.45-3.45pm Mon-Fri) Has an exchange office.

First aid (☎ 0921 42 36 23; Via Mazzini 8)

Hospital (☎ 0921 92 01 11; Contrada da Pietra Pietrapollastra) On the main road out of town in the direction of Palermo.

Police station (☎ 0921 92 60 11; Via Roma 15)

Post office (Via Vazzana 2; ⏱ 8.30am-6.30pm Mon-Fri, 8.30am-12.30pm Sat) Right down the *lungomare*.

Presidio Parco delle Madonie (☎ 0921 92 33 27; www .parcodellemadonie.it; Corso Ruggero 116; ⏱ 8.30am-1.30pm & 4.30-7.30pm Mon-Sat) The official office for the Madonie park, with leaflets on walking and driving tours in the park.

Tourist office (☎ 0921 42 10 50; www.cefalu-tour.pa.it; Corso Ruggero 77; ⏱ 8am-7.30pm Mon-Sat, 9am-1.30pm Sun) English-speaking staff with lots of leaflets and good maps.

Sights

Looming over the town, the craggy mass of **La Rocca** appears a suitable home for the race of giants that are said to have been the first inhabitants of Sicily. It was here that the Arabs built their citadel until the Norman conquest in 1063 brought the people down from the mountain to the port below. An enormous staircase, the **Salita Saraceno** winds up through three tiers of city walls in a 30-minute climb, nearly to the summit. From here you have stunning views of the town below, while nearby the ruined 4th-century **Tempio di Diana** provides a quiet and romantic getaway for young lovers.

Cefalù's **Cathedral** (☎ 0921 92 20 21; Piazza del Duomo; ⏱ 8am-noon & 3.30-7pm) is the final jewel in the Arab-Norman crown alongside the Cappella Palatina and Monreale. Inside, a towering figure of Christ Pantocrator is the focal point of the elaborate 12th-century Byzantine mosaics. Framed by the steep cliff, the twin pyramid towers of the Cathedral stand out over the **Piazza del Duomo**, making this an enjoyable place for a morning coffee or evening apéritif (it's crowded in summer).

Off Piazza del Duomo is the private **Museo Mandralisca** (☎ 0921 42 15 47; Via Mandralisca 13; adult/ concession €4.50/2; ⏱ 9am-7pm). The museum has a rather faded collection of Greek ceramics and Arab pottery with the one standout being the *Portrait of an Unknown Man* by Antonello da Messina.

Activities

Cefalù's crescent-shaped beach is one of the most popular along the whole coast. In summer it is packed so be sure to get down early to get a good spot.

You can also arrange boat tours along the coast or further afield to the Aeolian Islands during the summer months. This can be done through **Turismez Viaggi** (☎ 0921 42 12 64; Corso Ruggero 83; tour half day adult/child €20/10, full day to Alicudi incl lunch €50/25).

Sleeping

Cheap accommodation is like gold dust in Cefalù. Between July and August prices are exorbitant and there is no such thing as value for money. Bookings are essential in summer.

Marjolein Mees (☎ 0921 42 33 65; www.sunseasicily .com; 2-person apt per week €375) These apartments are recommended for longer stays. They are located above the town with fab views, but you will need a car to enjoy them. Log onto the website for details of how to reach the different apartments.

Hotel Kalura (☎ 0921 42 13 54; www.hotel-kalura .com; Via Vincenzo Cavallaro 13, Località Caldura; s/d €70/ 130; P ⊠ ⊠) A small resort-style hotel that has been managed by the same family for over 30 years. It is a good choice for families, even if it is fairly commercialised, as there are tons of activities and a large pool. It is situated on a rocky outcrop overlooking its own beach. Try to avoid the rooms at the back which overlook at parking lot.

Cangelosi Rosaria (☎ 0921 42 15 91; Via Umberto I 26; s/d €25/40) A private house, this is the only really cheap option in town and with only four rooms (there are another four nearby) you will have to book in advance. Rooms are clean and simple; there are communal bathrooms and a shared TV room.

La Giara (☎ 0921 42 15 62; fax 0921 42 25 18; Via Veterani 40; s/d €75/94; ⊠) This is one of the only hotels tucked in the tiny cobbled streets of the historic centre within spitting distance of Piazza del Duomo. It is a bit spartan for the price (and the beds are hard!) but it is central and the reception is efficient and friendly. It's better value out of season.

Costa Ponente Internazionale (☎ 0921 42 00 85; Località Contrada Ogliastrillo; person/tent €5.50/4.50; ⊠) This camp site is situated 4km west of the town. It has a tennis court and swimming pool but security is very lax. To reach it take the bus (€1) from the train station heading for La Spisa.

Eating

There are dozens of restaurants along Via Vittorio Emanuele – but the food can be surprisingly mundane and the ubiquitous tourist menus unimaginative.

Ostaria del Duomo (☎ 0921 42 18 38; Via Seminario 5, Piazza del Duomo; meals €20-25; ☺ Tue-Sun) Right on Piazza del Duomo, with outdoor tables facing the Cathedral, you might think that this would be the most overpriced restaurant of them all. But it serves up beautifully prepared fresh food at very reasonable prices.

Trattoria La Botte (☎ 0921 42 43 15; Via Veterani 6; meals €15-20; ☺ Tue-Sun) Despite not having a sexy beachfront location, this eatery just off Corso Ruggero continues to send out excellent antipasti and pasta dishes. The house special, *casarecce alla botte* (pasta with a meat sauce), is a nice change from fish.

La Vecchia Marina (☎ 0921 42 03 88; Via Vittorio Emanuele; tourist menus €18; ☺ Wed-Mon Dec-Oct) Overlooking a cute little fishermen's beach,

this restaurant serves an array of freshly caught beauties, which you can enjoy with a delightful view.

Shopping

Like Taormina, Cefalù has a maze of streets lined with trendy shops. Alongside some interesting jewellery shops specialising in work in coral and turquoise, you can stock up on some fruity Madonie cheeses at **Gatta Gaetano** (☎ 0921 42 31 56; Corso Ruggero 152).

Getting There & Away

Buses run from outside the train station. **SAIS** (☎ 091 617 11 41) buses service Palermo (€4.20, one hour, two daily Monday to Saturday) and Tèrmini Imerese (€1.80, 30 minutes, three daily Monday to Saturday).

The best way of getting to and from Cefalù is by train. The line links Cefalù with Palermo (€3.85, one hour, half-hourly) and virtually every other town on the coast.

You can also get a hydrofoil from Cefalù to the Aeolian Islands from 1 June to 30 September. **Ustica Lines** (www.usticalines.it) hydrofoils depart Cefalù for Alicudi at 8.10am (€14.50, one hour, one daily). During the same period, there are hydrofoils to and from Palermo (€12.60, one hour, one daily). You can buy tickets at **Pietro Barbaro** (☎ 0921 42 15 95; Corso Ruggero 82).

MILAZZO
pop 32,100

It's hardly Sicily's prettiest town, and Milazzo's eastern perimeter is hemmed in with industrial development and oil refineries that can make even the most determined visitor run for the nearest hydrofoil. Indeed, the prime reason for setting foot in this town is to get off the main island and head for the Aeolian archipelago. But away from the refinery and busy dock, Milazzo's Spanish quarter is actually very pretty and the isthmus which juts out to the north is an area of great natural beauty.

Information

All the ferry-company offices are directly opposite the port, along Via dei Mille.

Tabacchi Edicola (Via dei Mille) A better source of Aeolian maps and books than the tourist office is this newsagent.

Tourist office (☎ 090 922 28 65; Piazza C Duilio 10; ☺ 8am-2pm & 4-7pm Mon-Fri, 8am-2pm Sat) Behind Via Crispi but has very limited information.

Sights & Activities

If you have time on your hands in Milazzo head straight for the enormous **Spanish Castle** (☎ 090 922 12 91; Via Impallomeni; admission free; ☽ 10am-noon & 3-5pm Tue-Sun Sep-May, 10am-noon & 5-7pm Tue-Sun Jun-Aug); it has guided tours on the hour. It is a lovely site to clamber around, full of flowers and crumbling structures with great views of the Aeolians. To reach the castle climb the **Salita Castello** which rises up through the atmospheric Spanish quarter.

There is good swimming to be had at **Capo Milazzo** (6km north of the city) at the tip of the spit of land that stretches out towards the Aeolian Islands, but the most accessible pebble beach is at the end of Via Colombo.

Sleeping & Eating

Petit Hotel (☎ 090 928 67 84; www.petithotel.it; Via dei Mille; s/d €70/100; P ⊠ ☒) The hotel of choice in Milazzo, right opposite the hydrofoil dock. The hotel serves up a delicious homemade breakfast and organic food. You can also leave luggage and your car here (for €10 per day) while you visit the islands.

Hotel Garibaldi (☎ 090 924 01 89; www.hotelgaribaldi.net; Via Lungomare Garibaldi 160; s/d €80/120; P ☒) Not as convenient as the Petit Hotel, and it's better if you have a car. Still the Garibaldi, situated on the edge of the historic town, has more character and very swish rooms. It also has its own private beach.

Hotel Capitol (☎ 090 928 32 89; Via Giorgio Rizzo 91; s/d €34/60; ☒) Cheap, clean and simple, and close to the hydrofoil dock. You can park at Eolie Garage next door. Credit cards are not accepted.

Salamone a Mare (☎ 090 928 12 33; Strada Panoramica; meals €25; ☽ Tue-Sun) A wonderful seafood restaurant, north along the isthmus. It is wonderfully sited right on the cliff edge and its terrace juts out over the water, giving it fantastic views of the Aeolians.

Al Pescatore (☎ 090 928 65 95; Via Marina Garibaldi 176; meals €20; ☽ Wed-Mon) Good seafood dishes and swift service. The staff are efficient and used to dealing with people about to catch boats.

Also recommended is the popular pizzeria **Il Covo del Pirata** (☎ 090 928 44 37; Via San Francesco 1; pizzas €6-8; ☽ Thu-Tue).

Getting There & Away

Milazzo is easy to reach by bus or train from Palermo and Messina. **Giuntabus** (☎ 090 67 37 82) runs a service from Messina (€3.40, 50 minutes, half-hourly). All intercity buses run from Piazza della Repubblica along the quayside. Trains are more frequent, with two departures and arrivals hourly for both Palermo (€9.20, 2½ to three hours) and Messina (€2.65, 45 minutes). The train station is very far away on Piazza Marconi, connected to the port by AST buses (€0.85, half-hourly).

If you fancy leaving your car here while you island-hop, you can park long term at the **Eolie Garage** (Via Giorgio Rizzo; per day €10).

See below for details of travel to and from the Aeolian Islands.

AEOLIAN ISLANDS

Stunning cobalt sea, windswept mountains and steaming volcanoes go some way to explaining why the Aeolians (Isole Eolie) are the European Holy Grail for island-lovers. Part of a huge volcanic ridge stretching 200km north from the coast of Sicily near Milazzo, the seven islands of Lìpari, Vulcano, Salina, Panarea, Stromboli, Alicudi and Filicudi represent the very pinnacle of this 3000m-high outcrop that was formed a million years ago. Collectively, the islands exhibit a unique range of volcanic characteristics, which earnt them a place on Unesco's World Heritage list in 2000. These days their natural beauty and extraordinary variety of landscapes attract nature-lovers and modern hedonists, including stars such as Robert de Niro and Madonna. The best time to come is in May and early June or late September and October to avoid the heaving summer crowds.

Getting There & Away

In summer, ferries and hydrofoils leave regularly from Milazzo and Messina. In Milazzo, all the ticket offices are along Via dei Mille, at the port, and in Messina the office is halfway up Via Vittorio Emanuele II. Hydrofoils are twice as frequent and faster than the ferries although they're more expensive. Peak season is from June to September with winter services much reduced and sometimes cancelled due to heavy seas. All of the following prices are one-way high-season fares.

FERRY

Siremar runs car ferries from Milazzo to the islands (€7.30, two hours, small cars €24.40,

CONCRETE CATASTROPHE

Despite its catalogue of World Heritage sites – 40 sites in total – Italy may become the first country to have a site struck off the UN's prestigious list. The Aeolian archipelago, one of the few remaining natural wildernesses left in Italy, is in danger of falling into the clutches of developers as plans for eight new hotels gained approval in October 2004.

The controversial plans are part of a €50 million development project aimed at increasing the tourism capacity of the islands, providing extra beds for some of the 200,000 visitors that land on the islands every summer. Lìpari would be worst affected with seven new hotels, the eighth being planned for Vulcano.

Understandably, the plans have met with fierce opposition, from environmentalists right up to the Italian culture minister, Giuliano Urbani, who has promised to put an end to this 'Sicilian scheming'. Hopefully, he will be successful and the wild beauty of the Aeolian archipelago will be preserved.

five daily), but they are slower and less regular. **NGI Traghetti** (☎ 090 928 40 91; Via dei Mille 26, Milazzo) also runs a thrice-daily car ferry for the same rates.

HYDROFOIL

Both Ustica Lines and Siremar run hydrofoils from Milazzo to Lìpari (€11.30, 40 minutes), and then on to the other islands. From 1 June to 30 September hydrofoils depart almost hourly (from around 7am to 8pm) to Lìpari, and also stop at Vulcano (€11.60, 45 minutes) and either Santa Marina or Rinella (€12.80, 1½ to two hours) on Salina. Services to the other islands are less frequent unless you change boats in Lìpari; there are a combined nine departures daily for Panarea (€14.40, two hours) and Stromboli (€17.30, 2½ hours). There are four daily departures for Alicudi (€21.30, three hours) and Filicudi (€17.50, two hours 20 minutes).

Ustica Lines hydrofoils also connect the islands with Messina (€16.50, 1½ hours from Lìpari, three daily) and Reggio di Calabria (€17.50, two hours from Lìpari, five daily), as well as Naples (€75, 5½ hours, one daily,

summer only) and Palermo (€32, four hours, one daily, summer only).

Getting Around
AIR

For some real Aeolian style book yourself an excursion around the islands in your very own helicopter with **Air Panarea** (☎ 090 983 44 28; www.airpanarea.com; Via Iditella, Panarea). Tours over Stromboli costs €140 per person for a group of five.

BOAT

Regular hydrofoil and ferry services operate between the islands. On Lìpari nearly all hydrofoil and ferry services arrive at and depart from Marina Lunga. Siremar and Ustica Lines have ticket offices in a cabin opposite the port. Full timetable information is available at all offices. On the other islands, ticket offices are at or close to the docks.

The following table lists destinations, fares and approximate sailing times from Lìpari.

Destination	Cost (€) (hydrofoil/ferry)	Duration (hydrofoil/ferry)
Alicudi	14.10/8.95	2/3¾hr
Filicudi	11.30/6.40	1½/2¾hr
Panarea	6.90/3.85	50min/2hr
Salina (Rinella)	6.10/3.40	45min/1½hr
Salina (Santa Marina)	5.30/3	35/45min
Stromboli	13.30/7.70	1/3¾hr
Vulcano	2.50/1.30	10/25min

CAR & MOPED

If you're visiting the islands for a couple of days it's not worth the expense of taking a car. You can garage it in Milazzo for €10 per day (see opposite). However, for longer trips it works out cheaper than hiring. You can take cars on to Lìpari, Vulcano and Salina, all of which have scooter- and car-hire outlets.

LÌPARI
pop 10,500 / elev 602m

Difficult as it is to imagine amid the sandals and sunshades, Lìpari has actually been inhabited for 6000 years, having been settled in the 4th millennium BC by Sicily's first known inhabitants, the Stentillenians. Why, you may wonder, did they hike all the way out here instead of remaining on the main island? The answer is Lìpari's obsidian, a glassy volcanic rock that became the basis

SICILY

of the island's economy. Commerce also attracted the Greeks, who used the islands as ports on the east–west trade route between the Aegean and Tyrrhenian Seas. They built their acropolis on the promontory where you can still root around the Neolithic and classical ruins.

The soaring castle that surrounds the ruins only came later when the harbour was the regular victim of pirates, like Barbarossa (or Redbeard) who was eager to get his hands on Lìpari's lucrative obsidian and pumice mines.

At the centre of the archipelago, Lìpari, well-served with a good variety of hotels and restaurants, remains the best-equipped base for island-hopping.

Orientation

Lìpari's two harbours, Marina Lunga and Marina Corta, are on either side of the cliff-top citadel, surrounded by 16th-century walls. The town centre extends between them. The main street, Corso Vittorio Emanuele, runs roughly north–south to the west of the castle. From Marina Corta, walk across the piazza to Via Garibaldi; follow the 'centro' signs for Corso Vittorio Emanuele.

Information

The *farmacie di turno*, a timetable showing which pharmacy is on duty each night, is displayed in the window of each pharmacy.

Corso Vittorio Emanuele is lined with ATMs. The other islands do not have such good facilities so it is best to sort out your finances here before moving on. Outside of banking hours you can change cash at the post office and travel agencies.

Ambulance (☎ 090 988 52 67)

Farmacia Internazionale (☎ 090 981 15 83; Corso Vittorio Emanuele 128; ☽ 9am-1pm & 5-9pm Mon-Fri) Pharmacy.

Internet point (☎ 090 981 34 94; Via Vittorio Emanuele 53; per hr from €5; ☽ 10.30am-1.30pm & 6.30-11.30pm)

Net C@fe (090 981 35 27; Via Garibaldi 61; per hr from €5; ☽ 10am-late) Open all day, this café serves snacks and regularly screens football matches.

Ospedale Civile di Lìpari Centralino (☎ 090 988 51 11; Via Sant'Anna) Operates a first-aid service.

Police station (☎ 090 981 13 33; Via G Marconi)

Post office (Corso Vittorio Emanuele 207; ☽ 8.30am-6.30pm Mon-Fri, 8.30am-1.20pm Sat)

Siremar ticket office (Marina Lunga; per bag per hr €3; ☽ 8am- 8pm) Left-luggage facilities.

Tourist office (☎ 090 988 00 95; www.aasteolie.info; Corso Vittorio Emanuele 202; ☽ 8.30am-1.30pm & 4.30-8pm Mon-Fri year-round, 8.30am-1.30pm Sat & Sun Jul-Aug) This office provides information for all the islands and can assist you with finding accommodation. Pick up a free copy of *Ospitalità in blu*, which contains details of accommodation and services on all the islands. Off peak the office is randomly closed in the afternoon.

Sights

After the mercenary Barbarossa rampaged through the town in 1544 murdering most of the citizens, enslaving the women and desecrating the relics of St Bartholomew, the Spaniards rebuilt and fortified Lìpari with the **citadel** (☽ 9am-7pm). Within these fortifications you will find the fabulous **Museo Archeologico Eoliano** (☎ 090 988 01 74; Castello di Lìpari; admission €4.50; ☽ 9am-1.30pm & 3-6pm Mon-Sat), one of the very best museums in Sicily, tracing the volcanic and human history of the islands. It is divided into three sections: an archaeological section devoted to artefacts from the Neolithic and Bronze Ages to the Roman era; a classical section with finds from Lìpari's necropolis (including the most complete collection of sensational miniature Greek theatrical masks in the world); and a section on finds from the other islands.

Nearby is the **Chiesa di San Bartolo** (☽ 9am-noon & 4-7pm), built in 1654 to replace the Norman church that Barbarossa destroyed. The only part of the original structure to survive the raids was the 12th-century Benedictine **cloisters** (admission €1; ☽ 9am-1pm & 4-7pm).

The southern part of the citadel contains viewable **archaeological ruins** dating from the Neolithic period to the Roman era, which have given archaeologists valuable clues to the prehistoric civilisations that flourished in the Mediterranean.

Activities

Sunbathers and swimmers head for Canneto, a few kilometres north of Lìpari town, to bask on the pebbly **Spiaggia Bianca** (White Beach). Further north are the **pumice mines** of Pomiciazzo and Porticello, where there is another beach, **Spiaggia della Papesca**, dusted white by the fine pumice dust that gives the sea its limpid turquoise colour.

Given the crystal-clear waters, snorkelling and scuba diving are also incredibly popular. For details of courses or to rent equipment, contact **Diving Center La Gorgonia** (☎ 090 981

20 60; www.lagorgoniadiving.it; Salita San Giuseppe, Marina Corta; dive/beginners courses €30/60, mask & fin rental per day €9).

You can rent out boats from **Roberto Foti** (☎ 090 981 23 52; www.robertofoti.it; Via F Crispi; 3-/6-seat motorised rubber dinghy per day €70/120), which is a great way to view the islands and have a taste of the jet-set lifestyle.

Tours
Gruppo di Navigazione (☎ 090 982 22 37; www.navi gazioniregina.com; Via Garibaldi; ❧ Mar-Oct) conducts boat tours including one to Stromboli by night (€25) to see the Sciara del Fuoco (Trail of Fire; p774).

Sleeping
Lìpari provides plenty of options for a comfortable stay. However, prices soar in summer (increasing on average by 30%). In peak season, if all else fails, the staff at the tourist office will billet new arrivals in private homes on the island. Don't dismiss offers by touts when you arrive, as they usually have decent rooms in private houses. To rent an apartment, contact the tourist office for a list of establishments.

Prices for the high and low seasons are listed below as there is such a variation.

BUDGET
Diana Brown (☎ 090 981 25 84; www.dianabrown.it; Vico Himera 3; d low/high season €40/100; ❂) Diana Brown's spotless rooms are in great demand due to Diana's friendly, hands-on management and the services on offer, including washing, a book exchange and small kitchenettes. The 1st-floor rooms are lighter and more cheerful.

Casa Vittorio (☎ 090 981 15 23; www.eolnet.it/casa vittorio; Vico Sparviero 15; d low/high season €36/70) These comfortable rooms, some of which sleep up to five people, are off Via Garibaldi near Marina Corta. You'll find the owner (unless he finds you first) at Via Garibaldi 78. There is a communal kitchen and two terraces with views.

Baia Unci (☎ /fax 090 981 19 09; www.campeggita lia.it/sicilia/baiaunci; Marina Garibaldi 2, Località Canneto; person/tent high season €10/12; ❧ 15 Mar–15 Oct) The island's only camp site is at Canneto, about 2km out of Lìpari town. It is well organised and tent sites are beneath shady eucalyptus trees. There is a self-service restaurant. In August you'll need to reserve.

MIDRANGE
Giardino sul Mare (☎ 090 981 10 04; www.netnet .it/conti; Via Maddalena 65; half board per person low/high season €70/120; ❧ Mar-Nov; ❂ ❂) A small hotel with 1970s décor – cane furniture and the like. However, the poolside terrace, situated on a cliff edge, is one of the best on the island. It is family run and has an easy-going atmosphere.

Casajanca (☎ 090 988 02 22; www.casajanca.it; Marina Garibaldi 115, Località Canneto; d low/high season €102/180; ❂) Once the home of Aeolian poet Ruccio Carbone, this cute hotel has only 10 rooms. Silvia and Massimo have taken great care to decorate it with authentic antiques and the dappled courtyard is a relaxing place to enjoy breakfast.

Villa Diana (☎ 090 981 14 03; www.isole-eolie.com; 1 Via Tufo; d low/high season €70/130; ❂) An Aeolian house converted by the Swiss artist Edwin Hunziker in the 1950s into this bohemian-spirited hotel. It stands above Lìpari town in a garden of citrus trees and olives and there are panoramic views from its terrace.

Also recommended is **Enzo Il Negro** (☎ /fax 090 981 31 63; www.enzoilnegro.altervista.org; Via Garibaldi 29; d low/high season €92/123; ❂).

TOP END
Villa Meligunis (☎ 090 981 24 26; www.villamelingunis .it; Via Marte 7; d low/high season €120/290; ❂) A converted 18th-century villa, the Meligunis is Lìpari's top hotel, offering luxurious accommodation, extensive facilities and a scenic rooftop terrace. Diving and watersports can also be arranged at reception.

Eating
Fish abound in the waters of the archipelago and include tuna, mullet, cuttlefish and sole, all of which end up on restaurant tables at the end of the day. Try *pasta all'eoliana*, a simple blend of the island's excellent capers with olive oil and basil. In summer, reservations are recommended .

Filippino (☎ 090 981 10 02; Piazza Municipio; meals €40-50; ❧ daily Apr-Sep, Tue-Sun Oct-Mar) Occupying a big chunk of Piazza Municipio, Filippino remains Lìpari's most classy restaurant. The menu is based on old-fashioned Sicilian cooking and is full of surprising tastes – veal in sweet Malvasia wine or bass with salsa. Dress appropriately and reserve a table.

Kasbah (☎ 090 981 10 75; Via Maurolico 25; pizzas €8, meals €25-30; ❧ 7pm-3am Mar-Oct) The Kasbah has a sleek, new look and enlarged dining area. White banquettes line the walls and a vine-covered garden twinkles out back. The food is as good as ever – delicious pizzas and delicacies such as linguine with *bottarga* (dried pressed fish roe).

La Nassa (☎ 090 981 13 19; Via G Franza; meals €20-25; ☑ daily Apr-Oct, Tue-Sun Nov-Mar) Genuine Aeolian cuisine is served in this family-run trattoria away from the main drag. Favourites include the Aeolian sausages, which are a speciality of the house.

La Cambusa (☎ 349 476 60 61; Via Garibaldi 72; meals €15) A tiny one-room restaurant with tasty, unpretentious cooking. Although it specialises in fish it also does a mean pasta and lasagne.

La Piazzetta (☎ 090 981 25 22; pizzas €4-7; ☑ 7-11pm Sep-Jun) A popular pizzeria restaurant that has served the likes of Audrey Hepburn. Great location and lively atmosphere. It's off Corso Vittorio Emanuele, behind Pasticceria Subba.

People with access to a kitchen can shop for supplies at the **SISA supermarket** (Corso Vittorio Emanuele).

Drinking

If you fancy a late-night drink or want to be in the right place for crowd-gazing during *passeggiata* (evening stroll), **Bar La Precchia** (☎ 090 981 13 03; Corso Vittorio Emanuele 191) is a local favourite. It has an enormous menu of drinks from *caffè frappé* and fruit milkshakes to cocktails and wine. In summer it's open until 3am and often has live music.

Shopping

You simply can't leave these islands without a small pot of capers and a bottle of sweet Malvasia wine (see the boxed text, p772). You can get both plus lots of other delicious goodies at **F.lli Laise** (☎ 090 981 27 31; Corso Vittorio Emanuele 118).

Getting There & Around

See p766 for ferry and hydrofoil details.

Autobus Urso Guglielmo (☎ 090 981 12 62, 090 981 10 26; Via Cappuccini 9) runs a frequent service around the island departing from Marina Lunga. There are departures for Canneto (€1.30, nine daily), Acquacalda, Porticello and Quattrocchi. If you plan on using the bus a lot buy a booklet of 10 tickets (€9.80) which you can use as and when you like.

The company also offers tours of the island. These trips (€3.70, one hour) depart at 9.30am, 11.30am and 5pm daily from 1 July to 30 September.

Roberto Foti (☎ 090 981 23 52; Via F Crispi 31) rents out scooters (low/high season €15/30 per day) and cars (Fiat Panda/Uno €50/55 per 24 hours).

VULCANO

pop 720 / elev 500m

Vulcano is the least attractive of the Aeolian Islands, with the cone of Fossa di Vulcano (or Gran Cratere, 'Large Crater') rising like a malodorous carbuncle above the tiny port. Still, the island is worshipped by Italians for its therapeutic mud baths and hot springs. Its weird steaming landscape, oozing psychedelic minerals, black beaches and a noticeable absence of greenery make the island an interesting day trip once you overcome the vile smell of sulphurous gases. Mind you, if you're allergic to sulphur, this island may well play havoc with your sinuses and digestion.

Orientation

Boats dock at Porto di Levante. To the right, as you face the island, is the small Vulcanello peninsula. To reach the mud baths walk right along the *lungomare* and at the end, hidden behind a small hillock, are the pools. All facilities are concentrated between Porto di Levante and Porto di Ponente, where you will find the Spiaggia Sabbia Nera (Black Sand Beach).

Information

Emergency doctor (☎ 090 985 22 20; Via Lentia)
Thermessa Agency (☎ 090 985 22 30; Via Provinciale) Changes money and sells tickets for Ustica Lines hydrofoils.
Tourist office (☎ 090 985 20 28; Via Provinciale 41; ☑ 8am-2pm Jun-Oct) A dome-like building on the main street, 50m back from the dock. It provides information on rented rooms.

Activities

The top attraction on Vulcano is the trek up the **Fossa di Vulcano** (391m). Follow the signs south along Via Provinciale out of town. It's about an hour's demanding scramble to the lowest point of the crater's edge (290m), but once you reach the top the sight of the steaming crater encrusted with red and yellow crystals is reward enough. The bottom of the crater is clearly visible from the rim and you can take a steep trail down to the bottom for a walk along the crater floor. If you don't feel like such a daredevil, walk clockwise around the crest for stunning 360-degree views of all the islands lined up to the north. The walk is best done early in the day and you will need to wear sturdy boots, take plenty to drink and a hat is a must. If you want to hire a guide, contact the **Gruppo Nazionale Vulcanologia** (☎ 090 985 25 28) or **Gruppo Trekking Vulcano** (☎ 339 418 58 75). The latter has a stand by the restaurant Da Maurizio (for details, see right).

Mud-bath enthusiasts should head for the **Laghetto di Fanghi** (admission €1.50), a large mud pit of thick, smelly, sulphurous gloop that has long been considered an excellent treatment for arthritis, rheumatism and skin disorders. Whatever you do, don't wear your best bathing costume (you'll never get the smell out) or any silver jewellery (it will tarnish). Once you've had enough you can hop into the water at the adjacent beach where acquacalda (hot springs) create a natural Jacuzzi effect.

On the far side of the peninsula from Porto di Levante at Porto di Ponente is the **Spiaggia Sabbia Nera** (Black Sand Beach), curving around a very pretty bay now mildly commercialised. It is one of the few sandy beaches in the archipelago. A similar, quieter beach, **Spiaggia dell'Asina** (Donkey Beach), can be found on the island's southern side near Gelso.

Tours

Pino & Giuseppe (☎ 090 985 24 19; Via Comunale Levante), in front of the tobacconist, and **Gente di Mare** (☎ 333 457 74 46; Via Comunale Levante) organise boat trips around the island (€13 per person).

The proprietor of **Gioielli del Mare** (☎ 090 985 21 70; Porto di Levante) organises bus tours (€13 per person, about two hours) around the island in his red transit Ford. Make a booking and wait for a group of 10 people to form.

Sleeping

Vulcano is not a great place to stay for any extended period of time; the town has little character, the hotels are expensive and the mud baths really smell. If you do decide to stay, the best hotels are situated around Spiaggia Sabbia Nera.

Les Sables Noirs (☎ 090 985 24 54; www.framon-hotels.com; Porto di Ponente; B&B per person low/high season €65/110; ☺ Apr-Oct; ☒ ☒) The best hotel on the island, with a beachfront location. The large pool is surrounded by gardens and palms, creating a small oasis in Vulcano's unforgiving landscape.

Hotel Arcipelago (☎ 090 985 20 02; www.hotel arcipelago.it; s/d €85/130; ☺ Apr-Sep; ☒ ☒) One of the smaller big hotels, 2km from the village on Vulcanello. Bright breezy rooms have views over the gardens and sea.

Hotel Torre (☎ /fax 090 985 23 42; www.portaledelle eolie.it/hoteltorre; Via Favaloro 1; d low/high season €38/75; ☒) Very good value for Vulcano, and the rooms are large and bright. They also come with a kitchen and a terrace. Its proximity to the beach at Laghetto di Fanghi may prove too potent for some.

Eating

Vulcano has a few overpriced restaurants where you eat some very average food. The following are some of the few exceptions.

Da Maurizio (☎ 090 985 24 26; Via Porto di Levante; tourist menus €15.50, mains €13-20; ☺ Apr-Oct) This is a pleasant restaurant in an attractive garden setting. It's very pricey but is considered to be the best restaurant on the island. Try the excellent cuttlefish pasta.

Trattoria Maniaci Pina (☎ 090 985 22 42; Gelso; meals €20-25; ☺ Apr-Oct) Right on the south side of the island, this down-to-earth trattoria serves ubiquitous Sicilian dishes and has the best atmosphere of any restaurant on the island.

Cantine Stevenson (☎ 090 985 32 47; Porto Levante; pizzas €6-8) Scotsman James Stevenson bought most of Vulcano in the 19th century and planted the first vineyards. His cellars are now this neat little wine bar and restaurant.

Getting There & Around

Vulcano is an intermediate stop between Milazzo and Lìpari and a good number of vessels go both ways throughout the day. See p766 for more details.

Scooters, bikes and small motorised cars can be rented from **Da Paolo** (☎ 090 985 21 12) or **Sprint** (☎ 090 985 22 08) at the intersection of Via Provinciale and Via Porto Levante. Scooters cost around €25 per day although this varies with season and demand.

You can hire boats at **Centro Nautico Baia di Levante** (☎ 090 982 21 97, 0339 337 27 95). A four-/

eight-person zodiac costs €60/80 for the whole day. You will find it in a shed on the beach to the left of the hydrofoil dock.

SALINA

pop 2300 / elev 962m

In stark contrast to Vulcano's barren landscape, Salina's twin craters of Monte dei Porri and Monte Fossa delle Felci are lushly wooded – a result of the numerous freshwater springs on the island. Wildflowers, thick yellow gorse bushes and serried ranks of vines carpet the hillsides in vibrant colours and cool greens while its high coastal cliffs plunge into dramatic beaches. The famous Aeolian capers grow plentifully here, as do the grapes used to make Malvasia wine.

Orientation

Most boats dock at Santa Marina Salina. The main road, Via Risorgimento, runs parallel to the lungomare and is filled with small boutiques. Accommodation can be found in Salina's three main towns: Santa Marina Salina, Malfa and Rinella, a fishing hamlet on the southern coast.

Information

In summer, tourist booths operate in all three towns; the rest of the year, contact the Lìpari office. You will find public phones at the island's ports.

Banco Antoveneta Santa Marina (Via Lungomare Notar Giuffre; ☑ 8.40am-1.20pm Mon-Sat); Malfa (Via Provinciale 2) The Santa Marina branch has an ATM and is to the right along the lungomare.

Emergency doctor (☎ 090 984 40 05)
Police (☎ 090 984 30 19)
Post office (☎ 090 984 30 28; Via Risorgimento, Santa Marina Salina) Can also change money.

Sights & Activities

If you are feeling energetic, you could climb the **Fossa delle Felci** (962m) and visit the nature reserve. At Valdichiesa, in the valley that separates Salina's two volcanoes, is the **Santuario della Madonna del Terzito** (Sanctuary of the Madonna of Terzito), which is a place of pilgrimage, particularly around the Feast of the Assumption on 15 August. From the church, you can follow the track (signposted) all the way to the peak (about two hours). Once you've reached the top (the last 100m are particularly tough), you have unparalleled views of the entire archipelago. You can get to the sanctuary by taking a bus from Santa Marina Salina to Rinella or Leni, and asking the driver to let you off.

You can also make the climb from **Lingua**, walking through some of the acres of vineyards that cover the island. **Rinella**, on the south side of the island, is a popular spot for spear-gun fishing. For information, contact the tourist booths. Boats are available for hire from June to August at **Nautica Levante** (☎ 090 984 30 83; Via Risorgimento, Santa Marina Salina).

Don't miss a trip to the beach at **Pollara**, one of the locations in the film Il Postino. The climb down is a bit tricky but the beach itself, with its backdrop of volcanic cliffs, is absolutely unbeatable (visit in the afternoon as the beach is in shadow in the morning).

A TASTE OF HONEY

Salina's fortune is in its freshwater springs. The islanders have put them to good use in producing their own brand of wine, Malvasia. It is thought that the grapes were brought to the islands by the Greeks in 588 BC, and certainly the name is derived from Monenvasìa, the name of a Greek city.

Although the local industry has suffered greatly due to competition from the Sicilian mainland, a few cultivators still practise traditional techniques using the Malvasia grape and the now rare red Corinthian grape. The harvest generally occurs in the second week of September when the grapes are picked and laid out to dry on woven cane mats. The drying process is crucial; the grapes must dry out enough to concentrate the sweet flavour but not too much, which would result in caramelisation.

The result is a dark golden or light amber wine that tastes, some say, of honey. It is usually drunk in very small glasses and goes well with cheese, sweet biscuits and almond pastries.

To experience a working vineyard you can stay at the luxurious **Capo Faro** (☎ 090 984 43 30; www.capofaro.com; Via Faro 3, Malfa; d low/high season €190/400; ⬚ ⬚), a small, chic resort of Aeolian-style cottages on the 13-acre Tasca d'Almerita vineyard.

Tours

Eolie Adventure (☎ 090 984 41 34, 333 469 95 30; www.eolieadventure.com) organises excellent nature hikes on Salina, as well as the other islands. Hikes cost €20 per person per day; a three-day hike to Filicudi including tent and sleeping bag costs €75. The tour company has a table at Santa Marina Salina harbour (where the hydrofoils dock) during summer where they take bookings.

Sleeping

Salina remains relatively undisturbed by mass tourism and offers some gorgeous upmarket accommodation in a few small hotels.

Hotel Signum (☎ 090 984 42 22; www.hotelsignum.it; Via Scalo 15, Malfa; d low/high season €100/190; ☒ ☒) Surrounded by vineyards, the Signum is actually a series of interlinking Aeolian houses, clustered around the stunning swimming pool with its invisible edge and views straight out to smoking Stromboli. The interior is decorated with stylish and valuable antiques.

Pensione Mamma Santina (☎ 090 984 30 54; www.mammasantina.it; Via Sanità 40, Santa Marina; d low/high season €90/180; ☒ ☒) A family atmosphere, colourful rooms with typically tiled floors and a restaurant featured in *Cucina Italiana* all make Mamma Santina another favourite. Head for Via Risorgimento (the narrow main street) and walk north for a few hundred metres.

Hotel L'Ariana (☎ 090 980 90 75; www.hotelariana.it; Via Rotabile 11; d half board per person low/high season €85/170) A patrician villa overlooking the sea at Rinella. The huge terrace is the place to be for sundowners as the sun sets on this side of the island. It also has good deals on half/full board in summer.

Campeggio Tre Pini (☎ 090 980 91 55; www.trepini.com; Frazione Rinella-Leni; person/tent €8/8; ☺ Mar-Oct) This camp site has terraced sites overlooking the sea. Reserve in July and August as it is popular. There is also a market, bar and restaurant although most people decamp to nearby Hotel L'Ariana for sundowners.

Eating

The majority of restaurants on Salina are located in hotels (which you can eat in if you make a reservation). The following are two notable exceptions.

Portobello (☎ 090 984 31 25; Via Bianchi 1, Santa Marina Salina; meals €26; ☺ Tue-Sat) Without doubt the best restaurant in town, where you can tuck into the daily catch for a reasonable price. The terrace looks out over the sea.

A Cannata (☎ /fax 090 984 31 61; www.netnet.it /salina/cannata; Via Umberto 1; meals €25-30) Situated on a wild, green bluff A Cannata is an excellent restaurant overlooking an unruly garden shaded by pines; there are also 10 rooms (doubles €110). You'd be advised to book in advance in summer.

Getting There & Around

Hydrofoils and ferries service Santa Marina Salina and Rinella from Lìpari. You'll find ticket offices in both places.

Regular **Citis** (☎ 090 984 41 50) buses run from Santa Marina Salina to Lingua, Malfa, Rinella, Pollara, Valdichiesa and Leni (€1.80). Timetables are posted at the ports.

Motorcycles and scooters (€24 per day) can be hired from **Antonio Bongiorno** (☎ 090 984 34 09; Via Risorgimento 240, Santa Marina Salina). If you feel like hiring a scooter in Rinella (and given the steepness of the road from here to the rest of the island, it's a good idea), check out **Eolian Service** (☎ 090 980 92 03) at the port, where you can hire a scooter from €18 per day.

PANAREA

pop 320 / elev 421m

Tiny Panarea is just 3km long and 2km wide and feels like a Greek island with its adobe-style whitewashed houses. Exclusive and expensive, it is the smallest and most fashionable of the Aeolians, attracting the international jet set for a little taste of *dolce far niente* (sweet nothing). In the summer luxury yachts fill the tiny harbour while flocks of day-trippers dock at San Pietro, where you will find most of the expensive accommodation.

Sights & Activities

Originally a bigger island, Panarea is now a mini archipelago of its own – the original volcano is long gone. The other five islets of Basiluzzo, Dàttilo, Lisca Bianca, Bottaro and Lisca Nera are located off the eastern shore and can only be reached by boat. **Tesoriero Roberto** (☎ 090 98 30 33; Via San Pietro) does all kinds of boat rentals. Expect to pay around €52 for half a day. **Amphibia** (☎ 335 613 85 29), at the port, organises scuba dives.

On Panarea you will find the remains of a **Bronze Age village** at the rocky outcrop

SICILY

of Punta Milazzese (it's about a 30-minute walk). Other than these and the exclusive hotel pools you can sun yourself on the tiny beaches of Cala Junco and Spiaggia Fumarola.

Sleeping & Eating

Finding accommodation can be an expensive nightmare in the high season of July and August. Out of season, however, prices drop dramatically.

Hotel Raya (☎ 090 98 30 13; www.hotelraya.it; Via San Pietro; d low/high season €298/440; ☒ ☒) This is *the* hotel on Panarea. A complex of low-lying villas climbing up the hillside, the Raya is pure understated luxury. Each room has its own sunbathing terrace with views of Stromboli. In the evening diners eat by the intimate light of oil lamps, and tables are in such demand that you need to reserve them. Its disco (open July to August) is known all over the islands.

Trattoria da Pina (☎ 090 98 30 32; Via San Pietro; meals €30; ☒ Tue-Sat) A cult restaurant just up from the harbour where tables spill out onto a large covered terrace. Try the unusual house speciality *gnocchi di melanzane* (aubergine dumplings). Da Pina attracts a stylish crowd in season and is definitely worth a try.

Da Francesco (☎ 090 98 30 23; Via San Pietro; meals €25) Good value for Panarea, this restaurant overlooks the dock. Try the speciality *spaghetti con le cozze* (spaghetti with mussels). In summer, they also rent out some good-value rooms (B&B/half board is €50/80 per person).

Getting There & Away

In summer there are at least six daily hydrofoils and a daily ferry that link the island with Stromboli to the northeast and Salina (and onto Lìpari and Milazzo) to the west.

STROMBOLI

pop 400 / elev 924m

Stromboli has a special kind of magic, not least because it is the only island to have a permanently active volcano, which draws experts and amateurs alike, like moths to a massive flame. Volcanic activity has scarred and blackened one side of the island, while the eastern side is ruggedly green and dotted with white houses. The youngest of all the Aeolians, Stromboli was formed a mere 40,000 years ago and its gases continue to send up an almost constant spray of liquid magma. The most recent volcanic eruptions took place in April 2003.

Orientation

Boats arrive at Scari/San Vincenzo, downhill from the town. Accommodation is a short walk up the Scalo Scari to Via Roma, or, if you plan to head straight for the crater, follow the road along the waterfront.

Information

ATM (Ficogrande, Via Nunziante; ☒ Jun-Sep)
Emergency doctor (☎ 090 98 60 97; Via Vittorio Emanuele)
Police station (☎ 090 98 60 21; Via Roma) Just on the left as you walk up Via Roma.
Post office (☎ 090 98 60 27; Via Roma; ☒ 8.20am-1.20pm Mon-Sat)
Totem Trekking (Piazza San Vincenzo 4; per 15min €2; ☒ 10am-1pm & 4-8pm) For Internet.
Vulcanalogical Information Centre (Porto Scari; ☒ 10.30am-1pm & 5-7.30pm) 150m to the right of the port, an information centre dedicated to the volcano. A video (in Italian) is shown in the afternoon.

Activities

Climbing the volcano without a guide is generally discouraged, especially given the eruptions in 2003. Many people do, although it must be said that treks with a knowledgeable guide really do enhance one's awareness of the dramatic environment.

After a closure of two years, the path to the summit (920m) is once again open. It is a demanding six- to seven-hour trek (rest stops every 40 minutes), but it is terribly exciting, rewarding you with tremendous views of the **Sciara del Fuoco** (Trail of Fire) and the constantly exploding crater. These explosions usually occur every 20 minutes or so and are preceded by a loud belly-roar as gases force the magma into the air. From March to June and September to October the treks head off at 3.30pm, but in the hot summer months the departure time is delayed until 6pm. You can also undertake a seven- to eight-hour night trek which involves camping on the volcano, a breakfast on the beach and a leisurely boat trip back to town.

To undertake the climb you will need heavy shoes and clothing for cold wet weather, a torch (flashlight) if you're climbing at night and a good supply of water. **Totem Trekking** (☎ 090 986 57 52; Piazza San Vincenzo 4) hires out all the necessary equipment, from torches to trekking boots. The cost of the whole kit is €14.50 for 24 hours.

For the less ambitious you can follow the road leading right along the waterfront to the **Osservatorio di Punta Labronzo** (follow the signs), the observatory from where you have good views of the volcano. The ascent to the summit starts here.

Make your way to the beach of rocks and black volcanic sand at **Ficogrande** to swim and sunbathe. **La Sirenetta Diving Center** (☎ 090 98 60 25, 0347 353 47 14; La Sirenetta Park Hotel, Via Marina 33) offers diving courses and accompanied dives.

Tours

Magmatrek (☎ 090 98 65 768; www.magmatrek.it; Via Vittorio Emanuele) has experienced, multilingual volcanological guides that take groups of 10 people up to the crater (afternoon trek €21, night excursions €34). Contact the office around noon to make a booking. They can also put together tailor made treks for individual groups.

AGAI (Associazione Guide Alpine Italiane; ☎ 090 98 62 63; Via Pola 1; ☾ Apr-Oct), down the steps from Piazzale San Vincenzo, is the volcano's own information office. They also take groups to the crater.

Società Navigazione Pippo (☎ 090 98 61 35; Via Roma 47) and **Bortolo** (☎ 090 98 60 65; www.strombolitour.it; Porto Scari) take visitors for a 2½-hour gander at the Sciara del Fuoco from the sea (€15 per person). Both leave at 10pm from the port.

Sleeping

There is limited accommodation on Stromboli. An alternative is one of the half-dozen *affittacamere*, which charge from €45 for doubles.

Locanda del Barbablù (☎ 090 98 61 18; www.barbablu.it; Via Vittorio Emanuele 17; d low/high season €110/170; ☾ Apr-Oct) This dusky-pink Aeolian house is an inn in the true sense of the word. It not only has a fabulous restaurant in which to dine but also has some eccentrically decorated rooms with painted ceilings, antique tiles and silk coverlets.

Park Hotel La Sirenetta (☎ 090 98 60 25; www.sirenetta.it; Via Marina 33; d low/high season €100/134; ☾ Apr-Oct; ☒ ☒) The Park Hotel is perfectly sited on the beach at Ficogrande in front of Strombolicchio. Although the décor is

rather dated – think floor-to-ceiling posters of sunsets – the hotel is well known as a diving centre.

Eating

The island's best restaurant is **Locanda del Barbablù** (meals €25-30).

Ai Gechi (☎ 090 98 62 13; Vico Salina 12, Porto Scari; meals €25; ☾ 6.30-11pm) A favourite with the locals, serving traditional food in a typical Aeolian house. As you walk up from the port you will see a sign pointing down a small lane to your left. The restaurant is right at the end of the lane.

Ritrovo Ingrid (☎ 090 98 63 85; Piazza San Vincenzo; ☾ 8am-midnight Sep-Jun, 8am-3am Jul-Aug) Situated at the high point of Piazza San Vincenzo with scenic views all around from its terrace, Ritrovo Ingrid is the heart of Stromboli. Trekkers come here for sundowners and pizza as well as the day's gossip.

Also recommended is the noisy, vine-draped terrace of **La Lampara** (☎ 090 98 64 09; Via Vittorio Emanuele 27; meals €20-25; ☾ 6pm-late). You will find it beyond Locanda del Barbablù.

Getting There & Away

It takes four hours by ferry to reach the island from Lìpari, 1½ to two hours by hydrofoil. Ticket offices for **Ustica Lines** (☎ 090 98 60 03) and **Siremar** (☎ 090 98 60 16) are at the port.

Motonautica Mandarano (☎ 090 98 62 12; Via Marina) has scooters for hire or €20 per day. To get there, from the port follow the road to your left; you will find them after about 300m.

FILICUDI & ALICUDI
pop 300

Filicudi is arguably the wildest and the prettiest of the Aeolian Islands, with crystal-clear waters and deep grottoes. The most attractive of these is **Grotta del Bue Marino** (Grotto of the Monk Seal). If you want to explore the grotto, boats are available for hire (€21) from the main port as well as from **I Delfini** (☎ 090 988 9077; Via Pecorini, Pecorini Mare). To the northwest, **Scoglio della Canna** (Cane Reef) towers 71m out of the sea. On Capo Graziano, located south of the port, are the remains of a **prehistoric village** dating from 1800 BC.

For real isolation escapists should head for Alicudi, the furthest island from Lìpari and the least developed of all the Aeolians, home only to a handful of fishermen.

While on the island, walk up **Monte Filo dell'Arpa** (String of the Harp; 672m) to see the crater of the extinct Montagnola volcano and the **Timpone delle Femmine**, huge fissures where women are said to have taken refuge during pirate raids.

Sleeping & Eating
FILICUDI
Filicudi has just two hotels and a B&B, all of which serve meals and offer half-board options.

La Canna (☎ 090 988 99 56; www.lacannahotel.it; Via Rosa 43; d low/high season €120/250; 🗗 🗷) After an exhausting walk uphill (you can be picked up from the port) the Hotel Canna appears like a private paradise. Minimalist white rooms, magnificent panoramic views as well as some wonderful home cooking.

Villa La Rosa (☎ 090 988 99 65; www.villalarosa.it; Via Rosa; d half board low/high season €90/140) Villa La Rosa is a splash of rust-red against a verdant backdrop. It is a private house and as such the rooms are lovingly furnished with romantically draped mosquito nets. The restaurant is excellent and the disco is the only nightlife on the island.

Hotel Phenicusa (☎ 090 988 99 46; Via Porto; s/d half board €76/152; 🕑 May-Sep) This boxy modern hotel dominates the port and provides accommodation that's pleasant enough. Some rooms have sea views.

ALICUDI
Ericusa (☎ 090 988 99 02; www.alicudihotel.it; Via Regina Elena; d half board low/high season €120/150; 🕑 Jun-Sep) This pleasant 12-room hotel is the only place to stay on the island. Bookings are strongly recommended.

For longer stays consider renting the gorgeous **Casa Ibiscus** (www.alicudi.net; per week low/high season €800/1250). Rentals run from Saturday and bookings are via the website. It sleeps up to four.

IONIAN COAST

Magnificent, overdeveloped and unruly, the Ionian coast is Sicily's most popular tourist destination, its commercial engine room and home to 20% of the island's population. Moneyed entrepreneurs have built their villas and hotels up and down the coastline, eager to bag a spot on Sicily's version of the Amalfi Coast. Above it all towers the muscular peak of Etna (3323m), puffs of smoke billowing from its snow-covered cone. It's surrounded by the huge Parco dell'Etna, the largest, unspoilt wilderness left in Sicily.

MESSINA
pop 250,000
Looking out to mainland Italy, Messina is all about the straits that separate them, now a veritable highway of seafaring traffic. The Greeks mythologised the clashing currents in the straits as the twin monsters of Charbydis (the whirlpool) and Scylla (the six-headed monster), and strong currents still lurk in the attractive waters, making swimming inadvisable.

Messina is still defined by the straits. Beneath the choppy surface of the sea this geological faultline has brought both prosperity and adversity to the city. In 1908 it was responsible for one of the worst natural disasters to hit the island – an earthquake sank the shore by half a metre and killed 84,000 people – but the narrow waterway is also the secret of Messina's economic success. Messina looks poised for more seismic changes – the building of the world's largest suspension bridge spanning the straits between Sicily and the mainland (see the boxed text, p742).

Orientation
Wide boulevards and a practical grid system make Messina an easy and pleasant city to navigate. The main transport hub is Piazza della Repubblica, at the southern end of the long waterfront. You will find the train station here, and the Trenitalia ferries arrive here. The main intercity bus station is outside the train station, to the left on the piazza. To get to the city centre from Piazza della Repubblica, walk either straight across the piazza and directly ahead along Via I Settembre to the Piazza del Duomo, or turn left into Via La Farina and take the first right into Via Tommaso Cannizzaro to reach Piazza Cairoli.

Those visitors coming by hydrofoil from Reggio di Calabria arrive about 1km north of the city on Corso Vittorio Emanuele II, while drivers on the private car ferry from Villa San Giovanni land a few kilometres further along, just north of the trade-fair area (Fiera).

Information

There are numerous banks in the centre – most with ATMs – and a currency-exchange booth at the train station.

There are public telephones on Piazza Cairoli and at Paritel Telecommunicazioni.

CTS (☎ 090 292 67 61; Via Ugo Bassi 93) Student travel group with special deals for students and those under 26. Messina has many other travel agencies.

Ospedale Piemonte (☎ 090 222 42 38; Viale Europa) Has a casualty service.

Paritel Telecommunicazioni (Via Centonze 74; per hr €3; ☒ 9am-8pm) Telephones and Internet connection.

Post office (Piazza Antonello, Corso Cavour; ☒ 8.30am-6.30pm Mon-Sat)

Tourist office (☎ 090 67 42 36; www.aapitme.it; Via Calabria 301; ☒ 9am-1.30pm & 3-5pm Mon-Thu, 9am-1.30pm Fri) To the right of the station. Friendly, English-speaking staff with good information about Messina and onward travel.

Sights

Messina's Norman **Cathedral** (Piazza del Duomo; ☒ 8am-6pm) is one of the most attractive in Sicily and if it hadn't been for its unfortunate history it would undoubtedly be on a par with the cathedrals of Cefalù and Monreale. Built in the 12th century, it suffered its first disaster in 1254 at the funeral of Conrad IV (son of Frederick II), when a mass of candles set the church on fire. Devastating earthquakes in 1783 and 1908, and a WWII incendiary bomb in 1943, put paid to the rest. True to their patrician nature, the Messinese rebuilt it faithfully in the style of the original basilica with its mosaic apses. The lovely stripy marble inlay, and tracery of the façade and the Catalan-Gothic portal with its sculpted columns, are some of the few original elements that were salvaged.

The magnificent 1668 *Golden Mantle* (a cloth that's draped around an image of the Virgin at key religious festivals), designed by Innocenzo Mangani, is kept in the Cathedral **treasury** (admission €3; ☒ 9am-1pm Mon-Sat). Outside, the elegant **campanile** (bell tower; admission €3.50; ☒ 9am-1pm Mon-Sat) houses the world's largest astronomical clock. It strikes at noon, setting in motion a procession of slow-moving bronze automata which sets off a comical roaring lion and crowing cockerel. You can climb the *campanile* and see the enormous figures up close.

Below the tower, the pale marble **Fontana di Orione** (1553) commemorates Orion, the mythical founder of Messina. It was constructed by Giovanni Angelo Montorsoli (a pupil to Michelangelo) to commemorate the construction of Messina's first aqueduct, making the city's houses the first in Sicily to receive running water.

Picking up the free city tram at Piazza Cairoli (or the train station), you can take a laid-back ride up the sickle-shaped harbour. Halfway up is Messina's other great fountain, the 16th-century **Fontana del Nettuno**. Get off here to enjoy views over the harbour and admire the huge golden statue of the **Madonnino del Porto**. Alternatively, continue on to the end of the tramline to the **Museo Regionale** (☎ 090 36 12 92; Viale della Libertà 465; adult/concession €4.50/2; ☒ 9am-1.30pm Mon, Wed & Fri, 9am-1.30pm & 3pm-5.30pm Tue, Thu & Sat, 9am-12.30pm Sun). It houses works of art including the *Virgin and Child with Saints* by Antonello da Messina (born here in 1430) and two masterpieces by Caravaggio – *L'Adorazione dei Pastori* and *Resurrezione di Lazzaro*.

If you have your own transport, the drive north along the coast from Messina to Capo Peloro and then round to the east is pretty, and there are some reasonable beaches between the Cape and Acquarone. Alternatively, you can take bus No 79 or 80 to the lighthouse at **Torre del Faro** (8km north) and the popular summer resort of **Mortelle**.

Sleeping

Despite being a major transport hub, Messina is not a tourist city. Hotels and restaurants cater for businesspeople and tend to lack charm.

   Grand Hotel Liberty (☎ 090 640 94 36; www.framon-hotels.com; Via I Settembre 15; d/ste €170/224; P ☒) The most comfortable hotel in Messina, the Grand is a renovated Liberty-style villa with luxurious rooms and efficient English-speaking staff.

   Royal Palace Hotel (☎ 090 6503; www.framonhotels.com; Via Tommaso Cannizzaro 224; s/d €104/126; P ☒) Messina's most popular hotel is big, central and ramshackle. James Bond would love the buttons on the bedhead and the electric shutters.

   Hotel Cairoli (☎ 090 67 37 55; www.hotel-cairoli.com; Viale San Martino 63; s/d €46/77; ☒) Just off Piazza Cairoli, this is Messina's most reasonably priced and centrally located accommodation, even if the beds are rock hard and the décor is dated.

SICILY

Messina's two budget hotels, the **Touring** (☎ 090 293 88 51; Via N Scotto 17; s/d €40/60; ✷) and the **Mirage** (☎ 090 293 88 44; Via N Scotto 3; d €40, with bathroom €55) are both near the station. There's not much to choose between them.

Eating

Messina is most famous for its quality swordfish. It is typically served with *agghiotta*, a mouthwatering dish flavoured with pine nuts, sultanas, garlic, basil and tomatoes.

Da Piero (☎ 090 71 83 65; Via Ghibellina 121; meals €25-40; ✷ 8-11pm Mon-Sat) A classy restaurant frequented by well-heeled Messinese. It is an excellent place to try the swordfish *agghiotta*. Make a reservation and dress appropriately.

Duck Pub (☎ 090 71 27 72; Via E L Pellegrino 107a; sandwiches/meals €4/20; ✷ Mon-Sat) The most authentic pub in Sicily, with a long wooden bar crammed full of young professionals, and a well-priced menu. Steaks are the big thing here; it is a mistake to order anything else.

Le Due Sorelle (☎ 090 4 47 20; Piazza Municipio 4; meals €20-25; ✷ lunch & dinner Mon-Fri, dinner Sat & Sun Sep-Jul) For something a tad different – traditional Mediterranean cooking with some exotic adaptations from North Africa such as couscous. In summer, you can eat out on the piazza, something not often possible in Messina.

Mario's (☎ 090 4 24 77; Via Vittorio Emanuele; meals €20; ✷ Tue-Sun Oct-Aug) Opposite the hydrofoil dock, this is a specialist fish restaurant serving a delicious array of vegetable and seafood antipasti. It is a great place to enjoy lunch before the hydrofoil leaves.

Getting There & Away
BOAT

Messina is the main point of arrival for ferries and hydrofoils from the Italian mainland, only a 20-minute trip across the straits.

Trenitalia (090 66 16 74; www.trenitalia.com; Stazione Marittima) runs at least 20 fast boats a day to Reggio di Calabria (10 on Sunday). The trip costs €2.80/4.50 one way/return for passengers and a small car (such as a Fiat Punto) costs €18. There are also services to Villa San Giovanni on the Italian mainland.

Caronte (☎ 090 371 83 24; www.ferriesonline.com; Viale della Libertà) runs ferries for Salerno (foot passengers/cars €26/73, 7½ hours, one daily).

Ustica Lines (☎ 090 36 40 44; www.usticalines.it; Via Vittorio Emanuele II) runs hydrofoils to Reggio di Calabria (€2.80, 15 minutes, five daily) daily and summer-only hydrofoils to the Aeolian Islands (Lìpari, €16.50, 1½ hours, five daily).

BUS
Interbus (☎ 090 66 17 54; www.interbus.it; Piazza della Reppublica 6) runs a regular service to Taormina (€2.60, 1½ hours, hourly Monday to Saturday) and has a weekly connection to Rome (€33, 9½ hours, one Saturday).

SAIS Autolinee (☎ 090 77 19 14; Piazza della Reppublica 6) serves Palermo (€13.30, two hours, nine daily Monday to Friday, two daily Saturday and Sunday) and Catania (€6.70, 1½ hours, half-hourly Monday to Saturday, five on Sunday). The Catania bus travels via Taormina, Giardini-Naxos, Giarre and Acireale.

Giuntabus (☎ 090 67 37 82; Via Terranova 8) runs a service to Milazzo (€3.40, 45 minutes, half-hourly Monday to Saturday, one Sunday) to catch the ferries and hydrofoils to the Aeolian Islands.

CAR & MOTORCYCLE
If you arrive by Trenitalia ferry with a vehicle it is simple to make your way out of town. For Palermo (or Milazzo and the Aeolian Islands), turn right from the docks and follow Via Garibaldi along the waterfront. After about 1km, turn left into Viale Boccetta and follow the green autostrada signs for Palermo. To reach Taormina and Syracuse, turn

---

THE HIGH ROAD

Sicily has one real autostrada running between Catania Nord and Messina and continuing to Sant'Agata di Militello. Here you must get off the autostrada and onto the SS113 to complete the journey to Cefalù. To access the autostrada you will have to pass through an unstaffed ticket barrier (press the button and take a ticket). You pay at the barrier where you exit (when the staff aren't on strike, that is).

You don't have to take the autostrada; you can make the same journeys along the traffic-logged SS113 (north to Milazzo) and the SS114 (south to Taormina).

Motorway costs are: Messina–Catania, €3; Messina–Milazzo, €1.70; Messina–Sant' Agata di Militello, €5.50; Messina–Taormina, €1.70.

left from the docks into Via La Farina and follow the autostrada signs for Catania.

If you arrive by private ferry, turn right along Viale della Libertà for Palermo and Milazzo and left for Taormina and Catania – follow the green autostrada signs. Streets in Messina are well signposted

If you arrive on foot and want to hire a car the usual companies are represented.

Avis (☎ 090 67 91 50; Via Garibaldi 109)

Hertz (☎ 090 36 37 40; Via Vittorio Emanuele II 75)

Sicilcar (☎ 090 4 69 42; Via Garibaldi 187)

TRAIN

Hourly *diretto* (direct) trains connect Messina with Catania (1st/2nd class €10/8, 1½ to two hours, hourly), Taormina (€7.25/6, 40 minutes, hourly), Syracuse (€17/12 intercity, 2½ to three hours, hourly) and Palermo (€20/15 intercity, €10.50 regional, 3½ hours). You can also get the train to Milazzo (€2.65, one hour, 10 daily, hourly), but buses are generally faster. The train stations for Milazzo and Taormina are inconveniently located some distance from their respective town centres.

From Messina you can also take the train across the straits for Rome and Milan (for details, see p748).

Getting Around

An electric tram runs up and down the length of the town from Piazza Cairoli via the train station (Piazza della Repubblica) up to the Museo Regionale. You can buy a ticket (€0.90, valid for two hours) from the ticket conductor at the stop.

City buses (€0.90, valid for two hours) run from outside the train station to Ganzirri (Nos 79 and 81) and Mortelle (Nos 79 and 80).

TAORMINA
pop 10,800 / elev 204m

Spectacularly located on a terrace of Monte Tauro with views westwards to Mt Etna, it is difficult to exaggerate the beauty of Taormina, Sicily's glitziest resort. Over the centuries Taormina has seduced an exhaustive line of writers and artists, aristocrats and royalty, and these days it is host to a summer arts festival (p782) that packs the town with international visitors.

Perched on its eyrie, sophisticated and chic, Taormina is very far removed from the banal economic realities of other Sicilian cities, comfortably cushioned by some serious wealth. But the charm is not manufactured. The capital of Byzantine Sicily in the 9th century, Taormina is an almost perfectly preserved medieval town, and if you can tear yourself away from the shopping and sunbathing it has a wealth of small but quite perfect tourist sites.

In July and August the town is *flooded* with tourists; it is difficult to find accommodation and even dining can be a problem without a reservation.

Orientation

The train station (Taormina-Giardini) is at the bottom of Monte Tauro. You'll need to hop on an Interbus (€0.80) to the bus station (for local and intercity services) on Via Pirandello. You will arrive here anyway if you come by bus. A short walk uphill from there brings you to the old city entrance and Corso Umberto I, which traverses the town.

Information

There are lots of banks in Taormina along Corso Umberto I; all have ATMs. You'll also find currency-exchange places along the same street – check the commissions. Public telephones are dotted around town, and on Piazza IX Aprile.

British Pharmacy (☎ 0942 62 58 66; Piazza IX Aprile; ☒ 8.30am-1pm & 4.30-8.30pm) Offers a night call-out service on ☎ 338 15 87 988.

L@s Veg@s (☎ 0942 2 40 59; Salita Alexander Humboldt; per 20min €2; ☒ 8am-1pm & 7pm-2am Tue-Sun) A slick Internet bar with a bunch of fast computers and cocktails.

Mazza Giuseppe (Corso Umberto I 9) A big newsagent selling all the foreign newspapers and a selection of foreign-language books.

Ospedale San Vincenzo (☎ 0942 5 37 45; Piazza San Vincenzo) Call the same number for an ambulance. It is just outside Porta Catania.

Police station (☎ 0942 61 11 11; Corso Umberto I)

Post office (Piazza Sant'Antonio Abate; ☒ 8.30am-6.30pm Mon-Sat)

Tourist first aid (☎ 0942 62 54 19; Piazza San Francesco di Paola) 24-hour, free medical service available from 16 June to 15 September.

Tourist office (☎ 0942 2 32 43; www.gate2taormina.com; Palazzo Corvaja, Corso Umberto I; ☒ 8.30am-2pm & 4-7pm Mon-Sat) Very busy tourist office with multilingual staff. Loads of informative brochures but you may have to queue to speak to someone.

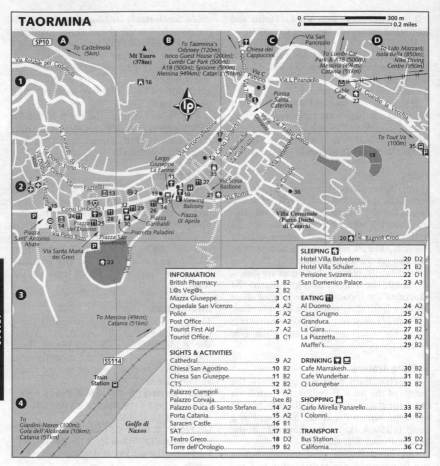

TAORMINA

INFORMATION		
British Pharmacy	1	B2
L@s Veg@s	2	B2
Mazza Giuseppe	3	C1
Ospedale San Vicenzo	4	A2
Police	5	A2
Post Office	6	A2
Tourist First Aid	7	A2
Tourist Office	8	C1

SIGHTS & ACTIVITIES		
Cathedral	9	A2
Chiesa San Agostino	10	B2
Chiesa San Giuseppe	11	B2
CTS	12	B2
Palazzo Ciampoli	13	A2
Palazzo Corvaja	(see 8)	
Palazzo Duca di Santo Stefano	14	A2
Porta Catania	15	A2
Saracen Castle	16	B1
SAT	17	B2
Teatro Greco	18	D2
Torre dell'Orologio	19	B2

SLEEPING		
Hotel Villa Belvedere	20	D2
Hotel Villa Schuler	21	B2
Pensione Svizzera	22	D1
San Domenico Palace	23	A3

EATING		
Al Duomo	24	A2
Casa Grugno	25	A2
Granduca	26	B2
La Giara	27	B2
La Piazzetta	28	A2
Maffei's	29	B2

DRINKING		
Cafe Marrakesh	30	B2
Cafe Wunderbar	31	B2
Q Loungebar	32	B2

SHOPPING		
Carlo Mirella Panarello	33	B2
I Colonni	34	B2

TRANSPORT		
Bus Station	35	D2
California	36	C2

Sights

One of the chief delights of Taormina is wandering along its medieval main drag, browsing among the antique and craft shops, delis and designer boutiques. More serious tourists should head straight for **Teatro Greco** (☎ 0942 2 32 20; Via Teatro Greco; adult/concession €4.50/2; ⏰ 9am-7pm Apr-Oct, 9am-4.30pm Nov-Mar), Taormina's premiere attraction. This perfect horseshoe theatre, suspended between sea and sky, was built in the 3rd century BC and is the second largest in Sicily (after Syracuse), although its lofty position makes it the most dramatically situated Greek theatre in the world. In summer the theatre is used as the venue for the international arts festival, Taormina Arte (p782).

In peak season the site is best explored early in the morning to avoid the crowds.

When the shops and the sights have exhausted their charms most folk retire to Piazza IX Aprile, from where you can enjoy stunning panoramic views of Etna and pop your head into the cutest rococo church, **Chiesa San Giuseppe** (Piazza IX Aprile; ⏰ 9am-7pm).

On the western side of Piazza IX Aprile is the 12th-century clock tower, **Torre dell' Orologio**, which leads you through into the Borgo Medievale, the oldest quarter of the town. Head down here to Piazza del Duomo, where teenagers congregate around the ornate baroque fountain (built 1635), which sports a two-legged centaur with the bust of an angel, the symbol of Taormina. On the eastern side of this piazza is the 13th-century **Cathedral** (Piazza del Duomo; ✆ 8am-noon & 4-7pm). It survived much of the Renaissance remodelling undertaken throughout the town by the Spanish aristocracy in the 15th century. This is better illustrated in various palaces like **Palazzo Duca di Santo Stefano** with its Norman-Gothic windows, **Palazzo Corvaja** (the tourist office) and **Palazzo Ciampoli** (now the Hotel Palazzo Vecchio).

To get away from the crowds, wander down to **Villa Comunale** (Parco Duchi di Cesarò; Via Bagnoli Croci; admission free; ✆ 9am-midnight summer, 9am-10pm winter). Created by Englishwoman Florence Trevelyan, these hanging gardens are a lush paradise of tropical plants and delicate flowers. There's also a children's play area.

Panorama fanatics should head 5km up Via Leonardo da Vinci to **Castelmola**, literally the high point of the area, with a ruined castle and sweeping views of, well, everything. Interbus runs an hourly service (€1.30) up the hill.

Activities

Many visitors to Taormina come only for the beach scene. To reach **Lido Mazzarò**, directly under Taormina, take the **cable car** (Via L Pirandello; one way/return €1.80/3; ✆ 8am-1am). This beach is well serviced with bars and restaurants, and private operators charge a fee for umbrellas and deckchairs (€5 per person per day). To the right of the beach past the Sant'Andrea hotel is the minuscule **Isola Bella**, set in a stunning cove. You can walk here in a few minutes but it's more fun to rent a small boat from Mazzarò to paddle round Capo Sant'Andrea.

Nike Diving Centre (✆ 0942 4 75 34, 339 19 61 559; www.divenike.com; Contrada Isola Bella Spiaggia) can be found on the beach opposite the Isola Bella. It offers a whole range of courses. A single dive costs €35 and snorkelling equipment is €10 per day.

For a sandy beach you will have to go to **Spisone**, just beneath the autostrada exit (left from the cable-car station). When you reach the Le Capinera restaurant, take the staircase on the right which will take you through a tunnel and out onto the large sandy beach.

Other activities involve short excursions around Taormina, one of the most popular being to the **Gole dell'Alcàntara**, a series of vertiginous lava gorges swirling with rapids. The Gole dell'Alcàntara runs **tours** (✆ 0942 98 50 10; adult €4.50) onsite and hires out the necessary wellies and wetsuits (€5). Take the bus from Taormina (€4.70 return, one hour, four daily Monday to Saturday). It is forbidden to enter the gorges from around November to May due to flooding.

Tours

It is possible to take any number of coach excursions from Taormina. They are time-saving and hassle-free but it may be cheaper to rent a car for the day as the quoted prices do not include admission charges to the museums and archaeological sites.

CST (✆ 0942 62 60 88; www.cts.it; Corso Umberto I 101) Coach excursions to Mt Etna (€27), Piazza Armerina (with the Roman Villa, €50), Palermo (with Monreale, €45) and Panarea and Stromboli in the Aeolian Islands (€75).

A GAY RESORT

Among its many reputations, Taormina has long been famous as a haven of homosexuality, due in part to an illustrious list of gay celebrities and artists, including photographer Wilhelm von Gloeden and Oscar Wilde who both lived there. Gloeden, who arrived in 1880, did more than anyone else to put Taormina on the tourist map. His photographs of nude young colts draped in tropical foliage set the heart of every old queen in Europe racing and it wasn't long before they were all racing down to Taormina. The flavour of the resort was gay glamour, epitomised by Oscar Wilde, who often helped Gloeden set up his compositions. Wilde was followed by Truman Capote and Tennessee Williams, Somerset Maugham and Jean Cocteau, all of whom came to see the 'boys with the almond eyes'.

True to this fine Taorminese tradition is the congenial and gay-friendly **Isoco Guest House** (✆ 0942 2 36 79; www.isoco.it; Via Salita Branco 2; s/d €90/105; 🅿 🖳). Each of its five rooms (soon to be six) is dedicated to an artist – the sculpted buttocks and pant-popping thighs on the walls of the Herb Ritts room will give you the general idea. **Q Loungebar** (✆ 0942 2 12 96; Piazzetta F Paladini 6; cocktails €5.50-7; ✆ Tue-Sun) is a gay-friendly bar.

SAT (Sicilian Airbus Travel; ☎ 0942 2 46 53; www.sat -group.it; Corso Umberto I 73) Almost identical tours to CST for very similar prices.

Festivals & Events

The **Taormina Arte festival** (☎ 0942 2 11 42; www .taormina-arte.com) in July/August includes films, theatrical events and music concerts from an impressive list of international names.

Raduno del Costume e del Carretto Siciliano is a parade featuring traditional Sicilian carts and folkloric groups. It's usually held in autumn; ask at the tourist office for details and dates

Sleeping

Taormina has plenty of (expensive) accommodation and in summer it is essential to reserve well in advance. You will also need to book your parking place at most hotels. This usually incurs an extra charge of €10 to €15 per day.

Hotel Villa Belvedere (☎ 0942 2 37 91; www.villa belvedere.it; Via Bagnoli Croce 79; s/d €164/198; ⊗ 11 Mar–19 Nov; Ⓟ ✗ ☔) The jaw-droppingly pretty Villa Belvedere is one of the original grand hotels, fantastically sited with views to die for and a luxuriant garden, which is a particular highlight.

San Domenico Palace (☎ 0942 61 31 11; www.thi .it; Piazza San Domenico 5; d without/with sea view €360 /480; Ⓟ ✗ ☐ ☔) Converted into a hotel in 1896, the San Domenico Palace is Italy's oldest monastery hotel and is utterly luxurious. Over the years it has hosted an illustrious list of names including King Edward VII, François Mitter and and Audrey Hepburn. Despite its achingly pretty décor and situation, it has a rather claustrophobic air of exclusivity – all hushed tones and creeping footsteps.

Hotel Villa Schuler (☎ 0942 2 34 81; www.villa schuler.com; Piazzetta Bastione, Via Roma 1; s/d €90/130; Ⓟ ✗) The rose-pink Villa Schuler is family owned and preserves a homely atmosphere although the standard rooms can be a bit stingy in size. Breakfast is served on the terrace where you enjoy uninterrupted views of smoky Etna.

Pensione Svizzera (☎ 0942 2 37 90; www.pensione svizzera.com; Via Pirandello 26; d without/with sea view €90 /120; Ⓟ ✗ ☐) A popular B&B teetering on the edge of the cliff with views over Mazzaro bay. Many of the rooms have balconies. The hotel can also organise tennis and diving.

Taormina's Odyssey (☎ 0942 2 45 33; www.taorm inaodyssey.com; 2 Traversa A, Via G Martino; dm/d €15/50; Ⓟ) A new hostel which has earned a flurry of complimentary letters from LP readers who highly rate its warm, friendly atmosphere, lack of curfew and open kitchen. A seven-minute walk from the town centre.

Eating

Eating out in Taormina goes hand-in-hand with posing. There are some excellent restaurants serving very good food but it is essential to make a reservation. Be aware that Taormina's cafés charge extraordinarily high prices even for coffee.

Casa Grugno (☎ 0942 2 12 08; Via Santa Maria dei Greci; meals €40) With an Austrian chef in the kitchen don't expect typical Sicilian fare. The food at Casa Grugno is international in the best sense of the word, making this Taormina's most fashionable eatery.

La Giara (☎ 0942 2 33 60; Vico la Floresta 1; meals €35-45; ⊗ 8.15-11pm Tue-Sun Sep-Jul) This stylish Art Deco restaurant and piano bar serves up perfectly grilled fish dishes and delicate pasta with inventive sauces. It has a well-heeled clientele and the sniffy maître d' won't hesitate to turn you away if you aren't dressed appropriately.

Granduca (☎ 0942 2 49 83; Corso Umberto I 172; pizzas/meals €10/30; ⊗ Thu-Tue) Eating delicious pizza *al forno* on the terrace of Granduca is an experience that is not easily forgotten. A reservation is highly recommended if you want to be sure of getting a table on the terrace.

Al Duomo (☎ 0942 62 56 56; Vico Ebrei 11; meals €30-40; ⊗ Mon-Sat) Completely different from the above restaurants but no less attractive is the discreet Al Duomo. The intimate terrace overlooks the Cathedral and the restaurant is a real celebrity haunt. It has an excellent selection of seafood and more rustic dishes like stewed lamb.

Maffei's (☎ 0942 2 40 55; Via San Domenico de Guzman 1; meals €35) A small restaurant with a pretty courtyard garden and some of the best fish dishes in Taormina. Here you can enjoy a cornucopia of fish cooked to your liking. It is always a good bet to go for the house special.

Also recommended is **La Piazzetta** (☎ 0942 62 63 17; Via Paladini 5; mains €10-14; ⊗ Tue-Sun winter, daily summer), tucked in the corner of the very pretty Piazzetta Paladini.

Drinking

Cafe Wunderbar (Piazza IX Aprile 7; alcoholic drinks €5.50-7, coffee €3.50) A poseur's paradise on Piazza IX Aprile serving the most delicious *latte di mandorla* (almond milk). Perfect for a warm summer's evening.

Cafe Marrakesh (☎ 0942 62 56 92; Piazza Garibaldi 2; cocktails €5.50; ☺ 6pm-3am) An Arabian-themed cocktail bar with candlelit, mosaic-topped tables. Its outdoor tables draw a cosmopolitan crowd in summer.

Tout Va (☎ 0942 2 38 24; Via Pirandello 70; ☺ 6pm-3.30am) Down by the water, this open-air club sees the hottest summer action. It also serves up food late into the night on its panoramic terrace.

Shopping

Taormina is a shopper's paradise, absolutely choked with smart boutiques, quaint antique shops, stylish jewellers and tempting delis. The quality in most places is high but don't come here expecting a bargain – instead think of purchasing one or two memorable items such as a piece of exquisitely hand-crafted jewellery from **I Colonni** (☎ 0942 2 36 80; Corso Umberto I 164) or some quality ceramic art with delightful naive designs from **Carlo Mirella Panarello** (Via A Marziani).

Getting There & Around

BUS

The bus is the easiest way to reach Taormina. **Interbus** (☎ 0942 62 53 01; Via Pirandello) services leave daily for Messina (€2.60, 1½ hours, five daily Monday to Saturday) and Catania (€4.20, 1½ hours, hourly). The Catania bus also services the train station and Giardini-Naxos (€1.60). There are also services to the Alcantara Gorge (€4.70 return, four daily) and up to Castelmola (€1.30, 15 minutes, four daily).

CAR & MOTORCYCLE

Taormina is on the A18 motorway and the SS114 between Messina and Catania. Parking is a complete nightmare and Corso Umberto I is closed to traffic. The only real place to park is the **Lumbi car park** (☎ 0942 2 43 45; ☺ 24hr), north of the town centre. There is a shuttle service to the centre from Porta Messina.

California (☎ 0942 23 7 69; Via Bagnoli Croce 86) rents out cars and scooters at reasonable prices. A Fiat Punto with air-con costs €78/339 per day/week. A Vespa 125 costs €30/189.

TRAIN

There are regular trains to and from Messina (1st/2nd class €7.25/6, 40 minutes, half-hourly) and Catania (1st/2nd class €4.25/3, 45 minutes, half-hourly), but the awkward location of Taormina's station is a strong disincentive. If you arrive this way, catch an Interbus service up to the town. They run roughly every 30 to 90 minutes (much less frequently on Sunday).

CATANIA

pop 310,000

Catania is a true city of the volcano, much of it constructed from the lava that poured down the mountain and engulfed the city in the 1669 eruption when nearly 12,000 people lost their lives. It is also lava-black, as if a fine dusting of soot permanently covers its elegant buildings, most of which are the work of baroque master Giovanni Vaccarini who almost single-handedly rebuilt the civic centre into an elegant modern city of spacious boulevards and set-piece piazzas.

However, Catania's shades and shadows run deep, right into the heart of a murky local government which shamefully neglects large portions of the decaying historic centre. It's therefore surprising to find out that Catania is Sicily's second commercial city, a thriving, entrepreneurial centre with a large university and a tough and resilient local population which adheres very much to the motto of *carpe diem* ('seize the day').

Orientation

The main train station is near the port at Piazza Giovanni XXIII, and the intercity bus terminal is one block up at Via d'Amico. From here, Corso Martiri della Libertà heads west towards the city centre, about a 15-minute walk (1km). Follow the road to Piazza della Repubblica and continue along Corso Sicilia to Via Etnea, the main thoroughfare running north off Piazza del Duomo. Most sights are concentrated around and west of Piazza del Duomo, while the commercial centre of Catania is further north around Via Pacini and Via Umberto I.

Information

Banks are concentrated along Corso Sicilia, and several have currency exchanges. There is also an exchange office at the train station. Plenty of ATMs can be found along

SICILY

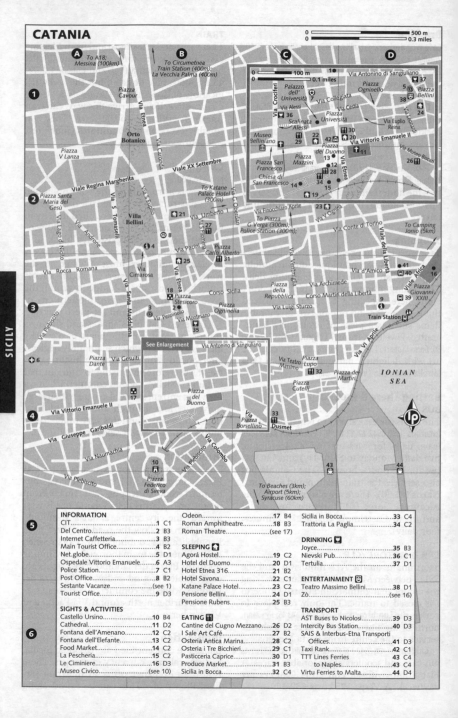

CATANIA

0 — 500 m
0 — 0.3 miles

SICILY

Via Etnea. There are public phones dotted around town and at the train station.

Ambulance (☎ 118)

CIT (☎ 095 31 35 77; Via Antonino di San Giuliano 205) Book train, ferry and air tickets.

Del Centro (☎ 095 31 36 85; Via Etnea 107) Late-night pharmacy.

Internet Caffetteria (Via Penninello 44; per hr from €2.50; ⏰ 10am-8pm) A nice café serving snacks and drinks with speedy computers.

Net.globe (Via Michele Rapisardi 10; per hr from €2.50; ⏰ 5pm-1am) Small café right next to Teatro Massimo Bellini.

Ospedale Vittorio Emanuele (☎ 091 743 54 52; Via Plebiscito 628) Has a 24-hour emergency doctor.

Police station (☎ 095 736 71 11; Piazza San Nicolella)

Post office (Via Etnea 215; ⏰ 8am-6.30pm Mon-Fri, 8.30am-12.30pm Sat)

Sestante Vacanze (☎ 095 31 35 17; Via Antonino di San Giuliano 208) For train, ferry and air tickets.

Tourist office (⏰ 8am-8pm Mon-Fri, 8am-2pm Sat); airport (☎ 095 730 62 66); train station (☎ 095 730 62 55); Via Cimarosa 10-12 (☎ 095 730 62 22, 095 730 62 11; www.apt.catania.it in Italian) The Via Cimarosa main office is very inconveniently located and not very helpful. Some English is spoken.

Train station (per bag per 12hr €3.90; ⏰ 24hr) Left luggage.

Sights

Catania's central square, **Piazza del Duomo**, is a World Heritage site. It's a set piece of sinuous buildings and a grand cathedral all built in Catania's own style of baroque, with its contrasting lava and limestone. In the centre of the piazza is Catania's most memorable monument, the smiling **Fontana dell'Elefante** (Fountain of the Elephant; built in 1736). The statue is composed of a naive black-lava elephant, dating from the Roman period, surmounted by an improbable Egyptian obelisk. The elephant, with its comical upturned trunk, is the symbol of the city. Legend has it that it belonged to the 8th-century-AD magician Eliodorus, who reputedly made his living turning men into animals. It is believed to possess magical powers that help to calm the restless activity of Mt Etna.

Facing the statue is Catania's other defence against Mt Etna, St Agata's **Cathedral** (☎ 095 32 00 44; Piazza del Duomo; ⏰ 8am-noon & 4-7pm), with its impressive marble façade. Inside the cool, vaulted interior lies the remains of the city's patron saint, the young virgin Agata, who resisted the advances of the

nefarious Quintian (AD 250) and was horribly mutilated (her breasts were hacked off and her body was rolled in hot coals). The saint's jewel-drenched effigy is ecstatically venerated on 5 February in one of Sicily's largest *festas* (see p786).

A few blocks northeast you'll stumble onto the shabby Piazza Bellini. Its centrepiece is the **Teatro Massimo Bellini** (☎ 095 730 61 11; Via Perrotta 12; ⏰ performances only), named after the composer Vincenzo Bellini, the father of Catania's vibrant modern musical scene. There is a small museum, **Museo Belliniano** (☎ 095 715 05 35; Piazza San Francesco d'Assisi; admission free; ⏰ 9am-1.30pm Mon-Sat, 9am-12.30pm Sun & holidays), which houses a collection of memorabilia from the composer's life.

However, the best show in town is the bustling **La Pescheria** (fish market; ⏰ 5-11am) and adjoining **food market** (⏰ 8-9am & 6-7pm) where carcasses of meat, silvery fish, skinned sheep's heads, rolls of sausages, huge cartwheels of cheese and piles of luscious vegetables are all rolled together in a few noisy, jam-packed alleyways. The **Fontana dell'Amenano** marks the entrance to the market and is Tito Angelini's commemoration of the River Amenano, which once ran overground and on whose banks the Greeks first founded the city of Katáne.

Catania also has a number of ruinous Roman remains dotted throughout the city. West along Via Vittorio Emanuele II is the **Roman theatre** and a small rehearsal theatre, the **Odeon** (Via Vittorio Emanuele II 266; admission ind Roman theatre €2; ⏰ 9am-1.30pm & 3-7pm). North of Piazza del Duomo, more leftovers from Roman days include a modest **amphitheatre** on Piazza Stesicoro. For relief from the madding crowd, continue north along Via Etnea to the lovely gardens of **Villa Bellini** (⏰ 8am-8pm) with its views of Mt Etna.

Catania's **Museo Civico** (☎ 095 34 58 30; Piazza Federico II di Svevia; admission free) is housed in the grim-looking **Castello Ursino**. The museum is the repository of the valuable Biscari archaeological collection. However it has been closed for years and many fear that the collection, so long hidden from the public gaze, may have been looted.

If you have some extra time another curious site is the renovated sulphur refineries, **Le Ciminiere** (☎ 095 734 99 11; Viale Africa), which now constitute a cultural centre with a cool restaurant.

Festivals & Events

There's hysterical celebrations during **Festa di Sant'Agata** (3 to 5 February), where one million Catanians follow as the Fercolo (a silver reliquary bust of the saint) is carried along the main street of the city accompanied by spectacular fireworks.

Held in July are **Catania Musica Estate**, a classical music festival; **Settimana Barocca**, a week of baroque concerts, pageants and other performances; and **Etna Jazz** – ask at the tourist office for information on this jazz festival.

Sleeping

Catania is served by a good range of reasonably priced places to stay, making it an excellent base for exploring the Ionian coast and Etna. Quality top-end hotels, however, are thin on the ground.

BUDGET

Pensione Rubens (☎ 095 31 70 73; fax 095 715 17 13; Via Etnea 196; s/d €45/78; ⊠) Signor Caviezel continues to stand head and shoulders above the competition with his seven comfortable rooms and tip-top service, and his advice on his home town makes for a rewarding and enjoyable stay. You will do well to book in advance.

Agorá Hostel (☎ 095 723 30 10; www.agorahostel .com; Piazza Currò 6; dm/d €20/50; 🖳) A classic hostel with rooms of six to 10 beds and some doubles. There is no lock-out, an Internet point is provided (€4 per hour) and you can do laundry (€5 per wash). Its location near La Pescheria makes it a great base for self-caterers, although its restaurant/bar is also fabulous. The hostel is a mine of information about trips to Etna and around Catania.

Pensione Bellini (☎ 095 715 09 69; Via Landolini 41; s/d €32/46; ⊠) A friendly budget option providing comfortable accommodation. The young couple who run it try their utmost to be helpful. Breakfast is included if requested.

Camping Jonio (☎ 095 49 11 39; www.camping.it/sicilia /jonio; Via Villini a Mare 2; adult/tent €6.20/18.10, 4-person bungalow €76) This place is about 5km north of Catania, close to a rocky beach. To get there, catch bus No 334 from Via Etnea. It also has bungalows.

MIDRANGE

Hotel del Duomo (☎ 095 250 31 77; www.hoteldel duomo.it; Via Etnea 28; s/d €110/140; ⊠) Can't be beaten for location right on the Piazza del Duomo. The hotel actually occupies a whole wing of an ancient palazzo and the rooms are generally cosy and comfortable. Best of all, however, are the views over the floodlit piazza at night.

Hotel Savona (☎ 095 32 69 82; www.hotelsavona .it; Via Vittorio Emanuele 210; s/d €80/100; ⊠) Another reliable hotel located just off the Piazza del Duomo. Recent renovations make it a comfortable midrange option and the staff speak impeccable English. Back rooms overlook a quiet inner courtyard.

La Vecchia Palma (☎ 095 43 20 25; www.lavecchia palma.com; Via Etnea 668; s/d €70/100; ⊠ 🖳) This beautifully renovated palazzo adds a touch of style to the rather bland Catanian hotel scene. The 14 rooms are simply gorgeous, with frescoed ceilings, panelled walls and antique tiled floors. The very grand baroque furnishings complement the grandeur of the place and the summer garden is delightful.

Also recommended is the **Hotel Etnea 316** (☎ 095 250 30 76; www.hoteletnea316.com; Via Etnea 316; s/d €55/90; ⊠ 🖳), located opposite the Bellini gardens.

TOP END

Katane Palace Hotel (☎ 095 747 07 02; www.katane palace.it; Via Finocchiaro Aprile 10; s/d €160/189; P ⊠ 🖳) Catania's only real quality hotel in a restored palazzo. It is discreet and elegant, and offers top-class service. The rooms are warmly furnished and the restaurant, Il Cuciniere, is excellent, with a menu drawn from local ingredients and wines.

Eating

Catanians love to eat, and aside from some very good restaurants, the city has a number of street-facing bar counters serving *arancini* (fried rice balls usually filled with meat, cheese or tomatoes), *cartocciate* (bread which is stuffed with ham, mozzarella, olives and tomato) and *pasta alla Norma* (with basil, aubergine and ricotta), a dish that originated here.

A note of warning: some restaurants in Catania randomly refuse to accept credit cards, so make sure you take enough cash for an evening out.

RESTAURANTS

I Sale Art Café (☎ 095 31 68 88; Via S Filomena 10-12; meals €15; ⏰ 8pm-12.30am Wed-Mon Aug-Jun) Located in an old art gallery, this great-value restaurant still hosts artistic and cultural events. The small, informal dining area is busy and popular with locals. Good pizza and beer as well as some fine cooking.

Osteria i Tre Bicchieri (☎ 095 715 35 40; Via S Giuseppe al Duomo 31; cheese plates €10, fondues €20; ☾ 8pm-midnight Tue-Sun) The dark wood-panelled interior creates the perfect atmosphere for this classy wine bar which stocks over 1000 different labels. The fondue is great fun on evenings of live jazz.

Osteria Antica Marina (☎ 095 34 81 97; Via Pardo 29; meals €20-25; ☾ Wed-Mon) A rustic-style trattoria behind the fish market, this is the restaurant to come to for fish – try the local favourite, a raw anchovy salad. The décor is solid wooden tables and rough stone walls. Reservations are essential.

Cantine del Cugno Mezzano (☎ 095 715 87 10; Via Museo Biscari 8; meals €22; ☾ 7-11pm Mon-Sat Sep-Jul) Located in the former stables of Palazzo Biscari, this restaurant (really more a wine bar that serves food) has a great atmosphere. It places a high value on quality and all the food on its very limited menu is organic.

Sicilia in Bocca Piazza Lupo 16-18 (☎ 095 746 31 61; mains €8-16; ☾ lunch & dinner Thu-Tue, closed Wed & lunch Sun); Via Dusmet 31-35 (☎ 095 250 02 08; meals €20-25; ☾ Tue-Sun) A favourite of the bohemian crowd who flock to this restaurant for its traditional fish recipes. The Piazza Lupo branch is the original.

Trattoria La Paglia (☎ 095 34 68 38; Via Pardo 23; meals €15; ☾ Mon-Sat) This is a great, cheap trattoria with an in-your-face view of the action around La Pescheria market.

CAFÉS & PASTICCERIA

Pasticceria Caprice (Via Etnea 30) An old-style *pasticceria*, this is the perfect place to come during *passeggiata*. Try a selection of mini tarts filled with fresh fruit.

SELF-CATERING

Every morning except Sunday, Piazza Carlo Alberto is flooded by the chaos of a **produce market**, (La Fiera; ☾ 7am-noon Mon-Sat). The other major market is La Pescheria (p785).

Drinking

Not surprisingly for a busy university town, Catania has a reputation for its great nightlife. Most nightspots are closed on Monday and opening hours are generally from around 9pm to 2am.

Tertulia (Via M Rapisardi 1-3; ☾ 4.30pm-1.30am Sep-Jul) A nocturnal bookshop and cafeteria, that's a mix between a stylish teahouse and bar. There is occasional live music, literary evenings and book presentations, as well as Internet access.

Nievski Pub (☎ 095 31 37 92; www.nievski.it; Scalinata Alessi 15; meals €10-15; ☾ 1-4pm & 8pm-2am Tue-Sat) On the heaving Scalinata Alessi, this is a good place to mingle with Catania's alternative crowd. Cuban revolutionary posters adorn the walls, and the menu uses fair-trade produce for its Greek and Cuban dishes.

Agorá Hostel (☎ 095 723 30 10; www.agorahostel.com; Piazza Currò 6; meals €15) The bar and restaurant of the Agorà Hostel are a great venue for a drink. It's a neon-lit, subterranean cave 60 feet below ground where a stream bubbles to the surface. The Romans used it as a spa and now a cosmopolitan crowd lingers over drinks in the cavern.

Joyce (☎ 0349 810 78 96, Via Montesano 46; ☾ 9pm-2am Tue-Sun) An Irish pub where you can enjoy pints of Guinness in a pleasant courtyard. It's a popular place (Italians think Irish culture is really glamorous) and, quite frankly, it can really go off – in a good way.

Entertainment

To see what's going on pick up a copy of *Lapis* (it's free, and available throughout the city).

Teatro Massimo Bellini (☎ 095 730 61 11; www.teatromassimobellini.it; Via Perrotta 12) Ernesto Basile's Art Nouveau theatre stages opera, ballet and music concerts. Its programme runs from October to May. You can book tickets online.

Zò (☎ 095 53 38 71; www.zoculture.it; Piazzale Asia 6; ☾ 1-3pm & 8.30pm-12.30am Tue-Sat) This bar/café/restaurant serves good food in an impressive venue – the converted sulphur works, Le Ciminiere (p785). Weekends are the best time as there is live music and dancing.

Getting There & Away

AIR

Catania's airport, **Fontanarossa** (☎ 095 30 45 05; www.aeroporto.catania.it) is 7km southwest of the city centre. To get to the airport, take the special Alibus No 457 (€0.85) from outside the train station. There is also a regular shuttle from the airport to Taormina (€5, hourly, 7am to 8pm). All the big car-hire companies are represented here.

Catania is well served by international carriers such as Air Malta, British Airways and Lufthansa, as well as Alitalia. It is also the airport of choice for a host of charter flights.

Air Berlin (☎ 848 39 00 54; www.airberlin.com) Direct flights from Berlin.

British Midland (☎ 0870 607 05 55; www.flybmi.com) Summer-only charters.

Hapag-Lloyd Flug (www.hapagfly.com in German) Flights through Nuernberg.

JMC (☎ 0870 75 05 711; www.jmc.com) Summer-only charters.

BOAT

The ferry terminal is located south of the train station along Via VI Aprile.

Virtu Ferries (☎ 095 53 57 11; www.virtuferries.com) has express ferries from Catania to Malta. Ferries depart Catania's Molo Centrale (one departure a week March to May and four weekly departures between 24 July and 3 September). The trip takes three hours and tickets cost €61/91 one way/return and €105 for a car.

TTT Lines (☎ 095 746 21 87; www.tttlines.it in Italian) has a daily ferry from Naples to Catania (10½ hours, armchair/car/double cabin tickets cost €55/90/170).

BUS

Intercity buses terminate in the area around Piazza Giovanni XXIII, in front of the train station, and depart from Via d'Amico one block up. Catania's bus station is super-efficient, far surpassing the rather plodding train service.

AST (☎ 095 746 10 96; Via L Sturzo 230) runs similar services to SAIS and Interbus, as well as to many smaller provincial towns around the Catania region, including to Nicolosi (€3.55, 50 minutes, half-hourly).

Interbus (☎ 095 53 27 16; www.interbus.it; Via d'Amico 181) runs buses to Syracuse (€4.10, 1¼ hours, half-hourly Monday to Saturday, eight on Sunday), Piazza Armerina (€19.30, 1½ hours, nine daily Monday to Saturday) and Taormina (€4.20, 1½ hours, four daily Monday to Friday).

SAIS Autolinee (☎ 095 53 62 01; Via d'Amico 181-187) serves Palermo (€12.50, 2½ hours, 17 daily), Agrigento (€11, three hours, 14 daily Monday to Friday, seven daily Saturday and Sunday) and Messina (€6.70, 1½ hours, half-hourly Monday to Saturday, two on

Sunday). It also has a service to Rome (€43, 14 hours) that leaves at 8pm.

CAR & MOTORCYCLE

Catania is easily reached from Messina on the A18 autostrada (see the boxed text, p778) and from Palermo on the A19. From the autostrada, signs for the centre of Catania will bring you to Via Etnea.

TRAIN

Frequent trains connect Catania with Messina (1st/2nd class €10/8, two hours, half-hourly) and Syracuse (€4.65, 1½ hours, 18 daily) and there are less frequent services to Palermo (€11.25, 3½ hours, six daily) and Agrigento (€11.25, 4½ hours, five daily).

The private Ferrovia Circumetnea train line circles Mt Etna, stopping at the towns and villages on the volcano's slopes; for details, see p790.

Getting Around

Many of the more useful **AMT city buses** (☎ 095 736 01 11) terminate in front of the train station. These include Alibus No 457 (station to airport every 20 minutes), Nos 1 to 4 (station to Via Etnea) and Nos 4 to 7 (station to Piazza del Duomo). A two-hour ticket costs €0.85. In summer, a special service (D) runs from Piazza G Verga to the sandy beaches.

For a taxi, call **CST** (☎ 095 33 09 66).

For drivers, some words of warning: there are complicated one-way systems around the city and the centre has now been pedestrianised. This means that the narrow streets get terribly clogged during rush hours and parking is a problem.

MT ETNA
elev 3350m

Dominating the landscape of eastern Sicily, Mt Etna is Europe's largest volcano and one of the world's most active. Eruptions occur frequently, both from the four craters at the summit and on the slopes of the volcano, which is littered with fissures and old craters. The volcano's most devastating eruptions occurred in 1669 and lasted 122 days. A huge river of lava poured down its southern slope, engulfing a good part of Catania and dramatically altering the landscape.

Since 1987 the volcano and its slopes have been part of a national park, the Parco dell'Etna, a territory which encompasses a

A SLEEPING GIANT

Italy's southern coast with its three volcanoes – Etna, Stromboli and Vesuvius – forms Europe's biggest pressure cooker. In July 2001 Etna began to stir once more, spitting ash 700m into the skies and releasing rivers of molten rock down its southern side. As lava flowed from the Cratere Sud-Est the road leading to Rifugio Sapienza was cut off and a heavy layer of ash covered Catania's airport, forcing it to close. While it was not a serious eruption, the residents of Nicolosi, 10km from the lava's source, took to the streets with the best form of spiritual insurance, an effigy of Sant'Agata. By the time things had calmed down in August, an impressive 50 million cu metres of lava had been launched out of the crater.

Not quite finished, Etna started up once again in October 2002, this time tragically sweeping away a huge swathe of ancient pine forests on the northern slope and the whole of the Piano Provenzano resort with it. The steaming remains of these eruptions are now contained in the deep Valle del Bove. You can trek in the valley with Gruppo Guide Alpine Etna Sud (see p790).

fascinatingly varied natural environment, from the severe, almost surreal summit to deserts of lava and alpine forests.

Orientation & Information

The two main approaches to Etna are from Piano Provenzano on the northern flank and Rifugio Sapienza on the southern flank. You can pick up information at a number of sources, the most convenient being the main tourist office in Catania (p785).

On Etna the office of the **Parco Regionale dell'Etna** (☎ 095 82 11 11; www.parcoetna.ct.it; Via Etnea 107a; ⊙ 9am-2pm & 4-7.30pm) is in Nicolosi on the southern side. Near the summit at Rifugio Sapienza, you will find the **Etna Sud Tourist Office** (☎ 095 91 63 56; ⊙ 9am-4pm).

On the northern side of the mountain the local **tourist office** (☎ 095 64 73 52; www.proloco linguaglossa.it; Piazza Annunziata 5; ⊙ 9am-3pm) in Linguaglossa is the best source of information.

For up-to-date information on eruptions and weather forecasts, and for a detailed account of the mountain's geology and history, take a look at www.etnaonline.it.

Sights

With a daily bus link from Catania via Nicolosi, the southern side of the volcano presents the easier ascent to the **craters**. The AST bus drops you off at the **Rifugio Sapienza** (1923m; p790) from where **Funivia dell'Etna** (☎ 095 91 42 09; www.funiviaetna.com; cable car €23, incl bus & guide €42.50; ⊙ 9am-4.30pm) runs a cable car up the mountain to 2500m (the ticket office accepts credit cards).

Once out of the cable car you can attempt the long walk (3½ to four hours return) up the winding track to the authorised crater

zone (2920m). If you plan on doing this make sure you leave yourself enough time to get up *and* down before the last cable car leaves. Otherwise hop on one of the Mercedes Benz trucks (with obligatory guide, €19.50).

On a clear day the landscape above the cable-car station is simply stunning – the perfect black cone of the Cratere Sud-Est offset by a bright-blue sky. The guided tour takes you on a 45-minute walk around the Bocca Nuova. On the eastern edge of the volcano, the Valle del Bove falls away in a precipitous 1000m drop, smoke billowing up from its depths and enveloping you on the ridge above.

On the northern flank of the volcano, you can also make an ascent from the **Piano Provenzano** (1800m). Previously Etna's main ski resort, the entire infrastructure of *refugi*, ski lifts and hotels was wiped out during the 2001–02 eruptions. Now a temporary portacabin has been set up and sells tickets for the regular truck excursions to the summit (€37). To reach this side of the volcano you will need a car as there is no public transport from Linguaglossa, 16km away.

Tours

Ferrovia Circumetnea (FCE; ☎ 095 54 12 50; www .circumetnea.it; Via Caronda 352a, Catania; ⊙ 8am-5pm) has some good tours to Mt Etna and the surrounding region. The Catania–Giarre–Linguaglossa–Etna tour (€25) includes transport to Linguaglossa and Piano Provenzano, and lunch.

Gruppo Guide Alpine Etna Nord (☎ 095 64 78 33; Piazza Santa Caterina 24, Linguaglossa) run a similar tour service to the group below, taking in the north side of the volcano.

SICILY

Gruppo Guide Alpine Etna Sud (☎ 095 791 47 55; Via Etnea 49, Nicolosi) are the official guide service on the mountain, running day or multiday itineraries with a guide. They also have a hut at Rifugio Sapienza from where they run a daily trek into the Valle del Bove (€55, four hours, departs 9am).

Natura e Turismo (☎ 095 91 15 05; Via R Quartararo 11, Catania) does tours of the volcano with expert, multilingual guides or volcanologists.

Sleeping

Accommodation around Mt Etna is scant. If you plan to stay on the mountain, be sure to book in advance.

B&B La Giara (☎ 095 731 90 22; www.giara.it; Viale della Regione 12a; s/d €45/67; P ☒) This reader-recommended place is an elegant patrician villa in Nicolosi. The rooms are decorated with verve, wrought-iron and rattan in one, colourful prints and embroideries in another. Your hostess, Patricia, can help arrange excursions and bike rental and can also arrange rental in a small cottage on the wooded slopes of Etna (€200/400 per week low/high season, sleeps four).

Rifugio Sapienza (☎ 095 91 63 56; Piazzale Funivia; s/d €60/100) Completely refurbished since the last eruptions, the Sapienza refuge now offers comfortable accommodation right next to the cable car. It also has a restaurant.

Ostello della Gioventù Etna (☎ 095 791 46 86; fax 095 791 47 01; etnahostel@hotmail.com; Via della Quercia 7; dm €26; ☼ year-round) If you don't fancy camping but need a cheap bed, this hostel in Nicolosi is the answer to your prayers.

Rifugio Brunek (☎ 095 64 30 15; Bosco Ragabo; B&B/half board per person €26/39) A rustic refuge situated in the tranquil Ragabo pine forest on the eastern slopes of Etna. Designed as a chalet, it has pleasant rooms and a dedicated and helpful host.

Getting There & Away

Having your own transport will make life much easier around Mt Etna, but there are some public transport options.

BUS

AST (☎ 095 53 17 56) runs buses from Catania to Rifugio Sapienza (€3.55, one hour). It leaves from the car park in front of the main train station in Catania at 8.15am, travelling via Nicolosi. It returns from Rifugio Sapienza at 4.45pm.

TRAIN

You can circle Etna on the private **Ferrovia Circumetnea** (FCE; ☎ 095 54 12 50; www.circumetnea .it; Via Caronda 352a) train line. You can catch the metro from Catania's main train station to the FCE station at Via Caronda (metro stop Borgo) or catch bus No 429 or 432 going up Via Etnea and ask to be let off at the Borgo metro stop.

The train follows a 114km trail around the base of the volcano from where you get great views of the mountain. It also passes through many of Etna's unique towns like Adrano, Bronte and Randazzo (€3.85, two hours). To continue from here you will need to get another train for Giarre on the coast (another hour).

SOUTHEASTERN SICILY

The writer Gesualdo Bufalino described the southeast as an 'island within an island', and certainly this pocket of Sicily has a more remote and genteel air about it, undoubtedly the lingering legacy of its glorious Greek heritage.

Inland a checkerboard of stonewalled fields and river valleys embrace a series of richly baroque market towns – Ragusa, Mòdica and Noto. Shattered by a devastating earthquake in January 1693, they were rebuilt in the ornate and much-lauded style known as Sicilian baroque, a style that lends the region a honey-coloured cohesion and collective beauty.

SYRACUSE
pop 122,900

Nowhere is the aesthetic unity of the southeast more visible than in Syracuse, one of Sicily's most visited cities. Settled by colonists from Corinth in 734 BC, Syracuse was considered by Cicero to be the most beautiful city of the ancient world, rivalling Athens in power and prestige. Under the demagogue Dionysius the Elder the city reached its zenith, attracting luminaries, such as Livy, Plato, Aeschylus and Archimedes, who flocked to his capital, cultivating the sophisticated urban culture that was to see the birth of comic Greek theatre. As the sun set on ancient Greece, Syracuse became a Roman colony and was looted of its treasures. Lacking the drama of Palermo and the energy of Catania, Syracuse still manages to seduce visitors with its quiet decrepitude, excellent hotels and fascinating sites.

Orientation

The main sights of Syracuse are in two areas: on the island of Ortygia and 2km across town in the Neapolis Archaeological Park. The train station is located to the west of the busy shopping street, Corso Gelone. If you arrive by bus, you'll be dropped in or near Piazza della Posta in Ortygia. Stay on Ortygia for atmosphere, great restaurants and good-quality hotels.

Information

Numerous banks (all with ATMs) line Corso Umberto. There are others on Corso Gelone and on Ortygia around Via XX Settembre and on Via Roma. There are plenty of public phones on the streets.

Internet Train (☎ 0931 46 87 97; Via Roma 122, Ortygia; per hr €4; ☺ 7.30pm-midnight Tue-Sat) There's 15 fast computers, colour printing, digital downloads and scanning.

Main tourist office (☎ 0931 48 12 00; www.apt-siracusa .it in Italian; Via San Sebasiano 43; ☺ 8.30am-1.30pm & 3.30-6.30pm Mon-Sat) Multilingual staff and a useful city map – ask about the cumulative tickets for the sites.

Ortygia tourist office (☎ 0931 46 42 55; Via Maestranza 33; ☺ 8am-2pm & 2.30-5.30pm Mon-Fri, mornings Sat) English-speaking staff and lots of good information.

Ospedale Generale Provinciale (☎ 0931 72 41 11; Via Testaferrata 1)

Police station (☎ 0931 46 35 56; Via San Sebastiano)

Post office (Piazza della Posta 15; ☺ 8am-6.30pm Mon-Fri, 8.30am-1pm Sat) Also offers currency exchange.

Syrako Porta Marina Tourist Point (☎ 0931 2 41 33; Largo Porta Marina; ☺ 9am-1pm & 3-8pm Mon-Sat) This information/tourist centre can help travellers without cars see more of the province.

Sights

ORTYGIA

Despite its baroque veneer, the Greek essence of Syracuse is everywhere in evidence, from the formal civility of the people to disguised architectural relics. The most obvious of these is the **Cathedral** (Piazza del Duomo; ☺ 8am-noon & 4-7pm), which is in fact a Greek temple converted into a church when the island was evangelised by St Paul. The baroque carapace, designed by Andrea Palma, barely hides the solid Temple of Athena beneath and the huge 5th-century-BC Doric columns are still visible both inside and out.

Just down the winding main street from the Cathedral is the **Fontana Aretusa**, where fresh water bubbles up just as it did in ancient times when it was the city's main water supply. Legend has it that the goddess Artemis transformed her beautiful handmaiden Aretusa into the spring to protect her from the unwelcome attention of the river god Alpheus. Now populated by ducks, grey mullet and papyrus plants, the fountain is *the* place to hang out on summer evenings.

Just up Via Capodieci from the fountain is **Museo Regionale d'Arte Medioevale e Moderna** (☎ 0931 6 96 17; Via Capodieci 14; adult/concession €4.50/2; ☺ 9am-1.30pm Mon-Sat, 9am-12.30pm Sun), housing a respectable collection of sculpture and paintings dating from the Middle Ages to the 20th century. Highlights of the museum include Byzantine icons and lots of blood-thirsty religious paintings, the most famous of which is Caravaggio's *La Sepoltura di Santa Lucia* (The Burial of St Lucy; 1609). The palazzo itself is Ortygia's finest Catalan-Gothic mansion.

Simply walking through the tangled maze of alleys that characterises Ortygia is an atmospheric experience, especially down the narrow lanes of **Via Maestranza**, the heart of the old guild quarter, and the crumbling Jewish ghetto of **Via della Giudecca**. Recent renovations of the Alla Giudecca hotel (see the boxed text, p794) uncovered an ancient Jewish **miqwe** (ritual bath; ☎ 0931 2 22 55; Alla Giudecca, Via GB Alagona 52; admission €5; ☺ 10am-7pm) some 20m below ground level. The baths were blocked up in 1492 when the Jewish community was expelled from the island and hadn't been seen since then!

Also in the Jewish quarter is Syracuse's own thriving puppet theatre, **Piccolo Teatro dei Pupi** (☎ 0931 46 55 40; www.pupari.it; Via della Giudecca 17; admission €5; ☺ shows 9.30pm Tue, Thu & Sat, 5pm Sun; ▨). The workshop, where you can buy puppets, is at number 19.

PARCO ARCHEOLOGICO DELLA NEAPOLIS

For the classicist, Syracuse's real attraction is the **Parco Archeologico della Neapolis** (Neapolis Archaeological Park; ☎ 0931 6 62 06; Viale Paradisa; adult/concession €4.50/2; ☺ 9am-2hr before sunset), with its pearly white, 5th-century-BC **Teatro Greco** (Greek Theatre), completely hewn out of the rock overlooking the city. It saw the last tragedies of Aeschylus (including *The Persians*), which were first performed here in his

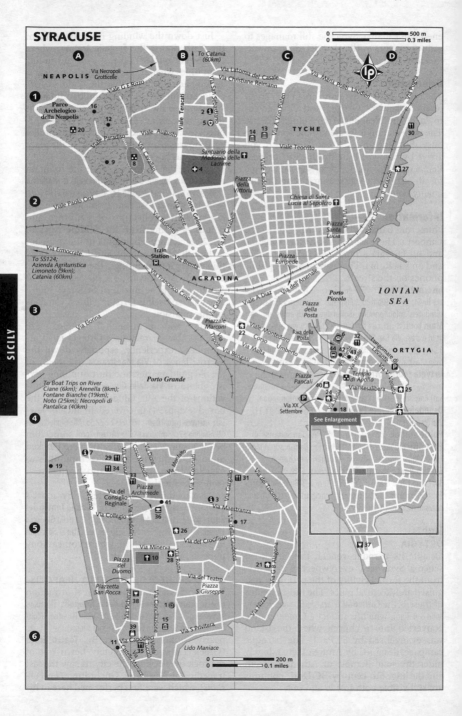

SICILY

presence. Every summer it is brought to life again with a host of classical dramas.

Just beside the theatre is the mysterious **Latomia del Paradiso** (Garden of Paradise); deep, precipitous limestone quarries out of which the stone for the ancient city was extracted. These quarries, riddled with catacombs and filled with citrus and magnolia trees, are where the 7000 survivors of the 413 BC Syracuse–Athens war were imprisoned. The **Orecchio di Dionisio** (Ear of Dionysius), a grotto 23m by 3m deep, was named by Caravaggio after the tyrant, who is said to have used the almost perfect acoustics of the quarry to eavesdrop on his prisoners.

Back outside this area and opposite the tourist office you'll find the entrance to the 2nd-century-AD **Anfiteatro Romano**. The amphitheatre was used for gladiatorial combats and horse races. The Spaniards, little interested in archaeology, largely destroyed the site in the 16th century, using it as a quarry to build the city walls of Ortygia. West of the amphitheatre is the 3rd-century-BC **Ara di Gerone II** (Altar of Hieron II). The monolithic sacrificial altar was a kind of giant abattoir where 450 oxen could be killed at one time.

To get there, take bus No 4, 5, 6, 8, 11, 12 or 15 from Piazza della Posta to Corso Gelone/Viale Teracati. The walk from Ortygia will take about 30 minutes. If you have a car, you can park along Viale Augusto for €1 (as long as you like).

MUSEO ARCHEOLOGICO PAOLO ORSI & MUSEO DEL PAPIRO

Located in the grounds of Villa Landolina, about 500m east of the archaeological park, is the **Museo Archeologico Paolo Orsi** (☎ 0931 46 40 22; Viale Teocrito; admission €4.50; 🕙 9am-2pm Tue-

Sat). It contains the best-organised and most interesting archaeological collection in Sicily (and one of the most extensive archaeological collections in Europe) and certainly merits a visit. The opening hours are all over the place and often get extended in summer; check with one of the tourist offices. The museum is wheelchair accessible.

Around the corner, the **Museo del Papiro** (☎ 0931 6 16 16; Viale Teocrito 66; admission free; 🕙 9am-1.30pm Tue-Sun) includes papyrus documents and products. The plant grows in abundance around the Ciane River, near Syracuse, and was used to make paper in the 18th century.

Activities

Syracuse is all about urban pleasures and there are few activities for those with itchy feet. You can book yourself a pew on Syracuse's tiny **Lido Maniace** (www.lidomaniace.it), a platform crowded with sunbeds and shades (€10 for two people) where you can dip into the water. Ortygia can become a cauldron in summer so this is useful to know. Bigger, sandy beaches can be found at **Arenella** (bus No 23) and the **Fontana Bianche** (bus No 21 or 22 from Piazza della Posta), but note that they are very busy and as with many Sicilian beaches there are charges on certain sections.

One of the best activities is to take a boat trip on one of the gorgeous rigs rented out by **Sailing Team** (☎ 0931 6 08 08, 335 78 50 344; www.sailingteam.biz; Via Savoia 14). The whole day costs €250 (four to six people), departing at 10am and returning at 6pm, enabling you to explore the coastline and snorkel to your heart's content.

Landlubbers should definitely take an excursion with **Ente Fauna Siciliana** (☎ 0931 71 73 35, 328 88 57 092; www.entefaunasiciliana.it; Viale Montedoro 79).

SICILY

Itineraries include mountain-bike trips to the Cava Cardinale (€10 per person), trekking on Etna (€6 per person) and archaeological and botanical itineraries. Booking numbers and departure points are all on their website. Most of the tours are in Italian only.

Tours

Syracuse has a wealth of professional tour guides. The guides generally escort groups so prices are steep (€110 for half a day to €155 for a whole day). The tourist office has a list of guides with whom you can negotiate directly for smaller groups.

Selene (per person €10; ☉ 12.30pm & 1.30pm Apr–Oct) runs a one-hour cruise that takes passengers around Ortygia. It departs from the dock opposite the Grand Hotel; don't forget to bring along a picnic lunch.

Syrako Porta Marina Tourist Point (p791) can help you to arrange guides, and runs good tours with varying themes from classical to baroque itineraries.

Festivals & Events

In May and June Syracuse hosts the **Ciclo di Spettacoli Classici** (Festival of Greek Theatre; ☎ 0931 44 93 58; www.indafondazione.org). Syracuse boasts the only school of classical Greek drama outside Athens and the performances (in Italian) attract Italy's finest performers. Tickets (€15 to €35) are available online, from the tourist office or at the booth at the entrance to the theatre.

During the **Festa di Santa Lucia** (13 December) the enormous silver statue of the city's patron saint wends its way from the Cathedral to Piazza Santa Lucia accompanied by fireworks.

Sleeping

Syracuse prides itself on discerning tourism and this is certainly reflected in its excellent hotels. The best options are on Ortygia. All the cheaper options cluster around the train station.

BUDGET

Hotel L'Acanto (☎ /fax 0931 46 11 29; www.bebsicilia.it; Via Roma 15; s/d €50/75; 🅿 💻) The family-run L'Acanto is a very popular, value-for-money *albergo*. It has delightful and well-decorated rooms set around a pretty internal courtyard. The service and attention to detail and comfort are excellent.

B&B Casa Mia (☎ 0931 46 33 49; www.bbcasamia.it; Corso Umberto 112; s/d €45/75; 🅿 💻) This home away from home is a great choice on the mainland, situated in an old mansion on Corso Umberto. Its three rooms are furnished with family antiques and there is a lovely breakfast area in the internal patio. You can borrow bikes and use the Internet for free.

Hotel Riviera (☎ 0931 6 70 50; www.hotelrivierasiracusa.com; Via Eucleida 7; s/d €61/80; 🅿 🅿) One of the only hotels in Syracuse with a seafront location, giving it lovely views from the 1st-floor terrace and some of its rooms. It is a friendly family-run hotel (English is spoken) and the rooms are slowly being renovated. Better if you have a car.

MIDRANGE & TOP END

Hotel Gutkowski (☎ 0931 46 58 61; www.guthotel.it; Lungomare Vittorini 26; s/d €65/95; 🅿 💻) This charming pastel-blue hotel with crisp minimalist rooms continues to lead the way. It now offers some excellent excursions (€40 per person) to natural beauty spots as well as Italian lessons. Ask for sea-view rooms and book several weeks in advance.

Hotel Roma (☎ 0931 46 56 26; www.hotelroma.sr.it; Via Minerva 10; s/d €123.95/195; 🅿 🅿) Right in the centre of Ortygia just behind the Cathedral is a restored palazzo which now houses the Hotel Roma. Intimate, efficient and convenient, this is an excellent luxury option with helpful staff.

Domus Mariae (☎ 0931 2 48 54; www.sistemia.it/domusmariae; Via V Veneto 76; s/d €105/135; 🅿 🅿) A former school for nuns transformed into an elegant hotel. More formal than the Gut-kowski, it has great character and sea views. It is still run by the nuns, who know how to turn out an impeccable room.

Hotel Gran Bretagne (☎ 0931 6 87 65; Via Savoia 21; s/d €73/100; ⊠) This handsome, small hotel has friendly management and is situated in a great location on Ortygia. The dark, de-signer colour scheme – petrol-blue fittings and black-and-white striped bedspreads – makes some of the rooms a touch gloomy.

Azienda Agrituristica Limoneto (☎ 0931 71 73 52; www.emmeti.it/Limoneto; Via del Platano 3; d €90; P ⊠) A big country farm set amid attractive cit-rus and olive groves, noted for its organic produce and excellent restaurant. A lovely alternative to the city and a great base for exploring the countryside. You will find it 9km from Syracuse along the SS124.

Eating

There is no shortage of restaurants on Orty-gia, where all the best eateries are located.

Jonico – A Rutta 'e Ciauli (☎ 0931 6 55 40; Riviera Dioisio il Grande 194; pizzas €3.50-8, meals €35; ⊠ Wed-Mon) Very inconvenient but worth the trek or taxi ride, Jonico is right on the sea with a wonderful terrace, a quirky Art Deco In-terior and an exquisite Syracusan menu, which includes swordfish rolled in raisins and pine nuts, and steak in a white wine salsa. The roof garden serves pizza in the evenings.

Trattoria la Foglia (☎ 0931 6 62 33; www.lafoglia .it; Via Capodieci 21; meals €25) Here the eccentric owner/chef and her vegetarian husband serve whatever seafood and vegetables are fresh that day. The ambience is delightful, with hand-embroidered tablecloths and fine porcelain plates.

Trattoria Archimede (☎ 0931 697 01; Via Gemellaro 8; meals €20-25; ⊠ Aug-Jun) The most authentic restaurant on Ortygia, with black-and-white photographs of the island as it once was. There are three formal dining rooms and the menu changes constantly so you never get bored. Typical, traditional trattoria food – pastas and straightforward seafood and meat dishes.

Le Baronie (☎ 0931 6 88 84; Via Gargallo 24; meals €25-30; ⊠ Tue-Sun) A boisterous atmosphere in an old Catalan-Gothic mansion. Le Bar-onie prides itself on traditional cuisine with a twist, such as swordfish with a pepper and brandy sauce.

Il Gattopardo (Via Cavour 67a; pizzas €3.50-7, meals €10-15) This hugely popular, unpretentious restaurant is easy to miss. The cooking is simple and delicious (there is no menu at lunchtime) and in the evenings everyone comes here for a pizza.

Quelli della Trattoria (Via Cavour 28; pastas €6-8; ⊠ Mon-Sat) A tiny rustic restaurant that spe-cialises in all manner of fresh pasta dishes (try the speciality of the house, seafood ravi-oli). It fills up quickly in the evenings so reservations are advised.

The **produce market** (Antico Mercato; www.antico mercato.it) is in the streets near the post office. The market is busy until about 1pm daily; there is also a market restaurant.

Drinking

Syracuse is a big university town and at the weekends students are out and about in force.

There are dozens of small bars, but three recommended spots are the literary **Biblios Cafe** (Via del Consiglio Reginale 11; ⊠ 10am-1.30pm & 5-9pm Mon, Tue & Thu-Sat Oct-Aug), the cosy wine bar **Peter Pan** (☎ 0931 46 89 37; Via Castello Maniace 46-48; glass of wine €4-7) and the more boisterous **San Rocca** (Piazzetta San Rocca, Ortygia; cocktails €5).

Shopping

Ortygia is full of quirky little shops like **Circo Fortuna** (☎ 0931 6 26 81; Via Capodieci 42), which produces lots of cheeky ceramics. Another good ceramicist can be found at **Lecomarí** (Via Salvatore Chindemi 21).

Getting There & Away

BUS

Unless you're coming from Catania or Mes-sina, you'll almost always find buses faster and more convenient than trains. **Interbus** (☎ 0931 6 67 10; Via Trieste 28) buses leave from Riva della Posta (also known as Piazza della Posta), or near the Interbus office a block in. They connect with Catania (€4.10, 1¼ hours, 19 daily Monday to Friday, eight on Sunday) and its airport, and Palermo (€13.40, four hours, four daily Monday to Saturday, three on Sunday).

AST (☎ 0931 46 27 11; Riva della Posta 9) runs buses to Palermo (€13.40, four hours, six daily Monday to Saturday, three Sunday) and a local network to Piazza Armerina (€7.75, four hours, one daily), Noto (€2.75, one hour, 12 daily Monday to Saturday) and Ragusa

(€5.80, two hours, nine daily Monday to Saturday) from their office.

CAR & MOTORCYCLE
If arriving from the north, you will enter Syracuse on Viale Scala Greca. To reach the centre of the city, turn left at Viale Teracati and follow it around to the south; it eventually becomes Corso Gelone. The road between Catania and Syracuse is the SS114 and between Syracuse and Noto it's the SS115. A motorway is supposed to connect the SS114 and SS115, but it starts and ends in the middle of nowhere some kilometres out of Syracuse.

There is a large underground car park on Via V Veneto on Ortygia where you can park for free.

TRAIN
More than a dozen trains depart daily for Messina (1st/2nd class €20.10/15.35, 2½ to three hours) via Catania (€12/9, 1¼ hours). Some go onto Rome, Turin and Milan, plus other long-distance destinations. For Palermo (€16.40, five to six hours) you will have to change at either Catania or Messina. There are several slow trains from Syracuse to Noto (€2.65, 30 minutes) and Ragusa (€5.85, 2¼ hours).

Getting Around
If you arrive by bus, you'll be dropped on or near Piazza della Posta in Ortygia. Bus Nos 1 and 4 make the trip from Piazza della Posta to the archaeological park. All city buses cost €0.85 for two hours, irrespective of the number of buses you take.

To hire a bicycle (€10 per day) or scooter (€30 per day) ask at **Allakatalla** (☎ 0931 6 74 52; Via Roma 10) travel agency. They get very busy so try to book in advance.

NOTO
pop 23,100 / elev 160m
Flattened by the 1693 earthquake, Noto was rebuilt by its noble families in the grand baroque style and is now the finest baroque town in Sicily. The florid architecture is the work of Rosario Gagliardi and his assistant Vincenzo Sinatra, local architects who also worked in Ragusa and Mòdica. Recently added to Unesco's list of World Heritage sites, Noto is currently undergoing extensive restoration. In 1996 the town was shocked when

the roof of the Cathedral collapsed after a thunderstorm. Since then major works have been implemented to stabilise the church and fix the dome.

Intercity buses drop you in the Porta Reale, which is at the beginning of Corso Vittorio Emanuele, the town's main street.

Information
Ambulance (☎ 0931 89 02 35)
Police station (☎ 0931 83 52 02; Via Maiore) On the eastern extension of Via Aurispa.
Tourist office (☎ 0931 57 37 79; www.comune.noto.sr.it; Piazza XVI Maggio; ⊙ 8am-2pm & 3.30-6.15pm Mon-Sat) An excellent and busy information office with multilingual staff and a free map.

Sights
The **San Nicoló Cathedral** (still clad in scaffolding) stands in the centre of Noto's most graceful square, Piazza Municipio. The restoration work on the roof continues slowly although this has its up side; at the time of research it was possible to watch the complicated process of craftsmen creating a new dome around a skeletal framework of scaffolding.

The cathedral is surrounded by elegant townhouses such as Palazzo Ducezio (Town Hall) and Palazzo Landolina, once home to Noto's oldest noble family. However, the only palazzo that has been restored to its former glory is the **Palazzo Villadorata** (Palazzo Nicolaci; ☎ 0931 83 50 05; Via Corrado Nicolaci; adult/concession €3/1.50; ⊙ 10am-1pm & 3-7pm Tue-Sun), where wrought-iron balconies are supported by a swirling pantomime of grotesque figures. Inside, richly brocaded walls and frescoed ceilings give an idea of the sumptuous lifestyle of Sicilian nobles brought to life in the Tomasi di Lampedusa novel, *Il Gattopardo* (The Leopard; see p57).

Two other piazzas break up the long corso: Piazza dell'Immacolata to the east and more notably Piazza XVI Maggio to the west. The latter is overlooked by the beautiful **Chiesa di San Domenico** and the adjacent Dominican monastery, both designed by Rosario Gagliardi. On the way up to Piazza XVI Maggio, climb up the **campanile** (admission €1.55; ⊙ 9am-12.30pm & 4-7pm) of the Chiesa di San Carlo al Corso for some pretty views.

Festivals & Events
Infioraci, held on the third Sunday of May, is Noto's colourful flower festival, when artists

line the length of Via Corrada Nicolaci with
artwork made entirely of flower petals.

Sleeping
Noto has very limited hotel accommodation,
but there are a plethora of good B&Bs. Ask
at the tourist office for a detailed list, otherwise check out www.notobarocca.com.

Hotel della Ferla (☎ 0931 57 60 07; www.hotelferla
.it; Via A Gramsci; s/d €40/70; Ⓟ ▒) A new addition to Noto, this small hotel with 15 rooms
is modern, efficient and within easy walking distance of the historic centre. Its garage
is a big bonus.

B&B Montandòn (☎ 0931 83 57 93; www.b-bmont
andon.com; Via A Sofia 50; s/d €40/70; Ⓟ ▒) A beautiful B&B in a crumbling palazzo – real old
Noto. Upper rooms have panoramic views
and are light and elegantly furnished.

Il Castello Youth Hostel (☎ /fax 0931 57 15 34;
ostellodinoto@tin.it; Via Fratelli Bandiera; dm €14.50)
Right in the centre of things in a beautiful
old building, this place is the pride of Noto
and great value for money. There are 68 beds
and an open-all-day policy.

Eating
The people of Noto are serious about their
food, so take time to enjoy a meal and follow
it up with a visit to one of the town's excellent
ice-cream shops.

Il Barocco (☎ 0931 83 59 99; Via Cavour 8; mains €7-
12) Located in the stable block of the Palazzo
Astuto-Barresi. The eccentric character of the
owner and chef is everywhere in evidence
from the graffitied walls to the spaghetti with
limpets.

Ristorante Neas (☎ 0931 57 35 38; Via Rocco Pirri 30;
mains €8-12; Ⓨ Tue-Sun) You'll find a high standard of food and service at this place, which
opens up its lovely terrace in summer.

Caffè Sicilia (☎ 0931 83 50 13; Corso Vittorio Emanuele 125), operating since 1892, and **Corrado
Costanzo** (☎ 0931 83 52 43; Via Silvio Spaventa 9),
around the corner, are neck and neck when
it comes to the best ice cream and cakes in
Noto. Both make superb *dolci di mandorla*
(almond cakes and sweets), real *cassata* cake
(made with ricotta cheese, chocolate and
candied fruit) and *torrone* (nougat).

Getting There & Around
Noto is easily accessible by AST and Interbus buses from Catania (€5.75, 2¼ hours,
12 daily Monday to Saturday, seven on Sun-

day) and Syracuse (€2.75, one hour, 12 daily
Monday to Saturday). From June to August
only, buses run frequently between Noto
and Noto Marina (in the winter there is a
school-bus service). Trains from Syracuse are
frequent (€2.65, 30 minutes, 11 daily), but
the station is located 1.5km south of the bus
station area.

MÒDICA
pop 52,900 / elev 296m
Once a powerhouse in the region, Mòdica
has now lost its pre-eminent position to
Ragusa. Still, its sun-bleached colour, faded
baroque structures and the best chocolate
on the island make it worth a visit.

The multilayered town – divided into
Mòdica Alta (High Mòdica) and Mòdica
Bassa (Low Mòdica) – tumbles into a deep
valley, where once a raging river flowed.
Today, following a devastating flood in 1902,
the water has been transformed into Corso
Umberto and Via Giarrantana (the river was
dammed and diverted). These are the main
axes of the town, lined with shabby palazzi
and higgledy-piggledy houses.

The highlight of a trip to Mòdica is the
Chiesa di San Giorgio (Mòdica Alta; Ⓨ 9am-noon & 4-
7pm), easily one of the most extraordinary
baroque churches on the island. Gagliardi's
masterpiece, it is a vision of pure rococo
splendour perched at the top of a majestic
250-step staircase. Viewed from below, the
swirling confection looks as if it might float
away. Its counterpoint in Mòdica Bassa is the
Cattedrale di San Pietro (Corso Umberto I), another
impressive church atop a rippling staircase
lined with life-size statues of the apostles.

Mòdica is also famous for its confectionary, a legacy of the town's Spanish overlords
who imported cocoa from their South American colonies. To taste the crunchy black
stuff – flavoured with cinnamon, vanilla and
orange peel – head straight for **Antica Dolceria
Bonajuto** (☎ 0932 94 12 25; www.bonajuto.it; Corso
Umberto I 159).

Mòdica is slowly developing into a wonderful base for discerning travellers. The few
accommodation options in town, such as
Hotel Relais (☎ 0932 75 44 51; www.hotelrelaismodica
.it; Via Tommaso Campanella, Mòdica Bassa; s/d €60/95; ▒)
and **Albergo Il Tetti di Siciliano** (☎ 0932 94 28 43;
www.siciliando.it; Via Cannata 24, Mòdica Alta; s/d €30/50),
are both of a high standard, while **Fattoria
delle Torri** (☎ 0932 75 12 86; Vico Napolitano 14, Mòdica

SICILY

Alta; meals €25-30; ✷ lunch Tue-Sun) is one of the best restaurants in the region.

There are plenty of buses and trains to Mòdica from Syracuse (€6.60, five buses daily Monday to Saturday) and to Ragusa (€1.35, 30 minutes, four buses daily Monday to Saturday, two on Sunday).

RAGUSA

pop 69,700 / elev 502m

Classic, quiet, dignified and decrepit, Ragusa is a delightful provincial town completely overlooked by tourists. Like every other town in the region Ragusa collapsed after the 1693 earthquake and a new town was built on a high plateau above the original settlement, which now forms Ragusa Superiore. But the old aristocracy were loathe to leave their tottering palazzi and rebuilt Ragusa Ibla on exactly the same spot. The two towns were only merged in 1927.

Undoubtedly, Ragusa Ibla remains the heart and soul of the town, and it's where all the best restaurants and the majority of sights are. Everything else, including the majority of hotels, are up in the newer town. A perilous bus ride or some very steep steps connect the two towns. A good map and information booklet is available from the **tourist office** (☎ 0932 22 15 11; www.ragusaturismo .it; Via Capitano Bocchieri 33; ✷ 9am-1.30pm & 3.30-6pm Tue-Sun).

Aside from the grand churches and palazzi that literally line your route wherever you go, the best thing about the town is

---

AUTHOR'S CHOICE

Ristorante Duomo (☎ 0932 65 12 65; Via Capitano Bochieri 31; menu degustazione €50; ✷ lunch Tue-Sun) One of the reasons to come to Ragusa is to eat at 'Il Duomo'. It has been called the best restaurant in Sicily, and boy is it good. Inside, a quintet of small rooms are outfitted like private parlours, keeping the atmosphere romantically intimate. The cuisine of chef Ciccio Sultana is intensely patriotic and dishes, although unconventional, stick close to the Sicilian culinary roots of cherry tomatoes, pistachios, bitter almonds, wild fennel and mint. The *menu degustazione* (tasting menu) is insanely good and for foodies this may well be the highlight of their trip.

---

simply wandering through its narrow streets and sun-drenched squares. If you continue east along Via del Mercato (which has excellent views of the valley below) you'll get your first view of palm-planted Piazza del Duomo, the western end of which is dominated by the **Cattedrale di San Giorgio** (built in 1744; it was under scaffolding at the time of research), an elegant Gagliardi church. The smaller **Chiesa di San Giuseppe** (also currently under scaffolding) is on Piazza Pola, east of Piazza del Duomo.

At the eastern end of the old town is the **Giardino Ibleo** (✷ 8am-8pm), a pleasant public garden laid out in the 19th century that is perfect for a picnic lunch.

Sleeping & Eating

Most of Ragusa's large hotels are found in the upper town, but recently a rash of B&Bs have opened in Ragusa Ibla, where there are a number of exceptional restaurants.

Il Barocco (☎ 0932 65 23 97; www.ilbarocco.it; Via S Maria La Nuova; s/d €65/110; ✷) This hotel has been newly opened by the Cabibbo family, who own the massively popular restaurant of the same name. Once a carpenter's workshop, the rooms are unfussy and comfortable.

Il Barocco (Via Orfanatrofio 29; meals €20) This restaurant is so popular that reservations are essential. You simply must try the delicious grilled meat and mushroom platter (€22 for two people).

Also recommended, **Locanda Don Serafino** (☎ 0932 24 87 78; Via Orfanotrofio 39; mains €12-18; ✷ Wed-Mon) is in the atmospheric barrel-vaulted caverns of an old stable block.

Getting There & Around

Ragusa is accessible by train from Syracuse (€5.70, 2¼ hours, eight daily) and Noto (€4.25, 1¾ hours, eight daily).

Interbus (Viale Tenente Lena 42) runs daily buses to Catania (€6.60, 1¾ hours, 10 daily Monday to Friday, five daily Saturday and Sunday); information and tickets are available at Caffè del Viale. **AST** (☎ 0932 68 18 18) runs the local network to Syracuse (€5.80, 2½ hours, six daily Monday to Saturday). An AST timetable is posted on Piazza Gramsci where AST and SAIS buses stop.

City bus Nos 1 and 3 run from Piazza del Popolo in the upper town to Piazza Pola and the Giardino Ibleo in the lower town of Ragusa Ibla.

CENTRAL & SOUTHERN SICILY

The most rural parts of Sicily, the southern coastline and centre of the island are full of perplexing juxtapositions: undulating fields and severe mountain ridges; shabby hilltop towns and superb sandy beaches; and the busiest and most famous classical site set against acres of brutal modern development. But persevere in this ancient landscape and you will be rewarded with an insight into a more authentic Sicily not yet sanitised for tourists.

ENNA

pop 28,800 / elev 948m

A rich agricultural centre, Enna has long been the seat of a sacred cult of Demeter (the goddess of fertility), and throughout the Greek, Roman and Arab periods it supplied far-flung places with grain, wheat, cotton and cane – a tradition it continues on a smaller scale today.

Information

Main tourist office (☎ 0935 52 82 88; www.apt-enna .com; Via Roma 413; ☺ 9am-1pm & 3.30-6.30pm Mon-Sat) Provides a good map and information about the province. Helpful staff.

Sights

Jealously guarded, Enna's massive **Castello di Lombardia** (☎ 0935 50 09 62; Piazza Mazzini; admission free; ☺ 9am-8pm) is the most obvious physical manifestation of the inward-looking nature of Sicily's mountain villages. It is hardly surprising given the waves of invaders who sought to possess this mountain eyrie. This history is perfectly illustrated in the hotchpotch architecture of the **Cathedral** (☺ 9am-1pm & 4-7pm), a catalogue of Graeco-Roman remains, medieval walls, Gothic doors and apses, Renaissance artwork and baroque carvings. Behind the Cathedral is the **Museo Alessi** (☎ 0935 50 31 65; Via Roma; adult/concession €2.60/1.50; ☺ 9am-8pm Tue-Sun), which houses the contents of the treasury.

To enjoy a gorgeous sunset on the rust-red town of Calascibetta situated on the opposite hill, head for Piazza Francesco Crispi and its spectacular **belvedere** (viewing point).

Festivals & Events

Holy Week is celebrated at Easter. Thousands of people wearing hoods and capes representing the town's different religious confraternities participate in a solemn procession to the Cathedral.

The **Festa di Maria Santissim della Visitazione** is held on 2 July. An effigy of Enna's patron saint was traditionally dragged through the town by farmers wearing just a white band over their hips! Today the band has been replaced by a long sheet.

Sleeping & Eating

Grande Albergo Sicilia (☎ 0935 50 08 50; fax 0935 50 04 88; Piazza Colaianni 7; s/d €63/91; P) Enna Alta's only hotel has a crude concrete façade disguising the kitschy Art Nouveau interior decorated with lots of coloured glass and gold-framed pictures.

San Gennaro Da Gino (☎ 0935 2 40 67; Viale Marconi 6; pizzas €6-8; ☺ Thu-Tue) This historic pizzeria is located right on the belvedere with outdoor seating, and is absolutely buzzing with teenagers. Good atmosphere and great views.

Ristorante Centrale (☎ 0935 50 09 63; Piazza VI Dicembre 9; meals €20; ☺ 12.30-3.30pm & 8-11pm) This place has friendly service and dishes up traditional mountain food, including the local *castrato* (charcoal-grilled castrated ram) and *polpettone* (stuffed lamb or meatballs).

There is a morning **market** (Via Mercato Sant' Antonio; ☺ Mon-Sat) where you can find fresh produce.

Getting There & Away

There is a **bus station** (☎ 0935 50 09 05; Viale Diaz) in the historic town from where the company **SAIS Autolinee** (☎ 0935 50 09 02) runs services to Catania (€10.30, 1½ to two hours, 10 daily Monday to Saturday) and Palermo (€8.30, 1¾ hours, two daily Monday to Saturday). It is possible to reach Agrigento via Caltanissetta (€3.30, one hour, three daily Monday to Friday) and regular buses also run to Piazza Armerina (€2.75, 45 minutes, two daily Monday to Saturday). There is usually only one bus on Sunday.

The train station is inconveniently located at the bottom of a steep hill 3.5km northeast of Enna Alta. Trains service Catania (€4.65, seven daily) and Palermo (€7.50, four daily) and you can purchase tickets from the machine on the platform. Local buses (€1.35, day pass €2.10) make the run to town hourly

SICILY

(except Sunday, when you might have to wait a couple of hours between buses). You can call for a taxi on ☎ 0935 50 09 05.

VILLA ROMANA DEL CASALE

Situated 35km southeast of Enna and 5km southwest of Piazza Armerina is the **Villa Imperiale** (☎ 0935 68 00 36; www.villaromanadelcasale .it; adult/concession €4.50/2; ♥ 8am-6.30pm), a stunning 3rd-century Roman villa and one of the few remaining sites of Roman Sicily. The sumptuous hunting lodge is thought to have belonged to Diocletian's co-emperor Marcus Aurelius Maximianus. Buried under mud in a 12th-century flood, it remained hidden for 700 years before its magnificent floor mosaics were discovered in the 1950s. It is worth arriving early or during the lunch hour (1pm to 2pm) to avoid the hordes of tourist groups (some 2000 visitors per day in summer) that descend on the villa.

The mosaics cover almost its entire floor (3500 sq metres) and are considered unique for their narrative style, the range of subject matter and variety of colour – many of them clearly influenced by African themes. Along the eastern end of the internal courtyard is the wonderful **Corridor of the Great Hunt** depicting chariots, rhinos, cheetahs and lions in rich golden colours. The stylised animals seem ready to jump out of the scene, watched by the voluptuously beautiful Queen of Sheba. On the other side of the corridor is a series

of apartments, where floor illustrations reproduce scenes from Homer. But perhaps the most captivating of the mosaics include the erotic depictions in what was probably a private apartment on the northern side of the great peristyle (colonnaded garden).

The **tourist office** (☎ 0935 68 02 01; www.comune .piazzaarmerina.en.it; Via Cavour 15; ♥ 8.30am-12.30pm & 3-7pm Mon-Fri) in Piazza Armerina hands out brochures of the villa with a floor plan and an explanation of the mosaics. Otherwise you can get hold of a copy at one of the many souvenir stalls that line the road.

Autolinee Urbane runs buses from Piazza Armerina to the villa (€0.70, 30 minutes, six daily 1 May to 30 September). Buses depart from the Piazza on the hour (9am to 11am and 3pm to 5pm) and return on the half-hour (9.30am to 11.30am and 3.30pm to 5.30pm).

Outside summer you will have to walk (an easygoing 5km downhill), drive or get a taxi. Taxis (parked all over town) will take you there, wait for an hour and drive you back to Piazza Armerina for about €20. If you have your own car, head south along the SS117.

AGRIGENTO

pop 55,900 / elev 230m

Busy, brutish, beleaguered Agrigento is Sicily's oldest tourist site, first put on the map by Goethe in the 18th century. In ancient

---

A REGION BLIGHTED

By the end of the 19th century Sicily was officially the chief area of emigration in the world, with nearly 1.5 million Sicilians trying their luck elsewhere. Although it was an island-wide problem, the effect of the depopulation was greatest in the southwestern interior. Novelist Leonardo Sciascia captured the huge emigration with his stories *The Long Crossing* and *The Test*. You can find them, with other great stories about Sicily, in his collection *The Wine Dark Sea.*

It is hardly surprising that Sciascia was able to capture the Sicilian longing for a better life so vividly. He grew up in Racalmuto, and his own grandfather worked in the sulphur mines that surround Caltanissetta. By 1900 Italy had a world monopoly on the trade, but for the 16,000 miners working in 300 mines life was not so rosy. At the age of nine, Sciascia's grandfather went to work down the mine – children were used as they were the only ones small enough to crawl through the suffocating 60m-deep galleries. Naked, maltreated, clawing the sulphur out of the pits with their bare hands, they must have had a hellish existence, and many only saw the light of day once a week.

The grandfather of Sicily's greatest novelist taught himself to read and write in the evenings, enabling his son (Sciascia's father) to become a mine clerk who could afford shoes for the young Leonardo to go to school. By the end of the 19th century American sulphur was beginning to dominate the markets and the consequent collapse of the Sicilian industry started the huge exodus of rural poor.

times Pindar declared that the people of Akragas were 'built for eternity but feasted as if there were no tomorrow' – nowadays the modern town, with its savvy inhabitants, has more in common with the character rather than the aesthetics of its ancient counterpart. Overshadowed by modern apartment blocks on the hill above, the splendid Valle dei Templi (Valley of the Temples) loses much of its immediate impact and it is only when you get down among the ruins that you can appreciate their monumentality. Still, the modern town – encasing its medieval predecessor – is one of the most lively and aggressive in Sicily and harbours a number of notorious crime families who are reputedly key players in the multi-billion-dollar narcotics trade.

Orientation

Intercity buses arrive on Piazza Rosselli and the train station is slightly south on Piazza Marconi. Lying between Piazzale Aldo Moro and Piazza Pirandello is the main street of the medieval town, Via Atenea. Frequent city buses run to the Valley of the Temples below the town (see p804).

Information

There are banks on Piazza Vittorio Emanuele I and along the high street, Via Atenea. Out of hours, there's an exchange office at the post office and another at the train station, although the rates are mediocre.

Ambulance (☎ 0922 40 13 44)

Internet Train (☎ 0922 40 27 83; www.Internettrain.it; Cortile Contarini 7; per hr €4.30; ⊕ 9am-11pm Mon-Fri, 10am-8pm Sat, noon-8pm Sun) Has 10 fast computers.

Ospedale Civile San Giovanni di Dio (☎ 0922 40 13 44; Via Giovanni XXII)

Police station (☎ 0922 59 63 22; Piazzale Aldo Moro 2)

Post office (Piazza Vittorio Emanuele I; ⊕ 8.30am-6.30pm Mon-Fri, 8.30am-12.30pm Sat)

Tourist information booth Piazzale Aldo Moro (⊕ 9am-1pm & 3-7pm) Maps, and a little information if pushed; Valle dei Templi (⊕ 8am-7.30pm summer) Adjacent to the car park; has maps of the archaeological park and information on guides.

Tourist office (☎ 0922 2 04 54; www.agrigentosicilia.it; Via Cesare Battisti 15; ⊕ 8.30am-1.30pm Mon-Fri) Staff have maps and brochures and little else besides.

Sights

VALLEY OF THE TEMPLES

The Valley of the Temples (Valle dei Templi) is one of Sicily's premier attractions. A Unesco World Heritage site incorporating a complex of temples and old city walls from the ancient Greek city of Akragas. Despite the name the five Doric temples stand along a ridge, designed as a beacon to homecoming sailors. Although in varying states of ruin, the temples give a tantalising glimpse of what must truly have been one of the most luxurious cities in Magna Graecia. The most scenic time to come is from February to March when the valley is awash with almond blossom.

The **archaeological park** (☎ 0922 49 72 26; admission €4.50, incl archaeological museum €6; ⊕ Temples of Hera, Concord & Hercules 8.30am-10pm, Temples of Zeus & Dioscuri & Sanctuary of Chtonic deities 8.30am-7pm) is divided into two main sections. East of Via dei Templi are the most spectacular temples, the first of which is the **Tempio di Ercole** (Temple of Hercules), built towards the end of the 6th century BC and believed to be the oldest of the temples. Eight of its 38 columns were raised in 1924 to reveal a structure that was roughly the same size as the Parthenon. The magnificent **Tempio della Concordia** (Temple of Concord) is the only one to survive relatively intact. Built around 440 BC, it was transformed into a Christian church in the 6th century AD. The **Tempio di Giunone** (Temple of Juno) stands high on the edge of the ridge, a five-minute walk to the east. Part of its colonnade remains and there is an impressive sacrificial altar.

Across Via dei Templi, to the west, is what remains of the massive **Tempio di Giove** (Temple of Jupiter), never actually completed and now totally in ruins. It covered an area 112m by 56m with columns 20m high. Between the columns stood *telamoni* (colossal statues), one of which was reconstructed and is now in the Museo Archeologico. A copy lies on the ground among the ruins, gives an idea of the immense size of the structure. Work began on the temple around 480 BC and it was probably destroyed during the Carthaginian invasion in 406 BC. The nearby **Tempio di Castore e Polluce** (Temple of Castor and Pollux) was partly reconstructed in the 19th century, although probably using pieces from other constructions. All the temples are atmospherically lit up at night.

The **Museo Archeologico** (☎ 0922 40 1 11; adult/concession €4.50/2; ⊕ 9am-1.30pm, 2-6pm Wed & Sat), north of the temples, has a huge collection

SICILY

AGRIGENTO

INFORMATION
Internet Train.................................1 C2
Ospedale Civile San Giovanni di
Dio...2 D3
Police Station.................................3 D3
Post Office....................................4 D2
Tourist Information Booth............5 A4
Tourist Information Booth............6 D3
Tourist Office.................................7 C3

SIGHTS & ACTIVITIES
Cathedral......................................8 A1
Chiesa di Santa Maria dei Greci.....9 B2
Entrance & Ticket Office..............10 B4
Ethnographic Museum............(see 11)
Monastero del Santo Spirito......11 C2
Museo Archeològico...................12 B3
Tempio della Concordia.............13 B4
Tempio di Castore e Polluce.....14 A4

Tempio di Ercole........................15 A4
Tempio di Giove.........................16 A4
Tempio di Giunone....................17 B4
Valley of the Temples Main
Entrance..............................(see 5)

SLEEPING
Camere a Sud.............................18 C2
Colleverde Park Hotel.................19 B3
Corte dei Greci............................20 A2
Villa Athena................................21 B4

EATING
La Forchetta...............................22 C3
La Promenade dei Templi...........23 B3
Produce Market..........................24 C3

DRINKING
Café Girasole..............................25 C3
Tempio di Vino...........................26 C3

TRANSPORT
Bus Ticket Booth........................27 D2
Intercity Bus Station..................28 D2

of clearly labelled artefacts from the excavated site. It also has wheelchair access.

MEDIEVAL AGRIGENTO

Roaming around the town's lively, winding
streets is relaxing after a day among the temples. The **Chiesa di Santa Maria dei Greci** (Salita
Santa Maria dei Greci; 8am-noon & 3-6pm Mon-Sat),
uphill from Piazza Lena (at the end of Via
Atenea), is an 11th-century Norman church
built on the site of a 5th-century-BC Greek
temple. Note the remains of the wooden
Norman ceiling and some Byzantine frescoes. If the church is closed, check with the
custodian at Salita Santa Maria dei Greci 1,
who will open the doors for you (with a tip
expected).

Further up the hill is the fragile-looking
Cathedral (Via Duomo; 9am-noon & 4-7pm). Built
in AD 1000, it has been restructured many
times, and is dedicated to the Norman San
Gerlando. Back towards the Piazza Vittorio
Emanuele I, the **Monastero del Santo Spirito**
was founded by Cistercian nuns at the end
of the 13th century. Giacomo Serpotta is
responsible for the stuccoes in the chapel.
There is a small **ethnographic museum** (0922
59 03 71; Via Fodera; admission free; 9am-1.30pm &
4.30-6.30pm Mon-Sat) above the old church. The
nuns here will sell you cakes and pastries,
including *dolci di mandorla*, *cuscusu* (couscous made of almonds and pistachio) and
bucellati (rolled sweet dough with figs). Press
the doorbell, say '*Vorrei comprare qualche*

dolce' ('I'd like to buy a few cakes') and see how you go.

Activities

Siculmarè (☎ 0925 90 53 43; www.leminicrociere.it; May-Jun €29.50, Jul-Aug €33; ☺ bookings 9am-3.30pm) runs a boat along the spectacular coastline, taking in the Scale dei Turchi, a stunning cliff of stratified white marl. The trip takes five hours, departing at 1pm from San Leone.

Tours

The tourist office can provide you with a list of multilingual guides. The official rate is €84 for half a day.

Michele Gallo (☎ 0922 40 22 57, 0360 39 37 30; www.sicilytravel.net; Via Dante 49; per half day €80, temples & museum €100) is an excellent English-speaking guide who can organise individual and group itineraries according to travellers' specific interests.

Festivals & Events

The **Sagra del Mandorlo in Fiore** (Festival of the Almond Blossom) is a huge folk festival held on the first Sunday in February, when the Valley of Temples is cloaked in almond blossom.

Festa di San Calògero (Feast of St Calògero) is held on the first Sunday in July. It's a week-long festival in which the statue of St Calògero (who saved Agrigento from the plague) is carried through the town while spectators throw spiced loaves at the saint.

Sleeping

Rapacious tourism has made the modern town expensive and the services lousy. Most of Agrigento's better hotels are out of town around the Valle dei Templi or near the sea.

Camere a Sud (☎ 349 638 44 24; www.camereasud.it; Via Ficani 6; s/d €40/54, with bathroom €45/70) This cute B&B is run by three sparky Agrigentans; Ignazio, Elvira and Filippo. Apart from the cheerful rooms and delightful roof-terrace breakfast, they organise personal tours, including a swim at the Scala dei Turchi. Payment is cash only.

Foresteria Baglio della Luna (☎ 0922 51 10 61; www.bagliodellaluna.com; Contrada Maddalusa; s/d €175/245; P ☒) This handsome converted *baglio* 2km southwest of the Valley of the Temples is Agrigento's best hotel. It is full of character and extremely comfortable and

the restaurant is rated as one of the best in Sicily.

Villa Athena (☎ 0922 2 69 66; www.athenahotels.com; Via Ugo La Malfa 3; s/d €140/190; P ☒ ☒) Agrigento's most famous hotel and the only one situated inside the archaeological park, it was once the home of Alexander Hardcastle, who devoted his life to the excavations. It has a peerless position overlooking the temples.

Corte dei Greci (☎ 339 422 04 76; www.cortedeigreci.it; Cortile Zeta 3; s/d €35/70) Located high up in the old Arab quarter of the town, this B&B is a series of renovated old houses surrounding a quaint internal courtyard. Each room is really a suite, charmingly decorated with traditional Sicilian furniture. Breakfast is served in the old stables.

Colleverde Park Hotel (☎ 0922 2 95 55; www.colleverde-hotel.it; Via Panoramica dei Templi 21; s/d €120/145; P ☒) A good choice if you have a car as the hotel is located halfway between the town and the valley. Set in lushly planted gardens, it is a pleasant family option.

There are some very average camp sites by the sea at San Leone, 5km south of Agrigento. Try **Camping Nettuno** (☎ 0922 41 62 68; Viale Le Dune, San Leone; person/tent €5/5) although it is likely to be very busy.

Eating

Leon d'Oro (☎ 0922 41 44 00; Viale Emporium 102; mains €10-15; ☺ Tue-Sun) An excellent restaurant that warrants its high prices, perfectly mixing the fish and fowl that typify Agrigento cuisine. Try the *coniglio in agrodolce* (rabbit in a sweet sauce) or the *triglia e macco di fave* (mullet with broad beans).

La Forchetta (☎ 0922 59 45 87; Piazza San Francesco 9; mains €5-8; ☺ Mon-Sat) One of the cheapest meals in town can be found here. The cramped dining room is popular with locals who come for the ever-changing daily specials.

Kokalos (☎ 0922 60 64 27; Viale Magazzeni 3; pizzas €6-8) If you have your own car, head for this trattoria/pizzeria on the road to San Leone, where they dish up great pizza. They also serve the local *cavatelli* pasta, which look like little shells.

La Promenade dei Templi (☎ 0922 2 37 15; Via dei Templi; tourist menus €15) A good café/restaurant popular with locals for a morning coffee, this is really the best eatery near the temples away from the crowds.

SICILY

Drinking

Tempio di Vino (☎ 0922 59 67 86; Piazza San Francesco 11-13; ☺ Mon-Sat) A trendy *enoteca* (wine bar) in a pretty piazza. Enjoy a cool white Inzolia, as you listen to laid-back jazz, munching on olives and spicy salami.

Café Girasole (Via Atenea 68-70; ☺ 11am-midnight Mon-Sat) A popular wine bar in the heart of the medieval town. Light table snacks are served with cocktails and wine and it has a busy atmosphere and some outdoor seating.

Getting There & Away

BUS

For most destinations, bus is the easiest way to get to and from Agrigento. The intercity bus station is located on Piazza Rosselli, just off Piazza Vittorio Emanuele I, and the ticket booth (with timetables) is in the same piazza. **Autoservizi Cuffaro** (☎ 0922 41 82 31) runs daily buses to Palermo (€7.25, two hours, seven daily Monday to Saturday, two on Sunday). **Lumia** (☎ 0922 2 04 14) has departures to Tràpani (€10, four hours, three daily Monday to Saturday, one on Sunday) and **SAIS** (☎ 0922 59 52 60) runs buses to Catania (€11, three hours, half-hourly).

CAR & MOTORCYCLE

The SS189 links Agrigento with Palermo, while the SS115 runs along the coast, northwest towards Tràpani and southeast to Syracuse. To get to Enna, take the SS640 via Caltanissetta.

Driving in the medieval town is nearly impossible. The main street is pedestrianised from 9am to 1.30pm and 5.30pm to 8.30pm when traffic is re-routed around Via Gioieni. There is metered parking at the train station (Piazza Marconi) and Piazza Fratelli Rosselli.

TRAIN

There are plenty of trains daily to and from Palermo (€6.70, two hours, 11 daily) and Catania (€9.20, 3½ hours, six daily). Although trains serve other destinations as well, you're better off taking the bus. The train station has left-luggage lockers (€2.50 per 12 hours).

Getting Around

City buses run down to the Valley of the Temples from in front of the train station. Take bus No 1, 2 or 3 and get off at either the museum or a bit further downhill at the Piazzale dei Templi. No 1 continues to Porto Empèdocle (€1.70). No 2 continues to San Leone (€0.85). The Linea Verde (green line) bus runs every hour from the train station to the Cathedral, for those who prefer not to make the uphill walk.

SELINUNTE

The ruins of Selinunte are the most impressively sited ruins in Sicily. The huge city was built in 628 BC on a promontory immediately overlooking the sea, and for two-and-a-half centuries it was one of the richest and most powerful in the world. It was destroyed by the Carthaginians in 409 BC and finally fell to the Romans in about 350 BC when it went into rapid decline and disappeared from historical accounts.

The city's past is so remote that the names of the various temples have been forgotten and they are now identified by the letters A to G, M and O. The most impressive, **Temple E**, has been partially rebuilt, its columns pieced together from their fragments with part of its tympanum. Many of the carvings, particularly from **Temple C**, are now on display in the archaeological museum in Palermo (see p753). Their quality is on a par with the Parthenon Marbles and clearly demonstrates the high cultural levels reached by many Greek colonies in Sicily.

No visit to Selinunte is complete without a walk along the beach below the city, from where there are marvellous views of the temples. The path down is to the left of the parking area near the acropolis.

The **ticket office** (☎ 0924 4 62 51; adult/concession €4.50/2; ☺ 9am-1hr before sunset Mon-Sat, 9am-noon & 3-6pm Sun) is located near the eastern temples. Just behind the ticket office you can pick up an electric cart (€5 per person) to tour the enormous site.

Sleeping & Eating

Selinunte is close to the village of Marinella di Selinunte, where you should be able to find accommodation.

Garzia (☎ 0924 4 60 24; www.hotelgarzia.com; Via Antonio Pigafetta 6; s/d €60/100) This is a modern hotel situated right on the seafront next to numerous restaurants, and is very close to the ruins.

Villa Anna Bed & Breakfast 'Il Gattopardo' (☎ 0924 4 68 81; www.gattopardobb.it; SS115 136; s/d €45/80; P ✷) Also highly recommended is the highly surreal experience (check out the website to see what we mean) at this mock-Palladian villa located on the main road into Selinunte (about 2km before the village). It is very friendly and there are good facilities for children.

Al Ristorante Pierrot (☎ 0924 4 62 05; Via Marco Polo 108; meals €15-20) This place is very popular; you can hear the contented hubbub down the road. It does a fantastic buffet and good fish.

Getting There & Away

Regular AST buses link Selinunte and Marinella di Selinunte to Castelvetrano (€0.77, 20 minutes, five daily), which can be reached by bus from Agrigento, Marsala and Tràpani. Very slow trains also run from Palermo and Tràpani to Castelvetrano.

If travelling by car, take the Castelvetrano exit off the A29 and follow the brown signs for about 6km. If you're driving from Agrigento, take the SS115 and follows the signposts.

WESTERN SICILY

For decades Western Sicily has been written off as a remote and uninteresting corner of the island, but to ignore the west is to miss out on a smorgasbord of delights, ranging from unpretentious fishing towns to one of Sicily's finest nature reserves, the Riserva Naturale dello Zingaro. Offshore a cluster of islands; Pantelleria and the Egadi archipelago, share some 15,000 years of history between them – the latter was once a land bridge between Italy and north Africa.

MARSALA

pop 78,000

Best known for its sweet dessert wines, Marsala is an elegant town full of stately baroque buildings and bookshops.

It was founded by the Phoenicians who escaped the Roman onslaught at Mòzia. Not taking any chances, they fortified their city with 7m-thick walls, which ensured it was the last Punic settlement to fall to the Romans. In AD 830 it was conquered by the Arabs, who gave it its current name, Marsa Allah (Port of God).

It was here, in 1860, that Garibaldi landed in his rickety old boats with his 1000-strong army, a claim to fame that finds its way into every tourist brochure.

Information

Ospedale San Biagio (☎ 0923 71 60 31; Piazza San Francesco)
Police station (☎ 0923 92 43 71; Via Gramsci)
Post office (Via Garibaldi; ☯ 8am-6.30pm Mon-Sat) Just southeast of Piazza della Repubblica.
Tourist office (☎ 0923 71 40 97; Via XI Maggio 100; ☯ 8am-2pm & 3-8pm Mon-Sat, 9am-noon Sun) A friendly tourist office with a good map and brochures.

Sights & Activities

Marsala's finest treasure is the partially reconstructed remains of a Carthaginian *liburna* (warship) in the **Museo Archeologico Regionale Baglio Anselmi** (☎ 0923 95 25 35, Lungomare Boeo; admission €2; ☯ 9am-1.30pm, plus 4-6.30pm Wed & Fri-Sun). Sunk off the Egadi Islands during the First Punic War nearly 3000 years ago, this strangely delicate remnant is the only remaining physical evidence of the Phoenicians' seafaring superiority in the 3rd century BC. The ship resonates with history – especially if you see it after you visit the excavations on San Pantaleo (p807) – giving a glimpse of a civilisation that was quite literally extinguished by the Romans.

Marsala's other sights are limited to the **Museo degli Arazzi Fiammingi** (☎ 0923 71 29 03; Via Giuseppe Garraffa 57; admission €1; ☯ 9am-1pm & 4-6pm Tue-Sun), which displays eight 16th-century Flemish tapestries woven for Spanish King Philip II, and the adjoining **Cathedral** (under scaffolding at the time of writing) on Piazza della Repubblica. Although the Cathedral was built in the 17th century it wasn't actually completed until 1956 when a returning emigrant donated some much-needed cash.

If you're travelling with small children, you might enjoy a break at **Villa Cavalotti**, a large park just outside the Porta Nuova with a playground and acres of space for a relaxing walk.

Festivals & Events

The **Processione del Giovedì Santo** (Holy Thursday Procession) is a centuries-old tradition, where actors depict the events leading up to Christ's crucifixion.

The **Marsala Jazz Festival** is held in the historic centre in July. It's sponsored by Marsala wine companies and increasingly attracts major artists.

THE BOY OF MÒZIA

In 1979 the statue of a young boy was discovered on the island of San Pantaleo, lying on its back in the dirt, headless, armless and legless. The head was found nearby, and its restoration completed one of the greatest surviving Greek sculptures in the world, *Il Giovinetto di Mòzia*. You can view the statue at the Whitaker Museum (opposite) on the island.

Carved in the early 5th century BC from imported Anatolian marble, the statue of the young boy is unique, namely because he is clothed in a sensual long tunic, cinched around his chest with a wide band. Hundreds of delicate vertical grooves render the gossamer fabric realistic as it clings to his muscular body. Compared with the usual robust nudity of other Greek sculpture of the period (witness the Bronzi di Riace in Calabria, p739) the boy is extraordinarily graceful and sensuous, capturing the ineffable physical ease of a young boy on the brink of manhood.

The enigma for scholars is that nothing comparable was to come out of ancient Greece for hundreds of years and, when it did, the delicate tension between grace and strength visible in the Boy of Mòzia had vanished.

Sleeping

Marsala has few hotels within the centre.

Villa Sparta (☎ 0923 98 00 00; www.villasparta .com; Contrada Amabilina 3; s/d €90/130; P) This cubist-style villa boasts rustic-chic rooms with handsome marble bathrooms (some with sea views!). The palm-planted garden is a shock of welcoming green and the view from the terrace is just blue, blue sea.

Baglio Vajarassa (☎ /fax 0923 96 86 28; Contrada Spagnola 176; s/d €45/75) This traditional manor house 6km north of Marsala is a great choice if you have your own car. Lots of good food, wine and formal furnishings.

Hotel Garden (☎ /fax 0923 98 23 20; Via Gambini 36; s/d €35/45, d with bathroom €55; P) An ugly exterior disguises this good old-fashioned *pensione* with neat, clean rooms full of mismatched furnishings. Very friendly.

Eating

Fonte d'Oro (☎ 0923 71 95 86; Via Curatolo; meals €20-25; ☽ Mon-Sat) It is surprisingly hard to find good restaurants in Marsala, but this trendy restaurant is an exception. It specialises in super-fresh fish; the catch of the day is always good, or try the crisp *fritto misto* (mixed fry-up).

Divino...Rosso (☎ 0923 71 17 70; Via XI Maggio; meals €20; ☽ 7-11pm) An excellent option in the historic centre is this restaurant/wine bar. Dine out on the pavement overlooked by the imposing Palazzo Fici.

Trattoria Garibaldi (☎ 0923 95 30 06; Via Rubbino 35; meals €15; ☽ lunch Tue-Sun) This reliable trattoria is not much to look at but it serves hearty Sicilian fare and receives good word of mouth from the locals.

When everywhere else is closed you can always count on **Caffetteria Grand Italia** (☎ 0923 95 68 28; Piazza della Repubblica 3; sandwiches €3.50).

Shopping

Tipplers should head to **Cantine Florio** (☎ 0923 78 11 11; fax 0923 98 23 80; Lungomare Florio; ☽ 3-5pm Mon-Thu, 10am-noon Fri) on the road to Mazara del Vallo (bus No 16 from Piazza del Popolo). Florio opens its doors to visitors to explain the process of making Marsala wine and to give you a taste of the goods (fax to make a reservation for one of the free tours). Pellegrino, Rallo, Mavis and Intorcia are four of the other producers in the same area (which are usually open from about 9am to 12.30pm). Booking is recommended; ask the tourist office.

You can sample and buy the wine in town at several *enoteche*.

Getting There & Away

There are buses from Tràpani (on AST or Lumia, €2.60, 55 minutes, four daily Monday to Saturday), Agrigento (Lumia, €7.75, 3½ hours, three daily) and Palermo (Salemi, €7.75, 2½ hours), but the best way to travel along this coast is by train.

Regular trains serve Marsala from Tràpani (€2.65, 30 minutes, 20 daily) and Palermo (€7.90, three hours, six daily).

Between June and September, **Sandokan** (☎ 0923 71 20 60, 0923 95 34 34) runs a boat service from Molo Dogana to the Egadi Islands (€5.30 to Favignana). Ustica Lines also runs daily hydrofoils (€5.30 to Favignana and Lèvanzo, €11.80 to Maréttimo).

SALINE DI TRÀPANI

Drive along the SS115 coast road between Marsala and Tràpani and you will find yourself in a bleached landscape of shallow *saline* (salty pools) and softly shimmering heaps of salt. The salt from these pans is considered the best in Italy and has been big business since the 12th century. Now, however, only a cottage industry remains, providing for Italy's more discerning dinner tables.

The most attractive spot along the coast is the **Riserva Naturale di Stagnone**, a shallow lagoon and noted wetlands area. In the foreground floats the site of ancient **Mòzia** (also known as Motya or Mothia), on the tiny island of **San Pantaleo**, connected to the mainland by a Phoenician road which can still be seen at a depth of 3ft below the water. The island is accessible by private boat (€3 return) which operates from 9am to around 6pm (mornings only in winter).

The island (5km north of Marsala) was bought by the amateur archaeologist, Joseph Whitaker, who spent decades excavating and assembling the unique collection of Phoenician artefacts that now appear in the **Whitaker Museum** (☎ 0923 71 25 98; admission €5.50; ☼ 9am-1pm & 3pm-6.30pm Mar-Sep). Its main treasure is *Il Giovinetto di Mòzia* (see the boxed text, opposite).

On the mainland near the pier is the small **Museo Saline Ettore e Inferza** (☎ 0923 96 69 36; admission €3; ☼ 9.30am-1.30pm & 3-7pm), a salt museum housed in an old windmill. Ask at the reception about renting canoes (€5 per hour, summer only).

There is a busy café, **La Finestra sul Sale** (☎ 0923 73 30 03; Contrada Ettore Infersa 55; d €129; ☒), opposite the pier with outdoor tables overlooking the lagoon. It is a lovely place for an evening drink as the sun turns the saltpans rosy pink. Above the café are three attractive rooms with views over the saltpans.

To reach the Stagnone islands and the embarkation point for San Pantaleo from Marsala, take bus No 4 from the Piazza del Popolo (€4.25, 25 minutes, Monday to Saturday).

TRÀPANI

pop 68,400

Arriving in Tràpani through extensive and unattractive suburbs, one's first impression is of an uninspiring town that has suffered some of the worst abuses of unchecked Mafia construction. However, once ensconced in the tight-knit historic centre it is easy to be charmed by the laid-back atmosphere of what is, essentially, a large Arab fishing village. Once situated at the heart of a powerful trading network that stretched from Carthage to Venice, the sickle-shaped spit of land hugs the precious harbour, nowadays busy with the steady stream of tourists and traffic to and from Tunisia, Pantelleria and the Egadi Islands.

Orientation

The main bus station is on Piazza Montalto, with the train station around the corner on Piazza Umberto I. The cheaper hotels are in the heart of the old centre, about 500m west. Make for Piazza Scarlatti down Corso Italia. The narrow streets of the old part of town can be a nightmare to negotiate if you're driving, so head for the port and park near there.

Information

There are dozens of banks in Tràpani and nearly all of them have ATMs. Public telephone booths can be found in front of the ferry terminal. The terminal also has a phone centre on the 1st floor.

Egatours (☎ 0923 2 17 54; Via Ammiraglio Staiti 13) Travel agency for bus and ferry tickets.

Emergency doctor (☎ 0923 2 96 29; Piazza Generale Scio 1)

Main post office (Piazza Vittoria Veneto; ☼ 8am-6.30pm Mon-Sat)

Ospedale Sant'Antonio Abate (☎ 0923 80 91 11, casualty ☎ 0923 80 94 50; Via Cosenza)

Police station (☎ 0923 59 81 11; Piazza Vittoria Veneto)

Salvo Viaggi (☎ 0923 54 54 55; Corso Italia 48) Travel agency for boat and air tickets to Pantelleria.

Tourist office (☎ 0923 2 90 00; www.apt.trapani.it in Italian; Piazzetta Saturno 1-2; ☼ 8am-8pm Mon-Sat, 9am-noon Sun) A friendly tourist office with bags of information on the province and a good town map.

World Sport Line (Via Regina Elena 26-28; per hr €4; ☼ 10.30am-1pm & 4-10pm Mon-Sat) Has up-to-date computers and fast connection to the Internet.

Sights

The narrow network of streets in Tràpani's historic centre remains a Moorish labyrinth, although it takes much of its character from the fabulous 18th-century baroque of the Spanish period – a catalogue of examples can be found down the pedestrianised **Via**

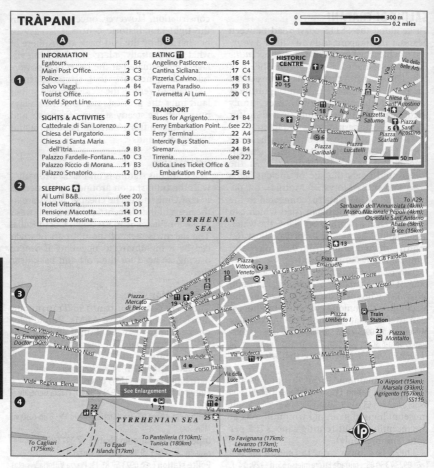

TRÀPANI

INFORMATION
Egatours...1 B4
Main Post Office.............................2 C3
Police...3 C3
Salvo Viaggi..................................4 B4
Tourist Office................................5 D1
World Sport Line...........................6 C2

SIGHTS & ACTIVITIES
Cattedrale di San Lorenzo.............7 C1
Chiesa del Purgatorio....................8 C1
Chiesa di Santa Maria
    dell'Itria..................................9 B3
Palazzo Fardelle-Fontana..............10 C3
Palazzo Riccio di Morana..............11 B3
Palazzo Senatorio..........................12 D1

SLEEPING
Ai Lumi B&B..........................(see 20)
Hotel Vittoria...............................13 D3
Pensione Maccotta........................14 D1
Pensione Messina..........................15 C1

EATING
Angelino Pasticcere........................16 B4
Cantina Siciliana...........................17 C4
Pizzeria Calvino.............................18 C1
Taverna Paradiso...........................19 B3
Tavernetta Ai Lumi........................20 C1

TRANSPORT
Buses for Agrigento.......................21 B4
Ferry Embarkation Point...........(see 22)
Ferry Terminal...............................22 A4
Intercity Bus Station......................23 D3
Siremar...24 B4
Tirrenia...................................(see 22)
Ustica Lines Ticket Office &
    Embarkation Point....................25 B4

Garibaldi. The best time to walk down here is in the early evening (around 7pm) when the *passeggiata* is in full swing.

Tràpani's other main street is Corso Vittorio Emanuele, punctuated by the huge **Cattedrale di San Lorenzo** (Corso Vittorio Emanuele; 🕙 8am-4pm), with its baroque façade and stuccoed interior. Facing off the east end of the corso is another baroque confection, the **Palazzo Senatorio**.

Just off the corso, south along Via Generale Dom Giglio, is the **Chiesa del Purgatorio** (☎ 0923 56 28 82; Via D'Assisi; 🕙 4pm-6.30pm), which houses the impressive 18th-century *Misteri*, 20 life-size wooden effigies depicting the story of Christ's Passion (used in I Misteri; see opposite).

Tràpani's major sight is the 14th-century **Santuario dell'Annunziata** (Via Conte Agostino Pepoli 179; 🕙 8am-noon & 4-7pm), some way from the centre on Via A Pepoli. The Cappella della Madonna, behind the high altar, contains the venerated *Madonna di Tràpani*, carved, it's thought, by Nino Pisano.

Adjacent to the Santuario dell'Annunziata, in a former Carmelite monastery, is the **Museo Nazionale Pepoli** (☎ 0923 55 32 69; Via Conte Agostino Pepoli 200; admission €2.50; 🕙 9am-1.30pm Tue-Sat, 9am-12.30pm Sun). It houses the collection of Conte Pepoli, who made it his business to salvage much of Tràpani's local arts and crafts, not least the garish coral carvings, once all the rage in Europe before the banks of coral off Tràpani were decimated. The museum also has a respectable collection of Gagini sculptures, silverwork, archaeological artefacts and religious artwork.

Festivals & Events

I Misteri (Easter Holy Week), Sicily's most venerated Easter procession, is a four-day festival of extraordinary religious fervour. Nightly processions, bearing life-size wooden effigies, make their way through the old quarter to a specially erected chapel in Piazza Lucatelli. The high point is on Good Friday when the celebrations reach fever pitch.

Sleeping

Tràpani has a limited choice of small hotels and *pensioni*. The best options are in the historic centre.

Ai Lumi B&B (☎ 0923 87 24 18; www.ailumi.it; Corso Vittorio Emanuele 71; s/d €55/70; ✗) Right on the main drag surrounded by swirling baroque architecture is this 18th-century palazzo. Opened in 2004, the rooms and small apartments are excellent value and well furnished. Guests receive a 15% discount at the Ai Lumi Tavernetta (right).

Pensione Maccotta (☎ 0923 2 84 18; albergomac cota@comeg.it; Via degli Argentieri 4; s/d €30/55; ✗) The Maccotta continues to maintain good standards at reasonable prices. Rooms are clean and comfortable although you need shades for the blindingly white corridors. It also hires out bicycles for €5 per day.

Hotel Vittoria (☎ 0923 87 30 44; www.hotelvittoria trapani.it; Via Francesco Crispi 40; s/d €58/89; ✗) Completely refurbished in 2003, the Hotel Vittoria is now the biggest hotel in the historic centre with a total of 104 rooms. The rooms are comfortable and modern and more spacious than the average but they lack the character of some of the other acommodation options.

Pensione Messina (☎ 0923 2 11 98; Corso Vittorio Emanuele 71; s/d with shared bathroom €20/35) The hilarious Pensione Messina is run by an ancient Tràpanesi couple. It is cheap and basic but a real insight into 1950s Italy. Beware of being answered by an irascible old guy in his dressing gown – he's your host! Breakfast costs an extra €3.50.

Eating

Sicily's Arab heritage and Tràpani's unique position on the sea route to Tunisia has made couscous ('*cuscus*' or '*kuscus*' as they spell it around here) something of a speciality, particularly when served with a fish sauce that includes tomatoes, garlic and parsley.

Taverna Paradiso (☎ 0923 87 37 51; Lungomare Dante Alighieri 24; meals €35; ✗ Feb-Dec) This is Tràpani's best restaurant, where Dolce & Gabbana–clad women and bejewelled men gorge themselves on succulent seafood specialities. The atmosphere here is heavily charged by influential patrons and during the *mattanza* season (see the boxed text, p812) the tables are cleared for live traditional music. Reservations are essential, as is dressing appropriate.

Cantina Siciliana (☎ 0923 2 86 73; Via Giudecca 52; meals €15) Hidden in the old Jewish ghetto, where scaffolding prevents the alley from collapsing in on itself, is this rustic trattoria with its fine-tuned menu. It sports the Slow Food Movement badge of approval.

Tavernetta Ai Lumi (☎ 0923 87 24 18; Corso Vittorio Emanuele 15; mains €8-14; ✗ Mon-Sat) Converted from an 18th-century stable block, this tavern is rustic to the core. Exposed brickwork and huge arches lend the dining room great character and the menu is full of mostly unpretentious country fare.

Pizzeria Calvino (☎ 0923 2 14 64, Via N Nasi 77, pizzas €3.50-7; ✗ 7pm-midnight Wed-Mon) You can't get a much better recommendation than being told this place is the town's favourite takeaway pizza place.

Angelino Pasticcere (☎ 0923 2 80 64; Via A Staiti 87; cakes €2.50-3.50) A heavenly café serving a delicious array of cakes, chocolates, Sicilian sweets and light savoury meals. It is a great place to pick up a snack before heading off to the islands.

An open-air **fish market** (Piazza Mercato di Pesce) is held Monday to Saturday morning on the northern waterfront.

Getting There & Around

AIR

Tràpani's small **Vincenzo Florio Airport** (TPS; ☎ 0923 84 25 02) is located 16km south of town at Birgi. Flights head to Pantelleria, Rome and Tunis. AST buses connect the Tràpani bus station with the airport (€3.35, 20 minutes, 10 daily Monday to Saturday, two on Sunday).

BOAT

Tràpani's **Stazione Marittima** (ferry terminal; ☎ 0923 54 54 11) is located opposite Piazza Garibaldi.

Inside you will find a money exchange, the Tirrenia and Siremar ticket offices and clean toilets. For the embarkation point of Ustica Lines hydrofoils you will need to head down Via Ammiraglio Staiti.

Siremar (☎ 0923 54 54 55; www.siremar.it in Italian; Via Ammiraglio Staiti 61) runs ferries/hydrofoils to Favignana (€3.15/5.30, 20 minutes), Lèvanzo (€3.15/5.30, 35 minutes) and Marèttimo (€7/ 11.80, one hour). The same company runs a daily ferry to Pantelleria (€28 for an airline-style seat, five hours) at midnight from June to September.

Ustica Lines (☎ 0923 2 22 00; www.usticalines.it in Italian; Via Ammiraglio Staiti 23) runs hydrofoils to Favignana, Lèvanzo and Marèttimo for similar prices, as well as summer-only services to Ùstica (€19, 2½ hours, one daily), Naples (€83, seven hours, one daily) and Pantelleria (€34, 2½ hours, one daily).

Tirrenia (☎ 0923 52 18 96; www.tirrenia.it; Stazione Marittima) runs weekly ferries to Tunisia (€52 for an airline-style seat, €64 for a bed in a 2nd-class cabin), leaving at 9am on Monday. There is also a service to Cagliari (€38 airline-style seat, €52 2nd-class cabin, 11½ hours, one weekly).

BUS

All intercity buses arrive and depart from the bus station on Piazza Montalto. Tickets can be bought from kiosks in the station.

Segesta (☎ 0923 2 17 54) runs express buses connecting Tràpani with Palermo (€7.80, two hours, eight daily). **AST** (☎ 0923 232 22) buses serve Èrice (€1.80, 45 minutes, 10 daily Monday to Saturday) and Marsala (€2.60, 30 minutes, eight daily Monday to Friday). **Autoservizi Tarantola** runs a bus service to Segesta (€2.60, 25 minutes, five daily June to September).

Lumia (☎ 0923 2 17 54) buses serve Agrigento (€10, three hours, two daily). You can pick up these buses outside Egatours where you purchase the tickets.

A free bus (No 11) does a circular trip through Tràpani, leaving from the bus station and stopping at the train station on the return leg.

TRAIN

Tràpani is linked to Palermo (€6.25, 2½ hours, 10 to 12 daily) and Marsala (€2.65, 30 minutes, 20 daily). The train is the best option for travelling along this coast.

ÈRICE

pop 28,900 / elev 751m

Èrice sits on the legendary Mt Eryx (750m) and despite its rather puritanical appearance – all forts and churches – it has a notorious history as a centre for the cult of Venus. Settled by the mysterious Elymians, Èrice was an obvious abode for the goddess of love, and the town followed the peculiar ritual of sacred prostitution, with the prostitutes themselves accommodated in the temple. Needless to say, despite countless invasions the temple remained inviolate – no guesses why.

Information

The **tourist office** (☎ 0923 86 93 88; Via Tommaso Guarrasi 1; ⏰ 8am-2pm Mon-Sat) is in the centre of town.

Sights

The best views can be had from the quaint **Giardino del Balio**, which overlooks rugged turrets and wooded hillsides down to the saltpans of Tràpani and the sea. Adjacent to the gardens is the Norman **Castello di Venere** (Castle of Venus; Via Castello di Venere; admission by donation; ⏰ 8am-7pm), built in the 12th and 13th centuries over the temple of Venus where those ancients were busy in their devotions. Not much more than a ruin, the castle is upstaged by the panoramic vistas.

Of the several churches and monuments in the small, quiet town, the 14th-century **Chiesa Matrice** (Via Vito Carvini; ⏰ 9.30am-1pm & 3pm-5.15pm), just inside Porta Tràpani, is probably the most interesting by virtue of its separate *campanile* (admission €1). The interior of the church was remodelled in the 19th century with the heavy use of decorative stucco.

Sleeping & Eating

Èrice has some excellent hotels and a quiet night in this medieval stronghold can be an attraction in itself.

Elimo (☎ 0923 86 93 77; www.charmerelax.com; Via Vittorio Emanuele 75; s/d €90/130; 🅿 🖳) A wonderfully character-filled hotel with enticing communal rooms full of intimate alcoves, low-beamed ceilings and marble fireplaces. All the rooms have breathtaking views as does the hotel terrace.

Baglio Santa Croce (☎ 0923 89 11 11; www.baglio santacroce.it; Contrada Ragosia da Santa Croce, Valderice;

s/d €56/112; (P 🛏)) A converted 17th-century *baglio*, located 9km east of Èrice in Valderice. It is set amid citrus groves and lush gardens and the pool is a great treat.

Hotel Moderno (☎ 0923 86 93 00; www.pippocata lano.it; Via Vittorio Emanuele 63; s/d €80/115; 🛏) Despite the name, Hotel Moderno surprises with an eclectic mix of mismatched pieces that somehow work together. The restaurant prepares homemade food (some of the best in town) and the hotel has a good *enoteca*.

Monte San Giuliano (☎ 0923 86 95 95; Vicolo San Rocco 7; meals €20-25; 🕙 Tue-Sun) You enter this restaurant through a crumbling arch into a cool patio graced with drooping hydrangeas. The terrace is canopied with a roof of vines and the food lives up to the heady surroundings.

Èrice has a tradition of *dolci ericini* and there are numerous pastry shops in town, like **Caffè Maria** (Via Vittorio Emanuele 4 & 14).

Getting There & Away

There is a regular AST bus service to and from Tràpani (€1.80/2.85 one way/return, 45 minutes, 10 daily Monday to Saturday, four on Sunday). Metered parking is available along Viale Conte Pepoli and costs €1 per hour.

SEGESTA
elev 304m

The ancient Elymians must have been great aesthetes if their choice of sites for cities is any indication. Along with Èrice, they founded Segesta. Set on the edge of a deep canyon in the midst of wild, desolate mountains, this huge 5th-century-BC temple is a magical site. On windy days its 36 giant columns are said to act like an organ, producing mysterious notes.

The city was in constant conflict with Selinunte in the south, whose destruction it sought with dogged determination and singular success. Time, however, has done to Segesta what violence inflicted on Selinunte, and little remains, save the **theatre** and the never-completed **Doric temple** (☎ 0924 95 23 56; adult/concession €4.50/2; 🕙 9am-4pm Nov-Mar, 9am-7pm Apr-Aug), the latter dating from around 430 BC and remarkably well preserved. A shuttle bus (€1.20) runs every 30 minutes from the entrance 1.5km uphill to the theatre.

During July and August, performances of Greek plays are staged in the theatre. For information, contact the tourist office in Tràpani (p807).

Segesta is accessible by **AST bus** (☎ 0924 3 10 20) from Piazza Montalto in Tràpani (€2.60, 25 minutes, five daily in summer). Otherwise catch a train from Tràpani (€2.65 return, 25 minutes, 10 daily) or Palermo (€5, one hour 40 minutes, three daily) to Segesta Tempio; the site is then a 20-minute walk away. There are signs to direct you.

GOLFO DI CASTELLAMMARE

Saved from development and road projects by local protests, the tranquil **Riserva Naturale dello Zingaro** (☎ 0923 2 61 11; www.riservazingaro.it; adult/child €3/2; 🕙 7am-9pm Apr-Sep, 8am-4pm Oct-Mar) is the star attraction on the gulf. Sicily's, and Italy's, first nature reserve, Zingaro's wild coastline is a haven for the rare Bonelli eagle along with 40 other species of bird. Mediterranean flora dusts the hillsides with wild carob and bright-yellow euphorbia, and hidden coves, like Marinella Bay, provide tranquil swimming spots. The main entrance of the park is 2km from Scopello. There are several walking trails, which are detailed on maps available for free at the park's two entrances. You can also download these from the website (Italian only).

Cetaria Diving Centre (☎ 0924 54 10 73; www.cet aria.com; Via Marco Polo 3) in Scopello organises dives and underwater tours of the nature reserve from the Tonnara di Scopello in summer.

Once home to tuna fishers, **Scopello** now mainly hosts tourists, although its sleepy village atmosphere remains unspoiled. Its port is extremely picturesque, with an rust-red *tonnara* (tuna processing plant) in the foreground and *faraglione* (rock towers) rising out of the sea.

AST buses run to San Vito lo Capo and Castellammare del Golfo from Tràpani's Piazza Montalto. From Castellammare, it is possible to catch a bus to Scopello (€1.80/2.85 one way/return). There is no road through the Zingaro park.

EGADI ISLANDS

For centuries the Egadi islanders have lived from the sea – and more famously from the tuna harvest in the spring. The lucrative industry caused successive conquerors to fortify the islands until the 17th century, when they were sold to Genovese bankers

---

LA MATTANZA

A centuries-old tradition, the Egadi Islands' *mattanza* (the ritual slaughter of tuna) only just survives. For centuries, shoals of tuna have used the waters around western Sicily as a mating ground. Locals recall the golden days when it wasn't uncommon to catch giant breeding tuna of between 200kg and 300kg.

Now that the slaughter of tuna can no longer support the economy of the islands, it has reinvented itself as a tourist attraction. From around 20 May to 10 June, tourists flock to the Egadi Islands to witness the event. For a fee you can join the fishers in their boats (ask at the tourist office on Favignana) and watch them catching the tuna – you'll need a strong stomach for this. It is no ordinary fishing expedition; the fishers organise their boats and nets in a complex formation designed to channel the tuna into a series of enclosures that culminate in the *camera della morte* (chamber of death). Once enough tuna are imprisoned here, the fishers close in and the *mattanza* begins. It is a bloody affair – up to eight or more fishers at a time will sink huge hooks into a tuna and drag it aboard. Anyone who has seen Rossellini's classic film *Stromboli* will no doubt recall the famous *mattanza* scene.

---

and ultimately passed into the hands of business tycoon Ignazio Florio, who made his fortune from them. Nowadays, the waters around the islands have been overfished and the tuna fishery (once the only cannery in Europe) is long closed. Tourism has become the main earner – even the *mattanza*, the ritual slaughtering of tuna, has become a spectator sport (see the boxed text, above), although the future of this is by no means certain.

Ferries and hydrofoils run between the islands and to Tràpani. See p809 for details.

Lèvanzo, Favignana & Marèttimo

Closest to Tràpani lies Lèvanzo, the smallest island of the archipelago, inhabited by a handful of people and the site of ancient rock carvings at **Grotta del Genovese**. The huge cave exhibits Mesolithic and Neolithic etchings, 'painted' on the walls using animal fat and carbon. Fittingly, there is one image of the tuna that even then must have been revered. The cave can be visited by sea (if you negotiate with one of the fishermen at the port). Contact the custodian **Signor Natale Castiglione** (☎ 0923 92 40 32, 339 741 88 00; ncasti@tin .it; foot/boat €5.50/12; ☒ 10am-1pm & 3-6pm).

The largest of the islands is butterfly-shaped Favignana, dominated by the Monte Santa Caterina. It is pleasant to explore on bicycle as it's almost completely flat, and around the coast tufa quarries are carved out of the crystal-clear waters – most notably around **Cala Rossa** and **Cala Cavallo**. Wander around the **tonnara** (tuna processing plant) at the port. It was closed at the end of the

1970s due to the general crisis in the local tuna fishing industry.

Given the history, this is unsurprisingly an excellent place to pick up tuna-related products. **Casa del Tonno** (☎ 0923 92 22 27; 12 Via Roma) is a great little deli filled to the rafters with smoked and canned bluefin tuna, and a host of other fishy delicacies like *bottarga* (roe) and sardines.

There is a **tourist office** (☎ 0923 92 16 47; www .egadi.com; Piazza Matrice 8; ☒ 9am-12.30pm & 4.30-7pm Mon-Sat, plus 9.30am-12.30pm Sun Jun-Sep) in Favignana town. You will find dive-hire outlets and bicycles or scooters for rent around the town and at the small harbour.

The last of the islands and the most distant is Marèttimo. A few hundred people live mostly in the tiny village on the eastern coast and there are no roads. However, it is the island's crystal-clear waters that are the main attraction for divers. Alternatively, you can explore some of the 400 grottoes along the rocky coast by arranging an excursion with one of the local fishermen at the port.

SLEEPING & EATING

There is good accommodation on Favignana and two hotels on Lèvanzo. There are no hotels on Marèttimo, but you should be able to dig up a room with the locals.

During the *mattanza* and in August you will have trouble finding a bed without an advance booking.

Albergo Egadi (☎ /fax 0923 92 12 32; www.albergo egadi.com; Via Colombo 17, Favignana; s/d €60/120) Run by the Guccione sisters, this small *albergo* has 12 princess-pink rooms with wafting chiffon curtains. It also has the best restaurant on the islands (meals €25 to €30, open Thursday to Tuesday from March to January). Advance bookings are essential in summer.

Albergo Aegusa (☎ 0923 92 24 30; www.aegusa hotel.it; Via Garibaldi 11; d low/high season €69/108; ☒) An attractive hotel with comfortable, well-furnished rooms right in the centre of Favignana. There is also a good restaurant in an outdoor courtyard.

Lèvanzo has only two hotels, the best of which is **Albergo Paradiso** (☎ 0923 92 40 80; Via Lungomare; s/d half board €60/120; ☒) with its geranium-clad terrace where you will eat well (mains €8 to €15).

PANTELLERIA

Known to the Arabs as 'daughter of the winds', this volcanic outcrop is Sicily's biggest offshore island, although it lies closer to Tunisia than it does to Sicily. Buffeted by winds, even in August, the island is characterised by jagged lava stone, low-slung caper bushes, dwarf vines, steaming fumaroles and the **Bagno dell'Aqua** (Lago di Venere) mud baths near Bugeber. Near Siba, at the summit of Montagna Grande (836m), there are also steaming natural saunas, **Stufa del Bagno di Arturo**.

However, the island is more famous for its secluded coves, which are perfect for snorkelling and diving. The northeastern end of the island provides the best spots with a popular **acquacalda** at Gadir. Here you can while away your day wallowing like a walrus in the hot, shallow springs. Slightly further down the coast you will find ever more scenic spots such as **Cala di Tramontana** and **Cala di Levante**. Boat excursions are available at the dock; contact **Minardi Adriano** (☎ 0923 91 15 02; Via Borgo Italia 5) for day trips costing €20 per person.

The only archaeological site on the island is at **Mursia**, where the remnants of *sesi* (ancient funerary monuments) are the only remaining evidence of a Bronze Age settlement. Many of the tombs have been destroyed and the lava rock was used to build the famous domed *dammusi* (houses with thick, whitewashed walls and shallow cupolas). The exotic and remote atmosphere of Pantelleria has long made it a favourite with celebrities from Truman Capote and Henry Cartier-Bresson to the likes of Madonna and Giorgio Armani, who has his own *dammusi* here.

There is a small **tourist office** (☎ 0923 91 18 38; www.pantelleria.com; Piazza Cavour; ⏱ 9.30am-12.30pm & 5.30pm-6.30pm Mon-Sat, 9-11am Sun) in the corner of the Municipal Hall.

Sleeping & Eating

Summer accommodation bookings should be made at least a month in advance.

Zubeb Resort (☎ 0923 91 36 53; www.zubebi.it; Contrada Zubebi; 2-/4-person apt €800/1600; P ☒ ▨) A complex made up of traditional *dammusi*. Inside the décor is austere minimalism, smooth concrete walls and Indian furnishings. There is also an über-stylish crescent-shaped pool and on-site scooters.

Also recommended are the sweet B&B, **Albergo Papuscia** (☎ 0923 91 54 63; www.papuscia.com; Corso da Sopra Portella 48, Tracino; d low/high season €59/89; ☒), and the convenient and newly renovated **Port Hotel** (☎ 0923 91 12 99; fax 0923 91 22 03; Via Borgo Italia 6, Pantelleria town; s/d €80/102; P ☒).

Getting There & Away

Pantelleria is 30 minutes by airplane with **Gandalf Air** (☎ 848 80 14 24; www.gandalfair.it) from Tràpani (€27, 50 minutes, three daily). Air Sicilia flies from Palermo (€28.50, one hour 20 minutes, one daily), and **Air One** (☎ 848 84 88 80) and Alitalia from Rome (from €172). The local bus connects the airport with Pantelleria Town.

All boats arrive at the port in Pantelleria Town. Ustica Lines has hydrofoils departing from Tràpani daily from June to September (€34, 2½ hours, one daily). Siremar runs a daily ferry from Tràpani (€22.50, 5 hours, one daily). There are reduced services from October to May.

You can purchase ferry and hydrofoil tickets from **Agenzia Rizzo** (☎ 0923 91 11 04; http://pantelleria.it/agenziarizzo; Via Borgo Italia 12) and plane tickets from **La Cossira** (☎ 0923 91 10 78; www .lacossira.it; Via Borgo Italia 19), both in Pantelleria town.

Local buses depart from Piazza Cavour in Pantelleria town at regular intervals each day (except Sunday) and service all the towns on the island. Alternatively you can rent scooters (€10 per day from September to June, €25 per day from July to August) and cars (Fiat Panda €15 per day from September to June, €40 per day from July to August) from **Autonoleggio Policardo** (☎ 0923 91 28 44; Vicolo Messina 35), just down the alley to the left of the Port'Hotel.

Sardinia

Nature has been kind to Sardinia (Sardegna). The scenery is stunning even away from the much-touted coast, with plunging valleys, forested slopes and mountain ranges that are tantalisingly impenetrable and dusted with snow in winter. And most of the coastal resorts *are* worthy of all that hype with white sandy beaches, a turquoise sea and a refreshingly slim choice of souvenir T-shirts for sale. Only a few hours by ferry from mainland Italy, Sardinia can seem a world apart: subjected to a history of domination by outside forces, the proud Sardinians have never lost their sense of identity.

The island has an extraordinary history. Across the landscape are scattered 7000 *nuraghi,* strange conical stone fortresses, some extended into grand settlements that predate the arrival of the Romans by more than 1000 years. Curious temples, *domus de janas* (fairy houses), *tombe dei giganti* (giants' tombs), mysterious menhirs and remains of entire Bronze Age villages complete this ancient picture. Phoenicians, Carthaginians and finally Romans landed here, leaving their mark in Nora and Tharros. Later masters also left reminders. The northwest is strewn with Pisan-Romanesque churches, and Cagliari and Alghero retain a palpable Spanish feel. The island distinguishes itself in the kitchen, with hearty pastas and a love for suckling pig, kid and lamb. Sardinians produce notable wines and a head-splitting firewater, *filu e ferru.*

Avoid visiting during the broiling, crowded months of July and August, as well as in the depths of winter when much of the island goes into hibernation and many restaurants and hotels are closed.

HIGHLIGHTS

- Saunter around the *centro storico* (historic centre) in the coastal Catalan town of **Alghero** (p834), a medieval tangle of narrow alleys and atmospheric piazze

- Island-hop around the **Arcipelago di La Maddalena** (p842) in a speedboat tour or whiz past the **Golfo di Orosei's** (p845) beguiling beaches and coves

- Stroll, sunbathe or swim at one of the stunning beaches on the unspoilt **Costa Verde** (p828)

- Feast on a traditional meal of *porcetto* (roast suckling pig) washed down with a glass of the local Cannonau red tipple at **Osteria Macchiavello** (p836) in Alghero

- Enjoy sweeping city views with a backdrop of sea and mountains from Cagliari's ancient citadel, the **Bastione San Remy** (p819)

★ Arcipelago di La Maddalena

★ Alghero

★ Golfo di Orosei

★ Costa Verde

★ Cagliari

- POPULATION: 1.6 million
- AREA: 24,090 sq km

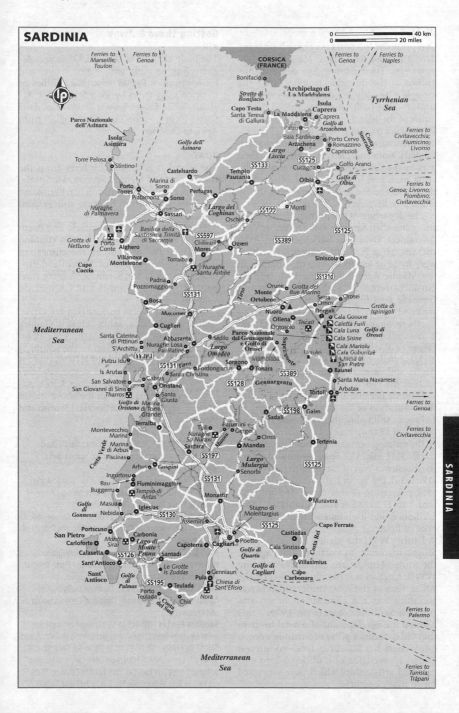

SARDINIA

0   40 km
0   20 miles

Ferries to Marseille; Toulon
Ferries to Genoa

CORSICA (FRANCE)
Bonifacio

Ferries to Genoa
Ferries to Naples

Stretto di Bonifacio
Archipelago di La Maddalena
Tyrrhenian Sea

Capo Testa
Santa Teresa di Gallura
La Maddalena
Isola Caprera
Caprera

Parco Nazionale dell'Asinara
Isola Asinara

Golfo dell' Asinara

Golfo di Arzachena
Baia Sardinia
Arzachena
Porto Cervo
Romazzino
Capriccioli

Ferries to Civitavecchia; Fiumicino; Livorno

Torre Pelosa
Stintino

Castelsardo
Tempio Pausania
Palau
Cucagna
Olbia
Golfo di Olbia
Golfo Aranci

Costa Smeralda

SS133
SS125

Marina di Sorso
Perfugas

Largo Liscia

Ferries to Genoa; Livorno; Piombino; Civitavecchia

Porto Torres
Platamona
Sorso
Largo del Coghinas
Oschiri
Monti

SS199
SS125

Nuraghe di Palmavera
Sassari

Basilica della Santissima Trinità di Saccargia
Chilivani
Mores
Ozieri

SS597
SS389

Grotta di Nettuno
Porto Conte
Alghero

Villanova Monteleone
Torralba
Siniscola

SS125

Capo Caccia
Padria
Pozzomaggiore

Nuraghe Santu Antine
SS131d

Mediterranean Sea
Bosa
Macomer
Orune
Grotta del Bue Marino
Serra Orrios
Orosei

SS131
Monte Ortobene
Nuoro
Dorgali
Grotta di Ispinigoli

Cuglieri
Oliena
Orgosolo
Tiscali
Cala Gonone
Caletta Fuili
Cala Luna
Cala Sisine
Golfo di Orosei

Santa Caterina di Pittinuri
S'Archittu
Abbasanta
Sédilo
Parco Nazionale del Gennargentu e Golfo di Orosei
Urzulei

Cala Mariolu
Cala Goloritzè
Chiesa di San Pietro
Baunei

Nuraghe Losa
Paulilatino

SS131
Largo Omodeo
Sorgono
Aritzo

Putzu Idu
Is Arutas
San Salvatore
Cabras
Santa Christina
Fordongianus
Tonara

SS389
Gennargentu
Santa Maria Navarrese
Arbatax

San Giovanni di Sinis
Tharros
Oristano
Santa Giusta

SS128
Tortolì
Ferries to Genoa

Golfo di Oristano
Marina di Torre Grande
Barumini
Gergei
Sadali

SS198
Gairu
Ferries to Civitavecchia

Montevecchio Marina
Terralba
Tuili
Nuraghe Su Nuraxi
Sardara
Orroli
Mandas
Tertenia

SS125

Marina di Arbus
Piscinas
Arbus
Guspini

SS197
Largo Mulargia
Senorbi

Costa Verde
Ingurtosu
Bau
Buggerru

SS131
Muravera

Golfo di Gonnessa
Masua
Nebida
Fluminimaggiore
Tempio di Antas
Monastir
Stagno di Molentargius
Capo Ferrato

Iglesias
SS130
Assemini
SS125
Castiadas
Costa Rei

Portscuso
San Pietro
Carloforte
Carbonia
Monte Sirai
Lago di Monte Pranu
Capoterra
Cagliari
Poetto
Cala Sinzias
Villasimius

Calasetta
SS126
Santadì
Le Grotte Is Zuddas
Golfo di Quartu
Capo Carbonara

Sant'Antioco
Sant' Antioco
Golfo di Palmas
SS195
Teulada
Gennauri
Pula
Chiesa di Sant'Efisio
Golfo di Cagliari

Porto Teulada
Costa del Sud
Chia
Nora

Ferries to Palermo

Mediterranean Sea

Ferries to Tunisia; Trápani

SARDINIA

History

Our primitive forebears may have been wandering around Sardinia as long as 400,000 years ago. Their Bronze Age descendants, known as the nuraghic peoples (after the *nuraghi* – bewildering stone towers and fortresses – they built), long dominated the interior of the island, even after the arrival of Phoenician traders around 850 BC. Phoenician settlements (such as Karalis, or modern Cagliari, Nora and Tharros) were later taken over by the Carthaginians and Romans. The latter managed to take control of much of the island and the indigenous people slowly faded into history.

The departure of the Romans and the ensuing chaos left Sardinia at the mercy of Vandal raiders, Byzantine occupiers and Arab corsairs. Four *giudicati* (kingdoms), which were more or less independent, emerged in the Middle Ages but by the 13th century outsiders were again at the door. Pisans and Genoese vied for control but were finally replaced by the Catalano-Aragonese from northern Spain. They arrived in 1323 and only snuffed out the last resistance in 1478. Eleonora d'Arborea (1340–1404) offered the greatest challenge against them and to this day is still revered as Sardinia's very own Joan of Arc (p828).

Sardinia became a Spanish territory after the unification of the Spanish kingdoms in 1479 and, still today, there is a tangible Hispanic feel to towns such as Alghero (p834). In the ensuing centuries Sardinia decayed as the fleeting might of Spain crumbled. After the disastrous War of the Spanish Succession (1701–14), the north Italian Savoy kingdom took possession of this rough and difficult island in 1720. After Italian unity in 1861, Sardinia found itself under the disinterested boot of Rome.

During WWI the island's Sassari Brigade fought heroically in northern Italy against the Austro-Hungarians and in 1943, during WWII, Cagliari was heavily bombed by the Allies. One of the most important postwar successes was the elimination of malaria from the Sardinian coast in the 1950s – this allowed the development of coastal tourism that today forms a pillar of Sardinia's economy. There has also been renewed interest in and appreciation of traditional Sard culture and artisanship, which were repressed for so many centuries.

Getting There & Away

AIR

The main airports at Cagliari, Olbia and Alghero link Sardinia with major Italian and European cities. **Ryanair** (www.ryanair.com) flies up to twice a day from London Stansted to Alghero, while **Easyjet** (www.easyjet.com) has daily flights from London Luton to Cagliari from April to October.

BOAT

The island is accessible by ferry from the Italian ports of Genoa, Savona, La Spezia, Livorno, Piombino, Civitavecchia, Fiumicino and Naples, and from Palermo and Tràpani in Sicily.

Ferries also run from Bonifacio and Porto Vecchio in Corsica. French ferries running from Marseilles and Toulon sometimes call in at the Corsican ports of Ajaccio and Propriano en route for Sardinia. A ferry runs between Tunis in Tunisia and Cagliari via Tràpani.

The arrival points in Sardinia are Olbia, Golfo Aranci, Palau, Santa Teresa di Gallura and Porto Torres in the north; Arbatax on the east coast; and Cagliari in the south.

Italy's main ferry company is **Tirrenia** (☎ 199 12 31 99; www.tirrenia.it). It runs year-round ferries to Port Torres, Golfo Aranci, Olbia, Arbatax and Cagliari from all the above Italian ports, except Savona, La Spezia, Livorno and Piombino.

Other companies:

Enermar (☎ 899 20 00 01; www.enermar.it) Runs between the northern ports of Genoa, Savona and La Spezia to Palau (some via Corsica).

Grandi Navi Veloci (Grimaldi; ☎ 010 25 465; www1 .grimaldi.it) Has year-round luxury ferry services from Genoa to Porto Torres and Olbia.

Linea dei Golfi (☎ 0565 22 23 00; www.lineadeigolfi.it) Operates from Livorno to Cagliari and Olbia, and Piombino to Olbia from April to September.

Med Mar (☎ 081 551 33 52; www.medmargroup.it) Has two weekly boats from Naples to Palau and Porto Vecchio, which increases to four weekly during August.

Moby Lines (☎ 010 254 15 13; www.mobylines.it) Operates year-round between Olbia and Genoa, Livorno and Civitavecchia.

Sardinia Ferries (☎ 019 21 55 11; www.corsicaferries .com) Operates from Civitavecchia and Livorno to Golfo Aranci.

SNCM (in France ☎ 08 91 70 18 01, in Sardinia ☎ 079 51 44 77; www.sncm.fr) Operates ferries from Marseilles to Porto Torres (via Corsica) from April to October. There are two to four sailings weekly, but in July and August some leave from Toulon instead. Crossing time is 12 to 16 hours (12½ hours from Toulon) depending on the vessel. A return fare for two people plus car starts at €330 in high season (July and August). A basic cabin for two costs up to €325 return.

For tickets and information in Porto Torres, go to **Agenzia Paglietti** (☎ 079 51 44 77; fax 079 51 40 63; Corso Vittorio Emanuele 19).

There are regular ferry links between Sardinia (Santa Teresa di Gallura) and Bonifacio, across the straits in Corsica. **Saremar** (☎ 0789 75 41 56; www.saremar.it in Italian) has two to four daily departures each way depending on the season. Adult one-way fares go up to €8.70, depending on the season. A small car costs up to €28.70. The trip takes one hour. Sardinia Ferries (see opposite) have a similar timetable and fares.

Moby Lines (☎ 010 254 15 13) has 10 crossings per day in July and August and four during the rest of the year.

For an idea of the fares you might pay, see the boxed text, right.

Getting Around
BUS
The main bus company is **Azienda Regionale Sarda Trasporti** (ARST; ☎ 800 86 50 42; www.arst.sardegna.it in Italian), which operates extensive services throughout the island. **PANI** (☎ 070 65 23 26, 079 23 69 83) operates a faster service linking Cagliari, Oristano, Sassari, Nuoro and Porto Torres.

Other companies include Ferrovie della Sardegna (FdS) and Ferrovie Meridionale Sardegna (FMS). Buses are generally faster than trains.

CAR & MOTORCYCLE
The only way to really explore Sardinia is by road. For details about rental agencies in Cagliari, see p823. There are also rental agencies at some of the other towns around the island.

TRAIN
The main **Trenitalia** (www.trenitalia.it) train lines link Cagliari with Oristano, Sassari and Olbia, and are generally reliable but they can be fairly slow. The FdS links some of the smaller towns with even slower narrow-gauge trains. In summer several *Trenino Verde* steam-train services use the scenic lines that have long since gone out of standard commercial

action. Some lines are very pretty, especially Arbatax–Mandas. The others include Palau–Tempio Pausania; Tempio Pausania–Nulvi (from where you can connect with a regular service to Sassari); Bosa–Macomer (which links with the Macomer–Nuoro line); and Isili–Sorgono.

CAGLIARI

pop 175,200
A cultural hot pot and historically rich city, Cagliari is a real class act which hums with cosmopolitan charm yet retains a palpable old-fashioned feel.

The hilly labyrinth of the sandy-coloured medieval Castello district, the bright pastel colours of restored façades, the taverns and restaurants spilling out onto the cobbled piazze, all attribute to the city's classic Mediterranean visual appeal. Two thousand years of history has also left its mark, with

---

MAINLAND ITALY–SARDINIA FERRY CROSSINGS

The following table has sample fares on a selection of the main routes. The fares are standard high-season one-way fares (in an armchair, one up from deck class, which is around €5 less). Children aged four to 12 generally pay around half and those under four travel free. Also included here is the high-season cost of transporting a small car. Port taxes of a few euros (per person; it varies from port to port) have to be added onto these fares.

Destination	Adult/ car (€)	Duration (hr)
Civitavecchia-Arbatax	32.70/65.60	10½
Civitavecchia-Olbia	26.20/75.05	8
Civitavecchia-Olbia*	35.75/92.15	4
Genoa-Arbatax	48/92	19
Genoa-Porto Torres/Olbia	45/92	8-11
Genoa-Porto Torres/Olbia*	79/99.40	8-11
Livorno-Golfo Aranci	48/115	10
Naples-Cagliari	41.90/78.90	16¼
Palermo-Cagliari	39.45/79	13½
Piombino-Olbia	39.25/80	8
Tràpani-Cagliari	26.20/75.05	11

*fast ferries

CAGLIARI

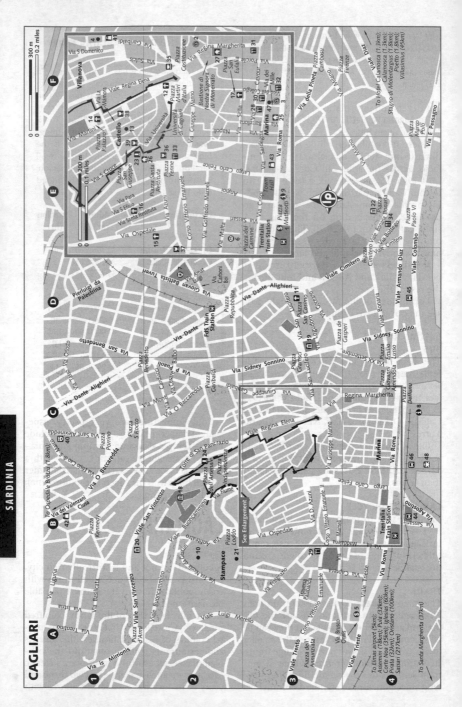

INFORMATION		
Banco di San Paolo	**1**	E3
Intermedia Point	**2**	F2
Le Liberie della Costa	**3**	F3
Libreria Dattena	**4**	F1
Mail Boxes Etc	**5**	A4
Main Post Office	**6**	E2
Police Station	**7**	D2
Tourist Office	**8**	C4
Tourist Office	**9**	E3

SIGHTS & ACTIVITIES		
Anfiteatro Romano	**10**	B2
Basilica di San Saturno	**11**	D3
Bastione San Remy	**12**	F2
Castello	**13**	F1
Cattedrale di Santa Maria	**14**	F1
Chiesa di San Michele	**15**	E2
Chiesa di Sant'Efisio	**16**	E1
Chiesa di Sant'Eulalia	**17**	F2
Citadela dei Musei	**18**	B2
Exma	**19**	D3
Galleria Comunale d'Arte	**20**	B1

Mostra di Cere Anatomiche	(see 18)	
Museo Archeologico	(see 18)	
Museo d'Arte Siamese	(see 18)	
Museo del Tesoro e Area Archeologica di Sant'Eulalia	(see 17)	
Orto Botánico	**21**	B2
Pinacoteca	(see 18)	
Santuario & Basilica di Nostra Signora di Bonaria	**22**	E4
Torre dell'Elefante	**23**	E1
Torre di San Pancrazio	**24**	C2

SLEEPING		
Hotel A&R Bundes Jack	**25**	F3
Hotel Aurora	**26**	E2
Hotel Regina Margherita	**27**	F2

EATING		
Antica Hostaria	**28**	F3
Crackers	**29**	B3
Da Lillicu	**30**	F3
Dal Corsaro	**31**	F3
Il Buongustaio	**32**	F3

Isola del Gelato	**33**	E2
Ristorante Royal	**34**	E4

DRINKING		
Antico Caffè	**35**	F2
Forum Caffè	**36**	E2
Il Merlo Parlante	**37**	D2
Old Coffee	**38**	F1
Sotto La Torre	**39**	F1

ENTERTAINMENT		
Teatro Comunale	**40**	C1

SHOPPING		
Grand Wazoo	**41**	F1
Isola	**42**	B1
La Rinascente	**43**	E3

TRANSPORT		
ARST Intercity Bus Station	**44**	B4
FMS Bus Station	**45**	D4
PANI Bus Station	**46**	C4
Ruvioli	**47**	F3
Stazione Marittima	**48**	C4

archaeological remains, several fine museums and superb churches, including Museo Archeologico with its priceless nuraghic collection. Nearby, the city's long Poetto beach is good for a city-side splash, while the salt marshes are preferred by such magnificent feathered friends as brilliant bright pink flamingos, cranes and cormorants.

ORIENTATION

The main port, bus and train stations are near Piazza Matteotti, which is also home to the tourist office. Running through the square is Via Roma, part of the principal route to Poetto and Villasimius in the east and Pula and the south coast to the west.

The warren of lanes just inland from Via Roma is known as the Marina, home to most of the cheaper and midrange hotels and a plethora of eateries of all categories.

INFORMATION
Bookshops
Libreria Dattena (☎ 070 67 02 20; Via Garibaldi 175) Novels plus other books in languages other than Italian.

Emergency
Police station (☎ 070 49 21 69; Via Amat Luigi 9) The main police station; located behind the imposing law courts.

Internet Access
Intermedia Point (Via Eleonora d'Arborea 4; per hr €3.50; ☯ 10am-1pm & 4-9pm Mon-Fri, 11am-1pm & 5-9pm Sat)
Le Librerie della Costa (Via Roma 63-5; per hr €5; ☯ 9am-8.30pm Mon-Sat, 10am-1.30pm & 5.30-9pm Sun) Also has a range of English-language books.

Medical Services
Guardia Medica (☎ 070 50 29 31) For a night-time emergency call-out doctor.
Ospedale Brotzu (☎ 070 54 32 66; Via Peretti 21) This hospital is northwest of the city centre. Take Bus No 1 from Via Roma if you need to make a nonemergency visit.

Money
Banco di San Paolo (Piazza Matteotti) Handily located next to the main train station. There are also ATMs inside the station.
Mail Boxes Etc (☎ 070 67 37 04; Viale Trieste 65b) You can send or receive money via Western Union here.

Post
Main post office (Piazza del Carmine; ☯ 8.10am-6.40pm Mon-Fri, 8.10am-1.20pm Sat) Has a fax service and *fermo posta* (poste restante). Closes at 4pm on the last day of the month.

Tourist Information
Tourist office Piazza Matteotti (☎ 070 66 92 55; ☯ 8am-8pm Mon-Sat Apr-Sep, 8am-2pm Sun Jul-Aug, 9am-2pm & 3-6pm Mon-Fri, 9am-2pm Sat Oct-Mar); Stazione Marittima (☎ 070 66 83 52; ☯ 8.30am-1.30pm & 3-6pm)

SIGHTS
Castello
The precipitous white stone walls of medieval Cagliari, with two of the grand-looking Pisan towers still standing watch, enclose the **castello** (castle), a once virtually impregnable fortress town. The walls are best admired from afar – one good spot is the Anfiteatro Romano (Roman amphitheatre) to the west.

You can catch bus No 7 from Piazza Matteotti to the castle or approach via the grand steps leading to the **Bastione San Remy**,

SARDINIA

which is well worth the puff-out climb for the fabulous views across the city.

A brisk march north brings you to Piazza Palazzo and face to face with the 1938 neo–Pisan-Romanesque façade of the **Cattedrale di Santa Maria** (☎ 070 66 38 37; Piazza Palazzo 4; ☀ 8am-12.30pm & 4-7pm). Little remains of the original 13th-century church, which was buried in a heavy baroque remake in the 17th century. Then from 1933 to 1938 they tried to turn the clocks back with the reasonably successful throwback façade. The square-based bell tower *does*, however, date from the 13th century. Inside are two magnificent stone pulpits on either side of the central entrance, sculpted by Guglielmo da Pisa and donated by Pisa to Cagliari in 1312.

The grand white **Torre di San Pancrazio** (Piazza Indipendenza; admission €2; ☀ 9am-1pm & 3.30-7.30pm Tue-Sun Apr-Oct, 9am-4.30pm Tue-Sun Nov-Mar), to the right of the northern city gate, is one of two medieval Pisan defensive towers still standing. Under the Catalano-Aragonese it became an austere office block (with a view) for civil servants before being downgraded to a prison in the 17th century.

Beyond the city gate you are in Piazza dell'Arsenale. Cross the square into what was once the city's arsenal (the Regio Arsenale). Four museums constituting the **Citadella dei Musei**, including the island's most important archaeological and art collections, are located here amid remains of the old arsenal and city walls.

The **Museo Archeologico** (☎ 070 68 40 00; admission €4, incl Pinacoteca €5; ☀ 9am-8pm Tue-Sun) contains material dating from pre-nuraghic to late Roman times found at sites across Sardinia. Without doubt, the single most impressive part of the collection is the *bronzetti*, astonishing bronze figurines that (in the absence of any written record) provide one of the few clues to the nuraghic people. There are two separate displays of the statuettes on the ground and 2nd floors. Of all the figures, the 'chieftain' stands out with his flowing mantle, staff and sword. Roman artefacts include mosaics, statuary, jewellery and coins.

The **Pinacoteca** (☎ 070 68 40 00; admission €2, incl Museo Archeologico €5; ☀ 9am-8pm Tue-Sun) is the place to acquaint yourself with Sardinian art history, especially works from the 15th to the 17th centuries. The four works by Pietro Cavaro, father of the so-called Stampace school and possibly Sardinia's most important art-

ist, are outstanding. They include a moving *Deposizione* (Deposition) and portraits of Sts Peter, Paul and Augustine.

The city's other museums are far more obscure. **Mostra di Cere Anatomiche** (admission €1.55; ☀ 9am-1pm & 4-7pm Tue-Sun) contains some fairly gruesome 19th-century anatomical wax models, while the **Museo d'Arte Siamese** (☎ 070 65 18 88; admission €2; ☀ 9am-1pm & 4-8pm Tue-Sun Jun-Sep, 9am-1pm & 3.30-7.30pm Tue-Sun Oct-May) houses an impressive former private collection of Southeast Asian art, crafts and weaponry.

Return to Piazza Indipendenza and head south along Castello's canyon-like streets to the **Torre dell'Elefante**, the other Pisan watchtower which takes its name from a small sculpted elephant at the tower's base as you enter from Via Università.

Marina, Stampace & Around

Just south of Piazza Costituzione a maze of lanes should – with the help of a compass – eventually lead you to the Cagliari waterfront. Known as Marina, this area has the highest concentration of restaurants and hotels in town, and is also remarkably blessed with lots of churches. The **Chiesa di Sant'Eulalia** is most interesting for its attached **Museo del Tesoro e Area Archeologica di Sant'Eulalia** (MUTSEU; ☎ 070 66 37 24; Piazza Sant'Eulalia; admission €3; ☀ 10am-1pm & 5-11pm Jul-Sep, 10am-1pm & 5-8pm Tue-Sun Oct-Jun). In the underground area you can see evidence of Roman roads discovered when restoration work began on the church. Upstairs is the treasury, containing a rich collection of religious art and artefacts.

From Marina head up Largo Carlo Felice to the busy Piazza Yenne and veer west along Via Azuni into the centuries-old working-class district of Stampace. Of the various churches here the most impressive one is the triple-arched **Chiesa di San Michele** (Via Ospedale 2; ☀ 7.30-11am & 7-8pm), the most opulent example of rococo in Sardinia and scene of a rousing pre-war speech by Habsburg Emperor Carlos V before he set off on a fruitless campaign against Arab corsairs in Tunisia in 1535.

Of the few reminders of the Roman presence in Cagliari the most important is the **Anfiteatro Romano** (admission €3; ☀ 10am-1pm & 3-6pm Tue-Sun Apr-Oct, 10am-4pm Tue-Sun Nov-Mar). It's a bit of a climb to this marvellous 2nd-century outdoor theatre largely carved out of the hillside, but it's well worth the effort.

Although much of the original theatre was cannibalised for other constructions, over the centuries enough has survived to pique your imagination. In summer the amphitheatre regains something of its original vocation when it is used as the venue for a series of annual outdoor concerts. Just south of here is the leafy retreat of the **Orto Botanico** (admission €0.50; ⊗ 8am-1.30pm & 3-7pm Apr-Oct, 8am-1.30pm Nov-Mar), the city's botanical gardens.

From here you can head further north for a slug of contemporary culture at the **Galleria Comunale d'Arte** (☎ 070 49 07 27; Viale San Vincenzo; adult/child €3.10/1.05; ⊗ 9am-1pm & 5-9pm Wed-Mon) dedicated to the Collezione Ingrao, and where there are more than 650 works of Italian art from the mid-19th century to the late 20th century on display.

Villanova

Although exhaust fumes and soulless modern apartment blocks typify Cagliari's new town of Villanova, this area east of Viale Regina Margherita has some worthy sites. Readily visible between the concrete towers are such curiosities as the **Basilica di San Saturno** (Piazza San Cosimo; ⊗ 9am-1pm Mon-Sat), the site of a 6th-century church, one of the island's oldest. Inside excavations of the necropolis continue and you can clearly see several tombs. Nearby, the former abattoir now serves as the **Exma** (☎ 070 66 63 99; Via San Lucifero 11; exhibition admission about €3; ⊗ 10am-2pm & 5pm-midnight Tue-Sun Jun-Sep, 9am-8pm Tue-Sun Oct-May), both an art exhibition space and a venue for classical and jazz concerts.

The **Santuario & Basilica di Nostra Signora di Bonaria** (Viale Bonaria; ⊗ 6.30am-noon & 4.30-7.30pm Apr-Oct, 6.30am-noon & 4-6.30pm Nov-Mar) houses the miraculous statue of the Virgin Mary and Christ child that allegedly washed ashore from a shipwreck in the 14th century. The sanctuary is dwarfed by the basilica to its right. It was bombed in 1943 and restoration was only completed in 1998.

Beaches

You can easily kick back for a day at either the little **Calamosca** or longer **Poetto** beaches, about 1.5km east of the centre. There are several small bars with outside tables where you can sip a cool beer with sand between your toes. Alternatively, head over to the **Stagno di Molentargius**, just west of Poetto, where you may spy pink flamingos on the salt lake.

FESTIVALS & EVENTS

The **Festa di Sant'Efisio** has been held annually in May since the 17th century. For more information, see the boxed text, p831. Cagliari is also known for its lively **Carnevale** in February.

SLEEPING

Hotel A&R Bundes Jack (☎ /fax 070 66 79 70; Via Roma 75; s/d €43/70, with bathroom €54/82) Agreeably showing its age, this grand old-fashioned place has high ceilings and is better than most in this euro range. Choose a room above the arches with five-star views of the port. The helpful owners can advise you on what's on, providing you speak the lingo.

Hotel Aurora (☎ 0/0 65 86 25; www.albergoaurora .3000.it; Salita Santa Chiara 19; s/d €38/51) A pleasantly shabby old palazzo just up from the cheerful bustle of Piazza Yenne. The rooms are small but the pastel colour scheme, city views and smiley service help to compensate. During peak season book your bed a month in advance.

Hotel Regina Margherita (☎ 070 67 03 42; www .hotelreginamargherita.com; Via Regina Margherita 44; s/d €120/170; ✘ Ⓟ) Close your eyes until you are inside the lobby at this slick modern hotel with its disappointingly bland exterior. Rooms are predictably plush, with marshmallow-soft pillows and all the latest gizmos. The breakfast buffet has eggs and bacon – a real treat for anyone suffering withdrawals.

Hotel Calamosca (☎ 070 37 16 28; www.hotelcala mosca.it; Viale Calamosca 50; s/d €54/84; ✘ Ⓟ) A great option right by the sea at this, the nearest beach to Cagliari's city centre. The modern rooms are warmly designed using a subdued colour palette accented by sunny-coloured furnishings and lovely views over a secluded cove near the lighthouse on Capo Sant'Elia.

EATING

The Marina area is peppered with good restaurants providing a culinary balance of traditional cheap eats and more gourmet options designed to blow minds and budgets.

Da Lillicu (☎ 070 65 29 70; Via Sardegna 78; meals about €25; ⊗ Mon-Sat Sep-Jul) This down-to-earth trattoria has shiny marble tables and a gratifyingly brief menu of fish and meat mains and tasty antipasti. Attracts a regular deluge of locals, so be prepared to wait.

SARDINIA

AUTHOR'S CHOICE

Antica Hostaria (☎ 070 66 58 60; Via Cavour 60; meals €45; ☼ Sep-Jul) Without doubt this is one of the strongholds of fine dining in Cagliari. Antique furnishings create a warm ambience and set the scene for simple but classic Italian cooking, as well as rare treats such as those dishes served *al tartufo* (with truffles).

Buongustaio (☎ 070 66 81 24; Via Concezione 7; meals €25-30; ☼ Wed-Sun & lunch Mon) Sensory overload comes with every meal at this spiffed-up trattoria. The menu changes according to the season. If available, try the handmade pasta with prawns and jumbo crab meat for a real taste-bud treat.

Dal Corsaro (☎ 070 66 43 18; Via Regina Margherita 28; meals €45-55; ☼ Mon-Sat) A classic of Cagliari's fine-dining scene, Dal Corsaro attracts the glad-rag scenesters who want to be seen. Eat à la carte or choose from a range of set-meal options starting at €45. The white-smocked waiters provide impeccable service.

Crackers (☎ 070 65 39 12; Corso Vittorio Emanuele II 193; meals about €25; ☼ Thu-Tue) Crackers has a big creamy coloured vault beneath which you sit down to enjoy northern Italian specialities, including a variety of yummy risottos. It attracts an effortlessly stylish crowd.

Ristorante Royal (☎ 070 34 13 13; Via Bottego 24; meals €25-30; ☼ Tue-Sat & lunch Sun) Tuck into a succulent Florentine steak or choose from a range of other meat and vegetable dishes at this restaurant which offers a window on Tuscany. There's not much fishy fare available but there's plenty of lip-smacking desserts, including exemplary *seadas* (light pastries filled with cheese and covered with honey).

Isola del Gelato (☎ 070 65 98 24; Piazza Yenne 35; ☼ 9am-2am Tue-Sun) A boggling 280 variations on the ice-cream theme, including homemade yoghurt with fresh fruit and the vegan variety made with soy milk.

DRINKING

Antico Caffè (☎ 070 65 82 06; Piazza Costituzione) The city's most elegant café is located next to the Bastione San Remy. If the traffic puts you off the terrace, head for the charming interior with its marble-topped tables and a meet-and-greet vibe.

Sotto La Torre (Piazza San Giuseppe 2; ☼ 8am-3am Thu-Tue) Trip through the centuries as you sip anything from coffee and tea to grappa. The décor is 17th century, with several rooms and elegant beams. You can step back in time further still by peering into a couple of cisterns here that date back to Roman and Punic times.

Il Merlo Parlante (☎ 070 65 39 81; Via Portoscalas 69; ☼ Tue-Sun) Expect grizzled old geezers and students on the razzle at this boisterous *birreria* (bar serving beer) shoe-horned into a narrow alley off Corso Vittorio Emanuele II. Well-stuffed *panini* (bread rolls with simple fillings) are available for the peckish.

Forum Caffè (Piazza Yenne; ☼ Tue-Sun) This is a funky watering hole in the nerve centre of Cagliari's pre-club doings. The funseekers are firmly in control here until the wee hours.

Old Coffee (Via La Mámora 91) A good-looking traditional bar right across from the cathedral equals suitably soul-stirring views. Avoid the pucker-making house wine and go for a beer or long spirit drink instead. You can get snacks here, too.

ENTERTAINMENT

For nine months of the year, the bulk of the club action takes place in six locales in Assemini, 16km northwest of Cagliari. Most of the clubs shut down in summer as the seaside action takes over. Cagliaritani and visitors make for the beachside clubs, many of which are open air, along the coast as far east as Villasimius and west to Pula and Santa Margherita. Clubs include Pirata, along the SS195 in Pula (km29.5), and Corte Noa, 3km further along.

Teatro Comunale (☎ 070 408 22 30; Via Sant'Alexinedda) is the main stage for classical music concerts and opera.

SHOPPING

For Sardinian crafts blow your budget at the one-stop regional crafts shop, **Isola** (☎ 070 49 27 56; Via O Baccaredda 176-178), where you can take a look at a range of quality products. It has other branches around the island.

Cagliari is the only place in Sardinia to do big-city shopping. Italy's quality department store, **La Rinascente** (Via Roma 141) has one retail-therapy branch here.

A good outlet for Sardinian music is **Grand Wazoo** (☎ 070 66 60 39; Via Garibaldi 143).

SARDINIA

GETTING THERE & AWAY
Boat
Boats run from Cagliari's Stazione Marittima (ferry terminal) to Civitavecchia, Livorno and Naples on the Italian mainland, as well as to Palermo and Tràpani in Sicily.

Bus
The main ARST intercity bus station is on Piazza Matteotti.

PANI buses to Oristano (€5.95, one hour 35 minutes), Nuoro (€11.31, 3½ hours) and Sassari (€13.60, 3¼ hours nonstop) leave from outside the Stazione Marittima. The ticket office is in the port building itself.

For Iglesias (€3, one to 1½ hours), Carbonia, Portovesme (€4.50, two hours) and the Sulcis area, FMS buses leave from Via Colombo 24. Buy tickets from the nearby Bar Mura.

Some FdS buses leave from the FdS train station.

Car & Motorcycle
The SS131 Carlo Felice highway links the capital with Porto Torres via Oristano and Sassari. It is the island's main dual-carriage artery. Another highway, the SS130, scoots east to Iglesias.

Train
The main Trenitalia station is found on Piazza Matteotti. Trains service both Iglesias (€2.75, 1½ hours) and Carbonia (€3.50, 1¼ hours) in the southwest, while the main line proceeds northwards as far as Sassari (€12.10, 4¼ hours) and Porto Torres via the towns of Oristano (€4.75, one to two hours) and Macomer. A branch line from Chilivani heads out for Olbia (€13, four hours) and Golfo Aranci.

The FdS train station for trains travelling north to Dolianova, Mandas and Isili is on Piazza Repubblica. In the summer, a *Trenino Verde* scenic service runs between Mandas and Arbatax on the east coast – this is quite a slow ride through some wild country, mostly in the province of Nuoro. A similar line runs north from Isili to Sorgono.

GETTING AROUND
To/From the Airport
Cagliari's **Elmas airport** (CAG; ☎ 070 2 10 51) is 6km northwest of the centre. Up to 24 daily buses connect with the city centre (ARST station in Piazza Matteotti). The trip normally takes 10 to 15 minutes and costs €0.80. A taxi will cost up to €15.

Bus
CTM (☎ 070 209 12 10) buses have routes across the city and surrounding area. They come in handy for the Calamosca and Poetto beaches. A single ticket costs €0.80, while a *biglietto giornaliero* (day ticket) costs €2.10.

Car & Motorcycle
Parking in the city centre generally means paying. Parking in blue zones costs €0.55 for the first hour and €1.05 for each hour thereafter. Either buy special tickets to leave on the dashboard of your car from newspaper stands or pay one of the attendants.

The big international car-rental agencies are represented at the airport and there are also several at the port. You'll also find a few local outfits. **Ruvioli** (☎ 070 65 89 55; www.ruvioli .it; Via dei Mille 9) charges €120.85 to hire a Fiat Panda for two days.

Taxi
There are taxi ranks at Piazza Matteotti, Piazza della Repubblica and on Largo Carlo Felice. You can call for one on ☎ 070 40 01 01 from 5.30am to 2am. Outside those times you might have difficulty.

AROUND CAGLIARI

Once past the sandy strip of Poetto, the road east hugs the coast prettily (if precariously) all the way around to Villasimius and then north along the Costa Rei.

The landscape is bare and hilly and the more clicks you put between yourself and Cagliari the more enticing the beaches become. Numerous nondescript hotels beyond Poetto can put you up, but you are better off pushing onto Villasimius and the Costa Rei.

VILLASIMIUS & COSTA REI
A few kilometres short of Villasimius, the heart of the tourist coast in these parts, a road veers south along the peninsula that leads to **Capo Carbonara**, the most southeasterly point of Sardinia. On the way is a camp site and what remains of a square Spanish tower. South of the tower are a few stretches of beach, including the lovely sandy stretch of **Spiaggia**

SARDINIA

del Riso, lapped by the azure-coloured sea. The east side is dominated by the **Stagno Notteri** lagoon, which is seasonally frequented by flamingos. On its seaward side is yet another sweeping beach, the **Spiaggia del Simius**.

Villasimius is the most developed town in this area and has a swanky new yachting port on the Golfo di Carbonara.

The only camp site nearby is **Spiaggia del Riso** (☎ 070 79 10 52; www.villaggiospiaggiadelriso.it; person/site €7.75/28, 4-person bungalows €110; ☺ May-Oct; **P**) on the beach of the same name, about halfway down the west side of the Capo Carbonara peninsula. It has excellent facilities for families and gets hellishly crowded in midsummer.

Albergo Stella d'Oro (☎ 070 79 12 55; fax 070 79 26 32; Via Vittorio Emanuele 25; s/d €35/70; ☒ **P**) is a charming and casual small hotel about 50m east off Piazza Gramsci. Rooms are of a reasonable size and all but the one single have their own bathroom. There's a good seafood restaurant here, too, complete with a pretty inner courtyard.

Ristorante Carbonara (☎ 070 79 12 70; Via Umberto I 60; meals about €30; ☺ Thu-Tue) is seaside chic with a sunny blue-and-white colour scheme and a good standard range of seafood dishes. The watery critters are on display for you to choose the subject of your main course.

In the summertime, ARST has up to nine buses daily from Cagliari (€3, 1½ hours) to Villasimius.

To take the wonderful high coastal road west and then north towards the Costa Rei, head *south* out of Villasimius and follow the

signs. About 25km out of Villasimius you hit **Cala Sinzias**, a lovely sandy strand that has two camp sites. About 6km north you hit the resort of **Costa Rei**, with villas, shops and bars. Like those to its south and north, the **Spiaggia Costa Rei** is a dazzling white sandy beach lapped by impossibly clear blue-green water.

Camping Capo Ferrato (☎ /fax 070 99 10 12; www .campingcapoferrato.it; person/tent €9/8.60, 4-person bungalow €79; ☺ Mar-Oct) is a shady good-value camp ground at the southern entrance to the Costa Rei resort, 7km from **Capo Ferrato**.

North of the resort scene, **Spiaggia Piscina Rei** has blinding white sand and turquoise water, and there's a camp site fenced in just behind it. More beaches fill the remaining length of coast up to Capo Ferrato, beyond which driveable dirt trails lead north.

The same ARST buses from Cagliari to Villasimius continue around to Costa Rei (€3.55, 30 minutes).

NORA

Possibly founded by the Phoenicians as long ago as the 11th century, the port town of Nora was later occupied by Carthaginians and Romans and only finally abandoned in the Middle Ages. What you see at the **ancient site** (adult/child incl Pula museum €5.50/2.50; ☺ 9am-7pm) mostly dates back to ancient Roman times. Upon entry to the site you pass by a single standing column of a former temple, and then the small **theatre** (www.lanottedeipoeti.it in Italian), which makes a wonderfully evocative setting for the annual summer season

---

MYSTERY TOWERS, FAIRY HOUSES & SACRED WELLS

As early as 1800 BC Sardinians started raising *nuraghi* (rudimentary defensive towers). These Bronze Age structures, usually made of great slabs of dark basalt or trachyte, have defied explanation throughout the centuries, but one thing is for certain – their creators were fine engineers. In their more complex form, these conical towers, consisting of several levels, are held together by the force of gravity.

Even before they started building *nuraghi*, the Sardinians were busy digging tombs into the rock across the island. These cavities were later known to the superstitious as *domus de janas* (fairy houses). More elaborate were the common graves fronted by what appeared to be great ceremonial entrances known as *tombe dei giganti* (giants' tombs).

From about 1100 BC the island's people began to construct elaborate *pozzi sacri*, or sacred well temples. Those that have been discovered display many common traits. This includes a keyhole-shaped opening in the ground with a triangular stairwell leading down to a well. The wells always face the sun and are so oriented that during solstice the sun shines directly down the stairs. The building techniques were more refined than those employed in the *nuraghi* and nowhere is this more evident than in the Santa Cristina site (p832), northeast of Oristano.

of performances, including theatre, music and poetry readings. Towards the west are the substantial remains of the **Terme al Mare** (Baths by the Sea). Four columns (a tetrastyle) stand at the heart of what was a patrician villa whose surrounding rooms retain their mosaic floor decoration.

In nearby Pula, the **Civico Museo Archeologico** (☎ 070 920 96 10; Corso Vittorio Emanuele 67; adult/child incl Nora site €5.50/2.50; ⏰ 9am-8pm Sep-Jul, 9am-midnight Aug), near the central Piazza Municipio, has selected finds taken from Nora – mostly ceramics found in Punic and Roman tombs, a few bits of gold and bone jewellery, Roman glassware and the like.

The best sleeping option here is **Hotel Su Guventuddu** (☎ 070 920 90 92; fax 070 920 94 68; s/d €68/114; **P**), 2km from the Nora site on the road leading around to the Su Guventeddu beach. It is a comfortable country house, with pleasant modern rooms and a decent restaurant.

Zio Dino (☎ 070 920 91 59; Viale Segni 14; meals €30; ⏰ Mon-Sat) is one of central Pula's best eateries, serving robust portions of seafood and meat. The atmosphere is cranked up on Saturdays when wooing couples swoop in to dine on such dishes as *spaghetti allo Zio Dino*, a seafood special.

Regular ARST buses run from Cagliari to Pula (€2.05, 50 minutes). The last one back to Cagliari leaves at 9.30pm. Up to 16 local shuttle buses circulate between Pula and Nora; alternatively it's a 3km walk.

COSTA DEL SUD & AROUND

The small town and beach of **Chia** marks the start of the beautiful Costa del Sud (Southern Coast). The coast winds its way west to Porto Teulada and offers several enticing beaches en route, such as Cala Teuradda. Make sure to stop for the magnificent views at the lookout point high above Capo Malfatano.

Campeggio Torre Chia (☎ 070 923 00 54; www .campeggiotorrechia.it; person/tent €8/9.50, 4-person villas to €120) is a few hundred metres back from Spiaggia Su Portu, so there's no surprises in the lack of tent-peg space in busy August. Facilities include a tennis court, pizzeria and children's playground. Turn right at the Chia junction and follow the signs.

ARST buses to/from Chia run along the Costa del Sud a couple of times daily in summer. Up to eight buses run between Cagliari and Chia daily (€2.89, 1¼ hours).

Inland you could visit **Le Grotte Is Zuddas** (☎ 0781 95 57 41; adult/child €6.50/3.65; ⏰ 9.30am-noon & 2.30-6pm Apr-Sep, noon-4pm Mon-Sat, 9.30am-noon & 2.30-7pm Sun & holidays Oct-Mar) one of the island's many spectacular caves. The largely limestone rock lends the stalactites and stalagmites a particularly translucent quality. There are hourly tours with English spoken.

SOUTHWESTERN SARDINIA

IGLESIAS
pop 29,750

Despite the ghostly remains of a huge mine that closed in the 1970s, Iglesias is a lively and atmospheric working town. The Spaniards are long gone but the place retains an Iberian feel, with chatter in the air, deep summer heat, Aragonese-style wrought-iron balconies and that sun-bleached shabbiness you find in many a Spanish town. Visit at Easter to experience a quasi-Seville experience during the extraordinary drum-beating processions.

The Romans called the town Metalla, after the precious metals mined here, especially lead and silver. Mining equipment dating back to the Carthaginian era was discovered in the 19th century.

Information

Tourist office (☎ 0781 4 17 95; www.prolocoiglesias.it in Italian; Via Gramsci 11-13; ⏰ 9.30am-1pm & 4-7pm Mon-Fri, 9.30am-12.30pm Sat) The Pro Loco office has information on the town and the surrounding Iglesiente region.

Sights

The grand Piazza Sella, laid out in the 19th century, is the stop-and-chat centre for locals. Just off the piazza, amid pleasant hillside sculpted gardens, stand the remains of **Castello Salvaterra**, a Pisan fortress finished under Catalano-Aragonese rule. A stretch of the 14th-century northwestern perimeter wall survives along Via Campidano.

The **duomo** (cathedral) dominates the east flank of Piazza del Municipio and retains its Pisan-flavoured Romanesque-Gothic façade, as does the bell tower with its chequerboard variety of stone. At the time of writing the cathedral was closed for long-term restoration work.

The **Museo dell'Arte Mineraria** (☎ 333 447 99 80; www.museoartemineraria.it; Via Roma 17; admission free; ☼ 7-10.30pm Wed-Sun Jun-Aug, 6-8.30pm Sat & Sun Sep-May) was a mining school and is designed to recreate the reality of the mines. Many of the materials and displays downstairs were used by the school to train senior mine workers.

Sleeping & Eating

Hotel Artu (☎ 0781 2 24 92; www.hotelartuiglesias.it; Piazza Sella 15; s/d €42/72; P ❊) The only central option, this hotel's exterior ugliness grates with the rest of the square. Thankfully, once inside, the rooms are well appointed and bright. Ask for a view of the square, although on Saturdays this could mean sleeping with a pillow over your head.

Volters & Murion (☎ 0781 3 37 88; Piazza Collegio 1; meals €25) This cheerful eatery is tucked into an elbow of lively Piazza del Collegio. Enjoy lavish plates of pasta with a choice of toppings, including a superb spicy tomato sauce. Mains are conventional – rather than conveyor belt – meat and fish dishes. Rumbling tummies aside, this place doubles as a great venue for an evening tipple in summer.

Getting There & Away

Intercity buses arrive at the Via Oristano side of the Giardini Pubblici (Public Gardens). You can get information and tickets from Bar Giardini across the road. As many as 10 FMS buses run daily from Cagliari to Iglesias (€3, 1½ hours), and as many as 16 trains go between Iglesias and Cagliari (€2.75, one hour). The **train station** (Via Garibaldi) is about a 15-minute walk along Via Matteotti from the town centre.

TEMPIO DI ANTAS

This Carthaginian-Roman **temple** (☎ 347 817 49 89; adult/child €2.60/1.30; ☼ 9am-1pm & 3-8pm May-Sep, 9am-1pm & 3-6pm Sat, Sun & holidays Oct-Apr), about 15km north of Iglesias on the twisting road towards Fluminimaggiore, is set in a wide, picturesque valley. What you see, including the eight resurrected columns, dates back to Roman times. To get here, take the FMS bus (€1.78, 45 minutes) from Iglesias for Fluminimaggiore and get off just after the village of Sant'Angelo. The temple is a further 3km walk along a dirt road.

Nearby, and only reached by car, is the **Grotta de Su Mannau** (☎ 0781 58 01 89; admission €6; ☼ 9.30am-6.30pm), which is an 8km-long cave

with otherworldly rock formations; advance reservations are essential from October to April.

IGLESIENTE COAST

Just 8km west of Iglesias is the local golden beach of **Funtanamare**, facing the Golfo di Gonnesa. Swing north from Funtanamare along the coast road, which quickly climbs the rocky walls of the Iglesiente coast to give you spectacular views northwards. Even before you reach the former mining settlement of Nebida, 5.5km away, three *faraglioni* (craggy outcrops jutting out of the sea) and the bizarre **Scoglio Pan di Zucchero** (Sugarloaf Rock) islet come into view against a majestic backdrop of sheer rugged cliffs.

Nebida is a sprawling place with great views and a useful hotel. **Pan di Zucchero** (☎ /fax 0781 4 71 14; Via Centrale 366; s/d €38/48) has neat spartan rooms, some with balconies and stunning coastal views. Right next to the hotel, a narrow lane descends to a pretty sandy cove. The restaurant serves up copious helpings from a limited menu of mostly seafood pasta dishes (try the fish-stuffed *ravioli al pomodoro*).

A few kilometres north, **Masua** boasts wonderful close-up views of the Scoglio Pan di Zucchero and the chance to visit a singular mining 'port'. In 1924 a 600m twin tunnel was dug into the cliff here towards the open sea. An ingenious mobile 'arm' shoved the raw minerals from a conveyor belt to ships moored directly below. **Porto Flavia** (☎ 348 661 51 92; adult/child €8/4.50) can be visited daily for one-hour tours (the staff provide the hard hats!) in July and August (four or five visits a day depending on demand). In other months it is generally only possible for groups to visit by calling ahead.

Up to 11 FMS buses run between Iglesias and Masua, just up from Nebida (€1.20, 30 minutes).

Beach-lovers should call in at the deepset **Cala Domestica** on the way north to the former mining town of Buggerru and the broad **Spiaggia Portixeddu** beach at the northern end of the Iglesiente coast.

CARBONIA & AROUND
pop 32,775

The listless grid-plan town of Carbonia was to have been the pride and joy of the island. In 1936 work began on the island's coal capital (*carbone* means coal). Unfortunately, the idea of attaining self-sufficiency in coal had no chance and today the town is barely worth stopping for. However, palaeontology fans may enjoy the **Museo Paleontologico-Speleologico** (☎ 0781 6 43 82; Piazza Garibaldi; admission €1.60; ☒ 9am-1pm & 4-8pm Tue-Sun May-Sep, 9am-1pm & 3-7pm Tue-Sun Oct-Apr), with its exhibits of fossils, rock specimens and other ancient goodies found in caves.

About 4km northwest of Carbonia is **Monte Sirai** (admission €2.60; ☒ 9am-5pm Oct-Apr, 9am-1pm & 4-8pm May-Sep). The high plateau was a natural spot for a fort and the Phoenicians built one here in 650 BC. They were dislodged by local Sardinian tribes and later replaced by the Carthaginians. You can still make out the placement of the Carthaginian acropolis and defensive tower, a necropolis and *tophet* (where deceased children were interred).

SANT'ANTIOCO & SAN PIETRO

These islands, off the southwestern coast of Sardinia, have sandy beaches and quiet coves, as well as the cheerful towns of Calasetta (Sant'Antioco) and Carloforte (San Pietro), both with whitewashed or pastel-coloured houses lining narrow streets. The town of Sant'Antioco is more developed but parts still have a delightful dilapidated feel.

Information

Tourist office San Pietro (☎ 0781 85 40 09; Piazza Carlo Emanuele III 19; ☒ 9.30am-12.30pm & 5-8pm Mon-Sat, 10am-noon Sun); Sant'Antioco (☎ 0781 8 20 31; Piazza Repubblica 31a; ☒ 9am-noon & 5.30-9pm Mon-Fri)

Sights & Activities

In Sant'Antioco the **Chiesa di Sant'Antioco** is worth visiting for its **catacombs** (admission €2.50; ☒ 9am-noon & 3-6pm Mon-Sat, 10-11am & 3-6pm Sun), where the early Christians buried their dead and sometimes held Mass. A few doors down is a small archaeology museum, while across town some Carthaginian sites are scattered.

A couple of beaches worth bucket and spading it to are **Maladroixa** and **Spiaggia Coa Quaddus** along the eastern coast. The town of Calasetta on the northwest of the island is a sleepy place, and there's a boat here that heads across to the Isola San Pietro, whose main resort, **Carloforte**, is relaxed yet elegant with some fine restaurants and cafés.

The tourist offices can point you in the direction of **sailing** and **diving** outfits, especially on the Carloforte waterfront.

Sleeping

On both islands you will find a few camping grounds and a handful of hotels outside the main towns.

Hotel Eden (☎ 0781 84 07 68; Piazza Parrocchia 15, Sant'Antioco; s/d €50/80; ☒) A charming option in a modest mansion opposite the Chiesa di Sant'Antioco. Rooms make up for their swing-a-cat size by being big on atmosphere with homy décor and attention to detail.

Hotel Hieracon (☎ 0781 85 40 28; Corso Cavour 63, San Pietro; s/d €57/98; ☒) Carloforte's faded jewel, this hotel is a grey Art Nouveau mansion at the northern end of the waterfront. There's a something-for-everyone choice of rooms, including a family-sized room with up to four beds.

Eating

Ristorante Sette Nani (☎ 0781 84 09 00; Via Garibaldi 139, Calasetta, Sant'Antioco; meals €25-30) Spread out over several floors indoors or mellow out with a table in the garden dining area. Sette Nani delivers the goods with unfussy seafood dishes, topped off with a selection of Sardinian sweets and a complimentary glass of *mirto* (the local liqueur) to send you on your way.

Tonno di Corsa (☎ 0781 85 51 06; Via Marconi 47, Carloforte, San Pietro; meals €35-40; ☒ Tue-Sun) Up a few blocks from the seaside along Via Caprera (then turn right), this place is paradise for tuna-lovers. Push the boat out with the delicious *ventresca di tonno*, a sublime cut of what is possibly the best tuna you will ever have.

Dau Bobba (☎ 0781 85 40 37; Lungocanale delle Saline, Carloforte, San Pietro; meals €45-50; ☒ Wed-Mon) Dau Bobba, 500m south of the main waterfront, has a little courtyard garden that creates an inviting ambience in which to sample anything from a great pesto to the fresh catch of the day.

Getting There & Around

Sant'Antioco is connected to the mainland by a land bridge and is accessible by FMS bus from Cagliari and Iglesias. Regular ferries connect Calasetta and Carloforte. From Carloforte boats run to Portovesme on the mainland. The one-way trip on any of these boats costs approximately €2.50 per person. Local buses run around Sant'Antioco, and limited summertime services operate on San Pietro.

SARDINIA

COSTA VERDE

From Capo Pecora in the south to Capo Frasca in the north, the Costa Verde (Green Coast) boasts some of the least spoiled and most beautiful beaches in Sardinia.

From the south, head inland along the SS126 and turn west at the turn-off for Bau and Gennamari. A high hill road winds out towards the coast. Keep an eye out for signs to **Spiaggia Scivu**, a spectacular golden strand. Almost 4km north of the Bau and Gennamari turn-off is another for the ghost town of **Ingurtosu**. Follow this and the track that winds out west to the coast to reach the magnificent dune-backed **Spiaggia Piscinas**.

In summer a few kiosk/cafés and freshwater showers are set up on the beach. People park their campervans here or stay in the stylish and appropriately sand-coloured **Hotel Le Dune** (☎ 070 97 71 30; www.leduneingurtosu .it; d from €165) nearby, which is a restored 19th-century mining structure.

From Spiaggia Piscinas the road winds north through green *macchia* bush and pine stands past several beaches until you reach the attractive, low-key Torre dei Corsari resort. The broad beach that sweeps its way north below this high promontory is another gem. At its northern end the beach is also known as **Pistis**.

B&B Brezza Marina (☎ 338 367 68 86; Viale della Torre; s/d €30-50) is a real winner run by a charming English-speaking Sardinian couple fresh from a stint in London. The place has a friendly spare-room feel and there's a small garden complete with barbecue. They also offer cooking courses three times a week for a reasonable €15 (including the meal). Aside from the B&B, the couple rent out a couple of apartments in town with sea views.

It is difficult to get around the Costa Verde by public transport. A couple of buses run to Ingurtosu from the inland town of Guspini (reached in turn from Cagliari or Oristano), but from there you have to walk. Your own car is the only seriously workable option.

ORISTANO & THE WEST

The focal point for most visitors is the ancient site of Tharros on the Sinis Peninsula and the beaches to the north. But the sleepy capital, Oristano, which was only created as a province in 1974, has a pleasant centre for

strolling and a tangible sense of history, only spoilt (again) by the mindless graffiti. It is well worth a stopover, together with several towns and nuraghic sites in the interior.

ORISTANO

pop 33,000

Oristano was founded in the early Middle Ages as the inhabitants of Tharros wearied of repeated raids by North African corsairs. By the 11th century it had become the capital of the Giudicato d'Arborea (which encompasses the same area as the modern province), one of four such entities into which Sardinia was divided in the Middle Ages prior to its takeover by the Crown of Aragón. Eleonora d'Arborea (1340–1404) became the head of the *giudicato* in 1383 and has gone down in history for her wise administration and resistance to the Catalano-Aragonese. Eleonora's death in 1404 led to capitulation but her Carta de Logu, an extraordinary law code, outlived her. You can see her statue in the namesake piazza.

Information

Guardia Medica (☎ 0783 7 43 33; Via Carducci) For medical assistance.

Hospital (Viale Fondazione Rockefeller) The main hospital is south of the town centre.

La Pergomena (☎ /fax 0783 7 50 58; Via Vittorio Emanuele II 24) An excellent range of books on all aspects of Sardinia, plus a handful of novels in English, French and German.

Pharmacy (Corso Umberto 51)

Post office (Via Mariano IV d'Arborea; ⏲ 8.15am-6.15pm Mon-Fri, 8.15am-noon Sat)

Search Interpoint (Via Cagliari 288; per hr €5; ⏲ 9.30am-1pm & 3.30-7.30 Mon-Fri) Internet access.

Tourist information point (Piazza Roma; ⏲ 9am-1pm & 4-9pm Mon-Sat, 9am-1pm & 4-10pm Sun & holidays Jul–mid-Sep)

Tourist office Piazza Eleonora d'Arborea 19 (☎ 0783 3 68 31; enturismo.oristano@tiscali.it; ⏲ 8am-2pm & 4-7pm Mon-Sat); Via Ciutadella di Menorca 14 (☎ 0783 7 06 21; ⏲ 9am-noon & 4.30-7.30pm Mon-Fri)

Sights

The 13th-century **Torre di Mariano II** (Piazza Roma) is one of the only vestiges of Oristano's medieval walls. The shopping street of Corso Umberto leads from Piazza Roma to **Piazza Eleonora d'Arborea**, presided over by a 19th-century **statue** of Oristano's heroine. The neoclassical **Chiesa di San Francesco** (Via Sant'Antonio;

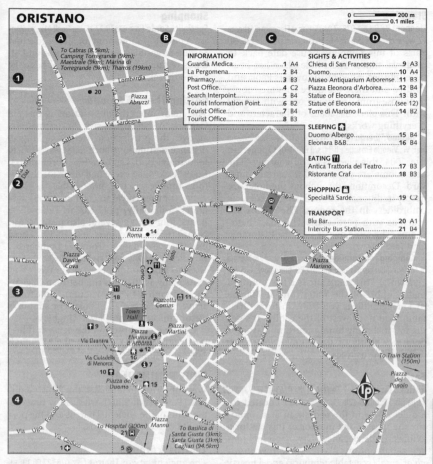

ORISTANO

0 ——— 200 m
0 ——— 0.1 miles

INFORMATION
Guardia Medica................................**1** A4
La Pergomena..................................**2** B4
Pharmacy...**3** B3
Post Office.......................................**4** C2
Search Interpoint..............................**5** B4
Tourist Information Point..................**6** B2
Tourist Office...................................**7** B4
Tourist Office...................................**8** B3

SIGHTS & ACTIVITIES
Chiesa di San Francesco...................**9** A3
Duomo..**10** A4
Museo Antiquarium Arborense......**11** B3
Piazza Eleonora d'Arborea...............**12** B4
Statue of Eleonora..........................**13** B3
Statue of Eleonora...................(see 12)
Torre di Mariano II.........................**14** B2

SLEEPING
Duomo Albergo..............................**15** B4
Eleonara B&B..................................**16** B4

EATING
Antica Trattoria del Teatro..............**17** B3
Ristorante Craf...............................**18** B3

SHOPPING
Specialità Sarde...............................**19** C2

TRANSPORT
Blu Bar...**20** A1
Intercity Bus Station.......................**21** B4

8am-noon & 5-7pm Mon-Sat, 8am-noon Sun) is home to the *Crocifisso di Nicodemoa*, which is a 14th-century wooden sculpture made by an unknown Catalan artist.

Follow Via Duomo to the **Duomo** (Piazza del Duomo; 7am-noon & 4-7pm Mon-Sat, 8am-1pm Sun), built in the 13th century but remodelled in the 18th century. Its baroque bell tower is topped by a multicoloured dome.

Museo Antiquarium Arborense (0783 79 12 62; Piazzetta Corrias; adult/child €3/1; 9am-1.30pm & 3-8pm), in the heart of the town, contains one of the most important collections found on the island. Artefacts dug up at Tharros and on the Sinis Peninsula range from pre-nuraghic items to early medieval pieces. A section of the museum hosts a small collec-tion of *retablos* (painted altarpieces). One series of panels, the *Retablo del Santo Cristo*, painted by the workshop of Cagliari's Pietro Cavaro in 1533, depicts a decorative series of Franciscan saints.

Around 3km south of Oristano at Santa Giusta is the **Basilica di Santa Giusta**. Built from 1135 to 1145, it's one of the earliest Tuscan-style Romanesque churches built on the island. The basilica is easily accessible by local ARST buses.

Festivals & Events

Oristano bursts into life with **Sa Sartiglia**, held on the last Sunday of Carnevale (late February or early March) and repeated on Shrove Tuesday (see the boxed text, p831).

SARDINIA

Sleeping

Eleonora B&B (☎ 0783 7 04 35; Piazza Eleonora d'Arborea 12; www.eleonora-bed-and-breakfast.com; s/d from €35/60) Parts of this rambling house date back to medieval times. The whole place has been tastefully decorated by the owners Paola and Andrea and there are three en-suite rooms to choose from, including one with Jacuzzi bath. This place has loads of character (and everything works).

Duomo Albergo (☎ 0783 77 80 61; www.hotelduomo .net; Via Vittorio Emanuele II 34; s/d €70/140) Opened in late 2004, this place is a real charmer. The best rooms are set around a central courtyard. Decorations throughout the hotel are deeply traditional, with wall hangings of local embroidery in the rooms. The rooms are spacious with particularly chic tiled bathrooms. The same owner runs the Ristorante Craf (see below).

Camping Torregrande (☎ /fax 0783 2 22 28; Marina di Torregrande; person/tent €5.20/7.80, bungalows €65.50; ☯ May-Sep) This camp site is a few hundred metres short of the waterfront at Marina di Torregrande as you come in from Oristano, 9km northwest of the centre. It's got the lot, including tennis court, mini-soccer field and plenty of shade under lofty pine and eucalyptus trees.

Eating

Antica Trattoria del Teatro (☎ 0783 7 16 72; Via Parpaglia 11; meals €28-35; ☯ Thu-Tue) Located on a quiet elbow in the pedestrian area, opposite the theatre, the interior of this trattoria exudes subtle elegance. The menu includes vegetarian options like *tempura di verduras all'oriental* (vegetable tempura) and a hearty minestrone.

Ristorante Craf (☎ 0783 37 06 89; Via de Castro 34; meals €30; ☯ Mon-Sat) There's carafe loads of atmosphere at this former 17th-century granary with its vaulted brick-faced dining rooms and folksy clutter. The menu includes a delicious *panne frattau* (Sardinian bread soup), fish dishes and, if you're game, *asinello in padella ai funghi* (donkey with mushrooms). Unfortunately, vegetarians will find slim pickings.

Maestrale (☎ 0783 2 21 21; Lungomare Torregrande; meals €35; ☯ Tue-Sun) The pick of the culinary crop in this strip of restaurants and cafés, Maestrale fronts the palm-flanked promenade. The emphasis is firmly on fishy fare, including a recommended seafood risotto.

Shopping

Specialità Sarde (☎ 0783 7 27 25; Via Figoli 41; ☯ Mon-Sat) A one-stop showroom for all the gourmet Sardinian goodies, including cheese and all kinds of fancy fare in jars. Typical basketry is also on sale.

Getting There & Around

The main intercity bus station is on Via Cagliari. ARST buses leave for destinations all over the province, as well as to longer-distance destinations such as Sassari (€7.25, four daily) and Cagliari (€6, three daily). Buses leave once every half-hour for the 10- to 15-minute trip to Santa Giusta.

PANI buses travel to Cagliari (€5.95, 1¾ hours, four daily) plus Sassari (€7.59, 2½ hours, four daily); several also head east to Nuoro (€5.84, two hours, four daily). These buses arrive and leave from Via Lombardia. Buy tickets at **Blu Bar** (Via Lombardia 30; ☯ 6am-10pm Mon-Sat) or on the bus on Sunday.

As many as 20 trains run between Cagliari and Oristano (€4.75, two hours). Some trains arrive from Sassari and Olbia. The station is west of the centre on Piazza Ungheria.

Oristano city buses on the *azzurra* (blue) line run from Via Cagliari to the Marina di Torregrande.

SINIS PENINSULA

West of Oristano stretches the Sinis Peninsula (Penisola di Sinis), with sandy beaches, the ruins of the ancient Tharros and the possibility of seeing flamingos.

Tharros & Around

The ancient city of **Tharros** (☎ 0783 37 00 19; admission incl Museo Civico in Cabras €4; ☯ 9am-sunset), set impeccably against the sea at the southern extreme of the peninsula, reached the height of its importance under the Carthaginians. What is visible today, however, largely dates back to the Roman era, when the city got a thorough overhaul, particularly in the 2nd and 3rd centuries AD, when the city's basalt streets were laid, and the aqueduct, baths and other major monuments were built.

Just before Tharros is the settlement of **San Giovanni di Sinis**, with its 6th-century Byzantine church of the same name; it's one of the oldest in Sardinia. Some 4km north, in a tiny village of pastel-coloured houses once used for spaghetti westerns, is the tiny church of **San Salvatore**, built over a pagan temple.

FEAST OF FESTIVALS

Sardinia has hung on more tenaciously to its traditions than almost anywhere else in Italy and this is borne out in the rich calendar of festivals held around the island. A few of the more important ones are listed here.

January

Festa di Sant'Antonio Abate (16 Jan) With the winter solstice passed, people of many towns and villages across Sardinia, especially in the Nuoro province, seem intent on giving the chilly weather a push towards spring with great bonfires lit up in central squares on the evening of 16 January. After the blessing of the fire and perhaps a procession, townsfolk turn to the serious business of drinking. Among the places where you can be sure of seeing a good bonfire are Orosei, Orgosolo, Mamoiada, Sedilo and Paulilatino.

Mamuthones (16 & 17 Jan) Warranting special mention are the celebrations that take place in the otherwise nondescript town of Mamoiada, south of Nuoro. Here, traditional costumes are used in processions to represent the *mamuthones*, disturbing animal-like characters in fearsome masks, wearing a heavy belt of cowbells with which they create an infernal din. They generally come out to play again during Carnevale.

February

Carnevale (Carnival) During the period running up to Ash Wednesday, many towns stage carnivals and enjoy their last opportunity to indulge before Lent. Traditionally processions and parties take place from Thursday to *martedì grasso* ('fat Tuesday' – the last chance to eat and drink whatever you want before Ash Wednesday).

Sa Sartiglia This is the highlight of Carnevale celebrations at Oristano, held on the Sunday and Tuesday before Lent. It involves a medieval tournament of horsemen in masquerade.

March/April

Pasqua (Easter) Holy Week (any time from 22 March to 25 April, depending on the lunar calendar) is marked by solemn processions and Passion plays all over the island. The people of Iglesias celebrate Easter with Iberian vigour. The most engaging Easter procession is probably Castelsardo's Lunissanti (Monday of Holy Week), an evocative torch-lit parade through the old town.

May

Festa di Sant'Efisio (1 & 4 May) One of the island's most colourful festivals takes place to honour the memory of Sardinia's patron saint in Cagliari. On 1 May the saint's effigy is paraded around the city on a bullock-drawn carriage amid a colourful costume procession. It is then accompanied out of the city to the ancient site of Nora, where St Ephisius, a Roman commander who converted to Christianity, is said to have been decapitated on Emperor Diocletian's orders in AD 303. On 4 May the effigy is returned to Cagliari by the same road.

Cavalcata Sarda (Sardinian Cavalcade; 2nd-last Sun in May) Hundreds of Sardinians wearing colourful traditional costumes gather at Sassari to mark a victory over the Saracens in the year 1000. They are followed by horsemen who make a spirited charge through the streets at the end of the parade.

July

Ardia (6 & 7 Jul) More dangerous than Siena's famed Il Palio horse race, this impressive and mostly chaotic equestrian event at Sedilo celebrates the victory of the Roman emperor Constantine over Maxentius in AD 312 (the battle took place at the Ponte Milvio in Rome). An unruly pack of skilled horsemen race around a dusty track not far from the chapel erected in Constantine's name (Santu Antine) just outside the town. Onlookers drink, hoot and fire their guns into the air.

August

I Candelieri (The Candlesticks; 14 Aug) Held in Sassari, I Candelieri features town representatives in medieval costume bearing huge wooden columns (the 'candlesticks') through the town. The celebrations are held to honour a vow made in 1652 for deliverance from a plague but are also connected with the Feast of the Assumption (15 August).

Festa del Redentore (Last week of Aug) What is possibly the island's grandest procession of traditional Sardinian costume, the parade dominates this festival in Nuoro. Groups from towns and villages all over the island proudly parade their festive dress on the last or second-last Sunday of the month. Joining them in the parade are horsemen and dance groups. The religious side of the festivities has its roots in the placement of a statue of Christ at the top of Monte Ortobene at the turn of the 20th century. A torchlit procession winds through the city on the evening of 28 August and an early morning pilgrimage to Monte Ortobene occurs the following day.

September

Festa di San Salvatore (1st Sun of Sep) Hundreds of young fellows in white set off on the Corsa degli Scalzi (Barefoot Race), an 8km run to the hamlet and sanctuary of San Salvatore. They carry an effigy of the Saviour, and the whole event commemorates an episode in 1506, when townspeople raced to the San Salvatore sanctuary to collect the effigy and save it from Moorish sea raiders.

SARDINIA

In summer, four ARST buses a day head to Tharros from Oristano (€1.45, 20 to 30 minutes).

Cabras

This straggling lagoon town is really only worth stopping for the **Museo Civico** (☎ 783 29 06 36; Via Tharros 121; admission incl Tharros €4; ☼ 9am-1pm & 4-8pm Tue-Sun Jun-Sep, 9am-1pm & 3-7pm Tue-Sun Oct-May) at the southern end of the town. It has Carthaginian and Roman artefacts from Tharros, as well as prehistoric items from the nearby archaeological site of Cuccuru is Arrius. Regular ARST buses run from Oristano (€0.70, 15 minutes).

Beaches

The **Spiaggia di San Giovanni di Sinis**, the golden strand nearest to Tharros has the advantage over most of the more northern beaches of being relatively free of rocks and algae, which can equal a definite lack of sun-bronzing space in summer.

Of the many beaches further north, **Is Arutas** is interesting. Mingled in with the pebbles and sand is a good quantity of quartz – walking along the beach is like getting a foot massage (but making a souvenir of some of the quartz is illegal, enforceable by law). The beach is signposted and is 5km west off the main road leading north from the church of San Salvatore.

At **Putzu Idu** a long and sandy, if untidy, strand of beach is backed by a motley set of holiday homes and beach bars. The lagoon inland from Putzu Idu often hosts some of Sardinia's flamingo population.

You can find accommodation in Putzu Idu, Mandriola and Su Pallosu, and a handful of restaurant/pizzerias keep hunger at bay. Up to three ARST buses run from Oristano to Putzu Idu (€1.55, 30 minutes) in summer. The summer service to Tharros goes on as far as Is Arutas.

NORTH ORISTANO COAST

Further north of the Sinis Peninsula are some even better beaches around the low-key resort of **Santa Caterina di Pittinuri**. The town itself has a decent beach surrounded by dramatic cliffs. The emerald waters in the cove of **S'Archittu** are tempting, or you could head a few kilometres south for the long expanse of the **Is Arenas** beach, which you reach along tracks threading past three camp sites. Buses between Oristano and Bosa stop at Santa Caterina, S'Archittu and Cuglieri. They will stop on request at the camp sites.

LAGO OMEDEO CIRCUIT

Following the SS131 highway north out of Oristano you come across the **Santa Cristina** (admission incl Paulilatino archaeological museum €3.10; ☼ 8.30am-11pm May-Sep, 8.30am-9pm Oct-Apr), site of a small pilgrims' church, nuraghic village and, most importantly, an ancient nuraghic well temple whose lines are so perfect it looks like it was made yesterday. Finds from the Santa Cristina site can be seen at a small archaeological museum in **Paulilatino**, a few kilometres north. Just north of Paulilatino is one of the island's most important *nuraghi*, the **Nuraghe Losa** (☎ 0785 5 48 23; admission €3.50; ☼ 9am-1pm & 3-7pm).

About 14km northeast of the Nuraghe Losa, past Lago Omedeo, is the unremarkable rural town of **Sedilo**, which crackles to life for the **Ardia** festival (for details, see the boxed text, p831).

About 30km south of Sedilo on the banks of the Tirso River is the strange red-coloured town of **Fordongianus**, where everything seems to be made of the local trachyte stone except the **Terme Romane** (☎ 0783 6 01 57; admission €3; ☼ 9.30am-1pm & 3-7.30pm summer, 9.30am-1pm & 3-5.30pm winter). From below these Roman baths, piping hot water still bubbles forth into the river.

Your own transport is needed to get to and around most of these sights, although several ARST buses run from Oristano to Fordongianus (€1.80, 40 minutes). Buses from Oristano to Abbasanta (€2.40, 55 minutes), via Paulilatino, put you within walking distance of the Nuraghe Losa.

BARUMINI & AROUND

One of the most important and most visited of the island's *nuraghi* is the **Nuraghe Su Nuraxi** (adult/under 25 €4.20/3.10; ☼ 9am-8pm), barely half a kilometre to the west of the village of Barumini on the road to Tuili. The hulk of the central tower of the complex stands as a prominent landmark; however, what makes it impressive is not so much the central tower but the extent of the village ruins around it. It's a veritable beehive of circular buildings, most not more than a metre high.

Albergo Sa Lolla (☎ 070 936 84 19; fax 070 936 11 07; Via Cavour 49; s/d €42/57; 🅿) is a striking ranch-style hotel with seven freshly decorated rooms and a welcoming home-sweet-home vibe. The restaurant here pumps out exquisite home-cooked food and there's a pool and tennis court for working off any extra pounds. The location is excellent, a few hundred metres east of the Chiesa di Santa Tecla.

To the *albergo's* north is the high **Giara di Gesturi** plateau, home to some 500 wild *cavallini* ('minihorses', or ponies), most likely seen by shallow *pauli* (seasonal lakes) at daybreak or dusk.

About 24km by road to the east (you have to double-back through Serrior you'll miss it) is the **Santuario Santa Vittoria di Serri** (adult/child €4/2; 9am-7pm), the most extensive nuraghic settlement unearthed in Sardinia.

You definitely need your own transport to get around this area as buses are rare and could leave you stranded.

BOSA
pop 7856

Bosa lies within the fat finger of Nuoro province, which slips its way to the western coast between the provinces of Sassari and Oristano. The only important Sardinian town on a river, Bosa is a picturesque place with washed-out pastel houses that combine the old-fashioned appeal of the medieval town with the broad sweep of sandy beach nearby. It is largely untainted by tourism, although planned-for new hotels will inevitably mean less towel space on the sand in future.

Information
Medical services (0785 37 46 15; Viale Italia) Just off the beach at Bosa Marina.

Tourist office Bosa Marina train station (0785 37 71 08; 10am-1pm & 7-10pm Jun-Sep); cnr Via Alberto Azuni & Via F Romagna (0785 37 61 07; www.infobosa .it in Italian; 9.30am-1pm & 6-8.30pm May-Sep)

Sights & Activities
Bosa's old centre, known as Sa Costa and bunched on a hillside, is all narrow lanes, little squares and a sprinkling of elegant baroque churches. The medieval **castle** was built in 1112 by the Malaspina, a noble Tuscan family, to control the Temo Valley. The Temo River, with its 8km of navigable waters, made a local tanning industry possible. Also of interest is the Romanesque church of **San Pietro Extramuros** (10am-7pm May-Sep), 2km from the old bridge on the south bank of the Temo.

Bosa Marina's broad, sandy **beach** is the perfect place to end a tough morning's sightseeing. Wind and kite surfers like this spot and it is possible to hire gear on the beach. There are spectacular coral reefs offshore. To organise **dives**, contact **Malesh** (0785 37 56 49; Via Colombo).

The coastline between Bosa and Alghero is stunning, with rugged cliffs dropping down to coves. It's a protected area and a breeding ground for several rare bird species.

Sleeping & Eating
Hotel Sa Pischedda (0785 37 30 65; fax 0785 37 70 54; www.hotelsapischedda.it; Via Roma 2; s/d €70/86; P) The apricot-coloured façade of this aesthetically restored house greets you just as you reach the south side of the Ponte Vecchio. This place is a real gem; several rooms have original frescoed ceilings, while others are split level. There are terraces overlooking the river and satellite TV if you tire of the view. The restaurant is exceptional (see below).

Hotel Al Gabbano (0785 37 41 23; Viale Mediterraneo; s/d €56/78; P) The main draw here is the location, a Frisbee throw from the beach. The rooms don't exactly sparkle, but are spacious and comfy enough. Guests have their own sunbed space on the beach, and rooms with balconies and sea views cost the same as regular rooms.

Sa Pischedda (0785 37 30 65; Via Roma 8; meals €25-30; closed Tue in winter) Recognised by both the Slow Food Movement and the Michelin guide, this kitchen is run with passion by the son of the owner (his brother runs the hotel). The dishes have plenty of aesthetic wow factor but they taste good, too. Try the *anguleddas porcini e bottarga* (homemade pasta with mushrooms and mullet roe), followed by one of the seductive desserts.

La Pulce Rossa (0785 37 56 57; Via Lungo Temo Amendola; meals €24; Tue-Sun) Across from the river, this restaurant's menu is unwaveringly authentic, with delicious pasta made daily by chef Vincenzo. For undecided taste buds, there's more than 47 pizzas to choose from.

Getting There & Away
All buses stop at Piazza Zanetti. Most services are run by FdS, which has a ticket office on the square. Up to four buses run to/from Alghero. The quicker ones take the scenic coastal route (€2.90, 55 minutes). Sassari takes double the time (€5.85, 2¼ hours).

SARDINIA

NORTHERN SARDINIA

ALGHERO
pop 43,387

In the years after their arrival in Sardinia in 1323, the conquerors of the Crown of Aragón tried to 'ethnically cleanse' several Sardinian cities, replacing the local populace with Catalan colonists. These attempts largely failed, except in the northwestern port town of Alghero, where even today the Catalan tongue is still spoken. The medieval centre, with its sea walls hugging the coast, is colourful and picturesque and you may well feel as if you have landed somewhere in Spain. Alghero makes an agreeable base for exploring the northwest but can get crowded in summer and at weekends due, in part, to the steady stream of tourists arriving on cut-price Ryanair flights from the UK and Germany.

Orientation

Alghero's historic centre is on a small promontory jutting into the sea, with the new town stretching out behind it and along the coast to the north. Intercity buses arrive in Via Catalogna, just outside the historic centre. The train station is about 1km north, on Via Don Minzoni.

Information

Bar Miramare (☎ 079 973 10 27; Via Gramsci 2; per hr €5; ☯ 8.30am-1pm & 4.30-2am) Surf your way through a cappuccino while checking your emails at this gruff, old-fashioned bar.

Farmacia Bulla (Via Garibaldi 13) Pharmacy.

Farmacia Cabras (Piazza Sulis 11) Pharmacy.

Ospedale Civile (☎ 079 99 62 00; Via Don Minzoni) The main hospital.

Post office (Via Carducci 35; ☯ 8.15am-6.15pm Mon-Fri, 8.15am-1pm Sat)

Tourist office Piazza Porta Terra 9 (☎ 079 97 90 54; www.infoalghero.it in Italian; ☯ 8am-8pm Mon-Sat, 9am-1pm Sun Apr-Oct, 8am-2pm Mon-Sat Nov-Mar); airport (☎ 079 93 51 24; ☯ 8.30am-2.30pm & 5-10pm)

Sights & Activities

The cobbled lanes and honey-coloured walls of this former outpost of the Catalan merchant empire preserve more than a whiff of the centuries of Catalan presence here.

The **Cattedrale di Santa Maria** has been ruined by constant remodelling, but its **bell tower** (admission €1.50; ☯ 7-9.30pm Jul-Sep) remains a fine

example of Catalan-Gothic architecture. Next door the **Museo Diocesano** (Piazza Duomo; admission €2.50; ☯ 10am-12.30pm year-round, 5-8pm Mar-May, Oct & Nov-Dec, 6-9pm Jun & Sep, 7-11pm Jul-Aug) houses religious treasures in a former chapel.

On the old town's main street is the engaging **Chiesa di San Francesco** (Via Carlo Alberto; ☯ 9.30am-noon & 5-7.30pm Mon-Sat, 5-7.30pm Sun), a combination of Romanesque and Gothic styles with an austere stone façade.

Several landward towers remain, including what was the main land entrance, or **Torre Porta a Terra**, now an information office, and the **Torre di San Giovanni**, which houses a small multimedia display on the town's history (it's currently closed for restoration, check at the tourist office for an update). To the north the **Bastione della Maddalena**, with its eponymous tower, form the only extant remnant of the city's former land battlements. The Mediterranean Sea crashes up against the seaward walls of the **Bastioni di San Marco** and **Bastioni di Cristoforo Colombo**. Along these seaward bulwarks are some inviting restaurants and bars where you can camera-snap the sunset over a drink.

North of Alghero's port, which is jammed with yachts, Via Garibaldi sweeps up to the town's beaches, **Spiaggia di San Giovanni** and the adjacent **Spiaggia di Maria Pia**. Indeed, the sands continue pretty much uninterrupted around the coast to Fertilia.

Courses

If you fancy a course in Sardinian cuisine (or want to brush up on your Italian), **Stroll & Speak** (☎ 328 765 54 77; info@strollandspeak.com; Via Cavour 4) organises year-round culinary courses. A one-week, 13-hour session is €200. Shorter courses are also available.

Festivals & Events

The **Estate Musicale Internazionale di Alghero** (International Summer of Music) is staged in July and August, and features classical music concerts in the evocative setting of the Chiesa di San Francesco cloister.

Sleeping

It is virtually impossible to find a room in August unless you book in advance.

Mario & Giovanna's B&B (☎ 339 890 35 63; www.marioandgiovanna.com; Via E Porrino 17; s/d €30/50, d with bathroom €55) Run by an affable couple, this place has homy rooms lovingly furnished

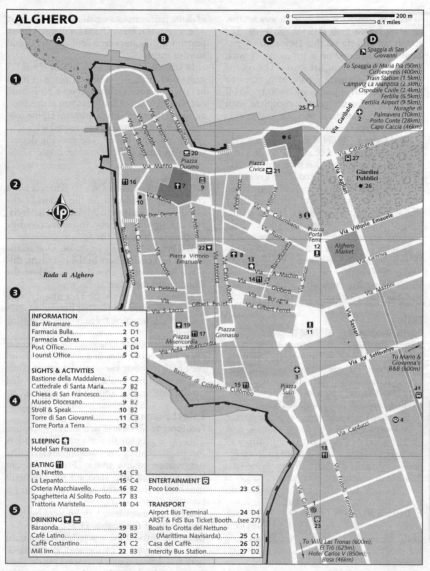

ALGHERO

SARDINIA

with pictures and ornaments. Mario worked as a chef in England and guests are welcomed with a glass of wine and titbits while he practises his English with a friendly chat. Located in the blander modern part of town, it's about a 10-minute stroll to the historic centre.

Hotel San Francesco (☎ /fax 079 98 03 30; www .sanfrancescohotel.com; Via Ambrogio Machin 2; s/d with breakfast €55/90; ✷) The only place to stay in the old town, and alone in exuding historic charm. Housed in the former convent of the Chiesa di San Francesco, the hotel's rooms are five star in monastic terms, but still nothing fancy – aside from the satellite TV. Go for a room overlooking the lovely medieval cloisters if you can.

Villa Las Tronas (☎ 079 98 18 18; www.hvlt.com; Lungomare Valencia 1; s/d €215/140; 🅿 P 🖳 🖵) Splash out and stay at this 19th-century palatial hotel situated on a promontory with balconies overlooking the waves. The rooms are pure *fin de siècle* plush, with acres of brocade, elegant antiques and moody old oil paintings. A beauty centre, complete with indoor pool, Hammam massage and gym is a welcome recent addition.

Hotel Carlos V (☎ 079 97 95 01; www.hotelcarlosv .it; Lungomare Valencia 24; d €95; 🅿 🖵 P 🖳) In a fine seafront position, this pleasant low-rise hotel has recently benefited from a revamp. The exec-style rooms are slickly furnished with dark blue fabrics and plenty of shiny wood. The best have views of the palm-fringed pool with the ocean beyond. There are large terraces and tennis courts.

Camping La Mariposa (☎ 079 95 03 60; Via Lido 22; person/tent €10.50/5; bungalows to €72; 🌣 Apr-Oct) About 2km north of the centre, approaching Via Il Lido, this camp site is on the beach and has plenty of mature shady trees.

Eating

Osteria Macchiavello (☎ 079 98 06 28; Bastioni di San Marco 57; meals €20-25; 🌣 Wed-Mon) A restaurant for those wanting full-on meaty flavours. Grilled meats include horse, beef – and donkey. Alternatively, there's a tasty wild-boar *ragú* (meat sauce) and a few fishy dishes, including *zuppa di polpi e patate* (octopus and potato soup) as a whet-your-appetite starter.

Da Ninetto (☎ 079 97 80 62; Via Gioberti 4; meals €30-35; 🌣 Wed-Mon) A bright hole-in-the-wall arrangement and *the* best place in town for reasonably priced lobster dishes. Note that it is a costly delicacy everywhere, so get it weighed first to avoid possible indigestion when you come to pay the bill.

Trattoria Maristella (☎ 079 97 81 72; Via Fratelli Kennedy 9; meals €22-25; 🌣 Mon-Sat & lunch Sun) One of the best deals in town if you are looking for moderately priced but innovative fare. The sunny yellow décor is classic modern Mediterranean and in summer you can sit outside. There is plenty of vegetarian choice, including our favourite: pasta shells with tomatoes, rocket and smoked ricotta cheese.

Spaghetteria Al Solito Posto (☎ 328 913 37 45; Piazza Misericordia; meals €20-25; 🌣 Fri-Wed) The corner TV and plastic tablecloths create an underwhelming ambience but the freebie plate of smoked ricotta and olives and toothsome *al dente* pasta choices equal excellent dining. The *seadas con miele* (fried Sardinian cheese pastries with honey) are a soul-satisfying end to your meal.

La Lepanto (☎ 079 97 91 16; Via Carlo Alberto 135; meals €35-40; 🌣 Tue-Sun) The best place in town to fatten up your credit card on a posh meal out. Grand tanks of fish greet you at the door, although the speciality is *aragosta* (spiny lobster) flavoured with orange, tossed with spaghetti or simply boiled. The enticing dessert trolley means a definite waddle home.

Drinking

Caffè Costantino (Piazza Civica 31) The classiest coffee stop in town is on the ground floor of the Gothic Palazza d'Albis. Alternatively, you can sip your cappuccino *al fresco* while people-watching on the square.

Mill Inn (Via Maiorca 37; 🌣 Thu-Tue) One of the busiest and cosiest bars in the old town, this place has punters crowding in below the stone vaults for a Guinness.

Baraonda (Via P Umberto 75) This moody wine bar for swooning couples has burgundy walls and just a few tables; there is outside seating as well.

Café Latino (Bastioni Magellano 10) An elegant cocktail or coffee spot in a prime waterfront spot with harbour views. Kick back in comfort in the stone-vaulted interior or outside on the promenade among the strollers.

Entertainment

Poco Loco (☎ 079 973 10 34; Via Gramsci 8; 🌣 7pm-1am) This place gets the thumbs up from readers for its cavernous atmosphere and regular programme of live music. Frothy draught beer and pizza help stave off the midnight munchies. There's the added surprise of a bowling alley upstairs.

El Tró (Lungomare Valencia 3; 🌣 Tue-Sun) Less than 1km south of the centre, El Tró is a kind of beach bar without the beach (but settled right on a rocky outcrop by the sea). People flock here and, late at night, start working on their moves on the dance floor. On Friday and Saturday it's a steamy dance pit until dawn.

Getting There & Away
AIR
Fertilia airport (AHO; ☎ 079 93 50 39) is around 9.5km north of Alghero. Domestic flights from Italy, and Ryanair flights from London and Frankfurt, land here.

BUS

Intercity buses stop at Via Catalogna, by the Giardini Pubblici. Buy tickets for ARST and FdS buses at the booth in the gardens.

Up to 18 buses (ARST and FdS) depart daily to/from Sassari and take 50 minutes to an hour depending on the route (€2.35 to €2.60). ARST runs up to eight buses to Porto Torres (€3, 50 minutes). Other routes include two buses daily to Bosa (€2.90, 55 minutes) and three buses daily to Olbia, direct and via Sassari (€3.75 to €5.90, 2½ hours).

TRAIN

The train station is 1.5km north of the old town on Via Don Minzoni. Up to 11 trains run to and from Sassari (€1.85, 35 minutes, daily).

Getting Around

Eight FdS buses a day travel between Piazza della Mercede in Alghero and the airport (€0.60, 20 minutes). The timetable is outside the tourist office. A taxi to the airport costs €24 or more.

Line AO runs from Via Cagliari (via the Giardini Pubblici) to the beaches. Urban buses also operate to Fertilia as well as several places beyond. You can pick up these buses at stops around the Giardini Pubblici. Tickets (€0.60) are available at Casa del Caffè in the park and most *tabacchi* (tobacconists) outlets.

Cicloexpress (☎ 079 98 69 50; Via Garibaldi), on the port side of the road, has bicycles and mountain bikes for hire from €8 to €13 a day and scooters for up to €35 a day.

AROUND ALGHERO

About 10km northwest of Alghero on the road to Porto Conte is **Nuraghe di Palmavera** (admission €3, incl Necropoli di Anghelu Ruiu €5; ☻ 9am-7pm Apr-Oct, 9.30am-4pm Nov-Mar). At the heart of this 3500-year-old nuraghic village stands a central limestone tower and an elliptical building with a secondary sandstone tower that was added later. The AF local bus from Alghero to Porto Conte passes through here (€0.60, 15 to 20 minutes).

About 7km north of Alghero, just to the left (west) of the road to Porto Torres, lie scattered the ancient burial chambers of the **Necropoli di Anghelu Ruiu**. The 38 tombs carved into the rock date from between 2700 BC and 3300 BC. This sort of tomb came to be

known as *domus de janas*. You need your own vehicle to get here. Just 2km further up the road are the beautiful vineyards of the **Tenute Sella & Mosca** (☻ 8.30am-8pm), the island's best-known wine-makers. Join a tour of the **cellars** (☎ 079 99 77 00; admission free; ☻ tours 5.30pm Mon-Sat mid-Jun–mid-Oct).

The road west from the *nuraghe* heads to **Porto Conte**, a lovely bay, and on around to **Capo Caccia**, a dramatic cape jutting out high above the Mediterranean. The end of the road is marked by the entrance to the **Grotta di Nettuno** (☎ 079 94 65 40; adult/child €10/5; ☻ 9am-7pm Apr-Sep, 9am-6pm Oct, 9am-2pm Nov-Mar); to get there, climb down several hundred steps along the seaward face of Capo Caccia – worthwhile in itself. The grotto is an underground fairyland that can also be accessed by sea. **Traghetti Navisarda** (☎ 079 95 06 03) runs several boats a day from April to October and allows you a fish-eye view of the coast from Alghero to Capo Caccia before depositing you at the grotto. The round-trip costs €11 (not including entry to the grotto) and takes about 2½ hours. Otherwise, there is the FdS bus that leaves daily from Via Catalogna in Alghero (€3.25 return, 9.15am, 3.10pm and 5.10pm from June to September, 9.15am only the rest of the year, 50 minutes).

Those with transport should explore the coast north of Capo Caccia. Just a few kilometres north of the turn-off for Alghero, the road continues north. After 2km turn west for the delightful bay of **Torre di Porticciolo** (which has a decent camping site). Around 7km further north is **Porto Ferro**, an unspoiled beach that even gets a few small waves on wilder days.

SASSARI

pop 121,600

Sardinia's second-biggest city has the gritty individuality of a Sardinian working town. The outer shell of the town is drab with grid-system streets and building-block apartments, but the medieval kernel remains and is well worth a wander about if you have some time. Two grand churches, the cathedral and Santa Maria di Betlem, are impressive and the important archaeological museum is a must-see. Stick around for lunch and dinner, too, as the old city hides some wonderful traditional locales.

Sassari rose to importance as its coastal counterpart, Porto Torres, began to decline.

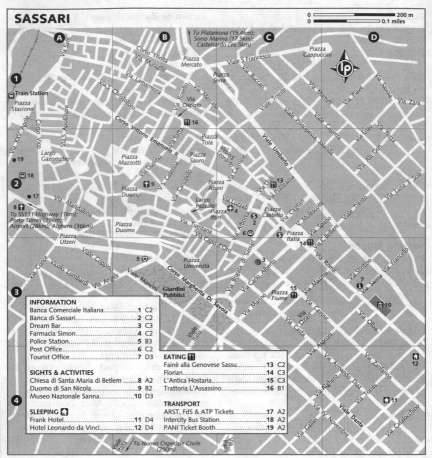

SASSARI

INFORMATION
Banca Comerciale Italiana.............1 C2
Banca di Sassari............................2 C2
Dream Bar...................................3 C3
Farmacia Simon..........................4 C2
Police Station..............................5 B3
Post Office..................................6 C2
Tourist Office..............................7 D3

SIGHTS & ACTIVITIES
Chiesa di Santa Maria di Betlem....8 A2
Duomo di San Nicola....................9 B2
Museo Nazionale Sanna...............10 D3

SLEEPING
Frank Hotel.................................11 D4
Hotel Leonardo da Vinci..............12 D4

EATING
Fainè alla Genovese Sassu............13 C2
Florian.......................................14 C3
L'Antica Hostaria........................15 C3
Trattoria L'Assassino...................16 B1

TRANSPORT
ARST, FdS & ATP Tickets.............17 A2
Intercity Bus Station....................18 A2
PANI Ticket Booth.......................19 A2

The capital of the medieval Giudicato di Logudoro, Sassari resisted both Genoese and Catalano-Aragonese rule. A university was set up here in the 16th century, but this could not arrest the city's slow decline. More recently, Sassari has been a breeding ground for lawyers and politicians, among them former Italian presidents Antonio Segni and Francesco Cossiga. Communist leader, Enrico Berlinguer (1922–84), was another notable Sassarese.

Orientation

Sassari has a compact centre concentrated around its cathedral, but most services are in the busy newer part of town in the area around the vast 18th-century Piazza Italia.

The main bus and train stations are just west of the centre.

Information

Banca Comerciale Italiana (Piazza Italia 23)
Banca di Sassari (Piazza Castello 8) Western Union representative.
Dream Bar (Via Cavour 15; per hr €3.50; 7am-9.30pm & 5-8pm Mon-Sat) Internet access.
Farmacia Simon (Piazza Castello) Pharmacy.
Nuovo Ospedale Civile (☎ 079 206 10 00; Viale Italia) Hospital.
Police station (☎ 079 283 55 00, Via Angioi 16)
Post office (Via Brigata di Sassari; 8.15am-6.15pm Mon-Fri, 8.15am-1pm Sat)
Tourist office (☎ 079 23 17 77; www.regione.sardegna .it/azstss; Via Roma 62; 9am-1.30pm & 4-6pm

Mon-Thu, 9am-1.30pm Fri) Information is patchy and the website outdated.

Sights
In the heart of the medieval quarter stands the extraordinary baroque façade of Sassari's cathedral, the **Duomo di San Nicola**, seems to emanate its own radiant light. Busy with bulging sculptural caprice, it bears an uncanny resemblance to the ebullient baroque style of Apulia, in southeastern Italy.

Just beyond what were once the city walls stands the **Chiesa di Santa Maria di Betlem**. The mostly Romanesque façade betrays Gothic and vaguely Oriental touches. Inside, the Catalan-Gothic vaulting has been preserved but much baroque silliness has crept in.

Located in the new part of the city, the **Museo Nazionale Sanna** (☎ 079 27 22 03; Via Roma 64; adult/under 25 €2/1; ☒ 9am-8pm Tue-Sun) holds one of the island's most important archaeological collections, with in-depth coverage of the nuraghic period.

Festivals & Events
The **Cavalcata Sarda** in May and **I Candelieri** on 14 August are the city's big festivals. For more details, see the boxed text, p831.

Sleeping
Frank Hotel (☎ 079 27 64 56; Via Armando Diaz 20; s/d €50/75; ☒ P) A solid no-surprises hotel with the real bonus of private parking. Rooms are in better nick than the tired-looking lobby and they have plenty of space, colourful rugs, minibars and balconies. The view is pretty pedestrian so the satellite TV is a welcome addition.

Hotel Leonardo da Vinci (☎ 079 28 07 44; www.leonardodavincihotel.it; Via Roma 79; s/d €80/110; ☒ ▣ P) The rooms here have been revamped with stylish wallpaper, salmon-coloured marble floors and shiny modern bathrooms, half of which have actual bathtubs. There's also Internet access in the lobby.

Eating
Eating is a pleasure in Sassari and all tastes and budgets are catered for. A local curiosity is *fainè*, a cross between a crepe and a pizza with a base made from chickpea flour. It was introduced by the Genoese and is similar to their *farinata*.

Fainè alla Genovese Sassu (Via Usai 17; ☒ dinner Mon-Sat) Sassari's original purveyor of fine

fainè. Toppings vary from onions to sausage and, with prices starting at €3.50, this is a filling option if you're suffering from wallet stress.

Trattoria L'Assassino (☎ 079 23 50 41; Via Ospizio Cappuccini 1a; set lunches €8; ☒ Mon-Sat) This trattoria is hidden away in a back alley off Piazza Tola. The more adventurous will step beyond the set meal and try a selection of 10 starters (€18). These can include classics like *funghi arrosto* (roasted mushrooms) and *lumaconi* (big snails). If you get really lucky you may find calf's testicles on the menu as well.

Florian (☎ 079 200 80 56; Via Capitano Bellieni 27; meals €35-40; ☒ Mon-Sat) A classic, with an unwaveringly authentic menu and elegant dining area flanked by mirrors and stained glass. The adjacent café is similarly swanky with Toulouse Lautrec-style murals and girth-expanding cakes.

L'Antica Hostaria (☎ 079 20 00 60; Via Mazzini 27; meals €40-45; ☒ Mon-Sat) L'Antica enjoys a reputation as one of Sassari's top addresses. In intimate surroundings with vaulted ceilings and butter-coloured walls you are treated to inventive cuisine rooted in local tradition. Meat-lovers should try the *tagliata di manzo* (beef).

Getting There & Away
The **intercity bus station** (Via XXV Aprile) is near the train station. ARST, FdS, PANI and some ATP local buses travelling beyond the city leave from here. Tickets for all but PANI can be bought at the bar next to the AGIP petrol station. PANI has a separate ticket booth at the other end of the bus station.

PANI has up to nine services to/from Cagliari (€13.60 to €14.45, 3¾ hours). Four buses run to Nuoro (€7, 2½ hours) and seven to Oristano (€7.60, 2½ hours).

Plenty of ARST and FdS buses depart to Alghero (€2.35 to €2.60, 50 to 60 minutes), Porto Torres (€1.45, 35 minutes) and also Castelsardo (€2, one hour).

Three direct trains link the city with Cagliari (€12.10, 4¼ hours).

AROUND SASSARI
The northwestern Sardinian countryside is peppered with delightful Romanesque churches built in a rough Tuscan style by the Pisans. One of the more impressive is the **Basilica della Santissima Trinità di Saccargia**,

about 18km southeast of Sassari on the SS597 road to Olbia.

About 2.5km back towards Sassari, where the SS597 branches off the SS131, head south along the latter about 23km to Torralba, where, just outside, stands one of the island's major ancient sites, the **Nuraghe Santu Antine** (☎ 079 84 72 96; admission €3; ✆ 8.30am-sunset). Set in the so-called Valle dei Nuraghi (Nuraghes Valley), it is a unique blast from the past – at least 1600 years BC. If you only see one *nuraghe* in Sardinia, see this one, which rivals Su Nuraxi at Barumini. Not far off to the northwest, just outside the village of Borutta, is another fine Romanesque church, **Chiesa di San Pietro Sorres**. ARST buses from Sassari stop at Torralba.

North of Sassari stretch the locals' favourite beaches, such as **Platamona** and **Marina di Sorso**. The coast road leads northeast to the coastal bastion of **Castelsardo**, a confusion of tiny lanes wrapped around a high promontory that juts defiantly out to sea. ARST buses run from Sassari (€2.10, one hour) and Santa Teresa di Gallura (€4.50, 1½ hours).

PORTO TORRES
pop 21,440

This port town and petrochemical centre is unlikely to hold your attention for long, but a couple of sites are worth the effort if you're in sightseeing mode.

The Pro Loco **tourist office** (☎ 079 51 50 00; Piazza Garibaldi; ✆ 8.30am-1pm & 6-8pm Mon-Sat) is a couple of streets back from the port.

Just a five-minute walk from the main port, towards where Grimaldi's ferries dock, is the **Antiquarium** (admission €2; ✆ 9am-8pm Tue-Sat), which houses artefacts discovered in Turris Libisonis, the present city's Roman predecessor. More interesting is what's outside: the excavated remains of the Roman city's public baths, plus remnants of Roman streets and mosaics.

Of greater interest is the limestone Romanesque **Basilica di San Gavino** (✆ 8.30am-1pm & 3-7pm), about 1.5km inland on Corso Vittorio Emanuele, the town's main road. Built in 1050 to honour three Roman-era Christian martyrs, it is an extraordinary church, notable among other things for the apses on either end; note that you can only enter the church by side doors.

You can almost drop anchor at **Hotel Elisa** (☎ 079 51 32 60; fax 079 51 37 68; Via Mare 2; s/d with breakfast €50/73; ❄), a small but neat hotel a block back from the port. The rooms are painted an appropriate nautical blue and have all the mod cons, including TV, phone and minibar. Most rooms have sea views.

Cristallo (☎ 079 51 49 09; Piazza XX Settembre 11; meals €35; ✆ Tue-Sun) is a sprawling modern restaurant with a terrace on the town's main shopping street. Exercise your tastebuds with good seafood and a selection of Sardinian favourites, such as lamb. Sweet treats include *pan a spagila con crema,* a decadent cream-cake affair.

Most buses leave from Piazza Colombo, virtually at the port. Plenty head to Sassari (€1.45, 35 minutes). As many as to six buses per day head for Alghero (€3, 50 minutes) and another six to Stintino (€2.10, 30 minutes). Trains also run south to Sassari (€1.25, 15 minutes) and beyond.

For information on ferries, see the boxed text, p817.

STINTINO & ISOLA ASINARA

Stintino, a small fishing village, lies at the core of this peninsula resort area. Above all, people come here for the magnificent azure waters of the **Spiaggia della Pelosa** towards the northern end of the peninsula. The area's main island stretching off to the north is **Isola Asinara** (Donkey Island), named after the remarkable white donkeys which are native there.

Until recently the island was off limits as a penitentiary but now has been converted to a national park, the **Parco Nazionale dell' Asinara**. You can join organised visits; **Agenzia La Nassa** (☎ 079 52 00 60; www.stintinoincoming.com; Via Sassari 6) in Stintino and the tourist office in Porto Torres sell tickets to the park. You can also book by calling ☎ 800 56 11 66, or going online at www.parcoasinara.it. Bring lunch as there is nowhere on the island to buy anything. Agenzia La Nassa also offers **Internet access** (per 30min €3.50).

There are three hotels and one B&B in Stintino and another dozen mostly mid- to upper-range places dotted along the coast.

Albergo Silvestrino (☎ 079 52 34 73; www.silvestrino.it; Via XXI Aprile 4; s/d €56/98; ❄) is a tastefully spruced-up hotel near the port with good-sized if slightly spare rooms. Go for the top floor if you can – the spacious terraces are well worth the stairs. The restaurant is a notch above the norm.

Ristorante L'Ancora (☎ 079 527 90 09; meals €35; ☒ Jun-Sep) has a charming veranda with magnificent sea views where you can indulge in good seafood. It's north of Stintino on the way to Spiaggia della Pelosa – turn right into the Ancora residential complex and follow the signs.

Up to eight buses run from Sassari to Stintino and Spiaggia della Pelosa in summer (€3.15, one hour and 10 minutes). As many as six run from Porto Torres (€2, 30 minutes).

SANTA TERESA DI GALLURA
pop 4500

Together with Palau, about 20km to the east, this pleasing seaside resort is a cheaper alternative to the higher-profile resorts on the Costa Smeralda. Head for the surreal, windsculpted granite rock forms of the nearby Capo Testa. You can see Corsica across the Stretto di Bonifacio or even catch a ferry to Bonifacio for a day trip.

The town was founded in 1808 by the island's Savoy rulers to combat smugglers – the neat grid streets were designed by an army officer. Beyond it, tourism-boom housing has spread since the 1960s. In summer as many as 50,000 tourists arrive in town.

The **tourist office** (☎ 0789 75 41 27; Piazza Vittorio Emanuele I 24) has information on the town and surrounding area. You can pedal the streets by renting a bike from **Global** (☎ 0789 75 50 80; Piazza San Vittorio 7; per day €5) in front of the church.

After wandering the tidy streets, head for the 16th-century Spanish watchtower, the **Torre Longonsardo** (admission €1.50; ☒ 10am-12.30pm & 4-7pm Jun-Sep) and kick back on the local beach, the **Spiaggia Rena Bianca**.

About 5km west of Santa Teresa, the granite headland of **Capo Testa** seems more like a divine sculpture garden. The place also has a couple of beaches (and a resident cat colony). Five daily buses run here from Santa Teresa from June to September only. If you have

---

A MEATY SUBJECT

Sardinia's cuisine was born of poverty and is traditionally based on what is local, practical and cost effective.

Broths (*minestra* or *minestrone*) are common starters. On the coast this often comes in the form of fish soup or stews, such as *brodetto* and *burrida*.

Another fishy speciality is *bottarga* – dried, pressed tuna roe – which is served finely grated over piping hot spaghetti. Traditional pasta dishes tend to be on the heavy side and include *culurgiones*, delicious parcels of pasta filled with potato and wild mint. Also common are *mallodoreddus*, a dense seashell-shaped pasta usually served with *salsa alla campidanese* (a sausage and tomato sauce). *Maccarones de busa*, or just plain *busa*, are shaped by wrapping the pasta around knitting needles. Thus 'pierced', the pasta soaks up as much sauce or broth as possible.

A long history of invasion and coastal malaria turned most Sardinians away from the sea. As a result, traditional Sardinian cuisine is based on meat dishes. Locals love *porcetto* (also called *porcheddu* or *porchetto*), which is roast suckling pig, *capretto* (kid) and *agnello* (lamb, a pre-Christmas special). Demand for these, especially in high tourist season is such that the quality is often poor. Horse and donkey meat are also sometimes on the menu, especially in little eateries in Sassari. Sardinians are also great lovers of tripe and other innards. And what about *granelle*, or sliced calf's testicles?

Seafood is now a common element along the coast but has more to do with tourism than Sardinian tradition.

The most common bread, especially in the north, is the crisp, paper-thin *pane carasau* (often sprinkled with oil and salt). Shepherds would carry it with them for weeks at a time. When soaked, *pane carasau* becomes malleable. Topped with tomato, soft-boiled egg and *pecorino* (the ever-present ewe's-milk cheese), it becomes *pane frattau*, a cheap and protein-filled meal.

Sardinia produces about 80% of Italy's *pecorino. Pecorino romano* (originally from Lazio) is a dense pale cheese with a pale crust and is the cheese of choice for accompanying pasta. *Pecorino sardo* is a semi-cooked, nutty-flavoured cheese.

The most widespread dessert is *seadas* (or *sebadas*), a delightfully light pastry (vaguely like a turnover) filled with ricotta or sheep's cheese and drenched in honey.

transport, you could follow the coast road west towards Castelsardo and choose any of a number of wild and barely visited beaches.

There are plenty of hotels although most only open from about Easter to October. In August you may have to pay *mezza pensione* (half board).

Camping La Liccia (☎ /fax 0789 75 51 90; person/ tent €11/15.70, 4-person bungalows €88; ☼ late Apr–Sep) is a pleasant spot about 8km west of town overlooking the sea and with a nearby sandy beach. It has a restaurant, playground and entertainment.

Hotel Funtana (☎ 0789 74 10 25; www.hotellafun tana.com; Via Nazionale s/n; s/d €52/104, ste €57-114; P ☒ ☒) is a low-rise hacienda-style hotel with acres of terracotta tiles, earthy colours and live music by the pool in summer. The suites have kitchenettes and cost a little more for the self-catering privilege.

Ristorante Papè Satan (☎ 0789 75 50 48; Via Lamarmora 20; pizzas to €9; ☼ late Apr–Sep), with its wood-fired oven, is one of the best pizza options in town and has earned the Vera Pizza recognition to prove it. The internal courtyard is a pleasant place to linger and the service is smiley and quick.

Ristorante La Torre (☎ 0789 75 46 00; Via del Mare 36; meals €30) has seagull views with a vast picture window, plus an outside terrace. Go for the robust portions of risotto or seafood dishes. Locals rate this place – always a good sign.

Buses stop at Via Eleonora d'Arborea, near the post office. ARST buses operate up to seven times a day between Olbia and Santa Teresa (€3.75, one hour 50 minutes) and five times daily to/from Sassari (€5.85, 2½ hours). Get tickets from Bar Central opposite.

For information on the frequent ferries across to Bonifacio in Corsica, see p816.

PALAU & ARCIPELAGO DI LA MADDALENA

Close to the Costa Smeralda, **Palau** is not an exciting place but makes a good base if you can't afford the glitzier resorts on this coast. You can also catch a ferry from Palau to the **Isola della Maddalena**, the principal island of an archipelago of seven islands and 40 islets, which is classified as a national park: **Parco Nazionale dell'Arcipelago di La Maddalena**. The magic lies in exploring these islands by boat, although the two main islands deserve more time.

Palau's **tourist office** (☎ 0789 70 85 56; Via Nazionale 107; ☼ 8.30am-1pm & 8pm) can advise on accommodation. You can check the Internet at **Bar Frizzante** (Via Capo D'Orso 20; per 30min €3.50). La Maddalena's **tourist office** (☎ 0789 73 63 21; Cala Cavetta; ☼ 8.30am-1pm & 4.30-7.30 Jun-Sep, shorter hrs Oct-May) has information on the entire archipelago.

The town is worth a wander about and the island has some reasonable beaches.

Sights & Activities

Linked to La Maddalena by a narrow causeway is **Isola Caprera**, where legendary revolutionary Giuseppe Garibaldi made his home. You can visit his **Compendio Garibaldi** (admission €2; ☼ 9am-1.30pm & 4-7pm Tue-Sun Jun-Sep, 9am-1.30pm Tue-Sun Oct-May), which remains an object of pilgrimage for many Italians; guided visits are in Italian only. Garibaldi, professional revolutionary and apotheosised in the folklore of Italian unification, bought half of the island in 1855 (he purchased the rest 10 years later). He made the island his home and refuge, and it was the place he would return to after yet another daring campaign in the pursuit of liberty and Italian unification. It is filled with personal memorabilia. A walking trail north of Garibaldi's pad leads down to the secluded **Cala Coticcio** beach.

The five remaining main islands can only be reached by boat. Numerous excursions leave from Isola della Maddalena and Palau. Or you can hire motorised dinghies and do it yourself. The three northernmost islands are **Isola Budelli**, **Isola Razzoli** and **Isola di Santa Maria**.

Wind and kite surfers go to town on the windswept waters of Porto Pollo. You can hire the gear at several shops near Camping Isola dei Gabbiani on the peninsula of the same name.

Sleeping

Hotel Piccada (☎ 0789 70 93 44; www.hotelpiccada.com; Via degli Asfodeli 6; s/d €65/85; P ☒) A cheerful hotel in Palau with bright primary colours in the rooms and some terraces with sea views. Those suffering from world-news deprivation can catch up via the American Forces Network station beamed in courtesy of the nearby NATO base.

Hotel Il Gabbiano (☎ 0789 72 25 07; Via Giulio Cesare 20; r €65-104; P) It could be tempting to dive into the waves from your balcony here. Isola della Maddalena's oldest hotel juts into the sea and has mooring space. Family run, the rooms are a little thrifty but the downstairs bar has a welcoming home-hearth feel complete with maritime memorabilia and dog basket.

Camping Abbatoggia (☎ 0789 73 91 73; www.campingabbatoggia.it in Italian; per person €10.50; ☼ Jun-Sep) The best of Isola della Maddalena's handful of camping grounds is in the north of the island in Località Abbatoggia. It has access to a couple of good beaches, including Lo Strangolato, and can arrange the rental of canoes and windsurfing equipment.

Eating

La Maddalena has a few worthwhile dining options.

Osteria Enoteca da Liò (☎ 0789 73 75 07; Corso Vittorio Emanuele 2-6; meals €10-20) This rare open-all-year choice is fronted by an earthy bar full of crusty locals. The menu is tummy filling rather than wallet slimming, with a €10 lunch menu or à la carte options such as *carpaccio di salmone* (very thin slices of raw salmon). Tables sprawl out onto the street in summer.

Ristorante Garden (☎ 0789 73 88 25; Via Garibaldi 65; meals €20-25) Good for pleasing the tots and teens, this restaurant offers lots of choice, including bruschette from €4, antipasti including a recommended clam soup, and mains such as seafood spaghetti and pizza. There's slouchy seating upstairs with cosy alcoves and tanks of fish.

La Taverna (☎ 0789 70 92 89; Via Rossini 6; meals €25; ☼ Wed-Mon) In Palau, try La Taverna, which is a cosy sidestreet dining option with unfussy, lovingly prepared food. Pop in for some *risotto marinaro* (seafood risotto) or go for a grilling with a choice of lobster, bass or red mullet.

Getting There & Around

ARST buses connect Palau with destinations around the north and east coast, including Olbia (€2.70, one hour) and Santa Teresa di Gallura (€1.65, 30 minutes). **Caramelli** (☎ 0789 70 94 95; ☼ May-Sep) buses run frequently to nearby destinations such as the Costa Smeralda, Isola dei Gabbiani and Capo d'Orso. All buses leave from the port.

The **Trenino Verde** (☎ 079 24 57 40; www.treninoverde.com in Italian) is an old-world train (some-

times of the steam variety) that runs from Palau twice a day inland to Tempio Pausania (€13 return, 1¾ hours, from mid-June to mid-September).

Several companies have regular car ferries to Isola della Maddalena. **Enermar** (☎ 0789 70 84 84; www.enermar.it) runs from 7.10am to 10.20pm (€2, 20 minutes); a small car costs €5.50. **Saremar** (☎ 0789 70 93 70) and **Tremar** (☎ 0789 73 00 32) also operate regular services. The latter has an hourly late-night service until dawn. Ticket prices are similar on all vessels.

COSTA SMERALDA & AROUND

Back in 1961 the Aga Khan and some pals bought a strip of beautiful Sardinian coast from struggling farmers and created the Costa Smeralda (Emerald Coast). Its 'capital' is in the yachtie haven of **Porto Cervo**, which is distinctive for its troglodyte-style architecture in pastel colours that were favoured back in the sixties (but look a tad dated today).

Visit out of season and this is a sad place with more seagulls than celebrities around and most places are closed rather than open. From June through to September, though, the resort throbs with footballers' wives and Italian sophisticates. There *are* some lovely beaches around which are wonderful all year-round, such as **Capriccioli**, **Spiaggia Liscia Ruia** (both near the exclusive Moorish-style Hotel Cala di Volpe, 6km south of Porto Cervo) and the **Spiaggia del Principe**, a couple of kilometres further around the headland near Romazzino. The oft-crowded beach of **Baia Sardinia**, 5km west of Porto Cervo, outside the Costa Smeralda area, boasts waters of an incredible blue hue.

Cervo Hotel (☎ 0789 93 11 11; Porto Cervo; www.sheraton.com/cervo; d from €226; ☒ P ☐) overlooks the old marina has a courtyard-style setting. There's beauty salons, restaurants and chic boutiques a short swagger away. Recently refurbished throughout, the rooms are luxurious and large. Extras include squash and tennis courts, as well as a private secluded beach.

Mama Latina (☎ 0789 9 13 12; Porto Cervo Marina; meals €25-35) is a rare year-round choice with an elegant dining room and café in front where you can chomp on a pizza for around €8 – or go for one of the more costly à la carte options.

Inland it is another world. **Arzachena**, a sprawling town 19km inland from Porto Cervo, is the launching pad for a driving tour to explore the ancient nuraghic sites. Among the most interesting of a series of *nuraghi* and burial grounds is **Coddu Ecchju** (☎ 0789 8 15 37; admission €2; ⏰ 9am-8pm Jun-Sep), a so-called *tomba dei giganti* that is in fact an ancient burial ground fronted by what indeed seems like a giant's door. To get here take the Arzachena–Luogosanto road south out of Arzachena and follow the signs.

As if in defiance of all the wealth on the Costa Smeralda, a highly strategic camp site has been placed on the road running along the south side of Golfo di Cugnana, between Porto Rotondo and the north–south road leading to Porto Cervo. **Villaggio Camping La Cugnana** (☎ 0789 3 31 84; www.campingcugnana.it; Località Cugnana; 2 people & car €33.60, 2-person bungalows per week €526; ⏰ May-Sep) has a convenient supermarket, backs onto the sea and, perhaps best of all, puts on a free shuttle bus to Costa Smeralda beaches such as Capriccioli, Spiaggia Liscia Ruia and Spiaggia del Principe.

OLBIA
pop 60,000

For many, this chaotic port and industrial centre is their first sight of Sardinia. It's not a pretty place, although Piazza Regina Margherita has a certain charm and the street that leads to it – Corso Umberto – is good for shops and restaurants.

Orientation

Ferries arrive at the Stazione Marittima (terminal) 1km east of town and a local bus (No 9) goes to the centre. Trains run from the station to the port to coincide with ferry departures. Intercity buses stop at the end of Corso Umberto, next to the main train station. A handful of hotels and eateries are clustered in the narrow streets around Corso Umberto.

Information

Inter Smeraldo (☎ 0789 2 53 66; Via Porto Romano 8b; per 15min €1.25) Internet connection.
Tourist office (☎ 0789 2 14 53; fax 0789 2 22 21; Via Catello Piro 1; ⏰ 8am-2pm & 4-8pm Mon-Sat, 8.30am-12.30pm & 5-7pm Sun Jun-Sep, 8am-2pm & 3.30-6.30pm Mon-Sat Oct-May) Handily located just off the port end of Corso Umberto.

Sights

There's precious little to visit in Olbia apart from the **Chiesa di San Simplicio** (Via San Simplicio; ⏰ 9-noon & 4-7pm), a Romanesque jewel set aside from the town hubbub. Built entirely of granite, it is a curious mix of Tuscan and Lombard styles.

Sleeping & Eating

Hotel Terranova (☎ 0789 2 23 95; www.hotelterranova.it; Via Garibaldi 6; s/d €55/110; ✂ P) Right in the middle of town, the rooms here are small but plush, with terracotta tiles and classy marbled bathrooms. Most have balconies overlooking the narrow cobbled lane below.

Hotel Cavour (☎ 0789 20 40 33; www.cavourhotel.it; Via Cavour 22; s/d €65/90; ✂ P) These rooms sparkle with lots of fresh white paint and pastel colours. The double-glazed windows are a godsend on a Saturday night. Boat excursions can be arranged.

Ristorante Gallura (☎ 0789 2 46 48; Corso Umberto I 145; meals €25-35; ⏰ Tue-Sun) The menu reads like an Italian culinary dictionary. There are at least 20 different risottos to choose from, plus several polenta and homemade pasta dishes. The atmosphere here is nicely low key and traditional. It's recommended that you book ahead.

Barbagia (☎ 0789 5 16 40; Via Galvani 94; meals €30) Out of the centre you'll find one of the best spots in Olbia to get a taste of authentic Sardinian lush tuck. All sorts of odd names in Sardinian can mean a gamble when it comes to ordering time – rest assured, you can't go far wrong whatever the choice.

Getting There & Away
AIR

Olbia's **Aeroporto di Costa Smeralda** (OLB; ☎ 0789 6 90 00; www.olbiairport.it) is about 5km southeast of the centre and handles flights from most important Italian mainland destinations, as well as international flights from London, Paris and Frankfurt.

BOAT

Regular ferries arrive in Olbia from Genoa, Civitavecchia and Livorno. For more details, see the boxed text, p817.

BUS

You can buy tickets from the bus or train station. ARST has buses travelling from Olbia to destinations all over the island:

SARDINIA

Destination	Cost (€)	Frequency (daily)
Arzachena	1.75	11
Dorgali	6.30	3
Golfo Aranci (summer only)	1.20	8
Nuoro	6.30	7
Porto Cervo	2.60	5
Santa Teresa di Gallura	3.75	6

There's a half-hourly bus service from the airport to Piazza Regina Margherita (€0.60).

CAR & MOTORCYCLE

Holiday Car (☎ 0789 2 84 96; Via Genova 71) will rent you a Fiat Panda from €40 a day in high season, or a Fiat Punto for €45. This includes 150km and insurance.

TRAIN

The Trenitalia station lies parallel to Via Gabriele d'Annunzio – walk through the bus station. One direct train a day runs to Cagliari (€13, four hours). Otherwise you have to change at Chilivani (and sometimes Macomer too). Up to three trains run to Sassari (€5.90, one hour 50 minutes) and up to seven to Golfo Aranci (€1.85, 25 minutes).

GOLFO ARANCI

Sardinia Ferries and Tirrenia run ferries from Livorno, Civitavecchia and Fiumicino to this ferry terminal located on the promontory northeast of Olbia. There's not a great deal else to say about this place, although there are some pleasant enough beaches on the coastal route to Olbia. Regular buses and trains connect the two places.

NUORO & THE EAST

If Sardinia is a world apart from the Italian mainland, Nuoro is an island within the island. Much of Sardinia's most rugged mountain territory is concentrated in this defiant and inward-looking province filling up the central eastern part of the island. More than anywhere else in Sardinia the people of this region are firmly attached to their traditions. You will never hear so much Sardinian spoken as here and it is in the remoter villages of Nuoro that you are most likely to come across the occasional local still sporting traditional dress.

The dark majesty of the Supramonte and Gennargentu Mountains and the inland Barbagia region (also known as the Barbagie, a plural collective noun indicating the several distinct areas that make it up) is matched by the extraordinary beauty of the Golfo di Orosei coast, a series of magical coves and beaches accessible only by sea or long inland treks. The breathtaking gorges of the Gola Su Gorroppu are a hiker's delight and indeed the entire mountainous province presents some of Sardinia's best walking country.

The people of this proud territory can be reserved but, once the ice is broken, they are also incredibly hospitable. When visiting the villages and countryside, do so with respect.

Fine country restaurants of all classes purvey heaped dishes of solid comfort food, best washed down with a robust Cannonau red.

Larger towns are accessible by bus, but you need your own transport to truly get to grips with this part of the island. If you have time, hire a guide for long walking excursions.

NUORO
pop 37,600
Despite the urban sprawl, a handful of museums and churches and the town's pleasant hilly position in the shadow of Monte Ortobene make Nuoro worth a stopover. Relax in the birthplace of Sardinia's most celebrated writer, Grazia Deledda. Mind you Deledda would surely turn in his grave if he could see all the graffiti that blights the town today.

By the end of the 18th century Nuoro barely numbered 3000 inhabitants but was the only real 'urban' centre in a world of subsistence farming and banditry that had changed little in the preceding centuries. The town took off after being made provincial capital in 1927.

Orientation
The old centre of the town is bunched in the northeast corner of the city on a high spur of land that swings eastward to become Monte Ortobene. The heart of the town is contained in the warren of tidy streets and lanes around Piazza San Giovanni and Corso Garibaldi, the main street. The train and main bus stations are west of the city centre.

SARDINIA

Information

Tourist office Corso Garibaldi 155 (☎ 0784 3 87 77; ☾ 9am-1pm & 3.30-7pm Mon-Sat); Piazza Italia 19 (☎ 0784 3 00 83; ☾ 9am-1pm & 4-7pm Mon-Sat)

Sights

The **Museo della Vita e delle Tradizioni Sarde** (☎ 0784 25 70 35; Via Antonio Mereu 56; adult/child €3/0.65; ☾ 9am-8pm Tue-Sat, 9am-1pm Sun mid-Jun–Sep, 9am-1pm & 3-7pm Oct–mid-Jun) is the most interesting sight in town. The emphasis here is on the richly embroidered costumes from all over the province. Textiles, traditional musical instruments and photographs of a bygone age offer a fascinating step into the culture and folklore of the past.

The **Museo Archeologico Nazionale** (Via Mannu 1; admission free; ☾ 9am-1.30pm & 3-6pm Wed & Fri, 9am-1.30pm Tue, Thu & Sat) has a collection of artefacts ranging from ancient ceramics and fine *bronzetti* to a drilled skull from 1600 BC and early medieval finds.

Around 7km out of Nuoro rises **Monte Ortobene**, a favourite picnic spot with locals. The No 8 local bus runs up to the mountain seven times a day from Piazza Vittorio Emanuele.

Festivals & Events

For more on the remarkably colourful **Festa del Redentore** held at the end of August, see the boxed text, p831.

Sleeping & Eating

Casa Solotti (☎ 0784 3 39 54; www.casasolotti.it; s/d €29/50) Set in a rambling garden on Monte Ortobene, this charming house is surrounded by woods and walking trails. The accommodation is suitably relaxed, with a friendly family atmosphere and the family's pets. Three of the five rooms have balconies with views and you can use the kitchen. Call ahead to arrange a free pick-up from town.

Hotel Grillo (☎ 0784 3 86 78; fax 0784 3 20 05; Via Monsignor Melas 14; s/d €55/65) On the edge of town near the Museo della Vita e delle Tradizioni Sarde, Hotel Grillo's rooms are compact but manage to squeeze in every mod con (including MTV on the telly); you pay an extra €10 for more space and a balcony. The restaurant is convenient if it's raining, otherwise eat elsewhere.

Ciusa (☎ 0784 25 70 52; Viale Ciusa 55; pizzas to €8, meals €24; ☾ Wed-Mon) Ciusa pulls in punters with its excellent pizzas, tempting pasta

dishes such as *maccarones de busa al ragú* (macaroni in a duck sauce) and a lusciously rich risotto with melted cheese and wine.

Il Rifugio (☎ 0784 23 23 55; Via Antonio Mereu 28-36; meals €25-30; ☾ Thu-Tue) An age-old trattoria in a modern new locale. Grab a table in front of the entertaining *pizzaioli* (pizza makers) if you can. We recommend the pizzas here, or try one of the inventive pasta dishes like the house speciality, *culurgiones, basilico e mandorle* (pasta with fresh basil and ground almonds). A favourite with locals, it's worth waiting for a table.

Getting There & Away

PANI buses run from Cagliari (€11.30, 3½ hours) four times a day via Oristano (€5.85, two hours), and from Sassari (€7, 2½ hours) up to six times a day. There is a ticket office at Via Brigata di Sassari 19, where the buses stop.

ARST buses run from the station on Viale Sardegna. There are two or three daily runs to places such as Baunei (€4.90), Santa Maria Navarrese (€5.40), Olbia (€6.30) and Tortolì-Arbatax (€5.85). Regular buses make the trip to Oliena (€0.90, 20 minutes) and Orgosolo (€1.45, 30 minutes). Up to nine buses run to/from Dorgali (€2, 45 minutes).

AROUND NUORO
Fonte Sacra Su Tempiesu

The **Fonte Sacra Su Tempiesu** (☎ 0784 27 67 16; adult/child €2/1; ☾ 9am-6pm) is unique among the nuraghic temples for its A-shaped housing rising above the typical keyhole-shaped well. It is a masterpiece of ancient engineering and was only unearthed in 1953. You need transport to get here. Head for **Orune**, 18km northeast of Nuoro (buses come this far), from where it is a 7km drive southeast down a narrow country route (signposted).

Oliena

From Nuoro you can see the fetching town of Oliena across a deep valley to the south. Behind it rises the magnificent spectacle of Monte Corrasi.

In Piazza Santa Maria, the site of the Saturday market and the 13th-century Santa Maria church, you will find **Servizi Turistici Corrasi** (☎ 0784 28 71 44; Piazza Santa Maria 30), which has information on the town and mountains. It organises treks to Tiscali, the Gola Su Gorroppu and elsewhere.

Hotel Cikappa (☎ /fax 0784 28 87 33; Corso Martin Luther King; s/d €38/50; ☒) is a cheerful hikers' hotel with tidy, functional rooms. Go for a room in the front with a balcony overlooking the town and mountain backdrop views beyond. There's a scruffy local bar downstairs and a surprisingly good restaurant with dishes that change according to what's in season.

Hotel Monte Maccione (☎ 0784 28 83 63; www.coopenis.it; s/d €33.50/55; P), also known as Co-operativa Eris, is 21 hairpin bends (4km) up in the woods south of Oliena. The rooms are suitably rustic with leafy views, while the reasonably priced restaurant gets packed with boisterous families at weekends. Oliena is a centre of good Cannonau reds, so always ask for a local drop.

Orgosolo

Some 18km further south and backed by the dramatic grey wall of the Supramonte, The town of Orgosolo means sheep-rustlers and bandits to most people. More recently this dusty, insular town has gained a little fame for its *murales*, lively wall paintings that express the social and political concerns of locals. They range from Sardinian issues to world politics and new ones still appear every now and then, 30 years after the first ones were done. The leftist murals were the brainchild of Francesco del Casino, an art teacher from Siena who has lived in Orgosolo for many years.

Petit Hotel (☎ /fax 0784 40 20 09; Via Mannu; s/d €30/40; ☷ May-Oct) is easy to find – just follow the signs through the centre of town and turn right at Bar Candela. The rooms are well dusted but basic with balconies and flower-filled window boxes. This place is family run and friendly – especially if you speak some Italian.

Mamoiada

Just 14km south of Nuoro, this undistinguished town is the scene of a remarkable winter celebration that dates back to pagan times.

For the **Festa di Sant'Antonio Abate** on 16 and 17 January the townspeople turn out to behold the frightful *mamuthones* as they parade about the town. For more, see the boxed text, p831.

For an up-close look at the local masks and costumes, check out the **Museo delle Maschere** (☎ 0784 56 90 18; www.museodellemaschere.it; Piazza Europa 15; adult/child €4/2.60; ☷ 9am-1pm & 3-7pm Tue-Sun) on the northwestern side of town.

Regular buses service Mamoiada from Nuoro (€1.25, 20 minutes).

DORGALI & AROUND

Dorgali is an unexceptional small provincial town, but it makes a handy base as it lies at the crossroads for traffic south to Arbatax and beyond; north to the coast and Olbia; east 10km to Cala Gonone; and west towards Oliena and Nuoro.

The **tourist office** (☎ 0784 9 62 43; Via La Marmora 108b) can book rooms in hotels and B&Bs in Dorgali and Cala Gonone on the coast – convenient when things fill up in summer.

Dorgali is also well cited for hiking excursions. Several groups can take you on 4WD excursions, hikes and caving expeditions. **Gennargentu Escursioni** (☎ 0784 9 43 85; www.gennargentu.it; Via La Marmora 204) organises one-day trips into the Gola Su Gorroppu (€25) and into the Supramonte (€41). **Escursioni Ghivine** (☎ 349 442 55 52; www.ghivine.com; Via La Marmora 69e) offers horse-trekking trips.

Hotel S'Adde (☎ 0784 9 44 12; fax 0784 9 41 35; Via Concordia; s/d with breakfast €60/108; ☒ P) is an attractive Alpine-style hotel at the northeastern end of the town. Family-run with kiddies around, the hotel's rooms are appropriately pine-clad with terraces and nice views. The restaurant/pizzeria opens out onto a 1st-floor terrace.

Ristorante Colibrì (☎ 0784 9 60 54; Via Gramsci 14; meals €27-30; ☷ Mon-Sat) is tucked away in a residential area with a baffling signposting system. Persevere as this is the real McCoy for meat eaters with dishes like *cinghiale al* romarino (wild boar with rosemary) and the like. Don't expect atmosphere – you are here for the food.

Grotta di Ispinigoli

Mexico is home to the world's tallest stalagmite (40m) but you shouldn't worry about settling for second best here – the natural spectacle of its slightly shorter counterpart is every bit as awe-inspiring. **Grotta di Ispinigoli** (adult/child €7/4.50; ⊙ 9am-7pm Aug, shorter hrs Apr-Jul & Sep-Nov) is just 4km north of Dorgali.

Serra Orrios & Thomes

The nuraghic village of **Serra Orrios** (adult/child €5/2; ⊙ hourly visits 9am-1pm & 4-6pm), while not as remarkable as the site at Santa Vittoria di Serri, is still worth a stop. The remnants of more than 70 huts are clustered around what is left of two temples. The site lies 11km northwest of Dorgali (3km north off the Dorgal–Oliena road).

From Sierra Orrios you could continue north to see a fine example of a *tomba dei giganti*. Continue 3km north of the crossroads with the Nuoro–Orosei route; the **Tomba dei Giganti S'Ena e Thomes** (⊙ sunrise-sunset) is signposted to the right. Just open the gate and walk on for about 200m. The stone monument is dominated by a central oval-shaped stone stele that once closed off an ancient burial chamber.

OGLIASTRA

The southeastern sector of Nuoro province is known as the Ogliastra. From Dorgali, the SS125 (Orientale Sarda) highway winds southwards through the high mountain terrain of the eastern end of the **Parco Nazionale del Gennargentu e Golfo di Orosei**. The 18km stretch southwards to the Genna 'e Silana pass (1017m) is the most breathtaking. A useful local website for this area is **Welcome in Ogliastra** (www.turinforma.it).

Tiscali

A first detour comes a few kilometres south of Dorgali with a road dropping off to the southwest past Monte Sant'Elene towards the nuraghic village of **Tiscali** (adult/child €5/2; ⊙ 9am-7pm May-Sep, 9am-5pm Oct-Apr). The village is thought to date back to the 3rd or 4th century BC, and was built in the white limestone *dolina* (sinkhole) inside the modest Monte Tiscali (515m) at an altitude of 360m.

From Dorgali, you drive about 14km to a bridge where a walking trail (1.5km) to the site is signposted. Another, tougher approach for walkers is from the north down the Valle di Lanaitto. If you're on a 4WD tour, you will be transported down this valley and to within about an hour's walk of the site.

Gola Su Gorroppu

When you reach the **Genna 'e Silana** pass you could stop for a morning's hike to the **Gola Su Gorroppu** (Gorroppu Gorge). The trail is signposted to the right (east) side of the road and is easy to follow. You reach the gorge with its claustrophobically tight high walls after about two hours' hiking. There is nothing to stop you from wandering a little either way along the Rio Fluminedda riverbed, but beyond that you will need harnesses and proper equipment to get in any deeper.

To get to the gorge entrance by car, head south off Dorgali along the SS125 and turn right for the Hotel Sant'Elene. Follow this dirt road into the valley for about 8km (don't head uphill for the hotel) and you'll get to a small bridge. Here you will have to park the car and continue along on foot. Walk for about 1½ hours to two small lakes and the entrance to the gorge – one of the most spectacular and romantic landscapes in Sardinia. The huge boulders scattered around the entrance are a reminder that nature can be harsh as well as beautiful. Allow a full day for the expedition, which will give you time for the walk, a picnic and a swim in the lakes.

Cooperativa Gorropu (☎ 0782 64 92 82; Via Sa Preda Lada 2, Urzulei), in the Sa Domu 'e S'Orcu building on the SS125, just north of the Urzulei turn-off, guides trekkers into the gorge and on other walks around the Golfo di Orosei and the Supramonte. It also organises meals with shepherds in the countryside and might be able to swing rooms in private houses for you.

For more tips on hiking in this area, see Lonely Planet's *Walking in Italy* guide.

Hotel Sant'Elene (☎ 0784 9 45 72; fax 0784 9 53 85; Località Sant'Elene; d with breakfast €56.50; ⊙ Mar-Oct; P) is a wonderful choice of place to stay. The hotel is a cosy spot with comfortable rooms and fine views stretching across the valley. The restaurant here is also excellent for its Sardinian specialities.

Baunei & the Altopiano del Golgo

Around 28km south of the Genna 'e Silana pass you roll into the town of **Baunei**. There is nothing of particular interest to hold you up long here but you could sit at Bar Belvedere for a drink and soak in the mountain-valley views to the west.

However, what is seriously worth your while in Baunei is a 10km detour up to the mountain plateau known as the **Altopiano del Golgo**, signposted from the middle of town. A steep 2km (10 degree incline) set of switchbacks gets you up to the plateau and sailing north through heavily wooded terrain. After 8km you see a sign to your right to Su Sterru (Il Golgo). Follow the sign (for less than 1km), leave your vehicle and head for this remarkable feat of nature – a 270m abyss just 40m wide at its base. Its funnel-like opening is now fenced off but, knowing the size of the drop, just peering into the dark and damp opening of this eroded karst phenomenon is enough to bring on a case of vertigo. Cavers who like abseiling just love it.

At the end of the dirt trail is the **Locanda Il Rifugio** (☎ /fax 0782 61 05 99, ☎ 368 702 89 80; d from €40), which the Cooperativa Goloritzè has carved out of a one-time shepherd's farmstead. You can opt for full board and take your meals in the excellent restaurant, where the staff prepare such specialities as *capretto* and *porcetto*. All the meat is raised by the shepherds' cooperative – the place is surrounded by cattle, pigs and donkeys. The cooperative organises horse riding, 4WD excursions and hiking. From the plateau, 4WD trails lead to within 20 minutes' hiking distance of the marvellous Cala Goloritzè and Cala Sisine beaches. Roughly speaking, the place opens for spring and summer. The staff can arrange to pick you up in Baunei if you don't have your own transport.

Just beyond their stables is the late 16th-century **Chiesa di San Pietro**, a humble affair flanked to one side by some even humbler *cumbessias* – rough, largely open stone affairs which are not at all comfortable for the passing pilgrims who traditionally sleep here to celebrate the saint's day.

Santa Maria Navarrese

At the southern end of the Golfo di Orosei, the unpretentious and attractive small town of Santa Maria Navarrese is a tempting alternative to its busier northern counterpart, Cala Gonone. Basque sailors shipwrecked here built a small church in 1052, dedicated to Santa Maria di Navarra on the orders of the Princess of Navarra, who happened to be one of the survivors. The church was built in the shade of a grand olive tree that still thrives today.

Lofty pines and eucalyptus trees back this lovely beach lapped by transparent water (with more sandy stretches to the south). Offshore are several islets, including the **Isola dell'Ogliastra**. The leafy northern end of the beach is topped by a watchtower built to look out for raiding Saracens.

About 500m further north is the small pleasure port, where **Nautica Centro Sub** (☎ 0782 61 55 22) organises dives and rents out *gommoni* (high-speed dinghies) for exploring the Golfo di Orosei coast to the north. They start at €145 a day for up to 10 people (see the boxed text, p850). Out of season, prices plummet to around a third. Similar excursions to those heading out of Cala Gonone (see p850) to some or all of these beauty spots also depart from here. Inquire at the kiosks at the port or at the **Tourpass office** (☎ 0782 61 53 30; Piazza Principessa di Navarra; ☿ 8.30am-1pm & 5-8pm Sep-Jun, 8.30am-1pm & 5-11.30pm Jul-Aug) in the centre of town.

Three hotels lie within 200m of one another. **Hotel Plammas** (☎ 0782 61 51 30; www.hotel plammas.com in Italian; Viale Plammas 59; d to €76) is the cheapest deal and, while it won't blow your socks off, is pleasant enough and conveniently placed about 200m up the hill from the central square. The rooms are sparsely furnished but sport balconies with distant sea views. The restaurant is popular for its pasta dishes (try the fish-based *culurgiones*) and seafood mains.

You'll find several other eateries and a handful of bars within strolling distance of the centre. At the northern end of the beach, **Bar L'Olivastro** dishes up *panini*, ice cream and drinks on its shady terraces below the gnarled ancient branches of a couple of huge olive trees.

A handful of buses (sometimes only one a day) link Santa Maria Navarrese with Tortolì (€0.70, 15 minutes), Arbatax (€0.90, 30 minutes), Dorgali (€3.50, 1½ hours), Nuoro (€5.40, 2½ hours) and even Cagliari (€7.65, four hours).

SARDINIA

Tortolì & Arbatax

The rather dispiriting sprawl of Tortolì and, 4km east, its industrial outgrowth and port Arbatax will be unlikely to enthral you. If you have to kill time here, head across the road from the port and behind the petrol station to the *rocce rosse* (red rocks). These bizarre, weather-beaten rock formations dropping into the sea are well worth a camera shot or two. In the distance your gaze is attracted by the imperious cliffs of the southern Ogliastra and Golfo di Orosei.

Just by the port is the terminus for the FdS *Trenino Verde* summer tourist train to/from Mandas (4¾ hours, two daily) – one of the most scenic rides. The train station also houses the tourist office, whose opening hours vary with ferry arrival times.

Local bus Nos 1 and 2 run from Arbatax to Tortolì and, in the case of the latter service, to the beach and hotels at nearby **Porto Frailis**. If you want to stay here and are all set to splurge, the luxurious **La Bitta** (☎ 0782 66 70 80; www.arbataxhotels.com; Porto Frailis; s/d €99/200; ⊠ 🖳 P 🖳) is right on the beach and has palatial rooms complete with columns, arches and seamless sea views.

A few buses run from both these destinations to Santa Maria Navarrese, Dorgali, Nuoro and Cagliari, as well as many inland villages. Frequency is generally low, with sometimes only one departure a day.

CALA GONONE & AROUND

The fast-developing seaside resort of **Cala Gonone**, just 10km east of Dorgali, is in a stunning position and makes an excellent base from which to explore the coves along the most startling stretch of the Golfo di Orosei's coastline.

Cala Gonone's port is also a launch pad for boat excursions to the magical coves and cliffs to the south.

At the **tourist office** (☎ 0784 9 36 96; Viale Bue Marino 1a; ⊠ 9am-6pm Apr-Oct, 9am-11pm Jul & Aug) there is plenty of info on the area. Click on www.calagonone.com for comprehensive information on the area.

Sights & Activities

Several decent beaches stretch to the immediate south of the port. Some better ones, including the sugar-white strand of the **Cala Cartoe** are accessible only by car – take Via Marco Polo away from the port and then follow the signs.

Don't miss out on one of Sardinia's most memorable experiences – taking an excursion to explore the magical coves along a 20km stretch south of Cala Gonone. The first stop is **Grotta del Bue Marino**, touted as the last island refuge of the monk seal, although none have been seen around here for a long time. The watery gallery is certainly impressive, with shimmering light playing on the

---

BOATING ALONG THE COAST

There are several ways to approach the coastal wonders from Cala Gonone. A fleet of boats, from large high-speed dinghies to small cruise boats and graceful sailing vessels are on hand, and there's a broad range of excursions on offer. The most basic option would see you joining a band of punters to be transported to one of the beaches along the coast.

The basic cost of such trips starts at €8.50 for the return trip only from Cala Luna (for those who elect to walk there). The return trip to Cala Luna or Grotta del Bue Marino is €14.50. Both Cala Luna and Grotta del Bue Marino costs €24.50. The return trip to Cala Mariolu costs €23. Prices drop in the slower months.

Full-day cruises, with visits to various (but usually not all) beaches and other beauty spots can cost from €23 for a minicruise. Much nicer is the day-long trip on a sailing boat, costing €67 a head. If you want lunch on board (instead of taking your own), add €18. Contact **Cala Gonone Charter** (☎ 0784 9 37 37; Via S'Abba Irde 3).

The final option is the most tempting and the most expensive. Consider hiring a *gommone* (a big motorised dinghy). They start at €150 plus a further €10 to €15 for petrol. Nothing beats the freedom this offers you.

Boats operate from March until about November – dates depend a lot on demand. Prices vary dramatically according to the time of year and can plummet in low season. 'Very high season' is around 11 to 25 August. You can get information at agencies around town or at a series of booths directly at the port.

strange shapes within the cave. Guided visits take place up to seven times a day.

From there follows a string of coves and beaches, from the crescent moon–shaped **Cala Luna** and **Cala Sisine**, backed by a green valley, through to the incredible cobalt blue waters of **Cala Mariolu** and **Cala Goloritzè**. Indeed, the waters along this coast cover an exquisite spectrum from deep purple through emerald green to cerulean blue.

You can also walk to Cala Luna from Cala Gonone. The track starts at **Cala Fuili**, 3.5km from Cala Gonone. It's then 4km (about 1½ hours) between the two coves on rocky terrain but with breathtaking coastal views. Longer inland treks to some of these beaches can also be organised. Several local excursion and hiking outfits will put you onto this and other trails (on foot or in a 4WD), including descents of the Gola Su Gorroppu gorge and visits to the Tiscali nuraghic village (see p848). Try **Dolmen** (☎ 0784 9 33 45; www.sardegna dascoprire.it; Via Vasco da Gama 18).

Several operators offer diving courses and trips in the Golfo di Orosei, including **Sea Charter** (☎ 328 487 57 46; Porto Cala; cruises €35) and **Argonauta** (☎ /fax 0784 9 30 46; www.argonauta .it; Via dei Lecci 10), which also offers Professional Association of Diving Instructors (PADI) courses.

Sleeping & Eating

Pensione L'Oasi (☎ 0784 9 31 11; fax 0784 9 34 44; Via G Lorca; s/d to €92/114; ☎ Mar-Oct) High up above the centre, this place is tucked away on the road to Cala Cartoe, but a shortcut path means you can reach the sea in 10 minutes or so. The rooms are light and airy with balconies and superb views of the gardens against a backdrop of blue.

Camping Cala Gonone (☎ 0784 9 31 65; fax 0784 9 32 56; per person €16, bungalows to €134; ☎ Apr-Oct) This camp site is a little way back from the waterfront along the main road from Dorgali. The

facilities are excellent and include a tennis court, playground, bar, restaurant, pizzeria and barbecue grills.

Hotel Miramare (☎ 0784 9 31 40; fax 0784 9 34 69; Piazza Giardini; s/d to €67/120; ☎ Apr-Oct) The first hotel to be built here in 1955 has a charming, if slightly faded, appeal. All the rooms have balconies and sea views, satellite TV, phone/fax and minibar. The shady front terrace has a timeless elegance, while the restaurant serves reliably tasty, and traditional, Sardinian dishes. There are plenty of other hotels on or near the waterfront, but you will definitely need to book ahead in July and August.

Piccolo Hotel (☎ 0784 9 32 32; fax 0784 9 32 35; Viale Colombo; s/d €31/51) With its institutional grey exterior, this is the cheapest place in town – and looks it. The rooms are predictably no-frills basic but the location is convenient, only a short schlep from the port.

Bar Gelateria Fronte del Porte (Via Acqua Dolce 5; pizzas from €3.50) Not the place for a cosy head-to-head, this bright and breezy bar-restaurant has lots of snacks on offer, including good pizza and sandwiches, plus ice creams. It's also open year-round – a rarity in these parts.

Ristorante Acquarius (☎ 0784 9 34 28; Lungomare Palmasera 34; meals €35; ☎ Apr-Sep) On the waterfront, this is one of the best dining options in Cala Gonone, with the added bonuses of a bar and an ice-cream counter. You can sit on the front terrace and choose between a mix of Sardinian and standard Italian dishes. Try the *anzelottos* (ricotta-filled ravioli) or the *cozze alla marinara* (mussels).

Getting There & Away

In summer, as many as 10 ARST buses travel from Dorgali (€0.70, 20 minutes, 10km) and pull up at Via Marco Polo, near the port. Seven of these come in from Nuoro (€2.60, 70 minutes).

Directory

CONTENTS

ACCOMMODATION

Accommodation in Italy can range from the sublime to the ridiculous with prices to match. Hotels and *pensioni* (guesthouses) make up the bulk of accommodation, covering a rainbow of options from cheap, nasty and ill-lit dosshouses near stations to luxury hotels considered among the best on the planet. Youth hostels and busy camping grounds are scattered across the country. A rapidly growing array of good, characterful B&B-style, villa rentals and *agriturismo* (farm stay) options broaden the choice away from hotels. Mountain walkers will find *rifugi* (Alpine huts) handy, and it is possible to overnight in some of Italy's many monasteries.

In this book high-season prices are quoted and are intended as a guide only. Hotels are listed according to three categories (budget, midrange and top end), and further within those categories by author preference. Half board equals breakfast and either lunch or dinner; full board includes breakfast, lunch and dinner.

Prices can fluctuate enormously depending on the season, with Easter, summer and the Christmas–New Year period being peak tourist times. Expect to pay peak prices in the mountains during the ski season. There are many variables on these general rules. Summer is clearly high season on the coast and at the beaches, but in the cities summer can equal low season. In August especially, while sunbathers are paying through the nose for their handkerchief-sized piece of *costa* (coast), visitors to, say, Milan, Venice or Florence will find many hotels charge as little as half price. It is always worth considering booking ahead in high season (although in the urban centres you can usually find something if you trust it to luck).

There is no set rule on raising or lowering prices by season. Some hotels barely alter prices throughout the year. This is especially true of the lower-end places, although in low season there is no harm in trying to bargain for a discount even in the cheapest place. You may find hoteliers especially receptive to this sort of thing if you intend to stay for several days.

To make a reservation, hotels usually require confirmation by fax or, more commonly, a credit card number. In the latter case, if you don't show up you will be docked a night's accommodation.

Agriturismo & B&Bs

Holidays on working farms, or *agriturismo*, are increasingly popular, both with travellers and property owners looking for extra revenue. Accommodation can range from simple, rustic affairs to luxury locations where little farming is done and the swimming pool sparkles. *Agriturismo* business booms in Tuscany and Umbria, but is also steadily gaining ground in Trentino-Alto Adige, Sicily and Sardinia. Indeed, you can find options from

PRACTICALITIES

■ Use the metric system for weights and measures.

■ Buy or watch videos on the PAL system.

■ Plugs have two or three round pins so bring an international adapter. The electric current is 220V, 50Hz but older buildings may still use 125V.

■ If your Italian's up to it, try the following newspapers: *Corriere della Sera,* the country's leading daily; *Il Messaggero,* a popular Rome-based broadsheet; *L'Unità,* the former left-wing mouthpiece; or *La Repubblica,* a centre-left daily with a flow of Mafia conspiracies and Vatican scoops. For the Church's view, try the *Osservatore Romano.*

■ Tune into: Vatican Radio (1530AM, 93.3 FM and 105 FM) for a run-down on what the pope is up to; state-owned Italian RAI-1 (1332AM or 89.7 FM), RAI-2 (846AM or 91.7 FM) and RAI-3 (93.7 FM) for classical and light music with news broadcasts; and commercial stations such as Radio Centro Suono (101.3 FM), the Naples-based Radio Kiss Kiss (97.25 FM) and Radio Città Futura (97.7 FM) for contemporary music.

■ Switch on the box to watch Italy's commercial stations Canale 5, Italia 1, Rete 4 and La 7, as well as the state-run RAI 1, RAI 2 and RAI 3.

the Veneto to Basilicata. Local tourist offices can usually supply lists of operators. For detailed information on *agriturismo* facilities throughout Italy check out the website of **Agriturist** (www.agriturist.com). Several other sites also offer information. One that concentrates on the Tuscany area is **Agriturismo.com** (☎ 0575 616091; www.agriturismo.com).

Another increasingly popular option in Italy is B&B (bed and breakfast). Options include everything from restored farmhouses, city *palazzi* and seaside bungalows to rooms in family houses. Tariffs cover a wide price range typically in the €50 to €150 bracket. For more information, call **Bed & Breakfast Italia** (Map pp98-9; ☎ 06 688 01 513; www.bbitalia .it; Corso Vittorio Emanuele II 282, 00186 Rome).

Camping

Most camping grounds in Italy are major complexes with swimming pools, restaurants and supermarkets. Like hotels, they are graded according to a star system. Charges range from €5 to €12 per adult, €4 to €10 for children aged under 12, and from €5 to €12 for a site. In the major cities, grounds are often a long way from the historic centres. Many camping grounds offer the alternative of bungalows or even simple, self-contained flats.

Independent camping is not permitted in protected areas but, out of the main tourist season, independent campers who choose spots that aren't visible from the road and who don't light fires shouldn't have too much trouble. Make sure to always get permission from the landowner if you want to camp on private property.

Lists of camping grounds are available from local tourist offices or can be looked up on various sites including www.campeggi.com and www.camping.it. The Touring Club Italiano (TCI) annually publishes the book, *Campeggi in Italia* (Camping in Italy), listing all camping grounds, and the Istituto Geografico de Agostini publishes the annual *Guida ai Campeggi in Europa* (Guide to Camping in Europe), sold together with *Guida ai Campeggi in Italia*. Both books are available in major bookshops.

Other sites worth looking up:

Canvas Holidays (www.canvasholidays.com)
Eurocamp (www.eurocamp.co.uk)
Keycamp (www.keycamp.co.uk)
Select Sites (www.select-site.com) It's possible to make individual site bookings.

Convents & Monasteries

A less usual accommodation option can be a night or two staying in a convent or monastery. Some convents and monasteries let out cells or rooms as a modest revenue-making exercise and happily take in tourists, while others are single sex and only take in pilgrims or people who are on a spiritual retreat or seeking to participate in monastic life for a short while. Many do not take in guests at all. Convents and monasteries are not for party animals and generally impose a fairly early curfew. Charges hover around €35/70/100 for a single/double/triple.

As a starting point, take a look at the website of the **Chiesa di Santa Susana** (www.santasusanna.org/comingToRome/convents.html), an American Catholic church in Rome. Here, they have searched out options around the country. Getting a spot is generally up to you contacting the individual institution – there are no central booking agencies for convents and monasteries (yet!). Another site worth a look is www.initaly.com/agri/convents.htm, for options in Lazio, Liguria, Puglia, Emilia-Romagna and Abruzzo. At www.realrome.com/accommconvents.html you will find a list of Roman convents that generally take in young single women. **Dolce Vita Travel** (www.dolcevita.com/travel) lists a top 10 of convents and monasteries in Italy. A useful publication is Eileen Barish's *The Guide to Lodging in Italy's Monasteries*.

Hostels

Ostelli per la Gioventù (youth hostels) are run by the Associazione Italiana Alberghi per la Gioventù (AIG), which is, in turn, affiliated to **Hostelling International** (HI; www.hihostels.com). A valid HI card is required in all associated youth hostels in Italy. You can get this in your home country or direct at many hostels.

Pick up a booklet on Italian hostels, with details of prices, locations and so on, from the national head office of **AIG** (Map pp102-3; ☎ 06 487 11 52; www.ostellionline.org; Via Cavour 44, Rome). Nightly rates vary from around €14 to €20, which usually includes a buffet breakfast. You can often get lunch or dinner for around €9.

Accommodation is in segregated dormitories and it can be very basic, although many hostels offer doubles or family rooms (usually at a higher price per person). Some readers have reported difficulties getting access to such rooms. Hostels will sometimes have a lock-out period between about 9am and 1.30pm. Check-in is usually not before 1pm, although some hostels will allow you a morning check-in before they close for the day. In many hostels, there is a curfew from around 11pm. It is usually necessary to pay before 9am on the day of departure, otherwise you could be charged for another night.

Hotels & Pensioni

There is often very little difference between a *pensione* and an *albergo* (hotel). However, a *pensione* will generally be of one- to three-star quality and traditionally it has been a family-run operation, while an *albergo* can be awarded up to five stars. *Locande* (inns) long fell into much the same category as *pensioni*, but the term has become a trendy one in some parts and reveals little about the quality of a place. *Affittacamere* are rooms for rent in private houses. They are generally cheapish and simple affairs although in some of the more heavily touristed areas can boast a high standard.

Quality can vary enormously, but one-star hotels/*pensioni* tend to be basic and usually do not offer private bathrooms. Standards at two-star places are often only slightly better but rooms will generally have a private bathroom. Once you arrive at three stars you can assume that standards will be reasonable. Four- and five-star hotels offer facilities such as room service, laundry and dry-cleaning. In recent years in some of the more important tourist centres (Venice is a case in point) a flood of new and attractive accommodation (often boutique spots) on the market has obliged all establishments to smarten up their act or lose custom.

Prices are highest in major tourist destinations. They also tend to be higher in northern Italy. A *camera singola* (single room) costs from €25. A *camera doppia* (twin beds) or *camera matrimoniale* (double room with a double bed) will cost from around €40. As a rough guide, a budget double can cost up to about €80, a midrange option from €80 to about €180 and a top-end option anything from there to thousands for a suite in one of the country's premier establishments. This depends greatly on where you are looking. A bottom-end budget choice in Venice or Milan will set you back the price of a decent midrange option in, say, Puglia. For more on costs, see p20.

Tourist offices usually have booklets with local accommodation listings. Many hotels are also signing up with (steadily proliferating) online accommodation-booking services. You could start your search at:

All Hotels in Italy (www.hotelsitalyonline.com)
Bookings (www.bookings.it)
Italy Hotels Discount (www.italy-hotels-discount.com)
Travel to Italy (www.travel-to-italy.com)

Mountain Refuges

The network of *rifugi* in the Alps, Apennines and other mountains in Italy are usually only open from July to September. Accommodation is generally in dormitories but some of the larger refuges have doubles. The price per person (which usually includes breakfast) ranges from €16 to €26 depending on the quality of the refuge (it's more for a double room). A hearty post-walk dinner will set you back another €15 to €20.

Rifugi are marked on good walking maps. Some are close to chair lifts and cable-car stations, which means they are usually expensive and crowded. Others are at high altitude and involve hours of hard walking. It is important to book in advance. Additional information can be obtained from the local tourist offices.

The **Club Alpino Italiano** (CAI; www.cai.it in Italian) owns and runs many of the mountain huts. Members of organisations such as the Australian Alpine Club and British Mountaineering Council can enjoy discounted rates for accommodation and meals by obtaining (for a fee) a reciprocal rights card.

Rental Accommodation

Finding rental accommodation in the major cities can be difficult and time-consuming – rental agencies (local and foreign) can assist, for a fee. Rental rates are higher for short-term leases. A small apartment or a studio anywhere near the centre of Rome will cost around €1000 per month and it is usually necessary to pay a deposit (generally one month in advance). Expect to spend similar amounts in cities such as Florence, Milan, Naples and Venice. Apartments and villas for rent are listed in local publications such as Rome's weekly *Porta Portese* and the fortnightly *Wanted in Rome*. Another option is to answer an advertisement in a local publication to share an apartment. If you are staying for a few months and don't mind sharing, check out university noticeboards for student flats with vacant rooms.

If you're looking for an apartment or studio to rent for a short stay (such as a week or two) the easiest option is to check out the websites of agencies dealing in this kind of thing:

Carefree Italy (www.carefree-italy.com)
Euroflats (www.ccrsrl.com) Has flats sleeping six from €650 to €1800 per week.

Guest in Italy (www.guestinitaly.com) An online agency, with apartments ranging from about €100 to €320 a night.
Interhome (www.interhome.co.uk)
Wotspot (www.wotspot.com) Has apartments that generally go for around US$900 to $1500 per week, sleeping two to four people.

In major resort areas, such as popular coastal areas in summer and the ski towns in winter, the tourist offices have lists of apartments and villas for rent. Most tourist offices will be more than cooperative if you telephone beforehand for information on how to book an apartment.

Villa Rentals

Long the preserve of the Tuscan sun, the villa-rental scene in Italy has taken off in recent years, with agencies offering villa accommodation, often in splendid rural locations not far from enchanting medieval towns or Mediterranean beaches, up and down the country. More eccentric options include renting *trulli*, the conical traditional houses of southern Puglia or *dammusi* (houses with thick, whitewashed walls and a shallow cupola), on the island of Pantelleria, south off the Sicilian mainland. You can start off your search with the following agencies but there are dozens of operators out there.

For villas in the time-honoured and most popular central regions, particularly Tuscany and Umbria, check out the following:

Cottages and Castles (www.cottagesandcastles.com.au) The Australian associate of Cuendet.

Cottages to Castles (www.cottagestocastles.com)

Cuendet (www.cuendet.com) One of the old hands in this business; operates from the heart of Siena province in Tuscany.

Ilios Travel (www.iliostravel.com) Has villas, apartments and castles in Tuscany, Umbria, Lazio and the south.

Invitation to Tuscany (www.invitationtotuscany.com)
Summer's Leases (www.summerleases.com)
Thomson (www.thomson.co.uk)
Tuscany Now (www.tuscanynow.com)

Some agencies concentrate their energies on the south (especially Campania and Puglia) and the islands of Sicily and Sardinia. Have a look at:

Costa Smeralda Holidays (www.costasmeralda-holidays .com)

Long Travel (www.long-travel.co.uk)
Think Sicily (www.thinksicily.com)
Voyages Ilena (www.voyagesilena.co.uk) For Sardinia.

DIRECTORY

Operators offering villas and other short-term let properties across the country:

Carefree Italy (www.carefree-italy.com)
Italian Life (www.italianlife.co.uk)
Italian Retreats (www.italianretreats.com)
Magic of Italy (www.magictravelgroup.co.uk)
Parker Villas (www.parkervillas.co.uk)
Simpson (www.simpson-travel.com)
Veronica Tomasso Cotgrove (www.vtcitaly.com)

ACTIVITIES

Although Italy is justly famous for its cultural, artistic and historical treasures, you could get into any number of outdoorsy activities as well. The stunning scenery, from the rolling hills of Tuscany and Umbria to dramatic mountain ranges and sinister volcanoes, offer a wealth of exciting activities off the beaten tourist track.

Cycling

Tourist offices will be able to offer information on mountain-bike trails and guided rides. For information on hiring or buying a bike and on travelling around Italy with one, see p880.

The hills of Tuscany are popular for cycling, particularly around the cities of Florence and Siena, from where you can explore the countryside around Fiesole, San Gimignano and Chianti. Try the tours offered in Chianti by **Bicycle Tuscany** (www.bicycletuscany.com) and **Florence By Bike** (www.florencebybike.it), among others. In Umbria, areas like the Valnerina and the Piano Grande at Monte Vettore have beautiful trails and quiet country roads to explore and a bike could be particularly useful for getting around Sardinia. Serious cyclists will know where to go for the most challenging routes – the tortuous, winding road up to the Passo Stelvio is one of the most famous. At the end of May, the prestigious Giro d'Italia takes place and attracts a host of international participants.

If you plan to make cycling a focus of your trip, try to get hold of a copy of Lonely Planet's *Cycling Italy*.

Diving & Water Sports

Windsurfing and sailing are popular in Italy and at most beach resorts, as well as around the northern lakes, it is possible to hire boats and equipment. Canoeing and kayaking are also increasingly indulged in, especially in the north – the Turin-based

Amici del Fiume (www.amicidelfiume.it in Italian) has information.

Some of the best snorkelling and diving spots are in the south – Campania, Calabria, Sardinia and Sicily – where the volcanic geology makes for rich marine life. The small island of Ústica is almost entirely devoted to diving and holds an annual marine festival from mid-June to August. It is also a popular pastime in the Aeolians and around Taormina. Check out:

Dive-centers.Net (www.dive-centers.net)
Dive Italy (www.diveitaly.com in Italian)

Walking & Hiking

Italy is a walker's paradise with thousands of kilometres of *sentieri* (marked trails). The **Club Alpino Italiano** (CAI; www.cai.it in Italian) is a useful source of information if you understand some Italian. The Dolomites is the most popular area with a multitude of stunning peaks. The Parco Nazionale Gran Paradiso in Valle d'Aosta has a magnificent network of *sentieri* over high passes and through beautiful valleys. The Matterhorn (Monte Cervino) and Monte Rosa lie north of Valle d'Aosta – you can enjoy the mountains from below along paths linking the fringing valleys.

For wild and remote mountains, try the Maritime Alps in southwest Piedmont and both the Carniche and Giulie Alps in Friuli-Venezia Giulia. The long Apennines chain has some high-level walks, especially in Tuscany's Apuane Alps and the Parco Nazionale d'Abruzzo. Sicily also has a number of parks, which are rapidly improving their infrastructure and provide some wonderful seaside walks, particularly in the Riserva Naturale dello Zingaro. You can also brave the active volcanoes on foot – Vesuvius near Naples, Etna in Sicily and Stromboli and Vulcano on the Aeolian Islands.

Walking in the mountains and the valleys around the northern lakes of Garda, Como and Maggiore is superb. Tuscany and Sicily offer incomparable opportunities for combining scenic walks with fine food and wine stops. Two great areas by the sea are the Cinque Terre in Liguria and the Amalfi-Sorrento peninsula in Campania, where age-old paths follow precipitous hillsides.

Consult Lonely Planet's *Walking in Italy* for detailed descriptions of more than 50 walks. Guided walks are organised in many national parks but generally you need to understand Italian (inquire at local tourist offices for details).

Skiing

Numerous excellent ski resorts dot the Italian Alps and the Dolomites provide the most dramatic scenery. Options include *sci alpino* (downhill skiing) and *sci di fondo* (cross-country skiing), as well as *sci-alpinismo* (ski mountaineering).

Skiing in Italy is as expensive as anywhere in Western Europe but a *settimana bianca* (winter-sports holiday, literally 'white week') package can reduce the costs.

The snow season in Italy generally runs from December to late March. There is year-round skiing in areas such as the Marmolada glacier in Trentino-Alto Adige and on Mont Blanc (Monte Bianco) and the Matterhorn in the Valle d'Aosta.

The five major (read: most fashionable and expensive) ski resorts in Italy are Cortina d'Ampezzo in the Veneto; Madonna di Campiglio, San Martino di Castrozza and Canazei in Trentino; and Courmayeur in the Valle d'Aosta.

BUSINESS HOURS

Generally shops open from 9am to 1pm and 3.30pm to 7.30pm (or 4pm to 8pm) Monday to Saturday. Many close on Saturday afternoon and some close on a Monday morning or afternoon, and sometimes again on a Wednesday or Thursday afternoon. In major towns most department stores and supermarkets have continuous opening hours from 10am to 7.30pm Monday to Saturday. Some even open from 9am to 1pm on Sunday.

Banks tend to open from 8.30am to 1.30pm and 3.30pm to 4.30pm Monday to Friday. They are closed at weekends but it is always possible to find a bureau de change open in the larger cities and in major tourist areas.

Central post offices open from 8.30am to 6.30pm from Monday to Saturday. Some main branches close at 1pm on Saturday, while most smaller branches only open from Monday to Friday. All close two hours earlier than normal on the last business day of each month (not including Saturday).

Farmacie (pharmacies) are open 9am to 12.30pm and 3.30pm to 7.30pm. Most shut on Saturday afternoon, Sunday and holidays but a handful remain open on a rotation basis for emergency purposes. All closed

pharmacies are obliged to display a list of the nearest ones open.

Many bars and cafés open from about 8am to 8pm, serving workaday customers. Others then go on into the night serving a more nocturnal crowd while still others, dedicated more exclusively to evening diversion, don't get started until the early evening (even if they officially open in the morning). Few bars remain open anywhere beyond 1am or 2am. Clubs (known as *discoteche* in Italy) might open around 10pm (or even earlier if they happen to have eateries on the premises) but things don't get moving until after midnight. Restaurants open noon to 3pm and 7.30pm to 11pm (later in summer and in the south). Restaurants and bars are required to close for one day each week with the day varying between establishments.

The opening hours of museums, galleries and archaeological sites vary enormously, although there is a trend towards continuous opening at the more important sites from around 9.30am to 7pm. Many close on Monday. Some of the major national museums and galleries remain open until 10pm in summer.

CHILDREN
Practicalities

Italians love children but there are few special amenities for them. Always make a point of asking staff at tourist offices if they know of any special family activities or have suggestions on hotels that cater for kids. Discounts are available for children (usually aged under 12 but sometimes based on the child's height) on public transport and for admission to sites.

If you have kids, book accommodation in advance to avoid any inconvenience and when travelling by train make sure to reserve seats to avoid finding yourselves standing up for the entire journey. You can hire car seats for infants and children from most car-rental firms, but you should always book them in advance.

You can buy baby formula in powder or liquid form, as well as sterilising solutions such as Milton, at all pharmacies. Disposable nappies (diapers) are widely available at supermarkets and pharmacies. A pack of around 30 disposable nappies costs about €10. Fresh cow's milk is sold in cartons in supermarkets and in bars that have a 'Latteria'

DIRECTORY

sign. UHT milk is popular and in many out-of-the-way areas the only kind available.

Sights & Activities

Successful travel with children can require a special effort. Don't try to overdo things and make sure activities include the kids – older children could help in the planning of these. Try to think of things that might capture their imagination like the sites at Pompeii (p654), the Colosseum (p110) and the Forum (p113) in Rome, and Greek temples in the south and Sicily. Another good bet are the volcanoes in the south.

Water activities, from lolling on a beach to snorkelling or sailing are always winners. When choosing museums to visit, throw in the odd curio that may be more likely to stir a young 'un's fascination than yet another worthy art gallery! Boys will probably like such things as Turin's Museo dell'Automobile (p229), while girls might enjoy the idea of a little fashion shopping with Mum in Milan's Golden Quad (p275) district. If you are travelling in northern Italy, you might want to make a stopover at Gardaland (p304), the amusement park near Lago di Garda in Lombardy, or at Italia in Miniatura (p451) at Viserba near Rimini in Emilia-Romagna.

Always remember to allow some free-time for kids to play, and make sure treats such as a whopping *gelati* (ice cream) or a slice of their favourite pizza are included in the bag of tricks.

For more information, see Lonely Planet's *Travel with Children* or the websites www.travelwithyourkids.com and www.familytravelnetwork.com.

CLIMATE CHARTS

Situated in the temperate zone and jutting deep into the Mediterranean, Italy is regarded by many tourists as a land of sunny, mild weather. However, due to the north–south orientation of the peninsula and the fact that it is largely mountainous, the country's climate is actually quite variable. See p20 for more information on when to go.

In the Alps, temperatures are lower and winters can be long and severe. Generally the weather is warm from July to September, although rainfall can be high in September. While the first snowfall is usually in November, light snow sometimes falls in mid-September and the first heavy falls can occur

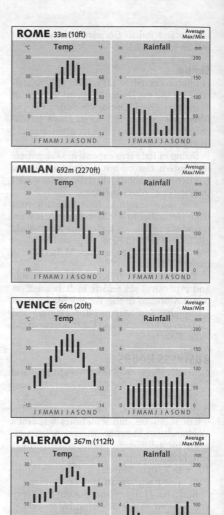

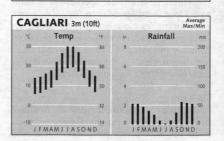

in early October. Freak snowfalls in June are not unknown at high altitudes.

The Alps shield northern Lombardy and the Lakes area, including Milan, from the extremes of the northern European winter, and Liguria enjoys a mild, Mediterranean climate similar to that in southern Italy because it is protected by both the Alps and the Apennine range.

Winters are severe and summers very hot in the Po valley. Venice can be hot and humid in summer and, although not too cold in winter, it can be unpleasant if wet or when the sea level rises and *acque alte* (literally 'high waters') inundate the city. This is most likely in November and December. Along the Po Valley and in Venice especially, January and February can be crisp and stunning.

Further south in Florence, which is encircled by hills, the weather can be quite extreme but, as you travel towards the tip of the boot, temperatures and weather conditions become milder. Rome, for instance, has an average July and August temperature in the mid-20°Cs (Celsius), although the impact of the sirocco (a hot, humid wind blowing from Africa) can produce stiflingly hot weather in August, with temperatures in the high 30°Cs for days on end. Winters are moderate and snow is rare in Rome, although winter clothing (or at least a heavy overcoat) is still a requirement.

The south of Italy and the islands of Sicily and Sardinia have a Mediterranean climate. Summers are long, hot and dry, and winter temperatures tend to be relatively moderate, with daytime averages not too far below 10°C. These regions are also affected by the humid sirocco in summer.

COURSES

Holiday courses are a booming section of the Italian tourist industry and they cover everything from painting, art, sculpture, wine, food, photography, scuba diving and even hang-gliding. You will find details on various local courses throughout this book. US students looking to sign up for courses in Italy might want to check out the offerings at **Study Abroad Italy** (www.studyabroad-italy.com).

Cooking

Many people come to Italy just for the food so it is hardly surprising that cookery courses are among the most popular. The useful website www.italycookingschools.com can help you evaluate hundreds of possibilities; see also p86 for details on specific courses.

Language

Courses are run by private schools and universities throughout the country and are a great way to learn Italian while enjoying the opportunity to live in an Italian city or town. Among the more popular and reasonably priced options, are the **Università per Stranieri di Perugia** (www.unistrapg.it) and the **Università per Stranieri di Siena** (www.unistrasi.it), both set in beautiful medieval cities. Frequently these schools offer extracurricular or full-time courses in painting, art history, sculpture and architecture, too. One school much praised by Lonely Planet readers is **Saenaiulia** (☎ 0577 441 55; www.saenaiulia.it) in Siena. Florence and Rome are teeming with Italian-language schools, while Venice has hardly any. Turn to the relevant chapters for suggestions.

The Istituto Italiano di Cultura (IIC), which has branches all over the world, is a government-sponsored organisation aimed at promoting Italian culture and language. This is a good place to start your search for places to study in Italy. The institute has branches all over the world, including in Australia (Sydney), Canada (Montreal), the UK (London) and the USA (Los Angeles, New York and Washington). The website of the **Italian foreign ministry** (www.esteri.it) has a full list of institutions; click on Diplomatic Representations and then on Italian Cultural Institutes.

Painting

Art and painting courses also abound in Italy, especially in cities such as Florence. The **Accademia del Giglio** (www.adg.it) is one of several organisations that offers art courses as part of their offerings to foreigners who are sojourning in the city.

Yoga

It will always be hard to close your senses to the food and drink of Italy, but another way to enjoy the country is with a little gentle bodywork. **Yoga in Italy** (☎ 0445 48 02 98; www.yogainitaly.com) offers a variety of week-long holidays combining yoga with anything from walks in the Chianti countryside to white-water rafting.

CUSTOMS

There is no limit on the amount of euros brought into the country. Goods brought in and exported within the EU incur no additional taxes, provided duty has been paid somewhere within the EU and the goods are for personal consumption.

Duty-free sales within the EU no longer exist. Visitors coming into Italy from non-EU countries can import, duty free: 1L of spirits, 2L wine, 60mL perfume, 250mL eau de toilette, 200 cigarettes and other goods up to a total of €175.50; anything over this limit must be declared on arrival and the appropriate duty paid. On leaving the EU, non-EU citizens can reclaim any Value Added Tax (VAT) on expensive purchases.

DANGERS & ANNOYANCES

It requires patience to deal with the Italian concept of service. What for Italians is simply a way of everyday life can be a real pain for foreigners. Anyone in a uniform or behind a counter (including police officers, waiters and shop assistants) is likely to regard you with imperious contempt or supreme indifference.

Long queues are the norm in banks, post offices and government offices.

Pollution

Noise and air pollution are problems in the major cities, caused mainly by heavy traffic. A headache after a day of sightseeing in Rome is likely to be caused by breathing in carbon monoxide and lead, rather than simple tiredness.

In the summer (and occasionally at other times during the year) there are periodic pollution alerts in cities such as Rome, Milan, Naples and Florence. The elderly, children and people who have respiratory problems are warned to stay indoors. If you fit into one of these categories, keep yourself informed through the tourist office or your hotel. Often traffic is cut in half during these alerts by obliging drivers with odd and even number plates to drive only on alternate days.

Keep an eye where you step as dog poop on the pavements is a big city irritation. Italian dog-owners are catching onto the idea of cleaning up their best friend's daily doings, but it's by no means a universal courtesy.

Italy's beaches can be polluted by industrial waste, sewage and oil spills from the Mediterranean's considerable sea traffic. The best and cleanest beaches are on Sardinia, Sicily in less-populated areas of the south and around Elba.

Smoking

For some smoking is heaven, for others it's torture. Since early 2005 smoking in all closed public spaces (from bars to elevators, offices to trains) has been banned – and believe it or not, the ban is being enforced.

Theft

Pickpockets and bag-snatchers operate in most cities, especially Naples and Rome. The best way to avoid being robbed is to wear a moneybelt under your clothing. Keep all important items, such as money, passport, other documents and tickets, in your moneybelt and wear bags or cameras slung across the body.

You should also watch out for groups of dishevelled-looking women and children asking you for money. Their favourite haunts are train stations, tourist sights and shopping areas. If you've been targeted by a group take evasive action (such as crossing the street) or shout 'Va via!' (Go away!). You should also be cautious of sudden friendships, particularly if your new-found *amico* or *amica* wants to sell you something.

Parked cars, particularly those with foreign number plates or rental-company stickers, are prime targets. Try not to leave anything in the car and certainly not overnight. Car theft is a problem in Rome, Campania and Puglia. Use supervised car parks. Motorway service stations, especially in the south, can be the haunt of thieves.

In case of theft or loss, always report the incident at the police station within 24 hours and ask for a statement, otherwise your travel-insurance company won't pay out.

Traffic

Italian traffic can at best be described as chaotic, at worst it's downright dangerous for the unprepared outsider. Drivers are not keen to stop for pedestrians, even at pedestrian crossings, and are more likely to swerve. Italians simply step off the footpath and walk through the (swerving) traffic with determination. Follow the locals!

In many cities, roads that appear to be for one-way traffic have lanes for buses travelling in the opposite direction – look both ways before stepping onto the road.

DISABLED TRAVELLERS
Italy is not an easy country for disabled travellers and getting around can be a problem for wheelchair users. Even a short journey in a city or town can become a major expedition if cobblestoned streets have to be negotiated. Although many buildings have lifts, they are not always wide enough for wheelchairs. Not an awful lot has been done to make life for the deaf and/or blind any easier either.

The Italian National Tourist Office (see p871) in your country may be able to provide advice on Italian associations for the disabled and information on what help is available. It may also carry a small brochure, *Services for Disabled Passengers*, published by Italian railways, which details facilities at stations and on trains.

Some organisations that may help:

Accessible Italy (☎ +378 0549 94 11 08; www.access ibleitaly.com) A San Marino–based company that specialises in holiday services for the disabled, ranging from tours to the hiring of adapted transport.

Accessible Travel & Leisure (☎ 01452-729739; www .accessibletravel.co.uk; Avionics House, Naas Lane, Gloucester GL2 2SN) This group claims to be the biggest UK travel agent dealing with travel for the disabled. The company encourages the disabled to travel independently.

Consorzio Cooperative Integrate (COIN; ☎ 06 2326 9231; www.coinsociale.it) Based in Rome, COIN is the best reference point for disabled travellers. It provides information on the capital (including transport and access) and is happy to share its contacts throughout Italy. It publishes a multilingual guide, *Roma Accessibile*, which lists available facilities at museums, shops and theatres. It is available by mail order and from some tourist offices.

Holiday Care (☎ 0845 124 9971; www.holidaycare.org .uk; 7th fl, Sunley House, 4 Bedford Park, Croydon, Surrey CR0 2AP) Has information on hotels with disabled access, where to hire equipment and tour operators dealing with the disabled.

DISCOUNT CARDS
At museums and galleries, never hesitate to ask if there are discounts available for students, young people, children, families or the elderly. When sightseeing and wherever possible buy a *biglietto cumulativo*, a ticket which allows admission to a number of associated sights for less than the combined cost of separate admission fees.

Senior Cards
Senior citizens are often entitled to public-transport discounts but usually only for monthly passes (not daily or weekly tickets); the minimum qualifying age is 65 years.

For rail travel, seniors (over 60) can get a 30% reduction on full 2nd-class fares and 40% off 1st-class fares by purchasing an annual seniors' pass called the Carta Argento (€30); purchase these at major train stations.

Admission to most museums in Rome is free for over-60s but in other cities (such as Florence) often no concessions are made for nonresidents. In numerous places EU seniors have free entry to sights. Always ask.

Student & Youth Cards
Free admission to some galleries and sites is available to under 18s. Discounts (usually half the normal fee) are available for some sights to EU citizens aged between 18 and 25 (you will need to produce proof of age). An ISIC (International Student Identity Card) is no longer sufficient at many tourist sites as prices are usually based on age so a passport, driver's licence or **Euro<26** (www.euro26 .org) card is preferable. An ISIC card will still, however, prove useful for cheap flights and theatre and cinema discounts; similar cards are available to teachers (ITIC). For non-student travellers who are under 25, there is the **International Youth Travel Card** (IYTC; www.isic .org), which offers the same benefits.

Student cards are issued by student unions, hostelling organisations as well as some youth travel agencies. In Italy, the **Centro Turistico Studentesco e Giovanile** (CTS; www.cts.it) youth travel agency can issue ISIC, ITIC and Euro<26 cards.

EMBASSIES & CONSULATES
Italian Embassies & Consulates
The following is a selection of Italian diplomatic missions abroad. Bear in mind that Italy maintains consulates in additional cities in many of the countries listed here.

Australia Canberra (☎ 02-6273 3333; www.ambitalia.org .au; 12 Grey St, Deakin ACT 2600); Melbourne (☎ 03-9867 5744; itconmel@netlink.com.au; 509 St Kilda Rd VIC 3004); Sydney (☎ 02-9392 7900; itconsydn@itconsyd.org; Lvl 45, The Gateway, 1 Macquarie Place NSW 2000)

Austria (☎ 01-712 51 21; www.ambitaliavienna.org; Metternichgasse 13, Vienna, 1030)

Canada Ottawa (☎ 613-232 2401; www.italyincanada .com; 21st fl, 275 Slater St, Ontario, K1P 5H9); Montreal

(☎ 514-849 83 51; www.italconsul.Montreal.qc.ca; 3489 Drummond St, Montreal, H3G 1X6); Vancouver (☎ 604-684 7288; www.italianconsulate.bc.ca; Standard Bldg, 1100-510 West Hastings St, BC V6B 1L8)

France (☎ 01 49 54 03 00; www.amb-italie.fr; 47 Rue de Varenne, Paris 75343)

Germany (☎ 030-254 40 0; www.botschaft-italien.de; Hiroshima Strasse 1, Berlin, 10785)

Ireland (☎ 01-660 1744; www.italianembassy.ie; 63-65 Northumberland Rd, Dublin 4)

Japan (☎ 03-3453 5291; www.embitaly.jp; 2-5-4 Mita, Minato-ku, Tokyo, 108-8302)

Netherlands (☎ 070-302 10 30; www.italy.nl; Alexanderstraat 12, The Hague, 2514 JL)

New Zealand (☎ 04-473 5339; www.italy-embassy.org .nz; 34-38 Grant Rd, Thorndon, Wellington)

Switzerland (☎ 031 350 07 77; http://sedi.esteri.it/berna; Elfenstrasse 14, Bern, 3006)

UK London (☎ 020-7312 2200; www.embitaly.org.uk; 14 Three Kings Yard, W1K 4EH); Edinburgh (☎ 0131-2263 631; 32 Melville St, EH3 7HA)

USA Washington (☎ 202-612 4400; www.italyemb.org; 3000 Whitehaven St, NW Washington, DC 20008); Los Angeles (☎ 310-826 6207; la.italcons@itwash.org; Suite 300, 12400 Wilshire Blvd, 90025); New York (☎ 212-737 9100; www.italconsulnyc.org; 690 Park Ave, 10021)

Embassies & Consulates in Italy

For other foreign embassies and consulates in Italy that are not listed here, look under 'Ambasciate' or 'Consolati' in the telephone directory. Alternatively, tourist offices generally have a list. In addition to the following, some countries run honorary consulates in other cities.

Australia Rome (Map p95; ☎ 06 85 27 21, emergencies ☎ 800 877 790; www.australian-embassy.it; Via Antonio Bosio 5, 00161); Milan (☎ 02 7770 4217; www.austrade.it; Via Borgogna 2, 20122)

Austria (☎ 06 844 01 41; www.austria.it; Via Pergolesi 3, Rome, 00198)

Canada Rome (Map p95; ☎ 06 44 59 81; www.dfait-maeci .gc.ca/canadaeuropa/italy; Via G B de Rossi 27, 00161); Milan (☎ 02 6 75 81; www.dfait-maeci.gc.ca/canadaeuropa/italy/ milan_consul-en.asp; Via Vittorio Pisani 19, 20124)

France Rome (Map p104; ☎ 06 68 60 11; www.france -italia.it; Piazza Farnese 67, 00186); Milan (Map pp260-1; ☎ 02 655 91 41; Via della Moscova 12, 20121); Naples (☎ 081 598 07 11; Via Francesco Crispi 86, 80121); Venice (Map pp352-3)

Germany Rome (Map pp102-3; ☎ 06 49 21 31; www .rom.diplo.de; Via San Martino della Battaglia 4, 00185); Florence (Map pp462-3; ☎ 055 29 47 22; Lungarno Amerigo Vespucci 30, 50123); Milan (☎ 02 623 11 01; www.mailand.diplo.de; Via Solferino 40, 20121); Naples

(☎ 081 248 85 11; Via Francesco Crispi 69, 80121); Venice (Map pp352-3)

Ireland Rome (Map pp98-9; ☎ 06 697 91 21; www .ambasciata-irlanda.it; Piazza Campitelli 3, 00186)

Japan Rome (Map pp102-3; ☎ 06 48 79 91; www.it .emb-japan.go.jp; Via Quintino Sella 60, 00187); Milan (☎ 02 624 11 41; Via Privata Cesare Mangili 2/4, 20121)

Netherlands Rome (☎ 06 322 11 41; www.olanda.it; Via Michele Mercati 8, 00197); Milan (☎ 02 4855 8421; Via San Vittore 45, 20123); Naples (☎ 081 551 30 03; Via Agostino Depretis 114, 80133); Palermo (☎ 091 58 15 21; Via Roma 489, 90139)

New Zealand Rome (Map p95; ☎ 06 441 71 71; www .nzembassy.com; Via Zara 28, 00198); Milan (☎ 02 4801 2544; Via Guido d'Arezzo 6, 20145)

Switzerland Rome (Map p95; ☎ 06 80 95 71; Via Barnarba Oriani 61, 00197); Milan (☎ 02 777 91 61; Via Palestro 2, 20121); Naples (☎ 081 761 45 33; Via Pergolesi 1, 80122)

UK Rome (☎ 06 4220 0001; www.britishembassy.gov.uk; Via XX Settembre 80a, 00187); Florence (Map p466; ☎ 055 28 41 33; Lungarno Corsini 2, 50123); Milan (p262; ☎ 02 72 30 01; Via S Paolo 7, 20121); Naples (☎ 081 423 89 11; Via dei Mille 40, 80121); Palermo (Map p750); Venice (☎ 041 505 59 90; Piazzale Donatori di Sangue 2, Mestre, 30171)

USA Rome (Map pp102-3; ☎ 06 467 41; www.usis.it; Via Vittorio Veneto 119a-121, 00187); Florence (☎ 055 266 951; Lungarno Vespucci 38, 50123); Milan (p262; ☎ 02 29 03 51; Via Principe Amedeo 2/10, 20121); Naples (☎ 081 583 81 11; Piazza della Repubblica, 80122)

FESTIVALS & EVENTS

Italy's calendar bursts with cultural events ranging from colourful traditional celebrations, with a religious and/or historical flavour, through to festivals of the performing arts, including opera, music and theatre.

Among the important opera seasons are those at Verona's Arena, Venice's Teatro La Fenice and La Scala in Milan. There are also significant opera seasons in Palermo and Catania. Major music festivals include **Umbria Jazz** (p548) in Perugia (July) and the **Umbria Jazz Winter** (p576) in Orvieto (late December/ early January), which hosts a fantastic party on New Year's Eve. Look out also for Siena Jazz, Vicenza Jazz and Florence's Maggio Musicale Fiorentino. International orchestras play annually at the **Festivale Musicale di Ravello** (www.ravelloarts.org).

February, March & April

Festa di Sant'Agata (p786; 3-5 Feb) Hysterical celebrations where one million Catanians and tourists follow as a silver reliquary bust of the saint covered in marvellous jewels is carried along the main street of Catania.

Sagra del Mandorlo in Fiore (Festival of the Almond Blossoms; p803; 1st Sun in Feb) A folk festival in Agrigento with open-air performances of drama and music.

Carnevale (Carnival) During the period before Ash Wednesday, many towns stage carnivals and enjoy their last opportunity to indulge before Lent. The carnival held in Venice (p364) during the 10 days before Ash Wednesday is the most famous.

Sa Sartiglia (p829; Sun & Tue before Lent) The highlight of carnival celebrations at Oristano. It involves a medieval tournament of horsemen in masquerade.

Settimana Santa (Holy Week) Holy Week in Italy is marked by solemn processions and Passion plays. Notable processions take place in Taranto (Puglia), Chieti (Abruzzo) and Tràpani (Sicily). On Good Friday evening the pope leads a candlelit procession to the Colosseum and on Easter Sunday he gives his traditional blessing.

Scoppio del Carro (Explosion of the Cart; p477; Easter Sat) A cartful of fireworks is exploded in the Piazza del Duomo in Florence – a tradition dating back to the crusades.

May

Festa di Sant'Efisio (p821; 1 May) An effigy of Sardinia's patron saint is paraded around Cagliari on a bullock-drawn carriage amid a colourful procession.

Festa di San Nicola (p700; 2-3 May) A procession in Bari follows a statue of the saint for a ceremony out at sea.

Processione dei Serpari (Snake-Charmers' Procession; p607; 1st Thu in May) Held at Cocullo, a statue of Saint Domenico is draped with live snakes and carried in procession.

Festa di San Gennaro (p628; 1st Sun in May, 19 Sep & 16 Dec) The faithful gather in Naples' cathedral to wait for the blood of San Gennaro to liquefy.

Corsa dei Ceri (Candles Race; p567; 15 May) Three teams, each carrying a *cero* (massive wooden pillars weighing about 400kg, bearing the statue of a rival saint) race through Gubbio's streets in commemoration of Sant'Ubaldo, the city's patron saint.

Cavalcata Sarda (Sardinian Cavalcade; p839; 2nd-last Sun in May) Hundreds of Sardinians wearing colourful traditional costume gather at Sassari to mark a victory over the Saracens in the year 1000.

Palio della Balestra (Crossbow Contest; p567; last Sun in May) Held in Gubbio this contest is between the men of Gubbio and neighbouring Sansepolcro, who dress in medieval costume and use antique weapons.

Ciclo di Spettacoli Classici (Festival of Greek Theatre; p794; mid-May–mid-Jun) During this unique yearly festival the works of Aristophanes, Euripides and other classical playwrights, bring the stones of Syracuse's ancient 5th-century-BC amphitheatre back to life. The festivals attract some of Italy's finest performers.

June

Gioco del Ponte (Game of the Bridge; p504; last Sun in Jun) Two groups in medieval costume contend for the Ponte di Mezzo in Pisa.

Infiorata (Flower Festival; 21 Jun) To celebrate Corpus Domini some towns (including Bolsena and Genzano near Rome, Spello in Umbria and Noto in Sicily) decorate a street with colourful designs made with flower petals.

Festa di San Giovanni (p477; 24 Jun) Celebrated with the lively Calcio Storico, a series of medieval football–style matches played on Florence's Piazza di Santa Croce.

Festival dei Due Mondi (Festival of Two Worlds; p571) An international arts event held in June and July in Spoleto, featuring music, theatre, dance and art.

Palio delle Quattro Antiche Repubbliche Marinare (Regatta of the Four Ancient Maritime Republics) A procession of boats and a race between the four historical maritime rivals: Pisa, Venice, Amalfi and Genoa. The event rotates between the four towns: Pisa in 2006, Venice in 2007, Genoa in 2008 and Amalfi in 2009. Although usually held in June, it has been known to be delayed as late as September.

July

Il Palio (p518; 2 Jul) A dangerous bareback horse race around the piazza in Siena, preceded by a parade of supporters in traditional costume.

Ardia (p831; 6-7 Jul) More dangerous than Il Palio, this impressive and chaotic horse race (accompanied by gunshots) at Sedilo celebrates the victory of the Roman Emperor Constantine over Maxentius in AD 312.

Festa del Redentore (p364; 3rd weekend In Jul) One of Venice's most popular traditional festivities, marked with an extraordinary fireworks display over the Bacino di San Marco. A pontoon bridge is built to connect the Giudecca (the Chiesa del Redentore) with the rest of Venice.

Festival Internazionale del Balleto (International Ballet Festival) This festival held in Nervi, near Genoa features international performers.

Taormina Arte (p782) Films, theatrical events and music concerts from an impressive list of international names are on show in Sicily.

August

Quintana (p594; Medieval Joust; 1st Sun in Aug) A parade of hundreds of people in 15th-century costume, followed by a jousting tournament, is held at Ascoli Piceno.

I Candelieri (The Candlesticks; p839; 14 Aug) Town representatives in Sassari dress in medieval costume and carry huge wooden columns through the town.

Il Palio (p518; 16 Aug) A repeat of the famous horse race is held in Siena.

Festa del Redentore (p846; 28-29 Aug) Held in Nuoro, this folk festival is attended by thousands of people, dressed in traditional costume, from all over the island.

Mostra del Cinema di Venezia (Venice International Film Festival; p364) Held at the Lido, the festival attracts the international film glitterati and is when Venetians do a year's cinema-going in a couple of weeks.

September
Palio della Balestra (1st Sun Sep) Sansepolcro in Tuscany hosts a rematch with crossbow sharpshooters from Gubbio.
Regata Storica (Historic Regatta; p364; 1st Sun in Sep) A magnificent parade of boats in period dress followed by gondola and other boat races along the Grand Canal in Venice.

October
Salone Internazionale del Gusto (p232; biennially every Oct) Turin is the stage for this celebration of good food, quality products and fine cooking. The home-grown anti–fast food organisation, the Slow Food Movement, hosts this international sybarites' get-together.

November
Festa della Madonna della Salute (p364; 21 Nov) A procession – over a pontoon bridge – to the Chiesa di Santa Maria della Salute in Venice gives thanks for the city's deliverance from plague in 1630.
Festa di Santa Cecilia (p518) A series of concerts and exhibitions in Siena to honour the patron saint of musicians.

December
Natale (Christmas) During the weeks preceding Christmas there are numerous processions and religious events. Many churches set up elaborate cribs or nativity scenes known as *presepi* – Naples is famous for these. From the first week in December there is a toy fair in Piazza Navona (Rome) where you can buy handmade nativity scenes.

FOOD
Eating is one of life's great pleasures for Italians, and if it wasn't already for you, it soon will be. Be adventurous and don't be intimidated by eccentric waiters or indecipherable menus and you will agree with the locals that nowhere in the world has food as good as Italy. For some mouth-watering information on what's cooking, see p80.

For large cities and towns, restaurant listings in this book are given in the order: budget (up to €20), midrange (€20 to €45) and top end (over €45). These figures are arbitrary and represent a halfway point between the very expensive cities of Milan and Venice and the considerably cheaper towns across the south. Indeed, a restaurant rated as midrange in one place might be considered as cheap as chips in Milan! Within each section the restaurants are listed in order of preference, for small towns, listings are given in order of best first.

GAY & LESBIAN TRAVELLERS
Homosexuality is legal in Italy and well tolerated in the major cities. However, overt displays of affection by homosexual couples could attract a negative response in the more conservative south and in the smaller towns. The legal age of consent is 16. A few years ago the gay capitals of Italy were Milan and Bologna, but Rome is now giving both cities some strong competition.

There are gay clubs in Rome, Milan and Bologna, and a handful in places such as Florence. Some coastal towns and resorts (such as the Tuscan town of Viareggio) have more action in summer. For clues, track down local gay organisations or publications such as *Pride*, a national monthly magazine, and *AUT* published by Circolo Mario Mieli in Rome. The useful website http://it.gay.com (in Italian) lists gay bars and hotels across the country. A worthy organisation is: **Arci-Gay & Arci-Lesbica** (☎ 051 649 3055; www.arcigay.it; Via Don Minzoni 18, Bologna), a national organisation for gay men and lesbians.

HOLIDAYS
Most Italians take their annual holiday in August. This means that many businesses and shops close for at least a part of that month. Larger cities, notably Milan and Rome, are left to the tourists, who may be frustrated that many restaurants and shops are closed until early September. One advantage is that hotels often drop their rates considerably! The *Settimana Santa* (Easter Week) is another busy holiday period for Italians. Beware of school holiday periods (especially Easter), when large groups of children noisily prowl the cultural sights.

Individual towns have public holidays to celebrate the feasts of their patron saints (see p862). National public holidays include the following:
New Year's Day (Capodanno or Anno Nuovo) 1 January
Epiphany (Epifania or Befana) 6 January
Easter Monday (Pasquetta or Lunedì dell'Angelo) March/April
Liberation Day (Giorno della Liberazione) April 25 – marks the Allied Victory in Italy, and the end of the German presence and Mussolini, in 1945
Labour Day (Festa del Lavoro) 1 May
Republic Day (Festa della Repubblica) 2 June

Feast of the Assumption (Assunzione or Ferragosto) 15 August
All Saints' Day (Ognissanti) 1 November
Feast of the Immaculate Conception (Immaculata Concezione) 8 December
Christmas Day (Natale) 25 December
Boxing Day (Festa di Santo Stefano) 26 December

INSURANCE

A travel-insurance policy to cover theft, loss and medical problems is a good idea. It may also cover you for cancellation or delays to your travel arrangements. Paying for your ticket with a credit card can often provide limited travel accident insurance and you may be able to reclaim the payment if the operator doesn't deliver. Ask your credit-card company what it will cover.

All foreigners have the same right as Italians to free emergency medical treatment in a public hospital. The E111 was replaced in 2005 by the European Health Insurance Card (EHIC). EU citizens (and those of Switzerland, Norway and Iceland) are entitled to the full range of healthcare services in public hospitals free of charge, but you will need to present your EHIC form (inquire at your national health service before leaving home). Australia has a reciprocal arrangement with Italy that entitles Australian citizens to free public healthcare – carry your Medicare card.

INTERNET ACCESS

If you plan to carry your notebook or palmtop computer with you, carry a universal AC adaptor for your appliance (most are sold with these). If using a modem, the Italian phone jack is the standard RJ-11 type.

Major Internet service providers such as **AOL** (www.aol.com) and **CompuServe** (www.compuserve.com) have dial-in nodes in Rome and Milan; download a list before you leave home. If you access your Internet email account at home through a smaller ISP or your office or school network, your best option is either to open an account with a global ISP, like those mentioned above, or to rely on Internet cafés to collect your mail.

If you intend to rely on Internet cafés, you'll need to carry three pieces of information: your incoming (POP or IMAP) mail server name, your account name and your password. Your ISP or network supervisor will be able to give you these.

You will find Internet cafés throughout Italy; prices hover around the €5 to €8 mark per hour. For some useful Internet addresses, see p22.

LEGAL MATTERS

For many Italians, finding ways to get around the law (any law) is a way of life. Few people pay attention to speed limits; most motorcyclists and many drivers don't stop at red lights. No-one bats an eyelid about littering or dogs pooping in the middle of the pavement, although many municipal governments have introduced laws against these things. But these are only minor transgressions when measured against the country's organised crime, tax evasion and corruption in government and business.

The average tourist will only have a brush with the law if they are robbed by a bagsnatcher or pickpocket.

Drink & Drugs

Although Italy's drug laws are relatively lenient, drugs are seriously frowned upon, in part due to the heroin problem (most notable in Naples and the poorer south) created by the Mafia's lucrative business. Although a 'few' grams of cannabis or marijuana are permissible for personal use, there is nothing to say how much a few grams is and it is better to avoid the risks altogether given the fact that the police can hold you for as long as it takes to analyse your case. If the police further decide that you are a dealer you could end up in prison.

The legal limit for blood-alcohol level is 0.05% and random breath tests do occur.

Police

If you run into trouble in Italy, you are likely to end up dealing with either the *polizia statale* (state police) or the *carabinieri* (military police).

The *polizia* are a civil force, take their orders from the Ministry of the Interior, and generally deal with thefts, visa extensions and permissions. They wear powder-blue trousers with a fuchsia stripe and a navy-blue jacket. Details of police stations, or *questure*, are given throughout this book.

The *carabinieri* are more concerned with civil obedience. They deal with general crime, public order and drug enforcement. They wear a black uniform with a red stripe and

DIRECTORY

drive dark-blue cars also with a red stripe. They are based in a *caserma* (barracks), a reflection of their military status. One of the big differences between the police and *carabinieri* is the latter's reach – even many villages have a *carabinieri* post.

Other police include the *vigili urbani*, basically local traffic police. You will have to deal with them if you get a parking ticket or your car is towed away. The *guardia di finanza* are responsible for fighting tax evasion and drug smuggling. The *guardia forestale*, aka *corpo forestale*, are responsible for enforcing laws concerning forests and the environment in general.

For national emergency numbers, see the inside front cover.

Your Rights

Italy still has antiterrorism laws on its books that could make life difficult if you are detained. You can be held for 48 hours without a magistrate being informed and you can be interrogated without the presence of a lawyer. It is difficult to obtain bail and you can be held legally for up to three years without being brought to trial.

MAPS
City Maps

The city maps in this book, combined with tourist office maps, are generally adequate. More detailed maps are available in Italy at good bookshops, such as Feltrinelli. De Agostini, Touring Club Italiano (TCI) and Michelin all publish detailed city maps. TCI publishes *200 Piante di Città*, a handy book of street plans covering pretty much any city. Lonely Planet publishes City Maps to Rome and Venice.

Road Atlases

If you are driving around Italy, the Automobile Association's (AA) *Road Atlas Italy*, available in the UK, is scaled at 1:250,000 and includes 39 town maps. Just as good is

Michelin's *Tourist and Motoring Atlas Italy*, scaled at 1:300,000, with 78 town maps.

In Italy, the Istituto Geografico de Agostini publishes a comprehensive *Atlante Turistico Stradale d'Italia* (1:250,000), which includes 145 city maps. TCI publishes an *Atlante Stradale d'Italia* (1:200,000) divided into three parts – Nord, Centro and Sud (€18 each). It also publishes *Autoatlante d'Italia*, a road/street directory for the whole country on a scale of 1:1,350,000. It includes 206 city maps.

Small-Scale Maps

Michelin has a series of good fold-out country maps. No 988 covers the whole country on a scale of 1:1,000,000. You could also consider the series of area maps at 1:400,000 – Nos 428 to 431 cover the mainland, 432 covers Sicily and 433 Sardinia. TCI publishes a decent map covering Italy, Switzerland and Slovenia at 1:800,000, as well as a series of regional maps at 1:200,000 (€7).

Walking Maps

Maps of walking trails in the Alps and Apennines are available at all major bookshops in Italy, but the best by far are the TCI bookshops.

The best walking maps are the 1:25,000 scale series published by Tabacco (mainly covering the north). Kompass publishes 1:25,000 scale maps of various parts of Italy, as well as a 1:50,000 series and several in other scales (including one at 1:7500 of Capri). Edizioni Multigraphic Florence produces a series of walking maps concentrating mainly on the Apennines.

The series of *Guide dei Monti d'Italia*, grey hardbacks published by the TCI and Club Alpino Italiano, are exhaustive walking guides with maps.

MONEY

As in the 11 other EU nations (Austria, Belgium, Finland, France, Germany, Greece, Ireland, Luxembourg, Netherlands, Portugal and Spain), the euro has been Italy's currency since 2002. By mid-2005 it had risen to record levels against the US dollar. The seven euro notes come in denominations of €500, €200, €100, €50, €20, €10 and €5, in different colours and sizes. The eight euro coins are in denominations of €2 and €1, and 50, 20, 10, five, two and one cents.

Exchange rates are given on the inside front cover of this book. For the latest rates, check out www.oanda.com. For some hints on costs in Italy, turn to p20.

Cash

There is little advantage in bringing foreign cash into Italy. True, exchange commissions are often lower than for travellers cheques but the danger of losing the lot far outweighs such gains.

Credit & Debit Cards

Credit and debit cards can be used in a *bancomat* (ATM) displaying the appropriate sign – Visa and MasterCard are among the most widely recognised, but others such as Cirrus and Maestro are also well covered. Only some banks give cash advances over the counter, so you will be much better off using ATMs armed with your PIN. Cards are also good for payment in most hotels, restaurants, shops, supermarkets and highway tollbooths.

Check any charges with your bank. Most banks now build in a fee of around 2.75% into every foreign transaction. In addition, ATM withdrawals can attract a further fee, usually around 1.5%.

It is not uncommon for ATMs in Italy to reject foreign cards. Try a few more ATMs displaying your card's logo before assuming the problem lies with your card.

If your card is lost, stolen or swallowed by an ATM, you can telephone toll free to have an immediate stop put on its use. For MasterCard the number in Italy is ☎ 800 870 866, for Visa it's ☎ 800 819 014. For Diners Club, call either ☎ 06 357 53 33 (in Rome) or reverse-charges to the country of issue (☎ 702 797 55 32 in the USA).

American Express (Amex) is also widely accepted (although not as commonly as Visa or MasterCard). If you lose your Amex card, call ☎ 800 864 046.

Moneychangers

You can change money in banks, at the post office or in a *cambio* (exchange office). Post offices and most banks are reliable and tend to offer the best rates. Commission fluctuates and depends on whether you are changing cash or cheques. Generally post office commissions are lowest and the exchange rate reasonable. The main advantage of exchange offices is the longer hours they keep, but watch for absurdly high commissions and inferior rates.

Taxes & Refunds

A value-added tax of around 19%, known as IVA (Imposta di Valore Aggiunto), is slapped onto just about everything in Italy. If you are a non-EU resident and spend more than €155 on a purchase, you can claim a refund when you leave. The refund only applies to purchases from affiliated retail outlets that display a 'tax free for tourists' (or similar) sign. You have to complete a form at the point of sale, then get it stamped by Italian customs as you leave. At major airports you can then get an immediate cash refund; otherwise it will be refunded to your credit card. For information, pick up a pamphlet on the scheme from participating stores.

Tipping

You are not expected to tip on top of restaurant service charges but you can leave a little extra if you feel service warrants it. If there is no service charge, the customer should consider leaving a 10% tip, but this is not obligatory. In bars, Italians often leave small change as a tip, maybe only €0.10. Tipping taxi drivers is not common practice, but you are expected to tip the porter at top-end hotels.

Travellers Cheques

Traditionally a safe way to carry money and possibly not a bad idea as a backup, travellers cheques have been outmoded by plastic. Various readers have reported having trouble changing travellers cheques in Italy and it seems most banks now apply hefty commissions, even on cheques denominated in euros.

If you wish to carry cheques, Visa, Travelex and Amex are widely accepted. The best idea is probably to spread funds across one or more debit/credit cards and a fistful of cheques for emergencies.

Strangely, several readers have reported having more problems with cheques denominated in euros than in US dollars. Whatever they are in, cheques can be difficult to change in smaller towns.

Get most of your cheques in fairly large denominations to save on per-cheque commission charges. Amex exchange offices do not charge commission to exchange travellers cheques (even other brands) or cash equivalent of US$500 or above.

It's vital to keep your initial receipt, along with a record of your cheque numbers and the ones you have used, separate from the cheques themselves. Take along your passport as identification when you go to cash travellers cheques.

For lost or stolen cheques, call:

Amex (☎ 800 72 000)
MasterCard (☎ 800 870 866)
Travelex (☎ 800 335 511)
Visa (☎ 800 874 155)

POST

Le Poste (☎ 803160; www.poste.it), Italy's postal system, is not as reliable as it could be but has improved much down the years. The most efficient mail service is *posta prioritaria* (priority mail).

Francobolli (stamps) are available at post offices and authorised tobacconists (look for the official *tabacchi* sign: a big 'T', usually white on black). Since letters often need to be weighed, what you get at the tobacconist's for international air mail will occasionally be an approximation of the proper rate. Tobacconists keep regular shop hours.

Postal Rates & Services

The cost of sending a letter by *via aerea* (airmail) depends on its weight and where it is being sent. For regular post, letters up to 20g cost €0.45 within Europe, €0.65 to Africa, Asia, North and South America and €0.70 to Australia and New Zealand. Postcards cost the same.

Few people use the regular post, preferring the slightly more expensive *posta prioritaria*, guaranteed to deliver letters sent to Europe within three days and to the rest of the world within four to eight days. Letters up to 20g sent *posta prioritaria* cost €0.62 within Europe, €0.80 to Africa, Asia, the Americas and €1 to Australia and New Zealand. Letters weighing 21g to 50g cost €0.85/1.45 (standard/priority) within Europe, €1/1.50 to Africa, Asia and the Americas, and €1.20/1.80 to Australia and New Zealand.

Receiving Mail

Poste restante (general delivery) is known as *fermo posta* in Italy. Letters marked thus will be held at the counter of the same name in the main post office in the relevant town. Poste restante mail to Verona, for example, should be addressed as follows:

John SMITH,
Fermo Posta,
37100 Verona,
Italy

You will need to pick up your letters in person and you must present your passport or national ID.

Amex card or travellers cheque holders can use the free client mail-holding service at Amex offices. You can obtain a list of these from any Amex office. Take your passport with you when you go to pick up mail.

SHOPPING

Italy is a shopper's paradise, so bring your plastic well charged up and even an empty bag for your purchases (or just buy a new one while in Italy).

Fashion is probably one of the first things that springs to the mind of the serious retail lover. The big cities and tourist centres, especially Milan, Rome and Florence, are home to countless designer boutiques spilling over with clothes, shoes and accessories by all the great Italian names, and many equally enticing unknowns!

Foodies and wine-lovers will want to bring home some souvenirs for the kitchen ranging from fine Parma ham to aromatic cheeses, from class wines (especially from Tuscany, Piedmont and the Veneto) to local tipples (such as Benevento's La Strega, grappa from Bassano del Grappa, or *limoncello*, the lemon-based liquor common in Naples and Sicily as well as other parts of the south).

Many cities and provinces offer specialised products. Sicily springs to mind for its ceramics, as does the town of Gubbia in Umbria. Shoes and leather goods are one of Florence's big calling cards. In Venice, seek out beautifully handmade Carnevale masks, along with the famous Murano glass and Burano lace.

SOLO TRAVELLERS

The main disadvantage for solo travellers in Italy is the higher price they generally pay for accommodation. A single room in a hotel or *pensione* usually costs around two-thirds of the price of a double.

TELEPHONE
Domestic Calls

Rates, particularly for long-distance telephone calls, are among the highest in Europe. From private phones, local calls cost between €0.01 and €0.02 per minute depending on the time of day. National calls are between €0.03 and €0.11. A *comunicazione urbana* (local call) from a public payphone costs €0.10 every minute and 12.5 seconds. For a *comunicazione interurbana* (long distance) call within Italy you pay €0.10 when the call is answered and then €0.10 every 57 seconds thereafter.

Telephone area codes all begin with 0 and consist of up to four digits. The area code is followed by a number of anything from four to eight digits. Area codes, including the 0, are an integral part of all telephone numbers in Italy. Mobile phone numbers begin with a three-digit prefix such as 330. Toll-free (free-phone) numbers are known as *numeri verdi* and usually start with 800. National call rate numbers start with 848 or 199. Some six-digit national rate numbers are also in use (such as those for rail and postal information).

For national directory inquiries, telephone ☎ 12.

International Calls

Direct international calls can easily be made from public telephones by using a phonecard. Dial ☎ 00 to get out of Italy, then the relevant country and area codes, followed by the telephone number.

A three-minute call from a payphone to most European countries and North America will cost about €2.10. Australasia would cost €2.80. Calling from a private phone is cheaper. You are better off using your country's direct-dialling services paid for at home-country rates (such as AT&T in the USA and Telstra in Australia). Get the access numbers before you leave home.

To make a reverse-charges (collect) international call from a public telephone, dial ☎ 170. All phone operators speak English. In Italy, the number for international directory inquiries is ☎ 176.

To call Italy from abroad call the international access number (usually 00), Italy's country code (☎ 39) and then the area code of the location you want, including the leading 0.

TAKING YOUR MOBILE PHONE

Italy uses GSM 900/1800, which is compatible with the rest of Europe and Australia but not with North American GSM 1900 or the totally different Japanese system (though some GSM 1900/900 phones do work here). If you have a GSM phone, check with your service provider about using it in Italy and beware of calls being routed internationally (very expensive for a 'local' call).

Mobile Phones

Italy has one of the highest levels of mobile phone penetration in Europe, and there are four main companies through which you can get a temporary or prepaid account if you already own a GSM, dual- or tri-band cellular phone. You will usually need your passport to open an account. Always check with your mobile service provider in your home country to ascertain whether your handset allows use of another SIM card (usually they do not). If yours does, it can cost as little as €10 to activate a local prepaid SIM card (sometimes with €10 worth of calls on the card!).

Of the four main mobile phone companies TIM (Telecom Italia Mobile) and Vodafone-Omnitel have the densest networks of outlets across the country.

Payphones & Phonecards

Partly privatised Telecom Italia is the largest telecommunications organisation in Italy and its orange public payphones are liberally scattered about the country. The most common accept only *carte/schede telefoniche* (phonecards), although you'll still find some that take cards and coins. A few cardphones accept credit cards.

Telecom payphones can be found in the streets, train stations and some stores as well as in Telecom offices. Where these offices are staffed, it is possible to make international calls and pay at the desk afterwards. You can buy phonecards (€1, €2.50, €3, €5 or €7.50) at post offices, tobacconists and newsstands. You must break off the top left-hand corner of the card before you can use it. Phonecards have an expiry date, usually this is 31st December or 30th June depending on when you purchase the card.

Public phones operated by the private telecommunications companies Infostrada

DIRECTORY

and Albacom can be found in airports and at stations. These phones accept Infostrada or Albacom phonecards (available from post offices, tobacconists and newspaper stands). The rates are slightly cheaper than Telecom's for long-distance and international calls.

You will find cut-price call centres in all of the main cities. Rates can be considerably lower than from Telecom payphones for international calls. You simply place your call from a private booth inside the centre and pay for it when you've finished. Alternatively, ask about international calling cards at newsstands and tobacconists. They can be hit and miss but are sometimes good value.

TIME

Italy is one hour ahead of GMT. Daylight-saving time, when clocks are moved forward one hour, starts on the last Sunday in March. Clocks are put back an hour on the last Sunday in October. Italy operates on a 24-hour clock.

TOURIST INFORMATION
Local Tourist Offices

The quality of tourist offices in Italy varies dramatically. One office might have enthusiastic staff but no useful printed information, while indifferent staff in another might have a gold mine of brochures.

Three tiers of tourist office exist: regional, provincial and local. They have different names, but roughly offer the same services, with the exception of regional offices, which are generally concerned with promotion, planning and budgeting. Throughout this book, offices are referred to as tourist offices rather than by their more elaborate titles. Most tourist offices will respond to written and telephone requests for information.

Azienda Autonoma di Soggiorno e Turismo
(AAST) The local tourist office in many towns and cities of the south. They have town-specific information and should also know about bus routes and museum opening times.

Azienda di Promozione Turistica (APT) The provincial (ie main) tourist office should have information on the town you are in and the surrounding province.

Informazione e Assistenza ai Turisti (IAT) Local tourist office branches in towns and cities, mostly in the northern half of Italy.

Pro Loco This is the local office in small towns and villages and is similar to the AAST office.

Tourist offices are generally open 8.30am to 12.30pm or 1pm and 3pm to 7pm Monday to Friday. Hours are usually extended in summer, when some offices also open on Saturday or Sunday. In the more popular tourist destinations hours in some offices can be more generous.

Information booths at most major train stations tend to keep similar hours but in some cases operate only in summer. Staff can usually provide a city map, list of hotels and information on the major sights.

English, and sometimes French or German, is spoken at tourist offices in larger towns and major tourist areas. German is spoken in Alto Adige and French in much of the Valle d'Aosta. Printed information is generally provided in a variety of languages.

Regional Tourist Authorities

As a rule, the regional tourist authorities are more concerned with planning and marketing than offering a public information service, with work done at a provincial and local level. Addresses of local tourist offices appear throughout the guide. Following are some useful regional websites, allowing you to get to know the regions and access provincial and local tourist offices, as well as host of other tourism-related links. In some cases you need to look for the Tourism or Turismo link within the regional site. At the website of the **Italian National Tourist Office** (www.enit .it) you can find details of all provincial and local tourist offices across the country.

Abruzzo (www.regione.abruzzo.it in Italian)
Basilicata (www.basilicatanet.it in Italian)
Calabria (www.turismo.regione.calabria.it)
Campania (www.turismoregionecampania.it)
Emilia-Romagna (www.emiliaromagnaturismo.it)
Friuli-Venezia Giulia (www.turismo.fvg.it)
Lazio (www.turislazio.it)
Le Marche (www.le-marche.com)
Liguria (www.turismo.liguriainrete.it)
Lombardy (www.turismo.regione.lombardia.it)
Molise (www.regione.molise.it in Italian)
Piedmont (www.regione.piemonte.it/turismo in Italian)
Puglia (www.pugliaturismo.com)
Sardinia (www.regione.sardegna.it/tematiche/turismo in Italian)
Sicily (www.regione.sicilia.it/turismo)
Trentino-Alto Adige (www.trentino.to, www.provincia .bz.it)
Tuscany (www.turismo.toscana.it)
Umbria (www.umbria.org)

Valle d'Aosta (www.regione.vda.it/turismo)
Veneto (http://turismo.regione.veneto.it)

Tourist Offices Abroad

Information on Italy is available from the **Italian National Tourist Office** (ENIT; ☎ 06 4 97 11; www.enit.it; Via Marghera 2, Rome 00185) in the following countries.

Australia (☎ 02-9262 1666; italia@italiantourism.com.au; Level 4, 46 Market St, Sydney, NSW 2000)

Austria (☎ 01-505 16 30 12; delegation.wien@enit.at; Kaerntnerring 4, Vienna, A-1010)

Canada (☎ 416-925 4882; www.italiantourism.com; Suite 907, South Tower, 175 Bloor St East, Toronto, M4W 3R8)

France (☎ 01 42 66 03 96; www.enit-france.com in French; 23 rue de la Paix, Paris, 75002)

Germany Berlin (☎ 030-83 98; www.enit.de in German; Kontorhaus Mitte, Friedrichstrasse 187, 10117); Frankfurt (☎ 069-259 126; Kaiserstrasse 65, 60329); Munich (☎ 089-531 317; Lenbachplatz 2, 80336)

Japan (☎ 03-3478 2051; 2-7-14 Minamiayoama, Minato-ku, Tokyo, 107)

The Netherlands (☎ 020-616 82 44; enitams@wirehub .nl; Stadhouderskade 2, Amsterdam, 1054 ES)

Switzerland (☎ 043 466 40 40; info@enit.ch; Urania-strasse 32, Zurich, 8001)

UK (☎ 020-7408 1254; italy@italiantouristboard.co.uk; 1 Princes St, London, W1B 9AY)

USA Chicago (☎ 312-644 0996; www.italiantourism.com; 500 North Michigan Avenue, Suite 2240, IL 60611); Los Angeles (☎ 310-820 1898; 12400 Wilshire Blvd, Suite 550, CA 90025); New York (☎ 212-245 4822; 630 Fifth Ave, Suite 1565, NY 10111)

VISAS

Italy is among the 15 countries that have signed the Schengen Convention, an agreement whereby 13 EU member countries (excluding the UK, Ireland and the 10 new members that entered the union in 2004) plus Iceland and Norway agreed to abolish checks at common borders. Legal residents of one Schengen country do not require a visa for another. Citizens of the remaining 12 EU countries are also exempt. Nationals of some other countries, including Australia, Brazil, Canada, Israel, Japan, New Zealand, Switzerland and the USA, do not require visas for tourist visits of up to 90 days.

All non-EU nationals entering Italy for any reason other than tourism (such as study or work) should contact an Italian consulate, as they may need a specific visa. They should also insist on having their passport stamped on entry as, without a stamp, they could encounter problems when trying to obtain a residence permit (*permesso di soggiorno*).

The standard tourist visa is valid for up to 90 days. A Schengen visa issued by one Schengen country is generally valid for travel in other Schengen countries. However, individual Schengen countries may impose additional restrictions on certain nationalities. It is therefore worth checking visa regulations with the consulate of each country you plan to visit.

You must apply for a Schengen visa in your country of residence. You can apply for no more than two Schengen visas in any 12-month period and they are not renewable inside Italy. If you are going to visit more than one Schengen country, you should apply for the visa at a consulate of your main destination country or the first country you intend to visit.

For more information on the wonderful world of Schengen visas, check out www .eurovisa.info/SchengenCountries.htm.

EU citizens do not require any permits to live or work in Italy. They are, however, required to register with a police station if they take up residence and obtain a *permesso di soggiorno* (see below).

Copies

All important documents (passport data page and visa page, credit cards, travel insurance policy, tickets, driver's licence etc) should be photocopied before you leave home. Leave a copy with someone at home and keep one with you, separate from the originals.

Permesso di Soggiorno

If you are planning to stay at the same address for more than one week you are supposed to report to the police station to receive a *permesso di soggiorno* (a permit to remain in the country). Tourists staying in hotels are not required to do this.

A *permesso di soggiorno* only really becomes a necessity if you plan to study, work (legally) or live in Italy. Obtaining one is never a pleasant experience; it involves long queues and the frustration of arriving at the counter only to find you don't have the necessary documents.

Even EU citizens who decide to stay in Italy for any length of time are supposed to have a permit, although for them the bureaucracy is greatly eased.

The exact requirements, such as specific documents and *marche da bollo* (the official stamps), can change from year to year. In general you will need: a valid passport (if possible containing a visa stamp indicating your date of entry into Italy), a special visa issued in your own country if you are planning to study (for non-EU citizens), four passport-size photographs and proof of your ability to support yourself financially. You can apply at the *ufficio stranieri* (foreigners' bureau) of the police station closest to where you are staying.

Study Visas

Non-EU citizens who want to study at a university or language school in Italy must have a study visa. These visas can be obtained from your nearest Italian embassy or consulate. You will normally require confirmation of your enrolment, proof of payment of fees and adequate funds to support yourself before a visa is issued. The visa covers only the period of the enrolment. This type of visa is renewable within Italy but, again, only with confirmation of ongoing enrolment and proof that you are able to support yourself (bank statements are preferred).

WOMEN TRAVELLERS

Italy is not a dangerous country for women to travel in. Clearly, as with anywhere in the world, women travelling alone need to take certain precautions and, in some parts of the country, be prepared for more than their fair share of unwanted attention. Eye-to-eye contact is the norm in Italy's daily flirtatious interplay. Eye contact can become outright staring the further south you travel.

Lone women may simply find it difficult to remain alone. In many places, local lotharios will try it on with exasperating insistence. This can be flattering, or a pain, especially the latter if persistent. Foreign women are particular objects of male attention in tourist towns like Florence and more generally in the south. Usually the best response to undesired advances is to ignore them. If that doesn't work, politely tell your undesired interlocutors that you are waiting for your *marito* (husband) or *fidanzato* (boyfriend) and, if necessary, walk away. Avoid becoming aggressive as this may result in an unpleasant confrontation. If all else fails, approach the nearest member of the police.

Watch out for men with wandering hands on crowded buses. Either keep your back to the wall or make a loud fuss if someone starts fondling your backside. A loud '*Che schifo!*' (How disgusting!) will usually do the trick. If a more serious incident occurs, make a report to the police, who are then required to press charges.

Women travelling alone should use their common sense. Avoid walking alone in dark streets, and look for hotels that are central (unsafe areas are noted in this book). Women should avoid hitchhiking alone. Use some dress sense, too. Skimpy beachwear is not a good idea in the south (except perhaps at the beach!), and especially in more conservative areas, such as the smaller towns.

WORK

It is illegal for non-EU citizens to work in Italy without a *permesso di lavoro* (work permit), but trying to obtain one can be time consuming. EU citizens are allowed to work in Italy but they still need a *permesso di soggiorno* from the main police station in the town and a *codice fiscale* (tax-file number).

Immigration laws require foreign workers to be 'legalised' through their employers, and this applies even to cleaners and babysitters. The employers then pay pension and health-insurance contributions. This doesn't mean there aren't employers willing to take people without the right papers.

Work options depend on a number of factors (eg location, length of stay, nationality and qualifications) but, in the major cities at least, job possibilities for English speakers can be surprisingly plentiful. Go armed with a CV (if possible in Italian) and be persistent.

Jobs are advertised in local newspapers and magazines, such as Rome's *Porta Portese* (weekly) and *Wanted in Rome* (fortnightly) or *Secondamano* in Milan, and you can also place an ad yourself. A useful guide is *Living, Studying and Working in Italy* by Travis Neighbor Ward and Monica Larner.

The most easily secured jobs are short-term work in bars, hostels, on farms, babysitting and even volunteering (in return for accommodation and some expenses paid). The other obvious work source for English-speaking foreigners is teaching English. However, most of the more reputable language schools will only hire people who hold a work permit. The more professional schools will require you to have a TEFL (Teaching English as a Foreign Language) certificate.

Some useful organisations to start the job hunt:

Au Pair International (☎ 051 26 75 75; www.au-pair -international.com; Via Santo Stefano 32, Bologna) Organises au pair jobs in Italian families for women aged 18 to 30. EU citizens are preferred, but citizens of countries such as Australia, Canada and the USA can be placed for up to three months.

British Institutes (☎ 02 7209 4595; www.british institutes.it; Via Carducci 5, Milan) Recruits English-speaking teachers. Italian essential.

Center for Cultural Exchange (☎ 630-377 2272; www.cci-exchange.com; 17 North Second Ave, St Charles, Illinois 60174) A nonprofit cultural-exchange organisation that offers short-term internships in Italy.

Concordia International Volunteer Projects (☎ 01273 422218; www.concordia-iye.org.uk; 20-22 Boundary Rd, Hove, UK) Short-term community-based projects covering the environment, archaeology and the arts. UK applicants only.

European Youth Portal (http://europa.eu.int/youth /working/index_eu_en.html) Has various links suggesting

work options across Europe. You can narrow down the Europewide search to Italy, where you will find pages of general work links and more specific links on things like au pair opportunities and seasonal work.

Italian Association for Education, Exchanges & Intercultural Activities (AFSAI; ☎ 06 537 03 32; www.afsai.it; Viale dei Colli Portuensi 345, B2) Financed by the EU, this voluntary programme runs projects of six to 12 months for those aged between 16 and 25 years. Knowledge of Italian is required.

Mix Culture Au Pair Service (☎ 06 47 88 22 89; Via Nazionale 204, Rome) Posts from six months to a year. Enrolment in a language school is necessary to obtain the required visa.

Recruitaly (www.recruitaly.it) For graduates looking for long-term employment in Italy, this useful website links up to professional employers.

The Cambridge School (☎ 045 800 31 54; www .cambridgeschool.it; Via Rosmini 6, Verona) Another major employer of English teachers.

World Wide Organisation of Organic Farming (www.wwoof.org) For a membership fee of €25 this organisation provides a list of farms looking for volunteer workers who receive food and board in exchange for labour.

Transport

TRANSPORT

GETTING THERE & AWAY

Competition between the airlines means you should be able to pick up a reasonably priced fare to Italy, even if you are coming from as far away as Australia. If you live in Europe, you can also travel overland by car, bus or train.

WARNING

The information in this chapter is particularly vulnerable to change: prices for international travel are volatile, routes are introduced and cancelled, schedules change, special deals come and go, and rules and visa requirements are amended. You should check directly with the airline or a travel agent to make sure you understand how a fare (and the ticket you may buy) works and be aware of the security requirements for international travel.

You should get quotes from as many airlines and travel agents as possible. The details given in this chapter should be regarded as pointers and not a substitute for your own careful, up-to-date research.

ENTERING THE COUNTRY

Entering Italy is relatively simple. Airport customs have tightened up a bit since 9/11, but land crossings from neighbouring EU countries don't require a passport check.

Passport

Citizens of the EU member states can travel to Italy with their national identity cards. People from countries that do not issue ID cards, such as the UK or USA, must carry a valid passport. All non-EU nationals must have a full valid passport. If applying for a visa, check that the expiry date of your passport is at least some months off. See p871 for more information about obtaining a visa and permits for longer stays.

AIR

High season for air travel to Italy is June to September. Shoulder season will often run from mid-September to the end of October and again in April. Low season is generally November to March, but fares around Christmas and Easter often increase or are sold out well in advance.

Airports & Airlines

Italy's main intercontinental gateway is the **Leonardo da Vinci Airport** (Fiumicino; Map p179; ☎ 06 659 51; www.adr.it) in Rome, but regular intercontinental flights also serve Milan's **Malpensa airport** (Map p257; ☎ 02 748 522 00; www.sea-aeroporti milano.it). Plenty of flights from other European cities also go direct to regional capitals around the country.

Many European and international airlines compete with the country's national carrier, Alitalia. If an airline has intercontinental routes, it most likely flies to Fiumicino airport. From Aeroflot to Air Gabon, all planes truly do lead to Rome.

Following are some of the more frequent carriers:

Air Canada (AC; ☎ 06 55 1112, 800 919091; www.air canada.com)

Air France (AF; ☎ 848 88 44 66; www.airfrance.com)

Air Malta (KM; ☎ 06 488 4685; www.airmalta.com)

Air One (AP; ☎ 199 207080; www.flyairone.it)

Alitalia (AZ; ☎ 848 86 56 41, in Rome ☎ 06 6 56 41; www.alitalia.it)

American Airlines (AA; ☎ 06 6605 3169; www.aa.com)
British Airways (BA; ☎ 199 712 266; www.britishair
ways.com)
British Midland (BD; in UK ☎ 44-1332 854 000; www
.flybmi.com)
Delta Air Lines (DL; ☎ 800-477-999; www.delta.com)
EasyJet (U2; ☎ 848 887766; www.easyjet.com)
Emirates Airlines (EK; ☎ 06 4520 6060; www.emi
rates.com)
KLM (KL; ☎ 02 218 981; www.klm.com)
Lufthansa (LH; ☎ 06 6568 4004; www.lufthansa.com)
Meridiana (IG; ☎ 199 111 333; www.meridiana.it)
Qantas (QF; ☎ 06 5248 2725; www.qantas.com.au) Via
Hong Kong only.
Ryanair (FR; ☎ 899 678 910; www.ryanair.com)
Singapore Airlines (SQ; ☎ 06 478 55 360; www.singa
poreair.com)
Thai Airways International (TG; ☎ 064 781 3304;
www.thaiair.com)
United Airlines (UA; ☎ 848 800 629; www.united.com)
Virgin Express (TV; ☎ 800 097 097; www.virgin
-express.com)

Tickets

World aviation has never been so competitive and the Internet is fast becoming the
easiest way to locate and book reasonably
priced seats.

Full-time students and those under 26
years of age have access to discounted fares.
You have to show a document proving your
date of birth or a valid International Student Identity Card (ISIC) when buying your
ticket. Other cheap deals are the discounted
tickets released to travel agents and specialist
discount agencies. Most major cities carry
a Sunday travel section with ads for these
agencies, often known as brokers, consolidators or bucket shops. Also check the websites
directly for deals on low-cost carriers, such as
Ryanair and Easyjet.

Many of the major travel websites can
offer competitive fares, such as:
Booking Buddy (www.bookingbuddy.com)
Expedia (www.expedia.com)
Kayak (www.kayak.com)
Travelocity (www.travelocity.com)

Africa

From South Africa there are a host of major
airlines that fly to Italy, most notably: British
Airways from Cape Town and Johannesburg
through the UK; Air France with connections throughout Europe; and Lufthansa
from Cape Town, Durban and Johannesburg

connecting through Germany. Ethiopian
Airlines flies from Johannesburg through
Addis Ababa to Rome. Emirates Air flies
through Dubai to Rome. **Flight Centre** (☎ 0860
400 727; www.flightcentre.co.za) has offices in Johannesburg, Cape Town and Durban, while **STA
Travel** (www.statravel.co.za) has them in Johannesburg, Pretoria and Bloemfontein.

In Nairobi, **Flight Centre** (☎ 02-21 00 24) has
been in business for many years.

Asia

Bangkok, Singapore and Hong Kong are
the best places to shop around for discount
tickets. Cathay Pacific flies nonstop between
Hong Kong to Rome. **STA Travel** (www.statravel
.com) has offices in Hong Kong, Singapore,
Taiwan and Thailand. In Hong Kong many
travellers use the **Hong Kong Student Travel
Bureau** (☎ 2730 3269; www.hkst.com.hk in Chinese).

Singapore Air and Thai Airways both
serve most of Western Europe and also
have connecting flights with Australia and
New Zealand. Singapore Air flies direct to
Rome on Sunday, Tuesday and Friday from
May to October. Thai Airways runs a Bang-
kok to Rome nonstop flight Wednesday to
Monday March to October. In the off sea-
son, the frequency drops to Wednesday and
Friday only. They also have a nonstop to
Milan Malpensa from Bangkok on Sunday,
Tuesday and Friday year-round.

Similarly, discounted fares can be picked
up from Qantas which usually transits in
Kuala Lumpur, Bangkok or Singapore.

Australia

Cheap flights from Australia to Europe generally go via Southeast Asian capitals. Qantas, along with Alitalia, offer the only direct
flights from Melbourne and Sydney to Rome
but also try the Star Alliance carriers (such
as Thai Air, Singapore Airlines or Austrian
Air) or Malaysian Air. Flights from Perth are
generally a few hundred dollars cheaper.

Quite a few travel offices specialise in discount air tickets. Some travel agencies, particularly the smaller ones, advertise cheap
air fares in the travel sections of weekend
newspapers, such as the *Age* in Melbourne
and the *Sydney Morning Herald*.

STA Travel and Flight Centre are well
known for cheap fares. **STA Travel** (☎ 1300 733
035; www.statravel.com.au) has offices in all major
cities and on many university campuses.

Flight Centre (☎ 131 600; www.flightcentre.com.au) has dozens of offices throughout Australia.

Canada

Alitalia has direct flights to Rome and Milan from Toronto. Air Transat flies nonstop from Montreal to Rome in the summer months. Scan the budget travel agencies' advertisements in the *Toronto Globe & Mail*, the *Toronto Star* and the *Vancouver Province*.

Air Canada flies daily from Toronto to Rome, direct and via Montreal. British Airways, Air France, KLM and Lufthansa all fly to Italy via their respective home countries. Canada's main student travel organisation is **Travel Cuts** (☎ 800 667 2887; www.travelcuts.com), which has offices in all major cities.

Continental Europe

All national European carriers offer services to Italy. The largest of these, Air France, Lufthansa and KLM, have representative offices in major European cities. Italy's national carrier, Alitalia, has a huge range of offers on all European destinations. Several airlines, including Alitalia, Qantas and Air France, offer cut-rate fares between cities on the European legs of long-haul flights.

In France, both the student travel agencies **OTU Voyages** (☎ 0820 817 817; www.otu.fr in French) and **Travel Club Voyages** (☎ 0892 888 888; www .travelclub-voyages.com in French) are a safe bet for cut-price travel. In Germany, Munich is a haven of budget travel outlets such as **STA Travel** (www.statravel.de in German), which is one of the best and has offices throughout the country. **Kilroy Travel Group** (www.kilroygroups.com) offers discounted travel to people aged 16 to 33, and has representative offices in Denmark, Sweden, Norway, Finland and the Netherlands. In Athens, **ISYTS** (☎ 010 322 12 67; www.travelling.gr/isyts/) is the official International Student Youth Travel Service. **Virgin Express** (www.virgin-express.com) has a whole host of flights out of Brussels, including five daily flights to Rome. Details of its offices in Belgium, Denmark, France, Germany and Greece can be found on the website. If you are searching online, try www.budgettravel .com. Getting cheap flights between Spain and Italy is difficult – frequently the best-value flights are routed through another European city (such as Munich). In Madrid, one of the most reliable budget travel agencies is **Viajes Zeppelin** (☎ 902 38 42 53; www.viajeszep

pelin.com in Spanish), which also offers onward flights to South American destinations. The Italian airline, **Meridiana** (☎ 199 111 333; www .meridiana.it) has direct flights to Florence from Barcelona and Madrid.

New Zealand

Singapore Air flies from Auckland through Singapore to Rome's Fiumicino on Sunday, Tuesday and Friday from May to October. On New Zealand Air, you'll have to make at least two stops. The *New Zealand Herald* has a travel section in which travel agencies advertise fares. **Flight Centre** (☎ 0800 24 35 44; www.flightcentre.co.nz) has a large central office in Auckland and many other branches throughout the country. **STA Travel** (☎ 0800 24 35 44; www.statravel.co.nz) has offices in Auckland, as well as in Hamilton, Palmerston North, Wellington, Christchurch and Dunedin.

The UK & Ireland

Discount air travel is big business in London. Advertisements for many travel agencies appear in the travel pages of the weekend newspapers, such as the *Independent* and the *Guardian* on Saturday and the *Sunday Times*, as well as in publications such as *Time Out*, *The Big Issue* and *Exchange & Mart*.

STA Travel (☎ 0870 160 0599; www.statravel.co.uk) and **Trailfinders** (☎ 020 7292 18 88; www.trailfinders .com), both of which have offices throughout the UK, sell discounted and student tickets. Other good sources of discounted fares are: **Discount-Tickets.com** (www.discount-tickets.com) **Ebookers.com** (www.ebookers.com) **Flynow.com** (www.flynow.com)

No-frills airlines are increasingly big business for travel between the UK and Ireland and Italy. EasyJet, having taken over British Airways' Go, is now the biggest operator. Their main competitor is the Irish Ryanair, although British Midland also offers some excellent deals. Prices vary wildly according to season and depend on how far in advance you can book them.

The two national airlines linking the UK and Italy are British Airways and Alitalia. They both operate regular flights to Rome, Milan, Venice, Florence, Naples, Palermo, Turin and Pisa.

Most British travel agents are registered with the Association of British Travel Agents (ABTA). If you have paid for your flight with an ABTA-registered agent who then goes bust, ABTA will guarantee a refund or an alternative.

USA

Delta Airlines and Alitalia have nonstop daily flights from New York's JFK airport to Rome Fiumicino and Milan Malpensa, while Continental flies nonstop to both from Newark. American Airlines flies from Chicago and JFK to Rome from May to October.

Discount travel agencies in the USA are known as consolidators. San Francisco is the ticket consolidator capital of America although some good deals can be found in other big cities. The *New York Times*, the *Los Angeles Times*, the *Chicago Tribune* and the *San Francisco Chronicle* all produce weekly travel sections. Be careful when you purchase from a company you find on the Internet or in the back of newspaper. Do your homework.

STA Travel (☎ 800 781 40 40; www.statravel.com) has offices in Boston, Chicago, Los Angeles, New York, Philadelphia and San Francisco. Fares vary wildly depending on season, availability and a little luck. **Discover Italy** (☎ 866 878 74 77; www.discoveritaly.com) offers flight-, hotel- and villa-booking services.

Discount and rock-bottom options from the USA include charter, stand-by and courier flights. Stand-by fares are often sold at 60% of the normal price for one-way tickets. **Courier Travel** (☎ 303 570 75 86; www.couriertravel .org) is a comprehensive searchable database for courier and stand-by flights.

LAND

There are plenty of options for entering Italy by train, bus or private vehicle. Bus is the cheapest option but services are less frequent, less comfortable and significantly longer than the train. Take care to check whether you require a visa to pass through any countries on your way.

Border Crossings

The main points of entry to Italy are the Mont Blanc Tunnel from France at Chamonix which connects with the A5 for Turin and Milan; the Grand St Bernard tunnel from Switzerland, which also connects with the A5; and the Brenner Pass from Austria, which connects with the A22 to Bologna. All three are open year-round. Mountain passes

are often closed in winter and sometimes even in autumn and spring, making the tunnels a more reliable option. Make sure you have snow chains if driving in winter.

Regular trains on two lines connect Italy with the main cities in Austria and on into Germany, France or Eastern Europe. Those crossing the frontier at the Brenner Pass go to Innsbruck, Stuttgart and Munich. Those crossing at Tarvisio in the east proceed to Vienna, Salzburg and Prague. Trains from Milan head for Switzerland and on into France and the Netherlands. The main international train line to Slovenia crosses near Trieste.

In 2007 the world's largest land tunnel will open in Switzerland, providing a rail link under the Alps. The tunnel will be 34km long and carry passenger trains at 150km/h, cutting the time to cross from Germany to Milan from 3½ hours to two hours.

Bus

Eurolines (www.eurolines.com) is a consortium of European coach companies that operates across Europe with offices in all major European cities. Italy-bound buses head to Milan, Rome or Florence and all come equipped with on-board toilet facilities (necessary for journeys such as London to Rome, which takes about 30 hours). You can contact them in your own country or in Italy and their multilingual website gives comprehensive details of prices, passes and travel agencies where you can book tickets.

Another option is the backpacker-friendly **Busabout** (☎ 020 7950 1661; www.busabout.com), which covers at least 60 European cities and towns with a hop-on, hop-off pass. It also books three- and four-day short-break itineraries, including a weekend out of Rome along the Amalfi Coast (a tough place to get to by public transport). Their season runs from May to October and buses usually leave between large cities every other day. In Italy, it covers Rome, Florence, Siena, Pisa, Ancona, Venice and La Spezia (for the Cinque Terre). You can book onward travel and accommodation on the bus or on their website.

Car & Motorcycle

CONTINENTAL EUROPE

When driving in Europe always carry proof of ownership of a private vehicle. Third-

TRANSPORT

RAIL PASSES

Eurail Passes are for non-European residents and are supposed to be bought outside Europe. They are available from travel agencies and websites worldwide. You can review passes, buy directly or check out special deals on the website of **Eurail International** (www .eurail.com). To qualify for a Youth pass, passengers must be under 26 years old on the first day of the validity of the pass.

The InterRail Pass is available to EU residents or people who've lived in Europe for at least six months. They can be bought at most major stations and student travel outlets.

Eurail Passes

Eurail offers three types of pass: the Eurailpass, the Eurail Selectpass and the Eurail Regional Pass. People aged over 26 pay for a 1st-class pass and, if there are two to five people travelling together, a Saver version is available, offering about 15% discount. All types of pass also come in a youth version, available for those aged under 26. As of January 2005 the Eurailpass and Eurail Selectpass youth prices are now about 35% cheaper than the adult passes (a saving of 5% over the previous year). Eurail Passes also allow its holders to receive discounts or free passage on a variety of travel services.

Eurailpass

Eurailpasses are good for travel in 17 European countries in the Eurail network (including the Republic of Ireland but not the UK and much of Eastern Europe). They can be a good deal if you're planning on visiting several countries. However, if you're just planning on travelling within Italy, it's not worth the money.

Pass	Adult 1st class (US$)	Saver 1st class (US$)	Youth 2nd class (US$)
15 days	588	498	382
21 days	762	648	495
1 month	946	804	615
2 months	1338	1138	870
3 months	1654	1408	1075

There's also a Eurailpass Flexi which is available for 10 or 15 days within two months. Instead of paying for days when you're not travelling, you choose which days out of the two months you'd like to travel. It's available in the same countries as the Eurailpass.

Eurail Selectpass

The Eurail Selectpass is a good bet for travellers who are planning on visiting less than a

---

party motor insurance is also a minimum requirement in Italy and throughout Europe. Ask your insurer for a European Accident Statement (EAS) form which can simplify matters in the event of an accident. A European breakdown-assistance policy is a good investment. In Italy, assistance can be obtained through the **Automobile Club Italiano** (ACI; ☎ 06 4 99 81, 24hr information ☎ 166 664 477; www.aci .it in Italian).

Every vehicle travelling across an international border should display a nationality plate of its country of registration.

You can either prebook a car before you leave home (multinational car-rental agencies are listed on p883) or you can often find a better deal by contacting the agency directly (check out the individual chapters for contact information). Check with your credit-card company to see if they offer a Collision Damage Waiver, which covers you for additional damage if you use that card

to pay for the car. Many car-rental agencies request that you bring the car back with the tank filled, and will charge you astronomically if it's not. Young drivers should call ahead, as many companies do not rent cars or bikes to drivers aged 25 and younger.

Italy is made for motorcycle touring and motorcyclists swarm into the country in summer to tour the scenic roads. With a bike you rarely have to book ahead for ferries and can enter restricted traffic areas in cities. Crash helmets are compulsory. **Beach's Motorcycle Adventures** (☎ 1 716 773 4960; www.beachs-mca.com) can arrange two-week tours within Italy in early May and early October. Riders need to have a motorcycle licence – an international one is best.

One interesting way to get around Italy (and Europe) is to rent or buy a camper van. If you are travelling for more than a few weeks, it's much more cost effective to purchase and then sell back the camper van, as half-dozen countries that connect via either rail or shipping line. You get to choose the three, four or five adjacent countries you'd like to visit and how many days within two months you'd like to travel – five, six, eight, 10 or 15 (five-country passes only) – and pay accordingly. For Italy, the available adjoining countries are Austria, France, Switzerland, Greece and Spain, and Slovenia and Croatia (which are counted as one country).

For an adult 1st-class Selectpass, prices range from US$370 for three countries in five days over two months to US$826 for five countries in 15 days over two months. The Selectpass Saver, for two to five people travelling together, costs about 15% less, running from US$316 to US$702. Eurail Selectpass Youth for 2nd-class travel for those 26 and under cost US$241 to US$537.

Eurail Regional Pass

There are nine different Eurail Regional Passes available that consist of two (or in some cases more) bordering countries. The 1st-class version is available for each pass and, in some cases, the 2nd-class pass is also available for adults.

You can get two Eurail Regional Passes that include Italy – the Eurail France & Italy pass and the Eurail Greece & Italy pass.

Both the France & Italy pass and the Greece & Italy pass offer four to 10 days of travel in a two-month period. Prices quoted here are for four- and 10-day passes.

The prices listed here for the Eurail France & Italy pass are for four-/10-day passes, but you can select any number of days in between: US$269–449/US$309–513 (1st-class adult), US$239–395/269–449 (2nd-class adult) and US$199–337 (2nd-class youth).

The Eurail Greece & Italy pass costs US$299–479/255–405 (1st-class adult), US$239–383/204–324 (2nd-class adult) and US$200–320 (2nd-class youth).

InterRail Pass

The InterRail Pass is only for people who have lived in Europe for at least six months. The French railway system manages this system, which covers 29 countries divided into eight zones, but tickets are available at many travel agents and on a plethora of websites all over Europe. Children under 12 pay half the adult fare.

Pass	Under 26s (£)	Adult (£)
1 zone - 16 days	145	215
2 zones - 22 days	185	295
All zones - 1 month	205	405

rental fees start at about €60 per day. Check www.ideamerge.com.

THE UK

Coming from the UK, you can take your car across to France by ferry or via the Channel Tunnel on **Eurotunnel** (☎ 08705 35 35 35; www .eurotunnel.com). The latter runs four crossings (35 minutes) an hour between Folkestone and Calais in the high season. You pay for the vehicle only and fares vary according to time of day, season and advance purchase, but start at UK£49 each way.

For breakdown assistance both the **RAC** (☎ 0800 0156 638; www.rac.co.uk) and **Automobile Association** (AA; ☎ 0870 600 03 71; www.theaa.com) offer comprehensive cover in Europe.

Train

CONTINENTAL EUROPE

The *Thomas Cook European Timetable* has a complete listing of train schedules. The time-

table is updated monthly and available from Thomas Cook offices worldwide for around €20. It is always advisable, and sometimes compulsory, to book seats on international trains to and from Italy. Some of the main international services include transport for private cars. Consider taking long journeys overnight as the €20 or so extra for a sleeper costs substantially less than Italian hotels.

THE UK

The passenger-train service **Eurostar** (☎ 0870 518 61 86; www.eurostar.com) travels between London and Paris and London and Brussels. Alternatively you can get a train ticket that includes crossing the Channel by ferry, Sea-Cat or hovercraft.

For the latest fare information on journeys to Italy, including Eurostar fares, contact the **Rail Europe Travel Centre** (☎ 0870 84 88 48; www.raileurope.co.uk). A Trenitalia Pass can be purchased in advance in the UK from **Rail**

Pass Direct (☎ 0870 120 1606; www.railpassdirect.co.uk) or **Rail Choice** (www.railchoice.com).

SEA

Dozens of ferry companies connect Italy with virtually every other Mediterranean country. The incredibly helpful search engine **Traghettionline** (☎ 010 58 20 80; www.traghettionline.com) covers all the ferry companies in the Mediterranean; you can also book online. Tickets are the most expensive in summer and prices for vehicles vary according to their size. Eurail and InterRail passholders pay only a supplement on the Italy to Greece routes from Ancona and Bari.

Ferry companies and their destinations:

Blue Star Ferries (www.bluestarferries.com) Services Venice, Brindisi and Ancona from Igoumenitsa, Corfu or Patras.

Fragline Ferries (☎ 0831 548 540 www.fragline.gr) Connects Corfu to Brindisi.

Grandi Navi Veloci (☎ 010 209 45 91; www.gnv.it) Heads from Genoa to Barcelona.

Grimaldi Ferries (☎ 081 496 444; www.grimaldi-ferries.com) Plies the Mediterranean between Civitavecchia, Livorno, Salerno and Palermo to Tunisia and Barcelona (the Spain routes are part of the Eurail pass system).

Jadrolinija (☎ 071 20 13 09; www.jadrolinija.hr) Makes the rounds from Ancona along the Croatian coast, including Split and Zadar and from Bari to Dubrovnik.

Marmara Lines (☎ 071 2076165; www.marmaralines.com) A Turkish company connecting Cesme to Brindisi and Ancona.

Minoan Lines (☎ 071 201708; www.minoan.gr) Services Venice, Brindisi and Ancona from Igoumenitsa, Corfu or Patras.

Tirrenia Navigazione (☎ 800 83 49 52; www.tirrenia.it) Connects all major Italian ports, including on Sicily and Sardinia.

Virtu Ferries (☎ 095 53 57 11; www.virtuferries.com) This Maltese company has ferries from Malta to Catania between March and October.

GETTING AROUND

You can reach almost any destination in Italy by train, bus or ferry and services are efficient and cheap; for longer distances there are plenty of domestic air services. Your own wheels give you the most freedom. However, be aware that *benzina* (petrol) and autostrada (highway) tolls are quite expensive and that the stress of driving and parking your car in a big Italian city could easily ruin your trip. The best bet is to take public transport between large cities and use a car only for country drives.

AIR

Domestic airlines in Italy:

Air One (☎ 199 207080; www.flyairone.it)

Alitalia (☎ 848 86 56 41, in Rome ☎ 06 6 56 41; www.alitalia.it)

Meridiana (☎ 199 111 333; www.meridiana.it)

The secondary airports are found in Rome (Ciampino), Pisa, Milan (Linate), Naples, Palermo, Catania, Venice, Florence, Bologna and Cagliari; there are other, smaller airports throughout the country. Domestic flights can be booked through any travel agency (listed throughout this guide).

Alitalia offers a range of discounts for young people, families, seniors and weekend travellers, as well as advance purchase deals. A one-way fare is generally half the cost of the return fare.

All applicable airport taxes are factored into the price of your ticket.

BICYCLE

Cycling is a national pastime in Italy. There are no special road rules for cyclists but you would be wise to equip yourself with a helmet and lights. You cannot take bikes onto the autostrade. If you plan to bring your own bike, check with your airline for any additional costs. The bike will need to be disassembled and packed for the journey. Make sure you include a few tools, spare parts and a bike lock and chain.

Bikes can be taken on any train carrying the bicycle logo. The cheapest way to do this is to buy a separate bicycle ticket (usually around €3.50), available even at the self-service kiosks. You can use this ticket for 24 hours, making a day trip quite economical. Bikes dismantled and stored in a bag can be taken for free, even on night trains, and all ferries allow free bicycle passage.

In the UK, **Cyclists' Touring Club** (☎ 0870 873 00 60; www.ctc.org.uk) can help you plan your own bike tour or organise guided tours for you. Membership costs as little as £12.

Hire

Bikes are available for hire in most Italian towns and many places have both city and mountain bikes. Rental costs for a city bike start at €8/25 per day/week.

Purchase

If you shop around, bargain prices for bikes range from about €100 for a standard ladies' bike without gears to €210 for a mountain bike with 16 gears. A good place to shop for bargains is **Tacconi Sport** (www.tacconisport.com), which buys in bulk. It has large outlets near Perugia, Arezzo, Trento and in San Marino.

BOAT

Navi (large ferries) service Sicily and Sardinia, and *traghetti* (smaller ferries) and *aliscafi* (hydrofoils) service the smaller islands. The main embarkation points for Sardinia are Genoa, Livorno, Civitavecchia and Naples; for Sicily the main points are Naples and Villa San Giovanni in Calabria. The main points of arrival in Sardinia are Cagliari, Arbatax, Olbia and Porto Torres; in Sicily they are Palermo and Messina.

For a comprehensive guide to all ferry services into and out of Italy, check out **Traghettionline** (www.traghettionline.com in Italian). The website lists every route and includes links to ferry companies, where you can purchase tickets or search for deals.

Tirrenia Navigazioni (☎ 800 83 49 52; www.tirrenia .it) services nearly all Italian ports. Other companies include Trans Tirreno Express, Moby Lines, and Grandi Navi Veloci. The state railway service, Trenitalia operates ferries to Sicily and Sardinia. Detailed information on ferry companies, prices and times for Sicily can be found on p747, and for Sardinia on p816. For other relevant destinations, see the Getting There & Away sections of the individual destination chapters.

Many ferry services travel overnight and travellers can choose between cabin accommodation or a *poltrona*, which is an airline-type armchair. Deck class (which allows you to sit/sleep in the general lounge areas or on deck) is available only on some ferries. Almost all ferries carry vehicles.

BUS

Bus services within Italy are provided by numerous companies and vary from local routes linking small villages to fast and reliable intercity connections. As a rule, buses are not always cheaper than the train, but can be invaluable getting to smaller towns.

It is usually possible to get bus timetables from local tourist offices. In larger cities most of the intercity bus companies have ticket offices or operate through agencies. In some villages and even good-sized towns, tickets are sold in bars or on the bus. Note that buses almost always leave on time.

Although it is usually not necessary to make reservations on buses, it is advisable in the high season for overnight or long-haul trips.

CAR & MOTORCYCLE

There is an excellent network of autostrade in Italy, represented by a white A followed by a number on a green background. The main north–south link is the Autostrada del Sole, which extends from Milan to Reggio di Calabria (called the A1 from Milan to Rome, the A2 from Rome to Naples and the A3 from Naples to Reggio di Calabria).

There's a toll to use most of Italy's autostrade. You can pay by cash or credit card as you leave the autostrada; to avoid lengthy queues buy a prepaid card (Telepass or Viacard) from banks and ACI offices in denominations of €25, €50 or €75, which you can use all over Italy. For information on road tolls and passes, check online at www .autostrade.it, or call the **Società Autostrade** (☎ 06 436 31).

However, off the beaten path you'll be doing most of your travelling on the larger system of *strade statali*. On maps they'll be represented by 'S' or 'SS' and can vary from four-lane highways (no tolls) to two-lane roads. These can be extremely slow, especially in mountainous regions. The third category is the *strade provinciali*, which you'll find on maps in rural areas and connecting small villages and, finally *strade locali*, which might not even be paved. You'll often find the most beautiful scenery off the provincial and local roads.

Automobile Associations

The ever-handy **Automobile Club d'Italia** (ACI; ☎ 06 42 12, 24hr ☎ 800 116 80; www.aci.it; Via Colombo 261, Rome) is a driver's best resource in Italy. They have a dedicated 24-hour phone line for foreigners in need of emergency assistance, weather conditions or even tourist information.

To reach the ACI in a roadside emergency, dial ☎ 116 from a land line or ☎ 800 116 80 from a mobile phone. Foreigners do not have to join, but instead pay a per-incident fee.

Road Distances (km)

	Bari	Bologna	Florence	Genoa	Milan	Naples	Palermo	Perugia	Reggio di Calabria	Rome	Siena	Trent	Trieste	Turin	Venice	Verona
Bari	---															
Bologna	681	---														
Florence	784	106	---													
Genoa	996	285	268	---												
Milan	899	218	324	156	---											
Naples	322	640	534	758	858	---										
Palermo	734	1415	1345	1569	1633	811	---									
Perugia	612	270	164	432	488	408	1219	---								
Reggio di Calabria	490	1171	1101	1325	1389	567	272	816	---							
Rome	482	408	302	526	626	232	1043	170	664	---						
Siena	714	176	70	296	394	464	1275	103	867	232	---					
Trent	892	233	339	341	218	874	1626	459	1222	641	375	---				
Trieste	995	308	414	336	420	948	1689	543	1445	715	484	279	---			
Turin	1019	338	442	174	139	932	1743	545	1307	702	460	349	551	---		
Venice	806	269	265	387	284	899	799	394	1296	567	335	167	165	415	---	
Verona	808	141	247	282	164	781	1534	377	1139	549	293	97	250	295	120	---

Note

Distances between Palermo and mainland towns do not take into account the ferry from Reggio di Calabria to Messina. Add an extra hour to your journey time to allow for this crossing.

Bring Your Own Vehicle

Cars entering Italy from abroad need a valid national licence plate and an accompanying registration card. A car imported from a country that does not use the Latin alphabet will need to have their registration card translated at the nearest Italian consulate before entering the country.

If you plan to ship your car, be aware that you must have less than a one-quarter tank of petrol. Unfortunately, you can't use your vehicle as a double for luggage storage; it is supposed to be empty apart from any necessary car-related items. All vehicles must be equipped with any necessary adjustments for the Italian market; for example, left-side drive cars will need to have their headlamps adjusted.

Driving Licence

All EU member states' driving licences are fully recognised throughout Europe. Those with a non-EU licence are supposed to obtain an International Driving Permit (IDP) to accompany their national licence which your national automobile association can

issue. It is valid for 12 months and must be kept with your proper licence. People who have held residency in Italy for one year or more must apply for an Italian driving licence. If you want to hire a car or motorcycle you will need to produce your driving licence.

Fuel & Spare Parts

Italy is covered by a good network of petrol stations. You will have three choices at the tank – *benzina* (petrol), *benzina senza piombo* (unleaded petrol) and *gasolio* (diesel).

For spare parts, call the 24-hour ACI motorist assistance number ☎ 06 4212. You'll almost always get connected to an operator who speaks English.

Hire

CARS

Most tourist offices and hotels can provide information about car or motorcycle rental. To rent a car in Italy you have to be age 25 or over and you have to have a credit card. Most firms will accept your standard licence or IDP.

The most competitive multinational car rental agencies:

Avis (☎ 199 100 133; www.avis.com)
Budget (☎ 800 472 33 25; www.budget-italy.com)
Europcar (☎ 800 014 410; www.europcar.com)
Hertz (☎ 091 213 112; www.hertz.com)
Italy by Car (☎ 800 846 083) Partners with Thrifty.
Maggiore (☎ 848 867 067; www.maggiore.com)

MOTORCYCLE

You'll have no trouble hiring a small Vespa or moped. There are numerous rental agencies in cities where you'll also be able to hire larger motorcycles for touring. The average cost for a 50cc scooter (per person) is around €20/150 per day/week.

Most agencies will not rent motorcycles to people aged under 18. Note that many places require a sizeable deposit and that you could be responsible for reimbursing part of the cost of the bike if it is stolen.

Insurance

To drive your own vehicle in Italy you need an International Insurance Certificate, also known as a Carta Verde (Green Card); your car-insurance company will issue this.

Purchase

Rock-bottom prices for a reasonable car that won't break down instantly will run about €2000 to €3000. The cost of a second-hand Vespa ranges from €200 to €700.

To find vehicles for sale, look in the classified sections of newspapers or go to an online auction site such as www.ebay.it.

Road Rules

In Italy, as in the rest of continental Europe, drive on the right side of the road and overtake on the left. Unless otherwise indicated, you must always give way to cars entering an intersection from a road on your right. It is compulsory to wear front seat belts, as well as rear seat belts if the car is fitted with them. If you are caught not wearing a seat belt, you will be required to pay an on-the-spot fine.

A warning triangle (to be used in the event of a breakdown) is compulsory throughout Europe. Recommended accessories are a first-aid kit, spare-bulb kit and fire extinguisher. If your car breaks down at night, take note if you get out of the vehicle. You could be fined up to €138 unless you wear an approved yellow or orange safety vest (available at bicycle shops and outdoor stores).

Random breath tests now take place in Italy. If you're involved in an accident while under the influence of alcohol, the penalties can be severe. The blood-alcohol limit is 0.05%.

Speed limits on the autostrade are 130km/h, and on all non-urban highways 110km/h. In built-up areas the limit is 50km/h. Speeding fines follow EU standards and are proportionate with the number of kilometres that you are caught driving over the speed limit, reaching up to €260.

You don't need a licence to ride a moped under 50cc but you should be aged 14 or over and you can't carry passengers or ride on the autostrade. The autostrada is no place for a moped or scooter, and those in the know recommend at least a 150cc engine to venture forth. On all two-wheeled transport, helmets are required. The speed limit for a moped is 40km/h. To ride a motorcycle or scooter up to 125cc, you must be aged 16 or over and have a licence (a car licence will do). Helmets are compulsory. For motorcycles over 125cc you will need a motorcycle licence.

You will be able to enter restricted traffic areas in Italian cities on a motorcycle without any problems, and traffic police generally turn a blind eye to motorcycles or scooters parked on footpaths. There is no lights-on requirement for motorcycles during the day.

Motoring organisations in various countries have publications that detail road rules for foreign countries. If you get an IDP, it should also include a road rules booklet.

HITCHING

Hitching is extremely uncommon in Italy. Public transport is surprisingly reliable (save for the ubiquitous train strike every few months) and most Italians would rather give up an arm than their car. This makes it quite easy to pick up rides once you've befriended a few *amici*, but hitchhikers could get stranded for hours and women alone should take great, great caution.

LOCAL TRANSPORT

All the major cities have good transport systems, with bus and underground-train networks usually integrated. However, in Venice your only options are by *vaporetti* (small passenger ferries) or on foot.

TRANSPORT

TRANSPORT

VALIDATE, VALIDATE, VALIDATE!

Almost every train (and several bus) journeys require passengers to validate their tickets *before* boarding. You simply punch them in the yellow *convalida* machines installed at the entrance to all train platforms. On local buses and some private railway companies, you validate your ticket on the bus or train itself. Getting caught with a ticket that hasn't been validated risks a hefty fine of up to €50, paid on the spot to an inspector who will be kind enough to escort you to an ATM if you don't have the cash on hand. Don't even think about trying the '*Ma sono una turista!*' line; it hasn't worked for at least 15 years.

Bus & Underground Trains

You must buy bus tickets before you board the bus and validate them once on board. If you get caught with an unvalidated ticket you will be fined on the spot (up to €30 in most cities).

There are *metropolitane* (underground systems) in Rome, Milan and Naples, as well as an in-progress new line in Turin (Metro-Torino). You must buy tickets and validate them before getting on the train. You can get a map of the network from tourist offices in the relevant city.

Every city or town of any size has an efficient *urbano* (city) and *extraurbano* (intercity) system of buses that reaches even the tiniest and most remote of villages. Call ahead if you want to travel on a Sunday, though, as services come to a virtual halt.

Tickets can be bought at most *tabacchi* (tobacconists), newsstands, from ticket booths or dispensing machines at bus stations and in underground stations. Tickets cost around €0.80 to €0.90. Most large cities offer good-value 24-hour or daily tourist tickets.

Taxi

You can usually find taxi ranks at train and bus stations or you can telephone for radio taxis. It's best to go to a designated taxi stand, as it's illegal for them to stop in the street if hailed.

With a minimum charge of approximately €3.10 (covering the first 3km) most short city journeys end up costing between €10

and €15. In Rome, there's a supplement of €7.80 on travel to and from the airports, because they are outside of the city limits. No more than four or five people are allowed in one taxi.

TRAIN

Trenitalia (☎ 800 89 20 21 in Italian; www.trenitalia .com) is the partially privatised state train system which runs most of the services in Italy. Other private Italian train lines are noted throughout this book.

There are several types of trains. Some stop at all stations, such as Regionale or Interregionale trains, while faster trains, such as the Intercity (IC) or the very fast Eurostar Italia (ES), stop only at major cities. It is cheaper to buy all local train tickets in Italy.

Almost every train station in Italy has either a guarded left-luggage office or self-service lockers. The guarded offices are usually open 24 hours or from 6am to midnight. They charge around €3 per for each piece of luggage.

Classes & Costs

There are 1st and 2nd classes on most Italian trains; a 1st-class ticket costs just under double the price of a 2nd-class ticket.

To travel on Intercity and Eurostar trains you are required to pay a supplement (€3 to €16) determined by the distance you are travelling. On the Eurostar the cost of the ticket includes the supplement and booking fee. If you are simply heading over a town or two, make sure you check whether your 40-minute journey requires a supplement. You might arrive 10 minutes earlier but pay €5 more for the privilege. Check up-to-date prices of routes on the Trenitalia website.

On overnight trips within Italy it can be worth paying extra for a *cuccetta* – a sleeping berth in a six- or four-bed compartment – which can cost just €20 more but save you the cost of a hotel.

Reservations

Reservations on trains are not essential but without one you may not be able to find a seat. Bookings can be made when you buy your ticket, and usually cost an extra €2.50. Reservations are obligatory for many of the Eurostar trains.

You can make train bookings at most travel agencies or you can simply buy your

TRAIN ROUTES

Principal Train Lines
Local Train Lines

---

ticket on arrival at the station (allow plenty of time for this). There are special booking offices for Eurostar trains at the relevant train stations.

Train Passes

Trenitalia offers its own discount passes for foreigners travelling within Italy. These in-clude the Carta Verde (€25, valid one year), which offers a 20% discount for people aged from 12 to 26 years of age. Similarly, the Carta d'Argento (€25, valid one year) offers the same discount to people aged 60 years and over. Children aged between four and 12 years are entitled to a 50% discount; those aged under four travel free.

The Trenitalia Pass allows for four to 10 days of travel within a two-month period. Passes should be available from all major train stations or bought through a travel agent in your home country. Prices are detailed in the table, right.

For information on Eurail Passes, see the boxed text, p878.

Category	4 days	6 days	8 days	10 days
1st class	€217	€261	€305	€349
2nd class	€174	€210	€246	€282
Youth				
(2nd class)	€145	€175	€205	€235
Groups (2-5)				
2nd class	€149	€179	€209	€239

Health

CONTENTS

BEFORE YOU GO

While Italy has excellent health care, prevention is the key to staying healthy while abroad. A little planning before departure, particularly for pre-existing illnesses, will save trouble later. Bring medications in their original, clearly labelled, containers. A signed and dated letter from your physician describing your medical conditions and medication, including generic names, is also a good idea. If carrying syringes or needles, be sure to have a physician's letter documenting their medical necessity. If you are embarking on a long trip, make sure your teeth are OK (dental treatment is expensive in Italy) and take your optical prescription with you.

INSURANCE

If you're an EU citizen, a European Health Insurance Card (EHIC; formerly the E111) covers you for most medical care but not for emergency repatriation home or non-emergencies. The card is available from health centres and post offices in the UK. Citizens from other countries should find out if there is a reciprocal arrangement for free medical care between their country and Italy (Australia, for instance, has such an agreement). If you do need health insurance, make sure you get a policy that covers you for the worst possible scenario, such as an accident requiring an emergency flight home. Find out in advance if your insurance plan will make payments directly to providers or reimburse you later for overseas health expenditures.

RECOMMENDED VACCINATIONS

No jabs are required to travel to Italy. The World Health Organization (WHO), however, recommends that all travellers should be covered for diphtheria, tetanus, the measles, mumps, rubella and polio, as well as hepatitis B.

INTERNET RESOURCES

The WHO's publication *International Travel and Health* is revised annually and is available online at www.who.int/ith.

Other useful websites:

www.ageconcern.org.uk Advice on travel for the elderly.

www.fitfortravel.scot.nhs.uk General travel advice for the layperson.

www.mariestopes.org.uk Information on women's health and contraception.

www.mdtravelhealth.com Travel health recommendations for every country; updated daily.

IN TRANSIT

DEEP VEIN THROMBOSIS (DVT)

Blood clots may form in the legs during a plane flight, chiefly because of prolonged immobility (the longer the flight, the greater the risk).

The chief symptom of DVT is swelling or pain of the foot, ankle, or calf, usually but not always on just one side. When a blood clot travels to the lungs, it may cause chest pain and breathing difficulties. Travellers with any of these symptoms should immediately seek medical attention.

To prevent the development of DVT on long-haul flights you should walk about the cabin, contract the leg muscles while sitting, drink plenty of fluids and avoid alcohol and tobacco.

HEALTH

JET LAG

To avoid jet lag try drinking plenty of non-alcoholic fluids and eating light meals. Upon arrival, get exposure to natural sunlight and readjust your schedule (for meals, sleep etc) as soon as possible.

IN ITALY

AVAILABILITY & COST OF HEALTH CARE

If you need an ambulance anywhere in Italy, call ☎ 118. For emergency treatment, head straight to the *pronto soccorso* (casualty) section of a public hospital, where you can also get emergency dental treatment.

Excellent health care is readily available throughout Italy but standards can vary significantly. Pharmacists can give you valuable advice and sell over-the-counter medication for minor illnesses. They can also advise you when more specialised help is required and point you in the right direction. In major cities you are likely to find English-speaking doctors or a translator service available.

TRAVELLER'S DIARRHOEA

If you develop diarrhoea, be sure to drink plenty of fluids, preferably in the form of an oral-rehydration solution such as Dioralyte. If diarrhoea is bloody, persists for more than 72 hours or is accompanied by fever, shaking, chills or severe abdominal pain you should seek medical attention.

ENVIRONMENTAL HAZARDS
Bites, Stings & Insect-Borne Diseases

Italian beaches are occasionally inundated with jellyfish. Their stings are painful but not dangerous. Dousing in vinegar will deactivate any stingers that have not fired. Calamine lotion, antihistamines and analgesics may reduce the reaction and relieve pain.

Italy's only dangerous snake, the viper, is found throughout the country except on Sardinia. To minimise the possibilities of being bitten, always wear boots, socks and long trousers when walking through undergrowth where snakes may be present. Don't put your hands into holes and crevices, and be careful when collecting firewood. Viper bites do not cause instantaneous death and an antivenin is widely available in pharmacies. Keep the victim calm and still, wrap the bitten limb tightly, as you would for a sprained ankle, and attach a splint to immobilise it. Seek medical help, if possible with the dead snake for identification. Don't attempt to catch the snake if there is a possibility of being bitten again. Tourniquets and sucking out the poison are now comprehensively discredited.

Always check all over your body if you have been walking through a potentially tick-infested area as ticks can cause skin infections and other more serious diseases such as Lyme disease and tick-borne encephalitis. If a tick is found attached, press down around the tick's head with tweezers, grab the head and gently pull upwards. Avoid pulling the rear of the body as this may squeeze the tick's gut contents through the attached mouth parts into the skin, increasing the risk of infection and disease. Lyme disease begins with the spreading of a rash at the site of the bite, accompanied by fever, headache, extreme fatigue, aching joints and muscles and severe neck stiffness. If untreated, symptoms usually disappear but disorders of the nervous system, heart and joints can develop later. Treatment works best early in the illness – medical help should be sought. Symptoms of tick-borne encephalitis include blotches around the bite, which is sometimes pale in the middle, and headaches, stiffness and other flu-like symptoms (as well as extreme tiredness) appearing a week or two after the bite. Again, medical help must be sought.

Rabies is still found in Italy but only in isolated areas of the Alps. Any bite, scratch or even lick from a mammal in an area where rabies does exist should be scrubbed with soap and running water immediately and then cleaned thoroughly with an alcohol solution. Medical help should be sought.

Leishmaniasis is a group of parasitic diseases transmitted by sandflies and found in coastal parts of Italy. Cutaneous leishmaniasis affects the skin tissue and causes ulceration and disfigurement; visceral leishmaniasis affects the internal organs. Avoiding sandfly bites by covering up and using repellent is the best precaution against this disease.

Heatstroke

Heatstroke occurs following excessive fluid loss with inadequate replacement of fluids and salt. Symptoms include headache, dizziness and tiredness. Dehydration is already happening by the time you feel thirsty – aim to drink sufficient water to produce pale, diluted urine. To treat heatstroke drink water and/or fruit juice, and cool the body with cold water and fans.

Hypothermia

Hypothermia occurs when the body loses heat faster than it can produce it. As ever, proper preparation will reduce the risks of getting it. Even on a hot day in the mountains, the weather can change rapidly so carry waterproof garments, warm layers and a hat, and inform others of your route. Hypothermia starts with shivering, loss of judgment and clumsiness. Unless re-warming occurs, the sufferer deteriorates into apathy, confusion and coma. Prevent further heat loss by seeking shelter, warm dry clothing, hot sweet drinks and shared bodily warmth.

TRAVELLING WITH CHILDREN

Make sure children are up to date with routine vaccinations and discuss possible travel vaccines well before your departure as some vaccines are not suitable for children under a year. Lonely Planet's *Travel with Children* includes travel health advice for younger children.

WOMEN'S HEALTH

Emotional stress, exhaustion and travelling through different time zones can all contribute to an upset in a woman's menstrual pattern.

If using oral contraceptives, remember some antibiotics, diarrhoea and vomiting can stop the pill from working. Time zones, gastrointestinal upsets and antibiotics do not affect injectable contraception.

Travelling during pregnancy is usually possible but always consult your doctor before planning your trip. The most risky times for travel are during the first 12 weeks of pregnancy and after 30 weeks.

SEXUAL HEALTH

Condoms are readily available but emergency contraception is not, so take the necessary precautions.

HEALTH

Language

CONTENTS

Italian is a Romance language related to French, Spanish, Portuguese and Romanian. The Romance languages belong to the Indo-European group of languages, which includes English. Indeed, as English and Italian share common roots in Latin, you will recognise many Italian words.

Modern literary Italian began to develop in the 13th and 14th centuries, predominantly through the works of Dante, Petrarch and Boccaccio, who wrote chiefly in the Florentine dialect. The language drew on its Latin heritage and many dialects to develop into the standard Italian of today. Although many dialects are spoken in everyday conversation, standard Italian is the national language of schools, media and literature, and is understood throughout the country.

If you've managed to gain more than the most fundamental grasp of the language you will need to be aware that many older Italians still expect to be addressed by the third person polite, that is, *lei* instead of *tu*. Also, it is not considered polite to use the greeting *ciao* when addressing strangers, unless they use it first; it's better to say *buon giorno* (or *buona sera*, as the case may be) and *arrivederci* (or the more polite form, *arrivederla*). We have used the polite address for most of the phrases in this guide.

Use of the informal address is indicated by (inf). Italian also has both masculine and feminine forms (in the singular they often end in 'o' and 'a' respectively). Where both forms are given in this guide, they are separated by a slash, the masculine form first.

If you'd like a more comprehensive guide to the language, pick up a copy of Lonely Planet's *Italian Phrasebook*.

PRONUNCIATION

Italian pronunciation isn't very difficult to master once you learn a few easy rules. Although some of the more clipped vowels and stress on double letters require careful practice for English speakers, it's easy enough to make yourself understood.

Vowels

Vowels sounds are generally shorter than English equivalents:

a	as in 'art', eg *caro* (dear); sometimes short, eg *amico/a* (friend)
e	short, as in 'let', eg *mettere* (to put); long, as in 'there', eg *mela* (apple)
i	short, as in 'it', eg *inizio* (start); long, as in 'marine', eg *vino* (wine)
o	short, as in 'dot', eg *donna* (woman); long, as in 'port', eg *ora* (hour)
u	as the 'oo' in 'book', eg *puro* (pure)

Consonants

The pronunciation of most Italian consonants is similar to that of their English counterparts. Pronunciation of some consonants depends on certain rules:

c	as the 'k' in 'kit' before **a**, **o** and **u**; as the 'ch' in 'choose' before **e** and **i**
ch	as the 'k' in 'kit'
g	as the 'g' in 'get' before **a**, **o**, **u** and **h**; as the 'j' in 'jet' before **e** and **i**
gli	as the 'lli' in 'million'
gn	as the 'ny' in 'canyon'
h	always silent
r	a rolled 'rr' sound
sc	as the 'sh' in 'sheep' before **e** and **i**; as 'sk' before **a**, **o**, **u** and **h**
z	at the beginning of a word, as the 'dz' in 'adze'; elsewhere as the 'ts' in 'its'

Note that when **ci**, **gi** and **sci** are followed by **a**, **o** or **u**, the 'i' is not pronounced unless the accent falls on the 'i'. Thus the name 'Giovanni' is pronounced joh-*vahn*-nee.

A double consonant is pronounced as a longer, more forceful sound than a single consonant. This can directly affect the meaning of a word, eg *sono* (I am), *sonno* (sleep), but the context of a sentence will usually get the message across.

Word Stress

Stress is indicated in our pronunciation guide by italics. Word stress generally falls on the second-last syllable, as in spa-*ghet*-ti, but when a word has an accent, the stress falls on that syllable, as in cit-*tà* (city).

ACCOMMODATION

I'm looking	Cerco ...	cher·ko ...
for a ...		
guesthouse	una pensione	oo·na pen·syo·ne
hotel	un albergo	oon al·ber·go
youth hostel	un ostello per	oon os·te·lo per
	la gloventù	la jo·ven·too

Where is a cheap hotel?
Dov'è un albergo   do·ve oon al·ber·go
a buon prezzo?   a bwon pre·tso

What is the address?
Qual'è l'indirizzo?   kwa·le leen·dee·ree·tso

Could you write the address, please?
Può scrivere l'indirizzo,   pwo skree·ve·re leen·dee·ree·tso
per favore?   per fa·vo·re

Do you have any rooms available?
Avete camere libere?   a·ve·te ka·me·re lee·be·re

I'd like (a) ...	Vorrei ...	vo·ray ...
bed	un letto	oon le·to
single room	una camera	oo·na ka·me·ra
	singola	seen·go·la
double room	una camera	oo·na ka·me·ra
	matrimoniale	ma·tree·mo·nya·le
room with two	una camera	oo·na ka·me·ra
beds	doppia	do·pya
room with a	una camera	oo·na ka·me·ra
bathroom	con bagno	kon ba·nyo
to share a	un letto in	oon le·to een
dorm	dormitorio	dor·mee·to·ryo

How much is	Quanto costa ...?	kwan·to ko·sta ...
it ...?		
per night	per la notte	per la no·te
per person	per persona	per per·so·na

May I see it?
Posso vederla?   po·so ve·der·la

Where is the bathroom?
Dov'è il bagno?   do·ve eel ba·nyo

I'm/We're leaving today.
Parto/Partiamo oggi.   par·to/par·tya·mo o·jee

CONVERSATION & ESSENTIALS

Hello.	Buon giorno	bwon jor·no
	Ciao. (inf)	chow
Goodbye.	Arrivederci.	a·ree·ve·der·chee
	Ciao. (inf)	chow
Yes.	Sì.	see
No.	No.	no
Please.	Per favore/	per fa·vo·re/
	Per piacere.	per pya·chay·re
Thank you.	Grazie.	gra·tsye
That's fine/	Prego.	pre·go
You're welcome.		
Excuse me.	Mi scusi.	mee skoo·zee
I'm sorry.	Mi scusi/	mee skoo·zee/
	Mi perdoni.	mee per·do·nee

What's your name?
Come si chiama?   ko·me see kya·ma
Come ti chiami? (inf)   ko·me tee kya·mee

My name is ...
Mi chiamo ...   mee kya·mo ...

Where are you from?
Da dove viene?   da do·ve vye·ne
Di dove sei? (inf)   dee do·ve se·ee

I'm from ...
Vengo da ...   ven·go da ...

I (don't) like ...
(Non) Mi piace ...   (non) mee pya·che ...

LANGUAGE

Just a minute.
  Un momento.   oon mo-*men*-to

DIRECTIONS

Where is ...?
  Dov'è ...?   do-*ve* ...
Go straight ahead.
  Si va sempre diritto.   see va *sem*-pre dee-*ree*-to
  Vai sempre diritto. (inf)   va-ee *sem*-pre dee-*ree*-to
Turn left.
  Giri a sinistra.   *jee*-ree a see-*nee*-stra
Turn right.
  Giri a destra.   *jee*-ree a *de*-stra
at the next corner
  al prossimo angolo   al *pro*-see-mo *an*-go-lo
at the traffic lights
  al semaforo   al se-*ma*-fo-ro

SIGNS

Ingresso/Entrata	Entrance
Uscita	Exit
Informazione	Information
Aperto	Open
Chiuso	Closed
Proibito/Vietato	Prohibited
Camere Libere	Rooms Available
Completo	Full/No Vacancies
Polizia/Carabinieri	Police
Questura	Police Station
Gabinetti/Bagni	Toilets
Uomini	Men
Donne	Women

behind	*dietro*	*dye*-tro
in front of	*davanti*	da-*van*-tee
far (from)	*lontano (da)*	lon-*ta*-no (da)
near (to)	*vicino (di)*	vee-*chee*-no (dee)
opposite	*di fronte a*	dee *fron*-te a
beach	*la spiaggia*	la *spya*-ja
bridge	*il ponte*	eel *pon*-te
castle	*il castello*	eel kas-*te*-lo
cathedral	*il duomo*	eel *dwo*-mo
island	*l'isola*	*lee*-so-la
(main) square	*la piazza*	la *pya*-tsa
	(principale)	(preen-chee-*pa*-le)
market	*il mercato*	eel mer-*ka*-to
old city	*il centro*	eel *chen*-tro
	storico	*sto*-ree-ko
palace	*il palazzo*	eel pa-*la*-tso
ruins	*le rovine*	le ro-*vee*-ne
sea	*il mare*	eel *ma*-re
tower	*la torre*	la *to*-re

EMERGENCIES

Help!
  Aiuto!   a-*yoo*-to
There's been an accident!
  C'è stato un   che *sta*-to oon
  incidente!   een-chee-*den*-te
I'm lost.
  Mi sono perso/a.   mee *so*-no per-so/a
Go away!
  Lasciami in pace!   la-sha-mi een *pa*-che
  Vai via! (inf)   va-ee *vee*-a

Call ...!   *Chiami ...!*   kee-*ya*-mee ...
  a doctor   *un dottore/*   oon do-*to*-re/
     un medico   oon me-*dee*-ko
  the police   *la polizia*   la po-lee-*tsee*-ya

HEALTH

I'm ill.   *Mi sento male.*   mee *sen*-to *ma*-le
It hurts here.   *Mi fa male qui.*   mee fa *ma*-le kwee

I'm ...   *Sono ...*   *so*-no ...
  asthmatic   *asmatico/a*   az-*ma*-tee-ko/a
  diabetic   *diabetico/a*   dee-a-*be*-tee-ko/a
  epileptic   *epilettico/a*   e-pee-*le*-tee-ko/a

I'm allergic ...   *Sono*   *so*-no
   allergico/a ...   a-*ler*-jee-ko/a ...
  to antibiotics   *agli antibiotici*   a-lyee an-tee-
     bee-o-tee-chee
  to aspirin   *all'aspirina*   a-*la*-spe-*ree*-na
  to penicillin   *alla penicillina*   a-la pe-nee-see-
     lee-na
  to nuts   *ai noci*   a-ee *no*-chee

antiseptic	*antisettico*	an-tee-*se*-tee-ko
aspirin	*aspirina*	as-pee-*ree*-na
condoms	*preservativi*	pre-zer-va-*tee*-vee
contraceptive	*contraccetivo*	kon-tra-che-*tee*-vo
diarrhoea	*diarrea*	dee-a-*re*-a
medicine	*medicina*	me-dee-*chee*-na
sunblock cream	*crema solare*	*kre*-ma so-*la*-re
tampons	*tamponi*	tam-*po*-nee

LANGUAGE DIFFICULTIES

Do you speak English?
  Parla inglese?   *par*-la een-*gle*-ze
Does anyone here speak English?
  C'è qualcuno che   che kwal-*koo*-no ke
  parla inglese?   *par*-la een-*gle*-ze
How do you say ... in Italian?
  Come si dice ... in   *ko*-me see *dee*-che ... een
  italiano?   ee-ta-*lya*-no

What does ... mean?

	Che vuol dire ...?	ke vwol *dee*·re ...

I understand.

	Capisco.	ka·*pee*·sko

I don't understand.

	Non capisco.	non ka·*pee*·sko

Please write it down.

	Può scriverlo, per favore?	pwo *skree*·ver·lo per fa·*vo*·re

Can you show me (on the map)?

	Può mostrarmelo	pwo mos·*trar*·me·lo
	(sulla pianta)?	(*soo*·la *pyan*·ta)

NUMBERS

0	*zero*	*dze*·ro
1	*uno*	*oo*·no
2	*due*	*doo*·e
3	*tre*	tre
4	*quattro*	*kwa*·tro
5	*cinque*	*cheen*·kwe
6	*sei*	say
7	*sette*	*se*·te
8	*otto*	*o*·to
9	*nove*	*no*·ve
10	*dieci*	*dye*·chee
11	*undici*	oon·*dee*·chee
12	*dodici*	do·*dee*·chee
13	*tredici*	tre·*dee*·chee
14	*quattordici*	kwa *tor* dee chee
15	*quindici*	*kween*·dee·chee
16	*sedici*	se·dee·chee
17	*diciassette*	dee·cha·*se*·te
18	*diciotto*	dee·*cho*·to
19	*diciannove*	dee·cha·*no*·ve
20	*venti*	*ven*·tee
21	*ventuno*	ven·*too*·no
22	*ventidue*	ven·tee·*doo*·e
30	*trenta*	*tren*·ta
40	*quaranta*	kwa·*ran*·ta
50	*cinquanta*	cheen·*kwan*·ta
60	*sessanta*	se·*san*·ta
70	*settanta*	se·*tan*·ta
80	*ottanta*	o·*tan*·ta
90	*novanta*	no·*van*·ta
100	*cento*	*chen*·to
1000	*mille*	*mee*·le
2000	*due mila*	*doo*·e *mee*·la

PAPERWORK

name	*nome*	*no*·me
nationality	*nazionalità*	na·tsyo·na·lee·*ta*
date/place of	*data/luogo di*	*da*·ta/*lwo*·go de
birth	*nascita*	*na*·shee·ta
sex (gender)	*sesso*	*se*·so
passport	*passaporto*	pa·sa·*por*·to
visa	*visto*	*vee*·sto

QUESTION WORDS

Who?	*Chi?*	kee
What?	*Che?*	ke
When?	*Quando?*	*kwan*·do
Where?	*Dove?*	*do*·ve
How?	*Come?*	*ko*·me

SHOPPING & SERVICES

I'd like to buy ...

	Vorrei comprare ...	vo·*ray* kom·*pra*·re ...

How much is it?

	Quanto costa?	*kwan*·to *ko*·sta

I don't like it.

	Non mi piace.	non mee *pya*·che

May I look at it?

	Posso dare	*po*·so *da*·re
	un'occhiata?	oo·no·*kya*·ta

I'm just looking.

	Sto solo guardando.	sto *so*·lo gwar·*dan*·do

It's cheap.

	Non è caro/cara.	non e *ka*·ro/*ka*·ra

It's too expensive.

	È troppo caro/a.	e *tro*·po *ka*·ro/*ka*·ra

I'll take it.

	Lo/La compro.	lo/la *kom*·pro

Do you accept	*Accettate carte*	a·che·*ta*·te *kar*·te
credit cards?	*di credito?*	dee *kre*·dee·to

I want to	*Voglio*	*vo*·lyo
change ...	*cambiare ...*	kam·*bya*·re ...
money	*del denaro*	del de·*na*·ro
travellers	*assegni di*	a·*se*·nyee dee
cheques	*viaggio*	vee·*a*·jo

more	*più*	pyoo
less	*meno*	*me*·no
smaller	*più piccolo/a*	pyoo *pee*·ko·lo/la
bigger	*più grande*	pyoo *gran*·de

I'm looking for ...	*Cerco ...*	*cher*·ko ...
a bank	*un banco*	oon *ban*·ko
the church	*la chiesa*	la *kye*·za
the city centre	*il centro*	eel *chen*·tro
the ... embassy	*l'ambasciata*	lam·ba·*sha*·ta
	di ...	dee ...
the market	*il mercato*	eel mer·*ka*·to
the museum	*il museo*	eel moo·*ze*·o
the post office	*la posta*	la *po*·sta
a public toilet	*un gabinetto*	oon ga·bee·*ne*·to
the telephone	*il centro*	eel *chen*·tro
centre	*telefonico*	te·le·fo·*nee*·ko
the tourist	*l'ufficio*	loo·*fee*·cho
office	*di turismo*	dee too·*reez*·mo

TIME & DATES

What time is it?	Che ore sono?	ke o·re so·no
It's (8 o'clock).	Sono (le otto).	so·no (le o·to)

in the morning	di mattina	dee ma·tee·na
in the afternoon	di pomeriggio	dee po·me·ree·jo
in the evening	di sera	dee se·ra
When?	Quando?	kwan·do
today	oggi	o·jee
tomorrow	domani	do·ma·nee
yesterday	ieri	ye·ree

Monday	lunedì	loo·ne·dee
Tuesday	martedì	mar·te·dee
Wednesday	mercoledì	mer·ko·le·dee
Thursday	giovedì	jo·ve·dee
Friday	venerdì	ve·ner·dee
Saturday	sabato	sa·ba·to
Sunday	domenica	do·me·nee·ka

January	gennaio	je·na·yo
February	febbraio	fe·bra·yo
March	marzo	mar·tso
April	aprile	a·pree·le
May	maggio	ma·jo
June	giugno	joo·nyo
July	luglio	loo·lyo
August	agosto	a·gos·to
September	settembre	se·tem·bre
October	ottobre	o·to·bre
November	novembre	no·vem·bre
December	dicembre	dee·chem·bre

TRANSPORT
Public Transport

What time does the ... leave/ arrive?	A che ora parte/ arriva ...?	a ke o·ra par·te/ a·ree·va ...
boat	la nave	la na·ve
(city) bus	l'autobus	low·to·boos
(intercity) bus	il pullman	eel pool·man
plane	l'aereo	la·e·re·o
train	il treno	eel tre·no

I'd like a ... ticket.	Vorrei un biglietto ...	vo·ray oon bee·lye·to ...
one way	di solo andata	dee so·lo an·da·ta
return	di andata e ritorno	dee an·da·ta e ree·toor·no
1st class	di prima classe	dee pree·ma kla·se
2nd class	di seconda classe	dee se·kon·da kla·se

I want to go to ...

Voglio andare a ...	vo·lyo an·da·re a ...

The train has been cancelled/delayed.

Il treno è soppresso/ in ritardo.	eel tre·no e so·pre·so/ een ree·tar·do

the first	il primo	eel pree·mo
the last	l'ultimo	lool·tee·mo
platform (two)	binario (due)	bee·na·ryo (doo·e)
ticket office	biglietteria	bee·lye·te·ree·a
timetable	orario	o·ra·ryo
train station	stazione	sta·tsyo·ne

Private Transport

I'd like to hire a/an ...	Vorrei noleggiare ...	vo·ray no·le·ja·re ...
car	una macchina	oo·na ma·kee·na
4WD	un fuoristrada	oon fwo·ree·stra·da
motorbike	una moto	oo·na mo·to
bicycle	una bici(cletta)	oo·na bee·chee·(kle·ta)

Is this the road to ...?

Questa strada porta a ...?	kwe·sta stra·da por·ta a ...

Where's a service station?

Dov'è una stazione di servizio?	do·ve oo·na sta·tsyo·ne dee ser·vee·tsyo

Please fill it up.

Il pieno, per favore.	eel pye·no per fa·vo·re

I'd like (30) litres.

Vorrei (trenta) litri.	vo·ray (tren·ta) lee·tree

diesel	gasolio/diesel	ga·zo·lyo/dee·zel
leaded petrol	benzina con piombo	ben·dzee·na kon pyom·bo
unleaded petrol	benzina senza piombo	ben·dzee·na sen·dza pyom·bo

(How long) Can I park here?

(Per quanto tempo) Posso parcheggiare qui?	(per kwan·to tem·po) po·so par·ke·ja·re kwee

ROAD SIGNS

Dare la Precedenza	Give Way
Deviazione	Detour
Divieto di Accesso	No Entry
Divieto di Sorpasso	No Overtaking
Divieto di Sosta	No Parking
Entrata	Entrance
Passo Carrabile	Keep Clear
Pedaggio	Toll
Pericolo	Danger
Rallentare	Slow Down
Senso Unico	One Way
Uscita	Exit

Where do I pay?
Dove si paga?   do·ve see pa·ga
I need a mechanic.
Ho bisogno di un   o bee·zo·nyo dee oon
meccanico.   me·ka·nee·ko
The car/motorbike has broken down (at ...).
La macchina/moto   la ma·kee·na/mo·to
si è guastata (a ...).   see e gwas·ta·ta (a ...)
The car/motorbike won't start.
La macchina/moto   la ma·kee·na/mo·to
non parte.   non par·te
I have a flat tyre.
Ho una gomma bucata.   o oo·na go·ma boo·ka·ta
I've run out of petrol.
Ho esaurito la benzina. o e·zo·ree·to la ben·dzee·na
I've had an accident.
Ho avuto un incidente.   o a·voo·to oon een·chee·den·te

TRAVEL WITH CHILDREN

Is there a/an ...? *C'è ...?*   che ...
I need a/an ...   *Ho bisogno di ...* o bee·zo·nyo dee ...
  baby change   *un bagno con*   oon ba·nyo kon
  room   *fasciatoio*   fa·sha·to·yo

car baby seat	*un seggiolino*	oon se·jo·lee·no
	per bambini	per bam·bee·nee
child-minding	*un servizio*	oon ser·vee·tsyo
service	*di babysitter*	dee be·bee·see·ter
children's menu	*un menù per*	oon me·noo per
	bambini	bam·bee·nee
(disposable)	*pannolini*	pa·no·lee·nee·
nappies/diapers	*(usa e getta)*	(oo·sa e je·ta)
formula (milk)	*latte in polvere*	la·te in pol·ve·re
(English-	*un/una*	oon/oo·na
speaking)	*babysitter (che*	be·bee·see·ter
babysitter	*parli inglese)*	(ke par·lee
		een·gle·ze)
highchair	*un seggiolone*	oon se·jo·lo·ne
potty	*un vasino*	oon va·zee·no
stroller	*un passeggino*	oon pa·se·jee·no

Do you mind if I breastfeed here?
Le dispiace se allatto il/la bimbo/a qui?
le dees·pya·che se a·la·to eel/la beem·bo/a kwee
Are children allowed?
I bambini sono ammessi?
ee bam·bee·nee so·no a·me·see

Also available from Lonely Planet:
Italian Phrasebook

LANGUAGE

Glossary

AAST – Azienda Autonoma di Soggiorno e Turismo; city or town tourist office (mostly in southern Italy)
abbazia – abbey
ACI – Automobile Club Italiano (Italian Automobile Association)
affittacamere – rooms for rent in private houses
affresco – fresco
agriturismo – tourist accommodation on working farms
AIG – Associazione Italiana Alberghi per la Gioventù (Italian Youth Hostel Association)
al taglio – by the slice
albergo, alberghi (pl) – hotel
alimentari – grocery shop
aliscafo, aliscafi (pl) – hydrofoil
Alleanza Nazionale – National Alliance; neo-Fascist political party
alto – high
ambasciata – embassy
ambulanza – ambulance
anfiteatro – amphitheatre
APT – Azienda di Promozione Turistica; local town or city tourist office
autonoleggio – car hire
autostazione – bus station/terminal
autostrada, autostrade (pl) – motorway; highway
autunno – autumn

bambino, bambini (pl) – child
battistero – baptistry
bene – well; good
benzina – petrol
benzina senza piombo – unleaded petrol
bianco – white
biglietto – ticket
biglietto cumulativo – a cumulative ticket that allows entrance to a number of associated sights
borgo, borghi (pl) – archaic name for small town, village or town sector (often dating to Middle Ages)
Brigate Rosse – BR; Red Brigades (terrorist group)

campanile – bell tower
campo – field; also a square in Venice
cappella – chapel
carabinieri – police with military and civil duties
Carnevale – carnival period between Epiphany and Lent
carretto – cart
carta – menu
carta d'identità – identity card
carta geografica – map
casa – house

castello – castle
cattedrale – cathedral
cena – evening meal
centro – city centre
centro storico – historic centre
certosa – monastery belonging to or founded by Carthusian monks
chiesa, chiese (pl) – church
chiostro – cloister; covered walkway, usually enclosed by columns, around a quadrangle
cima – summit
città – town; city
colle – hill
colonna – column
comune – equivalent to a municipality or county; a town or city council; historically, a self-governing town or city
consolato – consulate
contrada – district
convalida – validation (eg of train ticket)
coperto – cover charge in restaurants
corso – main street
CTS – Centro Turistico Studentesco e Giovanile; student/youth travel agency
cuccetta – couchette (bed in train carriage)
cupola – dome

Democratici di Sinistra – DS; Left Democrats; political party
Democrazia Cristiana – DC; Christian Democrats; former Italian political party
deposito bagagli – left luggage
diretto – direct, slow train
duomo – cathedral

ENIT – Ente Nazionale Italiano per il Turismo; Italian National Tourist Board
enoteca – wine bar
ES – Eurostar; very fast train
espresso – express mail; express train; short black coffee
estate – summer

fermo posta – poste restante (general delivery)
ferramenta – hardware store
ferrovia – railway
festa – feast day; holiday
Feste di Pasqua – Easter Holy Week
fiume – river
fontana – fountain
fornaio – bakery
foro – forum

Forza Italia – Go Italy; political party
francobollo – postage stamp
frazione – municipal division
funicolare – funicular railway
funivia – cable car

gabinetto – toilets; WC
gasauto, GPL – liquid petroleum gas (LPG)
gasolio – diesel
gelateria, gelaterie (pl) – ice-cream shop
giardino, giardini (pl) – gardens
golfo – gulf
grotta – cave
guardia forestale – forest ranger

IAT – Informazione e Assistenza ai Turisti; local tourist office
IC – Intercity; fast train
IDP – International Driving Permit
interregionale – long-distance train that stops frequently
inverno – winter
isola – island
IVA – Imposta di Valore Aggiunto; value-added tax of around 19%

lago – lake
largo – small square
lavanderia – laundrette
Lega Nord – Northern League; political party
lido – beach
lingua originale – original language
locanda – inn; small hotel
loggia – covered area on the side of a building; porch; lodge
lo sci – skiing
lungomare – seafront road/promenade

mar, mare – sea
mercato – market
Metropolitana – the Rome and Naples underground transport systems
Mezzogiorno – literally 'midday'; name for the south of Italy
MM – Metropolitana Milano; Milan's underground transport system
monte – mountain
motorini – scooters
motoscafo – motorboat
municipio – town hall

Natale – Christmas
nave, navi (pl) – large ferry/ship
necropoli – ancient name for cemetery/burial site
nuraghe, nuraghi (pl) – megalithic stone fortress (Sardinia)

oggetti smarriti – lost property
ostello per la gioventù – youth hostel
osteria – simple, trattoria-style restaurant, often with a bar

Pagine Gialle – Yellow Pages; phone directory
palazzo, palazzi (pl) – mansion; palace; large building of any type, including an apartment block
palio – contest
panetteria – bakery
paninoteca – sandwich bar
parco – park
Partito Rifondazione Comunista – PRC; Refounded Communist Party; political party
passeggiata – traditional evening stroll
pasticceria – cake/pastry shop
patrician – a member of the hereditary aristocracy of ancient Rome
pellicola – camera film
pensione, pensioni (pl) – guesthouse
permesso di lavoro – work permit
permesso di soggiorno – resident permit
piazza – square
piazzale – large open square
pietà – literally 'pity' or 'compassion'; sculpture, drawing or painting of the dead Christ supported by the Madonna
pinacoteca – art gallery
Polo per le Libertà – Freedom Alliance; right-wing political coalition
poltrona – airline-type chair on a ferry
ponte – bridge
pontile – jetty
porta – gate; door
portico – covered walkway, usually attached to the outside of buildings
porto – port
posta – post office
presepio – nativity scene
primavera – spring
pronto soccorso – first aid

quartiere, quartieri (pl) – district
questura – police station

reale – royal
regionale – slow local train
rifugio, rifugi (pl) – mountain hut; accommodation in the Alps
riparto di pronto soccorso – casualty/emergency ward
riserva marina – marine reserve
riva – river bank
rocca – fortress
ronda – roundabout
rosticceria – shop selling roast meats

sala – room; hall
salumeria – delicatessen
santuario – sanctuary
sassi – literally 'stones'; stone houses built in two ravines in Matera, Basilicata
scala mobile – escalator; moving staircase
scalinata – staircase
scavi – excavations
sci alpinismo – ski mountaineering
sci alpino – downhill skiing
sci di fondo – cross-country skiing
servizio – service charge in restaurants
sestiere, sestieri (pl) – city district (Venice)
settimana bianca – literally 'white week'; winter-sports holiday
soccorso alpino – mountain rescue
soccorso stradale – highway rescue
spiaggia – beach
stazione – station
stazione di servizio – petrol/service station
stazione marittima – ferry terminal
strada – street; road
strada provinciale – main provincial road; sometimes just a country lane
strada statale – main road; toll free and sometimes multi-lane
superstrada – expressway; highway with divided lanes
supplemento – supplement; payable on a fast train

tabaccheria, tabaccaio – tobacconist's shop; tobacconist
tavola calda – literally 'hot table'; pre-prepared meat, pasta and vegetable selection, often self-service
teatro – theatre
tempietto – small temple
tempio – temple
terme – thermal baths
tesoro – treasury
torre – tower
torrente – stream
traghetto, traghetti (pl) – ferry
trattoria – simple restaurant
Trenitalia – Italian State Railways; used to be known as Ferrovie dello Stato (FS)

ufficio postale – post office
ufficio stranieri – foreigners' bureau

vaporetto – small passenger ferry (Venice)
via – street; road
viale – avenue
vico – alley; alleyway
vigili del fuoco – fire brigade
vigili urbani – local police; traffic police
villa – townhouse; country house; also the park surrounding the house

Zona Rimozione – Vehicle Removal Zone

Behind the Scenes

THIS BOOK

The 1st edition of Lonely Planet's *Italy* was written by Helen Gillman and John Gillman. Helen Gillman and Damien Simonis updated the 2nd edition. The 3rd edition was revised and expanded by Helen Gillman, Damien Simonis and Stefano Cavedoni. The 4th edition was updated by Helen Gillman, Damien Simonis, Sally Webb and Stefano Cavedoni. The 5th edition was worked on by Damien Simonis, Sally Webb, Fiona Adams, Miles Roddis and Nicola Williams, while the 6th was revised by Damien Simonis, Duncan Garwood, Paula Hardy, Wendy Owen, Miles Roddis and Nicola Williams. This mammoth 7th edition was updated by Damien Simonis, Duncan Garwood, Paula Hardy, Alex Leviton, Josephine Quintero, Miles Roddis and Richard Watkins.

THANKS from the Author

Damien Simonis Returning to Venice is like coming home, a rich stage whose characters are very real, warm and engaging. As always, Irina Freguia and Vladi Salvan kindly gave me access to their home, a fine base by the Rialto for exploring the city and the region.

Other friends and acquaintances, old and new, all helped render my research time in the lagoon and around as pleasant as it was profitable. Thanks go to: Antonella Bampa, Etta Lisa Basaldella, Federica Centulani, Caterina de Cesero, Luisa De Salvo, Antonella Dondi dall'Orologio, 'Seba' Giorgi, Bernhard Klein, Francesco Lobina, Lucialda Lombardi, Alessandra Magistretti, Lee Marshall, Marta at the Fondazione Giorgio Cini, Thom Price, Federica Rocco, Susanne Sagner, Laura Scarpa, Michela Scibilia, Alberto Stassi and Francesca Piro, Alberto Toso Fei and Olivia Alighieri, Manuel Vecchina and Angela Colonna, and Ottobrina Voccoli.

Thanks also to the staff of tourist offices in Venice and throughout the Veneto for their time-saving help.

My co-authors on this tome deserve a round of applause for their enthusiasm – it's great working with people who clearly love their territory. Michala Green, our champion commissioning editor, should have statues made to her.

Finally, this book is dedicated to Janique, who convinced me to buy the mask and tricorn and, thus attired, accompanied me on forays into Venice of the Carnevale.

Duncan Garwood I'd like to thank staff at tourist offices throughout Abruzzo, Molise and Lazio. In particular to Barbara and Rachele in Viterbo, Stefania Tirabassi, Franca Leone and the team at the Council Tourist Office in Sulmona, and to the very helpful lady at Tivoli who was too modest to give out her name.

In London thanks to Michala Green and Sam Trafford at Lonely Planet and to Damien Simonis, wherever he is, who clearly shares my enjoyment of a certain much-maligned Italian politician.

On a family front, as always grazie to Lidia, without whose support I couldn't do the job, to my ever-generous in-laws, and to little Ben for taking my mind off museum opening times, map keys and impending deadlines.

THE LONELY PLANET STORY

The story begins with a classic travel adventure: Tony and Maureen Wheeler's 1972 journey across Europe and Asia to Australia. There was no useful information about the overland trail then, so Tony and Maureen published the first Lonely Planet guidebook to meet a growing need.

From a kitchen table, Lonely Planet has grown to become the largest independent travel publisher in the world, with offices in Melbourne (Australia), Oakland (USA) and London (UK). Today Lonely Planet guidebooks cover the globe. There is an ever-growing list of books and information in a variety of media. Some things haven't changed. The main aim is still to make it possible for adventurous travellers to get out there – to explore and better understand the world.

At Lonely Planet we believe travellers can make a positive contribution to the countries they visit – if they respect their host communities and spend their money wisely. Every year 5% of company profit is donated to charities around the world.

Paula Hardy Southern Italy is a paradox of warm welcomes, hopeless tourist offices and those special individuals who will cancel their whole day's plans to take you on a tour of their town. This trip has been no exception, from the lonely man in the Reggio tourist office to the military efficiency of Angela and Silvana at Il Frantoio.

Particular thanks go to Amy Weideman, Michele and Dora Cappiello and Vincenzo for all their information and onward contacts. Thanks, too, Renata in Lecce, and John and Cindy for fantastic lunchtime company. To Ugo Sergi and Giuseppe Cosenza, guides who know their mountains, thank you for showing me the way. And thank you to Susi Travisano in Maratea for such smiling efficiency at the end of a very long day. Also, a big thank you to Rafaelle and Esther Ripoli for sharing their enthusiasm for Calabria's many eccentricities – it was inspiring. In Sicily, thanks to Marjolein Wortmann for taking time out to show me new aspects of old Palermo. Also, thank you Magmatrek for the update on Stromboli.

Thank you to readers who sent in some great tips, including Loes Massaro, Ans Compaijen, Davide Torsello, Andrew Smith, Gill Few and Patricia Ponte. Last, but never least, thank you Michala Green for effortlessly managing a chaotic author and setting me on the sunny southern road once again.

Alex Leviton Endless thanks go to Len Amaral – driver, sherpa, muffin. *Tante grazie* to my dear friends in Italy: Fabiano, Katya and Iona Spagnoli; Mario Santoro; Zach Nowak; Alessia, Teresa and Aldo Alessi; Allan Whyte; Carlo Rocchi Bilancini and Leo Pretelli. Thanks to the tourist officials who were actually helpful: Nicole Danner in Perugia, Massimo Evangelisti in Spoleto and Laura in Urbino. Rachel Young at Eurail: thank you for helping me make sense at 3.30am. In the Lonely Planet world, my appreciation goes out to tireless commissioning editor Michala Green and fellow author Miles Roddis. Back home, thanks to Rah Bickley and Greg DeWitt for their support and Angelita Nitti for help with my Italian.

Josephine Quintero Firstly many thanks to Robin Chapman for his sense of humour, map reading and sharing his expertise in photography and Italian wines. Also a mega–thank you to my Italy-based daughter, Isabel, for some insider's tips. Also thanks to the staff of the tourist offices and to Michala Green and Duncan Garwood for their compassion and support when a family crisis threatened to throw me off course.

Miles Roddis Huge thanks, as ever, to Ingrid, who drove me the length and breadth of my patch, then proofed with a sharp eagle's eye. And to Paola Lazzarini who, once again, chased up fleeting facts so efficiently. A long overdue tribute to fellow Florence-savvy author Damien Simonis, in whose sure footsteps I've so often trodden. Book after book, he's been my ideal hands-off, leave-you-alone, unobtrusive coordinating author. In Florence, Marco was generous with budget hospitality and Maurizio Piegaja of Victoria Hotel, Pisa, gave me some useful leads.

Tourist office staff were, as ever and almost without exception, helpfulness itself. Special thanks to: Sabrina Mafara and Maria Laura Billeri, a hugely efficient pair in Florence, Daniela and Roberta (Modena), Antonella Arnesano (Fiesole), Chiara Marcucci (Livorno), Mariarosario Aliboni (Viareggio), Lucia (Pisa), Roberta (Volterra), Claudia (San Gimignano), Emanuela Lorenzetti (Siena), Barbara (Montalcino), Elisa (Montepulciano), Andrea (Pienza), Anna (Porto Santo Stefano), Marÿke van der Weide (Pitigliano), Silvia (Cortona), Giampaolo (Arezzo), Felicia (Parma), Massimo Campobianchi (Reggio Emiliana), Elisabetta (Ferrara), Maria Luisa (Bologna), Chiara Ravaioli (Ravenna) and Grazia (Rimini).

Lastly, and risking taunts of toadiness, a hug for Michala, the most efficient, understanding and cooperative commissioning editor an author could dream of.

Richard Watkins Many thanks go to all the helpful and professional tourist office staff who assisted me in my research across northern Italy. Special thanks go to Paola Musolino and her ever enthusiastic colleagues at Turismo Torino, and to my guide in that city, Lina Brun. A big thank you is also due to Fabio Marzano of Studio Mailander, who went out of his way to show me some of the hidden corners of Piedmont and Valle d'Aosta. Thanks also go to Paolo Enria and Anna Eastman at the Università di Scienze Gastronomiche in Pollenzo for the informative tour and the excellent meal, Alessandra Abbona from Slow Food in Bra, Daniela and Mauro Veglio for the wine, Roberta Rossetti in Bardonechia and Antonella Migliazza and Micaela Gotelli at APT Genova.

CREDITS

Commissioning Editors: Michala Green, Stefanie Di Trocchio, Imogen Franks and Sam Trafford
Coordinating Editors: Nancy Ianni and Charlotte Harrison
Coordinating Cartographer: Csanad Csutoros

Coordinating Layout Designer: Yvonne Bischofberger
Managing Cartographer: Mark Griffiths
Assisting Editors: Nigel Chin, Adrienne Costanzo, Emma Gilmour, Kate James, Piers Kelly, Kim Noble and Charlotte Orr
Assisting Cartographers: Julie Dodkins, Jack Gavran, Corey Hutchison, Kusnandar, Malisa Plesa and Sarah Sloane
Assisting Layout Designers: Wibowo Rusli
Cover Designer: Annika Roojun
Colour Designer: Jacqui Saunders
Project Manager: Rachel Imeson
Language Content Coordinator: Quentin Frayne

Thanks to Melanie Dankel, Martin Heng and Darren O'Connell; managing layout designers Sally Darmody and Celia Wood; and Rebecca Lalor and Nick Stebbing for their guidance on all things technical.

THANKS from Lonely Planet

Many thanks to the following travellers who used the last edition and wrote to us with helpful hints, useful advice and interesting anecdotes.

A Louise Albertella, Virginia Allen, Mauricio Alvarez, Joe Alvaro, Santina Ampt, Sue Anderson, Hugh Annand, Mimmo e Silvana & Paolo Arese, Larry Arthur, Silvia Ascarelli, Robert Ashcroft **B** Chris Bachovchin, Peter Badame, Chris Bailey, Yvonne Balchin, Teresa Barber, Denise Bardan, Max Bar-Lev, Mark Bauer, Melda Beanette, David Beattie, F W Betts, Patrick Bijsmans, Janine Bird, Dean Biron, Jullian Blight, Federico Bonino, Alessandro Borgogna, Hans Bot, Leslie Branckaute, Floris Brandriet, Anita Brands, Svea Breckberg, Valerie Bridgeman, Peter Briggs, Claire Brooklyn, Joan Brown, Madeline Brown, Sarah Buchanan, Michael Buckley, Guy Burchett **C** Norman Cain, Massimo Calamelli, Peter Calder, Anne Campbell, Jill Carbone, Jim Carr, Dianne Caulkett, Scott Charity, Pam Cheadle, Angela Cirelli, Richard Clayton, Ruth Clowes, Loyola Colebeck, Ben Coleman, Iain Colquhoun, Ans Compaijen, Chiara Confalonieri, Stuart Conger, Simon Cope, Martin Corroy, Kate Crane, Eva Creel, Pietro Crivelli, Louise Crowe **D** Suzanne Dalton, Hans Damli, Richard Darlow, Michael Dawson, Cormac de Barra, David de Kleine, Silvia de Lorenzo, Katrijn de Ronde, Shena Deadman, Andrew Dean, Manuela del Boca, Vittorio del Duca, Katie Deluca, Alexandra Demiralp, Elena Dezani, Richard Dickens, Bill Douillet, Rachael Downham, Martin Senftleben, Linda Drath, Susan Duca, Alan Dunn, Heather Dunn, Caroline Dussault **E** Laura Elvin, Marianne en Leen Van Brink, Nick Evans **F** Careema Farms, Enzo Fassinelli, Capodici Fatima, Claire Featherstone, Gill Few, Usha Fitch, Daniel Fleming, Fortunato & Franca, Grahame Foster, Victor Fraser, Elena Frazzoni, Marjolein Fredrix, Daniel Friedrich, Mike Frost, Geer Furtjes **G** Sophie Gee, Catina & Bill Gillian, Francesca Giorgi, Brad Goodsell, Evan Gorman, Emily Gravett, Charles Greenless, Cindy Gregory, Luca Gricinella, Alison Grimsdell, Erik Gronvall, Christina Gustavsson, Patricio Gutierrez, David & Alison Gyger **H** Trevor Hamersley, Liv Hamilton, Clare Hampton, Siobhan Hanbury-Aggs, Graham Hannaford, Richard Hanson, Lucy Hardwick, Chris Hartman, Paul Harvey, Kristine Hasle Overby, Henry & Sandra Hatch, Patricia Havekost, Sandi Heimlich, Dane Henderson, Ernesto Hernandez, Rocío Viciana, Benjamin Hetzel, Georgina Hewes, Amy Hewitson, John Hillyard, Martine Hofstede, Lesley Hollinger, Holly Hooper, Edward Hotte, Margaret Huggett, J Hunter, Russell Huntington, D Hurlin, Iqbal Husain, Sarah Hussey **I** Vigdis Isachsen **J** Neil Jackson, Neil Jacobs, David Jacopin, Ted James, David Ji, Tim Johnson, Gabrielle Jones, Hester Jones **K** Kirsten Kammermeyer, Minte Kamphuis, John Kappenburg, S Karry, Glen Kearney, Lindsay Keed, Lisa Keeley, Dan Keller, Gayle Keller, David Kemp, Gael Kennedy, Jodi Kensley, David Kerlick, Kai Klinge, Jehangir Kohiyar, Katie Koprinik, Maxene Kupperman-Guinals **L** Andrea La Fratta, Gaetano La Rocca, Marion La Torella, Erin Lagoudakis, E Lambert, Niels Lassen, Mick Lauson, John Lee, Karen Lee, Victor Lee, Michael Leonard, Stephen Leong, Paul Levatino, M Levine, Moore Lia, Anne-Mette Lilleoore, Matthew Line, Michael Liska, Chris Lisowski, Yoni Livne, Rosa Lopez, Desmond Low **M** Jason M, Al MacInnes, Kelley Malcher, Alison Malzahn, Joanne Marshall, Tessa Marshall-Denton, Bernhard Marti, Ugo Masala, Marica Massai, Loes Massaro, Nick Massey, Paola Mazzuco, Alastair McCall, Chandra McCann, Shaun McCann, Nicola McCoy, Dave McGreal, Robert McIntire, Robert McManamon, Tim Meddings, Cesar Megina, John Meredith, Barbara Merlo, Kimberly Merris, Michaela Messner, David Michelson, Raoul Middelmann, Jacqueline Miedema, Jo Miller, Joe Milum, Darlene Moak, Heather Monell, Seamus Moran, Mary Moreira, Charlotte Morton, Barbara Mottl, Edyta Mrugalska, Lorenzo Mugnai, Peter Mulino, Jennifer Mundy, Noelle Myers **N** Patrick Naughter,

Ellen Navratil, Thomas Neuman, Michaela Newell, Judy Ng, Larry North **O** Samanta O'Laary, Mel O'Brien, Tim O'Brien, Romina Ochner, Eoin O'Cinneide, Torlach O'Connor, Shane O'Neill, Sean O'Reilly, Marie Orsted, Arthur Oudhuis **P** Rolf Palmberg, Andrea Panno, Barbara Paradise, Fleur Paris, Barbara Parrini, Federico Pastrone, Lance Patford, John Paton, Douglas Patterson, Maurice Peel, James Perry-Keene, Giovanni Pesce, Rob Philibert, Susan Philippi, Paul Pickering, Stefano Pierantozzi, Lorenzo Pilati, Tal Pol, Katharina Polatschek, Christopher Polkinghome, Laura Pontiggia, Pascal Portelli, Chris Porter, Neale Prescott, Vassilis Psarianos, Marilú Pugliese, Siomonn Pulla **R** Emanuele Ramella, Joel Ramilrez, Ute Ramseger, Vibeke Ranum, Karen & John Reilly, Anke Riccio, Alan Richardson, Marina Rizzetto, Katherine Robertson, Margaret Robinson, Sam Rob-King, Hilary Rock-Gormley, Arcelia Rodriguez, Anna Ruisniemi **S** Robert Sanders, Richard Sanderson, Marcello Sannucci, Karen Sarah, Lone Scherfig, Alex Schooten, Linda Schulman, Nanette Schuppers, Ami Schwab, Arthur Schwartz, Giambattista Scivoletto, Robin & Peter Scott, Richard Scotton, Anne Sear, May Sharman, Maria Sherry, Andrea Sita, Dan Skelton, Andrew Smith, Chris Smith, Sue Smith, Mark Snyder, Claudia Spener, Edith Springveld, Robert Stagg, Claire Stalker-Booth, Marianne Stam, Anne Steigerwald, Eivind Stene, Andrew Stephenson, Barbara Stynen **T** Marissa Tabbada, Deborah Taylor, Shaun Taylor, Terry Taylor, David Teevan, Laz Teleky, Malla Tennila, Laura Theng, Jeremy Thomas, Christopher Thompson, Jeanette Thompson, Janet Thomson, Nienke Thönissen, Maria Tillett, Debbie Tindall, Tiziana Tirelli, Davide Torsello, Richard Totik, Mike Treacy, Nicole Trombley, Liz Turner, Marty Turner **V** Paolo Valbusa, Desiree van Schaick, Bart Verhallen, Mathias Viaene, Pilar Villasana, Wilko Graf von Hardenberg, Joost Vullings **W** Jessica Wade-Murphy, Raoul Wainwright, Carl Walasek, Catherine Waldby, Ulrich Walter, Neta Weber, Christine Welch, Corinna Wenger, Carmen Werner Davidson, Hugh Westacott, Karen Weston, Andreas Willi, Linda Williamson, Bob Willyams, Jean Willyams, Jan Wiznerowicz, Ken Wong, Ling Heng Wong, Sharon Wood, Caroline Woodgate, Antoine Wyss **Z** Ang Jian Zhong, Kathrin Zingerle

ACKNOWLEDGMENTS

Many thanks to the following for the use of their content:

Globe on back cover © Mountain High Maps 1993 Digital Wisdom, Inc.

Rome Metro Map © 2005 ATAC S.p.A.

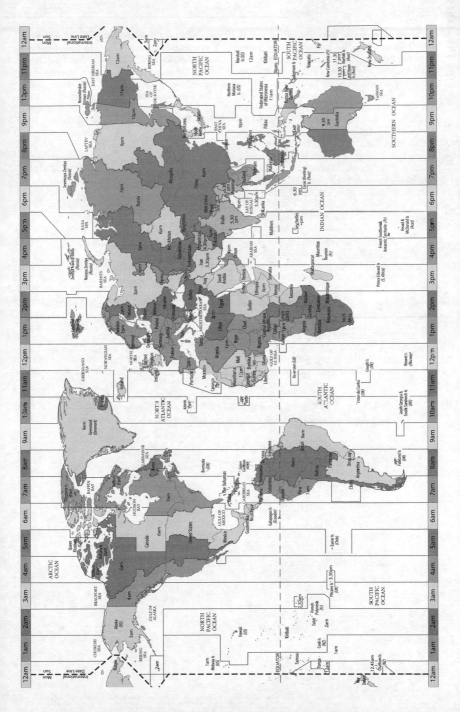

Index

INDEX

INDEX

000 Map pages
000 Location of colour photographs

INDEX

INDEX

000 Map pages
000 Location of colour photographs

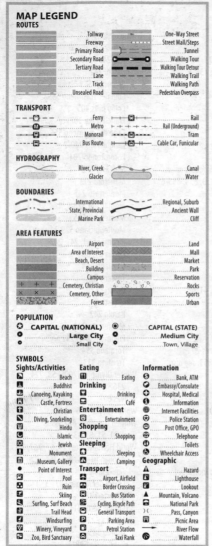

MAP LEGEND

ROUTES

Tollway
Freeway
Primary Road
Secondary Road
Tertiary Road
Lane
Track
Unsealed Road
One-Way Street
Street Mall/Steps
Tunnel
Walking Tour
Walking Tour Detour
Walking Trail
Walking Path
Pedestrian Overpass

TRANSPORT

Ferry
Metro
Monorail
Bus Route
Rail
Rail (Underground)
Tram
Cable Car, Funicular

HYDROGRAPHY

River, Creek
Glacier
Canal
Water

BOUNDARIES

International
State, Provincial
Marine Park
Regional, Suburb
Ancient Wall
Cliff

AREA FEATURES

Airport
Area of Interest
Beach, Desert
Building
Campus
Cemetery, Christian
Cemetery, Other
Forest
Land
Mall
Market
Park
Reservation
Rocks
Sports
Urban

POPULATION

⊙ **CAPITAL (NATIONAL)**
● **Large City**
● Small City
◉ CAPITAL (STATE)
● Medium City
○ Town, Village

SYMBOLS

Sights/Activities
Beach
Buddhist
Canoeing, Kayaking
Castle, Fortress
Christian
Diving, Snorkeling
Hindu
Islamic
Jewish
Monument
Museum, Gallery
Point of Interest
Pool
Ruin
Skiing
Surfing, Surf Beach
Trail Head
Windsurfing
Winery, Vineyard
Zoo, Bird Sanctuary

Eating
Eating

Drinking
Drinking
Café

Entertainment
Entertainment

Shopping
Shopping

Sleeping
Sleeping
Camping

Transport
Airport, Airfield
Border Crossing
Bus Station
Cycling, Bicycle Path
General Transport
Parking Area
Petrol Station
Taxi Rank

Information
Bank, ATM
Embassy/Consulate
Hospital, Medical
Information
Internet Facilities
Police Station
Post Office, GPO
Telephone
Toilets
Wheelchair Access

Geographic
Hazard
Lighthouse
Lookout
Mountain, Volcano
National Park
Pass, Canyon
Picnic Area
River Flow
Waterfall

LONELY PLANET OFFICES

Australia
Head Office
Locked Bag 1, Footscray, Victoria 3011
☎ 03 8379 8000, fax 03 8379 8111
talk2us@lonelyplanet.com.au

USA
150 Linden St, Oakland, CA 94607
☎ 510 893 8555, toll free 800 275 8555
fax 510 893 8572, info@lonelyplanet.com

UK
72-82 Rosebery Ave,
Clerkenwell, London EC1R 4RW
☎ 020 7841 9000, fax 020 7841 9001
go@lonelyplanet.co.uk

Published by Lonely Planet Publications Pty Ltd
ABN 36 005 607 983

© Lonely Planet 2006

© photographers as indicated 2006

Cover photographs: Detail, Palazzo dei Conservatori, Rome, Jon Arnold Images/Alamy (front); Gondolas, Venice, Jon Davison/Lonely Planet Images (back). Many of the images in this guide are available for licensing from Lonely Planet Images: www.lonelyplanetimages.com.

Printed through The Bookmaker International Ltd.
Printed in China